Financial Accounting Standards Board

ORIGINAL

PRONOUNCEMENTS

1997/98 EDITION

ACCOUNTING STANDARDS

AS OF JUNE 1, 1997

VOLUME I

FASB STATEMENTS OF STANDARDS

JOHN WILEY & SONS, INC.

New York • Chichester • Brisbane • Toronto • Singapore

NOTICE TO USERS OF THE *ORIGINAL PRONOUNCEMENTS*

This year's edition of the Financial Accounting Standards Board's (FASB) *Original Pronouncements* has been updated to include the following new pronouncements:

FAS 125: Accounting for Transfers and Servicing of Financial Assets and Extinguishments of Liabilities

Statement 125 provides standards for transfers and servicing of financial assets and extinguishing liabilities. The Statement uses a "financial-components" approach that focuses on control to determine the proper accounting for financial asset transfers. Under that approach, an entity recognizes the financial and servicing assets it controls and the liabilities it has incurred, derecognizes financial assets when control has been surrendered, and derecognizes liabilities when extinguished.

Statement 125 requires that servicing assets and liabilities be subsequently measured by (a) amortization in proportion to and over the period of estimated net servicing income or loss and (b) assessment for asset impairment or increased obligation based on their fair values.

Statement 125 requires that liabilities and derivatives incurred or obtained by transferors as part of a transfer of financial assets be initially measured at fair value, if practicable. Statement 125 also requires that servicing assets and other retained interests in the transferred assets be measured by allocating the previous carrying amount between the assets sold, if any, and retained interests, if any, based on their relative fair values at the date of transfer. In addition, Statement 125 requires that debtors reclassify financial assets pledged as collateral and that secured parties recognize those assets and their obligation to return them in certain circumstances in which the secured party has taken control of those assets.

Statement 125 requires that a liability be derecognized if and only if either (a) the debtor pays the creditor and is relieved of its obligation for the liability or (b) the debtor is legally released from being the primary obligor under the liability either judicially or by the creditor.

FAS 126: Exemption from Certain Required Disclosures about Financial Instruments for Certain Nonpublic Entities

Statement 126 exempts nonpublic entities with less than $100 million in assets on the date of the financial statements and that have not held or issued any derivative financial instruments, other than loan commitments, during the reporting period from the requirements of FASB Statement No. 107, *Disclosures about Fair Value of Financial Instruments.*

FAS 127: Deferral of the Effective Date of Certain Provisions of FASB Statement No. 125 (an amendment of FASB Statement No. 125)

Statement 127 defers for one year the effective date (a) of paragraph 15 of FASB Statement No. 125, *Accounting for Transfers and Servicing of Financial Assets and Extinguishments of Liabilities,* and (b) for repurchase agreement, dollar-roll, securities lending, and similar transactions, of paragraphs 9 through 12 and 237(b) of Statement 125, until January 1, 1998.

FAS 128: Earnings per Share

Statement 128 has been issued in an effort to simplify the current standards in the United States for computing earnings per share (EPS) and to make them compatible with international standards. Statement 128 applies to entities with publicly held common stock or potential common stock and is effective for financial instruments issued for periods ending after December 15, 1997, including interim periods. Earlier application is not permitted.

Statement 128 replaces the presentation of primary EPS with a presentation of basic EPS. The Statement also requires dual presentation of basic and diluted EPS by entities with complex capital structures and requires a reconciliation of the numerator and denominator of the basic EPS computation to the numerator and denominator of the diluted EPS computation. Basic EPS includes no dilution and is computed by dividing income available to common stockholders by the weighted-average number of common shares outstanding for the period. Diluted EPS reflects the potential dilution of securities that could share in the earnings of an entity, similar to fully diluted EPS.

FAS 129: Disclosure of Information about Capital Structure

Statement 129 consolidates existing capital structure disclosure requirements for ease of retrieval. Statement 129 applies to all entities. Statement 129 contains no change in disclosure requirements for companies that were subject to the previously existing requirements.

FIN 42: Accounting for Transfers of Assets in Which a Not-for-Profit Organization Is Granted Variance Power

Interpretation 42 interprets paragraph 4 of FASB Statement No. 116, *Accounting for Contributions Received and Contributions Made.* This Interpretation clarifies that a not-for-profit organization that receives assets acts as a donee and a donor rather than an agent, trustee, or intermediary, if the asset provider specifies a third-party beneficiary and explicitly grants the recipient organization the power to redirect the use of the assets.

Acknowledgments

Deborah L. Monroe, FASB project manager, compiled the *Original Pronouncements* with the assistance of Jennifer A. Berkowitz, FASB project research associate. Glen Kudlicki, production supervisor, and Ana Dolan, assistant production supervisor, and the production staff provided invaluable production assistance in the preparation of these volumes.

Norwalk, Connecticut   Timothy S. Lucas
June 1997   Director of Research
                  and Technical Activities

Volume I

ORIGINAL PRONOUNCEMENTS

(as of June 1, 1997)

TABLE OF CONTENTS

FASB Statements (FAS)

Table of Contents

Table of Contents

Table of Contents

Table of Contents

Table of Contents

Table of Contents

Table of Contents

(Refer to Volume II of the *Original Pronouncements* for the appendixes and topical index.)

Statements of

Financial Accounting Standards

Statement of Financial Accounting Standards No. 1
Disclosure of Foreign Currency Translation Information

STATUS

Issued: December 1973

Effective Date: For fiscal periods ending after November 30, 1973

Affects: No other pronouncements

Affected by: Superseded by FAS 8
Superseded by FAS 52

Statement of Financial Accounting Standards No. 2
Accounting for Research and Development Costs

STATUS

Issued: October 1974

Effective Date: For fiscal years beginning on or after January 1, 1975

Affects: Amends APB 17, paragraph 6
Amends APB 22, paragraph 13

Affected by: Paragraph 14 superseded by FAS 71
Paragraph 31 amended by FAS 86

Other Interpretive Pronouncements: FIN 4
FIN 5 (Superseded by FAS 7)
FIN 6
FTB 79-2 (Superseded by FAS 86)

Issues Discussed by FASB Emerging Issues Task Force (EITF)

Affects: No EITF Issues

Interpreted by: No EITF Issues

Related Issue: EITF Issue No. 86-14

Statement of Financial Accounting Standards No. 2
Accounting for Research and Development Costs

CONTENTS

INTRODUCTION

1. This Statement establishes standards of financial accounting and reporting for research and development costs with the objectives of reducing the number of alternative accounting and reporting practices presently followed and providing useful financial information about research and development costs. This Statement specifies:

a. Those activities that shall be identified as research and development for financial accounting and reporting purposes.
b. The elements of costs that shall be identified with research and development activities.
c. The accounting for research and development costs.
d. The financial statement disclosures related to research and development costs.

2. Accounting for the costs of research and development activities conducted for others under a contractual arrangement is a part of accounting for contracts in general and is beyond the scope of this Statement. Indirect costs that are specifically reimbursable under the terms of a contract are also excluded from this Statement.

3. This Statement does not apply to activities that are unique to enterprises in the extractive industries, such as prospecting, acquisition of mineral rights, exploration, drilling, mining, and related mineral development. It does apply, however, to research and development activities of enterprises in the extractive industries that are comparable in nature to research and development activities of other enterprises, such as development or improvement of processes and techniques including those employed in exploration, drilling, and extraction.

4. *APB Opinion No. 17,* "Intangible Assets," is

hereby amended to exclude from its scope those research and development costs encompassed by this Statement.

5. Paragraph 13 of *APB Opinion No. 22,* "Disclosure of Accounting Policies," is amended to delete "research and development costs (including basis for amortization)" as an example of disclosure "commonly required" with respect to accounting policies.

6. Standards of financial accounting and reporting for research and development costs are set forth in paragraphs 7-16. The basis for the Board's conclusions, as well as alternatives considered by the Board and reasons for their rejection, are discussed in Appendix B to this Statement. Background information is presented in Appendix A.

STANDARDS OF FINANCIAL ACCOUNTING AND REPORTING

Activities Constituting Research and Development

7. Paragraphs 8-10 set forth broad guidelines as to the activities that shall be classified as research and development.

8. For purposes of this Statement, research and development is defined as follows:

a. *Research* is planned search or critical investigation aimed at discovery of new knowledge with the hope that such knowledge will be useful in developing a new product or service (hereinafter "product") or a new process or technique (hereinafter "process") or in bringing about a significant improvement to an existing product or process.
b. *Development* is the translation of research find-

ings or other knowledge into a plan or design for a new product or process or for a significant improvement to an existing product or process whether intended for sale or use. It includes the conceptual formulation, design, and testing of product alternatives, construction of prototypes, and operation of pilot plants. It does not include routine or periodic alterations to existing products, production lines, manufacturing processes, and other on-going operations even though those alterations may represent improvements and it does not include market research or market testing activities.

9. The following are examples of activities that typically would be included in research and development in accordance with paragraph 8 (unless conducted for others under a contractual arrangement—see paragraph 2):

a. Laboratory research aimed at discovery of new knowledge.
b. Searching for applications of new research findings or other knowledge.
c. Conceptual formulation and design of possible product or process alternatives.
d. Testing in search for or evaluation of product or process alternatives.
e. Modification of the formulation or design of a product or process.
f. Design, construction, and testing of pre-production prototypes and models.
g. Design of tools, jigs, molds, and dies involving new technology.
h. Design, construction, and operation of a pilot plant that is not of a scale economically feasible to the enterprise for commercial production.
i. Engineering activity required to advance the design of a product to the point that it meets specific functional and economic requirements and is ready for manufacture.

10. The following are examples of activities that typically would be excluded from research and development in accordance with paragraph 8:

a. Engineering follow-through in an early phase of commercial production.
b. Quality control during commercial production including routine testing of products.
c. Trouble-shooting in connection with breakdowns during commercial production.
d. Routine, on-going efforts to refine, enrich, or otherwise improve upon the qualities of an existing product.
e. Adaptation of an existing capability to a particular requirement or customer's need as part of a continuing commercial activity.
f. Seasonal or other periodic design changes to existing products.

g. Routine design of tools, jigs, molds, and dies.
h. Activity, including design and construction engineering, related to the construction, relocation, rearrangement, or start-up of facilities or equipment other than (1) pilot plants (see paragraph 9(h)) and (2) facilities or equipment whose sole use is for a particular research and development project (see paragraph 11(a)).
i. Legal work in connection with patent applications or litigation, and the sale or licensing of patents.

Elements of Costs to Be Identified with Research and Development Activities

11. Elements of costs shall be identified with research and development activities as follows:

a. *Materials, equipment, and facilities.* The costs of materials (whether from the enterprise's normal inventory or acquired specially for research and development activities) and equipment or facilities that are acquired or constructed for research and development activities and that have alternative future uses (in research and development projects or otherwise) shall be capitalized as tangible assets when acquired or constructed. The cost of such materials consumed in research and development activities and the depreciation of such equipment or facilities used in those activities are research and development costs. However, the costs of materials, equipment, or facilities that are acquired or constructed for a particular research and development project and that have no alternative future uses (in other research and development projects or otherwise) and therefore no separate economic values are research and development costs at the time the costs are incurred.
b. *Personnel.* Salaries, wages, and other related costs of of personnel engaged in research and development activities shall be included in research and development costs.
c. *Intangibles purchased from others.* The costs of intangibles that are purchased from others for use in research and development activities and that have alternative future uses (in research and development projects or otherwise) shall be capitalized and amortized as intangible assets in accordance with *APB Opinion No. 17*. The amortization of those intangible assets used in research and development activities is a research and development cost. However, the costs of intangibles that are purchased from others for a particular research and development project and that have no alternative future uses (in other research and development projects or otherwise) and therefore no separate economic values are research and development costs at the time the costs are incurred.

erally similar to or broader than the NSF definition. The Board agreed that a broad definition including research and development activities in the social sciences such as those conducted by service-type business enterprises is appropriate for financial accounting and reporting purposes. Accordingly, the definition in paragraph 8 has been adopted.

29. The Exposure Draft had included research and development activities conducted for others under a contractual arrangement within the definition of research and development and had proposed that all research and development costs not directly reimbursable by others be charged to expense when incurred. Some respondents to the Exposure Draft contended that costs incurred in research and development activities conducted for others under a contractual arrangement should continue to be accounted for in accordance with financial accounting standards for contracts in general rather than as research and development costs. The Board agrees with this view and the change is reflected in paragraph 2.

30. The examples in paragraphs 9-10 incorporate certain changes, many of which were recommended by respondents to the Exposure Draft. The Board believes that those paragraphs as changed more clearly reflect its intent regarding the inclusion or exclusion of particular types of activities within the definition of research and development.

31. Several respondents to the Exposure Draft raised questions about the inclusion or exclusion of the development of various types of computer software within the definition of research and development. Computer software is developed for many and diverse uses. Accordingly, in each case the nature of the activity for which the software is being developed should be considered in relation to the guidelines in paragraphs 8-10 to determine whether software costs should be included or excluded. For example, efforts to develop a new or higher level of computer software capability intended for sale (but not under a contractual arrangement) would be a research and development activity encompassed by this Statement.

ELEMENTS OF COSTS TO BE IDENTIFIED WITH RESEARCH AND DEVELOPMENT ACTIVITIES

32. To achieve a reasonable degree of comparability among enterprises, the Board concluded that broad guidelines are appropriate to identify the elements of costs that should be included as research and development. Those guidelines are in paragraph 11.

33. Consideration was given to the alternative that

the costs of materials, equipment, or facilities that are acquired or constructed for a particular research and development project and that have no alternative future uses (in other research and development projects or otherwise) be apportioned over the life of the project rather than treated as research and development costs when incurred. The Board reasoned, however, that if materials, equipment, or facilities are of such a specialized nature that they have no alternative future uses, even in another research and development project, those materials, equipment, or facilities have no separate economic values to distinguish them from other types of costs such as salaries and wages incurred in a particular project. Accordingly, all costs of those materials, equipment, and facilities should be treated as research and development costs when incurred.

34. Paragraph 11(c) reflects certain changes from the Exposure Draft to treat the costs of intangibles purchased from others in a manner similar to that in paragraph 11(a) for the costs of materials, equipment, or facilities. Paragraph 11(c) is not intended to alter the conclusions in paragraphs 87-88 of *APB Opinion No. 16,* "Business Combinations," regarding allocation of cost to assets acquired in a business combination accounted for by the purchase method.

35. The conclusion that general and administrative costs not be allocated to research and development activities (unless clearly related) conforms to present accounting practice, which generally treats such costs as expenses when incurred.

36. One question in the Discussion Memorandum was whether interest or other cost of capital should be allocated to research and development activities. At present, interest or other cost of capital generally is not allocated to the cost of assets or specific activities for financial accounting purposes. The Board believes that allocation of interest or other cost of capital to research and development activities is part of a broader question beyond the scope of this Statement.

ACCOUNTING FOR RESEARCH AND DEVELOPMENT COSTS

37. The Board considered four alternative methods of accounting at the time research and development costs are incurred:

a. Charge all costs to expense when incurred.
b. Capitalize all costs when incurred.
c. Capitalize costs when incurred if specified conditions are fulfilled and charge all other costs to expense.
d. Accumulate all costs in a special category until

the existence of future benefits can be determined.

38. In concluding that all research and development costs be charged to expense when incurred (see paragraph 12), Board members considered the factors discussed in paragraphs 39-59. Individual Board members gave greater weight to some factors than to others.

Uncertainty of Future Benefits

39. There is normally a high degree of uncertainty about the future benefits of individual research and development projects, although the element of uncertainty may diminish as a project progresses. Estimates of the rate of success of research and development projects vary markedly—depending in part on how narrowly one defines a "project" and how one defines "success"—but all such estimates indicate a high failure rate. For example, one study of a number of industries found that an average of less than 2 percent of new product ideas and less than 15 percent of product development projects were commercially successful.[3]

40. Even after a project has passed beyond the research and development stage, and a new or improved product or process is being marketed or used, the failure rate is high. Estimates of new product failures range from 30 percent to 90 percent, depending on the definition of failure used.[4] One study concludes that "for about every three products emerging from research and development departments as technical successes, there is an average of only one commercial success."[5] That study goes on to say that "of all the dollars of new product expense, almost three-fourths go to unsuccessful products; about two-thirds of these . . . dollars are in the 'development stage.'"[6]

Lack of Causal Relationship between Expenditures and Benefits

41. A direct relationship between research and development costs and specific future revenue generally has not been demonstrated, even with the benefit of hindsight. For example, three empirical research studies, which focus on companies in industries intensively involved in research and development activities, generally failed to find a significant correlation between research and development expenditures and increased future benefits as measured by subsequent sales,[7] earnings,[8] or share of industry sales.[9]

Accounting Recognition of Economic Resources

42. In paragraph 57 of *APB Statement No. 4,* "Basic Concepts and Accounting Principles Underlying Financial Statements of Business Enterprises," economic resources are defined as the scarce means for carrying on economic activities. The economic resources of a particular enterprise are generally regarded as those *scarce* resources for which there is an *expectation of future benefits to the enterprise* either through use or sale.

43. Not all of the economic resources of an enterprise are recognized as assets for financial accounting purposes. However, criteria for identifying those economic resources that should be recognized as the assets of an enterprise for accounting purposes have not been specified in the official accounting literature. One criterion that has been suggested in published research studies and articles and in position papers, letters of comment, and oral presentations the Board received in connection with the public hearing is that of *measurability.*

44. The criterion of measurability would require that a resource not be recognized as an asset for accounting purposes unless at the time it is acquired or developed its future economic benefits can be identified and objectively measured.

45. Paragraphs 39-40 indicate that at the time most research and development costs are incurred the future benefits are at best uncertain. In other words, there is no indication that an economic resource has been created. Moreover, even if at some point in the progress of an individual research and development project the expectation of future benefits becomes sufficiently high to indicate that an economic resource has been created, the question remains whether that resource should be recognized as an asset for financial accounting purposes. Although future benefits from a particular research and devel-

---

[3]Booz-Allen & Hamilton, Inc., *Management of New Products* (Chicago: Booz-Allen & Hamilton, Inc., 1968), p. 12.

[4]John T. Gerlach and Charles Anthony Wainwright, *Successful Management of New Products* (New York: Hastings House, Publishers, Inc., 1968), p. 126.

[5]Booz-Allen & Hamilton, Inc., *Management of New Products,* p. 2.

[6]*Ibid.,* p. 11.

[7]Maurice S. Newman, "Equating Return from R & D Expenditures," *Financial Executive,* April 1968, pp. 26-33.

[8]Orace Johnson, "A Consequential Approach to Accounting for R & D," *Journal of Accounting Research,* Autumn 1967, pp. 164-172.

[9]Alex J. Milburn, "An Empirical Study of the Relationship of Research and Development Expenditures to Subsequent Benefits" (Unpublished Research Study, Department of Accountancy of the University of Illinois, 1971).

opment project may be foreseen, they generally cannot be measured with a reasonable degree of certainty. According to the research data cited in paragraph 41, there is normally little, if any, direct relationship between the amount of current research and development expenditures and the amount of resultant future benefits to the enterprise. Research and development costs therefore fail to satisfy the suggested measurability test for accounting recognition as an asset.

46. The criterion of exchangeability, which was discussed in the Exposure Draft, was not considered a significant factor by the Board in reaching its final conclusion on accounting for research and development costs. The Board believes that exchangeability needs further study and at this time the Board neither accepts nor rejects exchangeability as a criterion for accounting recognition of an economic resource.

Expense Recognition and Matching

47. *APB Statement No. 4* explicitly avoids using the term "matching" because it has a variety of meanings in the accounting literature. In its broadest sense, matching refers to the entire process of income determination—described in paragraph 147 of *APB Statement No. 4* as "identifying, measuring, and relating revenues and expenses of an enterprise for an accounting period." Matching may also be used in a more limited sense to refer only to the process of expense recognition or in an even more limited sense to refer to the recognition of expenses by associating costs with revenue on a cause and effect basis. In the following discussion, matching is used in its most limited sense to refer to the process of recognizing costs as expenses on a cause and effect basis.

48. Three pervasive principles for recognizing costs as expenses are set forth in paragraphs 156-160 of *APB Statement No. 4* as follows:

Associating Cause and Effect. Some costs are recognized as expenses on the basis of a presumed direct association with specific revenue. . . . recognizing them as expenses accompanies recognition of the revenue.

Systematic and Rational Allocation. . . . If an asset provides benefits for several periods its cost is allocated to the periods in a systematic and rational manner in the absence of a more direct basis for associating cause and effect.

Immediate Recognition. Some costs are associated with the current accounting period as expenses because (1) costs incurred during the period provide no discernible future benefits, (2)

costs recorded as assets in prior periods no longer provide discernible benefits, or (3) allocating costs either on the basis of association with revenue or among several accounting periods is considered to serve no useful purpose. . . . The principle of immediate recognition also requires that items carried as assets in prior periods that are discovered to have no discernible future benefit be charged to expense, for example, a patent that is determined to be worthless.

49. As noted in paragraph 41, evidence of a direct causal relationship between current research and development expenditures and subsequent future benefits generally has not been found. Also, there is often a high degree of uncertainty about whether research and development expenditures will provide any future benefits. Thus, even an indirect cause and effect relationship can seldom be demonstrated. Because there is generally no direct or even indirect basis for relating costs to revenues, the Board believes that the principles of "associating cause and effect" and "systematic and rational allocation" cannot be applied to recognize research and development costs as expenses. That is, the notion of "matching"—when used to refer to the process of recognizing costs as expenses on any sort of cause and effect basis—cannot be applied to research and development costs. Indeed, the general lack of discernible future benefits at the time the costs are incurred indicates that the "immediate recognition" principle of expense recognition should apply.

Usefulness of Resulting Information

50. *APB Statement No. 4* indicates that certain costs are immediately recognized as expenses because allocating them to several accounting periods "is considered to serve no useful purpose." There is general agreement that two of the basic elements in the decision models of many financial statement users are (a) expected return—the predicted amount and timing of the return on an investment—and (b) risk—the variability of that expected return. The data cited in paragraphs 39-41, the views of security analysts and other professional investors submitted to the Board in connection with the public hearing, and FASB interviews with selected analysts and bankers suggest that the relationship between current research and development costs and the amount of resultant future benefits to an enterprise is so uncertain that capitalization of any research and development costs is not useful in assessing the earnings potential of the enterprise. Therefore, it is unlikely that one's ability to predict the return on an investment and the variability of that return would be enhanced by capitalization.

Capitalization of All Costs When Incurred

51. Enterprises undertake research and development activities with the hope of future benefits. If there were no such hope, the activities would not be conducted. Some persons take the position that the accounting treatment for research and development costs should be determined by considering in the aggregate all of the research and development activities of an enterprise. In their view, if there is a high probability of future benefits from an enterprise's total research and development program, the entire cost of those activities should be capitalized without regard to the certainty of future benefits from individual projects.

52. The Board believes, however, that it is not appropriate to consider accounting for research and development activities on an aggregate or total-enterprise basis for several reasons. For accounting purposes the expectation of future benefits generally is not evaluated in relation to broad categories of expenditures on an enterprise-wide basis but rather in relation to individual or related transactions or projects. Also, an enterprise's total research and development program may consist of a number of projects at varying stages of completion and with varying degrees of uncertainty as to their ultimate success. If research and development costs were capitalized on an enterprise-wide basis, a meaningful method of amortization could not be developed because the period of benefit could not be determined. Moreover, over 90 percent of the respondents to a survey reported in AICPA *Accounting Research Study No. 14* indicated that their company's philosophy is that research and development expenditures are intended to be recovered by current revenues rather than by revenue from new products.[10]

Selective Capitalization

53. Selective capitalization—capitalizing research and development costs when incurred if specified conditions are fulfilled and charging to expense all other research and development costs—requires establishment of conditions that must be fulfilled before research and development costs are capitalized. The Board considered a number of factors on which prerequisite conditions might be based, including the following:

a. *Definition of product or process.* The new or improved product or process must be defined.
b. *Technological feasibility.* The new or improved product or process must be determined to be technologically feasible.

c. *Marketability/Usefulness.* The marketability of the product or process or, if it is to be used internally rather than sold, its usefulness to the enterprise must be substantially assured.
d. *Economic feasibility.* Probability of future economic benefits sufficient to recover all capitalized costs must be high. Encompassed by the notion of economic feasibility is measurability of future benefits. Also implicit is the ability to associate particular future benefits with particular costs.
e. *Management action.* Management must have definitely decided to produce and market or use the new product or process or to incorporate the significant improvement into an existing product or process.
f. *Distortion of net income comparisons.* Capitalization or immediate charging to expense of research and development costs must be determined on the basis of whether interperiod comparisons of net income would be materially distorted.

54. None of those factors, however, lends itself to establishing a condition that could be objectively and comparably applied by all enterprises. Considerable judgment is required to identify the point in the progress of a research and development project at which a new or improved product or process is "defined" or is determined to be "technologically feasible," "marketable," or "useful." Nor can the "probability of future benefits" be readily assessed. A "management decision" to proceed with production does not necessarily assure future benefits. The Board does not believe that "distortion of net income comparisons," which a few respondents to the Discussion Memorandum suggested, is an operable criterion by which to decide whether research and development costs should be capitalized because the point at which net income comparisons might be "distorted" cannot be defined. Moreover, in assessing risk, financial statement users have indicated that they seek information about the variability of earnings.

55. The Board has concluded that no set of conditions that might be established for capitalization of costs could achieve the comparability among enterprises that proponents of "selective capitalization" cite as a primary objective of that approach.

56. If selective capitalization were applied only to costs incurred after fulfillment of the specified conditions, only a portion of the total costs of a particular research and development project would be capitalized and amortized. Thus, the capitalized amount would not indicate the total costs incurred

---

[10]Oscar S. Gellein and Maurice A. Newman, *Accounting Research Study No. 14,* "Accounting for Research and Development Expenditures" (New York: AICPA, 1973), p. 100.

to produce future benefits; nor would the amount of periodic amortization of capitalized costs represent a "matching" of costs and benefits.

57. Selective capitalization might involve retroactive capitalization of previously incurred costs in addition to capitalization of costs incurred after fulfillment of the specified conditions. However, many research and development costs incurred before fulfillment of the conditions are not likely to be directly identifiable with the particular new or improved product or process for which costs would be capitalized. Moreover, retroactive capitalization of costs previously charged to expense is contrary to present accounting practice for other transactions whose initial accounting is not altered as a result of hindsight. The preparation of periodic financial statements requires many estimates and judgments for which restatements are not made in retrospect.

Accumulation of Costs in a Special Category

58. The Board considered the proposal that all research and development costs be accumulated in a special category distinct from assets and expenses until a determination can be made about whether future benefits exist. That special category might be reported either below the asset section of the balance sheet (with segregation of a corresponding amount of stockholders' equity) or as a negative (contra) element of stockholders' equity. Ultimately, the accumulated costs would be transferred to assets (if future benefits become reasonably established) or written off (if it were reasonably established that no significant future benefits would ensue).

59. A feature cited by proponents of this approach is that it draws attention to the uncertainty surrounding most research and development costs and it enables postponement of the capitalize vs. expense decision. This alternative was rejected, however, for the following reasons. First, financial analysts and others have indicated that costs accumulated in that special category would not be useful in assessing the earning power of an enterprise because of the uncertainties involved, and the research data cited earlier tend to support that view. Second, use of a special category would alter the nature of the basic financial statements and would complicate the computation of ratios and other financial data.

DISCLOSURE

60. Regardless of their position on the accounting treatment for research and development costs, respondents to the Discussion Memorandum generally pointed out that current disclosure practices for research and development costs vary and that

requirements for informative disclosure need to be established. The disclosures specified in paragraphs 13-14 reflect the Board's general agreement with that view.

61. The Exposure Draft had proposed that disclosure also be required of (a) the accounting policy for research and development costs, (b) the amount of directly reimbursable research and development costs incurred, (c) the costs of research and development conducted in behalf of the enterprise by others, and (d) the amounts and classifications in the income statement of research and development costs charged to expense during the period. The Board has accepted the recommendation of some respondents to the Exposure Draft that disclosure of accounting policy not be required[11] because this Statement permits only one method of accounting for research and development costs. Some letters of comment on the Exposure Draft indicated that data related to items (b), (c), and (d) above are frequently difficult to obtain and that those disclosures generally would not be meaningful. The Board agrees with this view; this Statement does not require those disclosures.

62. The Board recognizes that disclosure of additional information about an enterprise's research and development activities might be useful to some financial statement users. However, many respondents to the Discussion Memorandum contended that certain kinds of information should not be required to be included in financial statements because the information is not sufficiently objective, is confidential in nature, or is beyond the scope of financial accounting information. For that reason, the Board concluded that disclosure of (a) the nature, status, and costs of individual research and development projects, (b) the nature and status of patents, (c) projections about new or improved products or processes, and (d) an enterprise's philosophy regarding research and development, all of which were included in the Discussion Memorandum as disclosure possibilities, should not be required. In addition, most respondents said that forecasts of research and development expenditures should not be considered in this project, and the Board agrees with that view. Disclosure of research and development costs by line of business is a matter included in "Financial Reporting for Segments of a Business Enterprise," another project presently on the Board's agenda.

EFFECTIVE DATE AND TRANSITION

63. The Board considered three alternative approaches to reporting a change in the method of accounting for research and development costs: (1)

---

[11]That disclosure is required by this Statement for certain government-regulated enterprises (see paragraph 14).

prior period adjustment, (2) the "cumulative effect" method described in *APB Opinion No. 20*, "Accounting Changes," and (3) continued amortization of previously capitalized costs. The Board concluded that the prior period adjustment method will provide the most useful information about research and development costs for comparing financial data for periods after the effective date of this Statement with data presented for earlier periods.

64. Upon consideration of all circumstances, the Board judged that the effective date specified in paragraph 15, which had been proposed in the Exposure Draft, is advisable.

Statement of Financial Accounting Standards No. 3
Reporting Accounting Changes in
Interim Financial Statements

an amendment of APB Opinion No. 28

STATUS

Issued: December 1974

Effective Date: For interim periods ending on or after December 31, 1974

Affects: Amends APB 28, paragraph 31
Supersedes APB 28, paragraph 27 and footnote 5

Affected by: No other pronouncements

Statement of Financial Accounting Standards No. 3
Reporting Accounting Changes in Interim Financial Statements

an amendment of APB Opinion No. 28

CONTENTS

INTRODUCTION AND BACKGROUND INFORMATION

1. As a result of numerous inquiries concerning the appropriate procedures for reporting a change to the LIFO method of inventory pricing in interim financial reports, the FASB has examined certain conclusions of *APB Opinion No. 28,* "Interim Financial Reporting," with respect to two aspects of reporting accounting changes in interim financial reports:

a. Reporting a cumulative effect type accounting change (as described in *APB Opinion No. 20,* "Accounting Changes") including a change to the LIFO method of inventory pricing for which a cumulative effect cannot be determined.

b. Reporting an accounting change made during the fourth quarter of a fiscal year by a company whose securities are publicly traded.

2. *APB Opinion No. 28* became effective for interim periods relating to fiscal years beginning on or after January 1, 1974, and paragraphs 23-29 of that Opinion set forth standards for reporting accounting changes in interim financial reports. Those paragraphs provide that, in general, an accounting change made in an interim period should be reported in accordance with the provisions of *APB Opinion No. 20.*

3. Paragraphs 9-14 of this Statement establish standards of financial accounting and reporting that address the matters identified in paragraph 1. The Appendices to this Statement contain examples of application of *APB Opinion No. 28* (as amended by this Statement) and the requirements of *APB Opinion No. 20* as they are incorporated by reference in *APB Opinion No. 28.*

4. An Exposure Draft of a proposed Statement on "Reporting Accounting Changes in Interim Financial Statements" was issued on November 11, 1974. Fifty-five letters were received in response to the request for comments. This Statement incorporates a number of changes suggested by those respondents. The principal change is to require that, if an accounting change is made in other than the first interim period of an enterprise's fiscal year, the cumulative effect of the change on retained earnings at the beginning of that year shall be included in the determination of net income of the first interim period of the year of change (by restatement of that period's financial information).

5. The Board has concluded that it can make an informed decision on the matters identified in paragraph 1 of this Statement without a public hearing. It has also concluded that the effective date in paragraph 16 of this Statement is advisable to permit application of the provisions of this Statement before divergent interpretations of *APB Opinion No. 28* develop in practice.

Cumulative Effect Type Accounting Changes

6. Paragraph 27 of *APB Opinion No. 28* provides that "a change in accounting principle or practice adopted in an interim period that requires an adjustment for the cumulative effect of the change to the beginning of the current fiscal year should be reported in the interim period in a manner similar to that to be followed in the annual report. . . . The effect of the change from the beginning of the annual period to the period of change should be reported as a determinant of net income in the interim period in which the change is made." That paragraph goes on to require, however, that when information is subsequently presented for the period in which the change is made or for pre-change interim periods of that year, that information should be restated to give effect to the accounting change.

7. As a result of those requirements, if a cumulative effect type accounting change is made, the cumulative effect of the change on retained earnings at the beginning of that fiscal year is a component of net income of the interim period in which the change is adopted. If a change is made in other than the first interim period, since the cumulative effect remains a component of that interim period's income when financial information for that period is subsequently reported, reissued pre-change interim period balance sheets would not reflect the cumulative effect of the change on retained earnings at the beginning of the fiscal year on a retroactive basis, whereas reissued pre-change interim period income statements would be restated. In addition, an enterprise may issue interim financial information knowing that the information will subsequently have to be revised. For example, during the second quarter of its fiscal year an enterprise may make an accounting change as of the beginning of that quarter. If, subsequently during that second quarter, the enterprise issues first quarter financial information (perhaps in a report to its securityholders, in a report to a bank, or in a filing with the SEC), that first quarter information would be prepared on the basis of the old accounting principle—not the newly adopted one. When that enterprise later issues second quarter information, both the cumulative effect of the change up to the beginning of the fiscal year and the effect from the beginning of the second quarter would be included in the determination of second quarter net income. However, in any subsequent report that separately presents information either for that first quarter or that second quarter, the first quarter information would be retroactively restated on the basis of the newly adopted accounting principle, and the effect of the change from the beginning of the year to the beginning of the second quarter would no longer be included in second quarter net income. Thus the enterprise issued both first and second quarter information that had to be restated in subsequent periods. A similar situation arises if the accounting change were made during the third or fourth quarters.

Fourth Quarter Accounting Changes Made by Publicly Traded Companies

8. Paragraphs 30-33 of *APB Opinion No. 28* set forth special requirements for disclosure of summarized financial data by publicly traded companies (as defined in footnote 1 to that Opinion). Some publicly traded companies are required by paragraph 31 of the Opinion to disclose certain fourth quarter information in a note to the annual financial statements. Information about the effects of an accounting change made during the fourth quarter is not explicitly identified as one of the items for which disclosure is required.

STANDARDS OF FINANCIAL ACCOUNTING AND REPORTING

Cumulative Effect Type Accounting Changes Other Than Changes to LIFO

9. If a cumulative effect type accounting change is made during the *first* interim period of an enterprise's fiscal year, the cumulative effect of the change on retained earnings at the *beginning of that fiscal year* shall be included in net income of the first interim period (and in last-twelve-months-to-date financial reports that include that first interim period).

10. If a cumulative effect type accounting change is made in *other than the first* interim period of an enterprise's fiscal year, *no* cumulative effect of the change shall be included in net income of the period of change. Instead, financial information for the pre-change interim periods of the fiscal year in which the change is made shall be restated by applying the newly adopted accounting principle to those pre-change interim periods. The cumulative effect of the change on retained earnings at the *beginning of that fiscal year* shall be included in restated net income of the first interim period of the fiscal year in which the change is made (and in any year-to-date or last-twelve-months-to-date financial reports that include the first interim period). Whenever financial information that includes those pre-change interim periods is presented, it shall be presented on the restated basis.

11. The following disclosures about a cumulative effect type accounting change shall be made in interim financial reports:

a. In financial reports for the interim period in which the new accounting principle is adopted, disclosure shall be made of the nature of and justification for the change.

b. In financial reports for the interim period in which the new accounting principle is adopted, disclosure shall be made of the effect of the change on income from continuing operations, net income, and related per share amounts for the interim period in which the change is made. In addition, when the change is made in other than the first interim period of a fiscal year, financial reports for the period of change shall also disclose (i) the effect of the change on income from continuing operations, net income, and related per share amounts for each pre-change interim period of that fiscal year and (ii) income from continuing operations, net income, and related per share amounts for each pre-change interim period restated in accordance with paragraph 10 of this Statement.

c. In financial reports for the interim period in

which the new accounting principle is adopted, disclosure shall be made of income from continuing operations, net income, and related per share amounts computed on a pro forma basis for (i) the interim period in which the change is made and (ii) any interim periods of prior fiscal years for which financial information is being presented. If no financial information for interim periods of prior fiscal years is being presented, disclosure shall be made, in the period of change, of the actual and pro forma amounts of income from continuing operations, net income, and related per share amounts for the interim period of the immediately preceding fiscal year that corresponds to the interim period in which the change is made. In all cases, the pro forma amounts shall be computed and presented in conformity with paragraphs 19, 21, 22, and 25 of *APB Opinion No. 20*.

d. In year-to-date and last-twelve-months-to-date financial reports that include the interim period in which the new accounting principle is adopted, the disclosures specified in the first sentence of subparagraph (b) above and in subparagraph (c) above shall be made.

e. In financial reports for a subsequent (postchange) interim period of the fiscal year in which the new accounting principle is adopted, disclosure shall be made of the effect of the change on income from continuing operations, net income, and related per share amounts for that postchange interim period.

Changes to the LIFO Method of Inventory Pricing and Similar Situations

12. Paragraph 26 of *APB Opinion No. 20* indicates that in rare situations—principally a change to the LIFO method of inventory pricing[1]—neither the cumulative effect of the change on retained earnings at the beginning of the fiscal year in which the change is made nor the pro forma amounts can be computed. In those situations, that paragraph requires an explanation of the reasons for omitting (a) accounting for a cumulative effect and (b) disclosure of pro forma amounts for prior years. If a change of that type is made in the *first* interim period of an enterprise's fiscal year, the disclosures specified in paragraph 11 of this Statement shall be

made (except the pro forma amounts for interim periods of prior fiscal years called for by paragraph 11(c) will not be disclosed).

13. If the change is made in *other than* the first interim period of an enterprise's fiscal year, the disclosure specified in paragraph 11 of this Statement shall be made (except the pro forma amounts for interim periods of prior fiscal years called for by paragraph 11(c) will not be disclosed) and in addition, financial information for the pre-change interim periods of that fiscal year shall be restated by applying the newly adopted accounting principle to those pre-change interim periods. Whenever financial information that includes those prechange interim periods is presented, it shall be presented on the restated basis.

Fourth Quarter Accounting Changes Made by Publicly Traded Companies

14. When a publicly traded company that regularly reports interim information to its securityholders makes an accounting change during the fourth quarter of its fiscal year and does not report the data specified by paragraph 30 of *APB Opinion No. 28* in a separate fourth quarter report or in its annual report[2] to its securityholders, the disclosures about the effect of the accounting change on interim periods that are required by paragraphs 23-26 of *APB Opinion No. 28* or by paragraphs 9-13 of this Statement, as appropriate, shall be made in a note to the annual financial statements for the fiscal year in which the change is made.

Amendments to Existing Pronouncement

15. Paragraph 27 of *APB Opinion No. 28* is superseded by paragraphs 9-13 of this Statement. Paragraph 31 of that Opinion is amended by this Statement to require the additional disclosures set forth in paragraph 14.

Effective Date

16. The provisions of this Statement shall apply to accounting changes made in interim periods ending on or after December 31, 1974.

The provisions of this Statement need not be applied to immaterial items.

---

[1] In making disclosures about changes to the LIFO method, enterprises should be aware of the limitations the Internal Revenue Service has placed on such disclosures.
[2] See footnote 1.

This Statement was adopted by the unanimous vote of the seven members of the Financial Accounting Standards Board:

Marshall S. Armstrong,	Arthur L. Litke	Walter Schuetze
Chairman	Robert E. Mays	Robert T. Sprouse
Donald J. Kirk	John W. Queenan	

Appendix A

REPORTING A CUMULATIVE EFFECT TYPE ACCOUNTING CHANGE (OTHER THAN A CHANGE TO LIFO)

The following are examples of application of *APB Opinion No. 28* (as amended by this Statement) and the requirements of *APB Opinion No. 20* as they are incorporated by reference in *APB Opinion No. 28*. The examples do not encompass all possible circumstances and are not intended to indicate the Board's preference for a particular format.

FACTS

In the year 19x5, ABC Company decides to adopt the straight-line method of depreciation for plant equipment. The straight-line method will be used for new acquisitions as well as for previously acquired plant equipment for which depreciation had been provided on an accelerated method.

These examples assume that the effects of the change are limited to the effect on depreciation, incentive compensation, and related income tax provisions and that the effect on inventories is not material. The pro forma amounts have been adjusted for an assumed 10% pre-tax effect of the change on the provisions for incentive compensation and an assumed 50% income tax rate. The per share amounts are computed assuming that throughout the two years 19x4 and 19x5, 1,000,000 shares of common stock were issued and outstanding with no potential dilution. Other data assumed for these examples are:

Period	Net Income on the Basis of Old Accounting Principle (Accelerated Depreciation)	Gross Effect of Change to Straight-Line Depreciation	Gross Effect Less Income Taxes	Net Effect After Incentive Compensation and Related Income Taxes
Prior to first quarter 19x4		$20,000	$10,000	$9,000
First quarter 19x4	$1,000,000	30,000	15,000	13,500
Second quarter 19x4	1,200,000	70,000	35,000	31,500
Third quarter 19x4	1,100,000	50,000	25,000	22,500
Fourth quarter 19x4	1,100,000	80,000	40,000	36,000
Total at beginning of 19x5	$4,400,000	$250,000	$125,000	$112,500
First quarter 19x5	$1,059,500	$90,000	$45,000	$40,500
Second quarter 19x5	1,255,000	100,000	50,000	45,000
Third quarter 19x5	1,150,500	110,000	55,000	49,500
Fourth quarter 19x5	1,146,000	120,000	60,000	54,000
	$4,611,000	$420,000	$210,000	$189,000

EXAMPLE 1

The change in depreciation method is made in the first quarter of 19x5. The manner of reporting the change in the first quarter of 19x5, with comparative information for the first quarter of 19x4, is as follows:

	Three Months Ended March 31,	
	19x5	**19x4**
Income before cumulative effect of a change in accounting principle	$1,100,000	$1,000,000
Cumulative effect on prior years (to December 31, 19x4) of changing to a different depreciation method (Note A)	125,000	
Net income	$1,225,000	$1,000,000
Amounts per common share:		
Income before cumulative effect of a change in accounting principle	$1.10	$1.00
Cumulative effect on prior years (to December 31, 19x4) of changing to a different depreciation method (Note A)	.13	
Net income	$1.23	$1.00
Pro forma amounts assuming the new depreciation method is applied retroactively (Note A):		
Net income	$1,100,000	$1,013,500
Net income per common share	$1.10	$1.01

NOTE A: Change in Depreciation Method for Plant Equipment

In the first quarter of 19x5, the method of computing depreciation of plant equipment was changed from the . . . (state previous method) . . . used in prior years, to the straight-line method . . . (state justification for the change in method) . . . and the new method has been applied to equipment acquisitions of prior years. The $125,000 cumulative effect of the change on prior years (after reduction for income taxes of $125,000) is included in income of the first quarter of 19x5. The effect of the change on the first quarter of 19x5 was to increase income before cumulative effect of a change in accounting principle $40,500 ($.04 per share) and net income $165,500 ($.17 per share). The pro forma amounts reflect the effect of retroactive application on depreciation, the change in provisions for incentive compensation that would have been made in 19x4 had the new method been in effect, and related income taxes.

EXAMPLE 2

Assume the same facts as in Example 1, except that the change is made in the third quarter of 19x5.

The manner of reporting the change in the third quarter of 19x5, with year-to-date information and comparative information for similar periods of 19x4, is as follows:

	Three Months Ended September 30,		Nine Months Ended September 30,	
	19x5	**19x4**	**19x5**	**19x4**
Income before cumulative effect of a change in accounting principle	$1,200,000	$1,100,000	$3,600,000	$3,300,000
Cumulative effect on prior years (to December 31, 19x4) of changing to a different depreciation method (Note A)			125,000	
Net income	$1,200,000	$1,100,000	$3,725,000	$3,300,000
Amounts per common share:				
Income before cumulative effect of a change in accounting principle	$1.20	$1.10	$3.60	$3.30
Cumulative effect on prior years (to December 31, 19x4) of changing to a different depreciation method (Note A)			.13	
Net income	$1.20	$1.10	$3.73	$3.30
Pro forma amounts assuming the new depreciation method is applied retroactively (Note A):				
Net income	$1,200,000	$1,122,500	$3,600,000	$3,367,500
Net income per common share	$1.20	$1.12	$3.60	$3.37

24

The effect of the change on the first and second quarters of 19x5 is as follows:

	Three Months Ended	
	March 31, 19x5	**June 30, 19x5**
Net income as originally reported*	$1,095,500	$1,295,000
Effect of change to LIFO method of inventory pricing	(40,500)	(45,000)
Net income as restated	$1,055,000	$1,250,000
Per share amounts:		
Net income as originally reported*	$1.10	$1.30
Effect of change to LIFO method of inventory pricing	(.04)	(.05)
Net income as restated	$1.06	$1.25

*Disclosure of net income as originally reported is not required.

Statement of Financial Accounting Standards No. 4
Reporting Gains and Losses from Extinguishment of Debt

an amendment of APB Opinion No. 30

STATUS

Issued: March 1975

Effective Date: For extinguishments after March 31, 1975

Affects: Amends APB 26, paragraph 20
Amends APB 30, paragraph 20

Affected by: Paragraph 7 superseded by FAS 71
Paragraph 8 and footnote 2 amended by FAS 64

Other Interpretive Pronouncement: FTB 80-1

Issues Discussed by FASB Emerging Issues Task Force (EITF)

Affects: No EITF Issues

Interpreted by: Paragraph 8 interpreted by EITF Issue No. 95-15

Related Issues: EITF Issues No. 86-15 and 90-19

Statement of Financial Accounting Standards No. 4
Reporting Gains and Losses from Extinguishment of Debt

an amendment of APB Opinion No. 30

CONTENTS

INTRODUCTION AND BACKGROUND INFORMATION

1. *APB Opinion No. 26,* "Early Extinguishment of Debt," became effective for extinguishment of debt occurring on or after January 1, 1973. Paragraph 19 of that Opinion states "that all extinguishments of debt before scheduled maturities are fundamentally alike. The accounting for such transactions should be the same regardless of the means used to achieve the extinguishment." Paragraph 20 of the same Opinion states that "a difference between the reacquisition price and the net carrying amount of the extinguished debt should be recognized currently in income of the period of extinguishment as losses or gains and identified as a separate item.... The criteria in *APB Opinion No. 9* ['Reporting the Results of Operations'] should be used to determine whether the losses or gains are ordinary or extraordinary items. Gains and losses should not be amortized to future periods."

2. *APB Opinion No. 30,* "Reporting the Results of Operations," became effective for events and transactions occurring after September 30, 1973 and superseded *APB Opinion No. 9* with respect to the determination of extraordinary items. *APB Opinion No. 30* and the related Accounting Interpretation issued by the AICPA staff (see *The Journal of Accountancy,* November 1973, pages 82-84) can be read literally to preclude classifying most if not all gains or losses from early extinguishment of debt as an extraordinary item in the income statement. The Board has observed that in those cases coming to its attention where a gain or loss from early extinguish-

ment of debt has been reported in an income statement to which *APB Opinion No. 30* was applicable, the gain or loss was included in income before extraordinary items.

3. Since the effective date of *APB Opinion No. 30,* the Board has had inquiries regarding that Opinion because application of the criteria, especially as illustrated in the related AICPA Accounting Interpretation, appears to preclude classifying gains or losses from most transactions or events as extraordinary items in the income statement. Many respondents to the Board's July 12, 1973 request for views concerning APB Opinions and Accounting Research Bulletins suggested that the conclusions of *APB Opinion No. 26* relating to *early* extinguishment of debt be reconsidered. Since that time, concern also has been expressed to the Board with respect to the accounting for extinguishment of debt at its *scheduled maturity date or later* because the authoritative accounting pronouncements do not address that issue. In addition, the Securities and Exchange Commission and others have expressed concern to the Board about including gains and losses from extinguishment of debt in the determination of income before extraordinary items in the income statement.

4. The Board considered carefully the suggestions that *APB Opinion No. 26* be reconsidered and concluded that the issues extend beyond *APB Opinion No. 26* and could involve *APB Opinion No. 14,* "Accounting for Convertible Debt and Debt Issued with Stock Purchase Warrants," and *APB Opinion No. 21,* "Interest on Receivables and Payables,"

and could extend to exchanges or sales and related purchases of similar monetary assets. The Board concluded that the pervasiveness of those issues makes broad reconsideration of all these Opinions and the other related issues a more comprehensive undertaking than can be accomplished in the near future. The Board also considered carefully the questions raised with respect to *APB Opinion No. 30* and concluded that there is insufficient experience under that Opinion to warrant a general reconsideration of the criteria set forth therein at this time.

5. Prior to the issuance of the Exposure Draft of this Statement, the Board had been considering an Interpretation of *APB Opinion No. 26* that would have specified disclosure requirements regarding gains and losses from extinguishment of debt, but that course of action was changed when it became clear to the Board that the income statement classification of gains or losses on extinguishment of debt also required attention. The Board believes that an immediate response is needed to the concern expressed regarding income statement classification of gains and losses from certain extinguishments of debt. Further, the Board continues to believe that guidelines are needed regarding disclosures related to certain debt extinguishments because a review of a number of financial statements by the FASB staff indicates that disclosures often have been unclear, particularly with regard to the income tax effects.

6. The Board has concluded that on the basis of existing data it can make an informed decision on the narrow issues identified in paragraph 5 without a public hearing and that the effective date and transition requirements set forth in paragraphs 11 and 12 are advisable.

7. This Statement applies to regulated enterprises in accordance with the provisions of the Addendum to *APB Opinion No. 2*, "Accounting for the 'Investment Credit.'"

STANDARDS OF FINANCIAL ACCOUNTING AND REPORTING

Income Statement Classification

8. Gains and losses from extinguishment of debt that are included in the determination of net income shall be aggregated and, if material,[1] classified as an extraordinary item, net of related income tax effect.

That conclusion shall apply whether an extinguishment is early or at scheduled maturity date or later. The conclusion does not apply, however, to gains or losses from cash purchases of debt made to satisfy current or future sinking-fund requirements.[2] Those gains and losses shall be aggregated and the amount shall be identified as a separate item.

Disclosure

9. Gains or losses from extinguishment of debt that are classified as extraordinary items should be described sufficiently to enable users of financial statements to evaluate their significance. Accordingly, the following information, to the extent not shown separately on the face of the income statement, shall be disclosed in a single note to the financial statements or adequately cross-referenced if in more than one note:

a. A description of the extinguishment transactions, including the sources of any funds used to extinguish debt if it is practicable to identify the sources.
b. The income tax effect in the period of extinguishment.
c. The per share amount of the aggregate gain or loss net of related income tax effect.

Amendment to Existing Pronouncement

10. This Statement amends *APB Opinion No. 30* only to the extent that classification of gains or losses from extinguishment of debt as an extraordinary item pursuant to the first two sentences of paragraph 8 of this Statement shall be made without regard to the criteria in paragraph 20 of that Opinion.

Effective Date and Transition

11. This Statement shall be effective for extinguishments occurring after March 31, 1975, except that it need not be applied to extinguishments occurring on or after April 1, 1975 pursuant to the terms of an offer or other commitment made prior to that date. Application to *all* extinguishments occurring during a fiscal year in which April 1, 1975 falls is encouraged. Retroactive application to extinguishments occurring in prior fiscal years is encouraged but not required.

12. Although the requirements of this Statement may be applied retroactively, such application is not

---

[1]See the first sentence of paragraph 24 of *APB Opinion No. 30*.

[2]Some obligations to acquire debt have the essential characteristics of sinking-fund requirements, and resulting gains or losses are not required to be classified as extraordinary items. For example, if an enterprise is required each year to purchase a certain percentage of its outstanding bonds before their scheduled maturity, the gain or loss from such purchase is not required to be classified as an extraordinary item. Debt maturing serially, however, does not have the characteristics of sinking-fund requirements, and gain or loss from extinguishment of serial debt shall be classified as an extraordinary item.

intended to change the accounting for amounts deferred on refundings of debt that occurred prior to the effective date of *APB Opinion No. 26* or the income statement classification of the amortization of those amounts.

> **The provisions of this Statement need not be applied to immaterial items.**

This Statement was adopted by the affirmative votes of six members of the Financial Accounting Standards Board. Mr. Kirk dissented.

Mr. Kirk dissents because he believes that extinguishments of debt are reportable transactions that seldom, if ever, warrant extraordinary item treatment. In many cases, extinguishments are neither unusual nor infrequent. In most cases, they are certainly no more extraordinary than other infrequent gains or losses for which *APB Opinion No. 30* prohibits extraordinary item classification. That Opinion sharply restricted—for good reasons—the types of gains and losses that may be identified as extraordinary items and reported on a net-of-tax basis, and Mr. Kirk can see no inherent characteristic of debt extinguishments that justifies overriding the criteria in *APB Opinion No. 30.* He believes that disclosures, like those required by paragraph 20 of *APB Opinion No. 26* and paragraph 26 of *APB Opinion No. 30,* are sufficient to prevent a financial statement user from being misled. In his view, accounting standards cannot satisfy everyone's perception of economic reality, but they should at least be logically consistent in their result. Mr. Kirk believes that this Statement fails in that regard and may well encourage piecemeal erosion of *APB Opinion No. 30.*

Members of the Financial Accounting Standards Board:

Marshall S. Armstrong,	Donald J. Kirk	Walter Schuetze
Chairman	Arthur L. Litke	Robert T. Sprouse
Oscar S. Gellein	Robert E. Mays	

Appendix A

SUMMARY OF CONSIDERATION OF COMMENTS ON EXPOSURE DRAFT

13. In response to the request for comments on the Exposure Draft issued January 31, 1975, the FASB received and considered 120 letters in its deliberations on this Statement. Certain of the comments and the FASB's consideration of them are summarized in paragraphs 14-17.

14. For a variety of reasons, many respondents recommended that the FASB not adopt the Exposure Draft as a final Statement. Some respondents recommended that *APB Opinion No. 26* and related issues be reconsidered. Others recommended that the criteria for determining extraordinary items as set forth in *APB Opinion No. 30* be reconsidered. The Board concluded not to address these issues for the reasons stated in paragraph 4.

15. Some respondents suggested that the proposals in the Exposure Draft, if adopted, would result in erosion of the criteria in *APB Opinion No. 30* for determining extraordinary items. However, this Statement is neither an amendment nor an interpretation of the criteria for classifying and reporting an event or transaction as an extraordinary item as set forth in paragraph 20 of that Opinion. Rather, the Board is proscribing the application of those criteria to certain extinguishments of debt in the same way that the application of those criteria has been proscribed with respect to the realization of tax benefits from an operating loss carryforward and to certain profits or losses resulting from the disposal of a significant part of the assets or a separable segment acquired in a business combination accounted for as a pooling of interests.[3] The Board recognizes that the application of the criteria in *APB Opinion No. 30* to extinguishments of debt would seldom, if ever, require that resulting gains and losses be classified as extraordinary items. In issuing this Statement requiring that a gain or loss from certain debt extinguishments be classified as an extraordinary item in the income statement, the Board is neither modifying the criteria set forth in that Opinion nor intending to start a piecemeal revision of those criteria. Although as a result of this Statement questions may be raised regarding the application of the criteria for determining extraordinary items pursuant to *APB Opinion No. 30,* the Board has concluded that, on balance, this Statement represents a practical and reasonable solution to the question regarding income statement classification of gains or losses

---

[3]See paragraph 7 of *APB Opinion No. 30.*

from extinguishment of debt until such time as the broader issues involved can be addressed.

16. Many respondents argued that gains and losses from extinguishment of debt pursuant to sinking-fund requirements should not be required to be classified as extraordinary items. The Board agrees primarily because acquisitions for sinking-fund purposes are made to meet continuing contractual requirements assumed in connection with the incur-

rence of the debt.

17. In addition to the fact that many respondents recommended that the Exposure Draft not be issued as a final Statement, some respondents objected to the proposal that the Statement be applied retroactively. On further consideration of all the circumstances, the Board concluded that application of the Statement should be required only on a prospective basis although retroactive application is encouraged.

Statement of Financial Accounting Standards No. 5
Accounting for Contingencies

STATUS

Issued: March 1975

Effective Date: For fiscal years beginning on or after July 1, 1975

Affects: Supersedes ARB 43, Chapter 6
Supersedes ARB 50

Affected by: Paragraph 7 amended by FAS 87, FAS 112, and FAS 123
Paragraph 13 superseded by FAS 71
Paragraph 18 amended by FAS 111
Paragraph 20 amended by FAS 11
Paragraph 23 amended by FAS 114
Paragraphs 41 and 102 amended by FAS 60
Paragraph 44 amended by FAS 113
Footnote 3 superseded by FAS 16

Other Interpretive Pronouncements: FIN 14
FIN 34

Issues Discussed by FASB Emerging Issues Task Force (EITF)

Affects: No EITF Issues

Interpreted by: Paragraph 8 interpreted by EITF Issues No. 87-22 and 92-13 and Topics No. D-47 and D-57
Paragraph 9 interpreted by EITF Issue No. 92-13
Paragraph 45 interpreted by EITF Issue No. 93-14

Related Issues: EITF Issues No. 86-12, 91-10, 93-6, 94-3, 95-14, and 97-1 and Topic No. D-35

Statement of Financial Accounting Standards No. 5
Accounting for Contingencies

CONTENTS

INTRODUCTION

1. For the purpose of this Statement, a contingency is defined as an existing condition, situation, or set of circumstances involving uncertainty as to possible gain (hereinafter a "gain contingency") or loss[1] (hereinafter a "loss contingency") to an enterprise that will ultimately be resolved when one or more future events occur or fail to occur. Resolution of the uncertainty may confirm the acquisition of an asset or the reduction of a liability or the loss or impairment of an asset or the incurrence of a liability.

2. Not all uncertainties inherent in the accounting process give rise to contingencies as that term is used in this Statement. Estimates are required in financial statements for many on-going and recurring activities of an enterprise. The mere fact that an estimate is involved does not of itself constitute the type of uncertainty referred to in the definition in paragraph 1. For example, the fact that estimates are used to allocate the known cost of a depreciable asset over the period of use by an enterprise does not make depreciation a contingency; the eventual expiration of the utility of the asset is not uncertain. Thus, depreciation of assets is not a contingency as defined in paragraph 1, nor are such matters as recurring repairs, maintenance, and overhauls, which interrelate with depreciation. Also, amounts owed for services received, such as advertising and utilities, are not contingencies even though the accrued amounts may have been esti-

mated; there is nothing uncertain about the fact that those obligations have been incurred.

3. When a loss contingency exists, the likelihood that the future event or events will confirm the loss or impairment of an asset or the incurrence of a liability can range from probable to remote. This Statement uses the terms *probable, reasonably possible,* and *remote* to identify three areas within that range, as follows:

a. *Probable.* The future event or events are likely to occur.
b. *Reasonably possible.* The chance of the future event or events occurring is more than remote but less than likely.
c. *Remote.* The chance of the future event or events occurring is slight.

4. Examples of loss contingencies include:

a. Collectibility of receivables.
b. Obligations related to product warranties and product defects.
c. Risk of loss or damage of enterprise property by fire, explosion, or other hazards.
d. Threat of expropriation of assets.
e. Pending or threatened litigation.
f. Actual or possible claims and assessments.
g. Risk of loss from catastrophes assumed by property and casualty insurance companies including reinsurance companies.
h. Guarantees of indebtedness of others.

---

[1] The term *loss* is used for convenience to include many charges against income that are commonly referred to as *expenses* and others that are commonly referred to as *losses.*

i. Obligations of commercial banks under "standby letters of credit."[2]

j. Agreements to repurchase receivables (or to repurchase the related property) that have been sold.

5. Some enterprises now accrue estimated losses from some types of contingencies by a charge to income prior to the occurrence of the event or events that are expected to resolve the uncertainties while, under similar circumstances, other enterprises account for those losses only when the confirming event or events have occurred.

6. This Statement establishes standards of financial accounting and reporting for loss contingencies (see paragraphs 8-16) and carries forward without reconsideration the conclusions of *Accounting Research Bulletin (ARB) No. 50,* "Contingencies," with respect to gain contingencies (see paragraph 17) and other disclosures (see paragraphs 18-19). The basis for the Board's conclusions, as well as alternatives considered and reasons for their rejection, are discussed in Appendix C. Examples of application of this Statement are presented in Appendix A, and background information is presented in Appendix B.

7. This Statement supersedes both *ARB No. 50* and Chapter 6, "Contingency Reserves," of *ARB No. 43.* The conditions for accrual of loss contingencies in paragraph 8 of this Statement do not amend any other present requirement in an Accounting Research Bulletin or Opinion of the Accounting Principles Board to accrue a particular type of loss or expense. Thus, for example, accounting for pension cost, deferred compensation contracts, and stock issued to employees are excluded from the scope of this Statement. Those matters are covered, respectively, in *APB Opinion No. 8,* "Accounting for the Cost of Pension Plans," *APB Opinion No. 12,* "Omnibus Opinion—1967," paragraphs 6-8, and *APB Opinion No. 25,* "Accounting for Stock Issued to Employees." Accounting for other employment-related costs, such as group insurance, vacation pay, workmen's compensation, and disability benefits, is also excluded from the scope of this Statement. Accounting practices for those types of costs and pension accounting practices tend to involve similar considerations.

STANDARDS OF FINANCIAL ACCOUNTING AND REPORTING

Accrual of Loss Contingencies

8. An estimated loss from a loss contingency (as defined in paragraph 1) shall be accrued by a charge to income[3] if *both* of the following conditions are met:

a. Information available prior to issuance of the financial statements indicates that it is probable that an asset had been impaired or a liability had been incurred at the date of the financial statements.[4] It is implicit in this condition that it must be probable that one or more future events will occur confirming the fact of the loss.

b. The amount of loss can be reasonably estimated.

Disclosure of Loss Contingencies

9. Disclosure of the nature of an accrual[5] made pursuant to the provisions of paragraph 8, and in some circumstances the amount accrued, may be necessary for the financial statements not to be misleading.

10. If no accrual is made for a loss contingency because one or both of the conditions in paragraph 8 are not met, or if an exposure to loss exists in excess of the amount accrued pursuant to the provisions of paragraph 8, disclosure of the contingency shall be made when there is at least a reasonable possibility that a loss or an additional loss may have

---

[2]As defined by the Federal Reserve Board, "standby letters of credit" include "every letter of credit (or similar arrangement however named or designated) which represents an obligation to the beneficiary on the part of the issuer (1) to repay money borrowed by or advanced to or for the account of the account party or (2) to make payment on account of any evidence of indebtedness undertaken by the account party or (3) to make payment on account of any default by the account party in the performance of an obligation." A note to that definition states that "as defined, 'standby letter of credit' would not include (1) commercial letters of credit and similar instruments where the issuing bank expects the beneficiary to draw upon the issuer and which do not 'guaranty' payment of a money obligation or (2) a guaranty or similar obligation issued by a foreign branch in accordance with and subject to the limitations of Regulation M [of the Federal Reserve Board]." Regulations of the Comptroller of the Currency and the Federal Deposit Insurance Corporation contain similar definitions.

[3]Paragraphs 23-24 of *APB Opinion No. 9,* "Reporting the Results of Operations," describe the "rare" circumstances in which a prior period adjustment is appropriate. Those paragraphs are not amended by this Statement.

[4]*Date of the financial statements* means the end of the most recent accounting period for which financial statements are being presented.

[5]Terminology used shall be descriptive of the nature of the accrual (see paragraphs 57-64 of *Accounting Terminology Bulletin No. 1,* "Review and Resume").

been incurred.[6] The disclosure shall indicate the nature of the contingency and shall give an estimate of the possible loss or range of loss or state that such an estimate cannot be made. Disclosure is not required of a loss contingency involving an unasserted claim or assessment when there has been no manifestation by a potential claimant of an awareness of a possible claim or assessment unless it is considered probable that a claim will be asserted and there is a reasonable possibility that the outcome will be unfavorable.

11. After the date of an enterprise's financial statements but before those financial statements are issued, information may become available indicating that an asset was impaired or a liability was incurred after the date of the financial statements or that there is at least a reasonable possibility that an asset was impaired or a liability was incurred after that date. The information may relate to a loss contingency that existed at the date of the financial statements, e.g., an asset that was not insured at the date of the financial statements. On the other hand, the information may relate to a loss contingency that did not exist at the date of the financial statements, e.g., threat of expropriation of assets after the date of the financial statements or the filing for bankruptcy by an enterprise whose debt was guaranteed after the date of the financial statements. In none of the cases cited in this paragraph was an asset impaired or a liability incurred at the date of the financial statements, and the condition for accrual in paragraph 8(a) is, therefore, not met. Disclosure of those kinds of losses or loss contingencies may be necessary, however, to keep the financial statements from being misleading. If disclosure is deemed necessary, the financial statements shall indicate the nature of the loss or loss contingency and give an estimate of the amount or range of loss or possible loss or state that such an estimate cannot be made. Occasionally, in the case of a loss arising after the date of the financial statements where the amount of asset impairment or liability incurrence can be reasonably estimated, disclosure may best be made by supplementing the historical financial statements with pro forma financial data giving effect to the loss as if it had occurred at the date of the financial statements. It may be desirable to present pro forma statements, usually a balance sheet only, in columnar form on the face of the historical financial statements.

12. Certain loss contingencies are presently being disclosed in financial statements even though the possibility of loss may be remote. The common characteristic of those contingencies is a guarantee, normally with a right to proceed against an outside party in the event that the guarantor is called upon to satisfy the guarantee. Examples include (a) guarantees of indebtedness of others, (b) obligations of commercial banks under "standby letters of credit," and (c) guarantees to repurchase receivables (or, in some cases, to repurchase the related property) that have been sold or otherwise assigned. The Board concludes that disclosure of those loss contingencies, and others that in substance have the same characteristic, shall be continued. The disclosure shall include the nature and amount of the guarantee. Consideration should be given to disclosing, if estimable, the value of any recovery that could be expected to result, such as from the guarantor's right to proceed against an outside party.

13. This Statement applies to regulated enterprises in accordance with provisions of the Addendum to *APB Opinion No. 2,* "Accounting for the 'Investment Credit.'" If, in conformity with the Addendum, a regulated enterprise accrues for financial accounting and reporting purposes an estimated loss without regard to the conditions in paragraph 8, the following information shall be disclosed in its financial statements:

a. The accounting policy including the nature of the accrual and the basis for estimation.
b. The amount of any related "liability" or "asset valuation" account included in each balance sheet presented.

General or Unspecified Business Risks

14. Some enterprises have in the past accrued so-called "reserves for general contingencies." General or unspecified business risks do not meet the conditions for accrual in paragraph 8, and no accrual for loss shall be made. No disclosure about them is required by this Statement.

Appropriation of Retained Earnings

15. Some enterprises have classified a portion of retained earnings as "appropriated" for loss contingencies. In some cases, the appropriation has been shown outside the stockholders' equity section of the balance sheet. Appropriation of retained earnings is not prohibited by this Statement provided that it is shown within the stockholders' equity section of the balance sheet and is clearly identified as an appropriation of retained earnings. Costs or

---

[6]For example, disclosure shall be made of any loss contingency that meets the condition in paragraph 8(a) but that is not accrued because the amount of loss cannot be reasonably estimated (paragraph 8(b)). Disclosure is also required of some loss contingencies that do not meet the condition in paragraph 8(a)—namely, those contingencies for which there is a *reasonable possibility* that a loss may have been incurred even though information may not indicate that it is *probable* that an asset had been impaired or a liability had been incurred at the date of the financial statements.

losses shall not be charged to an appropriation of retained earnings, and no part of the appropriation shall be transferred to income.

Examples of Application of This Statement

16. Examples of application of the conditions for accrual of loss contingencies in paragraph 8 and the disclosure requirements in paragraphs 9-11 are presented in Appendix A.

Gain Contingencies

17. The Board has not reconsidered *ARB No. 50* with respect to gain contingencies. Accordingly, the following provisions of paragraphs 3 and 5 of that Bulletin shall continue in effect:

a. Contingencies that might result in gains usually are not reflected in the accounts since to do so might be to recognize revenue prior to its realization.
b. Adequate disclosure shall be made of contingencies that might result in gains, but care shall be exercised to avoid misleading implications as to the likelihood of realization.

Other Disclosures

18. Paragraph 6 of *ARB No. 50* required disclosure of a number of situations including "unused letters of credit, long-term leases, assets pledged as security for loans, pension plans, the existence of cumulative preferred stock dividends in arrears, and commitments such as those for plant acquisition or an obligation to reduce debts, maintain working capital, or restrict dividends." Subsequent Opinions issued by the Accounting Principles Board established more explicit disclosure requirements for a number of those items, i.e., leases (see *APB Opinions No. 5* and *31*), pension plans (see *APB Opinion No. 8*), and preferred stock dividend arrearages (see *APB Opinion No. 10,* paragraph 11(b)).

19. Situations of the type described in the preceding paragraph shall continue to be disclosed in financial statements, and this Statement does not alter the present disclosure requirements with respect to those items.

Effective Date and Transition

20. This Statement shall be effective for fiscal years beginning on or after July 1, 1975, although earlier application is encouraged. A change in accounting principle resulting from compliance with paragraph 8 or 14 of this Statement shall be reported in accordance with *APB Opinion No. 20,* "Accounting Changes." Accordingly, except in the special circumstances referred to in paragraphs 29-30 of *APB Opinion No. 20,* the cumulative effect of the change on retained earnings at the beginning of the year in which the change is made shall be included in net income of the year of the change, and the disclosures specified in *APB Opinion No. 20* shall be made. Reclassification of an appropriation of retained earnings to comply with paragraph 15 of this Statement shall be made in any financial statements for periods before the effective date of this Statement, or financial summaries or other data derived therefrom, that are presented after the effective date of this Statement.

The provisions of this Statement need not be applied to immaterial items.

This Statement was adopted by the unanimous vote of the seven members of the Financial Accounting Standards Board:

Marshall S. Armstrong, *Chairman*	Donald J. Kirk	Walter Schuetze
Oscar S. Gellein	Arthur L. Litke	Robert T. Sprouse
	Robert E. Mays	

Appendix A

EXAMPLES OF APPLICATION OF THIS STATEMENT

21. This Appendix contains examples of application of the conditions for accrual of loss contingencies in paragraph 8 and of the disclosure requirements in paragraphs 9-11. Some examples have been included in response to questions raised in letters of comment on the Exposure Draft. It should be recognized that no set of examples can encompass all possible contingencies or circumstances. Accordingly, accrual and disclosure of loss contingencies should be based on an evaluation of the facts in each particular case.

Collectibility of Receivables

22. The assets of an enterprise may include receivables that arose from credit sales, loans, or other transactions. The conditions under which receivables exist usually involve some degree of uncertainty about their collectibility, in which case a

contingency exists as defined in paragraph 1. Losses from uncollectible receivables shall be accrued when both conditions in paragraph 8 are met. Those conditions may be considered in relation to individual receivables or in relation to groups of similar types of receivables. If the conditions are met, accrual shall be made even though the particular receivables that are uncollectible may not be identifiable.

23. If, based on available information, it is probable that the enterprise will be unable to collect all amounts due and, therefore, that at the date of its financial statements the net realizable value of the receivables through collection in the ordinary course of business is less than the total amount receivable, the condition in paragraph 8(a) is met because it is probable that an asset has been impaired. Whether the amount of loss can be reasonably estimated (the condition in paragraph 8(b)) will normally depend on, among other things, the experience of the enterprise, information about the ability of individual debtors to pay, and appraisal of the receivables in light of the current economic environment. In the case of an enterprise that has no experience of its own, reference to the experience of other enterprises in the same business may be appropriate. Inability to make a reasonable estimate of the amount of loss from uncollectible receivables (i.e., failure to satisfy the condition in paragraph 8(b)) precludes accrual and may, if there is significant uncertainty as to collection, suggest that the installment method, the cost recovery method, or some other method of revenue recognition be used (see paragraph 12 of *APB Opinion No. 10,* "Omnibus Opinion—1966"); in addition, the disclosures called for by paragraph 10 of this Statement should be made.

Obligations Related to Product Warranties and Product Defects

24. A warranty is an obligation incurred in connection with the sale of goods or services that may require further performance by the seller after the sale has taken place. Because of the uncertainty surrounding claims that may be made under warranties, warranty obligations fall within the definition of a contingency in paragraph 1. Losses from warranty obligations shall be accrued when the conditions in paragraph 8 are met. Those conditions may be considered in relation to individual sales made with warranties or in relation to groups of similar types of sales made with warranties. If the conditions are met, accrual shall be made even though the particular parties that will make claims under warranties may not be identifiable.

25. If, based on available information, it is probable that customers will make claims under warranties relating to goods or services that have been sold, the condition in paragraph 8(a) is met at the date of an enterprise's financial statements because it is probable that a liability has been incurred. Satisfaction of the condition in paragraph 8(b) will normally depend on the experience of an enterprise or other information. In the case of an enterprise that has no experience of its own, reference to the experience of other enterprises in the same business may be appropriate. Inability to make a reasonable estimate of the amount of a warranty obligation at the time of sale because of significant uncertainty about possible claims (i.e., failure to satisfy the condition in paragraph 8(b)) precludes accrual and, if the range of possible loss is wide, may raise a question about whether a sale should be recorded prior to expiration of the warranty period or until sufficient experience has been gained to permit a reasonable estimate of the obligation; in addition, the disclosures called for by paragraph 10 of this Statement should be made.

26. Obligations other than warranties may arise with respect to products or services that have been sold, for example, claims resulting from injury or damage caused by product defects. If it is probable that claims will arise with respect to products or services that have been sold, accrual for losses may be appropriate. The condition in paragraph 8(a) would be met, for instance, with respect to a drug product or toys that have been sold if a health or safety hazard related to those products is discovered and as a result it is considered probable that liabilities have been incurred. The condition in paragraph 8(b) would be met if experience or other information enables the enterprise to make a reasonable estimate of the loss with respect to the drug product or the toys.

Risk of Loss or Damage of Enterprise Property

27. At the date of an enterprise's financial statements, it may not be insured against risk of future loss or damage to its property by fire, explosion, or other hazards. The absence of insurance against losses from risks of those types constitutes an existing condition involving uncertainty about the amount and timing of any losses that may occur, in which case a contingency exists as defined in paragraph 1. Uninsured risks may arise in a number of ways, including (a) noninsurance of certain risks or co-insurance or deductible clauses in an insurance contract or (b) insurance through a subsidiary or investee[7] to the extent not reinsured with an inde-

[7]The effects of transactions between a parent or other investor and a subsidiary or investee insurance company shall be eliminated from an enterprise's financial statements (see paragraph 6 of *ARB No. 51,* "Consolidated Financial Statements," and paragraph 19(a) of *APB Opinion No. 18,* "The Equity Method of Accounting for Investments in Common Stock").

pendent insurer. Some risks, for all practical purposes, may be noninsurable, and the self-assumption of those risks is mandatory.

28. The absence of insurance does not mean that an asset has been impaired or a liability has been incurred at the date of an enterprise's financial statements. Fires, explosions, and other similar events that may cause loss or damage of an enterprise's property are random in their occurrence.[8] With respect to events of that type, the condition for accrual in paragraph 8(a) is not satisfied prior to the occurrence of the event because until that time there is no diminution in the value of the property. There is no relationship of those events to the activities of the enterprise prior to their occurrence, and no asset is impaired prior to their occurrence. Further, unlike an insurance company, which has a contractual obligation under policies in force to reimburse insureds for losses, an enterprise can have no such obligation to itself and, hence, no liability.

Risk of Loss from Future Injury to Others, Damage to the Property of Others, and Business Interruption

29. An enterprise may choose not to purchase insurance against risk of loss that may result from injury to others, damage to the property of others, or interruption of its business operations.[9] Exposure to risks of those types constitutes an existing condition involving uncertainty about the amount and timing of any losses that may occur, in which case a contingency exists as defined in paragraph 1.

30. Mere exposure to risks of those types, however, does not mean that an asset has been impaired or a liability has been incurred. The condition for accrual in paragraph 8(a) is not met with respect to loss that may result from injury to others, damage to the property of others, or business interruption that may occur after the date of an enterprise's financial statements. Losses of those types do not relate to the current or a prior period but rather to the *future* period in which they occur. Thus, for example, an enterprise with a fleet of vehicles should not accrue for injury to others or damage to the property of others that may be caused by those vehicles in the future even if the amount of those losses may be reasonably estimable. On the other hand, the conditions in paragraph 8 would be met with respect to uninsured losses resulting from injury to others or damage to the property of others that took place prior to the date of the financial statements, even though the enterprise may not

become aware of those matters until after that date, if the experience of the enterprise or other information enables it to make a reasonable estimate of the loss that was incurred prior to the date of its financial statements.

Write-Down of Operating Assets

31. In some cases, the carrying amount of an operating asset not intended for disposal may exceed the amount expected to be recoverable through future use of that asset even though there has been no physical loss or damage of the asset or threat of such loss or damage. For example, changed economic conditions may have made recovery of the carrying amount of a productive facility doubtful. The question of whether, in those cases, it is appropriate to write down the carrying amount of the asset to an amount expected to be recoverable through future operations is not covered by this Statement.

Threat of Expropriation

32. The threat of expropriation of assets is a contingency within the definition of paragraph 1 because of the uncertainty about its outcome and effect. If information indicates that expropriation is imminent and compensation will be less than the carrying amount of the assets, the condition for accrual in paragraph 8(a) is met. Imminence may be indicated, for example, by public or private declarations of intent by a government to expropriate assets of the enterprise or actual expropriation of assets of other enterprises. Paragraph 8(b) requires that accrual be made only if the amount of loss can be reasonably estimated. If the conditions for accrual are not met, the disclosures specified in paragraph 10 would be made when there is at least a reasonable possibility that an asset has been impaired.

Litigation, Claims, and Assessments

33. The following factors, among others, must be considered in determining whether accrual and/or disclosure is required with respect to pending or threatened litigation and actual or possible claims and assessments:

a. The period in which the underlying cause (i.e., the cause for action) of the pending or threatened litigation or of the actual or possible claim or assessment occurred.
b. The degree of probability of an unfavorable outcome.

---

[8]The Board recognizes that, in practice, experience regarding loss or damage to depreciable assets is in some cases one of the factors considered in estimating the depreciable lives of a group of depreciable assets, along with such other factors as wear and tear, obsolescence, and maintenance and replacement policies. This Statement is not intended to alter present depreciation practices (see paragraph 2).

[9]As to injury or damage resulting from products that have been sold, see paragraph 26.

c. The ability to make a reasonable estimate of the amount of loss.

34. As a condition for accrual of a loss contingency, paragraph 8(a) requires that information available prior to the issuance of financial statements indicate that it is probable that an asset had been impaired or a liability had been incurred at the date of the financial statements. Accordingly, accrual would clearly be inappropriate for litigation, claims, or assessments whose underlying cause is an event or condition occurring after the date of financial statements but before those financial statements are issued, for example, a suit for damages alleged to have been suffered as a result of an accident that occurred after the date of the financial statements. Disclosure may be required, however, by paragraph 11.

35. On the other hand, accrual may be appropriate for litigation, claims, or assessments whose underlying cause is an event occurring on or before the date of an enterprise's financial statements even if the enterprise does not become aware of the existence or possibility of the lawsuit, claim, or assessment until after the date of the financial statements. If those financial statements have not been issued, accrual of a loss related to the litigation, claim, or assessment would be required if the probability of loss is such that the condition in paragraph 8(a) is met and the amount of loss can be reasonably estimated.

36. If the underlying cause of the litigation, claim, or assessment is an event occurring before the date of an enterprise's financial statements, the probability of an outcome unfavorable to the enterprise must be assessed to determine whether the condition in paragraph 8(a) is met. Among the factors that should be considered are the nature of the litigation, claim, or assessment, the progress of the case (including progress after the date of the financial statements but before those statements are issued), the opinions or views of legal counsel and other advisers, the experience of the enterprise in similar cases, the experience of other enterprises, and any decision of the enterprise's management as to how the enterprise intends to respond to the lawsuit, claim, or assessment (for example, a decision to contest the case vigorously or a decision to seek an out-of-court settlement). The fact that legal counsel is unable to express an opinion that the outcome will be favorable to the enterprise should not necessarily be interpreted to mean that the condition for accrual of a loss in paragraph 8(a) is met.

37. The filing of a suit or formal assertion of a claim or assessment does not automatically indicate that accrual of a loss may be appropriate. The degree of probability of an unfavorable outcome must be assessed. The condition for accrual in paragraph 8(a) would be met if an unfavorable outcome is determined to be probable. If an unfavorable outcome is determined to be reasonably possible but not probable, or if the amount of loss cannot be reasonably estimated, accrual would be inappropriate, but disclosure would be required by paragraph 10 of this Statement.

38. With respect to unasserted claims and assessments, an enterprise must determine the degree of probability that a suit may be filed or a claim or assessment may be asserted and the possibility of an unfavorable outcome. For example, a catastrophe, accident, or other similar physical occurrence predictably engenders claims for redress, and in such circumstances their assertion may be probable; similarly, an investigation of an enterprise by a governmental agency, if enforcement proceedings have been or are likely to be instituted, is often followed by private claims for redress, and the probability of their assertion and the possibility of loss should be considered in each case. By way of further example, an enterprise may believe there is a possibility that it has infringed on another enterprise's patent rights, but the enterprise owning the patent rights has not indicated an intention to take any action and has not even indicated an awareness of the possible infringement. In that case, a judgment must first be made as to whether the assertion of a claim is probable. If the judgment is that assertion is not probable, no accrual or disclosure would be required. On the other hand, if the judgment is that assertion is probable, then a second judgment must be made as to the degree of probability of an unfavorable outcome. If an unfavorable outcome is probable and the amount of loss can be reasonably estimated, accrual of a loss is required by paragraph 8. If an unfavorable outcome is probable but the amount of loss cannot be reasonably estimated, accrual would not be appropriate, but disclosure would be required by paragraph 10. If an unfavorable outcome is reasonably possible but not probable, disclosure would be required by paragraph 10.

39. As a condition for accrual of a loss contingency, paragraph 8(b) requires that the amount of loss can be reasonably estimated. In some cases, it may be determined that a loss was incurred because an unfavorable outcome of the litigation, claim, or assessment is probable (thus satisfying the condition in paragraph 8(a)), but the range of possible loss is wide. For example, an enterprise may be litigating an income tax matter. In preparation for the trial, it may determine that, based on recent decisions involving one aspect of the litigation, it is probable that it will have to pay additional taxes of $2 million. Another aspect of the litigation may, however, be open to considerable interpretation, and depending on the interpretation by the court the enterprise may have to pay taxes of $8 million over and above the $2 million. In that case, paragraph 8 requires

the Discussion Memorandum were used "as examples to assist in the evaluation and development of criteria for accounting for future losses," and other examples were discussed. The Board has concluded that loss contingencies such as those given as examples in paragraph 4 of this Statement have common characteristics and that questions about accounting for and reporting of those contingencies should be resolved comprehensively. It is for that reason, also, that the Board believes it inappropriate to deal with catastrophe losses in a separate Statement.

58. A question has been raised whether uncollectibility of receivables and product warranties constitute contingencies within the scope of this Statement. The Board recognizes that uncertainties associated with uncollectibility of some receivables and some product warranties are likely to be, in part, inherent in making accounting estimates (described in paragraph 2) as well as, in part, the type of uncertainties that give rise to a contingency (described in paragraph 1). The Board believes that no useful purpose would be served by attempting to distinguish between those two types of uncertainties for purposes of establishing conditions for accrual of uncollectible receivables and product warranties. Consequently, those matters are deemed to be contingencies within the definition of paragraph 1 and should be accounted for pursuant to the provisions of this Statement.

ACCRUAL OF LOSS CONTINGENCIES

59. Paragraph 8 requires that a loss contingency be accrued if the two specified conditions are met. The purpose of those conditions is to require accrual of losses when they are reasonably estimable and relate to the current or a prior period. The requirement that the loss be reasonably estimable is intended to prevent accrual in the financial statements of amounts so uncertain as to impair the integrity of those statements. The Board has concluded that disclosure is preferable to accrual when a reasonable estimate of loss cannot be made. Further, even losses that are reasonably estimable should not be accrued if it is not probable that an asset has been impaired or a liability has been incurred at the date of an enterprise's financial statements because those losses relate to a future period rather than the current or a prior period. Attribution of a loss to events or activities of the current or prior periods is an element of asset impairment or liability incurrence.

60. In establishing the conditions in paragraph 8, Board members considered the factors discussed in paragraphs 61-101. Individual Board members gave greater weight to some factors than to others.

Accounting Accruals Do Not Provide Protection against Losses

61. Accrual of a loss related to a contingency does not create or set aside funds to lessen the possible financial impact of a loss, although some respondents to the Discussion Memorandum and the Exposure Draft argued to the contrary. The Board believes that confusion exists between accounting accruals (sometimes referred to as "accounting reserves") and the reserving or setting aside of specific assets to be used for a particular purpose or contingency. Accounting accruals are simply a method of allocating costs among accounting periods and have no effect on an enterprise's cash flow. An enterprise may choose to maintain or have access to sufficient liquid assets to replace or repair lost or damaged property or to pay claims in case a loss occurs. Alternatively, it may transfer the risk to others by purchasing insurance. Those are financial decisions, and if enterprise management decides to do neither, the presence or absence of an accrued credit balance on the balance sheet will have no effect on the consequences of that decision. The accounting standards set forth in this Statement do not affect the fundamental business economics of that decision.

62. In that regard, some respondents to the Discussion Memorandum and the Exposure Draft contended that an accounting standard that does not permit periodic accrual of so-called "self-insurance reserves" and, in the case of insurance companies, so-called "catastrophe reserves" will force enterprises to purchase insurance or reinsurance because the "protection" afforded by the accrual would no longer exist. Those accruals, however, in no way protect the assets available to replace or repair uninsured property that may be lost or damaged, or to satisfy claims that are not covered by insurance, or, in the case of insurance companies, to satisfy the claims of insured parties. Accrual, in and of itself, provides no financial protection that is not available in the absence of accrual.

63. The sole result of accrual, for financial accounting and reporting purposes, is allocation of costs among accounting periods. Some respondents to the Discussion Memorandum and the Exposure Draft took the position that estimated losses from loss contingencies should be accrued even before available information indicates that it is probable that an asset has been impaired or a liability has been incurred to avoid reporting net income that fluctuates widely from period to period. In their view, financial statement users may be misled by those fluctuations. They believe that estimated losses should be accrued without regard to whether the loss relates to the current period if, based on experience, it is reasonable to expect losses sometime in the future.

64. Financial statement users have indicated, however, that information about earnings variability is important to them. Two elements often cited as basic to the decision models of many financial statement users are (a) expected return—the predicted amount and timing of the return on an investment—and (b) risk—the variability of that expected return. If the nature of an enterprise's operations is such that irregularities in the incurrence of losses cause variations in periodic net income, that fact should not be obscured by accruing for anticipated losses that do not relate to the current period.

65. The Board recognizes that some investors may have a preference for investments in enterprises having a stable pattern of earnings, because that indicates lesser uncertainty or risk than fluctuating earnings. That preference, in turn, is perceived by many as having a favorable effect on the market prices of those enterprises' securities. If accruals for such matters as future uninsured losses and catastrophes were prohibited, some respondents contended, enterprises would be forced to purchase insurance or reinsurance to achieve the more stable pattern of reported earnings that tends to accompany the use of an "accounting reserve." Insurance or reinsurance reduces or eliminates risks and the inherent earnings fluctuations that accompany risks. Unlike insurance and reinsurance, however, the use of "accounting reserves" does not reduce or eliminate risk. The Board rejects the contention, therefore, that the use of "accounting reserves" is an alternative to insurance and reinsurance in protecting against risk. Earnings fluctuations are inherent in risk retention, and they should be reported as they occur. The Board cannot sanction the use of an accounting procedure to create the illusion of protection from risk when, in fact, protection does not exist.

66. The Board has also considered the argument that periodic accrual of losses without regard to whether an asset has been impaired or liability incurred is justified on grounds of comparability of financial statements among enterprises. Some respondents contended, for example, that accrual is necessary to make the financial statements of enterprises that do not purchase insurance comparable to those of enterprises that do purchase insurance (and report the premiums as expenses) and to make the financial statements of property and casualty insurance companies comparable regardless of the extent to which reinsurance has been purchased. In the Board's view, however, to report activity when there has been none would obscure a fundamental difference in circumstance between enterprises that transfer risks to others and those

that do not.

Financial Accounting and Reporting Reflects Primarily the Effects of Past Transactions and Existing Conditions

67. Financial accounting and reporting reflects primarily the effects of past transactions and existing conditions, not future transactions or conditions. For example, paragraph 35 of *APB Statement No. 4,* "Basic Concepts and Accounting Principles Underlying Financial Statements of Business Enterprises," states:

> Financial accounting and financial statements are primarily historical in that information about events that have taken place provides the basic data of financial accounting and financial statements.

68. The first condition in paragraph 8—that a loss contingency not be accrued until it is probable that an asset has been impaired or a liability has been incurred—is consistent with this concept of financial accounting and financial statements. That condition is not so past-oriented that accrual of a loss must await the occurrence of the confirming future event, for example, final adjudication or settlement of a lawsuit. The condition requires only that it be probable that the confirming future event will occur. The condition is intended to prohibit the recognition of a liability when it is not probable that one has been incurred and to prohibit the accrual of an asset impairment when it is not probable that an asset of an enterprise has been impaired.

The Concept of a Liability

69. In many cases, the accrual of a loss contingency results in the recording of a liability, for example, accruals for a probable tax assessment, a warranty obligation, or a probable loss resulting from the guarantee of indebtedness of others. In the course of its deliberations, therefore, the Board found it relevant to consider the concept of a liability as expressed in accounting literature.

70. The economic obligations of an enterprise are defined in paragraph 58 of *APB Statement No. 4* as "its present responsibilities to transfer economic resources or provide services to other entities in the future." Two aspects of that definition are especially relevant to accounting for contingencies: first, that liabilities are *present* responsibilities and, second, that they are obligations to *other entities*. Those notions are supported by other definitions of liabilities in published accounting literature, for example:

Liabilities are claims of creditors against the enterprise, arising out of past activities, that are to be satisfied by the disbursement or utilization of corporate resources.[11]

A liability is the result of a transaction of the past, not of the future.[12]

71. The condition in paragraph 8(a)—that a loss contingency shall be accrued if it is probable that a liability has been incurred—is intended to proscribe recognition of losses that relate to future periods but to require accrual of losses that relate to the current or a prior period (assuming the amount of loss can be reasonably estimated—see paragraph 8(b)).

72. Liability definitions also generally require that the amount of an economic obligation be known or susceptible of reasonable estimation before it is recorded as a liability. For example:

[Liabilities] are measured by cash received, by the established price of noncash assets or services received, or by estimates of a definitive character when the amount owing cannot be measured more precisely.[13]

The amount of the liability must be the subject of calculation or of close estimation.[14]

73. The condition in paragraph 8(b)—that an estimated loss from a loss contingency not be accrued until the amount of loss can be reasonably estimated—is consistent with this feature of the liability concept.

Accounting for Impairment of Value of Assets

74. The accrual of some loss contingencies may result in recording the impairment of the value of an asset rather than in recording a liability, for example, accruals for expropriation of assets or uncollectible receivables. Accounting presently recognizes impairments of the value of assets such as the following:

a. Paragraph 9 of Chapter 3A, "Current Assets and Current Liabilities," of *ARB No. 43* provides that "in the case of marketable securities where market value is less than cost by a substantial amount and it is evident that the decline in market value is not due to a mere temporary condition, the amount to be included as a current asset should not exceed the market value."

b. Statement 5 of Chapter 4, "Inventory Pricing," of *ARB No. 43* states that "a departure from the cost basis of pricing the inventory is required when the utility of the goods is no longer as great as its cost. . . . A loss of utility is to be reflected as a charge against the revenues of the period in which it occurs."

c. Paragraph 19(h) of *APB Opinion No. 18*, "The Equity Method of Accounting for Investments in Common Stock," states that "a loss in value of an investment which is other than a temporary decline should be recognized the same as a loss in value of other long-term assets."

d. Paragraph 15 of *APB Opinion No. 30*, "Reporting the Results of Operations," states that "if a loss is expected from the proposed sale or abandonment of a segment, the estimated loss should be provided for at the measurement date. . . ." Paragraph 14 states that the measurement date is the date on which management "commits itself to a formal plan to dispose of a segment of the business, whether by sale or abandonment."

e. Paragraph 183 of *APB Statement No. 4* states that "when enterprise assets are damaged by others, asset amounts are written down to recoverable costs and a loss is recorded."

75. A recurring principle underlying all of these references to asset impairments in the accounting literature is that a loss should not be accrued until it is probable that an asset *has been* impaired and the amount of the loss can be reasonably estimated. As indicated by those references, impairment is recognized, for instance, when a non-temporary decline in the market price of marketable securities below cost *has taken place,* when the utility of inventory *is no longer* as great as its cost, when a commitment, in terms of a formal plan, *has been made* to abandon a segment of a business or to sell a segment at less than its carrying amount, when enterprise assets *are damaged,* and so forth. The condition in paragraph 8(a) is intended to proscribe accrual of losses that relate to future periods, and the condition in paragraph 8(b) further requires that the amount of loss be reasonably estimable before it is accrued.

The Matching Concept

76. A number of respondents to the Discussion Memorandum and the Exposure Draft noted that losses from certain types of contingencies are likely to occur irregularly over an extended period of time encompassing a number of accounting periods. In their view, the matching process in accounting

---

[11] American Accounting Association, *Accounting and Reporting Standards for Corporate Financial Statements and Preceding Statements and Supplements* (Sarasota, Fla.: AAA, 1957), p. 16.

[12] Maurice Moonitz, "The Changing Concept of Liabilities," *The Journal of Accountancy,* May 1960, p. 44.

[13] American Accounting Association, *Accounting and Reporting Standards for Corporate Financial Statements,* p. 16.

[14] Maurice Moonitz, "The Changing Concept of Liabilities," p. 44.

requires that estimated losses from those types of contingencies be accrued in each accounting period even if not directly related to events or activities of the period.

77. *APB Statement No. 4* explicitly avoids using the term "matching" because it has a variety of meanings in the accounting literature. In its broadest sense, matching refers to the entire process of income determination—described in paragraph 147 of *APB Statement No. 4* as "identifying, measuring, and relating revenue and expenses of an enterprise for an accounting period." Matching may also be used in a more limited sense to refer only to the process of expense recognition or in an even more limited sense to refer to the recognition of expenses by associating costs with revenue on a cause and effect basis.

78. Three pervasive principles for recognizing costs as expenses are set forth in paragraphs 156-160 of *APB Statement No. 4* as follows:

> *Associating Cause and Effect.* . . . Some costs are recognized as expenses on the basis of a presumed direct association with specific revenue . . . recognizing them as expenses accompanies recognition of the revenue.

> *Systematic and Rational Allocation.* . . . If an asset provides benefits for several periods its cost is allocated to the periods in a systematic and rational manner in the absence of a more direct basis for associating cause and effect.

> *Immediate Recognition.* Some costs are associated with the current accounting period as expenses because (1) costs incurred during the period provide no discernible future benefits, (2) costs recorded as assets in prior periods no longer provide discernible benefits or (3) allocating costs either on the basis of association with revenue or among several accounting periods is considered to serve no useful purpose.

79. Some who believe that matching requires accrual of losses that are likely to occur irregularly over an extended period of time encompassing a number of accounting periods cite the systematic and rational allocation principle of expense recognition as justification for their position. That principle, however, involves the systematic and rational allocation of the cost of an asset (an asset that *has been* acquired) throughout the estimated periods that the asset provides benefits or the systematic and rational accrual of the amount of some obligations (obligations that *have been* incurred) throughout the estimated periods that the obligations are incurred. The customary depreciation of plant and equipment is an example of the former; when reasonably esti-

mable, the accrual of vacation pay is an example of the latter. The systematic and rational allocation principle has no application to assets that are expected to be acquired in the future or to obligations that are expected to be incurred in the future.

80. Matching, in the sense of recognizing expenses by associating costs with specific revenue on a cause and effect basis, is a consideration in relation to accrual for such matters as uncollectible receivables and warranty obligations. For example, most enterprises that make credit sales or warrant their products or services regularly incur losses from uncollectible receivables and warranty obligations. Frequently, those losses can be associated with revenue on a cause and effect basis. If the amount of those losses can be reasonably estimated, paragraph 8 of this Statement requires accrual if it is probable that an asset has been impaired (estimated uncollectible receivables) or that a liability has been incurred (estimated warranty claims).

Spreading the Burden of Irregularly Occurring Costs to Successive Generations of Customers and Shareholders

81. Some respondents to the Discussion Memorandum and the Exposure Draft contended that all costs of doing business should be accrued in each accounting period so that successive generations of customers and shareholders would bear their share of all costs including those that occur irregularly. It would seem, however, that those irregularly occurring costs are usually borne by customers through pricing policy and that pricing is not necessarily dependent upon financial accounting and reporting practices. With regard to accrual on grounds that it enables successive generations of shareholders to bear their share of irregularly occurring costs, see paragraphs 63-65.

Conservatism

82. On the grounds of conservatism, some respondents supported accrual of estimated losses from loss contingencies before available information indicates that it is probable that an asset has been impaired or a liability has been incurred. Conservatism is indicated as one of the "characteristics and limitations" of financial accounting in paragraph 35 of *APB Statement No. 4* as follows:

> *Conservatism.* The uncertainties that surround the preparation of financial statements are reflected in a general tendency toward early recognition of unfavorable events and minimization of the amount of net assets and net income.

83. Conservatism is further discussed in paragraph 171 of *APB Statement No. 4:*

Conservatism. Frequently, assets and liabilities are measured in a context of significant uncertainties. Historically, managers, investors, and accountants have generally preferred that possible errors in measurement be in the direction of understatement rather than overstatement of net income and net assets. This has led to the convention of conservatism. . . .

84. The conditions for accrual in paragraph 8 are not inconsistent with the accounting concept of conservatism. Those conditions are not intended to be so rigid that they require virtual certainty before a loss is accrued. They require only that it be *probable* that an asset has been impaired or a liability has been incurred and that the amount of loss be *reasonably* estimable. In the absence of that probability or estimability, however, the Board has concluded that disclosure is preferable to accruing in the financial statements amounts so uncertain as to impair the integrity of the financial statements.

Risk of Future Loss or Damage of Enterprise Property, Injury to Others, Damage to the Property of Others, and Business Interruption

85. Some persons contend that the decision not to purchase insurance against losses that can be reasonably expected some time in the future (such as risk of loss or damage of enterprise property, injury to others, damage to the property of others, and business interruption) justifies periodic accrual for those losses without regard to whether it is probable that an asset has been impaired or a liability incurred at the date of the financial statements. As a basis for their position, they frequently cite the following factors: matching of revenue and expense, spreading the burden of irregularly occurring costs to successive generations of customers, and conservatism. They also believe that accrual of estimated losses from those types of risks improves the comparability of the financial statements of enterprises that do not insure with those of enterprises that purchase insurance. Some contend that a prohibition against periodic accrual for uninsured losses will force enterprises to purchase insurance coverage that would not otherwise be purchased.

86. In the Board's judgment, however, the mere existence of risk, at the date of an enterprise's financial statements, does not mean that a loss should be accrued. Anticipation of asset impairments or liabilities or losses from business interruption that do not relate to the current or a prior period is not justified by the matching concept.

87. The Board's views regarding the contention that periodic accrual for uninsured losses is a way of providing protection against loss and improving comparability among enterprises that do and do not purchase insurance, and the contention that prohibition of accrual will force enterprises to purchase insurance, are discussed in paragraphs 61-66. The Board's position regarding periodic accrual for uninsured risks and other loss contingencies on the grounds of spreading the burden of irregularly occurring costs to successive generations of customers or on the grounds of conservatism is discussed in paragraphs 81-84.

88. Some respondents to the Exposure Draft said that prohibition against periodic accrual for uninsured losses would be detrimental to government contractors because requirements of Federal government agencies in auditing costs subject to procurement regulations currently allow reimbursement for periodic accruals for uninsured losses only if they are included in the contractor's financial statements. Contract reimbursement and financial accounting and reporting may well have different objectives. Accordingly, the provisions of this Statement may not be appropriate for contract reimbursement purposes.

Catastrophe Losses of Property and Casualty Insurance Companies

89. At the time that a property and casualty insurance company or reinsurance company issues an insurance policy covering risk of loss from catastrophes, a contingency arises. The contingency is the risk of loss *assumed* by the insurance company, that is, the risk of loss from catastrophes that may occur *during the term of the policy.*

90. Some respondents to the Discussion Memorandum and the Exposure Draft proposed that insurance companies accrue estimated losses from catastrophes including both those that may occur during the terms of insurance policies in force and those that may occur beyond the terms of policies in force. Other respondents proposed that some portion of the premium revenue of a property and casualty insurance company be deferred beyond the terms of insurance policies in force to provide what, in substance, is an estimated liability for future catastrophe losses. Some respondents proposed that accrual of estimated losses or deferral of premiums be permitted but not required. On the other hand, some respondents to the Discussion Memorandum and the Exposure Draft were opposed to any accrual for future catastrophe losses by means of an estimated liability or deferral of premium revenue. Because those estimated liabilities and revenue deferrals have come to be referred to as "catastrophe reserves," that term will be used in paragraphs 91-101 for convenience.

91. In response to the Exposure Draft, it was recommended that the FASB appoint a special commit-

tee to study further the matter of catastrophe reserve accounting and to make recommendations thereon. The Board has concluded, however, that its own research and that of others (mentioned in Appendix B to this Statement and summarized in the Discussion Memorandum), the written responses received to the Discussion Memorandum, the presentations made at the public hearing, and the letters of comment on the Exposure Draft provide the Board with sufficient information with which to reach a conclusion.

92. Proponents of catastrophe reserve accounting generally cite the following reasons for their position:

a. *Catastrophes certain to occur.* Over the long term, catastrophes are certain to occur; therefore, they are not contingencies.
b. *Predictability of catastrophe losses.* On the basis of experience and by application of appropriate statistical techniques, catastrophe losses can be predicted over the long term with reasonable accuracy.
c. *Matching.* Some portion of property and casualty insurance premiums is intended to cover losses that usually occur infrequently and at intervals longer than both the terms of the policies in force and the financial accounting and reporting period. Catastrophe losses should, therefore, be accrued when the revenue is recognized (or premiums should be deferred beyond the terms of policies in force to periods in which the catastrophes occur) to match catastrophe losses with the related revenue.
d. *Stabilization of reported income.* Catastrophe reserve accounting stabilizes reported income and avoids erratic variations caused by irregularly occurring catastrophes.
e. *Comparability.* Reinsurance premiums paid by a prime insurer are said to be similar to accrual of catastrophe losses prior to their occurrence because the reinsurance premiums paid reduce income before a catastrophe loss occurs. Accrual of catastrophe losses as an expense prior to occurrence of a catastrophe makes the financial statements of property and casualty insurance companies comparable regardless of the extent to which reinsurance has been purchased.
f. *Non-accrual would force purchase of reinsurance.* Non-accrual of catastrophe losses will force property and casualty insurance companies to purchase reinsurance.
g. *Generations of policyholders.* Periodic accrual of estimated catastrophe losses charges each generation of policyholders with its share of the loss through the premium structure.

93. The Board does not find those arguments persuasive. The fact that over the long term catas-trophes are certain to occur does not justify accrual before the catastrophes occur. As stated in paragraph 59, the purpose of the conditions for accrual in paragraph 8 is to require accrual of losses if they are reasonably estimable *and relate to the current or a prior period.* An enterprise may know with certainty, for example, next year's administrative salaries, but that does not justify accrual in the current accounting period because those salaries do not relate to that period. As indicated in paragraphs 67-68, financial accounting and reporting reflects primarily the effects of past transactions and existing conditions, not future transactions or conditions; accrual for losses from catastrophes that are expected to occur *beyond the terms of insurance policies in force* would amount to accrual of a liability before one has been incurred. Existing policyholders are insured only during the period covered by their insurance contracts; an insurance company is not presently obligated to policyholders for catastrophes that may occur after expiration of their policies. Accrual for those catastrophe losses would record a liability that is inconsistent with the concept of a liability discussed in paragraphs 69-73.

94. The Board recognizes that the costs of catastrophes to insurance companies are large and are incurred irregularly and that insurance companies recoup those costs in the long run through periodic adjustments in the premiums charged to policyholders. It is the view of the Board, however, that the long-run nature of pricing of premiums should not be a determinant of the time when a liability is recorded.

95. The AICPA Industry Audit Guide, "Audits of Fire and Casualty Insurance Companies," describes accounting for premiums as follows (pp. 24-25):

As soon as a policy is issued promising to indemnify for loss, the insurance company incurs a potential liability. The company may be called upon to pay the full amount of the policy, a portion of the policy, or nothing. It would be impossible to try to measure the liability under a single policy. However, since insurance is based on the law of averages, one may estimate from experience the loss on a large number of policies.

As state supervision of insurance developed, the insurance departments set about providing a legal basis for determining the potential liability under outstanding policies in order to establish an ample reserve for the protection of policyholders and provide a uniform method of calculation. It was recognized that, since the premium is expected to pay losses and expenses, and provide a margin of profit over the term of the policy, the portion measured by the unexpired term should be adequate to pay policy liabilities (principally losses and loss expenses) and return premiums during the unexpired term on a uniform basis for all companies. Therefore the unearned premium was adopted as the basis for computing the unknown liability on unexpired policies.

96. Because unearned premiums represents the "unknown liability," the Board is of the view that it is inappropriate to accrue an additional amount as an estimate for that same unknown liability. Further, in the Board's view, deferral of premiums beyond the terms of policies in force is inconsistent with the concept of revenue recognition set forth in the Audit Guide and is without any conceptual basis. Moreover, the Board believes that its conclusion regarding the time at which accruals shall be made for catastrophic losses is consistent with the Audit Guide. It should be noted that this Statement does not prohibit (and, in fact, requires) accrual of a *net* loss (that is, a loss in excess of deferred premiums) that probably will be incurred on insurance policies that are in force, provided that the loss can be reasonably estimated, just as accrual of net losses on long-term construction-type contracts is required (see *ARB No. 45,* "Long-Term Construction-Type Contracts").

97. With respect to catastrophes that may occur within the terms of policies in force, to satisfy the conditions for accrual in paragraph 8, the occurrence of catastrophes would have to be probable during the terms of those policies, and the amounts of losses therefrom would have to be reasonably estimable. The letters of comment and position papers received in response to the Discussion Memorandum and the Exposure Draft and presentations at the public hearing lead the Board to conclude that neither the timing of catastrophes nor the amounts of losses therefrom are reasonably predictable within the terms of policies in force.

98. The Board is of the view that accrual of losses from catastrophes is not justified by the accounting concept of matching. Systematic and rational allocation does not apply to costs that have not been incurred. The Board recognizes that large and irregularly occurring costs must of necessity be considered in systematically and rationally determining premiums to be charged to customers but does not believe that pricing considerations should dictate the accrual of losses for financial accounting purposes. The Board also does not believe that matching in the sense of recognizing expenses by associating losses with specific revenue on a cause and effect basis is, in and of itself, a basis for accrual of catastrophe losses prior to the event causing the loss. The Board believes that, for the reasons stated in paragraphs 94-96, there can be no presumed direct association with specific revenue prior to the event causing the catastrophe loss.

99. The Board's views regarding justification of periodic accrual of catastrophe reserves on grounds of (a) stabilizing reported income, (b) improving comparability among financial statements of insurance companies, and (c) preventing the "forced" purchase of reinsurance are discussed in paragraphs 61-66.

100. The argument that accrual of catastrophe reserves enables each generation of policyholders to bear its share of the losses through the premiums that it is charged is also questionable because amounts established for premiums are not necessarily dependent on financial accounting and reporting practices.

101. The Board considered the proposal that catastrophe reserve accounting be permitted but not made mandatory. Whether it is probable that an asset has been impaired or a liability incurred is determined by the circumstances, not by choice. Accordingly, the conditions for accrual in paragraph 8 apply to all loss contingencies, including risk of loss from catastrophes assumed by property and casualty insurance companies and reinsurance companies. In the Board's view, the use of different methods to report catastrophe losses in similar circumstances cannot be justified.

APPLICABILITY TO LIFE INSURANCE COMPANIES

102. Some respondents to the Exposure Draft inquired as to whether the conditions for accrual in paragraph 8 are intended to change accounting practices of life insurance companies. This Statement does not amend the AICPA Industry Audit Guide, "Audits of Stock Life Insurance Companies."

DISCLOSURE OF NONINSURANCE

103. A number of respondents to the Exposure Draft inquired as to whether it is the Board's intent to require disclosure of noninsurance or underinsurance. Some recommended that the Board require disclosures with respect to uninsured risks that enterprises ordinarily insure against. Others said that they were unable to define risks that would ordinarily be insured against because the insurance practices of enterprises are so varied. Because of the problems involved in developing operational criteria for disclosure of noninsured or underinsured risks, this Statement does not require disclosure of uninsured risks. However, the Board does not discourage those disclosures in appropriate circumstances.

EFFECTIVE DATE AND TRANSITION

104. The Board considered three alternative approaches to a change in the method of accounting for contingencies: (1) prior period adjustment, (2) the "cumulative effect" method described in *APB Opinion No. 20,* "Accounting Changes," and (3) retention of amounts accrued for contingencies that do not meet the conditions for accrual in paragraph 8 until those amounts are exhausted by actual losses charged thereto. The Exposure Draft had proposed the change be effected by the prior period adjust-ment method. A large number of respondents to the Exposure Draft, however, opposed the prior period adjustment method for a number of reasons, including significant difficulties involved in determining the degree of probability and estimability that had existed in prior periods as would have been required if the conditions in paragraph 8 were applied retroactively. On further consideration of all the circumstances, the Board has concluded that use of the "cumulative effect" method described in *APB Opinion No. 20* represents a satisfactory solution and has concluded that the effective date in paragraph 20 is advisable.

ance sheets dated on or after that date and to related statements of changes in financial position. Reclassification in financial statements for periods ending prior to December 31, 1975 is permitted but not required.

> **The provisions of this Statement need not be applied to immaterial items.**

This Statement was adopted by the affirmative votes of six members of the Financial Accounting Standards Board. Mr. Mays dissented.

Mr. Mays dissents because this Statement permits the exclusion of short-term obligations from current liabilities under circumstances in which, in his view, such exclusion is unwarranted. He believes that the criteria for exclusion set forth in the Statement tend to blur rather than to sharpen the accounting concept of working capital.

He is of the opinion that more restrictive criteria would result in a more meaningful portrayal of current and long-term cash requirements. He believes that information concerning management's ability and intent to refinance certain of its obligations can be communicated in financial statements by footnote disclosure or by disclosures within the current liabilities section of the balance sheet. However, those considerations, while important, should not be permitted to obscure the nature of the obligations themselves.

In Mr. Mays' opinion, classification of an obligation as a current liability or as a long-term liability should be based on the maturity date of the obligation, and only in exceptional circumstances should the existence of a financing agreement affect that classification. Those circumstances would be (1) the agreement is noncancelable by the lender (whereas the Statement provides for reclassifica-

tion even though the lender may cancel if a provision of the agreement is violated); and (2) the agreement is entered into for the stated purpose of refinancing the particular short-term obligation (whereas the Statement requires merely that the agreement not prohibit such refinancing); and (3) the enterprise fully intends to refinance the obligation on a long-term basis under the agreement (whereas the Statement provides for reclassification even if the enterprise intends to seek other sources of financing).

In Mr. Mays' view, since the Statement permits general lines of bank credit to be used to justify the exclusion of unrelated short-term debt from current liabilities, logic would suggest that any solvent corporation with sufficient unused borrowing capacity should be permitted to exclude from current liabilities any kind of short-term obligation that it intends to refinance on a long-term basis. While not in agreement with the criteria that the Statement establishes, given those criteria, he sees no logical basis for denying their application to any short-term obligation, including those payables for which reclassification is ruled out by paragraph 8 of the Statement.

Members of the Financial Accounting Standards Board:

Marshall S. Armstrong, *Chairman*	Donald J. Kirk	Walter Scheutze
Oscar S. Gellein	Arthur L. Litke	Robert T. Sprouse
	Robert E. Mays	

Appendix A

BASIS FOR CONCLUSIONS

18. This Appendix discusses factors deemed significant by members of the Board in reaching the conclusions in this Statement. Individual Board members gave greater weight to some factors than to others. The Appendix also sets forth suggestions made by those responding to the Exposure Draft and reasons for accepting some and rejecting others.

SCOPE OF THIS STATEMENT

19. Some respondents indicated that the Exposure Draft appeared to require all enterprises to prepare a classified balance sheet regardless of normal industry practice or other justification for adopting a balance sheet format that does not identify current assets and current liabilities. The question of whether it is appropriate for an enterprise to present an unclassified balance sheet is beyond the scope of this Statement. Accordingly, paragraph 7 indicates that the standards established by this Statement

apply only if an enterprise is preparing a classified balance sheet.

20. The Board also concluded that it should not, as part of this project, re-examine the accounting concept of working capital described in detail in Chapter 3A of *ARB No. 43*. Paragraph 7 of Chapter 3A defines current liabilities as those whose liquidation "is reasonably expected to require the use of existing resources properly classified as current assets, or the creation of other current liabilities." That paragraph goes on to say that the current liabilities classification "is intended to include obligations for items which have entered into the operating cycle. . . . and debts which arise from operations directly related to the operating cycle. . . ." Accordingly, paragraph 8 of this Statement requires that short-term obligations arising from transactions in the normal course of business that are to be paid in customary terms shall be included in current liabilities. On the other hand, short-term obligations arising from the acquisition or construction of noncurrent assets would be excluded from current liabilities if the conditions in paragraphs 10 and 11 are met. Similarly, short-term obligations not directly related to the operating cycle—for example, a note given to a supplier to replace an account payable that originally arose in the normal course of business and had been due in customary terms—would be excluded if the conditions in paragraphs 10 and 11 are met. This Statement does not specify disclosures relating to short-term obligations that are *included* in current liabilities, although the Statement does make explicit that a total of current liabilities shall be presented in classified balance sheets (see paragraph 15).

BALANCE SHEET CLASSIFICATION

21. The alternative solutions considered by the Board with regard to the question of how to classify a short-term obligation that is expected to be refinanced on a long-term basis (see paragraph 2) ranged between:

a. A *strict maturity-date* approach under which all obligations scheduled to mature within one year (or, in certain cases, within an enterprise's operating cycle) would be classified as current liabilities regardless of any intention to refinance on a long-term basis.
b. An approach based *solely* on management's intention to seek refinancing on a long-term basis without requiring evidence of the enterprise's ability to do so.

22. The Board also considered alternatives within that range. Those alternatives all require that the *intent* of the enterprise to refinance a short-term

obligation on a long-term basis be demonstrated by an *ability* to consummate the refinancing, but they differ in terms of the conditions required to demonstrate that ability.

23. The Board rejected a strict maturity-date approach because the scheduled maturity date of an obligation is not necessarily indicative of the point in time at which that obligation will require the use of the enterprise's funds. Inclusion of all short-term obligations within the current liability classification ignores the fact that enterprises, for sound economic reasons, often use commercial paper and other short-term debt instruments as means of long-term financing or that they often replace the currently maturing portion of long-term debt with other long-term debt. Borrowings under long-term revolving credit agreements and borrowings backed by long-term stand-by credit agreements are commonplace. A strict maturity-date approach would deny that these borrowings are sometimes, in substance, long-term financing. That approach would also result in a major change in the concept of current liabilities described in paragraph 7 of Chapter 3A of *ARB No. 43* as "obligations whose liquidation is reasonably expected to require the use of existing resources properly classifiable as current assets, or the creation of other current liabilities."

24. The Board also rejected classification based solely on an enterprise's intention to seek refinancing on a long-term basis. The Board concluded that intent, while essential, is insufficient to justify excluding a short-term obligation from current liabilities. The intent of an enterprise is an essential condition because without intent to refinance there is a presumption that liquidation of the short-term obligation would require the use of current assets or the creation of other current liabilities. The existence of a financing agreement, even one that requires that funds obtained thereunder be used to liquidate the short-term obligation, is irrelevant if the enterprise does not intend to refinance on a long-term basis. In the Board's judgment, however, intent alone does not provide sufficiently objective evidence to overcome the presumption that a short-term obligation will require the use of funds at its scheduled maturity date. The intent must be supported by a demonstrated ability to carry out that intent.

25. The two conditions set forth in this Statement for exclusion of a short-term obligation from current liabilities—intent and ability—are essentially the same as the requirements proposed in the Exposure Draft. That draft had proposed that a short-term obligation be classified as a current liability unless all of the following conditions were met:

a. The borrower has a noncancelable binding agreement to refinance the obligation from a source reasonably expected to be financially capable of honoring the agreement.

b. The maturity date of the new obligation expected to be incurred by the borrower as a result of the refinancing under the agreement will be more than one year from the date of the financial statements.

c. The borrower intends to exercise its rights under the agreement.

26. Many respondents to the Exposure Draft indicated that the requirement of a "noncancelable binding agreement" was unrealistic because lenders generally do not make unqualified commitments. Financing agreements often include provisions that could restrict borrowing under the agreement. As indicated by the conditions in paragraphs 11(b)(i) and 11(b)(ii) of this Statement, the inclusion of a restrictive covenant, representation, warranty, or other provision in a financing agreement does not prevent a short-term obligation from being excluded from current liabilities provided that compliance with the provision can be objectively determined or measured and provided that there is no evidence of a violation for which a waiver has not been obtained. In the Board's view, inability to objectively determine or measure compliance, or the existence of a violation of a provision for which a waiver has not been obtained, raises a serious doubt about the enterprise's ability to consummate an intended refinancing to avoid the use of working capital and, consequently, requires classification of the short-term obligation as a current liability. The existence of a situation that permits the lender to cancel the agreement or otherwise to prevent the enterprise from exercising its rights thereunder after expiration of a grace period or after notice to the enterprise or both is also considered a violation of a provision that will, in the absence of a waiver, require classification of the short-term obligation as a current liability.

27. The Board has concluded that exclusion of a short-term obligation from current liabilities should not be precluded as long as the financing agreement *clearly permits* the enterprise to replace the short-term obligation with a long-term obligation or with equity securities or to renew, extend, or replace the short-term obligation with another short-term obligation for an uninterrupted period extending beyond one year (or operating cycle). The Board considered and rejected the proposal that a short-term obligation should be excluded from current liabilities only if a financing agreement is *specifically linked* to the short-term obligation, either by specifically permitting or requiring that funds obtained thereunder be used to liquidate the short-term obligation. In the Board's judgment, that proposal places undue emphasis on the form of an agreement

rather than on its substance. It is neither practicable nor realistic to trace specific funds to their ultimate use. The financial position of an enterprise that has refinanced under a linked agreement will be indistinguishable from the financial position of an enterprise that has entered into the same transactions under an agreement that is not linked but clearly permits refinancing the short-term obligation. Moreover, whether or not a financing agreement is specifically linked to a particular short-term obligation, the enterprise is not precluded from issuing another short-term obligation at approximately the same time as the old obligation is refinanced under the agreement. The potential effect of such a transaction can be avoided only if a strict maturity-date approach is adopted, but the Board rejected that alternative for the reasons stated in paragraph 23. The Board believes that the requirement in paragraph 10 that the enterprise intend to refinance on a long-term basis and thus not to use working capital to repay the maturing short-term obligation more closely comports with the spirit of this Statement and Chapter 3A of *ARB No. 43* than would a requirement for specific linkage.

28. Respondents to the Exposure Draft indicated that many enterprises enter into agreements that assure their ability to refinance short-term obligations although they might not intend to exercise their rights under the agreement if an alternative source of financing becomes available. One of the conditions in the Exposure Draft was that the enterprise intend to exercise its rights under the agreement (see paragraph 25(c)). A footnote in the Exposure Draft indicated that this condition would be met if the enterprise intended to exercise its rights under the agreement when the short-term obligations could not continue to be refinanced on a short-term basis. Respondents asked the Board to clarify the intent of the condition in the Exposure Draft and the related footnote. The Board believes that the justification for excluding a short-term obligation from current liabilities is not negated simply because an enterprise may intend to seek a more advantageous source of financing (including, perhaps, short-term financing) than that provided under the financing agreement in existence when the balance sheet is issued. However, the condition in paragraph 11(b)(i) requires that the agreement extend beyond one year (or operating cycle) from the date of the enterprise's balance sheet to demonstrate clearly the enterprise's ability to avoid using working capital to repay the short-term obligation. Moreover, paragraph 13 requires that the enterprise intend to exercise its rights under the agreement if another source of financing does not become available.

29. A number of respondents to the Exposure Draft asked whether events occurring after the date

of the balance sheet but before the balance sheet is issued should be considered in assessing an enterprise's ability to consummate the refinancing of a short-term obligation on a long-term basis. In particular, the two types of post-balance-sheet-date events cited were (a) actual issuance of a long-term obligation or equity securities for the purpose of refinancing the short-term obligation on a long-term basis and (b) entering into a financing agreement after the balance-sheet date but before the balance sheet is issued. In the Board's judgment, both of those types of post-balance-sheet-date events should be considered in determining liability classification and in assessing an enterprise's ability to consummate an intended refinancing, and they are explicitly provided for in paragraphs 11(a) and 11(b).

30. Several respondents to the Exposure Draft asked whether a short-term obligation could be excluded from current liabilities if it is intended to be replaced (or, in fact, has been replaced after the balance sheet date) by issuing equity securities. A short-term obligation will not require the use of working capital regardless of whether refinancing on a long-term basis is accomplished by issuing debt securities or equity securities. Accordingly, *refinancing on a long-term basis* is defined in paragraph 2 to include issuance of equity securities, and a short-term obligation intended to be refinanced in that manner would be excluded from current liabilities if the conditions in paragraphs 10 and 11 are met. Although it is appropriate to exclude the short-term obligation from current liabilities when those conditions are met, the Board concluded that it is not appropriate to include the short-term obligation in owners' equity (see footnote 2 to paragraph 11(a)). The intent of an enterprise to refinance a short-term obligation on a long-term basis and its ability to do so relate to the question of whether the obligation is expected to require the use of working capital, not whether it is a liability. The obligation is a liability and not owners' equity at the date of the balance sheet.

EFFECTIVE DATE AND TRANSITION

31. Many respondents opposed the proposal in the Exposure Draft that balance sheets for dates prior to the effective date of the Statement be restated to conform to the provisions of the Statement. They indicated that restatement would not achieve comparability of balance sheets for dates prior to the effective date of the Statement with balance sheets for subsequent dates because of the new conditions established by paragraph 11. After considering all of the circumstances, the Board concluded that prospective application of this Statement is appropriate, with restatement permitted but not required,

and that the effective date in paragraph 17 is advisable.

Appendix B

EXAMPLES OF APPLICATION OF THIS STATEMENT

32. The following examples provide guidance for applying this Statement. It should be recognized that these examples do not comprehend all possible circumstances and do not include all the disclosures that would typically be made regarding long-term debt or current liabilities.

GENERAL ASSUMPTIONS

33. The assumptions on which the examples are based are:

a. ABC Company's fiscal year end is December 31, 19x5.
b. The date of issuance of the December 31, 19x5 financial statements is March 31, 19x6; the Company's practice is to issue a classified balance sheet.
c. At December 31, 19x5, short-term obligations include $5,000,000 representing the portion of 6% long-term debt maturing in February 19x6 and $3,000,000 of 9% notes payable issued in November 19x5 and maturing in July 19x6.
d. The Company intends to refinance on a long-term basis both the current maturity of long-term debt and the 9% notes payable.
e. Accounts other than the long-term debt maturing in February 19x6 and the notes payable maturing in July 19x6 are:

Current assets	$30,000,000
Other assets	$50,000,000
Accounts payable and accruals	$10,000,000
Other long-term debt	$25,000,000
Shareholders' equity	$37,000,000

f. Unless otherwise indicated, the examples also assume that the lender or prospective lender is expected to be capable of honoring the agreement, that there is no evidence of a violation of any provision, and that the terms of borrowings available under the agreement are readily determinable.

EXAMPLE 1

34. The Company negotiates a financing agreement with a commercial bank in December 19x5 for a maximum borrowing of $8,000,000 at any time through 19x7 with the following terms:

a. Borrowings are available at ABC Company's request for such purposes as it deems appropriate and will mature three years from the date of borrowing.

b. Amounts borrowed will bear interest at the bank's prime rate.

c. An annual commitment fee of 1/2 of 1% is payable on the difference between the amount borrowed and $8,000,000.

d. The agreement is cancelable by the lender only if:

  (i) The Company's working capital, excluding borrowings under the agreement, falls below $10,000,000.

  (ii) The Company becomes obligated under lease agreements to pay an annual rental in excess of $1,000,000.

  (iii) Treasury stock is acquired without the prior approval of the prospective lender.

  (iv) The Company guarantees indebtedness of unaffiliated persons in excess of $500,000.

35. The enterprise's intention to refinance meets the condition specified by paragraph 10. Compliance with the provisions listed in paragraph 34(d) is objectively determinable or measurable; therefore, the condition specified by paragraph 11(b)(i) is met. The proceeds of borrowings under the agreement are clearly available for the liquidation of the 9% notes payable and the long-term debt maturing in February 19x6. Both obligations, therefore, would be classified as other than current liabilities.

36. Following are the liability section of ABC Company's balance sheet at December 31, 19x5 and the related footnote disclosures required by this Statement, based on the information in paragraphs 33 and 34. Because the balance sheet is issued subsequent to the February 19x6 maturity of the long-term debt, the footnote describes the refinancing of that obligation.

	December 31, 19x5
Current Liabilities:	
Accounts payable and accruals	$10,000,000
Total Current Liabilities	10,000,000
Long-Term Debt:	
9% notes payable (Note A)	3,000,000*
6% debt due February 19x6 (Note A)	5,000,000*
Other long-term debt	25,000,000
Total Long-Term Debt	33,000,000
Total Liabilities	$43,000,000

Note A

The Company has entered into a financing agreement with a commercial bank that permits the Company to borrow at any time through 19x7 up to $8,000,000 at the bank's prime rate of interest. The Company must pay an annual commitment fee of 1/2 of 1% of the unused portion of the commitment. Borrowings under the financing agreement mature three years after the date of the loan. Among other things, the agreement prohibits the acquisition of treasury stock without prior approval by the bank, requires maintenance of working capital of $10,000,000 exclusive of borrowings under the agreement, and limits the annual rental under lease agreements to $1,000,000. In February 19x6, the Company borrowed $5,000,000 at 8% and liquidated the 6% long-term debt, and it intends to borrow additional funds available under the agreement to refinance the 9% notes payable maturing in July 19x6.

EXAMPLE 2

37. A foreign subsidiary of the enterprise negotiates a financing agreement with its local bank in December 19x5. Funds are available to the subsidiary for its unrestricted use, including loans to affiliated companies; other terms are identical to those cited in paragraph 34. Local laws prohibit the transfer of funds outside the country.

38. The requirement of paragraph 11(b)(i) is met because compliance with the provisions of the agreement is objectively determinable or measurable. Because of the laws prohibiting the transfer of funds, however, the proceeds from borrowings under the agreement are not available for liquidation of the debt maturing in February and July 19x6. Accordingly, both the 6% debt maturing in February 19x6 and the 9% notes payable maturing in July 19x6 would be classified as current liabilities.

---

*These obligations may also be shown in captions distinct from both current liabilities and long-term debt, such as "Interim Debt," "Short-Term Debt Expected to Be Refinanced," and "Intermediate Debt."

EXAMPLE 3

39. Assume that instead of utilizing the agreement cited in paragraph 34, the Company issues $8,000,000 of ten-year debentures to the public in January 19x6. The Company intends to use the proceeds to liquidate the $5,000,000 debt maturing February 19x6 and the $3,000,000 of 9% notes payable maturing July 19x6. In addition, assume the debt maturing February 19x6 is paid prior to the issuance of the balance sheet, and the remaining proceeds from the sale of debentures are invested in a U.S. Treasury note maturing the same day as the 9% notes payable.

40. Since the Company refinanced the long-term debt maturing in February 19x6 in a manner that meets the conditions set forth in paragraph 11 of this Statement, that obligation would be excluded from current liabilities. In addition, the 9% notes payable maturing in July 19x6 would also be excluded because the Company has obtained funds expressly intended to be used to liquidate those notes and not intended to be used in current operations. In balance sheets after the date of sale of the debentures and before the maturity date of the notes payable, the Company would exclude the notes payable from current liabilities if the U.S. Treasury note is excluded from current assets (see paragraph 6 of Chapter 3A of *ARB No. 43,* which is not altered by this Statement).

41. If the debentures had been sold prior to January 1, 19x6, the $8,000,000 of obligations to be paid would be excluded from current liabilities in the balance sheet at that date if the $8,000,000 in funds were excluded from current assets.

42. If, instead of issuing the ten-year debentures, the Company had issued $8,000,000 of equity securities and all other facts in this example remained unchanged, both the 6% debt due February 19x6 and the 9% notes payable due July 19x6 would be classified as liabilities other than current liabilities, such as "Indebtedness Due in 19x6 Refinanced in January 19x6."

EXAMPLE 4

43. In December 19x5 the Company negotiates a revolving credit agreement providing for unrestricted borrowings up to $10,000,000. Borrowings will bear interest at 1% over the prevailing prime rate of the bank with which the agreement is arranged but in any event not less than 8%, will have stated maturities of ninety days, and will be continuously renewable for ninety-day periods at the Company's option for three years provided there is compliance with the terms of the agreement. Pro-

visions of the agreement are similar to those cited in paragraph 34(d). Further, the enterprise intends to renew obligations incurred under the agreement for a period extending beyond one year from the balance-sheet date. There are no outstanding borrowings under the agreement at December 31, 19x5.

44. In this instance, the long-term debt maturing in February 19x6 and the 9% notes payable maturing in July 19x6 would be excluded from current liabilities because the Company consummated a financing agreement meeting the conditions set forth in paragraph 11(b) prior to the issuance of the balance sheet.

EXAMPLE 5

45. Assume that the agreement cited in Example 4 included an additional provision limiting the amount to be borrowed by the Company to the amount of its inventory, which is pledged as collateral and is expected to range between a high of $8,000,000 during the second quarter of 19x6 and a low of $4,000,000 during the fourth quarter of 19x6.

46. The terms of the agreement comply with the conditions required by this Statement; however, because the minimum amount expected to be available from February to December 19x6 is $4,000,000, only that amount of short-term obligations can be excluded from current liabilities (see paragraph 12). Whether the obligation to be excluded is a portion of the currently maturing long-term debt or some portions of both it and the 9% notes payable depends on the intended timing of the borrowing.

47. If the Company intended to refinance only the 9% notes payable due July 19x6 and the amount of its inventory is expected to reach a low of approximately $2,000,000 during the second quarter of 19x6 but be at least $3,000,000 in July 19x6 and thereafter during 19x6, the $3,000,000 9% notes payable would be excluded from current liabilities at December 31, 19x5 (see paragraph 12).

EXAMPLE 6

48. In lieu of the facts given in paragraphs 33(c) and 33(d), assume that during 19x5 the Company entered into a contract to have a warehouse built. The warehouse is expected to be financed by issuance of the Company's commercial paper. In addition, the Company negotiated a stand-by agreement with a commercial bank that provides for maximum borrowings equal to the expected cost of the warehouse, which will be pledged as collateral.

Statement of Financial Accounting Standards No. 7
Accounting and Reporting by Development Stage Enterprises

CONTENTS

INTRODUCTION

1. This Statement specifies the guidelines for identifying an enterprise in the development stage and the standards of financial accounting and reporting applicable to such an enterprise. The transition requirements of this Statement are also applicable to certain established operating enterprises.[1]

2. Some development stage enterprises have adopted special financial accounting and reporting practices, including special forms of financial statement presentation or types of disclosure, that are different from those used by established operating enterprises. Some of the special practices have resulted from applying regulations of the Securities and Exchange Commission; other practices appear simply to have evolved. Special accounting practices have included (a) deferral of all types of costs without regard to their recoverability, (b) nonassignment of dollar amounts to shares of stock issued for consideration other than cash, and (c) offset of revenue against deferred costs. Special reporting formats have included statements of (a) assets and unrecovered preoperating costs, (b) liabilities, (c) capital shares, and (d) cash receipts and disbursements. Sometimes, a balance sheet or a statement of operations is presented in conjunction with one or more special formats. Other development stage enterprises issue financial statements like those of established operating enterprises that present financial position, changes in financial position, and results of operations in conformity with generally accepted accounting principles.

3. No special standards of financial accounting and reporting were established for development stage enterprises by the AICPA Accounting Principles Board or its predecessor, the Committee on

Accounting Procedure. In 1973, the AICPA Committee on Companies in the Development Stage issued an exposure draft of a proposed Audit Guide recommending special financial statements and accounting methods, but no action was taken on the exposure draft and the matter was referred to the FASB. *FASB Statement No. 2,* "Accounting for Research and Development Costs," issued in October 1974, has been interpreted by the FASB to apply to "the accounting for research and development costs of development stage enterprises whose financial statements present financial position, changes in financial position, or results of operations in conformity with generally accepted accounting principles."[2] However, pending the issuance of a Statement on the subject of accounting and reporting by development stage enterprises, the FASB Interpretation stated that "a development stage enterprise that issues financial statements that do not purport to present financial position, changes in financial position, or results of operations in conformity with generally accepted accounting principles need not apply *Statement No. 2* in accounting for its research and development costs."[3]

4. The standards of financial accounting and reporting set forth in this Statement apply to any separate financial statements of a development stage subsidiary or other investee[4] of an established operating enterprise, as well as to the financial statements of a separate development stage enterprise (or of a group of companies that, as a whole, is considered to be in the development stage). Hereinafter, the term "development stage enterprise" is used to include a development stage subsidiary or other investee that is issuing separate financial statements.

5. This Statement applies to development stage enterprises in all industries. This Statement applies

---

[1]See paragraphs 14-16.

[2]*FASB Interpretation No. 5*, "Applicability of FASB Statement No. 2 to Development Stage Enterprises," para. 6.

[3]Ibid., para. 7

[4]The terms *subsidiary* and *investee* are defined in paragraph 3 of *APB Opinion No. 18,* "The Equity Method of Accounting for Investments in Common Stock."

to development stage enterprises in regulated industries in accordance with the provisions of the Addendum to *APB Opinion No. 2,* "Accounting for the 'Investment Credit.'" However, paragraphs 11-12 of this Statement, which require disclosure of additional information, apply to development stage enterprises in regulated industries in all cases.

6. This Statement supersedes *FASB Interpretation No. 5,* "Applicability of FASB Statement No. 2 to Development Stage Enterprises." It does not supersede, alter, or amend any other present requirement in an Accounting Research Bulletin (ARB), Accounting Principles Board (APB) Opinion, or FASB Statement or Interpretation. Neither does this Statement change generally accepted accounting principles that are currently applicable to established operating enterprises but that are not explicitly stated in an ARB, APB Opinion, or FASB Statement or Interpretation. For example, this Statement does not change generally accepted accounting principles applicable to (a) established operating enterprises generally in expanding their existing businesses, (b) established operating enterprises in the extractive industries in their exploration and development activities, and (c) established operating enterprises in the real estate industry in developing their properties.

7. Standards of financial accounting and reporting for development stage enterprises are set forth in paragraphs 8-16. Appendix B sets forth the basis for the Board's conclusions, including alternatives considered and reasons for accepting some and rejecting others. Appendix A provides background information.

STANDARDS OF FINANCIAL ACCOUNTING AND REPORTING

Guidelines for Identifying a Development Stage Enterprise

8. For purposes of this Statement, an enterprise shall be considered to be in the development stage if it is devoting substantially all of its efforts to establishing a new business and either of the following conditions exists:

a. Planned principal operations have not commenced.
b. Planned principal operations have commenced, but there has been no significant revenue therefrom.

9. A development stage enterprise will typically be devoting most of its efforts to activities such as financial planning; raising capital; exploring for natural resources; developing natural resources; research and development;[5] establishing sources of supply; acquiring property, plant, equipment, or other operating assets, such as mineral rights; recruiting and training personnel; developing markets; and starting up production.

Financial Accounting and Reporting

10. Financial statements issued by a development stage enterprise shall present financial position, changes in financial position, and results of operations in conformity with the generally accepted accounting principles that apply to established operating enterprises and shall include the additional information required by paragraphs 11-12. Special accounting practices and reporting formats, such as those described in paragraph 2 of this Statement, that are based on a distinctive accounting for development stage enterprises are no longer acceptable. Generally accepted accounting principles that apply to established operating enterprises shall govern the recognition of revenue by a development stage enterprise and shall determine whether a cost incurred by a development stage enterprise is to be charged to expense when incurred or is to be capitalized or deferred. Accordingly, capitalization or deferral of costs shall be subject to the same assessment of recoverability that would be applicable in an established operating enterprise. For a development stage subsidiary or other investee, the recoverability of costs shall be assessed within the entity for which separate financial statements are being presented.

11. In issuing the same basic financial statements as an established operating enterprise, a development stage enterprise shall disclose therein certain additional information. The basic financial statements to be presented[6] and the additional information shall include the following:

a. A balance sheet, including any cumulative net losses reported with a descriptive caption such as "deficit accumulated during the development stage" in the stockholders' equity section.
b. An income statement, showing amounts of revenue and expenses for each period covered by the income statement and, in addition, cumulative amounts from the enterprise's inception.[7]
c. A statement of changes in financial position,

---

[5] *Research and development* is defined in paragraph 8 of *FASB Statement No. 2,* "Accounting for Research and Development Costs."

[6] Under some circumstances, an established operating enterprise may issue less than a full set of financial statements, for example, only a balance sheet. This Statement does not preclude that possibility for development stage enterprises. Also, different titles or formats used by some established operating enterprises may be used provided that the prescribed information is included.

[7] For a dormant enterprise that is reactivated to undertake development stage activities, the disclosure of cumulative amounts required by this paragraph shall be from inception of the development stage.

showing the sources and uses of financial resources for each period for which an income statement is presented[8] and, in addition, cumulative amounts from the enterprise's inception.

d. A statement of stockholders' equity, showing from the enterprise's inception:[9]

1. For each issuance, the date and number of shares of stock, warrants, rights, or other equity securities issued for cash and for other consideration.

2. For each issuance, the dollar amounts (per share or other equity unit and in total) assigned to the consideration received for shares of stock, warrants, rights, or other equity securities. Dollar amounts shall be assigned to any noncash consideration received.

3. For each issuance involving noncash consideration, the nature of the noncash consideration and the basis for assigning amounts.

12. The financial statements shall be identified as those of a development stage enterprise and shall include a description of the nature of the development stage activities in which the enterprise is engaged.

13. The financial statements for the first fiscal year in which an enterprise is no longer considered to be in the development stage shall disclose that in prior years it had been in the development stage. If financial statements for prior years are presented for comparative purposes, the cumulative amounts and other additional disclosures required by paragraphs 11-12 need not be shown.

Effective Date and Transition

14. This Statement shall be effective for fiscal periods beginning on or after January 1, 1976, although earlier application is encouraged. Thereafter, when financial statements, or financial summaries or other data derived therefrom, are presented for periods prior to the effective date of this Statement, they shall be restated, where necessary, to conform to the provisions of this Statement. Accordingly, any items that would have been accounted for differently by a development stage enterprise if the provisions of paragraph 10 had then been applicable shall be accounted for by prior period adjustment (described in paragraphs 18 and 26 of *APB Opinion No. 9*, "Reporting the Results of Operations").

15. An established operating enterprise that during its development stage would have accounted for any items differently if the provisions of paragraph 10 had then been applicable shall account for those items by prior period adjustment. In some cases, those items will have been amortized or otherwise included in an income statement in periods prior to the effective date of this Statement. Financial statements, or financial summaries or other data derived therefrom, for those periods shall be restated when they are included for comparative purposes with financial data for periods after the effective date of this Statement.

16. The nature of any adjustment or restatement resulting from application of paragraphs 14-15 and, where appropriate, its effect on income before extraordinary items, net income, and related per share amounts shall be disclosed in the period of change for all periods presented. Any related income tax effects shall be recognized and disclosed.

The provisions of this Statement need not be applied to immaterial items.

This Statement was adopted by the affirmative votes of six members of the Financial Accounting Standards Board. Mr. Schuetze dissented.

Although he agrees with the basic conclusions in this Statement that development stage enterprises should use the same accounting principles and prepare the same basic financial statements as established operating enterprises, Mr. Schuetze dissents because he believes that the Board should have addressed the question of accounting for start-up costs before issuing this Statement. Paragraph 10 states that "capitalization or deferral of costs [in a development stage enterprise] shall be subject to the same assessment of recoverability that would be applicable in an established operating enterprise." A substantial portion of the costs incurred by many development stage enterprises falls into the broad category that most persons would regard as start-up costs. In Mr. Schuetze's view, neither this Statement

---

[8]Subject to the exceptions described in paragraphs 7 and 16 of *APB Opinion No. 19*, "Reporting Changes in Financial Position."

[9]Separate issuances of equity securities within the same fiscal year for the same type of consideration and for the same amount per equity unit may be combined in the statement of stockholders' equity. Appropriate modification of the statement of stockholders' equity may be required for (a) a combined group of companies that, as a whole, is considered to be in the development stage and (b) in unincorporated development stage enterprise.

nor any other authoritative pronouncement furnishes adequate guidance as to how the recoverability of start-up costs should be assessed or as to how those start-up costs that are capitalized or deferred should be accounted for thereafter. Mr. Schuetze believes that until such a pronouncement is issued the accounting practices of development stage enterprises will vary significantly. In this regard, Mr. Schuetze is particularly concerned as to how the recoverability test in paragraph 10 would be applied by development stage enterprises in the extractive industries.

Members of the Financial Accounting Standards Board:

Marshall S. Armstrong, *Chairman*	Donald J. Kirk	Walter Schuetze
Oscar S. Gellein	Arthur L. Litke	Robert T. Sprouse
	Robert E. Mays	

Appendix A

BACKGROUND INFORMATION

17. In April 1973, the FASB placed on its technical agenda a project on "Accounting for Research and Development and Similar Costs." The scope of the project also encompassed accounting and reporting by development stage enterprises, the subject of this Statement.

18. A task force of sixteen persons from industry, government, public accounting, the financial community, and academe was appointed in July 1973 to provide counsel to the Board in preparing a Discussion Memorandum analyzing issues related to the project.

19. The FASB did not undertake a major research effort in connection with the project but rather relied primarily on published research studies and articles that are cited in the Discussion Memorandum. Especially important in this regard was *Accounting for Companies in the Development Stage,* an exposure draft of an Audit Guide originally issued for comment in 1973 by the Committee on Companies in the Development Stage of the American Institute of Certified Public Accountants.

20. The Discussion Memorandum was issued by the Board on December 28, 1973, and a public hearing on the subject was held on March 15, 1974. Seventy-four position papers, letters of comment, and outlines of oral presentations were received by the Board in response to the Discussion Memorandum. Thirty-nine of those responses included recommendations about development stage enterprises. Fourteen oral presentations were made at the public hearing.

21. In the course of its deliberations following the hearing, the Board concluded that accounting and reporting by development stage enterprises should be addressed in a separate Statement of Financial Accounting Standards. An Exposure Draft of a proposed Statement on "Accounting and Reporting by Development Stage Companies, Subsidiaries, Divisions and Other Components" was issued on July 19, 1974. The Board received 138 letters of comment on the Exposure Draft. In November 1974, the Board announced that "because of questions raised in many of the comment letters received during exposure of the proposed Statement on development stage companies, the Standards Board is continuing its consideration of that subject and a final Statement is not expected to be issued before April or May of 1975."[10]

Appendix B

BASIS FOR CONCLUSIONS

22. This Appendix discusses factors deemed significant by members of the Board in reaching the conclusions in this Statement, including various alternatives considered and reasons for accepting some and rejecting others.

SCOPE OF THIS STATEMENT

23. As indicated by the title, the Exposure Draft, "Accounting and Reporting by Development Stage Companies, Subsidiaries, Divisions and Other Components," explicitly encompassed a development stage subsidiary, division, or other component of an established operating enterprise as well as a separate development stage enterprise. A number of respondents to the Exposure Draft interpreted the inclusion of subsidiaries, divisions, or other components of an established operating enterprise to mean that new financial accounting standards were being proposed for the costs incurred by established operating enterprises in expanding their existing businesses. Those respondents suggested that any changes called for by the proposed new standards in

---

[10]*FASB Status Report,* No. 19, November 16, 1974.

applicability of generally accepted accounting principles to them.

SEC Regulations and AICPA Committee Proposal

34. Both the regulations of the Securities and Exchange Commission (SEC) and the proposed Audit Guide issued by the AICPA Committee on Companies in the Development Stage provide for the use by development stage enterprises of certain accounting practices that differ from those appropriate for established operating enterprises.

35. Article 5A of SEC *Regulation S-X* prescribes the form and content of financial statements filed with the SEC by development stage enterprises. It provides for separate statements of (a) assets and unrecovered promotional, exploratory, and development costs; (b) liabilities; (c) capital shares; (d) other securities; and (e) cash receipts and disbursements. Among the types of costs indicated as includible in *unrecovered promotional, exploratory, and development costs* are:

> (a) development expenses, (b) plant and equipment maintenance expenses, (c) rehabilitation expenses, (d) general administrative expenses incurred in a period when there was little or no actual mining and (e) other expenses.... General administrative expenses incurred in connection with subcaptions (a), (b) and (c) should be included therein. Any other general administrative expenses not chargeable to those subcaptions nor written off as costs or other operating charges (including taxes, protection and conservation of property when inactive) shall be included under subcaption (d).[17]

Rule 12-06a of *Regulation S-X* allows for the offset of certain proceeds and other income against promotional, exploratory, and development costs.

36. The AICPA Committee proposed the presentation of cumulative cost outlays, together with assets, liabilities, and investment by stockholders, in a special statement referred to as a "preoperating accountability statement." Cumulative cost outlays would have been deferred and amortized by charges against income when operations commenced. Incidental revenue received during the development stage would have been deducted from the cumulative cost outlays.

37. The AICPA Committee stated the basis for its conclusion as follows:

A company in the development stage is engaged in building an enterprise, and the expenditures it makes are in the nature of investments for the future. Costs incurred during the development stage are accumulated because they have been incurred in the expectation that they will generate future revenues or otherwise benefit periods after the company reaches the operating stage. Accumulating costs is consistent with the business fact that for many companies a development stage must precede the attainment of ordinary business operations. . . . The only outlays that should not be carried as accumulated costs during the preoperating period are those relating to known losses. . . .

For a company in the development stage there is from inception a presumption that uncertainty as to cost recovery will both exist and persist. (By contrast, the presumption for an operating company is that cost recoverability can be reasonably evaluated.) It would be unrealistic and arbitrary to write off immediately the costs incurred during the development stage simply because of this predictable uncertainty.[18]

38. Both the SEC and AICPA Committee approaches draw attention to the uncertainty about cost recovery surrounding most development stage costs by segregating them in a special category and a special financial statement (or group of statements) similar to the conventional balance sheet. Those costs are not reported as "assets," and they need not be subjected to the assessment of recoverability that is applied to costs incurred by established operating enterprises. The Board believes, however, that the distinction between costs that would be reported as "assets" and costs that would be reported as "unrecovered costs" or "cumulative cost outlays" under the SEC and AICPA Committee approaches is one that is likely to be overlooked by many financial statement users. In addition, as indicated in paragraphs 30-33, the Board believes that all costs of a development stage enterprise should be subjected to the same assessment of recoverability applicable to costs incurred by established operating enterprises. In the Board's view, the nature of development stage activities and their related costs can best be indicated by the additional financial statement disclosures required by paragraphs 11-12, rather than by accumulation or deferral of costs that would be charged to expense when incurred if generally accepted accounting principles applicable to established operating enterprises were applied.

---

[17]U.S. Securities and Exchange Commission, *Regulation S-X*, Rule 5a-02, "Statement of Assets and Unrecovered Promotional, Exploratory, and Development Costs," item 14.

[18]American Institute of Certified Public Accountants, Committee on Companies in the Development Stage, *Accounting for Companies in the Development Stage,* an exposure draft of an Audit Guide (New York: AICPA, March 1973), pp. 25-26, 28.

39. Accumulation or deferral of development stage costs requires amortization after operations commence. Article 5A does not address the question of amortization, and the AICPA Committee noted that "while the current practices are anything but uniform, the most prevalent policy noted is to amortize such costs over a short period of time, usually not more than five years."[19] The Board believes that the difficulty in reasonably relating subsequent revenue to accumulated or deferred costs that would not be deferred under generally accepted accounting principles applicable to established operating enterprises limits the usefulness of the data that would result from such accumulation or deferral by a development stage enterprise. Moreover, the initial operating periods of such an enterprise would include both the amortization of those costs incurred during the development stage and the charging to expense of certain costs incurred currently.

40. Some respondents to the Discussion Memorandum and to the Exposure Draft supported the SEC approach, the proposed approach of the AICPA Committee, or similar approaches. The reasons offered were generally similar to those stated by the AICPA Committee (see paragraph 37). A number of respondents to the Discussion Memorandum and to the Exposure Draft recommended that development stage enterprises follow the same accounting standards as established operating enterprises. The reasons given by the respondents were generally similar to those specified in paragraph 30.

Relationship to "Similar Costs"

41. The Exposure Draft stated that the Board was considering an additional pronouncement on the "similar costs" identified in the Discussion Memorandum. A number of respondents to the Exposure Draft indicated that because, in their view, many costs incurred by development stage enterprises are within a broader category of costs that include start-up costs generally, the Board should address accounting for those "similar costs" before issuing a final Statement on development stage enterprises. The Board considered those suggestions, but concluded that it could reach an informed decision on the issues covered in this Statement without first addressing the more pervasive issues associated with accounting for "similar costs." In the Board's view, this Statement will significantly improve financial accounting and reporting for development stage enterprises.

FINANCIAL STATEMENT PRESENTATION AND ADDITIONAL DISCLOSURES

42. The Board believes that a development stage enterprise should present the same basic financial statements as any other enterprise. The conventional balance sheet, income statement, statement of changes in financial position, and statement of stockholders' equity are sufficiently adaptable to provide the distinctive information that might be considered useful for development stage enterprises. Unique financial statements for development stage enterprises might imply that the nature and results of the transactions entered into by those enterprises are unique, but many established operating enterprises have similar transactions. Further, unique financial statements would not be readily comparable with financial statements issued after an enterprise has emerged from the development stage. Also, the conclusion that the same accounting principles are appropriate for the transactions of development stage enterprises suggests that conventional basic financial statements should be presented.

43. A development stage enterprise typically will be incurring substantial costs in connection with development stage activities and will not have significant revenue. Development stage activities are likely to extend into two or more financial reporting periods. To reflect the significance of development stage activities, the Board believes that the basic financial statements presented by a development stage enterprise should be expanded to provide cumulative financial information since its inception, as well as current information. The Board concluded that disclosure of cumulative revenue and expenses and cumulative amounts of funds obtained from various sources to finance the development effort and initial operations will provide useful information about the activities of development stage enterprises without sacrificing the advantages of retaining the familiar format and content of the basic financial statements of established operating enterprises. Those additional disclosures are specified in paragraphs 11-12.

44. Some respondents to the Discussion Memorandum and Exposure Draft suggested that the differences between established operating enterprises and development stage enterprises are so fundamental as to require unique financial statements for development stage enterprises. The AICPA Committee concluded that, because of the absence of revenue, a conventional income statement would be

---

[19]Ibid., p. 11

inappropriate for a development stage enterprise; unique financial statements were deemed necessary to emphasize accountability for financial resources received and expended and to direct attention to accumulated costs rather than to measurement of performance. To accomplish those objectives, the Committee recommended the following special statements:

Preoperating accountability statement—to show the assets and cumulative cost outlays, the liabilities, and the investment by stockholders.

Statement of preoperating financial activities—to show the sources and uses of financial resources, preferably cumulative since an enterprise's inception along with data for the current period.

Statement of investment by stockholders—to show the classes and numbers of shares authorized, issued, and outstanding and the types of amounts of consideration received for the shares issued.

45. The AICPA Committee proposed extensive disclosures emphasizing that the enterprise is in the development stage, calling attention to the uncertainties that surround the enterprise and making clear that the financial statements do not purport to present financial position and results of operations.

46. Other respondents to the Discussion Memorandum and to the Exposure Draft took the position that different basic financial statements or additional disclosures are not necessary for a development stage enterprise. Still others asserted that the same basic financial statements are appropriate but should be supplemented by additional disclosures relevant to the distinctive features of a development stage enterprise.

Other Suggestions

47. The Board considered other presentation and disclosure possibilities for a development stage enterprise (including forecasts, disclosure of liquidation priorities and values, and a description of the business environment) and concluded that they should not be required solely for development stage enterprises. The Board also considered the possibility of a statement of cash receipts and disbursements and concluded that the statement of changes in financial position including amounts on a cumulative basis required by paragraph 11(c) would fulfill that need.

POTENTIAL ECONOMIC IMPACT

48. Some respondents to the Exposure Draft expressed concern that requiring development stage

enterprises to present the same basic financial statements and to apply the same generally accepted accounting principles as established operating enterprises might make it difficult, if not impossible, for development stage enterprises to obtain capital. They suggested that those requirements would likely cause many development stage enterprises to report periodic losses in an income statement and a cumulative deficit in a balance sheet. Because those results would not be fully understood, suppliers of capital would be disinclined to invest in those enterprises.

49. During the course of developing the Discussion Memorandum and preparing the Exposure Draft, the FASB solicited information about the potential economic impact of applying to development stage enterprises the same generally accepted accounting principles that apply to established operating enterprises. Responses of financial statement users to the Discussion Memorandum and to the Exposure Draft provided only limited information about the potential economic impact. To obtain additional information, the FASB arranged for discussions with officers of fifteen venture capital enterprises. The consensus of those officers was that whether a development stage enterprise defers or expenses preoperating costs has little effect on (a) the amount of any venture capital to be provided to that enterprise and (b) the terms under which any venture capital is provided. According to those officers, the venture capital investor typically relies on an investigation of the technological, marketing, management, and financial aspects of an enterprise. That investigation provides a basis for estimating potential cash flows and the probabilities of achieving them. Whether a development stage enterprise defers or expenses its preoperating costs does not affect those estimates. Based on their experience, those officers also expressed the opinion that the accounting treatment of preoperating costs would have minimal impact on the availability of short-term credit from commercial banks, but might have impact on the investment and credit decisions of unsophisticated investors.

50. In January 1975, the U.S. Department of Commerce issued a report of a study entitled "Impact of FASB's Rule Two Accounting for Research and Development Costs on Small/Developing Stage Firms." The study involved interviews with forty lenders and investors, eleven small, high-technology firms, eleven accountants, and selected government agencies. It focused primarily on the impact on investment and credit decisions concerning development stage enterprises if they were required to charge research and development costs to expense when incurred. That issue is related to the issue at hand—that is, the potential economic impact on development stage enterprises of requiring certain

costs to be expensed when incurred rather than deferred. The conclusions of the Department of Commerce study were generally consistent with the FASB findings described in paragraph 49 of this Statement. Specifically, the study concluded that "FASB's Statement Two should not have a significant impact on those firms who have heretofore capitalized R&D."[20]

51. In summary, the Board has concluded that the cumulative income statement information and the cumulative information about changes in financial position required in paragraph 11 of this Statement will provide the cumulative information about pre-operating costs that is typically provided by development stage enterprises currently when using special reporting formats and special accounting practices, such as those cited in paragraph 2. In addition, this Statement requires such information to be presented in financial statements whose formats are familiar and, therefore, less likely to be misinterpreted. As for the concerns of some respondents, the results of FASB discussions and the Department of Commerce study suggest that this Statement will have no significant adverse effect on the ability of development stage enterprises to obtain capital.

ISSUANCE OF SHARES OF STOCK OTHER THAN FOR CASH

52. Under the provisions of Article 5A of SEC *Regulation S-X,* dollar amounts are not assigned to shares of stock issued by a development stage enterprise for noncash consideration, or to the consideration received, unless the noncash consideration has a "fixed or objectively determinable value."

53. The proposed AICPA Audit Guide would have required assignment of dollar amounts to shares of stock issued for noncash consideration, and to the consideration received, at the time of issuance.

54. The Board agrees with the conclusion of the AICPA Committee, and of a number of respondents to the Discussion Memorandum and Exposure Draft who addressed this question, that those transactions should be accounted for when the shares are issued in accordance with the guidelines applicable to acquisition of assets or issuance of shares in general. The transactions are not unique to development stage enterprises and should not be accounted for differently by those enterprises, even if estimates and judgments are required to determine their values.

EFFECTIVE DATE AND TRANSITION

55. The Board adopted the restatement provisions set forth in paragraphs 14-16 because, in its view, this approach provides the most useful information about development stage enterprises and about those previously in the development stage in comparing financial data for periods after the effective date of this Statement with data presented for earlier periods.

---

[20]U.S. Department of Commerce, "Impact of FASB's Rule Two Accounting for Research and Development Costs on Small/Developing Stage Firms" (Washington, D.C.: U.S. Department of Commerce, January 20, 1975), p. 3.

Statement of Financial Accounting Standards No. 8
Accounting for the Translation of Foreign Currency
Transactions and Foreign Currency Financial Statements

STATUS

Issued: October 1975

Effective Date: For fiscal years beginning on or after January 1, 1976

Affects: Amends ARB 43, Chapter 12, paragraph 5
Supersedes ARB 43, Chapter 12, paragraphs 7 and 10 through 22
Supersedes APB 6, paragraph 18
Amends APB 22, paragraph 13
Supersedes FAS 1

Affected by: Paragraphs 27 and 35 amended by FAS 20
Superseded by FAS 52

Other Interpretive Pronouncements: FIN 15 (Superseded by FAS 52)
FIN 17 (Superseded by FAS 52)

(This page intentionally left blank.)

Statement of Financial Accounting Standards No. 9
Accounting for Income Taxes—Oil and Gas Producing Companies

an amendment of APB Opinions No. 11 and 23

STATUS

Issued: October 1975

Effective Date: For financial statements issued on or after December 1, 1975

Affects: Supersedes APB 11, paragraph 40
Amends APB 23, paragraph 2

Affected by: Superseded by FAS 19

(This page intentionally left blank.)

Statement of Financial Accounting Standards No. 10
Extension of "Grandfather" Provisions for Business Combinations

an amendment of APB Opinion No. 16

STATUS

Issued: October 1975

Effective Date: November 1, 1975

Affects: Amends APB 16, paragraph 99
Amends AIN-APB 16, Interpretations No. 15, 17, and 24

Affected by: No other pronouncements

Statement of Financial Accounting Standards No. 10

Extension of "Grandfather" Provisions for Business Combinations

an amendment of APB Opinion No. 16

CONTENTS

INTRODUCTION AND BACKGROUND INFORMATION

1. *APB Opinion No. 16,* "Business Combinations," which became effective for business combinations initiated after October 31, 1970, establishes conditions that must be met for a business combination to be accounted for by the pooling of interests method. Paragraph 99 of that Opinion, however, provides an exemption from certain of those conditions for a business combination between two companies with certain intercorporate investments at October 31, 1970 if "the combination is completed within five years after October 31, 1970." That exemption has been referred to as a "grandfather clause." AICPA Accounting Interpretations No. 15, 16, 17, and 26 of *APB Opinion No. 16* relate to that grandfather clause.

2. In addition, AICPA Accounting Interpretation No. 24 of *APB Opinion No. 16* contains a grandfather provision related to paragraph 46(a) of that Opinion and permits certain subsidiaries to account for business combinations by the pooling of interests method. In part, the Interpretation states:

> Subsidiaries which had a *significant* outstanding minority interest at October 31, 1970 may take part in a pooling combination completed within five years after that date providing the significant minority also exists at the initiation of the combination. In addition, the combination must meet all of the other pooling conditions specified in paragraphs 46 through 48. . . .
>
> For purposes of this Interpretation, a sig-

nificant minority means that at least 20 percent of the voting common stock of the subsidiary is owned by persons not affiliated with the parent company.

This "grandfathering" is consistent with paragraph 99 of the Opinion and applies both to combinations where the subsidiary with a significant minority interest is the issuing corporation and those where it is the other combining company. However, it does not permit a pooling between a subsidiary and its parent.

3. The FASB presently has on its technical agenda a project entitled "Accounting for Business Combinations and Purchased Intangibles," which involves a reconsideration of *APB Opinion No. 16.* Consequently, accounting practices that would change if the grandfather provisions of that Opinion expire on October 31, 1975 might, once again, be changed as a result of the FASB's reconsideration of the Opinion. The Board believes that because it is reconsidering *APB Opinion No. 16* the grandfather provisions of the Opinion and related AICPA Accounting Interpretations should continue in effect so as to maintain the status quo during the Board's reconsideration of that Opinion.

4. An Exposure Draft of a proposed Statement on "Extension of 'Grandfather' Provisions for Business Combinations" was issued on September 8, 1975. Twenty-two letters were received in response to that Exposure Draft. No substantive changes were suggested by respondents, and this Statement contains no substantive changes from the Exposure Draft.

5. The Board concluded that on the basis of existing data it could make an informed decision on the matter addressed in this Statement without a public hearing and that the effective date set forth in paragraph 8 is advisable.

STANDARDS OF FINANCIAL ACCOUNTING AND REPORTING

6. The five-year limitation in the grandfather provisions contained in paragraph 99 of *APB Opinion No. 16* and in the AICPA Accounting Interpretations cited in paragraphs 1-2 of this Statement is eliminated.

Amendment to Existing Pronouncement

7. The wording "the combination is completed within five years after October 31, 1970 and" in paragraph 99 of *APB Opinion No. 16* and similar wording in the AICPA Accounting Interpretations cited in paragraphs 1-2 of this Statement, imposing an October 31, 1975 expiration date for the grandfather provisions, are deleted.

Effective Date

8. This Statement shall be effective on November 1, 1975.

> **The provisions of this Statement need**
> **not be applied to immaterial items.**

This Statement was adopted by the unanimous vote of the seven members of the Financial Accounting Standards Board:

Marshall S. Armstrong,
  Chairman
Oscar S. Gellein

Donald J. Kirk
Arthur L. Litke
Robert E. Mays

Walter Schuetze
Robert T. Sprouse

(This page intentionally left blank.)

financial data for periods after the adoption of the Statement with prior periods.

4. The Board recently issued *FASB Statement No. 8,* "Accounting for the Translation of Foreign Currency Transactions and Foreign Currency Financial Statements." With respect to that Statement's effective date and transition, paragraphs 35 and 36 of that Statement read as follows:

This Statement shall be effective for fiscal years beginning on or after January 1, 1976,[14] although earlier application is encouraged. Thereafter, if financial statements for periods before the effective date, and financial summaries or other data derived therefrom, are presented, they shall be restated, if practicable, to conform to the provisions of paragraphs 7-31 of this Statement. In the year that this Statement is first applied, the financial statements shall disclose the nature of any restatement and its effect on income before extraordinary items, net income, and related per share amounts for each period restated.

If restatement of financial statements or summaries for all prior periods presented is not practicable, information presented shall be restated for as many consecutive periods immediately preceding the effective date of this Statement as is practicable, and the cumulative effect of applying paragraphs 7-31 on the retained earnings at the beginning of the earliest period restated (or at the beginning of the period in which the Statement is first applied if it is not practicable to restate any prior periods) shall be included in determining net income of that period (see paragraph 20 of *APB Opinion No. 20,* "Accounting Changes").[15] The effect on income before extraordinary items, net income, and related per share amounts of applying this Statement in a period in which the cumulative effect is included in determining net income shall be disclosed for that period, and the reason for not restating all of the prior periods presented shall be explained.

[14]For enterprises having fiscal years of 52 or 53 weeks instead of the calendar year, this Statement shall be effective for fiscal years beginning in late December 1975.

[15]Pro forma disclosures required by paragraphs 19(d) and 21 of *APB Opinion No. 20* are not applicable.

5. Although the Exposure Draft of *FASB Statement No. 8* indicated that transition under that State-

ment would be required in accordance with paragraphs 19-21, 25, and 39 of *APB Opinion No. 20* (viz., to include in the determination of net income in the year of change the effect of the accounting change), in the final Statement, the Board concluded that prior period restatement is the preferable method to provide useful information about foreign currency transactions and foreign operations for comparing financial data for a number of periods. In Appendix D, "Basis for Conclusions," of that Statement, paragraphs 240 and 241 read as follows:

The Board concluded that because of the various methods of translation or of recognition of exchange gains and losses now followed in practice and because of the complex nature of the translation process, a prospective method of transition is not feasible. The Board considered whether the transition should be by prior period restatement or by cumulative effect adjustment (the method specified in the Exposure Draft). The Board concluded that prior period restatement is the preferable method to provide useful information about foreign currency transactions and foreign operations for purposes of comparing financial data for periods after the effective date of this Statement with data presented for earlier periods.

The Board recognizes, however, that the procedures called for by this Statement may sometimes differ significantly from procedures followed in previous periods. In addition, restatement requires the availability of records or information that an enterprise may no longer have or that its past procedures did not require. Therefore, if the effect of the restatement on all individual periods presented cannot be computed or reasonably estimated, the cumulative effect adjustment method shall be used in accordance with paragraph 36.

Reconsideration of the Transition Method of FASB Statement No. 5

6. In considering and resolving the issue of transition in *FASB Statement No. 8,* the Board was mindful that there were similarities in characteristics of certain accounts affected by *FASB Statement No. 8* and *FASB Statement No. 5.* As indicated in paragraph 104 of *FASB Statement No. 5,* one of the factors that led the Board to conclude that use of the cumulative effect

method would be preferable to restatement of financial statements for prior periods was its concern about the cases in which there might be significant difficulties in determining the degree of probability and estimability that existed in the prior periods. After reconsideration of the differences in the transition methods required by *FASB Statements No. 5* and *8* and the factors that led the Board to reach different conclusions on transition in those two Statements, the Board has concluded that the cumulative effect method should not be required as it now is by *FASB Statement No. 5* in those cases in which the difficulties of determining probability and estimability retroactively are not present. On reconsideration of all the circumstances, the Board has concluded that in order to provide the most useful information, it is preferable for an enterprise adopting *FASB Statement No. 5* to restate its financial statements for as many immediately preceding periods as is practicable in accordance with the revised transition method set forth in paragraph 10 of this Statement.

7. Some enterprises elected to apply *FASB Statement No. 5* prior to its effective date (as encouraged in paragraph 20 of the Statement) and issued annual or interim financial statements or financial summaries or other data derived therefrom using the cumulative effect method of transition. The Board considered whether those enterprises should now be required to conform to the method of transition to *FASB Statement No. 5* specified by this Statement. Although the Board strongly encourages those enterprises to restate their financial statements in a manner similar to that required of enterprises that did not elect early application, it has concluded that it should not require them to do so.

8. An Exposure Draft of a proposed Statement on "Accounting for Contingencies—Transition Method" was issued on October 31, 1975. Forty-five letters were received in response to that Exposure Draft.

9. The Board concluded that on the basis of existing data it could make an informed decision on the matter addressed in this Statement without a public hearing and that the effective date in paragraph 11 is advisable.

STANDARDS OF FINANCIAL ACCOUNTING AND REPORTING

Amendment to FASB Statement No. 5

10. Paragraph 20 of *FASB Statement No. 5* is amended to read as follows:

FASB Statement No. 5 shall be effective for fiscal years beginning on or after July 1, 1975, although earlier application is encouraged. Thereafter, if financial statements for periods before the effective date, and financial summaries or other data derived therefrom, are presented, they shall be restated, if practicable, to conform to the provisions of paragraph 8 or 14 of *FASB Statement No. 5*.* In the year that the Statement is first applied, the financial statements shall disclose the nature of any restatement and its effect on income before extraordinary items, net income, and related per share amounts for each period restated. If restatement of financial statements or summaries for all prior periods presented is not practicable, information presented shall be restated for as many consecutive periods immediately preceding the effective date of *FASB Statement No. 5* as is practicable, and the cumulative effect of applying paragraph 8 or 14 on the retained earnings at the beginning of the earliest period restated (or at the beginning of the period in which the Statement is first applied if it is not practicable to restate any prior periods) shall be included in determining net income of that period (see paragraph 20 of *APB Opinion No. 20*).** The effect on income before extraordinary items, net income, and related per share amounts of applying *FASB Statement No. 5* in a period in which the cumulative effect is included in determining net income shall be disclosed for that period, and the

Statement of Financial Accounting Standards No. 13
Accounting for Leases

STATUS

Issued: November 1976

Effective Date: For leasing transactions and revisions entered into on or after January 1, 1977

Affects: Supersedes APB 5
Supersedes APB 7
Supersedes APB 18, paragraphs 15 and footnote 5
Supersedes APB 27
Supersedes APB 31

Affected by: Paragraph 3 superseded by FAS 71
Paragraphs 5, 5(j)(i), 12, 16(a)(iv), 17(b), and 18(b) amended by FAS 29
Paragraphs 5, 6(b)(i), 7(a), 8, 17(a), 19, 25, 26(a), and 26(b)(ii)(b) amended by FAS 98
Paragraph 5(b) superseded by FAS 23
Paragraphs 5(f), 6(b)(iv), 8(a), 18(a), 18(b), 26(a)(ii), and 26(b)(i)(b) superseded by FAS 98
Paragraph 5(m) superseded by FAS 17
Paragraphs 5(m), 23(a)(i), and 23(a)(iii) superseded by FAS 91
Paragraphs 6(b)(i), 6(b)(ii), and 17(f)(ii) amended by FAS 27
Paragraphs 8(b), 10, 17(a), 18(a), 26(a)(i), and 43(c) amended by FAS 23
Paragraph 8 amended by FAS 26
Paragraph 12 amended by FAS 34
Paragraphs 14 and 17(f) amended by FAS 22
Paragraphs 18(a) and 18(b) amended by FAS 91
Paragraph 20 amended by FAS 77 and FAS 125
Paragraphs 32 and 33 superseded by FAS 28
Paragraph 47 amended by FAS 96 and FAS 109
Footnote 13 superseded by FAS 29

Other Interpretive Pronouncements: FIN 19
FIN 21
FIN 23
FIN 24
FIN 26
FIN 27
FTB 79-10
FTB 79-11 (Superseded by FAS 98)
FTB 79-12
FTB 79-13
FTB 79-14
FTB 79-15
FTB 79-16 (Superseded by FTB 79-16(R))
FTB 79-16(R)
FTB 79-17
FTB 85-3
FTB 86-2
FTB 88-1

Issues Discussed by FASB Emerging Issues Task Force (EITF)

Affects: No EITF Issues

Interpreted by: Paragraphs 1 and 5(j) interpreted by EITF Issue No. 95-1
      Paragraphs 5(j)(i) and 5(n) interpreted by EITF Issue No. 86-33
      Paragraph 7 interpreted by EITF Issue No. 97-1
      Paragraph 7(d) interpreted by EITF Issue No. 96-21
      Paragraphs 21 and 22 interpreted by EITF Issue No. 95-4
      Paragraph 26(b)(ii) interpreted by EITF Issue No. 92-1
      Paragraph 34 interpreted by EITF Issue No. 88-21
      Paragraph 42(c) interpreted by EITF Issue No. 85-16
      Paragraph 46 interpreted by EITF Issue No. 86-43

Related Issues: EITF Issues No. 84-37, 85-27, 86-17, 86-44, 87-7, 88-10, 89-16, 89-20, 90-15, 93-8, 95-6, and 95-17 and Topics No. D-8 and D-14

(This page intentionally left blank.)

Statement of Financial Accounting Standards No. 13
Accounting for Leases

CONTENTS

INTRODUCTION

1. This Statement establishes standards of financial accounting and reporting for leases by lessees and lessors. For purposes of this Statement, a lease is defined as an agreement conveying the right to use property, plant, or equipment (land and/or depreciable assets) usually for a stated period of time. It includes agreements that, although not nominally identified as leases, meet the above definition, such as a "heat supply contract" for nuclear fuel.[1] This definition does not include agreements that are contracts for services that do not transfer the right to use property, plant, or equipment from one contracting party to the other. On the other hand, agreements that do transfer the right to use property, plant, or equipment meet the definition of a lease for purposes of this Statement even though substantial services by the contractor (lessor) may be called for in connection with the operation or maintenance of such assets. This Statement does not apply to lease agreements concerning the rights to explore for or to exploit natural resources such as oil, gas, minerals, and timber. Nor does it apply to licensing agreements for items such as motion picture films, plays, manuscripts, patents, and copyrights.

2. This Statement supersedes *APB Opinion No. 5,* "Reporting of Leases in Financial Statements of Lessee"; *APB Opinion No. 7,* "Accounting for Leases in Financial Statements of Lessors"; paragraph 15 of *APB Opinion No. 18,* "The Equity Method of Accounting for Investments in Common Stock"; *APB Opinion No. 27,* "Accounting for Lease Transactions by Manufacturer or Dealer Lessors"; and *APB Opinion No. 31,* "Disclosure of Lease Commitments by Lessees."

3. This Statement applies to regulated enterprises in accordance with the provisions of the Addendum to *APB Opinion No. 2,* "Accounting for the 'Investment Credit'."

4. Appendix A provides background information. Appendix B sets forth the basis for the Board's conclusions, including alternatives considered and reasons for accepting some and rejecting others. Illustrations of the accounting and disclosure requirements for lessees and lessors called for by this Statement are contained in Appendixes C and D. An example of the application of the accounting and disclosure provisions for leveraged leases is provided in Appendix E.

---

[1] Heat supply (also called "burn-up") contracts usually provide for payments by the user-lessee based upon nuclear fuel utilization in the period plus a charge for the unrecovered cost base. The residual value usually accrues to the lessee, and the lessor furnishes no service other than the financing.

STANDARDS OF FINANCIAL ACCOUNTING AND REPORTING

Definitions of Terms

5. For purposes of this Statement, certain terms are defined as follows:

a. *Related parties in leasing transactions.* A parent company and its subsidiaries, an owner company and its joint ventures (corporate or otherwise) and partnerships, and an investor (including a natural person) and its investees, provided that the parent company, owner company, or investor has the ability to exercise significant influence over operating and financial policies of the related party, as significant influence is defined in *APB Opinion No. 18,* paragraph 17. In addition to the examples of significant influence set forth in that paragraph, significant influence may be exercised through guarantees of indebtedness, extensions of credit, or through ownership of warrants, debt obligations, or other securities. If two or more entities are subject to the significant influence of a parent, owner company, investor (including a natural person), or common officers or directors, those entities shall be considered related parties with respect to each other.

b. *Inception of the lease.* With the exception noted below, the date of the lease agreement or commitment, if earlier. For purposes of this definition, a commitment shall be in writing, signed by the parties in interest to the transaction, and shall specifically set forth the principal terms of the transaction. However, if the property covered by the lease has yet to be constructed or has not been acquired by the lessor at the date of the lease agreement or commitment, the inception of the lease shall be the date that construction of the property is completed or the property is acquired by the lessor.

c. *Fair value of the leased property.* The price for which the property could be sold in an arm's-length transaction between unrelated parties. (See definition of related parties in leasing transactions in paragraph 5(a).) The following are examples of the determination of fair value:

i. When the lessor is a manufacturer or dealer, the fair value of the property at the inception of the lease (as defined in paragraph 5(b)) will ordinarily be its normal selling price, reflecting any volume or trade discounts that may be applicable. However, the determination of fair value shall be made in light of market conditions prevailing at the time, which may indicate that the fair value of the property is less than the normal selling price and, in some instances, less than the cost of the property.

ii. When the lessor is not a manufacturer or dealer, the fair value of the property at the inception of the lease will ordinarily be its cost, reflecting any volume or trade discounts that may be applicable. However, when there has been a significant lapse of time between the acquisition of the property by the lessor and the inception of the lease, the determination of fair value shall be made in light of market conditions prevailing at the inception of the lease, which may indicate that the fair value of the property is greater or less than its cost or carrying amount, if different. (See paragraph 6(b).)

d. *Bargain purchase option.* A provision allowing the lessee, at his option, to purchase the leased property for a price which is sufficiently lower than the expected fair value of the property at the date the option becomes exercisable that exercise of the option appears, at the inception of the lease, to be reasonably assured.

e. *Bargain renewal option.* A provision allowing the lessee, at his option, to renew the lease for a rental sufficiently lower than the fair rental[2] of the property at the date the option becomes exercisable that exercise of the option appears, at the inception of the lease, to be reasonably assured.

f. *Lease term.* The fixed noncancelable term of the lease plus (i) all periods, if any, covered by bargain renewal options (as defined in paragraph 5(e)), (ii) all periods, if any, for which failure to renew the lease imposes a penalty on the lessee in an amount such that renewal appears, at the inception of the lease, to be reasonably assured, (iii) all periods, if any, covered by ordinary renewal options during which a guarantee by the lessee of the lessor's debt related to the leased property is expected to be in effect, (iv) all periods, if any, covered by ordinary renewal options preceding the date as of which a bargain purchase option (as defined in paragraph 5(d)) is exercisable, and (v) all periods, if any, representing renewals or extensions of the lease at the lessor's option; however, in no case shall the lease term extend beyond the date a bargain purchase option becomes exercisable. A lease which is cancelable (i) only upon the occurrence of some remote contingency, (ii) only with the permission of the lessor, (iii) only if the lessee enters into a new lease with the same lessor, or (iv) only upon payment by the lessee of a penalty in an amount such that continuation of the lease appears, at inception, reasonably assured shall be considered "noncancelable" for purposes of this definition.

---

[2]"Fair rental" in this context shall mean the expected rental for equivalent property under similar terms and conditions.

g. *Estimated economic life of leased property.*
The estimated remaining period during which
the property is expected to be economically usable by one or more users, with normal repairs
and maintenance, for the purpose for which it
was intended at the inception of the lease,
without limitation by the lease term.

h. *Estimated residual value of leased property.*
The estimated fair value of the leased property
at the end of the lease term (as defined in paragraph 5(f)).

i. *Unguaranteed residual value.* The estimated
residual value of the leased property (as defined in paragraph 5(h)) exclusive of any portion guaranteed by the lessee[3] or by a third
party unrelated to the lessor.[4]

j. *Minimum lease payments.*

  i. From the standpoint of the lessee: The payments that the lessee is obligated to make or
  can be required to make in connection with
  the leased property. However, a guarantee
  by the lessee of the lessor's debt and the lessee's obligation to pay (apart from the
  rental payments) executory costs such as insurance, maintenance, and taxes in connection with the leased property shall be excluded. If the lease contains a bargain
  purchase option, only the minimum rental
  payments over the lease term (as defined in
  paragraph 5(f)) and the payment called for
  by the bargain purchase option shall be included in the minimum lease payments.
  Otherwise, minimum lease payments include the following:

   (a) The minimum rental payments called
   for by the lease over the lease term.

   (b) Any guarantee by the lessee[5] of the residual value at the expiration of the
   lease term, whether or not payment of
   the guarantee constitutes a purchase of
   the leased property. When the lessor
   has the right to require the lessee to purchase the property at termination of the
   lease for a certain or determinable
   amount, that amount shall be considered a lessee guarantee. When the lessee
   agrees to make up any deficiency below
   a stated amount in the lessor's realization of the residual value, the guarantee
   to be included in the minimum lease
   payments shall be the stated amount,
   rather than an estimate of the deficiency to be made up.

   (c) Any payment that the lessee must make
   or can be required to make upon failure
   to renew or extend the lease at the expiration of the lease term, whether or not
   the payment would constitute a purchase of the leased property. In this
   connection, it should be noted that the
   definition of lease term in paragraph
   5(f) includes "all periods, if any, for
   which failure to renew the lease imposes
   a penalty on the lessee in an amount
   such that renewal appears, at the inception of the lease, to be reasonably assured." If the lease term has been extended because of that provision, the
   related penalty shall not be included in
   minimum lease payments.

  ii. From the standpoint of the lessor: The payments described in (i) above plus any guarantee of the residual value or of rental payments beyond the lease term by a third
  party unrelated to either the lessee[6] or the
  lessor,[7] provided the third party is financially capable of discharging the obligations that may arise from the guarantee.

k. *Interest rate implicit in the lease.* The discount
rate that, when applied to (i) the minimum
lease payments (as defined in paragraph 5(j)),
excluding that portion of the payments representing executory costs to be paid by the lessor,
together with any profit thereon, and (ii) the
unguaranteed residual value (as defined in
paragraph 5(i)) accruing to the benefit of the
lessor,[8] causes the aggregate present value at
the beginning of the lease term to be equal to
the fair value of the leased property (as defined
in paragraph 5(c)) to the lessor at the inception
of the lease, minus any investment tax credit
retained by the lessor and expected to be realized by him. (This definition does not necessarily purport to include all factors that a lessor
might recognize in determining his rate of return, e.g., see paragraph 44.)

l. *Lessee's incremental borrowing rate.* The rate
that, at the inception of the lease, the lessee
would have incurred to borrow over a similar
term the funds necessary to purchase the leased
asset.

m. *Initial direct costs.* Those incremental direct
costs incurred by the lessor in negotiating and
consummating leasing transactions (e.g., commissions and legal fees).

---

[3]A guarantee by a third party related to the lessee shall be considered a lessee guarantee.

[4]If the guarantor is related to the lessor, the residual value shall be considered as unguaranteed.

[5]See footnote 3.

[6]See footnote 3.

[7]See footnote 4.

[8]If the lessor is not entitled to any excess of the amount realized on disposition of the property over a guaranteed amount, no unguaranteed residual value would accrue to his benefit.

Classification of Leases for Purposes of This Statement

6. For purposes of applying the accounting and reporting standards of this Statement, leases are classified as follows:

a. Classifications from the standpoint of the lessee:
   i. *Capital leases.* Leases that meet one or more of the criteria in paragraph 7.
   ii. *Operating leases.* All other leases.
b. Classifications from the standpoint of the lessor:
   i. *Sales-type leases.* Leases that give rise to manufacturer's or dealer's profit (or loss) to the lessor (i.e., the fair value of the leased property at the inception of the lease is greater or less than its cost or carrying amount, if different) and that meet one or more of the criteria in paragraph 7 and both of the criteria in paragraph 8. Normally, sales-type leases will arise when manufacturers or dealers use leasing as a means of marketing their products. Leases involving lessors that are primarily engaged in financing operations normally will not be sales-type leases if they qualify under paragraphs 7 and 8, but will most often be direct financing leases, described in paragraph 6(b)(ii) below. However, a lessor need not be a dealer to realize dealer's profit (or loss) on a transaction, e.g., if a lessor, not a dealer, leases an asset that at the inception of the lease has a fair value that is greater or less than its cost or carrying amount, if different, such a transaction is a sales-type lease, assuming the criteria referred to are met. A renewal or an extension[9] of an existing sales-type or direct financing lease shall not be classified as a sales-type lease; however, if it qualifies under paragraphs 7 and 8, it shall be classified as a direct financing lease. (See paragraph 17(f).)
   ii. *Direct financing leases.* Leases other than leveraged leases that do not give rise to manufacturer's or dealer's profit (or loss) to the lessor but that meet one or more of the criteria in paragraph 7 and both of the criteria in paragraph 8. In such leases, the cost or carrying amount, if different, and fair value of the leased property are the same at the inception of the lease. An exception arises when an existing lease is renewed or extended.[10] In such cases, the fact that the carrying amount of the property at the end of the original lease term is different from its fair value at that date shall not preclude the classification of the renewal or extension as a direct financing lease. (See paragraph 17(f).)

   iii. *Leveraged leases.* Leases that meet the criteria of paragraph 42.
   iv. *Operating leases.* All other leases.

Criteria for Classifying Leases (Other Than Leveraged Leases)

7. The criteria for classifying leases set forth in this paragraph and in paragraph 8 derive from the concept set forth in paragraph 60. If at its inception (as defined in paragraph 5(b)) a lease meets one or more of the following four criteria, the lease shall be classified as a capital lease by the lessee. Otherwise, it shall be classified as an operating lease. (See Appendix C for an illustration of the application of these criteria.)

a. The lease transfers ownership of the property to the lessee by the end of the lease term (as defined in paragraph 5(f)).
b. The lease contains a bargain purchase option (as defined in paragraph 5(d)).
c. The lease term (as defined in paragraph 5(f)) is equal to 75 percent or more of the estimated economic life of the leased property (as defined in paragraph 5(g)). However, if the beginning of the lease term falls within the last 25 percent of the total estimated economic life of the leased property, including earlier years of use, this criterion shall not be used for purposes of classifying the lease.
d. The present value at the beginning of the lease term of the minimum lease payments (as defined in paragraph 5(j)), excluding that portion of the payments representing executory costs such as insurance, maintenance, and taxes to be paid by the lessor, including any profit thereon, equals or exceeds 90 percent of the excess of the fair value of the leased property (as defined in paragraph 5(c)) to the lessor at the inception of the lease over any related investment tax credit retained by the lessor and expected to be realized by him. However, if the beginning of the lease term falls within the last 25 percent of the total estimated economic life of the leased property, including earlier years of use, this criterion shall not be used for purposes of classifying the lease. A lessor shall compute the present value of the minimum lease payments using the interest rate implicit in the lease (as defined in paragraph 5(k)). A lessee shall compute the present value of the minimum lease payments using his incremental borrowing rate (as defined in paragraph 5(l)), unless (i) it is practicable for him to learn the implicit rate computed by the lessor and (ii) the implicit rate computed by the lessor is less than the lessee's incremental borrowing rate. If both

---

[9]As used here, renewal or extension includes a new lease under which the lessee continues to use the same property.
[10]See footnote 9.

of those conditions are met, the lessee shall use the implicit rate.

8. From the standpoint of the lessor, if at inception a lease meets any one of the preceding four criteria and in addition meets both of the following criteria, it shall be classified as a sales-type lease or a direct financing lease, whichever is appropriate (see paragraphs 6(b)(i) and 6(b)(ii)). Otherwise, it shall be classified as an operating lease.

a. Collectibility of the minimum lease payments is reasonably predictable. A lessor shall not be precluded from classifying a lease as a sales-type lease or as a direct financing lease simply because the receivable is subject to an estimate of uncollectibility based on experience with groups of similar receivables.

b. No important uncertainties surround the amount of unreimbursable costs yet to be incurred by the lessor under the lease. Important uncertainties might include commitments by the lessor to guarantee performance of the leased property in a manner more extensive than the typical product warranty or to effectively protect the lessee from obsolescence of the leased property. However, the necessity of estimating executory costs such as insurance, maintenance, and taxes to be paid by the lessor (see paragraphs 17(a) and 18(a)) shall not by itself constitute an important uncertainty as referred to herein.

9. If at any time the lessee and lessor agree to change the provisions of the lease, other than by renewing the lease or extending its term, in a manner that would have resulted in a different classification of the lease under the criteria in paragraphs 7 and 8 had the changed terms been in effect at the inception of the lease, the revised agreement shall be considered as a new agreement over its term, and the criteria in paragraphs 7 and 8 shall be applied for purposes of classifying the new lease. Likewise, except when a guarantee or penalty is rendered inoperative as described in paragraphs 12 and 17(e), any action that extends the lease beyond the expiration of the existing lease term (see paragraph 5(f)), such as the exercise of a lease renewal option other than those already included in the lease term, shall be considered as a new agreement, which shall be classified according to the provisions of paragraphs 6-8. Changes in estimates (for example, changes in estimates of the economic life or of the residual value of the leased property) or changes in circumstances (for example, default by the lessee), however, shall not give rise to a new classification of a lease for accounting purposes.

Accounting and Reporting by Lessees

Capital Leases

10. The lessee shall record a capital lease as an asset and an obligation at an amount equal to the present value at the beginning of the lease term of minimum lease payments during the lease term, excluding that portion of the payments representing executory costs such as insurance, maintenance, and taxes to be paid by the lessor, together with any profit thereon. However, if the amount so determined exceeds the fair value of the leased property at the inception of the lease, the amount recorded as the asset and obligation shall be the fair value. If the portion of the minimum lease payments representing executory costs, including profit thereon, is not determinable from the provisions of the lease, an estimate of the amount shall be made. The discount rate to be used in determining present value of the minimum lease payments shall be that prescribed for the lessee in paragraph 7(d). (See Appendix C for illustrations.)

11. Except as provided in paragraphs 25 and 26 with respect to leases involving land, the asset recorded under a capital lease shall be amortized as follows:

a. If the lease meets the criterion of either paragraph 7(a) or 7(b), the asset shall be amortized in a manner consistent with the lessee's normal depreciation policy for owned assets.

b. If the lease does not meet either criterion 7(a) or 7(b), the asset shall be amortized in a manner consistent with the lessee's normal depreciation policy except that the period of amortization shall be the lease term. The asset shall be amortized to its expected value, if any, to the lessee at the end of the lease term. As an example, if the lessee guarantees a residual value at the end of the lease term and has no interest in any excess which might be realized, the expected value of the leased property to him is the amount that can be realized from it up to the amount of the guarantee.

12. During the lease term, each minimum lease payment shall be allocated between a reduction of the obligation and interest expense so as to produce a constant periodic rate of interest on the remaining balance of the obligation.[11] (See Appendix C for illustrations.) In leases containing a residual guarantee by the lessee or a penalty for failure to renew the lease at the end of the lease term,[12] following the above method of amortization will result in a bal-

---

[11]This is the "interest" method described in the first sentence of paragraph 15 of *APB Opinion No. 21*, "Interest on Receivables and Payables," and in paragraphs 16 and 17 of *APB Opinion No. 12*, "Omnibus Opinion—1967."

[12]Residual guarantees and termination penalties that serve to extend the lease term (as defined in paragraph 5(f)) are excluded from minimum lease payments and are thus distinguished from those guarantees and penalties referred to in this paragraph.

ance of the obligation at the end of the lease term that will equal the amount of the guarantee or penalty at that date. In the event that a renewal or other extension of the lease term or a new lease under which the lessee continues to lease the same property renders the guarantee or penalty inoperative, the asset and the obligation under the lease shall be adjusted by an amount equal to the difference between the present value of the future minimum lease payments under the revised agreement and the present balance of the obligation. The present value of the future minimum lease payments under the revised agreement shall be computed using the rate of interest used to record the lease initially. In accordance with paragraph 9, other renewals and extensions of the lease term shall be considered new agreements, which shall be accounted for in accordance with the provisions of paragraph 14. Contingent rentals,[13] including rentals based on variables such as the prime interest rate, shall be charged to expense when actually incurred.

13. Assets recorded under capital leases and the accumulated amortization thereon shall be separately identified in the lessee's balance sheet or in footnotes thereto. Likewise, the related obligations shall be separately identified in the balance sheet as obligations under capital leases and shall be subject to the same considerations as other obligations in classifying them with current and noncurrent liabilities in classified balance sheets. Unless the charge to income resulting from amortization of assets recorded under capital leases is included with depreciation expense and the fact that it is so included is disclosed, the amortization charge shall be separately disclosed in the financial statements or footnotes thereto.

14. Prior to the expiration of the lease term, a change in the provisions of a lease, a renewal or extension[14] of an existing lease, and a termination of a lease shall be accounted for as follows:

a. If the provisions of the lease are changed in a way that changes the amount of the remaining minimum lease payments and the change either (i) does not give rise to a new agreement under the provisions of paragraph 9 or (ii) does give rise to a new agreement but such agreement is also classified as a capital lease, the present balances of the asset and the obligation shall be adjusted by an amount equal to the difference between the present value of the future minimum lease payments under the revised or new agreement and the present balance of the obligation. The

present value of the future minimum lease payments under the revised or new agreement shall be computed using the rate of interest used to record the lease initially. If the change in the lease provisions gives rise to a new agreement classified as an operating lease, the asset and obligation under the lease shall be removed, gain or loss shall be recognized for the difference, and the new lease agreement shall thereafter be accounted for as any other operating lease.

b. Except when a guarantee or penalty is rendered inoperative as described in paragraph 12, a renewal or an extension[15] of an existing lease shall be accounted for as follows:
   i. If the renewal or extension is classified as a capital lease, it shall be accounted for as described in subparagraph (a) above.
   ii. If the renewal or extension is classified as an operating lease, the existing lease shall continue to be accounted for as a capital lease to the end of its original term, and the renewal or extension shall be accounted for as any other operating lease.

c. A termination of a capital lease shall be accounted for by removing the asset and obligation, with gain or loss recognized for the difference.

Operating Leases

15. Normally, rental on an operating lease shall be charged to expense over the lease term as it becomes payable. If rental payments are not made on a straight-line basis, rental expense nevertheless shall be recognized on a straight-line basis unless another systematic and rational basis is more representative of the time pattern in which use benefit is derived from the leased property, in which case that basis shall be used.

Disclosures

16. The following information with respect to leases shall be disclosed in the lessee's financial statements or the footnotes thereto (see Appendix D for illustrations).

a. For capital leases:
   i. The gross amount of assets recorded under capital leases as of the date of each balance sheet presented by major classes according to nature or function. This information may be combined with the comparable information for owned assets.
   ii. Future minimum lease payments as of the date of the latest balance sheet presented, in

---

[13]The term "contingent rentals" includes all or any portion of the stipulated rental that is contingent.
[14]See footnote 9.
[15]See footnote 9.

the aggregate and for each of the five succeeding fiscal years, with separate deductions from the total for the amount representing executory costs, including any profit thereon, included in the minimum lease payments and for the amount of the imputed interest necessary to reduce the net minimum lease payments to present value (see paragraph 10).

iii. The total of minimum sublease rentals to be received in the future under noncancelable subleases as of the date of the latest balance sheet presented.

iv. Total contingent rentals (rentals on which the amounts are dependent on some factor other than the passage of time) actually incurred for each period for which an income statement is presented.

b. For operating leases having initial or remaining noncancelable lease terms in excess of one year:

i. Future minimum rental payments required as of the date of the latest balance sheet presented, in the aggregate and for each of the five succeeding fiscal years.

ii. The total of minimum rentals to be received in the future under noncancelable subleases as of the date of the latest balance sheet presented.

c. For all operating leases, rental expense for each period for which an income statement is presented, with separate amounts for minimum rentals, contingent rentals, and sublease rentals. Rental payments under leases with terms of a month or less that were not renewed need not be included.

d. A general description of the lessee's leasing arrangements including, but not limited to, the following:

i. The basis on which contingent rental payments are determined.

ii. The existence and terms of renewal or purchase options and escalation clauses.

iii. Restrictions imposed by lease agreements, such as those concerning dividends, additional debt, and further leasing.

Accounting and Reporting by Lessors

Sales-Type Leases

17. Sales-type leases shall be accounted for by the lessor as follows:

a. The minimum lease payments (net of amounts, if any, included therein with respect to executory costs such as maintenance, taxes, and insurance to be paid by the lessor, together with any profit

thereon) plus the unguaranteed residual value (as defined in paragraph 5(i)) accruing to the benefit of the lessor shall be recorded as the gross investment in the lease.

b. The difference between the gross investment in the lease in (a) above and the sum of the present values of the two components of the gross investment shall be recorded as unearned income. The discount rate to be used in determining the present values shall be the interest rate implicit in the lease. The net investment in the lease shall consist of the gross investment less the unearned income. The unearned income shall be amortized to income over the lease term so as to produce a constant periodic rate of return on the net investment in the lease.[16] However, other methods of income recognition may be used if the results obtained are not materially different from those which would result from the prescribed method. The net investment in the lease shall be subject to the same considerations as other assets in classification as current or noncurrent assets in a classified balance sheet. Contingent rentals, including rentals based on variables such as the prime interest rate, shall be credited to income when they become receivable.

c. The present value of the minimum lease payments (net of executory costs, including any profit thereon), computed at the interest rate implicit in the lease, shall be recorded as the sales price. The cost or carrying amount, if different, of the leased property, plus any initial direct costs (as defined in paragraph 5(m)), less the present value of the unguaranteed residual value accruing to the benefit of the lessor, computed at the interest rate implicit in the lease, shall be charged against income in the same period.

d. The estimated residual value shall be reviewed at least annually. If the review results in a lower estimate than had been previously established, a determination must be made as to whether the decline in estimated residual value is other than temporary. If the decline in estimated residual value is judged to be other than temporary, the accounting for the transaction shall be revised using the changed estimate. The resulting reduction in the net investment shall be recognized as a loss in the period in which the estimate is changed. An upward adjustment of the estimated residual value shall not be made.

e. In leases containing a residual guarantee or a penalty for failure to renew the lease at the end of the lease term,[17] following the method of amortization described in (b) above will result in a balance of minimum lease payments receivable at the end of the lease term that will equal the amount of the guarantee or penalty at that date.

---

[16]See footnote 11.
[17]See footnote 12.

In the event that a renewal or other extension[18] of the lease term renders the guarantee or penalty inoperative, the existing balances of the minimum lease payments receivable and the estimated residual value shall be adjusted for the changes resulting from the revised agreement (subject to the limitation on the residual value imposed by subparagraph (d) above) and the net adjustment shall be charged or credited to unearned income.

f. Prior to the expiration of the lease term, a change in the provisions of a lease, a renewal or extension[19] of an existing lease, and a termination of a lease shall be accounted for as follows:

   i. If the provisions of a lease are changed in a way that changes the amount of the remaining minimum lease payments and the change either (a) does not give rise to a new agreement under the provisions of paragraph 9 or (b) does give rise to a new agreement but such agreement is classified as a direct financing lease, the balance of the minimum lease payments receivable and the estimated residual value, if affected, shall be adjusted to reflect the change (subject to the limitation on the residual value imposed by subparagraph (d) above), and the net adjustment shall be charged or credited to unearned income. If the change in the lease provisions gives rise to a new agreement classified as an operating lease, the remaining net investment shall be removed from the accounts, the leased asset shall be recorded as an asset at the lower of its original cost, present fair value, or present carrying amount, and the net adjustment shall be charged to income of the period. The new lease shall thereafter be accounted for as any other operating lease.

   ii. Except when a guarantee or penalty is rendered inoperative as described in subparagraph (e) above, a renewal or an extension[20] of an existing lease shall be accounted for as follows:

     (a) If the renewal or extension is classified as a direct financing lease, it shall be accounted for as described in subparagraph (f)(i) above.

     (b) If the renewal or extension is classified as an operating lease, the existing lease shall continue to be accounted for as a sales-type lease to the end of its original term, and the renewal or extension shall be accounted for as any other operating lease.

   iii. A termination of the lease shall be accounted for by removing the net investment from the accounts, recording the leased asset at the lower of its original cost, present fair value, or present carrying amount, and the net adjustment shall be charged to income of the period.

Direct Financing Leases

18. Direct financing leases shall be accounted for by the lessor as follows (see Appendix C for illustrations):

   a. The minimum lease payments (net of amounts, if any, included therein with respect to executory costs such as maintenance, taxes, and insurance to be paid by the lessor, together with any profit thereon) plus the unguaranteed residual value accruing to the benefit of the lessor shall be recorded as the gross investment in the lease.

   b. The difference between the gross investment in the lease in (a) above and the cost or carrying amount, if different, of the leased property shall be recorded as unearned income. The net investment in the lease shall consist of the gross investment less the unearned income. Initial direct costs (as defined in paragraph 5(m)) shall be charged against income as incurred, and a portion of the unearned income equal to the initial direct costs shall be recognized as income in the same period. The remaining unearned income shall be amortized to income over the lease term so as to produce a constant periodic rate of return on the net investment in the lease.[21] However, other methods of income recognition may be used if the results obtained are not materially different from those which would result from the prescribed method in the preceding sentence. The net investment in the lease shall be subject to the same considerations as other assets in classification as current or noncurrent assets in a classified balance sheet. Contingent rentals, including rentals based on variables such as the prime interest rate, shall be credited to income when they become receivable.

   c. In leases containing a residual guarantee or a penalty for failure to renew the lease at the end of the lease term,[22] the lessor shall follow the accounting procedure described in paragraph 17 (e). The accounting provisions of paragraph 17(f) with respect to renewals and extensions not dealt with in paragraph 17(e), terminations, and other changes in lease provisions shall also be fol-

---

[18]See footnote 9.

[19]See footnote 9.

[20]See footnote 9.

[21]See footnote 11.

[22]See footnote 12.

lowed with respect to direct financing leases.

d. The estimated residual value shall be reviewed at least annually and, if necessary, adjusted in the manner prescribed in paragraph 17(d).

Operating Leases

19. Operating leases shall be accounted for by the lessor as follows:

a. The leased property shall be included with or near property, plant, and equipment in the balance sheet. The property shall be depreciated following the lessor's normal depreciation policy, and in the balance sheet the accumulated depreciation shall be deducted from the investment in the leased property.

b. Rent shall be reported as income over the lease term as it becomes receivable according to the provisions of the lease. However, if the rentals vary from a straight-line basis, the income shall be recognized on a straight-line basis unless another systematic and rational basis is more representative of the time pattern in which use benefit from the leased property is diminished, in which case that basis shall be used.

c. Initial direct costs shall be deferred and allocated over the lease term in proportion to the recognition of rental income. However, initial direct costs may be charged to expense as incurred if the effect is not materially different from that which would have resulted from the use of the method prescribed in the preceding sentence.

Participation by Third Parties

20. The sale or assignment of a lease or of property subject to a lease that was accounted for as a sales-type lease or direct financing lease shall not negate the original accounting treatment accorded the lease. Any profit or loss on the sale or assignment shall be recognized at the time of the transaction except that (a) when the sale or assignment is between related parties, the provisions of paragraphs 29 and 30 shall be applied, or (b) when the sale or assignment is with recourse, the profit or loss shall be deferred and recognized over the lease term in a systematic manner (e.g., in proportion to the minimum lease payments).

21. The sale of property subject to an operating lease, or of property that is leased by or intended to be leased by the third-party purchaser to another party, shall not be treated as a sale if the seller or any party related to the seller retains substantial risks of ownership in the leased property. A seller may by various arrangements assure recovery of the investment by the third-party purchaser in some operating lease transactions and thus retain substantial risks in connection with the property. For example, in the case of default by the lessee or termination of the lease, the arrangements may involve a formal or informal commitment by the seller to (a) acquire the lease or the property, (b) substitute an existing lease, or (c) secure a replacement lessee or a buyer for the property under a remarketing agreement. However, a remarketing agreement by itself shall not disqualify accounting for the transaction as a sale if the seller (a) will receive a reasonable fee commensurate with the effort involved at the time of securing a replacement lessee or buyer for the property and (b) is not required to give priority to the re-leasing or disposition of the property owned by the third-party purchaser over similar property owned or produced by the seller. (For example, a first-in, first-out remarketing arrangement is considered to be a priority.)

22. If a sale to a third party of property subject to an operating lease or of property that is leased by or intended to be leased by the third-party purchaser to another party is not to be recorded as a sale because of the provisions of paragraph 21 above, the transaction shall be accounted for as a borrowing. (Transactions of these types are in effect collateralized borrowings.) The proceeds from the "sale" shall be recorded as an obligation on the books of the "seller." Until that obligation has been amortized under the procedure described herein, rental payments made by the lessee(s) under the operating lease or leases shall be recorded as revenue by the "seller," even if such rentals are paid directly to the third-party purchaser. A portion of each rental shall be recorded by the "seller" as interest expense, with the remainder to be recorded as a reduction of the obligation. The interest expense shall be calculated by application of a rate determined in accordance with the provisions of *APB Opinion No. 21*, "Interest on Receivables and Payables," paragraphs 13 and 14. The leased property shall be accounted for as prescribed in paragraph 19(a) for an operating lease, except that the term over which the asset is depreciated shall be limited to the estimated amortization period of the obligation. The sale or assignment by the lessor of lease payments due under an operating lease shall be accounted for as a borrowing as described above.

Disclosures

23. When leasing, exclusive of leveraged leasing, is a significant part of the lessor's business activities in terms of revenue, net income, or assets, the following information with respect to leases shall be disclosed in the financial statements or footnotes thereto (see Appendix D for illustrations):

a. For sales-type and direct financing leases:

   i. The components of the net investment in sales-type and direct financing leases as of

lessee and lessor are related. In such cases the classification and/or accounting shall be modified as necessary to recognize economic substance rather than legal form. The nature and extent of leasing transactions with related parties shall be disclosed.

30. In consolidated financial statements or in financial statements for which an interest in an investee is accounted for on the equity basis, any profit or loss on a leasing transaction with the related party shall be accounted for in accordance with the principles set forth in *ARB No. 51*, "Consolidated Financial Statements," or *APB Opinion No. 18*, whichever is applicable.

31. The accounts of subsidiaries (regardless of when organized or acquired) whose principal business activity is leasing property or facilities to the parent or other affiliated companies shall be consolidated. The equity method is not adequate for fair presentation of those subsidiaries because their assets and liabilities are significant to the consolidated financial position of the enterprise.

Sale-Leaseback Transactions

32. Sale-leaseback transactions involve the sale of property by the owner and a lease of the property back to the seller.

33. If the lease meets one of the criteria for treatment as a capital lease (see paragraph 7), the seller-lessee shall account for the lease as a capital lease; otherwise, as an operating lease. Except as noted below, any profit or loss on the sale shall be deferred and amortized in proportion to the amortization of the leased asset,[23] if a capital lease, or in proportion to rental payments over the period of time the asset is expected to be used, if an operating lease. However, when the fair value of the property at the time of the transaction is less than its undepreciated cost, a loss shall be recognized immediately up to the amount of the difference between undepreciated cost and fair value.

34. If the lease meets the criteria in paragraphs 7 and 8, the purchaser-lessor shall record the transaction as a purchase and a direct financing lease; otherwise, he shall record the transaction as a purchase and an operating lease.

Accounting and Reporting for Subleases and Similar Transactions

35. This section deals with the following types of leasing transactions:

a. The leased property is re-leased by the original lessee to a third party, and the lease agreement between the two original parties remains in effect (a sublease).
b. A new lessee is substituted under the original lease agreement. The new lessee becomes the primary obligor under the agreement, and the original lessee may or may not be secondarily liable.
c. A new lessee is substituted through a new agreement, with cancellation of the original lease agreement.

Accounting by the Original Lessor

36. If the original lessee enters into a sublease or the original lease agreement is sold or transferred by the original lessee to a third party, the original lessor shall continue to account for the lease as before.

37. If the original lease agreement is replaced by a new agreement with a new lessee, the lessor shall account for the termination of the original lease as provided in paragraph 17(f) and shall classify and account for the new lease as a separate transaction.

Accounting by the Original Lessee

38. If the nature of the transaction is such that the original lessee is relieved of the primary obligation under the original lease, as would be the case in transactions of the type described in paragraphs 35(b) and 35(c), the termination of the original lease agreement shall be account for as follows:

a. If the original lease was a capital lease, the asset and obligation representing the original lease shall be removed from the accounts, gain or loss shall be recognized for the difference, and, if the original lessee is secondarily liable, the loss contingency shall be treated as provided by *FASB Statement No. 5*, "Accounting for Contingencies." Any consideration paid or received upon termination shall be included in the determination of gain or loss to be recognized.
b. If the original lease was an operating lease and the original lessee is secondarily liable, the loss contingency shall be treated as provided by *FASB Statement No. 5*.

39. If the nature of the transaction is such that the original lessee is not relieved of the primary obligation under the original lease, as would be the case in transactions of the type described in paragraph 35(a), the original lessee, as sublessor, shall account for the transaction as follows:

a. If the original lease met either criterion (a) or (b) of paragraph 7, the original lessee shall classify the new lease in accordance with the criteria of

---

[23]If the leased asset is land only, the amortization shall be on a straight-line basis over the lease term.

paragraphs 7 and 8. If the new lease meets one of the criteria of paragraph 7 and both of the criteria of paragraph 8, it shall be accounted for as a sales-type or direct financing lease, as appropriate, and the unamortized balance of the asset under the original lease shall be treated as the cost of the leased property. If the new lease does not qualify as a sales-type or direct financing lease, it shall be accounted for as an operating lease. In either case, the original lessee shall continue to account for the obligation related to the original lease as before.

b. If the original lease met either criterion (c) or (d) but not criterion (a) or (b) of paragraph 7, the original lessee shall, with one exception, classify the new lease in accordance with the criteria of paragraphs 7(c) and 8 only. If it meets those criteria, it shall be accounted for as a direct financing lease, with the unamortized balance of the asset under the original lease treated as the cost of the leased property; otherwise, as an operating lease. In either case, the original lessee shall continue to account for the obligation related to the original lease as before. The one exception arises when the timing and other circumstances surrounding the sublease are such as to suggest that the sublease was intended as an integral part of an overall transaction in which the original lessee serves only as an intermediary. In that case, the sublease shall be classified according to the criteria of paragraphs 7(c) and 7(d), as well as the criteria of paragraph 8. In applying the criterion of paragraph 7(d), the fair value of the leased property shall be the fair value to the original lessor at the inception of the original lease.

c. If the original lease is an operating lease, the original lessee shall account for both it and the new lease as operating leases.

Accounting by the New Lessee

40. The new lessee shall classify the lease in accordance with the criteria of paragraph 7 and account for it accordingly.

Accounting and Reporting for Leveraged Leases

41. From the standpoint of the lessee, leveraged leases shall be classified and accounted for in the same manner as non-leveraged leases. The balance of this section deals with leveraged leases from the standpoint of the lessor.

42. For purposes of this Statement, a leveraged lease is defined as one having all of the following characteristics:

a. Except for the exclusion of leveraged leases from the definition of a direct financing lease as set forth in paragraph 6(b)(ii), it otherwise meets that definition. Leases that meet the definition of sales-type leases set forth in paragraph 6(b)(i) shall not be accounted for as leveraged leases but shall be accounted for as prescribed in paragraph 17.

b. It involves at least three parties: a lessee, a long-term creditor, and a lessor (commonly called the equity participant).

c. The financing provided by the long-term creditor is nonrecourse as to the general credit of the lessor (although the creditor may have recourse to the specific property leased and the unremitted rentals relating to it). The amount of the financing is sufficient to provide the lessor with substantial "leverage" in the transaction.

d. The lessor's net investment, as defined in paragraph 43, declines during the early years once the investment has been completed and rises during the later years of the lease before its final elimination. Such decreases and increases in the net investment balance may occur more than once.

A lease meeting the preceding definition shall be accounted for by the lessor using the method described in paragraphs 43-47; an exception arises if the investment tax credit is accounted for other than as stated in paragraphs 43 and 44,[24] in which case the lease shall be classified as a direct financing lease and accounted for in accordance with paragraph 18. A lease not meeting the definition of a leveraged lease shall be accounted for in accordance with its classification under paragraph 6(b).

43. The lessor shall record his investment in a leveraged lease net of the nonrecourse debt. The net of the balances of the following accounts shall represent the initial and continuing investment in leveraged leases:

a. Rentals receivable, net of that portion of the rental applicable to principal and interest on the nonrecourse debt.

b. A receivable for the amount of the investment tax credit to be realized on the transaction.

c. The estimated residual value of the leased asset.

d. Unearned and deferred income consisting of (i) the estimated pretax lease income (or loss), after deducting initial direct costs, remaining to be allocated to income over the lease term and (ii) the investment tax credit remaining to be allocated to income over the lease term.

---

[24]It is recognized that the investment tax credit may be accounted for other than as prescribed in this Statement, as provided by Congress in the Revenue Act of 1971.

The investment in leveraged leases less deferred taxes arising from differences between pretax accounting income and taxable income shall represent the lessor's net investment in leveraged leases for purposes of computing periodic net income from the lease, as described in paragraph 44.

44. Given the original investment and using the projected cash receipts and disbursements over the term of the lease, the rate of return on the net investment in the years[25] in which it is positive shall be computed. The rate is that rate which when applied to the net investment in the years in which the net investment is positive will distribute the net income to those years (see Appendix E, Schedule 3) and is distinct from the interest rate implicit in the lease as defined in paragraph 5(k). In each year, whether positive or not, the difference between the net cash flow and the amount of income recognized, if any, shall serve to increase or reduce the net investment balance. The net income recognized shall be composed of three elements: two, pretax lease income (or loss) and investment tax credit, shall be allocated in proportionate amounts from the unearned and deferred income included in net investment, as described in paragraph 43; the third element is the tax effect of the pretax lease income (or loss) recognized, which shall be reflected in tax expense for the year. The tax effect of the difference between pretax accounting income (or loss) and taxable income (or loss) for the year shall be charged or credited to deferred taxes. The accounting prescribed in paragraph 43 and in this paragraph is illustrated in Appendix E.

45. If the projected net cash receipts[26] over the term of the lease are less than the lessor's initial investment, the deficiency shall be recognized as a loss at the inception of the lease. Likewise, if at any time during the lease term the application of the method prescribed in paragraphs 43 and 44 would result in a loss being allocated to future years, that loss shall be recognized immediately. This situation might arise in cases where one of the important assumptions affecting net income is revised (see paragraph 46).

46. Any estimated residual value and all other important assumptions affecting estimated total net income from the lease shall be reviewed at least annually. If during the lease term the estimate of the residual value is determined to be excessive and the decline in the residual value is judged to be other than temporary or if the revision of another important assumption changes the estimated total net income from the lease, the rate of return and the allocation of income to positive investment years shall be recalculated from the inception of the lease following the method described in paragraph 44 and using the revised assumption. The accounts constituting the net investment balance shall be adjusted to conform to the recalculated balances, and the change in the net investment shall be recognized as a gain or loss in the year in which the assumption is changed. An upward adjustment of the estimated residual value shall not be made. The accounting prescribed in this paragraph is illustrated in Appendix E.

47. For purposes of presenting the investment in a leveraged lease in the lessor's balance sheet, the amount of related deferred taxes shall be presented separately (from the remainder of the net investment), as prescribed in *APB Opinion No. 11*, "Accounting for Income Taxes," paragraphs 57, 59, and 64. In the income statement or the notes thereto, separate presentation (from each other) shall be made of pretax income from the leveraged lease, the tax effect of pretax income, and the amount of investment tax credit recognized as income during the period. When leveraged leasing is a significant part of the lessor's business activities in terms of revenue, net income, or assets, the components of the net investment balance in leveraged leases as set forth in paragraph 43 shall be disclosed in the footnotes to the financial statements. Appendix E contains an illustration of the balance sheet, income statement, and footnote presentation for a leveraged lease.

Effective Date and Transition

48. The preceding paragraphs of this Statement shall be effective for leasing transactions and lease agreement revisions (see paragraph 9) entered into on or after January 1, 1977. However, leasing transactions or revisions of agreements consummated on or after January 1, 1977 pursuant to the terms of a commitment made prior to that date and renewal options exercised under agreements existing or committed prior to that date shall not be considered as leasing transactions or lease agreement revisions entered into after January 1, 1977 if such commitment is in writing, signed by the parties in interest to the transaction, including the financing party,[27] if any, when specific financing is essential to the transaction, and specifically sets forth the principal terms

---

[25]The use of the term "years" is not intended to preclude application of the accounting prescribed in this paragraph to shorter accounting periods.

[26]For purposes of this paragraph, net cash receipts shall be gross cash receipts less gross cash disbursements exclusive of the lessor's initial investment.

[27]For purposes of this paragraph, the term "financing party" shall include an interim lender pending long-term financing.

of the transaction. The disclosures called for in the preceding paragraphs of this Statement shall be included in financial statements for calendar or fiscal years ending after December 31, 1976.[28] Earlier application of the preceding paragraphs of this Statement, including retroactive application to all leases regardless of when they were entered into or committed is encouraged but, until the effective date specified in paragraph 49, is not required. If applied retroactively, financial statements presented for prior periods shall be restated according to the provisions of paragraph 51.

49. For purposes of financial statements for calendar or fiscal years beginning after December 31, 1980, paragraphs 1-47 of this Statement shall be applied retroactively, and any accompanying financial statements presented for prior periods shall be restated as may be required by the provisions of paragraph 51.

50. If paragraphs 1-47 are not applied initially on a retroactive basis, as permitted by paragraph 48, those leases existing or committed at December 31, 1976 shall be subject to the following provisions until such time as paragraphs 1-47 are applied retroactively to all leases.

a. For purposes of applying the presentation and disclosure requirements of this Statement applicable to lessees, those leases existing or committed at December 31, 1976 that are capitalized in accordance with the provisions of superseded *APB Opinion No. 5* shall be considered as capital leases, and those leases existing or committed at December 31, 1976 that are classified and accounted for as operating leases shall be considered as operating leases. For those leases that are classified and accounted for as operating leases but that meet the criteria of paragraph 7 for classification as capital leases, separate disclosure of the following information shall be made for purposes of financial statements for the year ending December 31, 1977 and for years ending thereafter:

  i. The amounts of the asset and the liability that would have been included in the balance sheet had those leases been classified and accounted for in accordance with the provisions of paragraphs 1-47. This information shall also be disclosed for balance sheets as of December 31, 1976 and thereafter when such balance sheets are included in the financial statements referred to in paragraph 50(a) above.

  ii. The effect on net income that would have resulted if those leases had been classified and

accounted for in accordance with the provisions of paragraphs 1-47. This information shall also be disclosed for income statements for periods beginning after December 31, 1976 when such income statements are included in the aforementioned financial statements.

b. For purposes of applying the presentation and disclosure requirements of this Statement applicable to lessors, those leases existing or committed at December 31, 1976 that are accounted for as sales, financing leases, and as operating leases in accordance with superseded *APB Opinions No. 7* and *27* shall be considered as sales-type leases, as direct financing leases, and as operating leases, respectively. (Refer to (c) below for provisions applicable to leveraged leases.) For those leases existing or committed at December 31, 1976 that are classified and accounted for as operating leases but that meet the criteria of paragraphs 7 and 8 for classification as direct financing leases or sales-type leases, separate disclosure of the following information shall be made for purposes of financial statements for the year ending December 31, 1977 and for years ending thereafter:

  i. The amount of the change in net worth that would have resulted had the leases been classified and accounted for in accordance with the provisions of paragraphs 1-47. This information shall also be disclosed for balance sheets as of December 31, 1976 and thereafter when such balance sheets are included in the foregoing financial statements referred to in paragraph 50(b) above.

  ii. The effect on net income that would have resulted if the leases had been classified and accounted for in accordance with the provisions of paragraphs 1-47. This information shall also be disclosed for income statements for periods beginning after December 31, 1976 when such income statements are included in the aforementioned financial statements.

c. For those leases that meet the criteria of paragraph 42 (leveraged leases) but that are accounted for other than as prescribed in paragraphs 1-47, separate disclosure of the following information shall be made for purposes of lessors' financial statements for the year ending December 31, 1977 and for years ending thereafter:

  i. The amounts of the net changes in total assets and in total liabilities that would have resulted had the leases been classified and accounted for in accordance with the provisions of paragraphs 1-47. This information shall also be

---

[28]For an enterprise having a fiscal year of 52 or 53 weeks ending in the last seven days in December or the first seven days in January, references to December 31 in paragraphs 48-51 shall mean the date in December or January on which the fiscal year ends.

disclosed for balance sheets as of December 31, 1976 and thereafter when such balance sheets are included in the financial statements referred to in paragraph 50(c) above.

ii. The effect on net income that would have resulted if the leases had been classified and accounted for in accordance with the provisions of paragraphs 1-47. This information shall also be disclosed for income statements for periods beginning after December 31, 1976 when such income statements are included in the aforementioned financial statements.

51. Paragraph 49 requires retroactive application of paragraphs 1-47 for purposes of financial statements for calendar or fiscal years beginning after December 31, 1980, and paragraph 48 encourages earlier retroactive application. If after retroactive application is adopted, financial statements for earlier periods and financial summaries or other data derived from them are presented, they shall be restated in accordance with the following requirements to conform to the provisions of paragraphs 1-47:

a. Such restatements shall include the effects of leases that were in existence during the periods covered by the financial statements even if those leases are no longer in existence.

b. Balance sheets presented as of December 31, 1976 and thereafter and income statements presented for periods beginning after December 31, 1976 and financial summaries and other data derived from those financial statements shall be restated to conform to the provisions of paragraphs 1-47.

c. Balance sheets as of dates before December 31, 1976 and income statements for periods beginning before December 31, 1976 shall, when presented, be restated to conform to the provisions of paragraphs 1-47 for as many consecutive periods immediately preceding December 31, 1976 as is practicable. Summaries or other data presented based on such balance sheets and income statements shall be treated in like manner.

d. The cumulative effect of applying paragraphs 1-47 on the retained earnings at the beginning of the earliest period restated shall be included in determining net income of that period (see paragraph 20 of *APB Opinion No. 20* , "Accounting Changes").[29]

The effect on net income of applying paragraphs 1-47 in the period in which the cumulative effect is included in determining net income shall be disclosed for that period, and the reason for not restating the prior periods presented shall be explained.

The provisions of this Statement need not be applied to immaterial items.

This Statement was adopted by the affirmative votes of five members of the Financial Accounting Standards Board. Mr. Kirk dissented.

Mr. Kirk dissents primarily because he does not believe that the front-ending of lease income required by paragraph 44 for leveraged leases versus the method of lease income recognition required by paragraph 18(b) for direct financing leases is justified by any significant economic (i.e., cash flow) differences between the two types of leases. The front-ending of leveraged lease income results from treating the related debt and deferred tax benefits (principally the latter) as valuation accounts, and Mr. Kirk believes that the treatment as valuation accounts is unwarranted.

The leasing business is a leveraged business. Many leases are partially financed by recourse debt; some leases are partially financed by nonrecourse debt. Mr. Kirk believes the cash inflows from the lessee and the outflows to the creditor can be similar whether the debt is recourse or nonrecourse, and he does not believe that a difference in the method of financing a lease should be a factor in determining the pattern of recognizing lease income (and interest

expense) as is required by this Statement. Mr. Kirk also objects to the inconsistent classification of nonrecourse debt required by this Statement (i.e., if the lease meets the criteria of paragraph 42, the nonrecourse debt financing the lease is a valuation account and *not* a liability; if the lessor is the manufacturer of the leased asset or if the lease does not meet all the criteria of paragraph 42, the nonrecourse debt *is* a liability).

The amount and timing of the cash flow benefits resulting from the tax attributes of a leased asset are the same to the lessor whether he finances the asset with recourse debt, with nonrecourse debt, or with equity. A difference in the method of financing the lease should not, in the opinion of Mr. Kirk, result in a difference in accounting for deferred taxes. This Statement, however, requires that deferred income tax balances arising from tax timing differences be accounted for as a valuation account (for purposes of computing periodic lease income) only if (a) the lease is financed with *substantial* nonrecourse debt

---

[29]Pro forma disclosures required by paragraphs 19(d) and 21 of *APB Opinion No. 20* are not applicable.

and (b) the lessor accounts for the benefit from the investment tax credit as a valuation account. The special treatment of these deferred tax benefits as valuation accounts results in a net investment that declines in the early years and rises during the later years; that result then requires the front-ending of lease income. Also, Mr. Kirk can see no reason why the method of accounting for the investment tax credit should determine the accounting for deferred income taxes and, therefore, the pattern of lease income recognition.

Mr. Kirk also believes the treatment of deferred taxes and the required method of accounting for changes in assumptions (paragraph 46) result in the deferred taxes related to leveraged leases being accounted for by the *liability method*, which is not in conformity with the requirements of *APB Opinion No. 11*, "Accounting for Income Taxes," and the accounting for deferred taxes related to other leases.

In order to avoid having (a) the method of financing, (b) the debt repayment schedule, and (c) the method of accounting for deferred tax benefits

influence the pattern of recognition of lease income, interest expense, and initial direct costs (as is the case for those leases meeting the criteria of paragraph 42), Mr. Kirk believes it is necessary to use the ordinary financing lease method (paragraph 109(a)) for all financing leases, including those financed with nonrecourse debt. However, in view of the present inconsistencies in accounting for nonrecourse debt, Mr. Kirk would not have dissented to a requirement that the three-party financing lease method (paragraph 109(b)) be used for financing leases financed with nonrecourse debt. Both methods avoid the inconsistent treatment of nonrecourse debt and the front-ending of lease income.

Mr. Kirk also dissents because he objects to the exemption in paragraph 28 that applies to certain facilities leased from governmental units because of special provisions *normally* present in those leases. Mr. Kirk believes the classification of all leases, regardless of the nature of the asset or lessor, should be determined by application of the criteria in paragraphs 7 and 8.

Members of the Financial Accounting Standards Board:

Marshall S. Armstrong,	Donald J. Kirk	Robert E. Mays
Chairman	Arthur L. Litke	Robert T. Sprouse
Oscar S. Gellein		

Appendix A

BACKGROUND INFORMATION

52. The growing importance of leasing as a financing device was recognized by the accounting profession as early as 1949, when the AI[CPA] issued *Accounting Research Bulletin No. 38*, "Disclosure of Long-Term Leases in Financial Statements of Lessees." In early 1960, the newly formed APB recognized the importance of the matter by including lease accounting as one of the first five topics to be studied by the AICPA's Accounting Research Division. That project culminated in 1962 with the publication of *Accounting Research Study No. 4*, "Reporting of Leases in Financial Statements," and shortly thereafter the APB took up the subject. In all, during the ten years ending June 30, 1973, the APB issued four Opinions (No. 5, 7, 27, and 31) dealing with leases. They were supplemented by three AICPA Accounting Interpretations. The last of the APB Opinions, *APB Opinion No. 31*, "Disclosure of Lease Commitments by Lessees," as its name implies, dealt only with disclosure. The APB had previously acknowledged that certain questions remained in connection with Opinions 5 and 7 and had publicly announced its intention to give those questions further consideration. The APB decided, however, to deal only with additional disclosure

requirements. In paragraph 5 of *APB Opinion No. 31*, which was approved in June 1973, the APB noted that:

. . . disclosure of lease commitments is part of the broad subject of accounting for leases by lessees, a subject which has now been placed on the agenda of the Financial Accounting Standards Board. The Board [APB] also recognizes that the forthcoming report of the Study Group on the Objectives of Financial Statements may contain recommendations which will bear on this subject and which the FASB may consider in its deliberations. Accordingly, the Board is refraining from establishing any disclosure requirements which may prejudge or imply any bias with respect to the outcome of the FASB's undertaking, particularly in relation to the questions of which leases, if any, should be capitalized and how such capitalization may influence the income statement. Nevertheless, in the meantime the Board recognizes the need to improve the disclosure of lease commitments in order that users of financial statements may be better informed.

53. The SEC, too, has issued a number of pronouncements on accounting for leases, including three Accounting Series Releases: No. 132, 141, and 147, adopted on October 5, 1973. The latter Release

imposes essentially the same disclosure requirements with respect to total rental expense and minimum rental commitments as *APB Opinion No. 31*. However, it makes mandatory the disclosure of the present value of certain lease commitments (defined differently from the optional present value disclosure included in *APB Opinion No. 31*). In addition, it requires disclosure of the impact on net income had "financing" leases been capitalized, a disclosure not called for by *APB Opinion No. 31*.

54. Despite the attention that the accounting profession has given to the matter of accounting for leases, inconsistencies remain in lease accounting practices, and differences of opinion as to what should be done about them remain. In recognition of that fact, the FASB placed on its initial agenda a project on Accounting for Leases. In October 1973, a task force of 11 persons from industry, government, public accounting, the financial community, and academe was appointed to provide counsel to the Board in preparing a Discussion Memorandum analyzing issues related to the project.

55. As indicated above, accounting for leases is a subject which has been thoroughly studied over a long period of time and on which numerous pronouncements have been made. Extensive research has been carried out; several public hearings have been held for which position papers were filed by many interested parties and groups; especially appointed committees, not only of the Accounting Principles Board, but of a number of other organizations, have analyzed and debated the issues. A considerable number of the studies and articles on lease accounting were available to the Board, many of which are summarized or identified in the Discussion Memorandum. In addition, the FASB staff surveyed the accounting and reporting practices of a number of lessee and lessor companies, the results of which are set forth in Appendix C to the Discussion Memorandum. The staff also met on a number of occasions with representatives of various organizations interested in leasing for the purpose of obtaining specialized information helpful to the Board's consideration of the various issues involved in accounting for leases.

56. The Board issued its Discussion Memorandum on July 2, 1974, and on November 18-21, 1974 held a public hearing on the subject. The Board received 306 position papers, letters of comment, and outlines of oral presentations in response to the Discussion Memorandum, and 32 presentations were made at the public hearing.

57. On August 26, 1975, the Financial Accounting Standards Board issued an Exposure Draft of a Proposed Statement of Financial Accounting Standards on Accounting for Leases that, if adopted, would

have been effective for leasing transactions entered into on or after January 1, 1976. Two hundred and fifty letters of comment were received in response to that Exposure Draft. The Board announced on November 25, 1975 that, because of the need to analyze the large number of responses and the complexity of the issues involved, it would be unable to issue a final Statement in 1975 but expected to do so early in 1976. A further announcement made by the Board on June 2, 1976 stated that a number of modifications were being made to the Exposure Draft and that a second Exposure Draft would be issued for public comment preparatory to the expected issuance of a final Statement in 1976.

58. The Board issued the second Exposure Draft of a Proposed Statement of Financial Accounting Standards on Accounting for Leases on July 22, 1976. Two hundred and eighty-two letters of comment were received in response to that Exposure Draft.

Appendix B

BASIS FOR CONCLUSIONS

59. This Appendix discusses factors deemed significant by the Board in reaching the conclusions in this Statement, including various alternatives considered and reasons for accepting some and rejecting others.

60. The provisions of this Statement derive from the view that a lease that transfers substantially all of the benefits and risks incident to the ownership of property should be accounted for as the acquisition of an asset and the incurrence of an obligation by the lessee and as a sale or financing by the lessor. All other leases should be accounted for as operating leases. In a lease that transfers substantially all of the benefits and risks of ownership, the economic effect on the parties is similar, in many respects, to that of an installment purchase. This is not to say, however, that such transactions are necessarily "in substance purchases" as that term is used in previous authoritative literature.

61. The transfer of substantially all the benefits and risks of ownership is the concept embodied in previous practice in lessors' accounting, having been articulated in both *APB Opinion No. 7*, "Accounting for Leases in Financial Statements of Lessors," and *APB Opinion No. 27*, "Accounting for Lease Transactions by Manufacturer or Dealer Lessors," as a basis for determining whether a lease should be accounted for as a financing or sale or as an operating lease. However, a different concept has existed in the authoritative literature for lessees' accounting, as evidenced by *APB Opinion No. 5*, "Reporting of Leases in Financial Statements of Lessee."

That Opinion required capitalization of those leases that are "clearly in substance installment purchases of property," which it essentially defined as those leases whose terms "result in the creation of a material equity in the property." Because of this divergence in both concept and criteria, a particular leasing transaction might be recorded as a sale or as a financing by the lessor and as an operating lease by the lessee. This difference in treatment has been the subject of criticism as being inconsistent conceptually, and some of the identifying criteria for classifying leases, particularly those applying to lessees' accounting, have been termed vague and subject to varied interpretation in practice.

62. The Board believes that this Statement removes most, if not all, of the conceptual differences in lease classification as between lessors and lessees and that it provides criteria for such classification that are more explicit and less susceptible to varied interpretation than those in previous literature.

63. Some members of the Board who support this Statement hold the view that, regardless of whether substantially all the benefits and risks of ownership are transferred, a lease, in transferring for its term the right to use property, gives rise to the acquisition of an asset and the incurrence of an obligation by the lessee which should be reflected in his financial statements. Those members nonetheless support this Statement because, to them, (i) it clarifies and improves the guidelines for implementing the conceptual basis previously underlying accounting for leases and (ii) it represents an advance in extending the recognition of the essential nature of leases.

Definition of a Lease

64. Some respondents took the position that nuclear fuel leases, sometimes called "heat supply" or "burn up" contracts, should be excluded from the definition of a lease on the grounds that such agreements are of the same nature as take-or-pay contracts to supply other types of fuel such as coal or oil which are excluded. The Board's conclusion that nuclear fuel leases meet the definition of a lease as expressed in paragraph 1 is based on the fact that under present generally accepted accounting principles a nuclear fuel installation constitutes a depreciable asset. Thus, a nuclear fuel lease conveys the right to use a depreciable asset whereas contracts to supply coal or oil do not. The fact that the latter contracts may be take-or-pay, in the Board's view, is irrelevant to this central point.

Classification of Leases

65. The Board believes that the characteristics of a leasing transaction should determine its classification in terms of the appropriate accounting treat-

ment by both the lessee and lessor; this is to say that the characteristics that identify a lease as a capital lease, as distinct from an operating lease, from the standpoint of the lessee should, with certain exceptions identified in this Statement, be the same attributes that identify a direct financing or sales-type lease, as distinct from an operating lease, from the standpoint of the lessor. The principal exceptions referred to are those stated in paragraph 8.

66. The Board considered and rejected, for the reason set forth in paragraph 65, the argument that the difference in the nature of the lessor's and lessee's businesses is often sufficient to warrant different classification of a lease by the two parties.

67. Some respondents to the Discussion Memorandum and Exposure Drafts, while agreeing generally with the premise that the nature of the transaction should govern its classification by both the lessee and lessor, pointed out that there is no assurance that the transaction will be discerned identically by both parties. However, the Board believes that by adopting essentially the same criteria for classification of leases by both parties (see paragraph 65), as contrasted with the difference in criteria previously existing between *APB Opinion No. 5*, concerning lessee accounting, and *APB Opinions No. 7 and 27*, concerning lessor accounting, and, by virtue of the fact that the criteria adopted are in some respects more explicit than those referred to in those Opinions, that a significant improvement in consistency of classification can be achieved.

68. A large number of respondents favored capitalization by lessees of only those leases that they would classify as "in substance installment purchases." A wide range of preferences was expressed as to the criteria to be used to identify such leases. Most prominent among these was the "material equity" criterion that is the basic criterion of *APB Opinion No. 5* and that is discussed in paragraph 73. Most of those favoring this concept would apply it only to the lessee rather than to both parties.

69. The Board considered the concept for capitalization by the lessee of those leases that are "in substance installment purchases." Such leases, if identifiable, would be encompassed within the concept described in paragraph 60, but, by itself, the installment purchase concept, in the Board's view, is too limiting as a basis for lease capitalization. Taken literally, the concept would apply only to those leases that automatically transfer ownership. All other leases contain characteristics not found in installment purchases, such as the reversion of the property to the lessor at the termination of the lease.

70. Some respondents advocated capitalization of leases that give rise to what they term "debt in a

strict legal sense." A number of the respondents in this group were also represented in the group referred to in paragraph 68, indicating that they view the two concepts as not being mutually exclusive. The argument advanced is essentially that some leases contain clauses that make the lessee's obligation absolute and unconditional, and because the obligation is absolute, such clauses should be made the determinant for capitalization of leases containing them. Those advancing this view generally appeared to be focusing on the liability aspect of the transaction rather than on the nature of the corresponding asset to be recorded. Few had any comment to offer concerning cases in which the "legal debt" assumed by the lessee represents only a portion of the asset's cost; nor was it clear from the comments how, if at all, the concept of "legal debt" standing alone should affect accounting for the lease by the lessor.

71. The Board noted that the determination of whether a lease obligation represents debt in the strict legal sense would of necessity rest primarily on court decisions, and that such decisions have arisen almost entirely from litigation involving bankruptcy, reorganization, or taxation. The Board concluded that legal distinctions of this nature were apt to be neither relevant nor practical in application to the accounting issue of lease capitalization. The Board believes further that, in most instances where the lessee has assumed an unconditional obligation that the courts might hold to be legal debt, it is reasonable to assume that he will have protected his interest through other features in the agreement that are likely to meet one or more of the criteria for capitalization stated in paragraph 7. The Board accordingly rejected the concept of "legal debt" as a determinant for lease capitalization.

Criteria for Classification

72. The Discussion Memorandum listed 14 criteria as having some support for use in classifying leases by lessees. A number of criteria, including some of the 14, were also listed for possible use in classifying leases by lessors. Among the respondents, opinion was divided as to the criteria that identify leases that should be capitalized by the lessee as well as to those criteria that identify leases that should be recorded as sales or financing leases by lessors. The Board concluded that many of the listed criteria were overlapping, i.e., that the basic idea contained in one also was embodied in others designed to identify the same attribute. The Board believes that the criteria stated in paragraphs 7 and 8 contain the essence of the listed criteria except those that the Board did not consider relevant or suitable. The basis for the Board's adoption or rejection of individual criteria is the concept discussed in paragraph 60, namely, the transfer of substantially all of the benefits and risks

incident to the ownership of property. The following discusses the Board's conclusions with respect to each of the 14 criteria listed in the lessee section of the Discussion Memorandum together with 5 other criteria that were dealt with in the lessor section. These last 5 are discussed in paragraphs 87-90.

73. *Lessee builds up a material equity in the leased property.* Many of the respondents favored the material equity criterion as contained in *APB Opinion No. 5* as the principal basis for lease capitalization by the lessee. Of the criteria selected by the Board, the criterion stated in paragraph 7(b) wherein the lease contains a bargain purchase option is evidential that a material equity is being established. The criterion stated in paragraph 7(a) wherein ownership is transferred by the end of the lease term may in some circumstances be evidential that a material equity is being established. However, in relating material equity to the concept discussed in paragraph 60, the Board concluded that leases in which no material equity is established by the lessee may effectively transfer substantially all of the benefits and risks of ownership. For example, a lease whose term extends over the entire economic life of the asset and thus transfers all of the benefits and risks of ownership need not give rise to a material equity. Accordingly, the Board rejected material equity as a separate criterion and considered it too limiting to represent the central basis for lease capitalization by lessees.

74. *Leased property is special purpose to the lessee.* The Board rejected this criterion for two reasons. First, "special purpose property" is a relative concept that is hard to define objectively. Second, the fact that the leased property is special purpose does not, of itself, evidence a transfer of substantially all of the benefits and risks of asset ownership. Although it is expected that most lessors would lease special purpose property only under terms that transfer substantially all of those benefits and risks to the lessee, nothing in the nature of special purpose property necessarily entails such lease terms. The Board concluded that, if the lease, in fact, contains such terms, it is likely that one or more of the adopted criteria in paragraph 7 would be met.

75. *Lease term is substantially equal to the estimated useful life of the property.* This criterion was modified as adopted in criterion (c) of paragraph 7 as follows:

The lease term (as defined in paragraph 5(f)) is equal to 75 percent or more of the estimated economic life of the leased property (as defined in paragraph 5(g)).

In the Board's view, the fact that the lease term need be for only 75 percent of the economic life of the property is not inconsistent with the concept discussed in paragraph 60 for the following reasons:

Although the lease term may represent only 75 percent of the economic life of the property in terms of years, the lessee can normally expect to receive significantly more than 75 percent of the total economic benefit to be derived from the use of the property over its life span. This is due to the fact that new equipment, reflecting later technology and in prime condition, can be assumed to be more efficient, and hence yield proportionately more use benefit, than old equipment which has been subject to obsolescence and the wearing-out process. Moreover, that portion of use benefit remaining in the equipment after the lease term, in terms of the dollar value that may be estimated for it, when discounted to present worth, would represent a still smaller percentage of the value of the property at inception.

As a result of comments received in response to the second Exposure Draft, the following qualification has been added to paragraph 7(c):

However, if the beginning of the lease term falls within the last 25 percent of the total estimated economic life of the leased property, including earlier years of use, this criterion shall not be used for purposes of classifying the lease.

The Board found persuasive the argument that it would be inconsistent to require that a lease covering the last few years of an asset's life be recorded as a capital lease by the lessee and as a sales-type or direct financing lease by the lessor when a lease of the asset for a similar period earlier in its life would have been classified as an operating lease. Without the above qualification, in the case of a tank car having an estimated economic life of 25 years and placed under five successive 5-year leases, the first four leases would be classified as operating leases under this criterion and the last lease would be classified as a capital lease. The Board considered such a result illogical.

76. *Lessee pays costs normally incident to ownership.* This criterion was rejected by the Board since it can be presumed that, one way or another, the lessee bears the costs of ownership in virtually all lease agreements.

77. *Lessee guarantees the lessor's debt with respect to the leased property.* The Board concluded that this criterion does not necessarily evidence a lease that transfers substantially all of the benefits and risks of property ownership; the amount guaranteed may represent only a portion of the fair value of the property. When there is a guarantee, the Board

believes it likely that the lessee will have protected his interest through other features in the agreement that may meet one or more of the adopted criteria stated in paragraph 7. In this regard, any periods covered by renewal options in which a lessee guarantee is expected to be outstanding are to be included in the lease term, as provided by paragraph 5(f), and the corresponding renewal rentals are to be included in minimum lease payments, as provided by paragraph 5(j). Thus, such periods would be recognized in applying criterion 7(c) to the property's economic life, and both the periods and the corresponding rentals would be recognized in applying the 90 percent recovery criterion (paragraph 7(d)).

78. *Lessee treats the lease as a purchase for tax purposes.* The Board rejected this criterion. There are many instances in which tax and financial accounting treatments diverge, and the question of a possible need for conformity between them is beyond the scope of this Statement.

79. *Lease is between related parties.* The Board did not consider this criterion as suitable, in itself, for determining lease classification. Leases between related parties are discussed in paragraphs 29-31.

80. *Lease passes usual risks and rewards to lessee.* The Board considered this to be a concept rather than a criterion. It is closely related to the basic concept underlying the conclusions of this Statement, described in paragraph 60.

81. *Lessee assumes an unconditional liability for lease rentals.* This criterion was rejected by the Board for the reasons given in paragraph 71.

82. *Lessor lacks independent economic substance.* The Board considered the argument advanced by some that, if the lessor has no economic substance, the lessor serves merely as a conduit in that the lender looks to the lessee for payment and thus, it is asserted, the lessee is, in fact, the real debtor and purchaser. Whether the lessee is judged to be a debtor does not, in the Board's view, constitute a suitable criterion for determining lease classification for the reasons expressed in paragraph 71. The Board finds unpersuasive the argument that the lessee's accounting for a leasing transaction should be determined by the economic condition of an unrelated[30] lessor. If a lease qualifies as an operating lease because it does not meet the criteria in paragraph 7, the Board finds no justification for requiring that it be accounted for as a capital lease by the lessee simply because an unrelated lessor lacks independent economic substance. In such a case, it probably means that someone else, presumably the lender, is in substance the lessor, but this circumstance, per se, should not alter the lessee's accounting. Accordingly, the Board rejected this criterion.

---

[30]If the lessee and the lessor are related parties, the provisions of paragraphs 29-31 apply.

83. *Residual value at end of lease is expected to be nominal.* Some respondents recommended that such a criterion, if adopted, should be based on the present value of the residual, which, because of the long-term nature of many leases, would represent a much smaller percentage of asset value at inception than the undiscounted residual value. However, other respondents who favored the addition of a recovery criterion based on the relationship of the present value of the lease payments to the fair value of the leased property argued that a criterion based on residual value would be redundant in that it would essentially measure the complement of that relationship. Since, for the reasons set forth in paragraph 84 below, the Board favored the recovery criterion, it was adopted in lieu of a criterion based on residual values.

84. *Lease agreement provides that the lessor will recover his investment plus a fair return (a) guaranteed by the lessee or (b) not so guaranteed.* A variation of this criterion was adopted as criterion (d) of paragraph 7. In the form adopted, the criterion is met when the present value of the minimum lease payments, defined in paragraph 5(j), excluding executory costs, equals or exceeds 90 percent of the excess of the fair value of the leased property, defined in paragraph 5(c), to the lessor at the inception of the lease over any related investment tax credit retained by the lessor and expected to be realized by him. The Board concluded that if the present value of the contractual receipts of the lessor provide for recovery of substantially all (defined as 90 percent or more) of his net investment in the fair value of the leased asset, the lessor has transferred substantially all of the benefits and risks of asset ownership. Likewise, if the present value of the lessee's lease obligations provide for that degree of recovery by the lessor, the conclusion was that the lessee has acquired those benefits and risks. Some respondents pointed out that a recovery criterion more clearly evidences the transfer of risks than of benefits since a substantial residual value may revert to the lessor at the end of the lease term. However, the Board concluded that, in leases meeting the recovery criterion, the residual amount, when discounted to its present value at the inception of the lease, is likely to represent only a small percentage of the fair value of the property. For the reasons cited above, the Board adopted a criterion based on recovery of substantially all (defined as 90 percent or more) of the fair value of the leased property. A lessee guarantee of recovery to the lessor is recognized through inclusion in the definition of minimum lease payments. Thus, such guarantees are taken into account in the application of the 90 percent recovery criterion. As a result of comments received in response to the second Exposure Draft, the following qualification has been added to paragraph 7(d):

However, if the beginning of the lease term falls within the last 25 percent of the total estimated economic life of the leased property, including earlier years of use, this criterion shall not be used for purposes of classifying the lease.

The above qualification is the same as that added to criterion 7(c) and the reasons are the same as those discussed in paragraph 75.

85. *Lessee has the option at any time to purchase the asset for the lessor's unrecovered investment.* The Board concluded that the existence of a purchase option is significant only if it is a bargain purchase option as defined in paragraph 5(d) and as adopted in paragraph 7(b); otherwise, there is no presumption that the lessee will exercise the option. Accordingly, the Board rejected this criterion.

86. *Lease agreement is noncancelable for a "long term."* This criterion was rejected by the Board in favor of criterion (c) of paragraph 7.

87. *Lease transfers title (ownership) to the lessee by the end of the lease term.* This criterion was adopted by the Board as criterion (a) of paragraph 7. Such a provision effectively transfers all of the benefits and risks of ownership and, thus, the criterion is consistent with the concept discussed in paragraph 60.

88. *Lease provides for a bargain purchase or a renewal option at bargain rates.* The existence of a bargain purchase option was adopted by the Board as criterion (b) of paragraph 7. Such a provision effectively transfers all of the benefits and risks of ownership and, thus, the criterion is consistent with the concept discussed in paragraph 60. The period covered by a bargain renewal option is included in the lease term, as defined in paragraph 5(f), and the option rentals are included in minimum lease payments, as defined in paragraph 5(j). Thus, a bargain renewal option enters into the determination of whether the lease meets either criterion (c) or criterion (d) of paragraph 7. Accordingly, the Board rejected the existence of a bargain renewal option as a separate criterion.

89. *Collection of the rentals called for by the lease is reasonably assured.* This criterion relates only to lessors. It has been restated as follows and adopted by the Board as a necessary criterion (paragraph 8(a)): "Collectibility of the minimum lease payments is reasonably predictable." The wording change reflects the Board's view that lessors should not be precluded from classifying leases as direct financing or sales-type leases, when they meet one of the criteria for such classification in paragraph 7, if losses are reasonably predictable based on experience with groups of similar receivables. When other than normal credit risks are involved in a leasing transaction,

it was the Board's conclusion that collectibility is not reasonably predictable and classification as a sales-type or direct financing lease, in such cases, is therefore not appropriate.

90. *No important uncertainties surround costs yet to be incurred by lessor.* The matter of uncertainties surrounding future costs was dealt with in the Discussion Memorandum as one of the risks of ownership relevant to the classification of leases by lessors. This criterion is essentially equivalent to one of the criteria set forth in *APB Opinion No. 27*, paragraph 4, as a requirement for treating a lease by a manufacturer or dealer lessor as a sale. In adopting this as a necessary criterion, the Board believes that if future unreimbursable costs to be incurred by the lessor under the lease are not reasonably predictable, the risks under the lease transaction may be so great that it should be accounted for as an operating lease instead of as a sales-type or direct financing lease.

Accounting by Lessees

91. *APB Opinion No. 5*, paragraph 15, prescribed accounting for leases that were to be capitalized as "in substance installment purchases" as follows:

> Leases which are clearly in substance installment purchases of property . . . should be recorded as purchases. The property and the obligation should be stated in the balance sheet at an appropriate discounted amount of future payments under the lease agreement. . . . The method of amortizing the amount of the asset to income should be appropriate to the nature and use of the asset and should be chosen without reference to the period over which the related obligation is discharged.

As stated in paragraph 60, the concept underlying this Statement is that a lease that transfers substantially all of the benefits and risks incident to the ownership of property should be accounted for as the acquisition of an asset and the incurrence of an obligation by the lessee, and as a sale or financing by the lessor. The concept for capitalization by the lessee of only those leases that are "in substance installment purchases" was rejected by the Board as too limiting a basis for lease capitalization (see paragraph 69).

92. Despite this difference in the concept for capitalization, the Board viewed the accounting prescribed by *APB Opinion No. 5* for capitalized leases as generally appropriate. While respondents expressed varying opinions as to the characteristics of leases that should be capitalized, there was little opposition to the method of accounting for such leases prescribed by *APB Opinion No. 5*. The

accounting provisions of this Statement applicable to lessees, with the exceptions noted below, generally follow that Opinion; however, these provisions are more specific with respect to implementation.

93. With respect to the rate of interest to be used in determining the present value of the minimum lease payments for recording the asset and obligation under a capital lease, the Board concluded the rate should generally be that which the lessee would have incurred to borrow for a similar term the funds necessary to purchase the leased asset (the lessee's incremental borrowing rate). An exception to that general rule occurs when (a) it is practicable for the lessee to ascertain the implicit rate computed by the lessor and (b) that rate is less than the lessee's incremental borrowing rate; if both of those conditions are met, the lessee shall use the implicit rate. However, if the present value of the minimum lease payments, using the appropriate rate, exceeds the fair value of the leased property at the inception of the lease, the amount recorded as the asset and obligation shall be the fair value. A number of respondents pointed out that in many instances, the lessee does not know the implicit rate as computed by the lessor. Also, since the implicit rate is affected by the lessor's estimate of the residual value of the leased property in which the lessee will usually have no interest, and may also be affected by other factors extraneous to the lessee, it may, if higher than the lessee's incremental borrowing rate, produce a result that is less representative of the transfer of use benefit to the lessee than would be obtained from use of the lessee's incremental borrowing rate. For those reasons, the Board concluded that the lessee's use of the implicit rate for discounting purposes should be limited to circumstances in which he is able to ascertain that rate, as computed by the lessor, and it is less than his incremental borrowing rate. In the revised Exposure Draft, the Board had defined this rate as that which "the lessee would have incurred to borrow the funds necessary to buy the leased asset on a secured loan with repayment terms similar to the payment schedule called for in the lease." A number of respondents objected to this definition pointing out that they would not have financed the asset on a secured loan basis and, hence, would be unable to determine such a theoretical rate. Those respondents suggested that the definition be revised to allow the lessee to use a rate consistent with the type of financing that would have been used in the particular circumstances. The Board found merit in those suggestions because it intended that the rate should be both determinable and reasonable. The definition of the lessee's incremental borrowing rate has been revised accordingly. Some respondents pointed out that the use of the lessee's incremental rate, however determined, would in some cases produce an amount to be capitalized that would be greater than the known fair value of the leased asset.

It was suggested that in such cases the amount to be capitalized be limited to the fair value. The Board agreed with that recommendation.

94. The method of amortization of the capitalized asset prescribed in this Statement (see paragraph 11) differs from that called for in *APB Opinion No. 5* in that, except for those leases that meet criterion 7(a) or 7(b), the period of amortization is limited to the lease term. *APB Opinion No. 5* did not so limit the period of amortization since the leases to be capitalized were those that were considered "in substance installment purchases." The Board concluded that, for leases which are capitalized under criterion 7(c) or 7(d) of this Statement, the amortization period should be the lease term. It is presumed for accounting purposes that, in such leases, the lessee's period of use of the asset will end at the expiration of the lease term.

95. Some respondents asked for clarification and more specific treatment in the Statement with respect to the accounting to be followed in connection with the situations referred to in paragraph 9 having to do with changes in lease provisions that would have resulted in a different classification of the lease at its inception and renewals and extensions of existing leases. The clarification requested has been incorporated in paragraph 14. Additionally, respondents asked for clarification with respect to the accounting to be followed when a guarantee or penalty provision in a lease is rendered inoperative by a renewal or extension. That clarification has been provided in paragraph 12.

Disclosure by Lessees

96. Users of financial statements have indicated a strong desire for disclosure by lessees of information concerning leasing transactions whether leases are capitalized or not. In some cases, the information desired was similar to that now provided in accordance with *APB Opinion No. 31* or *SEC Accounting Series Release No. 147*. However, some respondents objected to the requirement to disclose future minimum rental payments by periods beyond the next succeeding five years. It was contended that any such projections are apt to be misleading since the accumulating effect of new leases and lease renewals on future payments in those periods is not reflected. In addition, some users and many other respondents opposed requiring disclosure of the estimated effect on net income had certain leases been capitalized. The Board agreed with both of those views except that during the transition period until full retroactive application of this Statement is required, the Board decided that the disclosure called for in paragraph 50 is needed by users of financial statements pending retroactive application. The Board concluded that the disclosures called for in paragraph 16(a) with respect to capital leases would provide information helpful to users of financial statements in assessing the financial condition and results of operations of lessees. In the Board's view, such disclosures are consistent with the information presently required to be disclosed with respect to owned property and to long-term obligations in general. The Board further concluded that users' assessments would be facilitated by the disclosures called for in paragraphs 16(b) and 16(c) with respect to operating leases. The requirement to disclose information concerning commitments for rental payments under operating leases during the succeeding five years is consistent with the similar requirement for capital leases.

Accounting by Lessors

97. As stated in paragraph 61, the concept underlying the accounting for leases by lessors in this Statement is essentially the same as the concept embodied in *APB Opinions No. 7* and *27*; that is, a lease that transfers substantially all of the benefits and risks incident to the ownership of property should be accounted for as a sale or financing by the lessor. Accordingly, the accounting provisions of this Statement applicable to lessors, with the principal exceptions noted below, generally follow those of the two APB Opinions.

98. In computing the manufacturer's or dealer's profit on a sales-type lease, the cost of the property leased will be reduced by the present value of the estimated residual value. This represents a liberalization of the provisions of *APB Opinion No. 27*, which did not permit recognition of any residual value in determining manufacturer's or dealer's profit. Some respondents favored continuing the provisions of Opinion 27 in this regard. Others believed that the present value of the residual should be recognized in profit determination and that the accounting for the financing element of a leasing transaction should be essentially the same in a sales-type lease as in a direct financing lease. The Board agreed with this latter view and concluded that the difference between the estimated residual and its present value should be included in unearned income and recognized in income over the lease term.

99. This Statement calls for the estimated residual value, along with rentals and other minimum lease payments receivable, to be included in the balance sheet presentation of the investment in sales-type and in direct financing leases. Under *APB Opinion No. 7*, the estimated residual value was to be included with property, plant, and equipment. Several respondents contended that inclusion of the residual with depreciable assets of the lessor would blur the distinction between property on lease and

property used in the lessor's internal operations. Others pointed out that, in the vast majority of leases, the estimated residual value is realized by a sale or re-lease of the property and, for that reason, the residual should be looked upon as a last payment similar to the minimum lease payments. In addition, it was contended, presentation of the estimated residual value as part of the lease investment rather than as part of property, plant, and equipment is necessary to portray the proper relationship between the gross investment in leases and the related unearned income, since a portion of the unearned income relates to the residual value. The Board agreed with those views.

100. This Statement requires that the selling price in a sales-type lease be determined by computing the present value of payments required under the lease. In this respect, it follows Opinion 27. However, this Statement is more specific than Opinion 27 in identifying the payments that are to be included in the computation, and it requires use of the rate of interest implicit in the lease for discounting instead of an interest rate determined in accordance with the provisions of *APB Opinion No. 21*, as called for by Opinion 27. Use of the latter rate was rejected by the Board on the grounds that it would yield an amount to be recorded as the sales price that would be at variance with the known fair value of the leased asset (after adjusting that price for the present value of any investment tax credit or residual retained).

101. This Statement requires different treatment of initial direct costs (see paragraph 5(m)) as between sales-type leases and direct financing and leveraged leases. In the case of sales-type leases, initial direct costs are to be charged against income of the period in which the sale is recorded, which is consistent with the general practice of accounting for similar costs incurred in connection with installment sales on the basis that such costs are incurred primarily to produce sales revenue. In this respect, the Statement follows *APB Opinion No. 27*, which, although not mentioning initial direct costs specifically, in paragraph 6 called for estimated "future costs" related to leases accounted for as sales to be charged to income of the period in which the sale is recorded. The second Exposure Draft called for initial direct costs incurred in connection with direct financing leases to be accounted for in the manner that *APB Opinion No. 7*, paragraph 11, described as preferred, that is, to be deferred and allocated to future periods in which the related financing income is reported. This requirement recognized that, unlike the initial direct costs in sales-type leases, such costs in direct financing leases are not primarily related to income of the period in which the costs are incurred. A number of respondents objected to the deferral of initial direct costs incurred in connection with direct financing leases because it is at variance with pre-dominant industry practice and would, it was reported, necessitate a major revision of existing record systems and computer programs with no appreciable effect on net income over the lease term. The predominant industry practice as cited by those respondents consists of expensing such costs as incurred and recognizing as income in the same period a portion of unearned income equal to the amount of the costs expensed. It was pointed out that this method produces essentially the same income effect as if the initial direct costs were deferred and amortized separately, as was called for by the revised Exposure Draft, or as if these costs were charged to unearned income, as is called for in the case of leveraged leases. The Board accepted this recommendation for practical considerations and has revised the accounting prescribed for initial direct costs incurred in connection with direct financing leases accordingly. In the case of leveraged leases, the accounting for initial direct costs is consistent with the central concept underlying the accounting for leveraged leases by the investment with separate phases method, that concept being that the net income should be recognized at a level rate of return on the investment in the lease in the years in which the investment is positive.

102. As was the case with lessee accounting, respondents requested clarification and more specific guidance as to the accounting to be followed by lessors with respect to the situations referred to in paragraph 95. The requested guidance for lessor accounting for those situations has been provided in paragraphs 17(e) and 17(f). In addition, respondents objected to the provisions of the revised Exposure Draft allowing, in some instances, gain to be recognized immediately on renewals or extensions of sales-type or direct financing leases. Those who objected contended that gain recognition in those circumstances was equivalent to allowing upward revisions of residual value estimates, a practice specifically prohibited in the Statement. The Board found those objections persuasive and, accordingly, revised the accounting for renewals or extensions of sales-type or direct financing leases to prohibit immediate recognition of gain.

Disclosure by Lessors

103. A number of those respondents who addressed the question of what information should be disclosed by lessors thought that the disclosures called for by *APB Opinion No. 7* were adequate. Some, however, thought there should be consistency, where relevant, between the disclosure requirements for lessors and those for lessees and noted that disclosure requirements for lessees had been recently made more extensive by *APB Opinion No. 31* and SEC *Accounting Series Release No. 147*. The Board agreed with this latter view. As in the case of lessees,

the Board believes that the information required to be disclosed by paragraph 23 will be helpful to users of financial statements in assessing the financial condition and results of operations of lessors. Several respondents to the second Exposure Draft objected to the limitation of lessor disclosure requirements to those lessors for which leasing is the predominant activity. It was contended that the disclosures should be required whenever leasing is a significant part of the lessor's business activities rather than only when leasing is predominant. Other respondents thought that a single test of predominance based on revenues was inappropriate and pointed to the difference in the nature of lease rentals as compared to sales revenue of a manufacturing concern. It was recommended that significance be determined in terms of revenue, net income, or assets as separate indicators. The Board found merit in these recommendations and revised the disclosure limitation accordingly.

104. Some respondents recommended the elimination of the requirement in the Exposure Drafts that the cost or carrying amount of property on operating leases and that of property held for lease be separately disclosed. They contended that in companies having thousands of operating leases it would be difficult, if not impossible, to make such a split. Since the information would be based on one particular point in time, it may well be unrepresentative. The Board found those arguments persuasive and believes, moreover, that a better indication of the productivity of property on or held for lease is its relationship to the minimum future rentals by years and in the aggregate from noncancelable operating leases, which latter information is required by the Statement.

Leases Involving Real Estate

105. The second Exposure Draft provided that criteria 7(c) and 7(d) were not applicable to leases of land and that, unless criterion 7(a) or 7(b) was met, leases of land should be accounted for as operating leases. In a lease involving both land and building, if the land element represented 15 percent or more of the total fair value of the leased property, the land and building elements of the lease were required to be separated and each classified and accounted for as if it were a separate lease. Some respondents objected to this, contending that the recovery criterion, 7(d), should be applicable to land leases the same as to other leases. Others objected to the required separate treatment of the land and building elements in a lease involving both, contending that the property should be classified and accounted for as a unit and that to require separation would be inconsistent with the economic substance of the transaction. Some, particularly in the case of retail leases, cited the difficulties and cost involved in separating the land and building elements for companies with large numbers of such leases. They recommended that separation not be required and that all such leases be classified as operating leases. However, if separation were to continue to be required, some suggested that the 15 percent limitation be raised to permit treating as a unit a greater number of leases in which land would still not represent a major element. The Board's conclusion that, unless criterion 7(a) or 7(b) was met, leases of land should be classified as operating leases is based on the concept that such leases do not transfer substantially all the benefits and risks of ownership. Land normally does not depreciate in value over time, and rental payments for the use of land are not predicated on compensation for depreciation plus interest, as is the case with leases of depreciable assets, but are in the nature of interest only or, as some may prefer to say, interest plus whatever additional profit element may be included. The requirement for separation of the land and building elements in a lease involving both is based on this distinction. The Board found merit, however, in the recommendation that the 15 percent limitation be raised in order to reduce the practical problems involved in separating the land and building elements for large numbers of leases. The Board concluded that the 15 percent limitation established in the second Exposure Draft should accordingly be raised to 25 percent.

106. A number of respondents pointed out that leases of facilities such as airport and bus terminals and port facilities from governmental units or authorities contain features that render the criteria of paragraph 7 inappropriate for classifying such leases. Leases of such facilities do not transfer ownership or contain bargain purchase options. By virtue of its power to abandon a facility during the term of a lease, the governmental body can effectively control the lessee's continued use of the property for its intended purpose, thus making its economic life essentially indeterminate. Finally, since neither the leased property nor equivalent property is available for sale, a meaningful fair value cannot be determined, thereby invalidating the 90 percent recovery criterion. For those reasons, the Board concluded that such leases shall be classified as operating leases by both the lessee and lessor.

Sale-Leaseback Transactions

107. Of those respondents who addressed the issues of accounting for sale-leaseback transactions, opinions were divided between those who favored (a) treatment as a single transaction with deferral of profit on the sale and (b) treatment as two independent transactions unless the lease meets criteria for capitalization by the lessee. Generally, those favoring treatment as a single transaction would make

certain exceptions, such as "leasebacks to accommodate a short-term property requirement of the seller" and "leasebacks of only a relatively small part of the property sold." The Board noted that most sale-leasebacks are entered into as a means of financing, for tax reasons, or both and that the terms of the sale and the terms of the leaseback are usually negotiated as a package. Because of this interdependence of terms, no means could be identified for separating the sale and the leaseback that would be both practicable and objective. For that reason, the Board concluded that the present general requirement that gains and losses on sale-leaseback transactions be deferred and amortized should be retained. An exception to that requirement arises when the fair value of the property at the time of the transaction is less than its undepreciated cost. In that case, the Board decided that the loss should be recognized up to the amount of the difference between the undepreciated cost and fair value.

Accounting for Leveraged Leases by Lessors

108. The first issue concerning leveraged leases in the Discussion Memorandum asked whether leveraged leases are unique in the sense that special standards are required to recognize their economic nature. The affirmative responses to this issue generally gave as reasons the arguments stated in the Discussion Memorandum. The essence of those arguments is that the combination of nonrecourse financing and a cash flow pattern that typically enables the lessor to recover his investment in the early years of the lease and thereafter affords him the temporary use of funds from which additional income can be derived produces a unique economic effect. Those respondents who did not agree that leveraged leases are unique generally cited the contra argument in the Discussion Memorandum, namely, that each of the attributes of leveraged leases that serve to support the uniqueness claim has its counterpart in other types of business transactions. Information communicated by respondents, as well as that obtained through staff investigation, indicates that the use of a variety of accounting methods for leveraged leases has grown rapidly. The methods in use generally correspond, although frequently with variations, to those illustrated in the Discussion Memorandum. The Board noted with concern the increasing disparity in practice in accounting for leveraged leases. Despite the fact that each of the attributes of a leveraged lease is found in other types of transactions, the Board believes that in a leveraged lease those attributes are combined in a manner that produces an overall economic effect that is distinct from that of other transactions. Accordingly, the Board concluded that a leveraged lease, as defined in paragraph 42, should be accounted for in a manner that recognizes this over-all economic effect. However, the Board emphasizes that the qualification "as defined in paragraph 42" is an important one since the term "leveraged lease" is used by some respondents to refer to any lease involving nonrecourse debt. There is further discussion of this distinction in paragraph 110.

109. The Discussion Memorandum described and illustrated four different methods of accounting for leveraged leases. Three of those methods are designed to recognize what their adherents see as the economic effect of a leveraged lease, while the other method, the ordinary financing lease method, is that presently prescribed for financing leases by *APB Opinion No. 7*. The Board's conclusions and the reasons therefor concerning the four methods are as follows:

a. *The ordinary financing lease method.* This accounting method makes no distinction between a leveraged lease and an ordinary two-party financing lease. Even though the debt is nonrecourse to the lessor and the lessor has no claim on the debt service payments, the transaction is recorded "gross" with the lessor's investment based on the present value of the gross rentals plus the residual value as prescribed by *APB Opinion No. 7*. In fact, however, the lessor's real investment is not a function of the amount of the future rental payments, which amount represents neither the funds he has at risk nor the asset from which he derives earnings. Further, no recognition is given to the separate investment phases of a leveraged lease as defined in paragraph 42. This method was rejected by the Board because it is incompatible with the essential features of the transaction.

b. *The three-party financing lease method.* This method does reflect the three-party nature of the transaction in that the lessor's investment is recorded net of the nonrecourse debt, and rental receipts are reduced by the debt service payments. However, it gives no recognition to the fact that a leveraged lease has separate investment phases, which is one of the characteristics included in the definition (see paragraph 42(d)). The lessor's unrecovered investment balance declines during the early years of a leveraged lease from the strong cash inflow in that period. Typically, the cumulative cash inflow during the early years exceeds the investment, producing a negative investment balance during the middle years. The investment returns to a positive balance again in the later years as funds are reinvested and then goes to zero with realization of the residual value at the termination of the lease. This pattern of cash flow results from the fact that income tax reductions from the investment tax credit, accelerated depreciation, and greater interest deductions in earlier years are replaced by additional income taxes in the later years after the investment tax credit has been utilized and as tax benefits from depreciation and interest diminish. By ignoring these separate investment phases, the three-party financing method shows a gradually declining investment balance throughout the years of the lease, with income recognized at a level rate of return on the declining balance. The Board believes that the accounting treatment for a leveraged lease should reflect these separate investment phases, which have different economic effects, and should provide for the recognition of income in appropriate relation to them. To do otherwise, in the Board's view, is to negate the reason for having a separate standard for leveraged leases, that reason being that leveraged leases have a distinct combination of economic features that sets them apart from ordinary financing leases. While the three-party financing lease method reflects the three-party nature of the transaction, it fails to recognize the other economic features referred to above; as a consequence, it produces results that are inconsistent with the manner in which the lessor-investor views the transaction. For those reasons, the Board rejected the three-party financing lease method.

c. *The investment with separate phases method.* This method recognizes the separate investment phases and the reversing cash flow pattern of a leveraged lease. By recognizing income at a level rate of return on net investment in the years in which the net investment is positive, it associates the income with the unrecovered balance of the earning asset in a manner consistent with the investor's view of the transaction. In the middle years of the lease term, the investment balance is generally negative, indicating that the lessor has not only recovered his initial investment but has the temporary use of funds that will be reinvested in the later years. The earnings on these temporary funds are reflected in income as and if they occur in the years in which the investment is negative. The income that is recognized at a level rate of return in the years in which the net investment balance is positive consists only of the so-called "primary" earnings from the lease, as distinct from the earnings on temporary funds to be reinvested, sometimes referred to as "secondary" earnings. The lessor-investor looks upon these secondary earnings from the temporarily held funds as one of the economic benefits inherent in the transaction. The integral investment method discussed in (d) below allocates both the primary and secondary earnings to annual income on a level rate of return basis. It is asserted by some that because of this feature, the integral investment method is more consistent with the manner in which the lessor-investor views the transaction. However, this feature

involves estimation of the secondary earnings and recognition of a substantial portion of them in advance of their occurrence, which the Board did not favor for reasons stated below in the discussion of the integral investment method. The Board believes that secondary earnings should be recognized in income only as they occur (in the negative investment years), and that this treatment, coupled with the recognition of primary earnings in the positive investment years, appropriately portrays the economic effects of the separate investment phases. Accordingly, the Board concluded that the investment with separate phases method as prescribed in paragraphs 43-47 is the appropriate method for accounting for leveraged leases.

d. *The integral investment method.* Several variations of the method illustrated in Schedule 7, page 126, of the Discussion Memorandum were suggested by respondents who supported its concept. That concept looks upon the earnings from the use of temporarily held funds (discussed in (c) above) as constituting an integral part of the lease income, rather than as secondary earnings to be accounted for as they occur (the treatment called for in the separate phases method). Advocates of the integral method point out that the equity participant (lessor) in a leveraged lease is actually buying a series of cash flows consisting not only of the equity portion of the rental payments, the investment tax credit and other tax benefits, and the amount to be realized from the sale of the residual, but also including the earnings to be obtained from the use of temporarily held funds. Failure to include the latter in the calculation and recognition of lease income, in their view, understates lease income and is inconsistent with the manner in which the lessor-investor views the transaction. In considering these arguments, the Board noted (1) that the earnings in question, in effect, represent an estimate of interest expected to be earned (or interest cost to be saved) in future years through the application of the temporarily held funds; (2) although these earnings will not be realized until future years, their inclusion in lease income under the integral investment method would result in their recognition in substantial amounts beginning with the first year of the lease; and (3) the actual occurrence and amount of those earnings cannot be verified because this would involve tracing the source of specific investment dollars, generally acknowledged to be impractical. The Board noted further that the other cash flows that constitute the source of the primary earnings, with the exception of the residual value, are either contractual or based on existing tax law and thus provide a firmer basis for income recognition than the secondary earnings. Admittedly, there is uncertainty involved in the estimate of residual value to be realized; however, the Board noted that recognition of residual value is consistent with the accounting prescribed for ordinary financing leases, whereas the anticipation of future interest on funds expected to be held temporarily has no support in present generally accepted accounting principles. For the foregoing reasons, the Board rejected the integral investment method.

110. Some respondents who objected to the inclusion of paragraph 42(d) in the definition of a leveraged lease argued that leveraged leases can have a variety of rental payment arrangements, some of which would not produce the separate investment phases specified as part of the definition, but that, nevertheless, such leases should be accorded the accounting method prescribed in the Statement. The Board did not agree with this view, since the method prescribed is designed to recognize the unique economic aspects of the separate investment phases. It concluded that leases not having this characteristic should not be accounted for as leveraged leases and that the presence of nonrecourse debt in a leasing transaction is not by itself justification for special accounting treatment. Nonrecourse debt occurs in many types of transactions other than leases and, as discussed in paragraph 108, it is only the combination of attributes, not the presence of nonrecourse debt alone, that produces an overall economic effect that is distinct from that of other transactions.

111. Some have contended that the inclusion of deferred taxes in the determination of the lessor's unrecovered investment is what gives rise to the separate investment phases, which is then used to justify the Board's adoption of the separate phases method and its rejection of the three-party financing method. The Board believes that the essential difference between the three-party financing method and the separate phases method is that the latter method closely follows the cash flow of the transaction, whereas the former does not. The three-party financing method portrays a gradually declining investment balance over the entire lease term, thus failing to recognize the short-term nature of the lessor's initial investment, which is typically recovered through the cash flow in the early years of the lease. That this early cash flow comes in large part from tax benefits does not alter the fact that the lessor has recovered his investment and is then provided with the temporary use of funds by which additional income can be generated. It is this feature which provides much of the incentive for the lessor to enter into the transaction in the first place and, in fact, without those tax benefits some leveraged leases would yield negative results. The Board concluded that leveraged leases should be accounted for in a manner that recognizes this cash flow pattern, both in determining the lessor's unrecovered invest-

ment balance and in the allocation of income relating to it. The assertion by some that the separate phases method results in an unwarranted "front ending" of income, in the Board's view, fails to take into account that the economic benefits of the transaction are themselves "front-ended," as has been described above. It is precisely this feature and the lack of recognition given it by the three-party financing method that caused the Board to reject that method.

112. A number of respondents to the second Exposure Draft objected to the exclusion of the 90 percent recovery criterion, 7(d), in determining whether or not a lease meets the requirement of paragraph 42(a) as part of the definition of a leveraged lease. These respondents pointed out that the majority of leveraged leases would not meet any of the other criteria of paragraph 7 and that, if criterion 7(d) was not to be applicable, few leases would meet the definition of a leveraged lease. They took exception to the Board's reasons for having excluded criterion 7(d) as expressed in the second Exposure Draft. In their view, the determination of whether the lease would qualify as a direct financing lease, as required by paragraph 42(a), should be made in the same manner as with any other lease and that the presence of nonrecourse debt should thus not enter into such determination. The Board agreed with this reasoning and has changed the requirement of paragraph 42(a) accordingly.

113. Some respondents asked that the Board reconsider its decision reflected in the second Exposure Draft that leases meeting the definition of sales-type leases should not be accounted for as leveraged leases. The argument was advanced that manufacturers and dealers often engaged in leasing transactions that, except for the exclusion of sales-type leases, would otherwise meet the definition of a leveraged lease as set forth in paragraph 42. Specifically, it was asked why should not a manufacturer record manufacturing profit for a sales-type lease and then also account for it as a leveraged lease, if it otherwise meets the definition? In the Board's view, the recognition of manufacturing profit by the lessor at the beginning of the lease is incompatible with the concept underlying the accounting method prescribed by this Statement for leveraged leases. As stated in paragraph 109(c), that method recognizes income at a level rate of return on the lessor's net investment in the years in which the net investment is positive. The annual cash flow is thus allocated between that portion recognized as income and that applied as a reduction of net investment. Net investment at any point is considered to represent the lessor's unrecovered investment. If manufacturing profit is recognized at the beginning of the lease, an element of the overall profit in the transaction has been abstracted at the outset, thus changing the pat-

tern of income recognition contemplated. The lessor's investment as recorded after recognition of manufacturing profit would not represent his unrecovered investment. That fact plus the deferral of income taxes related to the manufacturing profit recognized would alter both the investment base and the income to be allocated, thus departing from the cash flow concept on which the prescribed method is based. For these reasons, the Board did not accept the recommendation.

114. For much the same reason, the Board concluded that if the investment tax credit is accounted for other than as described in paragraphs 43 and 44, the leveraged lease should not be accounted for by the investment with separate phases method but, instead, by the method prescribed for a direct financing lease. Accounting for the credit other than as prescribed by the investment with separate phases method would abstract an important element of the overall profit in the transaction, thereby changing the lessor's net investment and the pattern of income recognition contemplated by the investment with separate phases method and thus, in the Board's view, rendering the use of that method inappropriate.

Effective Date and Transition

115. The Board considered three methods of transition in the application of the Statement:

a. Retroactive application with restatement of prior period financial statements
b. Retroactive application without restatement
c. Prospective application

The first alternative maximizes comparability of a company's financial statements with those of other companies and with its own statements for prior periods. However, respondents expressed concern that it would require the accumulation of a considerable amount of information about existing and expired leases and that some companies might have problems relating to restrictive covenants in loan indentures and other contracts. In addition, it requires estimates that in some cases would be made with after-the-fact knowledge. The second alternative reduces the problem of data accumulation but at the cost of impairing interperiod comparability of a company's financial statements before and after the date of retroactive application. Depending on the particular circumstances, it may or may not mitigate the possible problems relating to loan indenture covenants. The third alternative avoids most of the problems of the other two but would result in noncomparability of financial statements, both as among different companies and those of the same company for different periods, for years in the future.

116. While the majority of respondents favored prospective application, others strongly urged that the Statement be applied retroactively with restatement. The long period of time that would ensue before comparability would be achieved was given as the prime reason by those advocating retroactivity. Some preparers, on the other hand, cited problems involving loan indenture restrictions should the Statement require retroactive application. Some companies with large numbers of leases stated in their responses that the task of gathering the necessary data for retroactive application would be onerous as well as time consuming for existing leases, and that it would be more difficult, if not impossible, to obtain the information on expired leases necessary for restatement.

117. Included in the responses was the suggestion that a transition period be established during which companies would be given time both for the purpose of accumulating the necessary data for retroactive application and for taking steps toward resolving problems that might arise in connection with restrictive clauses in loan indentures or other agreements.

118. In considering these conflicting recommendations, the Board was sympathetic to the problems of data accumulation for companies with large numbers of leases and to the problems that some companies believe might be associated with indenture restrictions. On the other hand, the objections raised, particularly by users of financial statements, to the long period of noncomparability of financial statements that would be entailed by prospective application concerned the Board. The Board concluded that the use of a transition period at the end of which full retroactive application would be required would best meet the needs of users while at the same time giving significant recognition to the problems referred to by preparers.

119. The procedure adopted by the Board calls for immediate prospective application of the Statement (see paragraph 48), with retroactive restatement required after a four-year transition period (see paragraph 49). Thus, companies that might have problems arising from loan indenture restrictions are given at least four full years in which, depending on the nature of the restrictions, resolution of such problems may be possible. Further, restatement is required for periods beginning before December 31, 1976 only to the extent that it is practicable (see paragraph 51), in recognition of the fact that some companies may be unable to obtain or reconstruct the necessary information about leases expiring in prior years. Finally, interim disclosures (see paragraph 50) are called for to facilitate comparability before retroactive application of the Statement is required; however, since the Board recognizes that the accumulation of information to make such dis-

closures may require time, companies are given at least one full year before such disclosure is called for. Although the Board recognizes that the period of time provided for transition will not completely eliminate the problems of retroactive restatement, it believes that those problems will be alleviated under the method outlined above and that the benefit to be gained through comparability of financial statements is substantial.

120. Upon consideration of the relevant circumstances, the Board concluded that the interests of users of financial statements would be best served by making the statement effective for leasing transactions and lease agreement revisions entered into on or after January 1, 1977, as provided by paragraph 48.

Appendix C

ILLUSTRATIONS OF ACCOUNTING BY LESSEES AND LESSORS

121. This Appendix contains the following schedules illustrating the accounting requirements of this Statement as applied to a particular example (an automobile lease):

1. Lease example—terms and assumptions, Schedule 1
2. Computation of minimum lease payments (lessee and lessor) and lessor's computation of rate of interest implicit in the lease, Schedule 2
3. Classification of the lease, Schedule 3
4. Journal entries for the first month of the lease as well as for the disposition of the leased property at the end of the lease term, Schedule 4

SCHEDULE 1

Lease Example
Terms and Assumptions

Lessor's cost of the leased property (automobile)	$5,000
Fair value of the leased property at inception of the lease (1/1/77)	$5,000
Estimated economic life of the leased property	5 years

Lease terms and assumptions: The lease has a fixed noncancelable term of 30 months, with a rental of $135 payable at the beginning of each month. The lessee guarantees the residual value at the end of the 30-month lease term in the amount of $2,000. The lessee is to receive any excess of sales price of property over the guaranteed amount at the end of the lease term. The lessee pays executory costs. The lease is renewable periodically based on a schedule of rentals and guarantees of the residual values decreasing over time. The rentals specified are deemed to be fair rentals (as distinct from bargain rentals), and the guarantees of the residual are expected to approximate realizable values. No investment tax credit is available.

The residual value at the end of the lease term is estimated to be $2,000. The lessee depreciates his owned automobiles on a straight-line basis. The lessee's incremental borrowing rate is 10½% per year. There were no initial direct costs of negotiating and closing the transaction. At the end of the lease term the asset is sold for $2,100.

SCHEDULE 2

Computation of Minimum Lease Payments
(Lessee and Lessor)

In accordance with paragraph 5(j), minimum lease payments for both the lessee and lessor are computed as follows:

Minimum rental payments over the lease term ($135 × 30 months)	$4,050
Lessee guarantee of the residual value at the end of the lease term	2,000
Total minimum lease payments	$6,050

Lessor's Computation of Rate of Interest
Implicit in the Lease

In accordance with paragraph 5(k), the interest rate implicit in the lease is that rate implicit in the recovery of the fair value of the property at the inception of the lease ($5,000) through the minimum lease payments (30 monthly payments of $135 and the lessee's guarantee of the residual value in the amount of $2,000 at the end of the lease term). That rate is 12.036% (1.003% per month).

SCHEDULE 3

Classification of the Lease

Criteria set forth
 in paragraph

7(a)   *Not met*. The lease does not transfer ownership of the property to the lessee by the end of the lease term.

7(b)   *Not met*. The lease does not contain a bargain purchase option.

7(c)   *Not met*. The lease term is not equal to 75% or more of the estimated economic life of the property. (In this case, it represents only 50% of the estimated economic life of the property.)

7(d)   *Met*. In the lessee's case, the present value ($5,120) of the minimum lease payments using his incremental borrowing rate (10 1/2%) exceeds 90% of the fair value of the property at the inception of the lease. (See computation below.) Even if the lessee knows the implicit rate, he uses his incremental rate because it is lower. The lessee classifies the lease as a capital lease. In the lessor's case, the present value ($5,000) of the minimum lease payments using the implicit rate also exceeds 90% of the fair value of the property. (See computation below.) Having met this criterion and assuming that the criteria of paragraph 8 are also met, the lessor will classify the lease as a direct financing lease (as opposed to a sales-type lease) because the cost and fair value of the asset are the same at the inception of the lease. (See paragraph 6(b)(ii).)

	Present Values	
	Lessee's computation using his incremental borrowing rate of 10 1/2% (.875% per month)*	Lessor's computation using the implicit interest rate of 12.036% (1.003% per month)
Minimum lease payments:		
Rental payments	$3,580	$3,517
Residual guarantee by lessee	1,540	1,483
Total	$5,120	$5,000
Fair value of the property at inception of the lease	$5,000	$5,000
Minimum lease payments as a percentage of fair value	102%	100%

---

*In this case, the lessee's incremental borrowing rate is used because it is lower than the implicit rate. (See paragraph 7(d).)

SCHEDULE 4

**Journal Entries for the First Month of the Lease as Well as for the
Disposition of the Leased Property at the End of the Lease Term**

First Month of the Lease

LESSEE

1/1/77	Leased property under capital leases	5,000	
	Obligations under capital leases		5,000
	To record capital lease at the fair value of the property. (Since the present value of the minimum lease payments using the lessee's incremental borrowing rate as the discount rate (see paragraph 7(d) for selection of rate to be used) is greater than the fair value of the property, the lessee capitalizes only the fair value of the property. (See paragraph 10.))		
1/1/77	Obligations under capital leases	135	
	Cash		135
	To record first month's rental payment.		
1/31/77	Interest expense	49	
	Accrued interest on obligations under capital leases		49*
	To recognize interest expense for the first month of the lease. Obligation balance outstanding during month $4,865 ($5,000 − $135) × 1.003% (rate implicit in the liquidation of the $5,000 obligation through (a) 30 monthly payments of $135 made at the beginning of each month and (b) a $2,000 guarantee of the residual value at the end of 30 months) = $49. (See paragraph 12.)		
1/31/77	Depreciation expense	100	
	Leased property under capital leases		100
	To record first month's depreciation on a straight-line basis over 30 months to a salvage value of $2,000, which is the estimated residual value to the lessee. (See paragraph 11(b).)		

LESSOR

1/1/77	Minimum lease payments receivable	6,050	
	Automobile		5,000
	Unearned income		1,050
	To record lessor's investment in the direct financing lease. (See paragraphs 18(a) and (b).)		
1/1/77	Cash	135	
	Minimum lease payments receivable		135
	To record receipt of first month's rental payment under the lease.		
1/31/77	Unearned income	49	
	Earned income		49
	To recognize the portion of unearned income that is earned during the first month of the lease. Net investment outstanding for month $4,865 (gross investment $5,915 ($6,050 − $135) less unearned income ($1,050) × 1.003% (monthly implicit rate in the lease) = $49. (See paragraph 18(b).)		

---

*In accordance with paragraph 12, the February 1, 1977 rental payment of $135 will be allocated as follows: $86 (principal reduction) against obligations under capital leases and $49 against accrued interest on obligations under capital leases.

The following is a schedule by years of future minimum lease payments under capital leases together with the present value of the net minimum lease payments as of December 31, 1976:

Year ending December 31:

1977	$ XXX
1978	XXX
1979	XXX
1980	XXX
1981	XXX
Later years	XXX
Total minimum lease payments[1]	XXX
Less: Amount representing estimated executory costs (such as taxes, maintenance, and insurance), including profit thereon, included in total minimum lease payments	(XXX)
Net minimum lease payments	XXX
Less: Amount representing interest[2]	(XXX)
Present value of net minimum lease payments[3]	$ XXX

Note 3—Operating Leases

The following is a schedule by years of future minimum rental payments required under operating leases that have initial or remaining noncancelable lease terms in excess of one year as of December 31, 1976:

Year ending December 31:

1977	$ XXX
1978	XXX
1979	XXX
1980	XXX
1981	XXX
Later years	XXX
Total minimum payments required*	$ XXX

The following schedule shows the composition of total rental expense for all operating leases except those with terms of a month or less that were not renewed:

	Year ending December 31,	
	1976	1975
Minimum rentals	$ XXX	$ XXX
Contingent rentals	XXX	XXX
Less: Sublease rentals	(XXX)	(XXX)
	$ XXX	$ XXX

---

[1]Minimum payments have not been reduced by minimum sublease rentals of $XXX due in the future under noncancelable subleases. They also do not include contingent rentals which may be paid under certain store leases on the basis of a percentage of sales in excess of stipulated amounts. Contingent rentals amounted to $XXX in 1976 and $XXX in 1975.

[2]Amount necessary to reduce net minimum lease payments to present value calculated at the Company's incremental borrowing rate at the inception of the leases.

[3]Reflected in the balance sheet as current and noncurrent obligations under capital leases of $XXX and $XXX, respectively.

*Minimum payments have not been reduced by minimum sublease rentals of $XXX due in the future under noncancelable subleases.

LESSOR'S DISCLOSURE (Other Than for Leveraged Leases)

Company X
BALANCE SHEET

	December 31,	
ASSETS	**1976**	**1975**
Current assets:		
Net investment in direct financing and sales-type leases (Note 2)	XXX	XXX
Noncurrent assets:		
Net investment in direct financing and sales-type leases (Note 2)	XXX	XXX
Property on operating leases and property held for leases (net of accumulated depreciation of $XXX and $XXX for 1976 and 1975, respectively) (Note 3)	XXX	XXX

Footnotes appear [below and] on the following pages.

FOOTNOTES

Note 1—Description of Leasing Arrangements

The Company's leasing operations consist principally of the leasing of various types of heavy construction and mining equipment, data processing equipment, and transportation equipment. With the exception of the leases of transportation equipment, the bulk of the Company's leases are classified as direct financing leases. The construction equipment and mining equipment leases expire over the next ten years and the data processing equipment leases expire over the next eight years. Transportation equipment (principally trucks) is leased under operating leases that expire during the next three years.

Note 2—Net Investment in Direct Financing and Sales-Type Leases

The following lists the components of the net investment in direct financing and sales-type leases as of December 31:

	1976	1975
Total minimum lease payments to be received*	$ XXX	$ XXX
Less: Amounts representing estimated executory costs (such as taxes, maintenance, and insurance), including profit thereon, included in total minimum lease payments	(XXX)	(XXX)
Minimum lease payments receivable	XXX	XXX
Less: Allowance for uncollectibles	(XXX)	(XXX)
Net minimum lease payments receivable	XXX	XXX
Estimated residual values of leased property (unguaranteed)	XXX	XXX
Less: Unearned income	(XXX)	(XXX)
Net investment in direct financing and sales-type leases	$ XXX	$ XXX

---

*Minimum lease payments do not include contingent rentals which may be received under certain leases of data processing equipment on the basis of hours of use in excess of stipulated minimums. Contingent rentals amounted to $XXX in 1976 and $XXX in 1975. At December 31, 1976, minimum lease payments for each of the five succeeding fiscal years are as follows: $XXX in 1977, $XXX in 1978, $XXX in 1979, $XXX in 1980, and $XXX in 1981.

**Note 3—Property on Operating Leases and
Property Held for Lease**

The following schedule provides an analysis of the
Company's investment in property on operating
leases and property held for lease by major classes
as of December 31, 1976:

Construction equipment	$ XXX
Mining equipment	XXX
Data processing equipment	XXX
Transportation equipment	XXX
Other	XXX
	XXX
Less: Accumulated depreciation	(XXX)
	$ XXX

Note 4—Rentals under Operating Leases

The following is a schedule by years of minimum
future rentals on noncancelable operating leases as
of December 31, 1976:

Year ending December 31:	
1977	$ XXX
1978	XXX
1979	XXX
1980	XXX
1981	XXX
Later years	XXX
Total minimum future rentals*	$ XXX

Appendix E

**ILLUSTRATIONS OF ACCOUNTING AND
FINANCIAL STATEMENT PRESENTATION
FOR LEVERAGED LEASES**

123. This Appendix illustrates the accounting
requirements of this Statement and one way of
meeting its disclosure requirements as applied to a
leveraged lease. The illustrations do not encompass
all circumstances that may arise in connection with
leveraged leases; rather, the illustrations are based
on a single example of a leveraged lease, the terms
and assumptions for which are stated in Schedule
1. The elements of accounting and reporting illustrated for this example of a leveraged lease are as
follows:

a. Leveraged lease example—terms and assumptions, Schedule 1

b. Cash flow analysis by years, Schedule 2
c. Allocation of annual cash flow to investment
   and income, Schedule 3
d. Journal entries for lessor's initial investment and
   first year of operation, Schedule 4
e. Financial statements including footnotes at end
   of second year
f. Accounting for a revision in the estimated residual value of the leased asset assumed to occur in
   the eleventh year of the lease (from $200,000 to
   $120,000):
   i. Revised allocation of annual cash flow to
      investment and income, Schedule 5
   ii. Balances in investment accounts at beginning
       of the eleventh year before revised estimate,
       Schedule 6
   iii. Journal entries, Schedule 7
   iv. Adjustment of investment accounts, Sched-
       ule 8

---

*This amount does not include contingent rentals which may be received under certain leases of data processing equipment on the basis
of hours of use in excess of stipulated minimums. Contingent rentals amounted to $XXX in 1976 and $XXX in 1975.

SCHEDULE 1

Leveraged Lease Example
Terms and Assumptions

Cost of leased asset (equipment)	$1,000,000
Lease term	15 years, dating from January 1, 1975
Lease rental payments	$90,000 per year (payable last day of each year)
Residual value	$200,000 estimated to be realized one year after lease termination. In the eleventh year of the lease the estimate is reduced to $120,000.
Financing:	
Equity investment by lessor	$400,000
Long-term nonrecourse debt	$600,000, bearing interest at 9% and repayable in annual installments (on last day of each year) of $74,435.30
Depreciation allowable to lessor for income tax purposes	Seven-year ADR life using double-declining-balance method for the first two years (with the half-year convention election applied in the first year) and sum-of-years digits method for remaining life, depreciated to $100,000 salvage value
Lessor's income tax rate (federal and state)	50.4% (assumed to continue in existence throughout the term of the lease)
Investment tax credit	10% of equipment cost or $100,000 (realized by the lessor on last day of first year of lease)
Initial direct costs	For simplicity, initial direct costs have not been included in the illustration.

SCHEDULE 2

Cash Flow Analysis by Years

Year	1 Gross lease rentals and residual value	2 Depreciation (for income tax purposes)	3 Loan interest payments	4 Taxable income (loss) (col. 1 − 2 − 3)	5 Income tax credits (charges) (col. 4 × 50.4%)	6 Loan principal payments	7 Investment tax credit realized	8 Annual cash flow (col. 1 − 3 + 5 − 6 + 7)	9 Cumulative cash flow
Initial investment	—			—	—			$(400,000)	(400,000)
1	$ 90,000	$ 142,857	$ 54,000	$(106,857)	$ 53,856	$ 20,435	$100,000	169,421	(230,579)
2	90,000	244,898	52,161	(207,059)	104,358	22,274	—	119,923	(110,656)
3	90,000	187,075	50,156	(147,231)	74,204	24,279	—	89,769	(20,887)
4	90,000	153,061	47,971	(111,032)	55,960	26,464	—	71,525	50,638
5	90,000	119,048	45,589	(74,637)	37,617	28,846	—	53,182	103,820
6	90,000	53,061	42,993	(6,054)	3,051	31,442	—	18,616	122,436
7	90,000	—	40,163	49,837	(25,118)	34,272	—	(9,553)	112,883
8	90,000	—	37,079	52,921	(26,672)	37,357	—	(11,108)	101,775
9	90,000	—	33,717	56,283	(28,367)	40,719	—	(12,803)	88,972
10	90,000	—	30,052	59,948	(30,214)	44,383	—	(14,649)	74,323
11	90,000	—	26,058	63,942	(32,227)	48,378	—	(16,663)	57,660
12	90,000	—	21,704	68,296	(34,421)	52,732	—	(18,857)	38,803
13	90,000	—	16,957	73,043	(36,813)	57,478	—	(21,248)	17,555
14	90,000	—	11,785	78,215	(39,420)	62,651	—	(23,856)	(6,301)
15	90,000	—	6,145	83,855	(42,263)	68,290	—	(26,698)	(32,999)
16	200,000	100,000	—	100,000	(50,400)	—	—	149,600	116,601
Totals	$1,550,000	$1,000,000	$516,530	$ 33,470	$ (16,869)	$600,000	$100,000	$ 116,601	

SCHEDULE 3

Allocation of Annual Cash Flow to Investment and Income

Year	1 Lessor's net investment at beginning of year	2 Annual Cash Flow Total (from Schedule 2, col. 8)	3 Annual Cash Flow Allocated to investment	4 Annual Cash Flow Allocated to income[1]	5 Pretax income	6 Components of Income[2] Tax effect of pretax income	7 Components of Income[2] Investment tax credit
1	$400,000	$169,421	$134,833	$34,588	$9,929	$(5,004)	$29,663
2	265,167	119,923	96,994	22,929	6,582	(3,317)	19,664
3	168,173	89,769	75,227	14,542	4,174	(2,104)	12,472
4	92,946	71,525	63,488	8,037	2,307	(1,163)	6,893
5	29,458	53,182	50,635	2,547	731	(368)	2,184
6	(21,177)	18,616	18,616	—	—	—	—
7	(39,793)	(9,553)	(9,553)	—	—	—	—
8	(30,240)	(11,108)	(11,108)	—	—	—	—
9	(19,132)	(12,803)	(12,803)	—	—	—	—
10	(6,329)	(14,649)	(14,649)	—	—	—	—
11	8,320	(16,663)	(17,382)	719	206	(104)	617
12	25,702	(18,857)	(21,079)	2,222	637	(321)	1,906
13	46,781	(21,248)	(25,293)	4,045	1,161	(585)	3,469
14	72,074	(23,856)	(30,088)	6,232	1,789	(902)	5,345
15	102,162	(26,698)	(35,532)	8,834	2,536	(1,278)	7,576
16	137,694	149,600	137,694	11,906	3,418	(1,723)	10,211
Totals		$516,601	$400,000	$116,601	$33,470	$(16,869)	$100,000

[1] Lease income is recognized as 8.647% of the unrecovered investment at the beginning of each year in which the net investment is positive. The rate is that rate which when applied to the net investment in the years in which the net investment is positive will distribute the net income (net cash flow) to those years. The rate for allocation used in this Schedule is calculated by a trial and error process. The allocation is calculated based upon an initial estimate of the rate as a starting point. If the total thus allocated to income (column 4) differs under the estimated rate from the net cash flow (Schedule 2, column 8) the estimated rate is increased or decreased, as appropriate, to derive a revised allocation. This process is repeated until a rate is selected which develops a total amount allocated to income that is precisely equal to the net cash flow. As a practical matter, a computer program is used to calculate Schedule 3 under successive iterations until the correct rate is determined.

[2] Each component is allocated among the years of positive net investment in proportion to the allocation of net income in column 4.

SCHEDULE 4

Illustrative Journal Entries for Year Ending December 31, 1975

Lessor's Initial Investment

Rentals receivable (Schedule 2, total of column 1 less residual value, less totals of columns 3 and 6)	233,470	
Investment tax credit receivable (Schedule 2, column 7)	100,000	
Estimated residual value (Schedule 1)	200,000	
Unearned and deferred income (Schedule 3, totals of columns 5 and 7)		133,470
Cash		400,000
Record lessor's initial investment		

First Year of Operation

Journal Entry 1

Cash	15,565	
Rentals receivable (Schedule 2, column 1 less columns 3 and 6)		15,565
Collection of first year's net rental		

Journal Entry 2

Cash *	100,000	
Investment tax credit receivable (Schedule 2, column 7)		100,000
Receipt of investment tax credit		

Journal Entry 3

Unearned and deferred income	9,929	
Income from leveraged leases (Schedule 3, column 5)		9,929

Recognition of first year's portion of pretax income allocated in the same proportion as the allocation of total income

$$\left(\frac{34,588}{116,601}\right) \times 33,470 = 9,929$$

Journal Entry 4

Unearned and deferred income	29,663	
Investment tax credit recognized (Schedule 3, column 7)		29,663

Recognition of first year's portion of investment tax credit allocated in the same proportion as the allocation of total income

$$\left(\frac{34,588}{116,601}\right) \times 100,000 = 29,663$$

Journal Entry 5

Cash (Schedule 2, column 5) *	53,856	
Income tax expense (Schedule 3, column 6)	5,004	
Deferred taxes		58,860

To record receipt of first year's tax credit from lease operation, to charge income tax expense for tax effect of pretax accounting income, and to recognize as deferred taxes the tax effect of the difference between pretax accounting income and the tax loss for the year, calculated as follows:

Tax loss (Schedule 2, column 4)	$(106,857)
Pretax accounting income	9,929
Difference	$(116,786)
Deferred taxes ($116,786 × 50.4%)	$ 58,860

---

*Receipts of the investment tax credit and other tax benefits are shown as cash receipts for simplicity only. Those receipts probably would not be in the form of immediate cash inflow. Instead, they likely would be in the form of reduced payments of taxes on other income of the lessor or on the combined income of the lessor and other entities whose operations are joined with the lessor's operations in a consolidated tax return.

ILLUSTRATIVE PARTIAL FINANCIAL STATEMENTS INCLUDING FOOTNOTES

BALANCE SHEET

ASSETS			LIABILITIES		
	December 31,			December 31,	
	1976	1975		1976	1975
Investment in leveraged leases	$334,708	$324,027	Deferred taxes arising from leveraged leases	$166,535	$58,860

INCOME STATEMENT
(Ignoring all income and expense items other than those relating to leveraged leasing)

	1976	1975
Income from leveraged leases	$ 6,582	$ 9,929
Income before taxes and investment tax credit	6,582	9,929
Less: Income tax expense*	(3,317)	(5,004)
	3,265	4,925
Investment tax credit recognized*	19,664	29,663
Net income	$22,929	$34,588

FOOTNOTES

Investment in Leveraged Leases

The Company is the lessor in a leveraged lease agreement entered into in 1975 under which mining equipment having an estimated economic life of 18 years was leased for a term of 15 years. The Company's equity investment represented 40 percent of the purchase price; the remaining 60 percent was furnished by third-party financing in the form of long-term debt that provides for no recourse against the Company and is secured by a first lien on the property. At the end of the lease term, the equipment is turned back to the Company. The residual value at that time is estimated to be 20 percent of cost. For federal income tax purposes, the Company receives the investment tax credit and has the benefit of tax deductions for depreciation on the entire leased asset and for interest on the long-term debt. Since during the early years of the lease those deductions exceed the lease rental income, substantial excess deductions are available to be applied against the Company's other income. In the later years of the lease, rental income will exceed the deductions and taxes will be payable. Deferred taxes are provided to reflect this reversal.

The Company's net investment in leveraged leases is composed of the following elements:

	December 31,	
	1976	1975
Rentals receivable (net of principal and interest on the nonrecourse debt)	$202,340	$217,905
Estimated residual value of leased assets	200,000	200,000
Less: Unearned and deferred income	(67,632)	(93,878)
Investment in leveraged leases	334,708	324,027
Less: Deferred taxes arising from leveraged leases	(166,535)	(58,860)
Net investment in leveraged leases	$168,173	$265,167

---

*These two items may be netted for purposes of presentation in the income statement, provided that the separate amounts are disclosed in a note to the financial statements.

SCHEDULE 5

**Allocation of Annual Cash Flow to Investment and Income
Revised to Include New Residual Value Estimate**

	1	2	3	4	5	6	7
			Annual Cash Flow			**Components of Income**	
Year	Lessor's net investment at beginning of year	Total	Allocated to investment	Allocated to income[1]	Pretax loss	Tax effect of pretax loss	Investment tax credit
1	$400,000	$169,421	$142,458	$26,963	$(16,309)	$ 8,220	$ 35,052
2	257,542	119,923	102,563	17,360	(10,501)	5,293	22,568
3	154,979	89,769	79,323	10,446	(6,319)	3,184	13,581
4	75,656	71,525	66,425	5,100	(3,085)	1,555	6,630
5	9,231	53,182	52,560	622	(377)	190	809
6	(43,329)	18,616	18,616	—	—	—	—
7	(61,945)	(9,553)	(9,553)	—	—	—	—
8	(52,392)	(11,108)	(11,108)	—	—	—	—
9	(41,284)	(12,803)	(12,803)	—	—	—	—
10	(28,481)	(14,649)	(14,649)	—	—	—	—
11	(13,832)	(16,663)	(16,663)	—	—	—	—
12	2,831	(18,857)	(19,048)	191	(115)	58	248
13	21,879	(21,248)	(22,723)	1,475	(892)	450	1,917
14	44,602	(23,856)	(26,862)	3,006	(1,819)	916	3,909
15	71,464	(26,698)	(31,515)	4,817	(2,914)	1,469	6,262
16	102,979	109,920	102,979	6,941	(4,199)	2,116	9,024
Totals		$476,921	$400,000	$76,921	$(46,530)	$23,451	$100,000

[1]The revised allocation rate is 6.741%.

SCHEDULE 6

Balances in Investment Accounts before
Revised Estimate of Residual Value

	1	2	3	4	5	6	7
	Rentals receivable[1]	Estimated residual value	Investment tax credit receivable	Unearned & Deferred Income — Pretax income (loss)[2]	Investment tax credit[3]	Deferred taxes[4]	Net investment (col. 1 + 2 + 3) less (col. 4 + 5 + 6)
Initial investment	$233,470	$200,000	$100,000	$33,470	$100,000	$ —	$400,000
Changes in year of operation							
1	(15,565)	—	(100,000)	(9,929)	(29,663)	58,860	(134,833)
2	(15,565)	—	—	(6,582)	(19,664)	107,675	(96,994)
3	(15,565)	—	—	(4,174)	(12,472)	76,308	(75,227)
4	(15,565)	—	—	(2,307)	(6,893)	57,123	(63,488)
5	(15,565)	—	—	(731)	(2,184)	37,985	(50,635)
6	(15,565)	—	—	—	—	3,051	(18,616)
7	(15,565)	—	—	—	—	(25,118)	9,553
8	(15,564)	—	—	—	—	(26,672)	11,108
9	(15,564)	—	—	—	—	(28,367)	12,803
10	(15,565)	—	—	—	—	(30,214)	14,649
Balances, beginning of eleventh year	$ 77,822	$200,000	$ —	$ 9,747	$ 29,124	$230,631	$ 8,320

[1]Schedule 2, column 1, excluding residual value, less columns 3 and 6.
[2]Schedule 3, column 5.
[3]Schedule 3, column 7.
[4]50.4% of difference between taxable income (loss), Schedule 2, column 4, and pretax accounting income (loss), Schedule 3, column 5.

SCHEDULE 7

Illustrative Journal Entries
Reduction in Residual Value in Eleventh Year

Journal Entry 1		
Pretax income (or loss)		60,314
Unearned and deferred income		27,450
Pretax income (loss):		
Balance at end of 10th year	9,747[1]	
Revised balance	(9,939)[2]	
Adjustment	(19,686)	
Deferred investment tax credit:		
Balance at end of 10th year	29,124[3]	
Revised balance	21,360[4]	
Adjustment	(7,764)	
Investment tax credit recognized		7,764
Estimated residual value		80,000

To record:

i. The cumulative effect on pretax income and the effect on future income resulting from the decrease in estimated residual value:

Reduction in estimated residual value	$80,000
Less portion attributable to future years (unearned and deferred income)	(19,686)
Cumulative effect (charged against current income)	$60,314

ii. The cumulative and future effect of the change in allocation of the investment tax credit resulting from the reduction in estimated residual value

Journal Entry 2		
Deferred taxes	30,398	
Income tax expense		30,398

To recognize deferred taxes for the difference between pretax accounting income (or loss) and taxable income (or loss) for the effect of the reduction in estimated residual value.

Pre-tax accounting loss per journal entry 1	$(60,314)
Tax income (or loss)	—
Difference	$(60,314)
Deferred taxes ($60,314 × 50.4%)	$(30,398)

---

[1]Schedule 6, column 4.
[2]Schedule 5, total of column 5 less amounts applicable to the first 10 years.
[3]Schedule 6, column 5.
[4]Schedule 5, total of column 7 less amounts applicable to the first 10 years.

SCHEDULE 8

Adjustment of Investment Accounts for Revised Estimate of Residual Value in Eleventh Year

	1	2	3	4	5	6
			Unearned & Deferred Income			Net investment
	Rentals receivable	Estimated residual value	Pretax income (loss)	Investment tax credit	Deferred taxes	(col. 1 + 2) less (col. 3 + 4 + 5)
Balances, beginning of eleventh year (Schedule 6)	$77,822	$200,000	$ 9,747	$29,124	$230,631	$ 8,320
Adjustment of estimated residual value and unearned and deferred income (Schedule 7 – journal entry 1)	—	(80,000)	(19,686)	(7,764)	—	(52,550)
Adjustment of deferred taxes for the cumulative effect on pretax accounting income (Schedule 7 – journal entry 2)	—	—	—	—	(30,398)	30,398
Adjusted balances, beginning of eleventh year	$77,822	$120,000	$ (9,939)	$21,360	$200,233	$(13,832)[1]

[1]Schedule 5, column 1.

Statement of Financial Accounting Standards No. 14
Financial Reporting for Segments of a
Business Enterprise

STATUS

Issued: December 1976

Effective Date: For fiscal years beginning after December 15, 1976 and interim periods within
those years (but amended by FAS 18, FAS 21, and FAS 24)

Affects: No other pronouncements

Affected by: Paragraphs 3 and 7 amended by FAS 95
Paragraphs 4 and 73 and footnote 15 superseded by FAS 18
Paragraph 7 amended by FAS 24
Paragraph 27(c) amended by FAS 111
Paragraph 39 superseded by FAS 30
Paragraph 41 amended by FAS 18 and FAS 21

Other Interpretive Pronouncements: FTB 79-4
FTB 79-5

Statement of Financial Accounting Standards No. 14
Financial Reporting for Segments of a Business Enterprise

CONTENTS

INTRODUCTION

1. In recent years, many business enterprises have broadened the scope of their activities into different industries, foreign countries, and markets. This Statement requires that the financial statements of a business enterprise (hereinafter enterprise) include information about the enterprise's operations in different industries, its foreign operations and export sales, and its major customers. This Statement also requires that an enterprise operating predominantly or exclusively in a single industry identify that industry.

2. Appendix A contains background information. Appendix B sets forth the basis for the Board's conclusions, including alternatives considered and reasons for accepting some and rejecting others. Appendix C describes two systems that have been developed for classifying business activities, and Appendix D describes a number of factors to be considered in grouping products and services by industry lines. An illustration of applying paragraph 15(b) is presented in Appendix E, and illustrations of the disclosures required by this Statement are presented in Appendix F.

STANDARDS OF FINANCIAL ACCOUNTING AND REPORTING

Inclusion in Financial Statements

3. When an enterprise issues a complete set of financial statements that present financial position at the end of the enterprise's fiscal year and results of operations and changes in financial position for that fiscal year in conformity with generally accepted accounting principles, those financial statements shall include certain information relating to:

a. The enterprise's operations in different industries —paragraphs 9-30.
b. Its foreign operations and export sales— paragraphs 31-38.
c. Its major customers—paragraph 39.

If such statements are presented for more than one fiscal year, the information required by this Statement shall be presented for each such year, except as provided in paragraph 41.

4. If an enterprise issues for an interim period a complete set of financial statements that are expressly described as presenting financial position, results of operations, and changes in financial position in conformity with generally accepted accounting principles, this Statement requires that the information referred to in paragraph 3 be included in those interim financial statements. If an enterprise issues for an interim period financial statements that are not a complete set or are otherwise complete but not expressly described as presenting financial position, results of operations, and changes in financial position in conformity with generally accepted accounting principles, this Statement does not require that the information referred

to in paragraph 3 be included in those interim financial statements.

Purpose of Segment Information

5. The purpose of the information required to be reported by this Statement is to assist financial statement users in analyzing and understanding the enterprise's financial statements by permitting better assessment of the enterprise's past performance and future prospects. As noted in paragraph 76, information prepared in conformity with this Statement may be of limited usefulness for comparing a segment of one enterprise with a similar segment of another enterprise.

Accounting Principles Used in Preparing Segment Information

6. The information required to be reported by this Statement is a disaggregation of the consolidated financial information[1] included in the enterprise's financial statements. The accounting principles underlying the disaggregated information should be the same accounting principles as those underlying the consolidated information, except that most intersegment transactions that are eliminated from consolidated financial information are included in segment information (see paragraph 8). For example, a segment for which information is required to be reported by this Statement may include a consolidated subsidiary that prepares separate financial statements. Amounts reported in the subsidiary's financial statements sometimes differ from amounts included in consolidation for reasons other than intersegment transactions, for instance, because the subsidiary was acquired in a business combination accounted for by the purchase method. In that event, the segment information required to be reported by this Statement with respect to the consolidated financial statements shall be based on the amounts included in consolidation, not on the amounts reported in the subsidiary's financial statements.

7. Enterprises are not required by this Statement to disaggregate financial information pertaining to unconsolidated subsidiaries or other unconsolidated investees. Unconsolidated subsidiaries and investments in corporate joint ventures and 50 percent or less owned companies are normally accounted for by the equity method, and financial information about equity method investees is required to be disclosed in the investor's financial statements in accordance with paragraph 20 of *APB Opinion No. 18,* "The Equity Method of Accounting for Investments in Common Stock." In addition, *ARB No.*

43, Chapter 12, "Foreign Operations and Foreign Exchange," requires the disclosure of certain financial information about foreign subsidiaries of an enterprise. This Statement does not amend those disclosure requirements. However, in addition to those disclosures, identification shall be made of both the industries and the geographic areas in which the equity method investees operate. Also, paragraph 27(c) of this Statement requires special disclosures with respect to an equity method investee whose operations are vertically integrated with those of a reportable segment of the enterprise. Disaggregation of financial information pertaining to unconsolidated subsidiaries and other unconsolidated equity method investees is encouraged when that is considered to be desirable for an understanding of the enterprise's operations. When a complete set of financial statements that present financial position, results of operations, and changes in financial position in conformity with generally accepted accounting principles is presented for a subsidiary, corporate joint venture, or 50 percent or less owned investee, each such entity is considered to be an enterprise as that term is used in this Statement and thus is subject to its requirements whether those financial statements are issued separately or included in another enterprise's financial report.

8. Transactions between a parent and its subsidiaries or between two subsidiaries are eliminated in preparing consolidated financial statements (see paragraph 6 of *ARB No. 51,* "Consolidated Financial Statements"). In preparing the information required to be reported by this Statement, however, transactions between the segments of an enterprise shall be included in the segment information. Thus, for example, revenue reported for a segment includes both sales to unaffiliated customers (i.e., customers outside the enterprise) and intersegment sales or transfers. Similarly, expenses relating both to sales to unaffiliated customers and to intersegment sales or transfers are deducted in measuring a segment's profitability. Exceptions to the general rule that intersegment transactions are not eliminated from segment information are provided in paragraphs 10(c)-10(e) for certain intersegment advances and loans and related interest revenue and expense. Paragraphs 30 and 38 require reconciliation of segment information with amounts reported in consolidated financial statements.

Information about an Enterprise's Operations in Different Industries

9. The financial statements of an enterprise shall include certain information about the industry seg-

---

[1]The term "consolidated financial information" is used herein to refer to aggregate information relating to an enterprise as a whole whether or not the enterprise has consolidated subsidiaries.

ments of the enterprise. Criteria for determining industry segments for which information shall be reported are in paragraphs 11-21. The type of information to be presented for each reportable industry segment is specified in paragraphs 22-27. Requirements for presenting that information in financial statements are in paragraphs 28-30.

Definitions

10. Certain terms are defined for purposes of this Statement as follows:

a. *Industry segment.*[2] A component of an enterprise engaged in providing a product or service or a group of related products and services primarily to unaffiliated customers (i.e., customers outside the enterprise) for a profit.[3] By defining an industry segment in terms of products and services that are sold primarily to unaffiliated customers, this Statement does not require the disaggregation of the vertically integrated operations of an enterprise.

b. *Reportable segment.* An industry segment (or, in certain cases, a group of two or more closely related industry segments—see paragraph 19) for which information is required to be reported by this Statement.

c. *Revenue.* The revenue of an industry segment includes revenue both from sales[4] to unaffiliated customers (i.e., revenue from customers outside the enterprise as reported in the enterprise's income statement) and from intersegment sales or transfers, if any, of products and services similar to those sold to unaffiliated customers.[5] Interest from sources outside the enterprise and interest earned on intersegment trade receivables is included in revenue if the asset on which the interest is earned is included among the industry segment's identifiable assets (see paragraph 10(e)), but interest earned on advances or loans to other industry segments is not included.[6] For purposes of this Statement, revenue from intersegment sales or transfers shall be accounted for on the basis used by the enterprise to price the intersegment sales or transfers.

d. *Operating profit or loss.* The operating profit or loss of an industry segment is its revenue as defined in paragraph 10(c) minus all operating expenses. As used herein, operating expenses include expenses that relate to both revenue from sales to unaffiliated customers and revenue from intersegment sales or transfers; those operating expenses incurred by an enterprise that are not directly traceable to an industry segment shall be allocated on a reasonable basis among those industry segments for whose benefit the expenses were incurred (see paragraph 24). For purposes of this Statement, intersegment purchases shall be accounted for on the same basis as intersegment sales or transfers (i.e., on the basis used by the enterprise to price the intersegment sales or transfers—see the last sentence of paragraph 10(c)). None of the following shall be added or deducted, as the case may be, in computing the operating profit or loss of an industry segment: revenue earned at the corporate level and not derived from the operations of any industry segment; general corporate expenses;[7] interest expense;[8] domestic and foreign income taxes; equity in income or loss from unconsolidated subsidiaries and other unconsolidated investees; gain or loss on discontinued operations (as defined in *APB Opinion No. 30,* "Reporting the Results of Operations"); extraordinary items; minority interest; and the cumulative effect of a change in accounting principles (see *APB Opinion No. 20,* "Accounting Changes").

e. *Identifiable assets.* The identifiable assets of an industry segment are those tangible and intangible enterprise assets that are used by the industry segment, including (i) assets that are used exclu-

---

[2]The meaning of the term "industry segment" as it is used in this Statement is different from the use of the term "segment" in pronouncements of the Cost Accounting Standards Board.

[3]In some industries, it is normal practice for an enterprise to purchase and sell substantially identical commodities to minimize transportation or other costs. In those situations, sales and purchases of substantially identical commodities shall be netted for the purpose of determining whether a product or service or a group of related products and services is sold primarily to unaffiliated customers. Although those sales and purchases are netted for the purpose of identifying an industry segment, it is not intended that this rule change an enterprise's accounting practice with respect to determining the revenue of the enterprise or any of its industry segments.

[4]For convenience, the term "sales" is used in this Statement to include the sale of a product, the rendering of a service, and other types of transactions by which revenue is earned.

[5]Intersegment billings for the cost of shared facilities or other jointly incurred costs do not represent intersegment sales or transfers as that term is used in this Statement.

[6]Interest earned on advances or loans to other industry segments is included in computing the operating profit or loss of an industry segment whose operations are principally of a financial nature (e.g., banking, insurance, leasing, or financing).

[7]Some of the expenses incurred at an enterprise's central administrative office may not be general corporate expenses, but rather may be operating expenses of industry segments that should therefore be allocated to those industry segments. The nature of an expense rather than the location of its incurrence shall determine whether it is an operating expense. Only those expenses identified by their nature as operating expenses shall be allocated as operating expenses in computing an industry segment's operating profit or loss.

[8]Interest expense is deducted in computing the operating profit or loss of an industry segment whose operations are principally of a financial nature (e.g., banking, insurance, leasing, or financing).

sively by that industry segment and (ii) an allocated portion of assets used jointly by two or more industry segments. Assets used jointly by two or more industry segments shall be allocated among the industry segments on a reasonable basis. Because the assets of an industry segment that transfers products or services to another industry segment are not used in the operations of the receiving segment, no amount of those assets shall be allocated to the receiving segment. Assets that represent part of an enterprise's investment in an industry segment, such as goodwill, shall be included in the industry segment's identifiable assets.[9] Assets maintained for general corporate purposes (i.e., those not used in the operations of any industry segment) shall not be allocated to industry segments. The identifiable assets of an industry segment shall not include advances or loans to or investments in another industry segment, except that advances or loans to other industry segments shall be included in the identifiable assets of a financial segment because the income therefrom is included in computing the financial segment's operating profit or loss (see footnote 6). Asset valuation allowances such as the following shall be taken into account in computing the amount of an industry segment's identifiable assets: allowance for doubtful accounts, accumulated depreciation, and marketable securities valuation allowance.

Determining Reportable Segments

11. The reportable segments of an enterprise shall be determined by (a) identifying the individual products and services from which the enterprise derives its revenue, (b) grouping those products and services by industry lines into industry segments (see paragraphs 12-14), and (c) selecting those industry segments that are significant with respect to the enterprise as a whole (see paragraphs 15-21).

Grouping Products and Services by Industry Lines

12. Several systems have been developed for classifying business activities, such as the Standard Industrial Classification (SIC) and the Enterprise Standard Industrial Classification (ESIC). (The SIC and ESIC systems are described in Appendix C to this Statement.) The Board has examined those systems and has judged that none is, by itself, suitable to determine industry segments for purposes of this Statement. Moreover, although certain characteristics can be identified that assist in differentiating among industries (such as those discussed in Appendix D to this Statement), no single set of characteristics is universally applicable in determining the

industry segments of all enterprises, nor is any single characteristic determinative in all cases. Consequently, determination of an enterprise's industry segments must depend to a considerable extent on the judgment of the management of the enterprise.

13. Many enterprises presently accumulate information about revenue and profitability on a less-than-total-enterprise basis for internal planning and control purposes. Frequently, that type of information is maintained by profit centers for individual products and services or for groups of related products and services, particularly with respect to an enterprise's domestic operations. The term "profit center" is used in this Statement to refer only to those components of an enterprise *that sell primarily to outside markets* and *for which information about revenue and profitability is accumulated.* An enterprise's existing profit centers—the smallest units of activity for which revenue and expense information is accumulated for internal planning and control purposes—represent a logical starting point for determining the enterprise's industry segments. If an enterprise's existing profit centers cross industry lines, it will be necessary to disaggregate existing profit centers into smaller groups of related products and services (except as provided in paragraph 14). If an enterprise operates in more than one industry but does not presently accumulate any information on a less-than-total-enterprise basis (i.e., its only profit center is the enterprise as a whole), it shall disaggregate its operations along industry lines (except as provided in paragraph 14).

14. Industry segmentation on a worldwide basis is a desirable objective but it may be impracticable for some enterprises. To the extent that revenue and profitability information is accumulated along industry lines for an enterprise's foreign operations, as defined in paragraph 31, or that it would be practicable to do so, industry segments shall be determined on a worldwide basis. To the extent that it is impracticable to disaggregate part or all of its foreign operations along industry lines, the enterprise shall disaggregate along industry lines its domestic operations and its foreign operations for which disaggregation is practicable and shall treat the aggregate of its foreign operations for which disaggregation is not practicable as a single industry segment. When that segment qualifies as a reportable industry segment (see paragraphs 15-21), disclosure shall be made of the types of industry operations included in the foreign operations that have not been disaggregated.

Selecting Reportable Segments

15. Each industry segment that is significant to an

---

[9]Any related depreciation or amortization expense is deducted in determining the operating profit of the industry segment.

enterprise as a whole shall be identified as a reportable segment. For purposes of this Statement, an industry segment shall be regarded as significant— and therefore identified as a reportable segment (see paragraph 16)—if it satisfies one or more of the following tests. The tests shall be applied separately for each fiscal year for which financial statements are presented, except as provided in paragraph 41.

a. Its revenue (including both sales to unaffiliated customers and intersegment sales or transfers) is 10 percent or more of the combined revenue (sales to unaffiliated customers and intersegment sales or transfers) of all of the enterprise's industry segments.
b. The absolute amount of its operating profit or operating loss is 10 percent or more of the greater, in absolute amount, of:
   (i) The combined operating profit of all industry segments that did not incur an operating loss, or
   (ii) The combined operating loss of all industry segments that did incur an operating loss. (Appendix E illustrates the application of paragraph 15(b).)
c. Its identifiable assets are 10 percent or more of the combined identifiable assets of all industry segments.

Revenue, operating profit or loss, and identifiable assets relating to those foreign operations that have not been disaggregated along industry lines on grounds of impracticability (see paragraph 14) shall be included in computing the combined revenue, combined operating profit or operating loss, and combined identifiable assets of the enterprise's industry segments.

16. The results of applying the percentage tests in paragraph 15 shall be evaluated from the standpoint of interperiod comparability before final determination of an enterprise's reportable segments is made. For instance, interperiod comparability would most likely require that an industry segment that has been significant in the past and is expected to be significant in the future be regarded as a reportable segment even though it fails to satisfy the tests in paragraph 15 in the current year. Conversely, a relatively insignificant industry segment may happen to satisfy the tests in paragraph 15 in the current fiscal year because its revenue or operating profit or loss is abnormally high or the combined revenue or operating profit or loss of all industry segments is abnormally low. In that case, it may be inappropriate to regard it as a reportable segment. Appropriate explanation of such circumstances shall be included as a part of the enterprise's segment information.

17. The reportable segments of an enterprise shall represent a substantial portion of the enterprise's total operations. The following test shall be applied to determine whether a substantial portion of an enterprise's operations is explained by its segment information: The combined revenue from sales to unaffiliated customers of all reportable segments (that is, revenue not including intersegment sales or transfers) shall constitute at least 75 percent of the combined revenue from sales to unaffiliated customers of all industry segments. The test shall be applied separately for each fiscal year for which financial statements are presented, except as provided in paragraph 41. Revenue relating to those foreign operations that have not been disaggregated along industry lines on grounds of impracticability shall be included in the denominator of the computation required by this paragraph and will be included in the numerator if those operations have been identified (in accordance with paragraphs 14 and 15) as a reportable segment.

18. If the industry segments identified as reportable in accordance with paragraphs 15 and 16 do not satisfy the 75-percent test in paragraph 17, additional industry segments shall be identified as reportable segments (subject to the provisions of paragraph 19) until the 75-percent test is met.

19. The Board recognizes the need for a practical limit to the number of industry segments for which an enterprise reports information; beyond that limit, segment information may become overly detailed. Without attempting to define that limit precisely, the Board suggests that as the number of industry segments that would be identified as reportable segments in accordance with paragraphs 15-18 increases above 10, the question of whether a practical limit has been reached comes increasingly into consideration, and combining the most closely related industry segments into broader reportable segments may be appropriate. Combinations shall be made, however, only to the extent necessary to contain the number of reportable segments within practical limits while still meeting the 75-percent test.

20. An enterprise may operate exclusively in a single industry or a dominant portion of an enterprise's operations may be in a single industry segment with the remaining portion in one or more other industry segments. The Board has concluded that the disclosures required by paragraphs 22-30 of this Statement need not be applied to a dominant industry segment, except that the financial statements of an enterprise that operates predominantly or exclusively in a single industry shall identify that industry. An industry segment may be regarded as dominant if its revenue, operating profit or loss, and identifiable assets (as defined in paragraphs 10(c)-(e)) each constitute more than 90 percent of related combined totals for all industry segments,

and no other industry segment meets any of the 10-percent tests in paragraph 15.

21. Paragraphs 11-20 and the guidelines for grouping products and services into industry segments set forth in Appendix D are not intended to prohibit a more detailed disaggregation if that is considered to be desirable for an understanding of the enterprise's operations.

Information to Be Presented

22. The following shall be presented for each of an enterprise's reportable segments determined in accordance with paragraphs 11-21 (including those foreign operations that have not been disaggregated along industry lines on grounds of impracticability—see paragraph 14) and in the aggregate for the remainder of the enterprise's industry segments not deemed reportable segments:

a. Revenue information as set forth in paragraph 23.
b. Profitability information as set forth in paragraphs 24 and 25.
c. Identifiable assets information as set forth in paragraph 26.
d. Other related disclosures as set forth in paragraph 27.

In addition, the types of products and services from which the revenue of each reportable segment is derived shall be identified, and the accounting policies relevant to the information reported for industry segments shall be described to the extent not adequately explained by the disclosures of the enterprise's accounting policies required by *APB Opinion No. 22,* "Disclosure of Accounting Policies." Presentation of additional information for some or all of an enterprise's reportable segments beyond that specified in paragraphs 23-27 may be considered to be desirable, and this Statement does not preclude those additional disclosures.

23. *Revenue.* Sales to unaffiliated customers and sales or transfers to other industry segments of the enterprise shall be separately disclosed in presenting revenue of a reportable segment. As indicated in paragraph 10(c), for purposes of this Statement sales or transfers to other industry segments shall be accounted for on the basis used by the enterprise to price the intersegment sales or transfers. The basis of accounting for intersegment sales or transfers shall be disclosed. If the basis is changed, disclosure shall be made of the nature of the change and its effect on the reportable segments' operating profit or loss in the period of change.

24. *Profitability.* Operating profit or loss as defined in paragraph 10(d) shall be presented for each re-

portable segment. As part of its segment information, an enterprise shall explain the nature and amount of any unusual or infrequently occurring items (see paragraph 26 of *APB Opinion No. 30*) reported in its consolidated income statement that have been added or deducted in computing the operating profit or loss of a reportable segment in accordance with paragraph 10(d). Methods used to allocate operating expenses among industry segments in computing operating profit or loss should be consistently applied from period to period (but, if changed, disclosure shall be made of the nature of the change and its effect on the reportable segments' operating profit or loss in the period of change).

25. *Other profitability information.* In addition to presenting operating profit or loss as required by paragraph 24, an enterprise may choose to present some other measure of profitability for some or all of its segments. If the enterprise elects to present a measure of contribution to operating profit or loss, the enterprise shall describe the differences between contribution and operating profit or loss. If the enterprise elects to present net income or a measure of profitability between operating profit or loss and net income, the nature and amount of each category of revenue or expense that was added or deducted and the methods of allocation, if any, shall be disclosed. Those methods should be consistently applied from period to period (but, if changed, disclosure shall be made of the nature and effect of the change in the period of change).

26. *Identifiable assets.* The aggregate carrying amount of identifiable assets as defined in paragraph 10(e) shall be presented for each reportable segment.

27. *Other related disclosures.* Disclosures relating to the information for reportable segments shall be made as follows:

a. Disclosure shall be made of the aggregate amount of depreciation, depletion, and amortization expense for each reportable segment.
b. Disclosure shall be made of the amount of each reportable segment's capital expenditures, i.e., additions to its property, plant, and equipment.
c. For each reportable segment disclosure shall be made of the enterprise's equity in the net income from and investment in the net assets of unconsolidated subsidiaries and other equity method investees whose operations are vertically integrated with the operations of that segment. Disclosure shall also be made of the geographic areas in which those vertically integrated equity method investees operate.
d. Paragraph 17 of *APB Opinion No. 20* requires that the effect on income of a change in accounting principle be disclosed in the financial state-

ments of an enterprise in the period in which the change is made. Disclosure shall also be made of the effect of the change on the operating profit of reportable segments in the period in which the change is made.[10]

Methods of Presentation

28. Information about the reportable segments of a business enterprise shall be included in the enterprise's financial statements in any of the following ways:

a. Within the body of the financial statements, with appropriate explanatory disclosures in the footnotes to the financial statements.
b. Entirely in the footnotes to the financial statements.
c. In a separate schedule that is included as an integral part of the financial statements. If, in a report to securityholders, that schedule is located on a page that is not clearly a part of the financial statements, the schedule shall be referenced in the financial statements as an integral part thereof.

29. Financial information such as revenue, operating profit or loss, and identifiable assets of reportable segments shall be presented as dollar amounts. Corresponding percentages may be shown in addition to dollar amounts.

30. The information required to be presented by paragraphs 22-27 for individual reportable segments and in the aggregate for industry segments not deemed reportable shall be reconciled to related amounts in the financial statements of the enterprise as a whole, as follows: Revenue shall be reconciled to revenue reported in the consolidated income statement, and operating profit or loss shall be reconciled to pretax income from continuing operations (before gain or loss on discontinued operations, extraordinary items, and cumulative effect of a change in accounting principle) in the consolidated income statement. Also, identifiable

assets shall be reconciled to consolidated total assets, with assets maintained for general corporate purposes separately identified in the reconciliation. An illustration is presented in Appendix F to this Statement.

Information about Foreign Operations and Export Sales

31. The financial statements of an enterprise shall include information about its foreign operations. The features that identify an operation as foreign vary among enterprises. Thus, the identification of foreign operations will depend on the facts and circumstances of the particular enterprise. For purposes of this Statement, an enterprise's foreign operations include those revenue-producing operations (except for unconsolidated subsidiaries and other unconsolidated investees (see paragraph 7)) that (a) are located outside of the enterprise's home country (the United States for U.S. enterprises)[11] and (b) are generating revenue either from sales to unaffiliated customers or from intraenterprise sales or transfers between geographic areas.[12] Similarly, an enterprise's domestic operations include those revenue-producing operations of the enterprise located in the enterprise's home country that generate revenue either from sales to unaffiliated customers or from intraenterprise sales or transfers between geographic areas. Operations, either domestic or foreign, (and regardless of whether part of a branch or a division of the enterprise or part of a consolidated subsidiary) should have identified with them the revenues generated by those operations, the assets employed in or associated with generating those revenues, and the costs and expenses incurred in generating those revenues or employing those assets.

32. The information specified in paragraph 35 shall be presented for (1) an enterprise's foreign operations, either in the aggregate or, if appropriate under paragraph 33, by geographic area, and (2) its domestic operations,[13] if either of the following conditions is met:

---

[10]The pro forma effects of retroactive application, which are required to be disclosed on a consolidated basis by paragraph 21 of *APB Opinion No. 20*, need not be disclosed for individual reportable segments. Also, the pro forma supplemental information relating to a business combination accounted for by the purchase method required to be presented by paragraph 96 of *APB Opinion No. 16*, "Business Combinations," need not be presented for individual reportable segments.

[11]An enterprise whose home country is other than the United States but that prepares financial statements in conformity with U.S. generally accepted accounting principles shall classify operations outside of its home country as foreign operations.

[12]Difficulties may arise in classifying the activities of certain types of enterprises. The following examples may provide useful guidelines: (1) Determination of whether the employment of an enterprise's mobile assets, such as off-shore drilling rigs or ocean-going vessels, constitutes foreign operations should depend on whether such assets are normally identified with operations located and generating revenue from outside the home country. If they are normally identified with the enterprise's foreign operations, revenue generated from abroad would be considered foreign revenue. If they are normally identified with the enterprise's domestic operations, revenue generated from abroad would be considered export sales; (2) Services rendered by the foreign offices of a service enterprise, such as a consulting firm, having offices or facilities located both in the home country and in foreign countries would be considered foreign operations, and the revenue should be considered foreign revenue. Revenue generated abroad from services provided by domestic offices should be considered export sales.

[13]Separate information about domestic operations need not be presented if domestic operations' revenue from sales to unaffiliated customers and domestic operations' identifiable assets are less than 10 percent of related consolidated amounts.

a. Revenue generated by the enterprise's foreign operations from sales to unaffiliated customers is 10 percent or more of consolidated revenue as reported in the enterprise's income statement.
b. Identifiable assets of the enterprise's foreign operations are 10 percent or more of consolidated total assets as reported in the enterprise's balance sheet.

33. If an enterprise's foreign operations are conducted in two or more geographic areas as defined in paragraph 34, the information specified in paragraph 35 shall be presented separately for each significant foreign geographic area, and in the aggregate for all other foreign geographic areas not deemed significant. A geographic area shall be regarded as *significant,* for the purpose of applying this paragraph, if its revenue from sales to unaffiliated customers or its identifiable assets are 10 percent or more of related consolidated amounts.

34. For purposes of this Statement, foreign *geographic areas* are individual countries or groups of countries as may be determined to be appropriate in an enterprise's particular circumstances. No single method of grouping the countries in which an enterprise operates into the geographic areas can reflect all of the differences among international business environments. Each enterprise shall group its foreign operations on the basis of the differences that are most important in its particular circumstances. Factors to be considered include proximity, economic affinity, similarities in business environments, and the nature, scale, and degree of interrelationship of the enterprise's operations in the various countries.

35. The following information shall be presented for an enterprise's foreign operations and for its domestic operations as appropriate in accordance with paragraphs 32-34:

a. Revenue as defined in paragraph 10(c), with sales to unaffiliated customers and sales or transfers between geographic areas shown separately. For purposes of this Statement, intraenterprise sales or transfers between geographic areas shall be accounted for on the basis used by the enterprise to price the intraenterprise sales or transfers. The basis of accounting for intraenterprise sales or transfers shall be disclosed. If the basis is changed, disclosure shall be made of the nature of the change and its effect in the period of change.
b. Operating profit or loss as defined in paragraph 10(d) *or* net income *or* some other measure of profitability between operating profit or loss and net income. A common level of profitability shall be reported for all geographic areas,

although an enterprise may choose to report additional profitability information for some or all of its geographic areas of operations.
c. Identifiable assets as defined in paragraph 10(e).

36. With respect to an enterprise's *domestic* operations, sales to unaffiliated customers include both (a) sales to customers within the enterprise's home country and (b) sales to customers in foreign countries, i.e., export sales. If the amount of export sales from an enterprise's home country to unaffiliated customers in foreign countries is 10 percent or more of total revenue from sales to unaffiliated customers as reported in the enterprise's consolidated income statement, that amount shall be separately reported, in the aggregate and by such geographic areas as are considered appropriate in the circumstances. The disclosure required by this paragraph shall be made even if the enterprise is not required by this Statement to report information about its operations in different industries or foreign operations.

37. Information about the foreign operations and export sales of a business enterprise may be included in the enterprise's financial statements in any of the ways identified in paragraph 28 of this Statement. Financial information shall be presented as U.S. dollar amounts; corresponding percentages may be shown in addition to dollar amounts. The geographic areas into which an enterprise's foreign operations have been disaggregated shall be identified.

38. The information about revenue, profitability, and identifiable assets required to be presented for foreign operations shall be reconciled to related amounts in the financial statements of the enterprise as a whole, in a manner similar to that described in paragraph 30. An illustration is presented in Appendix F to this Statement.

Information about Major Customers

39. If 10 percent or more of the revenue of an enterprise is derived from sales to any single customer, that fact and the amount of revenue from each such customer shall be disclosed. (For this purpose, a group of customers under common control shall be regarded as a single customer.) Similarly, if 10 percent or more of the revenue of an enterprise is derived from sales to domestic government agencies in the aggregate or to foreign governments in the aggregate, that fact and the amount of revenue shall be disclosed. The identity of the industry segment or segments making the sales shall be disclosed. The disclosures required by this paragraph shall be made even if the enterprise is not required by this Statement to report information about operations in different industries or foreign operations.

Restatement of Previously Reported Segment Information

40. When prior period information about an enterprise's reportable industry segments, its foreign operations and export sales, and its major customers is being presented with corresponding information for the current period, the prior period information shall be retroactively restated (at least as far back as the effective date of this Statement—see paragraph 41) in the following circumstances, with appropriate disclosure of the nature and effect of the restatement:

a. When the financial statements of the enterprise as a whole have been retroactively restated, for example, for a change in accounting principle of the type described in paragraphs 27 and 29 of *APB Opinion No. 20* or for a business combination accounted for by the pooling-of-interests method.
b. When there has been a change in the way the enterprise's products and services are grouped into industry segments or a change in the way the enterprise's foreign operations are grouped[14] into

geographic areas and such changes affect the segment or geographic area information being reported.

Effective Date and Transition

41. The provisions of this Statement shall be effective for financial statements for fiscal years beginning after December 15, 1976 and for interim periods[15] within those fiscal years. Earlier application is encouraged in financial statements for periods beginning before December 16, 1976 that have not previously been issued. Information of the type required by this Statement need not be included in financial statements for periods beginning before the effective date of this Statement that are being presented for comparative purposes with financial statements for periods after the effective date, but if included, that information shall be prepared and presented in conformity with the provisions of this Statement to the extent practicable with appropriate explanation if the information for periods before the effective date is not comparable to that for periods after the effective date.

> **The provisions of this Statement need not be applied to immaterial items.**

This Statement was adopted by the unanimous vote of the six members of the Financial Accounting Standards Board:

Marshall S. Armstrong,	Donald J. Kirk	Robert E. Mays
Chairman	Arthur L. Litke	Robert T. Sprouse
Oscar S. Gellein		

Appendix A

BACKGROUND INFORMATION

42. Although the authoritative accounting literature has heretofore dealt principally with financial statements prepared on a consolidated or total-enterprise basis, several pronouncements of the Accounting Principles Board and its predecessor, the Committee on Accounting Procedure, have required business enterprises to report information on a less-than-total-enterprise basis in a limited number of areas. For example, Chapter 12 of *ARB No. 43* requires certain disclosures related to an enterprise's foreign operations; *APB Opinion No. 18* requires disclosure of information about companies accounted for by the equity method; and

APB Opinion No. 30 requires information about the discontinued operations of a segment of a business.

43. Starting in the mid-1960s, a number of professional organizations, including the Financial Analysts Federation, the Financial Executives Research Foundation, and the National Association of Accountants, sponsored research studies to assess the desirability and feasibility of disclosing information for line-of-business segments in external financial reports. Several professional organizations have issued pronouncements that generally support segment reporting, including the APB (its Statement No. 2, "Disclosure of Supplemental Financial Information by Diversified Companies," issued in 1967, urged companies to report segment information voluntarily), the Financial Accounting Policy Com-

---

[14]Restatement is not required when an enterprise's reportable segments change as a result of a change in the nature of an enterprise's operations or as a result of applying the tests in paragraphs 15-20.

[15]See paragraph 4.

mittee of the Financial Analysts Federation, the Financial Executives Institute, the Committee on Management Accounting Practices of the National Association of Accountants, and the Accountants International Study Group.

44. In 1969, the Securities and Exchange Commission issued requirements for reporting line-of-business information in registration statements. In 1970, those requirements were extended to annual reports filed with the SEC on Form 10-K, and in October 1974 they were extended to the annual reports to securityholders of companies filing with the SEC.

45. In 1973, the New York Stock Exchange issued a "white paper" urging that line-of-business information at least as extensive as that required in SEC Form 10-K be included in annual reports to securityholders.

46. In 1974, the Federal Trade Commission initiated an annual line-of-business reporting program to enable it to publish aggregate data on corporations engaged in commerce in the United States. Under the FTC program, large manufacturing companies are required to report detailed financial information for each line of business as defined by the FTC.[16]

47. In recognition of the broadened scope of operations of many business enterprises, the need for disaggregation of enterprise-wide information expressed by many financial statement users, and the variety of present reporting practices in reports to securityholders, in April 1973 the FASB placed on its technical agenda a project on Financial Reporting for Segments of a Business Enterprise.

48. A task force of 16 persons from industry, government, public accounting, the financial community, and academe was appointed in May 1973 to counsel the Board in preparing a Discussion Memorandum analyzing issues related to the project.

49. A considerable number of research studies and articles on the subject were available to the Board, many of which were summarized or identified in the Discussion Memorandum. In addition, two research reports were prepared by the FASB staff. One was a survey of the existing reporting practices of 100 companies disclosing segment information in annual reports to shareholders. The other, involving field interviews of corporate executives of 30 companies, was directed primarily at identifying the decision criteria used by management for purposes of internal and external segmentation. Those research reports were included as appendixes to the Discussion Memorandum.

50. The Board issued the Discussion Memorandum on May 22, 1974 and held a public hearing on the subject on August 1 and 2, 1974. The Board received 144 position papers, letters of comment, and outlines of oral presentations in response to the Discussion Memorandum. Twenty-one presentations were made at the public hearing.

51. An Exposure Draft of a proposed Statement on "Financial Reporting for Segments of a Business Enterprise" was issued on September 30, 1975. The Board received 233 letters of comment on the Exposure Draft.

52. In June 1976, the Organization for Economic Cooperation and Development (OECD) adopted a "Declaration on International Investment and Multinational Enterprises," recommending certain guidelines for a code of conduct for multinational corporations. Those guidelines include, but are not limited to, the following disclosures:

a. The geographical areas where operations are carried out and the principal activities carried on therein by the parent company and the main affiliates.
b. The operating results and sales by geographical area and the sales in the major lines of business for the enterprise as a whole.
c. Significant new capital investment by geographical area and, as far as practicable, by major lines of business for the enterprise as a whole.
d. The policies followed in respect of intergroup pricing.
e. The accounting policies, including those on consolidation, observed in compiling the published information.

The OECD is made up of representatives of the governments of 24 economically developed nations of Western Europe, North America, Asia, and the South Pacific.

Appendix B

BASIS FOR CONCLUSIONS

53. This Appendix discusses factors deemed significant by members of the Board in reaching the conclusions in this Statement, including alternatives considered and reasons for accepting some and rejecting others.

Inclusion in Financial Statements

54. The Board concluded that information relating to an enterprise's industry segments, foreign operations, export sales, and major customers is useful to

---

[16]A number of companies are challenging the FTC's line-of-business reporting program through legal proceedings.

analyze and understand the financial statements of the enterprise. Reasons for that conclusion are discussed in paragraphs 55-74.

55. The financial statements of an enterprise are usually prepared on a consolidated or total-enterprise basis, aggregating the financial data of the various activities of the enterprise. The principal exception to the rule of consolidation is that financial subsidiaries (such as banks, insurance companies, and finance companies) of a manufacturing company usually are not consolidated (see *ARB No. 51,* "Consolidated Financial Statements," especially paragraphs 1-5). Another exception to the rule of consolidation is that foreign subsidiaries sometimes are not consolidated (see *ARB No. 43,* Chapter 12, "Foreign Operations and Foreign Exchange," especially paragraphs 8 and 9).

56. Investors and lenders who acquire equity interests in or extend credit to an enterprise as a whole recognize the importance of consolidated financial statements for reporting the overall performance of the enterprise. At the same time, however, investors, credit grantors, and other financial statement users have indicated that disaggregation of total-enterprise financial data to provide information about the various segments of an enterprise, in addition to aggregate data for the enterprise, is useful to them.

57. Those financial statement users point out that the evaluation of risk and return is the central element of investment and lending decisions—the greater the perceived degree of risk associated with an investment or lending alternative, the greater is the required rate of return to the investor or lender. If return is defined as expected cash flows to the investor or creditor, the evaluation of risk involves assessment of the uncertainty surrounding both the timing and the amount of the expected cash flows to the enterprise, which in turn are indicative of potential cash flows to the investor or creditor. Users of financial statements indicate that uncertainty results, in part, from factors unique to the particular enterprise in which an investment may be made or to which credit may be extended. Uncertainty also results, in part, from factors related to the industries and geographic areas in which the enterprise operates and, in part, from national and international economic and political factors. Investors and lenders analyze factors at all of those levels to evaluate the risk and return associated with an investment or lending alternative.

58. Information contained in an enterprise's financial statements constitutes an important input to that analysis. Financial statements provide information about conditions, trends, and ratios that assist in predicting cash flows. In analyzing an enterprise,

a financial statement user often compares information about the enterprise with information about other enterprises, with industry-wide information, and with national or international economic information in general. Those comparisons are helpful in determining whether a given enterprise's operations may be expected to move with, against, or independently of developments in its industry and in the economy within which it operates.

59. The broadening of an enterprise's activities into different industries or geographic areas complicates the analysis of conditions, trends, and ratios and, therefore, the ability to predict. The various industry segments or geographic areas of operations of an enterprise may have different rates of profitability, degrees and types of risk, and opportunities for growth. There may be differences in the rates of return on the investment commitment in the various industry segments or geographic areas and in their future capital demands.

60. Consequently, many financial statement users have said that consolidated financial information, while important, would be more useful if supplemented with disaggregated information to assist them in analyzing the uncertainties surrounding the timing and amount of expected cash flows—and, therefore, the risks—related to an investment in or a loan to an enterprise that operates in different industries or areas of the world. Since the progress and prospects of a diversified enterprise are composits of the progress and prospects of its several parts, financial statement users regard financial information on a less-than-total-enterprise basis as also important.

61. Although many business enterprises presently include disaggregated financial information in reports to securityholders, in filings with the Securities and Exchange Commission and in other types of reports, the nature and extent of the information disclosed and the methods of presentation vary, and that information generally is not included in the financial statements.

62. A few respondents to the Discussion Memorandum and the Exposure Draft contended that information on a less-than-total-enterprise basis is not useful to investors and creditors. They generally argued that investors and lenders who acquire equity interests in or extend credit to an enterprise as a whole should be concerned only with overall enterprise results as reported in its consolidated financial statements. For the reasons expressed in paragraphs 55-61, however, the Board concluded that investors and creditors find segment information to be useful in analyzing and understanding consolidated statements and therefore in analyzing overall enterprise results.

63. Although most respondents agreed that information on a less-than-total-enterprise basis is useful for investment and credit decisions, some said that the information should not be included in the financial statements of an enterprise, principally on two grounds:

a. Some said that while segment information may indeed be useful to investors and credit grantors, it is too analytical or interpretive to be classified as accounting information and, thus, does not belong in financial statements.
b. Others said that disaggregated information is not susceptible to the same degree of verifiability as consolidated information.

64. The Board has given careful consideration to those points of view because inclusion of segment information in financial statements is an important question to be resolved in this project. The Board does not agree that segment information of the type required to be reported by this Statement is too analytical or interpretive to be properly classified as accounting information. The information called for by this Statement is a rearrangement (that is, a disaggregation) of information included in an enterprise's consolidated financial statements, as is the information required in the statement of changes in financial position a rearrangement of information reported in or underlying the balance sheet and income statement. Thus, in the Board's judgment, this Statement does not go beyond or enlarge the boundaries of accounting, as some have contended.

65. As to the question of verifiability, the Board recognizes that disaggregated information is subject to certain limitations and that some of it may not be susceptible to the *same degree* of verifiability as some of the consolidated information. The Board believes, however, that the more critical question to be addressed is whether the disaggregated information is *sufficiently* verifiable to warrant its inclusion in an enterprise's financial statements.

66. Verifiability is identified in *APB Statement No. 4,* "Basic Concepts and Accounting Principles Underlying Financial Statements of Business Enterprises," as one of the qualitative objectives of financial accounting. Paragraph 90 of that Statement says:

> Verifiable financial accounting information provides results that would be substantially duplicated by independent measures using the same measurement methods.

That paragraph further states:

> Measurements cannot be completely free

from subjective opinions and judgments. The process of measuring and presenting information must use human agents and human reasoning and therefore is not founded solely on an "objective reality." Nevertheless, the usefulness of information is enhanced if it is verifiable, that is, if the attribute or attributes selected for measurement and the measurement methods used provide results that can be corroborated by independent measures.

67. Other qualitative objectives set forth in paragraphs 87-93 of *APB Statement No. 4* are relevance (described as "the primary qualitative objective"), understandability, neutrality, timeliness, and comparability. Paragraph 94 sets forth a final qualitative objective, completeness: "Complete financial accounting information includes all financial accounting data that reasonably fulfill the requirements of the other qualitative objectives." Paragraph 94 goes on to say that the qualitative objectives are not absolute but, rather, must be met "in reasonable degree." That is, an appropriate balance must be maintained among the objectives. For example, some degree of verifiability might have to be sacrificed to improve the relevance of information included in financial statements. In the Board's judgment, the information required to be reported by this Statement meets the objective of verifiability in reasonable degree and is useful for analyzing and understanding an enterprise's financial statements. Moreover, consistency from period to period in the methods by which an enterprise's segment information is prepared and presented is as important as consistency in the application of the accounting principles used in preparing the enterprise's consolidated financial statements. Consistency is a quality that is comprehended by the objective of comparability and is an important aspect of segment reporting that does lend itself to objective verification. For those reasons, the Board concluded that the information required to be reported by this Statement shall be included as an integral part of an enterprise's financial statements.

68. Some respondents contended that the costs of compiling and processing the type of information called for by this Statement would be overly burdensome to many enterprises, particularly those that are relatively small or whose securities are not publicly traded. Many enterprises, however, already accumulate information similar to the type required to be reported by this Statement for various purposes, such as inclusion in filings with the SEC or internal planning and control. Those enterprises will be able to provide the information required to be reported by this Statement by using existing records.

69. To lessen the information processing costs to enterprises, the Board has modified the proposal in

the Exposure Draft that an enterprise's industry segments be determined by grouping its products and services by industry lines on a *worldwide* basis. Some respondents to the Exposure Draft felt that disaggregation of *foreign* operations was an especially burdensome requirement. Accordingly, this Statement does not require an enterprise to disaggregate its foreign operations to the extent that it is impracticable to do so (see paragraph 14).

70. In the Exposure Draft, the Board proposed that any requirement to include segment information in financial statements be applicable to all enterprises regardless of their size or whether their securities are publicly traded. The Board continues to believe that there are no fundamental differences in the types of decisions and the decision-making processes of those who use the financial statements of smaller or privately held enterprises. Many small or privately held enterprises operate in more than one industry or country or rely significantly on a single or a few major customers or export sales. Information of the type required to be disclosed by this Statement is as important to users of the financial statements of those enterprises as it is to users of the financial statements of larger or publicly held enterprises. Accordingly, this Statement applies to all enterprises, regardless of their size or whether their securities are publicly traded. In reaching that conclusion, the Board neither rejects nor accepts the recommendations of the AICPA Committee on Generally Accepted Accounting Principles for Smaller and/or Closely Held Businesses, in its August 1976 report.

71. Several respondents cited harm to an enterprise's competitive position as a basis for opposing disclosures about industry segments such as this Statement requires. However, the required disclosures about an industry segment are no more detailed or specific than the disclosures typically provided by an enterprise that operates in a single industry. The information required to be reported is intended primarily to permit users to make a better assessment of the past performance and future prospects of an enterprise operating in more than one industry. In the Board's judgment, the information specified by this Statement is useful in making that assessment and, therefore, the information should be required.

72. Some respondents recommended that the disclosure requirement of this Statement should apply only to annual financial statements and not to any interim financial statements. They said that an interim reporting requirement would be unnecessarily burdensome for many enterprises, particularly those enterprises not heretofore reporting any information of the type required by this Statement. Also, some said that for many enterprises, seasonal fluctuations could cause significant changes from quarter to quarter in the composition of an enterprise's significant industry segments, diminishing the interperiod comparability of segment information. On the other hand, some respondents took the position that segment information should be included in all interim reports, including those that present only condensed financial statements or selected financial data and that do not purport to present financial position, results of operations, and changes in financial position in conformity with generally accepted accounting principles. Those respondents contended that segment information is needed on a more timely basis than annually and that the difficulties of preparing it on an interim basis can be overcome.

73. After considering both views, the Board has concluded that segment information should not be required in interim financial statements or interim financial reports unless they are *expressly described* as presenting financial position, results of operations, and changes in financial position in conformity with generally accepted accounting principles. When an enterprise issues for an interim period a complete set of financial statements that are *expressly described* as presenting financial position, results of operations, and changes in financial position in conformity with generally accepted accounting principles, those financial statements should include all of the disclosures required by this Statement in similar financial statements for an entire fiscal year. Users have the right to expect that financial statements so described, even though for an interim period, would contain all of the disclosures required in similarly described financial statements for an entire fiscal year.

74. A number of respondents to both the Discussion Memorandum and the Exposure Draft said that differences among enterprises in the nature of their operations and in the extent to which components of the enterprise share common facilities, equipment, materials and supplies, or labor force make unworkable the prescription of highly detailed rules and procedures that must be followed by all enterprises. Moreover, they pointed out that differences in the accounting systems of business enterprises are a practical constraint on the degree of specificity with which standards of financial accounting and reporting for disaggregated information can be established. The Board agrees, in general, with those views. In the Board's judgment, the standards set forth in this Statement are sufficiently broad that when they are applied in the context of the objective stated in paragraph 5 they will result in reporting information that is useful in analyzing and understanding the financial statements of an enterprise that operates in different industries or geographic areas or that derives significant revenue

from export sales or from a single or a few major customers.

Purpose of Segment Information

75. As stated in paragraph 5, the purpose of the information required to be disclosed by this Statement about an enterprise's operations in different industries and different areas of the world and about the extent of its reliance on export sales or major customers is to assist financial statement users in analyzing and understanding the enterprise's financial statements by permitting better assessment of the enterprise's past performance and future prospects. The standards of financial accounting and reporting set forth in paragraphs 3-40 derive from that purpose.

76. Information prepared in conformity with those standards may be of limited usefulness for comparing an industry segment of one enterprise with a similar industry segment of another enterprise (i.e., for interenterprise comparison). Interenterprise comparison of industry segments would require a fairly detailed prescription of the basis or bases of disaggregation to be followed by all enterprises, as well as specification of the basis of accounting for intersegment transfers and methods of allocating costs common to two or more segments. As explained in paragraph 74, the Board concluded that it is not appropriate to specify rules and procedures in that degree of detail. Moreover, differences in the bases of accounting for intersegment sales or transfers may also militate against comparison of a segment of an enterprise with extensive intersegment transactions with a similar but autonomous segment of another enterprise or with a unitary enterprise in the same industry.

Information Required to Be Presented

77. This Statement requires that sales to outsiders be reported separately from sales or transfers to other segments because different types of uncertainties and measurement bases affect those two sources of a reportable segment's revenue. The Exposure Draft proposed that intersegment sales or transfers be accounted for at amounts that are consistent with the objective of determining segment profitability "as realistically as practicable." A number of respondents to the Exposure Draft asked the Board whether, under the draft, intersegment sales or transfers could be accounted for at other than market price, for example, at cost. The Board has concluded that for purposes of this Statement revenue from intersegment sales or transfers shall be accounted for on whatever basis is used by the enterprise to price the intersegment sales or transfers. No single basis is prescribed or proscribed, but disclosure of the basis of accounting for intersegment sales or transfers is required.

78. The Exposure Draft proposed that two specified levels of profitability—profit or loss contribution and operating profit or loss—be presented for each reportable segment. The former was defined as revenue less only those operating expenses that were directly traceable to the segment, and the latter was defined (as it is in paragraph 10(d) of this Statement) as revenue less all operating expenses including those allocated to segments on a reasonable basis as well as those that are directly traceable. This Statement, however, requires presentation of only operating profit or loss for reportable segments. In the Exposure Draft, the Board stated that "presenting profitability both before and after allocation of common costs and expenses highlights the extent to which the computation of operating profit or loss is affected by allocations." Although most respondents to the Exposure Draft did not disagree with the requirement that operating profit or loss be disclosed for individual reportable segments, many made the point that it is not practicable to distinguish between those operating expenses that may be said to be *directly traceable* to a segment and those that may be said only to be *allocable*. Some respondents pointed out that traceability often depends on the sophistication of an enterprise's internal record-keeping system. They noted that traceability depends on the degree to which management of an enterprise's operations is decentralized. Some said that location of incurrence should not govern the attribution of a cost to a particular segment. In view of the problems cited by those who responded to the Exposure Draft, the Board has judged that disclosure of profit or loss contribution should not be required, although this Statement does not proscribe that disclosure if an enterprise wishes to include it.

79. The Board continues to believe that certain items of revenue and expense either do not relate to segments or cannot *always* be allocated to segments on the basis of objective evidence, and for that reason this Statement does not require that net income be disclosed for reportable segments. Those items are revenue earned at the corporate level and not derived from operations of any industry segment, general corporate expenses, interest expense, domestic and foreign income taxes, and equity in income or loss from unconsolidated subsidiaries and other unconsolidated investees. The Board also has not required that the following (which are normally reported net of income taxes) be allocated: extraordinary items, gain or loss on discontinued operations, minority interest, and the cumulative effect of a change in accounting principle. However, paragraph 25 permits additional disclosure of some other measure of profitability for some or all of an enterprise's reportable segments in addition to operating profit or loss, with appropriate disclosure of the nature and amount of each type of item allocated to segments and the method of allocation.

80. Disclosure of identifiable assets is required, as proposed in the Exposure Draft, to allow financial statement users to assess the relative investment commitment in an enterprise's various segments and to assess the results obtained by the various segments in relation to the investment committed. Some respondents to the Exposure Draft stated that the definition of a segment's identifiable assets as proposed in the Exposure Draft was inconsistent with the proposed definition of a segment's operating profit or loss. They indicated that although allocation of all operating expenses common to two or more segments was required to compute operating profit or loss, allocation of all assets used jointly by two or more segments was not required. In response to that view, the definition of identifiable assets in paragraph 10(e) of this Statement requires that a portion of assets used jointly by two or more industry segments be allocated among the industry segments on a reasonable basis.

81. To provide information useful in understanding the operating profit or loss and the identifiable assets of an industry segment, paragraph 27 requires disclosure of the aggregate amount of each reportable segment's depreciation, depletion, and amortization and of each reportable segment's capital expenditures. The Exposure Draft had identified certain additional disclosures that "may be important" in certain circumstances, including property, plant, and equipment and related accumulated depreciation, receivables and inventories, loans, deposits, or other monetary amounts, and research and development costs. A number of respondents to the Exposure Draft recommended that the final Statement not identify those disclosures as possibly "important" unless the circumstances were clearly specified. Some said the disclosures were overly detailed and would be of questionable benefit in many cases. The Board found those arguments persuasive and decided to delete them in the final Statement. As stated in paragraph 22, presentation of additional information beyond that required to be reported by this Statement may be considered to be desirable, and this Statement does not preclude those additional disclosures.

82. The Exposure Draft proposed that operating profit or loss and identifiable assets of an industry segment or geographic area of consolidated operations include, respectively, the income from and the investment in unconsolidated investees operating in the same industry or the same geographic area. Some respondents stated that, due to the complexity of many enterprises' unconsolidated operations, information called for by the Exposure Draft (i.e., operating profit or loss and identifiable assets) may

not be available for some of those investees, especially for those investees in which the enterprise has less than a 50 percent ownership. Other respondents considered it inappropriate to combine the after-tax net income from the unconsolidated investees with operating profit of the consolidated operations. They also considered it inappropriate to combine the investment in the net assets of unconsolidated investees with identifiable assets of the consolidated operations. Such combinations, in their view, would distort the operating results and financial ratios for the industry segments and geographic areas and thereby make the reported information less useful in some cases and misleading in others. The Board found merit in those arguments and accordingly eliminated the requirement. The Board continues to believe, however, that if the operations of an unconsolidated investee are closely related with those of a reportable segment, information about the segment would be incomplete and therefore subject to possible misinterpretation without information about the relationship. For that reason, the Board concluded that disclosure should be made for each reportable segment of the enterprise's equity in the net income from and investment in the net assets of unconsolidated subsidiaries and other equity method investees whose operations are vertically integrated with the operations of that segment.[17] The Board further concluded that disclosure should also be made of the geographic areas in which those vertically integrated equity method investees operate.

Information about Foreign Operations and Export Sales

83. Several respondents to the Exposure Draft indicated that for their particular industries the distinction between domestic and foreign operations was very difficult to make and requested that the Board develop guidelines and allow judgment in determining the distinction between the two. The Board's intention had been to allow judgment and that intention is made explicit and guidelines are furnished in paragraph 31 and footnote 12 of this Statement.

84. With respect to reporting information about an enterprise's operations in different geographic areas, some respondents to the Exposure Draft requested that the Board clarify or elaborate on a number of matters, including (a) whether the Statement would require disclosure of information on an individual country-by-country basis and (b) how should significance be determined for an enterprise's foreign operations in the aggregate or in any geographic area. The Board's conclusion on each of those matters is clarified or elaborated on in paragraphs 32 and 33 of this Statement.

---

[17]If the operations of two or more equity method investees are vertically integrated with a reportable segment, the amounts required to be disclosed may be combined respectively.

85. The Board recognized in the Exposure Draft and in this Statement that the variety of ways in which foreign operations are conducted made it impossible to define appropriate geographic areas for all enterprises. Therefore, only general guidelines for that determination are set forth in paragraph 34 of this Statement. For those enterprises conducting foreign operations in two or more geographic areas, the Board considered several methods of associating foreign revenue, a measure of profitability, and identifiable assets with a particular geographic area. Those methods include associating this information with geographic areas in terms of the location of the accounting records, the location of the assets, the location of the risks associated with the assets and liabilities, and the location of the customers. However, the Board concluded that none of those methods would necessarily correlate the profitability and identifiable assets of a geographic area in a manner consistent with the objective expressed in paragraph 31. The Board believes that the description of geographic areas of foreign operations in paragraph 34 is sufficiently broad to permit management to accomplish that objective by determining the scope of its operations in each area and then identifying (i) the revenue generated from those operations, (ii) the assets employed in or associated with generating those revenues, and (iii) the costs and expenses related to those revenues and assets. The Board believes that disclosing a measure of assets or assets and liabilities that can be related to a measure of profitability for each significant geographic area will provide users of financial statements with useful financial information about an enterprise's foreign operations consistent with the purpose set forth in paragraph 5.

86. Some respondents to the Exposure Draft recommended that the Statement not require disclosure of operating profit or loss for each geographic area of an enterprise's operations if it is determined instead to present a level of profitability below operating profit or loss. They said that in many cases an after-tax profitability measure is more informative than a pretax measure and that because of significant differences in income tax rates among different geographic areas a pretax measure could at times be misinterpreted. They also said that many enterprises can more easily determine net income or another measure of profitability below operating profit or loss by geographic area than by industry segment. The Board found those arguments convincing, and paragraph 35(b) requires presentation of operating profit or loss, or net income, or some other measure of profitability between operating profit or loss and net income.

87. The Board considered whether this Statement should supersede any part of *ARB No. 43,* Chapter 12, "Foreign Operations and Foreign Exchange,"

especially paragraph 9 thereof. Since paragraph 9 of Chapter 12 deals with consolidation of foreign subsidiaries which is a subject beyond the scope of this Statement, the Board concluded that it should not be superseded. However, this Statement provides definitions and guidelines that may also be useful in applying that Bulletin.

88. The Board has determined that disclosure of working capital and property, plant, and equipment and related accumulated depreciation should not be required by geographic area. Those disclosures had been proposed in the Exposure Draft, but a number of respondents said, and the Board agreed, that the volume of detail that would be required would be excessive. However, as noted in paragraph 87, this Statement does not supersede the requirements of paragraph 9, Chapter 12, *ARB No. 43,* for certain disclosures with respect to the assets and liabilities of foreign subsidiaries.

89. A number of respondents to the Exposure Draft requested that the Board provide guidance as to when export sales should be considered significant, and paragraph 36 of this Statement provides a test of significance. The Board also was asked to clarify certain matters with respect to the disclosures about major customers, including a guideline as to significance and an elaboration on the type of information required to be presented. Paragraph 39 of this Statement reflects the appropriate revisions. Because many respondents argued that identification of the major customer could be competitively harmful to either the enterprise or the customer, the proposal for disclosure of the name of the customer has been dropped.

Effective Date and Transition

90. On considering all circumstances, the Board determined that prospective application of the standards set forth in this Statement effective for periods beginning after December 15, 1976 as stated in paragraph 41, is appropriate because enterprises may not have accumulated in prior years all of the information required to be disclosed by this Statement; the Board also determined that the effective date is advisable in the circumstances.

Appendix C

STANDARD INDUSTRIAL CLASSIFICATIONS

91. As indicated in paragraph 12, the Board has examined several systems that have been developed for classifying business activities, such as the Standard Industrial Classification and the Enterprise Standard Industrial Classification systems and has

judged that none is, by itself, suitable to determine industry segments as that term is used in this Statement. Nonetheless, those systems may provide guidance for the exercise of the judgment required to group an enterprise's products and services by industry lines.

92. As set forth in the *Standard Industrial Classification Manual* prepared by the Statistical Policy Division of the U.S. Office of Management and Budget, SIC is a system for classifying business establishments (generally, individual plants, stores, banks, etc.) by the type of economic activity in which they are engaged. An establishment is not necessarily identical with a business enterprise, which may consist of one or more establishments.

93. The 649-page manual contains one-digit, two-digit, three-digit, and four-digit SIC industry codes, each of which is described in detail. At the one-digit level, the SIC classifies business activities into 11 divisions:

A Agriculture, forestry, and fishing.
B Mining.
C Construction.
D Manufacturing.
E Transportation, communications, electric, gas, and sanitary services.
F Wholesale trade.
G Retail trade.
H Finance, insurance, and real estate.
I Services.
J Public administration.
K Nonclassifiable establishments.

94. Each of those divisions is subdivided into two-digit major groups. There is a total of 84 two-digit groups. For example, the 20 major groups in manufacturing are:

1. Food and kindred products.
2. Tobacco manufacturers.
3. Textile mill products.
4. Apparel and other finished products made from fabrics and similar materials.
5. Lumber and wood products, except furniture.
6. Furniture and fixtures.
7. Paper and allied products.
8. Printing, publishing, and allied products.
9. Chemicals and allied products.
10. Petroleum refining and related industries.
11. Rubber and miscellaneous plastics products.
12. Leather and leather products.
13. Stone, clay, glass, and concrete products.
14. Primary metal industries.
15. Fabricated metal products, except machinery and transportation equipment.
16. Machinery, except electrical.

17. Electrical and electronic machinery, equipment, and supplies.
18. Transportation equipment.
19. Measuring, analyzing, and controlling instruments; photographic, medical, and optical goods; watches and clocks.
20. Miscellaneous manufacturing industries.

95. Each of the two-digit SIC major groups, in turn, is further subdivided into three-digit industry groups. There are 421 three-digit industry groups. For example, the "machinery, except electrical" group includes the following industry groups:

1. Engines and turbines.
2. Farm and garden machinery and equipment.
3. Construction, mining, and materials handling machinery and equipment.
4. Metalworking machinery and equipment.
5. Special industry machinery, except metalworking machinery.
6. General industry machinery and equipment.
7. Office, computing, and accounting machines.
8. Refrigeration and service industry machinery.
9. Miscellaneous machinery, except electrical.

96. The three-digit SIC industry groups are still further subdivided by product lines into over 1,000 narrower four-digit industry groups. Metalworking machinery and equipment (a three-digit industry group), for example, is divided into metal cutting machine tools, metal forming machine tools, power driven hand tools, rolling mill machinery and equipment, and so on.

97. The *Standard Industrial Classification Manual* is revised periodically, most recently in 1972. It is available for sale by the Superintendent of Documents, U.S. Government Printing Office.

98. The *Enterprise Standard Industrial Classification Manual,* like the *SIC Manual,* is prepared by the Statistical Policy Division of the U.S. Office of Management and Budget. It classifies enterprises (companies, firms, partnerships, etc.) rather than establishments (plants, stores, banks, etc.). The structure of ESIC follows closely the structure of the SIC codes. It includes eight classes of enterprises at the one-digit level, 67 at the two-digit level, 216 at the three-digit level, and 252 at the four-digit level.

Appendix D

FACTORS TO BE CONSIDERED IN DETERMINING INDUSTRY SEGMENTS

99. This Appendix identifies a number of factors to be considered in grouping products and services by

industry lines into industry segments. As indicated in paragraph 12, although certain characteristics can be identified that assist in differentiating among industries, no single set of characteristics is universally applicable to determine the industry segments of all business enterprises. Nor is any single characteristic determinative in all cases.

100. Among the factors that should be considered in determining whether products and services are related (and, therefore, should be grouped into a single industry segment) or unrelated (and, therefore, should be separated into two or more industry segments) are the following:

a. *The nature of the product.* Related products or services have similar purposes or end uses. Thus, they may be expected to have similar rates of profitability, similar degrees of risk, and similar opportunities for growth.
b. *The nature of the production process.* Sharing of common or interchangeable production or sales facilities, equipment, labor force, or service group or use of the same or similar basic raw materials may suggest that products or services are related. Likewise, similar degrees of labor intensiveness or similar degrees of capital intensiveness may indicate a relationship among products or services.
c. *Markets and marketing methods.* Similarity of geographic marketing areas, types of customers, or marketing methods may indicate a relationship among products or services. For instance, the use of a common or interchangeable sales force may suggest a relationship among products or services. The sensitivity of the market to price changes and to changes in general economic conditions may also indicate whether products or services are related or unrelated.

101. Broad categories such as *manufacturing, wholesaling, retailing,* and *consumer products* are not per se indicative of the industries in which an enterprise operates, and those terms should not be used without identification of a product or service to describe an enterprise's industry segments.

Appendix E

ILLUSTRATION OF APPLYING PARAGRAPH 15(b)

102. Under paragraph 15(b), an industry segment is to be regarded as significant if the absolute amount of its operating profit or operating loss is 10 percent or more of the greater, in absolute amount, of:

(i) The combined operating profit of all industry segments that did not incur an operating loss, or

(ii) The combined operating loss of all industry segments that did incur an operating loss.

103. To illustrate how that paragraph is applied, assume that an enterprise has seven industry segments some of which incurred operating losses, as follows:

Industry Segment	Operating Profit or (Operating Loss)	
A	$ 100	
B	500	} $1,000
C	400	
D	(295)	
E	(600)	
F	(100)	} (1,100)
G	(105)	
	$(100)	

104. The combined operating profit of all industry segments that did not incur a loss (A, B, and C) is $1,000. The absolute amount of the combined operating loss of those segments that did incur a loss (D, E, F, and G) is $1,100. Under paragraph 15(b), therefore, Industry Segments B, C, D, and E are significant because the absolute amount of their individual operating profit or operating loss equals or exceeds $110 (10 percent of $1,100). Additional industry segments might, of course, also be deemed significant under the revenue and identifiable assets tests in paragraphs 15(a) and 15(c).

Appendix F

ILLUSTRATIONS OF FINANCIAL STATEMENT DISCLOSURES

105. This Appendix contains examples of disclosures of the type that this Statement requires to be included in the financial statements of an enterprise. The illustrations do not encompass all possible circumstances, nor do the formats used indicate a particular preference of the Board.

106. Exhibit A presents the consolidated income statement of a hypothetical company for the year ended December 31, 1977. Exhibit B illustrates how the company might present information about its operations in different industries and its reliance on major customers. Exhibit C illustrates how the company might present information about its foreign operations in different geographic areas and its export sales.

EXHIBIT A

X Company
Consolidated Income Statement
Year ended December 31, 1977

Sales		$4,700
Cost of sales	$3,000	
Selling, general, and administrative expense	700	
Interest expense	200	3,900
		800
Equity in net income of Z Co. (25% owned)		100
Income from continuing operations before income taxes		900
Income taxes		400
Income from continuing operations		500
Discontinued operations:		
Loss from operations of discontinued West Coast division (net of income tax effect of $50)	70	
Loss on disposal of West Coast division (net of income tax effect of $100)	130	200
Income before extraordinary gain and before cumulative effect of change in accounting principle		300
Extraordinary gain (net of income tax effect of $80)		90
Cumulative effect on prior years of change from straight-line to accelerated depreciation (net of income tax effect of $60)		(60)
Net income		$ 330

EXHIBIT B

X Company
Information about the Company's Operations in Different Industries
Year ended December 31, 1977

	Industry A	Industry B	Industry C	Other Industries	Adjustments and Eliminations	Consolidated
Sales to unaffiliated customers	$1,000	$2,000	$1,500	$ 200		$ 4,700
Intersegment sales	200		500		$(700)	
Total revenue	$1,200	$2,000	$2,000	$ 200	$(700)	$ 4,700
Operating profit	$ 200	$ 290	$ 600	$ 50	$ (40)	$ 1,100
Equity in net income of Z Co.						100
General corporate expenses						(100)
Interest expense						(200)
Income from continuing operations before income taxes						$ 900
Identifiable assets at December 31, 1977	$2,000	$4,050	$6,000	$1,000	$ (50)	$13,000
Investment in net assets of Z Co.						400
Corporate assets						1,600
Total assets at December 31, 1977						$15,000

See accompanying note.

Note

The Company operates principally in three industries, A, B, and C. Operations in Industry A involve production and sale of (describe types of products and services). Operations in Industry B involve production and sale of (describe types of products and services). Operations in Industry C involve production and sale of (describe types of products and services). Total revenue by industry includes both sales to unaffiliated customers, as reported in the Company's consolidated income statement, and intersegment sales, which are accounted for by (describe the basis of accounting for intersegment sales).

Operating profit is total revenue less operating expenses. In computing operating profit, none of the following items has been added or deducted: general corporate expenses, interest expense, income taxes, equity in income from unconsolidated investee, loss from discontinued operations of the West Coast division (which was a part of the Company's operations in Industry B), extraordinary gain (which relates to the Company's operations in Industry A), and the cumulative effect of the change from straight-line to accelerated depreciation (of which $30 relates to the Company's operations in Industry A, $10 to Industry B, and $20 to Industry C). Depreciation for Industries A, B, and C, respectively, was $80, $100, and $150. Capital expenditures for the three industries were $100, $200, and $400, respectively.

The effect of the change from straight-line to accelerated depreciation was to reduce the 1977 operating profit of Industries A, B, and C, respectively, by $40, $30, and $20.

Identifiable assets by industry are those assets that are used in the Company's operations in each industry. Corporate assets are principally cash and marketable securities.

The Company has a 25 percent interest in Z Co., whose operations are in the United States and are vertically integrated with the Company's operations in Industry A. Equity in net income of Z Co. was $100; investment in net assets of Z Co. was $400.

To reconcile industry information with consolidated amounts, the following eliminations have been made; $700 of intersegment sales; $40 relating to the net change in intersegment operating profit in beginning and ending inventories; and $50 intersegment operating profit in inventory at December 31, 1977.

Contracts with a U.S. government agency account for $1,100 of the sales to unaffiliated customers of Industry B.

EXHIBIT C

X Company
Information about the Company's Operations in Different Geographic Areas
Year ended December 31, 1977

	United States	Geographic Area A	Geographic Area B	Adjustments and Eliminations	Consolidated
Sales to unaffiliated customers	$3,000	$1,000	$ 700		$ 4,700
Transfers between geographic areas	1,000			$(1,000)	
Total revenue	$4,000	$1,000	$ 700	$(1,000)	$ 4,700
Operating profit	$ 800	$ 400	$ 100	$ (200)	$ 1,100
Equity in net income of Z Co.					100
General corporate expenses					(100)
Interest expense					(200)
Income from continuing operations before income taxes					$ 900
Identifiable assets at December 31, 1977	$7,300	$3,400	$2,450	$ (150)	$13,000
Investment in net assets of Z Co.					400
Corporate assets					1,600
Total assets at December 31, 1977					$15,000

See accompanying note.

Note

Transfers between geographic areas are accounted for by (describe the basis of accounting for such transfers). Operating profit is total revenue less operating expenses. In computing operating profit, none of the following items has been added or deducted: general corporate expenses, interest expense, income taxes, equity in income from unconsolidated investee, loss from discontinued operations of West Coast division (which was part of the Company's U.S. operations), extraordinary gain (which relates to the Company's operations in Geographic Area B), and the cumulative effect of the change from straight-line to accelerated depreciation (which relates entirely to the Company's operations in the United States).

Identifiable assets are those assets of the Company that are identified with the operations in each geographic area. Corporate assets are principally cash and marketable securities.

Of the $3,000 U.S. sales to unaffiliated customers, $1,200 were export sales, principally to Geographic Area C.

Statement of Financial Accounting Standards No. 15
Accounting by Debtors and Creditors for Troubled Debt Restructurings

STATUS

Issued: June 1977

Effective Date: For troubled debt restructurings consummated after December 31, 1977

Affects: Amends APB 26, paragraphs 2 and 3(a)
Supersedes FIN 2

Affected by: Paragraph 1 amended prospectively by FAS 114
Paragraph 9 superseded by FAS 71
Paragraphs 28 and 33 amended by FAS 121
Paragraphs 30 through 32, 35 through 37, 40(a), and 41 and footnotes 18, 19, 21, 24, and 25
superseded prospectively by FAS 114
Paragraphs 33, 34, and 42 amended prospectively by FAS 114
Footnote 20 superseded by FAS 111
Footnote 26 amended by FAS 111

Other Interpretive Pronouncements: FTB 79-6 (Superseded by FAS 114)
FTB 79-7 (Superseded by FAS 114)
FTB 80-1
FTB 80-2
FTB 81-6
FTB 94-1

Issues Discussed by FASB Emerging Issues Task Force (EITF)

Affects: No EITF Issues

Interpreted by: Paragraphs 16 through 18 interpreted by EITF Issue No. 89-15
Paragraphs 28 and 34 interpreted by EITF Issues No. 87-18 and 87-19
Footnote 1 interpreted by EITF Issue No. 91-2

Related Issues: EITF Issues No. 84-19, 85-44, 89-14, and 94-8 and Topic No. D-4

Statement of Financial Accounting Standards No. 15
Accounting by Debtors and Creditors for Troubled Debt Restructurings

CONTENTS

INTRODUCTION

1. This Statement establishes standards of financial accounting and reporting by the debtor and by the creditor for a troubled debt restructuring. The Statement does not cover accounting for allowances for estimated uncollectible amounts and does not prescribe or proscribe particular methods for estimating amounts of uncollectible receivables.

2. A restructuring of a debt constitutes a *troubled debt restructuring* for purposes of this Statement if the creditor for economic or legal reasons related to the debtor's financial difficulties grants a concession to the debtor that it would not otherwise consider. That concession either stems from an agreement between the creditor and the debtor or is imposed by law or a court. For example, a creditor may restructure the terms of a debt to alleviate the burden of the debtor's near-term cash requirements, and many troubled debt restructurings involve modifying terms to reduce or defer cash payments required of the debtor in the near future to help the debtor attempt to improve its financial condition and eventually be able to pay the creditor. Or, for example, the creditor may accept cash, other assets, or an equity interest in the debtor in satisfaction of the debt though the value received is less than the amount of the debt because the creditor concludes that step will maximize recovery of its investment.[1]

3. Whatever the form of concession granted by the creditor to the debtor in a troubled debt restructuring, the creditor's objective is to make the best of a difficult situation. That is, the creditor expects to obtain more cash or other value from the debtor, or to increase the probability of receipt, by granting the concession than by not granting it.

4. In this Statement, a *receivable* or *payable* (collectively referred to as *debt*) represents a contractual right to receive money or a contractual obligation to pay money on demand or on fixed or determinable dates that is already included as an asset or liability in the creditor's or debtor's balance sheet at the time of the restructuring. Receivables or payables that may be involved in troubled debt restructurings commonly result from lending or borrowing of cash, investing in debt securities that were previously issued, or selling or purchasing goods or services on credit. Examples are accounts receivable or payable, notes, debentures and bonds (whether those receivables or payables are secured or unsecured and whether they are convertible or nonconvertible), and related accrued interest, if any. Typically, each receivable or payable is negotiated separately, but

---

[1]Although troubled debt that is fully satisfied by foreclosure, repossession, or other transfer of assets or by grant of equity securities by the debtor is, in a technical sense, not restructured, that kind of event is included in the term *troubled debt restructuring* in this Statement.

sometimes two or more receivables or payables are negotiated together. For example, a debtor may negotiate with a group of creditors but sign separate debt instruments with each creditor. For purposes of this Statement, restructuring of each receivable or payable, including those negotiated and restructured jointly, shall be accounted for individually. The substance rather than the form of the receivable or payable shall govern. For example, to a debtor, a bond constitutes one payable even though there are many bondholders.

5. A troubled debt restructuring may include, but is not necessarily limited to, one or a combination of the following:

a. Transfer from the debtor to the creditor of receivables from third parties, real estate, or other assets to satisfy fully or partially a debt (including a transfer resulting from foreclosure or repossession).

b. Issuance or other granting of an equity interest to the creditor by the debtor to satisfy fully or partially a debt unless the equity interest is granted pursuant to existing terms for converting the debt into an equity interest.

c. Modification of terms of a debt, such as one or a combination of:

1. Reduction (absolute or contingent) of the stated interest rate for the remaining original life of the debt.
2. Extension of the maturity date or dates at a stated interest rate lower than the current market rate for new debt with similar risk.
3. Reduction (absolute or contingent) of the face amount or maturity amount of the debt as stated in the instrument or other agreement.
4. Reduction (absolute or contingent) of accrued interest.

6. Troubled debt restructurings may occur before, at, or after the stated maturity of debt, and time may elapse between the agreement, court order, etc. and the transfer of assets or equity interest, the effective date of new terms, or the occurrence of another event that constitutes consummation of the restructuring. The date of consummation is the *time of the restructuring* in this Statement.

7. A debt restructuring is not necessarily a troubled debt restructuring for purposes of this Statement even if the debtor is experiencing some financial difficulties. For example, a troubled debt restructuring is not involved if (a) the fair value[2] of cash, other assets, or an equity interest accepted by a creditor from a debtor in full satisfaction of its receivable at least equals the creditor's recorded investment in the

receivable;[3] (b) the fair value of cash, other assets, or an equity interest transferred by a debtor to a creditor in full settlement of its payable at least equals the debtor's carrying amount of the payable; (c) the creditor reduces the effective interest rate on the debt primarily to reflect a decrease in market interest rates in general or a decrease in the risk so as to maintain a relationship with a debtor that can readily obtain funds from other sources at the current market interest rate; or (d) the debtor issues in exchange for its debt new marketable debt having an effective interest rate based on its market price that is at or near the current market interest rates of debt with similar maturity dates and stated interest rates issued by nontroubled debtors. In general, a debtor that can obtain funds from sources other than the existing creditor at market interest rates at or near those for nontroubled debt is not involved in a troubled debt restructuring. A debtor in a troubled debt restructuring can obtain funds from sources other than the existing creditor in the troubled debt restructuring, if at all, only at effective interest rates (based on market prices) so high that it cannot afford to pay them. Thus, in an attempt to protect as much of its investment as possible, the creditor in a troubled debt restructuring grants a concession to the debtor that it would not otherwise consider.

8. For purposes of this Statement, troubled debt restructurings do not include changes in lease agreements (the accounting is prescribed by *FASB Statement No. 13*, "Accounting for Leases") or employment-related agreements (for example, pension plans and deferred compensation contracts). Nor do troubled debt restructurings include debtors' failures to pay trade accounts according to their terms or creditors' delays in taking legal action to collect overdue amounts of interest and principal, unless they involve an agreement between debtor and creditor to restructure.

9. The Addendum to *APB Opinion No. 2*, "Accounting for the 'Investment Credit'," states that "differences may arise in the application of generally accepted accounting principles as between regulated and nonregulated businesses, because of the effect in regulated businesses of the rate-making process" and discusses the application of generally accepted accounting principles to regulated industries. FASB Statements and Interpretations should therefore be applied to regulated companies that are subject to the rate-making process in accordance with the provisions of the Addendum.

10. This Statement supersedes *FASB Interpretation No. 2*, "Imputing Interest on Debt Arrangements Made under the Federal Bankruptcy Act," and shall

---

[2]Defined in paragraph 13.

[3]Defined in footnote 17.

be applied to the types of situations that were covered by that Interpretation. Thus, it shall be applied to troubled debt restructurings consummated under reorganization, arrangement, or other provisions of the Federal Bankruptcy Act or other Federal statutes related thereto.[4] It also amends *APB Opinion No. 26,* "Early Extinguishment of Debt," to the extent needed to exclude from that Opinion's scope early extinguishments of debt through troubled debt restructurings.

11. Appendix A provides background information. Appendix B sets forth the basis for the Board's conclusions, including alternatives considered and reasons for accepting some and rejecting others.

STANDARDS OF FINANCIAL ACCOUNTING AND REPORTING

Accounting by Debtors

12. A debtor shall account for a troubled debt restructuring according to the type of the restructuring as prescribed in the following paragraphs.

Transfer of Assets in Full Settlement

13. A debtor that transfers its receivables from third parties, real estate, or other assets to a creditor to settle fully a payable shall recognize a gain on restructuring of payables (see paragraph 21). The gain shall be measured by the excess of (i) the carrying amount of the payable settled (the face amount increased or decreased by applicable accrued interest and applicable unamortized premium, discount, finance charges, or issue costs) over (ii) the fair value of the assets transferred to the creditor.[5] The fair value of the assets transferred is the amount that the debtor could reasonably expect to receive for them in a current sale between a willing buyer and a will-

ing seller, that is, other than in a forced or liquidation sale. Fair value of assets shall be measured by their market value if an active market for them exists. If no active market exists for the assets transferred but exists for similar assets, the selling prices in that market may be helpful in estimating the fair value of the assets transferred. If no market price is available, a forecast of expected cash flows may aid in estimating the fair value of assets transferred, provided the expected cash flows are discounted at a rate commensurate with the risk involved.[6]

14. A difference between the fair value and the carrying amount of assets transferred to a creditor to settle a payable is a gain or loss on transfer of assets.[7] The debtor shall include that gain or loss in measuring net income for the period of transfer, reported as provided in *APB Opinion No. 30,* "Reporting the Results of Operations."

Grant of Equity Interest in Full Settlement

15. A debtor that issues or otherwise grants an equity interest to a creditor to settle fully a payable shall account for the equity interest at its fair value.[8] The difference between the fair value of the equity interest granted and the carrying amount of the payable settled shall be recognized as a gain on restructuring of payables (see paragraph 21).

Modification of Terms

16. A debtor in a troubled debt restructuring involving only modification of terms of a payable—that is, not involving a transfer of assets or grant of an equity interest—shall account for the effects of the restructuring prospectively from the time of restructuring, and shall not change the carrying amount of the payable at the time of the restructuring unless the carrying amount exceeds the total

---

[4]This Statement does not apply, however, if under provisions of those Federal statutes or in a quasi-reorganization or corporate readjustment (*ARB No. 43,* Chapter 7, Section A, "Quasi-Reorganization or Corporate Readjustment . . .") with which a troubled debt restructuring coincides, the debtor restates its liabilities generally.

[5]Paragraphs 13, 15, and 19 indicate that the fair value of assets transferred or the fair value of an equity interest granted shall be used in accounting for a settlement of a payable in a troubled debt restructuring. That guidance is not intended to preclude using the fair value of the payable settled if more clearly evident than the fair value of the assets transferred or of the equity interest granted in a full settlement of a payable (paragraphs 13 and 15). (See paragraph 67 of *APB Opinion No. 16,* "Business Combinations.") However, in a partial settlement of a payable (paragraph 19), the fair value of the assets transferred or of the equity interest granted shall be used in all cases to avoid the need to allocate the fair value of the payable between the part settled and the part still outstanding.

[6]Some factors that may be relevant in estimating the fair value of various kinds of assets are described in paragraphs 88 and 89 of *APB Opinion No. 16,* paragraphs 12-14 of *APB Opinion No. 21,* "Interest on Receivables and Payables," and paragraph 25 of *APB Opinion No. 29,* "Accounting for Nonmonetary Transactions."

[7]The carrying amount of a receivable encompasses not only unamortized premium, discount, acquisition costs, and the like but also an allowance for uncollectible amounts and other "valuation" accounts, if any. A loss on transferring receivables to creditors may therefore have been wholly or partially recognized in measuring net income before the transfer and be wholly or partly a reduction of a valuation account rather than a gain or loss in measuring net income for the period of the transfer.

[8]See footnote 5.

future cash payments specified by the new terms.[9] That is, the effects of changes in the amounts or timing (or both) of future cash payments designated as either interest or face amount shall be reflected in future periods.[10] Interest expense shall be computed in a way that a constant effective interest rate is applied to the carrying amount of the payable at the beginning of each period between restructuring and maturity the "interest" method prescribed by paragraph 15 of *APB Opinion No. 21*). The new effective interest rate shall be the discount rate that equates the present value of the future cash payments specified by the new terms (excluding amounts contingently payable) with the carrying amount of the payable.

17. If, however, the total future cash payments specified by the new terms of a payable, including both payments designated as interest and those designated as face amount, are less than the carrying amount of the payable, the debtor shall reduce the carrying amount to an amount equal to the total future cash payments specified by the new terms and shall recognize a gain on restructuring of payables equal to the amount of the reduction (see paragraph 21).[11] Thereafter, all cash payments under the terms of the payable shall be accounted for as reductions of the carrying amount of the payable, and no interest expense shall be recognized on the payable for any period between the restructuring and maturity of the payable.[12]

18. A debtor shall not recognize a gain on a restructured payable involving indeterminate future cash payments as long as the maximum total future cash payments may exceed the carrying amount of the payable. Amounts designated either as interest or as face amount by the new terms may be payable contingent on a specified event or circumstance (for example, the debtor may be required to pay specified amounts if its financial condition improves to a specified degree within a specified period). To determine whether the debtor shall recognize a gain

according to the provisions of paragraphs 16 and 17, those contingent amounts shall be included in the "total future cash payments specified by the new terms" to the extent necessary to prevent recognizing a gain at the time of restructuring that may be offset by future interest expense. Thus, the debtor shall apply paragraph 17 of *FASB Statement No. 5*, "Accounting for Contingencies," in which probability of occurrence of a gain contingency is not a factor, and shall assume that contingent future payments will have to be paid. The same principle applies to amounts of future cash payments that must sometimes be estimated to apply the provisions of paragraphs 16 and 17. For example, if the number of future interest payments is flexible because the face amount and accrued interest is payable on demand or becomes payable on demand, estimates of total future cash payments shall be based on the maximum number of periods possible under the restructured terms.

Combination of Types

19. A troubled debt restructuring may involve partial settlement of a payable by the debtor's transferring assets or granting an equity interest (or both) to the creditor and modification of terms of the remaining payable.[13] A debtor shall account for a troubled debt restructuring involving a partial settlement and a modification of terms as prescribed in paragraphs 16-18 except that, first, assets transferred or an equity interest granted in that partial settlement shall be measured as prescribed in paragraphs 13 and 15, respectively, and the carrying amount of the payable shall be reduced by the total fair value of those assets or equity interest.[14] A difference between the fair value and the carrying amount of assets transferred to the creditor shall be recognized as a gain or loss on transfer of assets. No gain on restructuring of payables shall be recognized unless the remaining carrying amount of the payable exceeds the total future cash payments (including amounts contingently payable) specified by the

---

[9]In this Statement, *total future cash payments* includes related accrued interest, if any, at the time of the restructuring that continues to be payable under the new terms.

[10]All or a portion of the carrying amount of the payable at the time of the restructuring may need to be reclassified in the balance sheet because of changes in the terms, for example, a change in the amount of the payable due within one year after the date of the debtor's balance sheet. A troubled debt restructuring of a short-term obligation after the date of a debtor's balance sheet but before that balance sheet is issued may affect the classification of that obligation in accordance with *FASB Statement No. 6*, "Classification of Short-Term Obligations Expected to Be Refinanced."

[11]If the carrying amount of the payable comprises several accounts (for example, face amount, accrued interest, and unamortized premium, discount, finance charges, and issue costs) that are to be continued after the restructuring, some possibly being combined, the reduction in carrying amount may need to be allocated among the remaining accounts in proportion to the previous balances. However, the debtor may choose to carry the amount designated as face amount by the new terms in a separate account and adjust another account accordingly.

[12]The only exception is to recognize interest expense according to paragraph 22.

[13]Even if the stated terms of the remaining payable, for example, the stated interest rate and the maturity date or dates, are not changed in connection with the transfer of assets or grant of an equity interest, the restructuring shall be accounted for as prescribed by paragraph 19.

[14]If cash is paid in a partial settlement of a payable in a troubled debt restructuring, the carrying amount of the payable shall be reduced by the amount of cash paid.

terms of the debt remaining unsettled after the restructuring. Future interest expense, if any, shall be determined according to the provisions of paragraphs 16-18.

Related Matters

20. A troubled debt restructuring that is in substance a repossession or foreclosure by the creditor or other transfer of assets to the creditor shall be accounted for according to the provisions of paragraphs 13, 14, and 19.

21. Gains on restructuring of payables determined by applying the provisions of paragraphs 13-20 of this Statement shall be aggregated, included in measuring net income for the period of restructuring, and, if material, classified as an extraordinary item, net of related income tax effect, in accordance with paragraph 8 of *FASB Statement No. 4*, "Reporting Gains and Losses from Extinguishment of Debt."

22. If a troubled debt restructuring involves amounts contingently payable, those contingent amounts shall be recognized as a payable and as interest expense in future periods in accordance with paragraph 8 of *FASB Statement No. 5*. Thus, in general, interest expense for contingent payments shall be recognized in each period in which (a) it is probable that a liability has been incurred and (b) the amount of that liability can be reasonably estimated. Before recognizing a payable and interest expense for amounts contingently payable, however, accrual or payment of those amounts shall be deducted from the carrying amount of the restructured payable to the extent that contingent payments included in "total future cash payments specified by the new terms" prevented recognition of a gain at the time of restructuring (paragraph 18).

23. If amounts of future cash payments must be estimated to apply the provisions of paragraphs 16-18 because future interest payments are expected to fluctuate—for example, the restructured terms may specify the stated interest rate to be the prime interest rate increased by a specified amount or proportion—estimates of maximum total future payments shall be based on the interest rate in effect at the time of the restructuring. Fluctuations in the effective interest rate after the restructuring from changes in the prime rate or other causes shall be accounted for as changes in estimates in the periods the changes occur. However, the accounting for those fluctuations shall not result in recognizing a gain on restructuring that may be offset by future cash payments (paragraphs 18 and 22). Rather, the carrying amount of the restructured payable shall

remain unchanged, and future cash payments shall reduce the carrying amount until the time that any gain recognized cannot be offset by future cash payments.

24. Legal fees and other direct costs that a debtor incurs in granting an equity interest to a creditor in a troubled debt restructuring shall reduce the amount otherwise recorded for that equity interest according to paragraphs 15 and 19. All other direct costs that a debtor incurs to effect a troubled debt restructuring shall be deducted in measuring gain on restructuring of payables or shall be included in expense for the period if no gain on restructuring is recognized.

Disclosure by Debtors

25. A debtor shall disclose, either in the body of the financial statements or in the accompanying notes, the following information about troubled debt restructurings that have occurred during a period for which financial statements are presented:

a. For each restructuring:[15] a description of the principal changes in terms, the major features of settlement, or both.
b. Aggregate gain on restructuring of payables and the related income tax effect (paragraph 21).
c. Aggregate net gain or loss on transfers of assets recognized during the period (paragraphs 14 and 19).
d. Per share amount of the aggregate gain on restructuring of payables, net of related income tax effect.

26. A debtor shall disclose in financial statements for periods after a troubled debt restructuring the extent to which amounts contingently payable are included in the carrying amount of restructured payables pursuant to the provisions of paragraph 18. If required by paragraphs 9-13 of *FASB Statement No. 5*, a debtor shall also disclose in those financial statements total amounts that are contingently payable on restructured payables and the conditions under which those amounts would become payable or would be forgiven.

Accounting by Creditors

27. A creditor shall account for a troubled debt restructuring according to the type of the restructuring as prescribed in the following paragraphs. Paragraphs 28-42 do not apply to a receivable that the creditor is accounting for at market value in accordance with the specialized industry practice (for example, a marketable debt security accounted

---

[15]Separate restructurings within a fiscal period for the same category of payables (for example, accounts payable or subordinated debentures) may be grouped for disclosure purposes.

for at market value by a mutual fund). Estimated cash expected to be received less estimated costs expected to be incurred is not market value in accordance with specialized industry practice as that term is used in this paragraph.

Receipt of Assets in Full Satisfaction

28. A creditor that receives from a debtor in full satisfaction of a receivable either (i) receivables from third parties, real estate, or other assets or (ii) shares of stock or other evidence of an equity interest in the debtor, or both, shall account for those assets (including an equity interest) at their fair value at the time of the restructuring (see paragraph 13 for how to measure fair value).[16] The excess of (i) the recorded investment in the receivable[17] satisfied over (ii) the fair value of assets received is a loss to be recognized according to paragraph 35.

29. After a troubled debt restructuring, a creditor shall account for assets received in satisfaction of a receivable the same as if the assets had been acquired for cash.

Modification of Terms

30. A creditor in a troubled debt restructuring involving only modification of terms of a receivable—that is, not involving receipt of assets (including an equity interest in the debtor)—shall account for the effects of the restructuring prospectively and shall not change the recorded investment in the receivable at the time of the restructuring unless that amount exceeds the total future cash receipts specified by the new terms.[18] That is, the effects of changes in the amounts or timing (or both) of future cash receipts designated either as interest or as face amount shall be reflected in future periods.[19] Interest income shall be computed in a way that a constant effective interest rate is applied

to the recorded investment in the receivable at the beginning of each period between restructuring and maturity (in substance the "interest" method prescribed by paragraph 15 of *APB Opinion No. 21*).[20] The new effective interest rate shall be the discount rate that equates the present value of the future cash receipts specified by the new terms (excluding amounts contingently receivable) with the recorded investment in the receivable.

31. If, however, the total future cash receipts specified by the new terms of the receivable, including both receipts designated as interest and those designated as face amount, are less than the recorded investment in the receivable before restructuring, the creditor shall reduce the recorded investment in the receivable to an amount equal to the total future cash receipts specified by the new terms. The amount of the reduction is a loss to be recognized according to paragraph 35. Thereafter, all cash receipts by the creditor under the terms of the restructured receivable, whether designated as interest or as face amount, shall be accounted for as recovery of the recorded investment in the receivable, and no interest income shall be recognized on the receivable for any period between the restructuring and maturity of the receivable.[21]

32. A creditor shall recognize a loss on a restructured receivable involving indeterminate future cash receipts unless the minimum future cash receipts specified by the new terms at least equals the recorded investment in the receivable. Amounts designated either as interest or as face amount that are receivable from the debtor may be contingent on a specified event or circumstance (for example, specified amounts may be receivable from the debtor if the debtor's financial condition improves to a specified degree within a specified period). To determine whether the creditor shall recognize a loss according to the provisions of paragraphs 30 and 31, those

---

[16]Paragraphs 28 and 33 indicate that the fair value of assets received shall be used in accounting for satisfaction of a receivable in a troubled debt restructuring. That guidance is not intended to preclude using the fair value of the receivable satisfied if more clearly evident than the fair value of the assets received in full satisfaction of a receivable (paragraph 28). (See paragraph 67 of *APB Opinion No. 16*.) However, in a partial satisfaction of a receivable (paragraph 33), the fair value of the assets received shall be used in all cases to avoid the need to allocate the fair value of the receivable between the part satisfied and the part still outstanding.

[17]*Recorded investment in the receivable* is used in paragraphs 28-41 instead of *carrying amount of the receivable* because the latter is net of an allowance for estimated uncollectible amounts or other "valuation" account, if any, while the former is not. The recorded investment in the receivable is the face amount increased or decreased by applicable accrued interest and unamortized premium, discount, finance charges, or acquisition costs and may also reflect a previous direct write-down of the investment.

[18]In this Statement, total future cash receipts includes related accrued interest, if any, at the time of the restructuring that continues to be receivable under the new terms. Uncertainty of collection of noncontingent amounts specified by the new terms (see paragraph 32 for inclusion of contingent amounts) is not a factor in applying paragraphs 30-32 but should, of course, be considered in accounting for allowances for uncollectible amounts.

[19]All or a portion of the recorded investment in the receivable at the time of restructuring may need to be reclassified in the balance sheet because of changes in the terms.

[20]Some creditors—for example, finance companies (*AICPA Industry Audit Guide*, "Audits of Finance Companies," Chapter 2)—use methods that recognize less revenue in early periods of a receivable than does the "interest" method. The accounting for restructured receivables described in this Statement is not intended to change creditors' methods of recognizing revenue to require a different method for restructured receivables from that for other receivables.

[21]The only exception is to recognize interest income according to paragraph 36.

contingent amounts shall be included in the "total future cash receipts specified by the new terms" only if at the time of restructuring those amounts meet the conditions that would be applied under the provisions of paragraph 8 of *FASB Statement No. 5* in accruing a loss. That is, a creditor shall recognize a loss unless contingent future cash receipts needed to make total future cash receipts specified by the new terms at least equal to the recorded investment in the receivable both are probable and can be reasonably estimated. The same principle applies to amounts of future cash receipts that must sometimes be estimated to apply the provisions of paragraphs 30 and 31. For example, if the number of interest receipts is flexible because the face amount and accrued interest is collectible on demand or becomes collectible on demand after a specified period, estimates of total future cash receipts should be based on the minimum number of periods possible under the restructured terms.

Combination of Types

33. A troubled debt restructuring may involve receipt of assets (including an equity interest in the debtor) in partial satisfaction of a receivable and a modification of terms of the remaining receivable.[22] A creditor shall account for a troubled debt restructuring involving a partial satisfaction and modification of terms as prescribed in paragraphs 30-32 except that, first, the assets received shall be accounted for at their fair values as prescribed in paragraph 28 and the recorded investment in the receivable shall be reduced by the fair value of the assets received.[23] No loss on the restructuring shall be recognized unless the remaining recorded investment in the receivable exceeds the total future cash receipts specified by the terms of the receivable remaining unsatisfied after the restructuring. Future interest income, if any, shall be determined according to the provisions of paragraphs 30-32.

Related Matters

34. A troubled debt restructuring that is in substance a repossession or foreclosure by the creditor, or in which the creditor otherwise obtains one or more of the debtor's assets in place of all or part of the receivable, shall be accounted for according to the provisions of paragraphs 28 and 33 and, if appropriate, 39.

35. Losses determined by applying the provisions of paragraphs 28-34 of this Statement shall, to the extent that they are not offset against allowances for uncollectible amounts or other valuation accounts, be included in measuring net income for the period of restructuring and reported according to *APB Opinion No. 30*. Although this Statement does not address questions concerning estimating uncollectible amounts or accounting for the related valuation allowance (paragraph 1), it recognizes that creditors use allowances for uncollectible amounts. Thus, a loss from reducing the recorded investment in a receivable may have been recognized before the restructuring by deducting an estimate of uncollectible amounts in measuring net income and increasing an appropriate valuation allowance. If so, a reduction in the recorded investment in the receivable in a troubled debt restructuring is a deduction from the valuation allowance rather than a loss in measuring net income for the period of restructuring. A valuation allowance can also be used to recognize a loss determined by applying paragraphs 28-34 that has not been previously recognized in measuring net income. For example, a creditor with an allowance for uncollectible amounts pertaining to a group of receivables that includes the restructured receivable may deduct from the allowance the reduction of recorded investment in the restructured receivable and recognize the loss in measuring net income for the period of restructuring by estimating the appropriate allowance for remaining receivables, including the restructured receivable.

36. If a troubled debt restructuring involves amounts contingently receivable, those contingent amounts shall not be recognized as interest income in future periods before they become receivable—that is, they shall not be recognized as interest income before both the contingency has been removed and the interest has been earned.[24] Before recognizing those amounts as interest income, however, they shall be deducted from the recorded investment in the restructured receivable to the extent that contingent receipts included in "total future cash receipts specified by the new terms" avoided recognition of a loss at the time of restructuring (paragraph 32).

37. If amounts of future cash receipts must be estimated to apply the provisions of paragraphs 30-32 because future interest receipts are expected to

---

[22]Even if the stated terms of the remaining receivable, for example, the stated interest rate and the maturity date or dates, are not changed in connection with the receipt of assets (including an equity interest in the debtor), the restructuring shall be accounted for as prescribed by paragraph 33.

[23]If cash is received in a partial satisfaction of a receivable, the recorded investment in the receivable shall be reduced by the amount of cash received.

[24]*FASB Statement No. 5*, paragraph 17 (which continued without reconsideration certain provisions of *ARB No. 50*, "Contingencies"), states, in part: "Contingencies that might result in gains usually are not reflected in the accounts since to do so might be to recognize revenue prior to its realization."

fluctuate—for example, the restructured terms may specify the stated interest rate to be the prime interest rate increased by a specified amount or proportion—estimates of the minimum total future receipts shall be based on the interest rate in effect at the time of restructuring. Fluctuations in the effective interest rate after the restructuring from changes in the prime rate or other causes shall be accounted for as changes in estimates in the periods the changes occur except that a creditor shall recognize a loss and reduce the recorded investment in a restructured receivable if the interest rate decreases to an extent that the minimum total future cash receipts determined using that interest rate fall below the recorded investment in the receivable at that time.

38. Legal fees and other direct costs incurred by a creditor to effect a troubled debt restructuring shall be included in expense when incurred.

39. A receivable from the sale of assets previously obtained in a troubled debt restructuring shall be accounted for according to *APB Opinion No. 21* regardless of whether the assets were obtained in satisfaction (full or partial) of a receivable to which that Opinion was not intended to apply. A difference, if any, between the amount of the new receivable and the carrying amount of the assets sold is a gain or loss on sale of assets.

Disclosure by Creditors

40. A creditor shall disclose, either in the body of the financial statements or in the accompanying notes, the following information about troubled debt restructurings as of the date of each balance sheet presented:

a. For outstanding receivables whose terms have been modified in troubled debt restructurings, by major category:[25] (i) the aggregate recorded investment; (ii) the gross interest income that would have been recorded in the period then ended if those receivables had been current in accordance with their original terms and had been outstanding throughout the period or since origination, if held for part of the period; and (iii) the amount of interest income on those

receivables that was included in net income for the period. A receivable whose terms have been modified need not be included in that disclosure if, subsequent to restructuring, its effective interest rate (paragraph 30) has been equal to or greater than the rate that the creditor was willing to accept for a new receivable with comparable risk.

b. The amount of commitments, if any, to lend additional funds to debtors owing receivables whose terms have been modified in troubled debt restructurings.

41. A financial institution, or other creditor, may appropriately disclose the information prescribed by paragraph 40, by major category, for the aggregate of outstanding reduced-earning and nonearning receivables rather than separately for outstanding receivables whose terms have been modified in troubled debt restructurings.

Substitution or Addition of Debtors

42. A troubled debt restructuring may involve substituting debt of another business enterprise, individual, or government unit[26] for that of the troubled debtor or adding another debtor (for example, as a joint debtor). That kind of restructuring should be accounted for according to its substance. For example, a restructuring in which, after the restructuring, the substitute or additional debtor controls, is controlled by, or is under common control[27] with the original debtor is an example of one that shall be accounted for by the creditor according to the provisions of paragraphs 30-32. Those paragraphs shall also apply to a restructuring in which the substitute or additional debtor and original debtor are related after the restructuring by an agency, trust, or other relationship that in substance earmarks certain of the original debtor's funds or funds flows for the creditor although payments to the creditor may be made by the substitute or additional debtor. In contrast, a restructuring in which the substitute or additional debtor and the original debtor do not have any of the relationships described above after the restructuring shall be accounted for by the creditor according to the provisions of paragraphs 28 and 33.

---

[25]The appropriate major categories depend on various factors, including the industry or industries in which the creditor is involved. For example, for a commercial banking enterprise, at a minimum, the appropriate categories are investments in debt securities and loans. Information need not be disclosed, however, for non-interest-bearing trade receivables; loans to individuals for household, family, and other personal expenditures; and real estate loans secured by one-to-four family residential properties.

[26]Government units include, but are not limited to, states, counties, townships, municipalities, school districts, authorities, and commissions. See page 4 of *AICPA Industry Audit Guide*, "Audits of State and Local Governmental Units."

[27]"Control" in this paragraph has the meaning described in paragraph 3(c) of *APB Opinion No. 18*, "The Equity Method of Accounting for Investments in Common Stock": "The usual condition for control is ownership of a majority (over 50%) of the outstanding voting stock. The power to control may also exist with a lesser percentage of ownership, for example, by contract, lease, agreement with other stockholders or by court decree."

Effective Date and Transition

43. The preceding paragraphs of this Statement, other than paragraphs 39-41, shall be effective for troubled debt restructurings consummated after December 31, 1977.[28] Earlier application is encouraged for those consummated on or before December 31, 1977 but during fiscal years for which annual financial statements have not previously been issued. The paragraphs shall not be applied to those consummated during fiscal years for which annual financial statements have previously been issued.

44. Paragraph 39 shall be effective for receivables resulting from sales of assets after December 31, 1977 regardless of whether the provisions of this Statement were applied to the related troubled debt restructuring. Earlier application is encouraged for receivables from sales of assets on or before December 31, 1977 but during fiscal years for which annual financial statements have not previously been issued. It shall not be applied to those from sales of assets during fiscal years for which annual financial statements have previously been issued.

45. The information prescribed by paragraphs 40 and 41 shall be disclosed in financial statements for fiscal years ending after December 15, 1977. Earlier application is encouraged in financial statements for fiscal years ending before December 16, 1977. For the purpose of applying paragraph 40, "receivables whose terms have been modified in troubled debt restructurings" shall encompass not only (a) receivables whose terms have been modified in troubled debt restructurings to which the other provisions of this Statement have been applied in accordance with paragraph 43 but also (b) those whose terms have been modified in earlier restructurings that constitute troubled debt restructurings (paragraphs 2-8) but have been excluded from its other provisions because of the timing of the restructurings.

> **The provisions of this Statement need not be applied to immaterial items.**

This Statement was adopted by the affirmative votes of five members of the Financial Accounting Standards Board. Messrs. Gellein and Kirk dissented.

Messrs. Kirk and Gellein dissent because they disagree with the conclusions in paragraphs 16 and 30 (which are also in paragraphs 19 and 33) about prospective treatment of the effect of a reduction of the face amount or maturity amount of debt. They would apply the fair value accounting required in paragraphs 13, 15, and 28 to reductions in the face amount of restructured debt. They point to the incontrovertible fact that a modification of terms that reduces the face amount or interest rate or extends the maturity date, without equivalent consideration, is a relinquishment of rights by the creditor and a corresponding benefit to the debtor, and note that debtors and creditors currently record a reduction in face amount when it occurs. They believe that this Statement takes a backward step in reversing, for the sake of consistency, the practice of current recognition, though not based on fair value. They do not accept the argument implicit in paragraphs 140-144, especially paragraph 144, that consistency in accounting for various modifications of terms should govern. They find no virtue in theoretical consistency if it means now ignoring a substantive consequence of an event—in this case relinquishment of rights—that prior to the issuance of this Statement was being recognized. Messrs. Kirk and Gellein accept prospective recognition of the relinquishment by the creditor and the contra benefit to the debtor associated with interest rate reductions and extensions of maturity dates pending further consideration of other aspects of accounting for interest.

Messrs. Kirk and Gellein believe that their proposal to apply fair value accounting (required in paragraphs 13, 15, and 28 of this Statement) to reduction in the face amount would eliminate a significant difference between the accounting required by this Statement and that required by *APB Opinion No. 26* for debt exchanges that involve changes in the face amount. They also believe that their proposal would result in a more conventional and understandable measure of gain or loss than that which results from the application of paragraphs 17, 19, 31, and 33. They believe that in situations considered to be recordable events, any gain or loss should be determined by comparing fair value, not an undiscounted amount of future cash flows, with previously recorded amounts.

Messrs. Kirk and Gellein also dissent because of disagreement with the guidelines in paragraph 42 for determining when a restructuring that involves a substitution of debtors is a recordable event. First, they believe that from the viewpoint of the creditor, there is no significant difference between a change from the original debtor to one under or to one not under the same control as the original debtor. To the

---

[28]For an enterprise having a fiscal year of 52 or 53 weeks ending in the last seven days in December or the first seven days in January, references to December 31, 1977 in paragraphs 43 and 44 shall mean the date in December 1977 or January 1978 on which the fiscal year ends.

creditor both are changes to a new and different credit risk that should be accounted for in the same way. Second, they believe the guideline in that paragraph concerning a substitute debtor and original debtor who are "related after the restructuring by an agency, trust, or other relationship that in substance earmarks certain of the original debtor's funds or funds flows for the creditor although payments to the creditor may be made by the substitute . . . debtor," is an unworkable criterion and is irrelevant if the right, or asset that gives rise to those funds flows, is irrevocably transferred. In the latter event, from the creditor's viewpoint, the transfer changes the risk and, in effect, results in a different asset—similar in substance to that described in paragraph 28. Further, they find insufficient guidance about the kind of relationship between the parties intended to govern. As an example, they disagree with the interpretation of that guideline in paragraph 161 where recent exchanges of bonds of the Municipal Assistance Corporation (the Corporation) for notes of the City of New York (the City) are noted as examples of debt substitutions whose substance to

creditors is modification of terms of an existing receivable rather than an acquisition of a new asset. They believe the relationship in that case goes beyond that of an agency, trust, or other relationship that earmarks funds. They note that the Corporation is a corporate governmental agency and an instrumentality of the State of New York (the State), not the City; that bonds of the Corporation do not constitute an enforceable obligation, or a debt, of either the State or the City and neither the State nor the City shall be liable thereon; and that neither the faith and credit nor the taxing power of the State or City is pledged to the payment of principal of or interest on the bonds. They note, too, that the Corporation is empowered to issue and sell bonds and notes and to pay or lend funds received from such sale to the City and to exchange the Corporation's obligations for obligations of the City. Those characteristics in their minds establish sufficient independence of the Corporation from the City to take the exchanges out from under the guidelines of paragraph 42.

Members of the Financial Accounting Standards Board:

Marshall S. Armstrong,	Donald J. Kirk	Robert T. Sprouse
Chairman	Arthur L. Litke	Ralph E. Walters
Oscar S. Gellein	Robert E. Mays	

Appendix A

BACKGROUND INFORMATION

46. There has been a substantial increase in recent years in the number of debtors that are unable to meet their obligations on outstanding debt because of financial difficulties. Sometimes the debtor and the creditor have restructured the debt to enable the debtor to avoid bankruptcy proceedings or other consequences of default, and the number of troubled debt restructurings receiving publicity has also increased. Although many of the most publicized troubled debt restructurings have involved debtors that are real estate companies or real estate investment trusts, debtors in other industries have also been involved in troubled debt restructurings.

47. *APB Opinion No. 26,* "Early Extinguishment of Debt," established the accounting by a debtor for debt extinguished before its scheduled maturity. A number of commentators have observed, however, that not all troubled debt restructurings are "extinguishments" as that term is used in *APB Opinion No. 26.* Also, since many troubled debt restructurings have occurred on or after the scheduled maturity of the debt, questions have arisen about accounting for debt restructurings that are not early extinguishments. It has been suggested that troubled

debt restructurings should be considered separately from restructurings, including early extinguishments, that do not involve the economic or legal pressure to restructure on the creditor that characterizes troubled debt restructurings.

48. Concern over the lack of guidance in the authoritative literature on accounting for troubled debt restructurings, accentuated by their increasing number, led to requests that the Financial Accounting Standards Board consider the matter. The Board submitted the question to the Screening Committee on Emerging Problems and weighed its recommendations in deciding to proceed with a project limited in scope to accounting and reporting by a debtor whose debt is restructured in a troubled loan situation. The Board issued an Exposure Draft of a Proposed Statement, "Restructuring of Debt in a Troubled Loan Situation," dated November 7, 1975, and held a public hearing on December 12, 1975. The Board received 63 written responses to the Exposure Draft and heard five oral presentations at the public hearing. A number of respondents objected to the accounting prescribed by the Exposure Draft, but they held divergent views about the appropriate accounting. Major issues of concern centered on (a) whether certain kinds of troubled debt restructurings require reductions of carrying amounts of debt, (b) if they do, whether the effect of the reduction should be included in measuring

current net income, be deferred, or be considered a contribution to capital, and (c) whether interest that is contingently payable on restructured debt should be recognized before it becomes payable.

49. During the same period, uncertainties arose about the abilities of some state and local government units to pay their obligations when due. Some of those obligations have also been restructured, for example, by continuing the existing obligation for a designated period at a reduced interest rate or by substituting obligations with later maturities of the same or a related issuer. Questions about accounting and reporting by creditors for those restructured securities led various individuals and organizations to urge the Board to consider that matter.

50. The Board considered (a) the lack of authoritative guidance and divergent views about accounting and reporting by debtors for troubled debt restructurings and by creditors for restructured securities of state and local government units and (b) the similarities of the issues for debtors and creditors and concluded that the accounting and reporting issues affecting both debtors and creditors should be considered in a single project. The Board therefore announced on January 7, 1976, that it had added to its agenda a project to determine accounting and reporting by both debtors and creditors. At the same time the Board announced that since the new project concerned accounting by both debtors and creditors, the Board would not issue a Statement covering the limited topic of the November 7, 1975 Exposure Draft.

51. The Securities and Exchange Commission issued, also on January 7, 1976, *Accounting Series Release No. 188,* "Interpretive Statement by the Commission on Disclosure by Registrants of Hold-

ings of Securities of New York City and Accounting for Securities Subject to Exchange Offer and Moratorium." The Commission did not require a particular accounting method because of the divergent views on accounting for the securities held and "the fact that the Financial Accounting Standards Board has agreed to undertake a study of the accounting problems . . . with the intention of developing standards which can be applied to year-end statements in 1976."

52. The Board appointed a task force in January 1976 to provide counsel in preparing a Discussion Memorandum. Its sixteen members included individuals from academe, the financial community, industry, law, and public accounting. The Board issued a Discussion Memorandum, "Accounting by Debtors and Creditors When Debt Is Restructured," dated May 11, 1976, comprehending accounting and reporting by debtors and creditors for "any change in the amount or timing of cash payments otherwise required under the terms of the debt at the date of restructuring." It received 894 written responses to the Discussion Memorandum and heard 37 oral presentations at a public hearing on July 27-30, 1976.

53. In addition, the FASB staff reviewed the accounting and reporting practices of a number of debtors and creditors involved in troubled debt restructurings and interviewed a limited number of individuals who were directly associated with some of those restructurings.

54. The Board issued an Exposure Draft of a proposed Statement on "Accounting by Debtors and Creditors for Troubled Debt Restructurings," dated December 30, 1976. It received 96 letters of comment on the Exposure Draft.

Appendix B

BASIS FOR CONCLUSIONS

CONTENTS

BASIS FOR CONCLUSIONS

55. This Appendix discusses factors deemed significant by members of the Board in reaching the conclusions in this Statement, including various alternatives considered and reasons for accepting some and rejecting others.

SCOPE OF THIS STATEMENT

56. Paragraph 1 states that this Statement establishes standards of financial accounting and reporting by the debtor and by the creditor for a troubled debt restructuring. In contrast, the Discussion Memorandum comprehended all restructurings that changed "the amount or timing of cash payments otherwise required under the terms of the debt at the date of the restructuring." The broader scope of the Discussion Memorandum, which encompassed nontroubled as well as troubled debt restructurings, was due to several factors. The Board considered it necessary to obtain additional information about accounting practices and problems for both troubled and nontroubled debt restructurings. Some respondents to the November 7, 1975 Exposure Draft of a Proposed Statement, "Restructuring of Debt in a Troubled Loan Situation," expressed concern that to apply its guidelines for identifying troubled loan situations would require considerable judgment. Some Task Force members and other commentators advised the Board to comprehend all restructurings accomplished by exchanges of debt for debt or of equity securities for debt that may not be covered by *APB Opinion No. 26*.[29]

---

[29]See paragraph 47 of this Statement.

57. Most respondents to the Discussion Memorandum that commented on the matter, however, recommended that a Statement at this time should be limited to accounting for troubled debt restructurings. Numerous respondents indicated that restructurings of debt in nontroubled situations present no significant or unusual accounting problems that merit consideration or require new accounting and reporting standards. Many respondents contended that the kinds of major changes that might result from new standards on accounting for all restructurings should be deferred pending progress on the FASB's existing projects on accounting for interest costs and the conceptual framework for financial accounting and reporting. Some respondents argued that a useful distinction between troubled and nontroubled restructurings of debt can be made and that the need to use judgment in some circumstances should not be a deterrent to making that distinction in a Statement. A number of respondents to the Exposure Draft[30] made similar comments.

58. The Board found persuasive the views described in the preceding paragraph and decided to limit the scope of this Statement to troubled debt restructurings. The Board also decided that conclusions in this Statement should not attempt to anticipate results of considering the issues in its Discussion Memorandum, "Conceptual Framework for Financial Accounting and Reporting: Elements of Financial Statements and Their Measurement," dated December 2, 1976. Rather, the Board believes that, to the extent possible, the accounting for troubled debt restructurings prescribed in this Statement should be consistent and compatible with the existing accounting framework.

59. Paragraph 1 also states that the Statement does not establish standards of financial accounting and reporting for allowances for uncollectible amounts and does not prescribe or proscribe particular methods for estimating amounts of uncollectible receivables. Several respondents to the Exposure Draft urged the Board to adopt the method of accounting for uncollectible amounts based on the net realizable value of collateral property set forth in *Statement of Position 75-2*, "Accounting Practices of Real Estate Investment Trusts," issued June 27, 1975 by the Accounting Standards Division of the American Institute of Certified Public Accountants. Others noted potential conflicts between the Exposure Draft and the AICPA publication and requested clarification. Still others urged the Board to reject the method for estimating amounts of uncollectible receivables in *Statement of Position 75-2*.

60. Since this Statement neither prescribes nor proscribes particular methods for estimating uncollectible amounts of receivables, it takes no position on whether the net realizable value of collateral is a proper basis for estimating allowances for uncollectible amounts of receivables. However, the accounting prescribed in this Statement for assets received in troubled debt restructurings differs from that in *Statement of Position 75-2*, for reasons given in paragraphs 65-105, and the accounting prescribed in this Statement governs.

61. Paragraphs 2-8 identify debt restructurings that fall within the scope of this Statement. This paragraph and the next are intended to clarify further the meaning of *troubled debt restructuring* for purposes of this Statement. The description of a troubled debt restructuring is based generally on that in the November 7, 1975 Exposure Draft, which many respondents to that Exposure Draft and the Discussion Memorandum found satisfactory. It focuses on the economic and legal considerations related to the debtor's financial difficulties that in effect compel the creditor to restructure a receivable in ways more favorable to the debtor than the creditor would otherwise consider. The creditor participates in a troubled debt restructuring because it no longer expects its investment in the receivable to earn the rate of return expected at the time of investment and may view loss of all or part of the investment to be likely unless the receivable is restructured. Thus, a troubled debt restructuring involves a receivable whose risk to the creditor has greatly increased since its acquisition, and if the creditor were not faced with the need to restructure to protect itself, it would require a much higher effective interest rate to invest in the same receivable currently. If the receivable has a market price, the effective interest rate based on that market price will have increased because of that increased risk to the creditor—that is, it will have increased more than market interest rates generally (or fallen less than market rates or increased while interest rates generally have fallen).

62. Although the broad description of a troubled debt restructuring in paragraphs 2-8 includes settlements of debt by transfers of assets and grants of equity interests in debtors, *troubled debt restructuring* refers in particular to modifications of terms intended to continue an existing debt by making the terms more favorable to the debtor to protect the creditor's investment. For purposes of this Statement, troubled debt restructurings do not include changes in terms resulting in an effective interest rate based on market price of the debt that is comparable to effective interest rates applicable to debt

---

[30]References to "Exposure Draft" in this Appendix are to "Accounting by Debtors and Creditors for Troubled Debt Restructurings," dated December 30, 1976, unless the reference specifically identifies the earlier Exposure Draft, "Restructurings of Debt in a Troubled Loan Situation," dated November 7, 1975.

issued by nontroubled debtors, for example, a situation in which a debtor is able to exchange for its outstanding debt new marketable debt with an effective interest rate at or near the market interest rates for debt issued by nontroubled debtors generally. The fact that the debtor can obtain that interest rate only by including a "sweetener," such as a conversion privilege, does not make that transaction a troubled debt restructuring because (a) the debtor is sufficiently strong financially that the kind of economic compulsion on the creditor described earlier is not present, (b) the "sweetener" represents so drastic a change in the terms of the debt that the transaction is in substance the exchange of new debt for outstanding debt rather than merely a modification of terms to continue an existing debt, or (c) some combination of both factors.

63. Some respondents to the Discussion Memorandum advocated that the scope of this Statement specifically exclude restructurings of receivables related to consumer finance activities or to all or certain residential properties. Their reasons focused primarily on the individual insignificance of those receivables in a creditor's financial position and on the cost involved to account for reductions in recorded investments in large numbers of receivables that may be restructured. The Board concluded that accounting for restructurings of those receivables in troubled situations should in general be the same as for other troubled debt restructurings. However, grouping like items or using statistical measures may be appropriate for receivables that are not individually material.

64. Some respondents to the Exposure Draft suggested that the *time of a troubled debt restructuring* be clarified because several dates or events may be involved. The time may be significant in matters relating to recognizing gains or losses from restructuring or to the effective date of the Statement. Paragraph 6 specifies the time of a restructuring to be the date of consummation, that is, the time that assets are transferred, new terms become effective, and the like. A debtor should not recognize a gain on restructuring before consummation of the restructuring; a creditor should record receipt of an asset or equity interest at that date or should formally write down a restructured receivable, but may already have recognized a loss on restructuring through estimated uncollectible amounts.

DIVERGENT VIEWS OF TROUBLED DEBT RESTRUCTURINGS

65. Respondents to the Discussion Memorandum expressed divergent views about the substance of various types of troubled debt restructurings and appropriate accounting for them within the existing accounting framework. Those views fall generally into three categories:

a. All troubled debt restructurings constitute events that are part of continuing efforts by creditors to recover amounts invested and obtain a return on investment despite debtors' financial difficulties; therefore, troubled debt restructurings may require certain disclosures, but usually do not require changes in carrying amounts of payables or recorded investments in receivables or recognition of gains or losses.

b. All debt restructurings, troubled and nontroubled, constitute transactions whose financial effect on assets or liabilities (receivables or payables) should be recognized, including recognition of gains or losses.

c. Accounting for a troubled debt restructuring depends on the characteristics of the restructuring. Some troubled debt restructurings constitute transactions requiring recognition of changes in receivables or payables and related gains or losses; other troubled debt restructurings do not.

Recognition of Changes Not Appropriate

66. Respondents who contended that troubled debt restructurings constitute events for which recognition of changes in assets or liabilities is usually not appropriate within the existing accounting framework generally focused on accounting by creditors. They reasoned that a troubled debt restructuring commonly involves a concession granted unilaterally by the creditor to increase its prospects of recovering the amount invested. The debtor is usually a passive beneficiary of the effects of the restructuring. Troubled debt restructurings typically result from the debtor's financial difficulties that existed before restructuring, and in the existing accounting framework the creditor should have considered the debtor's financial difficulties in estimating an allowance for uncollectible amounts regardless of whether those difficulties were likely to culminate in a restructuring. According to those respondents, the restructuring event in itself has no accounting significance except to sometimes provide more definitive evidence of the effect of the debtor's financial difficulties on the creditor's ability to recover the recorded investment in the receivable.

67. According to that view, the creditor should record no change in a receivable restructured in a troubled debt restructuring and no gain or loss whether the restructuring involves (i) transfer of receivables, real estate, or other noncash assets from the debtor to the creditor to satisfy the receivable, (ii) grant to the creditor of an equity interest in the debtor to satisfy the receivable, (iii) modification of the terms of the receivable, or (iv) some combina-

tion of transfer of assets or grant of equity interests (or both) and modification of terms. The normal, expected course of events in a creditor's activities is to invest cash, earn interest on the cash invested, and eventually recover the cash. Although a creditor initiates or agrees to a restructuring to protect the amount invested, not to acquire noncash assets, the creditor may accept noncash assets (including an equity interest) as a necessary intermediate step. The creditor previously held a claim on the debtor's assets, either through a receivable secured by specific collateral or through an unsecured general claim against the debtor's assets. Accepting noncash assets in a restructuring represents the exercise of that claim; the assets stand in the place of the receivable. According to that view, the creditor's recorded investment in the receivable should become the recorded investment in the surrogate assets obtained. Then, since whether the creditor recovers that investment depends on the cash received for the assets that replaced the receivable, recoverability of that recorded investment as a result of obtaining the surrogate assets should be assessed. An expected failure, if any, to recover all of the recorded investment should be recognized as a loss by the creditor to the extent not previously recognized. However, transfer of the assets to the creditor should not precipitate recognition of a loss that was not inherent in the receivable before the restructuring; at most, the transfer provides evidence of the existence and amount of a loss.

Recognition of Changes Appropriate for All Debt Restructurings

68. Some respondents advocated for virtually all debt restructurings, troubled and nontroubled, the accounting normally required in the existing accounting framework for initial recognition of assets and liabilities. They reasoned that each restructuring is an exchange resulting in a new asset for the creditor or liability for the debtor in place of the old one. According to that view, the presence or absence of financial difficulties does not affect the appropriate accounting for a restructuring; at most, a debtor's financial difficulties may affect the terms of the exchange. Those respondents contended that all assets and liabilities exchanged in debt restructurings should be measured at their fair values at the time of the restructuring by both debtors and creditors. They considered continued use of recorded amounts derived from previous exchange transactions to be inappropriate for restructured receivables and payables because it ignores a current exchange transaction and may ignore gains or losses that have occurred and should be recognized.

Accounting Depends on Circumstances

69. Some respondents contended that the control-

ling criterion in determining appropriate accounting for a debt restructuring within the existing accounting framework is whether the restructuring involves transfer of resources, obligations, or both between debtor and creditor. According to that view, a troubled debt restructuring involving transfer of resources, obligations, or both should be accounted for the same as other transfers of resources and obligations in the existing accounting framework and may involve recognizing a gain or loss. A troubled debt restructuring involving no transfer of resources or obligations requires no accounting for changes in assets or liabilities, except to recognize losses in accordance with *FASB Statement No. 5.*

70. Some respondents distinguished debt restructurings involving transfers of resources, obligations, or both from those involving no transfers on the basis of whether the debtor transferred assets or granted an equity interest to the creditor to satisfy the debt or the restructuring involved modification of terms only. Other respondents classified modifications of terms involving reduction of face amount of the debt with transfers of assets or grants of equity interests (discussed further in paragraphs 106-155).

Board Conclusions about Recognizing Changes in Assets or Liabilities

71. *APB Statement No. 4,* "Basic Concepts and Accounting Principles Underlying Financial Statements of Business Enterprises," describes relevant parts of the existing accounting framework. That Statement defines "economic resources" as "the scarce means (limited in supply relative to desired uses) available for carrying on economic activities" and identifies "claims to receive money" as an economic resource. It defines "economic obligations" as "present responsibilities to transfer economic resources or provide services to other entities in the future" and identifies "obligations to pay money" as an economic obligation. It also states that "events that change resources, obligations, and residual interest are the basis for the basic elements of results of operations . . . and other changes in financial position with which financial accounting is concerned." (See *APB Statement No. 4,* paragraphs 57, 58, and 61.)

72. According to *APB Statement No. 4,* almost all of the events that in the existing accounting framework normally change assets and liabilities and also affect net income for the period of change are either "exchanges" or "nonreciprocal transfers," the two classes that comprise "transfers of resources or obligations to or from other entities." The other classes of events—"external events other than transfers of resources or obligations to or from other entities" (price changes, interest rate changes, technological

changes, vandalism, etc.) and "internal events" (production and casualties)—result in revenues or gains only through "exceptions" and result in expenses or losses only because some produce losses by definition or by applying the "modifying convention" of conservatism. (See *APB Statement No. 4*, paragraphs 62 and 180-187.)

73. An exchange is a reciprocal transfer between the enterprise and another entity in which "the enterprise either sacrifices resources or incurs obligations in order to obtain other resources or satisfy other obligations." "Exchanges between the enterprise and other entities (enterprises or individuals) are generally recorded in financial accounting when the transfer of resources or obligations takes place or services are provided." Nonreciprocal transfers are "transfers in one direction of resources or obligations, either from the enterprise to other entities or from other entities to the enterprise." In nonreciprocal transfers between the enterprise and entities other than owners, "one of the two entities is often passive, a mere beneficiary or victim of the other's actions." Nonreciprocal transfers between the enterprise and entities other than owners "are recorded when assets are acquired (except that some noncash assets received as gifts are not recorded), when assets are disposed of or their loss is discovered, or when liabilities come into existence or are discovered." (See *APB Statement No. 4*, paragraphs 62, 181, and 182.)

74. The Board rejected the view that virtually all troubled debt restructurings have the same substance in the existing accounting framework. It therefore rejected both the view that accounting for all troubled debt restructurings should involve recognition of changes in assets or liabilities and perhaps gains and losses and the view that no troubled debt restructurings should require recognition of changes in assets or liabilities or gains or losses.

75. The Board concluded that a troubled debt restructuring that involves transfer of resources or obligations requires accounting for the resources or obligations transferred whether that restructuring involves an exchange transaction or a nonreciprocal transfer. Both kinds of transfers are accounted for in the existing accounting framework on essentially the same basis (exchange price received or paid or fair value received or given). In this Statement, therefore, the Board found it unnecessary to decide whether the transfer of resources and obligations in various types of troubled debt restructurings is reciprocal (an exchange) or nonreciprocal as those terms are used in paragraph 62 of *APB Statement No. 4*.

76. The Board also concluded that a troubled debt

restructuring that does not involve a transfer of resources or obligations is a continuation of an existing debt. It is neither an event that results in a new asset or liability for accounting purposes nor an event that requires a new measurement of an existing asset or liability.

77. The Board noted that guidance regarding the types of troubled debt restructurings that involve transfers of resources, obligations, or both is sparse in existing accounting pronouncements, and various views exist. The Board concluded that to the extent a troubled debt restructuring involves (i) transfer of receivables, real estate, or other assets from debtor to creditor to satisfy debt or (ii) grant to the creditor of an equity interest in the debtor to satisfy debt (or a combination of both), a transfer of resources or obligations has occurred that in the existing accounting framework should be accounted for at fair value. The debtor has given up assets or granted an equity interest to settle a payable, and the creditor has received the assets or equity interest in satisfaction of a receivable. In contrast, to the extent a troubled debt restructuring involves only modification of terms of continuing debt, no transfer of resources or obligations has occurred. The substance of troubled debt restructurings involving modifications of continuing debt is discussed in paragraphs 106-155.

78. Several respondents to the Exposure Draft disagreed with the Board's distinction between troubled debt restructurings involving transfers of assets or grants of equity interests in debtors and those involving only modifications of terms. Some respondents wished to have fewer kinds of troubled debt restructurings accounted for as transactions between debtors and creditors and thus disagreed with the Exposure Draft's conclusions on accounting for transfers of assets; their views are noted in the next section. Others wished to account for more kinds of troubled debt restructurings as transactions between debtors and creditors and thus disagreed with the Exposure Draft's conclusions on accounting for modifications of terms; their views are noted in paragraphs 150-153.

ACCOUNTING FOR RESTRUCTURINGS INVOLVING TRANSFERS

Accounting by Debtors and Creditors for Transfer of Assets

Concept of Fair Value

79. Some respondents to the Exposure Draft continued to argue that all troubled debt restructurings should be accounted for as modifications of terms of debt and that none should be accounted for as

transfers of assets (paragraphs 66 and 67). Others accepted the need to account for some troubled debt restructurings as asset transfers but held that obtaining assets through foreclosure or repossession under terms included in lending agreements should be distinguished from obtaining assets in exchange for cash or in other "asset swaps." They contended that (a) only the form of the asset is changed by foreclosure or repossession, (b) the substance of a secured loan is that the lender may choose either to postpone receipt of cash or take the asset to optimize cash receipts and recovery of its investment, and (c) foreclosure or repossession is not the completion of a lending transaction but merely a step in the transaction that begins with lending cash and ends with collecting cash.

80. The Board rejected those arguments for the reasons given in paragraphs 71-77, emphasizing that an event in which (a) an asset is transferred between debtor and creditor, (b) the creditor relinquishes all or part of its claim against the debtor, and (c) the debtor is absolved of all or part of its obligation to the creditor is the kind of event that is the basis of accounting under the existing transaction-based accounting framework. To fail to recognize an event that fits the usual description of a transaction and to recognize only the lending and collection of cash as transactions would significantly change the existing accounting framework.

81. Use of the fair value of an asset transferred to measure the debtor's gain on restructuring and gain or loss on the asset's disposal or the creditor's cost of acquisition is not adopting some kind of "current value accounting." On the contrary, that use of fair value is common practice within the existing accounting framework. Paragraph 13 of this Statement explains briefly the meaning of *fair value* and refers to *APB Opinions No. 16, No. 21,* and *No. 29,* which use *fair value* in the same way and provide guidance about determining fair values within the existing accounting framework. The term *fair value* is used in essentially the same way as *market value* was used in the Discussion Memorandum to denote a possible attribute to be measured at the time a debt is restructured. *Fair value* is defined in paragraph 181 of *APB Statement No. 4* as "the approximation of exchange price in transfers in which money or money claims are not involved." Although a "money claim" is necessarily involved in transferring assets to settle a payable in a troubled debt restructuring, the troubled circumstances in which the transfer occurs make it obvious that the amount of the "money claim" does not establish an exchange price. Determining the fair value of the assets transferred in a troubled debt restructuring is usually necessary to approximate an exchange price

for the same reasons that determining fair value is necessary to account for transfers of assets in nonmonetary transactions (*APB Opinion No. 29*).

82. That point is emphasized in this Appendix because some respondents to the Exposure Draft apparently misunderstood the concept of fair value (paragraph 11 of the Exposure Draft and paragraph 13 of this Statement) and the discounting of expected cash flows specified in those paragraphs. Paragraph 13 permits discounting of expected cash flows from an asset transferred or received in a troubled debt restructuring to be used to estimate fair value only if no market prices are available either for the asset or for similar assets. The sole purpose of discounting cash flows in that paragraph is to estimate a current market price as if the asset were being sold by the debtor to the creditor for cash. That estimated market price provides the equivalent of a sale price on which the debtor can base measurement of a gain on restructuring and a gain or loss on disposal of the asset and the equivalent of a purchase price on which the creditor can measure the acquisition cost of the asset. To approximate a market price, the estimate of fair value should use cash flows and discounting in the same way the marketplace does to set prices—in essence, the marketplace discounts expected future cash flows from a particular asset "at a rate commensurate with the risk involved" in holding the asset. An individual assessment of expected cash flows and risk may differ from what the marketplace's assessment would be, but the procedure is the same.

83. In contrast to the purpose of paragraph 13, *AICPA Statement of Position No. 75-2*[31] is concerned with different measures—net realizable value to a creditor of a receivable secured by real property and net realizable value of repossessed or foreclosed property. Its method of accounting for assets obtained by foreclosure or repossession thus differs from the method specified in this Statement. It proposes discounting expected cash flows at a rate based on the creditor's "cost of money" to measure the "holding cost" of the asset until its realizable value is collected in cash. The concept of fair value in paragraph 13 does not involve questions of whether interest is a "holding cost" or "period cost" because it is concerned with estimating market price, not net realizable value, however defined. Accounting for transfers of assets in troubled debt restructurings and for the assets after transfer is, of course, governed by this Statement.

84. Several respondents to the Exposure Draft suggested that the Statement should explicitly state that troubled debt restructurings that are in substance transfers of assets should be accounted for accord-

---

[31]See paragraphs 59 and 60 of this Statement.

ing to that substance. The Board agreed that a restructuring may be in substance a foreclosure, repossession, or other transfer of assets even though formal foreclosure or repossession proceedings are not involved. Thus, the Statement requires accounting for a transfer of assets if, for example, the creditor obtains control or ownership (or substantially all of the benefits and risks incident to ownership) of one or more assets of the debtor and the debtor is wholly or partially relieved of the obligations under the debt, or if both the debt and one or more assets of the debtor are transferred to another debtor that is controlled by the creditor.

Debtor's Recognition of Gain or Loss

85. Responses to the November 7, 1975 Exposure Draft, the May 11, 1976 Discussion Memorandum, and the Exposure Draft included two general procedures for a debtor to account for a gain or loss from a troubled debt restructuring involving a transfer of assets to settle a payable:

a. The debtor recognizes a difference, if any, between the carrying amount of assets transferred and the carrying amoung of the payable settled as a gain on restructuring of a payable.
b. The debtor (1) recognizes a difference, if any, between the fair value and carrying amount of assets transferred as a gain or loss on transfer of assets and (2) recognizes a difference, if any, between the fair value of assets transferred and the carrying amount of the payable settled, as a gain on restructuring of a payable.

86. Some respondents contended that debtors should not recognize the difference between the carrying amount and fair value of assets transferred to settle a payable as a gain or loss on assets. Instead, the net difference, if any, between the carrying amount of assets transferred and the carrying amount of a payable settled should be recognized as a gain or loss on restructuring of a payable. They argued that to measure the fair value of assets transferred would be costly and subjective in certain circumstances and that distinctions in the debtor's income statement between a gain or loss on disposition of assets and a gain on settlement of payables in the same troubled debt restructuring would probably not be helpful and might be arbitrary.

87. Other respondents who addressed the question emphasized the desirability of being able to assess separately the debtor's performance with respect to the transferred assets. They suggested that measuring the fair values of the transferred assets is essential to that assessment and conveys significant information that is obscured if fair values are not measured. For example, the fair values of some assets transferred (such as real estate) may often exceed their carrying amounts, while the fair values of other assets transferred (such as receivables) may sometimes be less than their face amounts. In the existing accounting framework, the first kind of difference is not recognized before disposal of the asset, but the second kind of difference is likely to have been recognized before restructuring by some debtors but not recognized by others for various reasons. Failure to include a gain or loss for the difference between the fair values and carrying amounts of assets transferred in troubled debt restructurings is likely to obscure differences and similarities between restructurings, according to that view, and respondents who advocated separate recognition of a debtor's gains or losses on assets transferred and gains on restructuring argued that separate recognition is required to provide consistent information about a single debtor for different periods and comparable information about different debtors for the same periods. The need for separate recognition is accentuated if gains and losses on transfer of assets are classed differently from gains on restructuring in the debtor's income statement (that is, if the latter are classified as extraordinary items).

88. The Board concluded that the fair value of the assets transferred in a troubled debt restructuring constitutes the best measure of the debtor's sacrifice to settle the payable and therefore that the fair value of assets transferred should be used to measure the gain on restructuring of the payable. In the existing accounting framework, gains, and losses on certain kinds of noncurrent assets, are usually recognized on assets only when the assets are sold or otherwise disposed of. For many assets, that gain or loss on sale or disposal is the only indication of whether the enterprise did well or poorly by having the asset. That indication is lost if the gain or loss on disposition is buried in a gain on restructuring of troubled debt, and the effect of the restructuring itself is also obscured. Further, unless fair value of the asset transferred is used to account for the transaction, the proportion of a payable settled by the transfer can usually be determined only by arbitrary and complicated allocations if the transfer settles only part of the payable and the terms are modified on the remainder (paragraph 19).

89. Since a gain or loss recognized by a debtor on the assets transferred to settle a payable in a troubled debt restructuring is closely related to a gain recognized by a debtor on restructuring of a payable, the Board concluded that the aggregate amount of each should be disclosed for restructurings that have occurred during a period for which financial statements are presented (paragraph 25).

Creditor's Subsequent Accounting

90. The Board considered two proposals for a creditor's accounting for assets received in full satisfaction of a receivable in a troubled debt restructuring: (a) the creditor accounts for the assets received at their fair value and recognizes as a loss a difference, if any, between the total fair value of assets received and the recorded investment in the receivable satisfied or (b) the creditor accounts for the assets received at the recorded investment in the receivable satisfied and recognizes no loss. Those alternatives are described in paragraphs 65-70, and the Board's reasons for adopting the first proposal are given in paragraphs 71-78.

91. Several respondents to the Exposure Draft requested guidance on a creditor's accounting after a troubled debt restructuring for assets received in the restructuring. Some asked the Board to require or permit creditors to accrue interest on all assets acquired through repossession or foreclosure. In response, paragraph 29 states that "after a troubled debt restructuring, a creditor shall account for assets received in satisfaction of a receivable the same as if the assets had been acquired for cash." The fair value at the time of transfer of an asset transferred to a creditor in a troubled debt restructuring is a measure of its cost to the creditor and generally remains its carrying amount (except for depreciation or amortization) until sale or other disposition if the asset is inventory, land, building, equipment, or other nonmonetary asset. That is, under the present accounting framework, interest is accrued only on some receivables and other monetary assets. Except for the effects of a few specialized rules that permit interest cost to be added to the cost of some assets under construction, etc., interest is not accrued on nonmonetary assets. That framework governs accounting for assets acquired in a troubled debt restructuring. The method of accounting for assets received through foreclosure, repossession, or other asset transfer to satisfy a receivable proposed by *Statement of Position 75-2* is not compatible with the accounting specified in this Statement.

Debtor's Accounting for Grant of Equity Interest

92. The Board considered three proposals for a debtor's accounting for an equity interest granted to a creditor to settle a payable in a troubled debt restructuring:

a. The debtor directly increases its owners' equity by the fair value of the equity interest granted[32] and recognizes the difference between that fair value and the carrying amount of the payable settled as a gain included in measuring net income.

b. Same as (a) except that the resulting gain is included directly in the owners' equity of the debtor.

c. The debtor directly increases its owners' equity by the carrying amount of the payable settled, recognizing no gain.

93. Respondents favoring use of fair value to record a grant of an equity interest contended that the increase in the owners' equity of the debtor as a result of a troubled debt restructuring should be measured by the consideration received for the equity interest granted, not by the carrying amount of the payable settled because that carrying amount has no current economic significance. They also contended that a separate measure of a gain on restructuring of payables provides useful information.

94. Among those who advocated use of fair value to record an equity interest granted to settle debt in a troubled debt restructuring and recognition of a resulting gain on restructuring, some advocated including that gain in measuring net income and others advocated including it directly in the debtor's equity accounts. Those favoring inclusion in net income argued that all gains from troubled debt restructurings are components of net income whether they arise from transfer of assets or grant of equity interests. Those favoring direct inclusion in owners' equity argued that, to the extent an equity interest is involved, the restructuring is a capital transaction and gains resulting from capital transactions should be recognized as direct increases in paid-in or contributed owners' equity rather than as components of net income.

95. Those who advocated that the debtor's increase in equity for an equity interest granted should be the carrying amount of the debt settled also argued that granting an equity interest is essentially a capital transaction to which the notion of a gain does not apply. That solution was proposed in the November 7, 1975 Exposure Draft. Advocates of that view noted that paragraph 187 of *APB Statement No. 4* states that, among other sources, increases in owners' equity arise from investments in an enterprise by its owners. According to that view, a creditor that accepts an equity interest in the debtor in satisfaction of a receivable becomes an owner; the debtor's measure of the owners' investment is the carrying amount of the payable settled.

96. After considering the comments received in response to the November 7, 1975 Exposure Draft,

---

[32]"Fair value" in this context normally means the fair value of the liability satisfied or the fair value of the equity interest granted, whichever is the more clearly evident (*APB Opinion No. 16*, paragraph 67 and *APB Statement No. 4*, paragraph 182).

the May 11, 1976 Discussion Memorandum, and the Exposure Draft, the Board concluded that a debtor should record an equity interest in the debtor granted to a creditor to settle a payable in a troubled debt restructuring at its fair value, and the difference between that fair value and the carrying amount of the payable settled should be recognized as a gain in measuring net income. The Board recognizes that, for some debtors involved in troubled debt restructurings, estimating either fair value of the equity interest granted or the fair value of the payable settled may be difficult. That estimate is necessary, however, to measure separately the consideration received for the equity interest and the gain on restructuring. To include the gain on restructuring in contributed equity would violate a clear principle for accounting for issues of stock—capital stock issued is recorded at the fair value of the consideration received (*APB Statement No. 4,* paragraph 182). The consideration received for the stock issued in that kind of troubled debt restructuring is cancellation of the payable (or part of it), but the fair value of the consideration received is not measured by the carrying amount of the payable. Whether the consideration received is measured by the fair value of the stock issued or the fair value of the payable cancelled, the consideration is less than the carrying amount of the payable. To record the stock issued at the carrying amount of the payable thus results in recording the stock at an amount in excess of the consideration received; to include the gain in restructuring in contributed equity instead of net income gives the same result.

97. To recognize a gain on restructuring acknowledges that the creditor accepted something less than the carrying amount of the payable to settle it. Since that is the essential result whether the restructuring is in the form of a transfer of assets from debtor to creditor or the form of a grant to the creditor of an equity interest in the debtor, the Board believes that essentially the same accounting applies in the existing accounting framework to both kinds of restructurings. Although the creditor becomes an owner of the debtor to the extent that the creditor accepts an equity interest in the debtor, that is a consequence of the kind of consideration used to settle a payable in a restructuring. The restructuring itself is an agreement between a debtor and a creditor, and the gain to the debtor results because the creditor accepted less consideration than the carrying amount of the debt.

Classification of Debtor's Gain on Restructuring

98. Alternatives considered by the Board for classifying gain on a troubled debt restructuring in the debtor's financial statements were that the gain is: (a) always included in measuring net income in accordance with *APB Opinion No. 30,* (b) always

included in measuring net income as an extraordinary item, and (c) always included as a direct addition to paid-in capital. Most respondents addressing the question recommended classifying a gain on restructuring debt as an extraordinary item, primarily because they perceived it to be similar to gains or losses on extinguishment of debt that, according to *FASB Statement No. 4,* shall be aggregated and, if material, classified as an extraordinary item, net of related income tax effect. Some respondents recommended classifying the gain as a direct increase in paid-in capital, contending that since the gain results from a unilateral action by the creditor, the debtor has in effect received a contribution to equity from the creditor.

99. The Board concluded that a gain on restructuring (net of related income tax effect), if material, should always be classified as an extraordinary item in measuring the debtor's net income. The Board recognized that to apply the criteria in *APB Opinion No. 30* to a particular debtor's gain on restructuring would not necessarily result in its classification as an extraordinary item. The Board concluded, however, that a gain on restructuring of a payable in a troubled debt restructuring is indistinguishable from a gain or loss on other extinguishments of debt, and the same classification in financial statements is appropriate. Since *FASB Statement No. 4* classifies a gain or loss on extinguishment of debt as an extraordinary item, the classification is appropriate for a gain on restructuring of a payable.

100. Some respondents suggested that "legal fees and other direct costs that a debtor incurs in granting an equity interest to a creditor in a troubled debt restructuring" (paragraph 24) always be included as extraordinary items whether or not the debtor recognizes a gain on restructuring. Issuing equity interests is not an extraordinary event for a business enterprise, however, and related costs are not extraordinary items under any existing authoritative literature. Deducting those costs from the proceeds of issue has been customary practice, and this Statement does not change that custom. But only costs of issuing the equity interest may be accounted for that way. All other direct costs of a troubled debt restructuring are expenses of the period of restructuring but shall be deducted from a gain, if any, on restructuring.

Creditor's Accounting for Loss on Restructuring

101. Some respondents to the Discussion Memorandum, especially financial institutions, indicated that they hold and manage broad groups of earning assets (primarily loans and investments) as portfolios rather than as individual assets. According to them, their primary consideration in making a new loan or investment is to recover the amount

invested, and the rate of return on the amount invested is a secondary consideration. Although one objective is to obtain an appropriate rate of return for the particular credit risk, changes in market conditions and general economic conditions as well as changes affecting the individual asset or debtor may cause the actual return from a loan or investment to vary from that originally anticipated. Therefore, the objective is to maintain a portfolio with an average yield that provides an adequate margin over the cost of funds and that has risk, maturity, marketability, and liquidity characteristics that are appropriate for the particular institution. To achieve that objective, the contractual rate of return required on individual loans and investments must include a factor to offset the probability that some of them will become nonearning assets, some will ultimately recover amounts invested only with difficulty, and some will involve loss of at least a portion of the amounts invested.

102. The financial difficulties of a debtor that lead to a troubled debt restructuring usually require the creditor to consider those difficulties carefully in determining whether to recognize a loss on the existing receivable. Typically, before restructuring occurs, the creditor has determined the need for a related allowance for uncollectible amounts in light of those difficulties. An allowance for uncollectible amounts may have been based on individual receivables, on groups of similar receivables without necessarily attempting to identify particular receivables that may prove uncollectible, or both. The creditor typically has numerous lending transactions and expects loan losses to recur as a consequence of customary and continuing business activities. Almost all respondents who commented on the classification of a creditor's loss on restructuring recommended that the loss be accounted for in a manner consistent with the enterprise's method of accounting for other losses related to its receivables. Usually that involves recognizing specific losses as they are identified and periodically adjusting the allowance for uncollectible amounts based on an assessment of its adequacy for losses not yet specifically identified. Respondents recommended that the net effect of recognizing specific losses and adjusting the valuation allowance be included in measuring net income in accordance with the provisions of *APB Opinion No. 30.*

103. The Board considered the varied frequency and significance for creditors of troubled debt restructurings in the light of the discussion in *APB Opinion No. 30,* and agreed that (a) a creditor should account for a loss from a troubled debt restructuring in the same manner as a creditor's other losses on receivables (that is, as deductions in measuring net income or as reductions of an allowance for uncollectible amounts), and (b) *APB Opin-*

ion No. 30 should apply to losses on restructuring that are included in measuring net income.

Creditor's Sale of Assets Received in Restructuring

104. A creditor whose customary business activities include lending may sell an asset that was previously acquired in a troubled debt restructuring. The consideration received in that sale may be represented, in whole or in part, by a receivable. The Board considered whether a receivable received in that way is exempt from the provisions of *APB Opinion No. 21* because paragraph 3(d) of that Opinion states that, except for one paragraph, the Opinion does not apply to several kinds of receivables or payables or activities, including "the customary cash lending activities and demand or savings deposit activities of financial institutions whose primary business is lending money." Some respondents to the Exposure Draft held that acquiring and disposing of those assets is part of "the customary cash lending activities" of certain financial institutions.

105. The "lending activities" referred to in paragraph 3(d) of *APB Opinion No. 21* are modified by the words "customary" and "cash," and the Board concluded that the sale of an asset, such as real estate, by a financial institution is distinguishable from its customary cash lending activities. The view that the customary cash lending activities of a financial institution include repossession or foreclosure and resale of assets is part of the argument that repossessions and foreclosures are not transactions to be accounted for but merely changes in the form of the asset (paragraphs 66, 67, and 79-84). The Board rejected that contention and also rejected this part of it. *APB Opinion No. 21* focuses primarily on the possible misstatement of the exchange price (sale price or purchase price) in an exchange of a noncash asset for a receivable or payable, with consequent misstatement in the period of the transaction of gain or loss on sale or acquisition cost and misstatement in later periods of interest income or interest expense. The resale of repossessed or foreclosed assets is that kind of transaction and involves the same questions. Accordingly, the Board concluded that a receivable resulting from sale of an asset received in a troubled debt restructuring is covered by that Opinion, including paragraph 12, which prescribes the measurement of a note (receivable) exchanged "for property, goods, or service in a bargained transaction entered into at arm's length."

ACCOUNTING FOR RESTRUCTURINGS INVOLVING MODIFICATION OF TERMS

Background Information

106. A creditor holds a receivable with the expecta-

tion that the future cash receipts, both those designated as interest and those designated as face amount, specified by the terms of the agreement will provide a return of the creditor's investment in that receivable and a return on the investment (interest income).[33] That essential nature of a creditor's investment in a receivable is the same whether the creditor invested cash (for example, a cash loan to a debtor or a cash purchase of debt securities) or exchanged assets or services (for example, a sale of the creditor's services, product, or other assets) for the receivable.

107. Similarly, a debtor expects the future cash payments specified by the terms of a payable to include a cost (interest expense) for the privilege of deferring repayment of funds borrowed or deferring payment for goods or services acquired. The essential nature of a debtor's payable is the same whether the debtor received cash in exchange for the payable (for example, a cash loan or the issue of debt securities for cash) or received other assets or services (for example, a purchase of services, materials, or other assets from the creditor).

108. The difference between the amount a creditor invests in a receivable and the amount it receives from the debtor's payments of interest and face amount is the return on the investment (interest income) for the entire period the receivable is held. Similarly, the difference between the amount a debtor receives and the amount it pays for interest and face amount is the cost of deferring payment (interest expense) for the entire period the payable is outstanding. The question that must be answered to account for a debt (a receivable or payable) and related interest is how that total interest income or expense is to be allocated to the accounting periods comprising the entire period that the receivable is held or the payable is outstanding.

109. That allocation of interest income or expense to periods is normally accomplished in present accounting practices by the interest method, which measures the interest income or expense of each period by applying the effective interest rate implicit in the debt to the amount of the debt at the beginning of the period, assuming that all cash receipts or payments will occur as specified in the agreement. The effective interest rate implicit in the debt may be the same as or different from the interest rate stated in the agreement (the stated interest rate). The effective and stated rates are the same if the amount invested or borrowed equals the face amount; the rates differ if the amount invested or borrowed is greater or less than the face amount.

110. Thus, the recorded investment in a receivable or the carrying amount of a payable, both at the time of the originating transaction and at the beginning of each period comprising the entire period a receivable is held or a payable is outstanding, is the sum of the present values of (a) the amounts of periodic future cash receipts or payments that are designated as interest and (b) the face amount of cash due at maturity, both discounted at the effective interest rate implicit in the debt. If the effective interest rate differs from the stated interest rate, the recorded investment in the receivable or carrying amount of the payable in financial statements is the face amount plus unamortized premium or less unamortized discount, and that amount is used to measure the interest income or expense, as described in the preceding paragraph.

111. Numerous references to and descriptions of the concepts and procedures referred to in paragraphs 108-110 are found in the pronouncements of the Accounting Principles Board and the Financial Accounting Standards Board, for example, on accounting for leases *(FASB Statement No. 13);* accounting for the cost of pension plans *(APB Opinion No. 8);* accounting for interest on receivables and payables *(APB Opinions No. 12* and *No. 21);* accounting for early extinguishment of debt *(APB Opinion No. 26);* recording receivables and payables of a company acquired in a business combination (*APB Opinion No. 16,* paragraphs 87-89); and translating receivables and payables denominated in a foreign currency *(FASB Statement No. 8,* paragraph 39).

112. Pronouncements of the Accounting Principles Board also include several specific statements of broad principle. They include: "The general principles to apply the historical-cost basis of accounting to an acquisition of an asset depend on the nature of the transaction: . . . b. An asset acquired by incurring liabilities is recorded at cost—that is, at the present value of the amounts to be paid" (*APB Opinion No. 16,* paragraph 67); "Conceptually, a liability is measured at the amount of cash to be paid discounted to the time the liability is incurred" (*APB Statement No. 4,* paragraph 181 [M-1C]; and ". . . upon issuance, a bond is valued at (1) the present value of the future coupon interest payments plus (2) the present value of the future principal payments (face amount) . . . discounted at the prevailing market rate of interest . . . at the date of issuance of the debt" and ". . . the difference between the present value and the face amount should be treated as discount or premium and amortized as interest expense or income over the life of

---

[33]The terms of some short-term receivables and payables (for example, trade accounts receivable or payable) may not be expected to result in interest income or interest expense to the creditor or debtor except as it may be implicit in the transaction (for example, implicit in the price of a product sold or purchased on account).

the note in such a way as to result in a constant rate of interest when applied to the amount outstanding at the beginning of any given period. This is the 'interest' method described in and supported by paragraphs 16 and 17 of *APB Opinion No. 12"* (*APB Opinion No. 21,* paragraphs 18 [Appendix] and 15).

Kinds of Modifications and Accounting Issues

113. Agreements between a creditor and a debtor that modify the terms of an existing debt may affect (i) only the *timing* of future cash receipts or payments specified by the agreement—the timing of periodic interest, the maturity date, or both, (ii) only the *amounts* of cash to be received or paid—the amounts of interest, face amount, or both, or (iii) *both* timing and amounts of cash to be received or paid.

114. Two major issues arise in accounting for an existing debt whose terms are modified in a troubled debt restructuring. One issue involves whether to: (a) continue the same recorded investment for the receivable or carrying amount for the payable and recognize the effects of the new terms prospectively as reduced interest income or expense or (b) recognize a loss or gain by changing the recorded amount. The interest method (paragraph 109) is used in both (a) and (b) to allocate interest income or expense to periods between restructuring and maturity, but in general, the implicit annual interest rate will be higher, and the resulting interest income or expense will be larger in each of the remaining periods, if a loss (creditor) or gain (debtor) is recognized at the time of a troubled debt restructuring, as in (b), than if the effects of the new terms are recognized prospectively, as in (a).

115. The other issue involves two related questions: Should the same accounting (either (a) or (b) in paragraph 114) apply both to modifications of *timing* and to modifications of *amounts* to be received or paid under the agreement? And should the same accounting apply both to modifications of *interest* and to modifications of *face amount?* The following paragraphs explain and illustrate those issues and summarize the arguments advanced for various proposed solutions.

116. Modifications of terms that affect only the *timing* of amounts to be received or paid do not change the total amount to be received or paid. However, changes in timing of the amounts to be received or paid on a debt change its present value determined by discounting at the prerestructuring effective interest rate or a current market interest rate or change the effective interest rate needed to

discount the amounts to the prerestructuring present value (recorded investment in receivable or carrying amount of payable) or market value. Modifications that affect only the *amount* of interest or face amount (or both unless they are exactly offsetting) to be received or paid change total amounts as well as present values, effective interest rates, or both. Modifications of *both timing and amount* to be received or paid combine those effects. A hypothetical case illustrates those kinds of modifications and their effects.

117. A creditor holds a receivable calling for receipt of $100 at the end of each year for five more years and receipt of the $1,000 face amount at the end of those five years. The stated interest rate is 10 percent, compounded annually. The recorded investment in the receivable is $1,000, and the effective annual interest rate implicit in the investment is also 10 percent. If all amounts are received as agreed, the creditor will receive total interest income of $500—the difference between the total amount to be received ($1,500) and the recorded investment in the receivable ($1,000)—and the effective interest rate on the $1,000 investment will be 10 percent. However, the terms of the receivable are to be modified in a troubled debt restructuring. The four modifications that follow are examples of the three kinds of modifications described in paragraphs 113 and 116 (change in amount of interest and change in face amount are both illustrated; change in timing of face amount raises no issues different from change in timing of interest and is not illustrated):

1. *Timing of interest only*—Terms modified to defer collection of interest until the receivable matures (a single collection of $500 at the end of five years is substituted for five annual collections at $100).
2. *Amount of interest only*—Terms modified to leave unchanged the timing of interest and the timing and amount of the face amount but reduce the annual interest from $100 to $60.
3. *Amount of face amount only*—Terms modified to leave unchanged the amounts and timing of interest but reduce the face amount to $800 due at the end of five years.
4. *Both timing of interest and amount of face amount*—Terms modified to defer collection of interest until the receivable matures and reduce the face amount to $800 (modifications 1 and 3 combined).

118. The following chart lists several factual observations that can be made about the effects on the creditor's receivable of each of those restructurings. In general, the same observations apply to the debtor's payable.

designating a proportion of the future receipts or payments under the new terms as interest and designating another proportion as face amount. If those designations were to dictate the accounting, a creditor desiring to recognize a loss on restructuring and to recognize higher interest income for later periods could restructure terms in one way, while a creditor desiring to avoid recognizing a loss on restructuring and to recognize lower interest income for later periods could restructure the terms in another way, even though the underlying cash receipts specified by the new terms were the same, both in timing and amount, for both creditors. A creditor desiring to recognize a gain on restructuring could conceivably increase the amount designated as face amount to an amount higher than the present recorded investment and reduce the amounts designated as receipt of interest; a debtor might agree to that arrangement if it were financially troubled at the time of restructuring but expected to be able to pay the higher face amount later.

Change in Face Amount View

126. Some respondents distinguished modifications of face amounts from modifications affecting only amounts or timing of receipts or payments designated as interest or timing of the maturity date. They would neither reduce recorded investment in a receivable or carrying amount of a payable nor recognize loss or gain in a troubled debt restructuring if a modification of terms of a debt changed only the *amounts or timing* of receipts or payments designated as interest or changed the *timing* of receipts or payments designated as face amount. They held, however, that if a troubled debt restructuring *reduces the face amount* of a debt, the creditor should recognize a loss, and the debtor should recognize a gain.[35]

127. To record a modification of terms involving reduction of face amount of a debt, proponents of that view would reduce the recorded investment in the receivable or carrying amount of the payable by the same proportion as the reduction of the face amount and recognize a loss (creditor) or gain (debtor) for that amount. If the restructuring changed the effective interest rate on the remaining recorded investment or carrying amount, they would allocate interest income or expense to the remaining periods between restructuring and maturity using that new effective interest rate. That rate would be implicit in the difference between the new recorded investment in the receivable or carrying amount of the payable and the future cash receipts or payments specified by the new terms. That rate would be higher for a debt whose face amount had

been reduced, and would therefore result in more interest income or expense for those periods, than the rate described in paragraph 121.

128. Respondents who distinguished between modifications of terms that change the face amount of a debt and other kinds of modifications generally agreed with the view expressed in paragraphs 120 and 122 that the existing accounting framework does not recognize losses or gains from events that change the profitability of existing assets but requires a loss to be recognized if the event causes part or all of an investment in an asset to become unrecoverable. Those respondents gave several reasons for concluding that reduction of face amount of a debt in a troubled debt restructuring requires proportionate reduction of the recorded investment in the receivable or carrying amount of the payable and recognition of a resulting loss or gain.

129. Some respondents who favored accounting based on a distinction between modifications of face amount and other modifications argued that to the extent that the face amount of a debt is reduced, the debtor-creditor relationship has been terminated, and the accounting should recognize that termination. In other words, the face amount adjusted by a premium or discount, if any, measured in the market at the time a receivable or payable was created is recognized in the existing accounting framework as an asset for the creditor or liability for the debtor; reducing that face amount therefore reduces an asset or liability proportionately, and the reduction must be recognized. In their view, to the extent the face amount is reduced, a transfer of resources or obligations occurs.

130. Some respondents described the analogy between a creditor's investment in a receivable and an investment in "capital assets" that is noted in paragraph 122 and contended that reductions of face amounts of receivables in troubled debt restructurings are analogous to events that reduce the amount, rather than the future profitability, of capital assets. Both they and the respondents whose view is described in the preceding paragraph held that the act of reducing the face amount showed that the creditor and debtor agreed that the receivable and payable had been decreased.

131. Some respondents contended in effect that accounting for receivables and payables in the existing accounting framework is based on the face amount of a receivable or payable, or perhaps on the face amount plus a premium or minus a discount at the date of acquisition or issue, and a change in the face amount is a change in an asset

---

[35]Some proponents of this view opposed recognizing gains from troubled debt restructurings not involving transfers of assets or grants of equity interests.

(receivable) or liability (payable). They implicitly assumed or concluded that the present value concepts described in the pronouncements noted in paragraphs 111 and 112 did not apply to receivables or payables involved in troubled debt restructurings. Thus, they contended that the distinction between the face amount due at maturity and the amounts designated as interest to be received or paid periodically until maturity is vital in determining proper accounting for a troubled debt restructuring. According to that view, the face amount due at maturity (sometimes referred to as the "principal") is the basis of the recorded investment in a receivable or carrying amount of a payable; that investment or carrying amount does not include the present value of future receipts or payments designated as interest. That is, a creditor or debtor records the face amount (perhaps increased by premium or decreased by discount) when a receivable is obtained or a payable is incurred, and no value is ascribed in the accounts to rights to receive or obligations to pay amounts designated as interest; rather, cash receipts or payments designated as interest are recognized in the accounts only as they become receivable or payable in future periods. Some respondents holding that view added that to record a loss (creditor) or gain (debtor) because future cash receipts or payments designated as interest are modified in a troubled debt restructuring would represent abandonment of the existing historical cost framework and constitute piecemeal implementation of current value accounting.

132. Several respondents who supported the views described in paragraphs 126-131 held that the accounting required by those views is presently used, at least by some financial institutions. Some banker respondents indicated that troubled debt restructurings involving reductions in face amount or "principal" are exceedingly rare, but that most bankers would probably recognize a loss of "principal" in recording one in which their institution was the creditor.

133. Differences between the view that focuses on the effect of a troubled debt restructuring on face amount (paragraphs 126-132) and the view that focuses on its effect on the effective interest rate (paragraphs 120-125) pertain wholly to troubled debt restructurings that reduce the amount designated as face amount. Both views lead to the same accounting for troubled debt restructurings involving other kinds of modification of terms.

Present Value at Prerestructuring Rate View

134. Some respondents contended that accounting for troubled debt restructurings should recognize the revised pattern of cash receipts or payments under the new terms of the restructured debt. That is, they would continue to use the effective interest rate established when the receivable was acquired or payable was incurred and would reduce the recorded investment or carrying amount to the present value of the future cash receipts or payments specified by the new terms.

135. Those respondents in effect supported the accounting proposed in the FASB Exposure Draft, "Restructuring of Debt in a Troubled Loan Situation" (November 7, 1975): a debtor should account for a troubled debt restructuring that involves modification of terms of debt by adjusting the carrying amount of the payable to the present value of the cash payments (both those designated as interest and those designated as face amount) required of the debtor after restructuring, discounted at the prerestructuring effective interest rate, and recognizing a gain on restructuring of the payable equal to the difference, if any, between that present value and the carrying amount of the payable before restructuring (paragraph 6 of that Exposure Draft). Since a troubled debt restructuring almost invariably involves stretching out or deferring the debtor's payments, and may involve reducing amounts due as well, the present value of a restructured payable is almost invariably less than its carrying amount (both are determined by discounting at the same interest rate); a debtor would thus normally recognize a gain on the restructuring. The November 7, 1975 Exposure Draft dealt only with accounting by debtors, but if the counterpart accounting were adopted by creditors, the creditor would normally recognize a loss equal to the difference between its recorded investment in the receivable before restructuring and the present value at the prerestructuring effective interest rate. Interest expense or income in future periods would continue to be based on the prerestructuring interest rate.

136. Some respondents who held the view described in paragraphs 134 and 135 agreed with the view in paragraphs 124 and 125 that no economic basis exists for distinguishing between modifications of face amounts and other kinds of modifications. The major difference between the two views is that the accounting for one view (paragraphs 134 and 135) retains the same effective interest rate as before restructuring and changes the present value of the future cash receipts or payments specified by the new terms, while the other view (paragraphs 124 and 125) retains the same present value as before restructuring (the recorded investment in a receivable or carrying amount of a payable)[36] and changes the effective interest rate for the periods remaining between restructuring and maturity.

---

[36]Unless the restructuring causes the effective interest rate to fall below zero.

Fair Value View

137. Some respondents contended that modifying terms in a troubled debt restructuring results in an exchange of new debt for the previous debt. The new debt should be recorded at its fair value—usually the present value of the future cash receipts or payments specified by the new terms (whether designated as interest or face amount) discounted at the current market rate of interest for receivables or payables with similar terms and risk characteristics. Those respondents contended that every debt restructuring is an exchange transaction (paragraph 68), and they would recognize a loss (creditor) and gain (debtor) to the extent of the difference between the recorded investment in the receivable or carrying amount of the payable before restructuring and the fair value of the receivable or payable after restructuring. Interest income and expense in future periods would be based on the market rate of interest at the time of restructuring.

138. Respondents who supported the view just described agreed that designations of amounts as face amount or interest should not determine whether a loss or gain should be recognized (paragraphs 124 and 125) because only the amounts and timing of cash receipts or payments, and not their names, affect the present value of a receivable or payable. They disagreed with other respondents by contending that the current market interest rate—which gives the fair value of a receivable or payable—should be used because an exchange transaction had occurred.[37]

139. Some of the responding financial analysts indicated a preference for accounting that does not use a current interest rate to determine whether a creditor should recognize a loss in a troubled debt restructuring involving modification of terms. According to them, to use a current interest rate to discount future cash receipts only for receivables that have been restructured would not result in meaningful information about the earning potential of a creditor's entire loan or investment portfolio and might be confusing because receivables that were not restructured would continue to reflect the various historical interest rates at the time of each investment.

Conclusions on Modification of Terms

140. After considering the information received in connection with (i) the Exposure Draft, "Restructuring of Debt in a Troubled Loan Situation" (November 7, 1975), and·the public hearing based on it (paragraph 48), (ii) the Discussion Memoran-

dum, "Accounting By Debtors and Creditors When Debt Is Restructured" (May 11, 1976), and the public hearing based on it (paragraph 52), and (iii) the Exposure Draft, the Board concluded that the substance of all modifications of a debt in a troubled debt restructuring is essentially the same whether they are modifications of timing, modifications of amounts designated as interest, or modifications of amounts designated as face amounts. All of those kinds of modifications affect future cash receipts or payments and therefore affect (a) the creditor's total return on the receivable, its effective interest rate, or both and (b) the debtor's total cost on the payable, its effective interest rate, or both. The Board believes that accounting for restructured debt should be based on the substance of the modifications—the effect on cash flows—not on the labels chosen to describe those cash flows.

141. The Board thus rejected views that modifications involving changes in face amounts should be distinguished from and accounted for differently from modifications involving amounts of future cash receipts or payments designated as interest and modifications involving timing of future cash receipts or payments. The major reason for that rejection is given in the preceding paragraph: the substance of a troubled debt restructuring lies in its effect on the *timing and amounts* of cash receipts or payments due in the future. Whether an amount due at a particular time is described as face amount or interest is of no consequence to either the present value of the receivable or payable or its effective interest rate.

142. The Board considered the views described in paragraphs 129-132 and rejected them to the extent they conflict with the Board's conclusions. In the Board's view, a debtor-creditor relationship is described by the entire agreement between the debtor and creditor and not merely by the face amount of the debt. Changes in that relationship therefore encompass changes in timing and changes in amounts designated as interest as well as changes in an amount designated as face amount. The same reasoning applies to the analogy between debt and investment in "capital assets." A reduction in a troubled debt restructuring of an amount designated as face amount is not, in the Board's view, analogous to the loss or destruction of a portion of a capital asset. Indeed, the economic impact of reducing an amount designated as face amount is essentially the same as that of reducing by the same amount an amount designated as interest that is due at the same time. Thus, although an analogy between investment in a receivable and investment in a capital asset may have merit, an analogy between an amount des-

---

[37]Some respondents contended that the fair value of the receivable or payable after restructuring should be measured by discounting the future cash flows specified by the new terms at the cost of capital to the creditor or debtor, as appropriate.

ignated as the face amount of a receivable and the physical entirety of a capital asset does not.

143. The Board also rejected the view that accounting is based on the face amount or "principal" in the existing accounting framework. That view is not consistent with the weight of the pronouncements noted in paragraphs 111 and 112 to the effect that the recorded investment in a receivable or carrying amount of a payable is the present value of the future cash receipts or payments specified by the terms of the debt discounted at the effective interest rate that is implicit in the debt at its inception. That accounting explicitly excludes from the recorded investment in a receivable or carrying amount of a payable the interest income or expense to be recognized in future periods. The interest method recognizes that interest income or expense as a constant percent (the effective interest rate) of the recorded investment or carrying amount at the beginning of each future period as the interest income or expense becomes receivable or payable. The method is not a "current value method" as that term is generally used in the accounting literature, unless the effective interest rate used to determine present value and interest income or expense each period is the current market interest rate for the period.

144. The Board noted the argument that current practice in some financial institutions is to record losses based on reductions in troubled debt restructurings of amounts designated as face amount. The Board also noted that several respondents indicated that modifications of terms of that kind almost never occur. Presumably, a creditor would generally prefer to alleviate the debtor's cash difficulties by deferring payment of the amount designated as face amount rather than by reducing it because deferring payment preserves a creditor's maximum claim in the event of the debtor's bankruptcy. The Board decided that accounting for reductions in troubled debt restructurings of amounts designated as face amounts, although occurring only rarely, should be made consistent with accounting for other modifications of future cash receipts or payments in troubled debt restructurings and with the accounting pronouncements referred to in paragraphs 111 and 112.

145. The Board also considered the views described in paragraphs 134-139 and rejected them to the extent they conflict with the Board's conclusions. The Board concluded that since a troubled debt restructuring involving modifications of terms of debt does not involve transfers of resources or obligations (paragraph 77), restructured debt should continue to be accounted for in the existing accounting framework, on the basis of the recorded investment in the receivable or carrying amount of the payable before the restructuring. The effective interest rate on that debt should be determined by the relation of the recorded investment in the receivable or carrying amount of the payable and the future cash receipts or payments specified by the new terms of the debt.

146. To introduce the current market interest rate to provide a new measure of the recorded investment in a restructured receivable or carrying amount of a restructured payable is inappropriate in the existing accounting framework in the absence of a transfer of resources or obligations, that is, if only the terms of a debt are modified in a troubled debt restructuring. Moreover, since the new terms are not negotiated on the basis of the current market rates of interest, there is little or no reason to believe that a current market rate of interest applied to the restructured debt reflects the effective return to the creditor or the effective cost to the debtor. On the contrary, the circumstances of a troubled debt restructuring give every reason to believe that, except by coincidence, it does not. Similarly, there is little or no reason to believe that a restructured debt continues to earn or cost the same effective interest rate as before the restructuring. The restructuring reflected the creditor's recognition that its investment in the receivable no longer could earn that rate and that a lower effective rate was inevitable. In other words, the effect of the restructuring was to decrease the effective interest rate on a continuing debt, and the accounting should show that result.

147. The Board found persuasive the arguments that a creditor in a troubled debt restructuring is interested in protecting its unrecovered investment (represented in the accounts by the recorded investment in the receivable) and, if possible, obtaining a return. To the creditor, therefore, the effect of a restructuring that provides for recovery of the investment is to reduce the rate of return (the effective interest rate) between the restructuring and maturity. Similarly, the effect of that kind of restructuring to the debtor is to reduce the cost of credit (the effective interest rate) between the restructuring and maturity.

148. Thus, the Board concluded that no loss (creditor) or gain (debtor) should be recognized in a troubled debt restructuring if the total future cash receipts or payments (whether designated as interest or face amount) specified by the new terms at least equals the recorded investment or carrying amount of the debt before the restructuring. The creditor should reduce the recorded investment in the receivable and recognize a loss and the debtor should reduce the carrying amount of the payable and recognize a gain to the extent that the recorded investment or carrying amount exceeds the total cash receipts or payments specified by the new terms. Some respondents to the Exposure Draft apparently

misunderstood the reason for using *total* future cash receipts or payments to compare with the recorded investment in a receivable or the carrying amount of a payable to determine whether to recognize a loss or gain on restructuring. Some wondered if the failure to discount the future cash flows implied changes in pronouncements that require discounting or de-emphasis or abandonment by the Board of discounting methods. On the contrary, the Statement is based solidly on the need to consider the effect of interest. Indeed, the Board's conclusion is that a troubled debt restructuring affects primarily the effective interest rate and results in no loss or gain as long as the effective rate does not fall below zero. It requires recognition of a loss to prevent the effective rate from falling below zero. The effective interest rate inherent in the unrecovered receivable or unpaid payable and the cash flows specified by the modified terms is then used to recognize interest income or interest expense between restructuring and maturity.

149. The Board also concluded that the fair values of assets transferred or equity interest granted in partial settlement of debt in a troubled debt restructuring should be accounted for the same as a partial cash payment. The recorded investment in the receivable or carrying amount of the payable should be reduced by the amount of cash or fair value transferred, and the remaining receivable or payable should be accounted for the same as a modification of terms. That accounting avoids basing losses or gains on restructuring on arbitrary allocations otherwise required to determine the amount of a receivable satisfied or payable settled by transfer of assets or grant of an equity interest.

150. Several respondents to the Exposure Draft disagreed with its proposed conclusions on accounting for modifications of terms in troubled debt restructurings. One group, which favored accounting for all troubled debt restructurings at fair value as exchanges of debt, criticized the Exposure Draft for failing to recognize losses and gains from decreases in present values of receivables and payables, for being inconsistent with *APB Opinions No. 21* and *No. 26,* and for elevating form over substance. Another group, which agreed with the Exposure Draft except for restructurings in which face amounts of receivables are reduced, criticized it for failing to recognize losses and gains from decreases in face amounts, for changing existing practice, and for elevating form over substance. Both views are discussed individually in earlier paragraphs (126-139) and are there shown to be virtually opposite views to each other, but they have some similarities when compared to the accounting in the Exposure Draft and this Statement.

151. For example, both criticisms of the Exposure Draft noted in the preceding paragraph result from rejection of fundamental conclusions in the Exposure Draft. Thus, respondents who favor accounting for all troubled debt restructurings as exchanges of debt disagreed with the conclusions that "a troubled debt restructuring that does not involve a transfer of resources or obligations is a continuation of an existing debt" and "to the extent that a troubled debt restructuring involves only a modification of terms of continuing debt, no transfer of resources or obligations has occurred" (paragraphs 76 and 77). Respondents with that view presumably saw troubled debt restructurings as of the same essence as exchanges covered by *APB Opinions No. 21* and *No. 26* and found the Exposure Draft inconsistent with those Opinions. If, however, the conclusions quoted earlier in this paragraph are accepted, modifications of terms of continuing debt are different in substance from exchanges of resources or obligations, and the Exposure Draft is consistent with the Opinions.

152. Similarly, some respondents who favor recognizing losses and gains from reducing face amounts in troubled debt restructurings disagreed with the conclusion that "the substance of all modifications of a debt in a troubled debt restructuring is essentially the same whether they are modifications of timing, modifications of amounts designated as interest, or modifications of amounts designated as face amounts" (paragraph 140). That is, they think that financial institutions' customary distinctions between principal and interest have more substance than the effects of modifications on future cash flows, although they admit that changes in practice would be minimal because few troubled debt restructurings involve changes in face amounts (paragraph 144).

153. The fact that elevating form over substance is a criticism common to the arguments of respondents who fundamentally disagreed with the Exposure Draft emphasizes that various views on proper accounting depend on varying perceptions of the substance of modification of terms in a troubled debt restructuring. The preceding paragraphs note three different views of that substance: the view on which the Exposure Draft and this Statement are based and two other views that differ significantly not only from the view adopted but from each other. The Board carefully analyzed all three views before issuing the Exposure Draft and decided on one of them for the reasons stated in paragraphs 106-152.

154. Some respondents who agreed generally with the accounting for modifications of terms specified in the Exposure Draft and some who preferred to recognize debtors' gains and creditors' losses from decreases in face amounts expressed concern that a debtor's prepayment may result in recognizing a

creditor's loss in the wrong period (they are silent about a debtor's gain). That is, if a debtor may prepay a reduced face amount without penalty, total future cash receipts may actually be less than the recorded investment in the receivable even though the total future amounts specified by the restructured terms are at least equal to the recorded investment, and no loss is recognized by the creditor at the time of restructuring under paragraph 16. The loss would be recorded in the period of prepayment rather than the period of restructuring. They propose that a creditor be required to recognize a loss on restructuring in the period of restructuring to the extent that a reduction of face amount is not protected by a prepayment penalty.

155. This Statement does not include that kind of test based on prepayment penalties. The proposed test rests on the assumption that a loss resulting from prepayment necessarily is a loss on restructuring, and that presumption is questionable. At the time of restructuring, the most probable estimate of future cash receipts is usually that the debtor will not prepay, even if there is no prepayment penalty, because (a) prepayment of a debt with a relatively low effective interest rate is to the creditor's advantage, not the debtor's, (b) initiative for prepayment lies wholly with the debtor, and (c) the debtor is clearly unable to prepay at the time of a troubled debt restructuring and may never be able to prepay. If that most probable estimate later proves incorrect, and the debtor does prepay, a change of estimate should be recorded in the period of prepayment.

CREDITOR'S ACCOUNTING FOR SUBSTITUTION OR ADDITION OF DEBTORS

156. A change between the Exposure Draft and this Statement is that the Exposure Draft dealt with substitutions of debtors only if the debtors were government units. Several respondents to the Exposure Draft suggested that the principles developed there applied to substitutions or additions of nongovernment debtors as well.

157. The general principle developed in earlier paragraphs is that the accounting for a troubled debt restructuring depends on its substance. The issues raised if a creditor in a troubled debt restructuring accepts, or is required to accept, a new receivable from a different debtor to replace an existing receivable from a debtor experiencing financial difficulties pertains to the circumstances, if any, in which the substitution or addition is in substance similar to a transfer of assets to satisfy a receivable

and the circumstances, if any, in which that kind of restructuring is in substance similar to a modification of terms only.

158. One view expressed by respondents was that the substitution of a receivable from a different debtor for an existing receivable or the addition of another debtor is always a transaction requiring accounting by the creditor for a new asset at its fair value, recognizing gain or loss to the extent that the fair value of the new asset differs from the recorded investment in the receivable it replaces. To some proponents, that view holds regardless of the relationship between the original debtor and the new debtor.

159. Another view expressed was that the kind of substitution involved in each restructuring must be considered, and the accounting depends on the relationship between the original and new debtors and between the original and new terms.

160. The Board rejected the view that the substitution or addition of a new debtor is always a transaction requiring recognition of a new asset by the creditor. In some troubled debt restructurings, the substitution or addition may be primarily a matter of form while the underlying debtor-creditor relationship, though modified, essentially continues. For example, to enhance the likelihood that the modified terms of a troubled debt restructuring will be fulfilled, a new legal entity may be created to serve as a custodian or trustee to collect designated revenues and disburse the cash received in accordance with the new debt agreement. The role of that new unit may be similar to that of a sinking fund trustee in an untroubled debt situation. The source of the funds required to fulfill the agreement may be the same, but some or all of those funds may be earmarked to meet specific obligations under the agreement. Similarly, if the new debtor controls, is controlled by, or is under common control with the original debtor, the substance of the relationship is not changed. Each troubled debt restructuring involving a substitution or addition of a debtor should be carefully examined to determine whether the substitution or addition is primarily a matter of form to facilitate compliance with modified terms or primarily a matter of substance.

161. The Board considers the exchanges of bonds of the Municipal Assistance Corporation (Corporation) for notes of the City of New York (City) described in recent exchange offers[38] to be examples of troubled debt restructurings whose substance to creditors for accounting purposes is a modification of the terms of an existing receivable rather than an

---

[38]Municipal Assistance Corporation for the City of New York, "Exchange Offer[s] to Holders of Certain Short-Term Notes of the City of New York," November 26, 1975, May 21, 1976, and March 22, 1977.

acquisition of a new asset (receivable). According to those exchange offers:

> The Corporation . . . was created in June 1975 . . . for the purposes of assisting the City in providing essential services to its inhabitants without interruption and in creating investor confidence in the soundness of the obligations of the City. To carry out such purposes, the Corporation is empowered, among other things, to issue and sell bonds and notes and to pay or lend funds received from such sale to the City and to exchange the Corporation's obligations for obligations of the City.[39]

The Board's understanding is that: (a) the Corporation receives its funds to meet debt service requirements and operating expenses from tax allocations from New York State's collections of Sales Taxes imposed by the State within the City, Stock Transfer Taxes, and Per Capita Aid (revenue sources previously available to the City); (b) Tax and Per Capita Aid amounts not allocated to the Corporation for its requirements are available to the City under the terms of the applicable statutes; and (c) the primary purpose in creating the Corporation was to enhance the likelihood that the City's debt will be paid, not to introduce new economic resources and activities.

RELATED MATTERS

162. Several respondents commenting on accounting for contingent future cash payments or receipts indicated a need for some clarification of the accounting described in the Exposure Draft. Accounting for contingent payments or receipts is complicated because it involves four separate situations—(1) accounting by the debtor at the time of restructuring, (2) accounting by the debtor after the time of restructuring, (3) accounting by the creditor at the time of restructuring, and (4) accounting by the creditor after the time of restructuring. It is further complicated because the view of both debtor and creditor shifts between "gain" contingencies and "loss" contingencies as the accounting shifts from the time of restructuring to after the time of restructuring. The accounting in the Exposure Draft and this Statement is governed by the following general principles:

a. Paragraph 17 (gain contingencies) of *FASB Statement No. 5* governs a debtor's accounting for contingent cash payments at the time of restructuring (paragraph 18) and a creditor's accounting for contingent cash receipts after the time of restructuring (paragraph 36). Since gain

contingencies are not recognized until a gain is realized, (1) a *debtor* should not recognize a gain at the time of restructuring that may be offset by future contingent payments, which is equivalent to assuming that contingent future payments will be paid, and (2) a *creditor* should not recognize contingent cash receipts as interest income until they become unconditionally receivable, that is, until both the contingency has been removed and the interest has been earned.
b. Paragraph 8 (loss contingencies) of *FASB Statement No. 5* governs a debtor's accounting for contingent cash payments after the time of restructuring (paragraph 22) and a creditor's accounting for contingent cash receipts at the time of restructuring (paragraph 32). Since two conditions must be met to recognize an estimated loss, (1) a *debtor* should recognize an interest expense and payable for contingent payments when it is probable that a liability has been incurred and the amount can be reasonably estimated, and (2) a *creditor* should recognize a loss unless offsetting contingent cash receipts are probable and the amount can be reasonably estimated. Contingent cash receipts are unlikely to be probable at the time of restructuring.

163. The principles described in the preceding paragraph also apply to other situations in which future cash payments or receipts must be estimated to apply the provisions of the Statement, for example, future interest payments or receipts that are expected to fluctuate because they are based on the prime interest rate or indeterminate total interest payments or receipts because the debt is payable or collectible on demand or becomes payable or collectible on demand after a specified period (paragraphs 18 and 32).

DISCLOSURE

Disclosure by Debtors

164. Most respondents to the Discussion Memorandum commenting on disclosure by debtors for restructurings advocated essentially the disclosure prescribed for gains or losses from extinguishment of debt in *FASB Statement No. 4.* Paragraph 99 gives the Board's reasons for adopting for gains on troubled debt restructurings the guidelines for income statement classification prescribed in that Statement for gains from extinguishment of debt. Since troubled debt restructurings for which gains are recognized and extinguishments of debts thus use the same guidelines for income statement classification and are similar for disclosure purposes, the

---

[39]Municipal Assistance Corporation for the City of New York, "Exchange Offer to Holders of Certain Short-Term Notes of the City of New York," November 26, 1975, p. 15.

Board concluded that the kind of information prescribed in paragraph 9 of *FASB Statement No. 4* is generally appropriate for disclosing troubled debt restructurings involving recognition of gains. Since some of those restructurings involve transfers of assets to creditors to settle payables, the Board believes that it is appropriate also to disclose the aggregate net gain or loss recognized on transfers of assets. However, since several respondents to the Exposure Draft indicated that problems would arise in attempting to determine when a debtor's current difficulties began and perhaps in obtaining amounts of earlier losses, this Statement omits a requirement in the Exposure Draft to disclose also "the aggregate loss, if any, recognized on those assets in earlier periods in connection with the debtor's current financial difficulties."

165. Restructurings not involving recognition of gain or loss at the time of restructuring usually modify the timing, amounts, or both, of interest or face amount the debtor is to pay under the debt's terms (paragraphs 16-18). In the Board's view, the principal changes in terms should be disclosed to permit an understanding of the financial effects of those modifications.

166. Paragraph 26, specifying disclosure of the extent to which inclusion of contingent future cash receipts prevented recognizing a gain on restructuring was added in response to suggestions by respondents to the Exposure Draft. The Board agreed that information would be useful in assessing the relation between future cash payments and future interest expenses of the debtor.

Disclosure by Creditors

167. Most banking and other financial institutions responding to the Discussion Memorandum that commented on disclosure by creditors argued against separate disclosures about restructured receivables. They emphasized that to be the most meaningful to financial statement users information about receivables should disclose the interest rate characteristics of each broad group of earning assets (primarily loan or investment portfolios), by major category. They argued that information limited to receivables that have been restructured would not only be less meaningful than information about entire portfolios of receivables but also could be confusing because the same information is also needed about other receivables, particularly those that are earning no return but have not been restructured (nonearning receivables). Several of those institutions referred to the requirements of the Securities and Exchange Commission and of the banking regulatory agencies, which recently became effective, both concerning disclosure about categories of loan and investment portfolios—including

their maturities, interest rates, and nonearning loans and investments—and the allowance for uncollectible amounts. They indicated that those requirements provide adequate information about the financial effects of restructurings, troubled or nontroubled. Financial analysts responding also recommended disclosure focusing on the characteristics of each broad group of earning assets. They expressed a desire for information about past and expected yields of entire portfolios, by major category, to enable them to make informed judgments about recent and prospective earnings performance.

168. Some respondents to the Discussion Memorandum that are not financial institutions recommended that the Board require information to be disclosed about each significant troubled debt restructuring in the period that it occurs, primarily the terms of the restructuring, gain or loss recognized, if any, and the related income tax effect. Most of those respondents focused on individual receivables rather than on groups of receivables and proposed that debtors and creditors disclose similar information.

169. The Board concluded that the information prescribed by paragraph 40 should be disclosed, by major category, for outstanding receivables whose terms have been modified in troubled debt restructurings. The information may be disclosed either separately for those receivables or as part of the disclosure about reduced-earning and nonearning receivables. The Board believes that the appropriate format for that disclosure depends primarily on the characteristics and number of receivables, including the proportion of those receivables that have reduced earning potential. It believes the argument has merit that the most meaningful disclosure about earnings potential for a financial institution typically should focus on entire portfolios of receivables, by major category, rather than only on receivables that have been restructured in troubled situations, but the Board acknowledges that determining appropriate disclosure for receivables in general is beyond the scope of this Statement. Accordingly, paragraphs 40 and 41 specify types of information that shall be disclosed and permit that information to be provided by major category for the aggregate of outstanding reduced-earning and nonearning receivables, by major category for outstanding receivables whose terms have been modified in troubled debt restructurings, or for each significant outstanding receivable that has been so restructured, depending on the circumstances.

170. This Statement contains three changes from the Exposure Draft concerning disclosure by creditors, all made in response to comments or suggestions from respondents to the Exposure Draft and all in paragraph 40, which was paragraph 34 of the

Exposure Draft: (1) disclosure of information more in conformity with SEC Guides 61 and 3[40] replaces disclosure of the weighted average effective interest rate and the range of maturities, (2) disclosure of the allowance for uncollectible amounts or other valuation allowance applicable to restructured receivables is deleted, and (3) disclosure of a commitment to lend additional funds to debtors owing restructured receivables is added.

171. Disclosure of commitments to lend additional funds was chosen instead of a penalty suggested by some respondents to the Exposure Draft. They expressed concern that a creditor might avoid recognizing a loss under paragraphs 30-32 by restructuring a troubled receivable in a way that the specified future cash receipts exceed the recorded investment in the receivable and then agree to lend funds to the debtor to meet those terms. They proposed that irrevocable commitments to lend to the debtor be included in the creditor's recorded investment to determine whether the creditor should recognize a loss at the time of restructuring. Since that test is equivalent to saying that a creditor must recognize a loss unless the restructured terms provide not only for recovery of the outstanding receivable but also for recovery of future loans to the same debtor (because future cash receipts from future loans are ignored), the test is excessively punitive. The Board decided that disclosure of those commitments is adequate. That disclosure may already be required by paragraphs 18 and 19 of *FASB Statement No. 5,* but paragraph 40(b) makes the disclosure explicit.

172. Some respondents who advocated that the scope of this Statement exclude restructurings of receivables related to consumer financing activities or to all or certain residential properties (paragraph 63) also argued that, if those restructurings were embraced by this Statement, applicable requirements for disclosure would likely be burdensome and not very meaningful to financial statement users. They point out that the accounting, including information normally disclosed in financial statements or in other reports, for those types of receivables has been tailored to fit special characteristics of the receivables, such as large numbers of relatively small balances, interest rates fixed by state law rather than in a fluctuating market, and numerous accounts on which collections are past due. The Board noted the special characteristics of those types of receivables and, since the scope of this Statement does not encompass appropriate disclosure for receivables generally, concluded that para-

graphs 40 and 41 should not necessarily apply to those types of receivables that have been restructured.

ACCOUNTING SYMMETRY BETWEEN DEBTORS AND CREDITORS

173. The Discussion Memorandum contained several questions on whether particular accounting by debtors and creditors should be symmetrical. Most respondents considered a criterion of symmetry between debtors and creditors an insignificant factor in accounting for troubled debt restructurings. Many noted that existing accounting principles for accounting by creditors for receivables after their initial recording and for recognizing losses already differ from those for accounting by debtors for payables and for recognizing gains. Some respondents also noted that differences usually exist between the debtor and creditor in a particular restructuring (for example, differences in the industry or industries in which they are involved, in their financial viability, and in the significance and frequency of that kind of event for them). The accounting for troubled debt restructurings prescribed in this Statement is symmetrical between debtors and creditors in most matters. However, the Board considered the types of differences described above, among other factors, in concluding that different accounting is appropriate for debtors and creditors in matters such as classifying gains or losses recognized at the time of troubled debt restructurings, accounting for contingent interest, and disclosing information about troubled debt restructurings.

EFFECTIVE DATE AND TRANSITION

174. The Board concluded that prospective application of this Statement is appropriate and that the effective dates in paragraphs 43-45 are advisable. In the Board's view, comparability of financial statements would not be greatly enhanced by restating past, nonrecurring troubled debt restructurings. Further, difficulties in retroactive application of the provisions of this Statement include identifying restructurings for which fair values would need to be determined and determining those fair values. A number of enterprises that in recent years have had several restructurings of those types would be unlikely to have information available to restate retroactively.

---

[40]SEC, *Securities Exchange Act of 1934 Release No. 12748,* "Guides for Statistical Disclosure by Bank Holding Companies," August 31, 1976.

Statement of Financial Accounting Standards No. 16
Prior Period Adjustments

STATUS

Issued: June 1977

Effective Date: For fiscal years beginning after October 15, 1977

Affects: Amends APB 9, paragraph 18
Supersedes APB 9, paragraphs 23 and 24
Supersedes APB 20, footnote 9
Amends APB 30, paragraph 25
Supersedes FAS 5, footnote 3

Affected by: Paragraph 9 superseded by FAS 71
Paragraph 11 and footnote 5 superseded by FAS 96 and FAS 109
Paragraph 13 and footnotes 3 and 4 amended by FAS 96 and FAS 109

Statement of Financial Accounting Standards No. 16
Prior Period Adjustments

CONTENTS

INTRODUCTION AND BACKGROUND INFORMATION

1. The AICPA Committee on SEC Regulations and others have requested that the FASB consider the criteria for prior period adjustments stated in paragraph 23 of *APB Opinion No. 9*, "Reporting the Results of Operations," and provide further guidelines for the application of those criteria. Paragraph 23 of *APB Opinion No. 9* states:

Adjustments related to prior periods—and thus excluded in the determination of net income for the current period—are limited to those material adjustments which (a) can be specifically identified with and directly related to the business activities of particular prior periods, and (b) are not attributable to economic events occurring subsequent to the date of the financial statements for the prior period, and (c) depend primarily on determinations by persons other than management and (d) were not susceptible of reasonable estimation prior to such determination. Such adjustments are rare in modern financial accounting. They relate to events or transactions which occurred in a prior period, the accounting effects of which could not be determined with reasonable assurance at that time, usually because of some major uncertainty then existing. Evidence of such an uncertainty would be disclosure thereof in the financial statements of the applicable period, or of an intervening period in those cases in which the uncertainty became apparent during a subsequent period. Further, it would be expected that, in most cases, the opinion of the reporting independent auditor on such prior period would have contained a qualification because of the uncertainty. Examples are material, nonrecurring adjustments or settlements of income taxes, of renegotiation proceedings or of utility revenue under rate processes. Settlements of significant amounts resulting from litigation or similar claims may also constitute prior period adjustments.

2. The requests referred to in paragraph 1 were prompted by Securities and Exchange Commission staff administrative interpretations of *APB Opinion No. 9* during 1975 limiting prior period adjustments for out-of-court settlements of litigation. The view of the SEC staff was later explained in *Staff Accounting Bulletin No. 8* (see Appendix C). In addition, differing interpretations of the criteria of paragraph 23 and of the provisions of paragraph 24 of *APB Opinion No. 9* have been cited as a basis for requesting a reconsideration of the concept of prior period adjustments.

3. Paragraph 24 of *APB Opinion No. 9* elaborates on paragraph 23 by giving examples of items that do not qualify as prior period adjustments. Paragraph 24 states:

Treatment as prior period adjustments should not be applied to the normal, recurring corrections and adjustments which are the natural result of the use of estimates inherent in the accounting process. For example, changes in the estimated remaining lives of fixed assets affect the computed amounts of depreciation, but these changes should be considered prospective in nature and not prior period adjustments. Similarly, relatively immaterial adjustments of provisions for liabilities (including income taxes) made in prior periods should be considered recurring items to be reflected in operations of the current period. Some uncertainties, for example those relating to the realization of assets (collectibility of accounts receivable, ultimate recovery of deferred costs or realizability of inventories or other assets), would not qualify for prior period adjustment treatment, since economic events subsequent to the date of the financial statements must of necessity enter into the elimination of any previously-existing uncertainty. Therefore, the effects of such matters are considered to be elements in the determination of net income for the period in which the uncertainty is eliminated. Thus, the Board [APB] believes that prior period adjustments will be rare.

4. *APB Opinion No. 20,* "Accounting Changes," affirmed the conclusions of paragraph 24 of *APB Opinion No. 9* by requiring that "a change in an estimate should not be accounted for by restating amounts reported in financial statements of prior periods . . . unless the change meets all the conditions for a prior period adjustment (paragraph 23 of *APB Opinion No. 9*)."

5. *FASB Statement No. 5,* "Accounting for Contingencies," (effective for fiscal years beginning on or after July 1, 1975) establishes the conditions for accrual of an estimated loss from a loss contingency and prohibits accrual before those conditions are met. The two conditions for accrual of an estimated loss from a loss contingency set forth in paragraph 8 of Statement No. 5 are that "(a) information available prior to issuance of the financial statements indicates that it is probable that an asset had been impaired or a liability had been incurred at the date of the financial statements . . ." and "(b) the amount of loss can be reasonably estimated." Paragraph 8 of the Statement requires that "an estimated loss from a loss contingency . . . shall be accrued by a charge to income. . . ." A footnote to that paragraph states that "paragraphs 23-24 of *APB Opinion No. 9* . . . describe the 'rare' circumstances in which a prior period adjustment is appropriate" and indicates that "those paragraphs are not amended" by Statement No. 5.

6. The Board has, among other things, (a) reviewed an FASB staff survey of prior period adjustments made in recent years pursuant to the criteria of *APB Opinion No. 9,* (b) considered the relationship of the criteria of *APB Opinion No. 9* for prior period adjustments to the rationale of subsequent APB Opinions (see paragraphs 29-36), and (c) examined the relationship of the criteria of *APB Opinion No. 9* for prior period adjustments to the conditions of *FASB Statement No. 5* for accrual of estimated losses from loss contingencies (see paragraph 37).

7. An Exposure Draft of a proposed Statement on "Prior Period Adjustments" was issued July 29, 1976, and a public hearing based on the Exposure Draft was held on October 15, 1976. The Board received 162 position papers and letters of comment in response to the Exposure Draft. Ten presentations were made at the public hearing. On April 12, 1977 the FASB announced that it was unable to

attain the necessary five assenting votes for issuance of a final Statement on Prior Period Adjustments. That announcement stated that four FASB members agreed to support the position in the Exposure Draft, modified in certain respects for interim reporting, and that the other three Board members dissented for varied reasons. On June 21, 1977 the Trustees of the Financial Accounting Foundation announced that they had approved the implementation of a number of the recommendations made by the Trustees' Structure Committee in its April 1977 report, "The Structure of Establishing Financial Accounting Standards." The recommendations approved included amending the Foundation's bylaws to change the voting requirement for adoption of pronouncements by the FASB from five affirmative votes among the seven members to a simple majority. Subsequent to the action by the Trustees, the Board reconsidered the subject and voted to issue this Statement.

8. The Board concluded that, with limited exceptions, items of profit and loss recognized during a period shall be included in the determination of net income of that period. Paragraphs 11 and 13-15 describe the exceptions that shall be accounted for and reported as prior period adjustments. The basis for the Board's conclusions, as well as alternatives considered and reasons for their rejection, are discussed in Appendix A to this Statement. The results of the FASB staff survey of prior period adjustments made pursuant to the criteria of *APB Opinion No. 9* in annual financial statements for fiscal years ending from July 1973 through June 1975 are summarized in Appendix B to this Statement.

9. The Addendum to *APB Opinion No. 2,* "Accounting for the 'Investment Credit'," states that "differences may arise in the application of generally accepted accounting principles as between regulated and nonregulated businesses, because of the effect in regulated businesses of the rate-making process," and discusses the application of generally accepted accounting principles to regulated industries. FASB Statements and Interpretations should therefore be applied to regulated companies that are subject to the rate-making process in accordance with the provisions of the Addendum.

STANDARDS OF FINANCIAL ACCOUNTING AND REPORTING

10. Except as specified in paragraph 11 and in paragraphs 13 and 14 with respect to prior interim periods of the current year, all items of profit and loss recognized during a period,[1] including accruals of estimated losses from loss contingencies, shall be

---

[1] As used in this Statement, the term "period" refers to both annual and interim reporting periods.

included in the determination of net income for that period.[2]

11. Items of profit and loss related to the following shall be accounted for and reported as prior period adjustments[3] and excluded from the determination of net income for the current period:

a. Correction of an error in the financial statements of a prior period[4] and
b. Adjustments that result from realization of income tax benefits of pre-acquisition operating loss carryforwards of purchased subsidiaries.[5]

12. This Statement does not affect the manner of reporting accounting changes required or permitted by an FASB Statement, an FASB Interpretation, or an APB Opinion.[6]

Adjustments Related to Prior Interim Periods of the Current Fiscal Year

13. For purposes of this Statement, an "adjustment related to prior *interim* periods of the current fiscal year" is an adjustment or settlement of litigation or similar claims, of income taxes, of renegotiation proceedings, or of utility revenue under rate-making processes provided that the adjustment or settlement meets each of the following criteria:

a. The effect of the adjustment or settlement is material in relation to income from continuing operations of the current fiscal year or in relation to the trend of income from continuing operations or is material by other appropriate criteria, and
b. All or part of the adjustment or settlement can be specifically identified with and is directly related to business activities of specific prior interim periods of the current fiscal year, and
c. The amount of the adjustment or settlement could not be reasonably estimated prior to the current interim period but becomes reasonably estimable in the current interim period.

Criterion (b) above is not met solely because of inci-

dental effects such as interest on a settlement. Criterion (c) would be met by the occurrence of an event with currently measurable effects such as new retroactive tax legislation or a final decision on a rate order. Treatment as adjustments related to prior interim periods of the current fiscal year shall not be applied to the normal recurring corrections and adjustments that are the result of the use of estimates inherent in the accounting process. Changes in provisions for doubtful accounts shall not be considered to be adjustments related to prior interim periods of the current fiscal year even though the changes result from litigation or similar claims.

14. If an item of profit or loss occurs in *other than the first* interim period of the enterprise's fiscal year and all or a part of the item of profit or loss is an adjustment related to prior interim periods of the current fiscal year, as defined in paragraph 13 above, the item shall be reported as follows:

a. The portion of the item that is directly related to business activities of the enterprise during the current interim period, if any, shall be included in the determination of net income for that period.
b. Prior interim periods of the current fiscal year shall be restated to include the portion of the item that is directly related to business activities of the enterprise during each prior interim period in the determination of net income for that period.
c. The portion of the item that is directly related to business activities of the enterprise during prior fiscal years, if any, shall be included in the determination of net income of the first interim period of the current fiscal year.

15. The following disclosures shall be made in interim financial reports about an adjustment related to prior interim periods of the current fiscal year. In financial reports for the interim period in which the adjustment occurs, disclosure shall be made of (a) the effect on income from continuing operations, net income, and related per share amounts for each prior interim period of the current fiscal year, and (b) income from continuing opera-

---

[2]Many items that would previously have been reported as prior period adjustments will be subject to existing disclosure requirements when that type of item is included in the determination of current net income. For example, *APB Opinion No. 28,* "Interim Financial Reporting," specifies certain disclosures for interim reporting periods and *APB Opinion No. 30,* "Reporting the Results of Operations," specifies disclosures for certain types of items discussed by that Opinion.

[3]The reporting of prior period adjustments is described in paragraph 18 of *APB Opinion No. 9,* as modified by paragraph 16 of this Statement, and in paragraph 26 of *APB Opinion No. 9.*

[4]As defined in paragraph 13 of *APB Opinion No. 20.* That paragraph also describes the distinction between a correction of an error and a change in accounting estimate.

[5]See paragraph 49 of *APB Opinion No. 11,* "Accounting for Income Taxes," and paragraph 88 of *APB Opinion No. 16,* "Business Combinations."

[6]In addition to transition requirements of these pronouncements, accounting changes resulting in restatement of previously issued financial statements of prior periods include a change in accounting method permitted by paragraph 52 of *APB Opinion No. 16,* a change in the reporting entity described in paragraph 34 of *APB Opinion No. 20,* and special changes in accounting principle described in paragraphs 27 and 29 of *APB Opinion No. 20.* See also footnote 5 to *APB Opinion No. 20.*

tions, net income, and related per share amounts for each prior interim period restated in accordance with paragraph 14 of this Statement.

Amendments to Existing Pronouncements

16. The conclusions of this Statement require the following amendments to existing pronouncements:

a. *APB Opinion No. 9.* Delete paragraphs 23 and 24. The first sentence of paragraph 18 is modified to read as follows:

> Those items that are reported as prior period adjustments shall, in single period statements, be reflected as adjustments of the opening balance of retained earnings.

b. *APB Opinion No. 20.* Delete footnote 9 to paragraph 31.
c. *APB Opinion No. 30.* Delete the following words from the second and third sentences of paragraph 25: "should not be reported as a prior period adjustment unless it meets the criteria for a prior period adjustment as defined in paragraph 23 of APB Opinion No. 9. An adjustment that does not meet such criteria," and combine

the remainder of the two sentences into one sentence as follows:

> Each adjustment in the current period of a loss on disposal of a business segment or of an element of an extraordinary item that was reported in a prior period should be separately disclosed as to year of origin, nature, and amount and classified separately in the current period in the same manner as the original item.

d. *FASB Statement No. 5.* Delete footnote 3 to paragraph 8.

Effective Date and Transition

17. This Statement shall be effective for financial statements for fiscal years beginning after October 15, 1977. Application in financial statements for fiscal years beginning before October 16, 1977 that have not been previously issued, and in interim periods within those fiscal years, is encouraged but not required. This Statement shall not be applied retroactively to previously issued annual financial statements.

> **The provisions of this Statement need not be applied to immaterial items.**

This Statement was adopted by the affirmative votes of four members of the Financial Accounting Standards Board. Messrs. Sprouse, Litke, and Walters dissented.

Mr. Sprouse and Mr. Litke dissent primarily because the effect of this Statement is to include in the current year's *income from continuing operations* adjustments related to prior years that previously would have been excluded in the determination of the current year's *net income*. In their opinion this is a quantum leap that detracts from the usefulness of the measure of income from continuing operations and that should not be undertaken without comprehensive consideration of the presentation of information about earnings activities. Mr. Sprouse and Mr. Litke believe that application of this Statement produces anomalous results including (i) reporting tax benefits of loss carryforwards as extraordinary items when realized (a practice with which they concur) but including other adjustments or settlements of income taxes related to prior periods in income from continuing operations, (ii) reporting gains and losses from extinguishing debt during the current period as extraordinary items (a practice with which they concur) but including adjudications and out-of-court settlements of litigation, results of renegotiation proceedings, and other financial results related to prior periods in income from continuing operations, and (iii) exclud-

ing adjustments related to prior interim periods from the net income of the current interim period (except that such adjustments made during the first interim period are included in that period's income from continuing operations) because the Board is reconsidering interim reporting and some respondents to the Exposure Draft argued that the inclusion of those adjustments would detract from the usefulness of interim reporting (paragraph 46) but rejecting similar considerations related to annual reporting (paragraphs 23 and 52). If, without comprehensive consideration of the presentation of information about earnings activities, certain adjustments related to prior periods that previously were excluded in the determination of net income for the current period are now to be included in that determination, Mr. Sprouse and Mr. Litke believe that, as a minimum, those adjustments should be specifically designated (as they are in paragraph 13) and be reported as extraordinary items.

Further, Mr. Litke would provide an additional specific exception in paragraph 11 (as is now provided by paragraph 23 of *APB Opinion No. 9*) for cost-of-service regulated utility companies in those instances where revenues collected subject to refund are required to be refunded. He believes that the circumstances applicable to regulated utility companies in those instances are sufficiently different from circumstances applicable to other industries to warrant such special treatment.

With respect to current practice for such companies, the amount of the refund generally is attributed to the year of collection and not to the year of the refund. Mr. Litke agrees with this practice. He notes that when management believes a reasonable estimate can be made of the amount of revenues currently being collected which are likely to be refunded, they generally record a reserve against revenue for that amount in accordance with *FASB Statement No. 5*. However, management is often unable to make a reasonable estimate as to what, if any, refunds may be required. In that case, all revenues resulting from such rate increases collected but subject to refund are frequently recorded as current revenue in the determination of the current period's income (even though the revenue and the income are subject to final adjudication), and the auditor's report is normally qualified. When the amount of the refund is determined, it generally is attributed to the year(s) of collection by prior period adjustment.

Mr. Litke believes that, if prior period adjust-

ments were not permitted for a regulated company required to refund amounts previously collected subject to refund, the revenue, operating profit, and net income for prior periods could be materially misstated based on what the rate regulatory body finally allowed.

In addition, Mr. Litke believes that a specific exception is necessary because this Statement does not specifically respond to the questions raised by many as to the applicability of the Addendum to *APB Opinion No. 2* to refunds of utility revenues for which a reasonable estimate cannot be made.

Mr. Walters dissents because he does not believe the elimination of prior period adjustments improves financial reporting. To the contrary, he believes that there are clearly valid items, admittedly somewhat rare, whose inclusion in prior periods with which they are specifically identified, enhances the relevance, comparability, and understandability of financial statements and therefore their usefulness. He also does not believe the Board should tinker with this narrow, but basic, issue outside the conceptual framework project. As a minimum, it should be part of a broader project dealing with the meaning and presentation of results of operations.

Members of the Financial Accounting Standards Board:

Marshall S. Armstrong, *Chairman*	Donald J. Kirk	Robert T. Sprouse
Oscar S. Gellein	Arthur L. Litke	Ralph E. Walters
	Robert E. Mays	

Appendix A

BASIS FOR CONCLUSIONS

18. This Appendix contains a discussion of the factors deemed significant by members of the Board in reaching the conclusions in this Statement, including various alternatives considered and reasons for accepting some and rejecting others. Individual Board members gave greater weight to some factors than to others.

Scope

19. The initial request referred to in paragraph 1 was for clarification of the application of criterion (b)[7] and criterion (c)[8] of paragraph 23 of *APB Opinion No. 9* to negotiated settlements of litigation. Paragraph 23 of *APB Opinion No. 9* included "settlements of significant amounts resulting from

litigation or similar claims" as an example of items that may qualify as prior period adjustments. SEC *Staff Accounting Bulletin No. 8* states the SEC staff's conclusion that "litigation is inevitably an 'economic event' and that settlements would constitute 'economic events' of the period in which they occur. Accordingly, it would seem that charges or credits relating to settlements would also not meet" criterion (b).[9] *Staff Accounting Bulletin No. 8* also states the view that when litigation is settled, management must make a number of significant judgments, and, hence, criterion (c)[10] has not been met.

20. As described in Appendix B, the FASB staff searched approximately 6,000 annual reports for fiscal years ended from July 1973 through June 1975 and identified 191 annual reports that showed prior period adjustments that appeared to have been made pursuant to the criteria of paragraph 23 of *APB Opinion No. 9*. The purpose of the research

---

[7]Criterion (b) of paragraph 23 of *APB Opinion No. 9* requires that the adjustments "are not attributable to economic events occurring subsequent to the date of the financial statements for the prior period."

[8]Criterion (c) of paragraph 23 of *APB Opinion No. 9* requires that the adjustment "depend primarily on determinations by persons other than management."

[9]See footnote 7.

[10]See footnote 8.

was to determine the extent and nature of those prior period adjustments and the possible interpretative problems the Board would face if it decided to clarify the criteria in paragraph 23 of *APB Opinion No. 9.* Over one-third of the identified adjustments resulted from litigation and similar claims, and most of these were negotiated. Income tax settlements also represented over one-third of the identified adjustments. Because of the similarity of the process involved in settling litigation and income taxes, and because they constitute most of the identified prior period adjustments made pursuant to the criteria of paragraph 23 of *APB Opinion No. 9,* the Board concluded that this Statement should not be limited to the area of negotiated settlements of litigation, but rather, should address all items reported as prior period adjustments pursuant to the criteria of paragraph 23 of *APB Opinion No. 9.*

21. Some respondents to the Exposure Draft questioned whether this Statement was intended to change the reporting of adjustments that are required by *APB Opinions No. 9, 11,* and *16* to be reported as adjustments to paid-in capital, goodwill, or other assets. This Statement is not intended to require those adjustments to be included in the determination of net income of the current period. This Statement is also not intended to proscribe restatements of earnings per share that are required by *APB Opinions No. 15,* "Earnings Per Share," and *16* or by other APB Opinions and FASB Statements.

Summary

22. In considering possible clarification of the criteria in paragraph 23 of *APB Opinion No. 9* (see paragraph 24), the purpose of the criteria (see paragraph 25), and the effect on prior period adjustments of subsequent pronouncements (see paragraphs 29-37), the Board determined that an amendment of *APB Opinion No. 9* was needed. The Board concluded for the reasons indicated in paragraphs 24-39 that all items of profit and loss recognized during a period, with the limited exceptions indicated in paragraphs 11 and 13-15 and explained in paragraphs 41-46, shall be included in the determination of net income for that reporting period. The Board also concluded, for the reasons indicated in paragraphs 47-51, that the manner of reporting accounting changes should not be modified at this time (see paragraph 12).

23. Some respondents recommended that this project be included in or deferred pending completion of the Board's agenda project entitled "Conceptual Framework for Financial Accounting and Reporting." The Board determined that this problem required resolution at this time and could be resolved in the existing accounting framework. As outlined in paragraphs 29-37, the all-inclusive income statement is predominant in the existing accounting framework.

Possible Clarification of Criteria

24. Relating the criteria of paragraph 23 of *APB Opinion No. 9* and the examples given in that paragraph to prior period adjustments identified in the FASB staff survey (see Appendix B) led to the conclusion that any attempted clarification could result in an amendment of *APB Opinion No. 9* and that the problem could not be satisfactorily resolved by an Interpretation as indicated by the following examples:

a. Settlements of income taxes and litigation constitute the majority of identified prior period adjustments. The former is included in paragraph 23 as an example of a prior period adjustment when material and nonrecurring and the latter is included as an example of an item that *may* qualify as a prior period adjustment. Such settlements are usually negotiated and often do not depend *primarily* on determinations by *any* single party. Accordingly, for out-of-court settlements of both income taxes and litigation to qualify as prior period adjustments, the phrase "depend primarily on determinations by persons other than management" (criterion (c)) would have to be amended to read "*not* depending primarily on management."

b. The term "economic events" in criterion (b)[11] has been interpreted in significantly different ways (see paragraph 19 and Appendix C). Refining the definition of this term could result in an effective amendment.

c. Refining the requirement that prior period adjustments be "material" or of the word "nonrecurring" in the examples in paragraph 23 would likely be an effective amendment.

Purpose of the Criteria of Paragraph 23 of APB Opinion No. 9

25. Paragraph 17 of *APB Opinion No. 9* states that "net income should reflect all items of profit and loss recognized during the period with the sole exception of . . . prior period adjustments. . . ." *APB Opinion No. 9* requires restatement of affected prior periods only if the statements of the affected prior periods are presented; otherwise, only the effect on beginning retained earnings of the earliest period presented is required. The Board believes that a decision to exclude certain items of profit and loss recognized during a period from the determina-

---

[11]See footnote 7.

tion of net income for that period should be based on a determination that some expected user or class of users would be benefited. Items of profit and loss clearly related to prior period operations and unrelated to the current period operations, for example, might be excluded from the determination of net income for the current period because existing and potential investors might be misled by their inclusion. The criteria of paragraph 23 of *APB Opinion No. 9* do not serve this purpose because they do not comprehend many other items of profit and loss related to prior periods and unrelated to the current period operations. The Board concluded that users will not be benefited by special treatment for some items of profit and loss recognized during a period but not for other similar items. The reasons for the limited exceptions indicated in paragraphs 11 and 13-15 are explained in paragraphs 41-46.

The Matching Concept

26. A number of respondents to the Exposure Draft noted that adjustments that are reported as prior period adjustments are unrelated to operations of the current period. In their view, inclusion in net income of the current period of costs or revenues that are directly related to business activities of prior periods distorts net income in the current period by matching revenue of one period with costs of another period.

27. *APB Statement No. 4,* "Basic Concepts and Accounting Principles Underlying Financial Statements of Business Enterprises," explicitly avoids using the term "matching" because it has a variety of meanings in the accounting literature. In its broadest sense, matching refers to the entire process of income determination—described in paragraph 147 of *APB Statement No. 4* as "identifying, measuring, and relating revenue and expenses of an enterprise for an accounting period." Matching may also be used in a more limited sense to refer only to the process of expense recognition or in an even more limited sense to refer to the recognition of expenses by associating costs with revenue on a cause and effect basis.

28. The Board reviewed items that were reported as prior period adjustments in recent years. The results of that review are summarized in Appendix B. Based on that review, the Board concluded that the items that were reported as prior period adjustments were not sufficiently different from other items that were included in the determination of net income in the current period to justify their exclusion.

Relationship to Subsequent Pronouncements

29. *APB Opinion No. 9* was issued in December 1966. Since then, other APB Opinions and FASB Statements have changed the standards of accounting for some items related to prior periods. The following paragraphs refer to certain of those changes and their relationship to prior period adjustments.

30. Paragraph 23 of *APB Opinion No. 9* includes "material, nonrecurring adjustments or settlements of income taxes" as an example of items that would meet the criteria for prior period adjustments. Paragraph 24 of Opinion No. 9 states that "relatively immaterial adjustments of provisions for liabilities (including income taxes) made in prior periods should be considered recurring items to be reflected in operations of the current period." *APB Opinion No. 11,* issued in December 1967, requires the use of comprehensive allocation in accounting for income taxes. Prior to the issuance of that Opinion, some enterprises applied partial allocation, a method that did not require taxes to be allocated for certain timing differences. Many settlements of income taxes involve timing differences. With the use of comprehensive allocation, tax settlements relating to timing differences normally do not affect income; thus, *APB Opinion No. 11* probably has reduced the income effect of some settlements of income tax and accordingly the number of settlements that would be accounted for as prior period adjustments.

31. Paragraph 45 of *APB Opinion No. 11* requires that the benefits of prior year tax loss carryforwards not recognized in the year of the loss be recognized as an extraordinary item in the year in which the benefits are realized. Previously, Chapter 10B, "Income Taxes," of *ARB No. 43* provided that ". . . where it is believed that misleading inferences would be drawn from such inclusion, the tax reduction should be credited to surplus." Thus, *APB Opinion No. 11* requires that an item that is related to specific prior periods be included in the determination of current income.

32. Paragraph 50 of *APB Opinion No. 11* requires that realized tax benefits of loss carryforwards arising prior to a "quasi-reorganization" be added to contributed capital if not recognized prior to the "quasi-reorganization." Thus, *APB Opinion No. 11* requires inclusion of an item that relates to specific prior periods as an addition to contributed capital in the current period. (See paragraph 34.)

33. Paragraphs 79-83 of *APB Opinion No. 16* require that adjustments resulting from resolution of certain contingencies be accounted for as adjustments of the cost of the acquired enterprise. The required accounting is prospective rather than retroactive. Thus, *APB Opinion No. 16* requires that resolution of certain contingencies relating to specific prior periods be reported as an adjustment of the purchase price of assets in the current period. (See paragraph 34.)

34. *APB Opinion No. 19,* "Reporting Changes in Financial Position," established the statement of changes in financial position as a new basic financial statement. This statement purports to present all changes in financial position that occur during the period. The interaction of Opinion No. 19, *APB Opinion No. 9,* and other APB Opinions results in the following anomalies:

a. Realized tax benefits of loss carryforwards arising prior to a "quasi-reorganization" are considered related to prior operations and are added to contributed capital, but are reported as changes in financial position in the current period (see paragraph 32); whereas settlements of income taxes, when they meet the criteria of paragraph 23 of *APB Opinion No. 9,* are reported as changes in financial position in the prior period.
b. Adjustments arising from resolution of certain pre-acquisition contingencies of acquired subsidiaries, considered unrelated to current operations and thus reported as adjustments to the cost of the acquired enterprise, are reported as changes in financial position in the current period (see paragraph 33); whereas adjustments of contingencies that meet the criteria of paragraph 23 of *APB Opinion No. 9* are reported as changes in financial position in the prior period.

The Board concluded that all items of profit and loss recognized in a period, with the limited exceptions indicated in paragraphs 11 and 13-15 and explained in paragraphs 41-46, shall be included in the determination of net income and accordingly shall be reported as changes in financial position in that reporting period.

35. Paragraph 31 of *APB Opinion No. 20* requires that the effect of changes in accounting estimates be accounted for in the current period, or the current and future periods if the change affects both. Restatement of amounts reported in prior periods and reporting of pro forma amounts for prior periods are prohibited. However, the Opinion includes a footnote that states:

Financial statements of a prior period should not be restated for a change in estimate resulting from later resolution of an uncertainty which may have caused the auditor to qualify his opinion on previous financial statements unless the change meets all the conditions for a prior period adjustment (paragraph 23 of *APB Opinion No. 9*).

Thus, Opinion No. 20 requires that most items related to prior periods be included in the determination of current net income without disclosure of the pro forma effect of those items on prior periods but continues the requirements of paragraph 23 of *APB Opinion No. 9* that a few similar items be reported as prior period adjustments.

36. In addition to establishing criteria for prior period adjustments, which were expected to be rare, *APB Opinion No. 9* also established criteria for "extraordinary items," which were to be reported separately in net income of the current period. *APB Opinion No. 30,* "Reporting the Results of Operations," issued in June 1973, established new criteria for extraordinary items, including a change of "would not be expected to recur frequently" in *APB Opinion No. 9* to "not reasonably expected to recur in the foreseeable future" in *APB Opinion No. 30.* Although *APB Opinion No. 30* did not address prior period adjustments, it significantly restricted the eligibility for classification as an extraordinary item. Under Opinion No. 9 the statement that prior period adjustments would be *nonrecurring* adjustments was often interpreted in practice to mean adjustments that would not be expected to recur frequently, but in the current accounting environment, including *APB Opinion No. 30,* nonrecurring would be defined as "not reasonably expected to recur in the foreseeable future."

37. Paragraph 8 of *FASB Statement No. 5,* issued in March 1975, establishes two conditions for accrual of an estimated loss from a loss contingency and prohibits accrual before those conditions are met. The Board did not reexamine the concept of prior period adjustments at that time. Consideration in this Statement of the kinds of items, if any, to be accounted for as prior period adjustments led to the following questions: If pursuant to *FASB Statement No. 5* a loss cannot be accrued in the period when it is probable that an asset had been impaired or a liability had been incurred because the amount of loss cannot be reasonably estimated, should the loss be charged retroactively to that period when it can be reasonably estimated in a subsequent period? Does the loss accrue to the earlier period, when it was probable that an asset had been impaired or a liability had been incurred, or to the later period, when the amount of loss can be reasonably estimated? The Board believes that the requirement under *APB Opinion No. 9* that certain losses, when they can be reasonably estimated in a later period, be charged retroactively to an earlier period is inconsistent with the intent of *FASB Statement No. 5* in prohibiting accrual of an estimated loss when the amount of loss cannot be reasonably estimated, even though it is probable that an asset has been impaired or a liability has been incurred. The Board concluded that all estimated losses for loss contingencies should be charged to income rather than charging some to income and others to retained earnings as prior period adjustments.

Consideration of Specific Types of Adjustments

38. A number of respondents questioned the appropriateness of a rate-regulated utility's reporting refunds in the period in which the refunds are ordered if the refunded amounts were originally collected subject to refund. Upon request, several of those respondents furnished additional data that further explained the effect of those refunds. The Board is aware that there are differing views about the reporting of both the contingently refundable revenue when it is billed and the subsequent refunds. Determining the reporting that would be appropriate for the contingently refundable revenue when it is billed is outside the scope of this Statement. Except for the possible effect of the rate-making process, the Board does not believe that the reporting of any adjustment at the time that a subsequent refund is determined is sufficiently different from the reporting of other adjustments that result from previous uncertainties to justify special treatment in this Statement. However, the Board did not consider whether the effect of the rate-making process might permit or require special treatment for those refunds. (See also paragraphs 46, concerning adjustments related to prior interim periods of the current fiscal year, and 55, concerning the Addendum to *APB Opinion No. 2.*)

39. A number of respondents recommended that this Statement be modified to provide that specific types of adjustments, such as renegotiation, continue to be reported as prior period adjustments. The Board rejected this recommendation because none of the items cited is sufficiently different from other adjustments that are included in the determination of net income of the current period to justify special treatment. (However, see paragraph 46 concerning adjustments related to prior interim periods of the current fiscal year.)

Prior Period Adjustments That Are Not Affected by This Statement

40. The Board reviewed other kinds of items reported as prior period adjustments, described in paragraphs 41-45. In each case, the Board concluded that the accounting for these items should not be modified at this time.

Correction of an Error

41. Paragraph 13 of *APB Opinion No. 20* states:

Errors in financial statements result from mathematical mistakes, mistakes in the application of accounting principles, or oversight or misuse of facts that existed at the time the financial statements were prepared. In contrast, a change in accounting estimate results from new information or subsequent developments and accordingly from better insight or improved judgment. Thus, an error is distinguishable from a change in estimate. A change from an accounting principle that is not generally accepted to one that is generally accepted is a correction of an error for purposes of applying this Opinion.

A major distinguishing feature of a correction of an error is that the financial statements of the affected prior period, when originally issued, should have reflected the adjustment. In contrast, a prior period adjustment that meets the criteria of paragraph 23 of *APB Opinion No. 9* could not have been determined when the financial statements were originally issued. The Board concluded that a correction of an error, as defined above, should continue to be reflected by restating the financial statements of the affected prior period.

42. Some respondents contended that the distinction between a correction of an error and a change in estimate is too vague to be a basis for different accounting. The Board noted that *APB Opinion No. 20* used that same distinction as the basis for different accounting for corrections of errors and changes in estimates that did not meet the criteria of Opinion No. 9 for prior period adjustments. No problems of application resulting from that requirement of Opinion No. 20 have been brought to the Board's attention.

43. Several respondents stated that an exception to permit the reporting of corrections of errors as prior period adjustments is not justified. The Board concluded that the normal procedures of revising and reissuing financial statements promptly when an error is discovered or otherwise advising users that the financial statements contain erroneous data appear to satisfy the interest of financial statement users. Those procedures also permit enterprises to disclose the inaccuracies on as timely a basis as is practicable in the circumstances.

Income Tax Benefits of Pre-Acquisition Operating Loss Carryforwards of Purchased Subsidiaries

44. Paragraph 88 of *APB Opinion No. 16* states that "an acquiring corporation should reduce the acquired goodwill retroactively for the realized tax benefits of loss carry-forwards of an acquired company not previously recorded by the acquiring corporation." The corresponding reduction in the amount of goodwill amortization in prior years is reported as a prior period adjustment as described in paragraph 49 of *APB Opinion No. 11*. The FASB presently has on its technical agenda a project entitled "Accounting for Business Combinations and Purchased Intangibles" that includes a re-

consideration of *APB Opinion No. 16.* The Board believes that because it is reconsidering *APB Opinion No. 16* the requirements of that Opinion should continue in effect so as to maintain the status quo during the Board's reconsideration.

45. Some respondents recommended that the acquired goodwill be reduced *in the current year* for the realized tax benefits of loss carryforwards of an acquired company not previously recorded by the acquiring corporation. The adjustment would thus in effect be amortized only prospectively rather than both retroactively, as a prior period adjustment, and prospectively. Accounting for realized tax benefits of loss carryforwards of an acquired company is addressed as Problem 2 of Technical Issue Two at paragraphs 512-520 of the August 19, 1976 FASB Discussion Memorandum, "Accounting for Business Combinations and Purchased Intangibles." As indicated in paragraph 44 above, the Board believes that the status quo should be maintained on that project during the Board's deliberations.

Adjustments Related to Prior Interim Periods of the Current Fiscal Year

46. A number of respondents to the Exposure Draft and to the October 7, 1976 Exposure Draft on "Accounting for Income Taxes in Interim Periods" recommended that this Statement be applied to annual financial statements only, rather than to annual and interim financial statements. Several of those respondents noted that the APB concluded in paragraph 9 of *APB Opinion No. 28* that "the usefulness of such [interim financial] information rests on the relationship that it has to the annual results of operations." In those respondents' view, restatement of interim periods is necessary to make interim data relate in a meaningful way to anticipated annual results. Several other of those respondents observed that the Board has on its technical agenda a project entitled "Interim Financial Reporting" that includes a reconsideration of *APB Opinion No. 28* and contended that, because Opinion No. 28 was issued when the criteria of Opinion No. 9 for prior period adjustments were in effect, the Board should not change interim reporting during its reconsideration of Opinion No. 28 by proscribing adjustments to prior interim periods. While not necessarily agreeing with these arguments, the Board decided to continue the practice of interim period restatements in the current fiscal year on a limited basis for the present. To avoid the interpretation problems that have resulted from the criteria of paragraph 23 of Opinion No. 9, the Board (a) limited such restatements to the specific examples cited in paragraph 23 of Opinion No. 9, (b) required that the adjustments meet the definition of materiality for extraordinary items (paragraph 24 of *APB Opinion No. 30*), and (c) required that the adjustments meet the two criteria of paragraph 23 of Opinion No. 9 that have not created interpretation problems in the past. The Board believes that application of the criteria in paragraph 13 will substantially continue existing practice for interim periods of the current fiscal year. Some Board members believe that this exception is inconsistent with some of the other conclusions of this Statement; however, they are willing to accept the provisions of paragraphs 13-15 during the Board's consideration of its project on interim financial reporting.

Accounting Changes

47. Paragraph 25 of *APB Opinion No. 9* addressed the subject of accounting changes as follows:

A change in the application of accounting principles may create a situation in which retroactive application is appropriate. In such situations *these changes should receive the same treatment as that for prior period adjustments.* [Emphasis added]

While distinguishing a retroactive accounting change from the prior period adjustments covered by paragraph 23 of that Opinion, the APB did prescribe the same accounting treatment for both.

48. Accounting changes (but not prior period adjustments covered by paragraph 23 of *APB Opinion No. 9*) were subsequently dealt with in *APB Opinion No. 20.* Paragraph 5 of Opinion No. 20 states:

Paragraph 25 of *APB Opinion No. 9* is superseded. Although the conclusion of that paragraph is not modified, this Opinion deals more completely with accounting changes.

49. The Board believes that retroactive accounting changes, whether specified in transition requirements of FASB Statements and Interpretations and APB Opinions or in the requirements of *APB Opinion No. 20,* differ significantly in nature from the prior period adjustments covered by paragraph 23 of *APB Opinion No. 9,* as described in the following paragraph. For that reason, the Board concluded that it should not, in this standard, reexamine existing requirements for retroactive accounting changes or proscribe the use of retroactive accounting changes in future Statements or Interpretations.

50. Requirements for restatements of prior periods to reflect changes in accounting principles address categories of transactions that are usually recurring and pervasive. Those restatements provide useful information for purposes of comparing financial data for periods after initial application of the

accounting principles with data presented for earlier periods. In contrast, the criteria of paragraph 23 of *APB Opinion No. 9* address isolated adjustments that are stated to be "rare in modern financial accounting." The purpose of restatement of prior periods for nonrecurring items cannot be to make the affected prior period comparable to subsequent periods because comparability cannot be accomplished by shifting nonrecurring items among periods. Instead, the purpose is to exclude material items directly related to prior periods from the determination of net income in the current period to avoid impairing the significance of net income of the current period (see paragraphs 10-12 of *APB Opinion No. 9*). As previously stated, the Board concluded that purpose is not accomplished by paragraph 23 of *APB Opinion No. 9* (see paragraph 25 above).

51. Paragraph 52 of *APB Opinion No. 16* states that a change in accounting method of one of the combining enterprises in a pooling of interests that is made to conform the accounting methods of the combining enterprises shall be applied retroactively. Like the item discussed in paragraph 44, this provision will be reconsidered as a part of the current FASB technical agenda project entitled "Accounting for Business Combinations and Purchased Intangibles," and the Board believes the status quo should be maintained in the meantime.

Income Statement Classification

52. Some respondents noted that most adjustments that would have been reported as prior period adjustments prior to the issuance of this Statement will not meet the criteria of *APB Opinion No. 30* for classification as extraordinary items. Some of those respondents recommended that this Statement require adjustments to be classified in the future as extraordinary items if they meet the present criteria of paragraph 23 of *APB Opinion No. 9*. Others contended that inclusion of such adjustments in income from continuing operations would obscure current income from ongoing operations. Considerations of income statement classification under Opinion No. 30 are not different for items previously classified as prior period adjustments and for other changes in estimates. The Board concluded that income statement classification is too pervasive to be dealt with in this project and that it probably should be considered in some phase of the FASB agenda project entitled "Conceptual Framework for Financial Accounting and Reporting."

53. A number of respondents observed that the "average" investor relies primarily on earnings per share data or earnings summaries in the financial press and thus might be misled by the inclusion of adjustments that are related to prior periods in

income from continuing operations in the current period. The effect of random, irregular, or unpredictable events may make periodic earnings per share data unrepresentative of an enterprise's earning activities during that period. For example, completed contract accounting for long-term contracts may result in an enterprise's reporting activities of one period in a subsequent period. However, the Board does not believe that investors are served by excluding the effects of such events from reported earnings. Disclosure of the effects of such events is required by certain APB Opinions and FASB Statements. Thus, reliance on a single earnings per share amount or a summary in the financial press may not be a sound basis for investment decisions.

54. Some respondents to the Exposure Draft contended that this Statement substitutes a narrow rule for managements' and auditors' judgments. The Board agrees that judgment is necessary in financial reporting but does not believe that judgment should result in special treatment for some items of profit and loss recognized during a period but not for other similar items unless special treatment is justified by different circumstances. On the other hand, management's judgment may indicate that disclosure should be furnished to allow a user to properly evaluate the enterprise's earnings. For example, *APB Opinion No. 30* requires disclosure of the effect of "unusual" or "infrequently occurring" items. Similar disclosure for items that are not "unusual" or "infrequently occurring," as defined in that Opinion, may also be appropriate if management feels that such disclosure is needed.

Addendum to APB Opinion No. 2

55. A number of respondents requested that the FASB clarify how the Addendum to *APB Opinion No. 2* applies to prior period adjustments. The Board is aware that differing applications of the Addendum exist in practice and has not addressed that issue.

Effective Date and Transition

56. Some respondents recommended that the Statement not apply to certain categories of preexisting contingencies. Those respondents suggested a variety of criteria for determining the preexisting contingencies to be exempted, including prior disclosure of the contingency, prior partial settlements of the same or of a related matter that were reported as prior period adjustments, and qualifications of auditors' earlier reports with respect to the contingency. The Board concluded that there was no equitable basis for exempting certain preexisting contingencies and not others.

57. The Exposure Draft proposed that the State-

ment be applied to fiscal years beginning on or after December 15, 1976. Several respondents recommended earlier application to avoid an interim period of confusion. Several others recommended a delay in the effective date because management may have disclosed in good faith that an anticipated adjustment would be reported as a prior period adjustment and might as a result be charged with having misled investors if the adjustment is reported in income of the current period. Following further consideration the Board concluded that it was appropriate to modify the effective date of this Statement to fiscal years beginning after October 15, 1977.

Applicability to Interim Periods

58. Some respondents questioned whether this Statement was intended to apply to interim as well as annual financial statements. As a result the Board added footnote 1 to paragraph 10. In addition, as explained in paragraph 46, paragraphs 13-15 were added.

Disclosure

59. Some respondents recommended that this Statement specify the disclosures that should be made for an adjustment that would previously have been reported as a prior period adjustment under the criteria of *APB Opinion No. 9*. The Board concluded that existing disclosure requirements that have been applied to other similar items included in the determination of current net income also apply to items that would previously have been reported as prior period adjustments. For example, *APB Opinion No. 30* specifies the disclosure requirements for "unusual items," "infrequently occurring items," and "extraordinary items"; *APB Opinion No. 28* specifies the disclosure requirements for various categories of adjustments in interim financial reports; and other pronouncements specify disclosures that apply to certain types of items.

Appendix B

SUMMARY OF FASB STAFF RESEARCH

Other Studies Available

60. A recent survey of the annual reports of 600 industrial and commercial corporations contained the following summary of adjustments to the opening balances of retained earnings during the four fiscal years of those enterprises ended not later than February 2, 1975:[12]

Reasons for adjustment	1974	1973	1972	1971
Poolings of interests	30	56	67	69
Research and development expenditures charged to operations	23	—	—	—
Litigation or income tax settlements	12	29	26	15
Other	18	36	89	87
Total adjustments	83	121	182	171

Investigation revealed that the "other" category consisted principally of accounting changes (adopting tax allocation, adopting recommendations of AICPA Industry Audit Guides that required retroactive application, etc.) and changes in the reporting entity. The items categorized as "litigation or income tax settlements" were prior period adjustments made pursuant to the criteria of paragraph 23 of *APB Opinion No. 9*. Since the adjustments represented by this caption were few in number, the broader study described in the following paragraphs was undertaken. The adjustments in the above table that were determined to have been made pursuant to paragraph 23 of *APB Opinion No. 9* were used as a control to ensure that the selection procedures were adequate to locate substantially all of such adjustments made by enterprises included in the study.

---

[12]American Institute of Certified Public Accountants, *Accounting Trends & Techniques—1975*, 29th ed. (New York: AICPA, 1975), p. 363.

Methodology

61. The research by the FASB staff utilized the National Automated Accounting Research System (NAARS).[13] NAARS includes a file of annual reports of publicly held enterprises. Enterprises reporting or referring to prior period adjustments in either the footnotes or the retained earnings statement were identified. The control group referred to in paragraph 60 was used to provide assurance that no substantial number of items was omitted. Complete reliability of the results of such a search could not be assured because of the variety of ways that enterprises disclose such adjustments. Adjustments were located in approximately 1,200 reports and those adjustments were reviewed in detail, and the adjustments made pursuant to paragraph 23 of *APB Opinion No. 9* were identified. If it was unclear whether the adjustment belonged in this category, it was included, except that in a few instances where there was virtually no disclosure of the nature or circumstances of the adjustment, the adjustment was excluded from the study because no meaningful conclusions could be derived. Subsidiary companies that reported the same prior period adjustment reported in consolidated statements were excluded to avoid duplication. At the time the research was conducted, the NAARS system included:

Year*	Total reports including subsidiaries	Approximate total enterprises
1973	3,617	3,350
1974	3,150	2,800
1975	650	600
Total	7,417	6,750

The detail summaries following are limited to 1974 and 1973; 1975 was reviewed to determine whether significant trends were apparent (none were noted) but the file was considered not sufficiently complete to justify any further conclusions. In addition, later 1975 results, if available, would probably have reflected the effect of the recent SEC staff interpretations.

Overall Results

62. The following table compares 1974 and 1973 identified prior period adjustments:

	1974		1973	
Category	Number of enterprises reporting adjustments	Percentage of enterprises	Number of enterprises reporting adjustments	Percentage of enterprises
Income taxes	30	1.1%	53	1.6%
Litigation and similar claims	37	1.3%	37	1.1%
Utility rate and similar matters	13	0.5%	13	0.4%
Renegotiation	—	0.0%	6	0.2%
Economic stabilization	1	0.0%	2	0.1%
Other	—	0.0%	5	0.1%
Total†	81		116	
Total enterprises	79	2.8%	112	3.3%

---

[13]NAARS is a computer-assisted accounting retrieval system developed by the American Institute of Certified Public Accountants in conjunction with Mead Data Central, Inc.

*The NAARS system classifies fiscal year-ends from July through June as a "year" (e.g., 1974 includes fiscal years ended July 1974 through June 1975).

†Individual categories add to more than the total enterprises shown because some enterprises reported prior period adjustments in more than one category.

63. The following table compares the relative size of the identified adjustments reported for 1974 and 1973:

| Range of prior period adjustment as a percentage of net income or loss in the year reported | | Number of enterprises reporting adjustments in the range | | | |
Over	But not over	Income taxes	Litigation and similar claims	Utility rate and similar matters	All other
0%	5%	13	18	7	4
5%	10%	29	7	6	3
10%	20%	17	17	6	3
20%	50%	16	19	4	1
50%	100%	5	8	—	—
100%		2	5	2	3
Not determinable		1	—	1	—
Total		83	74	26	14

64. Investigation of the adjustments relating to income taxes and litigation disclosed the following circumstances:

| Apparent circumstances of the adjustment, based on financial statement disclosures | Adjustments relating to | |
	Income taxes	Litigation and similar claims
Negotiated settlements	56	45*
Adjudicated settlements	5	14
Combination of negotiated and adjudicated settlements	—	5
Not settled at the date the financial statements were issued	8	7
Negotiated by outside parties without participation by the enterprise	—	1
Change in estimate, with no other party involved	5	—
Not determinable	9	2
Total	83	74

Other Findings

65. Paragraphs 66-70 describe other findings of the survey.

Changes in Accounting Estimates

66. *APB Opinion No. 20* prohibits restatement of amounts reported in prior periods as a result of changes in accounting estimates except for adjustments that meet all of the criteria of paragraph 23 of *APB Opinion No. 9* (see paragraph 35). Twenty of the 197 identified 1974 and 1973 prior period adjustments were changes in previously recorded accounting estimates. These consisted of seven reversals of income tax accruals, six adjustments of prior year provisions for loss on disposal of discontinued

operations, and seven adjustments of prior year provisions for other litigation and similar claims.

Frequency of Occurrence

67. Paragraph 23 of *APB Opinion No. 9* stated that prior period adjustments would be "nonrecurring." Paragraph 24 of Opinion No. 9 stated that "treatment as prior period adjustments should not be applied to the normal, recurring corrections. . . ." The term "nonrecurring" is discussed in paragraph 36 above. Many of the identified prior period adjustments appeared to be of a nature that would be reasonably expected to recur in the foreseeable future in the enterprise's operating environment. Nine enterprises reported similar or related prior period adjustments in both 1974 and 1973.

*17 required court approval.

218

Application of Criterion (a)

68. Criterion (a) of paragraph 23 of *APB Opinion No. 9* requires that an item "can be specifically identified with and directly related to the business activities of particular prior periods." Most of the identified prior period adjustments for settlements of litigation were charged to the period in which the underlying event that gave rise to the litigation occurred. Some, however, were charged or credited to a prior period subsequent to the underlying event, including (a) the period the litigation was initiated, (b) the period of a prior criminal conviction for the alleged acts, or (c) the period that an amount was accrued in excess of the eventual cost of the settlement.

Utility Rate and Similar Matters

69. Utility rate making processes sometimes allow rates to customers to be increased on a provisional basis prior to the regulatory commission's final action on a requested rate increase. If a portion of the requested increase is subsequently disallowed, the utility is required to refund the disallowed portion. Of the 26 identified adjustments relating to utility rate and similar matters, 14 relate to this process.

Income Taxes

70. Identified adjustments for income tax matters included 12 settlements for which the underlying basis of the settlement was recorded (e.g., retroactive adjustment of depreciation to reflect longer useful lives). These may have been corrections of errors. As explained in paragraph 61, these adjustments were included because it was unclear whether the adjustments were made pursuant to paragraph 23 of *APB Opinion No. 9*.

Appendix C

EXCERPTS FROM SEC STAFF ACCOUNTING BULLETIN NO. 8

71. On June 4, 1976 the SEC published *Staff Accounting Bulletin No. 8*. This Bulletin included a statement of the SEC staff's interpretation and application of the criteria of *APB Opinion No. 9* for prior period adjustments.

72. Staff Accounting Bulletins contain the following statement concerning their authoritative status:

The statements in the Bulletin are not rules or interpretations of the Commission nor are they published as bearing the Commission's official approval; they represent interpretations and practices followed by the Division [of Corporation Finance] and the Chief Accountant in administering the disclosure requirements of the federal securities laws.

73. *Staff Accounting Bulletin No. 8* included the following:

H. Prior Period Adjustments

Facts:

Accounting Principles Board Opinion No. 9, paragraph 23, limits treatment as a prior period adjustment "to those material adjustments which (a) can be specifically identified with and directly related to the business activities of particular prior periods, and (b) are not attributable to economic events occurring subsequent to the date of the financial statements for the prior period, and (c) depend primarily on determinations by persons other than management and (d) were not susceptible of reasonable estimation prior to such determination."

It is not uncommon for parties to litigation to reach settlement of the matter at issue in an out-of-court settlement.

Question:

Do out-of-court settlements meet the criteria for prior period adjustments?

Interpretative Response:

The staff has been extremely reluctant to permit registrants to charge items to retained earnings as prior period adjustments in the light of the clear intent expressed in APB 9 to limit such charges severely. That opinion effectively adopted an all-inclusive approach to the measurement of periodic income. While such an approach may not result in the best matching of costs and revenues, it does provide assurance that all items will at some time be accounted for as elements of income and it prevents the abuses which were noted prior to the adoption of APB 9 whereby adverse circumstances could be at least partially obscured through the vehicle of a direct charge to retained earnings. If unusual items and items related to matters arising in prior years are properly isolated and described in the income statement, we believe that investors will be able to interpret results in an intelligent fashion. Were the Financial Accounting Standards Board to revise the basic accounting philosophy of the all-inclusive income statement, the staff would, of course, review its position in the light of that revision.

In the meantime, however, the staff intends to

continue to apply the four restrictive tests set forth in paragraph 23 of Accounting Principles Board Opinion No. 9 strictly. In this connection, the issue which has arisen most frequently is the treatment of litigation settlements. It is the staff's view that when litigation is settled, the management must make a number of significant judgments and, hence, the test that the amounts must "depend primarily on determinations by persons other than management" (criterion (c) above) has not been met. In addition, in a business world increasingly characterized by litigation to an extent far in excess of that when

Accounting Principles Board Opinion No. 9 was adopted (1966), it seems that litigation is inevitably an "economic event" and that settlements would constitute "economic events" of the period in which they occur. Accordingly, it would seem that charges or credits relating to settlements would also not meet the second test (criterion (b) above) set forth in paragraph 23 of Opinion 9 that they not be "attributable to economic events occurring subsequent to the date of the financial statements for the prior period."

Statement of Financial Accounting Standards No. 17
Accounting for Leases—Initial Direct Costs

an amendment of FASB Statement No. 13

STATUS

Issued: November 1977

Effective Date: For leasing transactions and revisions entered into on or after January 1, 1978

Affects: Supersedes FAS 13, paragraph 5(m)

Affected by: Superseded by FAS 91

Other Interpretive Pronouncement: FTB 79-18

(This page intentionally left blank.)

Statement of Financial Accounting Standards No. 18
Financial Reporting for Segments of a Business Enterprise—Interim Financial Statements

an amendment of FASB Statement No. 14

STATUS

Issued: November 1977

Effective Date: December 1, 1977 retroactive to effective date of FAS14

Affects: Amends FAS 14, paragraph 41
      Supersedes FAS 14, paragraphs 4 and 73 and footnote 15

Affected by: No other pronouncements

Statement of Financial Accounting Standards No. 18
Financial Reporting for Segments of a Business Enterprise— Interim Financial Statements

an amendment of FASB Statement No. 14

CONTENTS

INTRODUCTION AND BACKGROUND INFORMATION

1. Paragraph 4 of *FASB Statement No. 14,* "Financial Reporting for Segments of a Business Enterprise," issued by the Board in December 1976, provides for the inclusion of segment information in interim financial statements as follows:

> If an enterprise issues for an interim period a complete set of financial statements that are expressly described as presenting financial position, results of operations, and changes in financial position in conformity with generally accepted accounting principles, this Statement requires that the information referred to in paragraph 3 be included in those interim financial statements. If an enterprise issues for an interim period financial statements that are not a complete set or are otherwise complete but not expressly described as presenting financial position, results of operations, and changes in financial position in conformity with generally accepted accounting principles, this Statement does not require that the information referred to in paragraph 3 be included in those interim financial statements.

The alternatives considered by the Board and the basis for its conclusions are set forth in paragraphs 72 and 73 of the Statement.

2. Since the issuance of *FASB Statement No. 14,* the Board has received a number of questions about when the information specified in the Statement is required in financial statements for interim periods. On March 2, 1977, the Board submitted a proposed Interpretation of paragraph 4 of the Statement to the members of the Financial Accounting Standards Advisory Council for comment. That proposed Interpretation included examples of situations in which the "expressly described" test of paragraph 4 was met and segment information was required and other situations in which the "expressly described" test was not met and segment information was not required. A number of the comment letters received from Council members indicated that the proposed Interpretation did not provide adequate clarification and that an amendment of Statement No. 14 was necessary.

3. The Board has the subject of interim financial reporting on its technical agenda. The issues addressed in that project include consideration of the type of financial information that should be reported for interim periods.

4. The Board has reconsidered the question of whether segment information shall be included in interim financial statements and has decided to eliminate any requirement to report the information specified by *FASB Statement No. 14* in interim period financial statements pending completion of the interim financial reporting project.

5. An Exposure Draft of a proposed Statement on "Financial Reporting for Segments of a Business Enterprise—Interim Financial Statements" was issued on September 20, 1977. Sixty-five letters were received in response to that Exposure Draft, virtually all of which expressed agreement.

6. The Board concluded that on the basis of existing data it can reach an informed decision without a public hearing and that the effective date and transition specified in paragraph 9 are advisable in the circumstances.

STANDARDS OF FINANCIAL ACCOUNTING AND REPORTING

Amendment to FASB Statement No. 14

7. The information specified in paragraph 3 of *FASB Statement No. 14* is not required in financial statements for interim periods. Accordingly, Statement No. 14 is amended as follows:

a. Paragraphs 4 and 73 and footnote 15 to paragraph 41 are deleted.

b. The words "and for interim periods[15] within those fiscal years" are deleted from the first sentence of paragraph 41 and that sentence is modified to read as follows:

> The provisions of this Statement shall be effective for financial statements for fiscal years beginning after December 15, 1976.

8. Although segment information is not required in financial statements for interim periods, any segment information that is presented in interim period financial statements shall be consistent with the requirements of *FASB Statement No. 14.*

Effective Date and Transition

9. This amendment to *FASB Statement No. 14* shall be effective December 1, 1977, retroactive to the effective date of that Statement. Segment information presented in interim period financial statements issued prior to December 1, 1977 need not be included if those interim period financial statements are subsequently presented for comparative purposes after the effective date of this Statement.

> **The provisions of this Statement need not be applied to immaterial items.**

This Statement was adopted by the affirmative votes of the seven members of the Financial Accounting Standards Board.

Marshall S. Armstrong,
Chairman
Oscar S. Gellein

Donald J. Kirk
Arthur L. Litke
Robert E. Mays

Robert T. Sprouse
Ralph E. Walters

Statement of Financial Accounting Standards No. 19
Financial Accounting and Reporting by Oil and Gas Producing Companies

STATUS

Issued: December 1977

Effective Date: For fiscal years beginning after December 15, 1978 and interim periods within those years (but amended by FAS 25)

Affects: Supersedes FAS 9

Affected by: Paragraph 9 superseded by FAS 71
Paragraphs 48 through 59 superseded by FAS 69
Paragraphs 48 and 63 amended by FAS 25
Paragraph 61 amended by FAS 96 and FAS 109
Paragraph 62 amended by FAS 96, FAS 109, and FAS 121
Paragraph 271 and footnotes 11 and 12 superseded by FAS 25

Other Interpretive Pronouncements: FIN 33
FIN 36

Statement of Financial Accounting Standards No. 19
Financial Accounting and Reporting by Oil and Gas Producing Companies

CONTENTS

INTRODUCTION

1. This Statement establishes standards of financial accounting and reporting for the oil and gas producing activities of a business enterprise. Those activities involve the acquisition of mineral interests in properties, exploration (including prospecting), development, and production of crude oil, including condensate and natural gas liquids, and natural gas (hereinafter collectively referred to as oil and gas producing activities).

2. Existing authoritative accounting pronouncements do not explicitly or comprehensively establish standards of financial accounting and reporting for

those activities. Numerous alternative accounting practices are presently followed by oil and gas producing companies, and the nature and extent of the information they disclose in their financial statements about their oil and gas producing activities vary considerably from company to company. The Board is issuing this Statement to address the financial accounting and reporting issues that led to the alternative practices.

3. Appendix A contains background information. Appendix B sets forth the basis for the Board's conclusions, including alternatives considered and reasons for accepting some and rejecting others. Appendix C is a glossary of terms.

4. The accounting standards in this Statement adhere to the traditional historical cost basis. Although the Board considered both *discovery value* and *current value* as alternative bases of accounting for oil and gas reserves, it determined for the reasons discussed in paragraphs 133-141 that any decision on applying value accounting to oil and gas companies should await resolution of the broader issue of the general applicability of value accounting in the Board's project, "Conceptual Framework for Financial Accounting and Reporting."

5. This Statement supersedes *FASB Statement No. 9,* "Accounting for Income Taxes—Oil and Gas Producing Companies."

SCOPE

6. This Statement applies only to *oil and gas producing* activities; it does not address financial accounting and reporting issues relating to the transporting, refining, and marketing of oil and gas. Also, this Statement does not apply to activities relating to the production of other wasting (nonregenerative) natural resources; nor does it apply to the production of geothermal steam or to the extraction of hydrocarbons as a by-product of the production of geothermal steam and associated geothermal resources as defined in the *Geothermal Steam Act of 1970;* nor does it apply to the extraction of hydrocarbons from shale, tar sands, or coal.

7. Accounting for interest on funds borrowed to finance an enterprise's oil and gas producing activities is excluded from consideration in this Statement because the broader subject of accounting for interest costs in general is a project presently on the Board's technical agenda.

8. This Statement prescribes disclosures related to an enterprise's oil and gas producing activities that are considered necessary for fair presentation of the enterprise's financial position, results of operations, and changes in financial position in conformity with generally accepted accounting principles. Those disclosures are only part of the information that may be needed for investment, regulatory, or national economic planning and energy policy decisions.

9. The Addendum to *APB Opinion No. 2,* "Accounting for the 'Investment Credit'," states that "differences may arise in the application of generally accepted accounting principles as between regulated and nonregulated businesses, because of the effect in regulated businesses of the rate-making process" and discusses the application of generally accepted accounting principles to regulated industries. Accordingly, the provisions of the Addendum shall govern the application of this Statement to those oil and gas producing operations of a company that are regulated for rate-making purposes on an individual-company-cost-of-service basis.

STANDARDS OF FINANCIAL ACCOUNTING AND REPORTING

Definitions

10. The glossary in Appendix C defines the following terms as they are used in this Statement:

a. Proved reserves.
b. Proved developed reserves.
c. Proved undeveloped reserves.
d. Field.
e. Reservoir.
f. Exploratory well.
g. Development well.
h. Service well.
i. Stratigraphic test well.
   i. Exploratory-type.
   ii. Development-type.
j. Proved area.

Basic Concepts

11. An enterprise's oil and gas producing activities involve certain special types of assets. Costs of those assets shall be capitalized when incurred. Those types of assets broadly defined are:

a. *Mineral interests in properties* (hereinafter referred to as *properties*), which include fee ownership or a lease, concession, or other interest representing the right to extract oil or gas subject to such terms as may be imposed by the conveyance of that interest. Properties also include royalty interests, production payments payable in oil or gas, and other nonoperating interests in properties operated by others. Properties include those agreements with foreign governments or authorities under which an enterprise participates in the operation of the related properties or otherwise serves as "producer" of the underlying reserves (see paragraph 53); but properties do not include other supply agreements or contracts that represent the right to *purchase* (as opposed to *extract*) oil and gas. Properties shall be classified as proved or unproved as follows:
   i. *Unproved properties*—properties with no proved reserves.
   ii. *Proved properties*—properties with proved reserves.

b. *Wells and related equipment and facilities,*[1] the costs of which include those incurred to:

   i. Drill and equip those exploratory wells and exploratory-type stratigraphic test wells that have found proved reserves.

   ii. Obtain access to proved reserves and provide facilities for extracting, treating, gathering, and storing the oil and gas, including the drilling and equipping of development wells and development-type stratigraphic test wells (whether those wells are successful or unsuccessful) and service wells.

c. *Support equipment and facilities used in oil and gas producing activities,* such as seismic equipment, drilling equipment, construction and grading equipment, vehicles, repair shops, warehouses, supply points, camps, and division, district, or field offices.

d. *Uncompleted wells, equipment, and facilities,* the costs of which include those incurred to:

   i. Drill and equip wells that are not yet completed.

   ii. Acquire or construct equipment and facilities that are not yet completed and installed.

12. The costs of an enterprise's wells and related equipment and facilities and the costs of the related proved properties shall be amortized as the related oil and gas reserves are produced. That amortization plus production (lifting) costs become part of the cost of oil and gas produced. Unproved properties shall be assessed periodically, and a loss recognized if those properties are impaired.

13. Some costs incurred in an enterprise's oil and gas producing activities do not result in acquisition of an asset and, therefore, shall be charged to expense. Examples include geological and geophysical costs, the costs of carrying and retaining undeveloped properties, and the costs of drilling those exploratory wells and exploratory-type stratigraphic test wells that do not find proved reserves.

14. The basic concepts in paragraphs 11-13 are elaborated on in paragraphs 15-41.

Accounting at the Time Costs Are Incurred

Acquisition of Properties

15. Costs incurred to purchase, lease, or otherwise acquire a property (whether unproved or proved) shall be capitalized when incurred. They include the costs of lease bonuses and options to purchase or lease properties, the portion of costs applicable to

minerals when land including mineral rights is purchased in fee, brokers' fees, recording fees, legal costs, and other costs incurred in acquiring properties.

Exploration

16. Exploration involves (a) identifying areas that may warrant examination and (b) examining specific areas that are considered to have prospects of containing oil and gas reserves, including drilling exploratory wells and exploratory-type stratigraphic test wells. Exploration costs may be incurred both before acquiring the related property (sometimes referred to in part as prospecting costs) and after acquiring the property.

17. Principal types of exploration costs, which include depreciation and applicable operating costs of support equipment and facilities (paragraph 26) and other costs of exploration activities, are:

a. Costs of topographical, geological, and geophysical studies, rights of access to properties to conduct those studies, and salaries and other expenses of geologists, geophysical crews, and others conducting those studies. Collectively, those are sometimes referred to as geological and geophysical or "G&G" costs.

b. Costs of carrying and retaining undeveloped properties, such as delay rentals, *ad valorem* taxes on the properties, legal costs for title defense, and the maintenance of land and lease records.

c. Dry hole contributions and bottom hole contributions.

d. Costs of drilling and equipping exploratory wells.

e. Costs of drilling exploratory-type stratigraphic test wells.[2]

18. Geological and geophysical costs, costs of carrying and retaining undeveloped properties, and dry hole and bottom hole contributions shall be charged to expense when incurred.

19. The costs of drilling exploratory wells and the costs of drilling exploratory-type stratigraphic test wells shall be capitalized as part of the enterprise's uncompleted wells, equipment, and facilities pending determination of whether the well has found proved reserves. If the well has found proved reserves (paragraphs 31-34), the capitalized costs of drilling the well shall become part of the enterprise's wells and related equipment and facilities (even

---

[1] Often referred to in the oil and gas industry as "lease and well equipment" even though, technically, the property may have been acquired other than by a lease.

[2] While the costs of drilling stratigraphic test wells are sometimes considered to be geological and geophysical costs, they are accounted for separately under this Statement for reasons explained in paragraphs 200-202.

though the well may not be completed as a producing well); if, however, the well has not found proved reserves, the capitalized costs of drilling the well, net of any salvage value, shall be charged to expense.

20. An enterprise sometimes conducts G&G studies and other exploration activities on a property owned by another party, in exchange for which the enterprise is contractually entitled to receive an interest in the property if proved reserves are found or to be reimbursed by the owner for the G&G and other costs incurred if proved reserves are not found. In that case, the enterprise conducting the G&G studies and other exploration activities shall account for those costs as a receivable when incurred and, if proved reserves are found, they shall become the cost of the proved property acquired.

Development

21. Development costs are incurred to obtain access to proved reserves and to provide facilities for extracting, treating, gathering, and storing the oil and gas. More specifically, development costs, including depreciation and applicable operating costs of support equipment and facilities (paragraph 26) and other costs of development activities, are costs incurred to:

a. Gain access to and prepare well locations for drilling, including surveying well locations for the purpose of determining specific development drilling sites, clearing ground, draining, road building, and relocating public roads, gas lines, and power lines, to the extent necessary in developing the proved reserves.
b. Drill and equip development wells, development-type stratigraphic test wells, and service wells, including the costs of platforms and of well equipment such as casing, tubing, pumping equipment, and the wellhead assembly.
c. Acquire, construct, and install production facilities such as lease flow lines, separators, treaters, heaters, manifolds, measuring devices, and production storage tanks, natural gas cycling and processing plants, and utility and waste disposal systems.
d. Provide improved recovery systems.

22. Development costs shall be capitalized as part of the cost of an enterprise's wells and related equipment and facilities. Thus, all costs incurred to drill and equip development wells, development-type stratigraphic test wells, and service wells are development costs and shall be capitalized, whether the well is successful or unsuccessful. Costs of drilling those wells and costs of constructing equipment and facilities shall be included in the enterprise's uncompleted wells, equipment, and facilities until drilling or construction is completed.

Production

23. Production involves lifting the oil and gas to the surface and gathering, treating, field processing (as in the case of processing gas to extract liquid hydrocarbons), and field storage. For purposes of this Statement, the production function shall normally be regarded as terminating at the outlet valve on the lease or field production storage tank; if unusual physical or operational circumstances exist, it may be more appropriate to regard the production function as terminating at the first point at which oil, gas, or gas liquids are delivered to a main pipeline, a common carrier, a refinery, or a marine terminal.

24. Production costs are those costs incurred to operate and maintain an enterprise's wells and related equipment and facilities, including depreciation and applicable operating costs of support equipment and facilities (paragraph 26) and other costs of operating and maintaining those wells and related equipment and facilities. They become part of the cost of oil and gas produced. Examples of production costs (sometimes called lifting costs) are:

a. Costs of labor to operate the wells and related equipment and facilities.
b. Repairs and maintenance.
c. Materials, supplies, and fuel consumed and services utilized in operating the wells and related equipment and facilities.
d. Property taxes and insurance applicable to proved properties and wells and related equipment and facilities.
e. Severance taxes.

25. Depreciation, depletion, and amortization of capitalized acquisition, exploration, and development costs also become part of the cost of oil and gas produced along with production (lifting) costs identified in paragraph 24.

Support Equipment and Facilities

26. The cost of acquiring or constructing support equipment and facilities used in oil and gas producing activities shall be capitalized. Examples of support equipment and facilities include seismic equipment, drilling equipment, construction and grading equipment, vehicles, repair shops, warehouses, supply points, camps, and division, district, or field offices. Some support equipment or facilities are acquired or constructed for use exclusively in a single activity—exploration, development, or production. Other support equipment or facilities may serve two or more of those activities and may also serve the enterprise's transportation, refining, and marketing activities. To the extent that the support

equipment and facilities are used in oil and gas producing activities, their depreciation and applicable operating costs become an exploration, development, or production cost, as appropriate.

Disposition of Capitalized Costs

27. The effect of paragraphs 15-26, which deal with accounting at the time costs are incurred, is to recognize as assets: (a) unproved properties; (b) proved properties; (c) wells and related equipment and facilities (which consist of all development costs plus the costs of drilling those exploratory wells and exploratory-type stratigraphic test wells that find proved reserves); (d) support equipment and facilities used in oil and gas producing activities; and (e) uncompleted wells, equipment, and facilities. Paragraphs 28-41 which follow deal with disposition of the costs of those assets after capitalization. Among other things, those paragraphs provide that the acquisition costs of proved properties and the costs of wells and related equipment and facilities be amortized to become part of the cost oil and gas produced; that impairment of unproved properties be recognized; and that the costs of an exploratory well or exploratory-type stratigraphic test well be charged to expense if the well is determined not to have found proved reserves.

Assessment of Unproved Properties

28. Unproved properties shall be assessed periodically to determine whether they have been impaired. A property would likely be impaired, for example, if a dry hole has been drilled on it and the enterprise has no firm plans to continue drilling. Also, the likelihood of partial or total impairment of a property increases as the expiration of the lease term approaches if drilling activity has not commenced on the property or on nearby properties. If the results of the assessment indicate impairment, a loss shall be recognized by providing a valuation allowance. Impairment of individual unproved properties whose acquisition costs are relatively significant shall be assessed on a property-by-property basis, and an indicated loss shall be recognized by providing a valuation allowance. When an enterprise has a relatively large number of unproved properties whose acquisition costs are not individually significant, it may not be practical to assess impairment on a property-by-property basis, in which case the amount of loss to be recognized and the amount of the valuation allowance needed to provide for impairment of those properties shall be determined by amortizing those properties, either in the aggregate or by groups, on the basis of the experience of the enterprise in similar situations and other information about such factors as the primary lease terms of those properties, the average holding period of unproved properties, and the relative proportion of such properties on which proved reserves have been found in the past.

Reclassification of an Unproved Property

29. A property shall be reclassified from unproved properties to proved properties when proved reserves are discovered on or otherwise attributed to the property; occasionally, a single property, such as a foreign lease or concession covers so vast an area that only the portion of the property to which the proved reserves relate—determined on the basis of geological structural features or stratigraphic conditions—should be reclassified from unproved to proved. For a property whose impairment has been assessed individually in accordance with paragraph 28, the *net* carrying amount (acquisition cost minus valuation allowance) shall be reclassified to proved properties; for properties amortized by providing a valuation allowance on a group basis, the gross acquisition cost shall be reclassified.

Amortization (Depletion) of Acquisition Costs of Proved Properties

30. Capitalized acquisition costs of proved properties shall be amortized (depleted) by the unit-of-production method so that each unit produced is assigned a pro rata portion of the unamortized acquisition costs. Under the unit-of-production method, amortization (depletion) may be computed either on a property-by-property basis or on the basis of some reasonable aggregation of properties with a common geological structural feature or stratigraphic condition, such as a reservoir or field. When an enterprise has a relatively large number of royalty interests whose acquisition costs are not individually significant, they may be aggregated, for the purpose of computing amortization, without regard to commonality of geological structural features or stratigraphic conditions; if information is not available to estimate reserve quantities applicable to royalty interests owned (paragraph 50), a method other than the unit-of-production method may be used to amortize their acquisition costs. The unit cost shall be computed on the basis of the total estimated units of proved oil and gas reserves. (Joint production of both oil and gas is discussed in paragraph 38.) Unit-of-production amortization rates shall be revised whenever there is an indication of the need for revision but at least once a year; those revisions shall be accounted for prospectively as changes in accounting estimates—see paragraphs 31-33 of *APB Opinion No. 20*, "Accounting Changes."

Accounting When Drilling of an Exploratory Well Is Completed

31. As specified in paragraph 19, the costs of drilling an exploratory well are capitalized as part of the

enterprise's uncompleted wells, equipment, and facilities pending determination of whether the well has found proved reserves. That determination is usually made on or shortly after completion of drilling the well, and the capitalized costs shall either be charged to expense or be reclassified as part of the costs of the enterprise's wells and related equipment and facilities at that time. Occasionally, however, an exploratory well may be determined to have found oil and gas reserves, but classification of those reserves as proved cannot be made when drilling is completed. In those cases, one or the other of the following subparagraphs shall apply depending on whether the well is drilled in an area requiring a major capital expenditure, such as a trunk pipeline, before production from that well could begin:

a. *Exploratory wells that find oil and gas reserves in an area requiring a major capital expenditure, such as a trunk pipeline, before production could begin.* On completion of drilling, an exploratory well may be determined to have found oil and gas reserves, but classification of those reserves as proved depends on whether a major capital expenditure can be justified which, in turn, depends on whether additional exploratory wells find a sufficient quantity of additional reserves. That situation arises principally with exploratory wells drilled in a remote area for which production would require constructing a trunk pipeline. In that case, the cost of drilling the exploratory well shall continue to be carried as an asset pending determination of whether proved reserves have been found only as long as both of the following conditions are met:
    i. The well has found a sufficient quantity of reserves to justify its completion as a producing well if the required capital expenditure is made.
    ii. Drilling of the additional exploratory wells is under way or firmly planned for the near future.
    Thus if drilling in the area is not under way or firmly planned, or if the well has not found a commercially producible quantity of reserves, the exploratory well shall be assumed to be impaired, and its costs shall be charged to expense.
b. *All other exploratory wells that find oil and gas reserves.* In the absence of a determination as to whether the reserves that have been found can be classified as proved, the costs of drilling such an exploratory well shall not be carried as an asset for more than one year following completion of drilling. If, after that year has passed, a determination that proved reserves have been found cannot be made, the well shall be assumed to be impaired, and its costs shall be charged to expense.

32. Paragraph 31 is intended to prohibit, in all cases, the deferral of the costs of exploratory wells that find some oil and gas reserves merely on the chance that some event totally beyond the control of the enterprise will occur, for example, on the chance that the selling prices of oil and gas will increase sufficiently to result in classification of reserves as proved that are not commercially recoverable at current prices.

Accounting When Drilling of an Exploratory-Type Stratigraphic Test Well Is Completed

33. As specified in paragraph 19, the costs of drilling an exploratory-type stratigraphic test well are capitalized as part of the enterprise's uncompleted wells, equipment, and facilities pending determination of whether the well has found proved reserves. When that determination is made, the capitalized costs shall be charged to expense if proved reserves are not found or shall be reclassified as part of the costs of the enterprise's wells and related equipment and facilities if proved reserves are found.

34. Exploratory-type stratigraphic test wells are normally drilled on unproved offshore properties. Frequently, on completion of drilling, such a well may be determined to have found oil and gas reserves, but classification of those reserves as proved depends on whether a major capital expenditure—usually a production platform—can be justified which, in turn, depends on whether additional exploratory-type stratigraphic test wells find a sufficient quantity of additional reserves. In that case, the cost of drilling the exploratory-type stratigraphic test well shall continue to be carried as an asset pending determination of whether proved reserves have been found only as long as both of the following conditions are met:

a. The well has found a quantity of reserves that would justify its completion for production had it not been simply a stratigraphic test well.
b. Drilling of the additional exploratory-type stratigraphic test wells is under way or firmly planned for the near future.

Thus if associated stratigraphic test drilling is not under way or firmly planned, or if the well has not found a commercially producible quantity of reserves, the exploratory-type stratigraphic test well shall be assumed to be impaired, and its costs shall be charged to expense.

Amortization and Depreciation of Capitalized Exploratory Drilling and Development Costs

35. Capitalized costs of exploratory wells and exploratory-type stratigraphic test wells that have

found proved reserves and capitalized development costs shall be amortized (depreciated) by the unit-of-production method so that each unit produced is assigned a pro rata portion of the unamortized costs. It may be more appropriate, in some cases, to depreciate natural gas cycling and processing plants by a method other than the unit-of-production method. Under the unit-of-production method, amortization (depreciation) may be computed either on a property-by-property basis or on the basis of some reasonable aggregation of properties with a common geological structural feature or stratigraphic condition, such as a reservoir or field. The unit cost shall be computed on the basis of the total estimated units of proved *developed* reserves, rather than on the basis of all proved reserves, which is the basis for amortizing acquisition costs of proved properties. If significant development costs (such as the cost of an off-shore production platform) are incurred in connection with a planned group of development wells before all of the planned wells have been drilled, it will be necessary to exclude a portion of those development costs in determining the unit-of-production amortization rate until the additional development wells are drilled. Similarly it will be necessary to exclude, in computing the amortization rate, those proved developed reserves that will be produced only after significant additional development costs are incurred, such as for improved recovery systems. However, in no case should future development costs be anticipated in computing the amortization rate. (Joint production of both oil and gas is discussed in paragraph 38.) Unit-of-production amortization rates shall be revised whenever there is an indication of the need for revision but at least once a year; those revisions shall be accounted for prospectively as changes in accounting estimates—see paragraphs 31-33 of *APB Opinion No. 20.*

Depreciation of Support Equipment and Facilities

36. Depreciation of support equipment and facilities used in oil and gas producing activities shall be accounted for as exploration cost, development cost, or production cost, as appropriate (paragraph 26).

Dismantlement Costs and Salvage Values

37. Estimated dismantlement, restoration, and abandonment costs and estimated residual salvage values shall be taken into account in determining amortization and depreciation rates.

Amortization of Costs Relating to Oil and Gas Reserves Produced Jointly

38. The unit-of-production method of amortization requires that the total number of units of oil or

gas reserves in a property or group of properties be estimated and that the number of units produced in the current period be determined. Many properties contain both oil and gas reserves. In those cases, the oil and gas reserves and the oil and gas produced shall be converted to a common unit of measure on the basis of their approximate relative energy content (without considering their relative sales values). However, if the relative proportion of gas and oil extracted in the current period is expected to continue throughout the remaining productive life of the property, unit-of-production amortization may be computed on the basis of one of the two minerals only; similarly, if either oil or gas clearly dominates both the reserves and the current production (with dominance determined on the basis of relative energy content), unit-of-production amortization may be computed on the basis of the dominant mineral only.

Information Available after the Balance Sheet Date

39. Information that becomes available after the end of the period covered by the financial statements but before those financial statements are issued shall be taken into account in evaluating conditions that existed at the balance sheet date, for example, in assessing unproved properties (paragraph 28) and in determining whether an exploratory well or exploratory-type stratigraphic test well had found proved reserves (paragraphs 31-34).

Surrender or Abandonment of Properties

40. When an unproved property is surrendered, abandoned, or otherwise deemed worthless, capitalized acquisition costs relating thereto shall be charged against the related allowance for impairment to the extent an allowance has been provided; if the allowance previously provided is inadequate, a loss shall be recognized.

41. Normally, no gain or loss shall be recognized if only an individual well or individual item of equipment is abandoned or retired or if only a single lease or other part of a group of proved properties constituting the amortization base is abandoned or retired as long as the remainder of the property or group of properties continues to produce oil or gas. Instead, the asset being abandoned or retired shall be deemed to be fully amortized, and its cost shall be charged to accumulated depreciation, depletion, or amortization. When the *last* well on an individual property (if that is the amortization base) or group of properties (if amortization is determined on the basis of an aggregation of properties with a common geological structure) ceases to produce and the entire property or property group is abandoned, gain or loss shall be recognized. Occasionally, the partial abandonment or retirement of a proved property or group of

proved properties or the abandonment or retirement of wells or related equipment or facilities may result from a catastrophic event or other major abnormality. In those cases, a loss shall be recognized at the time of abandonment or retirement.

Mineral Property Conveyances and Related Transactions

42. Mineral interests in properties are frequently conveyed to others for a variety of reasons, including the desire to spread risks, to obtain financing, to improve operating efficiency, and to achieve tax benefits. Conveyances of those interests may involve the transfer of all or a part of the rights and responsibilities of operating a property (operating interest). The transferor may or may not retain an interest in the oil and gas produced that is free of the responsibilities and costs of operating the property (a non-operating interest). A transaction may, on the other hand, involve the transfer of a nonoperating interest to another party and retention of the operating interest.

43. Certain transactions, sometimes referred to as conveyances, are in substance borrowings repayable in cash or its equivalent and shall be accounted for as borrowings. The following are examples of such transactions:

a. Enterprises seeking supplies of oil or gas sometimes make cash advances to operators to finance exploration in return for the right to purchase oil or gas discovered. Funds advanced for exploration that are repayable by offset against purchases of oil or gas discovered, or in cash if insufficient oil or gas is produced by a specified date, shall be accounted for as a receivable by the lender and as a payable by the operator.

b. Funds advanced to an operator that are repayable in cash out of the proceeds from a specified share of future production of a producing property, until the amount advanced plus interest at a specified or determinable rate is paid in full, shall be accounted for as a borrowing. The advance is a payable for the recipient of the cash and a receivable for the party making the advance. Such transactions, as well as those described in paragraph 47(a) below, are commonly referred to as production payments. The two types differ in substance, however, as explained in paragraph 47(a).

44. In the following types of conveyances, gain or loss shall not be recognized at the time of the conveyance:

a. A transfer of assets used in oil and gas producing activities (including both proved and unproved properties) in exchange for other assets also used in oil and gas producing activities.

b. A pooling of assets in a joint undertaking intended to find, develop, or produce oil or gas from a particular property or group of properties.

45. In the following types of conveyances, gain shall not be recognized at the time of the conveyance:

a. A part of an interest owned is sold and substantial uncertainty exists about recovery of the costs applicable to the retained interest.

b. A part of an interest owned is sold and the seller has a substantial obligation for future performance, such as an obligation to drill a well or to operate the property without proportional reimbursement for that portion of the drilling or operating costs applicable to the interest sold.

46. If a conveyance is not one of the types described in paragraphs 44 and 45, gain or loss shall be recognized unless there are other aspects of the transaction that would prohibit such recognition under accounting principles applicable to enterprises in general.

47. In accordance with paragraphs 44-46, the following types of transactions shall be accounted for as indicated in each example.[3] No attempt has been made to include the many variations of those arrangements that occur, but paragraphs 44-46 shall, where applicable, determine the accounting for those other arrangements as well.

a. Some production payments differ from those described in paragraph 43(b) in that the seller's obligation is not expressed in monetary terms but as an obligation to deliver, free and clear of all expenses associated with operation of the property, a specified quantity of oil or gas to the purchaser out of a specified share of future production. Such a transaction is a sale of a mineral interest for which gain shall not be recognized because the seller has a substantial obligation for future performance. The seller shall account for the funds received as unearned revenue to be recognized as the oil or gas is delivered. The purchaser of such a production payment has acquired an interest in a mineral property that shall be recorded at cost and amortized by the unit-of-production method as delivery takes place. The related reserve estimates and production data shall be reported as those of the purchaser of the production payment and not of the seller (paragraphs 50-56).

---

[3] Costs of unproved properties are always subject to an assessment for impairment as required by paragraph 28.

b. An assignment of the operating interest in an unproved property with retention of a non-operating interest in return for drilling, development, and operation by the assignee is a pooling of assets in a joint undertaking for which the assignor shall not recognize gain or loss. The assignor's cost of the original interest shall become the cost of the interest retained. The assignee shall account for all costs incurred as specified by paragraphs 15-41 and shall allocate none of those costs to the mineral interest acquired. If oil or gas is discovered, each party shall report its share of reserves and production (paragraphs 50-56).

c. An assignment of a part of an operating interest in an unproved property in exchange for a "free well" with provision for joint ownership and operation is a pooling of assets in a joint undertaking by the parties. The assignor shall record no cost for the obligatory well; the assignee shall record no cost for the mineral interest acquired. All drilling, development, and operating costs incurred by either party shall be accounted for as provided in paragraphs 15-41 of this Statement. If the conveyance agreement requires the assignee to incur geological or geophysical expenditures instead of, or in addition to, a drilling obligation, those costs shall likewise be accounted for by the assignee as provided in paragraphs 15-41 of this Statement. If reserves are discovered, each party shall report its share of reserves and production (paragraphs 50-56).

d. A part of an operating interest in an unproved property may be assigned to effect an arrangement called a "carried interest" whereby the assignee (the carrying party) agrees to defray all costs of drilling, developing, and operating the property and is entitled to all of the revenue from production from the property, excluding any third party interest, until all of the assignee's costs have been recovered, after which the assignor will share in both costs and production. Such an arrangement represents a pooling of assets in a joint undertaking by the assignor and assignee. The carried party shall make no accounting for any costs and revenue until after recoupment (payout) of the carried costs by the carrying party. Subsequent to payout the carried party shall account for its share of revenue, operating expenses, and (if the agreement provides for subsequent sharing of costs rather than a carried interest) subsequent development costs. During the payout period the carrying party shall record all costs, including those carried, as provided in paragraphs 15-41 and shall record all revenue from the property including that applicable to the recovery of costs carried. The carried party shall report as oil or gas reserves only its share of proved reserves estimated to remain after payout, and unit-of-

production amortization of the carried party's property cost shall not commence prior to payout. Prior to payout the carrying party's reserve estimates and production data shall include the quantities applicable to recoupment of the carried costs (paragraphs 50-56).

e. A part of an operating interest owned may be exchanged for a part of an operating interest owned by another party. The purpose of such an arrangement, commonly called a joint venture in the oil and gas industry, often is to avoid duplication of facilities, diversify risks, and achieve operating efficiencies. Such reciprocal conveyances represent exchanges of similar productive assets, and no gain or loss shall be recognized by either party at the time of the transaction. In some joint ventures which may or may not involve an exchange of interests, the parties may share different elements of costs in different proportions. In such an arrangement a party may acquire an interest in a property or in wells and related equipment that is disproportionate to the share of costs borne by it. As in the case of a carried interest or a free well, each party shall account for its own cost under the provisions of this Statement. No gain shall be recognized for the acquisition of an interest in joint assets, the cost of which may have been paid in whole or in part by another party.

f. In a unitization all the operating and nonoperating participants pool their assets in a producing area (normally a field) to form a single unit and in return receive an undivided interest (of the same type as previously held) in that unit. Unitizations generally are undertaken to obtain operating efficiencies and to enhance recovery of reserves, often through improved recovery operations. Participation in the unit is generally proportionate to the oil and gas reserves contributed by each. Because the properties may be in different stages of development at the time of unitization, some participants may pay cash and others may receive cash to equalize contributions of wells and related equipment and facilities with the ownership interests in reserves. In those circumstances, cash paid by a participant shall be recorded as an additional investment in wells and related equipment and facilities, and cash received by a participant shall be recorded as a recovery of cost. The cost of the assets contributed plus or minus cash paid or received is the cost of the participant's undivided interest in the assets of the unit. Each participant shall include its interest in reporting reserve estimates and production data (paragraphs 50-56).

g. If the entire interest in an unproved property is sold for cash or cash equivalent, recognition of gain or loss depends on whether, in applying paragraph 28 of this Statement, impairment had been assessed for that property individually or by amortizing that property as part of a group. If impairment was assessed individually, gain or loss shall be recognized. For a property amortized by providing a valuation allowance on a group basis, neither gain nor loss shall be recognized when an unproved property is sold unless the sales price exceeds the original cost of the property, in which case gain shall be recognized in the amount of such excess.

h. If a part of the interest in an unproved property is sold, even though for cash or cash equivalent, substantial uncertainty usually exists as to recovery of the cost applicable to the interest retained. Consequently, the amount received shall be treated as a recovery of cost.[4] However, if the sales price exceeds the carrying amount of a property whose impairment has been assessed individually in accordance with paragraph 28 of this Statement, or exceeds the original cost of a property amortized by providing a valuation allowance on a group basis, gain shall be recognized in the amount of such excess.

i. The sale of an entire interest in a proved property that constitutes a separate amortization base is not one of the types of conveyances described in paragraph 44 or 45. The difference between the amount of sales proceeds and the unamortized cost shall be recognized as a gain or loss.

j. The sale of a part of a proved property, or of an entire proved property constituting a part of an amortization base, shall be accounted for as the sale of an asset, and a gain or loss shall be recognized, since it is not one of the conveyances described in paragraph 44 or 45. The unamortized cost of the property or group of properties a part of which was sold shall be apportioned to the interest sold and the interest retained on the basis of the fair values of those interests. However, the sale may be accounted for as a normal retirement under the provisions of paragraph 41 with no gain or loss recognized if doing so does not significantly affect the unit-of-production amortization rate.

k. The sale of the operating interest in a proved property for cash with retention of a nonoperating interest is not one of the types of conveyances described in paragraph 44 or 45. Accordingly, it shall be accounted for as the sale of an asset, and any gain or loss shall be recognized. The seller shall allocate the cost of the proved property to the operating interest sold and the nonoperating interest retained on the basis of the fair values of those interests.[5]

l. The sale of a proved property subject to a retained production payment that is expressed as a fixed sum of money payable only from a specified share of production from that property, with the purchaser of the property obligated to incur the future costs of operating the property, shall be accounted for as follows:

  i. *If satisfaction of the retained production payment is reasonably assured.* The seller of the property, who retained the production payment, shall record the transaction as a sale, with recognition of any resulting gain or loss. The retained production payment shall be recorded as a receivable, with interest accounted for in accordance with the provisions of *APB Opinion No. 21,* "Interest on Receivables and Payables." The purchaser shall record as the cost of the assets acquired the cash consideration paid plus the present value (determined in accordance with *APB Opinion No. 21*) of the retained production payment, which shall be recorded as a payable. The oil and gas reserve estimates and production data, including those applicable to liquidation of the retained production payment, shall be reported by the purchaser of the property (paragraphs 50-56).

  ii. *If satisfaction of the retained production payment is not reasonably assured.* The transaction is in substance a sale with retention of an overriding royalty that shall be accounted for in accordance with paragraph 47(k).

m. The sale of a proved property subject to a retained production payment that is expressed as a right to a specified quantity of oil or gas out of a specified share of future production shall be accounted for in accordance with paragraph 47(k).

Disclosure

48. An enterprise engaged in oil and gas producing activities shall include in a complete set of annual financial statements the disclosures specified in paragraphs 50-59. Those disclosures may be made within the body of the financial statements, in the notes thereto, or in a separate schedule that is an integral part of the financial statements.

49. Disclosure of capitalized costs (paragraph 57) shall also be included in a complete set of interim financial statements that present financial position, results of operations, and changes in financial position in conformity with generally accepted accounting principles. Disclosures of reserve quantities and of costs incurred as set forth in paragraphs 50-56 and 58 and 59 are not required in such interim financial statements, though the Board encourages disclosure in those financial statements of information

---

[4]The carrying amount of the interest retained shall continue to be subject to the assessment for impairment as required by paragraph 28.

[5]A retained production payment denominated in money is not a mineral interest (see paragraphs 11(a) and 43).

about a major discovery or other favorable or adverse event that causes a significant change from the reserve data reported in the most recent annual financial statements.

Disclosure of Reserve Quantities

50. Net quantities of an enterprise's interests in proved reserves and proved developed reserves of (a) crude oil (including condensate and natural gas liquids) and (b) natural gas shall be reported as of the beginning and the end of each year for which a complete set of financial statements is presented. "Net" quantities of reserves include those relating to the enterprise's operating and nonoperating interests in properties as defined in paragraph 11(a). Quantities of reserves relating to royalty interests owned shall be included in "net" quantities if the necessary information is available to the enterprise; if reserves relating to royalty interests owned are not included because the information is unavailable, that fact and the enterprise's share of oil and gas produced for those royalty interests shall be reported for each year for which a complete set of financial statements is presented. "Net" quantities shall not include reserves relating to interests of others in properties owned by the enterprise.

51. Changes in the net quantities of an enterprise's proved reserves of oil and of gas during each year for which a complete set of financial statements is presented shall be reported. Changes resulting from each of the following shall be separately shown with appropriate explanation of significant changes:

a. *Revisions of previous estimates.* Revisions represent changes in previous estimates of proved reserves, either upward or downward, resulting from new information (except for an increase in proved acreage) normally obtained from development drilling and production history or resulting from a change in economic factors.
b. *Improved recovery.* Changes in reserve estimates resulting from application of improved recovery techniques shall be separately shown if significant. If not significant, such changes shall be included in revisions of previous estimates.
c. *Purchases of minerals-in-place.*
d. *Extensions, discoveries, and other additions.* Additions to an enterprise's proved reserves that result from (i) extension of the proved acreage of previously discovered (old) reservoirs through additional drilling in periods subsequent to discovery and (ii) discovery of new fields with proved reserves or of new reservoirs of proved reserves in old fields.
e. *Production.*
f. *Sales of minerals-in-place.*

52. If an enterprise's proved reserves of oil and gas

are located entirely within its home country, that fact shall be disclosed. If some or all of its reserves are located in foreign countries, the disclosures of net quantities of reserves of oil and of gas and changes in them required by paragraphs 50 and 51 shall be separately reported for (a) the enterprise's home country (if significant reserves are located there) and (b) each foreign geographic area in which significant reserves are located. Foreign geographic areas are individual countries or groups of countries as appropriate for meaningful disclosure in the circumstances.

53. Net quantities disclosed in conformity with paragraphs 50-52 shall not include oil or gas subject to purchase under long-term supply, purchase, or similar agreements and contracts, including such agreements with foreign governments or authorities. However, quantities of oil or gas subject to such agreements with foreign governments or authorities as of the end of each year for which a complete set of financial statements is presented, and the net quantity of oil or gas received under the agreements during each such year, shall be separately disclosed if the enterprise participates in the operation of the properties in which the oil or gas is located or otherwise serves as the "producer" of those reserves, as opposed, for example, to being an independent purchaser, broker, dealer, or importer.

54. In determining the reserve quantities to be reported in conformity with paragraphs 50-53:

a. If the enterprise issues consolidated financial statements, 100 percent of the *net* reserve quantities attributable to the parent company and 100 percent of the *net* reserve quantities attributable to its consolidated subsidiaries (whether or not wholly owned) shall be included.
b. If the enterprise's financial statements include investments that are proportionately consolidated, the enterprise's reserve quantities shall include its proportionate share of the investee's net oil and gas reserves.
c. If the enterprise's financial statements include investments that are accounted for by the equity method, the investee's net oil and gas reserves shall *not* be included in the disclosures of the enterprise's reserves. However, the enterprise's (investor's) share of the investee's net oil and gas reserves shall be separately reported as of the end of each year for which a complete set of financial statements is presented.

55. In reporting reserve quantities and changes in them, oil reserves (which include condensate and natural gas liquids) shall be stated in barrels, and gas reserves in cubic feet. Disclosures of the type called for by paragraphs 50-54 are diagrammed on page 238.

	Total Worldwide		United States		Foreign Geographic Area A		Foreign Geographic Area B		Other Foreign Geographic Areas	
	Oil	*Gas*	*Oil*	*Gas*	*Oil*	*Gas*	*Oil*	*Gas*	*Oil*	*Gas*
Proved developed and undeveloped reserves:										
Beginning of year	X	X	X	X	X	X	X	X	X	X
Revisions of previous estimates	X	X	X	X	X	X	X	X	X	X
Improved recovery	X	X	X	X	X	X	X	X	X	X
Purchases of minerals-in-place	X	X	X	X	X	X	X	X	X	X
Extensions, discoveries, and other additions	X	X	X	X	X	X	X	X	X	X
Production	(X)	(X)	(X)	(X)	(X)	(X)	(X)	(X)	(X)	(X)
Sales of minerals-in-place	(X)	(X)	(X)	(X)	(X)	(X)	(X)	(X)	(X)	(X)
End of year	X	X	X	X	X	X	X	X	X	X
Proved developed reserves:										
Beginning of year	X	X	X	X	X	X	X	X	X	X
End of year	X	X	X	X	X	X	X	X	X	X
Oil and gas applicable to long-term supply agreements with foreign governments or authorities in which the company acts as producer:										
Proved reserves at end of year	X	X			X	X	X	X	X	X
Received during the year	X	X			X	X	X	X	X	X
Company's proportional interest in reserves of investees accounted for by the equity method, end of year	X		X		X		X		X	

56. If important economic factors or significant uncertainties affect particular components of an enterprise's proved reserves, explanation shall be provided. Examples include unusually high expected development or lifting costs; the necessity to build a major pipeline or other major facilities before production of the reserves can begin; or contractual obligations to produce and sell a significant portion of reserves at prices that are substantially below those at which the oil or gas could otherwise be sold in the absence of the contractual obligation.

Disclosure of Capitalized Costs

57. The aggregate amount of capitalized costs relating to an enterprise's oil and gas producing activities (paragraph 11) and the aggregate amount of the related accumulated depreciation, depletion, amortization, and valuation allowances shall be reported as of the end of each period for which financial statements are presented. Paragraph 5 of *APB Opinion No. 12*, "Omnibus Opinion—1967," requires disclosure of "balances of major classes of depreciable assets, by nature or function." Thus, separate disclosure of the amount of capitalized costs for one or more of asset categories (a) to (d) in paragraph 11 or for a combination of two or more of those categories often may be appropriate.

Disclosure of Costs Incurred in Oil and Gas Producing Activities

58. The financial statements of an oil and gas producing company shall disclose the amounts of each of the following types of costs for each year for which a complete set of financial statements is presented (whether those costs are capitalized or charged to expense at the time they are incurred under the provisions of paragraphs 15-26). As defined in the paragraphs cited, exploration, development, and production costs *include* depreciation of support equipment and facilities used in those activities and *do not include* the expenditures to acquire support equipment and facilities. Also, as stated in paragraph 25, production (lifting) costs do not include depreciation, depletion, and amortization of capitalized acquisition, exploration, and development costs.

a. Property acquisition costs (paragraph 15).
b. Exploration costs (paragraph 17).
c. Development costs (paragraph 21).
d. Production (lifting) costs (paragraph 24).

59. If some or all of those costs are incurred in foreign countries, the amounts shall be disclosed separately for each of the geographic areas for which reserve quantities are disclosed (paragraph 52).

Accounting for Income Taxes

60. Some costs incurred in an enterprise's oil and gas producing activities enter into the determination of taxable income and pretax accounting income in different periods. A principal example is intangible drilling and development costs, which are deductible in determining taxable income when incurred but which, for successful exploratory wells and for all development wells, are capitalized and amortized for financial accounting purposes under the provisions of this Statement. As another example, some geological and geophysical costs, which are charged to expense when incurred under the provisions of this Statement, are deferred and deducted in subsequent periods for income tax purposes.

61. Comprehensive interperiod income tax allocation by the deferred method, as described in *APB Opinion No. 11*, "Accounting for Income Taxes," shall be followed by oil and gas producing companies for intangible drilling and development costs and other costs incurred that enter into the determination of taxable income and pretax accounting income in different periods.

62. In applying the comprehensive interperiod income tax allocation provision of the preceding paragraph, the possibility that statutory depletion in future periods will reduce or eliminate the amount of income taxes otherwise payable shall not be taken into account. That is, the so-called *interaction* of book/tax timing differences with any anticipated future excess of statutory depletion allowed as a tax deduction over the amount of cost depletion otherwise allowable as a tax deduction shall not be recognized in determining the appropriate periodic provision for income taxes. Accordingly, the excess of statutory depletion over cost depletion for tax purposes shall be accounted for as a permanent difference in the period in which the excess is deducted for income tax purposes; it shall not be anticipated by recognizing interaction.

Effective Date and Transition

63. This Statement shall be effective for financial statements for fiscal years beginning after December 15, 1978 and for interim periods within those fiscal years. Accounting changes adopted to conform to the provisions of this Statement, including changes to apply comprehensive interperiod income tax allocation (paragraph 61) and to eliminate the recognition of the interaction of book/tax timing differences with the excess of statutory depletion over cost depletion for tax purposes (paragraph 62), shall be made retroactively by restating the financial statements of prior periods. Financial statements for

the fiscal year in which this Statement is first applied, and for interim periods of that year, shall disclose the nature of those accounting changes and their effect on income before extraordinary items, net income, and related per share amounts for each period restated. The disclosures specified by paragraphs 50-59 shall be included in complete sets of financial statements that have been restated pursuant to the provisions of this paragraph.

64. Retroactive application of the provisions of this Statement requires the use of estimates and approximations; a provision that would not have a significant effect on prior years' financial statements need not be retroactively applied. Further, retroactive application of some provisions of this Statement may require the use of estimates of a type that the enterprise had not previously made; information that may have become available some time after the year being restated may be taken into account in making those estimates, except that estimates of quantities of oil and gas reserves that had been made in prior years shall not currently be revised in retrospect.

> **The provisions of this Statement need not be applied to immaterial items.**

This Statement was adopted by the affirmative votes of four members of the Financial Accounting Standards Board. Messrs. Litke, Mays, and Walters dissented.

Messrs. Litke and Walters dissent because this Statement endorses accounting measurements that in their opinion do not portray the unique economic characteristics of oil and gas exploration and discovery. As a result, it does not measure up to the fundamental objective of financial statements, as enunciated by the Trueblood Committee, that they be "useful for making economic decisions."

Conceptually, they believe it is necessary to account for mineral reserves at fair value for the financial statements to appropriately emphasize certain economic characteristics of the industry, which include:

1. The principal assets are the mineral reserves.
2. The most significant economic event is discovery of reserves.
3. There is no necessary correlation between finding costs and values of reserves found.

No historical cost method adequately emphasizes these facts; both full cost and successful efforts accounting in their traditional forms have significant defects.

In their view, the conceptual case for accounting for mineral reserves at fair value is so strong that it should be rejected only if it is infeasible to derive amounts meeting an acceptable standard of reliability. They are not satisfied that it is infeasible. The public record on this project indicates that many creditors and investors find value information relevant and useful and either obtain it from the enterprise or approximate it themselves. Nonetheless, the record further indicates most respondents may not be ready to accept the perceived sacrifice in reliability necessary to achieve relevance.

Under any approach that is not based on fair value accounting, Messrs. Litke and Walters believe that the estimated quantities and values of the mineral reserves should be disclosed as supplemental information. While recognizing that the Board has taken a positive step in requiring disclosure of the quantities of, and changes in, mineral reserves, they believe the Board failed to go far enough. Research included in the public record indicates that investment and lending decisions in the oil and gas industry are heavily dependent on information about the quantity and value of mineral reserves, as well as about expected cash flows. For reserve information to be useful to investors and creditors, they must assign values to the quantities of estimated reserves. The values of reserves can vary greatly, even within the same overall market price structure, because of differences in quality and in costs of developing, lifting, and transporting to market.

Messrs. Litke and Walters believe that the enterprise is in a better position to evaluate its own reserves than the users of its financial statements. Accordingly, they believe the company should disclose a measure of fair value attributable to its proven mineral reserves, together with the methods and principal assumptions used to develop that information. They believe that discounted cash flow procedures can be developed based on methodologies that are already widely used and understood. Though this information may not be perceived by some as reliable enough to be used as the basis for accounting for mineral reserves in the balance sheet or for recognizing income, they believe a lesser degree of reliability can be accepted for informative supplemental disclosures which have such a high degree of relevance.

If the Board will not adopt the conceptually superior value approach at this time, whether because that approach may be impracticable or ahead of its time, Messrs. Litke and Walters would have accepted an area-of-interest approach, supplemented by disclosure of mineral reserve values. The approach acceptable to them would be a modified full cost approach in which costs of prospecting, acquisition, exploration, and development in an area-of-interest where proven reserves are discovered would be capitalized as the cost of discovering and developing the reserves found in that area-of-interest, subject to a discounted cash flow ceiling. Similar costs in an area-of-interest where no reserves were found would be written off. This method:

1. Measures the costs incurred in each area-of-interest, and reflects "success or failure" with a decision model that would most commonly be used by management.
2. Avoids the worst fault of "pure" full costing—that of charging reserves with costs which are unrelated either temporally or geographically.
3. Avoids the worst faults of "pure" successful efforts accounting—the failures to recognize the principal asset and to capitalize costs that are logically and integrally related to the discovery and development of that asset.

Some say that it is not possible to define an area-of-interest with enough precision that it would be interpreted the same in each case by every company. While Messrs. Litke and Walters believe this concern is overstated, it has some validity if uniformity is the primary objective. While they agree that uniformity is an appropriate consideration and that "free choice" accounting alternatives should be narrowed or eliminated, Messrs. Litke and Walters believe some room for judgment, guided by relevant criteria, is both appropriate and necessary. They do not believe that uniformity for its own sake can be used to justify accounting standards. They observe that unless the uniform accounting and reporting provides *more meaningful economic* information to users of financial statements, the fact that the financial accounting and reporting is on a uniform basis is largely irrelevant.

Mr. Litke further dissents because he believes the Board should not impose successful efforts accounting upon the industry without having provided conceptual support for the superiority of that method in the Basis for Conclusions. Based on the public record (including FASB research) which strongly indicates that *neither* successful efforts *nor* full costing is sufficient to portray the economic substance of an enterprise's financial position or results of operations, he believes merely summarizing the faults of *either* method is not a sufficient basis for imposing the other method. He observes that because neither traditional method of accounting communicates the necessary and relevant investment and return-on-investment information to investors, creditors, regulators or other users of financial statements, an accounting method that adopts the strengths and minimizes the weaknesses of each method must be considered. He believes an area-of-interest method, with certain supplemental disclosures, would satisfy these criteria.

In addition to being unconvincing, Mr. Litke believes the arguments that are presented in the Basis for Conclusions are internally inconsistent. They represent, in his view, a series of inconsistent and unsupported assertions. Mr. Litke believes the need for such inconsistencies has not been supported. Some of those inconsistencies are discussed in the following paragraphs.

• The Statement emphasizes that full cost accounting obscures failures and risks in the search for oil and gas reserves and that successful efforts accounting highlights such failures and risks. This assertion evades the real issues. Mr. Litke observes that neither success nor failure, however defined, is satisfactorily measured based solely on the costs incurred. Success is most appropriately measured by the discovery and development of mineral reserves in sufficient quantity and of sufficient value to result in a return of the amounts invested, as well as a return on the amounts invested. Failure is a result of not discovering and developing sufficient reserves. Further, in Mr. Litke's view the purpose of accounting is neither to obscure nor to highlight "risks" or "failures" or "success." The purpose is to reflect the facts in the most meaningful and useful manner. Under the historical cost basis of accounting, the most meaningful and useful manner would be based on an area-of-interest approach, with certain supplemental disclosures.

• Mr. Litke finds substantial evidence in the accounting literature that an enterprise's assets include its natural resource deposits, including oil and gas reserves. The Statement does not define "assets" in a manner fully consistent with the accounting literature. Nor does the Statement choose to account for or determine the cost of all the enterprise's assets. By identifying only the individual properties, wells, equipment, and facilities as assets to be accounted for, it excludes oil and gas reserves-in-place from the assets to be accounted for and for which costs must be determined. Mr. Litke believes such an exclusion results in an inappropriate and unnecessary distinction between the economic substance of the enterprise's oil and gas operations and the method of accounting for them. Furthermore, some costs that meet the Statement's capitalization criteria are expensed because the criteria are not uniformly applied to all exploration and development costs, including G&G costs. Because of this inconsistent application of criteria, the Statement fails to recognize the benefits derived from the costs of geological and geophysical testing performed on the enterprise's own properties but requires capitalization of such costs, when contractually reimbursable, on G&G testing performed on property owned by another party. G&G costs are often a meaningful element of cost in the acquisition and development of productive properties. They are an integral part of the costs of acquiring and developing an oil and gas property. It is therefore theoretically correct and both practicable and appropriate to capitalize G&G costs applicable to oil and gas properties, especially to the extent that expenditures are specifically identifiable with retained acreage in specific areas-of-interest. Such costs should be capitalized and amortized in the same manner as other acquisition, drilling, and development costs.

• The Statement requires that the costs of exploratory dry holes be expensed as incurred while the costs of development dry holes be capitalized and amortized. In other words, the accounting for these exploratory and development costs in an area may be different even though the costs of drilling the exploratory dry holes in the area are just as much a part of the costs invested as are the costs of drilling the development dry holes in that area. Further, the fact that a well may be classified as a development well, based on the definitions provided in this Statement, may depend on whether it is the first well drilled or whether it is drilled after a successful well. Mr. Litke observes that the cost of drilling both exploratory and development wells is an integral part of the cost of exploring and developing oil and gas properties. Mr. Litke believes such conflicting accounting requirements are not conceptually sound and will not necessarily result in uniform accounting and reporting. Such requirements will, however, result in such illogical results as having the amounts capitalized depend on the sequence in which the wells were drilled.

• Mr. Litke believes the costs of drilling exploration and development dry holes are integrally related to the other reasonable and necessary costs that are incurred in discovering and developing mineral reserves. He believes therefore that all such reasonable and necessary costs incurred in or related to the acquisition or enhancement of an asset in an area-of-interest in which commercially recoverable reserves are discovered and developed, or that result in increased discernible future benefits, should be deferred (temporarily capitalized) pending evaluation of the results of the exploration and development activities in that area-of-interest.

This Statement, however, prescribes that the costs of exploratory dry holes and certain stratigraphic wells be expensed as incurred. It also requires that the costs of development dry holes and certain other stratigraphic wells be capitalized. Mr. Litke observes that each of those types of wells has the same expected future benefits, but they are accounted for differently. The Statement also permits deferral of the costs of drilling in progress even though those wells on which those costs were incurred may prove

to provide no discernible future benefits either. While Mr. Litke agrees that those costs should be capitalized, he believes the logical conceptual basis under which such costs should be capitalized also results in the capitalization of other costs under an area-of-interest approach—an approach which he believes is appropriate but which the Statement specifically rejects. He further observes that the reasons supporting these capitalization policies are inconsistent with the reasoning behind *FASB Statement No. 2,* "Accounting for Research and Development Costs."

Mr. Mays dissents because he considers some of the conclusions reached conceptually inconsistent with others. Mr. Mays believes that in adopting successful efforts accounting a choice must be made between two basic and distinct concepts. In the first concept, each well drilled is an individual "effort," the success or failure of which determines the capital/expense treatment. Thus, a well that is not capable of commercial production, whether it be exploratory, development, or stratigraphic, is expensed. In the second concept, a group of wells with a common geological objective is a collective "effort," and the capital/expense decision is based on the success or failure of the group as a whole. Although he prefers the first, Mr. Mays would accept either of these concepts but not a mixing of the two. In his view, the Statement contains elements of both concepts resulting in inconsistencies such as the following:

While affirming that the nature of a cost rather than a cost center should govern the capital/expense decision, the Statement uses the producing system as a collective asset, in effect a cost center, to justify the capitalization of development dry holes and certain nonproducible stratigraphic test wells. At the same time, the Statement excludes an exploratory dry hole having the same geological objective from capitalization even though that well also was intended to form part of the producing system and represents just as much a part of its cost as the development dry hole. The fact that the development location was not drilled first in the drilling program, and would thus have been an exploratory dry hole, may well be pure chance; in Mr. Mays's view, capital/expense decisions should not depend on sequential happenstance. Similar inconsistencies result from the distinction for capital/expense purposes that the Statement draws with respect to "successful" and "unsuccessful" stratigraphic wells, and the further distinction drawn between "unsuccessful development type" and "unsuccessful exploratory type" stratigraphic wells. Mr. Mays believes that, since none of such wells are to be produced, they should either all be expensed under the first concept or all be capitalized, assuming collective success, under the second concept.

Mr. Mays also dissents with respect to the changes

in accounting for income taxes promulgated by this Statement. The changes, which he views as major, represent a reversal of the Board's position taken only two years ago with the issuance of *FASB Statement No. 9,* and he points to the fact that nothing has happened in the interim to justify such a rever-

sal. Mr. Mays considers these changes especially untimely in view of the Board's current consideration of the definition of the elements of financial statements, including the definition of a liability, in the conceptual framework project.

Members of the Financial Accounting Standards Board:

Marshall S. Armstrong, *Chairman* Oscar S. Gellein	Donald J. Kirk Arthur L. Litke Robert E. Mays	Robert T. Sprouse Ralph E. Walters

Appendix A

BACKGROUND INFORMATION

65. Financial accounting and reporting for oil and gas producing companies has been debated for many years in the United States by the accounting profession, regulatory agencies, industry groups, and the companies themselves. The principal focus in recent years has been on the two widely different methods of accounting followed by those companies—the full cost method and the successful efforts method.

66. In 1964, the American Institute of Certified Public Accountants commissioned Robert E. Field, a partner of Price Waterhouse & Co., to study the various accounting methods used by companies in the extractive industries and to make recommendations for consideration by the AICPA Accounting Principles Board in formulating a pronouncement. The study was published by the AICPA in 1969 as *Accounting Research Study No. 11,* "Financial Reporting in the Extractive Industries." The recommendations in *ARS No. 11* essentially supported the successful efforts method of accounting.

67. In 1970, the APB asked its Committee on Extractive Industries to (a) study the recommendations in *ARS No. 11* and (b) "determine the appropriate accounting practices with the intent of narrowing the different accounting practices in the extractive industries." In mid-1971, the Committee drafted a proposed APB Opinion dealing only with determination of the appropriate *cost center,* on the belief that issues associated with the cost center question were at the heart of the full cost/successful efforts controversy. The full APB decided, however, that limiting an Opinion to the cost center question was inappropriate. The APB directed its Committee to prepare a paper containing recommendations on (a) determination of the cost center, (b) accounting for prediscovery and postdiscovery costs, (c) disposition of capitalized costs, and (d) disclosure of supplementary information in financial reports.

68. The APB Committee paper was published in the fall of 1971 under the title "Accounting and Reporting Practices in the Petroleum Industry." The paper recommended using the *field* as the cost center and capitalizing all prediscovery and postdiscovery costs that could be directly associated with oil and gas reserves, including reinstatement of the costs of exploratory dry holes initially written off but later determined to be in a field. The APB scheduled a public hearing for November 1971, with the Committee paper to serve as the basis for the hearing.

69. While the APB Committee was deliberating and preparing its paper, the Federal Power Commission was studying the accounting practices of natural gas producing companies subject to its jurisdiction. In October 1970, the FPC issued a proposal to require application of the full cost concept in FPC filings by natural gas companies. During the following thirteen months, the FPC weighed arguments for and against its proposal, including a request from the APB that the FPC delay final action until an APB Opinion could be issued. On November 5, 1971, the FPC issued Order No. 440 adopting the full cost method for mineral leases acquired after October 6, 1969 with each country as a cost center. Petitions for rehearing, which were filed on December 5, 1971, were denied by the FPC in Order No. 440-A issued January 5, 1972.

70. The APB's public hearing was held on November 22 and 23, 1971. At the hearing, the recommendations in the APB Committee paper were opposed not only by advocates of the full cost method, who viewed the proposal to use the field as the cost center as effectively banning the full cost concept, but also by many advocates of successful efforts accounting, who disagreed with various aspects of the recommendations including, among other things, the capitalization of the costs of development dry holes and those exploratory dry holes determined to be in a field. After the hearing, the APB Committee on Extractive Industries continued to work on a proposed Opinion. The testimony given at that public hearing and the written submissions to the APB have been studied by the FASB.

71. On July 1, 1973, the FASB succeeded the APB as the private sector accounting standards-setting body. The APB Committee prepared for the FASB a detailed report on its activities entitled "Accounting and Reporting Practices in the Oil and Gas Industry." That report is reprinted as an appendix to the FASB Discussion Memorandum on the project.

72. In January 1973, a group of oil and gas producing companies that use the full cost method formed the Ad Hoc Committee (Petroleum Companies) on Full Cost Accounting. That Committee commissioned a research study by John H. Myers, Professor of Accounting at Indiana University. The study, entitled *Full Cost vs. Successful Efforts in Petroleum Accounting: An Empirical Approach,* was published in 1974. Dr. Myers simulated the results of accounting for various types of transactions under each of the two methods and concluded that full cost accounting together with disclosure of data on oil and gas reserves better serves the needs of users of financial statements.

73. In 1975, Congress substantially reduced or eliminated the percentage depletion deduction for many oil and gas producing companies, which led to the issuance in October 1975 of *FASB Statement No. 9.*

74. The FASB did not place accounting and reporting in the extractive industries on its initial technical agenda in 1973, but the foreign oil embargo of that year and the resulting substantial increases in world oil prices aroused great interest in the oil and gas industry on the part of both the American public and the federal government. With other energy legislation enacted or under active consideration by Congress, the FASB decided that accounting by oil and gas producing companies should receive high priority. In October 1975, it added to its technical agenda a project entitled "Financial Accounting and Reporting in the Extractive Industries."

75. In December 1975, President Gerald R. Ford signed Public Law 94-163, the *Energy Policy and Conservation Act* [42 U.S. Code, Sec. 6383]. Title V, Section 503 of the Act empowers the Securities and Exchange Commission either:

> to prescribe rules applicable to persons engaged in the production of crude oil or natural gas, or make effective by recognition, or by other appropriate means indicating a determination to rely on, accounting practices developed by the Financial Accounting Standards Board, if the Securities and Exchange Commission is assured that such practice will be observed by persons engaged in the production of crude oil or natural gas to the same extent as would result if the Securities and Exchange Commission had prescribed such practices by rule.

76. The effect of Section 503 is to require that the contemplated accounting practices be developed by December 22, 1977 (24 months after the Act was signed into law) for all persons engaged either exclusively or partially in the production of crude oil or natural gas in the United States. The Act requires the SEC to provide an opportunity for interested persons to submit written comments on whether the Commission should recognize or otherwise rely on the standards developed by the FASB. That comment period can be after December 22, 1977.

77. The Act further provides that the SEC shall assure that the accounting practices developed pursuant to Section 503 will, to the greatest extent practicable, permit the compilation of a national energy data base consisting of the following data with domestic and foreign operations treated separately:

(1) The separate calculation of capital, revenue, and operating cost information pertaining to—
   (A) prospecting,
   (B) acquisition,
   (C) exploration,
   (D) development, and
   (E) production,
including geological and geophysical costs, carrying costs, unsuccessful exploratory drilling costs, intangible drilling and development costs on productive wells, the cost of unsuccessful development wells, and the cost of acquiring oil and gas reserves by means other than development. Any such calculation shall take into account disposition of capitalized costs, contractual arrangements involving special conveyance of rights and joint operations, differences between book and tax income, and prices used in the transfer of products or other assets from one person to any other person, including a person controlled by, controlling, or under common control with such person.
(2) The full presentation of the financial information of persons engaged in the production of crude oil or natural gas, including—
   (A) disclosure of reserves and operating activities, both domestic and foreign, to facilitate evaluation of financial effort and result; and
   (B) classification of financial information by function to facilitate correlation with reserve and operating statistics, both domestic and foreign.
(3) Such other information, projections, and relationships of collected data as shall be necessary to facilitate the compilation of such data base.

78. The Board is issuing this Statement under its authority, which exists entirely apart from the Act, and also to assist the SEC in carrying out its obliga-

tions as contemplated by Congress under the Act as well as under the federal securities laws.

79. The FASB appointed a task force of 18 persons in December 1975 to counsel the Board in preparing a Discussion Memorandum analyzing issues related to the project. Members of the task force came from the oil and gas industry, petroleum geology and engineering, other extractive industries, public accounting, banking, securities underwriting, and academe. Professor Horace R. Brock of North Texas State University was engaged by the Board to serve as chairman of the task force and consultant to the Board during the preparation of the Discussion Memorandum. Meetings of the task force were attended by observers from the following federal agencies and Congressional committee:

a. Cost Accounting Standards Board.
b. Federal Energy Administration.
c. Federal Power Commission.
d. Securities and Exchange Commission.
e. Oversight and Investigations Subcommittee of the Committee on Interstate and Foreign Commerce, United States House of Representatives.
f. United States General Accounting Office.

80. The task force held its initial meeting in January 1976. Three additional meetings were held during that year. Much of the work of the task force was accomplished by correspondence, with task force members providing the Board with a significant amount of input concerning the accounting and reporting issues that they believed should be addressed in this project. Drafts of all sections of the Discussion Memorandum were sent to task force members and observers for written comment. Although the chairman of the task force and members of the staff of the FASB assumed primary responsibility for drafting the Discussion Memorandum, some sections were initially drafted by task force members expert on the particular matter being discussed.

81. In February 1976, the FASB concluded, on the basis of a task force recommendation, that the Discussion Memorandum should not be restricted to only the oil and gas industry, but should cover accounting and reporting issues relevant to companies engaged in the search for and production of all wasting (nonregenerative) natural resources. That recommendation was not unanimously supported by the task force. Some members believed that it would be preferable to focus initially on the oil and gas industry, as the APB Committee on Extractive Industries had done. Those members were also concerned that broadening the study could blur important distinctions between oil and gas companies and other extractive industries. The FASB, in accepting the recommendation of a majority of the task force

members, concluded that apparent similarities of operations among extractive industries warranted the inclusion of all such industries in the scope of the Discussion Memorandum. The Board noted in the Discussion Memorandum, however, that inclusion of all extractive industries within the scope of the project at that stage did not mean that the Board intended to issue a single Statement covering all of those industries.

82. On March 23, 1976, the SEC issued *Accounting Series Release No. 190* amending Regulation S-X to require companies that meet specified size tests to disclose certain replacement cost data relating to "inventories" and "productive capacity" in financial statements filed with the Commission for fiscal years ending on or after December 25, 1976. In that Release, the SEC delayed for one year the effective date of the required replacement cost disclosures for "mineral resource assets." SEC *Staff Accounting Bulletin No. 10* defines mineral resource assets as "those costs shown on the balance sheet representing assets which are directly associated with and which derive value from mineral reserves." In June 1977, the American Petroleum Institute published and submitted to the SEC a study by Professors Glenn A. Welsch and Edward B. Deakin, of the University of Texas at Austin, entitled *Measuring and Reporting the "Replacement" Cost of Oil and Gas Reserves.* In transmitting the study to the SEC, the API stated its view that "the concept of replacement cost as envisioned in ASR 190 is not applicable to oil and gas reserves" and urged the SEC to "permanently exempt oil and gas reserves from replacement cost disclosure."

83. On May 12, 1976, the SEC issued *Securities Act Release No. 5706,* which requires that information relating to oil and gas properties, reserves, and production be disclosed in registration statements, proxy statements, and reports filed with the Commission.

84. In preparing the Discussion Memorandum, the task force and the Board considered many research studies and other publications in addition to *ARS No. 11* and the study by Dr. Myers, including the proceedings of the APB's public hearing and studies of accounting and reporting practices in the extractive industries by public accounting firms and industry associations. Approximately 100 recent (generally post-1968) publications on accounting and reporting in the extractive industries were reviewed by the FASB staff; a bibliography is included as an appendix to the Discussion Memorandum. Copies of those publications are in the FASB library.

85. The Board issued the Discussion Memorandum on December 23, 1976 with written comments due

by March 7, 1977. In response to the Discussion Memorandum, the Board received 140 position papers, letters of comment, and outlines (totalling approximately 2,600 pages), copies of which have been available for inspection at the Board's offices since March 14, 1977 and are available for purchase. Copies were made available to each of the observer groups identified in paragraph 79.

86. On January 31, 1977, in *Securities Act Release No. 5801*, the SEC called attention to publication of the FASB Discussion Memorandum and encouraged interested parties to obtain and comment on the Memorandum and to participate in the FASB public hearing. The Release states that "the Commission, consistent with its policy most recently expressed in Accounting Series Release No. 150, contemplates that the Financial Accounting Standards Board (FASB) will be providing the leadership in establishing financial accounting principles and standards for producers of oil and gas." A part of one of the chapters in the Discussion Memorandum was prepared by the staff of the SEC. It considers matters relating to the SEC's responsibilities regarding the national energy data base.

87. The Board held a public hearing on the subject on March 30 and 31 and April 1 and 4, 1977. Thirty-nine presentations were made at the hearing. A transcript of the hearing (nearly 1,000 pages in length) is available for inspection or purchase. Copies were made available to each of the observer groups identified in paragraph 79.

88. Seven days of concentrated preparatory sessions were held by the Board prior to deliberations on the issues. Those sessions were devoted to detailed examination of (a) the nature of acquisition, exploration, development, and production activities in the oil and gas industry; (b) the features and variations of the full cost method, the successful efforts method, discovery value accounting, and current value accounting; (c) reserve definitions and measurement; (d) reserve valuation; and (e) mineral property conveyances and contracts. Outside experts were invited to make presentations or otherwise assist the Board's staff in conducting the sessions. Those experts, eight of whom were task force members, included petroleum engineers and geologists, public accountants, corporate executives from the oil and gas industry, and academicians.

89. Subsequent to issuance of the Discussion Memorandum, the Board and its staff have maintained close contact with representatives of the SEC who, in turn, have been in contact with the other government agencies concerned with implementing the *Energy Policy and Conservation Act* and other federal energy legislation, with the mutual objective of keeping all parties informed of the others' activities

regarding accounting and reporting by oil and gas producing companies. That close contact has continued after issuance of the FASB's Exposure Draft.

90. In addition to the Discussion Memorandum and the research studies and other publications mentioned earlier in paragraph 84, two other research efforts were undertaken at the Board's request during its deliberations on the Exposure Draft:

a. Academic consultants conducted interviews to ascertain how investment and credit decisions regarding oil and gas producing companies are reached. The 24 interviewees included loan officers of large and small banks that make loans to large and small oil and gas companies, bank trust department officers, institutional securities underwriters for both large and small companies, securities analysts, and an officer of a bond rating agency. The selection of interviewees from both the Northeast and the Southwest was designed to include organizations that invest or recommend investments in small as well as large companies. While the limited number of interviews did not provide conclusive evidence, the majority of interviewees indicated that the method of accounting would not affect their investment and credit decisions regarding oil and gas producing companies. The key factor in the decisions of a number of interviewees was their own valuations of oil and gas reserves and other assets; others relied heavily on cash flow data rather than earnings; still others took into consideration the method of accounting when evaluating earnings. Several interviewees believed that reduced earnings from accounting changes probably affected some investors and thus could adversely affect some stock prices.

b. A study was made of how *FASB Statement No. 9* was applied in practice. The study found no relationship between the way that Statement was applied and the method of accounting employed or company size.

91. On June 20, 1977, the SEC issued *Securities Act Release No. 5837* soliciting comments in connection with the Commission's responsibilities under the *Energy Policy and Conservation Act* to assure the development and observance of accounting practices to be followed by U.S. producers of crude oil and natural gas. That Release not only raised questions relating to the reporting of financial and operating data to the Federal Energy Administrator but also solicited comments about the extent to which that data should be "included in filings with the Commission in a manner which would require independent public accountants reporting on registrants' financial statements to be associated with the data." The Release indicated that "the Commission recognizes that the FASB is considering for inclusion

in its proposed standard the disclosure of functional financial data and information on oil and gas reserves. The Commission will be cognizant of the FASB's conclusions in this area and will attempt to coordinate the reporting requirements pursuant to the Act and any revisions proposed to the disclosure requirements under the Securities Acts with the disclosures required in financial statements by the FASB. Reporting pursuant to the Act and any changes to the Commission's disclosure rules may encompass matters . . . in addition to or in greater detail than those required by the FASB."

92. The Board issued an Exposure Draft of a proposed Statement on "Financial Accounting and Reporting by Oil and Gas Producing Companies" on July 15, 1977. It received letters of comment on the Exposure Draft from 195 respondents (totalling approximately 1,300 pages). Copies of the letters were made available to each of the observer groups identified in paragraph 79.

93. After the Exposure Draft was issued, two additional research studies were conducted at the Board's request:

a. A research consultant, with assistance from the FASB staff, studied the effect of the Exposure Draft on the market prices of common stock issued by both full cost and successful efforts oil and gas producing companies. The research was conducted by Professor Thomas R. Dyckman of Cornell University, using data part of which was supplied by the FASB staff. Two research methodologies were employed. The first required two samples of equal size and was applied to companies that derive more than 50 percent of their revenue from exploration and production activities. The market prices of common shares issued by 22 full cost companies and 22 successful efforts companies were studied for the 11 weeks before and the 11 weeks after the Exposure Draft was issued. The study did not find statistically significant evidence that issuance of the Exposure Draft affected the market prices of securities issued by the full cost companies as compared to those of the successful efforts companies—except for some possible effect on the full cost companies during the week preceding and the week of issuance of the Exposure Draft, but the market soon adjusted, and evidence of a permanent or lingering effect was not found. The second methodology employed different underlying statistical procedures and was applied to broader samples. Those samples were not limited to companies engaged primarily in exploration and production but were limited to oil and gas companies with annual revenues less than $1 billion each. The samples included 65 full cost companies and 40 successful efforts companies.

Again, the evidence did not support the hypothesis that the prices of shares issued by full cost companies were adversely affected, other than for a very brief period, by issuance of the Exposure Draft. Both Professor Dyckman and the Board recognize that statistical testing may not necessarily be conclusive. Following issuance of this Statement, the Board will undertake a similar study with respect to whether this Statement adversely affects the market prices of securities of oil and gas producing companies that heretofore had been using the full cost method as compared to those that had been using the successful efforts method.

b. The Board commissioned a telephone interview survey of senior executive officers of 27 relatively small and medium sized, publicly traded, successful efforts oil and gas producing companies (with annual revenues ranging from $1 million to $441 million, average $68 million). No large integrated oil and gas companies were included. The study was conducted under the direction of Professor Horace R. Brock of North Texas State University. The purpose of the survey was to ascertain whether, in the judgment of those corporate officers, the use of the successful efforts method of accounting has had any negative effect on the ability of their companies to raise the capital necessary to finance their exploration and production activities. Most of the surveyed companies have raised capital externally during the past 10 years from one or more of the following sources: public issue of debt securities, public issue of equity securities, private placement of securities, special conveyances, borrowing from a local bank, international bank, or insurance company, and sale of participations in individual projects. None of the executive officers surveyed indicated that the company's use of successful efforts accounting had hindered its ability to raise capital. Four of the officers did indicate an uncertainty as to whether their continued use of the successful efforts method would affect their ability to raise capital in the future.

94. On August 31, 1977, the SEC issued *Securities Act Release No. 5861* proposing to amend the Commission's regulations to incorporate therein the accounting standards set forth in the FASB Exposure Draft. The Commission stated that the reason for the proposal is to place the Commission in a position to adopt by December 22, 1977 financial accounting and reporting standards for oil and gas producing activities in the unlikely event that the FASB has not adopted final standards by that date. The Release states that the proposed standards would be applicable to both (1) persons filing reports with the Department of Energy and (2) filings with the Commission under federal securities

laws. The Commission stated that it proposed the rules pursuant to its authority under the *Energy Policy and Conservation Act* and the federal securities laws. The Release deals only with accounting standards and does not address disclosure matters.

95. On October 26, 1977, the SEC issued two Releases dealing with disclosures by oil and gas producing companies. The first Release, *Securities Act Release No. 5877,* proposes to amend the Commission's regulations to provide for disclosure in financial statements of certain operating and financial data relating to oil and gas producing activities. Like the proposal mentioned in the preceding paragraph, the disclosure standards proposed in this Release would apply both to (1) filings with the Commission pursuant to federal securities laws and (2) reports filed with the Department of Energy pursuant to the *Energy Policy and Conservation Act*. The SEC's proposed disclosures are generally the same as those proposed in the FASB Exposure Draft.

96. The second SEC Release of October 26, 1977,

Securities Act Release No. 5878, deals with replacement cost disclosures for mineral resource assets. The Release proposes (1) to rescind the requirement adopted in *ASR No. 190* for certain registrants to disclose replacement cost information about their mineral resource assets employed in oil and gas producing activities (see paragraph 82 of this Statement) and (2) to require, instead, that registrants with mineral resource assets employed in oil and gas producing activities disclose information based on the present value of future net revenues from estimated production of proved oil and gas reserves. The Release points out that "the proposed disclosures cannot be described as replacement cost information; however, they would provide information on the differences between the historical costs associated with proved oil and gas reserves shown in the financial statements and the future net revenues to be derived from these reserves." That proposal would be effective in filings covering fiscal years ending on or after December 25, 1978. Comments on the proposal are to be submitted to the Commission by March 31, 1978.

Appendix B

BASIS FOR CONCLUSIONS

CONTENTS

Appendix B

BASIS FOR CONCLUSIONS

97. This Appendix discusses factors deemed significant by members of the Board in reaching the conclusions in this Statement, including alternatives considered and reasons for accepting some and rejecting others.

Scope

98. Although the Discussion Memorandum for this project analyzed issues and solicited comments on accounting and reporting by companies in all extractive industries, this Statement applies only to the oil and gas producing industry as had been proposed in the Exposure Draft. Some respondents to the Discussion Memorandum and the Exposure Draft said that the mining industries are sufficiently different from the oil and gas industry to warrant separate pronouncements. For instance, some said that in the mining industries the principal emphasis is on the development and operation of existing mines and known deposits whereas in the oil and gas industry the principal emphasis is on the search for new mineral deposits. Also, some respondents said that mining operations involve substantially lower exploration and acquisition costs and substantially higher development and production costs relative to the oil and gas industry, which, they claimed, is characterized by high finding costs and a high proportion of unsuccessful search activities. In the view of those respondents, *discovery* is the critical event

leading to the production of oil and gas whereas *development* and *extraction* are the critical events for most other minerals. Many who favored separating the oil and gas industry from other extractive industries pointed out also that the full cost versus successful efforts controversy has little significance in the mining industry while it is the primary issue for the oil and gas industry. Still others noted that there is greater uniformity in current accounting practices within the mining industries than within the oil and gas industry. Thus, they took the position that current generally accepted accounting principles are adequate for the mining industries and do not require the attention of the FASB at this time. The Board has not yet examined in depth those and other claimed dissimilarities between the oil and gas industry and other extractive industries; nor has it decided whether there is a need to address the other extractive industries in a separate pronouncement.

99. In response to questions raised in letters of comment on the Exposure Draft, paragraph 7 indicates that this Statement does not deal with accounting for interest costs because that matter is being addressed in another Board agenda project.

The Four Basic Accounting Alternatives

100. Four basic methods of accounting for a company's oil and gas producing activities were considered by the Board:

a. Full costing.
b. Successful efforts costing.
c. Discovery value accounting.
d. Current value accounting.

The principal features of each of those four methods, and variations within each method, are described in paragraphs 104-127.

101. Both full costing and successful efforts costing have been considered as conforming to generally accepted accounting principles, and both, in various forms, are widely used today. Discovery value accounting and current value accounting are both proposals that are not presently followed by oil and gas producing companies or by other companies (except in a few specialized industries and then only for certain assets with readily determinable market prices) in preparing their financial statements. The full costing method came into use around 1960 and only since the late 1960s has become widely used. A 1973 survey of nearly 300 oil and gas companies found that roughly half used full cost accounting and half used successful efforts costing.[6] A 1972 survey showed that companies employing the successful efforts method account for approximately 87 percent of U.S. oil and gas production, indicating that full costing has been adopted by relatively more small and medium sized companies than large companies.[7] Testimony given at the Board's public hearing by a spokesperson for an association of independent petroleum producers indicated that many independent oil and gas companies follow federal income tax accounting practices in preparing their financial statements; income tax accounting is a variation of successful efforts accounting.

Basic Differences between Full Costing and Successful Efforts Costing

102. The principal difference between full costing and successful efforts costing concerns costs that cannot be directly related to the discovery of specific oil and gas reserves. Under full costing those costs are carried forward to future periods as costs of oil and gas reserves generally; under successful efforts costing those costs are charged to expense. Full costing regards the costs of unsuccessful acquisition and exploration activities as necessary for the discovery of reserves. All of those costs are incurred with the knowledge that many of a company's prospects will not result directly in the discovery of reserves. However, the company expects that the benefits obtained from those prospects that do prove successful together with the benefits from past discoveries will be adequate to recover the costs of all activities, both successful and unsuccessful, and will result in an ultimate profit. Thus, all costs incurred in oil and gas producing activities are regarded as integral to the acquisition, discovery, and development of

whatever reserves ultimately result from the efforts as a whole, and are thus associated with the company's reserves. Establishing a direct cause-and-effect relationship between costs incurred and specific reserves discovered is not relevant to full costing. Under successful efforts costing, however, except for acquisition costs of properties, a direct relationship between costs incurred and specific reserves discovered is required before costs are identified with assets; costs of acquisition and exploration activities that are known not to have resulted in the discovery of reserves are charged to expense.

103. Although many variations exist within the successful efforts method, two principal approaches can be identified. One approach relies on an "area-of-interest" (or "project" or "prospect") as a cost center because the oil and gas reserves in that area-of-interest are deemed to represent the asset for which cost is determined. Under that approach, all costs incurred within that cost center are capitalized; if the area-of-interest is abandoned, the costs are charged to expense; if the area-of-interest proves successful, the capitalized costs are amortized as the reserves are produced. The second approach does not rely on a cost center for capitalization purposes; the accounting treatment is determined by the nature of the costs at the time they are incurred. This approach does not assign costs to oil and gas reserves until they are extracted; prior to then, this approach regards properties, wells, equipment, and facilities as the assets to which costs relate. Under one variation of this approach, all exploratory costs are charged to expense when incurred, but the cost of an exploratory well is later capitalized by reinstatement if the well is successful. Under the other variation, all exploration costs except the costs of exploratory wells are charged to expense when incurred; the costs of exploratory wells are capitalized as "construction-in-progress" when incurred, to be expensed later if the well is determined to be unsuccessful.

Principal Features of Full Costing

104. Under the full cost concept, all costs incurred in acquiring, exploring, and developing properties within a relatively large geopolitical (as opposed to geological) cost center (such as a country) are capitalized when incurred and are amortized as mineral reserves in the cost center are produced, subject to a limitation that the capitalized costs not exceed the value of those reserves.

105. Many variations of the full cost method exist,

---

[6]Ginsburg, Feldman and Bress, Attorneys for Ad Hoc Committee (Petroleum Companies), *Comments of the Ad Hoc Committee (Petroleum Companies) on Full Cost Accounting,* File No. S7-464, presented to the Securities and Exchange Commission, 14 March 1973, p. 31.

[7]Porter, Stanley P., *"Full Cost" Accounting: The Problem It Poses for the Extractive Industries* (New York: Arthur Young & Company, 1972), p. 6.

one of which is in the selection of the cost center. Under the broadest concept of full costing, all acquisition, exploration, and development costs wherever and whenever incurred are capitalized and amortized on a pro rata basis over the production of all of the company's oil and gas reserves wherever and whenever discovered, subject to the aforementioned limitation. This approach is referred to as using a company-wide cost center. Most companies that use full costing, however, adopt a country or a continent as the cost center.

106. If full costing is applied on a less-than-company-wide basis, the limitation (sometimes called a ceiling) on capitalized costs generally is applied separately to each cost center, though sometimes the comparison of unamortized capitalized costs and reserve values is made on the basis of groups of cost centers or on a company-wide basis. Variations also exist in the categories of reserves used in computing the limitation and in the methods of valuing those reserves.

107. Under the full cost concept, acquisition, exploration, and development costs are sometimes included in the pool of capitalized costs associated with a cost center when incurred, so that if the cost center is producing, those costs are subject to amortization at once. In some cases, however, certain significant costs, such as those associated with offshore U.S. operations, are deferred separately without amortization until the specific property to which they relate is found to be either productive or nonproductive, at which time those deferred costs and any reserves attributable to the property are included in the computation of amortization in the cost center.

108. Although most proponents of full costing indicate that the reserve value limitation is an essential condition for use of that method, preproduction costs incurred in a nonproducing cost center (for example, a country or continent in which the company has only recently begun its first exploration activity) are sometimes capitalized without regard to a limitation or ceiling test, based on the expectation that reserves will be discovered in the future sufficient to assure recovery of the capitalized costs.

109. Under full costing and in many cases under successful efforts costing (if the amortization base comprises a number of properties), the unamortized costs relating to a property that is surrendered, abandoned, or otherwise disposed of are accounted for as an adjustment of accumulated amortization, rather than as a gain or loss that enters into the determination of net income, until *all* of the properties constituting the amortization base are disposed of, at which point gain or loss is recognized. Under full costing, the amortization base is normally a

very large cost center—country or continent—whereas under successful efforts costing it is usually either individual properties or groups of properties with a common geological structural feature or stratigraphic condition. Therefore, recognition of gain or loss on abandonment of properties is more likely to be delayed under full costing than under successful efforts costing, although some proponents of full costing would recognize certain unusual or significant losses even before activities in an entire country or continent are discontinued.

110. Variations within both the full cost method and the successful efforts method exist in (a) the categories of reserves used in computing amortization, (b) whether future development costs are anticipated if capitalized acquisition, exploration, or development costs are amortized on the basis of all proved reserves, (c) the extent to which properties are aggregated for amortization purposes, (d) the bases for determining amortization rates if oil and gas are jointly produced, (e) the categories of reserves and methods of valuation used in computing a limitation on capitalized costs, and (f) allocation of overhead.

Principal Features of Successful Efforts Costing

111. Under successful efforts costing, except for acquisition costs of properties, a direct relationship between costs incurred and specific reserves discovered is required before costs are identified with assets. An acquired property is regarded as an asset until either a determination is made that it does not contain oil and gas reserves or the property is surrendered. Capitalized costs relating to producing properties are amortized as the reserves underlying those properties are produced.

112. Many variations of successful efforts accounting exist. As noted in paragraph 103, a conceptual difference centers around the role of the cost center—whether a cost center is needed for cost capitalization purposes or only to compute amortization. For example, some proponents of successful efforts accounting would capitalize all geological and geophysical costs and, possibly, all carrying costs relating to a cost center, such as an area-of-interest, on grounds that any mineral reserves in the cost center represent the asset with which the costs are associated. If mineral reserves are found in that area-of-interest, those capitalized costs are carried forward as the costs of those reserves; otherwise, they are charged to expense. Those proponents of successful efforts thus rely in part on the concept of a cost center for the capitalize/expense decision. Others who favor successful efforts accounting would use a cost center, such as a field or a lease, only for purposes of amortizing costs. They would let the nature of the cost govern the capitalize/

expense decision. For example, they might charge all G&G costs and all carrying costs to expense, based on the belief that such costs result in no identifiable future benefits, but they would capitalize all lease bonus expenditures on the basis that an asset (the right to explore for and extract oil and gas) has been acquired.

113. With respect to property acquisition costs, relatively minor variations exist within the successful efforts method concerning the extent to which such items as brokers' fees, recording fees, legal costs, other direct costs, and allocations of indirect costs are considered acquisition costs. Those minor variations aside, virtually all advocates of successful efforts accounting capitalize all property acquisition costs when incurred, though different accounting methods are used to dispose of those costs subsequent to capitalization.

114. Under successful efforts accounting, different methods are sometimes used to account for *pre*acquisition and *post*acquisition geological and geophysical costs. With respect to preacquisition G&G, some expense all such costs when incurred; others capitalize preacquisition G&G to the extent that those costs can be related to acquired properties and expense all other such costs. Some follow a practice of reinstating costs charged to expense in a prior period based on events and experience in subsequent periods. Others do not. With respect to postacquisition G&G, alternatives include (a) capitalize all postacquisition G&G as part of the cost of the acquired properties to which the G&G costs relate; (b) charge it all to expense when incurred; and (c) charge it all to expense when incurred but reinstate those costs that relate to reserves that are found. Some persons would capitalize only post*discovery* G&G while expensing when incurred all other postacquisition G&G as well as the preacquisition G&G.

115. At least two variations can be identified in accounting for the costs of carrying undeveloped properties (delay rentals, *ad valorem* taxes, etc.) under successful efforts accounting: (a) charge all to expense as incurred and (b) charge to expense as incurred but reinstate if subsequently associable with an area-of-interest in which reserves are found.

116. Some proponents of the successful efforts method defer all exploratory drilling costs as "construction-in-progress" for a period of time until a determination has been made whether reserves have been found, at which time the costs of dry holes are charged to expense. Others expense all exploratory drilling costs as incurred but reinstate costs relating to any reserves that are discovered. The costs of drilling a stratigraphic test well, which is drilled solely to obtain geological information and

is not customarily intended to be completed as a producing well, are sometimes charged to expense when incurred; alternatively, those costs are sometimes capitalized to the extent that reserves are found (even though the well is not intended to be used to produce those reserves), with the costs of such wells that did not find reserves charged to expense when that determination is made.

117. The principal alternative with respect to accounting for development costs within a successful efforts framework concerns the treatment of development dry holes. Some proponents of successful efforts accounting capitalize the costs of drilling unsuccessful development wells on grounds that those costs were incurred as part of the capital investment required to extract reserves that were previously discovered. On the other hand, many successful efforts proponents take the position that those costs should be charged to expense on the basis that any dry hole, whether exploratory or development, has no future benefit. With respect to other development costs, some companies capitalize all while other companies—principally the smaller and closely held companies—follow the income tax accounting treatment under which intangible development costs are charged to expense as incurred.

118. Whether capitalized preproduction costs are amortized or otherwise written off before production begins is another area of difference within the successful efforts method. Some companies do not amortize any capitalized costs until production of the related reserves begins. If reserves are not found, the entire cost is written off when the property is surrendered. A variety of methods is used by those companies that do amortize costs before production begins. A distinction normally is made between (a) acquisition costs of unproved properties and (b) preproduction costs relating to properties that become proved. Some companies amortize the acquisition costs of unproved properties or provide an allowance for impairment; other companies carry unproved properties at their cost without regard to diminution of value until either reserves are found or the property is surrendered. With respect to the capitalized preproduction costs relating to proved properties, amortization generally does not begin until production commences. Reinstatement of costs is another accounting alternative, and whether to establish a limitation on capitalized costs of proved properties is yet another area of difference.

119. A number of other variations within the successful efforts method (which are also variations within full costing) were noted in paragraph 110.

Principal Features of Discovery Value Accounting

120. Under discovery value accounting as it has

generally been proposed, mineral reserves would be recorded at their estimated *value* when the reserves are discovered or, alternatively, when the reserves are developed. Property acquisition costs and other prediscovery costs generally would be deferred and written off when the areas to which the costs apply have been explored and the underlying reserves, if any, evaluated. Subsequent to discovery, the carrying amount of the reserves would not be adjusted for changes in prices; however, the carrying amount would be adjusted for revisions of estimated reserve quantities. The discovery value would be treated as revenue from the oil and gas exploration activities of the enterprise and would become the recorded value ("cost") of reserves for future accounting purposes. Those discovery value amounts would then be amortized against the revenues resulting from the production and sale of the minerals.

121. Several variations of discovery value accounting have been proposed. If only proved developed reserves are included in the value computation, generally all development costs associated with the reserves will have been incurred; if additional development costs are incurred, the value of any incremental quantity of reserves discovered is recorded and, simultaneously, the related costs are written off. If undeveloped reserves are included in the value computation, an adjustment must be made for the expected future development costs (generally by reducing the value otherwise attributable to the reserves in the ground). When the development costs are eventually incurred, it is generally proposed that they be added to the carrying value of the reserves.

122. Determination of the value of oil and gas reserves is critical to both discovery value accounting and current value accounting. Four principal valuation methods that might be used to measure the value of reserves (and other assets) were discussed at length in paragraphs 436-466 of the Discussion Memorandum. Briefly summarized, they are:

a. *Current cost.* Current cost is the amount of cash or its equivalent that would have to be paid if the same asset were acquired currently. The "same asset" may be an identical asset (current reproduction cost or current cost of replacement in kind) or an asset with equivalent productive capacity (current replacement cost).

b. *Current exit value in orderly liquidation.* Current exit value in orderly liquidation is the net amount of cash that could be obtained currently by selling the asset in orderly liquidation (current market value, if a market exists). The value of mineral reserves on a current exit value basis would equal the price at which the reserves could be sold in place by a willing seller to a willing

buyer, neither being under any compulsion to sell or buy, both being competent and having reasonable knowledge of the facts.

c. *Expected exit value in due course of business.* Expected exit value in due course of business is the nondiscounted amount of cash or its equivalent into which an asset is expected to be converted in the due course of business less the direct costs necessary to make that conversion (sometimes referred to as net realizable value). The value of mineral reserves on this basis would be an amount equal to the estimated net cash flows attributable to the reserves.

d. *Present value of expected cash flows.* The present value of expected cash flows is the present value of future cash inflows into which an asset is expected to be converted in the due course of business, less the present value of cash outflows necessary to obtain those inflows. Present value measurements require information about estimated amounts of future cash inflows and outflows, the timing of those expected cash flows, and the appropriate discount rate. Various discount rates that have been proposed include the (i) rate applicable to long-term government bonds issued by the government of the country in which the reserves are located, (ii) prime rate, (iii) company's weighted average or incremental long-term borrowing rate, (iv) company's weighted average cost of capital, and (v) discount rate used by company management internally to make individual investment decisions.

123. Considerable disagreement exists as to which of those methods, if any, are suitable for valuation of oil and gas reserves, either at the time of discovery or subsequently. Also, under discovery value accounting, a decision must be made as to which categories of reserves enter into the value computation.

124. Some discovery value accounting proponents would report the value of periodic discoveries of reserves as operating income. Others would segregate the discovery value from realized revenues and gains reported in the income statement. Still others would report the discovery values in a special unrealized income section of stockholders' equity in the balance sheet until realized through the actual production and sale of oil and gas.

Principal Features of Current Value Accounting

125. Current value accounting involves the continuous use in the financial statements of one of the four methods of valuation identified in paragraph 122, or some other method. (Current value accounting could, of course, be applied to all of an enterprise's assets and liabilities, not just oil and gas reserves, but applying current value accounting beyond oil

and gas reserves was not included in the scope of this project. Alternative methods of measurement are to be considered in the Board's project to develop a conceptual framework for financial accounting and reporting.)

126. Most proponents of current value accounting for oil and gas reserves believe that the reserves should be valued at each financial statement date using the most current information available. Some proponents suggest that periodic changes in reserve values should be reflected directly in the income statement; others would report value changes directly in the stockholders' equity section of the balance sheet, perhaps by segregating or otherwise separately identifying the realized and unrealized amounts. Under current value accounting, separate data might be presented for (a) value increases resulting from new discoveries, (b) value changes resulting from adjustment of reserve quantities, and (c) holding gains and losses resulting from revaluing end-of-period reserve quantities to reflect the change in unit value during the period.

127. As with discovery value accounting, decisions must be made as to which method of valuation should be used and which reserve categories should be included in the current value computations.

A Single Accounting Method

128. The proposal that the two presently accepted accounting methods, full costing and successful efforts costing, be allowed to continue as optional alternatives received little support in the letters of comment submitted to the Board in response to the Discussion Memorandum or in the oral presentations made at the public hearing conducted by the Board before the Exposure Draft was issued. It was principally after the Exposure Draft was issued proposing to proscribe the full costing method that support for retaining both methods was expressed to the Board.

129. The Board has considered the question of accounting alternatives at length, not only in connection with its oil and gas project but also for other projects on its agenda, and has concluded that differences in accounting may be appropriate when significant differences in facts and circumstances exist, but different accounting among companies for the same types of facts and circumstances impedes comparability of financial statements and significantly detracts from their usefulness to financial statement users.

130. In the Board's judgment, the facts and circumstances surrounding the search for and development and production of oil and gas do not differ because of the size of the company or whether its securities are publicly traded. Similar types of risks of failure and potential rewards of success prevail among all companies engaged in oil and gas producing activities; only the magnitude and number of projects vary. Although the scale or location of operations may differ among companies, that should not affect the principles underlying recognition of assets, measurement of the cost of those assets, and measurement of earnings. The costs of exploratory dry holes or abandonded properties, for example, should not be included in the costs of assets for some companies and reported as losses by other companies. Yet if full costing and successful efforts costing were both retained as optional accounting alternatives, different principles of asset recognition and measurement and earnings measurement would be regarded as appropriate for companies whose circumstances are substantially similar.

131. Some respondents to the Exposure Draft cited the existence of other accounting alternatives—for instance, the use of both the last-in, first-out and the first-in, first-out methods in accounting for inventories—as justification for retaining full costing and successful efforts costing as optional alternatives. The Board does not believe that the availability of alternatives in unrelated areas of accounting should bear on a decision that the Board must make for a project on its agenda. In the Board's judgment, accounting for similar circumstances similarly and for different circumstances differently is a desirable objective in establishing standards of financial accounting and reporting. For that reason, the Board rejected the proposal, made by some respondents to the Exposure Draft, that intercompany comparability be achieved by footnote disclosure with retention of both full costing and successful efforts costing. Also, for that reason, the Board rejected the proposal that it simply "clean up" the many variations in full costing and the many variations in successful efforts costing presently used in practice by mandating only one acceptable approach to full costing and one acceptable approach to successful efforts costing and allowing companies to choose one of those two approaches.

132. One of the principal criticisms of the work of the FASB's predecessors that led to creation of the FASB was that they did not sufficiently narrow or eliminate free choice accounting alternatives. A report entitled *Federal Regulation and Regulatory Reform* (the "Moss Report") issued in 1976 by the Subcommittee on Oversight and Investigations of the U.S. House of Representatives and a report entitled *The Accounting Establishment* (the "Metcalf Report") prepared in 1976 by the staff of the Subcommittee on Reports, Accounting and Management of the U.S. Senate were both strongly critical of the availability of alternative accounting

principles. In its November 1977 report, "Improving the Accountability of Publicly Owned Corporations and Their Auditors," Senator Metcalf's Subcommittee concluded that "uniformity in the development and application of accounting standards must be a major goal of the standard-setting system." Moreover, two major financial statement user groups—the Financial Accounting Policy Committee of the Financial Analysts Federation (the national professional association of security analysts) and the Robert Morris Associates (the national professional association of bank lending officers)—have endorsed elimination of optional accounting alternatives not only for oil and gas producing companies but for other industries as well. The Securities and Exchange Commission, in *Securities Act Release No. 5877* (October 26, 1977), took a similar position, stating that the Board's oil and gas project "is expected to result in significant improvement in financial reporting through the establishment of uniform accounting standards so that investors are provided with a valid basis for comparing the financial statements of different companies." In the Board's judgment, when the same or similar facts and circumstances exist, as they do in the search for and development of oil and gas reserves, intercompany comparability requires a single method of accounting. Comparable reporting by companies competing for capital is, in the Board's judgment, in the public interest (see paragraphs 157-174).

Reasons for Rejecting Discovery Value Accounting

133. The Board concluded that financial statements of an oil and gas producing company should not be prepared on a discovery value basis for a number of reasons. One group of reasons relates to problems in measuring the value of reserves with reasonable accuracy at the point of discovery. Measurements of discovery value require estimates of (a) the quantity of reserves, (b) the amount and timing of costs to develop the reserves, (c) the timing of production of the reserves, (d) the production costs and income taxes, (e) selling prices, and (f) (for some valuation methods) appropriate discount rates that reflect both an interest element and a risk factor. Those estimates, in turn, might be based on predictions of changes in government regulations and restrictions (both domestic and foreign), technological changes (including not only the technology involved in oil and gas producing activities but also the technology of transportation, refining, and marketing of oil and gas products), and domestic and international economic conditions; or current regulations, technology, and conditions might be assumed to continue indefinitely. The uncertainties inherent in those estimates and predictions tend to make estimates of reserve values highly subjective and relatively unreliable for the purpose of providing the

basis on which to prepare financial statements of an oil and gas producing company.

134. Under generally accepted accounting principles followed by companies in nearly all industries, revenue is normally recognized only when the earning process is complete or virtually complete and, then, only after an exchange transaction has taken place. The earning process is the continuum of profit-directed activities by which revenue is earned—purchasing, manufacturing, selling a product or rendering a service, delivery, cash collection, etc. The exchange transaction is the specific point at which the earning process is normally regarded as sufficiently complete to justify accounting recognition of revenue.

135. Discovery value accounting recognizes revenue from exploration activities at the point of discovery even though it may be many years until the property is developed and the oil and gas are produced and sold. That is, the earning process is far from complete, at least as completion of that process is generally determined for other industries. Discovery is certainly a critical event in the search for and extraction of oil and gas, but there are many uncertainties standing between discovery of reserves and the ultimate realization of related revenues. Often many years pass, very substantial amounts of money are spent, and significant revisions are made to estimated quantities of reserves discovered.

136. Exceptions to the general rule for revenue recognition are found in practice today. *APB Statement No. 4,* "Basic Concepts and Accounting Principles Underlying Financial Statements of Business Enterprises," paragraph 152, states:

> Sometimes revenue is recognized at the completion of production and before a sale is made. Examples include certain precious metals and farm products with assured sales prices. The assured price, the difficulty in some situations of determining costs of products on hand, and the characteristic of unit interchangeability are reasons given to support this exception.

137. As noted earlier, reserves often are discovered many years before they are produced, and many dollars often are spent for development and production costs before the oil and gas reserves are extracted. Moreover, while oil and gas may to some extent be regarded as fungible, sales prices, particularly in the present domestic and international economic and regulatory environments, are anything but assured. Thus, the reasons given in support of the special revenue recognition principles for precious metals and farm products that have been produced and have assured sales prices do not apply to oil and gas producing activities.

138. Proponents of discovery value accounting argue that it provides better information about the success or failure of exploration activities, which activities are the most important ones in oil and gas production. However, discovery value accounting represents a fundamental change from the traditional, historical cost basis of preparing financial statements. Various alternatives to the historical cost measurement basis are under examination as part of the Board's conceptual framework project. Although covered in the Discussion Memorandum for the extractive industries project, valuation methods were addressed by relatively few respondents, and discovery value accounting received only very limited support among respondents. On balance, the Board concluded that estimated discovery values do not provide a satisfactory basis of accounting for oil and gas producing activities for the reasons that (a) values that were current when initially recorded quickly become out-of-date and (b) the mixture of values of minerals measured at different dates of discovery lacks both the verifiability of historical costs and the relevance of current values. The Board believes that issues relating to the accounting measurement basis should await resolution in the conceptual framework project.

Reasons for Rejecting Current Value Accounting

139. Like discovery value accounting, current value accounting for oil and gas reserves requires estimation of reserve values. The uncertainties inherent in those estimates (discussed in paragraph 133) tend to make them subjective and relatively unreliable for the purpose of providing the underlying basis on which the financial statements of an oil and gas producing company are prepared.

140. As noted in paragraph 138, the historical cost basis of accounting and certain alternative measurement bases are currently under examination as part of the Board's project on a conceptual framework for financial accounting and reporting. The Board has concluded that it should not attempt to resolve those issues in the narrow context of the extractive industries project.

141. Moreover, as with discovery value accounting, adoption of current value accounting for oil and gas reserves would require reconsideration of the accounting concept of earnings (discussed in paragraphs 134-137). Decisions would have to be made as to whether the periodic value changes should be reflected in determining earnings or only in the stockholders' equity section of the balance sheet, and whether realized value changes should be treated differently from unrealized. Those issues, too, are part of the Board's conceptual framework project.

Reasons for Accepting Successful Efforts Accounting and for Rejecting Full Costing

142. None of the assenting or dissenting members of the Board consider it appropriate to capitalize costs of exploration efforts in a geological area in which no reserves are found simply because the company previously discovered valuable reserves in an unrelated geological area.

Successful Efforts Accounting Is Consistent with the Present Accounting Framework

143. In the presently accepted financial accounting framework, an asset is an economic resource that is expected to provide future benefits, and nonmonetary assets generally are accounted for at the cost to acquire or construct them. Costs that do not relate directly to specific assets having identifiable future benefits normally are not capitalized—no matter how vital those costs may be to the ongoing operations of the enterprise. If costs do not give rise to an asset with identifiable future benefits, they are charged to expense or recognized as a loss.

144. In the Board's judgment, successful efforts costing is consistent with that accounting framework, and full costing is not. Under full costing, even costs that are known *not* to have resulted in identifiable future benefits are nonetheless capitalized as part of the cost of assets to which they have no direct relationship.

145. In the oil and gas industry, ultimately the expected future benefits that an enterprise is attempting to obtain through its acquisition, exploration, and development activities are represented by oil and gas reserves. But, other than by purchasing minerals-in-place, an enterprise does not acquire reserves directly. Rather, it acquires properties (rights to extract any reserves that may be discovered in the future) and it acquires (develops) systems capable of producing the oil and gas reserves that are discovered. Costs that are known *not* to relate directly to the discovery of oil and gas reserves or in the development of a system for the extraction of previously discovered reserves should not be capitalized. To capitalize them is inconsistent with the presently accepted accounting framework based on measuring the historical cost of an asset.

146. Present accounting concepts place boundaries on the assets to be accounted for—boundaries determined by the transaction in which the asset was acquired, by physical attributes of the asset, by legal attributes of the asset, or by the way in which the asset is used. Full costing aggregates all oil and gas reserves within very broad cost centers (countries or continents), wherever those reserves may be located

in the cost center and whenever discovered, and accounts for that aggregation as a single asset. All acquisition, exploration, and development costs incurred in that cost center are deemed to be the cost of the aggregate asset, even if those costs relate to activities that are known *not* to have been successful in acquiring, discovering, or developing reserves.

147. The successful efforts method, on the other hand, circumscribes the boundaries of, and accounts separately for, individual assets. Under the "area-of-interest" approach to successful efforts costing, oil and gas reserves located in an individual area-of-interest are the assets accounted for. Under the approach to successful efforts in which no cost center is used for the capitalize/expense decision, individual properties or groups of geologically related properties and wells, equipment, and facilities are the assets accounted for. Either way, boundaries are placed on the assets being accounted for. Only those exploration and development costs that relate directly to specific oil and gas reserves are capitalized; costs that do not relate directly to specific reserves are charged to expense. The successful efforts method of accounting conforms to the traditional concept of the historical cost of an asset.

148. Under the successful efforts method, certain types of costs may be capitalized as "construction-in-progress" pending further information about the existence of future benefits, but as soon as the additional information becomes available, and it is known whether future benefits exist, those costs are either reclassified as an amortizable asset or charged to expense.

Financial Statements Should Reflect Risk and Unsuccessful Results

149. The function of the nation's capital markets is to direct capital to companies and institutions through decisions to invest and lend. Financial accounting and reporting provides one important source of information on which investment, lending, and related decisions are made.

150. Enterprises seeking capital operate in varying circumstances of possible success or failure. That is, they offer varying degrees of risk and opportunity to those supplying capital. Although investors and lenders differ among themselves with regard to the risks they are willing to accept, they have one thing in common: They seek a higher expected return for accepting higher risk. Business enterprises seeking capital offer different risks. Capital is equitably allocated if the prices paid are commensurate with the risk.

151. In the production of oil and gas, significant risks and returns arise in the search for reserves. In other words, discovery of oil and gas reserves is a critical event in determining failure or success, for assessing risks and returns. Because it capitalizes the costs of unsuccessful property acquisitions and unsuccessful exploratory activities as part of the costs of successful acquisitions and activities, full costing tends to obscure failure and risk. Successful efforts accounting, on the other hand, highlights failures and the risks involved in the search for oil and gas reserves by charging to expense costs that are known not to have resulted in identifiable future benefits.

152. Neither full costing nor successful efforts costing reflects success at the time of discovery. Under both methods, success is reported at the time of sale. It might be said, therefore, that both methods tend to obscure, or at least delay, the reporting of success, but that is the consequence of the historical cost basis of accounting, and its adherence to the realization concept. The obscuring of failure, however, results only from the full cost method. Under successful efforts accounting, unsuccessful costs are charged to expense and not carried forward as assets. In the Board's judgment, financial statements prepared on the successful efforts basis, including disclosures (as required by this Statement) of capitalized costs and costs incurred in oil and gas producing activities (to provide an indication of effort) and of reserve quantities and changes therein (to provide an indication of accomplishment) will provide investors with important information about success as well as failure.

153. Investors and creditors look to financial statements as an important source of information about companies' risks and returns. Investors and creditors focus on earnings—and in particular on earnings variability—as an indicator of risks and returns. As the Board noted in summarizing its *Tentative Conclusions on Objectives of Financial Statements of Business Enterprises:*[8]

> Earnings (or profits or net income) of a business enterprise are the focal point of the information communicated in financial statements. Earnings are a major motivating force in the economic activities of business enterprises and a major motivating force in the economic activities of those who lend to business enterprises, those who invest in them, and those who manage them. In general, earnings reduce the risk of those who lend funds to an enterprise or acquire its debt securities.
>
> Earnings also enable an enterprise to pay cash

---

[8]FASB Discussion Memorandum, "Conceptual Framework for Financial Accounting and Reporting: Elements of Financial Statements and Their Measurement," December 2, 1976, paragraph 4.

dividends to those who invest in its equity securities and enhance the prospects for increases in the market price of its stock. Thus, investors and creditors are generally more willing to commit funds to profitable enterprises than to unprofitable ones. Expectations of earnings, often based on a history of earnings, enable an enterprise to obtain both equity and debt financing.

154. Some persons criticize successful efforts accounting on grounds that a company's earnings tend to fluctuate more under that method than under full cost accounting, depending on the level and degree of success or failure of the company's acquisition and exploration activities in a given accounting period. While fluctuating earnings may, indeed, be a *characteristic* of successful efforts accounting, it is not a *fault*. The successful efforts method enables investors and lenders to observe the impact of the risks inherent in oil and gas producing activities on a company's results of operations from period to period.

155. A similar issue arose in connection with the Board's project on accounting by enterprises in the development stage. The Board concluded in *FASB Statement No. 7*, "Accounting and Reporting by Development Stage Enterprises," that a development stage enterprise should not be permitted to capitalize costs that would be charged to expense when incurred by an established operating enterprise because to do so would tend to obscure, in financial statements, the impact of risks inherent in starting up a new company.

156. The same issue has arisen in a number of other Board projects, for example, the projects on self-insurance, catastrophe losses, expropriations, and other contingencies and on foreign currency translation. A basic issue in each of those projects, as it is in the oil and gas project, was whether financial accounting standards should be adopted to normalize or average the effects of events that are inevitable over extended periods but occur at infrequent and relatively unpredictable intervals. Consistent with its conclusion in this Statement, the Board concluded in those projects that financial statements should report the effects of risk and not attempt to normalize them.

Ability to Raise Capital

157. Many proponents of full costing have said, in written submissions in response to the Discussion Memorandum, at the public hearing, and in comment letters on the Exposure Draft, that adoption of the successful efforts method of accounting will inhibit the ability of oil and gas producing companies to raise capital to finance their exploration activities. In particular, they contend, small explora-

tion companies will have special difficulties in obtaining capital because, under a successful efforts approach, their income statements will be more likely to report earnings fluctuations and in some cases net losses, and their balance sheets could even show cumulative deficits. Potential suppliers of capital will not understand those fluctuations, losses, and deficits, it is argued, and sources of capital will diminish or be more costly. Those results, they say, are at variance with national economic goals. A particular national economic goal they cite is to encourage additional oil and gas exploration.

158. In the Board's judgment, the arguments put forth by those who say that adoption of successful efforts accounting and proscription of full costing will prevent them from raising the capital needed to finance their exploration and production activities are not persuasive. In a free enterprise economy in which capital is allocated among enterprises largely on the basis of individual investors' decisions, if a company is an economically successful enterprise, it will continue to attract capital. Its financial statements should provide those who supply capital with information that assists them in determining whether the expected returns on that capital are commensurate with the risks involved. In the Board's judgment, financial statements that are prepared in conformity with the provisions of this Statement will provide investors and creditors with that type of information. Many small oil and gas producing companies use the successful efforts method, not full costing; have done so for many years; and have generally been able to obtain capital to finance their exploration activities. Indeed, full costing is a relatively recent development in accounting for oil and gas producing activities. The 1973 survey (cited in paragraph 101 of this Statement), which was sponsored by a group of full costing petroleum companies, identified only *one* instance of its use prior to 1960, and it was not until the late 1960s that the use of full costing became relatively widespread.

159. In examining the ability-to-raise-capital issue, the Board focused in particular on three distinct types of small exploration companies:

a. Privately owned exploration companies. (A representative of the Independent Petroleum Association of America at the Board's public hearing estimated that there are 10,000 such companies in the United States.)
b. Publicly owned exploration companies. (A 1977 list of companies whose securities are registered with the SEC identifies 214 companies in "petroleum and natural gas extraction" Standard Industrial Classification.)
c. Oil and gas exploration subsidiaries and divisions of companies that are mainly in other lines of business.

160. As noted in paragraphs 101 and 117, a great many *privately* owned exploration companies follow federal income tax accounting practices in preparing their financial statements. Income tax accounting is a variation of successful efforts accounting. Those companies have for many years been able to obtain capital from external sources, including loans from local and international banks and insurance companies, from knowledgeable individual investors, and from private placements of securities.

161. Many publicly owned oil and gas exploration companies follow the successful efforts method. In connection with the research study described in paragraph 93(a) of this Statement, the staff of the FASB identified 79 oil and gas companies that (a) have securities currently traded on a securities exchange or in the over-the-counter market and (b) derive more than 50 percent of their revenue from exploration and production. (The latter criterion eliminates virtually all of the major integrated companies from the group.) Of the publicly owned companies so identified, 41 percent use successful efforts accounting.

162. Some responses to the Exposure Draft were from companies that are mainly in lines of business other than oil and gas but that have oil and gas exploration subsidiaries and divisions that use the full cost method. A number of the responses came from electric and gas public utility companies with oil and gas exploration subsidiaries recently formed or under active consideration. Those respondents urged retention of full costing for their subsidiaries and divisions on grounds that investors and lenders who supply capital to the enterprise do not regard the enterprise as an oil and gas producing company and thus would not understand the fluctuations of reported earnings or losses that, in their view, would more likely result from using successful efforts accounting, especially by a newly formed exploration subsidiary. In the Board's judgment, however, that is not an appropriate reason for allowing those subsidiaries and divisions to adopt or continue to use full costing. By choosing to seek the rewards of engaging in oil and gas exploration activities, those enterprises have assumed the risks associated with the search for oil and gas reserves, and their financial statements should provide information about those risks and not obscure them. Investors and creditors seek a return on their capital commensurate with the risks involved, and financial statements should assist them in assessing those risks. One would expect that those who supply capital for a high-risk activity such as oil and gas exploration would demand a higher return than for capital invested in less risky activity.

163. The telephone interview survey described in paragraph 93(b) provides additional evidence about the ability of small, publicly owned, successful efforts companies to raise capital. Professor Horace R. Brock of North Texas State University, or a person working under his direction, asked a senior executive officer of each of 27 small, publicly owned, successful efforts companies whether, in the officer's opinion, use of the successful efforts method has affected the company's ability to obtain the capital necessary to finance its exploration and production activities. None of the executive officers surveyed felt that the company's use of successful efforts accounting had hindered its ability to raise capital. Most of the surveyed companies raised capital externally during the past 10 years from public sales of equity and debt securities, loans from banks and insurance companies, private placements, investments by individual investors, or other outside sources. Those corporate officers were also asked whether they felt that their companies were denied access to any particular source of capital and, if so, whether the company's accounting method was a significant factor in any such situation. Again, they said that successful efforts accounting did not adversely affect their companies' ability to obtain capital from a desired source.

164. Interviews with suppliers of capital to oil and gas producing companies resulted in a similar finding. As described in paragraph 90(a), 24 bank loan officers, bank trust department officers, and securities underwriters, all of whom work directly with oil and gas companies, were interviewed to ascertain how investment and credit decisions regarding such companies are reached. The majority of interviewees indicated that the method of accounting would not affect their investment and credit decisions regarding oil and gas producing companies.

165. Some who favor retention of full costing argue that use of that method by newly formed exploration companies is essential to their viability, because investors will be disinclined to provide capital to those companies if their financial statements report net losses from operations and cumulative deficits. The Board found, however, in the course of its deliberations on *FASB Statement No. 7,* that those who supply capital to companies in the development stage understand the special circumstances of those companies and the possibility that their financial statements will report losses and deficits. In connection with that project, the Board surveyed officers of 15 venture capital companies that provide capital to development stage enterprises (though not necessarily to oil and gas ventures). Those officers said that whether a development stage enterprise defers preoperating costs or charges them to expense has little effect on (a) the amount of venture capital to be provided to that enterprise and (b) the terms under which any venture capital is provided. That

survey and related economic impact considerations were supported by a study conducted by the U.S. Department of Commerce, which is described in paragraph 50 of Statement No. 7.

166. Most proponents of full costing indicate that the reserve value ceiling on capitalized costs is an essential condition for use of that method. Except for those new companies that find relatively large quantities of proved reserves in their initial exploration efforts or that purchase interests in proved properties, it seems likely that many new exploration companies would be reporting operating losses and cumulative deficits under full costing as well as under successful efforts costing.

167. A few respondents to the Exposure Draft have said that their own companies' property acquisition and exploratory drilling programs would be sharply curtailed if they were forced to change from the full cost method of accounting to the successful efforts method. However, since the prospects of finding commercially recoverable reserves, the prices at which those reserves would be sold, the costs that would be incurred, and the income taxes that would be paid are totally unaffected by the method of accounting for the costs incurred, a decision not to go ahead with an otherwise commercially attractive project simply because successful efforts reporting is required would seem to be unlikely for the vast majority of companies. Conversely, a venture that is not otherwise commercially attractive does not become so simply because a particular method will be used to account for that venture in the company's financial statements. While a few respondents representing full cost companies did say that their companies would expect to reduce their exploration efforts because successful efforts accounting would reduce reported earnings, other companies that use full costing have said that an FASB Statement mandating successful efforts accounting will not affect their exploration plans. For example, one such company has publicly stated that while a mandated change to successful efforts accounting would have a substantial effect on previously reported earnings, it would not change the value of the company's assets, its reserves, or its cash flow, and that the company had decided not to change its exploration program if successful efforts accounting is required.

168. In support of their claim that adopting the successful efforts method will impair their companies' ability to raise capital and thereby reduce exploration activity, some persons have said that in November 1971 the Federal Power Commission adopted its Order No. 440 (which supports the full cost concept) to stimulate the search for and development of new natural gas supplies. (Order No. 440

is described in paragraph 69 of this Statement.) The petitions for rehearing of that Order that were filed with the FPC in December 1971 alleged, among other things, that the Commission had failed to reach any conclusion on what was stated to be the primary factor resulting in issuance of Order No. 440—namely, how full cost accounting would provide a stimulus for companies under the FPC's jurisdiction to conduct a search for and develop new gas supplies. In its Order No. 440-A denying the request for rehearing, the FPC stated: "Since we concluded that full-cost accounting on its merits should be adopted, it is not necessary for us to proceed further and reach a finding as to whether the accounting, as such, would provide a stimulus to discover and develop new gas supplies." (The Federal Power Commission is now the Federal Energy Regulatory Commission, a part of the Department of Energy.)

169. Some advocates of full costing apparently feel that the securities markets, which bring together those who provide capital and those who seek it, will not understand financial results reported by the successful efforts method. They imply that investors' willingness to provide capital to a given company or industry is affected by that company's or industry's use of a particular method of accounting. However, a number of research studies indicate that the securities markets generally recognize and compensate for intercompany differences in accounting practices for the same or similar events and transactions. In a 1973 summary of the findings of the then-extant research, Stanford University Professor William H. Beaver noted:[9]

> The prevailing opinion in the accounting profession is that the market reacts naively to financial statement information. This view is reinforced by the anecdotal data of the sort described earlier, and by the obvious fact that the market is populated with several million uninformed, naive investors, whose knowledge or concern for the subtleties of accounting matters is nil. However, in spite of this obvious fact, the formal research in this area is remarkably consistent in finding that the market, at least as manifested in the way in which security prices react, is quite sophisticated in dealing with financial statement data.

170. The research undertaken at the Board's request to examine the effect of the oil and gas Exposure Draft on the market prices of common stock issued by both full cost and successful efforts companies (described in paragraph 93(a) of this Statement) corroborates that the securities markets are generally able to assimilate financial information and to understand the underlying economics of

---

[9]Beaver, William H., "What Should Be the FASB's Objectives?," *The Journal of Accountancy,* August 1973, pp. 49-56.

the oil and gas exploration and production industry. That study did not find statistically significant evidence that issuance of the Exposure Draft affected the market prices of common shares issued by full cost companies as compared to successful efforts companies—except for some possible effect on the full cost companies during the week preceding and the week of issuance of the Exposure Draft, but the market soon adjusted, and evidence of a permanent or lingering effect was not found. (As noted in paragraph 93(a), the Board will undertake a similar study of the impact of this Statement following its issuance.)

171. The Board acknowledges that not all empirical evidence supports the view that the securities markets are entirely able to take into account the differences in accounting methods used by different companies. The studies referred to in paragraph 169 provide evidence only with respect to the securities markets as a whole; those researchers readily admit (and other research substantiates) the likelihood that decisions of individual investors in individual securities can be affected by accounting differences. As noted in paragraph 170, a Board-sponsored study found that the oil and gas Exposure Draft may have affected the prices of full cost companies' securities during the two weeks surrounding its issuance, though the effect was of brief duration. That finding supports the conclusions of other researchers that investors are sometimes unable to properly evaluate the impact of alternative accounting methods. Further, in situations in which accounting changes may have had a long-term effect on securities prices (as opposed to a temporary disruption), that result might well be viewed as an equitable adjustment of the cost of capital.[10]

172. Some respondents to the Exposure Draft said that adopting the successful efforts method and proscribing the full costing method would likely have anticompetitive effects and would be contrary to national economic or policy goals. Any national economic or policy goal that involves the use of data reported in or derived from financial statements can, in the Board's judgment, be best pursued if the relevant financial statements are prepared on a common basis, so that lenders, investors, government regulators, and others involved directly or indirectly in allocating capital can analyze and reach informed decisions on the basis of consistent and comparable financial data. To the extent that furtherance of

competition in oil and gas exploration and production and the availability of increased capital resources to finance those efforts are perceived as national economic or policy goals and in the interest of the general public, those goals can best be fostered—and the likelihood of their attainment substantially increased—if all competitors disclose financial data in a marketplace free from the burdens of inconsistency, noncomparability, and misunderstanding, a marketplace in which risks and rewards are reported as objectively and as evenhandedly as possible.

173. Financial accounting should attempt to report the results of business decisions as nearly as those results can be determined in accordance with the accepted framework of accounting for all enterprises. If an enterprise's operations are subject to economic influences that are manifested in fluctuating earnings, financial statements should report those fluctuations and not obscure them. If the economic influences that affect an enterprise's operations are manifested in only minor fluctuations, that too should be portrayed. Otherwise, accounting is not evenhanded, for it fails to distinguish different characteristics of enterprises that investors may perceive as involving different risks. That evenhandedness becomes especially important for equitable allocation of capital. If financial reporting obscures differences that may be perceived as representing differences in risk or creates differences where none exist, it may contribute to channeling some capital into enterprises with expected returns and risks that are disparate—in effect, subsidizing the cost of capital to some companies at the expense of other companies.

174. As explained in paragraphs 157-173, the Board has not been presented with or able to obtain persuasive information indicating that adoption of successful efforts accounting and proscription of full costing will inhibit competition in exploration for and production of oil and gas reserves or in financing those activities. Indeed, the Board is of the view that, far from inhibiting competition, the removal of one or two significantly different optional alternative methods of accounting in similar situations will facilitate competition. The weight of the evidence before the Board is that independent oil and gas producing companies using successful efforts accounting do compete successfully and conduct effective exploration and production programs

---

[10]The contradictory conclusions of the various studies on accounting and securities prices and the implications of those conclusions are discussed in considerable depth in *Tentative Conclusions on Objectives of Financial Statements of Business Enterprises,* which was issued by the Board in December 1976. A number of specific studies are cited in Chapter 2, "Investors and Creditors," of *Tentative Conclusions;* additional studies are identified in the bibliography of the extractive industries Discussion Memorandum. Chapter 2 of *Tentative Conclusions* discusses both the traditional view of investors' and creditors' information needs (which concentrates on analysis of individual securities and enterprises that issue them) and the more recent capital market theory (which concentrates on portfolios and the extent to which individual securities increase or decrease the level of risk of a portfolio). An appendix to *Tentative Conclusions* provides an even more technical discussion of recent capital market theory.

that they are able to finance through a variety of capital sources.

The "Cover" Concept Is Inconsistent with the Present Accounting Framework

175. Under the full cost method, all costs incurred in acquiring, exploring, and developing properties within a relatively large geopolitical cost center (usually a country or a continent) are capitalized when incurred as costs of obtaining whatever reserves have been found in that cost center as long as the aggregate capitalized costs do not exceed the aggregate value of those reserves. If the value of previously discovered reserves exceeds the aggregate unamortized capitalized costs, unsuccessful acquisition and exploration costs are said to be adequately "covered" by the value of the previously discovered reserves, and a loss need not be recognized. In other words, current failures are "covered" and are not reported to the extent of past successes. Further, an increase in the market prices of previously discovered reserves in a cost center can enhance the amount of "cover" and further delay recognition of failures (losses) in that cost center.

176. In the Board's judgment, the "cover" concept is inconsistent with the present accounting framework, and it also obscures risk (see paragraphs 149-156). Reserves that may have been discovered ten, twenty, thirty, forty, or more years ago by a company under completely different management, with very different technology, and in very different domestic and international economic and political circumstances, should not be used, as they are under the full cost method, to justify nonrecognition of current failures. Similarly, reserves located in, say, West Texas should not be used to "cover" unsuccessful acquisition and exploration efforts in Louisiana, Alaska, or Canada, or in the offshore U.S. waters.

Successful Efforts Is Comparable to Accounting in Other Extractive Industries

177. Although not usually labeled as such, successful efforts accounting generally is followed in extractive industries other than the oil and gas industry. Because of its wide acceptance in those industries, requiring it for all oil and gas producing companies is likely to bring about greater comparability of financial statements among companies in the various extractive industries.

The Matching Concept Does Not Justify Full Costing

178. Some persons contend that full costing is justified because a "better matching" of revenues and expenses is achieved if all costs incurred in acquisition, exploration, and development activities are amortized on a pro rata basis as total reserves are produced. Proponents of full costing argue that it is impossible to discover oil and gas reserves without incurring the costs of some unsuccessful acquisition, exploration, and development activities, and they sometimes compare those activities with manufacturing operations in which spoilage or breakage is unavoidable. They argue that "proper matching" requires that the costs incurred in unavoidable unsuccessful efforts be accounted for as reasonable and necessary costs of successful efforts in the same way that the costs of unavoidable spoilage or breakage are accounted for as costs of good products.

179. Three pervasive principles by which revenues and expenses are matched are described in paragraphs 156-160 of *APB Statement No. 4,* as follows:

> *Associating Cause and Effect.* Some costs are recognized as expenses on the basis of a presumed direct association with specific revenue . . . recognizing them as expenses accompanies recognition of the revenue.
>
> *Systematic and Rational Allocation.* . . . If an asset provides benefits for several periods its cost is allocated to the periods in a systematic and rational manner in the absence of a more direct basis for associating cause and effect.
>
> *Immediate Recognition.* Some costs are associated with the current accounting period as expenses because (1) costs incurred during the period provide no discernible future benefits, (2) costs recorded as assets in prior periods no longer provide discernible benefits, or (3) allocating costs either on the basis of association with revenue or among several accounting periods is considered to serve no useful purpose.

180. A direct cause and effect justification for associating unsuccessful acquisition and exploration costs with revenues derived from successful activities has not been demonstrated. A direct cause and effect association can be said to exist between the costs of nonproductive fields and the revenues from reserves in productive fields, or between costs applicable to unsuccessful ventures and costs applicable to successful ventures, if there is a *reliable* association between total costs and reserves discovered as a direct result of incurring those costs. Only then could it be said that a cost gives rise to revenues, that is, causes revenues. Although some persons claim that *industry-wide* statistics indicate a general predictable relationship between total number of wells or total footage drilled and total reserves added, those relationships have not been constant, particularly over a relatively short period of time such as a year, and there can be no assurance that they will apply to the future. More importantly, to the best of the Board's knowledge no such relationship has

been demonstrated to be predictable for an *individual company.* Accounting is done for individual companies, not for an industry as a whole, and for companies a direct association between finding costs and mineral reserves emerges only at the level of an individual property unit or within a given field or other localized geological structure. Even that association often is not evident at the time the costs are incurred, and that is when accounting decisions must be made.

181. Systematic and rational allocation likewise does not justify attributing unsuccessful acquisition and exploration costs to the results of successful activities. As *APB Statement No. 4* states, allocation of an asset's cost is justified "if an asset provides benefits for several periods." In the full costing versus successful efforts costing controversy, the question is not whether or how to allocate capitalized costs but which costs to capitalize.

182. The "immediate recognition" principle referred to in *APB Statement No. 4* is appropriate for unsuccessful acquisition and exploration costs. According to that principle, costs are associated with the current period as expenses if they provide no discernible future benefits (for example, geological and geophysical costs) or, if previously capitalized, they no longer provide discernible benefits (for example, acquisition costs of abandoned properties). The application of the immediate recognition principle in this Statement is consistent with its application by the Board in other pronouncements. In paragraph 49 of *FASB Statement No. 2,* "Accounting for Research and Development Costs," for example, the Board stated that "the general lack of discernible future benefits at the time the costs are incurred indicates that the 'immediate recognition' principle of expense recognition should apply."

183. In *FASB Statement No. 2,* moreover, the Board considered and rejected the argument that research and development costs be capitalized when incurred and amortized on a company-wide basis. Paragraphs 51 and 52 state:

> 51. Enterprises undertake research and development activities with the hope of future benefits. If there were no such hope, the activities would not be conducted. Some persons take the position that the accounting treatment for research and development costs should be determined by considering in the aggregate all of the research and development activities of an enterprise. In their view, if there is a high probability of future benefits from an enterprise's total research and development program, the entire cost of those activities should be capitalized without regard to the certainty of future benefits from individual projects.

> 52. The Board believes, however, that it is not appropriate to consider accounting for research and development activities on an aggregate or total-enterprise basis for several reasons. For accounting purposes the expectation of future benefits generally is not evaluated in relation to broad categories of expenditures or an enterprise-wide basis but rather in relation to individual or related transactions or projects. . . .

Value Ceiling Is Subjective

184. Limiting capitalized costs to the estimated value of reserves, which is an integral part of the full cost method of accounting, requires estimation of reserve quantities, development costs, production costs, the timing of development and production, selling prices, and appropriate discount rates. The uncertainties inherent in those estimates and projections tend to make estimates of reserve values highly subjective, and estimates of value made by trained experts can differ markedly. Under the successful efforts method, the need to limit capitalized costs is much less crucial because the costs of unsuccessful efforts, which may represent a large part of the total capitalized costs under the full cost method, will have been charged to expense as incurred or recognized as a loss when the effort was determined to be unsuccessful.

Full Costing Does Not Represent
Current Value on the Balance Sheet

185. Some persons contend that by using full costing, asset carrying amounts reported in the balance sheet will be closer to the current values of most companies' oil and gas reserves than they would under successful efforts costing. In the Board's judgment, however, under neither method do the *costs* to acquire, explore, and develop mineral properties indicate the *values* of reserves discovered. Those values change continually, depending on revisions of estimates of reserve quantities, development costs, production costs, income taxes, the timing of future development and production, selling prices, and appropriate discount rates. The capitalized costs, however, do not change. Neither full costing nor successful efforts costing is intended to portray current values; both of those methods are based on historical costs.

The Ability to Manage Earnings Is Not
Unique to Successful Efforts Accounting

186. Some proponents of full costing contend that the ability of management to subjectively influence reported earnings is reduced under full costing. In their view, under successful efforts accounting,

management may be inclined to smooth or average periodic reported earnings by (a) deciding to delay final determination of the outcome of a project or to delay the write-off of an unsuccessful venture, thus postponing loss recognition, (b) incurring larger or smaller amounts of costs that are charged to expense as incurred, such as in exploration, and (c) postponing or moving forward the times at which such costs are to be incurred.

187. While a transaction-oriented accounting framework—which is the presently accepted framework—allows opportunities to postpone or accelerate earnings effects, those opportunities are not unique to the oil and gas industry. Nor are they unique to successful efforts accounting since full costing itself may be viewed as a method for averaging reported earnings over long periods of time. Most importantly, the Board does not believe that the potential actions described in the preceding paragraph should bear importantly on the accounting decisions confronting the Board in this project. Even if accounting results were to influence some managers' decisions, it does not follow that accounting standards should be designed to accomplish or prevent an action by management. That type of accounting standard would require a judgment by the Board as to which potential actions are desirable and which are undesirable. Accounting should evenhandedly report economic actions taken, regardless of motivation. Accounting should not obscure the effect of actions and events in order to prevent what some believe to be "uneconomic" actions.

Simplicity Is Not the Overriding Criterion for Selection of Accounting Method

188. Some persons advocate full costing on grounds that it reduces the amount of procedural and mechanical accounting work, thus saving time, effort, and cost in maintaining accounting records. They claim that since all costs incurred in acquisition, exploration, and development are capitalized, there is less need to make arbitrary cost allocations or to prepare separate computations of amortization on individual properties. The Board disagrees. Firstly, individual property records must be maintained for purposes of determining royalties, computing taxable income, and making management decisions to commit funds, abandon properties, and so forth, so the amount of additional effort that may be required under successful efforts accounting is not expected to be burdensome. More importantly, in the Board's judgment, accounting simplicity should not justify nonrecognition of losses at the time they are incurred.

Reasons for Specific Conclusions within the Successful Efforts Method

189. Paragraphs 142-188 set forth the Board's reasons for rejecting full cost accounting and accepting successful efforts accounting. As explained in paragraphs 111-119, however, there are many variations within the successful efforts method. Paragraphs 190-214 which follow explain the Board's conclusions regarding the principal variations considered.

Rejection of Area-of-Interest Approach

190. Some proponents of successful efforts accounting believe that a cost center (such as an area-of-interest) has a central role in accumulating certain types of prediscovery costs prior to the time that a reasonable determination can be made as to whether future benefits will result from having incurred those costs. They would capitalize some or all prediscovery costs relating to an area-of-interest until it is determined whether that area contains proved reserves. If it is determined that the area-of-interest does not contain reserves, the costs are written off and a loss is recognized. Even among proponents of the area-of-interest approach there are differences as to which prediscovery costs relating to an area-of-interest should be capitalized. Some proponents would capitalize prediscovery drilling costs but not G&G; others would capitalize the G&G as well. Other successful efforts proponents use a cost center only for computing amortization rates. They believe that the nature of a cost, and not the nature of a cost center, should be the primary consideration in the capitalize/expense decision (discussed further in paragraph 103).

191. The Board has adopted the latter view. Until discovery, delineation of the boundaries of a cost center such as an area-of-interest is arbitrary, and intercompany differences in defining cost centers are likely to be significant and unavoidable. Many years often elapse before reserves are discovered in an area-of-interest, if they are discovered at all. Thus, depending on the extent to which an area-of-interest proponent would capitalize prediscovery costs, exploration costs that have no identifiable future benefits may be carried forward as assets potentially for many years. The Board concluded that exploration expenditures that do not directly result in the acquisition of an asset having identifiable future benefits should not be capitalized simply because they fall within lines drawn on a map by individual companies, that is, lines drawn to circumscribe an area-of-interest or, as some would say, a project.

192. Some persons who advocate capitalization of all costs associated with an area-of-interest say that doing so is essential for financial statements to reflect the total "historical cost" of a project that ultimately proves successful. Many projects, however, do not ultimately prove successful, and determination of success or failure of an area-of-interest often takes a number of years. In the Board's judgment, periodic reporting of financial position and results of operations to investors and creditors is an overriding consideration that precludes the indefinite accumulation of costs of unknown future benefit. The Board reached a similar conclusion in *FASB Statement No. 2*, "Accounting for Research and Development Costs," in which the Board rejected the indefinite deferral of R&D costs on a project basis pending determination of success or failure of the project.

Charging G&G to Expense

193. This Statement requires that geological and geophysical costs, whether incurred before or after acquisition of the related property, be charged to expense when incurred. Those costs are information costs very much like research costs. To a considerable extent, G&G costs are incurred before any properties are acquired, and in the majority of cases the acreage surveyed is either never acquired or, if acquired, is ultimately abandoned or surrendered. It is difficult, and in many cases impossible, to correlate geological and geophysical expenditures with a specific discovery made many months or years later, even with the benefit of hindsight; such correlation clearly cannot be done at the time the G&G expenditures are incurred, which is when accounting decisions are made. For those reasons, the Board has concluded that G&G costs shall be charged to expense when incurred. While the costs of drilling stratigraphic test wells are sometimes considered to be geological and geophysical costs, they are accounted for separately under this Statement for reasons explained in paragraphs 200-202.

194. In response to recommendations made by commentators on the Exposure Draft, this Statement makes clear that dry hole contributions and bottom hole contributions are included in exploration costs (paragraph 17(c)). Also, in response to comments on the Exposure Draft, paragraph 20 has been added to provide for capitalization of contractually reimbursable G&G and other exploration costs.

Charging Carrying Costs to Expense

195. Costs of carrying and retaining undeveloped properties do not increase the potential of those properties to contain oil and gas reserves. Carrying costs are incurred to *maintain* an enterprise's rights, not to *acquire* those rights. In a sense, they are penalties for having delayed drilling and development activities and, thereby, having delayed potential production of oil and gas. Because carrying costs do not enhance the future benefits from the enterprise's properties and other assets, they are charged to expense when incurred under the provisions of this Statement.

Charging the Costs of Drilling Unsuccessful Exploratory Wells to Expense

196. Charging the costs of drilling unsuccessful exploratory wells to expense is generally regarded as an inherent part of the successful efforts method of accounting. Not all successful efforts proponents agree, however, on what constitutes unsuccessful exploratory wells, and there is also disagreement over the timing of expense recognition. Under this Statement, success is defined in terms of whether proved oil and gas reserves have been found. As to timing, under this Statement the costs of drilling exploratory wells are initially capitalized when incurred and are subsequently either charged to expense or reclassified as part of the enterprise's wells and related equipment and facilities when the determination is made as to whether proved reserves have been found. Further, this Statement establishes guidelines for determining whether the costs of drilling exploratory wells may continue to be carried as an asset pending determination of whether proved reserves have been found.

197. Several alternatives regarding the timing of expense recognition are proposed by successful efforts advocates. Some persons, on grounds that the majority of all exploratory wells (73 percent for the U.S. as a whole in 1976) are unsuccessful, would charge all costs of drilling exploratory wells to expense when incurred, rather than regard them as "construction-in-progress" pending determination of success or failure. Some would subsequently "reinstate" the costs of drilling an exploratory well that is determined to have been successful. In the Board's judgment, however, reinstatement of costs previously charged to expense is inconsistent with generally accepted accounting principles for other industries. For example, the Board has previously rejected the notion of cost reinstatement with respect to research and development costs (paragraph 57 of *FASB Statement No. 2*). Consequently, the Board concluded that a method of accounting for oil and gas producing activities based on cost reinstatement is inappropriate.

198. The best accounting, in the Board's judgment, is to capitalize as "construction-in-progress" the costs of drilling all exploratory wells pending determination of success or failure, that is, pending determination of whether proved reserves are found. The

length of time it takes to drill an exploratory well is relatively short—generally a matter of weeks or months, although a few occasionally take a year or longer—so the period during which costs of undetermined future benefit are capitalized usually is relatively brief, and this Statement requires that the costs be charged to expense as soon as a determination is made that proved reserves have not been found. In the Board's judgment, it is appropriate that the costs of drilling exploratory wells be treated differently from G&G and similar exploration costs because, first, determination of success or failure is much more clear-cut for exploratory drilling than it is for G&G and similar exploration costs, and, second, because successful exploratory wells result directly in the discovery of proved reserves whereas G&G does not.

199. The quantity of oil and gas reserves found by an exploratory well is normally estimated on or shortly after completion of drilling; occasionally that assessment takes a matter of weeks or months, rarely longer. If, however, a major capital expenditure is required before production could begin—such as for construction of a trunk pipeline—the reserves found may not be classifiable as proved unless sufficient quantities of additional reserves are found as a result of additional exploratory drilling. The additional exploratory drilling might take several years to complete. Paragraph 31 of this Statement therefore divides exploratory wells that find oil and gas reserves into two types: Those that are not drilled in an area requiring a major capital expenditure such as a trunk pipeline before production could begin and those that are drilled in such an area. For the former type, when classification of the reserves that are found cannot be made at the time drilling is completed, a one-year capitalization period is provided if that is necessary to allow a reasonable period of time for determining whether to classify those reserves as proved. Recognizing, however, that the decision to make a major capital expenditure, such as for a trunk pipeline, must sometimes await the results of additional exploratory wells, the Board concluded not to impose the one-year presumption of impairment on exploratory wells drilled in areas requiring a major capital expenditure before production could begin. Instead, paragraph 31(a) establishes two conditions for continued capitalization that take into account the realities and economics of exploratory drilling in remote areas and, at the same time, prohibit the indefinite deferral of the costs of exploratory wells merely on the hope that the selling prices of oil and gas will increase or on the possibility that unplanned exploratory drilling activity in the indefinite future might find additional quantities of reserves.

Stratigraphic Test Wells Treated Similarly to Exploratory Wells and Development Wells

200. Stratigraphic test wells are drilled to obtain information. They are not normally intended to be completed for hydrocarbon production and are customarily abandoned after drilling is completed and the information is obtained. Normally, stratigraphic test wells are drilled offshore to determine whether an offshore property contains sufficient reserves to justify the cost of constructing and installing a production platform and to determine where to locate such a platform.

201. Under this Statement, stratigraphic test wells are divided into two types—exploratory-type and development-type—and the standards of accounting for the two types parallel the accounting for exploratory wells and development wells, respectively. Thus, an exploratory-type stratigraphic test well is accounted for in a manner similar to an exploratory well drilled in an area requiring a major capital expenditure before production could begin: The costs of drilling the exploratory-type stratigraphic test well are capitalized pending determination of whether proved reserves are found, subject to the condition that those costs not continue to be carried as assets indefinitely if stratigraphic test drilling activity in the area has ceased or if the quantity of reserves found would not justify completion of the well for production had it not been simply a stratigraphic test well. The capitalized costs either are reclassified as part of the cost of the enterprise's wells and related equipment and facilities if proved reserves are found or are charged to expense if proved reserves are not found. Thus if an exploratory-type stratigraphic test well discovers reserves that are classified as proved and facilities are to be installed to produce those reserves, the cost of the exploratory-type stratigraphic test well is accounted for as part of the cost of the facilities even though the particular well itself may be abandoned. Accounting for the other type of stratigraphic test well—development-type—is identical to accounting for development wells and other development costs generally: capitalize as part of the cost of an enterprise's wells and related equipment and facilities (reasons therefor discussed in paragraph 207).

202. The method of accounting for exploratory-type stratigraphic test wells described in the preceding paragraph represents a change from the Exposure Draft, which had proposed that the costs of all stratigraphic test wells be charged to expense when incurred on grounds that they are similar to G&G costs. A number of respondents to the Expo-

sure Draft pointed out that an important difference exists between the costs of stratigraphic test wells and G&G costs: G&G information, no matter how persuasive, does not provide sufficient evidence to classify reserves as proved; reserves are classified as proved only after an exploratory well or a stratigraphic test well has been drilled. Thus a stratigraphic test well can result directly in the discovery of proved reserves whereas information obtained from geological and geophysical studies cannot. Discovery of proved reserves establishes the existence of future benefits and justifies the continued capitalization of the costs of those stratigraphic test wells that find proved reserves. Because of the foregoing differences, the costs of exploratory-type stratigraphic test wells are more like the costs of drilling exploratory wells than they are like G&G costs. The Board agrees with that view, and this Statement reflects the appropriate modification from the Exposure Draft. Further, paragraph 34 provides for deferral of the costs of exploratory-type stratigraphic test wells that find commercially producible quantities of reserves, even though those wells cannot be used to produce the reserves. That provision reflects the realities and economics of offshore drilling. Producible exploratory wells often are prohibitively expensive in offshore waters, and offshore exploratory drilling generally involves nonproducible, expendable wells.

All Development Costs Capitalized

203. Under this Statement, discovery of oil and gas reserves is viewed as the single most critical event in the search for and extraction of oil and gas. Discovery of proved reserves establishes the existence of future benefits and justifies the capitalization of the costs of successful exploratory wells and exploratory-type stratigraphic test wells as amortizable assets. After discovery, development costs are incurred to obtain additional access to those proved reserves and to provide facilities for extracting, treating, gathering, and storing the oil and gas. Those development costs result in the creation of a producing system of wells and related equipment and facilities—a system much like the production system of a manufacturing company.

204. After discovery, all costs incurred to build that producing system, including the costs of drilling unsuccessful development wells and development-type stratigraphic test wells, are capitalized as part of the cost of that system under the provisions of this Statement. With respect to development dry holes, some persons take the position that no costs incurred in drilling a dry hole—exploratory or development—can provide future benefits, and therefore the costs of all dry holes, including development dry holes, should be charged to expense.

205. In the Board's judgment, however, there is an important difference between exploratory dry holes and development dry holes. The purpose of an exploratory well is to search for oil and gas. The existence of future benefits is not known until the well is drilled. Future benefits depend on whether reserves are found. A development well, on the other hand, is drilled as part of the effort to build a producing system of wells and related equipment and facilities. Its purpose is to extract previously discovered proved oil and gas reserves. By definition (Appendix C, paragraph 274), a development well is a well drilled *within the proved area* of a reservoir to a *depth known to be productive.* The existence of future benefits is discernible from reserves already proved at the time the well is drilled. An exploratory well, because it is drilled outside a proved area, or within a proved area but to a previously untested horizon, is not directly associable with specific proved reserves until completion of drilling. An exploratory well must be assessed on its own, and the direct discovery of oil and gas reserves can be the sole determinant of whether future benefits exist and, therefore, whether an asset should be recognized. Unlike an exploratory well, a development well by definition is associable with known future benefits before drilling begins. The cost of a development well is a part of the cost of a bigger asset—a producing system of wells and related equipment and facilities intended to extract, treat, gather, and store known reserves.

206. Moreover, because they are drilled only in proved areas to proved depths, the great majority of development wells are successful; a much smaller percentage (22 percent in the United States in 1976), as compared to exploratory wells (73 percent in the United States in 1976) are dry holes. Development dry holes occur principally because of a structural fault or other unexpected stratigraphic condition or because of a problem that arose during drilling, such as tools or equipment accidentally dropped down the hole, or simply the inability to know precisely the limits and nature of a proven reservoir. Development dry holes are similar to normal, relatively minor "spoilage" or "waste" in manufacturing or construction. The Board believes that there is a significant difference between the *exploration for* and the *development of* proved reserves. Therefore, in the Board's judgment, it is appropriate to account for the costs of development dry holes different from exploratory dry holes.

207. For similar reasons, the Board believes that the costs of development-type stratigraphic test wells should be accounted for as other development costs. Development-type stratigraphic test wells are drilled *after* proved reserves have been discovered, and they are drilled *within* the proved area, generally either to

assess more accurately the quantity of reserves that has been found or to provide information as to where best to locate the production platform. The existence of future benefits is discernible from reserves already proved at the time the development-type stratigraphic test well is drilled. The costs of drilling the well are part of the costs of developing a system that will produce those reserves. In the Board's judgment, it is inappropriate to account for the costs of development-type stratigraphic test wells different from other development costs. As explained in paragraph 202, the method of accounting for stratigraphic test wells in this Statement represents a change from the proposal in the Exposure Draft as a result of comments made by respondents to the Exposure Draft.

Impairment Test for Unproved Properties

208. When unproved properties are acquired, their acquisition costs are capitalized when incurred. Whether the unproved property will ultimately provide future benefits—that is, whether it contains proved oil and gas reserves—is unknown at the time of acquisition. However, a *property right* is acquired. That property right, and the underlying *right to search for and extract* oil and gas reserves, in themselves are in the Board's judgment a sufficient future benefit to justify capitalizing the acquisition cost of an unproved property at the time it is incurred. Because a purchase price has been paid, there is a presumption that the property right has an independent market value at the time equivalent to the purchase price. Thereafter, either as a result of unsuccessful exploration activities including those of other parties on nearby or adjacent properties or as the expiration of the property right approaches, the future benefits inherent in the right to search for and extract oil and gas in an unproved property may diminish or disappear entirely, with no offsetting benefits in terms of oil and gas discovered. Consequently, this Statement requires that unproved properties be assessed periodically and a loss recognized if those properties have been impaired. Many respondents to the Exposure Draft recommended that for practical reasons the Board should permit recognition of impairment of individually insignificant properties by amortizing their costs, either in the aggregate or by groups, on the basis of the experience of the enterprise and other information. This Statement reflects the appropriate modification of the Exposure Draft to permit amortization of individually insignificant properties.

Question of a Limitation Test for Proved Properties and Capitalized Exploration and Development Costs

209. As explained in paragraphs 190 and 191, a cost center is not the primary consideration in the capitalize/expense decision under the approach to successful efforts accounting adopted by the Board in this Statement. Under that approach, the assets to which the capitalized acquisition, exploratory drilling, and development costs relate are *properties, wells, equipment, and facilities*. The question of whether to write down the carrying amount of productive assets to an amount expected to be recoverable through future use of those assets is unsettled under present generally accepted accounting principles. This is a pervasive issue that the Board has not addressed. Consequently, this Statement is not intended to change practice by either requiring or prohibiting an impairment test for proved properties or for wells, equipment, and facilities that constitute part of an enterprise's oil and gas producing systems.

Unit-of-Production Amortization

210. Nearly all respondents to the Discussion Memorandum and the Exposure Draft favored unit-of-production amortization for capitalized acquisition, exploratory drilling, and development costs. There was some disagreement, however, as to the appropriate reserve categories on which to base amortization. Some persons favor using the same reserve categories for all amortizations. Within that group, some would use only *proved developed* reserves while others would use *all proved* reserves. Some who would use all proved reserves would include estimated future development costs in the amortization computation; others would use only actual costs incurred. Some persons would use different reserve categories for different types of capitalized costs.

211. The Board believes that using estimated future development costs to compute amortization rates introduces an unnecessary and subjective element into the financial accounting and reporting process. Only development costs incurred to date should be amortized. Further, in the Board's judgment, costs should be amortized on the basis of estimates of quantities of proved reserves to which those costs relate. Proved developed reserves, by definition, relate to the costs of wells and related equipment and facilities. Acquisition costs relating to proved properties, on the other hand, were incurred to obtain not only the proved reserves that are already developed but also those proved reserves remaining to be developed. Accordingly, this Statement requires that acquisition costs of proved properties be amortized on the basis of all proved reserves, developed and undeveloped, and that capitalized exploratory drilling and development costs (wells and related equipment and facilities) be amortized on the basis of proved developed reserves.

212. Respondents to the Exposure Draft cited three

important aspects of its provisions regarding unit-of-production amortization that, in their view, required clarification or modification. The Board agrees that clarification or modification is needed for each of those matters, and the following changes have been made in this Statement:

a. Paragraph 29 has been modified to permit reclassification from unproved to proved of only a portion of an unusually large property to which proved reserves have been attributed. The acquisition cost of the portion remaining as unproved will therefore not be subject to unit-of-production amortization, though it will continue to be subject to assessment for impairment.
b. Paragraph 35 has been modified to permit amortization of natural gas cycling and processing plants by other than the unit-of-production method if another method is deemed more appropriate in the circumstances.
c. Paragraph 35 has been modified to provide for exclusion of certain large front-end development costs that relate to an entire planned group of wells as a whole from immediate early amortization pending completion of drilling the additional wells; similarly, that paragraph now provides for exclusion from the amortization rate determination those proved developed reserves that will be produced only after significant expenditures are made.

213. Two principal approaches were considered by the Board for equating, in computing amortization rates, oil and gas that are jointly produced from a property or group of properties. One is to equate the oil and gas on the basis of their relative energy content—their heat content based on the British Thermal Unit (BTU). The other approach is to equate oil and gas on the basis of their relative sales values.

214. The relative energy content approach stresses the physical relationship of oil and gas. The relative sales value method is intended to emphasize their economic relationship. The Board rejected the relative sales value method principally because of problems in determining and using relative sales values. For example, because market prices of much of the oil and gas sold are regulated, sometimes with widely disparate prices prevailing for the same commodity and with relatively significant year-to-year fluctuations, the economic relationship as of a given date could be quite artificial and quite different from a similar determination made for the same reserves as of some prior or future date. Consequently, the Board rejected the relative sales value method.

Importance of the Definition of Proved Reserves

215. Under the provisions of this Statement, capi-

talization and asset classification decisions hinge on whether *proved* reserves have been found. For that reason, the definition of proved reserves in Appendix C of this Statement assumes great importance. That definition is the one set forth in the rules and regulations of the Securities and Exchange Commission. The Board chose that definition, rather than definitions proposed by others and rather than creating a definition of its own, because the SEC definition is already required to be used in practice by oil and gas producing companies whose securities are publicly traded. The Board believes that conformity of the reserve definitions used in filings with the SEC, in information reported to the Department of Energy for the national energy data base, and in financial statements prepared in conformity with generally accepted accounting principles is desirable.

216. Under paragraph 11 of this Statement, properties are classified as either unproved or proved depending on whether those properties have proved reserves. Although some oil and gas producing companies currently make a developed/undeveloped or producing/nonproducing distinction among properties, in the Board's judgment *discovery,* rather than development or production, is the single most critical event in an enterprise's oil and gas producing activities. The Board recognizes that some companies presently refer to properties with no proved reserves as *undeveloped* or *nonproducing,* for disclosure purposes; conversely, some companies heretofore have referred to properties with proved reserves as *developed* or *producing* properties even though some or all of a property's proved reserves may not be developed or producing.

Information Available after the Balance Sheet Date

217. In response to questions raised in letters of comment on the Exposure Draft, paragraph 39 has been added to this Statement to clarify that information that becomes available after the balance sheet date but before the financial statements are issued shall be taken into account in evaluating conditions that existed at the balance sheet date, for example, in assessing unproved properties and in determining whether a well has found proved reserves. The Board believes that this position is consistent with the concepts in *FASB Statement No. 5,* "Accounting for Contingencies."

Mineral Property Conveyances and Related Transactions

218. Mineral property conveyances and related transactions may be classified according to their nature as a sale, a borrowing, an exchange of nonmonetary assets, a pooling of assets in a joint undertaking, or some combination thereof. In the Board's

judgment, the accounting principles set forth in the authoritative accounting literature and otherwise generally accepted in current practice for similar transactions in other industries should apply to the oil and gas industry. Paragraphs 43 and 47 apply accepted accounting practices to some of the more common types of conveyances.

219. The transactions described in paragraph 43(a) are classified as borrowings because the funds advanced are repayable in cash or its equivalent. Although the purpose of advancing funds for exploration is to obtain future supplies, successful exploration is not assured, and to the extent production is inadequate to satisfy the obligation, the balance is payable in cash. Accordingly, the transaction is in substance a borrowing.

220. A production payment repayable in cash out of the proceeds from a specified share of production until the amount advanced has been recovered with interest (paragraph 43(b)), is in substance a borrowing. Some hold the view that the recipient of the advance has no liability except to the extent that oil or gas is produced and that, accordingly, the recipient should account for the advance as deferred revenue. The Board did not find that reasoning persuasive. Normally, the advances are made by banks (often through an intermediary) or by other lenders under conditions that leave little doubt that the proved reserves are more than adequate to recover the funds advanced plus interest. The intent of the transaction is to obtain funds and not to sell oil or gas for future delivery. The recipient of the advance is at risk for any change in the price of oil or gas and for the cost of operating the property. The transaction is in substance a loan secured by reserves and is without recourse to other assets of the party receiving the advance. The reserves and production involved are reported by the recipient, not by the lender.

221. The Exposure Draft had proposed that neither gain nor loss be recognized at the time of conveyance if a part of an interest owned is sold and either (a) substantial uncertainty exists about recovery of the costs applicable to the retained interest or (b) the seller has a substantial obligation for future performance. While agreeing that because of those uncertainties recognition of a *gain* is not appropriate in those situations, some respondents to the Exposure Draft said that recognition of a *loss* should not be prohibited. The Board agrees, and paragraph 45 of this Statement prohibits only the recognition of a gain in those situations. In addition, the phrase "substantial obligation for future performance" in paragraph 45(b) has been expanded to include examples, as suggested by some respondents to the Exposure Draft.

222. A production payment to be satisfied by

delivery of a specified quantity of oil or gas out of a specified share of production (paragraph 47(a)) is a sale for which income is not recognized because the earning process is not complete. The seller still has to perform the production and delivery function. Unlike the production payment payable in cash, the amount payable is not fixed, there is no specified or determinable rate of interest, and the risks of price changes rest with the purchaser rather than the seller. The purchaser, not the seller, reports the reserves and production because the substance of the transaction is the purchase of a mineral interest rather than the lending of cash.

223. In some transactions, the owner of an operating interest in an unproved property arranges for another party to assume some or all of the exploration, drilling, development, and operating obligations in return for a share of the rewards if those efforts are successful. This Statement addresses three types of such arrangements: (a) assignment of the operating interest with retention of a nonoperating interest in return for which the assignee assumes the drilling, development, and operating obligations (paragraph 47(b)); (b) assignment of a part of an operating interest in return for assumption by the assignee of the obligation to drill one or more exploratory wells at assignee's cost, after which the property is to be jointly owned and operated if the drilling is successful (paragraph 47(c)); and (c) a carried interest arrangement by which the assignee assumes all the exploration drilling and development risk in return for a fractional operating interest but recovers the cost incurred, if the venture is successful, before the assignor shares in the production from the property (paragraph 47(d)).

224. While the three types of conveyances described in the preceding paragraph have different features, in each instance one party has provided the property and the other party has agreed to incur certain high risk costs, and the benefits, if any, are to be shared in agreed proportions. The Board concluded that all those transactions represent a pooling of assets in a joint undertaking. The investment of each party in the joint operations consists of the carrying amount of the assets contributed by it. Each party will share in the resulting benefits, if any, according to the terms of the agreement. The cost of those benefits to the recipient is the amount of its investment. At the time of the transaction the earning process is incomplete and no gain or loss has been realized by either party. Each party records only its own costs and revenues and does not make a reassignment of costs to reflect the interest that it obtains, or may obtain, in assets contributed by the other party. Each party looks upon its earning assets as those contributed by it.

225. Some support the view that when part of an

interest in an unproved property is relinquished to obtain another type of interest in the same property or an interest in wells and equipment, both parties to the transaction should reassign the cost each has incurred so that their accounts will reflect some cost for each type of asset. The Board rejected that view because there is no true exchange of assets in this type of transaction. As stated above each party's earning assets are those contributed by it, and the carrying amounts of those assets should be retained at their historical cost.

226. In applying the above conclusions to carried interests, the Board recognizes that before payout a carried party will reflect no income and that at payout the carried party will own an interest in wells and related equipment and facilities, but its accounts will reflect only the original investment in the property. The Board believes, however, that the pooling concept best reflects the substance of the agreement between the parties. At the time expenditures are made it is not known whether payout will occur, and many carried interests, even in properties where production is obtained, do not pay out. The Board's conclusions in respect to accounting for this type of transaction are that a carried party has no revenue until payout and no cost of assets beyond the original leasehold cost; a carrying party's accounts reflect the investment, operating costs, and revenue that are at its risk or for its benefit; and the disclosures of reserves and production should be consonant with that basis of accounting.

227. Because an exchange of fractional operating interests in undeveloped mineral properties upon formation of a joint venture (paragraph 47(e)) is a nonmonetary exchange of similar productive assets, accounting as prescribed in *APB Opinion No. 29,* "Accounting for Nonmonetary Transactions," paragraph 21(b) is appropriate. In response to requests for clarification of gain or loss recognition in disproportional cost sharing arrangements paragraph 47(e) was expanded to provide that each party to a joint venture shall record its cost and that gain shall not be recognized if an interest in a property or other assets is acquired without cost or at a cost disproportionate to the interest acquired. This accounting is compatible with that prescribed for a free well or a carried interest.

228. The Board considered the transactions carried out to effect the unitization of oil and gas properties (paragraph 47(f)) to be a pooling of assets for which the earning process is incomplete. Unitizations result in a group of separate properties being combined and operated as a single property. Each participant normally has essentially the same quantity of oil and gas reserves immediately following the unitization as before. A payment of money to equalize the contributions of wells, equipment, and facilities

does not in the Board's judgment change the substance of the transaction.

229. Paragraph 47(g) has been added to this Statement to clarify the appropriate accounting for the sale of an entire interest in an unproved property. Recognition of gain or loss on the sale of a property whose impairment has been assessed individually is consistent with accounting for the sales of assets generally. Nonrecognition of gain or loss on the sale of a property whose impairment has been assessed by amortizing its cost as part of a group is compatible with the normal accounting for a partial retirement of assets subject to group depreciation; paragraph 47(g) also provides for recognizing gain when the sales price exceeds the original cost of the property sold, a circumstance that does not normally arise in the usual group depreciation situation for other types of assets.

230. The sale of a part of an interest in an unproved property for cash (paragraph 47(h)) is viewed by some as the sale of an asset that results in a gain or loss. The Board does not agree with that view. The objective of the parties in this type of transaction is generally to diversify risks and jointly participate in any future costs and benefits. Since this Statement requires continuing evaluation of unproved properties for impairment, no loss need be recognized as stemming directly from the sale of a fractional interest. The Board concluded that because of the uncertainty of the recovery of costs applicable to the interest retained in an unproved property, the transaction should be accounted for as a recovery of cost and that a gain should be recognized only to the extent that proceeds from the fractional interest sold exceed the carrying amount of the property. The proposal in the Exposure Draft has been revised to clarify the question of gain recognition if the unproved property in which part or all of an interest is sold is part of a group for which an impairment allowance is provided in the aggregate.

231. The risk of nonrecovery of the remaining cost is usually not significant if proved properties or parts of interests in proved properties are sold (paragraph 47(i)-(m)). Accordingly, the Board concluded that gain or loss should normally be recognized in those transactions consistent with other sales of capital assets.

232. Paragraphs 47(l) and 47(m) have been added to clarify that accounting for the sale of a property with retention of a production payment shall be compatible with the accounting for the sale of production payments with retention of the operating interest. A retained production payment expressed in money may sometimes be so large that it is highly improbable that the production payment will be satisfied before the reserves are fully depleted. In

those situations, therefore, paragraph 47(l) provides that the retained production payment shall be treated as an overriding royalty interest rather than as a receivable or payable.

Disclosure

233. In establishing the disclosure standards in paragraphs 48-59 of this Statement, the Board relied on the following general guidelines:

a. The disclosures in financial statements do not and cannot include all information that may be needed for investment, credit, regulatory, or national economic planning and energy policy decisions, although the accounting standards established by this Statement should contribute importantly to the reliability and uniformity of financial data used in those types of decisions. Financial statements are intended to present fairly an enterprise's financial position, results of operations, and changes in financial position in conformity with generally accepted accounting principles. Thus, financial statement disclosures are those disclosures that are considered necessary for such a fair presentation. Criteria such as relevance, reliability, verifiability, freedom from bias, and comparability provide guidance in considering which disclosures are necessary for fair financial statement presentation.

b. Oil and gas producing companies currently disclose a considerable amount of information about their oil and gas producing activities in annual reports to shareholders, in published statistical summaries, in filings with the SEC, Department of Energy, and other regulatory agencies, and in other publicly available documents. Most of that information is currently presented outside the scope of the companies' financial statements. This Statement will result in some of that information being included in financial statements and, for many companies, will result in changes in the bases of preparing the information.

c. The disclosures required by this Statement relate only to those activities (acquisition, exploration, development, and production) for which this Statement establishes accounting standards; therefore, this Statement does not prescribe disclosures related to transporting, refining, and marketing of oil and gas or other activities of an oil and gas producing company.

d. As a general proposition, disclosures required for companies engaged in oil and gas producing activities should be similar to those required for companies in other industries.

e. As elaborated on in paragraphs 149-152, financial statements by themselves do not adequately portray the success of a company in finding and developing oil and gas reserves under either of the two historical cost methods of accounting for oil and gas producing activities—full costing or successful efforts costing. Under both methods, earnings are recognized at the time of sale, not at the time of discovery or production. Therefore, an important objective of the disclosures included in financial statements prepared by either of those historical cost methods should be to help the user of those statements relate a company's *efforts* (in terms of costs incurred in searching for and developing oil and gas reserves) and *accomplishments* (in terms of reserves discovered and developed).

f. The disclosure requirements must be consistent with and derived from the accounting standards established by this Statement. That is, a principal purpose of the disclosures should be to aid in understanding of the information *shown* in the financial statements of an oil and gas producing company. The disclosures should not be designed to present information that *might have been shown* in the financial statements had different accounting standards been established by this Statement.

Disclosures in Interim Financial Statements

234. This Statement does not require that the disclosures of reserve quantities and of acquisition, exploration, development, and production costs be included in interim financial statements, though they are required in annual financial statements. The Board reached that conclusion principally because problems in gathering data of that type on a timely basis become especially acute at interim reporting dates and, for some companies, the costs of that effort may be unduly burdensome. The Board presently has on its agenda a project on interim financial reporting in which the nature and extent of disclosures in interim financial statements are issues.

Disclosure of Information about Reserves

235. Most of the respondents to the Discussion Memorandum and most of the interviewees in the research effort described in paragraph 90(a) of Appendix A said that information about quantities of oil and gas reserves is essential to understand and interpret the financial statements of an oil and gas producing company. Many felt that reserve information is the single most important type of disclosure that could be required of an oil and gas producing company. They said that discovery of reserves is the critical event in the oil and gas production cycle and that reserves and changes in reserves are key indicators of the success of a company. In general, the Board agrees with those views. None of the methods of accounting considered by the Board in this project, not even discovery value

or current value accounting, would, in the Board's judgment, result in financial statements that would not need to be accompanied by disclosures of reserves and reserve changes. This Statement requires disclosure of information with respect to a company's oil and gas reserves.

236. The Board does not agree with the view, expressed by some, that mineral reserve information is not accounting information and, if disclosed at all, should not be included in financial statements. Those who take that position argue that while reserve information may indeed be important, it is too subjective, too frequently revised, too unreliable, too "soft" to be reported in financial statements. In the Board's judgment, however, certain reserve information has the qualities of verifiability, reliability, freedom from bias, comparability, and the like to a sufficiently reasonable degree to warrant its inclusion in financial statements. Accordingly, the Board concluded that reserve information is so helpful and essential to an understanding of the financial position, results of operations, and changes in financial position of an oil and gas producing company that the added relevance of the financial statements from including the information more than compensates for the lack of precision of estimates of reserves.

237. The Board considered the following broad areas of disclosure of information regarding oil and gas reserves:

a. Disclosure of reserve quantities:
  i. Estimated reserve quantities, by categories and types of reserves.
  ii. Changes in estimated reserve quantities, by categories and types of reserves.
  iii. Other disclosures relating to estimated reserve quantities, such as geographic locations, ownership characteristics, quality of reserves, and unusual risks and uncertainties.
b. Disclosure of reserve values:
  i. Estimated value of reserves.
  ii. Changes in estimated reserve values.
c. Description of assumptions and difficulties in estimating quantities or values of oil and gas reserves.

Disclosure of Reserve Quantities

238. This Statement relies on estimates of proved reserves and proved developed reserves for a number of capitalization and amortization determinations, and for the reasons discussed in paragraphs 235 and 236 disclosure of quantities of those categories of reserves, and of changes in those quantities, is required. In the Board's judgment, the constraints imposed on the estimator by the definitions of proved reserves and proved developed reserves in

paragraph 271 of Appendix C will keep the subjectivity of the estimates to an acceptably low level for financial reporting purposes.

239. Reserve increases that result from successful exploration and development efforts and from purchases of minerals-in-place, net of decreases from production and sales of minerals-in-place, represent the *physical* expansion or contraction of the quantity of the company's reserves from the beginning to the end of the period. Revisions of previous estimates, on the other hand, represent a change to the quantity that was *perceived* to have existed at the beginning of the period. The categories of changes in reserve quantities required to be separately reported by paragraph 51 are intended to reflect those differences. Some respondents to the Exposure Draft disagreed with the inclusion of changes in reserves resulting from application of improved recovery techniques among other additions; they pointed out that such changes are normally classified by industry practice as revisions of previous estimates. This Statement reflects a change from the Exposure Draft in response to the foregoing concerns. Paragraph 51 provides for separate disclosure of changes resulting from improved recovery techniques if significant and for inclusion of those changes as revisions of previous estimates if not significant. Also, in response to comments on the Exposure Draft, paragraph 50 provides for exclusion of reserves relating to royalty interests owned if the reserve information is not available to the royalty owner. Also, paragraph 54(c) reflects a modification of the Exposure Draft to provide for separate disclosure of the investor's share of oil and gas reserves owned by an investee accounted for by the equity method.

240. Because enterprises' interests in foreign oil and gas reserves are affected by political, economic, and environmental risks and considerations that are often significantly different from the risks associated with domestic reserves, this Statement requires that reserve quantities and changes in them be reported separately for each geographic area in which significant reserves are located. That requirement comports with the conclusions of the Board in *FASB Statement No. 14*, "Financial Reporting for Segments of a Business Enterprise," which requires that the financial statements of a company that operates in different geographic areas report certain key information by geographic area.

241. Some persons propose that disclosure be required of estimated future development costs relating to proved undeveloped reserves. In the Board's view, disclosure of cost projections of that nature and tentativeness should not be required in financial statements of oil and gas producing companies. The question is not unique to the oil and gas

industry—indeed, the whole area of disclosure of forecasts is unsettled. To provide some indication of the extent to which development of proved reserves has been accomplished, paragraph 50 requires the separate reporting of year-end quantities of proved developed reserves. Further, the Board believes that estimates of reserves that are not classified as proved but that are regarded as probable reserves or possible reserves are too subjective to be required for inclusion in financial statements. Some persons have suggested that disclosure of those quantities be required.

242. Some foreign governments have nationalized or otherwise taken over, in whole or in part, certain properties in which oil and gas producing companies previously had mineral interests. Some of those interests have been converted into long-term supply, purchase, or similar agreements with the foreign government or a government authority. In some countries, oil and gas producing companies can obtain access to oil and gas reserves only through such agreements, and not through direct acquisition of a traditional type of mineral interest in a property. If an oil and gas producing company participates in the operation of a property subject to such an agreement or otherwise serves as "producer" of the reserves from the property, it is the Board's judgment that the reserve quantities identified with, and quantities of oil or gas received under, agreements with foreign governments or authorities should be disclosed in the company's financial statements. In view of the different nature of those agreements, however, paragraph 53 requires that those reserve quantities be separately reported from the company's regular proved reserves. The fact that the reserves are available to the company under agreements that differ from domestic agreements does not justify excluding those reserves from the accounting and disclosure provisions of this Statement as long as the foreign agreements, in substance, represent the right to *extract* oil and gas.

243. Although the Exposure Draft had proposed to include in an investor's reserve quantities, for purposes of the disclosures required by paragraphs 50-56 of this Statement, the investor's share of reserves owned by an investee accounted for by the equity method, some respondents to the Exposure Draft pointed out that the investor's financial statements do not include the investee's individual assets, liabilities, revenues, or expenses. They questioned therefore the propriety of including the investee's reserves in the investor's. The Board is persuaded that the better approach is not to commingle the investee's and investor's reserves in the investor's disclosures but, rather, to require separate disclosure of the investee's reserves at year-end. Paragraph 54(c) reflects the revised requirement.

244. Some persons believe that information about ownership characteristics (for example, whether reserves are owned in fee, by domestic lease agreement, or by concession from a foreign government) and about quality of reserves (for example, sulphur or paraffin content or specific gravity) should accompany disclosure of reserve quantities. Because of differences from property to property in those types of characteristics, for many companies the disclosures either would be so broad and general that they would be of little or no value to financial statement users or they would be so detailed and voluminous that they could overwhelm or confuse financial statement users rather than inform them. Consequently, the Board believes that explanations of that type should not be required in general purpose financial statements. For similar reasons, this Statement does not require a description of the assumptions used and difficulties involved in estimating quantities of oil and gas reserves.

Disclosure of Reserve Values

245. The fact that the Board rejected both discovery value and current value as bases of accounting for oil and gas reserves did not, of itself, mean that the Board automatically had rejected estimated reserve values as additional financial statement disclosures. The Board viewed the use of estimated reserve values as the basis of accounting for oil and gas producing companies and the disclosure of estimated reserve values as part of the financial statements of those companies as separable decisions, although, of course, many common considerations are involved.

246. The measurement problems discussed in paragraph 133 were important reasons for not requiring disclosure of estimated reserve values, as they were for not accepting discovery value or current value accounting. They were not, however, the only reasons.

247. As noted in paragraphs 138 and 140, various bases of accounting measurement, including both historical cost and current value measurements, are under consideration as part of the Board's conceptual framework project. The Discussion Memorandum on "Financial Accounting and Reporting in the Extractive Industries" did raise issues relating to methods of valuing mineral reserves. Relatively few respondents supported the use of discovery value or current value accounting or the disclosure of estimated reserve values, and the Board received only limited response to the valuation issues. The Board has decided not to resolve those issues for the limited purpose of this Statement.

248. The SEC's consideration of whether replacement cost disclosures or other reserve value disclo-

Opinion No. 11. Although the recognition of interaction is consistent, in some respects, to the "partial allocation" theory discussed in paragraphs 26-28 of that Opinion, the APB rejected the partial allocation theory in favor of comprehensive income tax allocation by the deferred method (paragraphs 29-32 of that Opinion).

264. The concept of interaction is, essentially, a "cover" concept: Deferred income taxes that otherwise relate to *current* period pretax accounting income need not be recognized to the extent of offsetting possible *future* income tax benefits from excess statutory depletion. The Board has expressly rejected the "cover" concept in reaching certain decisions in this Statement (see paragraphs 175 and 176) and in *FASB Statement No. 8,* "Accounting for the Translation of Foreign Currency Transactions and Foreign Currency Financial Statements" (see paragraphs 174-180 of that Statement).

Effective Date and Transition

265. This Statement was made effective for fiscal years beginning after December 15, 1978 to allow an oil and gas producing company sufficient time to gather the necessary data, modify its accounting systems, and otherwise prepare for transition to the accounting standards established by this Statement. The Exposure Draft had proposed a June 15, 1978 effective date; the change to December 15, 1978 is intended to give all companies at least one year to prepare for the change and to explain any impact it may have to investors and creditors. Voluntary adoption of the provisions of this Statement prior to its effective date is not prohibited by this Statement.

266. For several reasons, the Board has concluded that the provisions of this Statement should be applied retroactively by restating the financial statements of prior periods. First, unlike FASB pronouncements that deal with a comparatively narrow accounting question, the standards established by this Statement prescribe the fundamental basis by which the financial statements of an oil and gas producing company shall be prepared. Moreover, because many variations of successful efforts accounting have heretofore been applied in practice, this Statement is likely to have an impact on the financial statements of a great many oil and gas producing companies, not just those companies presently using the full cost method. In the Board's judgment, because of the magnitude and pervasiveness of the impact of this Statement, restatement will result in the most meaningful and comparable financial statements of all oil and gas producing companies.

267. Further, in paragraph 27 of *APB Opinion No. 20,* the Accounting Principles Board cited a change to or from the full cost method of accounting in the extractive industries as one of three special types of changes in accounting principle that should be reported by applying retroactively the new method in restatements of prior periods.

268. The Board recognizes that some companies may encounter some difficulties in accumulating the necessary data or in making after-the-fact estimates or judgments to apply the provisions of this Statement retroactively. The Board believes, however, that the added interperiod and intercompany comparability thus obtained outweighs any cost-saving advantages of prospective application or the cumulative effect method. Further, because of (a) the diversity of cost capitalization and amortization practices heretofore followed by both full cost and successful efforts companies and (b) the fact that amortization of some previously capitalized costs could continue for ten, twenty, thirty, forty, or more years, the Board concluded that prospective application of the standards established by this Statement is inappropriate.

269. With regard to some of the restatement problems cited by some respondents to the Exposure Draft, paragraph 64 points out that a provision of this Statement that would not have a significant effect on prior years' financial statements need not be retroactively applied. Also, in response to questions raised in letters of comment on the Exposure Draft, paragraph 64 allows the use of "hindsight" information in making the retroactive restatements except that reserve estimates should not now be revised in retrospect.

Appendix C

GLOSSARY

270. This glossary defines certain terms as they are used in this Statement.

271. The definitions of categories of *reserves* used in this Statement are those set forth in the regulations of the Securities and Exchange Commission:[11]

> *Proved reserves.* Those quantities of crude oil, natural gas, and natural gas liquids which, upon analysis of geologic and engineering data, appear with reasonable certainty to be recoverable in the future from known oil and gas reservoirs under existing economic and operating conditions. Proved reserves are limited to those

---

[11] Adopted May 12, 1976, in Securities Act Release No. 5706, which deals with disclosure of estimates of oil and gas reserves in registration statements, proxy statements, and reports filed with the Commission.

quantities of oil and gas which can be expected, with little doubt, to be recoverable commercially at current prices[12] and costs, under existing regulatory practices and with existing conventional equipment and operating methods. Depending upon their status of development, such proved reserves are subdivided into "proved developed reserves" and "proved undeveloped reserves."

Proved developed reserves. Reserves which can be expected to be recovered through existing wells with existing equipment and operating methods. Proved developed reserves include both (a) proved developed *producing* reserves (those that are expected to be produced from existing completion intervals now open for production in existing wells) and (b) proved developed *nonproducing* reserves (those that exist behind the casing of existing wells, or at minor depths below the present bottom of such wells, which are expected to be produced through these wells in the predictable future, where the cost of making such oil and gas available for production should be relatively small compared to the cost of a new well). Additional oil and gas expected to be obtained through the application of fluid injection or other improved recovery techniques for supplementing the natural forces and mechanisms of primary recovery should be included as "proved developed reserves" only after testing by a pilot project or after the operation of an installed program has confirmed through production response that increased recovery will be achieved.

Proved undeveloped reserves. Reserves which are expected to be recovered from new wells on undrilled acreage, or from existing wells where a relatively major expenditure is required for recompletion. Reserves on undrilled acreage shall be limited to those drilling units offsetting productive units, which are reasonably certain of production when drilled. Proved reserves for other undrilled units can be claimed only where it can be demonstrated with certainty that there is continuity of production from the existing productive formation. Under no circumstances should estimates for proved undeveloped reserves be attributable to any acreage for which an application of fluid injection or other improved recovery technique is contemplated, unless such techniques have been proved effective by actual tests in the area and in the same reservoir.

272. The following is the definition of a *field* used in this Statement:

Field. An area consisting of a single reservoir or multiple reservoirs all grouped on or related to the same individual geological structural feature and/or stratigraphic condition. There may be two or more reservoirs in a field which are separated vertically by intervening impervious strata, or laterally by local geologic barriers, or by both. Reservoirs that are associated by being in overlapping or adjacent fields may be treated as a single or common operational field. The geological terms "structural feature" and "stratigraphic condition" are intended to identify localized geological features as opposed to the broader terms of basins, trends, provinces, plays, areas-of-interest, etc.

273. The foregoing definition of a field relies, in turn, on the definition of a reservoir. The following definition shall be used for purposes of this Statement:

Reservoir. A porous and permeable underground formation containing a natural accumulation of producible oil or gas that is confined by impermeable rock or water barriers and is individual and separate from other reservoirs.

274. For purposes of this Statement, the following definitions of wells shall be used:

Exploratory well. An exploratory well is a well that is not a development well, a service well, or a stratigraphic test well as those terms are defined below.

Development well. A development well is a well drilled within the proved area of an oil or gas reservoir to the depth of a stratigraphic horizon known to be productive.

Service well. A service well is a well drilled or completed for the purpose of supporting production in an existing field. Wells in this class are drilled for the following specific purposes: gas injection (natural gas, propane, butane, or flue gas), water injection, steam injection, air injection, salt-water disposal, water supply for injection, observation, or injection for in-situ combustion.

Stratigraphic test well. A stratigraphic test is a

---

[12]The term *current prices* is elaborated on by the SEC in *Securities Act Release No. 5837* as follows: "Current prices include consideration of changes in existing prices provided by contractual arrangements, by law, or by regulatory agencies, where applicable; and for changes in prices for gas to be produced subsequent to termination or expiration of existing contracts, which latter prices should be based on current prices plus escalation for similar production subject to the entity's or other entities' recent contracts." The term "escalation" is further elaborated on in *SEC Release No. 5877* as follows: "The 'escalation' referred to in these releases is limited to specific escalation provisions in recent contracts. Escalations to reflect future price expectations are not permitted."

drilling effort, geologically directed, to obtain information pertaining to a specific geologic condition. Such wells customarily are drilled without the intention of being completed for hydrocarbon production. This classification also includes tests identified as core tests and all types of expendable holes related to hydrocarbon exploration. For purposes of this Statement, stratigraphic test wells (sometimes called "expendable wells") are classified as follows:

1. *Exploratory-type stratigraphic test well.* A stratigraphic test well not drilled in a proved area.

2. *Development-type stratigraphic test well.* A stratigraphic test well drilled in a proved area.

275. The term *proved area* is used in the foregoing definitions of development well, exploratory-type stratigraphic test well and development-type stratigraphic test well. As used therein, a *proved area* is the part of a property to which proved reserves have been specifically attributed.

(This page intentionally left blank.)

Statement of Financial Accounting Standards No. 20
Accounting for Forward Exchange Contracts

an amendment of FASB Statement No. 8

STATUS

Issued: December 1977

Effective Date: January 1, 1978

Affects: Amends FAS 8, paragraphs 27 and 35

Affected by: Superseded by FAS 52

Statement of Financial Accounting Standards No. 21
Suspension of the Reporting of Earnings per Share and Segment Information by Nonpublic Enterprises

an amendment of APB Opinion No. 15 and FASB Statement No. 14

STATUS

Issued: April 1978

Effective Date: April 30, 1978 retroactive to fiscal years beginning after December 15, 1976

Affects: Amends APB 15, paragraph 45
        Amends FAS 14, paragraph 41

Affected by: Footnote 3 amended by FAS 123
           Footnote 4 amended by FAS 95

Other Interpretive Pronouncement: FTB 79-8

Statement of Financial Accounting Standards No. 21
Suspension of the Reporting of Earnings per Share and Segment Information by Nonpublic Enterprises

an amendment of APB Opinion No. 15 and FASB Statement No. 14

CONTENTS

INTRODUCTION AND BACKGROUND INFORMATION

1. The Accounting Standards Division of the AICPA began a study of the application of generally accepted accounting principles (GAAP) to smaller or closely held enterprises in 1974 and issued its report on that study in August 1976. One of the major recommendations in that report states:

> The Financial Accounting Standards Board should develop criteria to distinguish disclosures that should be required by GAAP, which is applicable to the financial statements of all entities, from disclosures that merely provide additional or analytical data. (Some of these latter disclosures may, however, still be required in certain circumstances for certain types of entities.) The criteria should then be used in a formal review of disclosures presently considered to be required by GAAP and should also be considered by the Board in any new pronouncements.

The report also recommends that the FASB amend *APB Opinion No. 15,* "Earnings per Share," to require disclosure of earnings per share information only by enterprises whose securities are publicly traded. In addition to the recommendation contained in the AICPA report, a number of respondents to the FASB agenda project, "Conceptual Framework for Financial Accounting and Reporting: Objectives of Financial Reporting and Elements of Financial Statements of Business Enterprises," have expressed the view that the Board should distinguish between the information that should be included in financial statements and the so-called predictive, interpretive, or "soft" data that should be provided by financial reporting other than financial statements. Further, since the issuance in December 1976 of *FASB Statement No. 14,* "Financial Reporting for Segments of a Business Enterprise," the Board has received a number of suggestions that nonpublic enterprises be exempted from the requirements of that Statement. Others have suggested that segment information is an example of the type of interpretive or analytical information that should be presented outside the financial statements.

2. *APB Opinion No. 15* requires that earnings per share data be presented on the face of an enterprise's income statement and requires certain other disclosures in specified situations. *FASB Statement No. 14* requires disclosure of certain information relating to (a) the operations of an enterprise in different industries, (b) its foreign operations and export sales, and (c) its major customers. In its deliberations leading to the issuance of Statement No. 14, the Board considered whether certain enterprises should be exempted from disclosing segment information based on the size of the enterprise or whether its securities are publicly traded and concluded, for the reasons set forth in paragraph 70 of the Statement, that segment information should be included in the financial statements of all business enterprises.

3. The members of the Financial Accounting Standards Advisory Council and the FASB Screening Committee on Emerging Problems were consulted in January 1978 about the possibility of different applications of generally accepted accounting principles to small or closely held enterprises and large or public enterprises. Many of the members of the Advisory Council and the Screening Committee who advised the Board on this matter indicated that there should be a differentiation between disclosures required of small or closely held enterprises and disclosures required of large publicly traded enterprises and recommended that the Board add a project to its agenda to develop criteria for such a differentiation. Further, many of the members of the Advisory Council and the Screening Committee who advised the Board on this matter cited earnings per share and segment information as examples of disclosures that they believe should be optional for certain enterprises.

4. On February 23, 1978, the Board added to its agenda a major project to consider whether guidelines should be established for (a) distinguishing between information that should be disclosed in financial statements and information that should be disclosed in financial reporting otherwise and (b) distinguishing between information that all enterprises should be required to disclose and information that only designated types of enterprises should be required to disclose. Special attention will be given in that project to the financial statements and financial reporting of small or closely held enterprises.

5. In recognition of (a) the apparent pervasive public concern about the burden on small or closely held enterprises of compliance with certain financial statement disclosure requirements, (b) the recommendations of the AICPA report on "Generally Accepted Accounting Principles for Smaller and/or Closely Held Businesses," and (c) the recommendations of the members of the Board's Screening Committee on Emerging Problems and the Board's Advisory Council, the Board has concluded that application of *APB Opinion No. 15* and *FASB Statement No. 14* to nonpublic enterprises should be suspended, pending completion of the project referred to in paragraph 4. The Board will consider whether the disclosure requirements in pronouncements issued while that project is underway should be applicable to all enterprises.

6. An Exposure Draft of a proposed Statement of Financial Accounting Standards, "Suspension of the Reporting of Earnings per Share and Segment Information by Nonpublic Enterprises," was issued on February 27, 1978. The Board received 126 letters of comment in response to the Exposure Draft, most of which expressed agreement.

7. Some respondents recommended that the Board clarify whether the definition of "nonpublic" applies to a subsidiary, corporate joint venture, or other investee. The Board has a project on its agenda addressing the question of whether a complete set of financial statements of a parent company, a subsidiary, a corporate joint venture, or other investee accounted for by the equity method should include segment information when those financial statements are presented with consolidated financial statements. That project involves a recon-

sideration of the requirements of the last sentence of paragraph 7 of *FASB Statement No. 14*.[1] The Board concluded that it should not delay issuance of this Statement pending completion of its deliberations on that project. This Statement applies to a complete set of separately issued financial statements of a subsidiary, corporate joint venture, or other investee that is nonpublic as that term is used in this Statement. This Statement does not extend to those financial statements when presented in the financial report of another enterprise, as that matter is included in the scope of the project involving reconsideration of the last sentence of paragraph 7 of Statement No. 14 referred to above. An Exposure Draft of a proposed Statement of Financial Accounting Standards addressing that matter will be issued in the near future.

8. Some respondents noted that defining a nonpublic enterprise as an enterprise other than one whose debt or equity securities trade in a public market would exempt other kinds of enterprises with public participation from the requirements of *FASB Statement No. 14*. Those exempted enterprises include certain mutual associations, cooperatives, nonbusiness organizations, and partnerships that often make their financial statements available to a broad class, such as, insurance policyholders, depositors, members, contributors, or partners. The Board concluded that it should not delay the issuance of this Statement to refine the meaning of the term "nonpublic" at this time. Accordingly, the suspensions in paragraph 12 apply for the present to enterprises with a broad class of public participants that meet the "nonpublic" definition in paragraph 13. Those suspensions, however, should not be construed as an indication that the Board has decided that the information requirements for those enterprises are significantly different from those for an enterprise whose debt or equity securities are publicly traded.

9. Some respondents stated that the requirement of paragraph 39 of *FASB Statement No. 14* to disclose information about major customers should not be suspended. Those respondents believe that disclosure is necessary if an enterprise sells much of its output to one or relatively few other enterprises. Although this Statement suspends the application of Statement No. 14 to the financial statements of nonpublic enterprises, the Board notes that it does not

---

[1]The last sentence of paragraph 7 of *FASB Statement No. 14* states:

When a complete set of financial statements that present financial position, results of operations, and changes in financial position in conformity with generally accepted accounting principles is presented for a subsidiary, corporate joint venture, or 50 percent or less owned investee, each such entity is considered to be an enterprise as that term is used in this Statement and thus is subject to its requirements whether those financial statements are issued separately or included in another enterprise's financial report.

affect the disclosure of information about economic dependency when such disclosure may be necessary for a fair presentation.[2]

10. Some respondents stated that the effective date and transition set forth in the Exposure Draft of the proposed Statement were too restrictive. They noted that financial statements issued prior to the effective date of this Statement may be reissued subsequent to its effective date for other than comparative purposes and recommended that disclosure of earnings per share and segment information for fiscal years ended prior to the effective date of this Statement should not be required in financial statements of nonpublic enterprises that are reissued for any reason subsequent to the effective date of this Statement. The Board accepted those views, and the provisions of this Statement are retroactive to fiscal years beginning after December 15, 1976, the effective date of *FASB Statement No. 14*.

11. The Board has concluded that on the basis of existing information it can reach an informed decision without a public hearing and the effective date and transition specified in paragraph 16 are advisable in the circumstances.

STANDARDS OF FINANCIAL ACCOUNTING AND REPORTING

12. This Statement suspends the requirements of *APB Opinion No. 15*[3] and *FASB Statement No. 14* in the financial statements of nonpublic enterprises as defined in paragraph 13. Therefore, this Statement suspends any requirement to disclose the information specified by Opinion No. 15 and Statement No. 14 in a complete set of separately issued financial statements of a subsidiary, corporate joint venture, or other investee that is a nonpublic enterprise.[4]

13. For purposes of this Statement, a nonpublic enterprise is an enterprise other than one (a) whose debt or equity securities trade in a public market on a foreign or domestic stock exchange or in the over-the-counter market (including securities quoted only locally or regionally) or (b) that is required to file financial statements with the Securities and Exchange Commission. An enterprise is no longer considered a nonpublic enterprise when its financial statements are issued in preparation for the sale of any class of securities in a public market.

14. Although the presentation of earnings per share and segment information is not required in the financial statements of nonpublic enterprises, any such information that is presented in the financial statements shall be consistent with the requirements of *APB Opinion No. 15* and *FASB Statement No. 14*.

Amendments to Existing Pronouncements

15. The following footnote is added to the end of the first sentence of paragraph 45 of *APB Opinion No. 15* and to the end of the first sentence of paragraph 41 of *FASB Statement No. 14* (as amended by *FASB Statement No. 18*, "Financial Reporting for Segments of a Business Enterprise—Interim Financial Statements: an amendment of FASB Statement No. 14"):

> The provisions of this [Opinion/Statement] were suspended by *FASB Statement No. 21* and need not be applied by a nonpublic enterprise as defined in that Statement pending further action by the FASB.

Effective Date and Transition

16. This Statement shall be effective April 30, 1978 retroactive to fiscal years beginning after December 15, 1976.

---

[2]Paragraph .05 of section 335, "Related Party Transactions," of *Statements on Auditing Standards* states:

> An entity may be economically dependent on one or more parties with which it transacts a significant volume of business, such as a sole or major customer, supplier, franchisor, franchisee, distributor, general agent, borrower, or lender. Such parties should not be considered related parties solely by virtue of economic dependency unless one of them clearly exercises significant management or ownership influence over the other. Disclosure of economic dependency may, however, be necessary for a fair presentation of financial position, results of operations, or changes in financial position in conformity with generally accepted accounting principles.

[3]This Statement does not suspend or modify other generally accepted accounting principles or practices (such as those specified in paragraph 15 of Chapter 13B, "Compensation Involved in Stock Option and Stock Purchase Plans," of *ARB No. 43* and paragraphs 10 and 11, "Liquidation Preference of Preferred Stock," of *APB Opinion No. 10*) that require disclosure of information concerning the capital structure of an enterprise.

[4]As mentioned in paragraph 7, the Board has a project on its agenda addressing the question of whether a complete set of financial statements of a parent company, a subsidiary, a corporate joint venture, or other investee accounted for by the equity method should include segment information when those financial statements are presented with consolidated financial statements.

> **The provisions of this Statement need
> not be applied to immaterial items.**

This Statement was adopted by the affirmative votes of five members of the Financial Accounting Standards Board. Messrs. Mosso and Walters dissented.

Although Messrs. Mosso and Walters agree with the suspension of the application of *APB Opinion No. 15* and *FASB Statement No. 14* to the financial statements of small, closely held enterprises, they dissent because this amendment suspends the standards for many enterprises that do not meet reasonable tests of "small" or "closely held." Some are large complex enterprises whose financial reports are widely distributed. They may be in direct competition with enterprises whose securities are traded in public markets. The dissenters believe that suspension of Statement No. 14 for some of the large enterprises in an industry but not for others is not sustainable on the basis solely of differences in the form of ownership.

Members of the Financial Accounting Standards Board:

Donald J. Kirk,
    Chairman
Oscar S. Gellein

John W. March
Robert A. Morgan
David Mosso

Robert T. Sprouse
Ralph E. Walters

Statement of Financial Accounting Standards No. 22
Changes in the Provisions of Lease Agreements
Resulting from Refundings of Tax-Exempt Debt

an amendment of FASB Statement No. 13

STATUS

Issued: June 1978

Effective Date: For lease agreement revisions entered into on or after July 1, 1978

Affects: Amends FAS 13, paragraphs 14 and 17(f)

Affected by: Footnote 1 amended by FAS 76 and FAS 125
Paragraph 11 superseded by FAS 71

Other Interpretive Pronouncement: FTB 79-18

Statement of Financial Accounting Standards No. 22
Changes in the Provisions of Lease Agreements
Resulting from Refundings of Tax-Exempt Debt

an amendment of FASB Statement No. 13

CONTENTS

INTRODUCTION AND BACKGROUND INFORMATION

1. The FASB has been asked to reconcile an apparent inconsistency between *FASB Statement No. 13*, "Accounting for Leases," and *APB Opinion No. 26*, "Early Extinguishment of Debt," arising from refundings of tax-exempt debt, including advance refundings[1] that are accounted for as early extinguishments of debt. In some situations tax-exempt debt is issued to finance construction of a facility, such as a plant or hospital, that is transferred to a user of the facility by either lease or sale. A lease or, in the case of sale, a mortgage note generally serves as collateral for the guarantee of payments equivalent to those required to service the tax-exempt debt. Payments required by the terms of the lease or mortgage note are essentially the same, as to both amount and timing, as those required by the tax-exempt debt. In practice, a liability equivalent to the amount of the tax-exempt debt often has been included in the accounts of the lessee or the mortgagor. Some issuers of tax-exempt debt recently have entered into refundings and, concurrently, the terms of the related lease or mortgage note have been changed to conform with the terms of the refunding issue. If a refunding of tax-exempt debt results in a change in the provisions of a lease and the revised lease is classified as a capital lease by a lessee or a direct financing lease by a lessor, gain or loss is not recognized under Statement No. 13 (see paragraphs 14(a) and 17(f)(i) of the Statement). If a refunding of tax-exempt debt results in a change in the terms of a mortgage note, any gain or loss arising from the transaction because of the change in the carrying amount of the debt would be recognized currently in accordance with the provisions of Opinion No. 26.

Lessee Accounting

2. Paragraph 14(a) of *FASB Statement No. 13* sets forth the accounting by a lessee for a change in the provisions, a renewal, or an extension of an existing lease if the revised lease agreement is classified as a capital lease as follows:

> If the provisions of the lease are changed in a way that changes the amount of the remaining minimum lease payments and the change either (i) does not give rise to a new agreement . . . or (ii) does give rise to a new agreement but such agreement is also classified as a capital lease, the present balances of the asset and the obligation shall be adjusted by an amount equal to the difference between the present value of the future minimum lease payments under the revised or new agreement and the present balance of the obligation. The present value of the future minimum lease payments under the revised or new agreement shall be computed using the rate of interest used to record the lease initially.

3. In accounting for an early extinguishment of debt, paragraph 20 of *APB Opinion No. 26* requires that "a difference between the reacquisition price

---

[1] An advance refunding involves the issuance of new debt to replace existing debt with the proceeds from the new debt placed in trust or otherwise restricted to retire the existing debt at a determinable future date or dates. Descriptions of advance refundings that are and are not accounted for as early extinguishments of debt are presented in the AICPA Statement of Position on "Accounting for Advance Refundings of Tax-Exempt Debt."

and the net carrying amount of the extinguished debt should be recognized currently in income of the period of extinguishment as losses or gains. . . ." In this regard, paragraph 8 of *FASB Statement No. 4* , "Reporting Gains and Losses from Extinguishment of Debt," requires that "gains and losses from extinguishment of debt that are included in the determination of net income shall be aggregated and, if material, . . . classified as an extraordinary item, net of related income tax effect."

4. If a refunding of tax-exempt debt results in a change in the provisions of a capital lease that passes the perceived economic advantages of the refunding through to the lessee, paragraph 14(a) of *FASB Statement No. 13* requires the lessee to adjust both the asset and related obligation for any difference caused by a change in the provisions of a lease. If the perceived economic advantages of the same refunding had been passed through by a change in the terms of a mortgage note, the accounting specified by *APB Opinion No. 26* would result in the recognition of a gain or loss.

5. The Board considered the possibility of amending *APB Opinion No. 26* to defer recognition of gain or loss. That would not completely eliminate the inconsistency unless the gain or loss were included as an adjustment to the cost of the related property, because *FASB Statement No. 13* specifies that any difference resulting from a change in the provisions of a capital lease should be accounted for as an adjustment of the leased asset. In the interest of a timely resolution of the conflict, the Board decided that paragraph 14 of Statement No. 13 should be amended so that the accounting will be compatible with that specified by Opinion No. 26.

Lessor Accounting

6. Paragraph 17(f)(i) of *FASB Statement No. 13* specifies the accounting by a lessor for a change in the provisions, a renewal, or an extension of an existing lease if the revised lease agreement is classified as a direct financing lease as follows:

> If the provisions of a lease are changed in a way that changes the amount of the remaining minimum lease payments and the change either (a) does not give rise to a new agreement . . . or (b) does give rise to a new agreement but such agreement is classified as a direct financing lease, the balance of the minimum lease payments receivable and the estimated residual value, if affected, shall be adjusted to reflect the change . . . and the net adjustment shall be charged or credited to unearned income.

7. If a refunding of tax-exempt debt results in a change in the provisions of a lease that passes the perceived economic advantages of the refunding through to the lessee and the revised agreement is classified as a direct financing lease, paragraphs 18 (c) and 17(f)(i) of *FASB Statement No. 13* require the lessor to adjust the balance of the minimum lease payments receivable and unearned income. The lessor, on the other hand, would look to *APB Opinion No. 26* for guidance in accounting for a refunding. That Opinion requires recognition of a gain or loss concurrent with early extinguishments of debt. The Board has concluded that the accounting for changes in the provisions of a lease in connection with a refunding of tax-exempt debt should be compatible with the accounting for the refunding of the debt itself. The Board has, therefore, decided to amend paragraph 17 (f) of Statement No. 13 so that any gain or loss resulting from a change in the provisions of a lease agreement in connection with a refunding of tax-exempt debt is recognized when the tax-exempt debt is considered to have been extinguished.

Other Matters

8. An Exposure Draft of a proposed Statement on "Accounting for Leases: Changes in the Provisions of Lease Agreements Resulting from Refundings of Tax-Exempt Debt" was issued on December 19, 1977. The Board received 26 letters of comment in response to the Exposure Draft, most of which expressed general agreement.

9. Several respondents recommended that the final Statement should apply to all types of refundings and not be limited to refundings involving only tax-exempt debt. The Board noted that, typically, lessors in tax-exempt debt refundings are governmental or quasi-governmental agencies that are not affected by state or federal income tax regulations. For the most part, the governmental lessor's borrowing serves only to obtain necessary financing for the construction of the leased facilities. Refundings that do not involve tax-exempt debt may involve considerations beyond those normally present in the lessor/lessee relationship discussed above. The Board considered these recommendations and concluded that further consideration of the subject of refundings should not delay the issuance of this Statement.

10. The Board has concluded that on the basis of existing information it can reach an informed decision without a public hearing, and the effective date and transition specified in paragraph 16 are advisable in the circumstances.

11. The Addendum to *APB Opinion No. 2*, "Accounting for the 'Investment Credit'," states that "differences may arise in the application of generally accepted accounting principles as between reg-

ulated and nonregulated businesses, because of the effect in regulated businesses of the rate-making process" and discusses the application of generally accepted accounting principles to regulated industries. Accordingly, the provisions of the Addendum shall govern the application of this Statement to those operations of a company that are regulated for rate-making purposes on an individual-company-cost-of-service basis.

STANDARDS OF FINANCIAL ACCOUNTING AND REPORTING

12. If prior to the expiration of the lease term a change in the provisions of a lease results from a refunding by the lessor of tax-exempt debt, including an advance refunding,[2] in which the perceived economic advantages of the refunding are passed through to the lessee and the revised agreement is classified as a capital lease by the lessee or a direct financing lease by the lessor, the change shall be accounted for as follows:

a. Lessee accounting:

   i. If a change in the provisions of a lease results from a refunding by the lessor of tax-exempt debt, including an advance refunding that is accounted for as an early extinguishment of debt, the lessee shall adjust the lease obligation to the present value of the future minimum lease payments under the revised lease using the effective interest rate applicable to the revised agreement and shall recognize any resulting gain or loss currently as a gain or loss on early extinguishment of debt. Any gain or loss so determined shall be classified in accordance with *FASB Statement No. 4.*

   ii. If the provisions of a lease are changed in connection with an advance refunding by the lessor of tax-exempt debt that is not accounted for as an early extinguishment of debt at the date of the advance refunding and the lessee is obligated to reimburse the lessor for any costs related to the debt to be refunded that have been or will be incurred, such as unamortized discount or issue costs or a call premium, the lessee shall accrue those costs by the "interest" method[3] over the period from the date of the advance refunding to the call date of the debt to be refunded.

b. Lessor accounting:[4]

   i. If a change in the provisions of a lease results from a refunding of tax-exempt debt, including an advance refunding that is accounted for as an early extinguishment of debt, the lessor shall adjust the balance of the minimum lease payments receivable and the estimated residual value, if affected (i.e., the gross investment in the lease) in accordance with the requirements of paragraphs 18(c) and 17(f)(i) of *FASB Statement No. 13*. The adjustment of unearned income shall be the amount required to adjust the net investment in the lease to the sum of the present values of the two components of the gross investment based on the interest rate applicable to the revised lease agreement. The combined adjustment resulting from applying the two preceding sentences shall be recognized as a gain or loss in the current period.

   ii. If a change in the provisions of a lease results from an advance refunding that is not accounted for as an early extinguishment of debt at the date of the advance refunding, the lessor shall systematically recognize, as revenue, any reimbursements to be received from the lessee for costs related to the debt to be refunded, such as unamortized discount or issue costs or a call premium, over the period from the date of the advance refunding to the call date of the debt to be refunded.

13. The accounting prescribed in subparagraphs 12(a)(i) and 12(b)(i) for a refunding of tax-exempt debt is illustrated in Appendix A.

Amendments to FASB Statement No. 13

14. The introduction to paragraph 14 of *FASB Statement No. 13* is amended to read as follows:

Except for a change in the provisions of a lease that results from a refunding by the lessor of tax-exempt debt, including an advance refunding, in which the perceived economic advantages of the refunding are passed through to the lessee by a change in the provisions of the lease agreement and the revised agreement is classified as a capital lease (see *FASB Statement No. 22*), a change in the provisions of a lease, a renewal or extension[14] of an existing lease, and a termina-

---

[2]See footnote 1.

[3]See paragraph 12 of *FASB Statement No. 13* and footnote 11 thereto.

[4]This paragraph prescribes the accounting for a direct financing lease by governmental units that classify and account for leases of that kind.

tion of a lease prior to the expiration of the lease term shall be accounted for as follows:

15. The introduction to paragraph 17(f) of *FASB Statement No. 13* is amended to read as follows:

Except for a change in the provisions of a lease that results from a refunding by the lessor of tax-exempt debt, including an advance refunding, in which the perceived economic advantages of the refunding are passed through to the lessee by a change in the provisions of the lease agreement and the revised agreement is classified as a direct financing lease (see *FASB Statement No. 22*), a change in the provisions of a lease, a renewal or extension[19] of an existing lease, and a termination of a lease prior to the expiration of

the lease term shall be accounted for as follows:

Effective Date and Transition

16. This Statement shall be effective for lease agreement revisions entered into on or after July 1, 1978. Earlier application is encouraged. In addition, the provisions of this Statement shall be applied retroactively at the same time and in the same manner as the provisions of *FASB Statement No. 13* are applied retroactively (see paragraphs 49 and 51 of Statement No. 13). Enterprises that have already applied the provisions of Statement No. 13 retroactively and have published annual financial statements based on the retroactively adjusted accounts before the effective date of this Statement may, but are not required to, apply the provisions of this Statement retroactively.

> **The provisions of this Statement need not be applied to immaterial items.**

This Statement was adopted by the affirmative votes of five members of the Financial Accounting Standards Board. Messrs. March and Sprouse dissented.

Mr. March dissents because he believes the Statement will encourage differing treatment of similar transactions based merely on legal form rather than real substance. As stated in paragraph 1 of this Statement, tax-exempt debt refundings arise in situations where the user of a facility acquires that use by either a lease or sale. In either case, the governmental unit or authority often, if not usually, has no real liability to the holder of the debt who must look entirely to the resources of the lessee or mortgagor-purchaser. It is not logical to conclude that *FASB Statement No. 13* is even applicable under these circumstances. The logic of the provisions of paragraphs 7, 9, and 12(a) of this Statement rests on the substance of the lessee's obligations being the equivalent of debt.

The AICPA Statement of Position on "Accounting for Advance Refundings of Tax-Exempt Debt," referred to in footnote 1 of this Statement, requires users of such a facility that are mortgagors to record their obligations for both the refunding issue and the debt to be refunded in the future when the latter issue is not accounted for as an early extinguishment of debt. This Statement fails to state specific acceptance or rejection of the existing practice, referred to in paragraph 1, which recognizes the reality of the transaction by accounting for a lessee's obligations as debt in the same manner as a mortgagor. The

Statement also fails to require presentation of the lessee's obligations under both the original and refunding debt issues still outstanding, in a manner parallel to the mortgagor; by such silence inviting the development of alternative practices.

Mr. Sprouse dissents because he believes that a loss related to an advance refunding is the result of past events (see paragraphs 8 and 9 of *APB Opinion No. 26*) and should be recognized at the time the refunding commitment is made and the loss becomes measurable (see paragraph 8 of *FASB Statement No. 5*). Despite identical changes in the cash flows required by a lease agreement, subparagraph 12(a)(i) of this Statement requires the lessee to immediately recognize a gain or loss while subparagraph 12(a)(ii) requires the lessee to spread the amount of that gain or loss over the period between the advance refunding and call date, depending on the way in which the lessor accounts for the related advance refunding of tax-exempt debt. Subparagraph 12(b)(i) and subparagraph 12(b)(ii) call for counterpart immediate recognition or systematic accrual by the lessor, respectively. Mr. Sprouse believes that a loss related to an advance refunding is not a function of future passage of time and therefore it should be recognized when it becomes known and measurable rather than spread over a future period of time.

Members of the Financial Accounting Standards Board:

Donald J. Kirk,	John W. March	Robert T. Sprouse
Chairman	Robert A. Morgan	Ralph E. Walters
Oscar S. Gellein	David Mosso	

Appendix A

ILLUSTRATION OF LESSOR AND LESSEE ACCOUNTING REQUIRED BY PARAGRAPH 12 OF THIS STATEMENT

17. The following example illustrates the application of the requirements of subparagraphs 12(a)(i) and 12(b)(i) of this Statement when a refunding of tax-exempt debt results in a change in the provisions of a lease agreement and the revised lease is classified as a direct financing lease by the lessor and as a capital lease by the lessee.

Computation Information

The following table summarizes the total debt service requirements of the serial obligation to be refunded and of the refunding obligation. It is presumed that the perceived economic advantages of the refunding results from the lower interest rate applicable to the refunding obligation. The resulting reduction in total debt service requirements will be passed through to the lessee by changing the terms of the related lease to conform with the debt service requirements of the refunding obligation. All costs that have been or that will be incurred by the lessor in connection with the refunding transaction will be passed through to the lessee.

Fifteen Year Serial Debt Service Requirements ($000 omitted):

Obligation to Be Refunded			Refunding Obligation*			
Face Amount	Interest 7%	Total	Face Amount	Interest 5%	Total	Difference
$50,000	$32,300	$82,300	$52,000	$23,150	$75,150	$7,150

LESSOR ACCOUNTING

Computation of Required Adjustments to Reflect Changes in the Terms of a Lease Resulting from a Refunding of Tax-Exempt Debt

Adjustment to Balance of Minimum Lease Payments Receivable:

Present balance of minimum lease payments receivable (equal to debt service requirements of obligation to be refunded)	$82,300,000
Minimum lease payments receivable under revised agreement (equal to debt service requirements of refunding obligation)	75,150,000
Adjustment to reflect reduction in minimum lease payments receivable	$ 7,150,000

Adjustment to Unearned Income:

Change in the sum of the present value of the two components of the gross investment using the interest rate applicable to each agreement	$ 2,000,000
Change in the balance of minimum lease payments receivable	7,150,000
Adjustment to reflect reduction in balance of unearned income	$ 9,150,000

Summary of Adjustments ($000 omitted):

	Minimum Lease Payments Receivable	Unearned Income	Net Investment
Balance before Refunding	$82,300	$32,300	$50,000
Adjustment	(7,150)	(9,150)	2,000
Balance after Refunding	$75,150	$23,150	$52,000

---

*The face amount of the refunding obligation ($52,000,000) is equal to the face amount of the obligation to be refunded ($50,000,000) plus the redemption premium applicable to the obligation to be refunded ($1,500,000) and the costs of issuance ($500,000).

Journal Entries to Record the Refunding and the Changes in the Terms of the Lease Resulting from the Refunding of Tax-Exempt Debt

Recoverable deferred issue costs	500,000	
Loss resulting from refunding of tax-exempt debt	1,500,000	
7% Outstanding obligation	50,000,000	
5% Refunding obligation		52,000,000

To record loss from refunding $50,000,000 — 7% obligation with $52,000,000 — 5% refunding obligation in accordance with the provisions of *APB Opinion No. 26*

Unearned income	9,150,000	
Minimum lease payments receivable		7,150,000
Gain resulting from adjustment of lease terms		1,500,000
Recoverable deferred issue costs		500,000

To adjust unearned income by the amount required to adjust the net investment in the lease to the sum of the present values of the two components of the gross investment based on the interest rate applicable to the revised lease agreement in accordance with *FASB Statement No. 22*.

LESSEE ACCOUNTING

Computation of Required Adjustment to Lease Obligation to Reflect Changes in the Terms of the Lease Resulting from a Refunding of Tax-Exempt Debt

Adjustment to Balance of Lease Obligation:

Present balance of lease obligation under original agreement	$50,000,000
Present value of future minimum lease payments under revised agreement	51,500,000
Adjustment to Lease Obligation	$ 1,500,000

Journal Entry to Record Adjustment to Lease Obligation Resulting from a Refunding of Tax-Exempt Debt

Loss resulting from revision to lease agreement	1,500,000	
Obligation under capital lease		1,500,000

To record the loss resulting from changes in the lease terms resulting from a refunding of tax-exempt debt. For purposes of calculating the present value of the future minimum lease payments, deferred issue costs were considered as additional interest in determining the effective interest rate applicable to the revised agreement. (The loss shall be classified in accordance with *FASB Statement No. 4*.)

FAS23

Statement of Financial Accounting Standards No. 23
Inception of the Lease

an amendment of FASB Statement No. 13

STATUS

Issued: August 1978

Effective Date: For leasing transactions and revisions recorded as of December 1, 1978

Affects: Supersedes FAS 13, paragraph 5(b)
Amends FAS 13, paragraphs 8(b), 10, 17(a), 18(a), 26(a)(i), and 43(c)

Affected by: No other pronouncements

Other Interpretive Pronouncement: FTB 79-18

SUMMARY

Under *FASB Statement No. 13*, "Accounting for Leases," the *inception of the lease* is the date on which the classification of a lease is determined. The lease is recorded at the beginning of the lease term using the classification that was determined at the date of the inception of the lease. If property covered by a lease is yet to be constructed or has not yet been acquired by the lessor at the date of the lease agreement or any earlier commitment, this Statement:

- Changes the "inception of the lease" from the date that construction is completed or the property is acquired by the lessor to the date of the lease agreement or any earlier commitment. This change is intended to result in a lease classification that more closely reflects the substance of the transaction.
- Changes the lessee's determination of "fair value of the leased property" for a lease with a cost-based or similar escalator provision from the amount estimated on the inception date to an amount that is escalated to give effect to increases under the escalator clause, when:

  a. Fair value is used as a limitation on the amount of the asset to be recorded, or
  b. Fair value is used as a basis for allocation of recorded amounts between land and buildings.

This change is intended to base the lessee's accounting on amounts that relate to the finally determined lease payments.

If the redefined "inception of the lease" is a date before the beginning of the lease term, with limited exceptions this Statement prohibits the recording of increases in estimated residual value that may occur between those two dates.

Statement of Financial Accounting Standards No. 23
Inception of the Lease

an amendment of FASB Statement No. 13

CONTENTS

INTRODUCTION AND BACKGROUND INFORMATION

1. The FASB has been asked to reconsider the application of *FASB Statement No. 13*, "Accounting for Leases," for a leasing transaction in which the lessor and lessee agree on lease terms prior to the construction of the asset to be leased. Paragraph 2 describes circumstances in which a literal application of Statement No. 13 can result in a lease classification that does not reflect the economic considerations that entered into the agreement.

2. A lease that is, in effect, a financing transaction might be classified as an operating lease by both parties rather than as a capital lease to the lessee and a direct financing lease to the lessor. That classification would result from application of the 90 percent recovery criterion in *FASB Statement No. 13* at the date of completion of construction instead of the earlier date of the agreement or commitment. If the fair value of the leased asset increases during the construction period, it is possible that the present value of the minimum lease payments at the beginning of the lease term could be more than 90 percent of the estimated fair value of the leased asset at the earlier agreement date but less than 90 percent of the fair value of the leased asset at the later date that construction is completed. On the other hand, if the fair value of the leased asset decreases during the construction period, a lease that would otherwise have been classified as a direct financing lease by the lessor might meet the criteria for classification as a sales-type lease, requiring recognition of a loss even though the terms of the lease were designed to provide full recovery of cost and a reasonable rate of return on net investment to the lessor.

3. In view of the matters discussed above, the Board concluded that it should amend the definition of "inception of the lease" in *FASB Statement No. 13* to make it the date of the lease agreement or any earlier commitment in all cases. Previously, if a lease

were for property to be constructed or to be acquired by the lessor, the "inception of the lease" would have been the date that construction was completed or the property was acquired by the lessor. The purpose of the change is to make the classification of a lease, which is determined at its inception date, better reflect the economic considerations that entered into the agreement. This Statement also amends two paragraphs of Statement No. 13 to provide that, if a lease has a cost-based or similar construction period escalator clause, "fair value at the inception of the lease," for purposes of the lessee's recording of the lease, is escalated to reflect any increases under that clause.

4. An Exposure Draft of a proposed Statement on "Accounting for Leases—Inception of the Lease" was issued on December 19, 1977. The Board received 30 letters of comment in response to the Exposure Draft. Certain of the comments received and the Board's consideration of them are discussed in Appendix A, "Summary of Consideration of Comments on Exposure Draft."

5. The Board concluded that on the basis of existing information it can make an informed decision on the matters addressed by this Statement without a public hearing and that the effective date and transition specified in paragraph 11 are advisable in the circumstances.

STANDARDS OF FINANCIAL ACCOUNTING AND REPORTING

Amendments to FASB Statement No. 13

6. Paragraph 5(b) of *FASB Statement No. 13* is superseded by the following:

> *Inception of the lease.* The date of the lease agreement or commitment, if earlier. For purposes of this definition, a commitment shall be

in writing, signed by the parties in interest to the transaction, and shall specifically set forth the principal provisions of the transaction. If any of the principal provisions are yet to be negotiated, such a preliminary agreement or commitment does not qualify for purposes of this definition.

7. The following footnote is added to the end of the first sentence of paragraph 8(b) of *FASB Statement No. 13*:

If the property covered by the lease is yet to be constructed or has not been acquired by the lessor at the inception of the lease, the classification criterion of paragraph 8(b) shall be applied at the date that construction of the property is completed or the property is acquired by the lessor.

8. The following footnote is added to the end of the second sentence of paragraph 10 of *FASB Statement No. 13* and to the end of the second sentence of paragraph 26(a)(i) of Statement No. 13:

If the lease agreement or commitment, if earlier, includes a provision to escalate minimum lease payments for increases in construction or acquisition cost of the leased property or for increases in some other measure of cost or value, such as general price levels, during the construction or pre-acquisition period, the effect of any increases that have occurred shall be considered in the determination of "fair value of the leased property at the inception of the lease" for purposes of this paragraph.

9. Paragraphs 17(a) and 18(a) of *FASB Statement No. 13* are amended by adding the following final sentence and related footnote to each paragraph:

The estimated residual value used to compute the unguaranteed residual value accruing to the benefit of the lessor shall not exceed the amount estimated at the inception of the lease except as provided in footnote*.

---

*If the lease agreement or commitment, if earlier, includes a provision to escalate minimum lease payments for increases in construction or acquisition cost of the leased property or for increases in some other measure of cost or value, such as general price levels, during the construction or pre-acquisition period, the effect of any increases that have occurred shall be considered in the determination of "the estimated residual value of the leased property at the inception of the lease" for purposes of this paragraph.

10. Paragraph 43(c) of *FASB Statement No. 13* is amended by adding the following final sentence and related footnote:

The estimated residual value shall not exceed the amount estimated at the inception of the lease except as provided in footnote†.

---

†If the lease agreement or commitment, if earlier, includes a provision to escalate minimum lease payments for increases in construction or acquisition cost of the leased property or for increases in some other measure of cost or value, such as general price levels, during the construction or pre-acquisition period, the effect of any increases that have occurred shall be considered in the determination of "the estimated residual value of the leased property at the inception of the lease" for purposes of this paragraph.

Effective Date and Transition

11. The provisions of this amendment to *FASB Statement No. 13* shall be effective for leasing transactions recorded and lease agreement revisions (see paragraph 9 of Statement No. 13) recorded as of December 1, 1978 or thereafter. Earlier application is encouraged. In addition, except as provided in the next sentence, the provisions of this Statement shall be applied retroactively at the same time and in the same manner as the provisions of Statement No. 13 are applied retroactively (see paragraphs 49 and 51 of Statement No. 13). Enterprises that have already applied the provisions of Statement No. 13 retroactively and have published annual financial statements based on the retroactively adjusted accounts before the effective date of this Statement may, but are not required to, apply the provisions of this Statement retroactively.

> **The provisions of this Statement need not be applied to immaterial items.**

This Statement was adopted by the unanimous vote of the seven members of the Financial Accounting Standards Board:

Donald J. Kirk,	John W. March	Robert T. Sprouse
Chairman	Robert A. Morgan	Ralph E. Walters
Oscar S. Gellein	David Mosso	

Appendix A

SUMMARY OF CONSIDERATION OF COMMENTS ON EXPOSURE DRAFT

12. The December 19, 1977 Exposure Draft proposed a complex amendment of the definition of *inception of the lease* in paragraph 5(b) of *FASB Statement No. 13*. The amended definition would have modified various determinations used for both classification of and accounting for a lease. The Exposure Draft also would have, in most cases, limited the amount recorded by the lessor for the residual value of the leased property to an amount not greater than the lessor's estimate as of inception of the lease.

13. Many respondents indicated that the proposed amendment was too complicated and requested clarification or simplification. Some respondents suggested that the Board separate lease classification from lease recording. Based on those comments, the Board made this final Statement a series of individual amendments that, in total, have approximately the same result as the Exposure Draft. The individual amendments are:

a. The definition of *inception of the lease* in paragraph 5(b) of *FASB Statement No. 13* is amended to make it the date of the lease agreement or any earlier commitment. This modification should result in a lessee's classification of a lease that reflects the economic considerations that entered into the agreement.
b. A footnote was added to paragraph 8(b) of Statement No. 13 to permit a lease of property that is to be constructed or acquired by the lessor to be classified as a sales-type lease or direct financing lease (providing it otherwise meets the criteria for those classifications) if there are no important uncertainties about unreimbursable costs yet to be incurred by the lessor at the date that the property is completed or acquired by the lessor, although there may have been such uncertainties at the inception of the lease. This modification and the modification described in paragraph 13(a) above, in combination, should result in a lessor's classification of a lease that reflects the economic considerations that entered into the agreement.
c. Footnotes were added to paragraphs 10 and 26(a)(i) of Statement No. 13 to require a lessee to escalate the "fair value at the inception of the lease," used as a limitation for amounts to be recorded and as a basis for allocation between land and buildings in a real estate lease, for the effects of an escalator provision. The footnotes apply only to leases that include cost-based or similar construction period or pre-acquisition period escalator provisions.
d. Paragraphs 9 and 10 of this Statement modify paragraphs 17(a), 18(a), and 43 of Statement No. 13 to limit the amount recorded by the lessor for the residual value of the leased property to an amount not greater than the estimate as of the inception of the lease. Footnotes were added to provide a limited exception to this requirement in the event that a lease includes a cost-based or similar construction period or pre-acquisition period escalator provision.
e. If a lease calls for adjustment of a lease provision because of specified changes occurring during a construction or pre-acquisition period, a new determination related to that occurrence may be appropriate if Statement No. 13 requires a determination at the inception of the lease for recording purposes. The Exposure Draft specified formula adjustments that would have applied to any lease provisions that call for adjustments. For simplicity, this Statement addresses only the usual cost-based or similar construction or pre-acquisition period escalator provisions (see paragraph 13(c) above). The parties to the lease should make the appropriate adjustments to record a lease if other types of construction period or pre-acquisition period contingency provisions are present. However, no adjustments should be made to reflect the effect of contingency provisions that continue during the lease term.

14. Some respondents questioned the application of the amended definition of inception of the lease to multiple "takedowns" of equipment under a master lease agreement. If a master lease agreement specifies that the lessee must take a minimum number of units or dollar value of equipment and if all other principal provisions are stated, the inception of the lease is the date of the master lease agreement with respect to the specified minimum. The inception of the lease for equipment "takedowns" in excess of the specified minimum is the date that the lessee orders the equipment because the lessee does not agree to lease the equipment until that date. To the extent that lease payments for required "takedowns" are based on value at the date of the "takedown," the lease, in effect, has a pre-acquisition period escalator provision based on value. Paragraphs 8-10 of this Statement address that situation. If a master lease agreement does not require the lessee to "takedown" any minimum quantity or dollar value of equipment, the agreement is merely an offer by the lessor to rent equipment at an agreed price and the inception of the lease is the date that the lessee orders the equipment.

15. Some respondents stated that retroactive application of the proposed Statement would require extensive recomputations to classify and account for

existing leases and questioned whether the cost would be justified. Many respondents, on the other hand, stated that retroactive application of the amended definition in the proposed Statement was necesary to reflect the economic considerations that entered into existing leases. The Board considered the problems of data accumulation and reconsidered whether to require retroactive application or to permit prospective application of this Statement. Paragraphs 115-119 of *FASB Statement No. 13* discuss the considerations that resulted in the requirement for retroactive application of that Statement. The same considerations influenced the Board in its decision to adopt the transition requirements in this Statement. This Statement permits, but does not require, retroactive application for enterprises that have already applied Statement No. 13 retroactively *and* have published *annual* financial statements based on the retroactively adjusted accounts. All other enterprises are required to apply the provisions of this Statement retroactively at the same time as they apply the provisions of Statement No. 13 retroactively. Companies with a large number of leases that are affected may be able to use aggregate computations or statistical sampling techniques to compute the required adjustments.

Statement of Financial Accounting Standards No. 24
Reporting Segment Information in
Financial Statements That Are Presented in
Another Enterprise's Financial Report

an amendment of FASB Statement No. 14

STATUS

Issued: December 1978

Effective Date: January 1, 1979 retroactive to fiscal years beginning after December 15, 1976

Affects: Amends FAS 14, paragraph 7

Affected by: Paragraphs 1 and 5 and footnote 2 amended by FAS 95

SUMMARY

If consolidated or combined financial statements are accompanied by a complete set of separate parent company or investee company (or group of investee companies) financial statements, this Statement eliminates the requirement to disclose segment information in the separate financial statements of:

- The parent company or affiliated companies that have been consolidated or combined in that financial report.
- Certain foreign investee companies.
- Investee companies accounted for by the cost or equity method if that segment information is not significant in relation to the consolidated or combined financial statements.

Statement of Financial Accounting Standards No. 24
Reporting Segment Information in
Financial Statements That Are Presented in
Another Enterprise's Financial Report

an amendment of FASB Statement No. 14

CONTENTS

INTRODUCTION AND BACKGROUND INFORMATION

1. The FASB has been asked whether *FASB Statement No. 14,* "Financial Reporting for Segments of a Business Enterprise," requires segment information[1] to be disclosed in a complete set of parent company financial statements that are presented with the consolidated financial statements of that company. That question was raised apparently because of uncertainty about the intention of the last sentence of paragraph 7 of Statement No. 14, which states:

> When a complete set of financial statements that present financial position, results of operations, and changes in financial position in conformity with generally accepted accounting principles is presented for a subsidiary, corporate joint venture, or 50 percent or less owned investee, each such entity is considered to be an enterprise as that term is used in this Statement and thus is subject to its requirements whether those financial statements are issued separately or included in another enterprise's financial report.

The Board expanded this question and also considered the need for segment information in a complete set of financial statements[2] of a subsidiary, corporate joint venture, or other investee when those financial statements are presented in the parent's or investor's financial report.[3]

2. *FASB Statement No. 21,* "Suspension of the Reporting of Earnings per Share and Segment Information by Nonpublic Enterprises," suspended the requirement to disclose segment information in a complete set of separately issued financial statements of a subsidiary, corporate joint venture, or other investee that is a nonpublic enterprise (as that term is defined in Statement No. 21).

3. An Exposure Draft of a proposed Statement on "Reporting Segment Information in Financial Statements That Are Presented with Another Enterprise's Financial Report" was issued on July 19, 1978. Thirty-five letters of comment were received in response to the Exposure Draft. Virtually all respondents expressed or implied agreement with the proposal to eliminate the requirement to disclose segment information in the financial statements of a parent company or affiliated companies if those financial statements also are consolidated or combined in other financial statements that are presented in the same financial report. Many respondents also recommended that the Board reduce or eliminate the requirement to disclose segment information in the financial statements of other investees that are presented in the same finan-

---

[1] The term "segment information" as used in this Statement, is the information required to be disclosed by *FASB Statement No. 14* concerning:
a. The enterprise's operations in different industries.
b. Its foreign operations and export sales.
c. Its major customers.

[2] The term "complete set of financial statements," as used in this Statement, refers to a set of financial statements (including necessary footnotes) that present financial position, results of operations, and changes in financial position in conformity with generally accepted accounting principles.

[3] The term "financial report" as used in this Statement, includes any compilation of information that includes one or more complete sets of financial statements, such as in an annual report to stockholders or in a filing with the Securities and Exchange Commission.

cial report. The Board considered those recommendations and concluded that the exemption proposed in the Exposure Draft should be expanded in certain respects.

4. The Board has concluded that it can reach an informed decision on the basis of existing information without a public hearing and that the effective date and transition specified in paragraph 6 are advisable in the circumstances.

STANDARDS OF FINANCIAL ACCOUNTING AND REPORTING

Amendment to FASB Statement No. 14

5. The last sentence of paragraph 7 of *FASB Statement No. 14* is deleted and the following sentences and footnotes are added to the end of that paragraph:

If a complete set of financial statements that present financial position, results of operations, and changes in financial position in conformity with generally accepted accounting principles is presented for a parent company, subsidiary, corporate joint venture, or 50 percent or less owned investee, each such entity or a combined group of such entities is considered to be an enterprise as that term is used in this Statement [Statement No. 14] and thus is subject to its requirements if those financial statements are *issued separately.* * However, disclosure of the information that would otherwise be required by this Statement [Statement No. 14] need not be made in a complete set of financial statements that is presented in another enterprise's financial report (i.e., the primary reporting enterprise):

a. If those financial statements are also consolidated or combined in a complete set of financial statements and both sets of financial statements are presented in the same financial report, or
b. If those financial statements are presented for a foreign investee that is not a subsidiary of the primary reporting enterprise† unless that foreign investee's *separately issued* financial state-

ments disclose the information required by this Statement [Statement No. 14], for example, because the investee prepares its *separately issued* financial statements in accordance with United States generally accepted accounting principles, or
c. If those financial statements are presented in the financial report of an enterprise that is not subject to the requirements of *FASB Statement No. 14* because of the suspension provided by *FASB Statement No. 21*.

Unless exempted above, if a complete set of financial statements for an investee (i.e., subsidiary, corporate joint venture, or 50 percent or less owned investee) accounted for by the cost or equity method is presented in another enterprise's financial report, the information required by this Statement [Statement No. 14] shall be presented for the investee if that information is significant in relation to the financial statements of the primary reporting entity in that financial report (e.g., the consolidated or combined financial statements). To determine the information required by this Statement [Statement No. 14] to be disclosed for an investee in such situations, the percentage tests specified in paragraphs 15, 32, and 39 of this Statement [Statement No. 14] shall be applied as specified in those paragraphs in relation to the financial statements of the primary reporting entity without adjustment for the revenues, operating profit or loss, or identifiable assets of the investee.

---

*FASB Statement No. 21 suspends the requirements of this Statement [Statement No. 14] for the *separately issued* financial statements of a nonpublic enterprise as defined by that Statement.

†The term "foreign investee that is not a subsidiary of the primary reporting enterprise," as used in this Statement [Statement No. 14] refers to an enterprise incorporated or otherwise organized and domiciled in a foreign country if fifty percent or more of that enterprise's voting stock is owned by residents of a foreign country.

Effective Date and Transition

6. This Statement shall be effective January 1, 1979 retroactive to fiscal years beginning after December 15, 1976. Earlier application is encouraged.

> The provisions of this Statement need not be applied to immaterial items.

This Statement was adopted by the affirmative votes of five members of the Financial Accounting Standards Board. Messrs. Kirk and Gellein dissented.

Messrs. Kirk and Gellein dissent from the Statement because the exemption in paragraph 5b fails tests of usefulness and evenhandedness. Pursuant to that paragraph, the furnishing of segment information for an enterprise whose financial statements conform with generally accepted accounting principles depends on factors such as the extent to which the enterprise is owned by others, where it is incorporated, where it is domiciled, and where its shareholders reside. Those factors, in the view of Messrs. Kirk and Gellein, are not relevant to the usefulness of financial statements. Further, in their view, it is not evenhanded to single out for exemption a specified class of investees.

Mr. Gellein also disagrees with that aspect of the Statement that applies the tests for segment significance by comparing amounts in the separate financial statements with amounts in the consolidated statements, as reported. He believes it illogical to omit from the denominator of the ratios amounts for the segment being tested. The results may be irrational depending on the mix of industry segments among the enterprises and the extent of interenterprise transfers.

Members of the Financial Accounting Standards Board:

Donald J. Kirk,	John W. March	Robert T. Sprouse
Chairman	Robert A. Morgan	Ralph E. Walters
Oscar S. Gellein	David Mosso	

Statement of Financial Accounting Standards No. 25
Suspension of Certain Accounting Requirements for Oil and Gas Producing Companies

an amendment of FASB Statement No. 19

STATUS

Issued: February 1979

Effective Date: For fiscal years beginning after December 15, 1978

Affects: Amends FAS 19, paragraphs 48 and 63
　　　　Supersedes FAS 19, paragraph 271 and footnotes 11 and 12

Affected by: Paragraphs 6 and 8 superseded by FAS 111

SUMMARY

FASB Statement No. 19, "Financial Accounting and Reporting by Oil and Gas Producing Companies," requires the use of a form of the successful efforts method of accounting and disclosure of reserve quantities, costs incurred, and capitalized costs. The Securities and Exchange Commission (SEC) has incorporated into its rules all the substantive provisions of Statement No. 19 except that the Commission's rules permit, as an acceptable alternative for its reporting purposes, the use of a prescribed form of the full cost method of accounting. In light of this conflict between Statement No. 19 and the SEC's regulations, this Statement:

* Suspends the effective date for applying the requirements of Statement No. 19 related to the successful efforts method of accounting. Oil and gas producing companies not subject to SEC reporting requirements thus are permitted to continue their present methods of accounting.
* Retains, with revision of the effective date, the income tax allocation requirements of Statement No. 19. Those requirements supersede *FASB Statement No. 9,* "Accounting for Income Taxes—Oil and Gas Producing Companies."
* Retains, with revision of the effective date, the requirement of Statement No. 19 to classify production payments payable in cash as debt.
* Retains, with revision of the effective date, the requirements of Statement No. 19 related to disclosure of reserve quantities, costs incurred, and capitalized costs, but permits the required disclosure of reserve quantities to be made outside the financial statements.
* Requires disclosure of the method of accounting for costs incurred in oil and gas producing activities.
* Rescinds the reserve definitions as contained in Statement No. 19 and requires, for financial reporting purposes, the use of the reserve definitions developed by the Department of Energy for its Financial Reporting System and adopted by the SEC for its reporting purposes.

Statement of Financial Accounting Standards No. 25
Suspension of Certain Accounting Requirements for
Oil and Gas Producing Companies

an amendment of FASB Statement No. 19

CONTENTS

INTRODUCTION AND BACKGROUND INFORMATION

1. *FASB Statement No. 19,* "Financial Accounting and Reporting by Oil and Gas Producing Companies," was issued in December 1977. That Statement was to have become effective for financial statements for fiscal years beginning after December 15, 1978 and for interim periods within those years.

2. By its issuance of *Accounting Series Release (ASR) No. 253,* "Adoption of Requirements for Financial Accounting and Reporting Practices for Oil and Gas Producing Activities," on August 31, 1978, the Securities and Exchange Commission (SEC): (a) adopted the form of successful efforts accounting and the disclosures prescribed by *FASB Statement No. 19;* (b) indicated its intention to develop a form of the full cost accounting method as an alternative acceptable for SEC reporting purposes; (c) concluded that both the full cost and successful efforts methods of accounting, based essentially on historical costs, fail to provide sufficient information on the financial position and operating results of oil and gas producing companies and, accordingly, that steps should be taken to develop an accounting method based on a valuation of proved oil and gas reserves; (d) adopted rules that require financial statement disclosure of certain financial and operating data regardless of the method of accounting followed; and (e) adopted definitions of proved reserves different from those in effect at the time Statement No. 19 was issued. On December 19, 1978, the SEC issued *ASR No. 257,* "Requirements for Financial Accounting and

Reporting Practices for Oil and Gas Producing Activities," and *ASR No. 258,* "Oil and Gas Producers—Full Cost Accounting Practices," in which the SEC reaffirmed its conclusions reflected in *ASR No. 253,* adopted definitions of proved reserves developed by the Department of Energy (DOE) for its Financial Reporting System, and prescribed the form of full cost accounting acceptable as an alternative to successful efforts accounting for the SEC's reporting purposes. Those requirements are effective initially for fiscal years ending after December 25, 1978 that are contained in filings that include fiscal years ending after December 25, 1979.

3. After considering the foregoing, the Board has decided to suspend the effective date of *FASB Statement No. 19* for certain provisions related to the basic method of accounting while retaining certain requirements of that Statement related to tax allocation, production payments, and disclosure. Appendix A to this Statement sets forth the basis for the Board's conclusions.

STANDARDS OF FINANCIAL ACCOUNTING AND REPORTING

Amendment of FASB Statement No. 19

4. The effective date for application of paragraphs 11-41, 44-47, and 60 of *FASB Statement No. 19* is suspended insofar as those paragraphs pertain to a *required* form of successful efforts accounting. Those paragraphs are not suspended insofar as they provide definitions of terms in paragraph 11 or pro-

304

vide direction and guidance for financial statement disclosures required by paragraphs 57-59. Statement No. 19, including paragraphs 11-47, continues in effect as a Statement issued by the FASB for the purpose of applying paragraph 16 of *APB Opinion No. 20,* "Accounting Changes."[1]

5. If accounting changes are made to adopt the provisions of paragraphs 11-47 of *FASB Statement No. 19,* they shall be made by retroactive restatement as provided in paragraphs 63 and 64 of that Statement. Enterprises that presently follow a form of the full cost accounting method and that subsequently adopt accounting changes to conform to the form of the full cost accounting method specified by the SEC also shall make those changes retroactively by restating the financial statements of prior periods.

6. The disclosure requirements of *FASB Statement No. 19* are amended to permit the disclosures of reserve quantities to be made as supplementary information accompanying but outside the financial statements. The last sentence of paragraph 48 of Statement No. 19 is revised to read as follows: "Those disclosures shall be made within the body of the financial statements, in the notes thereto, or in a separate schedule that is an integral part of the financial statements, except that the disclosures of reserve quantities required by paragraphs 50-56 may be made as supplementary information accompanying but outside the financial statements." The last sentence of paragraph 63 is revised to read as follows: "The disclosures specified by paragraphs 50-59 shall be made when presenting complete sets of financial statements that have been restated pursuant to the provisions of this paragraph."

7. Paragraph 271 of *FASB Statement No. 19,* in which various categories of *reserves* are defined, is rescinded. For the purpose of applying this Statement and Statement No. 19, the definitions of proved reserves, proved developed reserves, and proved undeveloped reserves shall be the definitions adopted by the SEC for its reporting purposes that are in effect on the date(s) as of which reserve disclosures are to be made.[2] Previously reported quantities shall not be revised retroactively if the SEC definitions are changed.

8. An enterprise engaged in oil and gas producing activities shall disclose in its financial statements the method of accounting for costs incurred in those activities and the manner of disposing of capitalized costs related to those activities.

9. Paragraph 63 of *FASB Statement No. 19* is amended to change the effective date from "fiscal years beginning after December 15, 1978 and for interim periods within those fiscal years" to "fiscal years ending after December 25, 1979, although earlier application is encouraged." The provision of paragraph 4 of this Statement suspending application of a certain form of the successful efforts method of accounting is an indefinite suspension of that method as a mandatory requirement.

Effective Date

10. This Statement shall be effective for fiscal years beginning after December 15, 1978.

The provisions of this Statement need not be applied to immaterial items.

This Statement was adopted by the affirmative votes of four members of the Financial Accounting Standards Board. Messrs. March and Mosso dissented.

Mr. Mosso and Mr. March dissent because they think that this action at least partially abdicates the Board's standard-setting responsibility. By suspending *FASB Statement No. 19,* the Board passes an opportunity to significantly narrow the range of accounting alternatives in the oil and gas industry and steps aside while the federal government attempts to resolve the issues. They think the Board should have retained Statement No. 19 as the duly adopted private-sector accounting standard, with an

exemption for those companies (registered or nonregistered) electing to use the alternative full cost method permitted under SEC-prescribed rules. Although they disagree with the SEC decision that fails to adopt a standard for uniform use, in their view the Board's failure to narrow the numerous alternatives available to nonregistered companies to at least the two methods that registered companies must follow is not in the public interest. The absence of effective FASB-adopted standards may limit the

---

[1]Paragraph 16 of *APB Opinion No. 20* states in part: "The presumption that an entity should not change an accounting principle may be overcome only if the enterprise justifies the use of an alternative acceptable accounting principle on the basis that it is preferable. . . . The issuance of [a Statement of Financial Accounting Standards] that creates a new accounting principle, that expresses a preference for an accounting principle, or that rejects a specific accounting principle is sufficient support for a change in accounting principle. The burden of justifying other changes rests with the entity proposing the change."

[2]The definitions of proved reserves, proved developed reserves, and proved undeveloped reserves adopted by the SEC on December 19, 1978 in *Accounting Series Release No. 257* are presented in Appendix B to this Statement.

Board from any significant role in the maintenance of these standards, including the successful efforts method of Statement No. 19. Mr. March and Mr. Mosso also believe more affirmative action would have placed the Board in a better position to maintain an active presence in this critical area of national concern and to reassert leadership in setting accounting standards for the oil and gas industry.

Mr. March also dissents because he believes the last sentence of paragraph 4, which asserts that *FASB Statement No. 19* continues in effect for the

purpose of controlling accounting changes under *APB Opinion No. 20*, is not warranted in view of the Board's decision to suspend the effectiveness of that Statement. Since the Securities and Exchange Commission decided to permit two alternative accounting methods for companies subject to its jurisdiction and the Board declined to adopt the approach supported by the dissenting members for all companies, the matter of the justification for accounting changes for both registered and nonregistered companies cannot be guided by the Board.

Members of the Financial Accounting Standards Board:

Donald J. Kirk,	Robert A. Morgan	Robert T. Sprouse
Chairman	David Mosso	Ralph E. Walters
John W. March		

Appendix A

BASIS FOR CONCLUSIONS

Scope

11. For many years oil and gas producing companies generally have followed various forms of each of two accounting methods, commonly called successful efforts and full cost. In December 1977 the Board issued *FASB Statement No. 19*, "Financial Accounting and Reporting by Oil and Gas Producing Companies," which specified one form of the successful efforts method to be used by all oil and gas producing companies. That Statement was to have become effective for fiscal years beginning after December 15, 1978. The SEC reviewed the Board's decision and decided that, for the present, oil and gas producing companies subject to its reporting requirements should follow either the successful efforts method as provided by Statement No. 19 or a form of the full cost method specified by the SEC in *ASR No. 258*. Reporting to the SEC based on one of those two methods is effective initially for fiscal years ending after December 25, 1978 that are contained in filings that include fiscal years ending after December 25, 1979 as provided by *ASR No. 257*. This Statement addresses conflicts arising because of the differences between Statement No. 19 and the SEC's regulations.

12. The SEC also has concluded that, because it believes neither the full cost nor the successful efforts method provides sufficient information on the financial position and operating results of oil and gas producing companies, an accounting method based on valuations of proved oil and gas reserves should be developed. The proposed method is referred to by the SEC as Reserve Recognition Accounting (RRA). This Statement does not address RRA.

13. The Board issued an Exposure Draft of an amendment of *FASB Statement No. 19* on November 7, 1978 with a 60-day comment period. Letters of comment were received from 27 respondents.

Alternatives Considered

14. The Board considered the following four approaches for resolving conflicts between *FASB Statement No. 19*'s requirements and the SEC's decision to accept the continued use of alternative accounting methods while it considers the development of RRA:

a. Amend Statement No. 19 to suspend its effective date with respect to either the entire Statement or only portions of it.
b. Amend Statement No. 19 so as to permit all oil and gas producing companies (including those not subject to SEC reporting requirements) an election to follow the full cost method prescribed by the SEC for as long as the SEC permits that method to be an acceptable alternative for its reporting purposes.
c. Rescind Statement No. 19.
d. Take no action and let the American Institute of Certified Public Accountants (AICPA) amend or interpret its standards of reporting on financial statements or its rules of professional conduct to resolve the conflicts created by the different standards established by the FASB and the SEC.

15. For the reasons set forth in this Appendix, the Board decided to suspend the effective date for certain provisions of *FASB Statement No. 19*.

Reasons for Suspending the Effective Date for Certain Paragraphs of FASB Statement No. 19

16. The Board considered, during the deliberations that preceded the issuance of *FASB Statement No.*

19, the issue of whether oil and gas producing companies should be permitted to continue to choose between the full cost method and the successful efforts method. The Board rejected the continued use of alternative accounting methods by oil and gas producing companies for the reasons set forth in paragraphs 128-132 of that Statement. Paragraph 129 states:

> The Board has considered the question of accounting alternatives at length, not only in connection with its oil and gas project but also for other projects on its agenda, and has concluded that differences in accounting may be appropriate when significant differences in facts and circumstances exist, but different accounting among companies for the same types of facts and circumstances impedes comparability of financial statements and significantly detracts from their usefulness to financial statement users.

17. In the Board's view, the reasons cited in those paragraphs for not embracing alternatives continue to be valid. While the Board acknowledges the SEC's statutory authority to differ with the Board on substantive matters, such as in connection with the continued use of alternative methods of accounting for oil and gas producing companies subject to SEC reporting requirements while it considers the development of RRA, the Board sees no basis for reversing its earlier decision reached on the basis of extensive due process procedures.

18. The Board's recognition of the form of the full cost method as adopted by the SEC as an acceptable alternative would provide companies not subject to SEC reporting requirements with the same alternatives granted to companies that are subject to those requirements. Companies not subject to SEC reporting requirements are usually small, and the burden of implementing an accounting change can be particularly heavy for them. The Board was willing to impose that burden when it adopted *FASB Statement No. 19* because of the advantage of comparable reporting by all oil and gas producing companies. Now that two alternative methods are to be permitted for companies subject to SEC reporting requirements and the Commission is considering eventually replacing both of those methods with a completely different method based on RRA, the Board concluded that, at this time, it should not require companies not subject to SEC reporting requirements to adopt either alternative.

19. In addition, the Board's recognition of the form of the full cost method adopted by the SEC as an acceptable alternative would impose on companies not otherwise subject to SEC reporting requirements the regulations, rules, and interpretations of the SEC. The Board believes it is inappropriate for a private sector standard-setting body to impose requirements determined by a governmental agency.

20. Paragraph 4 of this Statement explains that *FASB Statement No. 19,* including paragraphs 11-47, continues in effect as an FASB Statement for the purpose of applying paragraph 16 of *APB Opinion No. 20,* "Accounting Changes." Statement No. 19 "expresses a preference for" the successful efforts method of accounting provided in paragraphs 11-47 and "rejects" other methods of accounting for oil and gas producing activities; accordingly, the Board considers it appropriate to indicate that paragraph 16 of Opinion No. 20 requires that entities proposing to change to an accounting method other than that provided in paragraphs 11-47 of Statement No. 19 bear the burden of justifying that change.

21. The SEC has indicated that, even though its judgment differs from that of the Board in certain respects in this instance, it reaffirms its basic policy of looking to the FASB for the initiative in establishing and improving accounting standards. The SEC has incorporated into its rules the provisions of *FASB Statement No. 19* related to the successful efforts method of accounting, conveyances, income tax allocation, and disclosure. The Board believes that rescinding Statement No. 19 would invalidate its intention to monitor the Statement and provide interpretations of it as they may be needed.

22. The Board considers it essential that it accept responsibility to resolve any problems that arise in implementing its standards. The conflicts between *FASB Statement No. 19* and the SEC's regulations do result in an implementation problem. Therefore, taking no action and letting the AICPA amend or interpret its standards of reporting on financial statements or its rules of professional conduct was not considered to be an acceptable alternative.

23. The Exposure Draft proposed to suspend the applicability of all of the conveyance requirements of paragraphs 42-47 of *FASB Statement No. 19.* It also discussed the possible retention of those conveyance requirements that did not appear to conflict with the form of full cost accounting then proposed by the SEC, but the limited provisions that might have been retained did not appear to have broad applicability, and it was possible that new conflicts could arise if the SEC's final requirements for full cost accounting differed from the proposed requirements. After considering the requirements for full cost accounting adopted by the SEC in *ASR No. 258,* the Board concluded that it should not suspend the applicability of paragraphs 42 and 43 of Statement No. 19, which address accounting for production payments payable in cash and funds advanced for exploration. The Board believes the conclusion

stated in Statement No. 19 that production payments payable in cash and funds advanced for exploration are, in substance, borrowings is consistent with the SEC's final regulations on accounting for those transactions under either the full cost or the successful efforts method of accounting. In other respects, the Board has decided to suspend the applicability of the conveyance requirements in paragraphs 44-47 of Statement No. 19 as proposed in the Exposure Draft because some of those requirements conflict with the full cost method of accounting.

Reasons for Retaining or Revising Certain Provisions of FASB Statement No. 19

24. The SEC has incorporated into its rules the requirements of *FASB Statement No. 19* that pertain to income tax allocation and to disclosures of costs incurred and capitalized costs. The retention of these requirements of Statement No. 19 does not conflict with the SEC's rules.

25. The income tax allocation provisions of *FASB Statement No. 19* superseded *FASB Statement No. 9,* "Accounting for Income Taxes—Oil and Gas Producing Companies," which had permitted different methods of accounting for income tax allocations. The Board believes the income tax allocation provisions of Statement No. 19 to be as appropriate for companies using the full cost method as they are for companies using the successful efforts method.

26. Many observers have advised the Board that information about quantities of oil and gas reserves is essential to understand and interpret the financial statements of oil and gas producing companies and that reserve information is the single most important type of disclosure that could be required. In general, the Board concurs with those views. In the Board's judgment, disclosure of reserve quantities and changes in reserve quantities should be required under any method of accounting.

27. The Board considered suspending the effective date for applicability of the disclosure requirements because they are effectively incremental disclosures only to companies not subject to SEC reporting requirements. However, information about reserves is essential, in the Board's judgment, for assessing the financial position and results of operations of an oil and gas producing company. Some, but not all, users of financial statements of companies not subject to SEC reporting requirements are in a position to obtain reserve information. The Board understood from responses to its Discussion Memorandum, "Financial Accounting and Reporting in the Extractive Industries," and testimony at its public hearing that the principal burden on companies not subject to SEC reporting requirements concerns

accounting requirements rather than disclosure requirements. The suspension provision of paragraph 4 permits companies not subject to SEC reporting requirements to continue their present methods of accounting if they so desire.

28. The Exposure Draft proposed the retention of *FASB Statement No. 19*'s requirement to disclose information about reserve quantities in the financial statements. Some respondents suggested, however, that those disclosures be made outside the financial statements. Their concerns generally related to the cost, time, or difficulty of obtaining an independent verification of reserve quantity information that may be necessary if disclosure were made in the financial statements. Many companies have *staff* engineers who prepare estimates of proved reserves quantities, but questions have been raised as to whether there are enough *independent* professional engineers to verify those estimates on a timely basis or whether generally accepted engineering standards exist whereby an engineer can verify the work of another. The Board considered those comments in light of several recent developments. The issuance of *FASB Statement of Financial Accounting Concepts No. 1,* "Objectives of Financial Reporting by Business Enterprises," indicates that the Board intends to establish standards for reporting information outside financial statements, and the Board has issued a proposed Statement that would require disclosure *outside* financial statements of information about the effects of changing prices. In addition, as part of the Board's conceptual framework project, progress is being made in the development of distinctions between financial reporting and financial statements. The Board also understands that the petroleum engineering profession is initiating studies to develop uniform guidelines for estimating quantities of proved reserves and to develop standards whereby an independent professional engineer can verify the work of another engineer. Finally, the Board understands that the auditing profession is in the process of developing standards that establish an independent accountant's responsibility to review and verify compliance with a required disclosure permitted to be made outside the financial statements. In view of the evolutionary and experimental nature of deciding where information should be disclosed and the degree of independent verification, the Board believes that, for the present, permitting the required disclosure of reserve quantities to be made outside the financial statements will ensure the provision of this essential information without excessive burden.

29. The Board also reviewed the reasons given in Appendix B of *FASB Statement No. 19* for the requirements to disclose costs incurred and capitalized costs and found them equally valid for a full cost company as for a successful efforts company.

30. Because of the SEC action and the suspension of the effective date for the accounting requirements of *FASB Statement No. 19,* there will not be a single, uniform method of accounting used by all oil and gas producing companies. Therefore, the Board concluded that it is desirable to add a requirement to disclose in the financial statements the method of accounting for costs incurred in oil and gas producing activities and the manner of disposition of capitalized costs relating to those activities. Since the provision of this Statement suspending portions of Statement No. 19 allows companies not reporting to the SEC to apply various forms of successful efforts and full cost accounting, reference to those terms alone may not provide an adequate description of the method followed.

31. Paragraph 7 of this Statement rescinds the definitions of proved reserves, proved developed reserves, and proved undeveloped reserves contained in paragraph 271 of *FASB Statement No. 19* and requires the use of definitions adopted by the SEC for its reporting purposes. As stated in Statement No. 19, the Board believes that conformity of the reserve definitions used in filings with the SEC, in information reported to the DOE for its Financial Reporting System, and in financial statements prepared in conformity with generally accepted accounting principles is desirable. On December 19, 1978, the SEC adopted in *ASR No. 257* the definitions developed by the DOE for its Financial Reporting System. For convenience purposes, the definitions adopted by the SEC and DOE are reprinted in Appendix B to this Statement.

32. *ASR No. 257* provides an exemption from its disclosure requirements if a company's oil and gas operations represent 10 percent or less of total revenue, total earnings, and total assets, as defined. The Board considered whether more specific guidance for applying its general materiality provision should be presented in this Statement. The Board concluded that it would be inappropriate to resolve pervasive materiality issues in the context of this project and that more specific guidance should be provided only after having considered those issues on a comprehensive basis. The provisions of this Statement, as with all the Board's standards, need not be applied to immaterial items.

33. Paragraph 9 of this Statement amends paragraph 63 of *FASB Statement No. 19* to change its effective date to "fiscal years ending after December 25, 1979, although earlier application is encouraged." The SEC's accounting requirements are "effective initially for fiscal years ending after December 25, 1978 that are contained in filings that include fiscal years ending after December 25, 1979, although earlier application is encouraged." The Board believes that it would be unreasonable to

impose on companies subject to SEC reporting requirements certain standards related to accounting for oil and gas producing activities, such as Statement No. 19's tax allocation provisions, prior to the time those companies are required to make accounting changes in accordance with the SEC's regulations.

Appendix B

DEFINITIONS OF PROVED RESERVES

34. The following definitions of proved reserves are those developed by the Department of Energy for its Financial Reporting System and adopted by the Securities and Exchange Commission on December 19, 1978 in *ASR No. 257.* Reference should be made to the SEC's reporting requirements for revisions that may have been made since the issuance of *ASR No. 257.*

> *Proved oil and gas reserves.* Proved oil and gas reserves are the estimated quantities of crude oil, natural gas, and natural gas liquids which geological and engineering data demonstrate with reasonable certainty to be recoverable in future years from known reservoirs under existing economic and operating conditions, i.e., prices and costs as of the date the estimate is made. Prices include consideration of changes in existing prices provided only by contractual arrangements, but not on escalations based upon future conditions.
>
> 1. Reservoirs are considered proved if economic producibility is supported by either actual production or conclusive formation test. The area of a reservoir considered proved includes (a) that portion delineated by drilling and defined by gas-oil and/or oil-water contacts, if any, and (b) the immediately adjoining portions not yet drilled, but which can be reasonably judged as economically productive on the basis of available geological and engineering data. In the absence of information on fluid contacts, the lowest known structural occurrence of hydrocarbons controls the lower proved limit of the reservoir.
> 2. Reserves which can be produced economically through application of improved recovery techniques (such as fluid injection) are included in the "proved" classification when successful testing by a pilot project, or the operation of an installed program in the reservoir, provides support for the engineering analysis on which the project or program was based.
> 3. Estimates of proved reserves do not include the following: (a) oil that may become avail-

able from known reservoirs but is classified separately as "indicated additional reserves"; (b) crude oil, natural gas, and natural gas liquids, the recovery of which is subject to reasonable doubt because of uncertainty as to geology, reservoir characteristics, or economic factors; (c) crude oil, natural gas, and natural gas liquids, that may occur in undrilled prospects; and (d) crude oil, natural gas, and natural gas liquids, that may be recovered from oil shales, coal, gilsonite and other such sources.

Proved developed oil and gas reserves. Proved developed oil and gas reserves are reserves that can be expected to be recovered through existing wells with existing equipment and operating methods. Additional oil and gas expected to be obtained through the application of fluid injection or other improved recovery techniques for supplementing the natural forces and mechanisms of primary recovery should be included as "proved developed reserves" only after testing by a pilot project or after the operation of an installed program has confirmed through production response that increased recovery will be achieved.

Proved undeveloped reserves. Proved undeveloped oil and gas reserves are reserves that are expected to be recovered from new wells on undrilled acreage, or from existing wells where a relatively major expenditure is required for recompletion. Reserves on undrilled acreage shall be limited to those drilling units offsetting productive units that are reasonably certain of production when drilled. Proved reserves for other undrilled units can be claimed only where it can be demonstrated with certainty that there is continuity of production from the existing productive formation. Under no circumstances should estimates for proved undeveloped reserves be attributable to any acreage for which an application of fluid injection or other improved recovery technique is contemplated, unless such techniques have been proved effective by actual tests in the area and in the same reservoir.

Statement of Financial Accounting Standards No. 26
Profit Recognition on Sales-Type Leases of Real Estate

an amendment of FASB Statement No. 13

STATUS

Issued: April 1979

Effective Date: For leasing transactions and revisions recorded as of August 1, 1979

Affects: Amends FAS 13, paragraph 8

Affected by: Paragraph 7 amended by FAS 66
Superseded by FAS 98

Other Interpretive Pronouncement: FTB 79-18

(The next page is 314.)

Statement of Financial Accounting Standards No. 27
Classification of Renewals or Extensions of Existing Sales-Type or Direct Financing Leases

an amendment of FASB Statement No. 13

STATUS

Issued: May 1979

Effective Date: For lease agreement renewals and extensions recorded as of September 1, 1979

Affects: Amends FAS 13, paragraphs 6(b)(i), 6(b)(ii), and 17(f)(ii)

Affected by: No other pronouncements

Other Interpretive Pronouncements: FTB 79-18
FTB 88-1

SUMMARY

This Statement modifies *FASB Statement No. 13*, "Accounting for Leases," to require a lessor to classify a renewal or an extension of a sales-type or direct financing lease as a sales-type lease if the lease would otherwise qualify as a sales-type lease and the renewal or extension occurs at or near the end of the lease term. If the renewal or extension occurs at other times during the lease term, the prohibition in Statement No. 13 against classifying the renewal or extension as a sales-type lease continues in effect. Furthermore, this Statement does not affect the classification of a lease that results from a change in the provisions of an existing lease or the accounting for changes in the provisions of a lease if those changes occur during the lease term.

Statement of Financial Accounting Standards No. 27
Classification of Renewals or Extensions of Existing Sales-Type or Direct Financing Leases

an amendment of FASB Statement No. 13

CONTENTS

INTRODUCTION AND BACKGROUND INFORMATION

1. The FASB has been asked to reconsider the provision of paragraph 6(b)(i) of *FASB Statement No. 13,* "Accounting for Leases," that states "a renewal or an extension[9] of an existing sales-type or direct financing lease shall not be classified as a sales-type lease; however, if it qualifies under paragraphs 7 and 8, it shall be classified as a direct financing lease." According to footnote 9 to paragraph 6(b)(i), a renewal or extension includes a new lease under which the lessee continues to use the same property. If the provisions of a sales-type or direct financing lease are changed, the revised agreement might be considered a new agreement under the provisions of paragraph 9 of Statement No. 13.

2. Those making the request described above stated that leases that have the same characteristics are classified and accounted for differently because of the prohibition in paragraph 6(b)(i) of *FASB Statement No. 13*. They noted that the prohibition against classifying a renewal or extension of an existing sales-type or direct financing lease is only applicable if the original lease was classified as a sales-type or direct financing lease and the same lessee continues to use the leased property. On the other hand, the prohibition is not applicable if the original lease was classified as an operating lease or if the property is leased to a different lessee. In their opinion, different lease classification and accounting should not be based on the identity of the lessee or the classification of an original or existing lease.

3. An Exposure Draft of a proposed Statement on "Classification of Renewals or Extensions of Existing Sales-Type or Direct Financing Leases" was issued for public comment on February 13, 1979. The Board received 25 letters of comment in response to the Exposure Draft.

4. The Exposure Draft made a distinction between renewals or extensions of existing sales-type or direct financing leases that occur during the lease term and those that occur at or near the end of the lease term. Several respondents stated that the timing of a renewal or an extension of an existing sales-type or direct financing lease should not affect the classification or the accounting for a revised or extended lease. They suggested completely eliminating the prohibition against recording a "second sale" for renewals or extensions of existing sales-type or direct financing leases. The Board considered that alternative but concluded that the prohibition against recording a "second sale" should continue if a renewal or extension occurs *during the term* of a lease. In limited circumstances, *FASB Statement No. 13* recognizes "partial sales" of leased property. In accounting for a sales-type lease, a "partial sale" is recognized by including only the present value of the minimum lease payments in "sales" revenue and excluding the present value of the unguaranteed residual value from the cost of the leased property charged against that revenue. Recognition of "partial sales" under Statement No. 13 is a liberalization of prior practice in accounting for leases, which did not permit recognition of "partial sales." This Statement extends those limited circumstances to certain renewals or extensions of existing sales-type or direct financing leases that occur at or near the end of the lease term. A further extension of those circumstances to permit recognition of a "partial sale" for a renewal or extension that occurs during the term of an existing lease would require significant modifications to many of the accounting and reporting provisions of Statement No. 13, and the Board does not believe that problem warrants the additional effort that would be required.

5. The Board has concluded that it can reach an informed decision on the basis of existing data without a public hearing and that the effective date

and transition specified in paragraph 9 are advisable in the circumstances.

STANDARDS OF FINANCIAL ACCOUNTING AND REPORTING

Amendments to FASB Statement No. 13

6. The last sentence of paragraph 6(b)(i) of *FASB Statement No. 13* is superseded by the following:

> A renewal or extension[9] of an existing sales-type or direct financing lease that otherwise qualifies as a sales-type lease shall be classified as a direct financing lease unless the renewal or extension occurs at or near the end of the original term* specified in the existing lease, in which case it shall be classified as a sales-type lease. (See paragraph 17(f).)

*A renewal or extension that occurs in the last few months of an existing lease is considered to have occurred at or near the end of the existing lease term.

7. The third sentence of paragraph 6(b)(ii) of *FASB Statement No. 13* is superseded by the following sentence:

> An exception arises when an existing sales-type or direct financing lease is renewed or extended[10] during the term of the existing lease.

8. The following subparagraph is added to paragraph 17(f)(ii) of *FASB Statement No. 13*:

> c. If a renewal or extension that occurs at or near the end of the term† of the existing lease is classified as a sales-type lease, the renewal or extension shall be accounted for as a sales-type lease.

†A renewal or extension that occurs in the last few months of an existing lease is considered to have occurred at or near the end of the existing lease term.

Effective Date and Transition

9. The provisions of this amendment to *FASB Statement No. 13* shall be effective for lease agreement renewals and extensions (see paragraph 9 of Statement No. 13) recorded as of September 1, 1979 or thereafter. Earlier application is encouraged. In addition, except as provided in the next sentence, the provisions of this Statement shall be applied retroactively at the same time and in the same manner as the provisions of Statement No. 13 are applied retroactively (see paragraphs 49 and 51 of Statement No. 13). Enterprises that have already applied the provisions of Statement No. 13 retroactively and have published annual financial statements based on the retroactively adjusted accounts before the effective date of this Statement may, but are not required to, apply the provisions of this Statement retroactively.

The provisions of this Statement need not be applied to immaterial items.

This Statement was adopted by the affirmative votes of six members of the Financial Accounting Standards Board. Mr. Walters dissented.

Mr. Walters dissents to this amendment because, while it properly removes one inconsistency in accounting for similar transactions, it substitutes another inconsistency based solely on timing. If one accepts that a transaction styled as a lease that does not transfer title is substantively a sale, one necessarily accepts the notion of a partial sale; that is, a sale of something less than all the rights to a property for all of its economic life. If one can sell a portion of the whole, one can also sell a portion or all of the remainder, and the accounting for a transaction that meets the criteria of a sale should not differ based solely on its proximity to the end of the original lease term.

Members of the Financial Accounting Standards Board:

Donald J. Kirk, *Chairman*	John W. March	Robert T. Sprouse
Frank E. Block	Robert A. Morgan	Ralph E. Walters
	David Mosso	

Statement of Financial Accounting Standards No. 28
Accounting for Sales with Leasebacks

an amendment of FASB Statement No. 13

STATUS

Issued: May 1979

Effective Date: For leasing transactions and revisions recorded as of September 1, 1979

Affects: Supersedes FAS 13, paragraphs 32 and 33

Affected by: Paragraphs 3 and 23 through 25 amended by FAS 66

Other Interpretive Pronouncements: FTB 79-18
FTB 88-1

Issues Discussed by FASB Emerging Issues Task Force (EITF)

Affects: No EITF Issues

Interpreted by: Paragraph 2 interpreted by EITF Issues No. 88-21 and 93-8
Paragraph 3 interpreted by EITF Issues No. 86-17, 88-21, 89-16, and 93-8

Related Issues: EITF Issues No. 84-37, 87-7, and 89-20

SUMMARY

Paragraph 33 of *FASB Statement No. 13,* "Accounting for Leases," generally treats a sale-leaseback as a single financing transaction in which any profit or loss on the sale is deferred and amortized by the seller, who becomes the lessee. This Statement requires the seller to recognize some profit or loss in either of the following limited circumstances:

- If the seller retains the use of only a minor part of the property or a minor part of its remaining useful life through the leaseback, the sale and the lease would be accounted for based on their separate terms. However, if the rentals called for by the lease are unreasonable in relation to current market conditions, an appropriate amount would be deferred or accrued by adjusting the profit or loss on the sale. The amount deferred or accrued would be amortized as an adjustment of those rentals.
- If the seller retains more than a minor part but less than substantially all of the use of the property through the leaseback and the profit on the sale exceeds the present value of the minimum lease payments called for by the leaseback for an operating lease or the recorded amount of the leased asset for a capital lease, that excess would be recognized as profit at the date of the sale.

Statement of Financial Accounting Standards No. 28
Accounting for Sales with Leasebacks

an amendment of FASB Statement No. 13

CONTENTS

INTRODUCTION

1. The FASB has been asked whether the description of sale-leaseback transactions in paragraph 32 of *FASB Statement No. 13*, "Accounting for Leases," is intended to mean that any sale with a leaseback of all or any part of the property for all or part of its remaining life is subject to the sale-leaseback provisions of Statement No. 13. Paragraph 32 of Statement No. 13 states that "sale-leaseback transactions involve the sale of property by the owner and a lease of the property back to the seller." Those making the inquiry noted that deferral of the profit on a sale and amortization of that profit over the term of the leaseback would appear to be inappropriate in some cases in which the leaseback covers only a relatively small part of the property sold or the leaseback is for only a relatively short period of time. They noted that in some cases the profit on the sale might exceed the total rentals under the leaseback, resulting in a negative rental if the accounting provisions of Statement No. 13 were followed. Appendix A provides additional background information about this matter. Appendix B provides illustrations of accounting for sales with leasebacks.

STANDARDS OF FINANCIAL ACCOUNTING AND REPORTING

Amendments to FASB Statement No. 13

2. Paragraph 32 of *FASB Statement No. 13* is superseded by the following:

Sale-leaseback transactions involve the sale of property by the owner and a lease of the property back to the seller. A sale of property that is accompanied by a leaseback of all or any part of the property for all or part of its remaining economic life shall be accounted for by the seller-lessee in accordance with the provisions of paragraph 33 [of Statement No. 13] and shall be accounted for by the purchaser-lessor in accordance with the provisions of paragraph 34 [of Statement No. 13].

3. Paragraph 33 of *FASB Statement No. 13* is superseded by the following:

If the lease meets one of the criteria for treatment as a capital lease (see paragraph 7 [of Statement No. 13]), the seller-lessee shall account for the lease as a capital lease; otherwise as an operating lease. Any profit or loss on the sale* shall be deferred and amortized in proportion to the amortization of the leased asset,[23] if a capital lease, or in proportion to the related gross rental charged to expense over the lease term, if an operating lease, unless:

a. The seller-lessee relinquishes the right to *substantially all* of the remaining use of the property sold (retaining only a *minor* portion of such use),† in which case the sale and the leaseback shall be accounted for as separate transactions based on their respective terms.

---

*"Profit or loss on the sale" is used in this paragraph to refer to the profit or loss that would be recognized on the sale if there were no leaseback. For example, on a sale of real estate subject to the *AICPA Industry Accounting Guide*, "Accounting for Profit Recognition on Sales of Real Estate," the profit on the sale to be deferred and amortized in proportion to the leaseback would be the profit that could otherwise be recognized in accordance with the Guide.

†"Substantially all" and "minor" are used here in the context of the concepts underlying the classification criteria of *FASB Statement No. 13*. In that context, a test based on the 90 percent recovery criterion of Statement No. 13 could be used as a guideline; that is, if the present value of a reasonable amount of rental for the leaseback represents 10 percent or less of the fair value of the asset sold, the seller-lessee could be presumed to have transferred to the purchaser-lessor the right to substantially all of the remaining use of the property sold, and the seller-lessee could be presumed to have retained only a minor portion of such use.

However, if the amount of rentals called for by the lease is unreasonable under market conditions at the inception of the lease, an appropriate amount shall be deferred or accrued, by adjusting the profit or loss on the sale, and amortized as specified in the introduction of this paragraph to adjust those rentals to a reasonable amount.

b. The seller-lessee retains more than a minor part but less than substantially all‡ of the use of the property through the leaseback and realizes a profit on the sale** in excess of (i) the present value of the minimum lease payments over the lease term, if the leaseback is classified as an operating lease, or (ii) the recorded amount of the leased asset, if the leaseback is classified as a capital lease. In that case, the profit on the sale in excess of either the present value of the minimum lease payments or the recorded amount of the leased asset, whichever is appropriate, shall be recognized at the date of the sale. For purposes of applying this provision, the present value of the minimum lease payments for an operating lease shall be computed using the interest rate that would be used to apply the 90 percent recovery criterion of paragraph 7(d) [of Statement No. 13].

c. The fair value of the property at the time of the transaction is less than its undepreciated cost, in which case a loss shall be recognized immediately up to the amount of the difference between undepreciated cost and fair value.

Effective Date and Transition

4. The provisions of this amendment to *FASB Statement No. 13* shall be effective for leasing transactions recorded and lease agreement revisions (see paragraph 9 of Statement No. 13) recorded as of September 1, 1979 or thereafter. Earlier application is encouraged. In addition, except as provided in the next sentence, the provisions of this Statement shall be applied retroactively at the same time and in the same manner as the provisions of Statement No. 13 are applied retroactively (see paragraphs 49 and 51 of Statement No. 13). Enterprises that have already applied the provisions of Statement No. 13 retroactively and have published annual financial statements based on the retroactively adjusted accounts before the effective date of this Statement may, but are not required to, apply the provisions of this Statement retroactively.

> **The provisions of this Statement need not be applied to immaterial items.**

This Statement was adopted by the unanimous vote of the seven members of the Financial Accounting Standards Board:

Donald J. Kirk,	John W. March	Robert T. Sprouse
Chairman	Robert A. Morgan	Ralph E. Walters
Frank E. Block	David Mosso	

Appendix A

BACKGROUND INFORMATION

5. Paragraph 33 of *FASB Statement No. 13* requires that with one stated exception any profit or loss on the sale in a sale-leaseback transaction be deferred by the seller-lessee and amortized. Paragraph 33 states:

> Except as noted below, any profit or loss on the sale shall be deferred and amortized in proportion to the amortization of the leased asset, . . . if a capital lease, or in proportion to rental payments over the period of time the asset is

expected to be used, if an operating lease. However, when the fair value of the property at the time of the transaction is less than its undepreciated cost, a loss shall be recognized immediately up to the amount of the difference between undepreciated cost and fair value.

6. Paragraph 107 of *FASB Statement No. 13* explains that the seller-lessee's accounting for a sale-leaseback transaction, described in paragraph 5 above, was prescribed because no means could be identified for separating the sale and the leaseback that would be both practicable and objective, with one exception. The one exception was that if an asset had a fair value less than its undepreciated cost at the time of the transaction, a loss should be recog-

---

‡"Substantially all" is used here in the context of the concepts underlying the classification criteria of *FASB Statement No. 13*. In that context, if a leaseback of *the entire property sold* meets the criteria of Statement No. 13 for classification as a capital lease, the seller-lessee would be presumed to have retained substantially all of the remaining use of the property sold.
**See footnote *.

nized up to the amount of the difference between undepreciated cost and fair value. Upon further consideration, the Board has concluded that it should provide two additional exceptions.

7. Paragraph 34 of *FASB Statement No. 13* requires the purchaser-lessor in a sale-leaseback transaction to classify the lease as a direct financing lease or an operating lease, based on the criteria of Statement No. 13 for those classifications. The principal effect of that paragraph is to prohibit the purchaser-lessor from classifying the lease to the seller-lessee as a sales-type lease. Paragraph 34 states:

> If the lease meets the criteria in paragraphs 7 and 8, the purchaser-lessor shall record the transaction as a purchase and a direct financing lease; otherwise, he shall record the transaction as a purchase and an operating lease.

8. The Board concluded that the provisions of paragraph 34 of *FASB Statement No. 13* should not be modified to permit a purchaser-lessor in a sale and leaseback transaction to classify the lease as a sales-type lease.

9. An Exposure Draft of a proposed Statement on "Accounting for Sales with Leasebacks" was issued on December 21, 1978. The Board received 37 letters of comment in response to the Exposure Draft. Certain of the comments received and the Board's consideration of them are discussed in paragraphs 10-21 below.

Sales with "Minor" Leasebacks

10. This Statement requires that sales with minor leasebacks be accounted for based on the separate terms of the sale and of the leaseback except when the rentals called for by the leaseback are unreasonable in relation to current market conditions. If the rentals called for by the leaseback are unreasonable, the rentals would be adjusted to a reasonable amount by adjusting the profit or loss on the sale. Some respondents asked why the Statement requires sales with minor leasebacks to be accounted for based on the separate terms of the sale and of the leaseback but prohibits that same accounting for sales with more significant leasebacks.

11. To the extent that the seller-lessee's use of the asset sold continues after the sale, the sale-leaseback transaction is in substance a method of financing that continuing use, and no profit or loss should result from that transaction. To the extent that the seller-lessee gives up the right to the use of the asset sold, the transaction is in substance a sale, and profit or loss recognition might be appropriate; however, the extent of the seller-lessee's continuing

use of the asset would have to be evaluated to determine whether that continuing involvement is so major that no profit should be recognized. Paragraph 107 of *FASB Statement No. 13* states the Board's conclusion that no means could be identified for separating the sale and the leaseback that would be both practical and objective. That conclusion was arrived at after considering comments received in response to an Exposure Draft on "Accounting for Leases." The Board has not modified that general conclusion. However, if the leaseback is minor, the overall sale-leaseback transaction clearly is in substance a sale of the property. The Board concluded that accounting for the sale and the leaseback based on their respective terms, using the reasonableness of the rentals as a control, is appropriate for a sale with a minor leaseback because it reflects the overall nature of the transaction. However, if the leaseback is more than a minor one, accounting for the sale and the leaseback based on their terms would permit the seller-lessee to recognize a profit on the portion of the transaction that is in substance a financing. Recognition of a sales-type profit on a financing would be equivalent to profit recognition on a company's sale to itself. Therefore, the Board concluded that the terms of the sale and of the leaseback, using the reasonableness of the leaseback rentals as a control, should not be used as a basis for accounting for other sale-leaseback transactions.

Definition of a "Minor" Leaseback

12. Footnote† indicates that a test based on the 90 percent criterion of *FASB Statement No. 13* could be used as a guideline to distinguish a "minor" leaseback. In that context, if the present value of the leaseback based on reasonable rentals is 10 percent or less of the fair value of the asset sold, the leaseback could be presumed to be minor. Some respondents suggested that "minor" be defined using a test based on the 75 percent of economic life criterion of Statement No. 13. In that context, if the leaseback encompassed less than 25 percent of the remaining economic life of the asset sold, the leaseback could be presumed to be minor.

13. Paragraph 75 of *FASB Statement No. 13* explains that 75 percent of economic life was considered to be substantially all of the benefits and risks incident to the ownership of the property because (a) new equipment, reflecting later technology and in prime condition, can be assumed to be more efficient, and hence yield proportionately more use benefit, than old equipment which has been subject to obsolescence and the wearing-out process, and (b) the present worth, at inception of the lease, of the last 25 percent of the remaining economic life of the property would represent less than 25 percent of the fair value of the asset at the inception of the

lease. Both of those arguments indicate that the first 25 percent of an asset's economic life is more than a minor part of the asset's value. The Board decided to severely limit the minor leaseback exception from the usual sale-leaseback accounting, and accordingly, it used the 90 percent recovery criterion as a guideline to indicate the Board's intent for determination of a "minor" leaseback.

Sales with Other Than "Minor" Leasebacks

14. If a seller-lessee retains more than a minor part but less than substantially all of the use of an asset through a leaseback, this Statement requires the seller-lessee to recognize an amount of profit on the sale equal to the excess, if any, of the realized profit on the sale over the present value of the minimum lease payments (or the recorded amount of the leased asset if the leaseback is classified as a capital lease). Some respondents to the Exposure Draft suggested that the Board permit recognition of a pro rata portion of the realized profit on the sale for those sale-leaseback transactions, i.e., if the present value of the leaseback were equal to 60 percent of the fair value of the asset sold, 40 percent of the profit realized on the sale would be recognized, and the remaining 60 percent would be deferred and amortized over the leaseback term.

15. Paragraph 107 of *FASB Statement No. 13* states that the Board concluded that the present general requirement that gains and losses on sale-leaseback transactions be deferred and amortized should be retained. As discussed in paragraph 13 above, this Statement provides an exception for a minor leaseback because in that case the substance of the overall transaction is apparent. For sales with leasebacks that are not minor, the Board decided to limit profit recognition to amounts that could not represent borrowings to be repaid. Thus, any profits up to the amount of the present value of the leaseback rentals (the maximum amount of borrowing that could be repaid) must be deferred and amortized. The recorded amount of the leased asset is usually the present value of the minimum lease payments. Accordingly, if the leaseback of part of the asset sold is classified as a capital lease, any profit on the sale up to the recorded amount of the leased asset must be deferred and amortized.

16. In the Exposure Draft, the Board proposed to limit recognition of profits on sales with other than minor leasebacks to the excess of the realized profit over the aggregate rental payments for an operating leaseback. Some respondents noted that the purchaser-lessor would expect to receive interest on any amount of sales proceeds that was in substance a borrowing; thus, the present value of those payments would be a more appropriate measure of the borrowing that could be repaid through leaseback rentals. The Board agreed with those respondents and modified this Statement to reflect their suggestion.

17. If the seller-lessee retains, through a leaseback, substantially all of the benefits and risks incident to the ownership of the property sold, the sale-leaseback transaction is merely a financing. The Board concluded that the seller-lessee should not recognize any profit on the sale of an asset if the substance of the sale-leaseback transaction is merely a financing. Accordingly, the Statement does not permit any profit to be recognized on a sale if a related leaseback *of the entire property sold* meets one of the criteria of *FASB Statement No. 13* for classification as a capital lease.

Indicated Losses

18. This Statement continues the requirement of *FASB Statement No. 13* that an indicated loss on the sale in a sale-leaseback be recognized up to the amount of the excess of the carrying amount of the asset sold over its fair value and does not permit an indicated loss on the sale in a sale-leaseback to be deferred and amortized as prepaid rent without some evidence that the indicated loss is in substance a prepayment of rent. If the fair value of the asset sold is more than its carrying amount, any indicated loss on the sale is probably in substance a prepayment of rent, and thus, deferral of that indicated loss to be amortized as prepaid rent would be appropriate.

Amortization of Deferred Amounts

19. Some respondents asked why the profit or loss that is deferred on the sale should be amortized over the period of expected use of the leased asset for an operating leaseback. They noted that any borrowing to be repaid through leaseback rentals would be repaid during the lease term, as defined in *FASB Statement No. 13,* to ensure recovery to the purchaser-lessor. Any reduction of sales proceeds that was in substance a prepayment of rent would result in bargain rentals during the affected period, and the lease term includes any option periods with bargain rentals. The Board agreed and modified paragraph 3 of this Statement to require that the amount deferred or accrued be amortized over the lease term.

Classification of Leasebacks

20. A few respondents asked whether special classification criteria should be provided for leasebacks. They suggested a criterion based on 90 percent recovery of the sales price called for by the related sale rather than 90 percent recovery of fair value of the leased asset. They also suggested that any

deferred profit or loss be considered an adjustment of minimum lease payments for application of that criterion. This Statement addresses a narrow issue that was identified as a problem requiring urgent resolution. The Board concluded that it should not expand the scope of this Statement to provide special criteria for classification of a leaseback.

21. The Board concluded that on the basis of existing information it can make an informed decision on the matters addressed by this Statement without a public hearing and that the effective date and transition specified in paragraph 4 are advisable in the circumstances.

Appendix B

ILLUSTRATIONS OF ACCOUNTING FOR SALES WITH LEASEBACKS

22. The examples in this Appendix illustrate the accounting for certain sales with leasebacks but do not encompass all possible circumstances. Accordingly, each situation should be resolved based on an evaluation of the facts, using the examples in this Appendix as guidance to the extent that they are applicable to the facts of the individual sale and leaseback.

Minor Leaseback

23. An enterprise constructs a regional shopping center and sells it to a real estate management firm. The sale meets the criteria of the *AICPA Industry Accounting Guide*, "Accounting for Profit Recognition on Sales of Real Estate," for full and immediate profit recognition. At the same time, the seller leases back for 40 years a part of the facility, estimated to be approximately 8 percent of the total rental value of the center. Pertinent data are:

Sales price	$11,200,000
Cost of shopping center	$10,000,000

The rental called for by the lease appears to be reasonable in view of current market conditions. The seller-lessee would record the sale and recognize $1,200,000 profit. The seller-lessee would account for the leaseback as though it were unrelated to the sale because the leaseback is minor as indicated in

paragraph 3(a).

24. An enterprise sells real estate, consisting of land and a factory. The factory has an estimated remaining life of approximately 40 years. The sale meets the criteria of the *AICPA Industry Accounting Guide*, "Accounting for Profit Recognition on Sales of Real Estate," for full and immediate profit recognition. The seller negotiates a leaseback of the factory for one year because its new facilities are under construction and approximately one year will be required to complete the new facilities and relocate. Pertinent data are:

Sales price	$20,000,000
Carrying value of real estate	$ 6,000,000
Annual rental under leaseback	$ 900,000
Estimated annual market rental	$ 1,800,000

The leaseback is minor as indicated in paragraph 3(a) because the present value of the leaseback ($1,800,000) is less than 10 percent of the fair value of the asset sold (approximately $20,900,000, based on the sales price and the prepaid rental that apparently has reduced the sales price). Accordingly, the seller-lessee would record the sale and would recognize profit. An amount of $900,000 would be deferred and amortized as additional rent expense over the term of the leaseback to adjust the leaseback rentals to a reasonable amount.†† Accordingly, the seller-lessee would recognize $14,900,000 as profit on the sale ($14,000,000 of profit based on the terms of the sale increased by $900,000 to adjust the leaseback rentals to a reasonable amount).

Leasebacks That Are Not Minor but Do Not Cover Substantially All of the Use of the Property Sold

25. An enterprise sells an existing shopping center to a real estate management firm. The sale meets the criteria of the *AICPA Industry Accounting Guide*, "Accounting for Profit Recognition on Sales of Real Estate," for full and immediate profit recognition. At the same time, the seller leases back the "anchor" store (with corresponding use of the related land), estimated to be approximately 30 percent of the total rental value of the shopping center, for 20 years, which is substantially all of the remaining economic life of the building. Pertinent data are:

---

††If the term of a prepayment of rent were significant, the amount deferred would be the amount required to adjust the rental to the market rental for an equivalent property if that rental were also prepaid.

Sales price of shopping center	$3,500,000
Estimated to consist of:	
Land	$1,000,000
Buildings and improvements	2,500,000
	$3,500,000
Carrying value of shopping center	$1,000,000
Monthly rentals called for by leaseback	$ 12,600
*Seller-lessee's incremental borrowing rate	10%

*Believed to be approximately the same as the implicit rate calculated by the lessor.

The seller-lessee estimates the ratio of land to building for the leaseback to be the same as for the property as a whole. The seller-lessee would apply paragraph 26(b)(ii)(a) of *FASB Statement No. 13* because the land value exceeds 25 percent of the total fair value of the leased property and would account for the leaseback of the land as a separate operating lease. The seller-lessee would account for $2,500 as monthly land rental (10 percent annual rate applied to the $300,000 value of the land leased back—30 percent of the land value of the shopping center). The balance of the monthly rental ($10,100) would be allocated to the building and improvements and would be accounted for as a capital lease pursuant to the 75 percent of economic life criterion of Statement No. 13. The leased building and improvements would be recorded at the present value of the $10,100 monthly rentals for 20 years at the seller-lessee's 10 percent incremental borrowing rate, or $1,046,608. The seller-lessee would compute the profit to be recognized on the sale as follows:

Profit on the sale		$2,500,000
Recorded amount of leased asset (capital lease)	$1,046,608	
Present value of operating lease rentals at 10% rate	259,061	
Profit to be deferred and amortized		1,305,669
Profit to be recognized		$1,194,331

The deferred profit would be amortized in relation to the separate segments of the lease. The amount attributable to the capital lease ($1,046,608) would be amortized in proportion to the amortization of the leased asset over the term of the lease. The amount attributable to the operating lease ($259,061) would be amortized on a straight line basis over the term of the lease.

26. An enterprise sells an airplane with an estimated remaining economic life of 10 years. At the same time, the seller leases back the airplane for three years. Pertinent data are:

Sales price	$600,000
Carrying value of airplane	$100,000
Monthly rental under leaseback	$ 6,330
*Interest rate implicit in the lease as computed by the lessor	12%

*Used because it is lower than the lessee's incremental borrowing rate.

The leaseback does not meet any of the criteria for classification as a capital lease; hence, it would be classified as an operating lease. The seller-lessee would compute the profit to be recognized on the sale as follows:

Profit on the sale	$500,000
Present value of operating lease rentals ($6,330 for 36 months at 12%)	190,581
Profit to be recognized	$309,419

The $190,581 deferred profit would be amortized in equal monthly amounts over the lease term because the leaseback is classified as an operating lease.

Leaseback That Covers Substantially All of the Use of the Property Sold

27. An enterprise sells equipment with an estimated remaining economic life of 15 years. At the same time, the seller leases back the equipment for 12 years. All profit on the sale would be deferred and amortized in relation to the amortization of the leased asset because the leaseback of *all* of the property sold covers a period in excess of 75 percent of the remaining economic life of the property, and thus, meets one of the criteria of *FASB Statement No. 13* for classification as a capital lease.

(This page intentionally left blank.)

Statement of Financial Accounting Standards No. 29
Determining Contingent Rentals

an amendment of FASB Statement No. 13

STATUS

Issued: June 1979

Effective Date: For leasing transactions and revisions recorded as of October 1, 1979

Affects: Amends FAS 13, paragraphs 5, 5(j)(i), 12, 16(a)(iv), 17(b), and 18(b)
Supersedes FAS 13, footnote 13

Affected by: Paragraph 13 amended by FAS 98

Other Interpretive Pronouncements: FTB 79-18
FTB 85-3

Issues Discussed by FASB Emerging Issues Task Force (EITF)

Affects: No EITF Issues

Interpreted by: Paragraphs 10 and 11 interpreted by EITF Issue No. 86-33

Related Issues: No EITF Issues

SUMMARY

The Board has been asked to reconsider the definition of contingent rentals in *FASB Statement No. 13*, "Accounting for Leases," because differing views about the meaning of that definition result in similar leases being accounted for differently, for example, as a capital lease by one lessee and as an operating lease by another lessee. This Statement defines contingent rentals as the increases or decreases in lease payments that result from changes occurring subsequent to the inception of the lease in the factors on which lease payments are based. Lease payments that depend on a factor that exists and is measurable at the inception of the lease, such as the prime interest rate, would be included in minimum lease payments based on the factor at the inception of the lease. Lease payments that depend on a factor that does not exist or is not measurable at the inception of the lease, such as future sales volume, would be contingent rentals in their entirety and, accordingly, would be excluded from minimum lease payments and included in the determination of income as they accrue.

Statement of Financial Accounting Standards No. 29
Determining Contingent Rentals

an amendment of FASB Statement No. 13

CONTENTS

INTRODUCTION AND BACKGROUND INFORMATION

1. The FASB has been asked whether lease payments that depend on changes in a factor that is measurable at the inception of the lease should be included in minimum lease payments for purposes of lease classification, accounting, and reporting under *FASB Statement No. 13,* "Accounting for Leases." Examples of factors upon which lease payments can be based include sales volume in a leased facility, an interest rate such as the prime rate, or an index such as a construction cost index or consumer price index.

2. Paragraph 16(a)(iv) of *FASB Statement No. 13* refers to contingent rentals as "rentals on which the amounts are dependent on some factor other than the passage of time." Footnote 13 of Statement No. 13 further states that "the term 'contingent rentals' includes all or any portion of the stipulated rental that is contingent."

3. In specifying the accounting for capital leases by lessees, paragraph 12 of *FASB Statement No. 13* states that "contingent rentals, . . . including rentals based on variables such as the prime interest rate, shall be charged to expense when actually incurred." Paragraphs 17(b) and 18(b) of Statement No. 13 include similar reference to contingent rentals in specifying the accounting by lessors for sales-type leases and direct financing leases.

4. The Board has been advised that diverse accounting practices have developed with respect to determining contingent rentals. The following three practices have been identified: (a) all lease payments that depend on factors that can change are considered contingent rentals and are excluded from minimum lease payments in their entirety, (b) lease payments that depend on such factors are included in minimum lease payments to the extent that pay-

ment by the lessee is assessed as probable, and (c) only the amounts based on a measurable factor existing at the inception of the lease are included in minimum lease payments. Under the last approach, lease payments that depend on a factor like future sales volume of a leased facility are contingent rentals in their entirety and are excluded from minimum lease payments because future sales do not exist at the inception of the lease. Supporters of this approach point out that lease payments based on future sales should be excluded from minimum lease payments because those payments would terminate if the lessee discontinues use of the leased facility.

5. The diverse accounting practices described in the preceding paragraph cause different amounts to be included in minimum lease payments for similar leases. Because the amount of minimum lease payments affects the classification and accounting for leases, such diverse practices result in similar leases being classified and accounted for differently. For example, a lease may be classified as a capital lease by one lessee and a similar lease classified as an operating lease by another lessee because of differing views about the definition of contingent rentals.

6. An Exposure Draft of a proposed Statement on "Determining Contingent Rentals" was issued for public comment on December 21, 1978. The Board received 37 letters of comment in response to the Exposure Draft.

7. Several respondents stated that contingent rentals should be included in minimum lease payments to the extent that payment by the lessee is probable. The Board rejected that approach primarily because of the subjectivity inherent in estimating probable contingent rentals. However, the Board noted that, if certain rental payments to the lessor were required rather than probable under the terms of the lease or other agreement, *FASB Statement*

No. 13 requires that such payments be included in minimum lease payments.

·8. The Board has considered various accounting practices with respect to determining contingent rentals and has concluded that lease payments that depend on factors that exist and are measurable at the inception of the lease should be included in minimum lease payments. The Board believes that the term *contingent rentals* contemplates an uncertainty about **future changes** in the factors on which lease payments are based. Accordingly, the Board has concluded that *FASB Statement No. 13* should be amended to identify the contingency in that way.

9. The Board has concluded that it can reach an informed decision on the basis of existing data without a public hearing and that the effective date and transition specified in paragraph 14 are advisable in the circumstances.

STANDARDS OF FINANCIAL ACCOUNTING AND REPORTING

Amendments to FASB Statement No. 13

10. The following footnote is added to the end of the first sentence of paragraph 5(j)(i) of *FASB Statement No. 13:*

> Contingent rentals as defined by paragraph 5(n) of *FASB Statement No. 13* shall be excluded from minimum lease payments.

11. Paragraph 5 of *FASB Statement No. 13* is amended by adding the following subparagraph:

> n. *Contingent rentals.* The increases or decreases in lease payments that result from changes occurring subsequent to the inception of the lease in the factors (other than the passage of time) on which lease payments are based, except as provided in the following sentence. Any escalation of minimum lease payments relating to increases in construction or acquisition cost of the leased property or for increases in some measure of cost or value during the construction or pre-construction period, as discussed in *FASB*

Statement No. 23, "Inception of the Lease," shall be excluded from contingent rentals. Lease payments that depend on a factor directly related to the future use of the leased property, such as machine hours of use or sales volume during the lease term, are contingent rentals and, accordingly, are excluded from minimum lease payments in their entirety. However, lease payments that depend on an existing index or rate, such as the consumer price index or the prime interest rate, shall be included in minimum lease payments based on the index or rate existing at the inception of the lease; any increases or decreases in lease payments that result from subsequent changes in the index or rate are contingent rentals and thus affect the determination of income as accruable.

12. Footnote 13 and the parenthetical phrase following *contingent rentals* in paragraph 16(a)(iv) of *FASB Statement No. 13* are deleted.

13. The last sentence of paragraphs 12, 17(b), and 18(b) of *FASB Statement No. 13* is superseded by the following:

> Contingent rentals shall be included in the determination of income as accruable.

Effective Date and Transition

14. The provisions of this amendment to *FASB Statement No. 13* shall be effective for leasing transactions recorded and lease agreement revisions (see paragraph 9 of Statement No. 13) recorded as of October 1, 1979 or thereafter. Earlier application is encouraged. In addition, except as provided in the next sentence, the provisions of this Statement shall be applied retroactively at the same time and in the same manner as the provisions of Statement No. 13 are applied retroactively (see paragraphs 49 and 51 of Statement No. 13). Enterprises that have already applied the provisions of Statement No. 13 retroactively and have published annual financial statements based on the retroactively adjusted accounts before the effective date of this Statement may, but are not required to, apply the provisions of this Statement retroactively.

> **The provisions of this Statement need not be applied to immaterial items.**

This Statement was adopted by the unanimous vote of the seven members of the Financial Accounting Standards Board:

Donald J. Kirk,	John W. March	Robert T. Sprouse
Chairman	Robert A. Morgan	Ralph E. Walters
Frank E. Block	David Mosso	

Appendix A

ILLUSTRATIONS OF THE APPLICATION OF THE PROVISIONS OF THIS STATEMENT

15. This Appendix illustrates the application of the provisions of paragraphs 10-13 of this Statement in determining contingent rentals. The examples do not comprehend all possible combinations of circumstances.

16. Paragraph 11 of this Statement indicates that lease payments that depend on an existing index or rate, such as the prime interest rate, shall be included in minimum lease payments based on the index or rate existing at the inception of the lease. As an example, an equipment lease could stipulate a monthly base rental of $2,000 and a monthly supplemental rental of $15 for each percentage point in the prime interest rate in effect at the beginning of each month. If the prime interest rate at the inception of the lease is 10 percent, minimum lease payments would be based on a monthly rental of $2,150 [$2,000 + ($15 × 10) = $2,150]. If the lease term is 48 months and no executory costs are included in the rentals, minimum lease payments would be $103,200 [$2,150 × 48]. If the lease is classified as a capital lease and the prime interest rate subsequently increases to 11 percent, the $15 increase in the monthly rentals would be a contingent rental included in the determination of income as it accrues. If the prime interest rate subsequently decreases to 9 percent, the $15 reduction in the monthly rentals would affect income as accruable. In the case of either the increase or decrease, minimum lease payments would continue to be $103,200.

17. Paragraph 11 of this Statement also indicates that lease payments that depend on a factor directly related to the future use of the leased property, such as machine hours of use or sales volume during the lease term, are contingent rentals and, accordingly, are excluded from minimum lease payments in their entirety. For example, a lease agreement for retail store space could stipulate a monthly base rental of $200 and a monthly supplemental rental of one-fourth of one percent of monthly sales volume during the lease term. Even if the lease agreement is a renewal for store space that had averaged monthly sales of $25,000 for the past 2 years, minimum lease payments would include only the $200 monthly base rental; the supplemental rental is a contingent rental that is excluded from minimum lease payments. The future sales for the lease term do not exist at the inception of the lease, and future rentals would be limited to $200 per month if the store were subsequently closed and no sales were made thereafter.

Statement of Financial Accounting Standards No. 30
Disclosure of Information about Major Customers

an amendment of FASB Statement No. 14

STATUS

Issued: August 1979

Effective Date: For fiscal years beginning after December 15, 1979

Affects: Supersedes FAS 14, paragraph 39

Affected by: No other pronouncements

Other Interpretive Pronouncement: FTB 79-5

SUMMARY

Paragraph 39 of *FASB Statement No. 14,* "Financial Reporting for Segments of a Business Enterprise," requires disclosure of the amount of revenue derived from sales to domestic governmental agencies in the *aggregate* or to foreign governments in the *aggregate* when those revenues are 10 percent or more of the enterprise's revenues. The Board was requested to consider the usefulness of disclosing aggregate amounts and concluded that such disclosure has limited general usefulness and should not be required. Therefore, this Statement amends that paragraph to require disclosure of the amount of sales to an individual domestic government or foreign government when those revenues are 10 percent or more of the enterprise's revenues. Consequently, disclosure of sales to a governmental customer is now the same as disclosure of sales to any other customer.

Statement of Financial Accounting Standards No. 30
Disclosure of Information about Major Customers

an amendment of FASB Statement No. 14

CONTENTS

INTRODUCTION AND BACKGROUND INFORMATION

1. Paragraph 39 of *FASB Statement No. 14,* "Financial Reporting for Segments of a Business Enterprise," requires disclosure of information about major customers as follows:

> If 10 percent or more of the revenue of an enterprise is derived from sales to any single customer, that fact and the amount of revenue from each such customer shall be disclosed. (For this purpose, a group of customers under common control shall be regarded as a single customer.) Similarly, if 10 percent or more of the revenue of an enterprise is derived from sales to domestic government agencies in the aggregate or to foreign governments in the aggregate, that fact and the amount of revenue shall be disclosed. The identity of the industry segment or segments making the sales shall be disclosed. The disclosures required by this paragraph shall be made even if the enterprise is not required by this Statement to report information about operations in different industries or foreign operations.

2. The Board has received a number of questions concerning the disclosure of revenue derived from sales to domestic governmental agencies in the aggregate or to foreign governments in the aggregate. The questions pertain to the usefulness of disclosing aggregate amounts, such as aggregate revenue derived from sales to federal, state, and county agencies when there is no apparent relationship, such as common control. Similar questions have been asked about aggregating sales to foreign governments.

3. The purpose of the major customer disclosure requirement of *FASB Statement No. 14* is to inform financial statement users of the extent of an enterprise's reliance on a customer. Accordingly, the Board has concluded that disclosure of revenue derived from sales to domestic governmental agencies in the *aggregate* or to foreign governments in the *aggregate* has limited general usefulness and should not be required. Instead, the major customer disclosure requirements of Statement No. 14 should apply for sales to domestic governmental agencies and foreign governments. Therefore, if 10 percent or more of the revenue of an enterprise is derived from sales to a domestic government or a foreign government, that fact and the amount of revenue from each such source should be disclosed.

4. An Exposure Draft of a proposed Statement on "Disclosure of Information about Major Customers" was issued on March 29, 1979. The Board received 36 letters of comment in response to that Exposure Draft, virtually all of which expressed agreement with the proposed Statement.

5. The Board has concluded that it can reach an informed decision on the basis of existing information without a public hearing and that the effective date and transition specified in paragraph 7 are advisable in the circumstances.

STANDARDS OF FINANCIAL ACCOUNTING AND REPORTING

Amendment to FASB Statement No. 14

6. Paragraph 39 of *FASB Statement No. 14* is superseded by the following:

> An enterprise shall disclose information about the extent of the enterprise's reliance on its major customers. If 10 percent or more of the revenue of an enterprise is derived from sales to any single customer, that fact and the amount of revenue from each such customer shall be disclosed. For this purpose, a group of entities under common control shall be regarded as a single customer, and the federal government, a state government, a local government (for

example, a county or municipality), or a foreign government shall each be considered as a single customer.* The identity of the customer need not be disclosed, but the identity of the industry segment or segments making the sales shall be disclosed. The disclosures required by this paragraph shall be made by an enterprise subject to this Statement [Statement No. 14] even if the enterprise operates only in one industry or has no foreign operations.

---

*If sales are concentrated in a particular department or agency of government, disclosure of

that fact and the amount of revenue derived from each such source is encouraged.

Effective Date and Transition

7. This Statement shall be effective for fiscal years beginning after December 15, 1979. Earlier application is encouraged in financial statements for fiscal years beginning before December 16, 1979. This Statement may be, but is not required to be, applied retroactively to previously issued financial statements.

> The provisions of this Statement need
> not be applied to immaterial items.

This Statement was adopted by the unanimous vote of the seven members of the Financial Accounting Standards Board:

Donald J. Kirk,	John W. March	Robert T. Sprouse
Chairman	Robert A. Morgan	Ralph E. Walters
Frank E. Block	David Mosso	

(This page intentionally left blank.)

Statement of Financial Accounting Standards No. 31
Accounting for Tax Benefits Related to U.K. Tax
Legislation concerning Stock Relief

STATUS

Issued: September 1979

Effective Date: For annual or interim financial statements issued after
September 30, 1979 for periods ending on or after July 26, 1979

Affects: No other pronouncements

Affected by: Superseded by FAS 96 and FAS 109

(This page intentionally left blank.)

Statement of Financial Accounting Standards No. 32
Specialized Accounting and Reporting Principles and Practices in AICPA Statements of Position and Guides on Accounting and Auditing Matters

an amendment of APB Opinion No. 20

STATUS

Issued: September 1979

Effective Date: October 31, 1979

Affects: Supersedes APB 20, footnote 5

Affected by: Appendix A amended (SOP 74-6) by FAS 77
Appendix A amended (SOPs 74-12 and 76-2) by FAS 65
Appendix A amended (SOP 75-1) by FAS 48
Appendix A amended (SOP 75-5) by FAS 63
Appendix A amended (SOPs 75-6 and 78-4 and Real Estate) by FAS 66
Appendix A amended (SOP 76-1) by FAS 50
Appendix A amended (SOP 78-3) by FAS 67
Appendix A amended (SOP 78-5) by FAS 76
Appendix A amended (SOPs 78-6 and 79-3 and Insurance) by FAS 60
Appendix A amended (SOP 78-8) by FAS 49
Appendix A amended (SOP 79-2) by FAS 51
Appendix A amended (SOP 79-4 and Motion Picture Films) by FAS 53
Appendix A amended (Franchise Fee Revenue) by FAS 45
Appendix A amended (Construction Contractors) by FAS 56
Appendix A amended (Banks, Brokers and Dealers in Securities, Employee Health and Welfare Benefit Funds, and Personal Financial Statements) by FAS 83
Appendix B amended by FAS 56, FAS 60, and FAS 67
Appendix B superseded by FAS 83
Superseded by FAS 111

(The next page is 341.)

(This page intentionally left blank.)

Statement of Financial Accounting Standards No. 33
Financial Reporting and Changing Prices

STATUS

Issued: September 1979

Effective Date: For fiscal years ending on or after December 25, 1979

Affects: No other pronouncements

Affected by: Paragraphs 22, 29(a), 30, 31, 34, 35, 35(c), 36, 39, 41, 50, 53, 56, 59, and 66 amended by FAS 70
Paragraph 22(c) superseded by FAS 70
Paragraph 23 amended by FAS 54
Paragraphs 29(a) and 35(b) superseded by FAS 82
Paragraphs 30(a) through (c), 35(c)(1) through (4), and 52 amended by FAS 39
Paragraph 31 amended by FAS 82
Paragraphs 33, 40, 42 through 46, 66(a), 70, 224, 225, 227, 229, 239, and 240 changed by FAS 82
Paragraphs 51(b), 52(b), and 53 superseded by FAS 39
Paragraphs 51(b) and 52(b) superseded by FAS 69
Paragraph 53 superseded by FAS 40
Paragraph 53 superseded by FAS 41
Paragraph 53 amended by FAS 46
Paragraph 53(a) superseded by FAS 69
Superseded by FAS 89

Other Interpretive Pronouncements: FTB 79-8
FTB 81-4 (Superseded by FAS 89)

(This page intentionally left blank.)

Statement of Financial Accounting Standards No. 34
Capitalization of Interest Cost

STATUS

Issued: October 1979

Effective Date: For fiscal years beginning after December 15, 1979

Affects: Amends APB 21, paragraphs 15 and 16
Amends FAS 13, paragraph 12

Affected by: Paragraph 5 superseded by FAS 71
Paragraphs 8 and 9 amended by FAS 42
Paragraphs 9, 10, and 20 amended by FAS 58
Paragraphs 10, 13, and 17 amended by FAS 62
Paragraph 19 amended by FAS 121

Other Interpretive Pronouncements: FIN 33
FTB 81-5 (Superseded by FAS 62)

SUMMARY

This Statement establishes standards for capitalizing interest cost as part of the historical cost of acquiring certain assets. To qualify for interest capitalization, assets must require a period of time to get them ready for their intended use. Examples are assets that an enterprise constructs for its own use (such as facilities) and assets intended for sale or lease that are constructed as discrete projects (such as ships or real estate projects). Interest capitalization is required for those assets if its effect, compared with the effect of expensing interest, is material. If the net effect is not material, interest capitalization is not required. However, interest cannot be capitalized for inventories that are routinely manufactured or otherwise produced in large quantities on a repetitive basis.

The interest cost eligible for capitalization shall be the interest cost recognized on borrowings and other obligations. The amount capitalized is to be an allocation of the interest cost incurred during the period required to complete the asset. The interest rate for capitalization purposes is to be based on the rates on the enterprise's outstanding borrowings. If the enterprise associates a specific new borrowing with the asset, it may apply the rate on that borrowing to the appropriate portion of the expenditures for the asset. A weighted average of the rates on other borrowings is to be applied to expenditures not covered by specific new borrowings. Judgment is required in identifying the borrowings on which the average rate is based.

Statement of Financial Accounting Standards No. 34
Capitalization of Interest Cost

CONTENTS

INTRODUCTION

1. This Statement establishes standards of financial accounting and reporting for capitalizing interest cost as a part of the historical cost of acquiring certain assets. For the purposes of this Statement, *interest cost* includes interest recognized on obligations having explicit interest rates,[1] interest imputed on certain types of payables in accordance with APB Opinion No. 21, *Interest on Receivables and Payables,* and interest related to a capital lease determined in accordance with FASB Statement No. 13, *Accounting for Leases.*

2. Paragraphs 15 and 16 of Opinion 21 provide that the discount or premium that results from imputing interest for certain types of payables should be amortized as interest expense over the life of the payable and reported as such in the statement of income. Paragraph 12 of Statement 13 provides that, during the term of a capital lease, a portion of each minimum lease payment shall be recorded as interest expense. This Statement modifies Opinion 21 and Statement 13 in that the amount chargeable to interest expense under the provisions of those paragraphs is eligible for inclusion in the amount of interest cost capitalizable in accordance with this Statement.

3. Some enterprises now charge all interest cost to expense when incurred; some enterprises capitalize

interest cost in some circumstances; and some enterprises, primarily public utilities, also capitalize a cost for equity funds in some circumstances. This diversity of practice and an observation that an increasing number of nonutility registrants were adopting a policy of capitalizing interest led the Securities and Exchange Commission to impose, in November 1974, a moratorium on adoption or extension of such a policy by most nonutility registrants until such time as the FASB established standards in this area.[2]

4. Appendix A provides additional background information. Appendix B sets forth the basis for the Board's conclusions, including alternatives considered and reasons for accepting some and rejecting others.

5. The Addendum to APB Opinion No. 2, *Accounting for the 'Investment Credit',* states that "differences may arise in the application of generally accepted accounting principles as between regulated and nonregulated businesses, because of the effect in regulated businesses of the rate-making process," and discusses the application of generally accepted accounting principles to regulated industries. Accordingly, the provisions of the Addendum shall govern the application of this Statement to those operations of an enterprise that are regulated for rate-making purposes on an individual-company-cost-of-service basis.

---

[1]Interest cost on these obligations includes amounts resulting from periodic amortization of discount or premium and issue costs on debt.

[2]Securities and Exchange Commission, ASR No. 163, *Capitalization of Interest by Companies Other Than Public Utilities* (Washington: November 14, 1974).

STANDARDS OF FINANCIAL ACCOUNTING AND REPORTING

6. The historical cost of acquiring an asset includes the costs necessarily incurred to bring it to the condition and location necessary for its intended use.[3] If an asset requires a period of time in which to carry out the activities[4] necessary to bring it to that condition and location, the interest cost incurred during that period as a result of expenditures for the asset is a part of the historical cost of acquiring the asset.

7. The objectives of capitalizing interest are (a) to obtain a measure of acquisition cost that more closely reflects the enterprise's total investment in the asset and (b) to charge a cost that relates to the acquisition of a resource that will benefit future periods against the revenues of the periods benefited.

8. In concept, interest cost is capitalizable for all assets that require a period of time to get them ready for their intended use (an "acquisition period"). However, in many cases, the benefit in terms of information about enterprise resources and earnings may not justify the additional accounting and administrative cost involved in providing the information. The benefit may be less than the cost because the effect of interest capitalization and its subsequent amortization or other disposition, compared with the effect of charging it to expense when incurred, would not be material. In that circumstance, interest capitalization is not *required* by this Statement.

Assets Qualifying for Interest Capitalization

9. Subject to the provisions of paragraph 8, interest shall be capitalized for the following types of assets ("qualifying assets"):

a. Assets that are constructed or otherwise produced for an enterprise's own use (including assets constructed or produced for the enterprise by others for which deposits or progress payments have been made)
b. Assets intended for sale or lease that are constructed or otherwise produced as discrete projects (e.g., ships or real estate developments).

10. However, interest cost shall not be capitalized for inventories that are routinely manufactured or otherwise produced in large quantities on a repetitive basis because, in the Board's judgment, the informational benefit does not justify the cost of so

doing. In addition, interest shall not be capitalized for the following types of assets:

a. Assets that are in use or ready for their intended use in the earning activities of the enterprise
b. Assets that are not being used in the earning activities of the enterprise and that are not undergoing the activities necessary to get them ready for use.

11. Land that is not undergoing activities necessary to get it ready for its intended use is not a qualifying asset. If activities are undertaken for the purpose of developing land for a particular use, the expenditures to acquire the land qualify for interest capitalization while those activities are in progress. The interest cost capitalized on those expenditures is a cost of acquiring the asset that results from those activities. If the resulting asset is a structure, such as a plant or a shopping center, interest capitalized on the land expenditures is part of the acquisition cost of the structure. If the resulting asset is developed land, such as land that is to be sold as developed lots, interest capitalized on the land expenditures is part of the acquisition cost of the developed land.

The Amount of Interest Cost to Be Capitalized

12. The amount of interest cost to be capitalized for qualifying assets is intended to be that portion of the interest cost incurred during the assets' acquisition periods that theoretically could have been avoided (for example, by avoiding additional borrowings or by using the funds expended for the assets to repay existing borrowings) if expenditures for the assets had not been made.

13. The amount capitalized in an accounting period shall be determined by applying an interest rate(s) ("the capitalization rate") to the average amount of accumulated expenditures for the asset during the period. The capitalization rates used in an accounting period shall be based on the rates applicable to borrowings outstanding during the period. If an enterprise's financing plans associate a specific new borrowing with a qualifying asset, the enterprise may use the rate on that borrowing as the capitalization rate to be applied to that portion of the average accumulated expenditures for the asset that does not exceed the amount of that borrowing. If average accumulated expenditures for the asset exceed the amounts of specific new borrowings associated with the asset, the capitalization rate to be applied to such excess shall be a weighted average of the rates applicable to other borrowings of the enterprise.

---

[3]The term *intended use* embraces both readiness for use and readiness for sale, depending on the purpose of acquisition.
[4]See paragraph 17 for a definition of those activities for purposes of this Statement.

14. In identifying the borrowings to be included in the weighted average rate, the objective is a reasonable measure of the cost of financing acquisition of the asset in terms of the interest cost incurred that otherwise could have been avoided. Accordingly, judgment will be required to make a selection of borrowings that best accomplishes that objective in the circumstances. For example, in some circumstances, it will be appropriate to include all borrowings of the parent company and its consolidated subsidiaries; for some multinational enterprises, it may be appropriate for each foreign subsidiary to use an average of the rates applicable to its own borrowings. However, the use of judgment in determining capitalization rates shall not circumvent the requirement that a capitalization rate be applied to all capitalized expenditures for a qualifying asset to the extent that interest cost has been incurred during an accounting period.

15. The total amount of interest cost capitalized in an accounting period shall not exceed the total amount of interest cost incurred by the enterprise in that period. In consolidated financial statements, that limitation shall be applied by reference to the total amount of interest cost incurred by the parent company and consolidated subsidiaries on a consolidated basis. In any separately issued financial statements of a parent company or a consolidated subsidiary and in the financial statements (whether separately issued or not) of unconsolidated subsidiaries and other investees accounted for by the equity method, the limitation shall be applied by reference to the total amount of interest cost (including interest on intercompany borrowings) incurred by the separate entity.

16. For the purposes of this Statement, *expenditures* to which capitalization rates are to be applied are capitalized expenditures (net of progress payment collections) for the qualifying asset that have required the payment of cash, the transfer of other assets, or the incurring of a liability on which interest is recognized (in contrast to liabilities, such as trade payables, accruals, and retainages on which interest is not recognized). However, reasonable approximations of net capitalized expenditures may be used. For example, capitalized costs for an asset may be used as a reasonable approximation of capitalized expenditures unless the difference is material.

The Capitalization Period

17. The capitalization period shall begin when three conditions are present:

a. Expenditures (as defined in paragraph 16) for the asset have been made.
b. Activities that are necessary to get the asset ready for its intended use are in progress.
c. Interest cost is being incurred.

Interest capitalization shall continue as long as those three conditions are present. The term *activities* is to be construed broadly. It encompasses more than physical construction; it includes all the steps required to prepare the asset for its intended use. For example, it includes administrative and technical activities during the preconstruction stage, such as the development of plans or the process of obtaining permits from governmental authorities; it includes activities undertaken after construction has begun in order to overcome unforeseen obstacles, such as technical problems, labor disputes, or litigation. If the enterprise suspends substantially all activities related to acquisition of the asset, interest capitalization shall cease until activities are resumed. However, brief interruptions in activities, interruptions that are externally imposed, and delays that are inherent in the asset acquisition process shall not require cessation of interest capitalization.

18. The capitalization period shall end when the asset is substantially complete and ready for its intended use. Some assets are completed in parts, and each part is capable of being used independently while work is continuing on other parts. An example is a condominium. For such assets, interest capitalization shall stop on each part when it is substantially complete and ready for use. Some assets must be completed in their entirety before any part of the asset can be used. An example is a facility designed to manufacture products by sequential processes. For such assets, interest capitalization shall continue until the entire asset is substantially complete and ready for use. Some assets cannot be used effectively until a separate facility has been completed. Examples are the oil wells drilled in Alaska before completion of the pipeline. For such assets, interest capitalization shall continue until the separate facility is substantially complete and ready for use.

19. Interest capitalization shall not cease when present accounting principles require recognition of a lower value for the asset than acquisition cost; the provision required to reduce acquisition cost to such lower value shall be increased appropriately.

Disposition of the Amount Capitalized

20. Because interest cost is an integral part of the total cost of acquiring a qualifying asset, its disposition shall be the same as that of other components of asset cost.

Disclosures

21. The following information with respect to interest cost shall be disclosed in the financial statements or related notes:

a. For an accounting period in which no interest cost is capitalized, the amount of interest cost incurred and charged to expense during the period

b. For an accounting period in which some interest cost is capitalized, the total amount of interest cost incurred during the period and the amount thereof that has been capitalized.

Effective Date and Transition

22. This Statement shall be applied prospectively in fiscal years beginning after December 15, 1979. Earlier application is permitted, but not required, in financial statements for fiscal years begining before December 16, 1979 that have not been previously issued. With respect to qualifying assets in existence at the beginning of the fiscal year in which this Statement is first applied for which interest cost has not been previously capitalized, interest capitalization shall begin at that time. With respect to qualifying assets for which interest cost has been capitalized according to a method that differs from the provisions of this Statement, no adjustment shall be made to the amounts of interest cost previously capitalized, but interest cost capitalized after this Statement is first applied shall be determined according to the provisions of this Statement. With respect to assets in existence when this Statement is first applied for which interest cost has been capitalized but which do not qualify for interest capitalization according to the provisions of this Statement, no adjustments shall be made, but no additional amounts of interest cost shall be capitalized.

23. If early application is adopted in financial reports for interim periods of a fiscal year beginning before December 16, 1979, previously issued financial information for any interim periods of that fiscal year that precede the period of adoption shall be restated to give effect to the provisions of this Statement, and any subsequent presentation of that information shall be on the restated basis. This Statement shall not be applied retroactively for previously issued annual financial statements.

> **The provisions of this Statement need not be applied to immaterial items.**

This Statement was adopted by the affirmative votes of four members of the Financial Accounting Standards Board. Messrs. Block, Kirk, and Morgan dissented.

Messrs. Block, Kirk, and Morgan dissent to this Statement because, in their opinion, it is founded on a view of interest cost that does not meet the needs of users of financial statements, because it makes the requirement to capitalize interest dependent on meeting an undefined test of materiality, and because it is not evenhanded in the application of its requirements.

Messrs. Block, Kirk, and Morgan consider interest to be a cost of a different order from the costs of materials, labor, and other services in two respects. First, cash—the resource obtained by the payment of interest on debt—has unique characteristics. It is fungible. It is obtained from a variety of sources (principally, earning activities, borrowings, issuance of equity securities, and sales of economic resources), only one of which (borrowings) gives rise to a cost that is recognized in the present accounting framework. The amount of cash (or cash equivalent) given in exchange for a noncash resource provides the basis for measuring the cost of a noncash resource. Because of those characteristics of cash, interest on debt cannot be assigned or allocated to noncash resources in the same way as material, labor, and overhead costs, and association of interest on debt with a particular category of noncash resources, such as assets undergoing a construction or production process, is inherently arbitrary. Second, interest cost is the return to lenders on capital provided by them to an enterprise for a certain period. In the view of Messrs. Block, Kirk, and Morgan, interest cost, like dividends, is more directly associable with the period during which the capital giving rise to it is outstanding than with the material, labor, and other resources into which capital is converted. They acknowledge that the conversion of cash into a nonearning asset entails the sacrifice of the return that the cash could otherwise have earned, but they do not believe that a measure of that sacrifice is a proper addition to the cost of acquiring the asset. In addition, they note that, by attaching an interest cost to all expenditures for a qualifying asset, the prescribed method in this Statement in effect imputes an interest cost to any equity funds that may have been used for it.

Information about the return earned by an enterprise during an accounting period on the capital existing during that period is important to investors and creditors in assessing the enterprise's periodic performance, in assessing the risks of financial leverage, and in assessing their prospects of receiving both return on and return of their investment. Users of financial statements often compute the return earned on the total of debt and equity capital by adding interest expense to reported earnings. Interest capitalization, however, merges interest cost into the costs of assets, with the result that, when the costs of those assets are charged to income in subsequent periods, the interest cost component cannot be distinguished. Thus, the return on total capital in those periods yielded by that computation is misstated. The disclosure requirements of this Statement do not provide the information needed to correct that misstatement.

Messrs. Block, Kirk, and Morgan conclude that charging interest on debt to expense when incurred results in information in the financial statements of all companies that allows the return earned on capital during a period to be readily related on a comparable basis to the capital existing during that period. They believe that information to be more useful in making rational investment, credit, and similar decisions than that provided by including interest cost in the cost of assets.

Messrs. Block, Kirk, and Morgan also believe the discussion of materiality in this Statement will cause confusion. All FASB Statements have contained the sentence, "the provisions of this Statement need not be applied to immaterial items." Heretofore, they believe, FASB standards generally have been followed whenever there was a possibility that noncompliance would have a material effect. In their opinion, paragraph 8 and the amplification of that paragraph in paragraphs 46 and 47 could be viewed as an invitation to search for a new but undefined

test of materiality. They believe that search, with the attendant arguments between preparers and auditors and explanations to users as to why interest was not capitalized, will result in more cost, in terms of credibility as well as in a monetary sense, than would compliance with the concept of interest capitalization. They also believe that it is untimely for the Board to elaborate on materiality in a Statement on interest capitalization when an Exposure Draft, *Qualitative Characteristics: Criteria for Selecting and Evaluating Financial Accounting and Reporting Policies,* covering the subject of materiality is out for public comment.

Messrs. Block, Kirk, and Morgan believe a goal of standards is similar accounting for similar situations. In their opinion, because this Statement prescribes interest capitalization for certain inventories, even when the effect is material, and does not define those inventories clearly, this Statement will fail to achieve that goal.

Mr. Morgan also dissents because he believes that the application of this Statement may result in unfavorable economic consequences of significance, such as (a) restructuring of analysis models by financial analysts and other users of financial statements, and (b) possible changes in laws and regulations as a result of reaction to the more liberal profitability concept embodied in this Statement.

Members of the Financial Accounting Standards Board:

Donald J. Kirk,	John W. March	Robert T. Sprouse
Chairman	Robert A. Morgan	Ralph E. Walters
Frank E. Block	David Mosso	

Appendix A

BACKGROUND INFORMATION

24. Accounting for interest cost was the subject of considerable discussion in accounting literature during the first quarter of this century, but, apart from discussion in accounting textbooks and some articles in regulatory periodicals, relatively little was written on the subject during the next 40 years. The sharp rise in interest rates and increased use of borrowed funds in the last 10 years, however, resulted in renewed attention to the subject.

25. The question of capitalizing interest cost has never been resolved by an authoritative pronouncement of a standard-setting body.[5] In 1971, the

Accounting Principles Board (APB) appointed a committee to study the subject. The committee prepared a comprehensive working paper setting forth the principal issues to be considered, but the APB terminated its activities before a pronouncement could be issued. Accounting for interest cost was also among the many topics originally suggested to the FASB by its Advisory Council and others; however, it was not included on the Board's initial technical agenda.

26. In 1974, the Securities and Exchange Commission became concerned with accounting for interest cost when it noted an increase in the number of nonutility registrants that were adopting a policy of capitalizing interest as part of the cost of certain assets. On June 21, 1974, the SEC issued a release that proposed a moratorium on adoption or exten-

---

[5]In 1917, the American Institute of Accountants (as it was then known) set up a Special Committee on Interest in Relation to Cost. The Committee concluded that interest on investment should not be included in production cost. At the Institute's 1918 annual meeting, the members in attendance voted their acceptance and approval of the Committee's report. Although the vote of the Institute's membership is of historical interest, it has not been incorporated into the body of authoritative pronouncements currently in force.

sion of a policy of capitalizing interest by registrants other than public utilities that had not, as of June 21, 1974, publicly disclosed such a policy. On November 14, 1974, the moratorium was imposed by ASR No. 163, *Capitalization of Interest by Companies Other Than Public Utilities.* "Public utilities" was defined to include electric, gas, water, and telephone utilities; registrants covered by AICPA Guides *Accounting for Retail Lands Sales* and *Audits of Savings and Loan Associations* were also excluded from the moratorium. In explaining its action, the SEC noted that:

. . . it does not seem desirable to have an alternative practice grow up through selective adoption by individual companies without careful consideration of such a change by the Financial Accounting Standards Board, including the development of systematic criteria as to when, if ever, capitalization of interest is desirable.

Accordingly, the Commission concludes that companies other than electric, gas, water and telephone utilities and those companies covered by the two exceptions in the authoritative literature described above which had not, as of June 21, 1974, publicly disclosed an accounting policy of capitalizing interest costs shall not follow such a policy in financial statements filed with the Commission covering fiscal periods ending after June 21, 1974. At such time as the Financial Accounting Standards Board develops standards for accounting for interest cost, the Commission expects to reconsider this conclusion. Until such time, companies which have publicly disclosed such a policy may continue to apply it on a consistent basis but not extend it to new types of assets. Return on equity invested shall not be capitalized by companies other than electric, gas, water and telephone utilities.

The Release amended *Regulation S-X* to require the disclosure of certain information by registrants continuing to capitalize interest.

27. At its meeting on September 18, 1974, the FASB's Advisory Council agreed that this matter should be considered by the FASB, and on November 25, 1974, the Board added the project to its technical agenda. In September 1975, a task force of 16 persons from academe, the financial community, industry, and public accounting was appointed to provide counsel to the Board in preparing a Discussion Memorandum.

28. The project began with a broad scope. It was to deal not only with accounting for interest on debt, but also to explore the proposal to give comprehensive accounting recognition to an imputed interest cost for equity capital. According to proponents of that proposal, accounting should recognize such imputed interest whether it is to be capitalized or not. The total of debt interest and imputed equity interest, they believe, should be allocated to enterprise assets and operations, just as material, labor, and overhead costs are presently allocated. However, as the project proceeded, the Board came to the conclusion that, because it could involve fundamental changes in the measurement of earnings and asset values—a subject that properly belongs in the Board's conceptual framework project—the Statement resulting from the interest cost project should not deal with that proposal. Accordingly, the scope of the project was narrowed to focus on accounting alternatives that are found in practice under the present accounting model.

29. Presently, some companies account for interest on debt as an expense of the period in which it is incurred. Some companies, on the other hand, capitalize interest on debt as part of the cost of certain kinds of assets, such as construction work in progress, land held for future development, and real estate in process of development; and some companies, notably public utility companies, capitalize a cost of equity funds as well as interest on debt as part of the cost of certain assets. Thus, the basic issue to be resolved by this project was stated in the Discussion Memorandum, *Accounting for Interest Costs,* to be a determination as to which of those accounting alternatives should be applied.

30. In addition to presenting arguments for and against each of the accounting alternatives, the Discussion Memorandum identified 10 implemental issues relating to interest capitalization and three implemental issues relating to information disclosures and application of this Statement. A chapter was devoted to the proposal for comprehensive accounting recognition of imputed equity interest to assist the reader to relate the basic issue being considered to the broader aspects of the subject but, because of the Board's decision not to deal with the proposal at the present time, the related issues were described as "advisory" issues.

31. The Board issued the Discussion Memorandum on December 16, 1977 and held a public hearing in New York on April 4 and 5, 1978. The Board received 145 position papers, letters of comment, and outlines of oral presentations in response to the Discussion Memorandum, and 18 presentations were made at the public hearing.

32. An Exposure Draft of a proposed Statement on *Capitalization of Interest Cost* was issued on December 15, 1978. The Board received 269 letters of comment in response to the Exposure Draft.

Appendix B

BASIS FOR CONCLUSIONS

33. This appendix discusses factors deemed significant by members of the Board in reaching the conclusions in this Statement, including various alternatives considered and reasons for accepting some and rejecting others. Individual assenting Board members gave greater weight to some factors than to others.

Scope

34. Some respondents to the Discussion Memorandum recommended that regulated enterprises be exempt from the provisions of this Statement because the rate-making process creates a special set of circumstances and because most regulatory agencies prescribe when and how interest shall be capitalized by companies subject to their jurisdiction. The Board concluded that the applicability of this Statement should not differ from that of other FASB Statements. Moreover, the effect of the rate-making process on accounting and reporting by regulated enterprises is the subject of another project on the Board's technical agenda, and the Board concluded that this Statement should not prejudge the outcome of that project.

35. Some respondents to the Exposure Draft urged that the scope of this Statement be expanded to include other costs, such as insurance and property taxes, that are sometimes capitalized in the same circumstances as interest cost. The Board did not adopt that suggestion because special considerations apply to interest cost and expansion of the scope of this Statement at that stage would have significantly delayed its issuance. The scope of the project was considered at length during the Discussion Memorandum stage, as indicated in Appendix A.

The Accounting Alternatives

36. As indicated in Appendix A, the Board considered three basic methods of accounting for interest cost:

a. Account for interest on debt as an expense of the period in which it is incurred.
b. Capitalize interest on debt as part of the cost of an asset when prescribed conditions are met.
c. Capitalize interest on debt and imputed interest on stockholders' equity as part of the cost of an asset when prescribed conditions are met.

The Board concluded that the second of those methods should be adopted. The reasons for that conclusion are presented in paragraphs 37-57.

Interest as a Cost of Acquiring an Asset

37. The Board determined that the primary question to be addressed was whether there are any circumstances in which interest cost should be considered to be part of the historical cost of *acquiring* an asset. The focus on the historical cost of acquiring an asset followed from the Board's decision, in developing the scope of this project, that the accounting alternatives that would be considered for this Statement should be limited to those found in practice based on the present accounting model, as stated in Appendix A. In the present accounting model, nonmonetary assets are generally carried at acquisition cost or some unexpired or unamortized portion of it.[6] The cost "at which assets are carried and expenses are measured in financial accounting today usually means historical or acquisition cost because of the conventions of initially recording assets at acquisition cost and of ignoring increases in assets until they are exchanged (the realization convention)."[7]

38. Some believe that interest should be capitalized as a cost of holding assets, but, in general, in the present accounting model, costs are not added to assets subsequent to their readiness for use. Consideration of that proposal would require a comprehensive reexamination of a fundamental principle underlying present practice. One of the consequences of restricting the focus to acquisition cost was that capitalization of interest as a holding cost was rejected. Thus, earning assets and nonearning assets not undergoing the activities necessary to get them ready for use do not qualify for interest capitalization under this Statement.

39. The Board concluded that interest cost is a part of the cost of acquiring an asset if a period of time is required to carry out the activities necessary to get it ready for its intended use. In reaching this conclusion, the Board considered that the point in time at which an asset is ready for its intended use is critical in determining its acquisition cost. Assets are expected to provide future economic benefits, and the notion of expected future economic benefits implies fitness for a particular purpose. Although assets may be capable of being applied to a variety of possible uses, the use intended by the enterprise in deciding to acquire an asset has an important bearing on the nature and value of the economic benefits that it will yield.

---

[6]APB Statement No. 4, *Basic Concepts and Accounting Principles Underlying Financial Statements of Business Enterprises*, par. 163.
[7]Ibid., par. 164.

40. Some assets are ready for their intended use when purchased. Others are constructed or otherwise developed for a particular use by a series of activities whereby diverse resources are combined to form a new asset or a less valuable resource is transformed into a more valuable resource. Activities take time for their accomplishment. During the period of time required, the expenditures for the materials, labor, and other resources used in creating the asset must be financed. Financing has a cost. The cost may take the form of explicit interest on borrowed funds, or it may take the form of a return foregone on an alternative use of funds, but regardless of the form it takes, a financing cost is necessarily incurred. On the premise that the historical cost of acquiring an asset should include all costs necessarily incurred to bring it to the condition and location necessary for its intended use, the Board concluded that, in principle, the cost incurred in financing expenditures for an asset during a required construction or development period is itself a part of the asset's historical acquisition cost.

41. Some assenting Board members believe that the informational value of historical cost as an indicator of an asset's cash flow potential is also a reason for capitalizing interest cost. At the time of the decision to acquire an asset, they point out, the enterprise believes that the present value of its cash flow service potential is at least as great as the sum of the costs that will have to be incurred to acquire it. Otherwise, the enterprise presumably would not acquire the asset. Accordingly, the enterprise's commitment of cash or other resources to acquire the asset provides the best available objective evidence of an asset's cash flow service potential at the time of acquisition.

42. Those Board members believe acquisition cost provides the most reliable measure of cash flow potential when assets are self-constructed or produced as well as when they are purchased in arms-length transactions. Measuring the acquisition cost of a self-constructed or produced asset is not as simple as measuring the acquisition cost of a purchased asset, but, those Board members believe, the objective should be the same—to obtain a measure of cash flow service potential that is supported by objective evidence. For such assets, therefore, acquisition cost should include all the cost components envisioned by the enterprise as being necessary to acquire the asset. The cost of financing the asset during the period of its construction or production is one of those cost components. Since the cash flow potential of an enterprise's assets is significant information in assessing the future net cash flows of the enterprise and hence the prospective cash receipts of

investors and creditors,[8] a measure of acquisition cost that includes interest cost is likely to be more useful to investors and creditors than one that does not.

43. Some assenting Board members believe that a case could be made for allocating interest cost to all nonmonetary assets, whether being developed for use or in use. It could be argued that, since assets are *future* economic benefits, the historical cost of an asset at any point in time should be the unexpired portion of *all* costs incurred in relation to the asset prior to that time. All assets require financing, and therefore the cost of financing (interest) should be included in the historical cost of all nonmonetary assets. Those Board members, however, concluded that allocation of interest cost to assets in use or ready for use is not appropriate at present. The broad issue of dividing the long-term service potential of an asset into the services associated with periods of use would have to be reexamined before such an extension of the historical cost concept could be made. Further, allocation of interest cost to all nonmonetary assets often would have a relatively small effect on periodic earnings because the amount of interest capitalized in a period would tend to be offset by amortization of interest capitalized in prior periods. The incremental informational benefit would not be commensurate with the additional accounting and administrative costs. They concluded that interest cost should be capitalized only when it is part of the original acquisition cost of an asset.

44. The reasoning in the foregoing paragraphs would lead to the conclusion that interest should be included in the acquisition cost of all assets that are derived from a production, construction, or other time-consuming development process. However, in considering the circumstances in which interest capitalization should be required, the Board weighed the expected benefit in terms of information about enterprise resources and earnings against the expected cost of providing that information. With that consideration in mind when developing the Exposure Draft, the Board had concluded that interest should not be included in the cost of manufactured inventories that turn over relatively quickly and that interest capitalization should be confined to assets whose required development period is significant. But respondents to the Exposure Draft identified a number of problems with the proposal to delineate qualifying assets by the length of the development period. In particular, it was pointed out that a judgment about the benefit of interest capitalization in a given set of circumstances should focus on the significance of the amount of interest

---

[8]FASB Concepts Statement No. 1, *Objectives of Financial Reporting by Business Enterprises,* especially par. 37.

cost associable with an asset, and that the length of the development period is only one of the factors to be considered. Other factors include the amount of expenditures, the timing of expenditures, the capitalization rate, and the criterion by which significance is judged (e.g., periodic earnings). In addition, some respondents said that a review of their operations showed that, in any given year, a very large number of assets would meet the "significant period" test. They said that considerable costs would be involved in continually identifying assets that meet the test and the borrowings to be associated with each asset, and in additional recordkeeping.

45. Other respondents expressed concern that inventory items that require an extended maturation period (such as aging whiskeys and tobacco) would qualify for interest capitalization according to the Exposure Draft. They said that aging is not part of the production process. Moreover, such inventories are often accounted for on the last-in, first-out basis (LIFO), which would present special difficulties in concept, in implementation, and in application of "LIFO conformity" requirements for income tax purposes. Finally, it was observed that, although an individual batch of whiskey or tobacco may be held in inventory for a significant period, there is a constant flow of product into and out of inventory. Hence, the effect on earnings of capitalizing interest on maturing inventories usually would not be significant in the long run.

46. In the light of respondents' comments, the Board decided that cost/benefit considerations indicated that the circumstances in which interest capitalization is required should be more restricted than those set forth in the Exposure Draft and that those circumstances should be delineated by criteria other than the length of the required development period. The significance of the effect of interest capitalization in relation to enterprise resources and earnings is the most important consideration in assessing its benefit. The ease with which qualifying assets and related expenditures can be separately identified and the number of assets subject to interest capitalization are important factors in assessing the cost of implementation. Interest capitalization should be required only when the balance of the informational benefit and the cost of implementation is favorable. The Board judged that a favorable balance is most likely to be achieved where an asset is constructed or produced as a discrete project for which costs are separately accumulated and where construction of the asset takes considerable time, entails substantial expenditures, and hence is likely to involve a significant amount of interest cost. A favorable balance is unlikely in the case of inventory items that are routinely manufactured or otherwise produced in large quantities on a repetitive basis. Accordingly, this Statement proscribes interest capitalization on those types of inventories and provides for interest capitalization on assets that are constructed or produced as discrete projects. (Some Board members believe that another reason for not capitalizing interest on inventories generally is that, because variations presently exist in the methods of costing inventories, inclusion of interest cost would do little to improve comparability of inventory costs among enterprises.)

47. The Board recognized that, in many cases, the effect of interest capitalization and its subsequent amortization or other disposition, compared with the effect of charging it to expense when incurred, would not be material. Some assenting Board members noted that the primary factor in making materiality judgments in current practice usually is the relation to the level or trend of earnings. Accordingly, they anticipate that such a factor will be primary in making materiality judgments about the requirement for interest capitalization in accordance with this Statement.

48. Some respondents to the Discussion Memorandum and the Exposure Draft expressed the view that interest is a unique cost that cannot be allocated to cost objectives in the same way as material, labor, and overhead costs. The Board rejected that view. As explained in paragraph 51, the Board concluded that the cause-and-effect relationship between acquiring an asset and the incurrence of interest cost makes interest cost analogous to a direct cost that is readily and objectively assignable to the acquired asset. The Board believes that failure to capitalize the interest cost associated with the acquisition of qualifying assets improperly reduces reported earnings during the period of acquisition and increases reported earnings in later periods.

The Amount of Interest Cost to Be Capitalized

49. Some Board members believe that there is a valid conceptual argument for measuring the cost of financing acquisition of qualifying assets on the basis of the enterprise's cost of capital, which would include imputed interest on equity capital as well as interest on borrowed capital. Such a measure would recognize that both borrowed capital and equity capital provide funds to the enterprise and that, due to the fungible nature of cash, it is usually impossible to determine objectively the proportion of the funds expended for a particular purpose that was derived from each source. It would also recognize the interrelationship between an enterprise's cost of borrowing and its cost of equity. Some assenting Board members believe that it may be appropriate at some time in the future to consider whether the cost

of equity capital should be recognized within a framework for financial reporting that continues to be based primarily on historical cost. Accordingly, they think that the standards prescribed in this Statement should not be incompatible with that possible development. Other assenting Board members do not share that view. Nevertheless, all Board members agreed that recognition of the cost of equity capital does not conform to the present accounting framework. In the present accounting framework, the cost of a resource is generally measured by the historical exchange price paid to acquire it. However, funds are an unusual kind of resource in that, although an enterprise obtains funds from various sources, only borrowed funds give rise to a cost that can be described as a historical exchange price. Although a historical exchange transaction may occur when equity securities are issued, that transaction is not the basis generally advocated for measuring the cost of equity capital. It is generally agreed that use of equity capital entails an economic cost, but in the absence of a historical exchange price, the cost of equity capital is not reliably determinable. The Board concluded, therefore, that the cost of financing expenditures for a qualifying asset should be measured by assigning to the asset an appropriate portion of the interest cost incurred on borrowings during the period of its acquisition. (As a result of that conclusion, the issue presented in the Discussion Memorandum regarding the appropriate method of accounting for the credit corresponding to imputed interest on equity capital did not have to be addressed.)

50. The Board considered several methods of determining the amount of interest cost to be capitalized. Some suggested that the amount capitalized be limited to the interest incurred on specific borrowings associated with the qualifying asset by the enterprise. However, in the Board's view, association of sources and uses of funds is primarily subjective. If that suggestion had been adopted, the enterprise's identification of the source of the funds used for the asset would determine not only the amount of interest capitalized but also whether *any* interest is capitalized. Some suggested that interest cost be allocated to qualifying assets on a basis such as total assets or the total of debt and owner's equity. That method would be based on an assumption that funds used for all assets are obtained from borrowings and other sources proportionately. However, in many cases, it would result in an amount of capitalized interest that was unrealistically low as a measure of the economic cost of financing acquisition of the qualifying asset.

51. The Board concluded that the amount of interest cost to be capitalized should be the amount that theoretically could have been avoided during the acquisition period if expenditures for the asset had not been made. Clearly, interest cost can be avoided by repaying existing borrowings as well as by not borrowing additional funds. When an enterprise is contemplating investment in an asset, both those alternatives are available. When the decision to invest in the asset is made, those alternatives are rejected and the incurrence of interest cost during the acquisition period is a consequence of that decision. That cause-and-effect relationship between the investment in the asset and the incurrence of interest cost makes interest cost analogous to a direct cost in those circumstances. Also, the amount of interest cost that could have been avoided is one measure of the opportunity cost incurred. Admittedly, investment of funds in the asset also entails rejection of a wide range of other possible uses of funds, and therefore interest cost avoided is only one of several possible measures of opportunity cost. But it is the measure that can be recognized in the present accounting framework. (In adopting the notion of interest on borrowings as an avoidable cost, the Board does not intend that the practicability of repaying individual borrowings has to be considered.)

52. In the Exposure Draft, the Board proposed a method of associating interest on borrowings with qualifying assets that gave priority to recent borrowings. Respondents criticized that method on a number of grounds, most of which related to its complexity in practice and hence the cost of implementation. The Board concluded that the method should be simplified in order to reduce that cost. Two methods considered were (a) a general measure of the current cost of money, such as the prime rate and (b) the enterprise's incremental borrowing rate. However, the Board rejected those methods on the grounds that the historical exchange price convention requires that the interest rate used for capitalization purposes be based on rates actually being paid by the enterprise. The Board also considered a weighted average of the rates being paid on all borrowings. But it concluded that, despite the element of subjectivity, if an enterprise borrows additional funds with the intention of using them to finance a qualifying asset, the enterprise should not be prevented from using the rate on that borrowing as a capitalization rate. That rate would provide a readily determined measure of a major part of the interest cost that could have been avoided if funds had not been invested in the asset. This Statement therefore permits use of the rate(s) on specific new borrowing(s) associated with a qualifying asset and provides that an average rate shall be applied to expenditures not covered by specific new borrowings. Judgment is to be used in determining the borrowings on which the average rate is based. Thus, for example, depending on the facts and circumstances, it might be appropriate to include all borrowings of the parent company and consolidated

subsidiaries or to include only the borrowings of the corporate entity constructing the qualifying asset. It should be noted, however, that the provisions regarding capitalization rates are intended to allow an enterprise to determine a relevant measure of the cost of financing acquisition of the asset while minimizing the cost of implementing this Statement. Exclusion of borrowings from the computation of the average rate is not to circumvent the requirement to capitalize interest cost to the extent that interest cost has been incurred during a qualifying asset's acquisition period.

53. Some respondents to the Exposure Draft observed that, by attaching an interest cost to all of the expenditures for a qualifying asset, the prescribed method of determining the amount of interest capitalized in effect imputes an interest cost to any equity funds that may have been used. Board members' responses to that observation differ. Some would agree, arguing that the prescribed method uses the cost of borrowings as a surrogate measure of enterprise cost of capital. In their view, the prescribed method is an appropriate compromise between the conceptually desirable and the constraints of the present accounting framework. Other Board members do not share that view. They believe that the essence of this Statement is that interest on borrowings is a cost, which, like any other cost, is capitalizable in certain circumstances. In their view, the notion of interest on borrowings as an avoidable cost incurred as a consequence of the decision to acquire the qualifying asset supports the position that the capitalization method does not impute a cost to equity funds.

54. Some respondents to the Discussion Memorandum and to the Exposure Draft observed that limiting capitalized interest to interest on borrowings would preclude the "all-equity" enterprise from capitalizing interest, even though it incurs an economic cost of the same order as an enterprise that has borrowed funds. The Board concluded that, despite that consequence, capitalization of interest on borrowings in the circumstances specified in this Statement is preferable to the alternatives of (a) excluding interest from asset acquisition cost in all circumstances or (b) imputing interest on equity capital. In the Board's view, the fact that the present accounting framework does not recognize all economic costs should not control accounting for the costs that are recognized. Moreover, an "all-equity" enterprise is not the same as an enterprise that has borrowed funds. (Similarly, an enterprise that is making substantial expenditures for asset construction differs from one that is not.) Those who assert that comparability among enterprises would be greater if all interest cost were expensed would create an illusion of comparability that may disguise the differences in facts.

55. Some respondents disagreed with the conclusion in the Exposure Draft that the total amount of interest cost available for capitalization should be the amount recognized in the present accounting framework and hence include interest cost imputed on certain types of payables in accordance with Opinion 21 and interest cost related to a capital lease determined in accordance with Statement 13. In their view, interest cost determined in accordance with Opinion 21 and Statement 13 clearly relates to transactions other than the acquisition of qualifying assets. However, as previously indicated, the Board's conclusions in this Statement rest on an assumption that association of sources and uses of funds is primarily subjective. The Board believes that, just as association of a particular borrowing with a qualifying asset is an insufficiently objective basis for determining whether any interest cost should be capitalized, the form of financing transactions covered by Opinion 21 and Statement 13 is an inadequate basis for excluding interest cost recognized on those transactions from the pool of interest cost available for capitalization.

56. The Board concluded that, in determining the expenditures with which interest cost is associated, amounts corresponding to liabilities on which interest cost is not recognized (such as trade payables, accruals, and retainages) should be excluded. The Board does not intend that enterprises try to determine precisely when those liabilities are liquidated. Capitalized costs may be used as a reasonable approximation of expenditures unless the difference is material.

57. One of the issues raised in the Discussion Memorandum was whether capitalized interest should be compounded. The Board concluded that compounding is conceptually consistent with its conclusion that interest on expenditures for the asset is a cost of acquiring the asset. Admittedly, some portion of the interest incurred during an accounting period may be unpaid at the end of the period, but that complication usually may be ignored to simplify practical application.

The Capitalization Period

58. The capitalization period is determined by the definition of the circumstances in which interest is capitalizable. Essentially, the capitalization period covers the duration of the activities required to get the asset ready for its intended use, provided that expenditures for the asset have been made and interest cost is being incurred. Interest capitalization continues as long as those activities and the incurrence of interest cost continue. The capitalization period ends when the asset is substantially complete and ready for its intended use. The words "substantially complete" are used to prohibit continuation of

interest capitalization in situations in which completion of the asset is intentionally delayed. For example, it is customary for a condominium developer to defer installation of certain fixtures and fittings until units are sold, so that buyers may choose the types and colors they want. An intentional delay of that kind is related more to marketing of the asset than to the exigencies of the asset acquisition process. Similarly, interest is not to be capitalized during periods when the enterprise intentionally defers or suspends activities related to the asset. Interest cost incurred during such periods is a holding cost, not an acquisition cost. However, delays that are inherent in the asset acquisition process and interruptions in activities that are imposed by external forces are unavoidable in acquiring the asset and as such do not call for a cessation of interest capitalization. Brief interruptions may be disregarded on immateriality grounds.

59. Some respondents to the Exposure Draft asked for confirmation that interest capitalization is not restricted to times when physical change is taking place. Most cited the example of land development. Many activities, they pointed out, must be undertaken before work on the land itself can begin. In response to those requests, an explanation that the term *activities* is to be construed broadly in this context has been included in paragraph 17.

60. Some respondents to the Exposure Draft asked for clarification concerning the end of interest capitalization when an asset is completed in parts and the individual parts are capable of being used while work continues on other parts. Paragraph 18 now explains that interest capitalization stops on each part as it is completed.

61. Some respondents took issue with the conclusion in Appendix C to the Exposure Draft that interest capitalization on mineral interests should stop when the first well capable of producing oil or gas is completed. They argued that the oil or gas producing system is not ready for its intended use until the means of transporting the oil or gas from the well (e.g., a pipeline) is in place. The Board agreed, and that conclusion has been added to paragraph 18.

62. Some respondents to the Discussion Memorandum expressed the view that capitalization of interest for an asset intended for sale should end when the accumulated costs of the asset equal its net realizable value. The Board concluded that that view is inconsistent with the conclusion that interest is a cost of acquiring the asset. Capitalization of material, labor, and overhead costs does not end

when a net realizable value limit is reached; interest cost should not be treated differently. The present accounting requirements for recognizing a lower asset value than acquisition cost should apply when total asset cost includes capitalized interest and when it does not.

Disposition of Capitalized Interest

63. Some companies that presently capitalize interest amortize it over a shorter period than the life of the related asset. The Board believes that the conclusion that interest is part of the cost of acquiring a qualifying asset requires that capitalized interest should not be accounted for differently from other components of asset cost.

Disclosures

64. Disclosure of the total amount of interest cost incurred in an accounting period is required because lenders, security analysts, and others may wish to know that amount in order to compute certain fixed-charge coverage ratios, etc. The amount of interest cost incurred and capitalized during a period is required because that amount is not included in the determination of earnings.

65. The Board concluded that the other possible disclosures listed in the Discussion Memorandum were not required. Descriptions of the method of accounting for interest, the circumstances in which interest is capitalized, and the method of determining the amount of interest capitalized are unnecessary because those matters are dealt with in this Statement. Information about amortization of capitalized interest is unnecessary; such disclosure is not required for other components of asset cost.

66. Some respondents to the Discussion Memorandum suggested that the net effect on periodic earnings of capitalizing interest as opposed to charging it to expense should be disclosed. The Board decided that such disclosure was unnecessary once accounting alternatives had been eliminated.

Effective Date and Transition

67. The Board concluded that this Statement should be applied prospectively. Inevitably, prospective application of a Statement entails some impairment of comparability among enterprises' financial statements during the periods immediately following its adoption. Retroactive application in this instance, however, would require greater accounting effort than would be justified by the resulting informational benefits.

Statement of Financial Accounting Standards No. 35
Accounting and Reporting by Defined Benefit
Pension Plans

STATUS

Issued: March 1980

Effective Date: For plan years beginning after December 15, 1980 (but deferred indefinitely by
FAS 75 for plans sponsored by state or local governments)

Affects: No other pronouncements

Affected by: Paragraph 11 amended by FAS 110
Paragraph 12 superseded by FAS 110
Paragraph 30 amended by FAS 59 and FAS 75
Footnote 6 superseded by FAS 110

SUMMARY

Standards

This Statement establishes standards of financial accounting and reporting for the annual financial statements of a defined benefit pension plan (*plan*). It applies both to plans in the private sector and to plans of state and local governmental units. It does not require the preparation, distribution, or attestation of financial statements for any plan.

The primary objective of a plan's financial statements is to provide financial information that is useful in assessing the plan's present and future ability to pay benefits when due. To accomplish that objective, the financial statements will include information regarding (a) the net assets available for benefits as of the end of the plan year, (b) the changes in net assets during the plan year, (c) the actuarial present value of accumulated plan benefits as of either the beginning or end of the plan year, and (d) the effects, if significant, of certain factors affecting the year-to-year change in the actuarial present value of accumulated plan benefits. If the date as of which the benefit information ((c) above) is presented (the *benefit information date*) is the beginning of the year, additional information is required regarding both the net assets available for benefits as of that date and the changes in net assets during the preceding year. Flexibility in the manner of presenting benefit information and changes therein (items (c) and (d) above) is permitted. Either or both of those categories of information may be presented on the face of one or more financial statements or in accompanying notes.

Information regarding net assets is to be prepared on the accrual basis of accounting. Plan investments (excluding contracts with insurance companies) are to be presented at fair value. Contracts with insurance companies are to be presented the same way as in the plan's annual report to certain governmental agencies pursuant to the Employee Retirement Income Security Act of 1974 (*ERISA*). Plans not subject to ERISA are to account for their contracts with insurance companies as though they also filed that annual report.

The primary information regarding participants' accumulated plan benefits reported in plan financial statements will be their actuarial present value. This Statement defines participants' accumulated plan benefits as those future benefit payments that are attributable under the plan's provisions to employees' service rendered to the benefit information date. Their measurement is primarily based on employees' history of pay and service and other appropriate factors as of that date. Future salary changes are not considered. Future years of service are considered only in determining employees' expected eligibility for particular types of benefits, for example, early retirement, death, and disability benefits. To measure their actuarial present value, assumptions are used to adjust those accumulated plan benefits to reflect the time value of money (through discounts for interest) and the probability of payment (by means of decrements such as for death, disability, withdrawal, or retirement) between the benefit information date and the expected date of payment. An assumption of an ongoing plan underlies those assumptions.

The use of averages and other methods of approximation consistent with recommended actuarial practice is permitted, provided the results are substantially the same as those contemplated by this Statement. Such simplified techniques may be particularly useful for plans sponsored by small employers.

Plan financial statements are required to include certain information about (a) the plan, (b) the results of transactions and other events that affect the information presented regarding net assets and participants' benefits, and (c) other factors necessary for users to understand the information provided.

This Statement is effective for plan years beginning after December 15, 1980.

Basis for Conclusions

In developing the foregoing standards, the Board first identified both the users of plan financial statements and the objectives of those statements. The Board believes that the content of plan financial statements should focus on the needs of participants because pension plans exist primarily for their benefit. However, plan financial statements should also be useful to others who either advise or represent participants, are present or potential investors or creditors of the employer(s), are responsible for funding the plan, or for other reasons have a derived or indirect interest in the plan's financial status.

Because employees render service long before they receive the benefits to which they are entitled as a result of that service, they are concerned with whether the plan will be able to pay their future benefits. Therefore, the Board concluded that the primary objective of plan financial statements should be to provide financial information that is useful in assessing the plan's present and future ability to pay benefits when due. However, plan financial statements do not provide all the information necessary for that assessment. They should be used in combination with other pertinent information, including information about the financial condition of the employer(s) and, for plans subject to ERISA, the guaranty of the Pension Benefit Guaranty Corporation. Also, financial statements for several plan years can provide information more useful in assessing the plan's future ability to pay benefits than can the financial statements for a single plan year.

Because a plan's net assets are the existing means by which it may provide benefits, information about them (the *net asset information*) is considered essential in assessing a plan's ability to pay benefits when due. The Board believes that measuring a plan's investments (other than contracts with insurance companies) at fair value will provide the most relevant information about those assets consistent with the primary objective of plan financial statements.

Insurance companies offer plans a wide variety of contracts. Because of their complexity, several difficult issues arise in recognizing and measuring the elements of such contracts that constitute plan assets. The Board decided that sufficient information was not available at this time to enable it to reach definitive conclusions about certain conceptual and implementation issues. It therefore chose the practical solution of requiring contracts with insurance companies to be reported in plan financial statements in the same way they are reported (for ERISA plans) or would have been reported (for non-ERISA plans) in the annual report required by ERISA to be filed with certain governmental agencies. That approach may result in such contracts being presented at other than fair value.

To be useful in assessing a plan's present and future ability to pay benefits when due, plan financial statements must also present information about the benefits to be paid. The Board believes that information (the *benefit information*) should relate to the benefits reasonably expected to be paid in exchange for employees' service to the benefit information date. Because the Board did not deem it essential at this time to resolve the issue of the accounting nature of the benefit information, this Statement does not prescribe its location in the financial statements.

The initial Exposure Draft required that both the benefit and net asset information be determined as of the same date. Thus, if the plan's annual financial statements were as of the end of the plan year, end-of-year benefit information was required. A number of respondents expressed the view that determination of end-of-year benefit information on a timely basis was not practical and would cause increased actuarial fees. They indicated that most actuarial valuations are performed during the year using data as of the beginning of the year. Changing that practice at this time might create significant timing problems in terms of scheduling the actuaries' workload and, in some cases, obtaining necessary end-of-year data.

The Board concluded that the perceived costs of requiring end-of-year benefit information at this time may exceed the potential benefits of such information. Therefore, this Statement provides for the presentation of benefit information as of either the beginning or end of the year. However, the Board continues to believe that presenting both net asset and benefit information as of the same date is necessary to present the financial status of the plan. Therefore, if benefit information is presented as of the beginning of the year, this Statement requires that net asset information also be presented as of that date.

The information about a plan's ability to pay benefits when due that is provided by its financial statements is affected whenever transactions and other events affect the net asset or benefit information presented in those statements. Normally, a plan's ability to pay participants' benefits does not remain constant. Therefore, users of the financial statements are concerned with assessing the plan's ability to pay participants' benefits not only as of a point in time but also on a continuing basis. To facilitate that latter assessment, users need to know the reasons for changes in the net asset and benefit information reported in successive financial statements. Therefore, the Board concluded that plan financial statements should include (a) information regarding the year-to-year change in the net assets available for benefits and (b) disclosure of the effects, if significant, of certain factors affecting the year-to-year change in the benefit information.

If the benefit information date is the beginning of the year, the required disclosure regarding the year-to-year change in the benefit information will relate to the preceding year. Presenting information regarding changes in both the net asset and benefit information for the same period is necessary to present the changes in the plan's financial status for that period. Therefore, if the benefit information date is the beginning of the year, information regarding the changes in net assets during the preceding year is also required.

Determination of the net asset and benefit information may be affected by estimates and judgment. The Board believes users can better evaluate that information if the underlying assumptions and methods are disclosed. In addition, certain explanations may be needed for users to understand the information provided by a plan's financial statements. Therefore, this Statement requires certain disclosures regarding the plan, the effects of certain transactions and events, and other factors necessary for users to understand the information provided.

Statement of Financial Accounting Standards No. 35
Accounting and Reporting by Defined Benefit Pension Plans

CONTENTS

INTRODUCTION

1. This Statement establishes standards of financial accounting and reporting for the annual financial statements of a **defined benefit pension plan (pension plan** or **plan**).* Plans covered are those that principally provide **pension benefits** but may also provide **benefits** on death, disability, or termination of employment.

2. This Statement applies to an ongoing plan that provides pension benefits for the **employees** of one or more employers, including state and local governments, or for the members of a trade or other employee association. Such a plan may have no intermediary **funding agency** or it may be financed through one or more trust funds, one or more contracts with insurance companies, or a combination thereof. This Statement applies to plans that are subject to the provisions of the Employee Retirement Income Security Act of 1974 (**ERISA** or the **Act**) as well as to those that are not. It is not intended to apply to a plan that is expected to be terminated, nor to a government-sponsored social security plan. This Statement does not require the preparation, distribution, or attestation of any plan's financial statements (paragraph 51).

3. Standards of financial accounting and reporting for defined benefit pension plans are presented in

paragraphs 4-30. Background information for this Statement is presented in Appendix A. The basis for the Board's conclusions, as well as alternatives considered and reasons for their rejection, are discussed in Appendix B. Illustrations of certain applications of the requirements of this Statement appear in Appendixes D and E.

STANDARDS OF FINANCIAL ACCOUNTING AND REPORTING

Existing Generally Accepted Accounting Principles

4. Existing generally accepted accounting principles other than those discussed in this Statement may apply to the financial statements of defined benefit pension plans. The financial accounting standards discussed in this Statement are those of particular importance to pension plans or that differ from existing generally accepted accounting principles for other types of entities.

Primary Objective of Plan Financial Statements

5. The primary objective of a pension plan's financial statements is to provide financial information that is useful in assessing the plan's present and future ability to pay benefits when due.[1] To accomplish that objective, a plan's financial statements

---

*Terms defined in the Glossary (Appendix C) are in boldface type the first time they appear in this Statement.

[1]The Board recognizes that (a) information in addition to that contained in a plan's financial statements is needed in assessing the plan's present and future ability to pay benefits when due and (b) financial statements for several plan years can provide information more useful in assessing the plan's future ability to pay benefits than can the financial statements for a single plan year (paragraphs 58-63).

should provide information about (a) plan resources and how the stewardship responsibility for those resources has been discharged, (b) the **accumulated plan benefits** of **participants**, (c) the results of transactions and events that affect the information regarding those resources and benefits, and (d) other factors necessary for users to understand the information provided.

Financial Statements

6. The annual financial statements of a plan shall include:

a. A statement that includes information regarding the **net assets available for benefits** as of the end of the plan year
b. A statement that includes information regarding the changes during the year in the net assets available for benefits
c. Information regarding the **actuarial present value of accumulated plan benefits** as of either the beginning[2] or end of the plan year
d. Information regarding the effects, if significant, of certain factors affecting the year-to-year change in the actuarial present value of accumulated plan benefits.

7. The primary objective set forth in paragraph 5 is satisfied only if (a) information regarding both the net assets available for benefits and the actuarial present value of accumulated plan benefits is presented as of the same date and (b) information regarding both the changes in net assets available for benefits and the changes in the actuarial present value of accumulated plan benefits is presented for the same period. Therefore, if the **benefit information date** pursuant to paragraph 6(c) is the beginning of the year, a statement that includes information regarding the net assets available for benefits as of that date and a statement that includes information regarding the changes during the preceding year in the net assets available for benefits shall also be presented. Use of an end-of-year benefit information date is considered preferable. Plans are encouraged to develop procedures to enable them to use that date (paragraph 29).

8. The Board believes it is desirable to allow certain flexibility in presenting the information regarding the actuarial present value of accumulated plan benefits and the year-to-year changes therein.

Therefore, either or both of those categories of information may be presented on the face of one or more financial statements or in notes thereto. Regardless of the format selected, each category of information shall be presented in its entirety in the same location. If a statement format is selected for either category, a separate statement may be used to present that information or, provided the information is as of the same date or for the same period, that information may be presented together with information regarding the net assets available for benefits and the year-to-year changes therein.

Net Assets Available for Benefits

9. The accrual basis of accounting[3] shall be used in preparing information regarding the net assets available for benefits. The information shall be presented in such reasonable detail as is necessary to identify the plan's resources that are available for benefits.

Contributions Receivable

10. Contributions receivable are the amounts due as of the **reporting date** to the plan from the employer(s), participants, and other sources of funding (for example, state subsidies or federal grants—which shall be separately identified). Amounts due include those pursuant to formal commitments as well as legal or contractual requirements. With respect to an employer's contributions, evidence of a formal commitment may include (a) a resolution by the employer's governing body approving a specified contribution, (b) a consistent pattern of making payments after the plan's year-end pursuant to an established **funding policy** that attributes such subsequent payments to the preceding plan year, (c) a deduction of a contribution for federal tax purposes for periods ending on or before the reporting date, or (d) the employer's recognition as of the reporting date of a contribution payable to the plan.[4]

Investments

11. Plan investments, whether equity or debt securities, real estate, or other (excluding contracts with insurance companies) shall be presented at their fair value at the reporting date. The fair value of an investment is the amount that the plan could reasonably expect to receive for it in a current sale between a willing buyer and a willing seller, that is, other than

---

[2]Financial information presented as of the beginning of the year shall be the amounts as of the end of the preceding year.

[3]The accrual basis requires that purchases and sales of securities be recorded on a trade-date basis. However, if the settlement date is after the reporting date and (a) the fair value of securities purchased or sold just before the reporting date does not change significantly from the trade date to the reporting date, and (b) the purchases or sales do not significantly affect the composition of the plan's assets available for benefits, accounting on a settlement-date basis for such sales and purchases is acceptable.

[4]The existence of accrued pension costs does not, by itself, provide sufficient support for recognition of a contribution receivable (paragraph 92).

in a forced or liquidation sale. Fair value shall be measured by the market price if there is an active market for the investment. If there is not an active market for an investment but there is such a market for similar investments, selling prices in that market may be helpful in estimating fair value. If a market price is not available, a forecast of expected cash flows may aid in estimating fair value, provided the expected cash flows are discounted at a rate commensurate with the risk involved.[5]

12. Contracts with insurance companies shall be presented in the same manner as that contained in the annual report filed by the plan with certain governmental agencies pursuant to ERISA.[6] A plan not subject to ERISA shall similarly present its contracts with insurance companies, that is, as if the plan were subject to the reporting requirements of ERISA.

13. Information regarding a plan's investments shall be presented in enough detail to identify the types of investments and shall indicate whether reported fair values have been measured by quoted prices in an active market or are fair values otherwise determined. (Paragraphs 28(g) and 28(h) require certain additional disclosures related to investments.)

Operating Assets

14. Plan assets used in plan operations (for example, buildings, equipment, furniture and fixtures, and leasehold improvements) shall be presented at cost less accumulated depreciation or amortization.

Changes in Net Assets Available for Benefits

15. Information regarding changes in net assets available for benefits shall be presented in enough detail to identify the significant changes during the year. Minimum disclosure shall include:

a. The net appreciation (depreciation)[7] in fair value for each significant class of investments, segregated between investments whose fair values have been measured by quoted prices in an active market and those whose fair values have been otherwise determined

b. Investment income (exclusive of (a) above)

c. Contributions from the employer(s), segregated between cash and noncash contributions[8]

d. Contributions from participants, including those transmitted by the **sponsor**

e. Contributions from other identified sources (for example, state subsidies or federal grants)

f. Benefits paid to participants

g. Payments to insurance companies to purchase contracts that are excluded from plan assets[9]

h. Administrative expenses.

Actuarial Present Value of Accumulated Plan Benefits

16. Accumulated plan benefits are those future benefit payments that are attributable under the plan's provisions to employees' **service** rendered to the benefit information date. Accumulated plan benefits comprise benefits expected to be paid to (a) retired or terminated employees or their beneficiaries, (b) beneficiaries of deceased employees, and (c) present employees or their beneficiaries.

17. To the extent possible, plan provisions shall apply in measuring accumulated plan benefits. In some plans, benefits are a specified amount for each year of service. Even if a plan does not specify a benefit for each year of service, another of its provisions (for example, a provision applicable to terminated employees or to termination of the plan—if independent of funding patterns) may indicate how to measure accumulated plan benefits. If the benefit for each year of service is not stated by or clearly determinable from the provisions of the plan, the benefit shall be considered to accumulate in proportion to (a) the ratio of the number of years of service completed to the benefit information date to the number that will have been completed when the benefit will first be fully vested, if the type of benefit is includable in **vested benefits** (for example, a supplemental early retirement benefit that is a vested benefit after a stated number of years of service), or (b) the ratio of completed years of service to projected years of service upon anticipated separation from covered employment, if the type of benefit is not includable in vested benefits (for example, a death or disability benefit that is payable only if death or disability occurs during active service).

18. In measuring accumulated plan benefits, the following shall apply:

a. Except as indicated in (b) and (c) below, accumu-

---

[5]For an indication of factors to be considered in determining the discount rate, see paragraphs 13 and 14 of APB Opinion No. 21, *Interest on Receivables and Payables*. If significant, the fair value of an investment shall reflect the brokerage commissions and other costs normally incurred in a sale.

[6]For 1979 plan years, the pertinent governmental reporting requirements relate to item 13 of either Form 5500 or Form 5500-C.

[7]Realized gains and losses on investments that were both bought and sold during the year shall be included.

[8]A noncash contribution shall be recorded at fair value. The nature of noncash contributions shall be described, either parenthetically or in a note.

[9]Paragraph 28(e) requires disclosure of the plan's dividend income related to excluded contracts and permits that income to be netted against item (g).

lated plan benefits shall be based on employees' history of pay and service and other appropriate factors as of the benefit information date.[10]

b. Projected years of service shall be a factor only in determining employees' expected eligibility for particular benefits, such as:

   i. Increased benefits that are granted provided a specified number of years of service are rendered (for example, a pension benefit that is increased from $9 per month to $10 per month for each year of service if 20 or more years of service are rendered)

   ii. Early retirement benefits

   iii. Death benefits

   iv. Disability benefits.

c. Automatic benefit increases specified by the plan (for example, automatic cost-of-living increases) that are expected to occur after the benefit information date shall be recognized.

d. Benefits to be provided by means of contracts excluded from plan assets for which payments to the insurance company have been made shall be excluded.

e. Plan amendments adopted after the benefit information date shall not be recognized.

f. If it is necessary to take future compensation into account in the determination of Social Security benefits, employees' compensation as of the benefit information date shall be assumed to remain unchanged during their assumed future service. Increases in the wage base or benefit level pursuant to either the existing Social Security law or possible future amendments of the law shall not be recognized.

19. The actuarial present value of accumulated plan benefits is that amount as of the benefit information date that results from applying actuarial assumptions to the benefit amounts determined pursuant to paragraphs 16-18, with the actuarial assumptions being used to adjust those amounts to reflect the time value of money (through discounts for interest) and the probability of payment (by means of decrements such as for death, disability, withdrawal, or retirement) between the benefit information date and the expected date of payment.

20. An assumption of an ongoing plan shall underlie the other assumptions used in determining the actuarial present value of accumulated plan benefits. Every other significant assumption used in that determination and disclosed pursuant to paragraph 27(b) shall reflect the best estimate of the plan's future experience solely with respect to that individual assumption. As to certain assumptions, the following shall apply:

a. Assumed rates of return shall reflect the expected rates of return during the periods for which payment of benefits is deferred and shall be consistent with returns realistically achievable on the types of assets held by the plan and the plan's investment policy. To the extent that assumed rates of return are based on values of existing plan assets, the values used in determining assumed rates of return shall be the values presented in the plan's financial statements pursuant to the requirements of this Statement.

b. Expected rates of inflation assumed in estimating automatic cost-of-living adjustments shall be consistent with the assumed rates of return.

c. Administrative expenses expected to be paid by the plan (not those paid by the sponsor) that are associated with providing accumulated plan benefits shall be reflected either by appropriately adjusting the assumed rates of return or by assigning those expenses to future periods and discounting them to the benefit information date. If the former method is used, the adjustment of the assumed rates of return shall be separately disclosed (paragraph 27(b)).

21. In selecting certain assumptions to be used in determining the actuarial present value of accumulated plan benefits, an acceptable alternative to that discussed in paragraph 20 is to use those assumptions that are inherent in the estimated cost at the benefit information date to obtain a contract with an insurance company to provide participants with their accumulated plan benefits. Those other assumptions that are necessary but are not inherent in that estimated cost shall be selected pursuant to the requirements in paragraph 20.

Presentation of the Actuarial Present Value of Accumulated Plan Benefits

22. The total actuarial present value of accumulated plan benefits as of the benefit information date shall be segmented into at least the following categories:

a. Vested benefits of participants currently receiving payments

b. Other vested benefits

c. Nonvested benefits.

Category (a) shall include those benefits due and payable as of the benefit information date. Present employees' accumulated contributions as of the benefit information date (including interest, if any) shall be disclosed. If interest has been credited on employees' contributions, the rate(s) shall be disclosed.

---

[10]An example of the application of paragraphs 18(a) and 18(b) appears in Appendix E.

> **The provisions of this Statement need
> not be applied to immaterial items.**

This Statement was adopted by the affirmative votes of four members of the Financial Accounting Standards Board. Messrs. March, Morgan, and Walters dissented.

Messrs. March, Morgan, and Walters dissent to this Statement because, in their opinion, it establishes an unattainable objective for a plan's financial statements, it improperly includes what they consider to be actuarial statements within the financial statements rather than as supplementary information outside the financial statements, and it prescribes detailed reporting beyond reasonable usefulness to plan participants. They share an overriding concern that, taken as a whole, these provisions invite comparison of items that do not possess enough common properties to be directly comparable and lend an unjustified aura of reliability to estimates of the future.

They believe that the stated primary objective of a pension plan's financial statements, ". . . to provide financial information that is useful in assessing the plan's *present* and *future* ability to pay benefits when due," promises more than can be achieved and will foster unreasonable expectations. In most cases, the plan's ability to pay benefits will depend primarily on the continuing support and financial health of the plan sponsor far into the future. In their view, users are not well served by an objective and a presentation that suggest that a *spot comparison* of the estimated present value of benefits to the current market valuation of assets held is a relevant or reliable indicator of a plan's ability to pay benefits when due. The benefit information is a product of estimates of events and conditions and payments over decades; the asset information necessarily relates to specific assets existing and values prevailing at a specific moment, often emphasizing temporary or short-run conditions. The trend *over time* of accumulated assets and benefits payable may indicate funding progress and the historical record of the investment policy and actuarial assumptions, but even that has limited value in assessing ability to make remote benefit payments.

They believe the primary objective of a pension plan's financial reporting should be to provide financial information about resources and financial activities of the plan that is useful in assessing the stewardship of the plan's administrators; an appropriate supplemental objective is to provide information about plan benefits and the trends *over time* in the accumulation of resources and benefits.

They believe the total effect of the following factors creates a powerful presumption that the information regarding the actuarial present value of accumulated plan benefits, changes in such actuarial values, and related disclosures (paragraphs 6(c), 6(d), 7, 8, and 16-26) should not be designated as part of the financial statements of the plan:

1. The essence of the information presented is based on estimates of probabilities, conditions, and events that may happen far into the future, vulnerable to all kinds of uncertainties and less reliable than financial statement measurements in general. Although actuarial estimates and judgments are often used in accounting measurements, they are only a part of an accounting presentation and not, as here, the totality of the information content.

2. Accumulated benefits have not been identified as liabilities or other elements of financial statements of pension plans. Trustees and plan administrators are responsible for stewardship of the funds entrusted to them and payment of benefits in compliance with the plan, but only to the extent of those funds.

3. Independent auditors are not trained to perform a substantive audit (that is, make an expert challenge) of the actuarial findings.

4. Congress, in adopting ERISA, identified the financial statements of a plan (Statements of Assets and Liabilities and Changes in Net Assets Available for Plan Benefits) to be covered by the opinion of an independent accountant as separate and distinct from actuarial statements to be covered by the opinion of an enrolled actuary.

They conclude that this presumption has not been overcome and disagree with the Board's determination that what are effectively actuarial statements are to be included within the financial statements. This is not just a theoretical distinction. It has potentially significant cost/benefit implications if the financial statements are audited. If the actuarial data are considered to be within financial statements, there is a presumption that they will be covered by the report of the independent auditor. In their view, the benefits of an auditor's opinion on these actuarial statements are doubtful, but the costs of the audit are real. They believe that a plan's financial report should consist of financial statements accompanied by the report of the independent auditor and actuarial information accompanied by the report of the actuary, if expert opinions are desired.

Messrs. March, Morgan, and Walters believe that the active cooperation between the Board and the actuarial profession in this project is a significant milestone toward more consistent reporting of actuarial data. They believe, however, that the Board has dealt in this Statement with choices of details and refinements in actuarial determinations (paragraphs 17-21) that should be left to the actuarial profession as long as their guidelines produce information relevant to the objectives of financial reporting.

They also are not convinced that plan participants need the detailed disclosures prescribed by this Statement, particularly as to actuarial methods, changes, and assumptions (paragraph 27) and as to the matters in paragraph 28. Users wishing such details for large private plans can obtain them from the annual reports filed with the Department of Labor which are available to participants on request. It should be sufficient to provide summarized benefit information as of the most recent actuarial valuation for plans with fewer than 100 participants, rather than to require an update for each annual report. They understand that less statistical reliability can be expected from actuarial data for these small plans.

Members of the Financial Accounting Standards Board:

Donald J. Kirk,
Chairman
Frank E. Block

John W. March
Robert A. Morgan
David Mosso

Robert T. Sprouse
Ralph E. Walters

Appendix A

BACKGROUND INFORMATION

31. Financial reporting by defined benefit pension plans in the private sector was generally quite limited before 1976. A few companies included a report of their pension plans in their annual reports to stockholders. Those financial statements that were distributed to participants were frequently limited to summary statements of assets and often did not purport to conform with generally accepted accounting principles.

32. The Employee Retirement Income Security Act of 1974 established minimum standards for participation, vesting, and funding for employee benefit plans of private enterprises. It also requires annual reporting of certain information to particular governmental agencies and summarized information to plan participants. For many plans, the reporting requirements include financial statements prepared in conformity with generally accepted accounting principles.

33. The House Pension Task Force Report indicates that many public employee retirement systems do not report important financial and actuarial information to participants, public officials, and taxpayers.[18] Although ERISA does not apply to those plans, interest in financial information about them has increased since enactment of ERISA, and proposed legislation[19] to establish reporting requirements for them was introduced during the 1978 and 1980 congressional sessions.

34. Prior to this Statement, no authoritative accounting pronouncement issued by the FASB or its predecessor bodies addressed financial accounting and reporting standards specifically for defined benefit pension plans.

35. In recognition of the broadened financial reporting requirements for most employee benefit plans, the significance of both the assets held by pension plans and the benefits accumulated by participants in those plans, and the diversity of existing accounting and reporting practices of employee benefit plans, the FASB placed on its technical agenda in November 1974 a project on accounting and reporting for employee benefit plans.

36. A 10-member task force, composed of individuals from academe, the financial community, government, industry, organized labor, and the public accounting and actuarial professions, was appointed in February 1975 to counsel the Board in preparing a Discussion Memorandum analyzing issues related to the project.

37. In preparing the Discussion Memorandum, the FASB primarily relied on the published research studies and articles that are cited in that document. The additional research undertaken in connection with this project included (a) a review of relevant literature, (b) an examination of selected published annual reports of employee benefit plans and trust funds, and annual reports to stockholders of corporations that included information about pension plans, (c) interviews with actuaries and employee benefit consultants, and (d) analysis of the provisions of ERISA and its related regulations.

38. The Board issued the Discussion Memorandum on October 6, 1975 and held a public hearing on February 4 and 5, 1976. The Board received 104 position papers, letters of comment, and outlines of

---

[18]U.S. Government Printing Office, *House of Representatives Committee on Education and Labor Pension Task Force Report on Public Employee Retirement Systems* (Washington, D.C., 1978), p. 3.

[19]H.R. 14138, *Public Employee Retirement Income Security Act of 1978*, September 20, 1978, and H.R. 6525, *Public Employee's Retirement Income Security Act of 1980*, February 13, 1980.

oral presentations in response to the Discussion Memorandum, and 23 presentations were made at the public hearing.

39. In its deliberations following the public hearing, the Board concluded for the reason expressed in paragraph 71 that the scope of the initial Statement of Financial Accounting Standards resulting from the project should be limited to financial accounting and reporting by defined benefit pension plans.

40. On April 14, 1977, an FASB Exposure Draft, *Accounting and Reporting by Defined Benefit Pension Plans*, was issued that, if adopted, would have been effective for plan years beginning on or after December 15, 1977. Approximately 700 letters of comment were received in response to that Exposure Draft. The Board announced on September 30, 1977 that because of the need to analyze the large number of responses and the complexity of the issues involved it would be unable to issue a final Statement in 1977.

41. Throughout the project, the FASB worked with the United States Department of Labor, the actuarial profession, and others in an attempt to avoid conflicts, duplication, and confusion in providing meaningful financial reporting. In conjunction with that cooperative effort, the Board decided in the first quarter of 1979 to expose to task force members and certain other interested parties a staff draft of standards that incorporated previously announced tentative conclusions. The Board considered the comments received on that draft. It then concluded that a revised Exposure Draft should be issued for public comment because of the significant changes that had been made to the proposed standards in the April 14, 1977 Exposure Draft.

42. A revised Exposure Draft, *Accounting and Reporting by Defined Benefit Pension Plans*, was issued on July 9, 1979. The Board received approximately 300 letters of comment in response to that Exposure Draft.

Appendix B

BASIS FOR CONCLUSIONS

CONTENTS

Appendix B

BASIS FOR CONCLUSIONS

43. This appendix discusses factors deemed significant by members of the Board in reaching the conclusions in this Statement, including various alternatives considered and reasons for accepting some and rejecting others. Individual Board members gave greater weight to some factors than to others.

REPORTING ENTITY

44. Deciding whether the plan or **pension fund** is the reporting entity is related to the objectives of the financial statements, and many respondents[20] who addressed the issue of the reporting entity did so in that context. Thus, the views expressed in paragraphs 45-47 should be considered together with those expressed in paragraphs 48-69.

45. Arguments presented by proponents of the plan as the reporting entity include the view that a plan has many attributes of a legal entity. It gives rise to participants' rights, plan resources, and employer obligations. That view is reinforced for plans subject to ERISA (**ERISA plans**) by certain sections of

the Act.[21] Further, and more importantly, to report only pension fund activities omits reporting the significant information about participants' benefits.

46. Supporting the pension fund as the reporting entity is the view that the pension plan consists only of a set of documents used by various entities, such as the sponsor, trust funds, and insurance companies, to assist in carrying out the terms of the agreement between the employer(s) and the employees. The fact that the plan may possess certain attributes of a legal entity is not viewed as sufficient reason for characterizing it as a reporting entity. Many respondents who supported the pension fund as the reporting entity linked that choice with the impropriety, in their view, of presenting quantitative information about plan benefits in the financial statements.

47. After considering the alternatives, the Board concluded that the needs of financial statement users and the related primary objective of the financial statements (as set forth in following paragraphs) necessitate establishing the plan, rather than the fund, as the reporting entity. The Board believes that financial information about both the promise to provide benefits and any assets committed to fulfill that promise are essential to present financial statements that are most meaningful to users (paragraphs 48-53).

---

[20]This appendix identifies the specific document on which respondents commented only if such comments are limited in their application to that document. Otherwise, the term *respondents* refers to those who responded to one or more documents preceding this Statement, that is, the Discussion Memorandum and the initial and revised Exposure Drafts.

[21]For example, Section 502(d)(1) includes the following statement: "An employee benefit plan may sue or be sued under this title as an entity." Any claims for pension benefits are enforceable against the pension plan as an entity, as provided for in Section 502(d)(2) of the Act: "Any money judgment under this title against an employee benefit plan shall be enforceable only against a plan as an entity and shall not be enforceable against any other person unless liability against such person is established in his individual capacity under this title." The view that the pension plan should be accounted for as if it were a separate accounting entity is also viewed as being compatible with reporting provisions of the Act. For example, Section 103(a)(3)(A) states, in part: ". . . the administrator of an employee benefit plan shall engage, on behalf of all plan participants, an independent qualified public accountant, who shall conduct such an examination of any financial statements of the plan, and of other books and records of the plan, as the accountant may deem necessary to enable the accountant to form an opinion as to whether the financial statements and schedules required to be included in the annual report by subsection (b) of this section are presented fairly in conformity with generally accepted accounting principles applied on a basis consistent with that of the preceding year."

PRIMARY OBJECTIVE OF PLAN FINANCIAL STATEMENTS

Users of Financial Statements

48. Potential users of plan financial statements include those who have an existing or potential relationship with either the plan or the employer(s). The initial Exposure Draft identified plan participants as the primary users of plan financial statements. Many respondents to that Exposure Draft expressed the view that the "typical" plan participant would be uninterested in or unable to properly assimilate the information presented in plan financial statements and thus would be confused and possibly misled.[22] Other respondents thought that Exposure Draft gave insufficient attention to the needs of other users, for example, employers, their investors and creditors, plan administrators, and governmental authorities responsible for regulating pension plans.

49. In response to such comments, the primary objective of plan financial statements as it appeared in that Exposure Draft was revised. Those revisions are intended only as clarifications and shifts in emphasis. For example, the phrase "useful in assessing the plan's present and future ability to pay benefits when due" now appears in place of "useful to plan participants in assessing the security with respect to receipt of their accumulated benefits." Although this Statement does not identify any one group as the primary users, the Board believes that the content of plan financial statements should focus on the needs of plan participants because pension plans exist primarily for their benefit. The Act provides additional support for that view. For example, Section 103(a)(3)(A), quoted in footnote 21, refers to an examination of plan financial statements by an independent accountant engaged on behalf of all plan participants. The Board recognizes, however, that plan financial statements should also be useful to others who either advise or represent participants, are present or potential investors or creditors of the employer(s), are responsible for funding the plan (for example, state legislators), or for other reasons have a derived or indirect interest in the financial status of the plan.

50. The Board recognizes that participants who have not had previous exposure to financial statements may need to be educated regarding the information presented in plan financial statements. However, the Board does not believe that a possible need to educate some users justifies disregarding the financial information needs of other users who have a reasonable understanding of financial reporting and economic activities and are willing to study the information with reasonable diligence. Financial statements should not exclude relevant information merely because it may be difficult for some to understand or because some members of the expected audience choose not to use it. To enhance their usefulness, **plan administrators** may wish to supplement the statements with a brief explanation that highlights those matters expected to be of most interest to participants. Including summary financial information for a period of years in such supplementary information, and thereby disclosing trends, may also be helpful.

51. Some respondents to the initial Exposure Draft who expressed concern regarding the usefulness of plan financial statements to participants presumed that it required that plan financial statements be distributed to all participants. Others interpreted that document as requiring plan financial statements to be audited. This Statement does not require the preparation, distribution, or attestation of any financial statements, but only establishes standards of accounting and reporting to be followed in the preparation of plan financial statements that purport to be in accordance with generally accepted accounting principles.

52. The accounting and reporting standards established by this Statement are intended to result in general purpose external financial statements. To include in financial statements designed to serve many the specialized information needed by a few who can otherwise obtain that information may be uneconomical. For example, the plan administrator may need many kinds of specialized and detailed information to decide day-to-day matters and establish policies. But the plan administrator controls the plan's accounting system, and much of the accounting effort may be managerial accounting designed to help the plan administrator manage and control operations. Similarly, the information needed by the sponsor of a single-employer plan to evaluate potential plan amendments or to determine current minimum funding requirements under the Act is specialized information. But sponsors usually have the ability to acquire the specific information they

---

[22]Most respondents commented from the perspective of an employer rather than an employee. Thus, those comments may not reflect the views of the "typical" plan participant. A recent nationwide study of attitudes toward pensions and retirement commissioned by Johnson & Higgins and conducted by Louis Harris and Associates surveyed the views of both employers and employees. It found that ". . . business leaders widely misjudge the importance employees place on certain types of information about their pension plans. Among employees who read their most recent pension report, substantial majorities believe it is 'very important' that they receive information about the current financial status of their plan (83%). . . . However, among business leaders whose employees receive annual reports, just 38% feel it is 'very important' that the report contain [that] information. . . ." (Johnson & Higgins, *1979 Study of American Attitudes Toward Pensions and Retirement*, pp. vii and viii.)

need. To the extent that governmental authorities responsible for regulating plans wish to indicate their needs for financial information by requiring submitted financial statements to be prepared in accordance with generally accepted accounting principles, it seems appropriate to consider the needs of those authorities in establishing generally accepted accounting principles for plans (provided those needs do not conflict with the needs of participants and do not entail an adverse cost/benefit relationship). To the extent that governmental authorities need specialized information, they can probably obtain it.

53. Information consistent with the primary objective of plan financial statements (set forth in subsequent paragraphs) is likely to be useful to participants and others who are interested in essentially the same financial aspects of the plan, including those who have an existing or potential relationship with the employer(s). Although information presented in plan financial statements may fulfill certain needs of those who have a relationship with the employer(s), the Board believes that an in-depth consideration of their needs is more appropriately a part of another Board project.[23]

Objectives

54. The Board considered those user needs that could be reasonably satisfied within the constraints of the characteristics and limitations of financial accounting.

55. Because employees generally render service long before they receive the benefits to which they are entitled as a result of that service, they are concerned with the security[24] for their future benefits. Thus, the primary objective of plan financial statements stated in the initial Exposure Draft was to provide information that is useful to plan participants in assessing the security with respect to receipt of their accumulated benefits.

56. A number of respondents thought that primary objective was too narrow. Although the initial Exposure Draft was based on an assumption of an ongoing plan, certain aspects (primarily those relating to measuring the actuarial present value of accumulated plan benefits) were seen as emphasizing the security of participants' benefits in the event of plan termination. Many respondents thought participants and other users should be interested not only in immediate security but in whether adequate pro-

gress is being made toward achieving security for the benefits participants expect to receive upon retirement or other termination of service. The Board agreed. Therefore, to emphasize the assumption of an ongoing plan, the phrase "plan's present and future ability to pay benefits when due" was substituted for "security with respect to receipt of [participants'] accumulated benefits."

57. Some respondents to the initial Exposure Draft also expressed the view that providing information useful in assessing the performance of pension plan administrators and other fiduciaries in managing the assets they control should be a part of the primary objective of plan financial statements. The Board believes that providing information useful in an assessment of stewardship is inherent in providing information useful in assessing **benefit security**. However, because of the importance of stewardship to a plan's ability to pay benefits, the Board concluded that that interrelationship should be explicitly indicated. (Paragraph 67 further discusses the use of financial statements in assessing stewardship.)

Other Information Needed in Assessing Benefit Security

58. Some respondents to the Exposure Drafts expressed the view that (a) the continued viability of the employer as an entity willing and able to meet the funding requirements of the plan and (b) (for ERISA plans) the guaranty of the PBGC were more important to long-range benefit security than the assets held by the plan at any given date. In their view, the Exposure Drafts either ignored or dealt inadequately with those factors, and thus the objective of providing information useful in assessing benefit security would not be achieved.

59. As indicated in the Exposure Drafts, the Board recognizes that information beyond that presented in plan financial statements is needed to assess benefit security. Whether participants receive their benefits when due depends not only on the existing relationship between plan resources and accumulated plan benefits but also on (a) the commitment and financial ability of the employer(s) to make future contributions to the plan and (b) (for an ERISA plan) the extent to which payment of benefits is insured by the PBGC. Although the commitment and financial ability of the employer(s) to make future contributions to the plan are primary factors in assessing benefit security, that kind of

---

[23]Another project on the Board's technical agenda, accounting by employers for pensions, encompasses a reconsideration of present generally accepted accounting principles regarding employer accounting for pension plans.

[24]That view of participants' informational needs appears to be supported by the results of the Harris survey. That survey found that 93 percent of the employees who read the last report thought it was very important that they know how certain it is that they will be paid their pension. (Johnson & Higgins, *1979 Study of American Attitudes Toward Pensions and Retirement*, p. 53.)

information is not within the limits of financial accounting for the plan itself.

60. However, a primary purpose of funding a pension plan is to enhance the plan's present and future ability to pay benefits when due. If a funding program is in effect, participants can look to funds that are irrevocably committed to the payment of benefits. Other factors being equal, the higher the ratio of those funds to the actuarial present value of accumulated plan benefits, the greater is the assurance that present accumulated plan benefits will be paid. With the information presented in plan financial statements, users can assess the extent to which the plan itself is able to pay participants' benefits and the extent to which payment of benefits is dependent on other factors, namely, the commitment and financial ability of the employer(s), and, for ERISA plans, the security provided by the PBGC.

61. The existence of the PBGC guaranty as an element of benefit security was not, as some respondents contended, ignored in the Exposure Drafts. Both drafts required, as does this Statement, that financial statements of ERISA plans include a brief, general description of the PBGC guaranty. However, the initial Exposure Draft's requirement was expanded to require an explanation of the application of the PBGC guaranty to any recent plan amendments (paragraph 265).

62. There is also the view that the primary objective is unattainable because a comparison of the net asset and benefit information as presented in a plan's annual financial statements is not sufficient for an assessment of the plan's future ability to pay benefits when due. The Board recognizes that information regarding the trend of the relationship over time between plan resources and accumulated plan benefits, on both an absolute and a relative basis, can be more useful than information about that relationship at any given date. Information over time is, however, an aggregation of information as of a series of dates. Without annual information, trend information over a period of years cannot be ascertained. Therefore, the Board believes it is appropriate for the primary objective to indicate that the information provided by plan financial statements should be *useful in assessing* (as contrasted with *portraying*) the plan's future as well as present ability to pay benefits when due. Paragraph 50 acknowledges that the usefulness of annual financial statements may be enhanced by supplementing them with summary financial information for a period of years.

63. To summarize, the Board does not believe that

the need for information beyond that provided by annual plan financial statements implies that the stated objective of providing information useful in assessing the plan's present and future ability to pay benefits when due is either unattainable or inappropriate. An analogous situation exists with regard to financial reporting by business enterprises. The objectives stated in FASB Concepts Statement No. 1, *Objectives of Financial Reporting by Business Enterprises,* focus on providing "information that is useful to present and potential investors and creditors and other users in making rational investment, credit, and similar decisions."[25] That document recognizes, however, that financial reporting is but one source of economic information about business enterprises. The financial information provided by financial reporting for business enterprises should be used in combination with pertinent information from other sources, for example, information about general economic conditions or expectations, political events and political climate, or industry outlook.[26] Similarly, financial information presented in plan financial statements should be used in combination with other pertinent information, including information about the financial condition of the employer(s) and, for ERISA plans, the guaranty of the PBGC. Concepts Statement 1 also implicitly recognizes that financial reporting by a business enterprise for any one period may be insufficient to fulfill users' needs. For example, paragraph 48 indicates that ". . . procedures such as averaging or normalizing reported earnings for several periods . . . are commonly used in estimating 'earning power'." Users of plan financial statements may likewise need financial information for several years in assessing benefit security.

Alternatives Considered

64. Alternatives suggested by respondents primarily focused on the objectives presented in the Discussion Memorandum, namely:

a. To provide information useful for assessing the aggregate future benefits payable to participants and the resources available to meet those payments

b. To provide information useful to individual pension plan participants for assessing the degree of risk that may be associated with the future receipt of their pension benefits

c. To provide information useful for assessing, in terms of amount, timing, and related uncertainty, the aggregate future benefits payable to participants should the pension plan be terminated

d. To provide information useful for assessing the

---

[25]Concepts Statement 1, par. 34.
[26]Ibid., par. 22.

performance of pension plan administrators and other fiduciaries in discharging their various responsibilities

e. To provide information useful for assessing the performance of pension plan administrators and other fiduciaries solely with regard to managing the assets that they control

f. To provide information useful for assessing the need for future contributions to the pension plan in terms of amount and timing

g. To provide information useful for assessing future earnings of the pension plan in terms of amount and timing.

65. As was indicated in the Discussion Memorandum and the Exposure Drafts, selection of a particular objective does not necessarily mean exclusion of an alternative; rather, selection of objectives determines the matters to be emphasized.

66. The Board views objectives (a)-(c) as falling within the broad objective of providing financial information that is useful in assessing the plan's present and future ability to pay benefits when due. However, each of those objectives and the views of respondents supporting them suggest an alternative manner of either measuring or displaying particular elements of the financial information. Accordingly, those alternatives are addressed in subsequent paragraphs that deal with the determination and presentation of benefit information.

67. Objectives (d) and (e) are concerned with whether the financial statements should be primarily oriented toward reporting what the plan administrator and other fiduciaries have done to carry out their duties. As indicated in paragraph 57, objective (e) is, to a significant degree, considered inherent in the broad objective adopted by the Board. In accomplishing that objective, plan financial statements will provide information regarding the management of plan assets together with information pertaining to participants' accumulated plan benefits as well as the results of transactions and events that affect those assets and benefits. Although that information should be useful in assessing performance, factors that are beyond the control of plan management, such as the financial condition of the employer(s), participants' longevity, and general economic conditions, may contribute to plan performance. Plan financial statements provide information about a plan when it was under the direction of a particular management but cannot separate the effect of management performance from the effects of other factors. Users therefore need to form their own assessment of the effect of management performance on plan performance. Further, to focus solely on objectives relating to performance might, based on certain respondents' views, result in the exclusion of benefit information. The Board does

not believe such exclusion would result in meaningful financial statements. Therefore, the Board does not believe that an objective relating to performance should, by itself, constitute the primary objective of plan financial statements.

68. Objectives (f) and (g) were rejected as primary objectives for reasons somewhat similar to those expressed in paragraph 67. To the extent that users' expectations about future plan performance are based on past plan performance, information about existing plan assets and the income from those assets together with information about present accumulated plan benefits may be useful in assessing the need for future contributions to the plan and future earnings of the plan. However, plan financial statements cannot provide information about assets or benefits that do not currently exist. Users need to assess the possible impact of factors that may cause change and form their own expectations about the future and its relation to the past.

69. Some respondents suggested another objective, namely that the financial statements for ERISA plans provide only the information required by ERISA and its related regulations. In their view, Congress established that pension plan financial statements serve plan participants and prescribed the information that it deemed appropriate for that purpose. The Board noted, however, that Section 103(a)(3)(A) (quoted in footnote 21) refers to financial statements "presented fairly in conformity with generally accepted accounting principles." The Board sees no indication in the Act that those principles of accounting are intended to be found in the Act's requirements or in regulations to be issued thereunder. It is the purpose of, and the Board believes Congress recognized the need for, financial accounting standards to determine the content of plan financial statements.

SCOPE OF THIS STATEMENT

70. This Statement establishes standards of financial accounting and reporting for defined benefit pension plans. In contrast, the Discussion Memorandum comprehended various types of employee benefit plans. However, most respondents to the Discussion Memorandum directed their attention to accounting and reporting for defined benefit pension plans—presumably the area of most concern to them. Some respondents to the Exposure Drafts suggested that the scope of this Statement should be expanded to include other types of employee benefit plans. Although requested to do so by paragraph 43 of the initial Exposure Draft, very few respondents to that document identified specific aspects of the accounting and reporting by other types of employee benefit plans that they believed the Board should focus on.

71. Because of respondents' overriding interest in reporting by defined benefit pension plans, the Board concluded that this Statement should focus on those plans. That focus is not intended to imply that the Board has concluded that the standards of financial accounting and reporting for other types of employee benefit plans should be the same as or different from those described in this Statement.

72. Some respondents to the initial Exposure Draft suggested that the scope of this Statement include interim as well as annual financial statements. Because few, if any, plans publish complete interim financial statements and because the consideration of related issues would delay issuance of this Statement, the Board did not consider interim financial statements.

73. Defined benefit pension plans of state and local governmental units are included in the scope of this Statement. Certain respondents suggested that because of the unique characteristics of governmental units, such as their taxing power and perpetual life, their plans are inherently different from private plans and therefore should be excluded. Others contended that governmental plans should be excluded because they may differ from private plans with respect to funding requirements, vesting and benefit provisions, or both.

74. Some respondents to the Exposure Drafts expressed the view that plans of state and local governmental units should be excluded because the stated primary objective of plan financial statements was not appropriate for such plans. In their view, because public plans are less likely to terminate than private plans, providing information useful in assessing benefit security is not relevant. The view was also expressed that the initial Exposure Draft's identification of participants as the primary users of plan financial statements was not appropriate for governmental plans. Those respondents thought the financial statements of such plans should be directed specifically to users other than plan participants (for example, public officials, state legislators, taxpayer groups, bond underwriters, potential investors, etc.) and that those users might have objectives other than assessing benefit security.

75. The Board recognizes that there are distinctions between business enterprises and governmental units. The Board also recognizes that the financial condition of the employer is of extreme importance for benefit security. However, the Board believes that only the characteristics of the plans themselves, not the characteristics of their sponsors, should affect the accounting and reporting by pension plans. The Board also did not find persuasive the argument that plans of state and local governmental units should be excluded because their vesting and benefit provisions may differ from those of private plans. The vesting and benefit provisions of private plans are not all the same. Such differences will be reflected in plan financial statements prepared in accordance with this Statement. (Paragraph 165 discusses how the basic method for determining the benefit information accommodates differences in such factors as plan provisions.)

76. The Board also believes that there is a need, as evidenced by the increasing interest[27] in financial information about public plans and by the House Pension Task Force Report on Public Employee Retirement Systems,[28] to establish standards of financial accounting and reporting for plans of state and local governmental units. That report states: "Serious deficiencies exist among public employee retirement systems at all levels of government regarding the extent to which important information is reported and disclosed to plan participants, public officials, and taxpayers."[29] It also states that participants in such plans "do face the risk of pension benefit reductions or other benefit curtailments due to reasons other than plan termination," and that "the financing of many pension plans covering local government employees lacks stability and predictability due to state imposed taxing restrictions as well as to the indeterminate amount of funds available from federal revenue sharing, state insurance premium taxes, etc."[30] In view of the foregoing, the Board concluded that the primary objective of providing information useful in assessing the plan's ability to pay benefits when due is as appropriate for plans of state and local governmental units as it is for private plans.

77. Views regarding the needs of financial statement users other than participants were previously addressed (paragraph 49). Further, the primary objective adopted by the Board does not necessarily deny other objectives that are associated with those users. However, to the extent that certain users need specialized or detailed information and can otherwise obtain that information, the Board con-

---

[27]The recent Harris survey (footnote 22) provides evidence of that interest. That survey found that public plan compliance with private plan regulations is favored by 68 percent of current and retired employees (14 percent opposed) and by 93 percent of business leaders. Moreover, such compliance is favored by a sizeable 65 percent majority of employees currently covered by public plans and opposed by only 18 percent. (Johnson & Higgins, *1979 Study of American Attitudes Toward Pensions and Retirement*, p. xi.)

[28]U.S. Government Printing Office, *House of Representatives Committee on Education and Labor Pension Task Force Report on Public Employee Retirement Systems* (Washington, D.C., 1978).

[29]Ibid., p. 3.

[30]Ibid., p. 102.

cluded (paragraph 52) that such information should not be required in general purpose external financial statements.

78. Government-sponsored social security plans (for example, the U.S. Social Security program and similar plans of foreign countries) are not included in the scope of this Statement. The scope of the Discussion Memorandum did not include those plans nor did the Board consider them in its deliberations.

79. This Statement does not differentiate among plans based on plan size. Some respondents to the initial Exposure Draft suggested that the cost of implementing that document would be excessive for small plans, and therefore such plans should be exempted. (Paragraphs 272-279 discuss certain changes made to that Exposure Draft's requirements to reduce the perceived implementation costs.) Other respondents objected because they interpreted the inclusion of small plans as requiring them to issue audited annual financial statements. As indicated in paragraph 2, this Statement does *not* require the preparation, distribution, or attestation of any plan's financial statements. The Board recognizes that ERISA plans with fewer than 100 participants are not required to have their annual financial statements audited and are subject to less detailed requirements regarding their annual reports to governmental agencies.

80. The Board believes that small plans should be included in the scope of this Statement. The financial information needed in assessing a plan's ability to pay benefits is not dependent on its size. Further, any size criterion selected for excluding plans would be arbitrary. To exclude small plans from the scope of this Statement would be justified only if the usefulness of the required information did not justify its cost. However, that cost/benefit relationship is difficult to determine. It is recognized that the incremental cost per participant to implement this Statement will be generally higher for smaller plans. Accordingly, the Board considered how the provisions of the Statement, primarily those relating to benefit information, might be modified to apply to small plans. The Board noted that the American Academy of Actuaries in its Interpretation 2, *Interpretation of Recommendations Concerning the Calculation of the Actuarial Present Value of Accrued Benefits under an Active Plan,* does not differentiate among plans based on plan size. Although their basic method is the same for large and small plans, the Board is aware that certain actuaries use simplified techniques in applying that method to minimize the costs for small plans. As indicated in paragraph 29, this Statement permits the use of averages or other methods of approximation, including those consistent with recommended actuarial practice, provided the results obtained are

substantially the same as the results contemplated by this Statement. That paragraph also notes that such approaches may be particularly useful for plans sponsored by small employers.

81. The revised Exposure Draft requested respondents, particularly those associated with small plans that intended to issue financial statements in accordance with generally accepted accounting principles, to express their views regarding whether the provisions of that document should be modified for small plans and, if so, to what extent. Of those relatively few respondents who thought modifications should be made, most suggested exempting small plans from the requirement to present benefit information. For such an exemption to be appropriate, it would be necessary to conclude that the primary objective of financial statements for a small plan is different from that for a large plan. The Board does not support that conclusion (paragraph 80).

82. The Board considered the American Society of Pension Actuaries' response to the revised Exposure Draft regarding specific simplified techniques that, in the Society's view, should be permitted in valuing small plans' ancillary benefits. Paragraph 29 of this Statement permits the use of such simplified techniques. Further, one reason for the delayed effective date of this Statement is so that small plans that intend to adopt this Statement will have additional time to develop the necessary procedures, which may include appropriate simplified techniques.

83. For plans maintained outside the United States that are similar to plans maintained in the United States, this Statement applies only when financial statements of such plans are intended to conform with U.S. generally accepted accounting principles.

84. The scope of this Statement excludes a plan that has been or is expected to be terminated. The event of termination, particularly for an ERISA plan, would make various requirements of this Statement inappropriate because they are based on the assumption of an ongoing plan.

85. This Statement applies to an unfunded plan. Although principally limited to the information required by paragraphs 6(c) and 6(d), the Board nevertheless considers that financial information useful in assessing such a plan's ability to pay benefits when due.

INFORMATION REGARDING NET ASSETS AVAILABLE FOR BENEFITS

86. Because a plan's net assets are the existing means by which it may provide benefits, **net asset information** is necessary in assessing a plan's ability

to pay benefits when due. This Statement requires that information to be presented as of the end of the plan year. If the benefit information date is the beginning of the year, a statement that includes net asset information as of that date is also required. (Paragraphs 244-246 discuss the Board's conclusions regarding the format for presenting that information.)

Basis of Accounting

87. The Discussion Memorandum referred to the following bases of accounting for the net assets of a pension plan: cash basis, accrual basis, and a modified cash or modified accrual basis. Most respondents who addressed the issue indicated a preference for the accrual basis. Some who favored either the cash basis or a modified basis cited the administrative convenience of such an approach and noted that, in many instances, the difference from the accrual basis would not be material. Respondents favoring the accrual basis generally indicated that it is the only basis that provides complete financial information relating to transactions and events occurring during the period. The Board agreed with the latter argument and believes that basis is the only one that is consistent with the primary objective.

88. Some respondents to the Discussion Memorandum objected to the accrual basis because it would require that purchases and sales of securities be recorded on a trade-date basis. They contended that present recordkeeping is geared to a settlement-date basis, that a change in reporting would be an administrative burden, and that the information produced by the two methods would not be significantly different for most plans. The Board concluded that, subject to materiality considerations, the accrual basis should be used. Therefore, if the results are not significantly different from the results on a trade-date basis, accounting for sales and purchases of securities on a settlement-date basis is acceptable (footnote 3).

Receivables from Employer(s) and Others

89. This Statement requires reporting as contributions receivable those amounts that, as of the reporting date, are due the plan from the employer(s), participants, and other sources of funding. Amounts due include those pursuant to formal commitments as well as legal or contractual requirements.

90. The initial Exposure Draft did not address receivables from sources other than the employer(s) and participants. However, certain other sources

(for example, state subsidies and federal grants) constitute a significant source of financing for many plans of state and local governmental units.[31] Accordingly, receivables from such sources should be included and separately identified. However, funds from sources such as federal revenue-sharing programs that are used for plan funding purposes at the employer's discretion are, in effect, employer contributions and should be reported as such.

91. The initial Exposure Draft limited employer contributions receivable to amounts legally or contractually due the plan. A number of respondents indicated that some employers (but not employers participating in collectively bargained multi-employer plans) contribute amounts in excess of legal or contractual minimums and, in some cases, those contributions are made after the plan's year-end. Respondents questioned the appropriateness of excluding those "excess" amounts from plan receivables. Some indicated that determining the amounts that are "legally or contractually" due could be burdensome if such amounts are less than actual contributions. The Board agreed and concluded that contributions receivable should include amounts evidenced by a formal commitment. Paragraph 10 indicates certain factors that may provide evidence of a formal commitment. The revised Exposure Draft did not include the employer's recognition as of the reporting date of a contribution payable to the plan as possible evidence of a formal commitment. Certain respondents suggested that that factor be added. The Board agreed that such a factor could provide *additional* support for the existence of a formal commitment. (Paragraph 92 indicates that the existence of accrued pension costs does not, by itself, provide sufficient support.) Receipt of formally committed amounts soon after the plan's year-end provides additional evidence of the existence of a receivable at year-end. In accordance with existing generally accepted accounting principles applicable to receivables, an adequate allowance should be provided for estimated uncollectible amounts.

92. Certain respondents favored treating as receivables all amounts reported as accrued pension costs by the employer(s). That position was generally founded on the belief that there should be symmetry in the financial reporting of the employer(s) and the plan. The Board has on its technical agenda a project on accounting by employers for pensions. The Board intends to consider further the issue of symmetry in that project. While neither accepting nor rejecting the concept of symmetry at this time (paragraph 163), the Board concluded that present practices of employers in accounting for pension costs are not a sufficient basis on which to account for

---

[31]U.S. Government Printing Office, *House of Representatives Committee on Education and Labor Task Force Report on Public Employee Retirement Systems,* p. 141.

employer contributions receivable. For various reasons, amounts recorded as accrued pension costs by an employer may differ from amounts formally committed to the plan. For example, the method used for measurement of periodic pension costs for the employer's financial statements may differ from the method used for determining the amount and incidence of employer contributions.

93. A few respondents to the initial Exposure Draft questioned whether the entire amount of "unfunded **prior service costs**" is a receivable of the plan. Because at the reporting date that amount is not due from the employer(s), it is not a receivable of the plan. The employer(s) may or may not intend to eventually contribute amounts sufficient to eliminate the "unfunded prior service costs." Until such payments are formally committed to the plan, "unfunded prior service costs" do not constitute a recordable resource of the plan. For similar reasons, any existing excess of the actuarial present value of accumulated plan benefits over the net assets available for benefits (excluding contributions receivable) is not a plan receivable unless at the reporting date that amount is legally, contractually, or pursuant to a formal commitment due the plan.

Alternatives Considered for Measuring Investments (Other Than Contracts with Insurance Companies)

94. Alternatives presented in the Discussion Memorandum encompassed the following approaches to measuring plan investments: fair value, historical cost, and certain hybrid methods. Opinion was divided among respondents as to whether a single method should be used for all investments.

Single Method

95. Most respondents to the Discussion Memorandum who favored a single method advocated fair value. In their view, the fair value of plan investments is the most relevant information that can be provided for assessing (a) the security within the plan for participants' benefits and (b) the plan's investment performance. Further, for ERISA plans, a number of respondents noted that there would be no additional administrative burden caused by requiring its use because fair value is presently required in financial data filed with certain governmental agencies.

96. Some respondents favoring use of only one method advocated historical cost. Generally, they emphasized the high degree of objectivity associated with that method and that its use does not result in the recognition of unrealized gains or losses as do other methods. Certain respondents who advocated that the primary objective of plan financial state-

ments be limited to portraying stewardship responsibility considered historical cost to be the most useful measure for achieving that objective. Many who supported historical cost nevertheless advocated supplemental disclosure of fair value.

97. A number of respondents preferred a method other than fair value or historical cost. Two such methods were the moving-average-market-value method and the long-range-appreciation method. Support for those methods generally was based on the view that the effects of short-term market fluctuations on financial position and investment performance should be avoided. In addition, because investments are normally held for a long time, the current fair value of those investments is not necessarily indicative of the amount to be ultimately realized.

98. Some respondents to the Exposure Drafts favored a method other than fair value based on their perceptions of the possible effects that disclosing fluctuations in fair values might have on a plan's investment policy. In their view, measurement of investments at fair value is undesirable because plan sponsors or administrators might attempt to avoid the financial statement effects of fluctuating fair values by adopting a more conservative investment policy or by avoiding certain types of investments whose fair values may be subject to wide fluctuations. Some who expressed that view favored historical cost for either all or certain types of investments; others favored some type of averaging method.

99. To avoid additional administrative costs and possible confusion of users of plan financial statements, some respondents argued in favor of using whatever method was used in determining the **actuarial asset value.**

Different Methods

100. Some respondents favored use of different methods for different types of investments. The principal investment categories addressed were fixed-income securities, not-readily-marketable investments, and contracts with insurance companies. (Paragraphs 112-126 discuss the last category.) The views supporting particular methods for marketable equity securities were basically the same as those indicated in paragraphs 95-99.

101. Regardless of the method(s) used to measure other types of investments, certain respondents advocated use of (amortized) historical cost for long-term, fixed-income investments that the plan had both the intent and ability to hold to maturity. They argued that measuring those investments at fair value does not reflect the amounts ultimately

expected to be received. Further, any appreciation or depreciation that is recognized using fair value will ultimately be reversed in subsequent periods.

102. Certain respondents focused on investments that are not readily marketable. They advocated use of historical cost for those investments. In their view, if market quotations are not available, determining fair value is highly subjective. Because users of plan financial statements might be misled by subjective measurements, historical cost should be used.

Conclusions on Measuring Investments (Other Than Contracts with Insurance Companies)

103. The Board concluded that plan investments (excluding contracts with insurance companies) should be measured at fair value. The Board believes that basis provides the most relevant information about the resources of a plan consistent with the primary objective of the financial statements. The Board recognizes that there may be practical problems in determining the fair value of certain types of investments. Notwithstanding those difficulties, the Board believes that the relevance of fair value is so great as to override any objections to its use.

104. If available, the Board considers quoted market prices to be the most objective and relevant measure of fair value. Paragraph 11 provides certain guidelines for determining fair value if no active market exists. The use of independent experts who are qualified to estimate fair value may be necessary for certain investments.

105. The Board rejected using historical cost because prices in past exchanges do not provide the most relevant information about the present ability of the plan's assets to provide participants' benefits. Further, the Board does not believe that historical cost is the most appropriate measure for use in assessing how the stewardship responsibility for plan assets has been discharged. Plan administrators or other fiduciaries who manage plan assets are accountable not only for the custody and safekeeping of those assets but also for their efficient and profitable use in producing additional assets for use in paying benefits. Investment performance is an essential element of stewardship responsibility. Measuring changes in fair value provides information necessary for assessing annual investment performance and stewardship responsibility. Historical cost provides that information only when investments are sold.

106. The Board does not consider perceived effects on investment policies to be an appropriate factor on which to base conclusions concerning measurement of investments. The Board has considered and rejected similar arguments regarding perceived effects of accounting standards on management decisions in conjunction with other projects on its agenda. Even if accounting results were to influence some managers' decisions, it does not follow that accounting standards should be designed to encourage or discourage an action by management. Developing accounting standards on that basis would require a judgment by the Board as to which actions are desirable and which are undesirable. The role of financial reporting is to provide neutral, evenhanded, or unbiased information that is useful to those (including management) who make economic decisions. It is not a function of financial reporting to try to influence those decisions. Even if an approach based on an attempt to avoid possible effects on investment decisions were deemed appropriate, an equally valid argument might be made against the use of historical cost. That is, if investments were presented at historical cost, decisions regarding timing of disposition of investments might be influenced by the effect on reported gains or losses.

107. For fixed-income investments held to maturity, the Board recognizes that market fluctuations will reverse before maturity (assuming no defaults). However, at the reporting date, it is the fair value, not the historical cost or the expected value at maturity, that is relevant to an assessment of the plan's ability to pay benefits. Changes in value from period to period are relevant to an assessment of investment performance and discharge of stewardship responsibility. Presenting fixed-income investments at historical cost (whether or not the intent is to hold them to maturity) does not provide essential information about the effect on investment performance of the decision to hold. Further, it may be difficult to determine whether the plan has both the intent and ability to hold a particular fixed-income investment to maturity.

108. At least two additional issues would need to be considered if fixed-income investments were to be presented at historical cost. First, some respondents contended that recognizing a gain or loss (based on historical cost) is inappropriate for a bond swap, that is, when one bond is sold and replaced by a similar investment-grade bond. Those respondents consider such gains and losses to be, in effect, modifications of future interest income. Therefore, to accomplish the desired results, gain/loss deferral and amortization approaches have been used. Those approaches, however, result in a measure of historical cost of fixed-income investments that other respondents believe is inconsistent with the generally accepted notion that historical cost represents exchange price at date of acquisition. The second issue is that the historical cost of a fixed-income

investment reflects the effective interest rate at the date the plan acquired the investment rather than current and prospective interest rates which are considered more relevant for purposes of measuring the actuarial present value of accumulated plan benefits. The use of historical cost would necessitate resolving that inconsistency in order for the net asset and benefit information to be comparably measured. Presenting fixed-income investments at fair value eliminates any need to address those issues.

109. To address the concerns expressed about the subjectivity of fair value determinations for certain investments, this Statement requires that information regarding a plan's investments indicate whether their fair values have been measured by quoted prices in an active market or are fair values otherwise determined. That requirement replaces the initial Exposure Draft's requirement to segment investments into those that are readily marketable and those that are not. Some respondents expressed the view that a criterion of "readily marketable" would be difficult to apply and would not necessarily be interpreted on a consistent basis among plans. The Board agreed and concluded that the intent of that requirement, namely to provide an indication of (a) the relative degree of subjectivity in the valuation of plan investments and (b) the relative liquidity of the investments, could be achieved by substituting the revised requirement.

110. Because the Board believes that quoted market prices, or in their absence other methods (for example, discounted cash flows or appraisals), are more relevant indicators of fair value than are any of the measures produced by hybrid methods, it rejected those methods for measuring investments.

111. For reasons similar to those expressed in paragraphs 165 and 166, the Board concluded that the measure of investments reported in financial statements should not be dependent on actuarial asset valuations. The Board believes that actuarial asset valuation methods are used in conjunction with objectives, principally determining measures of pension costs for purposes of financial reporting by the employer(s) and for determining periodic funding requirements, that differ from the primary objective of plan financial statements.

Alternatives Considered for Measuring Contracts with Insurance Companies

112. A plan may enter into various contractual agreements with an insurance company. Such agreements may be distinguished based on whether related payments to the insurance company are currently used to purchase immediate or deferred annuities for participants (**allocated contracts**) or

are accumulated in an unallocated fund (**unallocated contracts**) to be used to meet benefit payments when employees retire, either directly or through the purchase of annuities. Funds in an unallocated contract may also be withdrawn and otherwise invested.

113. Under an allocated contract (for example, a group deferred annuity contract), the insurance company has a legal obligation to make all benefit payments for which it has received the premiums or consideration requested.

114. An example of an unallocated contract is a group deposit administration *(DA)* contract. Under a DA contract, payments to the insurance company that are intended to provide future benefits to present employees are credited to an account. For investment purposes, the monies in the account are commingled with other assets of the insurance company. The account is credited with interest at the rate specified in the contract; it is charged with the purchase price of annuities when employees retire and with any incidental benefits (death, disability, and withdrawal) disbursed directly from the account.

115. The immediate participation guarantee *(IPG)* contract is a variation of the DA contract. In an IPG contract, the account is credited with the contributions received during the contract period plus its share of the insurance company's actual investment income. The IPG contract is written in two forms. Under either form the insurance company is obligated to make lifetime benefit payments to retired employees. One form provides for the actual purchase of annuities as employees retire. There is an annual adjustment to the account to reflect the insurance company's experience under the annuities. In the other form, the IPG contract may accomplish the same objective through a different technique. When an employee retires, pension payments are made directly from the account without the purchase of an annuity. However, the balance of the account must be maintained at the amount required, according to a premium schedule in the contract, to provide for the remaining pension benefits for all current retirees. That portion of the account is referred to as the **retired life fund.** Thus, if necessary, the account could always be used to buy all annuities in force.

116. Allocated contracts may or may not provide for plan participation in the investment performance and experience (for example, mortality experience) of the insurance company. Under those that do (**participating contracts**), the right to receive future dividends is referred to as a **participation right.**

117. The initial Exposure Draft prescribed that contracts whereby an insurance company was required

to pay certain specified benefits were to be excluded from plan assets. If no such obligation existed, the contracts were to be included in plan assets.

118. Certain respondents to that Exposure Draft favored excluding allocated contracts from plan assets and including unallocated contracts. Others favored excluding contracts under which funds were *assigned* to provide benefits that the insurance company is obligated to pay. Presumably, both proposals are based on the view that when an insurance company agrees to provide certain benefits, it incurs (and removes from the plan) the obligation to pay those benefits. To assess the security for those benefits, one should look to the financial statements of the insurance company rather than those of the plan. By paying premiums for the purchase of annuities, the plan has fulfilled its obligation to provide those benefits and ceases to be the focal point for financial information about those particular benefits and the assets that will be used to pay them.

119. Although the preceding proposals are similar, there may be a significant distinction between them regarding the retired life fund of an IPG contract. Although an IPG contract is an unallocated contract, the retired life fund could be viewed as having been effectively and permanently transferred to the insurance company (that is, the funds have been assigned) in return for the insurance company's agreement to provide certain benefits. Because no annuities are purchased while the contract is active, the funds are not physically transferred. However, because the plan is required to maintain the retired life fund at a level sufficient to purchase annuity contracts to provide the retired participants' remaining benefits, it could be argued that the insurance company has control of that fund.

120. Certain respondents favored including in plan assets all contracts with insurance companies. Some expressed the view that all contracts represent plan assets and to exclude certain contracts would be inconsistent with the reporting of assets and liabilities by other types of entities. Others favor such an approach because they believe the value of participation rights under allocated contracts should be included in plan assets. Presumably, those respondents believe that when a plan purchases a participating contract at a cost that is higher than that for a nonparticipating contract, it purchases an asset (the participation right) in exchange for the incremental cost because under either contract the insurance company is obligated to provide the same benefits. Presumably, subsequent values for the participation right can be determined, for example, upon cancellation of the contract. Thus, an asset with a determinable value (the participation right) seems to be created when the contract is purchased. A subse-

quent valuation of the participation right may be more or less objective depending on when it is made.

121. The initial Exposure Draft required that contracts included in plan assets be measured at fair value. Certain respondents preferred to measure those contracts at amounts determined by the insurance company in accordance with the terms of the contract. For purposes of this Statement, those values are referred to as **contract values.** Those respondents argued that, except for investments held in an insurance company's **separate account,** it is impossible for anyone other than the insurance company to determine a value for those contracts. They also argued that requiring a fair value approach for contracts under which the plan's investment is maintained in an insurance company's **general account** would necessitate extra calculations, whereas the information for determining contract values is readily available. Some respondents requested guidance as to how fair value should be determined for specific types of contracts, for example, IPG contracts and deposit administration contracts.

122. In view of certain respondents' comments, the Board solicited additional information from certain persons, including members of the project's task force and members of the insurance industry, before issuing the revised Exposure Draft. The issues raised were (a) what criteria should be used to determine the elements of contracts with insurance companies that constitute assets to be recognized in plan financial statements and (b) how to measure those elements that do constitute assets. Views regarding whether it was feasible to determine the value of participation rights were specifically requested. Some respondents indicated such valuation could be very difficult. Others indicated that it could be done.

Conclusions on Measuring Contracts with Insurance Companies

123. The initial Exposure Draft's requirements regarding contracts with insurance companies were changed to require that those contracts be presented in the same manner as that contained in the annual report filed by the plan with certain governmental agencies pursuant to ERISA. A plan not subject to ERISA is required to similarly present its contracts, that is, as if it were subject to the reporting requirements of ERISA. For 1979 plan years, the pertinent governmental reporting requirements relate to item 13 of either Form 5500 or Form 5500-C. Essentially, allocated contracts are excluded from, and unallocated contracts are included in, plan assets.

124. The Board believes that certain aspects of contracts with insurance companies might be appro-

priately accounted for in a manner different from the regulatory reporting requirements. For example, the applicable instructions for the 1979 Form 5500 and Form 5500-C appear to result in the inclusion of retired life funds under IPG contracts as plan assets and the exclusion of participation rights from plan assets. As discussed in paragraphs 119 and 120, it *may* be conceptually more appropriate to exclude retired life funds and include participation rights. Further, Form 5500 and Form 5500-C permit unallocated contracts recognized as plan assets to be measured at either fair value or at amounts determined by the insurance company (that is, contract value). The Board recognizes that presenting contracts with insurance companies at contract value is inconsistent with requiring all other plan investments to be presented at fair value. However, as previously discussed, the information required for determining contract value is readily available, whereas a fair value approach would necessitate extra calculations that, according to information the Board received (paragraph 122), might be extremely complex. The Board concluded that it did not have sufficient information at this time to enable it to reach definitive conclusions concerning matters such as the recognition of retired life funds and participation rights as plan assets and the feasibility of determining a contract's fair value. Moreover, obtaining the information considered necessary to properly assess both the conceptual and the cost/benefit considerations involved would unduly delay the issuance of this Statement. During the Board's deliberations, it was noted that the PBGC and the IRS had proposed certain regulations.[32] Before reaching definitive conclusions, it was thought advisable to consider any final regulations relating to contracts with insurance companies. For the present, the Board concluded that it should adopt the practical solution stated in paragraph 123.

125. Certain respondents to the revised Exposure Draft objected to inclusion of a reference to governmental reporting requirements in a Statement of Financial Accounting Standards and suggested that the pertinent instructions to Form 5500 be incorporated into this Statement. Because the Board has not concluded that those instructions contain the conceptually appropriate treatment of contracts with insurance companies, it rejected that suggestion.

126. Some respondents asked whether benefits to be provided by contracts excluded from plan assets should be excluded from the benefit information.

Paragraph 18(d) provides an affirmative response to that query. As discussed in paragraph 118, the insurance company rather than the plan may be viewed as the principal obligor of such benefits. Nevertheless, the fact that contracts excluded from plan assets exist is considered useful information. Accordingly, the Board concluded that the plan's policy with regard to the purchase of excluded contracts should be disclosed. The Board believes that information together with the required disclosure of payments to insurance companies to purchase contracts that are excluded from plan assets (paragraph 15(g)) will adequately inform users that certain benefits will be provided by means of excluded contracts. To inform users that a plan has participation rights and that plan assets reflect dividend income but not the source of that income, the Board concluded that disclosure of the year's income that is related to excluded contracts should be required.

Assets Employed in Operations

127. Certain respondents who advocated use of fair value to measure investments also advocated measuring assets employed in operations at fair value. In their view, a consistent measurement basis should be used for all plan assets. They also noted that fair value is presently required in the financial data filed with governmental agencies pursuant to ERISA.

128. Other respondents favored using historical cost (adjusted for any depreciation or amortization). Some argued that measuring operating assets at historical cost and appropriately allocating that cost to each plan year is the appropriate manner for recognizing that portion of the administrative expenses incurred to provide benefits. Expenditures for operating assets are in the nature of advance payments for future administrative services; in that respect they differ from investments which are expected to generate future cash flows that will be used to provide benefits. Others noted that ERISA reporting requirements are not applicable to plans of state and local governmental units and that requiring fair value could increase their administrative costs.

129. The Board considered the foregoing views together with the objective of the financial statements and concluded that operating assets should be measured at historical cost less accumulated depreciation or amortization.

---

[32]Pension Benefit Guaranty Corporation [29 CFR Parts 2608 and 2611], *Federal Register,* Vol. 42 (April 18, 1977), pp. 20156-20162; Department of the Treasury, Internal Revenue Service [26 CFR Part 1], *Federal Register,* Vol. 43 (August 25, 1978), pp. 38027-38029. Shortly before the issuance of this Statement, the PBGC announced that it had dropped its proposals [*Federal Register,* Vol. 44 (December 20, 1979), pp. 75405 and 75406].

INFORMATION REGARDING ACTUARIAL PRESENT VALUE OF ACCUMULATED PLAN BENEFITS

The Need to Present Benefit Information

130. To be useful in assessing a plan's present and future ability to pay benefits when due, it is essential that the financial statements present information about both the net assets available for benefits and the benefits to be paid.

131. Some respondents opposed disclosure of any benefit information on the basis that it was outside the scope of financial statements. They asserted that the information is appropriately the province of the actuarial report. In their view, to include such information would at least duplicate information available elsewhere (the actuary's report) and might be confusing and misleading if it differed from amounts reported by the actuary.

132. Similarly, some respondents interpreted certain provisions of the Act to mean that any disclosure of benefits for an ERISA plan is an issue that should be resolved independently of the plan's financial statements. Some who expressed that view thought that excluding benefit information from the financial statements is preferable because it alleviates the possibility of conflicts between the responsibilities of auditors and those of actuaries in the certifications required by the Act.

133. The Board considered whether the need to involve members of the actuarial profession in the development of financial information should be a factor that constrains the content of financial statements. From the project's inception, the Board has recognized the essential role of actuaries in developing any required benefit information. It undertook an extensive cooperative effort with the American Academy of Actuaries *(Academy)* to develop a basic method of determining benefit information that would be both meaningful and implementable. The Board appreciates the Academy's willingness to undertake that effort. The substantial agreement reached (discussed further in subsequent paragraphs of this appendix) should enhance the necessary ongoing cooperative effort among those who have a responsibility regarding the development or dissemination of plan financial information.

134. The Board believes that actuaries are best qualified to develop the benefit information required by this Statement because of their unique professional qualifications and their existing relationship with plans on other matters (for example, funding policy and measurement of pension costs). Although it acknowledges the role of the actuarial profession in developing certain financial information, the Board does not accept the notion that if the preparation of information does not fall within the professional qualifications of accountants, it is outside the scope of financial accounting. Certain financial information presently disclosed in financial statements of business enterprises is prepared exclusively by or with the assistance of professionals other than accountants. For example, the aggregate reserves for life, accident, and health policies of stock life insurance companies that appear in those entities' financial statements and measurements of pension costs in employers' financial statements are prepared by actuaries. The use of appraisers is common in establishing the value of nonmonetary assets acquired in a business combination accounted for as a purchase and may be necessary in conjunction with accounting for certain troubled debt restructurings. (With respect to plan reporting, paragraph 104 of this Statement recognizes that appraisers may be needed to determine the fair value of certain plan investments.) Information oriented to engineering and law may also enter into the preparation of financial accounting information. Thus, the Board rejected the view that the need, by itself, to involve actuaries should be a constraint on the content of financial statements.

135. The Board believes that unnecessary differences between the benefit information presented in plan financial statements and related information presented in schedules filed by ERISA plans pursuant to the Act could result in additional costs being incurred by preparers of the information and might also cause some confusion to those who use the information. Therefore, the Board worked closely with the Department of Labor *(Department)* in an attempt to avoid such unnecessary differences. As discussed further in subsequent paragraphs, that cooperative effort was successful in developing a basic method of determining benefit information that will satisfy both financial reporting requirements and Form 5500 reporting requirements.

136. The Board recognizes that there will be available other actuarial information concerning a plan that may differ from the benefit information in plan financial statements. The Board recognizes (and believes that both the Academy and the Department also recognize) that such differences are unavoidable when the information is intended to serve different purposes. For example, information that is useful in assessing the plan's ability to pay benefits may not be the most useful for determining periodic cost measurements or establishing minimum funding requirements pursuant to ERISA. The Board acknowledges that care needs to be exercised in the presentation of financial accounting information to mitigate any confusion that might result from the presence of other information about the plan. If other information that is made available to users of

plan financial statements is accompanied by appropriate disclosure of its nature and purpose, possible confusion on the part of certain users may be avoided.

137. The view expressed in paragraph 132 apparently reflects a concern that inclusion of benefit information will involve auditors in actuarial matters because of their examination of the plan's financial statements in accordance with generally accepted auditing standards. This Statement does not mandate auditor involvement in financial statements; matters relating to the attest function are not within the scope of the Board's authority. The Board recognizes, however, that both the auditing and actuarial professions have responsibilities under the Act and that their respective professional bodies have promulgated standards or recommendations regarding the conduct of their members. It is not within the Board's authority to attempt to resolve any issues relating to the relationship between those professions. The Board is aware of ongoing efforts by the interested parties to resolve certain such issues and is hopeful that those efforts will result in prompt solutions that are acceptable to all involved. The Board does not agree, however, that the proper manner of resolution is to omit from the financial statements information that is essential to users of those statements. Further, the Board does not believe that considerations relating to whether or by whom certain information should be audited are, of themselves, relevant to a determination of whether the information should be presented in financial statements. For example, Section 2520.103-8 of Department of Labor regulations provides that the auditor's examination need not include any statement or information regarding plan assets held by a bank or insurance carrier if the bank or insurance company is regulated, supervised, and subject to periodic examination by a state or federal agency and the bank or insurance company certifies to the correctness of the statement or information. In the absence of such regulations, it would be equally inappropriate to exclude information regarding those assets from plan financial statements to avoid attestation by an auditor.

Alternatives Considered for Determining Benefit Information

138. Having concluded that benefit information should be in the financial statements, the Board considered how that information should be determined. Respondents' recommendations can be broadly categorized as follows:

a. Some focused on benefit information that would represent those benefits to which employees would be entitled if they terminated their employment at the benefit information date. For present employees, the benefit information would include only that portion of the benefits accumulated under the plan's benefit accrual provision that is vested at that date.

b. Some focused on benefit information that would represent those benefits that are at risk at the benefit information date. The benefit information would include the benefits accumulated by present employees under the plan's benefit accrual provision, without adjustment for future withdrawal. This method is independent of the plan's vesting provision.

c. Some focused on benefit information that would represent the benefits attributable to employees' service to the benefit information date. Respondents' recommendations for determining those benefits can be broadly categorized as follows:

i. Some would include the benefits of present employees determined as in (a) above (vested benefits) plus that portion of present employees' accumulated plan benefits, determined in accordance with the benefit accrual provision, that is expected to become vested. Some proponents of this approach believe that the benefit information should differ from that determined in (b) above only in that future withdrawal should be recognized. Others would include some portion of certain types of benefits (for example, death and disability benefits) for which the plan does not clearly specify the amount attributable to each year of service.

ii. Others would measure the benefits as some pro rata portion of the expected benefits to be received by present employees who retire or terminate in a vested status after the benefit information date. That pro rata portion would relate in some manner the service rendered to date with total service expected to be rendered.

d. Some focused on the amount that is assigned by the **actuarial cost method** to periods before the benefit information date.

139. Categories (a)-(c) above refer to present employees; there is little, if any, difference of opinion about how to determine the accumulated plan benefits of employees who have retired or terminated before reaching retirement age. Accordingly, paragraphs 140-168 primarily focus on determining the accumulated plan benefits of present employees. Those paragraphs elaborate on the preceding alternatives. They do not focus on other measurement factors, such as various assumptions (other

than withdrawal)[33] used in determining the benefit information. Paragraphs 169-204 address that aspect of the measurement process.

Vested Benefits

140. Some respondents emphasized that only **vested benefit information** should be presented. Nonvested benefits are forfeitable if certain conditions (primarily age and length of service) are not met, whereas vested benefits are not. Thus, some believe that only vested benefit information could be properly presented as a plan liability. Some respondents to the initial Exposure Draft (which required presentation of information about both vested and nonvested benefits) believe that ERISA supports their view. Under ERISA the legal obligation of the plan upon plan termination cannot exceed vested benefits except to the extent that plan assets are available to provide benefits in excess of vested benefits.

141. Certain respondents to the Exposure Drafts expressed the view that participants would be confused and unduly alarmed by the fluctuations in the security for nonvested benefits that, in their view, are a likely result of the combination of the subordinate status of nonvested benefits and the presentation of plan investments at fair value. However, others argued that employees do not expect any security until they have met the plan's vesting requirements. It was also suggested that presenting **nonvested benefit information** might affect management decisions about plan funding. Respondents who expressed the foregoing views believed that presenting only vested benefit information would avoid such perceived effects and is therefore preferable.

Benefits at Risk

142. Some respondents recommended that the benefit information represent potential claims of employees in the event of plan termination. A defined benefit pension plan normally contains a formula or schedule that specifies the rate at which employees accumulate their benefits. That benefit accrual provision is necessary primarily to determine the benefits attributable to service rendered by an employee who separates from service before retirement. In the view of some, that provision best defines the benefits that are at risk at any time. Because nonvested benefits become vested to the extent of available assets upon plan termination, they are considered equally at risk as vested benefits and therefore could be included in the benefit infor-

mation under this approach. Because future service is not a factor in measuring benefits at risk, those who support this approach would not adjust the benefit information for future withdrawal. Some view this approach as providing benefit information that is most useful to participants because of its comparability with the computational basis used to prepare the individual statements of accrued benefits that participants in an ERISA plan are entitled to receive. In their view, reflecting future withdrawal would decrease the usefulness of the resulting benefit information. Supporters of this approach do not consider it inconsistent with the concept of an ongoing plan. Providing the specified benefit information is not the same as providing a measure of the benefits that would be paid assuming plan termination. Providing the latter measure would be consistent with the assumption that the plan had, in fact, terminated.

Benefits Attributable to Service Already Rendered

143. Some respondents recommended that the benefit information represent the benefits to which employees are entitled as a result of their service to the benefit information date. For purposes of this Statement, the two basic approaches to determining those benefits are referred to as (a) vested benefits and those accumulated plan benefits expected to become vested and (b) pro rata allocation of projected benefits.

Vested benefits and those expected to become vested

144. Some respondents recommended that the benefit information include benefits presently vested plus that portion of employees' accumulated plan benefits at the benefit information date that is expected to become vested. Those holding this view object to presenting only vested benefit information because that information fails to recognize the benefits that may be reasonably expected to be paid for services already rendered. Adjusting the benefit information for future withdrawal is inherent in the notion of benefits expected to become vested. Thus, this approach differs in that respect from a benefits-at-risk approach. Some holding this view would include in the benefit information a portion of certain nonvested benefits for which the plan does not clearly specify the amount attributable to each year of service, for example, death and disability benefits. The benefits-at-risk approach, on the other hand, would include such benefits only to the extent that employees presently have vested rights to them.

---

[33]All approaches to determining benefit information discussed in this Statement utilize various assumptions to estimate the probability that benefits will be paid. The approaches differ somewhat with respect to which assumptions are recognized. For convenience, the discussion in paragraphs 140-168 refers to certain assumptions only when necessary to distinguish between approaches. Assumptions relating to the probability of payment of benefits are discussed in more detail in paragraphs 180-186.

Pro rata allocation of projected benefits

145. Some respondents recommended that the benefit information be determined on the basis of the relationship between the total benefits expected to be ultimately paid to present employees and the service rendered in exchange for those benefits. Inherent in this view is the projection of future benefits determined in accordance with employees' projected future pay, service, or both. The relationship between projected benefits and service rendered can be determined by various methods. For purposes of this Statement, those methods are referred to as:

a. The benefit-compensation-correlation method
b. The cost-compensation-correlation method
c. The benefit-years of service-correlation method
d. The cost-years of service-correlation method.

Benefit-compensation-correlation method

146. One method of relating benefits to service is to relate the *benefits* (rather than the cost of such benefits) to compensation. Under that method, the percentage of (a) the actuarial present value at retirement date (or date of termination, if earlier) of the total estimated benefits to (b) the total estimated compensation to retirement (or termination, if earlier) is first determined for each employee.[34] That percentage is then applied to the employee's compensation each year to determine the *benefits* attributable to that year's service. The benefits so determined are then discounted to reflect the time value of money. The benefit information would be the aggregate of those discounted benefits attributable to all present employees' years of service to the benefit information date, increased for interest for the period from the year of service to the benefit information date.

Cost-compensation-correlation method

147. Under the method in which the *cost* of providing benefits (rather than the benefits) is correlated with compensation, a determination is made for each employee[35] of the percentage relationship of (a) the actuarial present value at retirement date (or date of termination, if earlier) of the total estimated benefits to (b) the total estimated compensation to retirement (or termination, if earlier) adjusted to reflect an interest factor from the period that service is rendered to that date. The resulting percentage is then applied to each year's compensation to allocate the employer's *cost* of providing benefits attributable, on the basis of compensation, to that year's service. This method results in each year's cost allocation remaining a constant percentage of each year's compensation. (That is not the case under the benefit-compensation-correlation method.) The benefit information would be the aggregate cost of benefits attributable to all present employees' years of service to the benefit information date, increased for interest for the period from the year of service to the benefit information date.

Years of service-correlation methods

148. The years of service-correlation methods are basically the same as the compensation-correlation methods described in paragraphs 146 and 147 except for the basis of allocation. Similar to the benefit-compensation-correlation method, the benefit-years of service-correlation method allocates a constant percentage of total estimated benefits to each year of service and discounts that amount to reflect the time value of money. Likewise, the cost-years of service-correlation method allocates to each year of service a constant dollar cost for providing the estimated total benefits.

Actuarial Cost Methods

149. Actuarial cost methods are primarily used to determine annual pension cost estimates; those cost estimates may be used for determining the amount and incidence of employer contributions, establishing tax deductibility of the amounts funded, determining pension expense for recognition in the employer's financial statements, determining the minimum funding required by the Act, and possibly other purposes. The view discussed here is not whether the use of actuarial cost methods is appropriate for financial reporting by the employer but whether actuarial cost methods, in general, produce measures that are acceptable for determining the benefit information to be presented in plan financial statements.

150. Certain respondents recommended that determination of any benefit information be left to the discretion of the actuary and that all actuarial cost methods acceptable under the Act be acceptable for plan financial statement purposes. In their view, the actuary is best qualified by training to select the appropriate measure. Certain respondents to the Exposure Drafts (which rejected actuarial cost methods for determining the benefit information) objected to the cost of requiring a method for determining benefit information that might differ from the actuarial cost method. In their view, requiring plans to incur such costs for financial reporting purposes alone would be inappropriate. It was also sug-

---

[34]In practice, the approach probably would be applied to all employees as a group, or to particular groups of employees, rather than on an individual employee basis.

[35]See footnote 34.

gested that the apparent comparability among plans achieved by the initial Exposure Draft's requirement for use of both a uniform basic method and uniform assumptions would be illusory because differences in plan provisions, characteristics of participants, and investment strategies would not be reflected. Other respondents thought use of the actuarial cost method used for funding purposes was appropriate because the resulting benefit information would be determined in the same way as employer contributions.

Conclusions on Determining Benefit Information

151. The Board concluded that the benefit information should include vested benefits plus employees' nonvested benefits expected to become vested as determined by the plan's benefit accrual provision using primarily employees' history of pay and service to the benefit information date. Projected service should be a factor only in determining employees' expected eligibility for particular benefits such as those listed in paragraph 18(b). The actuarial present value of those benefits should then be determined using appropriate actuarial assumptions to reflect the time value of money (through discounts for interest) and the probability of payment (by means of decrements such as for death, disability, withdrawal, or retirement) between the benefit information date and the expected date of payment.

152. The benefit information required by the initial Exposure Draft was based entirely on employees' history of pay and service and other appropriate factors at the benefit information date. Therefore, benefits such as those listed in paragraph 18(b) were not included, except to the extent that employees' eligibility for them at the benefit information date was not dependent on future service. That method of determining benefit information was primarily based on the benefits-at-risk approach. A number of respondents expressed the view that that approach was not as useful in an assessment of benefit security on an ongoing plan basis as would be an approach that included estimated amounts for benefits such as those listed in paragraph 18(b) for all employees expected to receive such benefits, to the extent those benefits related to service already rendered. For reasons discussed in the following paragraphs, the Board agreed.

153. The Board believes that the benefit information should relate to the benefits reasonably expected to be paid in exchange for employees' ser-

vice to the benefit information date. In the Board's view, vested benefits and nonvested benefits expected to become vested, determined primarily in accordance with the benefit accrual provision and employees' history of pay and service to the benefit information date, best represent the benefits attributable to service already rendered. For example, if a plan provides a benefit of 2 percent of final 5-year average salary per year of service, the accumulated pension benefit for an employee with 10 years of service would be 10 times 2 percent of the employee's average salary for the 5 years immediately preceding the benefit information date.

154. In the Board's view, future service should be considered only in determining employees' expected eligibility for certain benefits. The need to consider projected service for that purpose can be illustrated by assuming an employee[36] becomes eligible for a disability benefit in the 15th year of service pursuant to a plan that provides disability benefits when an active employee with 10 or more years of service becomes totally and permanently disabled. If projected disability in a future year of service is not considered during the first 14 years of service in determining that employee's expected eligibility for the disability benefit, the entire incremental actuarial present value of that benefit (that is, the excess, if any, over the actuarial present value of the normal retirement benefit previously recognized) is recognized in the 15th year of service, as if it were all attributable to that year of service. In the Board's view, the disability benefit should be related to the service rendered during the employee's entire career. A portion of the disability benefit should thus be attributed to each of the employee's 15 years of service. Similar illustrations could be developed for other types of benefits. For example, future service should be considered for determining an employee's expected eligibility for an early retirement benefit in order to appropriately relate that benefit to each year of service rendered; not doing so would result in attributing the entire incremental actuarial present value of the early retirement benefit to years after the employee initially becomes eligible for an early retirement benefit.

155. In the Board's view, the approach discussed in paragraphs 153 and 154 results in a measure of accumulated plan benefits that is most useful in assessing the plan's present and future ability to pay, when due, the benefits to which employees will ultimately be entitled as a result of their service to the benefit information date. Therefore, the approach is consis-

---

[36]For purposes of illustration, the discussion is in terms of an individual employee. In practice, such benefits would be recognized on an aggregate rather than individual basis because it is usually not possible to predict whether and when an individual employee will become disabled (or elect early retirement, die in active service, etc.). It is, however, possible to estimate the disability (or early retirement, death, etc.) benefits expected to become payable for a group of employees through the application of appropriate probability factors. The basic principle, however, is the same whether the computations are performed on an aggregate or an individual basis.

tent with the primary objective of plan financial statements.

156. For certain types of benefits, the amount attributable to each year of service cannot be directly determined from the plan's provisions. The manner in which such benefits should be considered to accumulate depends on whether the benefit is includable in vested benefits. To illustrate, assume a plan provides a supplemental early retirement benefit of $200 per month upon early retirement at age 55 with at least 25 years of service, payable from the date of early retirement until age 62 (the eligibility age for collecting Social Security benefits). If that benefit becomes a vested benefit after 25 years of service, it should be considered to accumulate in proportion to the ratio of the number of years of service completed to the benefit information date to the projected number of years of service that will have been completed when the benefit first becomes fully vested. Therefore, 1/25 of the $200 benefit (that is, $8) is attributed to each year of service (assuming the employee is expected to render at least 25 years of service).[37] In the case of a benefit that does not become a vested benefit (for example, a $5,000 death benefit that is payable only if death occurs during active service), the benefit should be considered to accumulate in proportion to the ratio of the number of years of service completed at the benefit information date to the number of years of service completed at the estimated time of separation from covered employment. For example, if the foregoing $5,000 death benefit is expected to be paid after the 20th year of service (that is, the employee is expected to die at the end of the 20th year of service), 1/20 of the benefit should be attributed to each year of service. Thus, after 5 years of service, the employee's accumulated death benefit is $1,250.[38]

157. Because the Board considered vested benefit information to be too restrictive of the benefits reasonably expected to be paid as a result of service rendered to the benefit information date, it rejected the views expressed in paragraphs 140 and 141. As further discussed in subsequent paragraphs regarding the location of benefit information, the Board concluded that it need not decide whether any part or all of the benefit information is a plan liability. Therefore, views regarding the liability nature of vested benefit information were not considered relevant.

158. The Board also did not find persuasive the views regarding perceived effects of presenting non-vested benefit information. If participants are properly educated in the use of financial statements (paragraph 50), the Board believes that they should not be confused or unduly alarmed if the portion of nonvested benefits that is covered by plan assets changes between periods. Further, information about such fluctuations, if they occur, is pertinent to an assessment of the plan's ability to pay benefits. (The Board also notes that the view that participants will be alarmed by information about such fluctuations in security for nonvested benefits and the view that participants do not expect security for nonvested benefits appear somewhat contradictory.) Arguments similar to the views regarding perceived effects on funding decisions were discussed in paragraph 106. As stated in that paragraph, the Board does not believe that accounting standards should be designed to encourage or discourage an action by management.

159. The initial Exposure Draft's approach to determining benefit information was primarily a benefits-at-risk approach. For reasons discussed in preceding paragraphs, the Board concluded that the method required by this Statement would result in more useful benefit information for assessing benefit security on an ongoing plan basis. Further, the revised approach is believed to be consistent both with the views of the Department of Labor as reflected in the revised Schedule B, "Actuarial Information," of Form 5500 (footnote 41) and with the views of the American Academy of Actuaries as reflected in its Interpretation 2 (paragraph 80). That Interpretation was developed during the previously mentioned cooperative effort between the Board and the Academy. Paragraphs 17-20 essentially reiterate the recommendations contained in Interpretation 2 and also provide certain additional guidance to ensure that the resulting benefit information is relevant for financial reporting purposes.

160. The Board also rejected the pro rata allocation methods discussed in paragraphs 145-148. In the Board's view, benefit information intended to be useful in assessing the plan's ability to pay benefits attributable to service already rendered should be based primarily on pay already earned and service already rendered. One significant difference between the method adopted by the Board and the pro rata allocation methods relates to whether future salary increases are considered in measuring benefits attributable to service already rendered. Because that difference relates to the assumptions to be considered in determining the benefit information, it is addressed in subsequent paragraphs that

---

[37]Footnote 36 discusses the estimation of benefits for a group of employees through application of appropriate probability factors. In determining the benefit information, such probability factors are used to estimate whether an employee will render at least 25 years of service, and whether and when that employee will elect early retirement.

[38] See footnotes 36 and 37.

focus on that aspect of the measurement process.

161. The Board recognizes that financial accounting measures are rarely exact and that the uncertainty that surrounds economic activities often requires use of approximations or predictions of various amounts and judgment about their inclusion and disclosure in financial statements. The foregoing is particularly true in determining benefit information. However, because the method it adopted does not necessitate subjective assumptions about future salary increases, the Board believes that method results in benefit information that is more objective and verifiable than the benefit information that results from the pro rata allocation methods.

162. It was also apparent from the responses of certain supporters of the pro rata allocation methods that their views were significantly affected by the view that there should be symmetry in the accounting by the employer(s) and the plan regarding the measure of *earned* benefits.

163. The Board considered and rejected the view that symmetrical reporting should be a necessary factor in selecting the method for determining benefit information for purposes of plan reporting. The information that is useful in assessing the plan's ability to pay benefits may differ from the information that would best serve the objectives of accounting by employers for pensions. The Board will consider those objectives in another project.[39] Further, those who support symmetrical reporting are presumably influenced by the view that if benefit information is presented as a liability in the financial statements of both the employer(s) and the plan, the liability should be determined in the same manner by both parties. Because the Board concluded that the benefit information need not be presented as a plan liability (paragraph 231), the issue of symmetry may not be pertinent even though some amount may appear as a liability in financial statements of the employer(s).

164. The Board rejected the two cost-correlation methods for an additional reason. Those methods focus solely on the principle of income statement cost-allocation rather than on attributing *benefits* to service rendered. Therefore, the Board does not believe that the measures that are by-products of those methods provide information useful in achieving the primary objective of plan financial statements.

165. For similar reasons, the Board rejected use of actuarial cost methods. APB Opinion No. 8,

Accounting for the Cost of Pension Plans, recognizes several actuarial cost methods as acceptable for determining employers' costs. Likewise, a number of actuarial cost methods are recognized by ERISA as acceptable for funding purposes. Each of those methods is designed to allocate the expected ultimate cost of the plan to particular time periods. (The pro rata allocation methods discussed in preceding paragraphs are, in effect, applications of allocation approaches employed under certain actuarial cost methods.) The portion allocated to periods before a valuation date, formerly identified as *prior service costs,* the *accrued liability,* or *prior service liability,* but now described as the **supplemental actuarial value,**[40] will vary widely from method to method. Although that variation may be appropriate for funding purposes, the Board considers it inappropriate for plan financial reporting. The Board has previously considered the question of accounting alternatives and has concluded that using different accounting methods for the same types of facts and circumstances impairs the comparability of financial statements and thus significantly detracts from their usefulness. Use of actuarial cost methods for determining the benefit information could result in two plans with essentially the same benefit provisions, participant populations, etc., reporting widely differing benefit information because different actuarial cost methods were used. Further, the Board does not believe that differences in factors such as benefit provisions, participant populations, and investment policies constitute different facts and circumstances that justify use of a different basic method for determining the benefit information. Differences in such factors are appropriately accommodated by the method adopted by the Board. For example, that method requires that employees' accumulated plan benefits be determined in accordance with the individual plan's benefit provisions. Differences in factors such as rates of disability, withdrawal, or mortality and differences in investment policies are reflected in the selection of assumptions that reflect the best estimate of the plan's expected experience with respect to those factors.

166. The Board also rejected the view that using the actuarial cost method used for determining employer contributions would result in an appropriate comparison of net asset and benefit information. Determination of benefit information in accordance with the actuarial cost method used for funding purposes might produce a measure that would be useful in assessing the progress of the funding program relative to the actuarial cost method. However, because most actuarial cost methods are not designed to attribute benefits to

---

[39]See footnote 23.

[40]Interprofessional Pension Actuarial Advisory Group, *Pension Terminology Final Report,* January 1978, p. 17.

service rendered, such an approach would not, in most cases, produce benefit information that would be useful in achieving the primary objective of plan financial statements. Further, that view taken to its logical conclusion would mean that no benefit information would be presented by an unfunded plan.

167. The Board's conclusions with respect to the appropriate method of determining the benefit information are based solely on plan accounting considerations. It recognizes that other methods, including actuarial cost methods and specifically the cost-correlation methods discussed above, are widely used by actuaries in establishing pension funding programs; the Board is not concerned with, nor does it question, their appropriateness for that purpose.

168. In rejecting the use of actuarial cost methods, the Board is *not* rejecting the use of actuarial expertise in determining the benefit information. On the contrary, the Board recognizes that it is critical to the measurement process.

Assumptions Used in Determining Benefit Information

169. The following paragraphs discuss the Board's conclusions regarding the more significant assumptions that may be used in determining the actuarial present value of accumulated plan benefits.

Future Salary Increases

170. As previously indicated, some believe that an assumption regarding present employees' future salary increases should be considered in measuring benefits attributable to service already rendered (at least when benefits are stated in terms of future salary as, for example, in a final-pay plan).[41] In rejecting that view, some Board members gave greater weight to some factors than to others.

171. Certain Board members believe that benefits attributable to future salary increases should not be considered "earned" until the related compensation is earned. That view holds that the total increase in an employee's accumulated plan benefit attributable to compensation earned in a given year of service is properly considered to have been earned in that year, not in an earlier year.

172. Certain Board members also believe that future salary increases are not unlike certain other

future price changes, the accounting effects of which are recognized in the periods in which the price changes occur. Future salary increases may be related to employees' future productivity levels, as well as to changes in wage levels (either as a result of general price changes or changes in the factors of supply and demand). This view considers it inappropriate to reflect salary increases due to either changing levels of productivity or changes in the exchange prices for constant levels of productivity until the economic conditions giving rise to those changes are also present. However, this view distinguishes those prices to be paid in exchange for future service and future price increases that will affect the exchange prices for past service. Thus, this view does not consider it inconsistent to reflect automatic cost-of-living adjustments (which affect the price paid for past service) and not reflect future salary increases (which are prices paid for future service). (The Board's conclusions regarding automatic cost-of-living adjustments are discussed in paragraphs 176-178.)

173. The American Academy of Actuaries' position in its Interpretation 2 was an additional factor that influenced certain Board members' conclusions. For both conceptual and practical reasons, the Academy opposes considering future salary increases. Because of the actuary's important role in developing the benefit information, those Board members gave particular weight to the Academy's views. As a result of not considering future salary increases, the Board's and the Academy's views on the basic method for determining employees' accumulated plan benefits appear to be substantially the same. Therefore, those Board members believe that not considering future salary increases will not only result in benefit information that is meaningful for an assessment of benefit security but will also enhance the necessary ongoing cooperative relationship among those who have a responsibility regarding the development or dissemination of plan financial information.

174. To a lesser degree, some Board members are concerned about certain implementation problems that might arise were it necessary to consider both past and future salary in determining the benefits attributable to service already rendered. Such potential problems include the availability of historical salary information needed to apply a compensation-allocation basis and the possible need to develop detailed guidelines for applying that allocation basis for various types of benefit formulas and fact situations.

---

[41]On September 26, 1978, the Department of Labor proposed such an approach for determining the benefit information to be reported by ERISA plans on the revised Schedule B ("Actuarial Information") of Form 5500. The Board testified in support of the method required by this Statement at hearings concerning the Schedule B proposals held by the Department on November 20, 1978; in that testimony the Board expressed its views regarding future salary increases. The Board is pleased that the revised Schedule B subsequently issued by the Department requires a method that is believed to be consistent with that required by this Statement.

175. Certain respondents to the Exposure Drafts linked the propriety of considering future salary increases with funding considerations. For example, the view was expressed that not considering future salary increases for a public plan would be inconsistent with assumptions used for funding purposes and might therefore influence the decisions of those responsible for allocating public funds to the plan. As previously stated, the Board's conclusions are based solely on plan accounting considerations. The benefit information presented in plan financial statements is intended to be useful in assessing benefit security. Other measurement methods may be more useful for determining periodic funding requirements. Further, as previously discussed, the Board does not consider it appropriate to establish accounting and reporting standards based on the perceived effects on management decisions. Regarding future salary increases, certain Board members consider it appropriate to note that the concept of long-term funding requirements should not be confused with the concept of benefits accumulated by employees. The former may require projections based on all relevant future factors, including future salary increases. The latter, however, carries with it a notion of "what has occurred to date" to determine the benefits attributable to service rendered to date.

Automatic Cost-of-Living Adjustments

176. Unlike future salary increases, automatic benefit increases specified by the plan, such as automatic cost-of-living adjustments, may be appropriately considered a part of the benefits exchanged for employee service already rendered. The propriety of that view can be illustrated with an example of a plan that provides that a retiree's monthly benefit will be increased on each January 1 by the percentage increase reflected in the change in the Consumer Price Index from the preceding January 1, up to a maximum increase of three percent in a single year. Recognizing amounts payable to a retiree pursuant to that plan provision only as benefits are increased would result in attributing the effect of the cost-of-living adjustment to periods after the employee's retirement, that is, *after* all service had been rendered. The Board considers that result inappropriate. The effects of automatic cost-of-living adjustments should be attributed in an appropriate manner to each year during which an employee renders service.

177. The initial Exposure Draft proscribed recognizing automatic cost-of-living adjustments in determining the benefit information. Some respondents expressed the view that exclusion of such amounts was inappropriate for purposes of providing information useful in assessing benefit security on an ongoing plan basis. As indicated in the preceding paragraph, the Board agreed.

178. This Statement requires that assumed rates of inflation used in measuring benefits attributable to automatic cost-of-living adjustments be consistent with those inherent in assumed rates of return (that is, interest rates). (Paragraphs 187-197 address the Board's conclusion regarding assumed rates of return.) Interest rates are generally perceived as comprising several factors, including a factor to compensate the lender for expected inflation during the life of the loan. The assumed rates of return required by this Statement relate to the periods for which payment of benefits is deferred and therefore encompass the periods on which automatic cost-of-living adjustments are based. Thus, the inflation assumptions for such periods used to reflect automatic cost-of-living adjustments should be consistent with the inflation assumptions inherent in the assumed rates of return for those periods. If an automatic cost-of-living adjustment is subject to a maximum annual percentage increase (sometimes referred to as a "cap"), the assumed rate of benefit increase may differ from the assumed rate of inflation. For example, in the illustration discussed in paragraph 176, which has a three percent "cap," the assumed annual rate of benefit increase would not exceed three percent regardless of the assumed rate of inflation.

Social Security Payments

179. Certain plans integrate pension benefits with payments provided under the federal Social Security program. That integration may take a variety of forms. Whatever the form, certain provisions of the Social Security law are used in determining the benefit information. Therefore, an issue arises regarding whether the benefit information should reflect (a) the Social Security provisions in effect at the benefit information date, (b) the provisions of the present Social Security law scheduled to be in effect at employees' assumed dates of retirement or other termination, or (c) the provisions of possible amendments to the Social Security law in effect at employees' assumed dates of retirement or other termination. This Statement requires that Social Security provisions in effect at the benefit information date be used ((a) above). Because both levels of Social Security payments and taxable wage bases are related to employees' salary, the Board concluded that use of presently effective provisions of the Social Security law is consistent with use of historical salary information.

Certain Assumptions Relating to the Probability and Timing of Benefit Payments

180. Among the more significant assumptions relating to whether and when benefits will initially become payable and for how long they will be paid are (a) pre- and post-retirement mortality, (b) with-

drawal, (c) disability, and (d) ages at which employees will retire.

Mortality

181. Pension benefits are not paid unless employees live to retirement, and they cease upon death unless there is a co-annuitant, as in the case of a joint and survivor option. Therefore, accumulated plan benefits should be adjusted to reflect participants' longevity. If a plan provides death benefits, those benefits should also be reflected in the benefit information.

182. The initial Exposure Draft required that certain plans use the mortality and interest rates prescribed by the PBGC to value benefits upon plan termination. Because most respondents' comments focused on PBGC interest rates rather than mortality rates, their use is discussed in that context (paragraphs 188 and 189).

Withdrawal

183. For reasons other than death or disability (which are addressed in paragraphs 181 and 185, respectively), employees may cease rendering service. If they do so before their pension benefits become fully vested, some or all of those benefits (depending on the plan's vesting provision) are forfeited. For multiemployer plans, withdrawal includes termination of service resulting from withdrawal of a participating employer from the plan. For reasons discussed in paragraph 142, the initial Exposure Draft proscribed adjusting the benefit information for those benefits that may be so forfeited in the future.

184. Although not necessarily disagreeing on a conceptual basis with the views stated in that Exposure Draft about the relationship between future withdrawal and benefits at risk, certain respondents nevertheless felt that nonrecognition of future withdrawal overstated the benefits reasonably expected to become payable. The Board agreed. It also believes that consideration of future withdrawal is consistent with consideration of future service in determining employees' expected eligibility for increased benefits (paragraph 154).

Disability

185. Certain plans provide disability benefits. Because it primarily focused on a benefits-at-risk approach, the initial Exposure Draft required that the benefit information exclude those benefits expected to become payable if an employee became disabled while in service. Some respondents thought excluding such benefits understated the benefits reasonably expected to become payable as a result of

service already rendered. As previously indicated, the Board agreed.

Early retirement

186. Certain plans provide that an employee may retire early, subject to the attainment of a specified age, typically 55. Additional conditions may also be imposed. As previously discussed, the Board concluded that the benefit information should reflect the estimated early retirement benefits to be paid to those employees expected to become eligible for and to elect early retirement. The initial Exposure Draft's requirements and respondents' comments regarding early retirement benefits were similar to those regarding disability benefits. In addition, a few respondents asked whether rates of early retirement should be assumed based on an ongoing or a terminating plan. This Statement requires that all assumptions be consistent with an ongoing plan.

Rates of Return

187. To be of use in assessing benefit security, the net asset and benefit information must be determined on a comparable basis. Therefore, accumulated plan benefits must be discounted to reflect the time value of money in order for the benefit information to be on a basis comparable to the net asset information, which is stated in terms of present dollars. Few, if any, respondents who advocated presenting benefit information in the financial statements disagreed. To increase the comparability of the net asset and benefit information, this Statement requires that assumed rates of return used to discount the accumulated plan benefits reflect the expected rates of return on plan investments applicable to the periods for which payment of benefits is deferred.

188. A principal factor behind the initial Exposure Draft's requirement that certain plans use PBGC interest (and mortality) rates to determine the benefit information was that the initial interest rates used by the PBGC were derived from annuity price data obtained from the private insurance industry. PBGC rates therefore represented currently available interest rates, and their use resulted in benefit information that was comparable with the net asset information. Certain respondents objected to the use of PBGC rates. They viewed those rates as relating to a "guaranty" basis rather than a "best estimate" basis and thus unduly conservative for an ongoing plan. The view was also expressed that requiring the use of the same interest and mortality rates by a wide divergency of plans was inappropriate. Questions also were raised about the feasibility of mandatory use of PBGC rates; those questions primarily related to the timeliness of their availability.

189. Because of (a) inherent differences among plans as to investment policies and participants' longevity and (b) questions about the appropriateness of using PBGC rates (that is, the view that their use implies plan termination), the Board concluded that requiring use of assumptions that reflect the plan's expected experience would result in more appropriate benefit information than would requiring the use of PBGC interest and mortality rates.

190. The determination of assumed rates of return for most plans is, to a significant degree, a matter of judgment. Thus, various factors should be considered in estimating rates of return to be used in determining the actuarial present value of accumulated plan benefits. Among them are (a) rates of return expected from investments currently held or available in the marketplace, (b) rates of return expected from the reinvestment of actual returns from those investments, and (c) the investment policy of the plan, including the diversity of investments currently held and expected to be held in the future.

191. Accordingly, accumulated plan benefits will generally not be discounted solely at rates of return expected on existing investments, and changes in assumed rates of return will probably not equal the change during the reporting period in either short-term or long-term interest rates.[42] However, to the extent that assumed rates of return are affected by the rates of return expected from existing investments, this Statement requires that those expected rates be based on the values presented for those investments in the plan's financial statements. Further, the assumed rates of return at which accumulated plan benefits are discounted should be reconsidered in light of changes in the fair values of investments between one period and another.

192. Some believe that year-to-year changes in reported benefit information as a result of changes in assumed rates of return should be avoided to the maximum extent possible. In their view, some averaging technique should be used to smooth out potential year-to-year changes so that assumed rates of return are changed only when it is apparent that the long-term trend has changed. The Board recognizes that long-term rates of return must be considered in determining appropriate assumed rates of return. However, it rejects the view that apparent material changes in long-term rates should be ignored on an annual basis solely to avoid annually adjusting assumed rates of return. Over a period of years, plan financial statements may display a trend of assumed rates of return. However, the Board believes that an assessment of that trend should be based on information determined in a neutral manner rather than on information that is biased so as to produce a presumed trend.

193. Some who object to potential year-to-year changes in assumed rates of return are apparently influenced by funding considerations. An approach to selecting assumed rates of return designed to avoid changing the size of annual contributions may be appropriate for funding purposes. However, the Board does not believe that such a smoothing approach is appropriate for purposes of determining the benefit information to be presented in plan financial statements. As discussed in paragraph 187, determining the benefit and net asset information on a consistent basis is necessary for an appropriate assessment of benefit security. Therefore, to employ a smoothing approach to determining assumed rates of return would require employing a similar approach (for example, certain actuarial asset valuation methods) to determining the values at which investments are presented in plan financial statements. As discussed in paragraph 111, the Board rejected such asset valuation methods for purposes of plan financial statements.

194. Certain respondents to the revised Exposure Draft expressed the view that if it was inappropriate to recognize future salary increases in determining the accumulated plan benefits under plans whose benefit formulas include employees' compensation (for example, final-pay plans), it was equally inappropriate to discount those benefits at rates of return that inherently reflect anticipated future inflation. Those respondents would prefer to recognize future salary increases (at least the inflation component thereof) in determining employees' accumulated plan benefits. However, as a less preferable alternative, they suggested excluding any inflation component from the rates of return used to discount benefits.

195. As acknowledged by its supporters, excluding the inflation component from the assumed rates of return is essentially an attempt to compensate for the exclusion of future salary increases in determining accumulated plan benefits. For the reasons discussed in paragraphs 170-175, the Board rejected considering future salary increases in determining accumulated plan benefits. The Board rejected the suggested approach because it attempts to nullify that decision.

196. In the Board's view, the appropriate method of determining accumulated plan benefits and the selection of assumed rates of return at which to discount those benefits are separate issues. The pur-

---

[42]A factor to consider in assessing the extent to which short-term and long-term interest rates should impact assumed rates of return is the degree to which the timing of cash inflows from related existing or potential investments matches the timing of payments of accumulated plan benefits.

pose of the former is to determine the benefits attributable under a plan's benefit formula to the service employees have rendered. The latter, however, is designed to present the net asset and benefit information on comparable bases and is independent of the plan's benefit formula. That is, the purpose of the discounting process is the same regardless of a plan's benefit formula, for example, whether it is a final-pay or flat-benefit plan. Given the purpose of the discounting process, the Board believes the appropriate relationship is between the measurement bases for plan investments and assumed rates of return, not between the method of determining accumulated plan benefits and assumed rates of return. Rates of return on plan investments are economic factors related to the plan's existing investments and investment policy, not to its benefit formula. Further, to be consistent, the suggested approach might make it necessary to attempt to exclude the effects of future inflation from all factors[43] used in determining the actuarial present value of accumulated plan benefits, and perhaps also from the values of plan investments. The Board believes that such potential modifications, if adopted, would result in financial information that is less useful in achieving the primary objective of plan financial statements.

197. The suggested approach of discounting benefits at assumed rates of return that exclude future inflation seems inappropriate for additional reasons. For example, future salary increases are a factor only in determining nonvested benefits. Therefore, to achieve the result desired by its supporters (that is, to compensate for the nonrecognition of future salary increases), it would seem necessary to modify the approach so that it would affect only the determination of the actuarial present value of nonvested benefits. Also, the period for which salary increases due to inflation might be a factor (that is, an employee's service period) is less than the period for which payment of benefits is deferred. Therefore, without certain modifications, the suggested approach would not result in the same total actuarial present value of accumulated plan benefits as that which would result from incorporating future salary increases into the measurement process. Modifications of the suggested approach that might be necessary for it to accomplish its intended purpose could be impractical to implement as well as difficult for users of plan financial statements to understand.

Administrative Expenses

198. Because administrative expenses are incurred when making benefit payments, those expenses should be considered in determining the benefit information. That is commonly done by reducing assumed rates of return by an appropriate factor. The initial Exposure Draft required use of that method. Certain respondents expressed the view that assigning anticipated administrative expenses to future periods and discounting them to the benefit information date should also be acceptable. Because the Board is not aware of any conceptual arguments supporting the preferability of either method and because the resulting benefit information should be the same, the Board concluded that both methods are acceptable. However, in similar circumstances, their use results in the disclosure (pursuant to paragraph 27(b)) of different rates of return. The Board therefore concluded that the adjustment of assumed rates of return should be disclosed if that method is used.

Explicit Approach

199. This Statement requires that each significant assumption used in determining the benefit information reflect the best estimate of the plan's future experience solely with respect to that assumption. That method of selecting assumptions is referred to as an *explicit approach*. An *implicit approach*, on the other hand, means that two or more assumptions do not individually represent the best estimate of the plan's future experience with respect to those assumptions. Rather, the aggregate effect of their combined use is presumed to be approximately the same as that of an explicit approach. The Board believes that an explicit approach results in more useful information regarding (a) components of the benefit information, (b) changes in the benefit information, and (c) the choice of significant assumptions used to determine the benefit information.

200. The following illustrates the preferability of an explicit approach as it relates to measuring components of the benefit information (that is, vested benefits of participants currently receiving payments, other vested benefits, and nonvested benefits). Under an implicit approach, it might be assumed that the net result of assuming no withdrawal before vesting and increasing assumed rates of return by a specified amount would approximate the same actuarial present value of total accumulated plan benefits as that which would result from using assumed rates of return and withdrawal rates determined by an explicit approach. Even if that were true, increasing assumed rates of return to compensate for withdrawal before vesting might sig-

---

[43]Factors that may be directly or indirectly affected by future inflation are discussed in "Recognition of Inflation in the Calculation of Actuarial Present Values under Pension Plans," American Academy of Actuaries, *Bylaws, Guide to Professional Conduct, Standards of Practice, February 1, 1978* (Chicago: American Academy of Actuaries), pp. 98-103.

nificantly misstate components of the benefit information. Withdrawal before vesting relates only to nonvested benefits. Therefore, discounting vested benefits at rates of return that have been adjusted to implicitly reflect that withdrawal understates that component of the benefit information and correspondingly overstates the nonvested benefit information.

201. The disadvantage of an implicit approach with respect to information regarding changes in the benefit information can be similarly illustrated. Assume that under an implicit approach, assumed rates of return are decreased to implicitly reflect the effects of a plan's provision for an automatic cost-of-living adjustment (COLA). In that situation, the effect of a plan amendment relating to the automatic COLA, for example, an amendment to increase the "cap" on the COLA from three percent to four percent, might be obscured. If significant, the effect of such an amendment should, pursuant to the requirements of this Statement, be disclosed as the effect of a plan amendment. If an implicit approach is used, however, assumed rates of return would be adjusted to reflect the effect of that amendment and accordingly, some part or all of the effect might be presented as the effect of a change in an actuarial assumption rather than as the effect of a plan amendment (particularly if assumed rates of return are also changed for other reasons).

202. In addition to the foregoing possible disadvantages, an implicit approach might result in less meaningful disclosure of the significant assumptions used to determine the benefit information. For example, disclosure of the assumed rates of return resulting from the implicit approaches described in paragraphs 200 and 201 could mislead users of the financial statements regarding the plan's investment return expectations and could result in noncomparable reporting for two plans with the same investment return expectations. Users might also draw erroneous conclusions about the relationship between the plan's actual and assumed rates of return.

Insurance Company Premium Rates

203. Paragraph 21 provides that in selecting certain assumptions, an acceptable alternative to the requirements in paragraph 20 is to use those assumptions that are inherent in the estimated cost at the benefit information date to obtain a contract with an insurance company to provide participants with their accumulated plan benefits. Those other assumptions that are necessary but are not inherent in that estimated cost should be selected pursuant to the requirements in paragraph 20. For plans below a certain size, that alternative may be preferable to selection of certain assumptions (for example, mor-

tality rates) appropriate for the participant group because the validity of actuarial assumptions is dependent on the law of large numbers. It has also been suggested that use of insurance company premium rates might reduce for some plans the cost of implementing this Statement. Because the alternative approach results in benefit information that is useful in assessing benefit security and because it also appears desirable on a practical basis, the Board concluded that it should be allowed.

204. The revised Exposure Draft requested those plans that used or intended to use the alternative approach to comment about the difficulty of obtaining information about the significant assumptions inherent in premium rates. The few respondents who commented expressed differing views regarding the difficulty of obtaining that information. It should be noted that paragraph 21 merely establishes an alternative; it does not require any plan to use that alternative. Because some plans apparently wish to use the alternative and expect to be able to obtain the necessary information, the insurance company premium rate approach has been retained.

Date of Required Benefit Information

205. The initial Exposure Draft required that the benefit information and net asset information be determined as of the same date. Thus, if the plan's annual financial statements were as of the end of the plan year, end-of-year benefit information was required. A number of respondents expressed the view that determination of end-of-year benefit information on a timely basis was not practical and would cause increased actuarial fees. They indicated that most actuarial valuations are performed during the year using data as of the beginning of the year. Changing that practice at this time might create significant timing problems in terms of scheduling the actuaries' workload and, in some cases, obtaining necessary end-of-year data.

206. Schedule B of Form 5500, as revised, requires that both net asset and benefit information be presented as of the beginning of the plan year. As originally proposed, the revised Schedule B would have required end-of-year benefit information. In response to that proposal, the Department received comments similar to those received by the Board in response to the initial Exposure Draft.

207. After considering the letters of comment on the initial Exposure Draft and certain of those received by the Department on the Schedule B proposal, the Board concluded that, at present, the perceived costs of requiring end-of-year benefit information may exceed the potential benefits of such information. Among the costs considered was

the cost to ERISA plans of financial reporting requirements that would differ from Schedule B requirements. Therefore, this Statement provides for the presentation of benefit information as of either the beginning or end of the year. However, the Board continues to believe that presenting both net asset and benefit information as of the same date is necessary for a presentation of the financial status of the plan. Therefore, if the benefit information date is the beginning of the year, only the net asset and benefit information presented as of that date may be considered to present the financial status of the plan. In that situation, the year-end net asset information required by paragraph 6(a) is an incomplete presentation of the plan's financial status.

208. The Board considered allowing the benefit information date to be any date within the year. However, presentation of benefit information as of an interim date would necessitate presentation of net asset information, at least the aggregate amount thereof, as of that interim date if the financial statements were to be useful in assessing the plan's ability to pay benefits. The Board believes that (a) requiring net asset information as of an interim date might cause certain difficulties (for example, determining contributions receivable at that date) and could cause plans to incur additional expense (for example, determining fair values of investments more often than annually) and (b) use of benefit information dates other than the beginning or end of the year is not a common practice. Accordingly, the Board decided not to permit interim benefit information dates.

209. The revised Exposure Draft encouraged respondents that used a benefit information date other than the beginning or end of the year to comment on whether disallowing interim benefit information dates would cause substantial problems. Follow-up discussions with most of those respondents who indicated that such action would cause them substantial problems revealed that the majority had interpreted the revised Exposure Draft as disallowing the roll-back to the beginning of the year of detailed employee data as of a date within the year. Paragraph 29 indicates that that method of approximating beginning-of-year benefit information is acceptable, provided the results obtained are substantially the same as those that would be determined using employee data as of the beginning of the year.

210. Although the Board decided not to require end-of-year benefit information, it considers presentation of such information to be a desirable goal. Plans are encouraged to develop procedures to enable them to use an end-of-year benefit information date. In that regard, paragraph 29 of this Statement provides, as did the Exposure Drafts, that

detailed service-related data for individual employees as of a date preceding the end of the year may be projected to that latter date, provided the results obtained are substantially the same as those that would be determined using data as of the end of the year.

211. Because ERISA permits benefit valuations for funding purposes to be performed on a triennial rather than annual basis, certain respondents opposed requiring annual benefit valuations for financial reporting purposes. This Statement permits detailed service-related data for individual employees collected at an earlier date to be projected to the benefit information date. However, based on testimony by certain actuaries at hearings held by the Department of Labor regarding the proposed revision of Schedule B of Form 5500 (footnote 41), projecting beginning-of-year employee data to year-end would be difficult. Therefore, it is expected that only in unusual circumstances will projecting the data collected during a triennial valuation to a benefit information date in a subsequent year satisfy the criterion of providing results that are substantially the same as those that would be obtained using data as of that latter date. An example of such unusual circumstances might be a small plan with a stable participant population.

Minimum Required Display of Benefit Information

212. Unless all participants' benefits represent claims against plan assets of equal status and timing, any assessment of benefit security for an individual participant or group of similarly situated participants would be impaired to the extent it was based solely on the relationship between total net assets available for benefits and the actuarial present value of all accumulated plan benefits. (Paragraph 219 discusses required disclosure regarding the priority order of participants' claims to plan assets.) It seems reasonable to assume, however, that the benefits of participants who are already receiving payments *(benefits in pay status)* will generally be paid sooner than will the benefits of present or terminated employees. In determining their respective actuarial present values, fewer subjective assumptions are required for benefits in pay status than are required for benefits not in pay status. For example, assumptions regarding when benefit payments will begin are required for the latter but not for the former. Thus, the actuarial present value of benefits in pay status is a more objective measurement. Similar relationships exist between other vested benefits and nonvested benefits.

213. Some respondents view vested and nonvested benefits differently. As previously indicated, some believe that only vested benefits are a plan liability.

For an ERISA plan, nonvested benefits do not enter into the determination of an employer's contingent liability to the PBGC upon plan termination. That contingent liability relates to the value of PBGC-guaranteed benefits, and that value will probably differ from the vested benefit information presented in plan financial statements. Nevertheless, in the absence of more accurate information, some consider vested benefit information useful in assessing an employer's potential liability in the event of plan termination.

214. This Statement requires that the benefit information be segmented into at least the following categories:

a. Vested benefits of participants currently receiving payments
b. Other vested benefits
c. Nonvested benefits.

The Board concluded that such minimum segmentation would be useful in assessing a plan's near-term vs. long-range liquidity requirements. It might also provide some indication of the relative degree of objectivity or subjectivity inherent in determining the benefit information and would provide information needed by those who wish to make certain judgments or wish to compute certain financial ratios, for example, net asset information to vested benefit information. (Paragraph 221 discusses another ratio sometimes used.) Certain actuaries with whom the Board consulted indicated that the required segmentation could be provided at minimal cost.

215. The initial Exposure Draft required similar benefit segmentation. However, it also required further segmentation if that would provide information particularly useful in assessing the security for the benefits of a significant number of participants. That additional requirement was consistent with that Exposure Draft's focus on a benefits-at-risk approach and its requirement that certain plans use PBGC rates to determine the benefit information.

216. Only in the event of plan termination is the security for each participant's benefits actually determined. Should that event occur, the degree of risk that particular participants bear depends on their benefits' priority position in the allocation of plan assets. For most **noncontributory plans**, benefits in pay status generally have the highest priority, followed by other vested benefits and then nonvested benefits. (In contributory plans, benefits derived from participants' contributions normally have the highest priority.) Additional priority positions may be specified within those broad classifications. In an ERISA plan, for example, vested benefits that are insured by the PBGC generally

have a higher priority than do vested benefits that are not so insured.

217. The initial Exposure Draft recognized that, particularly for ERISA plans, segmenting the benefit information by plan termination priority class could be a complex procedure, and its intent was to require that procedure only in certain limited circumstances. Because termination priorities govern the allocation of plan assets upon plan termination, those priorities are an essential element in assessing benefit security. Further, when an ERISA plan terminates, PBGC rates are used to value participants' benefits for purposes of determining plan sufficiency and allocating the assets of an insufficient plan. Thus, for ERISA plans, that Exposure Draft's requirement for the use of PBGC rates would (when the further segmentation provisions applied) generally have allocated to each applicable termination priority category the same actuarial present value that would have been allocated to it if the plan had been terminated at the benefit information date.

218. Many respondents objected to the benefit segmentation requirements of the initial Exposure Draft. Some objected to the basic segmentation. However, most objections focused on the possible additional segmentation requirement. Reasons for those objections included (a) the complexity and expense of making the termination priority allocations pursuant to Section 4044 of ERISA, (b) the view that termination priorities are irrelevant for an ongoing plan, and (c) concern that employers might become reluctant to improve benefits because of the resulting disclosure of the effect that plan amendments have in reallocating available assets among various categories of benefits in the event of plan termination.

219. Because (a) this Statement places more emphasis than did the initial Exposure Draft on providing information useful in assessing future rather than immediate security and (b) the requirement for use of PBGC rates was deleted, the Board concluded that the further segmentation requirement should not be retained. If the benefit information for an ERISA plan is determined using other than PBGC rates, the amount allocated to a given termination priority category may differ significantly from the amount that would be allocated to that category in the event of plan termination. However, because the primary objective adopted by the Board encompasses both the present and future ability of the plan to pay benefits (that is, both immediate and future security) the Board does not agree that disclosure of termination priorities is irrelevant for an ongoing plan. Therefore, this Statement requires that plan financial statements include a brief, general description of the priority order of participants' claims to the assets of the plan upon plan termination. The

Board concluded that such a description will serve to alert participants that a comparison of total net assets with the total actuarial present value of accumulated plan benefits (or with the three minimum required categories of benefit information) does not necessarily indicate which benefits would be covered by plan assets in the event of plan termination. However, the Board believes that unnecessary duplication of disclosures should be avoided. Therefore, if a description of termination priorities is otherwise published and made available to participants, the required description may be omitted if both a reference to such other source and a statement such as that illustrated in footnote 16 are made.

220. For reasons similar to those in paragraph 106, respondents' views regarding perceived effects on employers' decisions were rejected. Even if they had been accepted, the Board believes that at least as strong a case might be made that disclosure of termination priorities is appropriate because both employers and participants should understand the effect of plan amendments on benefit security.

221. Certain respondents to the initial Exposure Draft indicated that disclosure of present employees' accumulated contributions (including interest, if any) would provide useful information. Terminating employees are generally entitled to return of their accumulated contributions (sometimes with interest). Therefore, regardless of their overall view on the accounting nature of the benefit information, some view present employees' accumulated contributions as a plan liability. Others consider present employees' accumulated contributions to be a contingent liability that should be disclosed. It has been suggested that the relationship between net assets and the sum of accumulated employee contributions (including interest, if any) and the actuarial present value of benefits in pay status provides a useful measure for assessing minimum funding adequacy. That is, some believe that net assets available for benefits should, at a minimum, be adequate to provide all benefits in pay status and to refund present employees' accumulated contributions. The recommended disclosure would also provide some indication of relative amounts of plan assets that originated from employee contributions. Based on the foregoing, the Board concluded that disclosure of present employees' accumulated contributions (including interest, if any) should be required. Because the rate of interest credited on employees' contributions may vary among plans, disclosure of that interest rate is also required. Because plans generally maintain records of employee contributions, the Board believes that the benefits of the required disclosure can be obtained at minimal incremental cost.

222. If some or all employee contributions have been used to purchase contracts with insurance companies that are excluded from plan assets, comparison of the total amount of present employees' accumulated contributions with plan assets might be misleading as an indication of relative amounts of plan assets that originated from employee contributions. Therefore, employee contributions that have been so used should be excluded when making the required disclosure. The revised Exposure Draft asked respondents that have used employee contributions in the manner described to comment on the feasibility of determining the amount to be excluded. Responses generally indicated that that determination would be feasible.

Alternatives Considered for Location of Benefit Information

223. Respondents suggested the following alternative locations for presenting benefit information: as a liability, as an equity interest, as supplemental disclosure, or as a combination of the foregoing.

224. Certain respondents contended that a liability should be recognized to the extent that participants have legally enforceable rights to their benefits. They argued that generally accepted accounting principles require other accounting entities to recognize as liabilities those claims that are legally enforceable against them and that there is no reason to apply a different standard to pension plans. Other respondents advocated a liability presentation because they believed that, regardless of the legal relationship, benefits are an equitable obligation of the plan. In their view, participants earn their benefits as they perform services. Therefore, the financial statements should present as a liability those benefits considered earned by participants.

225. Certain respondents advocated presentation of benefit information as participants' equity in the net assets of the plan. Some did not believe that the benefit information satisfied present criteria for recognizing an accounting liability. Because they considered it necessary to display the measure in a prominent manner so users could focus on the relationship between the plan's resources and the benefits accumulated under the plan, they favored presentation of benefit information as an equity interest. Others considered that presentation appropriate because they view the relationship between the plan and its participants primarily as a fiduciary one. In their view, the plan's resources are held in trust for participants who have a beneficial interest in those resources.

226. Some respondents favored presenting benefit information in the notes to the financial statements. Others preferred a separate financial statement. For some, presenting the benefit information as either a

liability or an equity interest limited the information to less than that considered necessary in assessing the plan's ability to pay benefits. Others did not view benefit information as satisfying the criteria for either a liability or an equity interest. Certain respondents who expressed that view nevertheless felt that the benefit and net asset information should be combined and presented in a single financial statement. Those respondents believed that the relationship between the net assets available for benefits and the actuarial present value of accumulated plan benefits should be made explicit.

227. Certain respondents advocated some combination of the foregoing. Generally, those recommendations were based on what was perceived to be (a) an appropriate measure of a liability for an ongoing plan and (b) information necessary in assessing benefit security. Thus, certain respondents advocated presenting vested benefit information as a liability in the basic financial statements and nonvested benefit information in the accompanying notes.

228. For reasons similar to those discussed in paragraphs 131 and 132, other respondents favored presenting the benefit information as supplemental information, that is, in a financial report but outside of the financial statements.

Conclusions on Location of Benefit Information

229. Certain Board members are not convinced that the benefit information required by this Statement satisfies the criteria for presentation as a liability *of the plan.* Employees render services *to the employer* in exchange for their benefits. Therefore, if any liability exists, it is more likely that of the employer(s) rather than that of the plan.[44] Other Board members believe that the benefit information does represent a liability of the plan. Certain Board members believe that provided the benefit information is located in the financial statements, the primary objective is satisfied; that is, it is not necessary to resolve whether the benefit information constitutes a liability of the plan or the employer(s).

230. Although there is a fiduciary relationship between a plan and its participants, an equity presentation would have the disadvantage of limiting the net equity of participants to the plan's net assets available for benefits.

231. Notwithstanding the divergence of individual Board members' views regarding the accounting nature of the benefit information, the Board concluded that that issue need not be resolved at this time. As part of its ongoing effort to develop a conceptual framework for financial accounting and reporting, another project on the Board's agenda addresses the definitions of elements of financial statements.[45] If in the future it becomes necessary to readdress the accounting nature of the benefit information, that effort should be facilitated by the existence of a Statement of Financial Accounting Concepts that contains definitions of assets, liabilities, and equity interests. Because of its decision not to resolve the issue at this time, the Board concluded that this Statement should not restrict the location of the benefit information within the financial statements. However, because the primary objective of plan financial statements focuses on providing information useful in assessing the plan's ability to pay, when due, the aggregate benefits attributable to service already rendered, the Board concluded that the benefit information (that is, categories (a), (b), and (c) identified in paragraph 22) should be presented together. The Board believes that the usefulness of the financial statements in assessing benefit security might be impaired if the user had to extract portions of the benefit information from various locations. Further, those who favored a combination approach (paragraph 227) generally did so because of their views about the liability nature of certain components of the benefit information. Although it decided not to resolve the issue of whether some part or all of the benefit information is a plan liability, the Board considered it inappropriate to have differing views on that issue serve as a basis for allowing portions of the benefit information to be presented in different locations.

232. The Board decided not to restrict the location of the benefit information within the financial statements, but it did conclude that the benefit information should not be presented as supplemental information outside of the financial statements. To require presentation outside of the financial statements, the Board believes it would be necessary to conclude that no part of the benefit information is an essential element of plan financial statements, that is, that the benefit information, either in part or in total, is neither a liability of nor an equity interest in the plan. The Board did *not* reach that conclusion; rather, it decided that it was not necessary at this time to resolve the nature of the benefit information.

233. The Board has on its agenda a project to develop guidelines for determining where information that meets the objectives of financial reporting should be disclosed—either within or outside of

---

[44]Board members did not focus on the issue of what is the appropriate measure of the employer's obligation. That issue is presently covered by Opinion 8 and will be reconsidered in another Board project (footnote 23).

[45]An FASB revised Exposure Draft, *Elements of Financial Statements of Business Enterprises,* was issued on December 28, 1979.

financial statements. In the absence of such guide-lines, the Board compared the benefit information with the types of information that it has previously decided should be presented outside of financial statements (for example, the current cost and his-torical cost/constant dollar information required by FASB Statement No. 33, *Financial Reporting and Changing Prices*). It noted that other information permitted to be reported outside of financial state-ments was supplemental to the primary information about elements presented in an enterprise's financial statements (that is, the enterprise's assets, liabilities, owners' equity, revenues, expenses, etc.). Such sup-plemental information is not the only information about those elements that appears in the financial report of the enterprise. In the absence of that sup-plemental information, the information contained in the financial statements would still present the enterprise's financial condition and results of opera-tions. An analogous situation does not exist with regard to the benefit information. The benefit infor-mation does not supplement other information about an element in a plan's financial statements. It is the only information required to be presented about the benefits attributable to the service ren-dered by employees—which information is neces-sary to present the plan's financial status and to achieve the primary objective of plan financial state-ments. The Board believes that distinction supports requiring the benefit information to be presented within the financial statements.

234. Some who favored reporting the benefit infor-mation outside of the financial statements expressed views similar to those discussed in paragraphs 131 and 132. That is, they thought the benefit informa-tion was appropriately the province of actuaries rather than accountants. Some also wished to exclude the benefit information from the scope of an independent accountant's audit. As discussed in paragraph 134, the Board does not accept the notion that if the preparation of financial information is not within the professional qualifications of accoun-tants, it is outside the scope of financial statements. Further, inclusion of the benefit information within plan financial statements does not necessarily require it to be audited by an independent accoun-tant. A plan administrator's assessment of various factors, including the needs of particular users of the plan's financial statements, may determine the extent of auditor involvement. For example, as allowed by ERISA regulations, some plan adminis-trators are presently choosing to exclude certain plan investments from the scope of an audit (para-graph 137). The Board does not believe it is appro-priate or necessary to exclude the benefit information from plan financial statements solely for the purpose of avoiding auditor involvement.

CHANGES IN NET ASSET AND BENEFIT INFORMATION

235. The information about a plan's ability to pay benefits when due that is provided by the plan's financial statements is affected whenever transac-tions and other events affect the net asset or benefit information presented in those statements. Nor-mally, a plan's ability to pay participants' benefits does not remain constant. Therefore, users of the financial statements are concerned with assessing the plan's ability to pay participants' benefits not only as of a point in time but also on a continuing basis. To facilitate that latter assessment, users need to know whether perceived changes in the plan's ability to pay benefits result from changes in invest-ment performance, levels of contributions, improvements of benefits, changes in assumptions, or other factors. Further, as previously indicated, information regarding changes in the value of plan assets is essential in assessing stewardship responsi-bility. Accordingly, this Statement requires that plan financial statements include (a) a statement that contains information regarding changes during the year in the plan's net assets and (b) disclosure of the effects, if significant, of certain factors affecting the year-to-year change in the benefit information. Pre-senting information regarding both the changes in the net assets available for benefits and the changes in the actuarial present value of accumulated plan benefits for the same period is necessary to present the changes in the plan's financial status for that period. Therefore, if the benefit information date is the beginning of the year, this Statement requires that information regarding changes in the net asset information for the preceding year also be pre-sented. In that situation, information regarding changes in the net asset information during the cur-rent year is an incomplete presentation of the changes in the plan's financial status during that year.

Changes in Net Asset Information

236. Information regarding changes in net assets available for benefits is to be presented in enough detail to identify the significant changes during the year. Paragraph 15 indicates particular items to be separately identified. The Board considered those items to be of such significance that they are required, to the extent applicable, for all plans. Paragraph 15 is not intended to limit the amount of detail or manner of presenting information regard-ing changes in the net asset information. Subclassifi-cations and additional classifications may be useful. For example, separately reporting refunds of termi-nated employees' contributions may be useful. Alternatively, such refunds may be netted against

contributions received from participants or included in benefits paid. The Board has not considered issues relating to detailed application of the general guidance provided in paragraph 15. Accordingly, plan administrators should use their best judgment in light of the relevant circumstances.

237. The initial Exposure Draft required separate disclosure of (a) the net change in the fair value of investments sold during the year and (b) the net change in the fair value of investments held at year-end. Some respondents suggested that combining those two amounts would provide a sufficiently informative measure of the change in the fair value of the plan's investments during the year and would avoid substantial detailed calculations. The Board agreed.

238. That Exposure Draft also required disclosure of the net gain or loss realized during the year on sales of investments. Some respondents expressed the view that disclosure of realized gains and losses is not relevant in a fair value reporting environment. The Board is not convinced that disclosing the net gain or loss realized on investments sold during the year would enhance an assessment of the plan's ability to pay benefits when due. The Board believes that the basic rationale for requiring a fair value reporting basis for plan investments (excluding contracts with insurance companies) does not support *requiring* disclosure of realized gains and losses. Such disclosure, however, is not proscribed.

239. To further assist users in understanding the changes in net assets during the year, this Statement requires disclosure of the net change in fair value for each significant class of investment, segregated between investments whose fair values have been measured by quoted prices in an active market and those whose fair values have been otherwise determined. The Board believes that information may be useful in assessing the relative degree of objectivity or subjectivity in measuring the plan's investments and the relationship thereof to investment performance during the year. Disclosure of the change in fair value for each significant class of investments provides useful information because different types of investments may perform differently and those differences may be assessed differently. For example, a decrease in the fair value of bonds during a period of rising interest rates may be assessed differently than a decrease or an increase in the fair value of equity securities during the same period.

Changes in Benefit Information

240. The initial Exposure Draft required that the effects of all significant factors affecting the year-to-year change in the benefit information be presented in a statement format. Although such presentation remains acceptable, that requirement has been modified to permit disclosure of only the significant effects of certain factors such as plan amendments and changes in actuarial assumptions. A number of respondents expressed concern about the perceived complexity and expense of developing the information required by the initial Exposure Draft. However, certain respondents and certain actuaries with whom the Board consulted, including representatives of the American Academy of Actuaries and the American Society of Pension Actuaries, agreed that disclosure of at least certain factors having significant effects is important in understanding the year-to-year change in the benefit information. The Board concluded that the minimum required disclosure specified in paragraph 25 would provide that information. The Board believes that each of those factors is distinct in nature. Therefore, their effects should be separately disclosed. The minimum required disclosure may be presented either in a statement format (with the addition of an unidentified "other" category to reconcile beginning and ending balances) or elsewhere in the financial statements.

241. The Board believes that identification of the significant effects of all factors affecting the year-to-year change in the benefit information provides additional information useful in understanding that change. Therefore, disclosure of the effects of the additional factors identified in paragraph 25 is encouraged. The items specified in paragraph 25 are not intended to be an exhaustive list of all factors that may affect the change in the benefit information during the year. If additional information regarding that change is presented, it need not be limited to nor include all other factors identified in paragraph 25.

242. Certain respondents expressed concern that disclosing the effects of plan amendments might affect union negotiations or result in pitting one group of participants against another, as in the case of a benefit increase for retirees that present employees believe decreases the security for their benefits. Similar arguments regarding perceived effects of accounting and reporting standards on the decisions of those responsible for managing plan assets, plan funding, or deciding whether to amend the plan were addressed in preceding paragraphs (paragraphs 106, 158, and 220). The Board considers the reasons stated in those paragraphs for rejecting such arguments to be equally applicable to this concern.

243. Certain respondents to the Exposure Drafts suggested that the Board prescribe a uniform order for calculating the effects of individual factors on the change in the benefit information. They indicated that the effects of factors such as those enu-

merated in paragraph 25 are not all independent and that the order in which they are calculated will vary among plans. The Board recognizes that the determined effects of factors comprising the net change in the benefit information will vary depending on the order in which the effects are calculated. The Board solicited additional information from certain sources for use in considering the order in which the effects of individual factors should be determined; such information, however, was not forthcoming. Because the Board is not aware of any conceptual basis supporting a particular approach to determining the effects of individual factors, any prescribed order would be somewhat arbitrary. Thus, the Board concluded that at this time it would not prescribe an order.

FORMAT FOR PRESENTING FINANCIAL INFORMATION

244. The Board recognizes that divergent views exist about the appropriate format for presenting the net asset and benefit information (and changes therein) required by this Statement. Certain of those views have been previously discussed. In addition, many respondents to the Discussion Memorandum favored presenting net asset information in the format of a statement of net assets available for benefits because that is the statement that ERISA plans presently file with governmental agencies.

245. In view of the Board's conclusion not to restrict the location of benefit information in the financial statements, this Statement permits certain flexibility in presenting the benefit information and changes therein required by paragraphs 6(c) and 6(d). Net asset and benefit information may be presented with equal prominence but in separate financial statements, or benefit information may be presented in notes to a statement of net assets available for benefits. A statement that combines net asset and benefit information is also acceptable. Similar alternative methods of presenting information regarding changes in benefit information are permitted.

246. All financial information presented in a single financial statement is generally understood to be determined as of the same date or for the same period. For a comparison of two amounts or a deduction of one amount from the other to be valid, both amounts must be determined on a comparable basis. Therefore, this Statement permits a single statement that combines benefit and net asset information only if the benefit information is determined as of the same date as the net asset information. Likewise, a single statement that combines information regarding changes in the benefit and net asset information is permitted only if the respective change information is for the same period.

DISCLOSURES

247. The Board concluded that the financial statements should provide (a) information about the results of transactions and events that affect the net asset and benefit information and (b) other factors necessary for users to understand the information provided. Disclosure of underlying methods, assumptions, and estimates, including an indication of their objective/subjective nature, aids users in evaluating the information provided.

248. The Discussion Memorandum considered 4 broad areas of disclosure and within those areas 23 possible disclosures. A number were of the type required for business enterprises; others were specifically enumerated by ERISA as worthy of consideration for disclosure in financial statements filed pursuant to the Act. Opinion was divided among respondents who addressed the issue as to which specific disclosures should be required. The basis for the Board's conclusions regarding certain disclosures required by paragraphs 28(c) and 28(e) were previously discussed (paragraphs 219 and 126, respectively). The following paragraphs discuss the Board's conclusions with respect to other disclosure requirements. As indicated in paragraph 4, the financial accounting standards dealt with in this Statement are those of particular importance to pension plans or that differ from existing generally accepted accounting principles. Accordingly, this Statement does not address all disclosures required by generally accepted accounting principles for other types of entities that are also applicable to pension plans.

Plan Description

249. The Board concluded that a brief plan description could assist users, particularly nonparticipants, in understanding the financial statements. Of those who addressed the issue, many respondents favored that disclosure. Others were opposed because, for many plans, that information is available from other sources. The view was also expressed that it would be difficult to describe briefly but adequately the possibly numerous and complex provisions of a plan. The Board did not find those arguments persuasive. The Board believes that the usefulness of plan financial statements will be increased with a brief description of the plan and that, although there may be some difficulty in initially preparing that information, there should be little, if any, difficulty in presenting it in subsequent plan financial statements. Additionally, for plans not covered by ERISA, a summary plan description may not be readily available. However, the Board also believes that unnecessary duplication of disclosures should be avoided. Accordingly, the Board concluded that if a plan agreement or a description thereof providing the required information is otherwise published

and made available, the plan description required by this Statement may be omitted provided reference to such other source is made.

Methods and Assumptions Used to Determine Fair Value of Investments and Reported Value of Contracts with Insurance Companies

250. This Statement requires that the plan's accounting policy disclosure include a description of the methods and assumptions used to determine the fair value of investments and the reported value of contracts with insurance companies. Investments are normally the principal resource of a plan. Therefore, their measurement can significantly affect an assessment of the plan's ability to pay benefits when due. Most respondents who addressed the issue urged disclosure of the methods and assumptions used for measuring investments. The Board agreed.

Significant Investments

251. Some respondents to the initial Exposure Draft favored disclosure of significant investments. Presumably, they believe that such information is useful in assessing stewardship and investment performance and the degree of risk related to future changes in the fair value of a plan's investments. Because (a) certain securities' market prices may fluctuate more than others and (b) determination of the fair value of investments by means other than quoted prices in an active market may be subjective, the degree of risk related to changes in the fair value of a plan's investments may depend, to some extent, on the degree of diversification and the nature of a plan's investment portfolio.

252. Presumably, the more information that is disclosed about plan investments, the more useful are the financial statements in assessing the plan's ability to pay benefits when due. However, there is a cost associated with detailed disclosure. Therefore, this Statement requires only identification of significant investments, that is, those that represent five percent or more of the net assets available for benefits. Identification of other investments, however, is not proscribed. Because no more than 20 investments need be identified, the Board believes the incremental cost to provide the information will not be significant.

Cost Basis of Investments Presented at Fair Value

253. The initial Exposure Draft required that the historical cost of investments, at least for each significant category, be disclosed. A number of respondents urged deleting that requirement because, in their view, historical cost information is not relevant in a fair value reporting environment and does not provide information useful in assessing benefit secu-

rity. Questions were raised regarding how to determine historical cost, including its application to bond swaps (paragraph 108). The Board is not convinced that knowledge of the historical cost of significant classes of plan investments would necessarily enhance a user's assessment of the plan's ability to pay benefits when due. Thus, it concluded that such disclosure should not be required. However, it is not proscribed. Given the Board's conclusion, it was not deemed necessary to resolve issues relating to determination of historical cost.

Transactions with Certain Related Parties

254. A number of respondents advocated disclosure of investments in, or transactions with, related parties—primarily the plan sponsor, the employer(s), and the employee organization(s). An investment in an employer is viewed as increasing the degree to which a plan's ability to pay participants' benefits depends on the financial condition of the employer. Accordingly, disclosure is considered necessary to allow financial statement users to evaluate the relative significance of such investments. Because the sponsor, employer(s), and employee organization(s) may have close relationships with the plan, disclosure of transactions with those parties may provide information useful in assessing stewardship responsibility.

255. Because this Statement requires identification of investments that represent five percent or more of the net assets available for benefits, the Board concluded that it need not specifically require disclosure of investments in the employer(s). However, disclosure of other significant transactions with the employer(s), the sponsor (if not the employer), or the employee organization(s) is required.

Method and Assumptions Used to Determine the Benefit Information

256. The actuarial present value of accumulated plan benefits is an essential factor for assessing a plan's ability to pay benefits when due. Many users will be unaware of this Statement's requirements regarding how that amount is calculated. Therefore, the Board concluded that the usefulness of the financial statements would be enhanced by requiring disclosure of the method and significant assumptions used to determine the benefit information.

257. Numerous assumptions are used in determining the benefit information. A given percentage variation in certain of those assumptions may be expected to result in a greater percentage variation in the actuarial present value of accumulated plan benefits than would the same variation in other assumptions (that is, the benefit information is

more sensitive with respect to certain assumptions than to others). The Board believes that users of financial statements should be aware of the degree to which financial information is affected by estimates and judgment. Accordingly, the Board believes that the usefulness of plan financial statements would be enhanced by disclosure of the estimated effect on the benefit information, or on the difference between the net asset information and the benefit information, of a given variation in the assumptions to which that information is most sensitive. Examples of such assumptions are assumed rates of return and, for plans that provide automatic cost-of-living adjustments, assumed inflation rates. However, the Board does not have sufficient information to assess the cost/benefit implications of *requiring* that disclosure. Therefore, at this time it is only encouraging plans to experiment with such disclosure.

Changes in the Plan, Methods of Measurement, or Assumptions

258. The requirement that plan financial statements include (a) a description of significant plan amendments made during the year ending on the latest benefit information date and (b) a description of significant changes in assumptions stems from the conclusion that the financial statements should include information about other factors necessary for users to understand the information provided. The Board believes that users' understanding of the significant effects of plan amendments and changes in actuarial assumptions will be enhanced if descriptions of those events are provided. In addition, users need to know what plan provisions serve as a basis for the benefit information. Accordingly, the Board concluded that if any significant amendments are adopted between the latest benefit information date and year-end, the financial statements should indicate that the benefit information does not reflect those amendments.

259. Some respondents to the initial Exposure Draft opposed requiring a description of significant plan amendments because such information is included in the ERISA-required summary plan description. The Board recognizes that a supplement to the summary plan description concerning any "material modifications" to the plan must be provided to participants by 210 days after the end of the plan year during which the modification became effective. However, because of the potential significance of plan amendments to the year-to-year change in the actuarial present value of accumulated plan benefits and thus to an assessment of the plan's ability to pay benefits, the Board concluded that providing a brief description of the plan amendment in the notes is preferable to incorporating by reference that supplement to the summary plan description in the financial statements. Further, for plans not subject to ERISA, a description of the plan amendment may not be readily available elsewhere.

260. The Board concluded that disclosure of changes in methods or assumptions used to determine the net asset information should be in accordance with existing generally accepted accounting principles. For example, a change from contract value to fair value for measuring contracts with insurance companies should be viewed as a change in accounting principles pursuant to APB Opinion No. 20, *Accounting Changes.*

Funding Policy

261. Many respondents advocated disclosure of the funding policy. A primary purpose of funding is to enable a plan to pay benefits when due. Assessment of the plan's ability to pay benefits is therefore enhanced if information about the pattern of funding adopted by the employer(s) and, if applicable, participants and other sources is also disclosed. Accordingly, this Statement requires disclosure of the funding policy and any changes therein. Some respondents to the initial Exposure Draft suggested that the disclosure for ERISA plans indicate whether the minimum funding requirements of the Act have been met. The Board agreed that such information could be useful in assessing benefit security. Thus, that disclosure is required.

262. Certain respondents to that Exposure Draft suggested that the requirement for disclosure of the funding policy be more specific about the nature of the required information. For example, it was suggested that the actuarial cost method and the amortization period for the unfunded supplemental actuarial value be disclosed. Other respondents suggested that the funding policy be specifically related to the benefit information, to any existing difference between the net asset and benefit information, or to both. Although the Board believes it unlikely that a funding policy disclosure incorporating the technical name of the actuarial cost method and the amortization period for the unfunded supplemental actuarial value would be meaningful to most users, such disclosure is not proscribed. The Board believes that a brief description, in general terms and in layman's language, of how contributions are determined pursuant to the actuarial cost method would be more understandable and therefore more useful. Thus, the latter disclosure is considered preferable.

263. The Board agreed that information regarding the estimated future impact of the funding policy on an existing difference between the net asset and benefit information would be useful in assessing the plan's future ability to pay benefits. However, at this

time, sufficient information to develop and evaluate specific requirements regarding that type of disclosure has not been received. Therefore, it is not required. However, the Board encourages plans to experiment with such disclosures.

Tax Status of the Plan

264. A principal reason for funding a pension plan through a qualified trust or contract with an insurance company is to avoid having participants or the plan pay current federal income taxes on employer contributions and the plan's investment earnings. Virtually all defined benefit pension plans are designed to qualify for exemption from income taxes. Failure to obtain, or to maintain, an exempt status could have a significant effect on a plan. Because of its significance, some respondents recommended that the tax status of the plan be disclosed in all cases. However, because (a) the vast majority of private defined benefit pension plans receive favorable letters of determination from the IRS as to their tax-exempt status, (b) it is the *lack* or *loss* of an exempt status that could have a significant effect on a plan's ability to pay benefits, and (c) the Board believes that disclosures required annually for all plans should be kept to a minimum, the Board concluded that disclosure of a plan's tax status should be required only if the plan has not received a favorable letter of determination, or if that letter has not been maintained. However, disclosure of the plan's tax status is not proscribed in other circumstances.

Description of Benefits Guaranteed by the PBGC

265. For plans that are subject to Title IV of ERISA, the guaranty of the PBGC provides an additional source of security for certain participants' benefits. Providing information about that guaranty enhances the usefulness of the financial statements in assessing benefit security. Accordingly, the Board concluded that ERISA plans should provide a brief description of the benefits guaranteed by the PBGC. Because coverage by the PBGC of increased benefits resulting from plan amendments is phased-in over a period of years, the Board also concluded that the description should include an indication of the application of the PBGC guaranty to any recent plan amendments. For the same reason as that stated in paragraph 219, if the required disclosure is otherwise published and made available, it may be omitted from the financial statements provided the statements make reference to such other source.

266. Some respondents favored placing more emphasis on the PBGC guaranty, and a few favored disclosure of quantified amounts of PBGC-guaranteed benefits. Others, however, contended that calculation of the benefits guaranteed by the PBGC would be administratively burdensome for an ongoing plan. The Board has not assessed the additional cost of measuring the benefits guaranteed by the PBGC, but has concluded that requiring that disclosure is not necessary to achieve the primary objective of plan financial statements.

Unusual or Infrequent Events

267. The benefit information presented in plan financial statements is intended to provide information as of a specific date, that is, the benefit information date. Measures of that information at subsequent dates will necessarily change as events (for example, service rendered) affect the measurement basis. This Statement does not contemplate disclosure of normal changes after the benefit information date, such as benefits attributable to service rendered after that date. However, the Board recognizes that an unusual or infrequent event or transaction that might significantly affect an assessment of the plan's ability to pay participants' benefits may occur after the latest benefit information date and therefore should be disclosed. For example, a plan amendment that significantly increases benefits for service rendered before the latest benefit information date should be disclosed. If reasonably determinable, the effects of such an event or transaction should be disclosed.

EFFECTIVE DATE AND TRANSITION

268. The effective date in paragraph 30 is one year later than that proposed in the revised Exposure Draft. ERISA plans with at least 100 participants are presently required to prepare benefit information for Form 5500 reporting purposes that is similar to that required by this Statement. The Board believes that many of those plans should be able to comply with this Statement in financial statements prepared for the 1980 plan year, and they are encouraged to do so. However, the Board recognizes that small plans and plans of state and local governmental units are not presently required to prepare the benefit information. Those that choose to issue financial statements in accordance with this Statement may need additional time to develop the necessary procedures. Accordingly, the Board concluded that the effective date specified in paragraph 30 is appropriate.

269. In the Board's view, the usefulness of the financial statements in assessing benefit security and changes therein over time will be enhanced by restating the financial statements of prior years if those prior years' statements are presented together with financial statements for plan years that are subject to this Statement. Accordingly, the Board concluded

that retroactive application of this Statement is appropriate.

270. Certain respondents to the initial Exposure Draft expressed the view that restating the financial statements of prior years could be difficult and expensive and suggested that the requirement be eliminated. The Board believes that some respondents misinterpreted that Exposure Draft as *requiring presentation* of restated prior years' statements, rather than as requiring only that such statements be restated *if they are presented*. This Statement does *not* require presentation of the financial statements of prior years.

271. A few respondents to the Exposure Drafts suggested that information regarding changes in the net asset and benefit information not be required for the initial year of compliance with this Statement. Regarding changes in net asset information, the Board notes that ERISA plans presently file similar information with governmental agencies. For plans not subject to ERISA, it does not appear that initially providing that information should be that difficult. Because of the Board's conclusions that (a) beginning-of-year benefit information is acceptable, (b) a statement of changes in benefit information that identifies the effects of all significant factors is not required, and (c) the Statement is not effective until the 1981 plan year, the Board concluded that there should be sufficient time to develop the required information regarding changes in the benefit information. Accordingly, the Board concluded that an exemption for the initial year of compliance should not be provided.

REDUCTIONS IN PERCEIVED COST OF IMPLEMENTING INITIAL EXPOSURE DRAFT

272. Many respondents to the initial Exposure Draft were concerned that compliance with its requirements would impose a substantial and inappropriate cost burden on plans. Those concerns primarily related to the required benefit information and the changes therein, although some concerns addressed other requirements, including the required net asset information and the changes therein. Certain of those concerns were apparently based at least partially on misinterpretations of the requirements. For example, some respondents apparently interpreted that Exposure Draft as requiring that annual financial statements for a plan, regardless of its size, be prepared, audited, and distributed to all participants. Others thought that restated financial statements for one or more prior years were required. This Statement does not require the preparation, attestation, or distribution of any financial statements. It is applicable only to

financial information that purports to be in accordance with generally accepted accounting principles. Whether a plan prepares such information; who; if anyone, attests to that information, either in part or in total; and who receives that information are issues that are not within the scope of this Statement.

273. The Board recognizes that certain other concerns were not based on misinterpretations. The Board agrees that the benefits of providing financial information should be expected to exceed (or at least equal) the cost involved. A number of changes made to the initial Exposure Draft's requirements were directly related to the Board's desire to reduce the perceived implementation costs.

274. Most concerns about implementing the requirements regarding the net asset information and the changes therein related to (a) determination of the fair value of contracts with insurance companies and (b) segregating the net change in fair value of investments during the year into the net change in fair value of investments held at year-end and the net change in fair value of investments sold during the year. Those requirements have been deleted. This Statement permits contracts with an insurance company to be measured at amounts determined by the insurance company. It also provides for disclosing in a single amount the net change during the year in the fair value of investments.

275. Rather extensive changes were made to the initial Exposure Draft's requirements relating to benefit information and the changes therein. In response to concerns that determination of end-of-year benefit information would impose a substantial cost burden for many plans, this Statement permits a benefit information date that is either the beginning or the end of the year. Because of the cooperative effort between the Board and the Department of Labor, it appears that the benefit information determined pursuant to this Statement should serve both financial reporting purposes and, for ERISA plans, Form 5500 reporting purposes. The Board's desire to avoid unnecessary differences between those requirements was a significant factor that influenced its conclusion regarding the benefit information date.

276. Another concern regarding the benefit information was the requirement that certain plans use PBGC interest and mortality rates in determining that information. Some viewed that requirement as creating timing problems and causing plans to incur additional costs. They indicated that issuance of PBGC rates has, in the past, generally been subject to a lag of several months. If those rates were not available when other aspects of the benefit information were determined, plans might incur additional

costs when the determination process was completed at a later date. For that reason and others previously discussed, this Statement does not require use of PBGC rates.

277. Many respondents objected to the complexity and resulting expense relating to the initial Exposure Draft's requirement that the benefit information be segmented beyond certain categories if that would provide information particularly useful to a significant class of participants in their assessment of the security for their benefits. Although some objections were apparently based on a misinterpretation that such further segmentation would be required annually for all plans, that requirement has been deleted upon consideration of respondents' concerns and other reasons indicated in paragraph 219.

278. Many respondents contended that it would be complex and costly to comply with the initial Exposure Draft's requirement for a statement of changes in benefit information that identified the effects of all significant factors. As an alternative, this Statement permits disclosing only the significant effects of certain factors affecting the year-to-year change in the benefit information.

279. The Board believes that the changes discussed in the preceding paragraphs, on an individual and aggregate basis, should significantly reduce the perceived incremental costs that were of concern to respondents. The Board believes that the implementation of this Statement will have a favorable cost/benefit relationship. The Board recognizes that neither all benefits from nor all costs of financial information can be measured objectively; different persons may honestly disagree about whether the benefits of providing certain information justify the related costs.

Appendix C

GLOSSARY

280. This appendix defines certain terms, acronyms, and phrases used for convenience in this Statement.

Accumulated plan benefits
Benefits that are attributable under the provisions of a pension plan to employees' service rendered to the benefit information date.

Act
The Employee Retirement Income Security Act of 1974.

Actuarial asset value
A value assigned by an actuary to the assets of a

plan generally for use in conjunction with an actuarial cost method.

Actuarial cost method
A recognized actuarial technique used for establishing the amount and incidence of employer contributions or accounting charges for pension cost under a pension plan.

Actuarial present value of accumulated plan benefits
The amount as of a benefit information date that results from applying actuarial assumptions to the benefit amounts determined pursuant to paragraphs 16-18 of this Statement (that is, the accumulated plan benefits), with the actuarial assumptions being used to adjust those amounts to reflect the time value of money (through discounts for interest) and the probability of payment (by means of decrements such as for death, disability, withdrawal, or retirement) between the benefit information date and the expected date of payment.

Allocated contract
A contract with an insurance company under which related payments to the insurance company are currently used to purchase immediate or deferred annuities for individual participants.

Benefit information
The actuarial present value of accumulated plan benefits.

Benefit information date
The date as of which the actuarial present value of accumulated plan benefits is presented.

Benefit security
The plan's present and future ability to pay benefits when due.

Benefits
Payments to which participants may be entitled under a pension plan, including pension benefits, disability benefits, death benefits, and benefits due on termination of employment.

Contract value
The value of an unallocated contract that is determined by the insurance company in accordance with the terms of the contract.

Contributory plan
A pension plan under which participants bear part of the cost.

Defined benefit pension plan
A pension plan that specifies a determinable pension benefit, usually based on factors such as

age, years of service, and salary. Even though a plan may be funded pursuant to periodic agreements that specify a fixed rate of employer contributions (for example, a collectively bargained multiemployer plan), such a plan may nevertheless be a defined benefit pension plan as that term is used in this Statement. For example, if the plan prescribes a scale of benefits and experience indicates or it is expected that employer contributions are or will be periodically adjusted to enable such stated benefits to be maintained, this Statement considers such a plan to be a defined benefit pension plan. Further, a plan that is subject to ERISA and considered to be a defined benefit pension plan under the Act is a defined benefit pension plan for purposes of applying this Statement.

Employee
A person who has rendered or is presently rendering service.

ERISA
The Employee Retirement Income Security Act of 1974.

ERISA plan
A plan that is subject to ERISA.

Funding agency
An organization or individual, such as a specific corporate or individual trustee or an insurance company, that provides facilities for the accumulation of assets to be used for paying benefits under a pension plan; an organization, such as a specific life insurance company, that provides facilities for the purchase of such benefits.

Funding policy
The program regarding the amounts and timing of contributions by the employer(s), participants, and any other sources (for example, state subsidies or federal grants) to provide the benefits a pension plan specifies.

General account
An undivided fund maintained by an insurance company that commingles plan assets with other assets of the insurance company for investment purposes. That is, funds held by an insurance company that are not maintained in a separate account are in its general account.

Net asset information
Information regarding the net assets available for benefits.

Net assets available for benefits
The difference between a plan's assets and its liabilities. For purposes of this definition, a plan's liabilities do not include participants' accumulated plan benefits.

Noncontributory plan
A pension plan under which participants do not make contributions.

Nonvested benefit information
The actuarial present value of nonvested accumulated plan benefits.

Participant
Any employee or former employee, or any member or former member of a trade or other employee association, or the beneficiaries of those individuals, for whom there are accumulated plan benefits.

Participating contract
An allocated contract that provides for plan participation in the investment performance and experience (for example, mortality experience) of the insurance company.

Participation right
A plan's right under a participating contract to receive future dividends from the insurance company.

PBGC
The Pension Benefit Guaranty Corporation.

Pension benefits
Periodic (usually monthly) payments made to a person who has retired from employment.

Pension fund
The assets of a pension plan held by a funding agency.

Pension plan
See **defined benefit pension plan**.

Plan
See **defined benefit pension plan**.

Plan administrator
The person or group of persons responsible for the content and issuance of a plan's financial statements in much the same way that *management* is responsible for the content and issuance of a business enterprise's financial statements.

Prior service costs
See **supplemental actuarial value**.

Reporting date
The date as of which information regarding the net assets available for benefits is presented.

Retired life fund

That portion of the funds under an immediate participation guarantee contract that is designated as supporting benefit payments to current retirees.

Separate account

A special account established by an insurance company solely for the purpose of investing the assets of one or more plans. Funds in a separate account are not commingled with other assets of the insurance company for investment purposes.

Service

Periods of employment taken into consideration under a pension plan.

Sponsor

In the case of a pension plan established or maintained by a single employer, the employer; in the case of a plan established or maintained by an employee organization, the employee organization; in the case of a plan established or maintained jointly by two or more employers or by one or more employers and one or more employee organizations, the association, committee, joint board of trustees, or other group of representatives of the parties who have established or who maintain the pension plan.

Supplemental actuarial value

The amount assigned under the actuarial cost method in use to years before a given date.

Unallocated contract

A contract with an insurance company under which related payments to the insurance company are accumulated in an unallocated fund to be used to meet benefit payments when employees retire, either directly or through the purchase of annuities. Funds in an unallocated contract may also be withdrawn and otherwise invested.

Vested benefit information

The actuarial present value of vested accumulated plan benefits.

Vested benefits

Benefits that are not contingent on an employee's future service.

Appendix D

ILLUSTRATION OF FINANCIAL STATEMENTS

281. This appendix illustrates certain applications of the requirements of this Statement that are applicable for the 1981 annual financial statements of a hypothetical plan, the C&H Company Pension Plan. It does not illustrate other requirements of this Statement that might be applicable in circumstances other than those assumed for the C&H Company Pension Plan. The formats presented and the wording of accompanying notes are only illustrative and do not necessarily reflect a preference of the Board. Further, the circumstances assumed for the C&H Company Pension Plan are designed to facilitate illustration of many of this Statement's requirements. Therefore, the notes to the illustrative financial statements probably are more extensive than would be expected for a typical plan.

282. Included are illustrations of the following alternatives permitted by paragraphs 6, 8, 25, and 26:

a. An end-of-year vs. beginning-of-year benefit information date
b. Separate vs. combined statements for presenting information regarding (a) the net assets available for benefits and the actuarial present value of accumulated plan benefits and (b) changes in the net assets available for benefits and changes in the actuarial present value of accumulated plan benefits
c. A separate statement that reconciles the year-to-year change in the actuarial present value of accumulated plan benefits vs. presenting the effects of a change in actuarial assumptions on the face of the statement of accumulated plan benefits.

Although not illustrated, paragraph 8 of this Statement permits the information regarding actuarial present value of accumulated plan benefits and changes therein to be presented as notes to the financial statements.

CONTENTS

Exhibit D-1

C&H COMPANY PENSION PLAN
STATEMENT OF NET ASSETS AVAILABLE FOR BENEFITS

	December 31 1981
Assets	
Investments, at fair value (Notes B(1) and E)	
United States government securities	$ 350,000
Corporate bonds and debentures	3,500,000
Common stock	
C&H Company	690,000
Other	2,250,000
Mortgages	480,000
Real estate	270,000
	7,540,000
Deposit administration contract, at contract value (Notes B(1) and F)	1,000,000
Total investments	8,540,000
Receivables	
Employees' contributions	40,000
Securities sold	310,000
Accrued interest and dividends	77,000
	427,000
Cash	200,000
Total assets	9,167,000
Liabilities	
Accounts payable	70,000
Accrued expenses	85,000
Total liabilities	155,000
Net assets available for benefits	$9,012,000

The accompanying notes are an integral part of the financial statements.

Exhibit D-2

C&H COMPANY PENSION PLAN
STATEMENT OF CHANGES IN NET ASSETS
AVAILABLE FOR BENEFITS

	Year Ended December 31 1981
Investment income	
Net appreciation in fair value of investments (Note E)	$ 207,000
Interest	345,000
Dividends	130,000
Rents	55,000
	737,000
Less investment expenses	39,000
	698,000
Contributions (Note C)	
Employer	780,000
Employees	450,000
	1,230,000
Total additions	1,928,000
Benefits paid directly to participants	740,000
Purchases of annuity contracts (Note F)	257,000
	997,000
Administrative expenses	65,000
Total deductions	1,062,000
Net increase	866,000
Net assets available for benefits	
Beginning of year	8,146,000
End of year	$9,012,000

The accompanying notes are an integral part of the financial statements.

Exhibit D-3

C&H COMPANY PENSION PLAN
STATEMENT OF ACCUMULATED PLAN BENEFITS

	December 31 1981
Actuarial present value of accumulated plan benefits (Notes B(2) and C)	
Vested benefits	
Participants currently receiving payments	$ 3,040,000
Other participants	8,120,000
	11,160,000
Nonvested benefits	2,720,000
Total actuarial present value of accumulated plan benefits	$13,880,000

The accompanying notes are an integral part of the financial statements.

Exhibit D-4

C&H COMPANY PENSION PLAN
STATEMENT OF CHANGES IN ACCUMULATED PLAN BENEFITS

	Year Ended December 31 1981
Actuarial present value of accumulated plan benefits at beginning of year	$11,880,000
Increase (decrease) during the year attributable to:	
Plan amendment (Note G)	2,410,000
Change in actuarial assumptions (Note B(2))	(1,050,500)
Benefits accumulated	895,000
Increase for interest due to the decrease in the discount period (Note B(2))	742,500
Benefits paid	(997,000)
Net increase	2,000,000
Actuarial present value of accumulated plan benefits at end of year	$13,880,000

The accompanying notes are an integral part of the financial statements.

Exhibit D-5

**C&H COMPANY PENSION PLAN
STATEMENT OF ACCUMULATED PLAN BENEFITS AND
NET ASSETS AVAILABLE FOR BENEFITS
[An alternative for Exhibits D-1 and D-3]**

	December 31 1981
Accumulated Plan Benefits (Notes B(2) and C)	
Actuarial present value of vested benefits	
Participants currently receiving payments	$ 3,040,000
Other participants	8,120,000
	11,160,000
Actuarial present value of nonvested benefits	2,720,000
Total actuarial present value of accumulated plan benefits	13,880,000
Net Assets Available for Benefits	
Investments, at fair value (Notes B(1) and E)	
United States government securities	350,000
Corporate bonds and debentures	3,500,000
Common stock	
C&H Company	690,000
Other	2,250,000
Mortgages	480,000
Real estate	270,000
	7,540,000
Deposit administration contract, at contract value (Notes B(1) and F)	1,000,000
Total investments	8,540,000
Receivables	
Employees' contributions	40,000
Securities sold	310,000
Accrued interest and dividends	77,000
	427,000
Cash	200,000
Total assets	9,167,000
Accounts payable	70,000
Accrued expenses	85,000
Total liabilities	155,000
Net assets available for benefits	9,012,000
Excess of actuarial present value of accumulated plan benefits over net assets available for benefits	$ 4,868,000

The accompanying notes are an integral part of the financial statements.

Exhibit D-6

C&H COMPANY PENSION PLAN
STATEMENT OF CHANGES IN ACCUMULATED PLAN BENEFITS
AND NET ASSETS AVAILABLE FOR BENEFITS
[An alternative for Exhibits D-2 and D-4]

	Year Ended December 31 1981
Net Increase in Actuarial Present Value of Accumulated Plan Benefits	
Increase (decrease) during the year attributable to:	
Plan amendment (Note G)	$ 2,410,000
Change in actuarial assumptions (Note B(2))	(1,050,500)
Benefits accumulated	895,000
Increase for interest due to the decrease in the discount period (Note B(2))	742,500
Benefits paid	(997,000)
Net increase	2,000,000
Net Increase in Net Assets Available for Benefits	
Investment income	
Net appreciation in fair value of investments (Note E)	207,000
Interest	345,000
Dividends	130,000
Rents	55,000
	737,000
Less investment expenses	39,000
	698,000
Contributions (Note C)	
Employer	780,000
Employees	450,000
	1,230,000
Total additions	1,928,000
Benefits paid directly to participants	740,000
Purchases of annuity contracts (Note F)	257,000
	997,000
Administrative expenses	65,000
Total deductions	1,062,000
Net increase	866,000
Increase in excess of actuarial present value of accumulated plan benefits over net assets available for benefits	1,134,000
Excess of actuarial present value of accumulated plan benefits over net assets available for benefits	
Beginning of year	3,734,000
End of year	$ 4,868,000

The accompanying notes are an integral part of the financial statements.

Exhibit D-7

C&H COMPANY PENSION PLAN
STATEMENT OF NET ASSETS AVAILABLE FOR BENEFITS
[If a beginning-of-year benefit information date is selected]

	December 31	
	1981	1980
Assets		
Investments, at fair value (Notes B(1) and E)		
United States government securities	$ 350,000	$ 270,000
Corporate bonds and debentures	3,500,000	3,670,000
Common stock		
C&H Company	690,000	880,000
Other	2,250,000	1,860,000
Mortgages	480,000	460,000
Real estate	270,000	240,000
	7,540,000	7,380,000
Deposit administration contract, at contract value (Notes B(1) and F)	1,000,000	890,000
Total investments	8,540,000	8,270,000
Receivables		
Employees' contributions	40,000	35,000
Securities sold	310,000	175,000
Accrued interest and dividends	77,000	76,000
	427,000	286,000
Cash	200,000	90,000
Total assets	9,167,000	8,646,000
Liabilities		
Accounts payable		
Securities purchased	—	400,000
Other	70,000	60,000
	70,000	460,000
Accrued expenses	85,000	40,000
Total liabilities	155,000	500,000
Net assets available for benefits	$9,012,000	$8,146,000

The accompanying notes are an integral part of the financial statements.

Exhibit D-8

C&H COMPANY PENSION PLAN
STATEMENT OF CHANGES IN NET ASSETS AVAILABLE FOR BENEFITS
[If a beginning-of-year benefit information date is selected]

	Year Ended December 31	
	1981	1980
Investment income		
Net appreciation (depreciation) in fair value of investments (Note E)	$ 207,000	$ (72,000)
Interest	345,000	320,000
Dividends	130,000	110,000
Rents	55,000	43,000
	737,000	401,000
Less investment expenses	39,000	35,000
	698,000	366,000
Contributions (Note C)		
Employer	780,000	710,000
Employees	450,000	430,000
	1,230,000	1,140,000
Total additions	1,928,000	1,506,000
Benefits paid directly to participants	740,000	561,000
Purchases of annuity contracts (Note F)	257,000	185,000
	997,000	746,000
Administrative expenses	65,000	58,000
Total deductions	1,062,000	804,000
Net increase	866,000	702,000
Net assets available for benefits		
Beginning of year	8,146,000	7,444,000
End of year	$9,012,000	$8,146,000

The accompanying notes are an integral part of the financial statements.

Exhibit D-9

C&H COMPANY PENSION PLAN
STATEMENT OF ACCUMULATED PLAN BENEFITS
[If a beginning-of-year benefit information date is selected]

	December 31 1980
Actuarial present value of accumulated plan benefits (Notes B(2) and C)	
Vested benefits	
Participants currently receiving payments	$ 2,950,000
Other participants	6,530,000
	9,480,000
Nonvested benefits	2,400,000
Total actuarial present value of accumulated plan benefits	$11,880,000

The accompanying notes are an integral part of the financial statements.

At December 31, 1979, the total actuarial present value of accumulated plan benefits was $10,544,000. During 1980, the actuarial present value of accumulated plan benefits increased $700,000 as a result of a change in actuarial assumptions (Note B(2)). Also see Note G.

C&H COMPANY PENSION PLAN

NOTES TO FINANCIAL STATEMENTS[46]

A. Description of Plan

The following brief description of the C&H Company Pension Plan *(Plan)* is provided for general information purposes only. Participants should refer to the Plan agreement for more complete information.

1. *General.* The Plan is a defined benefit pension plan covering substantially all employees of C&H Company *(Company)*. It is subject to the provisions of the Employee Retirement Income Security Act of 1974 *(ERISA)*.
2. *Pension Benefits.* Employees with 10 or more years of service are entitled to annual pension benefits beginning at normal retirement age (65) equal to 1 1/2% of their final 5-year average annual compensation for each year of service. The Plan permits early retirement at ages 55-64. Employees may elect to receive their pension benefits in the form of a joint and survivor annuity. If employees terminate before rendering 10 years of service, they forfeit the right to receive the portion of their accumulated plan benefits attributable to the Company's contributions. Employees may elect to receive the value of their accumulated plan benefits as a lump-sum distribution upon retirement or termination, or they may elect to receive their benefits as a life annuity payable monthly from retirement. For each employee electing a life annuity, payments will not be less than the greater of (a) the employee's accumulated contributions plus interest or (b) an annuity for five years.
3. *Death and Disability Benefits.* If an active employee dies at age 55 or older, a death benefit equal to the value of the employee's accumulated pension benefits is paid to the employee's beneficiary. Active employees who become totally disabled receive annual disability benefits that are equal to the nor-

mal retirement benefits they have accumulated as of the time they become disabled. Disability benefits are paid until normal retirement age at which time disabled participants begin receiving normal retirement benefits computed as though they had been employed to normal retirement age with their annual compensation remaining the same as at the time they became disabled.

B. Summary of Accounting Policies

The following are the significant accounting policies followed by the Plan:

1. *Valuation of Investments.* If available, quoted market prices are used to value investments. The amounts shown in Note E for securities that have no quoted market price represent estimated fair value. Many factors are considered in arriving at that fair value. In general, however, corporate bonds are valued based on yields currently available on comparable securities of issuers with similar credit ratings. Investments in certain restricted common stocks are valued at the quoted market price of the issuer's unrestricted common stock less an appropriate discount. If a quoted market price for unrestricted common stock of the issuer is not available, restricted common stocks are valued at a multiple of current earnings less an appropriate discount. The multiple chosen is consistent with multiples of similar companies based on current market prices.

   Mortgages have been valued on the basis of their future principal and interest payments discounted at prevailing interest rates for similar instruments. The fair value of real estate investments, principally rental property subject to long-term net leases, has been estimated on the basis of future rental receipts and estimated residual values discounted at interest rates commensurate with the risks involved.

   The Plan's deposit administration contract with the National Insurance Company *(National)* (Note F) is valued at contract value. Contract value represents contributions made under the contract, plus interest at the contract rate, less funds used to purchase annuities and pay administration expenses charged by National. Funds under the contract that have been allocated and

---

[46]The notes are for the accompanying illustrative financial statements that use an end-of-year benefit information date. Modifications necessary to accompany the illustrative financial statements that use a beginning-of-year benefit information date are presented in brackets.

applied to purchase annuities (that is, National is obligated to pay the related pension benefits) are excluded from the Plan's assets.

2. *Actuarial Present Value of Accumulated Plan Benefits.* Accumulated plan benefits are those future periodic payments, including lump-sum distributions, that are attributable under the Plan's provisions to the service employees have rendered. Accumulated plan benefits include benefits expected to be paid to (a) retired or terminated employees or their beneficiaries, (b) beneficiaries of employees who have died, and (c) present employees or their beneficiaries. Benefits under the Plan are based on employees' compensation during their last five years of credited service. The accumulated plan benefits for active employees are based on their average compensation during the five years ending on the date as of which the benefit information is presented (the *valuation date*). Benefits payable under all circumstances—retirement, death, disability, and termination of employment—are included, to the extent they are deemed attributable to employee service rendered to the valuation date. Benefits to be provided via annuity contracts excluded from plan assets are excluded from accumulated plan benefits.

The actuarial present value of accumulated plan benefits is determined by an actuary from the AAA Company and is that amount that results from applying actuarial assumptions to adjust the accumulated plan benefits to reflect the time value of money (through discounts for interest) and the probability of payment (by means of decrements such as for death, disability, withdrawal, or retirement) between the valuation date and the expected date of payment. The significant actuarial assumptions used in the valuations as of December 31, 1981 [1980] and December 31, 1980 [1979] were (a) life expectancy of participants (the 1971 Group Annuity Mortality Table was used), (b) retirement age assumptions (the assumed average retirement age was 60), and (c) investment return. The 1981 [1980] and 1980 [1979] valuations included assumed average rates of return of 7% [6.25%] and 6.25% [6.75%], respectively, including a reduction of .2% to reflect anticipated administrative expenses associated with providing benefits. The foregoing actuarial assumptions are based on the presumption that the Plan will continue. Were the Plan to terminate, different actuarial assumptions and other factors might be applicable in determining the actuarial present value of accumulated plan benefits.

C. Funding Policy

As a condition of participation, employees are required to contribute 3% of their salary to the Plan. Present employees' accumulated contributions at December 31, 1981 [1980] were $2,575,000 [$2,325,000], including interest credited at an interest rate of 5% compounded annually. The Company's funding policy is to make annual contributions to the Plan in amounts that are estimated to remain a constant percentage of employees' compensation each year (approximately 5% for 1981 [and 1980]), such that, when combined with employees' contributions, all employees' benefits will be fully provided for by the time they retire. Beginning in 1982, the Company's contribution is expected to increase to approximately 6% to provide for the increase in benefits attributable to the Plan amendment effective July 1, 1981 (Note G). The Company's contributions for 1981 [and 1980] exceeded the minimum funding requirements of ERISA.

Although it has not expressed any intention to do so, the Company has the right under the Plan to discontinue its contributions at any time and to terminate the Plan subject to the provisions set forth in ERISA.

D. Plan Termination

In the event the Plan terminates, the net assets of the Plan will be allocated, as prescribed by ERISA and its related regulations, generally to provide the following benefits in the order indicated:

a. Benefits attributable to employee contributions, taking into account those paid out before termination.

b. Annuity benefits former employees or their beneficiaries have been receiving for at least three years, or that employees eligible to retire for that three-year period would have been receiving if they had retired with benefits in the normal form of annuity under the Plan. The priority amount is limited to the lowest benefit that was payable (or would have been payable) during those three years. The amount is further limited to the lowest benefit that would be payable under plan provisions in effect at any time during the five years preceding plan termination.

c. Other vested benefits insured by the Pension Benefit Guaranty Corporation (*PBGC*) (a U.S. governmental agency) up to the applicable limitations (discussed below).

d. All other vested benefits (that is, vested benefits not insured by the PBGC).

e. All nonvested benefits.

Benefits to be provided via contracts under which National (Note F) is obligated to pay the benefits would be excluded for allocation purposes.

Certain benefits under the Plan are insured by the PBGC if the Plan terminates. Generally, the PBGC guarantees most vested normal age retirement benefits, early retirement benefits, and certain disability and survivor's pensions. However, the PBGC does not guarantee all types of benefits under the Plan, and the amount of benefit protection is subject to certain limitations. Vested benefits under the Plan are guaranteed at the level in effect on the date of the Plan's termination. However, there is a statutory ceiling on the amount of an individual's monthly benefit that the PBGC guarantees. For plan terminations occurring during 1981 and 1980, that ceiling which is adjusted periodically was $ X,XXX.XX and $1,159.09 per month, respectively. That ceiling applies to those pensioners who elect to receive their benefits in the form of a single-life annuity and are at least 65 years old at the time of retirement or plan termination (whichever comes later). For younger annuitants or for those who elect to receive their benefits in some form more valuable than a single-life annuity, the corresponding ceilings are actuarially adjusted downward. Benefit improvements attributable to the Plan amendment effective July 1, 1981 (Note G) may not be fully guaranteed even though total

benefit entitlements fall below the aforementioned ceilings. For example, none of the improvement would be guaranteed if the plan were to terminate before July 1, 1982. After that date, the PBGC would guarantee 20% of any benefit improvements that resulted in benefits below the ceiling, with an additional 20% guaranteed each year the plan continued beyond July 1, 1982. If the amount of the benefit increase below the ceiling is also less than $100, $20 of the increase (rather than 20%) becomes guaranteed by the PBGC each year following the effective date of the amendment. As a result, only the primary ceiling would be applicable after July 1, 1986.

Whether all participants receive their benefits should the Plan terminate at some future time will depend on the sufficiency, at that time, of the Plan's net assets to provide those benefits and may also depend on the level of benefits guaranteed by the PBGC.

E. Investments Other Than Contract with Insurance Company

Except for its deposit administration contract (Note F), the Plan's investments are held by a bank-administered trust fund. The following table presents the fair values of those investments. Investments that represent 5% or more of the Plan's net assets are separately identified.

	December 31, 1981		December 31, 1980	
	Number of Shares or Principal Amount	Fair Value	Number of Shares or Principal Amount	Fair Value
Investments at Fair Value As Determined by Quoted Market Price				
United States government securities		$ 350,000		$ 270,000
Corporate bonds and debentures				
National Locomotive 6% series C bonds due 1990	$600,000	480,000	$600,000	492,000
General Design Corp. 5 1/2% convertible debentures due 1993	$700,000	520,000	$350,000	250,000
Other		2,260,000		2,618,000
Common stocks				
C&H Company	25,000	690,000	25,000	880,000
Reliable Manufacturing Corp.	12,125	625,000	9,100	390,000
American Automotive, Inc.	5,800	475,000	6,800	510,000
Other		680,000		500,000
		6,080,000		5,910,000
Investments at Estimated Fair Value				
Corporate bonds and debentures		240,000		310,000
Common stocks		470,000		460,000
Mortgages		480,000		460,000
Real estate		270,000		240,000
		1,460,000		1,470,000
		$7,540,000		$7,380,000

During 1981 [and 1980], the Plan's investments (including investments bought, sold, as well as held during the year) appreciated [(depreciated)] in value by $207,000 [and ($72,000), respectively], as follows:

Net Appreciation (Depreciation) in Fair Value

	Year Ended December 31 1981	Year Ended December 31 1980
Investments at Fair Value as Determined by Quoted Market Price		
United States Government securities	$ (10,000)	$ 8,000
Corporate bonds and debentures	(125,000)	50,000
Common stocks	228,000	(104,000)
	93,000	(46,000)
Investments at Estimated Fair Value		
Corporate bonds and debentures	(11,000)	9,000
Common stocks	100,000	(49,000)
Mortages	(5,000)	4,000
Real estate	30,000	10,000
	114,000	(26,000)
	$ 207,000	$ (72,000)

F. Contract with Insurance Company

In 1978, the Company entered into a deposit administration contract with the National Insurance Company under which the Plan deposits a minimum of $100,000 a year. National maintains the contributions in an unallocated fund to which it adds interest at a rate of 8%. The interest rate is guaranteed through 1983 but is subject to change for each succeeding five-year period. When changed, the new rate applies only to funds deposited from the date of change. At the direction of the Plan's administrator, a single premium to buy an annuity for a retiring employee is withdrawn by National from the unallocated fund. Purchased annuities are contracts under which National is obligated to pay benefits to named employees or their beneficiaries. The premium rates for such annuities to be purchased in the future and maximum administration expense charges against the fund are also guaranteed by National on a five-year basis. The annuity contracts provide for periodic dividends at National's discretion on the basis of its experience under the contracts. Such dividends received by the Plan for the year[s] ended December 31, 1981 [and 1980] were $25,000 [and $24,000, respectively]. In reporting changes in net assets, those dividends have been netted against amounts paid to National for the purchase of annuity contracts.

G. Plan Amendment

Effective July 1, 1981, the Plan was amended to increase future annual pension benefits from 1 1/4% to 1 1/2% of final 5-year average annual compensation for each year of service, including service rendered before the effective date. The retroactive effect of the Plan amendment, an increase in the actuarial present value of accumulated plan benefits of $2,410,000, was accounted for in the year ended December 31, 1981. [The actuarial present values of accumulated plan benefits at December 31, 1980 and December 31, 1979 do not reflect the effect of that Plan amendment. The Plan's actuary estimates that the amendment's retroactive effect on the actuarial present value of accumulated plan benefits at December 31, 1980 was an increase of approximately $1,750,000, of which approximately $1,300,000 represents an increase in vested benefits.]

H. Accounting Changes

In 1981, the Plan changed its method of accounting and reporting to comply with the provisions of Statement of Financial Accounting Standards No. 35 issued by the Financial Accounting Standards Board. Previously reported financial information pertaining to 1980 [and 1979] has been restated to present that information on a comparable basis.

Appendix E

ILLUSTRATION OF MEASUREMENT OF ACCUMULATED PLAN BENEFITS[47]

283. It is assumed that the actuary uses a full range of decrements including termination rates and disablement rates at ages below age 65, early retirement rates at ages when eligible below age 65, and normal retirement rates at ages 65 and over.

a. Given:
  i. Benefit rate of $10 per month per year of service.
  ii. Normal retirement at age 65, irrespective of service. Retirement not compulsory.
  iii. Unreduced immediate benefit upon early retirement from active employment at age 62 with 20 years of service.
  iv. Unreduced immediate benefit upon early retirement from active employment before age 62 with 30 years of service. Social Security make-up benefit of $200 per month payable until age 62.
  v. Reduced immediate benefit upon early retirement from active employment after age 55 and before age 62 with 20 years of service. Reduction is 4% for each year by which retirement precedes age 62.
  vi. Unreduced immediate benefit upon total and permanent disability before age 65 with 10 years of service.
  vii. Deferred vested benefit, commencing at age 65, upon termination with 10 years of service. Benefit payments (at full actuarially reduced value) may also be elected to commence as early as age 55 if 20 or more years of service have been completed.
  viii. Spouse's benefit upon death in service after meeting eligibility requirements for early or normal retirement (30 years of service, age 55 and 20 years of service, or age 65) equal to $5 per month per year of service.

b. [Follows on page 421.]

---

[47]This appendix illustrates the measurement of accumulated plan benefits pursuant to the provisions of paragraphs 18(a) and 18(b) of this Statement. The example has been reproduced from Interpretation 2: *Interpretation of Recommendations Concerning the Calculation of the Actuarial Present Value of Accrued Benefits under an Active Plan,* as presented in American Academy of Actuaries, *Bylaws, Guides to Professional Conduct, Standards of Practice, February 1, 1979* (Chicago: American Academy of Actuaries), pp. 106-113.

Type of Benefit	Payable upon Separation from Service at Ages	Amount of Benefit	Benefit Starts at	Duration of Benefit
Age 25 and 5 Years of Service				
(1) Deferred Vested	30-49	$50	Age 65	Life
(2) Unreduced Early	50-64	50	Retirement	Life
(3) Social Security				
Makeup	50-61	33*	Retirement	To Age 62
(4) Normal	65 and Over	50	Retirement	Life
(5) Spouse	50 and Over	25	Death in Service	Life of Spouse
(6) Disability	30-64	50	Disablement	Life
Age 40 and 5 Years of Service				
(1) Deferred Vested	45-54	$50	Age 65	Life
(2) Reduced Early	55-61	36 at Age 55 Increasing $2 a Year to Age 61	Retirement	Life
(3) Unreduced Early	62-64	50	Retirement	Life
(4) Normal	65 and Over	50	Retirement	Life
(5) Spouse	55 and Over	25	Death in Service	Life of Spouse
(6) Disability	45-64	50	Disablement	Life
Age 45 and 10 Years of Service				
(1) Deferred Vested	45-54	$100	Age 65	Life
(2) Reduced Early	55-61	72 at Age 55 Increasing $4 a Year to Age 61	Retirement	Life
(3) Unreduced Early	62-64	100	Retirement	Life
(4) Normal	65 and Over	100	Retirement	Life
(5) Spouse	55 and Over	50	Death in Service	Life of Spouse
(6) Disability	45-64	100	Disablement	Life
Age 50 and 20 Years of Service				
(1) Deferred Vested	50-54	$200	Age 65	Life
(2) Reduced Early	55-59	144 at Age 55 Increasing $8 a Year to Age 59	Retirement	Life
(3) Unreduced Early	60-64	200	Retirement	Life
(4) Social Security				
Makeup	60-61	133*	Retirement	To Age 62
(5) Normal	65 and Over	200	Retirement	Life
(6) Spouse	55 and Over	100	Death in Service	Life of Spouse
(7) Disability	50-64	200	Disablement	Life
Age 50 and 30 Years of Service				
(1) Unreduced Early	50-64	$300	Retirement	Life
(2) Social Security				
Makeup	50-61	200*	Retirement	To Age 62
(3) Normal	65 and Over	300	Retirement	Life
(4) Spouse	50 and Over	150	Death in Service	Life of Spouse
(5) Disability	50-64	300	Disablement	Life
Age 60 and 10 Years of Service				
(1) Deferred Vested	60-64	$100	Age 65	Life
(2) Normal	65 and Over	100	Retirement	Life
(3) Spouse	65 and Over	50	Death in Service	Life of Spouse
(4) Disability	60-64	100	Disablement	Life

*Because this benefit type is one which is includible in the computation of the present value of vested benefits, the $200 monthly benefit is assumed to accrue uniformly over the first 30 years of service (see I(b)(ii)). If, on the other hand, there had been specified a benefit which never is includible in the computation of the present value of vested benefits, such as a $200 monthly benefit payable in the event of the employee's death after 30 years of service, the accrued death benefit to be valued in the age 25 and 5 years of service example would have been $33 (5/30 of $200) for death at age 50, $32 (5/31 of $200) for death at age 51, etc.

c. If, in the example, there were a maximum service limit of 30 years applicable at normal or early retirement or disablement, with a pro-rata portion of the expected normal retirement benefit payable on vested termination, the only changes in the amount of benefit would be for the deferred vested benefit:

Age 25 and 5 Years of Service	$ 33	(5/45 of $300)
Age 50 and 20 Years of Service	171	(20/35 of $300)

Statement of Financial Accounting Standards No. 36
Disclosure of Pension Information

an amendment of APB Opinion No. 8

STATUS

Issued: May 1980

Effective Date: For fiscal years beginning after December 15, 1979 and for complete interim statements
issued after June 30, 1980 for interim periods within those fiscal years

Affects: Supersedes APB 8, paragraph 46

Affected by: Paragraph 8 amended by FAS 95
Superseded by FAS 87

Other Interpretive Pronouncement: FTB 81-3 (Superseded by FAS 111)

(The next page is 428.)

Statement of Financial Accounting Standards No. 37
Balance Sheet Classification of Deferred
Income Taxes

an amendment of APB Opinion No. 11

STATUS

Issued: July 1980

Effective Date: For periods ending after December 15, 1980

Affects: Amends APB 11, paragraph 57

Affected by: Superseded by FAS 96 and reinstated by FAS 109
    Paragraphs 4, 17, 18, and 26 through 29 and footnotes 1 through 3 and footnotes * and † of
        paragraph 4 superseded by FAS 109
    Paragraphs 19 through 25 amended by FAS 109

SUMMARY

This Statement specifies the basis for classification of deferred income taxes in a classified balance sheet. Deferred income taxes related to an asset or liability are classified the same as the related asset or liability. Deferred income taxes that are not related to an asset or liability are classified according to the expected reversal date of the timing difference.

Statement of Financial Accounting Standards No. 37
Balance Sheet Classification of Deferred Income Taxes

an amendment of APB Opinion No. 11

CONTENTS

INTRODUCTION

1. The FASB has been asked to clarify the classification of deferred income tax charges and credits related to the tax effects of certain timing differences (hereinafter referred to as "deferred income taxes"). The FASB also has been asked to clarify the balance sheet classification of the tax benefits related to "stock relief" under FASB Statement No. 31, *Accounting for Tax Benefits Related to U.K. Tax Legislation concerning Stock Relief.*

2. Paragraph 57 of APB Opinion No. 11, *Accounting for Income Taxes* (see paragraph 6 of this Statement), requires deferred income taxes to be classified in a balance sheet as current or noncurrent based on the classification of assets or liabilities related to the timing differences. Some timing differences, however, are not related to an asset or liability. Accordingly, the Board has concluded that it should amend paragraph 57 to clarify the classification of deferred income taxes when there is no asset or liability in the balance sheet related to the timing difference.

3. The Board also has concluded that it can reach an informed decision on the basis of existing data without a public hearing and that the effective date and transition specified in paragraph 5 are advisable in the circumstances.

STANDARDS OF FINANCIAL ACCOUNTING AND REPORTING

Amendment to APB Opinion No. 11

4. The last two sentences of paragraph 57 of Opin-
ion 11 are deleted and the following sentences and related footnotes are added to that paragraph:

> A deferred charge or credit is related to an asset or liability if reduction* of the asset or liability causes the timing difference to reverse. A deferred charge or credit that is related to an asset or liability shall be classified as current or noncurrent based on the classification of the related asset or liability. A deferred charge or credit that is not related to an asset or liability because (a) there is no associated asset or liability or (b) reduction of an associated asset or liability will not cause the timing difference to reverse shall be classified based on the expected reversal date of the specific timing difference.† Such classification disregards any additional timing differences that may arise and is based on the criteria used for classifying other assets and liabilities.

---

*As used here, the term "reduction" includes amortization, sale, or other realization of an asset and amortization, payment, or other satisfaction of a liability.

†Tax benefits related to "stock relief" that have been deferred under FASB Statement No. 31, *Accounting for Tax Benefits Related to U.K. Tax Legislation concerning Stock Relief,* are not timing differences and should be classified the same as other liabilities based on the period of potential recapture.

Effective Date and Transition

5. This Statement shall be effective for financial statements for periods ending after December 15, 1980, with earlier application encouraged. Reclassification in previously issued financial statements is permitted but not required.

> The provisions of this Statement need
> not be applied to immaterial items.

*This Statement was adopted by the unanimous vote of the seven members of the Financial Accounting
Standards Board.*

Donald J. Kirk,	John W. March	Robert T. Sprouse
Chairman	Robert A. Morgan	Ralph E. Walters
Frank E. Block	David Mosso	

Appendix A

BACKGROUND INFORMATION

6. Paragraph 57 of Opinion 11 states:

Deferred charges and deferred credits relating
to timing differences represent the cumulative
recognition given to their tax effects and as such
do not represent receivables or payables in the
usual sense. They should be classified in two
categories—one for the net current amount and
the other for the net noncurrent amount. This
presentation is consistent with the customary
distinction between current and noncurrent categories and also recognizes the close relationship
among the various deferred tax accounts, all of
which bear on the determination of income tax
expense. The current portions of such deferred
charges and credits should be those amounts
which relate to assets and liabilities classified as
current. Thus, if installment receivables are a
current asset, the deferred credits representing
the tax effects of uncollected installment sales
should be a current item; if an estimated provision for warranties is a current liability, the
deferred charge representing the tax effect of
such provision should be a current item.

7. Under Opinion 11, deferred income taxes are
classified as current and noncurrent on the basis of
how the related assets and liabilities are classified.
The Board concluded that it should amend paragraph 57 of Opinion 11 to address the classification
of deferred taxes when either (a) the timing difference is not related to an asset or liability because
reduction of the asset or liability does not result in
reversal of the timing difference or (b) there is no
asset or liability related to the deferred income taxes.

8. Paragraph 10 of Statement 31 states that the
Board believes U.K. "stock relief" does not have the
characteristics of a timing or permanent difference.
Therefore, the classification criterion of paragraph
57 of Opinion 11 does not apply. Those tax benefits
shall be classified the same as other liabilities based
on the period of potential recapture.

9. A proposed Interpretation, *Balance Sheet Classification of Deferred Income Taxes,* was released for
comment on June 22, 1979. The proposed Interpretation of Opinion 11 addressed the classification of
deferred income taxes related to timing differences
associated with long-term construction contracts,
undistributed earnings of subsidiaries, and a change
in method of accounting for income tax reporting
purposes. Fifty-one comment letters were received.
The Interpretation proposed to clarify that deferred
income taxes classified as current should be reclassified to noncurrent only if the related asset or liability
is reclassified to noncurrent. Many respondents to
the proposed Interpretation questioned the appropriate balance sheet classification when the timing
difference is not related to an asset or liability
because realization of the asset or liquidation of the
liability does not result in reversal of the timing difference. Others commented that there is no asset or
liability related to the deferred income taxes for certain timing differences.The Board concluded that it
should amend paragraph 57 of Opinion 11 to
address the balance sheet classification of deferred
income taxes in those circumstances.

10. An Exposure Draft of a proposed Statement,
on *Balance Sheet Classification of Deferred Income
Taxes,* an amendment of APB Opinion No. 11, was
issued for public comment on March 14, 1980.The
Board received 67 letters of comment in response to
the Exposure Draft.

11. Some respondents suggested classifying
deferred income taxes based on the net effect of (a)
reversals of existing timing differences and (b) any
additional timing differences that may arise. The
Board concluded that balance sheet classification of
deferred income taxes is based on the deferred
income taxes that exist at the balance sheet date.

12. Other respondents suggested classifying *all*
deferred income taxes based on when the timing differences reverse or classifying as current only those
deferred income taxes that will actually be paid. The
Board concluded, however, that such criteria would
involve a more fundamental change in paragraph 57
of Opinion 11 that should not be considered at this
time.

13. Several respondents to the Exposure Draft commented about the operating cycle in the illustration of construction contracts. The Board did not intend to address or change how an operating cycle is determined. Accordingly, that illustration has been revised to be consistent with the operating cycle concepts expressed in Chapter 3A, "Current Assets and Current Liabilities," of ARB 43.

14. Several comments were received on the capital lease illustration. Those comments suggested classifying the deferred income taxes like the asset or like the liability. The Board concluded that, based on the facts set forth in the capital lease illustration, the nature of lease timing differences and the classification of the associated deferred income taxes described in paragraph 27 are appropriate.

15. Some respondents of regulated utilities stated that regulatory accounting instructions for their industry required deferred income taxes to be classified with the associated asset or liability. Another respondent stated that their required system of accounts makes no provision for a current classification of deferred income taxes. This Statement clarifies classification of deferred income taxes when there is no asset or liability in the balance sheet related to the timing difference and does not otherwise change the classification criteria of Opinion 11. Also, this Statement does not modify the provision in paragraph 6 of Opinion 11 which states that Opinion 11 "does not apply . . . to regulated industries in those circumstances where the standards described in the Addendum (which remains in effect) to APB Opinion No. 2 are met. . . ."

Appendix B

ILLUSTRATIONS OF BALANCE SHEET CLASSIFICATION OF DEFERRED INCOME TAXES

16. The examples in this appendix illustrate the balance sheet classification of certain types of deferred income taxes but do not encompass all possible circumstances. Accordingly, each situation should be resolved based on an evaluation of the facts, using the examples in this appendix as guides to the extent that they are applicable.

Installment Receivables

17. An enterprise reports profit on installment sales for tax purposes on the installment basis as receivables are collected. For financial reporting purposes, profit on installment sales is reported when the merchandise is delivered. The enterprise uses a one-year time period as the basis for classifying current assets and current liabilities on its balance sheet. Deferred income taxes are computed on the net change method. At December 31, 19X1, the balances of receivables reported on the installment method for tax purposes and of related deferred income taxes are as follows:

Installment Receivables:	
Amounts Due within One Year	$1,491,560
Amounts Due after One Year	3,835,440
Total	$5,327,000
Accumulated Deferred Income Tax Credits Related to Installment Receivables	$1,065,000

18. The deferred income tax credits relate to the installment receivables because collection of the receivables will cause the timing differences to reverse.[1] Accordingly, the enterprise would classify the deferred income tax credits the same as the related trade receivables. The trade receivables due within the next year represent 28 percent of the total trade receivables ($1,491,560/$5,327,000). Therefore, 28 percent of the related deferred income tax credits would be classified as current ($298,200).

Accounting Change for Tax Purposes

19. Deferred income taxes associated with an accounting change for tax purposes would be classified like the associated asset or liability if reduction of that associated asset or liability will cause the timing difference to reverse. If there is no associated asset or liability or if the timing difference will reverse only over a period of time, the deferred income taxes would be classified based on the expected reversal date of the specific timing difference.

20. An enterprise changes its method of handling bad debts for tax purposes from the cash method to the reserve method. Ten percent of the effect of the change at the beginning of calendar year 19X1 will be included as a deduction from taxable income each year for 10 years. The enterprise uses a one-year time period as the basis for classifying current assets and current liabilities on its balance sheet. At

---

[1]Under the net change method, deferred income taxes are computed as though the timing differences at the end of the period were the same timing differences that existed at the beginning of the period except to the extent that the aggregate amount changes. That approach is not used for balance sheet classification because balance sheet classification is based on the nature of the specific timing differences that exist and that relate to the deferred income taxes at the balance sheet date.

December 31, 19X1, the amount of the effect of the change that is yet to be included as a deduction from taxable income and the balance of the related deferred income taxes are as follows:

Amount of the effect of the change that is yet to be included as a deduction from taxable income (9/10 of total effect of the change)	$5,125,000
Accumulated Deferred Income Tax Debits Related to Accounting Change	$2,357,500

21. The deferred income taxes do not relate to trade receivables or provisions for doubtful accounts because collection or write-off of the receivables will not cause the timing differences to reverse; the timing differences will reverse over time. Accordingly, the enterprise would classify the deferred income tax debits based on the scheduled reversal of the related timing differences. One-ninth of the remaining timing differences are scheduled to reverse in 19X2, so one-ninth of the related deferred income tax debits would be classified as current at December 31, 19X1 ($261,944).

Method of Reporting Construction Contracts

22. An enterprise reports profits on construction contracts on the completed contract method for tax purposes and the percentage-of-completion method for financial reporting purposes. The deferred income tax credits do not relate to an asset or liability that appears on the enterprise's balance sheet; the timing differences will only reverse when the contracts are completed. Receivables that result from progress billings can be collected with no effect on the timing differences; likewise, contract retentions can be collected with no effect on the timing differences, and the timing differences will reverse when the contracts are deemed to be complete even if there is a waiting period before retentions will be received. Accordingly, the enterprise would classify the deferred income tax credits based on the estimated reversal of the related timing differences. Deferred income tax credits related to timing differences that will reverse within the same time period used in classifying other contract-related assets and liabilities as current (for example, an operating cycle) would be classified as current.

Unremitted Foreign Earnings of Subsidiaries

23. An enterprise provides U.S. income taxes on the portion of its unremitted foreign earnings that are not considered to be permanently reinvested in its consolidated foreign subsidiary. The foreign earnings are included in U.S. taxable income in the year in which dividends are paid. The enterprise uses a one-year time period as the basis for classifying current assets and current liabilities on its balance sheet. At December 31, 19X1, the accumulated amount of unremitted earnings on which taxes have been provided and the balance of the related deferred income taxes are as follows:

Accumulated unremitted earnings on which taxes have been provided:	
Expected to be remitted within one year	$ 9,800,000
Not expected to be remitted within one year	2,700,000
Total	$12,500,000
Accumulated Deferred Income Tax Credits Related to Unremitted Earnings	$ 1,250,000

24. The deferred income tax credits do not relate to an asset or liability on the consolidated balance sheet; the timing difference will only reverse when the unremitted earnings are received from the foreign subsidiary by the parent. A payment between consolidated affiliates does not change the consolidated balance sheet, so no item on the consolidated balance sheet would be liquidated. Unremitted earnings expected to be remitted within the next year represent 78 percent of the total unremitted earnings for which tax has been provided ($9,800,000/ $12,500,000). Therefore, 78 percent of the related deferred income tax credits would be classified as current on the consolidated balance sheet ($975,000).

25. If the subsidiary were accounted for on the equity method rather than consolidated (e.g., a subsidiary reported on the equity method in separate parent company financial statements), the deferred income taxes would relate to the recorded investment in the subsidiary. The payment of dividends that causes the reversal of the timing difference would be accompanied by a reduction of the recorded investment in the subsidiary. Therefore, the deferred income tax credits would be classified the same as the related investment in the subsidiary.

Capital Lease

26. An enterprise is the lessee under one major lease that is reported as an operating lease for tax purposes and as a capital lease for financial reporting purposes. The enterprise uses a one-year time period as the basis for classifying current assets and current liabilities on its balance sheet. At December 31, 19X1, certain data related to the lease are as follows:

Accumulated Lease Timing Differences[2]		$1,020,900
Accumulated Deferred Income Tax Charges Related to Lease Timing Differences		410,000
Amounts relevant to 19X2:		
Rental expense for tax purposes		$579,000
Book expenses:		
Depreciation	$250,000	
Interest	210,500	460,500
Net Reversing Timing Differences		$ 118,500

27. The lease timing differences result from the difference between rental expense reported for tax purposes and the total of interest expense and depreciation expense for financial reporting. Therefore, the deferred income taxes could be considered to relate to both the capitalized leased asset and the recorded lease obligation and not to any specific asset or liability. Accordingly, the enterprise would classify the deferred income tax charges based on the estimated reversal of the related timing differences. The timing differences that will reverse within the next year amount to $118,500 or 12 percent of the total accumulated lease timing differences ($118,500/$1,020,900). Therefore, 12 percent of the related deferred tax charges would be classified as current ($49,200).

Depreciation

28. An enterprise computes its depreciation expense on accelerated methods for tax purposes. For financial reporting purposes, depreciation expense is computed on the straight-line method. The enterprise uses a one-year time period as the basis for classifying current assets and current liabilities on its balance sheet.

29. The deferred income tax credits relate to the fixed assets because sale of the assets would cause the timing differences to reverse.[3] Accordingly, the enterprise would classify the deferred income taxes the same as the related fixed assets. No portion of those deferred income tax credits would be classified as current.

---

[2]The accumulated timing differences related to a lease that is reported as a capital lease for financial reporting purposes and as an operating lease for tax purposes could be determined based on amounts in the balance sheet rather than based on the difference in amounts reported as expense for book and tax purposes in prior years. If there is no accrued or prepaid rent for tax purposes, the accumulated timing differences would be the difference between the present value of the lease obligation and the net book value of the leased asset, both as reported in the financial statements.

[3]See footnote 1.

Statement of Financial Accounting Standards No. 38
Accounting for Preacquisition Contingencies of Purchased Enterprises

an amendment of APB Opinion No. 16

STATUS

Issued: September 1980

Effective Date: For business combinations initiated after December 15, 1980

Affects: Amends APB 16, paragraph 88

Affected by: Paragraph 2 and footnote 2 amended by FAS 96
           Paragraphs 2 and 5 amended by FAS 109
           Footnote 2 superseded by FAS 109

Other Interpretive Pronouncement: FTB 81-2 (Superseded by FAS 96 and FAS 109)

Issues Discussed by FASB Emerging Issues Task Force (EITF)

Affects: No EITF Issues

Interpreted by: Paragraph 4(a) interpreted by EITF Issue No. 95-3
             Paragraph 5 interpreted by EITF Issues No. 90-6 and 93-7

Related Issues: No EITF Issues

SUMMARY

This Statement specifies how an acquiring enterprise should account for contingencies of an acquired enterprise that were in existence at the purchase date and for subsequent adjustments that result from those contingencies. Amounts that can be reasonably estimated for contingencies that are considered probable are recorded as a part of the allocation of the purchase price. Subsequent adjustments are included in net income when the adjustments are determined except in limited circumstances described in this Statement.

Statement of Financial Accounting Standards No. 38
Accounting for Preacquisition Contingencies of Purchased Enterprises

an amendment of APB Opinion No. 16

CONTENTS

INTRODUCTION

1. The FASB has been asked to specify the application of FASB Statements No. 5, *Accounting for Contingencies*, and 16, *Prior Period Adjustments*, and APB Opinion No. 16, *Business Combinations*, to preacquisition contingencies[1] of purchased enterprises and adjustments that result from resolution of those contingencies. For example, an acquired enterprise might have litigation pending at the acquisition date, or an unexpected lawsuit relating to events that occurred before the acquisition might be filed shortly after that date. In such cases, do the criteria of Statement 5 apply to the estimate recorded as a part of the purchase price allocation, or, if not, what criteria do apply? Also, does Statement 16 require that a subsequent adjustment that results from a settlement of that litigation or from an estimate of the cost of a future settlement of that litigation be reported by the acquiring enterprise as an item of profit or loss in the period in which the settlement occurs or can be estimated? Alternatively, does Opinion 16 require the subsequent adjustment to be reported by the acquiring enterprise as an adjustment of the purchase allocation?

2. The Board concluded that it should amend Opinion 16 to specify criteria for recording contingent assets, contingent liabilities, and contingent impairments of assets as a part of the allocation of the cost of an enterprise that is acquired in a business combination accounted for by the purchase method. This Statement requires either the fair value of contingencies or other amounts that can be reasonably estimated for contingencies that are considered probable to be used as the basis of allocation of the purchase price during the "allocation period" as defined in paragraph 4. Subsequent adjustments are included in the determination of net income in the period in which the adjustments are determined. This Statement does not apply to potential income tax benefits of preacquisition net operating loss carryforwards or adjustments that result from realization of those benefits. APB Opinion No. 11, *Accounting for Income Taxes*, and Opinion 16 specify the accounting for those items.

3. Appendix A provides additional background information on preacquisition contingencies. Appendix B explains the basis for the Board's conclusions. The Board has concluded that it can make an informed decision on the basis of existing information without a public hearing and that the effective date and transition specified in paragraphs 8-10 are advisable in the circumstances.

STANDARDS OF FINANCIAL ACCOUNTING AND REPORTING

Definitions

4. For purposes of applying this Statement, certain terms are defined as follows:

a. *Preacquisition contingency*. A contingency of an enterprise that is acquired in a business combination accounted for by the purchase method and that is in existence before the consummation of the combination. A preacquisition contingency can be a contingent asset, a contingent liability, or a contingent impairment of an asset.

---

[1]Statement 5 defines a contingency as an existing condition, situation, or set of circumstances involving uncertainty as to possible gain or loss to an enterprise that will ultimately be resolved when one or more future events occur or fail to occur.

b. *Allocation period.* The period that is required to identify and quantify the assets acquired and the liabilities assumed. The "allocation period" ends when the acquiring enterprise is no longer waiting for information that it has arranged to obtain and that is known to be available or obtainable. Thus, the existence of a preacquisition contingency for which an asset, a liability, or an impairment of an asset cannot be estimated does not, of itself, extend the "allocation period." Although the time required will vary with circumstances, the "allocation period" should usually not exceed one year from the consummation of a business combination.

Allocation of the Purchase Price

5. A preacquisition contingency other than the potential tax benefit of a loss carryforward[2] shall be included in the purchase allocation based on an amount determined as follows:

a. If the fair value of the preacquisition contingency can be determined during the "allocation period," that preacquisition contingency shall be included in the allocation of the purchase price based on that fair value.[3]
b. If the fair value of the preacquisition contingency cannot be determined during the "allocation period," that preacquisition contingency shall be included in the allocation of the purchase price based on an amount determined in accordance with the following criteria:

(1) Information available prior to the end of the "allocation period" indicates that it is probable that an asset existed, a liability had been incurred, or an asset had been impaired at the consummation of the business combination. It is implicit in this condition that it must be probable that one or more future events will occur confirming the existence of the asset, liability, or impairment.
(2) The amount of the asset or liability can be reasonably estimated.

The criteria of this subparagraph shall be applied using the guidance provided in Statement 5 and the related FASB Interpretation No. 14, *Reasonable Estimation of the Amount of a Loss,* for application of the similar criteria of paragraph 8 of Statement 5.[4]

Subsequent Adjustments

6. After the end of the "allocation period," an adjustment that results from a preacquisition contingency other than a loss carryforward[5] shall be included in the determination of net income in the period in which the adjustment is determined.

Amendment to APB Opinion No. 16

7. The following footnote is added to the end of the last sentence of paragraph 88 of Opinion 16:

Paragraphs 4 through 6 of FASB Statement No. 38, *Accounting for Preacquisition Contingencies of Purchased Enterprises,* specify how the general guidelines of this paragraph shall be applied to preacquisition contingencies.

Effective Date and Transition

8. The provisions of this Statement shall be effective for preacquisition contingencies assumed in business combinations initiated[6] after December 15, 1980.

9. Application of the provisions of this Statement to preacquisition contingencies assumed in business combinations initiated prior to December 16, 1980 is encouraged but not required. An enterprise electing to apply the provisions of this Statement to such preacquisition contingencies shall apply either the provisions of subparagraph (a) below or the provisions of subparagraphs (a) and (b) below:

a. The provisions of this Statement shall be applied to *all* preacquisition contingencies assumed in business combinations for which the "allocation

---

[2]Paragraph 49 of Opinion 11 and paragraph 88 of Opinion 16 (paragraphs 15 and 16 of this Statement) specify the accounting for the potential tax benefit of a loss carryforward of a purchased subsidiary. Opinion 11 specifies that such tax benefits are to be recognized as assets at the date of the purchase only if realization is assured beyond any reasonable doubt; otherwise, they are recognized only when realized. In the latter case, Opinion 16 specifies that those tax benefits retroactively reduce goodwill when realized.

[3]For example, if it can be demonstrated that the parties to a business combination agreed to adjust the total consideration by an amount as a result of a newly discovered contingency, that amount would be a determined fair value of that contingency.

[4]Interpretation 14 specifies the amount to be accrued if the reasonable estimate of the amount is a range. If some amount within the range appears at the time to be a better estimate than any other amount within the range, that amount is accrued. If no amount within the range is a better estimate than any other amount, however, the minimum amount in the range is accrued.

[5]See footnote 2.

[6]The date on which a business combination is "initiated" is defined in paragraph 46(a) of Opinion 16 as "the earlier of (1) the date that the major terms of a plan, including the ratio of exchange of stock, are announced publicly or otherwise formally made known to the stockholders of any one of the combining companies or (2) the date that stockholders of a combining company are notified in writing of an exchange offer."

period" *has not* ended at the date of initial application. If application of this Statement to such preacquisition contingencies requires adjustments of amounts previously recorded, those adjustments shall be reported the same as other adjustments of preliminary amounts recorded during the "allocation period." Also, if the enterprise so elects,

b. The provisions of this Statement shall be applied to *all other* unresolved preacquisition contingencies[7] at the date of initial application. If the application permitted by this subparagraph is elected, adjustments that result from resolution or revised estimates of *all other* unresolved preacquisition contingencies shall be reported in accordance with the provisions of paragraph 6 of this Statement. If the previous reporting of those preacquisition contingencies in the allocation of the purchase price was not in conformity with paragraph 5 of this Statement, the provisions of

this Statement may be applied retroactively at the date of initial application to *all other* unresolved preacquisition contingencies.

Except as provided in this paragraph, this Statement shall not be applied retroactively to previously issued annual or interim financial statements.

10. If the provisions of paragraph 6 of this Statement are not applied to all unresolved preacquisition contingencies as permitted by paragraph 9, financial statements for periods ending after December 15, 1980 shall include disclosure of the amount and nature of adjustments determined after December 15, 1980 that result from preacquisition contingencies and that are reported other than as specified in paragraph 6. The disclosure shall include a description of how those adjustments are reported and the effect of the adjustments on current or expected future cash flows of the enterprise.

> **The provisions of this Statement need**
> **not be applied to immaterial items.**

This Statement was adopted by the affirmative votes of five members of the Financial Accounting Standards Board. Messrs. March and Morgan dissented.

Messrs. March and Morgan dissent because they believe that the accounting for a business acquisition required by this Statement does not properly reflect the outcome of many preacquisition contingencies. They believe subsequent adjustments arising from such contingencies should be reflected as adjustments in the purchase allocation (the alternative summarized in paragraph 26) and not as an increase or decrease in net income of the period in which the adjustment is determined necessary (the requirement in paragraph 6 of this Statement). In their view, reporting the allocated cost of assets acquired and goodwill (positive or negative) based upon the best information obtainable, including hindsight, provides more reliable information to users. They do not agree that the fine distinction made in paragraphs 19 and 21 between an amount deemed paid for an item that includes an element of risk attribut-

able to an uncertainty and the outcome of that uncertainty is sufficiently substantive to require differences in accounting between the amount estimated for the contingency and its ultimate resolution. They also do not agree with paragraphs 4(b) and 5(b) which for all practical purposes require that the outcome be reasonably estimable within one year to be considered in the purchase allocation. The ability to predict the resolution of litigation and later-asserted claims within one year of an acquisition is often doubtful. Legal processes involve much longer time periods, particularly for more significant cases. Although they would oppose a time limit as a matter of principle, Messrs. March and Morgan believe approximately five years would be more realistic if a period were considered desirable for practical considerations.

Members of the Financial Accounting Standards Board:

Donald J. Kirk,	John W. March	Robert T. Sprouse
Chairman	Robert A. Morgan	Ralph E. Walters
Frank E. Block	David Mosso	

---

[7]"*All other* unresolved preacquisition contingencies" in this paragraph refers to all unresolved preacquisition contingencies assumed in business combinations for which the "allocation period" has ended at the date of initial application of this Statement.

Appendix A

BACKGROUND INFORMATION

11. The original request referred to in paragraph 1 was for an interpretation of Statement 16. The request indicated that the guidance of paragraphs 10 and 21 of Statement 16 could be considered to be in conflict. Paragraphs 12 and 13 of this appendix cite those provisions of Statement 16, and paragraphs 14-16 of this appendix cite the provisions of other authoritative literature that are referred to in paragraph 21 of Statement 16.

12. Paragraph 10 of Statement 16 requires that, with specified exceptions, ". . . items of profit and loss recognized during a period, . . . including accruals of estimated losses from loss contingencies, shall be included in the determination of net income for that period. . . ." The specified exceptions are described in paragraphs 11, 13, and 14 of Statement 16 and consist of:

a. Correction of an error in the financial statements of a prior period,
b. Adjustments that result from realization of income tax benefits of preacquisition operating loss carryforwards of purchased subsidiaries, and
c. Certain adjustments related to prior interim periods of the current fiscal year.

13. With respect to adjustments that are required by Opinions 9, 11, and 16 to be reported as adjustments to paid-in capital, goodwill, or other assets, paragraph 21 of Statement 16 states that "this Statement is not intended to require those adjustments to be included in the determination of net income of the current period." Paragraphs 14 and 15, below, cite the provisions of Opinions 9 and 11 that require adjustments to be reported as adjustments to paid-in capital, goodwill, or other assets. Paragraph 16, below, describes the provisions of Opinion 16 applicable to the purchase method of accounting for a business combination that require adjustments that result from preacquisition contingencies to be reported as adjustments to paid-in capital, goodwill, or other assets.

14. Paragraph 28 of APB Opinion No. 9, *Reporting the Results of Operations*, states that ". . . the following should be excluded from the determination of net income or the results of operations under all circumstances: (a) adjustments or charges or credits resulting from transactions in the company's own capital stock, . . . (b) transfers to and from accounts properly designated as appropriated retained earnings . . . and (c) adjustments made pursuant to a quasi-reorganization."

15. Paragraph 49 of Opinion 11 addresses reporting the tax effects of loss carryforwards of purchased subsidiaries, if not previously recognized. The paragraph states that those tax effects "should be recognized as assets at the date of purchase only if realization is assured beyond any reasonable doubt. Otherwise they should be recognized only when the tax benefits are actually realized and should be recorded as retroactive adjustments . . . of the purchase transactions. . . ." Paragraph 52 of Opinion 11 requires allocation of taxes to prior periods (or the opening balance of retained earnings) and to other stockholders' equity accounts in certain circumstances, none of which relate to preacquisition contingencies.

16. Paragraph 88 of Opinion 16 provides "general guides for assigning amounts to the individual assets acquired and liabilities assumed, except goodwill." The general guides in paragraph 88 include an acknowledgment that allowances for uncollectibility of receivables may be necessary and also include the statement that "an acquiring corporation should reduce the acquired goodwill retroactively for the realized tax benefits of loss carry-forwards of an acquired company not previously recorded by the acquiring corporation." Opinion 16 does not otherwise directly address preacquisition contingencies.

17. An Exposure Draft of a proposed Statement, *Accounting for Preacquisition Contingencies of Purchased Enterprises*, was issued on December 26, 1979. The Board received 59 letters of comment in response to the Exposure Draft.

Appendix B

BASIS FOR CONCLUSIONS

18. This appendix contains a discussion of the factors deemed significant by members of the Board in reaching the conclusions in this Statement, including various alternatives considered and reasons for accepting some and rejecting others. Individual Board members gave greater weight to some factors than to others.

Overall Approach Adopted by the Board

19. This Statement distinguishes between (a) an amount deemed to have been paid for an item that includes an element of risk and (b) the gain or loss that results from the risk assumed.

20. Paragraph 5 requires that the amount paid for the contingent asset or liability be estimated. If its fair value can be determined, that fair value is used as the basis for recording the asset or liability.

Otherwise, an amount determined on the basis of criteria drawn from Statement 5 is used as the best available estimate of fair value. In accordance with the rationale of Opinion 16 (which requires that all assets and liabilities of the acquired enterprise, whether recorded or unrecorded, be identified and recorded by the acquiring enterprise and that only the residual purchase price that cannot be allocated to specific assets and liabilities be allocated to goodwill), this Statement allows a period of time (the "allocation period") for discovery and quantification of preacquisition contingencies.

21. Paragraph 6 requires that subsequent adjustments of the amounts recorded as a part of the purchase allocation be included in the determination of net income in the period in which the adjustments are determined. In contrast to the amounts deemed paid for the asset or liability, those subsequent adjustments are gains or losses that result from the uncertainties and related risks assumed in the purchase.

Contingent Consideration

22. A number of respondents to the Exposure Draft questioned the difference in the accounting required for preacquisition contingencies by this Statement and the accounting required for contingent consideration by Opinion 16. Opinion 16 requires that contingent consideration be accounted for based on its nature. The following examples illustrate the relationship of the accounting for contingent consideration to the nature of the agreement and contrast the nature of each agreement with the nature of a preacquisition contingency:

a. If the contingent consideration is based on subsequent earnings, the additional consideration, when determinable, increases the purchase price because the increased value that was purchased has been demonstrated. Additional goodwill was proven to exist by the achievement of the specified level of earnings. In contrast, when an enterprise changes its estimate of a preacquisition contingent liability, there is nothing to indicate that additional value has been created. A payment is expected to be required, but the payment does not demonstrate that an asset exists or is more valuable than before the payment was anticipated.

b. If the contingent consideration represents payment of amounts withheld to insure against the existence of contingencies, neither the payment of the contingent consideration nor the payment of a liability that results from the contingency with the funds withheld affects the acquiring enterprise's accounting for the business combination. The escrow is a way of protecting the buyer against risk. The buyer has agreed to pay the amount either to the seller or to a third-party claimant; and thus, the only uncertainty to the buyer is the identity of the payee. The amount of the agreed consideration that is withheld would be recorded as part of the purchase price in the original allocation. In contrast, a change in an estimate of a preacquisition contingency for which the acquiring enterprise assumed responsibility represents a change in the total amount that will be paid out or received by the acquiring enterprise. The buyer assumed the risk and is subject to the results of that risk.

Contingencies That Result from a Purchase

23. A number of respondents to the Exposure Draft questioned whether this Statement should be applied to contingencies that arise from the acquisition and that did not exist prior to the acquisition. Examples provided included litigation over the acquisition and the tax effect of the purchase. The Board concluded that such contingencies are the acquiring enterprise's contingencies, rather than preacquisition contingencies of the acquired enterprise. Accordingly, Statement 16 applies to those contingencies after the initial purchase allocation.

Criteria for Inclusion in Purchase Allocation

24. Some believe that a distinction should be made based on whether contingencies were known to the acquiring enterprise at the date of the purchase. In their opinion, the initial recorded estimate for contingencies that were identified at the date of the purchase should be an adjustment of the purchase price and its allocation regardless of when that estimate becomes determinable. The acquiring enterprise agreed to assume those identified contingencies as a condition of the purchase, and presumably that assessment was considered directly in arriving at the purchase price; accordingly, they should be accounted for as part of the purchase. On the other hand, the discovery of contingent assets or liabilities that were *not* identified at the date of the purchase should not affect the allocation of a purchase price because unknown contingencies could not enter directly in the determination of the purchase price and discovery of unexpected assets or liabilities should not affect cost assigned to the other assets and liabilities acquired.

25. The Board rejected the approach outlined in paragraph 24 for a number of reasons, including the following:

a. An approach that would base the allocation of the purchase price on whether an item was known to the acquiring enterprise at the date of the purchase would conflict with the requirements of Opinion 16 for allocation of the cost of an enterprise accounted for by the purchase method. Paragraph 87 of Opinion 16 requires the acquiring enterprise to assign "a portion of the cost of the acquired company" to "all identifiable assets acquired . . . and liabilities assumed . . . , whether or not shown in the financial statements of the acquired company." The reference to "identifiable" does not indicate an intent to limit the allocation to items that were known at the date of the purchase.

b. A distinction based on whether contingencies were known to the acquiring enterprise at the date of the purchase could be viewed as only partially reflecting the economics of many purchase combinations. Many factors affect the purchase price in a business combination. Known contingencies would be one of those factors. Other factors might include amounts of earnings, demonstrated growth in earnings, and unknown preacquisition contingencies, the potential existence of which would nevertheless enter into an assessment of risk and affect the purchase price.

c. If all preacquisition contingencies that result from a cause that was identified at the date of the purchase were considered part of the purchase consideration, the distinction between an identified contingency and one that was not identified would be vague.

d. A requirement that initial recorded estimates for some contingencies be recorded as adjustments of the purchase allocation could discourage an enterprise from recording timely estimates.

26. Some believe that all adjustments that result from preacquisition contingencies should be excluded from income of the acquiring enterprise because they are not related to the acquiring enterprise's business operations. Some of those who hold this view would accept a time limit because they believe that the connection between the adjustment and any underlying event becomes less evident as the underlying event becomes more remote; however, the time limit would be an extended period of several years.

27. The Board rejected the approach outlined in paragraph 26 for a number of reasons, including the following:

a. The usual practice in the current accounting environment is for irregularly occurring costs that result from risks assumed by the enterprise to be reflected in income when they occur. The Board did not believe that it should differentiate between risks assumed by purchase and other business risks.

b. The distinction between an adjustment related to a preacquisition contingency and an adjustment that results from current events is not always clear. For example, an enterprise may settle litigation because the cost of a successful defense would exceed the cost of the settlement. The opinion of counsel may be that the case can be successfully defended. In that case, whether the cost of the settlement relates to the preacquisition event that is the stated cause of the litigation or to the current litigious environment is not clear.

28. Some believe that all adjustments related to preacquisition contingencies should be included in income of the acquired enterprise in the period in which the adjustments are determined. They note that Statement 16 requires accruals of estimated losses from loss contingencies to be included in income in the period in which they are determined, and they believe that contingencies assumed through purchase should be accounted for the same as other contingencies. Although the Board generally agreed, it concluded that an "allocation period" was needed to permit adequate time to make reasonable estimates for the purchase allocation required by Opinion 16.

29. Several respondents to the Exposure Draft stated that changes in an estimate should be accounted for the same as the original estimate. In examining the nature of a preacquisition contingency, the Board concluded that an estimate that can be made soon after the purchase likely would approximate the amount by which the purchase price reflected that contingency. If the eventual outcome of that contingency is significantly different, it is likely that the acquiring enterprise assumed a risk that turned out differently than expected. As indicated in paragraphs 19-21 above, the Board believes that it is appropriate for the result of a risk assumed by an enterprise to be accounted for differently than the transaction that resulted in the assumption of the risk.

Criteria for Amount to Be Included in Purchase Allocation

30. Paragraph 87 of Opinion 16 describes an acquiring enterprise's allocation of the cost of an acquired company to the assets acquired and liabilities assumed. That paragraph states:

First, all identifiable assets acquired, either individually or by type, and liabilities assumed in a business combination, whether or not shown in the financial statements of the acquired company, should be assigned a portion of the cost of the acquired company, normally equal to their fair values at date of acquisition.

Second, the excess of the cost of the acquired company over the sum of the amounts assigned to identifiable assets acquired less liabilities assumed should be recorded as goodwill.

If "identifiable assets" includes contingent assets, paragraph 87 could be viewed as inconsistent with the practice described in paragraph 17(a) of Statement 5 that "contingencies that might result in gains usually are not reflected in the accounts since to do so might be to recognize revenue prior to its realization." The Board concluded that this usual practice is not applicable to a purchase allocation because revenue does not result from such an allocation; rather, the question is whether to allocate amounts paid to identifiable assets that have value or to goodwill.

31. In the Exposure Draft, the Board proposed that all contingent assets, liabilities, and impairments of assets existing in an acquired enterprise at the acquisition date be recorded based on criteria similar to the criteria in Statement 5 for recognition of an estimated loss from a loss contingency. A number of respondents to the Exposure Draft stated that the fair value of a preacquisition contingency can sometimes be determined and that fair value might not equal the amount determined in accordance with the criteria based on Statement 5.

32. The Board did not intend to modify the general requirement of paragraph 87 of Opinion 16, cited in paragraph 30 above, that the purchase allocation be based on the fair value of the assets acquired and the liabilities assumed. Rather, the criteria were provided because fair value of a preacquisition contingency usually would not be determinable. Accordingly, the Board added paragraph 5(a) to this Statement, to permit recording a preacquisition contingency based on its fair value if that fair value can be determined. Otherwise, paragraph 5(b) requires that the amount recorded be based on the criteria included in the Exposure Draft.

33. Some respondents to the Exposure Draft inquired whether it would be appropriate to base the amount recorded on the present value of the amount determined in accordance with the criteria in paragraph 5(b) because the nature of the resulting amount would be a monetary asset or liability. The Board concluded that it should not specify such a requirement because the timing of payment or receipt of a contingent item seldom would be sufficiently determinable to permit the use of a present value technique on a reasonable basis. However, this Statement does not prohibit the use of a present value if appropriate.

Allocation Period

34. Opinion 16 provides the general principles of accounting for a business combination by the purchase method. The acquiring enterprise determines the value of the consideration given to the sellers, the present value of the liabilities assumed, and the value of the assets acquired. The total value of the consideration given and the liabilities assumed is then allocated among the identifiable assets acquired based on their value; and the balance, if any, is allocated to "goodwill."

35. The Board recognizes that completion of the allocation process that is required by Opinion 16 may sometimes require an extended period of time. For example, appraisals might be required to determine replacement cost of plant and equipment acquired, a discovery period may be needed to identify and value intangible assets acquired, and an actuarial determination may be required to determine the pension liability to be accrued.

36. If a business combination is consummated toward the end of an acquiring enterprise's fiscal year or the acquired enterprise is very large or unusually complex, the acquiring enterprise may not be able to obtain some of the data required to complete the allocation of the cost of the purchased enterprise for inclusion in its next annual financial report. In that case, a tentative allocation might be made using the values that have been determined and preliminary estimates of the values that have not yet been determined. The portions of the allocation that relate to the data that were not available subsequently are adjusted to reflect the finally determined amounts, usually by adjusting the preliminary amount with a corresponding adjustment of goodwill.

37. The Board considered specifying a time period during which estimates of preacquisition contingencies could be recorded as part of the purchase allocation. The Board concluded that it should relate the recording of preacquisition contingencies in the purchase allocation to the nature and process of the allocation, rather than to an arbitrary time limit. However, to indicate the Board's intent that the defined "allocation period" should not be unreasonably extended, paragraph 4(b) notes that the existence of a preacquisition contingency for which an amount cannot be estimated does not, of itself, extend the "allocation period." For example, the existence of litigation for which no estimate can be made in advance of the disposition by a court does not extend the "allocation period." That paragraph also notes that the "allocation period" should usually not exceed one year from the consummation date.

38. The "allocation period" is intended to differentiate between amounts that are determined as a result of the identification and valuation process required by Opinion 16 for all assets acquired and liabilities assumed and amounts that are determined because information that was not previously obtainable becomes obtainable. Thus, the "allocation

period" would continue while the acquiring enterprise's counsel was making an evaluation of a claim, but it would not continue if the counsel's evaluation were complete and resulted in the conclusion that no estimate could be made pending further negotiations with the claimant.

Preacquisition Net Operating Loss Carryforwards

39. A number of respondents cited the similarity of preacquisition net operating loss carryforwards to the other types of preacquisition contingencies that are addressed by this Statement and suggested that the accounting be conformed. The Board decided that it should not make that change in this Statement.

40. Some of those respondents asked whether the Board intended to completely exempt potential tax benefits of loss carryforwards from the provisions of this Statement or only to exempt them from the provisions that addressed the accounting for and reporting of subsequent changes in estimates. The Board did not intend to change the provisions of Opinions 11 and 16 with respect to preacquisition net operating loss carryforwards. Accordingly, paragraph 5 was modified to indicate the Board's intent.

Effective Date and Transition

41. A number of respondents to the Exposure Draft urged that the Statement be effective for adjustments resulting from purchases initiated after the effective date rather than for adjustments determined after that date. They indicated that, if the accounting required by this Statement had been in effect, the purchase price of some acquisitions would have been different or the acquisitions might not have been consummated. Several of those respondents indicated that they had disclosed the existence of a preacquisition contingency to their shareholders and had indicated that any resulting adjustment would be an adjustment of the purchase allocation.

42. The Board concluded that this Statement should be effective for preacquisition contingencies assumed in business combinations initiated after December 15, 1980. In arriving at that conclusion, the Board was concerned about the lack of comparability that may exist during a somewhat indefinite transition period, but it was influenced by expectations that may have existed at the time acquisitions were made (see preceding paragraph) and by the peculiar nature of the items in question. Disclosure of the nature of the items in question and their effect or potential effect on the enterprise's cash flows should provide adequate information for assessing the significance of those items. To ensure

that adjustments of contingencies not reported in accordance with the general provisions of this Statement are disclosed, the Board specified the disclosures that are required by paragraph 10.

43. To enhance comparability, the Board also concluded that it should encourage but not require application to preacquisition contingencies assumed in business combinations initiated prior to December 16, 1980. To enhance comparability, all similar preacquisition contingencies of an enterprise should be reported in a consistent manner. Therefore, an enterprise that elects to apply this Statement to such preacquisition contingencies must apply the Statement to *all* preacquisition contingencies assumed in business combinations for which the "allocation period" *has not* ended at the date of initial application of this Statement. With respect to other unresolved preacquisition contingencies, an enterprise making the above election may also elect to apply the provisions of the Statement that address reporting of adjustments after the end of the "allocation period" to those preacquisition contingencies. That election, if exercised, must also be applied to *all other* unresolved preacquisition contingencies.

44. The Board is aware that some enterprises may not have recorded amounts as a part of a purchase allocation because better estimates, when they became available, were expected to be recorded retroactively as a part of that allocation. Accordingly, the Board concluded that enterprises that elect to apply this Statement to existing unresolved preacquisition contingencies should be permitted to record those contingent items as they would have been recorded if this Statement had been in effect at the acquisition date. That procedure should alleviate any problems that would result from applying this Statement to existing preacquisition contingencies. However, that election must be applied to *all* unresolved preacquisition contingencies if it is exercised.

Other Matters

45. Several respondents to the Exposure Draft requested clarification of the accounting required by this Statement in the event that the "allocation period" extends beyond a fiscal year-end. For example, would a change in the purchase allocation determined in a subsequent fiscal year result in a corresponding retroactive restatement of previously recorded amortization or depreciation? The Board decided that the same question would arise whenever the valuations required by Opinion 16 are not finalized until a subsequent fiscal year. The issue is not created by the "allocation period" used in this Statement, and that larger issue should not be resolved in this limited-scope Statement. The Board also noted that the amounts involved usually are not material because they consist of amortization of long-lived assets for a short time period.

Statement of Financial Accounting Standards No. 39
Financial Reporting and Changing Prices:
Specialized Assets—Mining and Oil and Gas

a supplement to FASB Statement No. 33

STATUS

Issued: October 1980

Effective Date: For fiscal years ending on or after December 25, 1980

Affects: Amends FAS 33, paragraphs 30(a) through 30(c), 35(c)(1) through 35(c)(4), and 52
Supersedes FAS 33, paragraphs 51(b), 52(b), and 53

Affected by: Paragraph 10 superseded by FAS 69
Paragraph 11 superseded by FAS 69
Paragraph 12 superseded by FAS 40, FAS 41, and FAS 69
Paragraph 12 amended by FAS 46
Superseded by FAS 89

Statement of Financial Accounting Standards No. 40
Financial Reporting and Changing Prices:
Specialized Assets—Timberlands and Growing Timber

a supplement to FASB Statement No. 33

STATUS

Issued: November 1980

Effective Date: For fiscal years ending on or after December 25, 1980

Affects: Supersedes FAS 33, paragraph 53
Supersedes FAS 39, paragraph 12

Affected by: Paragraph 6 superseded by FAS 41
Paragraph 6 amended by FAS 46
Paragraph 6 superseded by FAS 69
Superseded by FAS 89

Statement of Financial Accounting Standards No. 41
Financial Reporting and Changing Prices:
Specialized Assets—Income-Producing Real Estate

a supplement to FASB Statement No. 33

STATUS

Issued: November 1980

Effective Date: For fiscal years ending on or after December 25, 1980

Affects: Supersedes FAS 33, paragraph 53
Supersedes FAS 39, paragraph 12
Supersedes FAS 40, paragraph 6

Affected by: Paragraph 7 amended by FAS 46
Paragraph 7 superseded by FAS 69
Superseded by FAS 89

(This page intentionally left blank.)

Statement of Financial Accounting Standards No. 42
Determining Materiality for Capitalization of Interest Cost

an amendment of FASB Statement No. 34

STATUS

Issued: November 1980

Effective Date: For fiscal years beginning after December 15, 1979, unless enterprise had already adopted FAS34; if so, effective for fiscal years beginning after October 15, 1980

Affects: Amends FAS 34, paragraphs 8 and 9

Affected by: No other pronouncements

SUMMARY

This Statement amends FASB Statement No. 34, *Capitalization of Interest Cost,* (1) to delete language that some believe allows capitalization of interest to be avoided under certain circumstances and (2) to make clear that Statement 34 does not establish new tests of materiality.

Statement of Financial Accounting Standards No. 42
Determining Materiality for Capitalization of Interest Cost

an amendment of FASB Statement No. 34

CONTENTS

INTRODUCTION

1. Paragraph 8 of FASB Statement No. 34, *Capitalization of Interest Cost,* states that:

> In concept, interest cost is capitalizable for all assets that require a period of time to get them ready for their intended use (an "acquisition period"). However, in many cases, the benefit in terms of information about enterprise resources and earnings may not justify the additional accounting and administrative cost involved in providing the information. The benefit may be less than the cost because the effect of interest capitalization and its subsequent amortization or other disposition, compared with the effect of charging it to expense when incurred, would not be material. In that circumstance, interest capitalization is not *required* by this Statement.

Paragraph 9 of Statement 34 begins as follows:

> Subject to the provisions of paragraph 8, interest shall be capitalized for the following types of assets ("qualifying assets"). . . .

2. The Board has received a number of questions concerning how paragraph 8 should be construed in deciding whether capitalization of interest is required. Some have stated that paragraph 8 appears to establish new tests of materiality that allow an enterprise to measure the effect of interest capitalization on income by a pro forma prospective or retroactive computation without also considering the effect on current year income. The Board has concluded that new tests of materiality should not be established for interest capitalization and has, accordingly, decided to amend paragraph 8 of Statement 34 to delete the language that gave rise to those questions.

3. The Board has concluded that it can reach an informed decision on the basis of existing information without a public hearing and that the effective date and transition specified in paragraph 5 are advisable in the circumstances.

STANDARDS OF FINANCIAL ACCOUNTING AND REPORTING

Amendment to FASB Statement No. 34

4. The last two sentences of paragraph 8 of Statement 34 are superseded and replaced by the following sentence:

> Accordingly, interest shall not be capitalized in the situations described in paragraph 10.

The introduction of paragraph 9 of Statement 34 is amended to read as follows:

> Interest shall be capitalized for the following types of assets ("qualifying assets"):

Effective Date and Transition

5. This Statement shall be effective for fiscal years beginning after December 15, 1979. The provisions of this Statement shall be applied at the same time as the provisions of Statement 34 are first applied. Enterprises that already have adopted the provisions of Statement 34 shall apply the provisions of this Statement in their next fiscal year beginning after October 15, 1980 and may, but are not required to, restate their financial statements for the year of initial adoption to reflect the provisions of this Statement.

> **The provisions of this Statement need
> not be applied to immaterial items.**

This Statement was adopted by the affirmative votes of five members of the Financial Accounting Standards Board. Messrs. March and Mosso dissented.

Messrs. March and Mosso dissent. They believe Statement 34 wisely introduced some flexibility to minimize the additional cost of implementing a new accounting procedure for many enterprises. They would not change the provisions or intent of paragraphs 8 and 9 of that Statement and would interpret it to permit the use of evaluations like the pro forma approaches described in paragraph 6 of this Statement in assessing materiality from a cost-benefit standpoint. In their view, the incremental gain in informational value from a requirement to capitalize interest on construction programs of a continuing level of activity involving many asset items may be insufficient to offset the accounting costs that would in many instances be involved.

Although this Statement acknowledges the appropriateness of minimum threshold policies, Messrs. March and Mosso would interpret Statement 34 as originally issued to permit a broader application of the same reasoning that supported the exclusion of routinely manufactured inventories as qualifying assets in paragraph 10 of Statement 34. Judgments on such cost-benefit evaluations should be left to those able to examine specific facts and circumstances.

Members of the Financial Accounting Standards Board:

Donald J. Kirk, *Chairman*	John W. March	Robert T. Sprouse
Frank E. Block	Robert A. Morgan	Ralph E. Walters
	David Mosso	

Appendix A

BACKGROUND AND BASIS FOR CONCLUSIONS

6. The Board received a number of questions concerning how paragraph 8 of Statement 34 should be construed in deciding whether capitalization of interest is required. Some asked whether capitalization is required if a pro forma prospective computation indicates that equilibrium between the amount of interest capitalized and amortized each period would be reached after a few years. If equilibrium would be reached ultimately, those favoring this approach believe the benefits perceived by the Board for interest capitalization would be small compared with the accounting and administrative costs involved in providing the information. Others inquired if paragraph 8 would permit an enterprise to make pro forma computations of (a) the effect that capitalizing interest in prior years and subsequently amortizing it would have on the level of earnings in the current year and on the trend of earnings of preceding, current, and future years and (b) the effect of always expensing interest on the level of earnings in the current year and on the trend of earnings over those years. Under that pro forma retroactive approach, they believe an enterprise would not be required to capitalize interest if a comparison of the computations showed no material difference in the effect on the current year's earnings or in the effect on the trend of earnings.

7. An Exposure Draft of a proposed Statement, *Determining Materiality for Capitalization of Interest Cost,* was issued on April 22, 1980. The Board received 63 letters of comment in response to the Exposure Draft. The Exposure Draft concluded that the pro forma prospective approach should not be adopted in Statement 34 because it focuses on expectations of future activities and developments rather than on measurement and reporting of current earnings from past events and transactions. The Exposure Draft also concluded that the pro forma retroactive approach should not be adopted because, among other reasons, the computations focus on avoiding the requirements of the Statement while at the same time incurring the costs of calculation. The Board, therefore, concluded that the usual materiality tests are sufficient for implementation of Statement 34. Some respondents stated that the views expressed above in paragraph 6 are consistent with the usual materiality tests. However, the Board believes those views are not consistent with the usual materiality tests for the reasons explained below in paragraphs 8 and 9.

8. The usual tests of materiality for accounting changes are set forth in APB Opinion No. 20, *Accounting Changes.* Paragraph 38 of Opinion 20 requires disclosure of an accounting change that has a material effect on income before extraordinary items or net income of the current period. In addition, paragraph 38 requires disclosure of an accounting change that has a material effect on the enterprise's trend of earnings. The views expressed

in paragraph 6 suggest that interest capitalization should not be required if the effect is material in the current year but immaterial to the trend of earnings because of the "roll-over" effect that would occur from amortizing previously capitalized interest. In effect, those views imply that immateriality to the trend of earnings in the future should negate materiality to the current year income statement. Opinion 20, however, requires determining the effect on the trend of earnings to provide disclosure of an accounting change that would otherwise not be disclosed because of its immaterial effect on current period income, not to eliminate disclosure of an accounting change for which disclosure would otherwise be required. In other words, the test of the effect on trend of earnings is an additional test of materiality that increases the probability that an accounting change will be deemed material.

9. Consistent with the approach of Opinion 20, pro forma retroactive or prospective computations might be used as part of the assessment of materiality to income in implementing Statement 34 but not as the overriding test of materiality. If the effect of capitalizing interest on current year income is not material, an enterprise might wish to use a pro forma prospective computation to determine whether the effect is likely to be material in future years. Likewise, if the effect of capitalizing interest on current year income is only marginally material, a pro forma prospective computation indicating that the effect will not be material in future years could aid a determination that the current effect is not material. Pro forma retroactive and prospective computations can confirm whether the effect of capitalizing interest is or is not material, but immateriality on a pro forma retroactive or prospective

test does not override a determination that an accounting change is material to current year income, the balance sheet, or other measures.

10. Some respondents expressed concern that paragraphs 5 and 6 of the Exposure Draft indicated that the Board opposes the use of minimum threshold levels in implementing Statement 34. That is not the case. Minimum threshold levels are common in inventory and property, plant, and equipment accounting. Many enterprises do not include the costs of minor items in inventory, and many enterprises do not capitalize individual items of property, plant, and equipment, the costs of which are less than a specified threshold. Such thresholds are designed to minimize the burden of capitalizing large numbers of assets and accounting for those costs as the assets are used. Those thresholds are justified on the grounds that the assets whose costs are charged to expense as purchased are immaterial both individually and in the aggregate. This Statement affirms the usual tests of materiality and does not affect threshold levels established in conformity with usual materiality tests.

11. Some respondents stated that the transition provisions did not address those enterprises that had elected early application of Statement 34 and might believe they were exempt from the provisions of this Statement. The Board intended that this Statement should apply to those enterprises and has clarified paragraph 5 to state that those who elected early application of Statement 34 are subject to the provisions of this Statement in the future. Those enterprises may, but are not required to, restate financial statements to the year of initial adoption of Statement 34.

Statement of Financial Accounting Standards No. 43
Accounting for Compensated Absences

STATUS

Issued: November 1980

Effective Date: For fiscal years beginning after December 15, 1980

Affects: No other pronouncements

Affected by: Paragraph 1 amended by FAS 112
Paragraph 2 superseded by FAS 112
Paragraph 2 amended by FAS 123
Paragraph 3 superseded by FAS 71

SUMMARY

This Statement requires an employer to accrue a liability for employees' rights to receive compensation for future absences when certain conditions are met. For example, this Statement requires a liability to be accrued for vacation benefits that employees have earned but have not yet taken; however, it generally does not require a liability to be accrued for future sick pay benefits, holidays, and similar compensated absences until employees are actually absent.

Statement of Financial Accounting Standards No. 43
Accounting for Compensated Absences

CONTENTS

INTRODUCTION AND BACKGROUND INFORMATION

1. The FASB has been asked to consider practices used by employers to account for employee absences, such as vacation, illness, and holidays, for which it is expected that employees will be paid (referred to in this Statement as *compensated absences*). The Board has been advised that the following alternative accounting practices exist with respect to compensated absences: (a) the cost is accrued over some period before payment or (b) the cost is recognized when paid. The Board has considered those alternative accounting practices and concluded that a liability for employees' rights to receive compensation for future absences should be accrued as specified by this Statement.

2. This Statement does not apply to severance or termination pay, postretirement benefits, deferred compensation, stock or stock options issued to employees, or other long-term fringe benefits, such as group insurance or long-term disability pay. This Statement does not address the allocation of costs of compensated absences to interim periods. Furthermore, because the appropriate structure for setting accounting standards for state and local governmental units is currently under discussion, the FASB is proposing no change with respect to the nature of its involvement with pronouncements in the governmental area until that matter is resolved. Consequently, the Board has deferred a decision regarding whether this Statement should apply to state and local governmental units.

3. The Addendum to APB Opinion No. 2, *Accounting for the "Investment Credit,"* states that ". . . differences may arise in the application of generally accepted accounting principles as between regulated and nonregulated businesses, because of the effect in regulated businesses of the rate-making process . . ." and discusses the application of generally accepted accounting principles to regulated industries. Accordingly, the provisions of the Addendum govern the application of this Statement to those operations of an employer that are regulated for rate-making purposes on an individual-company-cost-of-service basis.

4. An Exposure Draft of a proposed Statement, *Accounting for Compensated Absences*, was issued on December 17, 1979. The Board received 217 comment letters in response to the Exposure Draft. Certain of the comments received and the Board's consideration of them are discussed in Appendix A, "Summary of Consideration of Comments on Exposure Draft."

5. The Board has concluded that it can reach an informed decision on the basis of existing data without a public hearing and that the effective date and transition specified in paragraphs 8 and 9 are advisable in the circumstances.

STANDARDS OF FINANCIAL ACCOUNTING AND REPORTING

6. An employer shall accrue a liability for employees' compensation for future absences if *all* of the following conditions are met:

a. The employer's obligation relating to employees' rights to receive compensation for future absences is attributable to employees' services already rendered,
b. The obligation relates to rights that vest[1] or accumulate,[2]
c. Payment of the compensation is probable, and
d. The amount can be reasonably estimated.

If an employer meets conditions (a), (b), and (c) and

---

[1] In this Statement, *vested* rights are those for which the employer has an obligation to make payment even if an employee terminates; thus, they are not contingent on an employee's future service.

[2] For purposes of this Statement, *accumulate* means that earned but unused rights to compensated absences may be carried forward to one or more periods subsequent to that in which they are earned, even though there may be a limit to the amount that can be carried forward.

does not accrue a liability because condition (d) is not met, that fact shall be disclosed.

7. Notwithstanding the conditions specified in paragraph 6, an employer is not required to accrue a liability for nonvesting accumulating rights to receive sick pay benefits[3] (that is, compensation for an employee's absence due to illness) for the reasons stated in paragraph 15.

Effective Date and Transition

8. This Statement shall be effective for fiscal years beginning after December 15, 1980, with earlier application encouraged. Accounting changes adopted to conform to the provisions of this Statement shall be applied retroactively. In the year that this Statement is first applied, the financial statements shall disclose the nature of any restatement and its effect on income before extraordinary items, net income, and related per share amounts for each year restated.

9. If retroactive restatement of all years presented is not practicable, the financial statements presented shall be restated for as many consecutive years as practicable and the cumulative effect of applying the Statement shall be included in determining net income of the earliest year restated (not necessarily the earliest year presented). If it is not practicable to restate any prior year, the cumulative effect shall be included in net income in the year in which the Statement is first applied. (See paragraph 20 of APB Opinion No. 20, *Accounting Changes*.) The effect on income before extraordinary items, net income, and related per share amounts of applying this Statement in a year in which the cumulative effect is included in determining that year's net income shall be disclosed for that year.

The provisions of this Statement need not be applied to immaterial items.

This Statement was adopted by the affirmative votes of five members of the Financial Accounting Standards Board. Messrs. Kirk and Sprouse dissented.

Messrs. Kirk and Sprouse dissent because they believe the condition relating to "rights that vest or accumulate" (paragraph 6(b)) introduces unnecessary and irrelevant considerations in determining whether a liability for compensated absences has been incurred that should be recognized.

For benefits that have vesting provisions, the employee need not be absent to be compensated; therefore, services already rendered (condition 6(a)) is necessarily the past transaction or event that is referred to in the definition of liabilities as creating the obligation. For benefits that do not have vesting provisions, whether the benefits accumulate or are bestowed by outright grant by the employer is irrelevant and tends to detract from the central issue. The crucial question is whether the employer's liability is the result of employees rendering service (past presences) or being absent (future absences). Messrs. Kirk and Sprouse distinguish among the types of plans covered by this Statement believing, for example, that compensation for absences contingent on a specific event outside the control of the employer and employee, such as illness or jury duty, is attributable to those events. Compensation for absences that is not contingent on such events, for example vacations, is attributable to rendering service. Specifically, they believe the employer has a recordable liability for vacation pay and a contingency, but not a recordable liability for sick pay. Until illness occurs the employer has no liability; the employer does not owe anything until the contingent event, an illness, occurs.

Messrs. Kirk and Sprouse also are concerned that identical situations may continue to be accounted for differently because, under paragraph 7, a liability for nonvesting sick pay is not required but rather is permitted.

Members of the Financial Accounting Standards Board:

Donald J. Kirk,
Chairman
Frank E. Block

John W. March
Robert A. Morgan
David Mosso

Robert T. Sprouse
Ralph E. Walters

---

[3] In accounting for compensated absences, the form of an employer's policy for compensated absences should not prevail over actual practices. For example, if employees are customarily paid "sick pay" benefits even though their absences from work are not actually the result of illness or if employees are routinely allowed to take compensated "terminal leave" for accumulated unused sick pay benefits prior to retirement, such benefits shall not be considered sick pay benefits for purposes of applying the provisions of paragraph 7 but rather should be accounted for in accordance with paragraph 6.

Appendix A

ments Exposure Draft), which states:

SUMMARY OF CONSIDERATION OF COMMENTS ON EXPOSURE DRAFT

> Liabilities are probable future sacrifices of economic benefits stemming from present legal, equitable, or constructive obligations of a particular enterprise to transfer assets or provide services to other entities in the future as a result of past transactions or events affecting the enterprise.

10. Some respondents questioned the need for a project on accounting for compensated absences. They indicated that the informational benefits of requiring a liability for compensated absences to be accrued do not justify the costs of doing so. The accrual ordinarily would create a one-time significant adjustment with little financial statement effect among periods thereafter. The Accounting Standards Division of the AICPA asked the FASB to consider the alternative practices used by employers to account for compensated absences because of the potential for significant unrecorded or understated liabilities in certain cases. In view of the existence of significantly different alternative practices, the universality of the transactions, and the potential for understatement of liabilities, the Board concluded that a Statement on the subject should be issued (a) to affirm that generally accepted accounting principles require that compensated absences be accounted for on the accrual basis and (b) to clarify the accounting for those absences.

11. Some respondents requested guidance on how compensated absences should be accounted for in interim periods. Other respondents indicated that providing interim reporting guidance in this Statement would involve significant issues that are currently being addressed in the elements and recognition phases of the Board's conceptual framework project. Those respondents recommended that, in light of the Board's decision to defer further action on its interim reporting project until those conceptual issues are resolved, the Statement should specify that it does not change existing interim reporting practices and that the provisions of APB Opinion No. 28, *Interim Financial Reporting*, are still appropriate. The Board agreed; accordingly, this Statement is concerned with the accrual of a liability for compensated absences rather than with the allocation of the costs of such absences to interim periods.

12. Some respondents indicated that accrual of a liability for compensated absences should be limited to those absences for which the right to receive compensation is vested. The liability would then reflect only amounts that employees would be paid for their rights to compensated absences if their employment terminated. The Board believes that those respondents' comments generally reflect an approach that is more restrictive than called for by the Board's definition of a liability in paragraph 22 of the revised FASB Exposure Draft, *Elements of Financial Statements of Business Enterprises* (ele-

The Board believes that a liability for amounts to be paid as a result of employees' rights to compensated absences should be accrued, considering anticipated forfeitures, in the year in which earned. For example, if new employees receive vested rights to two-weeks' paid vacation at the beginning of their second year of employment with no pro rata payment in the event of termination during the first year, the two-weeks' vacation would be considered to be earned by work performed in the first year and an accrual for vacation pay would be required for new employees during their first year of service, allowing for estimated forfeitures due to turnover. Furthermore, the proposed definition of a liability does not limit an employer's liability for compensated absences solely to rights to compensation for those absences that eventually vest. The definition also encompasses a constructive obligation for reasonably estimable compensation for past services that, based on the employer's past practices, probably will be paid and can be reasonably estimated. Individual facts and circumstances must be considered in determining when nonvesting rights to compensated absences are earned by services rendered.

13. The requirement to accrue a liability for nonvesting rights to compensated absences depends on whether the unused rights (a) expire at the end of the year in which earned or (b) accumulate and are carried forward to succeeding years, thereby increasing the benefits that would otherwise be available in those later years. If the rights expire, the Board believes that a liability for future absences should not be accrued at year-end because the benefits to be paid in subsequent years would not be attributable to employee services rendered in prior years. (Jury duty and military leave benefits generally do not accumulate if unused and, unless they accumulate, a liability for those benefits would not be accrued at year-end.) On the other hand, if unused rights do accumulate and increase the benefits otherwise available in subsequent years, the Board believes a liability should be accrued at year-end to the extent that it is probable that employees will be paid in subsequent years for the increased benefits attributable to the accumulated rights and the amount can be reasonably estimated.

14. Board members' views differ regarding whether employees' rights to receive compensation for

unused sick days that accumulate for possible future use but do not vest qualify as a liability in terms of the definition in the elements Exposure Draft. Some Board members believe that the relevant "past transaction or event" that creates an obligation to transfer assets to (that is, compensate) employees is the illness and that only a potential liability (that is, a loss contingency) exists before the illness occurs. However, the Board concluded that the relevant event is the past event of working; permitting accumulated sick days to be carried forward for use in future periods represents part of the employees' compensation for past work performed. The accumulated amount at year-end is an obligation that leaves the employer with little or no discretion to avoid future payment. Therefore, a liability exists to the extent that some or all of the accumulated sick days are likely to be used. That view parallels the reasoning of FASB Statement No. 5, *Accounting for Contingencies*, which requires a loss contingency to be accrued if (a) it is probable that a liability has been incurred and that future events will confirm the fact of loss and (b) the amount of loss can be reasonably estimated.

15. Notwithstanding the Board's conclusion that accrual of a liability for the probable payment of accumulated unused sick days is appropriate under the liability definition in the elements Exposure Draft, the Board was influenced by respondents' comments that the amounts involved generally would not be large enough to justify the cost of computing the probable payments for nonvesting accumulating sick pay benefits. The Board concluded that accrual should not be required for an obligation related to employees' accumulating rights to receive compensation for future absences that are contingent on the absences being caused by an employee's future illness because, in the Board's judgment, the lower degree of reliability of estimates of future sick pay and the cost of making and evaluating those estimates do not justify a requirement for such accrual. Furthermore, the Board believes that the probable payments for accumulating sick pay benefits rarely would be material unless they vest or are otherwise normally paid without an illness-related absence (as discussed in the following paragraph), in which cases the benefits would not be dependent on an employee's future illness and the criteria of paragraph 6 would apply. On the other hand, this Statement does not prohibit an employer from accruing a liability for such nonvesting accumulating sick pay benefits, providing the criteria of paragraph 6 are met.

16. The Board believes that the employer's actual administration of sick pay benefits should determine the appropriate accounting. For example, if employees are customarily paid "sick pay" benefits even though their absences from work are not actually the result of illness or if employees are routinely allowed to take compensated "terminal leave" for nonvesting accumulated unused sick pay benefits prior to retirement, the Board believes such accumulated benefits should not be considered as sick pay benefits for purposes of the exclusion described in paragraph 7 but rather should be accounted for in accordance with paragraph 6.

17. Some respondents said that requiring employers to estimate and accrue a liability for compensated absences could be an undue burden for employers, particularly smaller enterprises with limited staff and resources. The Board believes that the accrual accounting specified in paragraph 6 ordinarily will not cause an additional significant record-keeping burden because it centers on employee rights that accumulate or vest. Records maintained by employers for the administration of employee benefits ordinarily will be adequate to provide information for such an accrual. By excluding nonvesting sick pay benefits from required accruals, the Board sought to minimize the estimating burden.

18. Some respondents questioned whether the Board intended this Statement to apply to a sabbatical leave. The Board believes that the appropriate accounting for a sabbatical leave depends on the purpose of the leave. If a sabbatical leave is granted only to perform research or public service to enhance the reputation of or otherwise benefit the employer, the compensation is not attributable to services already rendered (paragraph 6(a)); a liability should not be accrued in advance of the employee's services during such leave. If the leave is granted to provide compensated unrestricted time off for past service and the other conditions for accrual are met, a liability for sabbatical leave should be accrued.

19. Some respondents questioned whether the absence of a reference in the Exposure Draft to the Addendum to Opinion 2 indicated that the Statement would apply to rate-regulated industries. The Board currently is considering the effect of rate regulation on regulated companies in another project. In the meantime, paragraph 3 was added to acknowledge that the provisions of the Addendum govern the application of this Statement to those operations of a company that are regulated for rate-making purposes on a basis of individual company cost of service.

20. Some respondents requested guidance on how an employer should estimate its liability for compensated absences. The respondents asked (a) whether the liability should be based on current or on future rates of pay, (b) whether it should be discounted, and (c) when the effect of scheduled increases should be accrued. The Board noted that it expects to be studying similar issues in its project on

accounting by employers for pensions as well as in a possible project on discounting[4] and, accordingly, concluded to defer a decision on such issues at this time.

21. Some respondents viewed the transition provisions in the Exposure Draft as inconsistent with present generally accepted accounting principles proscribing direct charges to retained earnings. They also expressed the view that required methods of transition should not differ for material and immaterial adjustments. The Board considered those views and changed the transition provisions consistent with several prior FASB Statements.

---

[4]The AICPA is currently developing an issues paper on discounting for consideration by the FASB.

Statement of Financial Accounting Standards No. 44
Accounting for Intangible Assets of Motor Carriers

an amendment of Chapter 5 of ARB No. 43 and
an interpretation of APB Opinions 17 and 30

STATUS

Issued: December 1980

Effective Date: December 19, 1980 for financial statements for fiscal periods ending after
December 15, 1980

Affects: Amends ARB 43, Chapter 5, paragraphs 8 and 10

Affected by: Paragraph 6 amended by FAS 96 and FAS 109

Issues Discussed by FASB Emerging Issues Task Force (EITF)

Affects: No EITF Issues

Interpreted by: No EITF Issues

Related Issue: EITF Issue No. 91-9

SUMMARY

Enactment of the Motor Carrier Act of 1980, deregulating motor carriers, raises questions regarding whether certain intangible assets of motor carriers should continue to be reported as assets or charged to income. This Statement requires the unamortized costs of motor carrier intangible assets representing interstate rights to transport goods with limited competition to be charged to income and, if material, reported as an extraordinary item. This Statement does not affect the accounting for other intangible assets of motor carriers, such as goodwill.

Statement of Financial Accounting Standards No. 44
Accounting for Intangible Assets of Motor Carriers

an amendment of Chapter 5 of ARB No. 43 and
an interpretation of APB Opinions 17 and 30

CONTENTS

INTRODUCTION

1. The FASB has been asked to clarify the accounting for certain intangible assets of motor carriers because enactment of the Motor Carrier Act of 1980[1] (Act) on July 1, 1980 raises questions regarding whether those intangibles should continue to be reported as assets or charged to income. Appendix A provides additional background information and Appendix B provides the basis for the Board's conclusions.

2. The Board has concluded that it can reach an informed decision on the basis of existing data without a public hearing and that the effective date and transition specified in paragraph 8 are advisable in the circumstances.

STANDARDS OF FINANCIAL ACCOUNTING AND REPORTING

3. When acquired, intangible assets of motor carriers may have included costs[2] related to expected benefits from established routes or customers, marketing or operating efficiencies, knowledge of the business, and other elements of goodwill as well as from specifically identifiable intangible assets, such as customer lists, favorable leases, or operating rights.[3] The costs of intangible assets acquired may have been identified previously as operating rights or as goodwill. If not separately allocated in the past, the costs of intangible assets shall now be assigned to (a) interstate operating rights, (b) other

identifiable intangible assets (including intrastate operating rights[4]), and (c) goodwill; the cost of identifiable intangible assets (including operating rights) shall not be included in goodwill.

4. For purposes of identifying and assigning costs to interstate operating rights, other identifiable intangible assets, and goodwill, a motor carrier shall apply the criteria in paragraph 88 of APB Opinion No. 16, *Business Combinations*, and paragraphs 24-26 of APB Opinion No. 17, *Intangible Assets*, based on the circumstances existing when the assets were acquired. Costs assigned to intangible assets shall not reflect costs of developing, maintaining, or restoring those intangibles after they were acquired. Costs assigned to identifiable intangibles, including operating rights, shall not be merged with or be replaced by amounts relating to other identifiable intangibles or goodwill. Paragraphs 8 and 10 of Chapter 5, "Intangible Assets," of ARB No. 43 are amended by this paragraph and paragraph 3 of this Statement with regard to the intangible assets addressed by this Statement.

5. If a motor carrier cannot separately identify its interstate operating rights, other identifiable intangible assets, and goodwill and cannot assign costs to them as specified by this Statement or finds that it is impracticable to do so, that motor carrier shall presume that all of those costs relate to interstate operating rights.

6. Unamortized costs of interstate operating rights subject to the provisions of the Act shall be charged

---

[1] Public Law 96-296, 96th Congress, July 1, 1980.

[2] *Cost*, as used in this Statement, refers to the original cost or the unamortized cost of intangible assets as appropriate in the situation.

[3] An *operating right* (also known as an *operating authority*), as used in this Statement, is a franchise or permit issued by the Interstate Commerce Commission (ICC) or a similar state agency to a motor carrier to transport specified commodities over specified routes with limited competition. Those rights were either granted directly by the ICC or state agency, purchased from other motor carriers, or acquired through business combinations.

[4] See paragraph 7.

to income and, if material, reported as an extraordinary item in accordance with paragraph 11 of APB Opinion No. 30, *Reporting the Results of Operations.* Subsequently, the cost of any other identifiable intangible asset or goodwill that is charged to income for reasons attributable to the Act shall not be reported as an extraordinary item. Tax benefits, if any, relating to the costs of interstate operating rights charged to income shall be reported in accordance with the provisions of APB Opinion No. 11, *Accounting for Income Taxes,* and paragraph 25 of Opinion 30.

7. Other identifiable intangible assets and goodwill relating to motor carrier operations shall be accounted for in accordance with Chapter 5 of ARB 43 or Opinion 17, as appropriate. However, the cost

of intrastate operating rights shall be accounted for in accordance with the provisions of this Statement if a state deregulates motor carriers with effects similar to those of the Act.

Effective Date and Transition

8. The provisions of this Statement shall be effective on December 19, 1980 for financial statement for fiscal periods ending after December 15, 1980. Earlier application is encouraged for financial statements for fiscal periods ending before the effective date of this Statement that have not been issued before December 19, 1980. This Statement shall not be applied retroactively to previously issued financial statements.

> **The provisions of this Statement need not be applied to immaterial items.**

This Statement was adopted by the affirmative votes of five members of the Financial Accounting Standards Board. Messrs. March and Walters dissented.

Messrs. March and Walters dissent because they believe that the attempt in this Statement to differentiate between operating rights and other intangible assets is misplaced emphasis on form at the expense of substance. Operating rights represent a franchise to conduct business over a route with the objective of making a profit.

Because of the limited or exclusive nature of those rights in the past, their value often could be supported by reference to a resale market. The Act effectively eliminates this market. The fact that the rights have lost the value that attaches to exchangeability creates a presumption that their value has diminished. However, in the FASB Exposure Draft, *Elements of Financial Statements of Business Enterprises*, the Board said that exchangeability is not a necessary characteristic of an asset. A required characteristic of an asset is the capacity, either singly or in combination with other assets, to contribute to future net cash inflows. In some cases, there may be persuasive evidence that the real asset, the purchased opportunity to conduct business over a specific route with the objective of making a profit, is

in fact generating, and is expected to continue to generate, profits. In those cases, an immediate charge to income of the cost of operating rights is not consistent with the economic facts and does not measure properly either the operating resources or the return on investment of the enterprise.

Messrs. March and Walters further believe that the conclusion by the Board that all interstate operating rights have lost their value is a finding that substitutes the Board's judgment for the individual evaluations that should be made by the motor carriers and reviewed by their auditors. They believe that the Board should concern itself with setting standards. Application of standards to specific fact situations is a primary function of management. Existing accounting pronouncements are relatively clear in the requirements to charge to income the cost of intangible assets that no longer have value and to revise the periods of amortization when warranted by changed circumstances. At the very most, all that is needed is an interpretation of those pronouncements to demonstrate how they should apply to motor carriers.

Appendix A

BACKGROUND INFORMATION

9. The Board understands that the Motor Carrier

Act of 1980 provides for:

a. Easier entry into the motor carrier industry by new carriers and easier route expansion for existing carriers
b. Removal of most route restrictions and a

459

broadening of the classification of commodities that carriers are permitted to haul

c. Eventual freedom for motor carriers to change freight rates without the ICC's permission

d. Limitations on the scope of collective rate making exempt from antitrust considerations.

10. The Accounting Standards Division of the AICPA prepared an Issues Paper, *Accounting for Intangibles in the Motor Carrier Industry*, and asked the Board to consider the impact of the Act on accounting for intangible assets of motor carriers. The Board has considered the accounting issues relating to the impact of the Act on intangible assets and reached the conclusions presented in this Statement.

11. The Board understands that intangible assets of motor carriers consist principally of operating rights and goodwill. Most motor carriers have not distinguished among operating rights acquired (a) from the ICC or other licensing agency, (b) from other motor carriers, or (c) through business combinations, nor have they distinguished operating rights from other purchased intangibles, such as goodwill, in their financial statements. Intangible assets of motor carriers generally have been reported in general purpose financial statements at original cost, as permitted by Chapter 5 of ARB 43, or amortized over 40 years, the maximum life permitted by Opinion 17, depending on the date of acquisition of those assets.

12. An Exposure Draft of a proposed Statement, *Accounting for Intangible Assets of Motor Carriers*, was issued on October 24, 1980. The Board received 41 comment letters in response to the Exposure Draft. Certain of the comments received and the Board's consideration of them are discussed in Appendix B, "Basis for Conclusions."

Appendix B

BASIS FOR CONCLUSIONS

13. This appendix discusses the factors that the Board considered significant in reaching the conclusions in this Statement, including various alternatives considered and reasons for accepting some and rejecting others. Individual Board members gave greater weight to some factors than to others.

14. Some respondents questioned the need for a project on accounting for motor carrier intangible assets. They indicated that current accounting pronouncements (Chapter 5 of ARB 43, Opinions 11, 17, and 30, and FASB Statement No. 5, *Accounting for Contingencies*) provide adequate guidance for evaluating those intangibles. They also said that

those evaluations should be made on a case-by-case basis and that any uniform standard would fail to reflect the circumstances of individual motor carriers. The Board concluded that, although those existing pronouncements do provide some guidance with respect to the effect of passage of the Act on the costs of intangible assets of motor carriers, the provisions of paragraph 8 of Chapter 5 of ARB 43, which permits substitution or merging of intangible assets, should be modified and the other pronouncements should be clarified as discussed in paragraphs 15, 18, 19, and 21 of this Statement to ensure comparability in accounting for the impact of the Act. In addition, the Board concluded that motor carriers should allocate the costs of their intangible assets to identifiable intangible assets and goodwill. That allocation may not have been made in the past because paragraph 10 of Chapter 5 of ARB 43 does not require specific identification of intangible assets with no limited term of existence.

15. Operating rights generally have represented the right to haul specified commodities between two points with limited competition; that is, the rights included oligopolistic or monopolistic benefits. The past resale and collateral values of the rights support that view. Comments received from the motor carrier industry and other sources have convinced the Board that interstate operating rights have been substantially and permanently impaired as a result of the passage of the Act. The Board believes that this economic loss is evidenced further by the significant loss in resale and collateral values and the current nominal replacement cost of operating rights and that this loss should be reflected in the financial statements of motor carriers. Therefore, the Board has concluded that the unamortized costs of those operating rights should be charged to income immediately.

16. Some respondents stated that operating rights may continue to have value irrespective of the provisions of the Act and, in those cases, should not be charged to income. They indicated that operating rights are still required for motor carrier operations and that those rights principally represent a franchise to conduct business over a route with the objective of making a profit. They acknowledge that the value of operating rights often could be supported by reference to a resale market in the past, but they believe that the loss of exchangeability does not necessarily diminish the value of the asset. They believe that operating rights continue to qualify as assets as long as the rights, either singly or in combination with other assets, contribute to future net cash inflows. They believe that in those cases an immediate charge to income of the cost of operating rights is not consistent with economic facts and does not properly portray either the operating resources or the operating performance of the motor carrier.

Accounting for Intangible Assets of Motor Carriers — FAS44

The Board concluded, however, that operating rights no longer qualify as an asset because those rights no longer provide motor carriers with the benefit of protection from unlimited competition. Loss of exchange value is a consequence of the loss of that benefit.

17. Some respondents indicated that (a) time will be required to evaluate the impact of the Act on ICC actions and (b) the economic impact of increased competition resulting from the Act will take several years. They said that to date the ICC has not responded clearly to the provisions of the Act. They suggested that the uncertainty in the timing and amount of impairment of operating rights could be reflected best by amortizing the cost of the rights over an arbitrary short period, such as three years. They believe that amortization over a short period is consistent with the development of additional competition expected to result from the Act and with the transition provisions of the Act under which certain changes will be phased in over the next few years. The Board concluded that, in accordance with the provisions of Statement 5, a loss is both probable and reasonably estimable and that an arbitrarily short amortization period would defer recognition of the loss resulting from passage of the Act. Also, the Board believes that any arbitrary amortization period selected would not reflect either the general or specific impact of the Act.

18. Some respondents indicated that operating rights may include valuable benefits in addition to the right to provide transportation services with limited competition, such as the potential to increase a motor carrier's marketing or operating efficiency. They indicated that their purchases of operating rights were in combination with other benefits, such as a customer base, favorable leases on established freight terminals and equipment, and qualified and experienced personnel. The Board agrees that intangible assets acquired by motor carriers may have included benefits in addition to being able to operate with limited competition, for example, the potential to increase a motor carrier's operating efficiency. The Board concluded that an enterprise that has not done so should now assign costs to its identifiable intangible motor carrier assets, whether the assets were acquired before or after October 31, 1970, from the ICC, from other motor carriers, or through business combinations. The Board concluded that the cost assignment should be based on the circumstances existing when the assets were acquired. Some respondents indicated that the majority of motor carrier intangibles relate to operating rights. If identification and assignment cannot be made or if it is impracticable to do, the Board concluded that all unidentifiable intangible assets should be presumed to be interstate operating rights.

19. Other respondents indicated that their operating rights are as valuable today as they ever were because they have developed a customer base, favorable locations for operations, and qualified and experienced personnel. The Board recognizes that many enterprises build successful businesses and generate goodwill based on franchises such as operating rights; however, only purchased goodwill is capitalizable under present generally accepted accounting principles. The Board believes that costs assigned to intangible assets should not reflect costs of developing, maintaining, or restoring operating rights after they were acquired. The Board also believes that costs originally related to operating rights should not be merged with or be replaced by amounts relating to other identifiable intangibles or goodwill as would be permitted by paragraph 8 of Chapter 5 of ARB 43 for intangibles subject to the provisions of that chapter. Opinions 16 and 17 do not permit such combining or merging and the Board believes that paragraph 8 of Chapter 5 of ARB 43 should be amended to make it consistent with those Opinions.

20. The Board believes that, as long as intangible assets other than operating rights provide a motor carrier with continuing benefits, costs relating to those assets should continue to be subject to existing accounting pronouncements rather than be addressed by this Statement. Although other intangible assets may be impaired as a result of the Act, the Board believes that existing accounting pronouncements (Chapter 5 of ARB 43, Opinions 11, 17, and 30, and Statement 5) provide adequate guidance for accounting for those intangible assets.

21. The Board believes that the loss of limited competition resulting from the Act is both unusual and infrequent and that charging the costs of operating rights to income as an extraordinary item is appropriate under Opinion 30. The loss of the benefits of limited competition is unusual because the Act significantly alters the regulatory and operating environment of motor carriers. Also, the loss resulting from the Act is infrequent because it can happen only once. Therefore, the Board concluded that the charge to income of the cost of operating rights, if material, should be reported as an extraordinary item in accordance with Opinion 30.

22. Some respondents said that a requirement to charge operating rights to income could create an undue burden for some motor carriers because such a requirement could needlessly force some motor carriers to violate debt covenants. Those respondents recommended a grace period for those motor carriers. The Board believes that the significant loss in value of operating rights is an economic fact that should not be masked by deferring recognition of the loss.

461

23. Some respondents expressed concern that the Act would have significant impact on intrastate operating rights and that in many cases the unamortized cost of those rights also should be charged to income. This concern is based on increased competition from interstate carriers operating along intrastate routes. The Board decided to address in this Statement only the direct effects of the Act, that is, the effect on interstate operating rights. Intrastate operating rights may or may not continue to provide motor carriers with benefits. The Board believes that existing accounting pronouncements (Chapter 5 of ARB 43, Opinions 11, 17, and 30, and Statement 5) provide adequate guidance for accounting for those rights. However, if a state deregulates motor carriers with effects similar to those of the Act, the Board concluded that the cost of intrastate operating rights should be accounted for in accordance with the provisions of this Statement.

24. Some respondents said that the guidance in the Exposure Draft regarding any income tax benefits relating to the charge to income of the unamortized cost of operating rights was inadequate. The Board concluded that existing accounting pronouncements (particularly Opinion 11 and paragraph 25 of Opinion 30) provide adequate guidance regardless of how the income tax issue ultimately is resolved. In most cases, those pronouncements would require tax benefits related to the charge to income of operating rights to be considered an adjustment of the extraordinary item. Therefore, the Board believes that in most cases any material recognized tax benefits should be included in motor carriers' financial statements as an extraordinary item whenever reported.

25. Some respondents indicated that the disclosure requirements in the Exposure Draft already exist in other accounting pronouncements. After considering those comments, the Board agreed and concluded that the disclosure requirements in the Exposure Draft were unnecessary.

Statement of Financial Accounting Standards No. 45
Accounting for Franchise Fee Revenue

STATUS

Issued: March 1981

Effective Date: For fiscal years beginning after June 15, 1981

Affects: Amends FAS 32, Appendix A

Affected by: No other pronouncements

SUMMARY

This Statement extracts the specialized accounting principles and practices from the AICPA Industry Accounting Guide, *Accounting for Franchise Fee Revenue,* and establishes accounting and reporting standards for franchisors. It requires that franchise fee revenue from individual and area franchise sales be recognized only when all material services or conditions relating to the sale have been substantially performed or satisfied by the franchisor. This Statement also establishes accounting standards for continuing franchise fees, continuing product sales, agency sales, repossessed franchises, franchising costs, commingled revenue, and relationships between a franchisor and a franchisee.

Statement of Financial Accounting Standards No. 45
Accounting for Franchise Fee Revenue

CONTENTS

INTRODUCTION AND BACKGROUND INFORMATION

1. As discussed in FASB Statement No. 32, *Specialized Accounting and Reporting Principles and Practices in AICPA Statements of Position and Guides on Accounting and Auditing Matters,* the FASB is extracting the specialized[1] accounting and reporting principles and practices from AICPA Statements of Position (SOPs) and Guides on accounting and auditing matters and issuing them in FASB Statements after appropriate due process. This Statement extracts the specialized principles and practices from the AICPA Industry Accounting Guide, *Accounting for Franchise Fee Revenue* (Guide), and establishes accounting and reporting standards for franchise fee revenue that is obtained through a **franchise agreement.**[2]

2. The Board has not undertaken a comprehensive reconsideration of the accounting issues discussed in the Guide and has extracted the specialized accounting and reporting principles without significant change. Accordingly, some of the background material and discussion of accounting alternatives have not been carried forward from the Guide. The Board's conceptual framework project on accounting recognition criteria will address revenue recogni-

tion issues similar to those addressed in this Statement. A Statement of Financial Accounting Concepts resulting from that project in due course will serve as a basis for evaluating existing standards and practices. Accordingly, the Board may wish to evaluate the standards in this Statement when its conceptual framework project is completed.

3. The Guide was developed to clarify and standardize accounting by **franchisors,** particularly the timing of recognizing revenue from **initial franchise fees.** Before 1970, franchisors generally recognized revenue from initial franchise fees when franchises were sold. The Guide recommended that revenue from initial franchise fees be recognized when the franchise sale transaction was completed, that is, when all material services or conditions relating to the sale had been substantially performed or satisfied by the franchisor. In addition, the Guide stated a presumption that commencement of operations by the **franchisee** ordinarily would be the earliest point at which substantial performance could occur.

4. The Board has concluded that it can reach an informed decision on the basis of existing information without a public hearing and that the effective date and transition specified in paragraph 25 are advisable in the circumstances.

---

[1]The term *specialized* is used to refer to those accounting and reporting principles and practices in AICPA Guides and SOPs that are neither superseded by nor contained in Accounting Research Bulletins, APB Opinions, FASB Statements, or FASB Interpretations.

[2]Terms defined in the glossary (Appendix A) are in **boldface type** the first time they appear in this Statement.

STANDARDS OF FINANCIAL ACCOUNTING AND REPORTING

Individual Franchise Sales

5. Franchise fee revenue from an individual franchise sale ordinarily shall be recognized, with an appropriate provision for estimated uncollectible amounts, when all material services or conditions relating to the sale have been substantially performed or satisfied by the franchisor. Substantial performance for the franchisor means that (a) the franchisor has no remaining obligation or intent—by agreement, trade practice, or law—to refund any cash received or forgive any unpaid notes or receivables; (b) substantially all of the **initial services** of the franchisor required by the franchise agreement have been performed; and (c) no other material conditions or obligations related to the determination of substantial performance exist. If the franchise agreement does not require the franchisor to perform initial services but a practice of voluntarily rendering initial services exists or is likely to exist because of business or regulatory circumstances, substantial performance shall not be assumed until either the initial services have been substantially performed or reasonable assurance exists that the services will not be performed. The commencement of operations by the franchisee shall be presumed to be the earliest point at which substantial performance has occurred, unless it can be demonstrated that substantial performance of all obligations, including services rendered voluntarily, has occurred before that time.

6. Installment or cost recovery accounting methods[3] shall be used to account for franchise fee revenue only in those exceptional cases when revenue is collectible over an extended period and no reasonable basis exists for estimating collectibility.

7. Sometimes, large initial franchise fees are required but **continuing franchise fees** are small in relation to future services. If it is probable that the continuing fee will not cover the cost of the continuing services to be provided by the franchisor and a reasonable profit on those continuing services, then a portion of the initial franchise fee shall be deferred and amortized over the life of the franchise. The portion deferred shall be an amount sufficient to cover the estimated cost in excess of continuing franchise fees and provide a reasonable profit on the continuing services.

Area Franchise Sales

8. Initial franchise fees relating to **area franchise** sales shall be accounted for following the same principles described in paragraphs 5-7 for individual franchise sales, that is, revenue ordinarily shall be recognized when all material services or conditions relating to the sale(s) have been substantially performed or satisfied by the franchisor. If the franchisor's substantial obligations under the franchise agreement relate to the area franchise and do not depend significantly on the number of individual franchises to be established, substantial performance shall be determined using the same criteria applicable to individual franchises (paragraph 5). However, if the franchisor's substantial obligations depend on the number of individual franchises established within the area, area franchise fees shall be recognized in proportion to the initial mandatory services provided. Revenue that may have to be refunded because future services are not peformed shall not be recognized by the franchisor until the franchisee has no right to receive a refund.

9. The substance of an area franchise agreement shall determine when material services or conditions relating to a sale have been substantially performed or satisfied. Sometimes, the efforts and total cost relating to initial services are not affected significantly by the number of outlets opened in an area and, therefore, the area franchise sale is similar to an individual franchise sale. Conversely, when the efforts and total cost relating to initial services are affected significantly by the number of outlets opened in an area, it may be necessary to regard the franchise agreement as a divisible contract and to estimate the number of outlets involved so that revenue may be recognized in proportion to the outlets for which the required services have been substantially performed. Estimates shall consider the anticipated number of outlets based on the terms of the franchise agreement (for example, time limitations and any specified minimum or maximum number of outlets). Any change in estimate resulting from a change in circumstance shall result in recognizing remaining fees as revenue in proportion to remaining services to be performed.

Relationships between Franchisor and Franchisee

10. A franchisor may guarantee borrowings of a franchisee, have a creditor interest in the franchisee, or control a franchisee's operations by sales or other agreements to such an extent that the franchisee is, for all practical purposes, an affiliate of the franchisor. Sometimes, two franchisors may agree to pool their risks by selling their respective franchises to each other. In all those circumstances, revenue shall not be recognized if all material services, conditions, or obligations relating to the sale have not been substantially performed or satisfied (paragraph 5).

---

[3]See footnote 8 of APB Opinion No. 10, *Omnibus Opinion—1966.*

11. A franchise agreement may give the franchisor an option to purchase the franchisee's business. For example, a franchisor may purchase a profitable franchised outlet as a matter of management policy, or purchase a franchised outlet that is in financial difficulty or unable to continue in business to preserve the reputation and goodwill of the franchise system. If such an option exists, the likelihood of the franchisor's acquiring the franchised outlet shall be considered in accounting for the initial franchise fee. If at the time the option is given, an understanding exists that the option will be exercised or it is probable that the franchisor ultimately will acquire the franchised outlet, the initial franchise fee shall not be recognized as revenue but shall be deferred. When the option is exercised, the deferred amount shall reduce the franchisor's investment in the outlet.

Commingled Revenue

12. The franchise agreement ordinarily establishes a single initial franchise fee as consideration for the franchise rights and the initial services to be performed by the franchisor. Sometimes, however, the fee also may cover tangible property, such as signs, equipment, inventory, and land and building. In those circumstances, the portion of the fee applicable to the tangible assets shall be based on the fair value of the assets and may be recognized before or after recognizing the portion applicable to the initial services. For example, when the portion of the fee relating to the sale of specific tangible assets is objectively determinable, it would be appropriate to recognize that portion when their titles pass, even though the balance of the fee relating to services is recognized when the remaining services or conditions in the franchise agreement have been substantially performed or satisfied.

13. Although a franchise agreement may specify portions of the total fee that relate to specific services to be provided by the franchisor, the services usually are interrelated to such an extent that the amount applicable to each service cannot be segregated objectively. The fee shall not be allocated among the different services as a means of recognizing any part of the fee for services as revenue before all the services have been substantially performed unless actual transaction prices are available for individual services; for example, through recent sales of the separate specific services.

Continuing Franchise Fees

14. Continuing franchise fees shall be reported as revenue as the fees are earned and become receivable from the franchisee. Costs relating to continuing franchise fees shall be expensed as incurred. Although a portion of the continuing fee may be designated for a particular purpose, such as an advertising program, it shall not be recognized as revenue until the fee is earned and becomes receivable from the franchisee. An exception to the foregoing exists if the franchise constitutes an agency relationship under which a designated portion of the continuing fee is required to be segregated and used for a specified purpose. In that case, the designated amount shall be recorded as a liability against which the specified costs would be charged.

Continuing Product Sales

15. The franchisee may purchase some or all of the equipment or supplies necessary for its operations from the franchisor. Sometimes, the franchisee is given the right to make **bargain purchases** of equipment or supplies for a specified period or up to a specified amount, when the initial franchise fee is paid. If the bargain price is lower than the selling price of the same product to other customers or if the price does not provide the franchisor a reasonable profit on the equipment or supply sales, then a portion of the initial franchise fee shall be deferred and accounted for as an adjustment of the selling price when the franchisee purchases the equipment or supplies. The portion deferred shall be either (a) the difference between the selling price to other customers and the bargain purchase price or (b) an amount sufficient to cover any cost in excess of the bargain purchase price and provide a reasonable profit on the sale, as appropriate.

Agency Sales

16. Some franchisors engage in transactions in which they are, in substance, an agent for franchisees by placing orders for inventory and equipment and selling to franchisees at no profit. The franchisor shall account for such transactions as receivables and payables in its balance sheet and not as revenue and costs or expenses.

Franchising Costs

17. Direct (incremental) costs relating to franchise sales for which revenue has not been recognized ordinarily shall be deferred until the related revenue is recognized; however, the deferred costs shall not exceed anticipated revenue less estimated additional related costs. Indirect costs of a regular and recurring nature that are incurred irrespective of the level of sales, such as general, selling, and administrative costs, shall be expensed as incurred. Costs yet to be incurred shall be accrued and charged against income no later than the period in which the related revenue is recognized. Because of the concept of substantial performance (paragraph 5), such costs should be relatively minor.

Repossessed Franchises

18. A franchisor may recover franchise rights through repossession if a franchisee decides not to open an outlet. If, for any reason, the franchisor refunds the consideration received, the original sale is canceled, and revenue previously recognized shall be accounted for as a reduction in revenue in the period the franchise is repossessed. If franchise rights are repossessed but no refund is made, (a) the transaction shall not be regarded as a sale cancellation, (b) no adjustment shall be made to any previously recognized revenue, (c) any estimated uncollectible amounts resulting from unpaid receivables shall be provided for, and (d) any consideration retained for which revenue was not previously recognized shall be reported as revenue.

Business Combinations

19. A transaction in which a franchisor acquires the business of an operating franchisee ordinarily shall be accounted for as a business combination in accordance with APB Opinion No. 16, *Business Combinations,* assuming no relationship existed at the time of the franchise sale to preclude revenue recognition (paragraphs 10 and 11). If the transaction is accounted for as a pooling of interests, the financial statements of the two entities are retroactively combined and the original franchise sales transaction as well as any product sales shall be eliminated in the combined financial statements. If the transaction is accounted for as a purchase, the financial statements of the two entities are not retroactively combined and revenue shall not be adjusted. If such a transaction is, in substance, a cancellation of an original franchise sale, the transaction shall be accounted for in accordance with paragraph 18.

Disclosures

20. The nature of all significant commitments and obligations resulting from franchise agreements, including a description of the services that the franchisor has agreed to provide for agreements that have not yet been substantially performed, shall be disclosed.

21. If no basis for estimating the collectibility of specific franchise fees exists, the notes to the financial statements shall disclose whether the installment or cost recovery method is being used to account for the related franchise fee revenue. Furthermore, the sales price of such franchises, the revenue and related costs deferred (both currently and on a cumulative basis), and the periods in which such fees become payable by the franchisee shall be disclosed. Any amounts originally deferred but later recognized because uncertainties regarding the collectibility of franchise fees are resolved also shall be disclosed.

22. Initial franchise fees shall be segregated from other franchise fee revenue if they are significant. If it is probable that initial franchise fee revenue will decline in the future because sales predictably reach a saturation point, disclosure of that fact is desirable. Disclosure of the relative contribution to net income of initial franchise fees also is desirable if not apparent from the relative amounts of revenue.

23. Revenue and costs related to franchisor-owned outlets shall be distinguished from revenue and costs related to franchised outlets when practicable. That may be done by segregating revenue and costs related to franchised outlets. If there are significant changes in franchisor-owned outlets or franchised outlets during the period, the number of (a) franchises sold, (b) franchises purchased during the period, (c) franchised outlets in operation, and (d) franchisor-owned outlets in operation shall be disclosed.

Amendment to Other Pronouncement

24. The reference to the AICPA Industry Accounting Guide, *Accounting for Franchise Fee Revenue,* is deleted from Appendix A of Statement 32. The specialized accounting provisions of that Guide are superseded by this Statement.

Effective Date and Transition

25. This Statement shall be effective for financial statements for fiscal years beginning after June 15, 1981. Earlier application is encouraged. The provisions of this Statement shall be applied retroactively and any accompanying financial statements presented for prior periods shall be restated.

> **The provisions of this Statement need not be applied to immaterial items.**

This Statement was adopted by the unanimous vote of the seven members of the Financial Accounting Standards Board:

Donald J. Kirk, *Chairman* Frank E. Block	John W. March Robert A. Morgan David Mosso	Robert T. Sprouse Ralph E. Walters

Appendix A

GLOSSARY

26. This appendix defines certain terms that are used in this Statement.

Area franchise
An agreement that transfers franchise rights within a geographical area permitting the opening of a number of franchised outlets. Under those circumstances, decisions regarding the number of outlets, their location, and so forth are more likely made unilaterally by the franchisee than in collaboration with the franchisor. A franchisor may sell an area franchise to a franchisee who operates the franchised outlets or the franchisor may sell an area franchise to an intermediary franchisee who then sells individual franchises to other franchisees who operate the outlets.

Bargain purchase
A transaction in which the franchisee is allowed to purchase equipment or supplies for a price that is significantly lower than the fair value of the equipment or supplies.

Continuing franchise fee
Consideration for the continuing rights granted by the franchise agreement and for general or specific services during its life.

Franchise agreement[4]
A written business agreement that meets the following principal criteria:

a. The relation between the franchisor and franchisee is contractual, and an agreement, confirming the rights and responsibilities of each party, is in force for a specified period.
b. The continuing relation has as its purpose the distribution of a product or service, or an entire business concept, within a particular market area.
c. Both the franchisor and the franchisee contribute resources for establishing and maintaining the franchise. The franchisor's contribution may be a trademark, a company reputation, products, procedures, manpower, equipment, or a process. The franchisee usually contributes operating capital as well as the managerial and operational resources required for opening and continuing the franchised outlet.
d. The franchise agreement outlines and describes the specific marketing practices to be followed, specifies the contribution of

each party to the operation of the business, and sets forth certain operating procedures that both parties agree to comply with.
e. The establishment of the franchised outlet creates a business entity that will, in most cases, require and support the full-time business activity of the franchisee. (There are numerous other contractual distribution arrangements in which a local businessperson becomes the "authorized distributor" or "representative" for the sale of a particular good or service, along with many others, but such a sale usually represents only a portion of the person's total business.)
f. Both the franchisee and the franchisor have a common public identity. This identity is achieved most often through the use of common trade names or trademarks and is frequently reinforced through advertising programs designed to promote the recognition and acceptance of the common identity within the franchisee's market area.

The payment of an initial franchise fee or a continuing royalty fee is not a necessary criterion for an agreement to be considered a franchise agreement.

Franchisee
The party who has been granted business rights (the franchise) to operate the franchised business.

Franchisor
The party who grants business rights (the franchise) to the party (the franchisee) who will operate the franchised business.

Initial franchise fee
Consideration for establishing the franchise relationship and providing some initial services. Occasionally, the fee includes consideration for initially required equipment and inventory, but those items usually are the subject of separate consideration.

Initial services
Common provision of a franchise agreement in which the franchisor usually will agree to provide a variety of services and advice to the franchisee, such as the following:

a. Assistance in the selection of a site. The assistance may be based on experience with factors, such as traffic patterns, residential configurations, and competition.
b. Assistance in obtaining facilities, including related financing and architectural and engineering services. The facilities may be pur-

---

[4]This definition has been developed for purposes of this Statement and may not be appropriate for other uses.

chased or leased by the franchisee, and lease payments may be guaranteed by the franchisor.

c. Assistance in advertising, either for the individual franchisee or as part of a general program.

d. Training of the franchisee's personnel.

e. Preparation and distribution of manuals and similar material concerning operations, administration, and record keeping.

f. Bookkeeping and advisory services, including setting up the franchisee's records and advising the franchisee about income, real estate, and other taxes or about local regulations affecting the franchisee's business.

g. Inspection, testing, and other quality control programs.

Appendix B

SUMMARY OF CONSIDERATION OF COMMENTS ON EXPOSURE DRAFT

27. An Exposure Draft of a proposed Statement, *Accounting for Franchise Fee Revenue*, was issued December 1, 1980. The Board received 25 comment letters in response to the Exposure Draft. Certain of the comments received and the Board's consideration of them are discussed in this appendix.

28. Some respondents indicated that the requirement in the last sentence of paragraph 5 that the commencement of operations by the franchisee shall be presumed to be the earliest point at which substantial performance has occurred was too restrictive. They said that the Guide was less restrictive because it provided for recognition of revenue before the franchisee began operations when substantial performance could be demonstrated. The Board agrees with those respondents and has clarified paragraph 5 to state that the presumption may be overcome if the franchisor can demonstrate that it has substantially performed all of its obligations, including services rendered voluntarily, before the franchisee begins operations.

29. Some respondents requested that the phrase "portion of the initial franchise fee" in paragraphs 7 and 15 be clarified. They indicated that the phrase could be interpreted to mean either an amount necessary to cover net future costs only or an amount sufficient to cover net future costs plus a reasonable profit. The Board agrees with those respondents and has clarified those paragraphs to indicate that the appropriate portion represents cost and reasonable profit in excess of anticipated continuing franchise fees (paragraph 7) or bargain purchase price (paragraph 15).

30. Several individual respondents suggested various substantive changes to the Exposure Draft. Adoption of those suggestions would have required a reconsideration of the provisions of the Guide. Those suggestions were not adopted because such a reconsideration is beyond the scope of extracting the specialized accounting and reporting principles and practices from the Guide and because none of the changes was broadly supported.

Statement of Financial Accounting Standards No. 46
Financial Reporting and Changing Prices:
Motion Picture Films

a supplement to FASB Statement No. 33

STATUS

Issued: March 1981

Effective Date: For fiscal years ending on or after March 31, 1981

Affects: Amends FAS 33, paragraph 53
       Amends FAS 39, paragraph 12
       Amends FAS 40, paragraph 6
       Amends FAS 41, paragraph 7

Affected by: Paragraph 8 superseded by FAS 69
          Superseded by FAS 89

Statement of Financial Accounting Standards No. 47
Disclosure of Long-Term Obligations

STATUS

Issued: March 1981

Effective Date: For fiscal years ending after June 15, 1981

Affects: No other pronouncements

Affected by: Paragraph 10(c) superseded by FAS 129

Issues Discussed by FASB Emerging Issues Task Force (EITF)

Affects: No EITF Issues

Interpreted by: No EITF Issues

Related Issues: EITF Issues No. 91-6 and 96-17

SUMMARY

This Statement requires that an enterprise disclose its commitments under unconditional purchase obligations that are associated with suppliers' financing arrangements. Such obligations often are in the form of take-or-pay contracts and throughput contracts. This Statement also requires disclosure of future payments on long-term borrowings and redeemable stock. For long-term unconditional purchase obligations that are associated with suppliers' financing and are not recognized on purchasers' balance sheets, the disclosures include the nature of the obligations, the amount of the fixed and determinable obligation in the aggregate and for each of the next five years, a description of any portion of the obligation that is variable, and the purchases in each year for which an income statement is presented. For long-term unconditional purchase obligations that are associated with suppliers' financing and are recognized on purchasers' balance sheets, payments for each of the next five years shall be disclosed. For long-term borrowings and redeemable stock, the disclosures include maturities and sinking fund requirements (if any) for each of the next five years and redemption requirements for each of the next five years, respectively.

Statement of Financial Accounting Standards No. 47
Disclosure of Long-Term Obligations

CONTENTS

INTRODUCTION

1. The Board has received requests to consider the subjects of accounting for **project financing arrangements**[1] and accounting for **take-or-pay contracts, throughput contracts,** and other unconditional purchase obligations typically associated with project financing arrangements. Some have stated that certain of those arrangements and contracts result in acquisitions of ownership interests and obligations to make future cash payments that should be recognized as assets and liabilities on participants' balance sheets. Others consider such arrangements and contracts to result in commitments or contingent liabilities that should not be recognized on balance sheets.

2. The Board currently has on its agenda three topics that are part of the conceptual framework for financial accounting and reporting and that pertain to those requests:

a. Accounting recognition criteria for elements, which will address the types of transactions, events, and circumstances that should lead to recognition in financial statements of items that qualify as assets, liabilities, revenues, expenses, etc., under the definitions of elements of financial statements[2]
b. Measurement of the elements of financial statements, which will consider how assets, liabilities, and other elements should be measured
c. Funds flows, liquidity, and financial flexibility, which will determine the kinds of information that should be reported to facilitate assessments of an enterprise's flow of funds, liquidity, and ability to obtain cash to adapt to unexpected difficulties or opportunities

The Board believes that the questions raised in paragraph 1 can be addressed more readily after further work is completed on some or all of those conceptual framework projects.

3. The arrangements and contracts discussed in paragraph 1 and in the remainder of this Statement are sometimes recognized on balance sheets. If they are not recognized on balance sheets, they often are disclosed in the notes to financial statements. If disclosed, the disclosure sometimes quantifies the enterprise's rights and obligations. As an interim measure, pending further work on those conceptual framework projects identified in paragraph 2, the Board has concluded that unconditional purchase obligations associated with financing arrangements should be disclosed and quantified. The Board also has concluded that enterprises should disclose future cash payments in a manner similar to existing disclosures of capital lease obligations for long-term borrowings and capital stock with mandatory redemption requirements. This Statement provides standards of disclosure.

4. Appendix A provides additional background information and the basis for the Board's conclusions. Appendix C illustrates applications of this Statement.

5. The Board has concluded that it can reach an informed decision on the basis of existing data without a public hearing and that the effective date and transition specified in paragraph 11 are advisable in the circumstances.

---

[1] Terms defined in the glossary (Appendix B) are in **boldface type** the first time they appear in this Statement.

[2] The question of when rights and obligations that arise under contracts should be recognized as assets and liabilities in financial statements is addressed in an FASB Research Report, *Recognition of Contractual Rights and Obligations,* prepared by Professor Yuji Ijiri of Carnegie-Mellon University as part of the accounting recognition criteria project. The Research Report discusses several possible recognition points, including initiation of the contract, delivery of the contracted goods or services, and payment for those goods or services.

STANDARDS OF FINANCIAL ACCOUNTING AND REPORTING

Definition and Scope

6. An unconditional purchase obligation is an obligation to transfer funds in the future for fixed or minimum amounts or quantities of goods or services at fixed or minimum prices (for example, as in take-or-pay contracts or throughput contracts). An unconditional purchase obligation that has all of the following characteristics shall be disclosed in accordance with paragraph 7 (if not recorded on the purchaser's balance sheet) or in accordance with paragraph 10(a) (if recorded on the purchaser's balance sheet):

a. Is noncancelable, or cancelable only
   (1) Upon the occurrence of some remote contingency or
   (2) With the permission of the other party or
   (3) If a replacement agreement is signed between the same parties or
   (4) Upon payment of a penalty in an amount such that continuation of the agreement appears reasonably assured
b. Was negotiated as part of arranging financing for the facilities that will provide the contracted goods or services or for costs related to those goods or services (for example, carrying costs for contracted goods)
c. Has a remaining term in excess of one year

Future minimum lease payments under leases that have those characteristics need not be disclosed in accordance with this Statement if they are disclosed in accordance with FASB Statement No. 13, *Accounting for Leases*.

Unrecorded Obligations

7. A purchaser shall disclose unconditional purchase obligations that meet the criteria of paragraph 6 and that have not been recognized on its balance sheet. The disclosures shall include:

a. The nature and term of the obligation(s)
b. The amount of the fixed and determinable portion of the obligation(s) as of the date of the latest balance sheet presented in the aggregate and, if determinable, for each of the five succeeding fiscal years (paragraph 8)
c. The nature of any variable components of the obligation(s)
d. The amounts purchased under the obligation(s) (for example, the take-or-pay or throughput contract) for each period for which an income statement is presented

Disclosures of similar or related unconditional purchase obligations may be combined. These disclosures may be omitted only if the aggregate commitment for all such obligations not disclosed is immaterial.

8. Disclosure of the amount of imputed interest necessary to reduce the unconditional purchase obligation(s) to present value is encouraged but not required. The discount rate shall be the effective initial interest rate of the borrowings that financed the facility (or facilities) that will provide the contracted goods or services, if known by the purchaser. If not, the discount rate shall be the **purchaser's incremental borrowing rate** at the date the obligation is entered into.

Recorded Obligations and Redeemable Stock

9. Certain unconditional purchase obligations are presently recorded as liabilities on purchasers' balance sheets with the related assets also recognized. This Statement does not alter that accounting treatment or the treatment of future unconditional purchase obligations that are substantially the same as those obligations already recorded as liabilities with related assets, nor does it suggest that disclosure is an appropriate substitute for accounting recognition if the substance of an arrangement is the acquisition of an asset and incurrence of a liability.

10. The following information shall be disclosed for each of the five years following the date of the latest balance sheet presented:

a. The aggregate amount of payments for unconditional purchase obligations that meet the criteria of paragraph 6 and that have been recognized on the purchaser's balance sheet
b. The combined aggregate amount of maturities and sinking fund requirements for all long-term borrowings
c. The amount of redemption requirements for all issues of capital stock that are redeemable at fixed or determinable prices on fixed or determinable dates, separately by issue or combined.

Effective Date and Transition

11. This Statement shall be effective for financial statements for fiscal years ending after June 15, 1981. Earlier application is encouraged. The disclosures required by paragraph 7(d) need not be included in financial statements for periods beginning before the effective date of this Statement that are being presented for comparative purposes with financial statements for periods after the effective date.

> **The provisions of this Statement need
> not be applied to immaterial items.**

This Statement was adopted by the affirmative votes of six members of the Financial Accounting Standards Board. Mr. Morgan dissented.

Mr. Morgan dissents to issuance of this Statement because he believes it is not needed. In his opinion, conscientious preparers and auditors will disclose the existence of unconditional purchase obligations associated with financing arrangements if there is a reasonable possibility that a payment will be required without the purchaser receiving an asset of comparable value in return. Such disclosure seems to be required by FASB Statement No. 5, *Accounting for Contingencies*; if Statement 5 is ambiguous in that regard, an Interpretation would be sufficient. Mr. Morgan does not believe that there is a need for specific disclosure requirements for unconditional purchase obligations associated with financing arrangements, particularly if there is only a remote possibility that payment will be required without the purchaser receiving an asset of comparable value in return. Also, Mr. Morgan believes that the disclo-

sure of obligations for each of the next five years may convey a notion of a contractual period longer than is realistic. He believes that such agreements are renegotiated frequently in practice.

Mr. Morgan also disagrees with mandating disclosure of next-five-year repayment requirements on long-term borrowings and redemption requirements on redeemable stock. He does not recall any requests to the Board to consider such disclosures.

Mr. Morgan's preference would be to delay action on this Statement until completion of the Board's conceptual framework project on accounting recognition criteria. That project could provide the Board a basis to conclude that unconditional purchase obligations should be recorded on the balance sheet, disclosed in the notes to financial statements, or both.

The members of the Financial Accounting Standards Board:

Donald J. Kirk,	John W. March	Robert T. Sprouse
Chairman	Robert A. Morgan	Ralph E. Walters
Frank E. Block	David Mosso	

Appendix A

BACKGROUND INFORMATION AND BASIS FOR CONCLUSIONS

12. As noted in the introduction, the FASB was asked to consider accounting for project financing arrangements. The particular requests related to whether the unconditional purchase obligations and indirect guarantees of indebtedness of others typical of project financing arrangements result in participants acquiring ownership interests and obligations to make future cash payments that should be recognized as assets and liabilities on their balance sheets. The Board concluded, as noted in paragraph 2, that those accounting questions could be answered better after further progress is made on the conceptual framework for financial accounting and reporting.

13. Paragraphs 40 and 41 of FASB Concepts Statement No. 1, *Objectives of Financial Reporting by Business Enterprises*, state one objective of financial reporting:

    Financial reporting should provide information about the economic resources of an

enterprise, the claims to those resources (obligations of the enterprise to transfer resources to other entities and owners' equity), and the effects of transactions, events, and circumstances that change resources and claims to those resources. . . .

    Financial reporting should provide information about an enterprise's economic resources, obligations, and owners' equity. That information helps investors, creditors, and others identify the enterprise's financial strengths and weaknesses and assess its liquidity and solvency. Information about resources, obligations, and owners' equity also provides . . . direct indications . . . of the cash needed to satisfy many, if not most, obligations. . . . Many obligations are direct causes of cash payments by the enterprise, and reasonably reliable measures of . . . future net cash outflows are often possible for those . . . obligations.

Existing accounting for and disclosure of unconditional purchase obligations associated with financing arrangements are inconsistent among enterprises and often fail to satisfy that objective of financial reporting. In addition, as noted in paragraph 1, the unconditional purchase obligations discussed in this

Statement have some of the characteristics of liabilities. Accordingly, as an interim measure pending a decision on whether the obligations should be recognized on purchasers' balance sheets, the Board decided that disclosures of unconditional purchase obligations associated with financing arrangements should be expanded and standardized to satisfy that objective of financial reporting.

14. On March 31, 1980, the FASB released an Exposure Draft, *Disclosure of Guarantees, Project Financing Arrangements, and Other Similar Obligations* (March Exposure Draft). The FASB received 102 letters of comment on the March Exposure Draft. Based on the comments received, the content of the March Exposure Draft was separated into two documents that were exposed concurrently for comment on November 14, 1980: a revised Exposure Draft, *Disclosure of Unconditional Obligations*, and a proposed Interpretation, *Disclosure of Indirect Guarantees of Indebtedness of Others*.

15. The Board received 67 letters of comment on the revised Exposure Draft. Certain of the comments received and the Board's consideration of them are discussed in paragraphs 16-22.

16. Some respondents stated that the revised Exposure Draft did not distinguish clearly between the unconditional obligations that would have been required to be disclosed and the unconditional obligations that would have been excluded. The distinction between long-term purchase commitments and take-or-pay contracts was of particular concern. Other respondents suggested that the Board should limit the disclosures to unconditional obligations with clear financing elements. Based on those comments, the Board reconsidered the scope of this Statement. The Board's accounting recognition criteria project will consider criteria for balance sheet recognition of all contractual rights and obligations, whether or not unconditional and whether or not associated with financing arrangements. With respect to most contractual rights and obligations, the Board believes existing disclosures are adequate until the fundamental accounting concepts are resolved. Unconditional purchase obligations associated with financing arrangements, however, have many similarities to borrowings and to lease obligations, and the Board believes that existing disclosures often fail to adequately inform readers of the significance of those obligations. Accordingly, this Statement establishes standards of disclosure for unconditional purchase obligations associated with financing arrangements.

17. Some expressed concern that this Statement might impose on purchasers a burden of determining whether a supplier has used an unconditional purchase obligation to arrange financing without the purchaser's direct involvement or knowledge. The Board believes that, for most arrangements covered by this Statement, financing considerations are an integral part of negotiating the terms of the unconditional purchase obligation. There is no intent to require a purchaser to investigate whether a supplier used an unconditional purchase obligation to help secure financing, if the purchaser would otherwise be unaware of that fact.

18. Some respondents believe that FASB Statement No. 5, *Accounting for Contingencies*, already provides for adequate disclosure of unconditional purchase obligations associated with financing arrangements. They state that quantification of the obligation should be required only if a loss under the contract is reasonably possible. As stated in paragraph 13, however, the Board believes that existing disclosures of unconditional purchase obligations often fail to provide adequate information about an enterprise's economic resources and claims to those resources. Statement 5 contains requirements pertaining to accounting for and reporting loss contingencies, but does not otherwise address long-term unconditional obligations that are not required to be disclosed as loss contingencies but that nevertheless impose significant future financial commitments for which cash must be available. .

19. Some respondents stated that the disclosures required by this Statement might be misleading to readers of financial statements because the obligations are disclosed but the associated benefits are not disclosed. Some respondents described the approach of the revised Exposure Draft as a liquidation perspective rather than a going-concern approach. The Board has not included explicit requirements to disclose associated benefits because the expected benefits may be difficult to quantify and may not be assured of realization. Paragraph 7(a) of this Statement requires a description of the nature of the obligation, and each of the first three illustrations in Appendix C describes the obligation and the associated benefit (access to processing facilities, availability of needed pipeline capacity, and an assured supply of ammonia, respectively). The lack of explicit requirements to disclose associated benefits does not preclude an enterprise from describing those benefits.

20. Several respondents noted that the requirements in Statement 13 to disclose future lease obligations apply to leases with initial or remaining terms in excess of one year and suggested conforming the requirements in this Statement. The Board has adopted that suggestion both to conform with Statement 13 and to reduce the costs of applying this Statement by eliminating the need to review short-term unconditional purchase obligations.

21. The revised Exposure Draft and this Statement require quantification of the fixed and determinable portion of unrecorded purchase obligations and description, but not quantification, of the variable portion of unrecorded obligations. Several respondents noted that the variable portion is similar to contingent rentals on leases. They suggested that the purchases made in each period for which an income statement is presented should be disclosed, similar to the disclosure of contingent rental expense, to help readers of financial statements estimate future payments under the variable portions. The Board adopted that suggestion.

22. Paragraphs 7 and 10(a) of this Statement require purchasers to disclose future payments under long-term unconditional purchase obligations associated with financing arrangements, and Statement 13 requires lessees to disclose future payments under capital and operating leases. The Board believes it would be anomalous to require those disclosures but not to require disclosures of maturities and sinking fund requirements on long-term borrowings and of mandatory redemption requirements on capital stock that are similarly relevant in assessing future cash requirements. This Statement, therefore, includes standards of disclosure pertaining to long-term borrowings and capital stock with mandatory redemption features. Those standards are substantially the same as disclosures currently required by Regulation S-X of the Securities and Exchange Commission for publicly held enterprises.

Appendix B

GLOSSARY

23. For purposes of this Statement, certain terms are defined as follows:

a. *Project financing arrangement.* The financing of a major capital project in which the lender looks principally to the cash flows and earnings of the project as the source of funds for repayment and to the assets of the project as collateral for the loan. The general credit of the project entity is usually not a significant factor, either because the entity is a corporation without other assets or because the financing is without direct recourse to the owner(s) of the entity.
b. *Purchaser's incremental borrowing rate.* The rate that, at the inception of an unconditional purchase obligation, the purchaser would have incurred to borrow over a similar term the funds necessary to discharge the obligation.
c. *Take-or-pay contract.* An agreement between a purchaser and a seller that provides for the purchaser to pay specified amounts periodically in return for products or services. The purchaser must make specified minimum payments even if it does not take delivery of the contracted products or services.
d. *Throughput contract.* An agreement between a shipper (processor) and the owner of a transportation facility (such as an oil or natural gas pipeline or a ship) or a manufacturing facility that provides for the shipper (processor) to pay specified amounts periodically in return for the transportation (processing) of a product. The shipper (processor) is obligated to provide specified minimum quantities to be transported (processed) in each period and is required to make cash payments even if it does not provide the contracted quantities.

Appendix C

ILLUSTRATIONS OF THE APPLICATION OF THIS STATEMENT TO COMMON ARRANGEMENTS

Example 1

24. B Company has entered into a throughput agreement with a manufacturing plant providing that B will submit specified quantities of a chemical (representing a portion of plant capacity) for processing through the plant each period while the debt used to finance the plant remains outstanding. B's processing charges are intended to be sufficient to cover a proportional share of fixed and variable operating expenses and debt service of the plant. If, however, the processing charges do not cover such operating expenses and debt service, B must advance additional funds to cover a specified percentage of operating expenses and debt service. Such additional funds are considered advance payments for future throughput.

25. B's unconditional obligation to pay a specified percentage of the plant's fixed operating expenses and debt service is fixed and determinable, while the amount of variable operating expenses that B is obligated to pay will vary depending on plant operations and economic conditions.

26. B's disclosure might be as follows:

> To secure access to facilities to process chemical X, the company has signed a processing agreement with a chemical company allowing B Company to submit 100,000 tons for processing annually for 20 years. Under the terms of the agreement, B Company may be required to advance funds against future processing charges if the chemical company is unable to meet its financial obligations. The aggregate amount of required payments at December 31, 19X1 is as follows (in thousands):

19X2	$ 10,000
19X3	10,000
19X4	9,000
19X5	8,000
19X6	8,000
Later years	100,000
Total	145,000
Less: Amount representing interest	(45,000)
Total at present value	$100,000

In addition, the company is required to pay a proportional share of the variable operating expenses of the plant. The company's total processing charges under the agreement in each of the past 3 years have been $12 million.

Example 2

27. C Company has entered into a throughput agreement with a natural gas pipeline providing that C will provide specified quantities of natural gas (representing a portion of capacity) for transportation through the pipeline each period while the debt used to finance the pipeline remains outstanding. The tariff approved by the Federal Energy Regulatory Commission contains two portions, a demand charge and a commodity charge. The demand charge is computed to cover debt service, depreciation, and certain expected expenses. The commodity charge is intended to cover other expenses and provide a return on the pipeline company's investment. C Company must pay the demand charge based on the contracted quantity regardless of actual quantities shipped, while the commodity charge is applied to actual quantities shipped. Accordingly, the demand charge multiplied by the contracted quantity represents a fixed and determinable payment.

28. C's disclosure might be as follows:

C Company has signed an agreement providing for the availability of needed pipeline transportation capacity through 1990. Under that agreement, the company must make specified minimum payments monthly. The aggregate amount of such required payments at December 31, 19X1 is as follows (in thousands):

19X2	$ 5,000
19X3	5,000
19X4	5,000
19X5	4,000
19X6	4,000
Later years	26,000
Total	49,000
Less: Amount representing interest	(9,000)
Total at present value	$ 40,000

In addition, the company is required to pay additional amounts depending on actual quantities shipped under the agreement. The company's total payments under the agreement were (in thousands) $6,000 in 19W9 and $5,500 both in 19X0 and in 19X1.

Example 3

29. A subsidiary of F Company has entered into a take-or-pay contract with an ammonia plant. F's subsidiary is obligated to purchase 50 percent of the planned capacity production of the plant each period while the debt used to finance the plant remains outstanding. The monthly payment equals the sum of 50 percent of raw material costs, operating expenses, depreciation, interest on the debt used to finance the plant, and a return on the owner's equity investment.

30. F's disclosure might be as follows:

To assure a long-term supply, one of the company's subsidiaries has contracted to purchase half the output of an ammonia plant through the year 2005 and to make minimum annual payments as follows, whether or not it is able to take delivery (in thousands):

19X2 through 19X6 ($6,000 per annum)	$ 30,000
Later years	120,000
Total	150,000
Less: Amount representing interest	(65,000)
Total at present value	$ 85,000

In addition, the subsidiary must reimburse the owner of the plant for a proportional share of raw material costs and operating expenses of the plant. The subsidiary's total purchases under the agreement were (in thousands) $7,000, $7,100, and $7,200 in 19W9, 19X0, and 19X1, respectively.

Example 4

31. D Company has outstanding two long-term borrowings and one issue of preferred stock with mandatory redemption requirements. The first borrowing is a $100 million sinking fund debenture with annual sinking fund payments of $10 million in 19X2, 19X3, and 19X4, $15 million in 19X5 and 19X6, and $20 million in 19X7 and 19X8. The second borrowing is a $50 million note due in 19X5. The $30 million issue of preferred stock requires a 5 percent annual cumulative sinking fund payment of $1.5 million until retired.

32. D's disclosure might be as follows:

	Long-term debt	Preferred stock
19X2	$10,000	$1,500
19X3	10,000	1,500
19X4	10,000	1,500
19X5	65,000	1,500
19X6	15,000	1,500

Maturities and sinking fund requirements on long-term debt and sinking fund requirements on preferred stock subject to mandatory redemption are as follows (in thousands):

Statement of Financial Accounting Standards No. 48
Revenue Recognition When Right of Return Exists

STATUS

Issued: June 1981

Effective Date: For fiscal years beginning after June 15, 1981

Affects: Amends FAS 32, Appendix A

Affected by: No other pronouncements

SUMMARY

This Statement specifies how an enterprise should account for sales of its product in which the buyer has a right to return the product. Revenue from those sales transactions shall be recognized at time of sale only if *all* of the conditions specified by the Statement are met. If those conditions are not met, revenue recognition is postponed; if they are met, sales revenue and cost of sales reported in the income statement shall be reduced to reflect estimated returns and expected costs or losses shall be accrued.

Statement of Financial Accounting Standards No. 48
Revenue Recognition When Right of Return Exists

CONTENTS

INTRODUCTION

1. As discussed in FASB Statement No. 32, *Specialized Accounting and Reporting Principles and Practices in AICPA Statements of Position and Guides on Accounting and Auditing Matters,* the FASB is extracting the specialized[1] accounting and reporting principles and practices from AICPA Statements of Position (SOPs) and Guides on accounting and auditing matters and issuing them in FASB Statements after appropriate due process. This Statement extracts the specialized principles and practices from SOP 75-1, *Revenue Recognition When Right of Return Exists,* and establishes accounting and reporting standards for sales of an enterprise's product in which the buyer has a right to return the product.

2. The Board has concluded that it can reach an informed decision on the basis of existing information without a public hearing and that the effective date and transition specified in paragraphs 10-12 are advisable in the circumstances.

APPLICABILITY AND SCOPE

3. This Statement specifies criteria for recognizing revenue on a sale in which a product may be returned, whether as a matter of contract or as a matter of existing practice, either by the ultimate customer or by a party who resells the product to others. The product may be returned for a refund of the purchase price, for a credit applied to amounts owed or to be owed for other purchases, or in exchange for other products. The purchase price or credit may include amounts related to incidental services, such as installation.

4. This Statement does not apply to: (a) accounting for revenue in service industries if part or all of the service revenue may be returned under cancellation privileges granted to the buyer, (b) transactions involving real estate or leases, or (c) sales transactions in which a customer may return defective goods, such as under warranty provisions.

5. This Statement does not modify any of the provisions of FASB Statement No. 49, *Accounting for Product Financing Arrangements.* A product financing arrangement as defined in that Statement should be accounted for as a borrowing rather than as a sale.

STANDARDS OF FINANCIAL ACCOUNTING AND REPORTING

Criteria for Recognizing Revenue When Right of Return Exists

6. If an enterprise sells its product but gives the buyer the right to return the product, revenue from the sales transaction shall be recognized at time of sale only if *all* of the following conditions are met:

a. The seller's price to the buyer is substantially fixed or determinable at the date of sale.

b. The buyer has paid the seller, or the buyer is obligated to pay the seller and the obligation is not contingent on resale of the product.

c. The buyer's obligation to the seller would not be changed in the event of theft or physical destruction or damage of the product.

d. The buyer acquiring the product for resale has economic substance apart from that provided by the seller.[2]

---

[1] The term *specialized* is used to refer to those accounting and reporting principles and practices in AICPA Guides and SOPs that are neither superseded by nor contained in Accounting Research Bulletins, APB Opinions, FASB Statements, or FASB Interpretations.

[2] This condition relates primarily to buyers that exist "on paper," that is, buyers that have little or no physical facilities or employees. It prevents enterprises from recognizing sales revenue on transactions with parties that the sellers have established primarily for the purpose of recognizing such sales revenue.

e. The seller does not have significant obligations for future performance to directly bring about resale of the product by the buyer.

f. The amount of future returns[3] can be reasonably estimated (paragraph 8).

Sales revenue and cost of sales that are not recognized at time of sale because the foregoing conditions are not met shall be recognized either when the return privilege has substantially expired or if those conditions subsequently are met, whichever occurs first.

7. If sales revenue is recognized because the conditions of paragraph 6 are met, any costs or losses that may be expected in connection with any returns shall be accrued in accordance with FASB Statement No. 5, *Accounting for Contingencies.* Sales revenue and cost of sales reported in the income statement shall be reduced to reflect estimated returns.

8. The ability to make a reasonable estimate of the amount of future returns depends on many factors and circumstances that will vary from one case to the next. However, the following factors may impair the ability to make a reasonable estimate:

a. The susceptibility of the product to significant external factors, such as technological obsolescence or changes in demand

b. Relatively long periods in which a particular product may be returned

c. Absence of historical experience with similar types of sales of similar products, or inability to apply such experience because of changing circumstances, for example, changes in the selling enterprise's marketing policies or relationships with its customers

d. Absence of a large volume of relatively homogeneous transactions

The existence of one or more of the above factors, in light of the significance of other factors, may not be sufficient to prevent making a reasonable estimate; likewise, other factors may preclude a reasonable estimate.

Amendment to Statement 32

9. The reference to SOP 75-1, *Revenue Recognition When Right of Return Exists,* is deleted from Appendix A of Statement 32. The specialized accounting provisions of that SOP are superseded by this Statement.

Effective Date and Transition

10. This Statement shall be effective for fiscal years beginning after June 15, 1981, with earlier application encouraged. Accounting changes adopted to conform to the provisions of this Statement shall be applied retroactively. In the year that this Statement is first applied, the financial statements shall disclose the nature of any restatement and its effect on sales, income before extraordinary items, net income, and related per-share amounts for each year restated.

11. If retroactive restatement of all years presented is not practicable, the financial statements presented shall be restated for as many consecutive years as practicable and the cumulative effect of applying the Statement shall be included in determining net income of the earliest year restated (not necessarily the earliest year presented). If it is not practicable to restate any prior year, the cumulative effect shall be included in net income in the year in which the Statement is first applied. (Refer to paragraph 20 of APB Opinion No. 20, *Accounting Changes.*) The effect on sales, income before extraordinary items, net income, and related per-share amounts of applying this Statement in a year in which the cumulative effect is included in determining that year's net income shall be disclosed for that year.

12. Retroactive application of the provisions of paragraph 7 may require estimates of returns and costs or losses from returns that the enterprise has not previously made; information that may have become available after the year being restated may be considered in making those estimates.

The provisions of this Statement need not be applied to immaterial items.

This Statement was adopted by the unanimous vote of the seven members of the Financial Accounting Standards Board:

Donald J. Kirk, *Chairman* Frank E. Block	John W. March Robert A. Morgan David Mosso	Robert T. Sprouse Ralph E. Walters

---

[3]Exchanges by ultimate customers of one item for another of the same kind, quality, and price (for example, one color or size for another) are not considered returns for purposes of this Statement.

Appendix A

BACKGROUND INFORMATION

13. It is the practice in some industries for customers to be given the right to return a product to the seller under certain circumstances. In the case of sales to the ultimate customer, the most usual circumstance is customer dissatisfaction with the product. For sales to customers engaged in the business of reselling the product, the most usual circumstance is that the customer has not been able to resell the product to another party. (Arrangements in which customers buy products for resale with the right to return products often are referred to as *guaranteed sales.*)

14. Sometimes, the returns occur very soon after a sale is made, as in the newspaper and perishable food industries. In other cases, returns occur over a longer period, such as with book publishing and equipment manufacturing. The rate of returns varies considerably from a low rate usually found in the food industry to a high rate often found in the publishing industry.

15. Situations that pose particular problems occur when sales result in significant overstocking by customers acquiring product for resale. In those situations, the recognition of revenue in one period often is followed by substantial returns in a later period.

16. SOP 75-1 was developed to reduce diversity in the accounting for revenue when the right of return exists. The following alternative accounting practices were being used when the SOP was issued: (a) no sale was recognized until the product was unconditionally accepted, (b) a sale was recognized and an allowance for estimated returns was provided, and (c) a sale was recognized without providing an allowance for returns and, instead, sales returns were recognized when the product was returned. The SOP established criteria that had to be met before sales revenue could be recognized.

17. The Board has not undertaken a comprehensive reconsideration of the accounting issues discussed in SOP 75-1 and has extracted the specialized accounting and reporting principles without significant change. Accordingly, some of the background material and discussion of accounting alternatives have not been carried forward from the SOP. The Board's conceptual framework project on accounting recognition criteria will address revenue recognition issues that may pertain to those addressed in this Statement. A Statement of Financial Accounting Concepts resulting from that project in due course will serve as a basis for evaluating existing standards and practices. Accordingly, the Board may wish to evaluate the standards in this Statement when its conceptual framework project is completed.

Appendix B

SUMMARY OF CONSIDERATION OF COMMENTS ON EXPOSURE DRAFT

18. An Exposure Draft of a proposed Statement, *Revenue Recognition When Right of Return Exists,* was issued February 9, 1981. The Board received 36 comment letters in response to the Exposure Draft. Certain of the comments received and the Board's consideration of them are discussed in this appendix.

19. Some respondents requested that the Statement not apply to enterprises that account for inventory using the retail method of accounting. They recommended that sales returns of retailers be permitted to be recognized when merchandise actually is returned for refund or credit. They said that method is appropriate because accounting for sales returns at time of sale for each product sold is not cost justified, for three reasons. First, they believe that the results of recognizing sales returns when returns are made gives substantially the same results as applying the provisions of the Statement, that is, the Statement would have an insignificant effect on sales, gross margins, and earnings. Second, they state that enterprises using the retail method have not maintained historic data on sales returns. They believe that determining the percentage of sales of one accounting period returned in a later accounting period would be time-consuming and costly, because of the number of transactions to be reviewed. Third, if they were to follow the provisions of the Statement, providing for estimated returns for each product would be complex and costly. Others disagreed with the suggestion of exempting retailers from the Statement.

20. The Board believes that the fundamental issue is materiality. The Board recognizes that the provisions of this Statement may not materially affect the financial position and results of operations of some enterprises that currently account differently than specified by this Statement. Like other FASB Statements, the provisions of this Statement need not be applied to immaterial items. With respect to those enterprises for which this Statement would have a material effect, the Board recognizes that detailed record keeping for returns for each product line might be costly in some cases; this Statement permits reasonable aggregations and approximations of product returns.

21. Some respondents suggested that exchanges by ultimate customers of one item for another of the

same kind, quality, and price (for example, one color or size for another) should not be treated as sales returns for purposes of this Statement. They noted that retailers do not account for those exchanges as sales returns. The Board adopted that suggestion in footnote 3.

22. Several respondents, particularly in the publishing industry, expressed concern that the wording of the condition in paragraph 6(b) (paragraph 11(b) of the Exposure Draft) changed its meaning from the similar condition in SOP 75-1. The Board has refined the wording to clarify that the condition is met if the buyer pays the seller at time of sale or if the buyer does not pay at time of sale but is obligated to pay at a specified date or dates. If, however, the buyer does not pay at time of sale and the buyer's obligation to pay is contractually or implicitly excused until the buyer resells the product, then the condition is not met.

23. The transition provisions in the Exposure Draft proposed that either prospective application with cumulative effect of a change in accounting principles or retroactive restatement be permitted. The Notice for Recipients of the Exposure Draft requested respondents to comment on whether the proposed transition is appropriate or whether the transition provisions should be limited to one of the alternatives. Of those respondents who commented on the transition provisions, a substantial majority recommended that one method be specified, but they disagreed on which method. The Board believes that, for recurring revenue recognition issues, comparability is enhanced if enterprises apply accounting standards retroactively by restating the financial statements of previous periods, and the Board has, therefore, adopted that method in this Statement. This Statement, however, calls for enterprises that are unable to restate previous years' financial statements to include the cumulative effect of those years in the earliest year restated.

24. Several individual respondents suggested various substantive changes to the Exposure Draft. Adoption of those suggestions would have required a reconsideration of the provisions of SOP 75-1. Those suggestions were not adopted because such a reconsideration is beyond the scope of extracting the specialized accounting and reporting principles and practices from the SOP, none of the changes was broadly supported, and the Board believes the suggestions should not be adopted.

25. Several respondents requested guidance regarding specific implementation questions; for example, treatment of partial or limited refunds and balance sheet presentation of accruals for expected returns. SOP 75-1 did not provide specific guidance about those questions and the Board concluded that it should not address those questions at this time.

Statement of Financial Accounting Standards No. 49
Accounting for Product Financing Arrangements

STATUS

Issued: June 1981

Effective Date: For product financing arrangements entered into after June 15, 1981

Affects: Amends FAS 32, Appendix A

Affected by: Paragraph 7 superseded by FAS 71

SUMMARY

This Statement specifies criteria for determining when an arrangement involving the sale of inventory is in substance a financing arrangement. A product financing arrangement is a transaction in which an enterprise sells and agrees to repurchase inventory with the repurchase price equal to the original sale price plus carrying and financing costs, or other similar transactions. This Statement requires that a product financing arrangement be accounted for as a borrowing rather than as a sale.

Statement of Financial Accounting Standards No. 49
Accounting for Product Financing Arrangements

CONTENTS

INTRODUCTION

1. As discussed in FASB Statement No. 32, *Specialized Accounting and Reporting Principles and Practices in AICPA Statements of Position and Guides on Accounting and Auditing Matters,* the FASB is extracting the specialized[1] accounting and reporting principles and practices from AICPA Statements of Position (SOPs) and Guides on accounting and auditing matters and issuing them in FASB Statements after appropriate due process. This Statement extracts the specialized principles and practices from SOP 78-8, *Accounting for Product Financing Arrangements,* and establishes accounting and reporting standards for product financing arrangements.

2. The Board has concluded that it can reach an informed decision on the basis of existing information without a public hearing and that the effective date and transition specified in paragraph 11 are advisable in the circumstances.

APPLICABILITY AND SCOPE

3. Product financing arrangements include agreements in which a sponsor (the enterprise seeking to finance product pending its future use or resale):

a. Sells the product to another entity (the enterprise through which the financing flows), and in a related transaction agrees to repurchase the product (or a substantially identical product);

b. Arranges for another entity to purchase the product on the sponsor's behalf and, in a related transaction, agrees to purchase the product from the other entity; or

c. Controls the disposition of the product that has been purchased by another entity in accordance with the arrangements described in either (a) or (b) above.

In all of the foregoing cases, the sponsor agrees to purchase the product, or processed goods of which the product is a component, from the other entity at specified prices over specified periods or, to the extent that it does not do so, guarantees resale prices to third parties (paragraph 5(a)(1)). Appendix C illustrates each of the types of arrangements described in (a) and (b) above.

4. Other characteristics that commonly exist in product financing arrangements but that are not necessarily present in all such arrangements are:

a. The entity that purchases the product from the sponsor or purchases it directly from a third party on behalf of the sponsor was established expressly for that purpose or is an existing trust, nonbusiness organization, or credit grantor.

b. The product covered by the financing arrangement is to be used or sold by the sponsor, although a portion may be sold by the other entity directly to third parties.

c. The product covered by the financing arrangement is stored on the sponsor's premises.

d. The debt of the entity that purchases the product being financed is guaranteed by the sponsor.

5. This Statement applies to product financing arrangements for products[2] that have been produced by or were originally purchased by the sponsor or purchased by another entity on behalf of the sponsor and have both of the following characteristics:

a. The financing arrangement requires the sponsor

---

[1]The term *specialized* is used to refer to those accounting and reporting principles and practices in AICPA Guides and SOPs that are neither superseded by nor contained in Accounting Research Bulletins, APB Opinions, FASB Statements, or FASB Interpretations.

[2]Unmined or unharvested natural resources and financial instruments are not considered to be a product for purposes of this Statement.

to purchase the product, a substantially identical product, or processed goods of which the product is a component at specified prices. The specified prices are not subject to change except for fluctuations due to finance and holding costs. This characteristic of predetermined prices also is present if any of the following circumstances exists:

(1) The specified prices in the financing arrangement are in the form of resale price guarantees under which the sponsor agrees to make up any difference between the specified price and the resale price for products sold to third parties.

(2) The sponsor is not required to purchase the product but has an option to purchase the product, the economic effect of which compels the sponsor to purchase the product; for example, an option arrangement that provides for a significant penalty if the sponsor does not exercise the option to purchase.

(3) The sponsor is not required by the agreement to purchase the product but the other entity has an option whereby it can require the sponsor to purchase the product.

b. The payments that the other entity will receive on the transaction are established by the financing arrangement, and the amounts to be paid by the sponsor will be adjusted, as necessary, to cover substantially all fluctuations in costs incurred by the other entity in purchasing and holding the product (including interest).[3]

6. This Statement does not modify any of the provisions of FASB Statement No. 48, *Revenue Recognition When Right of Return Exists,* and does not apply to transactions for which sales revenue is recognized currently in accordance with the provisions of that Statement.

7. The Addendum to APB Opinion No. 2, *Accounting for the "Investment Credit,"* (paragraph 2) states that ". . . differences may arise in the application of generally accepted accounting principles as between regulated and nonregulated businesses, because of the effect in regulated businesses of the rate-making process . . ." and discusses the application of generally accepted accounting principles to regulated industries. Accordingly, the provisions of the Addendum govern the application of this Statement to those operations of an enterprise that are regulated for rate-making purposes on an individual-company-cost-of-service basis.

STANDARDS OF FINANCIAL ACCOUNTING AND REPORTING

8. Product and obligations under product financing arrangements that have both of the characteristics described in paragraph 5 shall be accounted for by the sponsor as follows:

a. If a sponsor sells a product to another entity and, in a related transaction, agrees to repurchase the product (or a substantially identical product) or processed goods of which the product is a component, the sponsor shall record a liability at the time the proceeds are received from the other entity to the extent that the product is covered by the financing arrangement. The sponsor shall not record the transaction as a sale and shall not remove the covered product from its balance sheet.

b. If the sponsor is a party to an arrangement whereby another entity purchases a product on the sponsor's behalf and, in a related transaction, the sponsor agrees to purchase the product or processed goods of which the product is a component from the entity, the sponsor shall record the asset and the related liability when the product is purchased by the other entity.

9. Costs of the product, excluding processing costs, in excess of the sponsor's original production or purchase costs or the other entity's purchase costs represent financing and holding costs. The sponsor shall account for such costs in accordance with the sponsor's accounting policies applicable to financing and holding costs as those costs are incurred by the other entity. For example, if insurance costs ordinarily are accounted for as period costs by the sponsor, similar costs associated with the product covered by financing arrangements shall be expensed by the sponsor as those costs are incurred by the other entity. Interest costs associated with the product covered by financing arrangements shall be identified separately and accounted for by the sponsor in accordance with FASB Statement No. 34, *Capitalization of Interest Cost,* as those costs are incurred by the other entity.

Amendment to Statement 32

10. The reference to SOP 78-8, *Accounting for Product Financing Arrangements,* is deleted from Appendix A of Statement 32. The specialized accounting provisions of that SOP are superseded by this Statement.

---

[3]The characteristic described in paragraph 5(b) ordinarily is not present in purchase commitments or contractor-subcontractor relationships. (Refer to paragraph 18.)

Effective Date and Transition

11. This Statement shall be applied prospectively to

product financing arrangements entered into after June 15, 1981.

> **The provisions of this Statement need
> not be applied to immaterial items.**

This Statement was adopted by the unanimous vote of the seven members of the Financial Accounting Standards Board:

Donald J. Kirk,	John W. March	Robert T. Sprouse
Chairman	Robert A. Morgan	Ralph E. Walters
Frank E. Block	David Mosso	

Appendix A

BACKGROUND INFORMATION

12. SOP 78-8 was developed to establish standards for product financing arrangements, such as transactions in which an enterprise sells and agrees to repurchase inventory (or substantially identical inventory) with the repurchase price equal to the original sale price plus carrying and financing costs. For example, an enterprise (sponsor) would sell a product and in a related transaction would agree to repurchase the product or processed goods of which the product was a component at a specified price over a specified period. The buyer, using the product and sometimes the financing arrangement as collateral, would borrow against the value of the product from a lending institution or other credit grantor and would remit the proceeds to the sponsor as payment for the product. As the terms of the financing arrangement were fulfilled by the sponsor, the buyer of the product would reduce its borrowing from the financial institution.

13. The following alternative accounting practices were being used when SOP 78-8 was issued: (a) product and obligations under product financing arrangements were reported as assets and liabilities in the sponsor's financial statements and (b) product and obligations under product financing arrangements were not reported as assets and liabilities in the sponsor's financial statements; instead, the obligations were disclosed as commitments. In addition, financing and holding costs incurred by the buyer often were not reported by the sponsor until the product was repurchased from the buyer.

14. The SOP concluded that (a) product financing arrangements, such as the one described in paragraph 12, did not transfer the risks and rewards of ownership of the product; (b) product financing arrangements are financing transactions rather than sales; and (c) a sponsor of an arrangement to finance product should account for the transaction

as a borrowing rather than as a sale and, accordingly, should report the asset and related liability resulting from the arrangement on its balance sheet.

15. The Board has not undertaken a comprehensive reconsideration of the accounting issues discussed in SOP 78-8 and has extracted the specialized accounting and reporting principles without significant change. Accordingly, some of the background material and discussion of accounting alternatives have not been carried forward from the SOP. The Board's conceptual framework project on accounting recognition criteria will address criteria for recognizing a transaction as a sale that may pertain to the issues addressed in this Statement. A Statement of Financial Accounting Concepts resulting from that project in due course will serve as a basis for evaluating existing standards and practices. Accordingly, the Board may wish to evaluate the standards in this Statement when its conceptual framework project is completed.

Appendix B

SUMMARY OF CONSIDERATION OF COMMENTS ON EXPOSURE DRAFT

16. An Exposure Draft of a proposed Statement, *Accounting for Product Financing Arrangements,* was issued February 9, 1981. The Board received 34 comment letters in response to the Exposure Draft. Certain of the comments received and the Board's consideration of them are discussed in this appendix.

17. In the Exposure Draft, the Board requested respondents to consider the implication of provisions of the proposed Statement on the accounting for certain contractor-subcontractor relationships, such as a contract in which specifications are provided by a customer for the manufacture of product. Some respondents indicated that the provisions of the proposed Statement were too broad and could result in certain contractor-subcontractor rela-

tionships, as well as purchase commitments, being accounted for inappropriately as product financing arrangements. They believe that the distinguishing characteristic of a product financing arrangement is that the sponsor retains the risks and rewards of ownership of the product while the buyer merely holds the product for the sponsor. They stated that the purpose of a purchase commitment is to assure the supply of product, rather than to provide the financing for an entity's inventory, and should not be considered a product financing arrangement. They believe that a product financing arrangement does not exist if a supplier has the risks and rewards of ownership until the product is transferred to the sponsor. They also noted that in a typical contractor-subcontractor relationship, the purchase of product by a subcontractor on behalf of a contractor ordinarily leaves a significant portion of the subcontractor's obligation unfulfilled. The subcontractor has the risks of ownership of the product until it has met all the terms of a contract. Accordingly, they believe that the typical contractor-subcontractor relationship also should not be considered a product financing arrangement.

18. The Board believes that SOP 78-8 was intended to apply only to arrangements in which the sponsor is in substance the owner of the product and the other entity holds the product to facilitate a financing arrangement. The Board does not believe that SOP 78-8 was intended to apply to (a) ordinary purchase commitments in which the risks and rewards of ownership are retained by the seller (for example, a manufacturer or other supplier) until the product is transferred to a purchaser or (b) typical contractor-subcontractor relationships in which the contractor is not in substance the owner of product held by the subcontractor and the obligation of the contractor is contingent on substantial performance on the part of the subcontractor. Accordingly, the Board has modified paragraph 5(b) to indicate that this Statement applies only to product financing arrangements in which the payments that the other entity will receive are established by the financing arrangement and the amounts to be paid will be adjusted, as necessary, to cover substantially all fluctuations in purchasing and holding costs. Most purchase commitments do not have that characteristic because the supplier's profit could fluctuate if the supplier's costs of fulfilling the commitment, including holding costs, change before the commitment is fulfilled. Most contractor-subcontractor relationships, including those having cost-plus-fixed-fee provisions, are not product financing arrangements as contemplated in this Statement. Paragraph 5(a) states that in product financing arrangements "the specified prices are not subject to change except for fluctuations due to finance and holding costs." Paragraph 5(b) states that the ". . . amounts to be paid by the sponsor will be adjusted, as necessary, to

cover substantially all fluctuations in costs incurred by the other entity in purchasing and holding the product. . . ." A cost-plus-fixed-fee contract typically provides for reimbursement of labor and other costs, not just finance and holding costs and, therefore, does not qualify as a product financing arrangement under paragraph 5(a). A fixed price contract typically is not adjusted to cover fluctuations in costs incurred by the subcontractor in purchasing and holding product and, therefore, does not qualify as a product financing arrangement under paragraph 5(b).

19. Some respondents suggested that arrangements involving the sale and repurchase of financial instruments be excluded from this Statement. The Board does not believe that SOP 78-8 was intended to encompass financial instruments as products. That conclusion is based, in part, on the existence of specialized accounting principles for agreements to sell and repurchase financial instruments in AICPA documents other than SOP 78-8. Accordingly, footnote 2 excludes financial instruments from the definition of product. In addition, footnote 2 carries forward from SOP 78-8 without change the exclusion of unmined or unharvested natural resources.

20. Some respondents requested the Board to explain why the accounting for product financing arrangements specified by this Statement differs from the accounting for long-term unconditional purchase obligations (for example, take-or-pay contracts) specified by FASB Statement No. 47, *Disclosure of Long-Term Obligations.* They noted that this Statement requires a sponsor to recognize an asset and a liability for a product financing arrangement; Statement 47 requires disclosure, but not necessarily balance sheet recognition of an asset and a liability for an unconditional purchase obligation by a purchaser.

21. There are similarities between a sponsor's rights and obligations under a product financing arrangement and a purchaser's rights and obligations under an unconditional purchase obligation. Both the sponsor and the purchaser obtain probable future economic benefits from the assured source of product. Both are obligated to make future cash payments to the other party to the agreement. Beyond those similarities, however, there is a substantial difference in the related accounting issues.

22. The accounting issue with respect to an unconditional purchase obligation is whether at the time the contract is entered into the purchaser should report rights to receive future product or services as an asset and obligations to make future payments for product or services as a liability. Under a product financing arrangement, the product already exists and the other entity's purchase cost is known. The

accounting issue addressed in this Statement is whether the sponsor should report the existing product currently held by the other entity as an asset and the obligation to pay the other entity as a liability. This Statement concludes that the sponsor is in substance the owner of the product and that the sponsor should, therefore, report the product as an asset and the related obligation as a liability. At the time a take-or-pay contract is entered into, by contrast, either the product does not yet exist (for example, electricity) or the product exists in a form unsuitable to the purchaser (for example, unmined coal); the purchaser has a right to receive future product but is not the substantive owner of existing product.

23. Some respondents questioned whether the absence of a reference in the Exposure Draft to the Addendum to Opinion 2 indicated that the Statement would apply to rate-regulated enterprises. The Board currently is considering the effect of rate regulation on regulated enterprises in another project. In the meantime, paragraph 7 was added to acknowledge that the provisions of the Addendum govern the application of this Statement to those operations of an enterprise that are regulated for rate-making purposes on a basis of individual company cost of service.

24. Several individual respondents suggested various substantive changes to the Exposure Draft. Adoption of those suggestions would have required a reconsideration of the provisions of SOP 78-8. Those suggestions were not adopted because such a reconsideration is beyond the scope of extracting the specialized accounting and reporting principles and practices from the SOP and because none of the changes was broadly supported.

Appendix C

ILLUSTRATIONS OF THE APPLICATION OF THIS STATEMENT TO COMMON PRODUCT FINANCING ARRANGEMENTS

25. This appendix illustrates how this Statement applies to two common product financing arrangements. The facts assumed in the examples are illustrative only and are not intended to modify or limit in any way the provisions of this Statement. The facts assumed in each case could vary in one or more respects without altering the application of the provisions of this Statement.

Example 1

26. An enterprise (sponsor) sells a portion of its inventory to another entity (the entity through which the financing flows), and in a related transaction agrees to repurchase the inventory (paragraph 3(a)).

Assumptions and Provisions of the Financing Arrangement

27. The sponsor arranges for the other entity to acquire a portion of the sponsor's inventory. The other entity's sole asset is the transferred inventory that is, in turn, used as collateral for bank financing. The proceeds of the bank financing are then remitted to the sponsor. The debt of the other entity is guaranteed by the sponsor. The inventory is stored in a public warehouse during the holding period. The sponsor, in connection with the "sale" (legal title passes to the entity), enters into a financing arrangement under which:

a. The sponsor agrees to pay all costs of the other entity associated with the inventory, including holding and storage costs.
b. The sponsor agrees to pay the other entity interest on the purchase price of the inventory equivalent to the interest and fees incurred in connection with the bank financing.
c. The sponsor agrees to repurchase the inventory from the other entity at a specified future date for the same price originally paid by the entity to purchase the inventory irrespective of changes in market prices during the holding period.
d. The other entity agrees not to assign or otherwise encumber the inventory during its ownership period, except to the extent of providing collateral for the bank financing.

Application of the Provisions of This Statement

28. In the product financing arrangement outlined above, both of the characteristics in paragraph 5 are present; accordingly, the sponsor neither records the transaction as a sale of inventory nor removes the inventory from its balance sheet. The sponsor recognizes a liability when the proceeds are received from the other entity. Financing and holding costs are accrued by the sponsor as incurred by the other entity and accounted for in accordance with the sponsor's accounting policies for such costs. Interest costs are separately identified and accounted for in accordance with Statement 34.

Example 2

29. A sponsor arranges for another entity to buy product on the sponsor's behalf with a related agreement to purchase the product from the other entity (paragraph 3(b)).

Assumptions and Provisions of the Financing Arrangement

30. The sponsor arranges for the other entity to purchase on its behalf an existing supply of fuel. In

a related agreement, the sponsor agrees to purchase the fuel from the other entity over a specified period and at specified prices. The prices established are adequate to cover all financing and holding costs of the other entity. The other entity finances the purchase of fuel using the fuel and the agreement as collateral.

**Application of the Provisions
of This Statement**

31. In the product financing arrangement described above, both of the characteristics in paragraph 5 are present; accordingly, the sponsor reports the asset (fuel) and the related liability on its balance sheet when the fuel is acquired by the other entity. Financing and holding costs are accrued by the sponsor as incurred by the other entity and accounted for in accordance with the sponsor's accounting policies for financing and holding costs. Interest costs are separately identified and accounted for in accordance with Statement 34.

Statement of Financial Accounting Standards No. 50
Financial Reporting in the Record and Music Industry

STATUS

Issued: November 1981

Effective Date: For fiscal years beginning after December 15, 1981

Affects: Amends FAS 32, Appendix A

Affected by: No other pronouncements

SUMMARY

This Statement extracts the specialized accounting principles and practices from AICPA Statement of Position 76-1, *Accounting Practices in the Record and Music Industry,* and establishes standards of financial accounting and reporting for licensors and licensees in the record and music industry. If a license agreement is, in substance, an outright sale and collectibility of the licensing fee is reasonably assured, this Statement requires the licensor to recognize the licensing fee as revenue. This Statement requires a licensee to record minimum guarantees as assets and charge them to expense in accordance with the terms of the license agreement. It also establishes accounting standards for artist compensation cost and cost of record masters.

Statement of Financial Accounting Standards No. 50
Financial Reporting in the Record and Music Industry

CONTENTS

INTRODUCTION AND BACKGROUND INFORMATION

1. As discussed in FASB Statement No. 32, *Specialized Accounting and Reporting Principles and Practices in AICPA Statements of Position and Guides on Accounting and Auditing Matters,* the FASB is extracting the specialized[1] accounting and reporting principles and practices from AICPA Statements of Position (SOPs) and Guides on accounting and auditing matters and issuing them in FASB Statements after appropriate due process. This Statement extracts the specialized principles and practices from SOP 76-1, *Accounting Practices in the Record and Music Industry,* and establishes financial accounting and reporting standards for the industry.

2. The Board has not undertaken a comprehensive reconsideration of the accounting issues discussed in SOP 76-1 and has extracted the specialized accounting and reporting principles without significant change. Accordingly, some of the background material, discussion of accounting alternatives, and general accounting guidance have not been carried forward from the SOP. The Board's conceptual framework project on accounting recognition criteria will address revenue recognition issues that may pertain to those addressed in this Statement. A Statement of Financial Accounting Concepts resulting from that project in due course will serve as a basis for evaluating existing standards and practices. Accordingly, the Board may wish to evaluate the standards in this Statement when its conceptual framework project is completed.

3. SOP 76-1 was developed to clarify and standardize accounting by the record and music industry, particularly when manufacturers and distributors should recognize revenue from sales. Before 1976, manufacturers and distributors usually recorded sales when inventory was shipped in accordance with normal trade terms and, because of the return or exchange privileges that characterize the industry, usually provided for the anticipated return of records from current and prior sales. The SOP notes that manufacturers and distributors in the record and music industry must be able to make a reasonable estimate of returns to account for shipments to customers as sales. The SOP also presents conclusions about the accounting by music publishers and other licensors when music copyrights or **record masters**[2] are licensed, for compensation to recording artists in the form of **royalties,** and for costs of record masters and about the accounting by licensees for various fees.

4. An Exposure Draft of a proposed Statement, *Financial Accounting and Reporting in the Record and Music Industry,* was issued June 12, 1981. The Board received 12 comment letters in response to the Exposure Draft. Several respondents suggested minor clarifications that were adopted. No substantive changes were made.

5. The conclusions in SOP 76-1 regarding recognition of sales revenue when right of return exists are based upon SOP 75-1, *Revenue Recognition When Right of Return Exists.* The FASB has issued FASB Statement No. 48, *Revenue Recognition When Right of Return Exists,* that extracts the specialized principles from SOP 75-1. Because the principles for revenue recognition when right of return exists are not unique to the record and music industry, this Statement does not address that subject.

6. The Board has concluded that it can reach an informed decision on the basis of existing information without a public hearing and that the effective date and transition specified in paragraph 17 are advisable in the circumstances.

---

[1] The term *specialized* is used to refer to those accounting and reporting principles and practices in AICPA Guides and SOPs that are neither superseded by nor contained in Accounting Research Bulletins, APB Opinions, FASB Statements, or FASB Interpretations.

[2] Terms defined in the glossary (appendix) are in **boldface type** the first time they appear in this Statement.

STANDARDS OF FINANCIAL ACCOUNTING AND REPORTING

Licensor Accounting

Revenues

7. Substantial revenues may be realized by the owner of a record master or music copyright by entering into **license agreements.** A license agreement may be, in substance, an outright sale. If the licensor has signed a noncancelable contract, has agreed to a fixed fee, has delivered the rights to the licensee who is free to exercise them, and has no remaining significant obligations to furnish music or records, the earnings process is complete and the licensing fee shall be reported as revenue if collectibility of the full fee is reasonably assured.

8. A **minimum guarantee** may be paid in advance by a licensee. The licensor shall report such a minimum guarantee as a liability initially and recognize the guarantee as revenue as the license fee is earned under the agreement. If the licensor cannot otherwise determine the amount of the license fee earned, the guarantee shall be recognized as revenue equally over the remaining performance period, which is generally the period covered by the license agreement.

9. Other fees (for example, for free records distributed by a record club in excess of a stipulated number) also may be required under the license agreement. Such other fees that are not fixed in amount prior to the expiration date of the agreement shall be recognized as revenue by the licensor only when reasonable estimates of such amounts can be made or the agreement has expired.

Artist Compensation Cost

10. The amount of royalties earned by artists, as adjusted for anticipated returns, shall be charged to expense of the period in which the sale of the record takes place. An **advance royalty** paid to an artist shall be reported as an asset if the past performance and current popularity of the artist to whom the advance is made provide a sound basis for estimating that the amount of the advance will be recoverable from future royalties to be earned by the artist. Advances shall be charged to expense as subsequent royalties are earned by the artist. Any portion of advances that subsequently appear not to be fully recoverable from future royalties to be earned by the artist shall be charged to expense during the period in which the loss becomes evident. Advance royalties shall be classified as current and noncurrent assets, as appropriate.

Cost of Record Masters

11. The portion of the cost of a record master borne by the record company shall be reported as an asset if the past performance and current popularity of the artist provides a sound basis for estimating that the cost will be recovered from future sales. Otherwise, that cost shall be charged to expense. The amount recognized as an asset shall be amortized over the estimated life of the recorded performance using a method that reasonably relates the amount to the net revenue expected to be realized.

12. The portion of the cost of a record master recoverable from the artist's royalties shall be accounted for as an advance royalty, as discussed in paragraph 10.

Disclosure

13. Commitments for artist advances payable in future years and future royalty guarantees shall be disclosed.

14. The portion of the cost of record masters borne by the record company that are recorded as assets shall be disclosed separately.

Licensee Accounting

15. If minimum guarantees are paid in advance by a licensee, such minimum guarantees shall be reported as an asset by the licensee and subsequently charged to expense in accordance with the terms of the license agreement. If all or a portion of the minimum guarantee subsequently appears not to be recoverable through future use of the rights obtained under the license, the nonrecoverable portion shall be charged to expense. Other fees, if any, required by the licensing agreement (for example, for free records distributed by a record club in excess of a stipulated number) that are not fixed in amount prior to the expiration date of the agreement shall be estimated and accrued on a license-by-license basis by the licensee.

Amendment to Statement No. 32

16. The reference to AICPA Statement of Position 76-1, *Accounting Practices in the Record and Music Industry,* is deleted from Appendix A of Statement 32.

Effective Date and Transition

17. This Statement shall be effective for financial statements for fiscal years beginning after December 15, 1981. Earlier application is encouraged. The provisions of this Statement shall be applied retroactively and any accompanying financial statements presented for prior periods shall be restated.

> **The provisions of this Statement need
> not be applied to immaterial items.**

*This Statement was adopted by the unanimous vote of the seven members of the Financial Accounting
Standards Board:*

Donald J. Kirk,   John W. March   Robert T. Sprouse
    Chairman   Robert A. Morgan   Ralph E. Walters
Frank E. Block   David Mosso

Appendix

GLOSSARY

18. This appendix defines certain terms that are
used in this Statement.

Advance Royalty
An amount paid to music publishers, record
producers, songwriters, or other artists in
advance of their earning royalties from record
or music sales. Such an amount is based on contractual terms and is generally nonrefundable.

License Agreements
Contractual arrangements entered into by an
owner (licensor) of a record master or music
copyright with a licensee granting the licensee
the right to sell or distribute records or music for
a fixed fee paid to the licensor or for a fee based
on sales of records or music. License agreements
are modifications of the compulsory provisions
of the copyright law.

Minimum Guarantee
An amount paid in advance by a licensee to a
licensor for the right to sell or distribute records
or music.

Record Master
The master tape resulting from the performance
of the artist. It is used to produce molds for
commercial record production and other tapes
for use in making cartridges, cassettes, and reel
tapes. The costs of producing a record master
include (a) the cost of the musical talent (musi-
cians, vocal background, and arrangements); (b)
the cost of the technical talent for engineering,
directing, and mixing; (c) costs for the use of the
equipment to record and produce the master;
and (d) studio facility charges. Under the standard type of artist contract, the record company
bears a portion of the costs and recovers a portion of the cost from the artist out of designated
royalties earned. However, either party may
bear all or most of the cost.

Royalties
Amounts paid to record producers, songwriters,
or other artists for their participation in making
records and to music publishers for their copyright interest in music. Amounts for artists are
determined by the terms of personal service contracts negotiated between the artists and record
companies and usually are determined based
upon a percentage of sales activity and license
fee income, adjusted for estimated sales returns.
Royalties for publishing are based on the copyright or other applicable laws, but the requirements of the law may be modified by licenses
issued by the publishers.

Statement of Financial Accounting Standards No. 51
Financial Reporting by Cable Television Companies

STATUS

Issued: November 1981

Effective Date: For fiscal years beginning after December 15, 1981

Affects: Amends FAS 32, Appendix A

Affected by: Paragraph 2 superseded by FAS 71
Paragraph 14 amended by FAS 121

SUMMARY

This Statement extracts the specialized accounting principles and practices from AICPA Statement of Position 79-2, *Accounting by Cable Television Companies,* and establishes standards of financial accounting and reporting for costs, expenses, and revenues applicable to the construction and operation of a cable television system. During a period while a cable television system is partially under construction and partially in service (the prematurity period), costs incurred that relate to both current and future operations shall be partially capitalized and partially expensed.

Statement of Financial Accounting Standards No. 51
Financial Reporting by Cable Television Companies

CONTENTS

INTRODUCTION

1. As discussed in FASB Statement No. 32, *Specialized Accounting and Reporting Principles and Practices in AICPA Statements of Position and Guides on Accounting and Auditing Matters,* the FASB is extracting the specialized[1] accounting and reporting principles and practices from AICPA Statements of Position (SOPs) and Guides on accounting and auditing matters and issuing them in FASB Statements after appropriate due process. This Statement extracts the specialized principles and practices from SOP 79-2, *Accounting by Cable Television Companies,* and establishes financial accounting and reporting standards for certain costs, expenses, and revenues related to cable television systems.

2. The FASB currently has a project under consideration for the effect of rate regulation on accounting for regulated enterprises. Under current practice, the Addendum to APB Opinion No. 2, *Accounting for the "Investment Credit,"* applies only to businesses that are regulated for rate-making purposes on an individual-company-cost-of-service basis and, therefore, does not apply to the financial statements of cable television companies.

3. The Board has concluded that it can reach an informed decision on the basis of existing information without a public hearing and that the effective date and transition specified in paragraph 16 are advisable in the circumstances.

STANDARDS OF FINANCIAL ACCOUNTING AND REPORTING

Prematurity Period

4. Before revenue is earned from the first subscriber, management shall establish the beginning and end of the **prematurity period,**[2] subject to a presumption that the prematurity period usually will not exceed two years. The prematurity period frequently will be shorter than two years; a longer period may be reasonably justified only in major urban markets. After the prematurity period is established by management, it shall not be changed except as a result of highly unusual circumstances.

5. A portion[3] of a cable television system that is in the prematurity period and can be clearly distinguished from the remainder of the system shall be accounted for separately. Such a portion would have most of the following characteristics:

a. Geographical differences, such as coverage of a noncontiguous or separately awarded franchise area
b. Mechanical differences, such as a separate head-end[4]
c. Timing differences, such as starting construction or marketing at a significantly later date
d. Investment decision differences, such as separate break-even and return-on-investment analyses or separate approval of start of construction

---

[1]The term *specialized* is used to refer to those accounting and reporting principles and practices in AICPA Guides and SOPs that are neither superseded by nor contained in Accounting Research Bulletins, APB Opinions, FASB Statements, or FASB Interpretations.

[2]Terms defined in the glossary (Appendix A) are in **boldface type** the first time they appear in this Statement.

[3]Some cable television companies have used the word *segment* to refer to a portion of a cable television system. In view of the use of *segment* in a different context in FASB Statement No. 14, *Financial Reporting for Segments of a Business Enterprise,* the word *portion* has been used here.

[4]Refer to paragraph 17 for a description of *head-end* in the definition of **cable television plant.**

e. Separate accounting records, separate budgets and forecasts, or other accountability differences

Costs incurred by the remainder of the system shall be charged to the portion in the prematurity period only if they are specifically identified with the operations of that portion. Separate projections for the portion shall be developed and the portion's capitalized costs shall be evaluated separately during the prematurity period for recoverability (paragraph 14).

6. During the prematurity period:

a. Costs of cable television plant, including materials, direct labor, and construction overhead shall continue to be capitalized in full.
b. **Subscriber-related costs** and general and administrative expenses shall be expensed as period costs.
c. Programming costs and other system costs[5] that are incurred in anticipation of servicing a fully operating system and that will not vary significantly regardless of the number of subscribers shall be allocated between current and future operations. The proportion attributable to current operations shall be expensed currently and the remainder shall be capitalized. The amount to be expensed currently shall be determined by multiplying the total of such costs for the month by the fraction described in paragraph 7 determined for that month.

7. The following fraction shall be determined each month of the prematurity period. The denominator of the fraction shall be the total number of subscribers expected at the end of the prematurity period. The numerator of the fraction shall be the greatest of (a) the average number of subscribers expected that month as estimated at the beginning of the prematurity period, (b) the average number of subscribers that would be attained using at least equal (that is, straight-line) monthly progress in adding new subscribers towards the estimate of subscribers at the end of the prematurity period, and (c) the average number of actual subscribers.

8. During the prematurity period, depreciation and amortization expense shall be determined by multiplying (a) the monthly depreciation and amortization of total capitalized costs expected on

completion of the prematurity period by (b) the fraction described in paragraph 7, using the depreciation method that will be applied by the company after the prematurity period.

9. The amount of interest cost that is capitalized during the prematurity period shall be determined in accordance with FASB Statement No. 34, *Capitalization of Interest Cost,* by applying an interest capitalization rate determined in accordance with paragraphs 13 and 14 of Statement 34 to the average amount of qualifying assets[6] for the system during the period. Qualifying assets shall be determined in accordance with the guidance in paragraphs 16 and 18 of Statement 34. The amount of interest cost capitalized shall not exceed the total amount of interest cost incurred by the cable television system in that period.

Amortization of Capitalized Costs

10. Costs that have been capitalized in accordance with paragraph 6(c) shall be amortized over the same period used to depreciate the main cable television plant.

Hookup Revenue and Costs

11. Initial hookup revenue shall be recognized as revenue to the extent of **direct selling costs**[7] incurred. The remainder shall be deferred and amortized to income over the estimated average period that subscribers are expected to remain connected to the system.

12. Initial subscriber installation costs, including material, labor, and overhead costs of the drop,[8] shall be capitalized and depreciated over a period no longer than the depreciation period used for cable television plant. The costs of subsequently disconnecting and reconnecting shall be charged to expense.

Franchise Costs

13. Costs of successful franchise applications shall be capitalized and amortized in accordance with the provisions of APB Opinion No. 17, *Intangible Assets.* Costs of unsuccessful franchise applications and abandoned franchises shall be charged to expense.

[5]Those costs include property taxes based on valuation as a fully operating system; pole, underground duct, antenna site, and microwave rental based on rental costs for a fully operating system; and local origination programming to satisfy franchise requirements.
[6]During the prematurity period, a portion of the system is in use in the earnings activity of the enterprise and is not eligible for interest capitalization. The portion of the cost of the system that represents a qualifying asset is the amount of accumulated expenditures in excess of the fraction specified in paragraph 7 of the total estimated cost of the system at the end of the prematurity period.
[7]Such costs are subscriber-related costs that are expensed in accordance with paragraph 6(b).
[8]Refer to paragraph 17 for a description of *drop* in the definition of *cable television plant.*

Recoverability

14. Capitalized plant and intangible assets shall be evaluated periodically to determine whether the costs are recoverable (through operations or sale of the system). If recoverability is doubtful, capitalized costs shall be written down to recoverable values. Capitalization of costs shall not cease when the total cost reaches an amount that is not fully recoverable. Capitalization of costs shall continue, and the provision required to reduce capitalized costs to recoverable value shall be increased.

Amendment to Statement No. 32

15. The reference to AICPA Statement of Position 79-2, *Accounting by Cable Television Companies,* is deleted from Appendix A of Statement 32.

Effective Date and Transition

16. The provisions of this Statement shall be effective for fiscal years beginning after December 15, 1981. Earlier application is permitted but not required. The provisions of this Statement may be, but are not required to be, applied retroactively for previously issued financial statements. If applied retroactively and if the estimates of subscribers needed to make the calculations required by some provisions of this Statement are not readily available, actual historical subscriber data may be used instead.

> **The provisions of this Statement need not be applied to immaterial items.**

This Statement was adopted by the unanimous vote of the seven members of the Financial Accounting Standards Board:

Donald J. Kirk, *Chairman*
Frank E. Block

John W. March
Robert A. Morgan
David Mosso

Robert T. Sprouse
Ralph E. Walters

Appendix A

GLOSSARY

17. This appendix defines certain terms that are used in this Statement.

Cable Television Plant

The cable television plant required to render service to the subscriber includes the following equipment:

a. *Head-end*—This includes the equipment used to receive signals of distant television or radio stations, whether directly from the transmitter or from a microwave relay system. It also includes the studio facilities required for operator-originated programming, if any.

b. *Cable*—This consists of cable and amplifiers (which maintain the quality of the signal) covering the subscriber area, either on utility poles or underground.

c. *Drops*—These consist of the hardware that provides access to the main cable, the short length of cable that brings the signal from the main cable to the subscriber's television set, and other associated hardware, which may include a trap to block particular channels.

d. *Converters and descramblers*—These devices are attached to the subscriber's television sets when more than 12 channels are provided or when special services are provided, such as "pay cable" or 2-way communication.

Direct Selling Costs

Direct selling costs include commissions, the portion of a salesperson's compensation other than commissions for obtaining new subscribers, local advertising targeted for acquisition of new subscribers, and costs of processing documents related to new subscribers acquired. Direct selling costs do not include supervisory and administrative expenses or indirect expenses, such as rent and costs of facilities.

Prematurity Period

During the prematurity period, the cable television system is partially under construction and partially in service. The prematurity period begins with the first earned subscriber revenue. Its end will vary with circumstances of the system but will be determined based on plans for completion of the first major construction period[9] or achievement of a specified predeter-

---

[9]The construction period of a cable television system varies with the size of the franchise area, density of population, and difficulty of physical construction. The construction period is not completed until the head-end, main cable, and distribution cables are installed, and includes a reasonable time to provide for installation of subscriber drops and related hardware. During the construction period, many system operators complete installation of drops and begin to provide service to some subscribers in some parts of the system while construction continues. Providing the signal for the first time is referred to as "energizing" the system.

mined subscriber level at which no additional investment will be required for other than cable television plant. The length of the prematurity period varies with the franchise development and construction plans. Such plans may consist of:

a. Small franchise that is characterized by the absence of free television signal and a short construction period. The entire system is "energized" at one time near the end of the construction period.
b. Medium-size franchise that is characterized by some direct competition from free television and by a more extensive geographical franchise area lending itself to incremental construction. Some parts of the system are "energized" as construction progresses.
c. Large metropolitan franchise that is characterized by heavy direct competition from free television and fringe area signal inadequacy, high cost, and difficult construction. Many parts of the system are "energized" as construction progresses.

Except in the smallest systems, programming is usually delivered to portions of the system and some revenues are obtained before construction of the entire system is complete. Thus, virtually every cable television system experiences a prematurity period during which it is receiving some revenue while continuing to incur substantial costs related to the establishment of the total system.

Subscriber-Related Costs

These are costs incurred to obtain and retain subscribers to the cable television system and include costs of billing and collection, bad debts, and mailings; repairs and maintenance of taps and connections; franchise fees related to revenues or number of subscribers; general and administrative system costs, such as salary of the system manager and office rent; programming costs for additional channels used in the marketing effort or costs related to revenues from, or number of subscribers to, per channel or per program service; and direct selling costs.

Appendix B

BACKGROUND INFORMATION AND SUMMARY OF CONSIDERATION OF COMMENTS ON EXPOSURE DRAFT

18. This Statement extracts the specialized accounting and reporting principles and practices from SOP 79-2 and codifies them as FASB standards without significant change. Board members have assented to the issuance of this Statement on the basis that it is an appropriate extraction of those existing specialized principles and practices and that a comprehensive reconsideration of those principles and practices was not contemplated in undertaking this FASB project. Some of the background material, discussion of accounting alternatives, and general accounting guidance have not been carried forward from the SOP. The Board's conceptual framework project on accounting recognition criteria will address revenue recognition issues that may pertain to those addressed in this Statement. A Statement of Financial Accounting Concepts resulting from that project in due course will serve as a basis for evaluating existing standards and practices. Accordingly, the Board may wish to evaluate the standards in this Statement when its conceptual framework project is completed.

19. SOP 79-2 was developed to clarify and standardize the diverse accounting practices being followed in the cable television industry, particularly the practices relating to accounting for costs during the prematurity period while the cable television system is partially under construction and partially in service. Before 1979, cable television companies differed as to the types of costs capitalized during the prematurity period and used different criteria to determine the date at which capitalization of some costs ceases and amortization of those costs begins. The SOP specified that all direct construction costs should be capitalized and that costs attributable to current operations and their administration should be charged to expense. For certain costs that relate to the cable television system and that benefit both current and future operations, the SOP specified that a proportion of such costs should be charged to current operations and the remainder should be capitalized.

20. An Exposure Draft of a proposed Statement, *Financial Accounting and Reporting by Cable Television Companies,* was issued June 12, 1981. The Board received 23 comment letters in response to the Exposure Draft. Certain of the comments received and the Board's consideration of them are discussed in this appendix.

21. The transition provisions in the Exposure Draft called for retroactive restatement except for companies that do not expect to have systems in the prematurity period in the future. These companies were permitted to continue their previous method of accounting for already mature systems. Several respondents from the cable television industry suggested that the transition provisions be modified to allow prospective application because retroactive application would require greater accounting effort than the resulting informational benefits. They believe that many cable television companies were

expensing some costs that SOP 79-2 recommended be capitalized. They recommended that prospective application be permitted because of the additional administrative burden that retroactive application would entail. The Board has considered these comments and the fact that major cable television companies have complied with SOP 79-2 and concluded that prospective application should be permitted.

22. Some respondents stated that paragraph 8(a) of the Exposure Draft implied that all interest cost incurred during the prematurity period should be capitalized, even though a portion of the cable television system is in use. The Board believes that paragraph 18 of Statement 34 prohibits capitalization of interest cost on the portion of the cable television system that is substantially complete and ready for its intended use. Accordingly, this Statement clarifies that all interest cost incurred during the prematurity period is not necessarily eligible to be capitalized.

23. Some respondents requested that guidance be included regarding accounting for costs of franchise applications. They indicated that practice varies with respect to the accounting for such costs and that additional guidance would enhance uniformity in practice. The Board has included such guidance to clarify the accounting for costs of franchise applications.

24. Some respondents suggested that the definition of direct selling costs be clarified regarding the circumstances under which advertising may be included. The Board believes that the intent of SOP 79-2 was to limit such costs to those pertaining to direct efforts to obtain new subscribers. Accordingly, the definition has been clarified to indicate that local advertising targeted for acquisition of new subscribers is a direct selling cost.

25. Several respondents suggested various substantive changes to the Exposure Draft (such as eliminating certain of the choices for the numerator of the capitalization fraction, reconsideration of provisions for deferral of hookup revenue and expensing of direct selling costs, changing the amortization period for costs capitalized during the prematurity period, and including certain general and administrative costs with other costs that are deferred during the prematurity period). Adoption of those suggestions would have required a reconsideration of some of the provisions of SOP 79-2. Such a reconsideration is not contemplated in the extraction project unless a proposed change meets one of the three criteria for change included in the "Notice for Recipients of This Exposure Draft" or is broadly supported. None of the proposed changes met the criteria for change and none was broadly supported. Accordingly, the Board did not adopt those suggestions.

Statement of Financial Accounting Standards No. 52
Foreign Currency Translation

STATUS

Issued: December 1981

Effective Date: For fiscal years beginning on or after December 15, 1982

Affects: Amends ARB 43, Chapter 12, paragraph 5
Supersedes ARB 43, Chapter 12, paragraphs 7 and 10 through 22
Supersedes APB 6, paragraph 18
Amends APB 22, paragraph 13
Supersedes FAS 1
Supersedes FAS 8
Supersedes FAS 20
Supersedes FIN 15
Supersedes FIN 17

Affected by: Paragraphs 22 through 24 and 48 amended by FAS 96 and FAS 109
Paragraph 26 effectively amended by FAS 94

Other Interpretive Pronouncement: FIN 37

Issues Discussed by FASB Emerging Issues Task Force (EITF)

Affects: No EITF Issues

Interpreted by: Paragraph 11 interpreted by EITF Topic No. D-55
Paragraph 15 interpreted by EITF Issues No. 93-10 and 96-15
Paragraph 19 interpreted by EITF Issue No. 87-2
Paragraph 20(a) interpreted by EITF Issue No. 87-26
Paragraph 21 interpreted by EITF Issues No. 91-1 and 95-2 and Topic No. D-16
Paragraph 26 interpreted by EITF Topic No. D-12
Paragraph 46 interpreted by EITF Issues No. 92-4 and 92-8 and Topic No. D-56

Related Issues: EITF Issues No. 87-1, 87-12, 88-18, 90-17, 91-4, and 96-11 and Topic No. D-4

SUMMARY

Application of this Statement will affect financial reporting of most companies operating in foreign countries. The differing operating and economic characteristics of varied types of foreign operations will be distinguished in accounting for them. Adjustments for currency exchange rate changes are excluded from net income for those fluctuations that do not impact cash flows and are included for those that do. The requirements reflect these general conclusions:

- The economic effects of an exchange rate change on an operation that is relatively self-contained and integrated within a foreign country relate to the net investment in that operation. Translation adjustments that arise from consolidating that foreign operation do not impact cash flows and are not included in net income.
- The economic effects of an exchange rate change on a foreign operation that is an extension of the parent's domestic operations relate to individual assets and liabilities and impact the parent's cash flows directly. Accordingly, the exchange gains and losses in such an operation are included in net income.

• Contracts, transactions, or balances that are, in fact, effective hedges of foreign exchange risk will be accounted for as hedges without regard to their form.

More specifically, this Statement replaces FASB Statement No. 8, *Accounting for the Translation of Foreign Currency Transactions and Foreign Currency Financial Statements,* and revises the existing accounting and reporting requirements for translation of foreign currency transactions and foreign currency financial statements. It presents standards for foreign currency translation that are designed to (1) provide information that is generally compatible with the expected economic effects of a rate change on an enterprise's cash flows and equity and (2) reflect in consolidated statements the financial results and relationships as measured in the primary currency in which each entity conducts its business (referred to as its "functional currency").

An entity's functional currency is the currency of the primary economic environment in which that entity operates. The functional currency can be the dollar or a foreign currency depending on the facts. Normally, it will be the currency of the economic environment in which cash is generated and expended by the entity. An entity can be any form of operation, including a subsidiary, division, branch, or joint venture. The Statement provides guidance for this key determination in which management's judgment is essential in assessing the facts.

A currency in a highly inflationary environment (3-year inflation rate of approximately 100 percent or more) is not considered stable enough to serve as a functional currency and the more stable currency of the reporting parent is to be used instead.

The functional currency translation approach adopted in this Statement encompasses:

a. Identifying the functional currency of the entity's economic environment
b. Measuring all elements of the financial statements in the functional currency
c. Using the current exchange rate for translation from the functional currency to the reporting currency, if they are different
d. Distinguishing the economic impact of changes in exchange rates on a net investment from the impact of such changes on individual assets and liabilities that are receivable or payable in currencies other than the functional currency

Translation adjustments are an inherent result of the process of translating a foreign entity's financial statements from the functional currency to U.S. dollars. Translation adjustments are *not* included in determining net income for the period but are disclosed and accumulated in a separate component of consolidated equity until sale or until complete or substantially complete liquidation of the net investment in the foreign entity takes place.

Transaction gains and losses are a result of the effect of exchange rate changes on transactions denominated in currencies other than the functional currency (for example, a U.S. company may borrow Swiss francs or a French subsidiary may have a receivable denominated in kroner from a Danish customer). Gains and losses on those foreign currency transactions are generally included in determining net income for the period in which exchange rates change unless the transaction hedges a foreign currency commitment or a net investment in a foreign entity. Intercompany transactions of a long-term investment nature are considered part of a parent's net investment and hence do not give rise to gains or losses.

Statement of Financial Accounting Standards No. 52
Foreign Currency Translation

CONTENTS

INTRODUCTION

1. FASB Statement No. 8, *Accounting for the Translation of Foreign Currency Transactions and Foreign Currency Financial Statements,* was issued in October 1975 and was effective for fiscal years that began on or after January 1, 1976. In May 1978, the Board issued an invitation for public comment on Statements 1-12, each of which had been in effect for at least two years. **Foreign currency translation**** was the subject of most of the comments received. In January 1979, the Board added to its agenda a project to reconsider Statement 8. This Statement is the result of that project.

2. This Statement establishes revised standards of financial accounting and reporting for **foreign currency transactions** in financial statements of a **reporting enterprise** (hereinafter, **enterprise**). It also revises the standards for translating foreign currency financial statements (hereinafter, **foreign currency statements**) that are incorporated in the financial statements of an enterprise by consolidation, combination, or the equity method of accounting. **Translation** of financial statements from one currency to another for purposes other than consolidation, combination, or the equity method is beyond the scope of this Statement. For example, this Statement does not cover translation of the financial statements of an enterprise from its **reporting currency** into another currency for the convenience of readers accustomed to that other currency.

3. This Statement supersedes FASB Statement No. 8, *Accounting for the Translation of Foreign Currency Transactions and Foreign Currency Financial Statements,*[1] FASB Statement No. 20, *Accounting for Forward Exchange Contracts,* FASB Interpretation No. 15, *Translation of Unamortized Policy Acquisition Costs by a Stock Life Insurance Company,* and FASB Interpretation No. 17, *Applying the Lower of Cost or Market Rule in Translated Financial Statements.*

---

*Terms defined in the glossary (Appendix E) are in **boldface type** the first time they appear in this Statement.

[1]The following pronouncements, which were superseded or amended by Statement 8, are also superseded or amended by this Statement: paragraphs 7 and 10-22 of Chapter 12, "Foreign Operations and Foreign Exchange," of ARB No. 43; paragraph 18 of APB Opinion No. 6, *Status of Accounting Research Bulletins;* and FASB Statement No. 1, *Disclosure of Foreign Currency Translation Information.* The last sentence of paragraph 5 of ARB 43, Chapter 12, is amended to delete "and they should be reserved against to the extent that their realization in dollars appears to be doubtful," and paragraph 13 of APB Opinion No. 22, *Disclosure of Accounting Policies,* is amended to delete "translation of foreign currencies" as an example of disclosure "commonly required with respect to accounting policies."

STANDARDS OF FINANCIAL ACCOUNTING AND REPORTING

Objectives of Translation

4. Financial statements are intended to present information in financial terms about the performance, financial position, and cash flows of an enterprise. For this purpose, the financial statements of separate **entities** within an enterprise, which may exist and operate in different economic and currency environments, are consolidated and presented as though they were the financial statements of a single enterprise. Because it is not possible to combine, add, or subtract measurements expressed in different currencies, it is necessary to translate into a single reporting currency[2] those assets, liabilities, revenues, expenses, gains, and losses that are measured or denominated in a **foreign currency.**[3] However, the unity presented by such translation does not alter the underlying significance of the results and relationships of the constituent parts of the enterprise. It is only through the effective operation of its constituent parts that the enterprise as a whole is able to achieve its purpose. Accordingly, the translation of the financial statements of each component entity of an enterprise should accomplish the following objectives:

a. Provide information that is generally compatible with the expected economic effects of a rate change on an enterprise's cash flows and equity
b. Reflect in consolidated statements the financial results and relationships of the individual consolidated entities as measured in their **functional currencies** in conformity with U.S. generally accepted accounting principles

The Functional Currency

5. The assets, liabilities, and operations of a **foreign entity** shall be measured using the functional currency of that entity. An entity's functional currency is the currency of the primary economic environment in which the entity operates; normally, that is the currency of the environment in which an entity primarily generates and expends cash. Appendix A provides guidance for determination of the functional currency. The economic factors cited in Appendix A, and possibly others, should be considered both individually and collectively when determining the functional currency.

6. For an entity with operations that are relatively self-contained and integrated within a particular country, the functional currency generally would be the currency of that country. However, a foreign entity's functional currency might not be the currency of the country in which the entity is located. For example, the parent's currency generally would be the functional currency for foreign operations that are a direct and integral component or extension of the parent company's operations.

7. An entity might have more than one distinct and separable operation, such as a division or branch, in which case each operation may be considered a separate entity. If those operations are conducted in different economic environments, they might have different functional currencies.

8. The functional currency (or currencies) of an entity is basically a matter of fact, but in some instances the observable facts will not clearly identify a single functional currency. For example, if a foreign entity conducts significant amounts of business in two or more currencies, the functional currency might not be clearly identifiable. In those instances, the economic facts and circumstances pertaining to a particular foreign operation shall be assessed in relation to the Board's stated objectives for foreign currency translation (paragraph 4). Management's judgment will be required to determine the functional currency in which financial results and relationships are measured with the greatest degree of relevance and reliability.

9. Once the functional currency for a foreign entity is determined, that determination shall be used consistently unless significant changes in economic facts and circumstances indicate clearly that the functional currency has changed. Previously issued financial statements shall not be restated for any change in the functional currency.

---

[2]For convenience, this Statement assumes that the enterprise uses the U.S. dollar (dollar) as its reporting currency. However, a currency other than the dollar may be the reporting currency in financial statements that are prepared in conformity with U.S. generally accepted accounting principles. For example, a foreign enterprise may report in its **local currency** in conformity with U.S. generally accepted accounting principles. If so, the requirements of this Statement apply.

[3]To measure in foreign currency is to quantify an **attribute** of an item in a unit of currency other than the reporting currency. Assets and liabilities are denominated in a foreign currency if their amounts are fixed in terms of that foreign currency regardless of exchange rate changes. An asset or liability may be both measured and denominated in one currency, or it may be measured in one currency and denominated in another. To illustrate: Two foreign branches of a U.S. company, one Swiss and one German, purchase identical assets on credit from a Swiss vendor at identical prices stated in Swiss francs. The German branch measures the cost (an attribute) of that asset in German marks. Although the corresponding liability is also measured in marks, it remains denominated in Swiss francs since the liability must be settled in a specified number of Swiss francs. The Swiss branch measures the asset and liability in Swiss francs. Its liability is both measured and denominated in Swiss francs. Although assets and liabilities can be measured in various currencies, rights to receive or obligations to pay fixed amounts of a currency are, by definition, denominated in that currency.

10. If an entity's books of record are not maintained in its functional currency, remeasurement into the functional currency is required. That remeasurement is required before translation into the reporting currency. If a foreign entity's functional currency is the reporting currency, remeasurement into the reporting currency obviates translation. The remeasurement process is intended to produce the same result as if the entity's books of record had been maintained in the functional currency. The remeasurement of and subsequent accounting for transactions denominated in a currency other than the functional currency shall be in accordance with the requirements of this Statement (paragraphs 15 and 16). Appendix B provides guidance for remeasurement into the functional currency.

The Functional Currency in Highly Inflationary Economies

11. The financial statements of a foreign entity in a highly inflationary economy shall be remeasured as if the functional currency were the reporting currency. Accordingly, the financial statements of those entities shall be remeasured into the reporting currency according to the requirements of paragraph 10. For the purposes of this requirement, a highly inflationary economy is one that has cumulative inflation of approximately 100 percent or more over a 3-year period.

Translation of Foreign Currency Statements

12. All elements of financial statements shall be translated by using a **current exchange rate.** For assets and liabilities, the exchange rate at the balance sheet date shall be used. For revenues, expenses, gains, and losses, the exchange rate at the dates on which those elements are recognized shall be used. Because translation at the exchange rates at the dates the numerous revenues, expenses, gains, and losses are recognized is generally impractical, an appropriately weighted average exchange rate for the period may be used to translate those elements.

13. If an entity's functional currency is a foreign currency, **translation adjustments** result from the process of translating that entity's financial statements into the reporting currency. Translation adjustments shall not be included in determining net income but shall be reported separately and accumulated in a separate component of equity.

14. Upon sale or upon complete or substantially complete liquidation of an investment in a foreign entity, the amount attributable to that entity and accumulated in the translation adjustment component of equity shall be removed from the separate component of equity and shall be reported as part of the gain or loss on sale or liquidation of the investment for the period during which the sale or liquidation occurs.

Foreign Currency Transactions

15. Foreign currency transactions are transactions denominated in a currency other than the entity's functional currency. Foreign currency transactions may produce receivables or payables that are fixed in terms of the amount of foreign currency that will be received or paid. A change in exchange rates between the functional currency and the currency in which a transaction is denominated increases or decreases the expected amount of functional currency cash flows upon settlement of the transaction. That increase or decrease in expected functional currency cash flows is a foreign currency **transaction gain or loss** that generally shall be included in determining net income for the period in which the exchange rate changes. Likewise, a transaction gain or loss (measured from the **transaction date** or the most recent intervening balance sheet date, whichever is later) realized upon settlement of a foreign currency transaction generally shall be included in determining net income for the period in which the transaction is settled. The exceptions to this requirement for inclusion in net income of transaction gains and losses are set forth in paragraphs 20 and 21 and pertain to certain intercompany transactions and to transactions that are designated as, and effective as, economic hedges of net investments and foreign currency commitments.

16. For other than **forward exchange contracts** (paragraphs 17-19), the following shall apply to all foreign currency transactions of an enterprise and its investees:

a. At the date the transaction is recognized, each asset, liability, revenue, expense, gain, or loss arising from the transaction shall be measured and recorded in the functional currency of the recording entity by use of the exchange rate in effect at that date (paragraphs 26-28).
b. At each balance sheet date, recorded balances that are denominated in a currency other than the functional currency of the recording entity shall be adjusted to reflect the current exchange rate.

Forward Exchange Contracts

17. A forward exchange contract (forward contract) is an agreement to exchange different currencies at a specified future date and at a specified rate (the **forward rate**). A forward contract is a foreign currency transaction. A gain or loss on a forward contract that does not meet the conditions described in paragraph 20 or 21 shall be included in determin-

ing net income in accordance with the requirements for other foreign currency transactions (paragraph 15). Agreements that are, in substance, essentially the same as forward contracts, for example, **currency swaps,** shall be accounted for in a manner similar to the accounting for forward contracts.

18. A gain or loss (whether or not deferred) on a forward contract, except a forward contract of the type discussed in paragraph 19, shall be computed by multiplying the foreign currency amount of the forward contract by the difference between the **spot rate** at the balance sheet date and the spot rate at the date of inception of the forward contract (or the spot rate last used to measure a gain or loss on that contract for an earlier period). The **discount or premium on a forward contract** (that is, the foreign currency amount of the contract multiplied by the difference between the contracted forward rate and the spot rate at the date of inception of the contract) shall be accounted for separately from the gain or loss on the contract and shall be included in determining net income over the life of the forward contract. However, if a gain or loss is deferred under paragraph 21, the forward contract's discount or premium that relates to the commitment period may be included in the measurement of the basis of the related foreign currency transaction when recorded. If a gain or loss is accounted for as a hedge of a net investment under paragraph 20, the forward contract's discount or premium may be included with translation adjustments in the separate component of equity.

19. A gain or loss on a speculative forward contract (that is, a contract that does not hedge an exposure) shall be computed by multiplying the foreign currency amount of the forward contract by the difference between the forward rate available for the remaining maturity of the contract and the contracted forward rate (or the forward rate last used to measure a gain or loss on that contract for an earlier period). No separate accounting recognition is given to the discount or premium on a speculative forward contract.

Transaction Gains and Losses to Be Excluded from Determination of Net Income

20. Gains and losses on the following foreign currency transactions shall not be included in determining net income but shall be reported in the same manner as translation adjustments (paragraph 13):

a. Foreign currency transactions that are designated as, and are effective as, economic hedges of a net investment in a foreign entity, commencing as of the designation date
b. Intercompany foreign currency transactions that are of a long-term-investment nature (that is, set-

tlement is not planned or anticipated in the foreseeable future), when the entities to the transaction are consolidated, combined, or accounted for by the equity method in the reporting enterprise's financial statements

21. A gain or loss on a forward contract or other foreign currency transaction that is intended to hedge an identifiable foreign currency commitment (for example, an agreement to purchase or sell equipment) shall be deferred and included in the measurement of the related foreign currency transaction (for example, the purchase or the sale of the equipment). Losses shall not be deferred, however, if it is estimated that deferral would lead to recognizing losses in later periods. A foreign currency transaction shall be considered a hedge of an identifiable foreign currency commitment provided both of the following conditions are met:

a. The foreign currency transaction is designated as, and is effective as, a hedge of a foreign currency commitment.
b. The foreign currency commitment is firm.

The required accounting shall commence as of the designation date. The portion of a hedging transaction that shall be accounted for pursuant to this paragraph is limited to the amount of the related commitment. If a hedging transaction that meets conditions (a) and (b) above exceeds the amount of the related commitment, the gain or loss pertaining to the portion of the hedging transaction in excess of the commitment shall be deferred to the extent that the transaction is intended to provide a hedge on an after-tax basis. A gain or loss so deferred shall be included as an offset to the related tax effects in the period in which such tax effects are recognized; consequently, it shall not be included in the aggregate transaction gain or loss disclosure required by paragraph 30. A gain or loss pertaining to the portion of a hedging transaction in excess of the amount that provides a hedge on an after-tax basis shall not be deferred. Likewise, a gain or loss pertaining to a period after the transaction date of the related commitment shall not be deferred. If a foreign currency transaction previously considered a hedge of a foreign currency commitment is terminated before the transaction date of the related commitment, any deferred gain or loss shall continue to be deferred and accounted for in accordance with the requirements of this paragraph.

Income Tax Consequences of Rate Changes

22. Interperiod tax allocation is required in accordance with APB Opinion No. 11, *Accounting for Income Taxes,* if taxable exchange gains or tax-deductible exchange losses resulting from an entity's foreign currency transactions are included in net

income in a different period for financial statement purposes from that for tax purposes.

23. Translation adjustments shall be accounted for in the same way as timing differences under the provisions of APB Opinions 11, 23, and 24. APB Opinion No. 23, *Accounting for Income Taxes—Special Areas,* provides that deferred taxes shall not be provided for unremitted earnings of a subsidiary in certain instances; in those instances, deferred taxes shall not be provided on translation adjustments.

24. Opinion 11 requires income tax expense to be allocated among income before extraordinary items, extraordinary items, adjustments of prior periods (or of the opening balance of retained earnings), and direct entries to other equity accounts. Some transaction gains and losses and all translation adjustments are reported in a separate component of equity. Any income taxes related to those transaction gains and losses and translation adjustments shall be allocated to that separate component of equity.

Elimination of Intercompany Profits

25. The elimination of intercompany profits that are attributable to sales or other transfers between entities that are consolidated, combined, or accounted for by the equity method in the enterprise's financial statements shall be based on the exchange rates at the dates of the sales or transfers. The use of reasonable approximations or averages is permitted.

Exchange Rates

26. The exchange rate is the ratio between a unit of one currency and the amount of another currency for which that unit can be exchanged at a particular time. If exchangeability between two currencies is temporarily lacking at the transaction date or balance sheet date, the first subsequent rate at which exchanges could be made shall be used for purposes of this Statement. If the lack of exchangeability is other than temporary, the propriety of consolidating, combining, or accounting for the foreign operation by the equity method in the financial statements of the enterprise shall be carefully considered (ARB 43, Chapter 12, paragraph 8).

27. The exchange rates to be used for translation of foreign currency transactions and foreign currency statements are as follows:

a. *Foreign Currency Transactions*—The applicable rate at which a particular transaction could be settled at the transaction date shall be used to translate and record the transaction. At a subsequent balance sheet date, the current rate is that rate at which the related receivable or payable could be settled at that date.

b. *Foreign Currency Statements*—In the absence of unusual circumstances, the rate applicable to **conversion** of a currency for purposes of dividend remittances shall be used to translate foreign currency statements.[4]

28. If a foreign entity whose balance sheet date differs from that of the enterprise is consolidated or combined with or accounted for by the equity method in the financial statements of the enterprise, the current rate is the rate in effect at the foreign entity's balance sheet date for purposes of applying the requirements of this Statement to that foreign entity.

Use of Averages or Other Methods of Approximation

29. Literal application of the standards in this Statement might require a degree of detail in record keeping and computations that could be burdensome as well as unnecessary to produce reasonable approximations of the results. Accordingly, it is acceptable to use averages or other methods of approximation. For example, the propriety of using average rates to translate revenue and expense amounts is noted in paragraph 12. Likewise, the use of other time- and effort-saving methods to approximate the results of detailed calculations is permitted.

Disclosure

30. The aggregate transaction gain or loss included in determining net income for the period shall be disclosed in the financial statements or notes thereto. For that disclosure, gains and losses on forward contracts determined in conformity with the requirements of paragraphs 18 and 19 shall be considered transaction gains or losses. Certain enterprises, primarily banks, are dealers in foreign exchange. Although certain gains or losses from dealer transactions may fit the definition of transaction gains or losses in this Statement, they may be disclosed as dealer gains or losses rather than as transaction gains or losses.

31. An analysis of the changes during the period in the separate component of equity for cumulative translation adjustments shall be provided in a sepa-

---

[4]If unsettled intercompany transactions are subject to and translated using preference or penalty rates, translation of foreign currency statements at the rate applicable to dividend remittances may cause a difference between intercompany receivables and payables. Until that difference is eliminated by settlement of the intercompany transaction, the difference shall be treated as a receivable or payable in the enterprise's financial statements.

rate financial statement, in notes to the financial statements, or as part of a statement of changes in equity. At a minimum, the analysis shall disclose:

a. Beginning and ending amount of cumulative translation adjustments
b. The aggregate adjustment for the period resulting from translation adjustments (paragraph 13) and gains and losses from certain hedges and intercompany balances (paragraph 20)
c. The amount of income taxes for the period allocated to translation adjustments (paragraph 24)
d. The amounts transferred from cumulative translation adjustments and included in determining net income for the period as a result of the sale or complete or substantially complete liquidation of an investment in a foreign entity (paragraph 14)

32. An enterprise's financial statements shall not be adjusted for a rate change that occurs after the date of the enterprise's financial statements or after the date of the foreign currency statements of a foreign entity if they are consolidated, combined, or accounted for by the equity method in the financial statements of the enterprise. However, disclosure of the rate change and its effects on unsettled balances pertaining to foreign currency transactions, if significant, may be necessary.

Effective Date and Transition

33. This Statement shall be effective for fiscal years beginning on or after December 15, 1982, although earlier application is encouraged. The initial application of this Statement shall be as of the beginning of an enterprise's fiscal year. Financial statements for fiscal years before the effective date, and financial summaries or other data derived therefrom, may be restated to conform to the provisions of paragraphs 5-29 of this Statement. In the year that this Statement is first applied, the financial statements shall disclose the nature of any restatement and its effect on income before extraordinary items, net income, and related per share amounts for each fiscal year restated. If the prior year is not restated, disclosure of income before extraordinary items and net income for the prior year computed on a pro forma basis is permitted.

34. The effect of translating all of a foreign entity's assets and liabilities from a foreign functional currency into the reporting currency at the current exchange rate as of the beginning of the year for which this Statement is first applied shall be reported as the opening balance of the cumulative translation adjustments component of equity. The effect of remeasuring a foreign entity's deferred income taxes and life insurance policy acquisition costs at the current exchange rate (paragraph 54) as

of the beginning of the year for which this Statement is first applied shall be reported as an adjustment of the opening balance of retained earnings.

35. Amounts deferred on forward contracts that (a) under Statement 8 were accounted for as hedges of identifiable foreign currency commitments to receive proceeds from the use or sale of nonmonetary assets translated at historical rates, and (b) are canceled at the time this Statement is first applied, shall be included in the opening balance of the cumulative translation adjustments component of equity up to the amount of the offsetting adjustment attributable to those nonmonetary assets.

36. Financial statements for periods beginning on or after the effective date of this Statement shall include the disclosures specified by paragraphs 30-32. To the extent practicable, those disclosures shall also be included in financial statements for earlier periods that have been restated pursuant to paragraph 33.

37. Financial statements of enterprises that first adopt this standard for fiscal years ending on or before March 31, 1982 shall disclose the effect of adopting the new standard on income before extraordinary items, net income, and related per share amounts for the year of the change. Those disclosures are not required for financial statements of enterprises that first adopt this standard for subsequent fiscal years.

38. The Board expects to issue an Exposure Draft proposing an amendment of FASB Statement No. 33, *Financial Reporting and Changing Prices,* to be consistent with the functional currency approach to foreign currency translation. Prior to issuance of a final amendment of Statement 33, enterprises that adopt this Statement and that are subject to the requirements of Statement 33 shall have either of the following options:

a. They may prepare the supplementary information based on this Statement and on the proposed amendment of Statement 33.
b. They may prepare the supplementary information based on the application of Statement 8 and on the provisions of existing Statement 33. (Under this option, historical cost information based on the application of Statement 8 shall be presented in the supplementary information for comparison with the constant dollar and current cost information.)

Enterprises that would become subject to the requirements of Statement 33 as a result of adopting this Statement are exempt from the requirements of Statement 33 until the effective date of this Statement.

> The provisions of this Statement need
> not be applied to immaterial items.

This Statement was adopted by the affirmative votes of four members of the Financial Accounting Standards Board. Messrs. Block, Kirk, and Morgan dissented.

Messrs. Block, Kirk, and Morgan dissent to the issuance of this Statement. They start from a premise different from that underlying this Statement. They believe that more meaningful consolidated results are attained by measuring costs, cost recovery, and exchange risk from a dollar perspective rather than from multiple functional currency perspectives. Accordingly, the dissenters do not believe that this Statement improves financial reporting. In their opinion, improved financial reporting would have resulted from an approach that:

a. Adopted objectives of translation that retained the concept of a single consolidated entity and a single **unit of measure** (that is, all elements of U.S. consolidated financial statements would be measured in dollars rather than multiple functional currencies)
b. Avoided creating direct entries to equity
c. Essentially retained Statement 8's translation method, with an exception being translation of locally sourced inventory at the current rate
d. Recognized all gains and losses in net income (that is, no separate and different accounting for transaction gains or losses and translation adjustments), but allowed for a separate and distinct presentation of those gains and losses within the income statement
e. Recognized additional contractual arrangements (for example, operating leases and take-or-pay contracts) that effectively hedged an exposed net monetary liability position

The dissenters recognize that such an approach would not satisfy all of the critics of Statement 8, but they believe it would have avoided the more far-reaching implications of the functional currency theory. They acknowledge that translating certain inventories at current rates departs from historical cost in dollars. However, they would accept that departure on pragmatic grounds as part of a solution to an exceedingly difficult problem.

As further discussed in subsequent paragraphs, the dissenting Board members do not support this Statement because in their opinion it:

a. Builds on two incompatible premises and, as a result, produces anomalies and a significant but unwarranted reporting distinction between transaction gains and losses and translation adjustments
b. Adopts objectives and methods that are at variance with fundamental concepts that underlie present financial reporting

c. Incorrectly assumes that an aggregation of the results of foreign operations measured in functional currencies and *expressed* in dollars, rather than consolidated results *measured* in dollars, assists U.S. investors and creditors in assessing future cash flows to them
d. Will not result in similar accounting for similar circumstances

Incompatibility of Underlying Premises

The standards for translating foreign currency financial statements set forth in this Statement stem from two premises that are incompatible with each other. The first premise is that it is a parent company's net investment in a foreign operation that is subject to exchange rate risk rather than the foreign operation's individual assets and liabilities. The second premise is that translation should retain the relationships in foreign currency financial statements as measured by the functional currency. The premise of a parent company's exposed net investment reflects a dollar perspective of exchange rate risk, and that calls for a dollar measure of the effects of exchange rate changes. The premise of retaining the relationships of measurements in functional currency financial statements calls for a functional currency measure of the effects of exchange rate changes.

The dissenting Board members note that although the translation process can retain certain intraperiod relationships reported in functional currency financial statements, it cannot retain interperiod functional currency relationships when exchange rates change. Further, when an exchange rate changes between the dollar and a foreign currency, the value of any holdings of that currency changes and, from a dollar perspective, the resulting gain or loss is either real, or unreal, in its entirety. However, to implement the functional currency perspective, the standards result in a division of that gain or loss into two components. One is considered in measuring consolidated net income and the other is considered a translation adjustment. Thus, the standards require a transaction gain in income on a foreign operation's holdings of a third currency when that currency strengthens in relation to the functional currency, even if the third currency has weakened in terms of dollars. That gain will be reported in consolidated net income despite the fact that it does not exist in dollar terms and can never provide increased dollar cash flows to U.S. investors and creditors. The standards inherently recognize that fact by requiring a compensating debit translation adjustment. (Examples that further illustrate these concerns are contained in paragraphs 111-113 of the August 28, 1980 Exposure Draft, *Foreign Currency Translation.*)

The dissenters believe that the need for a translation adjustment that adjusts consolidated equity to the same amount as would have resulted had all foreign currency transactions of foreign operations been measured in dollars demonstrates the incompatibility of the two underlying premises. They believe that incompatibility is further demonstrated by the differing views of the nature of translation adjustments described in paragraphs 113 and 114. In the dissenters' opinion, translation adjustments are, from a dollar perspective, gains and losses as defined in FASB Concepts Statement No. 3, *Elements of Financial Statements of Business Enterprises,* which should be reported in net income when exchange rates change. The dissenters believe that from a functional currency perspective, translation adjustments fail to meet any definition of an element of financial statements because they do not exist in terms of functional currency cash flows.

Relationship to Preexisting Fundamental Concepts

The dissenters believe the two premises underlying this Statement (discussed above) challenge and reject the dollar perspective that underlies existing theories of historical cost and capital maintenance, inflation accounting, consolidation, and realization. The rejection of the dollar perspective has ramifications far beyond this project and was unnecessary in a translation project.

While not explicitly stated, today's accounting model includes the capital maintenance concept that income of a consolidated U.S. entity exists only after recovery of historical cost measured in dollars. For example, prior to this Statement, the gain on the sale by a foreign operation of an internationally priced inventory item or a marketable security would have been measured by comparing the dollar equivalent sales price with the fixed dollar equivalent historical cost of the item. This Statement changes that. It remeasures the dollar equivalent cost while the item is held (measured by changes in the exchange rate between the foreign currency and the dollar) and treats that remeasurement as a translation adjustment, seldom if ever to be reported in net income. Under this Statement, consolidated net income, although expressed in dollars, does not represent the measure of income after maintaining capital measured in dollars. The dissenters believe that U.S. investors' and creditors' decisions are based on a dollar perspective of capital maintenance. Not only does this Statement change income measurement and capital maintenance concepts in the primary financial statements but it also implies the need to modify the measurement of changes in current costs (sometimes referred to as

holding gains or losses) in Statement 33 and, likewise, to change that Statement's requirements for constant dollar accounting to constant functional currency accounting.

This Statement abandons the long-standing principle that consolidated results should be measured from a single perspective rather than multiple perspectives. The dissenters believe (for the reasons set forth in paragraphs 83-95 of Statement 8) that a single perspective is essential for (a) valid addition and subtraction in the measurement of financial position and periodic net income and (b) the understandability and representational faithfulness of consolidated results presented in dollars and described as being prepared on the historical cost basis. The dissenters believe that readers of financial statements are better served by having consolidated financial statements prepared in terms of a common bench mark—a single unit of measure. This means to the dissenters that the translation process is one of remeasurement of the individual items of foreign financial statements (not net investments) into dollars—much in the same way as Statement 33 presently requires a remeasurement of individual items of financial statements (not net investments) from nominal dollar measures into constant dollars.

The Statement introduces a concept of realization (paragraphs 71, 111, 117, and 119) different from any previously applied in consolidated financial statements. It requires the results of foreign operations to be measured in various functional currencies and then translated into dollars and included in consolidated net income. It defers recognizing in net income the effects of exchange rate changes from a dollar perspective on the individual assets and liabilities of those same foreign operations until an indefinite future period that will almost always be beyond the point in time that those individual assets and liabilities have ceased to exist. As a result, the dollar effects of a rate change on current operating revenues are recognized when they occur by reporting in the translated income statement an increased or decreased dollar equivalent for those revenues versus the dollar equivalent of identical revenues generated before the rate change. However, the effects of the same rate change on the uncollected receivables from those previous revenue transactions are not included in net income until liquidation of the foreign operation. By not recognizing in net income the effects of exchange rate changes on existing receivables, this Statement results in sales denominated in a foreign currency being accounted for as if they had been denominated in dollars. That result is a focal point of the criticism made in this Statement (paragraph 75) about Statement 8. However, unlike this Statement, Statement 8 recognized that foreign currency sales are not denominated in dollars and therefore it required that the effects of exchange rate changes on all foreign currency denominated receivables be recognized in net income. To do otherwise places the enterprise in the anomalous position of having recognized the entire effect of the rate change on a current transaction while holding in suspense its effect on a previous transaction until liquidation of the foreign operation.

This Statement accepts the use of the Statement 8 methodology (that is, using the dollar as the functional currency) for some foreign operations (including all operations in highly inflationary economies), but at the same time criticizes that methodology. It asserts that the Statement 8 methodology results in accounting as if all transactions were conducted in the economic environment of the United States and in dollars (paragraphs 74, 75, and 86). The dissenters believe such views were convincingly rebutted in paragraphs 94 and 95 of Statement 8, as follows:

> Some respondents to the Exposure Draft criticized that objective as an attempt to account for local and foreign currency transactions of foreign operations as if they were dollar transactions or, to a few respondents, as if they were dollar transactions in the United States. In the Board's judgment, those criticisms are not valid. Neither the objective nor the procedures to accomplish it change the denomination of a transaction or the environment in which it occurs. The procedures adopted by the Board are consistent with the purpose of consolidated financial statements. The foreign currency transactions of an enterprise and the local and foreign currency transactions of its foreign operations are translated and accounted for as transactions of a single enterprise. The denomination of transactions and the location of assets are not changed; however, the separate corporate identities within the consolidated group are ignored. Translation procedures are merely a means of remeasuring in dollars amounts that are denominated or originally measured in foreign currency. That is, the procedures do *not* attempt to simulate what the cost of a foreign plant would have been had it been located in the United States; instead, they recognize the factors that determined the plant's cost in the foreign location and express that cost in dollars.
>
> If translation procedures were capable of changing the denomination of an asset or liability from foreign currency to dollars, no exchange risk would be present.

Effects on Cash Flow Assessments

The dissenters believe that U.S. investors and creditors should be provided with information about a multinational enterprise's performance measured in dollars because that is the currency in which, ultimately, the enterprise makes cash payments to them. Foreign exchange exposure to a U.S.

investor or creditor is the exposure to increased or decreased potential dollar cash flows caused by changes in exchange rates between foreign currencies and the dollar. Changes in exchange rates between two foreign currencies are not relevant, except to the extent that each such foreign currency's exchange rate for the dollar changes.

Supporting the functional currency perspective is the assenters' view (paragraphs 73, 75, 97, and elsewhere) that a translated functional currency income statement better provides U.S. investors and creditors with information necessary in assessing future cash flows than does an income statement whose components have been measured from a dollar perspective. The dissenting view is that a translated functional currency income statement is inappropriate because it can include items that (a) do not exist for the consolidated enterprise (for example, transaction gains on intercompany trade receivables or monetary items denominated in dollars) or (b) are incorrectly measured (for example, a gain on a holding of a third currency that significantly strengthens against the dollar but only moderately strengthens against the functional currency). It can also exclude items that do exist for the consolidated enterprise (for example, a gain on a monetary asset denominated in a foreign operation's functional currency when that currency strengthens against the dollar).

The dissenters see no persuasive reasoning to support the belief that external users want or need to know the amount of transaction gains or losses as measured from the perspective of the manager of the foreign operation (that is, in functional currency), while at the same time wanting a balance sheet that is measured from a dollar perspective—a balance sheet that denies the usefulness of the foreign perspective. (The previously referenced examples in the August 1980 Exposure Draft also further illustrate this concern.)

Similar Accounting for Similar Circumstances

The dissenters believe that the criteria in paragraph 42 for deciding between the Statement 8 translation method and the current rate method are inappropriate (for the reasons set forth in paragraphs 140-151 of Statement 8). They also believe that application of those criteria will not result in similar accounting for similar situations.

Likewise, the absence of effective criteria that would objectively indicate when foreign currency transactions (paragraph 20(a)) and forward exchange contracts (paragraph 21) are hedges creates the possibility that transaction gains or losses that should be reported in net income currently may instead be reported as translation adjustments or deferred as hedges of commitments.

The variety of permissible methods of transition from the existing Statement 8 requirements may also result in similar circumstances being accounted for differently. Mr. Morgan believes the transition paragraphs should have required that the amount necessary to adjust from the Statement 8 basis to the new basis be reported as the opening translation adjustment in equity for the first year in which the new Statement becomes effective. To restate any year prior to the effective date of this Statement may foster an inappropriate conclusion, namely, that those restated results are the results an entity might have experienced had the new Statement been in effect for earlier periods. There is considerable evidence that many enterprises alter their hedging of foreign exchange exposure depending on the accounting standards currently in effect. Thus, restated financial statements for those entities, whether required or done voluntarily, could not accurately reflect what might have happened had this Statement been in effect. Voluntary restatement also diminishes the comparability of financial reporting among companies. In Mr. Morgan's view, the Board should have prohibited restatement as a method of transition to this new Statement.

Members of the Financial Accounting Standards Board:

Donald J. Kirk,	John W. March	Robert T. Sprouse
Chairman	Robert A. Morgan	Ralph E. Walters
Frank E. Block	David Mosso	

Appendix A

DETERMINATION OF THE FUNCTIONAL CURRENCY

39. An entity's functional currency is the currency of the primary economic environment in which the entity operates; normally, that is the currency of the environment in which an entity primarily generates and expends cash. The functional currency of an entity is, in principle, a matter of fact. In some cases, the facts will clearly identify the functional currency; in other cases they will not.

40. It is neither possible nor desirable to provide unequivocal criteria to identify the functional currency of foreign entities under all possible facts and circumstances and still fulfill the objectives of foreign currency translation. Arbitrary rules that might dictate the identification of the functional currency in each case would accomplish a degree of superficial uniformity but, in the process, might diminish the relevance and reliability of the resulting information.

41. The Board has developed, with significant input from its task force and other advisors, the following general guidance on indicators of facts to be considered in identifying the functional currency. In those instances in which the indicators are mixed and the functional currency is not obvious, management's judgment will be required in order to determine the functional currency that most faithfully portrays the economic results of the entity's operations and thereby best achieves the objectives of foreign currency translation set forth in paragraph 4. Management is in the best position to obtain the pertinent facts and weigh their relative importance in determining the functional currency for each operation. It is important to recognize that management's judgment is essential and paramount in this determination, provided only that it is not contradicted by the facts.

42. The salient economic factors set forth below, and possibly others, should be considered both individually and collectively when determining the functional currency.

a. Cash flow indicators
  (1) Foreign Currency—Cash flows related to the foreign entity's individual assets and liabilities are primarily in the foreign currency and do not directly impact the parent company's cash flows.
  (2) Parent's Currency—Cash flows related to the foreign entity's individual assets and liabilities directly impact the parent's cash flows on a current basis and are readily available for remittance to the parent company.
b. Sales price indicators
  (1) Foreign Currency—Sales prices for the foreign entity's products are not primarily responsive on a short-term basis to changes in exchange rates but are determined more by local competition or local government regulation.
  (2) Parent's Currency—Sales prices for the foreign entity's products are primarily responsive on a short-term basis to changes in exchange rates; for example, sales prices are determined more by worldwide competition or by international prices.
c. Sales market indicators
  (1) Foreign Currency—There is an active local sales market for the foreign entity's products, although there also might be significant amounts of exports.
  (2) Parent's Currency—The sales market is mostly in the parent's country or sales contracts are denominated in the parent's currency.

d. Expense indicators
   (1) Foreign Currency—Labor, materials, and other costs for the foreign entity's products or services are primarily local costs, even though there also might be imports from other countries.
   (2) Parent's Currency—Labor, materials, and other costs for the foreign entity's products or services, on a continuing basis, are primarily costs for components obtained from the country in which the parent company is located.
e. Financing indicators
   (1) Foreign Currency—Financing is primarily denominated in foreign currency, and funds generated by the foreign entity's operations are sufficient to service existing and normally expected debt obligations.
   (2) Parent's Currency—Financing is primarily from the parent or other dollar-denominated obligations, or funds generated by the foreign entity's operations are not sufficient to service existing and normally expected debt obligations without the infusion of additional funds from the parent company. Infusion of additional funds from the parent company for expansion is not a factor, provided funds generated by the foreign entity's expanded operations are expected to be sufficient to service that additional financing.
f. Intercompany transactions and arrangements indicators
   (1) Foreign Currency—There is a low volume of intercompany transactions and there is not an extensive interrelationship between the operations of the foreign entity and the parent company. However, the foreign entity's operations may rely on the parent's or affiliates' competitive advantages, such as patents and trademarks.
   (2) Parent's Currency—There is a high volume of intercompany transactions and there is an extensive interrelationship between the operations of the foreign entity and the parent company. Additionally, the parent's currency generally would be the functional currency if the foreign entity is a device or shell corporation for holding investments, obligations, intangible assets, etc., that could readily be carried on the parent's or an affiliate's books.

43. In some instances, a foreign entity might have more than one distinct and separable operation. For example, a foreign entity might have one operation that sells parent-company-produced products and another operation that manufactures and sells foreign-entity-produced products. If those two operations are conducted in different economic environments, those two operations might have different functional currencies. Similarly, a single subsidiary of a financial institution might have relatively self-contained and integrated operations in each of several different countries. In circumstances such as those described above, each operation may be considered to be an entity as that term is used in this Statement; and, based on the facts and circumstances, each operation might have a different functional currency.

44. Foreign investments that are consolidated or accounted for by the equity method are controlled by or subject to significant influence by the parent company. Likewise, the parent's currency is often used for measurements, assessments, evaluations, projections, etc., pertaining to foreign investments as part of the management decision-making process. Such management control, decisions, and resultant actions may reflect, indicate, or create economic facts and circumstances. However, the exercise of significant management control and the use of the parent's currency for decision-making purposes do not determine, per se, that the parent's currency is the functional currency for foreign operations.

45. Once a determination of the functional currency is made, that decision shall be consistently used for each foreign entity unless significant changes in economic facts and circumstances indicate clearly that the functional currency has changed. (APB Opinion No. 20, *Accounting Changes,* paragraph 8, states that "adoption or modification of an accounting principle necessitated by transactions or events that are clearly different in substance from those previously occurring" is not a change in accounting principles.)

46. If the functional currency changes from a foreign currency to the reporting currency, translation adjustments for prior periods should not be removed from equity and the translated amounts for nonmonetary assets at the end of the prior period become the accounting basis for those assets in the period of the change and subsequent periods. If the functional currency changes from the reporting currency to a foreign currency, the adjustment attributable to current-rate translation of nonmonetary assets as of the date of the change should be reported in the cumulative translation adjustments component of equity.

Appendix B

REMEASUREMENT OF THE BOOKS OF RECORD INTO THE FUNCTIONAL CURRENCY*

Introduction

47. Paragraph 12 of this Statement requires that all of a foreign entity's assets and liabilities shall be translated from the entity's functional currency into the reporting currency using the current exchange rate. Paragraph 12 also requires that revenues, expenses, gains, and losses be translated using the rates on the dates on which those elements are recognized during the period. The specified result can be reasonably approximated by using an appropriately weighted average exchange rate for the period. If an entity's books of record are not maintained in its functional currency, this Statement (paragraph 10) requires remeasurement into the functional currency prior to the translation process. If a foreign entity's functional currency is the reporting currency, remeasurement into the reporting currency obviates translation. The remeasurement process should produce the same result as if the entity's books of record had been initially recorded in the functional currency. To accomplish that result, it is necessary to use historical exchange rates between the functional currency and another currency in the remeasurement process for certain accounts (the current rate will be used for all others), and this appendix identifies those accounts. To accomplish that result, it is also necessary to recognize currently in income all exchange gains and losses from remeasurement of monetary assets and liabilities that are not denominated in the functional currency (for example, assets and liabilities that are not denominated in dollars if the dollar is the functional currency).

48. The table below lists common nonmonetary balance sheet items and related revenue, expense, gain, and loss accounts that should be remeasured using historical rates in order to produce the same result in terms of the functional currency that would have occurred if those items had been initially recorded in the functional currency.

Accounts to Be Remeasured Using Historical Exchange Rates

Marketable securities carried at cost
- Equity securities
- Debt securities not intended to be held until maturity

Inventories carried at cost

Prepaid expenses such as insurance, advertising, and rent

Property, plant, and equipment

Accumulated depreciation on property, plant, and equipment

Patents, trademarks, licenses, and formulas

Goodwill

Other intangible assets

Deferred charges and credits, except deferred income taxes and policy acquisition costs for life insurance companies

Deferred income

Common stock

Preferred stock carried at issuance price

Examples of revenues and expenses related to nonmonetary items:
    Cost of goods sold
    Depreciation of property, plant, and equipment
    Amortization of intangible items such as goodwill, patents, licenses, etc.
    Amortization of deferred charges or credits except deferred income taxes and policy acquisition costs for life insurance companies

---

*The guidance in this appendix applies only to those instances in which the books of record are not maintained in the functional currency.

Inventories—Applying the Rule of Cost or Market, Whichever Is Lower, to Remeasure Inventory Not Recorded in the Functional Currency

49. The rule of cost or market, whichever is lower (as described in Statement 6 of Chapter 4, "Inventory Pricing," of ARB 43), requires special application when the books of record are not kept in the functional currency. Inventories carried at cost in the books of record in another currency should be first remeasured to cost in the functional currency using historical exchange rates. Then, historical cost in the functional currency is compared with market as stated in the functional currency. Application of the rule in functional currency may require write-downs to market in the functional currency statements even though no write-down has been made in the books of record maintained in another currency. Likewise, a write-down in the books of record may need to be reversed if market exceeds historical cost as stated in the functional currency. If inventory[5] has been written down to market in the functional currency statements, that functional currency amount shall continue to be the carrying amount in the functional currency financial statements until the inventory is sold or a further write-down is necessary.

50. Literal application of the rule of cost or market, whichever is lower, may require an inventory write-down[6] in functional currency financial statements for locally acquired inventory[7] if the value of the currency in which the books of record are maintained has declined in relation to the functional currency between the date the inventory was acquired and the date of the balance sheet. Such a write-down may not be necessary, however, if the replacement costs or selling prices expressed in the currency in which the books of record are maintained have increased sufficiently so that market exceeds historical cost as measured in functional currency. Paragraphs 51-53 illustrate this situation.

51. Assume the following:

a. When the rate is BR*1 = FC2.40, a foreign subsidiary of a U.S. company purchases a unit of inventory at a cost of BR500 (measured in functional currency, FC1,200).

b. At the foreign subsidiary's balance sheet date, the current rate is BR1 = FC2.00 and the current replacement cost of the unit of inventory is BR560 (measured in functional currency, FC1,120).

c. Net realizable value is BR630 (measured in functional currency, FC1,260).

d. Net realizable value reduced by an allowance for an approximately normal profit margin is BR550 (measured in functional currency, FC1,100).

Because current replacement cost as measured in the functional currency (FC1,120) is less than historical cost as measured in the functional currency (FC1,200), an inventory write-down of FC80 is required in the functional currency financial statements.

52. Continue to assume the same information in the preceding example but substitute a current replacement cost at the foreign subsidiary's balance sheet date of BR620. Because market as measured in the functional currency (BR620 × FC2.00 = FC1,240) exceeds historical cost as measured in the functional currency (BR500 × FC2.40 = FC1,200), an inventory write-down is not required in the financial statements.

53. As another example, assume the information in paragraph 51, except that selling prices in terms of the currency in which the books of record are maintained have increased so that net realizable value is BR720 and net realizable value reduced by an allowance for an approximately normal profit margin is BR640. In that case, because replacement cost measured in functional currency (BR560 × FC2.00 = FC1,120) is less than net realizable value reduced by an allowance for an approximately normal profit margin measured in functional currency (BR640 × FC2.00 = FC1,280), market is FC1,280. Because market as measured in the functional currency (FC1,280) exceeds historical cost as measured in the functional currency (BR500 × FC2.40 = FC1,200),

---

[5]An asset other than inventory may sometimes be written down from historical cost. Although that write-down is not under the rule of cost or market, whichever is lower, the approach described in this paragraph might be appropriate. That is, a write-down may be required in the functional currency statements even though not required in the books of record, and a write-down in the books of record may need to be reversed before remeasurement to prevent the remeasured amount from exceeding functional currency historical cost.

[6]This paragraph is not intended to preclude recognition of gains in a later interim period to the extent of inventory losses recognized from market declines in earlier interim periods if losses on the same inventory are recovered in the same year, as provided by paragraph 14(c) of APB Opinion No. 28, *Interim Financial Reporting*, which states: "Inventory losses from market declines should not be deferred beyond the interim period in which the decline occurs. Recoveries of such losses on the same inventory in later interim periods of the same fiscal year through market price recoveries should be recognized as gains in the later interim period. Such gains should not exceed previously recognized losses. Some market declines at interim dates, however, can reasonably be expected to be restored in the fiscal year. Such *temporary* market declines need not be recognized at the interim date since no loss is expected to be incurred in the fiscal year."

[7]An inventory write-down also may be required for imported inventory.

*BR = Currency in which the books of record are maintained

FC = Functional currency

515

an inventory write-down is not required in the functional currency financial statements.

Deferred Taxes and Policy Acquisition Costs

54. Statement 8 required certain deferred taxes that do not relate to assets or liabilities translated at current rates to be translated at historical rates.[8] Interpretation 15 required unamortized policy

acquisition costs of a stock life insurance company to be translated at historical rates.[9] In Statement 33, the Board decided that, because of the close relationship of those accounts to related monetary items, a monetary classification should be used for the purposes of constant dollar accounting. For similar reasons, the Board decided to retain the classification required by Statement 33 for the purposes of remeasurement of an entity's books of record into its functional currency.

Appendix C

BASIS FOR CONCLUSIONS

CONTENTS

Appendix C

BASIS FOR CONCLUSIONS

Introduction

55. This appendix reviews considerations that were deemed significant by members of the Board in reaching the conclusions in this Statement. The Board members who assented to this Statement did so on the basis of the overall considerations; individual members gave greater weight to some factors than to others.

Nature of the Problem

56. Operations and transactions of an enterprise are affected by the changing prices of goods and services it buys and sells relative to a unit of currency, which is usually also the measuring unit for financial reporting.

57. If the enterprise operates in more than one currency environment, it is affected by the changing prices of goods and services in more than one economic environment and, additionally, by changes in relative prices among the several units of currency in which it conducts its business.

---

[8]Statement 8, paragraphs 50-52.

[9]Interpretation 15, paragraph 4.

58. The accounting model, generally referred to as the historical cost model, does not generally recognize the effect of changing prices of goods and services until there has been an exchange transaction, usually a sale or purchase. In general, then, it does not recognize unrealized holding gains resulting from changes in the price of goods and services relative to the unit of currency.

59. For enterprises conducting activities in more than a single currency, the practical necessities of financial reporting in a single currency require that the changing prices between two units of currency be accommodated in some fashion. People generally agree on this practical necessity but disagree on concepts and details of implementation. As a result, there is significant disagreement among informed observers regarding the basic nature, information content, and meaning of results produced by various methods of translating amounts from foreign currencies into the reporting currency. Each method has strong proponents and severe critics.

60. In dealing with this dilemma, the Board was faced with the following basic choices:

a. Changing the accounting model to one that recognizes currently the effects of all changing prices in the primary financial statements
b. Deferring any recognition of changing currency prices until they are realized by an actual exchange of foreign currency into the reporting currency
c. Recognizing currently the effect of changing currency prices on the carrying amounts of designated foreign assets and liabilities
d. Recognizing currently the effect of changing currency prices on the carrying amounts of all foreign assets and liabilities

61. Alternative (a) runs counter to the Board's approach in Statement 33, which fosters experimentation with supplemental reporting to test the feasibility, usefulness, and cost of various techniques for reporting the effects of changing prices. Accordingly, the Board did not consider a change in the primary financial statement model to be a reasonable alternative for this project on foreign currency translation.

62. Alternative (b) has little or no support from the Board or its constituents. All transactions and balances would be translated at historical exchange rates—a formidable clerical task—until conversion to the parent's currency occurred. Postponing recognition would fail to reflect the effects of possibly very significant economic events at the time they occurred, particularly those that affect transactions that must be settled under changed currency prices. Most would consider this a retreat rather than an advance toward more useful financial reporting.

63. Alternative (c) is the approach taken in Statement 8. Although some believe this approach is conceptually consistent with the historical cost model, others do not agree. In any event, this approach has produced results that the Board and many constituents believe do not reflect the underlying economic reality of many foreign operations and thereby produces results that are not relevant. A summary of the more common criticisms of Statement 8 is included in paragraphs 153-156 of Appendix D.

64. Some constituents urged the Board to introduce a selective departure from the rationale of Statement 8 by simply adding selected assets to or deleting selected liabilities from the list of those for which the effect of changing currency prices is currently recognized under Statement 8. The most frequent proposals would translate all or some portion of inventory at current exchange rates. This approach would reduce the reported exchange gains and losses of many enterprises, but it would increase the reported exchange gains and losses of other enterprises. It would do nothing to lessen the impact of temporal method gains and losses on enterprises that have no significant amounts of inventory, such as financial institutions; nor would it resolve problems caused by large amounts of debt-financed property, plant, and equipment. Thus, it is not a general cure for the cited deficiencies and it has little or no conceptual basis.

65. Those who advocate a limited modification to translate inventories at the current rate generally oppose translating property, plant, and equipment and other nonmonetary assets on the same basis. As a result, depreciation allocated to inventory and cost of sales would be translated at the current rate, while depreciation allocated directly to expense would be translated at historical rates. This is inconsistent in concept and result. In the absence of any conceptual distinction among nonmonetary items, the list of modifications would be subject to requests for continuous revisions that could be assessed only on an arbitrary, ad hoc basis. Selective modifications of Statement 8 were rejected by the Board primarily on those grounds.

66. The Board decided that, of the practical alternatives available to it, alternative (d) has the most conceptual merit, particularly for foreign operations that are reasonably self-contained. It will result in reports of financial condition and results of operations that, within the constraints of the historical cost model, will most closely reflect economic effects.

67. The problem is complicated by the fact that foreign operations differ greatly in structure and substance. In some situations, only certain assets and liabilities are exposed to foreign exchange risk, whereas in others the entire foreign operation or net

investment is exposed to foreign exchange risk. These differences can significantly change the economic effect of exchange rate fluctuations.

68. The Board agreed that these variations in economic facts and circumstances should be recognized to the degree it is practical to do so and, accordingly, settled on the functional currency approach to translation as one that accommodates alternative (d) above, but recognizes situational differences. The nature of these differences and guidance for identifying the functional currency appears in paragraphs 41 and 42 of Appendix A.

69. A feature of the functional currency approach is the current rate translation method. The Board recognizes that the current rate method, although common in some other countries, has not been extensively used in the United States. Based on extensive study and due process, however, the Board believes that the functional currency approach best recognizes the substantive differences among foreign operations and best reflects the underlying economic effects of exchange rate changes in the consolidated financial statements. The functional currency approach encompasses:

a. Identifying the functional currency of the entity's economic environment
b. Measuring all elements of the financial statements in the functional currency
c. Using the current exchange rate for translation from the functional currency to the reporting currency, if they are different
d. Distinguishing the economic impact of changes in exchange rates on a net investment from the impact of such changes on individual assets and liabilities that are receivable or payable in currencies other than the functional currency

Objectives of Translation

70. The functional currency approach was adopted after considering the following objectives of foreign currency translation:

a. To provide information that is generally compatible with the expected economic effects of a rate change on an enterprise's cash flows and equity
b. To present the consolidated financial statements of an enterprise in conformity with U.S. generally accepted accounting principles
c. To reflect in consolidated financial statements the financial results and relationships of the individual consolidated entities as measured in their functional currencies

d. To use a "single unit of measure" for financial statements that include translated foreign amounts

71. Objective (a), to provide information that is generally compatible with the expected economic effects of a rate change, was adopted by the Board as the basic objective. This was responsive to the pervasive criticism that translation results under Statement 8 do not reflect the underlying reality of foreign operations. The Board focused on two aspects of accounting results and their compatibility with the economic effects of a rate change—changes in equity and cash flow consequences. Compatibility in terms of effect on equity is achieved, for example, if an exchange rate change that is favorable to an enterprise's exposed position produces an accounting result that increases equity. Compatibility in terms of cash flow consequences is achieved if rate changes that are reasonably expected to impact either functional or reporting currency cash flows are reflected as gains or losses in determining net income for the period, and the effect of rate changes that have only remote and uncertain implications for realization are excluded from determining net income for the period.

72. The Board believes that objective (b), conformity with U.S. generally accepted accounting principles, is implicit in and basic to the purpose of all the Board's activities on every technical project and need not be singled out as a separate objective for foreign currency translation.

73. The primary focus of financial reporting is information about an enterprise's performance provided by measures of income and its components. Those who are concerned with the prospects for net cash flows are especially interested in that information.[10] The prospects for net cash flows of a foreign entity are necessarily derived from its performance in terms of transactions and events that occur in its functional currency; in turn, prospects for net cash flows to the consolidated enterprise from the foreign entity are necessarily derived from reinvestment of those functional currency net cash flows or their conversion and distribution. Accordingly, the Board believes that the performance of a foreign entity is best measured by U.S. generally accepted accounting principles applied in terms of the functional currency in which the entity primarily conducts its business, generates and expends cash, and reinvests or converts and distributes cash to its parent.

74. The purpose of translating the functional currency to the reporting currency, if the two are different, is to restate the functional currency financial

---

[10]FASB Concepts Statement No. 1, *Objectives of Financial Reporting by Business Enterprises,* paragraph 43.

statements in terms of the reporting currency for inclusion in consolidated financial statements. The process should retain the financial results and relationships that were created in the economic environment of the foreign operations; it should not remeasure individual financial statement elements as if the operations had been conducted in the economic environment of the reporting currency. Only by retaining the functional currency relationships of each operating entity is it possible to portray aggregate performance in different operating environments for purposes of consolidation. Accordingly, in addition to adopting objective (a), the Board also adopted objectives (b) and (c) in combination.

75. Objective (d), to use a "single unit of measure" (for example, the dollar) for financial statements that include translated amounts, is the stated premise of the temporal method set forth in Statement 8. In the Board's view, that premise reflects in consolidated financial statements the transactions of the entire group, including foreign operations, as though all operations were extensions of the parent's domestic activities and all transactions were conducted and measured in the parent's reporting currency. That premise does not recognize that the assets, liabilities, and operations of foreign entities frequently exist, in fact, in other economic and currency environments and produce and consume foreign currency cash flows in those other environments. By requiring all foreign currency transactions to be remeasured as if they all had occurred in dollars, the "single unit of measure" approach obscures the fact that foreign entities acquire assets, incur and settle liabilities, and otherwise conduct their operations in multiple foreign currencies. Foreign operations are frequently conducted exclusively in foreign currencies, and the flow of dollars to the parent enterprise is dependent upon the foreign currency net cash flows generated by the foreign entity and remitted to the parent. Because it does not accord with relevant economic facts, reliance on a "single unit of measure" is not always compatible with the nature of foreign operations that is described and discussed in subsequent sections of this basis for conclusions. Accordingly, objective (d) was not adopted.

76. The Board also believes that, to the extent practicable, the accounting for the translation of foreign currency transactions and financial statements in the United States should harmonize with related accounting practices followed in other countries of the world. The Board maintained close liaison with representatives of the International Accounting Standards Committee and the accounting standards-setting bodies in Canada and the United Kingdom and Ireland as this Statement was developed. Representatives from each of those groups were active participants with the Board's foreign currency task force. The Accounting Standards Committee in the United Kingdom and Ireland has issued a proposed standard for foreign currency translation that is compatible with the standards set forth in this Statement.

The Functional Currency

77. An entity's functional currency is the currency of the primary economic environment in which the entity operates; normally, that is the currency of the environment in which an entity primarily generates and expends cash.

78. The Board believes that the most meaningful measurement unit for the assets, liabilities, and operations of an entity is the currency in which it primarily conducts its business, assuming that currency has reasonable stability.

79. Multinational enterprises may consist of entities operating in a number of economic environments and dealing in a number of foreign currencies. All foreign operations are not alike. In order to fulfill the objectives adopted by the Board, it is necessary to recognize at least two broad classes of foreign operations.

80. In the first class are foreign operations that are relatively self-contained and integrated within a particular country or economic environment. The day-to-day operations are not dependent upon the economic environment of the parent's functional currency; the foreign operation primarily generates and expends foreign currency. The foreign currency net cash flows that it generates may be reinvested or converted and distributed to the parent. For this class, the foreign currency is the functional currency.

81. In the second class are foreign operations that are primarily a direct and integral component or extension of the parent company's operations. Significant assets may be acquired from the parent enterprise or otherwise by expending dollars and, similarly, the sale of assets may generate dollars that are available to the parent. Financing is primarily by the parent or otherwise from dollar sources. In other words, the day-to-day operations are dependent on the economic environment of the parent's currency, and the changes in the foreign entity's individual assets and liabilities impact directly on the cash flows of the parent company in the parent's currency. For this class, the dollar is the functional currency.

82. The Board recognizes that some foreign operations will not fit neatly in either of the two broad classes described in paragraphs 80 and 81. Management's judgment will be required in order to select

the functional currency in those instances. Guidance for management in this process is included in Appendix A.

83. Experience with Statement 8, responses to both Exposure Drafts, and testimony at the public hearing repeatedly evidenced that no translation method can yield reliable or economically credible results if it fails to recognize differences in economic substance among different foreign currency operations. Statement 8 did not recognize those differences. Implicitly, the dollar was designated the functional currency for all foreign operations. For those operations for which the functional currency was, in fact, the foreign currency, the reported results created by exchange rate changes did not conform with the underlying economic facts and were, therefore, not understood or not credible.

84. Some allege that the functional currency approach does not "result in similar accounting for similar situations." The Board believes a significant virtue of that approach is that it provides different accounting for significantly different economic facts. Because the facts will sometimes give mixed signals, and because management's judgment will be required to identify, weigh, and interpret the facts within the objectives and guidance in this Statement, the Board acknowledges the possibility that, occasionally, situations that appear similar may be accounted for in different ways. That is always a risk when standards must be applied with judgment. The Board believes that risk is likely to do less damage to the usefulness of financial reporting than arbitrary rules that overlook economic differences and require different situations to be accounted for as though they were the same.

Consolidation of Foreign Currency Statements

85. Critics of the functional currency approach assert that it is not consistent with consolidation theory and that it violates the single entity and "single unit of measure" concepts that they believe underlie consolidated financial statements. The Board believes that, for an enterprise operating in multiple currency environments, a true "single unit of measure" does not, as a factual matter, exist.

86. As noted elsewhere, multiple units of currency are an economic fact of foreign operations, and a translation method cannot prevent the effects of multiple units from showing up in financial statements. The temporal method obscures the fact of multiple units by requiring all transactions to be measured as if the transactions occurred in dollars. As a result, it produces profit margins and earnings fluctuations that do not synchronize with the economic events that affect an entity's operations. All translation methods, including both the tem-

poral and current rate methods, involve multiple currency units at the foreign entity level and a single currency unit, the dollar, at the consolidated reporting level. They only differ in how they bridge from multiple units to the single unit.

87. Proponents of a "single unit of measure" would require the historical cost of inventories and property, plant, and equipment acquired by a foreign entity in a foreign currency to be measured in terms of the equivalent number of dollars at the date of acquisition; that is, they would translate the foreign currency acquisition cost using the historical exchange rate. Statement 8 is based on that proposition. At the same time, however, many of those same proponents recommend that present standards (that is, Statement 8) be improved by requiring the foreign currency acquisition cost of inventories to be translated using the current exchange rate. Whether that proposal is presented as a departure from their perception of generally accepted accounting principles that require inventories to be measured at historical cost or as a departure from their perception of a "single unit of measure" is not always clear. Whatever the nature of the exception, some of those recommending it would have it apply to all inventories acquired by a foreign entity, others only to inventories for which the last-in, first-out method is not used, others only for inventory acquired locally, and still others to various combinations of those possibilities. No matter how the proposal might be applied, it would be impossible to adopt it and retain both the "single unit of measure" and accounting for inventories at historical cost.

88. Statement 8 is frequently described as a faithful application of the "single unit of measure" and the historical cost principle. Most agree that the faithful application of the "single unit of measure" and the historical cost principle produces results that are not compatible with the expected economic effects of changes in exchange rates. The Board concluded that for many foreign entities, adhering to a "single unit of measure" was artificial and illusory.

89. The Board also considered the assertion made by some that the functional currency approach is inconsistent with the presentation of consolidated financial statements that include the individual financial statement elements (that is, assets, liabilities, revenues, expenses, gains, losses, etc.) of foreign entities. That assertion seems to be based on the notion that, because the functional currency approach generally considers the relevant economic effect of exchange rate changes to be on the net investment in a foreign entity rather than on certain of its individual financial statement elements, including in consolidated financial statements the individual elements that underlie that net investment is inappropriate. The Board believes that assertion is without merit.

90. As stated in paragraph 1 of ARB No. 51, *Consolidated Financial Statements:*

> The purpose of consolidated statements is to present, primarily for the benefit of the shareholders and creditors of the parent company, the results of operations and the financial position of a parent company and its subsidiaries essentially as if the group were a single company with one or more branches or divisions. There is a presumption that consolidated statements are more meaningful than separate statements and that they are usually necessary for a fair presentation when one of the companies in the group directly or indirectly has a controlling financial interest in the other companies.

91. The Board agrees with the presumption in ARB 51 that presenting in consolidated financial statements the individual assets, liabilities, revenues, expenses, and other elements that underlie a net investment in a foreign entity in which there is a controlling financial interest is indeed more meaningful than merely presenting the net investment as a single item, as in the parent company's separate financial statements. Nothing in the functional currency approach suggests that the various entities that are included in consolidated financial statements are not components of a single enterprise. The same individual financial statement elements are aggregated in consolidated financial statements using the functional currency approach as under the temporal method or any of the other methods found in practice prior to Statement 8. Measures of some of the elements presented in consolidated financial statements differ depending on the approach to translation, but the component entities and elements of the consolidated enterprise are the same.

92. Some have also suggested that adoption of the functional currency approach causes reporting currency measures of items presented in consolidated financial statements to depart from the historical cost model found in present practice. The Board has concluded that is not the case. Costs are incurred and exchange transactions take place in the functional currency; the functional currency approach preserves those historical costs and exchange prices. If the functional currency and reporting currency are different, translation of functional currency historical costs and exchange prices into their current dollar equivalent is essential to the process of consolidation, but the exchange rate changes affect the dollar equivalents of those historical costs and exchange prices, not the historical costs and exchange prices actually experienced by the foreign entity. As explained elsewhere, the Board concluded that the most relevant information about the performance and financial position of foreign entities is provided by the functional currency financial statements of those entities. Using the current exchange rate to restate those functional currency financial statements in terms of their current dollar equivalents preserves that most relevant information.

93. Those who believe that the functional currency approach is inconsistent with consolidation principles sometimes put the argument in terms of a U.S. perspective versus a local perspective. They contend that the local perspective incorrectly assumes that U.S. investors and creditors are interested in functional currency cash flows rather than in dollar cash flows. To the contrary, the Board has adopted the functional currency approach because it believes that approach provides the best basis for assessing an enterprise's dollar cash flows. The foreign entity's net cash flows are one source of dollar cash flows. However, it is only after a foreign entity has realized net cash flows in its functional currency that those cash flows can be converted to dollars. For example, the property, plant, and equipment of a foreign entity is used directly to produce functional currency revenues, and it is only indirectly through the entire earnings process of the foreign entity that the net functional currency cash flows become available for conversion into dollar cash flows.

Translation of Foreign Currency Statements

94. Fundamental to the functional currency approach to translation is the view that, generally, a U.S. enterprise is exposed to exchange risk to the extent of its net investment in a foreign operation. This view derives from a broad concept of economic hedging. An asset, such as plant and equipment, that produces revenues in the functional currency of an entity can be an effective hedge of debt that requires payments in that currency. Therefore, functional currency assets and liabilities hedge one another, and only the net assets are exposed to exchange risk.

95. If all of a foreign entity's assets and liabilities are measured in its functional currency and are translated at the current exchange rate, the net accounting effect of a change in the exchange rate is the effect on the net assets of the entity. That accounting result is compatible with the broad concept of economic hedging on which the net investment view is based. No gains or losses arise from hedged assets and liabilities and the dollar equivalent of the unhedged net investment increases or decreases when the functional currency strengthens or weakens.

96. If a foreign entity transacts business in a currency other than its functional currency, it is exposed to exchange risk on assets and liabilities denominated in those currencies. That risk will be reflected through gains and losses in the functional currency.

Those gains and losses affect the foreign entity's functional currency net cash flows that may be reinvested by it or converted and distributed to the parent. That is equally the case for transactions of the foreign entity denominated in the reporting currency.

97. Another aspect of the functional currency approach pertains to the financial results and relationships of a foreign entity. The functional currency approach views the parent company as having an investment in a foreign business whose foreign currency earnings are generated in its local economic, legal, and political environment and accrue to the benefit of the parent company in the amount of the dollar equivalent of those earnings. That concept views the accounts of the foreign business measured in its functional currency in accordance with U.S. generally accepted accounting principles as the best available indicators of its performance and financial condition.

98. A foreign entity's assets, liabilities, and operations exist in the economic environment of its functional currency. Its costs are incurred in its functional currency and its revenues are produced in its functional currency. Use of a current exchange rate retains those historical costs and other measurements but restates them in terms of the reporting currency, thereby preserving the relationships established in the entity's economic environment. Accordingly, use of the current exchange rate reflects in the consolidated financial statements the inherent relationships appearing in the functional currency financial statements. If a foreign entity is producing net income in its functional currency, the dollar equivalent of that net income will be reflected in the consolidated financial statements. If different exchange rates are used for monetary and nonmonetary items, as in Statement 8, the translated dollar results inevitably differ from the entity's functional currency results. At an extreme, if different rates are used for monetary and nonmonetary items, the results of operations for a foreign entity that, in fact, is operating profitably and is generating functional currency net cash flows may be converted to a loss merely as a result of the mechanical translation process. The Board believes that by preserving the actual indicators of performance and financial condition of each component entity, the consolidated financial statements will portray the best information about the enterprise as a whole.

99. Paragraph 12 of this Statement requires that a foreign entity's revenues, expenses, gains, and losses be translated in a manner that produces amounts approximately as if the underlying elements had been translated on the dates they were recognized (sometimes referred to as the weighted average exchange rate). This also applies to accounting allocations (for example, depreciation, cost of sales, and amortization of deferred revenues and expenses) and requires translation at the current exchange rates applicable to the dates those allocations are included in revenues and expenses (that is, not the rates on the dates the related items originated). The objectives of the functional currency approach, particularly as expressed in paragraph 70(c), might be best served by application of a single current rate, such as the rate at the end of the period, to those elements. This would, however, require restating prior interim periods or recording a catch-up adjustment in income if rates change. The Board therefore rejected this alternative on practical grounds.

100. Translation of the statement of changes in financial position was the subject of frequent comment on both Exposure Drafts on foreign currency translation. APB Opinion No. 19, *Reporting Changes in Financial Position,* permits some flexibility and judgment to meet the stated objectives of a statement of changes and the Board does not intend to change that either by prescribing the form and content of the statement of changes or by requiring a separate compilation of complete information for each foreign operation. However, Opinion 19 does require disclosure of all important changes in financial position regardless of whether cash or working capital is directly affected and that requirement is not changed in any way by this Statement.

101. The functional currency approach applies equally to translation of financial statements of foreign investees whether accounted for by the equity method or consolidated. It also applies to translation after a business combination. Therefore, the foreign statements and the foreign currency transactions of an investee that are accounted for by the equity method should be translated in conformity with the requirements of this Statement in applying the equity method. Likewise, after a business combination accounted for by the purchase method, the amount allocated at the date of acquisition to the assets acquired and the liabilities assumed (including *goodwill* or *an excess of acquired net assets over cost* as those terms are used in APB Opinion No. 16, *Business Combinations)* should be translated in conformity with the requirements of this Statement. Accumulated translation adjustments attributable to minority interests should be allocated to and reported as part of the minority interest in the consolidated enterprise.

Translation of Operations in Highly Inflationary Economies

102. Translation of operations in highly inflationary economies is frequently cited as a problem if

all assets and liabilities are translated using current exchange rates. In the historical cost model, a reasonably stable measuring unit is an essential ingredient to useful reporting of financial position and operating results over periods of time. Any degree of inflation affects the usefulness of information measured in nominal currency units. If historical costs are measured in nominal currency units in a highly inflationary environment, those measures of historical cost rapidly lose relevance.

103. Because it is a common condition, users of financial statements have developed tolerance for some inflation and in varying degrees compensate for it in their analyses. As inflation increases or persists, however, nominal currency units of the inflationary environment are not useful measures of performance or investment, and a more stable unit of measure must be found.

104. The point at which a substitute measuring unit is necessary is a subjective one. It depends on a number of factors, including the current and cumulative rates of inflation and the capital intensiveness of the operation. In principle, however, a more stable measuring unit is always preferable to a less stable one.

105. The Board has considered a number of alternative methods for restating to a more stable measuring unit. None of the methods is completely satisfactory at this time, either because they are deemed to be incompatible with the functional currency concept or because they involve some aspect of accounting for the effects of inflation in the basic financial statements. Statement 33 calls for experimentation with reporting the effects of inflation on a supplemental basis, not in the basic financial statements. Accordingly, in the 1980 Exposure Draft, the Board proposed not to specify special translation provisions for reporting on operations in highly inflationary economies, pending resolution of the issues being tested in supplemental reporting on the effects of inflation.

106. Virtually every respondent to the 1980 Exposure Draft who addressed translation of operations in highly inflationary economies pointed out that, unless special provisions are made, the proposed translation method could report misleading results. Accordingly, in the revised Exposure Draft, the Board proposed that the financial statements of a foreign entity with a functional currency of a country that has a highly inflationary economy be restated to reflect changes in the general price level in that country prior to translation. Many respondents objected to the revision, generally on one or more of the following grounds:

a. Information restated to reflect changes in the general price level should not be required in the primary financial statements until and unless the usefulness of that information has been adequately demonstrated in the Statement 33 experiment.

b. The primary financial statements should not mix information presented in constant measuring units that reflect changes in the general price level with information presented in nominal monetary units.

c. The lack of reliable and timely price-level indexes in some highly inflationary economies constitutes a significant obstacle to practical application of the proposal.

107. In view of the difficulties with the proposal, the Board decided that the practical alternative, recommended by many respondents, is to require that the financial statements of foreign entities in those economies that meet the definition of highly inflationary be remeasured as if the functional currency were the reporting currency. This is essentially a pragmatic decision. The Board nonetheless believes that a currency that has largely lost its utility as a store of value cannot be a functional measuring unit. If the reporting currency is more stable, it can be used as the functional currency without introducing a form of inflation accounting.

108. The revised Exposure Draft also allowed latitude for restatement of operations in economies that are less than highly inflationary. Many respondents believed that this flexibility would significantly reduce the consistency and comparability of reporting among companies. The Board agreed and removed the latitude in the final Statement.

109. The definition of a highly inflationary economy as one that has cumulative inflation of *approximately* 100 percent or more over a 3-year period is necessarily an arbitrary decision. In some instances, the trend of inflation might be as important as the absolute rate. It is the Board's intention that the definition of a highly inflationary economy be applied with judgment.

Translation Adjustments

110. Translation adjustments arise from either consolidation or equity method accounting for a net investment in another entity having a different functional currency from that of the investor.

111. Translation adjustments do not exist in terms of functional currency cash flows. Translation adjustments are solely a result of the translation process and have no direct effect on reporting currency cash flows. Exchange rate changes have an indirect effect on the net investment that may be realized upon sale or liquidation, but that effect is related to

the net investment and not to the operations of the investee. Prior to sale or liquidation, that effect is so uncertain and remote as to require that translation adjustments arising currently should not be reported as part of operating results.

112. Assenting Board members hold two views of the nature of translation adjustments. Since both views exclude these adjustments from net income and include them in equity, the Board did not consider it necessary to settle on which view should be accepted.

113. The first view is described in terms of a parent (investor) with the dollar as the reporting and functional currency and an investment position in another entity with a functional currency other than the dollar. A change in the exchange rate between the dollar and the other currency produces a change in the dollar equivalent of the net investment although there is no change in the net assets of the other entity measured in its functional currency. A favorable exchange rate change enhances the dollar equivalent; an unfavorable exchange rate change reduces the dollar equivalent. Accordingly, the translation adjustment reflects an economic effect of exchange rate changes. However, that change in the dollar equivalent of the net investment is an unrealized enhancement or reduction, having no effect on the functional currency net cash flows generated by the foreign entity which may be currently reinvested or distributed to the parent. For that reason, the translation adjustment is reported separately from the determination of net income. That adjustment is accumulated separately as part of equity. Concepts Statement 3 defines *comprehensive income* as the change in equity (net assets) of an entity during a period from transactions from non-owner sources. The first view considers the translation adjustment to be an unrealized component of comprehensive income that, for the reasons given above, should be reported separately from net income.

114. The second view regards the translation adjustment as merely a mechanical by-product of the translation process, a process that is essential to providing aggregated information about a consolidated enterprise. An analogy may be drawn between the cumulative foreign currency translation adjustment and the difference between equity (net assets) measured in constant dollars and the same net assets measured in nominal dollars. Viewed as such, the translation adjustment for a period should be excluded from the determination of net income, reported separately, and included as a separate component of equity. In this respect, it represents a restatement of previously reported equity similar to that developed in constant dollar accounting to restate equity in constant dollars from an earlier

date to a current date after a change in the constant dollar unit of measure has occurred. Concepts Statement 3, in paragraph 58, anticipated that such restatements would be made to equity without being included in current-period comprehensive income.

115. Both views of the nature of translation adjustments report the same measure of net income and the same information about equity. The Board believes its requirements for disposition and disclosure of translation adjustments are consistent with both views.

116. The Board considered whether at some time the separately reported component of equity should be included in net income. Under the first view, the adjustments have already been included in comprehensive income and should not be included again. Any elimination of the separate component of equity should be accomplished by combining the different classes of items in equity. Under the second view, the translation adjustments are a direct restatement of equity, a form of capital adjustment. It would be contrary to that view to include them in income at any time.

117. Some respondents suggested that the translation adjustments be amortized to income over the lives or maturities of the individual assets and liabilities of the investee, or some relatively long arbitrary period. The Board did not adopt that approach because, as previously stated, translation adjustments are unrealized and do not have the characteristics of items generally included in determining net income.

118. The 1980 Exposure Draft called for recognition of translation adjustments in determining net income based upon permanent impairment of a net investment. That proposal was reconsidered and rejected. The Board concluded that any required provisions for asset-impairment adjustments should be made prior to translation and consolidation.

119. Pending completion of its project on reporting comprehensive income, however, the Board decided to include the accumulated translation adjustments in net income as part of the net gain or loss from sale or complete or substantially complete liquidation of the related investment. Sale and complete or substantially complete liquidation were selected because those events generally cause a related gain or loss on the net investment to be recognized in net income at that time. That procedure recognizes the "unrealized" translation adjustment as a component of net income when it becomes "realized." Although the information is probably marginal, the Board believes that this disposition is desirable until the concepts of reporting all components of comprehensive income are further developed. This dis-

position also can be considered to be in line with the existing view that nonowner transactions or events that change equity should be recognized in net income at some point.

Transaction Gains and Losses

120. A foreign currency transaction is a transaction that is denominated (requires settlement) in a currency other than the functional currency of an entity. Foreign currency transactions typically result from the import or export of goods, services, or capital. Examples include a sale denominated in Swiss francs, a Swiss franc loan, and the holding of Swiss francs by an entity whose functional currency is the dollar. Likewise, a Swiss franc denominated transaction by a German entity or other entity whose functional currency is not the Swiss franc is a foreign currency transaction. For any entity whose functional currency is *not* the dollar, a dollar-denominated transaction is also a foreign currency transaction.

121. The Board has concluded that gains and losses from foreign currency transactions have a different economic nature and therefore require different accounting treatment from that applied to adjustments arising from translating the financial statements of foreign entities from their functional currencies into the reporting currency for the purposes of consolidation. Accordingly, the accounting requirements for disposing of transaction gains and losses and translation adjustments are different.

122. Transaction gains or losses arise when monetary assets and liabilities (cash, receivables, and payables) are denominated in a currency other than the functional currency and the exchange rate between those currencies changes. They can arise at either or both the parent and the subsidiary entity level.

123. Transaction gains and losses have direct cash flow effects when foreign-denominated monetary assets or liabilities are settled in amounts greater or less than the functional currency equivalent of the original transactions.

124. The Board has concluded that such gains or losses should be reflected in income when the exchange rates change rather than when the transaction is settled or at some other intermediate date or period. This is consistent with accrual accounting; it results in reporting the effect of a rate change that will have cash flow effects when the event causing the effect takes place.

125. Some have proposed that a transaction gain or loss should be deferred if the rate change that caused it might be reversed before the transaction is settled. The argument is that to recognize transaction gains

and losses from rate changes in determining net income creates needless fluctuations in reported income if those transaction gains and losses might be canceled by future reversals of rate changes. The Board rejected the proposal on both conceptual and practical grounds. Past rate changes are historical facts, and the Board believes that users of financial statements are best served by accounting for rate changes that affect the functional currency cash flows of a foreign entity as those rate changes occur. The proposal is also impractical; future changes, including reversals, cannot be reliably predicted. As a result, a transaction gain or loss might ultimately have to be recognized during a period in which rate changes are unrelated to the recognized gain or loss.

126. The Board saw no conceptual basis for an alternative proposal for recognition of transaction gains or losses when unsettled balances are classified as current assets and liabilities (or as they became due within one year). Such a requirement would place emphasis on the balance sheet classification or settlement date rather than on the economic effect of the exchange rate movement. It would also add a further accounting complexity without a compensating benefit.

127. Others have proposed that transaction gains and losses, particularly those related to long-term debt, should be deferred and amortized over the life of the related liabilities as part of the costs of borrowing. The Board agrees that transaction gains and losses on amounts borrowed in a different currency might be considered part of the cost of the borrowed funds. However, no rational procedure can be prescribed to accrue the total cost at an average effective rate because until the liability is settled that average rate cannot be objectively determined. Amortization of the effect of past exchange rate changes over the remaining life of the borrowing does not accomplish that result. It changes the pattern of gain or loss recognition in net income, but it may retain much of the volatility that advocates seek to eliminate. Further, amortization allocates the effect of an exchange rate change to periods not related in any way to changes in rates or other economic events affecting the enterprise.

Foreign Currency Transactions That Hedge a Net Investment

128. Paragraph 20(a) of this Statement provides that transaction gains and losses attributable to a foreign currency transaction that is designated as, and is effective as, an economic hedge of a net investment in a foreign entity shall be reported in the same manner as translation adjustments and that such accounting shall commence as of the designation date. If a foreign currency transaction is in fact an economic hedge of a net investment, then the

accounting for the effect of a rate change on the transaction should be the same as the accounting for the effect of the rate change on the net investment, that is, both of those partially or fully offsetting amounts should be included in the separate component of equity.

129. An example of the situation contemplated in paragraph 20(a) would be a U.S. parent company with a net investment in a subsidiary that is located in Switzerland and for which the Swiss franc is the functional currency. The U.S. parent might also borrow Swiss francs and designate the Swiss franc loan as a hedge of the net investment in the Swiss subsidiary. The loan is denominated in Swiss francs which are not the functional currency of the U.S. parent and, therefore, the loan is a foreign currency transaction. The loan is a liability, and the net investment in the Swiss subsidiary is an asset. Subsequent to a change in exchange rates, the adjustment resulting from translation of the Swiss subsidiary's balance sheet would go in the opposite direction from the adjustment resulting from translation of the U.S. parent company's Swiss franc debt. To the extent that the adjustment from translation of the Swiss franc loan (after tax effects, if any) is less than or equal to the adjustment from translation of the Swiss subsidiary's balance sheet, both adjustments should be included in the analysis of changes in the cumulative translation adjustment and reflected in the separate component of equity. However, any portion of the adjustment from translation of the U.S. parent company's Swiss franc debt (after tax effects, if any) that exceeds the adjustment from translation of the Swiss subsidiary's balance sheet is a transaction gain or loss that should be included in the determination of net income.

130. Ordinarily, a transaction that hedges a net investment should be denominated in the same currency as the functional currency of the net investment hedged. In some instances, it may not be practical or feasible to hedge in the same currency and, therefore, a hedging transaction also may be denominated in a currency for which the exchange rate generally moves in tandem with the exchange rate for the functional currency of the net investment hedged.

Transaction Gains and Losses Attributable to Intercompany Transactions

131. Paragraph 20(b) of this Statement addresses transaction gains and losses attributable to intercompany foreign currency transactions that are of a long-term investment nature. Transactions and balances for which settlement is not planned or anticipated in the foreseeable future are considered to be part of the net investment. This might include balances that take the form of an advance or a demand

note payable provided that payment is not planned or anticipated in the foreseeable future. Accordingly, related gains or losses are to be reported and accumulated in the same manner as translation adjustments when financial statements for those entities are consolidated, combined, or accounted for by the equity method. Transaction gains and losses attributable to other intercompany transactions and balances, however, affect functional currency cash flows; and increases or decreases in actual and expected functional currency cash flows should be included in determining net income for the period in which exchange rates change.

Foreign Currency Transactions That Hedge Foreign Currency Commitments

132. In response to the Board's invitation for public comment on Statements 1-12, most of the comments received that addressed accounting for forward exchange contracts requested that the Board reconsider the requirement that a forward contract must extend from the foreign currency commitment date to the anticipated transaction date or a later date if the forward contract is to be accounted for as a hedge of a foreign currency commitment. Other commentators have requested that transactions other than forward exchange contracts (for example, a cash balance) also should be accounted for as a hedge of a commitment.

133. The Board believes that if a foreign currency commitment is hedged by a forward contract or by any other type of foreign currency transaction, the accounting for the foreign currency transaction should reflect the economic hedge of the foreign currency commitment. The existence of an economic hedge is a question of fact, not of form. Therefore, the Board did not require any linkage of the date of the hedging transaction with the date of the hedged commitment. However, the foreign currency transaction must be designated as, and effective as, a hedge of a foreign currency commitment. In some instances, it may not be practical or feasible to hedge in the same currency and, therefore, a hedging transaction also may be denominated in a currency for which the exchange rate generally moves in tandem with the exchange rate for the currency in which the hedged commitment is denominated.

Income Tax Consequences of Rate Changes

134. The Board has concluded that interperiod tax allocation is required if transaction gains and losses from foreign currency transactions are included in income in a different period for financial statement purposes than for tax purposes. This is consistent with the requirements of Opinion 11.

135. The Board also has considered the possible need to provide deferred taxes related to translation adjustments resulting from translation of functional currency statements. Translation adjustments are accumulated and reported in a separate component of equity. Reported as such, translation adjustments do not affect pretax accounting income and most such adjustments also do not affect taxable income. Adjustments that do not affect either accounting income or taxable income do not create timing differences as defined by Opinion 11. However, reporting those adjustments as a component of equity does have the effect of increasing or decreasing equity, that is, increasing or decreasing an enterprise's net assets. Potential future tax effects related to those adjustments would partially offset the increase or decrease in net assets. Therefore, the Board decided that timing differences relating to translation adjustments should be accounted for in the same way as timing differences relating to accounting income. The need for and the amount of deferred taxes should be determined according to the other requirements of Opinions 11, 23, and 24. For example, paragraph 23 of this Statement provides that deferred taxes should not be provided for translation adjustments attributable to an investment in a foreign entity for which deferred taxes are not provided on unremitted earnings. Similarly, Opinions 11, 23, and 24 provide guidance as to how to compute the amount of deferred taxes. Deferred taxes on translation adjustments should be computed in the same manner.

Elimination of Intercompany Profits

136. An intercompany sale or transfer of inventory, machinery, etc., frequently produces an intercompany profit for the selling entity and, likewise, the acquiring entity's cost of the inventory, machinery, etc., includes a component of intercompany profit. The Board considered whether computation of the amount of intercompany profit to be eliminated should be based on exchange rates in effect on the date of the intercompany sale or transfer, or whether that computation should be based on exchange rates as of the date the asset (inventory, machinery, etc.) or the related expense (cost of sales, depreciation, etc.) is translated.

137. The Board decided that any intercompany profit occurs on the date of sale or transfer and that exchange rates in effect on that date or reasonable approximations thereof should be used to compute the amount of any intercompany profit to be eliminated. The effect of subsequent changes in exchange rates on the transferred asset or the related expense is viewed as being the result of changes in exchange rates rather than being attributable to intercompany profit.

Exchange Rates

138. The Board has concluded that if multiple rates exist, the rate to be used to translate foreign statements should be, in the absence of unusual circumstances, the rate applicable to dividend remittances. Use of that rate is more meaningful than any other rate because cash flows to the reporting enterprise from the foreign entity can be converted at only that rate, and realization of a net investment in a foreign entity will ultimately be in the form of cash flows from that entity.

139. If a foreign entity's financial statements are as of a date that is different from that of the enterprise and they are combined, consolidated, or accounted for by the equity method in the financial statements of the enterprise, the Board concluded that for purposes of applying the requirements of this Statement, the current rate is the rate in effect at the entity's balance sheet date. The Board believes that use of that rate most faithfully presents the dollar equivalent of the functional currency performance during the entity's fiscal period and position at the end of that period. Paragraph 4 of ARB 51 and paragraph 19(g) of APB Opinion No. 18, *The Equity Method of Accounting for Investments in Common Stock,* address consolidation and application of the equity method when a parent and a subsidiary have different fiscal periods. The Board believes its conclusion is consistent with those pronouncements.

Use of Averages or Other Methods of Approximation

140. Paragraph 12 permits the use of average rates to translate revenues, expenses, gains, and losses. Average rates used should be appropriately weighted by the volume of functional currency transactions occurring during the accounting period. For example, to translate revenue and expense accounts for an annual period, individual revenue and expense accounts for each quarter or month may be translated at that quarter's or that month's average rate. The translated amounts for each quarter or month should then be combined for the annual totals.

Disclosure

141. Paragraph 30 requires disclosure of the aggregate transaction gain or loss included in the determination of net income for the period. A transaction gain or loss does not measure, nor is it necessarily an indicator of, the full economic effect of a rate change on an enterprise. However, the Board believes that disclosing the aggregate transaction gain or loss may provide information about the effects of rate changes that is useful in evaluating and comparing reported results of operations.

142. Paragraph 31 requires an analysis of the separate component of equity in which translation adjustments, certain transaction gains and losses, and related tax effects are accumulated and reported. Generally accepted accounting principles presently require an analysis of changes in all equity accounts. Nevertheless, the Board has decided that it should specifically require an analysis of the separate component of equity disclosing the major changes in each period for which financial statements are presented. The analysis may be presented in a separate financial statement, in the notes to the financial statements, or as part of the statement of changes in equity. This separate component of equity might be titled "Equity Adjustment from Foreign Currency Translation" or given a similar title.

143. The Board considered whether an enterprise's financial statements should be adjusted for a change in rate subsequent to the date of the financial statements. The Board concluded that financial statements should not be adjusted for such rate changes. However, disclosure of the rate change and the estimated effect on unsettled balances pertaining to foreign currency transactions, if significant, may be necessary. If disclosed, the disclosure should include consideration of changes in unsettled transactions from the date of the financial statements to the date the rate changed. The Board recognizes that in some cases it may not be practicable to determine these changes; if so, that fact should be stated.

144. The Board considered a proposal for financial statement disclosure that would describe and possibly quantify the effects of rate changes on reported revenue and earnings. This type of disclosure might have included the mathematical effects of translating revenue and expenses at rates that are different from those used in a preceding period as well as the economic effects of rate changes, such as the effects on selling prices, sales volume, and cost structures. After considering information that it received on this matter, the Board has decided not to require disclosure of this type of information, primarily because of the wide variety of potential effects, the perceived difficulties of developing the information, and the impracticality of providing meaningful guidelines. However, the Board encourages management to supplement the disclosures required by this Statement with an analysis and discussion of the effects of rate changes on the reported results of operations. The purpose is to assist financial report users in understanding the broader economic implications of rate changes and to compare recent results with those of prior periods.

Effective Date and Transition

145. The Board considered and rejected both a completely prospective and a completely retroactive application of the accounting standards required by this Statement.

146. A completely prospective application was rejected because continued translation of previously acquired nonmonetary assets and related expenses at historical rates is inconsistent with the Board's other decisions regarding foreign currency translation. Regarding retroactive application, there are two possible effects resulting from the change to the accounting requirements of this Statement. Those effects are:

a. An increase or decrease in the enterprise's net assets resulting from translating all of a foreign entity's assets and liabilities at the current exchange rate for that entity's functional currency.
b. A reclassification between retained earnings and the new separate component of equity for cumulative translation adjustments so that retained earnings would equal an amount as if, since inception, translation adjustments had not been recognized in income and as if expenses related to nonmonetary items had not been translated at historical rates. (Such a reclassification between retained earnings and cumulative translation adjustments would have no effect on an enterprise's net assets or the total amount of equity.)

The Board has decided that the effect on net assets (first possible effect listed above) should be reported as the opening balance of the separate component of equity for cumulative translation adjustments as of the beginning of the year for which this Statement is first applied. Reclassification of amounts between retained earnings and the separate component of equity (second possible effect listed above) would require recomputation of amounts for all prior years for which an enterprise had foreign investments. The Board has decided that the benefits of such a recomputation, even if possible, would not justify the cost and should not be required.

147. The Board recognizes that Statement 8 accounting exposure has been hedged by the management of some enterprises and that different management actions might have been taken if Statement 8 had not been in effect. Therefore, restatement of financial statements presented for fiscal years prior to the effective date of this Statement is not required. However, restatement is permitted

and, if the prior fiscal year is not restated, disclosure of income before extraordinary items and net income for the prior year computed on a pro forma basis is permitted. If pro forma amounts are disclosed, such pro forma amounts should be computed in accordance with Opinion 20.

148. The Board's decision that this Statement should be effective for fiscal years beginning on or after December 15, 1982 is based on the belief that such an effective date will provide sufficient time for enterprises (a) to make any desired changes in financial policies that might be prompted by this Statement and (b) to prepare internally for the accounting requirements of this Statement. Enterprises that want to adopt the provisions of this Statement at an earlier date, however, are encouraged to do so. If adopted for a fiscal year ending on or before March 31, 1982, disclosure of the effect of adopting the new standard is required to provide comparability between those enterprises that do adopt and those that do not adopt the standard before the effective date. This disclosure is not required for fiscal years ending after March 31, 1982 because many enterprises will have terminated some or all hedges of the previous Statement 8 accounting exposure, thereby rendering any determination of the effect virtually impossible. Furthermore, the cost of requiring two systems of translation beyond early 1982 is not justified.

149. The Board is considering an amendment of Statement 33 to provide information that is compatible with the functional currency approach to foreign currency translation. The Board believes that the transition provisions of this Statement provide appropriate flexibility to accommodate any amendment of Statement 33.

Appendix D

BACKGROUND INFORMATION

150. The extensive currency realignments and the major revisions of the international monetary system in the early 1970s, together with the existence in practice of several significantly different methods of accounting for the translation of foreign currency transactions and financial statements, highlighted the need to address foreign currency translation at that time. Statement 8, which was issued in October 1975 and was effective for fiscal years that began on or after January 1, 1976, established standards of financial accounting and reporting for foreign currency translation and eliminated the use of alternative methods.

151. Responding to a recommendation by the Structure Committee of the Financial Accounting Foundation that it experiment with a more formal postenactment review process, the Board issued in May 1978 an invitation for public comment on FASB Statements 1-12, each of which had been in effect for at least two years. More than 200 letters were received, and Statement 8 was the subject of most of the comments received.

152. Respondents were nearly unanimous in their call for changes to Statement 8 but had conflicting views as to what those changes should be. Changes were suggested both in the method to be used in translating financial statements and in the method of disposition of the resulting translation adjustments and transaction gains and losses from foreign currency transactions. Most respondents who suggested changes in the translation method also suggested changes in the method of recognition of the resulting translation effects.

153. Respondents' concerns with Statement 8 reflect the perception that the results of translation under that Statement frequently do not reflect the underlying economic reality of foreign operations. The perceived failure of accounting results to portray the underlying economic circumstances is underscored heavily in two respects: (a) the volatility of reported earnings and (b) the abnormality of financial results and relationships. The sources of both problems are attributed to the requirements for (a) current recognition of unrealized exchange adjustments and (b) that inventories and fixed assets are translated at historical rates under Statement 8, whereas debt is translated at current rates.

154. Many respondents believe that the exchange risk exposure on foreign currency debt is effectively hedged in many cases by the foreign currency revenue potential of operating assets, but that this hedge is not recognized in the Statement 8 translation process. One result is large and frequent fluctuations in reported earnings, which many believe misrepresent the real performance of a company and obscure operating trends. Another result is said to be erratic operating margins and irregular financial relationships that make operating performance difficult to interpret.

155. Recommendations regarding changes in the method of translation of foreign currency statements were that some or all nonmonetary assets (primarily inventories and, less frequently, fixed assets) should be translated at current exchange rates or that long-term debt should be translated at historical rates.

156. The most frequently made recommendations regarding changes to Statement 8 were for some form of deferral or nonrecognition of the exchange adjustments that result from its application. Some

respondents stated that exchange rates are affected by rumor, politics, speculation, and other factors so that foreign currency exchange rates at any particular moment in time are temporary, and that changes over a relatively short time span are not likely to have a long-term effect on a company's earnings or financial position. Those respondents believe that exchange adjustments resulting from transitory rate changes are subject to misinterpretation because short-term rate fluctuations are poor indicators of long-term trends. Moreover, many of those respondents indicated that exchange adjustments from translation of foreign currency statements have not been realized and often will never be realized in amounts approximating the amounts reported in financial statements as required by Statement 8.

157. In January 1979, after considering the FASB staff's analysis of the comment letters, the Board added to its agenda a project to reconsider Statement 8. In February 1979, a task force was appointed to advise the Board during its deliberations on this project. The task force is composed of 22 members and observers from academe, the financial community, government, industry, and public accounting, as well as representatives from the International Accounting Standards Committee, the Accounting Standards Committee of the United Kingdom and Ireland, and the Canadian Institute of Chartered Accountants.

158. Subsequently, foreign currency translation was addressed at 18 public Board meetings and at 4 public task force meetings. In August 1980, the Board issued an Exposure Draft that set forth new proposals for foreign currency translation.

159. The Exposure Draft had a 3-month comment period, and more than 360 comment letters were received. The Board conducted a public hearing on the Exposure Draft in December 1980, and 47 organizations and individuals presented their views at the 4-day hearing.

160. Between January and June 1981, foreign currency translation was addressed at four additional public Board meetings and one public task force meeting. The Board's consideration of the issues resulted in modifications that the Board believed were significant in the aggregate. Accordingly, a revised Exposure Draft was issued on June 30, 1981.

161. The revised Exposure Draft had a 90-day comment period, and more than 260 comment letters were received. In October and November 1981, foreign currency translation was addressed at two additional public Board meetings and one public task force meeting. Consideration of the written comments resulted in further modifications as reflected in this Statement.

Appendix E

GLOSSARY

162. This appendix defines terms that are essential to clear comprehension of this Statement. They are set in **boldface type** the first time they appear in this Statement.

Attribute
The quantifiable characteristic of an item that is measured for accounting purposes. For example, historical cost and current cost are attributes of an asset.

Conversion
The exchange of one currency for another.

Currency Swaps
An exchange between two enterprises of the currencies of two different countries pursuant to an agreement to reexchange the two currencies at the same rate of exchange at a specified future date.

Current Exchange Rate
The current exchange rate is the rate at which one unit of a currency can be exchanged for (converted into) another currency. For purposes of translation of financial statements referred to in this Statement, the current exchange rate is the rate as of the end of the period covered by the financial statements or as of the dates of recognition in those statements in the case of revenues, expenses, gains, and losses. The requirements for applying the current exchange rate for translating financial statements are set forth in paragraph 12. Further information regarding exchange rates is provided in paragraphs 26-28.

Discount or Premium on a Forward Contract
The foreign currency amount of the contract multiplied by the difference between the contracted forward rate and the spot rate at the date of inception of the contract.

Enterprise
See Reporting Enterprise.

Entity
See Foreign Entity.

Foreign Currency
A currency other than the functional currency of the entity being referred to (for example, the dollar could be a foreign currency for a foreign entity). Composites of currencies, such as the Special Drawing Rights on the International

Monetary Fund (SDRs), used to set prices or denominate amounts of loans, etc., have the characteristics of foreign currency for purposes of applying this Statement.

Foreign Currency Statements

Financial statements that employ as the unit of measure a functional currency that is not the reporting currency of the enterprise.

Foreign Currency Transactions

Transactions whose terms are denominated in a currency other than the entity's functional currency. Foreign currency transactions arise when an enterprise (a) buys or sells on credit goods or services whose prices are denominated in foreign currency, (b) borrows or lends funds and the amounts payable or receivable are denominated in foreign currency, (c) is a party to an unperformed forward exchange contract, or (d) for other reasons, acquires or disposes of assets, or incurs or settles liabilities denominated in foreign currency.

Foreign Currency Translation

The process of expressing in the reporting currency of the enterprise those amounts that are denominated or measured in a different currency.

Foreign Entity

An operation (for example, subsidiary, division, branch, joint venture, etc.) whose financial statements (a) are prepared in a currency other than the reporting currency of the reporting enterprise and (b) are combined or consolidated with or accounted for on the equity basis in the financial statements of the reporting enterprise.

Forward Exchange Contract

An agreement to exchange at a specified future date currencies of different countries at a specified rate (forward rate).

Forward Rate

See Forward Exchange Contract.

Functional Currency

An entity's functional currency is the currency of the primary economic environment in which the entity operates; normally, that is the currency of the environment in which an entity primarily generates and expends cash. (See Appendix A.)

Local Currency

The currency of a particular country being referred to.

Reporting Currency

The currency in which an enterprise prepares its financial statements.

Reporting Enterprise

An entity or group whose financial statements are being referred to. In this Statement, those financial statements reflect (a) the financial statements of one or more foreign operations by combination, consolidation, or equity accounting; (b) foreign currency transactions; or (c) both of the foregoing.

Spot Rate

The exchange rate for immediate delivery of currencies exchanged.

Transaction Date

The date at which a transaction (for example, a sale or purchase of merchandise or services) is recorded in accounting records in conformity with generally accepted accounting principles. A long-term commitment may have more than one transaction date (for example, the due date of each progress payment under a construction contract is an anticipated transaction date).

Transaction Gain or Loss

Transaction gains or losses result from a change in exchange rates between the functional currency and the currency in which a foreign currency transaction is denominated. They represent an increase or decrease in (a) the actual functional currency cash flows realized upon settlement of foreign currency transactions and (b) the expected functional currency cash flows on unsettled foreign currency transactions.

Translation

See Foreign Currency Translation.

Translation Adjustments

Translation adjustments result from the process of translating financial statements from the entity's functional currency into the reporting currency.

Unit of Measure

The currency in which assets, liabilities, revenues, expenses, gains, and losses are measured.

Statement of Financial Accounting Standards No. 53
Financial Reporting by Producers and Distributors of Motion Picture Films

STATUS

Issued: December 1981

Effective Date: For fiscal years beginning after December 15, 1981

Affects: Amends FAS 32, Appendix A

Affected by: No other pronouncements

Issues Discussed by FASB Emerging Issues Task Force (EITF)

Affects: No EITF Issues

Interpreted by: Paragraph 6 interpreted by EITF Issue No. 87-10

Related Issues: No EITF Issues

SUMMARY

This Statement extracts the specialized accounting principles and practices from the AICPA Industry Accounting Guide, *Accounting for Motion Picture Films*, and AICPA Statement of Position 79-4, *Accounting for Motion Picture Films*, and establishes standards of financial accounting and reporting for producers and distributors of motion picture films. Exhibition rights transferred under license agreements for television program material shall be accounted for like sales by the licensor. The sale shall be recognized by the licensor when the license period begins and certain specified conditions have been met. Producers and distributors that license film exhibition rights to movie theaters generally shall recognize revenue when the films are shown. This Statement also describes how producers and distributors shall account for film costs and participation agreements.

Statement of Financial Accounting Standards No. 53
Financial Reporting by Producers and Distributors of Motion Picture Films

CONTENTS

INTRODUCTION

1. As discussed in FASB Statement No. 32, *Specialized Accounting and Reporting Principles and Practices in AICPA Statements of Position and Guides on Accounting and Auditing Matters,* the FASB is extracting the specialized[1] accounting and reporting principles and practices from AICPA Statements of Position (SOPs) and Guides on accounting and auditing matters and issuing them in FASB Statements after appropriate due process. This Statement extracts the specialized principles and practices from the AICPA Industry Accounting Guide, *Accounting for Motion Picture Films* (Guide), and SOP 79-4, *Accounting for Motion Picture Films,* and establishes financial accounting and reporting standards for **producers**[2] and **distributors** of **motion picture films** (films).

2. The Board has concluded that it can reach an informed decision on the basis of existing information without a public hearing and that the effective date and transition specified in paragraph 25 are advisable in the circumstances.

STANDARDS OF FINANCIAL ACCOUNTING AND REPORTING

Revenue

Films Licensed to Movie Theaters

3. Motion picture exhibition rights are generally sold (licensed) to theaters on the basis of a percentage of the box office receipts or for a flat fee in some markets. In certain instances, the licensor may receive a nonrefundable guarantee against a percentage of box office receipts. In some markets, for example in many foreign markets, those guarantees are essentially outright sales because the licensor has no reasonable expectations of receiving additional revenues based on percentages of box office receipts, particularly where there is a lack of control over distribution.

4. A licensor shall recognize revenues on the dates of exhibition for both percentage and flat fee engagements. In most cases, nonrefundable guarantees shall be deferred in the accounts and recognized

---

[1] The term *specialized* is used to refer to those accounting and reporting principles and practices in AICPA Guides and Statements of Position that are neither superseded by nor contained in Accounting Research Bulletins, APB Opinions, FASB Statements, or FASB Interpretations.

[2] Terms defined in the glossary (Appendix A) are in **boldface type** the first time they appear in this Statement.

as revenues on the dates of exhibition. Guarantees that are, in substance, outright sales, shall be recognized as revenue if the conditions specified in paragraph 6 are met.

Films Licensed to Television

5. Motion picture companies and **independent producers** and distributors (licensors) shall consider a **license agreement for television program material** as a sale of a right or a group of rights.

6. A licensor shall recognize revenue from a license agreement for television program material when the license period begins *and* all of the following conditions have been met:

a. The license fee for each film is known.
b. The cost of each film is known or reasonably determinable.
c. Collectibility of the full license fee is reasonably assured.
d. The film has been accepted by the licensee in accordance with the conditions of the license agreement.
e. The film is available for its first showing or telecast. Unless a conflicting license prevents usage by the licensee, restrictions under the same license agreement or another license agreement with the same licensee on the timing of subsequent showings shall not affect this condition.

7. Ordinarily, when the conditions specified in paragraph 6 are met, both the licensee and licensor are contractually obligated under a noncancelable license agreement and are able to perform in compliance with all the significant terms of the license agreement. If significant factors raise doubt about the obligation or ability of either party to perform under the agreement, revenue recognition shall be delayed until such factors no longer exist. Insignificant factors, such as the actual delivery of an existing print of a previously accepted film, are not a sufficient basis for delaying revenue recognition. Amendments to an existing license shall receive appropriate accounting recognition consistent with the accounting described in this Statement.

8. Revenues from the licensing of a film shall be recognized in the same sequence as the **market**-by-market exploitation of the film and at the time the licensee is able to exercise rights under the agreement. That time would be the later of the commencement of the license period (the right then being exercisable by the licensee) or the expiration of a conflicting license (the right then being deliverable by the licensor).

9. The amount of the license fee for each film ordinarily is specified in the contract, and the present value of that amount, computed in accordance with the provisions of APB Opinion No. 21, *Interest on Receivables and Payables,* generally shall be used as the sales price for each film.

Costs and Expenses

Production Costs

10. Costs to produce a film **(production costs)** shall be capitalized as film cost inventory and shall be amortized using the individual-film-forecast-computation method (paragraphs 11 and 12 and Appendix D). The periodic-table-computation method (paragraph 13) may be used if the result would approximate the result achieved using the individual-film-forecast-computation method. Amortization shall reasonably relate the film costs to the gross revenues reported and shall yield a constant rate of gross profit before period expenses. Amortization of film costs shall begin when a film is released and revenues on that film are recognized.

11. The individual-film-forecast-computation method amortizes film costs in the same ratio that current gross revenues bear to anticipated total gross revenues. That method requires the determination of a fraction, the numerator being gross revenues from the film for the period and the denominator being the anticipated total gross revenues from the film during its useful life, including future estimated total gross revenues from exploitation in all markets. Estimated revenues from the sale of long-term, noninterest-bearing television exhibition rights shall be included in the denominator in an amount equal to the total estimated present value of those revenues as of the date they are expected to be recognized, computed in accordance with the provisions of Opinion 21. Accordingly, in the period those revenues are recognized, the numerator shall include only that present value (not gross proceeds). The resulting fraction is applied to production and other capitalized film costs to determine the amortization for each period.

12. Due to the uncertainties in the estimating process, anticipated total gross revenues may vary from actual total gross revenues. Estimates of anticipated total gross revenues shall be reviewed periodically and revised when necessary to reflect more current information. When anticipated total gross revenues are revised, a new denominator shall be determined to include only the anticipated total gross revenues from the beginning of the current year; the numerator (actual gross revenues for the current period) is not affected. The revised fraction is applied to the unrecovered film costs (production and other capitalized film costs) as of the beginning of the current year.

13. The periodic-table-computation method amortizes film costs using tables prepared from the historic revenue patterns of a large group of films. That revenue pattern is assumed to provide a reasonable guide to the experience of succeeding groups of films produced and distributed under similar conditions. The periodic-table-computation method ordinarily is used only to amortize that portion of film costs relating to film rights licensed to movie theaters, and film costs accordingly shall be allocated between those markets for which the table is used and other markets. If that method is used to amortize film costs, the periodic tables shall be reviewed regularly and updated whenever revenue patterns change significantly. Such tables shall not be used for a film whose distribution pattern differs significantly from those used in compiling the table, for example, a film released for reserved seat theater exhibition.

Participations

14. If it is anticipated that compensation will be payable under a **participation** agreement, including residuals, the total expected participation shall be charged to expense in the same manner as amortization of production costs as described in paragraphs 10-13, that is, in the same ratio as current gross revenues bear to anticipated total gross revenues.

Exploitation Costs

15. Costs incurred to exploit a film **(exploitation costs)** that clearly benefit future periods shall be capitalized as film cost inventory and amortized as described in paragraphs 10-13. Examples of those costs are film prints, and prerelease and early release advertising that is expected to benefit the film in future markets. Cooperative or other forms of local advertising that are not clearly expected to benefit the film in future markets, and rent, salaries, and other expenses of distribution shall be charged to expense in the period incurred.

Inventory Valuation

16. Unamortized production and exploitation costs shall be compared with **net realizable value** each reporting period on a film-by-film basis. If estimated future gross revenues from a film are not sufficient to recover the unamortized film costs, other direct distribution expenses, and participations, the unamortized film costs shall be written down to net realizable value. Film costs that are written down to net realizable value during a fiscal year may be written back up during that same fiscal year in an amount not to exceed the current year write-down, if the motion picture company increases its estimate of future gross revenues. The adjustments shall be recorded in the interim period in which the revised

estimates are made; previously reported interim amounts shall not be restated. Film costs that are reduced to net realizable value at the end of a fiscal year shall not be written back up in subsequent fiscal years. In unusual cases, such as a change in public acceptance of certain types of films or actual costs substantially in excess of budgeted costs, a write-down to net realizable value may be required before the film is released.

Story Costs and Scenarios

17. The cost of film inventories ordinarily includes expenditures for properties, such as film rights to books, stage plays, original screenplays, etc. The stories and scenarios generally must be adapted to the production techniques for motion picture films. The cost of the adaptation is included in the cost of the particular property. Those properties shall be reviewed periodically and, if it is determined that a property will not be used in the production of a film, the cost shall be charged to production overhead in the current period. There is a presumption that story costs shall be charged to production overhead if the property has been held for three years and has not been set for production. Once charged off, story costs shall not be reinstated if subsequently set for production.

Investments in Films Produced by Independent Producers

18. Cash advances made by motion picture companies to independent producers shall be included in film cost inventory of the motion picture company. Amounts of loans to independent producers that are guaranteed by a motion picture company shall be recorded by the motion picture company as film cost inventory and as a liability when funds are disbursed. Revenues and expenses shall be accounted for and reported following the same principles described in paragraphs 3-17.

Balance Sheet Classification

19. A license agreement for sale of film rights for television exhibition shall not be reported on the balance sheet until the time of revenue recognition. Amounts received on such agreements prior to revenue recognition shall be reported as advance payments and included in current liabilities, if those advance payments relate to film cost inventory classified as current assets.

20. Either a classified or unclassified balance sheet may be presented. If a classified balance sheet is presented, film costs shall be segregated on the balance sheet between current and noncurrent assets. The following film costs shall be classified as current assets: unamortized costs of film inventory released

and allocated to the primary market, completed films not released (reduced by the portion allocated to secondary markets), and television films in production that are under contract of sale. All other capitalized film costs shall be classified as noncurrent assets.

21. The allocated portion of film costs expected to be realized from secondary television or other exploitation shall be reported as a noncurrent asset and amortized as revenues are recorded.

Home Viewing Market

22. Motion picture companies may earn additional revenues by licensing films to the **home viewing market.** Some of those transactions have characteristics similar to the transactions described in paragraph 3 of this Statement and some have characteristics similar to the transactions described in paragraph 5. Accordingly, programs licensed to the home viewing market shall be reported as described in paragraphs 3-21, as appropriate.

Disclosure

23. The components of film inventories (including films released, completed but not released, and in process and story rights and scenarios) shall be disclosed.

Amendment to FASB Statement No. 32

24. The references to the AICPA Industry Accounting Guide, *Accounting for Motion Picture Films,* and AICPA Statement of Position 79-4, *Accounting for Motion Picture Films,* are deleted from Appendix A of Statement 32.

Effective Date and Transition

25. This Statement shall be effective for financial statements for fiscal years beginning after December 15, 1981, with earlier application encouraged. Restatement of previously issued financial statements to conform to the provisions of this Statement is encouraged but not required.

> **The provisions of this Statement need not be applied to immaterial items.**

This Statement was adopted by the unanimous vote of the seven members of the Financial Accounting Standards Board:

Donald J. Kirk,
Chairman
Frank E. Block

John W. March
Robert A. Morgan
David Mosso

Robert T. Sprouse
Ralph E. Walters

Appendix A

GLOSSARY

26. This appendix defines certain terms that are used in this Statement.

Distributor
A film distributor owns the rights to distribute films, which are sold (licensed) to movie theaters, individual television stations, groups of stations, networks, or others. This definition excludes syndicators or other independent sales organizations that act only as sales agents for producers or owners of films under agreements that do not call for the sharing of profits.

Exploitation Costs
Exploitation costs are costs incurred during the final production phase and during the release periods of films in both primary and secondary markets. Examples of such costs are film prints, advertising, rents, salaries, and other distribution expenses.

Home Viewing Market
The home viewing market includes all means by which films are sold or otherwise made available to residential viewers for a fee. Examples are video cassettes and disks and all forms of pay television, including cable and over-the-air transmission.

Independent Producer
Motion picture companies frequently advance funds or guarantee loans for the production of films by independent producers. Certain legal rights of ownership, including the copyright, may be retained by the independent producer. The motion picture company frequently has a participation in the net revenues from the film and generally has additional attributes of ownership, such as the right to exploit the film and the risk of loss. The financing arrangement usually provides that the production loan by the motion picture company (or the guaranteed loan) is repayable only from the revenues from the particular film. The independent producer does not have general liability with respect to such a loan. Consequently, the motion picture company bears substantially all the risks of ownership.

License Agreement for Television Program Material

A typical license agreement for television program material covers several films (a package) and grants a broadcaster (licensee) the right to telecast either a specified number or an unlimited number of showings over a maximum period of time (license period) for a specified fee. Ordinarily, the fee is paid in installments over a period generally shorter than the license period. The agreement usually contains a separate license for each film in the package. The license expires at the earlier of the last allowed telecast or the end of the license period. The licensee pays the required fee whether or not the rights are exercised. If the licensee does not exercise the contractual rights, the rights revert to the licensor with no refund to the licensee. The license period generally is not intended to provide continued use of the film throughout that period but rather to define a reasonable period of time within which the licensee can exercise the limited rights to use the film.

Market

The first market in which a film is exploited is called the primary market because that is the market for which a film principally is produced. All other exploitation is in the secondary market. Generally, the markets are mutually exclusive; that is, a film cannot be exploited in more than one market at a time, because of the contract terms or sound marketing techniques.

There is only one first-run telecast of a particular film in a given market, and film rights are marketed in a manner to avoid conflict in a given market. For example, conflict may exist in a market between (a) theaters and television stations, (b) premium cable or broadcast subscription television and network television, (c) network television and local stations, and (d) two or more local stations within the market area. To avoid conflict between theaters and television, a producer may impose restrictions on distribution that would prohibit the licensing of the film for television while the film is being shown in movie theaters.

The market in which a film is exhibited is a prime determinant of the value of the film. A film's previous exposure in a market will generally have an effect on the price the exhibitor is willing to pay for exhibition rights. In addition, the size and demographics of a particular market and the audience's acceptance of the film affect the price that a telecaster can charge for advertising time.

Motion Picture Film (Film)

The term *film* refers to all types of films and video cassettes and disks, including features, television specials, series, and cartoons that are (a) exhibited in theaters; (b) licensed for exhibition by individual television stations, groups of stations, networks, cable television systems, or other means; or (c) licensed for the home viewing market.

Net Realizable Value

Net realizable value is the estimated selling price (rental value) in the ordinary course of business less estimated costs to complete and exploit in a manner consistent with realization of that income.

Participation

Frequently, persons involved in the production of a motion picture film are compensated, in part or in full, with a participation in the income from the film. Determination of the amount of compensation payable to the participant is usually based on percentages of revenues or profits from the film from some or all sources. Television residuals are comparable to participations and are generally based on the number of times the film is exhibited on television or as a percentage of revenues from such exhibition.

Producer

A film producer is an individual or a motion picture company that produces films for exhibition in movie theaters, on television, or elsewhere.

Production Costs

Production costs include the cost of a story and scenario to be used for a film and other costs to produce a film, for example, salaries of cast, directors, producers, extras, and miscellaneous staff; cost of set construction and operations, wardrobe, and all accessories; cost of sound synchronization; production overhead, including depreciation and amortization of studio equipment and leasehold improvements used in production; and rental of facilities on location. Production costs ordinarily are accumulated by individual films in four chronological steps: (a) acquisition of the story rights; (b) preproduction, which includes script development, costume design, and set design and construction; (c) principal photography, which includes shooting the film; and (d) postproduction, which includes sound synchronization, and editing, culminating in a completed master negative.

Appendix B

**BACKGROUND INFORMATION AND
SUMMARY OF CONSIDERATION OF
COMMENTS ON EXPOSURE DRAFT**

27. This Statement extracts the specialized accounting and reporting principles and practices from the Motion Picture Guide and SOP 79-4 and codifies them as FASB standards without significant change. Board members have assented to the issuance of this Statement on the basis that it is an appropriate extraction of those existing specialized principles and practices and that a comprehensive reconsideration of those principles and practices was not contemplated in the undertaking of this FASB project. Some of the background material and discussion of accounting alternatives have not been carried forward from the Guide and SOP. The Board's conceptual framework project on accounting recognition criteria will address revenue recognition issues that may pertain to those addressed in this Statement. A Statement of Financial Accounting Concepts resulting from that project in due course will serve as a basis for evaluating existing standards and practices. Accordingly, the Board may wish to evaluate the standards in this Statement when its conceptual framework project is completed.

28. The Guide was developed to clarify and standardize accounting by motion picture companies for revenues and costs, particularly the timing of revenue recognition and the treatment of production and exploitation costs. Before 1973, motion picture companies accounted for revenue from films licensed to television under several different methods, each of which resulted in recognizing revenue at a different point in time, ranging from the date the agreement was signed to apportioning the revenue over the license period. In addition, industry practice varied with respect to capitalization, amortization, and balance sheet classification of film costs. The Guide recommended that revenue from films licensed for telecasting be recognized when the license period began, the film became available to the licensee, and certain other specified conditions were met that, in effect, contractually obligated the licensor and licensee. The Guide also recommended the amortization of film costs by the individual-film-forecast-computation method and the write-down of those costs to net realizable value when estimated gross revenues were not sufficient to recover the film's unamortized costs.

29. An Exposure Draft of a proposed Statement, *Financial Accounting and Reporting by Producers and Distributors of Motion Picture Films,* was issued June 12, 1981. The Board received 23 letters of comment on the Exposure Draft. The Board's consideration of certain of the comments received are discussed in the following paragraphs.

30. Some respondents believe that a license agreement for television program material should not be considered as a sale of a right or a group of rights, but rather should be reported like an operating lease even though FASB Statement No. 13, *Accounting for Leases,* does not apply to license agreements. They believe that such an agreement has many characteristics of an operating lease. If a licensor accounted for a license agreement as an operating lease, revenues would be recognized over the license period and film costs would be amortized as revenue is recognized.

31. Other respondents believe that a license agreement differs from an operating lease and should not be reported like an operating lease. They believe that a license agreement is a sale of a right. They noted that the licensor has satisfied substantially all of its obligations at the date the film becomes available to the licensee and, accordingly, there is no basis for deferring recognition of revenue beyond that point. They further noted that each sale of a motion picture exhibition right constitutes the final step in the realization process and, accordingly, should be reported as income when the conditions specified in paragraph 6 (paragraph 8 of the Exposure Draft) have been met. The Board agrees with those respondents.

32. Paragraphs 22 and 23 of the Exposure Draft required the segregation of film costs between current and noncurrent assets. Generally, costs allocated to primary markets would be classified as current assets and costs allocated to secondary markets would be classified as noncurrent assets. Several respondents prefer an unclassified balance sheet because they believe that the distinction between primary and secondary markets has blurred in recent years. The Board agrees that a classified balance sheet should not be required (paragraph 20 of this Statement). However, the Board believes that if a classified balance sheet is presented, segregation between current and noncurrent based on primary and secondary markets continues to represent a more meaningful presentation for this industry than other possible methods.

33. Paragraph 17 of the Exposure Draft required exploitation costs that clearly benefit future periods to be capitalized and amortized using the individual-film-forecast-computation method. Costs to be capitalized would have included prerelease and early release national advertising. Cooperative and all other forms of local advertising and distribution expenses would have been charged to expense in the period incurred. Some respondents stated that, in recent years, cooperative and local advertising have

increased substantially, especially in major urban and local media centers. They believe that certain local advertising expenditures benefit future periods by developing a market for the film, thereby increasing its value in other markets. They believe that requiring those local advertising costs to be charged to expense as incurred may result in depressed operating results in the early release period of a film, even for a film expected to be commercially successful. Accordingly, they believe the reporting provisions in paragraph 17 of the Exposure Draft would have mismatched costs and revenues. The Board agrees with those respondents and has broadened the example of advertising costs that may be capitalized under paragraph 15 of this Statement.

34. Some respondents suggested that this Statement specify the accounting for films licensed to the home viewing market. They noted that recent technology has significantly expanded that market and that its increasing economic importance indicates a need for reporting guidance. They believe that some home viewing market transactions have characteristics similar to the transactions described in paragraph 3 (paragraph 5 of the Exposure Draft) and some have characteristics similar to the transactions described in paragraph 5 (paragraph 7 of the Exposure Draft). The Board agrees with those respondents. Accordingly, paragraph 22 has been added to this Statement to specify that films licensed to the home viewing market shall be reported in accordance with the principles described in paragraphs 3-21 of this Statement, as appropriate. A definition of the home viewing market also has been added to the glossary.

35. Paragraph 6 of the Exposure Draft stated that nonrefundable guarantees that are, in substance, outright sales, would be recognized as revenue on execution of a noncancelable contract. Some

respondents noted that film producers may sell off exhibition rights during film production and recognize revenue before the film is completed and available for exploitation. They suggested that such nonrefundable guarantees should not be recognized as revenue until the conditions specified in paragraph 6 (paragraph 8 of the Exposure Draft) have been met. The Board adopted that suggestion in paragraph 4 of this Statement.

36. Several respondents suggested other changes to the Exposure Draft. None of those proposed changes met the criteria for change included in the Notice for Recipients of the Exposure Draft. Accordingly, the Board did not adopt those suggestions.

Appendix C

ILLUSTRATION OF REVENUE RECOGNITION CONCEPT

37. This appendix illustrates when revenue shall be recognized under a license agreement for television program material in accordance with paragraphs 5-9 of this Statement.

38. Assumptions

a. End of Fiscal Year—December 31
b. Contract Execution Date—July 31, 19X1
c. Number of Films and Telecasts Permitted—4 films, 2 telecasts each
d. Payment Schedule—$1,000,000 at contract execution date, $6,000,000 on January 1, 19X2, 19X3, and 19X4
e. Appropriate Interest Rate for Imputation of Interest—12 percent per year
f. Fees, License Periods, and Film Availability Dates:

Film	Total Fee	Stated License Periods		Film Availability Dates
		From	To[3]	
A	$ 8,000,000	10/1/X1	9/30/X3	9/1/X1
B	5,000,000	10/1/X1	9/30/X3	9/1/X1
C	3,750,000	9/1/X2	8/31/X4	12/1/X1
D	2,250,000	9/1/X3	8/31/X5	12/1/X2
	$19,000,000			

For purposes of determining the present value of the payments in accordance with Opinion 21, it is assumed that the $1,000,000 payment on July 31, 19X1 and the $6,000,000 payments on January 1, 19X2 and 19X3 relate to films A and B and the

$6,000,000 payment on January 1, 19X4 relates to films C and D. Other simplifying assumptions or methods of assigning the payments to the films could be made.

---

[3]The actual license periods expire at the earlier of (a) the second telecast or (b) the end of the stated license period.

Film	Payment Date	Amount	Discounted Present Value (rounded to 000s) As of Date	Amount
A&B -	7/31/X1	$ 1,000,000	10/1/X1	$ 1,000,000
	1/1/X2	6,000,000	10/1/X1	5,825,000
	1/1/X3	6,000,000	10/1/X1	5,201,000
		$13,000,000		$12,026,000
C	1/1/X4	$ 3,750,000	9/1/X2	$ 3,219,000
D	1/1/X4	$ 2,250,000	9/1/X3	$ 2,163,000
		$ 6,000,000		

39. Income Recognition

Film	License Period From	To	Year of Income Recognition 19X1	19X2	19X3
A&B	10/1/X1	9/30/X3	$12,026,000(R)		
			331,000(I)(a)	$ 643,000(I)(b)	
C	9/1/X2	8/31/X4		3,219,000(R)	
				129,000(I)(c)	$ 402,000(I)(d)
D	9/1/X3	8/31/X5			2,163,000(R)
					87,000(I)(e)
			$12,357,000	$3,991,000	$2,652,000

(R) Revenue
(I) Imputed interest income
(a) Interest at 12 percent for 3 months on receivable of $11,026,000
(b) Interest at 12 percent for 1 year on receivable of $5,357,000 ($11,026,000 plus $331,000 less 1/1/X2 payment of $6,000,000)
(c) Interest at 12 percent for 4 months on receivable of $3,219,000
(d) Interest at 12 percent for 1 year on receivable of $3,348,000 ($3,219,000 plus $129,000)
(e) Interest at 12 percent for 4 months on receivable of $2,163,000

Appendix D

**ILLUSTRATION OF
INDIVIDUAL-FILM-FORECAST-COMPUTATION
METHOD OF AMORTIZATION**

40. This appendix illustrates the individual-film-forecast-computation method used by a licensor to amortize film costs.

41. Assumptions

• Film cost	$10,000,000
• Actual gross revenues:	
First year	12,000,000
Second year	3,000,000
Third year	1,000,000
• Anticipated total gross revenues:	
At end of first year	24,000,000
At end of second and third years	20,000,000

42. Amortization

Amount of
Amortization

First-year amortization

$$\frac{\$12,000,000}{\$24,000,000} \quad \times \quad \$10,000,000 \quad = \quad \underline{\$5,000,000}$$

Second-year amortization (anticipated total gross revenues reduced from \$24,000,000 to \$20,000,000) (a)

$$\frac{\$\,3,000,000}{\$\,8,000,000(b)} \quad \times \quad \$5,000,000(c) \quad = \quad \underline{\$1,875,000}$$

Third-year amortization

$$\frac{\$1,000,000}{\$8,000,000(d)} \quad \times \quad \$5,000,000(d) \quad = \quad \underline{\$\ \ 625,000}$$

(a) If there were no change in anticipated total gross revenues, the second-year amortization would be as follows:

$$\frac{\$\,3,000,000}{\$24,000,000} \quad \times \quad \$10,000,000 \quad = \quad \underline{\$1,250,000}$$

(b) \$20,000,000 minus \$12,000,000 or anticipated total gross revenues from beginning of period
(c) \$10,000,000 minus \$5,000,000 or cost less accumulated amortization at beginning of period
(d) The \$8,000,000 and \$5,000,000 need not be reduced by the second-year gross revenue (\$3,000,000) and second-year amortization (\$1,875,000), respectively, because anticipated gross revenues did not change from the second to the third year (paragraph 12). If such reduction were made, the amount of amortization would be the same as follows:

$$\frac{\$1,000,000}{\$5,000,000} \quad \times \quad \$3,125,000 \quad = \quad \underline{\$\ \ 625,000}$$

(This page intentionally left blank.)

Statement of Financial Accounting Standards No. 54
Financial Reporting and Changing Prices: Investment Companies

an amendment of FASB Statement No. 33

STATUS

Issued: January 1982

Effective Date: January 27, 1982 retroactive to fiscal years ending on or after December 25, 1979

Affects: Amends FAS 33, paragraph 23

Affected by: Superseded by FAS 89

Statement of Financial Accounting Standards No. 55
Determining whether a Convertible Security Is a Common Stock Equivalent

an amendment of APB Opinion No. 15

STATUS

Issued: February 1982

Effective Date: For convertible securities issued after February 28, 1982

Affects: Amends APB 15, paragraph 33 and footnote 10

Affected by: Superseded by FAS 111

Statement of Financial Accounting Standards No. 56
Designation of AICPA Guide and Statement of
Position (SOP) 81-1 on Contractor Accounting
and SOP 81-2 concerning Hospital-Related
Organizations as Preferable for Purposes of
Applying APB Opinion 20

an amendment of FASB Statement No. 32

STATUS

Issued: February 1982

Effective Date: For fiscal years beginning after December 31, 1981

Affects: Amends FAS 32, Appendixes A and B

Affected by: Superseded by FAS 111

(The next page is 552.)

Statement of Financial Accounting Standards No. 57
Related Party Disclosures

STATUS

Issued: March 1982

Effective Date: For fiscal years ending after June 15, 1982

Affects: No other pronouncements

Affected by: Paragraph 2 amended by FAS 96 and FAS 109
Footnote 2 amended by FAS 95

SUMMARY

This Statement establishes requirements for related party disclosures. The requirements of this Statement are generally consistent with those in Statement on Auditing Standards No. 6, *Related Party Transactions,* issued by the Auditing Standards Executive Committee of the American Institute of Certified Public Accountants.

Statement of Financial Accounting Standards No. 57
Related Party Disclosures

CONTENTS

INTRODUCTION

1. The FASB has been asked to provide guidance on disclosures of transactions between **related parties.**[1] Examples of related party transactions include transactions between (a) a parent company and its subsidiaries; (b) subsidiaries of a common parent; (c) an enterprise and trusts for the benefit of employees, such as pension and profit-sharing trusts that are managed by or under the trusteeship of the enterprise's **management;** (d) an enterprise and its **principal owners,** management, or members of their **immediate families;** and (e) **affiliates.** Transactions between related parties commonly occur in the normal course of business. Some examples of common types of transactions with related parties are: sales, purchases, and transfers of realty and personal property; services received or furnished, for example, accounting, management, engineering, and legal services; use of property and equipment by lease or otherwise; borrowings and lendings; guarantees; maintenance of bank balances as compensating balances for the benefit of another; intercompany billings based on allocations of common costs; and filings of consolidated tax returns. Transactions between related parties are considered to be related party transactions even though they may not be given accounting recognition. For example, an enterprise may receive services from a related party without charge and not record receipt of the services.

STANDARDS OF FINANCIAL ACCOUNTING AND REPORTING

Disclosures

2. Financial statements shall include disclosures of material related party transactions, other than compensation arrangements, expense allowances, and other similar items in the ordinary course of business. However, disclosure of transactions that are eliminated in the preparation of consolidated or combined financial statements is not required in those statements.[2] The disclosures shall include:[3]

a. The nature of the relationship(s) involved
b. A description of the transactions, including transactions to which no amounts or nominal amounts were ascribed, for each of the periods for which income statements are presented, and such other information deemed necessary to an understanding of the effects of the transactions on the financial statements
c. The dollar amounts of transactions for each of the periods for which income statements are presented and the effects of any change in the method of establishing the terms from that used in the preceding period
d. Amounts due from or to related parties as of the date of each balance sheet presented and, if not otherwise apparent, the terms and manner of settlement

---

[1] Terms defined in the glossary (Appendix B) are in **boldface type** the first time they appear in this Statement.

[2] The requirements of this Statement are applicable to separate financial statements of each or combined groups of each of the following: a parent company, a subsidiary, a corporate joint venture, or a 50-percent-or-less owned investee. However, it is not necessary to duplicate disclosures in a set of separate financial statements that is presented in the financial report of another enterprise (the primary reporting enterprise) if those separate financial statements also are consolidated or combined in a complete set of financial statements and both sets of financial statements are presented in the same financial report.

[3] In some cases, aggregation of similar transactions by type of related party may be appropriate. Sometimes, the effect of the relationship between the parties may be so pervasive that disclosure of the relationship alone will be sufficient. If necessary to the understanding of the relationship, the name of the related party should be disclosed.

3. Transactions involving related parties cannot be presumed to be carried out on an arm's-length basis, as the requisite conditions of competitive, free-market dealings may not exist. Representations about transactions with related parties, if made, shall not imply that the related party transactions were consummated on terms equivalent to those that prevail in arm's-length transactions unless such representations can be substantiated.

4. If the reporting enterprise and one or more other enterprises are under common ownership or management **control** and the existence of that con-

trol could result in operating results or financial position of the reporting enterprise significantly different from those that would have been obtained if the enterprises were autonomous, the nature of the control relationship shall be disclosed even though there are no transactions between the enterprises.

Effective Date and Transition

5. This Statement shall be effective for financial statements for fiscal years ending after June 15, 1982. Earlier application is encouraged but is not required.

> The provisions of this Statement need
> not be applied to immaterial items.

This Statement was adopted by the unanimous vote of the seven members of the Financial Accounting Standards Board:

Donald J. Kirk,	John W. March	Robert T. Sprouse
Chairman	Robert A. Morgan	Ralph E. Walters
Frank E. Block	David Mosso	

Appendix A

BACKGROUND INFORMATION AND BASIS FOR CONCLUSIONS

6. This appendix discusses the factors that the Board considered significant in reaching the conclusions in this Statement. Individual Board members gave greater weight to some factors than to others.

7. AICPA Statement on Auditing Standards No. 6, *Related Party Transactions* (SAS 6), and interpretations of SAS 6 provide guidance on related party financial statement disclosures. However, authoritative auditing pronouncements are intended to direct the activities of auditors, not of reporting enterprises.

8. As part of Accounting Series Release No. 280, *General Revisions of Regulation S-X,* the Securities and Exchange Commission integrated the disclosure requirements of SAS 6 pertaining to related party transactions into Regulation S-X. Regulation S-X, however, applies only to enterprises subject to the filing requirements of the SEC.

9. Because guidance for related party disclosures was not included in the authoritative literature on generally accepted accounting principles, the Accounting Standards Division of the AICPA asked the FASB to consider providing such guidance in a Statement of Financial Accounting Standards.

10. As discussed in paragraphs 12-18, the Board believes that it is appropriate to establish standards that apply to all enterprises for disclosure of information about related party transactions and certain control relationships. The Board has not undertaken a comprehensive reconsideration of the accounting and reporting issues discussed in SAS 6 and related interpretations thereof. The related party disclosure requirements contained in those documents have been extracted without significant change, except that this Statement does not address the issues pertaining to economic dependency. Other FASB projects may address issues related to those in this Statement, and the Board may reconsider the standards in this Statement when those projects are completed.

11. An Exposure Draft of a proposed Statement, *Related Party Disclosures,* was issued on November 6, 1981. The Board received 66 comment letters in response to that Exposure Draft. Certain of the comments received and the Board's consideration of them are discussed in paragraphs 19-22 of this appendix.

Usefulness of Related Party Disclosures

12. FASB Concepts Statement No. 2, *Qualitative Characteristics of Accounting Information,* examines the characteristics of accounting information that make it useful. That Statement concludes that for accounting information to be useful, it should be relevant (meaning that it has predictive or

feedback value) and reliable (meaning that it has representational faithfulness, verifiability, and neutrality). That Statement further concludes that information about an enterprise increases in usefulness if it can be compared with similar information about other enterprises and with similar information about the same enterprise for some other period or point in time.

13. Accounting information is relevant if it is "capable of making a difference in a decision by helping users to form predictions about the outcomes of past, present, and future events or to confirm or correct expectations."[4] Relationships between parties may enable one of the parties to exercise a degree of influence over the other such that the influenced party may be favored or caused to subordinate its independent interests. Related party transactions may be controlled entirely by one of the parties so that those transactions may be affected significantly by considerations other than those in arm's-length transactions with unrelated parties. Some related party transactions may be the result of the related party relationship and without the relationship may not have occurred or may have occurred on different terms. For example, the terms under which a subsidiary leases equipment to another subsidiary of a common parent may be imposed by the common parent and might vary significantly from one lease to another because of circumstances entirely unrelated to market prices for similar leases.

14. Sometimes two or more enterprises are under common ownership or management control but do not transact business with each other. The common control, however, may result in operating results or financial position significantly different from that which would have been obtained if the enterprises were autonomous. For example, two or more enterprises in the same line of business may be controlled by a party that has the ability to increase or decrease the volume of business done by each. Disclosure of information about certain control relationships and transactions with related parties helps users of financial statements form predictions and analyze the extent to which those statements may have been affected by that relationship.

15. Reliability of financial information involves "assurance that accounting measures represent what they purport to represent."[5] Without disclosure to the contrary, there is a general presumption that transactions reflected in financial statements have been consummated on an arm's-length basis

between independent parties. However, that presumption is not justified when related party transactions exist because the requisite conditions of competitive, free-market dealings may not exist. Because it is possible for related party transactions to be arranged to obtain certain results desired by the related parties, the resulting accounting measures may not represent what they usually would be expected to represent. Reduced representational faithfulness and verifiability of amounts used to measure transactions with related parties weaken the reliability of those amounts. That weakness cannot always be cured by reference to market measures because in many cases there may be no arm's-length market in the goods or services that are the subject of the related party transactions.

16. The Board believes that an enterprise's financial statements may not be complete without additional explanations of and information about related party transactions and thus may not be reliable. Completeness implies that ". . . nothing material is left out of the information that may be necessary to insure that it validly represents the underlying events and conditions."[6]

17. The Board also believes that relevant information is omitted if disclosures about significant related party transactions required by this Statement are not made. "Completeness of information also affects its relevance. Relevance of information is adversely affected if a relevant piece of information is omitted, even if the omission does not falsify what is shown."[7]

18. Information about transactions with related parties is useful to users of financial statements in attempting to compare an enterprise's results of operations and financial position with those of prior periods and with those of other enterprises. It helps them to detect and explain possible differences. Therefore, information about transactions with related parties that would make a difference in decision making should be disclosed so that users of the financial statements can evaluate their significance.

Consideration of Comments on Exposure Draft

19. Some respondents were troubled by the proposal in the Exposure Draft to require disclosure of only those transactions "that are necessary for users to understand the financial statements." They generally expressed the view that it would be difficult to apply such a criterion and that it was unclear how that criterion interacted with materiality judgments.

---

[4]Concepts Statement 2, paragraph 47.

[5]Ibid., paragraph 81.

[6]Ibid., paragraph 79.

[7]Ibid., paragraph 80.

In addition, some respondents also interpreted that language combined with the Exposure Draft's omission of the specific exclusion provided in SAS 6 for disclosure of compensation arrangements, expense allowances, and other similar items in the ordinary course of business as a requirement that such items be disclosed. The Board does not intend to imply that disclosure of related party transactions and certain control relationships is a separate objective of financial reporting, nor does the Board intend to introduce a new concept of materiality. Rather, disclosure of related party transactions and certain control relationships is required solely for the purpose of enhancing the understanding of the financial statements and the fact that such matters have, or could have, an effect on the financial statements. Disclosure of compensation arrangements, expense allowances, and other similar items in the ordinary course of business is not necessary for a user to understand the financial statements. The standard has been revised accordingly.

20. The Exposure Draft would have prohibited representations to the effect that related party transactions were consummated on an arm's-length basis. While recognizing the difficulty in many situations of determining the terms on which a transaction might have occurred if the parties were unrelated, many respondents pointed out that certain related party transactions occur on terms available to unrelated parties or on terms established by regulatory agencies. They believe that representations as to the terms of a related party transaction should not be prohibited if they can be substantiated. The Board agreed, and the requirement (paragraph 3) has been modified accordingly.

21. SAS 6 and interpretations thereof call for disclosure of the nature of common control relationships if the controlling party has the ability to affect the reporting enterprise in a manner that could lead to significantly different operating results or financial position than if the enterprises were autonomous. The Exposure Draft would have gone beyond those requirements to require disclosure of all control relationships. Some respondents expressed doubt about the usefulness of some of the disclosures that would result. They indicated that the requirement would be burdensome particularly for closely held enterprises that might have numerous relationships with owners and their families, lenders, and possibly others that might be deemed to be "control." The Board agreed that requiring disclosure of all control relationships might be of limited usefulness. Accordingly, the requirement (paragraph 4) was revised to conform more closely to that discussed in SAS 6.

22. Several respondents asked the FASB to provide additional guidance on disclosures about economic dependency but did not provide information to define the issues involved, nor did they provide evidence as to why additional guidance is needed. Therefore, the Board concluded that issuance of this Statement should not be delayed to consider that issue.

23. The Board has concluded that it can reach an informed decision on the basis of existing information without a public hearing and that the effective date and transition specified in paragraph 5 are advisable in the circumstances.

Appendix B

GLOSSARY

24. For purposes of this Statement, certain terms are defined as follows:

a. **Affiliate.** A party that, directly or indirectly through one or more intermediaries, controls, is controlled by, or is under common control with an enterprise.

b. **Control.** The possession, direct or indirect, of the power to direct or cause the direction of the management and policies of an enterprise through ownership, by contract, or otherwise.

c. **Immediate family.** Family members whom a principal owner or a member of management might control or influence or by whom they might be controlled or influenced because of the family relationship.

d. **Management.** Persons who are responsible for achieving the objectives of the enterprise and who have the authority to establish policies and make decisions by which those objectives are to be pursued. Management normally includes members of the board of directors, the chief executive officer, chief operating officer, vice presidents in charge of principal business functions (such as sales, administration, or finance), and other persons who perform similar policy-making functions. Persons without formal titles also may be members of management.

e. **Principal owners.** Owners of record or known beneficial owners of more than 10 percent of the voting interests of the enterprise.

f. **Related parties.** Affiliates of the enterprise; entities for which investments are accounted for by the equity method by the enterprise; trusts for the benefit of employees, such as pension and profit-sharing trusts that are managed by or under the trusteeship of management; principal owners of the enterprise; its management; members of the immediate families of principal owners of the enterprise and its management; and other parties with which the enterprise may deal if one party controls or can significantly influence the management or operating policies of the other to an extent that one of the transacting parties might be prevented from fully pursuing its own separate interests. Another party also is a related party if it can significantly influence the management or operating policies of the transacting parties or if it has an ownership interest in one of the transacting parties and can significantly influence the other to an extent that one or more of the transacting parties might be prevented from fully pursuing its own separate interests.

Statement of Financial Accounting Standards No. 58
Capitalization of Interest Cost in Financial Statements That Include Investments Accounted for by the Equity Method

an amendment of FASB Statement No. 34

STATUS

Issued: April 1982

Effective Date: For investments made after June 30, 1982 but optional for investments contracted for but not yet made at that date

Affects: Amends ARB 51, paragraph 10
Amends APB 18, paragraph 19(m)
Amends APB 20, paragraph 34
Amends FAS 34, paragraphs 9, 10, and 20

Affected by: No other pronouncements

SUMMARY

This Statement amends FASB Statement No. 34, *Capitalization of Interest Cost,* (1) to limit capitalization of consolidated interest cost to qualifying assets of the parent company and consolidated subsidiaries and (2) to include investments (equity, loans, and advances) accounted for by the equity method as qualifying assets of the investor while the investee has activities in progress necessary to commence its planned principal operations provided that the investee's activities include the use of funds to acquire qualifying assets for its operations. This Statement does not affect the accounting for and reporting of capitalized interest cost in the separate financial statements of investees.

Statement of Financial Accounting Standards No. 58
Capitalization of Interest Cost in Financial Statements That Include Investments Accounted for by the Equity Method

an amendment of FASB Statement No. 34

CONTENTS

INTRODUCTION

1. The FASB has received several inquiries concerning (a) the limitations of FASB Statement No. 34, *Capitalization of Interest Cost,* relating to capitalization of interest cost in situations involving investees accounted for by the equity method and (b) the inconsistent requirements between (i) the limitations of Statement 34 on the capitalization of interest cost in situations involving investees accounted for by the equity method and (ii) the requirement of APB Opinion No. 18, *The Equity Method of Accounting for Investments in Common Stock,* that income and owners' equity amounts should be the same whether a subsidiary is consolidated or accounted for by the equity method.

2. The basic issue is whether Statement 34 distinguishes qualifying assets owned by the parent and consolidated subsidiaries from those owned by unconsolidated subsidiaries, joint ventures, and other investees accounted for by the equity method for purposes of determining the amount of interest cost to be capitalized in the investor's financial statements. Although paragraph 15 of Statement 34 clearly limits the amount of interest available for capitalization in consolidated financial statements to that shown in those statements, neither paragraph 9 nor paragraph 15 of Statement 34 is explicit regarding any similar limitations on qualifying assets.

3. The Board has concluded that qualifying assets as described in Statement 34 are limited to those of the parent company and consolidated subsidiaries. The Board has also concluded that certain investments (equity, loans, and advances) accounted for by the equity method are qualifying assets of the investor (including parent company and consolidated subsidiaries). For the investment to be a qualifying asset, the investee must be undergoing activities in preparation for its planned principal operations provided that the investee's activities include the use of funds to acquire qualifying assets for its operations. The investment ceases to be a qualifying asset when those operations begin. Subsequent accounting for interest capitalized on the investment is specified by paragraph 19(b) of Opinion 18.

4. This Statement does not affect the accounting for and reporting of capitalized interest cost in the separate financial statements of investees.

STANDARDS OF FINANCIAL ACCOUNTING AND REPORTING

Amendments to FASB Statement No. 34

5. The following subparagraph is added to paragraph 9 of Statement 34, which specifies the qualifying assets for which interest is to be capitalized:

c. Investments (equity, loans, and advances) accounted for by the equity method while the investee has activities in progress necessary to commence its planned principal operations provided that the investee's activities include the use of funds to acquire qualifying assets for its operations.

6. The following subparagraphs are added to paragraph 10 of Statement 34, which specifies the types of assets for which interest is not capitalized:

c. Assets that are not included in the consolidated balance sheet of the parent company and consolidated subsidiaries

d. Investments accounted for by the equity method after the planned principal operations of the investee begin

e. Investments in regulated investees that are capitalizing both the cost of debt and equity capital

7. The following sentence is added to paragraph 20 of Statement 34, which specifies the accounting for interest after it is capitalized:

Interest capitalized on an investment accounted for by the equity method shall be accounted for in accordance with paragraph 19(b) of Opinion 18 which states: "A difference between the cost of an investment and the amount of underlying equity in net assets of an investee should be accounted for as if the investee were a consolidated subsidiary."

Amendments to Other Pronouncements

8. Paragraph 10 of ARB No. 51, *Consolidated Financial Statements,* requires accounting for a subsidiary on a step-by-step basis if control is obtained through purchase of two or more blocks of stock. Paragraph 19(m) of Opinion 18 requires retroactive adjustment for an investee that was previously accounted for on other than the equity method when that investee becomes qualified for use of the equity method. Paragraph 34 of APB Opinion No. 20, *Accounting Changes,* requires restatement of prior financial statements for changes in reporting entities. The following footnote is added to each of those paragraphs:

*The amount of interest cost capitalized through application of FASB Statement No. 58, *Capitalization of Interest Cost in Financial Statements That Include Investments Accounted for by the Equity Method,* shall not be changed when restating financial statements of prior periods.

Effective Date and Transition

9. This Statement shall be effective for investments made after June 30, 1982 except that investments contracted for but not yet made may be accounted for as specified in the next sentence. Investments existing at the effective date or date of earlier adoption of this Statement (a) may be accounted for according to the provisions of this Statement or (b) may continue to be accounted for by the method of interest capitalization previously used even though not in accordance with the provisions of this Statement. Earlier application is encouraged. This Statement may be applied retroactively for annual financial statements that have not been issued but shall not be applied retroactively for previously issued annual financial statements.

> **The provisions of this Statement need not be applied to immaterial items.**

This Statement was adopted by the affirmative votes of four members of the Financial Accounting Standards Board. Messrs. Block, Kirk, and Morgan dissented.

Messrs. Block, Kirk, and Morgan are not persuaded by the arguments in this Statement that an investor should consider an investment in certain types of investees accounted for by the equity method as a qualifying asset for purposes of applying Statement 34. They see merit in an approach that would permit the inclusion of the qualifying assets of the investee in the qualifying assets of the entity (parent company and consolidated subsidiaries) issuing consolidated financial statements. However, they are convinced that there are serious complications in application of such an approach (paragraph 19). They also acknowledge the validity of the argument (paragraph 11) that there is a fundamental distinction between (a) the individual assets acquired by subsidiaries that are considered to be an integral part of the entity issuing consolidated financial statements and (b) the individual assets acquired by other investees that are excluded from consolidated financial statements. Therefore, they favor an interpretation of Statement 34 that, for future transactions, consolidated interest should not be capitalized on the qualifying assets of investees accounted for by the equity method. They note that the investee is subject to Statement 34 and will capitalize its own interest on qualifying assets.

Members of the Financial Accounting Standards Board:

Donald J. Kirk,
Chairman
Frank E. Block

John W. March
Robert A. Morgan
David Mosso

Robert T. Sprouse
Ralph E. Walters

Appendix

BACKGROUND INFORMATION AND BASIS FOR CONCLUSIONS

10. As stated in paragraph 1, the Board has received several inquiries concerning (a) the limitations of FASB Statement No. 34, *Capitalization of Interest Cost,* relating to capitalization of interest cost in situations involving investees accounted for by the equity method and (b) the inconsistent requirements between (i) the limitations of Statement 34 on the capitalization of interest cost in situations involving investees accounted for by the equity method and (ii) the requirement of APB Opinion No. 18, *The Equity Method of Accounting for Investments in Common Stock,* that income and owners' equity amounts should be the same whether a subsidiary is consolidated or accounted for by the equity method.

11. Some believe that Statement 34 proscribes capitalization of consolidated interest cost on qualifying assets of investees accounted for by the equity method. They believe that there is a fundamental distinction between (a) the individual costs incurred and assets acquired by subsidiaries that are considered to be an integral part of the entity issuing consolidated financial statements and (b) the individual costs incurred and assets acquired by other investees that are excluded from consolidated financial statements. They believe that the individual assets, liabilities, revenues, and expenses reflected in consolidated financial statements should relate to only the entity defined by those consolidated statements (that is, to only the parent company and consolidated subsidiaries) and should be complete. They believe that the equity method of accounting for investees appropriately reflects only the consolidated entity's net investment in and share of net income of the investee. Otherwise, users cannot use the amounts reported in the consolidated financial statements for their assessments of financial trends and relationships of the consolidated economic entity (for example, sales, gross profit percentages, current ratios, returns on total assets, etc.). Those who would proscribe capitalization of consolidated interest cost on qualifying assets of investees accounted for by the equity method do not believe that Opinion 18 precludes differences in net income and owners' equity, depending on whether an investment in a subsidiary is accounted for under the equity method or the subsidiary is consolidated.

12. Others believe that Statement 34 properly does not distinguish between qualifying assets of the investor (parent company and consolidated subsidiaries) and those of investees accounted for by the equity method. They believe that Opinion 18 gener-

ally precludes differences in net income and owners' equity for investees accounted for by the equity method. Accordingly, they believe both qualifying assets and interest cost of all investees accounted for by the equity method should be included in the application of Statement 34. They believe that consistent application of Opinion 18 is necessary because changes in the form of a transaction could otherwise affect the amount of interest capitalized. For example, the amount of interest capitalized could be affected because of either differences in interest rates or amounts eliminated in preparation of the investor's financial statements if the parent were to borrow and lend to the investee instead of the investee's borrowing directly from an independent third party with the parent company's guarantee.

13. Still others believe that investments (equity, loans, and advances) in investees that have not begun their planned principal operations are qualifying assets. They believe those investments meet the intent of paragraph 7 of Statement 34 (which states that the objectives of capitalizing interest are (a) to obtain a measure of acquisition cost that more closely reflects the enterprise's total investment in the asset and (b) to charge a cost that relates to the acquisition of a resource that will benefit future periods against the revenues of the periods benefited) because the investor's funds have been invested in an asset that is not ready for its intended use until the investee commences those principal operations. They believe this is particularly evident in the case of projects organized by a limited number of investors to pool resources in developing production or other facilities. Others believe that investments in investees accounted for by the equity method are never qualifying assets because they believe that such investments do not meet the description of qualifying assets in paragraph 9 of Statement 34.

14. An Exposure Draft of a proposed Statement, *Capitalization of Interest Cost in Financial Statements That Include Investments Accounted for by the Equity Method,* was issued on September 30, 1981. The Board received 72 letters of comment in response to the Exposure Draft. Certain of the comments received and the Board's consideration of them, including various alternatives considered and reasons for accepting some and rejecting others, are discussed in the remaining paragraphs.

15. Several respondents to the Exposure Draft stated that investments in investees accounted for by the equity method should be considered qualifying assets only to the extent that the investments in the investee have been reinvested in qualifying assets as defined in Statement 34. The Board concluded, for the reasons cited in paragraph 11, above, that qual-

ifying assets as described in Statement 34 should be limited to those of the parent company and consolidated subsidiaries. The Board also concluded that an investment accounted for by the equity method that has not begun its planned principal operations should be a qualifying asset of the investor while the investee has activities in progress necessary to commence its planned principal operations provided that the investee's activities include the use of funds to acquire qualifying assets for its operations. An investment in an investee that is not undergoing activities necessary to commence planned principal operations is not intended to be a qualifying asset under this Statement. The Board believes these conclusions are consistent with the objectives included in paragraph 7 of Statement 34. The Board believes that consideration of the individual qualifying assets of investees accounted for by the equity method would contradict the rationale in paragraph 11, above, for exclusion from consolidated financial statements of the individual assets and liabilities of such investees.

16. Some respondents stated that including investments in investees accounted for by the equity method in qualifying assets of the investor is undesirable because it would result in an additional exception to paragraph 19 of Opinion 18 that states that net income and stockholders' equity are the same whether an investment in a subsidiary is accounted for under the equity method or the subsidiary is consolidated. The Board realizes that application of Statement 34 and this Statement may produce results that are an exception to paragraph 19 of Opinion 18; that is, consolidated net income and owners' equity may be affected by whether an investee entity is consolidated or accounted for by the equity method. The Board noted the existing exceptions in (a) paragraph 19(i) of Opinion 18 and (b) footnote 5 of FASB Statement No. 12, *Accounting for Certain Marketable Securities,* as establishing circumstances in which net income and stockholders' equity may differ, depending on whether an investment in a subsidiary is accounted for by the equity method or the subsidiary is consolidated. The Board believes paragraph 19 of Opinion 18 provides important general guidance but was not intended to be inviolable in specific circumstances.

17. Some respondents concluded that consolidated interest cost should not be capitalized on the investment in investees accounted for by the equity method. They believe that such investments do not meet the definition of a qualifying asset in Statement 34 because they are not constructed or produced for the consolidated enterprise's own use. The Board has concluded, for reasons cited in paragraphs 11 and 15, above, that the asset that is relevant for determining the qualifying assets of the consolidated group is the investment in the equity

method investee until the investee has begun its planned principal operations.

18. Several respondents suggested that subsequent investments in investees that have begun their planned principal operations should qualify for interest capitalization. They believe that allowing capitalization of interest cost on investments in investees accounted for by the equity method that have not begun their planned principal operations while prohibiting capitalization of interest cost on similar investments of an established investee that is undergoing substantial expansion creates a situation in which similar circumstances may be accounted for differently. If an investee has several distinct projects in process and each becomes operational at different times, these respondents believe that allocation of the investment by the investor should be allowed, with capitalization of interest cost taking place on those projects that have not begun their planned principal operations. The Board concluded that the investor's investment in the investee, not the individual assets or projects of the investee, is the qualifying asset for purposes of interest capitalization.

19. Some respondents suggested that the investor should capitalize interest in consolidation on its proportionate share of the equity method investee's average amount of qualifying assets on which the equity method investee has not capitalized interest. The Board considered and rejected this approach because it concluded that (a) the investment in the investee is the qualifying asset for purposes of interest capitalization, (b) only limited guidance is currently available for application of the method, and (c) it involves complex calculations using arbitrary assumptions. The Board recently added to its agenda a project that will consider issues regarding the proportionate method of consolidation and also believes that it would not be prudent to specify a method of accounting that is currently under consideration in a major agenda project and is not clearly defined in current accounting literature.

20. Some respondents asked for clarification of the term *when planned principal operations begin* to be able to determine when the investment in the investee that is the qualifying asset is "ready for its intended use" and interest capitalization ceases under Statement 34. The Board has used that term in this Statement to have the same meaning as in FASB Statement No. 7, *Accounting and Reporting by Development Stage Enterprises.* Statement 7 considers an enterprise to be in the development stage if planned principal operations have not commenced and if it is devoting substantially all of its efforts to establishing a new business through activities such as financial planning; raising capital; exploring for natural resources; developing natural

resources; research and development; establishing sources of supply; acquiring property, plant, and equipment or other operating assets, such as mineral rights; recruiting and training personnel; developing markets; and starting up production.

21. Some respondents stated that a form of "double counting" may result if the investor capitalizes interest on its investment in an equity method investee and that investment also includes the investor's share of the investee's earnings (losses) that, in turn, may reflect the investee's own capitalization of interest on its qualifying assets. The Board believes, however, that the interest capitalized by the investee is a cost like any other cost of acquiring a qualified asset and is not reflected in the investee's earnings any differently than those other costs (for example, materials and labor) that are included in acquisition cost rather than deducted as expenses in determining earnings. The Board also believes that in situations involving intercompany interest there should be little effect because capitalized intercompany interest should be eliminated in accordance with Opinion 18 and ARB 51.

22. A few respondents requested guidance regarding application of the proposed Statement to an investment by an investor in a regulated investee that is accounted for by the equity method while the investee is constructing qualifying assets. The regulated investee capitalizes both a cost of debt and a cost of equity capital during its construction period rather than the amount of interest that it would capitalize in accordance with Statement 34. That method imputes a cost to the investee's equity capital and recognizes that cost as part of the carrying amount of the asset under construction and as current earnings of the investee. Since the investor, by recognizing its equity in the investee's current earnings, includes its prorated share of that imputed cost in the carrying amount of its investment and in its current earnings, the investor should not capitalize an additional cost.

23. Some respondents requested clarification regarding the meaning of the term *goodwill* in paragraph 12 of the Exposure Draft. They suggested that the capitalized interest should be associated with the related assets of the investee and amortized on the basis of the estimated useful lives of those assets. The situation referred to in paragraph 12 of the Exposure Draft was generally limited to one in which the investee would not have underlying qualifying assets. The intent of this Statement is to require capitalization of interest cost on an investment accounted for by the equity method that has not begun its planned principal operations while the investee has activities in progress necessary to commence its planned principal operations provided that the investee's activities include the use of funds to acquire qualifying assets for its operations. Under those circumstances, capitalized interest cost may be associated with the estimated useful lives of the investee's assets and amortized over the same period as those assets. Interest capitalized on the investments accounted for by the equity method is amortized consistent with paragraph 19(b) of Opinion 18. This Statement therefore does not refer to goodwill.

24. Some respondents requested clarification regarding whether the transition provisions of the Exposure Draft permitted retroactive application in previously issued financial statements and whether a qualifying investment existing on the effective date may be included in qualifying expenditures. The Board has revised the transition provisions to indicate that retroactive application in previously issued annual financial statements is not permitted and to clarify that an investment existing or contracted for on the effective date or date of earlier adoption (a) may be accounted for according to the provisions of this Statement or (b) may continue to be accounted for by the method of interest capitalization previously used for those investments even though not in accordance with the provisions of this Statement. The Board concluded that an investor that made an investment or contracted to do so prior to the effective date of this Statement should not be required to change its method of accounting to conform to the provisions of this Statement.

25. The Board concluded that it can reach an informed decision on the basis of existing information without a public hearing and that the effective date and transition specified in paragraph 9 are advisable in the circumstances.

Statement of Financial Accounting Standards No. 59
Deferral of the Effective Date of Certain Accounting Requirements for Pension Plans of State and Local Governmental Units

an amendment of FASB Statement No. 35

STATUS

Issued: April 1982

Effective Date: April 1982 retroactive to fiscal years beginning after December 15, 1980

Affects: Amends FAS 35, paragraph 30

Affected by: Superseded by FAS 75

Statement of Financial Accounting Standards No. 60
Accounting and Reporting by Insurance Enterprises

STATUS

Issued: June 1982

Effective Date: For fiscal years beginning after December 15, 1982

Affects: Amends APB 11, paragraph 6
Supersedes APB 23, paragraphs 26 through 30 and footnote 11
Amends APB 30, footnote 8
Amends FAS 5, paragraphs 41 and 102
Amends FAS 32, Appendixes A and B
Amends FIN 15, paragraphs 2 and 4
Amends FIN 22, paragraph 7

Affected by: Paragraph 6 amended by FAS 97 and FAS 120
Paragraph 15 superseded by FAS 97
Paragraphs 38 through 40 and 60(f) superseded by FAS 113
Paragraph 45 superseded by FAS 115
Paragraph 45 amended by FAS 124
Paragraph 46 superseded by FAS 115 and FAS 124
Paragraph 47 amended by FAS 114
Paragraph 48 amended by FAS 121
Paragraph 49 superseded by FAS 91
Paragraph 50 amended by FAS 97
Paragraphs 50 and 51 amended by FAS 115
Paragraphs 55 through 58, 60(i), 60(j), and footnote 8 superseded by FAS 96 and FAS 109
Paragraph 59 amended by FAS 109
Footnote 7 superseded by FAS 115

Other Interpretive Pronouncements: FIN 40
FTB 84-3 (Superseded by FAS 96 and FAS 109)

Issues Discussed by FASB Emerging Issues Task Force (EITF)

Affects: No EITF Issues

Interpreted by: No EITF Issues

Related Issues: EITF Issues No. 92-9, 93-6, and 93-14 and Topics No. D-35, D-41, and D-54

SUMMARY

This Statement extracts the specialized principles and practices from the AICPA insurance industry related Guides and Statements of Position and establishes financial accounting and reporting standards for insurance enterprises other than mutual life insurance enterprises, assessment enterprises, and fraternal benefit societies.

Insurance contracts, for purposes of this Statement, need to be classified as short-duration or long-duration contracts. Long-duration contracts include contracts, such as whole-life, guaranteed renewable term life, endowment, annuity, and title insurance contracts, that are expected to remain in force for an extended period. All other insurance contracts are considered short-duration contracts and include most property and liability insurance contracts.

Premiums from short-duration contracts ordinarily are recognized as revenue over the period of the contract in proportion to the amount of insurance protection provided. Claim costs, including estimates of costs for claims relating to insured events that have occurred but have not been reported to the insurer, are recognized when insured events occur.

Premiums from long-duration contracts are recognized as revenue when due from policyholders. The present value of estimated future policy benefits to be paid to or on behalf of policyholders less the present value of estimated future net premiums to be collected from policyholders are accrued when premium revenue is recognized. Those estimates are based on assumptions, such as estimates of expected investment yields, mortality, morbidity, terminations, and expenses, applicable at the time the insurance contracts are made. Claim costs are recognized when insured events occur.

Costs that vary with and are primarily related to the acquisition of insurance contracts (acquisition costs) are capitalized and charged to expense in proportion to premium revenue recognized.

Investments are reported as follows: common and nonredeemable preferred stocks at market, bonds and redeemable preferred stocks at amortized cost, mortgage loans at outstanding principal or amortized cost, and real estate at depreciated cost. Realized investment gains and losses are reported in the income statement below operating income and net of applicable income taxes. Unrealized investment gains and losses, net of applicable income taxes, are included in stockholders' (policyholders') equity.

(This page intentionally left blank.)

Statement of Financial Accounting Standards No. 60
Accounting and Reporting by Insurance Enterprises

CONTENTS

INTRODUCTION

1. The primary purpose of insurance is to provide economic protection from identified risks occurring or discovered within a specified period. Some types of risks insured include death, disability, property damage, injury to others, and business interruption. Insurance transactions may be characterized generally by the following:

a. The purchaser of an insurance contract makes an initial payment or deposit to the insurance enterprise in advance of the possible occurrence or discovery of an insured event.

b. When the insurance contract is made, the insurance enterprise ordinarily does not know if, how much, or when amounts will be paid under the contract.

2. Two methods of premium revenue and contract liability recognition for insurance contracts have developed, which are referred to as short-duration and long-duration contract accounting in this Statement. Generally, the two methods reflect the nature of the insurance enterprise's obligations and policyholder rights under the provisions of the contract.

3. Premiums from short-duration insurance contracts, such as most property and liability insurance contracts, are intended to cover expected **claim**[1] costs resulting from insured events that occur during a fixed period of short duration. The insurance enterprise ordinarily has the ability to cancel the contract or to revise the premium at the beginning of each contract period to cover future insured events. Therefore, premiums from short-duration contracts ordinarily are earned and recognized as revenue evenly as insurance protection is provided.

4. Premiums from long-duration insurance contracts, including many life insurance contracts, generally are level even though the expected policy benefits and services do not occur evenly over the periods of the contracts. Functions and services provided by the insurer include insurance protection, sales, premium collection, claim payment, investment, and other services. Because no single function or service is predominant over the periods of most types of long-duration contracts, premiums are recognized as revenue over the premium-paying periods of the contracts when due from policyholders. Premium revenue from long-duration contracts generally exceeds expected policy benefits in

---

[1] Terms defined in the glossary (Appendix A) are in **boldface type** the first time they appear in this Statement.

the early years of the contracts and it is necessary to accrue, as premium revenue is recognized, a liability for costs that are expected to be paid in the later years of the contracts. Accordingly, a liability for expected costs relating to most types of long-duration contracts is accrued over the current and expected renewal periods of the contracts.

5. Title insurance contracts provide protection for an extended period and therefore are considered long-duration contracts. Premiums from title insurance contracts ordinarily are recognized as revenue on the effective date of the contract because most of the services associated with the contract have been rendered by that time. Estimated claim costs are recognized when premium revenue is recognized because the insurance provides protection against claims caused by problems with title to real estate arising out of ascertainable insured events that generally exist at that time.

APPLICABILITY AND SCOPE

6. This Statement establishes accounting and reporting standards for the general-purpose financial statements of stock **life insurance enterprises, property and liability insurance enterprises,**[2] and **title insurance enterprises.** Except for the sections on premium revenue and claim cost recognition and **acquisition costs** (paragraphs 9-11, 13-18, and 20-31), this Statement applies to **mortgage guaranty insurance enterprises.** It does not apply to mutual life insurance enterprises, **assessment enterprises,** or **fraternal benefit societies.**

STANDARDS OF FINANCIAL ACCOUNTING AND REPORTING

General Principles

7. Insurance contracts, for purposes of this Statement, shall be classified as short-duration or long-duration contracts depending on whether the contracts are expected to remain in force[3] for an extended period. The factors that shall be considered in determining whether a particular contract can be expected to remain in force for an extended period are:

a. *Short-duration contract.* The contract provides insurance protection for a fixed period of short duration and enables the insurer to cancel the contract or to adjust the provisions of the contract at the end of any contract period, such as

adjusting the amount of premiums charged or coverage provided.

b. *Long-duration contract.* The contract generally is not subject to unilateral changes in its provisions, such as a noncancelable or guaranteed renewable contract, and requires the performance of various functions and services (including insurance protection) for an extended period.

8. Examples of short-duration contracts include most property and liability insurance contracts and certain **term life insurance** contracts, such as **credit life insurance.** Examples of long-duration contracts include **whole-life contracts,** guaranteed renewable term life contracts, **endowment contracts, annuity contracts,** and title insurance contracts. Accident and health insurance contracts may be short-duration or long-duration depending on whether the contracts are expected to remain in force for an extended period. For example, individual and **group insurance** contracts that are noncancelable or guaranteed renewable (renewable at the option of the insured), or collectively renewable (individual contracts within a group are not cancelable), ordinarily are long-duration contracts.

9. Premiums from short-duration insurance contracts ordinarily shall be recognized as revenue over the period of the contract in proportion to the amount of insurance protection provided. A **liability for unpaid claims** (including estimates of costs for claims relating to insured events that have occurred but have not been reported to the insurer) and a **liability for claim adjustment expenses** shall be accrued when insured events occur.

10. Premiums from long-duration contracts shall be recognized as revenue when due from policyholders. A liability for expected costs relating to most types of long-duration contracts shall be accrued over the current and expected renewal periods of the contracts. The present value of estimated future policy benefits to be paid to or on behalf of policyholders less the present value of estimated future **net premiums** to be collected from policyholders **(liability for future policy benefits)** shall be accrued when premium revenue is recognized. Those estimates shall be based on assumptions, such as estimates of expected investment yields, **mortality, morbidity, terminations,** and expenses, applicable at the time the insurance contracts are made. In addition, liabilities for unpaid claims and claim adjustment expenses shall be accrued when insured events occur.

---

[2]Property and liability insurance enterprises, for purposes of this Statement, include stock enterprises, mutual enterprises, and **reciprocal or interinsurance exchanges.**

[3]*In force* refers to the period of coverage, that is, the period during which the occurrence of insured events can result in liabilities of the insurance enterprise.

11. Costs that vary with and are primarily related to the acquisition of insurance contracts (acquisition costs) shall be capitalized and charged to expense in proportion to premium revenue recognized. Other costs incurred during the period, such as those relating to investments, general administration, and policy **maintenance,** shall be charged to expense as incurred.

12. Accounting for investments by insurance enterprises presumes that (a) insurance enterprises have both the ability and the intent to hold long-term investments, such as bonds, mortgage loans, and redeemable preferred stocks, to maturity and (b) there is no decline in the market value of the investments other than a temporary decline. Accordingly, bonds, mortgage loans, and redeemable preferred stocks shall be reported at amortized cost. Common and nonredeemable preferred stocks shall be reported at market, and real estate shall be reported at depreciated cost.

Premium Revenue Recognition

Short-Duration Contracts

13. Premiums from short-duration contracts ordinarily shall be recognized as revenue over the period of the contract in proportion to the amount of insurance protection provided. For those few types of contracts for which the period of risk differs significantly from the contract period, premiums shall be recognized as revenue over the period of risk in proportion to the amount of insurance protection provided. That generally results in premiums being recognized as revenue evenly over the contract period (or the period of risk, if different), except for those few cases in which the amount of insurance protection declines according to a predetermined schedule.

14. If premiums are subject to adjustment (for example, retrospectively rated or other experience-rated insurance contracts for which the premium is determined after the period of the contract based on claim experience or reporting-form contracts for which the premium is adjusted after the period of the contract based on the value of insured property), premium revenue shall be recognized as follows:

a. If, as is usually the case, the ultimate premium is reasonably estimable, the estimated ultimate premium shall be recognized as revenue over the period of the contract. The estimated ultimate premium shall be revised to reflect current experience.

b. If the ultimate premium cannot be reasonably estimated, the **cost recovery method** or the **deposit method** may be used until the ultimate premium becomes reasonably estimable.

Long-Duration Contracts

15. Premiums from long-duration contracts, such as whole-life contracts (including limited-payment and single-premium life contracts), guaranteed renewable term life contracts, endowment contracts, annuity contracts, and title insurance contracts, shall be recognized as revenue when due from policyholders.

16. Premiums from title insurance contracts shall be considered due from policyholders and, accordingly, recognized as revenue on the effective date of the insurance contract. However, the binder date (the date a commitment to issue a policy is given) is appropriate if the insurance enterprise is legally or contractually entitled to the premium on the binder date. If reasonably estimable, premium revenue and costs relating to title insurance contracts issued by agents shall be recognized when the agents are legally or contractually entitled to the premiums, using estimates based on past experience and other sources. If not reasonably estimable, premium revenue and costs shall be recognized when agents report the issuance of title insurance contracts.

Claim Cost Recognition

17. A liability for unpaid claim costs relating to insurance contracts other than title insurance contracts, including estimates of costs relating to **incurred but not reported claims,** shall be accrued when insured events occur. A liability for estimated claim costs relating to title insurance contracts, including estimates of costs relating to incurred but not reported claims, shall be accrued when title insurance premiums are recognized as revenue (paragraphs 15 and 16).

18. The liability for unpaid claims shall be based on the estimated ultimate cost of settling the claims (including the effects of inflation and other societal and economic factors), using past experience adjusted for current trends, and any other factors that would modify past experience.[4] Changes in estimates of claim costs resulting from the continuous review process and differences between estimates and payments for claims shall be recognized in income of the period in which the estimates are changed or payments are made. Estimated recoveries on unsettled claims, such as **salvage, subroga-**

---

[4]Certain disclosures are required if the time value of money is considered in estimating liabilities for unpaid claims and claim adjustment expenses relating to short-duration contracts (paragraph 60(d)).

tion, or a potential ownership interest in real estate, shall be evaluated in terms of their estimated realizable value and deducted from the liability for unpaid claims. Estimated recoveries on settled claims other than mortgage guaranty and title insurance claims also shall be deducted from the liability for unpaid claims.

19. Real estate acquired in settling mortgage guaranty and title insurance claims shall be reported at fair value, that is, the amount that reasonably could be expected to be received in a current sale between a willing buyer and a willing seller. If no market price is available, the expected cash flows (anticipated sales price less maintenance and selling costs of the real estate) may aid in estimating fair value provided the cash flows are discounted at a rate commensurate with the risk involved. Real estate acquired in settling claims shall be separately reported in the balance sheet and shall not be classified as an investment. Subsequent reductions in the reported amount and realized gains and losses on the sale of real estate acquired in settling claims shall be recognized as an adjustment to claim costs incurred.

20. A liability for all costs expected to be incurred in connection with the settlement of unpaid claims (**claim adjustment expenses**) shall be accrued when the related liability for unpaid claims is accrued. Claim adjustment expenses include costs associated directly with specific claims paid or in the process of settlement, such as legal and adjusters' fees. Claim adjustment expenses also include other costs that cannot be associated with specific claims but are related to claims paid or in the process of settlement, such as internal costs of the claims function.[5]

Liability for Future Policy Benefits

21. A liability for future policy benefits relating to long-duration contracts other than title insurance contracts (paragraph 17) shall be accrued when premium revenue is recognized. The liability, which represents the present value of future benefits to be paid to or on behalf of policyholders and related expenses less the present value of future net premiums (portion of **gross premium** required to provide for all benefits and expenses), shall be estimated using methods that include assumptions, such as estimates of expected investment yields, mortality, morbidity, terminations, and expenses, applicable at the time the insurance contracts are made. The liability also shall consider other assumptions relating to guaranteed contract benefits, such as coupons, annual endowments, and conversion privileges. The assumptions shall include provision

for the **risk of adverse deviation.** Original assumptions shall continue to be used in subsequent accounting periods to determine changes in the liability for future policy benefits (often referred to as the "lock-in concept") unless a premium deficiency exists (paragraphs 35-37). Changes in the liability for future policy benefits that result from its periodic estimation for financial reporting purposes shall be recognized in income in the period in which the changes occur.

Investment Yields

22. Interest assumptions used in estimating the liability for future policy benefits shall be based on estimates of investment yields (net of related investment expenses) expected at the time insurance contracts are made. The interest assumption for each block of new insurance contracts (a group of insurance contracts that may be limited to contracts issued under the same plan in a particular year) shall be consistent with circumstances, such as actual yields, trends in yields, portfolio mix and maturities, and the enterprise's general investment experience.

Mortality

23. Mortality assumptions used in estimating the liability for future policy benefits shall be based on estimates of expected mortality.

Morbidity

24. Morbidity assumptions used in estimating the liability for future policy benefits shall be based on estimates of expected incidences of disability and claim costs. Expected incidences of disability and claim costs for various types of insurance (for example, noncancelable and guaranteed renewable accident and health insurance contracts) and other factors, such as occupational class, waiting period, sex, age, and benefit period, shall be considered in making morbidity assumptions. The risk of antiselection (the tendency for lower terminations of poor risks) also shall be considered in making morbidity assumptions.

Terminations

25. Termination assumptions used in estimating the liability for future policy benefits shall be based on anticipated terminations and **nonforfeiture benefits,** using anticipated **termination rates** and contractual nonforfeiture benefits. Termination rates may vary by plan of insurance, age at issue, year of issue, frequency of premium payment, and other factors. If composite rates are used, the rates shall be repre-

---

[5]Title insurance internal claim adjustment expenses, which generally consist of fixed costs associated with a permanent staff handling a variety of functions including claim adjustment, ordinarily are expensed as period costs because the costs are insignificant.

sentative of the enterprise's actual mix of business. Termination assumptions shall be made for long-duration insurance contracts without termination benefits because of the effects of terminations on anticipated premiums and claim costs.

Expenses

26. Expense assumptions used in estimating the liability for future policy benefits shall be based on estimates of expected nonlevel costs, such as termination or settlement costs, and costs after the premium-paying period. Renewal expense assumptions shall consider the possible effect of inflation on those expenses.

Costs Other Than Those Relating to Claims and Policy Benefits

27. Costs incurred during the period, such as those relating to investments, general administration, and policy maintenance, that do not vary with and are not primarily related to the acquisition of new and renewal insurance contracts shall be charged to expense as incurred.

Acquisition Costs

28. Acquisition costs are those costs that vary with and are primarily related to the acquisition of new and renewal insurance contracts. Commissions and other costs (for example, salaries of certain employees involved in the underwriting and policy issue functions, and medical and inspection fees) that are primarily related to insurance contracts issued or renewed during the period in which the costs are incurred shall be considered acquisition costs.

29. Acquisition costs shall be capitalized and charged to expense in proportion to premium revenue recognized. To associate acquisition costs with related premium revenue, acquisition costs shall be allocated by groupings of insurance contracts consistent with the enterprise's manner of acquiring, servicing, and measuring the profitability of its insurance contracts. Unamortized acquisition costs shall be classified as an asset.

30. If acquisition costs for short-duration contracts are determined based on a percentage relationship of costs incurred to premiums from contracts issued or renewed for a specified period, the percentage relationship and the period used, once determined, shall be applied to applicable unearned premiums

throughout the period of the contracts.

31. Actual acquisition costs for long-duration contracts shall be used in determining acquisition costs to be capitalized as long as gross premiums are sufficient to cover actual costs. However, estimated acquisition costs may be used if the difference is not significant. Capitalized acquisition costs shall be charged to expense using methods that include the same assumptions used in estimating the liability for future policy benefits.

Premium Deficiency

32. A probable loss on insurance contracts exists if there is a premium deficiency relating to short-duration or long-duration contracts. Insurance contracts shall be grouped consistent with the enterprise's manner of acquiring, servicing, and measuring the profitability of its insurance contracts to determine if a premium deficiency exists.

Short-Duration Contracts

33. A premium deficiency shall be recognized if the sum of expected claim costs and claim adjustment expenses, expected **dividends to policyholders,** unamortized acquisition costs, and maintenance costs exceeds related unearned premiums.[6]

34. A premium deficiency shall first be recognized by charging any unamortized acquisition costs to expense to the extent required to eliminate the deficiency. If the premium deficiency is greater than unamortized acquisition costs, a liability shall be accrued for the excess deficiency.

Long-Duration Contracts

35. Original policy benefit assumptions for long-duration contracts ordinarily continue to be used during the periods in which the liability for future policy benefits is accrued (paragraph 21). However, actual experience with respect to investment yields, mortality, morbidity, terminations, or expenses may indicate that existing contract liabilities, together with the present value of future gross premiums, will not be sufficient (a) to cover the present value of future benefits to be paid to or on behalf of policyholders and settlement and maintenance costs relating to a block of long-duration contracts and (b) to recover unamortized acquisition costs. In those circumstances, a premium deficiency shall be determined as follows:

---

[6]Disclosure is required regarding whether the insurance enterprise considers anticipated investment income in determining if a premium deficiency relating to short-duration contracts exists (paragraph 60(e)).

Present value of future payments for
benefits and related settlement and
maintenance costs, determined using
revised assumptions based on actual
and anticipated experience $XX

Less the present value of future gross
premiums, determined using revised
assumptions based on actual and
anticipated experience   XX
    Liability for future policy benefits
    using revised assumptions   XX

Less the liability for future policy
benefits at the valuation date,
reduced by unamortized acquisition
costs   XX

    Premium deficiency $XX

36. A premium deficiency shall be recognized by a charge to income and (a) a reduction of unamortized acquisition costs or (b) an increase in the liability for future policy benefits. If a premium deficiency does occur, future changes in the liability shall be based on the revised assumptions. No loss shall be reported currently if it results in creating future income. The liability for future policy benefits using revised assumptions based on actual and anticipated experience shall be estimated periodically for comparison with the liability for future policy benefits (reduced by unamortized acquisition costs) at the valuation date.

37. A premium deficiency, at a minimum, shall be recognized if the aggregate liability on an entire line of business is deficient. In some instances, the liability on a particular line of business may not be deficient in the aggregate, but circumstances may be such that profits would be recognized in early years and losses in later years. In those situations, the liability shall be increased by an amount necessary to offset losses that would be recognized in later years.

Reinsurance

38. Amounts that are recoverable from reinsurers and that relate to paid claims and claim adjustment expenses shall be classified as assets, with an allowance for estimated uncollectible amounts. Estimated amounts recoverable from reinsurers that relate to the liabilities for unpaid claims and claim adjustment expenses shall be deducted from those liabilities. Ceded unearned premiums shall be netted with related unearned premiums. Receivables and payables from the same reinsurer, including amounts withheld, also shall be netted. **Reinsurance** premiums ceded and reinsurance recoveries on claims

may be netted against related earned premiums and incurred claim costs in the income statement.

39. Proceeds from reinsurance transactions that represent recovery of acquisition costs shall reduce applicable unamortized acquisition costs in such a manner that net acquisition costs are capitalized and charged to expense in proportion to net revenue recognized (paragraph 29). If the ceding enterprise has agreed to service all of the related insurance contracts without reasonable compensation, a liability shall be accrued for estimated excess future servicing costs under the reinsurance contract. The net cost to the assuming enterprise shall be accounted for as an acquisition cost.

40. To the extent that a reinsurance contract does not, despite its form, provide for indemnification of the ceding enterprise by the reinsurer against loss or liability, the premium paid less the premium to be retained by the reinsurer shall be accounted for as a deposit by the ceding enterprise. Those contracts may be structured in various ways, but if, regardless of form, their substance is that all or part of the premium paid by the ceding enterprise is a deposit, the amount paid shall be accounted for as such. A net credit resulting from the contract shall be reported as a liability by the ceding enterprise. A net charge resulting from the contract shall be reported as an asset by the reinsurer.

Policyholder Dividends

41. Policyholder dividends shall be accrued using an estimate of the amount to be paid.

42. If limitations exist on the amount of net income from **participating insurance** contracts of life insurance enterprises that may be distributed to stockholders, the policyholders' share of net income on those contracts that cannot be distributed to stockholders shall be excluded from stockholders' equity by a charge to operations and a credit to a liability relating to participating policyholders' funds in a manner similar to the accounting for net income applicable to minority interests. Dividends declared or paid to participating policyholders shall reduce that liability; dividends declared or paid in excess of the liability shall be charged to operations. Income-based dividend provisions shall be based on net income that includes adjustments between general-purpose and statutory financial statements that will reverse and enter into future calculations of the dividend provision.

43. For life insurance enterprises for which there are no net income restrictions and that use life insurance dividend scales unrelated to actual net income, policyholder dividends (based on dividends anticipated or intended in determining gross premiums or

as shown in published dividend illustrations at the date insurance contracts are made) shall be accrued over the premium-paying periods of the contracts.

Retrospective and Contingent Commission Arrangements

44. If retrospective commission or experience refund arrangements exist under experience-rated insurance contracts, a separate liability shall be accrued for those amounts, based on experience and the provisions of the contract. Income in any period shall not include any amounts that are expected to be paid to agents or others in the form of experience refunds or additional commissions. Contingent commissions receivable or payable shall be accrued over the period in which related income is recognized.

Investments

45. Bonds shall be reported at amortized cost if the insurance enterprise has both the ability and the intent to hold the bonds until maturity and there is no decline in the market value of the bonds other than a temporary decline. If an insurance enterprise is a trader in bonds and does not intend to hold the bonds until maturity, bonds shall be reported at market and temporary changes in the market value of the bonds shall be recognized as unrealized gains or losses (paragraph 50).

46. Common and nonredeemable preferred stocks shall be reported at market and temporary changes in the market value of those securities shall be recognized as unrealized gains or losses (paragraph 50). Preferred stocks that by their provisions must be redeemed by the issuer shall be reported at amortized cost if the insurance enterprise has both the ability and the intent to hold the stocks until redemption and there is no decline in the market value of the stocks other than a temporary decline.

47. Mortgage loans shall be reported at outstanding principal balances if acquired at par value, or at amortized cost if purchased at a discount or premium, with an allowance for estimated uncollectible amounts, if any. Amortization and other related charges or credits shall be charged or credited to investment income. Changes in the allowance for estimated uncollectible amounts relating to mortgage loans shall be included in realized gains and losses.

48. Real estate investments shall be reported at cost less accumulated depreciation and an allowance for any impairment in value. Depreciation and other

related charges or credits shall be charged or credited to investment income. Changes in the allowance for any impairment in value relating to real estate investments shall be included in realized gains and losses.

49. Normal commitment fees received in connection with the placement of mortgage loans (less direct costs) shall be capitalized and recognized as revenue over the commitment period. Commitment fees that exceed current (normal) fees for mortgage loan commitments shall be considered an adjustment of the effective interest yield on the loan. Those excess fees shall be capitalized until the loan is made and then recognized as revenue over the period of the mortgage loan. If the mortgage loan is not ultimately made, the unamortized commitment fee shall be recognized as revenue at the end of the commitment period.

50. Realized gains and losses on all investments (including, but not limited to, stocks, bonds, mortgage loans, real estate, and joint ventures) shall be reported in the income statement below operating income and net of applicable income taxes. Realized gains and losses on the sale of assets other than investments, such as real estate used in the business, shall be reported in accordance with APB Opinion No. 30, *Reporting the Results of Operations.* Unrealized investment gains and losses, net of applicable income taxes, shall be reported as a separate component of stockholders' (policyholders') equity. Except as discussed in paragraph 51, unrealized gains or losses on common stocks, preferred stocks, or publicly traded bonds shall not be recognized in income until the sale, maturity, or other disposition of the investment.[7]

51. If a decline in the value of a common stock, preferred stock, or publicly traded bond below its cost or amortized cost is considered to be other than temporary, the investment shall be reduced to its net realizable value, which becomes the new cost basis. The amount of the reduction shall be reported as a realized loss. A recovery from the new cost basis shall be recognized as a realized gain only at the sale, maturity, or other disposition of the investment.

Real Estate Used in the Business

52. Real estate shall be classified either as an investment or as real estate used in the enterprise's operations, depending on its predominant use. Depreciation and other real estate operating costs shall be classified as investment expenses or operating expenses consistent with the balance sheet classification of the related asset. Imputed investment

---

[7]This paragraph is not intended to preclude the accrual of losses on private-placement bonds when both conditions in paragraph 8 of FASB Statement No. 5, *Accounting for Contingencies,* are met.

income and rental expense shall not be recognized for real estate used in the business.

Separate Accounts

53. Separate accounts represent assets and liabilities that are maintained by an insurance enterprise for purposes of funding fixed-benefit or **variable annuity contracts,** pension plans, and similar activities. The contract holder generally assumes the investment risk, and the insurance enterprise receives a fee for investment management, certain administrative expenses, and mortality and expense risks assumed.

54. Investments in separate accounts shall be reported at market except for separate account contracts with guaranteed investment returns. For those separate accounts, the related assets shall be reported in accordance with paragraphs 45-51. Separate account assets and liabilities ordinarily shall be reported as summary totals in the financial statements of the insurance enterprise.

Income Taxes of Life Insurance Enterprises

Deferred Income Taxes

55. Because of the provisions of the Life Insurance Company Income Tax Act of 1959 (Act),[8] timing differences (paragraph 13(e) of APB Opinion No. 11, *Accounting for Income Taxes*) of life insurance enterprises arising in the current period may not affect the determination of income taxes in future periods when those timing differences reverse. Amounts determined in the with-and-without calculation (paragraph 36 of Opinion 11) need to be considered further to determine whether the difference will reverse in the future. Deferred taxes need not be provided for the current tax effect of timing differences if circumstances indicate that the current tax effect will not reverse in the future. Similarly, a change in category of taxation (the basis on which the enterprise determines its income tax liability) resulting from the with-and-without calculation need not be recognized unless circumstances indicate that a change in category will result when the timing difference reverses. If the reversal of tax effects cannot be reasonably determined, deferred income taxes shall be provided based on the differential determined using the with-and-without

calculation as if the enterprise's tax return was filed on the basis on which financial statements are prepared, including any resulting change in category of taxation.

56. Although (a) special deductions (allowable only for income tax purposes) never enter into the determination of pretax accounting income in any period and (b) the amount of policyholder dividend deductions and special deductions may be limited on the tax return (the unused deductions cannot be carried forward to subsequent periods), the amount of policyholder dividend deductions and available special deductions and limitations on those deductions may properly be determined based on pretax accounting income. For example, unused policyholder dividend deductions and special deductions may be used to offset timing differences that affect taxable income to the extent that the limitations on those deductions change when based on pretax accounting income, unless known or anticipated circumstances indicate that future taxable income resulting from the reversal of timing differences will not be offset by like deductions. In the case of provisions for policyholder dividends (including policyholder dividends deducted as part of the change in the liability for future policy benefits), which may be timing differences themselves, statutory limitations shall not be applied to eliminate their current tax effect unless circumstances indicate that the dividends will be limited when the timing differences reverse. Special deductions that are directly affected by timing differences need to be redetermined in the with-and-without calculation unless circumstances indicate that future special deductions will not be directly affected by the timing differences when the timing differences reverse. If the reversal of tax effects cannot be reasonably determined, special deductions that are not affected by timing differences and, therefore, do not reverse shall be limited to amounts available in the tax return.

57. A life insurance enterprise's liability for future policy benefits and capitalization and amortization of acquisition costs indirectly affect the amount of taxable investment income used in determining the income tax provision for financial reporting purposes. Differences in taxable investment income caused by differences between the liability for future policy benefits and capitalization and amortization of acquisition costs for income tax and financial

---

[8]The Act contemplated taxation of total income of life insurance enterprises, but the determination of tax is complex because of the manner in which total taxable income is classified as investment income, gain from operations (including investment income and less special deductions for certain accident and health, group life, and nonparticipating insurance contracts), policyholders' surplus (gain from operations previously excluded from tax and the special deductions), and the interrelationship of those elements. Taxable income consists of (a) taxable investment income, (b) 50 percent of the amount by which gain from operations exceeds taxable investment income, and (c) any reductions in policyholders' surplus. If gain from operations is less than taxable investment income, the lesser amount, plus any reductions in policyholders' surplus, is taxable income. If a loss from operations occurs, there is no taxable income except to the extent that there are reductions in policyholders' surplus. Deductions from gain from operations for policyholder dividends and the special deductions are limited and unused deductions cannot be carried forward to subsequent periods.

reporting purposes shall be considered permanent differences (paragraph 13(f) of Opinion 11).

58. If deferred income taxes have not been provided on timing differences on the presumption that the timing differences will not have tax effects when they reverse and circumstances change so that it becomes apparent that tax effects will result, deferred income taxes attributable to those timing differences shall be accrued and reported as income tax expense in that period; those income taxes shall not be reported as an extraordinary item. If deferred income taxes have been provided on timing differences and circumstances change so that it becomes apparent that the tax effects will differ from those originally expected, income taxes previously deferred shall be included in income only as the related timing differences reverse, regardless of whether the life insurance enterprise uses the gross change or net change method (paragraph 37 of Opinion 11).

Policyholders' Surplus

59. A difference between taxable income and pretax accounting income attributable to amounts designated as policyholders' surplus of a life insurance enterprise may not reverse until indefinite future periods or may never reverse. The insurance enterprise controls the events that create the tax consequences, and the enterprise generally is required to take specific action before the initial difference reverses. Therefore, a life insurance enterprise shall not accrue income taxes on the difference between taxable income and pretax accounting income attributable to amounts designated as policyholders' surplus. However, if circumstances indicate that the insurance enterprise is likely to pay income taxes, either currently or in later years, because of a known or expected reduction in policyholders' surplus, income taxes attributable to that reduction shall be accrued as a tax expense of the current period; the accrual of those income taxes shall not be accounted for as an extraordinary item.

Disclosures

60. Insurance enterprises shall disclose the following in their financial statements:

a. The basis for estimating the liabilities for unpaid claims and claim adjustment expenses
b. The methods and assumptions used in estimating the liability for future policy benefits with disclosure of the average rate of assumed investment yields in effect for the current year encouraged
c. The nature of acquisition costs capitalized, the method of amortizing those costs, and the amount of those costs amortized for the period
d. The carrying amount of liabilities for unpaid

claims and claim adjustment expenses relating to short-duration contracts that are presented at present value in the financial statements and the range of interest rates used to discount those liabilities
e. Whether the insurance enterprise considers anticipated investment income in determining if a premium deficiency relating to short-duration contracts exists
f. The nature and significance of reinsurance transactions to the insurance enterprise's operations, including reinsurance premiums assumed and ceded, and estimated amounts that are recoverable from reinsurers and that reduce the liabilities for unpaid claims and claim adjustment expenses
g. The relative percentage of participating insurance, the method of accounting for policyholder dividends, the amount of dividends, and the amount of any additional income allocated to participating policyholders
h. The following information relating to stockholders' equity, statutory capital and surplus, and the effects of **statutory accounting practices** on the enterprise's ability to pay dividends to stockholders:
   (1) The amount of statutory capital and surplus
   (2) The amount of statutory capital and surplus necessary to satisfy regulatory requirements (based on the enterprise's current operations) if significant in relation to the enterprise's statutory capital and surplus
   (3) The nature of statutory restrictions on the payment of dividends and the amount of retained earnings that is not available for the payment of dividends to stockholders
i. For life insurance enterprises or a parent of a life insurance enterprise that is either consolidated or accounted for by the equity method:
   (1) The treatment of policyholders' surplus under the U.S. Internal Revenue Code and that income taxes may be payable if the enterprise takes certain specified actions, which shall be appropriately described
   (2) The accumulated amount of policyholders' surplus for which income taxes have not been accrued
j. For life insurance enterprises, any retained earnings in excess of policyholders' surplus on which no current or deferred federal income tax provisions have been made and the reasons for not providing the deferred taxes

Amendments to Other Pronouncements

61. The following footnote is added to the end of paragraph 6 of Opinion 11:

   For life insurance enterprises, also refer to paragraphs 55-59 and subparagraphs 60(i) and 60(j) of FASB Statement No. 60, *Accounting and Reporting by Insurance Enterprises.*

62. The provisions of APB Opinion No. 23, *Accounting for Income Taxes—Special Areas,* that discuss policyholders' surplus of life insurance enterprises have been included in this Statement without reconsideration, and paragraphs 26-30 and footnote 11 of Opinion 23 are superseded by this Statement.

63. The references to AICPA insurance industry related Guides in footnote 8 of Opinion 30, paragraphs 41 and 102 of FASB Statement No. 5, *Accounting for Contingencies,* paragraph 4 of FASB Interpretation No. 15, *Translation of Unamortized Policy Acquisition Costs by a Stock Life Insurance Company,* and paragraph 7 of FASB Interpretation No. 22, *Applicability of Indefinite Reversal Criteria to Timing Differences,* are replaced by a reference to FASB Statement No. 60, *Accounting and Reporting by Insurance Enterprises.* The references to AICPA Statements of Position (SOPs) 78-6, *Accounting for Property and Liability Insurance Companies,* and 79-3, *Accounting for Investments of Stock Life Insurance Companies,* and to the AICPA Industry Audit Guides, *Audits of Fire and Casualty Insurance Companies* and *Audits of Stock Life Insurance Companies,* are deleted from Appendix A of FASB Statement No. 32, *Specialized Accounting and Reporting Principles and Practices in AICPA Statements of Position and Guides on Accounting and Auditing Matters.*

The reference to the AICPA project on accounting by title insurance companies, which resulted in the issuance of SOP 80-1, *Accounting for Title Insurance Companies,* is deleted from Appendix B of Statement 32.

Effective Date and Transition

64. This Statement shall be effective for fiscal years beginning after December 15, 1982, with earlier application encouraged. Accounting changes adopted to conform to the provisions of this Statement shall be applied retroactively. In the year that this Statement is first applied, the financial statements shall disclose the nature of any restatement and its effect on income before extraordinary items, net income, and related per share amounts for each year presented. The individual effects of changing to conform to the provisions of this Statement shall be disclosed in the financial statements.

65. If retroactive restatement of all years presented is not practicable, the financial statements presented shall be restated for as many consecutive years as practicable and the cumulative effect of applying this Statement shall be included in determining net income of the earliest year restated (not necessarily the earliest year presented). If it is not practicable to restate any prior year, the cumulative effect shall be included in net income in the year in which this Statement is first applied. (Refer to paragraph 20 of APB Opinion No. 20, *Accounting Changes.*)

> The provisions of this Statement need
> not be applied to immaterial items.

This Statement was approved by the unanimous vote of the seven members of the Financial Accounting Standards Board:

Donald J. Kirk,	John W. March	Robert T. Sprouse
Chairman	Robert A. Morgan	Ralph E. Walters
Frank E. Block	David Mosso	

Appendix A

GLOSSARY

66. This appendix defines certain terms that are used in this Statement.

Acquisition costs
Costs incurred in the acquisition of new and renewal insurance contracts. Acquisition costs include those costs that vary with and are primarily related to the acquisition of insurance contracts (for example, agent and broker commissions, certain underwriting and policy issue

costs, and medical and inspection fees).

Annuity contract
A contract that provides fixed or variable periodic payments made from a stated or contingent date and continuing for a specified period, such as for a number of years or for life. Also refer to variable annuity contract.

Assessment enterprise
An insurance enterprise that sells insurance to groups with similar interests, such as church denominations or professional groups. Some assessment enterprises also sell insurance directly to the general public. If funds are not sufficient

to pay claims, then assessments may be made against members.

Claim

A demand for payment of a policy benefit because of the occurrence of an insured event, such as the death or disability of the insured; the maturity of an endowment; the incurrence of hospital or medical bills; the destruction or damage of property and related deaths or injuries; defects in, liens on, or challenges to the title to real estate; or the occurrence of a surety loss.

Claim adjustment expenses

Expenses incurred in the course of investigating and settling claims. Claim adjustment expenses include any legal and adjusters' fees, and the costs of paying claims and all related expenses.

Cost recovery method

Under the cost recovery method, premiums are recognized as revenue in an amount equal to estimated claim costs as insured events occur until the ultimate premium is reasonably estimable, and recognition of income is postponed until that time.

Credit life insurance

Life insurance, generally in the form of decreasing term insurance, that is issued on the lives of borrowers to cover payment of loan balances in case of death.

Deposit method

Under the deposit method, premiums are not recognized as revenue and claim costs are not charged to expense until the ultimate premium is reasonably estimable, and recognition of income is postponed until that time.

Dividends to policyholders

Amounts distributable to policyholders of participating insurance contracts as determined by the insurer. Under various state insurance laws, dividends are apportioned to policyholders on an equitable basis. The dividend allotted to any contract often is based on the amount that the contract, as one of a class of similar contracts, has contributed to the income available for distribution as dividends.

Endowment contract

An insurance contract that provides insurance from inception of the contract to the maturity date (endowment period). The contract specifies that a stated amount, adjusted for items such as policy loans and dividends, if any, will be paid to the beneficiary if the insured dies before the maturity date. If the insured is still living at the maturity date, the policyholder will receive the maturity amount under the contract after adjustments, if any. Endowment contracts generally mature at a specified age of the insured or at the end of a specified period.

Fraternal benefit society

An organization that provides life or health insurance to its members and their beneficiaries. Policyholders normally participate in the earnings of the society, and insurance contracts stipulate that the society has the power to assess its members if the funds available for future policy benefits are not sufficient to provide for benefits and expenses.

Gross premium

The premium charged to a policyholder for an insurance contract. Also refer to net premium.

Group insurance

Insurance protecting a group of persons, usually employees of an entity and their dependents. A single insurance contract is issued to their employer or other representative of the group. Individual certificates often are given to each insured individual or family unit. The insurance usually has an annual renewable contract period, although the insurer may guarantee premium rates for two or three years. Adjustments to premiums relating to the actual experience of the group of insured persons are common.

Incurred but not reported claims

Claims relating to insured events that have occurred but have not yet been reported to the insurer or reinsurer as of the date of the financial statements.

Liability for claim adjustment expenses

The amount needed to provide for the estimated ultimate cost required to investigate and settle claims relating to insured events that have occurred on or before a particular date (ordinarily, the balance sheet date), whether or not reported to the insurer at that date.

Liability for future policy benefits

An accrued obligation to policyholders that relates to insured events, such as death or disability. The liability for future policy benefits can be viewed as either (a) the present value of future benefits to be paid to or on behalf of policyholders and expenses less the present value of future net premiums payable under the insurance contracts or (b) the accumulated amount of net premiums already collected less the accumulated amount of benefits and expenses already paid to or on behalf of policyholders.

Liability for unpaid claims

The amount needed to provide for the estimated ultimate cost of settling claims relating to insured events that have occurred on or before a particular date (ordinarily, the balance sheet date). The estimated liability includes the amount of money that will be required for future payments on both (a) claims that have been reported to the insurer and (b) claims relating to insured events that have occurred but have not been reported to the insurer as of the date the liability is estimated.

Life insurance enterprise

An enterprise that can issue annuity, endowment, and accident and health insurance contracts as well as life insurance contracts. Life insurance enterprises may be either stock or mutual organizations.

Maintenance costs

Costs associated with maintaining records relating to insurance contracts and with the processing of premium collections and commissions.

Morbidity

The relative incidence of disability due to disease or physical impairment.

Mortality

The relative incidence of death in a given time or place.

Mortgage guaranty insurance enterprise

An insurance enterprise that issues insurance contracts that guarantee lenders, such as savings and loan associations, against nonpayment by mortgagors.

Net premium

As used in this Statement for long-duration insurance contracts, the portion of the gross premium required to provide for all benefits and expenses.

Nonforfeiture benefits

Those benefits in a life insurance contract that the policyholder does not forfeit, even for failure to pay premiums. Nonforfeiture benefits usually include cash value, paid-up insurance value, or extended-term insurance value.

Participating insurance

Insurance in which the policyholder is entitled to participate in the earnings or surplus of the insurance enterprise. The participation occurs through the distribution of dividends to policyholders.

Property and liability insurance enterprise

An enterprise that issues insurance contracts providing protection against (a) damage to, or loss of, property caused by various perils, such as fire and theft, or (b) legal liability resulting from injuries to other persons or damage to their property. Property and liability insurance enterprises also can issue accident and health insurance contracts. The term *property and liability insurance enterprise* is the current terminology used to describe a fire and casualty insurance enterprise. Property and liability insurance enterprises may be either stock or mutual organizations.

Reciprocal or interinsurance exchange

A group of persons, firms, or corporations commonly referred to as "subscribers" that exchange insurance contracts through an attorney-in-fact (an attorney authorized by a person to act in that person's behalf).

Reinsurance

A transaction in which a reinsurer (assuming enterprise), for a consideration (premium), assumes all or part of a risk undertaken originally by another insurer (ceding enterprise). However, the legal rights of the insured are not affected by the reinsurance transaction and the insurance enterprise issuing the insurance contract remains liable to the insured for payment of policy benefits.

Risk of adverse deviation

A concept used by life insurance enterprises in estimating the liability for future policy benefits relating to long-duration contracts. The risk of adverse deviation allows for possible unfavorable deviations from assumptions, such as estimates of expected investment yields, mortality, morbidity, terminations, and expenses. The concept is referred to as *risk load* when used by property and liability insurance enterprises.

Salvage

The amount received by an insurer from the sale of property (usually damaged) on which the insurer has paid a total claim to the insured and has obtained title to the property.

Statutory accounting practices

Accounting principles required by statute, regulation, or rule, or permitted by specific approval, that an insurance enterprise is required to follow when submitting its financial statements to state insurance departments.

Subrogation

The right of an insurer to pursue any course of recovery of damages, in its name or in the name of the policyholder, against a third party who is liable for costs relating to an insured event that have been paid by the insurer.

Term life insurance

Insurance that provides a benefit if the insured dies within the period specified in the contract. The insurance is for level or declining amounts for stated periods, such as 1, 5, or 10 years, or to a stated age. Term life insurance generally has no loan or cash value.

Termination

In general, the failure to renew an insurance contract. Involuntary terminations include death, expirations, and maturities of contracts. Voluntary terminations of life insurance contracts include lapses with or without cash surrender value and contract modifications that reduce paid-up whole-life benefits or term-life benefits.

Termination rate

The rate at which insurance contracts fail to renew. Termination rates usually are expressed as a ratio of the number of contracts on which insureds failed to pay premiums during a given period to the total number of contracts at the beginning of the period from which those terminations occurred. The complement of the termination rate is persistency, which is the renewal quality of insurance contracts, that is, the number of insureds that keep their insurance in force during a period. Persistency varies by plan of insurance, age at issue, year of issue, frequency of premium payment, and other factors.

Title insurance enterprise

An enterprise that issues title insurance contracts to real estate owners, purchasers, and mortgage lenders, indemnifying them against loss or damage arising out of defects in, liens on, or challenges to their title to real estate.

Variable annuity contract

An annuity in which the amount of payments to be made are specified in units, rather than in dollars. When payment is due, the amount is determined based on the value of the investments in the annuity fund.

Whole-life contract

Insurance that may be kept in force for a person's entire life by paying one or more premiums. It is paid for in one of three different ways: (a) ordinary life insurance (premiums are payable as long as the insured lives), (b) limited-payment life insurance (premiums are payable over a specified number of years), and (c) single-premium life insurance (a lump-sum amount paid at the inception of the insurance contract). The insurance contract pays a benefit (contrac-

tual amount adjusted for items such as policy loans and dividends, if any) at the death of the insured. Whole-life insurance contracts also build up nonforfeiture benefits.

Appendix B

BACKGROUND INFORMATION AND SUMMARY OF CONSIDERATION OF COMMENTS ON EXPOSURE DRAFT

67. As discussed in Statement 32, the FASB is extracting the specialized[9] accounting and reporting principles and practices from AICPA SOPs and Guides on accounting and auditing matters and issuing them as FASB Statements after appropriate due process. This Statement extracts without significant change the specialized principles and practices relating to insurance enterprises from the AICPA Industry Audit Guides, *Audits of Stock Life Insurance Companies* and *Audits of Fire and Casualty Insurance Companies;* AICPA SOPs 78-6, 79-3, and 80-1; and Opinion 23. Accounting and reporting standards that apply to enterprises in general also apply to insurance enterprises, and the standards in this Statement are in addition to those standards.

68. Board members have assented to the issuance of this Statement on the basis that it is an appropriate extraction of existing specialized principles and practices and that a comprehensive reconsideration of those principles and practices was not contemplated in undertaking this FASB project. Most of the background material and discussion of accounting alternatives have not been carried forward from the AICPA insurance industry related Guides and SOPs. The Board's conceptual framework project on accounting recognition criteria will address recognition issues relating to elements of financial statements. A Statement of Financial Accounting Concepts resulting from that project in due course will serve as a basis for evaluating existing standards and practices. Accordingly, the Board may wish to evaluate the standards in this Statement when its conceptual framework project is completed.

69. This Statement does not address issues that currently are being studied by the insurance industry and the accounting and actuarial professions. Some of those issues include:

a. What financial accounting and reporting principles should mutual life insurance enterprises, assessment enterprises, and fraternal benefit societies follow in their general-purpose financial statements?

---

[9]The term *specialized* is used to refer to those accounting and reporting principles and practices in AICPA Guides and SOPs that are neither superseded by nor contained in Accounting Research Bulletins, APB Opinions, FASB Statements, or FASB Interpretations.

b. How should universal life insurance contracts and similar products that have been developed since the AICPA insurance industry related Guides and SOPs were originally issued be accounted for?

c. For short-duration contracts:

(1) Should certain claim liabilities be discounted?

(2) Should anticipated investment income be considered in determining if a premium deficiency exists?

d. What circumstances constitute a transfer of economic risk under a reinsurance contract?

70. An Exposure Draft of a proposed FASB Statement, *Accounting and Reporting by Insurance Enterprises,* was issued on November 18, 1981. The Board received 56 comment letters in response to the Exposure Draft. Certain of the comments received and the Board's consideration of them are discussed in this appendix.

Criteria for Distinguishing between Short-Duration and Long-Duration Contracts

71. Respondents commented on the appropriateness of the proposed criteria for distinguishing between short-duration and long-duration contracts and on whether the criteria could be improved. Some respondents said that the criteria were not well defined and could result in unintended changes in current accounting principles or practices because the criteria focused too narrowly on whether an insurance contract can be expected to remain in force for an extended period. They suggested that the criteria be clarified so that the nature of the insurance enterprise's obligations and policyholder rights under the provisions of the contract is considered.

72. Other respondents recommended that (a) accounting for insurance contracts should depend on the type of insurance enterprise issuing the contract, (b) the criteria for distinguishing between the two types of contracts should be based on the period of the contract, or (c) contracts should be specified by type of insurance protection that should be considered short-duration or long-duration so that the Statement can be specifically applied without exception or ambiguity.

73. In extracting the specialized principles and practices from the AICPA insurance industry related Guides and SOPs, the Board decided to establish a framework for accounting by insurance enterprises based on the nature of insurance contracts rather than type of insurance enterprise. The Board concluded that the criteria for distinguishing between short-duration and long-duration contracts should be clarified so that the nature of the insurance

enterprise's obligations and policyholder rights under the provisions of the contract is considered, because that is consistent with (a) a general framework, (b) the principles in the AICPA insurance industry related Guides and SOPs, and (c) current practice.

Impairment in Value of Publicly Traded Securities

74. If an investment in a publicly traded security is reduced to its net realizable value, paragraph 51 requires that a gain not be recognized until the sale, maturity, or other disposition of the investment. Some respondents argued that permanent impairment is too absolute and often cannot be determined until after the event causing the impairment has occurred. In addition, they said that accounting for impaired amounts relating to publicly traded securities should be consistent with accounting for mortgage loans and real estate investments and reflective of an insurance enterprise's estimate of its ability to recover the carrying amount of those securities. They suggested that a standard consistent with Statement 5 be included to require adjustments of the carrying amount as circumstances change.

75. Other respondents agreed with paragraph 51 because it is an accurate extraction of SOPs 78-6, 79-3, and 80-1 and is consistent with principles and practices applicable to enterprises in other industries. Based on that reasoning, the Board concluded that adjustments for increases in value of previously impaired publicly traded securities should continue to be proscribed.

Acquisition Costs: Primarily versus Directly Related

76. Some respondents commented on the definition in paragraph 28 that states that acquisition costs are those costs that vary with and are *primarily* related to the acquisition of new and renewal insurance contracts. They pointed out that, while the term *primarily* currently is used in practice by life insurance enterprises, the term *directly* is used in practice by property and liability insurance enterprises. They said that using the term *primarily* for all insurance enterprises could produce a different result for property and liability insurance enterprises. They recommended that the distinction between *primarily* and *directly* be retained in prescribing accounting principles for acquisition costs.

77. The Board believes that accounting principles and practices should not be applied differently among insurance enterprises without differences in underlying circumstances. Because the term *primarily* encompasses *directly,* the Board acknowledges that use of the term *primarily* might allow property and liability insurance enterprises to adopt broader

guidelines in defining acquisition costs that are capitalizable. However, the Board believes that the use of the term *primarily* should not cause insurance enterprises to change their methods of defining acquisition costs to be capitalized.

Disclosure of the Average Rate of Assumed Investment Yields

78. Respondents commented on the benefits and costs of specifically requiring a disclosure of the average rate of assumed investment yields used in estimating the liability for future policy benefits. Some respondents said that disclosure of the average rate of assumed investment yields should be required because the disclosure would be relevant to users in assessing the reasonableness of estimated rates of return in relation to current investment yields and in comparing insurance enterprises. They also expressed the view that the cost to the reporting enterprise would be minimal and that the benefit to users of insurance enterprise financial statements would outweigh the related cost.

79. Other respondents said it is likely that the development of a single average interest rate would involve a time-consuming and costly process that would not be justified by the benefit. They also argued that the weighted average of interest rate assumptions has little meaning when there are other significant assumptions that also must be considered in estimating the liability for future policy benefits and that the disclosure would likely result in a general perception that the rate possessed more significance and value than deserved.

80. The Board agrees with those respondents that said disclosure of the average rate of assumed investment yields is useful in assessing the reasonableness of estimated rates of return in relation to current investment yields and in comparing insurance enterprises. However, because of uncertainties relating to the cost of providing that disclosure, the Board decided to encourage but not require disclosure of that yield rate.

Disclosure of Discounting Short-Duration Contract Claim Liabilities and Considering Anticipated Investment Income in Determining Premium Deficiencies

81. The Exposure Draft would have required disclosure of (a) the effects (including amounts) of discounting short-duration contract claim liabilities and (b) the effects (including amounts) of an enterprise's considering anticipated investment income in determining if a premium deficiency relating to short-duration contracts exists. Some respondents said that insurance enterprises generally are not disclosing *amounts* in their notes because

they believe disclosure of amounts is not required in the AICPA insurance industry related Guides and SOPs, which require disclosure of only the *effects*. Other respondents recommended that the Exposure Draft be revised to require disclosure of the carrying amount of claim liabilities carried at present value in the balance sheet, the range of interest rates used to discount the claim liabilities, and the period of years over which the claims are being paid.

82. The phrase *including amounts* was included in the Exposure Draft to clarify what the Board understands was meant by *effects on the financial statements* in SOP 78-6. The Board believes that quantitative disclosures relating to the discounting of short-duration claim liabilities is necessary and, accordingly, decided to require disclosure of the carrying amount of short-duration contract liabilities that are presented at present value and the range of discount rates. However, the Board agreed that disclosure of amounts relating to an insurance enterprise's consideration of anticipated investment income in determining whether a premium deficiency exists is not necessary, and decided to require disclosure of only whether the insurance enterprise considers anticipated investment income in making that determination.

Disclosure of Statutory Requirements

83. With respect to the proposed disclosure of information relating to statutory capital and surplus requirements, some respondents suggested that disclosure be limited to the amount of statutory capital and surplus, minimum statutory requirements when significant, and statutory limitations on the payment of dividends. Other respondents recommended that the proposed disclosures parallel those in the SEC's recent revision of Article 7 of Regulation S-X. The Board agreed that the disclosure relating to statutory requirements needed clarification and revised the disclosure in accordance with the first sentence of this paragraph.

Reconciliation Disclosure

84. Respondents commented on whether disclosure of a reconciliation between financial reporting and statutory capital and income should be required. Some respondents said the disclosure should be required because the differences between statutory accounting practices and generally accepted accounting principles are an important element in the analysis of an insurance enterprise's general-purpose financial statements. They pointed out that statutory accounting determines the amount of dividends that can be paid as well as the sufficiency of statutory capital and surplus for regulatory purposes and, therefore, is important to users of insurance enterprise financial statements.

85. Other respondents said the reconciliation disclosure should not be required because the original purpose of the reconciliation was intended principally to provide relevant information during the life insurance industry's transition from statutory reporting. They also said that the disclosure may cast doubt on the appropriateness of accounting principles used in the general-purpose financial statements.

86. The Board believes that the disclosure in paragraph 60(h) relating to statutory requirements is sufficient for the general-purpose financial statements of insurance enterprises.

Other Comments

87. Some respondents noted that paragraph 10 of the Exposure Draft would require a liability for claim adjustment expenses to be accrued when insured events occur and that life insurance enterprises currently are not accruing those costs. They said that accruing claim adjustment expenses associated with unpaid claims would require an accounting change for life insurance enterprises and that, although it may be appropriate to require life insurance enterprises to accrue a liability for those costs, those enterprises should be excluded from that requirement since the AICPA stock life insurance guide does not require that accrual. However, they acknowledged that the change is not likely to significantly affect the financial statements of life insurance enterprises. The Board believes that the requirement is appropriate and that it meets a criterion for change—that is, practices among insurance enterprises are different without differences in circumstances. In addition, the Board believes the requirement is consistent with the provisions of Statement 5.

88. Several respondents suggested various substantive changes to the Exposure Draft. Adoption of those suggestions would have required a reconsideration of some of the provisions of the Guides and SOPs. Such a reconsideration is not contemplated in the extraction project unless a proposed change meets one of the three criteria for change included in the "Notice for Recipients" of the Exposure Draft or is broadly supported. The proposed changes did not meet the criteria for change and were not broadly supported. Accordingly, the Board did not adopt those suggestions. However, based on suggestions from respondents to the Exposure Draft, the Board has made several other changes that it believes clarify the Statement.

89. The Board has concluded that it can reach an informed decision on the basis of existing information without a public hearing and that the effective date and transition specified in paragraphs 64 and 65 are advisable in the circumstances.

Statement of Financial Accounting Standards No. 61
Accounting for Title Plant

STATUS

Issued: June 1982

Effective Date: For fiscal years beginning after December 15, 1982

Affects: No other pronouncements

Affected by: Paragraph 6 amended by FAS 121

SUMMARY

This Statement extracts the specialized principles and practices for title plant from AICPA Statement of Position 80-1, *Accounting for Title Insurance Companies,* and applies to enterprises, such as title insurance enterprises, title abstract enterprises, and title agents, that use a title plant in their operations. This Statement requires that costs directly incurred to construct a title plant be capitalized until the enterprise can use the title plant to do title searches. This Statement also requires that capitalized costs of a title plant not be depreciated and that costs of maintaining a title plant and doing title searches be expensed as incurred.

Statement of Financial Accounting Standards No. 61
Accounting for Title Plant

CONTENTS

INTRODUCTION

1. A title plant consists of (a) indexed and catalogued information for a period concerning the ownership of, and encumbrances on, parcels of land in a particular geographic area; (b) information relating to persons having an interest in real estate; (c) maps and plats; (d) copies of prior title insurance contracts and reports; and (e) other documents and records. In summary, a title plant constitutes a historical record of all matters affecting title to parcels of land in a particular geographic area. The number of years covered by a title plant varies, depending on regulatory requirements and the minimum information period considered necessary to issue title insurance policies efficiently. Title plants are updated on a daily or other frequent basis by adding copies of documents on the current status of title to specific parcels of real estate.

APPLICABILITY AND SCOPE

2. This Statement applies to enterprises that use a title plant in their operations. Those enterprises include, but are not limited to, title insurance enterprises (underwriters), title abstract enterprises, and title agents.

STANDARDS OF FINANCIAL ACCOUNTING AND REPORTING

Capitalization of Title Plant

3. Costs incurred to construct a title plant, including the costs incurred to obtain, organize, and summarize historical information in an efficient and useful manner, shall be capitalized until the title plant can be used by the enterprise to do title searches. To qualify for capitalization, costs need to be directly related to, and properly identified with, the activities necessary to construct the title plant.

4. Purchased title plant, including a purchased undivided interest in title plant, shall be recorded at cost at the date of acquisition. For title plant acquired separately, cost shall be measured by the fair value of the consideration given.

5. An enterprise may decide to construct or purchase a title plant that antedates the period covered by its existing title plant (backplant). Costs to construct a backplant need to be identifiable to qualify for capitalization.

6. Capitalized costs of title plant shall not be depreciated or charged to income unless circumstances indicate that the value of the title plant has been impaired. The following circumstances may indicate that the value of title plant has been impaired:

a. Changes in legal requirements or statutory practices
b. Effects of obsolescence, demand, and other economic factors
c. Actions of competitors and others that may affect competitive advantages
d. Failure to maintain the title plant properly on a current basis
e. Abandonment of title plant or other circumstances that indicate obsolescence

If the value of a title plant decreases below its adjusted cost, that impairment shall be recognized in income.

Title Plant Maintenance and Title Searches

7. Costs incurred to maintain a title plant and to do title searches shall be expensed as incurred. Title plant maintenance involves the updating of the title

plant on a daily or other frequent basis by adding (a) reports on the current status of title to specific parcels of real estate and (b) other documents, such as records relating to security or other ownership interests. Title searches involve the process of searching through records for all recorded documents or updating information summarized in the most recently issued title report.

Storage and Retrieval

8. Costs incurred after a title plant is operational (a) to convert the information from one storage and retrieval system to another or (b) to modify or modernize the storage and retrieval system shall not be capitalized as title plant. Those costs, however, may be capitalized separately and charged to expense in a systematic and rational manner.

Sale of Title Plant

9. The sale of a title plant shall be reported separately as follows:

a. If the enterprise sells its title plant and relinquishes all rights to its future use, the reported amount shall be the amount received net of the adjusted cost of the title plant.
b. If the enterprise sells an undivided ownership interest in its title plant (that is, the right to its joint use), the reported amount shall be the amount received net of a pro rata portion of the adjusted cost of the title plant.

c. If the enterprise sells a copy of its title plant or the right to use it, the reported amount shall be the amount received. Ordinarily, no cost shall be allocated to the sale of a copy of or the right to use a title plant unless the value of the title plant decreases below its adjusted cost as a result of the sale (paragraph 6).

Effective Date and Transition

10. This Statement shall be effective for fiscal years beginning after December 15, 1982, with earlier application encouraged. Accounting changes adopted to conform to the provisions of this Statement shall be applied retroactively. In the year that this Statement is first applied, the financial statements shall disclose the nature of any restatement and its effect on income before extraordinary items, net income, and related per share amounts for each year presented.

11. If retroactive restatement of all years presented is not practicable, the financial statements presented shall be restated for as many consecutive years as practicable and the cumulative effect of applying this Statement shall be included in determining net income of the earliest year restated (not necessarily the earliest year presented). If it is not practicable to restate any prior year, the cumulative effect shall be included in net income in the year in which this Statement is first applied. (Refer to paragraph 20 of APB Opinion No. 20, *Accounting Changes*.)

> **The provisions of this Statement need
> not be applied to immaterial items.**

This Statement was approved by the unanimous vote of the seven members of the Financial Accounting Standards Board:

Donald J. Kirk,	John W. March	Robert T. Sprouse
Chairman	Robert A. Morgan	Ralph E. Walters
Frank E. Block	David Mosso	

Appendix

BACKGROUND INFORMATION AND SUMMARY OF CONSIDERATION OF COMMENTS ON EXPOSURE DRAFT

12. As discussed in FASB Statement No. 32, *Specialized Accounting and Reporting Principles and*

Practices in AICPA Statements of Position and Guides on Accounting and Auditing Matters, the FASB is extracting the specialized[1] accounting and reporting principles and practices from AICPA Statements of Position (SOPs) and Guides on accounting and auditing matters and issuing them as FASB Statements after appropriate due process. This Statement extracts the specialized principles and practices for title plant from SOP 80-1,

---

[1]The term *specialized* is used to refer to those accounting and reporting principles and practices in AICPA Guides and SOPs that are neither superseded by nor contained in Accounting Research Bulletins, APB Opinions, FASB Statements, or FASB Interpretations.

Accounting for Title Insurance Companies,[2] without significant change.

13. Board members have assented to the issuance of this Statement on the basis that it is an appropriate extraction of those existing specialized principles and practices and that a comprehensive reconsideration of those principles and practices was not contemplated in undertaking this FASB project. Some of the background material and discussion of accounting alternatives have not been carried forward from the SOP. The Board's conceptual framework project on accounting recognition criteria will address recognition issues relating to elements of financial statements. A Statement of Financial Accounting Concepts resulting from that project in due course will serve as a basis for evaluating existing standards and practices. Accordingly, the Board may wish to evaluate the standards in this Statement when its conceptual framework project is completed.

14. An Exposure Draft of a proposed FASB Statement, *Accounting for Title Plant,* was issued on November 18, 1981. The Board received 14 comment letters in response to the Exposure Draft, most of which expressed agreement. Certain of the comments received and the Board's consideration of them are discussed in this appendix.

15. Some respondents stated that title plant is unique to the title insurance industry and that all accounting principles for title insurance enterprises, including title plant, should be included in a separate FASB Statement. The Board has concluded that it is more appropriate to include accounting standards relating to all insurance enterprises in one Statement and that separate Statements for each type of insurance enterprise are unnecessary. The Board concluded that a separate Statement on accounting for title plant was necessary because enterprises that are not insurance enterprises, such as title abstract enterprises and title agents, may use a title plant in their operations.

16. The Board has concluded that it can reach an informed decision on the basis of existing information without a public hearing and that the effective date and transition specified in paragraphs 10 and 11 are advisable in the circumstances.

---

[2]Other specialized principles and practices from SOP 80-1 are included in FASB Statement No. 60, *Accounting and Reporting by Insurance Enterprises.*

Statement of Financial Accounting Standards No. 62
Capitalization of Interest Cost in Situations Involving Certain Tax-Exempt Borrowings and Certain Gifts and Grants

an amendment of FASB Statement No. 34

STATUS

Issued: June 1982

Effective Date: For tax-exempt borrowing arrangements entered into and gifts or grants received after August 31, 1982

Affects: Amends FAS 34, paragraphs 10, 13, and 17
Supersedes FTB 81-5

Affected by: No other pronouncements

SUMMARY

This Statement amends FASB Statement No. 34, *Capitalization of Interest Cost*, (a) to require capitalization of interest cost of restricted tax-exempt borrowings less any interest earned on temporary investment of the proceeds of those borrowings from the date of borrowing until the specified qualifying assets acquired with those borrowings are ready for their intended use and (b) to proscribe capitalization of interest cost on qualifying assets acquired using gifts or grants that are restricted by the donor or grantor to acquisition of those assets.

Statement of Financial Accounting Standards No. 62
Capitalization of Interest Cost in Situations Involving Certain Tax-Exempt Borrowings and Certain Gifts and Grants

an amendment of FASB Statement No. 34

CONTENTS

INTRODUCTION

1. The FASB has received a number of requests to reconsider the issue of offsetting interest income against interest cost in the application of FASB Statement No. 34, *Capitalization of Interest Cost,* for purposes of determining either capitalization rates or limitations on the amount of interest to be capitalized. FASB Technical Bulletin No. 81-5, *Offsetting Interest Cost to Be Capitalized with Interest Income,* states that Statement 34 does not permit such offsetting. Other requests have been received to consider the issue of capitalization of interest cost in situations in which qualifying assets are acquired using gifts and grants restricted to the purchase of the specified assets.

2. The Board has concluded that Statement 34 should be amended to require offsetting of interest income against interest cost in certain circumstances involving tax-exempt borrowings that are externally restricted as specified in paragraph 3. Those situations include many governmental borrowings and most governmentally sponsored borrowings (such as industrial revenue bonds and pollution control bonds). In such situations, interest earned generally is considered in and is significant to the initial decision to acquire the asset, and the capitalization of net interest cost provides a better measure of the entity's net investment in the qualifying assets. The Board believes that in those circumstances the association is direct and the funds flows from borrowing, temporary investment, and construction expenditures are so intertwined and restricted as to

require accounting for the total net cost of financing as a cost of the qualifying assets. The Board also concluded that in all other situations offsetting of interest income against interest cost is not appropriate. The Board further concluded that qualifying assets acquired with externally restricted gifts or grants should not be subject to capitalization of interest cost under Statement 34.

STANDARDS OF FINANCIAL ACCOUNTING AND REPORTING

3. Interest earned shall not be offset against interest cost in determining either capitalization rates or limitations on the amount of interest cost to be capitalized except in situations involving acquisition of qualifying assets financed with the proceeds of tax-exempt borrowings if those funds are externally restricted to finance acquisition of specified qualifying assets or to service the related debt.

4. The amount of interest cost capitalized on qualifying assets acquired with proceeds of tax-exempt borrowings that are externally restricted as specified in paragraph 3 shall be all interest cost of the borrowing less any interest earned on related interest-bearing investments acquired with proceeds of the related tax-exempt borrowings[1] from the date of the borrowing until the assets are ready for their intended use. Interest cost of a tax-exempt borrowing shall be eligible for capitalization on other qualifying assets of the entity when the specified qualifying assets are no longer eligible for interest capitalization.

---

[1]The interest cost and interest earned on any portion of the proceeds of the tax-exempt borrowings that are not designated for the acquisition of specified qualifying assets and servicing the related debt are excluded. The entire interest cost on that portion of the proceeds that is available for other uses (such as refunding of an existing debt issue other than a construction loan related to those assets) is eligible for capitalization on other qualifying assets.

Amendments to FASB Statement No. 34

5. The following subparagraph is added to paragraph 10 of Statement 34, which specifies the types of assets for which interest is not capitalized:

> f. Assets acquired with gifts and grants that are restricted by the donor or grantor to acquisition of those assets to the extent that funds are available from such gifts and grants. Interest earned from temporary investment of those funds that is similarly restricted shall be considered an addition to the gift or grant for this purpose.

6. The following footnote is added at the end of the first sentence of paragraph 13 of Statement 34, which deals with determining the amount of interest cost to be capitalized:

> *If qualifying assets are financed with the proceeds of tax-exempt borrowings and those funds are externally restricted to the acquisition of specified qualifying assets or to service the related debt, the amount of interest cost capitalized shall be determined in accordance with FASB Statement No. 62, *Capitalization of Interest Cost in Situations Involving Certain Tax-Exempt Borrowings and Certain Gifts and Grants.*

7. The following footnote is added to paragraph 17 of Statement 34, which specifies the period for interest capitalization:

> *In situations involving qualifying assets financed with the proceeds of tax-exempt borrowings that are externally restricted as specified in Statement 62, the capitalization period begins at the date of the borrowing.

Rescission of Technical Bulletin

8. FASB Technical Bulletin No. 81-5, *Offsetting Interest Cost to Be Capitalized with Interest Income,* is rescinded upon issuance of this Statement.

Effective Date and Transition

9. This Statement shall be effective for tax-exempt borrowing arrangements entered into and gifts or grants received after August 31, 1982, with earlier application encouraged in financial statements that have not been previously issued. This Statement may be, but is not required to be, applied retroactively to previously issued financial statements for fiscal years beginning after December 15, 1979. If previously issued financial statements are restated, the financial statements shall, in the year that this Statement is first applied, disclose the nature of any restatement and its effects on income before extraordinary items, net income, and related per share amounts for each restated year presented.

> The provisions of this Statement need not be applied to immaterial items.

This Statement was adopted by the affirmative votes of four members of the Financial Accounting Standards Board. Messrs. Block, Morgan, and Walters dissented.

Mr. Block does not support this standard because it merges the accounting for three dissimilar business activities into one: the borrowing of funds, the temporary investment of funds, and the acquisition of capital assets. Users of financial statements find it useful to calculate rates of return to providers of capital, such as return on equity, return on long-term capital, and return on total capital, as well as returns on various types of investment assets and operating assets. Under this standard, interest income will not be reported as a return on the investment asset, interest expense will not be reported as a return on borrowed funds, and a net amount of interest expense or income will be amortized over the life of a fixed asset as depreciation rather than recognized currently as interest. This obscures information significant to users, particularly to those who look upon depreciation as a return of capital,

interest cost as a return *on* capital, and interest income as a return on a financial asset. In addition, this standard calls for an unwarranted extension of the capitalization period to include a period when no acquisition activities are under way, contrary to two of the three requirements of paragraph 17 of Statement 34. The extension of the capitalization period is defended (paragraphs 2 and 14 of this Statement) on grounds that the investment and financing activities are generally considered in the decision to acquire the asset. Mr. Block believes that accounting should reflect the nature and circumstances of transactions and not the unverifiable motivations and expectations that led to them. He doubts that the deferred net interest credit generated during the preacquisition period meets the definition of any element other than revenue as set forth in FASB Concepts Statement No. 3, *Elements of Financial*

Statements of Business Enterprises, and is troubled by the possibility that in extreme cases the acquired asset could be carried at a negative cost.

Mr. Morgan and Mr. Walters believe that offsetting related interest income and expense during the acquisition period is appropriate and consistent with the avoidable-interest-cost notion that is embodied in Statement 34. They disagree with this Statement, however, because it restricts offsetting to tax-exempt borrowings. In their opinion, the reasoning for this narrow approach is based on a conclusion that only the tax-exempt situations are so closely intertwined with the asset acquisition as to require association when, in all likelihood, such intertwining may exist regardless of the tax status of the borrowings. In addition, they believe that it is inconsistent to view the borrowings as intertwined with the asset during the capitalization period and as part of the pool of fungible funds from which interest is available for capitalization on other assets after the capitalization period.

Members of the Financial Accounting Standards Board:

Donald J. Kirk,
Chairman
Frank E. Block

John W. March
Robert A. Morgan
David Mosso

Robert T. Sprouse
Ralph E. Walters

Appendix A

EXAMPLE OF APPLICATION OF THIS STATEMENT

10. The following example illustrates the application of this Statement in the situation described below:

a. The entity is committed to construct Project A at a cost of $10 million. Project A is to be financed from three sources:
   (1) $4 million government grant restricted to use for the specified construction project, payable $1 million per year
   (2) $4 million tax-exempt borrowing at an interest rate of 8 percent ($320,000 per year)
   (3) $2 million from operations
b. The entity has $10 million in other borrowings that are outstanding throughout the construction of Project A. The interest rate on those borrowings is 6 percent. Other qualifying assets of the entity never exceed $5 million during the construction of Project A.
c. The proceeds from the borrowing and the initial phase of the grant are received 1 year in advance of starting construction on Project A and are temporarily invested in interest-bearing investments yielding 12 percent. Interest income earned from temporary investments is not reinvested.
d. Project A will take 4 years after start of construction to complete.
e. The table on the following page sets forth the amount of interest to be capitalized as part of the entity's investment in Project A.
f. Over the course of construction the net cost of financing is $678,000, the sum of the interest capitalized for the 5 years. Accordingly, the entity's total net investment in Project A will be $10,678,000.

589

		Year				
		19X1	**19X2**	**19X3**	**19X4**	**19X5**
		(amounts in thousands)				
(1)	Assumed average qualifying assets	$ 0	$2,000	$5,000	$8,000	$9,000
(2)	Average funding received					
	borrowing	4,000	4,000	4,000	4,000	4,000
	grant	1,000	2,000	3,000	4,000	4,000
(3)	Average temporary investments ((2) − (1), not less than zero)*					
	borrowing	4,000	3,000	1,000	0	0
	grant	1,000	1,000	1,000	0	0
(4)	Interest earned ((3) × 12 percent)					
	(a) borrowing	480	360	120	0	0
	(b) grant	120	120	120	0	0
(5)	Average qualifying assets in excess of borrowing, grant, and interest earned on grant†	0	0	0	0	640
(6)	Interest cost capitalized— other borrowings ((5) × 6 percent)	0	0	0	0	38
(7)	Interest cost— tax-exempt borrowings	320	320	320	320	320
(8)	Interest capitalized ((6) + (7) − (4)(a))‡	(160)	(40)	200	320	358

---

*Balances of unexpended borrowings and unexpended grants can vary depending on the source from which the entity elects to disburse funds.

†That is, (1) average qualifying assets minus the sum of ((2) average funding received plus (4)(b) cumulative interest earned on grant), not less than zero.

‡Note that amounts in parentheses are reductions in the cost of the asset.

Appendix B

BASIS FOR CONCLUSIONS

11. An Exposure Draft of a proposed Statement, *Capitalization of Interest Cost in Situations Involving Tax-Exempt Borrowings and Certain Gifts and Grants,* was issued on December 22, 1981. The Board received 94 letters of comment in response to the Exposure Draft. This appendix discusses the factors that the Board considered significant in reaching the conclusions in this Statement. The Board members who assented to this Statement did so on the basis of the overall considerations. Individual Board members gave greater weight to some factors than to others.

Capitalization of Interest Cost in Situations
Involving Certain Tax-Exempt Borrowings and
Certain Gifts and Grants

FAS62

Tax-Exempt Borrowings

12. Many respondents recommended that offsetting interest income against interest expense be extended to situations in addition to tax-exempt borrowings. They believe that the tax status of the borrowings should not determine the accounting and that offsetting should be required in situations that involve borrowings that are externally restricted for use on particular projects specified under the terms of the borrowing agreement and that externally restrict the interest on temporary investment of the proceeds to finance construction or service the related debt. They believe that the association of such borrowings with the specified projects is direct and that offsetting is appropriate under those circumstances.

13. Some respondents stated that interest income earned prior to acquisition or construction is related to investment decisions and not to acquisition decisions. They would not offset the interest earned for the period from the date of the borrowing to the beginning of the acquisition period even in situations involving tax-exempt borrowings.

14. Statement 34 requires that interest cost be capitalized only on funds that actually have been expended in the process of acquiring a qualifying asset. Obviously, those expended funds cannot be earning interest income. Identifying a borrowing with a specific acquisition and requiring that interest income be offset against interest cost in determining the amount of interest to be capitalized necessarily involves extending the beginning of the capitalization period from the date actual expenditures are made to the date of the borrowing. The Board does not believe that extending the capitalization period in that way and thereby generally increasing the amount of capitalized interest is appropriate. As stated in paragraph 6 of Statement 34, "the historical cost of acquiring an asset includes the costs necessarily incurred to bring it to the condition and location necessary for its intended use." Borrowing for indeterminate periods in advance of actual expenditures cannot be said generally to be a necessary part of acquiring an asset. The Board is persuaded, however, that an exception should be made in the case of tax-exempt borrowings specified by this Statement. The timing and use of tax-exempt borrowings are generally an integral part of the decision to acquire the related asset, and the net interest cost from the date of borrowing to the time the acquired asset is substantially complete and ready for its intended use is an essential part of the cost of acquiring that asset.

15. Some respondents questioned the appropriateness of a net reduction in the cost of an asset that may occur if the interest earned from the date of borrowing is greater than the interest accrued on the debt during the capitalization period. The Board believes, for the reasons indicated in paragraph 14, that interest earned on the temporary investment of the proceeds of certain tax-exempt borrowings from the date of borrowing until the specified qualifying assets are ready for their intended use is a part of the net cost of financing that is properly included as a cost of the qualifying asset. This may result in a net reduction in the cost of an asset.

16. Some respondents stated that interest cost of a tax-exempt borrowing should not be eligible for capitalization on other qualifying assets of the entity if the specified qualifying asset is no longer eligible for capitalization. They believe that this conflicts with the notion of specific association between the tax-exempt borrowings and the assets acquired and that the initial association of the borrowing with the qualifying asset nullifies subsequent capitalization of interest cost of the borrowing. The Board believes that the avoidable-interest concept explained in paragraph 12 of Statement 34 requires that interest cost of tax-exempt borrowings be eligible for capitalization on other qualifying assets acquired after completion of the specified qualifying assets. For the same reason, the interest cost on funds provided from the tax-exempt borrowings that are not designated for the acquisition of qualifying assets and servicing the related debt during the capitalization period are eligible for capitalization on other qualifying assets.

Gifts and Grants

17. Nearly all of the respondents who commented on the proposed treatment for qualifying assets acquired with a restricted gift or grant and for interest earned on the temporary investment of those funds supported the Exposure Draft. They believe that qualifying assets acquired with restricted gifts and grants should not be subject to capitalization of interest cost under Statement 34 because they believe there is no economic cost of financing associated with a gift or grant. They believe such an exemption is appropriate only if the gift or grant is restricted by the donor or grantor to the acquisition of the specified asset (or otherwise required to be returned to the donor or grantor). Accordingly, they would capitalize no interest cost during the acquisition of the qualifying asset to the extent that funds are available from such gifts and grants. They would also consider restricted interest earned from temporary investment of the gift or grant as an enhancement to and consequently an integral part of the gift or grant. The Board concurred and has adopted those provisions of the Exposure Draft.

Transition

18. Some respondents requested that the transition provisions of the Exposure Draft be modified to permit retroactive application. They believe that permitting retroactive application would enable enterprises to eliminate problems of lack of comparability resulting from applying Statement 34 and Bulletin 81-5 that prohibit offsetting and the provisions of this Statement that require offsetting. The Board concurred and has revised the transition pro-

visions to permit retroactive application to the effective date of Statement 34. Statement 34 was effective prospectively for fiscal years beginning after December 15, 1979.

19. The Board concluded that it can reach an informed decision on the basis of existing information without a public hearing and that the effective date and transition specified in paragraph 9 are advisable in the circumstances.

Statement of Financial Accounting Standards No. 63
Financial Reporting by Broadcasters

STATUS

Issued: June 1982

Effective Date: For fiscal years beginning after December 15, 1982

Affects: Amends FAS 32, Appendix A

Affected by: No other pronouncements

SUMMARY

This Statement extracts and modifies the specialized accounting principles and practices contained in AICPA Statement of Position (SOP) 75-5, *Accounting Practices in the Broadcasting Industry*, and establishes standards of financial accounting and reporting for broadcasters. Exhibition rights acquired under a license agreement for program material shall be accounted for as a purchase of rights by the licensee. The asset and liability for a license agreement shall be reported by the licensee, at either the present value or the gross amount of the liability, when the license period begins and certain specified conditions have been met. This Statement also establishes standards of reporting by broadcasters for barter transactions and network affiliation agreements.

Statement of Financial Accounting Standards No. 63
Financial Reporting by Broadcasters

CONTENTS

INTRODUCTION

1. As discussed in FASB Statement No. 32, *Specialized Accounting and Reporting Principles and Practices in AICPA Statements of Position and Guides on Accounting and Auditing Matters,* the FASB is extracting the specialized[1] accounting and reporting principles and practices from AICPA Statements of Position (SOPs) and Guides on accounting and auditing matters and issuing them in FASB Statements after appropriate due process. This Statement extracts and modifies the specialized principles and practices contained in SOP 75-5, *Accounting Practices in the Broadcasting Industry,* and establishes accounting and reporting standards for **Broadcasters.**[2] Appendix C illustrates applications of this Statement.

STANDARDS OF FINANCIAL ACCOUNTING AND REPORTING

License Agreements for Program Material

Financial Statement Presentation

2. A broadcaster (licensee) shall account for a **license agreement for program material** as a purchase of a right or group of rights.

3. A licensee shall report an asset and a liability for the rights acquired and obligations incurred under a license agreement when the license period begins *and* all of the following conditions have been met:

a. The cost of each program is known or reasonably determinable.
b. The program material has been accepted by the licensee in accordance with the conditions of the license agreement.
c. The program is available for its first showing or telecast. Except when a conflicting license prevents usage by the licensee, restrictions under the same license agreement or another license agreement with the same licensor on the timing of subsequent showings shall not affect this availability condition.

The asset shall be segregated on the balance sheet between current and noncurrent based on estimated time of usage. The liability shall be segregated between current and noncurrent based on the payment terms.

4. A licensee shall report the asset and liability for a broadcast license agreement either (a) at the present value of the liability calculated in accordance with the provisions of APB Opinion No. 21, *Interest on Receivables and Payables,* or (b) at the gross amount of the liability. If the present value approach is used, the difference between the gross and net liability shall be accounted for as interest in accordance with Opinion 21.

Amortization

5. The capitalized costs to be amortized shall be determined under one of the methods specified in

---

[1]The term *specialized* is used to refer to those accounting and reporting principles and practices in AICPA Guides and Statements of Position that are neither superseded by nor contained in Accounting Research Bulletins, APB Opinions, FASB Statements, or FASB Interpretations.
[2]Terms defined in the glossary (Appendix A) are in **boldface type** the first time they appear in this Statement.

paragraph 4. Those costs shall be allocated to individual programs within a package on the basis of the relative value of each to the broadcaster, which ordinarily would be specified in the contract. The capitalized costs shall be amortized based on the estimated number of future showings, except that licenses providing for unlimited showings of cartoons and programs with similar characteristics may be amortized over the period of the agreement because the estimated number of future showings may not be determinable.

6. Feature programs shall be amortized on a program-by-program basis; however, amortization as a package may be appropriate if it approximates the amortization that would have been provided on a program-by-program basis. Program series and other syndicated products shall be amortized as a series. If the first showing is more valuable to a station than reruns, an accelerated method of amortization shall be used. However, the straight-line amortization method may be used if each showing is expected to generate similar revenues.

Valuation

7. The capitalized costs of rights to program materials shall be reported in the balance sheet at the lower of unamortized cost or estimated net realizable value on a program-by-program, series, package, or **daypart** basis, as appropriate. If management's expectations of the programming usefulness of a program, series, package, or daypart are revised downward, it may be necessary to write down unamortized cost to estimated net realizable value. A write-down from unamortized cost to a lower estimated net realizable value establishes a new cost basis.

Barter Transactions

8. Broadcasters may **barter** unsold advertising time for products or services. All barter transactions except those involving the exchange of advertising time for network programming[3] shall be reported at the estimated fair value of the product or service received, in accordance with the provisions of paragraph 25 of APB Opinion No. 29, *Accounting for Nonmonetary Transactions.* Barter revenue shall be reported when commercials are broadcast, and merchandise or services received shall be reported when received or used. If merchandise or services are received prior to the broadcast of the commercial, a liability shall be reported. Likewise, if the commercial is broadcast first, a receivable shall be reported.

Network Affiliation Agreements

9. Network affiliation agreements and other such items ordinarily are presented in the balance sheet of a broadcaster as intangible assets. If a network affiliation is terminated and not immediately replaced or under agreement to be replaced, the unamortized balance of the amount originally allocated to the network affiliation agreement shall be charged to expense. If a network affiliation is terminated and immediately replaced or under agreement to be replaced, a loss shall be recognized to the extent that the unamortized cost of the terminated affiliation exceeds the fair value of the new affiliation. Gain shall not be recognized if the fair value of the new network affiliation exceeds the unamortized cost of the terminated affiliation.

Disclosure

10. Disclose commitments for license agreements that have been executed but were not reported because they do not meet the conditions of paragraph 3.

Amendment to FASB Statement No. 32

11. The reference to AICPA Statement of Position (SOP) 75-5, *Accounting Practices in the Broadcasting Industry,* is deleted from Appendix A of Statement 32.

Effective Date and Transition

12. This Statement shall be effective for financial statements for fiscal years beginning after December 15, 1982, with earlier application encouraged. If application of this Statement results in a change in accounting, restatement of previously issued annual financial statements to conform to the provisions of this Statement is encouraged but not required. If it is not practicable or if the issuer of financial statements elects not to restate any prior year, the cumulative effect shall be included in net income in the year in which the Statement is first applied. (Refer to paragraph 20 of APB Opinion No. 20, *Accounting Changes.*) The effect on income before extraordinary items, net income, and related per share amounts of applying this Statement in a year in which the cumulative effect is included in determining that year's net income shall be disclosed for that year.

13. If previously issued financial statements are restated, the financial statements shall disclose, in

---

[3]As the definition of **network affiliation agreement** in the glossary to this Statement describes in further detail, a network affiliate does not incur program cost for network programming it carries; likewise, it does not sell the related advertising time but instead receives compensation from the network.

the year that this Statement is first applied, the nature of any restatement and its effects on income before extraordinary items, net income, and related per share amounts for each restated year presented. If retroactive restatement of all years presented is not practicable, the financial statements presented

shall be restated for as many consecutive years as practicable and the cumulative effect of applying the Statement shall be included in determining net income of the earliest year restated (not necessarily the earliest year presented).

> **The provisions of this Statement need not be applied to immaterial items.**

This Statement was adopted by the affirmative votes of six members of the Financial Accounting Standards Board. Mr. Sprouse dissented.

Mr. Sprouse dissents from the issuance of this Statement. In his opinion, this Statement is retrogressive in two important respects: (a) it flies in the face of Opinion 21 by permitting the asset and liability arising from a license agreement to be reported at the gross amount of future cash payments necessary to settle the obligation, and (b) it ignores the need for comparability, an important qualitative characteristic of accounting information, by designating as equally acceptable two different methods of accounting for the asset and liability arising from license agreements under identical facts and circumstances. Mr. Sprouse believes that the principles

enunciated in Opinion 21 are fundamental and sound. In FASB Statement No. 53, *Financial Reporting by Producers and Distributors of Motion Picture Films,* those principles were applied in measuring the receivable and revenue of the other party to a license agreement. Requiring the seller's receivable and revenue to be reported at the present value of the future license payments and permitting the purchaser's asset and payable to be reported at either the gross amount or present value of those future cash payments can only serve to detract from the credibility and usefulness of financial reporting.

Members of the Financial Accounting Standards Board:

Donald J. Kirk,	John W. March	Robert T. Sprouse
Chairman	Robert A. Morgan	Ralph E. Walters
Frank E. Block	David Mosso	

Appendix A

GLOSSARY

14. This appendix defines certain terms that are used in this Statement.

Barter

The exchange of unsold advertising time for products or services. The broadcaster benefits (providing the exchange does not interfere with its cash sales) by exchanging otherwise unsold time for such things as programs, fixed assets, merchandise, other media advertising privileges, travel and hotel arrangements, entertainment, and other services or products.

Broadcaster

An entity or an affiliated group of entities that transmits radio or television program material.

Daypart

An aggregation of programs broadcast during a

particular time of day (for example, daytime, evening, late night) or programs of a similar type (for example, sports, news, children's shows). Broadcasters generally sell access to viewing audiences to advertisers on a daypart basis.

License agreement for program material

A typical license agreement for program material (for example, features, specials, series, or cartoons) covers several programs (a package) and grants a television station, group of stations, network, pay television, or cable television system (licensee) the right to broadcast either a specified number or an unlimited number of showings over a maximum period of time (license period) for a specified fee. Ordinarily, the fee is paid in installments over a period generally shorter than the license period. The agreement usually contains a separate license for each program in the package. The license expires at the earlier of the last allowed telecast or the end of the license period. The licensee pays the required fee whether or not the rights are exercised. If the licensee does not exercise the contractual rights, the rights revert to the licensor with no refund to the licensee. The license period is not intended to provide continued use of the program material throughout that period but rather to define a reasonable period of time within which the licensee can exercise the limited rights to use the program material.

Network affiliation agreement

A broadcaster may be affiliated with a network under a network affiliation agreement. Under the agreement, the station receives compensation for the network programming that it carries based on a formula designed to compensate the station for advertising sold on a network basis and included in network programming. Program costs, a major expense of television stations, are generally lower for a network affiliate than for an independent station because an affiliate does not incur program costs for network programs.

Appendix B

BACKGROUND INFORMATION AND BASIS FOR CONCLUSIONS

15. SOP 75-5 was developed to narrow the range of acceptable alternative accounting practices among broadcasters, particularly accounting for program rights and related license fees. Before 1975, some broadcasters treated the unpaid fees stipulated in license agreements for program material as commitments and recorded neither the program rights nor the related obligations on their balance sheets. Other broadcasters recorded the program rights and the related obligations as assets and liabilities, respectively, but practice varied with respect to measuring the amount at which the asset and liability were reported and with respect to classification and method of amortizing the assets. SOP 75-5 concluded that assets and liabilities should be reported at the present value of the future license payments determined using an imputed discount rate, that interest should be accrued on the liability, that assets should be classified based on estimated usage, and that accelerated amortization based on estimated future showings generally should be used. The Board has been informed that the variety of practices in existence prior to the issuance of SOP 75-5 has continued to date.

16. The Board has extracted the specialized accounting and reporting principles of SOP 75-5 without significant change except for providing an option in paragraph 4 to report the asset and liability for a license agreement at the gross amount of the liability. Some of the background material, discussion of accounting alternatives, and general accounting guidance have not been carried forward from the SOP. The Board's conceptual framework project on accounting recognition criteria will address issues of recognizing contractual rights and obligations that may pertain to those addressed in this Statement. A Statement of Financial Accounting Concepts resulting from that project in due course will serve as a basis for evaluating existing standards and practices. Accordingly, the Board may wish to evaluate the standards in this Statement when its conceptual framework project is completed.

17. An Exposure Draft of a proposed Statement, *Financial Accounting and Reporting by Broadcasters,* was issued June 12, 1981 for a 90-day comment period. The Board received 45 letters of comment on the Exposure Draft. Two issues were addressed by the majority of respondents: (a) Should a license agreement for television program material be treated by a licensee as a purchase of a right or as an operating lease, and (b) if the license agreement is treated as a purchase of a right, and an asset and a liability are reported, should the liability be reported in accordance with Opinion 21 at its present value determined by discounting future license payments using an imputed rate of interest? This appendix discusses the factors deemed significant by the Board in reaching the conclusions of this Statement. The Board members who assented to this Statement did so on the basis of the overall considerations; individual members gave greater weight to some factors than to others.

Reporting the Asset and Liability

18. Many respondents believe that a license agreement for program material should be accounted for as an operating lease, that no receivable or payable should be reported at the inception of the agreement, and that footnote disclosure of program commitments is adequate. They believe that such an agreement has many characteristics of an operating lease, even though FASB Statement No. 13, *Accounting for Leases,* does not apply to license agreements. They further believe that if license agreements were classified in accordance with the criteria of paragraph 7 of Statement 13, a majority would be considered operating leases rather than capital leases. They note that if a license agreement were accounted for as an operating lease, no asset or liability would be reported by the licensee and Opinion 21 would not be applicable. A few respondents believe broadcast license agreements are similar to executory contracts and that an asset and liability should therefore not be reported.

19. Many other respondents believe that a license agreement for program material should be reported as a purchase of a right to broadcast that material.

Programs available under license agreements are an important source of future advertising revenue to a broadcaster. Those respondents believe that reporting an asset that will produce future revenues and a liability that will require future license payments is necessary for readers of financial statements to assess the resources, obligations, and future cash flows of the enterprise. They rejected accounting for license agreements as operating leases because under that approach the balance sheet of a broadcaster would reflect only a net debit or a net credit representing the difference between cumulative license payments and cumulative amortization of program costs to date.

20. Some respondents stated that reporting program license agreements as a purchase of a right and the incurrence of a liability is consistent with the definitions of an asset and a liability in FASB Concepts Statement No. 3, *Elements of Financial Statements of Business Enterprises.* The right to broadcast program material during the license period is an asset—a probable future economic benefit that is obtained by the broadcaster as a result of a past transaction—signing the license agreement. Similarly, the broadcaster's obligation to make future payments under the license agreement is a liability—a probable future sacrifice of cash that arises from a present obligation of the broadcaster as a result of a past transaction. They also believe that symmetry in accounting is desirable and that both parties to a contract generally should account for it similarly. Statement 53 considers a license agreement to be a sale of a right by a producer or distributor (licensor) of program material.

21. The Board concluded that exhibition rights acquired under a license agreement for program material should be accounted for as a purchase of rights by the licensee. The Board believes that reporting an asset and a liability for such an agreement is consistent with the definitions of an asset and a liability in Concepts Statement 3 and that information concerning the resources and obligations of the enterprise is necessary for readers of financial statements to assess future cash flows. It also believes that a broadcast license agreement differs from an executory contract because the obligation to make license payments is absolute and because the subject of the agreement—program material—is at hand and available for use.

Date of Recording the License Agreement

22. The Exposure Draft stated that a broadcaster should report the asset and liability for a license agreement when the license period begins, the program is available for its first broadcast, and other specified conditions have been met. A few respondents believe the asset and liability should be reported on the date the agreement is signed. They believe that signing the agreement is the event by which the licensee acquires rights to use the program material and that reporting the asset and liability on that date best portrays in the financial statements the broadcaster's rights to future program material and obligations for future cash payments.

23. The Board believes that an asset and a liability for a license agreement should be reported when the conditions specified in paragraph 3 are met. The Board believes that at the date of signing, a substantial degree of uncertainty about cost, acceptability, and availability exists, particularly if a license agreement is signed for program material that does not yet exist. The major uncertainties are eliminated when the conditions specified in paragraph 3 are met, and the asset and liability should be reported then.

Recognition of Imputed Interest

24. Many respondents in the broadcasting industry stated that if an asset and a liability for a license agreement are reported, the asset and liability should be reported at the gross amount of future license payments rather than at the present value of those future payments determined using an imputed discount rate. Some believe that accruing interest on the liability would not properly match revenue and expense. They believe that the gross amount of the license payments should be amortized to expense in the periods in which the program is broadcast and generates advertising revenue. Accruing interest on the liability would result in recognizing interest expense in different periods from those in which advertising revenue is earned. Other respondents believe that accruing interest results in timing of expense recognition similar to that which would exist if the broadcaster paid the cash equivalent amount of the liability at the outset of the arrangement using borrowed funds. They believe that interest expense arises from the way in which the license agreement asset is financed. In their opinion, recognizing interest expense in a different pattern from amortization of the asset is a faithful representation of the different patterns of license payments and utilization of the licensed rights.

25. Several respondents stated that, for many license agreements, accounting separately for interest expense would not have a material impact on the pattern of expense recognition. They believe that imputing interest is burdensome, especially when it must be applied to the large number of contracts a broadcaster may have. They infer from this that an accounting requirement that would call for the asset and liability to be reported initially at their present values is inappropriate. Others similarly observe that many individual contracts would be

excluded from the scope of Opinion 21 because they are short-term or because the timing of payments is based on the uncertain timing of future broadcasts.

26. Some respondents stated that they view the entire program cost as an operating expense. They do not recognize interest as a component of this cost, either during negotiations with licensors or later as payments are made. They believe the reporting of that "noncash" interest expense distorts operating results and segment disclosures and will confuse readers and management. Other respondents believe that a cash payment of interest is included in each cash payment for the license and that the concept of the time value of money, and therefore interest, is implicit to some degree in every license agreement, regardless of whether interest is specifically discussed during negotiations or separately identified as a component of license fee payments.

27. Some respondents believe that Opinion 21 excludes program license agreements from its scope. They believe that a license agreement is by its nature a prepayment because the payments are made over a period generally shorter than the broadcast period. Paragraph 3(b) of Opinion 21 excludes certain advance payments from the scope of that Opinion. Other respondents stated that a license agreement is not an advance payment because the licensor has fulfilled all of its responsibilities at the time the programs are made available to the licensee.

28. A few respondents believe that Opinion 21 does not apply because, even if a complete package or series of programs is made available to the broadcaster at the inception of a license agreement, it cannot use those programs all at once but will instead use them over an extended period of time as marketing and scheduling factors permit. They believe that, in substance, this is equivalent to delivery of the programs over time and that an ongoing flow of product in exchange for an ongoing payment stream does not involve a payment for interest.

29. Some Board members believe the asset and liability for a broadcast license agreement should be reported at the present value of the liability determined using an imputed interest rate, and that interest should be accrued on the liability in accordance with Opinion 21 and consistent with SOP 75-5. They believe that interest arises from the manner in which the acquisition of program materials is financed and that recognizing the difference between the gross and net liability as interest is a faithful representation of that cost.

30. Some Board members agree that the asset and liability for a license agreement should be reported at the present value of the liability. However, they believe that (a) in each period the amortization of discount on the liability should be accounted for as additional program cost rather than as interest cost as would be required under Opinion 21 and (b) program expense should be determined by amortizing undiscounted program cost, that is, the aggregate of all payments under the license. That approach was described in paragraph 31 of the Exposure Draft. The Board members who support the approach believe it should be followed whenever a normal business arrangement calls for later payment for supplies or services that is linked to use of the related specific assets in future operations. Those Board members believe such an approach should not be required in this Statement because in their opinion it would be premature to decide whether accounting for broadcast license agreements should reflect imputed interest on an interest method or on a program cost method like the one described in this paragraph until broader issues concerning recognition of contractual rights and obligations have been examined.

31. In the "Notice for Recipients" of the Exposure Draft, the Board stated that changes may be needed in the accounting principles and reporting practices to be extracted from SOP 75-5 if those principles and practices are not being followed. The Board has been advised by the FASB Task Force on Specialized Principles for the Entertainment Industry, and by many respondents, that for the reasons cited in paragraphs 18 and 24-28, (a) some broadcasters do not report an asset and a liability for rights acquired and obligations incurred under a license agreement and (b) few of those who report an asset and a liability recognize imputed interest. Some Board members support the view in paragraph 29; others support the view in paragraph 30. One Board member supports the view in paragraph 18. In addition, some Board members believe broadcasters should not be required to report the asset and liability for a license agreement at the present value of the liability until the broad subject of discounting has been considered by the Board. The assenting Board members have concluded that a standard is required, however, to reduce the number of reporting practices now used by broadcasters. Therefore, the Board believes that the option in this Statement that permits reporting the asset and liability for a license agreement at either the present value or gross amount of the liability will be an improvement in financial reporting by broadcasters.

Other Issues

32. SOP 75-5 concluded that broadcasting intangibles are subject to the amortization provisions of APB Opinion No. 17, *Intangible Assets.* Several respondents stated that this Statement should specifically exempt intangible assets such as network affil-

iation agreements and broadcasting licenses from the provisions of Opinion 17. They believe such intangibles are marketable assets whose values do not diminish over time and, therefore, the intangibles should not be required to be amortized.

33. The Board did not consider the accounting for broadcasting intangible assets because a reconsideration of the provisions of Opinion 17 is beyond the scope of this project.

34. Some respondents requested guidance regarding the treatment of changes in estimates of net realizable value during interim periods. SOP 75-5 did not provide guidance in that area and the Board concluded that it should not address that matter at this time.

35. The Board has concluded that it can reach an informed decision on the basis of existing information without a public hearing and that the effective date and transition specified in paragraphs 12 and 13 are advisable in the circumstances.

Appendix C

ILLUSTRATION OF ACCOUNTING FOR LICENSE AGREEMENTS FOR PROGRAM MATERIAL

36. This appendix illustrates accounting for a license agreement for television program material in accordance with this Statement.

37. Assumptions

a. End of Fiscal Year—December 31
b. Contract Execution Date—July 31, 19X1
c. Number of Films and Telecasts Permitted—4 films, 2 telecasts each
d. Payment Schedule—$1,000,000 at contract execution date, $6,000,000 on January 1, 19X2, 19X3, and 19X4
e. Appropriate Interest Rate for Imputation of Interest—12 percent per year
f. Fees, License Periods, and Film Availability Dates

		Stated License Periods		Film Availability
Film	Total Fee	From	To[4]	Dates
A	$ 8,000,000	10/1/X1	9/30/X3	9/1/X1
B	5,000,000	10/1/X1	9/30/X3	9/1/X1
C	3,750,000	9/1/X2	8/31/X4	12/1/X1
D	2,250,000	9/1/X3	8/31/X5	12/1/X2
	$19,000,000			

g. Telecast Dates and Revenues

	First Telecast		Second Telecast	
Film	Date	Percent of Total Revenue	Date	Percent of Total Revenue
A	3/1/X2	60%	6/1/X3	40%
B	5/1/X2	70%	7/1/X3	30%
C	6/1/X3	75%	6/1/X4	25%
D	12/1/X4	65%	8/1/X5	35%

38. For purposes of imputing interest in accordance with Opinion 21, it is assumed that the $1,000,000 payment on July 31, 19X1 and the $6,000,000 payments on January 1, 19X2 and 19X3 relate to films A and B and the $6,000,000 payment on January 1, 19X4 relates to films C and D. Other simplifying assumptions or methods of assigning the payments to the films could be made.

---

[4]The actual license periods expire at the earlier of (a) the second telecast or (b) the end of the stated license period.

Film	Payment		Discounted Present Value (rounded to 000s)	
	Date	Amount	As of Date	Amount
A&B	7/31/X1	$ 1,000,000	10/1/X1	$ 1,000,000
	1/1/X2	6,000,000	10/1/X1	5,825,000
	1/1/X3	6,000,000	10/1/X1	5,201,000
		$13,000,000		$12,026,000
C	1/1/X4	$ 3,750,000	9/1/X2	$ 3,219,000
D	1/1/X4	$ 2,250,000	9/1/X3	$ 2,163,000
		$ 6,000,000		

39. Asset and Liability Recognition (Present Value Approach)

Film	License Period		Year of Asset and Liability Recognition		
	From	To	19X1	19X2	19X3
A	10/1/X1	9/30/X3	$7,401,000(a)		
B	10/1/X1	9/30/X3	4,625,000(a)		
C	9/1/X2	8/31/X4		$3,219,000	
D	9/1/X3	8/31/X5			$2,163,000

(a) Discounted present value of $12,026,000 allocated 8/13 to film A and 5/13 to film B based on stated license fees.

40. Expense Recognition (Present Value Approach)

Film	Year of Expense Recognition				
	19X1	19X2	19X3	19X4	19X5
A	$204,000(I)(a)	$ 396,000(I)(b)			
		4,441,000(A)(c)	$2,960,000(A)(d)		
B	127,000(I)(e)	247,000(I)(f)			
		3,238,000(A)(g)	1,387,000(A)(h)		
C		129,000(I)(i)	402,000(I)(j)		
			2,414,000(A)(k)	$ 805,000(A)(l)	
D			87,000(I)(m)		
				1,406,000(A)(n)	$757,000(A)(o)
	$331,000	$8,451,000	$7,250,000	$2,211,000	$757,000

(I)   Accrued interest expense
(A)   Amortization of program cost
(a)   Interest at 12% for 3 months on liability of $11,026,000 allocated 8/13 to film A
(b)   Interest at 12% for 1 year on liability of $5,357,000 ($11,026,000 plus $331,000 less 1/1/X2 payment of $6,000,000) allocated 8/13 to film A
(c) $7,401,000 × 60%
(d) $7,401,000 × 40%
(e)   Interest at 12% for 3 months on liability of $11,026,000 allocated 5/13 to film B
(f)   Interest at 12% for 1 year on liability of $5,357,000 ($11,026,000 plus $331,000 less 1/1/X2 payment of $6,000,000) allocated 5/13 to film B
(g) $4,625,000 × 70%
(h) $4,625,000 × 30%
(i)   Interest at 12% for 4 months on liability of $3,219,000
(j)   Interest at 12% for 1 year on liability of $3,348,000 ($3,219,000 plus $129,000)
(k) $3,219,000 × 75%
(l) $3,219,000 × 25%
(m)   Interest at 12% for 4 months on liability of $2,163,000
(n) $2,163,000 × 65%
(o) $2,163,000 × 35%

41. Asset and Liability Recognition (Gross Approach)

Film	License Period From	To	Year of Asset and Liability Recognition 19X1	19X2	19X3
A	10/1/X1	9/30/X3	$8,000,000		
B	10/1/X1	9/30/X3	5,000,000		
C	9/1/X2	8/31/X4		$3,750,000	
D	9/1/X3	8/31/X5			$2,250,000

42. Expense Recognition (Gross Approach)

Film	Year of Expense Recognition(a) 19X1	19X2	19X3	19X4	19X5
A		$4,800,000(b)	$3,200,000(c)		
B		3,500,000(d)	1,500,000(e)		
C			2,813,000(f)	$ 937,000(g)	
D				1,463,000(h)	$787,000(i)
	$ —	$8,300,000	$7,513,000	$2,400,000	$787,000

(a)   Under the Gross Approach, all costs under a license agreement are recorded as amortization of program cost.
(b) $8,000,000 × 60%
(c) $8,000,000 × 40%
(d) $5,000,000 × 70%
(e) $5,000,000 × 30%
(f) $3,750,000 × 75%
(g) $3,750,000 × 25%
(h) $2,250,000 × 65%
(i) $2,250,000 × 35%

Statement of Financial Accounting Standards No. 64
Extinguishments of Debt Made to Satisfy
Sinking-Fund Requirements

an amendment of FASB Statement No. 4

STATUS

Issued: September 1982

Effective Date: For extinguishments of debt occurring after September 30, 1982

Affects: Amends FAS 4, paragraph 8 and footnote 2

Affected by: No other pronouncements

SUMMARY

This Statement amends FASB Statement No. 4, *Reporting Gains and Losses from Extinguishment of Debt,* so that (a) gains and losses from extinguishments of debt made to satisfy sinking-fund requirements that an enterprise must meet within one year of the date of the extinguishment are not required to be classifed as extraordinary items and (b) the classification of gains and losses from extinguishments of debt made to satisfy sinking-fund requirements are to be determined without regard to the means used to achieve the extinguishment.

Statement of Financial Accounting Standards No. 64
Extinguishments of Debt Made to Satisfy Sinking-Fund Requirements

an amendment of FASB Statement No. 4

CONTENTS

INTRODUCTION

1. The FASB has been requested to reconsider two provisions of FASB Statement No. 4, *Reporting Gains and Losses from Extinguishment of Debt,* regarding the classification of gains and losses from extinguishments of debt made to satisfy current or future sinking-fund requirements. Paragraph 8 of Statement 4 states:

> Gains and losses from extinguishment of debt that are included in the determination of net income shall be aggregated and, if material, . . . classified as an extraordinary item, net of related income tax effect. That conclusion shall apply whether an extinguishment is early or at scheduled maturity date or later. The conclusion does not apply, however, to gains or losses from cash purchases of debt made to satisfy current or future sinking-fund requirements.[2] Those gains and losses shall be aggregated and the amount shall be identified as a separate item.

---

[2]Some obligations to acquire debt have the essential characteristics of sinking-fund requirements, and resulting gains or losses are not required to be classified as extraordinary items. For example, if an enterprise is required each year to purchase a certain percentage of its outstanding bonds before their scheduled maturity, the gain or loss from such purchase is not required to be classified as an extraordinary item. Debt maturing serially, however, does not have the characteristics of sinking-fund requirements, and gain or loss from extinguishment of serial debt shall be classified as an extraordinary item.

2. With respect to the requirements of paragraph 8, the FASB has been asked:

a. Whether gains and losses from extinguishments of debt made to satisfy future sinking-fund requirements are exempt from the extraordinary-item classification requirement of Statement 4 regardless of when in the future those sinking-fund requirements have to be met

b. Whether the exemption from extraordinary-item classification also should apply to gains and losses resulting from noncash extinguishments of debt made to satisfy sinking-fund requirements

3. The Board has concluded that the exemption from the general extraordinary-item classification requirement of Statement 4 should be limited to gains and losses from extinguishments of debt made to satisfy sinking-fund requirements that an enterprise must meet within one year of the date of the extinguishment. The Board also has decided that the classification of gains and losses from extinguishments of debt made to satisfy sinking-fund requirements should be determined without regard to the means used to achieve the extinguishment. Accordingly, gains and losses resulting from noncash extinguishments of debt made to satisfy sinking-fund requirements shall be classified in the same manner as gains and losses from cash extinguishments.

STANDARDS OF FINANCIAL ACCOUNTING AND REPORTING

Amendment to FASB Statement No. 4

4. The third sentence of paragraph 8 of Statement 4 and the first sentence of footnote 2 to that paragraph are amended to read as follows:

> The conclusion does not apply, however, to gains or losses from extinguishments of debt made to satisfy sinking-fund requirements that an enterprise must meet within one year of the date of the extinguishment.[2]

---

[2]Some obligations to acquire debt have the essential characteristics of sinking-fund requirements, and resulting gains or losses are not required to be classified as extraordinary items if the obligations must be met within one year of the date of the extinguishment.

Effective Date and Transition

5. This Statement shall be effective for extinguishments of debt occurring after September 30, 1982 with earlier application encouraged in annual financial statements that have not previously been issued. The provisions of this Statement shall not be applied retroactively to previously issued annual financial statements.

> The provisions of this Statement need not be applied to immaterial items.

This Statement was adopted by the unanimous vote of the seven members of the Financial Accounting Standards Board:

Donald J. Kirk,	John W. March	Robert T. Sprouse
Chairman	Robert A. Morgan	Ralph E. Walters
Frank E. Block	David Mosso	

Appendix

BACKGROUND INFORMATION AND BASIS FOR CONCLUSIONS

6. As stated in paragraph 2, the Board was asked (a) whether gains and losses from extinguishments of debt made to satisfy future sinking-fund requirements are exempt from the extraordinary-item classification requirement of Statement 4 regardless of when in the future those sinking-fund requirements have to be met and (b) whether the exemption from extraordinary-item classification also should apply to gains and losses resulting from noncash extinguishments of debt made to satisfy sinking-fund requirements.

7. The Board has been advised that diverse accounting practices have developed as a result of different interpretations of the phrase *future sinking-fund requirements* in paragraph 8. Some have interpreted that paragraph to exempt all gains and losses from extinguishments of debt subject to future sinking-fund requirements from the extraordinary-item classification requirement regardless of when in the future those requirements have to be met. Others, however, have interpreted that phrase to mean only those future sinking-fund requirements that have to be met in the near future. In the Exposure Draft, the Board proposed that the exemption be limited to gains and losses from extinguishments of debt made to satisfy sinking-fund requirements that an enterprise must meet within the next year.

8. Paragraph 8 of Statement 4 specifically exempts from the extraordinary-item classification requirement those gains or losses resulting from *cash purchases* of debt made to satisfy current or future sinking-fund requirements. Those raising this ques-

tion believe that the method of achieving the extinguishment should not determine the manner in which the resulting gains and losses are classified in the financial statements. They point out that APB Opinion No. 26, *Early Extinguishment of Debt,* indicates that all extinguishments of debt before scheduled maturities are fundamentally alike and that the accounting for such transactions should be the same regardless of the means used to achieve the extinguishment. They believe that similar reasoning should be adopted in paragraph 8 of Statement 4 and that the classification of gains and losses resulting from extinguishments of debt made to satisfy sinking-fund requirements should not be based on the means used to effect the extinguishments. The Board agrees and deleted the reference to "cash purchases" in the third sentence of paragraph 8 of Statement 4.

9. An Exposure Draft of a proposed Statement, *Extinguishments of Debt Made to Satisfy Sinking-Fund Requirements,* was issued on February 23, 1982. The Board received 90 letters of comment in response to the Exposure Draft. Certain of the comments received and the Board's consideration of them, including various alternatives considered and reasons for accepting some and rejecting others, are discussed in the remaining paragraphs.

10. Many respondents to the Exposure Draft opposed issuance of a final Statement because they believe the extraordinary-item criteria in APB Opinion No. 30, *Reporting the Results of Operations,* are preferable to the provisions of Statement 4 for purposes of classifying gains and losses resulting from the extinguishment of *all* forms of debt. Those respondents recommended that the Board rescind, or consider rescinding, Statement 4 rather than proceeding with the proposal in the Exposure Draft. The Board notes that the general issue of how to report components of comprehensive income is

being considered in the Board's conceptual framework project on reporting income, cash flows, and financial position of business enterprises. The Board has concluded that the general requirement of Statement 4 (extraordinary-item classification of gains and losses from extinguishment of debt) should not be reconsidered until that conceptual framework project is completed.

11. Other respondents opposed the proposed amendment because they view it as a major extension of Statement 4. They viewed Statement 4 as removing all *nonsinking-fund* debt extinguishments from the classification criteria of Opinion 30, and they now view the proposed amendment as removing many *sinking-fund* debt extinguishments from those same criteria. They believe that the criteria of Opinion 30 should continue to be applied to gains and losses resulting from the extinguishment of sinking-fund debt. The Board believes that the exemption from extraordinary-item classification is appropriate in circumstances in which an enterprise extinguishes debt annually to meet its pending sinking-fund requirements. The Board notes, however, that extinguishments of debt made in anticipation of future sinking-fund requirements are not required to be made currently to meet continuing contractual requirements. Instead, the Board believes those extinguishments are similar in nature to extinguishments of debt not subject to sinking-fund requirements for which resulting gains and losses must be classified as extraordinary items. The Board recognizes, however, that, as a practical matter, an enterprise may extinguish debt somewhat in advance of a sinking-fund due date to satisfy the requirement at that date.

12. Many respondents stated that the proposed one-year time frame is too restrictive and could have adverse economic effects and suggested the time frame be extended. They argued that such a one-year limitation may induce enterprises to delay purchases of sinking-fund debt until one year from the due date to avoid extraordinary-item classification

of resulting gains and losses. They pointed out that sinking-fund debt often is extinguished several years in advance of its due date to take advantage of temporary changes in interest rates and believe that such a policy is a prudent and normal business practice that should not be discouraged by an accounting standard. Other respondents noted that some sinking-fund debt issues are held primarily by a small number of institutional investors and are not widely traded. Those respondents pointed out that the market price of sinking-fund debt will rise to a level higher than would prevail in a free market situation as the sinking fund due date approaches. They believe enterprises need flexibility to minimize the costs of their sinking-fund repurchase programs and also that the proposed amendment would, in effect, impair that flexibility. Those respondents who opposed the one-year time frame suggested various alternative limitations. Most recommended a three-year limitation.

13. The Board was not persuaded by the arguments summarized in the previous paragraph. The Board believes gains and losses from extinguishments of sinking-fund debt should be exempt from extraordinary-item classification only if those sinking-fund requirements for which the debt was acquired must be met currently. The Board acknowledges that an enterprise may determine that extinguishment of several years' sinking-fund requirements or an entire sinking-fund debt issue is advisable in the circumstances. However, the Board does not believe that fact should affect the classification of the resulting gains or losses. Further, several Board members rejected the arguments in paragraph 12 because they believe the sinking-fund exemption in Statement 4 should be eliminated completely.

14. The Board concluded that it can reach an informed decision on the basis of existing information without a public hearing and that the effective date and transition specified in paragraph 5 are advisable in the circumstances.

Statement of Financial Accounting Standards No. 65
Accounting for Certain Mortgage Banking Activities

STATUS

Issued: September 1982

Effective Date: For transactions entered into after December 31, 1982

Affects: Amends FAS 32, Appendix A

Affected by: Paragraphs 1 and 10 amended by FAS 122 and FAS 125
Paragraph 4 amended by FAS 115 and FAS 124
Paragraphs 5, 7, 8, 9(c), 12, 17, 28, and 29 amended by
  FAS 115
Paragraph 6 amended by FAS 91, FAS 115, and FAS 125
Paragraphs 8, 11, 19, and 30 and footnote 4 superseded by FAS 125
Paragraph 9(a) amended by FAS 115 and FAS 125
Paragraphs 14, 21, 25, and 26 and footnotes 2 and 7 superseded by FAS 91
Paragraph 15 amended by FAS 122 and FAS 125
Paragraphs 16 through 18 and footnote 6 superseded by FAS 122 and FAS 125
Paragraphs 19 and 30 amended by FAS 122
Paragraph 23 amended by FAS 91
Paragraph 34 amended by FAS 125

Other Interpretive Pronouncement: FTB 87-3

Issues Discussed by FASB Emerging Issues Task Force (EITF)

Affects: No EITF Issues

Interpreted by: Paragraph 3 interpreted by EITF Topic No. D-2

Related Issues: EITF Issues No. 84-4, 85-13, 87-34, 88-11, 90-21, and 95-5

SUMMARY

This Statement extracts the specialized accounting and reporting principles and practices from AICPA Statements of Position 74-12, *Accounting Practices in the Mortgage Banking Industry,* and 76-2, *Accounting for Origination Costs and Loan and Commitment Fees in the Mortgage Banking Industry,* and establishes accounting and reporting standards for certain mortgage banking activities.

Mortgage loans and mortgage-backed securities held for sale are reported at the lower of cost or market value. Origination costs associated with loan applications received directly from borrowers are expensed as period costs. The premium paid for the right to service loans in a purchase of mortgage loans ordinarily is capitalized as the cost of acquiring that right.

This Statement also establishes accounting and reporting standards for several different types of loan and commitment fees. Loan origination fees, to the extent they represent reimbursement of loan origination costs, are recognized as revenue when the loan is made. Loan commitment fees ordinarily are recognized as revenue or expense when the loans are sold to permanent investors. Fees for services performed by third parties and loan placement fees are recognized as revenue when all significant services have been performed. Land acquisition, development, and construction loan fees and standby and gap commitment fees are recognized as revenue over the combined commitment and loan periods.

Statement of Financial Accounting Standards No. 65
Accounting for Certain Mortgage Banking Activities

CONTENTS

INTRODUCTION

1. Mortgage banking activities primarily consist of two separate but interrelated activities: (a) the origination or acquisition of mortgage loans and the sale of the loans to **permanent investors**[1] and (b) the subsequent long-term **servicing** of the loans. Mortgage loans are acquired for sale to permanent investors from a variety of sources, including applications received directly from borrowers (in-house originations), purchases from realtors and brokers, purchases from investors, and conversions of various forms of interim financing to permanent financing.

2. A **mortgage banking enterprise** usually retains the right to service mortgage loans it sells to permanent investors. A servicing fee, usually based on a percentage of the outstanding principal balance of the mortgage loan, is received for performing loan administration functions. When servicing fees exceed the cost of performing servicing functions, the existing contractual right to service mortgage loans has economic value. Because of their value, rights to service mortgage loans frequently have been purchased and sold.

APPLICABILITY AND SCOPE

3. This Statement establishes accounting and reporting standards for certain activities of a mortgage banking enterprise. Other enterprises, such as commercial banks and thrift institutions, may conduct operations that are substantially similar to the primary operations of a mortgage banking enterprise (for example, through subsidiaries or divisions). In those circumstances, this Statement also applies to those operations. This Statement does not apply, however, to the normal lending activities of those other enterprises.

STANDARDS OF FINANCIAL ACCOUNTING AND REPORTING

Mortgage Loans and Mortgage-Backed Securities

4. Mortgage loans and mortgage-backed securities held for sale shall be reported at the lower of cost or market value, determined as of the balance sheet date. The amount by which cost exceeds market value shall be accounted for as a valuation allowance. Changes in the valuation allowances shall be included in the determination of net income of the period in which the change occurs.

5. Purchase discounts on mortgage loans and mortgage-backed securities shall not be amortized as interest revenue during the period the loans or securities are held for sale.

6. A mortgage loan or mortgage-backed security transferred to a long-term-investment classification shall be transferred at the lower of cost or market

---

[1]Terms defined in the glossary (Appendix A) are in **boldface type** the first time they appear in this Statement.

value on the transfer date. Any difference between the carrying amount of the loan or security and its outstanding principal balance shall be amortized to income over the estimated life of the loan or security using the interest method.[2] A mortgage loan or mortgage-backed security shall not be classified as a long-term investment unless the mortgage banking enterprise has both the ability and the intent to hold the loan or security for the foreseeable future or until maturity.

7. If ultimate recovery of the carrying amount of a mortgage loan or mortgage-backed security held as a long-term investment is doubtful and the impairment is considered to be other than temporary, the carrying amount of the loan or security shall be reduced to its expected collectible amount, which becomes the new cost basis. The amount of the reduction shall be reported as a loss. A recovery from the new cost basis shall be reported as a gain only at the sale, maturity, or other disposition of the loan or security.

8. As a means of financing its mortgage loans or mortgage-backed securities held for sale, a mortgage banking enterprise may transfer mortgage loans or mortgage-backed securities temporarily to banks or other financial institutions under formal repurchase agreements that indicate that control over the future economic benefits relating to those assets and risk of market loss are retained by the mortgage banking enterprise. Under those agreements, those same mortgage loans or mortgage-backed securities generally are reacquired from the banks or other financial institutions when the mortgage banking enterprise sells the loans or securities to permanent investors. Mortgage loans or mortgage-backed securities also may be transferred temporarily without a repurchase agreement but under circumstances that indicate a repurchase agreement exists on an informal basis, for example, when the mortgage banking enterprise (a) makes all of the necessary marketing efforts, (b) retains any positive or negative interest spread on the loans or securities, (c) retains the risk of fluctuations in loan or security market values, (d) reacquires any uncollectible loans, or (e) routinely reacquires all or almost all of the loans or securities from the bank or other financial institution and sells them to permanent investors. Mortgage loans and mortgage-backed securities held for sale that are transferred under formal or informal repurchase agreements of the nature described in this paragraph shall (1) be accounted for as collateralized financing arrangements and (2) continue to be reported by the transferor as being held for sale.

9. The market value of mortgage loans and mortgage-backed securities held for sale shall be determined by type of loan. At a minimum, separate determinations of market value for residential (one- to four-family dwellings) and commercial mortgage loans shall be made. Either the aggregate or individual loan basis may be used in determining the lower of cost or market value for each type of loan. Market value for loans subject to investor purchase commitments (committed loans) and loans held on a speculative basis (uncommitted loans)[3] shall be determined separately as follows:

a. *Committed Loans and Mortgage-Backed Securities.* Market value for mortgage loans and mortgage-backed securities covered by investor commitments shall be based on commitment prices. Any commitment price that provides for servicing fee rates materially different from current servicing fee rates shall be adjusted in accordance with paragraph 11.

b. *Uncommitted Loans.* Market value for uncommitted loans shall be based on the market in which the mortgage banking enterprise normally operates. That determination would include consideration of the following:
   (1) Commitment prices, to the extent the commitments clearly represent market conditions at the balance sheet date
   (2) Market prices and yields sought by the mortgage banking enterprise's normal market outlets
   (3) Quoted **Government National Mortgage Association (GNMA)** security prices or other public market quotations for long-term mortgage loan rates
   (4) **Federal Home Loan Mortgage Corporation (FHLMC)** and **Federal National Mortgage Association (FNMA)** current delivery prices

c. *Uncommitted Mortgage-Backed Securities.* Market value for uncommitted mortgage-backed securities that are collateralized by a mortgage banking enterprise's own loans ordinarily shall be based on the market value of the securities. If the trust holding the loans may be readily terminated and the loans sold directly, market value for the securities shall be based on the market value of the loans or the securities, depending on the mortgage banking enterprise's sales intent. Market value for other uncommitted mortgage-backed securities shall be based on published mortgage-backed securities yields.

10. Capitalized costs of acquiring rights to service mortgage loans, associated with the purchase of existing mortgage loans (paragraphs 16 through 19),

---

[2]The interest method is discussed in paragraph 15 of APB Opinion No. 21, *Interest on Receivables and Payables,* and paragraphs 16 and 17 of APB Opinion No. 12, *Omnibus Opinion—1967.*

[3]A mortgage loan shall be considered uncommitted for purposes of determining market value if the loan does not meet the specific terms of a commitment or if a reasonable doubt exists about the acceptance of the loan under a commitment.

shall be excluded from the cost of mortgage loans for the purpose of determining the lower of cost or market value.

Servicing Fees

11. If mortgage loans are sold with servicing retained and the stated servicing fee rate differs materially from a **current (normal) servicing fee rate,** the sales price shall be adjusted, for purposes of determining gain or loss on the sale, to provide for the recognition of a normal servicing fee in each subsequent year. The amount of the adjustment shall be the difference between the actual sales price and the estimated sales price that would have been obtained if a normal servicing fee rate had been specified.[4] The adjustment and any gain or loss to be recognized shall be determined as of the date the mortgage loans are sold. In addition, if normal servicing fees are expected to be less than estimated servicing costs over the estimated life of the mortgage loans, the expected loss on servicing the loans shall be accrued at that date.

Transactions with an Affiliated Enterprise[5]

12. The carrying amount of mortgage loans or mortgage-backed securities to be sold to an **affiliated enterprise** shall be adjusted to the lower of cost or market value of the loans or securities as of the date management decides that a sale to an affiliated enterprise will occur. The date shall be determined based on, at a minimum, formal approval by an authorized representative of the purchaser, issuance of a commitment to purchase the loans or securities, and acceptance of the commitment by the selling enterprise. The amount of any adjustment shall be charged to income.

13. If a particular class of mortgage loans or all loans are originated exclusively for an affiliated enterprise, the originator is acting as an agent of the affiliated enterprise, and the loan transfers shall be accounted for at the originator's acquisition cost. Such an agency relationship, however, would not exist in the case of "right of first refusal" contracts or similar types of agreements or commitments if the originator retains all the risks associated with ownership of the loans.

In-House Origination Costs

14. Costs associated with loan applications received directly from borrowers (in-house originations) shall be expensed as period costs. Those costs include (a) direct costs, such as personnel, financing, and marketing costs, and (b) general and administrative costs, such as occupancy and equipment rental costs.

Costs of Issuing Certain GNMA Securities

15. One month's interest cost, which is required to be paid to a trustee by issuers of GNMA securities electing the **internal reserve method,** shall be capitalized and amortized. The aggregate amount capitalized, including amounts capitalized under other provisions of this Statement, shall not exceed the present value of net future servicing income (paragraph 18).

Servicing Rights

16. The right to service mortgage loans for other than an enterprise's own account is an intangible asset that may be acquired separately, in a purchase of mortgage loans, or in a business combination. Subject to the limitations specified in paragraphs 17 and 18, the cost of acquiring that right from others shall be capitalized and amortized in accordance with the requirements of paragraph 19.

17. A mortgage banking enterprise acquiring the right to service loans in a purchase of mortgage loans shall capitalize the portion of the purchase price representing the cost of acquiring that right if a definitive plan for the sale of the mortgage loans exists when the transaction is initiated.[6] A definitive plan exists if (a) the mortgage banking enterprise has obtained, before the purchase date, commitments from permanent investors to purchase the mortgage loans or related mortgage-backed securities, or makes a commitment within a reasonable period (usually not more than 30 days after the purchase date) to sell the mortgage loans or related mortgage-backed securities to a permanent investor or underwriter, and (b) the plan includes estimates of the purchase price and selling price. The amount capitalized shall not exceed (1) the purchase price of

---

[4]The adjustment ordinarily will approximate the present value, based on an appropriate interest rate, of the difference between normal and stated servicing fees over the estimated life of the mortgage loans.

[5]This section on "Transactions with an Affiliated Enterprise" applies to only the separate financial statements of a mortgage banking enterprise. The provisions of FASB Statement No. 57, *Related Party Disclosures,* also apply to the separate financial statements of a mortgage banking enterprise. The provisions of ARB No. 51, *Consolidated Financial Statements,* and APB Opinion No. 18, *The Equity Method of Accounting for Investments in Common Stock,* apply when a mortgage banking enterprise is either consolidated or accounted for by the equity method.

[6]In the absence of a definitive plan for the sale of the related mortgage loans, the cost of acquiring the right to service mortgage loans generally is included as part of the cost of the loans for purposes of determining the lower of cost or market value.

the loans, including any transfer fees paid, in excess of the market value of the loans without servicing rights at the purchase date or (2) the present value of net future servicing income, determined in accordance with paragraph 18. The amount capitalized shall be reduced by any amount that the final sales price to the permanent investor exceeds the market value of the loans at the purchase date. All other costs, such as salaries and general and administrative expenses, shall be expensed as period costs.

18. The amount capitalized as the right to service mortgage loans shall not exceed the amount by which the present value of estimated future servicing revenue exceeds the present value of expected future servicing costs. Estimates of future servicing revenue shall include expected late charges and other ancillary revenue. Estimates of expected future servicing costs shall include direct costs associated with performing the servicing function and appropriate allocations of other costs. Estimated future servicing costs may be determined on an incremental cost basis. The rate used to determine the present value shall be an appropriate long-term interest rate.

19. The amount capitalized as the right to service mortgage loans and the amount capitalized by certain issuers of GNMA securities (paragraph 15) shall be amortized in proportion to, and over the period of, estimated net servicing income (servicing revenue in excess of servicing costs).

Loan and Commitment Fees

20. Mortgage banking enterprises may receive or pay nonrefundable loan and commitment fees representing compensation for a variety of services. Those fees may include components representing, for example, an adjustment of the interest yield on the loan, a fee for designating funds for the borrower, or an offset of loan origination costs. Loan and commitment fees shall be accounted for as set forth in paragraphs 21 through 27.

Loan Origination Fees

21. Fees representing reimbursement of the mortgage banking enterprise's costs of processing mortgage loan applications, reviewing legal title to real estate, and performing other loan origination procedures (loan origination fees) shall be recognized as revenue when the loan is made. If origination costs are not reasonably estimable, a portion of the fees, not to exceed the amount allowable by the Department of Housing and Urban Development and the Veterans Administration, may be recognized

as revenue when the loan is made because fees based on those rates generally do not exceed loan origination costs. Any fees in excess of the amount considered to be a reimbursement of loan origination costs shall be recognized as revenue in accordance with paragraphs 23 through 26.

Fees for Services Rendered

22. Fees representing reimbursement for the costs of specific services performed by third parties with respect to originating a loan, such as appraisal fees, shall be recognized as revenue when the services have been performed.

Fees Relating to Loans Held for Sale

23. Fees received for guaranteeing the funding of mortgage loans to borrowers, builders, or developers and fees paid to permanent investors to ensure the ultimate sale of the loans (residential or commercial loan commitment fees) shall be recognized as revenue or expense when the loans are sold to permanent investors or when it becomes evident the commitment will not be used. Because residential loan commitment fees ordinarily relate to blocks of loans, fees recognized as revenue or expense as the result of individual loan transactions shall be based on the ratio of the individual loan amount to the total commitment amount.

24. Fees for arranging a commitment directly between a permanent investor and a borrower (loan placement fees) shall be recognized as revenue when all significant services have been performed. In addition, if a mortgage banking enterprise obtains a commitment from a permanent investor before or at the time a related commitment is made to a borrower and if the commitment to the borrower will require (a) simultaneous assignment of the commitment to the investor and (b) simultaneous transfer to the borrower of the amount received from the investor, the related fees also shall be accounted for as loan placement fees.

Fees Relating to Loans Not Held for Sale

25. Fees for guaranteeing the funding of a mortgage loan to acquire or develop land or to construct residential or income-producing properties shall be recognized as revenue over the combined commitment and loan periods using the best estimate of that period. The straight-line method shall be used during the commitment period to recognize the fee revenue, and the interest method shall be used during the loan period to recognize the remaining fee revenue. If it is not practicable to apply the

interest method during the loan period,[7] the straight-line method shall be used. If the original estimate of the combined commitment and loan periods is revised significantly, the remaining commitment fee shall be recognized as revenue over the revised period. Additional fees received as a result of changes in the period shall be recognized as revenue over the revised period.

26. **Standby commitment** and **gap commitment** fees for issuing a commitment to fund a standby or gap loan for purposes such as interim or construction financing shall be recognized as revenue over the combined commitment and loan periods. The straight-line method shall be used during the commitment period to recognize the fee revenue, and the interest method shall be used during the loan period to recognize the remaining fee revenue. If it is not practicable to apply the interest method during the loan period, the straight-line method shall be used. Any additional fees received when the loan is made shall be recognized as revenue over the loan period.

Expired Commitments and Prepayments of Loans

27. If a loan commitment expires without the loan being made or if a loan is repaid before the estimated repayment date, any related unrecognized fees shall be recognized as revenue or expense at that time.

Balance Sheet Classification

28. Mortgage banking enterprises using either a classified or unclassified balance sheet shall distinguish between (a) mortgage loans and mortgage-backed securities held for sale and (b) mortgage loans and mortgage-backed securities held for long-term investment.

Disclosures

29. The method used in determining the lower of cost or market value of mortgage loans and mortgage-backed securities (that is, aggregate or individual loan basis) shall be disclosed.

30. The amount capitalized during the period in connection with acquiring the right to service mortgage loans (paragraph 16), the method of amortizing the capitalized amount, and the amount of amortization for the period shall be disclosed.

Amendments to Statement 32

31. The references to AICPA Statements of Position (SOPs) 74-12, *Accounting Practices in the Mortgage Banking Industry,* and 76-2, *Accounting for Origination Costs and Loan and Commitment Fees in the Mortgage Banking Industry,* are deleted from Appendix A of FASB Statement No. 32, *Specialized Accounting and Reporting Principles and Practices in AICPA Statements of Position and Guides on Accounting and Auditing Matters.*

Effective Date and Transition

32. The provisions of this Statement, other than those of paragraphs 4 and 28 through 30, shall be applied prospectively to transactions entered into after December 31, 1982, with earlier application encouraged. The provisions of paragraphs 4 and 28 through 30 shall be effective for financial statements for fiscal years beginning after December 15, 1982, with earlier application encouraged. If application of paragraph 4 of this Statement results in a change in accounting, restatement of previously issued annual financial statements to conform to the provisions of that paragraph is encouraged but not required. If it is not practicable or if the issuer of financial statements elects not to restate any prior year, the cumulative effect shall be included in net income in the year in which this Statement is first applied. (Refer to paragraph 20 of APB Opinion No. 20, *Accounting Changes.*) The effect on income before extraordinary items, net income, and related per share amounts of applying this Statement in a year in which the cumulative effect is included in determining that year's net income shall be disclosed for that year.

33. If previously issued financial statements are restated, the financial statements shall be restated for as many consecutive years as practicable. In the year that this Statement is first applied, the nature of any restatement and its effect on income before extraordinary items, net income, and related per share amounts for each restated year presented shall be disclosed. The cumulative effect of applying this Statement shall be included in determining net income of the earliest year restated (not necessarily the earliest year presented).

> **The provisions of this Statement need not be applied to immaterial items.**

---

[7] For example, if a construction loan is to be funded over time in proportion to the progress of the construction, the interest method may not be practicable to apply.

This Statement was approved by the unanimous vote of the seven members of the Financial Accounting Standards Board:

Donald J. Kirk,   John W. March   Robert T. Sprouse
  Chairman   Robert A. Morgan   Ralph E. Walters
Frank E. Block   David Mosso

Appendix A

GLOSSARY

34. This appendix defines certain terms that are used in this Statement.

Affiliated enterprise
An enterprise that directly or indirectly controls, is controlled by, or is under common control with another enterprise; also, a party with which the enterprise may deal if one party has the ability to exercise significant influence over the other's operating and financial policies as discussed in paragraph 17 of APB Opinion No. 18, *The Equity Method of Accounting for Investments in Common Stock.*

Current (normal) servicing fee rate
A servicing fee rate that is representative of servicing fee rates most commonly used in comparable servicing agreements covering similar types of mortgage loans.

Federal Home Loan Mortgage Corporation (FHLMC)
Often referred to as "Freddie Mac," FHLMC is a private corporation authorized by Congress to assist in the development and maintenance of a secondary market in conventional residential mortgages. FHLMC purchases mortgage loans and sells mortgages principally through mortgage participation certificates (PCs) representing an undivided interest in a group of conventional mortgages. FHLMC guarantees the timely payment of interest and the collection of principal on the PCs.

Federal National Mortgage Association (FNMA)
Often referred to as "Fannie Mae," FNMA is an investor-owned corporation established by Congress to support the secondary mortgage loan market by purchasing mortgage loans when other investor funds are limited and selling mortgage loans when other investor funds are available.

Gap commitment
A commitment to provide interim financing while the borrower is in the process of satisfying provisions of a permanent loan agreement, such as obtaining a designated occupancy level on an apartment project. The interim loan ordinarily finances the difference between the floor loan (the portion of a mortgage loan commitment that is less than the full amount of the commitment) and the maximum permanent loan.

Government National Mortgage Association (GNMA)
Often referred to as "Ginnie Mae," GNMA is a U.S. governmental agency that guarantees certain types of securities (mortgage-backed securities) and provides funds for and administers certain types of low-income housing assistance programs.

Internal reserve method
A method for making payments to investors for collections of principal and interest on mortgage loans by issuers of GNMA securities. An issuer electing the internal reserve method is required to deposit in a custodial account an amount equal to one month's interest on the mortgage loans that collateralize the GNMA security issued.

Mortgage-backed securities
Securities issued by a governmental agency or corporation (for example, GNMA or FHLMC) or by private issuers (for example, FNMA, banks, and mortgage banking enterprises). Mortgage-backed securities generally are referred to as *mortgage participation certificates* or *pass-through certificates* (PCs). A PC represents an undivided interest in a pool of specific mortgage loans. Periodic payments on GNMA PCs are backed by the U.S. government. Periodic payments on FHLMC and FNMA PCs are guaranteed by those corporations, but are not backed by the U.S. government.

Mortgage banking enterprise
An enterprise that is engaged primarily in originating, marketing, and servicing real estate mortgage loans for other than its own account. Mortgage banking enterprises, as local representatives of institutional lenders, act as correspondents between lenders and borrowers.

Permanent investor
An enterprise that invests in mortgage loans for its own account, for example, an insurance enterprise, commercial or mutual savings bank, savings and loan association, pension plan, real estate investment trust, or FNMA.

Servicing

Mortgage loan servicing includes collecting monthly mortgagor payments, forwarding payments and related accounting reports to investors, collecting escrow deposits for the payment of mortgagor property taxes and insurance, and paying taxes and insurance from escrow funds when due.

Standby commitment

A commitment to lend money with the understanding that the loan probably will not be made unless permanent financing cannot be obtained from another source. Standby commitments ordinarily are used to enable the borrower to obtain construction financing on the assumption that permanent financing will be available on more favorable terms when construction is completed. Standby commitments normally provide for an interest rate substantially above the market rate in effect when the commitment is issued.

Appendix B

BACKGROUND INFORMATION AND SUMMARY OF CONSIDERATION OF COMMENTS ON EXPOSURE DRAFT

35. As discussed in Statement 32, the FASB is extracting the specialized[8] accounting and reporting principles and practices (specialized principles) from AICPA SOPs and Guides on accounting and auditing matters and issuing them as FASB Statements after appropriate due process. This Statement extracts the specialized principles from SOPs 74-12 and 76-2. Accounting and reporting standards that apply to enterprises in general also apply to mortgage banking enterprises, and the standards in this Statement are in addition to those standards.

36. The Board has not undertaken a comprehensive reconsideration of the specialized principles in SOPs 74-12 and 76-2. Also, most of the background material and discussion of accounting alternatives have not been carried forward from the SOPs. The Board's conceptual framework project on accounting recognition criteria will address recognition issues relating to elements of financial statements. A Statement of Financial Accounting Concepts resulting from that project in due course will serve as a basis for evaluating existing standards and practices. Accordingly, the Board may wish to evaluate the standards in this Statement when its conceptual framework project is completed.

37. An Exposure Draft of a proposed FASB Statement, *Accounting for Certain Mortgage Banking Activities,* was issued on February 3, 1982. The Board received 42 comment letters in response to the Exposure Draft. Certain of the comments received and the Board's consideration of them are discussed in this appendix.

Applicability and Scope

38. Respondents commented on the appropriateness of this Statement's applying to the mortgage banking operations of other enterprises, such as commercial banks and thrift institutions, when those enterprises conduct operations that are substantially similar to the operations of a mortgage banking enterprise. Some respondents said that it would be difficult to define "substantially similar" operations and that the scope of the Statement could result in unintended changes in current accounting principles or practices followed by other enterprises, such as commercial banks and thrift institutions. Those enterprises may engage in some, but generally not all, of the activities of a mortgage banking enterprise. A mortgage banker primarily is engaged in originating, selling, and servicing mortgage loans for other than its own account. However, it also may originate loans for investment purposes and collect related loan fees. Commercial banks and thrift institutions may primarily be engaged in those latter activities and occasionally may sell mortgage loans to others for liquidity or other reasons. Those respondents questioned whether this Statement was intended to apply broadly to all activities discussed in the Statement regardless of the basic nature of the enterprise involved. Other respondents pointed out that commercial banks and thrift institutions originate many types of loans other than mortgage loans and questioned whether the Statement also would apply to activities relating to those loans. Still other respondents said that the scope of the Statement could be viewed as establishing broadly applicable standards with respect to the basis of carrying mortgage loans and to the accounting for servicing rights and loan and commitment fees. They suggested that the scope of the Statement be limited solely to mortgage banking enterprises.

39. In extracting the specialized principles from SOPs 74-12 and 76-2, the Board decided that those principles should apply to mortgage banking operations whether those operations are conducted by a mortgage banking enterprise or by another enterprise. That notion is consistent with the recommendations in SOP 76-2. However, the Board

---

[8]The term *specialized* is used to refer to those accounting and reporting principles and practices in AICPA Guides and SOPs that are neither superseded by nor contained in Accounting Research Bulletins, APB Opinions, FASB Statements, or FASB Interpretations.

decided not to establish in this project broadly applicable standards for each type of activity in which a mortgage banking enterprise generally is engaged because this project did not include a comprehensive consideration of whether the circumstances in other industries do or do not justify different reporting for those activities. Accordingly, the Board has clarified the scope to indicate that the Statement does not apply to the normal lending activities of those other enterprises.

Sales of Mortgage Loans to an Affiliated Enterprise

40. The "Notice for Recipients" of the Exposure Draft requested respondents to comment on whether the Statement should specify the amount at which sales of loans to an affiliated enterprise are to be reported in the separate financial statements of a mortgage banking enterprise. Of those respondents who commented, a majority recommended that the Statement specify how those sales should be reported. Some respondents noted that separate financial statements of mortgage banking enterprises are common in the mortgage banking industry and that guidance is necessary to ensure continued consistency of reporting among those enterprises. Those respondents pointed out that mortgage banking enterprises generally are required, by terms of their various selling and servicing contracts, to issue separate financial statements. Those financial statements are used for regulatory, credit, and other purposes and may be used by potential purchasers of loans to evaluate the mortgage banking enterprise's ability to perform required services under the servicing agreements.

41. Other respondents said that transactions with affiliated enterprises are not unique to mortgage banking enterprises and that issues relating to the accounting for transactions with an affiliated enterprise should be addressed in a separate Board project covering all enterprises. They also argued that transactions with an affiliated enterprise should not be addressed in this Statement because they believe that disclosures required by FASB Statement No. 57, *Related Party Disclosures,* provide financial statement users with sufficient information to understand and evaluate the significance of sales of mortgage loans to affiliated enterprises. They suggested that the section on transactions with an affiliated enterprise be deleted.

42. Primarily for the reasons given in paragraph 41, the Board has decided not to specify for mortgage banking enterprises a common basis of measuring transactions with affiliates, except as provided in paragraph 13. However, the Board decided to clarify in paragraph 12 that the carrying amount of mortgage loans or mortgage-backed securities to be sold to an affiliated enterprise must be adjusted to the lower of cost or market value. The Board believes the clarification is consistent with the intent of SOP 74-12. The Board also indicated in a footnote to paragraph 12 that the provisions of Statement 57 apply to the separate financial statements of a mortgage banking enterprise.

Transition

43. The Exposure Draft proposed that accounting changes adopted to conform to the provisions of this Statement be applied retroactively by restating financial statements for as many years as practicable, with the cumulative effect included in income of the earliest year restated. That method of transition was proposed on the premise that it would afford maximum comparability among financial statements. Some respondents disagreed with the proposed transition provisions because they believe the application of certain provisions of the Exposure Draft would be difficult to implement retroactively. In particular, they noted that the Statement specifies different methods of reporting loans and certain fees based on whether an enterprise intends to sell the applicable loans or hold them as investments. Those respondents noted that retroactive restatement may require an enterprise that was not following the provisions of SOPs 74-12 and 76-2 to reconstruct its intent as of the end of several prior reporting periods, a process that would be difficult and time-consuming. They also noted that the provisions of the Statement relating to the acquisition of servicing rights may be difficult to implement retroactively for enterprises that were following the SOPs because, as noted in the "Notice for Recipients" of the Exposure Draft, this Statement changes the reporting of certain acquisitions of servicing rights. They recommended that prospective application be required.

44. The Board considered those views and concluded that prospective application of the transaction-related provisions of this Statement is appropriate. Because the provisions of paragraph 4 relate to the measurement and reporting of mortgage loan and mortgage-backed security portfolios, the Board concluded that those portfolios should be reported by a single method, that is, the lower of cost or market value. The Board also concluded that comparability would be enhanced if enterprises apply the provisions of that paragraph retroactively by restating the financial statements of previous periods. Because the benefits of restatement may not justify the cost of restating in some cases, however, the Board decided to permit rather than require retroactive restatement in applying the provisions of paragraph 4.

Other Comments

45. Some respondents noted that the provisions of the Exposure Draft relating to sales of mortgage loans with servicing retained are not followed universally by enterprises in other industries, although those provisions currently are being followed by most mortgage banking enterprises. Paragraph 11 requires that, when mortgage loans are sold with servicing retained, the sales price should be adjusted, for purposes of determining gain or loss on the sale, if the stated servicing fee rate differs materially from normal servicing fee rates. The adjustment is determined by the difference between the actual sales price and the estimated sales price that would have been obtained if a normal servicing fee rate had been specified. Those respondents said that some financial institutions are recognizing in income the present value of all future servicing income (stated servicing fees in excess of estimated servicing costs) when mortgage loans are sold rather than over the period servicing is performed. The Board believes that the present value of excess servicing fees (the portion that exceeds normal servicing fees) should be recognized as an additional element of the sales price. However, the Board believes that it is inappropriate to recognize, in effect, the present value of all future servicing income as an element of the sales price when loan servicing is a primary revenue-producing activity of an enterprise. Accordingly, this Statement requires that a normal servicing fee be recognized as revenue when the servicing is performed.

46. The Exposure Draft proposed that commitment fees received for issuing floating-rate commitments for certain loans, such as land development and construction loans, should be recognized in income over the commitment period rather than over the combined commitment and loan periods as recommended in SOP 76-2. The provision was included so that the accounting for those fees would more closely parallel the accounting by other financial institutions for similar fees. Some respondents expressed concern about the proposed provision because it was not identical to existing practices of either banks or thrift institutions. Other respondents pointed out that a task force of the AICPA currently is studying issues relating to the accounting for loan origination and commitment fees by all enterprises.

They recommended that the current accounting for those fees not be changed until that task force completes its study and the resulting recommendations are sent to the FASB for consideration. Based on those respondents' comments, the Board concluded that the provisions of this Statement relating to fees on loans not held for sale (paragraphs 25 and 26) should be revised to conform more closely to the existing recommendations in SOP 76-2 (that is, commitment fees should be recognized as revenue over the combined commitment and loan periods regardless of whether the commitment is fixed or floating rate).

47. Several respondents suggested that this Statement address the accounting and reporting of certain transactions that are not covered by SOPs 74-12 and 76-2. Those respondents recommended that the Board (a) specify the accounting for interest rate futures contracts and forward commitments to purchase or sell mortgage loans and (b) address the issue of whether the issuance of a mortgage-backed security collateralized by the issuer's own loans should be reported as a sale of the mortage loans or as a borrowing. The Board notes that it currently has other projects in which those and related issues are being considered. For that reason and because the issues are not unique to mortgage banking enterprises, the Board decided not to adopt the suggestions.

48. Several respondents suggested various substantive changes to the Exposure Draft. Adoption of those suggestions would have required reconsideration of some of the provisions of SOPs 74-12 and 76-2. Those suggestions were not adopted because such a reconsideration is beyond the scope of extracting the specialized principles from the SOPs and because none of the changes was broadly supported. However, based on suggestions from respondents to the Exposure Draft, the Board has made several other changes that it believes clarify the Statement.

49. The Board has concluded that it can reach an informed decision on the basis of existing information without a public hearing and that the effective date and transition specified in paragraphs 32 and 33 are advisable in the circumstances.

Statement of Financial Accounting Standards No. 66
Accounting for Sales of Real Estate

STATUS

Issued: October 1982

Effective Date: For real estate sales transactions entered into after December 31, 1982

Affects: Amends FAS 26, paragraph 7
Amends FAS 28, paragraphs 3 and 23 through 25
Amends FAS 32, Appendix A

Affected by: Paragraph 40 superseded by FAS 98
Footnote 5 superseded by FAS 121
Footnote 34 amended FAS 98

Issues Discussed by FASB Emerging Issues Task Force (EITF)

Affects: No EITF Issues

Interpreted by: Paragraph 3, 4, and 6 interpreted by EITF Issue No. 88-24
Paragraph 5 interpreted by EITF Issues No. 86-7 and 88-24
Paragraph 9 interpreted by EITF Issues No. 87-9, 87-29, 88-12, and 88-24
Paragraph 10 interpreted by EITF Issues No. 87-9, 88-12, and 88-24
Paragraph 11 interpreted by EITF Issues No. 87-9 and 88-12
Paragraph 12 interpreted by EITF Issue No. 84-17
Paragraph 26 interpreted by EITF Issue No. 86-6
Paragraph 53 interpreted by EITF Issue No. 87-9
Paragraph 54 interpreted by EITF Issues No. 87-9 and 88-12

Related Issues: EITF Issues No. 84-37, 85-27, 85-37, 86-17, 88-14, 88-21, 89-14, 96-21, and 97-1

SUMMARY

This Statement establishes accounting standards for recognizing profit or loss on sales of real estate. It adopts the specialized profit recognition principles in the AICPA Industry Accounting Guides, *Accounting for Profit Recognition on Sales of Real Estate* and *Accounting for Retail Land Sales;* and AICPA Statements of Position 75-6, *Questions Concerning Profit Recognition on Sales of Real Estate,* and 78-4, *Application of the Deposit, Installment, and Cost Recovery Methods in Accounting for Sales of Real Estate.*

For retail land sales, this Statement requires that the seller's receivables from the land sales be collectible and that the seller have no significant remaining obligations for construction or development before profits are recognized by the full accrual method. Other sales in retail land sales projects are to be reported under either the percentage-of-completion or the installment method, for which the Statement establishes criteria based on the collectibility of the seller's receivables from the land sales and the seller's remaining obligations.

For other sales of real estate, this Statement provides for profit recognition by the full accrual and several other methods, depending on whether a sale has been consummated, the extent of the buyer's investment in the property being sold, whether the seller's receivable is subject to future subordination, and the degree of the seller's continuing involvement with the property after the sale. Paragraphs 3-5 set forth the general requirements for recognition of all the profit at the date of sale. Paragraphs 6-18 elaborate on those general rules. Paragraphs 19-43 provide more detailed guidance for a variety of more complicated circumstances if the criteria for immediate profit recognition are not met.

* * *

Certain provisions of this Statement that relate to accounting for sales of real estate are summarized in decision trees that appear on pages 655-59.

(This page intentionally left blank.)

Statement of Financial Accounting Standards No. 66
Accounting for Sales of Real Estate

CONTENTS

INTRODUCTION

1. This Statement establishes standards for recognition of profit on all real estate sales transactions without regard to the nature of the seller's business. The Statement distinguishes between retail land sales and other sales of real estate because differences in terms of sales and selling procedures lead to different profit recognition criteria and methods. Accounting for real estate sales transactions that are not retail land sales is specified in paragraphs 3-43. Accounting for retail land sales transactions is specified in paragraphs 44-50. This Statement does not cover exchanges of real estate for other real estate, the accounting for which is covered in APB Opinion No. 29, *Accounting for Nonmonetary Transactions.*

2. Although this Statement applies to all sales of real estate, many of the extensive provisions were developed over several years to deal with complex transactions that are frequently encountered in enterprises that specialize in real estate transactions. The decision trees on pages 655-59 highlight the major provisions of the Statement and will help a user of the Statement identify criteria that determine when and how profit is recognized. Those using this Statement to determine the accounting for relatively simple real estate sales transactions will need to apply only limited portions of the Statement. The general requirements for recognizing all of the profit on a nonretail land sale at the date of sale are set forth in paragraphs 3-5 and are highlighted on the decision tree on page 655. Paragraphs 6-18 elaborate on those general provisions. Paragraphs 19-43 provide more detailed guidance for a variety of more complex transactions.

STANDARDS OF FINANCIAL ACCOUNTING AND REPORTING

Real Estate Sales Other Than Retail Land Sales

Recognition of Profit by the Full Accrual Method

3. Profit shall be recognized in full when real estate is sold, provided (a) the profit is determinable, that is, the collectibility of the sales price is reasonably assured or the amount that will not be collectible can be estimated, and (b) the earnings process is virtually complete, that is, the seller is not obliged to perform significant activities after the sale to earn the profit. Unless both conditions exist, recognition of all or part of the profit shall be postponed. Recognition of all of the profit at the time of sale or at some later date when both conditions exist is referred to as the *full accrual method* in this Statement.

4. In accounting for sales of real estate, collectibility of the sales price is demonstrated by the buyer's commitment to pay, which in turn is supported by substantial initial and continuing investments that give the buyer a stake in the property sufficient that the risk of loss through default motivates the buyer to honor its obligation to the seller. Collectibility shall also be assessed by considering factors such as the credit standing of the buyer, age and location of the property, and adequacy of cash flow from the property.

5. Profit on real estate sales transactions[1] shall not be recognized by the full accrual method until all of the following criteria are met:

a. A sale is consummated (paragraph 6).
b. The buyer's initial and continuing investments are adequate to demonstrate a commitment to pay for the property (paragraphs 8-16).
c. The seller's receivable is not subject to future subordination (paragraph 17).
d. The seller has transferred to the buyer the usual risks and rewards of ownership in a transaction that is in substance a sale and does not have a substantial continuing involvement with the property (paragraph 18).

Paragraphs 19-43 describe appropriate accounting if the above criteria are not met.

Consummation of a Sale

6. A sale shall not be considered consummated until (a) the parties are bound by the terms of a contract, (b) all consideration has been exchanged, (c) any permanent financing for which the seller is responsible has been arranged, and (d) all conditions[2] precedent to closing have been performed. Usually, those four conditions are met at the time of closing or after closing, not when an agreement to sell is signed or at a preclosing.

Buyer's Initial and Continuing Investment

7. "Sales value" shall be determined by:

a. Adding to the stated sales price the proceeds from the issuance of a real estate option that is exercised and other payments that are in substance additional sales proceeds. These nominally may be management fees, points, or prepaid interest or fees that are required to be maintained in an advance status and applied against the amounts due to the seller at a later date.
b. Subtracting from the sale price a discount to reduce the receivable to its present value and by the net present value of services that the seller commits to perform without compensation or by the net present value of the services in excess of the compensation that will be received. Paragraph 31 specifies appropriate accounting if services are to be provided by the seller without compensation or at less than prevailing rates.

8. Adequacy of a buyer's initial investment shall be measured by (a) its composition (paragraphs 9-10) and (b) its size compared with the sales value of the property (paragraph 11).

9. The buyer's initial investment shall include only: (a) cash paid as a down payment, (b) the buyer's notes supported by irrevocable letters of credit from an independent established lending institution,[3] (c) payments by the buyer to third parties to reduce existing indebtedness on the property, and (d) other amounts paid by the buyer that are part of the sales value. Other consideration received by the seller, including other notes of the buyer, shall be included as part of the buyer's initial investment only when that consideration is sold or otherwise converted to cash without recourse to the seller.

10. The initial investment shall not include:

a. Payments by the buyer to third parties for improvements to the property
b. A permanent loan commitment by an independent third party to replace a loan made by the seller
c. Any funds that have been or will be loaned, refunded, or directly or indirectly provided to the buyer by the seller or loans guaranteed or collateralized by the seller for the buyer[4]

11. The buyer's initial investment shall be adequate to demonstrate the buyer's commitment to pay for the property and shall indicate a reasonable likelihood that the seller will collect the receivable. Lending practices of independent established lending institutions provide a reasonable basis for assessing the collectibility of receivables from buyers of real estate. Therefore, to qualify, the initial investment shall be equal to at least a major part of the difference between usual loan limits and the sales value of the property. Guidance on minimum initial investments in various types of real estate is provided in paragraphs 53 and 54.

12. The buyer's continuing investment in a real estate transaction shall not qualify unless the buyer is contractually required to pay each year on its total debt for the purchase price of the property an amount at least equal to the level annual payment that would be needed to pay that debt and interest on the unpaid balance over no more than (a) 20 years for debt for land and (b) the customary amortization term of a first mortgage loan by an indepen-

---

[1] Profit on a sale of a partial interest in real estate shall be subject to the same criteria for profit recognition as a sale of a whole interest.

[2] Paragraph 20 provides an exception to this requirement if the seller is constructing office buildings, condominiums, shopping centers, or similar structures.

[3] An "independent established lending institution" is an unrelated institution such as a commercial bank unaffiliated with the seller.

[4] As an example, if unimproved land is sold for $100,000, with a down payment of $50,000 in cash, and the seller plans to loan the buyer $35,000 at some future date, the initial investment is $50,000 minus $35,000, or $15,000.

dent established lending institution for other real estate. For this purpose, contractually required payments by the buyer on its debt shall be in the forms specified in paragraph 9 as acceptable for an initial investment. Except as indicated in the following sentence, funds to be provided directly or indirectly by the seller (paragraph 10(c)) shall be subtracted from the buyer's contractually required payments in determining whether the initial and continuing investments are adequate. If a future loan on normal terms from an established lending institution bears a fair market interest rate and the proceeds of the loan are conditional on use for specified development of or construction on the property, the loan need not be subtracted in determining the buyer's investment.

Release Provisions

13. An agreement to sell property (usually land) may provide that part or all of the property may be released from liens securing related debt by payment of a release price or that payments by the buyer may be assigned first to released property. If either of those conditions is present, a buyer's initial investment shall be sufficient both to pay release prices on property released at the date of sale and to constitute an adequate initial investment on property not released or not subject to release at that time in order to meet the criterion of an adequate initial investment for the property as a whole.

14. If the release conditions described in paragraph 13 are present, the buyer's investment shall be sufficient, after the released property is paid for, to constitute an adequate continuing investment on property not released in order to meet the criterion of an adequate continuing investment for the property as a whole (paragraph 12).

15. If the amounts applied to unreleased portions do not meet the initial and continuing-investment criteria as applied to the sales value of those unreleased portions, profit shall be recognized on each released portion when it meets the criteria in paragraph 5 as if each release were a separate sale.

16. Tests of adequacy of a buyer's initial and continuing investments described in paragraphs 8-15 shall be applied cumulatively when the sale is consummated and annually afterward. If the initial investment exceeds the minimum prescribed, the excess shall be applied toward the required annual increases in the buyer's investment.

Future Subordination

17. The seller's receivable shall not be subject to

future subordination. This restriction shall not apply if (a) a receivable is subordinate to a first mortgage on the property existing at the time of sale or (b) a future loan, including an existing permanent loan commitment, is provided for by the terms of the sale and the proceeds of the loan will be applied first to the payment of the seller's receivable.

Continuing Involvement without Transfer of Risks and Rewards

18. If a seller is involved with a property after it is sold in any way that results in retention of substantial risks or rewards of ownership, except as indicated in paragraph 43, the absence-of-continuing-involvement criterion has not been met. Forms of involvement that result in retention of substantial risks or rewards by the seller, and accounting therefor, are described in paragraphs 25-42.

Recognition of Profit When the Full Accrual Method Is Not Appropriate

19. If a real estate sales transaction does not satisfy the criteria in paragraphs 3-18 for recognition of profit by the full accrual method, the transaction shall be accounted for as specified in the following paragraphs.

Sale Not Consummated

20. The deposit method of accounting described in paragraphs 65-67 shall be used until a sale has been consummated (paragraph 6). "Consummation" usually requires that all conditions precedent to closing have been performed, including that the building be certified for occupancy. However, because of the length of the construction period of office buildings, apartments, condominiums, shopping centers, and similar structures, such sales and the related income may be recognized during the process of construction, subject to the criteria in paragraphs 41 and 42, even though a certificate of occupancy, which is a condition precedent to closing, has not been obtained.

21. If the net carrying amount of the property exceeds the sum of the deposit received, the fair value of the unrecorded note receivable, and the debt assumed by the buyer, the seller shall recognize the loss at the date the agreement to sell is signed.[5] If a buyer defaults, or if circumstances after the transaction indicate that it is probable the buyer will default and the property will revert to the seller, the seller shall evaluate whether the circumstances indicate a decline in the value of the property for which an allowance for loss should be provided.

---

[5]Paragraph 24 of FASB Statement No. 67, *Accounting for Costs and Initial Rental Operations of Real Estate Projects,* specifies the accounting for an excess of costs over net realizable value for property that has not yet been sold.

Initial or Continuing Investments Do Not Qualify

22. If the buyer's initial investment does not meet the criteria specified in paragraphs 8-11 for recognition of profit by the full accrual method and if recovery of the cost of the property is reasonably assured if the buyer defaults, the installment method described in paragraphs 56-61 shall be used. If recovery of the cost of the property is not reasonably assured if the buyer defaults or if cost has already been recovered and collection of additional amounts is uncertain, the cost recovery method (described in paragraphs 62-64) or the deposit method (described in paragraphs 65-67) shall be used. The cost recovery method may be used to account for sales of real estate for which the installment method would be appropriate.

23. If the initial investment meets the criteria in paragraphs 8-11 but the continuing investment by the buyer does *not* meet the criteria in paragraphs 12 and 16, the seller shall recognize profit by the reduced profit method described in paragraphs 68 and 69 at the time of sale if payments by the buyer each year will at least cover both of the following:

a. The interest and principal amortization on the maximum first mortgage loan that could be obtained on the property
b. Interest, at an appropriate rate,[6] on the excess of the aggregate actual debt on the property over such a maximum first mortgage loan

If the criteria specified in this paragraph for use of the reduced profit method are not met, the seller may recognize profit by the installment method (paragraphs 56-61) or the cost recovery method (paragraphs 62-64).

Receivable Subject to Future Subordination

24. If the seller's receivable is subject to future subordination as described in paragraph 17, profit shall be recognized by the cost recovery method (paragraphs 62-64).

Continuing Involvement without Transfer of Risks and Rewards

25. If the seller has some continuing involvement with the property and does not transfer substantially all of the risks and rewards of ownership, profit shall be recognized by a method determined by the nature and extent of the seller's continuing involvement. Generally, profit shall be recognized at the time of sale if the amount of the seller's loss of profit because of continued involvement with the property is limited by the terms of the sales contract. The profit recognized shall be reduced by the maximum exposure to loss. Paragraphs 26-43 describe some common forms of continuing involvement and specify appropriate accounting if those forms of involvement are present. If the seller has some other form of continuing involvement with the property, the transaction shall be accounted for according to the nature of the involvement.

26. *The seller has an obligation to repurchase the property, or the terms of the transaction allow the buyer to compel the seller or give an option[7] to the seller to repurchase the property.* The transaction shall be accounted for as a financing, leasing, or profit-sharing arrangement rather than as a sale.

27. *The seller is a general partner in a limited partnership that acquires an interest in the property sold (or has an extended, noncancelable management contract requiring similar obligations) and holds a receivable from the buyer for a significant[8] part of the sales price.* The transaction shall be accounted for as a financing, leasing, or profit-sharing arrangement.

28. *The seller guarantees[9] the return of the buyer's investment or a return on that investment for a limited or extended period.* For example, the seller guarantees cash flows, subsidies, or net tax benefits. If the seller guarantees return of the buyer's investment or if the seller guarantees a return on the investment for an extended period, the transaction shall be accounted for as a financing, leasing, or

---

[6]Paragraphs 13 and 14 of APB Opinion No. 21, *Interest on Receivables and Payables,* provide criteria for selecting an appropriate rate for present-value calculations.

[7]A right of first refusal based on a bona fide offer by a third party ordinarily is not an obligation or an option to repurchase.

[8]For this purpose, a significant receivable is a receivable in excess of 15 percent of the maximum first-lien financing that could be obtained from an independent established lending institution for the property. It would include:

a. A construction loan made or to be made by the seller to the extent that it exceeds the minimum funding commitment for permanent financing from a third party that the seller will not be liable for
b. An all-inclusive or wraparound receivable held by the seller to the extent that it exceeds prior-lien financing for which the seller has no personal liability
c. Other funds provided or to be provided directly or indirectly by the seller to the buyer
d. The present value of a land lease when the seller is the lessor (footnote 15)

[9]Guarantees by the seller may be limited to a specified period of time.

profit-sharing arrangement. If the guarantee of a return on the investment is for a limited period, the deposit method shall be used until operations of the property cover all operating expenses, debt service, and contractual payments. At that time, profit shall be recognized on the basis of performance of the services required, as illustrated in paragraphs 84-88.

29. *The seller is required to initiate or support operations or continue to operate the property at its own risk, or may be presumed to have such a risk, for an extended period, for a specified limited period, or until a specified level of operations has been obtained, for example, until rentals of a property are sufficient to cover operating expenses and debt service.* If support is required or presumed to be required[10] for an *extended* period of time, the transaction shall be accounted for as a financing, leasing, or profit-sharing arrangement. If support is required or presumed to be required for a *limited* time, profit on the sale shall be recognized on the basis of performance of the services required. Performance of those services shall be measured by the costs incurred and to be incurred over the period during which the services are performed. Profit shall begin to be recognized when there is reasonable assurance that future rent receipts will cover operating expenses and debt service including payments due the seller under the terms of the transaction. Reasonable assurance that rentals will be adequate would be indicated by objective information regarding occupancy levels and rental rates in the immediate area. In assessing whether rentals will be adequate to justify recognition of profit, total estimated future rent receipts of the property shall be reduced by one-third as a reasonable safety factor unless the amount so computed is less than the rents to be received from signed leases. In this event, the rents from signed leases shall be substituted for the computed amount. Application of this method is illustrated in paragraphs 84-89.

30. If the sales contract does not stipulate the period during which the seller is obligated to support operations of the property, support shall be presumed for at least two years from the time of initial rental unless actual rental operations cover operating expenses, debt service, and other contractual commitments before that time. If the seller is contractually obligated for a longer time, profit rec-

ognition shall continue on the basis of performance until the obligation expires. Calculation of profits on the basis of performance of services is illustrated in paragraphs 84-89.

31. If the sales contract requires the seller to provide management services relating to the property after the sale without compensation or at compensation less than prevailing rates for the service required (paragraph 7) or on terms not usual for the services to be rendered (footnote 10(d)), compensation shall be imputed when the sale is recognized and shall be recognized in income as the services are performed over the term of the management contract.

32. *The transaction is merely an option to purchase the property.* For example, undeveloped land may be "sold" under terms that call for a very small initial investment by the buyer (substantially less than the percentages specified in paragraph 54) and postponement of additional payments until the buyer obtains zoning changes or building permits or other contingencies specified in the sales agreement are satisfactorily resolved. Proceeds from the issuance of the option by a property owner shall be accounted for as a deposit (paragraphs 65-67). Profit shall not be recognized until the option either expires or is exercised. When an option to purchase real estate is sold by an option holder,[11] the seller of the option shall recognize income by the cost recovery method (paragraphs 62-64) to the extent nonrefundable cash proceeds exceed the seller's cost of the option if the buyer's initial and continuing investments are not adequate for profit recognition by the full accrual method (paragraphs 7-16).

33. *The seller has made a partial sale.* A sale is a partial sale if the seller retains an equity interest in the property or has an equity interest in the buyer. Profit (the difference between the sales value and the proportionate cost of the partial interest sold) shall be recognized at the date of sale if:

a. The buyer is independent of the seller.
b. Collection of the sales price is reasonably assured (paragraph 4).
c. The seller will not be required to support the operations of the property or its related obligations to an extent greater than its proportionate interest.

---

[10]Support shall be presumed to be required if: (a) a seller obtains an interest as a general partner in a limited partnership that acquires an interest in the property sold; (b) a seller retains an equity interest in the property, such as an undivided interest or an equity interest in a joint venture that holds an interest in the property; (c) a seller holds a receivable from a buyer for a significant part of the sales price and collection of the receivable depends on the operation of the property; or (d) a seller agrees to manage the property for the buyer on terms not usual for the services to be rendered, and the agreement is not terminable by either the seller or the buyer.

[11]When an option to purchase real estate is sold by an option holder, the sales value includes the exercise price of the option and the sales price of the option. For example, if the option is sold for $150,000 ($50,000 cash and a $100,000 note) and the exercise price is $500,000, the sales value is $650,000.

34. If the buyer is not independent of the seller, for example, if the seller holds or acquires an equity interest in the buyer, the seller shall recognize the part of the profit proportionate to the outside interests in the buyer at the date of sale. If the seller controls the buyer, no profit on the sale shall be recognized until it is realized from transactions with outside parties through sale or operations of the property.

35. If collection of the sales price is not reasonably assured, the cost recovery or installment method of recognizing profit shall be used.

36. If the seller is required to support the operations of the property after the sale, the accounting shall be based on the nature of the support obligation. For example, the seller may retain an interest in the property sold and the buyer may receive preferences as to profits, cash flows, return on investment, and so forth. If the transaction is in substance a sale, the seller shall recognize profit to the extent that proceeds from the sale, including receivables from the buyer, exceed all of the seller's costs related to the entire property. Other examples of support obligations are described in paragraphs 29-31.

37. If individual units in condominium projects[12] or time-sharing interests are being sold separately and all the following criteria are met, profit shall be recognized by the percentage-of-completion method on the sale of individual units or interests:

a. Construction is beyond a preliminary stage.[13]
b. The buyer is committed to the extent of being unable to require a refund except for nondelivery of the unit or interest.[14]
c. Sufficient units have already been sold to assure that the entire property will not revert to rental

property. In determining whether this condition has been met, the seller shall consider the requirements of state laws, the condominium or time-sharing contract, and the terms of the financing agreements.
d. Sales prices are collectible (paragraph 4).
e. Aggregate sales proceeds and costs can be reasonably estimated. Consideration shall be given to sales volume, trends of unit prices, demand for the units including seasonal factors, developer's experience, geographical location, and environmental factors.

If any of the above criteria is not met, proceeds shall be accounted for as deposits until the criteria are met.

38. *The seller sells property improvements and leases the underlying land to the buyer of the improvements.* In these circumstances, the transactions are interdependent and it is impracticable to distinguish between profits on the sale of the improvements and profits under the related lease. The transaction shall be accounted for as a lease of both the land and improvements if the term of the land lease to the buyer from the seller of the improvements either (a) does not cover substantially all of the economic life of the property improvements, thus strongly implying that the transaction is in substance a lease of both land and improvements, or (b) is not for a substantial period, for example, 20 years.

39. If the land lease described in paragraph 38 covers substantially all of the economic life of the improvements and extends for at least 20 years, the profit to be recognized on the sale of the improvements at the time of sale shall be (a) the present value of the rental payments[15] not in excess of the

---

[12]A condominium project may be a building, a group of buildings, or a complete project.

[13]Construction is not beyond a preliminary stage if engineering and design work, execution of construction contracts, site clearance and preparation, excavation, and completion of the building foundation are incomplete.

[14]The buyer may be able to require a refund, for example, if a minimum status of completion of the project is required by state law and that status has not been attained; if state law requires that a "Declaration of Condominium" be filed and it has not been filed, except that in some states the filing of the declaration is a routine matter and the lack of such filing may not make the sales contract voidable; if the sales contract provides that permanent financing at an acceptable cost must be available to the buyer at the time of closing and it is not available; or if the condominium units must be registered with either the Office of Interstate Land Sales Registration of the Department of Housing and Urban Development or the Securities and Exchange Commission, and they are not so registered.

[15]The present value of the specified rental payments is the present value of the lease payments specified in the lease over the term of the primary indebtedness, if any, on the improvements, or over the customary amortization term of primary debt instruments on the type of improvements involved. The present value is computed at an interest rate appropriate for (a) primary debt if the lease is not subordinated or (b) secondary debt if the lease is subordinated to loans with prior liens.

seller's cost of the land plus (b) the sales value of the improvements minus (c) the carrying value of the improvements and the land. Profit on (1) the buyer's rental payments on the land in excess of the seller's cost of the land and (2) the rent to be received on the land after the maturity of the primary indebtedness on the improvements or other customary amortization term shall be recognized when the land is sold or the rents in excess of the seller's cost of the land are accrued under the lease. Calculations of profit in those circumstances are illustrated in paragraphs 82 and 83.

40. *The sale of the property is accompanied by a leaseback to the seller of all or any part of the property for all or part of its remaining economic life.* Real estate sale and leaseback transactions shall be accounted for in accordance with the provisions of this Statement and FASB Statements No. 13, *Accounting for Leases,* and 28, *Accounting for Sales with Leasebacks.* Statement 13 as amended by Statement 28 provides criteria for determining if a leaseback is a capital lease or an operating lease. If the leaseback is a capital lease, the seller-lessee shall record an asset and an obligation as prescribed by Statement 13. Regardless of whether the leaseback is a capital lease or an operating lease, a sale shall be recorded, and the property sold and any related debt assumed by the buyer shall be removed from the seller-lessee's balance sheet. The criteria in this Statement then shall be used to determine the amount of profit that would be recognized at the date of sale, absent the leaseback provisions. The profit so determined shall be accounted for in accordance with the provisions of Statements 13 and 28 (usually deferred and amortized over the term of the lease) unless other provisions of this Statement require postponement of profit recognition until a later event.

41. *The sales contract or an accompanying agreement requires the seller to develop the property in the future, to construct facilities on the land, or to provide off-site improvements or amenities.* The seller is involved with future development or construction work if the buyer is unable to pay amounts due for that work or has the right under the terms of the arrangement to defer payment until the work is done. If future costs of development can be reasonably estimated at the time of sale, profit allocable to (a) performance before the sale of the land and (b) the sale of the land shall be recognized when the sale of the land meets the criteria in paragraph 5. Profit allocable to performance after the sale shall be recognized by the percentage-of-completion method as

development and construction proceed, provided that cost and profit can be reasonably estimated from the seller's previous experience.

42. The profit shall be allocated to the sale of the land and the later development or construction work on the basis of estimated costs of each activity; the same rate of profit shall be attributed to each activity. No profit shall be recognized at the time of sale if future costs of development cannot be reasonably estimated at that time.

43. *The seller will participate in future profit from the property without risk of loss (such as participation in operating profits or residual values without further obligation).* If the transaction otherwise qualifies for recognition of profit by the full accrual method, the transfer of risks and rewards of ownership and absence of continuing involvement criterion shall be considered met. The contingent future profits shall be recognized when they are realized.[16] All the costs of the sale shall be recognized at the time of sale; none shall be deferred to periods when the contingent profits are recognized.

Retail Land Sales

44. A single method of recognizing profit shall be applied to all sales transactions within a project[17] that have been consummated.[18] That method of recognizing profit shall be changed when certain conditions are met for the entire project (paragraph 49).

Recognition of Profit

45. The full accrual method of accounting described in paragraphs 70-72 shall be applied to a sale if *all* of the following conditions are met:

a. *Expiration of refund period.* The buyer has made the down payment and each required subsequent payment until the period of cancellation with refund has expired. That period shall be the longest period of those required by local law, established by the seller's policy, or specified in the contract.
b. *Sufficient cumulative payments.* The cumulative payments of principal and interest equal or exceed 10 percent of the contract sales price.
c. *Collectibility of receivables.* Collection experience for the project in which the sale is made or for the seller's prior projects indicates that at least 90 percent of the contracts in the project in which the sale is made that are in force 6 months after the criteria in paragraph 46 are met will be

---

[16]Paragraph 17 of FASB Statement No. 5, *Accounting for Contingencies,* addresses accounting for gain contingencies.

[17]A retail land sales "project" is a homogeneous, reasonably contiguous area of land that may, for development and marketing, be subdivided in accordance with a master plan.

[18]Retail land sales shall be considered consummated when all of the criteria in paragraph 47 are met.

collected in full.[19] The collection experience with the seller's prior projects may be applied to a new project if the prior projects:

(1) Had predominantly the same characteristics (type of land, environment, clientele, contract terms, sales methods)[20] as the new project.

(2) Had a sufficiently long collection period to indicate the percentage of current sales of the new project that will be collected to maturity.

A down payment of at least 20 percent shall be an acceptable indication of collectibility.

d. *Nonsubordination of receivables.* The receivable from the sale is not subject to subordination to new loans on the property except that subordination by an individual lot buyer for home construction purposes is permissible if the collection experience on those contracts is the same as on contracts not subordinated.

e. *Completion of development.* The seller is not obligated to complete improvements of lots sold or to construct amenities or other facilities applicable to lots sold.

Paragraphs 46-49 specify accounting methods that shall be used if the above criteria are not met.

46. The percentage-of-completion method of accounting[21] described in paragraphs 73-75 shall be applied to a sale that meets all of the following criteria:

a. *The period of cancellation with refund has expired* (paragraph 45(a)).

b. *Cumulative payments equal or exceed 10 percent* (paragraph 45(b)).

c. *Receivables are collectible* (paragraph 45(c)).

d. *Receivables are not subject to subordination* (paragraph 45(d)).

e. *There has been progress on improvements.* The project's improvements have progressed beyond preliminary stages, and there are indications that the work will be completed according to plan. Some indications of progress are:

(1) The expenditure of funds on the proposed improvements.

(2) Initiation of work on the improvements.

(3) Existence of engineering plans and work commitments relating to lots sold.

(4) Completion of access roads and amenities such as golf courses, clubs, and swimming pools.

In addition, there shall be no indication of significant delaying factors, such as the inability to obtain permits, contractors, personnel, or equipment, and estimates of costs to complete and extent of progress toward completion shall be reasonably dependable.

f. *Development is practical.* There is a reasonable expectation that the land can be developed for the purposes represented and the properties will be useful for those purposes at the end of the normal payment period. For example, it should be expected that legal restrictions, including environmental restrictions, will not seriously hamper development and that improvements such as access roads, water supply, and sewage treatment or removal are feasible within a reasonable time.

Paragraphs 47 and 48 specify accounting methods that shall be used if the above criteria are not met.

47. The installment method of accounting described in paragraphs 56-61 shall be applied to a sale that meets all of the following criteria:

a. *The period of cancellation with refund has expired* (paragraph 45(a)).

b. *Cumulative payments equal or exceed 10 percent* (paragraph 45(b)).

c. *The seller is financially capable.* The seller is clearly capable of providing both land improvements and off-site facilities promised in the contract and of meeting all other representations it has made. It is financially capable of funding or bonding the planned improvements in the project when required. That capability may be indicated by the seller's equity capitalization, its borrowing capacity, or its positive cash flow from operations.

48. If a retail land sale transaction does not meet the criteria for accounting by the methods described in paragraphs 45-47, that transaction shall be accounted for as a deposit as described in paragraphs 65-67.

Change from Installment to Percentage-of-Completion Method

49. When all of the conditions in paragraph 46 are satisfied on a retail land sales project originally reported by the installment method, the percentage-

---

[19]The six-month period is solely a test of eligibility for the accrual method and is not intended to restrict the recognition of profit before the six-month period expires.

[20]Examples of sales methods include telephone sales, broker sales, and site-visitation sales.

[21]In the AICPA Guide, *Accounting for Retail Land Sales,* this was called the "accrual method."

of-completion method of accounting may be adopted for the entire project (current and prior sales) and the effect accounted for as a change in accounting estimate.[22]

Financial Statement Presentation and Disclosures

50. In addition to disclosures otherwise required by generally accepted accounting principles, the financial statements of enterprises with retail land sales operations shall disclose:

a. Maturities of accounts receivable for each of the five years following the date of the financial statements
b. Delinquent accounts receivable and the method(s) for determining delinquency
c. The weighted average and range of stated interest rates of receivables
d. Estimated total costs and estimated dates of expenditures for improvements for major areas from which sales are being made over each of the five years following the date of the financial statements
e. Recorded obligations for improvements

Financial statement presentations of retail land sales transactions are illustrated in paragraphs 95-97.

Amendments to Other Pronouncements

51. The references to the AICPA Industry Accounting Guides, *Accounting for Profit Recognition on Sales of Real Estate* and *Accounting for Retail Land Sales,* and the AICPA Statements of Position (SOPs) 75-6, *Questions Concerning Profit Recognition on Sales of Real Estate* and 78-4, *Application of the Deposit, Inst.:llment, and Cost Recovery Methods in Accounting for Sales of Real Estate,* are deleted from Appendix A of FASB Statement No. 32, *Specialized Accounting and Reporting Principles and Practices in AICPA Statements of Position and Guides on Accounting and Auditing Matters.* The references to the profit recognition Guide in paragraph 7 of FASB Statement No. 26, *Profit Recognition on Sales-Type Leases of Real Estate,* and in footnote "*" and paragraphs 23-25 of Statement 28 are amended to refer to Statement No. 66, *Accounting for Sales of Real Estate.*

Effective Date and Transition

52. This Statement shall be applied to real estate sales transactions entered into after December 31, 1982 and to changes in methods of accounting for real estate sales transactions made after that date. Earlier application is encouraged but not required. The disclosures required by paragraph 50 shall be provided in financial statements for periods ending after December 15, 1982.

> **The provisions of this Statement need
> not be applied to immaterial items.**

This Statement was adopted by the affirmative votes of five members of the Financial Accounting Standards Board. Messrs. Morgan and Walters dissented.

Mr. Morgan dissents to the issuance of this Statement. Although he recognizes the Board's commitment to extract specialized principles and practices from SOPs and Guides and to issue them as FASB Statements, as stated in paragraph 2 of Statement 32, and the fact that issuance of this Statement is considered by a majority of Board members to be a fulfillment of part of that commitment, Mr. Morgan believes this Statement should be deferred until certain other projects are completed.

Incorporation of these detailed guidelines into accounting standards is inappropriate at this time in view of three projects in process that should bear on the nature and effect of accounting standards in this area:

a. The Board's conceptual framework project on accounting recognition, which should establish a

basic framework for all revenue recognition
b. The Board's project on financial reporting by private and small public companies
c. The August 1982 report of the Financial Accounting Foundation's Structure Committee, which acknowledges the comments of many respondents that the Board should deal primarily with broad accounting standards issues and charges the Board to develop a plan, for consideration by the Trustees, to provide timely *guidance* for implementation questions and emerging issues

Mr. Morgan believes that no urgent need for an FASB Statement on this subject has been demonstrated. Accordingly, he believes it more prudent to complete the broader, more general projects before further considering whether this Statement is needed.

---

[22]The credit to income resulting from the change is the profit not yet recognized less (a) a discount, if required, to reduce the receivable balances to their present values at the date of change to the percentage-of-completion method (using the appropriate interest rates, as specified in paragraphs 13 and 14 of Opinion 21, in effect at the time of the original sales) and (b) the liability (also discounted) for remaining future performance. The computation is illustrated in paragraph 97.

Mr. Walters dissents to the issuance of this Statement primarily because he objects to incorporating these complex, rigid, and detailed rules into accounting standards. Entirely aside from the conceptual merit of these rules, which is at least debatable, he believes the Board should focus at about the level expressed in paragraphs 3 and 4 of this Statement. Beyond that, he believes the accounting profession can serve its members by offering more specific *guidance* for applying the standards in particular specialized areas, but such detailed and arbitrary guidelines should not be dignified as accounting standards. To do so debases accounting standards and inevitably will diminish the stature and effectiveness of the accounting profession, whose strength and purpose arise from applying broad accounting and reporting objectives and standards to specific circumstances with professional judgment and objectivity. That judgment is the hallmark of a true profession.

Secondarily, he believes that incorporation of these detailed guidelines into accounting standards is particularly inappropriate at this time for the reasons cited by Mr. Morgan.

Members of the Financial Accounting Standards Board:

Donald J. Kirk,
Chairman
Frank E. Block

John W. March
Robert A. Morgan
David Mosso

Robert T. Sprouse
Ralph E. Walters

Appendix A

MINIMUM INITIAL INVESTMENTS

53. Minimum initial investment requirements for sales, other than retail land sales, that are to be accounted for by the full accrual method are specified in paragraph 11. The table of minimum initial investments in paragraph 54 is based on usual loan limits for various types of properties. However, lenders' appraisals of specific properties may differ. Therefore, if a recently placed permanent loan or firm permanent loan commitment for maximum financing of the property exists with an independent established lending institution, the minimum initial investment should be whichever of the following is greater:

a. The minimum percentage of the sales value (paragraph 7) of the property specified in paragraph 54
b. The lesser of:
   (1) The amount of the sales value of the property in excess of 115 percent of the amount of a newly placed permanent loan or firm permanent loan commitment from a primary lender that is an independent established lending institution
   (2) Twenty-five percent of the sales value

54. This table does not cover every type of real estate property. To evaluate initial investments on other types of property, enterprises may make analogies to the types of properties specified, or the risks of a particular property can be related to the risks of the properties specified. Use of this table is illustrated in paragraphs 77-83.

	Minimum Initial Investment Expressed as a Percentage of Sales Value

Land
Held for commercial, industrial, or residential development to commence within two years after sale 20
Held for commercial, industrial, or residential development to commence after two years 25

Commercial and Industrial Property
Office and industrial buildings, shopping centers, and so forth:
  Properties subject to lease on a long-term lease basis to parties with satisfactory credit rating; cash flow currently sufficient to service all indebtedness 10
  Single-tenancy properties sold to a buyer with a satisfactory credit rating 15
  All other 20
Other income-producing properties (hotels, motels, marinas, mobile home parks, and so forth):
  Cash flow currently sufficient to service all indebtedness 15
  Start-up situations or current deficiencies in cash flow 25

Multifamily Residential Property
Primary residence:
  Cash flow currently sufficient to service all indebtedness 10
  Start-up situations or current deficiencies in cash flow 15
Secondary or recreational residence:
  Cash flow currently sufficient to service all indebtedness 15
  Start-up situations or current deficiencies in cash flow 25

Single-Family Residential Property (including condominium or cooperative housing)
Primary residence of the buyer .... 5[a]
Secondary or recreational residence .... 10[a]

Appendix B

DESCRIPTION OF CERTAIN METHODS OF ACCOUNTING FOR REAL ESTATE SALES TRANSACTIONS

55. This appendix describes several of the methods of profit recognition that are provided for by this Statement.

Installment Method

56. The installment method apportions each cash receipt and principal payment by the buyer on debt assumed between cost recovered and profit. The apportionment is in the same ratio as total cost and total profit bear to the sales value. The calculation is illustrated in paragraph 90.

57. If the stated interest rate is equal to or less than an appropriate interest rate, it is acceptable not to reduce the receivable to its present value. This ordinarily results in reducing profit recognized in the earlier years.

58. Under the installment method, the receivable less profits not recognized does not exceed what the property value would have been if the property had not been sold.

59. The income statement, or related footnotes, for the period including the date of sale presents the sales value, the gross profit that has not yet been recognized, and the total cost of the sale. Revenue and cost of sales (or gross profit) are presented as separate items on the income statement or are disclosed in the footnotes when profit is recognized as earned. This presentation is illustrated in paragraph 96.

60. Paragraph 75 describes accounting for obligations for future improvement costs under the percentage-of-completion method. That description applies as well to accounting for those obligations under the installment method.

61. If after adoption of the installment method the transaction meets the requirements for the full accrual method (specified in paragraphs 3-18) of recognizing profit for real estate sales other than retail land sales, the seller may then change to the full accrual method. The remaining profit that was not recognized is recognized in income at that time.

---

[a]If collectibility of the remaining portion of the sales price cannot be supported by reliable evidence of collection experience, the minimum initial investment shall be at least 60 percent of the difference between the sales value and the financing available from loans guaranteed by regulatory bodies such as the Federal Housing Authority (FHA) or the Veterans Administration (VA), or from independent, established lending institutions. This 60-percent test applies when independent first-mortgage financing is not utilized and the seller takes a receivable from the buyer for the difference between the sales value and the initial investment. If independent first mortgage financing is utilized, the adequacy of the initial investment on sales of single-family residential property should be determined in accordance with paragraph 53.

Cost Recovery Method

62. Under the cost recovery method, no profit is recognized until cash payments by the buyer, including principal and interest on debt due to the seller and on existing debt assumed by the buyer, exceed the seller's cost of the property sold.[23] The receivable less profits not recognized, if any, does not exceed what the depreciated property value would have been if the property had not been sold.

63. The income statement for the period including the date of sale presents the sales value, the gross profit that has not yet been recognized, and the total cost of the sale. Gross profit not recognized is offset against the related receivable on the balance sheet. Principal collections reduce the related receivable, and interest collections on such receivables increase the unrecognized gross profit on the balance sheet. Gross profit is presented as a separate item of revenue on the income statement when it is recognized as earned.

64. If, after the adoption of the cost recovery method, the transaction meets the requirements for the full accrual method (specified in paragraphs 3-18), the seller may then change to the full accrual method. The remaining profit that was not recognized is recognized in income at that time.

Deposit Method

65. Under the deposit method, the seller does not recognize any profit, does not record notes receivable, continues to report in its financial statements the property and the related existing debt even if it has been assumed by the buyer, and discloses that those items are subject to a sales contract. The seller continues to charge depreciation to expense as a period cost for the property for which deposits have been received. Cash received from the buyer, including the initial investment and subsequent collections of principal and interest, is reported as a deposit on the contract except that, for sales that are not retail land sales, portions of cash received that are designated by the contract as interest and are not subject to refund offset carrying charges (property taxes and interest on existing debt) on the property. Interest collected that is subject to refund and is included in the deposit account before a sale is consummated is accounted for as part of the buyer's initial investment (paragraph 7) at the time the sale is consummated.

66. When a contract is canceled without a refund, deposits forfeited are recognized as income. When deposits on retail land sales are ultimately recognized as sales, the interest portion is recognized as interest income.

67. The seller's balance sheet presents nonrecourse debt assumed by the buyer among the liabilities; the debt assumed is not offset against the related property. The seller reports the buyer's principal payments on mortgage debt assumed as additional deposits with corresponding reductions of the carrying amount of the mortgage debt.

Reduced-Profit Method

68. A reduced profit is determined by discounting the receivable from the buyer to the present value of the lowest level of annual payments required by the sales contract over the maximum period specified in paragraph 12 and excluding requirements to pay lump sums. The present value is calculated using an appropriate interest rate,[24] but not less than the rate stated in the sales contract. This method permits profit to be recognized from level payments on the buyer's debt over the maximum term established in paragraph 12 and postpones recognition of other profits until lump sum or other payments are made.

69. To illustrate, assume a sale of land that cost the seller $800,000 and is being sold for $1,000,000 with the following financing:

Buyer's initial investment	$ 250,000
First mortgage note payable to an independent lending institution (Terms—15 percent interest payable annually over 20 years: $79,881 per year including principal and interest)	500,000
Second mortgage note payable to seller (Terms—12 percent interest payable annually over 25 years: $31,875 per year including principal and interest)	250,000
Total selling price	$1,000,000

The amortization term of the second mortgage (25 years) exceeds the term permitted by paragraph 12 (20 years for sales of land). It is assumed that the payments by the buyer each year will meet the requirement in paragraph 23, that the reduced-profit method is to be applied, and that the market interest rate is 16 percent.

---

[23]For an all-inclusive or "wrap-around" receivable held by the seller, interest collected is recognized as income to the extent of, and as an appropriate offset to, interest expense on prior-lien financing for which the seller remains responsible.

[24]Paragraphs 13 and 14 of Opinion 21 provide criteria for selecting an appropriate rate for present-value calculations.

The present value of $31,875 per year for 20 years at a market rate of 16 percent is $31,875 × 5.92884 = $188,982.

The profit to be recognized at the time of sale is reduced by the difference between the face amount of the seller's receivable ($250,000) and the reduced amount ($188,982), or $61,018. The profit recognized at the time of sale is $1,000,000 (sales price) minus $800,000 (cost) minus $61,018, or $138,982. Additional profit of $61,018 is recognized as the second mortgage payments are received in years 21 through 25.

Full Accrual Method—Retail Land Sales

70. Revenues and costs are accounted for under the accrual method as follows:

a. The net receivable is discounted to the present value of the payments required. The present value is determined using an appropriate interest rate,[25] not less than the rate stated in the sales contract. The objective is to value the net receivable at the amount at which it could be sold without recourse to the seller at the date of the sales contract.
b. An allowance is provided for receivables that are not expected to be collected because of cancellation in subsequent periods. Receivable balances applicable to canceled contracts are charged in their entirety to the allowance for contract cancellations when those contracts are canceled.
c. Costs of sales (land and improvement costs incurred, carrying costs, and so forth) are based on sales net of those sales expected to be canceled in future periods.

71. Historical data is evaluated to predict the collection of receivables from current sales. The historical data is selected from a representative sample of receivables that reflect the latest available collection data and cover an adequate period of time. The receivables in the sample are considered uncollectible and the allowance for contract cancellations provided for previously recognized sales (paragraph 70(b)) is appropriately adjusted if payments due are unpaid at the end of the sample period selected for the following delinquency periods:

Percent of Contract Price Paid	Delinquency Period
Less than 25 percent	90 days
25 percent but less than 50 percent	120 days
50 percent and over	150 days

The specified delinquency periods may be extended if the seller's recent experience has been better or if the buyer has accepted, or is willing to accept, personal liability on its debt, provided that the buyer's ability to complete payment on the contract can be determined.

72. Many sellers have programs to accelerate collections of receivables or contract provisions that encourage prepayment with a reduction of the principal as the major incentive for prepayment. If a seller expects to institute those or similar programs in the future, the amount of profit recognized at the date of sale is reduced through charges to income for anticipated discounts not otherwise recognized. Reductions that are given sporadically are charged to income in the period they occur.

**Percentage-of-Completion Method—
Retail Land Sales**

73. The earnings process is not complete if a seller is obliged to complete improvements of lots sold or to construct amenities and other facilities applicable to lots sold, if those obligations are significant in relation to total costs, and if they remain unperformed at the time the sale is recognized. Therefore, the amount of revenue recognized (the discounted contract price) at the time a sale is recognized is measured by the relationship of costs already incurred to total estimated costs to be incurred, including costs of the marketing effort. If performance[26] is incomplete, the portion of revenue related to costs not yet incurred is recognized as the costs are incurred.

74. The costs already incurred and total costs to be incurred include land cost, costs previously charged to expense, such as interest and project carrying costs incurred prior to sale, and selling costs[27] directly associated with a project. The accounting

---

[25]Paragraphs 13 and 14 of Opinion 21 provide criteria for selecting an appropriate rate for present-value calculations.

[26]*Performance* means completion of the improvements required under the sales contract by either the seller or contractors retained by the seller. However, payments made to municipalities or other governmental organizations not under the direct or joint control of the seller constitute performance by the seller if those organizations are not financed solely by liens on property in the project and they undertake to complete the improvements without further risk or obligation of the seller.

[27]Accounting for selling costs is addressed in FASB Statement No. 67, *Accounting for Costs and Initial Rental Operations of Real Estate Projects.*

described in this paragraph and paragraph 73 is illustrated in paragraphs 91-95.

75. If there is an obligation for future improvement costs that is recognized under the percentage-of-completion method:

a. Estimates are based on costs generally expected in the construction industry locally.
b. Unrecoverable costs of off-site improvements, utilities, and amenities are provided for. In determining the amount of unrecoverable costs, estimates of amounts to be recovered from future sale of the improvements, utilities, and amenities are discounted to present value as of the date the net unrecoverable costs are recognized.

76. Estimates of future improvement costs are reviewed at least annually. Changes in those estimates do not lead to adjustment of revenue applicable to future improvements that has been previously recorded unless the adjusted total estimated cost exceeds the applicable revenue. When cost estimates are revised, the relationship of the two elements included in the revenue not yet recognized—costs and profit—is recalculated on a cumulative basis to determine future income recognition as performance takes place. If the adjusted total estimated cost exceeds the applicable revenue previously recognized, the total anticipated loss is charged to income when it meets the criteria in paragraph 8 of Statement 5. When anticipated losses on lots sold are recognized, the enterprise also considers recognizing a loss on land and improvements not yet sold.

Appendix C

ILLUSTRATIONS OF CALCULATIONS FOR RECOGNITION OF PROFIT ON SALES OF REAL ESTATE OTHER THAN RETAIL LAND SALES[28]

Exhibits

Exhibit I—Illustration of Effect of Land Lease—New Multifamily Residential Property

77. Land improvements may be sold and concurrently the land under the improvements may be leased to the buyer of the improvements.

78. This exhibit illustrates the effect of loans issued in connection with long-term land leases on evaluations of the adequacy of a buyer's initial investment if improvements on the land are sold separately. In addition, it demonstrates the limit that a lease places on profit recognition if the leased land is owned by the seller of the improvements, making the lease of land and sale of improvements interdependent transactions.

79. The calculations are illustrated for four different circumstances: two examples with a primary land lease and two with a subordinated land lease.

---

[28]The financing and interest rate assumptions in this appendix are based on conditions at the time the profit recognition Guide was issued. They should not be considered as indicative of financing and interest rate assumptions that would be appropriate under different circumstances and at different times.

80. Primary Land Lease: Land Owned by Third Party Lessor—Nonqualifying

Assumptions:

Sales price of improvements	$875,000

Represented by proceeds of:

Cash down payment	$125,000
Loan by insurance company—lien on leasehold improvements, 28-year term, 8 1/2%, payable in equal monthly installments of principal and interest	657,000
Note received by seller from buyer: 12-year term, 9 1/2%, payable in equal monthly installments of principal and interest	93,000
	$875,000

Land lease for 99 years @ $19,000/year, net, payable monthly in advance
Cost of constructing improvements—$750,000
No continuing involvement by seller

Computations:

Present value of 336 monthly payments on land lease of $1,583.33 discounted at 8 1/2% (interest rate on loan from insurance company): $1,583.33 + ($1,583.33 × 127.9071)	$ 204,000
Loan from insurance company	657,000
Equivalent primary debt	861,000
Note receivable from buyer	93,000
Total debt or equivalent	954,000
Down payment	125,000
Sales value	$1,079,000

Because 15% of the sales value of the improvements is $161,850, the initial investment of $125,000 (about 12% of adjusted sales value) is inadequate to recognize profit on the sale of improvements. The second test is therefore irrelevant.

81. Primary Land Lease: Land Owned by Third Party Lessor—Qualifying

Assumptions:

Sales price of improvements	$875,000

Represented by proceeds of:

Cash down payment	$165,000
Loan by insurance company: lien on leasehold improvements, 28-year term, 8 1/2%, payable in equal monthly installments of principal and interest	657,000
Note received by seller from buyer: 12-year term, 9 1/2%, payable in equal monthly installments of principal and interest	53,000
	$875,000

Land lease for 99 years @ $17,880/year, net, payable monthly in advance
Cost of constructing improvements—$750,000
No continuing involvement by seller

Computations:

Present value of 336 monthly payments on land lease of $1,490 discounted at 8 1/2% (interest rate on loan from insurance company): $1,490 + ($1,490 × 127.9071)	$ 192,000
Loan from insurance company	657,000
Equivalent primary debt	849,000
Note receivable from buyer	53,000
Total debt or equivalent	902,000
Down payment	165,000
Sales value	$1,067,000

Because 15% of the sales value of the improvements is $160,050, the initial investment of $165,000 (15% of the sales value) is adequate to recognize profit on the sale of improvements. However, the second test must also be applied.

The initial investment required by the second test is:	
Sales value	$1,067,000
115% of $849,000 (loan from primary lender)	976,350
	$ 90,650

The initial investment of $165,000 exceeds the amount required, so recognition of profit on sale of improvements is appropriate. The second test may alternatively be applied as the ratio of total debt or equivalent to the equivalent primary debt: $902,000/$849,000 = 106%. Because 106% is less than 115%, the initial investment exceeds the difference between the sales value of the property and 115% of the equivalent primary debt.

Profit recognition:	
Sales price of improvements	$875,000
Less: Cost of improvements	750,000
Profit recognized at time of sale	$125,000

82. Subordinated Land Lease: Land Owned by Seller—Qualifying

Assumptions:	
Sales price of improvements	$914,000
Represented by proceeds of:	
Cash down payment	$154,000
Loan by insurance company: first lien on the fee or on subordinated leasehold, 28-year term, 8 1/4%, payable in equal monthly installments of principal and interest	760,000
	$914,000

Land lease for 99 years @ $11,580/year, net, payable monthly in advance, and 5% of gross rents
Cost of land—$200,000
Cost of constructing improvements—$750,000
No continuing involvement by seller

Computations:

Present value of 336 monthly payments on land lease at $965 discounted at 12% (imputed interest for a second lien receivable): $965 + ($965 × 96.432696)	$ 94,000
Loan from insurance company (primary debt)	760,000
Total debt or equivalent	854,000
Down payment	154,000
Sales value	$1,008,000

The initial investment ($154,000) is more than 15% of the sales value. (15% × $1,008,000 = $151,200).

The initial investment is also larger than the excess of the sales value over 115% of the primary debt.

Sales value	$1,008,000
115% of $760,000	874,000
Excess of sales value over 115% of debt	$ 134,000

Therefore, the initial investment of $154,000 is adequate, and recognizing profit on the sale of the improvements is appropriate.

Profit recognition:

Sales value		$1,008,000
Less: Cost of improvements	$750,000	
Cost of land	200,000	950,000
Profit recognized at time of sale		$ 58,000

The effect of including the present value of the lease is to reduce profit recognized by $106,000: $94,000 (present value of the land lease) − $200,000 (cost of land).

83. Subordinated Land Lease: Land Owned by Seller—Nonqualifying

Assumptions:

Sales price of improvements	$875,000

Represented by proceeds of:

Cash down payment	$132,000
Loan by insurance company: first lien on the fee or on subordinated leasehold, 28-year term, 8 1/4%, payable in equal monthly installments of principal and interest	743,000
	$875,000

Land lease for 99 years @ $19,332/year, net, payable monthly in advance
Cost of land—$200,000
Cost of improvements—$750,000
No continuing involvement by seller

Computations:

Present value of 336 monthly payments on land lease of $1,611 discounted at 12%		
(imputed interest for a second lien receivable): $1,611 + ($1,611 × 96.432696)		$ 157,000
Loan from insurance company (primary debt)		743,000
Total debt or equivalent		900,000
Down payment		132,000
Sales value		$1,032,000

The initial investment ($132,000) is less than 15% of the sales value (15% × $1,032,000 = $154,800), and therefore is inadequate to recognize profit on sale of improvements. Profit recognized at time of sale should not exceed that recognizable under the installment method as if the subordinated lease were an installment receivable.

Profit recognition on installment method:

Sales value		$1,032,000
Less: Cost of improvements	$750,000	
Cost of land	200,000	950,000
Anticipated profit on sale of improvements		$ 82,000

Cash received or to be received by the seller, other than the proceeds of the primary loan, is:

Down payment	$132,000
Present value of land lease payments	157,000
	$289,000

The percentage of profit in each collection is therefore:

$$\frac{\$ 82,000}{\$289,000} = 28.37\%$$

Profit recognizable in the period of sale is 28.37% of the down payment of $132,000, or $37,450. The remaining profit of $44,550 will be recognized at the rate of 28.37% of the portion of each lease payment that is equivalent to a reduction of principal on a loan of $157,000 for 28 years at 12%.

The effect of including the present value of the lease in the sales value of the improvements is to reduce the profit recognized on the improvements by $43,000: $157,000 (present value of the land lease) − $200,000 (cost of the land).

**Exhibit II—Illustration of Profit Recognition—
Sale of Property with Construction and
Support Obligations by Seller**

84. This exhibit illustrates the method of accounting required for a sale of property in which the seller is obligated to construct multifamily units and in which cash flow deficits are anticipated. The example applies to obligations of the seller specified in paragraphs 28-30.

85. Assumptions:

a. Company X develops and sells multifamily residential projects. The Company performs directly all developmental activities, including initial planning, site acquisition, obtaining of financing, and physical construction of the project.

b. During the year ended December 31, 19X1 the Company began a project of 100 units. The project was planned and substantial activity had been performed in 19X1 but physical construction had not started as of December 31, 19X1. However, all contracts had been let, and the Company had obtained construction financing.

c. On December 31, 19X1, the Company sold the project to a limited partnership syndication (fully formed) in which it is the sole general partner:

Sales value	$1,100,000
Represented by proceeds of:	
Cash down payment	$ 165,000
Permanent financing assumed by the buyer, consisting of a 28-year 8 1/2% fully amortizing first mortgage loan by a conventional lender, payable in equal monthly payments of principal and interest to maturity	825,000
Second mortgage note received by the Company payable in equal monthly installments including interest at 9 1/2% over 12 years	110,000
	$1,100,000

d. The closing occurred on December 31, 19X1 and included delivery or performance of the following:
   (1) The Company delivered to the buyer a legal title to the land and all existing improvements.
   (2) The Company delivered to the buyer a firm commitment from an outside lender for permanent financing, and the buyer assumed permanent financing formerly in the name of the Company.
   (3) The Company received from the buyer $165,000 cash and a second mortgage note for $110,000.
   (4) The Company signed a contract to deliver the completed project for a single price of $1,100,000.

e. Costs incurred by the Company and total costs estimated to complete the project, as of December 31, 19X1, were:

	Costs to Date	Estimated Costs to Complete	Total Estimated Costs
Land	$117,000		$117,000
Feasibility, zoning, architectural	35,000		35,000
Finance and other	85,000	$ 10,000	95,000
Site improvements	—	20,000	20,000
Building construction		571,000	571,000
Total	$237,000	$601,000	$838,000

f. The Company has completed an extensive market research and feasibility study analyzing its cost estimates, the rent-up incubation period, and subsequent rent levels. The initial rent-up will commence in 19X2. Accordingly, a support period of two years is presumed for 19X3 and 19X4.

g. Based on its market analysis, the projected results are as follows:

	19X2	19X3	19X4
Rental expense	$ 37,000	$ 58,000	$ 58,000
Debt service	93,000	93,000	93,000
Total	130,000	151,000	151,000
Rental revenue	(75,000)	(150,000)	(180,000)*
Anticipated net deficit (surplus) in cash flow	55,000	1,000	(29,000)
Safety factor of 1/3 of rental revenue	25,000	50,000	60,000
Adjusted anticipated net deficit in cash flow	$ 80,000	$ 51,000	$ 31,000

*$180,000 equals 95% of gross scheduled rents.

h. Initial cost estimates by the Company on previous projects have never varied from final costs by more than one-half of one % of total costs.

86. Calculations of Profit to Be Recognized:

Schedules A and B (paragraphs 87 and 88) illustrate calculations of profit to be recognized in the period of sale, in the period of construction, and in each period in which the seller will support operations (19X2-19X4). The following features should be noted:

a. The percentage of estimated total profit to be recognized each period is determined by the ratio of gross costs incurred to the end of the period to total estimated gross costs of the project, including gross costs during the period of support of operations. (Construction costs should be included even if construction is performed by parties other than the seller.)

b. The estimated total profit that is the basis of the calculation in each period (that is, the profit to which the percentage in (a) is applied) is determined by adding the sales value and two-thirds of the projected revenue during the period of support of operations and deducting the estimated total costs of the project, including costs of operating the property and debt service.

   (1) Actual amounts of revenue and costs are substituted for estimated amounts in the calculation as the actual amounts are known. However, in this illustration, remaining estimates of future revenue and expense are not changed because of actual results even though experience might indicate that projections of future amounts should be revised.

   (2) Projected and actual revenues in the calculation should exclude amounts that accrue to the buyer, for example, revenue in excess of the sum of operating expenses and debt service.

   (3) One-third of projected revenue should be excluded from the estimate of profit to provide a margin of safety (paragraph 85(g)). Actual results incorporated in the calculation need not be reduced by a safety factor.

   (4) The calculation illustrated should be applied only if objective information is available regarding occupancy levels and rental rates for similar property in the immediate area. This will provide reasonable assurance that rent revenue from the project will be sufficient to cover operating expenses and debt service, including payments due to the seller under the terms of the transaction. Unless that evidence is available, no profit should be recognized on the transaction until rent revenue actually reaches levels that assure coverage of those costs.

c. Schedule A shows calculation of profit to be recognized each period on the assumption that actual revenue and costs are the same as those projected in paragraph 85(g) *adjusted* for the safety margin of one-third of revenue.

d. Schedule B shows calculation of profit to be recognized each period on the assumption that actual revenue and costs are the same as those projected in paragraph 85(g) *before* adjustment for safety margin.

e. Schedule C illustrates the calculation of estimated future rent receipts by adjustment for a safety margin.

87. **Schedule A**

Example of Profit Calculation
(assuming actual rental revenue equals
adjusted projection)

REVENUES
Sales value	$1,100,000
Adjusted—projected rental revenue[29]	
19X2	50,000
19X3	100,000
19X4	120,000
	1,370,000

COSTS
Total estimated costs of project (paragraph 85(e))	838,000
Estimated rental expenses and debt service	
19X2	130,000
19X3	151,000
19X4	151,000
	1,270,000

TOTAL PROJECTED PROFIT $ 100,000

Profit to be recognized:

$$\frac{\text{Cost to date}}{\text{Total costs}} \times \text{projected profit}$$

Profit recognized in period of sale:

$$\frac{\$\ 237,000}{1,270,000} \times \$100,000 = \$18,661$$

Total profit to date	$ 18,661
Less profit previously reported	0
Current profit recognition	$ 18,661

Profit recognized in period of construction:

$$\frac{\$\ 838,000}{1,270,000} \times \$100,000 = \$65,984$$

Total profit to date	$ 65,984
Less profit previously recognized	18,661
Current profit recognition	$ 47,323

Profit recognized during support period (19X2):

$$\frac{\$\ 968,000}{1,270,000} \times \$100,000 = \$76,221$$

Total profit to date	$ 76,221
Less profit previously recognized	65,984
Current profit recognition	$ 10,237

Profit recognized during support period (19X3):

$$\frac{\$1,119,000}{1,270,000} \times \$100,000 = \$88,110$$

Total profit to date	$ 88,110
Less profit previously recognized	76,221
Current profit recognition	$ 11,889

Profit recognized during support period (19X4):

$$\frac{\$1,270,000}{1,270,000} \times \$100,000 = \$100,000$$

Total profit to date	$ 100,000
Less profit previously recognized	88,110
Current profit recognition	$ 11,890

---

[29]Two-thirds of projected revenue during periods of support of operations; this can also be calculated as projected rental expenses plus projected debt service less projected deficit cash flow.

88. **Schedule B**

Example of Profit Calculation
(assuming actual rental revenue equals *unadjusted* projection)
(in thousands)

	Profit Recognized in Period of Sale	Profit Recognized in Period of Construction	Profit Recognized during Support Period		
			19X2	**19X3**	**19X4**
REVENUES					
Sales value	$1,100	$1,100	$1,100	$1,100	$1,100
Adjusted—projected rental revenue*					
19X2	50	50	75[†]	75[†]	75[†]
19X3	100	100	100	150[†]	150[†]
19X4	120	120	120	150[§]	151[‡]
	1,370	1,370	1,395	1,475	1,476
COSTS					
Same as Schedule A	1,270	1,270	1,270	1,270	1,270
TOTAL PROJECTED PROFIT	$ 100	$ 100	$ 125	$ 205	$ 206

Profit to be recognized:

$$\frac{\text{Cost to date}}{\text{Total costs}} \times \text{projected profit}$$

Profit recognized in period of sale:

$$\frac{\$ \ 237,000}{1,270,000} \times \$100,000 = \$18,661$$

Total profit to date	$ 18,661
Less profit previously reported	0
Current profit recognition	$ 18,661

Profit recognized in period of construction

$$\frac{\$ \ 838,000}{1,270,000} \times \$100,000 = \$65,984$$

Total profit to date	$ 65,984
Less profit previously reported	18,661
Current profit recognition	$ 47,323

Profit recognized during support period (19X2):

$$\frac{\$ \ 968,000}{1,270,000} \times \$125,000 = \$95,276$$

Total profit to date	$ 95,276
Less profit previously reported	65,984
Current profit recognition	$ 29,292

---

*Two-thirds of projected revenue during periods of support of operation; this can also be calculated as projected rental expenses plus projected debt service less projected deficit cash flow.

†Actual rental revenue.

‡Because the property has attained a level of occupancy in excess of the original adjusted projection, and there is no reason to believe that such occupancy level cannot be sustained, the projected 19X4 rental revenue should be adjusted to 19X3 actual rental revenue.

§Actual rental revenue excluding amounts not needed to meet cash flow requirements of the property.

Profit recognized during support period (19X3):

$$\frac{\$1,119,000}{1,270,000} \times \$205,000 = \$180,626$$

Total profit to date	$180,626
Less profit previously reported	95,276
Current profit recognition	$ 85,350

Profit recognized during support period (19X4):

$$\frac{\$1,270,000}{1,270,000} \times \$206,000 = \$206,000$$

Total profit to date	$206,000
Less profit previously reported	180,626
Current profit recognition	$ 25,374

89. **Schedule C**

Calculation of Adjusted Projected Rental Revenue

Assume an office building under development is sold together with an agreement to support operations of the property for three years. The projected annual rent roll is $1,000,000 of which $350,000 is supported by signed lease agreements. The projected rental revenue for the first year of operation is $600,000; the second year $750,000; and the third year $1,000,000. At the time of sale, the amounts to be included in the calculation would be as follows:

Year	Projected Rental Revenue	Safety Factor (33-1/3%)	Adjusted Projected Rental Revenue
1	$ 600,000	$200,000	$400,000
2	750,000	250,000	500,000
3	1,000,000	333,333	666,667

If at the time of sale there were signed lease agreements for $450,000, then the $450,000 would be used in year 1 because it is greater than the adjusted projected rental revenue. The adjusted projected rental revenue for years 2 and 3 would remain $500,000 and $666,667, respectively.

Exhibit III—Illustration of Profit Recognition—Installment Method, with Debt Assumed by Buyer

90. Assumptions:

Cash down payment	$ 150,000
Second mortgage payable by buyer to seller (10-year amortization of principal plus interest)	350,000
Total cash to be received by seller	500,000
First mortgage assumed by buyer (20-year amortization of principal plus interest)	500,000
Total sales price and sales value	1,000,000
Cost	600,000
Total profit	$ 400,000

The initial investment is assumed to be inadequate for full profit recognition, and the installment method of accounting is assumed to be appropriate. It is also assumed that, after the down payment, the buyer pays $25,000 of principal on the first mortgage and $35,000 of principal on the second mortgage.

Profit recognition: Under the installment method, profit recognition attributable to the down payment is $60,000, representing 40% ($400,000/$1,000,000) of $150,000.

Profit recognition attributable to the principal payments by the buyer on the first and second mortgages is $24,000, representing 40% of $60,000 ($25,000 + $35,000).

Appendix D

ILLUSTRATIONS OF CALCULATIONS FOR RECOGNITION OF PROFIT ON RETAIL LAND SALES[30]

Exhibit I—Initial Measure of Consideration
(Percentage-of-Completion Method)
(amounts in thousands)

91. Assumptions:

Gross sales contracts recorded in year 1 (stated interest of 6%)	$1,000
Estimated uncollectible principal amount (sales contracts of $200* less estimated down payments to be forfeited of $20)	(180)
Net sales contracts receivable	820
Down payments and collections in year 1 relative to above sales contracts ($80 + $20)	100
Collections projected (principal amounts) for years 2 through 10	$ 720
Land cost (applicable to sales contracts of $800)	$ 60
Selling expenses in year 1	300
Future improvement costs (applicable to sales contracts of $800)	120
Minimum annual yield required on contracts receivable	12%

Discount Required:

Sales contracts receivable in year 1 (see above)	$ 720
Present value of 108 level monthly payments of $8.65 on sales contracts receivable (discounted at 12%) (Schedule A)	570
Discount required	$ 150

Computation of Revenue Applicable to Future Improvements:

$$\frac{\$120}{\$60 + \$300 + \$120} = 25\%$$

$$25\% \times \$650\ (\$1000 - \$200 - \$150) = \$163$$

---

[30]The financing and interest rate assumptions in this appendix are based on conditions at the time the retail land sales Guide was issued. They should not be considered as indicative of financing and interest rate assumptions that would be appropriate under different circumstances and at different times.
*It is assumed that experience shows that 90% of contracts in force 6 months after sales are recognized will ultimately be collected in full (paragraph 45).

Profit Recognition in Year 1:
  Revenue recognized:

Cash received in year 1	$100
Present value of balance of sales contracts receivable	570
(Net sales $820, less discount $150)	670
Less: Revenue applicable to future improvements	163
Net revenue	507
Less: Costs and expenses ($60 + $300)	360
Pretax income	$147

92. **Schedule A**

Present Value of Sales Contracts Receivable
(amounts in thousands)

	Receivable Collections		Annual Collections	Present Value @ 12%
Year	**Principal**	**Interest***		
2	$ 62	$ 42	$104	$ 97
3	66	38	104	87
4	70	34	104	77
5	75	29	104	68
6	79	25	104	60
7	84	20	104	53
8	89	15	104	47
9	95	9	104	43
10	100	4	104	38
	$720	$216	$936	$570

*Assumes no interest for year 1.

93. **Schedule B**

Computation of Interest Income for Financial Reporting Purposes
(amounts in thousands)

Year	Debit: Cash	Debit: Unamortized Valuation Discount	Credit: Contracts Receivable	Credit: Interest Income*
2	$104	$ 24	($ 62)	($ 66)
3	104	24	(66)	(62)
4	104	22	(70)	(56)
5	104	21	(75)	(50)
6	104	19	(79)	(44)
7	104	16	(84)	(36)
8	104	12	(89)	(27)
9	104	8	(95)	(17)
10	104	4	(100)	(8)
	$936	$150	($720)	($366)

*Total interest income equals $216 stated interest plus $150 discount, or $366.

94. Schedule C

Determination of Income Tax Payable
(amounts in thousands)

Year	Principal Receipts	Profit from Installment Sale	Interest Income from Receivable	Selling Expense	Taxable Income (Loss)	Tax	Tax Effect of Loss Carry-forward from Year 1	Net Tax
1	$100	$ 82*	$ 42	($300)	($218)	($ 43)		($ 23)
2	62	48	38		90	(43)	$ 43	(42)
3	66	51	34		89	(42)	43	(41)
4	70	54	29		88	(42)	19	(41)
5	75	58	25		87	(41)		(40)
6	79	61	20		86	(41)		(40)
7	84	65	15		85	(40)		(40)
8	89	69	9		84	(40)		
9	95	74	9		83	(40)		
10	100	78	4		82			
	$820	$640	$216	($300)	$556	($372)	$105†	($267)

Assumption: The installment method is used for income tax purposes.

*Profit on land sale computed on installment method as follows:

Gross profit = $800 − $180 = $620

Principal payment × profit margin: $80 × $\dfrac{\$620}{\$800}$ = $62

Forfeited down payments $\underline{\quad 20 \quad}$

$\underline{\underline{\$82}}$

†Carryforward amount is 48% of $218 = $105.

95. Schedule D

**Percentage-of-Completion Method—Illustration of Financial
Statement Presentation of Transactions
Assumed in Paragraph 91**
(amounts in thousands)

Balance Sheets	Beginning of Year 1	End of Year 1	2	3	4	5	6	7	8	9	10
Assets:											
Cash	$300	$100	$204	$308	$389	$451	$514	$547	$581	$615	$649
Contracts receivable		720	658	592	522	447	368	284	195	100	
Less: Allowance for contract cancellations*	—										
Unamortized valuation discount		(150)	(126)	(102)	(80)	(59)	(40)	(24)	(12)	(4)	
		570	532	490	442	388	328	260	183	96	
Land	75	15	15	15	15	15	15	15	15	15	15
	$375	$685	$751	$813	$846	$854	$857	$822	$779	$726	$664
Liabilities and equity:											
Deferred income taxes		$ 71	$103	$133	$137	$119	$100	$ 81	$ 59	$ 32	
Revenue applicable to future improvements†		163	163	163	163	163	163	122	81	40	
Capital stock	$375	375	375	375	375	375	375	375	375	375	$375
Retained earnings		76	110	142	171	197	219	244	264	279	289
	$375	$685	$751	$813	$846	$854	$857	$822	$779	$726	$664

Schedule D (Cont.)

Income Statements	1	2	3	4	5	6	7	8	9	10	Total
						Year					
Revenues:											
Gross Sales	$1,000										$1,000
Less:											
Estimated uncollectible sales	(180)										(180)
Revenue applicable to future improvements	(163)										(163)
Valuation discount	(150)										(150)
Net sales	507										507
Improvement revenue—prior sales							$41	$41	$41	$40	163
Interest income (Schedule B)		$66	$62	$56	$50	$44	36	27	17	8	366
	507	66	62	56	50	44	77	68	58	48	1,036
Costs and expenses:											
Cost of sales	60										60
Improvement costs—prior sales							30	30	30	30	120
Selling expenses	300										300
	360						30	30	30	30	480
Income before provision for income taxes	147	66	62	56	50	44	47	38	28	18	556
Provision for income taxes:											
Current	71	32	30	23	42	41	41	40	40	40	267
Deferred				4	(18)	(19)	(19)	(22)	(27)	(32)	
	71	32	30	27	24	22	22	18	13	8	267
Net Income	$76	$34	$32	$29	$26	$22	$25	$20	$15	$10	$289

*Assumes that all cancellations occurred in year 1 without refunds of down payments.

†Assumes that future performance occurred equally in years 7, 8, 9, and 10.

Note: The illustrative statements are not intended to represent retail land sales company financial statements because they include only items necessary to illustrate timing of revenue and income recognition.

Exhibit II—Installment Method

96. Schedule A

Illustration of Financial Statement Presentation
Based on Assumptions in Paragraph 91
(amounts in thousands)

Balance Sheets	Beginning of Year 1	1	2	3	4	5	6	7	8	9	10
Assets:											
Cash	$300	$100	$204	$308	$389	$451	$514	$547	$581	$615	$649
Contracts receivable		720	658	592	522	447	368	284	195	100	
Less: Profit applicable to future improvements		(342)	(313)	(282)	(249)	(213)	(175)	(135)	(93)	(48)	
		378	345	310	273	234	193	149	102	52	
Land	75	15	15	15	15	15	15	15	15	15	15
	$375	$493	$564	$633	$677	$700	$722	$711	$698	$682	$664
Liabilities and equity:											
Deferred income taxes			$ 33	$ 66	$ 75	$ 64	$ 54	$ 42	$ 29	$ 15	
Liability for future improvements		$120	120	120	120	120	120	90	60	30	
Capital stock	$375	375	375	375	375	375	375	375	375	375	$375
Retained earnings (deficit)		(2)	36	72	107	141	173	204	234	262	289
	$375	$493	$564	$633	$677	$700	$722	$711	$698	$682	$664

97. **Schedule B**

Installment Method Changed to Percentage-of-Completion Method at Beginning of Year 4
(amounts in thousands)

					End of Year					
Balance Sheets	1	2	3	4	5	6	7	8	9	10
Assets:										
Cash	$100	$204	$308	$389	$451	$514	$547	$581	$615	$649
Contracts receivable	720	658	592	522	447	368	284	195	100	
Less:										
Profit applicable to future improvements	(342)	(313)	(282)							
Unamortized valuation discount				(80)	(59)	(40)	(24)	(12)	(4)	
	378	345	310	442	388	328	260	183	96	
Land	15	15	15	15	15	15	15	15	15	15
	$493	$564	$633	$846	$854	$857	$822	$779	$726	$664
Liabilities and equity:										
Deferred income taxes		$33	$66	$137	$119	$100	$81	$59	$32	
Liability for future improvements (revenue applicable to future improvements after Year 3)	$120	120	120	163	163	163	122	81	40	
Capital stock	375	375	375	375	375	375	375	375	375	$375
Retained earnings (deficit)	(2)	36	72	171	197	219	244	264	279	289
	$493	$564	$633	$846	$854	$857	$822	$779	$726	$664

Schedule B (Cont.)

Income Statements

					Year						
Income Statements	1	2	3	4	5	6	7	8	9	10	Total
Revenues:											
Gross sales contracts recorded	$1,000										$1000
Improvement revenue—prior sales							$41	$41	$41	$40	163
Profit deferred	(427)										(427)
Profit recognized		$29	$31								60
Interest income*		42	38	$56	$50	$44	36	27	17	8	318
Income resulting from change from installment to percentage-of-completion method† (described fully in notes to financial statements)				137							137
	573	71	69	193	50	44	77	68	58	48	1,251
Costs and expenses:											
Cost of sales	225										225
Improvement costs—prior sales							30	30	30	30	120
Selling expenses	300										300
Loss on cancellations	50										50
	575						30	30	30	30	695
Income (loss) before provision for income taxes	(2)	71	69	193	50	44	47	38	28	18	556
Provision for income taxes:											
Current				23	42	41	41	40	40	40	267
Deferred		33	33	71	(18)	(19)	(19)	(22)	(27)	(32)	—
Net income (loss)	($ 2)	$38	$36	$99	$26	$22	$25	$20	$15	$10	$289

See Notes to Exhibit II, Schedule B, on next page.

Schedule B (Cont.)

Notes to Exhibit II, Schedule B:

*Interest at stated rate for Years 2 and 3; 12% after change from installment to percentage-of-completion method.

†Computation of effect of change from installment to percentage-of-completion method:

(Amounts in thousands)

Profit not yet recognized under installment method:		
Original	$427	
Recognized in prior years	(60)	
Applicable to canceled contracts	(85)	$282
Less, valuation discount required:		
Receivables at beginning of Year 4	592	
Present value of payments due (principal and interest) at 12%	(490)	102
		180
Less:		
Revenue to be recognized in future as performance takes place	163	
Costs to be recognized in future	(120)	43
Net amount credited to income (before taxes)		$137

Appendix E

BACKGROUND INFORMATION AND SUMMARY OF CONSIDERATION OF COMMENTS ON EXPOSURE DRAFT

98. As discussed in FASB Statement No. 32, *Specialized Accounting and Reporting Principles and Practices in AICPA Statements of Position and Guides on Accounting and Auditing Matters,* the FASB is extracting the specialized[31] accounting and reporting principles and practices from AICPA Statements of Position (SOPs) and Guides on accounting and auditing matters and issuing them as FASB Statements after appropriate due process. This Statement extracts the specialized sale and profit recognition principles and practices from the AICPA Industry Accounting Guides, *Accounting for Profit Recognition on Sales of Real Estate* and *Accounting for Retail Land Sales,* and SOPs 75-6, *Questions Concerning Profit Recognition on Sales of Real Estate,* and 78-4, *Application of the Deposit, Installment, and Cost Recovery Methods in Accounting for Sales of Real Estate.* The provisions of the retail land sales Guide that address costs have been included in FASB Statement No. 67, *Accounting for Costs and Initial Rental Operations of Real Estate Projects.*

99. Board members have assented to the issuance of this Statement on the basis that it is an appropriate extraction of existing specialized principles and practices and that a comprehensive reconsideration of those principles and practices was not contemplated in undertaking this FASB project. Most of the background material and discussion of accounting alternatives has not been carried forward from the Guides and SOPs. The Board's conceptual framework project on accounting recognition criteria will address recognition issues relating to elements of financial statements. A Statement of Financial Accounting Concepts resulting from that project in due course will serve as a basis for evaluating existing standards and practices. Accordingly, the Board may wish to evaluate the standards in this Statement when its conceptual framework project is completed. However, the Board concluded that this Statement should not be postponed indefinitely to await completion of a Statement of concepts on recognition issues.

100. Retail land sales are sales, on a volume basis, of lots that are subdivisions of large tracts of land. They are characterized by down payments so small that local banks and savings and loan institutions would not loan money on the property at market rates or purchase the buyer's note for the remaining purchase price without a substantial discount. The seller is unable to enforce the sales contract or the buyer's note against the buyer's general credit. If the buyer cancels the contract within an established cancellation period, its money is refunded. Defaults by the buyer after the cancellation period result in recovery of the land by the seller and forfeiture of at least some principal payments made by the buyer.[32]

---

[31]The term *specialized* is used to refer to those accounting and reporting principles and practices in AICPA Guides and Statements of Position that are neither superseded by nor contained in Accounting Research Bulletins, APB Opinions, FASB Statements, or FASB Interpretations.

[32]Federal and state laws may affect the amount that can be retained by the seller.

101. Examples of real estate sales transactions that are not retail land sales include sales of lots to builders; sales of homes, buildings, and parcels of land to builders and others; sales of corporate stock of enterprises with substantial real estate, sales of partnership interests,[33] and sales of time-sharing interests[34] if the sales are in substance sales of real estate; and sales of options to purchase real estate.

102. The retail land sales Guide was developed to clarify and standardize accounting for retail land sales, particularly the timing and methods of revenue and profit recognition. The Guide recommended conditions to be met by both the buyer and the seller before the seller reported a sale. It also recommended criteria for the use of the full accrual, percentage-of-completion, and installment methods for recognizing profit.

103. The profit recognition Guide addressed real estate sales transactions other than retail land sales. It was developed to standardize accounting for transactions that had become increasingly diverse and complex. The Guide addressed the timing of profit recognition and recommended criteria for determining appropriate methods for profit recognition. SOPs 75-6 and 78-4 clarified and elaborated on the recommendations of the Guide.

104. A draft of this Statement was reviewed by the FASB Task Force on Specialized Principles for the Real Estate Industry to ensure that the specialized principles in the Guides and SOPs had been extracted correctly. Based on the task force's comments, the Board believes that the specialized profit recognition principles in the Guides and SOPs have been correctly identified and included in this Statement.

105. An Exposure Draft of a proposed FASB Statement, *Accounting for Sales of Real Estate,* was issued on December 15, 1981. The Board received 47 comment letters in response to the Exposure Draft. Certain of the comments received and the Board's consideration of them are discussed in this appendix.

Accounting for Sales of Time-Sharing Interests

106. The Exposure Draft proposed that sales of time-sharing interests in real estate that represent either fee simple ownership or are sales-type leases under Statement 13 should be accounted for as sales of real estate other than retail land sales under the provisions of this Statement. Sales of time-sharing interests were not addressed in the Guides and SOPs whose principles are extracted in this Statement.

107. The majority of respondents commenting on this issue agreed that accounting for sales of time-sharing interests should be covered in this Statement and that the accounting proposed in the Exposure Draft is appropriate. Some respondents felt that accounting for sales of time-sharing interests in real estate should not be dealt with as part of this Statement because the Guides and SOPs being extracted did not deal with that subject. Other respondents believe that this Statement should provide additional guidance on accounting for revenue and costs of time-sharing interests.

108. The Board concurred with those respondents who believe that it is appropriate to require that sales of real estate time-sharing interests be accounted for in accordance with the provisions of this Statement but that additional guidance should not be provided as part of this extraction project.

Discount Rate for Valuation of Retail Land Sales Receivables

109. Paragraph 79(a) of the Exposure Draft proposed that a net retail land sales receivable be valued at an amount at which it could be sold on a volume basis without recourse to the seller at the time of the initial transaction. It referred to APB Opinion No. 21, *Interest on Receivables and Payables,* for guidance on selection of an appropriate interest rate. The retail land sales Guide had provided a more specific recommendation—that those receivables be discounted at a rate not less than the rate charged locally for financing installment purchases of soft goods and appliances.

110. Many respondents agreed that the guidance proposed in the Exposure Draft was appropriate. Others suggested that additional guidance be provided as to selection of a discount rate, such as the seller's incremental borrowing rate, the yield rate established by recent sales of Government National Mortgage Association (GNMA) securities, or an average rate charged by local savings and loan associations. Other respondents objected to the principle of valuing receivables at an amount at which they could be sold on a volume basis without recourse. They believe that there is not a market for this type of paper or an opportunity for nonrecourse discounting with lending institutions.

---

[33]An example of a sale of a partnership interest that is in substance a sale of real estate would be an enterprise forming a partnership, arranging for the partnership to acquire the property directly from third parties, and selling an interest in the partnership to investors who then become limited partners.

[34]For purposes of this Statement, a time-sharing interest that is in substance a sale of real estate is the exclusive right to occupy a specified dwelling unit for a designated period each year and represents (a) fee simple ownership of real estate or (b) a right-to-use time-sharing interest that is a sales-type lease as defined in Statement 13, as amended and interpreted.

111. The Board believes that determination of an appropriate interest rate should be governed by the principles of Opinion 21 and that designation of specific rates would be arbitrary. Therefore, the Board believes that the general guidance proposed in the Exposure Draft should be retained. However, the idea of valuation at the amount at which receivables could be sold without recourse has been expressed as an objective rather than as a prescribed methodology.

Condensed Disclosure Requirements

112. The Exposure Draft proposed that certain detailed disclosures that were recommended by the retail land sales Guide not be required by this Statement because they are already required by other authoritative literature. Most of the comment letters agreed with that proposal. A few respondents suggested adding specific disclosures or eliminating one or more specific items, but those suggestions were not generally supported. The Board considered those suggestions and determined that no significant changes should be made to the Exposure Draft.

Loans to Buyers by Sellers of Real Estate

113. The Exposure Draft noted that financing institutions occasionally sell land and make development or construction loans to the buyers. It proposed that the buyer's initial investment not include such funds and that anticipated future loans from the seller be subtracted from the initial and continuing investments.

114. Several respondents agreed with that provision. Others disagreed and suggested that it is not appropriate to subtract future loans from sellers that are established lending institutions if those loans will be used to add value to the property, especially if the future loan is on normal lending terms. They agreed, however, that the future loans should not be included as part of the buyer's initial investment.

115. The Board has considered those comments and concluded that future loans from an established lending institution need not be subtracted if (a) they are on normal terms, (b) they bear fair-market interest rates, and (c) the proceeds of the loans are conditional on use for specified development of or construction on the property. Those requirements are designed to preclude an effective reduction in the buyer's investment in the property to less than the minimum requirement by a subsequent loan from the seller.

Sale and Leaseback of Real Estate

116. Several respondents recommended that para-

graph 8 of the Exposure Draft clarify the relative applicability of this Statement and FASB Statements 13 and 28. Paragraph 40 of this Statement has been added to indicate that (a) recognition of a sale in a sale-leaseback shall be governed by Statements 13 and 28, (b) the amount of the profit on sale-leaseback transactions is to be determined by the provisions of this Statement, and (c) the profit so determined is to be accounted for in accordance with the provisions of Statements 13 and 28 unless other provisions of this Statement require postponement of profit recognition until a later event.

Due Process

117. Several respondents questioned the appropriateness of extracting specialized accounting principles from AICPA documents that had not been subjected to the FASB's extensive due process procedures. They noted the Guides and SOPs were promulgated through a process that did not include input from industry, academe, or the general public and that those documents were not exposed for comments before they were issued.

118. The extraction process is described in paragraph 98 of this Statement, paragraphs 1-9 of Statement 32, and the FASB's *Request for Written Comments on an FASB Proposal for Dealing with Industry Accounting Matters and Accounting Questions of Limited Application.* Input from the public has been received and carefully considered:

a. At a meeting of the Financial Accounting Standards Advisory Council in July 1978 at which the extraction process was discussed
b. In the form of 157 letters of comment on the request for written comments described above
c. In the form of 53 letters of comment in response to the Exposure Draft, *Specialized Accounting and Reporting Principles and Practices in AICPA Industry Accounting Guides, Industry Audit Guides, and Statements of Position*
d. At two meetings of the FASB Task Force on Specialized Principles for the Real Estate Industry held in 1981
e. In extensive oral and written comments from task force members on several drafts of the Exposure Draft, *Accounting for Sales of Real Estate,* and of this Statement
f. In the form of 47 letters of comment on the Exposure Draft

The Board believes it has followed its required due process procedures and that it is appropriate to issue this Statement.

Other

119. Several respondents suggested various sub-

stantive changes to the Exposure Draft. Adoption of those suggestions would have required a reconsideration of some of the provisions of the Guides and SOPs. Such a reconsideration is not contemplated in the extraction project unless a proposed change meets one of the three criteria for change included in the "Notice for Recipients" section of the Exposure Draft or is broadly supported. The proposed changes did not meet the criteria for change and were not broadly supported. Accordingly, the Board did not adopt those suggestions. However, based on suggestions from respondents to the Exposure Draft, the Board has made several other changes, including an internal reorganization of this Statement, that it believes clarify the Statement.

120. It was suggested that compliance with this Statement would be burdensome to small practitioners and enterprises that sell real estate infrequently. In response to that suggestion, the Board considered limiting the scope and applicability of this Statement, for example, to publicly held enterprises and privately owned real estate enterprises. However, the Board believes further consideration is necessary before income measurement standards such as those in this Statement are applied differently based on the size or form of ownership of an enterprise. The Board notes that its project on financial reporting by private and small public companies will consider characteristics of those enterprises and how their financial reporting needs differ from those of other business enterprises. The Board may reconsider the need for applying some or all of the provisions of this State-

ment to certain private and small public enterprises when that project is completed.

121. In its August 1982 report, the Structure Committee of the Financial Accounting Foundation recommended that the Board develop a plan to provide timely guidance for implementation questions (pages 18 and 19 of the report). The committee also said it believes the program to extract specialized accounting standards from AICPA pronouncements and issue them as FASB Statements is consistent with the Board's mission (page 18 of the report).

122. The Board has concluded that it can reach an informed decision on the basis of existing information without a public hearing and that the effective date and transition specified in paragraph 52 are advisable in the circumstances.

Appendix F

DECISION TREES

123. The following decision trees are intended to provide an overview of the major provisions in this Statement that relate to the accounting for sales of real estate. They should not be used without further reference to the Statement. Two decision trees are provided—one for retail land sales and a second for all other sales of real estate. The highlighted boxes on the next page describe the general requirements for recognizing all of the profit on a sale of real estate other than a retail land sale at the date of sale.

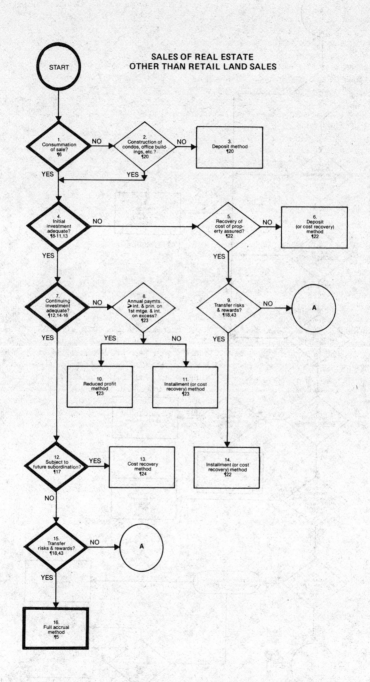

SALES OF REAL ESTATE
OTHER THAN RETAIL LAND SALES

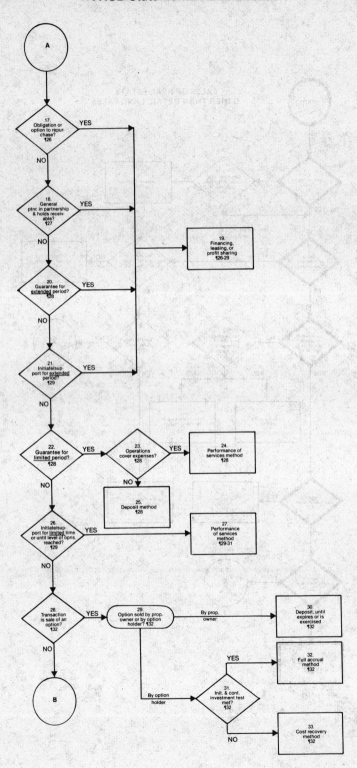

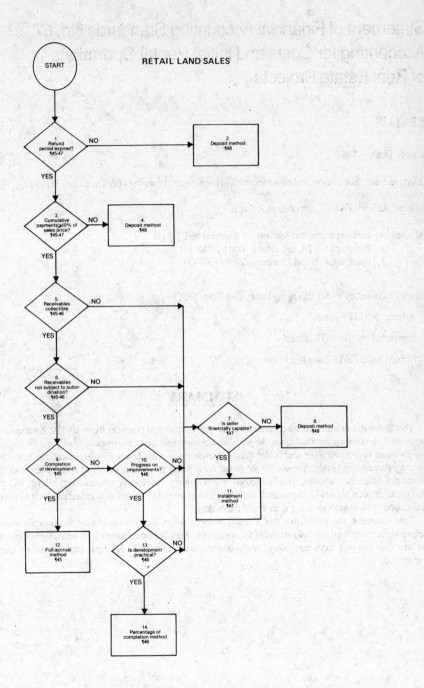

RETAIL LAND SALES

START

1. Refund period expired? 145-47
 — NO → 2. Deposit method 148
 YES ↓

3. Cumulative payments >10% of sales price? 145-47
 — NO → 4. Deposit method 148
 YES ↓

5. Receivables collectible 145-46
 — NO →
 YES ↓

6. Receivables not subject to subordination? 145-46
 — NO →
 YES ↓

7. Is seller financially capable? 147
 — NO → 8. Deposit method 148
 YES ↓
 11. Installment method 147

9. Completion of development? 145
 — NO → 10. Progress on improvements? 146
 YES ↓   — NO →
 12. Full accrual method 145

13. Is development practical? 146
 — NO →
 YES ↓

14. Percentage of completion method 146

Statement of Financial Accounting Standards No. 67
Accounting for Costs and Initial Rental Operations
of Real Estate Projects

STATUS

Issued: October 1982

Effective Date: For costs of real estate incurred in fiscal years beginning after December 31, 1982

Affects: Amends FAS 32, Appendixes A and B

Affected by: Paragraph 2(b) and footnote 10 amended by FAS 111
Paragraphs 3, 24, and 28 amended by FAS 121
Paragraphs 16 and 25 superseded by FAS 121

Issues Discussed by FASB Emerging Issues Task Force (EITF)

Affects: No EITF Issues

Interpreted by: No EITF Issues

Related Issue: EITF Issue No. 91-10

SUMMARY

This Statement extracts the specialized accounting principles and practices from AICPA Statements of Position 80-3, *Accounting for Real Estate Acquisition, Development, and Construction Costs,* and 78-3, *Accounting for Costs to Sell and Rent, and Initial Rental Operations of, Real Estate Projects,* and those in the AICPA Industry Accounting Guide, *Accounting for Retail Land Sales,* that address costs of real estate projects. This Statement establishes whether costs associated with acquiring, developing, constructing, selling, and renting real estate projects should be capitalized. Guidance also is provided on the appropriate methods of allocating capitalized costs to individual components of the project.

This Statement also establishes that a rental project changes from nonoperating to operating when it is substantially completed and held available for occupancy, that is, upon completion of tenant improvements but no later than one year from cessation of major construction activities. At that time, costs should no longer be capitalized.

Statement of Financial Accounting Standards No. 67
Accounting for Costs and Initial Rental Operations of Real Estate Projects

CONTENTS

INTRODUCTION

1. This Statement establishes accounting and reporting standards for acquisition, development, construction, selling, and rental costs associated with real estate projects. It also provides guidance for the accounting for initial rental operations and criteria for determining when the status of a rental project changes from nonoperating to operating.

SCOPE AND APPLICABILITY

2. This Statement does not apply to:

a. Real estate developed by an enterprise for use in its own operations,[1] other than for sale or rental.
b. "Initial direct costs" of sales-type, operating, and other types of leases, which are defined in FASB Statement No. 17, *Accounting for Leases—Initial Direct Costs.* The accounting for initial direct costs is prescribed in FASB Statement No. 13, *Accounting for Leases.*
c. Costs directly related to manufacturing, merchandising, or service activities as distinguished from real estate activities.

Paragraphs 20-23 of this Statement do not apply to real estate rental activity in which the predominant rental period is less than one month.

STANDARDS OF FINANCIAL ACCOUNTING AND REPORTING

General

3. Paragraphs 4-25 specify the accounting for the following as they relate to real estate projects: (a) **preacquisition costs,**[2] (b) taxes and insurance, (c) **project costs,** (d) **amenities,** (e) **incidental operations,** (f) allocation of capitalized costs to components of a real estate project, (g) revisions of estimates, (h) abandonments and changes in use, (i) selling costs, (j) rental costs, and (k) costs in excess of estimated **net realizable value.**

Acquisition, Development, and Construction Costs

Preacquisition Costs

4. Payments to obtain an option to acquire real property shall be capitalized as incurred. All other costs related to a property that are incurred before the enterprise acquires the property, or before the enterprise obtains an option to acquire it, shall be capitalized if all of the following conditions are met and otherwise shall be charged to expense as incurred:

a. The costs are directly identifiable with the specific property.

---

[1]In this context, "real estate developed by an enterprise for use in its own operations" includes real estate developed by a member of a consolidated group for use in the operations of another member of the group (for example, a manufacturing facility developed by a subsidiary for use in its parent's operations) when the property is reported in the group's consolidated financial statements. However, such property is not "real estate developed for use in the enterprise's operations" when reported in the separate financial statements of the entity that developed it.

[2]Terms defined in the glossary (Appendix A) are in **boldface type** the first time they appear in this Statement.

b. The costs would be capitalized if the property were already acquired.

c. Acquisition of the property or of an option to acquire the property is probable.[3] This condition requires that the prospective purchaser is actively seeking to acquire the property and has the ability to finance or obtain financing for the acquisition and that there is no indication that the property is not available for sale.

5. Capitalized preacquisition costs (a) shall be included as project costs upon the acquisition of the property or (b) to the extent not recoverable by the sale of the options, plans, etc., shall be charged to expense when it is probable that the property will not be acquired.

Taxes and Insurance

6. Costs incurred on real estate for property taxes and insurance shall be capitalized as property cost only during periods in which activities necessary to get the property ready for its intended use are in progress.[4] Costs incurred for such items after the property is substantially complete and ready for its intended use[5] shall be charged to expense as incurred.

Project Costs

7. Project costs clearly associated with the acquisition, development, and construction of a real estate project shall be capitalized as a cost of that project. **Indirect project costs** that relate to several projects shall be capitalized and allocated to the projects to which the costs relate. Indirect costs that do not clearly relate to projects under development or construction, including general and administrative expenses, shall be charged to expense as incurred.

Amenities

8. Accounting for costs of amenities shall be based on management's plans for the amenities in accordance with the following:

a. If an amenity is to be sold or transferred in connection with the sale of individual units, costs in excess of anticipated proceeds shall be allocated as **common costs** because the amenity is clearly associated with the development and sale of the project. The common costs include expected future operating costs to be borne by the developer until they are assumed by buyers of units in a project.

b. If an amenity is to be sold separately or retained by the developer, capitalizable costs of the amenity in excess of its estimated **fair value** as of the expected date of its substantial physical completion shall be allocated as common costs. For the purpose of determining the amount to be capitalized as common costs, the amount of cost previously allocated to the amenity shall not be revised after the amenity is substantially completed and available for use. A later sale of the amenity at more or less than its estimated fair value as of the date of substantial physical completion, less any accumulated depreciation, results in a gain or loss that shall be included in net income in the period in which the sale occurs.

Costs of amenities shall be allocated among land parcels[6] benefited and for which development is probable.

9. Before an amenity is substantially completed and available for use, operating income (or loss) of the amenity shall be included as a reduction of (or an addition to) common costs. When an amenity to be sold separately or retained by the developer is substantially completed and available for use, current operating income and expenses of the amenity shall be included in current operating results.

Incidental Operations

10. **Incremental revenue from incidental operations** in excess of **incremental costs of incidental operations** shall be accounted for as a reduction of capitalized project costs. Incremental costs in excess of incremental revenue shall be charged to expense as incurred, because the incidental operations did not achieve the objective of reducing the costs of developing the property for its intended use.

Allocation of Capitalized Costs to the Components of a Real Estate Project

11. The capitalized costs of real estate projects shall be assigned to individual components of the project based on specific identification. If specific identification is not practicable, capitalized costs shall be allocated as follows:

---

[3]*Probable* is defined in FASB Statement No. 5, *Accounting for Contingencies*, as "likely to occur" and is used in the same sense in this Statement.

[4]The phrase *activities necessary to get the property ready for its intended use are in progress* is used here with the same meaning as it has for interest capitalization in paragraph 17 of FASB Statement No. 34, *Capitalization of Interest Cost.*

[5]The phrase *substantially complete and ready for its intended use* is used here with the same meaning as it has for interest capitalization in paragraph 18 of Statement 34.

[6]A land parcel may be considered to be an individual lot or unit, an amenity, or a **phase.**

a. Land cost and all other common costs[7] (prior to construction) shall be allocated to each land parcel benefited. Allocation shall be based on the **relative fair value before construction.**

b. Construction costs shall be allocated to individual units in the phase on the basis of relative sales value of each unit.

If allocation based on relative value also is impracticable, capitalized costs shall be allocated based on area methods (for example, square footage) or other value methods as appropriate under the circumstances.

Revisions of Estimates

12. Estimates and cost allocations shall be reviewed at the end of each financial reporting period until a project is substantially completed and available for sale. Costs shall be revised and reallocated as necessary for material changes on the basis of current estimates.[8] Changes in estimates shall be reported in accordance with paragraph 31 of APB Opinion No. 20, *Accounting Changes.*

Abandonments and Changes in Use

13. If real estate, including rights to real estate, is abandoned (for example, by allowing a mortgage to be foreclosed or a purchase option to lapse), capitalized costs of that real estate shall be expensed. Such costs shall not be allocated to other components of the project or to other projects even if other components or other projects are capable of absorbing the losses.

14. Real estate donated to municipalities or other governmental agencies for uses that will benefit the project are not abandonments. The cost of the real estate donated shall be allocated as a common cost of the project.

15. Changes in the use of real estate comprising a project or a portion of a project may arise after significant development and construction costs have been incurred. If the change in use is made pursuant to a formal plan for a project that is expected to produce a higher economic yield (as compared to its yield based on use before change), the development and construction costs to be charged to expense shall be limited to the amount by which the capitalized costs incurred and to be incurred exceed the estimated value of the revised project when it is substantially complete and ready for its intended use.

16. In the absence of a formal plan for a project that is expected to produce a higher economic yield, the project costs to be charged to expense shall be limited to the amount by which total project costs exceed the estimated net realizable value of the property determined on the assumption it will be sold in its present state.

Costs Incurred to Sell and Rent Real Estate Projects, Including Initial Rental Operations

Costs Incurred to Sell Real Estate Projects

17. **Costs incurred to sell real estate projects** shall be capitalized if they (a) are reasonably expected to be recovered from the sale of the project or from incidental operations and (b) are incurred for (1) tangible assets that are used directly throughout the selling period to aid in the sale of the project or (2) services that have been performed to obtain regulatory approval of sales. Examples of costs incurred to sell real estate projects that ordinarily meet the criteria for capitalization are costs of model units and their furnishings, sales facilities, legal fees for preparation of prospectuses, and semipermanent signs.

18. Other costs incurred to sell real estate projects shall be capitalized as prepaid costs if they are directly associated with and their recovery is reasonably expected from sales that are being accounted for under a method of accounting other than full accrual.[9] Costs that do not meet the criteria for capitalization shall be expensed as incurred.

19. Capitalized selling costs shall be charged to expense in the period in which the related revenue is recognized as earned. When a sales contract is canceled (with or without refund) or the related receivable is written off as uncollectible, the related unrecoverable capitalized selling costs shall be charged to expense or an allowance previously established for that purpose.

Costs Incurred to Rent Real Estate Projects

20. If **costs incurred to rent real estate projects,** other than initial direct costs,[10] under operating leases are related to and their recovery is reasonably expected from future rental operations, they shall be capitalized. Examples of such costs are costs of model units and their furnishings, rental facilities, semipermanent signs, "grand openings," and unused rental brochures. Costs that do not meet the

---

[7]Including the costs of amenities to be allocated as common costs (paragraphs 8 and 9).

[8]Paragraph 76 of Statement No. 66, *Accounting for Sales of Real Estate,* discusses revisions of estimates relating to retail land sales accounted for by the percentage-of-completion method.

[9]FASB Statement 66 discusses the circumstances under which the appropriate accounting methods are to be applied, including the full accrual method.

[10]Initial direct costs are defined in Statement 17. The accounting for initial direct costs is prescribed in Statement 13.

criteria for capitalization shall be expensed as incurred, for example, rental overhead.

21. Capitalized rental costs directly related to revenue from a specific operating lease shall be amortized over the lease term. Capitalized rental costs not directly related to revenue from a specific operating lease shall be amortized over the period of expected benefit. The amortization period shall begin when the project is substantially completed and held available for occupancy.[11] Estimated unrecoverable amounts of unamortized capitalized rental costs associated with a lease or group of leases shall be charged to expense when it becomes probable that the lease(s) will be terminated.

Initial Rental Operations

22. When a real estate project is substantially completed and held available for occupancy, rental revenues and operating costs shall be recognized in income and expense as they accrue, all carrying costs (such as real estate taxes) shall be charged to expense when incurred, depreciation on the cost of the project shall be provided, and costs to rent the project shall be amortized in accordance with paragraph 21 of this Statement. A real estate project shall be considered substantially completed and held available for occupancy upon completion of tenant improvements by the developer but no later than one year from cessation of major construction activity (as distinguished from activities such as routine maintenance and cleanup).

23. If portions of a rental project are substantially completed and occupied by tenants or held available for occupancy and other portions have not yet reached that stage, the substantially completed portions shall be accounted for as a separate project. Costs incurred shall be allocated between the portions under construction and the portions substantially completed and held available for occupancy.

Recoverability

24. The carrying amount of a real estate project, or parts thereof, held for sale or development and sale shall not exceed net realizable value. If costs exceed net realizable value, capitalization of costs associated with development and construction of a property shall not cease, but rather an allowance shall be provided to reduce the carrying amount to estimated net realizable value, determined on the basis of an evaluation of individual projects. An individual project, for this purpose, consists of components that are relatively homogeneous, integral parts of a whole (for example, individual houses in a residential tract, individual units in a condominium complex, and individual lots in a subdivision and amenities). Therefore, a multiphase development consisting of a tract of single-family houses, a condominium complex, and a lot subdivision generally would be evaluated as three separate projects.

25. Evidence of insufficient rental demand for a rental project currently under construction may indicate an impairment of the carrying value. If it is probable that the insufficient rental demand is other than temporary, an allowance for losses shall be provided, whether or not construction is actually suspended.

Amendments to Other Pronouncement

26. The references to AICPA Statements of Position 78-3, *Accounting for Costs to Sell and Rent, and Initial Rental Operations of, Real Estate Projects,* and 80-3, *Accounting for Real Estate Acquisition, Development, and Construction Costs,* are deleted from Appendixes A and B of FASB Statement No. 32, *Specialized Accounting and Reporting Principles and Practices in AICPA Statements of Position and Guides on Accounting and Auditing Matters,* respectively.

Effective Date and Transition

27. This Statement shall be applied to costs of real estate projects incurred in fiscal years beginning after December 31, 1982. Earlier application is encouraged but not required.

> **The provisions of this Statement need not be applied to immaterial items.**

This Statement was adopted by the affirmative votes of six members of the Financial Accounting Standards Board. Mr. Morgan dissented.

Mr. Morgan dissents to the issuance of this Statement. Although he recognizes the Board's commitment, as stated in paragraph 2 of Statement 32, to extract specialized principles and practices from SOPs and Guides and to issue them as FASB Statements and the fact that issuance of this Statement is considered by a majority of Board members as a fulfillment of part of that commitment, Mr. Morgan believes this Statement should be deferred until certain other projects are completed.

---

[11]Refer to paragraph 22 for the definition of *substantially completed and held available for occupancy.*

Incorporation of these detailed guidelines into accounting standards is inappropriate at this time in view of two projects in process that should bear on the nature and effect of accounting standards in this area.

a. The Board's project on financial reporting by private and small public companies
b. The August 1982 report of the Financial Accounting Foundation Structure Committee, which acknowledges the comments of many respondents that the Board should deal primarily

with broad accounting standards issues and charges the Board to develop a plan, for consideration by the Trustees, to provide timely *guidance* for implementation questions and emerging issues

Mr. Morgan believes that no urgent need for an FASB Statement on this subject has been demonstrated. Accordingly, he believes it more prudent to complete the broader, more general projects before further considering whether this Statement is needed.

Members of the Financial Accounting Standards Board:

Appendix A

GLOSSARY

28. This glossary defines certain terms as they are used in this Statement.

Amenities
Examples of amenities include golf courses, utility plants, clubhouses, swimming pools, tennis courts, indoor recreational facilities, and parking facilities.

Common Costs
Costs that relate to two or more units within a real estate project.

Costs Incurred to Rent Real Estate Projects
Examples of such costs include costs of model units and their furnishings, rental facilities, semipermanent signs, rental brochures, advertising, "grand openings," and rental overhead including rental salaries.

Costs Incurred to Sell Real Estate Projects
Examples of such costs include costs of model units and their furnishings, sales facilities, sales brochures, legal fees for preparation of prospectuses, semipermanent signs, advertising, "grand openings," and sales overhead including sales salaries.

Fair Value
The amount in cash or cash equivalent value of other consideration that a real estate parcel would yield in a current sale between a willing buyer and a willing seller (i.e., selling price), that is, other than in a forced or liquidation sale. The fair value of a parcel is affected by its physical characteristics, its probable ultimate use, and the

time required for the buyer to make such use of the property considering access, development plans, zoning restrictions, and market absorption factors.

Incidental Operations
Revenue-producing activities engaged in during the holding or development period to reduce the cost of developing the property for its intended use, as distinguished from activities designed to generate a profit or a return from the use of the property.

Incremental Costs of Incidental Operations
Costs that would not be incurred except in relation to the conduct of incidental operations. Interest, taxes, insurance, security, and similar costs that would be incurred during the development of a real estate project regardless of whether incidental operations were conducted are not incremental costs.

Incremental Revenues from Incidental Operations
Revenues that would not be produced except in relation to the conduct of incidental operations.

Indirect Project Costs
Costs incurred after the acquisition of the property, such as construction administration (for example, the costs associated with a field office at a project site and the administrative personnel that staff the office), legal fees, and various office costs, that clearly relate to projects under development or construction. Examples of office costs that may be considered indirect project costs are cost accounting, design, and other departments providing services that are clearly related to real estate projects.

Net Realizable Value
The estimated selling price in the ordinary

course of business less estimated costs of completion (to the stage of completion assumed in determining the selling price), holding, and disposal.

Phase

A parcel on which units are to be constructed concurrently.

Preacquisition Costs

Costs related to a property that are incurred for the express purpose of, but prior to, obtaining that property. Examples of preacquisition costs may be costs of surveying, zoning or traffic studies, or payments to obtain an option on the property.

Project Costs

Costs clearly associated with the acquisition, development, and construction of a real estate project.

Relative Fair Value before Construction

The fair value of each land parcel in a real estate project in relation to the fair value of the other parcels in the project, exclusive of value added by on-site development and construction activities.

Appendix B

BACKGROUND INFORMATION AND SUMMARY OF CONSIDERATION OF COMMENTS ON EXPOSURE DRAFT

29. As discussed in Statement 32, the FASB is extracting the specialized[12] accounting and reporting principles and practices from AICPA SOPs and Guides on accounting and auditing matters and issuing them in FASB Statements after appropriate due process. This Statement extracts without significant changes the specialized principles and practices from AICPA SOPs 80-3, *Accounting for Real Estate Acquisition, Development, and Construction Costs,* and 78-3, *Accounting for Costs to Sell and Rent, and Initial Rental Operations of, Real Estate Projects,* and those from the AICPA Industry Accounting Guide (Guide), *Accounting for Retail Land Sales,* that address costs of real estate projects. Accounting and reporting standards that apply to costs in general also apply to real estate costs, and the standards in this Statement are in addition to those standards.

30. SOP 80-3 was developed to provide guidance in accounting for costs associated with real estate

acquisition, development, and construction. Trends in real estate development activities at the time SOP 80-3 was developed had dramatically increased the size of enterprises engaged in real estate development, the cost of individual projects, and the time required to complete the development of individual projects. Those trends focused attention on the need for guidance. SOP 80-3 specifies when costs related to a real estate project should be capitalized and how those costs should be allocated to the components of a real estate project.

31. SOP 78-3 was developed to eliminate the wide diversity in practice in accounting for costs to sell and rent real estate projects and the costs and revenues during the initial operating period of a rental project before occupancy stabilizes (sometimes referred to as the "rent-up" period).

32. The Guide was developed to clarify and standardize the accounting for retail land sales. The Guide discusses both the timing of revenue and income recognition and costs to be capitalized. This Statement incorporates only the principles addressing the accounting for costs. The specialized principles dealing with revenue and income recognition have been extracted into Statement 66.

33. Board members have assented to the issuance of this Statement on the basis that it is an appropriate extraction of existing specialized principles and practices and that a comprehensive reconsideration of those principles and practices was not contemplated in undertaking this FASB project. Most of the background material and discussion of accounting alternatives have not been carried forward from the AICPA real estate related SOPs and Guide. The Board's conceptual framework project on accounting recognition criteria will address recognition issues relating to elements of financial statements. A Statement of Financial Accounting Concepts resulting from that project in due course will serve as a basis for evaluating existing standards and practices. Accordingly, the Board may wish to evaluate the standards in this Statement when its conceptual framework project is completed.

34. An Exposure Draft of a proposed FASB Statement, *Accounting for Costs and Initial Rental Operations of Real Estate Projects,* was issued on December 15, 1981. The Board received 37 comment letters in response to the Exposure Draft. Certain of the comments received and the Board's consideration of them are discussed in this appendix.

---

[12]The term *specialized* is used to refer to those accounting and reporting principles and practices in AICPA Guides and SOPs that are neither superseded by nor contained in Accounting Research Bulletins, APB Opinions, FASB Statements, or FASB Interpretations.

Due Process

35. Several respondents questioned the appropriateness of extracting specialized accounting principles from AICPA documents that had not been subjected to the FASB's extensive due process procedures. They noted the Guides and SOPs were promulgated through a process that did not include input from industry, academe, or the general public and that those documents were not exposed for comments before they were issued.

36. The extraction process is described in paragraph 29 of this Statement, paragraphs 1-9 of FASB Statement 32, and the FASB's *Request for Written Comments on an FASB Proposal for Dealing with Industry Accounting Matters and Accounting Questions of Limited Application.* Input from the public has been received and carefully considered:

a. At a meeting of the Financial Accounting Standards Advisory Council in July 1978 at which the extraction process was discussed
b. In the form of 157 letters of comment on the request for written comments described above
c. In the form of 53 letters of comment in response to the Exposure Draft, *Specialized Accounting and Reporting Principles and Practices in AICPA Industry Accounting Guides, Industry Audit Guides, and Statements of Position*
d. At two meetings of the FASB Task Force on Specialized Principles for the Real Estate Industry in 1981
e. In extensive oral and written comments from task force members on several drafts of the Exposure Draft, *Accounting for Costs and Initial Rental Operations of Real Estate Projects,* and of this Statement
f. In the form of 37 letters of comment on the Exposure Draft

The Board believes it has followed its required due process procedures and that it is appropriate to issue this Statement. In addition, in its August 1982 report, the Structure Committee of the Financial Accounting Foundation said it believes the program to extract specialized accounting standards from AICPA pronouncements and issue them as FASB Statements is consistent with the Board's mission (page 18 of the report).

Initial Rental Operations

37. Respondents commented on the appropriateness of the proposed provision that a rental project changes from nonoperating to operating status when it is substantially completed and held available for occupancy. Some respondents said that the proposed provision was acceptable although they suggested that further clarification of the phrase

substantially completed and held available for occupancy was necessary, specifically, how tenant improvements should be treated. Some respondents suggested that a limit of one year be placed on the length of time a project that is substantially completed (other than tenant improvements) and held available for occupancy can remain in a nonoperating status.

38. Other respondents recommended that the "percentage-of-occupancy" method, or some variation thereof, be used to phase in depreciation and other operating costs. The Board considered the percentage-of-occupancy method but concurred with a majority of respondents that the method proposed in the Exposure Draft, modified by a one-year maximum period, was more appropriate. The Board has therefore modified the provisions of the Exposure Draft to state that a project shall be considered to be substantially completed and held available for occupancy upon completion of tenant improvements by the developer but no later than one year from cessation of major construction activity.

Amenities

39. With respect to the proposed accounting for amenities, some respondents indicated that the Exposure Draft appropriately extracted the relevant provisions of SOP 80-3. A few of those respondents also indicated that paragraph 13(b) of the Exposure Draft should be modified to indicate that downward revision of costs allocated to an amenity would be appropriate in the event of an impairment.

40. A few respondents believe that the provisions of the retail land sales Guide should have been extracted instead of the provisions of SOP 80-3. They believe those provisions would not have required any adjustment for fair value at the date of substantial physical completion.

41. Although the Board agrees that the provisions of the retail land sales Guide would not have required a fair value adjustment, it concluded that any excess of capitalizable costs over fair value should be allocated as common costs and no changes have been made to the provisions of the Exposure Draft.

Revisions of Estimates

42. Some respondents commented that the seller's performance of development and construction work is very similar to the long-term construction contracts discussed in SOP 81-1, *Accounting for Performance of Construction-Type and Certain Production-Type Contracts.* SOP 81-1 requires that revisions of estimates be accounted for by the cumu-

lative catch-up method and those respondents believed that the accounting for real estate should be consistent.

43. The provisions in the Exposure Draft extracted from SOP 80-3 are consistent with paragraph 31 of Opinion 20, which requires that a change in estimate should be accounted for in (a) the period of change if the change affects that period only or (b) the period of change and future periods if the change affects both. The Board has concluded that this Statement should rely on the general provisions of Opinion 20. The provisions of SOP 81-1 will be considered when the specialized accounting principles and practices from that AICPA document are extracted.

Interest as a Holding Cost

44. Some of the respondents indicated that the definition of net realizable value needed clarification, particularly whether interest not capitalized under Statement 34 should be considered as a holding cost in determining net realizable value.

45. The Board considered the need to address the issue of interest as a holding cost in this document. The Board concluded that it was not appropriate to address this issue within the real estate extraction project because the issue is not limited to real estate transactions.

Allocation of Capitalized Costs to the Components of Real Estate Projects

46. A number of respondents commented that the guidance in the Exposure Draft on allocation of

capitalized costs to the components of real estate projects precluded the use of "area" and "other value" methods as provided in the retail land sales Guide. Those respondents indicated that this omission would have a significant impact on the real estate industry.

47. The Board has agreed with those respondents. The paragraph has been revised to allow for area or other value methods to be used if specific identification or relative fair and sales value methods, as originally proposed, are impracticable.

Other Comments

48. Several respondents suggested various substantive changes to the Exposure Draft. Adoption of those suggestions would have required a reconsideration of some of the provisions of the Guide and SOPs. Such a reconsideration is not contemplated in the extraction project unless a proposed change meets one of the three criteria for change included in the "Notice for Recipients" of the Exposure Draft or is broadly supported. The proposed changes did not meet the criteria for change and were not broadly supported. Accordingly, the Board did not adopt those suggestions. However, based on suggestions from respondents to the Exposure Draft, the Board has made several other changes that it believes clarify the Statement.

49. The Board has concluded that it can reach an informed decision on the basis of existing information without a public hearing and that the effective date and transition specified in paragraph 27 are advisable in the circumstances.

Statement of Financial Accounting Standards No. 68
Research and Development Arrangements

STATUS

Issued: October 1982

Effective Date: For research and development arrangements entered into after December 31, 1982

Affects: No other pronouncements

Affected by: No other pronouncements

Other Interpretive Pronouncement: FTB 84-1

SUMMARY

This Statement specifies how an enterprise should account for its obligation under an arrangement for the funding of its research and development by others. The enterprise must determine whether it is obligated only to perform contractual research and development for others, or is otherwise obligated. To the extent that the enterprise is obligated to repay the other parties, it records a liability and charges research and development costs to expense as incurred.

Statement of Financial Accounting Standards No. 68
Research and Development Arrangements

CONTENTS

INTRODUCTION

1. The FASB has been asked how an enterprise should account for an arrangement through which research and development is funded by other parties. Some consider a research and development arrangement to be simply a contract to do research for others. Others believe that such arrangements are, in essence, borrowings by the enterprise. They believe the research and development expenditures should be reflected in the enterprise's financial statements as current expenses in accordance with FASB Statement No. 2, *Accounting for Research and Development Costs*. As a result of those different views, the reporting of similar arrangements has been inconsistent.

2. The legal structure of a research and development arrangement may take a variety of forms and often is influenced by federal and state income tax and securities regulations. An enterprise might have an equity interest in the arrangement, or its legal involvement might be only contractual (for example, a contract to provide services and an option to acquire the results of the research and development).

SCOPE

3. This Statement establishes standards of financial accounting and reporting for an enterprise that is a party to a research and development arrangement through which it can obtain the results of research and development funded partially or entirely by others. It applies whether the research and development is performed by the enterprise, the funding parties, or a third party. Although the limited-partnership form of arrangement is used for illustrative purposes in this Statement, the standards also apply for other forms. This Statement does not address reporting of government-sponsored research and development.

STANDARDS OF FINANCIAL ACCOUNTING AND REPORTING

4. An enterprise shall determine the nature of the obligation it incurs when it enters into an arrangement with other parties who fund its research and development. The factors discussed in paragraphs 5-11 and other factors that may be present and relevant to a particular arrangement shall be considered when determining the nature of the enterprise's obligation.

Obligation Is a Liability to Repay the Other Parties

5. If the enterprise is obligated to repay any of the funds provided by the other parties regardless of the outcome of the research and development, the enterprise shall estimate and recognize that liability. This requirement applies whether the enterprise may settle the liability by paying cash, by issuing securities, or by some other means.

6. To conclude that a liability does not exist, the transfer of the financial risk involved with research and development from the enterprise to the other parties must be substantive and genuine. To the extent that the enterprise is committed to repay any of the funds provided by the other parties regardless of the outcome of the research and development, all or part of the risk has not been transferred. The following are some examples in which the enterprise is committed to repay:

a. The enterprise guarantees, or has a contractual commitment that assures, repayment of the funds provided by the other parties regardless of the outcome of the research and development.

b. The other parties can require the enterprise to purchase their interest in the research and development regardless of the outcome.

c. The other parties automatically will receive debt or equity securities of the enterprise upon termination or completion of the research and development regardless of the outcome.

7. Even though the written agreements or contracts under the arrangement do not require the enterprise to repay any of the funds provided by the other parties, surrounding conditions might indicate that the enterprise is likely to bear the risk of failure of the research and development. If those conditions suggest that it is probable[1] that the enterprise will repay any of the funds regardless of the outcome of the research and development, there is a presumption that the enterprise has an obligation to repay the other parties. That presumption can be overcome only by substantial evidence to the contrary.

8. Examples of conditions leading to the presumption that the enterprise will repay the other parties include the following:

a. The enterprise has indicated an intent to repay all or a portion of the funds provided regardless of the outcome of the research and development.

b. The enterprise would suffer a severe economic penalty if it failed to repay any of the funds provided to it regardless of the outcome of the research and development. An economic penalty is considered "severe" if in the normal course of business an enterprise would probably choose to pay the other parties rather than incur the penalty. For example, an enterprise might purchase the partnership's interest in the research and development if the enterprise had provided the partnership with proprietary basic technology necessary for the enterprise's ongoing operations without retaining a way to recover that technology, or prevent it from being transferred to another party, except by purchasing the partnership's interest.

c. A significant related party[2] relationship between the enterprise and the parties funding the research and development exists at the time the enterprise enters into the arrangement.

d. The enterprise has essentially completed the project before entering into the arrangement.

9. An enterprise that incurs a liability to repay the other parties shall charge the research and development costs to expense as incurred. The amount of funds provided by the other parties might exceed the enterprise's liability. That might be the case, for example, if license agreements or partial buy-out provisions permit the enterprise to use the results of the research and development or to reacquire certain basic technology or other assets for an amount that is less than the funds provided. Those agreements or provisions might limit the extent to which enterprise is economically compelled to buy out the other parties regardless of the outcome. In those situations, the liability to repay the other parties might be limited to a specified price for licensing the results or for purchasing a partial interest in the results. If the enterprise's liability is less than the funds provided, the enterprise shall charge its portion of the research and development costs to expense in the same manner as the liability is incurred. For example, the liability might arise as the initial funds are expended, or the liability might arise on a pro rata basis.

Obligation Is to Perform Contractual Services

10. To the extent that the financial risk associated with the research and development has been transferred because repayment of any of the funds provided by the other parties depends *solely* on the results of the research and development having future economic benefit, the enterprise shall account for its obligation as a contract to perform research and development for others.

11. If the enterprise's obligation is to perform research and development for others and the enterprise subsequently decides to exercise an option to purchase the other parties' interests in the research and development arrangement or to obtain the exclusive rights to the results of the research and development, the nature of those results and their future use shall determine the accounting for the purchase transaction.[3]

Loan or Advance to the Other Parties

12. If repayment to the enterprise of any loan or advance by the enterprise to the other parties depends solely on the results of the research and development having future economic benefit, the

---

[1] *Probable* is used here consistent with its use in FASB Statement No. 5, *Accounting for Contingencies,* to mean that repayment is likely.

[2] *Related parties* are defined in FASB Statement No. 57, *Related Party Disclosures.*

[3] Paragraph 5 of FASB Interpretation No. 4, *Applicability of FASB Statement No. 2 to Business Combinations Accounted for by the Purchase Method,* states: ". . . the accounting for the cost of an item to be used in research and development activities is the same under paragraphs 11 and 12 of Statement 2 whether the item is purchased singly, or as part of a group of assets, or as part of an entire enterprise in a business combination accounted for by the purchase method." The accounting for other identifiable intangible assets acquired by the enterprise is specified in APB Opinion No. 17, *Intangible Assets.*

loan or advance shall be accounted for as costs incurred by the enterprise. The costs shall be charged to research and development expense unless the loan or advance to the other parties can be identified as relating to some other activity, for example, marketing or advertising, in which case the costs shall be accounted for according to their nature.

Issuance of Warrants or Similar Instruments

13. If warrants or similar instruments are issued in connection with the arrangement, the enterprise shall report a portion of the proceeds to be provided by the other parties as paid-in capital. The amount so reported shall be the fair value of the instruments at the date of the arrangement.

Disclosures

14. An enterprise that under the provisions of this Statement accounts for its obligation under a research and development arrangement as a contract to perform research and development for others shall disclose[4] the following:[5]
a. The terms of significant agreements under the research and development arrangement (including royalty arrangements, purchase provisions, license agreements, and commitments to provide additional funding) as of the date of each balance sheet presented
b. The amount of compensation earned and costs incurred under such contracts for each period for which an income statement is presented

Effective Date and Transition

15. The provisions of this Statement shall be effective for research and development arrangements covered by this Statement that are entered into after December 31, 1982 with earlier application encouraged in financial statements that have not been previously issued. This Statement may be, but is not required to be, applied retroactively to previously issued financial statements. If previously issued financial statements are restated, the financial statements shall, in the year that this Statement is first applied, disclose the nature of any restatement and its effects on income before extraordinary items, net income, and related per share amounts for each restated year presented.

The provisions of this Statement need not be applied to immaterial items.

This Statement was adopted by the unanimous vote of the seven members of the Financial Accounting Standards Board:

Donald J. Kirk,	John W. March	Robert T. Sprouse
Chairman	Robert A. Morgan	Ralph E. Walters
Frank E. Block	David Mosso	

Appendix A

BACKGROUND INFORMATION

16. Research and development arrangements have been used to finance the research and development of a variety of new products, such as information processing systems, medical technology, experimental drugs, electronic devices, and aerospace equipment. Enterprises may enter into arrangements for different reasons. The objectives of entering into an arrangement may be to:

a. Transfer all or part of the uncertainty and risk involved with the research and development to others
b. Obtain the benefit of funds that are made available because of tax incentives for investors
c. Attract qualified research and development personnel who otherwise might be concerned that funding might not be assured
d. Avoid expanding the ownership of the enterprise and the impact on earnings per share that would result from issuing equity securities
e. Avoid debt service expenditures and the impact on the enterprise's debt-to-equity ratio that would result from issuing debt securities
f. Avoid the impact on the enterprise's near-term earnings that would result if it incurred the related research and development expenses

17. Many arrangements have been formed as limited partnerships. In some, the enterprise or a related party is the general partner who manages the research and development activities. Sometimes, the limited partners are related to the enterprise. In some arrangements, the enterprise has the basic

---

[4]Statement 57 specifies additional disclosure requirements for related party transactions and certain control relationships.

[5]An enterprise that is a party to more than one research and development arrangement need not separately disclose each arrangement unless separate disclosure is necessary to understand the effects on the financial statements. Aggregation of similar arrangements by type may be appropriate.

technology needed for the research and development and has performed preliminary research and development work to determine the attractiveness of further work. The enterprise might contribute the preliminary research and development work and basic technology to the partnership for a minor equity interest or might license or give the rights to the preliminary work and basic technology to the partnership.

18. The terms of the arrangement usually contemplate, but do not guarantee, that the funds provided by the limited partners will be sufficient to complete the intended research and development. However, some agreements permit or require the general partner to sell additional limited-partnership interests or to use its own funds if the funds provided are insufficient to complete the research and development effort. The enterprise sometimes provides additional funds through loans or advances to the partnership. Repayment of the loans or advances sometimes is guaranteed by the partnership although repayment sometimes is contingent on realization of future economic benefits of the research and development; for example, repayment might be made through offsets against the purchase price for the results of the project or against royalty payments.

19. The enterprise or a related party of the enterprise usually performs the research and development work under a contract with the partnership. The compensation under the research and development contract usually is either a fixed fee or reimbursement of direct costs plus a fixed fee or fixed percentage of those costs. The work is performed on a best-efforts basis with no guarantee of either technological or commercial success. The partnership retains legal ownership of the results of the research and development and sometimes retains legal rights to the basic technology provided by the enterprise.

20. Either as part of the partnership agreement or through contracts with the partnership, the enterprise usually has an option either to purchase the partnership's interest in or to obtain the exclusive rights to the entire results of the research and development in return for a lump sum payment or royalty payments to the partnership. Some arrangements contain a provision that permits the enterprise to acquire complete ownership of the results for a specified amount of the enterprise's stock or cash at some future time. In some of those purchase agreements, the partnership has the option to receive either the enterprise's stock or cash; in others, the enterprise makes the decision. Sometimes, warrants or similar instruments to purchase the enterprise's stock are issued in connection with the arrangement.

21. An enterprise that is a party to an arrangement through which research and development is funded by other parties usually incurs an obligation when it enters into the arrangement. The nature and extent of the enterprise's obligation are sometimes difficult to determine and can range from an obligation to perform contract research and development work to an obligation to repay the other parties, with a return, for the funds provided.

22. If the results of the research and development are determined to have sufficient future economic benefit, the enterprise probably will exercise its option either to purchase the partnership's interests in or to obtain the exclusive rights to the entire results. If the results do not have future economic benefit, the enterprise usually is not legally required to exercise its option; however, there may be valid business reasons for the enterprise to acquire the results even though the original objectives of the research and development are not met. For example, the enterprise may want to obtain ownership of results that have value to the enterprise even though they do not meet the original objectives. Other reasons may be to maintain the ability to enter into another arrangement with the same parties or similar arrangements with other parties; to recover the ownership of or rights to the enterprise's basic technology or to prevent the partnership from providing that technology to others; to avoid any potential future claim against the use of the results; or to fulfill a moral obligation (for example, the enterprise is the general partner and due to a conflict of interest feels compelled to exercise its option).

23. Although the enterprise's legal liabilities will be specified in the various contracts and agreements under the arrangement, accounting representations should not necessarily be limited to legal requirements. Depending on the facts and circumstances involved in a particular research and development arrangement, future payments by the enterprise to the other parties ostensibly for royalties or to purchase the partnership's interests in or to obtain the exclusive rights to the research and development results might actually be any of the following: (a) the settlement of a borrowing, (b) the purchase price of an asset, or (c) royalties for the use of an asset. The financial reporting of an enterprise that is a party to a research and development arrangement should represent faithfully what it purports to represent and should not subordinate substance to form.

Appendix B

BASIS FOR CONCLUSIONS

24. An Exposure Draft of a proposed Statement, *Research and Development Arrangements,* was

issued on April 27, 1982. The Board received 37 letters of comment in response to that Exposure Draft. This appendix discusses the factors that the Board considered significant in reaching the conclusions in this Statement. Individual Board members gave greater weight to some factors than to others.

25. Several respondents to the Exposure Draft questioned the need for a project to specify how an enterprise that is a party to a research and development arrangement should account for its obligation under the arrangement. Although they generally agreed with the principles proposed in the Exposure Draft, they expressed the view that a careful reading of other Statements, such as FASB Statements No. 2, *Accounting for Research and Development Costs,* No. 5, *Accounting for Contingencies,* and No. 57, *Related Party Disclosures,* would lead to the correct answers. However, because information received by the Board showed significant diversity in the accounting practices of enterprises involved in similar research and development arrangements, the Board concluded that those Statements do not provide adequate guidance. Some enterprises accounted for the proceeds received from the other parties as contract revenues from performing research and development for others while other enterprises accounted for the proceeds from similar arrangements as borrowings. Various regulatory agencies raised questions about the diversity in accounting for similar arrangements, and industry and the accounting profession asked the FASB to provide guidance.

26. Some people believe that most, if not all, research and development arrangements are borrowing transactions. Those with that view believe that in most, if not all, cases the enterprise controls the right to the future economic benefits of the research and development and has in one form or another an obligation to repay principal and pay interest on the borrowed funds, even though those amounts may be paid in the form of royalties.

27. Others argue for contract accounting because they believe that in most, if not all, research and development arrangements the financial risk is transferred to others, the results of the research and development belong to the partnership, and the enterprise is not obligated to acquire the results or to acquire the partnership's interest therein. They believe that the enterprise has a liability only if it decides to exercise its option.

28. The Board believes that each of the above positions is appropriate in certain situations and that neither position is universally applicable to all research and development arrangements. The

Board's conclusions in this Statement are derived from FASB Concepts Statement No. 3, *Elements of Financial Statements of Business Enterprises,* which defines liabilities as:

> . . . Probable . . . future sacrifices of economic benefits arising from present obligations . . . of a particular entity to transfer assets or provide services to other entities in the future as a result of past transactions or events. [paragraph 28]

Concepts Statement 3 uses the term *obligation* to include duties imposed legally or socially; that is, what an enterprise is bound to do by contract, promise, or moral responsibility. Therefore, an enterprise may have a liability that is recognized for financial reporting even though it is not a legal liability.

29. Some respondents believed that the Board should have based its conclusions on the definition of a loss contingency in Statement 5 rather than on the definition of a liability in Concepts Statement 3. The Board concluded that Statement 5 does not address the primary issue involved in determining whether an enterprise involved in a research and development arrangement has a liability. Statement 5 deals with contingencies; that is, an existing condition, situation, or set of circumstances involving *uncertainty as to possible gain or loss* that will ultimately be resolved when one or more future events occur or fail to occur. This Statement deals with a transaction in which the issue is whether at the time an enterprise enters into a research and development arrangement (a) it is *committed* to repay any of the funds provided by the other parties regardless of the outcome of the research and development, (b) existing conditions indicate that it is likely that the enterprise will repay the other parties regardless of the outcome, or (c) the enterprise is obligated only to perform research and development work for others.

30. Some people consider the likelihood of success of the research and development as the key issue in who bears the risk of failure of those activities. However, even though future benefits from a particular project may be foreseen, the amount generally cannot be measured with a reasonable degree of certainty. The key question in determining who bears the risk of failure is whether the enterprise is obligated to repay any of the funds provided by the other parties regardless of the outcome of the research and development. Concepts Statement 3 states that "an enterprise is not obligated to sacrifice assets in the future if it can avoid the future sacrifice at its discretion without significant penalty."[6] A deter-

---

[6]Concepts Statement 3, paragraph 135.

mination must be made of the penalty, if any, that the enterprise will incur if it does not repay any of the funds provided.

31. If an enterprise is contractually committed to repay any of the funds provided or has guaranteed or assured the other parties of repayment of the funds provided, regardless of the outcome of the research and development, the enterprise clearly has a liability to repay the other parties. However, because of tax considerations, the agreements and contracts under the arrangement normally state that the enterprise is obligated only to perform services and generally do not require the enterprise to repay any of the funds provided if the research and development does not have future economic benefit. Nonetheless, the Board believes that substantive and genuine transfer of risk is essential for the enterprise's obligation to be limited to performing contractual services and that certain conditions create a presumption that the transfer of risk to the other parties may not be substantive or genuine. An enterprise involved in a research and development arrangement might incur equitable or constructive obligations through actions that bind the enterprise or by circumstances that change the nature of the enterprise's obligation from one to perform services for a fee to one to repay amounts provided by the other parties. For example, an enterprise might provide the partnership with basic technology necessary for the enterprise's ongoing operations without retaining a way to recover that technology, or to prevent it from being transferred to another party, except by purchasing the partnership's interest in the research and development. Another example might be that there is a conflict of interest and the limited partners could reasonably be expected to litigate successfully if the enterprise does not buy out the partnership.

32. Some respondents questioned whether the mere presence in a research and development arrangement of parties related to the enterprise should lead to a presumption that a liability has been incurred. In particular, they questioned the relevance of the enterprise's role as general partner. Although transactions between related parties commonly occur in the normal course of business, the conditions of competitive free-market dealings between independent parties may not exist. Accordingly, the enterprise might be influenced by considerations other than those that would exist in arm's-length transactions with unrelated parties. This is particularly true if the related parties can directly or indirectly influence the enterprise's decision whether or not to acquire the results of the research and development. The Board concluded that the com-

bined attractiveness of "off-balance-sheet" financing for the enterprise and tax incentives for related party investors may cause the substance of such an arrangement to differ from its form. However, the Board does not believe that the enterprise's obligation should be accounted for as a liability just because the enterprise is the general partner. The example in paragraph 8(c) has been revised accordingly.

33. The Board believes that the enterprise should account for the amount of any loan or advance to the partnership, the collection of which is contingent on the results of the research and development having future economic benefit, as costs incurred by the enterprise because of the uncertainty of recovery of those loans and advances. As discussed in the "Basis for Conclusions" of Statement 2, "estimates of the rate of success of research and development projects vary markedly—depending in part on how narrowly one defines a 'project' and how one defines 'success'—but all such estimates indicate a high failure rate."[7] Statement 2 further states that "even after a project has passed beyond the research and development stage, and a new or improved product or process is being marketed or used, the failure rate is high."[8] Statement 2 requires any research and development costs to be charged to expense as those costs are incurred. If the costs relate to some other activity, for example, marketing or advertising, the costs should be accounted for according to their nature.

34. If the enterprise exercises an option to purchase the partnership's interest in or to obtain the exclusive rights to the results of the research and development, a question arises as to whether the amount paid should be an expense or the purchase price of an intangible asset. If an intangible asset is developed, the Board believes that there is a distinction between an amount paid for the results of a known successful project and the costs incurred in ongoing research and development whose ultimate success or failure is unknown. An enterprise exercising a purchase option on a successful project has made a decision about the results of past research and development costs. The uncertainty usually has diminished to the point that an evaluation, comparable to an evaluation made when an intangible asset is acquired from an independent party, can be made about the future economic benefits of the results. If a purchase price is reported as the cost of an intangible asset, the provisions of FASB Interpretation No. 4, *Applicability of FASB Statement No. 2 to Business Combinations Accounted for by the Purchase Method,* or of APB Opinion No. 17, *Intangible Assets,* apply.

---

[7]Statement 2, paragraph 39.

[8]Ibid., paragraph 40.

35. If the enterprise's liability is less than the amount of funds provided by the other parties, the Exposure Draft would have required an enterprise to charge its portion of the research and development costs relating to the research and development to expense on a pro rata basis. Several respondents argued that a pro rata approach is appropriate only if the enterprise must repay on a pro rata basis. In some instances, the enterprise's liability might arise as the initial funds are spent. The Board agreed that a pro rata approach might not be appropriate in all circumstances. Paragraph 9 has been revised to require that the enterprise charge its portion of the research and development costs to expense in the same manner as the enterprise's liability is incurred.

36. Several respondents suggested that the final Statement provide detailed guidance for the various aspects of research and development arrangements. Most of the guidance sought deals with accounting in general or is addressed by other existing generally accepted accounting principles; for example, guidance for discounting a liability is contained in APB Opinion No. 21, *Interest on Receivables and Payables*, and guidance for recognition of losses on cost overruns is contained in Statement 5. Accordingly, the Board concluded that it is unnecessary to specify such detailed guidance in this Statement. Some respondents also requested that the final Statement specify the accounting and reporting for contract revenues and costs under a research and development arrangement. Those issues relate to accounting and reporting for contracts in general, which is beyond the scope of this Statement.

37. The Exposure Draft included a notice to recipients specifically requesting comments on the proposed disclosures. Several respondents said that the proposed disclosure requirements were excessive for an enterprise's obligation accounted for as a liability because adequate disclosures are required by other existing generally accepted accounting principles. The Board agreed with those respondents and, accordingly, the disclosure requirements for an obligation accounted for as a liability have not been carried forward from the Exposure Draft. Some respondents also disagreed with requiring the disclosures as of each balance sheet presented and about requiring that the disclosures be presented in the footnotes. The Board concluded that the disclosures required by this Statement should be provided for each balance sheet presented because the research and development activities often are long-term in nature and the disclosures are useful for comparison. The Board agreed that it is acceptable to present the disclosures either in the primary financial statements or in the footnotes and revised the disclosure requirements accordingly.

38. Some respondents requested that the transition provisions of the Exposure Draft be modified to permit retroactive restatement of previously issued financial statements. They believe that permitting retroactive restatement would enable enterprises that have used various accounting alternatives to report old and new arrangements consistently and thereby improve overall comparability. The Board agreed and revised the transition to permit retroactive restatement for previously issued financial statements.

39. The Board concluded that it can reach an informed decision on the basis of existing information without a public hearing and that the effective date and transition specified in paragraph 15 are advisable in the circumstances.

Statement of Financial Accounting Standards No. 69
Disclosures about Oil and Gas Producing Activities

an amendment of FASB Statements 19, 25, 33, and 39

STATUS

Issued: November 1982

Effective Date: For fiscal years beginning on or after December 15, 1982

Affects: Supersedes FAS 19, paragraphs 48 through 59
Supersedes FAS 33, paragraphs 51(b), 52(b), and 53(a)
Supersedes FAS 39, paragraphs 10, 11, and 12
Supersedes FAS 40, paragraph 6
Supersedes FAS 41, paragraph 7
Supersedes FAS 46, paragraph 8

Affected by: Paragraphs 7, 8, and 41 and footnote 3 amended by FAS 95
Paragraphs 26, 30(c), 40, and 41 amended by FAS 96 and FAS 109
Paragraphs 35 through 38 and footnote 10 superseded by FAS 89

SUMMARY

This Statement establishes a comprehensive set of disclosures for oil and gas producing activities and replaces requirements of several earlier Statements. The requirement to disclose the method of accounting for costs incurred in oil and gas producing activities and the manner of disposing of related capitalized costs is continued for both publicly traded and other enterprises. None of the other requirements in this Statement is extended to enterprises that are not publicly traded, thereby eliminating existing requirements for them to disclose information about proved oil and gas reserve quantities, capitalized costs, and costs incurred.

Publicly traded enterprises with significant oil and gas activities, when presenting a complete set of annual financial statements, are to disclose the following as supplementary information, but not as a part of the financial statements:

a. Proved oil and gas reserve quantities
b. Capitalized costs relating to oil and gas producing activities
c. Costs incurred in oil and gas property acquisition, exploration, and development activities
d. Results of operations for oil and gas producing activities
e. A standardized measure of discounted future net cash flows relating to proved oil and gas reserve quantities

This Statement eliminates a previous requirement to disclose capitalized costs in complete sets of interim financial statements.

In addition, this Statement permits historical cost/constant dollar measures to be used for oil and gas mineral interests when presenting current cost information under the provisions of FASB Statement No. 39, *Financial Reporting and Changing Prices: Specialized Assets—Mining and Oil and Gas.*

NOTE

Paragraph 5 of FAS 69 originally stated:

"(Amendments to Statements 19 and 33 contained in this Statement are indicated by shading.)"

This comment, and the shading described in the comment, have been deleted in the ensuing reprint because shading in this volume indicates paragraphs superseded or amended by subsequent pronouncements. No other changes have been made to FAS 69.

Statement of Financial Accounting Standards No. 69
Disclosures about Oil and Gas Producing Activities

an amendment of FASB Statements 19, 25, 33, and 39

CONTENTS

INTRODUCTION

1. This Statement amends FASB Statement No. 19, *Financial Accounting and Reporting by Oil and Gas Producing Companies,* by establishing disclosures about oil and gas producing activities[1] to be made for publicly traded enterprises[2] when presenting a complete set of annual financial statements.[3] Those disclosures include the information required by Statement 19 and FASB Statement No. 25, *Suspension of Certain Accounting Requirements for Oil and Gas Producing Companies,* concerning proved oil and gas reserve quantities, capitalized costs, costs incurred, and the method of accounting for costs incurred for an enterprise's oil and gas producing activities. Information about the results of operations for oil and gas producing activities, a standardized measure of discounted future net cash flows relating to proved oil and gas reserve quantities, and

summary information about oil and gas producing activities associated with equity investments and minority interests also is required to be disclosed. The accounting method shall be disclosed within the financial statements; the other disclosures are considered to be supplementary information.

2. This Statement also amends Statement 19 to eliminate, for enterprises that are not publicly traded, the requirement to disclose information concerning capitalized costs, costs incurred, and proved oil and gas reserve quantities. However, this Statement maintains the requirement of Statement 25 for all enterprises to disclose the method of accounting for costs incurred in oil and gas producing activities and the manner of disposing of capitalized costs relating to those activities.

3. In addition, this Statement permits historical

---

[1] Statement 19 defines oil and gas producing activities as "those activities [that] involve the acquisition of mineral interests in properties, exploration (including prospecting), development, and production of crude oil, including condensate and natural gas liquids, and natural gas . . ." (par. 1).

[2] For purposes of this Statement, a publicly traded enterprise is a business enterprise (a) whose securities are traded in a public market on a domestic stock exchange or in the domestic over-the-counter market (including securities quoted only locally or regionally) or (b) whose financial statements are filed with a regulatory agency in preparation for the sale of any class of securities in a domestic market.

[3] FASB Statement No. 24, *Reporting Segment Information in Financial Statements That Are Presented in Another Enterprise's Financial Report,* refers to a complete set of financial statements as "a set of financial statements (including necessary footnotes) that present financial position, results of operations, and changes in financial position in conformity with generally accepted accounting principles" (footnote 2).

cost/constant dollar measures to be used when presenting current cost information about oil and gas mineral interests under the provisions of FASB Statement No. 39, *Financial Reporting and Changing Prices: Specialized Assets—Mining and Oil and Gas.*

4. Appendix A contains summaries and illustrations of certain disclosures about oil and gas producing activities set forth in this Statement. Background information highlighting the pertinent events that preceded the issuance of this Statement is set forth in Appendix B. The basis for the Board's conclusions, including alternative approaches considered in developing the disclosures for oil and gas producing activities, is discussed in Appendix C.

STANDARDS OF FINANCIAL ACCOUNTING AND REPORTING

Amendments to Statements 19, 25, 33, and 39

5. Paragraphs 48-59 of Statement 19, as amended by Statement 25, are superseded by paragraphs 6-34 of this Statement. Paragraphs 51-53 of FASB Statement No. 33, *Financial Reporting and Changing Prices,* as amended by Statement 39, are amended by paragraphs 35-38 of this Statement.

Applicability and Scope

6. All enterprises engaged in oil and gas producing activities shall disclose in their financial statements the method of accounting for costs incurred in those activities and the manner of disposing of capitalized costs relating to those activities.

7. In addition, publicly traded enterprises that have significant oil and gas producing activities shall disclose with complete sets of annual financial statements the information required by paragraphs 10-34 of this Statement. Those disclosures relate to the following and are considered to be supplementary information:

a. Proved oil and gas reserve quantities
b. Capitalized costs relating to oil and gas producing activities
c. Costs incurred for property acquisition, exploration, and development activities
d. Results of operations for oil and gas producing activities

e. A standardized measure of discounted future net cash flows relating to proved oil and gas reserve quantities

8. For purposes of this Statement, an enterprise is regarded as having significant oil and gas producing activities if it satisfies one or more of the following tests. The tests shall be applied separately for each year for which a complete set of annual financial statements is presented.

a. Revenues from oil and gas producing activities, as defined in paragraph 25 (including both sales to unaffiliated customers and sales or transfers to the enterprise's other operations), are 10 percent or more of the combined revenues (sales to unaffiliated customers and sales or transfers to the enterprise's other operations) of all of the enterprise's industry segments.[4]
b. Results of operations for oil and gas producing activities, excluding the effect of income taxes, are 10 percent or more of the greater of:
(1) The combined operating profit of all industry segments that did not incur an operating loss
(2) The combined operating loss of all industry segments that did incur an operating loss
c. The identifiable assets, defined in a similar manner as in paragraph 10 of FASB Statement No. 14, *Financial Reporting for Segments of a Business Enterprise,* relating to oil and gas producing activities are 10 percent or more of the combined identifiable assets of all industry segments.

9. The disclosures set forth in this Statement are not required in interim financial reports. However, interim financial reports shall include information about a major discovery or other favorable or adverse event that causes a significant change from the information presented in the most recent annual financial report concerning oil and gas reserve quantities.

Disclosure of Proved Oil and Gas Reserve Quantities

10. Net quantities of an enterprise's interests in proved reserves and proved developed reserves of (a) crude oil (including condensate and natural gas liquids)[5] and (b) natural gas shall be disclosed as of the beginning and the end of the year. "Net" quantities of reserves include those relating to the enterprise's operating and nonoperating interests in properties as defined in paragraph 11(a) of Statement 19. Quantities of reserves relating to royalty

---

[4]FASB Statement No. 14, *Financial Reporting for Segments of a Business Enterprise,* defines an industry segment as "a component of an enterprise engaged in providing a product or service or a group of related products and services primarily to unaffiliated customers (i.e., customers outside the enterprise) for a profit" (par. 10).

[5]If significant, the reserve quantity information shall be disclosed separately for natural gas liquids.

interests owned shall be included in "net" quantities if the necessary information is available to the enterprise; if reserves relating to royalty interests owned are not included because the information is unavailable, that fact and the enterprise's share of oil and gas produced for those royalty interests shall be disclosed for the year. "Net" quantities shall not include reserves relating to interests of others in properties owned by the enterprise.

11. Changes in the net quantities of an enterprise's proved reserves of oil and of gas during the year shall be disclosed. Changes resulting from each of the following shall be shown separately with appropriate explanation of significant changes:

a. *Revisions of previous estimates.* Revisions represent changes in previous estimates of proved reserves, either upward or downward, resulting from new information (except for an increase in proved acreage) normally obtained from development drilling and production history or resulting from a change in economic factors.
b. *Improved recovery.* Changes in reserve estimates resulting from application of improved recovery techniques shall be shown separately, if significant. If not significant, such changes shall be included in revisions of previous estimates.
c. *Purchases of minerals in place.*
d. *Extensions and discoveries.* Additions to proved reserves that result from (1) extension of the proved acreage of previously discovered (old) reservoirs through additional drilling in periods subsequent to discovery and (2) discovery of new fields with proved reserves or of new reservoirs of proved reserves in old fields.
e. *Production.*
f. *Sales of minerals in place.*

12. If an enterprise's proved reserves of oil and of gas are located entirely within its home country, that fact shall be disclosed. If some or all of its reserves are located in foreign countries, the disclosures of net quantities of reserves of oil and of gas and changes in them required by paragraphs 10 and 11 shall be separately disclosed for (a) the enterprise's home country (if significant reserves are located there) and (b) each foreign geographic area in which significant reserves are located. Foreign geographic areas are individual countries or groups of countries as appropriate for meaningful disclosure in the circumstances.

13. Net quantities disclosed in conformity with paragraphs 10-12 shall not include oil or gas subject to purchase under long-term supply, purchase, or similar agreements and contracts, including such agreements with ~~foreign~~ governments or authorities. However, quantities of oil or gas subject to such agreements with ~~foreign~~ governments or authorities

as of the end of the year, and the net quantity of oil or gas received under the agreements during the year, shall be separately disclosed if the enterprise participates in the operation of the properties in which the oil or gas is located or otherwise serves as the "producer" of those reserves, as opposed, for example, to being an independent purchaser, broker, dealer, or importer.

14. In determining the reserve quantities to be disclosed in conformity with paragraphs 10-13:

a. If the enterprise issues consolidated financial statements, 100 percent of the net reserve quantities attributable to the parent company and 100 percent of the net reserve quantities attributable to its consolidated subsidiaries (whether or not wholly owned) shall be included. If a significant portion of those reserve quantities at the end of the year is attributable to a consolidated subsidiary(ies) in which there is a significant minority interest, that fact and the approximate portion shall be disclosed.
b. If the enterprise's financial statements include investments that are proportionately consolidated, the enterprise's reserve quantities shall include its proportionate share of the investees' net oil and gas reserves.
c. If the enterprise's financial statements include investments that are accounted for by the equity method, the investees' net oil and gas reserve quantities shall *not* be included in the disclosures of the enterprise's reserve quantities. However, the enterprise's (investor's) share of the investees' net oil and gas reserve quantities shall be separately disclosed as of the end of the year.

15. In reporting reserve quantities and changes in them, oil reserves and natural gas liquids reserves shall be stated in barrels, and gas reserves in cubic feet.

16. If important economic factors or significant uncertainties affect particular components of an enterprise's proved reserves, explanation shall be provided. Examples include unusually high expected development or lifting costs, the necessity to build a major pipeline or other major facilities before production of the reserves can begin, and contractual obligations to produce and sell a significant portion of reserves at prices that are substantially below those at which the oil or gas could otherwise be sold in the absence of the contractual obligation.

17. If a government restricts the disclosure of estimated reserves for properties under its authority, or of amounts under long-term supply, purchase, or similar agreements or contracts, or if the government requires the disclosure of reserves other than

proved, the enterprise shall indicate that the disclosed reserve estimates or amounts do not include figures for the named country or that reserve estimates include reserves other than proved.

Disclosure of Capitalized Costs Relating to Oil and Gas Producing Activities

18. The aggregate capitalized costs relating to an enterprise's oil and gas producing activities (paragraph 11 of Statement 19) and the aggregate related accumulated depreciation, depletion, amortization, and valuation allowances shall be disclosed as of the end of the year. Paragraph 5 of APB Opinion No. 12, *Omnibus Opinion—1967,* requires disclosure of "balances of major classes of depreciable assets, by nature or function." Thus, separate disclosure of capitalized costs for asset categories (a) through (d) in paragraph 11 of Statement 19 or for a combination of those categories often may be appropriate.

19. If significant, capitalized costs of unproved properties shall be separately disclosed. Capitalized costs of support equipment and facilities may be disclosed separately or included, as appropriate, with capitalized costs of proved and unproved properties.

20. If the enterprise's financial statements include investments that are accounted for by the equity method, the enterprise's share of the investees' net capitalized costs relating to oil and gas producing activities as of the end of the year shall be separately disclosed.

Disclosure of Costs Incurred in Oil and Gas Property Acquisition, Exploration, and Development Activities

21. Each of the following types of costs for the year shall be disclosed (whether those costs are capitalized or charged to expense at the time they are incurred under the provisions of paragraphs 15-22 of Statement 19):[6]

a. Property acquisition costs
b. Exploration costs
c. Development costs
d. Production (lifting) costs

22. If some or all of those costs are incurred in foreign countries, the amounts shall be disclosed separately for each of the geographic areas for which reserve quantities are disclosed (paragraph 12). If significant costs have been incurred to acquire mineral interests that have proved reserves, those costs shall be disclosed separately from the costs of acquiring unproved properties.

23. If the enterprise's financial statements include investments that are accounted for by the equity method, the enterprise's share of the investees' property acquisition, exploration, and development costs incurred in oil and gas producing activities shall be separately disclosed for the year, in the aggregate and for each geographic area for which reserve quantities are disclosed (paragraph 12).

Disclosure of the Results of Operations for Oil and Gas Producing Activities

24. The results of operations for oil and gas producing activities shall be disclosed for the year. That information shall be disclosed in the aggregate and for each geographic area for which reserve quantities are disclosed (paragraph 12). The following information relating to those activities shall be presented:[7]

a. Revenues
b. Production (lifting) costs
c. Exploration expenses[8]
d. Depreciation, depletion, and amortization, and valuation provisions
e. Income tax expenses
f. Results of operations for oil and gas producing activities (excluding corporate overhead and interest costs)

25. Revenues shall include sales to unaffiliated enterprises and sales or transfers to the enterprise's other operations (for example, refineries or chemical plants). Sales to unaffiliated enterprises and sales or transfers to the enterprise's other operations shall be disclosed separately. Revenues shall include sales to unaffiliated enterprises attributable to net working interests, royalty interests, oil payment interests, and net profits interests of the reporting enterprise. Sales or transfers to the enterprise's other operations

---

[6]As defined in the paragraphs cited, exploration and development costs include depreciation of support equipment and facilities used in those activities and do not include the expenditures to acquire support equipment and facilities.

[7]If oil and gas producing activities represent substantially all of the business activities of the reporting enterprise and those oil and gas activities are located substantially in a single geographic area, the information required by paragraphs 24-29 of this Statement need not be disclosed if that information is provided elsewhere in the financial statements. If oil and gas producing activities constitute a business segment, as defined by Statement 14, paragraph 10(a), and the business segment activities are located substantially in a single geographic area, the results of operations information required by paragraphs 24-29 of this Statement may be included with segment information disclosed elsewhere in the financial report.

[8]Generally, only enterprises utilizing the successful efforts accounting method will have exploration expenses to disclose, since enterprises utilizing the full cost accounting method generally capitalize all exploration costs when incurred and subsequently reflect those costs in the determination of earnings through depreciation, depletion, and amortization, and valuation provisions.

shall be based on market prices determined at the point of delivery from the producing unit. Those market prices shall represent prices equivalent to those that could be obtained in an arm's-length transaction. Production or severance taxes shall not be deducted in determining gross revenues, but rather shall be included as part of production costs. Royalty payments and net profits disbursements shall be excluded from gross revenues.

26. Income taxes shall be computed using the statutory tax rate for the period, applied to revenues less production (lifting) costs, exploration expenses, depreciation, depletion, and amortization, and valuation provisions. Calculation of income tax expenses shall reflect permanent differences and tax credits and allowances relating to the oil and gas producing activities that are reflected in the enterprise's consolidated income tax expense for the period.

27. Results of operations for oil and gas producing activities are defined as revenues less production (lifting) costs, exploration expenses, depreciation, depletion, and amortization, valuation provisions, and income tax expenses. General corporate overhead and interest costs[9] shall not be deducted in computing the results of operations for an enterprise's oil and gas producing activities. However, some expenses incurred at an enterprise's central administrative office may not be general corporate expenses, but rather may be operating expenses of oil and gas producing activities, and therefore should be reported as such. The nature of an expense rather than the location of its incurrence shall determine whether it is an operating expense. Only those expenses identified by their nature as operating expenses shall be allocated as operating expenses in computing the results of operations for oil and gas producing activities.

28. The amounts disclosed in conformity with paragraphs 24-27 shall include an enterprise's interests in proved oil and gas reserves (paragraph 10) and in oil and gas subject to purchase under long-term supply, purchase, or similar agreements and contracts in which the enterprise participates in the operation of the properties on which the oil or gas is located or otherwise serves as the producer of those reserves (paragraph 13).

29. If the enterprise's financial statements include investments that are accounted for by the equity method, the investees' results of operations for oil and gas producing activities shall not be included in the enterprise's results of operations for oil and gas producing activities. However, the enterprise's share of the investees' results of operations for oil and gas producing activities shall be separately disclosed for the year, in the aggregate and by each geographic area for which reserve quantities are disclosed (paragraph 12).

Disclosure of a Standardized Measure of Discounted Future Net Cash Flows Relating to Proved Oil and Gas Reserve Quantities

30. A standardized measure of discounted future net cash flows relating to an enterprise's interests in (a) proved oil and gas reserves (paragraph 10) and (b) oil and gas subject to purchase under long-term supply, purchase, or similar agreements and contracts in which the enterprise participates in the operation of the properties on which the oil or gas is located or otherwise serves as the producer of those reserves (paragraph 13) shall be disclosed as of the end of the year. The standardized measure of discounted future net cash flows relating to those two types of interests in reserves may be combined for reporting purposes. The following information shall be disclosed in the aggregate and for each geographic area for which reserve quantities are disclosed in accordance with paragraph 12:

a. *Future cash inflows.* These shall be computed by applying year-end prices of oil and gas relating to the enterprise's proved reserves to the year-end quantities of those reserves. Future price changes shall be considered only to the extent provided by contractual arrangements in existence at year-end.

b. *Future development and production costs.* These costs shall be computed by estimating the expenditures to be incurred in developing and producing the proved oil and gas reserves at the end of the year, based on year-end costs and assuming continuation of existing economic conditions. If estimated development expenditures are significant, they shall be presented separately from estimated production costs.

c. *Future income tax expenses.* These expenses shall be computed by applying the appropriate year-end statutory tax rates, with consideration of future tax rates already legislated, to the future pretax net cash flows relating to the enterprise's proved oil and gas reserves, less the tax basis of the properties involved. The future income tax expenses shall give effect to permanent differences and tax credits and allowances relating to the enterprise's proved oil and gas reserves.

d. *Future net cash flows.* These amounts are the result of subtracting future development and production costs and future income tax expenses from future cash inflows.

---

[9]The disposition of interest costs that have been capitalized as part of the cost of acquiring qualifying assets used in oil and gas producing activities shall be the same as that of other components of those assets' costs.

e. *Discount.* This amount shall be derived from using a discount rate of 10 percent a year to reflect the timing of the future net cash flows relating to proved oil and gas reserves.

f. *Standardized measure of discounted future net cash flows.* This amount is the future net cash flows less the computed discount.

31. If a significant portion of the economic interest in the consolidated standardized measure of discounted future net cash flows reported is attributable to a consolidated subsidiary(ies) in which there is a significant minority interest, that fact and the approximate portion shall be disclosed.

32. If the financial statements include investments that are accounted for by the equity method, the investees' standardized measure of discounted future net cash flows relating to proved oil and gas reserves shall not be included in the disclosure of the enterprise's standardized measure. However, the enterprise's share of the investees' standardized measure of discounted future net cash flows shall be separately disclosed for the year, in the aggregate and by each geographic area for which quantities are disclosed (paragraph 12).

33. The aggregate change in the standardized measure of discounted future net cash flows shall be disclosed for the year. If individually significant, the following sources of change shall be presented separately:

a. Net change in sales and transfer prices and in production (lifting) costs related to future production

b. Changes in estimated future development costs

c. Sales and transfers of oil and gas produced during the period

d. Net change due to extensions, discoveries, and improved recovery

e. Net change due to purchases and sales of minerals in place

f. Net change due to revisions in quantity estimates

g. Previously estimated development costs incurred during the period

h. Accretion of discount

i. Other—unspecified

j. Net change in income taxes

In computing the amounts under each of the above categories, the effects of changes in prices and costs shall be computed before the effects of changes in quantities. As a result, changes in quantities shall be stated at year-end prices and costs. The change in

computed income taxes shall reflect the effect of income taxes incurred during the period as well as the change in future income tax expenses. Therefore, all changes except income taxes shall be reported pretax.

34. Additional information necessary to prevent the disclosure of the standardized measure of discounted future net cash flows and changes therein from being misleading also shall be provided.

Disclosure of Current Cost Information

35. In applying the provisions of Statement 39 for presenting supplementary information on a current cost basis, this Statement permits enterprises to use historical cost/constant dollar measures of oil and gas mineral resource assets and related expense. As a result of this provision, together with the provision of paragraph 31 of Statement 33, an enterprise needs to present supplementary information on a current cost basis only if it has significant holdings of inventory and property, plant, and equipment apart from oil and gas producing activities or certain other specialized assets.

36. Paragraph 53(a) of Statement 33, as amended by Statements 39, 40, 41, and 46,[10] is superseded by the following:

a. When an enterprise presents information on a current cost basis for fiscal years ended on or after December 15, 1982, it shall measure:
(1) Oil and gas mineral resource assets and related expenses at either their historical cost/constant dollar amounts or current cost or lower recoverable amounts
(2) Mining mineral resource assets and related expenses at their current cost or lower recoverable amounts

37. Paragraph 51(b) of Statement 33, as amended by Statements 39, 40, 41, and 46, is superseded by the following:

b. Property, plant, and equipment at the current cost or lower recoverable amount (paragraphs 57-64) of the assets' remaining service potential at the measurement date. (This provision is qualified by paragraph 53 with respect to timberlands and growing timber, income-producing real estate, motion picture films, and oil and gas mineral resource assets.)

---

[10]FASB Statements No. 40, *Financial Reporting and Changing Prices: Specialized Assets—Timberlands and Growing Timber,* No. 41, *Financial Reporting and Changing Prices: Specialized Assets—Income-Producing Real Estate,* and No. 46, *Financial Reporting and Changing Prices: Motion Picture Films.*

38. Paragraph 52(b) of Statement 33, as amended by Statements 39, 40, 41, and 46, is superseded by the following:

  b. Depreciation, depletion, and amortization expense of property, plant, and equipment shall be measured on the basis of the average current cost or lower recoverable amount (paragraphs 57-64) of the assets' service potential during the period of use. (This provision is qualified by paragraph 53 with respect to timberlands and growing timber, income-producing real estate, motion picture films, and oil and gas mineral resource assets.)

Effective Date and Transition

39. This Statement shall be effective for fiscal years beginning on or after December 15, 1982. Earlier application is encouraged but is not required.

> The provisions of this Statement need
> not be applied to immaterial items.

This Statement was adopted by the affirmative votes of four members of the Financial Accounting Standards Board. Messrs. March, Morgan, and Sprouse dissented.

Messrs. March, Morgan, and Sprouse dissent to this Statement because they are opposed to requiring the disclosure of the computation and analysis of a standardized measure of discounted future net cash flows relating to proved oil and gas reserves (paragraphs 30-34). They believe that a requirement to disclose supplementary historical information about proved reserve quantities (paragraphs 10-17), capitalized and incurred costs (paragraphs 18-23), and results of producing activities (paragraphs 24-29) by significant geographic area is adequate to achieve the objectives of this Statement. Those disclosures are important for understanding oil and gas producing activities due to (a) the significance of oil and gas reserves as an economic resource; (b) the relatively long cycle from resource exploration to production, product sale, and ultimate cash flow; and (c) the risks related to geographic location. They help to fill a void caused by the absence of reliable measurements of the cost of finding and developing oil and gas reserves and the lack of a relationship between those costs and the revenues and cash inflows resulting from their disposition in the normal course of business.

Elsewhere, the Board has stated that relevance and reliability are the two primary qualities that make accounting useful for decision making and has adopted the position that if either of those qualities is completely missing, the information will not be useful (FASB Concepts Statement No. 2, *Qualitative Characteristics of Accounting Information*). The dissenting Board members believe that the proposed standardized measure of discounted future net cash flows is completely lacking in reliability. The reliability of a measure rests on the faithfulness with which it represents what it purports to represent (representational faithfulness), coupled with an assurance for the user that it has that representational quality (verifiability). Representational faithfulness is correspondence or agreement between a measure or description of an economic resource and the phenomenon that the measure or description purports to represent. The phenomenon being measured or described must be something that actually exists; the arithmetical results of a prescribed calculation that does not even purport to represent current cost, historical cost, fair market value, or any other real-world phenomenon cannot have representational faithfulness. Indeed, one of the concerns is that many users would not understand that the result of the standardized calculation itself is not intended to measure fair market value, the present value of future net cash flows, value to the business, or any other economic attribute (paragraphs 77 and 83) and might assume erroneously that it is some kind of an estimate of fair value.

Although it would be possible to provide assurance to users that the arithmetic involved in computing the standardized measure has been properly performed, it is impossible to verify the future. The standardized calculation depends largely upon management's forecasts of future production quantities, not only for the immediate future but for the entire period required to exhaust the existing estimated quantity of proved reserves. It is true that the discounting process automatically gives less weight to those forecasts the further into the future they extend, but the proposed disclosures do not provide adequate information for users, other than perhaps the most sophisticated, to assess the underlying production forecast itself.

Although the Board has not taken a position on reporting management forecasts generally, in Concepts Statement No. 1, *Objectives of Financial Reporting of Business Enterprises,* it characterizes financial statements and financial reporting as largely reflecting the financial effects of transactions and events that have already happened. Those who use the information provided by financial reporting may try to predict the future, but that is the essence of investment decision making, not the objective of financial reporting. The dissenting Board members are unconvinced that the case for a standardized measure of discounted future net cash flows that depends on management production forecasts is greater for enterprises engaged in oil and gas producing activities than for enterprises engaged in any other activity.

The dissenting Board members also are not convinced of the purported usefulness of the standardized measure as a benchmark to permit comparison of enterprises on a relative scale. The subjectivity of the estimates of quantities and production rates is too great. Each management's different expectations about what the future holds (for example, the future demand for energy, future use of alternative sources of energy, and future political stability among oil and gas producing nations) will be reflected in its critical production forecasts. Only if

a user reflects his or her own set of expectations in predicting the future activities and results of various enterprises is comparability possible.

Disclosures of historical information about revenues, costs, and production permit users to determine average unit prices received and average unit costs incurred in each significant geographic area and to make their own predictions about future production, prices, costs, net cash flows, and risks. Predicting the future is the users' responsibility; it is not an appropriate objective of financial reporting. The cost of calculating a standardized measure in which comprehensive management production forecasts are inextricably intermingled with current costs and prices and weighted with a prescribed 10-percent discount rate is likely to exceed the limited benefits of that disclosure.

Members of the Financial Accounting Standards Board:

Donald J. Kirk,
  Chairman
Frank E. Block

John W. March
Robert A. Morgan
David Mosso

Robert T. Sprouse
Ralph E. Walters

Appendix A

SUMMARIES AND ILLUSTRATIONS OF CERTAIN DISCLOSURES ABOUT OIL AND GAS PRODUCING ACTIVITIES

40. Following are summaries and illustrations of certain of the disclosure requirements for oil and gas producing activities required by this Statement.

**Disclosure
Illustration**

Accounting Method

Method of accounting for costs incurred and the manner of disposing of capitalized costs relating to oil and gas producing activities —

Capitalized Costs

Aggregate amount of capitalized costs and related accumulated depreciation, depletion, and amortization, and valuation allowances (If significant, capitalized costs of unproved properties shall be separately disclosed.) 1

Enterprise's share of equity method investees' capitalized costs in the aggregate at the end of the year 1

Costs Incurred in Oil and Gas Property Acquisition, Exploration, and Development

Cost incurred in oil and gas producing activities in the aggregate, by type, and by geographic area during the year (If significant, costs of acquiring existing mineral interests that have proved reserves shall be disclosed separately from the costs of acquiring unproved properties.) 2

Enterprise's share of equity method investees' costs incurred in the aggregate and by geographic area during the year 2

Results of Operations

Reserve Quantity Information

Standardized Measure of Discounted Future Net Cash Flows

41. The following illustrations present formats that may be used to disclose certain information required by this Statement when a complete set of annual financial statements is presented for one year.

Illustration 1

CAPITALIZED COSTS RELATING TO OIL AND GAS
PRODUCING ACTIVITIES
AT DECEMBER 31, 19XX

	Total
Unproved oil and gas properties	$X
Proved oil and gas properties	X
	X
Accumulated depreciation, depletion, and amortization, and valuation allowances	X
Net capitalized costs	$X
Enterprise's share of equity method investees' net capitalized costs	$X

Illustration 2

COSTS INCURRED IN OIL AND GAS PROPERTY ACQUISITION,
EXPLORATION, AND DEVELOPMENT ACTIVITIES
FOR THE YEAR ENDED DECEMBER 31, 19XX

	Total	United States	Foreign Geographic Area A	Foreign Geographic Area B	Other Foreign Geographic Areas
Acquisition of properties					
—Proved	$X	$X	$X	$X	$X
—Unproved	X	X	X	X	X
Exploration costs	X	X	X	X	X
Development costs	X	X	X	X	X
Enterprise's share of equity method investees' costs of property acquisition, exploration, and development	X	X	X	X	X

Illustration 3

**RESULTS OF OPERATIONS FOR PRODUCING ACTIVITIES
FOR THE YEAR ENDED DECEMBER 31, 19XX**

	Total	United States	Foreign Geographic Area A	Foreign Geographic Area B	Other Foreign Geographic Areas
Revenues					
Sales	$ X	$ X	$ X	$ X	$ X
Transfers	X	X	X	X	X
Total	X	X	X	X	X
Production costs	(X)	(X)	(X)	(X)	(X)
Exploration expenses	(X)	(X)	(X)	(X)	(X)
Depreciation, depletion, and amortization, and valuation provisions	(X)	(X)	(X)	(X)	(X)
	X	X	X	X	X
Income tax expenses	(X)	(X)	(X)	(X)	(X)
Results of operations from producing activities (excluding corporate overhead and interest costs)	$ X	$ X	$ X	$ X	$ X
Enterprise's share of equity method investees' results of operations for producing activities	$ X	$ X	$ X	$ X	$ X

Illustration 4

RESERVE QUANTITY INFORMATION*
FOR THE YEAR ENDED DECEMBER 31, 19XX

	Total		United States		Foreign Geographic Area A		Foreign Geographic Area B		Other Foreign Geographic Areas	
	Oil	Gas	Oil	Gas	Oil	Gas	Oil	Gas	Oil	Gas
Proved developed and undeveloped reserves:										
Beginning of year	X	X	X	X	X	X	X	X	X	X
Revisions of previous estimates	X	X	X	X	X	X	X	X	X	X
Improved recovery	X	X	X	X	X	X	X	X	X	X
Purchases of minerals in place	X	X	X	X	X	X	X	X	X	X
Extensions and discoveries	X	X	X	X	X	X	X	X	X	X
Production	(X)	(X)	(X)	(X)	(X)	(X)	(X)	(X)	(X)	(X)
Sales of minerals in place	(X)	(X)	(X)	(X)	(X)	(X)	(X)	(X)	(X)	(X)
End of year	X†	X	X	X	X	X	X	X	X	X
Proved developed reserves:										
Beginning of year	X	X	X	X	X	X	X	X	X	X
End of year	X	X	X	X	X	X	X	X	X	X

689

Illustration 4 (continued)

	Total		United States		Foreign Geographic Area A		Foreign Geographic Area B		Other Foreign Geographic Areas	
	Oil	Gas	Oil	Gas	Oil	Gas	Oil	Gas	Oil	Gas
Oil and gas applicable to long-term supply agreements with governments or authorities in which the enterprise acts as producer:										
Proved reserves— end of year	X	X			X	X				
Received during the year	X	X			X	X				
Enterprise's proportional interest in reserves of investees accounted for by the equity method— end of year	X	X	X	X	X	X	X	X	X	X

*Oil reserves stated in barrels; gas reserves stated in cubic feet.

†Includes reserves of X barrels attributable to a consolidated subsidiary in which there is an X-percent minority interest.

Illustration 5

STANDARDIZED MEASURE OF DISCOUNTED FUTURE NET CASH FLOWS AND CHANGES THEREIN RELATING TO PROVED OIL AND GAS RESERVES
AT DECEMBER 31, 19XX

	Total	United States	Foreign Geographic Area A	Foreign Geographic Area B	Other Foreign Geographic Areas
Future cash inflows*	$ X	$ X	$ X	$ X	$ X
Future production and development costs*	(X)	(X)	(X)	(X)	(X)
Future income tax expenses*	(X)/X	(X)/X	(X)/X	(X)/X	(X)/X
Future net cash flows					
10% annual discount for estimated timing of cash flows	(X)	(X)	(X)	(X)	(X)
Standardized measure of discounted future net cash flows	$ X †	$ X	$ X	$ X	$ X
Enterprise's share of equity method investees' standardized measure of discounted future net cash flows	$ X	$ X	$ X	$ X	$ X

691

Illustration 5 (continued)

The following are the principal sources of change in the standardized measure of discounted future net cash flows during 19XX:

	Total	United States	Foreign Geographic Area A	Foreign Geographic Area B	Other Foreign Geographic Areas
Sales and transfers of oil and gas produced, net of production costs	$(X)				
Net changes in prices and production costs	X				
Extensions, discoveries, and improved recovery, less related costs	X				
Development costs incurred during the period					
Revisions of previous quantity estimates	(X)				
Accretion of discount	X				
Net change in income taxes	X				
Other	X				

*Future net cash flows were computed using year-end prices and costs, and year-end statutory tax rates (adjusted for permanent differences) that relate to existing proved oil and gas reserves in which the enterprise has mineral interests, including those mineral interests related to long-term supply agreements with governments for which the enterprise serves as the producer of the reserves.

†Includes $X attributable to a consolidated subsidiary in which there is an X-percent minority interest.

Appendix B

BACKGROUND INFORMATION

42. In December 1977, Statement 19 was issued by the Board. That Statement adopted a form of successful efforts accounting and required disclosure of proved oil and gas reserve quantities, capitalized costs, and costs incurred in oil and gas producing activities.

43. Before Statement 19 became effective, the Securities and Exchange Commission (SEC) issued, in August 1978, ASR No. 253, *Adoption of Requirements for Financial Accounting and Reporting Practices for Oil and Gas Producing Activities.*[11] That release (a) adopted the form of successful efforts accounting prescribed by Statement 19, (b) indicated an intention to adopt the disclosures prescribed by Statement 19 (which was subsequently done), (c) indicated an intention to adopt a form of the full cost accounting method (which was subsequently done), (d) permitted the use of either (a) or (c) for SEC reporting purposes, and (e) adopted rules requiring disclosure of certain financial and operating information beyond that required in Statement 19. The SEC took those actions because it believed that neither the full cost nor the successful efforts method provided sufficient information on the financial position and operating results of oil and gas producing enterprises. Accordingly, the SEC concluded that a new method of accounting that is based on valuations of proved oil and gas reserves and that would replace both the successful efforts and full cost accounting methods should be developed for the primary financial statements. The SEC initiated the development of that new accounting method (which it referred to as reserve recognition accounting [RRA]) by requiring supplemental disclosures on that basis. The SEC also indicated (and subsequently carried out) its intention to require the disclosure of a supplemental earnings summary to reflect estimated additions to proved reserves and changes in valuation of estimated proved reserves, based on current prices and a 10-percent discount rate. All costs associated with finding and developing such additions and all costs determined to be nonproductive during the period are deducted in determining that supplemental measure of earnings.

44. In February 1979—because Statement 19 requirements would be imposed only on enterprises not subject to SEC reporting requirements and therefore would not achieve comparability—the Board issued Statement 25, which suspended the effective date of Statement 19 as to the accounting method to be used in financial statements but not as to the disclosure requirements.

45. Further supplemental information is presently required to be disclosed by Statements 33 and 39. Those Statements require large publicly held oil and gas enterprises to report the effects of changes in general prices and changes in specific prices of certain types of assets.

46. During the development of Statement 39, the Board recognized that the accumulation of both the Board's and the SEC's disclosure requirements placed a significant burden on oil and gas producing enterprises. It recognized that the disclosures made in response to those requirements may have become unnecessarily voluminous and complex without a corresponding increase in their usefulness to the users of financial statements. Furthermore, other information, frequently suggested by some financial analysts as useful, was not presented. Accordingly, the Board indicated that it would study the usefulness of the existing and proposed disclosures and would work with the oil and gas industry, the SEC, and users to develop a single, coherent set of disclosure requirements for oil and gas producing enterprises.

47. On February 26, 1981, the SEC issued ASR No. 289, *Financial Reporting by Oil and Gas Producers,* which states that the SEC no longer considers RRA to be a potential method of accounting in the primary financial statements of oil and gas producers. That release also announced the Commission's "support of an undertaking by the Financial Accounting Standards Board to develop a comprehensive package of disclosures for those engaged in oil and gas producing activities." The Commission indicated in that release that it expected to amend its rules to be consistent with the disclosure standards for oil and gas producers to be developed by the FASB for oil and gas producers.

48. The Board added a project on disclosures about oil and gas producing activities to its agenda on March 4, 1981.

49. A task force comprising 20 people from the oil and gas industry, petroleum engineering and geological consulting firms, the financial community, the public accounting profession, and academe was formed at the outset of the project to advise the staff on technical matters encompassed in the scope of the project.

50. On May 13, 1981, the Board published the

---

[11]In April 1982, the SEC codified the relevant ASRs concerning accounting and auditing matters in Financial Reporting Release No. 1, *Codification of Financial Reporting Policies.*

FASB Invitation to Comment, *Disclosures about Oil and Gas Producing Activities.* The Board received 120 letters in response to that Invitation to Comment.

51. In August 1981, the Board conducted a public hearing on the Invitation to Comment. Twenty-eight organizations and individuals presented their views at the two-day hearing.

52. On April 15, 1982, the Board issued an FASB Exposure Draft, *Disclosures about Oil and Gas Producing Activities.* The Board received 113 letters of comment on that Exposure Draft.

53. Since the project was added to the Board's agenda, the Board held 10 open meetings at which the project's issues were discussed. The Task Force on Disclosures about Oil and Gas Producing Activities met three times with the FASB staff, and individuals serving on the task force participated in open educational Board meetings held on the project's issues. Task force members provided the Board and its staff with comments on those issues.

Appendix C

BASIS FOR CONCLUSIONS

CONTENTS

Appendix C

BASIS FOR CONCLUSIONS

Introduction

54. This appendix reviews considerations that were deemed significant by members of the Board in reaching the conclusions in this Statement. It includes reasons for accepting certain views and rejecting others. Individual Board members gave greater weight to some factors than to others.

55. The underlying causes of the problem leading to this Statement relate to some significant and unusual economic characteristics of oil and gas producing activities:

a. The principal assets are oil and gas reserves.
b. There is no necessary correlation between the costs and the values of oil and gas reserves.
c. The costs of finding specific reserves are unique.

The costs of existing reserves, therefore, are not relevant indicators of either (a) cash inflows from production and sale of those reserves or (b) cash outflows necessary to replace those reserves.

56. An important quality of information that is useful in making rational investment, credit, and similar decisions is its predictive value—specifically, its usefulness in assessing the amounts, timing, and uncertainty of prospective net cash inflows to the enterprise. Historical cost based financial statements for oil and gas producing enterprises have limited predictive value. Their usefulness is further reduced because a uniform accounting method is not required to be used for costs incurred in oil and gas producing activities.

57. The inherent limitations involved in using historical cost based information relative to mineral interests in properties have long been recognized. Various attempts have been made to standardize the industry's method of accounting for costs incurred in oil and gas producing activities. Those attempts have not been successful.

58. Other attempts have been made by the FASB and the SEC (current cost accounting and RRA) to develop disclosures to assist the user to:

a. Assess future net cash flows
b. Estimate the values or replacement costs of mineral reserves
c. Compare financial positions and operating results of enterprises in the industry

59. Those attempts have resulted in a great volume

694

of additional disclosures, particularly for publicly owned oil and gas producing enterprises. The Board's project is an attempt, by agreement with the SEC, to analyze the problem, to sort out the reasonable needs of users, and to determine what information will help to meet those needs at a reasonable cost.

60. In summary, the primary objectives of this Statement are:

a. To develop disclosure requirements that are useful and in particular would compensate, in some measure, for recognized deficiencies in the comparability and predictive value of financial statement information of oil and gas enterprises
b. To consider cost-benefit relationships of alternative disclosures and to reduce the quantity and cost of existing disclosures

Alternatives Considered

61. The Board considered four basic approaches to developing comprehensive oil and gas disclosures:

A — Historical cost based information and reserve quantity information *only*
B — Historical cost based information and reserve quantity information *plus* future estimated costs and reserve production information
C — Historical cost based information and reserve quantity information *plus* information about estimated future net cash flows relating to oil and gas reserves
D — Historical cost based information and reserve quantity information plus information about estimated future net cash flows relating to oil and gas reserves *and* an alternative measure of income based on changes in those future net cash flows

62. Most respondents to the Invitation to Comment and the Exposure Draft support the Board's conclusion in Statement 19 that for users to understand and interpret an enterprise's financial statements, information about its oil and gas producing activities must be supplemented by information about its mineral interests. The discovery of proved oil and gas reserves is a critical event in the oil and gas producing cycle, and information about those reserves and changes in them are key indicators of the success of an enterprise. That information is considered so useful in decision making that the lack of precision associated with the estimate of proved oil and gas reserve quantities is more than compensated for by the added relevance to users.

63. All four alternatives considered by the Board provide historical cost based and reserve quantity information. However, they differ on the extent to which that information is considered sufficient to meet the objectives of financial reporting for oil and gas producing activities.

Historical Cost Based Information and Reserve Quantity Information

64. Some respondents to the Invitation to Comment and the Exposure Draft support disclosure of only historical cost based information and proved oil and gas reserve quantity information (Alternative A). They believe that users can apply current costs and prices or their own estimates of future costs and prices to an extrapolation of historical production trends to estimate future net cash flows related to the enterprise's proved oil and gas reserves. Supporters of this alternative generally believe that disclosure of fair market value, discounted future net cash flows, or projections of future events or conditions relating to an enterprise's proved oil and gas reserves should not be part of financial reporting.

65. In the Board's view, historical cost based financial information and proved oil and gas reserve quantity information are crude tools for any predictive analytical process for many reasons, the most notable of which are:

a. Mineral interests in proved oil and gas reserves may have significantly different economic values because of such features as location, qualitative properties, development status, and tax status. Reserve quantity information does not give a comparable base for comparison over time or among companies.
b. Historical production trends, even if determinable, may differ significantly from management's future production plans.

66. Alternative A, then, is subject (as are all alternatives considered) to the challenge of the reliability of the proved oil and gas reserve estimates and, in addition, does not add materially to users' ability to make comparisons and to assess the future net cash flows of oil and gas producing enterprises.

Estimated Future Costs and Reserve Production Information

67. A few respondents to the Invitation to Comment and the Exposure Draft support, in addition to historical cost based information and proved oil and gas reserve quantity information, disclosure of additional information about oil and gas producing activities that would provide forecasts of (a) estimated future costs of production (lifting) and development of existing proved oil and gas reserves and (b) estimated timing of future production of those reserves (Alternative B). Supporters of this alternative generally suggest limiting the disclosure requirements for that information to a period encompass-

ing the following three to five years. This alternative is intended to allow users of the financial reports of oil and gas producing enterprises to compute estimated near-term future cash flows using their own assumptions concerning future prices and risks.

68. The lack of broad support for Alternative B seems to reflect primarily three views:

a. An objection to presenting explicit forecasts of production and costs in financial reports
b. A concern that, for data to be useful, they would have to be presented separately for each significant field
c. A belief that the data would tend to be used by only the most sophisticated industry analysts

69. The Board was dissuaded from this alternative primarily by the combination of the large volume of data to be presented and the limited number of probable users.

Information about Future Net Cash Flows

70. Some respondents to the Invitation to Comment and to the Exposure Draft supported disclosure of summary information regarding the future net cash flows associated with an enterprise's existing proved oil and gas reserves (Alternative C). This Statement reflects an Alternative C approach to developing disclosure requirements for oil and gas producing activities.

71. The Board considered various means of providing relevant summary information:

a. Fair market value
b. Estimate of discounted net cash flows based on future prices and costs and an enterprise-specific discount rate
c. Standardized measure of discounted future net cash flows with major factors separately reported

Fair Market Value

72. *Fair market value* is usually defined as the exchange price that reasonably could be expected in an arm's-length transaction between a willing buyer and a willing seller. If ascertainable, fair market value would be better than historical cost for indicating future net cash flows relating to oil and gas properties. It also would have been better than the standardized discounted future net cash flow approach required by this Statement because, among other factors, the fair market value of mineral interests in properties includes the "value" of all the various categories of reserves (proved, possible, and probable) as well as undeveloped acreage.

73. Nevertheless, the Board concluded that a requirement to disclose fair market value would be impracticable because:

a. Relatively few exchanges of oil and gas mineral interests take place.
b. Mineral interests that are exchanged tend to be interests in smaller properties that principally involve undeveloped acreage.
c. The geological characteristics of each oil and gas property are unique to that individual mineral interest.
d. The amount of information concerning sales price and stratigraphic data available to parties not directly involved in the exchange is limited because that information usually is considered confidential.

Discounted Future Net Cash Flows

74. The Board considered the use of discounted future net cash flows based on estimated future prices and costs, production timing, and an enterprise-specific discount rate as a surrogate for fair market value. The Board rejected that approach, however, for a number of reasons.

75. As a practical matter, the estimate would have to be limited to proved reserves because information about probable and possible reserves and undeveloped acreage can be little more than conjectural. Limiting the estimate to proved reserves, however, would seriously detract from the estimate as a representation of fair market value.

76. Estimates of future costs and prices are highly subjective, depending on political events (for example, price controls, tax policy, embargoes, and political upheavals) in addition to supply and demand factors. Estimates of future production are also subject to a wide range of error, and selection of a discount rate is subjectively variable due to individual assessments of political, operating, and general business risks. This combination of subjective estimating variables could not result in information with the necessary degree of verifiability and comparability required for financial reporting.

Standardized Measure of Discounted Net Cash Flows

77. The Board finally settled on a standardized measure of discounted net cash flows to achieve some of the characteristics of a fair market value measure without the extreme subjectivity inherent in either direct estimation of market value or entity-specific discounted net cash flows. Although it cannot be considered an estimate of fair market value, the standardized measure of discounted net cash flows should be responsive to some of the key variables that affect fair market value, namely, changes

in reserve quantities, selling prices, production costs, and tax rates.

78. Some respondents to the Invitation to Comment and the Exposure Draft, including financial analysts who specialize in oil and gas securities and petroleum engineers, believe that the disclosure of a standardized measure of discounted future net cash flows associated with an enterprise's proved oil and gas reserves is useful.[12] In ASR 253, the SEC required a measure based on year-end prices and costs specific to the enterprise's proved oil and gas reserves, a standard discount rate of 10 percent, and an estimate of the production timing of those reserves. The Board has adopted that approach to requiring information about future net cash flows.

79. One criticism of a standardized measure of discounted net cash flows has been that it is limited to proved reserves, omitting probable and possible reserves. The Board believes, however, that limiting the estimate to proved reserves is appropriate because:

a. Only proved reserves have been defined in a manner that has gained general acceptance by the petroleum engineering profession.
b. Information on proved reserves is already used within the industry to describe and compare oil and gas mineral interests.

Further, proved reserves ordinarily will be produced sooner than other categories of reserves and are weighted more heavily than other types of reserves in calculating discounted net cash flows. Additionally, more risk is associated with other types of reserves, and consequently the cash flows relating to those reserves probably would be discounted at a higher rate than proved reserves. Those two factors would tend to mitigate the effects of limiting the estimated discounted future net cash flows disclosed to proved reserves.

80. Disclosure of the principal components of the standardized measure of discounted future net cash flows provides users with information concerning the factors involved in making the calculation. Users then have standardized data they can adjust as necessary for their own individual estimates of future changes and risks in order to prepare their own assessments of future cash flows. In addition, disclosing both undiscounted and discounted net cash flows provides a means of comparing proved oil and gas reserves both with and without the subjec-

tivity introduced by management's estimate of production timing, although management generally is in a better position than a user to forecast both the production timing and the recovery method of the enterprise's proved oil and gas reserves.

81. Government participation in oil and gas producing activities takes various forms, ranging from participation in production (royalties, either in cash or in kind) to income taxes. As governments devise different methods of participating, problems of classification arise. For example, excise taxes are based on production or revenue and are generally classified as a part of production costs. Other taxes are based on revenues less certain costs and are generally classified as income taxes. Because of those differences in classification, a standardized measure of discounted future net cash flows relating to proved reserves must reflect income taxes to reflect all forms of taxation (those considered as costs of production and those considered as income taxes). The Board also noted that several enterprises already disclose in their annual reports the effects of income taxes on a standardized measure of estimated net cash flows relating to proved reserves.

82. The Board decided not to require disclosure of the periods in which the calculated net cash flows are expected to be realized. That type of detailed information would add some predictive value to the disclosure, but the Board did not consider the added benefits to be sufficient to justify the additional volume of information that would be included in financial reports if that requirement were adopted. Based on respondents' comments to the Exposure Draft, the Board also decided not to require disclosure by geographic area of changes in the standardized measure that occurred during the period. The Board believes that the small reduction in the feedback value of the disclosure caused by the elimination of geographic area information for the types of changes is acceptable considering the resulting large reduction in volume of information from that initially proposed in the Exposure Draft.

83. The Board was persuaded by respondents' comments that the standardized information can be useful and is, in fact, being used. The Board is concerned, at the same time, that users of financial statements understand that it is neither fair market value nor the present value of future cash flows. It is a rough surrogate for such measures, a tool to allow for a reasonable comparison of mineral reserves and changes through the use of a standardized method

---

[12] A survey of 190 oil and gas financial analysts (conducted by Edward B. Deakin and James W. Deitrick of the University of Texas at Austin) shows that 90 percent supported disclosure of reserve values. Approximately 80 percent of those supporters indicated that the disclosures should be based on specified, uniform pricing and discounting assumptions. A survey of members of the Society of Petroleum Evaluation Engineers (conducted by B. P. Huddleston & Co., Inc.) indicated that over 70 percent of the 102 respondents believe that the "present value" of proved oil and gas reserves should be reported by publicly traded companies, based on current price information. Approximately 58 percent of those who responded support the use of a standard 10-percent discount rate in that calculation.

that recognizes qualitative, quantitative, geographic, and temporal characteristics. Absent such a tool, there is no reasonable basis for comparing these most important assets and activities; values are not determinable and quantities are not comparable. In addition, the standardized measure provides users with a common base upon which they can prepare their own estimates of future cash flows.

84. Largely because of the limitations of the standardized measure, the Board rejected the presentation of an alternative measure of income based on changes in the standardized cash flows (Alternative D).

Historical Cost Based Information and Reserve Quantity Information

85. This Statement sets forth disclosure requirements for historical cost based information and reserve quantity information about oil and gas producing activities of the type presently required by the FASB and the SEC. Some of those existing disclosure requirements have been continued in this Statement, while other requirements have either been reorganized or omitted from the Board's disclosure requirements. The Board's considerations of the principal disclosures of historical cost based information and reserve quantity information are discussed below.

Accounting Method

86. Because of past SEC action and the related FASB suspension of the effective date for the accounting requirements of Statement 19, all oil and gas producing enterprises do not use a single method of accounting for costs incurred in oil and gas producing activities. Therefore, the Board has continued the requirement in Statement 25 to disclose in the financial statements the method of accounting and the manner of disposition of capitalized costs.

Capitalized Costs

87. Separately disclosing capitalized costs related to proved and unproved properties will assist users in assessing the degree of risk associated with those two different types of assets. Unproved properties have a much higher degree of risk associated with them since many of them may never result in additions to an enterprise's proved oil and gas reserves. Disclosure of the costs associated with unproved properties also helps users of an oil and gas enterprise's financial statements to assess the enterprise's efforts to maintain an inventory of properties in which it seeks to find additional oil and gas reserves and thereby to maintain or increase its existing oil and gas production level. The Board and most respondents therefore believe that it is appro-

priate to continue the requirement in Statement 19 to disclose the aggregate amount of capitalized costs and to expand it to require separate disclosure of capitalized costs related to unproved properties.

88. Some respondents suggested that capitalized costs information be required to be disclosed by geographic area to allow an evaluation of an enterprise's risks by geographic area. The Board disagrees with that suggestion because information concerning the enterprise's risks by geographic area is provided to the users of the enterprise's financial reports by the reserve quantity and standardized measure information required to be disclosed.

Costs Incurred

89. The Board and most respondents believe that it is necessary to continue the requirement in Statement 19 to disclose information about costs incurred during the period because that information indicates management's efforts to replace its existing proved reserves. Disclosure of costs by type also allows users of the financial statements to assess the emphasis of the enterprise's oil and gas producing activities because the disclosure provides information about the enterprise's efforts to find new reserves, to develop existing proved reserves, or both. The accomplishments of those efforts over time are indicated by the reserve quantity disclosures and the analysis of changes in a standardized measure of discounted future net cash flows.

90. Several respondents to the Exposure Draft suggested that costs incurred to acquire proved reserves should be disclosed separately, if significant. They believe it is useful to report the costs of acquiring mineral interests in proved reserves separately from the costs of acquiring unproved mineral leases because of the implications and risks associated with each of those types of expenditures. The Board agreed and believes the data is readily obtainable.

91. Several respondents noted that the Exposure Draft proposed that production costs information should be disclosed in both the costs incurred and results of operations information. Those respondents believe that there is no need for this duplicative disclosure of production costs and suggested that the disclosure of production costs be eliminated from the schedule of costs incurred. The Board agreed and eliminated the requirement of Statement 19 to report production costs as part of costs incurred information.

Results of Operations

92. Disclosing the results of operations for oil and gas producing activities by geographic area is useful in evaluating historical results of operations, cash

flows, and risks associated with an important portion of a vertically integrated oil and gas enterprise's activities. It is also useful in comparing the historical performance of independent exploration and production enterprises with the producing activities of integrated enterprises and in comparing the performance of one integrated enterprise with that of another.

93. The November 1981 FASB Exposure Draft, *Reporting Income, Cash Flows, and Financial Position of Business Enterprises,* stresses the relevance of separately disclosing information about different activities within complex enterprises. Analysis aimed at predicting the amount, timing, and uncertainty of future cash flows is facilitated by segregating financial information into homogeneous groups. Oil and gas producing activities of an integrated oil and gas enterprise are subject to significantly different degrees of risk than are its other activities (for example, refining and marketing). Therefore, separately reporting the results of oil and gas producing activities is likely to enhance the predictive value of the information presented by vertically integrated oil and gas producing enterprises.

94. Disclosing the results of operations for oil and gas producing activities also complements the disclosure of the standardized measure of discounted future net cash flows and changes therein. The results of operations provide historical information that may help users to confirm or correct prior expectations about the factors involved in assessing the near-term cash flow potential of the proved reserves from the trends of the historical results of operations.

95. The reasons for requiring the results of operations for oil and gas producing activities to be reported on an after-tax basis are the same as those provided for the standardized measure of discounted future net cash flows (paragraph 81). That is, there are significant differences in the total governmental participation in oil and gas producing activities and differences in the methods by which that participation is achieved (for example, different mixes of royalties, excise taxes, income taxes, and so forth). The Board believes that to provide comparable information all forms of taxation must be reflected in the disclosure.

96. This Statement requires that general corporate expenses and interest expenses not be added to or deducted from the results of operations for an enterprise's oil and gas producing activities because the allocation of those expenses would be subjective and would tend to decrease the comparability of the disclosure.

97. Some Board members and respondents expressed concern about the reliability of using a transfer price between oil and gas producing activities and other internal operations (for example, refining) for vertically integrated enterprises. However, a reliable transfer price appears to be obtainable since local regulatory and taxation authorities ordinarily require separate information about an enterprise's oil and gas producing activities. The price used to prepare that information reflects the effective price after separation of the oil and gas found in the reserves. The requirement to use established prices will increase the comparability of the information in making comparisons of the revenues and results of operations of enterprises' oil and gas producing activities.

98. Another possible transfer-pricing method considered by the Board is the wellhead price, which is the market price established at the well location where the reserves are produced (lifted). The wellhead price ordinarily is comparable to the point-of-delivery price from the producing unit, except for reserves in remote locations for which the initial processing to separate gas from oil is delayed. The Board considers the wellhead price to be less satisfactory because wellhead prices generally do not exist for reserves in remote locations.

99. The Board agreed, however, with those respondents to the Exposure Draft who suggested separate disclosure of revenues from sales and transfers to other operations of the enterprise, and revenues from sales to unaffiliated customers. That disclosure would indicate the interrelationship between the oil and gas producing activities and the enterprise's other activities. The disclosure of that information makes the disclosure of revenues from oil and gas producing activities consistent with the Statement 14 requirements for business segments.

Reserve Quantity Information

100. As previously indicated, most respondents to the Invitation to Comment and to the Exposure Draft agreed with the Board's conclusions in Statement 19 that information about quantities of oil and gas reserves is useful to understanding and interpreting the financial statements of an oil and gas producing enterprise. The discovery of reserves is a critical event in the oil and gas producing cycle, and reserves and changes in them are key indicators of the success of an enterprise.

101. Respondents also agreed with the Board's conclusions in Statement 19 that reserve quantities and changes in them should be reported separately for each geographic area in which significant reserves are located since such reporting assists in assessing the risks associated with those reserves.

102. Some governments have nationalized or otherwise taken over, in whole or in part, certain properties in which oil and gas producing enterprises previously had mineral interests. Some of those interests have been converted into long-term supply, purchase, or similar agreements with a government or a governmental authority. In some countries, oil and gas producing enterprises can obtain access to oil and gas reserves only through such agreements and not through direct acquisition of mineral interests. If an oil and gas producing enterprise participates in the operation of a property subject to such an agreement or otherwise serves as "producer" of the reserves from the property, disclosure of the reserve quantities identified with, and quantities of oil or gas received under, that type of agreement with those governments or authorities provides useful information. The fact that the reserves are available to an enterprise requires their inclusion to give a complete presentation of the enterprise's reserve position. However, because of the different nature of those agreements (that is, they do not represent direct ownership interests in reserves), those reserve quantities are to be reported separately from the enterprise's own proved reserves.

103. The requirement of Statement 19 to disclose important economic factors and significant uncertainties affecting an enterprise's proved reserves is continued because it provides information that assists users in assessing the economic resources of an oil and gas producing enterprise. Examples of this type of disclosure include expectation of unusually high development or lifting costs, the necessity to build a major pipeline or other major facility before production of the reserves can begin, or contractual obligations to produce and sell a significant portion of reserves at prices that are substantially below those at which the oil and gas could otherwise be sold.

104. Certain governments restrict the disclosure of reserves located within their jurisdiction. Disclosure of restrictions informs users about the completeness and uniformity of the reserve information presented. Therefore, the Board decided to require disclosure of the existence of any governmental restrictions that affect the completeness of reporting the reserve information.

Equity Method Investees and Minority Interests

105. An enterprise may carry out significant operations through investees to share the high risks of exploration and the high costs of development in some areas. Respondents' comments indicate that such sharing of risks and costs is increasing and that they generally favor disclosing supplemental information about equity investees' oil and gas produc-

ing activities. It is most commonly achieved by joint participation agreements without formation of a separate entity. However, if a separate entity is formed and accounted for by the equity method, information needs to be provided about the enterprise's share of the equity investees' capitalized costs, costs incurred, results of operation, proved oil and gas reserve quantities, and standardized measure of discounted future net cash flows. That information should be disclosed for the same reasons that the Board requires disclosure of similar information about an enterprise's consolidated operations—so users can obtain a meaningful understanding of all the oil and gas operations of the enterprise.

106. Several respondents to the Exposure Draft also noted that an enterprise's consolidated financial statements may include subsidiaries with significant minority interests related to oil and gas producing activities. The Board believes that unless significant minority interests in reported oil and gas producing activities are disclosed, users may overestimate the portion of future cash flows that may accrue to an enterprise's shareholders. As indicated earlier, it is important to include disclosures about equity method investees; it is equally important to include disclosures about significant minority interests in consolidated subsidiaries.

107. The Board acknowledges that disclosures about equity investees and minority interests may have implications for other industries that operate through equity investees and that have significant minority interests. Therefore, the Board may reassess the requirements to report information about equity investments and minority interests contained in this Statement upon completion of a project on consolidated financial statements, the equity method, and other procedures for accounting for investments in or other relations with affiliated entities.

Reasons for Omitting Other Disclosures

108. Other disclosures of historical cost based information suggested by respondents or required by the SEC were rejected either because they do not assist in meeting the objectives of financial reporting in a cost-beneficial manner or because their usefulness would overlap that of the disclosures required by this Statement.

109. In the Exposure Draft, the Board specifically requested comment on the usefulness of requiring operational disclosures concerning acreage. Some respondents to the Invitation to Comment and the Exposure Draft expressed the view that disclosure of the quantity of undeveloped acreage would provide some indication of the enterprise's future explora-

tion and production efforts. However, most respondents to the Exposure Draft stated that disclosure of information about undeveloped acreage should not be required by this Statement principally because: (a) the quality of the acreage and its precise location are more important than its quantity, (b) that type of detailed information would be unduly voluminous and would be considered proprietary, and (c) information that describes general physical facilities is readily available outside of financial reports. Therefore, the Board did not require the disclosure of this type of operational information.

Interim Reporting

110. The Board and the majority of respondents to the Invitation to Comment and to the Exposure Draft believe that the disclosure requirements for oil and gas producing activities should apply to only complete sets of annual financial statements. Statement 19 specifically omits from its requirements for interim statements disclosure of information about reserve quantities and costs incurred. That Statement indicates that "the Board reached that conclusion principally because problems in gathering data of that type on a timely basis become especially acute at interim reporting dates and, for some companies, the costs of that effort may be unduly burdensome" (paragraph 234). The Board believes that those reasons for not requiring information about reserve quantities and costs incurred to be disclosed in interim reports are still valid. For the same reasons, information about the results of operations and discounted future net cash flows also should not be required in interim reports.

111. The Board rescinded the requirement in Statement 19 to report information about capitalized costs for oil and gas producing activities in interim financial statements or reports because that information is not essential for an understanding of the performance and financial position of the enterprise. That rescission is consistent with the provisions of FASB Statement No. 18, *Financial Reporting for Segments of a Business Enterprise—Interim Financial Statements.*

112. However, if interim financial statements or reports are presented, this Statement requires disclosure of information about a major discovery or other event that causes a significant change from the information reported in the most recent financial statements. That approach is consistent with Statement 19, paragraph 49, and APB Opinion No. 28, *Interim Financial Reporting*, paragraph 32, both of which seek commentary relating to the effects of significant events in interim financial statements or reports.

Applicability

113. If information about an enterprise's oil and gas producing activities meets the objectives of financial reporting and possesses the necessary degree of relevance and reliability, the Board believes that the only justification for excluding a particular enterprise (or group of enterprises) from the disclosure requirements would be that the costs of providing that information exceed the benefits. Respondents to the Invitation to Comment and to the Exposure Draft raised that argument concerning the application of this Statement's requirements to enterprises that are not publicly traded and to publicly traded enterprises that do not have significant oil and gas producing activities. Furthermore, responses to the Invitation to Comment and to the Exposure Draft and testimony received at the public hearing specified the following reasons for omitting enterprises that are not publicly traded from specialized disclosure requirements:

a. The users of financial statements of enterprises that are not publicly traded are generally its owners and creditors. Those users usually are knowledgeable about the individual enterprise and its industry and frequently are directly involved in the management of the enterprise or have the ability to demand and obtain the information they need (for example, creditors).
b. In assessing the creditworthiness of enterprises that are not publicly traded, lending institutions generally require that their own staffs prepare estimates of reserve quantities and information about estimated future net cash flows from the petroleum engineer's report. Therefore, to require enterprises that are not publicly traded to report that information cannot be cost justified since those lending institutions would not be expected to use the information.

114. As previously indicated, the informational needs of the users of financial reports are the same for enterprises that are publicly traded and enterprises that are not publicly traded. However, creditors of and investors in enterprises that are not publicly traded, if they do not already have the information they require, usually are able to obtain it. Therefore, a Board requirement to report specialized information about oil and gas producing activities would provide little additional benefit to the users of those financial reports. The Board acknowledges that there are instances in which certain investors in closely held businesses may not have the ability to get the information necessary for decision making. However, comments received in the course of this project do not indicate that this is a widespread problem. The Board may need to reassess a possible requirement for enterprises that are not publicly traded to provide the information after completion of the Board's project on financial reporting by private and small public companies.

Location of Information within Financial Reports

115. The requirement to report specialized information about oil and gas producing activities and the issue of where that information should be reported were considered by the Board in 1979 as part of its consideration of Statement 25 requirements. Since that time, the Board has issued an Exposure Draft on reporting income, which offers some guidance on the placement of information within financial reports.

116. That Exposure Draft indicates that information with a different perspective from that reported in the body of the financial statements (for example, other than historical cost based information) can be reported as supplementary information. Presenting information about proved reserve quantities and estimated discounted future net cash flows as supplementary disclosures would be consistent with that suggestion. In addition, cost-benefit considerations (as well as reliability considerations) indicate that information about the reserve quantities, estimated discounted future net cash flows, and results of operations should be supplementary because the placement of information outside the financial statements may result in lower auditing costs.

117. Also, that Exposure Draft indicates that detailed information or information useful for specialized analysis of financial reports can appropriately be considered supplementary. That supports the inclusion of the whole disclosure package for oil and gas producing activities—except for the disclosure of the enterprise's accounting method—as supplementary information. Reporting specialized information on oil and gas producing activities in a single location within a financial report is a desired objective of this Statement so as to make the relationship among the different types of information easier to analyze.

118. Since the industry does not use a uniform accounting method for costs incurred in oil and gas producing activities, this Statement retains the requirements of Statement 25 to disclose the accounting method within the financial statements.

Current Cost Information

119. Most comments received in response to the Exposure Draft's specific question concerning current cost for oil and gas producing activities addressed the decision usefulness of that information. The principal reason given by respondents who do not consider current cost information useful for oil and gas mineral interests is that it is not representationally faithful. That is, the amount does not represent the cost of replacing the enterprise's mineral interests. Respondents who supported disclosure of current cost information for oil and gas producing activities generally view it as a mechanical necessity to report current cost information in their consolidated operations. In addition, some supporters of current cost information for oil and gas producing activities believe that the information is useful since it provides information about part of the change in current cost—the part attributed to price changes—even though the uncertainty concerning future exploration and development defies measurement.

120. Respondents to the Invitation to Comment and to the Exposure Draft indicated that current cost measurements of oil and gas interests presented in annual reports for 1980 and 1981 usually reflected an indexed cost, in many cases the result of applying a general price index to past costs incurred to find oil and gas reserves, not a current finding cost of the same quantity and quality of mineral interests. Therefore, the Board has modified the requirements of Statement 39 to permit enterprises to use historical cost/constant dollar measures for oil and gas mineral resource assets in presenting supplementary information on a current cost basis.

121. The effect of the modification is to require enterprises to present information on a current cost basis only if the enterprise has significant holdings of inventory and property, plant, and equipment apart from its oil and gas mineral resource assets or certain other specialized assets. However, the modifications allow enterprises to continue experimenting with developing current cost information for oil and gas mineral interests, and also allow the use of the present value of future cash flows associated with those mineral interests for enterprises that would expect to replace their oil and gas mineral interests by purchase.

Statement of Financial Accounting Standards No. 70
Financial Reporting and Changing Prices:
Foreign Currency Translation

an amendment of FASB Statement No. 33

STATUS

Issued: December 1982

Effective Date: For fiscal years ending after December 15, 1982 for which an enterprise has applied
FAS 52

Affects: Supersedes FAS 33, paragraph 22(c)
Amends FAS 33, paragraphs 22, 29(a), 30, 31, 34, 35, 35(c), 36, 39, 41, 50, 53, 56, 59, and 66

Affected by: Paragraphs 7 and 8 changed by FAS 82
Superseded by FAS 89

Statement of Financial Accounting Standards No. 71
Accounting for the Effects of Certain Types of Regulation

STATUS

Issued: December 1982

Effective Date: For fiscal years beginning after December 15, 1983

Affects: Supersedes ARB 44 (Rev.), paragraphs 8 and 9
Amends ARB 51, paragraph 6
Supersedes APB 1, paragraph 7
Supersedes APB 2, paragraph 17 and Addendum
Supersedes APB 6, paragraph 20
Amends APB 11, paragraph 6
Supersedes APB 16, paragraph 6
Supersedes APB 17, paragraph 7
Amends APB 20, paragraph 3
Supersedes APB 23, paragraph 4
Supersedes APB 24, paragraph 3
Amends APB 26, paragraph 2
Amends APB 29, paragraph 4
Amends AIN- APB 11, Interpretation No. 4
Supersedes FAS 2, paragraph 14
Supersedes FAS 4, paragraph 7
Supersedes FAS 5, paragraph 13
Amends FAS 7, paragraph 5
Supersedes FAS 13, paragraph 3
Supersedes FAS 15, paragraph 9
Supersedes FAS 16, paragraph 9
Supersedes FAS 19, paragraph 9
Supersedes FAS 22, paragraph 11
Supersedes FAS 34, paragraph 5
Supersedes FAS 43, paragraph 3
Supersedes FAS 49, paragraph 7
Supersedes FAS 51, paragraph 2
Supersedes FIN 18, paragraph 4
Supersedes FIN 22, paragraph 8
Supersedes FIN 25, paragraph 9

Affected by: Paragraph 9 amended by FAS 90, FAS 92, and FAS 121
Paragraph 10 amended by FAS 90 and FAS 121
Paragraph 13 superseded by FAS 90 and FAS 92
Paragraph 14 superseded by FAS 92
Paragraph 15 amended by FAS 90
Paragraph 18 and footnote 12 superseded by FAS 96 and FAS 109
Paragraph 34 amended by FAS 90
Paragraph 46 amended by FAS 96 and FAS 109
Footnote 6 superseded by FAS 90

Other Interpretive Pronouncement: FTB 87-2

Issues Discussed by FASB Emerging Issues Task Force (EITF)

Affects: No EITF Issues

Interpreted by: Paragraph 9 interpreted by EITF Issues No. 92-12 and 93-4
Paragraph 11 interpreted by EITF Issue No. 92-7

Related Issues: EITF Issues No. 88-21 and 97-4

SUMMARY

This Statement provides guidance in preparing general-purpose financial statements for most public utilities. Certain other companies with regulated operations that meet specified criteria are also covered.

In general, the type of regulation covered by this Statement permits rates (prices) to be set at levels intended to recover the estimated costs of providing regulated services or products, including the cost of capital (interest costs and a provision for earnings on shareholders' investments).

For a number of reasons, revenues intended to cover some costs are provided either before or after the costs are incurred. If regulation provides assurance that incurred costs will be recovered in the future, this Statement requires companies to capitalize those costs. If current recovery is provided for costs that are expected to be incurred in the future, this Statement requires companies to recognize those current receipts as liabilities.

This Statement also requires recognition, as costs of assets and increases in net income, of two types of allowable costs that include amounts not usually accepted as costs in the present accounting framework for nonregulated enterprises, as follows:

- If rates are based on allowable costs that include an allowance for the cost of funds used during construction (consisting of an equity component and a debt component), the company should capitalize and increase net income by the amount used for rate-making purposes—instead of capitalizing interest in accordance with FASB Statement No. 34, *Capitalization of Interest Cost.*
- If rates are based on allowable costs that include reasonable intercompany profits, the company should not eliminate those intercompany profits in its financial statements.

Pending completion of the Board's current project on accounting for income taxes, this Statement continues current practices of most utilities with respect to accounting for deferred income taxes. Accordingly, if the current income tax benefits (or costs) of timing differences are passed through to customers in current prices and it is probable that any resulting income taxes payable in future years will be recovered through future rates, the company should not record deferred income taxes resulting from those timing differences. However, the company should disclose the cumulative net amounts of timing differences for which deferred taxes have not been recorded.

This Statement may require that a cost be accounted for in a different manner from that required by another authoritative pronouncement. In that case, this Statement is to be followed because it reflects the economic effects of the rate-making process—effects not considered in other authoritative pronouncements. All other provisions of that other authoritative pronouncement apply to the regulated enterprise.

This Statement clarifies the application of certain other authoritative pronouncements, which is expected to result in at least two changes in general-purpose financial statements of certain public utilities. First, expected refunds of revenue collected in prior years will be charged to income in the period in which those refunds are first recognized. Second, leases will be classified (as capital or operating leases) in accordance with FASB Statement No. 13, *Accounting for Leases,* as amended. Because Statement 13 has not been applied by some utilities in the past, this Statement provides a four-year transition period before retroactive application of lease capitalization is required. Statement 13 provided a similar transition period for unregulated enterprises.

Statement of Financial Accounting Standards No. 71
Accounting for the Effects of Certain Types of Regulation

CONTENTS

INTRODUCTION

1. Regulation of an enterprise's prices (hereinafter referred to as *rates*) is sometimes based on the enterprise's costs. Regulators use a variety of mechanisms to estimate a regulated enterprise's allowable costs,[1] and they allow the enterprise to charge rates that are intended to produce revenue approximately equal to those allowable costs. Specific costs that are allowable for rate-making purposes result in revenue approximately equal to the costs.

2. In most cases, allowable costs are used as a means of estimating costs of the period during which the rates will be in effect, and there is no intent to permit recovery of specific prior costs. The process is a way of setting prices—the results of the process are reported in general-purpose financial statements in accordance with the same accounting principles that are used by unregulated enterprises.

3. Regulators sometimes include costs in allowable costs in a period other than the period in which the costs would be charged to expense by an unregulated enterprise. That procedure can create assets (future cash inflows that will result from the rate-making process), reduce assets (reductions of future cash inflows that will result from the rate-making process), or create liabilities (future cash outflows that will result from the rate-making process) for the regulated enterprise. For general-purpose financial reporting, an incurred cost for which a regulator permits recovery in a future period is accounted for like an incurred cost that is reimbursable under a cost-reimbursement-type contract.

4. Accounting requirements that are not directly related to the economic effects of rate actions may be imposed on regulated businesses by orders of regulatory authorities and occasionally by court decisions or statutes. This does not necessarily mean that those accounting requirements conform with generally accepted accounting principles. For example, a regulatory authority may order an enterprise to capitalize[2] and amortize a cost that would be charged to income currently by an unregulated enterprise. Unless capitalization of that cost is appropriate under this Statement, generally accepted accounting principles require the regulated enterprise to charge the cost to income currently.

STANDARDS OF FINANCIAL ACCOUNTING AND REPORTING

Scope

5. This Statement applies to general-purpose

---

[1]The term *allowable costs* is used throughout this Statement to refer to all costs for which revenue is intended to provide recovery. Those costs can be actual or estimated. In that context, allowable costs include interest cost and amounts provided for earnings on shareholders' investments.

[2]*Capitalize* is used in this Statement to indicate that the cost would be recorded as the cost of an asset. That procedure is often referred to as "deferring a cost," and the resulting asset is sometimes described as a "deferred cost."

external financial statements of an enterprise that has regulated operations that meet all of the following criteria:

a. The enterprise's rates for regulated services or products provided to its customers are established by or are subject to approval by an independent, third-party regulator or by its own governing board empowered by statute or contract to establish rates that bind customers.[3]
b. The regulated rates are designed to recover the specific enterprise's costs of providing the regulated services or products.
c. In view of the demand for the regulated services or products and the level of competition, direct and indirect, it is reasonable to assume that rates set at levels that will recover the enterprise's costs can be charged to and collected from customers. This criterion requires consideration of anticipated changes in levels of demand or competition during the recovery period for any capitalized costs.

6. If some of an enterprise's operations are regulated and meet the criteria of paragraph 5, this Statement shall be applied to only that portion of the enterprise's operations.

7. Authoritative accounting pronouncements that apply to enterprises in general also apply to regulated enterprises. However, enterprises subject to this Statement shall apply it instead of any conflicting provisions of standards in other authoritative pronouncements.[4]

8. This Statement does not apply to accounting for price controls that are imposed by governmental action in times of emergency, high inflation, or other unusual conditions. Nor does it cover accounting for contracts in general. However, if the terms of a contract between an enterprise and its customer are subject to regulation and the criteria of paragraph 5 are met with respect to that contract, this Statement shall apply.

General Standards of Accounting for the Effects of Regulation

9. Rate actions of a regulator can provide reasonable assurance of the existence of an asset. An enterprise shall capitalize all or part of an incurred cost[5] that would otherwise be charged to expense if both of the following criteria are met:

a. It is probable[6] that future revenue in an amount at least equal to the capitalized cost will result from inclusion of that cost in allowable costs for rate-making purposes.
b. Based on available evidence, the future revenue will be provided to permit recovery of the previously incurred cost rather than to provide for expected levels of similar future costs. If the revenue will be provided through an automatic rate-adjustment clause, this criterion requires that the regulator's intent clearly be to permit recovery of the previously incurred cost.

10. Rate actions of a regulator can reduce or eliminate the value of an asset. If a regulator excludes all or part of a cost from allowable costs and it is not probable that the cost will be included as an allowable cost in a future period, the cost cannot be expected to result in future revenue through the rate-making process. Accordingly, the carrying amount of any related asset shall be reduced to the extent that the asset has been impaired. Whether the asset has been impaired shall be judged the same as for enterprises in general.

11. Rate actions of a regulator can impose a liability on a regulated enterprise. Such liabilities are usually obligations to the enterprise's customers. The following are the usual ways in which liabilities can be imposed and the resulting accounting:

a. A regulator may require refunds to customers.[7] Refunds that meet the criteria of paragraph 8 (accrual of loss contingencies) of FASB State-

---

[3]The appropriate structure for setting accounting standards for state and local governmental units is currently under discussion. The FASB is proposing no change with respect to the applicability or use of its pronouncements in the governmental area until that matter is resolved.

[4]For example, a regulator might authorize a regulated enterprise to incur a major research and development cost because the cost is expected to benefit future customers. The regulator might also direct that cost to be capitalized and amortized as an allowable cost over the period of expected benefit. If the criteria of paragraph 9 of this Statement were met, the enterprise would capitalize that cost even though FASB Statement No. 2, *Accounting for Research and Development Costs*, requires such costs to be charged to income currently. Statement 2 would still apply to accounting for other research and development costs of the regulated enterprise, as would the disclosure requirements of Statement 2.

[5]An *incurred cost* is "a cost arising from cash paid out or obligation to pay for an acquired asset or service, a loss from any cause that has been sustained and has been or must be paid for" (Eric L. Kohler, *A Dictionary for Accountants*, 5th ed. [Englewood Cliffs, N.J.: Prentice-Hall, Inc., 1975], p. 253).

[6]The term *probable* is used in this Statement with its usual general meaning, rather than in a specific technical sense, and refers to that which can reasonably be expected or believed on the basis of available evidence or logic but is neither certain nor proved (*Webster's New World Dictionary of the American Language*, 2d college ed. [New York and Cleveland: World Publishing Company, 1972], p. 1132). That is the meaning referred to by FASB Concepts Statement No. 3, *Elements of Financial Statements of Business Enterprises.*

[7]Refunds can be paid to the customers who paid the amounts being refunded; however, they are usually provided to current customers by reducing current charges.

ment No. 5, *Accounting for Contingencies,* shall be recorded as liabilities and as reductions of revenue or as expenses of the regulated enterprise.

b. A regulator can provide current rates intended to recover costs that are expected to be incurred in the future with the understanding that if those costs are not incurred future rates will be reduced by corresponding amounts. If current rates are intended to recover such costs and the regulator requires the enterprise to remain accountable for any amounts charged pursuant to such rates and not yet expended for the intended purpose,[8] the enterprise shall not recognize as revenues amounts charged pursuant to such rates. Those amounts shall be recognized as liabilities and taken to income only when the associated costs are incurred.

c. A regulator can require that a gain or other reduction of net allowable costs be given to customers over future periods. That would be accomplished, for rate-making purposes, by amortizing the gain or other reduction of net allowable costs over those future periods and reducing rates to reduce revenues in approximately the amount of the amortization. If a gain or other reduction of net allowable costs is to be amortized over future periods for rate-making purposes, the regulated enterprise shall not recognize that gain or other reduction of net allowable costs in income of the current period. Instead, it shall record it as a liability for future reductions of charges to customers that are expected to result.

12. Actions of a regulator can eliminate a liability only if the liability was imposed by actions of the regulator.

13. Appendix B illustrates the application of the general standards of accounting for the effects of regulation.

Specific Standards Derived from the General Standards

14. The following specific standards are derived from the general standards in paragraphs 9-12. The specific standards shall not be used as guidance for other applications of those general standards.

Allowance for Funds Used during Construction

15. In some cases, a regulator requires an enterprise subject to its authority to capitalize, as part of the cost of plant and equipment, the cost of financing construction as financed partially by borrowings and partially by equity. A computed interest cost and a designated cost of equity funds are capitalized, and net income for the current period is increased by a corresponding amount. After the construction is completed, the resulting capitalized cost is the basis for depreciation and unrecovered investment for rate-making purposes. In such cases, the amounts capitalized for rate-making purposes as part of the cost of acquiring the assets shall be capitalized for financial reporting purposes instead of the amount of interest that would be capitalized in accordance with FASB Statement No. 34, *Capitalization of Interest Cost.*[9] The income statement shall include an item of other income, a reduction of interest expense, or both, in a manner that indicates the basis for the amount capitalized.

Intercompany Profit[10]

16. Profit on sales to regulated affiliates shall not be eliminated in general-purpose financial statements[11] if both of the following criteria are met:

a. The sales price is reasonable.
b. It is probable that, through the rate-making process, future revenue approximately equal to the sales price will result from the regulated affiliate's use of the products.

17. The sales price usually shall be considered reasonable if the price is accepted or not challenged by the regulator that governs the regulated affiliate. Otherwise, reasonableness shall be considered in light of the circumstances. For example, reasonableness might be judged by the return on investment earned by the manufacturing or construction operations or by a comparison of the transfer prices with prices available from other sources.

Other Specific Standards

Accounting for Income Taxes

18. Items of revenue and expense are sometimes

---

[8]The usual mechanism used by regulators for this purpose is to require the regulated enterprise to record the anticipated cost as a liability in its regulatory accounting records.

[9]Statement 34 requires capitalization of interest cost on certain qualifying assets. The amount capitalized is the portion of the interest cost incurred during the period that theoretically could have been avoided if the expenditures had not been made.

[10]The term *intercompany profit* is used in this Statement to include both profits on sales from one company to another within a consolidated or affiliated group and profits on sales from one operation of a company to another operation of the same company.

[11]ARB No. 51, *Consolidated Financial Statements,* requires that profit on sales of assets remaining in the consolidated group be eliminated in consolidated financial statements. APB Opinion No. 18, *The Equity Method of Accounting for Investments in Common Stock,* effectively extends that requirement to affiliated entities reported on the equity method.

taxable or deductible in periods other than the periods in which those items are recognized for financial reporting purposes. In some cases, a regulator does not include the income tax effect of certain transactions in allowable costs in the period in which the transactions are reported but includes income taxes related to those transactions in allowable costs in the period in which the taxes become payable. In such cases, if it is probable that income taxes payable in future years because of net reversal of timing differences will be recovered through rates based on taxes payable at that time, the enterprise shall record neither the deferred income taxes[12] that result from those timing differences nor the related asset (the probable future benefits that will result from payment of the taxes). However, the enterprise shall disclose the cumulative net amount of income tax timing differences for which deferred income taxes have not been provided. That disclosure supplements the requirements of paragraph 63 of Opinion 11 for disclosure of operating loss carryforwards, significant amounts of other unused deductions or credits, and reasons for significant variations in the customary relationships between income tax expense and pretax accounting income. Except as provided in this paragraph, regulated enterprises shall apply the requirements of Opinion 11.

Other Disclosure

19. For refunds that are recognized in a period other than the period in which the related revenue was recognized and that have a material effect on net income, the enterprise shall disclose the effect on net income and indicate the years in which the related revenue was recognized. Such effect may be disclosed by including it, net of related income taxes, as a line item in the income statement. However, that item shall not be presented as an extraordinary item.

20. In some cases, a regulator may permit an enterprise to include a cost that would be charged to expense by an unregulated enterprise as an allowable cost over a period of time by amortizing that cost for rate-making purposes, but the regulator does not include the unrecovered amount in the rate base. That procedure does not provide a return on investment during the recovery period. If recovery of such major costs is provided without a return on investment during the recovery period, the enterprise shall disclose the remaining amounts of such assets and the remaining recovery period applicable to them.

Amendments to Existing Pronouncements

21. Appendix A lists the amendments to existing pronouncements that result from this Statement.

Effective Date and Transition

22. This Statement shall be effective for fiscal years beginning after December 15, 1983. Earlier application is encouraged. Accounting changes adopted to conform to the provisions of this Statement shall be applied retroactively, except that:

a. Previously issued financial statements shall not be restated for changes in accounting for refunds.
b. Leases for which the inception[13] is after December 31, 1982 shall be classified in accordance with FASB Statement No. 13, *Accounting for Leases,* in financial statements commencing with initial application of this Statement. Leases for which the inception of the lease is before January 1, 1983 may be classified as they would have been classified before this Statement was issued until fiscal years beginning after December 15, 1986. Commencing no later than the first fiscal year beginning after December 15, 1986, those leases shall be retroactively classified in accordance with Statement 13 as amended.

23. If leases are not retroactively classified in accordance with Statement 13 in financial statements for fiscal years beginning after December 15, 1983 and before December 15, 1986 as permitted by paragraph 22(b), lessees shall disclose the amounts of additional capitalized leased assets and lease obligations that would be included in each balance sheet presented if Statement 13 had been applied retroactively.

24. In the year that this Statement is first applied, the financial statements shall disclose the nature of any restatement and its effect on income before extraordinary items, net income, and related per-share amounts[14] for each year restated. If retroactive restatement of all years presented is not practicable, the financial statements shall be restated for as many consecutive years as is practicable, and the cumulative effect of applying this Statement shall be included in determining net income of the earliest year restated (not necessarily the earliest year presented). If it is not practicable to restate any prior year, the cumulative effect shall be included in net income in the year in which this Statement is first applied. (See paragraph 20 of APB Opinion No. 20,

---

[12]APB Opinion No. 11, *Accounting for Income Taxes,* requires comprehensive interperiod allocation of the income tax effect of timing differences, that is, differences between the timing of income or expense recognition in financial statements and in income tax returns.

[13]The inception of a lease is defined in FASB Statement No. 23, *Inception of the Lease.*

[14]The effect on related per-share amounts need not be disclosed if the enterprise does not disclose earnings per share.

Accounting Changes.) The effect on income before extraordinary items, net income, and related per-share amounts[15] of applying this Statement in a year in which the cumulative effect is included in determining that year's net income shall be disclosed for that year.

> The provisions of this Statement need
> not be applied to immaterial items.

This Statement was adopted by the affirmative votes of four members of the Financial Accounting Standards Board. Messrs. Block, Kirk, and Sprouse dissented.

Mr. Block dissents to the issuance of this Statement. He believes that the regulatory environment as it exists today does not provide the necessary assurance of realization of future revenues to justify the standards in this Statement.

In his opinion, the creation of an asset by a regulator requires, at a minimum, an exclusive franchise to deliver goods and services for which demand is insensitive to price. This means that the goods and services must be necessities and that no alternative goods and services exist as competition. Further, the creation of long-lived assets requires assurance that the regulatory environment will remain unchanged for long periods. The nature of assets created by a regulator (future amounts receivable from customers) would appear to require assurance that the customers will exist, the goods and services will be delivered to customers, and the customers will pay the decreed rates. Mr. Block does not believe that rate regulators can provide such assurances in the industries to which this Statement is likely to be applied. Because of those beliefs, Mr. Block concludes that the rate-making process should have no bearing on principles for cost capitalization and loss recognition. Those principles should be the same for rate-regulated enterprises as they are for unregulated enterprises.

Mr. Block further believes that the assets created by regulation under this Statement are merely future accounts receivable for future sales. While he is opposed to recognizing such receivables, he notes that APB Opinion No. 21, *Interest on Receivables and Payables,* requires discounting of long-term receivables on which there is no stated interest rate or the stated rate is unreasonable. Thus, in his view, if such receivables are to be recognized, discounting at market rates of return should be required.

Mr. Kirk dissents to the issuance of this Statement because he believes the immediate increases in income resulting from the capitalization of costs imputed for equity funds used during construction (paragraph 15) and intercompany profit (paragraphs 16 and 17) are not valid reflections of the economics of rate regulation or in accordance with other generally accepted accounting principles. Unlike other allowable costs, imputed costs have not been incurred. In Mr. Kirk's opinion, even if capitalization is deemed appropriate for financial reporting purposes, income should not be recognized. The income related to allowable but imputed costs should be recognized when the rates covering the costs are charged to customers, not before.

Mr. Sprouse dissents primarily because he does not agree with the thrust of paragraph 11 related to liabilities. He agrees that a regulator can impose a liability on a regulated enterprise by requiring the enterprise to make refunds to its customers (paragraph 11(a)). In his opinion, however, "refunds" involve reductions in existing assets—either cash settlements or lump-sum deductions from the amounts due from customers. Reductions in future rates do not "refund" anything and, therefore, do not create a liability. Indeed, reductions in future rates do not obligate a regulated enterprise to transfer assets or use them in any way that would not be required in the absence of those reductions. Of course, a sufficiently severe reduction in future rates might trigger the need to recognize impairment of assets.

In Mr. Sprouse's view, paragraph 11(b) tends to confuse the use of a formula that a regulator might properly use to set reasonably stable rates with real, often sporadic, economic events, the effects of which should be recognized in financial statements if and when they have actually occurred. In setting rates, a regulator may include a "provision for noninsurance" among the allowable costs, but that does not create a present obligation to repair unusual storm damage that has not yet occurred (paragraphs 11(b), 38, and 39). If over a period of time the amounts of uninsured losses are sufficiently less than the "provisions for noninsurance" included in allowable costs, the regulator may reduce or eliminate future allowed provisions and reduce rates accordingly. As explained in the previous paragraph, however, possible future rate reductions do not create a liability. The possibility that sometime in the future the regulator might require cash refunds to customers to reduce or eliminate the cumulative "provision for noninsurance" is too remote to be recognized as a liability.

Similarly, in a formula designed to maintain reasonably stable rates, a regulatory agency may wish

---

[15]See footnote 14.

to spread a gain on early extinguishment of debt over some arbitrary period, but that does not create a present obligation for the regulated enterprise to transfer assets or to use them in any way that would not be required in the absence of such a gain (paragraphs 11(c) and 35-37).

Mr. Sprouse does agree that, to the extent that there is adequate evidence that the rates set by a regulator will cause a specific cost or other amount to be recovered through future incremental revenues, the regulated enterprise has an asset or asset enhancement (a quasi-receivable) that is properly measured by that incurred cost or other amount. Accordingly, he agrees that those circumstances may call for capitalizing (a) unusual storm losses, prop-erty abandonments, plant conversions, and similar costs that have occurred (paragraph 9); (b) an imputed cost of equity funds (paragraph 15); and (c) intercompany profits included in transfer prices to affiliates (paragraphs 16 and 17).

Messrs. Kirk and Sprouse also dissent because they believe the amendment to APB Opinion 30 in paragraph 19 of this Statement that suggests that refunds be reported in income net of taxes but not as extraordinary items is unrelated to the economics of rate regulation and therefore inappropriate. They see no reason why a potentially recurring charge to income should be singled out from all other recurring or even unusual items for this special treatment.

Members of the Financial Accounting Standards Board:

Donald J. Kirk,	John W. March	Robert T. Sprouse
Chairman	Robert A. Morgan	Ralph E. Walters
Frank E. Block	David Mosso	

Appendix A

AMENDMENTS TO EXISTING PRONOUNCEMENTS

25. This Statement supersedes the Addendum, *Accounting Principles for Regulated Industries,* to APB Opinion 2.

26. Paragraph 7 provides for this Statement to be applied by enterprises that are subject to it instead of conflicting provisions of other authoritative pronouncements. The Board sees no need for references to this Statement in either existing pronouncements or future authoritative pronouncements. That conclusion requires the following amendments to existing pronouncements:

a. ARB No. 44 (Revised), *Declining-Balance Depreciation,* as amended by APB Opinion No. 6, *Status of Accounting Research Bulletins.* Delete paragraphs 8 and 9.

b. ARB 51. Delete the last sentence of paragraph 6.

c. APB Opinion No. 1, *New Depreciation Guidelines and Rules.* Delete paragraph 7.

d. APB Opinion No. 2, *Accounting for the "Investment Credit."* Delete paragraph 17.

e. APB Opinion 11. In the second sentence of paragraph 6, delete the words "(a) to regulated industries in those circumstances where the standards described in the Addendum (which remains in effect) to APB Opinion No. 2 are met and (b)."

f. APB Opinion No. 16, *Business Combinations.* Delete paragraph 6.

g. APB Opinion No. 17, *Intangible Assets.* Delete paragraph 7.

h. APB Opinion 20. Delete the last two sentences of paragraph 3.

i. APB Opinion No. 23, *Accounting for Income Taxes—Special Areas.* Delete paragraph 4.

j. APB Opinion No. 24, *Accounting for Income Taxes.* Delete paragraph 3.

k. APB Opinion No. 26, *Early Extinguishment of Debt.* Delete the last sentence of paragraph 2.

l. APB Opinion No. 29, *Accounting for Nonmonetary Transactions.* In the first sentence following subparagraph 4(d), delete the words "applies to regulated companies in accordance with the Addendum to APB Opinion No. 2, *Accounting for the Investment Credit,* 1962 and it."

m. FASB Statement No. 2, *Accounting for Research and Development Costs.* Delete paragraph 14.

n. FASB Statement No. 4, *Reporting Gains and Losses from Extinguishment of Debt.* Delete paragraph 7.

o. FASB Statement 5. Delete paragraph 13.

p. FASB Statement No. 7, *Accounting and Reporting by Development Stage Enterprises.* Delete the second sentence of paragraph 5.

q. FASB Statement 13. Delete paragraph 3.

r. FASB Statement No. 15, *Accounting by Debtors and Creditors for Troubled Debt Restructurings.* Delete paragraph 9.

s. FASB Statement No. 16, *Prior Period Adjustments.* Delete paragraph 9.

t. FASB Statement No. 19, *Financial Accounting and Reporting by Oil and Gas Producing Companies.* Delete paragraph 9.

u. FASB Statement No. 22, *Changes in the Provisions of Lease Agreements Resulting from Refundings of Tax-Exempt Debt.* Delete paragraph 11.

v. FASB Statement 34. Delete paragraph 5.

w. FASB Statement No. 43, *Accounting for Compensated Absences.* Delete paragraph 3.

x. FASB Statement No. 49, *Accounting for Product Financing Arrangements.* Delete paragraph 7.

y. FASB Statement No. 51, *Financial Reporting by Cable Television Companies.* Delete paragraph 2.

z. FASB Interpretation No. 18, *Accounting for Income Taxes in Interim Periods.* Delete paragraph 4.

aa. FASB Interpretation No. 22, *Applicability of Indefinite Reversal Criteria to Timing Differences.* Delete paragraph 8.

bb. FASB Interpretation No. 25, *Accounting for an Unused Investment Tax Credit.* Delete paragraph 9.

Appendix B

APPLICATION OF GENERAL STANDARDS TO SPECIFIC SITUATIONS

27. This appendix provides guidance for application of this Statement to some specific situations. The guidance does not address all possible applications of this Statement. All of the examples assume that the enterprise meets the criteria in paragraph 5 of this Statement; thus, recovery of any cost is probable if that cost is designated for future recovery by the regulator. The examples also assume that the items addressed are material. The provisions of this Statement need not be applied to immaterial items.

28. Specific situations discussed in this appendix are:

	Paragraph Numbers
Intangible assets	29—30
Accounting changes	31—32
Recovery of costs without return on investment	33—34
Early extinguishment of debt	35—37
Accounting for contingencies	38—39
Accounting for leases	40—43
Revenue collected subject to refund	44—45
Refunds to customers	46—47
Accounting for compensated absences	48—49

Intangible Assets

29. Opinion 17 requires that the cost of an intangible asset acquired after October 30, 1970 be amortized over the shorter of its estimated useful life or 40 years. That Opinion also requires that a company continually evaluate the period of amortization to determine whether later events and circumstances warrant a revised estimate of the useful life and whether the unamortized cost should be reduced significantly by a charge to income. For rate-making purposes, a regulator may permit an enterprise to amortize purchased goodwill over a specified period. In other cases, a regulator may direct an enterprise not to amortize goodwill acquired in a business combination after October 30, 1970 or to write off that goodwill.

30. If the regulator permits the goodwill to be amortized over a specific time period as an allowable cost for rate-making purposes, the regulator's action provides reasonable assurance of the existence of an asset (paragraph 9). The goodwill would then be amortized for financial reporting purposes over the period during which it will be allowed for rate-making purposes. If the regulator excludes amortization of goodwill from allowable costs for rate-making purposes, either by not permitting amortization or by directing the enterprise to write off the goodwill, the value of the goodwill may be reduced or eliminated (paragraph 10). If there is no indication that the amortization will be allowed in a subsequent period, the goodwill would be amortized for financial reporting purposes and continually evaluated to determine whether the unamortized cost should be reduced significantly by a charge to income in accordance with Opinion 17.

Accounting Changes

31. Opinion 20 defines various types of accounting changes and establishes guidelines for reporting each type. Other authoritative pronouncements specify the manner of reporting initial application of those pronouncements.

32. If a regulated enterprise changes accounting methods and the change does not affect costs that are allowable for rate-making purposes, the regulated enterprise would apply the change in the same manner as would an unregulated enterprise. Capitalization of leases with no income statement effect (paragraphs 40-43) is an example of that type of change. If a regulated enterprise changes accounting methods and the change affects allowable costs for rate-making purposes, the change generally would be implemented in the way that it is implemented for regulatory purposes. A change in the method of accounting for research and development costs, either from a policy of capitalization and amortization to one of charging those costs to expense as incurred or vice versa, is an example of that type of change.

Recovery of Costs without Return on Investment

33. In some cases, a regulator may approve rates that are intended to recover an incurred cost over an extended period without a return on the unrecovered cost during the recovery period.

34. The regulator's action provides reasonable assurance of the existence of an asset (paragraph 9). Accordingly, the regulated enterprise would capitalize the cost and amortize it over the period during which it will be allowed for rate-making purposes. That cost would not be recorded at discounted present value. If the amounts are material, the disclosures specified in paragraph 20 of this Statement would be furnished.

Early Extinguishment of Debt

35. Opinion 26 requires recognition in income of a gain or loss on an early extinguishment of debt in the period in which the debt is extinguished. For rate-making purposes, the difference between the enterprise's net carrying amount of the extinguished debt and the reacquisition price may be amortized as an adjustment of interest expense over some future period.

36. If the debt is reacquired for an amount in excess of the enterprise's net carrying amount, the regulator's decision to increase future rates by amortizing the difference for rate-making purposes provides reasonable assurance of the existence of an asset (paragraph 9). Accordingly, the regulated enterprise would capitalize the excess cost and amortize it over the period during which it will be allowed for rate-making purposes.

37. If the debt is reacquired for an amount that is less than the enterprise's net carrying amount, the regulator's decision to reduce future rates by amortizing the difference for rate-making purposes imposes a liability on the regulated enterprise (paragraph 11(c)). Accordingly, the enterprise would record the difference as a liability and amortize it over the period during which permitted rates will be reduced.

Accounting for Contingencies

38. Statement 5 specifies criteria for recording estimated losses from loss contingencies. A regulator may direct a regulated enterprise to include an amount for a contingency in allowable costs for rate-making purposes even though the amount does not meet the criteria of Statement 5 for recording. For example, a regulator may direct a regulated enterprise to include an amount for repairs of expected future uninsured storm damage.

39. If the regulator requires the enterprise to remain accountable for any amounts charged pursuant to such rates and not yet expended for the intended purpose, the resulting increased charges to customers create a liability (paragraph 11(b)). If a cost to repair storm damage is not subsequently incurred, the increased charges will have to be refunded to customers through future rate reductions. Accordingly, the regulated enterprise would recognize the amounts charged pursuant to such rates as liabilities rather than as revenues. If a cost to repair storm damage is subsequently incurred, the enterprise would charge that cost to expense and reduce the liabilities at that time by recognizing income in amounts equal to the cost.

Accounting for Leases

40. Statement 13, as amended, specifies criteria for classification of leases and the method of accounting for each type of lease. For rate-making purposes, a lease may be treated as an operating lease even though the lease would be classified as a capital lease under the criteria of Statement 13. In effect, the amount of the lease payment is included in allowable costs as rental expense in the period it covers.

41. For financial reporting purposes, the classification of the lease is not affected by the regulator's actions. The regulator cannot eliminate an obligation that was not imposed by the regulator (paragraph 12). Also, by including the lease payments as allowable costs, the regulator sets rates that will provide revenue approximately equal to the combined amount of the capitalized leased asset and interest on the lease obligation over the term of the lease and, thus, provides reasonable assurance of the existence of an asset (paragraph 9). Accordingly, regulated enterprises would classify leases in accordance with Statement 13 as amended.

42. The nature of the expense elements related to a capitalized lease (amortization of the leased asset and interest on the lease obligation) is not changed by the regulator's action; however, the timing of expense recognition related to the lease would be modified to conform to the rate treatment. Thus, amortization of the leased asset would be modified so that the total of interest on the lease obligation and amortization of the leased asset would equal the rental expense that was allowed for rate-making purposes.

43. The Board notes that generally accepted accounting principles do not require interest expense or amortization of leased assets to be classified as separate items in an income statement. For example, the amounts of amortization of capitalized leased nuclear fuel and interest on the related lease obliga-

tion could be combined with other costs and displayed as "fuel cost." However, the disclosure of total interest cost incurred, required by Statement 34, would include the interest on that lease obligation; and the disclosure of the total amortization charge, required by Statement 13, would include amortization of that leased asset.

Revenue Collected Subject to Refund

44. In some cases, a regulated enterprise is permitted to bill requested rate increases before the regulator has ruled on the request.

45. When the revenue is originally recorded, the criteria in paragraph 8 of Statement 5 would determine whether a provision for estimated refunds should be accrued as a loss contingency. That provision would be adjusted subsequently if the estimate of the refund changes (paragraph 11(a)).[16]

Refunds to Customers

46. Statement 16 limits prior period adjustments (other than those that result from reporting accounting changes) to corrections of errors, adjustments that result from realization of income tax benefits of preacquisition operating loss carryforwards of purchased subsidiaries, and adjustments related to prior interim periods of the current fiscal year.

47. In accordance with Statement 16, estimated refunds that were not previously accrued would be charged to income in the first period in which they meet the criteria for accrual (paragraph 8 of Statement 5). If the amounts are material, the disclosures specified in paragraph 19 of this Statement would be furnished.

Accounting for Compensated Absences

48. Statement 43 specifies criteria for accrual of a liability for employees' compensation for future absences. For rate-making purposes, compensation for employees' absences may be included in allowable costs when the compensation is paid.

49. The liability, if any, would be accrued in accordance with Statement 43 because rate actions of the regulator cannot eliminate obligations that were not imposed by the regulator (paragraph 12). By including the accrued compensation in future allowable costs on an as-paid basis, the regulator provides reasonable assurance of the existence of an asset. The asset is the probable future benefit (increased revenue) that will result from the regulatory treatment of the subsequent payment of the liability (paragraph 9). Accordingly, the enterprise also would record the asset that results from the regulator's actions.

---

[16]Revenue collected subject to refund is similar to sales with warranty obligations. Paragraph 25 of Statement 5 states that "inability to make a reasonable estimate of the amount of a warranty obligation at the time of sale because of significant uncertainty about possible claims . . . precludes accrual and, if the range of possible loss is wide, may raise a question about whether a sale should be recorded. . . ." Similarly, if the range of possible refund is wide and the amount of the refund cannot be reasonably estimated, there may be a question about whether it would be misleading to recognize the provisional revenue increase as income.

Appendix C

BASIS FOR CONCLUSIONS

CONTENTS

Appendix C

BASIS FOR CONCLUSIONS

Introduction

50. This appendix discusses factors deemed significant by members of the Board in reaching the conclusions in this Statement. It includes descriptions of the various alternatives considered and the Board's reasons for accepting some and rejecting others. Individual Board members gave greater weight to some factors than to others.

Relationship of Regulatory-Prescribed Accounting to Generally Accepted Accounting Principles

51. The FASB Discussion Memorandum, *Effect of Rate Regulation on Accounting for Regulated Enterprises,* presented a threshold issue: "Should accounting prescribed by regulatory authorities be considered in and of itself generally accepted for purposes of financial reporting by rate-regulated enterprises?"

52. Virtually all respondents to the Discussion Memorandum indicated that accounting prescribed by regulatory authorities should not be considered in and of itself generally accepted for purposes of

financial reporting by rate-regulated enterprises. Respondents noted that the function of accounting is to report economic conditions and events. Unless an accounting order indicates the way a cost will be handled for rate-making purposes, it causes no economic effects that would justify deviation from the generally accepted accounting principles applicable to business enterprises in general. The mere issuance of an accounting order not tied to rate treatment does not change an enterprise's economic resources or obligations. In other words, the economic effect of regulatory decisions—not the mere existence of regulation—is the pervasive factor that determines the application of generally accepted accounting principles.

53. Respondents also noted that regulatory-prescribed accounting has not been considered generally accepted per se in the past.

54. The Board concluded that regulatory-prescribed accounting should not be considered generally accepted per se, but rather that the Board should specify how generally accepted accounting principles apply in the regulatory environment.

55. Some respondents to the FASB Exposure Draft, *Accounting for the Effects of Regulation of an Enterprise's Prices Based on Its Costs,* suggested that the Board clarify the relationship of this State-

ment to an enterprise's regulatory accounting and to regulators' actions. This Statement does not address an enterprise's regulatory accounting. Regulators may require regulated enterprises to maintain their accounts in a form that permits the regulator to obtain the information needed for regulatory purposes. This Statement neither limits a regulator's actions nor endorses them. Regulators' actions are based on many considerations. Accounting addresses the effects of those actions. This Statement merely specifies how the effects of different types of rate actions are reported in general-purpose financial statements.

Economic Effects of Regulation

56. The second threshold issue in the Discussion Memorandum was: "Does rate regulation introduce an economic dimension in some circumstances that should affect the application of generally accepted accounting principles to rate-regulated enterprises?"

57. Most respondents to the Discussion Memorandum indicated that rate regulation does introduce such an economic dimension in some circumstances. Respondents cited the cause-and-effect relationship of costs and revenues as the principal economic effect of regulation that affects accounting for regulated enterprises. They noted that cost might be one factor used by unregulated enterprises to establish prices, but it would often not be the most important factor. Usually, prices are limited by the market. An unregulated enterprise might desire to price its goods or services at a level that would recover all costs and a reasonable profit; however, the market might not permit that price. Alternatively, an unregulated enterprise might be able to increase its prices and its profit if competition does not limit its prices. In either case, cost often is not the principal determinant of prices. In contrast, for an enterprise with prices regulated on the basis of its costs, allowable costs are the principal factor that influences its prices.

58. The economic effect cited by most respondents is the ability of a regulatory action to create a future economic benefit—the essence of an asset. For example, consider a regulated enterprise that incurs costs to repair damage caused by a major storm. If the regulator approves recovery of the costs through rates over some future period or is expected to do so, the rate action of the regulator creates a new asset that offsets the reduction in the damaged asset. The enterprise has probable future economic benefits—the additional revenue that will result from including the cost in allowable costs for rate-making purposes. The future benefits are obtained or controlled by the enterprise as a result of a past event—incurring the cost that results in the rate order. Thus, the criteria of Concepts Statement 3 for an asset are met.

59. Most respondents that opposed special accounting for the effects of regulation cited the need for comparability between regulated and unregulated enterprises. Paragraph 119 of FASB Concepts Statement No. 2, *Qualitative Characteristics of Accounting Information,* indicates that ". . . the purpose of comparison is to detect and explain similarities and differences." The Board concluded that comparability would not be enhanced by accounting as though regulation had no effect. Regulation creates different circumstances that require different accounting.

Scope

60. The Discussion Memorandum discussed regulation of various industries, and it asked whether a Board pronouncement should identify specific industries that are affected. Most respondents indicated that applicability of an FASB Statement on rate regulation should be specified by clearly describing the nature of the regulated operations to which it applies rather than by attempting to delineate specific industries. Some noted that changes in the political environment can cause changes in the nature of regulation. Accordingly, whether an industry meets the criteria for applicability might change over time. The Board agreed with those respondents and, accordingly, specified criteria that focus on the nature of regulation rather than on specific industries.

61. This Statement specifies the economic effects that result from the cause-and-effect relationship of costs and revenues in the rate-regulated environment and how those effects are to be accounted for. The nature of those effects led to the criteria for applicability of this Statement (paragraph 5).

62. The first criterion is the existence of third-party regulation. That criterion is intended to exclude contractual arrangements in which the government, or another party that could be viewed as a "regulator," is a party to a contract and is the enterprise's principal customer. For example, the normal Medicare and Medicaid arrangements are excluded from the scope of this Statement because they are contractual-type arrangements between the provider and the governmental agency that is responsible for payment for services provided.

63. Some respondents to the Exposure Draft indicated that cooperative utilities should be included in the scope of this Statement. They observed that some cooperative utilities' rates are subject to third-party regulation, but others' rates are set by their own governing board. The governing board is elected by the members of the cooperative, and it has the same authority as an independent, third-party regulator. In their view, the difference between

cooperative utilities that are subject to third-party regulation and those that are not does not justify different accounting. The Board agreed with those respondents, and modified the first criterion to include enterprises with rates established by their own governing board providing that board is empowered by statute or by contract to establish rates that bind customers.

64. A number of governmental utility respondents to the Exposure Draft asked that governmental utilities be included within the scope of this Statement. They noted that many governmental utilities have been guided by the same accounting practices and standards as investor-owned utilities in their general-purpose financial statements, and they expressed the view that users' emphasis on comparability supports continuation of that practice. In their view, the Board's decision not to address governmental utilities in this Statement should not preclude them from applying it. The Board agreed with those respondents and modified paragraph 5(a) so as not to preclude application by governmental utilities with rates set by their own governing board.

65. The second criterion is that the regulated rates are designed to recover the specific enterprise's costs of providing the regulated services or products. If rates are based on industry costs or some other measure that is not directly related to the specific enterprise's costs, there is no cause-and-effect relationship between the enterprise's costs and its revenues. In that case, costs would not be expected to result in revenues approximately equal to the costs; thus, the basis for the accounting specified in this Statement is not present under that type of regulation. That criterion is intended to be applied to the substance of the regulation, rather than its form. If an enterprise's regulated rates are based on the costs of a group of companies and the enterprise is so large in relation to the group of companies that its costs are, in essence, the group's costs, the regulation would meet the second criterion for that enterprise.

66. The last criterion requires that it be reasonable to assume that rates set at levels that will recover the enterprise's costs can be charged to and collected from customers. Regardless of the actions of the regulator, if the market for the enterprise's regulated services or products will not support a price based on cost, the enterprise's rates are at least partially controlled by the market. In that case, the cause-and-effect relationship of costs and revenues that is the basis for the accounting required by this Statement cannot be assumed to exist, and this Statement would not apply.

67. The Board does not intend the last criterion as a requirement that the enterprise earn a fair return on shareholders' investment under all conditions; an enterprise can earn less than a fair return for many reasons unrelated to the ability to bill and collect rates that will recover allowable costs.[17] For example, mild weather might reduce demand for energy utility services. In that case, rates that were expected to recover an enterprise's allowable costs might not do so. The resulting decreased earnings do not demonstrate an inability to charge and collect rates that would recover the enterprise's costs; rather, they demonstrate the uncertainty inherent in estimating weather conditions.

68. The last criterion also requires reasonable assurance that the regulated environment and its economic effects will continue. That requirement must be evaluated in light of the circumstances. For example, if the enterprise has an exclusive franchise to provide regulated services or products in an area and competition from other services or products is minimal, there is usually a reasonable expectation that it will continue to meet the other criteria. Exclusive franchises can be revoked, but they seldom are. If the enterprise has no exclusive franchise but has made the very large capital investment required to provide either the regulated services or products or an acceptable substitute, future competition also may be unlikely.

69. Some respondents to the Discussion Memorandum questioned whether, in light of recent events, it would ever be reasonable to assume that rates set at levels that will recover the enterprise's costs can be charged to and collected from customers. They cited recent developments—such as the use of solar devices as alternatives to certain energy utility services, increasing competition in the telecommunications industry, and deregulation of various transportation industries—as evidence that the environment of a regulated enterprise can change rapidly. The Board concluded that users of financial statements should be aware of the possibility of rapid, unanticipated changes in an industry, but accounting should not be based on such possibilities unless their occurrence is considered probable. However, changes of a long-term nature could modify the demand for an enterprise's regulated services sufficiently to affect its qualifying under the criterion of subparagraph 5(c).

70. The first scope limitation of paragraph 8—excluding accounting for price controls imposed by governmental action in times of emergency, high inflation, or other unusual conditions—was included in the Discussion Memorandum. Price

---

[17]As indicated in footnote 1, the term *allowable costs* is used here to include earnings permitted on shareholders' investment.

controls imposed in periods of unusual conditions are not expected to be applied consistently over an extended period. Indeed, their duration usually is limited by statute. In that environment, assurance of future benefits cannot be provided by probable future actions of the price control regulator because that regulator may not exist at a given future date.

71. Accounting for contracts in general was also excluded from the scope of the Discussion Memorandum. The economic effects of cost reimbursement contracts are in some respects similar to the economic effects of the type of regulation addressed by this Statement. However, most contracts tend to be relatively short-term, whereas regulation of enterprises covered by this Statement is expected to continue beyond the foreseeable future. The Board noted that other authoritative literature addresses contract accounting and concluded that it should exclude the general issue of contract accounting from the scope of this Statement.

72. The Discussion Memorandum described rate-making processes in several industries and asked whether each process justified the application of this Statement. As noted in paragraph 60, the Board concluded that applicability of this Statement should be specified by describing the nature of the regulated operations and the type of rate making to which it applies rather than by attempting to delineate specific industries.

73. In view of the nature of comments received, the Board concluded that the possible application of this Statement to the health care industry should be discussed. The Board does not intend to preclude application of the provisions of this Statement to the health care industry or to any other industry. Rather, application of this Statement is limited to regulated operations that meet the specified criteria for application.

74. In general, rates for services in the health care industry are not regulated based on the provider's costs. The federal Medicare and Medicaid programs usually are applied through a contractual-type arrangement (paragraph 62). Some states are applying comprehensive, prospective rate making to health care providers. In some cases, the rates set by state regulatory agencies are accepted for Medicare and Medicaid reimbursement purposes. There is some disagreement about the extent to which such rates are based on a provider's costs. If regulatory agencies in those states base rates on the provider's costs and adopt a permanent system of regulation, health care providers in those jurisdictions could be subject to the provisions of this Statement. However, the criterion in subparagraph 5(c) also would have to be considered to determine whether the Statement applies to the enterprise.

General Standards of Accounting for the Effects of Regulation

75. The Board concluded that, for general-purpose financial reporting, the principal economic effect of the regulatory process is to provide assurance of the existence of an asset or evidence of the diminution or elimination of the recoverability of an asset. The regulator's rate actions affect the regulated enterprise's probable future benefits or lack thereof. Thus, an enterprise should capitalize a cost if it is probable that future revenue approximately equal to the cost will result through the rate-making process.

76. A number of respondents to the Exposure Draft asked for clarification of the types of costs addressed by paragraph 9. Those respondents expressed the view that tangible assets should be capitalized based on the criteria used by unregulated companies; paragraph 9 should be limited to other assets. Paragraph 9 was intended to address only accounting for costs that would be charged to expense by an unregulated enterprise, and the Board modified the paragraph to so indicate.

77. The regulatory process, as usually practiced, has two aspects. First, either historical or projected test period costs are used to compute the revenues necessary to provide for similar costs during the period in which the rates will be in force. Second, test period costs are adjusted to provide for recovery or to prevent recovery of costs that are considered unusual or unpredictable. If unusual or unpredictable costs are not provided for in advance, they may be recovered after their incurrence through increased rates provided for that purpose. In some cases, rate orders do not specify whether costs are (a) included as normal test period costs, used to compute rates that are intended to provide for similar future costs, or (b) incurred costs designated for specific recovery. The Board concluded that costs should be capitalized only if the future revenue is expected to be provided to permit recovery of the previously incurred cost rather than merely to provide for recovery of higher levels of similar future costs.

78. If rates are designed to be adjusted automatically for changes in operating expenses (e.g., costs of purchased fuel), the regulator's intent could be either to permit recovery of the incurred cost or merely to provide for recovery of similar future costs. Normal operating expenses such as fuel costs usually are provided for in current rates. In that case, the presumption is that the rate increase is intended to permit recovery of similar future costs. That presumption, which would preclude capitalizing the incurred cost, can be overcome only if it is clear that the regulator's intent is to provide recovery of the incurred cost.

79. Rate actions of a regulator can also impose a liability on a regulated enterprise in the following ways:

a. A regulator can order a regulated enterprise to refund previously collected revenues.

b. A regulator can provide rates intended to recover costs that are expected to be incurred in the future. Paragraphs 38 and 39 illustrate that possibility. The resulting increased charges to customers are liabilities and not revenues for the enterprise—the enterprise undertakes to provide the services for which the increased charges were collected, and it is obligated to return those increased charges if the future cost does not occur. The obligation will be fulfilled either by refunding the increased charges through future rate reductions or by paying the future costs with no corresponding effect on future rates. The resulting increases in charges to customers are unearned revenues until they are earned by their use for the intended purpose.

c. For rate-making purposes, a regulator can recognize a gain or other reduction of overall allowable costs over a period of time. Paragraphs 35-37 illustrate that possibility. By that action, the regulator obligates the enterprise to give the gain or other reduction of overall allowable costs to customers by reducing future rates. Accordingly, the amount of the gain or cost reduction is the appropriate measure of the obligation.

80. A number of respondents to the Exposure Draft asked the Board to clarify whether paragraph 11(b), discussed in paragraph 79(b) above, was intended to apply to costs such as nuclear plant decommissioning costs. Decommissioning costs are incurred costs in the current accounting framework. Those costs and the related liabilities are imposed by regulation or statute, similar to the liability to restore the land after strip mining, discussed in paragraph 142 of Concepts Statement 3. Accordingly, paragraph 11(b) does not address those costs.

Specific Standards Derived from the General Standards

81. The specific standards derived from the general standards deal with recognition, as assets and increases in net income, of allowable costs that are not usually accepted as incurred costs in the present accounting framework. For the reasons explained below, the Board concluded that recognition is appropriate for those allowable costs. However, the Board does not intend them to be used as guidance for other applications of the general standards in paragraphs 9-12.

Allowance for Funds Used during Construction

82. Most respondents to the Discussion Memoran-

dum supported the present practices of public utilities in accounting for the allowance for funds used during construction. They noted that the current income statement display reflects the regulatory process used in determining the amount to be capitalized and, thus, aids the user in understanding the regulatory environment. They cited the regulator's determination of the "cost" of equity capital as a basis for accepting that amount as a cost, and they noted that unregulated enterprises do not have a similar basis. They also noted that most utilities have an obligation to construct the facilities necessary to provide regulated services. Thus, there is no option of not obtaining the required funds or using accumulated funds to retire debt instead of investing in construction, and there is no available "avoidable cost" to use as the measure of the cost of the funds used.

83. Respondents who opposed present practices of accounting for the allowance for funds used during construction indicated that the cost of equity funds should be excluded from that allowance. Those respondents cited paragraph 49 of Statement 34, which states that ". . . recognition of the cost of equity capital does not conform to the present accounting framework." However, the arguments presented by those respondents supported capitalization of interest in accordance with Statement 34. Capitalization of interest in accordance with Statement 34 would be based on actual interest rates on outstanding debt and limited to the total amount of interest cost incurred during the period. In most cases, the effect on net income would be similar to capitalizing an allowance that included a cost of equity funds.

84. Some Board members believe that the allowances for funds used during construction, computed under current utility practices, are appropriate measures of the costs of financing construction and that the regulators' actions provide reasonable assurance of the existence of assets that should be measured by the amount on which rates will be based. Other Board members believe that those amounts are acceptable substitutes for the amount of interest that would be capitalized in accordance with Statement 34 and that, absent a change in regulatory practices, the cost of a change in those accounting practices would exceed any perceived benefits. The Board concluded that the amounts capitalized for rate-making purposes also should be capitalized for financial reporting purposes.

Intercompany Profit

85. Most respondents to the Discussion Memorandum indicated that enterprises should not eliminate intercompany profits on sales to regulated affiliates if it is probable that, through the rate-making pro-

cess, future revenues in amounts approximately equal to the intercompany transfer price will be provided. That revenue would result from inclusion of the intercompany profits in the amount used by the regulator as allowable cost for purposes of depreciation and return on investment. They noted that an enterprise does not recognize profits on sales to unregulated affiliates because the profits are not validated by transactions with outside parties. According to those respondents, however, an enterprise should recognize profits on sales to a regulated affiliate to the extent that the profits are included in allowable costs in the rate-making process because the profits are validated by the rate actions of the regulator. The regulator's acceptance of the transfer price provides evidence of recoverability. For rate-making purposes, the intercompany profits will be included in the depreciation used as an allowable cost, and the undepreciated amount will be included in the investment on which a return is provided as an allowable cost. Those respondents noted that ARB 51 did not require elimination of intercompany profits on sales to regulated affiliates.

86. The Board concluded that intercompany profits on sales of assets to regulated affiliates should not be eliminated in consolidated financial statements if the transfer price is reasonable and it is probable that, through the rate-making process, future revenue approximately equal to the transfer price will result from the regulated affiliate's use of those assets. In view of existing regulatory practices, the Board further concluded that the transfer price usually should be considered reasonable if the price is accepted or not challenged by the regulator that governs the regulated affiliate. Otherwise, reasonableness should be considered in light of the circumstances. For example, reasonableness might be judged by the return on investment earned by the manufacturing or construction operations or by a comparison of the transfer prices with prices available from other sources.

Other Specific Standards

Accounting for Income Taxes

87. In the past, enterprises generally have not provided for deferred income taxes if regulated rates to customers were based on taxes currently payable. Most respondents to the Discussion Memorandum supported that practice based on the rationale of Opinion 11. Opinion 11 indicates that deferred taxes are the result of comprehensive interperiod allocation of income taxes to achieve a proper "matching" of revenues and expenses. Those respondents indicated that a provision for deferred income taxes does not achieve a proper "matching" if rates to customers are based on taxes currently payable. In that situation, the income tax expense should be

recorded in the future periods in which the taxes become payable and the regulator grants a resulting rate increase. Those respondents also noted that Concepts Statement 3 concluded that deferred taxes computed under the deferred method that is prescribed by Opinion 11 do not meet the definition of a liability. They expressed the view that the Board should not require utilities to commence to apply Opinion 11 when the Board may reconsider that Opinion in the near future.

88. Other respondents indicated that deferred income taxes should be recorded in all cases. However, if rates charged to customers are based on taxes currently payable, the recorded deferred taxes should also result in an asset—the future benefit that will result from treatment of the taxes as allowable costs for regulatory purposes in the period in which those taxes become payable.

89. Some Board members believe that the general standards (paragraphs 9-12) would require a regulated enterprise to record deferred income taxes. If it is probable that income taxes payable in future years because of net reversal of timing differences will be recovered through rates based on taxes payable at that time, the enterprise also would record an asset in an amount equal to the deferred income taxes. Offsetting those deferred income taxes against the related asset normally would not be appropriate because the asset will be realized through collections from customers and the deferred income taxes will not be paid to the customers. However, the Board concluded that any possible benefits of commencing to record deferred income taxes and an offsetting asset at this time probably would not exceed the cost. Accordingly, if rates are based on income taxes currently payable and it is probable that income taxes payable in future years because of net reversal of timing differences will be recovered through rates based on income taxes payable at that time, this Statement does not permit deferred income taxes to be computed or recorded in accordance with Opinion 11. However, it does require disclosure of the cumulative amount of timing differences for which deferred income taxes have not been provided. Approximate amounts of cumulative timing differences can be estimated without the complex calculations required by Opinion 11. That information, together with the disclosures required by Opinion 11, should help users in estimating the possible future income tax and rate effects of those timing differences. The Board will reconsider its conclusions on this matter in the course of its project on accounting for income taxes, which was added to the agenda in January 1982.

90. A number of respondents to the Exposure Draft indicated that the disclosures required by this Statement would be misunderstood by users. In

their view, users might attempt to estimate unrecorded deferred taxes as a charge to current income. The Board believes that users will understand the required disclosures if affected companies explain that deferred taxes are not provided because the method of rate making assures future recovery of future taxes. The Board believes that it is important to disclose those costs which have to be recovered from future customers through future rates.

Other Specific Accounting Matters

Recovery of Cost without Return on Investment

91. The Discussion Memorandum asked whether the recoverability criterion for capitalization of costs should be based on recovery of cost (which excludes a return on equity capital) or on recovery of cost of service (which includes a return on equity capital). In some cases, a regulator may provide rates intended to recover an incurred cost over an extended period without a return on the unrecovered cost during the recovery period. That issue was intended to elicit comments on whether the capitalized costs should be carried at the present value of the amount to be recovered in those cases. Most respondents interpreted that issue as asking whether any capitalization of costs was justified if the enterprise would recover its cost but would not realize a return on the unrecovered cost during the recovery period. Thus, many of the responses did not address the valuation of the resulting asset.

92. The Board concluded that capitalized costs not related to a tangible asset provide a measure of an intangible asset. Generally accepted accounting principles do not necessarily require the carrying amount of an intangible asset to be its discounted present value, nor do they necessarily require an enterprise to consider a return on investment when evaluating possible impairment of an intangible or depreciable asset. Accordingly, the Board concluded that it should not impose such a requirement on regulated enterprises.

93. Some respondents to the Exposure Draft indicated that disclosure should be required for capitalized costs that are recovered over an extended period without a return on investment during the recovery period. Those respondents indicated that regulated enterprises should provide the same types of disclosure for a given item as unregulated enterprises do.

94. The situations in question usually result from a problem encountered by a regulated enterprise—an abandoned plant, major storm damage, or a similar event. For troubled debt restructurings, which are similar to the events in question, Statement 15 requires creditors that agree to forego interest on outstanding loans to disclose the amounts of non-earning assets included in the balance sheet. The Board agreed that regulated enterprises with capitalized costs that are recovered over an extended period without a return on investment during the recovery period should provide similar disclosure and, thus, added the requirements of paragraph 20.

Accounting for Leases

95. Statement 13, as amended, specifies criteria for classification of leases and the method of accounting for each type of lease. For rate-making purposes, a regulator may include lease payments in allowable costs as rental expense even though the lease would be classified as a capital lease under the criteria of Statement 13. The Discussion Memorandum asked for views on the economic effects of that regulatory treatment and how to account for those effects.

96. A number of respondents indicated that the classification of a lease is not affected by the regulator's actions. In their view, rate actions of the regulator cannot eliminate obligations to third parties unless the obligations were created by the regulator. Also, they observed that, over the term of a capital lease, the aggregate lease payments are equal to aggregate amortization of the leased asset and aggregate interest on the lease obligation. Thus, the regulator, by including the lease payments in allowable costs, establishes the existence of probable future benefits approximately equal to the combined amount of the capitalized leased asset and interest on the lease obligation over the term of the lease. In their view, regulated enterprises should classify leases in accordance with Statement 13 as amended. The Board agrees with that view.

97. Other respondents indicated that the regulator's action establishes that there is no asset related to the lease. They indicated that an income statement display consisting of amortization and interest would mislead users if the regulatory process based rates on rental expense. In their view, regulated enterprises should classify leases in accordance with their classification for rate-making purposes. The Board concluded that such a view focuses on the mechanics of the rate-making process rather than on the economic effects of the process. This Statement requires that regulated enterprises account for the economic effects of the rate-making process; it does not attempt to portray the mechanics of that process in financial statements.

98. The Board concluded that the nature of the expense elements for a capitalized lease (amortization and interest) are not changed by the regulator's action; however, the timing of expense recognition related to the lease should be modified to conform with the rate treatment. Thus, amortization of the

leased asset would be modified so that the total interest and amortization recognized during a period would equal the rental expense included in allowable cost for rate-making purposes during that period. Although this Statement requires the expense elements of a capitalized lease to consist of amortization and interest regardless of the regulatory treatment, the Board notes that generally accepted accounting principles do not require interest expense or amortization expense to be shown as such in an income statement.

Revenue Collected Subject to Refund

99. In some jurisdictions, regulated enterprises are permitted to bill and collect requested rate increases before the regulator has ruled on the request.

100. Some respondents opposed reducing net income by the amount expected to be disallowed prior to the final rate action. In their view, if the enterprise requests the increase, the increase must be supported by the evidence. In that case, management could not take the position that some portion of the request is likely to be disallowed without providing the regulator a possible basis for disallowance. Other respondents supported application of the loss contingency provisions of Statement 5 to those rate increases. They indicated that utilities usually can predict the outcome of a rate hearing by considering recent actions of the regulator. They also indicated that it is misleading to include in net income revenue that is expected to be refunded.

101. The Board concluded that regulation does not have a unique economic effect that requires special accounting for anticipated refunds of revenue. Rather, regulation results in a contingency that should be accounted for in accordance with Statement 5, the same as other contingencies.

Refunds to Customers

102. The Discussion Memorandum asked whether the effects of rate-making transactions applicable to prior periods should be charged to income in the year in which they become estimable, as required by Statement 16 for other adjustments applicable to prior periods, or accounted for as prior period adjustments.

103. Some respondents opposed applying Statement 16 to utility refunds. Most of those respondents indicated that Statement 16 is not presently applied to significant refunds that could not be estimated in advance. They indicated that including refunds in a year other than that in which the amount refunded was included in income misstates both years, because the financial statements would not accurately reflect permitted rates of return,

trends, etc. They also noted that current earnings could be reduced to a level at which existing covenants or state regulations governing investments by certain institutional investors could preclude necessary financing.

104. Respondents who favored applying Statement 16 to refunds indicated that the regulatory process does not introduce unique economic effects that warrant different accounting. In their view, the arguments supporting prior period adjustments for regulated enterprises are the same arguments that were made by unregulated enterprises before Statement 16 was issued.

105. The Board concluded that regulation does not have a unique economic effect that requires special accounting for refunds. Rather, regulation results in resolution of a previous contingency that should be accounted for the same as resolution of contingencies by unregulated enterprises. Reconsideration of Statement 16 was not within the scope of this Statement.

106. The Exposure Draft would have required disclosure of the pro forma effect of refunds on net income of each period presented, computed as though the refunds were retroactively recorded in the prior periods in which the revenue was recognized. A number of respondents objected to that requirement on the basis that the proposed disclosure indicates a need for restatement.

107. The Board believes that users are interested in two aspects of refunds. They are concerned about the impact of the refund in the year of the refund, and they also are concerned about the effect of the refund on trends of permitted earnings. Neither prior period adjustment nor current income charge provides all of the needed information. The Board concluded that users' needs could be satisfied by disclosure of (a) the effect of the refund on net income of the current year and (b) the years in which the refunded revenue was recognized.

108. In making its determination, the Board considered whether the amount disclosed should be net of related taxes. APB Opinion No. 30, *Reporting the Results of Operations,* prohibits net-of-tax disclosure of unusual or infrequently occurring items that are not extraordinary items. The Board concluded that users would not be confused by a net-of-tax disclosure of the effect of refunds. Users understand that refunds occur from time to time in public utilities—and they are concerned with the net effect rather than the gross amounts refunded. Accordingly, the Board concluded that refunds should be disclosed net of their related tax effects. Based on comments received and its deliberations, the Board decided that a narrow amendment of

Opinion 30 for utility refunds was justified. However, the Board's action is limited to utility refunds, and it is not intended to otherwise modify or question the requirements of Opinion 30.

Rate Making Based on a Fair Value Rate Base

109. Some state regulatory commissions use a "fair value rate base" for determining allowable return *on* invested capital. Normally, those commissions do not permit recovery *of* the fair value of the enterprise's assets by including depreciation of the fair value in allowable cost; rather, depreciation is based on historical cost. The Discussion Memorandum asked whether that procedure provides a basis for accounting for utility plant at its "fair value" in financial statements prepared in accordance with generally accepted accounting principles.

110. Virtually all respondents opposed the use of fair value in financial statements. Respondents indicated that fair value would present the enterprise's assets at an amount in excess of the recoverable amount of those assets. The use of depreciation based on historical cost for rate-making purposes limits recovery to that historical cost. Respondents also noted that the realized rate of return based on historical cost is not proportionately greater in jurisdictions that base rates on a fair value rate base than in other jurisdictions; thus, they question whether there is substance to that special treatment.

111. The Board concluded that if the return on investment permitted in a jurisdiction is based on fair value but recovery of cost is based on historical cost, the fair value of the assets should not be recognized in general-purpose financial statements. The Board did not need to address the accounting implications if a commission were to use fair value to determine both recovery of cost and return on capital invested because that practice currently is not used by regulators.

Acquisition Adjustments

112. A number of respondents to the Exposure Draft asked the Board to address accounting for *acquisition adjustments*. Those adjustments are the differences between the amounts paid for an acquired utility and the acquired utility's book value of its assets and liabilities. Those respondents indicated that utilities do not have goodwill because a utility cannot realize excess profits. Thus, they considered the example of goodwill in Appendix B unnecessary.

113. Opinion 16 describes how the amount paid in a business combination is allocated to the assets obtained and the liabilities assumed. Acquisition adjustments are values in excess of book value of identifiable assets obtained, valuation adjustments applicable to liabilities assumed, or goodwill or a combination of those items. Opinion 16 does not allow another possibility. The example of accounting for intangibles in Appendix B of this Statement indicates the appropriate accounting for goodwill. Additional guidance should not be needed about accounting for any portions of acquisition adjustments that represent amounts allocable to identifiable assets or liabilities such as property and equipment or intangibles amortizable over specific benefit periods.

Evidence

114. Several issues in the Discussion Memorandum identified types of evidence that might be available before a rate order is received and asked whether each would provide sufficient assurance to warrant capitalizing costs. A number of respondents indicated that judgment is needed to determine the adequacy of available evidence. In their view, all of the available evidence has to be evaluated, and the resulting decision cannot be standardized. Other respondents indicated that specific items did or did not provide adequate evidence; however, their responses appeared to differ based on the regulator involved and on their assumptions about other related circumstances.

115. The Board concluded that it should not attempt to categorize types of evidence and the reliance that should be based on each. Rather, this Statement indicates the degree of assurance required, and judgment must be exercised to evaluate whether that degree of assurance is present in various circumstances. In general, the Board concluded that costs should be capitalized only if (a) it is probable that future revenue in an amount at least equal to the cost will result from inclusion of that cost in allowable costs for rate-making purposes and (b) the future revenue will be provided to permit recovery of the previously incurred cost rather than to provide for expected levels of similar future costs.

Effective Date and Transition

116. This Statement prescribes the circumstances in which regulation has an economic effect that affects the application of generally accepted accounting principles, and it outlines the accounting that should result. Accounting changes that result from initial application of this Statement will involve accounting for the effects of regulation that have not been accounted for in the past and revising previous accounting that was not in accordance with the provisions of this Statement. Those changes are not expected to cause changes in the methods or in the results of regulation.

117. The Exposure Draft proposed that the Statement be effective for fiscal years beginning after December 15, 1982. A number of respondents suggested that the effective date be delayed to provide time for companies to determine how the Statement would affect them. The Board agreed that the proposed effective date could cause some hardship. Accordingly, this Statement is effective for fiscal years beginning after December 15, 1983.

118. Implementation of this Statement is not expected to have major effects on the accounting of most regulated enterprises. This Statement is considerably more specific than the Addendum; however, its thrust is similar. Accordingly, the Board concluded that comparability would be best achieved if this Statement were applied retroactively to the extent practicable. The Board did not extend that general approach to application of Statement 16, because Statement 16 does not permit retroactive application.

119. A number of respondents to the Exposure Draft urged the Board to permit affected companies to defer retroactive application of Statement 13. They noted that Statement 13 did not require retroactive application until the fourth year after its effective date, and they urged the Board to afford regulated enterprises the same consideration.

120. Retroactive application of Statement 13 was delayed to permit affected enterprises time to work out any resulting problems, such as indenture covenant restrictions. The Board agreed that regulated enterprises might have the same problems; thus, retroactive application of Statement 13 is not required until the first fiscal year beginning after December 15, 1986. The Board also decided that, pending retroactive application of Statement 13, regulated enterprises should furnish the same disclosure as was required of unregulated enterprises under Statement 13. Retroactive application of Statement 13

should not affect a regulated enterprise's net income or shareholders' equity. Thus, only the effect of retroactive application on the balance sheet is required by this Statement.

Appendix D

BACKGROUND INFORMATION

121. The Addendum to APB Opinion 2, issued in December 1962, outlined the general approach that has been used for accounting by regulated enterprises. On November 18, 1977, in response to requests from the Acting Chief Accountant of the Securities and Exchange Commission and from the AICPA's Accounting Standards Division, the FASB initiated a project to consider the effects of rate regulation on accounting for regulated enterprises.

122. An FASB Discussion Memorandum on rate regulation was issued on December 31, 1979. The Board received 197 letters of comment in response to the Discussion Memorandum. In May 1980, the Board conducted a public hearing on the issues in the Discussion Memorandum. Twenty-four individuals and organizations presented their views at the two-day hearing.

123. An Exposure Draft of a proposed Statement was issued on March 4, 1982. The Board received 172 letters of comment in response to that Exposure Draft.

124. An FASB task force provided counsel in preparing the Discussion Memorandum and in preparing material for Board consideration during the course of Board deliberations concerning this Statement. The task force included persons from the investment community, industry, public accounting, academe, and regulatory authorities.

Statement of Financial Accounting Standards No. 72
Accounting for Certain Acquisitions of Banking
or Thrift Institutions

an amendment of APB Opinion No. 17,
an interpretation of APB Opinions 16 and 17,
and an amendment of FASB Interpretation No. 9

STATUS

Issued: February 1983

Effective Date: For business combinations initiated after September 30, 1982

Affects: Amends APB 17, paragraphs 29 through 31
       Amends FIN 9, paragraphs 8 and 9

Affected by: No other pronouncements

Issues Discussed by FASB Emerging Issues Task Force (EITF)

  Affects: No EITF Issues

  Interpreted by: Paragraph 5 interpreted by EITF Issues No. 85-8, 85-42, and 88-19
                  Paragraph 15 interpreted by EITF Issue No. 89-19

  Related Issue: EITF Issue No. 85-41

SUMMARY

This Statement amends APB Opinion No. 17, *Intangible Assets,* with regard to the amortization of the unidentifiable intangible asset (commonly referred to as goodwill) recognized in certain business combinations accounted for by the purchase method. If, and to the extent that, the fair value of liabilities assumed exceeds the fair value of identifiable assets acquired in the acquisition of a banking or thrift institution, the unidentifiable intangible asset recognized generally shall be amortized to expense by the interest method over a period no longer than the discount on the long-term interest-bearing assets acquired is to be recognized as interest income. This Statement also specifies that financial assistance granted to an enterprise by a regulatory authority in connection with a business combination shall be accounted for as part of the combination if receipt of the assistance is probable and the amount is reasonably estimable.

Statement of Financial Accounting Standards No. 72

Accounting for Certain Acquisitions of Banking or Thrift Institutions

**an amendment of APB Opinion No. 17,
an interpretation of APB Opinions 16 and 17,
and an amendment of FASB Interpretation No. 9**

CONTENTS

INTRODUCTION

1. The FASB has been asked to address the accounting for certain acquisitions of banking or thrift institutions. Those making the requests indicate that APB Opinions No. 16, *Business Combinations,* and No. 17, *Intangible Assets,* do not adequately address the conditions that have been present in some recent business combinations involving those institutions and that the use of the purchase method of accounting accompanied by the use of long amortization periods for purchased goodwill has produced postcombination operating results that are not reliable. Such combinations have recently become more frequent as a result of the economic climate, the move toward deregulation of certain financial institutions, and the involvement of financial institution regulators.

SCOPE AND APPLICABILITY

2. This Statement applies to the acquisition of a commercial bank, a savings and loan association, a mutual savings bank, a credit union, other depository institutions having assets and liabilities of the same types as those institutions, and branches of such enterprises. Paragraphs 5 and 6 of this Statement apply to only those acquisitions in which the fair value of liabilities assumed by the acquiring enterprise exceeds the fair value of tangible and identifiable intangible assets acquired, and those provisions specify an amortization method for the

portion of any unidentifiable intangible asset up to the amount of that excess. Opinion 17 and FASB Interpretation No. 9, *Applying APB Opinions No. 16 and 17 When a Savings and Loan Association or a Similar Institution Is Acquired in a Business Combination Accounted for by the Purchase Method,* also provide guidance as to the amortization of any additional unidentifiable intangible asset recognized in the acquisition. The provisions of paragraphs 4 and 7 apply to all acquisitions of banking and thrift institutions.

3. The provisions of paragraphs 8 through 11, which relate to the reporting of regulatory financial assistance, apply to all acquisitions of banking or thrift institutions. The Board understands that regulatory financial assistance agreements are not standardized and that the conditions under which assistance will be granted vary widely. As a result, this Statement does not specifically address all forms of regulatory financial assistance, but its provisions should serve as a general guide.

STANDARDS OF FINANCIAL ACCOUNTING AND REPORTING

Identified Intangible Assets

4. In a business combination accounted for by the purchase method involving the acquisition of a banking or thrift institution, intangible assets

acquired that can be separately identified shall be assigned a portion of the total cost of the acquired enterprise if the fair values of those assets can be reliably[1] determined. The fair values of such assets that relate to depositor or borrower relationships[2] shall be based on the estimated benefits attributable to the relationships that *exist* at the date of acquisition without regard to new depositors or borrowers that may replace them. Those identified intangible assets shall be amortized over the estimated lives of those existing relationships.

Unidentifiable Intangible Asset

5. If, in such a combination, the fair value of liabilities assumed exceeds the fair value of tangible and identified intangible assets acquired, that excess constitutes an unidentifiable intangible asset. That asset shall be amortized to expense over a period no greater than the estimated remaining life of the long-term interest-bearing assets[3] acquired. Amortization shall be at a constant rate when applied to the carrying amount[4] of those interest-bearing assets that, based on their terms, are expected to be outstanding at the beginning of each subsequent period. The prepayment assumptions, if any, used to determine the fair value of the long-term interest-bearing assets acquired also shall be used in determining the amount of those assets expected to be outstanding. However, if the assets acquired in such a combination do not include a significant amount of long-term interest-bearing assets, the unidentifiable intangible asset shall be amortized over a period not exceeding the estimated average remaining life of the existing customer (deposit) base acquired. The periodic amounts of amortization shall be determined as of the acquisition date and shall not be subsequently adjusted except as provided by paragraphs 6 and 7 of this Statement. Notwithstanding the other provisions of this paragraph, the period of amortization shall not exceed 40 years.

6. Paragraph 31 of Opinion 17 specifies, among other things, that an enterprise should evaluate the periods of amortization of intangible assets continually to determine whether later events and circumstances warrant revised estimates of useful lives. In no event, however, shall the useful life of the unidentifiable intangible asset described in paragraph 5 of this Statement be revised upward.

7. For purposes of applying paragraph 32 of Opinion 17,[5] if a large segment or separable group of the operating assets of an acquired banking or thrift institution, such as branches, is sold or liquidated, the portion of the unidentifiable intangible asset attributable to that segment or separable group shall be included in the cost of the assets sold. If a large segment or separable group of the interest-bearing assets of an acquired institution is sold or liquidated and if the benefits attributable to the unidentifiable intangible asset have been significantly reduced,[6] that reduction shall be recognized as a charge to income.

Regulatory-Assisted Combinations

8. In connection with a business combination, a regulatory authority may agree to pay amounts by which future interest received or receivable on the interest-bearing assets acquired is less than the interest cost of carrying those assets for a period by a stated margin. In such a case, the projected assistance, computed as of the date of acquisition based on the interest-rate margin existing at that date, shall be considered as additional interest on the interest-bearing assets acquired in determining their fair values for purposes of applying the purchase method (paragraphs 87 and 88 of Opinion 16). The carrying amount of those interest-bearing assets shall not be adjusted for subsequent changes in the estimated amount of assistance to be received. Actual assistance shall be reported in income of the period in which it accrues. Notwithstanding the above provisions, if an enterprise intends to sell all or a portion of the interest-bearing assets acquired, those assets shall not be stated at amounts in excess of their current market values.

9. Other forms of financial assistance may be granted to a combining enterprise or the combined enterprise by a regulatory authority in connection with a business combination accounted for by the purchase method. If receipt of the assistance is

---

[1]Reliability embodies the characteristics of representational faithfulness and verifiability, as discussed in FASB Concepts Statement No. 2, *Qualitative Characteristics of Accounting Information.*

[2]Examples of intangible assets related to depositor or borrower relationships are described in paragraphs 8(a) and 8(b) of Interpretation 9.

[3]For purposes of this Statement, long-term interest-bearing assets are interest-bearing assets with a remaining term to maturity of more than one year.

[4]*Carrying amount* is the face amount of the interest-bearing asset plus (or minus) the unamortized premium (or discount).

[5]Paragraph 32 of Opinion 17 states: "a large segment or separable group of assets of an acquired company or the entire acquired company may be sold or otherwise liquidated, and all or a portion of the unamortized cost of the goodwill recognized in the acquisition should be included in the cost of the assets sold."

[6]For example, if a sale of a large group of interest-bearing assets is accompanied by the loss of a significant and valuable customer base, a reduction in goodwill likely would be appropriate. On the other hand, if the proceeds of sale are reinvested in other forms of interest-bearing or other assets, no such reduction may be necessary.

probable and the amount is reasonably estimable, that portion of the cost of the acquired enterprise shall be assigned to such assistance. Assets and liabilities that have been or will be transferred to or assumed by a regulatory authority shall not be recognized in the acquisition. If receipt of the assistance is not probable or the amount is not reasonably estimable, any assistance subsequently recognized in the financial statements shall be reported as a reduction of the unidentifiable intangible asset, described in paragraph 5, that was recognized in the acquisition. Subsequent amortization shall be adjusted proportionally. Assistance recognized in excess of that intangible asset shall be reported in income.

10. Under certain forms of assistance granted in connection with a business combination, the combined enterprise may agree to repay all or a portion of the assistance if certain criteria related to the level of future revenues, expenses, or profits are met. Such a repayment obligation shall be recognized as a liability and as a charge to income at the time the conditions in paragraph 8 of FASB Statement No. 5, *Accounting for Contingencies,* are met. This paragraph does not address repayments of assistance granted in exchange for debt or equity instruments.

Disclosures

11. The nature and amounts of any regulatory financial assistance granted to or recognized by an enterprise during a period in connection with the acquisition of a banking or thrift institution shall be disclosed.

Amendments to Other Pronouncements

12. The following footnote is added to the end of (a) paragraph 29 of Opinion 17, (b) the first sentence of paragraph 30 of Opinion 17, (c) the second sentence of paragraph 31 of Opinion 17, and (d) paragraph 9 of Interpretation 9:

> *Paragraphs 5 and 6 of FASB Statement No. 72, Accounting for Certain Acquisitions of Banking or Thrift Institutions,* specify an exception to the provisions of this [Opinion/Interpretation] with respect to the amortization of goodwill recognized in certain acquisitions of banking or thrift institutions.

13. The second sentence of paragraph 8 of Interpretation 9 is amended to insert the word *reliably* and the related footnote as follows:

> If the amount paid for any such factor can be reliably* determined, that amount shall not be included in goodwill.

---

*Reliability embodies the characteristics of representational faithfulness and verifiability, as discussed in FASB Concepts Statement No. 2, *Qualitative Characteristics of Accounting Information.*

14. The following sentence is added to the end of paragraph 8 of Interpretation 9:

> The fair values of identified intangible assets that relate to depositor or borrower relationships (refer to paragraphs 8(a) and 8(b)) shall be based on the estimated benefits attributable to the relationships that *exist* at the date of acquisition without regard to new depositors or borrowers that may replace them. Those identified intangible assets shall be amortized over the estimated lives of those existing relationships.

Effective Date and Transition

15. This Statement shall be applied prospectively to business combinations initiated[7] after September 30, 1982 with earlier application encouraged. Retroactive application to a business combination initiated prior to October 1, 1982 is permitted but not required. If, prior to March 1, 1983, an enterprise has issued financial statements in which the provisions of this Statement have not been applied to a business combination initiated and consummated after September 30, 1982, those financial statements shall be restated when they are first presented with financial statements for subsequent periods, or the opening balance of retained earnings for that subsequent period shall be appropriately adjusted if they are omitted. In addition, the financial statements shall, in the year the standards are first applied, disclose the nature of any restatement and its effect on income before extraordinary items, net income, and related per share amounts for each restated year presented.

---

[7]Refer to Opinion 16, paragraph 46(a) and footnote 14 to paragraph 97. Planned combinations involving a banking or thrift institution may be subject to approval by a regulatory authority and to a final determination concerning the amount of regulatory financial assistance to be granted. Under those circumstances, a combination shall be considered initiated if an announcement or notification as required by paragraph 46(a) of Opinion 16 has been made. A plan of combination involving only mutual banking or thrift institutions often is communicated by an enterprise to the board of directors of an institution rather than to the owners of the institution. In those circumstances, notification to a board of directors constitutes notification to shareholders for purposes of determining the date a business combination is initiated.

> **The provisions of this Statement need not be applied to immaterial items.**

This Statement was adopted by the unanimous vote of the seven members of the Financial Accounting Standards Board:

Donald J. Kirk,
Chairman
Frank E. Block

Victor H. Brown
John W. March
David Mosso

Robert T. Sprouse
Ralph E. Walters

Appendix A

BACKGROUND INFORMATION

16. Business combinations involving banking or thrift institutions have become frequent. Such combinations have increased, in part, as a result of the relaxed restrictions on interstate banking, the involvement of financial institution regulators, and the current trend toward deregulation of those industries. Various accounting and reporting questions have been raised as a result of those combinations.

17. Banking and thrift institutions, whose primary assets and liabilities are interest-bearing instruments, generally are regulated under laws of the various states or the federal government, or both. The qualified deposits of most banking and thrift institutions are insured by regulatory agencies, and as a result, those institutions are subject to the rules and regulations of those agencies. Because of its position as an insurer, a regulatory agency may provide financial assistance to an institution to minimize the agency's risk of loss.

18. Current economic and competitive conditions have adversely affected the financial position and operations of many financial institutions, particularly savings and loan associations and mutual savings banks. In particular, continued high interest rates have eroded interest margins, and competitive pressures in some cases have resulted in depositors' transferring funds to other kinds of enterprises. Many savings and loan associations and mutual savings banks have reported net losses during recent periods and some have failed to meet the minimum net worth requirements established by regulatory agencies. Failure to meet those requirements may result in a regulator's arranging or encouraging a merger with another enterprise. In some cases, a regulatory authority such as the Federal Deposit Insurance Corporation, the Federal Savings and Loan Insurance Corporation, the National Credit Union Share Insurance Fund, or a state insurance fund may grant financial assistance to an enterprise

as an inducement for that enterprise to assume the assets, liabilities, and operations of a banking or thrift institution that has failed, or is about to fail, those minimum regulatory net worth requirements.

19. A majority of the recent business combinations referred to above were mergers of mutual thrift institutions. Most thrifts are mutual institutions, that is, they are owned by their depositors, rather than by stockholders. The combination of two mutual thrifts generally is effected without any payment of cash or other assets by either institution to the previously separate ownership interests. Instead, one institution absorbs the operations of the other institution, thereby obtaining the assets and assuming the liabilities of that institution. Prior to 1981, substantially all mergers of mutual thrifts were accounted for using the pooling-of-interests method described in Opinion 16. Recently, however, the majority of such mergers have been accounted for using the purchase method of accounting.

20. Opinion 16 and Interpretation 9 specify how an acquiring enterprise should allocate the cost of an acquired enterprise to the assets acquired and the liabilities assumed in applying the purchase method. Paragraph 88 of Opinion 16 indicates that, as a general guide, a portion of the cost should be assigned to intangible assets that can be identified and named based on appraised values. Paragraph 87 of that Opinion indicates that the cost of the acquired enterprise in excess of the sum of the amounts assigned to identifiable assets acquired less liabilities assumed should be reported as goodwill, which is an unidentifiable intangible asset. Opinion 17 and Interpretation 9 also apply to intangible assets acquired in business combinations accounted for by the purchase method.

21. Opinion 17 specifies that any intangible asset should be amortized by systematic charges to income over the period to be benefited, but that period may not exceed 40 years. That Opinion sets forth factors that should be considered in estimating the useful lives of intangible assets. Paragraph 27(c) of that Opinion specifies that the "effects of obsolescence, demand, competition, and other economic factors may reduce a useful life."

22. When banking or thrift institutions are acquired in periods of high interest rates, application of the purchase method and subsequent amortization of acquired intangibles over an extended period of time may produce a significant effect on the subsequent reported results of operations of the combined enterprise. In such periods, if low-rate interest-bearing assets are discounted to their fair values using current interest rates, the fair value of liabilities assumed may exceed by a substantial amount the fair value of tangible and identifiable intangible assets acquired. That excess often has been reported as goodwill in applying the purchase method under Opinion 16. The discount on the interest-bearing assets is amortized to income over the remaining lives of those assets using the interest method. If the goodwill is amortized straight-line over a period that exceeds the period the discount is amortized to income, the subsequent reported earnings for the combined enterprise may show a dramatic increase compared with the sum of the separate results of those enterprises absent the combination.

23. Some believe that the goodwill recognized in such circumstances generally does not represent a negotiated premium paid for intangible factors that are expected to enhance future profit levels. They contend that the amount recognized is often merely a function of current interest rates. Others believe that the current economic and competitive conditions facing the banking and thrift industries do not support the selection of a 40-year estimated useful life, especially in view of the anomalous effect on postcombination earnings that the use of such an extended life can produce. Still others believe that goodwill recognized in the acquisition of such institutions is not different in nature from goodwill recognized in other acquisitions and that the existing provisions of Opinion 17 provide adequate guidance in determining the estimated life.

24. In July 1982, the Accounting Standards Executive Committee of the AICPA requested the FASB to address the accounting for business combinations of mutual thrift institutions. The committee requested the Board to issue guidance that would produce meaningful results in accounting for these combinations and reduce the diversity in practice. On August 11, 1982, the Board added to its agenda a project to address the amortization of the unidentifiable intangible asset recognized in certain acquisitions of banking or thrift institutions. On October 7, 1982, the Board issued an FASB Exposure Draft, *Accounting for Certain Acquisitions of Banking or Thrift Institutions.* The Board received 80 letters of comment on that Exposure Draft. On December 13, 1982, the Board conducted a public hearing on the Exposure Draft. Thirteen organizations and individuals presented their views at the hearing.

Appendix B

BASIS FOR CONCLUSIONS

25. This appendix discusses the significant comments received on the Exposure Draft and the factors deemed significant by the Board in reaching the conclusions in this Statement, including alternatives considered and reasons for accepting some and rejecting others. Individual Board members gave greater weight to some factors than to others.

Scope

26. Many respondents to the Exposure Draft pointed out that the issues of purchase accounting and the recognition and amortization of intangible assets are not unique to acquisitions of banking and thrift institutions. They suggested that if the Board perceives a problem with respect to those issues, it should undertake a comprehensive project to readdress the accounting for business combinations by all types of enterprises. They stated that the Exposure Draft discriminated against thrift institutions in particular and that such an approach ran counter to the Board's general practice of promulgating standards that are evenhanded and applicable to all enterprises.

27. Board members agree that questions concerning purchase accounting and the recognition and amortization of intangible assets are not unique to acquisitions of banking and thrift institutions but believe that a comprehensive reconsideration of Opinions 16 and 17 should not be undertaken at this time. Accounting for business combinations and intangible assets are subjects with a long history of diverse views and controversy among standard setters and among others interested in financial reporting—preparers, users, auditors, academics, and the financial press. As one would expect, individual Board members have different views on those subjects, and it is neither feasible nor appropriate to reconsider the pervasive issues of business combinations and intangible assets in the context of this narrow, but significant and urgent, practice problem. Accordingly, the Board decided to restrict the scope of this Statement to certain combinations involving the acquisition of a banking or thrift institution in order to address that problem in a timely manner. However, most Board members believe that if goodwill is recognized in the acquisition of any enterprise having liabilities in excess of its assets it generally would be short-lived.

Unidentifiable Intangible Asset

28. Many respondents stated that the Board's proposal to equate the amortization period for an

unidentifiable intangible asset with the average life
of the interest-bearing assets acquired is arbitrary
and conceptually unsound, and they urged the
Board to abandon the project. They stated that
enterprises that acquire banking and thrift institutions pay a premium to gain entry into new markets,
to acquire established branches with existing customer relationships, to acquire an existing deposit
base, and for other factors. They also indicated that
goodwill recognized in a banking or thrift acquisition relates to the expectation of enhanced future
earnings just as it does in acquisitions of other types
of enterprises. They pointed out that the proposed
amortization method implies that an acquiring
enterprise has paid a premium to acquire an institution's interest-bearing assets, when in fact that
aspect of the acquisition is of least importance.
Most of those respondents stated that the existing
guidance in Opinion 17 is sufficient to allow
enterprises and auditors to reach reasonable conclusions about the useful life of the unidentifiable
intangible.

29. All Board members recognize that acquisitions
of banking and thrift institutions seldom, if ever, are
consummated for the purpose of acquiring a portfolio of interest-bearing assets. In both Interpretation
9 and this Statement, the Board has emphasized that
intangible factors of the nature referred to in the
preceding paragraph should be identified and recognized if their fair values can be reliably measured.
The Board understands that identified intangibles
have not always been separately recognized in the
past.

30. The Board believes that the use of a 40-year
maximum amortization period in the face of existing economic and competitive uncertainties confronting the banking and thrift industries is
inappropriate. That accounting for such combinations produces results that lack economic substance,
that destroy both consistency of reporting by the
enterprise and comparability among similar
enterprises, and that have the capacity to mislead
users and damage the credibility of financial reporting. Accordingly, the Board concluded that more
explicit guidance was needed to improve the relevance and reliability of financial reporting.

31. For a variety of reasons discussed below, the
Board believes that if the fair value of the liabilities
assumed in an acquisition exceeds the fair value of
tangible and identified intangible assets acquired,
the remaining life of the long-term interest-bearing
assets acquired is an appropriate maximum period
for amortizing the unidentifiable intangible asset
attributable to that excess. It is important to observe
that Board members support this industry-specific
standard primarily because they agree that a rapid
and pragmatic resolution of the problem is essential.

32. Most Board members believe that Opinion 16
requires that the amount by which the fair value of
liabilities assumed exceeds the fair value of identifiable assets acquired be recognized as an unidentifiable intangible asset. They also believe that this
excess should be amortized over a relatively short
period because of the uncertainty about the nature
and extent of the estimated future benefits related to
that asset. Ordinarily, the form of consideration
given in a business combination (for example, cash,
assumption of debt, or issuance of stock) does not
affect the reporting of the transaction. However, the
Board believes that a deficiency of identifiable
assets (determined using fair values) is indicative of
uncertainty as to the recoverability of any unidentifiable intangible and augments the uncertainty
inherent in the economic and competitive environment of banking and thrift institutions. In many
cases, the acquired banking or thrift institution has
incurred recent operating losses, and its prospects
for returning (or contributing) to profitable operations in the future depend in large part on the level
of future interest rates. The nature and extent of
future benefits related to the intangible asset also
may be impacted by the possible deregulation of the
banking and thrift industries.

33. Most Board members also support the amortization method specified in paragraph 5 as a practical solution for eliminating what they believe is an
unwarranted positive effect on earnings when a
troubled financial institution is acquired and an
unidentifiable intangible asset is recognized and
amortized over an extended period. They agree that
an increase in earnings may occur after a business
combination as a result of acquiring a profitable
enterprise or because of economic advantages that
the combination has produced, but they believe that
reporting a substantial increase in earnings without
any substantive change in the economic condition of
the combined enterprise is not representationally
faithful and that the frequency of such reporting has
harmed the credibility of financial reporting in
general. Some Board members also support an
amortization method based on the lives of the
interest-bearing assets acquired because they believe
that that period more closely approximates the useful life of a customer list or deposit base than does a
40-year period.

34. Some Board members also believe that the purchase method of accounting may be inappropriate
for most combinations of *mutual* banking and thrift
institutions and note that a majority of thrift institutions are organized under that form of ownership.
Combinations of those institutions generally do not
involve the transfer of cash, other assets, or equity
interests to the previous owners of the acquired institution. Those Board members further support the
amortization method specified in paragraph 5

because it often results in reporting approximately the same amount of postcombination net income that would have been reported if the combination had been accounted for by combining the previous carrying amounts of the two enterprises.

Nature of Problem

35. Several respondents said the Board should re-examine the applicability of Opinion 16 to a combination of mutual banking or thrift institutions instead of pursuing the tentative conclusions in the Exposure Draft. They stated that Opinion 16's criteria for using the pooling-of-interests method are difficult to apply in a combination of mutuals and indicated that those criteria were not designed with mutual institutions in mind. Some of those respondents recommended that the Board explain how the pooling-of-interests criteria should be applied in a combination of mutuals. Others stated that the Board should mandate the use of the pooling-of-interests method in such combinations. Still others indicated that purchase accounting should be used.

36. Board members considered addressing the question of whether the methods of accounting for a business combination specified in Opinion 16 (that is, the purchase method and the pooling-of-interests method) are appropriate for business combinations of mutual banking and thrift institutions. Most Board members believe that (a) the Accounting Principles Board in Opinion 16 did not specifically consider such combinations and (b) application of the criteria in paragraphs 46-48 of Opinion 16 to combinations of mutual institutions is not clear. Most Board members believe such a reconsideration would be time-consuming and would delay resolution of the pressing accounting question at hand. The Board also notes that the reporting problem being addressed is not limited to combinations of mutuals. Stockholder-owned banking and thrift institutions are also involved in business combinations. The Board concluded that a broad consideration of accounting for business combinations of mutuals should be included as part of any future project to readdress accounting for business combinations in general.

37. Some respondents stated that the reporting problems addressed in this project have resulted from the failure of enterprises and auditors to properly apply the existing guidance in Opinion 17. Some of those respondents said that a 40-year life for goodwill may not be appropriate in many circumstances but suggested that the Board view the current problem as an auditing or enforcement matter and not take on the role of a mediator. They believe that the existing principles of Opinion 17 are sound and should not be changed to address such a limited problem. Some of those respondents pro-

vided the Board with data indicating the problem was not as widespread as some others had asserted. However, research by the FASB staff indicated that the use of a 40-year life for goodwill has become common. The Board assessed both the severity of the problem and the adequacy of existing guidance and concluded that, on balance, more explicit guidance was needed to minimize diversity in practice and to improve the relevance and reliability of financial reporting.

Perceived Economic Consequences

38. Some respondents recommended that the Board withdraw the proposal because its adoption would have adverse economic consequences. Those respondents stated that the adoption of the provisions of the Exposure Draft in a final Statement would (a) prevent economically sound mergers from occurring, (b) put a strain on the resources of regulatory insurance agencies because potential acquiring enterprises would demand an increased amount of financial assistance, (c) frustrate the thrift industry's survival plans, or (d) impair an enterprise's ability to restructure and meet changing economic conditions. The Board was not persuaded by those arguments. The Board believes that this Statement will not affect an enterprise's ability to survive or restructure. Those abilities are a function of future cash flows, management action, and legal and regulatory restrictions rather than a function of accounting standards. In addition, the Board believes that the amortization provisions of this Statement will produce accounting information that is more relevant, reliable, and neutral for purposes of decision making. A primary focus of financial reporting is information about an enterprise's performance provided by measures of earnings and its components. The need for relevant and reliable measures of earnings following the acquisition of a banking or thrift institution was a major factor contributing to the Board's decision.

Subsequent Dispositions of Interest-Bearing Assets

39. Many respondents asked whether the proposed amortization method and the provision of paragraph 11(b) of the Exposure Draft were intended to require an enterprise to reduce goodwill proportionally when all or a portion of the acquired interest-bearing assets are sold subsequent to the acquisition date. Some of those respondents stated that such reporting may be appropriate, but only if the acquiring enterprise sells or liquidates a large segment or separable group of those assets (paragraph 32 of Opinion 17). They requested the Board to clarify the meaning of *large segment or separable group of assets* in the context of the banking and thrift industries. Other respondents also asked for clarification and stated that paragraph 32 of Opin-

ion 17 should not apply in *any* subsequent sale of acquired interest-bearing assets, such as mortgage loans and investment securities. They pointed out that some banking and thrift institutions sell and reinvest in interest-bearing assets every day and that the benefits attributable to goodwill are unaffected by the presence or absence of such fungible assets. The Board generally agreed with that latter view, and this Statement specifies that the sale of all or a portion of acquired interest-bearing assets does not automatically require a reduction in goodwill. A determination of whether a reduction in goodwill is appropriate should be based on the individual facts and circumstances. For example, if a sale of a large group of interest-bearing assets is accompanied by the loss of a significant and valuable customer base, a reduction in goodwill likely would be appropriate. On the other hand, if the proceeds of sale are reinvested in other forms of interest-bearing or other assets, no such reduction is necessary if there has been no reduction in the benefits attributable to goodwill.

Identified Intangibles

40. Several respondents stated that the adoption of a shorter useful life for goodwill recognized in certain acquisitions of banking or thrift institutions would induce affected enterprises to assign a greater portion (or all) of the excess purchase price to identified intangibles rather than to goodwill. Some of those respondents said that amounts often have not been assigned in the past to identified intangibles because (a) appraised values were not readily determinable, (b) those intangible factors often have indefinite lives, and (c) factors such as core deposits, branch networks, and territorial advantages represent the essence of goodwill. They questioned whether the benefits of separate identification would justify the costs. Other respondents said the Board should clarify Opinion 16 and Interpretation 9 to indicate that the measurements of such identified intangibles must be representationally faithful and verifiable. They stated that, without such guidance, unreliable amounts may be assigned to identified intangibles, thus circumventing this Statement's intent.

41. The Board reaffirms the principles in Opinion 16 and Interpretation 9 that require identified intangibles to be recognized apart from goodwill and amortized over their estimated useful lives. The Board does not view as undesirable any increased effort to identify and measure specific intangible assets acquired in a business combination. However, the Board agrees with those respondents who stated that such intangible assets should be recognized only when they can be separately identified and their fair values can be reliably measured. Accordingly, this Statement specifies that the measurements of identi-

fied intangible assets must be verifiable and representationally faithful. The Board disagrees with those respondents who stated that intangible assets attributed to deposit accounts and customer relationships generally have indefinite lives. Those respondents viewed such relationships as being constantly renewed and growing and, therefore, indicated that a 40-year useful life may often be appropriate. The Board notes that Interpretation 9 refers to intangible factors representing the capacity of *existing* accounts to generate future income or new business. The Board recognizes that many enterprises purchase a banking or thrift institution with the expectation of maintaining and even expanding the existing customer base and, thereby, the value of the related intangible asset; however, only purchased intangible assets are capitalizable under present generally accepted accounting principles. The Board believes that the cost and useful life of acquired intangible assets should not reflect the costs and expectations of developing, maintaining, or restoring such intangibles after they are acquired.

Other Matters

42. A few respondents requested the Board to explain how the provisions of the Exposure Draft should be applied when a combination does not involve the acquisition of a significant amount of interest-bearing assets, such as in the acquisition of a branch location. The Board understands that such acquisitions often involve the assumption of deposit liabilities by the acquiring enterprise in exchange for a cash payment in an amount less than the fair value of the deposit liabilities assumed. In such circumstances, the Board believes identifiable intangible assets should be recognized as provided in Opinion 16, Interpretation 9, and paragraph 4 of this Statement. If a portion of the purchase price is allocated to an unidentifiable intangible, the Board believes that amount should be amortized over a relatively short period of time, not to exceed the estimated average remaining life of the existing customer base acquired. The value of a customer base was cited most often by respondents as the primary factor acquired in such transactions.

43. Some respondents questioned portions of the Exposure Draft that dealt with reporting regulatory financial assistance granted to an enterprise as an inducement for that enterprise to acquire a banking or thrift institution. Some stated that subsequent repayments of regulatory assistance should not be charged to income automatically because such reporting may not be consistent with the initial reporting of the assistance. The Board understands that repayment requirements generally are related to future profitability levels or other criteria based on future revenues or expenses. In those cases, the Board believes the nature of the repayment is similar

to a profit-sharing arrangement and that the repayments should be charged to expense, regardless of the manner in which the assistance was initially reported.

44. A few respondents stated that estimates of regulatory reimbursements for any future operating losses should not be recognized at the time of combination because the amount of assistance cannot be reliably measured. The Board is in general agreement with those respondents. However, the Board believes that certain forms of regulatory assistance expected to be effective in indemnifying an enterprise from all or a portion of any losses that may result from holding certain low-rate interest-bearing assets acquired in a combination accounted for using the purchase method should be taken into consideration in determining the fair value of the assets acquired. Those forms of assistance represent probable future economic benefits that will result in future cash flows as a result of either (a) payment by a regulatory authority (if interest rates increase or remain constant) or (b) reduced cost of funds (if interest rates decline). The Board believes that reporting the effect of this benefit as part of the carrying amount of the interest-bearing assets acquired is a reasonable approach.

45. A few respondents suggested that this Statement should be effective for business combinations initiated after the issuance of the Statement rather than for combinations initiated after September 30, 1982. They argued that it is inappropriate to establish a retroactive effective date in a Statement that changes existing standards, especially when those standards have previously been acceptable. Although the Board hopes that the conditions that led to the reporting problems addressed by this Statement are temporary, the accounting for intangible assets may affect financial reporting for an extended period. The Board considered when this Statement should become effective and the transition method that should be applied by enterprises in adopting it in that light, weighing considerations of consistent, comparable, and credible reporting with fairness to preparers who have adopted or may yet adopt practices this Statement would change, fairness to those who did not, and fairness to users of financial reports. Those are subjective considerations and individual Board members attached differing weights. Accordingly, the effective date of September 30, 1982 and the prospective application reflect a compromise among Board members, some of whom would prefer an earlier effective date or retroactive application or both, and others who would prefer that the Statement become effective upon issuance.

Statement of Financial Accounting Standards No. 73
Reporting a Change in Accounting for
Railroad Track Structures

an amendment of APB Opinion No. 20

STATUS

Issued: August 1983

Effective date: For changes from retirement-replacement-betterment accounting to depreciation accounting made after June 30, 1983

Affects: Amends APB 20, paragraph 27

Affected by: No other pronouncements

SUMMARY

This Statement amends APB Opinion No. 20, *Accounting Changes,* to specify that a change to depreciation accounting for railroad track structures shall be reported by restating financial statements of all prior periods presented. The Statement is effective for changes made after June 30, 1983; however, earlier application is encouraged but not required. Prior to 1983, railroads generally followed betterment accounting for track structures in their general purpose financial statements. In 1983, the Interstate Commerce Commission (ICC) adopted changes requiring depreciation accounting in ICC filings. As a result, railroads and their accountants requested a determination of how best to report a voluntary change from betterment to depreciation accounting for general purpose financial reporting. This Statement is a response to that request.

Statement of Financial Accounting Standards No. 73
Reporting a Change in Accounting for Railroad Track Structures

an amendment of APB Opinion No. 20

CONTENTS

INTRODUCTION

1. This Statement amends APB Opinion No. 20, *Accounting Changes,* to specify that a change to depreciation accounting for railroad track structures should be reported by restating financial statements of all prior periods presented.

STANDARDS OF FINANCIAL ACCOUNTING AND REPORTING

Amendment to APB Opinion No. 20

2. A change from retirement-replacement-betterment accounting (RRB) to depreciation accounting is added to the last sentence of paragraph 27 of Opinion 20, which will read as follows:

The changes that should be accorded this treatment are: (a) a change from the LIFO method of inventory pricing to another method, (b) a change in the method of accounting for long-term construction-type contracts, (c) a change to or from the "full cost" method of accounting which is used in the extractive industries, and (d) a change from retirement-replacement-betterment accounting to depreciation accounting.

Effective Date and Transition

3. This Statement shall be effective for changes in accounting from RRB to depreciation accounting made after June 30, 1983. Earlier application is encouraged but is not required.

> **The provisions of this Statement need not be applied to immaterial items**

This Statement was adopted by the unanimous vote of the seven members of the Financial Accounting Standards Board:

Donald J. Kirk, *Chairman*	Victor H. Brown	Robert T. Sprouse
Frank E. Block	John W. March	Ralph E. Walters
	David Mosso	

Appendix

BACKGROUND INFORMATION AND BASIS FOR CONCLUSIONS

4. Railroads and their accountants requested a determination by the Board of how best to report a voluntary change from betterment to depreciation accounting for general purpose reporting.

5. On February 17, 1983, the Interstate Commerce Commission (ICC) ruled that railroads must use depreciation accounting for railroad track structures in reports to the ICC. The ruling is effective for 1983 annual filings, 1984 quarterly filings, and all filings thereafter with the ICC. The ICC previously had required RRB for railroad track structures in reports to the ICC.

6. Under RRB, the initial costs of installing track

are capitalized, not depreciated, and remain capitalized until the track is retired. The costs of replacing track are expensed unless a betterment (for example, replacing a 110-lb. rail with a 132-lb. rail) occurs. In that case, the amount by which the cost of the new part exceeds the current cost of the part replaced is considered a betterment and is capitalized but not depreciated, and the current cost of the part replaced is expensed. Railroads generally have used RRB for financial reporting.

7. The ICC ruling does not apply to financial reporting by railroads, but the Board has been informed that many railroads plan to adopt depreciation accounting for financial reporting. A change from RRB to depreciation accounting would be a change in accounting principle under Opinion 20.

8. Opinion 20 specifies that most changes in accounting principle should be reported by including the cumulative effect of the change in net income of the period of change. The Opinion provides for certain exceptions that should be reported by restating financial statements of all prior periods presented. Those exceptions are: (a) a change from the LIFO method of inventory pricing to another method, (b) a change in the method of accounting for long-term construction-type contracts, and (c) a change to or from the "full cost" method of accounting which is used in the extractive industries.

9. The Board believes that a change from RRB to depreciation accounting should be included among the exceptions noted in paragraph 8 because that change is another specific instance in which the advantages of comparability of financial statements resulting from restating financial statements outweigh the disadvantages. Therefore, the Board decided to amend Opinion 20 to specify that a change from RRB to depreciation accounting

should be reported by restating financial statements of all prior periods presented.

10. An Exposure Draft of a proposed Statement, *Reporting a Change in Accounting for Railroad Track Structures,* was issued on April 12, 1983. The Board received 28 comment letters in response to the Exposure Draft, most of which expressed agreement. Certain of the comments received and the Board's consideration of them are discussed in the remaining paragraphs.

11. Some respondents stated that the Board should reconsider all of the provisions of Opinion 20. Those respondents suggested that a reconsideration of Opinion 20 would eliminate the need to amend that Opinion for exceptions as they arise. The Board concluded that a separate Statement on reporting a change in accounting for railroad track structures is appropriate because a need for timely guidance was demonstrated and there is no evidence that Opinion 20 needs to be reconsidered in its entirety. Also, voluntary accounting changes are infrequent, and the Board sees little benefit in attempting to devise a new implementation method applicable to all such changes.

12. Some respondents indicated that a Statement should not be issued on reporting a change in accounting for railroad track structures because it is a narrow issue. The Board considered other means of addressing this issue, such as through a Technical Bulletin, but concluded that at this time a response to the issue should be effected through a Statement.

13. The Board concluded that it could reach an informed decision on the basis of existing information without a public hearing and that the effective date and transition specified in paragraph 3 are advisable in the circumstances.

Statement of Financial Accounting Standards No. 74
Accounting for Special Termination
Benefits Paid to Employees

STATUS

Issued: August 1983

Effective Date: For special termination benefits offered after June 30, 1983

Affects: Amends APB 8, paragraph 31

Affected by: Superseded by FAS 88

(The next page is 743.)

Appendix

BACKGROUND INFORMATION
AND BASIS FOR CONCLUSIONS

5. Statement 35 was issued in March 1980 and defines generally accepted accounting principles for general purpose external financial reports of defined benefit pension plans. It was intended to apply both to plans in the private sector and to plans sponsored by state and local governmental units. As originally issued, Statement 35 was to be effective for plan years beginning after December 15, 1980.

6. In April 1982, the Board issued Statement 59. That Statement amended Statement 35 by deferring its applicability until plan years beginning after June 15, 1982 for plans that are sponsored by and provide benefits for the employees of one or more state or local governmental units.

7. In November 1982, the Financial Accounting Foundation (FAF) reached agreement with the Municipal Finance Officers Association, the National Association of State Auditors, Comptrollers and Treasurers, and the American Institute of Certified Public Accountants regarding the establishment of a Governmental Accounting Standards Board (GASB). The Foundation's trustees have approved the formation of an FAF committee to oversee all aspects of implementation of the agreement. Among the questions that remain to be resolved is how standards should be set for government-related entities (such as hospitals, municipal utilities, universities, and pension plans) that are similar to entities in the private sector.

8. As indicated in paragraph 1, the Board has been requested to further extend the effective date of Statement 35 for pension plans of state and local governmental units. The Board believes that the current efforts to establish a new structure for setting accounting standards for state and local governmental units bear on the consideration to amend Statement 35. The Board believes that those efforts might be impaired by imposition of new standards at this time or by the existence of differing standards issued by different bodies.

9. On June 7, 1983, the FASB issued an Exposure Draft proposing deferral of the effective date for application of Statement 35 to pension plans of state and local governmental units until plan years beginning after June 15, 1985. The Exposure Draft was issued after the Board was informed by representatives of the National Council on Governmental Accounting (NCGA) that the NCGA would consider at its June 1983 meeting taking similar action regarding its recently issued Statement 6, *Pension Accounting and Financial Reporting: Public Employee Retirement Systems and State and Local Government Employers.* NCGA Statement 6 differs significantly from Statement 35 in the measurement of participants' benefits and the basis for valuing plan investments. The Board received 10 letters of comment in response to the Exposure Draft, all of which generally supported extending the period of mutual deferral of both Statement 35 and NCGA Statement 6. Subsequent to issuance of the Exposure Draft, the NCGA has taken various actions regarding the effective date of Statement 6. The Board understands that the NCGA will soon issue its Interpretation 8 which will extend indefinitely the effective date of Statement 6.

10. The Board believes that a mutual deferral of both Statement 35 and NCGA Statement 6 is appropriate while discussions relating to the formation and operation of the GASB are in progress. Accordingly, the Board decided to defer indefinitely the applicability of Statement 35 to pension plans of state and local governmental units pending further action by the Board.

11. The Board has concluded that it can reach an informed decision on the basis of existing information without a public hearing and that the effective date specified in paragraph 4 is advisable in the circumstances.

(This page intentionally left blank.)

Statement of Financial Accounting Standards No. 76
Extinguishment of Debt

an amendment of APB Opinion No. 26

STATUS

Issued: November 1983

Effective Date: For transactions entered into after December 31, 1983

Affects: Supersedes APB 26, paragraphs 2 and 3(a)
Amends APB 26, paragraphs 3(c), 19, and 21
Amends FAS 22, footnote 1
Amends FAS 32, Appendix A, SOP 78-5

Affected by: Paragraph 7 amended by FAS 111
Superseded by FAS 125

Other Interpretive Pronouncement: FTB 84-4 (Superseded by FAS 125)

(The next page is 755.)

(This page intentionally left blank.)

Statement of Financial Accounting Standards No. 77
Reporting by Transferors for Transfers
of Receivables with Recourse

STATUS

Issued: December 1983

Effective Date: For transfers of receivables with recourse entered into after December 31, 1983

Affects: Amends FAS 13, paragraph 20
    Amends FAS 32, Appendix A

Affected by: Paragraph 9 amended by FAS 105
    Superseded by FAS 125

Other Interpretive Pronouncement: FTB 85-2 (Superseded by FAS 125)

(The next page is 766.)

Statement of Financial Accounting Standards No. 78
Classification of Obligations That Are
Callable by the Creditor

an amendment of ARB No. 43, Chapter 3A

STATUS

Issued: December 1983

Effective Date: For financial statements for fiscal years beginning after December 15, 1983 and for interim accounting periods within those fiscal years

Affects: Amends ARB 43, Chapter 3A, paragraph 7

Affected by: No other pronouncements

Issues Discussed by FASB Emerging Issues Task Force (EITF)

Affects: No EITF Issues

Interpreted by: Paragraph 5 interpreted by EITF Issues No. 86-5 and 86-30

Related Issues: No EITF Issues

SUMMARY

This Statement amends ARB No. 43, Chapter 3A, "Current Assets and Current Liabilities," to specify the balance sheet classification of obligations that, by their terms, are or will be due on demand within one year (or operating cycle, if longer) from the balance sheet date. It also specifies the classification of long-term obligations that are or will be callable by the creditor either because the debtor's violation of a provision of the debt agreement at the balance sheet date makes the obligation callable or because the violation, if not cured within a specified grace period, will make the obligation callable. Such callable obligations are to be classified as current liabilities unless one of the following conditions is met:

a. The creditor has waived or subsequently lost the right to demand repayment for more than one year (or operating cycle, if longer) from the balance sheet date.
b. For long-term obligations containing a grace period within which the debtor may cure the violations, it is probable that the violation will be cured within that period, thus preventing the obligation from becoming callable.

Short-term obligations expected to be refinanced on a long-term basis, including those callable obligations discussed herein, continue to be classified in accordance with FASB Statement No. 6, *Classification of Short-Term Obligations Expected to Be Refinanced*. This Statement is effective for financial statements for fiscal years beginning after December 15, 1983 and for interim periods within those fiscal years.

Statement of Financial Accounting Standards No. 78
Classification of Obligations That Are Callable by the Creditor

an amendment of ARB No. 43, Chapter 3A

CONTENTS

INTRODUCTION

1. The FASB has been requested to clarify how obligations that are callable[1] by the creditor should be presented by the debtor in a balance sheet in which liabilities are classified as current or noncurrent. Specifically, the issue is whether an obligation should be classified as a current liability if the debtor is in violation of a provision[2] of a long-term debt agreement at the balance sheet date and (a) the violation makes the obligation callable by the creditor within one year from the balance sheet date or (b) the violation, if not cured within a specified grace period, will make the obligation callable within one year from the balance sheet date (or operating cycle in both cases, if longer). In considering that issue, the Board also decided to clarify whether an obligation should be classified as a current liability if the obligation, by its terms, is or will be due on demand within that period.

2. Some obligations, by their terms, are due on demand; that is, they are callable by the creditor. Other obligations have scheduled future maturities but nevertheless are callable if the debtor is in violation of certain provisions of the related debt agreement or if the creditor has the right to accelerate those maturities for other reasons. Some obligations with scheduled future maturities will become callable if an existing violation of a provision of the debt agreement is not cured within a specified grace period.

3. Paragraph 7 of ARB No. 43, Chapter 3A, "Current Assets and Current Liabilities," discusses obligations that should be considered current liabilities and states:

> The term *current liabilities* is used principally to designate obligations whose liquidation is reasonably expected to require the use of existing resources properly classifiable as current assets, or the creation of other current liabilities. . . .

FASB Statement No. 6, *Classification of Short-Term Obligations Expected to Be Refinanced*, amends ARB 43, Chapter 3A to require short-term obligations arising from transactions in the normal course of business that are due in customary terms (such as trade payables, advance collections, and accrued expenses) to be classified as current liabilities in all instances. Other short-term obligations are excluded from current liabilities under that Statement only if the enterprise intends to refinance the obligation on a long-term basis and such intent is supported by an ability to consummate the refinancing, demonstrated by either a financing agreement or the post-balance-sheet-date issuance of a long-term obligation or equity securities. Neither ARB 43, Chapter 3A nor Statement 6, however, discusses how obligations that are callable by the creditor should be presented in a classified balance sheet. As a result of differing views on such presentation, the same types of obligations have been classified differently by various entities in similar circumstances.

---

[1]An obligation is *callable* at a given date if the creditor has the right at that date to demand, or to give notice of its intention to demand, repayment of the obligation owed to it by the debtor.

[2]A *violation of a provision* is the failure to meet a condition in a debt agreement or a breach of a provision in the agreement for which compliance is objectively determinable, whether or not a grace period is allowed or the creditor is required to give notice of its intention to demand repayment.

APPLICABILITY AND SCOPE

4. This Statement applies to obligations reported in classified balance sheets and to disclosures made about maturities of obligations reported in both classified and unclassified balance sheets. It does not modify Statement 6 or FASB Statement No. 47, *Disclosure of Long-Term Obligations.*

STANDARDS OF FINANCIAL ACCOUNTING AND REPORTING

Amendment to ARB No. 43, Chapter 3A

5. The following sentences and footnotes are added to the end of paragraph 7 of ARB 43, Chapter 3A:

The current liability classification is also intended to include obligations that, by their terms, are due on demand or will be due on demand within one year (or operating cycle, if longer) from the balance sheet date, even though liquidation may not be expected within that period. It is also intended to include long-term obligations that are or will be callable by the creditor either because the debtor's violation of a provision of the debt agreement at the balance sheet date makes the obligation callable or because the violation, if not cured within a specified grace period, will make the obligation callable. Accordingly, such callable obligations shall be classified as current liabilities unless one of the following conditions is met:

a. The creditor has waived* or subsequently lost† the right to demand repayment for more than one year (or operating cycle, if longer) from the balance sheet date.

b. For long-term obligations containing a grace period within which the debtor may cure the violation, it is probable‡ that the violation will be cured within that period, thus preventing the obligation from becoming callable.

If an obligation under (b) above is classified as a long-term liability (or, in the case of an unclassified balance sheet, is included as a long-term liability in the disclosure of debt maturities), the circumstances shall be disclosed. Short-term obligations that are expected to be refinanced on a long-term basis, including those callable obligations discussed herein, shall be classified in accordance with FASB Statement No. 6, *Classification of Short-Term Obligations Expected to Be Refinanced.*

---

*If the obligation is callable because of violations of certain provisions of the debt agreement, the creditor needs to waive its right with regard only to those violations.
†For example, the debtor has cured the violation after the balance sheet date and the obligation is not callable at the time the financial statements are issued.
‡*Probable* is defined in FASB Statement No. 5, *Accounting for Contingencies,* as "likely to occur" and is used in the same sense in this paragraph.

Effective Date and Transition

6. This Statement shall be effective for financial statements for fiscal years beginning after December 15, 1983 and for interim accounting periods within those fiscal years. Earlier application is encouraged in financial statements that have not previously been issued. This Statement may be, but is not required to be, applied retroactively to previously issued financial statements.

> **The provisions of this Statement need not be applied to immaterial items.**

This Statement was adopted by the affirmative votes of four members of the Financial Accounting Standards Board. Messrs. Block, Brown, and Walters dissented.

Messrs. Block, Brown, and Walters dissent from this Statement because they see no demonstrated need for it and because it is a further step to supplant judgment in financial reporting with arbitrary rules.

The concept of current liabilities, which was adopted over 35 years ago, comprises obligations whose liquidation is *reasonably expected* to consume existing current assets within a certain time span—usually one year. The reasonable-expectation notion implies that judgment should be applied to known facts and circumstances to assess the probable timing of liquidation. Statement 6 pointed out that reasonable expectations in the cases it considered must be supported by intent and evidence of an ability to refinance; but the Board then specifically rejected a strict maturity date (or worst-case) approach "because . . . [it] is not necessarily indicative of the point in time at which that obligation will require the use of the enterprise's funds" and because "that approach would also result in a major change in the concept of current liabilities described in . . . *ARB No. 43* . . ." (Statement 6, paragraph

23). The Board should not now change that concept of current liabilities unless it is able to demonstrate clearly how information that will result from the new concept is expected to be more useful.

This standard is a major change in the concept of current liabilities. It is based on a notion that obligations should be classified as current when they are legally callable within one year, whether or not they are likely to be called. This is a worst-case notion, not a reasonable-expectation notion. While the two notions may often give the same answer, they will not in all cases. It is asserted that this amendment will improve comparability. It will, in fact, cause situations to appear the same even when underlying facts and circumstances are sufficiently different to justify different reasonable expectations. This is not comparability; it is substituting an arbitrary rule for judgment.

Not only will the amendment classify essentially different situations similarly but it will also cause essentially similar situations to be classified differently. For example, the dissenters do not perceive any substantive difference between a demand loan and a loan with a subjective acceleration clause. In each case there must be cause for repayment to be demanded and the lender must not be unreasonable in demanding repayment. Thus, essentially similar liabilities could be classified as current under this Statement and as noncurrent under FASB Technical Bulletin No. 79-3, *Subjective Acceleration Clauses in Long-Term Debt Agreements.*

Members of the Financial Accounting Standards Board:

Donald J. Kirk,
Chairman
Frank E. Block

Victor H. Brown
John W. March
David Mosso

Robert T. Sprouse
Ralph E. Walters

Appendix

BACKGROUND INFORMATION AND BASIS FOR CONCLUSIONS

Introduction

7. An Exposure Draft of a proposed Statement, *Classification of Obligations That Are Callable by the Creditor,* was issued on July 30, 1982. The Board received 85 comment letters in response to the Exposure Draft. This appendix discusses the significant comments received during the exposure period and the factors deemed significant by the Board in reaching the conclusions in this Statement, including alternatives considered and reasons for accepting some and rejecting others. Individual Board members gave greater weight to some factors than to others. The Board concluded that it could reach an informed decision on the basis of existing information without a public hearing and that the effective date and transition specified in paragraph 6 are advisable in the circumstances.

8. Some have questioned the value of the current asset and current liability classifications which they believe are, at best, crude and superficial indicators of liquidity. Some Board members share those concerns; nonetheless, they recognize that those classifications and the resulting terms and ratios are widely used by creditors and are often incorporated in financing agreements. In addition, they believe that any reconsideration of the broad issue of balance sheet classification should be addressed in the Board's major agenda project on the reporting of income, cash flows, and financial position. Accordingly, until other measures of liquidity or funds flow are determined to be preferable, those Board members agreed to clarify the classification of obligations under the present system by proceeding with this project.

9. Several respondents to the Exposure Draft questioned the need for a Statement to specify how an enterprise should classify an obligation that is callable by the creditor. They stated that the issues covered by the Exposure Draft are narrow, that adequate accounting guidance already exists, and that the exercise of judgment in the context of existing standards, such as ARB 43, Chapter 3A and Statement 6, provides satisfactory results. Other respondents said that the issues covered by the Exposure Draft are important practice problems that need an objective standard for resolution. Comments received on the Exposure Draft and other information received by the Board showed that, under similar facts and circumstances, significant diversity in reporting practices of enterprises exists with respect to the classification of obligations that are callable by the creditor. Accordingly, the Board concluded that this Statement should be issued.

Subjective Acceleration Clauses

10. The Exposure Draft disclosed the Board's intent not to address the effects of a subjective acceleration

clause[3] in classifying a debtor's obligation. However, some respondents recommended that the Statement be expanded to include that issue since they believe it is similar to those currently being addressed and should be resolved in a consistent manner. Other respondents disagreed with the assertion in paragraph 13 of the Exposure Draft that, in principle, a long-term obligation that contains a subjective acceleration clause is callable by the creditor. They indicated that although compliance with the conditions of a subjective acceleration clause may not, by definition, be objectively determinable, such clauses do require the occurrence of some event of noncompliance, regardless of how subjective the determination of that occurrence may be, before the obligation can be called. Furthermore, they stated that the creditor must be "reasonable" in making any subjective determination to sustain a demand for repayment.

11. In determining the effect of a subjective acceleration clause on classification, FASB Technical Bulletin No. 79-3, *Subjective Acceleration Clauses in Long-Term Debt Agreements,* indicates that a debtor should assess the likelihood that the creditor will accelerate the debt's maturity under that clause, whereas this Statement does not permit a debtor to use such an assessment in determining the classification of obligations with objectively determinable provisions. The Board understands, however, that long-term debt agreements containing subjective acceleration clauses also typically include objectively determinable provisions, such as working capital or net worth requirements. The Board believes that creditors and debtors perceive a substantive difference between the rights that a creditor has under such a subjective acceleration clause and the rights that a creditor has under either (a) an obligation that is due on demand or (b) an obligation that is callable because of a violation of an objectively determinable provision. Accordingly, the Board has concluded that this Statement should not modify Bulletin 79-3.

Classification of Various Callable Obligations

12. Most respondents generally favored the proposals in the Exposure Draft and stated that requiring all callable obligations to be classified as current liabilities will promote more comparable financial reporting among various entities. Some respondents, however, disagreed with the classifications that would be required for specific types of callable obligations and implied that classifying those obligations in a similar manner would create an unwarranted uniformity of presentation. Many of the latter respondents expressed the view that a callable obligation should be classified as a noncurrent liability if the creditor has not demanded repayment and there is no indication that the creditor intends to do so within the next year, a situation sometimes referred to as "continued forbearance." They maintained that classifying an obligation based on the discussion of current liabilities in ARB 43, Chapter 3A (particularly the phrase *reasonably expected to require the use of existing resources* in paragraph 7) would provide users of financial statements with the most useful information.

13. The Board believes that, for purposes of balance sheet classification, all obligations that are callable at the creditor's discretion are fundamentally alike and that the merits of setting an objective standard for determining classification outweigh the disadvantages. The Board further believes that assessments of liquidity and financial flexibility and comparisons of current liability positions may be obscured if the balance sheet classification of such callable obligations is based on the debtor's subjective expectations of the creditor's intent. Accordingly, the Board has concluded that, as a general principle, classification of debt in a debtor's balance sheet should be based on facts existing at the balance sheet date rather than on expectations. If the creditor has at that date, or will have within one year (or operating cycle, if longer) from that date, the unilateral right to demand immediate repayment of the debt under any provision of the debt agreement, the Board concluded that the obligation should be classified as a current liability unless (a) one of the conditions in paragraph 5 is met or (b) the obligation is expected to be refinanced on a long-term basis and the provisions of Statement 6 are met.

14. Some respondents disagreed with the provision of the Exposure Draft with respect to an obligation that is not currently callable but will become so within one year (or operating cycle, if longer) from the balance sheet date if an existing violation is not cured within a specified grace period. They stated that the obligation should be classified as a noncurrent liability because the creditor does not have the right to demand repayment at the balance sheet date and will not have that right within one year from the balance sheet date if the violation is cured or if the grace period will not expire within the next year (or operating cycle in both cases, if longer). They argued that requiring an obligation to be classified as a current liability in those circumstances negates the purpose of a grace period, which is to permit the debtor time to cure a violation without being subjected to its consequences. Other respondents agreed with the tentative conclusion of the Exposure Draft that would have required current classifica-

---

[3]A *subjective acceleration clause* is a provision in a debt agreement that states that the creditor may accelerate the scheduled maturities of the obligation under conditions that are not objectively determinable (for example, "if the debtor fails to maintain satisfactory operations" or "if a material adverse change occurs").

tion in all such circumstances. They stated that classification of such an obligation should not be based on an assessment of the likelihood of future changes in circumstances, that is, on the debtor's assessment of the likelihood that the violation will be cured before the grace period expires.

15. Because the violation will make the obligation callable if conditions existing at the balance sheet date do not change within the grace period, the Board considers such liabilities to be presumptively current. However, because the creditor does not have the right to call the obligation at the balance sheet date, the Board believes that the presumption for current classification can be overcome if it is also probable that the creditor will not obtain such a right under that provision of the debt agreement during the next year (or operating cycle, if longer). Accordingly, the Board concluded that such obligations should be classified as current liabilities unless it is probable that the violation will be cured within the grace period, thus preventing the obligation from becoming callable. This approach calls for an assessment of the probability that the debtor's own actions will prevent the creditor from *obtaining* the unilateral right to demand repayment within the next year; it differs from the approach favored by some respondents to assess the probability that another party (the creditor) will exercise an *existing* right. (Refer to paragraph 12.) Therefore, the Board believes that evaluating the probability that the violation will be cured within the grace period is not in conflict with the general principle described in paragraph 13 or with the classification required for the other types of callable obligations addressed by this Statement.

Other Matters

16. Some respondents suggested that the final Statement should distinguish between the consequences of significant violations of critical conditions and technical violations that are considered not to be of substance. They stated that implementation of the provisions of the Exposure Draft could result in serious and unintended consequences even in situations involving minor and easily correctible violations of debt agreement provisions. Other respondents said that the Exposure Draft substantially removes any auditor judgment in evaluating how an obligation should be classified when a violation exists. The Board believes that drawing a distinction between significant violations of critical conditions and technical violations is not practicable. A violation that a debtor considers to be technical may be considered critical by the creditor. Furthermore, a creditor may choose to use a technical violation as a means to withdraw from its lending relationship with the debtor. The Board believes that if the violation is considered insignificant by the creditor, then the debtor should be able to obtain a waiver as discussed in paragraph 5.

17. Some respondents recommended that the Statement be expanded to address the effect of a violation of a debt agreement that occurs between the balance sheet date and the date the financial statements are issued. Because accounting for events occurring after the balance sheet date is a pervasive issue that is beyond the scope of this project, the Board decided that consideration of that topic should not delay issuance of a final Statement.

18. Some respondents suggested that the Statement require specific disclosures when a debtor is in violation of a debt agreement provision. The Board concluded that existing disclosure practices for obligations classified as current liabilities are adequate. However, the Board decided to require disclosure of the circumstances for situations in which a debtor is in violation of a provision of the loan agreement but classifies the related debt as a long-term liability because it is probable that the violation will be cured within a specified grace period that extends beyond the date that the financial statements are to be issued.

19. Some respondents requested that additional time be provided for enterprises to implement this Statement to enable them to cure existing debt agreement violations or to renegotiate loan provisions that are likely to cause what they consider to be technical violations. The Board extended the effective date to include financial statements for fiscal years beginning after December 15, 1983 to be responsive to those concerns.

Statement of Financial Accounting Standards No. 79
Elimination of Certain Disclosures for
Business Combinations by Nonpublic Enterprises

an amendment of APB Opinion No. 16

STATUS

Issued: February 1984

Effective Date: For financial statements for fiscal years beginning after
December 15, 1983

Affects: Amends APB 16, paragraph 96

Affected by: No other pronouncements

SUMMARY

This Statement amends APB Opinion No. 16, *Business Combinations,* to eliminate the requirement for nonpublic enterprises to disclose pro forma results of operations for business combinations accounted for by the purchase method. Disclosure requirements for public enterprises are not changed by this Statement.

This Statement is a product of FASB research on financial reporting by private and small public companies. A number of participants in those research efforts cited accounting and disclosure requirements that they believe should not apply to nonpublic enterprises, including the pro forma disclosures prescribed by Opinion 16. The Board has concluded that the costs of providing the pro forma disclosures prescribed by Opinion 16 generally exceed the benefits for the users of nonpublic company financial statements.

This Statement is effective for financial statements for fiscal years beginning after December 15, 1983, with earlier application permitted in financial statements that have not previously been issued.

Statement of Financial Accounting Standards No. 79

Elimination of Certain Disclosures for Business Combinations by Nonpublic Enterprises

an amendment of APB Opinion No. 16

CONTENTS

INTRODUCTION

1. The FASB has undertaken research on financial reporting by private and small public companies to obtain information about the practices and views of managers, financial statement users, and public accountants involved with those companies.[1] A number of participants in those research efforts stated that the requirement to disclose pro forma results of operations for business combinations accounted for by the purchase method was unnecessary and too costly for private companies.

2. Paragraph 96 of APB Opinion No. 16, *Business Combinations,* requires an acquiring enterprise to disclose the following information in financial statements of the period in which a business combination accounted for by the purchase method occurs:

a. Results of operations for the current period as though the enterprises had combined at the beginning of the period, unless the acquisition was at or near the beginning of the period
b. Results of operations for the immediately preceding period as though the enterprises had combined at the beginning of that period if comparative financial statements are presented.

3. The Board has concluded that the disclosures prescribed by paragraph 96 of Opinion 16 should not be required in the financial statements of non-

public enterprises. The basis for the Board's conclusions is presented in the appendix to this Statement.

STANDARDS OF FINANCIAL ACCOUNTING AND REPORTING

4. Disclosures of pro forma results of operations prescribed in paragraph 96 of Opinion 16 for business combinations accounted for by the purchase method are not required for nonpublic enterprises.

5. For purposes of this Statement, a nonpublic enterprise is an enterprise other than one (a) whose debt or equity securities are traded in a public market, including those traded on a stock exchange or in the over-the-counter market (including securities quoted only locally or regionally), or (b) whose financial statements are filed with a regulatory agency in preparation for the sale of any class of securities.

Amendment to APB Opinion No. 16

6. The following footnote is added to the end of paragraph 96 of Opinion 16:

> *The disclosures prescribed by paragraph 96 are not required in the financial statements of nonpublic enterprises as defined by FASB Statement No. 79, *Elimination of Certain Disclosures for Business Combinations by Nonpublic Enterprises.*

---

[1]Refer to (a) FASB Invitation to Comment, *Financial Reporting by Private and Small Public Companies,* 1981; (b) FASB Special Report, *Financial Reporting by Privately Owned Companies: Summary of Responses to FASB Invitation to Comment,* 1983; and (c) FASB Research Report, *Financial Reporting by Private Companies: Analysis and Diagnosis,* prepared by A. Rashad Abdel-khalik, 1983.

Effective Date

7. This Statement shall be effective for financial statements for fiscal years beginning after December 15, 1983. Earlier application is permitted in financial statements that have not previously been issued.

This Statement was adopted by the unanimous vote of the seven members of the Financial Accounting Standards Board:

Donald J. Kirk,	Victor H. Brown	David Mosso
Chairman	Raymond C. Lauver	Robert T. Sprouse
Frank E. Block	John W. March	

Appendix

BACKGROUND INFORMATION AND BASIS FOR CONCLUSIONS

8. An Exposure Draft of a proposed Statement, *Elimination of Certain Disclosures for Business Combinations by Nonpublic Enterprises,* was issued on October 4, 1983. In response to the Exposure Draft the Board received 46 comment letters, most of which expressed agreement. This appendix discusses factors deemed significant by the Board in reaching the conclusions in this Statement. Individual Board members gave greater weight to some factors than to others. The Board concluded that it could reach an informed decision on the basis of existing information without a public hearing and that the effective date specified in paragraph 7 is advisable in the circumstances.

Responses to Invitation to Comment

9. Many public accountants who responded to the FASB Invitation to Comment, *Financial Reporting by Private and Small Public Companies,* criticized the requirement in Opinion 16 to disclose pro forma information as unnecessary and too costly for nonpublic companies. They stated that those companies are frequently unable to make the pro forma calculations themselves and that the public accountants frequently have to develop the information, which increases the costs of compliance. They also stated that they believe many users of nonpublic company financial statements do not use the information.

10. Responses to the Invitation to Comment indicate that bankers are the primary external users of the financial statements of most nonpublic companies. Bankers responding to the Invitation to Comment did not identify as unnecessary the requirement to disclose pro forma information. However, in follow-up discussions with the FASB's small business advisory group and others, bankers indicated that they do not believe the pro forma disclosures are always necessary.

Costs and Benefits of Providing Pro Forma Information

11. FASB Concepts Statements No. 1, *Objectives of Financial Reporting by Business Enterprises,* and No. 2, *Qualitative Characteristics of Accounting Information,* both recognize the constraint of costs in relation to benefits in considering the information required to be disclosed in financial statements. Paragraph 23 of Concepts Statement 1 states:

> The information provided by financial reporting involves a cost to provide and use, and generally the benefits of information provided should be expected to at least equal the cost involved.

12. The preparation of pro forma disclosures is usually costly because necessary information is not always readily available and the compilation of the disclosures is complex. Most nonpublic companies are relatively small and often do not have extensive accounting expertise. They usually obtain outside assistance to prepare financial reporting disclosures that are required only infrequently. Consequently, the Board believes that the disclosures of pro forma results of operations that are required in the event of business combinations are relatively costly for nonpublic enterprises.

13. The primary users of financial statements of nonpublic enterprises believe that the pro forma disclosures required by Opinion 16 are not always needed, and when the financial statement users want information about a significant business acquisition they frequently desire and obtain different information.

14. The Board's decision to eliminate the pro forma disclosure requirements in Opinion 16 for nonpublic enterprises is based on the assessment that the costs of requiring all nonpublic enterprises to provide those disclosures generally exceed the benefits to the users of nonpublic company financial statements. The disclosure requirements in paragraph 95 of Opinion 16 continue unchanged, including the

requirement to disclose the period for which results of operations of the acquired company are included in the income statement of the acquiring enterprise.

Mutual and Cooperative Organizations

15. Some Board members believe that the definition of nonpublic enterprises in paragraph 5 of this Statement inappropriately includes mutual and cooperative organizations whose financial statements are broadly distributed. Many of those organizations have large numbers of depositors, policyholders, patrons, and other interested parties whose primary source of financial information about the organization may be the financial statements. They believe that those organizations are public companies in a practical sense. They also note that those organizations are frequently involved in business combinations.

16. A few respondents to the Exposure Draft agreed with the Board members' views described in paragraph 15 and stated that the definition of a nonpublic enterprise in paragraph 5 should be changed to exclude mutual and cooperative organizations

whose financial statements are broadly distributed. The Board decided not to address mutual and cooperative organizations separately in this Statement because it would raise additional issues (including those referred to in paragraph 17) that might impede its efforts to provide timely relief from pro forma disclosure requirements for nonpublic enterprises.

Applicability to Public Enterprises

17. A few respondents to the Exposure Draft stated that the pro forma disclosures required by Opinion 16 are not cost effective for public enterprises, and should be eliminated for those enterprises also. The Board did not address the cost effectiveness of the pro forma disclosures required by Opinion 16 for public enterprises. Such an undertaking would necessarily involve broader issues, including a review of other disclosures required for business combinations by public companies. The Board believes that such a review would unnecessarily delay providing relief from pro forma disclosure requirements for nonpublic enterprises.

Statement of Financial Accounting Standards No. 80
Accounting for Futures Contracts

STATUS

Issued: August 1984

Effective Date: For futures contracts entered into after December 31, 1984. Disclosures required shall be made in financial statements for periods ending after December 15, 1984 for open futures contracts designated as hedges whether the other provisions of FAS 80 have been applied to those contracts or not.

Affects: Supersedes FTB 81-1

Affected by: Paragraph 5 amended by FAS 115

Other Interpretive Release: FASB *Highlights*, "Futures Contracts: Guidance on Applying Statement 80," June 1985 (Resolves EITF Issue No. 85-6)

Issues Discussed by FASB Emerging Issues Task Force (EITF)

Affects: No EITF Issues

Interpreted by: Paragraphs 4, 9, and 11 interpreted by EITF Issue No. 86-34

Related Issues: EITF Issues No. 84-7, 84-14, 84-36, 86-26, 86-28, 87-1, 87-2, 88-8, 90-17, 91-1, 91-4, 95-2, 95-11, 96-11, and 96-13 and Topic No. D-50

SUMMARY

This Statement establishes standards of accounting for exchange-traded futures contracts (other than contracts for foreign currencies). This project was undertaken to consider two AICPA Issues Papers that concern futures contracts and because the Board was aware of diversity in practice in accounting for futures contracts.

This Statement requires that a change in the market value of an open futures contract be recognized as a gain or loss in the period of the change unless the contract qualifies as a hedge of certain exposures to price or interest rate risk. Immediate gain or loss recognition is also required if the futures contract is intended to hedge an item that is reported at fair value (which frequently will be the case for futures contracts used as hedges by investment companies, pension plans, and broker-dealers).

If the hedge criteria specified in this Statement are met, a change in the market value of the futures contract is either reported as an adjustment of the carrying amount of the hedged item or included in the measurement of a qualifying subsequent transaction. Enterprises are required to cease accounting for a contract as a hedge if high correlation of changes in the market value of the futures contract and the effects of price or interest rate changes on the hedged item has not occurred.

This Statement is effective for futures contracts entered into after December 31, 1984, with earlier application encouraged in financial statements that have not been previously issued.

Statement of Financial Accounting Standards No. 80
Accounting for Futures Contracts

CONTENTS

INTRODUCTION AND SCOPE

1. This Statement establishes standards of financial accounting and reporting for **futures contracts**,[1] except for futures contracts for foreign currencies.[2] This Statement does not apply to forward placement or delayed delivery contracts and therefore does not prescribe or proscribe particular methods of accounting for such contracts.

2. The basic issue addressed in this Statement is how to account for a change in the market value of a futures contract. The general principle set forth in this Statement is that such a change is recognized in income when it occurs. However, for certain contracts, this Statement requires that the timing of recognition in income be related to the accounting for associated assets, liabilities, **firm commitments,** or transactions. Appendix B presents examples that illustrate the applicability of this Statement, and Appendix C contains background information and the basis for the Board's conclusions.

STANDARDS OF FINANCIAL ACCOUNTING AND REPORTING

Recognition of Changes in Market Value

3. A change in the market value of a futures contract[3] shall be recognized as a gain or loss in the period of the change unless the contract meets the criteria specified in this Statement to qualify as a hedge of an exposure to price or interest rate risk. If the hedge criteria are met, the accounting for the futures contract shall be related to the accounting for the hedged item so that changes in the market value of the futures contract are recognized in income when the effects of related changes in the price or interest rate of the hedged item are recognized.

Hedge Criteria

4. In applying this Statement, both of the following

---

[1]Terms defined in the glossary (Appendix A) are in **boldface type** the first time they appear in this Statement.

[2]The provisions of FASB Statement No. 52, *Foreign Currency Translation,* apply to accounting for foreign currency futures.

[3]For purposes of this Statement, the change in the market value of a futures contract equals the change in the contract's quoted market price multiplied by the contract size. For example, the change in the market value of a $100,000 U.S. Treasury bond futures contract whose price moves from 80-00 to 78-00 is $2,000.

conditions shall be met for a futures contract to qualify as a hedge:

a. *The item to be hedged exposes the enterprise to price (or interest rate) risk.* In this Statement, *risk* refers to the sensitivity of an enterprise's income for one or more future periods to changes in market prices or yields of existing assets, liabilities, firm commitments, or anticipated transactions. To meet this condition, the item or group of items intended to be hedged must contribute to the price or interest rate risk of the enterprise.[4] In determining if this condition is met, the enterprise shall consider whether other assets, liabilities, firm commitments, and anticipated transactions already offset or reduce the exposure.[5] An enterprise that cannot assess risk by considering other relevant positions and transactions for the enterprise as a whole because it conducts its risk management activities on a decentralized basis can meet this condition if the item intended to be hedged exposes the particular business unit that enters into the contract.

b. *The futures contract reduces that exposure and is designated*[6] *as a hedge.* At the inception of the hedge and throughout the hedge period, high correlation of changes in (1) the market value of the futures contract(s) and (2) the fair value of, or interest income or expense associated with, the hedged item(s) shall be probable[7] so that the results of the futures contract(s) will substantially offset the effects of price or interest rate changes on the exposed item(s). In addition to assessing information about the correlation during relevant past periods, the enterprise also shall consider the characteristics of the specific hedge, such as the degree of correlation that can be expected at various levels of higher or lower market prices or interest rates. A futures contract for a commodity or a financial instrument different from the item intended to be hedged may qualify as a hedge provided there is a clear economic relationship between the prices of the two commod-

ities or financial instruments, and provided high correlation is probable.

Hedges of Items Reported at Fair Value

5. If an enterprise includes unrealized changes in the fair value of a hedged item in income, a change in the market value of the related futures contract shall be recognized in income when the change occurs. The same accounting shall be applied to a futures contract that hedges an anticipated transaction if the asset to be acquired or liability to be incurred will be reported at fair value subsequent to acquisition or incurrence. Some enterprises report assets at fair value but include unrealized changes in that value in a separate component of stockholders' (or policyholders') equity pending sale or other disposition of the assets. A change in the market value of a futures contract that qualifies as a hedge of those assets also shall be included in that separate component of equity until sale or disposition of the assets unless paragraph 11 requires earlier recognition of a gain or loss in income because high correlation has not occurred.

Hedges of Existing Assets, Liabilities, and Firm Commitments

6. A change in the market value of a futures contract that qualifies as a hedge of an existing asset or liability shall be recognized as an adjustment of the carrying amount of the hedged item. A change in the market value of a futures contract that is a hedge of a firm commitment shall be included in the measurement of the transaction that satisfies the commitment. An enterprise may recognize the premium or discount on a hedge contract in income over the life of the contract if the commodity or financial instrument being hedged is deliverable under the terms of the futures contract, and if it is probable that both the hedged item and the futures contract will be retained to the delivery date specified in the contract. The premium or discount is computed at the inception of the hedge by reference

---

[4]An interest-bearing **financial instrument** that an enterprise will retain to maturity does not, in and of itself, create interest rate risk if the instrument's interest rate is fixed. The amount of cash inflows or outflows is certain (assuming no default) and is not affected by changes in market interest rates. Notwithstanding that the cash flows associated with the instrument are fixed, the enterprise may be exposed to interest rate risk if it has funded its assets with instruments having earlier maturities or repricing dates. Futures contracts may qualify as a hedge of a fixed-rate financial instrument the enterprise intends to hold to maturity if the maturity or repricing characteristics of the instrument contribute to the enterprise's overall asset-liability mismatch.

[5]For example, assets held for resale may subject the enterprise to price risk, but that risk already may be wholly or partially offset by firm fixed-price sales commitments. Floating-rate debt may result in interest rate risk for one enterprise but not for another because of differences in the maturity or repricing characteristics of the assets owned by each enterprise. As a further example, unpriced anticipated raw material requirements may be a risk in some industries because finished product and raw material prices do not move together. For other industries, such as commodity trading, an exposure to risk may exist only when the commodity is held or when there are firm fixed-price commitments.

[6]One or more futures contracts may be designated as a hedge of either an individual item or an identifiable group of essentially similar items (for example, government securities that have similar maturities and coupon rates).

[7]*Probable* is used here and in other parts of this Statement consistent with its use in FASB Statement No. 5, *Accounting for Contingencies,* to mean that a transaction or event is likely to occur.

to the contracted futures price and the fair value of the hedged item.

7. Recognition in income of the adjustment of the carrying amount of an asset or liability required by paragraph 6 shall be the same as other components of the carrying amount of that asset or liability.[8] An adjustment of the carrying amount of a hedged interest-bearing financial instrument that is otherwise reported at amortized cost shall be amortized as an adjustment of interest income or interest expense over the expected remaining life of the instrument. That amortization shall commence no later than the date that a particular contract is closed out, whether that contract is replaced by a similar contract for later delivery or not.

8. Some enterprises (for example, commodity dealers) may use futures contracts to hedge a net exposure comprising inventory held for sale and firm commitments to purchase and sell essentially similar assets. If associating individual futures contracts with the assets on hand or specific commitments is impractical because of the volume and frequency of transactions, reasonable allocations of the results of futures contracts between assets or commitments on hand at the end of a reporting period and assets sold during the period may be used. The method of allocation shall be consistent from period to period.

Hedges of Anticipated Transactions

9. A futures contract may relate to transactions (other than transactions involving *existing* assets or liabilities, or transactions necessitated by *existing* firm commitments) an enterprise expects, but is not obligated, to carry out in the normal course of business. A change in the market value of a futures contract that hedges the price or interest rate of such an anticipated transaction shall be included in the measurement of the subsequent transaction if the two conditions in paragraph 4 *and* both of the following conditions are met:

a. *The significant characteristics and expected terms of the anticipated transaction are identified.* The significant characteristics and expected terms include the expected date of the transaction, the commodity or type of financial instrument involved, and the expected quantity to be purchased or sold. For transactions involving interest-bearing financial instruments, the expected maturity of the instrument is also a significant term.
b. *It is probable that the anticipated transaction will occur.* Considerations in assessing the likeli-

hood that a transaction will occur include the frequency of similar transactions in the past; the financial and operational ability of the enterprise to carry out the transaction; substantial commitments of resources to a particular activity (for example, a manufacturing facility that can be used in the short run only to process a particular type of commodity); the length of time to the anticipated transaction date; the extent of loss or disruption of operations that could result if the transaction does not occur; and the likelihood that transactions with substantially different characteristics might be used to achieve the same business purpose (for example, an enterprise that intends to raise cash may have several ways of doing so, ranging from short-term bank loans to common stock offerings). Enterprises sometimes may determine that two or more approximately similar alternative transactions are equally likely to occur. For example, a financial institution that plans to issue short-term obligations at a particular future date may have the choice of issuing various types of such obligations in domestic or foreign markets. In such cases, futures contracts are not precluded from qualifying as a hedge if all hedge criteria are met regardless of which transaction will be undertaken.

10. The accounting for a futures contract that hedges an anticipated acquisition of assets or an anticipated issuance of liabilities shall be consistent with the enterprise's method of accounting for those types of assets or liabilities. For example, a loss shall be recognized for a futures contract that relates to an anticipated inventory purchase to the extent there is evidence that the amount will not be recovered through sales. If a futures contract that has been accounted for as a hedge is closed before the date of the anticipated transaction, the accumulated change in value of the contract shall continue to be carried forward (subject to the other considerations in this paragraph and paragraph 11) and included in the measurement of the related transaction. A pro rata portion of the futures results that would otherwise be included in the measurement of a subsequent transaction shall be recognized as a gain or loss when it becomes probable that the quantity of the anticipated transaction will be less than that originally hedged.

Ongoing Assessment of Correlation

11. An enterprise regularly shall assess the results of a futures contract designated as a hedge to determine if the high correlation required by paragraph 4(b) is being achieved. If that assessment indicates

---

[8]For example, an adjustment of the carrying amount of a hedged asset held for sale usually would be recognized in income when the asset is sold. However, earlier recognition may be necessary if other accounting standards, for example, ARB No. 43, Chapter 4, "Inventory Pricing," require that the adjusted carrying amount of the asset be written down to a lower amount.

high correlation has not occurred, the enterprise shall cease to account for the futures contract as a hedge and shall recognize a gain or loss to the extent the futures results have not been offset by the effects of price or interest rate changes on the hedged item since inception of the hedge. If the effects of price or interest rate changes on the hedged item are not readily determinable by reference to quoted market prices or rates, reasonable estimates may be used.

Disclosure

12. An enterprise that has entered into futures contracts that have been accounted for as hedges shall disclose (a) the nature of the assets, liabilities, firm commitments, or anticipated transactions that are hedged with futures contracts and (b) the method of accounting for the futures contracts. The disclosure of the method shall include a description of the events or transactions that result in recognition in income of changes in value of the futures contracts.

Rescission of Technical Bulletin

13. FASB Technical Bulletin No. 81-1, *Disclosure of Interest Rate Futures Contracts and Forward and Standby Contracts,* is rescinded.

Effective Date and Transition

14. The standards of financial accounting and reporting established by this Statement shall be effective for futures contracts entered into after December 31, 1984. Earlier application for futures contracts entered into during periods for which financial statements have not been issued is encouraged. The provisions of this Statement may be, but are not required to be, applied prospectively to all futures contracts open when this Statement is first adopted. Disclosures required by paragraph 12 shall be made in financial statements for periods ending after December 15, 1984 for open futures contracts designated as hedges whether the other provisions of this Statement have been applied to those contracts or not.

The provisions of this Statement need not be applied to immaterial items.

This Statement was adopted by the affirmative votes of six members of the Financial Accounting Standards Board. Mr. Lauver dissented.

Mr. Lauver dissents from this Statement because of the exception in paragraph 4(a), which permits some enterprises that conduct their risk management activities on a decentralized basis to follow hedge accounting without demonstrating that risk of the enterprise as a whole has been reduced. The cornerstone of the hedge accounting provisions of the Statement is the condition that enterprise risk be reduced. The exception would be appropriate, in Mr. Lauver's view, only under the assumption that the business unit that enters into the futures contract has risk of the same nature as the enterprise as a whole, an assumption that would not always be correct. To base the accounting on an arbitrarily assumed factual state without evidence that that is the factual state constitutes, he believes, abandonment of the essence of the hedge accounting provisions of the Statement. The exception permitted in paragraph 4(a) may result in a futures contract being accounted for as a hedge even though, as a result of that contract, risk of the reporting enterprise has been increased rather than reduced. When there is no knowledge of the nature and extent of risk existing within the enterprise as a whole, Mr. Lauver believes there is no basis for departing from the general method of accounting for futures contracts stated in paragraph 3.

Members of the Financial Accounting Standards Board:

Donald J. Kirk,	Frank E. Block	Victor H. Brown
Chairman	Raymond C. Lauver	John W. March
David Mosso	Robert T. Sprouse	

Appendix A

GLOSSARY

15. This appendix defines certain terms that are used in this Statement.

Financial Instrument
The term is used broadly in this Statement to include instruments usually considered to be securities (such as notes, bonds, debentures, and equities) as well as other evidences of indebtedness (such as money market instruments, certificates of deposit, mortgages, and commercial paper) that often are not referred to as securities.

Firm Commitment
An agreement, usually legally enforceable, under which performance is probable because of sufficiently large disincentives for nonperformance.

Futures Contract
A legal agreement between a buyer or seller and the clearinghouse of a futures exchange. The futures contracts covered by this Statement include those traded on regulated futures exchanges in the United States and contracts having similar characteristics that are traded on exchanges in other countries. Futures contracts covered by this Statement have the following characteristics: (a) They obligate the purchaser (seller) to accept (make) delivery of a standardized quantity of a commodity or financial instrument at a specified date or during a specified period, or they provide for cash settlement rather than delivery,[9] (b) they effectively can be canceled before the delivery date by entering into an offsetting contract for the same commodity or financial instrument, and (c) all changes in value of open contracts are settled on a regular basis, usually daily.

Appendix B

EXAMPLES OF APPLICATION OF THIS STATEMENT

16. This appendix presents examples that illustrate the application of this Statement. The examples do not address all possible uses of futures contracts. The facts assumed are illustrative only and are not intended to modify or limit in any way the provisions of this Statement. For simplicity, commissions and other transaction costs, initial margin (except in Example 1), and income taxes are ignored.

Example 1: Nonhedge Contract

17. On September 15, 19X4, B Company purchases 10 March 19X5 U.S. Treasury bill (T-bill) futures contracts at 87.50 as an investment. (Each contract is for a three-month $1,000,000 face amount T-bill.) On that date, B Company makes an initial cash margin deposit of $30,000 with its broker. B Company holds the contracts through November 15, 19X4, when it closes out all contracts. The quoted market price of March 19X5 T-bill contracts increases during September (to 88.00) and October (to 88.20) and declines in November (to 87.80 by November 15). B Company withdraws some funds from its margin account at various times in September and October, deposits additional funds in November to meet margin calls, and withdraws the entire balance in its account when the futures position is closed out. Changes in the company's margin account are summarized below.

	September	October	November
Beginning balance	$ 0	$32,500	$31,500
Deposit initial margin	30,000		
Change in the market value of the futures contracts[a]	12,500	5,000	(10,000)
Payments to (withdrawals from) account	(10,000)	(6,000)	8,500
Withdrawal of initial margin			(30,000)
Ending balance	$32,500	$31,500	$ 0

[a]Each basis point change in the price of a T-bill futures contract is equal to a $25 change in value. The gain for September is computed as follows:

September 30 price	88.00
September 15 price	87.50
	50 basis points
	× $25
	$1,250
Number of contracts	× 10
	$12,500

[9]Futures contracts for indexes of prices are considered to meet this condition even though there is no underlying commodity or financial instrument.

18. B Company's financial statements for the months ended September 30 and October 31 would show $32,500 and $31,500, respectively, due from its broker. (If B Company satisfied the initial margin requirements by depositing government securities, such as T-bills, rather than cash, the securities would not be classified as part of the balance due from the broker.) Gains of $12,500 for September and $5,000 for October and a loss of $10,000 for November would be recognized. The income statement display of the gains and loss would be consistent with how the company reports other investment gains and losses.

Example 2: Hedge of an Anticipated Purchase

19. On November 1, 19X3, C Company, an enterprise that produces a grain-based industrial product, determines that it will require 100,000 bushels of the necessary grain in the last week of February 19X4. The finished product is not sold forward under fixed-price contracts but is sold at the going market price at the date of sale. Market conditions indicate that finished product selling prices are not likely to be affected significantly during the next few months by changes in the price of the grain during that period. On November 1, the enterprise purchases 20 March 19X4 futures contracts (each contract is for 5,000 bushels of the grain) at $3.00 per bushel. On December 31, 19X3, the enterprise's fiscal year-end, the closing price of the March 19X4 contract is $2.80 per bushel. On February 24, 19X4, the enterprise purchases 100,000 bushels of the grain through its normal commercial channels and closes out the futures contracts at $3.10 per bushel.

20. The changes in the value of the contracts during 19X3 and 19X4 are as follows:

	November 1– December 31, 19X3	January 1– February 24, 19X4
Futures price at beginning of period	$ 3.00	$ 2.80
Futures price at end of period	2.80	3.10
Change in price, per bushel	(0.20)	0.30
Bushels under contract (20 contracts @ 5,000 bushels each)	× 100,000	× 100,000
	$(20,000)	$ 30,000

Unless this transaction qualifies as a hedge, C Company would report a $20,000 loss for the period ending December 31, 19X3 and a $30,000 gain in 19X4.

21. If, however, the hedge conditions in paragraphs 4 and 9 are met and evidence at December 31 indicates the $20,000 will be recovered on sale of the finished product, the enterprise would not recognize a loss in its 19X3 financial statements. On February 24, 19X4, the cumulative change in the market value of the contracts is a $10,000 increase ($20,000 decline to December 31, 19X3 plus $30,000 appreciation in 19X4). That amount would be shown as a reduction of the cost of the grain acquired.

Example 3: Hedge of Financial Instruments Held for Sale

22. M Company, a mortgage banking enterprise, holds $10 million of mortgage loans that will be packaged and sold as mortgage-backed securities. M Company is exposed to the risk that interest rates will rise (and, thus, the value of the mortgages will fall) before the securities are sold. On April 1, 19X4, the enterprise sells June 19X4 futures contracts for mortgage-backed securities. Interest rates decline in April and increase in May, resulting in a $520,000 unfavorable change in the market value of the futures in April and a $940,000 favorable change in May.

23. The futures contracts qualify as a hedge of the mortgage loans if both conditions in paragraph 4 are met. If those hedge conditions are met, and as long as the correlation required in paragraph 4(b) is being achieved, the mortgage banker would adjust the carrying amount of the mortgages for changes in the market value of the futures contracts. The carrying amount of the mortgages in M Company's financial statements would be as follows:

	April	May
Mortgages, beginning of period	$10,000,000	$10,520,000
Adjustment for futures results	520,000	(940,000)
Mortgages, end of period[a]	$10,520,000	$ 9,580,000

---

[a]Paragraph 4 of FASB Statement No. 65, *Accounting for Certain Mortgage Banking Activities,* requires mortgage banking enterprises to report mortgage loans held for sale at the lower of cost or market. Therefore, if the market value of the mortgages is less than the carrying amounts shown, a valuation allowance would be necessary.

24. If M Company decides to transfer the mortgage loans to a long-term investment classification on May 31 rather than sell the assets, the mortgages would be transferred at the lower of their new cost basis ($9,580,000) or market value, in accordance with FASB Statement No. 65, *Accounting for Certain Mortgage Banking Activities.* The difference between that amount and the outstanding principal balance would be amortized to income over the estimated remaining life of the mortgages.

Example 4: Hedge of the Interest Expense Related to Short-Term Deposits

25. The interest rate paid by a financial institution on its money market deposit accounts is revised every month and is a function of the current yield for three-month T-bills. On September 1, 19X4, the institution sells 30 futures contracts for three-month T-bills for the purpose of offsetting changes in the rate paid on the accounts for the 6 months commencing October 1. At each date the money market accounts are repriced, the enterprise closes out five of the contracts originally sold on September 1.

26. Changes in the market value of the futures contracts would be reported in income as those changes occur unless the hedge criteria of this Statement are met. In this situation, the futures contracts would have to qualify as "anticipatory hedges" because they relate to subsequent transactions—the payment of interest on the deposit accounts—that are not certain to occur. Therefore, in addition to meeting the hedge conditions in paragraph 4, the institution would also have to satisfy the conditions in paragraph 9 by demonstrating that it is probable that the deposits will be retained for the six-month period. Assuming the conditions in paragraphs 4 and 9 are met, changes in the value of the futures contracts would be reported as adjustments of interest expense. In this example, that would be accomplished by associating the change in value of the contracts closed with interest expense for the subsequent period. For example, changes in the market value of the contracts closed on October 1 would be amortized over the month of October as increases or decreases in interest expense on the deposits.

Appendix C

BACKGROUND INFORMATION AND BASIS FOR CONCLUSIONS

CONTENTS

Appendix C

BACKGROUND INFORMATION AND BASIS FOR CONCLUSIONS

Introduction

27. In November 1980, the FASB issued for public comment an Exposure Draft of a proposed Statement, *Disclosure of Interest Rate Futures Contracts and Forward and Standby Contracts.* The letters received in response to the Exposure Draft pointed out that it would be difficult for enterprises to collect the required information. Because of the apparent implementation problems and because it wished to consider the advisory conclusions contained in a December 1980 AICPA Issues Paper, *Accounting for Forward Placement and Standby Commitments and Interest Rate Futures Contracts,* the Board decided not to issue a final Statement requiring the specific disclosures called for by the Exposure Draft. However, Technical Bulletin 81-1 was issued in February 1981 to provide guidance for disclosure of accounting policies for futures and certain other contracts. That Bulletin is rescinded by this Statement, but the provisions of APB Opinion No. 22, *Disclosure of Accounting Policies,* continue to require the disclosures called for by the Bulletin for forward and standby contracts.

28. In November 1981, the Board added a project to its technical agenda to address the issues raised in the AICPA Issues Paper on interest rate futures contracts and, to the extent practicable, accounting for commodity futures contracts. Subsequently, the FASB received an AICPA Issues Paper, *Accounting by Agricultural Producers and Agricultural Cooperatives,* that indicated there was diversity among agricultural producers and agricultural cooperatives in accounting for futures contracts. The Board later expanded the scope of its project to include all futures contracts except foreign currency futures, which are already addressed by FASB Statement No. 52, *Foreign Currency Translation.*

29. An Exposure Draft of a proposed FASB Statement, *Accounting for Futures Contracts,* was issued on July 14, 1983. The Board received 153 responses to the Exposure Draft.

30. This appendix discusses the significant comments received on the Exposure Draft and the factors deemed significant by the Board in reaching the decisions in this Statement. It includes descriptions of the alternatives considered and the Board's reasons for accepting or rejecting them. Individual Board members gave greater weight to some factors than to others. The Board concluded that it could reach an informed decision on the basis of existing information without a public hearing and that the effective date and transition specified in paragraph 14 of this Statement are advisable in the circumstances.

Scope

31. The scope of this Statement is the same as that in the Exposure Draft. Some respondents said that other contractual agreements, such as forward placement and option contracts, should be included because such contracts sometimes may be used—in either hedge or investment transactions—as alternatives to futures. Some of those respondents stated that excluding forwards or options could lead to dissimilar accounting for instruments that may affect

the risk of an enterprise in essentially similar ways.

32. The Board believes that options and futures are different. Option holders acquire the right either to buy or to sell a commodity or financial instrument but have no obligation to do so; option writers have an obligation to sell or to buy the commodity or financial instrument if the buyer exercises the option. In contrast, futures contracts are "two-sided" in that buyers and sellers of futures both acquire a right and incur an obligation. Thus, the risk and return characteristics of options and futures are different, as is the system of margins in each market. The Board also notes that an AICPA task force currently is studying option accounting and plans to prepare an Issues Paper. In the absence of a compelling reason to do so, the Board believes it should not examine accounting for options at least until the task force has completed its Issues Paper.

33. The Board decided to exclude forward contracts from this project for two reasons. First, forwards differ from futures in at least some, and often all, of the following respects: amount and timing of cash flows, availability of liquid markets and reliable quoted prices, and potential for default. Second, forward contracts generally result in delivery of goods or services, whereas futures are almost exclusively hedging or investment vehicles. A large part of business activity is conducted by means of forward contracts. Although some forwards may be used as hedges and some may be entered into primarily as investments, most forward contracts are the traditional and accepted means by which enterprises carry out their normal commercial operations of purchasing and selling goods and services, issuing securities, making loans, and so forth. In the Board's view, it was neither necessary nor possible to deal with all such contracts in this Statement. To cover only a subset of those contracts (those that are judged on some basis to be "similar" to futures) would, in the Board's view, delay necessary guidance on accounting for futures and inevitably would result in an imprecise scope for the Statement.

34. Exclusion of forward contracts from the Statement should not be construed as either acceptance or rejection by the Board of current practice for such contracts, nor should the exclusion be interpreted as an indication that the general principles of this Statement might not be appropriate in some circumstances for certain forward contracts. At some future date, the Board may address the accounting for particular types of forward contracts, and it may address the conceptual aspects of accounting for executory contracts generally.

Accounting at the Inception of the Contract

35. The Board considered and rejected requiring enterprises to recognize an asset and a liability for the total amount of the commodity or financial instrument that underlies a futures contract. Most, but not all, futures contracts give the holder of a long position the right to acquire a specified amount of a commodity or financial instrument at a particular date and obligate the contract holder to pay for those goods; the holder of a short position has the obligation to deliver goods and the right to receive payment. However, those rights may be exercised, and the obligations become firm, only if the enterprise holds the futures contract at the end of the last day of trading, a circumstance that rarely occurs. In addition, the individual rights and obligations related to delivery under a futures contract are similar to those embodied in most other fully executory contracts, which normally are not recognized in financial statements.

General Method of Accounting

36. Paragraph 3 of this Statement requires that a change in the market value of a futures contract that does not qualify as a hedge be recognized as a gain or loss in the period the change occurs. That accounting applies to futures contracts used for investment purposes and, as noted in paragraph 5, to hedging transactions of some enterprises, such as pension plans, investment companies, and broker-dealers, that currently recognize changes in the fair value of most assets in the period those changes occur. A few respondents objected to immediate gain or loss recognition for futures contracts that do not qualify as hedges. They said the Board should at least permit, if not require, a type of "lower of cost or market" accounting whereby net gains on futures contracts are recognized only when the contracts are closed. The arguments made in support of that accounting and the reasons the Board did not find them persuasive are summarized in paragraphs 37–39.

37. Some respondents stated that the daily cash settlements on open futures positions are not sufficient evidence that a gain has been realized. They said those settlements should be viewed as collateral or financing transactions, similar to margin arrangements for purchasing securities, that need not have an influence on income recognition. The Board disagrees with that position because, unlike purchasing securities on margin, buying or selling futures contracts does not involve loans. A favorable change in the market value of a futures contract enhances the enterprise's assets because the amount due from its broker is increased immediately. Amounts on deposit with a broker in excess of initial margin requirements can be, and frequently are, withdrawn in cash without closing out the futures contract. The Board does not believe such an increase in the assets of the enterprise results in a corresponding liability or a reduction of another asset.

38. Some respondents viewed the immediate recognition of gains on open futures contracts that are not hedges as an unwarranted departure from what they consider to be the general accounting framework in place today. In addition, a few cited FASB Statement No. 12, *Accounting for Certain Marketable Securities,* as support for using a lower-of-cost-or-market method for investments generally, and futures contracts specifically. The Board does not believe that holding a futures position is sufficiently similar to owning equity securities to conclude that the accounting set forth in Statement 12 applies. Statement 12 has a narrow scope (*certain* marketable equity securities owned by *certain* enterprises) and does not purport to establish accounting principles for all instruments that might be labeled "investments."

39. As noted in paragraph 59 of the December 1983 FASB Exposure Draft, *Recognition and Measurement in Financial Statements of Business Enterprises,* items currently reported in financial statements are measured by different attributes depending on the nature of the item and the relevance and reliability of the attribute measured. The Board believes the relevance and reliability of changes in the market value of futures contracts and the unique feature of futures trading—daily settlement of gains and losses—support recognizing gains on open contracts. Earnings of an enterprise that invests or speculates in futures contracts may fluctuate between periods as a result of applying the provisions of this Statement. The Board believes those reported results will provide relevant and understandable information to the users of the financial statements and will faithfully portray the economics of the transactions. In requiring recognition of gains and losses on open futures contracts, the Board is not changing present practice for other investments.

Hedges

40. Because of the unique features of futures trading, the effects of price or interest rate changes are realized as those changes occur. If enterprises use futures contracts to hedge assets, liabilities, or commitments for which unrealized changes in value are recognized in income, concurrent recognition of a gain or loss on the futures contract is also appropriate. Reported earnings will faithfully represent the economics of the hedge and will reflect the effectiveness of the enterprise's hedging practices. However, the effects of price or interest rate changes on most existing assets, liabilities, and firm commitments are not recognized in income until realized in a later transaction. To recognize gains or losses immediately for futures contracts that are intended to hedge such items could result in reporting related, offsetting amounts in income of different reporting periods. Such reporting would tend to increase variability in income, implying increased exposure to price or interest rate changes when, in fact, exposure to price or interest rate changes would have been reduced. A somewhat similar result would occur if gains or losses were recognized for futures contracts entered into in anticipation of probable transactions not involving existing assets, liabilities, or firm commitments.

41. This Statement recognizes the underlying economic effects of hedging activities by providing for delayed recognition in income of the changes in the market value of futures contracts that meet certain hedge criteria. The Board decided that the project should not consider any change in current accounting practices for assets, liabilities, or commitments generally. Thus, the Board restricted this project to considering methods of accounting for futures contracts that, given current accounting for hedged items, would better reflect the economic effects of hedging.

Hedge Criteria

42. The word *hedge* is used in a variety of ways by futures traders, accountants, and regulators, and there appears to be no generally accepted definition that is useful in making practical decisions. However, most, but not all, definitions are based on the notion of reducing exposure to price or interest rate risk. The Board concluded that risk reduction—that is, reducing the sensitivity of an enterprise's income to changes in prices or interest rates—should be the basis for delaying income recognition of the results of futures contracts.

43. Most respondents agreed that reduction of risk is an appropriate prerequisite for "deferral" accounting for futures contracts. However, several respondents disagreed with the Exposure Draft's proposal that other assets, liabilities, commitments, and transactions be considered in the assessment of whether a particular item contributes to exposure. Many of those respondents said that enterprises should be required to demonstrate only that price or interest rate risk is reduced on an individual item or transaction basis. The Board rejected that approach because it ignores the fact that some exposures already are hedged effectively by other positions of an enterprise. It could result in accounting for a futures contract as a hedge when the contract in fact *increases,* rather than reduces, the enterprise's exposure. For example, futures contracts used to "fix" the interest rate on variable-rate obligations could be considered a hedge if other positions of the enterprise are ignored. However, if the financial assets of the enterprise also have variable interest rates, the enterprise may expose itself to greater interest rate risk by entering into the futures con-

tracts. If an enterprise chooses to assume greater risk via the futures markets, the Board believes that immediate recognition in income of the results of those futures transactions would provide relevant information for assessing the enterprise's performance.

44. The Board acknowledges that determining whether an exposure already is hedged effectively by another item sometimes may not be clear and may require judgment. The Board believes that such judgment is essential and must be exercised by those who have a thorough understanding of the enterprise's business and the specific circumstances. Detailed rules on how to assess risk might be perceived as providing comparability but would not be responsive to the complex and changeable risks faced by enterprises.

45. Some respondents stated that it could be impractical for some enterprises, particularly multinationals that operate in a decentralized manner, to comply with the "overall" risk assessment required in paragraph 4(a). Those respondents argued that hedge accounting should be permitted if the item to be hedged results in an exposure for the individual business unit that enters into the futures contracts. The shortcomings of a business unit approach to risk assessment are similar to, although much less severe than, those described in paragraph 43 for the strictly transactional approach. However, the Board notes that if an enterprise is unable to gather and disseminate information about relevant positions and transactions of the entire enterprise, condition 4(a) would require gains and losses on all future transactions of the enterprise to be reported in the period that futures prices change. In the Board's view, it is unlikely that such accounting would be a faithful representation of the extent to which the enterprise has modified its risk exposure. Therefore, although the "overall" approach to risk assessment is retained as the basic concept, the Board decided for practical reasons to permit risk to be assessed on a business unit basis when the decentralized nature of the enterprise's operations makes it impossible to consider other relevant positions and transactions of the entire enterprise.

46. Under the Exposure Draft, a futures contract that differed from the item intended to be hedged would meet the hedge condition on risk reduction only if it were not practicable to enter into a contract for the identical commodity or financial instrument. Comment letters indicate that respondents interpreted this "cross hedge" provision in a more restrictive manner than the Board intended. For example, some respondents thought the Exposure Draft proscribed hedge accounting unless a contract for the identical instrument was used even when that identical contract trades in volumes insufficient to

make it a practical hedging vehicle. Paragraph 4(b), which differs from the Exposure Draft, now indicates that a futures contract for a different commodity or financial instrument may qualify as a hedge provided there is a clear economic relationship between the item underlying the contract and the item intended to be hedged, and provided high price correlation is probable.

47. One of the hedge criteria in the Exposure Draft was that unrealized changes in the fair value of the hedged item are not included, or are included only in certain circumstances, in the determination of income. A few respondents disagreed with that condition because they believed it implied that futures contracts intended to hedge items reported at fair value could not be legitimate hedges. The Board agreed with those comments and has revised the criteria to avoid that implication. The accounting, however, is unchanged.

48. The Exposure Draft distinguished between hedges (futures contracts used to reduce the risk caused by *existing* assets, liabilities, and firm commitments) and futures contracts related to certain anticipated transactions not involving existing assets, liabilities, or commitments. In this Statement, *hedge* refers to both uses of futures contracts. The Exposure Draft also contained separate risk exposure conditions for the two uses of futures contracts. This Statement requires that a single risk condition (paragraph 4(a)) be satisfied for any futures transaction for which hedge accounting is being contemplated. The revisions noted above were made to improve the understandability of the Statement and, in the Board's view, are not a change from the substance of the Exposure Draft.

Hedges of Existing Assets, Liabilities, and Firm Commitments

49. Some respondents recommended a method of accounting for certain hedge and arbitrage transactions that differed in some respects from the method proposed in the Exposure Draft. They indicated that the prices of certain futures contracts may reflect a full "carrying charge" (primarily to cover interest costs) over spot prices. Those respondents suggested that when an enterprise is "long" in the commodity or financial instrument and "short" in futures (or short in the commodity and long in futures), the difference between the futures price and the spot price at the inception of the hedge should be amortized to income over the life of the futures contract in a manner similar to that required in some cases by Statement 52 for foreign currency forward contracts.

50. The Board agreed with those respondents and concluded that in the conditions now specified in paragraph 6 an enterprise may account separately

for the discount or premium identified at the inception of a contract that qualifies as a hedge. The Board notes that the net gain or loss (that is, the difference between results of the futures contracts and changes in the value of the hedged item) on such transactions will equal the identified premium or discount only if there is convergence of spot and futures prices by the delivery date of the futures contract. Therefore, paragraph 6 requires that the commodity or financial instrument involved be deliverable under the futures contract and that retention of both the spot and futures positions to the delivery date of the contract be probable. Relatively few hedges are likely to meet those conditions because most futures contracts are not held open up to the specified delivery date and because "cross hedges" will not qualify.

51. A few respondents, primarily financial institutions, suggested that changes in the market value of futures contracts deemed to be hedges should not be reported as adjustments of the carrying amount of the hedged items. They believe those amounts should be reported as "other" assets or liabilities, at least until the start of amortization, to avoid what were claimed to be distortions of the yield of the hedged item. As noted in paragraph 66, the Board believes futures contracts that hedge existing fixed-rate financial instruments effectively change the yield of those instruments. Separate presentation of such adjustments in the balance sheet would not reflect those changed yields. Thus, the Board did not adopt that suggestion.

52. A few respondents stated that a loss should be recognized on a futures contract that hedges an asset reported at cost if the adjusted carrying amount of the asset would be in excess of its fair value. If the carrying amount and fair value of the hedged asset are approximately equal at the inception of the hedge, the Board believes that the provisions of paragraph 11 of this Statement are adequate to ensure that the adjusted carrying amount and fair value of the hedged item will continue to be approximately the same. However, if the fair value is less than the carrying amount of the asset at the inception of the hedge, a fair value limitation on hedge adjustments effectively would preclude deferral of unfavorable futures results even when the hedge is fully effective. In the Board's view, the existence of the initial difference between the fair value and the carrying amount of the asset has no bearing on whether a hedge has been effective and should not influence the accounting for the hedge. Therefore, the Board decided that the fair value limitation suggested by some respondents was either unnecessary or inappropriate. This Statement does not, however, change any existing accounting requirements to report assets at the lower of cost or market.

Hedges of Anticipated Transactions

53. Paragraph 9 of this Statement requires that changes in the value of certain futures contracts that qualify as hedges of anticipated purchase or sale transactions be included in the measurement of those transactions. For example, a banking enterprise that anticipates issuing certificates of deposit (CDs) to replace CDs that will mature at a particular time may sell interest rate futures contracts at an earlier date. If the market is demanding a higher yield on such instruments by the time the CDs are issued, the enterprise expects that the change in the market value of the futures contracts will be favorable and will, to some extent, offset the increased borrowing costs. Many view such contracts as a form of hedging, and the futures positions are often referred to as "anticipatory hedges." The Board understands that some enterprises use futures contracts as "anticipatory hedges" of sales of grain that is expected to be harvested at a later date, expected acquisitions of interest-bearing investments, expected purchases of inventory, and expected sales of metals that will be extracted and refined at a later date.

54. Although, in a technical sense, the anticipated transactions referred to in the preceding paragraph may not expose an enterprise to risk in the same way as existing assets, liabilities, or firm commitments, the Board believes there may be risk from a practical perspective. Gross margins of certain enterprises that have not established a price for anticipated purchases (for example, probable raw material requirements for the next six months) may be as exposed to price risk as the gross margins of enterprises in other industries that have not covered their firm fixed-price sales commitments. However, not all unpriced anticipated transactions involve risk for an enterprise, and, therefore, not all futures contracts that some may consider to be "anticipatory hedges" will meet the hedge criteria in paragraph 4. As noted in footnote 5 to paragraph 4(a), because of differences in the pricing structure of various industries, some enterprises become exposed to risk only through owning a commodity or when the price of a transaction becomes fixed; others in effect are exposed when they have not established the price for an anticipated transaction. It follows that some futures contracts related to anticipated transactions actually increase an enterprise's exposure and should not be accounted for as hedges. Ignoring fundamental differences in the risks to which different enterprises are exposed by prescribing hedge accounting for every contract related to an anticipated transaction would not produce reliable financial reporting of the results.

55. The "Notice for Recipients" accompanying the

Exposure Draft asked respondents to comment specifically on the conditions proposed for a contract to qualify as a hedge of an anticipated transaction. Most comments pertained to the requirement that the anticipated transaction be sufficiently probable that "in the normal course of business, the enterprise has little discretion to do otherwise." Several respondents said that the Board should require only that the transaction's occurrence be *probable* because that term has support in current accounting literature unlike *little discretion,* which many respondents seemed to find confusing. Also, some respondents did not agree with a condition in the Exposure Draft that an anticipated transaction would not qualify if failure to carry out the transaction would result in little cost or disruption of operations. Most of those respondents agreed that the financial and other effects of not carrying out the transaction should be considered in assessing probability, but they stated it should not be an overriding condition. In addition, they noted that in some circumstances reliably measuring the cost of not doing something may be difficult or impossible.

56. The Board agreed with those respondents and modified paragraph 9(b); however, a high level of assurance that a transaction will occur is still necessary for the related futures contract to qualify as a hedge. As noted in the Exposure Draft, determination of the likelihood of a transaction's taking place should not, in the Board's opinion, be based solely on management's stated intent because that is not verifiable. Probability should be supported by observable facts and the attendant circumstances. The Board believes that the likelihood of a transaction's taking place can be supported by the frequency of similar past transactions, irreversible commitments of resources to a particular use, and other factors discussed in paragraph 9(b).

57. A few respondents interpreted the requirement to identify the anticipated transaction to be unduly restrictive. They believed the Exposure Draft would require identification of *specific* dates and quantities for the condition to be met; they recommended that the condition be broadened to require only that the amount of futures contracts be reasonably related to quantities of commodities or financial instruments that can be used, sold, or issued in the normal course of business over a reasonable period. The purpose of requiring identification of the significant terms is threefold. First, without some idea of the timing and amount of the anticipated transaction, it is impossible to assess whether there is price or interest rate risk (paragraph 4(a)). Second, the information is also necessary to assess the likelihood that the transaction will occur (paragraph 9(b)). Third, unless the expected terms of the transaction can be reasonably identified, it is unlikely that the correlation condition (paragraph 4(b)) can be met. Because

the circumstances of each enterprise are different, the information needed to satisfy those three purposes may vary. In the Board's view, paragraph 9(a) does not preclude the use of reasonable estimates, such as estimates of dates and quantities, if the risk, probability, and risk reduction conditions can be satisfied. Therefore, the Board did not change the requirement in that paragraph.

Hedge Effectiveness

58. Under the Exposure Draft, a gain or loss would have been recognized to the extent that futures contracts were not effective as a hedge of an existing asset, liability, or firm commitment. The Exposure Draft also indicated that effectiveness might be assessed by comparing the change in the market value of the futures contracts and the unrecognized changes in the fair value of the hedged item since inception of the hedge. Paragraph 11 of this Statement differs somewhat from the Exposure Draft in that it requires an enterprise to discontinue accounting for a futures contract as a hedge if a high degree of correlation has not been achieved. When that occurs, paragraph 11 also requires recognition of a gain or loss to the extent the futures results have not been offset by the effects of price or interest rate changes on the hedged item.

59. Most respondents objected to the proposed requirement for an ongoing assessment of hedge effectiveness. Many claimed that the initial assessment of whether risk would be reduced (paragraph 4(b)) was a sufficient condition for continuation of hedge accounting. The Board did not concur with that view. Paragraph 4(b) requires that it be *probable* that changes in the market value of the futures contract(s) will offset the effects of price or interest rate changes on the hedged item. In many cases the actual results of a hedge transaction may be approximately what was expected. However, even though high correlation may be probable at inception, it is not certain; actual price relationships over the hedge period may be significantly different from what was expected. Several respondents confirmed that fact. The Board concluded that the continuation of hedge accounting must be justified by what has actually happened rather than on the basis of expectations formed at an earlier date.

60. The Exposure Draft's lack of an explicit effectiveness test for "anticipatory hedges" was mentioned by several respondents, who stated that such an omission resulted in an inconsistency in the document. The Board agreed with those comments; the ongoing review of correlation required by paragraph 11 applies both to hedges of existing positions and to hedges of anticipated transactions. Many respondents also said that the cost of complying with the effectiveness test proposed in the Exposure

Draft could be high and generally would not be justified by the resulting benefits. In addition, several other respondents commented that estimates of the changes in the fair value of hedged items frequently are too unreliable to use as a basis for gain or loss recognition. The Board decided that the requirement in paragraph 11 would be a less costly and more easily implemented method of assessing effectiveness.

Financial Institutions

61. A financial institution may be exposed to interest rate risk when its assets and liabilities have different repricing or maturity characteristics. For example, a bank that owns primarily long-term fixed-rate loans receivable and that has issued primarily short-term obligations may be exposed to the risk of rising interest rates. Financial institutions that use futures contracts to reduce that risk may sell interest rate futures contracts. There are several different views about how such an institution should account for those contracts. One view is that the short futures positions are hedges of a portion of the loans receivable (assuming the necessary degree of price correlation is probable). Another view is that the futures contracts relate to the rollover or replacement of some of the short-term obligations (again assuming the necessary correlation is probable). Others maintain that the contracts need not necessarily be related to identifiable assets or obligations but instead should be considered "general" or "macro" hedges of the enterprise's net exposure. Comment letters from some financial institutions expressed a variation of those views; they consider the futures contracts to be a hedge of the interest margin ("spread") for a particular period determined by reference to the repricing characteristics of specified assets and liabilities.

62. This Statement permits futures contracts that reduce interest rate risks of financial institutions to qualify as hedges of either existing positions (the loans in the example in the preceding paragraph) or anticipated repricings or replacement of particular instruments (the short-term obligations in the preceding paragraph) provided the hedge criteria are met for the strategy selected. The Board concluded that hedge accounting should not be permitted for so-called macro hedges where the futures contracts are not linked with identifiable assets, obligations, commitments, or anticipated transactions. Without such linkage, there is no objective method of either gauging the effectiveness of the futures contracts or ultimately recognizing the futures results in income. The Board also did not adopt the suggestion that futures contracts be considered hedges of the interest spread between specifically identified assets and liabilities. The Board views the association of an asset with a specific funding source as an arbitrary

process. Moreover, interest spreads per se cannot be hedged directly; there are no futures contracts for interest spreads. Clearly, the intent of the institution may be to reduce uncertainty about future interest spreads, but that is accomplished with futures by changing the revenue or expense component of the spread through hedges of existing or anticipated asset or liability positions.

63. The Board understands that the determination and measurement of the interest rate risk of a financial institution may be complex and may involve significant estimates and judgments. The Board considered providing more specific guidance concerning when the risk condition in paragraph 4(a) is met by financial institutions but concluded that it was not feasible to do so at present. The analysis and determination of an institution's interest rate sensitivity (and compilation of the necessary information) is, the Board understands, an evolving process, and the approach followed may vary from institution to institution. It was noted that there is not a consensus among bankers and others about whether "gap" analysis, duration analysis, or some other method is the most appropriate way of assessing risk. The Board concluded that it should not attempt at this time to specify a single measure of interest rate sensitivity for use in applying the provisions of this Statement.

64. A few respondents questioned whether the hedge criteria could be met for a futures contract intended to hedge a fixed-rate financial instrument that an institution plans to hold to maturity. They argued that instruments held as long-term investments and reported at cost do not expose the enterprise to price or interest rate risk. Those respondents acknowledged that interest rate risk could exist because such assets may be funded by shorter-term liabilities; in that case, those respondents would support hedge accounting only for futures contracts related to the replacement or repricing of the shorter-term liabilities. The Board considered those comments and concluded that a futures contract should not be precluded from qualifying as a hedge solely because the enterprise plans to hold a fixed-rate financial instrument (asset or liability) to maturity; interest rate risk may exist irrespective of an institution's stated intention not to sell fixed-rate assets (or redeem fixed-rate liabilities) before maturity. Footnote 4 to paragraph 4(a) has been added to indicate when futures may qualify as hedges of such instruments.

65. The Exposure Draft proposed that adjustments to the carrying amount of hedged fixed-rate financial instruments referred to in the preceding paragraph be amortized over the remaining life of the instrument beginning at the termination of the hedge. Comment letters contained many conflicting

views about when amortization should commence and over what period. Some respondents would relate the amortization to the repricing date of a liability that was deemed to fund the hedged asset (or the repricing date of an asset that was deemed to be funded by the hedged liability). Most of those respondents would determine the amortization period at the inception of the hedge and subsequently would not change the start or length of that period. Other respondents argued that it was inappropriate to delay amortization until hedge termination because lengthy periods could elapse before any futures results were recognized in income. Also, a few respondents claimed that the remaining life of the hedged item could be too long a period over which to amortize hedge adjustments. Other respondents also asked the Board to clarify whether a "rollover" of a contract (closing out a contract and replacing it with a similar contract for a more distant delivery month) results in termination of a hedge and whether the start of amortization could be delayed if a hedge is continued by using instruments other than futures.

66. The Board believes that the results of hedging the fixed-rate instruments referred to in paragraph 64 can be viewed as an adjustment of the yield on the instrument over its expected remaining life. If there is an unfavorable change in the value of a futures contract that hedges such a fixed-rate asset, the carrying amount of the asset increases, and the effective yield on that instrument is lower. Conversely, favorable futures results can be viewed as increasing the asset's yield. The Board believes it is reasonable to recognize the changed yield over the life of the instrument. To relate income recognition to a specific liability that is deemed to fund the asset is inconsistent with the notion that the futures contracts are used to change the asset's yield. And, as noted earlier, the Board believes that associating an asset with a specific funding source is an essentially arbitrary process and should not be the basis for amortization.

67. In concept, amortization should commence as soon as the futures contracts change in value. However, such a process would usually be cumbersome because the amount of the hedge adjustment changes daily as the price of open futures contracts changes. Paragraph 7 of this Statement now requires that amortization commence no later than the date a particular contract is closed (whether it is "rolled over" or not). That approach is relatively simple and eliminates the uncertainty that would be introduced if the start of amortization depended on when the hedging strategy, as opposed to a particular contract, is terminated. It also eliminates the possibility that amortization could be delayed for extended periods merely because a hedge has not been terminated. Paragraph 7 also differs from the

Exposure Draft in that the amortization period is now the *expected* remaining life, rather than the stated maturity, of the hedged instrument. The Board made that change in response to comments that the actual remaining life of some instruments (for example, Government National Mortgage Association mortgage-backed securities) may be less than their stated maturity.

Disclosure

68. Under this Statement, the method of accounting for a particular futures contract depends on the circumstances. A futures contract could be an investment for one enterprise; a hedge of an existing asset, liability, or firm commitment for another; and an "anticipatory hedge" for a third. In addition, the accounting for futures contracts that are hedges will vary depending on the nature of the hedged items. The Board concluded that disclosure of the method(s) of accounting for futures contracts that qualify as hedges and the nature of the hedged items is necessary in such circumstances.

69. The Exposure Draft was accompanied by a "Notice for Recipients" that asked for specific comments on whether additional disclosures should be required. The Exposure Draft outlined three possible additional disclosures: the amount of futures contracts outstanding at the end of a reporting period, futures results recognized in income during a period, and the amount of futures results "deferred" at the end of a period. Most respondents restricted their comments to just those items and generally were not in favor of additional disclosures. The Board decided not to require additional disclosures for the reasons cited in the following paragraphs.

70. Some respondents recommended disclosure of the amount of futures contracts outstanding at the end of an accounting period because they believe it could help financial statement readers assess the extent to which an enterprise is either insulated from or exposed to the effects of subsequent price or interest rate changes. Knowledge about the degree to which an enterprise has reduced or has increased risk exposure may help financial statement users estimate the probable effects of subsequent price changes on the enterprise's earnings and its possible performance relative to other enterprises in the same industry. The Board concluded that the amount of futures contracts outstanding at a particular time is a very crude and possibly misleading measure of risk exposure or hedging activity. The number of contracts outstanding may vary considerably over time because of seasonal or other temporary changes in the enterprise's business, changes in interest rates and prices, changes in the enterprise's hedging policy, decisions to invest in instruments

other than futures, and other factors. Also, because buying and selling futures contracts is a relatively simple and inexpensive procedure, the amount of contracts outstanding at the end of a period could easily be manipulated.

71. The Exposure Draft pointed out that some support disclosure of the income effects of using futures because they believe such transactions are a separable and discretionary activity of an enterprise. Some respondents disagreed with that position and noted that hedging with futures may be an integral part of the business. Others claimed that the effect of hedging with futures was no more noteworthy than the effects of the many other discretionary activities of a business, which often are not separately disclosed in financial statements. Some respondents also pointed out that disclosure of offsetting changes in the items being hedged would be necessary to make the futures disclosures not misleading and that such disclosures typically are not required for items that are not hedged. The Board agreed and decided not to require disclosure of the income effects. For similar reasons, the Board decided not to require disclosure of the changes in the value of futures contracts that have yet to be recognized in income.

Statement of Financial Accounting Standards No. 81
Disclosure of Postretirement Health Care and Life Insurance Benefits

STATUS

Issued: November 1984

Effective Date: For financial statements issued for periods ending after December 15, 1984

Affects: No other pronouncements

Affected by: Superseded by FAS 106

Other Interpretive Pronouncement: FTB 87-1 (Superseded by FAS 106)

(The next page is 799.)

(This page intentionally left blank.)

Statement of Financial Accounting Standards No. 82
Financial Reporting and Changing Prices: Elimination of Certain Disclosures

an amendment of FASB Statement No. 33

STATUS

Issued: November 1984

Effective Date: For fiscal years ending on or after December 15, 1984

Affects: Supersedes FAS 33, paragraphs 29(a) and 35(b)
Amends FAS 33, paragraph 31
Changes FAS 33, paragraphs 33, 40, 42 through 46, 66(a), 70, 224, 225, 227, 229, 239, and 240
Changes FAS 70, paragraphs 7 and 8

Affected by: Superseded by FAS 89

Statement of Financial Accounting Standards No. 83 Designation of AICPA Guides and Statement of Position on Accounting by Brokers and Dealers in Securities, by Employee Benefit Plans, and by Banks as Preferable for Purposes of Applying APB Opinion 20

an amendment of FASB Statement No. 32 and APB Opinion No. 30 and a rescission of FASB Interpretation No. 10

STATUS

Issued: March 1985

Effective Date: March 31, 1985

Affects: Amends APB 30, footnote 8
Amends FAS 32, Appendixes A and B
Supersedes FIN 10

Affected by: Superseded by FAS 111

(The next page is 804.)

(This page intentionally left blank.)

Statement of Financial Accounting Standards No. 84
Induced Conversions of Convertible Debt

an amendment of APB Opinion No. 26

STATUS

Issued: March 1985

Effective Date: For conversions of convertible debt pursuant to inducements offered after March 31, 1985

Affects: Amends APB 26, paragraph 2

Affected by: No other pronouncements

Issues Discussed by FASB Emerging Issues Task Force (EITF)

   Affects: Nullifies EITF Issue No. 84-3

   Interpreted by: No EITF Issues

   Related Issue: EITF Issue No. 85-17

SUMMARY

This Statement amends APB Opinion No. 26, *Early Extinguishment of Debt.* This Statement specifies the method of accounting for conversions of convertible debt to equity securities when the debtor induces conversion of the debt by offering additional securities or other consideration to convertible debt holders. Such an offer has sometimes been called a convertible debt "sweetener." This Statement requires recognition of an expense equal to the fair value of the *additional* securities or other consideration issued to induce conversion.

This Statement is effective for conversions of convertible debt pursuant to inducements offered after March 31, 1985, with earlier application encouraged. Retroactive application for transactions occurring during periods for which financial statements have previously been issued is permitted.

Statement of Financial Accounting Standards No. 84

Induced Conversions of Convertible Debt

an amendment of APB Opinion No. 26

CONTENTS

INTRODUCTION

1. The FASB has been asked to address the applicability of APB Opinion No. 26, *Early Extinguishment of Debt,* to situations in which the conversion privileges in a convertible debt instrument are changed or additional consideration is paid to debt holders for the purpose of inducing prompt conversion of the debt to equity securities (sometimes referred to as a convertible debt "sweetener"). Opinion 26 applies to all extinguishments of debt except debt that is extinguished through a troubled debt restructuring and debt that is converted to equity securities of the debtor pursuant to conversion privileges included in terms of the debt at issuance.[1] This Statement amends Opinion 26 to exclude from its scope convertible debt that is converted to equity securities of the debtor pursuant to conversion privileges different from those included in terms of the debt at issuance when the change in conversion privileges is effective for a limited period of time, involves additional consideration, and is made to induce conversion. This Statement also specifies the method of accounting for such conversions. Examples of application of this Statement are presented in Appendix A, background information is presented in Appendix B, and the basis for the Board's conclusions is presented in Appendix C.

APPLICABILITY AND SCOPE

2. This Statement applies to conversions of convertible debt to equity securities pursuant to terms that reflect changes made by the debtor to the conversion privileges provided in the terms of the debt at issuance (including changes that involve the payment of consideration) for the purpose of inducing conversion. This Statement applies only to conversions[2] that both (a) occur pursuant to changed conversion privileges that are exercisable only for a limited period of time and (b) include the issuance of all of the equity securities issuable pursuant to conversion privileges included in the terms of the debt at issuance for each debt instrument that is converted. The changed terms may involve reduction of the original conversion price thereby resulting in the issuance of additional shares of stock, issuance of warrants or other securities not provided for in the original conversion terms, or payment of cash or other consideration to those debt holders who convert during the specified time period. This Statement does not apply to conversions pursuant to other changes in conversion privileges or to changes in terms of convertible debt instruments that are different from those described in this paragraph.

---

[1] The scope of Opinion 26 was also amended by FASB Statement No. 76, *Extinguishment of Debt.* Refer to paragraph 17 of this Statement.

[2] For purposes of this Statement, a conversion includes an exchange of a convertible debt instrument for equity securities or a combination of equity securities and other consideration, whether or not the exchange involves legal exercise of the contractual conversion privileges included in terms of the debt.

STANDARDS OF FINANCIAL ACCOUNTING AND REPORTING

Recognition of Expense upon Conversion

3. When convertible debt is converted to equity securities of the debtor pursuant to an inducement offer described in paragraph 2 of this Statement, the debtor enterprise shall recognize an expense equal to the fair value of all securities and other consideration transferred in the transaction in excess of the fair value of securities issuable pursuant to the original conversion terms. The expense shall not be reported as an extraordinary item.

4. The fair value of the securities or other consideration shall be measured as of the date the inducement offer is accepted by the convertible debt holder. Normally this will be the date the debt holder converts the convertible debt into equity securities or enters into a binding agreement to do so.

Amendment to APB Opinion No. 26

5. The following sentence is added to paragraph 2 of Opinion 26:

Also, this Opinion does not apply to conversions of convertible debt when conversion privileges included in terms of the debt at issuance are changed, or additional consideration is paid, to induce conversion of the debt to equity securities as described in FASB Statement No. 84, *Induced Conversions of Convertible Debt.*

Effective Date and Transition

6. This Statement shall be effective for conversions of convertible debt pursuant to inducements offered after March 31, 1985. Earlier application is encouraged. Retroactive application of this Statement to transactions occurring during periods for which financial statements have previously been issued is permitted, in which case the financial statements of all prior periods presented shall be restated. In addition, the financial statements shall, in the year this Statement is first applied, disclose the nature of any restatement and its effect on income before extraordinary items, net income, and related per-share amounts.

The provisions of this Statement need not be applied to immaterial items.

This Statement was adopted by the affirmative votes of six members of the Financial Accounting Standards Board. Mr. Sprouse dissented.

Mr. Sprouse dissents because he believes the provisions of this Statement should not apply in circumstances similar to those described in Example 2 (paragraphs 11-13 of Appendix A) in this Statement. He believes that the Statement fails to distinguish between induced conversions made under two distinctly different sets of facts and circumstances: (a) debt convertible into equity securities whose market values are greater than the conversion price (refer to Example 1, paragraphs 8 and 9) and (b) debt convertible into equity securities whose market values are less than the conversion price (refer to Example 2, paragraphs 11 and 12). In the circumstances described in (a), he agrees that the inducement is an expense incurred to obtain certain benefits, such as elimination of the interest payments that would otherwise be made before the debt holder chooses to convert. In the circumstances described in (b), however, the substance of the obligation is essentially the same as for debt that is not convertible. The essential nature of an induced conversion under those circumstances is no different from a limited tender offer of equity securities for nonconvertible debt. Accordingly, he believes that an enterprise that extinguishes debt by issuing securities and other assets whose aggregate fair value is less than the carrying amount of the debt should recognize a gain in the amount of the difference in the same way that it would if securities and other assets were exchanged for nonconvertible debt.

Members of the Financial Accounting Standards Board:

Donald J. Kirk,	Victor H. Brown	Robert T. Sprouse
Chairman	Raymond C. Lauver	Arthur R. Wyatt
Frank E. Block	David Mosso	

Appendix A

EXAMPLES OF APPLICATION OF THIS STATEMENT

7. This appendix presents examples that illustrate application of this Statement. The facts assumed are illustrative only and are not intended to modify or limit in any way the provisions of this Statement. For simplicity, the face amount of each security is assumed to be equal to its carrying amount in the financial statements (that is, no original issue premium or discount exists).

Example 1

8. On January 1, 19X4, Company A issues a $1,000 face amount 10 percent convertible bond maturing December 31, 20X3. The carrying amount of the bond in the financial statements of Company A is $1,000, and it is convertible into common shares of Company A at a conversion price of $25 per share. On January 1, 19X6, the convertible bond has a market value of $1,700. To induce convertible bondholders to convert their bonds promptly, Company A reduces the conversion price to $20 for bondholders who convert prior to February 29, 19X6 (within 60 days).

9. Assuming the market price of Company A's common stock on the date of conversion is $40 per share, the fair value of the incremental consideration paid by Company A upon conversion is calculated as follows for each $1,000 bond that is converted prior to February 29, 19X6:

Value of securities issued[a]	$2,000
Value of securities issuable pursuant to original conversion privileges[b]	1,600
Fair value of incremental consideration	$ 400

[a]Value of securities issued to debt holders is computed as follows:

Face amount	$1,000
÷ New conversion price	÷ $ 20 per share
Number of common shares issued upon conversion	50 shares
× Price per common share	× $ 40 per share
Value of securities issued	$2,000

[b]Value of securities issuable pursuant to original conversion privileges is computed as follows:

Face amount	$1,000
÷ Original conversion price	÷ $ 25 per share
Number of common shares issuable pursuant to original conversion privileges	40 shares
× Price per common share	× $ 40 per share
Value of securities issuable pursuant to original conversion privileges	$1,600

10. Therefore, Company A records debt conversion expense equal to the fair value of the incremental consideration paid as follows:

	Debit	Credit
Convertible debt	1,000	
Debt conversion expense	400	
Common stock		1,400

Example 2

11. On January 1, 19X1, Company B issues a $1,000 face amount 4 percent convertible bond maturing December 31, 20X0. The carrying amount of the bond in the financial statements of Company B is $1,000, and it is convertible into common shares of Company B at a conversion price of $25. On June 1, 19X4, the convertible bond has a market value of $500. To induce convertible bondholders to convert their bonds promptly, Company B reduces the conversion price to $20 for bondholders who convert prior to July 1, 19X4 (within 30 days).

12. Assuming the market price of Company B's common stock on the date of conversion is $12 per share, the fair value of the incremental consideration paid by Company B upon conversion is calculated as follows for each $1,000 bond that is converted prior to July 1, 19X4:

Value of securities issued[a]	$ 600
Value of securities issuable pursuant to original conversion privileges[b]	480
Fair value of incremental consideration	$ 120

[a]Value of securities issued to debt holders is computed as follows:

Face amount	$1,000
÷ New conversion price	÷ $ 20 per share
Number of common shares issued upon conversion	50 shares
× Price per common share	× $ 12 per share
Value of securities issued	$ 600

[b]Value of securities issuable pursuant to original conversion privileges is computed as follows:

Face amount	$1,000
÷ Original conversion price	÷ $ 25 per share
Number of common shares issuable pursuant to original conversion privileges	40 shares
× Price per common share	× $ 12 per share
Value of securities issuable pursuant to original conversion privileges	$ 480

13. Therefore, Company B records debt conversion expense equal to the fair value of the incremental consideration paid as follows:

	Debit	Credit
Convertible debt	1,000	
Debt conversion expense	120	
Common stock		1,120

The same accounting would apply if, instead of reducing the conversion price, Company B issued shares pursuant to a tender offer of 50 shares of its common stock for each $1,000 bond surrendered to the company before July 1, 19X4. Refer to footnote 2 to paragraph 2 of this Statement.

Appendix B

BACKGROUND INFORMATION

14. The FASB has received several requests that it address the applicability of Opinion 26 when the conversion privileges in a convertible debt instrument are changed, or when additional consideration is paid to debt holders, for the purpose of inducing prompt conversion of the debt to equity securities.

15. Prior to an induced conversion of a convertible debt instrument, a debtor has outstanding convertible debt that is (or will become) convertible to equity securities of the debtor at the option of the debt holder. Usually the conversion privileges are exercisable for an extended period of time, frequently up to the maturity date of the debt. During the period when the conversion privileges are exercisable, the securities issuable upon conversion may have a fair value that exceeds the face amount of the debt; however, convertible debt holders often do not exercise conversion privileges until the debt is called or the conversion privileges are about to expire.

16. A debtor sometimes wishes to induce prompt conversion of its convertible debt to equity securities to reduce interest costs, to improve its debt-equity ratio, or for other reasons. Thus, the debtor may offer additional consideration as an inducement for debt holders to convert promptly. This additional consideration can take many forms, including a temporary improvement of the conversion ratio (effected by a reduction of the conversion price), the issuance of warrants or other securities, or the payment of a cash incentive or other assets to debt holders who convert by a specified date.

17. The first sentence of paragraph 2 of Opinion 26, as amended by paragraph 7 of FASB Statement No. 76, *Extinguishment of Debt,* but prior to amendment by this Statement, described the applicability of Opinion 26 as follows:

> *Applicability.* This Opinion applies to all extinguishments of debt, whether early or not, except debt that is extinguished through a troubled debt restructuring and debt that is converted to equity securities of the debtor pursuant to conversion privileges provided in terms of the debt at issuance.

18. Paragraph 20 of Opinion 26 describes the accounting for an extinguishment of debt:

> . . . A difference between the reacquisition price and the net carrying amount of the extinguished debt should be recognized currently in income of the period of extinguishment as losses or gains and identified as a separate item. [Footnote reference omitted.]

19. Paragraph 8 of FASB Statement No. 4, *Reporting Gains and Losses from Extinguishment of Debt,* specifies the income statement classification of gains and losses on extinguishment of debt:

> Gains and losses from extinguishment of debt that are included in the determination of net income shall be aggregated and, if material, classified as an extraordinary item, net of related income tax effect. [Footnote reference omitted.]

Appendix C

BASIS FOR CONCLUSIONS

20. An Exposure Draft of a proposed Statement, *Induced Conversions of Convertible Debt,* was issued on December 6, 1984. The Board received 59 responses to the Exposure Draft, a majority of which agreed with its principal conclusions. The following paragraphs discuss factors considered significant by the Board in reaching the conclusions in this Statement. Individual Board members gave greater weight to some factors than to others.

21. As amended by Statement 76 but prior to amendment by this Statement, Opinion 26 required recognition of a gain or loss equal to the difference between the reacquisition price and the carrying amount of debt when convertible debt was converted to equity securities pursuant to terms different from the original conversion privileges, including situations in which a debtor offered to give additional consideration for the purpose of inducing prompt conversion. A few respondents to the Exposure Draft recommended that that

accounting should also be applicable to induced conversions of convertible debt, stating that conversions pursuant to terms different from the original conversion privileges should be recognized based on the fair value of all securities issued. The Board did not agree with those respondents for the reasons set forth in the paragraphs that follow. Some of those respondents also questioned whether all conversions of debt to equity securities, including conversions pursuant to the original conversion privileges, should be recognized based on the fair value of all securities issued. The Board did not address accounting for conversions in general, noting that such a project would be a major undertaking and would delay the issuance of this Statement.

22. Many of those who urged the Board to address this issue and most respondents to the Exposure Draft stated that they believe accounting for an induced conversion as an extinguishment rather than as a conversion of debt does not faithfully portray the substance of such a transaction. They stated that the payment of an incentive to a debt holder could require recognition of a loss on extinguishment that might exceed the value of the conversion incentive by a material amount. The Board generally agreed that extinguishment accounting is not representationally faithful for certain induced conversions of convertible debt instruments. APB Opinion No. 14, *Accounting for Convertible Debt and Debt Issued with Stock Purchase Warrants,* states that no portion of the proceeds from the issuance of convertible debt should be accounted for as attributable to the conversion feature. The amount recognized as a liability relating to convertible debt represents an obligation either to pay a stated amount of cash or to issue a stated number of shares of equity securities. The Board believes that the nature of that obligation does not change if an incentive is paid to a debt holder to induce the holder to exercise a right already held. Therefore, this Statement requires no recognition of gain or loss with respect to the shares issuable pursuant to the original conversion privileges of the convertible debt when additional securities or assets are transferred to a debt holder to induce prompt conversion of the debt to equity securities.

23. In a conversion pursuant to original conversion terms, debt is extinguished in exchange for equity pursuant to a preexisting contract that is already recognized in the financial statements, and no gain or loss is recognized upon conversion. Unlike a conversion pursuant to original terms, in an induced conversion transaction the enterprise issues securities or pays assets in excess of those provided in the preexisting contract between the parties. The Board believes that the enterprise incurs a cost when it gives up securities or assets not pursuant to a previous obligation and that the cost of those securities or assets should be recognized.

24. Some respondents contended that the cost associated with a conversion inducement is a cost of obtaining equity capital that should be recognized as a reduction of the equity capital provided in the transaction. The Board did not agree, noting that a conversion of debt to equity securities is a transaction that involves both issuance of equity securities and extinguishment of debt securities. Although the cost of issuing equity securities in a transaction to raise capital is usually recorded as a reduction of the equity capital provided, transactions that involve the issuance of equity securities for other purposes often require recognition of expense. The Board believes that expense recognition is appropriate in circumstances involving an induced conversion of convertible securities because the transaction is not solely a capital-raising transaction.

25. The Board believes that an induced conversion transaction is also different from an extinguishment of debt transaction as described in Opinion 26, in which any preexisting contract between the debtor and the debt holder is effectively voided and the debt is extinguished pursuant to newly negotiated terms. In those circumstances, an extraordinary gain or loss is recognized equal to the difference between the carrying amount of the debt extinguished and the fair value of the securities or assets given. Some respondents stated that any expense to be recognized under the provisions of the Exposure Draft similarly should be reported as an extraordinary item. However, in an induced conversion, the preexisting contract for conversion remains in effect and an inducement is paid in an attempt to cause the conversion option to be exercised. Although the Board believes that an enterprise should recognize the cost of an inducement offer, that cost is different from the gain or loss that is recognized according to the provisions of Opinion 26 for extinguishment transactions. Therefore, the Board concluded that the cost of a conversion inducement, as defined in paragraph 2 of this Statement, should not be reported as an extraordinary item.

26. Some respondents stated that no cost should be recognized on induced conversions of convertible debt instruments. They recommended that the original and incremental consideration be accounted for in the same manner as a conversion pursuant to original conversion terms. They reasoned that changes in the number of shares issuable to satisfy a preexisting obligation do not change the nature of that obligation and also noted that gains and losses are not recognized by an enterprise in certain types of transactions involving issuance of shares of ownership.

27. When a debtor induces a holder of its debt to act by transferring assets or by issuing securities to the debt holder, the Board believes that an exchange

has taken place. In exchange for the assets or securities given up in excess of those it was already committed to pay or issue, the enterprise receives performance. In the absence of such consideration, the conversion would not have occurred at that time. The Board believes that this type of an exchange of consideration for performance is a transaction that should be recognized as a cost of obtaining that performance.

28. Some respondents disagreed with the accounting proposed in the Exposure Draft in circumstances when conversion is induced on debt that is convertible into equity securities whose market value is less than the conversion price. They stated that such debt instruments are traded at amounts primarily attributable to the interest and principal payments, and would account for an induced conversion of such an instrument like an extinguishment of nonconvertible debt, recognizing a gain. The Board disagrees with both the assertion about the security's trading characteristics and the respondents' proposed accounting.

a. Even though the equity securities issuable upon conversion have a market value less than the conversion price, the market value of a convertible debt security may not be primarily attributable to its debt characteristics if interest rate levels have increased significantly since issuance, thereby reducing the market value of those debt characteristics. Furthermore, the Board believes it is impractical to attempt to determine on an evenhanded basis whether a convertible security is trading based primarily on its equity characteristics or on its debt characteristics. The Board believes that the market value of all convertible debt securities are simultaneously influenced by both interest rates and stock prices, even though the relative influence of those factors varies. The Board believes that it is inappropriate to require significantly different accounting for a convertible debt security based on the perceived prominence of only one of its characteristics.

b. The Board notes that changes in either market interest rate levels or the market value of the equity securities issuable upon conversion do not affect the financial reporting of convertible debt securities. Even when convertible securities are perceived as trading based primarily on their equity characteristics, and even if exercise of the conversion privilege is considered highly probable, they are classified as debt securities in the balance sheet, the return to investors is reported as interest expense, and the difference between carrying amount and cash paid to retire them is reported as gain or loss from extinguishment of debt.

Thus, the Board concluded that the use of different recognition or measurement principles for induced conversions of convertible debt, based on the underlying market value or trading characteristics of the convertible security, would be inconsistent with existing accounting for other transactions involving convertible securities. The Board further noted that, in all induced conversions of convertible debt described herein, the debtor corporation gives debt holders equity securities (or a combination of equity securities and other consideration) whose total fair value exceeds the value of the securities it was previously obligated to give upon conversion. The Board believes that a debtor's election to induce conversion, causing additional value to be given up, should result in recognition of the cost of that inducement and not in the recognition of a gain that could result from extinguishment accounting.

29. The Board is aware that some convertible debt instruments include provisions allowing the debtor to alter terms of the debt to the benefit of debt holders in a manner similar to transactions described in paragraph 2 of this Statement. Such provisions may be general in nature, permitting the debtor or trustee to take actions to protect the interests of the debt holders, or they may be specific, for example, specifically authorizing the debtor to temporarily reduce the conversion price for the purpose of inducing conversion. The Board concluded that conversions pursuant to amended or altered conversion privileges on such instruments, even though they are literally "provided in the terms of the debt at issuance," should be included within the scope of this Statement. The Board concluded that the substantive nature of the transaction should govern. The Board believes that the existence of provisions in terms of the debt permitting changes to the conversion privileges should not influence the accounting.

30. The Board also considered whether a change in conversion privileges of a convertible debt instrument to induce prompt conversion should be recognized when the change is made, that is, when the inducement is offered to debt holders. The Board rejected that approach. Until the debt holder accepts the offer, no exchange has been made between the debtor and the debt holder. The Board concluded that the transaction should not be recognized until the inducement offer has been accepted by the debt holder.

31. Some respondents stated that the fair value of a change in conversion privileges should be measured (but not recognized) as of the date the conversion inducement is offered. They reasoned that the fair value of the conversion inducement at the offer date is the basis for management's decision to make the offer and that the value as of that date is the best measure of the consideration paid.

32. The Board did not adopt that approach. The Board believes that the transaction should not be measured until the parties agree, that is, until the inducement offer has been accepted by the debt holder. The Board notes that in many cases the difference between the measurements of value of the inducement offer at the offer date and the acceptance date will be minimal due to the normal structure of conversion inducement offers and the requirement in paragraph 2 of this Statement that the inducement be offered for a limited period of time. However, in circumstances involving differences in values, the Board believes the fair value as of the acceptance date is the appropriate measure because that is the value of the inducement which presumably causes the transaction to occur.

33. Some respondents questioned the need for the requirement in paragraph 2(b) of the Exposure Draft that the induced conversion "include the issuance of all of the equity securities issuable pursuant to the original conversion privileges for each debt instrument that is converted." They noted that not all induced conversions would necessarily meet this requirement and that it could lead to significantly different accounting for substantially similar transactions. The Board disagreed with those respondents, noting that a transaction that does not include the issuance of all of the equity securities issuable pursuant to the conversion privileges should not be characterized as a conversion transaction. Therefore, paragraph 2(b) of this Statement requires that an induced conversion include the issuance of all of the equity securities issuable pursuant to conversion privileges included in the terms of the debt at issuance for each debt instrument that is converted.

34. Some respondents suggested that the final Statement specify a maximum time period that could be considered a "limited period of time" for purposes of applying the provisions of paragraph 2 of this Statement. The Board did not specify any time period, noting that any period so specified would be arbitrary and that the terms of conversion inducement offers may vary according to the circumstances. This Statement applies to conversion inducements that are offered for a limited period of time because inducements offered without a restrictive time limit on their exercisability are not, by their structure, changes made to induce prompt conversion.

35. Some respondents urged the Board to address other issues relating to the issuance, conversion, or reporting of convertible securities. The Board concluded that the scope of the project should remain narrow to permit the Board to resolve the primary issue at hand without unnecessary delay. This Statement does not change the accounting for the original issuance of convertible debt instruments or the accounting for changes in conversion privileges other than those described in paragraph 2 of this Statement. The Board decided that this project should not consider other issues relating to convertible securities.

36. Some respondents stated that the effective date specified in the Exposure Draft should be changed from transactions effected after March 31, 1985 to induced conversions offered after March 31, 1985. They observed that some inducements offered before March 31, 1985 may not be accepted until after that date and stated that such transactions should not be affected by a standard that did not apply at the time the offer was made. The Board agreed and modified the effective date accordingly.

37. Some respondents objected to the provisions of the Exposure Draft permitting, but not requiring, retroactive application of its provisions. They said that past financial statements properly reflect the accounting pronouncements in effect when those statements were issued and that they do not believe that the issuance of a new pronouncement should affect those statements. Other respondents urged the Board to permit retroactive application of the provisions of this Statement, noting that some induced conversions have already occurred and questions have been raised about the way those transactions have been reported. The Board concluded that permitting, but not requiring, retroactive application was an appropriate practical solution. The Board also noted that such application was expected to apply to relatively few companies.

Statement of Financial Accounting Standards No. 85
Yield Test for Determining whether a Convertible
Security Is a Common Stock Equivalent

an amendment of APB Opinion No. 15

STATUS

Issued: March 1985

Effective Date: Applied to convertible securities issued after March 31, 1985

Affects: Amends APB 15, paragraph 35
Supersedes APB 15, paragraph 33 and footnotes 9 and 10
Supersedes APB 15, Appendix D, definition of cash yield
Supersedes AIN-APB 15, Interpretations No. 34 and 35 and footnote 21
Amends AIN-APB 15, Interpretations No. 36 and 37

Affected by: Superseded by FAS 128

Note: Although superseded, this pronouncement is still applicable until the effective date of FAS 128.

Issues Discussed by FASB Emerging Issues Task Force (EITF)

Affects: Resolves EITF Issue No. 84-16

Interpreted by: No EITF Issues

Related Issue: EITF Issue No. 90-19

SUMMARY

This Statement amends APB Opinion No. 15, *Earnings per Share,* to replace the "cash yield test" with an "effective yield test" for determining whether convertible securities are common stock equivalents in the primary earnings per share computation.

The Board was asked to consider how the provisions of Opinion 15 should be applied to zero coupon convertible bonds. Since such bonds have no annual cash interest payments, application of the "cash yield test" in Opinion 15 always results in these securities' being considered common stock equivalents. This amendment applies the common stock equivalency test in a manner consistent with the objective of Opinion 15 for a convertible security that pays much or all of its yield at maturity.

The provisions of this Statement shall be applied to convertible securities issued after March 31, 1985, with earlier application encouraged in financial statements that have not previously been issued. Retroactive application for transactions occurring during periods for which financial statements have been issued is permitted.

Statement of Financial Accounting Standards No. 85

Yield Test for Determining whether a Convertible Security Is a Common Stock Equivalent

an amendment of APB Opinion No. 15

CONTENTS

INTRODUCTION

1. The FASB has been asked to consider how the provisions of APB Opinion No. 15, *Earnings per Share,* should be applied in determining whether a zero coupon convertible bond is a common stock equivalent in the primary earnings per share computation. Because zero coupon convertible bonds have no annual cash interest payments, application of the "cash yield test" in Opinion 15 to convertible securities always results in zero coupon convertible bonds' being considered common stock equivalents. Some contend that this result is inconsistent with both the economic substance of such securities and the objective of Opinion 15.

2. Some have further suggested that the Board not limit its consideration to zero coupon convertible bonds, contending that the same problem exists with "deep discount" convertible securities, including convertible preferred stock. They believe the Board should replace the "cash yield test" with an "effective yield test" for all convertible securities. The Board agrees and is amending Opinion 15 accordingly.

STANDARDS OF FINANCIAL ACCOUNTING AND REPORTING

Amendment to APB Opinion No. 15 and Related Pronouncements

3. Paragraph 33 of Opinion 15, as amended by FASB Statement No. 55, *Determining whether a Convertible Security Is a Common Stock Equivalent,* and this Statement, and its related footnotes are to read in their entirety as follows:

A convertible security shall be considered a common stock equivalent if, at the time of issuance, it has an effective yield* of less than 66 2/3% of the then current average Aa† corporate bond yield.‡ The effective yield§ shall be based on the security's stated annual interest or dividend payments,# any original issuance premium or discount, and any call premium or discount and shall be the lowest of the yield to maturity and the yields to all call dates. The computation of effective yield does not include considerations of put options or changing conversion rates.

---

*In computing effective yield, interest shall be compounded on the same basis as publicly traded bonds in the country that the convertible securities are sold or issued. In the United States, interest is generally compounded on a semiannual basis.

†The designation Aa refers to the quality of the individual bonds that make up the average yield applied in the yield test. In the context of this Statement, the Board intends Aa to refer to bonds of equal quality to those rated Aa by either *Moody's* or *Standard & Poor's*. Those two organizations define Aa bonds as being of high quality and as having a very strong capacity to pay interest and repay principal. Bond yield information is widely and regularly published by a number of financial institutions and investor information services.

For purposes of applying the yield test, the *average* bond yield shall be based on bond yields for a brief period of time, for example, one week, including or immediately preceding the date of issuance of the security being tested.

‡If convertible securities are sold or issued outside the United States, the most comparable long-term yield in the foreign country should be used for this test.

§Effective yield for a security that does not have a stated maturity date shall be computed as the ratio of the security's stated annual interest or dividend payments to its market price at issuance.

#If the security's stated annual interest or dividend payments are adjustable, effective yield shall be computed based on scheduled formula adjustments and formula information at issuance.

4. The definition of "cash yield" is deleted from Appendix D of Opinion 15, and the parenthetical reference to that definition is deleted from paragraph 35 of Opinion 15. AICPA Accounting Interpretations 34, "Determining a Convertible Security's Cash Yield," and 35, "Computing a Convertible's Cash Yield," of Opinion 15 are deleted. The word *cash* is deleted from the term *cash yield* in paragraph 35 of Opinion 15 and AICPA Accounting Interpretations 36, "Cash Yield of Convertible Security in a 'Package,'" and 37, "Property Included in Cash Yield," of that Opinion.

Effective Date and Transition

5. The provisions of this Statement shall be applied to convertible securities issued after March 31, 1985. Earlier application of this Statement is encouraged for transactions in fiscal periods for which annual financial statements have not previously been issued. Furthermore, retroactive application of this Statement to transactions occurring during fiscal periods for which annual financial statements have previously been issued is permitted, in which case the effects on restated per share amounts of prior periods shall be disclosed. In determining whether a security issued prior to the adoption of Statement 55 was a common stock equivalent at issuance, effective yield shall be compared to 66⅔% of the then current prime interest rate.

The provisions of this Statement need not be applied to immaterial items.

This Statement was adopted by the affirmative votes of six members of the Financial Accounting Standards Board. Mr. Block dissented.

Mr. Block dissents from this Statement because he believes that the timing, probability, and degree of dilution are a complex problem in financial analysis. In addition, empirical evidence suggests that a cash yield, effective yield, or any other simple test fails to identify convertible securities that are likely to be dilutive. He believes the appropriate Board response is to amend Opinion 15 to eliminate the notion of common stock equivalency. Primary earnings per share would then be calculated on average common shares actually outstanding. He also believes that fully diluted earnings per share should be retained as a useful warning signal.

Members of the Financial Accounting Standards Board:

Donald J. Kirk, *Chairman*	Victor H. Brown	Robert T. Sprouse
Frank E. Block	Raymond C. Lauver	Arthur R. Wyatt
	David Mosso	

Appendix

BACKGROUND INFORMATION AND BASIS FOR CONCLUSIONS

6. An Exposure Draft of a proposed Statement, *Yield Test for Determining whether a Convertible Security Is a Common Stock Equivalent,* was issued on December 6, 1984. In response to the Exposure Draft the Board received 53 comment letters, most of which expressed agreement. This appendix discusses the significant comments received during the exposure period and the factors deemed significant by the Board in reaching the conclusions in this Statement. Individual Board members gave greater weight to some factors than to others. The Board concluded that it could reach an informed decision on the basis of existing information without a public hearing and that the effective date specified in paragraph 5 is advisable in the circumstances.

7. Opinion 15 requires that earnings per share computations reflect the dilutive effect of convertible securities, which is computed by assuming that a convertible security was converted into common stock as of the beginning of the period (or at the time of issuance, if later). Conversion is assumed for purposes of computing primary earnings per share only if the convertible security is a common stock equivalent and the assumed conversion reduces earnings per share.

8. Paragraph 33 of Opinion 15, as amended by paragraph 7 of Statement 55, describes the specific terms of the cash yield test:

. . . A convertible security should be considered as a common stock equivalent at the time of issuance if, based on its market price, it has a cash yield of less than 66⅔% of the then current average Aa corporate bond yield. [Footnote references omitted.]

9. In recent years, debt instruments that do not pay any interest until maturity, known as zero coupon bonds, have emerged. In response to corporate and investor demand, the notion of zero coupon convertible securities has also emerged. This development raised the accounting question of whether zero coupon convertible securities should always be considered common stock equivalents in the computation of earnings per share of the issuer, as would be required in applying the "cash yield test" specified by paragraph 33 of Opinion 15.

10. The Board agrees that the result of applying the "cash yield test" to a zero coupon or a low coupon convertible security is inconsistent with the economic substance of the security. The Board believes that the objective of Opinion 15 was to identify securities that have a yield to the holder at issuance significantly below the yield of a similar security of the issuer without the conversion option.

11. The Board has decided to amend Opinion 15 and replace the "cash yield test" with an "effective yield test." The Board believes this change, which takes into account any original issuance premium or discount and any call premium or discount, is theoretically preferable. It also makes the test rate more comparable with the Aa benchmark rate adopted for the test by Statement 55, which is based on yield to maturity.

12. The Board recognizes that in certain instances a security's effective yield to a call date may be lower than its effective yield to maturity. The Board concluded that the lower of the yields should be used in this test when that occurs. Consideration was also given to whether effective yield to a "put" date should be part of this test. The Board agrees that a put option, a unilateral right of the holder to demand redemption, can affect the investment value of a convertible security. However, the Board believes that the nature of the option, a right to terminate the debt investment for cash, is not consistent with the notion of common stock equivalency. Additionally, the Board believes that determining the limited circumstances when use of effective yield to a put date is appropriate would be difficult in

practice. For those reasons, the Board concluded that effective yield to a put date should not be part of this test.

13. Opinion 15 discusses a convertible security that has a changing conversion rate. For example, an issue may be convertible into one share of common stock in the first year, 1.10 shares in the second year, and 1.20 shares in the third year, and so forth. Frequently, these securities receive little or no cash dividends. Therefore, their value is derived principally from their conversion feature and would be deemed to be a common stock equivalent under the "cash yield test." This Statement does not change that conclusion or any other conclusions or provisions of Opinion 15 not specifically addressed in this Statement. Yield associated with changing conversion rates does not enter into the computation of effective yield, and the Board has expressly excluded it.

14. Some respondents suggested that the Board respond to this issue by amending Opinion 15 to eliminate the notion of common stock equivalency. They believe that primary earnings per share should be calculated on average common shares actually outstanding. Some other respondents raised the concern about a determination that a security is a common stock equivalent based on relationships existing at the date of issuance, and that precludes consideration of subsequent relationships during the period the convertible securities are outstanding. The Board recognizes these recurrent concerns but believes that this narrow issue does not warrant a major re examination of Opinion 15 or the various methods of determining whether convertible securities are common stock equivalents. Further, the Board believes that an "effective yield test" is more appropriate than a "cash yield test," especially for convertible securities issued at a significant discount.

15. Several respondents suggested that the final Statement should permit, but not require, retroactive implementation and restatement of previously issued financial statements for transactions occurring in periods previously reported so that similar transactions can be reported similarly. The Board concurs with that recommendation and has modified the Statement accordingly.

Statement of Financial Accounting Standards No. 86
Accounting for the Costs of Computer Software to Be Sold, Leased, or Otherwise Marketed

STATUS

Issued: August 1985

Effective Date: For financial statements for fiscal years beginning after December 15, 1985

Affects: Amends FAS 2, paragraph 31
       Amends FIN 6, paragraphs 3, 6, and 8
       Supersedes FIN 6, paragraphs 7 and 9
       Supersedes FTB 79-2

Affected by: No other pronouncements

Other Interpretive Release: FASB *Highlights,* "Computer Software: Guidance on Applying Statement 86,"
                     February 1986

Issues Discussed by FASB Emerging Issues Task Force (EITF)

Affects: No EITF Issues

Interpreted by: No EITF Issues

Related Issues: EITF Issues No. 96-6 and 96-14

SUMMARY

This Statement specifies the accounting for the costs of computer software to be sold, leased, or otherwise marketed as a separate product or as part of a product or process. It applies to computer software developed internally and to purchased software. This FASB project was undertaken in response to an AICPA Issues Paper, "Accounting for Costs of Software for Sale or Lease," and an accounting moratorium imposed by the Securities and Exchange Commission precluding changes in accounting policies related to computer software costs pending FASB action.

This Statement specifies that costs incurred internally in creating a computer software product shall be charged to expense when incurred as research and development until technological feasibility has been established for the product. Technological feasibility is established upon completion of a detail program design or, in its absence, completion of a working model. Thereafter, all software production costs shall be capitalized and subsequently reported at the lower of unamortized cost or net realizable value. Capitalized costs are amortized based on current and future revenue for each product with an annual minimum equal to the straight-line amortization over the remaining estimated economic life of the product.

This Statement is applicable, on a prospective basis, for financial statements for fiscal years beginning after December 15, 1985. The conclusions reached in this Statement change the predominant practice of expensing all costs of developing and producing a computer software product.

Statement of Financial Accounting Standards No. 86

Accounting for the Costs of Computer Software to Be Sold, Leased, or Otherwise Marketed

August 1985

CONTENTS

INTRODUCTION

1. This project was undertaken in response to requests by the Securities and Exchange Commission (SEC) and the Accounting Standards Executive Committee (AcSEC) of the American Institute of Certified Public Accountants (AICPA) to clarify the accounting for the costs of internally developed and produced computer software to be sold, leased, or otherwise marketed. They indicated that existing accounting pronouncements contain only general guidance that has been interpreted inconsistently.

SCOPE

2. This Statement establishes standards of financial accounting and reporting for the costs of computer software to be sold, leased, or otherwise marketed as a separate product or as part of a product or process, whether internally developed and produced or purchased. It identifies the costs incurred in the process of creating a software product that are research and development costs and those that are production costs to be capitalized, and it specifies amortization, disclosure, and other requirements. As used in this Statement, the terms *computer software product, software product,* and *product* encompass a computer software program, a group of programs, and a **product enhancement**.[1] This Statement does not address the accounting and reporting of costs incurred for computer software created for internal use or for others under a contractual arrangement.

STANDARDS OF FINANCIAL ACCOUNTING AND REPORTING

Research and Development Costs of Computer Software

3. All costs incurred to establish the technological feasibility of a computer software product to be sold, leased, or otherwise marketed are research and development costs. Those costs shall be charged to expense when incurred as required by FASB Statement No. 2, *Accounting for Research and Development Costs.*

4. For purposes of this Statement, the technological feasibility of a computer software product is

---

[1] Terms defined in the glossary (Appendix C) are in **boldface type** the first time they appear in this Statement.

established when the enterprise has completed all planning, designing, **coding,** and **testing** activities that are necessary to establish that the product can be produced to meet its design specifications including functions, features, and technical performance requirements. At a minimum, the enterprise shall have performed the activities in either (a) or (b) below as evidence that technological feasibility has been established:

a. If the process of creating the computer software product includes a **detail program design:**
   (1) The **product design** and the detail program design have been completed, and the enterprise has established that the necessary skills, hardware, and software technology are available to the enterprise to produce the product.
   (2) The completeness of the detail program design and its consistency with the product design have been confirmed by documenting and tracing the detail program design to product specifications.
   (3) The detail program design has been reviewed for high-risk development issues (for example, novel, unique, unproven functions and features or technological innovations), and any uncertainties related to identified high-risk development issues have been resolved through coding and testing.
b. If the process of creating the computer software product does not include a detail program design with the features identified in (a) above:
   (1) A product design and a **working model** of the software product have been completed.
   (2) The completeness of the working model and its consistency with the product design have been confirmed by testing.

Production Costs of Computer Software

5. Costs of producing **product masters** incurred subsequent to establishing technological feasibility shall be capitalized. Those costs include coding and testing performed subsequent to establishing technological feasibility. Software production costs for computer software that is to be used as an integral part of a product or process shall not be capitalized until both (a) technological feasibility has been established for the software and (b) all research and development activities for the other components of the product or process have been completed.

6. Capitalization of computer software costs shall cease when the product is available for general release to customers. Costs of **maintenance** and **customer support** shall be charged to expense when related revenue is recognized or when those costs are incurred, whichever occurs first.

Purchased Computer Software

7. The cost of purchased computer software to be sold, leased, or otherwise marketed that has no alternative future use shall be accounted for the same as the costs incurred to develop such software internally, as specified in paragraphs 3-6. If that purchased software has an alternative future use, the cost shall be capitalized when the software is acquired and accounted for in accordance with its use.

Amortization of Capitalized Software Costs

8. Capitalized software costs shall be amortized on a product-by-product basis. The annual amortization shall be the greater of the amount computed using (a) the ratio that current gross revenues for a product bear to the total of current and anticipated future gross revenues for that product or (b) the straight-line method over the remaining estimated economic life of the product including the period being reported on. Amortization shall start when the product is available for general release to customers.

Inventory Costs

9. The costs incurred for duplicating the computer software, documentation, and training materials from the product masters and for physically packaging the product for distribution shall be capitalized as inventory on a unit-specific basis and charged to cost of sales when revenue from the sale of those units is recognized.

Evaluation of Capitalized Software Costs

10. At each balance sheet date, the unamortized capitalized costs of a computer software product shall be compared to the net realizable value of that product. The amount by which the unamortized capitalized costs of a computer software product exceed the net realizable value of that asset shall be written off. The net realizable value is the estimated future gross revenues from that product reduced by the estimated future costs of completing and disposing of that product, including the costs of performing maintenance and customer support required to satisfy the enterprise's responsibility set forth at the time of sale. The reduced amount of capitalized computer software costs that have been written down to net realizable value at the close of an annual fiscal period shall be considered to be the cost for subsequent accounting purposes, and the amount of the write-down shall not be subsequently restored.

Accounting for the Costs of Computer Software
to Be Sold, Leased, or Otherwise Marketed
FAS86

Disclosures

11. The following shall be disclosed in the financial statements:

a. Unamortized computer software costs included in each balance sheet presented
b. The total amount charged to expense in each income statement presented for amortization of capitalized computer software costs and for amounts written down to net realizable value.

12. The disclosure requirements for research and development costs in Statement 2 apply to the research and development costs incurred for a computer software product to be sold, leased, or otherwise marketed.

Amendments to Other Pronouncements

13. The following sentence in paragraph 31 of Statement 2 is deleted:

For example, efforts to develop a new or higher level of computer software capability intended for sale (but not under a contractual arrangement) would be a research and development activity encompassed by this Statement.

14. The following portions of FASB Interpretation No. 6, *Applicability of FASB Statement No. 2 to Computer Software,* are deleted:

a. The sentence in paragraph 3 that states:

For example, efforts to develop a new or higher level of computer software capability intended for sale (but not under a contractual arrangement) would be a research and development activity encompassed by this Statement.

b. The phrase in the first sentence of paragraph 6 that states:

or as a product or process to be sold, leased, or otherwise marketed to others for their use

c. Paragraphs 7 and 9

d. The two sentences in paragraph 8 that state:

Developing or significantly improving a product or process that is intended to be sold, leased, or otherwise marketed to others is a research and development activity (see paragraph 8 of Statement 2). Similarly, developing or significantly improving a process whose output is a product that is intended to be sold, leased, or otherwise marketed to others is a research and development activity.

15. This Statement supersedes FASB Technical Bulletin No. 79-2, *Computer Software Costs.*

Effective Date and Transition

16. This Statement shall be effective for financial statements for fiscal years beginning after December 15, 1985 and shall be applied to costs incurred in those fiscal years for all projects including those in progress upon initial application of this Statement. Earlier application in annual financial statements that have not previously been issued is permitted.

17. Costs incurred prior to initial application of this Statement, whether capitalized or not, shall not be adjusted to the amounts that would have been capitalized if this Statement had been in effect when those costs were incurred. However, the provisions of paragraphs 8 (amortization), 10 (net realizable value test), and 11 (disclosures) of this Statement shall be applied to any unamortized costs capitalized prior to initial application of this Statement that continue to be reported as assets after the effective date.

> The provisions of this Statement need not be applied to immaterial items.

This Statement was adopted by the affirmative votes of five members of the Financial Accounting Standards Board. Messrs. Kirk and Mosso dissented.

Mr. Kirk and Mr. Mosso dissent from this Statement because (a) it unduly restricts capitalization of software costs, (b) it extends the research and development classification of Statement 2 to a major class of routine production activities, and (c) it per-

mits significantly different amounts of capitalization depending upon a company's choice of production methods.

In discussing the first point, the requirement in this Statement that either a detail program design or a working model be completed before capitalization can begin is likely to result in expensing most computer software costs, even though software is a significant, and often the only, revenue-generating asset of many companies. Assessing the probability of future benefits from computer software is difficult in the software industry, but no more difficult than in some tangible output industries such as fashion clothing and oil and gas drilling, or even in other creative process industries such as motion pictures. In each of these cases, capitalization of costs is accepted despite the inherent uncertainties.

The second point is related. This Statement sets the stage for extending the reach of Statement 2, with its mandatory expensing requirement, to a broad sweep of routine production activities because it assigns the bulk of computer programming activities (detail program design, coding, and testing) to the classification of research and development. Certainly, much research and development-type activity does take place in the computer software industry. However, most detail program design and coding activities are not discovery- or design-oriented in the sense of Statement 2; they are just the meticulous execution of a plan—skilled craftsmen applying proven methods as in any production process.

The third point is that this Statement makes capitalization dependent upon how the programming process is arranged, that is, the extent to which detail program design is separated from or integrated with coding and testing. The amount capitalized could differ significantly for comparable program outputs and, within the range of permitted capitalization, results would be essentially a matter of choice of approach to the programming process.

Mr. Mosso's dissent is based on the view that computer software is a key element in the ongoing shift of emphasis in the U. S. economy from tangible outputs and physical processes to intangible outputs and creative processes. Changes of that nature are evident in both emerging and old-line industries. In his view, accounting should accommodate this transition by reporting the results of creative processes on the balance sheet when those results comprise reasonably probable future economic benefits. Otherwise, financial statements will lose relevance as creative activities proliferate.

Messrs. Kirk and Mosso would support capitalization of costs incurred after an entity had completed the software product design and determined that proven technology is available to produce a deliverable product. The research and development classification of Statement 2 would apply only to those costs of designing the product and determining the availability of proven technology.

Members of the Financial Accounting Standards Board:

Donald J. Kirk,	Victor H. Brown	Robert T. Sprouse
Chairman	Raymond C. Lauver	Arthur R. Wyatt
Frank E. Block	David Mosso	

Appendix A

BACKGROUND INFORMATION

18. The SEC imposed a moratorium effective April 14, 1983 that precluded an enterprise from capitalizing the costs of computer software that is internally developed and produced to be sold, leased, or otherwise marketed if that enterprise's financial statements had not previously disclosed a policy of capitalizing those costs. Enterprises that had capitalized software costs and had disclosed doing so were permitted to continue to capitalize. The SEC rule specified that the moratorium would be rescinded when the FASB provided guidance on the subject.

19. In February 1984, the FASB received an Issues Paper, "Accounting for Costs of Software for Sale or Lease," prepared by the AICPA Accounting Standards Division's Task Force on Accounting for the Development and Sale of Computer Software and approved by its Accounting Standards Executive Committee. The task force included members of ADAPSO—The Computer Software and Services Industry Association (formerly known as the Association of Data Processing Service Organizations) and the National Association of Accountants. That Issues Paper recommended that certain costs incurred in creating computer software for sale or lease be recorded as an asset. Subsequently, the Board expanded the scope of its project to encompass purchased software that is to be sold, leased, or otherwise marketed and reached somewhat different conclusions from the recommendations in the Issues Paper.

20. On August 31, 1984, the Board issued an Exposure Draft of a proposed Statement on the accounting for the costs of computer software to be sold, leased, or otherwise marketed as a separate product or as part of a product or process. That Exposure Draft proposed that the costs incurred internally in creating a computer software product would be charged to expense until cost recoverability had been established by determining market, technological, and financial feasibility for the product and management had or could obtain the resources to produce and market the product and was committed to doing so. Thereafter, the costs of the detail program design would have been charged to expense, and the costs of producing the product

Accounting for the Costs of Computer Software
to Be Sold, Leased, or Otherwise Marketed
FAS86

masters, including coding and testing, would have been capitalized. The capitalized costs would have been reviewed periodically for recoverability. All costs of planning, designing, and establishing the technological feasibility of a computer software product would have been research and development costs.

21. The Board received 210 letters of comment. Issues raised by respondents included the iterative nature of the software product process, the risks and uncertainty inherent in the software product process and industry, the costs of implementing the proposed Statement in relation to its benefits, the subjectivity and possible inconsistent application of the proposal, and the difficulty in implementing the portion of the proposed Statement related to software as part of a product or process.

22. As a result of the input received in the comment letters, the Board held two educational Board meetings during March and April 1985, which were open to public observation. Representatives from a total of nine software companies participated in those meetings. In May 1985, the Board held a public hearing on the Exposure Draft and the issues set forth in the public hearing notice. Thirty-four organizations and individuals presented their views.

23. After considering the comment letters and testimony received, the Board concluded that a final Statement should be issued. The principal changes in this Statement from the Exposure Draft are:

a. Completion of a detail program design or, if a company's software product process does not include a detail program design activity, completion of a working model is the minimum requirement to establish technological feasibility. The minimum requirement to establish technological feasibility under the Exposure Draft was the completion of a product design.

b. All software creation costs incurred prior to establishing technological feasibility are charged to expense when incurred as research and development costs. Under the Exposure Draft, the costs of coding and testing after establishing technological feasibility but prior to demonstrating recoverability would have been charged to expense as other than research and development.

c. All software creation costs incurred subsequent to establishing technological feasibility are capitalized and reported at the lower of cost or net realizable value. The Exposure Draft would have required capitalization of software production costs after meeting recoverability criteria consisting of technological, market, and financial feasibility and management commitment, with capitalized costs reviewed periodically for recoverability.

Appendix B

BASIS FOR CONCLUSIONS

CONTENTS

Appendix B

BASIS FOR CONCLUSIONS

Introduction

24. This appendix summarizes considerations that were deemed significant by members of the Board in reaching the conclusions in this Statement. It includes reasons for accepting certain views and rejecting others. Individual Board members gave greater weight to some factors than to others.

Scope

25. This Statement addresses concerns about internally developed computer software raised in SEC Release No. 33-6476, *Accounting for Costs of Internally Developing Computer Software for Sale or Lease to Others.* That Release prohibited future capitalization of costs incurred to develop a computer software product by SEC registrants that had not previously done so and disclosed their accounting policy. This Statement also addresses issues raised in the AcSEC Issues Paper, but it establishes a more stringent capitalization requirement for computer software costs than was recommended in that Issues Paper.

26. In March 1985, the Board received an Issues Paper submitted by the Management Accounting Practices Committee of the National Association of Accountants, "Accounting for Software Used Internally," proposing that the costs of internal use software should be capitalized in certain situations. As a result, the Board considered broadening the scope of this project to include costs incurred for an enterprise's development of computer software for its own use. After evaluation, the Board concluded that accounting for the costs of software used internally is not currently a significant problem and, therefore, decided not to broaden the scope of this project nor add a project on internal use software to its present agenda. The Board recognized that the majority of companies expense all costs of developing software for internal-use, and the Board was not persuaded that this current predominant practice is improper. Also, this Statement clarifies activities that are research and development activities and establishes a high capitalization threshold that is likely to be applied to costs incurred in developing software for internal use as well as for sale or lease to others.

27. The Board also considered broadening the scope to include guidance on recognizing revenue from the sale of computer software but decided to postpone a decision on whether to deal with that subject until the AcSEC task force completes its research thereon and submits an Issues Paper to the Board for its consideration.

Research and Development and Production Costs of Computer Software

28. The Board recognized that the process of creating a computer software product varies among companies. Reasons for the variations include management style and differences in the types of products being developed. In defining those activities in the software product process that are research and development, the Board used the following definition of development presented in paragraph 8 of Statement 2 as a frame of reference:

> . . . the translation of research findings or other knowledge into a plan or design for a new product or process or for a significant improvement to an existing product or process whether intended for sale or use. It includes the conceptual formulation, design, and testing of product alternatives, construction of prototypes, and operation of pilot plants. It does not include routine or periodic alterations to existing products, production lines, manufacturing processes, and other ongoing operations even though those alterations may represent improvements and it does not include market research or market testing activities.

Paragraph 9 of Statement 2 provides several examples of activities that would be included in research and development. The Board concluded that the specific example in paragraph 9(i) closely describes the activities that lead to the existence of a detail program design or in its absence, a working model. That example states:

> Engineering activity required to advance the design of a product to the point that it meets specific functional and economic requirements and is ready for manufacture.

The above definition of development and the relevant example formed the foundation for the Board's final conclusions on what activities in the software product process should be classified as research and development.

29. Some activities in the software product process closely correspond with the example in Statement 2 while the correspondence of other activities is less clear. Some respondents viewed nearly all software creation activities as research and development, and others viewed very few activities in the creation of a software product as research and development.

30. In the Exposure Draft, the detail program design activities were considered similar to the devel-

Accounting for the Costs of Computer Software
to Be Sold, Leased, or Otherwise Marketed
FAS86

opment activities described in Statement 2. The Exposure Draft generally considered coding and testing to be production activities and proposed that they be segregated from detail program design activities. However, a majority of respondents disagreed with that approach. Some asserted that coding and testing, as well as detail program design activities, are research and development and should therefore be charged to expense as incurred. Others stated that the detail program design is a production activity and, therefore, should be eligible for capitalization. Many respondents indicated that the costs involved to segregate the detail program design activities from coding and testing activities would far exceed the benefits derived from doing so. Others suggested that detail program design activities may cease to be required as future technological advances occur.

31. The Board considered the information received from respondents and concluded that requiring the segregation of the costs of the detail program design from the costs of coding and testing activities would not provide an objective point for evidence of a computer software product's technological feasibility and in some circumstances would be difficult to implement. The Board further concluded that, for purposes of applying this Statement, research and development activities should be considered incomplete until technological feasibility has been objectively established and that research and development activities in the software product process include (a) all planning and designing (both product design and detail program design) and (b) any coding and testing necessary to establish technological feasibility. Some respondents indicated that coding and testing activities that precede establishing technological feasibility should be considered production activities. However, the Board concluded that, until technological feasibility can be objectively established, the future economic benefits from such coding and testing activities are too uncertain to qualify for recognition as an asset and should be classified as research and development.

32. Some respondents suggested that the process of creating a particular software product may not involve the development of a detail program design. The Board decided that, absent a detail program design, the completion of the working model would be acceptable evidence of technological feasibility. That provision permits the application of this Statement if the detail program design activity is, for any reason, omitted from the software product process employed.

33. The Board recognized that some comparability may be lost if an enterprise's software process does not include a detail program design but concluded that virtually no comparability would be achieved if

capitalizing the costs of computer software were dependent upon a somewhat subjective determination of technological feasibility at an earlier, less well-defined stage of the development process. However, the Board concluded that objective evidence of technological feasibility must be available before the research and development phase can be considered to be complete and the production phase can begin. Consistency in applying Statement 2 among industries is an important consideration. In addition, the Board selected alternative criteria for evidence of technological feasibility to insure future applicability in the event that the software product process employed in the future does not include a detail program design.

34. The Board also recognized that the technological feasibility of some products cannot be established with completion of the detail program design because high-risk development issues remain. Resolution of all uncertainties related to identified high-risk development issues is therefore included as a requirement for establishing technological feasibility. The discussion of technological feasibility in the Basis for Conclusions of the Exposure Draft included the need to resolve all high-risk development issues. Several respondents encouraged the Board to incorporate that consideration into the standards section of the final Statement. The Board agreed with that suggestion and included the requirement in paragraph 4.

35. The Exposure Draft proposed that the recoverability of the cost of a product be established prior to capitalization. The four criteria used to establish a product's recoverability were technological, market, and financial feasibility and management commitment. Some respondents to the Exposure Draft suggested that those criteria were subjective and effectively would permit optional application of the proposed Statement. However, many respondents agreed that at some point in the computer software product process an asset exists and some costs should be capitalized.

36. The Board recognized that, in some cases, an enterprise may believe that a software product is technologically feasible before the criteria for establishing technological feasibility as set forth in this Statement are met. To provide a more objective measure of technological feasibility, the Board concluded that completion of a detail program design is the earliest point in the process that technological feasibility can be considered to be established for purposes of applying this Statement.

Purchased Computer Software

37. Some enterprises purchase software as an alternative to developing it internally. Purchased

computer software may be modified or integrated with another product or process. The Board concluded that the costs of purchased software should be accounted for on a consistent basis with the costs incurred to develop such software internally. The Board further agreed that the alternative future use provision of paragraph 11 of Statement 2 should apply to purchased software; that is, if the purchased software is not capitalizable under the provisions of this Statement but has an alternative future use, the portion of the cost attributed to the software's alternative future use should be capitalized and accounted for according to its use.

38. Applying the provisions of this Statement to the costs of purchased software will result in the capitalization of the software's total cost if the criteria specified in paragraph 4 are met at the time of purchase. Otherwise, the cost will be charged to expense as research and development. For example, if the technological feasibility of a software product as a whole (that is, the product that will be ultimately marketed) has been established at the time software is purchased, the cost of the purchased software will be capitalized and further accounted for in accordance with the other provisions of this Statement. The cost of software purchased to be integrated with another product or process will be capitalized only if technological feasibility was established for the software component and if all research and development activities for the other components of the product or process were completed at the time of purchase.

39. If the technological feasibility test for the software product as a whole is not met at the time that the software is purchased but the software being purchased has an alternative future use (for example, for use as a tool in developing another product or for direct resale), the cost will be capitalized and subsequently accounted for according to its use. The alternative future use test will also apply to purchased software that will be integrated with a product or process in which the research and development activities for the other components are not complete.

Internally Developed Computer Software to Be Used as Part of a Product or Process

40. Computer software may be developed as an integral part of a product or process and not marketed or marketable as a separate product. In that case, even though the software has been completely developed, there may be no assurance that a salable product will exist, and the software may have no alternative future use. The Exposure Draft proposed the establishment of cost recoverability for the product or process as a whole prior to capitalization of any software costs.

41. Some respondents to the Exposure Draft and participants in the educational sessions objected to that provision on both conceptual and practical grounds. They suggested that the requirement to demonstrate recoverability for the product or process as a whole conflicted with Statement 2, which defines research and development activities and requires those activities to be charged to expense when incurred. In their view, the cost of a product that has hardware and software components would be accounted for differently under the Exposure Draft than currently required under Statement 2. For a product with hardware and software components, certain costs of the software could be capitalized when recoverability of the product cost was established, but all costs of the hardware would be expensed until completion of a prototype. That accounting treatment would require maintenance of separate cost records for the hardware and software components of the product.

42. The Board concluded that both establishing technological feasibility of the software component and completing research and development activities for the hardware component are necessary for capitalization of software costs to begin. The intention of this provision is to achieve consistency with Statement 2, consistency with the accounting for other software costs included in the scope of this Statement, and recognition of the related risks and uncertainties involved in developing a product or process that has more than one component. This approach does not require maintaining separate cost records for the hardware and software components of the same product.

Amortization of Capitalized Costs

43. A key objective in requiring the capitalization of certain costs incurred to purchase or internally produce computer software is to recognize the asset representing future economic benefits created by incurring those costs. Because a net realizable value test, which considers future revenues and costs, must be applied to capitalized costs, the Board concluded that amortization should be based on estimated future revenues. In recognition of the uncertainties involved in estimating revenue, the Board further concluded that amortization should not be less than straight-line amortization over the product's remaining estimated economic life. The Board also concluded that amortization expense should be computed on a product-by-product basis and that amortization should begin when the product is available for general release to customers.

Inventory and Other Costs

44. The costs incurred for a computer software product after coding, testing, and producing the

Accounting for the Costs of Computer Software
to Be Sold, Leased, or Otherwise Marketed
FAS86

product masters are production costs similar to costs incurred to produce any other product. Thus, the Board concluded that unit-specific costs, such as making copies from the product masters and physical packaging of the product, should be accounted for as costs of inventory as they are for other products.

45. Paragraph 6 requires the costs of other activities, such as customer support, maintenance, and training, to be charged to expense when related revenue is recognized or when the costs are incurred, whichever occurs first. When the sales price of a product includes customer support for several periods and the price of that support is not separately stated, the estimated related costs should be accrued in the same period that the sales price is recognized.

Evaluation of Capitalized Software Costs

46. The Exposure Draft proposed that an enterprise establish the recoverability of the costs of a computer software product prior to capitalization of software costs. An assessment of the recoverability of capitalized costs was required in each reporting period. If recoverability was determined to be no longer established, capitalized costs were to be written down to an amount for which recoverability could be established.

47. Respondents indicated that the ongoing recoverability test used was described in terminology different from that used to describe a net realizable value test in accounting for other assets, such as motion picture films. The Board concluded that a net realizable value test should replace the recoverability test because the net realizable value test will accomplish the same objective and uses terminology consistent with other accounting literature. The Board agreed that the capitalized costs of each software product should be subsequently valued, in each reporting period, at the lower of its remaining unamortized cost or net realizable value.

48. The concept of net realizable value is similar to that discussed in paragraph 9 of ARB No. 43, Chapter 4, "Inventory Pricing," which addresses inventory valuation. The Board determined that a test of "cost or market, whichever is lower" is not entirely appropriate for capitalized software costs because a replacement cost for the product will not always be available.

Disclosures

49. Because of the significance of computer software costs to enterprises in the computer software industry and because some of those costs are required to be capitalized and some charged to expense when incurred, the Board concluded that the disclosures specified in paragraphs 11 and 12 are necessary. Those disclosures are intended to assist users of the financial statements in making their assessments of the operations, potential risks, and financial status of enterprises that produce computer software.

Amendments to Other Pronouncements

50. The portions of Interpretation 6 that remain after the amendments specified in this Statement pertain essentially to the costs of software for internal use. Paragraph 5 of that Interpretation states that "costs incurred to purchase . . . computer software . . . are not research and development costs . . . unless the software is for use in research and development activities." The phrase "for use in research and development activities" includes tools used to facilitate research and development or components of a product or process that are undergoing research and development activities. The aforementioned reference to purchased software in Interpretation 6 is consistent with the requirements of this Statement.

Transition

51. Most enterprises in the computer software industry currently expense all computer software development and production costs when those costs are incurred. Those that capitalize some computer software production costs apply criteria that differ among enterprises and differ from the criteria specified in this Statement. The information that would be necessary to determine the amounts that would be capitalized if this Statement were applied retroactively is not necessarily available. The Board concluded that the cost of requiring such a determination retroactively would exceed the benefits it might offer. The Board concluded that such a retroactive determination should not be made. However, the Board decided to permit, but not require, application in financial statements for a fiscal year for which financial statements have not been issued. The Board further concluded that costs capitalized before the application of this Statement should be subject to the net realizable value test specified in paragraph 10, but should not otherwise be adjusted to an amount that would have been capitalized had this Statement been applied. Classifying, amortizing, and disclosing previously capitalized costs in accordance with the provisions of this Statement should result in an acceptable level of comparability and understandability.

Appendix C

GLOSSARY

52. This appendix defines certain terms that are used in this Statement.

Coding

Generating detailed instructions in a computer language to carry out the requirements described in the detail program design. The coding of a computer software product may begin prior to, concurrent with, or subsequent to the completion of the detail program design.

Customer support

Services performed by an enterprise to assist customers in their use of software products. Those services include any installation assistance, training classes, telephone question and answer services, newsletters, on-site visits, and software or data modifications.

Detail program design

The detail design of a computer software product that takes product function, feature, and technical requirements to their most detailed, logical form and is ready for coding.

Maintenance

Activities undertaken after the product is available for general release to customers to correct errors or keep the product updated with current information. Those activities include routine changes and additions.

Product design

A logical representation of all product functions in sufficient detail to serve as product specifications.

Product enhancement

Improvements to an existing product that are intended to extend the life or improve significantly the marketability of the original product. Enhancements normally require a product design and may require a redesign of all or part of the existing product.

Product masters

A completed version, ready for copying, of the computer software product, the documentation, and the training materials that are to be sold, leased, or otherwise marketed.

Testing

Performing the steps necessary to determine whether the coded computer software product meets function, feature, and technical performance requirements set forth in the product design.

Working model

An operative version of the computer software product that is completed in the same software language as the product to be ultimately marketed, performs all the major functions planned for the product, and is ready for initial customer testing (usually identified as *beta testing*).

Statement of Financial Accounting Standards No. 87
Employers' Accounting for Pensions

STATUS

Issued: December 1985

Effective Date: For fiscal years beginning after December 15, 1986

Affects: Supersedes APB 8
Amends APB 12, paragraph 6
Amends APB 16, paragraph 88
Supersedes APB 16, footnote 13
Amends FAS 5, paragraph 7
Supersedes FAS 36
Supersedes FIN 3

Affected by: Paragraph 8 amended by FAS 106
Paragraph 37 amended by FAS 96 and FAS 109
Footnote 3 superseded by FAS 106

Other Interpretive Pronouncement: FTB 87-1 (Superseded by FAS 106)

Other Interpretive Release: FASB Special Report, *A Guide to Implementation of Statement 87 on Employers' Accounting for Pensions: Questions and Answers* (Resolves EITF Issue No. 87-13)

Issues Discussed by FASB Emerging Issues Task Force (EITF)

Affects: Partially resolves EITF Issue No. 84-35

Interpreted by: Paragraphs 24 through 28 interpreted by EITF Issue No. 91-7
Paragraph 64 interpreted by EITF Issue No. 86-27
Paragraph 68 interpreted by EITF Issue No. 90-3
Paragraph 198 interpreted by EITF Topic No. D-36

Related Issues: EITF Issue No. 88-1 and Topic No. D-27

SUMMARY

This Statement supersedes previous standards for employers' accounting for pensions. The most significant changes to past practice affect an employer's accounting for a single-employer defined benefit pension plan, although some provisions also apply to an employer that participates in a multiemployer plan or sponsors a defined contribution plan.

Measuring cost and reporting liabilities resulting from defined benefit pension plans have been sources of accounting controversy for many years. Both the Committee on Accounting Procedure, in 1956, and the Accounting Principles Board (APB), in 1966, concluded that improvements in pension accounting were necessary beyond what was considered practical at those times.

After 1966, the importance of information about pensions grew with increases in the number of plans and amounts of pension assets and obligations. There were significant changes in both the legal environment (for example, the enactment of ERISA) and the economic environment (for example, higher inflation and interest rates). Critics of prior accounting requirements, including users of financial statements, became aware that reported pension cost was not comparable from one company to another and often was not consistent from period to period for the same company. They also became aware that significant pension-related obligations and assets were not recognized in financial statements.

Funding and Accrual Accounting

This Statement reaffirms the usefulness of information based on accrual accounting. Accrual accounting goes beyond cash transactions to provide information about assets, liabilities, and earnings. The Board has concluded, as did the APB in 1966, that net pension cost for a period is not necessarily determined by the amount the employer decides to contribute to the plan for that period. Many factors (including tax considerations and availability of both cash and alternative investment opportunities) that affect funding decisions should not be allowed to dictate accounting results if the accounting is to provide the most useful information.

The conclusion that accounting information on an accrual basis is needed does not mean that accounting information and funding decisions are unrelated. In pensions, as in other areas, managers may use accounting information along with other factors in making financial decisions. Some employers may decide to change their pension funding policies based in part on the new accounting information. Financial statements should provide information that is useful to those who make economic decisions, and the decision to fund a pension plan to a greater or lesser extent is an economic decision. The Board, however, does not have as an objective either an increase or a decrease in the funding level of any particular plan or plans. Neither does the Board believe that the information required by this Statement is the only information needed to make a funding decision or that net periodic pension cost, as defined, is necessarily the appropriate amount for any particular employer's periodic contribution.

Fundamentals of Pension Accounting

In applying accrual accounting to pensions, this Statement retains three fundamental aspects of past pension accounting: *delaying recognition* of certain events, reporting *net cost,* and *offsetting* liabilities and assets. Those three features of practice have shaped financial reporting for pensions for many years, although they have been neither explicitly addressed nor widely understood, and they conflict in some respects with accounting principles applied elsewhere.

The *delayed recognition* feature means that changes in the pension obligation (including those resulting from plan amendments) and changes in the value of assets set aside to meet those obligations are not recognized as they occur but are recognized systematically and gradually over subsequent periods. All changes are ultimately recognized except to the extent they may be offset by subsequent changes, but at any point changes that have been identified and quantified await subsequent accounting recognition as net cost components and as liabilities or assets.

The *net cost* feature means that the recognized consequences of events and transactions affecting a pension plan are reported as a single net amount in the employer's financial statements. That approach aggregates at least three items that might be reported separately for any other part of an employer's operations: the compensation cost of benefits promised, interest cost resulting from deferred payment of those benefits, and the results of investing what are often significant amounts of assets.

The *offsetting* feature means that recognized values of assets contributed to a plan and liabilities for pensions recognized as net pension cost of past periods are shown net in the employer's statement of financial position, even though the liability has not been settled, the assets may be still largely controlled, and substantial risks and rewards associated with both of those amounts are clearly borne by the employer.

Within those three features of practice that are retained by this Statement, the Board has sought to achieve more useful financial reporting through three changes:

a. This Statement requires a standardized method for measuring net periodic pension cost that is intended to improve comparability and understandability by recognizing the compensation cost of an employee's pension over that employee's approximate service period and by relating that cost more directly to the terms of the plan.

b. This Statement requires immediate recognition of a liability (the minimum liability) when the accumulated benefit obligation exceeds the fair value of plan assets, although it continues to delay recognition of the offsetting amount as an increase in net periodic pension cost.

c. This Statement requires expanded disclosures intended to provide more complete and more current information than can be practically incorporated in financial statements at the present time.

Cost Recognition and Measurement

A fundamental objective of this Statement is to recognize the compensation cost of an employee's pension benefits (including prior service cost) over that employee's approximate service period. Many respondents to *Preliminary Views* and the Exposure Draft on employers' accounting for pensions agreed with that objective, which conflicts with some aspects of past practice under APB Opinion No. 8, *Accounting for the Cost of Pension Plans.*

The Board believes that the understandability, comparability, and usefulness of pension information will be improved by narrowing the past range of methods for allocating or attributing the cost of an employee's pension to individual periods of service. The Board was unable to identify differences in circumstances that would make it appropriate for different employers to use fundamentally different accounting methods or for a single employer to use different methods for different plans.

The Board believes that the terms of the plan that define the benefits an employee will receive (the plan's benefit formula) provide the most relevant and reliable indication of how pension cost and pension obligations are incurred. In the absence of convincing evidence that the substance of an exchange is different from that indicated by the agreement between the parties, accounting has traditionally looked to the terms of the agreement as a basis for recording the exchange. Unlike some other methods previously used for pension accounting, the method required by this Statement focuses more directly on the plan's benefit formula as the basis for determining the benefit earned, and therefore the cost incurred, in each individual period.

Statement of Financial Position

The Board believes that this Statement represents an improvement in past practices for the reporting of financial position in two ways. First, recognition of the cost of pensions over employees' service periods will result in earlier (but still gradual) recognition of significant liabilities that were reflected more slowly in the past financial statements of some employers. Second, the requirement to recognize a minimum liability limits the extent to which the delayed recognition of plan amendments and losses in net periodic pension cost can result in omission of certain liabilities from statements of financial position.

Recognition of a measure of at least the minimum pension obligation as a liability is not a new idea. Accounting Research Bulletin No. 47, *Accounting for Costs of Pension Plans,* published in 1956, stated that "as a minimum, the accounts and financial statements should reflect accruals which equal the present worth, actuarially calculated, of pension commitments to employees to the extent that pension rights have vested in the employees, reduced, in the case of the balance sheet, by any accumulated trusteed funds or annuity contracts purchased." Opinion 8 required that "if the company has a legal obligation for pension cost in excess of amounts paid or accrued, the excess should be shown in the balance sheet as both a liability and a deferred charge."

The Board believes that an employer with an unfunded pension obligation has a liability and an employer with an overfunded pension obligation has an asset. The most relevant and reliable information available about that liability or asset is based on the fair value of plan assets and a measure of the present value of the obligation using current, explicit assumptions. The Board concluded, however, that recognition in financial statements of those amounts in their entirety would be too great a change from past practice. Some Board members were also influenced by concerns about the reliability of measures of the obligation.

The delayed recognition included in this Statement results in excluding the most current and most relevant information from the statement of financial position. That information, however, is included in the required disclosures.

Information Needed

The Board believes that users of financial reports need information beyond that previously disclosed to be able to assess the status of an employer's pension arrangements and their effects on the employer's financial position and results of operations. Most respondents agreed, and this Statement requires certain disclosures not previously required.

This Statement requires disclosure of the components of net pension cost and of the projected benefit obligation. One of the factors that has made pension information difficult to understand is that past practice and terminology combined elements that are different in substance and effect into net amounts. Although the Board agreed to retain from past pension accounting practice the basic features of reporting net cost and offsetting liabilities and assets, the Board believes that disclosure of the components will significantly assist users in understanding the economic events that have occurred. Those disclosures also make it easier to understand why reported amounts change from period to period, especially when a large cost or asset is offset by a large revenue or liability to produce a relatively small net reported amount.

* * *

After considering the range of comments on *Preliminary Views* and the Exposure Draft, the Board concluded that this Statement represents a worthwhile improvement in financial reporting. Opinion 8 noted in 1966 that "accounting for pension cost is in a transitional stage." The Board believes that is still true in 1985. FASB Concepts Statement No. 5, *Recognition and Measurement in Financial Statements of Business Enterprises*, paragraph 2, indicates that "the Board intends future change [in practice] to occur in the gradual, evolutionary way that has characterized past change."

(This page intentionally left blank.)

Statement of Financial Accounting Standards No. 87

Employers' Accounting for Pensions

CONTENTS

INTRODUCTION

1. This Statement establishes standards of financial reporting and accounting for an employer that offers **pension benefits**[1] to its employees. The FASB added two pension projects to its agenda in 1974: (a) accounting and reporting by employee benefit plans and (b) employers' accounting for pensions. The first of those projects led to the issuance in 1980 of FASB Statement No. 35, *Accounting and Reporting by Defined Benefit Pension Plans;* this Statement is a result of the second project.

2. Measurement of cost and reporting of liabilities resulting from **defined benefit pension plans** have been a source of accounting controversy for many years. In 1956, the Committee on Accounting Procedure in Accounting Research Bulletin (ARB) No. 47, *Accounting for Costs of Pension Plans,* expressed a preference for accounting in which cost would be "systematically accrued during the expected period of active **service** of the covered employees . . ." (paragraph 5). The committee went on to state:

> However, the committee believes that opinion as to the accounting for pension costs has not yet crystallized sufficiently to make it possible at this time to assure agreement on any one method, and that differences in accounting for pension costs are likely to continue for a time. Accordingly, for the present, the committee believes that, as a minimum, the accounts and financial statements should reflect accruals which equal the present worth, actuarially calculated, of pension commitments to employees to the extent that pension rights have vested in the employees, reduced, in the case of the balance sheet, by any accumulated trusteed **funds** or **annuity contracts** purchased. [paragraph 7]

---
[1]Words that appear in the glossary are set in **boldface type** the first time that they appear.

3. The Accounting Principles Board (APB) issued Opinion No. 8, *Accounting for the Cost of Pension Plans,* in 1966. Opinion 8 described several views of pension cost supported by members of the APB. It concluded that "in the light of such differences in views and of the fact that accounting for pension cost is in a transitional stage, . . . the range of practices would be significantly narrowed if pension cost were accounted for at the present time within limits . . ." (paragraph 17).

4. After 1966, the importance of information about pensions grew with increases in the number of plans and the amounts of pension assets and obligations. There were significant changes in both the legal environment (for example, the enactment of **ERISA**) and the economic environment (for example, higher inflation and **interest rates**). Critics of past accounting, including users of financial statements, became aware that reported pension cost was not comparable from one company to another and often was not consistent from period to period for the same company. They also became aware that significant pension-related obligations and assets were not recognized in financial statements.

5. This Statement continues the evolutionary search for more meaningful and more useful pension accounting. The FASB believes that the conclusions it has reached are a worthwhile and significant step in that direction, but it also believes that those conclusions are not likely to be the final step in that evolution. Pension accounting in 1985 is still in a transitional stage. It has not yet fully crystallized, but the Board believes this Statement represents significant progress, especially in the measurement of **net periodic pension cost** and in the disclosure of useful information.

6. The Board's objectives for this Statement, in broad terms, are as follows:

a. To provide a measure of net periodic pension cost[2] that is more representationally faithful than those used in past practice because it reflects the terms of the underlying plan and because it better approximates the recognition of the cost of an employee's pension over that employee's service period
b. To provide a measure of net periodic pension cost that is more understandable and comparable and is, therefore, more useful than those in past practice

c. To provide disclosures that will allow users to understand better the extent and effect of an employer's undertaking to provide employee pensions and related financial arrangements
d. To improve reporting of financial position.

STANDARDS OF FINANCIAL ACCOUNTING AND REPORTING

Scope

7. This Statement establishes standards of financial accounting and reporting for an employer that offers pension benefits to its employees. Ordinarily, such benefits are periodic pension payments to retired employees or their survivors, but they may also include benefits payable as a single lump sum and, except as noted in the following paragraph, other types of benefits such as death benefits provided through a pension plan. An employer's arrangement to provide pension benefits may take a variety of forms and may be financed in different ways. This Statement applies to any arrangement that is similar in substance to a pension plan regardless of the form or means of financing. This Statement applies to a written plan and to a plan whose existence may be implied from a well-defined, although perhaps unwritten, practice of paying postretirement benefits.

8. This Statement does not apply to a plan that provides only life insurance benefits or health insurance benefits, or both, to retirees; employers are also not required to apply this Statement to postemployment health care benefits provided through a pension plan.[3] If the provisions of this Statement are not applied to postemployment health care benefits provided through a pension plan, obligations and assets related to such benefits shall not be considered to be pension obligations or **plan assets** for purposes of this Statement. This Statement does not change or supersede any of the requirements set forth in Statement 35 for the financial statements of a pension plan.

9. This Statement supersedes Opinion 8, as amended; FASB Statement No. 36, *Disclosure of Pension Information;* and FASB Interpretation No. 3, *Accounting for the Cost of Pension Plans Subject to the Employee Retirement Income Security Act of 1974.* Paragraphs 70 and 75 of this Statement amend FASB Statement No. 5, *Accounting for Contingencies* and APB Opinion No. 16, *Business Combinations.*

---

[2]This Statement uses the term *net periodic pension cost* rather than *net pension expense* because part of the cost recognized in a period may be capitalized along with other costs as part of an asset such as inventory.

[3]The Board has a separate project on its agenda to address accounting for postemployment benefits other than pensions. The fact that this Statement does not apply to postemployment health care benefits does not mean that the Board is proscribing or discouraging accrual of the cost of those benefits.

Use of Reasonable Approximations

10. This Statement is intended to specify accounting objectives and results rather than specific computational means of obtaining those results. If estimates, averages, or computational shortcuts can reduce the cost of applying this Statement, their use is appropriate, provided the results are reasonably expected not to be materially different from the results of a detailed application.

Single-Employer Defined Benefit Pension Plans

11. The most significant parts of this Statement involve an employer's accounting for a single-employer defined benefit pension plan. For purposes of this Statement, a defined benefit pension plan is one that defines an amount of pension benefit to be provided, usually as a function of one or more factors such as age, years of service, or compensation.

12. A pension benefit is part of the compensation paid to an employee for services. In a defined benefit pension plan, the employer promises to provide, in addition to current wages, retirement income payments in future years after the employee retires or terminates service. Generally, the amount of benefit to be paid depends on a number of future events that are incorporated in the **plan's benefit formula,** often including how long the employee and any survivors live, how many years of service the employee renders, and the employee's compensation in the years immediately before retirement or termination. In most cases, services are rendered over a number of years before an employee retires and begins collecting the pension. Even though the services rendered by an employee are complete and the employee has retired, the total amount of benefit that the employer has promised and the cost to the employer of the services rendered are not precisely determinable but can only be estimated using the **benefit formula** and estimates of the relevant future events, many of which the employer cannot control.

13. Any method of pension accounting that recognizes cost before the payment of benefits to retirees must deal with two problems stemming from the nature of the defined benefit pension contract. First, estimates or **assumptions** must be made concerning the future events that will determine the amount and timing of the benefit payments. Second, some approach to attributing the cost of pension benefits to individual years of service must be selected.

14. This Statement requires use of explicit assumptions, each of which individually represents the best estimate of a particular future event. This Statement also requires use of the terms of the pension plan itself, specifically the plan's benefit formula, as a basis for attributing benefits earned and their cost to periods of employee service.

Basic Elements of Pension Accounting

15. The assumptions and the **attribution** of cost to periods of employee service are fundamental to the measurements of net periodic pension cost and pension obligations required by this Statement. The basic elements of pension accounting are described in paragraphs 16-19; they are the foundation of the accounting and reporting requirements set forth in this Statement.

16. Net periodic pension cost has often been viewed as a single homogeneous amount, but in fact it is made up of several *components* that reflect different aspects of the employer's financial arrangements as well as the cost of benefits earned by employees. The cost of a benefit can be determined without regard to how the employer decides to finance the plan. The **service cost component** of net periodic pension cost is the **actuarial present value** of benefits attributed by the plan's benefit formula to services rendered by employees during the period. The service cost component is conceptually the same for an unfunded plan, a plan with minimal funding, and a well-funded plan. The other components of net periodic pension cost are **interest cost**[4] (interest on the **projected benefit obligation,** which is a discounted amount), **actual return on plan assets, amortization** of **unrecognized prior service cost,** and **gain or loss.** Both the return on plan assets and interest cost components are in substance financial items rather than employee compensation costs.

17. The projected benefit obligation as of a date is the actuarial present value of all benefits attributed by the plan's benefit formula to employee service rendered prior to that date. The projected benefit obligation is measured using an assumption as to future compensation levels if the **pension benefit formula** is based on those future compensation levels. Plans for which the pension benefit formula is based on future compensation are sometimes called pay-related, **final-pay,** final-average-pay, or **career-average-pay plans.** Plans for which the pension benefit formula is not based on future compensation levels are called non-pay-related or **flat-benefit plans.** The projected benefit obligation is a measure of benefits attributed to service to date assuming that the plan continues in effect and that estimated future events (including compensation increases, **turnover,** and **mortality**) occur.

---

[4]The interest cost component of net periodic pension cost shall not be considered to be interest for purposes of applying FASB Statement No. 34, *Capitalization of Interest Cost.*

18. The **accumulated benefit obligation** as of a date is the actuarial present value of benefits attributed by the pension benefit formula to employee service rendered prior to that date and based on current and past compensation levels. The accumulated benefit obligation differs from the projected benefit obligation in that it includes no assumption about future compensation levels. For plans with flat-benefit or non-pay-related pension benefit formulas, the accumulated benefit obligation and the projected benefit obligation are the same. The accumulated benefit obligation and the **vested benefit obligation** provide information about the obligation the employer would have if the plan were discontinued.

19. Plan assets are assets—usually stocks, bonds, and other investments—that have been segregated and restricted (usually in a trust) to provide for pension benefits. The amount of plan assets includes amounts contributed by the employer (and by employees for a **contributory plan**) and amounts earned from investing the contributions, less benefits paid. Plan assets ordinarily cannot be withdrawn by the employer except under certain circumstances when a plan has assets in excess of obligations and the employer has taken certain steps to satisfy existing obligations. Assets not segregated in a trust or otherwise effectively restricted so that they cannot be used by the employer for other purposes are not plan assets for purposes of this Statement even though it may be intended that such assets be used to provide pensions. Amounts accrued by the employer but not yet paid to the plan are not plan assets for purposes of this Statement. Securities of the employer held by the plan are includable in plan assets provided they are transferable.

Recognition of Net Periodic Pension Cost

20. The following components shall be included in the net pension cost recognized for a period by an employer **sponsoring** a defined benefit pension plan:

a. Service cost
b. Interest cost
c. Actual return on plan assets, if any
d. Amortization of unrecognized prior service cost, if any
e. Gain or loss (including the effects of changes in assumptions) to the extent recognized (paragraph 34)
f. Amortization of the unrecognized net obligation (and loss or cost) or unrecognized net asset (and gain) existing at the date of initial application of this Statement (paragraph 77).

Service cost

21. The service cost component recognized in a period shall be determined as the actuarial present value of benefits attributed by the pension benefit formula to employee service during that period. The measurement of the service cost component requires use of an attribution method and assumptions. That measurement is discussed in paragraphs 39-48 of this Statement.

Interest cost

22. The interest cost component recognized in a period shall be determined as the increase in the projected benefit obligation due to the passage of time. Measuring the projected benefit obligation as a present value requires accrual of an interest cost at rates equal to the assumed discount rates.

Actual return on plan assets

23. For a funded plan, the actual return on plan assets shall be determined based on the **fair value** of plan assets at the beginning and the end of the period, adjusted for contributions and benefit payments.

Prior service cost

24. **Plan amendments** (including initiation of a plan) often include provisions that grant increased benefits based on services rendered in prior periods. Because plan amendments are granted with the expectation that the employer will realize economic benefits in future periods, this Statement does not require the cost of providing such **retroactive benefits** (that is, **prior service cost**) to be included in net periodic pension cost entirely in the year of the amendment but provides for recognition during the future service periods of those employees active at the date of the amendment who are expected to receive benefits under the plan.

25. The cost of retroactive benefits (including benefits that are granted to retirees) is the increase in the projected benefit obligation at the date of the amendment. Except as specified in paragraphs 26 and 27, that prior service cost shall be amortized by assigning an equal amount to each future period of service of each employee active at the date of the amendment who is expected to receive benefits under the plan. If all or almost all of a plan's **participants** are inactive, the cost of retroactive plan amendments affecting benefits of inactive participants shall be amortized based on the remaining life expectancy of those participants instead of based on the remaining service period.

26. To reduce the complexity and detail of the computations required, consistent use of an alternative amortization approach that more rapidly reduces the unrecognized cost of retroactive amendments is acceptable. For example, a straight-line amortization of the cost over the average remaining service period of employees expected to receive benefits under the plan is acceptable. The alternative method used shall be disclosed.

27. In some situations a history of regular plan amendments and other evidence may indicate that the period during which the employer expects to realize economic benefits from an amendment granting retroactive benefits is shorter than the entire remaining service period of the active employees. Identification of such situations requires an assessment of the individual circumstances and the substance of the particular plan situation. In those circumstances, the amortization of prior service cost shall be accelerated to reflect the more rapid expiration of the employer's economic benefits and to recognize the cost in the periods benefited.

28. A plan amendment can reduce, rather than increase, the projected benefit obligation. Such a reduction shall be used to reduce any existing unrecognized prior service cost, and the excess, if any, shall be amortized on the same basis as the cost of benefit increases.

Gains and losses

29. **Gains and losses** are changes in the amount of either the projected benefit obligation or plan assets resulting from experience different from that assumed and from changes in assumptions. This Statement does not distinguish between those sources of gains and losses. Gains and losses include amounts that have been realized, for example by sale of a security, as well as amounts that are unrealized. Because gains and losses may reflect refinements in estimates as well as real changes in economic values and because some gains in one period may be offset by losses in another or vice versa, this Statement does not require recognition of gains and losses as components of net pension cost of the period in which they arise.[5]

30. The **expected return on plan assets** shall be determined based on the **expected long-term rate of return on plan assets** and the **market-related value of plan assets**. The market-related value of plan assets shall be either fair value or a calculated value that recognizes changes in fair value in a systematic and rational manner over not more than five years. Different ways of calculating market-related value may be used for different classes of assets (for example, an employer might use fair value for bonds and a five-year-moving-average value for equities), but the manner of determining market-related value shall be applied consistently from year to year for each asset class.

31. Asset gains and losses are differences between the actual return on assets during a period and the expected return on assets for that period. Asset gains and losses include both (a) changes reflected in the market-related value of assets and (b) changes not yet reflected in the market-related value (that is, the difference between the fair value of assets and the market-related value). Asset gains and losses not yet reflected in market-related value are not required to be amortized under paragraphs 32 and 33.

32. As a minimum, amortization of an **unrecognized net gain or loss** (excluding asset gains and losses not yet reflected in market-related value) shall be included as a component of net pension cost for a year if, as of the beginning of the year, that unrecognized net gain or loss exceeds 10 percent of the greater of the projected benefit obligation or the market-related value of plan assets. If amortization is required, the minimum amortization[6] shall be that excess divided by the average remaining service period of active employees expected to receive benefits under the plan. If all or almost all of a plan's participants are inactive, the average remaining life expectancy of the inactive participants shall be used instead of average remaining service.

33. Any systematic method of amortization of unrecognized gains and losses may be used in lieu of the minimum specified in the previous paragraph provided that (a) the minimum is used in any period in which the minimum amortization is greater (reduces the net balance by more), (b) the method is applied consistently, (c) the method is applied similarly to both gains and losses, and (d) the method used is disclosed.

34. The gain or loss component of net periodic pension cost shall consist of (a) the difference between the actual return on plan assets and the expected return on plan assets and (b) amortization of the unrecognized net gain or loss from previous periods.

---

[5]Accounting for **plan terminations** and **curtailments** and other circumstances in which recognition of gains and losses might not be delayed is addressed in FASB Statement No. 88, *Employers' Accounting for Settlements and Curtailments of Defined Benefit Pension Plans and for Termination Benefits.*

[6]The amortization must always reduce the beginning-of-the-year balance. Amortization of a net unrecognized gain results in a decrease in net periodic pension cost; amortization of a net unrecognized loss results in an increase in net periodic pension cost.

Recognition of Liabilities and Assets

35. A liability (**unfunded accrued pension cost**) is recognized if net periodic pension cost recognized pursuant to this Statement exceeds amounts the employer has contributed to the plan. An asset (**prepaid pension cost**) is recognized if net periodic pension cost is less than amounts the employer has contributed to the plan.

36. If the accumulated benefit obligation exceeds the fair value of plan assets, the employer shall recognize in the statement of financial position a liability (including unfunded accrued pension cost) that is at least equal to the **unfunded accumulated benefit obligation.** Recognition of an additional minimum liability is required if an unfunded accumulated benefit obligation exists and (a) an asset has been recognized as prepaid pension cost, (b) the liability already recognized as unfunded accrued pension cost is less than the unfunded accumulated benefit obligation, or (c) no accrued or prepaid pension cost has been recognized.

37. If an additional minimum liability is recognized pursuant to paragraph 36, an equal amount shall be recognized as an intangible asset, provided that the asset recognized shall not exceed the amount of unrecognized prior service cost.[7] If an additional liability required to be recognized exceeds unrecognized prior service cost, the excess (which would represent a net loss not yet recognized as net periodic pension cost) shall be reported as a separate component (that is, a reduction) of equity, net of any tax benefits that result from considering such losses as timing differences for purposes of applying the provisions of APB Opinion No. 11, *Accounting for Income Taxes.*

38. When a new determination of the amount of additional liability is made to prepare a statement of financial position, the related intangible asset and separate component of equity shall be eliminated or adjusted as necessary.

Measurement of Cost and Obligations

39. The service component of net periodic pension cost, the projected benefit obligation, and the accumulated benefit obligation are based on an attribution of pension benefits to periods of employee service and on the use of actuarial assumptions to calculate the actuarial present value of those benefits. Actuarial assumptions reflect the time value of money (**discount rate**) and the probability of payment (assumptions as to mortality, turnover, early retirement, and so forth).

Attribution

40. For purposes of this Statement, pension benefits ordinarily shall be attributed to periods of employee service based on the plan's benefit formula to the extent that the formula states or implies an attribution. For example, if a plan's formula provides for a pension benefit of $10 per month for life for each year of service, the benefit attributed to each year of an employee's service is $10 times the number of months of life expectancy after retirement, and the cost attributable to each year is the actuarial present value of that benefit. For plan benefit formulas that define benefits similarly for all years of service, that attribution is a **"benefit/ years-of-service" approach** because it attributes the same amount of the pension benefit to each year of service.[8] For final-pay and career-average-pay plans, that attribution is also the same as the "projected unit credit" or "unit credit with service prorate" actuarial cost method. For a flat-benefit plan, it is the same as the "unit credit" actuarial cost method.

41. In some situations a history of regular increases in non-pay-related benefits or benefits under a career-average-pay plan and other evidence may indicate that an employer has a present commitment to make future amendments and that the substance of the plan is to provide benefits attributable to prior service that are greater than the benefits defined by the written terms of the plan. In those situations, the substantive commitment shall be the basis for the accounting, and the existence and nature of the commitment to make future amendments shall be disclosed.

42. Some plans may have benefit formulas that attribute all or a disproportionate share of the total benefits provided to later years of service, thereby achieving in substance a delayed vesting of benefits. For example, a plan that provides no benefits for the first 19 years of service and a vested benefit of $10,000 for the 20th year is substantively the same as a plan that provides $500 per year for each of 20 years and requires 20 years of service before benefits vest. For such plans the total projected benefit shall be considered to accumulate in proportion to the ratio of the number of completed years of service to the number that will have been completed when the

---

[7]For purposes of this paragraph, an unrecognized net obligation existing at the date of initial application of this Statement (paragraph 77) shall be treated as unrecognized prior service cost.

[8]Some plans define different benefits for different years of service. For example, a step-rate plan might provide a benefit of 1 percent of final pay for each year of service up to 20 years and 1½ percent of final pay for years of service in excess of 20. Another plan might provide 1 percent of final pay for each year of service but limit the total benefit to no more than 20 percent of final pay. For such plans the attribution called for by this Statement will not assign the same amount of pension benefit to each year of service.

benefit is first fully vested. If a plan's benefit formula does not specify how a particular benefit relates to services rendered, the benefit shall be considered to accumulate as follows:

a. For benefits of a type includable in **vested benefits,**[9] in proportion to the ratio of the number of completed years of service to the number that will have been completed when the benefit is first fully vested
b. For benefits of a type not includable in vested benefits,[10] in proportion to the ratio of completed years of service to total projected years of service.

Assumptions

43. Each significant assumption used shall reflect the best estimate solely with respect to that individual assumption. All assumptions shall presume that the plan will continue in effect in the absence of evidence that it will not continue.

44. Assumed discount rates shall reflect the rates at which the pension benefits could be effectively settled. It is appropriate in estimating those rates to look to available information about rates implicit in current prices of annuity contracts that could be used to effect settlement of the obligation (including information about available annuity rates currently published by the Pension Benefit Guaranty Corporation). In making those estimates, employers may also look to rates of return on high-quality fixed-income investments currently available and expected to be available during the period to maturity of the pension benefits. Assumed discount rates are used in measurements of the projected, accumulated, and vested benefit obligations and the service and interest cost components of net periodic pension cost.

45. The expected long-term rate of return on plan assets shall reflect the average rate of earnings expected on the funds invested or to be invested to provide for the benefits included in the projected benefit obligation. In estimating that rate, appropriate consideration should be given to the returns being earned by the plan assets in the fund and the rates of return expected to be available for reinvestment. The expected long-term rate of return on plan assets is used (with the market-related value of assets) to compute the expected return on assets.

46. The service cost component of net periodic pension cost and the projected benefit obligation shall reflect future compensation levels to the extent that

the pension benefit formula defines pension benefits wholly or partially as a function of future compensation levels (that is, for a final-pay plan or a career-average-pay plan). Future increases for which a present commitment exists as described in paragraph 41 shall be similarly considered. Assumed compensation levels shall reflect an estimate of the actual future compensation levels of the individual employees involved, including future changes attributed to general price levels, productivity, seniority, promotion, and other factors. All assumptions shall be consistent to the extent that each reflects expectations of the same future economic conditions, such as future rates of inflation. Measuring service cost and the projected benefit obligation based on estimated future compensation levels entails considering indirect effects, such as changes under existing law in social security benefits or benefit limitations[11] that would affect benefits provided by the plan.

47. The accumulated benefit obligation shall be measured based on employees' *history* of service and *compensation* without an estimate of future compensation levels. Excluding estimated future compensation levels also means excluding indirect effects of future changes such as increases in the social security wage base. In measuring the accumulated benefit obligation, projected years of service shall be a factor only in determining employees' expected eligibility for particular benefits, such as:

a. Increased benefits that are granted provided a specified number of years of service are rendered (for example, a pension benefit that is increased from $9 per month to $10 per month for each year of service if 20 or more years of service are rendered)
b. Early retirement benefits
c. Death benefits
d. Disability benefits.

48. Automatic benefit increases specified by the plan (for example, automatic cost-of-living increases) that are expected to occur shall be included in measurements of the projected, accumulated, and vested benefit obligations, and the service cost component required by this Statement. Also, retroactive plan amendments shall be included in the computation of the projected and accumulated benefit obligations once they have been contractually agreed to, even if some provisions take effect only in future periods. For example, if a plan amendment grants a higher benefit level for employees retiring after a future date, the higher benefit

---

[9]For example, a supplemental early retirement benefit that is a vested benefit after a stated number of years.

[10]For example, a death or disability benefit that is payable only if death or disability occurs during active service.

[11]For example, those currently imposed by Section 415 of the Internal Revenue Code.

level shall be included in current-period measurements for employees expected to retire after that date.

Measurement of Plan Assets

49. For purposes of measuring the minimum liability required by the provisions of paragraph 36 and for purposes of the disclosures required by paragraph 54, plan investments, whether equity or debt securities, real estate, or other, shall be measured at their fair value as of the **measurement date.** The fair value of an investment is the amount that the plan could reasonably expect to receive for it in a current sale between a willing buyer and a willing seller, that is, other than in a forced or liquidation sale. Fair value shall be measured by the market price if an active market exists for the investment. If no active market exists for an investment but such a market exists for similar investments, selling prices in that market may be helpful in estimating fair value. If a market price is not available, a forecast of expected cash flows may aid in estimating fair value, provided the expected cash flows are discounted at a current rate commensurate with the risk involved.[12]

50. For purposes of determining the expected return on plan assets and accounting for asset gains and losses pursuant to paragraphs 29-34, a market-related asset value, defined in paragraph 30, is used.

51. Plan assets used in plan operations (for example, buildings, equipment, furniture and fixtures, and leasehold improvements) shall be measured at cost less accumulated depreciation or amortization for all purposes.

Measurement Dates

52. The measurements of plan assets and obligations required by this Statement shall be as of the date of the financial statements or, if used consistently from year to year, as of a date not more than three months prior to that date. Requiring that the pension measurements be as of a particular date is not intended to require that all procedures be performed after that date. As with other financial statement items requiring estimates, much of the information can be prepared as of an earlier date and projected forward to account for subsequent

events (for example, employee service). The additional minimum liability reported in interim financial statements shall be the same additional minimum liability (paragraph 36) recognized in the previous year-end statement of financial position, adjusted for subsequent accruals and contributions, unless measures of both the obligation and plan assets are available as of a more current date or a significant event occurs, such as a plan amendment, that would ordinarily call for such measurements.

53. Measurements of net periodic pension cost for both interim and annual financial statements shall be based on the assumptions used for the previous year-end measurements unless more recent measurements of both plan assets and obligations are available or a significant event occurs, such as a plan amendment, that would ordinarily call for such measurements.

Disclosures

54. An employer sponsoring a defined benefit pension plan shall disclose the following:

a. A description of the plan including employee groups covered, type of benefit formula, **funding policy,** types of assets held and significant nonbenefit liabilities, if any, and the nature and effect of significant matters affecting comparability of information for all periods presented
b. The amount of net periodic pension cost for the period showing separately the service cost component, the interest cost component, the actual return on assets for the period, and the net total of other components[13]
c. A schedule reconciling the funded status of the plan with amounts reported in the employer's statement of financial position, showing separately:
   (1) The fair value of plan assets
   (2) The projected benefit obligation identifying the accumulated benefit obligation and the vested benefit obligation
   (3) The amount of unrecognized prior service cost
   (4) The amount of unrecognized net gain or loss (including asset gains and losses not yet reflected in market-related value)

---

[12]For an indication of factors to be considered in determining the discount rate, refer to paragraphs 13 and 14 of APB Opinion No. 21, *Interest on Receivables and Payables.* If significant, the fair value of an investment shall reflect the brokerage commissions and other costs normally incurred in a sale.

[13]The net total of other components is the net effect during the period of certain delayed recognition provisions of this Statement. That net total includes:
a. The net asset gain or loss during the period deferred for later recognition (in effect, an offset or a supplement to the actual return on assets)
b. Amortization of the net gain or loss from earlier periods
c. Amortization of unrecognized prior service cost
d. Amortization of the unrecognized net obligation or net asset existing at the date of initial application of this Statement.

(5) The amount of any remaining unrecognized net obligation or net asset existing at the date of initial application of this Statement

(6) The amount of any additional liability recognized pursuant to paragraph 36

(7) The amount of net pension asset or liability recognized in the statement of financial position pursuant to paragraphs 35 and 36 (which is the net result of combining the preceding six items)

d. The weighted-average assumed discount rate and rate of compensation increase (if applicable) used to measure the projected benefit obligation and the weighted-average expected long-term rate of return on plan assets

e. If applicable, the amounts and types of securities of the employer and related parties included in plan assets, and the approximate amount of annual benefits of employees and retirees covered by annuity contracts issued by the employer and related parties. Also, if applicable, the alternative amortization methods used pursuant to paragraphs 26 and 33, and the existence and nature of the commitment discussed in paragraph 41.

Employers with Two or More Plans

55. An employer that sponsors two or more separate defined benefit pension plans shall determine net periodic pension cost, liabilities, and assets by separately applying the provisions of this Statement to each plan. In particular, unless an employer clearly has a right to use the assets of one plan to pay benefits of another, a liability required to be recognized pursuant to paragraph 35 or 36 for one plan shall not be reduced or eliminated because another plan has assets in excess of its accumulated benefit obligation or because the employer has prepaid pension cost related to another plan.

56. Except as noted below, disclosures required by this Statement may be aggregated for all of an employer's single-employer defined benefit plans, or plans may be disaggregated in groups so as to provide the most useful information. For purposes of the disclosures required by paragraph 54(c), plans with assets in excess of the accumulated benefit obligation shall not be aggregated with plans that have accumulated benefit obligations that exceed plan assets. Disclosures for plans outside the U.S. shall not be combined with those for U.S. plans unless those plans use similar economic assumptions.

Annuity Contracts

57. An annuity contract is a contract in which an insurance company[14] unconditionally undertakes a legal obligation to provide specified benefits to specific individuals in return for a fixed consideration or premium. An annuity contract is irrevocable and involves the transfer of significant risk from the employer to the insurance company. Some annuity contracts (participating annuity contracts) provide that the purchaser (either the plan or the employer) may participate in the experience of the insurance company. Under those contracts, the insurance company ordinarily pays dividends to the purchaser. If the substance of a participating contract is such that the employer remains subject to all or most of the risks and rewards associated with the benefit obligation covered and the assets transferred to the insurance company, that contract is not an annuity contract for purposes of this Statement.

58. To the extent that benefits currently earned are covered by annuity contracts, the cost of those benefits shall be the cost of purchasing the contracts, except as provided in paragraph 61. That is, if all the benefits attributed by the plan's benefit formula to service in the current period are covered by **nonparticipating annuity contracts,** the cost of the contracts determines the service cost component of net pension cost for that period.

59. Benefits provided by the pension benefit formula beyond benefits provided by annuity contracts (for example, benefits related to future compensation levels) shall be accounted for according to the provisions of this Statement applicable to plans not involving insurance contracts.

60. Benefits covered by annuity contracts shall be excluded from the projected benefit obligation and the accumulated benefit obligation. Except as provided in paragraph 61, annuity contracts shall be excluded from plan assets.

61. Some annuity contracts provide that the purchaser (either the plan or the employer) may participate in the experience of the insurance company. Under those contracts, the insurance company ordinarily pays dividends to the purchaser, the effect of which is to reduce the cost of the plan. The purchase price of a **participating annuity contract** ordinarily is higher than the price of an equivalent contract without **participation rights.** The difference is the cost of the participation right. The cost of the par-

---

[14]If the insurance company does business primarily with the employer and related parties (a **captive insurer**), or if there is any reasonable doubt that the insurance company will meet its obligations under the contract, the contract is not an annuity contract for purposes of this Statement. Some contracts provide for a refund of premiums if an employee for whom an annuity is purchased does not render sufficient service for the benefit to vest under the terms of the plan. Such a provision shall not by itself preclude a contract from being treated as an annuity contract for purposes of this Statement.

ticipation right shall be recognized at the date of purchase as an asset. In subsequent periods, the participation right shall be measured at its fair value if the contract is such that fair value is reasonably estimable. Otherwise, the participation right shall be measured at its amortized cost (not in excess of its net realizable value), and the cost shall be amortized systematically over the expected dividend period under the contract.

Other Contracts with Insurance Companies

62. Insurance contracts that are in substance equivalent to the purchase of annuities shall be accounted for as such. Other contracts with insurance companies shall be accounted for as investments and measured at fair value. For some contracts, the best available evidence of fair value may be contract value. If a contract has a determinable cash surrender value or conversion value, that is presumed to be its fair value.

Defined Contribution Plans

63. For purposes of this Statement, a **defined contribution pension plan** is a plan that provides pension benefits in return for services rendered, provides an individual account for each participant, and has terms that specify how contributions to the individual's account are to be determined rather than the amount of pension benefits the individual is to receive. Under a defined contribution plan, the pension benefits a participant will receive depend only on the amount contributed to the participant's account, the returns earned on investments of those contributions, and forfeitures of other participants' benefits that may be allocated to the participant's account.

64. To the extent that a plan's defined contributions to an individual's account are to be made for periods in which that individual renders services, the net pension cost for a period shall be the contribution called for in that period. If a plan calls for contributions for periods after an individual retires or terminates, the estimated cost shall be accrued during the employee's service period.

65. An employer that sponsors one or more defined contribution plans shall disclose the following separately from its defined benefit plan disclosures:

a. A description of the plan(s) including employee groups covered, the basis for determining contributions, and the nature and effect of significant matters affecting comparability of information for all periods presented
b. The amount of cost recognized during the period.

66. A pension plan having characteristics of both a defined benefit plan and a defined contribution plan requires careful analysis. If the *substance* of the plan is to provide a defined benefit, as may be the case with some "target benefit" plans, the accounting and disclosure requirements shall be determined in accordance with the provisions of this Statement applicable to a defined benefit plan.

Multiemployer Plans

67. For purposes of this Statement, a **multiemployer plan** is a pension plan to which two or more unrelated employers contribute, usually pursuant to one or more collective-bargaining agreements. A characteristic of multiemployer plans is that assets contributed by one participating employer may be used to provide benefits to employees of other participating employers since assets contributed by an employer are not segregated in a separate account or restricted to provide benefits only to employees of that employer. A multiemployer plan usually is administered by a board of trustees composed of management and labor representatives and may also be referred to as a "joint trust" or "union" plan. Generally, many employers participate in a multiemployer plan, and an employer may participate in more than one plan. The employers participating in multiemployer plans usually have a common industry bond, but for some plans the employers are in different industries, and the labor union may be their only common bond. Some multiemployer plans do not involve a union. For example, local chapters of a not-for-profit organization may participate in a plan established by the related national organization.

68. An employer participating in a multiemployer plan shall recognize as net pension cost the required contribution for the period and shall recognize as a liability any contributions due and unpaid.

69. An employer that participates in one or more multiemployer plans shall disclose the following separately from disclosures for a **single-employer plan:**

a. A description of the multiemployer plan(s) including the employee groups covered, the type of benefits provided (defined benefit or defined contribution), and the nature and effect of significant matters affecting comparability of information for all periods presented
b. The amount of cost recognized during the period.

70. In some situations, withdrawal from a multiemployer plan may result in an employer's having an obligation to the plan for a portion of its unfunded benefit obligations. If withdrawal under circumstances that would give rise to an obligation is either

probable or reasonably possible, the provisions of FASB Statement No. 5, *Accounting for Contingencies,* shall apply. Paragraph 7 of Statement 5 is amended to delete the references to accounting for pension cost and Opinion 8.

Multiple-Employer Plans

71. Some pension plans to which two or more unrelated employers contribute are not multiemployer plans. Rather, they are in substance aggregations of single-employer plans combined to allow participating employers to pool their assets for investment purposes and to reduce the costs of plan administration. Those plans ordinarily do not involve collective-bargaining agreements. They may also have features that allow participating employers to have different benefit formulas, with the employer's contributions to the plan based on the benefit formula selected by the employer. Such plans shall be considered single-employer plans rather than multiemployer plans for purposes of this Statement, and each employer's accounting shall be based on its respective interest in the plan.

Non-U.S. Pension Plans

72. Except for its effective date (paragraph 76), this Statement includes no special provisions applicable to pension arrangements outside the United States. To the extent that those arrangements are in substance similar to pension plans in the United States, they are subject to the provisions of this Statement for purposes of preparing financial statements in accordance with accounting principles generally accepted in the United States. The substance of an arrangement is determined by the nature of the obligation and by the terms or conditions that define the amount of benefits to be paid, not by whether (or how) a plan is funded, whether benefits are payable at intervals or as a single amount, or whether the benefits are required by law or custom or are provided under a plan the employer has elected to sponsor.

73. It is customary or required in some countries to provide benefits in the event of a voluntary or involuntary severance of employment (also called termination indemnities). If such an arrangement is in substance a pension plan (for example, if the benefits are paid for virtually all terminations), it is subject to the provisions of this Statement.

Business Combinations

74. When an employer is acquired in a business combination that is accounted for by the purchase method under Opinion 16 and that employer sponsors a single-employer defined benefit pension plan, the assignment of the purchase price to individual assets acquired and liabilities assumed shall include a liability for the projected benefit obligation in excess of plan assets or an asset for plan assets in excess of the projected benefit obligation, thereby eliminating any previously existing unrecognized net gain or loss, unrecognized prior service cost, or unrecognized net obligation or net asset existing at the date of initial application of this Statement. Subsequently, to the extent that those amounts are considered in determining the amounts of contributions, differences between the purchaser's net pension cost and amounts contributed will reduce the liability or asset recognized at the date of the combination. If it is expected that the plan will be terminated or curtailed, the effects of those actions shall be considered in measuring the projected benefit obligation.

Amendment to Opinion 16

75. The reference to accruals for pension cost in paragraph 88(h) of Opinion 16 and footnote 13 to that Opinion are deleted. The following footnote is added to the end of the last sentence of paragraph 88 of Opinion 16:

> Paragraph 74 of FASB Statement No. 87, *Employers' Accounting for Pensions,* specifies how the general guidelines of this paragraph shall be applied to assets and liabilities related to pension plans.

Transition and Effective Dates

76. Except as noted in the following sentences of this paragraph, this Statement shall be effective for fiscal years beginning after December 15, 1986. For plans outside the U.S. and for defined benefit plans of employers that (a) are **nonpublic enterprises** and (b) sponsor no defined benefit plan with more than 100 participants, this Statement shall be effective for fiscal years beginning after December 15, 1988. For all plans, the provisions of paragraphs 36-38 shall be effective for fiscal years beginning after December 15, 1988. In all cases, earlier application is encouraged. Restatement of previously issued annual financial statements is not permitted. If a decision to initially apply this Statement is made in other than the first interim period of an employer's fiscal year, previous interim periods of that year shall be restated.

77. For a defined benefit plan, an employer shall determine as of the measurement date (paragraph 52) for the beginning of the fiscal year in which this Statement is first applied, the amounts of (a) the projected benefit obligation and (b) the fair value of plan assets plus previously recognized unfunded accrued pension cost or less previously recognized

prepaid pension cost. The difference between those two amounts, whether it represents an unrecognized net obligation (and loss or cost) or an unrecognized net asset (and gain), shall be amortized on a straight-line basis over the average remaining service period of employees expected to receive benefits under the plan, except that, (a) if the average remaining service period is less than 15 years, the employer may elect to use a 15-year period, and (b) if all or almost all of a plan's participants are inactive, the employer shall use the inactive participants' average remaining life expectancy period. That same amortization shall also be used to recognize any unrecognized net obligation related to a defined contribution plan.

> **The provisions of this Statement need not be applied to immaterial items.**

This Statement was adopted by the affirmative votes of four members of the Financial Accounting Standards Board. Messrs. Brown, Sprouse, and Wyatt dissented.

Mr. Brown does not support either the pension cost determination or the minimum liability recognition provisions of this Statement. He supports the Board's conclusion that pension costs constitute employee compensation and that pension costs should be recognized over employee service lives. He also agrees that the disclosures called for will be helpful in fostering user understanding of the nature and status of employer pension obligations and of employer progress in providing for these obligations. In his view, however, the evidence available to the Board is insufficient to sustain the argument that a benefit/years-of-service method should be the sole required expense attribution method or that recognition of liabilities and assets beyond unfunded accrued or prepaid pension costs should be required.

Mr. Brown believes that considerations of comparability and understandability argue for a narrowing of accounting methods now used to allocate pension costs to accounting periods but observes that neither the benefit family nor the cost family of attribution methods is inherently and demonstrably superior. He believes, however, that the cost/compensation family of attribution methods has considerable appeal as a solution to the difficult problem of allocating the estimated lifetime cost of an employee's defined benefit pension to years of service. Cost/compensation methods allocate net pension cost to periods based on direct compensation—in his view, a reasonable and understandable allocation method—producing a net pension cost that is a constant percentage of compensation over the years of an employee's career. Mr. Brown also notes that cost/compensation methods are more commonly used for both pension cost determination and for funding in the United States than are benefit methods.

Despite the appeal of cost/compensation methods, Mr. Brown would not specify a single actuarial calculation method to be used for periodic attribution of pension costs. Rather, he would establish an objective that net pension cost be charged over the service lives of the existing work force such that the net pension cost would be a level percentage of current and expected compensation of this work force. (He notes that the aggregate method—a cost/compensation approach—is one practical way to meet that objective.)

He believes that stating the accounting objective rather than specifying a single computational method would be cost beneficial. Comparability and understandability would be improved if methods used aimed at a common objective. Attaining comparability of end result does not require standardization of the calculation method as evidenced by the fact that different actuarial calculation methods can produce very similar cost results and cost patterns for the same plan, depending on plan-specific circumstances. Mr. Brown notes that both the actuarial method and the assumptions used are critical in determining periodic pension costs. Differences in assumptions arise both because of different plan circumstances and because judgments are required in developing assumptions. Thus, standardization in method represents only one step, of undeterminable size, in achieving comparability in end result. Available evidence does not support a conclusion that the comparability achieved by method change alone is worth the costs inevitably involved in making the change.

Permitting flexibility in the specific calculations to be used in achieving the accounting objective would avoid the need for specifying detailed methods for amortizing prior service cost and unrecognized actuarial gains and losses, as is done in this Statement. Those detailed methods are necessarily arbitrary and produce a complex accounting standard. The detailed methodology and the insistence on using settlement rates to measure the service and interest cost components of net periodic pension cost are both, in his view, examples of the pursuit of a level of precision or exactness that is realistically unattainable in this case. Mr. Brown would leave implementation details to those who are aware of and can consider the circumstances of each plan situation.

Mr. Brown believes that an employer has an obligation under a defined benefit plan and that information about that obligation and the resources accumulated to meet it should be included in financial reports. In his view, however, the nature of point-in-time value measures of plan assets and of plan obligations (whether measured in terms of vested benefits, accumulated benefits, or projected benefit obligations) is such that they do not fall meaningfully and readily within the present structure of financial statements. Delayed recognition of price changes and of actuarial gains and losses is embodied in the methodology of this Statement for pension cost determination. To require balance sheet recognition of selected point-in-time market values and actuarial liability estimates—and this only when liabilities exceed assets—is inconsistent both internally and with expense recognition methodology. It would also, in Mr. Brown's view, be confusing to users. He does not believe that the proposed intangible assets and separate components of equity that would be recorded in tandem with additional liability recognition would add meaningful or understandable information. For these reasons, he believes that plan asset and pension obligation information is better presented in disclosures to financial statements.

Mr. Sprouse believes that, although this Statement provides some improvements in employers' accounting for pensions, those improvements are more than offset by certain important deficiencies. As explained below, he would support the requirements for determining net periodic pension cost and for disclosure, if those deficiencies were eliminated.

He starts from the basic position that only unfunded accumulated benefits qualify for accounting recognition as an employer's liability and that plan assets in excess of accumulated benefits qualify for accounting recognition as an employer's asset.

In Mr. Sprouse's view, an employer cannot have a present obligation for pension benefits related to salary increases that are contingent upon future events—future inflation, future promotions, future improved productivity. He believes that the decision to grant increases in wages and salaries, whatever the reason, is an event that has directly related consequences, including increases in employers' social security taxes and pension costs, as well as the wages and salaries themselves. Accounting should recognize all of those directly related consequences at the time the event occurs—when wages and salaries are increased because inflation has reduced the purchasing power of the dollars being paid, when wages and salaries are increased because the more valuable services recognized by promotion are being received, when wages and salaries are increased because the benefits of improved productivity are being realized. Anticipating the effects of those future events on pension cost in accounting for the current period

before dollars have lost their purchasing power and before the more valuable services related to promotion and productivity have been received is no more appropriate than anticipating the future higher wages and salaries themselves in accounting for the current period.

Mr. Sprouse believes that past practices in accounting for employers' pension cost that rely on forecasts of nominal salary levels were largely the product of certain actuarial methods that were designed for funding purposes to conform to the provisions of the Internal Revenue Code; those methods are not appropriate for financial accounting purposes. Nevertheless, he recognizes that those practices are firmly embedded in financial accounting and drastic changes in them could be disruptive. Accordingly, he would support the requirements for determining net periodic pension cost and for disclosure as significant improvements in practice. Considering the practical limits within which practice can be changed without undue disruption, he could also support the alternative approach described in paragraph 155.

Mr. Sprouse objects, however, to the unique recognition practices this Statement establishes for an "intangible asset." In certain situations, this Statement calls for an employer to recognize an intangible asset to offset the result of a loss on plan assets or to eliminate an intangible asset to offset the result of a gain on plan assets. Similar recognition or elimination of an intangible asset is required to offset the effects of changes in actuarial assumptions related to the accumulated benefit obligation. Those features are unacceptable to him. In his view, those recognition practices can be neither reconciled with the Board's conceptual framework nor readily understood by financial statement users. He believes they seriously diminish the credibility of employers' accounting for pension costs.

Mr. Sprouse also objects to this Statement's accounting for a business combination under the purchase method that calls for recognition of an asset or liability based on the projected benefit obligation as of the date of the combination. For the reasons given above, he holds that the excess of the *projected* benefit obligation over plan assets does not qualify for recognition as an employer's liability, and plan assets in excess of *accumulated* benefits do qualify for recognition as an employer's asset. In his view, the fallacy of the Statement's requirement is demonstrated by the need to recognize a different net pension obligation or asset if the acquirer plans to terminate the plan than is recognized if the acquirer plans to continue it.

Mr. Wyatt believes the projected benefit obligation, as defined in this Statement, should be the measure of the pension obligation reported in the financial statements. He believes that neither the excess of net periodic pension cost over amounts contributed (unfunded accrued cost) nor the accumulated benefit obligation is an appropriate measure of an entity's pension obligation. He also believes that the use of a market-related asset value base for effecting the delayed recognition of actuarial gains and losses unnecessarily perpetuates an unsound measure for plan assets. As a result, this Statement falls short of achieving the degree of improvement in accounting for pension costs that was attainable and that users of financial statements could justifiably expect from this project.

A majority of the Board concluded that the pension liability is not properly measured by the unfunded accrued cost. Mr. Wyatt agrees with that conclusion. He believes, however, that the accumulated benefit obligation cannot be a faithful presentation of the pension obligation because its determination involves a fundamental inconsistency. The scheduled future pension benefits under this notion exclude any estimates of salary progression, whether based on estimated inflation or other factors. As a result, the amounts that provide the basis for the measure of the obligation do not represent the actual estimated cash flows in future periods. The interest rate used to reduce those scheduled future pension benefits to a present value is a rate at which the pension benefits could effectively be settled. Such a rate incorporates an existing anticipation of future inflation. Thus, the discounting process effectively removes an estimated inflation factor from a series of scheduled future payments that have been measured by specifically excluding any estimate for future inflation. The resulting amount has estimated future inflation removed twice and therefore is not a faithful measure of a liability; in fact, it understates the appropriate measure of the liability, grossly so in some cases.

Mr. Wyatt believes that the use of a market-related asset value as a basis for delayed recognition of gains and losses compromises the rationale that supports use of fair value to measure assets for other aspects of this Statement. It perpetuates a notion ("actuarial asset value") that has no basis as an accounting concept. Furthermore, other approaches to implement the delayed recognition of unamortized gains and losses are available that could only be perceived as practical in nature and that would not carry over into future considerations of pension accounting a concept that persists in spite of its conceptual defects.

The use of a market-related asset value and an expected rate of return on assets to measure the amortization of unrecognized gains and losses introduces unnecessary flexibility into a process that could justifiably be made uniform because it is inherently a practical mechanism to mitigate volatility. Such flexibility diminishes the improvements in comparability, as related to practice under Opinion 8, achieved by adoption of a single attribution method and an assumed discount rate that reflects the rates at which pension benefits could effectively be settled.

Mr. Wyatt agrees with the assenters that, on an overall basis, the conclusions in this Statement will lead to improvements in accounting for and understanding of pension costs. He believes, however, that the degree of improvement is modest when related to the improvement that he believes should have been achieved. Thus, in his view the Statement's deficiencies represent a lost opportunity for improvement in financial reporting.

Members of the Financial Accounting Standards Board are:

Donald J. Kirk,	Victor H. Brown	Robert T. Sprouse
Chairman	Raymond C. Lauver	Arthur R. Wyatt
Frank E. Block	David Mosso	

Appendix A

BASIS FOR CONCLUSIONS

CONTENTS

Appendix A

BASIS FOR CONCLUSIONS

Fundamental Conclusions—Single-Employer Defined Benefit Pension Plans

78. This appendix summarizes considerations that were deemed significant by members of the Board in reaching the conclusions in this Statement. It includes reasons for accepting certain views and rejecting others. Individual Board members gave greater weight to some factors than to others. The most significant changes to past practice resulting from the Board's conclusions in this Statement relate to accounting for a single-employer defined benefit pension plan.

The Exchange

79. The Board's conclusions in this Statement derive from the basic idea that a defined benefit pension is an exchange between the employer and the employee. In exchange for services provided by the employee, the employer promises to provide, in addition to current wages and other benefits, an amount of retirement income. It follows from that

basic view that pension benefits are not gratuities but instead are part of an employee's compensation, and since payment is deferred, the pension is a type of deferred compensation. It also follows that the employer's obligation for that compensation is incurred when the services are rendered.

Funding and Accrual Accounting

80. In this Statement the Board reaffirms the usefulness of information based on accrual accounting. That does not negate the importance of information about cash flows or the funding of the plan. Accounting recognition of transactions in which cash is disbursed is not controversial. Accrual accounting, however, goes beyond cash transactions to provide information about assets, liabilities, and earnings.

81. Opinion 8 stated, ". . . it is important to keep in mind that the annual pension cost to be charged to expense . . . is not necessarily the same as the amount to be funded for the year" (paragraph 9). However, Opinion 8 allowed any of a range of funding methods to serve as the basis for determining net periodic pension cost, with the result that annual net pension cost and the amount to be funded for the year were commonly the same. This Statement reaffirms the APB's conclusion that funding decisions should not necessarily be used as the basis for accounting recognition of cost. The amount funded (however determined) is, of course, given accounting recognition as a use of cash, but the Board believes this is one of many areas in which information about cash flows alone is not sufficient, and information on an accrual basis is also needed. The question of when to fund the obligation is not an accounting issue. It is a financing question that is properly influenced by many factors (such as tax considerations and the availability of attractive alternative investments) that are unrelated to how the pension obligation is incurred.

82. Any accrual basis of accounting for a defined benefit pension plan inevitably requires estimates of future events because those events determine the amounts of benefits that will be paid. The Board is convinced that information based on such estimates is useful along with information about cash flows, and notes that similar estimates are required for all presently acceptable funding methods and previously permitted accounting methods.

83. The Board's conclusion that accounting information on an accrual basis is needed does not mean accounting information and funding decisions are unrelated. In pensions, as in other areas, managers may use accounting information along with other factors in making financial decisions. Some employers may decide to change their pension funding policies based in part on the new accounting information. The Board believes that financial statements should provide information that is useful to those who make economic decisions, and the decision to fund a pension plan to a greater or lesser extent is an economic decision. The Board, however, does not have as an objective either an increase or a decrease in the funding level of any particular plan or plans. Neither does the Board believe that the information required by this Statement is the only information needed to make a funding decision or that net periodic pension cost, as defined, is necessarily the appropriate amount for any particular employer's periodic contribution.

Fundamentals of Pension Accounting

84. In applying accrual accounting to pensions, this Statement retains three fundamental aspects of past pension accounting: *delaying recognition* of certain events, reporting *net cost,* and *offsetting* liabilities and assets. Those three features of practice have shaped financial reporting for pensions for many years even though they have been neither explicitly addressed nor widely understood and they conflict in some respects with accounting principles applied elsewhere.

85. The *delayed recognition* feature means that certain changes in the pension obligation (including those resulting from plan amendments) and changes in the value of assets set aside to meet those obligations are not recognized as they occur but are recognized systematically and gradually over subsequent periods. All changes are ultimately recognized except to the extent that they may be offset by subsequent changes, but at any point changes that have been identified and quantified await subsequent accounting recognition as net cost components and as liabilities or assets.

86. The *net cost* feature means that the recognized consequences of events and transactions affecting a pension plan are reported as a single net amount (net periodic pension cost) in the employer's financial statements. That approach aggregates at least three items that might be reported separately for any other part of an employer's operations: the compensation cost of benefits promised, interest cost resulting from deferred payment of those benefits, and the results of investing what are often significant amounts of assets.

87. The *offsetting* feature means that recognized values of assets contributed to a plan and liabilities for pensions recognized as net pension cost of past periods are shown net in the employer's statement of financial position, even though the liability has not been settled, the assets may be still largely controlled, and substantial risks and rewards associated

with both of those amounts are clearly borne by the employer.

88. Within those three features of practice that are retained by this Statement, the Board has sought to achieve more useful financial reporting through three changes:

a. This Statement requires a standardized method for measuring net periodic pension cost that is intended to improve comparability and understandability by recognizing the compensation cost of an employee's pension (including prior service cost) over that employee's approximate service period and by relating cost more directly to the terms of the plan.
b. This Statement requires immediate recognition of a liability (the minimum liability) in certain circumstances when the accumulated benefit obligation exceeds the fair value of plan assets, although it continues to delay recognition of the offsetting amount as an increase in net periodic pension cost.
c. This Statement requires expanded disclosures intended to provide more complete and more current information than can be practically incorporated in financial statements at the present time.

Components of Net Periodic Pension Cost

89. The Board concluded that an understanding of pension accounting is facilitated by considering the components of net periodic pension cost separately. The same components were included in net periodic pension cost in prior practice, but they were seldom explicitly or separately addressed. Those components are service cost, interest cost, actual return on plan assets, amortization of unrecognized prior service cost, and gain or loss. An additional component, temporarily, is the amortization of the unrecognized net obligation or asset existing at the date of initial application of this Statement.

90. A plan with no plan assets, no plan amendments, and no gains or losses would still have two components of cost. First, as employees work during the year and earn added benefits, a *service cost* (or compensation cost) accrues. Measurement of that component is difficult and is discussed below. If the service component and the related obligation are measured on a present value basis, a second component—*interest cost*—must also be accounted for. Measurement of that component is less difficult. The primary issue is the selection of appropriate discount rates.

91. A third component is required for a funded plan. The employer must recognize the *return* (or possibly loss) *on plan assets*. That component ordi-

narily reduces the net cost of providing a pension. If the amount of assets is relatively great and the return on assets is high, the result can be net pension income for a period instead of net pension cost. The interest cost and return-on-plan-asset components represent financial items rather than employee compensation cost. They can be changed or even eliminated by changes in the employer's financing arrangements. For example, an employer can increase return on assets by adding more assets to the fund and can decrease interest cost (and return on assets) by purchasing annuity contracts to settle part of the obligation.

92. The next two components arise from plan amendments and gains or losses, both of which are to be recognized as part of net periodic pension cost over a number of periods. The *amortization of unrecognized prior service cost* resulting from plan amendments (including initiation of a plan) ordinarily increases the net cost. This component reflects the compensation cost of pension benefits granted in amendments and attributed by the plan's benefit formula to periods prior to the amendment.

93. The *gain or loss component* may either decrease or increase net periodic pension cost depending on whether the net unrecognized amount is a gain or a loss and whether actual return on assets for a particular period is greater or less than expected return on assets. This component combines gains and losses of various types and therefore includes both compensation and financial items that are not readily separable.

The Principal Issues

94. Among the many issues considered by the Board in this project, three stand out as central to the Board's extensive deliberations and to the public debate. Those issues concern (a) the periods in which net periodic pension cost should be recognized, (b) the method(s) that should be used to allocate or attribute that cost to individual periods, and (c) whether current information about the funded status of a defined benefit pension plan should be included in the employer's statement of financial position.

Cost recognition period

95. The Board concluded that, conceptually, compensation cost should be recognized in the period in which the employee renders services. Although the complexity and uncertainty of the pension arrangement may preclude complete achievement of that goal, a fundamental objective of this Statement is to approximate more closely the recognition of compensation cost of an employee's pension benefits over that employee's service period. Many of the

respondents to previous documents issued as part of this project agreed with that objective, which conflicts with some aspects of past practice under Opinion 8.

Attribution method

96. The Board concluded that the understandability, comparability, and usefulness of pension information could be improved by narrowing the range of different methods for allocating or attributing the cost of an employee's pension to individual periods of service. The Board was significantly aided in its consideration of alternative attribution approaches by the work of several committees of the American Academy of Actuaries and by research conducted by that organization. The Board appreciates the efforts of the individuals and firms involved in those efforts and recognizes that most of them continue to prefer that accounting be based on any of several approaches. However, the Board was unable to identify differences in circumstances that would make it appropriate for different employers to use fundamentally different accounting methods or for a single employer to use different methods for different plans. Many respondents agreed that the number of acceptable methods at least should be reduced.

97. The Board concluded that the terms of the plan that define the benefits an employee will receive (the plan's benefit formula) provide the most relevant and reliable indication of how pension cost and pension obligations are incurred. In the absence of convincing evidence that the substance of an exchange is different from that indicated by the agreement between the parties, accounting has traditionally looked to the terms of the agreement as a basis for recording the exchange. All attribution methods used in the past consider the plan's benefit formula in estimating the benefit an employee will receive at retirement. However, unlike some other methods previously used for pension accounting, the method required by this Statement focuses more directly on the plan's benefit formula as the basis for determining the benefit earned, and therefore the cost incurred, in each individual period.

Statement of financial position

98. The Board believes that an employer with an unfunded pension obligation has a liability and an employer with an overfunded pension obligation has an asset. The most relevant and reliable information available about that liability or asset is based on the fair value of plan assets and a measure of the present value of the obligation using current, explicit assumptions.

99. Many respondents to the Preliminary Views, *Employers' Accounting for Pensions and Other Postemployment Benefits (Preliminary Views),* and the Exposure Draft, *Employers' Accounting for Pensions,* agreed that at least the obligation for unfunded vested benefits, or the obligation for unfunded accumulated benefits, conceptually represents a recognizable liability. Most respondents, however, did not agree with recognition of any liability in the statement of financial position beyond the amount of accrued but unfunded net periodic pension cost. Most also objected to recognition of any liability based on estimates of future compensation levels. Respondents also objected to recognizing an asset in the case of an overfunded plan, and views differed about how to recognize changes in both the fair value of plan assets and the present value of the obligation.

100. Some argued that the uncertainties inherent in predicting future interest rates and salary levels are sufficiently great that available measures of the projected benefit obligation fail to achieve the level of reliability needed for recognition in financial statements. They would prefer to disclose rather than recognize the obligation. Some Board members were sympathetic to that view.

101. This Statement requires recognition of net periodic pension cost based on the present value of the obligation (with consideration of future compensation levels for pay-related plans). This Statement also requires recognition of a liability or an asset (unfunded accrued or prepaid pension cost) when the amount of that net periodic pension cost is different from the amount of the employer's contribution to the plan. Over time, therefore, this Statement requires recognition of a liability for the employer's unfunded obligation, including that portion based on estimated future compensation levels for plans with pay-related benefit formulas. Most respondents who argued that a present liability could not include amounts based on future compensation nevertheless argued strongly that the measure of net periodic pension cost must not ignore that factor.

102. This Statement provides for delayed recognition, in net periodic pension cost and in the related liability (accrued unfunded pension cost) or asset (prepaid pension cost), of certain changes in the present value of the obligation and the fair value of plan assets. Those changes (that is, gains and losses and the effects of plan amendments) are recognized in net periodic pension cost on a systematic basis over future periods. The Board concluded that it is not practical at this time to require accelerated recognition of those changes in financial statements as they occur, although certain of those changes are recognized in the statement of financial position

through the minimum liability requirement of this Statement.

103. This Statement accepts the unfunded accrued or prepaid pension cost as the recognized liability or asset except when the accumulated benefit obligation (measured without considering future compensation levels) exceeds the fair value of plan assets. In that situation, the Board concluded that the recognized liability should be adjusted so that the statement of financial position would reflect at least the unfunded accumulated benefit obligation.

104. The Board acknowledges that the delayed recognition included in this Statement results in excluding the most current and most relevant information from the employer's statement of financial position. That information is, however, included in the disclosures required, and, as noted above, certain liabilities previously omitted will be recognized.

Information Needed

105. The Board concluded that users of financial reports need additional information to be able to assess the status of an employer's pension arrangements and their effect on the employer's financial position and results of operations. Most respondents agreed, and this Statement requires certain disclosures not previously required.

106. The components of net periodic pension cost and the net funded status of the obligation are among the more significant disclosure requirements of this Statement. One of the factors that made pension information difficult to understand was that past practice and terminology combined elements that are different in substance into net amounts (assets with liabilities and revenues and gains with expenses and losses). Although the Board agreed to retain from past practice the basic features of reporting net cost and offsetting liabilities and assets, the Board believes that disclosure of the components will significantly assist users in understanding the economic events that have occurred. Those disclosures also make it easier to understand why reported amounts change from period to period, especially when a large cost or asset is offset by a large revenue or liability to produce a relatively small net reported amount.

Evolutionary Changes in Accounting Principles

107. After considering the range of comments on *Preliminary Views* and the Exposure Draft, the Board concluded that the changes required by this Statement represent a worthwhile improvement in financial reporting. Opinion 8 noted in 1966 that "accounting for pension cost is in a transitional stage" (paragraph 17). The Board believes that is still true in 1985. FASB Concepts Statement No. 5, *Recognition and Measurement in Financial Statements of Business Enterprises,* paragraph 2, indicates that "the Board intends future change [in practice] to occur in the gradual, evolutionary way that has characterized past change." The Board realizes that the evolutionary change in some areas may have to be slower than in others. The Board believes that it would be conceptually appropriate and preferable to recognize a net pension liability or asset measured as the difference between the projected benefit obligation and plan assets, either with no delay in recognition of gains and losses, or perhaps with gains and losses reported currently in comprehensive income but not in earnings. However, it concluded that those approaches would be too great a change from past practice to be adopted at the present time. In light of the differences in respondents' views and the practical considerations noted, the Board concluded that the provisions of this Statement as a whole represent an improvement in financial reporting.

Other Conclusions—Single-Employer Defined Benefit Pension Plans

108. This section discusses additional reasons for the Board's conclusions and some of the positions advocated by respondents.

The Nature of the Exchange

109. Some respondents disagreed with the Board's basic view of the nature of the employer's obligation under a defined benefit pension plan. They argued that the employer's only obligation is to make periodic contributions sufficient to support the plan. In this view, it is the plan—as a distinct legal entity—that has an obligation for benefits promised to employees. They concluded that the schedule or budget for making contributions determines the amount of the present obligation and current period cost and that contributions scheduled for future periods, although based upon past events, are future obligations.

110. The Board concluded that viewing the obligation and the cost only in terms of scheduled contributions does not reflect the fundamental difference between the inherent promise and the resulting obligation under a defined benefit plan and the promise and obligation under a defined contribution plan. An employer that has undertaken an obligation to provide defined pension benefits based on service already rendered may view it as an obligation directly to the employees (looking through the funding arrangement) or as an obligation to make future contributions to the plan, but the employer has a present obligation based on the defined benefits either way.

111. The Board believes that creating a separate legal entity to receive and invest contributions and pay benefits does not change the nature of the employer's obligation to pay promised benefits to retirees. Viewing the plan as a truly separate economic entity raises the question of what consideration the plan received for making benefit promises to employees. Although legal requirements are only one factor to be considered in determining accounting standards, the Board also notes that Congress, in enacting ERISA, chose to base the definition of an employee's rights under a defined benefit pension plan on the benefits promised rather than on the amounts the employer has contributed or is scheduled to contribute.

112. Those who subscribe to the separate legal entity idea also argued that plan assets are not the assets of the employer. The Board noted that the employer's future contributions to the plan will be increased or decreased by the performance of the plan assets so that the employer bears the risks and reaps the rewards associated with those assets. The Board also observed that numerous recent situations in which significant amounts of assets have been withdrawn by employers provide compelling evidence that rebuts that argument.

113. Some respondents argued that the pension exchange is between the employer and a collective ongoing work force rather than between the employer and each individual employee. They focus on the open group, including employees to be hired in the future, rather than the closed group of current and past employees. They conclude that the obligation to the work force should be defined in terms of contributions necessary to maintain the plan rather than in terms of the aggregate benefits promised to individuals.

114. The Board recognizes that uncertainty in measuring the benefit obligation for a single employee is greater than for a group because the future events that affect the amount of benefits (such as longevity) cannot be as reliably estimated for a single individual. In the Board's view, however, the fact that a more reliable measurement is possible only for a group does not change the nature of the promise. The actuarial computation considers that some existing or future retirees will live longer than others and that some individuals will terminate before vesting or die before receiving any benefits. Those factors are properly considered in measuring the probable future sacrifice that will result from the presently existing promise of benefits to the employees.

115. The practical effect of the argument that the obligation is to the ongoing employee group is often to defer recognition of part of the cost of an individ-

ual's pension to periods after that individual retires. That open-group view provides no basis for recognizing the cost of pension benefits over any particular period. One of the objectives of accrual accounting is to match costs and revenues. The Board believes that application of the matching objective to pension accounting requires that pension cost be recognized in the period in which economic benefits are received (employee services are rendered). The alternative view is no more appropriate than an argument that a machine should be depreciated over years after its retirement because the machine will be replaced and the important thing is the cost of maintaining the ongoing plant. Employee compensation, whether paid currently or deferred, should be recognized as cost when the services are rendered. The Board concluded that, in concept, the employer's obligation to the existing employee group is the sum of its obligations to individual employees, adjusted to reflect the present value of the amount and the probability of payment (the "actuarial present value").

Recognition versus Disclosure

116. Some respondents agreed that better information about net periodic pension cost and the pension obligation is needed but argued that the information would be just as useful if it were disclosed in the footnotes and, therefore, that changes in the basic financial statements (changes which they believed would be costly) were not necessary. The Board is aware that costs are involved for both preparers and users whenever changes are made in accounting principles, but in the Board's view it is important that elements qualifying for recognition be recognized in the basic financial statements. Footnote disclosure is not an adequate substitute for recognition. The argument that the information is equally useful regardless of how it is presented could be applied to any financial statement element, but the usefulness and integrity of financial statements are impaired by each omission of an element that qualifies for recognition. Further, although the "equal usefulness" argument may be valid for some sophisticated users, the Board does not believe it holds for all or even most other users. Finally, if the argument were valid, the consequences of recognition would not be different from those of not recognizing but disclosing the same information; it is obvious from their arguments that many who assert that disclosure would be equally useful believe recognition would have different consequences.

Measurement of Plan Assets

117. The Board concluded that plan investments should be measured at fair value for purposes of this Statement (except as provided in paragraph 30 for purposes of determining the extent of delayed recog-

nition of asset gains and losses). Fair value provides the most relevant information that can be provided for assessing both the plan's ability to pay benefits as they come due without further contributions from the employer and the future contributions necessary to provide for benefits already promised to employees. The same reasons led to a similar decision in Statement 35.

118. The Board recognizes that there may be practical problems in determining the fair value of certain types of assets. Notwithstanding those difficulties, the Board believes that the relevance of fair value of pension assets is so great as to override objections to its use based on difficulty of measurement. In addition, most pension assets are invested in marketable securities and are priced regularly for investment management purposes.

119. The Board considered the use of an actuarial value of assets instead of fair value. A number of different methods of determining actuarial asset values are available, generally based on some kind of average of past market values or on long-range projections of market values intended to eliminate short-term market fluctuations. The Board concluded that those methods produce information about the assets that is less relevant and more difficult to understand than fair value. Specifically, if an actuarial asset value were used to measure the minimum net liability defined in paragraph 36, it would sometimes result in recognition of a liability when the fair value of the assets exceeds the obligation, and at other times it would result in no recognition when a net unfunded obligation exists based on the fair value.

120. The Board understands that measuring investments at fair value could introduce volatility into the financial statements as a result of short-term changes in fair values. Some respondents described that volatility as meaningless or even misleading, particularly in view of the long-run nature of the pension commitment and the fact that pension investments are often held for long periods, thus providing the opportunity for some gains or losses to reverse. The Board also recognizes that some changes in the fair value of investments are related to some changes in the measurement of the pension liability because they are affected by the same economic factors. For example, a change in the level of interest rates would be expected to affect the liability by changing the discount rates and would also affect the fair value of at least some types of investments (such as bonds). In many cases such fluctuations in the pension benefit obligation and in the fair value of plan investments would tend to offset each other.

121. The Board concluded that the difference between the actual return on assets and the expected return on assets could be recognized in net periodic pension cost on a delayed basis. Those effects include the gains and losses themselves. That conclusion was based on (a) the probability that at least some gains would be offset by subsequent losses and vice versa and (b) respondents' arguments that immediate recognition would produce unacceptable volatility and would be inconsistent with the present accounting model.

122. The Board also considered whether amounts accrued by the employer but not yet contributed or paid to the plan (that is, unfunded accrued pension cost) should be considered plan assets for purposes of this Statement, noting that Statement 35 does consider some such amounts to be plan assets for purposes of the plan's financial reporting. The Board concluded that including accrued pension cost as plan assets for purposes of the disclosure of funded status (paragraph 54(c)) would be inappropriate because that amount has not been funded (contributed), and would unnecessarily complicate the recognition and disclosure requirements of this Statement.

123. The Board discussed whether securities of the employer held by the plan should be eliminated from plan assets and from the employer's financial statements as, in effect, treasury securities. The Board concluded that elimination would be impractical and might be inappropriate absent a decision that the financial statements of the plan should be consolidated with those of the employer, but that disclosure of the amount of such securities held would be appropriate and should be required.

Measurement of Service Cost and the Obligation

124. Measurement of the service cost component has much in common with measurement of the pension obligation. The service cost is essentially the portion of the projected benefit obligation that is attributable to services rendered in a period. The Board concluded that (a) all employers should use a single measurement method and (b) that method should reflect the plan's benefit formula to the extent that the formula specifies how employees' benefits accrue.

Single method

125. Some respondents suggested that the Board should not require the use of a single method but should allow a choice among a number of acceptable alternatives. Many noted that choices among accounting methods are allowed in other areas, including accounting for inventory and depreciation. They also suggested that a standardized

method would not achieve comparability because of differences in assumptions or would impair comparability because it would obscure different circumstances that call for different approaches.

126. The Board was not convinced by those who made reference to other areas of accounting. The appropriateness of allowing a choice of methods for depreciation and inventory accounting is beyond the scope of this project. The Board also believes that the differences among methods available for pension measurements are significantly more complex and less well understood than other method differences. A knowledgeable user is more likely to understand the approximate difference between straight-line and accelerated depreciation than the difference between two actuarial funding methods.

127. The Board concluded that use of a standardized method would improve comparability. Differences in assumptions are intended, at least conceptually, to reflect real differences in circumstances. The Board noted that comparability is not a characteristic that is either completely present or absent. It concluded that improvements in comparability could be achieved, even though some differences that are not necessarily reflective of real differences will remain because of the exercise of judgment in the selection of assumptions.

128. The Board is not convinced that differences in circumstances among employers require fundamentally different methods for measuring the service component of net periodic pension cost. Differences such as expected rates of turnover and mortality would continue to be reflected. The Board concluded that use of a single method based on the terms of the plan would improve comparability and understandability of financial reporting by reflecting real differences among plans.

Choice of method

129. The 1981 FASB Discussion Memorandum, *Employers' Accounting for Pensions and Other Postemployment Benefits,* described two families of attribution approaches: the benefit approaches and the cost approaches. Benefit approaches determine an amount of pension benefits attributed to service in a period and then calculate the service cost component for the period as the actuarial present value of those benefits. Cost approaches project an estimated total benefit at retirement and then calculate the level contribution that, together with return on assets expected to accumulate at the assumed rates, would be sufficient to provide that benefit at retirement. (The amount allocated to each year may be level in dollar amount or level as a percentage of compensation.)

130. A number of respondents indicated a preference for the cost family of approaches, usually the approach defined in the 1981 Discussion Memorandum as cost/compensation. That preference was frequently based on the view that a pension is earned only over an employee's full period of employment with the result that measuring the obligation and the cost on an annual basis is less important than the pattern of net cost from period to period. Although all of the commonly used approaches may be described as systematic and rational, the cost/compensation approach is preferred by many because it is thought to produce a net periodic pension cost that is a level percentage of compensation. In fact, however, that desired pattern of net periodic pension cost will result only if amounts recognized as net periodic pension cost are also the amounts funded and if experience does not vary from assumptions.

131. The Board rejected the cost family of approaches because it believes that the terms of the plan provide a more relevant basis for relating benefits promised to services rendered. The benefit approaches are also more consistent with the Board's definition of liabilities. FASB Concepts Statement No. 3, *Elements of Financial Statements of Business Enterprises,* defines liabilities in terms of obligations, and an employer's obligation under a defined benefit plan as of a particular date is for pension benefits promised by the terms of the plan rather than for an accumulation of level costs. The Board believes that, although the "level percentage of compensation" pattern may be desirable for funding or for budgeting contributions, it does not necessarily reflect how cost is incurred or how a liability arises.

132. All attribution approaches measure service cost and the related obligation by discounting amounts payable in future periods to reflect the time value of money. No respondents advocated solutions that would not include such discounting. The way in which discounting is applied, however, is the fundamental difference between the cost approaches and the benefit approaches. The benefit approach adopted by the Board uses the terms of the plan to determine the benefits earned during a period (that is, the future cash flow) and then calculates the actuarial present value of those benefits. Under the cost approaches the amount attributed to a period is not the actuarial present value of a benefit earned in the period. Instead, the total cost of all the expected benefits is discounted and assigned to periods in a single mathematical step so that the net pension cost (the service cost, plus interest cost, less anticipated return on assets in the fund and to be added in future periods) is a constant amount or a constant percentage of salary.

133. In the Board's view, the benefit approaches reflect the promise of a defined benefit, and the present value of a dollar of benefit promised to a 60-year-old is greater than that of a dollar of benefit promised to a 25-year-old, if both are payable at age 65. Under the cost approaches, the cost charged in the early years of an employee's service will provide an amount of benefit at retirement much greater than the benefits earned in those years based on the plan formula. In the last years of an employee's service, the cost is less than the present value of benefits earned. The result is that at any point before retirement, the amount accrued for an individual under a cost approach will exceed the present value of benefits earned to that point based on the plan's benefit formula.

134. The Board concluded that the measurements of net periodic pension cost and the projected benefit obligation should reflect the terms of the plan under which they arose. Because a defined benefit pension plan specifies the employer's promise in terms of how benefits are earned based on service, rather than how contributions can be made to adhere to a desired funding pattern, the benefit approaches were preferred.

135. The Board also considered a benefit approach that would attribute benefits to periods based on compensation paid in those periods (a benefit/compensation approach). Some believe that compensation is the best available indicator of the value of the employee's services and, therefore, it is the most logical basis for allocation of benefits. In the Board's view, however, that approach less faithfully represents how the cost is incurred under the terms of the plan than the approach selected. The Board also noted that the benefit/compensation approach is not among those allowable under Internal Revenue Service regulations for funding purposes for certain types of plans.

Funding considerations

136. For purposes of funding a plan, using a cost approach to assign relatively large amounts to early years may be considered by some to be desirable because it allows more time for tax-free earnings on contributed assets to compound and because it provides additional benefit security. That basic funding approach may be particularly useful in achieving funding objectives if the cost of plan amendments is to be funded over a relatively long period after each amendment occurs. The relatively rapid funding of the obligation arising from service in the current and future periods may compensate for delayed funding of obligations arising from plan amendments.

137. Some respondents asserted that the cost of calculating amounts for accounting purposes on a basis different from that used for funding purposes would be high and would exceed the benefits of improved financial reporting. The Board notes, however, that a large part of the cost involved in an actuarial valuation is incurred in gathering and processing the input data and that the data used are largely the same for any computational approach. The Board concluded that the additional cost attributable to the requirements is unlikely to be excessive.

Future compensation levels

138. In response to the Exposure Draft and earlier documents issued as part of this project, some respondents argued that, based on the definition of a liability, pension benefits dependent on future increases in compensation cannot be a present obligation and, therefore, the liability measurement should be based only on actual compensation experience to date. They also noted that if the plan were terminated or if an employee with vested benefits did not render future services, the employer's obligation would be limited to amounts based on compensation to date.

139. Among those respondents who argued that obligations dependent on future compensation increases are excluded by the definition of a liability, very few were prepared to accept a measure of net periodic pension cost that was based only on compensation to date. The Board notes that under the double entry accounting system, recognition of an accrued cost as a charge against operations requires recognition of a liability for that accrued cost. Thus, excluding future compensation from the liability and including it in net periodic pension cost are conflicting positions.

140. The Board also considered the arguments of respondents who noted that it would be inconsistent (a) to measure pension cost or the obligation ignoring future compensation increases that reflect inflation and (b) to use discount rates that reflect expected inflation rates in making those measurements. In this view, discounting a benefit that does not include the effects of inflation amounts to removing the effect of inflation twice. Those respondents suggested that the effects of inflation should either be considered for both purposes or be eliminated from both. The latter approach would involve use of inflation-free (or "real") discount rates. The Board considered that possibility but concluded that the use of explicit rates observable in actual transactions ("nominal rates") would be more understandable and would present fewer implementation problems, as noted below.

141. The Board notes that at present few private pension plans in the U.S. provide benefits that are increased automatically after an employee retires

based on either compensation levels or inflation. If future compensation increases were incorporated *implicitly* by reducing the discount rates used to compute the present value of the benefit obligation, projected benefit increases during the postretirement period would be incorporated automatically at the same time unless different (explicit) discount rates were used for those periods. Using inflation-adjusted (implicit) discount rates would, in effect, anticipate postretirement benefit increases, which would be inconsistent with the Board's decision that future plan amendments should not be anticipated unless there is a present substantive commitment to make such amendments.

142. Other respondents disagreed with the argument that a measurement approach based only on current compensation would be inconsistent with use of nominal interest rates (paragraph 140). They argued that the assumed discount rates should reflect the rates at which the obligation could be settled—for example, by purchasing annuities or perhaps by dedicating a portfolio of securities. They argued that future interest rates (and therefore forecasts of future inflation) are irrelevant.

143. The Board concluded that the pension obligation created when employees render services is a liability under the definition in Concepts Statement 3. That definition, however, does not resolve the issue of whether the measurement of that liability should consider future compensation levels. After considering respondents' views, both practical and conceptual, the Board concluded that estimated future compensation levels should be considered in measuring the service cost component and the projected benefit obligation if the plan's benefit formula incorporates them. The Board perceives a difference between an employer's promise to pay a benefit of 1 percent of an employee's *final* pay and a promise to pay an employee a fixed amount that happens to equal 1 percent of the employee's *current* pay. Ignoring the future variable (final pay) on which the obligation in the first case is based would result in not recognizing that difference. The Board also concluded that the accumulated benefit obligation, which is measured *without* considering future compensation levels, should continue to be part of the required disclosure and should be the basis on which to decide whether a minimum liability needs to be recognized.

Liabilities

144. *Preliminary Views* proposed requiring recognition of a net pension liability or asset based on the difference between the projected benefit obligation and the fair value of plan assets. However, the net gain or loss not yet included in net periodic pension cost was also unrecognized for purposes of measuring the net pension liability or asset, thereby reducing the volatility of that balance. An intangible asset would have been recognized when a plan was amended, increasing the projected benefit obligation. Respondents objected to the proposal for a number of reasons, both conceptual and pragmatic. Some of those objections, based on doubts about the nature of the employer's obligation, were discussed previously.

145. A number of respondents argued that increased pension benefits granted in a plan amendment are exchanged for employees' *future* services, even when the amount of the benefit is computed based on prior service. In this view, the employer's liability for such benefits arises only as the future services are rendered. Some also argued that a plan amendment is a wholly executory contract and for that reason should not be recognized. The Board agrees that the obligation is undertaken by the employer with the expectation of future economic benefits but believes that does not provide a basis for not recognizing the obligation that arises from the event or for arguing that no obligation exists. The Board does not agree that a plan amendment is a wholly executory contract. To the extent that an amendment increases benefits that will be attributable to future services, neither party has performed. The Board has never proposed to recognize any liability for those benefits. However, to the extent the increased benefits are attributed by the benefit formula to services already rendered, the Board concluded that one party to the contract has performed and the agreement is at most only partially executory.

146. Some respondents argued that the obligation could not be measured with sufficient reliability (or precision) to justify recognition. The Board notes that the measurements of net periodic pension cost and unfunded accrued pension cost, which are based on the same assumptions, are no more or less precise than measurements of the accumulated and projected benefit obligations. In addition, insurance companies often undertake obligations that will be determined in amount by future events (although not by future compensation levels), and those obligations are recognized. When an insurance contract involves obligations similar to pension obligations (for example, an annuity contract), measurement of those obligations involves some of the same assumptions used in pension accounting. The Board concluded that information about pension cost and obligations based on best estimates of the relevant future events is sufficiently reliable to be useful. The Board recognizes that pension (and other postemployment benefit) liabilities are, as some respondents argued, different from the other recognized liabilities of most employers, but that is because most enterprises other than insurance companies do

not ordinarily take on obligations of comparable significance that depend on unknown and uncontrollable future events to define the amount of future sacrifice.

147. Those respondents who challenged the reliability of liability measures based on actuarial calculations generally supported recognition of part of that same liability based on unfunded accrued pension costs. FASB Concepts Statement No. 2, *Qualitative Characteristics of Accounting Information,* defines reliability as a combination of representational faithfulness and verifiability. In the Board's view, the obligation based on the terms of the plan and the unfunded accrued cost are equally difficult to verify, but the former is a more faithful representation of a liability because it is an estimate of a present obligation to make future cash outlays as a result of past transactions and events. The unfunded accrued cost does not purport to be a measure of an obligation; it is a residual resulting from an allocation process and, therefore, it cannot be a faithful representation of a liability.

148. A number of respondents argued that a pension liability must be limited either to the amount that would have to be paid on plan termination or to the amount of vested benefits. Those arguments were based on the view that the employer has discretion to avoid any obligations in excess of those limits. Some who preferred no recognition nevertheless agreed that it is difficult to argue that at least unfunded vested benefits are not a liability.

149. The Board concluded that, in the absence of evidence to the contrary, accounting should be based on a going-concern assumption that, as applied to pensions, assumes that the plan will continue in operation and the benefits defined in the plan will be provided. Under that assumption, the employer's probable future sacrifice is not limited to either the termination liability or amounts already vested. The Board believes that the actuarial measurement of the obligation encompasses the probability that some employees will terminate and forfeit nonvested benefits. Benefits that are expected to vest are probable future sacrifices, and the liability in an ongoing plan situation is not limited to vested benefits. However, the Board was influenced by respondents' views of the nature of vested and accumulated benefit obligations in its decision that a reported liability should not be less than the unfunded accumulated benefit obligation. Some Board members were also influenced by arguments that the accumulated benefit obligation, which requires no estimate of future salary levels, is more reliably measurable than is the projected benefit obligation.

150. Some respondents objected to the accounting proposed in *Preliminary Views* on the grounds that delaying the recognition of gains and losses as part of the measurement of the net pension liability or asset could cause an employer to report a net liability when the fair value of plan assets exceeded the projected benefit obligation, or to report a net asset when the projected benefit obligation exceeded the fair value of plan assets. The Board noted that delayed recognition of the effects of price changes is an inherent part of historical cost accounting and that the problem results from the Board's retention of the delayed recognition and offsetting features of past pension accounting.

151. The Board understands that the recognition of a minimum liability required by this Statement only updates the statement of financial position in some circumstances when plan obligations are not fully funded. Unlike *Preliminary Views,* this Statement does not update the liability for all amendments when they occur. Also, like past practice and *Preliminary Views,* this Statement will result in recognition of liabilities for certain plans with assets in excess of their projected benefit obligations. That will occur because of delayed recognition of gains and of unrecognized net assets existing at the date of initial application of this Statement, if net periodic pension cost is not funded (for example, because it is not currently tax deductible). The provisions of this Statement, however, will result in recognition of some liabilities not currently reflected and, in the Board's view, in more representationally faithful reporting in those situations. This Statement also requires disclosure of the current information about assets and liabilities that is not reflected in the statement of financial position.

152. The Board believes that this Statement represents an improvement in past practices for the reporting of financial position in two ways. First, recognition of the cost of pensions over employees' service periods will result in earlier (but still gradual) recognition of significant liabilities that were reflected more slowly in the past financial statements of some employers. Second, the requirement to recognize a minimum liability limits the extent to which the delayed recognition of plan amendments and losses can result in omission of liabilities from statements of financial position.

153. Recognition of a measure of at least a minimum pension obligation as a liability is not a new idea. ARB 47, published in 1956, stated that "as a minimum, the accounts and financial statements should reflect accruals which equal the present worth, actuarially calculated, of pension commitments to employees to the extent that pension rights have vested in the employees, reduced, in the case of the balance sheet, by any accumulated trusteed

funds or annuity contracts purchased" (paragraph 7). Paragraph 18 of Opinion 8 required that "if the company has a legal obligation for pension cost in excess of amounts paid or accrued, the excess should be shown in the balance sheet as both a liability and a deferred charge." Opinion 8 did not define the term *legal liability,* and the FASB concluded in Interpretation 3 that, pending completion of this project, ERISA should not be presumed to create a legal liability for purposes of applying paragraph 18.

154. The Board considered a minimum liability based on the vested benefit obligation but concluded that the time at which benefits vest should not be the primary point for recognition of either cost or liabilities.

155. The Board also considered an alternative proposal that would differ from the requirements of this Statement in two ways. First, while it would have recognized the same minimum liability, it would also have recognized a minimum asset when the fair value of plan assets exceeded the projected benefit obligation. Second, it would have recognized an intangible asset only when recognition of a minimum liability resulted directly from a plan amendment. Changes in the minimum liability or the minimum asset not resulting from plan amendments (that is, gains and losses) would have been recognized as a separate component of equity (and thus would have been included in comprehensive income but not in earnings of the current period). The Board rejected that alternative because of the volatility that it would introduce into financial statements and because of its added complexity.

Two or More Plans

156. Some respondents argued that an employer with two or more plans should combine or net all plans and report the funded status only on an overall basis. That would affect the required disclosure and minimum liability recognition provisions of this Statement. They suggested that differences between plans are not substantive because an employer could merge two or more plans. The Board believes that an employer with one well funded plan and another less well-funded or unfunded plan is in a different position than an employer with similar obligations and assets in a single plan. The Board was not convinced that combining plans would be easy or even possible in many cases. For example, the Board believes it would be difficult to combine a qualified plan with an unqualified plan or a flat benefit plan with a final-pay plan. Further, netting all plans would be inconsistent with other standards that pre-

clude offsetting assets and liabilities unless a right of offset exists. The Board concluded that the requirements of this Statement to show separately certain information for plans with assets less than accumulated benefits would provide more useful information than would allowing the netting of all plans.

Recognition of the Cost of Retroactive Plan Amendments

157. When a defined benefit pension plan is initiated or amended to increase benefits, credit is often given for employees' services rendered before the date of the amendment. After such an amendment the projected benefit obligation, based on benefits attributed to past services by the plan's new benefit formula, is greater than before. The Board concluded that the employer's obligation for pension benefits granted in a plan amendment and attributable under the terms of the plan to prior service is not significantly different from the obligation arising year by year in accordance with the plan terms in effect prior to the amendment and that, as a result, the incremental obligation created by a plan amendment should be reflected as an increase in the projected benefit obligation. The increase in obligation is substantive, not simply the result of a computation; for example, vested benefits are increased immediately.

158. A few respondents argued that the retroactive cost of a plan amendment should be recognized as net periodic pension cost in the year of the amendment. They agreed that the obligation for benefits attributed to past service represents a liability and they concluded that, although some intangible future economic benefit may also result, it would not qualify for recognition as an asset. In their view, the retroactive cost of past plan amendments should not be charged to future periods.

159. Most respondents agreed with the rationale in *Preliminary Views* and the Exposure Draft that a plan initiation or amendment is invariably made with a view to benefiting the employer's operations in future periods rather than in the past or only in the period of the change.[15] The Board believes that a future economic benefit exists, that the cost of acquiring that benefit can be determined, and that amortization of that cost over future periods is consistent with accounting practice in other areas. The Board also believes that a requirement to charge the cost of a retroactive plan amendment immediately to net periodic pension cost would not be representationally faithful and would represent an unacceptably radical change from current practice. The Board concluded that the increase in the projected

---

[15]The probable future economic benefits in a particular case may include reduced employee turnover, improved productivity, and reduced demands for increases in cash compensation. The cost of the benefits is measured at the date of the plan change by the discounted amount of the incremental obligation resulting from the change.

benefit obligation resulting from a plan change should be recognized as a component of net periodic pension cost over a number of future periods as the anticipated benefit to the employer is expected to be realized.

160. Some respondents argued that the intangible asset proposed in the Exposure Draft does not qualify for recognition. The Board acknowledges the fact that similar future benefits are not recognized as assets in some cases. The Board concluded, however, that the asset should be recognized to the extent that a liability in excess of unfunded accrued pension cost is recognized. The Board also concluded that the asset recognized should be limited to the amount of prior service cost not yet recognized in net periodic pension cost. A plan can have unfunded accumulated benefits in excess of unfunded accrued pension cost only as a result of either retroactive plan amendments or losses. Although the Board agreed to delay recognition of losses in net periodic pension cost, it believes recognition of a loss as an asset would be inappropriate. No respondents argued that unrecognized losses represent future economic benefits.

161. Some respondents suggested that an intangible asset should be recognized but should be grouped with or netted against the pension liability. The Board rejected that approach because the asset cannot be used directly to satisfy the liability. There is no right of offset. That is really an argument against recognizing any liability arising from a plan change. The Board's conclusions on liability recognition were discussed previously.

Amortization of the cost of retroactive plan amendments

162. The Board recognizes that the number of periods benefited by a retroactive plan amendment (or the amount of the benefit remaining at a subsequent date) is difficult to estimate and is not objectively determinable. However, the Board concluded that amortization based on the expected future service of plan participants who are active at the time of the plan amendment or plan adoption and who are expected to receive benefits under the plan provides a reasonable basis for allocating the cost of a plan amendment to the periods benefited. Amortization beyond that period would be inconsistent with the objective of recognizing the cost of an employee's pension over that individual's service period.

163. The Board concluded that, conceptually, amortization of prior service cost should recognize the cost of each individual's added benefits over that individual's remaining service period. In practice, the Board believes that the precision of such a com-

putation on an individual basis is unnecessary and might not be worth the cost. The Board viewed a method that allocates the same amount of prior service cost to each expected future year of each employee's service as a reasonable approximation of the results of an individual computation. Use of the more precise method is, of course, appropriate. The Board also concluded that interest on that part of the obligation arising in an amendment and the anticipated future return on assets contributed (or to be contributed) to provide for that part of the obligation are separate components. Neither of those components should affect the recognition of prior service cost.

164. The individual computation, like the method adopted by the Board, would result in a declining amortization charge for the cost of a particular plan amendment because some of the employees who were granted additional benefits in the plan change normally could be expected to retire or terminate each period. In fact, an amortization of prior service cost for each individual as a level amount over that individual's remaining service period would be somewhat more rapid than the method adopted because the individuals receiving the greatest amount of retroactive benefits will usually be those nearest retirement. The method adopted is also consistent with the idea that the benefits realized by the employer as a result of a retroactive plan change are likely to be greatest in the years immediately after the change. An illustration of the method is included in Appendix B.

165. Some respondents to the Exposure Draft argued that the proposed allocation of the same amount of prior service cost to each future year of service would be unnecessarily complex and would require employers to maintain detailed records for long periods. The Board noted that it intends this Statement, to the extent possible, to define accounting objectives rather than specific computational means of attaining those objectives. The Board agreed to allow alternative methods of amortization (explicitly including a straight-line amortization over the average remaining service period of participants expected to receive benefits) that would simplify computations and record keeping as long as such methods do not have the effect of delaying recognition of prior service cost to a greater extent than the method that was defined in the Exposure Draft.

166. Because the cost of an amendment is measured as a present value (an increase in the projected benefit obligation), an amendment also results in an increase in the interest cost component of net periodic pension cost. Opinion 8 permitted amortization of the cost of retroactive plan amendments between a minimum and maximum range (paragraphs 17(a) and (b)), which, in practice, resulted in

amortization periods ranging from 10 to 40 years. The method previously most often used in practice was an "interest method" or "mortgage method," which allocates the prior service cost and interest cost on the unamortized (or unfunded) balance as a level total amount. Because that method considers interest only on a net basis (interest on the *unfunded* balance), it actually has the effect of delaying recognition of the cost of retroactive benefits in anticipation of future contributions and the return on the fund expected to be accumulated. That method is often described as producing a level total amortization, but the total that is level is the sum of principal amortization and interest cost on the related portion of the obligation, less return on the funds that will be built up, assuming future contributions equal to the level total. Under that method small amounts of the cost of the retroactive benefits are recognized in the years immediately after an amendment when interest on the unamortized cost is high, and the largest amounts of the cost of the benefits are recognized in the last years of the amortization period. The Board concluded that method has the effect of deferring a major portion of the cost of pensions beyond the service period of employees receiving them.

167. Some respondents suggested that some plans (for example, those providing benefits that are not pay-related or are related to career-average-pay) are amended more often than plans with final-pay benefit formulas and that as a result, the cost of each amendment should be recognized more rapidly. The Board concluded that if those or other circumstances indicate that the benefits of a retroactive plan amendment have been impaired or will expire more rapidly than would be reflected by the minimum amortization specified, the cost should be recognized more rapidly.

Future amendments

168. Some respondents suggested that plan amendments should be anticipated or estimated before they are made, in which case increased benefits expected to be granted in the future would be included in determining current period cost. Under that approach plan amendments actually occurring during a period would be treated as changes in estimates to the extent they varied from the assumption. The Board rejected that approach for most situations because of concerns about the ability to make reasonable estimates of future plan amendments and because the Board does not believe that a present obligation ordinarily exists for benefits to be promised in future amendments. Anticipation of future plan amendments also is inconsistent with the basic view that the terms of the present plan provide the best basis for measuring the present obligation.

169. However, respondents to the Exposure Draft argued that in some situations the substance of a plan embodies a present substantive commitment to provide benefits beyond those defined in the written plan formula. One example cited was a career-average-pay plan that produces approximately the same results as a final-pay plan through regular updates. Another example was an unwritten but substantive commitment to increase regularly the benefits paid to retirees to reflect inflation. The Board noted that this Statement retains from Opinion 8 the requirement to account for the substance of an unwritten plan. The Board agreed that employers should account for the substance of such commitments and disclose their existence and nature.

Amendments affecting retirees

170. An amendment sometimes increases benefits for individuals already retired. Since those individuals are not expected to render future services, the cost of those benefits cannot be recognized over the individuals' remaining service periods.

171. Some respondents argued that such an amendment does not give rise to a future economic benefit and that its entire cost should be recognized as an expense in the period of the amendment. The Board sees some merit in that argument but concluded that it is reasonable to assume that a plan amendment is the result of an economic decision and that future economic benefits similar to those expected to result from a benefit increase for active employees are expected to result when retirees' benefits are increased. The Board noted that in at least some cases retirees' benefit increases are part of collective-bargaining agreements and that some may view those benefits as being exchanged for services of active employees. The Board agreed that it would be simpler and more practical to recognize the cost of all plan amendments similarly, that is, on a delayed basis.

Amendments that reduce benefits

172. The Board recognizes that a situation might exist in which a plan amendment reduces benefits attributed to prior service. The Board concluded that accounting for such amendments should be consistent with accounting for benefit increases and that the accounting specified in paragraph 28 would accomplish that objective.

Volatility and Delayed Recognition of Gains and Losses

173. Gains and losses, sometimes called actuarial gains and losses, are changes in either the value of the projected benefit obligation or the fair value of

plan assets arising from changes in assumptions and from experience different from that incorporated in the assumptions. Gains and losses include actual returns on assets greater than or less than the expected rate of return.

174. A number of respondents to the Exposure Draft and earlier documents issued as part of this project expressed concern about the volatility of an unfunded or overfunded pension obligation measure and the practical effects of incorporating that volatility into financial statements. The Board does not believe that reporting volatility per se is undesirable. If a financial measure purports to represent a phenomenon that is volatile, the measure must show that volatility or it will not be representationally faithful. The Board also notes that the volatility of the unfunded or overfunded obligation may be less than some expect if the explicit assumptions used in the valuation of the obligation are changed to reflect fully the changes in interest rate structures that affect the fair values of plan assets, because changes in the assets may tend to offset changes in the obligation.

175. However, in the case of pension liabilities, volatility may not be entirely a faithful representation of changes in the status of the obligation (the phenomenon represented). It may also reflect an unavoidable inability to predict accurately the future events that are anticipated in making period-to-period measurements. That is, the difference in periodic measures of the pension liability (and therefore the funded status of the plan) results partly from the inability to predict accurately for a period (or over several periods) compensation levels, length of employee service, mortality, retirement ages, and other pertinent events. As a result, actual experience often differs significantly from that which was estimated and that leads to changes in the estimates themselves. Recognizing the effects of revisions in estimates in full in the period in which they occur may result in volatility of the reported amounts that does not reflect actual changes in the funded status of the plan in that period.

176. Some respondents believe that some of the volatility is representationally faithful, for example, gains and losses that result from measuring investments at fair value. They also believe, however, that recognizing those gains and losses, and especially including them in earnings of the current period, would be inconsistent with the present accounting model applicable to employers' financial statements. They argued that such a major departure from the present model should not be made in this project.

177. The Board considered those views and concluded that it should not require that gains and losses be recognized immediately as a component of net periodic pension cost. Accordingly, this Statement provides for recognition of gains and losses prospectively over future periods to the extent they are not offset by subsequent changes. Based on the concerns expressed by many respondents to the Exposure Draft, the Board also concluded that the effects of changes in the fair value of plan assets, including the indirect effect of those changes on the return-on-assets component of net periodic pension cost, should be recognized on a basis that reduces the volatility more effectively than that proposed in the Exposure Draft. The Board believes that both the extent of volatility reduction and the mechanism adopted to effect it are essentially practical issues without conceptual basis. The Board does not believe that the market-related value of assets used in this Statement as a device to reduce the volatility of net periodic pension cost is as relevant as the fair value required for other purposes.

178. The Exposure Draft would have required use of the discount rate and the fair value of assets as the basis for calculating the return-on-assets component of net periodic pension cost. Many respondents argued that the return-on-assets component so determined would generate unacceptable volatility even if gains and losses were never amortized. The Board considered several approaches that would have further reduced volatility and concluded that the approach required by this Statement represents the best pragmatic solution.

179. This Statement requires use of an assumption, described as the expected long-term rate of return on plan assets, and of a market-related value of assets to calculate the expected return on plan assets. Actual returns greater than or less than the expected return are afforded delayed recognition. The Board anticipates that the expected return on assets defined in this Statement will be less volatile than either the actual return on assets or the return on assets that would have been recognized based on the Exposure Draft. The Board noted, however, that an expected long-term return-on-assets rate significantly below the rate at which the obligations could be settled implies that settlement would be economically advantageous.

180. The Board believes the approach required in this Statement has several advantages. First, it is very similar mechanically to past practices intended to achieve similar objectives. As a result, it should be easier for those familiar with the details of past practices to understand and apply. Second, it avoids the use of discount rates relevant primarily to the pension obligation as part of a calculation related to plan assets. As a result, it reflects more clearly than did the Exposure Draft the Board's basic conclusion that information about a pension plan is more

understandable if asset-related or financial aspects of the arrangement are distinguished from the liability-related and compensation cost aspects.

181. This Statement defines market-related asset value as either fair value or a calculated value that recognizes changes in fair value in a systematic and rational manner over not more than five years. The Board considered defining a more specific averaging method to be used by all employers, but it concluded that the definition adopted has the advantage of simplicity. It also allows the use of fair value for some classes of assets, and the Board believes that use of fair value for certain assets (for example, bonds) will reduce the volatility of net periodic pension cost. The Board also noted that the definition adopted is similar to (in fact, it was adapted from) that proposed in an Exposure Draft by the Canadian Institute of Chartered Accountants.

182. The Board also considered a number of respondents' suggestions that would have further reduced the volatility of net periodic pension cost by using a discount rate that would change less often and less significantly than the rate described in paragraph 44. Those respondents were primarily concerned that the service component of net cost would be volatile because of changes in the discount rate assumption. The Board concluded that the service component is the cost of benefits attributed to service in the current period and should reflect prices of that period. The Board noted that accounting generally recognizes the current prices rather than past or average prices in recording transactions of the current period. The Board also noted that the service component under the provisions of this Statement is essentially the same as net pension cost determined under the provisions of Opinion 8 for a plan that purchases annuities annually for all benefits attributed to service of that year.

183. The discount rate also has some effect on the interest cost component of net periodic pension cost, but that was less controversial among respondents because as the rate increases (or decreases) the present value of the obligation determined at that rate decreases (or increases) so that the effect on net periodic pension cost (the rate times the present value of the obligation) is less significant.

184. The Board noted that, if assumptions prove to be accurate estimates of experience over a number of years, gains or losses in one year will be offset by losses or gains in subsequent periods. In that situation, all gains and losses would be offset over time, and amortization of unrecognized gains and losses would be unnecessary. The Board was concerned, however, that the uncertainties inherent in assumptions could lead to gains or losses that increase rather than offset, and concluded that gains and

losses should not be ignored completely. Actual experience will determine the final net cost of a pension plan. Therefore, the Board concluded that some amortization, at least when the net unrecognized gain or loss becomes significant, should be required. The Board also noted that amortization of unrecognized gains or losses is part of current funding and past accounting practice.

185. In *Preliminary Views,* the Board proposed a simple amortization based on the average remaining service period of active plan participants. The amount amortized would have been equal to the net unrecognized gain or loss divided by the average remaining service. Many respondents commented that the proposed amortization did not sufficiently reduce the volatility of net periodic pension cost.

186. The Board concluded that once a decision is made to delay recognition of gains and losses, no demonstrably correct period is identifiable over which those items should be amortized. Accordingly, the Board concluded that less rapid amortization could be allowed but that some limit should be retained.

187. The Board was attracted to the "corridor" approach required by this Statement as a minimum amortization approach in part because it allows a reasonable opportunity for gains and losses to offset each other without affecting net periodic pension cost. The Board also noted that the corridor approach is similar in some respects to methods used by some to deal with gains and losses on plan assets for funding purposes.

188. Like the period of amortization of unrecognized gains and losses, a decision about the point at which it becomes necessary to begin amortizing (the width of the corridor) is not conceptually based. The Board believes it is appropriate to relate that requirement to the market-related value of plan assets and the amount of the projected benefit obligation because the gains and losses subject to amortization are changes in those two amounts. The Board concluded that a net gain or loss equal to 10 percent of the greater of those two amounts should not be required to be amortized. The width of the resulting corridor is 20 percent (from 90 percent to 110 percent of the greater balance).

189. The Board considered whether the changes made to the provisions of the Exposure Draft to reduce the volatility of net periodic pension cost obviated the need for the corridor approach to gain or loss amortization, either for all gains and losses or for those related to plan assets. The Board concluded that that approach should be retained as a reasonable way to avoid excessive volatility that might otherwise result from changes in the projected

benefit obligation, and that treating asset gains and losses similarly was a simple and reasonable solution to a practical problem.

190. Opinion 8 stated that ". . . actuarial gains and losses should be spread over the current year and future years . . ." (paragraph 30). The Board understands, however, that predominant past practice did not consider gains and losses until after the period in which they arose. *Preliminary Views* would have calculated net periodic pension cost including amortization of the year-end unrecognized net gain or loss. Participants in a field test conducted by the Board and a number of employers associated with the Financial Executives Institute suggested that that approach would unnecessarily complicate the preparation of interim financial statements. The Board agreed, and this Statement requires amortization of unrecognized net gains or losses based on beginning-of-the-year balances.

Assumptions

191. This Statement requires that each significant assumption used in determining the pension information reflect the best estimate of the plan's future experience solely with respect to that assumption. That method of selecting assumptions is referred to as an *explicit approach*. An *implicit approach,* on the other hand, means that two or more assumptions do not individually represent the best estimate of the plan's future experience with respect to those assumptions, but the aggregate effect of their combined use is presumed to be approximately the same as that of an explicit approach. The Board believes that an explicit approach results in more useful information regarding (a) components of the pension benefit obligation and net periodic pension cost, (b) changes in the pension benefit obligation, and (c) the choice of significant assumptions used to determine the pension measurements. The Board also believes that the explicit approach is more understandable. Most respondents who addressed the question agreed.

192. A number of respondents commented that differences in assumptions, especially the discount rates and the assumed compensation levels, would impair comparability. Some of those respondents concluded that the Board should require all employers to use the same assumptions. Others concluded that the Board could not fix the assumptions and, therefore, any attempt to improve comparability by making other changes in accounting for pensions was futile.

193. The Board concluded that requiring all employers to use the same assumptions is inappropriate. Concepts Statement 2 defines comparability as "the quality of information that enables users to identify similarities in and differences between two sets of economic phenomena." The Board noted that requiring all employers to use the same turnover assumption, for example, would *reduce* comparability to the extent that that assumption would otherwise reflect real differences in expected turnover among employers.

194. This Statement requires use of an assumption described as the expected long-term rate of return on plan assets to calculate the expected return on plan assets. That assumption would not have been required by the Exposure Draft. The Board's reasons for adopting that requirement are discussed in paragraphs 177-181.

195. Most respondents focused their comments on assumed discount rates and compensation levels. Those are generally cited as the assumptions that have the greatest effect on measures of pension cost and benefit obligations, and they are related because both are affected by some of the same economic factors (such as the expected future rates of inflation). Some respondents also believe those assumptions (particularly the discount rates) are less likely than others to reflect real differences among plans.

196. The Board considered a requirement that all employers use common benchmark discount rates, such as those published by the Pension Benefit Guaranty Corporation (PBGC). One reason for that consideration was its concern that rates previously used for disclosure purposes varied among employers over an unreasonable range. In spite of that concern, however, the Board concluded that requiring use of benchmark rates would be inappropriate, in part because no readily available rates seemed fully suitable. Instead, the Board decided that this Statement should describe more clearly the objective of selecting the discount rates with the expectation that a narrower range of rates used would result. Although the Board concluded that it should not require use of PBGC rates, it noted that certain of those rates, as currently determined, are one source of readily available information that might be considered in estimating the discount rates required by this Statement.

197. The Board notes that discount rates are used to measure the current period's service cost component and to determine the interest cost component of net periodic pension cost. Both of those uses relate to the liability side of pension accounting. From an accounting (as opposed to funding) perspective, they have nothing to do with plan assets. The same assumptions are needed for an unfunded plan.

198. The Board concluded that selection of the discount rates should be based on current prices for settling the pension obligation. Under this Statement,

the discount rates are used most significantly to calculate the present value of the obligation and the service cost component of net periodic pension cost. Both of those uses are conceptually independent of the plan's assets. If two employers have made the same benefit promise, the Board believes the service cost component and the present value of the obligation should be the same even if one expected to earn an annual return of 15 percent on its plan assets and the other had an unfunded plan. The Board concluded that a current settlement rate best meets that objective and also is consistent with measurement of plan assets at fair value for purposes of disclosing the plan's funded status.

199. Interest rates vary depending on the duration of investments; for example, U.S. Treasury bills, 7-year bonds, and 30-year bonds have different interest rates. Thus, the weighted-average discount rate (interest rate) inherent in the prices of annuities (or a dedicated bond portfolio) will vary depending on the length of time remaining until individual benefit payment dates. A plan covering only retired employees would be expected to have significantly different discount rates from one covering a work force of 30-year-olds. The disclosures required by this Statement regarding components of the pension benefit obligation will be more representationally faithful if individual discount rates applicable to various benefit deferral periods are selected. A properly weighted average rate can be used for aggregate computations such as the interest cost component of net pension cost for the period.

200. An insurance company deciding on the price of an annuity contract will consider the rates of return available to it for investing the premium received and the rates of return expected to be available to it for reinvestment of future cash flows from the initial investment during the period until benefits are payable. That consideration is indicative of a relationship between rates inherent in the prices of annuity contracts and rates available in investment markets. The Board concluded that it would be appropriate for employers to consider that relationship and information about investment rates in estimating the discount rates required for application of this Statement.

201. Some believe that year-to-year changes in pension information as a result of changes in assumed discount rates should be avoided to the maximum extent possible. In their view, some averaging technique should be used to smooth potential year-to-year changes so that assumed rates are changed only when it is apparent that the long-term trend has

changed. The Board recognizes that long-term interest rates must be considered in determining appropriate assumed discount rates. However, it rejects the view that material changes in long-term rates should be ignored solely to avoid adjusting assumed discount rates.

202. The Board also addressed assumed compensation levels and concluded that they should (a) reflect the best estimate of actual future compensation levels for the individuals involved and (b) be consistent with assumed discount rates to the extent that both incorporate expectations of the same future economic conditions.

203. Some respondents argued that only certain components[16] of future compensation increases should be considered. The Board concluded that the terms of the plan do not distinguish between compensation increments from different causes and that accounting should not do so either. The Board also is not convinced that a meaningful breakdown of a change in compensation levels into its components is practical.

Different Accounting for Smaller Employers

204. The 1983 FASB Discussion Memorandum, *Employers' Accounting for Pensions and Other Postemployment Benefits,* raised the question of whether certain smaller employers should have pension accounting requirements different from those for larger companies.

205. Some respondents argued that different requirements were needed because the costs of obtaining information are relatively more burdensome for smaller employers and because there is less benefit from improved accounting for those employers. In their view, the needs and interests of users of smaller employers' financial statements, especially those of employers that are not publicly held, are different from the needs and interests of users of public companies' financial statements.

206. The Board also considered arguments that certain defined benefit plans of small employers are substantively different from those of larger employers. In this view the smaller employer's plan is primarily a means of sheltering the income of key employees or manager-owners from taxation, and as a result, the nature of the obligation is different.

207. The Board concluded that the measurement of net periodic pension cost and the recognition of net pension liabilities or assets should not differ for

---

[16]The components have been defined as increases due to merit, productivity, and inflation. Merit increases are those that an individual employee will receive as that employee progresses through a career and that are theoretically based on the employee's ability to perform at a more competent or responsible level as the individual becomes older and accumulates more experience. The second component is labor's share of productivity gains. The third component attempts to anticipate general compensation increases that result from inflation.

smaller or nonpublic employers. Evidence from users of the financial statements of smaller employers (in particular, bankers) does not provide support for a different approach. In the Board's view, the existence of a separate set of measurement requirements or a range of alternatives for certain employers would probably not improve the cost-benefit relationship but would add complexity and reduce the comparability and usefulness of financial statements.

208. The Exposure Draft proposed to allow certain smaller and nonpublic employers to elect an alternative set of disclosure requirements less extensive than those proposed for other employers. Because changes to reduce the extent of required disclosure for all employers eliminated most of the items that would not have been required of smaller employers, the Board concluded that the same requirements should apply to all employers.

209. Some respondents argued that smaller employers would have a more difficult time than other employers with the initial application of this Statement, in part because advisors involved with pension accounting may put a higher priority on the needs of larger employers. The Board agreed that the transition provisions of this Statement, which allow an extra two years before application is required for certain smaller employers, would be a practical and appropriate means of facilitating its adoption by those employers.

Different Accounting for Certain Industries

210. Some respondents argued that accounting requirements should be different for employers subject to certain types of regulation (rate-regulated enterprises) or for employers that have certain types of government contracts for which reimbursement is a function of costs incurred. In both of those cases it was noted that a change in reported net periodic pension cost might have a direct effect on the revenues of the employer (lower cost would result in reduced revenues), or conversely, that increases in reported net periodic pension cost would not be recoverable. The Board understands the practical concerns of those respondents, but it concluded that the cost of a particular pension benefit is not changed by the circumstances described and that this Statement should include no special provisions relating to such employers. For rate-regulated enterprises, FASB Statement No. 71, *Accounting for the Effects of Certain Types of Regulation,* may require that the difference between net periodic pension cost as defined in this Statement and amounts of pension cost considered for rate-making purposes be recognized as an asset or a liability created by the actions of the regulator. Those actions of the regulator change the timing of recognition of net pension

cost as an expense; they do not otherwise affect the requirements of this Statement.

Disclosure

General considerations

211. Decisions on disclosure requirements involve evaluating and balancing considerations of relevance, reliability, and cost. Relevance and reliability are characteristics that make information useful for making decisions and that make it beneficial to require disclosure of some information. Benefits to users that are expected to result from required disclosures must be compared with the costs of providing and assimilating that information. Evaluating individual disclosures in relation to those criteria is generally a matter of judgment. Cost, for example, is affected by several factors, one of which is the fact that some employers have a large number of different plans and some disclosures are more difficult than others to aggregate or summarize meaningfully. Also, as the total amount of disclosure increases, the incremental cost to both preparers and users of additional disclosure may be greater than the benefit of the additional information.

212. Many respondents supported the basic idea that additional information about defined benefit pension plans was needed by users of financial reports. Respondents suggested a wide range of possible disclosures.

Specific Disclosure Requirements

Descriptive information

213. Respondents generally favored disclosure of information about plan provisions and employee groups. The Board concluded that a brief description of the plan and the type of benefit formula could assist users in understanding the financial statements, particularly in view of the fact that the measurement of net periodic pension cost is based on the benefit formula. Respondents and the Board agreed that financial statements should continue to disclose the nature and effects of significant changes in the factors affecting the computation of the net pension liability (or asset) and net periodic pension cost recognized in the financial statements and other significant or unusual matters necessary to an understanding of the impact of the plan on the employer's financial position and results of operations.

214. Respondents also favored disclosure of the funding policy. They noted that the disclosure required by Opinion 8 and Statement 36 had been helpful in understanding differences between fund-

ing a pension plan and accounting for it. Information that highlights changes in funding policies also can be useful in predicting future cash flows.

Pension cost information

215. Most respondents indicated that the disclosure of net periodic pension cost has been useful and favored continuing that disclosure requirement. The Board concurred and also decided to require disclosure of the components of net periodic pension cost. Some respondents argued that it is important to separate return on assets from the other components because they consider that return to be the result of the employer's financing decisions and not really a part of pension cost. The Board also believes that disclosure of the components will, over time, increase the general understanding of the nature of net periodic pension cost, the reasons for changes in that cost, and the relationship of financing activities and employee compensation cost.

216. The Exposure Draft proposed to require disclosure of both the expected return on assets (as a component of net periodic pension cost) and the actual return on assets (as part of a disclosure of changes in the fair value of plan assets). Respondents suggested that disclosure of two different measures of return on assets would be confusing. The Board agreed and concluded that, of the two, the actual return was more relevant and important.

Information about obligations and assets

217. Disclosure of information about the funded status of the plan was favored by most respondents who addressed that issue. The Board concluded that disclosure of certain components of the pension benefit obligation should be required. The Board believes that disclosure of that information is important to an understanding of the economics of the employer's pension plan. For example, disclosure of vested benefits provides important information about the firmness of the obligation (vested benefits are less avoidable than nonvested benefits). In addition, vested benefits may be a reasonable surrogate for a plan termination liability. The Board believes that this information is not particularly difficult or costly to obtain.

218. The Board concluded that users should also be provided general information about the major types of plan assets (and nonbenefit liabilities, if any) and the actual amount of return on plan assets for the period. Management has a stewardship responsibility for efficient use of plan assets just as it does for operating assets. The Board believes that disclosure of that information will be useful in assessing the profitability of investment policies and the degree of risk assumed.

219. The Board believes that a reconciliation of the amounts included in the employer's statement of financial position to the funded status of the plan's projected benefit obligation is essential to understanding the relationship between the accounting and the funded status of the plan. The Board acknowledges that the amount recognized in the financial statements as a net pension liability or asset under this Statement does not fully reflect the underlying funded status of the plan.

Information about assumptions

220. Respondents addressing the question generally favored disclosure of the weighted-average assumed discount rate. They noted that the discount rate is a significant assumption that materially affects the computation of the pension benefit information and the comparability of that information among employers. Respondents were divided on whether other assumptions should be disclosed. Some opposed disclosing other assumptions on the basis that additional information would not be understood by most users. Others suggested that for employers with numerous plans, certain of the disclosures (such as turnover and mortality) would be complex and difficult to aggregate or summarize.

221. The Board agreed that information about certain assumptions is useful and this Statement requires disclosure of the assumed weighted-average discount rate and rate of compensation increase. It noted that those two assumptions have the most significant impact on the amounts of net periodic pension cost and the projected benefit obligation and that those two assumptions are related. It also noted that their effect on reported amounts is relatively easy to understand. The Board concluded that information about those two assumptions is essential if users are to be able to make meaningful comparisons among employers using different assumptions. For the same reasons, when the Board decided to allow the use of an expected long-term rate of return on plan assets different from the discount rate, it concluded that disclosure of that assumption should be required.

222. Some respondents opposed disclosure of assumed future compensation levels because providing that information to employees could affect labor negotiations. The Board concluded that the information is likely to be available to labor negotiators from other sources and that the usefulness of the information to financial statement users justifies its disclosure.

Suggested Disclosures

223. The Exposure Draft would have required the following disclosures in addition to those noted in the preceding paragraphs:

a. The ratio of net periodic pension cost to covered payroll
b. The separate amounts of amortization of unrecognized prior service and amortization of unrecognized net gain or loss
c. Information about the cash flows of the plan separately showing employer contributions, other contributions, and benefits paid during the period
d. The amounts of plan assets classified by major asset category
e. The amounts of the vested benefit obligation owed to retirees and to others
f. The change in the projected benefit obligation that would result from a one-percentage-point change in (1) the assumed discount rate and (2) the assumed rate of compensation increase
g. The change in the service cost and interest cost components of net periodic pension cost that would result from a one-percentage-point change in (1) the assumed discount rate and (2) the assumed rate of compensation increase.

224. Those disclosures had been suggested by respondents to previous documents issued as part of this project and the Board had concluded in the Exposure Draft that they would provide useful information and would not be unduly costly to provide. However, many respondents to the Exposure Draft commented that the volume of the proposed disclosures was too great. The Board agreed and concluded that the disclosures described in the preceding paragraph should not be required. The Board believes those disclosures are relatively less useful or (in the case of the last two items listed) relatively more costly than the disclosures required by this Statement. The Board also believes it would be appropriate for employers to consider disclosing those items if they decide to disclose more information about pension plans than the minimum required by this Statement, for example, because their plans are large relative to their overall operations.

225. The Board also considered an approach that would have allowed reduced disclosures for employers with defined benefit plans not large enough to qualify in the aggregate to qualify as a segment of the business under FASB Statement No. 14, *Financial Reporting for Segments of a Business Enterprise*. The Board concluded that that approach would not be cost effective, in part because of the difficulty of defining how the provisions of Statement 14 should be applied to pension plans.

Other Disclosures Considered

226. Other disclosures noted in the following paragraphs were suggested by respondents and considered by the Board. The Board concluded that those suggested disclosures are less important than the disclosures discussed previously and should not be required because, in the Board's judgment, there is not sufficient evidence that the usefulness of that information is great enough to justify the costs involved.

227. Some respondents favored disclosing estimates of future contributions. They suggested that the information would be relevant to assessing near-term cash flows and would provide more timely information about changes in funding policy. That requirement was opposed by others who believed that presentation of forecasts of future funds flows should not be required for any specific activity. Opponents also suggested that the information would be too costly to produce if done properly and that it implies greater certainty than exists. Similar views were expressed for and against disclosure of estimates of future net periodic pension cost.

228. Disclosure of demographic information about the employee population was advocated by several respondents. They suggested that a limited amount of demographic information could be provided at minimal cost and would be useful. For example, disclosure of the number of covered employees, the number of retirees, and the average age of active employees might contribute to understanding the pension situation. Opponents suggested that those disclosures are outside the scope of financial reporting.

229. Others suggested disclosing the obligation for pension benefits that would be used in determining the PBGC or termination liability. The Board concluded that such information could be costly to determine if done properly and might not be substantially different from other disclosed information (vested and accumulated benefit obligations).

230. Information about the plan's actuary was suggested as another possible disclosure. Recommendations were to provide the name and professional qualifications of the actuary and comments of the actuary about any anticipated changes in plan costs or contribution rates. The Board concluded that such information is outside the scope of financial reporting.

Timeliness of Information

231. The 1983 Discussion Memorandum raised the question of whether the accounting measurements of pension obligations and plan assets should be as

of the date of the financial statements or as of an earlier date. Measuring pension assets as of the date of the financial statements does not present very significant or unusual problems; the issue relates primarily to the measures of the pension obligations.

232. Although many respondents preferred that the Board allow measurements as of a date earlier than the date of the financial statements, most of the arguments raised related to a perceived requirement to have an actuarial valuation performed after that date and completed before financial statements are issued. The Board concluded that it should be feasible in most situations to provide information as of the date of financial statements based on a valuation performed at an earlier date with adjustments for relevant subsequent events (especially employee service) after that date. The Board noted that a number of employers have used that approach to provide information previously required. The Board also believes that the benefits of having the information on a timely basis and consistent with other financial information provided would usually outweigh the incremental costs involved. However, the Board acknowledges that practical problems may make it costly in some situations to obtain information, especially that concerning obligations and related components of net periodic pension cost, as of the date of the financial statements. Accordingly, the Board concluded that the information required by this Statement should be as of a date not earlier than three months before the date of the financial statements. The Board also noted that ARB No. 51, *Consolidated Financial Statements,* allows consolidation of a subsidiary with an annual fiscal period ending not more than about three months earlier than the parent's.

233. The Board also considered respondents' requests for clarification of how to apply the provisions of the Exposure Draft to quarterly reports and comments on the practical difficulty of basing current period net pension cost on assumptions related to the current period. The Board concluded that the provisions of paragraphs 52 and 53 of this Statement are practical and responsive to those concerns.

Other Situations and Types of Plans

Contracts with Insurance Companies

234. The Board concluded that some contracts with insurance companies are in substance forms of investments and that the use of those funding arrangements should not affect the accounting principles for determining an employer's net periodic pension cost. Some respondents who agreed with that conclusion were concerned that fair value of those investments would be difficult or impossible to determine. They suggested that contract value be used instead of fair value. The Board concluded that fair value should be the measurement basis for all types of investments but agreed that for some contracts the best available estimate of fair value might be contract value.

235. The Board recognized that some contracts with insurance companies are in substance more than investment vehicles. Most respondents noted that some insurance contracts (for example, nonparticipating annuities) effectively transfer the primary obligation for payment of benefits from the employer to the insurance company. They argued that, in those circumstances, the premium paid is an appropriate measure of pension cost. The Board agreed that the purchase of nonparticipating annuities is in substance more like a settlement of the pension obligation than like an investment.

236. Under some annuity contracts, the purchaser (either the plan or the employer) acquires the right to participate in the investment performance or experience of the insurance company (participating annuities). Under those contracts, if the insurance company has favorable experience, the purchaser receives dividends. Participating annuities have some characteristics of an investment. However, the employer is as fully relieved of the obligation as with a nonparticipating annuity, and a separate actuarial computation ordinarily would not be performed. The Board concluded that, except as indicated in the following paragraph, it would be appropriate to treat a participating annuity contract the same as a nonparticipating annuity contract and to exclude the benefits covered from measures of the obligation.

237. The Board was concerned, however, that a contract could be structured in such a way that the premium would be materially in excess of the cost of nonparticipating annuities because of the expectation of future dividends. If the full amount of the premium were recognized as periodic cost in the year paid and dividends were recognized as reductions of cost when received, the resulting measures of net periodic pension cost would be unrelated to benefits earned by employees. If the employer had the ability to influence the timing of dividends, it would then be possible to shift cost among periods without regard to underlying economic events. The Board concluded that part of a participating contract is in substance an investment that should be recognized as an asset.

238. The Board believes that measurement of the participation right asset in periods subsequent to its acquisition should be, consistent with the measurement of other assets, at fair value to the extent that fair value can be reasonably determined. The Board understands, however, that some participating

annuity contracts may not provide a basis for an estimate of fair value better than that provided by amortized cost and concluded that in that situation amortized cost should be used. That conclusion is not intended to permit use of amortized cost if that amount is in excess of net realizable value.

239. The Exposure Draft would have treated annuity contracts purchased from an insurance company affiliated with the employer as investments (that is, it would have included such contracts and covered benefits in plan assets and the accumulated benefit obligation). Respondents argued that information needed to treat such contracts as investments, including the actuarial present value of the obligations covered by the contract, would be neither available nor cost beneficial. The Board agreed and this Statement requires only contracts purchased from a captive insurance subsidiary to be treated as investments. Because an employer remains indirectly at risk if annuities are purchased from an affiliate, however, the Board concluded that disclosure of the approximate amount of annual benefits covered by such contracts should be required.

Defined Contribution Plans

240. Most respondents supported the past accounting and disclosure requirements for defined contribution plans, and the Board concluded that no significant changes to those requirements were needed. The Board believes that in most cases the formula in a defined contribution plan unambiguously assigns contributions to periods of employee service. Accordingly, the employer's present obligation under the terms of the plan is fully satisfied when the contribution for the period is made, subject to the constraint that costs (defined contributions) should not be deferred and recognized in periods after the termination of service of the individual to whose account the contributions are to be made. Most of the questions that have been referred to the Board about defined contribution plans have dealt with the definition of those plans and how to treat plans that have some of the attributes of both defined benefit and defined contribution plans. The definition of a defined contribution plan in this Statement is similar to the definitions presently established by the Internal Revenue Code and ERISA.

241. The Board also concluded that defined contribution plans are sufficiently different from defined benefit plans that disclosures about them should not be combined. Opinion 8 did not specifically address combining disclosures, and practice has varied as some employers disclosed, for example, net periodic pension cost as a single amount including both types of plans.

Multiemployer Plans

242. The 1983 Discussion Memorandum raised the issue of whether an employer participating in a multiemployer pension plan that provides defined benefits should recognize cost or obligations other than those defined by contributions. Respondents' comments indicated substantial uncertainty as to the legal status of employers' obligations to multiemployer plans. Some noted that the obligation to a multiemployer plan can be changed by events affecting other participating employers and their employees. Respondents also expressed concern about the availability of information sufficiently reliable for accounting recognition.

243. Based on respondents' comments, the Board concluded that it was not appropriate to require changes in the accounting for multiemployer plans as part of this Statement. Many respondents also emphasized the substantive differences between a multiemployer plan and a single-employer plan. The Board concluded that those differences are such that separating disclosure for the two types of plans will enhance the understandability and usefulness of the information.

244. The Exposure Draft would have required certain disclosures intended to provide information about the extent of involvement with multiemployer plans, including available information about the withdrawal liability. Many respondents argued that the withdrawal liability is a contingent liability, which suggests that it should be disclosed. Other respondents, however, argued that information about the withdrawal liability would be difficult and expensive to obtain, would be unreliable and, to the extent readily available, out of date, and would be of limited value except in cases in which withdrawal was expected to occur under circumstances that would trigger the liability. The Board agreed and the proposed requirements are not included in this Statement. Instead, the Board concluded that the provisions of Statement 5 should determine when withdrawal liabilities are recognized or disclosed.

245. Several respondents to the Exposure Draft argued that some plans involve more than one employer, are in substance multiemployer plans because the assets cannot be attributed to particular employers, and do not involve unions. The Board concluded that it should modify the proposed definition of multiemployer plans to include those plans.

246. The 1983 Discussion Memorandum also inquired about other multiple-employer plans not classified as multiemployer plans under ERISA. The few that responded to that issue indicated that those plans are in substance more like single-

employer plans than like multiemployer plans. Accordingly, the definition of multiemployer plans in this Statement is similar to that in ERISA as amended by the Multiemployer Pension Plan Amendments Act of 1980.

Non-U.S. Pension Plans

247. Respondents' reactions to accounting issues concerning pension arrangements outside the United States (foreign plans) varied. Almost equal numbers of respondents supported and opposed special accounting provisions for those plans. Those supporting the position that special provisions should be required for foreign plans argued that either (a) the nature of the arrangement or the substance of the obligation is sufficiently different from that of plans in the United States to preclude similar treatment or (b) circumstances in other countries make it impractical or impossible to implement similar accounting principles.

248. The Board concluded that the substance of the arrangement and the nature of the employer's obligation should determine the appropriate accounting. For foreign plans that are in substance similar to plans in the United States, the Board was not convinced that application of the basic requirements of this Statement would be impractical. The Board is not aware of significant problems arising from the application of prior requirements to foreign plans, and those requirements were based on actuarial calculations and the same assumptions needed to apply this Statement.

249. The Board was convinced, however, that practical problems could arise in communicating the requirements and obtaining the information necessary for initial application of this Statement to plans outside the U.S. The Board concluded that allowing an extra two years before application is required would give employers time to make necessary arrangements in an orderly manner and would reduce the cost of transition.

250. Some respondents also argued that combined disclosures for U.S. plans and for plans in other countries with very different economic conditions would be difficult to understand. The Board agreed and concluded that disclosures for such plans should be presented separately.

Business Combinations

251. The Board is aware of diversity in practice relating to recognition of pension-related assets and liabilities in purchase business combinations. The Board has also been asked how the asset or liability, once recognized, should be subsequently reduced.

252. This Statement requires that in a business combination accounted for as a purchase under Opinion 16, the acquiring company should recognize a pension liability (or asset) if the acquired company has a projected benefit obligation in excess of (or less than) plan assets. It also requires that, if it is expected that the purchaser will restructure the plan, the effects of restructuring should be considered in valuing the projected benefit obligation. The Board concluded that those requirements are consistent with purchase accounting as defined by Opinion 16, which specifies a *new basis of accounting* reflecting bargained (fair) value of assets acquired and liabilities assumed whether or not previously reflected in the financial statements. The Board believes that the unfunded or overfunded projected benefit obligation defined by this Statement is a more appropriate measure of the net pension obligation or asset than the measure required by Opinion 16 in view of the other conclusions in this Statement. The Board also noted that Opinion 16 was predicated on pension accounting that involved alternative methods. One result of the accounting required by this Statement is that the effects of plan amendments and gains and losses of the acquired company's plan that occurred before the acquisition are not a part of future net periodic pension cost of the acquirer.

253. The Board also decided to avoid possible ambiguity and future diversity in practice by clarifying how Opinion 16 should apply to a multiemployer plan situation. The Exposure Draft would have required recognition of a withdrawal liability when the employer is acquired in a business combination accounted for as a purchase. Based on respondents' comments, however, the Board concluded that no recognition of withdrawal liabilities should be required unless withdrawal under conditions that would result in a liability is probable. The Board was led to that conclusion by doubts about the reliability of the measure of the liability in other circumstances. The Board was not convinced that there is an obligation for future contributions to a multiemployer plan or that an estimated withdrawal liability would provide useful information about such an obligation, absent a probable withdrawal.

Transition and Effective Dates

254. In *Preliminary Views* the Board concluded that transition was essentially a practical question and that providing a choice between two specified transition methods (prospective and retroactive) was appropriate. However, the choice of methods was not supported by most respondents principally due to the lack of comparability that would result. Required application of a retroactive approach also had little appeal among respondents because of the practical problems for some employers. In particular, a retroactive determination of the balance of the

pension benefit obligation as of a past date would often require a new actuarial valuation as of that date. Many argued that such an approach would have been costly and might have been impracticable in some cases because relevant data no longer existed. Finally, many argued that a retroactive approach would have adverse consequences for some employers because of the materiality of pension amounts and the wide range of practices used under Opinion 8.

255. The Exposure Draft would have required amortization of the unrecognized net obligation or net asset on a declining basis over the service periods of employees active at the date of transition. Respondents argued that a declining basis amortization of that amount created year-to-year changes in net periodic pension cost that would reflect only transition and that for some companies with short average remaining service periods the transition would be unduly severe. The Board agreed and decided that the amortization required by this Statement would mitigate those concerns. That approach has the additional advantage that the transition will be completed somewhat earlier than would have been the case under the approach proposed in the Exposure Draft.

256. The Board continues to believe that transition is a practical matter and that a major objective of transition is to minimize the cost and to mitigate the disruption involved, to the extent that is possible without unduly compromising the objective of enhancing the ability of financial statements to provide useful information. The transition problem in this Statement is different from some others in several respects. The unrecognized net obligation or net asset described in paragraph 77 is the net total of several components: (a) unrecognized costs of past retroactive plan amendments, (b) unrecognized net gain or loss from previous periods, and (c) the cumulative effect of past use of accounting principles different from those in this Statement. If those components could be treated separately, it would be consistent with other provisions of this Statement to treat the last component as the effect of an account-

ing change (and to recognize it when this Statement is first applied), but prospective accounting (or delayed recognition) of the first two components is continued by this Statement. As a practical matter, the Board is convinced that it is effectively impossible, at least in many cases, to identify those components separately. Accordingly, the Board concluded that the single method of transition required by this Statement should be used.

257. Some respondents suggested that unrecognized amounts existing at transition should continue to be amortized using past methodologies. The Board noted that such a transition approach would result in delaying recognition of significant amounts for as much as 30 years and concluded that a less-extended transition was practical and preferable.

258. The Board also considered respondents' requests to clarify the appropriate procedures for transition to this Statement in other than the first interim period of a fiscal year. The Board agreed to do so and concluded that requiring restatement of previous interim periods would be appropriate and consistent with existing guidance in other areas.

259. The Board decided to allow more than the normal time between issuance of this Statement and its required application to give time for employers and their advisors to assimilate the requirements and to obtain the information required. The Board believes that a one-year delay is adequate for those purposes.

260. The Board also decided to allow an additional two years before employers are required to apply the provisions of this Statement that require recognition of a minimum liability because of concerns expressed by some respondents that some employers would have to arrange to renegotiate or to obtain waivers of provisions of some legal contracts. As noted previously, the Board also decided to allow an additional two years before employers are required to apply the provisions of this Statement to plans outside the U.S. and before certain smaller employers are required to apply those provisions.

ILLUSTRATIONS

261. This appendix contains illustrations of the following requirements of this Statement:

1. Delayed recognition and reconciliation of funded status
2. Transition
3. Amortization of unrecognized prior service cost
4. Accounting for gain or loss and timing of measurements
5. Recognition of pension liabilities, including minimum liability
6. Disclosure
7. Accounting for a business combination

Illustration 1—Delayed Recognition and Reconciliation of Funded Status

This Statement provides for delayed recognition of the effects of a number of types of events that change the measures of the projected benefit obligation and the fair value of plan assets. Those events include retroactive plan amendments and gains and losses. Gains and losses as defined in this Statement include the effects of changes in assumptions.

This Statement also requires disclosure of a reconciliation of the funded status of a plan to the net pension liability or asset recognized in the employers' financial statements. This illustration shows how that reconciliation provides information about items that have not been recognized due to delayed recognition. The illustration starts with an assumed funded status at the date of initial application of this Statement and shows how a series of events that change the obligation or the plan assets are reflected in the reconciliation. (Throughout this illustration the fair value of plan assets exceeds the accumulated benefit obligation and, therefore, no recognition of an additional minimum liability is required.)

Case 1—Company T at Transition

The reconciliation as of the date of initial application of this Statement is as follows:

Projected benefit obligation	$ (10,000)
Plan assets at fair value	6,500
Funded status	(3,500)
Unrecognized net (gain) or loss	0
Unrecognized prior service cost	0
Unrecognized net obligation or (net asset) at date of initial application	3,500
(Accrued)/prepaid pension cost	$ 0

The unrecognized net gain or loss and the unrecognized prior service cost are both initially zero by definition. The unrecognized net obligation or asset at transition is defined in paragraph 77 as the difference between the funded status and the accrued or prepaid pension cost already recognized. If, as in this case, the past contributions were equal to amounts recognized as net pension cost in past periods, there is no recognized accrued or prepaid pension cost in the statement of financial position and, therefore, the unrecognized net obligation or asset at transition is equal to the funded status.

Case 2—Past Contributions Lower by $400

If Company T had not made a contribution of $400 for the last year before the date of initial application but had recognized the same net periodic pension cost as in Case 1, the situation would be as follows:

Projected benefit obligation	$ (10,000)
Plan assets at fair value	6,100
Funded status	(3,900)
Unrecognized net (gain) or loss	0
Unrecognized prior service cost	0
Unrecognized net obligation or (net asset) at date of initial application	3,500
(Accrued)/prepaid pension cost	$ (400)

The unrecognized net obligation at transition is unchanged. It is the amount of the projected benefit obligation not yet recognized in net periodic pension cost and is not directly affected by funding decisions.

Case 3—Past Contributions Greater by $800

If, instead, the employer had made a contribution in excess of net periodic pension cost of $800, but the company had recognized the same net periodic pension cost as in Case 1, the reconciliation would be as follows:

Projected benefit obligation	$ (10,000)
Plan assets at fair value	7,300
Funded status	(2,700)
Unrecognized net (gain) or loss	0
Unrecognized prior service cost	0
Unrecognized net obligation or (net asset) at date of initial application	3,500
(Accrued)/prepaid pension cost	$ 800

After Initial Application

At any date after initial application, any change in the projected benefit obligation or the plan assets (other than contributions and benefit payments) either is unrecognized or has been included in net pension cost for some period. Contributions decrease the accrued pension cost or increase the prepaid pension cost, and benefit payments reduce the obligation and the plan assets equally. Thus, all changes in either the obligation or the assets are reflected in the reconciliation. Using Case 1 above as the starting point, the following reconciliations illustrate the effect of various events that change either the projected benefit obligation or the plan assets.

Case 4—Fair Value of Assets Increases by $400

	Before	After
Projected benefit obligation	$ (10,000)	$ (10,000)
Plan assets at fair value	6,500	6,900
Funded status	(3,500)	(3,100)
Unrecognized net (gain) or loss	0	(400)
Unrecognized prior service cost	0	0
Unrecognized net obligation or (net asset) at date of initial application	3,500	3,500
(Accrued)/prepaid pension cost	$ 0	$ 0

Case 5—Increase in Discount Rate Reduces Obligation by $900

	Before	After
Projected benefit obligation	$ (10,000)	$ (9,100)
Plan assets at fair value	6,500	6,500
Funded status	(3,500)	(2,600)
Unrecognized net (gain) or loss	0	(900)
Unrecognized prior service cost	0	0
Unrecognized net obligation or (net asset) at date of initial application	3,500	3,500
(Accrued)/prepaid pension cost	$ 0	$ 0

Case 6—Plan Amendment Increases the Obligation by $1,500

	Before	After
Projected benefit obligation	$ (10,000)	$ (11,500)
Plan assets at fair value	6,500	6,500
Funded status	(3,500)	(5,000)
Unrecognized net (gain) or loss	0	0
Unrecognized prior service cost	0	1,500
Unrecognized net obligation or (net asset) at date of initial application	3,500	3,500
(Accrued)/prepaid pension cost	$ 0	$ 0

Case 7—Employer Accrues Net Pension Cost

Net pension cost includes:

Service cost	$ 600
Interest cost	1,000
Amortization of initial unrecognized net obligation	233
Return on assets	(650)
	$ 1,183

No contribution is made.

	Before	After
Projected benefit obligation	$ (10,000)	$ (11,600)
Plan assets at fair value	6,500	7,150
Funded status	(3,500)	(4,450)
Unrecognized net (gain) or loss	0	0
Unrecognized prior service cost	0	0
Unrecognized net obligation or (net asset) at date of initial application	3,500	3,267
(Accrued)/prepaid pension cost	$ 0	$ (1,183)

Illustration 2—Transition

Case 1

As of December 31, 1985, the projected benefit obligation and plan assets of a noncontributory defined benefit plan sponsored by Company A were:

Projected benefit obligation	$ (1,500,000)
Plan assets at fair value	1,200,000
Initial unfunded obligation	$ (300,000)

Company A elected to apply the provisions of this Statement for its financial statements for the year ending December 31, 1986. At December 31, 1985,

no prepaid or accrued pension cost had been recognized in Company A's statement of financial position (that is, all amounts accrued as net periodic pension cost had been contributed to the plan). The average remaining service period of active plan participants expected to receive benefits was estimated to be 16 years at the date of transition. In this situation the initial unrecognized net obligation (and loss or cost) of $300,000 is to be amortized (recognized as a component of net periodic pension cost) on a straight-line basis over the average remaining service period of 16 years (paragraph 77) as follows:

Year	Beginning-of-Year Balance	Amortization[a]	End-of-Year Balance
1986	300,000	18,750	281,250
1987	281,250	18,750	262,500
1988	262,500	18,750	243,750
1989	243,750	18,750	225,000
1990	225,000	18,750	206,250
1991	206,250	18,750	187,500
1992	187,500	18,750	168,750
1993	168,750	18,750	150,000
1994	150,000	18,750	131,250
1995	131,250	18,750	112,500
1996	112,500	18,750	93,750
1997	93,750	18,750	75,000
1998	75,000	18,750	56,250
1999	56,250	18,750	37,500
2000	37,500	18,750	18,750
2001	18,750	18,750	0

Case 2

As of December 31, 1985, the projected benefit obligation and plan assets of a noncontributory defined benefit plan sponsored by Company B were:

Projected benefit obligation	$ (1,400,000)
Plan assets at fair value	1,600,000
Initial overfunded obligation	$ 200,000

Company B elected to apply the provisions of this Statement for its financial statements for the year ending December 31, 1986. In previous periods, Company B's plan was deemed to be fully funded for tax purposes, and the company decided not to make contributions that would not have been currently tax deductible. As a result, contributions were less than net pension cost for those periods, and the company had recognized unfunded accrued pension cost (a liability) of $150,000 at December 31, 1985.

The unrecognized net asset at transition defined in paragraph 77 consists of amounts previously charged to net pension cost in excess of the projected benefit obligation. Amounts charged to net pension cost in past periods include amounts contributed (plan assets) and amounts unfunded. In this case, at December 31, 1985 those amounts were:

Plan assets in excess of obligation	$ 200,000
Unfunded accrued pension cost	150,000
Unrecognized net asset	$ 350,000

The average remaining service period of active plan participants expected to receive benefits was estimated to be 10 years at the date of transition. In this situation, the initial unrecognized net asset of $350,000 may be amortized on a straight-line basis over either 10 years or 15 years (paragraph 77). That amortization will result in an annual credit to net periodic pension cost of either $35,000 or $23,333.

---

[a]300,000/16 = 18,750.

Illustration 3—Amortization of Unrecognized Prior Service Cost

Case 1—Assigning Equal Amounts to Future Years of Service

Determination of expected future years of service

The amortization of unrecognized prior service cost defined in paragraph 25 is based on the expected future years of service of participants active at the date of the amendment who are expected to receive benefits under the plan. Calculation of the expected future years of service considers population decrements based on the actuarial assumptions and is not weighted for benefits or compensation. Each expected future service year is assigned an equal share of the initially determined prior service cost. The portion of prior service cost to be recognized in each of the future years is determined by the service years rendered in that year.

The following chart illustrates the calculation of the expected future years of service for the defined benefit plan of Company E. At the date of the amendment (January 1, 1987), the company has 100 employees who are expected to receive benefits under the plan. Five percent of that group (5 employees) are expected to leave (either retire or quit) in each of the next 20 years. Employees hired after that date do not affect the amortization. Initial estimates of expected future years of service related to each amendment are subsequently adjusted only for a curtailment.

Determination of Expected Years of Service

Service Years Rendered in Each Year

Individuals	Future Service Years	Year 1	2	3	4	5	6	7	8	9	10	11	12	13	14	15	16	17	18	19	20
A1-A5	5	5																			
B1-B5	10	5	5																		
C1-C5	15	5	5	5																	
D1-D5	20	5	5	5	5																
E1-E5	25	5	5	5	5	5															
F1-F5	30	5	5	5	5	5	5														
G1-G5	35	5	5	5	5	5	5	5													
H1-H5	40	5	5	5	5	5	5	5	5												
I1-I5	45	5	5	5	5	5	5	5	5	5											
J1-J5	50	5	5	5	5	5	5	5	5	5	5										
K1-K5	55	5	5	5	5	5	5	5	5	5	5	5									
L1-L5	60	5	5	5	5	5	5	5	5	5	5	5	5								
M1-M5	65	5	5	5	5	5	5	5	5	5	5	5	5	5							
N1-N5	70	5	5	5	5	5	5	5	5	5	5	5	5	5	5						
O1-O5	75	5	5	5	5	5	5	5	5	5	5	5	5	5	5	5					
P1-P5	80	5	5	5	5	5	5	5	5	5	5	5	5	5	5	5	5				
Q1-Q5	85	5	5	5	5	5	5	5	5	5	5	5	5	5	5	5	5	5			
R1-R5	90	5	5	5	5	5	5	5	5	5	5	5	5	5	5	5	5	5	5		
S1-S5	95	5	5	5	5	5	5	5	5	5	5	5	5	5	5	5	5	5	5	5	
T1-T5	100	5	5	5	5	5	5	5	5	5	5	5	5	5	5	5	5	5	5	5	5
	1,050																				
Service Years Rendered		100	95	90	85	80	75	70	65	60	55	50	45	40	35	30	25	20	15	10	5
Amortization Fraction		$\frac{100}{1,050}$	$\frac{95}{1,050}$	$\frac{90}{1,050}$	$\frac{85}{1,050}$	$\frac{80}{1,050}$	$\frac{75}{1,050}$	$\frac{70}{1,050}$	$\frac{65}{1,050}$	$\frac{60}{1,050}$	$\frac{55}{1,050}$	$\frac{50}{1,050}$	$\frac{45}{1,050}$	$\frac{40}{1,050}$	$\frac{35}{1,050}$	$\frac{30}{1,050}$	$\frac{25}{1,050}$	$\frac{20}{1,050}$	$\frac{15}{1,050}$	$\frac{10}{1,050}$	$\frac{5}{1,050}$

Amortization of unrecognized prior service cost

On January 1, 1987, Company E granted retroactive credit for prior service pursuant to a plan amendment. This amendment generated unrecognized prior service cost of $750,000. The amortization of the unrecognized prior service cost resulting from the plan amendment is based on the expected future years of service of active participants as discussed in the previous paragraph.

Amortization of Unrecognized Prior Service Cost

Year	Beginning-of-Year Balance	Amortization Rate	Amortization	End-of-Year Balance
1987	750,000	100/1050	71,429	678,571
1988	678,571	95/1050	67,857	610,714
1989	610,714	90/1050	64,286	546,428
1990	546,428	85/1050	60,714	485,714
1991	485,714	80/1050	57,143	428,571
1992	428,571	75/1050	53,571	375,000
1993	375,000	70/1050	50,000	325,000
1994	325,000	65/1050	46,429	278,571
1995	278,571	60/1050	42,857	235,714
1996	235,714	55/1050	39,286	196,428
1997	196,428	50/1050	35,714	160,714
1998	160,714	45/1050	32,143	128,571
1999	128,571	40/1050	28,571	100,000
2000	100,000	35/1050	25,000	75,000
2001	75,000	30/1050	21,429	53,571
2002	53,571	25/1050	17,857	35,714
2003	35,714	20/1050	14,286	21,428
2004	21,428	15/1050	10,714	10,714
2005	10,714	10/1050	7,143	3,571
2006	3,571	5/1050	3,571	0

Case 2—Using Straight-Line Amortization over Average Remaining Service Period

Determination of expected future years of service

To reduce the complexity and detail of the computations shown in Illustration 3, Case 1, alternative amortization approaches that recognize the cost of retroactive amendments more quickly may be consistently used (paragraph 26). For example, a straight-line amortization of the cost over the average remaining service period of employees expected to receive benefits under the plan is acceptable.

If Company E (Case 1) had elected to use straight-line amortization over the average remaining service period of employees expected to receive benefits (1,050 future service years/100 employees = 10.5 years), the amortization would have been as follows:

Amortization of Unrecognized Prior Service Cost

Year	Beginning-of-Year Balance	Amortization[a]	End-of-Year Balance
1987	750,000	71,429	678,571
1988	678,571	71,429	607,142
1989	607,142	71,429	535,713
1990	535,713	71,429	464,284
1991	464,284	71,429	392,855
1992	392,855	71,429	321,426
1993	321,426	71,429	249,997
1994	249,997	71,429	178,568
1995	178,568	71,429	107,139
1996	107,139	71,429	35,710
1997	35,710	35,710	0

[a]750,000/10.5 = 71,429.

Illustration 4—Accounting for Gains and Losses and Timing of Measurements

The following shows the funded status of Company 1's pension plan at December 31, 1986 and its assumptions and expected components of net periodic pension cost for the following year (all amounts are in thousands):

DECEMBER 1986—INITIAL SITUATION

Assumptions:

Discount rate	10.00%		
Expected long-term rate of return on plan assets	10.00%		
Average remaining service	10 years		

	Actual 12/31/86	For 1987	Projected 12/31/87
Projected benefit obligation	$ (1,000)		$ (1,060)
Plan assets at fair value	800		880
Funded status	(200)		(180)
Unrecognized net obligation existing at January 1, 1987	200		180
Unrecognized prior service cost	0		0
Unrecognized net (gain) or loss	0		0
(Accrued)/prepaid	$ 0		$ 0
Service cost component		$ 60[a]	
Interest cost component		100	
Expected return on assets		(80)	
Amortization of:			
Unrecognized net obligation existing at January 1, 1987		20	
Unrecognized prior service cost		0	
Unrecognized net (gain) or loss		0	
Net cost		$ 100	
Contribution		$ 100	
Benefits paid		$ 100	

Company 1 elected to apply the provisions of this Statement as of January 1, 1987 rather than as of an earlier date. Also, the company elected to measure pension-related amounts as of year-end. Alternatively, the company could have chosen to make the measurements as of another date not earlier than September 30. (Throughout this illustration it is assumed that the fair value of plan assets exceeds the accumulated benefit obligation and, therefore, no recognition of an additional minimum liability is required. For simplicity, all contributions and benefit payments are assumed to occur on the last day of the year.)

---

[a]Throughout this illustration the service cost component is assumed as an input rather than calculated as part of the illustration.

1987—LIABILITY LOSS

When Company I's plan assets and obligations were measured at December 31, 1987, the amount of the projected benefit obligation was not equal to the expected amount. Because the discount rate had declined to 9 percent and for various other reasons not specifically identified, the projected benefit obligation was higher than had been projected (a loss had occurred). The results were as follows:

Assumptions:

Discount rate	10.00%	9.00%
Expected long-term rate of return on plan assets	10.00%	10.00%
Average remaining service	10 years	10 years

	Actual 12/31/86	For 1987	Projected 12/31/87	Actual 12/31/87	For 1988	Projected 12/31/88
Projected benefit obligation	$ (1,000)		$ (1,060)	$ (1,200)		$ (1,266)[b]
Plan assets at fair value	800		880	880		968[c]
Funded status	(200)		(180)	(320)		(298)
Unrecognized net obligation existing at January 1, 1987	200		180	180		160
Unrecognized prior service cost	0		0	0		0
Unrecognized net (gain) or loss	0		0	140		138
(Accrued)/prepaid	$ 0		$ 0	$ 0		$ 0
Service cost component		$ 60			$ 72	
Interest cost component		100			108	
Expected return on assets		(80)			(88)	
Market-related value of assets	$ 800			$ 880		
Actual return on assets—(increase)/decrease				(80)		
Amortization of:						
Unrecognized net obligation existing at January 1, 1987		20			20	
Unrecognized prior service cost		0			0	
Unrecognized net (gain) or loss		0[d]			2[d]	
Net cost		$ 100			$ 114	
Contribution		$ 100			$ 114	
Benefits paid		$ 100			$ 114	

The 1987 financial statements will include the following disclosures:

Cost Components	
Service cost	$ 60
Interest cost	100
Actual return on assets	(80)
Net amortization and deferral	20[e]
Net cost	$ 100

Reconciliation of Funded Status	
Projected benefit obligation	$ (1,200)
Plan assets at fair value	880
Funded status	(320)
Unrecognized net obligation existing at January 1, 1987	180
Unrecognized prior service cost	0
Unrecognized net (gain) or loss	140
(Accrued)/prepaid	$ 0[f]

[b](Actual projected benefit obligation at 12/31/87) + (service component) + (interest component) − (benefits paid).

[c](Actual plan assets at 12/31/87) + (expected return on assets) + (contributions) − (benefits paid).

[d]Paragraph 32 provides that net periodic pension cost may be based on unrecognized net gain or loss as of the beginning of the period. In the year of transition (1987) the beginning balance of unrecognized net gain or loss is zero by definition. The minimum amortization of unrecognized net gain or loss is calculated as follows:

	1987	1988
Unrecognized net (gain) or loss at 1/1	$ 0	$ 140
Plus asset gain or less asset loss not yet in market-related value of assets at 1/1— (fair value of plan assets) − (market-related value of plan assets)	0	0
Unrecognized net (gain) or loss subject to amortization	0	140
Corridor = 10% of the greater of projected benefit obligation or market-related value of assets at 1/1	100	120
Unrecognized net gain or loss outside corridor	0	20
× 1/average remaining service	0.10	0.10
Amortization	$ 0	$ 2

[e]The "net amortization and deferral" consists of:

Amortization of unrecognized net obligation existing at January 1, 1987	$ 20
Amortization of unrecognized prior service cost	0
Amortization of unrecognized net (gain) or loss	0
Asset gain/(loss) deferred	0
	$ 20

[f]The (accrued)/prepaid is the amount included in the company's statement of financial position. If the accumulated benefit obligation had been greater than the plan assets, an additional minimum liability would have been required and would have been shown as an additional item in this reconciliation.

1988—ASSET GAIN

When Company I's plan assets and obligations were measured at December 31, 1988, the amount of plan assets was not equal to the expected amount because of market performance better than the expected or assumed 10 percent. The results were as follows:

	Actual 12/31/87	For 1988	Projected 12/31/88	Actual 12/31/88	For 1989	Projected 12/31/89
Assumptions:						
Discount rate		9.00%			9.00%	
Expected long-term rate of return on plan assets		10.00%			10.00%	
Average remaining service		10 years			10 years	
Projected benefit obligation	$ (1,200)		$ (1,266)	$ (1,266)		$ (1,345)
Plan assets at fair value	880		968	1,068		1,167
Funded status	(320)		(298)	(198)		(178)
Unrecognized net obligation existing at January 1, 1987	180		160	160		140
Unrecognized prior service cost	0		0	0		0
Unrecognized net (gain) or loss	140		138	38		38
(Accrued)/prepaid	$ 0		$ 0	$ 0		$ 0
Service cost component		$ 72			$ 76	
Interest cost component		108			114	
Expected return on assets		(88)			(99)[g]	
Market-related value of assets	$ 880			$ 988[h]		
Actual return on assets—(increase)/decrease	(80)			(188)		
Amortization of:						
Unrecognized net obligation existing at January 1, 1987		20			20	
Unrecognized prior service cost		0			0	
Unrecognized net (gain) or loss		2[i]			0[j]	
Net cost		$ 114			$ 111	
Contribution		$ 114			$ 111	
Benefits paid		$ 114			$ 111	

The 1988 financial statements will include the following disclosures:

Cost Components

Service cost	$ 72
Interest cost	108
Actual return on assets	(188)
Net amortization and deferral	122j
Net cost	$ 114

Reconciliation of Funded Status

Projected benefit obligation	$ (1,266)
Plan assets at fair value	1,068
Funded status	(198)
Unrecognized net obligation existing at January 1, 1987	160
Unrecognized prior service cost	0
Unrecognized net (gain) or loss	38
(Accrued)/prepaid	$ 0

gExpected return on plan assets = (expected long-term rate of return on plan assets) × (market-related value of plan assets). If contributions occurred other than at the end of the year, market-related value would consider those amounts.

hMarket-related asset values may be calculated in a variety of ways. This example uses an approach that adds in 20% of each of the last five years' gains and losses. The only objective of the market-related calculation is to reduce the volatility of net pension cost.

Market-related value of assets at 1/1	$ 880
Expected return on assets	88
Contributions	114
Benefits paid	(114)
20% of last five years' asset gains and (losses)	20
Market-related value of assets at 12/31	$ 988

iAmortization of unrecognized net gain or loss is calculated as follows:

	1988	1989
Unrecognized net (gain) or loss at 1/1	$ 140	$ 38
Plus asset gain or less asset loss not yet in market-related value of assets at 1/1— (fair value of plan assets) – (market-related value of plan assets)	0	80
Unrecognized net (gain) or loss subject to amortization	140	118
Corridor = 10% of the greater of projected benefit obligation or market-related value of assets at 1/1	120	127
Unrecognized net (gain) or loss outside corridor	20	0
× 1/average remaining service	0.10	0.10
Amortization	$ 2	$ 0

jThe "net amortization and deferral" consists of:

Amortization of unrecognized net obligation existing at January 1, 1987	$ 20
Amortization of unrecognized prior service cost	0
Amortization of unrecognized net (gain) or loss	2
Asset gain/(loss) deferred	100
	$ 122

1989—ASSET LOSS AND LIABILITY GAIN

When Company I's plan assets and obligations were measured at December 31, 1989, both an asset loss and a liability gain were discovered.

Assumptions:

	Actual 12/31/88	For 1989	Projected 12/31/89	Actual 12/31/89	For 1990	Projected 12/31/90
Discount rate		9.00%			9.25%	
Expected long-term rate of return on plan assets		10.00%			10.00%	
Average remaining service		10 years			10 years	
Projected benefit obligation	$ (1,266)		$ (1,345)	$ (1,320)		$ (1,409)
Plan assets at fair value	1,068		1,167	1,097		1,206
Funded status	(198)		(178)	(223)		(203)
Unrecognized net obligation existing at January 1, 1987	160		140	140		120
Unrecognized prior service cost	0		0	0		0
Unrecognized net (gain) or loss	38		38	83		83
(Accrued)/prepaid	$ 0		$ 0	$ 0		$ 0
Service cost component		$ 76			$ 79	
Interest cost component		114			122	
Expected return on assets		(99)			(109)	
Market-related value of assets	$ 988			$ 1,093 [k]		
Actual return on assets—(increase)/decrease	(188)			(29)		
Amortization of:						
Unrecognized net obligation existing at January 1, 1987		20			20	
Unrecognized prior service cost		0			0	
Unrecognized net (gain) or loss		0 [l]			0 [l]	
Net cost		$ 111			$ 112	
Contribution		$ 111			$ 112	
Benefits paid		$ 111			$ 112	

The 1989 financial statements will include the following disclosures:

Cost Components

Service cost	$ 76
Interest cost	114
Actual return on assets	(29)
Net amortization and deferral	(50)^m
Net cost	$ 111

Reconciliation of Funded Status

Projected benefit obligation	$ (1,320)
Plan assets at fair value	1,097
Funded status	(223)
Unrecognized net obligation existing at January 1, 1987	140
Unrecognized prior service cost	0
Unrecognized net (gain) or loss	83
(Accrued)/prepaid	$ 0

^{k}Market-related asset values may be calculated in a variety of ways. This example uses an approach that adds in 20% of each of the last five years' gains and losses. The only objective of the market-related calculation is to reduce the volatility of net pension cost.

Market-related value of assets at 1/1	$ 988
Expected return on assets	99
Contributions	111
Benefits paid	(111)
20% of last five years' asset gains and (losses) = .20 (100 − 70) =	6
Market-related value of assets at 12/31	$ 1,093

^{l}Amortization of unrecognized net gain or loss is calculated as follows:

	1989	1990
Unrecognized net (gain) or loss at 1/1	$ 38	$ 83
Plus asset gain or less asset loss not yet in market-related value of assets at 1/1— (fair value of plan assets) − (market-related value of plan assets)	80	4
Unrecognized net (gain) or loss subject to amortization	118	87
Corridor = 10% of the greater of projected benefit obligation or market-related value of assets at 1/1	127	132
Unrecognized net (gain) or loss outside corridor	0	0
× 1/average remaining service	0.10	0.10
Amortization	$ 0	$ 0

^{m}The "net amortization and deferral" consists of:

Amortization of unrecognized net obligation existing at January 1, 1987	$ 20
Amortization of unrecognized prior service cost	0
Amortization of unrecognized net (gain) or loss	0
Asset gain/(loss) deferred	(70)
	$ (50)

Illustration 5—Recognition of Pension Liability, Including Minimum Liability

Case 1—Minimum Liability Less Than Unrecognized Prior Service Cost

Company K elected to apply the provisions of this Statement, including those requiring recognition of minimum liability, for its 1986 financial statements. The funded status of its plan for the years 1988 through 1991 is shown below.

	As of December 31,			
	1988	**1989**	**1990**	**1991**
		(in thousands)		
FUNDED STATUS—COMPANY K				
Assets and obligations:				
Accumulated benefit obligation	$ (1,254)	$ (1,628)	$ (1,616)	$ (1,554)
Plan assets at fair value	1,165	1,505	1,622	1,517
Unfunded accumulated benefits	$ (89)	$ (123)		$ (37)
Overfunded accumulated benefits			$ 6	
Projected benefit obligation	$ (1,879)	$ (2,442)	$ (2,424)	$ (2,331)
Plan assets at fair value	1,165	1,505	1,622	1,517
Items not yet recognized in earnings:				
Unrecognized net obligation (net asset)				
at January 1, 1986	280	260	240	220
Unrecognized prior service cost	715	1,314	1,172	1,039
Unrecognized net gain	(251)	(557)	(460)	(476)
(Accrued)/prepaid pension cost	$ 30	$ 80	$ 150	$ (31)
DETERMINATION OF AMOUNTS TO BE RECOGNIZED				
(Accrued)/prepaid pension cost at				
beginning of year	$ 0	$ 30	$ 80	$ 150
Net periodic pension cost	(304)	(335)	(397)	(361)
Contribution	334	385	467	180
(Accrued)/prepaid pension cost at				
end of year	$ 30	$ 80	$ 150	$ (31)
Required minimum liability (unfunded				
accumulated benefits)	$ (89)	$ (123)	$ 0	$ (37)
Adjustment required to reflect				
minimum liability:				
Additional liability[a]	$ (119)	$ (84)	$ 203	$ (6)
Intangible asset (not to exceed				
unrecognized prior service cost)	$ 119	$ 84	$ (203)	$ 6
Balance of additional liability	$ (119)	$ (203)	$ 0	$ (6)
Balance of intangible asset	$ 119	$ 203	$ 0	$ 6

---

[a]This amount is equal to unfunded accumulated benefits, plus prepaid (or minus accrued) pension cost, minus the previous balance. For financial statement presentation, the additional liability is combined with the (accrued)/prepaid pension cost.

Journal Entries

The journal entries required to reflect the accounting for the company's pension plan for the years 1988 through 1991 are as follows (in thousands):

Year 1988

Journal entry 1

Net periodic pension cost	304	
Accrued/prepaid pension cost		304

To record net pension cost for the period (paragraph 35)

Journal entry 2

Accrued/prepaid pension cost	334	
Cash		334

To record contribution (paragraph 35)

Journal entry 3

Intangible asset	119	
Additional liability		119

To record an additional liability to reflect the required minimum liability (For financial statement presentation, the additional liability account balance is combined with the accrued/prepaid pension cost account balance. Since prepaid pension cost of $30 has been recognized, an additional liability of $119 is needed to reflect the required minimum liability of $89 [equal to unfunded accumulated benefits]. Because the additional liability is less than unrecognized prior service cost, an intangible asset also is recognized.) (paragraphs 36 and 37)

Year 1989

Journal entry 1

Net periodic pension cost	335	
Accrued/prepaid pension cost		335

To record net pension cost for the period (paragraph 35)

Journal entry 2

Accrued/prepaid pension cost	385	
Cash		385

To record contribution (paragraph 35)

Journal entry 3

Intangible asset	84	
Additional liability		84

To adjust the additional liability to reflect the required minimum liability (For financial statement presentation, the additional liability account balance is combined with the accrued/prepaid pension cost account balance. The required minimum liability is determined independently of any prior years' amounts. Since unfunded accumulated benefits are $123 and a prepaid pension cost of $80 has been recognized, the amount of the additional liability is $203 or an increase of $84 from the previous period. Because the balance of the additional liability is less than unrecognized prior service cost, an intangible asset also is recognized.) (paragraphs 36 and 37)

Year 1990

Journal entry 1

Net periodic pension cost	397	
Accrued/prepaid pension cost		397

To record net pension cost for the period (paragraph 35)

Journal entry 2

Accrued/prepaid pension cost	467	
Cash		467

To record contribution (paragraph 35)

Journal entry 3

Additional liability	203	
Intangible asset		203

To reverse additional liability no longer required (Since plan assets exceed accumulated benefits, no additional liability is necessary.) (paragraph 38)

Year 1991

Journal entry 1

Net periodic pension cost	361	
Accrued/prepaid pension cost		361

To record net pension cost for the period (paragraph 35)

Journal entry 2

Accrued/prepaid pension cost	180	
Cash		180

    To record contribution (paragraph 35)

Journal entry 3

Intangible asset	6	
Additional liability		6

    To record an additional liability to reflect the required minimum liability amount (For financial statement presentation, the additional liability account balance is combined with the accrued/prepaid pension cost account balance. Since unfunded accumulated benefits of $37 exceed unfunded accrued pension cost of $31, recognition of an additional liability of $6 is necessary. Because the balance of additional liability is less than unrecognized prior service cost, an intangible asset also is recognized.) (paragraphs 36 and 37)

Case 2—*Minimum Liability in Excess of Unrecognized Prior Service Cost*

    Company L elected to apply the provisions of this Statement, including those requiring recognition of minimum liability, for its 1986 financial statements. The funded status of its plan for the years 1988 and 1989 is shown below.

	As of December 31,	
	1988	**1989**
	(in thousands)	
FUNDED STATUS— COMPANY L		
Assets and obligations:		
Accumulated benefit obligation	$ (1,270)	$ (1,290)
Plan assets at fair value	1,200	1,304
Unfunded accumulated benefits	$ (70)	
Overfunded accumulated benefits		$ 14

Projected benefit obligation	$ (1,720)	$ (1,807)
Plan assets at fair value	1,200	1,304
Items not yet recognized in earnings:		
Unrecognized prior service cost	92	86
Unrecognized net loss	486	497
(Accrued)/prepaid pension cost	$ 58	$ 80

DETERMINATION OF AMOUNTS TO BE RECOGNIZED

(Accrued)/prepaid pension cost at beginning of year	$ 0	$ 58
Net periodic pension cost	(141)	(144)
Contribution	199	166
(Accrued)/prepaid pension cost at end of year	$ 58	$ 80
Required minimum liability (unfunded accumulated benefits)	$ 70	$ 0
Adjustment required to reflect minimum liability:		
Additional liability[a]	$ (128)	$ 128
Intangible asset (not to exceed unrecognized prior service cost)	$ 92	$ (92)
Charge to equity (excess of additional pension liability over unrecognized prior service cost)	$ 36	$ (36)
Balance of additional liability	$ (128)	$ 0
Balance of intangible asset	$ 92	$ 0
Balance of equity account	$ 36	$ 0

Journal Entries

    The journal entries required to reflect the

---

[a]This amount is equal to unfunded accumulated benefits, plus prepaid (or minus accrued) pension cost, minus the previous balance. For financial statement presentation, the additional liability is combined with the (accrued)/prepaid pension cost.

accounting for the company's pension plan for the years 1988 and 1989 are as follows (in thousands):

Year 1988

Journal entry 1

Net periodic pension cost	141	
Accrued/prepaid pension cost		141

To record net pension cost for the period (paragraph 35)

Journal entry 2

Accrued/prepaid pension cost	199	
Cash		199

To record contribution (paragraph 35)

Journal entry 3

Excess of additional pension liability over unrecognized prior service cost	36	
Intangible asset	92	
Additional liability		128

To record an additional liability to reflect the required minimum liability (For financial statement presentation, the additional liability account balance is combined with the accrued/prepaid pension cost account balance. Since prepaid pension cost of $58 has been recognized, an additional liability of $128 is needed to reflect the required minimum liability of $70 [equal to unfunded accumulated benefits]. Because the additional liability is greater than unrecognized prior service cost, an intangible asset is recognized for the amount of additional liability up to the amount of unrecognized prior service cost, and equity is charged for the excess of the additional liability over unrecognized prior service cost.) (paragraphs 36 and 37)

Year 1989

Journal entry 1

Net periodic pension cost	144	
Accrued/prepaid pension cost		144

To record net pension cost for the period (paragraph 35)

Journal entry 2

Accrued/prepaid pension cost	166	
Cash		166

To record contribution (paragraph 35)

Journal entry 3

Additional liability	128	
Excess of additional pension liability over unrecognized prior service cost		36
Intangible asset		92

To reverse additional liability no longer required (Since plan assets exceed accumulated benefits, no additional liability is necessary.) (paragraph 38)

Illustration 6—Disclosure Requirements

Case 1—Simple Case

The following illustrates the disclosure for a sponsor with a single-employer defined benefit pension plan presenting only one year's financial statements.

Note P: The company has a defined benefit pension plan covering substantially all of its employees. The benefits are based on years of service and the employee's compensation during the last five years of employment. The company's funding policy is to contribute annually the maximum amount that can be deducted for federal income tax purposes. Contributions are intended to provide not only for benefits attributed to service to date but also for those expected to be earned in the future.

The following table sets forth the plan's funded status and amounts recognized in the company's statement of financial position at December 31, 1988 (in thousands):

Actuarial present value of benefit obligations:	
Accumulated benefit obligation, including vested benefits of $287	$ (335)
Projected benefit obligation for service rendered to date	$ (500)
Plan assets at fair value, primarily listed stocks and U.S. bonds	475
Projected benefit obligation in excess of plan assets	(25)
Unrecognized net gain from past experience different from that assumed and effects of changes in assumptions	(53)
Prior service cost not yet recognized in net periodic pension cost	19
Unrecognized net obligation at January 1, 1986 being recognized over 15 years	77
Prepaid pension cost included in other assets	$ 18

Net pension cost for 1988 included the following components (in thousands):

Service cost—benefits earned during the period	$ 26
Interest cost on projected benefit obligation	39
Actual return on plan assets	(45)
Net amortization and deferral[a]	10
Net periodic pension cost	$ 30

The weighted-average discount rate and rate of increase in future compensation levels used in determining the actuarial present value of the projected benefit obligation were 9 percent and 6 percent, respectively. The expected long-term rate of return on assets was 10 percent.

Case 2—Disclosures for Multiple Plans

Note S: The company and its subsidiaries have a number of noncontributory pension plans covering substantially all U.S. employees. Plans covering salaried and management employees provide pension benefits that are based on the employee's compensation during the three years before retirement. The company's funding policy for those plans is to contribute annually at a rate that is intended to remain a level percentage of compensation for the covered employees (presently 12.9 percent). Plans covering hourly employees and union members generally provide benefits of stated amounts for each year of service and provide for significant supplemental benefits for employees who retire with 30 years of service before age 65. The company's funding policy for those plans is to make the minimum annual contributions required by applicable regulations.

Net periodic pension cost for 1988 and 1987 included the following components (in thousands):

	1988	1987
Service cost—benefits earned during the period	$ 66	$ 66
Interest cost on projected benefit obligation	100	96
Actual return on assets	(79)	(63)
Net amortization and deferral	88	78
Net periodic pension cost	$ 175	$ 177

Assumptions used in the accounting were:

	As of December 31,	
	1988	1987
Discount rates	9.0%	8.75%
Rates of increase in compensation levels	6.0%	6.0%
Expected long-term rate of return on assets	9.5%	9.5%

The following table sets forth the plan's funded status and amounts recognized in the company's statement of financial position at December 31, 1988 and 1987, for its U.S. pension plans (in thousands):

---

[a]The net effects of delayed recognition of certain events (for example, unanticipated investment performance) arising during the current period and amortization (recognition) of the net unrecognized effects of past similar events at a rate based on employees' average remaining service life.

	December 31, 1988		December 31, 1987	
	Assets Exceed Accumulated Benefits	Accumulated Benefits Exceed Assets	Assets Exceed Accumulated Benefits	Accumulated Benefits Exceed Assets
Actuarial present value of benefit obligations:				
Vested benefit obligation	$ (298)	$ (385)	$ (268)	$ (363)
Accumulated benefit obligation	$ (339)	$ (442)	$ (311)	$ (427)
Projected benefit obligation[a]	$ (502)	$ (620)	$ (470)	$ (640)
Plan assets at fair value[b]	604	228	548	205
Projected benefit obligation (in excess of) or less than plan assets	102	(392)	78	(435)
Unrecognized net (gain) or loss	(114)	30	(117)	41
Prior service cost not yet recognized in net periodic pension cost	120	292	132	321
Unrecognized net obligation at January 1, 1986	180	225	200	250
Adjustment required to recognize minimum liability	0	(369)	0	(399)
Prepaid pension cost (pension liability) recognized in the statement of financial position	$ 288	$ (214)	$ 293	$ (222)

Case 3—Disclosure for a Defined Contribution Plan

Note T: The company sponsors a defined contribution pension plan covering substantially all of its employees in both its engine parts and tire subsidiaries. Contributions and cost are determined as 1.5 percent of each covered employee's salary and totaled $231,000 in 1987 and $215,000 in 1986.

Case 4—Disclosure for a Multiemployer Plan

Note W: One of the company's subsidiaries participates in a multiemployer plan. The plan provides defined benefits to substantially all unionized workers in the company's trucking subsidiary. Amounts charged to pension cost and contributed to the plan in 1987 and 1986 totaled $598,000 and $553,000, respectively.

[a]The projected benefit obligation and plan assets at December 31, 1988 and 1987 do not include amounts related to an annuity contract purchased from an affiliated company covering annual benefits of approximately $42.

[b]Plan assets include common stock of the company of $50 and $45 at December 31, 1988 and 1987, respectively. About half of the plan assets are invested in listed stocks and bonds. The balance is invested in income-producing real estate.

Illustration 7—Accounting for a Business Combination

The following example illustrates how the liability (or asset) recognized by the acquiring firm at the date of a business combination accounted for as a purchase would be reduced in years subsequent to the date of the business combination.

Company R purchased Company S on January 1, 1987. Company S sponsors a single-employer defined benefit pension plan. The reconciliation of funded status of the Company S plan before and after the combination was as follows (in thousands):

	Precombination	Postcombination
Pension benefit obligation	$ (1,000)	$ (1,000)
Plan assets at fair value	500	500
Unrecognized loss	200	0
Unrecognized prior service cost	300	0
Liability recognized in the statement of financial position—unfunded accrued pension cost	$　0	$　(500)

In subsequent periods, net periodic pension cost would not include any amortization of either the unrecognized prior service cost or the unrecognized loss existing at the date of the combination. However, the funding of the plan is not directly affected by a business combination. Whatever the basis of funding, it will, over time, reflect the past amendments and losses that underlie those amounts. As they are reflected in the funding process, contributions will, in some periods, exceed the net pension cost, and that will reduce the liability (unfunded accrued pension cost) recognized at the date of acquisition.

Appendix C

BACKGROUND

262. The Board added two pensions projects to its agenda in 1974: accounting and reporting by employee benefit plans and employers' accounting for pensions. Those projects were added to the agenda in response to both the passage of ERISA and certain criticisms concerning perceived deficiencies in Opinion 8. ERISA introduced changes in the legal status and in the perceived nature of an employer's obligation for pension benefits. Critics of Opinion 8 asserted that pension cost was not comparably measured from company to company and often not even from period to period for the same company and that Opinion 8 did not portray adequately the effect of a pension plan on a company. The ability of users of financial reports to understand and assess net periodic pension cost and the funded status of the employer's obligation was challenged because those amounts were determined using a variety of measurement methods or assumptions. Concerns were expressed about the reporting of both unfunded obligations and excess assets, especially when obligations had to be settled and when assets were withdrawn.

263. The following briefly outlines the steps taken on the two major pensions projects:

a. In December 1974, the Board issued Interpretation No. 3, *Accounting for the Cost of Pension Plans Subject to the Employee Retirement Income Security Act of 1974.* That Interpretation was issued to clarify the accounting for employers' obligations for pension plans covered by the Act, pending completion of the major project on employers' accounting for pensions.

b. Task forces for both projects were formed in early 1975.

c. An FASB Discussion Memorandum, *Accounting and Reporting for Employee Benefit Plans,* was issued in October 1975.

d. In February 1976, the Board held a public hearing on the issues covered in the Discussion Memorandum. Twenty-three presentations were made at the hearing.

e. In 1976, the Board decided to focus first on the employee benefit plans project because of the lack of any standards in that area. By deferring action on the accounting by employers project, the Board also expected to benefit from further progress on its conceptual framework project.

f. An FASB Exposure Draft, *Accounting and Reporting by Defined Benefit Pension Plans,* was issued in April 1977. The Board received approximately 700 comment letters, which indicated the need to further consider the issues.

g. In July 1979, the Board issued a revised Exposure Draft, *Accounting and Reporting by Defined Benefit Pension Plans.*

h. Also in July 1979, the Board issued an Exposure Draft, *Disclosure of Pension and Other Post-Retirement Benefit Information.* It proposed amending the disclosure requirements of Opinion 8 pending the Board's comprehensive consideration of accounting and reporting by employers for pensions and similar benefits.

i. In March 1980, the Board issued Statement No. 35, *Accounting and Reporting by Defined Benefit Pension Plans,* which addresses financial reporting by plans rather than by sponsoring employers.

j. In March 1980, the FASB also published *Accounting for Pensions by Employers: A Background Paper,* which highlighted the changing pension environment, present accounting practices and concerns, and areas for consideration.

k. In May 1980, the Board issued Statement No. 36, *Disclosure of Pension Information.* Statement 36 amended Opinion 8 and required disclosure of certain information based on the requirements of Statement 35. Statement 36 made no change in the basic provisions of Opinion 8 that governed measurement of pension cost and pension liabilities. The Statement was an interim step pending completion of the major project on employers' accounting for pensions.

l. In February 1981, the Board issued a Discussion Memorandum, *Employers' Accounting for Pensions and Other Postemployment Benefits.* That memorandum analyzes basic issues related to accounting and reporting requirements for only single-employer, noninsured, defined benefit pension plans in the United States. One hundred ninety-three letters of comment were received in response to the Discussion Memorandum.

m. In July 1981, the Board held a public hearing on the issues covered in the February 1981 Discussion Memorandum. Thirty-seven presentations were made at the hearing.

n. In April 1982, the Board issued Statement No. 59, *Deferral of the Effective Date of Certain Accounting Requirements for Pension Plans of State and Local Governmental Units.* Statement 59 amended Statement 35 and deferred that Statement's effective date for plans sponsored by state or local governments.

o. In November 1982, the Board issued *Preliminary Views* on the issues addressed in the February 1981 Discussion Memorandum. That document was issued to obtain comments on the Board's tentative conclusions at that time before proceeding to an Exposure Draft.

p. In April 1983, the Board issued a Discussion Memorandum, *Employers' Accounting for Pensions and Other Postemployment Benefits,* on additional issues that were not addressed in the February 1981 Discussion Memorandum or in *Preliminary Views.* Over 500 comment letters were received on that document and *Preliminary Views.*

q. In cooperation with the Financial Executives Institute's Committee on Corporate Reporting, the Board conducted a field test of the accounting proposals in *Preliminary Views* and published a special report of the results in October 1983.

r. In November 1983, the Board issued FASB Statement No. 75, *Deferral of the Effective Date of Certain Accounting Requirements for Pension Plans of State and Local Governmental Units,* indefinitely deferring the requirements of Statement 35 for pension plans of state and local governments pending further action by the Board.

s. In January 1984, the Board held a public hearing on the issues covered in *Preliminary Views* and the April 1983 Discussion Memorandum. Fifty-nine presentations were made at the hearing.

t. In February 1984, accounting for postemployment benefits other than pensions was made a separate agenda project. Until that time, other postemployment benefits issues had been combined with the project on employers' accounting for pensions and were addressed in the documents issued as part of that project. In July 1984, the Board issued an Exposure Draft, *Disclosure of Postretirement Health Care and Life Insurance Benefits Information.*

u. In November 1984, as an interim measure pending completion of the project, the Board issued Statement No. 81, *Disclosure of Postretirement Health Care and Life Insurance Benefits.*

v. An FASB Exposure Draft, *Employers' Accounting for Pensions,* was issued in March 1985. It proposed standards of financial accounting and reporting for an employer that offers pension benefits to its employees. The Board received over 400 comment letters.

w. An FASB Exposure Draft, *Employers' Accounting for Settlements and Curtailments of Defined Benefit Pension Plans and for Termination Benefits,* was issued in June 1985. The Board received over 100 comment letters.

x. In July and August 1985, the Board held a public hearing on the issues covered in the March 1985 and June 1985 Exposure Drafts. Fifty-six presentations were made at the hearing.

Appendix D

GLOSSARY

264. This appendix contains definitions of certain terms used in accounting for pensions.

Accumulated benefit obligation
The actuarial present value of benefits (whether vested or nonvested) attributed by the pension benefit formula to employee service rendered before a specified date and based on employee service and compensation (if applicable) prior to that date. The accumulated benefit obligation differs from the projected benefit obligation in that it includes no assumption about future compensation levels. For plans with flat-benefit or non-pay-related pension benefit formulas, the accumulated benefit obligation and the projected benefit obligation are the same.

Actual return on plan assets component
(of net periodic pension cost)
The difference between fair value of plan assets at the end of the period and the fair value at the beginning of the period, adjusted for contributions and payments of benefits during the period.

Actuarial funding method
Any of several techniques that actuaries use in determining the amounts and incidence of employer contributions to provide for pension benefits.

Actuarial gain or loss
See **Gain or loss.**

Actuarial present value
The value, as of a specified date, of an amount or series of amounts payable or receivable thereafter, with each amount adjusted to reflect (a) the time value of money (through discounts for interest) and (b) the probability of payment (by means of decrements for events such as death, disability, withdrawal, or retirement) between the specified date and the expected date of payment.

Allocated contract
A contract with an insurance company under which payments to the insurance company are currently used to purchase immediate or deferred annuities for individual participants. See also **Annuity contract.**

Amortization
Usually refers to the process of reducing a recognized liability systematically by recognizing reve-nues or reducing a recognized asset systematically by recognizing expenses or costs. In pension accounting, amortization is also used to refer to the systematic recognition in net pension cost over several periods of previously *unrecognized* amounts, including unrecognized prior service cost and unrecognized net gain or loss.

Annuity contract
A contract in which an insurance company unconditionally undertakes a legal obligation to provide specified pension benefits to specific individuals in return for a fixed consideration or premium. An annuity contract is irrevocable and involves the transfer of significant risk from the employer to the insurance company. Annuity contracts are also called allocated contracts.

Assumptions
Estimates of the occurrence of future events affecting pension costs, such as mortality, with-drawal, disablement and retirement, changes in compensation and national pension benefits, and discount rates to reflect the time value of money.

Attribution
The process of assigning pension benefits or cost to periods of employee service.

Benefit approach
One of two groups of basic approaches to attrib-uting pension benefits or costs to periods of employee service. Approaches in this group assign a distinct unit of benefit to each year of credited service. The actuarial present value of that unit of benefit is computed separately and determines the cost assigned to that year. The accumulated benefits approach, benefit/compensation approach, and benefit/years-of-service approach are benefit approaches.

Benefit formula
See **Pension benefit formula.**

Benefits
Payments to which participants may be entitled under a pension plan, including pension bene-fits, death benefits, and benefits due on ter-mination of employment.

Benefit/years-of-service approach
One of three benefit approaches. Under this approach, an equal portion of the total esti-mated benefit is attributed to each year of ser-vice. The actuarial present value of the benefits is derived after the benefits are attributed to the periods.

Captive insurance subsidiary
An insurance company that does business primarily with related entities.

Career-average-pay formula (Career-average-pay plan)
A benefit formula that bases benefits on the employee's compensation over the entire period of service with the employer. A career-average-pay plan is a plan with such a formula.

Contributory plan
A pension plan under which employees contribute part of the cost. In some contributory plans, employees wishing to be covered must contribute; in other contributory plans, employee contributions result in increased benefits.

Cost approach
One of the two groups of basic approaches to attributing pension benefits or costs to periods of service. Approaches in this group assign net pension costs to periods as level amounts or constant percentages of compensation.

Cost/compensation approach
One of two cost approaches. Net pension costs under this approach are attributed to periods so that they are a constant percentage of compensation for each period.

Curtailment
See **Plan curtailment.**

Defined benefit pension plan
A pension plan that defines an amount of pension benefit to be provided, usually as a function of one or more factors such as age, years of service, or compensation. Any pension plan that is not a defined contribution pension plan is, for purposes of this Statement, a defined benefit pension plan.

Defined contribution pension plan
A plan that provides pension benefits in return for services rendered, provides an individual account for each participant, and specifies how contributions to the individual's account are to be determined instead of specifying the amount of benefits the individual is to receive. Under a defined contribution pension plan, the benefits a participant will receive depend solely on the amount contributed to the participant's account, the returns earned on investments of those contributions, and forfeitures of other participants' benefits that may be allocated to such participant's account.

Discount rate
The interest rate used to adjust for the time value of money. See also **Actuarial present value.**

ERISA
The Employee Retirement Income Security Act of 1974.

Expected long-term rate of return on plan assets
An assumption as to the rate of return on plan assets reflecting the average rate of earnings expected on the funds invested or to be invested to provide for the benefits included in the projected benefit obligation.

Expected return on plan assets
An amount calculated as a basis for determining the extent of delayed recognition of the effects of changes in the fair value of assets. The expected return on plan assets is determined based on the expected long-term rate of return on plan assets and the market-related value of plan assets.

Explicit approach to assumptions
An approach under which each significant assumption used reflects the best estimate of the plan's future experience solely with respect to that assumption. See also **Implicit approach to assumptions.**

Fair value
The amount that a pension plan could reasonably expect to receive for an investment in a current sale between a willing buyer and a willing seller, that is, other than in a forced or liquidation sale.

Final-pay formula (Final-pay plan)
A benefit formula that bases benefits on the employee's compensation over a specified number of years near the end of the employee's service period or on the employee's highest compensation periods. For example, a plan might provide annual pension benefits equal to 1 percent of the employee's average salary for the last five years (or the highest consecutive five years) for each year of service. A final-pay plan is a plan with such a formula.

Flat-benefit formula (Flat-benefit plan)
A benefit formula that bases benefits on a fixed amount per year of service, such as $20 of monthly retirement income for each year of credited service. A flat-benefit plan is a plan with such a formula.

Fund

Used as a verb, to pay over to a funding agency (as to fund future pension benefits or to fund pension cost). Used as a noun, assets accumulated in the hands of a funding agency for the purpose of meeting pension benefits when they become due.

Funding method

See **Actuarial funding method.**

Funding policy

The program regarding the amounts and timing of contributions by the employer(s), participants, and any other sources (for example, state subsidies or federal grants) to provide the benefits a pension plan specifies.

Gain or loss

A change in the value of either the projected benefit obligation or the plan assets resulting from experience different from that assumed or from a change in an actuarial assumption. See also **Unrecognized net gain or loss.**

Gain or loss component (of net periodic pension cost)

The sum of (a) the difference between the actual return on plan assets and the expected return on plan assets and (b) the amortization of the unrecognized net gain or loss from previous periods. The gain or loss component is the net effect of delayed recognition of gains and losses (the net change in the unrecognized net gain or loss) except that it does not include changes in the projected benefit obligation occurring during the period and deferred for later recognition.

Implicit approach to assumptions

An approach under which two or more assumptions do not individually represent the best estimate of the plan's future experience with respect to those assumptions. Instead, the aggregate effect of their combined use is presumed to be approximately the same as that produced by an explicit approach.

Interest cost component (of net periodic pension cost)

The increase in the projected benefit obligation due to passage of time.

Interest rate

See **Discount rate.**

Loss

See **Gain or loss.**

Market-related value of plan assets

A balance used to calculate the expected return on plan assets. Market-related value can be either fair market value or a calculated value that recognizes changes in fair value in a systematic and rational manner over not more than five years. Different ways of calculating market-related value may be used for different classes of assets, but the manner of determining market-related value shall be applied consistently from year to year for each asset class.

Measurement date

The date as of which plan assets and obligations are measured.

Mortality rate

The proportion of the number of deaths in a specified group to the number living at the beginning of the period in which the deaths occur. Actuaries use mortality tables, which show death rates for each age, in estimating the amount of pension benefits that will become payable.

Multiemployer plan

A pension plan to which two or more unrelated employers contribute, usually pursuant to one or more collective-bargaining agreements. A characteristic of multiemployer plans is that assets contributed by one participating employer may be used to provide benefits to employees of other participating employers since assets contributed by an employer are not segregated in a separate account or restricted to provide benefits only to employees of that employer. A multiemployer plan is usually administered by a board of trustees composed of management and labor representatives and may also be referred to as a "joint trust" or "union" plan. Generally, many employers participate in a multiemployer plan, and an employer may participate in more than one plan. The employers participating in multiemployer plans usually have a common industry bond, but for some plans the employers are in different industries and the labor union may be their only common bond.

Multiple-employer plan

A pension plan maintained by more than one employer but not treated as a multiemployer plan. Multiple-employer plans are not as prevalent as single-employer and multiemployer plans, but some of the ones that do exist are large and involve many employers. Multiple-employer plans are generally not collectively bargained and are intended to allow participating employers, commonly in the same industry, to pool their assets for investment purposes and reduce the costs of plan administration. A multiple-employer plan maintains separate accounts for each employer so that contributions provide benefits only for employees of the contributing employer. Some multiple-employer plans have features that allow participating employers to have different benefit formulas, with the employer's contributions to the plan based on the benefit formula selected by the employer.

Net periodic pension cost

The amount recognized in an employer's financial statements as the cost of a pension plan for a period. Components of net periodic pension cost are service cost, interest cost, actual return on plan assets, gain or loss, amortization of unrecognized prior service cost, and amortization of the unrecognized net obligation or asset existing at the date of initial application of this Statement. This Statement uses the term *net periodic pension cost* instead of *net pension expense* because part of the cost recognized in a period may be capitalized along with other costs as part of an asset such as inventory.

Nonparticipating annuity contract

An annuity contract that does not provide for the purchaser to participate in the investment performance or in other experience of the insurance company. See also **Annuity contract.**

Nonpublic enterprise

An enterprise other than one (a) whose debt or equity securities are traded in a public market, either on a stock exchange or in the over-the-counter market (including securities quoted only locally or regionally), or (b) whose financial statements are filed with a regulatory agency in preparation for the sale of any class of securities.

Participant

Any employee or former employee, or any member or former member of a trade or other employee association, or the beneficiaries of those individuals, for whom there are pension plan benefits.

Participating annuity contract

An annuity contract that provides for the purchaser to participate in the investment performance and possibly other experience (for example, mortality experience) of the insurance company.

Participation right

A purchaser's right under a participating contract to receive future dividends or retroactive rate credits from the insurance company.

PBGC

The Pension Benefit Guaranty Corporation.

Pension benefit formula (plan's benefit formula or benefit formula)

The basis for determining payments to which participants may be entitled under a pension plan. Pension benefit formulas usually refer to the employee's service or compensation or both.

Pension benefits

Periodic (usually monthly) payments made pursuant to the terms of the pension plan to a person who has retired from employment or to that person's beneficiary.

Plan amendment

A change in the terms of an existing plan or the initiation of a new plan. A plan amendment may increase benefits, including those attributed to years of service already rendered. See also **Retroactive benefits.**

Plan assets

Assets—usually stocks, bonds, and other investments—that have been segregated and restricted (usually in a trust) to provide benefits. Plan assets include amounts contributed by the employer (and by employees for a contributory plan) and amounts earned from investing the contributions, less benefits paid. Plan assets cannot ordinarily be withdrawn by the employer except in certain circumstances when a plan has assets in excess of obligations and the employer has taken certain steps to satisfy existing obligations. For purposes of this Statement, assets not segregated in a trust or otherwise effectively restricted so that they cannot be used by the employer for other purposes are not plan assets even though it may be intended that such assets be used to provide pensions. Amounts accrued by the employer as net periodic pension cost but not yet paid to the plan are not plan assets for purposes of this Statement. Securities of the employer held by the plan are includable in plan assets provided they are transferable. If a plan has liabilities other than for benefits, those non-benefit obligations may be considered as reductions of plan assets for purposes of this Statement.

Plan assets available for benefits

See **Plan assets.**

Plan curtailment

An event that significantly reduces the expected years of future service of present employees or eliminates for a significant number of employees the accrual of defined benefits for some or all of their future services.

Plan's benefit formula
See **Pension benefit formula.**

Plan suspension
An event in which the pension plan is frozen and no further benefits accrue. Future service may continue to be the basis for vesting of nonvested benefits existing at the date of suspension. The plan may still hold assets, pay benefits already accrued, and receive additional employer contributions for any unfunded benefits. Employees may or may not continue working for the employer.

Plan termination
An event in which the pension plan ceases to exist and all benefits are settled by purchase of annuities or other means. The plan may or may not be replaced by another plan. A plan termination with a replacement plan may or may not be in substance a plan termination for accounting purposes.

Prepaid pension cost
Cumulative employer contributions in excess of accrued net pension cost.

Prior service cost
The cost of retroactive benefits granted in a plan amendment. See also **Unrecognized prior service cost.**

Projected benefit obligation
The actuarial present value as of a date of all benefits attributed by the pension benefit formula to employee service rendered prior to that date. The projected benefit obligation is measured using assumptions as to future compensation levels if the pension benefit formula is based on those future compensation levels (pay-related, final-pay, final-average-pay, or career-average-pay plans).

Retroactive benefits
Benefits granted in a plan amendment (or initiation) that are attributed by the pension benefit formula to employee services rendered in periods prior to the amendment. The cost of the retroactive benefits is referred to as prior service cost.

Return on plan assets
See **Actual return on plan assets component** and **Expected return on plan assets.**

Service
Employment taken into consideration under a pension plan. Years of employment before the inception of a plan constitute an employee's past service; years thereafter are classified in relation to the particular actuarial valuation being made or discussed. Years of employment (including past service) prior to the date of a particular valuation constitute prior service; years of employment following the date of the valuation constitute future service; a year of employment adjacent to the date of valuation, or in which such date falls, constitutes current service.

Service cost component (of net periodic pension cost)
The actuarial present value of benefits attributed by the pension benefit formula to services rendered by employees during that period. The service cost component is a portion of the projected benefit obligation and is unaffected by the funded status of the plan.

Settlement
An irrevocable action that relieves the employer (or the plan) of primary responsibility for a pension benefit obligation and eliminates significant risks related to the obligation and the assets used to effect the settlement. Examples of transactions that constitute a settlement include (a) making lump-sum cash payments to plan participants in exchange for their rights to receive specified pension benefits and (b) purchasing nonparticipating annuity contracts to cover vested benefits.

Single-employer plan
A pension plan that is maintained by one employer. The term also may be used to describe a plan that is maintained by related parties such as a parent and its subsidiaries.

Sponsor
In the case of a pension plan established or maintained by a single employer, the employer; in the case of a plan established or maintained by an employee organization, the employee organization; in the case of a plan established or maintained jointly by two or more employers or by one or more employers and one or more employee organizations, the association, committee, joint board of trustees, or other group of representatives of the parties who have established or who maintain the pension plan.

Turnover
Termination of employment for a reason other than death or retirement.

Unallocated contract
A contract with an insurance company under which payments to the insurance company are accumulated in an unallocated fund (not allocated to specific plan participants) to be used either directly or through the purchase of

annuities, to meet benefit payments when employees retire. Funds held by the insurance company under an unallocated contract may be withdrawn and otherwise invested.

Unfunded accrued pension cost
Cumulative net pension cost accrued in excess of the employer's contributions.

Unfunded accumulated benefit obligation
The excess of the accumulated benefit obligation over plan assets.

Unfunded projected benefit obligation
The excess of the projected benefit obligation over plan assets.

Unrecognized net gain or loss
The cumulative net gain or loss that has not been recognized as a part of net periodic pension cost. See **Gain or loss.**

Unrecognized prior service cost
That portion of prior service cost that has not been recognized as a part of net periodic pension cost.

Vested benefit obligation
The actuarial present value of vested benefits.

Vested benefits
Benefits for which the employee's right to receive a present or future pension benefit is no longer contingent on remaining in the service of the employer. (Other conditions, such as inadequacy of the pension fund, may prevent the employee from receiving the vested benefit.) Under graded vesting, the initial vested right may be to receive in the future a stated percentage of a pension based on the number of years of accumulated credited service; thereafter, the percentage may increase with the number of years of service or of age until the right to receive the entire benefit has vested.

Statement of Financial Accounting Standards No. 88
Employers' Accounting for Settlements and
Curtailments of Defined Benefit Pension Plans
and for Termination Benefits

STATUS

Issued: December 1985

Effective Date: For events occurring in fiscal years beginning with the fiscal year in which Statement 87 is first applied

Affects: Supersedes FAS 74

Affected by: No other pronouncements

Other Interpretive Release: FASB Special Report, *A Guide to Implementation of Statement 88 on Employers' Accounting for Settlements and Curtailments of Defined Benefit Pension Plans and for Termination Benefits: Questions and Answers*

Issues Discussed by FASB Emerging Issues Task Force (EITF)

Affects: Nullifies EITF Issues No. 84-6 and 85-10
Resolves EITF Issue No. 84-44

Interpreted by: No EITF Issues

Related Issues: EITF Issues No. 91-7, 94-3, 95-14, and 96-5 and Topic No. D-27

SUMMARY

This Statement establishes standards for an employer's accounting for settlement of defined benefit pension obligations, for curtailment of a defined benefit pension plan, and for termination benefits. This Statement is closely related to FASB Statement No. 87, *Employer's Accounting for Pensions,* and should be considered in that context.

Statement 87 continues the past practice of delaying the recognition in net periodic pension cost of (a) gains and losses from experience different from that assumed, (b) the effects of changes in assumptions, and (c) the cost of retroactive plan amendments. However, this Statement requires immediate recognition of certain previously unrecognized amounts when certain transactions or events occur. It prescribes the method for determining the amount to be recognized in earnings when a pension obligation is settled or a plan is curtailed. Settlement is defined as an irrevocable action that relieves the employer (or the plan) of primary responsibility for an obligation and eliminates significant risks related to the obligation and the assets used to effect the settlement. A curtailment is defined as a significant reduction in, or an elimination of, defined benefit accruals for present employees' future services.

This Statement incorporates, with certain modifications, existing standards on employers' accounting for termination benefits paid to employees, and supersedes FASB Statement No. 74, *Accounting for Special Termination Benefits Paid to Employees.*

Prior to this Statement, an employer that entered into an asset reversion transaction involving the termination of one plan and establishment of a successor defined benefit plan was precluded from immediately recognizing any resulting gain in earnings. This Statement specifies how that employer should determine the gain to be recognized in earnings at the time of initial application of Statement 87.

Employers' Accounting for Settlements and
Curtailments of Defined Benefit Pension Plans **FAS88**
and for Termination Benefits

Statement of Financial Accounting Standards No. 88

Employers' Accounting for Settlements and Curtailments of Defined Benefit Pension Plans and for Termination Benefits

CONTENTS

INTRODUCTION

1. This Statement addresses an employer's accounting for a settlement or a curtailment of its defined benefit pension plan and for termination benefits. The conclusions reached in this Statement have been adopted within the general framework for accounting for pensions as set forth in FASB Statement No. 87, *Employers' Accounting for Pensions.*

STANDARDS OF FINANCIAL ACCOUNTING AND REPORTING

Scope

2. This Statement applies to an employer that sponsors a defined benefit pension plan accounted for under the provisions of Statement 87 if all or part of the plan's pension benefit obligation is settled or the plan is curtailed. It also applies to an employer that offers benefits to employees in connection with their termination of employment.

Definitions

Settlement

3. For purposes of this Statement, a *settlement* is defined as a transaction that (a) is an irrevocable action, (b) relieves the employer (or the plan) of primary responsibility for a pension benefit obligation, and (c) eliminates significant risks related to the obligation and the assets used to effect the settlement. Examples of transactions that constitute a settlement include (a) making lump-sum cash payments to plan participants in exchange for their rights to receive specified pension benefits and (b) purchasing nonparticipating annuity contracts to cover vested benefits.

4. A transaction that does not meet all of the above three criteria does not constitute a settlement for purposes of this Statement. For example, investing in a portfolio of high-quality fixed-income securities with principal and interest payment dates similar to the estimated payment dates of benefits may avoid or minimize certain risks. However, that does not constitute a settlement because the investment decision can be reversed and such a strategy does not relieve the employer (or the plan) of primary responsibility for a pension obligation nor does it eliminate significant risks related to the obligation.

Annuity Contract

5. An *annuity contract* is a contract in which an insurance company[1] unconditionally undertakes a

---

[1] If the insurance company is controlled by the employer, or if there is any reasonable doubt that the insurance company will meet its obligations under the contract, the purchase of the contract does not constitute a settlement for purposes of this Statement.

legal obligation to provide specified benefits to specific individuals in return for a fixed consideration or premium. An annuity contract is irrevocable and involves the transfer of significant risk from the employer to the insurance company. Some annuity contracts (participating annuity contracts) provide that the purchaser (either the plan or the employer) may participate in the experience of the insurance company. Under those contracts, the insurance company ordinarily pays dividends to the purchaser. If the substance of a participating annuity contract is such that the employer remains subject to all or most of the risks and rewards associated with the benefit obligation covered or the assets transferred to the insurance company, the purchase of the contract does not constitute a settlement.

Curtailment

6. For purposes of this Statement, a *curtailment* is an event that significantly reduces the expected years of future service of present employees or eliminates for a significant number of employees the accrual of defined benefits for some or all of their future services. Curtailments include:

a. Termination of employees' services earlier than expected, which may or may not involve closing a facility or discontinuing a segment of a business
b. Termination or suspension of a plan so that employees do not earn additional defined benefits for future services. In the latter situation, future service may be counted toward vesting of benefits accumulated based on past service.

Relationship of Settlements and Curtailments to Other Events

7. A settlement and a curtailment may occur separately or together. If benefits to be accumulated in future periods are reduced (for example, because half of a work force is dismissed or a plant is closed) but the plan remains in existence and continues to pay benefits, to invest assets, and to receive contributions, a curtailment has occurred but not a settlement. If an employer purchases nonparticipating annuity contracts for vested benefits and continues to provide defined benefits for future service, either in the same plan or in a successor plan, a settlement

has occurred but not a curtailment. If a plan is terminated (that is, the obligation is settled and the plan ceases to exist) and not replaced by a successor defined benefit plan, both a settlement and a curtailment have occurred (whether or not the employees continue to work for the employer).

8. Paragraphs 9-15 of this Statement describe the accounting for a settlement, a plan curtailment, and for termination benefits that are not directly related to a disposal of a segment of a business. Paragraph 16 addresses the accounting if those events are directly related to a disposal of a segment of a business.

Accounting for Settlement of the Pension Obligation

9. For purposes of this Statement, the maximum gain or loss subject to recognition in earnings when a pension obligation is settled is the unrecognized net gain or loss defined in paragraph 29 of Statement 87[2] plus any remaining unrecognized net asset existing at the date of initial application of Statement 87 (as discussed in paragraph 21 of this Statement). That maximum amount includes any gain or loss first measured at the time of settlement. The maximum amount shall be recognized in earnings if the entire projected benefit obligation is settled. If only part of the projected benefit obligation is settled, the employer shall recognize in earnings a pro rata portion of the maximum amount equal to the percentage reduction in the projected benefit obligation.

10. If the purchase of a participating annuity contract constitutes a settlement, the maximum gain (but not the maximum loss) shall be reduced by the cost of the participation right before determining the amount to be recognized in earnings.

11. If the cost of all settlements[3] in a year is less than or equal to the sum of the service cost and interest cost components of net periodic pension cost for the plan for the year, gain or loss recognition is permitted but not required for those settlements. However, the accounting policy adopted shall be applied consistently from year to year.

---

[2] Paragraph 29 of Statement 87 states:

> *Gains and losses* are changes in the amount of either the projected benefit obligation or plan assets resulting from experience different from that assumed and from changes in assumptions. This Statement does not distinguish between those sources of gains and losses. Gains and losses include amounts that have been realized, for example by sale of a security, as well as amounts that are unrealized. Because gains and losses may reflect refinements in estimates as well as real changes in economic values and because some gains in one period may be offset by losses in another or vice versa, this Statement does not require recognition of gains and losses as components of net pension cost of the period in which they arise. [Footnote reference omitted.]

[3] For the following types of settlements, the cost of the settlement is:
a. For a cash settlement, the amount of cash paid to employees
b. For a settlement using nonparticipating annuity contracts, the cost of the contracts
c. For a settlement using participating annuity contracts, the cost of the contracts less the amount attributed to participation rights. (Refer to paragraph 61 of Statement 87.)

Accounting for a Plan Curtailment

12. The unrecognized prior service cost associated with years of service no longer expected to be rendered as the result of a curtailment is a loss. For example, if a curtailment eliminates half of the estimated remaining future years of service of those who were employed at the date of a prior plan amendment and were expected to receive benefits under the plan, then the loss associated with the curtailment is half of the remaining unrecognized prior service cost related to that plan amendment. For purposes of applying the provisions of this paragraph, unrecognized prior service cost includes the cost of retroactive plan amendments (refer to paragraphs 24-25 of Statement 87) and any remaining unrecognized net obligation existing at the date of initial application of Statement 87 (as discussed in paragraph 21 of this Statement).

13. The projected benefit obligation may be decreased (a gain) or increased (a loss) by a curtailment.[4]

a. To the extent that such a gain exceeds any unrecognized net loss (or the entire gain, if an unrecognized net gain exists), it is a *curtailment gain.*
b. To the extent that such a loss exceeds any unrecognized net gain (or the entire loss, if an unrecognized net loss exists), it is a *curtailment loss.*

For purposes of applying the provisions of this paragraph, any remaining unrecognized net asset existing at the date of initial application of Statement 87 (as discussed in paragraph 21 of this Statement) shall be treated as an unrecognized net gain and shall be combined with the unrecognized net gain or loss arising subsequent to transition to Statement 87.

14. If the sum of the effects identified in paragraphs 12 and 13 is a net loss, it shall be recognized in earnings when it is probable that a curtailment will occur and the effects described are reasonably estimable. If the sum of those effects is a net gain, it shall be recognized in earnings when the related employees terminate or the plan suspension or amendment is adopted.

Termination Benefits

15. An employer may provide benefits to employees in connection with their termination of employment. They may be either *special termination benefits* offered only for a short period of time or *contractual termination benefits* required by the terms of a plan only if a specified event, such as a plant closing, occurs. An employer that offers special termination benefits to employees shall recognize a liability and a loss when the employees accept the offer and the amount can be reasonably estimated. An employer that provides contractual termination benefits shall recognize a liability and a loss when it is probable that employees will be entitled to benefits and the amount can be reasonably estimated. Termination benefits may take various forms including lump-sum payments, periodic future payments, or both. They may be paid directly from an employer's assets, an existing pension plan, a new employee benefit plan, or a combination of those means. The cost of termination benefits recognized as a liability and a loss shall include the amount of any lump-sum payments and the present value of any expected future payments. A situation involving termination benefits may also involve a curtailment to be accounted for under paragraphs 12-14.

Disposal of a Segment

16. If the gain or loss measured in accordance with paragraphs 9, 10, 12, 13, or 15 is directly related to a disposal of a segment of a business, it shall be included in determining the gain or loss associated with that event and recognized pursuant to the requirements of APB Opinion No. 30, *Reporting the Results of Operations—Reporting the Effects of Disposal of a Segment of a Business, and Extraordinary, Unusual and Infrequently Occurring Events and Transactions.*

Disclosure and Presentation

17. An employer that recognizes a gain or loss under the provisions of this Statement, whether directly related to the disposal of a segment of a business or otherwise, shall disclose the following:

a. A description of the nature of the event(s)
b. The amount of gain or loss recognized.

Supersession of FASB Statement 74

18. This Statement supersedes FASB Statement No. 74, *Accounting for Special Termination Benefits Paid to Employees.*

Effective Date and Transition

19. This Statement shall be effective for events occurring in fiscal years beginning with the fiscal year in which Statement 87 is first applied. Restatement of previously issued annual financial statements is not permitted. If a decision is made initially

---

[4]Increases in the projected benefit obligation that reflect termination benefits are excluded from the scope of this paragraph. (Refer to paragraph 15 of this Statement.)

to apply this Statement in other than the first interim period of an employer's fiscal year, previous interim periods of that year shall be restated.

20. Certain employers have settled significant portions of their pension obligations as part of transactions in which plan assets in excess of obligations reverted to the employer (asset reversion transactions). Consistent with prior standards, an employer that previously entered into an asset reversion transaction and continued to provide defined benefits recognized a credit on its statement of financial position for the amount withdrawn instead of recognizing a gain at the time of the withdrawal. Net periodic pension costs of subsequent periods were then reduced by amortization of the deferred gain (that is, the amount withdrawn). An employer that entered into such a transaction before the effective date of this Statement shall recognize a gain as the cumulative effect of a change in accounting principle at the time of initial application of Statement 87. The amount of gain recognized shall be the lesser of:

a. The unamortized amount related to the asset reversion

b. Any unrecognized net asset for the plan (or the successor plan) existing at the time of transition as defined in paragraph 77 of Statement 87.[5]

21. At the time of initial application of Statement 87, an employer may have an unrecognized net obligation or unrecognized net asset. For purposes of this Statement:

a. The portion of such an unrecognized net obligation remaining unamortized at the date of a subsequent curtailment shall be treated as unrecognized prior service cost before applying the provisions of paragraph 12.

b. The portion of such an unrecognized net asset remaining unamortized at the date of a subsequent settlement or curtailment shall be treated as an unrecognized net gain and shall be combined with the unrecognized net gain or loss arising subsequent to transition to Statement 87 before applying the provisions of paragraphs 9 and 13.

> **The provisions of this Statement need not be applied to immaterial items.**

This Statement was adopted by the affirmative votes of five members of the Financial Accounting Standards Board. Messrs. Mosso and Wyatt dissented.

Mr. Mosso dissents because the provisions of paragraph 14 of this Statement do not conform to the clear guidance of paragraphs 91-97 of FASB Concepts Statement No. 2, *Qualitative Characteristics of Accounting Information.* By recognizing curtailment losses and deferring curtailment gains, the Statement perpetuates the rule of conservatism in its most extreme form, that is, "anticipate no profits but anticipate all losses." Concepts Statement 2 unequivocally rejected that form of conservatism: "Conservatism in financial reporting should no longer connote deliberate, consistent understatement of net assets and profits." The clear thrust of Concepts Statement 2 was clouded by the guidance of FASB Concepts Statement No. 5, *Recognition and Measurement in Financial Statements of Business Enterprises,* but it was not amended. The conceptual framework was designed to raise the quality of accounting standard setting. It cannot achieve that goal if it is ignored without good and ample cause. Mr. Mosso finds no such cause in this case.

Paragraph 41 of this Statement cites FASB Statement No. 5, *Accounting for Contingencies,* and Opinion 30 as precedents to be followed. Both standards predated Concepts Statement 2. Paradoxically, therefore, a concepts Statement, the primary purpose of which is to provide guidance to the Board in setting standards, is nullified because it conflicts with preexisting standards.

Mr. Wyatt does not support the issuance of this Statement because he believes that its conclusions are inconsistent with the basic thrust of the policy of delayed recognition of gains and losses adopted in Statement 87. He believes that useful information is not provided by following delayed recognition in some circumstances and not following it in others. Settlements with employees in the absence of a plan curtailment are, in his view, in substance investment or funding transactions that may be as usual in the context of a pension plan as are the events that give rise to the gains and losses and prior service cost for which delayed recognition is provided in Statement 87. In those circumstances the plan continues and employees continue to earn benefits, and many times those benefits are identical to (or enhanced from) those earned prior to the settlement. If, as the Board concluded in Statement 87, it is appropriate

---

[5]Paragraph 77 of Statement 87 states:

    For a defined benefit plan, an employer shall determine as of the measurement date . . . for the beginning of the fiscal year in which this Statement is first applied, the amounts of (a) the projected benefit obligation and (b) the fair value of plan assets plus previously recognized unfunded accrued pension cost or less previously recognized prepaid pension cost. The difference between those two amounts . . . represents an unrecognized net obligation . . . or an unrecognized net asset. . . .

to delay recognition of gains and losses and prior service cost related to a defined benefit plan, then delayed recognition should not be discontinued while the plan is, in substance, continued.

Mr. Wyatt also disagrees with the conclusion that the purchase of participating annuity contracts should be deemed to be a settlement that creates gain or loss recognition. Participating annuity contracts are a type of investment of pension assets—an alternative to an investment in equity securities, long-term bonds, real estate, and so forth. Decisions to change investment vehicles, for example, from equity securities to bonds, are not a sufficient basis to recognize gains and losses under the delayed recognition philosophy adopted in Statement 87. He believes that the change in investment vehicle to participating annuity contracts likewise should not be viewed as sufficient to warrant gain or loss recognition.

Mr. Wyatt believes the conclusions in this Statement create the very volatility in earnings that the delayed recognition philosophy of Statement 87 was intended to mitigate, and that delayed recognition of gains and losses should be continued until both a settlement and a plan curtailment occurs.

Members of the Financial Accounting Standards Board:

Donald J. Kirk,	Victor H. Brown	Robert T. Sprouse
Chairman	Raymond C. Lauver	Arthur R. Wyatt
Frank E. Block	David Mosso	

Appendix A

BASIS FOR CONCLUSIONS

CONTENTS

Appendix A

BASIS FOR CONCLUSIONS

Introduction

22. In February 1985, the Board decided that issuing a separate Statement on an employer's accounting for a settlement of a pension obligation, a curtailment of a defined benefit pension plan, or termination benefits would provide a greater opportunity for both the Board and the public to identify and fully consider those issues than would including them in the scope of Statement 87. An Exposure Draft of a proposed Statement, *Employers' Accounting for Settlements and Curtailments of Defined Benefit Pension Plans and for Termination Benefits,* was issued on June 14, 1985. The Board received 110 letters of comment in response to the Exposure Draft. This appendix discusses the significant comments contained in those letters of comment and heard from commentators at the July and August 1985 public hearing on the Exposure Draft. This appendix also discusses the factors that were deemed significant by members of the Board in reaching the conclusions in this Statement. It includes reasons for accepting certain views and rejecting others. Individual Board members gave greater weight to some factors than to others.

Plan Termination and Delayed Recognition

23. Statement 87 provides for delayed recognition of gains or losses arising in the ordinary operations of a defined benefit pension plan. That Statement also provides for delayed recognition of the cost of retroactive plan amendments (prior service cost). As a consequence of delayed recognition, at any time amounts of net gain or loss and prior service cost ordinarily will remain unrecognized in the employer's financial statements.

24. This Statement defines the events that require certain previously unrecognized amounts to be recognized in earnings and as adjustments to liabilities or assets. It is clear that the previously unrecognized net gain or loss and the previously unrecognized prior service cost should be recognized in the period when all of the following conditions are met:

a. All pension obligations are settled.
b. Defined benefits are no longer accrued under the plan.
c. The plan is not replaced by another defined benefit plan.
d. No plan assets remain.
e. The employees are terminated.
f. The plan ceases to exist as an entity.

25. It is not uncommon for some, but not all, of the above conditions to exist in a particular situation. For example, the present obligation for benefits may be settled without terminating the plan, or a plan may be suspended so that no further benefits will accrue for future services but its obligations are not settled. In other situations one or more of the above conditions may apply to only part of a plan. For example, one plan may be divided into two plans, one of which is then terminated, or one-half of the employees in a plan may terminate employment and the obligation for their benefits may be settled. Those situations have raised accounting issues.

26. If recognition of previously unrecognized prior service cost and net gain or loss were required only when a plan is completely terminated and settled and if no recognition occurred when a plan is partially curtailed or an obligation is partially settled, certain anomalies and implementation problems would result. For example, if one employer had two plants with separate plans and another employer had two plants with a single plan, the accounting result of closing one plant and settling the related obligation would be a recognizable event for one employer but not for the other. Also, if recognition were an all-or-nothing proposition, it would be necessary to determine when the extent of settlement or curtailment is sufficient for recognition. If all employees but one from a large group are termi-

nated and obligations to the terminated employees are settled, presumably the accounting should reflect a plan termination. But it is not clear whether that accounting should apply if 5 percent, 10 percent, or 25 percent of the original group was to remain. Accordingly, the Board concluded that a complete plan termination and settlement need not occur in order to recognize previously unrecognized amounts.

Settlement of the Obligation

27. The Board concluded that settlement of all or part of the pension benefit obligation should be the event that requires recognition of all or part of the previously unrecognized net gain or loss. Most of the respondents to the Exposure Draft agreed. The Board noted that one basis for delayed recognition of gains and losses under Statement 87 is the possibility that gains or losses occurring in one period would be offset by losses or gains in subsequent periods. To the extent that the obligation has been settled, the possibility of future gains or losses related to that obligation and to the assets used to effect the settlement is diminished. The Board also noted that settlement of all or a large portion of an obligation could be viewed as realization of past gains or losses associated with that portion of the obligation and the assets used to effect the settlement. That realization would not be affected by the employer's subsequent decision to undertake or not to undertake future defined benefit obligations.

28. The Board acknowledges that other actions an employer can take, especially those related to plan assets, can affect the possibility of a subsequent net gain or loss. For example, an employer may avoid or minimize certain risks by investing in a portfolio of high-quality fixed-income securities with principal and interest payment dates similar to the estimated payment dates of benefits (as with a dedicated bond portfolio). However, settlement differs from other actions in that (a) it is irrevocable, (b) it relieves the employer (or the plan) of primary responsibility for the obligation, and (c) it eliminates significant risks related to the obligation (such as the risk that participants will live longer than assumed) and to the assets used to effect the settlement. The decision to have a dedicated bond portfolio can be reversed, it does not relieve the employer of primary responsibility for the obligation, and such a strategy does not eliminate mortality risk. The Board concluded that the circumstances requiring gain or loss recognition should be narrowly defined.

29. The Exposure Draft would have defined settlement as a discharge of the pension obligation by (a) making a lump-sum cash payment to plan participants in exchange for their rights to receive specified pension benefits or (b) purchasing annuity con-

Employers' Accounting for Settlements and
Curtailments of Defined Benefit Pension Plans
and for Termination Benefits

FAS88

tracts. Several respondents argued that the definition was event specific and therefore too restrictive. They noted that settlements could be accomplished by means other than those identified in the definition, such as by payments in noncash assets or by transfer of employee interests into a defined contribution plan. Those respondents suggested that criteria for a settlement should be set forth to describe characteristics of a settlement. The Board agreed that the Statement should establish criteria (as described in paragraph 28) rather than attempt to identify every transaction that might constitute a settlement.

30. The Board recognized that changes in the previously estimated value of the obligation and the assets may become evident at the time the obligation is settled. (For example, the interest rates inherent in the price actually paid for annuities may be different from the assumed discount rates.) Some respondents suggested that such changes should be recognized immediately in earnings as a gain or loss directly resulting from the settlement. The Board concluded that, based on the measurement principles adopted in Statement 87, such changes reflect factors expected to be considered in the measurement of the pension obligation and plan assets. Accordingly, the Board concluded that those amounts should be included with the previously unrecognized net gain or loss before a pro rata portion of that amount is recognized. Most of the respondents who addressed the issue agreed.

31. This Statement requires measurement of the pro rata portion of the unrecognized net gain or loss based on the decrease in the projected benefit obligation resulting from a settlement. The Board also considered basing that measurement in part on the decrease in plan assets resulting from the event. The Board acknowledges that a decrease in the amount of plan assets can affect the possibility of future gains and losses. The Board concluded that it would be simpler and more practical to base the measurement only on the obligation settled.

32. The Exposure Draft would have proscribed recognition of a previously unrecognized net gain or loss if the cost of settlements was less than or equal to the amount of obligation arising from the service cost and interest cost components of net periodic pension cost during the current year. This occurs, for example, when a plan regularly purchases annuities each year for benefits accumulated in that year. The basis for that proposal was that recognition of a previously unrecognized net gain or loss should not be required if the portion of the obligation settled is insignificant and that an obligation settled in the year in which it was incurred would not ordinarily give rise to significant gains or losses. Several respondents suggested that the benefits cov-

ered by the settlement may not relate to the obligation arising in the current year as in the case of settlement of pension obligations for employees upon retirement. The Board acknowledges that possibility and concluded that recognition of a previously unrecognized net gain or loss should be permitted, but not required, if the costs of the settlements do not exceed the limit described above. The Board believes that for many small plans, retaining that threshold for required recognition will reduce the cost of complying with this Statement.

Participating Annuity Contracts

33. As described in paragraph 5, a participating annuity contract (participating contract) allows the purchaser to participate in some way in the insurance company's experience subsequent to the purchase of the contract. That is, if the insurance company's investment return is better than anticipated, or perhaps if actual experience related to mortality or other assumptions is favorable, the purchaser will receive dividends that will reduce the cost of the contract. To that extent, a participating contract has some characteristics of an investment. However, many respondents agreed with the view in the Exposure Draft that the employer is as fully relieved of the obligation by the purchase of a participating contract as it is with the purchase of a nonparticipating contract. Except as indicated in paragraphs 34 and 35, the Board concluded that it would be appropriate to treat a participating contract the same as a nonparticipating contract and to consider purchases of participating contracts as settlements of pension obligations.

34. The Board realized that it is difficult to determine the extent to which a participating contract exposes the purchaser to the risk of unfavorable experience, which would be reflected in lower than expected future dividends. The Board also recognized that under some annuity contracts described as participating the purchaser might remain subject to all or most of the same risks and rewards related to future experience that would have existed had the contract not been purchased. The Board also is aware that some participating contracts may require or permit payment of additional premiums if experience is unfavorable. Accordingly, the Board concluded that if a participating contract requires or permits payment of additional premiums because of experience losses, or if the substance of the contract is such that the purchaser retains all or most of the related risks and rewards, the purchase of that contract does not constitute a settlement.

35. If the purchase of a participating contract constitutes a settlement for purposes of this Statement, recognition of a previously unrecognized net gain or loss is required (paragraph 9) except for small settle-

ments (paragraph 32). However, the possibility of a subsequent loss is not completely eliminated with a participating contract because realization of the participation right is not assured. Therefore, in recognition of the continuing risk related to the participation right, this Statement requires reduction of the maximum gain (paragraph 10) subject to pro rata recognition by an amount equal to the cost of the participation right.

Curtailment of the Plan

36. The Exposure Draft proposed and most respondents agreed that a plan curtailment should be the event that requires recognition of previously unrecognized prior service cost. One basis for delayed recognition of prior service cost is the likelihood of future economic benefits to the employer as a result of the amendment. Those benefits, in the Board's view, are derived from the future services of employees, and the amortization of unrecognized prior service cost is based on those services.

37. A curtailment, as defined in this Statement, is an event that significantly reduces the expected years of future service of present employees or eliminates for a significant number of employees the accrual of defined benefits for some or all of their future services. The Board concluded that either of those situations raises sufficient doubt about the continued existence of the future economic benefits to justify recognition of the prior service cost when it is probable that a curtailment will occur, the effects are reasonably estimable, and the net result of the curtailment (as described in paragraph 14) is a loss.

38. The Board also considered whether either a settlement or the termination of one plan and the adoption of a substantially equivalent replacement plan should trigger recognition of prior service cost. The Board concluded that neither of those events, absent a curtailment, raises sufficient doubt as to the existence of future economic benefits to trigger such recognition.

39. A curtailment may directly cause a decrease in the projected benefit obligation (a gain) or an increase in the projected benefit obligation (a loss). For example, an obligation based on employees' projected final compensation levels normally will be reduced if the employees leave earlier than expected (a gain). Also, an obligation based on estimated rates of acceptance of subsidized early retirement benefits[6] normally will be increased by an event that causes eligible employees to leave earlier than pre-

viously expected (a loss). Conceptually, the Board believes it would be appropriate to recognize such gains or losses immediately to the extent they represent adjustments of previously recognized net periodic pension cost (that is, to the extent they do not represent the reversal of previous unrecognized losses or gains). However, the obligation eliminated or created by a curtailment may not be independent of previously unrecognized losses or gains. For example, part of that obligation could relate to past changes in actuarial assumptions about projected compensation levels that produced gains or losses not yet fully recognized. To illustrate, if in year one the employer increases the estimated rate of increase in salaries from 6 percent to 8 percent, that creates an additional obligation and an unrecognized loss. If in year two the employer terminates those employees, the obligation related to their projected salaries is eliminated and a gain arises, which is, at least in part, a reversal of the previously unrecognized loss.

40. The Board concluded that a curtailment gain or loss as defined in paragraph 13 (which does not include recognition of prior service cost) should first be offset to the extent possible against the plan's previously existing unrecognized net loss or gain. Any remainder of the curtailment gain or loss cannot, at least in an overall sense, be a reversal of unrecognized amounts, and therefore, recognition of that remainder is appropriate.

41. The Exposure Draft would have required recognition of the results of a curtailment (which could be a net gain or net loss when combined with recognition of prior service cost) when it is probable that a curtailment will occur and the effects of the curtailment can be reasonably estimated. Several respondents objected to that provision. Those respondents suggested that recognition of a gain prior to termination of the related employees or adoption of the plan suspension or amendment may be inconsistent with the current literature as adopted in FASB Statement No. 5, *Accounting for Contingencies* (paragraph 17) and Opinion 30 (paragraph 15) which indicate that certain gains should not be reflected in earnings prior to realization.

42. Statement 87 continues the delayed recognition features of past practice so that gains or losses are not recognized as they occur (that is, when they are realized or when they are realizable as defined in paragraph 83 of FASB Concepts Statement No. 5, *Recognition and Measurement in Financial Statements of Business Enterprises*,) but are recognized

---

[6]Some plans provide for early retirement benefits that are reduced to reflect fully the fact that payments begin sooner and extend over more periods than normal retirement benefits. If the actuarial present value of the reduced benefits is the same as the actuarial present value of the accumulated benefits assuming payments beginning at normal retirement age, the benefits are said to be subject to "full actuarial reduction," and no loss results when an employee takes early retirement. Subsidized early retirement benefits are benefits not subject to full actuarial reduction so that a loss results when an employee unexpectedly takes early retirement.

paragraph 20 would provide more useful information than the alternative of applying the provisions of this Statement only to transactions occurring after a particular date.

Appendix B

ILLUSTRATIONS

57. This appendix contains separate illustrations of the following requirements of this Statement:

1. Accounting for a plan termination without a replacement defined benefit plan
2. Accounting for a settlement of a pension obligation
3. Accounting for a plan curtailment
4. Calculation of unrecognized prior service cost associated with services of terminated employees

5. Accounting for a plan curtailment when termination benefits are offered to employees
6. Transition for an employer that completed an asset reversion prior to the initial application of Statement 87

Illustration 1—Accounting for a Plan Termination without a Replacement Defined Benefit Plan

Company A sponsored a final-pay noncontributory defined benefit plan. On November 16, 1988, the employer terminated the plan, settled the accumulated benefit obligation of $1,500,000 (nonvested benefits became vested upon termination of the plan) by purchasing nonparticipating annuity contracts, and withdrew excess assets. Defined benefits were not provided under any successor plan. The plan ceased to exist as an entity.

As a result, Company A recognized a gain of $900,000, determined as follows:

	Company A (in thousands)		
	Before Termination	Effect of Termination	After Termination
Assets and obligations:			
Accumulated benefit obligation	$ (1,500)	$ 1,500[a]	$ 0
Effects of projected future compensation levels	(400)	400[b]	0
Projected benefit obligation	(1,900)	1,900	0
Plan assets at fair value	2,100	(1,500)[a] (600)[c]	0
Items not yet recognized in earnings:			
Unrecognized net asset at transition[d,e]	(200)	200	0
Unrecognized net gain subsequent to transition[e]	(300)	300	0
(Accrued)/prepaid pension cost on the statement of financial position	$ (300)	$ 300	$ 0

[a]The accumulated benefits of $1,500 were settled by using an equivalent amount of plan assets to purchase nonparticipating annuity contracts.

[b]The effects of projected future compensation levels ceased to be an obligation of the plan or the employer due to the termination of all plan participants. Under paragraph 13 of this Statement, the gain (that is, the decrease in the projected benefit obligation) resulting from the curtailment is first offset against any existing unrecognized net loss. Because the previously unrecognized amount in this case was a gain ($200 unrecognized net asset at transition plus $300 unrecognized net gain subsequent to transition), the $400 gain from the curtailment was recognized.

[c]Plan assets, in excess of the amount used to settle the pension benefits, were withdrawn from the plan.

[d]An unrecognized net asset at transition is treated as an unrecognized net gain for purposes of this Statement (paragraph 21).

[e]A pro rata amount of the maximum gain (paragraph 9), which includes the unrecognized net gain subsequent to transition ($300) and the unamortized net asset from transition ($200), is recognized due to settlement. The projected benefit obligation was reduced from $1,500 to $0 (the curtailment initially reduced the projected benefit obligation from $1,900 to $1,500 as described in footnote b), a reduction of 100 percent. Accordingly, the entire unrecognized net gain of $500 ($300 + $200) was recognized.

The journal entry required to reflect the accounting for the plan termination was:

Cash	600	
Accrued/prepaid pension cost	300	
Gain from plan termination		900

The gain from the plan termination without a replacement defined benefit plan was composed of the following:

Gain from curtailment	$ 400
Gain from settlement	500
Total gain	$ 900

Illustration 2—Accounting for a Settlement of a Pension Obligation

The following examples illustrate the accounting for a settlement of a pension obligation in three specific situations. The first example (Company B) had an unrecognized net obligation at the date of transition to Statement 87, and the second and third examples (Company C and Company D) each had unrecognized net assets at the date of transition. Each company settled a portion of the obligation subsequent to transition to Statement 87. Company

B had a retroactive plan amendment after transition; Company C and Company D did not.

Example 2A—Projected Benefit Obligation Exceeds Plan Assets

Company B sponsors a final-pay noncontributory defined benefit plan. On December 31, 1988, the plan settled the vested benefit portion ($1,300,000) of the projected benefit obligation through the purchase of nonparticipating annuity contracts.

As a result, Company B recognized a gain of $195,000, determined as follows:

	Company B (in thousands)		
	Before Settlement	Effect of Settlement	After Settlement
Assets and obligations:			
Vested benefit obligation	$ (1,300)	$ 1,300[a]	$ 0
Nonvested benefits	(200)		(200)
Accumulated benefit obligation	(1,500)	1,300	(200)
Effects of projected future compensation levels	(500)		(500)
Projected benefit obligation	(2,000)	1,300	(700)
Plan assets at fair value	1,400	(1,300)[a]	100
Items not yet recognized in earnings:			
Unrecognized net obligation at transition[b]	650		650
Unrecognized prior service cost from amendment subsequent to transition	150		150
Unrecognized net gain subsequent to transition[c]	(300)	195	(105)
(Accrued)/prepaid pension cost on the statement of financial position	$ (100)	$ 195	$ 95

---

[a]The vested benefits of $1,300 were settled by using plan assets to purchase nonparticipating annuity contracts.

[b]An unrecognized net obligation at transition is treated as unrecognized prior service cost and therefore is not affected by settlement of the obligation (paragraph 21).

[c]A pro rata portion of the maximum gain (paragraph 9), the unrecognized net gain subsequent to transition, is recognized due to settlement. The projected benefit obligation was reduced from $2,000 to $700, a reduction of 65 percent. Accordingly, 65 percent of the maximum gain of $300, a gain of $195, was recognized. The journal entry required to reflect the accounting for the plan settlement was:

| Accrued/prepaid pension cost | 195 | |
| Gain from settlement | | 195 |

Example 2B—Plan Assets Exceed the Projected Benefit Obligation

Company C sponsors a final-pay noncontributory defined benefit plan. On December 31, 1988, the plan settled the vested benefit portion ($1,300,000) of the projected benefit obligation through the purchase of nonparticipating annuity contracts.

As a result, Company C recognized a gain of $325,000, determined as follows:

Company C
(in thousands)

	Before Settlement	Effect of Settlement	After Settlement
Assets and obligations:			
Vested benefit obligation	$ (1,300)	$ 1,300[a]	$ 0
Nonvested benefits	(200)		(200)
Accumulated benefit obligation	(1,500)	1,300	(200)
Effects of projected future compensation levels	(500)		(500)
Projected benefit obligation	(2,000)	1,300	(700)
Plan assets at fair value	2,100	(1,300)[a]	800
Items not yet recognized in earnings:			
Unrecognized net asset at transition[b,c]	(200)	130	(70)
Unrecognized net gain subsequent to transition[c]	(300)	195	(105)
(Accrued)/prepaid pension cost on the statement of financial position	$ (400)	$ 325	$ (75)

---

[a]The vested benefits of $1,300 were settled by using plan assets to purchase nonparticipating annuity contracts.

[b]An unrecognized net asset at transition is treated as an unrecognized net gain for purposes of this Statement (paragraph 21).

[c]A pro rata amount of the maximum gain (paragraph 9), which includes the unrecognized net gain subsequent to transition ($300) and the unamortized net asset from transition ($200), is recognized due to settlement. The projected benefit obligation was reduced from $2,000 to $700, a reduction of 65 percent. Accordingly, 65 percent of the maximum gain of $500 ($300 + $200), a gain of $325, was recognized. The journal entry required to reflect the accounting for the plan settlement was:

Accrued/prepaid pension cost	325	
Gain from settlement		325

Example 2C—Plan Assets Exceed the Projected Benefit Obligation and a Participating Annuity Contract Is Purchased to Settle Benefits

Company D sponsors a final-pay noncontributory defined benefit plan. On December 31, 1988, the plan settled the vested benefit portion ($1,300,000) of the projected benefit obligation through the purchase of a participating annuity contract at a cost of $1,430,000. The plan could have purchased a nonparticipating contract covering the same benefits for $1,300,000. The participation features of the contract warranted a conclusion that its purchase constituted a settlement.

As a result, Company D recognized a gain of $240,000 (rounded), determined as follows:

| | Company D (in thousands) | | |
	Before Settlement	Effect of Settlement	After Settlement
Assets and obligations:			
Vested benefit obligation	$ (1,300)	$ 1,300[a]	$ 0
Nonvested benefits	(200)		(200)
Accumulated benefit obligation	(1,500)	1,300	(200)
Effects of projected future compensation levels	(500)		(500)
Projected benefit obligation	(2,000)	1,300	(700)
Plan assets at fair value:			
Participation right		130[a]	130
Other plan assets	2,100	(1,430)[a]	670
Items not yet recognized in earnings:			
Unrecognized net asset at transition[b,c]	(200)	130[d]	(70)
Unrecognized net gain subsequent to transition[c]	(300)	110[d]	(190)
(Accrued)/prepaid pension cost on the statement of financial position	$ (400)	$ 240	$ (160)

---

[a]The vested benefits of $1,300 were settled by using $1,430 of plan assets to purchase a participating annuity contract. However, a nonparticipating contract covering the same benefits could have been purchased for $1,300. The plan paid the additional $130 to obtain the participation right.

[b]An unrecognized net asset at transition is treated as an unrecognized net gain for purposes of this Statement (paragraph 21).

[c]A pro rata amount of the maximum gain (paragraph 9), which includes the unrecognized net gain subsequent to transition ($300) and the unamortized net asset from transition ($200), was recognized due to settlement. However, any gain on a settlement that uses a participating annuity contract shall be computed by first reducing the maximum gain by the cost of the participation right [$200 + ($300 − $130) = $370]. The projected benefit obligation was reduced from $2,000 to $700, a reduction of 65 percent. Accordingly, a gain of $240 (rounded) was recognized (.65 × $370). The journal entry required to reflect the accounting for the plan settlement was:

Accrued/prepaid pension cost	240	
Gain from settlement		240

[d]The amount of gain from settlement was allocated as follows (rounded):

Unrecognized net asset at transition (.65 × $200)	$ 130
Unrecognized net gain subsequent to transition [.65 × ($300 − $130)]	110
	$ 240

Employers' Accounting for Settlements and
Curtailments of Defined Benefit Pension Plans
and for Termination Benefits

FAS88

Illustration 4—Calculation of Unrecognized Prior Service Cost Associated with Services of Terminated Employees

Company S sponsors a final-pay noncontributory defined benefit plan. On January 1, 1988, the company had a retroactive plan amendment resulting in prior service cost of $800,000.

The unrecognized prior service cost that results from the plan amendment is amortized based on the expected future years of service of participants active as of January 1, 1988 who are expected to receive benefits under the plan.

As of January 1, 1988, the company had 100 employees who were expected to receive benefits under the plan. Based on the assumption that 5 percent of that group (5 employees) leaves (either quits or retires) in each of the next 20 years, the expected future years of service amounted to 1,050.

The amount of prior service cost associated with each expected future year of service is $762 ($800,000 ÷ 1,050). Exhibit A illustrates the originally expected expiration of the anticipated service years.

On December 31, 1990, Company S terminated 25 employees active at the date of the plan amendment. Immediately prior to the curtailment, 765 expected future years of service remained (1,050 less 285 years of service rendered in the previous 3 years). The curtailment reduced the total expected future years of service at December 31, 1990 from 765 to 555 (210) as illustrated in Exhibit B. Therefore, Company S will recognize $160,020 ($762 × 210) of prior service cost in conjunction with the curtailment.

Exhibit A

Determination of Expected Years of Service Rendered in Each Year

Before Curtailment

Individuals	Future Service Years	88	89	90	91	92	93	94	95	96	97	98	99	00	01	02	03	04	05	06	07
A1-A5	5	5																			
B1-B5	10	5	5																		
C1-C5	15	5	5	5																	
D1-D5	20	5	5	5	5																
E1-E5	25	5	5	5	5	5															
F1-F5	30	5	5	5	5	5	5														
G1-G5	35	5	5	5	5	5	5	5													
H1-H5	40	5	5	5	5	5	5	5	5												
I1-I5	45	5	5	5	5	5	5	5	5	5											
J1-J5	50	5	5	5	5	5	5	5	5	5	5										
K1-K5	55	5	5	5	5	5	5	5	5	5	5	5									
L1-L5	60	5	5	5	5	5	5	5	5	5	5	5	5								
M1-M5	65	5	5	5	5	5	5	5	5	5	5	5	5	5							
N1-N5	70	5	5	5	5	5	5	5	5	5	5	5	5	5	5						
O1-O5	75	5	5	5	5	5	5	5	5	5	5	5	5	5	5	5					
P1-P5	80	5	5	5	5	5	5	5	5	5	5	5	5	5	5	5	5				
Q1-Q5	85	5	5	5	5	5	5	5	5	5	5	5	5	5	5	5	5	5			
R1-R5	90	5	5	5	5	5	5	5	5	5	5	5	5	5	5	5	5	5	5		
S1-S5	95	5	5	5	5	5	5	5	5	5	5	5	5	5	5	5	5	5	5	5	
T1-T5	100	5	5	5	5	5	5	5	5	5	5	5	5	5	5	5	5	5	5	5	5
	1,050																				
Service Years Rendered		100	95	90	85	80	75	70	65	60	55	50	45	40	35	30	25	20	15	10	5
Amortization Fraction		$\frac{100}{1,050}$	$\frac{95}{1,050}$	$\frac{90}{1,050}$	$\frac{85}{1,050}$	$\frac{80}{1,050}$	$\frac{75}{1,050}$	$\frac{70}{1,050}$	$\frac{65}{1,050}$	$\frac{60}{1,050}$	$\frac{55}{1,050}$	$\frac{50}{1,050}$	$\frac{45}{1,050}$	$\frac{40}{1,050}$	$\frac{35}{1,050}$	$\frac{30}{1,050}$	$\frac{25}{1,050}$	$\frac{20}{1,050}$	$\frac{15}{1,050}$	$\frac{10}{1,050}$	$\frac{5}{1,050}$
Expected Future Years of Service Remaining at Year-End		950	855	765	680	600	525	455	390	330	275	225	180	140	105	75	50	30	15	5	0

Prior Service Cost $ 800,000

Total Expected Future Years of Service   1,050

Amortization Amount per Each Year of Service $ 762

Exhibit B

Determination of Expected Years of Service Rendered in Each Year

After Curtailment

Individuals	Year																			
	88	89	90	91	92	93	94	95	96	97	98	99	00	01	02	03	04	05	06	07
A1-A5	5																			
B1-B5	5	5																		
C1-C5	5	5	5																	
D1-D5*	5	5	5																	
E1-E5	5	5	5																	
F1-F5	5	5	5																	
G1-G5	5	5	5																	
H1-H5*	5	5	5																	
I1-I5	5	5	5	5	5															
J1-J5	5	5	5	5	5	5														
K1-K5	5	5	5	5	5	5	5													
L1-L5*	5	5	5	5	5	5	5	5	5											
M1-M5	5	5	5	5	5	5	5	5	5	5										
N1-N5	5	5	5	5	5	5	5	5	5	5	5									
O1-O5*	5	5	5	5	5	5	5	5	5	5	5	5	5							
P1-P5	5	5	5	5	5	5	5	5	5	5	5	5	5	5						
Q1-Q5	5	5	5	5	5	5	5	5	5	5	5	5	5	5	5	5				
R1-R3*	5	5	5	5	5	5	5	5	5	5	5	5	5	5	5	5	5			
S1-S5	5	5	5	5	5	5	5	5	5	5	5	5	5	5	5	5	5	5	5	
T1-T5	5	5	5	5	5	5	5	5	5	5	5	5	5	5	5	5	5	5	5	5
Service Years Rendered	100	95	90	60	60	55	50	45	45	40	35	30	30	25	20	20	15	10	10	5
Adjustment for Termination			210																	
Total	100	95	300	60	60	55	50	45	45	40	35	30	30	25	20	20	15	10	10	5
Amortization Fraction	100/1,050	95/1,050	300/1,050	60/1,050	60/1,050	55/1,050	50/1,050	45/1,050	45/1,050	40/1,050	35/1,050	30/1,050	30/1,050	25/1,050	20/1,050	20/1,050	15/1,050	10/1,050	10/1,050	1,050/1,050
Expected Future Years of Service Remaining at Year-End	950	855	555	495	435	380	330	285	240	200	165	135	105	80	60	40	25	15	5	0

*Terminated group of employees.

Illustration 5—Accounting for a Plan Curtailment When Termination Benefits Are Offered to Employees

Company G sponsors a final-pay noncontributory defined benefit plan. The company had an unrecognized net obligation at the date of transition to Statement 87 and did not have a retroactive plan amendment after that date. On May 11, 1990, the company offered for a short period of time (until June 30, 1990) special benefits to its employees in connection with their voluntary termination of employment (special termination benefits). The special termination benefit was a lump-sum payment to be made upon termination, payable in addition to the employee's regular plan benefits. The special ter-

mination benefit was paid directly from the employer's assets rather than from the plan assets.

On June 30, 15 percent of the employees accepted the offer. The amount of the special termination benefit payment was $125,000.

The portion of the projected benefit obligation based on the expected future compensation levels of the terminated employees amounted to $100,000, and all the employees terminated were fully vested in their accumulated benefits. The portion of the unrecognized net obligation at transition associated with the years of service no longer expected from the terminated employees was $150,000.

As a result, Company G recognized a loss of $175,000 that includes the cost of the special termination benefits and the loss* from the curtailment determined as follows:

	Company G (in thousands)		
	Before Curtailment	Effect of Curtailment	After Curtailment
Assets and obligations:			
Vested benefit obligation	$ (1,300)		$ (1,300)
Nonvested benefits	(200)		(200)
Accumulated benefit obligation	(1,500)		(1,500)
Effects of projected future compensation levels	(500)	$ 100	(400)
Projected benefit obligation	(2,000)	100[a]	(1,900)
Plan assets at fair value	1,400		1,400
Items not yet recognized in earnings:			
Unrecognized net obligation at transition[b]	800	(150)	650
Unrecognized net gain subsequent to transition	(300)		(300)
(Accrued)/prepaid pension cost on the statement of financial position	$ (100)	$ (50)	$ (150)
Loss on curtailment		$ 50	
Cost of special termination benefits (lump-sum payments to terminated employees)		125	
Total loss		$ 175[c]	

*Under paragraph 14 of this Statement, if the sum of the effects resulting from the curtailment is a net loss, it is to be recognized when it is probable that the curtailment will occur and the effects are reasonably estimable. In this example, the effects resulting from the curtailment were not reasonably estimable until June 30, 1990, the acceptance date for the offer of special termination benefits.

[a]Under paragraph 13 of this Statement, the curtailment gain (that is, the decrease in the projected benefit obligation) is first offset against any existing unrecognized net loss. Since the previously unrecognized amount was a gain ($300 unrecognized net gain subsequent to transition), the $100 gain from the curtailment was recognized.

[b]An unrecognized net obligation at the date of transition to Statement 87 is treated as unrecognized prior service cost for purposes of applying this Statement. The portion of unrecognized prior service cost associated with the years of service no longer expected from the terminated employees ($150) was recognized.

[c]The loss Company G recognized was $175, which includes the cost of the special termination benefits of $125, the gain related to salary progression of $100 and the recognition of prior service cost of $150. The journal entry required to reflect the accounting for this event was:

Loss on employee terminations	175	
Accrued/prepaid pension cost		50
Liability for termination benefits		125

If the company had paid the termination benefits from the pension plan (by amending the plan and using plan assets), the same loss would have been recognized, but $175 would have been credited to the accrued pension cost liability.

Illustration 6—Transition for an Employer That Completed an Asset Reversion Prior to the Initial Application of Statement 87

Company H sponsors a final-pay noncontributory defined benefit pension plan. On September 9, 1981, the company settled a portion of its pension obligation through the purchase of annuity contracts and withdrew excess assets. The company continued to provide defined benefits to its employees. No gain was recognized on the transaction, and Company H recognized a credit in its statement of financial position equal to the amount of cash withdrawn. For financial reporting purposes, that amount was grouped with accrued or prepaid pension cost. In subsequent periods the amount of the reversion (a deferred gain) was amortized as a reduction of net periodic pension cost. The company had no other past differences between net periodic pension cost and amounts contributed and,

therefore, had recognized no other accrued or prepaid pension cost.

As of January 1, 1985, the time of initial application of Statement 87, the unamortized amount of the reversion gain was $287,000. Company H's transition to Statement 87 would be accomplished as follows:

**Company H
Computation of
Unrecognized
Net Asset
(in thousands)**

Projected benefit obligation		$ (800)
Plan assets at fair value	$ 950	
Accrued pension cost on the statement of financial position	287	1,237
Unrecognized net asset		$ 437

**Company H
(in thousands)**

	Before Recognition of Reversion Gain	Effect of Recognition of Reversion Gain	After Recognition of Reversion Gain
Assets and obligations:			
Projected benefit obligation	$ (800)		$ (800)
Plan assets at fair value	950		950
Item not yet recognized in earnings:			
Unrecognized net asset at transition	(437)	$ 287a	(150)
(Accrued)/prepaid pension cost on the statement of financial position	$ (287)	$ 287a	$ 0

---

aUnder paragraph 20 of this Statement, an employer that completed an asset reversion prior to the effective date of this Statement should recognize a gain as the cumulative effect of a change in accounting principle at the time of initial application of Statement 87.

The gain recognized by Company H amounts to $287, which is the lesser of the unamortized amount of the reversion gain ($287) and the unrecognized net asset from transition ($437). The journal entry required to reflect the accounting as of January 1, 1985 was:

Accrued/prepaid pension cost	287	
Cumulative effect of a change in accounting principle		287

Statement of Financial Accounting Standards No. 89
Financial Reporting and Changing Prices

STATUS

Issued: December 1986

Effective Date: For financial reports issued after December 2, 1986

Affects: Supersedes FAS 33
　　　　 Supersedes FAS 39
　　　　 Supersedes FAS 40
　　　　 Supersedes FAS 41
　　　　 Supersedes FAS 46
　　　　 Supersedes FAS 54
　　　　 Supersedes FAS 69, paragraphs 35 through 38 and footnote 10
　　　　 Supersedes FAS 70
　　　　 Supersedes FAS 82
　　　　 Supersedes FTB 79-8, paragraph 3
　　　　 Amends FTB 79-8, paragraphs 1, 4, and 6
　　　　 Supersedes FTB 81-4

Affected by: Paragraphs 33 and 96 amended by FAS 96 and FAS 109

Issues Discussed by FASB Emerging Issues Task Force (EITF)

　 Affects: No EITF Issues

　 Interpreted by: No EITF Issues

　 Related Issue: EITF Issue No. 93-9

SUMMARY

　 This Statement supersedes FASB Statement No. 33, *Financial Reporting and Changing Prices*, and its subsequent amendments, and makes voluntary the supplementary disclosure of current cost/constant purchasing power information.
　 The Statement is effective for financial reports issued after December 2, 1986.

Statement of Financial Accounting Standards No. 89

Financial Reporting and Changing Prices

CONTENTS

INTRODUCTION AND SCOPE

1. In 1979, FASB Statement No. 33, *Financial Reporting and Changing Prices*, was issued as an experiment in requiring supplementary information on the effects of inflation and changes in specific prices. At that time the Board committed itself to review the results of the requirements within five years. The Board has completed that review and has concluded that further supplementary disclosures should be encouraged, but not required.

2. This Statement supersedes the following pronouncements:

a. FASB Statement No. 33, *Financial Reporting and Changing Prices*

b. FASB Statement No. 39, *Financial Reporting and Changing Prices: Specialized Assets—Mining and Oil and Gas*

c. FASB Statement No. 40, *Financial Reporting and Changing Prices: Specialized Assets—Timberlands and Growing Timber*

d. FASB Statement No. 41, *Financial Reporting and Changing Prices: Specialized Assets—Income-Producing Real Estate*

e. FASB Statement No. 46, *Financial Reporting and Changing Prices: Motion Picture Films*

f. FASB Statement No. 54, *Financial Reporting and Changing Prices: Investment Companies*

g. FASB Statement No. 69, *Disclosures about Oil and Gas Producing Activities*, paragraphs 35-38

h. FASB Statement No. 70, *Financial Reporting and Changing Prices: Foreign Currency Translation*

i. FASB Statement No. 82, *Financial Reporting and Changing Prices: Elimination of Certain Disclosures*

j. FASB Technical Bulletin No. 81-4, *Classification as Monetary or Nonmonetary Items*.

FASB Technical Bulletin No. 79-8, *Applicability of FASB Statements 21 and 33 to Certain Brokers and Dealers in Securities*, is amended to delete any reference to Statement 33.

STANDARDS OF FINANCIAL ACCOUNTING AND REPORTING

Disclosure

3. A business enterprise that prepares its financial statements in U.S. dollars and in accordance with U.S. generally accepted accounting principles is encouraged, but not required, to disclose supplementary information on the effects of changing prices. Appendix A provides measurement and presentation guidelines for disclosure. Entities are not discouraged from experimenting with other forms of disclosure.

Effective Date

4. This Statement is effective for financial reports issued after December 2, 1986.

This Statement was adopted by the affirmative vote of four members of the Financial Accounting Standards Board. Messrs. Lauver, Mosso, and Swieringa dissented.

Mr. Mosso dissented to the issuance of Statement 33 and he dissents to its recision, both for the same reason. He believes that accounting for the interrelated effects of general and specific price changes is the most critical set of issues that the Board will face in this century. It is too important either to be dealt with inconclusively as in the original Statement 33 or to be written off as a lost cause as in this Statement.

The basic proposition underlying Statement 33—that inflation causes historical cost financial statements to show illusory profits and mask erosion of capital—is virtually undisputed. Specific price changes are inextricably linked to general inflation, and the combination of general and specific price changes seriously reduces the relevance, the representational faithfulness, and the comparability of historical cost financial statements.

Although the current inflation rate in the United States is relatively low in the context of recent history, its compound effect through time is still highly significant. High inflation rates prevail in many countries where United States corporations operate. Rates from country to country vary from time to time. Those distortive influences on financial statements will now go unmeasured and undisclosed.

Although Statement 33 had obvious shortcomings, it was a base on which to build. It represented years of due process—research, debate, deliberations, decisions—and application experience. As last amended, it had made significant progress in eliminating alternative concepts and methodologies. Its recision means that much of that due process and application experience will have to be repeated in response to a future inflation crisis. That will entail great cost in terms of time, money, and creative talent and, because due process does not permit quick reaction to crises, it risks loss of credibility for the Board and loss of initiative in private sector standards setting.

Mr. Lauver shares the views expressed by Mr. Mosso. He believes that instead of rescinding Statement 33, a continuing effort should be undertaken to complete what was only begun by that Statement.

Statement 33 was not a completed product. First, it required adjustment of only two of the items known to be affected by price changes, cost of sales and depreciation. Second, two adjusted amounts for cost of sales and depreciation were required to be reported, one on a constant purchasing power basis and one on a specific price basis. Third, the adjusted amounts together with two new items required to be disclosed, gain or loss on monetary items and certain holding gains, were not required to be reported in an articulating set of adjusted statements of financial position and performance. Indeed, no determination was made about how those supplemental disclosures could or should be integrated into an alternate measure of enterprise performance.

Relative to most changes in financial reporting, the changes required by Statement 33 were monumental. Because most accountants and users of financial statements have been inculcated with a model of financial reporting that assumes stability of the monetary unit, accepting a change of this consequence would take a lengthy period of time under the best of circumstances. Given the incomplete and complex nature of the disclosures described in the preceding paragraph, Mr. Lauver believes that there is no reason to be concerned about or surprised by comments that the Statement 33 disclosures were not widely used after a period as short as five years. He acknowledges that improvement of disclosures about the effects of changing prices requires a number of complex and difficult decisions. However, the importance of those effects requires that the Statement 33 effort be continued to complete the development of an alternate measure of enterprise performance and that disclosures based on that measure be evaluated for a reasonable period of years before deciding to end the experiment.

Mr. Swieringa shares the views of Mr. Mosso and Mr. Lauver. In addition, he believes that Statement 33 should not be rescinded because an important opportunity exists now to reconsider the Statement 33 disclosures. Systems and data continuity will be lost by making these disclosures voluntary, and reinstating requirements to disclose the effects of changing prices on business enterprises when inflation rates increase will be difficult, time consuming, and costly.

The Statement 33 disclosures were developed in the late 1970s when double-digit inflation rates created considerable pressure for information about the effects of changing prices on enterprise financial position and performance. Since Statement 33 was issued, inflation rates have decreased dramatically and evidence has been obtained about the limited use of this information. Lower inflation rates and evidence of limited use are not independent events, but they provide a context in which a reconsideration of the Statement 33 disclosures can take place without the crisis atmosphere of the late 1970s. Mr. Swieringa believes that such a reconsideration could be based on the comments received on the December 1984 Exposure Draft and on evidence presented in several published articles and monographs.

Mr. Swieringa also believes that systems and data continuity will be lost by issuing this Statement. Statement 33 initially applied only to very large public enterprises, but the number of those enterprises increased over time because of growth and inflation. Those enterprises implemented systems to capture and report Statement 33 data. One concern is that those enterprises will remove their systems, thereby limiting their ability and inclination to provide the data when inflation rates increase. Another concern is that Statement 33 data will no longer be readily available from data service organizations in machine-readable form. In recent years, analysts and researchers have used those data for trend analysis and for model estimation and testing. The loss of those data may limit the ability and inclination of users and researchers to continue to assess the effects of changing prices on enterprise financial position and performance.

Finally, Mr. Swieringa believes that reinstating requirements to disclose the effects of changing prices on business enterprises when inflation rates increase will be as difficult, time consuming, and costly as the initial implementation of Statement 33 disclosures in 1979. The alternative approaches described in paragraph 120 and the criteria described in paragraphs 123-126 will have to be considered anew in any future project that considers reinstating those requirements.

Members of the Financial Accounting Standards Board:

Donald J. Kirk,
   Chairman
Victor H. Brown

Raymond C. Lauver
David Mosso
C. Arthur Northrop

Robert J. Swieringa
Arthur R. Wyatt

Appendix A

GUIDANCE FOR THE MEASUREMENT AND PRESENTATION OF SUPPLEMENTARY INFORMATION ON EFFECTS OF CHANGING PRICES

CONTENTS

Appendix A

GUIDANCE FOR THE MEASUREMENT AND PRESENTATION OF SUPPLEMENTARY INFORMATION ON EFFECTS OF CHANGING PRICES

Introduction

5. The Board and others expended considerable effort to develop the supplementary disclosures on the effects of changing prices required by Statement 33, as amended. The Board believes that those requirements are the best method devised to date for the presentation of those disclosures. Accordingly, those requirements have been combined[1] in this appendix for the benefit of those enterprises that wish to continue making those disclosures.

6. Although the U.S. economy is experiencing little inflation at the present time, that condition may not continue. If it does not, the Board again may need to require disclosure of the effects of changing prices. If so, this appendix is likely to serve as a starting point for the development of a standard on reporting the effects of changing prices.

Presentation

Five-Year Summary of Selected Financial Data

7. An enterprise shall disclose the following information[2] for each of the five most recent years[3] (paragraphs 36 and 37):

a. Net sales and other operating revenues
b. **Income from continuing operations**[4] on a current cost basis (paragraphs 32 and 33)

---

[1]The combining of prior requirements retains the editorial style of the relevant FASB Statements, for example, the use of "shall" is retained even though the presentations and measurements described are now voluntary.

[2]An enterprise that presents consolidated financial statements shall present the information required by this appendix on the same consolidated basis. The information required by this appendix need not be presented for a parent company, an investee company, or other enterprise in a financial report that includes the results for that enterprise in consolidated financial statements.

[3]The information required by this appendix shall be presented as supplementary information in any published annual report that contains the primary financial statements of the enterprise except that the information need not be presented in an interim financial report. The information required by this appendix need not be presented for segments of a business enterprise although such presentations are encouraged.

[4]Terms defined in paragraph 44 of this appendix are in **boldface type** the first time they appear in this appendix.

c. **Purchasing power gain or loss** on net monetary items (paragraphs 40-43)
d. Increase or decrease in the current cost or lower **recoverable amount** of inventory and property, plant, and equipment,[5] net of inflation (paragraphs 34 and 35)
e. The aggregate foreign currency **translation adjustment** on a current cost basis, if applicable (paragraphs 9, 38, and 39)
f. Net assets at year-end on a current cost basis (paragraphs 27 and 28)
g. Income per common share from continuing operations on a current cost basis
h. Cash dividends declared per common share
i. Market price per common share at year-end.

8. The information presented in the five-year summary shall be stated as either of the following:

a. In average-for-the-year or end-of-year units of constant purchasing power
b. In dollars[6] having a purchasing power equal to that of dollars of the base period used by the Bureau of Labor Statistics in calculating the Consumer Price Index for All Urban Consumers (CPI-U)[7] (currently 1967).

An enterprise shall disclose the level of the CPI-U used for each of the five most recent years.

9. If the enterprise has a significant foreign operation measured in a functional currency other than the U.S. dollar (dollar), it shall disclose whether adjustments to the current cost information to reflect the effects of general inflation are based on the U.S. general price level index (the **translate-restate** method, paragraph 38) or on a functional currency general price level index (the **restate-translate** method, paragraph 39).

10. The enterprise shall provide an explanation of the disclosures required by this appendix and a discussion of their significance in the circumstances of the enterprise. Disclosure and discussion of additional information to help users of the financial report understand the effects of changing prices on the activities of the enterprise are encouraged.

Additional Disclosures for the Current Year

11. In addition to the information required by paragraphs 7-10, an enterprise shall provide the information specified in paragraphs 12 and 13 if income from continuing operations on a **current cost/constant purchasing power** basis would differ significantly from income from continuing operations in the primary financial statements.

12. An enterprise shall disclose certain components of income from continuing operations for the current year on a current cost basis (paragraphs 32 and 33) applying the same constant purchasing power option used for presentation of the five-year summary. The information may be presented in a *statement format* (disclosing revenues, expenses, gains, and losses), in a *reconciliation format* (disclosing adjustments to the income from continuing operations that is shown in the primary income statement), or in notes to the five-year summary required by paragraph 7. Formats for presenting the supplementary information are illustrated in paragraph 45. Whichever format is used, the presentation shall disclose (for example, in a reconciliation format) or allow the reader to determine (for example, in a statement format) the difference between the amount in the primary statements and the current cost amount of the following items: cost of goods sold and depreciation, depletion, and amortization expense. If depreciation has been allocated among various expense categories in the supplementary computations of income from continuing operations (for example, among cost of goods sold and other functional expenses), the aggregate amount of depreciation on a current cost basis shall be included in the notes to the supplementary information. In addition to information about income from continuing operations, the enterprise may include the following items in a schedule of current year information: (a) the purchasing power gain or loss on net monetary items, (b) the increase or decrease in the current cost or lower recoverable amount of inventory and property, plant, and equipment, net of inflation, and (c) the translation adjustment. As illustrated in paragraph 45 and defined in the glossary in paragraph 44, income from

---

[5]For the purposes of this appendix, except where otherwise provided, "inventory" and "property, plant, and equipment" shall include land and other natural resources and capitalized leasehold interests but *not* goodwill or other intangible assets.

[6]As a practical matter, this option is not available to enterprises that measure a significant part of their operations in one or more functional currencies other than the U.S. dollar and that elect to use the restate-translate method (paragraph 39) for measuring inflation-adjusted current cost information.

[7]The index is published in *Monthly Labor Review.* Those desiring prompt and direct information may subscribe to the Consumer Price Index press release mailing list of the Department of Labor. If the level of the Consumer Price Index at the end of the year and the data required to compute the average level of the index over the year have not been published in time for preparation of the annual report, they may be estimated by referring to published forecasts based on economic statistics or by extrapolation based on recently reported changes in the index.

continuing operations does not include items (a), (b), or (c).

13. An enterprise shall also disclose:

a. Separate amounts for the current cost or lower recoverable amount at the end of the current year of inventory and property, plant, and equipment (paragraphs 16-26 and 29-31)

b. The increase or decrease in current cost or lower recoverable amount before and after adjusting for the effects of inflation of inventory and property, plant, and equipment for the current year (paragraphs 34 and 35)

c. The principal types of information used to calculate the current cost of inventory; property, plant, and equipment; cost of goods sold; and depreciation, depletion, and amortization expense (paragraphs 19-26)

d. Any differences between (1) the depreciation methods, estimates of useful lives, and salvage values of assets used for calculations of current cost/constant purchasing power depreciation and (2) the methods and estimates used for calculations of depreciation in the primary financial statements (paragraph 22).

Additional Disclosures by Enterprises with Mineral Resource Assets

14. For its mineral reserves other than oil and gas, an enterprise shall disclose the following additional information for each of its five most recent fiscal years:

a. Estimates of significant quantities of **proved mineral reserves** or proved and **probable mineral reserves** (whichever is used for cost amortization purposes) at the end of the year or at the most recent date during the year for which estimates can be made (If estimates are not made as of the end of the year, the disclosures shall indicate the dates of the estimates.)

b. The estimated quantity, expressed in physical units or in percentages of reserves, of each mineral product that is recoverable in significant commercial quantities if the mineral reserves included under subparagraph (a) include deposits containing one or more significant mineral products

c. The quantities of each significant mineral produced during the year (If the mineral reserves included under subparagraph (a) are ones that are milled or similarly processed, the quantity of each significant mineral product produced by the milling or similar process shall also be disclosed.)

d. The quantity of significant proved, or proved and probable, mineral reserves purchased or

sold in place during the year

e. For each significant mineral product, the average market price or, for mineral products transferred within the enterprise, the equivalent market price prior to use in a manufacturing process.

15. In determining the quantities to be reported in conformity with paragraph 14:

a. If the enterprise issues consolidated financial statements, 100 percent of the quantities attributable to the parent company and 100 percent of the quantities attributable to its consolidated subsidiaries (whether or not wholly owned) shall be included.

b. If the enterprise's financial statements include investments that are proportionately consolidated, the enterprise's quantities shall include its proportionate share of the investee's quantities.

c. If the enterprise's financial statements include investments that are accounted for by the equity method, the investee's quantities shall not be included in the disclosures of the enterprise's quantities. However, the enterprise's (investor's) share of the investee's quantities of reserves shall be reported separately, if significant.

Measurement

Inventory and Property, Plant, and Equipment

16. Current cost amounts of inventory and property, plant, and equipment are measured as follows:

a. Inventory at current cost or lower recoverable amount at the measurement date

b. Property, plant, and equipment at the current cost or lower recoverable amount of the assets' remaining service potential at the measurement date

c. Resources used on a partly completed contract at current cost or lower recoverable amount at the date of use on or commitment to the contract.

17. The current cost of inventory owned by an enterprise is the current cost of purchasing the goods concerned or the current cost of the resources required to produce the goods concerned (including an allowance for the current overhead costs according to the allocation bases used under generally accepted accounting principles), whichever would be applicable in the circumstances of the enterprise.

18. The current cost of property, plant, and equipment owned by an enterprise is the current cost of acquiring the same service potential (indicated by operating costs and physical output capacity) as embodied by the asset owned; the information used to measure current cost reflects whatever method of acquisition would currently be appropriate in the circumstances of the enterprise. The current cost of a used asset may be calculated:

a. By measuring the current cost of a new asset that has the same service potential as the used asset had when it was new (the current cost of the asset as if it were new) and deducting an allowance for depreciation
b. By measuring the current cost of a used asset of the same age and in the same condition as the asset owned
c. By measuring the current cost of a new asset with a different service potential and adjusting that cost for the value of the difference in service potential due to differences in life, output capacity, nature of service, and operating costs.

19. Various types of information may be used in the measurement methods described in paragraphs 17 and 18 to determine the current cost of inventory; property, plant, and equipment; cost of goods sold;[8] and depreciation, depletion, and amortization expense. The information may be applied to single items or broad categories, as appropriate in the circumstances. The following types of information are listed as examples of the information that may be used but are *not* listed in any order of preferability. The enterprise is expected to select types of information appropriate to its particular circumstances, giving due consideration to their availability, reliability, and cost:

a. Indexation
   (1) Externally generated price indexes for the class of goods or services being measured
   (2) Internally generated price indexes for the class of goods or services being measured
b. Direct pricing
   (1) Current invoice prices
   (2) Vendors' price lists or other quotations or estimates
   (3) Standard manufacturing costs that reflect current costs.

20. An enterprise may substitute **historical cost** amounts adjusted by an externally generated price index of a broad-based measure of general purchasing power (that is, **historical cost/constant purchasing power** amounts) for current cost amounts if that substitution would not result in a significantly different number for income from continuing operations than other means of estimating current cost amounts described in this appendix. For example, an enterprise with small amounts of inventory and property, plant, and equipment apart from certain specialized assets (paragraphs 23-26) may be able to report historical cost/constant purchasing power information. In such circumstances, disclosure of the increase or decrease in the current cost or lower recoverable amount of inventory and property, plant, and equipment, net of inflation (paragraphs 7(d) and 13(b)), is not required, but the discussions described in paragraphs 10 and 13(a), (c), and (d) are required.

21. Current cost measurements are to be based on production or purchase of the asset in whatever location or market would minimize total cost including transportation cost. For a U.S. operation, either (a) the purchase would be made in the United States and current cost would be estimated directly in dollars or (b) the purchase would be made in a foreign market and the current cost in that market would be translated into dollars at the current exchange rate. An enterprise may need to measure the current cost of inventory and property, plant, and equipment located outside the United States. That may be difficult depending upon the availability of information in the country concerned, and, accordingly, reasonable approximations are acceptable. If a foreign operation first measures current cost in a currency other than its functional currency, that amount is then translated into the functional currency at the current exchange rate.

22. There is a presumption that depreciation methods, estimates of useful lives, and salvage values of assets for purposes of the supplementary information are the same as the methods and estimates used for calculations in the primary financial statements. However, if the primary financial statements are based on methods and estimates that partly allow for price changes, different methods and estimates may be used for purposes of the supplementary information.

Specialized Assets

23. The current cost of **mineral resource assets** is determined by current market buying prices or by the current cost of finding and developing min-

[8]If turnover is rapid and material amounts of depreciation are not allocated to inventory, cost of goods sold measured on a Last-In, First-Out (LIFO) basis may provide an acceptable approximation of cost of goods sold, measured at current cost, provided that the effect of any LIFO inventory liquidations (that is, any decreases in earlier years' LIFO layers) is excluded.

eral reserves. The Board recognizes that no generally accepted approach exists for measuring the current finding cost of mineral reserves. To indicate the effects of changes in current costs, it may be impracticable to do more than adjust historical costs by an index of the changes in specific prices of the inputs concerned. That approach may fail to yield a close approximation of the current cost of finding and developing new reserves. In recognition of that difficulty, the requirements of this appendix are flexible regarding the approach used to measure current cost of mineral resource assets. The approach may include use of specific price indexes, direct information about market buying prices, and other statistical evidence of the cost of acquisitions.

24. Because Statement 69 requires an enterprise to disclose a standardized measure of discounted future net cash flows relating to proved oil and gas reserve quantities, the enterprise may follow the approach in paragraph 23 or in paragraph 25 for its oil and gas mineral resource assets. Paragraph 13(c) requires disclosure of the types of information that have been used to measure current costs.

25. Timberlands and growing timber, **income-producing real estate,** and **motion picture films** have certain special features that raise doubts about the applicability of the current cost measurement methods required for other assets. Accordingly, an enterprise may disclose historical cost amounts adjusted by an externally generated index of a broad-based measure of general purchasing power as substitutes for current cost amounts for such assets and their related expenses.

26. If an enterprise estimates the current cost of growing timber and timber harvested by adjusting historical cost for the changes in specific prices, those historical costs may either (a) be limited to the costs that are capitalized in the primary financial statements or (b) include all costs that are directly related to reforestation and forest management, such as planting, fertilization, fire protection, property taxes, and nursery stock, whether or not those costs are capitalized in the primary financial statements.

Net Assets

27. If the enterprise presents the minimum information required by this appendix, the amount of net assets (that is, shareholders' equity) is the amount of net assets reported in the primary financial statements, adjusted for the difference between the historical cost amounts and the current cost or lower recoverable amounts of inventory and property, plant, and equipment.

28. If the enterprise elects to present comprehensive current cost/constant purchasing power financial statements as supplementary information, the amount of net assets in the five-year summary is the amount reported in the supplementary balance sheet.

Recoverable Amount

29. Recoverable amount is the current worth of the net amount of cash expected to be recoverable from the use or sale of an asset. It may be measured by considering the **value in use** or **current market value** of the asset concerned. Value in use is used to determine recoverable amount of an asset if immediate sale of the asset is not intended. Current market value is used to determine recoverable amount only if the asset is about to be sold.

30. If the recoverable amount for a group of assets is judged to be materially and permanently lower than the current cost amount, the *recoverable amount* is used as a measure of the assets and of the expense associated with the use or sale of the assets. Decisions on the measurement of assets at their recoverable amounts need not be made by considering assets individually unless they are used independently of other assets.

31. An enterprise that is subject to rate regulation or another form of price control may be limited to a maximum recovery through its selling prices, based on the nominal currency amount of the historical cost of its assets. In that situation, historical costs measured in nominal currency may represent an appropriate basis for the measurement of the recoverable amounts associated with those assets. Recoverable amounts may also be lower than historical costs. Nevertheless, cost of goods sold and depreciation, depletion, and amortization expense are to be measured at current cost/constant purchasing power amounts provided that replacement of the service potential of the related assets would be undertaken, if necessary, in current economic conditions; if replacement would not be undertaken, those expenses are to be measured at recoverable amounts.

Income from Continuing Operations

32. An enterprise that presents the minimum information required by this appendix shall measure income from continuing operations on a current cost basis as follows:

a. Cost of goods sold at current cost or lower recoverable amount at the date of sale or at the date on which resources are used on or committed to a specific contract

b. Depreciation, depletion, and amortization expense of property, plant, and equipment on the basis of the average current cost of the assets' service potential or lower recoverable amount during the period of use.

Other revenues, expenses, gains, and losses may be measured at the amounts included in the primary income statement. (Refer to paragraphs 16-26 and 29-31 for discussions of current cost or lower recoverable amount measurements.)

33. The amount of income tax expense in computations of current cost/constant purchasing power income from continuing operations is the same as the amount of income tax expense charged against income from continuing operations in the primary financial statements. No adjustments are to be made to income tax expense for any timing differences that might be deemed to arise as a result of the use of current cost accounting methods. Income tax expense is not to be allocated between income from continuing operations and the increases or decreases in current cost amounts of inventory and property, plant, and equipment.

Increase or Decrease in the Current Cost Amounts of Inventory and Property, Plant, and Equipment, Net of Inflation

34. The increase or decrease in the current cost amounts of inventory and property, plant, and equipment represents the difference between the measures of the assets at their *entry dates* for the year and the measures of the assets at their *exit dates* for the year. *Entry dates* means the beginning of the year or the dates of acquisition, whichever is applicable; *exit dates* means the end of the year or the dates of use, sale, or commitment to a specific contract, whichever is applicable. For the purposes of this paragraph, assets are measured in accordance with the provisions of paragraphs 16-26 and 29-31.

35. For the current year, the increase or decrease in current cost amounts of inventory and property, plant, and equipment is reported both before and after eliminating the effects of general inflation (paragraph 13(b)). In the five-year summary, the increase or decrease is reported after elimination of the effects of each year's general inflation (paragraph 7(d)). An acceptable approximate method of calculating the increase or

decrease in current cost amounts and the inflation adjustment is illustrated in paragraphs 67-70.

Restatement of Current Cost Information into Units of Constant Purchasing Power

36. Enterprises that do not have significant foreign operations or that use the dollar as the functional currency for all significant foreign operations are to use the CPI-U to restate current costs into units of constant purchasing power. Acceptable approximate methods are illustrated in paragraph 82.

37. The effects of general inflation on current cost information for operations measured in a foreign functional currency are measured either (a) after translation and based on the CPI-U (the translate-restate method) or (b) before translation and based on a broad-based measure of the change in the general purchasing power of the functional currency (the restate-translate method).[9] The same method is to be used for all operations measured in functional currencies other than the dollar and for all periods presented. Acceptable approximate methods are illustrated in paragraphs 82, 83, 90, and 91.

Translation Adjustment

38. If current cost information for operations measured in functional currencies other than the dollar is based on the translate-restate method, the aggregate translation adjustment on the current cost basis is stated net of any income taxes allocated to the aggregate translation adjustment in the primary financial statements (FASB Statement No. 52, *Foreign Currency Translation,* paragraph 31(c)).

39. If current cost information for operations measured in functional currencies other than the dollar is based on the restate-translate method, the aggregate translation adjustment on the current cost basis is stated net of both any income taxes allocated to the aggregate translation adjustment in the primary financial statements and the aggregate **parity adjustment.** The parity adjustment is the amount needed to measure end-of-year net assets in (a) average-for-the-year dollars, if income from continuing operations is measured in average-for-the-year functional currency units, or (b) end-of-year dollars, if income

---

[9]The choice of a measure of functional currency purchasing power should take into account the availability, reliability, and timeliness of a general price level index and the frequency with which it is adjusted. It is anticipated that an appropriate index of the change in the general price level will be available for most functional currencies. Indexes are published in most countries, and some indexes are published periodically by organizations such as the International Monetary Fund, the Organisation for Economic Co-Operation and Development, and the United Nations. However, in some cases indexes may not be available on a timely basis or may not be sufficiently reliable. In those circumstances, management should estimate the change in the general price level.

from continuing operations is measured in end-of-year functional currency units.

Purchasing Power Gain or Loss on Net Monetary Items

40. The purchasing power gain or loss on net monetary items is the net gain or loss determined by restating in units of constant purchasing power the opening and closing balances of, and transactions in, **monetary assets** and **monetary liabilities.** Acceptable approximate methods of calculating the purchasing power gain or loss on net monetary items are illustrated in paragraphs 66, 83, and 90.

41. The economic significance of monetary assets and liabilities depends heavily on the general purchasing power of money, although other factors, such as creditworthiness of debtors, may affect their significance. The economic significance of nonmonetary items depends heavily on the value of specific goods and services. Nonmonetary assets include (a) goods held primarily for resale or assets held primarily for direct use in providing services for the business of the enterprise, (b) claims to cash in amounts dependent on future prices of specific goods or services, and (c) residual rights such as goodwill or equity interests. Nonmonetary liabilities include (a) obligations to furnish goods or services in quantities that are fixed or determinable without reference to changes in prices and (b) obligations to pay cash in amounts dependent on future prices of specific goods or services. Guidance on the classification of balance sheet items as monetary or nonmonetary is set forth in paragraphs 96-108.

42. If inflation-adjusted current cost information is based on the translate-restate method, the purchasing power gain or loss on net monetary items is equal to the net gain or loss determined by restating the opening and closing balances of, and transactions in, monetary assets and liabilities in units of constant purchasing power as measured by the CPI-U.

43. If inflation-adjusted current cost information is based on the restate-translate method, the purchasing power gain or loss on net monetary items is equal to the net gain or loss determined by restating the opening and closing balances of, and transactions in, monetary assets and liabilities in units of constant purchasing power as measured by the change in the general purchasing power of the functional currency. The purchasing power gain or loss computed in that manner is translated into its dollar equivalent at the average exchange rate for the period.

Glossary

44. This paragraph defines certain terms that are used in this appendix.

Current cost/constant purchasing power accounting
A method of accounting based on measures of current cost or lower recoverable amount in units of currency, each of which has the same general purchasing power. For operations in which the dollar is the functional currency, the general purchasing power of the dollar is used and the CPI-U is the required measure of purchasing power (paragraph 36). For operations in which the functional currency is other than the dollar, the general purchasing power of either the dollar or the functional currency is used (paragraph 37).

Current market value
The amount of cash, or its equivalent, expected to be derived from the sale of an asset net of costs required to be incurred as a result of the sale.

Historical cost accounting
The generally accepted method of accounting used in the primary financial statements that is based on measures of historical prices without restatement into units, each of which has the same general purchasing power.

Historical cost/constant purchasing power accounting
A method of accounting based on measures of historical prices in units of a currency, each of which has the same general purchasing power.

Income from continuing operations
Income after applicable income taxes but excluding the results of discontinued operations, extraordinary items, the cumulative effect of accounting changes, translation adjustments, purchasing power gains and losses on monetary items, and increases and decreases in the current cost or lower recoverable amount of nonmonetary assets and liabilities.

Income-producing real estate
Properties that meet all of the following criteria:

a. Cash flows can be directly associated with a long-term leasing agreement with unaffiliated parties.
b. The property is being operated. (It is not in a construction phase.)

c. Future cash flows from the property are reasonably estimable.

d. Ancillary services are not a significant part of the lease agreement.

Hotels, which have occupancy rates and related cash flows that may fluctuate to a relatively large extent, do not meet the criteria for income-producing real estate.

Mineral resource assets
Assets that are directly associated with and derive value from all minerals that are extracted from the earth. Such minerals include oil and gas, ores containing ferrous and non-ferrous metals, coal, shale, geothermal steam, sulphur, salt, stone, phosphate, sand, and gravel. Mineral resource assets include mineral interests in properties, completed and uncompleted wells, and related equipment and facilities and other facilities required for purposes of extraction (FASB Statement No. 19, *Financial Accounting and Reporting by Oil and Gas Producing Companies,* paragraph 11). This definition does not cover support equipment because that equipment is included in the property, plant, and equipment for which current cost measurements are required by this appendix.

Monetary asset
Money or a claim to receive a sum of money the amount of which is fixed or determinable without reference to future prices of specific goods or services.

Monetary liability
An obligation to pay a sum of money the amount of which is fixed or determinable without reference to future prices of specific goods and services.

Motion picture films
All types of films and videotapes and disks, including features, television specials, series, and cartoons that meet one of the following criteria:

a. Exhibited in theaters

b. Licensed for exhibition by individual television stations, groups of stations, networks, cable television systems, or other means

c. Licensed for commercial reproduction (for example, for the home viewing market).

Parity adjustment
The effect of the difference between local and U.S. inflation for the year on net assets (that is, shareholders' equity) measured in nominal

dollars. If only the differential rates of U.S. and local inflation are reflected in the exchange rates (parity), the parity adjustment and the translation adjustment net to zero. Therefore, the sum of the parity adjustment and the translation adjustment represents the effect of exchange rate changes in excess of (or less than) that needed to maintain purchasing power parity between the functional currency and the dollar.

Probable mineral reserves
In extractive industries other than oil and gas, the estimated quantities of commercially recoverable reserves that are less well defined than proved.

Proved mineral reserves
In extractive industries other than oil and gas, the estimated quantities of commercially recoverable reserves that, on the basis of geological, geophysical, and engineering data, can be demonstrated with a reasonably high degree of certainty to be recoverable in the future from known mineral deposits by either primary or improved recovery methods.

Purchasing power gain or loss on net monetary items
The net gain or loss determined by restating in units of constant purchasing power the opening and closing balances of, and transactions in, monetary assets and liabilities.

Recoverable amount
Current worth of the net amount of cash expected to be recoverable from the use or sale of an asset (paragraphs 29-31).

Restate-translate
An approach to converting current cost/nominal functional currency data of a foreign operation into units of constant purchasing power expressed in dollars. Using this approach, the current cost/nominal functional currency data are restated into units of constant purchasing power using a general price index for the foreign currency. After restatement into units of constant functional currency purchasing power, the current cost data are translated into dollars. This approach often necessitates a parity adjustment.

Translate-restate
An approach to converting current cost/nominal functional currency data of a foreign operation into units of constant purchasing power expressed in dollars. Using this approach, the current cost/nominal functional currency data are first translated into dollars

and then restated into units of constant purchasing power using the CPI-U.

Translation adjustment

The effect that results from the process of translating an entity's financial statements from its functional currency into the dollar (paragraphs 38 and 39).

Value in use

The amount determined by discounting the future cash flows (including the ultimate proceeds of disposal) expected to be derived from the use of an asset at an appropriate rate that allows for the risk of the activities concerned.

Illustrations of Disclosures

45. This paragraph illustrates formats that may be used to disclose the information required by this appendix for a manufacturing enterprise. An enterprise may choose to disclose the information required by paragraphs 7-13 of this appendix (a) in a schedule of annual information (for example, Schedule 1 or Schedule 2), in a five-year summary (for example, Schedule 3 or Schedule 4), and notes to those schedules or (b) in a five-year summary and notes to that summary (for example, Schedule 5). Many enterprises have included amounts reported in the primary statements alongside current cost/constant purchasing power amounts in the five-year summary. The Board encourages enterprises to continue to adapt the disclosure formats to enhance such comparisons. Schedule 4 illustrates a five-year summary with comparative data from the primary financial statements. The Board also encourages enterprises to provide more detailed discussions than the illustrative notes in this paragraph—especially discussion of the significance of the information in the circumstances of the enterprise (required by paragraph 10) and the principal types of information used to calculate current cost amounts (required by paragraph 13(c)). Illustrative calculations are given in paragraphs 46-95. In the schedules that follow, the CPI-U is expressed in average dollars.

Schedule 1

STATEMENT OF INCOME FROM CONTINUING OPERATIONS ADJUSTED FOR CHANGING PRICES[a]

For the Year Ended December 31, 19X6
In Thousands of Average 19X6 Dollars

Income from continuing operations, as reported in the primary income statement	$ 22,995
Adjustments to reflect current costs	
Cost of goods sold	(8,408)
Depreciation expense	(9,748)
Income from continuing operations adjusted for changes in specific prices	$ 4,839
Gain from decline in purchasing power of net amounts owed[b]	$ 2,449
Increase in specific prices (current cost) of inventory and property, plant, and equipment held during the year[c]	$ 25,846
Effect of increase in general price level	5,388
Excess of increase in specific prices over increase in the general price level	$ 20,458
Foreign currency translation adjustment[d]	$ (624)

[a]The condensed financial information in this schedule compares selected information from the primary financial statements with information that reflects effects of changes in the specific prices (current cost) of inventory and property, plant, and equipment expressed in units of constant purchasing power. The current cost amounts for inventory and cost of goods sold reflect actual manufacturing costs incurred in 19X6. The current cost amounts for major components of property, plant, and equipment were determined by applying specific price indexes to the applicable historical costs. For assets used in U.S. operations, Producer Price Indexes and Factory Mutual Building Indexes were used; for assets used in foreign operations, appropriate indexes for each country were used. The current cost information is expressed in average 19X6 dollars as measured by the CPI-U.

[b]The purchasing power gain on net amounts owed is an economic benefit to the enterprise that results from being able to repay those amounts with cheaper dollars.

[c]During 19X6, the specific prices (current cost) of inventory increased by $9,108 and of property, plant, and equipment by $16,738. The total increase of $25,846 exceeded the increase necessary to keep pace with general inflation. At December 31, 19X6, the current cost of inventory was $65,700 and of property, plant, and equipment, net of accumulated depreciation, was $89,335 (both measured in December 31, 19X6 units of purchasing power). Those amounts are higher than the amounts in the primary statements of $63,000 for inventory and $45,750 for property, plant, and equipment, net of accumulated depreciation; therefore, it is reasonable to expect income from continuing operations on a current cost basis for 19X7 to remain significantly below that reported in the primary statements.

[d]Current cost amounts for foreign operations are measured in their functional currencies, translated into dollar equivalents using the average exchange rate for the year, and restated into constant units of purchasing power using the CPI-U. Essentially, the foreign currency translation adjustment is the effect of changes in exchange rates during the year on shareholders' equity. The negative translation adjustment indicates that, overall, the dollar has increased in value relative to the functional currencies used to measure the foreign operations of the enterprise.

Schedule 2

STATEMENT OF INCOME FROM CONTINUING OPERATIONS
ADJUSTED FOR CHANGING PRICES[a]

For the Year Ended December 31, 19X6
In Thousands of Dollars

	As Reported in the Primary Statements	Adjusted for Changes in Specific Prices (Current Cost)
Net sales and other operating revenues	$ 275,500	$ 275,500
Cost of goods sold	197,000	205,408
Depreciation expense	10,275	20,023
Other operating expenses	14,685	14,685
Interest expense	7,550	7,550
Income tax expense	22,995	22,995
	252,505	270,661
Income from continuing operations	$ 22,995	$ 4,839
Gain from decline in purchasing power of net amounts owed[b]		$ 2,449
Increase in specific prices (current cost) of inventory and property, plant, and equipment held during the year[c]		$ 25,846
Effect of increase in general price level		5,388
Excess of increase in specific prices over increase in the general price level		$ 20,458
Foreign currency translation adjustment[d]	$ (295)	$ (624)

---

[a]The condensed financial information in this schedule compares selected information from the primary financial statements with information that reflects effects of changes in the specific prices (current cost) of inventory and property, plant, and equipment expressed in units of constant purchasing power. The current cost amounts for inventory and cost of goods sold reflect actual manufacturing costs incurred in 19X6. The current cost amounts for major components of property, plant, and equipment were determined by applying specific price indexes to the applicable historical costs. For assets used in U.S. operations, Producer Price Indexes and Factory Mutual Building Indexes were used; for assets used in foreign operations, appropriate indexes for each country were used. The current cost information is expressed in average 19X6 dollars as measured by the CPI-U.

[b]The purchasing power gain on net amounts owed is an economic benefit to the enterprise that results from being able to repay those amounts with cheaper dollars.

[c]During 19X6, the specific prices (current cost) of inventory increased by $9,108 and of property, plant, and equipment by $16,738. The total increase of $25,846 exceeded the increase necessary to keep pace with general inflation. At December 31, 19X6, the current cost of inventory was $65,700 and of property, plant, and equipment, net of accumulated depreciation, was $89,335 (both measured in December 31, 19X6 units of purchasing power). Those amounts are higher than the amounts in the primary statements of $63,000 for inventory and $45,750 for property, plant, and equipment, net of accumulated depreciation; therefore, it is reasonable to expect income from continuing operations on a current cost basis for 19X7 to remain significantly below that reported in the primary statements.

[d]Current cost amounts for foreign operations are measured in their functional currencies, translated into dollar equivalents using the average exchange rate for the year, and restated into constant units of purchasing power using the CPI-U. Essentially, the foreign currency translation adjustment is the effect of changes in exchange rates during the year on shareholders' equity. The negative translation adjustment indicates that, overall, the dollar has increased in value relative to the functional currencies used to measure the foreign operations of the enterprise.

Schedule 3

FIVE-YEAR COMPARISON OF SELECTED FINANCIAL DATA ADJUSTED FOR EFFECTS OF CHANGING PRICES

In Thousands of Average 19X6 Dollars, except for Per Share Amounts

	Year Ended December 31,				
	19X6	**19X5**	**19X4**	**19X3**	**19X2**
Net sales and other operating revenues	$ 275,500	$ 247,500	$ 240,000	$ 235,500	$ 265,000
Income (loss) from continuing operations	4,839	1,660	(2,102)	(4,663)	1,261
Gain from decline in purchasing power of net amounts owed	2,449	7,027	5,432	1,247	6,375
Excess of increase in specific prices of inventory and property, plant, and equipment over increase in the general price level	20,458	2,292	3,853	8,597	3,777
Foreign currency translation adjustment	(624)	(386)	(454)	(293)	127
Net assets at year-end[a]	92,027	67,905	60,409	56,966	55,705
Per share information:					
Income (loss) from continuing operations	$ 3.23	$ 1.11	$ (1.40)	$ (3.11)	$ .84
Cash dividends declared	2.00	2.06	2.19	2.42	2.75
Market price at year-end	35	39	43	27	32
Average consumer price index[b]	298.4	289.1	272.4	246.8	217.4

[a]Net assets include inventory and property, plant, and equipment at current cost and all other items as they are reported in the primary financial statements. No adjustment has been made for the lower tax basis applicable to the current cost amounts included in net assets.
[b]For purposes of this illustration, although the years for which information has been provided are nonspecific, the actual 1979-1983 average index numbers have been applied.

Schedule 4

FIVE-YEAR COMPARISON OF SELECTED FINANCIAL DATA

In Thousands of Dollars,
except for Per Share Amounts

	Year Ended December 31,				
	19X6	**19X5**	**19X4**	**19X3**	**19X2**
Total revenue					
As reported	$ 275,500	$ 239,800	$ 219,100	$ 194,800	$ 193,100
Adjusted for general inflation[a]	275,500	247,500	240,000	235,500	265,000
Income (loss) from operations					
As reported	22,995	11,097	4,756	9,977	11,847
Adjusted for specific price changes[a]	4,839	1,660	(2,102)	(4,663)	1,261
Purchasing power gain from holding net					
monetary liabilities[a]	2,449	7,027	5,432	1,247	6,375
Excess of increase in specific prices of assets					
over increase in the general price level[a]	20,458	2,292	3,853	8,597	3,777
Foreign currency translation adjustment					
As reported	(295)	(276)	(396)	(138)	76
Adjusted for specific price changes[a]	(624)	(386)	(454)	(293)	127
Net assets at year-end					
As reported	47,700	28,000	20,179	18,819	11,980
Adjusted for specific price changes[b]	92,027	67,905	60,409	56,966	55,705
Per share information:					
Income (loss) from operations					
As reported	$ 15.33	$ 7.40	$ 3.17	$ 6.65	$ 7.90
Adjusted for specific price changes[a]	3.23	1.11	(1.40)	(3.11)	.84
Cash dividends declared					
As reported	2.00	2.00	2.00	2.00	2.00
Adjusted for general inflation[a]	2.00	2.06	2.19	2.42	2.75
Market price at year-end					
As reported	36	38	41	23	25
Adjusted for general inflation[a]	35	39	43	27	32
Average consumer price index[c]	298.4	289.1	272.4	246.8	217.4

---

[a]In average 19X6 dollars.

[b]Net assets adjusted for specific price changes include inventory and property, plant, and equipment at current cost and all other items as they are reported in the primary financial statements. No adjustment has been made for the lower tax basis applicable to the current cost amounts included in net assets.

[c]For purposes of this illustration, although the years for which information has been provided are nonspecific, the actual 1979-1983 average index numbers have been applied.

Schedule 5

FIVE-YEAR COMPARISON OF SELECTED FINANCIAL DATA
ADJUSTED FOR EFFECTS OF CHANGING PRICES[a]

**In Thousands of Average 19X6 Dollars,
except for Per Share Amounts**

	Year Ended December 31,				
	19X6	**19X5**	**19X4**	**19X3**	**19X2**
Net sales and other operating revenues	$ 275,500	$ 247,500	$ 240,000	$ 235,500	$ 265,000
Income (loss) from continuing operations[b]	4,839	1,660	(2,102)	(4,663)	1,261
Gain from decline in purchasing power of net amounts owed[c]	2,449	7,027	5,432	1,247	6,375
Increase in specific prices of inventory and property, plant, and equipment[d]	20,458	2,292	3,853	8,597	3,777
Foreign currency translation adjustment[e]	(624)	(386)	(454)	(293)	127
Net assets at year-end[d]	92,027	67,905	60,409	56,966	55,705
Per share information:					
Income (loss) from continuing operations	$ 3.23	$ 1.11	$ (1.40)	$ (3.11)	$ .84
Cash dividends declared	2.00	2.06	2.19	2.42	2.75
Market price at year-end	35	39	43	27	32
Average consumer price index[f]	298.4	289.1	272.4	246.8	217.4

---

[a]The condensed financial information in this schedule presents selected information that reflects effects of changes in the specific prices (current cost) of inventory and property, plant, and equipment expressed in units of constant purchasing power. The current cost amounts for inventory and cost of goods sold reflect actual manufacturing costs incurred in 19X6. The current cost amounts for major components of property, plant, and equipment were determined by applying specific price indexes to the applicable historical costs. For assets used in U.S. operations, Producer Price Indexes and Factory Mutual Building Indexes were used; for assets used in foreign operations, appropriate indexes for each country were used. The current cost information is expressed in average 19X6 dollars as measured by the CPI-U.

[b]Income from continuing operations reported in the primary financial statements was $22,995 for 19X6. Current cost income reported in the five-year summary was only $4,839 because depreciation expense on a current cost basis exceeded depreciation expense in the primary statements by $9,748 and current cost of goods sold was $8,408 greater than the amount reported in the primary statements.

[c]The purchasing power gain on net amounts owed is an economic benefit to the enterprise that results from being able to repay those amounts with cheaper dollars.

[d]During 19X6, the specific prices (current cost) of inventory increased by $9,108 and of property, plant, and equipment by $16,738. The total increase exceeded the increase necessary to keep pace with general inflation by $20,458. Net assets include inventory and property, plant, and equipment at current cost and all other items as reported in the primary financial statements (restated into average-for-19X6 dollars). No adjustment has been made for the lower tax basis applicable to the current cost amounts included in net assets. At December 31, 19X6, the current cost of inventory was $65,700 and of property, plant, and equipment, net of accumulated depreciation, was $89,335 (both measured in December 31, 19X6 units of purchasing power). Those amounts are higher than the amounts in the primary statements of $63,000 for inventory and $45,750 for property, plant, and equipment, net of accumulated depreciation; therefore, it is reasonable to expect income from continuing operations on a current cost basis for 19X7 to remain significantly below that reported in the primary statements.

[e]Current cost amounts for foreign operations are measured in their functional currencies, translated into dollar equivalents using the average exchange rate for the year, and restated into constant units of purchasing power using the CPI-U. Essentially, the foreign currency translation adjustment is the effect of changes in exchange rates during the year on shareholders' equity. A negative (positive) translation adjustment indicates that, overall, the dollar increased (decreased) in value relative to the functional currencies used to measure the foreign operations of the enterprise.

[f]For purposes of this illustration, although the years for which information has been provided are nonspecific, the actual 1979-1983 average index numbers have been applied.

**Illustrative Calculations of Current
Cost/Constant Purchasing Power Information**

Introduction

46. Paragraphs 47-95 illustrate the methodology that might be used in calculating the disclosures in paragraph 45.

47. Computation of current cost information should be based on a detailed analysis of all transactions; however, the costs of preparing the information can be reduced with little loss of usefulness by simplifying the methods of calculation. Therefore, only cost of sales and depreciation expense need to be adjusted from the amounts shown in the primary income statement. Revenues, other expenses, and gains and losses need not be adjusted. Approximate methods of computation are acceptable for adjusting cost of sales and depreciation expense. The *measurement* of current cost is not illustrated.

48. The objective in making these calculations is to obtain a *reasonable degree* of accuracy—complete precision is not required. Preparers are encouraged to devise short-cut methods of calculation, appropriate to their individual circumstances.

49. If inventories and cost of sales are accounted for under the LIFO method in the primary financial statements, the only adjustment normally required in computing income from continuing operations would be to eliminate the effect of changing prices on any prior-period LIFO layer liquidation.

50. Seven basic steps to restate historical cost information into current cost/constant purchasing power information are illustrated in paragraphs 47-95:

a. Analyze inventory (at the beginning and end of the year) and cost of goods sold to determine when the costs were incurred
b. Restate inventory and cost of goods sold into current cost
c. Analyze property, plant, and equipment to determine when the related assets were acquired
d. Restate property, plant, and equipment and depreciation, depletion, and amortization expense into current cost

e. Identify the amount of net monetary items (paragraphs 96-108) at the beginning and end of the period and changes during the period
f. Compute the purchasing power gain or loss on net monetary items
g. Compute the change in current cost of inventory and property, plant, and equipment and the related effect of the increase in the general price level.

51. The methodology illustrated in paragraphs 47-95 has been developed for the hypothetical enterprise, Parent Company. Parent Company has a wholly owned foreign subsidiary, Sub Company. Sub Company measures its operations in a functional currency other than the dollar. The changing prices disclosures for Parent Company and Sub Company are developed separately. Merging the amounts calculated for each entity results in a consolidated disclosure:

a. Paragraphs 59-71 illustrate the minimum recommended calculations for the domestic operations of Parent Company. A method of checking the arithmetic accuracy of the calculations is included in paragraph 72.
b. Paragraphs 79-86 illustrate the translate-restate method for Sub Company, a foreign subsidiary that does not use the dollar as a functional currency. A method of checking the arithmetic accuracy of the calculations is included in paragraph 84.
c. The results of the calculations described in (a) and (b) are summarized in paragraph 87 and are reflected in the illustrative disclosures in paragraph 45.

52. Paragraphs 88-95 illustrate the restate-translate method for Sub Company. A method of checking the arithmetic accuracy of the calculations is included in paragraphs 92 and 93.

53. Throughout this appendix, $ indicates nominal dollars, C$ indicates average 19X6 constant dollars, FC indicates nominal functional currency, C$E indicates dollar equivalents of FC amounts using the translate-restate method, CFC indicates average 19X6 constant functional currency, and CFC$ indicates the translated dollar equivalents of CFC amounts using the restate-translate method.

Parent Company Information

54. Historical cost/nominal dollar financial statements

Parent Company Balance Sheet (Unconsolidated)
As of December 31, 19X6 and 19X5
(000s)

	19X6	19X5		19X6	19X5
Current assets:			Current liabilities:		
Cash	$ 1,000	$ 2,000	Accounts payable and accrued expenses	$ 47,000	$ 32,000
Accounts receivable	36,000	16,500	Income taxes payable	6,000	6,000
Inventories, at FIFO cost	63,000	56,000	Current portion of long-term debt	5,000	5,000
Total current assets	100,000	74,500	Total current liabilities	58,000	43,000
Property, plant, and equipment, at cost	100,000	85,000	Deferred income taxes	6,000	5,000
Less accumulated depreciation	56,000	46,000	Long-term debt	34,000	39,000
	44,000	39,000	Total liabilities	98,000	87,000
Investment in Sub Company*	1,500	1,500	Capital stock†	10,000	10,000
			Retained earnings	37,500	18,000
	$ 145,500	$ 115,000		$ 145,500	$ 115,000

*Investment in Sub Company is recorded at cost and is eliminated in consolidation. Parent Company does not issue separate unconsolidated statements.

†1,500,000 shares outstanding.

Parent Company (Unconsolidated)
Statement of Earnings and Retained Earnings
For the Year Ended December 31, 19X6

	(000s)
Sales	$ 270,000
Cost of goods sold, exclusive of depreciation	197,000
Selling, general, and administrative expenses	10,835
Depreciation	10,000
Interest	7,165
	225,000
Earnings before taxes	45,000
Income taxes	22,500
Net income	22,500
Retained earnings at beginning of year	18,000
	40,500
Dividends	3,000
Retained earnings at end of year	$ 37,500
Net income per share	$ 15

55. Inventory and production:

a. Inventory is accounted for on a First-In, First-Out (FIFO) basis and turns over four times per year. There is no significant amount of work in progress or raw materials.

b. At December 31, 19X6 and 19X5 inventory consisted of 900,000 units and 1,000,000 units respectively—representing production of the immediately preceding quarter. Management has measured the current cost of inventory at $73 per unit at December 31, 19X6 ($65,700,000) and $58 per unit at December 31, 19X5 ($58,000,000).

c. Costs were incurred and goods produced as follows:

	(000s)					
	19X5	19X6				
	4th	1st	2nd	3rd	4th	Total
Historical costs	$ 56,000	$ 39,560	$ 59,400	$ 42,040	$ 63,000	$ 204,000
Units produced	1,000	618	900	618	900	3,036
Units sold		1,000	618	900	618	3,136

d. At December 31, 19X6 the selling price per unit was $85.

e. There were no write-downs or disposals of inventory.

56. Property, plant, and equipment:

a. Details of fixed assets at December 31, 19X6 are as follows:

Date Acquired	Percent Depreciated	(000s) Historical Cost	Accumulated Depreciation
19W9	80	$ 50,000	$ 40,000
19X0	70	5,000	3,500
19X1	60	5,000	3,000
19X2	50	5,000	2,500
19X3	40	5,000	2,000
19X4	30	5,000	1,500
19X5	20	10,000	2,000
19X6	10	15,000	1,500
		$ 100,000	$ 56,000

b. Depreciation is calculated at 10 percent per annum, straight line. A full year's depreciation is charged in the year of acquisition.

c. There were no disposals.

d. Management has measured the current cost of property, plant, and equipment at December 31, 19X6 and 19X5 as follows:

	(000s)				
	December 31, 19X6			December 31, 19X5	
Date Acquired	**Current Cost**	**Accumulated Depreciation**		**Current Cost**	**Accumulated Depreciation**
19W9	$ 120,000	$ 96,000		$ 110,000	$ 77,000
19X0	10,000	7,000		6,000	3,600
19X1	15,000	9,000		7,000	3,500
19X2	18,000	9,000		12,000	4,800
19X3	12,000	4,800		10,000	3,000
19X4	17,000	5,100		15,000	3,000
19X5	12,000	2,400		10,000	1,000
19X6	16,000	1,600		—	—
	220,000	$ 134,900		170,000	$ 95,900
Accumulated depreciation	134,900			95,900	
Net current cost	$ 85,100			$ 74,100	

e. The recoverable amount has been determined by management to be in excess of current cost, net of accumulated depreciation.

57. Dividends were paid at the rate of $750,000 per quarter.

58. Consumer Price Index for All Urban Consumers (from the *Survey of Current Business,* U.S. Department of Commerce, Bureau of Economic Analysis, January 19X7):

December 19X5	292.4
Average 19X6	298.4
December 19X6	303.5

Parent Company Calculations

59. The objective is to express the supplementary information in average 19X6 dollars. As indicated in paragraph 27, nominal dollar measurements may be used for all elements of net assets other than inventory and property, plant, and equipment. As indicated in paragraph 32, nominal dollar measurements may be used for all elements of income from continuing operations other than cost of sales and depreciation.

Step 1: Analysis of inventory and cost of goods sold

60. Inventory is assumed to turn over four times per year. Therefore, inventory with a historical cost of $63,000,000 at December 31, 19X6 is assumed to have been acquired during the fourth quarter of 19X6, and inventory with a historical cost of $56,000,000 at December 31, 19X5 is assumed to have been acquired in the fourth quarter of 19X5.

Step 2: Current cost of inventory and cost of goods sold

61. Cost of goods sold, current cost:

Current cost at beginning of year	$ 58/unit
Current cost at end of year	73/unit
	$ 131/unit
Average current cost ($131 ÷ 2)	$ 65.5/unit
Units sold during the year (000s) (par. 55(c))	× 3,136
Average current cost of goods sold (000s)	$ 205,408

62. The current cost amounts should be compared with the recoverable amount. This is illustrated below:

Market price per unit at end of year	$ 85
Current cost per unit of inventory on hand at end of year	73
Excess—no write-down required	$ 12

Step 3: Analysis of property, plant, and equipment and depreciation

63. An analysis of property, plant, and equipment was given in paragraph 56.

Step 4: Current cost of property, plant, and equipment and depreciation

64. It will usually be appropriate to calculate current cost depreciation, depletion, and amortization expense by reference to average current cost of the related assets (current cost of assets at beginning of year + current cost of assets at end of year ÷ 2).

	(000s) Current Cost
Current cost—12/31/X5 (par. 56(d))	$ 170,000
Current cost—12/31/X6 (par. 56(d))	220,000
	390,000
	÷ 2
Average current cost	$ 195,000
Current cost depreciation: 10%, straight line	$ 19,500

In this example, management has determined that the recoverable amount is greater than net current cost of property, plant, and equipment and there is no write-down.

Step 5: Identification of net monetary items

65. Net monetary items (par. 54):

	(000s) Dec. 31, 19X6	Dec. 31, 19X5
Cash	$ 1,000	$ 2,000
Accounts receivable	36,000	16,500
Accounts payable and accrued expenses	(47,000)	(32,000)
Income taxes payable	(6,000)	(6,000)
Current portion of long-term debt	(5,000)	(5,000)
Deferred income taxes	(6,000)	(5,000)
Long-term debt	(34,000)	(39,000)
Net monetary liabilities	($ 61,000)	($ 68,500)

Step 6: Computation of the purchasing power gain or loss on net monetary items

66. The amount of net monetary items at the beginning of the year, changes in the net monetary items, and the amount at the end of the year are restated into average 19X6 dollars. The purchasing power gain or loss on net monetary items is then the balancing item as illustrated below:

	(000s) Nominal Dollars	Conversion Factor	(000s) Avg. 19X6 Dollars
Balance—1/1/X6	$ 68,500	298.4 (avg. 19X6) / 292.4 (Dec. 19X5)	C$ 69,906
Decrease in net monetary liabilities during the year	(7,500)	*	(7,500)
Balance—12/31/X6	$ 61,000	298.4 (avg. 19X6) / 303.5 (Dec. 19X6)	(59,975)
Purchasing power gain on net monetary items			C$ 2,431

*Assumed to be in average 19X6 dollars.

Step 7: Computation of the change in current cost of inventory and property, plant, and equipment and the effect of general price-level changes

67. Increase in current cost of inventories:

	(000s) Current Cost/ Nominal Dollars	Conversion Factor	(000s) Current Cost/ Average 19X6 Dollars
Balance—1/1/X6 (par. 55(b))	$ 58,000	298.4 (avg. 19X6) / 292.4 (Dec. 19X5)	C$ 59,190
Production (par. 55(c))	204,000	*	204,000
Cost of goods sold (par. 61)	(205,408)	*	(205,408)
Balance—12/31/X6 (par. 55(b))	(65,700)	298.4 (avg. 19X6) / 303.5 (Dec. 19X6)	(64,596)
Increase in current cost of inventories	$ 9,108		C$ 6,814

*Assumed to be in average 19X6 dollars.

68. The inflation component of the increase in current cost amount is the difference between the nominal dollar and constant dollar measures. Using the numbers from paragraph 67:

	(000s)
Increase in current cost (nominal dollars)	$ 9,108
Increase in current cost (constant dollars)	C$ 6,814
Inflation component	2,294

69. Increase in current cost of property, plant, and equipment:

	(000s) Current Cost/ Nominal Dollars	Conversion Factor	(000s) Current Cost/ Average 19X6 Dollars
Balance—1/1/X6 (par. 56(d))	$ 74,100	298.4 (avg. 19X6) / 292.4 (Dec. 19X5)	C$ 75,621
Additions (par. 56(a))	15,000	*	15,000
Depreciation (par. 64)	(19,500)	*	(19,500)
Balance—12/31/X6 (par. 56(d))	(85,100)	298.4 (avg. 19X6) / 303.5 (Dec. 19X6)	(83,670)
Increase in current cost of property, plant, and equipment	$ 15,500		C$ 12,549

*Assumed to be in average 19X6 dollars.

70. The inflation component of the increase in current cost amount is the difference between the nominal dollar and constant dollar measures. Using the numbers from paragraph 69:

	(000s)
Increase in current cost (nominal dollars)	$ 15,500
Increase in current cost (constant dollars)	C$ 12,549
Inflation component	2,951

Summary of increase in current cost amounts

71. Summarizing paragraphs 68 and 70 above:

	(000s)		
	Increase in Current Cost	**Inflation Component**	**Increase Net of Inflation**
Inventory	$ 9,108	2,294	C$ 6,814
Property, plant, and equipment	15,500	2,951	12,549
Total	$ 24,608	5,245	C$ 19,363

Check of calculations

72. A reconciliation of shareholders' equity[10] (net assets) on a current cost/constant purchasing power basis acts as a check on the arithmetic accuracy of the calculations. Changes in shareholders' equity during 19X6 in average 19X6 dollars appear below:

	Source Paragraph	**(000s)** Current Cost/ Average 19X6 Dollars
Equity at January 1, 19X6		
Inventory	67	C$ 59,190
Property, plant, and equipment—net	69	75,621
Net monetary items	66	(69,906)
		64,905
Income from continuing operations	87	4,592
Dividends	57	(3,000)
Gain from decline in purchasing power of net monetary liabilities	66	2,431
Excess of increase in specific prices over increase in the general price level	71	19,363
		C$ 88,291
Equity at December 31, 19X6		
Inventory	67	C$ 64,596
Property, plant, and equipment—net	69	83,670
Net monetary items	66	(59,975)
		C$ 88,291

---

[10]To facilitate the illustration of consolidated amounts in paragraph 87, investment in Sub Company has been excluded from net assets of Parent Company in this paragraph.

Sub Company Information

73. The functional currency financial statements of Sub Company[11] appear below:

Sub Company
Historical Cost/Nominal FC Balance Sheets

	(000s)	
	December 31,	
	19X6	**19X5**
Cash	FC2,550	FC1,250
Equipment	2,500	2,500
Accumulated depreciation	750	500
Net equipment	1,750	2,000
Total assets	FC4,300	FC3,250
Accounts payable	FC 600	FC 500
Long-term debt	2,000	1,500
Total liabilities	2,600	2,000
Capital stock	500	500
Retained earnings	1,200	750
Total equity	1,700	1,250
Total liabilities and equity	FC4,300	FC3,250

Sub Company
Historical Cost/Nominal FC Statement of Income and Retained Earnings For the Year Ended December 31, 19X6

	(000s)
Revenue	FC5,000
General and administrative expenses	3,500
Depreciation	250
Interest	350
	4,100
Income before taxes	900
Income taxes	450
Net income	450
Retained earnings—beginning of year	750
Retained earnings—end of year	FC1,200

74. The fixed asset was acquired on December 31, 19X4. It is depreciated on a straight-line basis over 10 years and is expected to have no salvage value. There were no acquisitions or disposals of assets during the year.

75. Exchange rates between the functional currency and the dollar are:

December 31, 19X5	FC1 = $1.20
Average 19X6	FC1 = $1.10
December 31, 19X6	FC1 = $1.00

76. Management has measured the current cost of equipment at December 31, 19X6 and 19X5 as follows:

	(000s)	
	19X6	**19X5**
Current cost	FC5,500	FC4,000
Accumulated depreciation	(1,650)	(800)
Net current cost	FC3,850	FC3,200

The recoverable amount has been determined to be in excess of net current cost at both dates.

77. Current cost equity in nominal FC at the beginning and end of the year may be computed by adding net monetary items and net property,

---

[11]For simplicity, Sub Company is assumed to have a fixed asset but no inventory. The mechanics of restating inventory and cost of goods sold on a current cost basis are essentially the same as those illustrated for property, plant, and equipment.

plant, and equipment at current cost. To determine current cost equity in nominal dollars, those

FC amounts are translated at the appropriate exchange rate:

		December 31				
		19X6			19X5	
	(000s) FC	Exchange Rate	(000s) $	(000s) FC	Exchange Rate	(000s) $
Monetary items (par. 73):						
Cash	FC2,550	$ 1	$ 2,550	FC1,250	$ 1.20	$ 1,500
Current liabilities	(600)	$ 1	(600)	(500)	$ 1.20	(600)
Long-term debt	(2,000)	$ 1	(2,000)	(1,500)	$ 1.20	(1,800)
Net monetary liabilities	FC (50)		$ (50)	FC (750)		$ (900)
Equipment—net (par. 76)	FC3,850	$ 1	$ 3,850	FC3,200	$ 1.20	$ 3,840
Equity at current cost	FC3,800		$ 3,800	FC2,450		$ 2,940

78. The U.S. and local general price level indexes are:

	Local	U.S.
December 19X5	144	292.4
Average 19X6	158	298.4
December 19X6	173	303.5

Sub Company Calculations: Translate-Restate Method

79. To apply the translate-restate method, amounts measured in nominal FC are first translated into their dollar equivalents. Changes in those dollar equivalent amounts are then restated to reflect the effects of U.S. inflation.

Current cost depreciation and income from continuing operations

80. The first step is to determine current cost depreciation for the year as follows:

	(000s)
Current cost—beginning of year (par. 76)	FC4,000
Current cost—end of year (par. 76)	5,500
	9,500
	÷ 2
Average current cost, gross	FC4,750

Current cost depreciation expense for the year is

FC475,000 (FC4,750,000 × 10%). Computation of current cost depreciation and income from continuing operations does not involve use of a general price level index if measurements are made in average-for-the-year currency units. Accordingly, reported current cost depreciation under the translate-restate method is C$E523,000 (FC475,000 × $1.10).

81. Income from continuing operations on a current cost basis is computed by simply replacing historical cost depreciation in income from continuing operations in the primary financial statements with the current cost amount. Accordingly, current cost income from continuing operations is:

> Net income + historical cost depreciation
> − current cost depreciation
> = FC450,000 (par. 73) + FC250,000 (par. 73)
> − FC475,000 (par. 80)
> = FC225,000.

Reported current cost income from continuing operations under the translate-restate method is C$E247,000[12] (FC225,000 × $1.10).

Excess of increase in specific prices over increase in general price level

82. The second step is to compute the change in the current cost of equipment and the effect of the increase in the general price level. To measure the increase in current cost of equipment in nominal FC dollar equivalents, the effect of the exchange rate change must be excluded. One way to accomplish this is to translate the December 31,

---

[12]Current cost income has been rounded down from $247,500 to $247,000. This is necessary because current cost depreciation was rounded up to $523,000 from $522,500 and current cost income is a remainder of this number.

19X5 and 19X6 FC current cost amounts to dollar equivalents at the average exchange rate and then restate those dollar amounts to average 19X6 constant dollar equivalents:

	(000s) Current Cost/FC	Exchange Rate	(000s) Current Cost/$	Conversion Factor	(000s) Current Cost/C$E
Current cost, net—12/31/X5 (par. 76)	FC3,200	$ 1.10	$ 3,520	298.4 (avg. 19X6) / 292.4 (Dec. 19X5)	C$E3,592
Depreciation (par. 80)	(475)	$ 1.10	(523)	*	(523)
Current cost, net—12/31/X6 (par. 76)	(3,850)	$ 1.10	(4,235)	298.4 (avg. 19X6) / 303.5 (Dec. 19X6)	(4,164)
Increase in current cost	FC1,125		$ 1,238		C$E1,095

---

*Assumed to be in average 19X6 C$E.

The inflation component of the increase in current cost amount is the difference between the nominal dollar and the constant dollar equivalent amounts:

	(000s)
Increase in current cost (nominal dollars)	$ 1,238
Increase in current cost (constant dollars)	C$E1,095
Inflation component	143

Purchasing power gain or loss on net monetary items

83. The third step is to compute the purchasing power gain or loss on net monetary items. Under the translate-restate method, the translated beginning and ending net monetary liabilities are restated to average 19X6 dollars. The U.S. purchasing power gain is then the balancing amount:

	(000s) FC	Exchange Rate	(000s) $
Net monetary liabilities—12/31/X5 (par. 77)	FC750	$ 1.20	$ 900
Net monetary liabilities—12/31/X6 (par. 77)	50	$ 1.00	50
Decrease during the year	FC700		$ 850

	(000s) $	Conversion Factor	(000s) C$E
Net monetary liabilities—12/31/X5	$ 900	298.4 (avg. 19X6) / 292.4 (Dec. 19X5)	C$E918
Decrease during the year	(850)	*	(850)
Net monetary liabilities—12/31/X6	$ 50	298.4 (avg. 19X6) / 303.5 (Dec. 19X6)	(49)
Purchasing power gain			C$E 19

---

*Assumed to be in average 19X6 C$E.

In some circumstances, the above procedure will include a part of the effect of exchange rate changes on net monetary items in the purchasing power gain or loss. A more precise computation that would completely exclude the effect of exchange rate changes would be to compute a sepa- rate purchasing power gain or loss for each functional currency operation in a manner simi- lar to that illustrated in paragraph 82 for the in- crease in specific prices. For Sub Company, that alternative method produces a purchasing power gain of C$E18:

	(000s) FC	Average Exchange Rate	(000s) $	Conversion Factor	(000s) C$E
Net monetary liabilities—12/31/X5 (par. 77)	FC750	$ 1.10	$ 825	298.4 (avg. 19X6) 292.4 (Dec. 19X5)	C$E842
Decrease during the year	(700)	$ 1.10	(770)	*	(770)
Net monetary liabilities—12/31/X6 (par. 77)	FC 50	$ 1.10	$ 55	298.4 (avg. 19X6) 303.5 (Dec. 19X6)	(54)
Purchasing power gain					C$E 18

*Assumed to be in average 19X6 C$E.

The first procedure illustrated is less costly be- cause it can be applied on a consolidated basis, and it generally provides a reasonable approxi- mation. Accordingly, that method is acceptable. For this exercise, the more precise computation is used.

Check of calculations

84. A reconciliation of equity serves as a check of the calculations and is a convenient way to compute the translation adjustment:

	(000s)
Equity at 12/31/X5 in average 19X6 C$— $2,940 (par. 77) × 298.4/292.4	C$ 3,000
Income from continuing operations (par. 81)	C$E247
Purchasing power gain (par. 83)	18
Excess of increase in specific prices over increase in general price level (par. 82)	1,095
Translation adjustment (par. 85)	(624)
Increase in equity in terms of U.S. purchasing power	736
	C$ 3,736
Equity at 12/1/X6 in average 19X6 C$—$3,800 (par. 77) × 298.4/303.5	C$ 3,736

Translation adjustment

85. The preceding paragraph shows that the translation adjustment is the amount needed to balance the reconciliation of equity. The transla- tion adjustment may be checked by computing the effect of changes in the exchange rate on beginning-of-year equity and on the increase or decrease in equity during the year. To check the translation adjustment determined under the translate-restate method: (a) translate the beginning- and end-of-year equity on a C$ basis into FC amounts and (b) use those FC amounts to compute the effect on equity of changes in the exchange rate.

	(000s) C$	Exchange Rate	(000s) FC
Equity at 12/31/X5 in average 19X6 C$ (par. 84)	C$ 3,000	$ 0.833*	FC2,499
Equity at 12/31/X6 in average 19X6 C$ (par. 84)	3,736	$ 1.00	3,736
Increase in equity	C$ 736		FC1,237

	(000s)
Beginning-of-year equity	FC2,499
Exchange rate change during 19X6 ($1.20 – $1.00)	× (.20) $ (500)
Increase in equity	FC1,237
Difference between ending exchange rate and average rate for 19X6 ($1.10 – $1.00)	× (.10)
	$ (124)
Translation adjustment	$ (624)

*FC1 – $1.20 = $0.833

946

If the short-cut method for determining the purchasing power gain or loss described in paragraph 83 were followed, the translation adjustment would be $(625).

Consolidation: Translate-Restate Method

86. Parent Company prepares its changing prices disclosures on a consolidated basis and complies with the minimum requirements in determining current cost income from continuing operations (paragraph 32). Accordingly, revenue, general and administrative expenses, interest, and income taxes (paragraph 33) are shown at amounts reported in the historical cost financial statements. For Sub Company, those amounts are translated into dollars as follows:

	(000s) FC Amount (Par. 73)	Exchange Rate	(000s) U.S. Dollars
Revenue	FC5,000	1.10	$ 5,500
General and administrative expenses	FC3,500	1.10	$ 3,850
Interest	FC 350	1.10	$ 385
Income taxes	FC 450	1.10	$ 495

87. The "Total" column of the following schedule provides the figures in Schedule 2 of paragraph 45, "Illustrations of Disclosures."

	Source Par.	(000s) Parent Company	Source Par.	(000s) Sub Company	Total
Average 19X6 Units of Purchasing Power					
Net sales & other revenues	54	$ 270,000	86	$ 5,500	$ 275,500
Cost of goods sold	61	205,408			205,408
Depreciation expense	64	19,500	80	523	20,023
Selling, general, and administrative expenses	54	10,835	86	3,850	14,685
Interest expense	54	7,165	86	385	7,550
Provision for taxes	54	22,500	86	495	22,995
		265,408		5,253	270,661
Income (loss) from operations		$ 4,592		$ 247	$ 4,839
Purchasing power gain (loss)	66	$ 2,431	83	$ 18	$ 2,449
Increase in specific prices					
Inventory	71	$ 9,108			$ 9,108
Property, plant, and equipment	71	15,500	82	$ 1,238	16,738
		24,608		1,238	25,846
Effect of increase in general price level	71	5,245	82	143	$ 5,388
Increase in specific prices— net of inflation	71	$ 19,363	82	$ 1,095	$ 20,458
Translation adjustment			85	$ (624)	$ (624)
Net assets	72	$ 88,291	84	$ 3,736	$ 92,027
December 31, 19X6 Units of Purchasing Power					
Inventory	55	$ 65,700			$ 65,700
Property, plant, and equipment— net of accumulated depreciation	56(d)	$ 85,100	82	$ 4,235	$ 89,335

Sub Company Calculations: Restate-Translate Method

88. To apply the restate-translate method, the steps illustrated in paragraphs 79-85 are followed except that all restatements to reflect the effects of general inflation are made using the local general price level index before translation to dollar equivalents.

Current cost depreciation and income from continuing operations

89. Current cost depreciation and income from

continuing operations are FC475,000 and FC225,000, respectively, as determined in paragraphs 80 and 81.

Purchasing power gain or loss on net monetary items

90. To apply the restate-translate method, the FC amount of net monetary items at the beginning of the year, changes in the net monetary items, and the amount at the end of the year are restated into average 19X6 CFC. The purchasing power gain or loss on net monetary items is then the balancing item:

	(000s) FC	Conversion Factor	(000s) CFC
Net monetary liabilities—12/31/X5 (par. 77)	FC750	158 (avg. 19X6) 144 (Dec. 19X5)	CFC823
Decrease during the year	(700)	*	(700)
Net monetary liabilities—12/31/X6 (par. 77)	FC 50	158 (avg. 19X6) 173 (Dec. 19X6)	(46)
Purchasing power gain			CFC 77

---

*Assumed to be in average 19X6 C$E.

Excess of increase in specific prices over increase in general price level

91. Under the restate-translate method, the local index is used to restate the beginning and ending current cost FC amounts into average 19X6 CFC:

	(000s) Current Cost/FC	Conversion Factor	(000s) Current Cost/ CFC
Current cost, net—12/31/X5 (par. 76)	FC3,200	158 (avg. 19X6) 144 (Dec. 19X5)	CFC3,511
Depreciation (par. 89)	(475)	*	(475)
Current cost, net—12/31/X6 (par. 76)	(3,850)	158 (avg. 19X6) 173 (Dec. 19X6)	(3,516)
Increase in current cost	FC1,125		CFC 480

---

*Assumed to be in average 19X6 CFC.

The inflation component of the increase in current cost amount is the difference between the nominal functional currency and constant functional currency amounts:

	(000s)
Increase in current cost (FC)	FC1,125
Increase in current cost (CFC)	CFC 480
Inflation component	645

Check of calculations

92. As with the translate-restate method, a reconciliation of equity acts as a check of the calculations. A reconciliation of equity also is a convenient point at which to translate the functional currency amounts determined in the preceding paragraphs into dollar equivalents and is a convenient way to compute the translation and parity adjustments.

93. If beginning and ending equity are restated to average 19X6 CFC using the local index, the reconciliation of equity under the restate-translate method would be:

	(000s) CFC	Exchange Rate	(000s) CFC$
Equity at 12/31/X5 in average 19X6 CFC (FC2,450 (par. 77) × 158/144)	CFC2,688	1.20	CFC$ 3,226
Income from continuing operations (par. 89)	225	1.10	247
Purchasing power gain (par. 90)	77	1.10	85
Excess of increase in specific prices over increase in general price level (par. 91)	480	1.10	528
Translation adjustment (par. 94)			(616)
	CFC3,470		CFC$ 3,470
Equity at 12/31/X6 in average 19X6 CFC (FC3,800 (par. 77) × 158/173)	CFC3,470	1.00	CFC$ 3,470

Translation adjustment

94. The translation adjustment is the amount needed to balance the CFC$ reconciliation of equity. The adjustment may be computed as (a) the change in exchange rates during the period multiplied by the restated amount of net assets at the beginning of the period plus (b) the difference between the average exchange rate for the period and the end-of-period exchange rate multiplied by the increase or decrease in restated net assets for the period. Accordingly, the translation adjustment under the restate-translate method is:

	(000s)	
Beginning-of-year equity (par. 93)	CFC2,688	
Exchange rate change during 19X6 ($1.20 − $1.00)	× .20	
		$ (538)
Increase in equity (3,470 − 2,688)	CFC 782	
Difference between ending exchange rate and average rate for 19X6 ($1.10 − $1.00)	× .10	
		(78)
Translation adjustment		$ (616)

Parity adjustment

95. The reconciliation of equity in paragraph 93, in which beginning-of-year and end-of-year equity are stated in average 19X6 CFC, is needed to calculate the translation adjustment in CFC$. However, beginning- and end-of-year equity and the increase in equity must be stated in average 19X6 constant dollars in the supplementary current cost information. Beginning- and end-of-year equity in average 19X6 constant dollars are C$3,000,000 and C$3,736,000, respectively, as computed in paragraph 84. Thus, the overall increase in U.S. purchasing power for the year is C$3,736,000 − C$3,000,000 = C$736,000. However, the reconciliation of equity in paragraph 93 indicates that the increase in equity for the year is CFC$244,000 (CFC$3,470,000 − CFC$3,226,000). The difference between C$736,000 and CFC$244,000 is the parity adjustment needed to adjust the ending net investment and the increase in the net investment to measures in average 19X6 constant dollars. Accordingly, the parity adjustment is C$736,000 − CFC$244,000 = $492,000. That amount represents (a) the effect of the difference between local and U.S. inflation from December 31, 19X5 average for 19X6 on the restatement of opening equity to average units plus (b) the effect of the

difference between local and U.S. inflation from average for 19X6 to December 31, 19X6 the re-

statement of ending nominal dollar equity to average units:

	(000s)
Beginning-of-year equity (par. 77)	$ 2,940
Difference between local and U.S. inflation from 12/31/X5 to average 19X6 (158/144 − 298.4/292.4)	× 0.0767
	$ 225
Equity at 12/31/X6 (par. 77)	3,800
Difference between local and U.S. inflation from average 19X6 to 12/31/X6 (158/173 − 298.4/303.5)	× 0.0699
	266
	491
Rounding difference	1
Parity adjustment	$ 492

For display purposes, the parity adjustment be combined with the $(616,000) translation adjustment (paragraph 94). Accordingly, the net translation adjustment disclosed in the supplementary current cost information prepared using the restate-translate method would be $(616,000) + $492,000 = $(124,000). The components of current cost information based on the restate-translate method thus would be:

		(000s)
Beginning-of-year equity— $2,940 (par. 77) × 298.4/292.4		C$ 3,000
Income from continuing operation— CFC225 (par. 89) × 1.10	CFC$ 247	
Purchasing power gain— CFC77 (par. 90) × 1.10	85	
Excess of increase in specific prices over increase in general price level— CFC480 (par. 91) × 1.10	528	
Translation and parity adjustments	(124)	
Increase in equity in terms of U.S. purchasing power		736
End-of-year equity— $3,800 (par. 77) × 298.4/303.5		C$ 3,736

Monetary and Nonmonetary Items

96. Paragraphs 96-108 provide guidance on the interpretation of paragraphs 40-43 for the classification of certain asset and liability items as monetary or nonmonetary. The following table illustrates the application of the definitions to common cases under typical circumstances. In other circumstances the classification should be resolved by reference to the definitions. Paragraphs 96-108 are not intended to provide answers that should be followed regardless of the circumstances of the case. (Footnote reference is at the end of the table.)

	Monetary	Nonmonetary
Assets		
Cash on hand and demand bank deposits (dollars)	X	
Time deposits (dollars)	X	
Foreign currency on hand and claims to foreign currency[a]	X	

	Monetary	Nonmonetary
Securities:		
Common stocks (not accounted for on the equity method)		X
Common stocks represent residual interests in the underlying net assets and earnings of the issuer.		
Preferred stock (convertible or participating)	Circumstances may indicate that such stock is either monetary or nonmonetary. Refer to convertible bonds.	
Preferred stock (nonconvertible, nonparticipating)	X	
Future cash receipts are likely to be substantially unaffected by changes in specific prices.		
Convertible bonds	If the market values the security primarily as a bond, it is monetary; if it values the security primarily as stock, it is nonmonetary.	
Bonds (other than convertibles)	X	
Trading account investments in fixed-income securities owned by banks, investment brokers, and others (paragraphs 97 and 98)		X
Accounts and notes receivable	X	
Allowance for doubtful accounts and notes receivable	X	
Variable-rate mortgage loans	X	
The terms of such loans do not link them directly to the rate of inflation. Also, there are practical reasons for classifying all loans as monetary.		
Inventories used on contracts		They are, in substance, rights to receive sums of money if the future cash receipts on the contracts will not vary due to future changes in specific prices. Goods used on contracts to be priced at market upon delivery are nonmonetary.
Inventories (other than inventories used on contracts) and commodity inventories (other than those described below)		X
Commodity inventories whose values are hedged by futures contracts whose contract amounts have not been recorded in the financial statements	Refer to paragraphs 99 and 100.	
Loans to employees	X	
Prepaid insurance, advertising, rent, and other prepayments		Claims to future services are nonmonetary. Prepayments that are deposits, advance payments, or receivables are monetary because the prepayment does not obtain a given quantity of future services, but rather is a fixed-money offset.

	Monetary	Nonmonetary
Long-term receivables	X	
Refundable deposits	X	
Advances to unconsolidated subsidiaries	X	
Equity investment in unconsolidated subsidiaries or other investees		X
Pension, sinking, and other funds under an enterprise's control	The specific assets in the fund should be classified as monetary or nonmonetary. Refer to listings under securities above.	
Property, plant, and equipment		X
Accumulated depreciation of property, plant, and equipment		X
The unguaranteed residual value of property owned by a lessor and leased under direct financing, sales-type, and leveraged leases	Refer to paragraphs 101 and 102.	
Investment tax credits that are deferred by a lessor as part of the unearned income of a leveraged lease	Refer to paragraphs 103 and 104.	
Portion of the carrying amount of lessors' assets leased under noncancellable operating leases that represent claims to fixed sums of money (paragraphs 105 and 106)		X
Cash surrender value of life insurance	X	
Purchase commitments—portion paid on fixed-price contracts An advance on a fixed-price contract is the portion of the purchaser's claim to nonmonetary goods or services that is recognized in the accounts; it is not a right to receive money.		X
Advances to supplier—not on a fixed-price contract Such advances are rights to receive credit for a sum of money, not claims to a specified quantity of goods or services.	X	
Deferred income tax charges[a] Offsets to prospective monetary liabilities	X	
Patents, trademarks, licenses, and formulas		X
Goodwill		X
Deferred life insurance policy acquisition costs[a] Such costs represent the portion of future cash receipts for premiums that is recognized in the accounts and are sometimes viewed as an offset to the policy reserve.	X	
Deferred property and casualty insurance policy acquisition costs related to unearned premiums		X
Other intangible assets and deferred charges		X

	Monetary	Nonmonetary
Liabilities		
Accounts and notes payable	X	
Accrued expenses payable (wages, and so forth)	X	
Accrued vacation pay		If to be paid at the wage rates as of the vacation dates and if those rates may vary, accrued vacation pay is nonmonetary.
Cash dividends payable	X	
Obligations payable in foreign currency	X	
Sales commitments—portion collected on fixed-price contracts An advance received on a fixed-price contract is the portion of the seller's obligation to deliver goods or services that is recognized in the accounts; it is not an obligation to pay money.		X
Advances from customers—not on a fixed-price contract Such advances are equivalent to loans from customers and are not obligations to furnish specified quantities of goods or services.	X	
Accrued losses on firm purchase commitments In essence, these are accounts payable.	X	
Deferred revenue		If an obligation to furnish goods or services is involved, deferred revenue is nonmonetary. Certain "deferred income" items of savings and loan associations are monetary.
Refundable deposits	X	
Bonds payable and other long-term debt	X	
Unamortized premium or discount and prepaid interest on bonds or notes payable Such items are inseparable from the debt to which they relate—a monetary item.	X	
Convertible bonds payable Until converted, these are obligations to pay sums of money.	X	
Accrued pension obligations		Fixed amounts payable to a fund are monetary; all other amounts are nonmonetary.
Obligations under warranties These are nonmonetary because they oblige the enterprise to furnish goods or services or their future price.		X
Deferred income tax credits[a] Cash requirements will not vary materially due to changes in specific prices.	X	

	Monetary	Nonmonetary
Deferred investment tax credits These are not to be settled by payment of cash and are related to nonmonetary assets.		X
Life insurance policy reserves These represent portions of policies' face values that are now deemed liabilities.	X	
Property and casualty insurance loss reserves	X	
Unearned property and casualty insurance premiums These are nonmonetary because they are principally obligations to furnish insurance coverage. The dollar amount of payments to be made under that coverage might vary materially due to changes in specific prices.		X
Deposit liabilities of financial institutions	X	
Minority interests in consolidated subsidiaries (paragraph 107)		X
Equity		
Capital stock of the enterprise or of its consolidated subsidiaries subject to mandatory redemption at fixed amounts (paragraph 108)	X	

---

^aAlthough classification of this item as nonmonetary may be technically preferable, the monetary classification provides a more practical solution for the purposes of computing the purchasing power gain or loss on a consolidated basis.

97. *Trading account investments in fixed-income securities owned by banks, investment brokers, and others.* Trading account securities are securities of all types carried in a dealer trading account that are held principally for resale to customers. The predominant practice by banks is to carry these securities at market value. Trading account investments include both fixed-income securities (for example, nonconvertible preferred stock, convertible bonds, and other bonds) and other securities (for example, common stock). Usually, trading account securities are held for extremely short periods of time—sometimes for only a few hours. Frequently, the enterprise buys and sells the securities expecting to make a profit on the difference between dealer and retail, or bid and ask, prices rather than on price changes during the period securities are held. However, the prices of the securities change with market forces.

98. Trading account investments in fixed-income securities are not claims to receive sums of money that are fixed or determinable. The market prices of the securities might and frequently do change while the securities are held. Generally, noncon-

vertible and nonparticipating preferred stock, convertible bonds that the market values primarily as bonds rather than as stocks, and nonconvertible bonds should be classified as monetary items. However, those classifications are based, in part, on the assumption that those securities would be held for long periods, if not to maturity. Trading account investments, on the other hand, are held for shorter periods and their value depends much less heavily on the general purchasing power of money and more on the specific values of the securities. Therefore, trading account investments in fixed-income securities should be classified as nonmonetary.

99. *Commodity inventories whose values are hedged by futures contracts.* Many enterprises hedge commodity inventories (such as grain or metals). *Short hedges* are designed to provide a degree of assurance that a decline in the price of the commodity would be offset by an increase in the value of the hedge contract. Short hedges thus tend to reduce the effects of price changes on the inventory that is hedged.

100. There are certain similarities between inventories that are hedged and inventories that are used on or committed to a fixed-price contract. In each case, the risk of gain or loss due to price changes before the inventory is sold is largely or entirely eliminated. To the extent that hedges fix the value of an inventory in dollars (or units of foreign functional currency, if appropriate), the inventory effectively becomes a monetary item.

101. *The unguaranteed residual value of property owned by a lessor and leased under direct financing, sales-type, and leveraged leases.* The unguaranteed residual value is included with the minimum lease payments, at present value, in the net investment in the lease.

102. The minimum lease payments are monetary items because they are claims to fixed sums of money. The residual value is not a claim to a fixed sum of money, so it is a nonmonetary item. Some assets and liabilities, of which the net investment in the lease is a good example, are combinations of claims to (or obligations of) fixed amounts and claims to (or obligations of) variable amounts. Ideally, those claims should be separated for purposes of classifying them as monetary and nonmonetary. However, if the information necessary to make the separation is not available or is impracticable to obtain, such items need not be divided into monetary and nonmonetary components and would be classified according to their dominant element. If the net investment in leases is principally claims to fixed amounts, it would be classified as monetary; it would be classified as nonmonetary if it is principally claims to residuals.

103. *Investment tax credits that are deferred by a lessor as part of the unearned income of a leveraged lease.* Under FASB Statement No. 13, *Accounting for Leases,* the deferred investment tax credit related to the leased asset is subtracted from rentals receivable and estimated residual value as part of the calculation of the lessor's investment in the leveraged lease. The investment, including the deferred investment tax credit related to the leveraged lease, is presented as one amount in the balance sheet. As indicated in paragraph 102, the investment in a leveraged lease would be classified as monetary or nonmonetary according to its dominant element.

104. As indicated in the table in paragraph 96, a deferred investment tax credit should be classified as nonmonetary but, if it is part of an investment in a leveraged lease and if the information necessary to separate its elements is not available or is impracticable to obtain, the investment would be classified according to its dominant element.

105. *Portion of the carrying amount of lessors' assets leased under noncancellable operating leases that represent claims to fixed sums of money.* These assets are carried at depreciated historical cost under generally accepted accounting principles and are classified with or near property, plant, and equipment, which are nonmonetary.

106. The classification of a lease as an operating lease under Statement 13 indicates that the lease has not transferred substantially all of the benefits and risks incident to ownership to the lessee. Thus, the economic significance of the asset continues to depend heavily on the value of the future lease rentals, residual values, and associated costs. Therefore, an asset subject to an operating lease should be classified as nonmonetary.

107. *Minority interests in consolidated subsidiaries.* The interests of minority shareholders in the earnings and equity of subsidiaries are, from the consolidated entity's point of view, claims that are not fixed. Rather, they are residuals that will vary based on the subsidiary's earnings, dividends, and other transactions affecting its equity and so are nonmonetary. (Refer to paragraph 108 as to classification of capital stock of the enterprise or of its consolidated subsidiaries subject to mandatory redemption at fixed amounts.)

108. *Capital stock of the enterprise or of its consolidated subsidiaries subject to mandatory redemption at fixed amounts.* Such securities are claims of the stockholders to a fixed sum of money and therefore are monetary. Classification as a monetary item called for in paragraphs 96-108 is only for purposes of determining a purchasing power gain or loss. Paragraphs 96-108 do not address how such securities should be classified in balance sheets or the accounting for dividends on those securities.

Appendix B

BACKGROUND INFORMATION AND BASIS FOR CONCLUSIONS

CONTENTS

Appendix B

BACKGROUND INFORMATION AND BASIS FOR CONCLUSION

Introduction

109. This appendix summarizes considerations that were deemed significant by members of the Board in reaching the conclusions in this Statement. It includes reasons for accepting certain views and rejecting others. Individual Board members gave greater weight to some factors than to others.

Statement 33

110. In September 1979, the FASB issued Statement 33 in response to a perceived need for information on effects of changing prices on the reported results of operations and on selected assets of business enterprises. The Board recognized that two methods of providing the information had been advocated by a significant number of preparers, users, and auditors, that no clear preference existed for one method, and that neither method had been used extensively enough to judge its relevance or reliability. Accordingly, the Board required certain large publicly held companies to provide on an experimental basis certain financial information based on each of those methods. The methods required were restatements of information from the primary financial statements to reflect changes in (a) general price levels (historical cost/constant purchasing power information) and (b) both specific prices and general price levels (current cost/constant purchasing power information).

111. The Basis for Conclusions of Statement 33 discusses (a) why the primary financial statements provide only a limited view of effects of changing prices, (b) why those effects may not be understood adequately unless they are directly reflected in financial reports, (c) how information on those effects might be used, and (d) why the current cost/constant purchasing power and the historical cost/constant purchasing power methods were selected over alternative measurement methods as the basis for an experiment in reporting certain effects of changing prices. Because the Board concluded that alternative measures of enterprise performance could be helpful in assessing the ability of an enterprise to maintain its operating capability and its financial capital, Statement 33 required a minimum set of disclosures that reflected effects of changing prices and provided users with sufficient information to assess alternative performance measures.

112. To enhance experimentation and learning by preparers, users, and the Board, Statement 33 permitted alternative methods for measuring and displaying the effects of specific and general price changes. To limit the cost of implementing the requirements, Statement 33 required information about only certain financial statement items that, for most of the enterprises covered, were likely to be most affected by changing prices. The Statement, therefore, required only selected data to be restated by the two methods.

Review of Statement 33

113. The Board committed itself to a comprehensive review of the experiment after a period of five years subsequent to the issuance date of Statement 33. In preparation for that review, the

956

Board encouraged a wide range of research studies to learn about the experiences of preparers, users, and auditors with both historical cost/constant purchasing power information and current cost/constant purchasing power information. In July 1983, a task force was appointed to assist the Board in evaluating whether to continue the requirements after the initial five-year period and, if continued, what changes should be considered. The task force assisted in the preparation of an FASB Invitation to Comment, *Supplementary Disclosures about the Effects of Changing Prices*, which was designed to supplement the research studies by soliciting the advice of users, preparers, and auditors. The Board received approximately 400 responses to that document.

114. The research studies and responses to the Invitation to Comment indicated that the Statement 33 information was not widely used. Both the number of users and the extent of use were limited. A large number of responses to the Invitation to Comment suggested that the costs of preparing the disclosures had outweighed the benefits. Some respondents stated that although inflation is considered in assessing the results of operations, mandatory disclosure requirements were unnecessary because users have developed their own methods for making those assessments. Others advocated alternative disclosures and criticized the methods but not the objectives adopted in Statement 33. Still others supported either historical cost/constant purchasing power or current cost/constant purchasing power disclosures but argued that the presentation of the data, especially using two methods, had discouraged and confused some users.

115. With the knowledge gained from the experiment, the Board concluded that reducing the number of disclosures and simplifying the remaining requirements might enhance the usefulness of the information. The Board decided to eliminate the historical cost/constant purchasing power disclosure requirements of Statement 33 because of evidence that reporting effects of changing prices using two different methods detracted from the usefulness of the information and that the historical cost/constant purchasing power information was less useful than the current cost/constant purchasing power information. Statement 70, issued in 1982, eliminated the requirement to disclose historical cost/constant purchasing power information for enterprises that did not use the dollar as the functional currency for all significant operations. Statement 82, issued in 1984, eliminated the requirement for other enterprises.

The Current Cost Exposure Draft

116. In December 1984, the Board issued an Exposure Draft, *Financial Reporting and Changing Prices: Current Cost Information*, that would have combined without significant changes all existing FASB pronouncements relating to reporting supplementary information on the effects of changing prices. Thus, it would have continued the disclosure of current cost information expressed in terms of constant monetary units. Certain disclosures related to mineral resource assets also would have been continued. Although the requirements for historical cost/constant purchasing power information were previously eliminated, such information could have been substituted for current cost/constant purchasing power information in certain circumstances. That proposed Statement would have differed from existing requirements in two respects. The five-year summary of selected financial data would have been stated in average-for-the-current-year units of purchasing power. The option in Statement 33 to use base-year dollars or the end-of-the-current-year U.S. Consumer Price Index would have been eliminated. In addition, a gain or loss on disposal or write-down of inventory or property, plant, and equipment that was included in income from continuing operations in the primary statements would have been adjusted to reflect the current cost basis of the item prior to its disposal or write-down when included in income from continuing operations on a current cost basis. The Board received comments from more than 100 respondents.

117. A large majority of respondents recommended that the Board discontinue the existing requirements. Many commented that the data did not appear to have been used by the institutional investment community, bankers, or investors in general. Numerous reasons were cited for nonuse. Some respondents believed that the data were not relevant or reliable (for reasons discussed further in paragraph 124). Others thought that comparisons of data between enterprises had been inhibited by the flexibility in methods of application, by differences in the quality of the raw data used to prepare the changing prices information, and by failure to disclose the assumptions used in preparing the data. Still other respondents expressed the view that the disclosures were overly complex and therefore difficult to understand. Some respondents commented that the manner of disclosing the information discouraged its use—the data were placed at the end of the financial information in annual reports, were labeled as supplementary and unaudited, were not adequately explained, and were not compre-

hensive. Further, some commented that the components of income adjusted for changing prices were not aggregated in a useful way. In addition to those views, the most frequently cited reason for discontinuing the supplementary disclosures was that the benefits derived from presenting that data had not been sufficient to justify the costs incurred. Although the Board is not persuaded that the cost of the disclosures required by Statement 33, as amended, *considered in isolation* was unduly burdensome, nevertheless, at the present time, the Board acknowledges that those disclosures did not achieve the cost-benefit relationship that had been anticipated for them.

118. Many respondents suggested that even an improved set of disclosures might not be useful because managements and investors had information better than or different from that required by Statement 33. Many respondents commented that the inflation rate had diminished and, therefore, interest in disclosures about the effects of inflation had decreased. Some commented that other factors were more important in investment decisions than information on changing prices, for example, the opportunity and ability to raise capital from outside sources to finance replacements of productive capacity or the effects of interest rates on monetary assets and liabilities.

119. A minority of respondents said that the supplementary disclosures required by Statement 33, as amended, should be continued. The central theme of supporters of those disclosures was the need to overcome the inherent weaknesses of historical cost financial statements in and following periods of changing prices. In their view, those financial statements must be adjusted for the effects of inflation to report performance in real terms to help in assessing an enterprise's ability to maintain its financial capital. The effects of past inflation carry over into current and future financial statements; therefore, even at the present low levels of inflation, a large cumulative effect remains. Also, higher levels of inflation may return. Some commented that it was too early to abandon the experiment. They believed that users had not had enough time to adapt their methods to the data, that more years of data would increase the utility of the data for trend analysis, and that the experimental label, dual disclosures, and temporary availability of the data had discouraged use. They suggested that changes in those areas should be made.

Alternative Approaches Considered

More Limited Disclosures

120. During the second and third quarters of 1985, the Board addressed the issue of whether to continue the disclosure requirements. It considered a number of alternatives suggested by respondents. The Board concluded that adoption of any of those alternatives, such as a current cost/nominal dollar approach, a condensed current cost approach, or a replacement cost approach based on ASR No. 190, *Notice of Adoption of Amendments to Regulation S-X Requiring Disclosure of Certain Replacement Cost Data* (now rescinded), would not significantly reduce the cost to prepare the data. A few respondents recommended that the Board retain only a modest statistical display of changing prices information, for example, a requirement to disclose in average-for-the-year or end-of-year units of constant purchasing power (a) net sales and other operating revenues, (b) cash dividends declared per common share, and (c) market price per common share at year-end. Those respondents said that approach would provide some limited data at a reasonable cost, warning readers about the effects of changing prices. The Board recognizes that a limited display of data could result in substantial cost savings, but it doubts whether users would gain much from such limited data. Further, most users could develop those data independently. Other respondents suggested that the Board rescind the requirements and urge preparers to disclose on a voluntary, experimental basis information thought to be useful for a particular enterprise.

A Continuing Project to Develop Improved Disclosures

121. In October 1985, the Board decided to continue (a) a project to develop more effective and useful disclosures of the effects of general inflation and specific price changes on enterprise performance, resources, obligations, and equity and (b) the requirements of Statement 33, as amended. Thus, enterprises were required to provide disclosures for 1985 pursuant to the same requirements that were in effect for 1984.

122. The principal goals of the project described in paragraph 121 would have been (a) to develop a comprehensive changing prices model that reflects both current price and general price-level adjustments of financial statement items and (b) to decide which aspects of that model were sufficiently relevant and reliable to be included as supplementary disclosures in financial reports. During early 1986, the Board considered the appropriate objectives, scope, and approach for that project in light of the four factors the Board generally considers in deciding whether to undertake a major technical project.

123. The first factor considered is the pervasiveness of the problem to be addressed. A determination is made concerning (a) the extent to which an issue is troublesome to users, preparers, auditors, or others, (b) the extent to which practice is diverse, and (c) the likely duration of the problem (that is, is it transitory or will it persist). The Board believes that the problems created by changing prices are pervasive. It is widely accepted that, in inflationary periods, historical cost financial statements for most capital-intensive enterprises show illusory profits, mask erosion of capital, and invalidate trend analysis. Although the Board believes current cost/constant purchasing power information may be useful, based on comment letters received, the information is of little interest at present, whether the problems are pervasive or not. Prior to the issuance of Statement 33, little information was disclosed about the effects of specific and general price changes on reported results of operations. During the period that pronouncement was effective, enterprises generally provided only the minimum disclosures required. In addition, since Statement 33 was designed as an experiment and permitted considerable flexibility, to some extent, diversity of practice was expected and accepted. Finally, interest in disclosures of the effects of changing prices on enterprise performance seems to build and to ebb depending on the severity of inflation. Despite the long-term effects of previous high inflation, during a period of low inflation, as exists now, the public has evidenced relatively little interest in the subject. As discussed previously in paragraphs 117 and 118, some respondents stated that the lack of interest in the supplementary disclosures stemmed from the inadequacies of the current cost disclosures and from preparers' and investors' ability to otherwise assess the effects of changing prices.

124. The second factor considered is the potential for developing an alternative solution—whether one or more alternatives that will improve the relevance, reliability, and comparability of financial reporting are likely to be developed. The Board believes a reason for the low level of acceptance of the current cost/constant purchasing power disclosures related to the perception that those disclosures were not sufficiently relevant or reliable for some or all enterprises. Some believe that the concept underlying current costs, that is, the cost of replacing existing service potential, is not relevant because many enterprises do not intend to, or physically cannot, replace an existing asset's service potential with another asset of comparable service potential. For example, an enterprise producing motion picture films or an enterprise exploring for oil and gas reserves could not duplicate its existing assets that have resulted from past successful efforts. In addition, some believe that applying a specific price index to a historical cost number to compute the current cost of inventory and property, plant, and equipment may not produce a reliable measure of current cost because of technological or other changes over time that affect particular assets but that may not affect or have a significantly different effect on the basket of goods or services on which a specific price index is based. Although Statement 33, as amended, provided for adjusting current costs for such changes, the difficulty of accomplishing that adjustment is acknowledged. Likewise, in the absence of specific guidelines, the determination that current cost did not exceed the lower recoverable amount of a unit of property, plant, and equipment required the application of considerable judgment. In some cases, enterprises reported current cost holding gains during periods in which losses from continuing operations on a current cost basis were incurred. Some have questioned the reliability of such results. Developing specific guidelines on how to determine the lower recoverable amount of a unit of property, plant, and equipment used in a production process is a complex technical issue and would be a principal consideration in any project that addresses impairment of assets in the context of the primary financial statements. To date, there is no acknowledged solution. The difficulties described above were acknowledged in Statement 33. Their existence is not the only reason for the Board's decision. Even though there is a wide range of views, even among Board members, on what changes might improve the relevance and reliability of the disclosures that were required by Statement 33, as amended, it is possible that a technical solution eventually could be developed notwithstanding the fact that research and investigation already performed both in the U.S. and abroad has not identified a solution generally acknowledged to be both relevant and reliable. However, the effort necessary to develop a solution would take significant time and significant Board resources and its results likely would be more costly for preparers to implement than were the requirements of Statement 33, as amended. Further, as noted in paragraph 126, there is sufficient uncertainty about whether the eventual technical solution would receive general acceptance among preparers, users, and auditors. Accordingly, it is the Board's belief that attempting to solve the existing problems at this time would not meet any reasonable cost-benefit test.

125. The third factor addresses the technical feasibility of a project, that is, the extent to which a technically sound solution can be developed or whether the project under consideration should

await completion of other projects. Statement 33 required presentation of an intermediate measure of performance (income from continuing operations) adjusted for certain effects of changing prices. It also required certain other disclosures (holding gains or losses and purchasing power gains or losses) that a user might consider in assessing aggregate enterprise performance. However, it did not require presentation of a "bottom line" alternative to net income. The further refinement of Statement 33 to require disclosure of an alternative "bottom line" measure of performance as envisioned by the project described in paragraph 122 would likely require the Board to readdress many complex issues of recognition and measurement that were considered as part of the conceptual framework, but that remain contentious and unresolved.

126. The last factor considers practical consequences, namely, whether an improved accounting solution is likely to be generally acceptable and whether not addressing a particular subject might cause others to act, that is, the SEC or Congress. Without a clearer indication of what the alternative accounting solution might be, it is difficult to assess its likely acceptability. However, as noted earlier, it is probable that the solution would be more costly for preparers to apply and, therefore, would likely be resisted by them, given their experience with, and assessment of, Statement 33. At present, governmental interest in any requirement to continue the disclosures required by Statement 33, as amended, seems to have diminished.

127. Based on the assessments discussed in paragraphs 123-126, the Board decided, in June 198′ not to proceed with a project to develop a com prehensive changing prices model that reflects both current price and general price-level adjustments of financial statement items and concluded that the supplementary disclosures required by Statement 33, as amended, should not be required. The Board expects to address (as it has in the past) the relevance of current prices of assets or liabilities as part of its deliberations on major accounting issues. Those projects may result in Statements that require measurement or disclosure in the primary financial statements of assets or liabilities based on current prices and the effects of changes in those prices. The Board's consideration of the complex issues surrounding the broad issue of specific price changes does not cease with the issuance of this Statement.

Voluntary Disclosure

128. An FASB Exposure Draft, *Financial Reporting and Changing Prices*, was issued on September 30, 1986 that proposed making voluntary the disclosure of supplementary information on the effects of inflation and changes in specific prices. The Board received over 200 letters of comment in response to the Exposure Draft. Reiterating many of the comments made in response to the 1983 Invitation to Comment and 1984 Exposure Draft, a substantial majority of the respondents to the most recent Exposure Draft supported the elimination of the requirement for supplementary disclosure of information on the effects of changing prices. A large number of the respondents reasserted that although inflation is considered in assessing the results of operations, mandatory disclosure requirements are unnecessary because users have developed their own methods of adjusting information in the primary financial statements for changing prices. A large majority of respondents also suggested that the costs of preparing the disclosures have outweighed the benefits to date.

129. A small minority of respondents disagreed with the Exposure Draft's recommendation to rescind Statement 33 for reasons similar to those previously discussed in paragraph 119. Some respondents believed that insufficient time had been allowed for information on the effects of changing prices to be incorporated into user evaluations and that additional years of data were needed to allow for the assimilation of this information into user methods. Other respondents stated that the effects of past high inflation carry over into future financial statements even in times of relatively low inflation and therefore affect such statements. Some noted that the experimental label and short-term availability of the data had discouraged use. Still other respondents believed that if inflation returns, the Board will need to reimplement the requirement. In that event, data comparison will be hampered by the lack of information on the effects of changing prices in the interim years. In addition, some respondents reiterated the view that one reason that the data were not used relates to the deficiencies of the current cost method.

130. The Board agrees with many of the concerns expressed by those few respondents that support continuance of a changing prices disclosure requirement. However, those concerns are not persuasive when considered in the light of what a large majority of respondents have stated about the general nonuse of the data. Further, the Board believes that any attempt to correct the deficiencies of the present changing prices disclosure requirements identified by many respondents would be so time-consuming and expensive that no reasonable cost-benefit relationship could be attained. That is especially true in view of the poor prospects that the Board believes now exist for increased use of supplementary changing prices data.

Statement of Financial Accounting Standards No. 90
Regulated Enterprises—Accounting for Abandonments and Disallowances of Plant Costs

an amendment of FASB Statement No. 71

STATUS

Issued: December 1986

Effective Date: For fiscal years beginning after December 15, 1987 and interim periods within those fiscal years

Affects: Amends FAS 71, paragraphs 9, 10, 15, and 34
Supersedes FAS 71, paragraph 13 and footnote 6

Affected by: Paragraph 9(d) superseded by FAS 92
Paragraphs 14 and 27 amended by FAS 96 and FAS 109
Paragraphs 16 through 25 superseded by FTB 87-2

Other Interpretive Pronouncement: FTB 87-2

Issues Discussed by FASB Emerging Issues Task Force (EITF)

Affects: EITF Topic No. D-5

Interpreted by: No EITF Issues

Related Issues: No EITF Issues

SUMMARY

This Statement amends FASB Statement No. 71, *Accounting for the Effects of Certain Types of Regulation*, for two types of events that recently have occurred in the electric utility industry—abandonments of plants and disallowances of costs of recently completed plants.

This Statement amends Statement 71 to require the future revenue that is expected to result from the regulator's inclusion of the cost of an abandoned plant in allowable costs for rate-making purposes to be reported at its present value when the abandonment becomes probable. If the carrying amount of the abandoned plant exceeds that present value, a loss would be recognized. Statement 71 previously required that asset to be reported at the lesser of the cost of the abandoned plant or the probable gross revenue.

This Statement also amends Statement 71 to require any disallowed costs of a recently completed plant to be recognized as a loss. Statement 71 previously required asset impairments to be recognized but did not specify what constitutes an impairment or provide specific guidance about how impairments should be measured.

Finally, this Statement amends Statement 71 to specify that an allowance for funds used during construction should be capitalized only if its subsequent inclusion in allowable costs for rate-making purposes is probable.

This Statement is effective for fiscal years beginning after December 15, 1987 unless (a) application of the Statement would cause a violation or probable future violation of a restrictive clause in an existing loan indenture or other agreement and (b) the enterprise is actively seeking to obtain modification of that restrictive clause. In that case, this Statement is effective for fiscal years beginning after December 15, 1988.

This Statement applies to the recorded costs of previously abandoned assets, the recorded costs of assets for which future abandonment is probable or becomes probable in the future, previously disallowed plant costs, and disallowances of plant costs that are probable or become probable in the future. Restatement of financial statements for prior fiscal years is encouraged but not required.

(This page intentionally left blank.)

Statement of Financial Accounting Standards No. 90

Regulated Enterprises—Accounting for Abandonments and Disallowances of Plant Costs

an amendment of FASB Statement No. 71

CONTENTS

INTRODUCTION

1. FASB Statement No. 71, *Accounting for the Effects of Certain Types of Regulation,* was issued in December 1982. Shortly after that Statement was issued, major events in the electric utility industry caused the Board to review the effects of the Statement on the accounting for those events. After considering the application of the Statement, the Board decided to amend Statement 71 to provide more specific guidance for some of those events and to change the accounting for others.

2. This Statement amends Statement 71 to specify accounting for plant abandonments and disallowances of costs of recently completed plants. It also provides guidance for the capitalization of an allowance for funds used during construction (AFUDC).

STANDARDS OF FINANCIAL ACCOUNTING AND REPORTING

Accounting for Abandonments

3. When it becomes probable[1] that an operating asset or an asset under construction will be abandoned, the cost of that asset shall be removed from construction work-in-process or plant-in-service. The enterprise shall determine whether recovery of any allowed cost is likely to be provided with (a) full return on investment during the period from the time when abandonment becomes probable to the time when recovery is completed or (b) partial or no return on investment during that period. That determination should focus on the facts and circumstances related to the specific abandonment and should also consider the past practice and current policies of the applicable regulatory jurisdiction on abandonment situations. Based on that determination, the enterprise shall account for the cost of the abandoned plant as follows:

a. *Full return on investment is likely to be provided.* Any disallowance of all or part of the cost of the abandoned plant that is both *probable* and *reasonably estimable,* as those terms are used in FASB Statement No. 5, *Accounting for Contingencies,* and the related FASB Interpretation No. 14, *Reasonable Estimation of the Amount of a Loss,* shall be recognized as a loss, and the carrying basis of the recorded asset shall be correspondingly reduced. The remainder of the cost of the abandoned plant shall be reported as a separate new asset.

---

[1] The term *probable* is used in this Statement consistent with its use in FASB Statement No. 5, *Accounting for Contingencies,* to mean that a transaction or event is likely to occur.

b. *Partial or no return on investment is likely to be provided.* Any disallowance of all or part of the cost of the abandoned plant that is both *probable* and *reasonably estimable,* as those terms are used in Statement 5 and Interpretation 14, shall be recognized as a loss. The present value of the future revenues expected to be provided to recover the allowable cost of that abandoned plant and return on investment, if any, shall be reported as a separate new asset. Any excess of the remainder of the cost of the abandoned plant over that present value also shall be recognized as a loss. The discount rate used to compute the present value shall be the enterprise's incremental borrowing rate, that is, the rate that the enterprise would have to pay to borrow an equivalent amount for a period equal to the expected recovery period. In determining the present value of expected future revenues, the enterprise shall consider such matters as (1) the probable time period before such recovery is expected to begin and (2) the probable time period over which recovery is expected to be provided. If the estimate of either period is a range, the guidance of Interpretation 14 shall be applied to determine the loss to be recognized. Accordingly, the most likely period within that range shall be used to compute the present value. If no period within that range is a better estimate than any other, the present value shall be based on the minimum time period within that range.

4. The recorded amount of the new asset shall be adjusted from time to time as necessary if new information indicates that the estimates used to record the separate new asset have changed. Those estimates include (a) the determination of whether full return on investment will be provided and, if not, the probable time period before recovery is expected to begin and the probable time period over which recovery is expected to be provided and (b) the amount of any probable and reasonably estimable disallowance of recorded costs of the abandoned plant. The amount of the adjustment shall be recognized in income as a loss or gain. Paragraphs 21, 22, and 24 of Appendix A illustrate how this paragraph applies to changes in the estimated time period before recovery begins and the time period over which recovery is expected to be provided. The recorded carrying amount of the new asset shall not be adjusted for changes in the enterprise's incremental borrowing rate.

5. During the period between the date on which the new asset is recognized and the date on which recovery begins, the carrying amount shall be increased by accruing a carrying charge. The rate used to accrue that carrying charge shall be as follows:

a. If full return on investment is likely to be provided, a rate equal to the allowed overall cost of capital in the jurisdiction in which recovery is expected to be provided shall be used.

b. If partial or no return on investment is likely to be provided, the rate that was used to compute the present value shall be used. Paragraphs 20 and 23 and Schedules 1 and 2 of Appendix A illustrate that procedure.

6. During the recovery period, the new asset shall be amortized as follows:

a. If full return on investment is likely to be provided, the asset shall be amortized in the same manner as that used for rate-making purposes.

b. If partial or no return on investment is likely to be provided, the asset shall be amortized in a manner that will produce a constant return on the unamortized investment in the new asset equal to the rate at which the expected revenues were discounted. Paragraph 25 and Schedule 3 of Appendix A illustrate that procedure.

Disallowances of Costs of Recently Completed Plants

7. When it becomes probable that part of the cost of a recently completed plant will be disallowed for rate-making purposes and a reasonable estimate of the amount of the disallowance can be made,[2] the estimated amount of the probable disallowance shall be deducted from the reported cost of the plant and recognized as a loss. If part of the cost is explicitly, but indirectly, disallowed (for example, by an explicit disallowance of return on investment on a portion of the plant), an equivalent amount of cost shall be deducted from the reported cost of the plant and recognized as a loss.

Allowance for Funds Used during Construction

8. Paragraph 15 of Statement 71 requires an allowance for funds used during construction, including a designated cost of equity funds, to be capitalized in specified circumstances as part of the acquisition cost of the related asset. That cost shall be capitalized under those circumstances only if its subsequent inclusion in allowable costs for rate-making purposes is probable.

---

[2]Interpretation 14 provides guidance for making a reasonable estimate of the amount of a loss.

Amendments to Statement 71

9. Statement 71 is amended as follows:

a. Footnote 6 to paragraph 9 is superseded by the following:

> [6]The term *probable* is used in this Statement consistent with its use in FASB Statement No. 5, *Accounting for Contingencies.* Statement 5 defines *probable* as an area within a range of the likelihood that a future event or events will occur. That range is from probable to remote, as follows:
>
> *Probable.* The future event or events are likely to occur.
> *Reasonably possible.* The chance of the future event or events occurring is more than remote but less than likely.
> *Remote.* The chance of the future event or events occurring is slight.

b. The following footnote is added at the end of the first sentence of paragraph 9:

> *Costs of abandoned plants shall be accounted for in accordance with paragraphs 3-6 of FASB Statement No. 90, *Regulated Enterprises—Accounting for Abandonments and Disallowances of Plant Costs.*

c. The following footnote is added to the end of paragraph 10:

> †Disallowances of costs of recently completed plants, whether direct or indirect, shall be accounted for in accordance with paragraph 7 of Statement 90.

d. Paragraph 13 is superseded by the following:

> Appendix B and Statement 90 illustrate the application of the general standards of accounting for the effects of regulation.

e. The following sentence is added preceding the last sentence of paragraph 15:

> Those amounts shall be capitalized only if their subsequent inclusion in allowable costs for rate-making purposes is probable.

f. The following footnote is added to the end of the third sentence of paragraph 34:

> ‡An exception to this general rule is provided for costs of abandoned plants. Paragraphs 16-25 of Statement 90 illustrate accounting for future revenues expected to result from the cost of an abandoned plant with a partial return or no return on investment during the recovery period.

Effective Date and Transition

10. Except as provided in paragraph 13, the provisions of this Statement shall be effective for fiscal years beginning after December 15, 1987 and interim periods within those fiscal years. Earlier application is encouraged. Retroactive application of this Statement in fiscal years for which financial statements have previously been issued is encouraged, in which case the financial statements of all prior periods presented shall be restated. In addition, the financial statements shall, in the year this Statement is first applied, disclose the nature of any restatement and its effect on income before extraordinary items, net income, and related per share amounts for each period presented and on retained earnings at the beginning of the earliest period presented.

11. If financial statements for prior fiscal years are not restated, the effects of applying this Statement to existing situations shall be reported as the cumulative effect of a change in accounting principle, as described in APB Opinion No. 20, *Accounting Changes,* and the nature of the change and the effect of adopting this Statement on income before extraordinary items, net income, and the related per share amounts shall be disclosed.

12. Initial application of this Statement will require the following adjustments to previously recorded assets with corresponding adjustments to reported net income of prior years or to the cumulative effect of an accounting change in the year of the change:

a. Amounts that were recorded in prior years for recoverable costs of abandoned plants shall be adjusted as indicated in paragraph 3. If partial or no return on investment is likely to be provided, the discount rate used to compute the present value shall be the regulated enterprise's incremental borrowing rate at the date on which the abandonment became probable.
b. Disallowed plant costs of the types described in paragraph 7 shall be deducted from the reported cost of the related asset.

13. If application of this Statement would cause a violation or probable future violation of a restrictive clause in an existing loan indenture or other agreement and the enterprise is actively seeking to obtain modification of that restrictive clause, that enterprise may delay application of this Statement for one additional year. In that

case, the enterprise shall disclose, in its financial statements for the first fiscal year beginning after December 15, 1987 and interim periods within that fiscal year, (a) the effects that application of this Statement would have had on assets, retained earnings at the end of that fiscal year or interim period, income before extraordinary items, net income, and related per share amounts, (b) the nature of the violation or probable future violation that would result from application of the Statement, and (c) the steps that the company is taking to eliminate the restrictions. That enterprise shall apply this Statement, as indicated in paragraphs 10-12 above, for fiscal years beginning after December 15, 1988 and interim periods within those fiscal years.

> **The provisions of this Statement need not be applied to immaterial items.**

This Statement was adopted by the affirmative votes of four members of the Financial Accounting Standards Board. Messrs. Brown, Kirk, and Northrop dissented.

Messrs. Brown and Northrop dissent to this Statement's provisions concerning accounting for abandonments and disallowances of plant costs. They see no reason to modify the applicability of generally accepted accounting principles to regulated enterprises beyond those departures specifically called for by Statement 71.

Messrs. Brown and Northrop disagree with the requirement to record recoverable costs of abandoned plants at their present value and subsequently to accrue the discount resulting from this present value computation. They would record the costs associated with abandoned plants at the lower of cost or gross recoverable amount (the undiscounted amount of such costs that will be allowed in future rates). They would amortize these costs over the period during which they will be allowed for rate-making purposes. In their view, this cost recovery approach, now specified

by Statement 71, should not be changed because it (l) conforms with accounting for enterprises in general and (2) is consistent with the Board's conclusion not to require recoverable costs of other regulator-created assets, such as storm damage costs, to be recorded at their present value. Further, they believe that recording recoverable costs at their present value results in inappropriate understatement of current period net income and overstatements of net income in subsequent periods.

Messrs. Brown, Kirk and Northrop object to the requirement to recognize disallowances of costs of newly completed operating plants as losses in all cases. In their view, a regulator's disallowance of part of the cost of a fixed asset is an event warranting disclosure but not accounting recognition, except to the extent that the asset has been impaired. They believe that, barring impairment, reflecting a disallowance as a loss inappropriately recognizes reduced future revenues as reductions in current period net income. This results in overstatement of net income in subsequent periods.

Members of the Financial Accounting Standards Board:

Donald J. Kirk, *Chairman*	Raymond C. Lauver	Robert J. Swieringa
Victor H. Brown	David Mosso	Arthur R. Wyatt
	C. Arthur Northrop	

Appendix A

EXAMPLES OF APPLICATION OF THIS STATEMENT TO SPECIFIC SITUATIONS

14. This appendix provides guidance for application of this Statement to some specific situations. The guidance does not address all possible applications of this Statement. All the examples assume that the enterprise meets the criteria in paragraph 5 of Statement 71 for the application of Statement 71 by the enterprise. Cases similar to those illustrated in this appendix may involve income tax effects that could accrue to the utility in question. Some of those tax effects may be recognized currently under the applicable authoritative literature (presently APB Opinion No. 11, *Accounting for Income Taxes*); others may not be recognized currently. Under Opinion 11, the tax effects of timing differences are measured by the differential between income taxes computed with and without inclusion of the transaction creating the difference between taxable income and pretax accounting income. For simplicity, the examples base the income tax effects on a 34 percent tax

rate and assume that those effects may be recognized.

15. Specific situations discussed in this appendix are:

Paragraph
Numbers

Accounting for an Abandonment

16. Assume that Utility A operates solely in a single-state jurisdiction that, in the past, has permitted recovery of amounts prudently invested in abandoned plants over an extended period of time without a return on unrecovered investment during the recovery period. Utility A decides to abandon a plant that has been under construction for some time. Although the possibility of abandoning the plant has been under consideration, abandonment was not considered probable before the actual decision was made. The recorded cost of the plant is $728 million; and the company estimates that it will incur additional contract cancellation penalties of approximately $22.5 million, which will be paid in approximately 6 months. Utility A's incremental borrowing rate at the date of the decision to abandon the plant is 14 percent, compounded monthly.

17. In view of the accumulated cost of the abandoned plant, Utility A believes that it is probable that recovery of cost without return on investment

during the recovery period will be granted over a period that will not be less than 5 years nor more than 10 years, but it has no basis for estimating the exact time period that will be selected by the regulator. In view of the rate-making process in Utility A's jurisdiction, it will take approximately 18 months to obtain a rate order covering the abandoned plant.

18. For income tax purposes, the abandoned plant has a basis of $500 million, including the contract cancellation penalties of $22.5 million. Utility A will deduct the cost of the abandoned plant as a loss on its income tax return in the year of the abandonment and will receive a tax benefit of 34 percent. All of the benefit of that loss will be recognized in the current year, partially through a reduction of current taxable income and carryback to prior years, the balance through offset of existing deferred taxes that will reverse during the carryforward period. Existing deferred taxes on timing differences relating to the abandoned plant total $35 million. For regulatory purposes, the tax benefit of the abandonment will be reflected as recovery of part of the cost of the abandoned plant.

19. When the abandonment becomes probable (in this case, at the date of the decision to abandon), Utility A would remove the plant from construction work-in-process. Any disallowance of the recorded cost that is probable and can be reasonably estimated would be recorded as a loss. This example assumes that no disallowance of recorded cost is anticipated. Utility A would record a separate new asset, representing the future revenues expected to result from the regulator's treatment of the cost of the abandoned plant, at the present value of those expected future revenues. The computation of the amount to be recovered would be as follows:

Recorded cost of abandoned plant		$ 728,000,000
Cancellation charges payable		22,500,000
Total		750,500,000
Less reduction of cost in an amount equal to the amounts designated by the regulator for current recovery:		
Current tax benefit of abandonment	$ 170,000,000	
Deferred taxes reversed	35,000,000	205,000,000
Net amount to be recovered in future rates		$ 545,500,000

The probable future revenues would be estimated at $9,091,667 per month for 5 years (based on an assumed straight-line recovery over the 5-year minimum period within the range), and those cash flows would be estimated to begin in 19 months. The computation of the amount to be recorded for the new asset and of the loss resulting from the abandonment would be as follows:

Present value of $9,091,667 per month at 14% for 60 months, starting at the end of the 19th month (amount to be recorded as new asset)		$ 317,107,016
Cost of abandoned plant:		
Net amount to be recovered in future rates for regulatory purposes (per table above)	$ 545,500,000	
Discount to reduce cancellation charges to present value ($22,500,000 discounted at 14% for 6 months)	(1,512,637)	543,987,363
Loss to be recognized at time of abandonment		226,980,347
Deferred tax benefit at 34%		77,139,318*
Net loss to be recognized at time of decision to abandon the plant		$ 149,741,029

*This amount consists of the following:

Deferred tax benefit of discount to reduce the expected recovery of abandonment to present value	$ 77,653,615
Deferred tax on discount to reduce cancellation charges to present value	(514,297)
Total	$ 77,139,318

The deferred tax benefit of the recovery would reverse in relation to the earnings on the unamortized asset. The deferred tax on the imputed interest on the cancellation charges would reverse as interest expense is accrued.

20. Pending receipt of a rate order, Utility A would accrue carrying charges on the recorded asset at a 14 percent annual rate. Schedule 1 shows that computation.

21. Assume that at the end of the 12th month Utility A determines that it is now probable, based on discussions with the regulator, that recovery of cost without return on investment will be granted over a period that will not be less than 7 years nor more than 15 years, but it still has no basis for estimating the exact time period that will be selected by the regulator. Utility A also estimates that it will take approximately another 12 months (that is, 24 months after the date of the decision to abandon rather than the 18 months previously assumed) to obtain a rate order.

22. When new evidence makes it possible to refine a previous estimate, Utility A would adjust the recorded amount of the asset to reflect its revised estimate. The probable future revenues now would be estimated at $6,494,048 per month for 7 years (based on an assumed straight-line recovery over the 7-year minimum period within the range), and those cash flows would be estimated to begin 25 months after the date of the decision to abandon. The computation of the adjustment to the carrying amount of the asset that results from the new estimate would be as follows:

Present value of $6,494,048 per month at 14% for 84 months, starting at the end of the 25th month, which is 13 months in the future (adjusted carrying amount of asset)	$ 301,506,272
Carrying amount of asset at end of 12th month (Schedule 1)	364,464,421
Pretax loss to be recognized at end of 12th month	62,958,149
Deferred tax benefit of loss at 34%	21,405,771
Net loss to be recognized at end of 12th month	$ 41,552,378

The discount rate would not be adjusted to reflect Utility A's current incremental borrowing rate. That new rate reflects current conditions rather than the conditions that prevailed at the time of the decision to abandon.

Schedule 1

Utility A

Accrual of Carrying Charges on Asset Resulting from Abandoned Plant

Month	Recorded Amount Beginning of Month	Carrying Charges Accrued*	Recorded Amount End of Month
1	$ 317,107,016	$ 3,699,582	$ 320,806,598
2	320,806,598	3,742,743	324,549,341
3	324,549,341	3,786,409	328,335,750
4	328,335,750	3,830,584	332,166,334
5	332,166,334	3,875,274	336,041,608
6	336,041,608	3,920,486	339,962,094
7	339,962,094	3,966,224	343,928,318
8	343,928,318	4,012,497	347,940,815
9	347,940,815	4,059,310	352,000,125
10	352,000,125	4,106,668	356,106,793
11	356,106,793	4,154,579	360,261,372
12	360,261,372	4,203,049	364,464,421

*As carrying charges are accrued, deferred income tax benefits would be reversed and income tax expense recognized in accordance with Opinion 11.

Schedule 2

Utility A

Accrual of Carrying Charges on Asset Resulting from Abandoned Plant Revised to Reflect a Change in Estimate

Month	Recorded Amount Beginning of Month	Carrying Charges Accrued*	Recorded Amount End of Month
13	$ 301,506,272	$ 3,517,573	$ 305,023,845
14	305,023,845	3,558,612	308,582,457
15	308,582,457	3,600,128	312,182,585
16	312,182,585	3,642,131	315,824,716
17	315,824,716	3,684,621	319,509,337
18	319,509,337	3,727,609	323,236,946
19	323,236,946	3,771,098	327,008,044
20	327,008,044	3,815,094	330,823,138
21	330,823,138	3,859,603	334,682,741
22	334,682,741	3,904,632	338,587,373
23	338,587,373	3,950,186	342,537,559
24	342,537,559	3,996,271	346,533,830

*As carrying charges are accrued, deferred income tax benefits would be reversed and income tax expense recognized in accordance with Opinion 11.

23. Pending receipt of a rate order, Utility A would continue to accrue carrying charges on the adjusted recorded asset at a 14 percent annual rate. Schedule 2 shows that revised computation.

24. Assume that the rate order is received at the end of the 24th month and specifies a recovery period of 8 years; the resulting revenues will start approximately 1 month after the rate order is received. The probable future revenues now would be estimated at $5,682,292 per month for 8 years (based on the regulator's decision to allow straight-line recovery over an 8-year period), and those cash flows would be estimated to begin 25 months after the abandonment occurred (1 month after the rate order is received). Utility A

968

would reflect that change by recognizing an additional loss, as follows:

Present value of $5,682,292 per
month at 14% for 96 months
(adjusted carrying amount of
asset) .... $ 327,104,260

Carrying amount of asset at end
of 24th month (Schedule 2) 346,533,830

Pretax loss to be recognized
at time of rate order 19,429,570

Deferred tax benefit of loss at
34% 6,606,054

Net loss to be recognized at
time of rate order .... $ 12,823,516

The discount rate would not be adjusted to reflect Utility A's current incremental borrowing rate.

That new rate reflects current conditions rather than the conditions that prevailed at the time of the abandonment.

25. As recovery occurs, the recorded asset would be amortized so as to reflect earnings on the unamortized asset at the 14 percent rate used to determine the present value of the asset. Schedule 3 shows the details of that computation.

Accounting for a Disallowance of Plant Cost

26. Assume that Utility B operates in two state jurisdictions. After an extensive "prudence investigation," the regulator in one of those state jurisdictions disallows $865 million of the $3.6 billion total cost of Utility B's recently completed nuclear generating plant. That state jurisdiction represents approximately 50 percent of Utility B's

Schedule 3

Utility A

Computation of Amortization of Asset Resulting from Abandoned Plant

Month	(1) Unamortized Balance Beg. of Month	(2) Return* at 14.00%	(3) Revenues	(4) Amortization of Cost (Col 3−Col 2)	(5) Unamortized Balance End of Month (Col 1−Col 4)
25	$ 327,104,260	$ 3,816,217	$ 5,682,292	$ 1,866,075	$ 325,238,185
26	325,238,185	3,794,445	5,682,292	1,887,847	323,350,338
27	323,350,338	3,772,421	5,682,292	1,909,871	321,440,467
28	321,440,467	3,750,139	5,682,292	1,932,153	319,508,314
29	319,508,314	3,727,597	5,682,292	1,954,695	317,553,619
30	317,553,619	3,704,792	5,682,292	1,977,500	315,576,119
31	315,576,119	3,681,721	5,682,292	2,000,571	313,575,548
32	313,575,548	3,658,382	5,682,292	2,023,910	311,551,638
33	311,551,638	3,634,769	5,682,292	2,047,523	309,504,115
34	309,504,115	3,610,881	5,682,292	2,071,411	307,432,704
35	307,432,704	3,586,715	5,682,292	2,095,577	305,337,127
.	.	.		.	.
.	.	.		.	.
.	.	.		.	.
110	58,342,320	680,661	5,682,292	5,001,631	53,340,689
111	53,340,689	622,308	5,682,292	5,059,984	48,280,705
112	48,280,705	563,275	5,682,292	5,119,017	43,161,688
113	43,161,688	503,553	5,682,292	5,178,739	37,982,949
114	37,982,949	443,134	5,682,292	5,239,158	32,743,791
115	32,743,791	382,011	5,682,292	5,300,281	27,443,510
116	27,443,510	320,174	5,682,292	5,362,118	22,081,392
117	22,081,392	257,617	5,682,292	5,424,675	16,656,717
118	16,656,717	194,328	5,682,292	5,487,964	11,168,753
119	11,168,753	130,302	5,682,292	5,551,990	5,616,763
120	5,616,763	65,529	5,682,292	5,616,763	0

*As earnings on the unamortized asset are recognized, deferred income tax benefits would be reversed and income tax expense recognized in accordance with Opinion 11.

operations, and approximately 50 percent of the output of the recently completed plant is expected to be used in that state. The tax basis of the plant is $2.4 billion. The regulator indicates that the tax benefit from a ratable portion of depreciation will be given to the shareholders as a result of the disallowance. After consultation with counsel, Utility B decides that it should not appeal the regulator's disallowance. The regulator in Utility B's other state jurisdiction has not participated in the "prudence investigation," and there is no indication that a similar disallowance is likely in that jurisdiction.

27. Utility B should recognize the effective disallowance as a loss. Because only 50 percent of the plant's cost will be recoverable from customers in the state, the effective disallowance is 50 percent of the amount disallowed, or $432.5 million. The disallowance should be recognized when the disallowance is probable and the amount of the disallowance can be reasonably estimated, and those conditions are met in this case. The tax benefit of the loss will be realized as future depreciation is taken for income tax purposes. Since the tax benefit of the plant is based on $2.4 billion and the cost of the plant prior to the disallowance is $3.6 billion, only two-thirds of the loss is available for tax benefit. A deferred tax benefit, based on two-thirds of the loss, can be recognized when the loss is recognized providing that benefit meets the criteria of Opinion 11 for recognition.

Accounting for a Disallowance of Plant Cost Resulting from a "Cost Cap"

28. Assume that Utility C, which operates solely in one state jurisdiction, is constructing a new electric generating plant. Completion is expected to take approximately one year. The cost of the plant, which was originally expected to be $1.25 billion, is now estimated to be as follows:

Costs capitalized to date	$ 2,700,000,000
AFUDC on above for 1 year at 11.25%	303,750,000
Remaining labor, materials, etc., to complete, expected to be spent ratably over the year	469,822,500
AFUDC on above for ½ year at 11.25%	26,427,500
Total estimated cost at completion	$ 3,500,000,000

Various parties have charged that certain cost increases were a result of imprudent management of the construction.

29. To avoid the cost and time delay that would be involved in a full-scale "prudence investigation" of the construction of the plant, Utility C and its regulator agree that the total cost of the plant that will be allowable in determining depreciation and that will be allowed in Utility C's rate base will be $3.4 billion. If the eventual cost of the plant exceeds that "cap," a ratable portion of the tax benefit of depreciation will accrue to the benefit of the shareholders. For tax purposes, the plant is expected to have a net depreciable basis of $2.0 billion.

30. The loss that results from the disallowance inherent in the "cost cap" would be computed as follows:

Total estimated cost at completion	$ 3,500,000,000
Maximum allowable cost	3,400,000,000
Difference	$ 100,000,000
Loss to be recognized (present value of difference at 11.25% AFUDC rate, based on 1 year to complete)	$ 89,887,600
Deferred tax benefit of loss (2.0/3.5 × $100,000,000 × 34%)	19,428,600
Net loss to be recognized when "cost cap" is agreed to	$ 70,459,000

After the loss is recognized, AFUDC would continue to be recorded based on the remaining recorded costs. Subsequently, if additional increases in the cost of the plant become probable and those costs are not allowable under the agreed "cost cap," those increases would also be recognized as losses from disallowances when they become probable.

31. If the regulator ordered a "cost cap" that Utility C did *not* agree to, Utility C would have to assess whether the criteria of Statement 5 for loss recognition are met. If those criteria are met, the accounting would be as indicated above. Otherwise, no loss would be recognized until that loss was probable and could be reasonably estimated. Because of the possible disallowance inherent in

the "cost cap," it may no longer be probable that some amount of AFUDC will be included in allowable costs in the future, and that amount may be reasonably estimable. In that case, that amount of AFUDC would not be capitalized.

Accounting for an Explicit, but Indirect, Disallowance

32. Assume that Utility D operates solely in a single-state jurisdiction. On January 1, 19X1, Utility D's new electric generating plant becomes operational. The cost of that plant is $1 billion.

33. Utility D's regulator concludes that part of the cost of the recently completed plant was imprudently incurred. However, rather than disallow the specific costs that were imprudent, the regulator instead excludes 10 percent ($100 million) of the plant from the rate base, thereby providing no return on investment on that portion of the plant. The regulator does not intend any part of the tax benefit of depreciation to accrue to the benefit of Utility D's shareholders. The regulator indicates that the exclusion of 10 percent of the

plant's cost from the rate base is intended to be permanent. The utility concludes that it will not appeal the disallowance after considering the likely outcome of an appeal.

34. Utility D should record the indirect disallowance as a loss and should estimate the amount of that loss using the best available information. If the regulator specifies the amount of cost that was imprudent, that amount may be the best estimate of the loss. Otherwise, Utility D would have to estimate the future cash flows that have been disallowed as a result of the order and determine the effective disallowance by computing the present value of those disallowed future cash flows. Since both the disallowed future cash flows and the appropriate discount rate to compute the present value would be estimates, those estimates should be calculated on a consistent basis. Accordingly, if the future cash flows are estimated based on the current weighted-average overall cost of Utility D's capital, that weighted-average overall cost of capital should also be used as the discount rate. The loss has no tax benefit to Utility D.

Appendix B

BASIS FOR CONCLUSIONS

CONTENTS

Appendix B

BASIS FOR CONCLUSIONS

Introduction

35. This appendix summarizes considerations that were deemed significant by members of the Board in reaching the conclusions in this Statement. It includes reasons for accepting certain views and rejecting others. Individual Board members gave greater weight to some factors than to others.

General Considerations

36. Many letters received as the Board was developing the conclusions in this Statement objected to the Board's conclusions about accounting for abandonments and disallowances of costs of recently completed plants on the basis that those decisions departed from the historical cost model of accounting for enterprises generally. The Board provided its view of the current accounting model in paragraphs 66-70 of FASB Concepts Statement No. 5, *Recognition and Measurement in Financial Statements of Business Enterprises.* Paragraph 66 acknowledges that the current

model is not a pure "historical cost" model, as follows:

> Items currently reported in financial statements are measured by different attributes, depending on the nature of the item and the relevance and reliability of the attribute measured. The Board expects the use of different attributes to continue.

37. The Board also noted that much of the accounting specified by Statement 71 is itself a departure from the accounting framework applied by nonregulated enterprises generally. That Statement recognizes that rate actions of a regulator can have economic effects and requires certain items that would be charged to expense by nonregulated enterprises to be capitalized by regulated enterprises solely because the regulator's rate actions can provide reasonable assurance of future revenue.

38. The accounting set forth in Statement 71 requires certain regulated enterprises to recognize probable increases in future revenues due to a regulator's actions as assets by capitalizing incurred costs that would otherwise be charged to expense. The Board believes those regulated enterprises should also recognize probable decreases in future revenues due to a regulator's actions as reductions of assets. General purpose financial statements that recognize asset enhancements but not asset decrements would lack representational faithfulness—a critical qualitative characteristic if financial statements are to be reliable. After reviewing the frequency and magnitude of recent plant abandonments and disallowances of plant costs in the electric utility industry, the Board concluded that it should require the resulting probable decreases in future revenues to be recognized as reductions in assets if financial statements are to be representationally faithful.

39. The Board also believes that the accounting for plant abandonments required by this Statement is consistent with the accounting followed by companies in general for monetary assets under APB Opinion No. 21, *Interest on Receivables and Payables.* Whatever asset remains after a utility plant is abandoned is essentially monetary in nature.

40. Many respondents to the Exposure Draft, *Regulated Enterprises—Accounting for Phase-in Plans, Abandonments, and Disallowances of Plant Costs,* urged the Board not to adopt some of the provisions in this Statement because they would reduce some companies' retained earnings to the extent that payment of dividends, future financing on favorable terms, or both would be

precluded. When a company incurs a loss, significant consequences may occur, and the Board is aware that some of the effects of the issues addressed in this Statement are major. The Board believes that those consequences result from the event that is being accounted for, not from the accounting itself. The Board believes that accounting should reflect major adverse occurrences that affect an enterprise even though the consequences of those major adverse occurrences may be significant.

41. Many respondents also urged the Board not to adopt certain provisions of this Statement because the regulated rates might decrease as a result of the accounting requirements. Others indicated that the regulated rates would increase if the accounting specified by this Statement were required. The Board believes that regulators will provide whatever rates they believe are justified; general-purpose financial reporting should not be designed to encourage or to discourage specific actions of regulators, and regulators can be expected to understand accounting that reflects the effects of their actions.

Accounting for Abandonments

42. Historically, utilities have usually abandoned plants in early stages of construction, rather than after incurring major construction costs. Prior to Statement 71, most regulated enterprises accounted for the costs of abandoned plants on a cost recovery basis; that is, no loss was recorded if revenues promised by a regulator were expected to recover the recorded costs. Statement 71 did not change that practice.

43. Recently, abandonments of plants under construction have become more common, and some utilities have abandoned plants during the later stages of construction. In many cases, the cost of abandoned plants is much greater than in the past.

44. Many respondents to the Exposure Draft indicated that the essential nature of the asset does not change when a plant is abandoned. In their view, cost-based regulation treats all assets the same; a plant under construction and an abandoned plant are both accumulated costs that will be recovered through revenues. The Board does not agree with that view and has concluded that an abandonment changes the nature of the asset. A plant under construction is expected to produce utility services that have value. An abandoned plant can produce no services. Any value that results from the abandoned plant is limited to the revenues that will be furnished through the sales of services provided by other plants.

45. Other respondents to the Exposure Draft urged the Board not to require loss recognition until the loss is probable. That is the basis for loss recognition that is provided by one of the criteria of Statement 5. The Board agrees that loss recognition should not occur until the loss is probable and reasonably estimable, consistent with Statement 5. However, some of those respondents equated *probable* with *certain*. The Board notes that the term *probable* is defined in Statement 5 and is used in the same sense in this Statement. That definition is not synonymous with *certain,* a term that connotes a much higher level of assurance than *probable.*

46. Regulators in many jurisdictions have provided recovery of the cost of abandoned plants without return on investment during the recovery period. That procedure has been described as a means of sharing the loss between customers and shareholders. A cost-recovery approach for accounting for abandonments was based on the view that the regulator was disallowing future earnings, rather than disallowing a portion of the cost of the abandoned plant. In reconsidering that issue in the context of today's environment, the Board concluded that a cost-recovery approach, in effect, delays recognition of losses that are known to have been incurred. Although that approach might have little significance when applied to relatively immaterial items, the significance of the amounts involved in recent cases indicates that recognition of losses resulting from abandonments should not be delayed beyond the date when they are probable and reasonably estimable.

47. The Board also concluded that the future revenue that will result from inclusion of the cost of an abandoned plant in allowable costs for rate-making purposes is essentially a monetary asset. In the Board's view, an abandoned plant should be written off when abandonment is probable. Unless it is probable that the cost of an abandoned plant will be entirely disallowed by the regulator, a new asset that is essentially a monetary asset should be recognized. That asset most closely resembles a long-term receivable that is recognized on the basis of (a) its cost, if the stated interest rate is reasonable, or (b) its present value, if the interest rate is not stated or if the stated rate is unreasonable. The Board believes that a similar measurement basis is appropriate for expected future revenue that will result from a regulator's treatment of the cost of an abandoned plant.

48. In the Exposure Draft, the Board proposed that the overall rate of return allowed in the regulated enterprise's last rate case in the jurisdiction in which recovery is expected to be received be used to measure the present value of the future revenue that will result from an abandoned plant. Respondents to the Exposure Draft pointed out that the actual disallowance is the overall rate of return in the future rate cases covering the period during which recovery will occur. That rate is not known at the time of the abandonment. The Board agreed that a surrogate rate should be used to compute the present value of the remaining future revenues, and it decided to require the enterprise to use its incremental borrowing rate at the date the abandonment becomes probable.

49. Some respondents suggested that the interest rate used should be changed whenever the allowed overall rate of return changes during the recovery period. The Board views that approach as a means of maintaining the asset in question at its fair value. Fair value often is used in accounting to measure a newly acquired asset when that fair value is more clearly evident than the value of the asset given up. However, with the exception of certain assets that are readily marketable, the present accounting model does not adjust the carrying basis of an existing asset when the fair value of that asset changes.

50. Some respondents to the Exposure Draft indicated that the rate used to value an abandonment should be a net-of-tax rate. Other respondents asked that the Board address the tax effects of the proposed accounting for abandonments. APB Opinion No. 11, *Accounting for Income Taxes,* does not permit accounting for items with tax effects on a net-of-tax basis. Rather, deferred income taxes are provided for timing differences when they occur, and those deferred taxes are reversed when the related timing differences reverse. Opinion 11 applies to taxable enterprises that apply Statement 71 except in the limited circumstances outlined in paragraph 18 of Statement 71. Accordingly, the loss recognized to reduce the asset resulting from an abandonment to its present value and the subsequent profit that results comprise a timing difference. The tax effects of that timing difference would be recognized when the timing difference originates if appropriate under the provisions of Opinion 11.

51. The Board concluded that accruing a carrying charge on, or recognizing accretion of, the present value of the expected future revenue related to an abandonment is appropriate for two reasons. First, the basis used to record that asset recognizes the effect of the regulator's disallowance of future return on investment as a loss in the period in which the loss becomes probable and the amount can be reasonably estimated. The disallowance that already has been recognized should not reduce the reported level of return on

investment in later years, and accrual of a carrying charge has the effect of maintaining the level of return on investment similar to what it would have been if there had been no disallowance. Second, the nature of the resulting asset is similar to a long-term receivable, even though Board members acknowledge that it lacks some of the characteristics of a receivable. Accordingly, they concluded that (a) the subsequent reporting should be consistent with that afforded a long-term receivable and (b) accrual of a carrying charge is consistent with accounting for a long-term receivable initially recognized at its present value.

52. A number of respondents to the Exposure Draft objected to the requirement that the amount recorded for the probable future revenue that would result from an abandonment be adjusted when a rate order is received. They indicated that the real process of regulation in some jurisdictions occurs in the courts. The Board viewed the rate order as the confirming event, permitting an estimate of the loss to be refined at that time, and it believes that will usually be the case. However, the Board agrees that a loss should not be recognized unless it is probable that a loss has occurred and the amount can be reasonably estimated. If those criteria are not met at the time of an initial rate order, the loss should not be recognized at that time.

53. The Board considered adopting a requirement that all assets representing solely the probable future revenue resulting from a regulator's actions be recorded at the present value of the future cash flows and decided not to adopt such a requirement at this time. Some Board members noted that the requirement of Statement 71 to recognize those other assets on a cost-recovery basis, which was a continuation of prior practice, does not seem to have caused major problems in practice. Other Board members noted that the rate treatment anticipated during construction, prior to abandonment of the asset under construction, was full recovery of both cost and return on investment, whereas the cost of repairing storm damage, which is sometimes afforded recovery over a period of time without return on investment, represents a cash outlay usually made with the anticipation of that rate treatment. Thus, if the Board were to conclude that recording that asset at the amount of the consideration paid is not appropriate, that conclusion would be based on considerations somewhat different from those that the Board applied to abandonments.

Disallowances of Costs of Recently Completed Plants

54. Paragraph 10 of Statement 71 addresses disallowances by a regulator. That paragraph indicates that when a disallowance occurs, "the carrying amount of any related asset shall be reduced to the extent that the asset has been impaired. Whether the asset has been impaired shall be judged the same as for enterprises in general."

55. Recently, several disallowances of major amounts of cost on recently completed plants have been well publicized. The AICPA Issues Paper, "Application of Concepts in FASB Statement of Financial Accounting Standards No. 71 to Emerging Issues in the Public Utility Industry," concludes that "the measure of whether an asset has been impaired [when part of the cost of that asset is disallowed for rate-making purposes] is whether net cash inflows (revenues less applicable expenses) are sufficient to cover the cost of the asset. In measuring expenses, interest applicable to the unit should be included, but equity return would not be included."

56. The Board concluded that the view described in the AICPA Issues Paper, which appears to describe some, but not all, of existing practice, is a narrower interpretation of an "impairment," as referred to in paragraph 10 of Statement 71, than is appropriate for the events in question. The Board believes that an impairment evaluation includes the estimation of losses in value that become determinable as a result of an identifiable event, and it concluded that a regulator's disallowance of part of the cost of a recently completed plant creates an impairment that warrants recognition.

57. Some Board members also believe that the stated reason for certain recent disallowances of plant costs—that the costs were not productive or were not necessary for the completion of the plant—indicates that those costs should not be included in the carrying amount of the related plant. Nonregulated enterprises do not continue to carry identified nonproductive costs as part of the cost of their fixed assets, and regulated enterprises also should not do so.

58. Many respondents to the Exposure Draft objected to what they considered to be a unique impairment evaluation. The Board believes that the event in question, disallowance of part of the cost of an operating plant by a regulator, is itself unique. Other enterprises do not have disallow-

ances of their plant costs resulting from actions of a regulator.

59. The Board believes that the credibility of financial reporting in general would be diminished by the failure to recognize a diminution in value and a corresponding loss that is generally agreed to have occurred. When a regulator disallows a significant part of the cost of a recently completed plant, financial statements that do not report that disallowance as a loss reflect adversely on the representational faithfulness of those financial statements and of financial statements generally. Accordingly, the Board decided to amend Statement 71 to require loss recognition for such a disallowance.

60. Some respondents to the Exposure Draft requested that the Board address "excess capacity" disallowances. Those disallowances relate to part of the cost of service of a recently completed plant and are based on a finding that the utility's reserve capacity exceeds an amount deemed to be reasonable. If an "excess capacity" disallowance is ordered by a regulator *without* a specific finding that the enterprise should not have constructed that capacity or should have delayed the construction of that capacity, the rate order raises questions about whether the enterprise meets the criteria for application of Statement 71, in that it is not being regulated based on its own cost of service. However, because such a rate order itself is neither a direct disallowance nor an explicit, but indirect, disallowance of part of the cost of the plant, this Statement does not specify the accounting for it. If an "excess capacity" disallowance is ordered by a regulator *with* a specific finding that the enterprise should not have constructed that capacity or should have delayed the construction of that capacity, the rate order may be an explicit, but indirect, disallowance of part of the cost of the plant, and the enterprise should account for the substance of that order as set forth in paragraph 7 of this Statement.

61. In a few recent cases, a regulator has included a recently completed plant in rates based on the assumed cost of another plant rather than based on the cost of the plant that exists. In those cases, the enterprise is not being regulated based on its own cost, and the criteria of application of Statement 71 do not appear to be met. If the rate order is based on a finding that, based on factors that were known during the construction, the utility should not have constructed the plant that it did construct, the order may be an explicit, but indirect, disallowance, and it should be accounted for as set forth in paragraph 7 of this Statement. Otherwise, unless the order is being appealed, the enterprise should consider discontinuing application of Statement 71.

62. A number of respondents indicated that it would often be impossible to determine whether an indirect disallowance had been made. They noted that regulators have considerable discretion in selecting a rate that represents a fair return on equity investment, and that specific matters included in a settlement agreement might not be apparent. The Board intends that explicit, but indirect, disallowances be reported as disallowances; it does not intend to require that an enterprise determine whether the terms of a settlement agreement or rate order contained a hidden, indirect disallowance. Accordingly, paragraph 7 of this Statement was modified to indicate the Board's intent.

63. The Board considered making a more sweeping amendment of Statement 71, to require loss recognition for all cost disallowances by a regulator, whether related to a recently completed plant or otherwise. For example, regulators in some jurisdictions disallow costs of acquired companies in excess of the acquired company's book value and a variety of other types of costs. After consideration, the Board decided to limit this Statement to the relatively narrow issues that caused the Board to add a project on regulated enterprises to its agenda.

Criteria for Capitalization of AFUDC

64. Paragraph 15 of Statement 71 requires an allowance for funds used during construction, including an allowance for equity funds, to be capitalized in lieu of capitalizing interest in accordance with FASB Statement No. 34, *Capitalization of Interest Cost,* if certain criteria are met. The AICPA Issues Paper cited a need for guidance on whether AFUDC should be capitalized in a number of different situations.

65. After considering the cases in which capitalization of AFUDC is controversial, the Board concluded that AFUDC should be capitalized only if subsequent inclusion of that AFUDC in plant cost for rate-making purposes is probable. That conclusion was based on paragraph 15 of Statement 71, which is derived from the general standards in paragraphs 9-12 of that Statement. Under those general standards, a cost may not be capitalized unless it is probable that the cost will be included in allowable cost in the future, and the Board concluded that the same criteria should apply to capitalization of AFUDC.

66. Some respondents to the Exposure Draft indicated that AFUDC is a cost, and it warrants capitalization whenever the general criteria of Statement 34, that interest cost is being incurred and construction is in progress, are met. The Board disagreed with this view of AFUDC. State-

ment 71 concluded that, if specific criteria in paragraph 15 are met, the AFUDC that will be the basis for future rates should be capitalized instead of interest computed in accordance with Statement 34. As noted above, that provision of Statement 71 was derived from the general standards in paragraphs 9-12 of that Statement. Those general standards require that inclusion of an amount in allowable cost in the future be probable for that amount to be capitalized. The Board believes that the intent of Statement 71, in accepting the amount of AFUDC that will be the basis for future rates instead of the usual capitalization of interest, was not solely to accept a surrogate computation, but also to accept a computation that was a better indicator of future cash flows for enterprises that meet both the criteria for application of Statement 71 and the criteria of paragraph 15 of the Statement for capitalization of AFUDC. The Board concluded that allowing capitalization of amounts for which future inclusion in allowable cost for rate-making purposes was not probable would make the resulting capitalized amounts poorer indicators of the future cash flows expected to result from utility plants. Accordingly, the Board concluded that if inclusion of that AFUDC in the cost that will become the basis for future rates is not probable, the enterprise should not capitalize it. The Board also concluded that, if the specific criteria in paragraph 15 of Statement 71 are met but AFUDC is not capitalized because its inclusion in the cost that will become the basis for future rates is not probable, the regulated enterprise may not alternatively capitalize interest cost in accordance with Statement 34.

67. The Board believes that the criteria for capitalization of AFUDC are particularly relevant to two situations that have occurred in practice. In the first situation, completion of a plant under construction is reasonably possible but no longer probable, and the regulator in the governing jurisdiction routinely disallows accumulated AFUDC on abandoned plants. In that situation, the criteria required to write off previously recognized AFUDC are not met since disallowance is not probable; thus, previously capitalized AFUDC should not be written off. However, because inclusion of AFUDC in the cost allowed for future rates is no longer probable, further capitalization of AFUDC is not warranted.

68. In the second situation, a prudence investigation is in process or has taken place, and a disallowance of cost (including subsequent AFUDC on those costs) is reasonably possible. The range of such disallowance is from zero to some maximum amount, and no point within the range is more likely than any other. In that situation, be-

cause a disallowance of the maximum amount in the range is reasonably possible and thus inclusion of that amount in rates is no longer probable, subsequent capitalization of AFUDC should be discontinued for an amount of costs equal to the maximum amount that is within the range.

Definition of Probable

69. The term *probable* was defined in Statement 71 differently from how it has been defined in other authoritative literature. The Board used a definition based on the definition used in FASB Concepts Statement No. 3, *Elements of Financial Statements of Business Enterprises,* because that definition was one of the criteria of an asset in Concepts Statement 3.

70. The AICPA Issues Paper questioned whether that definition was intended to be significantly different from the definition used in Statement 5 and indicated that the use of different definitions had caused some confusion in practice. The Board considered the concern expressed in the AICPA Issues Paper and decided to change the definition in Statement 71 to the definition in Statement 5.

71. Some respondents to the Exposure Draft indicated their belief that the definition included in this Statement was a more stringent one than that contained in FASB Concepts Statement No. 6, *Elements of Financial Statements,* and in Statement 71. In their view, the definition in this Statement is appropriate for loss recognition, but the definition that was originally included in Statement 71 was more appropriate for asset recognition. The Board believes that a single concept is involved, and one definition can be applied in practice more easily than two. Thus, the Board concluded that the change in definition in this Statement is appropriate.

Accounting for Phase-in Plans

72. The Exposure Draft proposed specific accounting for phase-in plans. After considering comments received, both in comment letters and during the public hearing, the Board concluded that additional consideration is necessary to resolve the accounting issues related to phase-in plans. Accordingly, the Board decided to issue this Statement on plant abandonments and disallowances of plant costs and to consider further how to address accounting for phase-in plans.

Effective Date and Transition

73. The Board considered whether this Statement should be applied only to events occurring

after the effective date or to all events of the types addressed. Applying this Statement only to events occurring after the effective date would diminish both comparability of the resulting financial statements among enterprises and consistency within an enterprise that had experienced such events both before and after the effective date. The events addressed by this Statement tend to have long-lasting effects on financial statements. For example, a decision whether to recognize a disallowance of plant cost as a loss affects reported depreciation and net income for the life of the related plant. Accordingly, the Board decided that this Statement should be applied to all abandoned plants and disallowed plant costs, regardless of whether those events occurred before or will occur after the effective date.

74. The Exposure Draft was proposed to be effective for fiscal years beginning after December 15, 1986. The Board requested respondents who believed that additional delay in that proposed effective date was warranted for their specific situations to describe their existing circumstances in detail and explain why a delay would be appropriate and what it would accomplish.

75. Most of the respondents who requested a de-lay in application of the proposed Statement cited phase-in plans that might be modified if this Statement were to address accounting for phase-in plans. Few respondents indicated that a regulator's disallowance might be reconsidered or that a regulator's decision about recovery on an abandoned plant might be reconsidered.

76. Many respondents to the Exposure Draft indicated that this Statement should not be applied to regulatory actions that occurred before the effective date. They indicated that covenants, entered into without knowledge of the accounting requirements of this Statement, may now result in unintended restrictions on companies' actions. The Board recognizes that creditors may be willing to modify existing covenants for some enterprises that will be affected by this Statement. Although the Board decided to make this Statement effective for fiscal years beginning after December 15, 1987, it also decided to permit enterprises to delay application of this Statement until fiscal years beginning after December 15, 1988 if (a) application of this Statement would cause a violation or probable future violation of a restrictive clause in an existing loan indenture or other agreement and (b) the enterprise is actively seeking to obtain modification of that restrictive clause.

Appendix C

BACKGROUND INFORMATION

77. Statement 71 was issued in December 1982, effective for financial statements for fiscal years beginning after December 15, 1983. In early 1984, several different circumstances caused the Board to question whether the application of Statement 71 in practice was what the Board had intended.

78. During 1984, representatives of some regulatory commissions began to question the cost of certain new plants and to discuss possible major disallowances. Also, several plants in advanced stages of construction were abandoned. In a few states, courts ruled that utilities could not recover the costs of those abandoned plants from customers.

79. As a result of Board member concerns, the Board asked the staff to investigate whether guidance on the application of Statement 71 was needed in practice. The staff met several times with committees of Edison Electric Institute (EEI), the National Association of Regulatory Utility Commissioners, and the Public Utilities Subcommittee of the American Institute of Certified Public Accountants (the AICPA Subcommittee). The Board also met with representatives of those groups and staff members of the Federal Energy Regulatory Commission.

80. In November 1984, the Board received an AICPA Issues Paper on emerging issues in the public utility industry. That paper listed 17 specific issues related to current problems in the electric utility industry identified by the the AICPA

Subcommittee. The Board also received a comment letter from EEI on the issues raised in the AICPA Issues Paper.

81. In April 1985, the Board's Task Force on Regulated Enterprises met and discussed a staff draft of a possible Exposure Draft that encompassed most of the conclusions included in this Statement.

82. Subsequent to the April 1985 task force meeting, the Board received 51 letters from 39 affected enterprises and other interested parties commenting on the positions proposed in the staff draft discussed at the task force meeting and on the Board's tentative conclusions reached at its public meetings subsequent to that task force meeting.

83. The Board issued an Exposure Draft in December 1985. More than 1,400 organizations and individuals responded to that Exposure Draft, many with multiple letters.

84. In June 1986, the Board held a public hearing on the proposals in the Exposure Draft. Sixty-six individuals and firms presented their views at the four-day public hearing.

85. After considering comments received in comment letters and at the public hearing, the Board concluded that additional consideration is necessary to resolve the accounting issues related to phase-in plans. After consideration, the Board decided to issue this Statement to address accounting for plant abandonments and disallowances of plant costs. The Board will consider accounting for phase-in plans further at a later date.

Statement of Financial Accounting Standards No. 91
Accounting for Nonrefundable Fees and Costs Associated with Originating or Acquiring Loans and Initial Direct Costs of Leases

an amendment of FASB Statements No. 13, 60, and 65 and a rescission of FASB Statement No. 17

STATUS

Issued: December 1986

Effective Date: For lending and leasing transactions entered into and commitments granted in fiscal years beginning after December 15, 1987 and interim periods within those fiscal years

Affects: Supersedes FAS 13, paragraphs 5(m), 23(a)(i), and 23(a)(iii)
Amends FAS 13, paragraphs 18(a) and 18(b)
Supersedes FAS 17
Supersedes FAS 60, paragraph 49
Amends FAS 65, paragraphs 6 and 23
Supersedes FAS 65, paragraphs 14, 21, 25, and 26 and footnotes 2 and 7

Affected by: Paragraph 3 amended by FAS 115 and FAS 124
Paragraph 14 amended by FAS 114
Paragraphs 25(a) through 25(c) superseded by FAS 98
Paragraph 27(a) amended by FAS 115

Other Interpretive Release: FASB Special Report, *A Guide to Implementation of Statement 91 on Accounting for Nonrefundable Fees and Costs Associated with Originating or Acquiring Loans and Initial Direct Costs of Leases: Questions and Answers*

Issues Discussed by FASB Emerging Issues Task Force (EITF)

Affects: Partially resolves EITF Issue No. 85-38

Interpreted by: Paragraphs 5 and 7 interpreted by EITF Issue No. 93-1
Paragraph 6 interpreted by EITF Issues No. 92-5 and 93-1
Paragraph 8 interpreted by EITF Issues No. 85-20 and 87-30
Paragraph 10 interpreted by EITF Issue No. 92-5
Paragraph 16 interpreted by EITF Issue No. 88-20
Paragraph 18 interpreted by EITF Issues No. 88-20, 92-5, and 93-1 and Topic No. D-10
Paragraphs 19 and 20 interpreted by EITF Issues No. 88-20, 92-5, and 93-1
Paragraph 23 interpreted by EITF Topic No. D-8

Related Issues: EITF Issues No. 84-4, 86-21, 87-25, 89-4, 95-6, 96-12, and 97-3 and Topic No. D-4

SUMMARY

This Statement establishes the accounting for nonrefundable fees and costs associated with lending, committing to lend, or purchasing a loan or group of loans. This project was undertaken in response to an AICPA Issues Paper that indicated a diversity in practice in the accounting for nonrefundable fees and costs associated with lending activities.

The provisions of this Statement apply to all types of loans (including debt securities) as well as to all types of lenders (including banks, thrift institutions, insurance companies, mortgage bankers, and other financial and nonfinancial institutions). This Statement also specifies the accounting for fees and initial direct costs associated with leasing.

The Statement specifies that:

- Loan origination fees shall be recognized over the life of the related loan as an adjustment of yield.
- Certain direct loan origination costs shall be recognized over the life of the related loan as a reduction of the loan's yield.
- All loan commitment fees shall be deferred except for certain retrospectively determined fees; commitment fees meeting specified criteria shall be recognized over the loan commitment period; all other commitment fees shall be recognized as an adjustment of yield over the related loan's life or, if the commitment expires unexercised, recognized in income upon expiration of the commitment.
- Loan fees, certain direct loan origination costs, and purchase premiums and discounts on loans shall be recognized as an adjustment of yield generally by the interest method based on the contractual terms of the loan. However, prepayments may be anticipated in certain specified circumstances.

This Statement changes the practice of recognizing loan origination and commitment fees at or prior to inception of the loan. It rescinds FASB Statement No. 17, *Accounting for Leases—Initial Direct Costs,* and amends FASB Statements No. 13, *Accounting for Leases;* No. 60, *Accounting and Reporting by Insurance Enterprises;* and No. 65, *Accounting for Certain Mortgage Banking Activities.*

This Statement shall be applied prospectively to all lending and leasing transactions entered into and commitments granted in fiscal years beginning after December 15, 1987 with earlier application encouraged in fiscal years for which annual financial statements have not previously been issued. Retroactive application with restatement of the financial statements for all prior years presented is encouraged but not required.

Accounting for Nonrefundable Fees and Costs
Associated with Originating or Acquiring Loans **FAS91**
and Initial Direct Costs of Leases

Statement of Financial Accounting Standards No. 91

Accounting for Nonrefundable Fees and Costs Associated with Originating or Acquiring Loans and Initial Direct Costs of Leases

an amendment of FASB Statements No. 13, 60, and 65 and a rescission of FASB Statement No. 17

CONTENTS

INTRODUCTION

1. This project was undertaken in response to a request by the Accounting Standards Executive Committee (AcSEC) of the AICPA to address the accounting for nonrefundable fees and costs associated with lending activities. AcSEC indicated that existing accounting pronouncements specify different guidance for similar transactions by various types of financial services entities.

SCOPE

2. This Statement establishes standards of financial accounting and reporting for nonrefundable fees and costs associated with lending activities and loan purchases. Lending, committing to lend, refinancing or restructuring loans, arranging standby letters of credit, syndicating loans, and leasing activities are "lending activities" for purposes of this Statement. The lender's activities that precede the disbursement of funds can generally be distinguished between (a) efforts to identify and attract potential borrowers and (b) efforts necessary to originate a loan or loan commitment after a potential borrower requests a loan or loan commitment. Nonrefundable fees have many different names in practice, such as **origination fees,**[1] points, placement fees, **commitment fees,** application fees, management fees, restructuring fees, and syndication fees, but, for purposes of this Statement, they are referred to as loan origination fees, commitment fees, or syndication fees.

3. This Statement addresses the recognition and the balance sheet classification of nonrefundable fees and costs associated with lending activities. The accounting for discounts, premiums, and commitment fees associated with the purchase of loans and other debt securities such as corporate

---

[1] Terms defined in the glossary (Appendix C) are in **boldface type** the first time they appear in this Statement.

bonds, Treasury notes and bonds, groups of loans, and loan-backed securities (such as pass-through certificates, collateralized mortgage obligations, and other so-called "securitized" loans) is also addressed by this Statement. This Statement does not apply to loan origination or commitment fees that are refundable; however, this Statement does apply when such fees subsequently become nonrefundable. It also does not apply to costs that are incurred by the lender in transactions with independent third parties if the lender bills those costs directly to the borrower. It does not apply to nonrefundable fees and costs associated with originating or acquiring loans that are carried at market value.

STANDARDS OF FINANCIAL ACCOUNTING AND REPORTING

General

4. An enterprise may acquire a loan by lending (originating the loan) or by purchasing (acquiring a loan from a party other than the borrower). This Statement applies to both a lender and a purchaser. This Statement shall be applied to individual loan contracts. Aggregation of similar loans for purposes of recognizing net fees or costs and purchase premiums or discounts is permitted if the provisions of paragraph 19 are met or if the resulting recognition does not differ materially from the amount that would have been recognized on an individual loan-by-loan basis.

Loan Origination Fees and Costs

5. Loan origination fees shall be deferred and recognized over the life of the loan as an adjustment of yield[2] (interest income). Likewise, direct loan origination costs defined in paragraph 6 shall be deferred and recognized as a reduction in the yield of the loan except as set forth in paragraph 14 (for a troubled debt restructuring). Loan origination fees and related direct loan origination costs for a given loan shall be offset and only the net amount shall be deferred and amortized. The practice of recognizing a portion of loan origination fees as revenue in a period to offset all or part of the costs of origination shall no longer be acceptable.

6. Direct loan origination costs of a completed loan shall include only (a) **incremental direct costs** of loan origination incurred in transactions with independent third parties for that loan and (b) certain costs directly related to specified activities performed by the lender for that loan. Those activities are: evaluating the prospective borrower's financial condition; evaluating and recording guarantees, collateral, and other security arrangements; negotiating loan terms; preparing and processing loan documents; and closing the transaction. The costs directly related to those activities shall include only that portion of the employees' total compensation and payroll-related fringe benefits directly related to time spent performing those activities for that loan and other costs related to those activities that would not have been incurred but for that loan.

7. All other lending-related costs, including costs related to activities performed by the lender for advertising, soliciting potential borrowers, servicing existing loans, and other ancillary activities related to establishing and monitoring credit policies, supervision, and administration, shall be charged to expense as incurred. Employees' compensation and fringe benefits related to those activities, unsuccessful loan origination efforts, and idle time shall be charged to expense as incurred. Administrative costs, rent, depreciation, and all other occupancy and equipment costs are considered indirect costs and shall be charged to expense as incurred.

Commitment Fees and Costs

8. Except as set forth in subparagraphs (a) and (b) below, fees received for a commitment to originate or purchase a loan or group of loans shall be deferred and, if the commitment is exercised, recognized over the life of the loan as an adjustment of yield or, if the commitment expires unexercised, recognized in income upon expiration of the commitment.

a. If the enterprise's experience with similar arrangements indicates that the likelihood that the commitment will be exercised is remote,[3] the commitment fee shall be recognized over the commitment period on a straight-line basis as service fee income. If the commitment is subsequently exercised during the commitment period, the remaining unamortized commitment fee at the time of exercise shall be recognized over the life of the loan as an adjustment of yield.

---

[2]Methods for recognition of deferred fees and direct loan origination costs over the life of the loan as an adjustment of yield are set forth in paragraphs 18-20.

[3]The term *remote* is used here, consistent with its use in FASB Statement No. 5, *Accounting for Contingencies*, to mean that the likelihood is slight that a loan commitment will be exercised prior to its expiration.

Accounting for Nonrefundable Fees and Costs
Associated with Originating or Acquiring Loans
and Initial Direct Costs of Leases   FAS91

b. If the amount of the commitment fee is determined retrospectively as a percentage of the line of credit available but unused in a previous period, if that percentage is nominal in relation to the stated interest rate on any related borrowing, and if that borrowing will bear a market interest rate at the date the loan is made, the commitment fee shall be recognized as service fee income as of the determination date.

9. Direct loan origination costs (described in paragraph 6) incurred to make a commitment to originate a loan shall be offset against any related commitment fee and the net amount recognized as set forth in paragraph 8.

10. Available lines of credit under credit card and similar charge card arrangements are loan commitments, and fees collected in connection with such cards (credit card fees) are viewed in part as being loan commitment fees. However, those fees generally cover many services to cardholders. Accordingly, fees that are periodically charged to cardholders shall be deferred and recognized on a straight-line basis over the period the fee entitles the cardholder to use the card. This accounting shall also apply to other similar card arrangements that involve an extension of credit by the card issuer.

Syndication Fees

11. The enterprise managing a loan syndication (the syndicator) shall recognize loan syndication fees when the syndication is complete unless a portion of the syndication loan is retained. If the yield on the portion of the loan retained by the syndicator is less than the average yield to the other syndication participants after considering the fees passed through by the syndicator, the syndicator shall defer a portion of the syndication fee to produce a yield on the portion of the loan retained that is not less than the average yield on the loans held by the other syndication participants.

Fees and Costs in Refinancings or Restructurings

12. If the terms of the new loan resulting from a loan refinancing or restructuring other than a troubled debt restructuring are at least as favorable to the lender as the terms for comparable loans to other customers with similar collection risks who are not refinancing or restructuring a loan with the lender, the refinanced loan shall be accounted for as a new loan. This condition would be met if the new loan's effective yield is at least equal to the effective yield for such loans.[4] Any unamortized net fees or costs and any prepayment penalties from the original loan shall be recognized in interest income when the new loan is granted.

13. If the refinancing or restructuring does not meet the condition set forth in paragraph 12 or if only minor modifications are made to the original loan contract, the unamortized net fees or costs from the original loan and any prepayment penalties shall be carried forward as a part of the net investment in the new loan. In this case, the investment in the new loan shall consist of the remaining net investment in the original loan,[5] any additional amounts loaned, any fees received, and direct loan origination costs set forth in paragraph 6 associated with the refinancing or restructuring.

14. Fees received in connection with a modification of terms of a troubled debt restructuring as defined in FASB Statement No. 15, *Accounting by Debtors and Creditors for Troubled Debt Restructurings*, shall be applied as a reduction of the recorded investment in the loan for purposes of applying paragraph 30 of that Statement. All related costs, including direct loan origination costs, shall be charged to expense as incurred.

Purchase of a Loan or Group of Loans

15. The initial investment in a purchased loan or group of loans shall include the amount paid to the seller plus any fees paid or less any fees received. The initial investment frequently differs from the related loan's principal amount at the date of purchase. This difference shall be recognized as an adjustment of yield over the life of the loan. All other costs incurred in connection with acquiring purchased loans or committing to purchase loans shall be charged to expense as incurred.

16. In applying the provisions of this Statement to loans purchased as a group, the purchaser may allocate the initial investment to the individual loans or may account for the initial investment in the aggregate. The cash flows provided by the un-

---

[4]The effective yield comparison considers the level of nominal interest rate, commitment and origination fees, and direct loan origination costs and would also consider comparison of other factors where appropriate, such as compensating balance arrangements.

[5]The net investment in the original loan includes the unpaid loan principal, any remaining unamortized net fees or costs, any remaining unamortized purchase premium or discount, and any accrued interest receivable.

derlying loan contracts shall be used to apply the interest method, except as set forth in paragraph 19. If prepayments are not anticipated pursuant to paragraph 19 and prepayments occur or a portion of the purchased loans is sold, a proportionate amount of the related deferred fees and purchase premium or discount shall be recognized in income so that the effective interest rate on the remaining portion of loans continues unchanged.

Other

17. Deferred net fees or costs shall not be amortized during periods in which interest income on a loan is not being recognized because of concerns about the realization of loan principal or interest.

Application of the Interest Method and Other Amortization Matters

18. Net fees or costs that are required to be recognized as yield adjustments over the life of the related loan(s) shall be recognized by the interest method except as set forth in paragraph 20. The objective of the interest method is to arrive at periodic interest income (including recognition of fees and costs) at a constant effective yield on the net investment in the receivable (that is, the principal amount of the receivable adjusted by unamortized fees or costs and purchase premium or discount). The difference between the periodic interest income so determined and the stated interest on the outstanding principal amount of the receivable is the amount of periodic amortization.[6] Under the provisions of this Statement, the interest method shall be applied as follows when the stated interest rate is not constant throughout the term of the loan:

a. If the loan's stated interest rate increases during the term of the loan (so that interest accrued under the interest method in early periods would exceed interest at the stated rate), interest income shall not be recognized to the extent that the net investment in the loan would increase to an amount greater than the amount at which the borrower could settle the obligation. Prepayment penalties shall be considered in determining the amount at which the borrower could settle the obligation only to the extent that such penalties are imposed throughout the loan term. (Refer to Appendix B.)

b. If the loan's stated interest rate decreases during the term of the loan, the stated periodic interest received early in the term of the loan would exceed the periodic interest income that is calculated under the interest method. In that circumstance, the excess shall be deferred and recognized in those future periods when the constant effective yield under the interest method exceeds the stated interest rate. (Refer to Appendix B.)

c. If the loan's stated interest rate varies based on future changes in an independent factor, such as an index or rate (for example, the prime rate, the London Interbank Offered Rate (LIBOR), or the U.S. Treasury bill weekly average rate), the calculation of the constant effective yield necessary to recognize fees and costs shall be based either on the factor (the index or rate) that is in effect at the inception of the loan or on the factor as it changes over the life of the loan.[7] (Refer to Appendix B.)

19. Except as stated in the following sentence, the calculation of the constant effective yield necessary to apply the interest method shall use the payment terms required by the loan contract, and prepayments of principal shall not be anticipated to shorten the loan term. If the enterprise holds a large number of similar loans for which prepayments are probable and the timing and amount of prepayments can be reasonably estimated, the enterprise may consider estimates of future principal prepayments in the calculation of the constant effective yield necessary to apply the interest method. If the enterprise anticipates prepayments in applying the interest method and a difference arises between the prepayments anticipated and actual prepayments received, the enterprise shall recalculate the effective yield to reflect actual payments to date and anticipated future payments. The net investment in the loans shall be adjusted to the amount that would have existed had the new effective yield been applied since the acquisition of the loans. The investment in the loans shall be adjusted to the new balance with a corresponding charge or credit to interest income. Enterprises that anticipate prepayments shall disclose that policy and the significant assumptions underlying the prepayment estimates. The practice of recognizing net fees over the estimated average life of a group of loans shall no longer be acceptable. (Refer to Appendix B.)

---

[6]The "interest" method is also described in paragraph 16 of APB Opinion No. 12, *Omnibus Opinion—1967*, in the first sentence of paragraph 15 of APB Opinion No. 21, *Interest on Receivables and Payables*, and in paragraphs 235-239 of FASB Concepts Statement No. 6, *Elements of Financial Statements*.

[7]A variable rate loan whose initial rate differs from the rate its base factor would produce is also subject to the provisions of paragraphs 18(a) and (b).

Accounting for Nonrefundable Fees and Costs
Associated with Originating or Acquiring Loans
and Initial Direct Costs of Leases

FAS91

20. Certain loan agreements provide no scheduled payment terms (demand loans); others provide the borrower with the option to make multiple borrowings up to a specified maximum amount, to repay portions of previous borrowings, and then reborrow under the same contract (revolving lines of credit).

a. For a loan that is payable at the lender's demand, any net fees or costs may be recognized as an adjustment of yield on a straight-line basis over a period that is consistent with (1) the understanding between the borrower and lender or (2) if no understanding exists, the lender's estimate of the period of time over which the loan will remain outstanding; any unamortized amount shall be recognized when the loan is paid in full.

b. For revolving lines of credit (or similar loan arrangements), the net fees or costs shall be recognized in income on a straight-line basis over the period the revolving line of credit is active, assuming that borrowings are outstanding for the maximum term provided in the loan contract. If the borrower pays all borrowings and cannot reborrow under the contract, any unamortized net fees or costs shall be recognized in income upon payment. The interest method shall be applied to recognize net unamortized fees or costs when the loan agreement provides a schedule for payment and no additional borrowings are provided for under the agreement.[8]

Balance Sheet Classification

21. The unamortized balance of loan origination, commitment, and other fees and costs and purchase premiums and discounts that is being recognized as an adjustment of yield pursuant to this Statement shall be reported on the enterprise's balance sheet as part of the loan balance to which it relates.

Income Statement Classification

22. Amounts of loan origination, commitment, and other fees and costs recognized as an adjustment of yield shall be reported as part of interest income. Amortization of other fees, such as commitment fees that are being amortized on a straight-line basis over the commitment period or included in income when the commitment expires, shall be reported as service fee income.

Application to Leasing Activities

23. The provisions of paragraphs 5-9 of this Statement shall apply to lessors in determining the net amount of *initial direct costs* as that term is used in FASB Statement No. 13, *Accounting for Leases*. Lessors shall account for initial direct costs as part of the investment in a direct financing lease. The practice of recognizing a portion of the unearned income at inception of the lease to offset initial direct costs shall no longer be acceptable.

Amendments to Other Pronouncements

24. This Statement rescinds FASB Statement No. 17, *Accounting for Leases—Initial Direct Costs* (which amended the definition of initial direct costs in Statement 13), and replaces the definition of initial direct costs in paragraph 5(m) of Statement 13 with the following:

Initial direct costs. * Only those costs incurred by the lessor that are (a) costs to originate a lease incurred in transactions with independent third parties that (i) result directly from and are essential to acquire that lease and (ii) would not have been incurred had that leasing transaction not occurred and (b) certain costs directly related to specified activities performed by the lessor for that lease. Those activities are: evaluating the prospective lessee's financial condition; evaluating and recording guarantees, collateral, and other security arrangements; negotiating lease terms; preparing and processing lease documents; and closing the transaction. The costs directly related to those activities shall include only that portion of the employees' total compensation and payroll-related fringe benefits directly related to time spent performing those activities for that lease and other costs related to those activities that would not have been incurred but for that lease. Initial direct costs shall not include costs related to activities performed by the lessor for advertising, soliciting potential lessees, servicing existing leases, and other ancillary activities related to establishing and monitoring credit policies, supervision, and administration. Initial direct costs shall not include administrative costs, rent, depreciation, any other occupancy and equipment costs and employees' compensation and fringe benefits related to activities described

---

[8]For example, if the loan agreement provides the borrower with the option to convert a one-year revolving line of credit to a five-year term loan, during the term of the revolving line of credit the lender would recognize the net fees or costs as income on a straight-line basis using the combined life of the revolving line of credit and term loan. If the borrower elects to convert the line of credit to a term loan, the lender would recognize the unamortized net fees or costs as an adjustment of yield using the interest method. If the revolving line of credit expires and borrowings are extinguished, the unamortized net fees or costs would be recognized in income upon payment.

in the previous sentence, unsuccessful origination efforts, and idle time.

Initial direct cost shall be offset by nonrefundable fees that are yield adjustments as prescribed in FASB Statement No. 91, Accounting for Nonrefundable Fees and Costs Associated with Originating or Acquiring Loans and Initial Direct Costs of Leases.

25. Statement 13 is further amended as follows for the accounting and disclosure of initial direct costs of direct financing leases:

a. The first sentence of paragraph 18(a) is amended to read as follows:

The sum of (i) the minimum lease payments (net of amounts, if any, included therein with respect to executory costs to be paid by the lessor, together with any profit thereon), (ii) the unguaranteed residual value accruing to the benefit of the lessor, and (iii) the initial direct costs shall be recorded as the gross investment in the lease.

b. The third sentence of paragraph 18(b), which reads as follows, is deleted:

Initial direct costs (as defined in paragraph 5(m)) shall be charged against income as incurred, and a portion of the unearned income equal to the initial direct costs shall be recognized as income in the same period.

c. The term *remaining* is deleted from the fourth sentence of paragraph 18(b), which then reads as follows:

The unearned income shall be amortized to income over the lease term so as to produce a constant periodic rate of return on the net investment in the lease.[21]

d. Subparagraph (a)(i) of paragraph 23 is superseded by the following to add disclosure of initial direct costs for direct financing leases:

The components of the net investment in sales-type and direct financing leases as of the date of each balance sheet presented:
   (a) Future minimum lease payments to be received, with separate deductions for (i) amounts representing executory costs, including any profit thereon, included in the minimum lease payments and (ii) the accumulated allowance for uncollectible minimum lease payments receivable.
   (b) The unguaranteed residual values accruing to the benefit of the lessor.
   (c) For direct financing leases only, initial direct costs (see paragraph 5(m)).
   (d) Unearned income (see paragraphs 17(b) and 18(b)).

e. Subparagraph (a)(iii) of paragraph 23 is deleted.

26. Paragraph 49 of FASB Statement No. 60, *Accounting and Reporting by Insurance Enterprises*, is superseded by the following:

Loan origination and commitment fees and direct loan origination costs shall be accounted for as prescribed in FASB Statement No. 91, *Accounting for Nonrefundable Fees and Costs Associated with Originating or Acquiring Loans and Initial Direct Costs of Leases*.

27. FASB Statement No. 65, *Accounting for Certain Mortgage Banking Activities*, is amended as follows:

a. The second sentence of paragraph 6 is superseded by the following:

Any difference between the carrying amount of the loan or security and its outstanding principal balance shall be recognized as an adjustment to yield by the interest method.[2]

b. Footnote 2 is superseded by the following:

[2]The interest method shall be applied as set forth in paragraphs 18 and 19 of FASB Statement No. 91, *Accounting for Nonrefundable Fees and Costs Associated with Originating or Acquiring Loans and Initial Direct Costs of Leases*.

c. Paragraph 21 and its heading are superseded by the following:

Loan Origination Fees and Costs

If the loan is held for resale, loan origination fees and the direct loan origination costs as specified in FASB Statement No. 91, *Accounting for Nonrefundable Fees and Costs Associated with Originating or Acquiring Loans and Initial Direct Costs of Leases*, shall be deferred until the related loan is sold. If the loan is held for investment, such fees and costs shall be deferred and recognized as an adjustment of yield as specified in paragraphs 18-20 of Statement 91.

d. The first sentence of paragraph 23 is superseded by the following:

Fees received for guaranteeing the funding of mortgage loans to borrowers, builders, or developers shall be accounted for as prescribed in paragraph 8 of Statement 91. Fees paid to permanent investors to ensure the ultimate sale of the loans (residential or commercial loan commitment fees) shall be recognized as expense when the loans are sold to permanent investors or when it becomes evident the commitment will not be used.

Accounting for Nonrefundable Fees and Costs
Associated with Originating or Acquiring Loans   **FAS91**
and Initial Direct Costs of Leases

e. Paragraph 25 and its heading are superseded by the following:

Fees and Costs Relating to Loans Not Held for Sale

Fees and costs associated with originating or acquiring or committing to originate or acquire loans for investment shall be accounted for as prescribed in Statement 91.

f. Paragraphs 14 and 26 and the heading for paragraph 14 are deleted.

Effective Date and Transition

28. This Statement shall be applied prospectively to lending and leasing transactions entered into and commitments granted in fiscal years beginning after December 15, 1987 and interim periods within those fiscal years. Retroactive application, by restating all prior years presented, is encouraged but not required. Earlier application is encouraged in fiscal years for which financial statements have not previously been issued. In the year that this Statement is first applied, the financial statements shall disclose the nature of accounting changes adopted to conform to the provisions of this Statement and their effect on income before extraordinary items, net income, and related per share amounts for the current year and for each restated year presented. If adopted prospectively, disclosure of the accounting change and the prior accounting policies shall be continued in financial statements of subsequent years in which outstanding loans accounted for under the prior policy are material.

> **The provisions of this Statement need not be applied to immaterial items.**

This Statement was adopted by the affirmative votes of six members of the Financial Accounting Standards Board. Mr. Wyatt dissented.

Mr. Wyatt dissents to issuance of this Statement because it provides for the deferral and amortization of various costs incurred by an entity that originates loans based on the nature of the parties to whom payments are made rather than on the nature of the costs incurred or the nature of the activities for which the costs are incurred. Paragraph 6 distinguishes between costs incurred in transactions with independent third parties and costs related to specified activities performed by the lender. The specified activities are intended to limit deferral to only those costs incurred directly on loan origination activities. No such limitation of activities is prescribed, however, for costs incurred in transactions with independent third parties. As a result, the attempt to limit deferral of costs to only specified loan origination activities is rendered ineffective by permitting deferral of a variety of nonorigination costs so long as payments for them are made to third parties. Costs incurred for advertising and solicitation activities (as well as for certain other activities) are deferred if payments for them are made to third parties but are charged to expense if paid to employees. That distinction is likely to encourage entities to engage third parties to undertake certain activities that are presently undertaken by employees to achieve an accounting result rather than for otherwise sound business reasons.

Mr. Wyatt believes that costs of origination to be deferred and amortized should be related to origination activities, as defined in paragraph 6, regardless of whether the payments for those services are made to outside third parties or to employees. In his view, such an approach would accomplish better the objective of accounting for similar activities in a similar, or consistent, fashion.

Those portions of the standard that provide guidance for accounting for fees received in connection with originating a loan or committing to lend will result in significantly improved reporting of revenues by more closely relating them to services provided than to receipts of cash. The guidance provided for the deferral and amortization of various costs incurred, however, is likely to counteract the improvements made in revenue recognition. As a result, little, if any, improvement is likely to result from this Statement for accounting for nonrefundable fees and costs associated with loan origination activities.

Mr. Wyatt also believes that the central thrust of the transition provisions is misplaced. The comparability of financial presentations achieved by applying new standards on a retroactive basis for all years presented is an objective that Board standards should strive to achieve. In some instances, practical considerations and costs to be incurred to restate may suggest that prospective application is also acceptable. Paragraph 28 implies that prospective application is preferable. Mr. Wyatt believes the transition should call for retroactive application, with prospective application permitted in this standard for practical reasons. While the net effect of such a transition would be the same as is likely to flow from application of paragraph 28, that transition approach would indicate better the most desirable transition priorities for new financial accounting standards.

Members of the Financial Accounting Standards Board:

Donald J. Kirk,	Raymond C. Lauver	Robert J. Swieringa
Chairman	David Mosso	Arthur R. Wyatt
Victor H. Brown	C. Arthur Northrop	

Appendix A

BACKGROUND INFORMATION AND BASIS FOR CONCLUSIONS

CONTENTS

Appendix A

BACKGROUND INFORMATION AND BASIS FOR CONCLUSIONS

Introduction

29. This appendix discusses factors deemed significant by members of the Board in reaching the conclusions in this Statement. It includes descriptions of alternatives considered by the Board with reasons for accepting some and rejecting others. Individual Board members gave greater weight to some factors than to others.

Background Information

30. Accounting guidance for loan fees and costs is provided in AICPA Audit and Accounting Guides and Statements of Position and FASB Statements. Each of those sources generally provides guidance for only a specific type of entity in the financial services industry.

31. In the late 1970s and early 1980s, AcSEC reviewed proposed revisions to the AICPA Audit and Accounting Guides for banks, savings and loan associations, and finance companies. During its review, AcSEC observed that the individual Guides contain differing guidance for accounting for fees and costs for similar lending transactions. Because of those inconsistencies, AcSEC formed a task force to study the issues applicable to all of the financial services industry. That task force prepared an Issues Paper, "Accounting for Nonrefundable Fees of Originating or Acquiring Loans and Acquisition Costs of Loan and Insurance Activities," which AcSEC submitted to the FASB. In September 1984, the Board issued an Invitation to Comment, *Accounting for Nonrefundable Fees and Costs Associated with Originating or Acquiring Loans*, incorporating the Issues Paper, to solicit information from interested parties prior to Board deliberations on the subject. The Board received 206 letters of comment in response to the Invitation to Comment. In December 1985, the Board issued an Exposure Draft, *Accounting for Nonre-*

Accounting for Nonrefundable Fees and Costs
Associated with Originating or Acquiring Loans FAS91
and Initial Direct Costs of Leases

fundable Fees and Costs Associated with Originating and Acquiring Loans, for a 120-day comment period. The Board received comments from 822 individuals and organizations and held a public hearing in July 1986 at which 55 of those organizations appeared.

Scope

32. After reviewing the nature of the lending process, the Board concluded that accounting for loan origination fees and costs should be consistent for all types of lending. That conclusion was generally supported by respondents to the Exposure Draft. No compelling arguments were made supporting a conclusion that the lending process for consumer, mortgage, commercial, and other loans or leases is fundamentally different. Nor were any substantive arguments made suggesting that different types of lenders should account for loans differently or that financial statement users for a particular industry or size of entity would be better served by accounting that differs from that of other lenders.

33. Some respondents urged that purchases of debt securities, such as corporate bonds, notes, debentures, and government debt instruments, should not be subject to this Statement. The Board did not agree. An enterprise may acquire an investment in a loan or other interest-earning asset by lending (originating the asset) or by purchasing. When a loan is purchased, the price paid to purchase the loan (including any fees received from the seller or paid by the buyer to take delivery of the loan, such as commitment or delivery fees) frequently differs from the loan's principal amount. The difference between the net cost and the principal amount adjusts the nominal rate on the loan to a yield that the purchaser is willing to accept. The Board concluded that premiums and discounts on purchased loans are fundamentally similar to net fees collected and costs incurred to originate a loan. Both must be considered to reflect accurately the asset's acquisition cost and income on the investment.

34. The Board concluded that this Statement should not apply to fees and costs and premiums or discounts associated with loans that are carried at market value, because carrying loans at market values obviates the need for accounting guidance for recognition of fees and costs and premiums or discounts associated with those loans.

Loan Origination Fees and Costs

35. The cost of originated loans is not limited to the net cash outflow to the borrower (principal amount of the loan less fees collected from the borrower in connection with the loan). The lender generally performs certain activities to process a borrower's request for credit. Those activities are: evaluating the prospective borrower's financial condition; evaluating and recording guarantees, collateral, and other security arrangements; negotiating loan terms; preparing and processing loan documents; and closing the transaction. The Board concluded that these activities are initiated upon the prospective borrower's request for credit, are for the benefit of the lender or subsequent investor, and relate directly to originating the loan; they are, therefore, integral to lending.

36. The Board received considerable comment about the variety of fees collected by a lender in connection with lending. The Board divided such fees for loan origination into two principal categories: (a) fees associated with origination of a loan and (b) fees associated with committing to lend. Origination fees consist of:

a. Fees that are being charged to the borrower as "prepaid" interest or to reduce the loan's nominal interest rate, such as interest "buy-downs" (explicit yield adjustments)
b. Fees to reimburse the lender for origination activities
c. Other fees charged to the borrower that relate directly to making the loan (for example, fees that are paid to the lender as compensation for granting a complex loan or agreeing to lend quickly)
d. Fees that are not conditional on a loan being granted by the lender that receives the fee but are, in substance, implicit yield adjustments because a loan is granted at rates or terms that would not have otherwise been considered absent the fee (for example, certain syndication fees addressed in paragraph 11).

Designation of a fee or cost as an origination fee or cost for a loan that is purchased is inappropriate because a purchased loan has already been originated by another party.

37. The Board concluded that loan origination fees and direct loan origination costs should be accounted for as components of a loan's acquisition cost and recognized as an adjustment to the yield of the related loan. The Board considered and rejected the argument that loan origination is a separate revenue-producing activity and concluded that originating loans is but one means of acquiring a loan. Revenue is not realized by the acquisition of a loan; it is only realized by holding or selling it. Furthermore, the Board disagreed with those respondents who argued that originating a loan is a separate service to the bor-

rower. The efforts of the lender to conclude that the borrower should be financially able to repay the loan and that the lender has satisfactory remedies in the event of default are for the benefit of the lender or subsequent investor rather than the borrower. The Board also rejected the argument that the fees represent a reimbursement for the costs the lender incurs in obtaining funds because the lending activity is not related to soliciting or obtaining funds to lend.

38. The Exposure Draft reflected the Board's tentative conclusions that certain origination costs should be deferred and recognized as an adjustment of yield over the life of the related loan. The Board limited the costs that should be deferred partly as a result of comments received from those respondents to the 1984 Invitation to Comment that asserted that they were unable to measure loan origination costs. The Exposure Draft proposed that costs to be deferred should be limited to those origination costs that are both incremental and direct to a specific lending transaction. Respondents to the Exposure Draft generally opposed deferral of only incremental direct costs. Respondents indicated that costs of origination, however defined, could be reliably measured, that deferral of only incremental direct costs treated costs of essentially similar activities differently, and that the way an enterprise carries out loan origination activities, for example, the way it compensates employees, should not determine the accounting for such costs. Based on comments received, the Board was persuaded that the conclusions of the Exposure Draft should be modified.

39. The Board concluded that deferral of the costs of origination activities set forth in paragraph 6 for completed loans is appropriate whether the activities are performed by the lender's employees or by independent third parties. The Board views those specified activities as integral to the lending transaction. The Board acknowledges that the lender may perform activities other than those specified in paragraph 6 to originate a loan and therefore incurs costs related to lending that do not meet the definition set forth in paragraph 6.

40. The Board concluded that costs associated with loan origination that are incurred by the lender in transactions with independent third parties should be deferred. The Board recognizes that this decision permits the deferral of a fee paid to a third party for solicitation related to a completed loan whereas, if that solicitation were performed by the lender's employees, paragraph 7 would proscribe the deferral of those costs. The Board considered whether costs incurred in trans-

actions with independent third parties should be deferred if those costs relate to activities other than those specified in paragraph 6. One approach was to defer all of those costs, because they represent a reliable measure of the lender's economic sacrifice that is incurred only if the lending transaction is completed. Another approach was to defer only the portion of those costs that relates to those specified origination activities and to charge the costs associated with other activities, such as solicitation, to expense. Under the latter approach, if the third party performed more than one activity for its fee, the lender would allocate the third party fee between specified origination activities and other activities. When origination activities are being performed by an independent third party, the Board believes that the lender is not in a position to determine the portion of time spent by the third party on each of the activities and therefore is unable to determine the amount of cost applicable to the origination activities. Because of that difficulty and because incremental direct costs incurred with an independent third party represent a reliable measure of the lender's economic sacrifice to acquire a specific loan, the Board concluded that the incremental direct costs of loan origination incurred in transactions with independent third parties should be deferred.

41. In requiring the deferral of incremental direct costs of loan origination incurred in transactions with independent third parties, the Board established certain conditions (refer to the definition of incremental direct costs in Appendix C) to have those costs qualify for deferral. Incremental direct costs of loan origination incurred with independent third parties must include only those costs that result directly from and are essential to the lending transaction and would not have been incurred by the lender had the lending transaction not occurred. The Board acknowledges that in some circumstances judgment will be necessary to conclude that a cost incurred with a third party is essential to the lending transaction and that the third party is, in fact, independent; however, the Board concluded that such judgments are both necessary and practicable.

42. The Board concluded that the costs associated with solicitation efforts by the lender's employees should be charged to expense as incurred because the nature of solicitation is such that it is impracticable to identify the extent of successful and unsuccessful solicitation efforts on a timely, reliable basis. The Board recognizes that commission-based compensation arrangements between a lender and its employees may be similar to arrangements a lender may have with independent third parties such as brokers. However,

Accounting for Nonrefundable Fees and Costs
Associated with Originating or Acquiring Loans
FAS91
and Initial Direct Costs of Leases

when origination activities are performed by the lender's employees, the Board believes that the lender can make reasonable estimates of the costs applicable to the activities specified in paragraph 6 based on the portion of time spent by employees. In making those cost allocations to a completed loan, the Board concluded that the lender should allocate the employee's total compensation, including payroll-related fringe benefits and amounts earned from solicitation, between origination activities and other activities, including solicitation, and only that portion of total compensation that relates to activities set forth in paragraph 6 should be deferred for that completed loan. The Board acknowledges that such allocations will be judgmental, but it believes that lenders can make such judgments based on measures of the activities performed by employees.

43. The Board also considered respondents' suggestions to permit allocation of indirect costs, such as supervision, occupancy, depreciation, and other costs, to completed loans. The Board views those as recurring indirect costs and concluded that all of those costs should be charged to expense as incurred, including occupancy costs for facilities that are dedicated solely to loan origination.

44. Many financial institutions have recognized as revenue fees equal to the approximate costs of origination when a loan is made. The Board rejected that approach because it believes that revenue recognition should not be based on the timing and amount of cost recognition. Likewise, the Board concluded that the practice of accelerating the recognition of lease finance revenues to offset initial direct costs or other costs of direct financing leases should no longer be acceptable.

Commitment Fees

45. The Board concluded that a loan commitment may be either integral to lending or a separate customer service depending on the nature of the commitment. Paragraph 8 of this Statement requires commitment fees to be deferred except in limited circumstances and, if the loan commitment is exercised, recognized by the interest method over the life of the loan as an adjustment of yield or recognized in income on expiration of the commitment if the loan commitment expires unexercised.

46. The Board considered two principal factors in reaching its conclusions about whether a commitment is principally a separate service or is integral to lending. The first was whether the commitment provides the customer with a benefit that is objectively distinguishable from a commitment that is expected to result in a lending transaction. The Board could find little substantive difference between the activities involved in loan origination and those involved in loan commitment when the enterprise reasonably expects the commitment to be exercised. Accordingly, the Board concluded that the accounting for fees for both activities should be the same unless the likelihood the commitment will be exercised is remote.

47. The second factor was whether the commitment provides the customer with a benefit that is not principally derived from the use of borrowed funds. Some respondents suggested that a fee received for granting a commitment constitutes a separate revenue-generating activity that should result in fee recognition over the commitment period. Those respondents indicated that the commitment fee compensates the enterprise for a variety of risks assumed during the commitment period. Those risks may include a liquidity risk, credit risk, or interest rate risk. Other respondents suggested that a commitment fee usually has both service and yield components and the accounting should reflect the substance of the fee. Some respondents, while noting that a commitment fee may have service and yield components, acknowledged that reliably measuring the separate components may be too difficult. As a result, they suggested that the commitment fee should be recognized over the combined commitment period and loan life. Recognition during the commitment period would be on a straight-line basis using a combined life approach; upon exercise, the remaining unamortized balance would be recognized under the interest method over the same period used for recognizing deferred origination fees and costs.

48. The Board rejected the suggestion of those respondents that the commitment fee be recognized over the commitment period or the combined commitment and loan period. The Board acknowledges that a fee received by an enterprise at the time a commitment is granted may be compensation to the enterprise for a variety of services provided and risks assumed. Those services and risks may include a guaranteed availability of funds and a guaranteed interest rate. To the extent that a commitment fee may compensate the enterprise for interest rate or credit risks assumed during the commitment period, the Board noted that the enterprise can suffer from those risks only if the loan is made. The related economic sacrifice is incurred by the lender over the term of the loan and not over the term of the commitment. Accordingly, the Board concluded that the lender should recognize the compensation related to those risks assumed over the period the enter-

prise incurs the economic sacrifice, that is, while the loan is outstanding. To the extent that a portion of the commitment fee represents a yield adjustment, recognition of the commitment fee over the combined commitment and loan period results in premature recognition of income. Further, even to the extent that a portion of the commitment fee is to compensate the enterprise for some service provided during the commitment period, the Board concluded that the separate components of a commitment fee cannot be identified and measured reliably enough to allow separate accounting recognition for each component part.

49. The Board concluded that if, at the inception of the commitment period, the likelihood of the commitment resulting in a loan is remote, the commitment fee should be recognized as service fee income over the commitment period. The Board decided that otherwise the fee should be deferred and, if the loan commitment is exercised, recognized by the interest method over the life of the loan as an adjustment of yield or, if the loan commitment expires unexercised, recognized in income upon expiration of the commitment.

50. The fees for some loan commitments are structured in a manner that precludes any part of the fee from being considered integral to lending because the amount of the commitment fee is based on the portion of a loan commitment that is not exercised. For example, a lending institution may grant its customer a commitment for a revolving line of credit, the fee for which is determined as a percentage of the unused line of credit. Since the percentage is applied only to the portion of the commitment that was not funded as a loan, the fee relates to the service of maintaining the availability of funds and is not considered to be principally integral to lending. Further, the level of fee for such commitments has historically been nominal in relation to the stated interest rate on any related borrowing. The Board concluded that if the amount of the commitment fee is determined retrospectively as a percentage of the line of credit available but unused in a previous period, if that percentage is nominal in relation to the stated interest rate on any related borrowing, and if that borrowing will bear a market interest rate at the date the loan is made, the commitment fee should be recognized as service fee income as of the determination date.

Credit Card and Similar Fees

51. The Board retained the provision in the Exposure Draft that called for recognition of credit card fees on a straight-line basis over the period the fee entitles the cardholder to use the credit card. Some respondents suggested that credit card fees are not related to the lending process and should be excluded from the scope of the Statement. The Board did not accept that view. While the amount of fee collected from each individual borrower may not be of the magnitude of other commitment fees collected by the lender on other loan arrangements, the Board concluded that the substance is the same. A credit card fee represents a payment by the cardholder to obtain the ability to borrow from the lender under predefined conditions. Such borrowings take place at the option of the borrower. The Board noted that such arrangements provide opportunities to lend and concluded that the related fees represent commitment fees. The Board recognized that application of the interest method to the outstanding balances of a credit cardholder would be impracticable in most instances. Accordingly, this Statement requires the fee to be recognized on a straight-line basis over the period the fee entitles the cardholder to use the card. The Board agreed with those respondents who suggested that the conclusion regarding credit card fees be extended to fees collected in similar arrangements that involve an extension of credit by the card issuer, such as charge cards and cash cards. The Board views the substance of these transactions as similar and has included fees received from such arrangements in the definition of credit card fees for purposes of applying this Statement.

Refinancings and Restructurings

52. The Exposure Draft required that all refinanced or restructured loans be accounted for as continuations of the prior loans. The Exposure Draft reflected the Board's concern about the practicality of establishing effective criteria for distinguishing between refinancings and restructurings that should be considered new loans and those that should be considered continuations of the prior loans. Respondents expressed the view that accounting for all refinanced or restructured loans as continuations of the prior loans would result in essentially identical loans having different effective yields and would not faithfully represent the substance of the transaction. Respondents acknowledged that establishing criteria that would be effective for all circumstances might not be possible but indicated that improvement could be achieved by permitting loans that can be demonstrated to possess terms that are comparable to new loans granted to comparable borrowers to be accounted for as new loans. The Board concluded that the lender should account for the loan as a new loan if the terms on the new loan are at least as favorable to the lender as the terms for comparable loans to other customers

Accounting for Nonrefundable Fees and Costs
Associated with Originating or Acquiring Loans
and Initial Direct Costs of Leases

FAS91

with similar collection risks who are not refinancing a loan with the lender; otherwise, the fees and costs associated with the prior loan are carried forward as part of the investment in the new loan. However, the Board also concluded that minor modifications to a loan agreement would not constitute a transaction that would result in a new loan and recognition of the prior loan's net fees or costs.

Amortization

53. The Board concluded that the interest method should be used to recognize fees and costs associated with originating and acquiring loans. The Board concluded that loan fees and costs and purchase premiums and discounts related to loans do not differ substantively and should be accounted for similarly. All are part of the net investment in the underlying asset, the loan. Using the interest method to recognize associated fees and costs, together with the loan's stated interest, appropriately reflects the effective interest on the loan.

54. When a loan's stated interest rate increases during the term of the loan, the periodic amortization calculated under the interest method early in the loan term would exceed the stated interest received. In such a case, an amount that would be recognized as income before it accrues under the contract would increase the net investment in the loan to an amount in excess of that at which the borrower could settle the obligation. The Board concluded that the recognition of interest income should not cause the net investment of a loan to exceed the amount at which the borrower could settle the obligation. Accordingly, paragraph 18(a) imposes a limit on the amount of periodic amortization that can be recognized. However, that limitation does not apply to the capitalization of costs incurred (such as direct loan origination costs and purchase premiums) that cause the investment in the loan to be in excess of the amount at which the borrower could settle the obligation. The Board concluded that the capitalization of costs incurred is different from increasing the net investment in a loan through accrual of interest income that is only contingently receivable.

55. In limiting the amount of interest income that can be recognized when a loan's stated interest rate increases during the term of the loan, paragraph 18(a) permits prepayment penalties to be considered only to the extent that such penalties are imposed on all prepayments occurring prior to maturity. Considering prepayment penalties has the effect of increasing the limit imposed on the recognition of interest income. Prohibiting

consideration of penalties that are not imposed throughout the term of the loan is, in the Board's view, a simplified and practical way of assuring that the net investment in the loan is not increased through accrual of interest to an amount in excess of that at which the borrower could settle the obligation.

56. If a loan contract establishes an interest rate that decreases over the loan term, the Board concluded that the interest method should be applied to recognize the fees and costs and the stated interest payment as specified in paragraph 18(b). The Board views the high initial rates as being substantively the installment payment of a loan fee during the early life of the loan.

57. The Board also decided that the interest method should be applied to recognize fees and costs associated with variable rate loans. The Board noted that the effect on the amortization as a result of subsequent changes in interest rates would not normally be significant and that the benefit of such subsequent calculations generally would not justify the additional cost. Therefore, paragraph 18(c) was added to simplify application of the interest method to those loans by eliminating the requirement to recalculate a new effective rate each time the index on the loan changes. However, the Board modified the provisions of the Exposure Draft to allow preparers the option of recalculating a new effective rate each time the index on the loan changes.

58. Respondents generally supported use of the interest method to recognize fees and costs and purchase premiums and discounts. However, most respondents disagreed with the provision of the Exposure Draft that precluded an entity from anticipating prepayments for purposes of applying the interest method. Respondents argued that the timing and amount of prepayments on loans such as mortgages can be reliably estimated and, therefore, prepayments should be anticipated for purposes of applying the interest method to recognize loan fees and costs. The Board acknowledges that in certain circumstances it may be possible to estimate reasonably an event beyond an enterprise's control, such as prepayments, if the population of loans is large and their characteristics are similar. The Board concluded that, in certain circumstances, anticipation of prepayments would be acceptable in applying the interest method. The Board concluded that an enterprise should be permitted but not required to anticipate prepayments of principal in applying the interest method to a large number of similar loans. The Board noted that loans grouped together should have sufficiently similar characteristics that prepayment experience of the loans

can be expected to be similar in a variety of interest rate environments. The Board also noted that loans that are grouped together for purposes of applying paragraph 19 should have sufficiently similar levels of net fees or costs so that, in the event that an individual loan is sold, recalculation of that loan's carrying amount will be practicable. Paragraph 19 sets forth conditions that must exist for an enterprise to anticipate prepayments in applying the interest method. Absent a reasonably large number of loans with similar characteristics, the Board believes the reliability of reasonably projecting cash flows is diminished to an unacceptable level.

59. When the conditions of paragraph 19 are not met, the Board concluded that anticipation of prepayments is not appropriate and that recognition of fees and costs and purchase premiums or discounts should be in accordance with the repayment terms provided in the loan contract, with any unamortized amount recognized in income if and when prepayment occurs.

Amendments to Other Pronouncements

60. The Board concluded that the activities involved in originating or acquiring leases are not substantively different from the activities involved in lending arrangements and, therefore, the costs involved in those activities should be determined similarly. In addition, nonrefundable fees and costs related to direct financing leases should be accounted for in a manner consistent with the accounting for lending activities.

Effective Date and Transition

61. The Exposure Draft would have been effective for fiscal years beginning after December 15, 1986 and would have required enterprises to adopt the provisions of the Statement by retroactively restating financial statements of prior years if practicable. If restatement of all years presented was not practicable, the provisions of the Statement were to be applied on a prospective basis to all lending and leasing transactions entered into and commitments granted in fiscal years beginning after December 15, 1986.

62. The Exposure Draft included a notice to recipients specifically requesting comments on a transition approach that would have involved retroactive application only to transactions occurring within the last three years. Some respondents suggested that any retroactive application would be too costly and time-consuming. Those respondents suggested that the Statement be applied prospectively. Historically, most lenders have charged acquisition costs to expense and recognized all or a portion of origination and commitment fees at the date a loan was funded. Respondents suggested the information that would be necessary to determine the amounts that would be deferred if this Statement were applied retroactively is not available. The Board noted that applying this Statement prospectively to transactions occurring after the effective date will diminish the comparability of an enterprise's financial statements for periods before and after the effective date and that, due to the types of transactions addressed by this Statement, the lack of comparability may exist for long periods of time. However, the Board is persuaded that the costs of requiring such a determination retroactively would place an excessive burden on many entities. Therefore, the Board modified the transition provision of this Statement to encourage, but not require, retroactive restatement.

63. Some respondents commented that the accounting system changes that would be required as a result of the Exposure Draft would require time for implementation and urged that the effective date of the Statement be delayed for a number of years. The Board acknowledges that certain changes in accounting systems will be required as a result of the provisions of this Statement. As a result, the Board changed the effective date of the Statement so as to require adoption in fiscal years beginning after December 15, 1987.

Accounting for Nonrefundable Fees and Costs
Associated with Originating or Acquiring Loans   **FAS91**
and Initial Direct Costs of Leases

Appendix B

EXAMPLES OF APPLICATION OF THIS STATEMENT

64. This appendix presents examples that illustrate the application of this Statement. The examples and estimates used are illustrative only and are not intended to modify or limit in any way the provisions of this Statement. All examples assume that principal and interest payments are made on the last day of the year.

Case 1—Amortization Based on Contractual Payment Terms

65. On January 1, 19X7, A Company originates a 10-year $100,000 loan with a 10 percent stated interest rate. The contract specifies equal annual payments of $16,275 through December 31, 19Y6. The contract also specifies that no penalty will be charged for prepayments of the loan. A

Company charges a 3 percent ($3,000) nonrefundable fee to the borrower and incurs $1,000 in direct loan origination costs (attorney fees, appraisal, title insurance, wages and payroll-related fringe benefits of employees performing origination activities, outside broker's fee). The carrying amount of the loan is computed as follows:

Loan principal	$ 100,000
Origination fees	(3,000)
Direct loan origination costs	1,000
Carrying amount of loan	$ 98,000

66. A Company accounts for this loan using contractual payments to apply the interest method of amortization. In calculating the effective rate to apply the interest method, the discount rate necessary to equate 10 annual payments of $16,275 to the initial carrying amount of $98,000 is approximately 10.4736 percent. The amortization if no prepayment occurs is shown in Table 1.

Table 1—Amortization Based on Contractual Payment Terms

Year	(1) Cash (Out) Inflow	(2) Stated Interest	(3) Amortization	(4) Interest Income	(5) Remaining Principal	(6) Unamortized Net Fees	(7) Carrying Amount
	$ (98,000)				$ 100,000		$ 98,000
1	16,275	$ 10,000	$ 264	$ 10,264	93,725	$ 1,736	91,989
2	16,275	9,373	262	9,635	86,823	1,474	85,349
3	16,275	8,682	257	8,939	79,230	1,217	78,013
4	16,275	7,923	248	8,171	70,878	969	69,909
5	16,275	7,088	234	7,322	61,691	735	60,956
6	16,275	6,169	215	6,384	51,585	520	51,065
7	16,275	5,159	189	5,348	40,469	331	40,138
8	16,275	4,047	157	4,204	28,241	174	28,067
9	16,275	2,824	116	2,940	14,790	58	14,732
10	16,275	1,485[a]	58	1,543	0	0	0
Total amortization			$ 2,000				

Computations:
Column (1)—Contractual payments
Column (2)—Column (5) for prior year × the loan's stated interest rate (10%)
Column (3)—Column (4) − Column (2)
Column (4)—Column (7) for prior year × the effective interest rate (10.4736%)[b]
Column (5)—Column (5) for prior year − (Column (1) − Column (2))
Column (6)—Initial net fees − amortization to date
Column (7)—Column (5) − Column (6)

---

[a]$6 rounding adjustment.
[b]The effective interest rate is the discount rate that equates the present value of the future cash inflows to the initial net cash outflow of $98,000.

Case 2—Amortization Based on Contractual Payment Terms with Full Prepayment in Year 3

67. On January 1, 19X7, B Company originates a 10-year $100,000 loan with a 10 percent stated interest rate. The contract specifies equal annual payments of $16,275 through December 31, 19Y6. The contract also specifies that no penalty will be charged for prepayments of the loan. B

Company charges a 3 percent ($3,000) nonrefundable fee to the borrower and incurs $1,000 in direct loan origination costs.

68. B Company accounts for this loan using contractual payments to apply the interest method of amortization. The amortization if the borrower prepays the remaining principal at the end of year 3 is shown in Table 2.

Table 2—Amortization Based on Contractual Payment Terms with Full Prepayment in Year 3

Year	(1) Cash (Out) Inflow	(2) Stated Interest	(3) Amortization	(4) Interest Income	(5) Remaining Principal	(6) Unamortized Net Fees	(7) Carrying Amount
	$ (98,000)				$ 100,000		$ 98,000
1	16,275	$10,000	$ 264	$ 10,264	93,725	$ 1,736	91,989
2	16,275	9,373	262	9,635	86,823	1,474	85,349
3	95,505	8,682	1,474	10,156	0	0	0
Total amortization			$ 2,000				

Computations:

Column (1)—Contractual payments + prepayments

Column (2)—Column (5) for prior year × the loan's stated interest rate (10%)

Column (3)—Column (4) − Column (2)

Column (4)—Column (7) for prior year × the effective interest rate (10.4736%) plus in year 3 an adjustment of $1,217 representing the unamortized net fees recognized when the loan is paid in full

Column (5)—Column (5) for prior year − (Column (1) − Column (2))

Column (6)—Initial net fees − amortization to date

Column (7)—Column (5) − Column (6)

Case 3—Amortization Based on Estimated Prepayment Patterns

69. On January 1, 19X7, C Company originates 1,000 10-year $10,000 loans with 10 percent stated interest rates. Each contract specifies equal annual payments through December 31, 19Y6. The contracts also specify that no penalty will be charged for prepayments. C Company charges each borrower a 3 percent ($300) fee and incurs $100 in direct origination costs for each loan. The carrying amount of the loans is computed as follows:

Loan principal amounts	$ 10,000,000
Origination fees	(300,000)
Direct loan origination costs	100,000
Carrying amount of loans	$ 9,800,000

70. C Company chooses to account for this large number of loans using anticipated prepayment patterns to apply the interest method of amortization. C Company estimates a constant prepayment rate of 6 percent per year, which is consistent with C Company's prior experience with similar loans and C Company's expectation of ongoing experience. The amortization when prepayments occur as anticipated is shown in Table 3.

Table 3—Amortization Based on Estimated Prepayment Patterns

Year	(1) Cash (Out) Inflow	(2) Stated Interest	(3) Amortization	(4) Interest Income	(5) Remaining Principal	(6) Unamortized Net Fees	(7) Carrying Amount
	$ (9,800,000)				$ 10,000,000		$ 9,800,000
1	2,227,454	$ 1,000,000	$ 35,141	$ 1,035,141	8,772,546	$ 164,859	8,607,687
2	2,049,623	877,255	31,946	909,201	7,600,178	132,913	7,467,265
3	1,880,619	760,018	28,724	788,742	6,479,577	104,189	6,375,388
4	1,719,716	647,958	25,453	673,411	5,407,819	78,736	5,329,083
5	1,566,144	540,782	22,111	562,893	4,382,457	56,625	4,325,832
6	1,419,028	438,246	18,677	456,923	3,401,675	37,948	3,363,727
7	1,277,230	340,168	15,131	355,299	2,464,613	22,817	2,441,796
8	1,138,934	246,461	11,458	257,919	1,572,140	11,359	1,560,781
9	1,000,180	157,214	7,646	164,860	729,174	3,713	725,461
10	802,091	72,917	3,713	76,630	0	0	0
Total amortization			$ 200,000				

Computations:
Column (1)—Contractual payments + 6% of Column (5) for the prior year (except in year 10)
Column (2)—Column (5) for prior year × the loan's stated interest rate (10%)
Column (3)—Column (4) − Column (2)
Column (4)—Column (7) for the prior year × the effective interest rate (10.5627%)
Column (5)—Column (5) for prior year − (Column (1) − Column (2))
Column (6)—Initial net fees − amortization to date
Column (7)—Column (5) − Column (6)

Case 4—Amortization Based on Estimated Prepayment Patterns Adjusted for Change in Estimate

71. On January 1, 19X7, D Company originates 1,000 10-year $10,000 loans with 10 percent stated interest rates. Each contract specifies equal annual payments through December 31, 19Y6. The contracts also specify that no penalty will be charged for prepayments. D Company charges each borrower a 3 percent ($300) fee and incurs $100 in direct origination costs for each loan.

72. D Company chooses to account for this portfolio of loans using anticipated prepayment patterns to apply the interest method of amortization. D Company estimates a constant prepayment rate of 6 percent per year, which is consistent with D Company's prior experience with similar loans and D Company's expectation of ongoing experience.

73. Table 4 illustrates the adjustment required by paragraph 19 of this Statement when an enterprise's actual prepayment experience differs from the amounts anticipated. The loans have actually prepaid at a rate of 6 percent in years 1 and 2 and 20 percent in year 3, and based on the new information at the end of year 3, D Company revises its estimate of prepayment experience to anticipate that 10 percent of the loans will prepay in year 4 and 6 percent of the loans will prepay in remaining years. The carrying amount of the loans at the end of year 3 is adjusted to the amount that would have existed had the new effective yield been applied since January 1, 19X7. Included in amortization in year 3 is an adjustment for the difference in the prior effective yield and the new effective yield applied to amounts outstanding in years 1 and 2. Amortization in years 4-10 assumes the new estimates of prepayment experience occur as anticipated.

Table 4—Amortization Based on Estimated Prepayment Patterns Adjusted for a Change in Estimate

Year	(1) Cash (Out) Inflow	(2) Stated Interest	(3) Amortization	(4) Interest Income	(5) Remaining Principal	(6) Unamortized Net Fees	(7) Carrying Amount
	$ (9,800,000)				$ 10,000,000		$ 9,800,000
1	2,227,454	$ 1,000,000	$ 35,141	$ 1,035,141	8,772,546	$ 164,859	8,607,687
2	2,049,623	877,255	31,946	909,201	7,600,178	132,913	7,467,265
3	2,944,644	760,018	41,951	801,969	5,415,552	90,962	5,324,590
4	1,653,939	541,555	23,294	564,849	4,303,168	67,668	4,235,500
5	1,246,229	430,317	18,998	449,315	3,487,256	48,670	3,438,586
6	1,129,164	348,726	16,050	364,776	2,706,818	32,620	2,674,198
7	1,016,331	270,682	13,005	283,687	1,961,169	19,615	1,941,554
8	906,285	196,117	9,849	205,966	1,251,001	9,766	1,241,235
9	795,875	125,100	6,574	131,674	580,226	3,192	577,034
10	638,249	58,023	3,192	61,215	0	0	0
	Total amortization		$ 200,000				

Computations:

Column (1)—Contractual payments + prepayments

Column (2)—Column (5) for prior year × the loan's stated interest rate (10%)

Column (3)—Column (4) – Column (2)

Column (4)—Column (7) for the prior year × the effective rate (10.5627% for years 1 and 2, and 10.6083% for years 3-10, + an adjustment of $8,876 in year 3 representing the cumulative effect[c] applicable to years 1 and 2 of changing the estimated effective rate)

Column (5)—Column (5) for prior year – (Column (1) – Column (2))

Column (6)—Initial net fees – amortization to date

Column (7)—Column (5) – Column (6)

---

[c]An adjustment would also be required if the level of prepayments realized was less than anticipated.

Accounting for Nonrefundable Fees and Costs
Associated with Originating or Acquiring Loans
and Initial Direct Costs of Leases   FAS91

Case 5—Application of Paragraph 18(a)—When the Loan's Prepayment Penalty Is Effective throughout the Entire Term

74. E Company grants a 10-year $100,000 loan with an 8 percent stated interest rate in year 1 and 10 percent in years 2-10. E Company receives net fees of $1,000 related to this loan. The contract

specifies that the borrower must pay a penalty equal to 1 percent of any principal prepaid. Application of the effective yield to recognize an amount in excess of net fees is appropriate for a loan with an increasing stated interest rate only to the extent that the loan agreement provides for a prepayment penalty that is effective throughout the loan term.

Table 5—Application of Paragraph 18(a)—When the Loan's Prepayment Penalty Is Effective throughout the Entire Term

Year	(1) Cash (Out) Inflow	(2) Stated Interest	(3) Amortization	(4) Interest Income	(5) Remaining Principal	(6) Unamortized Net Fees[d]	(7) Carrying Amount	(8) Settlement Amount
	$ (99,000)				$ 100,000		$ 99,000	
1	14,903	$ 8,000	$ 1,710	$ 9,710	93,097	$ (710)	93,807	$ 94,028
2	16,165	9,310	(108)	9,202	86,242	(602)	86,844	87,104
3	16,165	8,624	(106)	8,518	78,701	(496)	79,197	79,488
4	16,165	7,870	(102)	7,768	70,406	(394)	70,800	71,110
5	16,165	7,041	(97)	6,944	61,282	(297)	61,579	61,895
6	16,165	6,128	(88)	6,040	51,245	(209)	51,454	51,757
7	16,165	5,124	(78)	5,046	40,204	(131)	40,335	40,606
8	16,165	4,021	(65)	3,956	28,060	(66)	28,126	28,340
9	16,165	2,806	(47)	2,759	14,701	(19)	14,720	14,848
10	16,165	1,464[e]	(19)	1,445	0	0	0	0
Total amortization			$ 1,000					

Computations:
Column (1)—Contractual payments
Column (2)—Column (5) for prior year × the loan's stated interest rate (8% in year 1, 10% in years 2-10)
Column (3)—Column (4) – Column (2)
Column (4)—Column (7) for the prior year × the effective interest rate (9.8085%)
Column (5)—Column (5) for prior year – (Column (1) – Column (2))
Column (6)—Initial net fees – amortization to date
Column (7)—Column (5) – Column (6)
Column (8)—Column (5) × 1.01 (to calculate the settlement amount including prepayment penalty)

---

[d]Unamortized net fee and accrued interest.
[e]$6 rounding adjustment.

Case 6—Application of Paragraph 18(a)—With No Prepayment Penalty

75. F Company grants a 10-year $100,000 loan. The contract provides for 8 percent interest in year 1 and 10 percent interest in years 2-10. F Company receives net fees of $1,000 related to this loan. The contract specifies that no penalty will be charged for prepayment of principal.

76. The discount factor that equates the present value of the cash inflows in Column 1 with the initial cash outflow of $99,000 is 9.8085 percent. In year 1, recognition of interest income on the investment of $99,000 at a rate of 9.8085 percent would cause the investment to be $93,807, or $710 greater than the amount at which the borrower could settle the obligation. Because the condition set forth in paragraph 18(a) is not met, recognition of an amount greater than the net fee is not permitted.

Table 6—Application of Paragraph 18(a)—With No Prepayment Penalty

Year	(1) Cash (Out) Inflow	(2) Stated Interest	(3) Amortization	(4) Interest Income	(5) Remaining Principal	(6) Unamortized Net Fees	(7) Carrying Amount
	$ (99,000)				$ 100,000		$ 99,000
1	14,903	$ 8,000	$ 1,000	$ 9,000	93,097	$ 0	93,097
2	16,165	9,310	0	9,310	86,242	0	86,242
3	16,165	8,624	0	8,624	78,701	0	78,701
4	16,165	7,870	0	7,870	70,406	0	70,406
5	16,165	7,041	0	7,041	61,282	0	61,282
6	16,165	6,128	0	6,128	51,245	0	51,245
7	16,165	5,124	0	5,124	40,204	0	40,204
8	16,165	4,021	0	4,021	28,060	0	28,060
9	16,165	2,806	0	2,806	14,701	0	14,701
10	16,165	1,464[f]	0	1,464	0	0	0
Total amortization			$ 1,000				

Computations:
Column (1)—Contractual payments
Column (2)—Column (5) for prior year × the loan's stated interest rate (8% in year 1, 10% in years 2-10)
Column (3)—Column (4) – Column (2)
Column (4)—Column (7) for the prior year × the effective interest rate (9.8085%) as limited by paragraph 18(a) of this Statement
Column (5)—Column (5) for prior year – (Column (1) – Column (2))
Column (6)—Initial net fees – amortization to date
Column (7)—Column (5) – Column (6)

---
[f] $6 rounding adjustment.

Accounting for Nonrefundable Fees and Costs Associated with Originating or Acquiring Loans and Initial Direct Costs of Leases

FAS91

Case 7—Application of Paragraph 18(b)

77. G Company grants a 10-year $100,000 mortgage. G Company receives net fees of $1,000 related to this loan. The contract provides for an interest rate of 12 percent in year 1, 11 percent in year 2, and 10 percent thereafter.

Table 7—Application of Paragraph 18(b)

Year	(1) Cash (Out) Inflow	(2) Stated Interest	(3) Amortization	(4) Interest Income	(5) Remaining Principal	(6) Unamortized Net Fees[g]	(7) Carrying Amount
	$ (99,000)				$ 100,000		$ 99,000
1	17,698	$ 12,000	$ (1,259)	$ 10,741	94,302	$ 2,259	92,043
2	17,031	10,373	(388)	9,985	87,644	2,647	84,997
3	16,428	8,764	458	9,222	79,980	2,189	77,791
4	16,428	7,998	441	8,439	71,550	1,748	69,802
5	16,428	7,155	418	7,573	62,277	1,330	60,947
6	16,428	6,228	385	6,613	52,077	945	51,132
7	16,428	5,208	339	5,547	40,857	606	40,251
8	16,428	4,086	281	4,367	28,515	325	28,190
9	16,428	2,852	206	3,058	14,939	119	14,820
10	16,428	1,489[h]	119	1,608	0	0	0
Total amortization			$ 1,000				

Computations:

Column (1)—Contractual payments

Column (2)—Column (5) for prior year × the loan's stated interest rate (12% in year 1, 11% for year 2, and 10% in years 3-10)

Column (3)—Column (4) − Column (2)

Column (4)—Column (7) for the prior year × effective interest rate (10.8491%)

Column (5)—Column (5) for prior year − (Column (1) − Column (2))

Column (6)—Initial net fees − amortization to date

Column (7)—Column (5) − Column (6)

[g]Unamortized net fee and deferred interest.
[h]$5 rounding adjustment.

Case 8—Application of Paragraph 18(c)—Amortization Based on Factor at Inception

78. H Company grants a 10-year variable rate mortgage. The loan's interest rate and payment are adjusted annually based on the weekly Treasury bill index plus 1 percent. At the date the loan is granted, this index is 7 percent and does not change until the end of year 3. The first year loan interest rate is 8 percent (equal to the Treasury bill index plus 1 percent). H Company receives net fees of $3,000. At the end of year 3 the index changes to 9 percent and does not change again. Therefore, the loan's stated interest rate is 8 percent for years 1-3 and 10 percent for years 4-10. H Company chooses to determine the amortization based on the index at the date the loan is granted and to ignore subsequent changes in the factor.

Table 8—Application of Paragraph 18(c)—Amortization Based on Factor at Inception

Year	(1) Cash (Out) Inflow	(2) Stated Interest	(3) Amortization	(4) Interest Income	(5) Remaining Principal	(6) Unamortized Net Fees	(7) Carrying Amount
	$ (97,000)				$ 100,000		$ 97,000
1	14,903	$8,000	$ 420	$8,420	93,097	$2,580	90,517
2	14,903	7,448	410	7,858	85,642	2,170	83,472
3	14,903	6,851	395	7,246	77,590	1,775	75,815
4	15,937	7,759	375	8,134	69,412	1,400	68,012
5	15,937	6,941	347	7,288	60,416	1,053	59,363
6	15,937	6,042	314	6,356	50,521	739	49,782
7	15,937	5,052	272	5,324	39,636	467	39,169
8	15,937	3,964	221	4,185	27,663	246	27,417
9	15,937	2,766	160	2,926	14,492	86	14,406
10	15,937	1,445[i]	86	1,531	0	0	0
Total amortization			$ 3,000				

Computations:

Column (1)—Contractual payments

Column (2)—Column (5) for prior year × the loan's stated interest rate (8% in years 1-3, and 10% in years 4-10)

Column (3)—Calculated as if the index did not change—that is, the amount that would have been recognized for an 8%, 10-year $100,000 mortgage with no prepayments and a $3,000 net fee

Column (4)—Column (2) + Column (3)

Column (5)—Column (5) for prior year − (Column (1) − Column (2))

Column (6)—Initial net fees − amortization to date

Column (7)—Column (5) − Column (6)

---

[i]$4 rounding adjustment.

**Accounting for Nonrefundable Fees and Costs
Associated with Originating or Acquiring Loans
and Initial Direct Costs of Leases**   **FAS91**

Case 9—Application of Paragraph 18(c)—Amortization Recalculated for Subsequent Changes in Factor

79. I Company grants a 10-year variable rate mortgage. The loan's interest rate and payment are adjusted annually based on the weekly Treasury bill index plus 1 percent. At the date the loan is granted, this index is 7 percent and does not change until the end of year 3. The first year loan interest rate is 8 percent (equal to the Treasury bill index plus 1 percent). I Company receives net fees of $3,000. At the end of year 3 the index changes to 9 percent and does not change again. Therefore, the loan's stated interest rate is 8 percent for years 1-3 and 10 percent for years 4-10. I Company chooses to recalculate a new amortization schedule each time the loan's index changes.

Table 9—Application of Paragraph 18(c)—Amortization Recalculated for Subsequent Changes in Factor

Year	(1) Cash (Out) Inflow	(2) Stated Interest	(3) Amortization	(4) Interest Income	(5) Remaining Principal	(6) Unamortized Net Fees	(7) Carrying Amount
	$ (97,000)				$ 100,000		$ 97,000
1	14,903	$ 8,000	$ 420	$ 8,420	93,097	$ 2,580	90,517
2	14,903	7,448	410	7,858	85,642	2,170	83,472
3	14,903	6,851	395	7,246	77,590	1,775	75,815
4	15,937	7,759	358	8,117	69,412	1,417	67,995
5	15,937	6,941	340	7,281	60,416	1,077	59,339
6	15,937	6,042	311	6,353	50,521	766	49,755
7	15,937	5,052	275	5,327	39,636	491	39,145
8	15,937	3,964	227	4,191	27,663	264	27,399
9	15,937	2,766	168	2,934	14,492	96	14,396
10	15,937	1,445[j]	96	1,541	0	0	0
	Total amortization		$ 3,000				

Computations:

Column (1)—Contractual payments

Column (2)—Column (5) for prior year × the loan's stated interest rate (8% in years 1-3, and 10% in years 4-10)

Column (3)—Column (4) – Column (2)

Column (4)—Column (7) for the prior year × the effective interest rate (8.6809%) for years 1-3 and Column (7) for the prior year × the effective interest rate (10.7068%) for years 4-10

Column (5)—Column (5) for prior year – (Column (1) – Column (2))

Column (6)—Initial net fees – amortization to date

Column (7)—Column (5) – Column (6)

---

[j]$4 rounding adjustment.

Appendix C

GLOSSARY

80. This appendix defines certain terms that are used in this Statement.

Commitment fees

Fees charged for entering into an agreement that obligates the enterprise to make or acquire a loan or to satisfy an obligation of the other party under a specified condition. For purposes of this Statement, the term *commitment fees* includes fees for letters of credit and obligations to purchase a loan or group of loans and pass-through certificates.

Credit card fees

The periodic uniform fees that entitle cardholders to use credit cards. The amount of such fees generally is not dependent upon the level of credit available or frequency of usage. Typically the use of credit cards facilitates the cardholder's payment for the purchase of goods and services on a periodic, as-billed basis (usually monthly), involves the extension of credit, and, if payment is not made when billed, involves imposition of interest or finance charges. For purposes of this Statement, the term *credit card fees* includes fees received in similar arrangements, such as charge card and cash card fees.

Incremental direct costs

Costs to originate a loan that (a) result directly from and are essential to the lending transaction and (b) would not have been incurred by the lender had that lending transaction not occurred.

Origination fees

Fees charged to the borrower in connection with the process of originating, refinancing, or restructuring a loan. This term includes, but is not limited to, points, management, arrangement, placement, application, underwriting, and other fees pursuant to a lending or leasing transaction and also includes syndication and participation fees to the extent they are associated with the portion of the loan retained by the lender.

Statement of Financial Accounting Standards No. 92
Regulated Enterprises—Accounting for Phase-in Plans

an amendment of FASB Statement No. 71

STATUS

Issued: August 1987

Effective Date: For fiscal years beginning after December 15, 1987 and interim periods within those fiscal
years

Affects: Amends FAS 71, paragraph 9
Supersedes FAS 71, paragraphs 13 and 14
Supersedes FAS 90, paragraph 9(d)

Affected by: No other pronouncements

Issues Discussed by FASB Emerging Issues Task Force (EITF)

Affects: No EITF Issues

Interpreted by: Paragraphs 3(b) and 3(c) interpreted by EITF Topic No. D-21

Related Issue: EITF Issue No. 92-7

SUMMARY

This Statement amends FASB Statement No. 71, *Accounting for the Effects of Certain Types of Regulation,*
to specify the accounting for phase-in plans.
When a utility completes a new plant, conventional rate-making methods establish rates to recover the allowable costs of the plant. Those allowable costs include current operating costs, depreciation, interest on borrowed funds invested in the plant, and an allowance for earnings for the utility (an amount intended to represent a fair return on shareholders' investment in the plant).
The cost of electric utilities' plants constructed in recent years has been much greater than the cost of those
completed in earlier years, so that, for some utilities, conventional rate-making methods would result in significantly increased rates when a newly completed plant goes into service. In such cases, some regulators have
adopted phase-in plans to moderate the initial rate increase. The objective of those plans is to increase rates
more gradually than would be the case under conventional rate making, while providing the utility eventual
recovery of all of its allowable costs and a return on investment.
This Statement requires allowable costs deferred for future recovery under a phase-in plan related to plants
completed before January 1, 1988 and plants on which substantial physical construction has been performed
before January 1, 1988 to be capitalized if each of four criteria is met. Those criteria are (a) the plan has been
agreed to by the regulator, (b) the plan specifies when recovery will occur, (c) all allowable costs deferred under the plan are scheduled for recovery within 10 years of the date when deferrals begin, and (d) the percentage
increase in rates scheduled for each future year under the plan is not greater than the percentage increase in
rates scheduled for each immediately preceding year. If any of those criteria is not met, allowable costs deferred under the plan would not be capitalized. Instead, those costs would be recognized in the same manner as
if there were no phase-in plan.

This Statement also reiterates that Statement 71 does not permit an allowance for earnings on shareholders' investment to be capitalized in general-purpose financial statements when it is capitalized for rate-making purposes other than during construction and, with this Statement, as part of a phase-in plan.

This Statement is effective for fiscal years beginning after December 15, 1987, and it applies to existing and future phase-in plans. Application of this Statement to phase-in plans that do not meet the criteria of this Statement will be delayed if the regulated enterprise has filed a rate application to have those phase-in plans modified to meet the criteria of this Statement or intends to do so as soon as practicable and it is reasonably possible that the rate application will be successful. In that case, this Statement will be applied to those phase-in plans when the regulator amends or refuses to amend those plans.

(This page intentionally left blank.)

Statement of Financial Accounting Standards No. 92

Regulated Enterprises—Accounting for Phase-in Plans

an amendment of FASB Statement No. 71

CONTENTS

INTRODUCTION

1. FASB Statement No. 71, *Accounting for the Effects of Certain Types of Regulation,* was issued in December 1982. Shortly after the Statement was issued, major events in the electric utility industry caused the Board to review the effects of the Statement on the accounting for those events. After that review, the Board decided to amend Statement 71 to provide more specific guidance on the accounting for some of those events and to change the accounting for others.

2. FASB Statement No. 90, *Regulated Enterprises—Accounting for Abandonments and Disallowances of Plant Costs,* addresses the accounting for some of those events. This Statement amends Statement 71 to specify the accounting for phase-in plans.

STANDARDS OF FINANCIAL ACCOUNTING AND REPORTING

Accounting for Phase-in Plans

3. The term *phase-in plan* is used in this Statement to refer to any method of recognition of allowable costs[1] in rates that meets all of the following criteria:

a. The method was adopted by the regulator in connection with a major, newly completed plant of the regulated enterprise or of one of its suppliers or a major plant scheduled for completion in the near future (hereinafter referred to as "a plant").

b. The method defers the rates intended to recover allowable costs beyond the period in which those allowable costs would be charged to ex-

---

[1]The term *allowable costs* is used throughout this Statement to refer to all costs for which revenue is intended to provide recovery. Those costs can be actual or estimated. In that context, allowable costs include interest costs and an allowance for earnings on shareholders' investment.

pense under generally accepted accounting principles applicable to enterprises in general.

c. The method defers the rates intended to recover allowable costs beyond the period in which those rates would have been ordered under the rate-making methods routinely used prior to 1982 by that regulator for similar allowable costs of that regulated enterprise.

4. If a phase-in plan is ordered by a regulator in connection with a plant on which no substantial physical construction had been performed before January 1, 1988, none of the allowable costs that are deferred for future recovery by the regulator under the plan[2] for rate-making purposes shall be capitalized for general-purpose financial reporting purposes (hereinafter referred to as "financial reporting").

5. If a phase-in plan is ordered by a regulator in connection with a plant completed before January 1, 1988 or a plant on which substantial physical construction had been performed before January 1, 1988, the criteria specified below shall be applied to that plan. If the phase-in plan meets all of those criteria, all allowable costs that are deferred for future recovery by the regulator under the plan shall be capitalized for financial reporting as a separate asset (a deferred charge). If any one of those criteria is not met, none of the allowable costs that are deferred for future recovery by the regulator under the plan[3] shall be capitalized for financial reporting. The criteria to determine whether capitalization is appropriate are:

a. The allowable costs in question are deferred pursuant to a formal plan that has been agreed to by the regulator.
b. The plan specifies the timing of recovery of all allowable costs that will be deferred under the plan.
c. All allowable costs deferred under the plan are scheduled for recovery within 10 years of the date when deferrals begin.
d. The percentage increase in rates scheduled under the plan for each future year is no greater than the percentage increase in rates scheduled under the plan for each immediately preceding year. That is, the scheduled percentage increase in year two is no greater than the percentage increase granted in year one, the scheduled percentage increase in year three is no greater than the scheduled percentage increase in year two, and so forth.

Modifications of and Supplements to Phase-in Plans

6. Except as provided in paragraph 18 of this Statement, when an existing phase-in plan is modified or a new plan is ordered to replace or supplement an existing plan, the above criteria shall be applied to the combination of the original plan and the new plan. The date when deferrals begin, used in applying the criterion in paragraph 5(c), would be the date of the earliest deferral under either the new or the old plan, and the final recovery date would be the date of the last recovery of all amounts deferred under the plans.

Interrelationship of Phase-in Plans and Disallowances

7. A phase-in plan, as defined in paragraph 3, is a method of rate making intended to moderate a sudden increase in rates while providing the regulated enterprise with recovery of its investment and a return on that investment during the recovery period. A disallowance is a rate-making action that prevents the regulated enterprise from recovering either some amount of its investment or some amount of return on its investment. Statement 90 specifies the accounting for disallowances of plant costs. If a method of rate making that meets the criteria of this Statement for a phase-in plan includes an indirect disallowance of plant costs, that disallowance shall be accounted for in accordance with Statement 90.

Allowance for Earnings on Shareholders' Investment Capitalized for Rate-making Purposes

8. If specified criteria are met, paragraph 9 of Statement 71 requires capitalization of an incurred cost that would otherwise be charged to expense. An allowance for earnings on shareholders' investment[4] is not "an incurred cost that would otherwise be charged to expense." Accordingly, such an allowance shall not be capitalized pursuant to paragraph 9 of Statement 71.

9. In specified circumstances, paragraph 15 of Statement 71 requires capitalization of an allowance for earnings on shareholders' investment (a designated cost of equity funds) during construction. Paragraph 5 of this Statement requires capitalization of an allowance for earnings on shareholders' investment for qualifying phase-in plans. If an allowance for earnings on sharehold-

---

[2]"Allowable costs that are deferred for future recovery by the regulator under the plan" consist of all allowable costs deferred for rate-making purposes under the plan beyond the period in which those allowable costs would be charged to expense under generally accepted accounting principles applicable to enterprises in general.
[3]Refer to footnote 2.
[4]The phrase "an allowance for earnings on shareholders' investment," as used in this Statement, is intended to have the same meaning as the phrase "a designated cost of equity funds," used in paragraph 15 of Statement 71.

ers' investment is capitalized for rate-making purposes other than during construction or as part of a phase-in plan, the amount capitalized for rate-making purposes shall not be capitalized for financial reporting.

Financial Statement Classification of Amounts Capitalized under Phase-in Plans

10. Cumulative amounts capitalized under phase-in plans shall be reported as a separate asset in the balance sheet. The net amount capitalized in each period or the net amount of previously capitalized allowable costs recovered during each period shall be reported as a separate item of other income or expense in the income statement. Allowable costs capitalized shall not be reported as reductions of other expenses.

Disclosure

Phase-in Plans

11. The terms of any phase-in plans in effect during the year or ordered for future years shall be disclosed. This Statement does not permit capitalization for financial reporting of allowable costs deferred for future recovery by the regulator pursuant to a phase-in plan that does not meet the criteria of paragraph 5 of this Statement or a phase-in plan related to a plant on which substantial physical construction was not completed before January 1, 1988. Nevertheless, the financial statements shall include disclosure of the net amount deferred at the balance sheet date for rate-making purposes and the net change in deferrals for rate-making purposes during the year for those plans.

Allowance for Earnings on Shareholders' Investment Capitalized for Rate-making Purposes

12. The nature and amounts of any allowance for earnings on shareholders' investment capitalized for rate-making purposes but not capitalized for financial reporting shall be disclosed.

Amendments to Existing Pronouncements

13. This Statement amends Statements 71 and 90 as follows:

a. The following sentence is added to the end of the footnote, added by paragraph 9(b) of Statement 90, at the end of the first sentence of paragraph 9 of Statement 71:

Phase-in plans shall be accounted for in accordance with FASB Statement No. 92, *Regulated Enterprises—Accounting for Phase-in Plans.*

b. Paragraph 13 of Statement 71, as amended by Statement 90, is superseded by the following:

Appendix B, Statement 90, and Statement 92 illustrate the accounting for the effects of regulation.

c. Paragraph 14 of Statement 71 is superseded by the following:

The following specific standards and the standards in Statements 90 and 92 are derived from the general standards in paragraphs 9-12. The specific standards in paragraphs 15-17 and the standards in Statements 90 and 92 shall not be used as guidance for other applications of the general standards in paragraphs 9-12.

d. Paragraph 9(d) of Statement 90 is deleted.

Effective Date and Transition

14. Except as provided in paragraph 17 below, this Statement shall be effective for fiscal years beginning after December 15, 1987 and interim periods within those fiscal years. Earlier application is encouraged. At the date of initial application of this Statement, existing phase-in plans shall be evaluated under the criteria of paragraph 5 of this Statement. If those existing plans do not meet those criteria, all allowable costs deferred by the regulator under those phase-in plans[5] that have previously been capitalized shall be written off. The provisions of this Statement that address capitalization of an allowance for earnings on shareholders' investment other than during construction or as part of a phase-in plan (paragraphs 8 and 9) shall not be applied to amounts capitalized in fiscal years prior to the initial application of this Statement.

15. Retroactive application of the provisions of this Statement that address accounting for phase-in plans (paragraphs 5-7, 10, and 11), in fiscal years for which financial statements have previously been issued, is permitted. If those provisions are applied retroactively, the financial statements of all prior periods presented shall be restated. In addition, the restated financial statements shall, in

---

[5]Refer to footnote 2.

the year this Statement is first applied, disclose the nature of any restatement and its effect on income before extraordinary items, net income, and related per share amounts for each period presented and on retained earnings at the beginning of the earliest period presented.

16. If financial statements for prior fiscal years are not restated as permitted by paragraph 15, the effects of applying this Statement to existing phase-in plans shall be reported as the cumulative effect of a change in accounting principle, as described in APB Opinion No. 20, *Accounting Changes,* and the effect of adopting this Statement on income before extraordinary items, net income, and related per share amounts shall be disclosed.

17. Application of this Statement to an existing phase-in plan shall be delayed if both of the following conditions are met:

a. The enterprise has filed a rate application to have the plan amended to meet the criteria of paragraph 5 of this Statement or it intends to do so as soon as practicable.
b. It is reasonably possible that the regulator will change the terms of the phase-in plan so that it

will meet the criteria of paragraph 5 of this Statement.

If those conditions are met, the provisions of this Statement shall be applied to that existing phase-in plan on the earlier of the date when one of those conditions ceases to be met or the date when a final rate order is received, amending or refusing to amend the phase-in plan. However, if the enterprise delays filing its application for the amendment or the regulator does not process that application in the normal period of time, application of this Statement shall not be further delayed.

18. In applying the criteria of paragraph 5 to a plan that was in existence prior to the first fiscal year beginning after December 15, 1987 and that was revised to meet the criteria of this Statement pursuant to paragraph 17 above, the 10-year criterion (paragraph 5(c)) and the requirement that the percentage increase in rates scheduled under the plan in each future year be no greater than the percentage increase scheduled under the plan for each immediately preceding year (paragraph 5(d)) shall be measured from the date of the amendment rather than from the date of the first scheduled deferrals under the original plan.

The provisions of this Statement need not be applied to immaterial items.

This Statement was adopted by the affirmative votes of six members of the Financial Accounting Standards Board. Mr. Lauver dissented.

Mr. Lauver dissents from the issuance of this Statement because it permits including in income an imputed allowance for earnings on shareholders' investment during a phase-in period. He believes that accounting is inappropriate on conceptual grounds because the allowance should be included in income only at the time it is a component of prices charged to customers for services.

Further, he believes it is unwise policy, in the present environment, to authorize special accounting during a phase-in period. Phase-in plans are instigated because rates that would otherwise be charged are unacceptable to customers. Whatever might have been the case in a prior era, evidence now abounds, in the form of disallowances, temporary or indefinite omission of costs from rate

base, competition, actual and planned deregulation, and inability to earn allowed rates of return, that the relationship between present costs and future revenues is too tenuous to warrant accounting predicated on the assumption that the marketplace will accept charges tomorrow that it finds unacceptable today.

Mr. Lauver also dissents to the issuance of this Statement because it does not require elimination from balance sheets of certain amounts capitalized as an allowance for earnings on shareholders' investment even though not in compliance with unambiguous provisions of Statement 71 that have been reiterated in this Statement and even though inconsistent with the accounting required for nonqualifying phase-in plans. He believes it is unwise policy to grant an amnesty-like approval of accounting that was determined to be inappropriate in both Statement 71 and this Statement.

Members of the Financial Accounting Standards Board:

Dennis R. Beresford,	Raymond C. Lauver	Robert J. Swieringa
Chairman	David Mosso	Arthur R. Wyatt
Victor H. Brown	C. Arthur Northrop	

Appendix A

EXAMPLES OF APPLICATION OF THIS STATEMENT TO SPECIFIC SITUATIONS

19. This appendix provides guidance for application of this Statement to some specific situations. The guidance does not address all possible applications of this Statement. All examples assume that

the enterprise meets the criteria of paragraph 5 of Statement 71 for the application of Statement 71 by the enterprise.

20. Specific situations discussed in this appendix are:

Accounting for a Phase-in Plan That Includes an Indirect Disallowance

21. Utility A is an electric utility that operates solely in a single-state jurisdiction. On January 1, 19X1, Utility A's new electric generating plant becomes operational. The cost of that plant is $1 billion.

22. Utility A's regulator orders that the costs of the newly completed plant be phased in over a three-year period, as follows:

19X1—A portion of the return (interest and an allowance for earnings on shareholders' investment) on unrecovered investment is deferred by excluding 25 percent of the cost of the plant from the rate base.
19X2—All of the remaining cost of the plant is to be included in the rate base with no recovery of previously deferred amounts.
19X3—All of the remaining cost of the plant is to be included in the rate base. Also, additional revenue is to be provided equal to the return on unrecovered investment excluded from rates in year 1.

The order does not provide for recovery in any year of a return on Utility A's investment in the deferred amounts. Utility A's weighted-average cost of capital in its latest rate case was 11 percent.

23. The phase-in plan is partially a disallowance of plant costs because no return on investment is provided for the deferred amounts. That disallowance should be recognized in accordance with Statement 90 when it became probable. The

amount of equivalent cost disallowed should be determined as shown in Schedule 1. The recorded cost of the plant should be reduced by that amount, and a corresponding loss should be reported in 19X1.

24. The disallowance will reduce revenues only in years 1 through 3, so the depreciation charge that would otherwise be recognized for that plant in years 1 through 3 should be reduced by the amount of the effective disallowance attributable to those years (the amount in column 4 of Schedule 1). Amounts deferred under the plan (the amount for months 1-12 in column 1 of Schedule 1) should be capitalized as a separate asset, and that asset should be amortized as recovery occurs (in months 25-36), using the amounts in column 1 of Schedule 1.

Applications of the Definition of a Phase-in Plan

"Mirror CWIP"

25. "Mirror CWIP" is one means of moderating the sudden, one-time increase in rates that would otherwise result from placing a newly completed utility plant in service. Under "mirror CWIP," increasing amounts of construction work in progress (CWIP) are included in the current rate base in the periods before the plant goes into service, providing the utility with a current return on a portion of its investment in construction while the construction proceeds. After the plant is placed in service, a decreasing amount of plant-in-service is excluded from the rate base each year, "mirroring" the pattern in which the construction was included in the rate base. The result of this procedure is to increase

Schedule 1

Utility A
Determination of Effective Disallowance
Return on Investment Disallowed for Amounts Deferred under Phase-in Plan
(in thousands)

Month	(1) Cost Deferral (Recovery)	(2) Cumulative Amount Deferred	(3) R.O.I. on Cumulative Deferral	(4) Effective Disallowance
1	$ 2,292	$ 2,292	$ 21	$ 0
2	2,291	4,583	42	21
3	2,292	6,875	63	41
4	2,292	9,167	84	61
5	2,291	11,458	105	80
6	2,292	13,750	126	99
7	2,292	16,042	147	118
8	2,291	18,333	168	137
9	2,292	20,625	189	155
10	2,292	22,917	210	173
11	2,291	25,208	231	190
12	2,292	27,500	252	207
13	0	27,500	252	224
14	0	27,500	252	222
15	0	27,500	252	220
16	0	27,500	252	218
17	0	27,500	252	216
18	0	27,500	252	214
19	0	27,500	252	212
20	0	27,500	252	210
21	0	27,500	252	208
22	0	27,500	252	206
23	0	27,500	252	204
24	0	27,500	252	202
25	(2,292)	25,208	231	201
26	(2,291)	22,917	210	182
27	(2,292)	20,625	189	164
28	(2,292)	18,333	168	146
29	(2,291)	16,042	147	129
30	(2,292)	13,750	126	112
31	(2,292)	11,458	105	95
32	(2,291)	9,167	84	78
33	(2,292)	6,875	63	62
34	(2,292)	4,583	42	46
35	(2,291)	2,292	21	31
36	(2,292)	0	0	15

Total loss to be recognized in 19X1 $5,099

Computations:
Column (1)—Cost of plant ($1 billion) $\times$ .25 $\times$ 11% $\div$ 12
Column (2)—Column (2) for prior month + Column (1) for current month
Column (3)—Column (2) $\times$ 11% $\div$ 12
Column (4)—Present value (at beginning of month 1) at 11% (.9167 per month) of amount in Column (3)
        for prior month

rates while the plant is under construction and to reduce the increase in rates in the initial years of the plant's service life.

26. For rate-making purposes, no allowance for funds used during construction is recognized on the portion of the construction that is included in the rate base while the asset is under construction, and an allowance for funds used during construction is recognized on the portion of the plant-in-service that is subsequently excluded from the rate base after the plant is placed in service. The same total amount is capitalized as if no construction had been included in the current rate base. Is "mirror CWIP" a phase-in plan under the definition in this Statement? What financial reporting is appropriate for a "mirror CWIP" plan?

27. The "mirror CWIP" arrangement described above is not a phase-in plan under the definition used in this Statement because it does not defer recovery of costs that would not have been deferred under the methods of rate making used prior to 1982. Rather, it effectively provides a temporary loan from customers to the utility during construction and requires repayment of that loan after the plant is placed in service.

28. If the arrangement is known to be a "mirror CWIP" arrangement at the time of the construction (for example, if that arrangement is required by law or has been specifically ordered by the regulator), an allowance for funds used during construction should be accrued on the total cumulative construction cost in each period for financial reporting. The revenue collected as a result of inclusion of construction in the current rate base should be recorded as a liability to customers, with disclosure of the approximate timing of the repayment that will be required under the "mirror CWIP" arrangement.

29. If the arrangement is not known to be a "mirror CWIP" arrangement when the construction is included in the rate base but the regulator later orders a "mirror CWIP" arrangement, the accounting described in paragraph 28 should be implemented as soon as the nature of the arrangement becomes known. That will require an adjustment for the cumulative effect of the arrangement to date. An amount should be capitalized, with a corresponding accrual of an allowance for funds used during construction, when the "mirror CWIP" arrangement becomes known. Current revenues should be reduced by an equal amount, and a corresponding liability to customers should be recognized. That amount should be the amount that would have been capitalized if the arrangement had been known to be a "mirror CWIP" arrangement when the revenue was collected during

construction. That capitalized amount should be reported in the year in which the "mirror CWIP" arrangement becomes known in the same manner as if it had been capitalized during construction.

Sale with Leaseback—Capital Lease

30. Utility B sells its interest in a newly completed electric generating plant for an amount equal to its cost and leases that interest back under a lease that requires equal annual payments. The sale meets the criteria of FASB Statement No. 66, *Accounting for Sales of Real Estate,* for recognition as a sale, and the leaseback meets the criteria of FASB Statement No. 13, *Accounting for Leases,* for a capital lease. Utility B's regulator includes the lease rentals in allowable cost as they accrue. In the past, Utility B's regulator has treated other leases entered into by Utility B in the same manner, but those leases were for much less significant items of equipment—not for an interest in an electric generating plant. Is this rate-making method a phase-in plan under the definition in this Statement?

31. The rate-making method described is a phase-in plan under the definition in this Statement. Generally accepted accounting principles applicable to enterprises in general require a capital lease to be accounted for much like a purchase of the leased property. The resulting expense related to the lease consists of interest on the remaining lease obligation and depreciation based on the method used for similar owned property. In the early years of a lease, the lease rentals included in allowable cost as they accrue are significantly less than the sum of interest on the lease obligation and depreciation on the leased asset. Thus, significant deferrals will result. The method also defers recognition of expenses compared with the methods of expense recognition used by Utility B's regulator for similar assets of Utility B prior to 1982 because Utility B's interests in electric generating plants were included in allowable costs in the past based on current provisions for depreciation and for the cost of capital invested in the plants. The use of this rate-making method in the past for leases of equipment does not change this conclusion. The definition is based on the method of rate making used prior to 1982 for similar allowable costs. Similar allowable costs would be those resulting from electric generating plants.

Sale with Leaseback—Operating Lease

32. Utility C sells its interest in a newly completed electric generating plant for an amount equal to its cost and leases that interest back under a lease that requires equal annual payments. The sale meets the criteria of Statement 66 for recognition as a sale, and the leaseback meets the criteria of State-

ment 13 for an operating lease. Utility C's regulator includes the lease rentals in allowable cost as they accrue. In the past, Utility C's regulator has treated other leases entered into by Utility C in the same manner, but those leases were not for an interest in an electric generating plant. Is this rate-making method a phase-in plan under the definition in this Statement?

33. The rate-making method applied to Utility C is not a phase-in plan under the definition in this Statement because it recognizes rent expense for rate-making purposes in the same way as that expense would be recognized for enterprises in general for this type of lease.

Sale with Leaseback—Profit Recognition Accelerated

34. Utility D sells its interest in a 5-year-old electric generating plant for an amount that exceeds its undepreciated cost by $500,000 and leases that interest back. The leaseback term is 20 years, and there are no renewal options. The sale meets the criteria of Statement 66 for recognition as a sale with full profit recognition, and the leaseback meets the criteria of Statement 13 for an operating lease. Utility D's regulator includes the lease rentals in allowable cost as they accrue and orders Utility D to amortize the profit, for rate-making purposes, over 10 years. The sale occurred at a time when Utility D was about to place a newly completed plant in service. Utility D has not had any similar transactions in the past. Is this rate-making method a phase-in plan under the definition in this Statement?

35. The rate-making method described is a phase-in plan under the definition in this Statement. Generally accepted accounting principles applicable to enterprises in general require a profit on a sale-leaseback transaction to be amortized over the term of the leaseback. Amortization of that profit, for rate-making purposes, over 10 years when generally accepted accounting principles applicable to enterprises in general require amortization over the 20-year leaseback term is equivalent to a deferral of allowable costs. In view of the timing of the rate order on the sale-leaseback transaction, the presumption is that the order was issued in connection with the newly completed plant. The method cannot be compared with methods in use prior to 1982 because Utility D has had no previous transactions of this type.

Modified Depreciation Method

36. Utility E's regulator orders it to depreciate its new electric generating plant, for rate-making purposes, by using an annuity method. Under the method ordered, depreciation increases each year so that the total of depreciation and return on investment stays approximately level over the life of the plant. In the past, Utility E's regulator required the use of straight-line depreciation for electric generating plants. Is this rate-making method a phase-in plan under the definition in this Statement?

37. The rate-making method applied to Utility E is a phase-in plan under the definition in this Statement because (a) it defers depreciation expense compared with the depreciation methods that are acceptable under generally accepted accounting principles applicable to enterprises in general (annuity methods of depreciation are not acceptable under generally accepted accounting principles applicable to enterprises in general) and (b) it defers depreciation expense compared with the method of depreciation used by Utility E's regulator for Utility E's electric generating plants prior to 1982.

Deferral of Costs Before a Rate Order Is Issued

38. Utility F completes construction of a nuclear generating plant and places that plant in service. Utility F's regulator decides that it will complete its examination of the prudence of Utility F's construction cost before rates are adjusted to reflect the cost of operating the plant. During the examination and until rates are adjusted, the regulator orders Utility F to capitalize its net cost of operating the plant (operating costs, depreciation, allocable interest cost, and an allowance for earnings on shareholders' investment, all net of savings that result from operation of the new plant). Is the resulting deferral for rate-making purposes a phase-in plan? What accounting is required for financial reporting?

39. The resulting deferral is not a phase-in plan. The regulator's order to capitalize an amount pending completion of a rate hearing is designed to protect the utility from the effects of regulatory lag[6] in the absence of a rate order—a routine procedure on the part of regulators. The definition of a phase-in plan in this Statement is not intended to encompass actions of a regulator that are designed to protect a utility from the effects of regulatory

---

[6]*Regulatory lag* is the delay between a change in a regulated enterprise's costs and a change in rates ordered by a regulator as a result of that change in costs. A shortfall in a utility's net income can occur when regulators set rates prospectively and the estimated or test-period costs on which those rates were based are less than the actual costs that are incurred during the period covered by those rates. Regulators' actions that are designed to protect a utility from the effects of regulatory lag can occur during a rate case but before a rate order is issued, as in this example, and when no rate case is under active consideration. An accounting order to a utility to capitalize the cost of repairing storm damage would be an example of the latter situation. Those actions can also be a part of a rate order. An example of that type of action would be a fuel adjustment clause that is intended to protect the utility from the effects of unanticipated changes in fuel costs.

lag in the absence of a rate order, nor is it intended to encompass the regulator's subsequent treatment of any allowable costs that result from those actions.

40. Under paragraph 9 of Statement 71, Utility F should capitalize that portion of the amount capitalized for rate-making purposes that represents incurred costs that would otherwise be charged to expense, provided that it is probable that future revenue in an amount at least equal to the capitalized cost will result from inclusion of those costs in allowable costs for rate-making purposes. Otherwise, Utility F should not capitalize those costs.

41. Since the situation in this example is neither during construction nor a phase-in plan, Statement 71 does not permit capitalization of an allowance for earnings on shareholders' investment. Accordingly, Utility F should not capitalize, for financial reporting, the portion of the amount capitalized for rate-making purposes that represents an allowance for earnings on shareholders' investment. If recovery of that allowance subsequently occurs, increased earnings during the recovery period will result.

Interaction of Disallowance with Deferral of Costs Before a Rate Order Is Issued

42. Six months after the accounting order referred to in the previous example, Utility F's regulator approves part of the cost of the new plant but disallows $600,000,000—consisting of construction expenditures of $570,000,000 and amounts capitalized for rate-making purposes during this 6-month operating period prior to the rate order of $30,000,000. The recorded cost of the plant before consideration of the disallowance is $4,500,000,000. During this 6-month period, Utility F has capitalized $500,000,000 of net cost for rate-making purposes. This $500,000,000 consists of an allowance for earnings on shareholders' investment of $200,000,000 and incurred costs that would otherwise be charged to expense of $300,000,000. For rate-making purposes, the balance sheet accounts, before and after the disallowance, are as follows:

	Balance before Disallowance	Disallowance	Balance after Disallowance
		(in thousands)	
Plant in Service	$4,500,000	$(570,000)	$3,930,000
Amounts Capitalized Pending Rate Order	500,000	(30,000)	470,000
Combined totals	$5,000,000	$(600,000)	$4,400,000

For financial reporting, how should the disallowance be recognized?

43. Statement 90 requires a disallowance of plant costs to be recognized as a loss. Utility F should perform the following analysis to determine the loss that should be recognized and how it will be allocated:

a. Assuming that $300,000,000 of the $500,000,000 capitalized for rate-making purposes during the 6-month period was also capitalized for financial reporting (the $200,000,000 allowance for earnings on shareholders' investment would not be capitalized), the total loss recognized by Utility F for financial reporting should be the amount that reduces the combined total of Plant in Service and Amounts Capitalized Pending Rate Order ($4,800,000,000) to the combined total that will be honored for rate-making purposes ($4,400,000,000). The recognizable loss is $400,000,000.

b. Utility F should allocate to Plant in Service the lesser of the amount of the disallowance that was allocated to Plant in Service by the regulator ($570,000,000) or the total disallowance recognized for financial reporting ($400,000,000), or $400,000,000.

c. Utility F should allocate the rest of the disallowance recognized for financial reporting, if any, to Amounts Capitalized Pending Rate Order. In this case, no amount is allocated to that asset.

The recognition of the disallowance and the effect of that recognition on the financial reporting balance sheet accounts are as follows:

	Balance before Disallowance	Recognition of Disallowance	Balance after Disallowance
		(in thousands)	
Plant in Service	$4,500,000	$(400,000)	$4,100,000
Amounts Capitalized Pending Rate Order	300,000		300,000
Combined totals	$4,800,000	$(400,000)	$4,400,000

Interaction of Deferral of Costs Before a Rate Order Is Issued with a Subsequent Phase-in Plan

44. Utility G's fact situation is identical to that of Utility F, described in the above examples, except that Utility G's regulator approves all of the costs related to the newly completed plant. Utility G's regulator adopts a formal phase-in plan intended to provide recovery of amounts deferred under the plan and amounts capitalized, for rate-making purposes, during the six-month period from the plant's in-service date to the date of the rate order. How does the phase-in plan affect the financial re-porting of the costs deferred during the six-month period?

45. The phase-in plan does not affect the financial reporting of those previously deferred costs described in paragraphs 40 and 41, nor does the existence of those previously deferred costs affect the financial reporting of the phase-in plan. Accordingly, the allowance for earnings on shareholders' investment that was not capitalized previously during the period preceding issuance of the rate order may not be capitalized upon adoption of the phase-in plan.

Appendix B

BASIS FOR CONCLUSIONS

CONTENTS

Appendix B

BASIS FOR CONCLUSIONS

Introduction

46. This appendix summarizes considerations that were deemed significant by members of the Board in reaching the conclusions in this Statement. It includes reasons for accepting certain views and rejecting others. Individual Board members gave greater weight to some factors than to others.

Definition of Phase-in Plans

47. This Statement specifies a phase-in plan definition different from that specified in the December 19, 1985 Exposure Draft, *Regulated Enterprises—Accounting for Phase-in Plans, Abandonments, and Disallowances of Plant Costs.* Comments received on the definition in the Exposure Draft indicated that (a) the definition might encompass some methods of rate making that had been routinely followed for years, (b) the definition could be interpreted to encompass some methods of expense recognition that are accepted for enterprises in general, and (c) the definition was considered ambiguous for phase-in plans related to a supplier's newly completed plant. The Board adopted the definition in this Statement to avoid those problems. The definition now focuses on methods of rate making that defer recognition of allowable costs that would not be deferred under generally accepted accounting principles applicable to enterprises in general and that defer recognition of allowable costs that would not have been deferred by a regulator under the methods of rate making used by that regulator for that same utility in the past.

Accounting for Phase-in Plans

Origin and Nature of Phase-in Plans

48. When a utility places a newly completed plant in service, traditional rate-making procedures establish rates to recover the allowable costs of that plant. The allowable costs include an allowance for return on the utility's remaining investment in the plant, which is greatest in the first year of the plant's service life and decreases thereafter as the plant is depreciated.

49. In recent years, a combination of circumstances caused traditional rate-making procedures to result in a phenomenon called *rate spike.* Rate spike is a major, one-time increase in rates that can result from the inclusion of the cost of new plants in rates under traditional rate-making procedures. One cause of rate spike was the high cost of nuclear power plants. The cost of those plants escalated far beyond initial expectations. Another cause was the high cost of capital. Return on investment, which is based on the cost of capital, is a major part of the cost of operating a nuclear plant. Finally, demand for many utilities' services has not grown in recent years to the extent that was expected when the decision was made to construct many of the recently completed plants. As a result, plants that were expected to be needed to meet demand have created excess capacity. The increased efficiency of the new plants has not been sufficient to offset the high construction and capitalized capital costs of those plants and the return on investment that would have been included in rates under traditional rate-making procedures.

50. Phase-in plans were developed to alleviate the problem of rate spike. Those plans are intended to

moderate the initial increase in rates that would otherwise result from placing newly completed plants in service by deferring some of that rate increase to future years and providing the utility with return on investment for those deferred amounts. Instead of the traditional pattern of an increase in allowable costs followed by decreasing allowable costs for utility plants after the plants are placed in service, phase-in plans create a pattern of gradually increasing allowable costs for the initial years of the plant's service life.

Questions Raised by Phase-in Plans

51. Phase-in plans raise three questions under Statement 71. First, the very existence of a phase-in plan, whereby rate increases are postponed, calls into question whether future rates to be charged to and collected from customers will in fact be set at levels that will recover the enterprise's costs. Paragraph 5(c) of Statement 71 requires that such an assumption be reasonable as a threshold condition for application of that Statement.

52. Some phase-in plans have been discussed in public forums as ways of retaining major customers. Utility officials have stated that major industrial customers would leave their utility's service area or develop alternative sources of supply if rates were increased under normal rate-making procedures sufficiently to recover the costs of a newly completed plant. If rates cannot, immediately after a new plant is put in service, be set at levels to permit recovery of allowable costs, a question arises as to whether economic conditions or customer acceptance will permit collecting rates in the future that ultimately will recover costs.

53. The second question relates to paragraph 5(b) of Statement 71, which requires that rates be designed to recover the specific enterprise's costs of providing the regulated services or products as a condition for application of that Statement. In the past, regulators sometimes have provided rates to recover costs in periods other than the period in which the costs would be charged to expense under generally accepted accounting principles applicable to enterprises in general. The rationale for such differences has been that (a) costs like storm damage or plant abandonments were infrequently occurring and should be spread among customers of multiple years or (b) the regulator did not agree that the cost was a valid period cost of the period in which it would be recognized by nonregulated enterprises. Deferred income tax expense is an example of the latter category. Under phase-in plans, allowable costs that for years have been agreed to be costs of a period are charged to customers in a different period mainly *because otherwise rates are judged to be unacceptably high.*

54. If one accepted a premise that, in periods when rates would be unacceptably high, costs can be moved to a future period, the economic discipline inherent in a process of charging customers for the costs of the services they use would be absent. No constraint would exist on the rate-making process. In the extreme case, nothing would prevent a regulator from providing customers with free electricity and promising recovery of the costs of producing that electricity in future years when an improved local economy might be expected. Some Board members believe that the premise that rates in a given period are based on the cost of services provided to customers in that period provides a necessary constraint to accounting for the type of regulation that was addressed by Statement 71.

55. The third question raised by a phase-in plan is whether it is appropriate to capitalize an allowance for earnings on shareholders' investment after a plant begins operations. Paragraph 15 of Statement 71 requires capitalization of such an allowance as part of the acquisition cost of an asset *during construction.* Statement 71 does not permit capitalization of such an allowance under any other circumstances.

56. The Board notes that an allowance for earnings on shareholders' investment is different from other costs for which recovery is provided by regulators. An allowance for earnings on shareholders' investment is not an incurred cost but is a computed amount of earnings to which equity shareholders are deemed to be entitled if their capital is prudently employed in providing services to customers. Capitalizing such an allowance increases currently reported income. Some believe that this result is inappropriate and that income should not be recognized until revenues in the form of billable rates for services are realized. They acknowledge that a partial exception is permitted in Statement 71 for an allowance for funds used during construction but question whether that partial exception should be extended to the case of phase-in plans. They view the current recognition of that future income, by capitalizing an allowance for earnings on shareholders' investment, as recognition of income that is not yet earned. This view, in part, led to the Board's decision, in Statement 71, to permit capitalization of an allowance for earnings on shareholders' investment only as part of the acquisition cost during construction of an asset.

Board Conclusions about Phase-in Plans

57. After considering comments received in comment letters on the Exposure Draft, the Board considered the possibility of not permitting any capitalization of allowable costs deferred pursuant to phase-in plans. For the reasons outlined above,

the existence of phase-in plans calls into question the applicability of Statement 71. Observation of the actions of regulators over the past few years, since the first phase-in plan was initiated, suggests that some regulators did not view their actions or the resulting accounting to be constrained by the overriding principle that the cost of current services generally should be charged to current customers. Phase-in plans have evolved from a tightly controlled plan, which deferred recovery of some costs for a short number of years and promised recovery of those deferrals through an automatic rate adjustment mechanism within a brief time period, to open-ended plans that deferred costs indefinitely and promised recovery only when, and if, future demand grew to the point that the capacity in question was needed. The Board was concerned that such developments might undermine the credibility of financial reporting under Statement 71.

58. Despite those concerns, the Board decided against a blanket prohibition against capitalization, for financial reporting, of amounts capitalized for rate-making purposes under phase-in plans. Rather, the Board decided that capitalization of allowable costs deferred under some types of phase-in plans should be permitted. The Board believes that if any phase-in plans are to result in capitalization of the allowable costs that are deferred pursuant to the plans, those plans should meet stringent criteria so that they will not undermine the credibility of financial reporting under Statement 71. The Board adopted the four criteria in paragraph 5 as the minimum set of criteria that it believes would satisfy that objective.

59. Many respondents to the Exposure Draft urged the Board not to impose the 10-year criterion, which they view as an arbitrary limit. The Board recognizes that the 10-year period is arbitrary, but any other period (for example, the life of the plant) would be equally arbitrary. Cost of service regulation is based on implicit presumptions that (a) operating expenses should normally be recovered in the period in which the expenses are incurred and (2) an allowance for return on investment should normally be recovered in the period during which the investment is used to provide services to customers. Any departure from those norms requires an arbitrary decision about the appropriate time for recovery. The very existence of a phase-in plan indicates an inability to fully recover currently the allowable costs of delivering services to customers. Further, it represents a failure to realize normal expectations that return on prudent investments in operating plants would be recovered currently and that prudently incurred construction costs would begin to be recovered on a normal (usually straight-line) basis as soon as a plant was put in service. Although those departures from the norms of individual cost-of-service regulation are an adaptation to exceptional circumstances, they are such major departures that, if not tightly bounded, they could undermine the credibility of specialized accounting for regulated enterprises.

60. Some phase-in plans provided for deferral of extremely large amounts, such that phasing in those amounts and providing recovery of deferrals within 10 years was asserted to be not practicable. Board members are concerned that those costs might not be recoverable at all, and the phase-in plan might be nothing more than a means of delaying recognition of the fact that rates based on full cost of service cannot be charged to and collected from customers.

61. Board members were also concerned about changes that have occurred in the underlying environment of the electric utility industry. Cogeneration appears to be growing, some wholesale customers have changed suppliers, and the significant amounts of unused capacity presently in existence indicate that considerable competition, at least at the wholesale level, is possible. Also, some local regulators have not been inclined to support local franchise rights when the possibility of electric utility customers relocating is present. These uncertainties in the electric utility industry reinforced the Board's view that extraordinary solutions to temporary problems should themselves be temporary and that the 10-year criterion was appropriate.

62. Many respondents to the Exposure Draft urged the Board, if it concluded that the 10-year criterion was necessary, to permit partial application of that criterion. Under that approach, a utility with a phase-in plan that met all of the other criteria but extended beyond 10 years would capitalize the portion of the deferrals under the plan that would be recoverable under the plan within 10 years.

63. The Board considered and rejected partial application of and several alternatives to the 10-year criterion. Alternatives included other qualitative criteria and other quantitative criteria that specified different deferral periods and different methods and periods for recoveries. The Board concluded that it was important to specify a time period in which *all* deferred amounts must be recovered rather than a time period in which only *some* deferred amounts must be recovered. The Board concluded that the 10-year criterion, when considered with the other criteria of paragraph 5, was the maximum acceptable time that met the objective of a set of criteria that is sufficiently strin-

gent that the credibility of financial reporting under Statement 71 would not be compromised. Because the Board views those criteria as an interrelated set, it believes that it should not permit partial application for a phase-in plan that fails to meet one of those criteria.

64. Letters received before the Exposure Draft was issued and comments received on the Exposure Draft recommended that the regulator's selection of a specific allowable cost for deferral should not be important to accountants because any allowable cost can be selected with equal economic effect. The Board agrees that the regulator does have considerable discretion in identifying costs to be deferred under some phase-in plans because those plans merely defer a predetermined amount of allowable costs for a predetermined period of time. Since the Board decided to permit any allowable cost that is deferred for rate-making purposes under a qualifying phase-in plan to be capitalized for financial reporting, this issue became moot.

Limitation on Use of Accounting for Phase-in Plans

65. Some Board members agreed to permit the capitalization of allowable costs for plans meeting the specified criteria even though they believe that deferral of costs in those circumstances is not consistent with the premises that underlie the accounting provisions of Statement 71. Some viewed the regulators' decisions to approve phase-in plans as being driven more by market factors or competition than by the cost of the current services provided to customers. The Board concluded, however, that capitalization for financial reporting of amounts deferred pursuant to certain phase-in plans should be permitted because of the combination of circumstances experienced by electric utilities in recent years as set forth in paragraph 49. The Board views those circumstances as unusual and agreed to the accounting specified in this Statement as a means of addressing those unusual circumstances. On the other hand, the Board believes that the provisions of this Statement can be viewed as a departure from the premises of Statement 71. Accordingly, the Board decided to limit application of this Statement to phase-in plans adopted in connection with plants on which there was significant physical construction before January 1, 1988. The Board concluded that this limitation on the use of phase-in plans is appropriate because the provisions of this Statement are intended to apply in specific, known circumstances. One cannot predict the extent of future competition and deregulation in the electric utility industry or in other utility industries.

Distinction between Phase-in Plans and Disallowances

66. Some existing phase-in plans have deferred allowable costs for recovery in future periods for rate-making purposes and have not provided return on the investment in those deferred costs during the deferral period. The Board considered that type of phase-in plan and concluded that it is, in substance, partially a deferral and partially a disallowance. The environment of individual cost-of-service regulation provides an enterprise an opportunity to earn a fair return on capital invested for the benefit of the enterprise's customers. If no return is provided, the regulator has indirectly disallowed part of the cost of the related plant and the accounting should reflect that disallowance.

Allowance for Earnings on Shareholders' Investment Capitalized for Rate-making Purposes

67. An AICPA Issues Paper, *Application of Concepts in FASB Statement of Financial Accounting Standards No. 71 to Emerging Issues in the Public Utility Industry,* received by the Board in November 1984, recommended that the Board amend paragraph 9 of Statement 71 to require capitalization of any allowable cost when the criteria of that paragraph are met. Many respondents to the Exposure Draft made the same recommendation. Paragraph 9 requires capitalization only of "an incurred cost that would otherwise be charged to expense." Thus, paragraph 9 does not permit capitalization of an allowance for earnings on shareholders' investment—an allowable cost but not an incurred cost that would otherwise be charged to expense. An allowance for earnings on shareholders' investment provided by a regulator is an imputed cost. Capitalization of that cost would increase currently reported income, a result which some Board members believe is inappropriate. The Board believes that income related to an allowance for earnings on shareholders' investment generally should result from revenue realization, not from capitalization.

68. In the Exposure Draft, the Board proposed to require capitalization of the cost of equity funds (an allowance for earnings on shareholders' investment) in one other limited situation—when that allowance is deferred by the regulator in connection with a short-term cost deferral and recovery is expected either through an automatic rate adjustment clause or in the rates provided in the next rate case. Even though the situation was defined carefully, comments received about that provision of

the Exposure Draft indicated that any such requirement would be interpreted broadly. For example, some respondents interpreted the provision in question as contemplating a situation in which the regulator had ordered capitalization of the net cost of operating a newly completed plant during the period from the date of completion of the plant to the date of a later rate order placing the plant into rates even though recovery, if any, will be provided over the life of the newly completed plant rather than through rates provided in the next rate case.

69. After considering comments received, the Board agreed that recognition of a deferred allowance for earnings on shareholders' investment as income in other situations that were specifically mentioned in comment letters was not warranted. The Board decided that it was more appropriate to restrict capitalization, for financial reporting, of an allowance for earnings on shareholders' investment to construction and qualifying phase-in plans than to attempt to define limited other areas for which it would be permitted. That decision reflects both the Board's reluctance to permit premature recognition of income and the practical difficulties of defining situations that would warrant such capitalization. Accordingly, the Board decided not to amend Statement 71 to permit capitalization of an allowance for earnings on shareholders' investment for financial reporting in instances other than during construction or as part of a phase-in plan.

Effective Date and Transition

70. The Board considered whether this Statement should be applied only to phase-in plans ordered after the effective date or to all phase-in plans. Applying this Statement only to phase-in plans ordered after the effective date would diminish both the comparability of the resulting financial statements among enterprises and the year-to-year consistency of financial results of an enterprise that had phase-in plans ordered both before and after the effective date. Phase-in plans extend over a number of years. Applying the Statement only to phase-in plans ordered after the effective date would also permit financial-reporting recognition of phase-in plans that the Board believes could undermine the credibility of financial reporting under Statement 71. Accordingly, the Board decided that this Statement should be applied to all phase-in plans, regardless of whether they were ordered before or after the effective date.

71. In the Exposure Draft, the Board asked whether regulators would be likely to modify existing plans in order to meet the criteria of the final Statement. Comment letters received in response to the Exposure Draft indicated that such changes may well occur. Some respondents noted that their existing phase-in plans call for automatic reconsideration in the event that they do not meet the criteria of this Statement. In view of that response, this Statement provides special transition relief for certain existing phase-in plans. The Board decided that if the regulated enterprise has requested that its regulator amend the phase-in plan in order to meet the criteria of this Statement or intends to do so as soon as practicable and it is reasonably possible that the regulator will change the terms of the plan so that it will meet the criteria of this Statement, this Statement generally would not be applied to that plan until an order is received from the regulator, either revising or refusing to revise the plan. The Board also decided that the criteria of paragraph 5 should be modified for plans that are revised to meet the criteria of this Statement. For those plans, the 10-year limitation and the prohibition against increasing percentage rate increases would be measured from the date of the revision.

72. The Board also considered whether the provision in this Statement, that an allowance for earnings on shareholders' investment should not be capitalized for financial reporting other than during construction or as part of a phase-in plan, should be applied only to amounts accrued for rate-making purposes after the effective date or also to amounts previously capitalized for financial reporting. The Board concluded that although capitalization in circumstances other than construction and phase-in plans can result in questionable income recognition, retroactive restatement would be burdensome and would not be warranted in view of the relatively limited amounts or time periods involved in past practices. Also, the practice is not one that would be likely to undermine the credibility of financial reporting under Statement 71. Accordingly, the Board decided that this Statement should be applied to allowances for earnings on shareholders' investment deferred for rate-making purposes after initial application of the Statement. Retroactive application is not permitted for that item.

Appendix C

BACKGROUND INFORMATION

73. Statement 71 was issued in December 1982, effective for financial statements for fiscal years beginning after December 15, 1983. In early 1984, several different circumstances caused the Board to question whether the application of Statement 71 in practice was what the Board had intended.

74. Subsequent to issuing Statement 71, the Board became aware of several phase-in plans that involved capitalization of an allowance for earnings on shareholders' investment in an operating plant. The Board considered issuing an Interpretation or permitting issuance of a Technical Bulletin to point out that capitalization of such an allowance was not permitted by Statement 71. However, after discussing the nature of phase-in plans and the reasons for their adoption with an affected company and its auditor, the Board decided to explore the use of phase-in plans in more depth before addressing the accounting for those plans.

75. During 1984, rate problems related to new nuclear electric generating plants of several utilities were widely discussed in the financial press. Comments credited to executives of those utilities indicated considerable question whether the utilities could bill rates based on the cost of those plants to their customers without losing a major part of their customer base. Some articles indicated that phase-in plans were likely for certain of those utilities, but they raised significant questions about the assurance of recovery of costs that would be deferred.

76. As a result of Board member concerns, the Board asked the staff to investigate whether guidance about the application of Statement 71 was needed in practice. The staff met several times with committees of the Edison Electric Institute (EEI), the National Association of Regulatory Utility Commissioners, and the Public Utilities Subcommittee of the American Institute of Certified Public Accountants (the AICPA Subcommittee). The Board also met with representatives of those groups and the Federal Energy Regulatory Commission.

77. In November 1984, the Board received an AICPA Issues Paper on emerging issues in the public utility industry. That paper listed 17 specific issues related to current problems in the electric utility industry identified by the AICPA Subcommittee. The Board also received a comment letter from the EEI on the issues raised in the AICPA Issues Paper.

78. The Board issued an Exposure Draft on accounting for phase-in plans, abandonments, and disallowances in December 1985. More than 1,400 organizations and individuals responded to that Exposure Draft.

79. In June 1986, the Board held a public hearing on the proposals in the Exposure Draft. Sixty-six individuals and firms presented their views at the four-day public hearing.

80. After considering comments received in comment letters and at the public hearing, the Board concluded that additional consideration was necessary to resolve the accounting issues related to phase-in plans. In December 1986, the Board issued Statement 90 to address accounting for plant abandonments and disallowances of plant costs. Subsequently, the Board continued its deliberations on accounting for phase-in plans.

81. In March 1987, the Board met in an open meeting with representatives of the EEI and four public accounting firms that audit large numbers of electric utilities. Subsequent to that meeting, the Board decided to issue this Statement to address accounting for phase-in plans and capitalization of an allowance for earnings on shareholders' investment other than during construction or as part of a phase-in plan.

Statement of Financial Accounting Standards No. 93
Recognition of Depreciation by Not-for-Profit
Organizations

STATUS

Issued: August 1987

Effective Date: For fiscal years beginning after May 15, 1988

Affects: No other pronouncements

Affected by: Paragraph 7 amended by FAS 99

SUMMARY

This Statement requires all not-for-profit organizations to recognize the cost of using up long-lived tangible assets—depreciation—in general-purpose external financial statements. However, depreciation need not be recognized for certain works of art and certain historical treasures. The Statement also extends to not-for-profit organizations the requirements of APB Opinion No. 12, *Omnibus Opinion—1967,* to disclose information about depreciable assets and depreciation.

This Statement does not cover matters of financial statement display, recognition of assets, or measurement, such as how to measure the amount of depreciation to be recognized for a particular period.

This Statement is effective for financial statements issued for fiscal years beginning after May 15, 1988, with earlier application encouraged.

Statement of Financial Accounting Standards No. 93

Recognition of Depreciation by Not-for-Profit Organizations

CONTENTS

INTRODUCTION AND SCOPE

1. Generally accepted accounting principles for business enterprises have long required the recognition of depreciation expense in general-purpose external financial statements. Several not-for-profit organizations,[1] for example, health and welfare organizations, hospitals, private foundations, and trade associations, also have generally recognized depreciation expense. However, some not-for-profit organizations, for example, colleges, universities, and religious institutions, often have not recognized depreciation expense.

2. This Statement establishes standards of financial accounting and reporting that require all not-for-profit organizations to recognize the cost of using up long-lived tangible assets—depreciation—in general-purpose external financial statements. It also extends to those organizations the requirements of paragraph 5 of APB Opinion No. 12, *Omnibus Opinion—1967,* to disclose information about depreciable assets and depreciation.

3. FASB Statement No. 32, *Specialized Accounting and Reporting Principles and Practices in AICPA Statements of Position and Guides on Accounting and Auditing Matters,* designated the specialized accounting and reporting principles and practices contained in the AICPA Guides and SOPs listed in Appendix A as preferable accounting principles for purposes of justifying a change

in accounting principle under APB Opinion No. 20, *Accounting Changes.* This Statement considers provisions in two of the documents listed in that appendix:

a. Chapter 2, page 10, of AICPA Industry Audit Guide, *Audits of Colleges and Universities,* permits but does not require depreciation of certain assets.
b. Paragraph 108 of AICPA Statement of Position 78-10, *Accounting Principles and Reporting Practices for Certain Nonprofit Organizations,* exempts certain long-lived tangible assets from depreciation.

Since this Statement requires recognizing depreciation expense, those provisions are no longer acceptable accounting principles and cease to be specialized accounting principles under Statement 32.

4. This Statement does not cover matters of financial statement display, recognition of assets, or measurement, such as how to measure the amount of depreciation to be recognized for a particular period.

STANDARDS OF FINANCIAL ACCOUNTING AND REPORTING

Recognition and Disclosure

5. Not-for-profit organizations shall recognize the cost of using up the future economic benefits or

---

[1]The term *not-for-profit organizations* in this Statement encompasses all entities described by FASB Concepts Statement No. 4, *Objectives of Financial Reporting by Nonbusiness Organizations,* as possessing characteristics that distinguish them from business enterprises. Concepts Statement 4, paragraph 6, lists as the distinguishing characteristics of not-for-profit organizations (a) contributions of significant amounts of resources from resource providers who do not expect commensurate or proportionate pecuniary return, (b) operating purposes other than to provide goods or services at a profit, and (c) absence of ownership interests like those of business enterprises. Not-for-profit organizations have those characteristics in varying degrees. The term not-for-profit organizations encompasses the kinds of organizations covered by the AICPA specialized industry pronouncements: *Hospital Audit Guide* (1972), *Audits of Colleges and Universities* (1973), *Audits of Voluntary Health and Welfare Organizations* (1974), and Statement of Position 78-10, *Accounting Principles and Reporting Practices for Certain Nonprofit Organizations* (1978).

service potentials of their long-lived tangible assets—depreciation—and shall disclose the following:

a. Depreciation expense for the period
b. Balances of major classes of depreciable assets, by nature or function, at the balance sheet date
c. Accumulated depreciation, either by major classes of depreciable assets or in total, at the balance sheet date
d. A general description of the method or methods used in computing depreciation for major classes of depreciable assets.

6. Consistent with the accepted practice for land used as a building site, depreciation need not be recognized on individual works of art or historical treasures whose economic benefit or service potential is used up so slowly that their estimated useful lives are extraordinarily long. A work of art or historical treasure shall be deemed to have that characteristic only if verifiable[2] evidence exists demonstrating that (a) the asset individually has cultural, aesthetic, or historical value that is worth preserving perpetually and (b) the holder has the technological and financial ability to protect and preserve essentially undiminished the service potential of the asset and is doing that.

Effective Date and Transition

7. This Statement shall be effective for financial statements issued for fiscal years beginning after May 15, 1988, with earlier application encouraged. Accounting changes adopted to conform to the provisions of this Statement shall be applied retroactively by restating the financial statements of any prior years presented. This Statement shall be applied by adjusting the opening net asset balance for the earliest year presented, or if no prior years are presented, for the year this Statement is first applied. In the period that this Statement is first applied, the financial statements shall disclose the nature of any restatement and its effect on the change in net assets for each period presented.

8. Retroactive application of the provisions of this Statement requires estimates of useful lives and salvage values of all recognized long-lived tangible assets. Information that has become available after acquisition of the assets may be considered in making those estimates. For example, an estimate of an asset's useful life may be the sum of the number of years from acquisition to the date this Statement is adopted plus the estimated remaining years of life based on the current condition and planned use of the asset.

> **The provisions of this Statement need not be applied to immaterial items.**

This Statement was adopted by the unanimous vote of the seven members of the Financial Accounting Standards Board:

Dennis R. Beresford,	Raymond C. Lauver	Robert J. Swieringa
Chairman	David Mosso	Arthur R. Wyatt
Victor H. Brown	C. Arthur Northrop	

---

[2]*Verifiability* means that several measurers or observers are likely to obtain essentially the same measure or conclude that a description of an item faithfully represents what it purports to represent (FASB Concepts Statement No. 2, *Qualitative Characteristics of Accounting Information*, pars. 81-89).

Appendix A

BACKGROUND INFORMATION

9. In March 1986, the Board added a project to its agenda to establish standards of accounting for certain pervasive transactions of not-for-profit organizations for which inconsistencies exist in practice and in the authoritative specialized industry literature. The project includes accounting for depreciation and accounting for contributions. This Statement is about accounting for depreciation. Accounting for contributions will be considered separately at a later date.

10. Although depreciation expense has long been part of the financial statements of business enterprises, most not-for-profit organizations did not recognize depreciation in their accounting and financial reporting until relatively recently. Most not-for-profit organizations had been using a cash or "modified cash" (cash transactions plus accruals of some assets and liabilities) basis of accounting. A change from a cash or "modified cash" basis to accrual accounting occurred for most not-for-profit organizations in the 1960s. The use of accrual accounting—that is, recognizing transactions and other events and circumstances when they affect the entity rather than only when cash is received or paid—brought with it recognition of depreciation by many not-for-profit organizations. Some not-for-profit organizations, however, have not recognized depreciation expense. They use what some have called a "modified accrual" basis of accounting.

11. The four principal AICPA documents that focus on the specialized principles and practices of not-for-profit organizations are:

a. *Hospital Audit Guide,* 1972
b. *Audits of Colleges and Universities,* 1973
c. *Audits of Voluntary Health and Welfare Organizations,* 1974
d. Statement of Position 78-10, *Accounting Principles and Reporting Practices for Certain Nonprofit Organizations,* 1978.

In September 1979, Statement 32 designated the specialized accounting and reporting principles in those documents (among others) as preferable for purposes of applying Opinion 20.

12. The Audit Guides for hospitals and voluntary health and welfare organizations require depreciation of long-lived tangible assets. The Audit Guide for colleges and universities permits, but does not require, recognition of depreciation of the assets comprising the institutional plant; however, it requires recognition of depreciation of long-lived tangible assets that are held for investment of endowment. SOP 78-10 also requires depreciation of long-lived tangible assets (with exemptions for landmarks, monuments, cathedrals, historical treasures, and structures used primarily as houses of worship) but establishes no effective date for adoption of its recommendations. Many organizations have voluntarily adopted the recommendation of SOP 78-10 to recognize depreciation; other organizations have not.

13. The Board agreed in 1979, to extract the specialized accounting and reporting principles and practices in the AICPA's Guides and SOPs, including those for not-for-profit organizations, and to issue them as FASB Statements after appropriate due process. Before considering specific accounting standards for not-for-profit organizations, however, the Board chose to undertake a conceptual study of accounting and reporting for these organizations.

14. The Board's work on the concepts of financial accounting and reporting by not-for-profit organizations formally began in August 1977. An FASB Research Report, *Financial Accounting in Nonbusiness Organizations,* by Professor Robert N. Anthony, was published in May 1978. A related Discussion Memorandum and an Exposure Draft led to FASB Concepts Statement No. 4, *Objectives of Financial Reporting by Nonbusiness Organizations,* in December 1980. A subsequent project expanded FASB Concepts Statement No. 3, *Elements of Financial Statements of Business Enterprises,* to encompass not-for-profit organizations and reaffirmed the Board's tentative conclusion that the qualities of useful accounting information set forth in FASB Concepts Statement No. 2, *Qualitative Characteristics of Accounting Information* (May 1980), apply to not-for-profit organizations as well as to business enterprises. As part of that project, the Board issued an Exposure Draft, *Proposed Amendments to FASB Concepts Statements 2 and 3 to Apply Them to Nonbusiness Organizations,* in July 1983, held public hearings in November 1983, issued a revised Exposure Draft, *Elements of Financial Statements,* in September 1985, and issued Concepts Statement No. 6, *Elements of Financial Statements,* in December 1985. The concepts Statements provide a basis for considering the specialized accounting principles for not-for-profit organizations. That work is now being followed by Board projects to establish standards of accounting for depreciation of long-lived assets and for contributions.

15. An FASB Exposure Draft, *Recognition of Depreciation by Not-for-Profit Organizations,* was issued on December 23, 1986. The Board received 193 letters of comment in response to the Exposure Draft.

Appendix B

BASIS FOR CONCLUSIONS

CONTENTS

Appendix B

BASIS FOR CONCLUSIONS

Introduction

16. This appendix summarizes considerations that were deemed significant by members of the Board in reaching the conclusions in this Statement. It includes reasons for accepting certain views and rejecting others. Individual Board members gave greater weight to some factors than to others. The Board concluded that it could reach an informed decision without a public hearing.

Conclusions Underlying Recognition of Depreciation

Basic Concepts

17. Concepts Statements 2, 4, and 6 established the fundamental concepts that underlie the Board's conclusion that all not-for-profit organizations should recognize depreciation in general-purpose financial statements.

18. The conclusions in this Statement result from the Board's conclusions in Concepts Statement 4

that information about the amounts and kinds of inflows and outflows of resources during a period and the relations between them and information about service efforts and (to the extent possible) service accomplishments is useful to resource providers in assessing an organization's performance during a period. That information also is useful in assessing how an organization's managers have discharged their stewardship responsibilities, not only for the custody and safekeeping of the organization's resources, but also for their efficient and effective use.[3]

19. A not-for-profit organization produces and distributes goods and services by using resources. It obtains some of the resources it uses by paying cash, some by incurring liabilities, and some by contribution. Some of its resources (assets) are used up in providing services at the time they are received, others are used up at a later date, and still others are used up gradually over time (Concepts Statement 6, paragraphs 9-19).

20. Using up assets in providing services (or otherwise) has a cost whether those assets have been acquired in prior periods or in the current period and whether acquired by paying cash, incurring liabilities, or by contribution. In defining assets, para-

---

[3]Concepts Statement 4, pars. 9, 38, 41, and 47-53, and Concepts Statement 6, par. 19.

The Board's emphasis is on usefulness of financial reporting information to present and potential resource providers and others in making rational decisions about allocating resources to not-for-profit organizations. Those who make decisions about allocating resources to not-for-profit organizations include both (a) lenders, suppliers, employees, and the like who expect repayment or other direct pecuniary compensation from an entity and have essentially the same interest in and make essentially the same kinds of decisions about the entity whether it is a not-for-profit organization or a business enterprise and (b) members, contributors, donors, and the like who provide resources to not-for-profit organizations for reasons other than expectations of direct and proportionate pecuniary compensation (Concepts Statement 4, pars. 9, 15-19, and 29, and Concepts Statement 6, par. 9).

graph 26 of Concepts Statement 6 discusses the cost of acquiring assets and the cost of using up assets:

> . . . Assets may be acquired at a cost[19] and they may be tangible, exchangeable, or legally enforceable. However, those features are not essential characteristics of assets. Their absence, by itself, is not sufficient to preclude an item's qualifying as an asset. That is, assets may be acquired without cost. . . .

---

[19]*Cost* is the sacrifice incurred in economic activities—that which is given up or forgone to consume, to save, to exchange, to produce, and so forth. For example, the value of cash or other resources given up (or the present value of an obligation incurred) in exchange for a resource measures the cost of the resources acquired. Similarly, the expiration of future benefits caused by using up a resource in production is the cost of using it.

Using up assets acquired involves a cost to the organization because the economic benefits (or service potential) used up are no longer available to the organization. That is as true for assets acquired without cost as it is for assets acquired at a cost.

21. Accrual accounting is presently considered superior to the cash basis and the so-called "modified cash" and "modified accrual" bases because, among other things, those other bases do not faithfully represent costs incurred during a period.[4] Reporting on a cash basis omits all costs not incurred in cash during the period from cost of services provided and includes cash paid for resources used in other periods. Reporting on a "modified" basis includes some costs from incurring liabilities but excludes some costs of using up assets acquired in earlier periods.

22. Reliable information about the cost of assets used by a not-for-profit organization to provide services is useful to resource providers and others in assessing how the organization carried out its services. Resource providers are interested in that information because the services are the end for which the resources are provided and their assessment of whether an organization is efficient and effective in providing services is often significant in their decisions to provide resources to an organization.

Relevance of Information about the Maintenance of Net Assets

23. Some respondents to the December 1986 Exposure Draft argued that depreciation often is not relevant for not-for-profit organizations because those organizations have no need to measure income and thus no need to "match" expenses with related revenues. The Board believes that is not the issue. In Concepts Statement 6, the Board describes depreciation as a cost of using up assets, not as a technique for "matching" expenses with revenues. In discussing accrual accounting and related concepts, the concepts Statement distinguishes matching of costs and revenues from allocating expenses to periods.

> Matching of costs and revenues is simultaneous or combined recognition of the revenues and expenses that result directly and jointly from the same transactions or other events. In most entities, some transactions or events result simultaneously in both a revenue and one or more expenses. The revenue and expense(s) are directly related to each other and require recognition at the same time. In present practice, for example, a sale of product or merchandise involves both revenue (sales revenue) for receipt of cash or a receivable and expense (cost of goods sold) for sacrifice of the product or merchandise sold to customers. Other examples of expenses that may result from the same transaction and be directly related to sales revenues are transportation to customers, sales commissions, and perhaps certain other selling costs.
>
> Many expenses, however, are not related directly to particular revenues but can be related to a period on the basis of transactions or events occurring in that period or by allocation. Recognition of those expenses is largely independent of recognition of particular revenues, but they are deducted from particular revenues by being recognized in the same period.
>
> . . . Many assets yield their benefits to an entity over several periods, for example, prepaid insurance, buildings, and various kinds of equipment. Expenses resulting from their use are normally allocated to the periods of their estimated useful lives (the periods over which they are expected to provide benefits) by a "systematic and rational" allocation procedure, for example, by recognizing depreciation or other amortization. Although the purpose of expense allocation is the same as that of other expense recognition—to reflect the using up of assets as a result of transactions or other events or circumstances affecting an entity—allocation is applied if causal relations are generally, but not specifically, identified. For example, wear and tear

---

[4]Representational faithfulness is essential to reliable accounting information (Concepts Statement 2, pars. 58-97).

from use is known to be a major cause of the expense called depreciation, but the amount of depreciation caused by wear and tear in a period normally cannot be measured. Those expenses are not related directly to either specific revenues or particular periods. Usually no traceable relationship exists, and they are recognized by allocating costs to periods in which assets are expected to be used and are related only indirectly to the revenues that are recognized in the same period. [Paragraphs 146, 147, and 149, footnote references omitted.]

24. Concepts Statement 6 also indicates why an organization's using up of its assets is significant and why information about it is needed.

Although not-for-profit organizations do not have ownership interests or profit in the same sense as business enterprises, they nonetheless need a concept of capital maintenance or its equivalent to reflect "the relation between inflows and outflows of resources during a period." The activities of an organization during a period may draw upon resources received in past periods or may add resources that can be used in future periods.

Unless a not-for-profit organization maintains its net assets, its ability to continue to provide services dwindles; either future resource providers must make up the deficiency or services to future beneficiaries will decline. For example, use of an asset such as a building to provide goods or services to beneficiaries consumes part of the future economic benefits or service potential constituting the asset, and that decrease in future economic benefits is one of the costs (expenses) of using the asset for that purpose. The organization's net assets decrease as it uses up an asset unless its revenues and gains at least equal its expenses and losses, including the cost of consuming part of the asset during the period (depreciation). Even if that organization plans to replace the asset through future contributions from donors, and probably will be able to do so, it has not maintained its net assets during the current period. [Paragraphs 103 and 104, footnote references omitted.]

25. Those concepts reflect that a fair assessment of the costs of efforts expended is necessary to evaluate the results of economic activity that not-for-profit organizations undertake. Depreciation is an essential part of measuring the costs of services provided during a period. Omitting depreciation produces results that do not reflect all costs of services provided. That omission can result in a misunderstanding of the economics of providing services and may contribute to inefficiencies. The Board concluded that the potential cost of omission is too great and that depreciation should be recognized for all assets in use.

Depreciation of Contributed Assets

26. Some respondents to the Exposure Draft said that depreciation should not be an expense of a not-for-profit organization to the extent that the related assets were, and their replacements are expected to be, funded by contributions or special assessments. Those respondents do not consider assets obtained by contribution or special assessment to have a cost to be charged to future periods in the same sense as assets obtained by exchanging other assets or incurring liabilities.

27. The Board concluded that whether an organization's use of an asset results in an expense does not depend on how the asset was acquired (paragraph 20) and whether and how it will be replaced. APB Opinion No. 29, *Accounting for Nonmonetary Transactions,* and relevant AICPA industry pronouncements require donated assets to be recognized at their fair values at the date of receipt. Current practice also generally recognizes the cost of using up assets in the period of their use (the exception has been certain not-for-profit organizations).

28. Financial statements should report the effects of transactions and other events that have occurred and should be comparable[5] between entities. Therefore, accounting standards should result in accounting for similar transactions and circumstances similarly and for different transactions and circumstances differently. Long-lived tangible assets provide benefits to both business enterprises and not-for-profit organizations over several periods. Whether assets were acquired by purchase or by gift, using them up over several periods is a series of events—sacrifices of service potential—that result in costs of providing services in those periods. Failure to recognize depreciation for all or some long-lived tangible assets used denies the existence of those events and those costs. The Board concluded that the credibility and usefulness of general-purpose financial statements will be enhanced and the comparability of financial results between entities will be improved if those events and costs are recognized when they occur.

---

[5]Concepts Statement 2, pars. 111-22.

Expenses and Expenditures

29. Some respondents suggested that the Board allow colleges and universities to continue their practice of reporting current expenditures to maintain capital assets as an alternative to recognizing depreciation. Those respondents and others have argued that information about expenditures for long-lived tangible assets is more relevant to users of financial statements of not-for-profit organizations than information about the cost of using those assets for a period. The Board concluded that both of those kinds of information are relevant to users of financial statements of all not-for-profit organizations, including colleges and universities.

30. Information about the cost of using assets for a period determined by accrual accounting concepts is essential to assessing an entity's performance. Information about an organization's expenditures is needed in addition to, not in place of, information about expenses and other changes in net assets:

> Financial reporting should provide information about the performance of an organization during a period. [Concepts Statement 4, paragraph 47]
> Financial reporting should provide information about how an organization obtains and spends cash or other liquid resources, about its borrowing and repayment of borrowing, and about other factors that may affect its liquidity. [Concepts Statement 4, paragraph 54]

Exceptions Permitted by SOP 78-10

31. The Board considered and rejected in the December 1986 Exposure Draft the assertions in paragraph 108 of SOP 78-10 that landmarks, monuments, cathedrals, and historical treasures are not exhaustible and that neither those assets nor structures used primarily as houses of worship need be depreciated. Some respondents suggested that the Board continue to allow those exemptions. Others suggested that works of art and other "collections" commonly held by museums, art galleries, libraries, and other not-for-profit organizations also should be exempt from recognizing depreciation.

32. In rejecting assertions that specified groups of assets are not exhaustible and need not be depreciated, the Board observed that simply designating a structure or other object as, for example, a landmark or work of art, or using it for a particular purpose, for example, as a house of worship, does not preclude its service potential from being used up over time. That observation also applies to "collections" as the term is used in paragraphs 113-15 of SOP 78-10 because it is a broad and imprecise term that covers a variety of assets that differ from each other in how and at what rate their economic benefits or service potentials are used up.

33. The Board reaffirmed its conclusion that each organization needs to consider the characteristics of individual assets in making the estimates necessary to determine the amount of depreciation to be recognized. Measuring the extent to which the future economic benefits or service potential of a particular asset is used up during a period or in a particular use requires estimates of salvage values and useful lives and requires the exercise of judgment considering all the facts and circumstances. That estimation and evaluation process is not unique to particular assets or particular kinds of entities.

34. The asset broadly called land illustrates the need to consider the characteristics of individual assets in reporting depreciation. The process of using up the future economic benefit or service potential of land often takes place over a period so long that its occurrence is imperceptible—land used as a building site is perhaps the most common example—and whether depreciation is recognized is of no practical consequence. In contrast, however, that process also sometimes occurs much more rapidly—land used as a site for toxic waste, as a source of gravel or ore, or for farming under conditions in which fertility dissipates relatively quickly and cannot be restored economically are examples—and whether depreciation is recognized affects the representational faithfulness of financial statements.

35. The future economic benefits or service potentials of individual items comprising "collections" and of buildings and other structures—including those designated as landmarks, monuments, cathedrals, or historical treasures—are used up not only by wear and tear in intended uses but also by the continuous destructive effects of pollutants, vibrations, and so forth. The cultural, aesthetic, or historical values of those assets can be preserved, if at all, only by periodic major efforts to protect, clean, and restore them, usually at significant cost. Thus, the Board concluded that depreciation of those assets needs to be recognized.

36. The only assets described in the preceding paragraph for which depreciation need not be recognized are rare works of art and historical treasures

having a characteristic akin to land used as a building site—their economic benefit or service potential is used up so slowly that the amount related to a particular accounting period is of no consequence. Recognized cultural, aesthetic, or historical value and, generally, already long existence have established each of those assets as a member of a group of rare works with that characteristic. Most of them are acquired by purchase, gift, or discovery with that characteristic already having been demonstrated, and the holder or acquirer usually takes steps to protect and preserve it, for example, by keeping a work of art in a protective environment and limiting its use solely to display. While that characteristic is not limited to assets with an already long existence, an asset that has come into existence relatively recently cannot be assumed to have it in the absence of the verifiable evidence described in paragraph 6. For example, to put a painting in a protective environment is not by itself evidence of cultural, aesthetic, or historical value that is worth preserving perpetually.

37. Depreciation should be recognized, of course, on any capitalized costs of major preservation or restoration devices or efforts, which provide future economic benefits or service potentials until the next expected preservation or restoration, regardless of whether depreciation is recognized on the asset being protected or restored.

Other Considerations of Recognition, Measurement, and Display

Recognition of Assets

38. Some respondents questioned whether the Board implicitly intended to consider recognition of assets and, more specifically, to amend paragraph 113 of SOP 78-10. Paragraph 113 says "the [AICPA's Accounting Standards] division has concluded that it is often impracticable to determine a value for . . . collections [owned by museums, art galleries, botanical gardens, libraries, and similar entities] and accordingly has concluded that they need not be capitalized. If records and values do exist for the collections, the division encourages capitalization, at cost, if purchased, and at a fair value, if acquired by donation." Other respondents suggested that the Board should expand the scope of this Statement to require explicitly the recognition of assets. Still others suggested that the Board clarify that the Statement does not cover recognition of assets.

39. The Board reaffirmed its conclusion that this Statement need not cover recognition of assets because the four relevant AICPA pronouncements (paragraph 11) already require tangible assets (except "collections") to be recognized at cost if purchased or at fair value at date of contribution if contributed. The Board has decided to consider recognition of "collections," both contributed and purchased, as part of its project on accounting for contributions.

Relevant Attribute

40. Some respondents suggested that historical cost is not the most relevant attribute for measuring a not-for-profit organization's cost of using up long-lived assets. Ascertaining the appropriate attribute involves measurement questions that are not unique to not-for-profit organizations. Similar comments have been made by other respondents to various Board projects. The Board decided that the question of the appropriate attribute for measuring the cost of using up long-lived assets is a separate matter that, if considered, should be considered as part of a larger project applicable to all organizations.

Disclosure and Financial Statement Display

41. The depreciation method(s) used by an organization may significantly affect the information conveyed by its financial statements, including its reported financial position and results of operations. Not-for-profit organizations generally have disclosed, as required by APB Opinion No. 22, *Disclosure of Accounting Policies,* whether or not they recognize depreciation. Those recognizing depreciation generally have disclosed the information required of business enterprises by paragraph 5 of Opinion 12. The Board concluded that information about depreciable assets and depreciation policies and methods is useful to users of financial statements of not-for-profit organizations. Therefore, this Statement explicitly extends the requirements of Opinion 12 to not-for-profit organizations.

42. Some respondents to the Exposure Draft suggested that to increase comparability between financial statements the Board should not issue this Statement without providing additional guidance about how depreciation expense should be reported by organizations using fund accounting and reporting techniques. Others suggested the Board delay this Statement until an AICPA task force that is studying issues of financial statement display for not-for-profit organizations completes its study.

43. The Board reaffirmed its conclusion that this Statement need not provide additional guidance about how depreciation expense should be displayed because the three AICPA Audit Guides and

SOP 78-10 already provide it. For example, the Guide for colleges and universities says that depreciation expense related to depreciable assets comprising the physical plant is reported neither in the statement of current funds revenues, expenditures, and other changes nor in the statement of changes in unrestricted current funds balance. Rather, depreciation may be reported in a statement of changes in the balance of the investment-in-plant fund subsection of the plant funds group. Moreover, issues of display being studied by the AICPA task force are separate from issues of recognition of depreciation.

Applicability to Units of State and Local Government

44. Several respondents expressed concern that this Statement might lead to different standards of financial reporting for public and private-sector organizations. Some suggested that the Board clarify that the provisions of this Statement apply to units of government (for example, state universities, community colleges, municipal hospitals, public broadcasting stations, museums, and libraries) that issue financial statements in accordance with the generally accepted accounting principles applicable to their not-for-profit organization counterparts (paragraph 1, footnote 1). Others suggested that the Board explicitly exempt governmental units pending the results of certain projects undertaken by the Governmental Accounting Standards Board.

45. Under the "Agreement Concerning the Structure for a Governmental Accounting Standards Board (GASB)," dated January 16, 1984, "generally accepted accounting principles applicable to separately issued general purpose financial statements of certain entities or activities in the public sector should be guided by standards of the FASB except in circumstances where the GASB has issued a pronouncement applicable to such entities or activities. Those entities and activities include utilities, authorities, hospitals, colleges and univer-sities, and pension plans" (4(g)). Accordingly, because of this Agreement the Board concluded that no action in respect of governmental units is necessary or appropriate.

Effective Date and Transition

46. The Exposure Draft proposed that this Statement be effective for fiscal years beginning after May 15, 1987. Many respondents said that additional time was needed to develop measurement guidelines for various not-for-profit organizations and to gather necessary information. They suggested delaying the effective date of this Statement to allow for an efficient implementation of its provisions. The Board considered those requests and decided to change the effective date of this Statement to fiscal years beginning after May 15, 1988.

47. Some respondents said that the requirement for retroactive application was too burdensome. To minimize the implementation costs, some suggested that assets in use for an exceptionally long time, for which detailed historical cost records are often unavailable, should be exempted from this Statement. Others suggested that the final Statement should permit, but not require, retroactive implementation and restatement of previously issued financial statements or that the Statement be applied prospectively.

48. The Board considered those concerns about the cost of implementation and reaffirmed its conclusion that comparability would be best achieved if this Statement is applied retroactively. The Board understands that to apply this Statement retroactively to all assets may be very difficult if detailed records have not been maintained for assets that have been owned for very long periods of time. However, the Board expects that, in initially implementing the provisions of this Statement, not-for-profit organizations can make reasonable estimates that will be acceptable for the oldest assets, which probably represent the major problem area.

Statement of Financial Accounting Standards No. 94
Consolidation of All Majority-Owned Subsidiaries

an amendment of ARB No. 51, with related amendments of APB Opinion No. 18 and ARB No. 43, Chapter 12

STATUS

Issued: October 1987

Effective Date: For fiscal years ending after December 15, 1988

Affects: Supersedes ARB 43, Chapter 12, paragraphs 8 and 9
Supersedes ARB 51, paragraphs 2, 3, and 19 through 21
Amends APB 18, paragraphs 1, 16, 17, 19, 19(a), and 20(d)
Supersedes APB 18, paragraphs 14 and 20(c) and footnotes 1, 3, and 4
Effectively amends FAS 52, paragraph 26

Affected by: No other pronouncements

Issues Discussed by FASB Emerging Issues Task Force (EITF)

Affects: Resolves EITF Issues No. 84-41 and 85-28

Interpreted by: Paragraph 13 interpreted by EITF Issue No. 90-15

Related Issues: EITF Issues No. 84-23, 84-30, 84-33, 84-40, 85-21, 96-16, 96-20, 97-1, and 97-2 and Topic No. D-14

SUMMARY

This Statement amends ARB No. 51, *Consolidated Financial Statements,* to require consolidation of all majority-owned subsidiaries unless control is temporary or does not rest with the majority owner. This Statement requires consolidation of a majority-owned subsidiary even if it has "nonhomogeneous" operations, a large minority interest, or a foreign location.

This Statement also makes certain related amendments to APB Opinion No. 18, *The Equity Method of Accounting for Investments in Common Stock,* and to ARB No. 43, Chapter 12, "Foreign Operations and Foreign Exchange." Among other changes, those amendments preclude use of parent-company financial statements prepared for issuance to stockholders as the financial statements of the primary reporting entity.

This Statement requires that summarized information about the assets, liabilities, and results of operations (or separate statements) of previously unconsolidated majority-owned subsidiaries continue to be provided after those subsidiaries are consolidated.

This Statement is effective for financial statements for fiscal years ending after December 15, 1988. Restatement of comparative financial statements for earlier years is required.

Statement of Financial Accounting Standards No. 94

Consolidation of All Majority-Owned Subsidiaries

an amendment of ARB No. 51, with related amendments of APB Opinion No. 18 and ARB No. 43, Chapter 12

CONTENTS

INTRODUCTION

1. Accounting Research Bulletin No. 51, *Consolidated Financial Statements,* adopted by the Committee on Accounting Procedure of the AICPA in 1959, concisely describes the purpose of consolidated financial statements in its first paragraph.

> The purpose of consolidated statements is to present, primarily for the benefit of the shareholders and creditors of the parent company, the results of operations and the financial position of a parent company and its subsidiaries essentially as if the group were a single company with one or more branches or divisions. There is a presumption that consolidated statements are more meaningful than separate statements and that they are usually necessary for a fair presentation when one of the companies in the group directly or indirectly has a controlling financial interest in the other companies.

2. Similarly, the first sentence of paragraph 2 describes its general rule of consolidation policy.

> The usual condition for a controlling financial interest is ownership of a majority voting interest, and, therefore, as a general rule ownership by one company, directly or indirectly, of over fifty per cent of the outstanding voting shares of another company is a condition pointing toward consolidation.

3. While ARB 51's general rule is to consolidate all majority-owned subsidiaries, its paragraphs 2 and 3 describe "exceptions to that general rule."

4. Paragraph 2 precludes consolidation of a majority-owned subsidiary under two condi-

tions—"where control is likely to be temporary, or where it does not rest with the majority owners (as, for instance, where the subsidiary is in legal reorganization or in bankruptcy)." It also permits exclusion from consolidation of a subsidiary having a relatively large minority interest and of a foreign subsidiary.[1]

5. The exception in paragraph 3 of ARB 51 has become the basis for excluding from consolidation the greatest number of majority-owned subsidiaries. It has often been called exclusion of "nonhomogeneous" operations because of its wording:

> . . . even though a group of companies is heterogeneous in character, it may be better to make a full consolidation than to present a large number of separate statements. On the other hand, separate statements or combined statements would be preferable for a subsidiary or group of subsidiaries if the presentation of financial information concerning the particular activities of such subsidiaries would be more informative to shareholders and creditors of the parent company than would the inclusion of such subsidiaries in the consolidation. For example, separate statements may be required for a subsidiary which is a bank or an insurance company and may be preferable for a finance company where the parent and the other subsidiaries are engaged in manufacturing operations.

6. Business enterprises have increasingly used "nonhomogeneity" as a basis for excluding from consolidation majority-owned (even wholly owned) subsidiaries considered different in character from the parent and its other affiliates. Subsidiaries most commonly not consolidated on that basis have been finance, insurance, real estate, and leasing subsidiaries of manufacturing and merchandising enterprises.

7. However, certain diversified enterprises consolidate all of their majority-owned subsidiaries despite differences in their operations, and

significant questions about the "nonhomogeneity" exception have arisen. Present practice has been criticized not only because apparently similar enterprises use different consolidation policies but also because excluding some subsidiaries from consolidation results in the omission of significant amounts of assets, liabilities, revenues, and expenses from the consolidated statements of many enterprises. Omissions of large amounts of liabilities, especially those of finance and similar subsidiaries, have led to the criticism that not consolidating those subsidiaries is an important factor in what is often called "off-balance-sheet financing."

8. The "nonhomogeneity" exception has only relatively recently become the most prominent reason for excluding majority-owned subsidiaries from consolidation. When ARB 51 was issued, other restrictive consolidation policies—to consolidate only wholly owned subsidiaries, only subsidiaries owned to a specified degree (such as 66 2/3 percent, 75 percent, or 80 percent), only domestic subsidiaries, only North American subsidiaries, and the like—were more common. Those other restrictive policies have become less widely used while exclusion for "nonhomogeneity" has become more widespread.

Consolidation

9. This Statement eliminates three exceptions to the general rule that majority-owned subsidiaries should be consolidated: the exceptions for "nonhomogeneous" operations, for relatively large minority interests (which apparently is seldom used in practice), and for other restrictive policies. It amends ARB No. 43, Chapter 12, "Foreign Operations and Foreign Exchange," to narrow the exception for a majority-owned foreign subsidiary from one that permits exclusion from consolidation of any or all foreign subsidiaries to one that effectively eliminates distinctions between foreign and domestic subsidiaries.

10. The other exceptions noted in paragraph 4—control that is likely to be temporary and control

---

[1]Paragraph 2 permits omission of majority-owned foreign subsidiaries from consolidation by reference to the broad provisions of ARB No. 43, Chapter 12, "Foreign Operations and Foreign Exchange," paragraphs 8 and 9:

> In view of the uncertain values and availability of the assets and net income of foreign subsidiaries subject to controls and exchange restrictions and the consequent unrealistic statements of income that may result from the translation of many foreign currencies into dollars, careful consideration should be given to the fundamental question of whether it is proper to consolidate the statements of foreign subsidiaries with the statements of United States companies. Whether consolidation of foreign subsidiaries is decided upon or not, adequate disclosure of foreign operations should be made.
> The following are among the possible ways of providing information relating to such foreign subsidiaries:
>
> a. To exclude foreign subsidiaries from consolidation and to furnish (1) statements in which only domestic subsidiaries are consolidated and (2) as to foreign subsidiaries, a summary in suitable form of their assets and liabilities, their income and losses for the year, and the parent company's equity therein. . . .

that does not rest with the majority owner because of, for example, corporate reorganization or bankruptcy—have not been reconsidered in this Statement. They relate to the concept of control and its place in consolidation policy, which are not within the scope of this Statement but are part of a broader FASB project on the reporting entity, including consolidations and the equity method (paragraphs 19 and 20). Similarly, consolidation of subsidiaries controlled by means other than ownership of a majority voting interest—control by significant minority ownership, by contract, lease, or agreement with other stockholders, by court decree, or otherwise—has not been reconsidered in this Statement because that subject also is part of the project on the reporting entity.

Continued Disclosure

11. The FASB project on the reporting entity, including consolidations and the equity method, will consider what disaggregated information should be disclosed with consolidated financial statements. To prevent loss in the meantime of information about unconsolidated subsidiaries now required by APB Opinion No. 18, *The Equity Method of Accounting for Investments in Common Stock,* this Statement requires continued disclosure of that information for subsidiaries that are consolidated as a result of this Statement.

12. The time between issuance of this Statement and one that would require disclosure of specified disaggregated information provides an opportunity for business enterprises to explore ways to provide additional information that is useful to investors, creditors, and others in understanding and assessing the effects of the differing risks and returns of various activities. A number of enterprises have been providing information about consolidated subsidiaries that goes beyond that required by Opinion 18 and FASB Statement No. 14, *Financial Reporting for Segments of a Business Enterprise,* and the Board encourages them to continue with and to strive to improve that disclosure and encourages others to follow their example. That experimentation not only should result in improved disclosure but also will provide the Board and its constituents with experience on which to draw in considering the broad issue of disclosures of disaggregated information.

STANDARDS OF FINANCIAL ACCOUNTING AND REPORTING

Amendments of ARB No. 51, APB Opinion No. 18, and ARB No. 43, Chapter 12

13. Paragraphs 2 and 3 of ARB 51 are amended to read:[2]

2. The usual condition for a controlling financial interest is ownership of a majority voting interest, and, therefore, as a general rule ownership by one company, directly or indirectly, of over fifty percent of the outstanding voting shares of another company is a condition pointing toward consolidation. However, there are exceptions to this general rule. A majority-owned subsidiary shall not be consolidated if control is likely to be temporary or if it does not rest with the majority owner (as, for instance, if the subsidiary is in legal reorganization or in bankruptcy or operates under foreign exchange restrictions, controls, or other governmentally imposed uncertainties so severe that they cast significant doubt on the parent's ability to control the subsidiary).

3. All majority-owned subsidiaries—all companies in which a parent has a controlling financial interest through direct or indirect ownership of a majority voting interest—shall be consolidated except those described in the last sentence of paragraph 2.

14. The heading "Unconsolidated Subsidiaries in Consolidated Statements" and paragraphs 19-21 of ARB 51 are deleted and replaced by the following heading and new paragraph 19:

DISCLOSURE ABOUT FORMERLY UNCONSOLIDATED MAJORITY-OWNED SUBSIDIARIES

19. Information that was disclosed under APB Opinion No. 18, paragraph 20(c), about majority-owned subsidiaries that were unconsolidated in financial statements for fiscal years 1986 or 1987 shall continue to be disclosed for them after they are consolidated pursuant to the provisions of this pronouncement as amended by FASB Statement No. 94. That is,

[2]Details of the changes: Paragraph 2 of ARB 51 is amended to delete the fourth, fifth, and sixth sentences and to delete "For example," to change "should" to "shall," and to add an example in the parentheses in the third sentence. The deleted sentences read: "There may also be situations where the minority interest in the subsidiary is so large, in relation to the equity of the shareholders of the parent in the consolidated net assets, that the presentation of separate financial statements for the two companies would be more meaningful and useful. However, the fact that the subsidiary has a relatively large indebtedness to bondholders or others is not in itself a valid argument for exclusion of the subsidiary from consolidation. (Also, see Chapter 12 of Accounting Research Bulletin No. 43 for the treatment of foreign subsidiaries.)" Paragraph 3 (most of which is quoted in paragraph 5 of this Statement) is entirely deleted and replaced by a new paragraph 3.

1035

summarized information about the assets, liabilities, and results of operations (or separate statements) shall be provided for those subsidiaries, either individually or in groups, as appropriate, in the consolidated financial statements or notes.

15. Opinion 18 is amended to eliminate its requirement to use the equity method to account in consolidated financial statements for unconsolidated majority-owned subsidiaries and to eliminate its provisions applying to "parent-company financial statements prepared for issuance to stockholders as the financial statements of the primary reporting entity," which are precluded by this Statement.[3] The paragraphs primarily affected are 1, 14, 16, and 17 and the footnotes to them; changes in other paragraphs primarily remove "subsidiaries" or "unconsolidated subsidiaries" from expressions such as "subsidiaries, joint ventures, and other investees which qualify for the equity method" or remove other words or sentences that no longer apply.[4]

a. The second sentence of paragraph 1 is amended to read:

This Opinion extends the applicability of the equity method of accounting (paragraph 6(b)) to investments in common stock of corporate joint ventures and certain other investments in common stock.

The third sentence and footnote 1 are deleted.

b. Footnote 3 to paragraph 4 is amended to read:

See paragraphs 2 and 3 of ARB No. 51 as amended by FASB Statement No. 94.

c. Paragraph 14 is amended to read:

14. ARB No. 51, paragraphs 2 and 3 (as amended by FASB Statement No. 94), requires consolidation of all majority-owned subsidiaries except the few that meet conditions described in paragraph 2. The equity method is not a valid substitute for consolidation. Moreover, since ARB No. 51 as amended requires

the general-purpose financial statements of companies having one or more majority-owned subsidiaries to be consolidated statements, parent-company statements are not a valid substitute for consolidated financial statements.[4]

d. Paragraph 14, footnote 4, is amended to read:

Paragraphs 2 and 3 of ARB No. 51 (as amended by FASB Statement No. 94) describe the conditions under which a majority-owned subsidiary shall not be consolidated. The limitations in paragraphs 2 and 3 of ARB No. 51 (as amended by FASB Statement No. 94) should also be applied as limitations to the use of the equity method.

e. The second sentence of paragraph 16 is amended to read:

Therefore, investors should account for investments in common stock of corporate joint ventures by the equity method in consolidated financial statements.[6]

f. The last sentence of paragraph 17 is deleted.

g. The first two sentences of paragraph 19 are deleted.

h. In the third sentence of paragraph 19, the words "unconsolidated subsidiaries" are deleted.

i. In the first sentence of paragraph 19(a), the word "subsidiary" is deleted.

j. Paragraph 20(c) is deleted.

k. Paragraph 20(d) is amended to delete "of 50% or less" from the first sentence.

16. Paragraphs 8 and 9 of ARB 43, Chapter 12, "Foreign Operations and Foreign Exchange," are deleted. (Paragraph 8 and part of 9 are quoted in footnote 1 of this Statement.)

Effective Date and Transition

17. This Statement shall be effective for financial statements for fiscal years ending after December 15, 1988. Earlier application is encouraged. Application to interim financial statements for the year of adoption is not required at the time of their

---

[3]Opinion 18 was silent about parent-company financial statements prepared for purposes other than issuance as the general-purpose financial statements of the primary reporting entity. This Statement also does not consider that subject

[4]Details of major changes: *Paragraphs 1, 16, and 17*—The deleted parts of all three paragraphs pertain to "parent-company financial statements prepared for issuance to stockholders as the financial statements of the primary reporting entity." A similar provision is also deleted from paragraph 14. *Paragraph 14*—The first sentence, "The Board reaffirms the conclusion that investors should account for investments in common stock of unconsolidated domestic subsidiaries by the equity method in consolidated financial statements, and the Board now extends this conclusion to investments in common stock of all unconsolidated subsidiaries (foreign as well as domestic) in consolidated financial statements," and the third sentence (whose content was just described) are deleted and replaced by new sentences. In the second sentence the words "and should not be used to justify exclusion of a subsidiary when consolidation is otherwise appropriate" are deleted. *Paragraph 19*—The deleted sentences read: "The difference between consolidation and the equity method lies in the details reported in the financial statements. Thus, an investor's net income for the period and its stockholders' equity at the end of the period are the same whether an investment in a subsidiary is accounted for under the equity method or the subsidiary is consolidated (except as indicated in paragraph 19i)."

creasingly tenuous. The Board concluded that the increasingly diverse nature of business activity, and of business enterprises themselves, makes the fact that the business activity of a subsidiary is different from that of its parent and other subsidiaries an insufficient reason to exclude it from consolidation.

30. The managerial, operational, and financial ties that bind an enterprise into a single economic unit are stronger than the differences between its lines of business. Consolidated financial statements became common once it was recognized that boundaries between separate corporate entities must be ignored to report the business carried on by a group of affiliated corporations as the economic and financial whole that it actually is. Similarly, differences between the varied operations of a group of affiliated corporations that constitutes an economic and financial whole do not preclude including them all in consolidated financial statements.

31. Those differences also do not make the equity method a valid substitute for consolidation of majority-owned subsidiaries. Although the equity method described in Opinion 18 usually results in the same net income and the same net assets as consolidation, that method omits significant revenues and expenses from the income statement, omits significant assets and liabilities from the balance sheet, and omits significant receipts and payments from the statement of cash flows. For example, difference in operations has long been rejected as a basis for not consolidating so-called captive leasing subsidiaries. The decision and most of the language now in paragraph 31 of FASB Statement No. 13, *Accounting for Leases,* was in APB Opinion No. 10, *Omnibus Opinion—1966* (and was reaffirmed in Opinion 18):

> The accounts of subsidiaries (regardless of when organized or acquired) whose principal business activity is leasing property or facilities to the parent or other affiliated companies shall be consolidated. The equity method is not adequate for fair presentation of those subsidiaries because their assets and liabilities are significant to the consolidated financial position of the enterprise.

The same reasoning applies to other "nonhomogeneous" majority-owned subsidiaries, whether captive or not.

32. Other restrictive consolidation practices have been to exclude from consolidation, for example, all foreign subsidiaries, all subsidiaries that are not

wholly owned, or all subsidiaries that are not 80 percent owned. Those essentially arbitrary restrictions also are not sufficient reasons to exclude majority-owned subsidiaries from consolidation.

33. The central issue is whether financial statements that consolidate some majority-owned subsidiaries and report others as investments in the equity securities of other enterprises adequately report the operating results and financial position of the business enterprise of which all the subsidiaries are a part. The Board concluded that consolidated financial statements that include all majority-owned subsidiaries whose control is not in question better meet the objectives of financial reporting and more fully possess the qualitative characteristics of useful financial information described in FASB Concepts Statement No. 2, *Qualitative Characteristics of Accounting Information,* especially relevance, representational faithfulness, and comparability.

Objectives and Qualitative Characteristics

34. Investors, creditors, and others who use financial statements need information about a business enterprise that is useful in making investment, credit, or other similar decisions about it (FASB Concepts Statement No. 1, *Objectives of Financial Reporting by Business Enterprises,* paragraphs 34-40). Those who invest in the parent company of an affiliated group of corporations invest in the whole group, which constitutes the enterprise that is a potential source of cash flows to them as a result of their investment.

Relevance and Representational Faithfulness

35. Information that is most relevant to investors, creditors, and other users thus includes consolidated financial statements that "present, primarily for the benefit of the shareholders and creditors of the parent company, the results of operations and the financial position of a parent company and its subsidiaries essentially as if the group were a single company with one or more branches or divisions" (ARB 51, paragraph 1).

36. A set of consolidated financial statements that includes all majority-owned subsidiaries fits that description better than a set that excludes significant parts of an enterprise. If the assets, liabilities, revenues, expenses, and cash flows of "nonhomogeneous" subsidiaries are excluded from consolidation, the consolidated financial statements of

the enterprise do not faithfully represent[5] the operating results, financial status, and capital structure of the enterprise described in paragraph 35.

37. A significant aspect of both relevance and representational faithfulness is completeness—

> The inclusion in reported information of everything material that is necessary for faithful representation of the relevant phenomena.
> Freedom from bias . . . implies that nothing material is left out of the information that may be necessary to insure that it validly represents the underlying events and conditions.
> Relevance of information is adversely affected if a relevant piece of information is omitted, even if the omission does not falsify what is shown. [Concepts Statement 2, "Glossary," and paragraphs 79 and 80]

Consolidated financial statements that exclude some majority-owned subsidiaries provide an incomplete picture of an enterprise. If they are to see the complete picture, investors, creditors, and other users must themselves attempt to consolidate the excluded subsidiaries. Even then, a "do-it-yourself" consolidation can only be a rough approximation of one done by the enterprise itself because consolidation procedures require detailed information about current amounts and past transactions that is seldom provided by general-purpose financial reporting. The representational faithfulness of a user's consolidation is at least questionable, and its comparability with consolidated financial statements or "do-it-yourself" consolidations of other enterprises, or of the same enterprise for an earlier period, is at best doubtful.

38. Unconsolidated majority-owned subsidiaries usually have been accounted for by the equity method in accordance with Opinion 18. The equity method described by Opinion 18 normally results in the same net income and stockholders' equity as consolidation, but the information it provides about specific classes of assets, liabilities, revenues, and expenses is significantly different from, and is not a substitute for, information provided by consolidation. The equity method reports a parent's equity in the net assets of its unconsolidated subsidiaries as a single-line item in the consolidated statement of financial position and generally reports its share of the unconsolidated subsidiaries' reported net income as a single-line item in the consolidated income statement.

39. Although net income and total stockholders' equity are important factors in assessing the enterprise's performance and its financial position, the relative amounts of various assets, liabilities, revenues, and expenses and their relationships to other items in the consolidated financial statements also generally are essential factors in that analysis.

> Although . . . simplifications, condensations, and aggregations are both necessary and useful, the Board believes it is important to avoid focusing attention almost exclusively on "the bottom line," earnings per share, or other highly simplified condensations. Summary data, such as the amounts of net assets, comprehensive income, earnings, or earnings per share, may be useful as general indicators of the amount of investment or overall past performance and are often used in efforts to compare an entity with many other entities. But, in a complex business enterprise, summary amounts include many heterogeneous things and events. Components of a financial statement often reflect more homogeneous classes of items than the whole statement. The individual items, subtotals, or other parts of a financial statement may often be more useful than the aggregate to those who make investment, credit, and similar decisions. [FASB Concepts Statement No. 5, *Recognition and Measurement in Financial Statements of Business Enterprises,* paragraph 22]

40. The usefulness of information about amounts of various assets, liabilities, revenues, and expenses is also indicated by the fact that most summary indicators other than net income, earnings per share, and stockholders' equity are affected by whether a subsidiary is consolidated or accounted for by the equity method. Basic analytical tools such as the current ratio, receivables turnover, inventory turnover, times interest earned, and return on total assets are a few examples. The paramount example is the debt-equity ratio, which, for reasons already described, is much lower if finance or other highly leveraged subsidiaries are accounted for by the equity method rather than consolidated. That effect is one aspect of off-balance-sheet financing that has been criticized because transactions between affiliates and intercompany receivables and payables often make it unlikely that "do-it-yourself" consolidation can adequately approximate debt-equity ratios in consolidated financial statements provided by the enterprises themselves.

---

[5]"Representational faithfulness is correspondence or agreement between a measure or description and the phenomenon it purports to represent. In accounting, the phenomena to be represented are economic resources and obligations and the transactions and events that change those resources and obligations" (Concepts Statement 2, par. 63).

41. Use of the equity method for majority-owned subsidiaries that are significant parts of an enterprise diminishes the usefulness of and raises questions about the credibility of consolidated financial statements as those subsidiaries grow in significance. As enterprises become more diversified, the number and variety of their majority-owned subsidiaries that are not consolidated because of "nonhomogeneity" of operations often increase. Thus, the amounts reported as single-line items in consolidated financial statements not only become larger but also the information they convey diminishes—the resulting consolidated financial statements provide less and less information about the enterprise in which its stockholders have invested. Consolidated financial statements of some enterprises have excluded more assets and liabilities than they have included.

Comparability

42. Consolidation of all majority-owned subsidiaries will also improve comparability between enterprises. Investment and credit decisions involve comparing available alternative investment or credit opportunities. Thus:

> Information about an enterprise gains greatly in usefulness if it can be compared with similar information about other enterprises and with similar information about the same enterprise for some other period or some other point in time. The significance of information, especially quantitative information, depends to a great extent on the user's ability to relate it to some benchmark. [Concepts Statement 2, paragraph 111]

43. As Concepts Statement 2 also notes (paragraphs 113-119), comparison involves identifying, understanding, and assessing both similarities and differences. To the extent that similarities and differences stem from financial reporting rather than from the enterprises themselves, financial reporting hinders rather than helps investors and creditors in making their decisions. A significant problem in practice under ARB 51 is that large differences between consolidated financial statements of different business enterprises often have resulted from different consolidation policies rather than from significant differences between the enterprises.

Reporting of Cash Flows

44. Consolidated financial statements that include all majority-owned subsidiaries should also result in more relevant, representationally faithful, and comparable statements of cash flow. Although the equity method and consolidation may report the same net income and net assets, they do not report the same cash receipts and payments related to operating, investing, and financing activities. Potentially significant information about how an enterprise generates cash through operations, as well as information about its financing and investing activities, is not provided if subsidiaries are not consolidated.

Matters Raised in Comment Letters and at the Public Hearing

45. Many respondents who opposed the conclusion of the Exposure Draft argued that consolidation of "nonhomogeneous" subsidiaries would make the consolidated financial statements less useful. Many asserted that it would impair comparability of the financial data between enterprises and that it would confuse the expected debt-equity (and other) ratios of manufacturing and financial components of diverse business enterprises, resulting in ratios that would accurately reflect neither component. On the other hand, many respondents who supported the conclusion of the Exposure Draft did so because they thought comparability would be enhanced due to more comprehensive disclosure of financial results.

46. Before the Exposure Draft was issued, the Board recognized that opinions of respondents on whether consolidated financial statements were more useful probably would be divided. The Board considered the comments on usefulness with emphasis on comparability and noted that usefulness means more than comparability. The Board's conclusions rely on Concepts Statement 2, which emphasizes relevance and representational faithfulness as much as comparability. Thus, the Board concluded that consolidated financial statements that include all majority-owned subsidiaries whose control is not in question better meet the objectives of financial reporting.

47. Most respondents who opposed the elimination of the "nonhomogeneity" exception acknowledged that it needed some boundaries. Some proposed that finance and insurance subsidiaries ought to be excluded from consolidation by nonfinancial enterprises and suggested the Board establish criteria for excluding certain subsidiaries by examining differences in reported financial ratios or in the operating cycles. Respondents did not suggest a basis for determining threshold values for those criteria, and the Board observed that any choice necessarily would be arbitrary, would differ between industries, and could vary over time due to changes in business practices. Some measures that seem appropriate may not distinguish effectively between subsidiaries. For example, a high debt-equity ratio may reflect either poor financial condition, "nonhomogeneity," or both. The

Board concluded that establishing criteria for "nonhomogeneity" based on financial characteristics would be arbitrary and ineffective.

48. Other respondents suggested that the Board narrow the "nonhomogeneity" exception by requiring consolidation of all "captive" subsidiaries—that is, subsidiaries that conduct a majority of their transactions with their parent company. Those respondents argued that consolidating captive subsidiaries improves comparability with enterprises that have not formed subsidiaries but engage in like activities. They argued that consolidating noncaptive, "nonhomogeneous" subsidiaries impairs that comparability. Respondents suggested that the Board look to a subsidiary's relationship to the primary reporting entity to distinguish captive from noncaptive. The Board observed that as diversification increases so does the difficulty of identifying the primary business of an enterprise. Respondents were unable to provide substantive guidelines for that identification. The Board agreed with respondents that, if a subsidiary is captive, consolidation of that subsidiary improves comparability. However, the Board concluded that other arguments including improved representational faithfulness and relevance justify consolidating noncaptive subsidiaries.

49. Many respondents criticized the Exposure Draft's requirements as representing a "piecemeal" approach to establishing revised consolidation criteria. Most indicated that such an approach created a risk that future decisions by the Board may require the consolidation requirements of the Exposure Draft to be reversed. The Board recognizes that deliberation will continue on the reporting entity concept, which may lead to changed consolidation criteria based on control. However, the Board concluded that the risk of reversing the consolidation requirements of this Statement was minimal because the criteria for excluding subsidiaries from consolidation based on "nonhomogeneity" are unrelated to control.

50. Some respondents recommended that the Board provide guidance for various financial statement display questions that may arise, including how to consolidate a nonclassified statement of financial position used by a financial institution with a classified statement of financial position used by a manufacturing or merchandising company and how to display interest expense of both financial and manufacturing subsidiaries in a consolidated income statement. The Board noted that guidance might reduce diversity of display but concluded that some variety may be appropriate for reporting the financial position and results of diverse enterprises. The Board also noted that the issue is not new because some enterprises have consolidated subsidiaries with those characteristics

and have developed reporting formats to present consolidated results effectively.

51. Many respondents requested a delay in the effective date. The most compelling reasons offered for extending the effective date were the need to allow companies additional time to renegotiate loan covenants or other provisions of loan agreements and to familiarize investors, creditors, and other users with the effects of consolidation on financial statement ratios. Respondents indicated that the risk of increased cost of borrowing at the time loan covenants are renegotiated would be mitigated if additional time was available. Respondents also requested additional time to determine the most effective financial statement display. The Board accepted those arguments and delayed the effective date for one year.

52. Several respondents questioned whether direct financing and leveraged leases of a majority-owned leasing subsidiary accounted for under the equity method would be required to be reclassified as sales-type capital leases when the subsidiary is consolidated. Paragraph 19 of Opinion 18, which specifies how to account for those subsidiaries under the equity method prior to their being consolidated as required by this Statement, indicated that net income and stockholders' equity generally would be the same whether the subsidiary was accounted for under the equity method or whether it was consolidated. Thus, whether a leasing subsidiary was accounted for by the equity method or is now consolidated as required by this Statement, the distinction between a direct financing and a sales-type capital lease is based on application of Statement 13 as if the subsidiary were consolidated. Leases of a manufacturing company's equipment sold to a leasing subsidiary that are accounted for as direct financing leases on the subsidiary's financial statements normally would be sales-type capital leases in the consolidated financial statements. This Statement does not change that requirement.

53. The Exposure Draft's requirement to use the cost method for majority-owned subsidiaries that remain unconsolidated was intended to change Opinion 18 only to the extent necessary to avoid conflict with ARB 51 as amended. However, respondents said that the requirement would change practice because "significant influence" might remain even if control were lost and because of specialized industry practices for investment companies. The Board removed the requirement to use only the cost method, thereby leaving existing pronouncements in effect. The method to be used to account for those subsidiaries will be considered in the broad project described in paragraphs 19 and 20.

Need for Disaggregated Information

54. Some who favor consolidating all majority-owned subsidiaries whose control is not in question are nevertheless concerned that consolidating "nonhomogeneous" subsidiaries will obscure important information about the primary operations of an enterprise, producing less informative financial statements than those that exclude "nonhomogeneous" subsidiaries but append their separate financial statements or equivalent information. An example is a parent that is primarily a manufacturing enterprise that consolidates an insurance or bank subsidiary. That concern was expressed frequently in interviews conducted in the early stages of the FASB project on the reporting entity (paragraphs 19 and 20), both by those who use financial statements and by those who provide them.

55. The Board recognizes that aggregation of assets and liabilities resulting from operations with activities that differ from each other in profitability, risks, and returns can obscure important information about each of those activities. However, the Board also believes that disclosures required under FASB Statement No. 14, *Financial Reporting for Segments of a Business Enterprise,* can provide meaningful information about the different operations within a business enterprise. Consolidated financial statements and adequate disclosure of varied activities are not mutually exclusive.

56. The financial reporting that has followed the issuance of Statement 14 in 1976 has demonstrated that financial reporting can readily provide both consolidated and disaggregated information. For example, when the Securities and Exchange Commission eliminated its requirement to provide separate financial statements of consolidated subsidiaries engaged in "diverse financial-type" businesses in 1981, it said, "The Commission's decision to delete all requirements for additional financial information for consolidated finance-type subsidiaries . . . was significantly influenced by its conclusion that the disclosures required by [FASB Statement] 14 provide adequate information on these activities to most investors . . ." (Accounting Series Release No. 302, *Separate Financial Statements Required by Regulation S-X*).

57. The broad project on the reporting entity will consider disclosure of disaggregated information in consolidated financial statements. Business enterprises have the opportunity to experiment with providing additional information in the time between the issuance of this Statement and the completion of that portion of the broader project. The Board encourages experimentation to improve disclosure and better communicate to investors, creditors, and others. That experimentation should prove beneficial to the preparer and should provide the Board and others with experience that is useful when considering disclosure of disaggregated information in the future.

58. Opinion 18, paragraph 20(c) has required that summarized information about the assets, liabilities, and results of operations of unconsolidated subsidiaries should be presented in the notes of consolidated financial statements or in separate statements. Some of that information is not required by Statement 14. Many comments were received on the general issue of disclosing disaggregated information. Recommendations ranged from requiring no disclosure to requiring consolidating financial statements. Although opposition to the requirement to continue disclosure presently called for by Opinion 18 was substantial, some suggested less information should be required, while others said more, or at least different, information should be required. Users of financial statements expressed strong concern about the possible loss of information that was currently available.

59. The Board acknowledges that this Statement's disclosure requirement represents an expedient solution. The Board concluded, however, that alternatives were less attractive. Increasing disclosure requirements to eliminate what is perceived as this Statement's lack of evenhandedness without reconsidering the broad issue of disclosing disaggregated information probably would not result in meaningful requirements. Dropping that requirement would result in loss of information that users of financial statements urged the Board to retain. The Board concluded that to prevent loss of that information was important. The Board also noted that the requirement is reasonably evenhanded. Most enterprises with what generally have been called "nonhomogeneous" subsidiaries will be required to provide continued disclosure because most of those subsidiaries are not now consolidated. Moreover, the Board recognized that many enterprises would voluntarily provide the disaggregated information they thought necessary to meet concerns they expect to result from the revised consolidation policy. Those enterprises would incur no additional cost to implement the disclosure provision of this Statement. After assessing the matters set forth in this and the previous paragraph, the Board decided to continue Opinion 18's disclosure requirements for subsidiaries that are consolidated as a result of this Statement.

Benefits and Costs of Consolidating All Majority-Owned Subsidiaries

60. Paragraphs 25-44 discuss the benefits of requiring consolidation of all majority-owned subsidiaries whose control is not in question. The

Board recognizes that initial adoption of that requirement may cause some enterprises to incur certain costs, for example, to renegotiate debt covenants that are technically in default once highly leveraged finance and similar subsidiaries are consolidated and perhaps to educate some investors and creditors about the change in consolidation policy. However, the Board believes that those costs will be outweighed by the benefits of more relevant, representationally faithful, and comparable consolidated financial statements.

Parent-Company Financial Statements

61. Opinion 18, paragraphs 14, 16, and 17, re-

quires use of the equity method in "parent-company financial statements prepared for issuance to stockholders as the financial statements of the primary reporting entity." This Statement removes those provisions because, if an enterprise has one or more subsidiaries, consolidated rather than parent-company financial statements are the appropriate general-purpose financial statements. The Board is aware of no instances in which parent-company financial statements have been issued as general-purpose financial statements and believes the elimination of those provisions will result in little or no change in practice.

Statement of Financial Accounting Standards No. 95
Statement of Cash Flows

STATUS

Issued: November 1987

Effective Date: For fiscal years ending after July 15, 1988

Affects: Supersedes APB 19
Amends APB 20, paragraph 3
Amends APB 22, paragraphs 6, 7, 8, and 12
Amends APB 28, paragraphs 2 and 33
Supersedes AIN-APB 19, Interpretations No. 1 through 3
Amends FAS 7, paragraphs 10 and 11(c) and footnote 6
Supersedes FAS 7, footnote 8
Amends FAS 14, paragraphs 3 and 7
Amends FAS 21, footnote 4
Amends FAS 24, paragraphs 1 and 5 and footnote 2
Amends FAS 36, paragraph 8
Amends FAS 57, footnote 2
Amends FAS 69, paragraphs 7, 8, and 41 and footnote 3
Amends FTB 82-1, paragraph 4

Affected by: Paragraph 3 amended by FAS 102 and FAS 117
Paragraph 13 amended by FAS 104
Paragraphs 15, 16(a), 16(b), 17(a), 17(b), 22(a), 23(a), 147, 148, and 149(a) amended by FAS 102
Paragraphs 18, 19, 27(b), 28 through 30, 32, and 130 amended by FAS 117
Footnote 4 superseded by FAS 104
Footnote 12 amended by FAS 117

Issues Discussed by FASB Emerging Issues Task Force (EITF)

Affects: No EITF Issues

Interpreted by: Paragraph 20 interpreted by EITF Issue No. 95-13

Related Issues: No EITF Issues

SUMMARY

This Statement establishes standards for cash flow reporting. It supersedes APB Opinion No. 19, *Reporting Changes in Financial Position,* and requires a statement of cash flows as part of a full set of financial statements for all business enterprises in place of a statement of changes in financial position.

This Statement requires that a statement of cash flows classify cash receipts and payments according to whether they stem from operating, investing, or financing activities and provides definitions of each category.

This Statement encourages enterprises to report cash flows from operating activities directly by showing major classes of operating cash receipts and payments (the direct method). Enterprises that choose not to show operating cash receipts and payments are required to report the same amount of net cash flow from operating activities indirectly by adjusting net income to reconcile it to net cash flow from operating activities (the indirect or reconciliation method) by removing the affects of (a) all deferrals of past operating cash receipts and payments and all accruals of expected future operating cash receipts and payments and (b) all items that are included in net income that do not affect operating cash receipts and payments. If the direct method is used, a reconciliation of net income and net cash flow from operating activities is required to be provided in a separate schedule.

This Statement requires that a statement of cash flows report the reporting currency equivalent of foreign currency cash flows, using the current exchange rate at the time of the cash flows. The effect of exchange rate changes on cash held in foreign currencies is reported as a separate item in the reconciliation of beginning and ending balances of cash and cash equivalents.

This Statement requires that information about investing and financing activities not resulting in cash receipts or payments in the period be provided separately.

This Statement is effective for annual financial statements for fiscal years ending after July 15, 1988. Restatement of financial statements for earlier years provided for comparative purposes is encouraged but not required.

(This page intentionally left blank.)

Statement of Financial Accounting Standards No. 95

Statement of Cash Flows

CONTENTS

INTRODUCTION

1. This Statement establishes standards for providing a statement of cash flows in general-purpose financial statements. This Statement supersedes APB Opinion No. 19, *Reporting Changes in Financial Position,* and requires a business enterprise to provide a statement of cash flows in place of a statement of changes in financial position. It also requires that specified information about noncash investing and financing transactions and other events be provided separately.

2. Opinion 19 permitted but did not require enterprises to report cash flow information in the statement of changes in financial position. Since that Opinion was issued, the significance of information about an enterprise's cash flows has increasingly been recognized. In FASB Concepts Statement No. 5, *Recognition and Measurement in Financial Statements of Business Enterprises,* paragraph 13, the Board says, "A full set of financial statements for a period should show: . . . Cash flows during the period." Moreover, certain prob-

lems have been identified in current practice, including the ambiguity of terms such as *funds,* lack of comparability arising from diversity in the focus of the statement (cash, cash and short-term investments, quick assets, or working capital) and the resulting differences in definitions of funds flows from operating activities (cash or working capital), differences in the format of the statement (sources and uses format or activity format), variations in classifications of specific items in an activity format, and the reporting of net changes in amounts of assets and liabilities rather than gross inflows and outflows. The lack of clear objectives for the statement of changes in financial position has been suggested as a major cause of that diversity.

STANDARDS OF FINANCIAL ACCOUNTING AND REPORTING

Scope

3. A business enterprise that provides a set of financial statements that reports both financial po-

sition and results of operations shall also provide a statement of cash flows for each period for which results of operations are provided. This Statement supersedes or amends the accounting pronouncements listed in Appendix D.

Purpose of a Statement of Cash Flows

4. The primary purpose of a statement of cash flows is to provide relevant information about the cash receipts and cash payments of an enterprise during a period.

5. The information provided in a statement of cash flows, if used with related disclosures and information in the other financial statements, should help investors, creditors, and others to (a) assess the enterprise's ability to generate positive future net cash flows; (b) assess the enterprise's ability to meet its obligations, its ability to pay dividends, and its needs for external financing; (c) assess the reasons for differences between net income and associated cash receipts and payments; and (d) assess the effects on an enterprise's financial position of both its cash and noncash investing and financing transactions during the period.

6. To achieve its purpose of providing information to help investors, creditors, and others in making those assessments, a statement of cash flows should report the cash effects during a period of an enterprise's operations, its investing transactions, and its financing transactions. Related disclosures should report the effects of investing and financing transactions that affect an enterprise's financial position but do not directly affect cash flows during the period. A reconciliation of net income and net cash flow from operating activities, which generally provides information about the net effects of operating transactions and other events that affect net income and operating cash flows in different periods, also should be provided.

Focus on Cash and Cash Equivalents

7. A statement of cash flows shall explain the change during the period in cash[1] and cash equivalents. The statement shall use descriptive terms such as *cash* or *cash and cash equivalents* rather

than ambiguous terms such as *funds.* The total amounts of cash and cash equivalents at the beginning and end of the period shown in the statement of cash flows shall be the same amounts as similarly titled line items or subtotals shown in the statements of financial position as of those dates.

8. For purposes of this Statement, cash equivalents are short-term, highly liquid investments that are both:

a. Readily convertible to known amounts of cash
b. So near their maturity that they present insignificant risk of changes in value because of changes in interest rates.

Generally, only investments with original maturities[2] of three months or less qualify under that definition.

9. Examples of items commonly considered to be cash equivalents are Treasury bills, commercial paper, money market funds, and federal funds sold (for an enterprise with banking operations). Cash purchases and sales of those investments generally are part of the enterprise's cash management activities rather than part of its operating, investing, and financing activities, and details of those transactions need not be reported in a statement of cash flows.

10. Not all investments that qualify are required to be treated as cash equivalents. An enterprise shall establish a policy concerning which short-term, highly liquid investments that satisfy the definition in paragraph 9 are treated as cash equivalents. For example, an enterprise having banking operations might decide that all investments that qualify except for those purchased for its trading account will be treated as cash equivalents, while an enterprise whose operations consist largely of investing in short-term, highly liquid investments might decide that all those items will be treated as investments rather than cash equivalents. An enterprise shall disclose its policy for determining which items are treated as cash equivalents. Any change to that policy is a change in accounting principle that shall be effected by restating financial statements for earlier years presented for comparative purposes.

---

[1]Consistent with common usage, *cash* includes not only currency on hand but demand deposits with banks or other financial institutions. *Cash* also includes other kinds of accounts that have the general characteristics of demand deposits in that the customer may deposit additional funds at any time and also effectively may withdraw funds at any time without prior notice or penalty. All charges and credits to those accounts are cash receipts or payments to both the entity owning the account and the bank holding it. For example, a bank's granting of a loan by crediting the proceeds to a customer's demand deposit account is a cash payment by the bank and a cash receipt of the customer when the entry is made.

[2]*Original maturity* means original maturity to the entity holding the investment. For example, both a three-month U.S. Treasury bill and a three-year Treasury note purchased three months from maturity qualify as cash equivalents. However, a Treasury note purchased three years ago does not become a cash equivalent when its remaining maturity is three months.

Gross and Net Cash Flows

11. Generally, information about the gross amounts of cash receipts and cash payments during a period is more relevant than information about the net amounts of cash receipts and payments. However, the net amount of related receipts and payments provides sufficient information not only for cash equivalents, as noted in paragraph 9, but also for certain other classes of cash flows specified in paragraphs 12, 13, and 28.

12. For certain items, the turnover is quick, the amounts are large, and the maturities are short. For certain other items, such as demand deposits of a bank and customer accounts payable of a broker-dealer, the enterprise is substantively holding or disbursing cash on behalf of its customers. Only the net changes during the period in assets and liabilities with those characteristics need be reported because knowledge of the gross cash receipts and payments related to them may not be necessary to understand the enterprise's operating, investing, and financing activities.

13. Items that qualify for net reporting because their turnover is quick, their amounts are large, and their maturities are short are cash receipts and payments pertaining to (a) investments (other than cash equivalents), (b) loans receivable, and (c) debt, providing that the original maturity of the asset or liability is three months or less.[3]

Classification of Cash Receipts and Cash Payments

14. A statement of cash flows shall classify cash receipts and cash payments as resulting from investing, financing, or operating activities.[4]

Cash Flows from Investing Activities

15. Investing activities include making and collecting loans and acquiring and disposing of debt or equity instruments and property, plant, and equipment and other productive assets, that is, assets held for or used in the production of goods or services by the enterprise (other than materials that are part of the enterprise's inventory).

16. Cash inflows from investing activities are:[5]

a. Receipts from collections or sales of loans made by the enterprise and of other entities' debt instruments (other than cash equivalents) that were purchased by the enterprise
b. Receipts from sales of equity instruments of other enterprises and from returns *of* investment in those instruments
c. Receipts from sales of property, plant, and equipment and other productive assets.

17. Cash outflows for investing activities are:

a. Disbursements for loans made by the enterprise and payments to acquire debt instruments of other entities (other than cash equivalents)
b. Payments to acquire equity instruments of other enterprises
c. Payments at the time of purchase or soon before or after purchase[6] to acquire property, plant, and equipment and other productive assets.[7]

Cash Flows from Financing Activities

18. Financing activities include obtaining resources from owners and providing them with a return on, and a return of, their investment; borrowing money and repaying amounts borrowed, or otherwise settling the obligation; and obtaining and paying for other resources obtained from creditors on long-term credit.

19. Cash inflows from financing activities are:

a. Proceeds from issuing equity instruments
b. Proceeds from issuing bonds, mortgages,

---

[3]For this purpose, amounts due on demand are considered to have maturities of three months or less. For convenience, credit card receivables of financial services operations—generally, receivables resulting from cardholder charges that may, at the cardholder's option, be paid in full when first billed, usually within one month, without incurring interest charges and that do not stem from the enterprise's sale of goods or services—also are considered to be loans with original maturities of three months or less.

[4]Each cash receipt or payment is to be classified according to its nature without regard to whether it stems from an item intended as a hedge of another item. For example, the proceeds of a borrowing are a financing cash inflow whether or not the debt is intended as a hedge of an investment, and the purchase or sale of a futures contract is an investing activity without regard to whether the contract is intended as a hedge of a firm commitment to purchase inventory.

[5]Receipts from disposing of loans, debt or equity instruments, or property, plant, and equipment include directly related proceeds of insurance settlements, such as the proceeds of insurance on a building that is damaged or destroyed.

[6]Generally, only advance payments, the down payment, or other amounts paid at the time of purchase or soon before or after purchase of property, plant, and equipment and other productive assets are investing cash outflows. Incurring directly related debt to the seller is a financing transaction, and subsequent payments of principal on that debt thus are financing cash outflows.

[7]Payments to acquire productive assets include interest capitalized as part of the cost of those assets.

notes, and from other short- or long-term borrowing.

20. Cash outflows for financing activities are:

a. Payments of dividends or other distributions to owners, including outlays to reacquire the enterprise's equity instruments
b. Repayments of amounts borrowed
c. Other principal payments to creditors who have extended long-term credit.[8]

Cash Flows from Operating Activities

21. Operating activities include all transactions and other events that are not defined as investing or financing activities in paragraphs 15-20. Operating activities generally involve producing and delivering goods and providing services. Cash flows from operating activities are generally the cash effects of transactions and other events that enter into the determination of net income.

22. Cash inflows from operating activities are:

a. Cash receipts from sales of goods or services, including receipts from collection or sale of accounts and both short- and long-term notes receivable from customers arising from those sales
b. Cash receipts from returns *on* loans, other debt instruments of other entities, and equity securities—interest and dividends
c. All other cash receipts that do not stem from transactions defined as investing or financing activities, such as amounts received to settle lawsuits; proceeds of insurance settlements except for those that are directly related to investing or financing activities, such as from destruction of a building; and refunds from suppliers.

23. Cash outflows for operating activities are:

a. Cash payments to acquire materials for manufacture or goods for resale, including principal payments on accounts and both short- and long-term notes payable to suppliers for those materials or goods
b. Cash payments to other suppliers and employees for other goods or services

c. Cash payments to governments for taxes, duties, fines, and other fees or penalties
d. Cash payments to lenders and other creditors for interest
e. All other cash payments that do not stem from transactions defined as investing or financing activities, such as payments to settle lawsuits, cash contributions to charities, and cash refunds to customers.

24. Certain cash receipts and payments may have aspects of more than one class of cash flows. For example, a cash payment may pertain to an item that could be considered either inventory or a productive asset. If so, the appropriate classification shall depend on the activity that is likely to be the predominant source of cash flows for the item. For example, the acquisition and sale of equipment to be used by the enterprise or rented to others generally are investing activities. However, equipment sometimes is acquired or produced to be used by the enterprise or rented to others for a short period and then sold. In those circumstances, the acquisition or production and subsequent sale of those assets shall be considered operating activities.

Foreign Currency Cash Flows

25. A statement of cash flows of an enterprise with foreign currency transactions or foreign operations shall report the reporting currency equivalent of foreign currency cash flows using the exchange rates in effect at the time of the cash flows. An appropriately weighted average exchange rate for the period may be used for translation if the result is substantially the same as if the rates at the dates of the cash flows were used.[9] The statement shall report the effect of exchange rate changes on cash balances held in foreign currencies as a separate part of the reconciliation of the change in cash and cash equivalents during the period.

Content and Form of the Statement of Cash Flows

26. A statement of cash flows for a period shall report net cash provided or used by operating, investing, and financing activities[10] and the net effect of those flows on cash and cash equivalents during the period in a manner that reconciles beginning and ending cash and cash equivalents.

---

[8]Refer to footnote 6 which indicates that most principal payments on seller-financed debt directly related to a purchase of property, plant, and equipment or other productive assets are financing cash outflows.

[9]Paragraph 12 of FASB Statement No. 52, *Foreign Currency Translation,* recognizes the general impracticality of translating revenues, expenses, gains, and losses at the exchange rates on dates they are recognized and permits an appropriately weighted average exchange rate for the period to be used to translate those elements. This Statement applies that provision to cash receipts and cash payments.

[10]Separate disclosure of cash flows pertaining to extraordinary items or discontinued operations reflected in those categories is not required. An enterprise that nevertheless chooses to report separately operating cash flows of discontinued operations shall do so consistently for all periods affected, which may include periods long after sale or liquidation of the operation.

27. In reporting cash flows from operating activities, enterprises are encouraged to report major classes of gross cash receipts and gross cash payments and their arithmetic sum—the net cash flow from operating activities (the direct method). Enterprises that do so should, at a minimum, separately report the following classes of operating cash receipts and payments:[11]

a. Cash collected from customers, including lessees, licensees, and the like
b. Interest and dividends received
c. Other operating cash receipts, if any
d. Cash paid to employees and other suppliers of goods or services, including suppliers of insurance, advertising, and the like
e. Interest paid
f. Income taxes paid
g. Other operating cash payments, if any.

Enterprises are encouraged to provide further breakdowns of operating cash receipts and payments that they consider meaningful and feasible. For example, a retailer or manufacturer might decide to further divide cash paid to employees and suppliers (category (d) above) into payments for costs of inventory and payments for selling, general, and administrative expenses.

28. Enterprises that choose not to provide information about major classes of operating cash receipts and payments by the direct method as encouraged in paragraph 27 shall determine and report the same amount for net cash flow from operating activities indirectly by adjusting net income to reconcile it to net cash flow from operating activities (the indirect or reconciliation method). That requires adjusting net income to remove (a) the effects of all deferrals of past operating cash receipts and payments, such as changes during the period in inventory, deferred income, and the like, and all accruals of expected future operating cash receipts and payments, such as changes during the period in receivables and payables,[12] and (b) the effects of all items whose cash effects are investing or financing cash flows, such as depreciation, amortization of goodwill, and gains or losses on sales of property, plant, and equipment and discontinued operations (which relate to investing activities), and gains or losses on extinguishment of debt (which is a financing activity).

29. The reconciliation of net income to net cash flow from operating activities described in paragraph 28 shall be provided regardless of whether the direct or indirect method of reporting net cash flow from operating activities is used. That reconciliation shall separately report all major classes of reconciling items. For example, major classes of deferrals of past operating cash receipts and payments and accruals of expected future operating cash receipts and payments, including at a minimum changes during the period in receivables pertaining to operating activities, in inventory, and in payables pertaining to operating activities, shall be separately reported. Enterprises are encouraged to provide further breakdowns of those categories that they consider meaningful. For example, changes in receivables from customers for an enterprise's sale of goods or services might be reported separately from changes in other operating receivables. In addition, if the indirect method is used, amounts of interest paid (net of amounts capitalized) and income taxes paid during the period shall be provided in related disclosures.

30. If the direct method of reporting net cash flow from operating activities is used, the reconciliation of net income to net cash flow from operating activities shall be provided in a separate schedule. If the indirect method is used, the reconciliation may be either reported within the statement of cash flows or provided in a separate schedule, with the statement of cash flows reporting only the net cash flow from operating activities. If the reconciliation is presented in the statement of cash flows, all adjustments to net income to determine net cash flow from operating activities shall be clearly identified as reconciling items.

31. Except for items described in paragraphs 12 and 13, both investing cash inflows and outflows and financing cash inflows and outflows shall be reported separately in a statement of cash flows— for example, outlays for acquisitions of property, plant, and equipment shall be reported separately from proceeds from sales of property, plant, and equipment; proceeds of borrowings shall be reported separately from repayments of debt; and proceeds from issuing stock shall be reported separately from outlays to reacquire the enterprise's stock.

---

[11]Paragraphs 115-118 in Appendix B and paragraph 135 in Appendix C, respectively, discuss and illustrate a method by which those major classes of gross operating cash receipts and payments generally may be determined indirectly.

[12]Adjustments to net income to determine net cash flow from operating activities shall reflect accruals for interest earned but not received and interest incurred but not paid. Those accruals may be reflected in the statement of financial position in changes in assets and liabilities that relate to investing or financing activities, such as loans or deposits. However, interest credited directly to a deposit account that has the general characteristics described in paragraph 7, footnote 1, is a cash outflow of the payor and a cash inflow of the payee when the entry is made.

Information about Noncash Investing and Financing Activities

32. Information about all investing and financing activities of an enterprise during a period that affect recognized assets or liabilities but that do not result in cash receipts or cash payments in the period shall be reported in related disclosures. Those disclosures may be either narrative or summarized in a schedule, and they shall clearly relate the cash and noncash aspects of transactions involving similar items. Examples of noncash investing and financing transactions are converting debt to equity; acquiring assets by assuming directly related liabilities, such as purchasing a building by incurring a mortgage to the seller; obtaining an asset by entering into a capital lease; and exchanging noncash assets or liabilities for other noncash assets or liabilities. Some transactions are part cash and part noncash; only the cash portion shall be reported in the statement of cash flows.

Cash Flow per Share

33. Financial statements shall not report an amount of cash flow per share. Neither cash flow nor any component of it is an alternative to net income as an indicator of an enterprise's performance, as reporting per share amounts might imply.

Effective Date and Transition

34. The provisions of this Statement shall be effective for annual financial statements for fiscal years ending after July 15, 1988. Earlier application is encouraged. This Statement need not be applied in financial statements for interim periods in the initial year of application, but cash flow information for those interim periods shall be restated if reported with annual financial statements for that fiscal year. Restatement of comparative annual financial statements for earlier years is encouraged but not required.

The provisions of this Statement need not be applied to immaterial items.

This Statement was adopted by the affirmative votes of four members of the Financial Accounting Standards Board. Messrs. Lauver, Leisenring, and Swieringa dissented.

Messrs. Lauver, Leisenring, and Swieringa dissent to this Statement's requirements to classify interest and dividends received and interest paid as cash flows from operating activities. They believe that interest and dividends received are returns on investments in debt and equity securities that should be classified as cash inflows from investing activities. They believe that interest paid is a cost of obtaining financial resources that should be classified as a cash outflow for financing activities.

Messrs. Lauver, Leisenring, and Swieringa also dissent to this Statement's requirement to classify certain cash receipts and payments according to the nature of an earlier transaction rather than according to the nature of the cash receipts and payments. Under this Statement, an enterprise that sells merchandise in one year for an installment note receivable and receives principal payments on the note in subsequent years will classify those principal payments as operating cash inflows. They believe that those principal payments should be classified as cash inflows from investing activities because they represent a return of the enterprise's investment in the installment note. Classifying those principal payments as operating cash inflows denies receipt of the installment note as a noncash investing activity, is inconsistent with

the enterprise's recovery of its investment in that note, and is inconsistent with the treatment of the receipt of principal payments on other investments in debt instruments as cash inflows from investing activities. They also note that this Statement will result in similar inconsistencies for the purchase of inventory in exchange for a note payable.

Messrs. Lauver and Swieringa also dissent to this Statement's permitted use of the indirect method of reporting net cash flow from operating activities. They believe that by permitting the continued use of the indirect method, the Board has foregone the opportunity to make a significant contribution to the quality of financial reporting and to enhanced user understanding of cash flows from operating activities. Reporting information about cash received from customers, cash paid to suppliers and employees, income taxes paid, and other operating receipts and payments (the direct method) provides a description of the operating activities of an entity during a period that is both more informative and more consistent with the primary purpose of a statement of cash flows, which is described in paragraph 4 of this Statement as "to provide relevant information about the cash receipts and cash payments of an enterprise during a period."

Because the indirect method does not result in reporting separately major classes of gross operating cash flows, Messrs. Lauver and Swieringa believe that method is inconsistent with the conclusion in paragraph 11 that "generally, information about gross amounts of cash receipts and cash payments during a period is more relevant than information about the net amounts of cash receipts and payments." Further, permitting use of the indirect method makes this Statement internally inconsistent because major classes of gross cash flows from investing and financing activities are required to be reported separately while major classes of gross operating cash flows are not. In addition, presenting a reconciliation of net income and net cash flow from operating activities within the statement of cash flows rather than in a separate schedule results in including the effects of certain noncash transactions and other events within the statement of cash flows. Messrs. Lauver and Swieringa believe that is confusing and counter to the primary purpose of a statement of cash flows.

Mr. Lauver believes the internal inconsistencies in the provisions of this Statement concerning the classification of cash flows identified in the preceding paragraphs result from putting other objectives ahead of the Statement's stated objective of providing relevant information about cash receipts and payments. He believes that by adopting the view that the cash effects of transactions and events that enter into the determination of net in-

come are cash flows from operating activities (paragraph 21), this Statement, in spite of comments to the contrary (paragraph 33), attempts to establish net cash flow from operating activities as an alternative performance indicator, an objective that he believes is undesirable. Further, that objective makes each of the three categories misleading by excluding from investing and financing categories cash receipts and payments that stem from investing and financing activities and ought to be included in those categories. The result is that none of the three required categories of cash flows is aptly named and all of them are, therefore, likely to be misunderstood.

Mr. Lauver observes that a statement of cash flows involves no issues of recognition, measurement, or estimation; by definition it includes only the effects of identifiable, unquestioned transactions. In that circumstance, the financial reporting function involves only two tasks. The first is to aggregate similar cash receipts and payments to facilitate communication and understanding and to do so consistently. The second is to accurately characterize the various aggregations so that they are unlikely to be misunderstood. He believes this Statement fails to do either.

Members of the Financial Accounting Standards Board:

Dennis R. Beresford, *Chairman*	Raymond C. Lauver	C. Arthur Northrop
	James J. Leisenring	Robert J. Swieringa
Victor H. Brown	David Mosso	

Appendix A

BACKGROUND INFORMATION

35. As part of its work on the conceptual framework, the FASB issued a Discussion Memorandum in December 1980, *Reporting Funds Flows, Liquidity, and Financial Flexibility,* which discussed funds flow reporting issues. Major issues raised in the Discussion Memorandum relating to funds flow reporting included (a) the concept of funds that should be adopted as the focus of the funds flow statement, (b) the reporting of transactions that have no direct impact on funds, (c) the approaches for presenting information about funds flows, (d) the presentation of information about funds flows from operations, (e) the separation of funds flow information about investing activities into outflows for maintenance of operating capacity, expansion of operating capacity, or nonoperating purposes, and (f) summary indicators of funds flows. The Board received 190 letters of comment in response to the Discussion Memorandum. In May 1981, a public hearing was held to discuss the issues raised in the Discussion Memorandum.

Thirty-two individuals and organizations appeared at the hearing.

36. In November 1981, the Board issued an Exposure Draft of a proposed concepts Statement, *Reporting Income, Cash Flows, and Financial Position of Business Enterprises.* That Exposure Draft discussed the role of a funds statement and guides for reporting components of funds flows, concluding that funds flow reporting should focus on cash rather than on working capital. One hundred twenty-six comment letters were received in response to the November 1981 Exposure Draft. After considering those comment letters, the Board decided not to issue a final Statement on that subject. Instead, the Board chose to consider the subject in connection with its study of recognition and measurement concepts. In December 1983, the Board issued another Exposure Draft of a concepts Statement, *Recognition and Measurement in Financial Statements of Business Enterprises,* which also discussed the role of the cash flow statement. One hundred four comment letters were received on that Exposure Draft. In December 1984, the Board issued FASB Concepts Statement No. 5, *Recognition and Measurement in*

Financial Statements of Business Enterprises, which includes general guidance on a statement of cash flows and concludes that, in concept, a cash flow statement should be part of a full set of financial statements.

37. During its deliberations on the 1981 Exposure Draft, the FASB decided that detailed cash flow reporting issues should be addressed only at the standards level, but deferred consideration of the standards project until the results of a voluntary initiative by the Financial Executives Institute (FEI) were assessed. In late 1981, the FEI encouraged its members to change to a focus on cash and short-term investments in their funds statements. It also encouraged enterprises to experiment with alternative formats, such as grouping items by operating, investing, and financing activities. That experimentation with cash flow reporting in statements of changes in financial position was in keeping with the existing authoritative literature, Opinion 19, which allowed flexibility in the focus and form of the statement.

38. In 1984, the Financial Executives Research Foundation of the FEI published *The Funds Statement: Structure and Use,* a research study on funds statements that solicited views of both preparers and users on virtually all of the issues pertaining to funds flows discussed in the Discussion Memorandum and that analyzed the results of the experimentation encouraged by the FEI. The study pointed out several areas of diversity in current practice, including different definitions of *funds,* different definitions of *cash* and *cash flow from operations,* and different forms of presentation in the statement.

39. In April 1985, the Board added to its agenda a cash flow reporting project of limited scope to (a) establish the objectives of a statement of cash flows, (b) define the few major components of cash flows to be presented in the statement, and (c) decide whether to require a statement of cash flows as part of a full set of financial statements for all enterprises.

40. In May 1985, the FASB staff organized a Task Force on Cash Flow Reporting. In June 1985, the FASB staff met with the task force to discuss appropriate objectives for a statement of cash flows. In November 1985, the staff met again with the task force to discuss the identification and defini-

tion of the major elements of cash flows, the classification of certain transactions, the reporting of noncash transactions, and the methods for presenting cash flow from operating activities. In March 1986, an Advisory Group on Cash Flow Reporting by Financial Institutions was organized. In April 1986, the FASB staff met with the advisory group to discuss whether a statement of cash flows should be included in a complete set of financial statements of a financial institution as well as other cash flow reporting issues related to financial institutions. In March and April 1986, the staff communicated with the FASB Small Business Advisory Group and the Technical Issues Committee of the Private Companies Practice Section of the American Institute of Certified Public Accountants (AICPA) on whether a statement of cash flows should be required of small businesses as part of a full set of financial statements.

41. The Board issued an Exposure Draft, *Statement of Cash Flows,* in July 1986. It proposed standards for cash flow reporting to require a statement of cash flows as part of a full set of financial statements of all business enterprises in place of a statement of changes in financial position.

42. The Board received more than 450 comment letters in response to that Exposure Draft. In December 1986, the FASB staff met with an informal group of securities analysts who specialize in financial institutions to discuss users' needs for information about a financial institution's cash flows. In January 1987, the FASB staff held a special meeting to discuss the numerous comments received on the manner of reporting cash flows from operating activities. Representatives of the Financial Analysts Federation, the Financial Executives Institute, the National Association of Accountants, and the Robert Morris Associates participated in that meeting. In February 1987, the FASB staff met with the task force to discuss comments received on the Exposure Draft, and in March 1987, the staff met with the Advisory Group on Cash Flow Reporting by Financial Institutions.

43. The Board considered the comment letters and information obtained at those meetings in developing this Statement. Appendix B discusses the basis for the Board's conclusions, including changes made to the provisions of the 1986 Exposure Draft.

Appendix B

BASIS FOR CONCLUSIONS

CONTENTS

Appendix B

BASIS FOR CONCLUSIONS

Introduction

44. This appendix discusses factors deemed significant by members of the Board in reaching the conclusions in this Statement. It includes descriptions of alternatives considered by the Board with reasons for accepting some and rejecting others. Individual Board members gave greater weight to some factors than to others.

Need for Cash Flow Information

45. The Board decided to require a statement of cash flows as part of a full set of financial statements on the basis of the objectives and concepts set forth in FASB Concepts Statement No. 1, *Objectives of Financial Reporting by Business Enterprises,* and Concepts Statement 5.

46. Paragraph 37 of Concepts Statement 1 states that:

Financial reporting should provide information to help present and potential investors and creditors and other users in assessing the amounts, timing, and uncertainty of prospective cash receipts from dividends or interest and the proceeds from the sale, redemption, or maturity of securities or loans. The prospects for those cash receipts are affected by an enterprise's ability to generate enough cash to meet its obligations when due and its other cash operating needs, to reinvest in operations, and to pay cash dividends. . . .

Paragraph 39 states that:

. . . since an enterprise's ability to generate favorable cash flows affects both its ability to pay dividends and interest and the market prices of its securities, expected cash flows to investors and creditors are related to expected cash flows to the enterprise in which they have invested or to which they have loaned funds.

Paragraph 49 states that:

Financial reporting should provide information about how an enterprise obtains and spends cash, about its borrowing and repayment of borrowing, about its capital [equity] transactions, including cash dividends and other distributions of enterprise resources to owners, and about other factors that may affect an enterprise's liquidity or solvency.

47. Paragraph 13 of Concepts Statement 5 states that the "amount and variety of information that financial reporting should provide about an entity require several financial statements." A full set of financial statements for a period should show cash flows during the period. Paragraph 52 describes the role of information in the statement of cash flows as follows:

It provides useful information about an entity's activities in generating cash through operations to repay debt, distribute dividends, or reinvest to maintain or expand operating capacity; about its financing activities, both debt and equity; and about its investing or spending of cash. Important uses of information about an entity's current cash receipts and payments include helping to assess factors such as the entity's liquidity, financial flexibility, profitability, and risk.

Statements of Cash Flows and Other Information on Liquidity, Financial Flexibility, Profitability, and Risk

48. The statement of cash flows is not the only financial statement that provides information on liquidity, financial flexibility, profitability, and risk. Concepts Statement 5 discusses the complementary role of the other financial statements:

A statement of financial position provides information about an entity's assets, liabilities, and equity and their relationships to each other at a moment in time. The statement delineates the entity's resource structure—major classes and amounts of assets—and its financing structure—major classes and amounts of liabilities and equity. [paragraph 26]

Important uses of information about an entity's financial position include helping users to assess factors such as the entity's liquidity, financial flexibility, profitability, and risk. [paragraph 29]

Financial statements complement each other. For example:

a. Statements of financial position include information that is often used in assessing an entity's liquidity and financial flexibility, but a statement of financial position provides only an incomplete picture of either liquidity or financial flexibility unless it is used in conjunction with at least a cash flow statement. . . .

c. Statements of cash flows commonly show a great deal about an entity's current cash receipts and payments, but a cash flow statement provides an incomplete basis for assessing prospects for future cash flows because it cannot show interperiod relationships. Many current cash receipts, especially from operations, stem from activities of earlier periods, and many current cash payments are intended or expected to result in future, not current, cash receipts. Statements of earnings and comprehensive income, especially if used in conjunction with statements of financial position, usually provide a better basis for assessing future cash flow prospects of an entity than do cash flow statements alone. [paragraph 24, subparagraphs b and d and footnote references omitted]

Cash Instead of Working Capital

49. In light of those objectives and concepts, which were reinforced by the Board's observation of a trend in practice toward statements of changes in financial position that focused on cash flows, the Board concluded that a statement of cash flows should be required to help investors, creditors, and others assess future cash flows, provide feedback about actual cash flows, evaluate the availability of cash for dividends and investment and the enterprise's ability to finance growth from internal sources, and identify the reasons for differences between net income and net cash flows. Nearly all of the respondents to both the Discussion Memorandum and the Exposure Draft[13] agreed with those objectives of a statement of cash flows.

50. To achieve those objectives requires that the statement focus on flows of cash rather than flows of working capital. An overwhelming majority of

[13]Unless otherwise indicated, references throughout this appendix to *respondents* generally include respondents to both the Discussion Memorandum and the 1986 Exposure Draft.

respondents agreed with that focus. Many made negative comments on the usefulness of working capital as a concept of funds, generally questioning its relevance since positive working capital does not necessarily indicate liquidity nor does negative working capital necessarily indicate illiquidity.

Cash and Cash Equivalents

51. Cash is the most useful concept of funds because decisions of investors, creditors, and others focus on assessments of future cash flows. However, enterprises commonly invest cash in excess of immediate needs in short-term, highly liquid investments, and whether cash is on hand, on deposit, or invested in a short-term financial instrument that is readily convertible to a known amount of cash is largely irrelevant to users' assessments of liquidity and future cash flows. The Board therefore decided that a statement of cash flows should focus on the aggregate of cash and cash equivalents.

52. Respondents to the Exposure Draft generally agreed with the focus on cash and cash equivalents. Many, however, asked the Board to provide more guidance on which short-term, highly liquid investments qualify as cash equivalents. Others questioned whether particular instruments, such as marketable equity securities that management intends to hold for only a short period of time, might qualify.

53. The Board agreed to provide more guidance on the short-term, highly liquid investments that qualify as cash equivalents. In developing the guidance in paragraph 8 of this Statement, the Board noted that the objective of enterprises' cash management programs generally is to earn interest on temporarily idle funds rather than to put capital at risk in the hope of benefiting from favorable price changes that may result from changes in interest rates or other factors. Although any limit to the maturity of items that can qualify as cash equivalents is somewhat arbitrary, the Board decided to specify a limit of three months or less. The Board believes that that limit will result in treating as cash equivalents only those items that are so near cash that it is appropriate to refer to them as the "equivalent" of cash.

54. Some respondents to the Exposure Draft expressed concern that a reader of the financial statements might not be able to relate the amount of cash and cash equivalents in the statement of cash flows to a line item in the statement of financial position. The Board agreed that being able to trace the change in cash and cash equivalents in the statement of cash flows to related amounts in successive statements of financial position is desirable. It therefore decided to require that the total amounts of cash and cash equivalents at the beginning and end of the period shown in the statement of cash flows be the same amounts as similarly titled line items or subtotals in the statements of financial position as of those dates.

55. Banks and other financial institutions commonly carry three-month Treasury bills, commercial paper, and similar short-term financial instruments in their trading and investments accounts, in which they are commingled with longer term investments. Those institutions generally contend that purchases and sales of those items are part of their trading or investing activities—not part of their cash management program—and they prefer not to treat those items as cash equivalents in a statement of cash flows, which would require segregating them from other items in their trading and investment accounts.

56. The Board noted that the reason for focusing a statement of cash flows on cash and cash equivalents is to recognize and accommodate common practices in cash management. Accordingly, the Board agreed that items that meet the definition of cash equivalents that are part of a larger pool of investments properly considered investing activities need not be segregated and treated as cash equivalents. Because that decision will result in differences between enterprises in the items treated as cash equivalents, the Board decided that each enterprise should disclose its policy for treating items as cash equivalents.

Scope

57. Respondents from financial institutions, particularly commercial banks, generally said that a statement of cash flows would not be useful for their industry. Some commentators specifically mentioned that a statement of cash flows would be particularly useful for small businesses, but a few asked that small businesses be exempted from at least some provisions of the Exposure Draft. A few respondents to the Exposure Draft referred to the fact that investment companies were permitted to provide a statement of changes in net assets rather than a statement of changes in financial position and asked that they be exempted from a requirement to provide a statement of cash flows.

Financial Institutions

58. Financial institutions, particularly commercial banks, have long contended that their statements of changes in financial position are not meaningful. In response to the Exposure Draft, most asserted that a statement of cash flows would be

appropriate classification of items will not always be clear. In those circumstances, the appropriate classification generally should depend on the nature of the activity that is likely to be the predominate source of cash flows for the item. For example, the presumption is that the acquisition or production of productive assets is an investing activity. However, productive assets are sometimes acquired or produced to be a direct source of the enterprise's revenues, such as assets to be rented to others for a short period and then sold. In those circumstances, the nature of those assets may be similar to inventory in a retailing business. Accordingly, the acquisition or production and subsequent sale of such assets are appropriately classified as operating activities.

Interest Paid and Received

88. The Exposure Draft required interest paid and interest and dividends received to be classified as cash flows from operating activities. That classification is consistent with the view that, in general, cash flows from operating activities should reflect the cash effects of transactions and other events that enter into the determination of net income.

89. Some respondents to the Exposure Draft favored classifying interest paid as a cash outflow for financing activities and interest and dividends received as cash inflows from investing activities. Those respondents generally said that interest paid, like dividends paid, is a direct consequence of a financing decision and thus should be classified as a cash outflow for financing activities. That is, both interest and dividends are returns *on* the capital provided by creditors and investors, and both should be classified with returns *of* those amounts because the distinction between returns *of* and returns *on* investment is largely irrelevant in the context of cash flows. Respondents made similar comments for interest and dividends received.

90. The Board considered those views and, as mentioned in paragraph 86, noted that a reasonable case can be made for alternative classifications of certain items. However, the Board also noted that virtually all enterprises classified interest received and paid as operating cash flows under Opinion 19. In particular, interest received and paid were commonly considered to be operating cash flows of banks and other financial institutions. In addition, the Board perceived widespread support for the notion that operating cash flows should, insofar as possible, include items whose effects are included in determining net income to facilitate an understanding of the reasons for differences between net income and net cash flow from operating activities. The Board therefore was not convinced that changing the prevalent practice

in classifying interest received and paid would necessarily result in a more meaningful presentation of cash flows. This Statement does, however, require that the amount of interest paid during a period (net of amounts capitalized) be disclosed, which will permit users of financial statements who wish to consider interest paid as a financing cash outflow to do so.

Income Taxes Paid

91. The Exposure Draft required all income taxes paid to be classified as operating cash outflows. A few respondents suggested allocating income taxes paid to investing and financing transactions.

92. The Board decided that allocation of income taxes paid to operating, investing, and financing activities would be so complex and arbitrary that the benefits, if any, would not justify the costs involved. This Statement requires that the total amount of income taxes paid be disclosed for reasons discussed in paragraph 121.

Installment Sales and Purchases

93. A somewhat difficult classification issue arises for installment sales and purchases of inventory by an enterprise for which cash inflows or outflows may occur several years after the date of the transaction. Those transactions can be viewed as having aspects of both operating and investing activities (for a sale by the enterprise) or operating and financing activities (for a purchase by the enterprise). The Exposure Draft treated cash flows stemming from installment sales and purchases in accordance with that view. Only cash flows occurring "soon before or after" the time of sale or purchase would have been operating cash flows. Subsequent principal payments on the related notes would have been investing cash inflows or financing cash outflows.

94. Some respondents to the Exposure Draft suggested that the classification of a cash receipt or payment should be determined by the original purpose for which it is received or paid. Thus, all cash flows related to the sale or purchase of inventory would be operating cash flows regardless of when they were received or paid. Those respondents generally pointed out that, under the approach in the Exposure Draft, cumulative net cash flow from operating activities over the life of an enterprise that finances most of its sales under installment plans might be negative. They considered that to be an inappropriate and confusing result.

95. The Board agreed that all cash collected from customers or paid to suppliers from the sale or purchase of inventory should be classified as operating

cash flows. That classification is consistent with the notion that operating cash flows generally should include items that are included in net income.

96. A related issue involves principal payments on seller-financed mortgages on productive assets. Some have argued that all such principal payments should be classified as investing cash outflows rather than financing cash outflows. They said that they consider that classification to be more consistent with classifying all principal receipts and payments on sales and purchases of inventory as operating cash flows. The Board decided, however, that all principal payments on mortgages should be classified as financing cash outflows. The reason for that conclusion is largely pragmatic—the Board believes that it would be unduly burdensome to require enterprises to keep track of seller-financed versus third-party mortgages throughout the generally long period of time that a mortgage is outstanding. Some also consider all principal payments on mortgages to be financing cash outflows.

Maintenance and Expansion Investment Expenditures

97. The Board considered whether to require further classification of investment expenditures into expenditures for maintenance of existing capacity and expenditures for expansion into new capacity. That further classification would provide information designed to be used by investors, creditors, and others in calculating an amount sometimes described as "discretionary cash flow," with the idea that maintenance expenditures are nondiscretionary and only the cash remaining after such expenditures is free for discretionary purposes, such as paying dividends.

98. Most respondents said that the cash flows related to investing activities should not be allocated between those for maintenance of capacity and those for expansion. They said that those allocations would necessarily be arbitrary and the costs to compile the information would exceed the benefits provided.

99. The Board noted that substantial implementation difficulties would result if all enterprises were required to distinguish between expenditures for maintenance and those for expansion and that the subjectivity involved in making that distinction could result in numbers that would be unreliable. Accordingly, the Board decided not to require that disclosure.

Foreign Currency Cash Flows

100. The purpose of a statement of changes in financial position under Opinion 19 was to explain all important changes in financial position, regardless of whether they directly affected cash or working capital. That purpose suggested that the effects of changes in exchange rates on items reported in the statement of changes in financial position should be disclosed if material. Opinion 19 permitted a degree of flexibility in the statement of changes in financial position, and enterprises used alternative formats and terminology to report the effects of exchange rate changes.

101. The purpose of a statement of cash flows, on the other hand, is to report cash receipts and cash payments during a period, classified into meaningful categories. The effects of exchange rate changes on assets and liabilities denominated in foreign currencies, like those of other price changes, may affect the amount of a cash receipt or payment. But exchange rate changes do not themselves give rise to cash flows, and their effects on items other than cash thus have no place in a statement of cash flows. To achieve its objective, a statement of cash flows should reflect the reporting currency equivalent of cash receipts and payments that occur in a foreign currency. Because the effect of exchange rate changes on the reporting currency equivalent of cash held in foreign currencies affects the change in an enterprise's cash balance during a period but is not a cash receipt or payment, the Board decided that the effect of exchange rate changes on cash should be reported as a separate item in the reconciliation of beginning and ending balances of cash.

102. Some respondents to the Exposure Draft objected to the requirement to report the reporting currency equivalent of foreign currency cash receipts and payments. They generally said that they do not obtain cash flow information from their foreign subsidiaries but rather prepare the consolidated statement of changes in financial position from the consolidated balance sheet and income statement, perhaps supplemented by certain information about gross increases and decreases in asset and liability accounts after translation to U.S. dollars. Other respondents supported the Exposure Draft's requirement only for foreign subsidiaries whose functional currency is other than the reporting currency. For foreign subsidiaries whose functional currency is the reporting currency, they generally favored some variation of a method that would include in the statement of cash flows the effects of exchange rate changes on all items classi-

fied as cash flows from operating, investing, and financing activities.

103. The Board noted that exchange rate changes affect only the amount of a cash receipt or payment (that is, the effects of rate changes are not themselves cash flows) regardless of whether the asset or liability on which an effect arises is held directly by a domestic enterprise, by a foreign subsidiary whose functional currency is the reporting currency, or by a foreign subsidiary whose functional currency is other than the reporting currency. Accordingly, this Statement clarifies that the requirement to report the reporting currency equivalents of cash receipts and payments denominated in foreign currencies applies to all such cash flows.

104. The Board considered the assertions that the requirements concerning reporting cash receipts and payments that occur in a foreign currency would be unduly burdensome because they would require enterprises to obtain cash flow information from their foreign subsidiaries. Although Opinion 19 did not directly address how to report the effects of exchange rate changes, the Board noted that Opinion 19 did require the reporting of gross funds flows, including, for example, both outlays to acquire property, plant, and equipment and proceeds from disposing of property, plant, and equipment. That is, while Opinion 19 required that the effects of exchange rate changes be included in a statement of changes in financial position, it did not necessarily provide that those effects should be reported in a way that results in line items that are not funds flows but rather are net changes, or gross increases and decreases, in translated asset and liability accounts. The Board therefore believes that full compliance with Opinion 19 would require obtaining some information about the cash flows of foreign subsidiaries. As exchange rates change, the methods that some respondents advocate might report, for example, an asset acquisition or disposition in a period in which none occurred and might even report an asset acquisition when in fact a disposition occurred. Whether or not Opinion 19 intended that result, it is inappropriate in a statement intended to report cash receipts and payments.

105. The Board is aware that enterprises use various approximation techniques to meet the present requirements of reporting foreign-currency-denominated assets, liabilities, revenues, expenses, and other items in the income statement and the statement of financial position. For example, appropriately weighted average exchange rates generally are used to translate revenues and expenses. Such methods also are acceptable in complying with the provisions of this Statement concerning foreign-currency-denominated cash flows provided that it is reasonable to expect that the results are substantially the same as if more precise data were used.

Reporting Net Cash Flow from Operating Activities

106. The Board considered two principal alternatives for reporting net cash flow from operating activities. The *direct method* shows as its principal components operating cash receipts and payments, such as cash received from customers and cash paid to suppliers and employees, the sum of which is *net cash flow from operating activities*. The *indirect method* starts with net income and adjusts it for revenue and expense items that were not the result of operating cash transactions in the current period to reconcile it to *net cash flow from operating activities*. The indirect method thus does not disclose operating cash receipts and payments. Paragraph 10 of Opinion 19 permitted either method, but the indirect method prevailed in practice under that Opinion.

107. The principal advantage of the direct method is that it shows operating cash receipts and payments. Knowledge of the specific sources of operating cash receipts and the purposes for which operating cash payments were made in past periods may be useful in estimating future operating cash flows. The relative amounts of major classes of revenues and expenses and their relationship to other items in the financial statements are presumed to be more useful than information only about their arithmetic sum—net income—in assessing enterprise performance. Likewise, amounts of major classes of operating cash receipts and payments presumably would be more useful than information only about their arithmetic sum—net cash flow from operating activities—in assessing an enterprise's ability to generate sufficient cash from operating activities to pay its debt, to reinvest in its operations, and to make distributions to its owners.

108. The principal advantage of the indirect method is that it focuses on the differences between net income and net cash flow from operating activities. Concepts Statement 1, paragraph 43, states that:

> The primary focus of financial reporting is information about an enterprise's performance provided by measures of earnings [comprehensive income] and its components. Investors, creditors, and others who are concerned with assessing the prospects for enterprise net cash inflows are especially interested in that information. Their

interest in an enterprise's future cash flows . . . leads primarily to an interest in information about its earnings [comprehensive income] rather than information directly about its cash flows. Financial statements that show only cash receipts and payments during a short period, such as a year, cannot adequately indicate whether or not an enterprise's performance is successful.

Some investors and creditors may assess future cash flows in part by first estimating future income based in part on reports of past income and then converting those future income estimates to estimates of future cash flows by allowing for leads and lags between cash flows and income. Information about similar leads and lags in the past are likely to be helpful in that process. Identifying differences between income items and related cash flows also can assist investors and creditors who want to identify the differences between enterprises in the measurement and recognition of non-cash items that affect income.

109. Many providers of financial statements have said that it would be costly for their companies to report gross operating cash receipts and payments. They said that they do not presently collect information in a manner that will allow them to determine amounts such as cash received from customers or cash paid to suppliers directly from their accounting systems.

110. The Exposure Draft said that the Board recognized the advantages of both approaches and concluded that neither method provided benefits sufficient to justify requiring one and prohibiting the other. Enterprises therefore would have been permitted to use either method.

111. A majority of respondents to the Exposure Draft asked the Board to require use of the direct method. Those respondents, most of whom were commercial lenders, generally said that amounts of operating cash receipts and payments are particularly important in assessing an enterprise's external borrowing needs and its ability to repay borrowings. They indicated that creditors are more exposed to fluctuations in net cash flow from operating activities than to fluctuations in net income and that information on the amounts of operating cash receipts and payments is important in assessing those fluctuations in net cash flow from operating activities. They also pointed out that the direct method is more consistent with the objective of a statement of cash flows—to provide information about cash receipts and cash payments—than the indirect method, which does not report operat-

ing cash receipts and payments.

112. Both commercial lenders and equity analysts who responded to the Exposure Draft asked that more detail on cash flows from operating activities be required. Some said that degree of detail is more important than manner of presentation.

113. Most of the providers of financial statements who addressed the issue supported allowing a choice between the direct and indirect methods. They generally said that requiring the direct method would impose excessive implementation costs and that they believe that the indirect method provides more meaningful information.

114. Because of the extensive attention in the comment letters on the Exposure Draft to the manner of reporting operating cash flows, the Board gave particular consideration to that issue in its deliberations leading to the issuance of this Statement. As mentioned in paragraph 42, the FASB staff held a special meeting with representatives of interested groups of constituents to obtain more information about the benefits and costs of the direct and indirect methods. Because most enterprises said that they cannot now obtain amounts of gross operating cash receipts and payments directly from their accounting systems, the Board considered means by which those amounts might be determined indirectly. Together with other efforts, the FASB staff commissioned an informal interview survey of a limited number of enterprises concerning the potential costs they might incur in indirectly determining amounts of operating cash receipts and payments.

Indirectly Determining Amounts of Operating Cash Receipts and Payments

115. Given sufficiently detailed information, major classes of operating cash receipts and payments may be determined indirectly by adjusting revenue and expense amounts for the change during the period in related asset and liability accounts. For example, cash collected from customers may be determined indirectly by adjusting sales for the change during the period in receivables from customers for the enterprise's delivery of goods or services. Likewise, cash paid to suppliers and employees may be determined indirectly by adjusting cost of sales and expenses (exclusive of depreciation, interest, and income taxes) for the change during the period in inventories and payables for operating items. That procedure, of course, requires the availability of information concerning the change during the period in the appropriate

classes of receivables and payables.[17] The more detailed the categories of operating cash receipts and payments to be reported, the more complex the procedure for determining them.

116. Based on information available to the Board during its deliberations, it seems likely that amounts of operating cash receipts and payments at the minimum level of detail specified in paragraph 27 often may be determined indirectly without incurring unduly burdensome costs over those involved in appropriately applying the indirect method. For example, determining net cash flow from operating activities by the indirect method requires the availability of the total amount of operating receivables. That is, any receivables for investing or financing items must be segregated. Within the total amount of operating receivables, information on receivables from customers for an enterprise's delivery of goods or services may well be available separately from those for interest and dividends. Thus, it may be possible to determine indirectly cash collected from customers and interest and dividends received using much the same information needed to determine net cash flow from operating activities using the indirect method.

117. The same procedure may be used to determine cash paid to suppliers and employees. Determining net cash flow from operating activities by the direct method requires the availability of the total amount of payables pertaining to operating activities. Within that amount, payables to suppliers and employees may well be available separately from those for interest and taxes. The Board understands, however, that determining operating cash payments in more detail than the minimum specified in paragraph 27 might involve significant incremental costs over those already required to apply the indirect method because information on subcategories of payables to suppliers and employees may not be available.

118. The Board believes that many enterprises may well be able to determine amounts of operating cash receipts and payments at the minimum level of detail that this Statement encourages (paragraph 27) indirectly at reasonable cost by the procedure discussed in the foregoing paragraphs. But few, if any, companies have experimented with that procedure, and the degree of difficulty encountered in applying it undoubtedly would vary depending on the nature of an enterprise's operations and the features of its current accounting system.

Conclusion on Reporting Net Cash Flow from Operating Activities

119. The Board believes that both the direct and the indirect methods provide potentially important information. The more comprehensive and presumably more useful approach would be to use the direct method in the statement of cash flows and to provide a reconciliation of net income and net cash flow from operating activities in a separate schedule—thereby reaping the benefits of both methods while maintaining the focus of the statement of cash flows on cash receipts and payments. This Statement therefore encourages enterprises to follow that approach. But most providers and users of financial statements have little or no experience and only limited familiarity with the direct method, while both have extensive experience with the indirect method. Not only are there questions about the ability of enterprises to determine gross amounts of operating cash receipts and payments, as already discussed, but also little information is available on which specific categories of operating cash receipts and payments would be most meaningful.

120. Major change in financial reporting often is the result of an evolutionary process, which may involve interactions between the voluntary efforts of providers of financial statements and the actions of standards setters. Many areas of financial reporting, and reporting cash flows in particular, have benefited from the voluntary efforts of enterprises to improve their reporting practices. The Board decided that further movement toward a more comprehensive approach to reporting operating cash flows should be permitted to develop as both providers and users of financial statements gain experience with information on cash flows prepared in accordance with the provisions of this Statement.

121. To provide information about the gross amounts of at least those operating cash flows that are likely to be readily available, this Statement requires enterprises that use the indirect method of reporting net cash flow from operating activities to disclose amounts of interest and income taxes paid. The Board believes that that information usually will be readily available. This Statement also requires enterprises that use the indirect method to report separately changes in inventory, receivables, and payables. With that information, users may be able to make their own rough approximations of operating cash receipts and payments

---

[17]For the resulting operating cash receipts and payments to be accurate, the effects of all noncash entries to accounts receivable and payable, inventory, and other balance sheet accounts used in the calculation must be eliminated. For example, the change in accounts receivable would have to be determined exclusive of any bad debt write-offs and other noncash charges and credits to customer accounts during the period.

at a minimum level of detail using the indirect procedure discussed in paragraphs 116 and 117.

Cash Flow per Share

122. The Board considered whether cash flow per share should be reported. The Board concluded that reporting cash flow per share would falsely imply that cash flow, or some component of it, is a possible alternative to earnings per share as a measure of performance. The Board also noted other problems with calculating cash flow per share, including differing opinions about the appropriate numerator for the indicator (for example, whether it should be net cash flow from operating activities or an amount after deducting principal repayments on debt) and the appropriate denominator for the indicator (for example, whether it should be the same as the number of shares outstanding used for the earnings per share calculation).

123. A major problem in reporting cash flow per share data is investor understanding. Investors over many years have become accustomed to seeing operating data per share computed only for earnings. Moreover, the measurement problems associated with reporting earnings on a per share basis have been considered and largely settled. To report other data on a per share basis invites the danger that investors, creditors, and others may confuse those measures with the conventional accounting measure of earnings per share.

124. Earnings per share focuses attention on earnings available for common stockholders, and that concept guides the calculation of, and adjustments to, the numerator and denominator of the ratio. Earnings is suitable for the numerator of the ratio because the concepts underlying its calculation, such as capital maintenance (the distinction between the return *of* capital and return *on* capital), focus on return to stockholders *on* their investment. Net cash flow from operating activities is not comparable to net income because recovery of capital is not a factor in its calculation, and net cash flow from operating activities includes both returns *on* and returns *of* investment.

125. A majority of the respondents to the Exposure Draft who addressed the issue agreed that cash flow per share should not be reported. A few, however, asked whether the Board intended to preclude reporting of per unit amounts of cash flow distributable under the terms of a partnership agreement or other agreement between an enterprise and its owners. Reporting a contractually determined per unit amount is not the same as reporting a cash flow per share amount intended to

provide information useful to all investors and creditors and thus is not precluded by this Statement.

Effective Date and Transition

126. The Exposure Draft would have been effective for fiscal years ending after June 30, 1987 and would have required enterprises to effect the change in accounting by restating financial statements for earlier years presented for comparative purposes.

127. Some respondents to the Exposure Draft said that restatement of prior years' financial statements for their companies would be difficult and expensive, if not virtually impossible, because certain data on gross cash flows were not collected for earlier periods. The major problem areas mentioned were foreign subsidiaries' cash flows and gross cash flows pertaining to loans and deposits of banks. Because of the need to develop systems for gathering that information, those respondents generally asked that the effective date of a final Statement be deferred at least a year from that in the Exposure Draft. A few banks asked that the effective date be deferred until years ending after December 15, 1989. They said that they needed additional time to get data-gathering systems in place by the beginning of the year of adoption.

128. The Board recognizes that some enterprises will need to develop data-gathering systems and thus decided to make this Statement effective for fiscal years ending after July 15, 1988 and not to require its application in interim statements during the year of adoption. The Board, however, decided against a further delay of the effective date. The Board noted that reasonable approximations are generally acceptable.

129. The Board also was persuaded by respondents that requiring restatement of prior years' financial statements might be unduly burdensome for some enterprises and thus decided to encourage but not require restatement. However, not restating prior years' statements of changes in financial position to comply with the provisions of this Statement may result in a significant degree of noncomparability and may also make for an awkward presentation. For example, an enterprise that formerly presented its statement of changes in financial position in a sources and uses format and considered "funds" to be working capital might find it difficult to present those statements on the same page as a statement of cash flows. The Board therefore expects that enterprises with the ability to restate generally will do so.

Appendix C

ILLUSTRATIVE EXAMPLES

130. This appendix provides illustrations for the preparation of statements of cash flows. Example 1 illustrates a statement of cash flows under both the direct method and the indirect method for a domestic manufacturing company. Example 2 illustrates a statement of cash flows under the direct method for a manufacturing company with foreign operations. Example 3 illustrates a statement of cash flows under the direct method for a financial institution. These illustrations are intended as examples only. Also, the illustrations of the reconciliation of net income to net cash provided by operating activities may provide detailed information in excess of that required for a meaningful presentation. Other formats or levels of detail may be appropriate for particular circumstances.

Example 1

131. Presented below is a statement of cash flows for the year ended December 31, 19X1 for Company M, a U.S. corporation engaged principally in manufacturing activities. This statement of cash flows illustrates the direct method of presenting cash flows from operating activities, as encouraged in paragraph 27 of this Statement.

COMPANY M
CONSOLIDATED STATEMENT OF CASH FLOWS
FOR THE YEAR ENDED DECEMBER 31, 19X1
Increase (Decrease) in Cash and Cash Equivalents

Cash flows from operating activities:		
Cash received from customers	$13,850	
Cash paid to suppliers and employees	(12,000)	
Dividend received from affiliate	20	
Interest received	55	
Interest paid (net of amount capitalized)	(220)	
Income taxes paid	(325)	
Insurance proceeds received	15	
Cash paid to settle lawsuit for patent infringement	(30)	
Net cash provided by operating activities		$1,365
Cash flows from investing activities:		
Proceeds from sale of facility	600	
Payment received on note for sale of plant	150	
Capital expenditures	(1,000)	
Payment for purchase of Company S, net of cash		
acquired	(925)	
Net cash used in investing activities		(1,175)
Cash flows from financing activities:		
Net borrowings under line-of-credit agreement	300	
Principal payments under capital lease obligation	(125)	
Proceeds from issuance of long-term debt	400	
Proceeds from issuance of common stock	500	
Dividends paid	(200)	
Net cash provided by financing activities		875
Net increase in cash and cash equivalents		1,065
Cash and cash equivalents at beginning of year		600
Cash and cash equivalents at end of year		$1,665

Reconciliation of net income to net cash provided by operating activities:

Net income		$ 760
Adjustments to reconcile net income to net cash provided		
by operating activities:		
Depreciation and amortization	$ 445	
Provision for losses on accounts receivable	200	
Gain on sale of facility	(80)	
Undistributed earnings of affiliate	(25)	
Payment received on installment note receivable for		
sale of inventory	100	
Change in assets and liabilities net of effects from		
purchase of Company S:		
Increase in accounts receivable	(215)	
Decrease in inventory	205	
Increase in prepaid expenses	(25)	
Decrease in accounts payable and accrued expenses	(250)	
Increase in interest and income taxes payable	50	
Increase in deferred taxes	150	
Increase in other liabilities	50	
Total adjustments		605
Net cash provided by operating activities		$1,365

Supplemental schedule of noncash investing and financing activities:

The Company purchased all of the capital stock of Company S for $950. In conjunction with the acquisition, liabilities were assumed as follows:

Fair value of assets acquired	$1,580
Cash paid for the capital stock	(950)
Liabilities assumed	$ 630

A capital lease obligation of $850 was incurred when the Company entered into a lease for new equipment.

Additional common stock was issued upon the conversion of $500 of long-term debt.

Disclosure of accounting policy:

For purposes of the statement of cash flows, the Company considers all highly liquid debt instruments purchased with a maturity of three months or less to be cash equivalents.

132. Presented below is Company M's statement of cash flows for the year ended December 31, 19X1 prepared using the indirect method, as described in paragraph 28 of this Statement:

COMPANY M
CONSOLIDATED STATEMENT OF CASH FLOWS
FOR THE YEAR ENDED DECEMBER 31, 19X1
Increase (Decrease) in Cash and Cash Equivalents

Cash flows from operating activities:		
Net income		$ 760
Adjustments to reconcile net income to net cash provided by operating activities:		
Depreciation and amortization	$ 445	
Provision for losses on accounts receivable	200	
Gain on sale of facility	(80)	
Undistributed earnings of affiliate	(25)	
Payment received on installment note receivable for sale of inventory	100	
Change in assets and liabilities net of effects from purchase of Company S:		
Increase in accounts receivable	(215)	
Decrease in inventory	205	
Increase in prepaid expenses	(25)	
Decrease in accounts payable and accrued expenses	(250)	
Increase in interest and income taxes payable	50	
Increase in deferred taxes	150	
Increase in other liabilities	50	
Total adjustments		605
Net cash provided by operating activities		1,365
Cash flows from investing activities:		
Proceeds from sale of facility	600	
Payment received on note for sale of plant	150	
Capital expenditures	(1,000)	
Payment for purchase of Company S, net of cash acquired	(925)	
Net cash used in investing activities		(1,175)
Cash flows from financing activities:		
Net borrowings under line-of-credit agreement	300	
Principal payments under capital lease obligation	(125)	
Proceeds from issuance of long-term debt	400	
Proceeds from issuance of common stock	500	
Dividends paid	(200)	
Net cash provided by financing activities		875
Net increase in cash and cash equivalents		1,065
Cash and cash equivalents at beginning of year		600
Cash and cash equivalents at end of year		$1,665

Supplemental disclosures of cash flow information:

Cash paid during the year for:		
Interest (net of amount capitalized)	$ 220	
Income taxes	325	

Supplemental schedule of noncash investing and financing activities:

The Company purchased all of the capital stock of Company S for $950. In conjunction with the acquisition, liabilities were assumed as follows:

Fair value of assets acquired	$1,580
Cash paid for the capital stock	(950)
Liabilities assumed	$ 630

A capital lease obligation of $850 was incurred when the Company entered into a lease for new equipment.

Additional common stock was issued upon the conversion of $500 of long-term debt.

Disclosure of accounting policy:

For purposes of the statement of cash flows, the Company considers all highly liquid debt instruments purchased with a maturity of three months or less to be cash equivalents.

133. Summarized below is financial information for the current year for Company M, which provides the basis for the statements of cash flows presented in paragraphs 131 and 132:

COMPANY M
CONSOLIDATED STATEMENT OF FINANCIAL POSITION

	1/1/X1	12/31/X1	Change
Assets:			
Cash and cash equivalents	$ 600	$ 1,665	$1,065
Accounts receivable (net of allowance			
for losses of $600 and $450)	1,770	1,940	170
Notes receivable	400	150	(250)
Inventory	1,230	1,375	145
Prepaid expenses	110	135	25
Investments	250	275	25
Property, plant, and equipment, at cost	6,460	8,460	2,000
Accumulated depreciation	(2,100)	(2,300)	(200)
Property, plant, and equipment, net	4,360	6,160	1,800
Intangible assets	40	175	135
Total assets	$8,760	$11,875	$3,115
Liabilities:			
Accounts payable and accrued expenses	$1,085	$ 1,090	$ 5
Interest payable	30	45	15
Income taxes payable	50	85	35
Short-term debt	450	750	300
Lease obligation	—	725	725
Long-term debt	2,150	2,425	275
Deferred taxes	375	525	150
Other liabilities	225	275	50
Total liabilities	4,365	5,920	1,555
Stockholders' equity:			
Capital stock	2,000	3,000	1,000
Retained earnings	2,395	2,955	560
Total stockholders' equity	4,395	5,955	1,560
Total liabilities and stockholders' equity	$8,760	$11,875	$3,115

COMPANY M
CONSOLIDATED STATEMENT OF INCOME
FOR THE YEAR ENDED DECEMBER 31, 19X1

Sales	$13,965
Cost of sales	(10,290)
Depreciation and amortization	(445)
Selling, general, and administrative expenses	(1,890)
Interest expense	(235)
Equity in earnings of affiliate	45
Gain on sale of facility	80
Interest income	55
Insurance proceeds	15
Loss from patent infringement lawsuit	(30)
Income before income taxes	1,270
Provision for income taxes	(510)
Net income	$ 760

134. The following transactions were entered into by Company M during 19X1 and are reflected in the above financial statements:

a. Company M wrote off $350 of accounts receivable when a customer filed for bankruptcy. A provision for losses on accounts receivable of $200 was included in Company M's selling, general, and administrative expenses.

b. Company M collected the third and final annual installment payment of $100 on a note receivable for the sale of inventory and collected the third of four annual installment payments of $150 each on a note receivable for the sale of a plant. Interest on these notes through December 31 totaling $55 was also collected.

c. Company M received a dividend of $20 from an affiliate accounted for under the equity method of accounting.

d. Company M sold a facility with a book value of $520 and an original cost of $750 for $600 cash.

e. Company M constructed a new facility for its own use and placed it in service. Accumulated expenditures during the year of $1,000 included capitalized interest of $10.

f. Company M entered into a capital lease for new equipment with a fair value of $850. Principal payments under the lease obligation totaled $125.

g. Company M purchased all of the capital stock of Company S for $950. The acquisition was recorded under the purchase method of accounting. The fair values of Company S's assets and liabilities at the date of acquisition are presented as follows:

Cash	$ 25
Accounts receivable	155
Inventory	350
Property, plant, and equipment	900
Patents	80
Goodwill	70
Accounts payable and accrued expenses	(255)
Long-term note payable	(375)
Net assets acquired	$950

h. Company M borrowed and repaid various amounts under a line-of-credit agreement in which borrowings are payable 30 days after demand. The net increase during the year in the amount borrowed against the line-of-credit totaled $300.

i. Company M issued $400 of long-term debt securities.

j. Company M's provision for income taxes included a deferred provision of $150.

k. Company M's depreciation totaled $430, and amortization of intangible assets totaled $15.

l. Company M's selling, general, and administrative expenses included an accrual for incentive compensation of $50 that has been deferred by executives until their retirement. The related obligation was included in other liabilities.

m. Company M collected insurance proceeds of $15 from a business interruption claim that resulted when a storm precluded shipment of inventory for one week.

n. Company M paid $30 to settle a lawsuit for patent infringement.

o. Company M issued $1,000 of additional common stock of which $500 was issued for cash and $500 was issued upon conversion of long-term debt.

p. Company M paid dividends of $200.

135. Based on the financial data from the preceding example, the following computations illustrate a method of indirectly determining cash received from customers and cash paid to suppliers and employees for use in a statement of cash flows under the direct method:

Cash received from customers during the year:

Customer sales		$13,965
Collection of installment payment for sale of inventory		100
Gross accounts receivable at beginning of year	$2,370	
Accounts receivable acquired in purchase of Company S	155	
Accounts receivable written off	(350)	
Gross accounts receivable at end of year	(2,390)	
Excess of new accounts receivable over collections from customers		(215)
Cash received from customers during the year		$13,850

Cash paid to suppliers and employees during the year:

Cost of sales		$10,290
General and administrative expenses	$1,890	
Expenses not requiring cash outlay (provision for uncollectible accounts receivable)	(200)	
Net expenses requiring cash payments		1,690
Inventory at beginning of year	(1,230)	
Inventory acquired in purchase of Company S	(350)	
Inventory at end of year	1,375	
Net decrease in inventory from Company M's operations		(205)
Adjustments for changes in related accruals:		
Account balances at beginning of year		
Accounts payable and accrued expenses	$1,085	
Other liabilities	225	
Prepaid expenses	(110)	
Total	1,200	
Accounts payable and accrued expenses acquired in purchase of Company S	255	
Account balances at end of year		
Accounts payable and accrued expenses	1,090	
Other liabilities	275	
Prepaid expenses	(135)	
Total	(1,230)	
Additional cash payments not included in expense		225
Cash paid to suppliers and employees during the year		$12,000

139. Comparative statements of financial position for the parent company and for each of the foreign subsidiaries are presented below:

COMPARATIVE STATEMENTS OF FINANCIAL POSITION

	Parent Company			Subsidiary A Local Currency			Subsidiary A U.S. Dollars			Subsidiary B Local Currency			Subsidiary B U.S. Dollars		
	1/1/X1	12/31/X1	Change	1/1/X1	12/31/X1	Change	1/1/X1	12/31/X1	Change	1/1/X1	12/31/X1	Change	1/1/X1	12/31/X1	Change
Assets:															
Cash and cash equivalents	$255	$223	$(32)	LC 38	LC 25	LC (13)	$15	$11	$(4)	LC 100	LC 449	LC 349	$5	$9	$4
Accounts receivable	640	725	85	125	210	85	50	95	45	700	1,000	300	35	20	(15)
Intercompany loan receivable		15	15												
Inventory	550	630	80	400	625	225	160	281	121	2,900	3,200	300	203	96	(107)
Investments	730	730													
Property, plant, and equipment, net	3,280	3,305	25	3,075	3,202	127	1,230	1,441	211	6,200	5,900	(300)	930	816	(114)
Other assets	170	160	(10)	25	25		10	11	1						
Total assets	$5,625	$5,788	$163	LC3,663	LC4,087	LC424	$1,465	$1,839	$374	LC9,900	LC10,549	LC 649	$1,173	$941	$(232)
Liabilities:															
Accounts payable and accrued expenses	$570	$529	$(41)	LC 263	LC 300	LC 37	$105	$135	$30	LC2,100	LC 1,900	LC (200)	$105	$38	$(67)
Interest payable	40	35	(5)	15	24	9	6	11	5	200	200		10	4	(6)
Taxes payable	43	45	2	25	12	(13)	10	5	(5)		120	120		2	2
Short-term debt	140	160	20	125	300	175	50	135	85						
Intercompany debt											500	500		15	15
Long-term debt	1,300	1,100	(200)	550	700	150	220	315	95	3,000	2,000	(1,000)	150	40	(110)
Deferred taxes	252	342	90												
Total liabilities	2,345	2,211	(134)	978	1,336	358	391	601	210	5,300	4,720	(580)	265	99	(166)
Stockholders' equity:															
Capital stock	550	550		1,300	1,300		455	455		1,375	1,375		275	275	
Retained earnings	2,730	3,027	297	1,385	1,451	66	526	554	28	3,225	4,454	1,229	633	567	(66)
Cumulative translation adjustment							93	229	136						
Total stockholders' equity	3,280	3,577	297	2,685	2,751	66	1,074	1,238	164	4,600	5,829	1,229	908	842	(66)
Total liabilities and stockholders' equity	$5,625	$5,788	$163	LC3,663	LC4,087	LC424	$1,465	$1,839	$374	LC9,900	LC10,549	LC 649	$1,173	$941	$(232)

140. Statements of income in local currency and U.S. dollars for each of the foreign subsidiaries are presented below:

STATEMENTS OF INCOME
FOR THE YEAR ENDED DECEMBER 31, 19X1

| | Subsidiary A | | Subsidiary B | |
	Local Currency	U.S. Dollars	Local Currency	U.S. Dollars
Revenues	LC2,179	$925ᵃ	LC19,000	$570
Cost of sales	(1,458)	(615)ᵇ	(9,667)	(406)
Depreciation and amortization	(198)	(85)	(600)	(90)
General and administrative expenses	(256)	(110)	(2,167)	(65)
Interest expense	(209)	(90)	(4,500)	(135)
Gain (loss) on sale of equipment	–	–	150	(25)
Miscellaneous income (expense)	105	45	(167)	(5)
Exchange gain	–	–	–	115
Income before income taxes	163	70	2,049	(41)
Provision for income taxes	(47)	(20)	(820)	(25)
Net Income	LC 116	$ 50	LC 1,229	$ (66)

ᵃThis amount was computed as follows:

Sale to parent company at beginning of year	LC 400 @ .40 =	$160
Sales to customers	LC1,779 @ .43 =	765
Total sales in U.S. dollars		$925

ᵇThis amount was computed as follows:

Cost of sale to parent company at beginning of year	LC 400 @ .40 =	$160
Cost of sales to customers	LC1,058 @ .43 =	455
Total cost of sales in U.S. dollars		$615

141. The following transactions were entered into during the year by the parent company and are reflected in the above financial statements:

a. The parent company invested cash in excess of daily requirements in Treasury bills. Interest earned on such investments totaled $35.
b. The parent company sold excess property with a net book value of $35 for $150.
c. The parent company's capital expenditures totaled $450.
d. The parent company wrote down to its estimated net realizable value of $25 a facility with a net book value of $75.
e. The parent company's short-term debt consisted of commercial paper with maturities not exceeding 60 days.
f. The parent company repaid long-term notes of $200.
g. The parent company's depreciation totaled $340, and amortization of intangible assets to-

taled $10.
h. The parent company's provision for income taxes included deferred taxes of $90.
i. Because of a change in product design, the parent company purchased all of Subsidiary A's beginning inventory for its book value of $160. All of the inventory was subsequently sold by the parent company.
j. The parent company received a dividend of $22 from Subsidiary A. The dividend was credited to the parent company's income.
k. The parent company purchased from Subsidiary B $270 of merchandise of which $45 remained in the parent company's inventory at year-end. Intercompany profit on the remaining inventory totaled $15.
l. The parent company loaned $15, payable in U.S. dollars, to Subsidiary B.
m. Company F paid dividends totaling $120 to shareholders.

142. The following transactions were entered into during the year by Subsidiary A and are reflected in the above financial statements. The U.S. dollar equivalent of the local currency amount based on the exchange rate at the date of each transaction is included. Except for the sale of inventory to the parent company (transaction (a) below), Subsidiary A's sales and purchases and operating cash receipts and payments occurred evenly throughout the year.

a. Because of a change in product design, Subsidiary A sold all of its beginning inventory to the parent company for its book value of LC400 ($160).
b. Subsidiary A sold equipment for its book value of LC275 ($116) and purchased new equipment at a cost of LC600 ($258).
c. Subsidiary A issued an additional LC175 ($75) of 30-day notes and renewed the notes at each maturity date.
d. Subsidiary A issued long-term debt of LC400 ($165) and repaid long-term debt of LC250 ($105).
e. Subsidiary A paid a dividend to the parent company of LC50 ($22).

143. The following transactions were entered into during the year by Subsidiary B and are reflected in the above financial statements. The U.S. dollar equivalent of the local currency amount based on the exchange rate at the date of each transaction is included. Subsidiary B's sales and operating cash receipts and payments occurred evenly throughout the year. For convenience, all purchases of inventory were based on the weighted-average exchange rate for the year. Subsidiary B uses the FIFO method of inventory valuation.

a. Subsidiary B had sales to the parent company as follows:

	Local Currency	U.S. Dollars
Intercompany sales	LC9,000	$270
Cost of sales	(4,500)	(180)
Gross profit	LC4,500	$ 90

b. Subsidiary B sold equipment with a net book value of LC200 ($39) for LC350 ($14). New equipment was purchased at a cost of LC500 ($15).
c. Subsidiary B borrowed $15 (LC500), payable in U.S. dollars, from the parent company.
d. Subsidiary B repaid LC1,000 ($35) of long-term debt.

144. Statements of cash flows in the local currency and in U.S. dollars for Subsidiary A and Subsidiary B are presented below:

STATEMENTS OF CASH FLOWS
FOR THE YEAR ENDED DECEMBER 31, 19X1
Increase (Decrease) in Cash

	Subsidiary A		Subsidiary B	
	Local Currency	U.S. Dollars	Local Currency	U.S. Dollars
Cash flows from operating activities:				
Cash received from customers	LC2,094[a]	$888[a]	LC18,700[a]	$561[a]
Cash paid to suppliers and employees	(1,902)[a]	(806)[a]	(12,334)[a]	(370)[a]
Interest paid	(200)	(86)[b]	(4,500)	(135)[b]
Income taxes paid	(60)	(25)[b]	(700)	(21)[b]
Miscellaneous receipts (payments)	105	45[b]	(167)	(5)[b]
Net cash provided by operating activities	37	16	999	30
Cash flows from investing activities:				
Proceeds from sale of equipment	275	116[c]	350	14[c]
Payments for purchase of equipment	(600)	(258)[c]	(500)	(15)[c]
Net cash used in investing activities	(325)	(142)	(150)	(1)
Cash flows from financing activities:				
Net increase in short-term debt	175	75[c]	–	–
Proceeds from intercompany loan	–	–	500	15[c]
Proceeds from issuance of long-term debt	400	165[c]	–	–
Repayment of long-term debt	(250)	(105)[c]	(1,000)	(35)[c]
Payment of dividends	(50)	(22)c	–	–
Net cash provided by (used in) financing activities	275	113	(500)	(20)
Effect of exchange rate changes on cash	–	9[d]	–	(5)[d]
Net increase (decrease) in cash	(13)	(4)	349	4
Cash at beginning of year	38	15	100	5
Cash at end of year	LC 25	$ 11	LC 449	$ 9

---

[a]The computation of this amount is provided in paragraph 145.

[b]This amount represents the U.S. dollar equivalent of the foreign currency cash flow based on the weighted-average exchange rate for the year.

[c]This amount represents the U.S. dollar equivalent of the foreign currency cash flow based on the exchange rate in effect at the time of the cash flow.

[d]The computation of this amount is provided in paragraph 146.

Reconciliation of net income to net cash provided by operating activities:

	Subsidiary A		Subsidiary B	
	Local Currency	**U.S. Dollars**	**Local Currency**	**U.S. Dollars**
Net income	LC116	$50	LC1,229	$ (66)
Adjustments to reconcile net income to net cash provided by operating activities:				
Depreciation and amortization	198	85[a]	600	90[b]
(Gain) loss on sale of equipment	–	–	(150)	25[b]
Exchange gain	–	–	–	(115)[c]
Increase in accounts receivable	(85)	(37)[a]	(300)	(9)[a]
(Increase) decrease in inventory	(225)	(97)[a]	(300)	107[d]
Increase (decrease) in accounts payable and accrued expenses	37	16 [a]	(200)	(6)[a]
Increase (decrease) in interest and taxes payable	(4)	(1)[a]	120	4[a]
Net cash provided by operating activities	LC 37	$16	LC 999	$ 30

[a]This amount represents the U.S. dollar equivalent of the foreign currency amount based on the weighted-average exchange rate for the year.

[b]This amount represents the U. S. dollar equivalent of the foreign currency amount based on historical exchange rates.

[c]This amount represents the exchange gain included in net income as a result of remeasuring Subsidiary B's financial statements from the local currency to U.S. dollars.

[d]This amount represents the difference between beginning and ending inventory after remeasurement into U.S. dollars based on historical exchange rates.

145. Presented below is the computation of cash received from customers and cash paid to suppliers and employees as reported in the consolidating statement of cash flows for Company F appearing in paragraph 136:

	Parent Company	Subsidiary A Local Currency	Subsidiary A U.S. Dollars	Subsidiary B Local Currency	Subsidiary B U.S. Dollars
Cash received from customers during the year:					
Revenues	$4,695	LC2,179	$925	LC19,000	$570
Increase in accounts receivable	(85)	(85)	(37)	(300)	(9)
Cash received from customers	$4,610	LC2,094	$888	LC18,700	$561
Cash paid to suppliers and employees during the year:					
Cost of sales	$3,210	LC1,458	$615	LC 9,667	$406
Effect of exchange rate changes on cost of sales				–	(116)[a]
General and administrative expenses	425	256	110	2,167	65
Total operating expenses requiring cash payments	3,635	1,714	725	11,834	355
Increase (decrease) in inventory	80	225	97	300	9
(Increase) decrease in accounts payable and accrued expenses	41	(37)	(16)	200	6
Cash paid to suppliers and employees	$3,756	LC1,902	$806	LC12,334	$370

[a]This adjustment represents the difference between cost of sales remeasured at historical exchange rates ($406) and cost of sales translated based on the weighted-average exchange rate for the year ($290). This adjustment is necessary because cash payments for inventory, which were made evenly throughout the year, were based on the weighted-average exchange rate for the year.

146. Presented below is the computation of the effect of exchange rate changes on cash for Subsidiary A and Subsidiary B:

COMPUTATION OF EFFECT OF EXCHANGE RATE CHANGES ON CASH

	Subsidiary A		Subsidiary B	
Effect on beginning cash balance:				
Beginning cash balance in local currency	LC 38		LC100	
Net change in exchange rate during the year	× .05		× (.03)	
Effect on beginning cash balance		$ 2		$(3)
Effect from operating activities during the year:				
Cash provided by operating activities in local currency	LC 37		LC999	
Year-end exchange rate	× .45		× .02	
Operating cash flows based on year-end exchange rate	$ 16[a]		$ 20	
Operating cash flows reported in the statement of cash flows	16		30	
Effect from operating activities during the year		0		(10)
Effect from investing activities during the year:				
Cash used in investing activities in local currency	LC(325)		LC(150)	
Year-end exchange rate	× .45		× .02	
Investing cash flows based on year-end exchange rate	$(146)		$ (3)	
Investing cash flows reported in the statement of cash flows	(142)		(1)	
Effect from investing activities during the year		(4)		(2)
Effect from financing activities during the year:				
Cash provided by (used in) financing activities in local currency	LC 275		LC(500)	
Year-end exchange rate	× .45		× .02	
Financing cash flows based on year-end exchange rate	$124		$(10)	
Financing cash flows reported in the statement of cash flows	113		(20)	
Effect from financing activities during the year		11		10
Effect of exchange rate changes on cash		$ 9		$(5)

---

[a] This amount includes the effect of rounding.

Example 3

147. Presented below is a statement of cash flows for Financial Institution, Inc., a U.S. corporation that provides a broad range of financial services. This statement of cash flows illustrates the direct method of presenting cash flows from operating activities, as encouraged in paragraph 27 of this Statement.

FINANCIAL INSTITUTION, INC.
STATEMENT OF CASH FLOWS
FOR THE YEAR ENDED DECEMBER 31, 19X1
Increase (Decrease) in Cash and Cash Equivalents

Cash flows from operating activities:		
Interest received	$ 5,350	
Fees and commissions received	1,320	
Financing revenue received under leases	60	
Interest paid	(3,925)	
Cash paid to suppliers and employees	(795)	
Income taxes paid	(471)	
Net cash provided by operating activities		$ 1,539
Cash flows from investing activities:		
Proceeds from sales of trading and investment securities	22,700	
Purchase of trading and investment securities	(25,000)	
Net increase in credit card receivables	(1,300)	
Net decrease in customer loans with maturities		
of 3 months or less	2,250	
Principal collected on longer term loans	26,550	
Longer term loans made to customers	(36,300)	
Purchase of assets to be leased	(1,500)	
Principal payments received under leases	107	
Capital expenditures	(450)	
Proceeds from sale of property, plant, and equipment	260	
Net cash used in investing activities		(12,683)
Cash flows from financing activities:		
Net increase in demand deposits, NOW accounts,		
and savings accounts	3,000	
Proceeds from sales of certificates of deposit	63,000	
Payments for maturing certificates of deposit	(61,000)	
Net increase in federal funds purchased	4,500	
Net increase in 90-day borrowings	50	
Proceeds from issuance of nonrecourse debt	600	
Principal payment on nonrecourse debt	(20)	
Proceeds from issuance of 6-month note	100	
Proceeds from issuance of long-term debt	1,000	
Repayment of long-term debt	(200)	
Proceeds from issuance of common stock	350	
Payments to acquire treasury stock	(175)	
Dividends paid	(240)	
Net cash provided by financing activities		10,965
Net decrease in cash and cash equivalents		(179)
Cash and cash equivalents at beginning of year		6,700
Cash and cash equivalents at end of year		$ 6,521

Reconciliation of net income to net cash provided by operating activities:

Net income		$1,056
Adjustments to reconcile net income to net cash provided		
by operating activities:		
Depreciation	$100	
Provision for probable credit losses	300	
Provision for deferred taxes	58	
Gain on sale of trading and investment securities	(100)	
Gain on sale of equipment	(50)	
Increase in taxes payable	175	
Increase in interest receivable	(150)	
Increase in interest payable	75	
Decrease in fees and commissions receivable	20	
Increase in accrued expenses	55	
Total adjustments		483
Net cash provided by operating activities		$1,539

Supplemental schedule of noncash investing and financing activities:

Conversion of long-term debt to common stock	$ 500

Disclosure of accounting policy:

For purposes of reporting cash flows, cash and cash equivalents include cash on hand, amounts due from banks, and federal funds sold. Generally, federal funds are purchased and sold for one-day periods.

148. Summarized below is financial information for the current year for Financial Institution, Inc., which provides the basis for the statement of cash flows presented in paragraph 147:

FINANCIAL INSTITUTION, INC.
STATEMENT OF FINANCIAL POSITION

	1/1/X1	12/31/X1	Change
Assets:			
Cash and due from banks	$ 4,400	$ 3,121	$ (1,279)
Federal funds sold	2,300	3,400	1,100
Total cash and cash equivalents	6,700	6,521	(179)
Investment and trading securities	9,000	11,400	2,400
Credit card receivables	8,500	9,800	1,300
Loans	28,000	35,250	7,250
Allowance for credit losses	(800)	(850)	(50)
Interest receivable	600	750	150
Fees and commissions receivable	60	40	(20)
Investment in direct financing lease	–	421	421
Investment in leveraged lease	–	392	392
Property, plant, and equipment, net	525	665	140
Total assets	$52,585	$64,389	$11,804
Liabilities:			
Deposits	$38,000	$43,000	$ 5,000
Federal funds purchased	7,500	12,000	4,500
Short-term borrowings	1,200	1,350	150
Interest payable	350	425	75
Accrued expenses	275	330	55
Taxes payable	75	250	175
Dividends payable	0	80	80
Long-term debt	2,000	2,300	300
Deferred taxes	–	58	58
Total liabilities	49,400	59,793	10,393
Stockholders' equity:			
Common stock	1,250	2,100	850
Treasury stock	0	(175)	(175)
Retained earnings	1,935	2,671	736
Total stockholders' equity	3,185	4,596	1,411
Total liabilities and stockholders' equity	$52,585	$64,389	$11,804

FINANCIAL INSTITUTION, INC.
STATEMENT OF INCOME
FOR THE YEAR ENDED DECEMBER 31, 19X1

Revenues:		
Interest income	$5,500	
Fees and commissions	1,300	
Gain on sale of investment securities	100	
Lease income	60	
Gain on sale of equipment	50	
Total revenues		$7,010
Expenses:		
Interest expense	4,000	
Provision for probable credit losses	300	
Operating expenses	850	
Depreciation	100	
Total expenses		5,250
Income before income taxes		1,760
Provision for income taxes		704
Net income		$1,056

149. The following transactions were entered into by Financial Institution, Inc., during 19X1 and are reflected in the above financial statements:

a. Financial Institution sold trading and investment securities with a book value of $22,600 for $22,700 and purchased $25,000 in new trading and investment securities.

b. Financial Institution had a net decrease in short-term loans receivable (those with original maturities of 3 months or less) of $2,250. Financial Institution made longer term loans of $36,300 and collected $26,550 on those loans. Financial Institution wrote off $250 of loans as uncollectible.

c. Financial Institution purchased property for $500 to be leased under a direct financing lease. The first annual rental payment of $131 was collected. The portion of the rental payment representing interest income totaled $52.

d. Financial Institution purchased equipment for $1,000 to be leased under a leveraged lease. The cost of the leased asset was financed by an equity investment of $400 and a long-term nonrecourse bank loan of $600. The first annual rental payment of $90, of which $28 represented principal, was collected and the first annual loan installment of $74, of which $20 represented principal, was paid. Pretax income of $8 was recorded.

e. Financial Institution purchased new property, plant, and equipment for $450 and sold property, plant, and equipment with a book value of $210 for $260.

f. Customer deposits with Financial Institution consisted of the following:

	1/1/X1	12/31/X1	Increase
Demand deposits	$ 8,000	$ 8,600	$ 600
NOW accounts and savings accounts	15,200	17,600	2,400
Certificates of deposit	14,800	16,800	2,000
Total deposits	$38,000	$43,000	$5,000

Sales of certificates of deposit during the year totaled $63,000; certificates of deposit with principal amounts totaling $61,000 matured. For presentation in the statement of cash flows, Financial Institution chose to report gross cash receipts and payments for both certificates of deposit with maturities of three months or less and those with maturities of more than three months.

g. Short-term borrowing activity for Financial Institution consisted of repayment of a $200 90-day note and issuance of a 90-day note for $250 and a 6-month note for $100.

h. Financial Institution repaid $200 of long-term debt and issued 5-year notes for $600 and 10-year notes for $400.

i. Financial Institution issued $850 of common stock, $500 of which was issued upon conversion of long-term debt and $350 of which was issued for cash.

j. Financial Institution acquired $175 of treasury stock.

k. Financial Institution declared dividends of $320. The fourth quarter dividend of $80 was payable the following January.

l. Financial Institution's provision for income taxes included a deferred provision of $58.

m. In accordance with paragraph 7, footnote 1, of this Statement, interest paid includes amounts credited directly to demand deposit, NOW, and savings accounts.

Appendix D

AMENDMENTS TO EXISTING PRONOUNCEMENTS

150. This Statement supersedes Opinion 19 and the three AICPA Accounting Interpretations of Opinion 19.

151. This Statement amends the following pronouncements as follows:

a. APB Opinion No. 28, *Interim Financial Reporting.* In paragraph 33, the two references to the phrase *funds flow data* are replaced by the phrase *cash flow data.*

b. FASB Statement No. 7, *Accounting and Reporting by Development Stage Enterprises.* In paragraph 11(c), the phrase *A statement of changes in financial position, showing the sources and uses of financial resources* is replaced by the phrase *A statement of cash flows, showing the cash inflows and cash outflows.* Footnote 8 is deleted.

152. Many pronouncements issued by the Accounting Principles Board (APB) and the FASB contain references to the phrase (a) *a complete set of financial statements that present financial position, results of operations, and changes in financial position,* (b) *statement of changes in financial position,* or (c) *changes in financial position.* All such references appearing in paragraphs that establish standards or the scope of a pronouncement are hereby replaced by references to the phrase (a) *a complete set of financial statements that present financial position, results of operations, and cash flows,* (b) *statement of cash flows,* or (c) *cash flows,* respectively. That conclusion requires amendments to the following existing pronouncements:

a. APB Opinion No. 20, *Accounting Changes,* paragraph 3.

b. APB Opinion No. 22, *Disclosure of Accounting Policies,* paragraphs 6, 7, 8, and 12.

c. Opinion 28, paragraph 2.

d. Statement 7, paragraph 10.

e. FASB Statement No. 14, *Financial Reporting for Segments of a Business Enterprise,* paragraphs 3 and 7 (as amended by FASB Statement No. 24, *Reporting Segment Information in Financial Statements That Are Presented in Another Enterprise's Financial Report).*

f. Statement 24, paragraphs 1 and 5 and footnote 2.

g. FASB Statement No. 69, *Disclosures about Oil and Gas Producing Activities,* footnote 3.

h. FASB Technical Bulletin No. 82-1, *Disclosure of the Sale or Purchase of Tax Benefits through Tax Leases,* paragraph 4.

153. Some pronouncements issued by the APB or FASB contain references to the phrase (a) *a complete set of financial statements,* (b) *a full set of financial statements,* or (c) *a complete set of annual financial statements* without a specific reference to the phrase *changes in financial position.* Because this Statement redefines what constitutes a complete or full set of financial statements, this Statement effectively amends the intent of those pronouncements even though the terminology in those pronouncements was not changed. The affected pronouncements are as follows:

a. Statement 7, footnote 6.

b. FASB Statement No. 21, *Suspension of the Reporting of Earnings per Share and Segment Information by Nonpublic Enterprises,* footnote 4.

c. FASB Statement No. 36, *Disclosure of Pension Information,* paragraph 8.

d. FASB Statement No. 57, *Related Party Disclosures,* footnote 2.

e. Statement 69, paragraphs 7, 8, and 41.

Statement of Financial Accounting Standards No. 96
Accounting for Income Taxes

STATUS

Issued: December 1987

Effective Date: For fiscal years beginning after December 15, 1988

Affects: Amends ARB 43, Chapter 9C, paragraph 5
Supersedes ARB 43, Chapter 9C, paragraphs 11 through 13; Chapter 10B;
Chapter 11B, paragraph 8; and Chapter 15, paragraph 11
Supersedes ARB 44 (Revised) and related letter dated April 15, 1959
Supersedes ARB 51, paragraph 17
Supersedes APB 1
Supersedes APB 11
Amends APB 16, paragraphs 87 and 88
Supersedes APB 16, paragraph 89
Amends APB 17, paragraph 30
Amends APB 21, footnote 8*
Amends APB 23, paragraphs 9, 10,* 13,* 17, and 21 and footnotes 7* and 9
Supersedes APB 23, paragraphs 11, 14, and 24 and footnotes 4, 6, and 10
Supersedes APB 24
Amends APB 25, paragraph 17*
Amends APB 28, paragraphs 19* and 20 and footnotes 2 and 3
Amends APB 29, paragraph 27*
Amends APB 30, paragraph 7
Supersedes AIN-APB 4, Interpretations No. 4 and 6
Supersedes AIN-APB 11, Interpretations No. 1 through 25
Supersedes AIN-APB 15, Interpretations No. 13 and 16
Amends AIN-APB 18, Interpretations No. 1 and 2*
Supersedes AIN-APB 23, Interpretation No. 1
Amends AIN-APB 25, Interpretation No. 1
Amends FAS 12, paragraph 22*
Amends FAS 13, paragraph 47
Supersedes FAS 16, paragraph 11 and footnote 5
Amends FAS 16, paragraph 13 and footnotes 3 and 4
Amends FAS 19, paragraphs 61 and 62
Supersedes FAS 31
Supersedes FAS 37
Amends FAS 38, paragraph 2 and footnote 2
Amends FAS 44, paragraph 6*
Amends FAS 52, paragraphs 22,* 23,* 24,* and 48
Amends FAS 57, paragraph 2
Supersedes FAS 60, paragraphs 55 through 58, 60(i), and 60(j) and footnote 8
Amends FAS 69, paragraphs 26, 30(c), 40, and 41
Supersedes FAS 71, paragraph 18 and footnote 12
Amends FAS 71, paragraph 46
Amends FAS 87, paragraph 37*
Amends FAS 89, paragraphs 33* and 96

---

*Result of the amendment, at least in part, described in paragraph 204.

Amends FAS 90, paragraphs 14 and 27*
Supersedes FIN 18, paragraphs 14, 20, 23, 59 through 61, and 70 and footnotes 9 through 14, 18, 21 through 23, and 25
Amends FIN 18, paragraphs 6,* 15, 16, 18, 40 through 43,* 46 through 55, 58, 65, 66, and 68 and footnotes 2,* 19, and fn(*) of paragraph 47
Supersedes FIN 22
Supersedes FIN 25
Supersedes FIN 29
Amends FIN 30, paragraph 5*
Amends FIN 31, footnote 1
Supersedes FIN 32
Amends FTB 79-9, paragraph 3
Amends FTB 79-16 (Revised), paragraph 4
Supersedes FTB 81-2
Supersedes FTB 82-1, paragraph 5
Amends FTB 82-1, paragraph 7*
Supersedes FTB 83-1
Supersedes FTB 84-2
Supersedes FTB 84-3
Supersedes FTB 86-1
Supersedes FTB 87-2, paragraphs 9 through 11, 13, and 22 through 33 and footnotes 4 and 8
Amends FTB 87-2, paragraph 18

Affected by: Paragraph 32 amended by FAS 100, FAS 103, and FAS 108
          Superseded by FAS 109

Other Interpretive Release: FASB Special Report, *A Guide to Implementation of Statement 96 on Accounting for Income Taxes: Questions and Answers*

---

*Result of the amendment, at least in part, described in paragraph 204.

(The next page is 1160.)

(This page intentionally left blank.)

Statement of Financial Accounting Standards No. 97
Accounting and Reporting by Insurance Enterprises
for Certain Long-Duration Contracts and for
Realized Gains and Losses from the Sale of Investments

STATUS

Issued: December 1987

Effective Date: For fiscal years beginning after December 15, 1988

Affects: Supersedes APB 30, footnote 8
Amends FAS 60, paragraphs 6 and 50
Supersedes FAS 60, paragraph 15

Affected by: Paragraphs 6 and 11 amended by FAS 120
Paragraph 27 superseded by FAS 113
Paragraph 28 amended by FAS 115

Other Interpretive Pronouncement: FIN 40

Issues Discussed by FASB Emerging Issues Task Force (EITF)

Affects: No EITF Issues

Interpreted by: No EITF Issues

Related Issues: EITF Issues No. 87-1, 92-9, and 93-14 and Topic No. D-41

SUMMARY

This Statement establishes standards of accounting for certain long-duration contracts issued by insurance enterprises, referred to in this Statement as universal life-type contracts, that were not addressed by FASB Statement No. 60, *Accounting and Reporting by Insurance Enterprises*. The Statement also establishes standards of accounting for limited-payment long-duration insurance contracts and investment contracts and amends Statement 60 to change the reporting of realized gains and losses on investments.

New life insurance contracts have evolved since the development of specialized insurance industry accounting principles and practices in the early 1970s. Many of those new life insurance contracts have different provisions than do the life insurance contracts to which Statement 60 applies. Those new life insurance contracts are characterized by flexibility and discretion granted to one or both parties to the contract. Statement 60 identifies but does not address those contracts, noting that the accounting was under study by the insurance industry and the accounting and actuarial professions.

This Statement requires that the retrospective deposit method be used to account for universal life-type contracts. That accounting method establishes a liability for policy benefits at an amount determined by the account or contract balance that accrues to the benefit of the policyholder. Premium receipts are not reported as revenues when the retrospective deposit method is used. The Statement also requires that capitalized acquisition costs associated with universal life-type contracts be amortized based on a constant percentage of the present value of estimated gross profit amounts from the operation of a "book" of those contracts. Any gain or loss resulting from a policyholder's replacement of other life insurance contracts with universal life-type contracts is recognized in income of the period in which the replacement occurs.

Accounting and Reporting by Insurance Enterprises   **FAS97**
for Certain Long-Duration Contracts and for
Realized Gains and Losses from the Sale of Investments

This Statement requires that long-duration contracts issued by insurance enterprises that do not subject the enterprise to risks arising from policyholder mortality or morbidity (investment contracts) be accounted for in a manner consistent with the accounting for interest-bearing or other financial instruments. Payments received on those contracts are not reported as revenue.

This Statement also addresses limited-payment contracts that subject the insurance enterprise to mortality or morbidity risk over a period that extends beyond the period or periods in which premiums are collected and that have terms that are fixed and guaranteed. This Statement requires that revenue and income from limited-payment contracts be recognized over the period that benefits are provided rather than on collection of premiums.

This Statement amends the reporting by insurance enterprises of realized gains and losses on investments. Statement 60 previously required that realized gains and losses be reported in the statement of earnings on a separate line below operating income and net of applicable income taxes. This Statement requires that realized gains and losses now be reported on a pretax basis as a component of other income and precludes the deferral of realized gains and losses to future periods.

This Statement is effective for financial statements for fiscal years beginning after December 15, 1988. Accounting changes to adopt the Statement should be applied retroactively through restatement of all previously issued financial statements presented, or if restatement of all years presented is not practicable, the cumulative effect of applying this Statement is to be included in net income of the year of adoption.

Statement of Financial Accounting Standards No. 97

Accounting and Reporting by Insurance Enterprises for Certain Long-Duration Contracts and for Realized Gains and Losses from the Sale of Investments

CONTENTS

INTRODUCTION

1. FASB Statement No. 60, *Accounting and Reporting by Insurance Enterprises,* issued in June 1982, contains specialized accounting principles and practices based on AICPA insurance Industry Audit Guides and Statements of Position. Statement 60 identifies but does not address a number of areas that were being studied by the insurance industry and the accounting and actuarial professions when that Statement was issued. One of those areas is the accounting for universal life insurance and similar products that were developed after the issuance of the AICPA Guides and Statements of Position.

2. Statement 60 describes two methods of premium revenue and contract liability recognition, referred to as long-duration and short-duration contract accounting. Each method is designed to reflect the insurance enterprise's obligations and policyholder rights under the provisions of the contract. The insurance contracts addressed in this Statement are generally considered long-duration insurance contracts.

3. Recognition of premiums as revenue when due from policyholders and measurement of a liability for policyholder benefits based on a uniform percentage of anticipated premiums are distinguishing features of the accounting for long-duration insurance contracts specified in Statement 60. Because no single function or service is predominant over the periods of most long-duration insurance contracts, recognition of premiums as revenue over the premium-paying periods was considered a reasonable measure of service performed.

4. The differences between universal life insurance and the long-duration contracts described in Statement 60 led many to question the propriety of applying the accounting method described in Statement 60 to universal life insurance. Universal life insurance contracts lack the fixed and guaranteed terms that are typical for the contracts for which the accounting specified in Statement 60 was designed. Policyholders are frequently granted significant discretion over the amount and timing of premium payments. Insurers are frequently granted significant discretion over amounts that accrue to and that are assessed against policyholders.

Accounting and Reporting by Insurance Enterprises
for Certain Long-Duration Contracts and for
Realized Gains and Losses from the Sale of Investments

FAS97

5. Some long-duration insurance contracts that are addressed by Statement 60 have terms that are fixed and guaranteed but lack either the level premiums or the insurance protection characteristics contemplated in Statement 60. The increasing number of those contracts led the Board to reconsider the accounting for them at the same time it considered the accounting for universal life insurance.

APPLICABILITY AND SCOPE

6. This Statement applies to all insurance enterprises to which Statement 60 applies. The Statement establishes standards of financial accounting and reporting for three classes of long-duration contracts issued by those insurance enterprises and for reporting realized investment gains and losses. Those contracts are referred to in this Statement as *investment contracts, limited-payment contracts,* and *universal life-type contracts.* The accounting for long-duration contracts not otherwise addressed by this Statement is prescribed in Statement 60.

7. Long-duration contracts that do not subject the insurance enterprise to risks arising from policyholder mortality or morbidity are referred to in this Statement as investment contracts. A mortality or morbidity risk is present if, under the terms of the contract, the enterprise is required to make payments or forego required premiums contingent upon the death or disability (in the case of life insurance contracts) or the continued survival (in the case of annuity contracts) of a specific individual or group of individuals. A contract provision that allows the holder of a long-duration contract to purchase an annuity at a guaranteed price on settlement of the contract does not entail a mortality risk until the right to purchase is executed. If purchased, the annuity is a new contract to be evaluated on its own terms.

8. Annuity contracts may require the insurance enterprise to make a number of payments that are not contingent upon the survival of the beneficiary, followed by payments that are made if the beneficiary is alive when the payments are due (often referred to as *life-contingent payments*). Such contracts are considered insurance contracts under this Statement and Statement 60 unless (a) the probability that life-contingent payments will be made is remote[1] or (b) the present value of the expected life-contingent payments relative to the present value of all expected payments under the contract is insignificant.[2]

9. Long-duration insurance contracts with terms that are fixed and guaranteed, and for which premiums are paid over a period shorter than the period over which benefits are provided, are referred to in this Statement as limited-payment contracts. The period over which benefits are provided, as used in this Statement, includes the periods during which the insurance enterprise is subject to risk from policyholder mortality and morbidity and during which the insurance enterprise is responsible for administration of the contract. The benefit period does not include the subsequent period over which the policyholder or beneficiary may elect to have settlement proceeds disbursed.

10. Except as provided in paragraph 11, long-duration insurance contracts with terms that are not fixed and guaranteed are referred to in this Statement as universal life-type contracts. Universal life-type contracts include contracts that provide either death or annuity benefits and are characterized by any one of the following features:

a. One or more of the amounts assessed by the insurer against the policyholder—including amounts assessed for mortality coverage, contract administration, initiation, or surrender—are not fixed and guaranteed by the terms of the contract.

b. Amounts that accrue to the benefit of the policyholder—including interest accrued to policyholder balances—are not fixed and guaranteed by the terms of the contract.

c. Premiums may be varied by the policyholder within contract limits and without consent of the insurer.

11. This Statement does not apply to conventional forms of participating and nonguaranteed-premium contracts. Those contracts are addressed by Statement 60. A participating or nonguaranteed-premium contract is covered by this Statement, however, if the terms of the contract suggest that it is, in substance, a universal life-type contract. The determination that a contract is in substance a universal life-type contract requires judgment and a careful examination of all contract terms. Paragraphs 12 and 13 describe some cir-

---

[1]The term *remote* is defined in paragraph 3 of FASB Statement No. 5, *Accounting for Contingencies,* as "the chance of the future event or events occurring is slight."

[2]*Webster's New World Dictionary,* Second College Edition, defines the term *insignificant* as "having little or no importance; trivial."

cumstances in which a participating or nonguaranteed-premium contract shall be accounted for as a universal life-type contract. The provisions of paragraphs 12 and 13 are not intended to be either all-inclusive or limiting.

12. A participating contract that includes any of the following features shall be considered a universal life-type contract:

a. The policyholder may vary premium payments within contract limits and without consent of the insurer.
b. The contract has a stated account balance that is credited with policyholder premiums and interest and against which assessments are made for contract administration, mortality coverage, initiation, or surrender, and any of the amounts assessed or credited are not fixed and guaranteed.
c. The insurer expects that changes in any contract element will be based primarily on changes in interest rates or other market conditions rather than on the experience of a group of similar contracts or the enterprise as a whole.

13. A nonguaranteed-premium contract that includes either of the following features shall be considered a universal life-type contract:

a. The contract has a stated account balance that is credited with policyholder premiums and interest and against which assessments are made for contract administration, mortality coverage, initiation, or surrender, and any of the amounts assessed or credited are not fixed and guaranteed.
b. The insurer expects that changes in any contract element will be based primarily on changes in interest rates or other market conditions rather than on the experience of a group of similar contracts or the enterprise as a whole.

14. This Statement does not apply to the following types of long-duration insurance contracts:

a. Contracts with terms that are fixed and guaranteed and for which premiums are collected over the same period that benefits are provided
b. Contracts that provide benefits related only to illness, physical injury, or disability.

STANDARDS OF FINANCIAL ACCOUNTING AND REPORTING

Investment Contracts

15. Investment contracts issued by an insurance enterprise, as defined in this Statement, do not incorporate significant insurance risk as that concept is contemplated in Statement 60 and shall not be accounted for as insurance contracts. Amounts received as payments for such contracts shall not be reported as revenues. Payments received by the insurance enterprise shall be reported as liabilities and accounted for in a manner consistent with the accounting for interest-bearing or other financial instruments.

Limited-Payment Contracts

16. Limited-payment contracts subject the insurer to risks arising from policyholder mortality and morbidity over a period that extends beyond the period or periods in which premiums are collected. For those contracts, the liability for policy benefits shall be established in accordance with the provisions of Statement 60. The collection of premium does not, however, represent the completion of an earnings process. Any gross premium received in excess of the net premium[3] shall be deferred and recognized in income in a constant relationship with insurance in force (when accounting for life insurance contracts) or with the amount of expected future benefit payments (when accounting for annuity contracts).

Universal Life-Type Contracts

17. The liability for policy benefits for universal life-type contracts shall be equal to the sum of:

a. The balance that accrues to the benefit of policyholders at the date of the financial statements[4]
b. Any amounts that have been assessed to compensate the insurer for services to be performed over future periods (paragraph 20)
c. Any amounts previously assessed against policyholders that are refundable on termination of the contract
d. Any probable loss (premium deficiency) as described in paragraphs 35-37 of Statement 60.

---

[3]Statement 60 defines *gross premium* as "the premium charged to a policyholder for an insurance contract." That Statement defines *net premium* as "the portion of the gross premium required to provide for all benefits and expenses."

[4]Accounting methods that measure the liability for policy benefits based on policyholder balances are known as retrospective deposit methods.

Accounting and Reporting by Insurance Enterprises
for Certain Long-Duration Contracts and for **FAS97**
Realized Gains and Losses from the Sale of Investments

18. Amounts that may be assessed against policyholders in future periods, including surrender charges, shall not be anticipated in determining the liability for policy benefits. In the absence of a stated account balance or similar explicit or implicit contract value, the cash value, measured at the date of the financial statements, that could be realized by a policyholder upon surrender shall represent the element of liability described in paragraph 17(a). Provisions for adverse deviation shall not be made.

19. Premiums collected on universal life-type contracts shall not be reported as revenue in the statement of earnings of the insurance enterprise. Revenue from those contracts shall represent amounts assessed against policyholders and shall be reported in the period that the amounts are assessed unless evidence indicates that the amounts are designed to compensate the insurer for services to be provided over more than one period.

20. Amounts assessed that represent compensation to the insurance enterprise for services to be provided in future periods are not earned in the period assessed. Such amounts shall be reported as unearned revenue and recognized in income over the period benefited using the same assumptions and factors used to amortize capitalized acquisition costs. Amounts that are assessed against the policyholder balance as consideration for origination of the contract, often referred to as *initiation* or *front-end fees,* are unearned revenues.

21. Payments to policyholders that represent a return of policyholder balances are not expenses of the insurance enterprise and shall not be reported as such in the statement of earnings. Amounts reported as expenses shall include benefit claims in excess of the related policyholder balances, expenses of contract administration, interest accrued to policyholders, and amortization of capitalized acquisition costs.

22. Capitalized acquisition costs shall be amortized over the life of a book of universal life-type contracts at a constant rate based on the present value of the estimated gross profit amounts expected to be realized over the life of the book of contracts. The present value of estimated gross profits shall be computed using the rate of interest that accrues to policyholder balances (sometimes referred to as the *contract rate*). If significant negative gross profits are expected in any period, the present value of estimated gross revenues, gross costs, or the balance of insurance in force shall be substituted as the base for computing amortization.

23. *Estimated gross profit,* as the term is used in paragraph 22, shall include estimates of the following elements, each of which shall be determined based on the best estimate of that individual element over the life of the book of contracts without provision for adverse deviation:

a. Amounts expected to be assessed for mortality (sometimes referred to as the *cost of insurance*) less benefit claims in excess of related policyholder balances

b. Amounts expected to be assessed for contract administration less costs incurred for contract administration (including acquisition costs not included in capitalized acquisition costs as described in paragraph 24)

c. Amounts expected to be earned from the investment of policyholder balances less interest credited to policyholder balances

d. Amounts expected to be assessed against policyholder balances upon termination of a contract (sometimes referred to as *surrender charges*)

e. Other expected assessments and credits, however characterized.

24. The amortization method based on the present value of estimated gross profits described in paragraphs 22 and 23 of this Statement differs from that provided in Statement 60, which is based on expected premium revenues. This Statement does not define the costs to be included in acquisition costs but does describe those that are not eligible to be capitalized under this Statement. Acquisition costs are addressed in paragraphs 28-31 of Statement 60. Acquisition costs that vary in a constant relationship to premiums or insurance in force, are recurring in nature, or tend to be incurred in a level amount from period to period shall be charged to expense in the period incurred.

25. In computing amortization, interest shall accrue to the unamortized balance of capitalized acquisition costs and unearned revenues at the rate used to discount expected gross profits. Estimates of expected gross profit used as a basis for amortization shall be evaluated regularly, and the total amortization recorded to date shall be adjusted by a charge or credit to the statement of earnings if actual experience or other evidence suggests that earlier estimates should be revised. The interest rate used to compute the present value of revised estimates of expected gross profits shall be either the rate in effect at the inception of the book of contracts or the latest revised rate applied to the remaining benefit period. The approach selected to compute the present value of revised estimates shall be applied consistently in subsequent revisions to computations of expected gross profits.

Internal Replacement Transactions

26. Policyholders often purchase universal life-type contracts as replacements for other insurance contracts issued by the same enterprise (sometimes referred to as *internal replacement transactions*). In those cases, the policyholder often uses the cash surrender value of the previous contract to pay an initial lump-sum premium for the new contract. When surrender of a life insurance contract is associated with an internal replacement by a universal life-type contract, unamortized acquisition costs associated with the replaced contract and any difference between the cash surrender value and the previously recorded liability shall not be deferred in connection with the replacement contract.

Application of Statement 60

27. The provisions of Statement 60 dealing with loss recognition (premium deficiency), accounting for reinsurance, and financial statement disclosure shall apply to limited-payment and universal life-type contracts addressed by this Statement.

Reporting of Realized Investment Gains and Losses

28. Statement 60 required that insurance enterprises report realized gains and losses in the statement of earnings below operating earnings and net of applicable income taxes. This Statement precludes that practice. Realized gains and losses shall be reported in the statement of earnings as a component of other income, on a pretax basis, and shall not be deferred to future periods either directly or indirectly. The first sentence of paragraph 50 of Statement 60 is superseded by the following:

Realized gains and losses on all investments (except those that are accounted for as hedges as described in FASB Statements No. 52, *Foreign Currency Translation,* and No. 80, *Accounting for Futures Contracts*) shall be reported in the statement of earnings as a component of other income, on a pretax basis. Realized gains and losses shall be presented as a separate item in the statement of earnings or disclosed in the notes to the financial statements. Realized gains and losses shall not be deferred, either directly or indirectly.

Other Amendments to Statement 60

29. This Statement adds the following footnote to paragraph 6 of Statement 60:

*The accounting for certain long-duration insurance contracts referred to as investment contracts, limited-payment contracts, and universal life-type contracts is established by FASB Statement No. 97, *Accounting and Reporting by Insurance Enterprises for Certain Long-Duration Contracts and for Realized Gains and Losses from the Sale of Investments.*

30. Paragraph 15 of Statement 60 is superseded by the following:

Premiums from long-duration contracts, such as whole-life contracts, guaranteed renewable term life contracts, and title insurance contracts, shall be recognized as revenue when due from policyholders.

Amendments to Other Pronouncements

31. Footnote 8 of APB Opinion No. 30, *Reporting the Results of Operations—Reporting the Effects of Disposal of a Segment of a Business, and Extraordinary, Unusual and Infrequently Occurring Events and Transactions,* as amended by Statement 60, is deleted.

Effective Date and Transition

32. This Statement shall be effective for fiscal years beginning after December 15, 1988, with earlier application encouraged. Except as provided in paragraph 33, accounting changes to adopt the provisions of this Statement shall be applied retroactively through restatement of all previously issued financial statements presented. In the year that the Statement is first applied, the financial statements shall disclose the nature of the restatement and its effect on income before extraordinary items, net income, and related per share amounts for each year presented.

33. If restatement of all years presented is not practicable, the cumulative effect of applying this Statement shall be included in net income in the year the Statement is adopted. (Refer to paragraph 20 of APB Opinion No. 20, *Accounting Changes.*) In the year of adoption, the financial statements shall disclose the nature of the cumulative adjustment and the effect of applying this Statement on income before extraordinary items, net income, and related per share amounts.

The provisions of this Statement need not be applied to immaterial items.

This Statement was adopted by the affirmative votes of six members of the Financial Accounting Standards Board. Mr. Lauver dissented.

Mr. Lauver dissents to the issuance of this Statement because of the manner in which capitalized acquisition costs related to universal life-type contracts are required to be amortized. That amortization method, described in paragraphs 22-25, introduces an interest factor by requiring periodic accruals to the balance of capitalized acquisition costs, a nonmonetary, nonearning deferred charge. The Board found sufficient, relevant distinctions between universal life-type contracts and other long-duration insurance contracts to cause it to reject the Statement 60 model and require use of the retrospective deposit method to account for universal life-type contracts. Mr. Lauver agrees that those distinctions are significant and believes that they should also have precluded introducing an interest factor into the amortization of capitalized acquisition costs related to universal life-type contracts. A similar notion has regularly been rejected by the Board when advanced in the form of a sinking fund or annuity method of depreciating fixed assets.

Because the amortization of deferred costs is an area of accounting with pervasive application, Mr. Lauver believes it is inappropriate to have introduced an interest factor into the amortization method without first considering the broader implications of that action. The use of an interest factor as required herein is generally perceived as part of a general subject described as discounting. Although the Board has received many requests to consider that subject, it has not as yet evaluated those requests nor added the subject to its agenda. The precedent of the conclusion reached in this Statement can only complicate and make more difficult the inevitable evaluation of the appropriate circumstances in which interest factors should be introduced into accounting generally.

Members of the Financial Accounting Standards Board:

Dennis R. Beresford,
  Chairman
Victor H. Brown

Raymond C. Lauver
James J. Leisenring
David Mosso

C. Arthur Northrop
Robert J. Swieringa

Appendix A

BACKGROUND INFORMATION AND BASIS FOR CONCLUSIONS

CONTENTS

Appendix A

BACKGROUND INFORMATION AND BASIS FOR CONCLUSIONS

Introduction

34. This appendix discusses factors deemed significant by members of the Board in reaching conclusions in this Statement. It includes descriptions of alternatives considered by the Board with reasons for accepting some and rejecting others. Individual Board members gave greater weight to some factors than to others.

35. In the late 1970s, new insurance contracts were designed to address changing consumer needs. The accounting for one of those insurance contracts, universal life insurance, was identified in Statement 60 as an issue then being studied by the insurance industry and the accounting and actuarial professions. Statement 60 did not address the accounting for universal life insurance, pending the completion of that effort.

36. The American Academy of Actuaries released a Discussion Memorandum, *Accounting for Universal Life*, in September 1984. In November 1984, the AICPA released an Issues Paper, *Accounting by Stock Life Insurance Companies for Annuities, Universal Life Insurance, and Related Products and Accounting for Nonguaranteed-Premium Contracts.* The FASB added a project to its agenda in February 1985 to address the issues raised by those documents. In December 1986, the Board issued an Exposure Draft, *Accounting and Reporting by Insurance Enterprises for Certain Long-Duration Insurance Contracts and for Realized Gains and Losses from the Sale of Investments.* The Board received comment letters from 111 individuals and organizations and in June 1987 conducted a public hearing at which representatives of 21 of those organizations appeared.

Scope

37. After reviewing the nature of long-duration insurance contracts, the Board concluded that a general reconsideration of accounting by insurance enterprises is not necessary at this time. The Board concluded that the accounting for investment contracts, limited-payment contracts, and universal life-type contracts should be addressed. The Board concluded that consideration of those contracts separately from other long-duration contracts is justified because of the differences between each of those contracts and the traditional contracts to which Statement 60 applies.

38. The Board acknowledges that it is establishing accounting principles for three classes of long-duration contracts that differ from those applied to other long-duration insurance contracts. The Board believes, however, that the differences in accounting are warranted by the differences in the contractual relationships involved. The Board rejected suggestions that it either broaden the scope of this project to include all long-duration contracts or that the principles of Statement 60 should be applied to the contracts addressed in this Statement.

Accounting and Reporting by Insurance Enterprises
for Certain Long-Duration Contracts and for
Realized Gains and Losses from the Sale of Investments

FAS97

Investment Contracts

39. The Board concluded that contracts issued by insurance enterprises that do not incorporate significant risk from the death or disability of policyholders (mortality or morbidity risk) are more comparable to financial or investment instruments issued by other financial institutions than to the insurance contracts contemplated by Statement 60. While many investment contracts are issued primarily by insurance enterprises, the Board believes that similar financial instruments should be accorded similar treatment regardless of the nature of the issuing enterprise. Therefore, the Board concluded that the accounting for investment contracts issued by insurance enterprises should be consistent with the accounting for interest-bearing and other financial instruments.

40. Several respondents suggested that the presence of an annuity purchase option constitutes a mortality risk and that some contracts designated as investment contracts by the Board were therefore subject to Statement 60. The Board concluded that the obligation to make payments that are contingent upon the death or continued survival of a specific individual or group is the essence of a mortality risk. The risk that the guaranteed price of an annuity may prove to be unfavorable to the guaranteeing enterprise when the annuity is purchased is a price risk not unlike a guaranteed price of any commodity and does not create a mortality risk. A mortality risk does not arise until the purchase provision is executed and the obligation to make life-contingent payments is present in an annuity contract. A nominal mortality risk—a risk of insignificant amount or of remote probability—is not sufficient to permit that a contract be accounted for as an insurance contract.

Limited-Payment Contracts

41. The accounting for single-premium and limited-payment contracts was addressed in Statement 60 and in the AICPA Industry Audit Guide, *Audits of Stock Life Insurance Companies* (the AICPA Guide), which was extracted in Statement 60. Statement 60 requires that premiums be recognized as revenue when due. The liability for policy benefits is computed on the same basis as for other long-duration contracts, and net income is recognized, in part, as a residual percentage of premium revenue. Measurement of income as a residual percentage of premium thus leads to income recognition before services have been performed.

42. The Board concluded that limited-payment contracts with terms that are fixed and guaranteed are similar to other contracts addressed by Statement 60 in all respects except for the pattern of pre-

mium payment. The Board also concluded that income from insurance contracts is earned through the performance of contract services. The collection of a single premium or a limited number of premiums does not, in itself, represent the completion of an earnings process. The Board concluded that any amount of gross premium in excess of net premium, as those terms are defined in Statement 60, should be deferred and recognized over the period that services are provided.

43. The Board considered suggestions that it define a limited-payment contract in terms of a specified number of premiums or of a specific relationship between the present value of expected premiums and the present value of benefit and expense payments. The Board concluded that such a definition would necessarily be arbitrary and inconsistent with the proposition that contract services are provided over the entire benefit period.

Universal Life-Type Contracts

44. Most of the long-duration life insurance contracts to which Statement 60 applies have terms that are fixed and guaranteed. The purchaser of such a contract—having agreed to pay a fixed, usually level, premium in return for a guaranteed death benefit and schedule of cash value accumulations—cannot affect the individual elements of contract operation. Similarly, the insurer cannot unilaterally reduce the interest rate that is implicit in cash value increases or increase the amounts assessed for mortality, administration, and early termination that are inherent in the contract.

45. The purchaser of a universal life-type contract can often vary the amount and timing of premium payments, within limits set by the contract, without the approval of the insurer. Premium payments are credited to the policyholder balance, against which amounts are assessed for contract services and to which amounts are credited as income. The policyholder balance provides a base upon which interest accrues to the policyholder and, when compared with the death benefit amount, fixes the insurer's net amount at risk. The insurer can often adjust the schedule of amounts assessed for contract services and the rate at which interest is credited to the policyholder balance.

46. Some contracts may not possess all of the features described above. A contract might, for example, require payment of a fixed premium and provide a guaranteed death benefit while crediting interest to cash values at a rate established by reference to an external index. Several respondents suggested that the definition of universal life-type contracts should be based on only flexibility in pre-

mium payment or the presence of an explicit account balance. The Board concluded, however, that the elements of flexibility and discretion represent basic differences between universal life-type and other long-duration insurance contracts.

47. The Board acknowledges the view expressed by some respondents that the issuer of a universal life-type contract accepts many of the same risks that are present in other life insurance contracts. The Board also acknowledges that some enterprises employ the same aggregate pricing techniques for universal life-type contracts that are used for other life insurance contracts. The pooling of a large number of risks is essential to the life insurance industry, and accounting has historically considered the portfolio or book of contracts as the unit of accounting. The Board concluded, however, that there is a fundamental difference between the relationship of insurer and policyholder when risks are assumed in connection with a contract that is fixed and guaranteed and the relationship that exists when risks are assumed in connection with a contract that is flexible or discretionary. The Board further concluded that this difference is relevant and should be reflected in different accounting for universal life-type contracts.

48. Some respondents pointed out that participating life insurance and nonguaranteed-premium life insurance contracts provide a measure of discretion to the insurance enterprise that is similar to that found in universal life-type contracts. Participating life insurance contracts usually contemplate the sharing of favorable experience relative to contract guarantees rather than the market-related adjustments that are characteristic of universal life-type contracts. The policyholder is thus granted a right that is not present in universal life-type contracts. The operation of universal life-type contracts usually centers on an account or policy balance that is credited with interest and against which amounts are assessed for contract services. Participating and nonguaranteed-premium contracts usually lack this feature. The Board considered incorporating participating and nonguaranteed-premium contracts in the scope of this Statement but decided that the differences between the traditional forms of those contracts and universal life-type contracts justify their exclusion. However, the Board concluded that some participating and nonguaranteed-premium contracts may be, in substance, universal life-type contracts. The Board concluded that this Statement should apply to all contracts that have similar provisions, regardless of the name given to the contract.

49. Life insurance enterprises developed a number of approaches to the accounting for universal life-type contracts following the introduction of those contracts in the late 1970s. Some enterprises accounted for the new generation of contracts in a manner similar to that specified for other long-duration contracts in Statement 60. Others adopted accounting methods that measure the liability for policy benefits based on the balances that accrue to policyholders. The Board concluded that users of financial statements would be better served if insurance enterprises applied a single accounting method for universal life-type contracts.

50. An insurance enterprise agrees to provide two basic services to the policyholder when it enters into a long-duration life insurance contract. The first is to provide contract services, including assumption of mortality risk. The second is to manage the investment of the funds deposited by the policyholder. Statement 60 concluded that no predominant function or service was representative of the pooling or aggregation of services in a life insurance contract. In view of that conclusion and the usual level pattern of premium payments over the life of the contract, premiums were considered an appropriate measure of revenue. Under that approach, the liability for policy benefits accrues at a constant percentage of premiums received.

51. The variable terms of universal life-type contracts and the increased importance of the investment element led to a reexamination of the view that an insurance contract is a pool or aggregation of indistinguishable parts. The presence of a policyholder account balance in many universal life-type contracts and of separate amounts assessed for contract services that can change from time to time suggests that the advance funding and contract service functions can be measured and accounted for separately. In addition, the discretion in premium payment that is often granted to individual policyholders suggests that a liability based on the accounting method specified in Statement 60 may not be representationally faithful.

52. Paragraphs 35 and 36 of FASB Concepts Statement No. 6, *Elements of Financial Statements,* describe a liability in the following terms:

> Liabilities are probable future sacrifices of economic benefits arising from present obligations of a particular entity to transfer assets or provide services to other entities in the future as a result of past transactions or events.
> A liability has three essential characteristics: (a) it embodies a present duty or responsibility to one or more other entities that entails settlement by probable future transfer or use of assets at a specified or determinable

Accounting and Reporting by Insurance Enterprises
for Certain Long-Duration Contracts and for **FAS97**
Realized Gains and Losses from the Sale of Investments

date, on occurrence of a specified event, or on demand, (b) the duty or responsibility obligates a particular entity, leaving it little or no discretion to avoid the future sacrifice, and (c) the transaction or other event obligating the entity has already happened. [Footnote references omitted.]

53. After examining the characteristics of various long-duration insurance contracts, the Board concluded that the balance that accrues to the benefit of individual policyholders represents the minimum measure of an insurance enterprise's liability that is consistent with the definition above. For many universal life-type contracts, this amount takes the form of an account balance that, absent future action by the policyholder, will continue to fund operation of the contract until exhausted or reduced to a contract minimum. The insurer has a present obligation, arising from past transactions, to continue to maintain the contract and provide mortality protection as long as an adequate account balance exists. Other universal life-type contracts do not have an explicit policyholder account but do have a policyholder balance to which interest is accrued at a variable rate. In either case, future events and transactions will change the amount of the enterprise's obligation as policyholders make additional premium deposits and realize contract benefits. The present obligation, however, is fixed by the amount that has accrued to the benefit of the policyholder.

54. Some respondents suggested that the information provided by the insurer to individual policyholders does not represent the substance of the services provided under the contract. They maintained that services are provided ratably over the life of a contract and that amounts should be deferred or anticipated to produce a pattern of reported earnings that reflects a level pattern of service. The Board rejected that view. Accounting typically presumes that the terms and conditions of a contract entered into between two parties dealing at arm's length are representative of their agreement. This presumption can be overcome if evidence indicates that the substance of the agreement is not captured in the contract—for example, if the terms of contract financing differ from performance of contract services. The Board recognized that amounts assessed against policyholders might compensate the insurer for services to be provided in future periods. In those cases, this Statement requires that amounts be deferred and recognized over the period that service is provided.

55. Papers prepared by the AICPA and the American Academy of Actuaries suggested an accounting method for universal life-type contracts that has been termed the composite or balanced method. The composite method, which is an extension of the basic methods employed in Statement 60, requires that additional provisions for adverse deviation, beyond the amount that would otherwise be included under Statement 60, be incorporated into the measurement of universal life-type contracts. A portion of income would then be recognized in amounts that reflect release from management's estimate of the various risks assumed under the contract, with the balance recognized as a residual percentage of premiums collected.

56. The provision for adverse deviation is a convention unique to the accounting for long-duration insurance contracts. Adverse deviation is fundamentally a notion of subjective conservatism and requires an increase in the reported liability for policy benefits beyond management's best estimate of the enterprise's ultimate obligation to policyholders. Companies other than life insurers are proscribed from making similar provisions by FASB Statement No. 5, *Accounting for Contingencies.* While the Board concluded that the accounting for traditional long-duration insurance contracts should not be reconsidered at this time, it did not adopt accounting approaches that would incorporate provisions for adverse deviation in accounting for universal life-type contracts.

57. The Board rejected the view that the application of adverse deviation to universal life-type contracts represents an appropriately conservative approach to income recognition for flexible insurance contracts. FASB Concepts Statement No. 2, *Qualitative Characteristics of Accounting Information,* indicates that accounting conservatism is "a prudent reaction to uncertainty." Concepts Statement 2 articulates the principle that, while conservatism may suggest that the more conservative of two equally likely alternatives should be used in an accounting measurement, conservatism does not suggest that a less likely outcome should be used simply because it is less favorable to the enterprise.

Statement of Earnings Presentation

58. Statement 60 continued the industry practice of recognizing premiums from long-duration insurance contracts as revenue when due. This convention is based on the view that no single contract function is predominant over the periods of a long-duration contract and that individual functions are not readily measurable. Universal life-type contracts typically provide separate measures of the attributes of the contract that are communicated regularly to the policyholder. In addition, respondents indicated that separate measurements of the

advance funding and contract services functions are inherent in the provisions of long-duration contracts, even when those individual measurements are not communicated as such to policyholders.

59. The Board concluded that it is inappropriate to report total cash inflows (premiums) as revenues from universal life-type contracts. Concepts Statement 6 defines revenues as "inflows or other enhancements of assets of an entity or settlements of its liabilities (or a combination of both) from delivering or producing goods, rendering services, or other activities that constitute the entity's ongoing major or central operations" (paragraph 78). The portion of a premium that accrues directly to the policyholder balance—the advance funding function—does not satisfy that definition of revenue. Similarly, the Board concluded that payments that represent a return of policyholder balances are not expenses. The Board considered requiring separate disclosure of the total premiums received on universal life-type contracts. The Board concluded that an enterprise may voluntarily make such disclosure in footnotes or in the statement of cash flows but that requiring a disclosure would not be appropriate. Having concluded that premiums on certain contracts do not constitute revenues, the Board decided that requiring a disclosure of those premiums as if they were revenues would be confusing. Information about premiums may be useful to some financial statement users in evaluating volume or growth, just as is similar information about capacity or order backlog in other industries, but that information is not typically required in general-purpose financial statements.

60. The Board considered whether this Statement should provide additional guidance about circumstances in which amounts assessed against policyholders should be considered to have been collected in advance of having been earned. Some respondents suggested, for example, that amounts assessed for mortality protection often produce a much larger gross profit margin in early years than is produced from those same amounts assessed in later years. They maintained, therefore, that a portion of early mortality assessments represents compensation for services to be provided in future periods. The profit attributed to mortality assessments in early years, however, is usually the result of the recently completed underwriting process rather than of the collection of amounts assessed before they are earned.

61. The Board considered a number of circumstances that might suggest that an amount assessed against policyholders was collected before being earned. An amount assessed might be considered unearned, for example, if it is assessed only in certain contract periods or in a manner that is expected to result in current profits and future losses from a specific contract function. The Board concluded that those circumstances and others might lead to the determination that a particular amount assessed is unearned but that the determination must be based on the facts and circumstances of individual cases. The Board also concluded that amounts assessed against policyholder balances that are refundable and amounts that are assessed for initiation of a universal life-type contract are unearned revenues.

Capitalized Acquisition Costs

62. Statement 60 requires that capitalized acquisition costs be charged to expense in proportion to premium revenue recognized using methods that include the same assumptions used in estimating the liability for future policy benefits. The Board concluded that in accounting for universal life-type contracts it is appropriate to continue the practice of amortizing capitalized acquisition costs in a manner consistent with the accounting for performance under the contract. The retrospective deposit method adopted in this Statement, however, recognizes as revenue the amounts assessed against the policyholder accounts. Accordingly, capitalized policy acquisition costs are amortized based on the present value of the gross profit expected to be generated by the book of insurance.

63. Although capitalized acquisition costs are not, in themselves, monetary items, the requirements of Statement 60 link such costs to monetary liabilities and result in amortization methods that incorporate the same concepts of discounting and accrual of interest that are used in liability measurement. The Board has in the past also concluded that, in other limited situations, capitalized acquisition costs should be accounted for as if they were monetary because of their relationship to the measurement of the liability for future policy benefits in Statement 60.[5]

64. The Exposure Draft reflected the Board's conclusion that the retrospective deposit method breaks the linkage that exists in Statement 60 between the measurement of capitalized acquisition costs and the measurement of the liability for future policy benefits. The Board believed that the rationale for measuring and reporting capitalized acquisition costs as if they were monetary items was not appropriate when the retrospective deposit

---

[5]FASB Statements No. 33, *Financial Reporting and Changing Prices*, and No. 52, *Foreign Currency Translation*.

Accounting and Reporting by Insurance Enterprises for Certain Long-Duration Contracts and for Realized Gains and Losses from the Sale of Investments

FAS97

method is used to account for universal life-type contracts. The Board initially concluded, therefore, that interest should not accrue to the unamortized balance of capitalized acquisition costs associated with universal life-type contracts. A majority of respondents disagreed with that conclusion.

65. After considering the comments received, the Board concluded that the Exposure Draft provision should be changed. The assenting Board members hold two views of the basis for incorporating discounting techniques in the amortization of capitalized acquisition costs.

66. The first view is that the essential character of a long-duration insurance contract is that of a complex financial instrument incorporating both financial and service functions. The cash flows that arise from a book of universal life-type contracts are not as closely linked to the contract as are the cash flows from many other financial instruments. However, those cash flows are reasonably predictable and are sufficiently linked to capitalized acquisition costs to justify accounting that is appropriate for financial assets and liabilities.

67. The second view emphasizes the character of capitalized acquisition costs and existing industry practice. The commissions and other costs incurred to acquire universal life-type contracts are essentially the same as those incurred to acquire traditional long-duration contracts. The amortization of capitalized acquisition costs under Statement 60 is based on the present values of capitalized acquisition costs and accrual of interest to the unamortized balance of those costs. Insurance enterprises that adopted retrospective deposit methods carried forward this industry practice in the amortization of capitalized acquisition costs of universal life-type contracts. The Board members who hold this view acknowledge the similarity in costs and the established use of interest methods in amortizing costs on a variety of long-duration insurance contracts and concluded that the use of interest methods in amortizing capitalized acquisition costs should not be altered in this project.

Initiation Fees and Surrender Charges

68. Universal life-type contracts typically include an amount assessed against policyholders on inception of contracts (initiation fee) or an amount assessed against policyholders when contracts are terminated (surrender charge), or both. The Exposure Draft reflected the Board's conclusion that both initiation fees and surrender charges are assessed primarily to recover capitalized acquisition costs. Insurance enterprises that adopted retro-

spective deposit methods before the Exposure Draft was issued typically accounted for initiation fees as recoveries of capitalized acquisition costs. However, they accounted for surrender charges as revenues when realized. Most respondents supported that approach.

69. After considering the nature of amounts assessed against policyholders under universal life-type contracts, the Board concluded that all such amounts contribute proportionately to the profitability of a book of contracts. The fact that a particular event, for example, surrender of a contract, may trigger realization of an amount assessed does not alter that conclusion. The Board also concluded that some amounts are collected before being earned and that an initiation fee is one such amount. A surrender charge, on the other hand, is collected when the relationship between policyholder and insurer has been severed. The insurance enterprise has no remaining obligation, and, therefore, the surrender charge is earned when realized.

Internal Replacement Transactions

70. Universal life-type contracts are often purchased as replacements for traditional life insurance contracts issued by the same enterprise. In such cases, the policyholder often uses the cash surrender value of the previous contract to make an initial premium deposit for the new, universal life-type contract. This transaction is commonly referred to as an internal replacement. Insurance enterprises often conduct marketing programs aimed at retaining policyholders who might otherwise replace traditional contracts with universal life-type contracts issued by other insurance enterprises.

71. The replacement of a traditional life insurance contract with a universal life-type contract typically results in the need to account for an amount equal to the sum of (a) the unamortized acquisition costs associated with the replaced contract and (b) the difference between the cash surrender value and the previously recorded liability for policy benefits related to the replaced contract. The AICPA Issues Paper suggested that this net amount should be deferred and amortized as part of the capitalized acquisition costs of the new book of universal life-type contracts. The Issues Paper took the position that the universal life-type replacement contract represented a continuing relationship between the insurer and the policyholder, and maintained that the new contract represented only a change in the form of insurance protection. Some respondents also suggested that the incremental costs of replacement transactions are usually less than the costs of sales to new policyholders. In their view, the continued deferral

of net amounts related to replaced contracts more nearly equates the costs of contracts issued to different classes of policyholders.

72. The Board rejected those proposals. The Board recognizes that an insurance enterprise that conducts an internal replacement program may be motivated by a desire to retain its customer base and that the alternative to replacement may be loss of that base. That objective is not, however, different from the objectives of similar transactions undertaken by insurance enterprises and other enterprises for which continued deferral of costs is not permitted, including the refunding of debt. Paragraphs 19 and 20 of APB Opinion No. 26, *Early Extinguishment of Debt,* as amended by FASB Statement No. 76, *Extinguishment of Debt,* describe the accounting for extinguishment of debt, including extinguishments in which the old and new liability are to the same party:

> *Reduction of alternatives.* The [Accounting Principles] Board concludes that all extinguishments of debt are fundamentally alike. The accounting for such transactions should be the same regardless of the means used to achieve the extinguishment.
>
> *Disposition of amounts.* A difference between the reacquisition price and the net carrying amount of the extinguished debt should be recognized currently in income of the period of extinguishment as losses or gains and identified as a separate item. . . . Gains and losses should not be amortized to future periods. [Footnote reference omitted.]

Reporting of Realized Investment Gains and Losses

73. Statement 60 continued the insurance industry practice of reporting realized gains and losses from all investments on a separate line in the statement of earnings, below operating income and net of applicable income taxes. At the time Statement 60 was issued, banks reported realized gains and losses in a similar fashion. In 1983, the AICPA issued Statement of Position (SOP) 83-1, *Reporting by Banks Of Investment Securities Gains or Losses.* That Statement of Position amended the AICPA Industry Audit Guide, *Audits of Banks,* to require the presentation of realized gains or losses on investments on a pretax basis in the "other income" section of a bank's statement of earnings. As a result, only insurance enterprises and certain investment companies continued to report realized gains and losses separately from operating income.

74. The Board concluded that investment activities, including realized gains and losses, are an integral part of an insurance enterprise's operations and that operating income should include the results of all investment operations. The Board could find no compelling reason to continue the exception granted to the insurance industry from financial reporting practices that apply to most other financial institutions.

75. Some respondents, including many users of financial statements, suggested that presentation of realized gains and losses with operations provides an opportunity to manage reported income because the selection of securities sold and the timing of sales are at the discretion of management. The Board noted, however, that the ability to manage reported income through the selection and timing of sales is inherent in transaction-based historical-cost accounting because gains and losses are reported in income only when realized. The Board also noted instances in which the two-step statement of earnings presentation permits enterprises to enter into transactions designed to increase operating income with offsetting nonoperating realized losses.

76. Some respondents maintained that there is no reason to change because the present format has been in use for years and is well understood by users. The Board concluded, however, that realized gains and losses from investments are an integral part of the operating results of an insurance enterprise and cannot be considered incidental. The Board also noted that the two-step statement of earnings has been eliminated from financial reporting by most other financial institutions. The Board believes that financial reporting is enhanced when enterprises report similar transactions in a similar fashion.

77. Some respondents suggested that certain realized gains and losses should be deferred and recognized over the remaining life of the insurance contracts to which they maintain the gains are related. Some suggested that the deferral should be reflected directly—by excluding realized transactions from the statement of earnings—while others suggested that additional liabilities should be recorded. The objective of this practice, in their view, is the presentation of an appropriate investment yield over the life of the book of contracts. The Board notes that generally accepted accounting principles require that realized investment gains and losses be reflected in the period in which they occur. The Board acknowledges that some contracts with policyholders may entitle policyholders to an amount equal to a portion of specific investment performance. The recording of liabilities to reflect amounts to which those policyholders are entitled is appropriate, but the deferral of realized gains and losses is not justified.

Accounting and Reporting by Insurance Enterprises
for Certain Long-Duration Contracts and for
Realized Gains and Losses from the Sale of Investments

FAS97

Effective Date and Transition

78. The Board considered a solely prospective application of the accounting required by this Statement. The Board believes, however, that restatement of all financial statements presented for prior years will provide useful information about the relative importance of the various contracts addressed by this Statement. The Board concluded that restatement will provide useful information for comparing financial data for periods before and after the effective date of this Statement. Further, the provisions of this Statement establish a fundamentally different basis of liability measurement for universal life-type insurance contracts than for traditional long-duration insurance contracts. Continued recognition of the liability for policy benefits using other methods for some books of universal life-type contracts while applying the provisions of this Statement to newly issued contracts would result in inconsistent recognition of liabilities, revenues, and capitalized acquisition costs. The Board concluded, therefore, that restatement of only some financial statements presented while not restating others is not appropriate in this circumstance.

Appendix B

ILLUSTRATION OF ACCOUNTING FOR CAPITALIZED ACQUISITION COSTS

79. The accompanying schedules illustrate the accounting for capitalized acquisition costs incurred in connection with a portfolio or book of universal life-type contracts, projected over a 20-year period. The illustration displays the computations involved in (a) amortizing that amount as gross profits and surrender charges are realized and (b) revising estimates of gross profit expected to be realized (refer to paragraphs 22-25). During year one, actual experience is assumed to be the same as management's estimate. During year two, 20 percent of policyholders surrender their contracts. Management's original estimate was that 12 percent of policyholders would surrender their contracts in year two. Interest is credited to policyholder balances at 9 percent.

80. Schedule One—Computation of Estimated Gross Profit

Year	Surrender Charges (a)	Mortality Assessments (b)	Mortality Cost Incurred (c)	Expense Assessments (d)	Recurring Expenses Incurred (e)	Investment Income Related to Policy Balances (f)	Interest Credited to Policy Balances (g)	Estimated Gross Profit	Revised Gross Profit at Year 2
1	$13,298	$ 17,300	$ (3,685)	$ 11,700	$ (12,176)	$ 6,405	$ (5,490)	$ 27,352	$ 27,352
2	13,169	15,099	(3,541)	9,356	(9,669)	10,571	(9,061)	25,924	34,637
3	7,314	14,104	(3,627)	8,229	(8,476)	14,436	(12,374)	19,606	17,822
4	4,656	13,604	(3,866)	7,566	(7,781)	18,356	(15,734)	16,801	15,273
5	3,645	13,199	(4,107)	7,108	(7,309)	22,405	(19,204)	15,737	14,304
6	2,739	12,791	(4,330)	6,676	(6,866)	26,286	(22,531)	14,765	13,422
7	1,929	12,950	(4,513)	6,270	(6,449)	29,957	(25,677)	14,467	13,151
8	1,208	12,905	(4,690)	5,888	(6,057)	33,447	(28,669)	14,032	12,756
9	567	12,755	(4,865)	5,529	(5,688)	36,779	(31,525)	13,552	12,320
10	0	12,593	(5,003)	5,191	(5,340)	39,965	(34,256)	13,150	11,954
11-20	0	108,164	(55,512)	37,183	(38,270)	551,879	(473,039)	130,405	118,543
21-50	0	140,607	(88,833)	32,577	(33,712)	2,618,726	(2,244,622)	424,743	386,112
Total	$48,525	$386,071	$(186,572)	$143,273	$(147,793)	$3,409,212	$(2,922,182)	$730,534	$677,646
Present value								$180,944	$176,087

Explanation of columns:

(a) Surrender charges realized on termination of contracts.

(b) Amounts assessed against policyholder balances for mortality coverage.

(c) Benefit claims, less the amount in the related policyholder balances.

(d) Amounts assessed against policyholder balances for contract administration on either a percentage or a fixed amount per contract basis.

(e) Recurring expenses not included in capitalized acquisition costs.

(f) Investment income earned on policyholder deposits, computed by multiplying policyholder balances by the expected asset earning rate of 10.5 percent.

(g) Interest that is accrued to policyholder account balances at the expected crediting rate of 9 percent.

Accounting and Reporting by Insurance Enterprises
for Certain Long-Duration Contracts and for   **FAS97**
Realized Gains and Losses from the Sale of Investments

81. **Schedule Two—Computation of Amortization Rate**

		Original Estimate	Revised Estimate
Present value of estimated gross profit, years one to fifty, (from Schedule One)	(x)	$180,944	$176,087
Present value of capitalized acquisition costs	(y)	$ 90,986	$ 90,986
Amortization rate = (y) / (x)	(z)	50.284%	51.671%

82. **Schedule Three—Illustration of Amortization**

	Original Estimate	Revised Estimate
Capitalized costs, year one	$77,780	$77,780
Interest accrual at 9 percent	7,000	7,000
Amortization, year one		
Gross profit of $27,352 (from Schedule One) at rate (z) above	(13,754)	(14,133)
Balance, end of year one	71,026	70,647
Additional capitalized costs, year two	14,394	14,394
	85,420	85,041
Interest accrual at 9 percent	7,688	7,654
Amortization, year two		
Gross profit of $34,637 (from Schedule One) at 51.671% (revised rate from Schedule Two)	(17,897)	(17,897)
	$75,211	$74,798
Balance based on Original Estimate	$75,211	
Balance based on Revised Estimate	74,798	
Adjustment required	$ (413)	
Net amortization recognized		
In year one	$ 6,754	
In year two	$10,622	

Statement of Financial Accounting Standards No. 98
Accounting for Leases

- Sale-Leaseback Transactions Involving Real Estate
- Sales-Type Leases of Real Estate
- Definition of the Lease Term
- Initial Direct Costs of Direct Financing Leases

an amendment of FASB Statements No. 13, 66, and 91
and a rescission of FASB Statement No. 26 and
Technical Bulletin No. 79-11

STATUS

Issued: May 1988

Effective Date: For transactions entered into after June 30, 1988

Affects: Amends FAS 13, paragraphs 5, 6(b)(i), 7(a), 8, 17(a), 19, 25, 26(a), and 26(b)(ii)(b)
Supersedes FAS 13, paragraphs 5(f), 6(b)(iv), 8(a), 18(a), 18(b), 26(a)(ii), and 26(b)(i)(b)
Supersedes FAS 26
Amends FAS 29, paragraph 13
Amends FAS 66, footnote 34
Supersedes FAS 66, paragraph 40
Supersedes FAS 91, paragraphs 25(a) through 25(c)
Supersedes FTB 79-11

Affected by: No other pronouncements

Issues Discussed by FASB Emerging Issues Task Force (EITF)

Affects: Resolves EITF Topic No. D-9
Partially resolves EITF Issues No. 84-37 and 85-16
Affects EITF Issue No. 86-17

Interpreted by: Paragraph 10 interpreted by EITF Issues No. 90-14 and 90-20 and Topic No. D-24
Paragraph 11 interpreted by EITF Issues No. 90-14, 90-20, and 97-1 and Topic No. D-24
Paragraphs 12 and 13 interpreted by EITF Issues No. 90-14 and 90-20 and Topic No. D-24

Related Issues: EITF Issues No. 87-7, 88-21, 89-16, and 96-21

SUMMARY

This Statement specifies the accounting by a seller-lessee for a sale-leaseback transaction involving real estate, including real estate with equipment. In addition, this Statement modifies the provisions of FASB Statement No. 13, *Accounting for Leases,* that define the lease term, the accounting by a lessor for sales-type leases of real estate that provide for the transfer of title, and the accounting for initial direct costs of direct financing leases. This Statement provides that:

- A sale-leaseback transaction involving real estate, including real estate with equipment, must qualify as a sale under the provisions of FASB Statement No. 66, *Accounting for Sales of Real Estate,* as amended by this Statement, before it is appropriate for the seller-lessee to account for the transaction as a sale. If the transaction does not qualify as a sale under Statement 66, it should be accounted for by the deposit method or as a financing.
- A sale-leaseback transaction involving real estate, including real estate with equipment, that includes any continuing involvement other than a normal leaseback in which the seller-lessee intends to actively use the property during the lease should be accounted for by the deposit method or as a financing.
- The definition of lease term in paragraph 5(f) of Statement 13 is amended to include all renewal periods during which there will be a loan outstanding from the lessee to the lessor. This Statement also defines the term *penalty* as used in the lease term provisions of paragraph 5(f) of Statement 13 and thereby may cause lease terms to be longer than previously contemplated. Those modifications of the lease term provisions of Statement 13 apply to *all* leases, not just to sale-leaseback transactions involving real estate.
- A lease involving real estate may not be classified as a sales-type lease unless the lease agreement provides for the transfer of title to the lessee at or shortly after the end of the lease term. Sales-type leases involving real estate should be accounted for under the provisions of Statement 66.

This Statement supersedes paragraph 40 of Statement 66 and rescinds FASB Statement No. 26, *Profit Recognition on Sales-Type Leases of Real Estate,* and FASB Technical Bulletin No. 79-11, *Effect of a Penalty on the Term of a Lease.* This Statement is effective for transactions entered into after June 30, 1988 with earlier application encouraged.

This Statement also amends paragraph 25 of FASB Statement No. 91, *Accounting for Nonrefundable Fees and Costs Associated with Originating or Acquiring Loans and Initial Direct Costs of Leases,* and amends Statement 13 to reflect the amendment intended by Statement 91. The effective date of that amendment is the effective date of Statement 91.

Statement of Financial Accounting Standards No. 98

Accounting for Leases:
- **Sale-Leaseback Transactions Involving Real Estate**
- **Sales-Type Leases of Real Estate**
- **Definition of the Lease Term**
- **Initial Direct Costs of Direct Financing Leases**

an amendment of FASB Statements No. 13, 66, and 91 and a rescission of FASB Statement No. 26 and Technical Bulletin No. 79-11

CONTENTS

INTRODUCTION

1. The FASB has learned that practice varies in accounting by a seller-lessee for a sale-leaseback transaction involving real estate, including real estate with equipment (hereinafter referred to as a sale-leaseback transaction), such as manufacturing facilities, power plants, and office buildings with furniture and fixtures. Irrespective of the terms of the sale-leaseback agreement, some seller-lessees record the sale, remove all property and any related liabilities from the balance sheet, and recognize the profit in accordance with FASB Statement No. 13, *Accounting for Leases,* as amended by FASB Statement No. 28, *Accounting for Sales with Leasebacks.* That approach is hereinafter referred to as **sale-leaseback accounting.**[1] Others consider the provisions of the sale-leaseback agreement in evaluating compliance with the **sales recognition** criteria of FASB Statement No. 66, *Accounting for Sales of Real Estate.* In part, those differences result from differing interpretations of paragraph 40 of Statement 66. The FASB's Emerging Issues Task Force, the SEC staff, and others have asked the FASB to address the accounting for such transactions.

2. The FASB also has learned that diversity in practice exists in interpreting the definition of *lease term* in paragraph 5(f) of Statement 13. If the lessee provides financing to the lessor, some treat that loan the same as a guarantee by the lessee of the

---

[1] Terms defined in the glossary (Appendix C) are in **boldface type** the first time they appear in this Statement.

lessor's debt under paragraph 5(f) of Statement 13 and include all renewal periods during which the loan is expected to be in effect in the lease term. Others, however, do not include those periods in the lease term. This Statement amends paragraph 5(f) to address that circumstance.

3. Diversity also exists in interpreting the term *economic penalty* as used in FASB Technical Bulletin No. 79-11, *Effect of a Penalty on the Term of a Lease*. That Technical Bulletin clarifies that factors outside the lease agreement may be economic penalties. Some view an economic penalty as an agreement or other factor external to the lease that imposes a requirement on the lessee to pay a specified amount to a third party upon failure to renew the lease. Others view the loss of a future economic benefit, such as the loss of an enterprise's principal manufacturing or electric generating facility, as constituting an economic penalty and include the exercise of renewal rights related to that potential loss in determining the lease term. This Statement defines the term *penalty* to address those circumstances.

4. Statement 66 requires that a sale transaction be considered consummated before it is appropriate to recognize a sale. Consummation of a sale requires that (a) the parties are bound by the terms of a contract, (b) all consideration has been exchanged, (c) any permanent financing for which the seller is responsible has been arranged, and (d) all conditions precedent to closing have been performed. Statement 66 also requires that profit be recognized under other methods when a sale does not qualify for the full accrual method of profit recognition. The full accrual method of profit recognition requires that (i) the sale be consummated, (ii) the buyer's initial and continuing investments are adequate to demonstrate a commitment to pay for the property, (iii) the seller's receivable is not subject to future subordination, and (iv) the seller has transferred to the buyer the usual risks and rewards of ownership in a transaction that is in substance a sale and does not have a substantial continuing involvement with the property.

5. Consummation of a sale under Statement 66 would normally provide for the transfer of title to the buyer. Statement 13, on the other hand, allows a sale to be recognized in a sales-type lease of real estate even when title is *never* transferred provided that the transaction qualifies for the full accrual method of profit recognition. This Statement eliminates that inconsistency by requiring the transfer of title to the buyer for a transaction to qualify as a sales-type lease of real estate.

SCOPE

6. This Statement establishes standards of financial accounting and reporting with regard to the lease term for all leasing transactions (refer to paragraphs 22(a) and 22(b)), not just for sale-leaseback transactions involving real estate. In addition, this Statement establishes standards of financial accounting and reporting by a seller-lessee for sale-leaseback transactions involving real estate, including real estate with equipment, such as manufacturing facilities, power plants, and office buildings with furniture and fixtures. Under this Statement, a sale-leaseback transaction involving real estate with equipment includes any sale-leaseback transaction in which the equipment and the real estate are sold and leased back as a package, irrespective of the relative value of the equipment and the real estate. This Statement also addresses sale-leaseback transactions in which the seller-lessee sells property improvements or integral equipment[2] to a buyer-lessor and leases them back while retaining the underlying land.[3] In addition, this Statement applies to sale-leaseback transactions involving real estate with equipment that include separate sale and leaseback agreements (a) with the same entity or related parties and (b) that are consummated at or near the same time, suggesting that they were negotiated as a package. Except as specified in this paragraph and paragraph 22, this Statement does not address sale-leaseback or other leasing transactions involving *only* equipment.

---

[2]The terms *property improvements* or *integral equipment* as used in this Statement refer to any physical structure or equipment attached to the real estate, or other parts thereof, that cannot be removed and used separately without incurring significant cost. Examples include an office building, a manufacturing facility, a power plant, and a refinery.

[3]Paragraphs 38 and 39 of Statement 66 address transactions in which the seller sells property improvements to a buyer and leases the underlying land to the buyer of the improvements. Under certain circumstances, paragraph 38 of Statement 66 precludes sales recognition for such transactions and requires that they be accounted for as leases of both the land and improvements. It is not the intent of this Statement to modify paragraph 38; thus, it does not address a sale-leaseback transaction that does not qualify for sales recognition under the provisions of paragraph 38. However, this Statement does address a sale-leaseback transaction that qualifies for sales recognition under the provisions of paragraph 39 of Statement 66.

STANDARDS OF FINANCIAL ACCOUNTING AND REPORTING

Sale-Leaseback Transactions

Criteria for Sale-Leaseback Accounting

7. Sale-leaseback accounting shall be used by a seller-lessee only if a sale-leaseback transaction includes all of the following:

a. A normal leaseback as described in paragraph 8
b. Payment terms and provisions that adequately demonstrate the buyer-lessor's initial and continuing investment in the property (refer to paragraphs 8-16 of Statement 66)
c. Payment terms and provisions that transfer *all* of the other risks and rewards of ownership as demonstrated by the absence of *any* other continuing involvement by the seller-lessee described in paragraphs 11-13 of this Statement and paragraphs 25-39 and 41-43 of Statement 66.

8. A *normal leaseback* is a lessee-lessor relationship that involves the active use of the property by the seller-lessee in consideration for payment of rent, including contingent rentals that are based on the future operations of the seller-lessee,[4] and excludes other continuing involvement provisions or conditions described in paragraphs 11-13 of this Statement. The phrase *active use of the property by the seller-lessee* refers to the use of the property during the lease term[5] in the seller-lessee's trade or business, provided that subleasing of the leased back property is minor.[6] If the present value of a reasonable amount of rental for that portion of the leaseback that is subleased is not more than 10 percent of the fair value of the asset sold, the leased back property under sublease is considered minor. Active use of the property may involve the providing of services where the occupancy of the property is generally transient or short-term and is integral to the ancillary services being provided. Those ancillary services include, but are not limited to, housekeeping, inventory control, entertainment, bookkeeping, and food services. Thus, the use of property by a seller-lessee engaged in the hotel or bonded warehouse business or the operation of a golf course or a parking lot, for example, is considered active use.

Terms of the Sale-Leaseback Transaction

9. Terms of the sale-leaseback transaction that are substantially different from terms that an independent third-party lessor or lessee would accept represent an exchange of some stated or unstated rights or privileges. Those rights or privileges shall be considered in evaluating the continuing involvement provisions in paragraphs 11-13 of this Statement. Those terms or conditions include, but are not limited to, the sales price, the interest rate, and other terms of any loan from the seller-lessee to the buyer-lessor. The fair value of the property used in making that evaluation shall be based on objective evidence, for example, an independent third-party appraisal or recent sales of comparable property.

Continuing Involvement

10. A sale-leaseback transaction that does not qualify for sale-leaseback accounting because of any form of continuing involvement by the seller-lessee other than a normal leaseback shall be accounted for by the deposit method or as a financing, whichever is appropriate under Statement 66. The provisions or conditions described in paragraphs 11-13 of this Statement are examples of continuing involvement for the purpose of applying this Statement.

11. Paragraphs 25-39 and 41-43 of Statement 66 describe forms of continuing involvement by the seller-lessee with the leased property that result in the seller-lessee not transferring the risks or rewards of ownership to the buyer-lessor. Two examples of continuing involvement specified in those paragraphs that are frequently found in sale-leaseback transactions are provisions or conditions in which:

a. The seller-lessee has an obligation or an option[7] to repurchase the property or the buyer-lessor can compel the seller-lessee to repurchase the property.
b. The seller-lessee guarantees the buyer-lessor's investment or a return on that investment for a limited or extended period of time.

12. Other provisions or conditions that are guarantees and that do not transfer all of the risks of

---

[4]This Statement distinguishes between contingent rentals that are based on the future operations of the seller-lessee and those that are based on some predetermined or determinable level of future operations of the buyer-lessor. The latter type of contingent rental is addressed in paragraph 12(e) of this Statement.

[5]*Lease term* is used in this Statement in the context of the definition in paragraph 5(f) of Statement 13, as amended by this Statement.

[6]*Minor* is used in this Statement in the context of the definition in paragraph 33(a) of Statement 13, as amended by Statements 28 and 66 (hereinafter referred to collectively as Statement 13).

[7]A right of first refusal based on a bona fide offer by a third party ordinarily is not an obligation or an option to repurchase. An agreement that allows the seller-lessee to repurchase the asset in the event no third-party offer is made is an option to repurchase.

ownership shall constitute continuing involvement for the purpose of applying this Statement to sale-leaseback transactions and include, but are not limited to, the following:

a. The seller-lessee is required to pay the buyer-lessor at the end of the lease term for a decline in the fair value of the property below the estimated residual value on some basis other than excess wear and tear of the property levied on inspection of the property at the termination of the lease.
b. The seller-lessee provides **nonrecourse financing** to the buyer-lessor for any portion of the sales proceeds or provides recourse financing in which the only recourse is to the leased asset.
c. The seller-lessee is not relieved of the obligation under any existing debt related to the property.
d. The seller-lessee provides collateral on behalf of the buyer-lessor other than the property directly involved in the sale-leaseback transaction, the seller-lessee or a related party to the seller-lessee guarantees the buyer-lessor's debt, or a related party to the seller-lessee guarantees a return of or on the buyer-lessor's investment.
e. The seller-lessee's rental payment is contingent on some predetermined or determinable level of future operations of the buyer-lessor.[8]

13. The following provisions or conditions also shall be considered examples of continuing involvement for the purpose of applying this Statement to sale-leaseback transactions:

a. The seller-lessee enters into a sale-leaseback transaction involving property improvements or integral equipment[9] without leasing the underlying land to the buyer-lessor.[10]
b. The buyer-lessor is obligated to share with the seller-lessee any portion of the appreciation of the property.
c. Any other provision or circumstance that allows the seller-lessee to participate in any future profits of the buyer-lessor or the appreciation of the leased property, for example, a situation in which the seller-lessee owns or has an option to acquire any interest in the buyer-lessor.

Sale-Leaseback Transactions by Regulated Enterprises

14. The provisions of this Statement apply to sale-leaseback transactions of a regulated enterprise subject to FASB Statement No. 71, *Accounting for the Effects of Certain Types of Regulation,* as amended. That accounting may result in a differ-ence between the timing of income and expense recognition required by this Statement and the timing of income and expense recognition for rate-making purposes. That difference shall be accounted for as follows:

a. If the difference in timing of income and expense recognition constitutes all or a part of a phase-in plan, as defined in FASB Statement No. 92, *Regulated Enterprises—Accounting for Phase-in Plans,* it shall be accounted for in accordance with that Statement.
b. Otherwise, the timing of income and expense recognition related to the sale-leaseback transaction shall be modified as necessary to conform to Statement 71. That modification required for a transaction that is accounted for by the deposit method or as a financing is further described in paragraphs 15 and 16 of this Statement.

15. If a sale-leaseback transaction that is not part of a phase-in plan is accounted for by the deposit method but the sale is recognized for rate-making purposes, the amortization of the asset shall be modified to equal the total of the rental expense and the gain or loss allowable for rate-making purposes. Similarly, if the sale-leaseback transaction is accounted for as a financing and the sale is recognized for rate-making purposes, the total of interest imputed under the interest method for the financing and the amortization of the asset shall be modified to equal the total rental expense and the gain or loss allowable for rate-making purposes.

16. The difference between the amount of income or expense recognized for a transaction that is not part of a phase-in plan and that is accounted for by the deposit method or as a financing under this Statement and the amount of income or expense included in allowable cost for rate-making purposes shall be capitalized or accrued as a separate regulatory-created asset or liability, as appropriate, if that difference meets the criteria of Statement 71.

Financial Statement Presentation and Disclosure

17. In addition to the disclosure requirements of Statements 13 and 66, the financial statements of a seller-lessee shall include a description of the terms of the sale-leaseback transaction, including future commitments, obligations, provisions, or circumstances that require or result in the seller-lessee's continuing involvement.

18. The financial statements of a seller-lessee that

---

[8]Refer to footnote 4.

[9] Refer to footnote 2.

[10]Refer to footnote 3.

has accounted for a sale-leaseback transaction by the deposit method or as a financing according to the provisions of this Statement also shall disclose:

a. The obligation for future minimum lease payments as of the date of the latest balance sheet presented in the aggregate and for each of the five succeeding fiscal years
b. The total of minimum sublease rentals, if any, to be received in the future under noncancelable subleases in the aggregate and for each of the five succeeding fiscal years.

Other

19. Appendix A provides additional discussion and illustrations of how the provisions of this Statement shall be applied to specific aspects of accounting for sale-leaseback transactions. Appendix A constitutes an integral part of the requirements of this Statement.

Other Changes to the Accounting for Leases

20. Paragraph 22(a) of this Statement revises the definition of *lease term* for all leasing transactions to (a) include all periods, if any, during which a loan from the lessee to the lessor directly or indirectly related to the leased property is expected to be outstanding and (b) insert a cross-reference to the definition of *penalty* in new paragraph 5(o). Paragraph 22(b) defines penalty for *all* leasing transactions. Paragraphs 22(h) and 22(i) amend Statement 13 to reflect the amendment to that Statement intended by FASB Statement No. 91, *Accounting for Nonrefundable Fees and Costs Associated with Originating or Acquiring Loans and Initial Direct Costs of Leases*. The remainder of paragraph 22 modifies lessors' accounting for sales-type leases of real estate that provide for the transfer of title at or shortly after the lease term. Paragraphs 22(k)-(n) also clarify that a lease involving land or land and buildings may be classified as a leveraged lease.

Amendments to Existing Pronouncements

21. This Statement rescinds FASB Statement No. 26, *Profit Recognition on Sales-Type Leases of Real Estate,* and FASB Technical Bulletin No. 79-11, *Effect of a Penalty on the Term of a Lease.* This Statement also amends paragraph 13 of FASB Statement No. 29, *Determining Contingent Rentals,* by deleting the reference to paragraph 18(b) of Statement 13 and deletes paragraphs 25(a)-(c) of Statement 91.

22. This Statement amends Statement 13 as follows:

a. The definition of lease term in paragraph 5(f) is

superseded by the following:

Lease term. The fixed noncancelable term of the lease plus (i) all periods, if any, covered by bargain renewal options (as defined in paragraph 5(e)), (ii) all periods, if any, for which failure to renew the lease imposes a penalty (as defined in paragraph 5(o)) on the lessee in such amount that a renewal appears, at the inception of the lease, to be reasonably assured, (iii) all periods, if any, covered by ordinary renewal options during which a guarantee by the lessee of the lessor's debt directly or indirectly related to the leased property* is expected to be in effect or a loan from the lessee to the lessor directly or indirectly related to the leased property is expected to be outstanding, (iv) all periods, if any, covered by ordinary renewal options preceding the date as of which a bargain purchase option (as defined in paragraph 5(d)) is exercisable, and (v) all periods, if any, representing renewals or extensions of the lease at the lessor's option; however, in no case shall the lease term be assumed to extend beyond the date a bargain purchase option becomes exercisable. A lease that is cancelable (a) only upon the occurrence of some remote contingency, (b) only with the permission of the lessor, (c) only if the lessee enters into a new lease with the same lessor, or (d) only if the lessee incurs a penalty in such amount that continuation of the lease appears, at inception, reasonably assured shall be considered "noncancelable" for purposes of this definition.

---

*The phrase *indirectly related to the leased property* is used in this paragraph to describe provisions or conditions that in substance are guarantees of the lessor's debt or loans to the lessor by the lessee that are related to the leased property but are structured in such a manner that they do not represent a direct guarantee or loan. Examples include a party related to the lessee guaranteeing the lessor's debt on behalf of the lessee, or the lessee financing the lessor's purchase of the leased asset using collateral other than the leased property.

b. The definition of penalty is added in new paragraph 5(o) as follows:

Penalty. Any requirement that is imposed or can be imposed on the lessee by the lease agreement or by factors outside the lease agreement to disburse cash, incur or assume a liability, perform services, surrender or transfer an asset or rights to an asset or otherwise forego an economic benefit, or suffer an economic detriment. Factors to consider when determining if an economic detriment may be incurred include, but are not limited to, the uniqueness of purpose or location of the property, the availability of a comparable replacement property, the relative importance or significance of the property to the continuation of the lessee's line of business or service to its customers, the existence of leasehold improvements or other assets whose value would be impaired by the lessee vacating or discontinuing use of the leased property, adverse tax consequences, and the ability or willingness of the lessee to bear the cost associated with relocation or replacement of the leased property at market rental rates or to tolerate other parties using the leased property.

c. The first sentence of subparagraph 6(b)(i) is superseded by the following, thereby requiring that a lease involving real estate must transfer title by the end of the lease term for the lessor to classify the lease as a sales-type lease of real estate:

Sales-type leases. Leases that give rise to manufacturer's or dealer's profit (or loss) to the lessor (i.e., the fair value of the leased property at the inception of the lease is greater or less than its cost or carrying amount, if different) and that meet one or more of the criteria in paragraph 7 and both of the criteria in paragraph 8, except as indicated in the following sentence. A lease involving real estate shall be classified as a sales-type lease only if it meets the criterion in paragraph 7(a), in which case the criteria in paragraph 8 do not apply.

d. Subparagraph 6(b)(iv) is superseded by the following:

Operating leases. All other leases, including leases that involve real estate and give rise to manufacturer's or dealer's profit (or loss) to the lessor but do not meet the criterion in paragraph 7(a).

e. The following footnote is added to the end of paragraph 7(a):

*This criterion is met in situations in which the lease agreement provides for the transfer of title at or shortly after the end of the lease term in exchange for the payment of a nominal fee, for example, the minimum required by statutory regulation to transfer title.

f. The first two sentences of paragraph 8 and paragraph 8(a) are superseded by the following:

From the standpoint of the lessor, a lease involving real estate shall be classified as a sales-type lease only if it meets the criterion in paragraph 7(a) as appropriate under paragraph 6(b)(i). Otherwise, if the lease at inception

meets any one of the four criteria in paragraph 7 and in addition meets both of the following criteria, it shall be classified as a sales-type lease, a direct financing lease, a leveraged lease, or an operating lease as appropriate under paragraph 6(b). If the lease does not meet any of the criteria of paragraph 7 or both of the following criteria, the lease shall be classified as an operating lease.

a. Collectibility of the minimum lease payments is reasonably predictable. A lessor shall not be precluded from classifying a lease as a sales-type lease, a direct financing lease, or a leveraged lease simply because the receivable is subject to an estimate of uncollectibility based on experience with groups of similar receivables.

g. Paragraph 17(a) is amended by adding at the end of that paragraph the following sentence, which requires sales recognition in a sales-type lease of real estate in accordance with Statement 66:

However, if the sales-type lease involves real estate, the lessor shall account for the transaction under the provisions of *FASB Statement No. 66*, "Accounting for Sales of Real Estate," in the same manner as a *seller* of the same property.

h. Paragraph 18(a), as amended by FASB Statement No. 23, *Inception of the Lease*, and Statement 91, is superseded by the following to reflect the intent of the amendment made by Statement 91:

The sum of (i) the minimum lease payments (net of amounts, if any, included therein with respect to executory costs, such as maintenance, taxes, and insurance, to be paid by the lessor, together with any profit thereon) and (ii) the unguaranteed residual value accruing to the benefit of the lessor shall be recorded as the gross investment in the lease. The estimated residual value used to compute the unguaranteed residual value accruing to the benefit of the lessor shall not exceed the amount estimated at the inception of the lease.*

Footnote *, which was added to paragraph 18(a) by Statement 23, is unchanged by this Statement.

i. Paragraph 18(b), as amended by Statements 29 and 91, is superseded by the following to reflect the intent of the amendment by Statement 91:

The difference between the gross investment in the lease in (a) above and the cost or carrying amount, if different, of the leased property shall be recorded as unearned income. The net investment in the lease shall consist of the gross investment plus any unamortized initial direct costs less the unearned income. The unearned income and initial direct costs shall be amortized to income over the lease term so as to produce a constant periodic rate of return on the net investment in the lease.[21] However, other methods of income recognition may be used if the results obtained are not materially different from those that would result from the prescribed method in the preceding sentence. The net investment in the lease shall be subject to the same considerations as other assets in classification as current or noncurrent assets in a classified balance sheet. Contingent rentals shall be included in the determination of income as accruable.

Footnote 21 to paragraph 18(b) is unchanged by this Statement.

j. New paragraph 19(d) is added as follows:

If, at the inception of the lease, the fair value of the property in an operating lease involving real estate that would have been classified as a sales-type lease except that it did not meet the criterion in paragraph 7(a) is less than its cost or carrying amount, if different, then a loss equal to that difference shall be recognized at the inception of the lease.

k. The first two sentences of paragraph 25 are superseded by the following:

If land is the sole item of property leased and the criterion in either paragraph 7(a) or 7(b) is met, the lessee shall account for the lease as a capital lease, otherwise, as an operating lease. If the lease gives rise to manufacturer's or dealer's profit (or loss) and the criterion of paragraph 7(a) is met, the lessor shall classify the lease as a sales-type lease as appropriate under paragraph 6(b)(i) and account for the transaction under the provisions of Statement 66 in the same manner as a *seller* of the same property. If the lease does not give rise to manufacturer's or dealer's profit (or loss) and the criterion of paragraph 7(a) and both criteria of paragraph 8 are met, the lessor shall account for the lease as a direct financing lease or a leveraged lease as appropriate under paragraph 6(b). If the criterion of paragraph 7(b) and both criteria of paragraph 8 are met, the lessor shall account for the lease as a direct financing lease, a leveraged lease, or an operating lease as appropriate under paragraph 6(b). If the lease does not meet the criteria of paragraph 8, the lessor shall ac-

count for the lease as an operating lease.

l. Subparagraph 26(a)(ii) is superseded by the following two subparagraphs:

ii. Lessor's accounting if the lease meets criterion 7(a): If the lease gives rise to manufacturer's or dealer's profit (or loss), the lessor shall classify the lease as a sales-type lease as appropriate under paragraph 6(b)(i) and account for the lease as a single unit under the provisions of Statement 66 in the same manner as a *seller* of the same property. If the lease does not give rise to manufacturer's or dealer's profit (or loss) and meets both criteria of paragraph 8, the lessor shall account for the lease as a direct financing lease or a leveraged lease as appropriate under paragraph 6(b)(ii) or 6(b)(iii). If the lease does not give rise to manufacturer's or dealer's profit (or loss) and does not meet both criteria of paragraph 8, the lessor shall account for the lease as an operating lease.

iii. Lessor's accounting if the lease meets criterion 7(b): If the lease gives rise to manufacturer's or dealer's profit (or loss), the lessor shall classify the lease as an operating lease as appropriate under paragraph 6(b)(iv). If the lease does not give rise to manufacturer's or dealer's profit (or loss) and meets both criteria of paragraph 8, the lessor shall account for the lease as a direct financing lease or a leveraged lease as appropriate under paragraph 6(b)(ii) or 6(b)(iii). If the lease does not give rise to manufacturer's or dealer's profit (or loss) and does not meet both criteria of paragraph 8, the lessor shall account for the lease as an operating lease.

m. Subparagraph 26(b)(i)(b) is superseded by the following to remove the reference to *sales-type lease:*

Lessor's accounting: If either criterion (c) or (d) of paragraph 7 and both criteria of paragraph 8 are met, the lessor shall account for the lease as a single unit as a direct financing lease, a leveraged lease, or an operating lease as appropriate under paragraph 6(b). If the lease meets neither criterion (c) nor (d) of paragraph 7 or does not meet both criteria of paragraph 8, the lease shall be accounted for as an operating lease.

n. The first sentence in subparagraph 26(b)(ii)(b) is superseded by the following to remove the reference to *sales-type lease:*

Lessor's accounting: If the building element of the lease meets either criterion (c) or (d) of paragraph 7 and both criteria of paragraph 8, the building element shall be accounted for as a direct financing lease, a leveraged lease, or an operating lease as appropriate under paragraph 6(b).

23. Paragraph 40 of Statement 66 is superseded by the following:

The sale of the property is accompanied by a leaseback to the seller of all or any part of the property for all or part of its remaining economic life. Real estate sale-leaseback transactions shall be accounted for in accordance with FASB Statement No. 98, *Accounting for Leases: Sale-Leaseback Transactions Involving*

Real Estate, Sales-Type Leases of Real Estate, Definition of the Lease Term, and Initial Direct Costs of Direct Financing Leases.

Effective Date and Transition

24. Except as provided in paragraph 25, the provisions of this Statement shall be effective for transactions entered into[11] after June 30, 1988. Earlier application to transactions occurring in periods for which annual financial statements have not been issued is encouraged.

25. The effective date and transition provisions for paragraphs 22(h) and 22(i), which amend Statement 13 to reflect the amendments intended by Statement 91, shall be the same as the effective date and transition provisions of Statement 91.

> **The provisions of this Statement need not be applied to immaterial items.**

This Statement was adopted by the affirmative vote of four members of the Financial Accounting Standards Board. Messrs. Beresford, Lauver, and Swieringa dissented.

Messrs. Beresford, Lauver, and Swieringa dissent because this Statement prescribes different accounting for certain sale-leaseback transactions based on a distinction between active (as defined) and other use of leased property by a seller-lessee. That distinction is without economic substance and is used to arbitrarily preclude sale-leaseback accounting when a seller-lessee subleases the leased property.

Paragraph 48 acknowledges that a leaseback is a form of continuing involvement with leased property but argues that the form of that involvement is different if the seller-lessee intends to sublease that property. In a sale-leaseback transaction, the seller-lessee has exchanged ownership rights for lease rights, and the rights to use the leased property and to benefit from that use are the same regardless of how that property is used. Moreover, any guarantee of the cash flows related to the

leased property is lodged in the lease contract and is not altered by what the seller-lessee does with that property.

An objective of financial reporting is to achieve greater comparability of accounting information. Paragraph 119 of FASB Concepts Statement No. 2, *Qualitative Characteristics of Accounting Information,* states that this objective "is not to be attained by making unlike things look alike any more than by making like things look different. The moral is that in seeking comparability accountants must not disguise real differences nor create false differences."

Messrs. Beresford, Lauver, and Swieringa believe that this Statement makes like things look different by prescribing different accounting for certain sale-leaseback transactions based on the distinction between active and other use of leased property, a distinction not relevant to the accounting. Because that distinction arbitrarily limits the extent to which sale-leaseback accounting is permitted, the effects of accounting for identical sale-leaseback transactions will be different.

Members of the Financial Accounting Standards Board:

Dennis R. Beresford, *Chairman*
Victor H. Brown

Raymond C. Lauver
James J. Leisenring
C. Arthur Northrop

A. Clarence Sampson
Robert J. Swieringa

---

[11]For the purpose of applying the provisions of this Statement, *entered into* is used in the context of the term *inception of the lease* as defined in paragraph 5(b) of Statement 13, as amended by Statement 23.

Appendix A

APPLICATIONS OF THE STANDARDS TO SPECIFIC ASPECTS OF
ACCOUNTING FOR SALE-LEASEBACK TRANSACTIONS

CONTENTS

Appendix A

APPLICATIONS OF THE STANDARDS TO SPECIFIC ASPECTS OF ACCOUNTING FOR SALE-LEASEBACK TRANSACTIONS

Introduction

26. This appendix provides additional discussion and examples that illustrate applications of the standards to specific aspects of accounting for a sale-leaseback transaction. This appendix constitutes an integral part of the requirements of this Statement. A brief summary of the accounting guidance being demonstrated precedes each of the first three examples. All examples assume that the initial transaction occurs on the first day of the year and that subsequent transactions and payments are made on the last day of each year.

Sales Recognition

27. A sale-leaseback transaction that qualifies for sales recognition under the provisions of this Statement is accounted for using sale-leaseback ac-

counting by the seller-lessee whether the leaseback is classified as a capital lease or an operating lease in accordance with Statement 13.[12] The proper approach is first to determine the gain that would be recognized under Statement 66 as if the transaction were a sale without a leaseback and then to allocate that gain as provided by Statement 13 over the remaining lease term. Under the provisions of footnote * to paragraph 33 of Statement 13, the gain to be deferred and amortized in proportion to the leaseback is the gain that would otherwise be recognized in that year under the provisions of Statement 66, except for the amount that can be recognized currently under paragraph 33 of Statement 13. The total gain is recognized immediately if the leaseback is considered minor under the context of paragraph 33(a) of Statement 13. The gain to be recognized currently under paragraph 33(b) of Statement 13 is the amount of gain in excess of (a) the present value of the minimum lease payments if the leaseback is classified as an operating lease or (b) the recorded amount of the leased asset if the leaseback is classified as a capital lease.

---

[12]Statement 13, as used in this appendix, refers to Statement 13 as amended by Statement 28.

Example 1—Sale-Leaseback Transaction Accounted for as a Sale with Gain Recognized under the Installment Method and the Leaseback Classified as an Operating Lease

28. Company A (a seller-lessee) sells the building at its principal manufacturing facility with an estimated remaining life of 15 years and a cost less accumulated depreciation of $800,000 to a buyer-lessor for $950,000 (the fair value of the property as determined by an independent third-party appraisal) and enters into an agreement to lease back the building. In exchange for the building, the seller-lessee receives $50,000 and a 10-year $900,000 recourse note with a 10 percent annual interest rate with annual payments of $146,471. Under the terms of the agreement, the seller-lessee is required to lease the building back for $100,000 a year for an initial period of 5 years. In addition, the seller-lessee has the option to renew the lease for an additional 5 years at $110,000 (estimated to be the then fair-market rental).

29. The sale-leaseback transaction does not include any form of continuing involvement that would preclude the seller-lessee from using sale-leaseback accounting. The initial down payment is inadequate for the seller-lessee to account for the transaction under the full accrual method described in Statement 66. Under the provisions of Statement 66, the seller-lessee elects to use the installment method to recognize the gain on the transaction. The property and any related debt would be removed from the seller-lessee's balance sheet and the note receivable net of unamortized deferred profit would be reported on the balance sheet. The renewal of the lease is included in the lease term for purposes of classifying the lease and amortizing income because the loss of the property at the end of the initial lease term is considered to be a penalty. The leaseback is classified as an operating lease because none of the criteria of paragraph 7 of Statement 13 is met.

Illustration 1—Recognition of the Gain on the Transaction

Calculation of the Gain

Sales price	$950,000
Cost less accumulated depreciation	800,000
Total gain to be recognized	$150,000

Gain Recognition under Statement 66 (Installment Method Absent the Leaseback)

Day 1	$ 7,895
End of Year 1	8,916
Year 2	9,808
Year 3	123,381
Total	$150,000

**Gain Recognition for Sale-Leaseback
under Statement 13 and This Statement**

	Allocation of Annual Gain under the Installment Method with the Leaseback				
Period Recognized	Day 1 Gain	End of Year 1 Gain	Year 2 Gain	Year 3 Gain	Total Gain Recognized
Year 1	$ 789				$ 789
Year 2	789	$ 990			1,779
Year 3	789	990	$1,226		3,005
Year 4	789	990	1,226	$ 17,625	20,630
Year 5	789	991	1,226	17,626	20,632
Year 6	790	991	1,226	17,626	20,633
Year 7	790	991	1,226	17,626	20,633
Year 8	790	991	1,226	17,626	20,633
Year 9	790	991	1,226	17,626	20,633
Year 10	790	991	1,226	17,626	20,633
Total	$7,895	$8,916	$9,808	$123,381	$150,000

Note: The installment method as described in paragraph 56 of Statement 66 requires profit to be allocated to the down payment and subsequent collections on the buyer-lessor's note (principal portion only) by the percentage of profit inherent in the transaction (in this example, 15.79 percent). In addition, paragraph 61 of Statement 66 allows a seller to switch from the installment method to the full accrual method of recognizing profit when the transaction meets the requirements for the full accrual method on a cumulative basis. In this example, it is assumed that for the seller-lessee to recognize profit in year 3 under the full accrual method, the buyer-lessor must have an investment in the property of 20 percent of the sales price to meet the minimum investment requirement and that the seller-lessee elects to switch to the full accrual method in the first full year after the minimum initial and continuing investment criteria are met.

Deposit Method

30. Paragraphs 20-22, 28, and 32 of Statement 66 describe certain circumstances in which it is appropriate to account for a transaction using the deposit method (as described in paragraphs 65-67 of Statement 66). If a sale-leaseback transaction is accounted for by the deposit method, lease payments decrease and collections on the buyer-lessor's note, if any, increase the seller-lessee's deposit account. The property and any related debt continue to be included in the seller-lessee's balance sheet and the seller-lessee continues to depreciate the property. Under the provisions of paragraph 21 of Statement 66, a seller-lessee that is accounting for any transaction by the deposit method according to the provisions of this Statement shall recognize a loss if at any time the net carrying amount of the property exceeds the sum of the balance in the deposit account, the fair value of the unrecorded note receivable, and any debt assumed by the buyer.

31. If a sale-leaseback transaction accounted for by the deposit method subsequently qualifies for sales recognition under this Statement and Statement 66, the transaction is accounted for using sale-leaseback accounting, and the gain or loss is recognized in accordance with the provisions of paragraph 27 of this Statement. In addition, the leaseback is classified and accounted for in accordance with Statement 13 as if the sale had been recognized at the inception of the lease. If the leaseback meets one of the criteria for classification as a capital lease, the asset and liability accounts related to the leaseback, including accumulated amortization, are recorded as of the date that the sale is recognized to reflect amortization that would have been charged to expense had the lease been recorded as a capital lease at its inception. The change in the related lease accounts that would have been recorded from the inception of the lease had the transaction initially qualified for sale-leaseback accounting is included in computing the gain or loss recognized in accordance with paragraph 27 of this Statement.

Example 2—Sale-Leaseback Transaction Accounted for by the Deposit Method with Subsequent Sales Recognition and the Leaseback Classified as a Capital Lease

32. Company B (a seller-lessee) sells the building at one of its manufacturing facilities to a buyer-lessor for $950,000 (the fair value of the property as determined by an independent third-party appraisal) and enters into an agreement to lease the building back for 10 years at $150,000 per year. The property has a historical cost of $1,300,000

and accumulated depreciation at the date of the transaction of $400,000. Depreciation expense is $80,000 per year. In exchange for the building, the seller-lessee receives $50,000 and a 10-year $900,000 recourse note with a 10 percent annual interest rate with annual payments of $146,471.

33. The sale-leaseback transaction does not include any continuing involvement provisions, but the buyer-lessor has a questionable credit rating. Based on the poor credit standing of the buyer-lessor and the inadequate initial investment, the seller-lessee elects to account for the transaction by the deposit method. The initial and continuing investment must equal 20 percent of the sales price before it is appropriate to recognize profit by the full accrual method. Based on the amortization schedule of the buyer-lessor's note and assuming an improved credit rating of the buyer-lessor, income recognition under the full accrual method will be appropriate for the transaction at the end of year 3. The leaseback meets the criteria for classification as a capital lease in accordance with the provisions of paragraphs 7(c) and 7(d) of Statement 13.

Illustration 2—Recognition of the Gain on the Transaction

Calculation of the Gain

Sales price (at inception)	$950,000
Cost less accumulated depreciation (end of year 3)	660,000
	290,000
Adjustments required by the deposit method or provisions of this Statement:	
Amortization of capital asset not recognized	(285,000)
Interest income credited to the deposit account in years 1-3 (credited to the deposit account as part of note payments received)	252,495
Interest expense charged to the deposit account in years 1-3 (charged to the deposit account as part of lease payments)	(247,363)
Total gain to be recognized	$ 10,132

Under the provisions of Statement 66 and absent the leaseback, a gain of $10,132 would be recognized at the end of year 3 under the full accrual method.

Allocation of Gain Recognition under Statement 13 and This Statement

Period Recognized	Year 3 Gain
Year 4	$ 1,447
Year 5	1,447
Year 6	1,447
Year 7	1,447
Year 8	1,448
Year 9	1,448
Year 10	1,448
Total	$10,132

Illustration 3—Journal Entries

At inception:

Cash	50,000	
Deposit		50,000

To record the receipt of the down payment on the property

Recurring journal entries in years 1-3:

Cash	146,471	
Deposit		146,471

To record the receipt of collections on the buyer-lessor's note (the annual payment required for a 10-year $900,000 note)

Deposit	150,000	
Cash		150,000

To record the lease payments

Depreciation expense	80,000	
Accumulated depreciation		80,000

To record the depreciation expense

When the sale is recognized at end of year 3:

Deposit	39,413	
Capital asset	950,000	
Note receivable	713,082	
Accumulated depreciation	640,000	
Property, plant, and equipment		1,300,000
Capital lease obligation		747,363
Accumulated amortization of the capital asset		285,000
Deferred gain		10,132

To recognize the sale and to record the capitalization of the leased asset

Illustration 4—Annual Balances in the Related Balance Sheet Accounts

(1) Period	(2) Deposit Account	(3) Property, Plant, and Equipment	(4) Accum. Depr.	(5) Deferred Gain	(6) Deferred Interest Income	(7) Gross Note Receiv.	(8) Net Note Receiv.	Memo entries only in years 1-3				
								(9) Deferred Interest Expense	(10) Gross Lease Oblig.	(11) Net Lease Oblig.	(12) Capital Lease Asset	(13) Accum. Amort. Capital Lease
At inception	$50,000	$1,300,000	$400,000	$	$564,710	$1,464,710	$900,000	$550,000	$1,500,000	$950,000	$950,000	$ 0
Year 1	46,471	1,300,000	480,000		474,710	1,318,239	843,529	461,635	1,350,000	888,365	950,000	95,000
Year 2	42,942	1,300,000	560,000		390,357	1,171,768	781,411	379,003	1,200,000	820,997	950,000	190,000
Year 3	39,413	1,300,000	640,000		312,215	1,025,297	713,082	302,637	1,050,000	747,363	950,000	285,000
After sale is recognized	0	0	0	10,132	312,215	1,025,297	713,082	302,637	1,050,000	747,363	950,000	285,000
Year 4	0	0	0	8,685	240,907	878,826	637,919	233,120	900,000	666,880	950,000	380,000
Year 5	0	0	0	7,238	177,115	732,355	555,240	171,090	750,000	578,910	950,000	475,000
Year 6	0	0	0	5,791	121,591	585,884	464,293	117,242	600,000	482,758	950,000	570,000
Year 7	0	0	0	4,344	75,162	439,413	364,251	72,337	450,000	377,663	950,000	665,000
Year 8	0	0	0	2,896	38,736	292,942	254,206	37,209	300,000	262,791	950,000	760,000
Year 9	0	0	0	1,448	13,316	146,471	133,155	12,765	150,000	137,235	950,000	855,000
Year 10	0	0	0	0	0	0	0	0	0	0	950,000	950,000

Computations:

Column (2) Original deposit plus collections on the buyer-lessor's note net of payments on the lease.
Column (3) Plant balance at inception of lease.
Column (4) Accumulated depreciation at inception of lease plus annual depreciation expense.
Column (5) Deferred gain account less amount recognized annually per Illustration 2.
Column (6) Column 7 less column 8.
Column (7) Balance of remaining payments on the buyer-lessor's note.
Column (8) The present value of the remaining note payments discounted at 10 percent.
Column (9) Column 10 less column 11.
Column (10) Accumulated balance of the remaining payments on the seller-lessee's lease obligation.
Column (11) The present value of the remaining lease payments discounted at 9.301595 percent (assumed to be the seller-lessee's incremental borrowing rate).
Column (12) Balance of the capital lease asset.
Column (13) Accumulated balance of annual amortization of $95,000.

Financing Method

34. This Statement and paragraphs 25-39 and 41-43 of Statement 66 describe some common forms of continuing involvement with the property by the seller that preclude a sale-leaseback transaction from sale-leaseback accounting. Depending on the nature and duration of the continuing involvement with the property, those provisions may require a sale-leaseback transaction to be accounted for as a financing. If a sale-leaseback transaction is reported as a financing, lease payments, exclusive of an interest portion, decrease and collections on the buyer-lessor's note increase the seller-lessee's liability account with a portion of the lease payments being recognized under the interest method. The seller-lessee reports the sales proceeds as a liability, continues to report the real estate or the real estate and equipment as an asset, and continues to depreciate the property.

35. If a sale-leaseback transaction accounted for as a financing subsequently qualifies for sales recognition under this Statement and Statement 66, the transaction is then recorded using sale-leaseback accounting, and the cumulative change in the related balance sheet accounts is included in the computation of the gain recognized in accordance with the provisions of paragraph 27 of this Statement. In addition, the leaseback is classified and accounted for in accordance with paragraph 7 of Statement 13 as if the sale had been recognized at the inception of the lease. If the leaseback meets one of the criteria for classification as a capital lease, the related lease accounts, including accumulated amortization, are established as of the date the sale is recognized to reflect accumulated amortization and interest that would have been charged to expense had the lease been recorded at its inception. The change in the related lease accounts from the inception of the lease to the date the sale is recognized is included in the gain recognized in accordance with paragraph 27 of this Statement.

Example 3—Sale-Leaseback Transaction (with Seller-Lessee Providing Financing) Accounted for as a Financing with Subsequent Sales Recognition and the Leaseback Classified as an Operating Lease

36. Company C (a seller-lessee) sells one of its older special-purpose buildings at its principal manufacturing facility to a buyer-lessor for $950,000 (the fair value of the property as determined by an independent third-party appraisal) and enters into an agreement to lease the building back for 5 years at $100,000 per year. In addition, the agreement includes an option that allows the seller-lessee to renew the lease for an additional 5 years at $100,000 per year (estimated to be the then fair-market rental). The lease agreement also includes a fair value repurchase option during the initial lease term, and the seller-lessee guarantees that the residual value of the property will be no less than $920,000 at the end of the initial lease period. The special-purpose building has a historical cost of $3,510,000 and accumulated depreciation at the date of the transaction of $2,660,000. Depreciation expense is $70,000 per year. In exchange for the building, the seller-lessee receives $50,000 and a 10-year $900,000 recourse note with a 10 percent annual interest rate.

37. The seller-lessee accounts for this transaction as a financing because of the continuing involvement associated with the guarantee and the repurchase option. At the end of year 5, the seller-lessee exercises the renewal option, and the continuing involvement with the property is no longer at issue because the repurchase option and the guarantee no longer exist. The seller-lessee recognizes the transaction as a sale and classifies the leaseback as an operating lease because none of the criteria of paragraph 7 of Statement 13 is met.

Illustration 5—Recognition of the Gain on the Transaction

Calculation of the Gain

Sales price (at inception)	$950,000
Cost less accumulated depreciation (end of year 5)	500,000
	450,000
Adjustments required by the provisions of this Statement:	
Rent charged to the finance obligation account in years 1-5	(500,000)
Interest expense charged to income during years 1-5	82,405
Interest income credited to the finance obligation account in years 1-5	387,595
Total gain to be recognized	$420,000

Under the provisions of Statement 66 and absent the leaseback, a gain of $420,000 would be recognized at the end of year 5 under the full accrual method.

**Allocation of Gain Recognition
under Statement 13 and This Statement**

Period Recognized	Year 5 Gain
Year 5	$ 34,060*
Year 6	77,188
Year 7	77,188
Year 8	77,188
Year 9	77,188
Year 10	77,188
Total	$420,000

*Represents the amount by which the total gain to be recognized exceeds the present value of the future minimum lease payments discounted at the seller-lessee's incremental borrowing rate, assumed to be 9.301595 percent ($420,000 − $385,940 = $34,060).

Illustration 6—Journal Entries

At inception:

Cash	50,000	
Finance obligation		50,000

To record the receipt of the down payment on the property

Recurring journal entries in years 1-5:

Cash	146,471	
Finance obligation		146,471

To record the receipt of collections on the buyer-lessor's note (the annual payment required for a 10-year $900,000 note)

Depreciation expense	70,000	
Accumulated depreciation		70,000

To record the depreciation expense

Nonrecurring journal entries:

Year 1

Finance obligation	94,972	
Interest expense	5,028	
Cash		100,000

To record the lease payments (Interest expense is calculated under the interest method using an effective yield of 10.0562 percent and the guaranteed residual value as the last payment.)

Year 2

Finance obligation	89,793	
Interest expense	10,207	
Cash		100,000

To record the lease payments

Year 3

Finance obligation	84,093	
Interest expense	15,907	
Cash		100,000

To record the lease payments

Year 4

Finance obligation	77,820	
Interest expense	22,180	
Cash		100,000

To record the lease payments

Year 5

Finance obligation	70,917	
Interest expense	29,083	
Cash		100,000

To record the lease payments

When the sale is recognized:

Finance obligation	364,760	
Note receivable	555,240	
Accumulated depreciation	3,010,000	
Property, plant, and equipment		3,510,000
Deferred gain		385,940
Gain on sale		34,060

To record the transaction as a sale

Illustration 7—Annual Balances in the Related Balance Sheet Accounts

(1)	(2)	(3)	(4)	(5)	(6)	(7)	(8)
						Memo entries only in years 1-5	
Period	Finance Obligation	Property, Plant, and Equipment	Accumulated Depreciation	Deferred Gain	Deferred Interest Income	Gross Note Receivable	Net Note Receivable
At inception	$ 50,000	$3,510,000	$2,660,000	$ 0	$564,710	$1,464,710	$900,000
Year 1	101,499	3,510,000	2,730,000	0	474,710	1,318,239	843,529
Year 2	158,177	3,510,000	2,800,000	0	390,357	1,171,768	781,411
Year 3	220,555	3,510,000	2,870,000	0	312,215	1,025,297	713,082
Year 4	289,206	3,510,000	2,940,000	0	240,907	878,826	637,919
Year 5	364,760	3,510,000	3,010,000	0	177,115	732,355	555,240
After sale is recognized	0	0	0	385,940	177,115	732,355	555,240
Year 6	0	0	0	308,752	121,591	585,884	464,293
Year 7	0	0	0	231,564	75,162	439,413	364,251
Year 8	0	0	0	154,376	38,736	292,942	254,206
Year 9	0	0	0	77,188	13,316	146,471	133,155
Year 10	0	0	0	0	0	0	0

Computations:

Column (2) Collections on the buyer-lessor's note net of payments on the lease applied to the finance obligation account.
Column (3) Plant balance at inception of lease.
Column (4) Accumulated depreciation at inception of lease plus annual depreciation expense.
Column (5) Deferred gain less amounts recognized annually per Illustration 5.
Column (6) Column 7 less column 8.
Column (7) Balance of remaining payments on the buyer-lessor's note.
Column (8) The present value of the remaining note payments discounted at 10 percent.

Example 4—Sale-Leaseback Transaction (All Cash) Accounted for as a Financing with Subsequent Sales Recognition

38. Company D (a seller-lessee) sells the building at one of its manufacturing facilities to a buyer-lessor for $950,000 (the fair value of the property as determined by an independent third-party appraisal) and enters into an agreement to lease the building back for 5 years at $100,000 per year. In addition, the seller-lessee has an option to renew the lease for an additional 5 years at $110,000 (estimated to be the then fair-market rental). The lease agreement also includes a fair value repurchase option, and the seller-lessee guarantees that the residual value of the property will be no less than $950,000 at the end of the initial lease period. The property has a historical cost of $1,200,000 and accumulated depreciation at the date of the transaction of $400,000. Depreciation expense is $80,000 per year.

39. Because of the continuing involvement associated with the guarantee and the repurchase option, the seller-lessee accounts for this transaction as a financing in accordance with the provisions of this Statement. At the inception of the lease, it is known that the seller-lessee is developing a new manufacturing process that will require a different manufacturing facility. The new technology becomes available at the end of the initial lease term, and the seller-lessee vacates the property. The fair value of the property (as determined by an independent third-party appraisal) at that time is $915,000. The seller-lessee honors the $950,000 guarantee of the property by paying the buyer-lessor $35,000 and recognizes the sale of the property.

Illustration 8—Recognition of the Gain on the Transaction

Calculation of the Gain before the Effect of the Guarantee

Sales price (at inception)	$950,000
Cost less accumulated depreciation (end of year 5)	400,000
Total gain to be recognized	$550,000

Illustration 9—Journal Entries

At inception:

Cash	950,000	
Finance obligation		950,000

To record the receipt of the proceeds from the sale of the property

Recurring journal entries in years 1-5:

Depreciation expense	80,000	
Accumulated depreciation		80,000

To record the depreciation expense

Interest expense	100,000	
Cash		100,000

To record the lease payments (Interest expense is calculated under the interest method using an effective yield of 10.5263 percent and the guaranteed residual as the last payment.)

When the sale is recognized:

Accumulated depreciation	800,000	
Finance lease obligation	950,000	
Property, plant, and equipment		1,200,000
Cash		35,000
Gain on sale of property		515,000

To record the transaction as a sale

Under the provisions of this Statement, gain deferral is not required because the seller-lessee no longer occupies or otherwise benefits from the property and no longer has any guarantee or other continuing involvement.

Illustration 10—Annual Balances in the Related Balance Sheet Accounts

(1) Period	(2) Finance Obligation	(3) Property, Plant, and Equipment	(4) Accumulated Depreciation
At inception	$950,000	$1,200,000	$400,000
Year 1	950,000	1,200,000	480,000
Year 2	950,000	1,200,000	560,000
Year 3	950,000	1,200,000	640,000
Year 4	950,000	1,200,000	720,000
Year 5	950,000	1,200,000	800,000
When property is vacated	0	0	0

Appendix B

BASIS FOR CONCLUSIONS

CONTENTS

Appendix B

BASIS FOR CONCLUSIONS

Introduction

40. This appendix summarizes considerations that were deemed significant by members of the Board in reaching the conclusions in this Statement. It includes reasons for accepting certain views and rejecting others. Individual Board members gave greater weight to some factors than to others. The Board concluded that it could reach an informed decision on the basis of existing information without a public hearing.

General

41. An FASB Exposure Draft, *Sale and Lease-back Transactions Involving Real Estate, Sales-Type Leases of Real Estate, Definition of the Lease Term, and Initial Direct Costs of Direct Financing Leases,* was issued for public comment on August 31, 1987. The Board received 72 letters of comment in response to the Exposure Draft.

42. The provisions of this Statement that address sale-leaseback transactions are based on the view that those transactions should qualify for sales recognition before it is appropriate for the seller-lessee to use sale-leaseback accounting. Statement 66 establishes standards for profit recognition for sales of real estate. It also precludes sales recognition in certain circumstances and prescribes other methods to account for those transactions (paragraphs 20, 26-29, 32, and 38 of Statement 66). This Statement requires that a sale-leaseback transaction qualify for sales recognition under the provisions of Statement 66 before it is appropriate for

the seller-lessee to use sale-leaseback accounting.

Scope

43. Real estate sales transactions may be accounted for differently than sales of other assets. This Statement does not address a sale-leaseback transaction involving no real estate except for (a) modifying the definition of the lease term and the definition of a penalty and (b) precluding sale-leaseback accounting because of the continuing involvement in the circumstance in which the seller-lessee enters into a sale-leaseback transaction involving property improvements or integral equipment without leasing the underlying land to the buyer-lessor. However, this Statement does apply to a sale-leaseback transaction involving real estate with equipment. Paragraph 107 of Statement 13 states:

> The Board noted that most sale-leasebacks are entered into as a means of financing, for tax reasons, or both and that the terms of the sale and the terms of the leaseback are usually negotiated as a package. Because of this interdependence of terms, no means could be identified for separating the sale and the leaseback that would be both practicable and objective.

Similarly, because of the interdependence of terms in a sale-leaseback transaction involving real estate with equipment, no objective means could be identified for separating the real estate portion of the sale-leaseback transaction from that portion of the transaction relating to equipment. Therefore, the provisions of this Statement apply equally to a sale-leaseback transaction involving real estate with equipment or equipment integral to real estate and to a sale-leaseback transaction involving *only* real estate.

44. Some respondents to the Exposure Draft noted that separate accounting for the real estate and equipment portions of a transaction is required for income tax purposes and by paragraph 27 of Statement 13 and that objective methods to separate those portions of a transaction have been developed. Other respondents suggested that the Board develop a materiality test to exclude transactions that involve insignificant portions of real estate from the scope of this Statement.

45. The Board acknowledges that separate accounting for real estate and equipment portions of sales and leases of real estate with equipment are being made on the basis of applicable tax law or by whatever means is considered appropriate in the circumstance. While separate accounting for those portions may be appropriate for a transaction involving real estate with equipment structured either as a sale or as a lease, the Board believes separate accounting for those portions is not appropriate for determining profit recognition for a sale-leaseback transaction. That conclusion is based on (a) the interdependence of the contractual terms of the sale and the leaseback, (b) the physical interrelationship of the values associated with the equipment and the real estate, and (c) the significance of the values of some types of property, for example, power plants and refineries, in relation to the value of the underlying real estate.

Continuing Involvement

46. The Board believes that a leaseback in conjunction with a sale could be considered as constituting a form of continuing involvement that precludes a seller-lessee from using sale-leaseback accounting. Paragraph 28 of Statement 66 suggests the leaseback serves as a guarantee of the buyer-lessor's investment. That paragraph states:

> *The seller guarantees the return of the buyer's investment or a return on that investment for a limited or extended period.* For example, the seller guarantees cash flows, subsidies, or net tax benefits. If the seller guarantees return of the buyer's investment or if the seller guarantees a return on the investment for an extended period, the transaction shall be accounted for as a financing, leasing, or profit-sharing arrangement. If the guarantee of a return on the investment is for a limited period, the deposit method shall be used until operations of the property cover all operating expenses, debt service, and contractual payments. At that time, profit shall be recognized on the basis of performance of the services required. . . . [Footnote reference omitted.]

However, others have observed that paragraph 40 of Statement 66 clearly provides for sale-leaseback accounting and does not preclude sales recognition. That paragraph states:

> *The sale of the property is accompanied by a leaseback to the seller of all or any part of the property for all or part of its remaining economic life.* Real estate sale and leaseback transactions shall be accounted for in accordance with the provisions of this Statement and FASB Statements No. 13, *Accounting for Leases,* and 28, *Accounting for Sales with Leasebacks. . . .* Regardless of whether the leaseback is a capital lease or an operating lease, a sale shall be recorded, and the property sold

and any related debt assumed by the buyer shall be removed from the seller-lessee's balance sheet.

47. The principal objective of this Statement is to reconcile the inconsistency between Statements 13 and 66 described in the preceding paragraph without reconsidering the underlying principles of either document. To satisfy that objective, the Board considered whether there were any circumstances in which sale-leaseback accounting for real estate, including real estate with equipment, would be acceptable. The Exposure Draft proposed that sale-leaseback accounting be prescribed for a normal leaseback in which the seller-lessee intends to occupy the property. In adopting that approach, the Board accepted the continuing involvement and the form of guarantee that is inherent in a normal leaseback but limited that involvement to instances in which the seller-lessee intended to occupy the property. The Exposure Draft would have precluded sale-leaseback accounting for a sale-leaseback transaction in which the seller-lessee did not intend to occupy the property from the inception of the lease.

48. Some respondents to the Exposure Draft noted that the nature of the continuing involvement associated with a normal leaseback does not change because of the seller-lessee's intent to occupy the property. The Board acknowledges that the leaseback is a form of continuing involvement with the property that serves as support for the buyer-lessor's investment. Accordingly, the Board believes that transactions accounted for as sales should be limited when a sale-leaseback of property exists; otherwise, the effectiveness of paragraph 28 of Statement 66 would be compromised. Occupancy of the property by the seller-lessee provides a basis for distinguishing among sale-leaseback transactions involving real estate, including real estate with equipment. The Board believes that the intent to sublease the property represents a different form of continuing involvement than does the intent to occupy and use the property in the seller-lessee's trade or business. When the property is subleased, the form and consequences of the seller-lessee's continuing involvement are equivalent to those of a real estate investor or developer whose ultimate source, timing, and amount of cash flows from the use of the property are different from those realized by a tenant. Based on those differences, the Board decided to reaffirm the Exposure Draft's provision to allow sale-leaseback accounting when the seller-lessee occupies the leased property.

49. Some respondents suggested that sale-leaseback accounting also be allowed for certain sale-leaseback transactions involving property,

such as hotels, whose subsequent use by the seller-lessee involves some amount of subleasing integral to other ancillary services provided. The Board agreed and concluded that such transactions involve the active use of leased property in the seller-lessee's business in a manner similar to occupancy by the seller-lessee. The same reasoning should apply to other businesses in which the seller-lessee actively uses the property in its operations, as is the case with warehouse, golf course, and parking lot enterprises. Therefore, the Board revised the occupancy requirement of the Exposure Draft to one that prescribes sale-leaseback accounting when the leased back property is actively used by the seller-lessee.

50. The Exposure Draft precluded sale-leaseback accounting when any portion of the leaseback property was not occupied by the seller-lessee. Statement 28 provides for full profit recognition by the seller-lessee if the present value of a reasonable amount of rental for the leaseback represents 10 percent or less of the fair value of the property sold at the date of the transaction. Some respondents stated that it was inconsistent with that provision of Statement 28 to preclude sale-leaseback accounting for a leaseback that is minor, irrespective of whether the seller-lessee occupies the property. The Board agreed with those respondents. This Statement allows sale-leaseback accounting for a leaseback that is minor as defined by paragraph 33(a) of Statement 13.

51. Other respondents noted that some subleasing may be necessary to provide for the seller-lessee's future growth. Those respondents questioned whether some minor amount of subleasing should preclude a transaction from sale-leaseback accounting in situations in which the seller-lessee initially intends to occupy less than the entire leased property. The Board decided to allow sale-leaseback accounting for such transactions, provided that the portion of the leaseback that the seller-lessee intends to sublease is minor in relation to the fair value of the property sold at the date of the transaction. The term *minor* is used here in the context of its use in paragraph 33(a) of Statement 13.

52. The Board considered whether a normal leaseback should be considered in conjunction with the other continuing involvement provisions or conditions of the sale-leaseback transaction in analyzing the level of continuing involvement with the property. As mentioned in paragraphs 48-51, the Board decided to allow sale-leaseback accounting in certain limited circumstances involving a normal leaseback or a leaseback with a minor sublease. The Board concluded that any additional continuing involvement should preclude sale-leaseback accounting.

53. Many respondents noted that the Exposure Draft would preclude sales recognition for sale-leaseback transactions in which nonrecourse financing is provided by the seller-lessee to the buyer-lessor for the sales proceeds. They commented that this is inconsistent with Statement 66, which allows profit to be recognized on a sale involving seller financing. The Board considered those comments but decided to retain the nonrecourse provision in paragraph 12(b). The Board believes that because nonrecourse financing provided by the seller-lessee in a sale-leaseback transaction limits the buyer-lessor's risk of loss to the original investment, it is tantamount to a guarantee by the seller-lessee.

54. Several respondents to the Exposure Draft objected to precluding sale-leaseback accounting for a sale-leaseback transaction in which the seller-lessee provides additional collateral for or on behalf of the buyer-lessor or a party related to the seller-lessee guarantees a return of or on the buyer-lessor's investment. Those respondents suggested that such a provision should not apply to situations in which additional collateral or guarantees are provided solely in support of the leaseback payments and not to the leased asset's residual value. However, the Board believes that even in that circumstance the fair value of the additional collateral or the amount of the guarantee reduces the buyer-lessor's risk of loss and is substantially the same as a guarantee of some portion of the buyer-lessor's investment by the seller-lessee. Therefore, the Board decided to retain that requirement in paragraph 12(d).

55. Paragraph 43 of Statement 66 includes the following as an example of continuing involvement permitted by the seller:

> The seller will participate in future profit from the property without risk of loss (such as participation in operating profits or residual values without further obligation). If the transaction otherwise qualifies for recognition of profit by the full accrual method, the transfer of risks and rewards of ownership and absence of continuing involvement criterion shall be considered met. The contingent future profits shall be recognized when they are realized. All the costs of the sale shall be recognized at the time of sale; none shall be deferred to periods when the contingent profits are recognized. [Footnote reference omitted.]

Many respondents stated that the provision of the Exposure Draft that precluded the participation in future profits by the seller-lessee was inconsistent with the provisions of paragraph 43 of Statement

66 that allow the seller to participate in future profits if there is no risk of loss. The Board considered those comments and whether to allow sale-leaseback accounting when the seller-lessee retains an interest in the residual value of the property or will receive future profits from the residual value of the property. The Board decided that the practice permitted by paragraph 43 of Statement 66 should not apply to a sale-leaseback transaction because the continuing involvement inherent in the normal leaseback could represent sufficient continuing involvement to disqualify profit recognition by the seller-lessee. Therefore, the Board concluded that if the seller-lessee retains any portion of future profits or ownership interest in the residual value of the leased asset, retention of that interest represents continuing involvement with the property sufficient to preclude sales recognition.

56. The Board accepted the continuing involvement of a leaseback under certain circumstances, in part because that continuing involvement could be measured by the payment terms of the lease agreement. Some respondents also suggested allowing minor continuing involvement and requested that the Board develop a test to measure minor continuing involvement. The Board considered allowing sale-leaseback accounting for a sale-leaseback transaction that provides for minor continuing involvement other than the leaseback. However, the Board rejected that notion because it believes that many continuing involvement provisions are not measurable, so that there is no objective way to determine the amount of involvement.

57. Many respondents questioned why a fair value repurchase option should preclude a seller-lessee from using sale-leaseback accounting. Other respondents commented that Statement 66 precludes a seller from recognizing a sale if the agreement includes a repurchase option at any value and suggested that the Board reconsider the accounting for repurchase options under paragraph 26 of Statement 66. The Board currently has on its agenda a project addressing many issues relating to financial instruments and off-balance-sheet financing. The Board believes that it is inappropriate to reconsider the accounting for repurchase options until that project has proceeded further.

Sale-Leaseback Transactions by Regulated Enterprises

58. Paragraph 41 of Statement 71 states:

> For financial reporting purposes, the classification of the lease is not affected by the regulator's actions. The regulator cannot eliminate an obligation that was not imposed by the regulator. Also, by including

the lease payments as allowable costs, the regulator sets rates that will provide revenue approximately equal to the combined amount of the capitalized leased asset and interest on the lease obligation over the term of the lease and, thus, provides reasonable assurance of the existence of an asset. Accordingly, regulated enterprises would classify leases in accordance with Statement 13 as amended. [Paragraph references omitted.]

Similarly, the financial reporting of a sale-leaseback transaction may be considered to be of less consequence to the regulator. The regulator may continue to focus on the leaseback payments as allowable costs and continue to provide reasonable assurance of the existence of an asset.

59. Paragraph 42 of Statement 71 states:

> The nature of the expense elements related to a capitalized lease (amortization of the leased asset and interest on the lease obligation) is not changed by the regulator's action; however, the timing of expense recognition related to the lease would be modified to conform to the rate treatment. Thus, amortization of the leased asset would be modified so that the total of interest on the lease obligation and amortization of the leased asset would equal the rental expense that was allowed for rate-making purposes.

Similarly, the timing of expense recognition related to a sale-leaseback transaction accounted for by the deposit method (amortization of the asset) or as a financing (amortization of the asset and imputed interest on the financing) under the provisions of this Statement would be modified to conform to the rate treatment. Amortization of the asset would be modified so that the total of interest (if accounted for as a financing) and amortization of the asset would equal the rental expense net of the amortization of any gain allowable for rate-making purposes. Statement 92 addresses the accounting by regulated enterprises for phase-in plans. A regulator's treatment of a sale with lease-back for regulatory purposes may meet the definition of a phase-in plan under that Statement. In that case, Statement 92 may require different income and expense recognition for financial reporting purposes than that indicated above.

Financial Statement Presentation and Disclosure

60. The Board considered disclosure requirements for a sale-leaseback transaction accounted for by the deposit method, as a financing, or using sale-leaseback accounting under the provisions of this Statement and concluded that the significant terms and provisions of the transactions should be disclosed. The Board concluded that the amount charged to expense during the period for the transaction and the amount of the commitment or obligation to make future rental payments under the leaseback are relevant information irrespective of whether the sale-leaseback transaction is accounted for as a lease under Statement 13 or by the deposit method or as a financing under the provisions of this Statement and Statement 66. In the Board's view, those disclosures are consistent with the information required to be disclosed for owned property and long-term obligations in general. The Board concluded that the disclosure of a sale-leaseback transaction accounted for by the deposit method or as a financing under the provisions of this Statement should be similar to the disclosure that would have been required by Statements 13 and 66 had those transactions qualified for sale-leaseback accounting.

Lease Term Provisions

61. Subparagraph 5(f)(ii) of Statement 13 requires that the lease term include "all periods, if any, for which failure to renew the lease imposes a penalty on the lessee in an amount such that renewal appears, at the inception of the lease, to be reasonably assured." In addition, paragraph 3 of Technical Bulletin 79-11 states:

> The "penalty" referred to in paragraph 5(f) of Statement 13 is not limited to a penalty imposed by the lease agreement. Accordingly, the lease term would also include any periods for which failure to renew the lease would result in an *economic* penalty as a result of factors external to the lease so long as (a) the existence of the penalty were known at the inception of the lease and (b) the nature and estimated amount of the penalty at the inception of the lease were such that renewal would appear to be reasonably assured. [Emphasis added.]

62. Paragraph 22(b) of this Statement requires that the loss of a present or future economic benefit should be considered an economic penalty in the context of Technical Bulletin 79-11 and paragraph 5(f) of Statement 13. That loss is an economic penalty similar to a requirement to make a payment to the lessor at the end of the lease. Several respondents suggested that requiring an economic penalty to be considered in determining the lease term is too subjective and should not be required. However, the Board concluded that such penalties do affect the lessee's decision to renew the lease and any renewal period for which those penalties are present should be included in the lease

term under paragraph 5(f) of Statement 13.

63. Several respondents questioned why a loan from the lessee under usual terms and prevailing interest rates should affect the determination of the lease term. Subparagraph 5(f)(iii) of Statement 13 includes in the lease term "all periods, if any, covered by ordinary renewal options during which a guarantee by the lessee of the lessor's debt related to the leased property is expected to be in effect." The Board believes that a note from the buyer-lessor to the seller-lessee creates risks similar to a guarantee by the seller-lessee of the buyer-lessor's debt and concluded that the lease term should include all periods during which a loan from the seller-lessee to the buyer-lessor is outstanding.

Amendments to Other Pronouncements

64. Statement 66 precludes a sale of real estate from being recognized as a sale if the transaction gives the seller an option to repurchase the property. However, Statement 13, as amended by Statement 26, would allow a lessor (seller) to recognize *profit* under the full accrual method in a sales-type lease of real estate while retaining ownership of the property, provided that the transaction otherwise meets the requirements for full and immediate profit recognition under the full accrual method as described by Statement 66. This Statement amends Statement 13 to prohibit a lease involving real estate from being classified as a sales-type lease unless the lease transfers ownership of the property to the lessee by the end of the lease term.

65. Statement 13 also requires that a lessor recognize immediately a manufacturer's or dealer's loss in a sales-type lease. Statement 26 did not amend that requirement for sales-type leases involving real estate because it only applied to manufacturer's or dealer's *profit,* not loss. The Exposure Draft did not address recognition of a loss in a lease involving real estate that does not qualify as a sales-type lease because the title has not been transferred to the lessee by the end of the lease term. The Board did not intend to amend Statement 13 to allow the deferral of a loss in a sales-type lease in any circumstance. Therefore, this Statement clarifies that intent and requires that any applicable loss be recognized immediately in a lease involving real estate that would otherwise qualify as a sales-type lease but does not because of the requirements of this Statement.

66. Several respondents noted that some leases of real estate include provisions that transfer title at or shortly after the end of the lease term upon payment of some nominal or trifling amount, usually based on the minimum statutory amount necessary to transfer title. Those respondents suggested that such a provision be considered as meeting the criterion as a transfer of title during the lease term. The Board agreed with those respondents and added a footnote to paragraph 7(a) of Statement 13 to that effect.

67. Statement 66 recognizes that a sale of real estate may not qualify for full and immediate profit recognition under the full accrual method at inception. Thus, that Statement describes other profit recognition methods for such sales and allows for later qualification under the full accrual method. However, Statement 13, as amended by Statement 26, prohibits a lessor (seller) from recognizing profit under any of those other methods on a transaction involving real estate that would otherwise be classified at the inception of the transaction as a sales-type lease if that transaction does not qualify for profit recognition under the full accrual method and requires that the transaction be accounted for as an operating lease. This Statement amends Statement 13 to provide that a lessor should account for any sales-type lease of real estate under the provisions of Statement 66 in the same manner as a *seller* of the same property.

68. The objective of amending Statement 13 in Statement 91 was to achieve consistency between direct financing leases and loans for the capitalization of origination costs and recognition of income. In Statement 91, the Board concluded that the practice of recognizing a portion of loan origination fees as revenue in the period of origination to offset all or part of the cost of origination would no longer be acceptable. Prior to this amendment, Statement 91 required that initial direct costs of origination be included as part of the gross investment in a direct financing lease. Although this is consistent with the approach for a loan, the mechanics of lease accounting under Statement 13 are such that the effect of adding initial direct costs to the gross investment before calculating unearned income would cause overstatement of unearned income. This Statement corrects the amendment of Statement 13 by Statement 91 to reflect the Board's intent when Statement 91 was issued. Initial direct costs are capitalized separately from the gross investment.

Effective Date and Transition

69. The Board considered whether this Statement should be applied only to future transactions or retroactively to all transactions. The Board recognized that applying this Statement only to future transactions would diminish both comparability of the resulting financial statements among enterprises and consistency within an enterprise that had entered into similar transactions both before and after the effective date of this Statement.

While sale-leaseback and leasing transactions tend to have a long-term effect on the financial statements of an enterprise, the Board believes that transactions previously entered into might have been structured differently if the provisions of this Statement had been known at the time. Therefore, the Board concluded that this Statement should be applied prospectively except for the amendment to Statement 13 to reflect the intended amendment of that Statement by Statement 91, which should have an effective date and transition consistent with that of Statement 91.

Appendix C

GLOSSARY

70. This appendix defines certain terms as they are used in this Statement.

Nonrecourse financing
Lending or borrowing activities in which the creditor does not have general recourse to the debtor but rather has recourse only to the property used for collateral in the transaction or other specific property.

Sale-leaseback accounting
For purposes of this Statement, a method of accounting for a sale-leaseback transaction in which the seller-lessee records the sale, removes all property and related liabilities from its balance sheet, recognizes gain or loss from the sale in accordance with Statement 13 as amended by Statements 28 and 66 and this Statement, and classifies the leaseback in accordance with Statement 13, as amended by Statement 28.

Sales recognition
Any method that is described in Statement 66 as a method to record a transaction involving real estate, other than the deposit method, or the methods to record transactions accounted for as financing, leasing, or profit-sharing arrangements. Profit recognition methods described in Statement 66 commonly used to record transactions involving real estate include, but are not limited to, the full accrual method, the installment method, the cost recovery method, and the reduced profit method.

FAS99

Statement of Financial Accounting Standards No. 99
Deferral of the Effective Date of Recognition of
Depreciation by Not-for-Profit Organizations

an amendment of FASB Statement No. 93

STATUS

Issued: September 1988

Effective Date: September 1988

Affects: Amends FAS 93, paragraph 7

Affected by: No other pronouncements

SUMMARY

This Statement amends FASB Statement No. 93, *Recognition of Depreciation by Not-for-Profit Organizations.* It defers the effective date of Statement 93 to fiscal years beginning on or after January 1, 1990.

Statement of Financial Accounting Standards No. 99

Deferral of the Effective Date of Recognition of Depreciation by Not-for-Profit Organizations

an amendment of FASB Statement No. 93

CONTENTS

INTRODUCTION

1. In February 1988, the National Association of College and University Business Officers (NACUBO) and others asked the FASB to consider delaying the effective date of FASB Statement No. 93, *Recognition of Depreciation by Not-for-Profit Organizations,* pending the outcome of a Financial Accounting Foundation (FAF) reconsideration of the jurisdiction arrangement for standard setting. That reconsideration is scheduled to be completed early in 1989. The Board has concluded that, for the reasons presented in the appendix to this Statement, it is appropriate to defer the effective date of Statement 93.

STANDARDS OF FINANCIAL ACCOUNTING AND REPORTING

Amendment to Statement 93

2. The first sentence of paragraph 7 of Statement 93 is superseded by the following:

This Statement shall be effective for financial statements issued for fiscal years beginning on or after January 1, 1990.

Effective Date

3. This Statement shall be effective upon issuance.

This Statement was adopted by the affirmative votes of four members of the Financial Accounting Standards Board. Messrs. Brown, Lauver, and Northrop dissented.

Messrs. Brown, Lauver, and Northrop dissent from this Statement's delay of the effective date of Statement 93. They believe that since the formation of a separate Board for setting standards of governmental accounting, the FASB has been charged with improving financial reporting while operating under the terms of the jurisdiction arrangement for the two Boards. They believe it is inappropriate, at this time, to anticipate changes to the jurisdiction arrangement under which Statement 93 and other Statements were issued. Delaying the effective date of Statement 93, in their view, would not be consistent with the responsibilities of the Board.

Further, Messrs. Brown, Lauver, and Northrop believe that deferral of only Statement 93 is not an evenhanded response to concerns expressed by some constituents about similar entities' being required to follow different accounting standards because of the current jurisdiction arrangement. There is no reason to delay the applicability of one standard without delaying the effective date of all standards in circumstances in which possible new jurisdiction arrangements may result from the study now under way. Such a wholesale and potentially indefinite suspension of the applicability of standards would not further sound financial reporting.

Members of the Financial Accounting Standards Board:

Dennis R. Beresford,   Raymond C. Lauver   A. Clarence Sampson
   Chairman   James J. Leisenring   Robert J. Swieringa
Victor H. Brown   C. Arthur Northrop

Appendix

BACKGROUND INFORMATION AND BASIS FOR CONCLUSIONS

4. Statement 93 was issued in August 1987 and requires all not-for-profit organizations to recognize the cost of using up long-lived tangible assets—depreciation—in general-purpose external financial statements.[1] Statement 93 applies to charitable and religious organizations, colleges and universities, hospitals, and other not-for-profit organizations that issue general-purpose financial statements. As issued, Statement 93 is effective for financial statements issued for fiscal years beginning after May 15, 1988, with earlier application encouraged.

5. In January 1988, the Governmental Accounting Standards Board (GASB) issued its Statement No. 8, *Applicability of FASB Statement No. 93, "Recognition of Depreciation by Not-for-Profit Organizations," to Certain State and Local Governmental Entities,* which states that public colleges and universities and certain other governmental entities "should not change their accounting and reporting for depreciation of capital assets as a result of FASB Statement 93." Paragraph 18 of GASB Statement 8 states:

> . . . until its [GASB's] projects on measurement focus and basis of accounting, capital assets, capital reporting, and college and university user needs have been completed or advanced to a stage that will provide the Board with a clearer indication of how capital assets, depreciation, and related issues will be addressed, no useful purpose will be served by applying the provisions of FASB Statement 93 to . . . governmental entities. . . .

6. In February 1988, NACUBO reiterated its "serious reservations concerning the possibility of two sets of accounting standards for colleges and universities" (letter to the FAF, November 18, 1986). NACUBO and others asked the FAF, which oversees the FASB and the GASB, to reconsider the jurisdiction arrangement for standard setting, particularly for colleges and universities. They asked the FAF to determine if a single standard-setting body could be established for higher education to enhance the comparability of financial reporting.

7. The January 16, 1984 "Agreement Concerning the Structure for a Governmental Accounting Standards Board (GASB)" (the Structure Agreement) requires a review of the governmental accounting standard-setting structure after GASB has been in operation for approximately five years. The FAF, jointly with the Governmental Accounting Standards Advisory Council (GASAC), has formed the Committee to Review Structure for Governmental Accounting Standards (Five Year Review Committee) to conduct that review. The FAF Executive Committee has urged the Five Year Review Committee to consider, among other things, the possibility of recommending that the jurisdictional provisions of the Structure Agreement be revised to designate a single standard-setting body for the separately issued statements of both public and private colleges and universities. That consideration is not limited to institutions of higher education because other entities are similarly affected by the present jurisdiction arrangement. The Five Year Review Committee has commenced its work and is expected to complete its review in time for actions by the FAF by April 1989. January 1, 1990 is the target date for implementing any suggested changes to the Structure Agreement.

8. In light of the FAF review under way to reconsider the jurisdiction arrangement and the timetable for implementing changes emanating from that review, the Board concluded that it should defer the effective date of Statement 93. It is expected that such action will facilitate that review.

9. On June 6, 1988, the FASB issued an Exposure Draft proposing deferral of the effective date of Statement 93 until fiscal years beginning on or after January 1, 1990. The Board received 132 letters of comment in response to the Exposure Draft, a large majority of which supported the proposed deferral.

10. A few respondents, including some of those in support of the Exposure Draft, suggested that the Board use the deferral period as an opportunity to reconsider (and perhaps rescind) Statement 93. The Board disagreed reaffirming its conclusion in paragraph 25 of Statement 93, which states:

> . . . a fair assessment of the costs of efforts expended is necessary to evaluate the results of economic activity that not-for-profit organizations undertake. Depreciation is an essential part of measuring the costs of services provided during a period. Omitting depreciation produces results that do not reflect all costs of services provided. That omission can result in a misunderstand-

---

[1]Depreciation, however, need not be recognized for certain works of art and certain historical treasures. Statement 93 also extends to not-for-profit organizations the requirements of APB Opinion No. 12, *Omnibus Opinion—1967,* to disclose information about depreciable assets and depreciation.

ing of the economics of providing services and may contribute to inefficiencies.

The Board continues to believe that information about an entity's costs of using up assets is useful to users of its financial statements and that the interests of those who rely on financial information are best served by neutral standards that result in accounting for similar transactions and circumstances similarly and for different transactions and circumstances differently.

11. The Board expects not-for-profit organizations that under existing standards are required to depreciate long-lived assets to continue to do so. The Board also strongly encourages organizations that have been permitted, but not required, to depreciate long-lived assets to do so, particularly those that have already taken the steps necessary to implement Statement 93.

12. The Board concluded that it could reach an informed decision on the basis of existing information without a public hearing and that the effective date specified in paragraph 3 is advisable in the circumstances.

Statement of Financial Accounting Standards No. 100
Accounting for Income Taxes—Deferral of the
Effective Date of FASB Statement No. 96

an amendment of FASB Statement No. 96

STATUS

Issued: December 1988

Effective Date: December 15, 1988

Affects: Amends FAS 96, paragraph 32

Affected by: Superseded by FAS 103, FAS 108, and FAS 109

(The next page is 1211.)

Statement of Financial Accounting Standards No. 101
Regulated Enterprises—Accounting for the
Discontinuation of Application of FASB Statement No. 71

STATUS

Issued: December 1988

Effective Date: For discontinuations of application of Statement 71 occurring in fiscal years ending after December 15, 1988

Affects: Amends APB 30, paragraph 20

Affected by: Paragraph 6 amended by FAS 121
Paragraph 19 amended by FAS 109

Issues Discussed by FASB Emerging Issues Task Force (EITF)

Affects: No Issues

Interpreted by: No Issues

Related Issue: EITF Issue No. 97-4

SUMMARY

This Statement specifies how an enterprise that ceases to meet the criteria for application of FASB Statement No. 71, *Accounting for the Effects of Certain Types of Regulation,* to all or part of its operations should report that event in its general-purpose external financial statements.

An enterprise's operations can cease to meet those criteria for various reasons, including deregulation, a change in the method of regulation, or a change in the competitive environment for the enterprise's regulated services or products. Regardless of the reason, an enterprise whose operations cease to meet those criteria should discontinue application of that Statement and report that discontinuation by eliminating from its statement of financial position the effects of any actions of regulators that had been recognized as assets and liabilities pursuant to Statement 71 but would not have been recognized as assets and liabilities by enterprises in general. However, the carrying amounts of plant, equipment, and inventory measured and reported pursuant to Statement 71 should not be adjusted unless those assets are impaired, in which case the carrying amounts of those assets should be reduced to reflect that impairment. The net effect of the adjustments should be included in income of the period of the change and classified as an extraordinary item.

This Statement is effective for discontinuations of application of Statement 71 occurring in fiscal years ending after December 15, 1988, but its adoption may be delayed until the issuance of annual financial statements for the fiscal year that includes December 15, 1989. Retroactive application to discontinuations reported prior to fiscal years ending after December 15, 1988 by restatement of the financial statements for the period including the date of discontinuation and periods subsequent to the date of the discontinuation is permitted but not required.

Statement of Financial Accounting Standards No. 101

Regulated Enterprises—Accounting for the Discontinuation of Application of FASB Statement No. 71

CONTENTS

INTRODUCTION

1. FASB Statement No. 71, *Accounting for the Effects of Certain Types of Regulation,* requires that an enterprise's operations meet specific criteria for application of that Statement. Statement 71 does not address the accounting that should result when an enterprise's operations cease to meet those criteria. Since Statement 71 was issued, deregulation of certain industries and changes in the method of regulating others have caused several enterprises to discontinue application of Statement 71 for some or all of their operations.

2. The FASB has been informed that the methods used to account for those discontinuations have varied in practice. In its October 15, 1984 Issues Paper, *Application of Concepts in FASB Statement of Financial Accounting Standards No. 71 to Emerging Issues in the Public Utility Industry,* the AICPA Public Utility Subcommittee requested that the Board specify the appropriate accounting to reflect the discontinuation of application of Statement 71.

3. As a condition for its initial and continuing application, Statement 71 requires that an enterprise's operations meet the three criteria specified in paragraph 5 of Statement 71:

a. The enterprise's rates for regulated services or products provided to its customers are established by or are subject to approval by an inde-

pendent, third-party regulator or by its own governing board empowered by statute or contract to establish rates that bind customers.

b. The regulated rates are designed to recover the specific enterprise's costs of providing the regulated services or products.

c. In view of the demand for the regulated services or products and the level of competition, direct and indirect, it is reasonable to assume that rates set at levels that will recover the enterprise's costs can be charged to and collected from customers. This criterion requires consideration of anticipated changes in levels of demand or competition during the recovery period for any capitalized costs. [Footnote reference omitted.]

4. Failure of an enterprise's operations to continue to meet the criteria in paragraph 5 of Statement 71 can result from different causes. Examples include the following:

a. Deregulation
b. A change in the regulator's approach to setting rates from cost-based rate making to another form of regulation
c. Increasing competition that limits the enterprise's ability to sell utility services or products at rates that will recover costs
d. Regulatory actions resulting from resistance to rate increases that limit the enterprise's ability to sell utility services or products at rates that will recover costs if the enterprise is unable to

obtain (or chooses not to seek) relief from prior regulatory actions through appeals to the regulator or the courts.

Regardless of the reason for an enterprise's discontinuation of application of Statement 71, this Statement specifies how that discontinuation shall be reported in the enterprise's general-purpose external financial statements.

STANDARDS OF FINANCIAL ACCOUNTING AND REPORTING

Discontinuation of the Application of Statement 71

5. When an enterprise determines that its operations in a regulatory jurisdiction no longer meet the criteria for application of Statement 71, that enterprise shall discontinue application of that Statement to its operations in that jurisdiction. If a separable portion of the enterprise's operations within a regulatory jurisdiction ceases to meet the criteria for application of Statement 71, application of that Statement to that separable portion shall be discontinued. That situation creates a presumption that application of Statement 71 shall be discontinued for all of the enterprise's operations within that regulatory jurisdiction. That presumption can be overcome by establishing that the enterprise's other operations within that jurisdiction continue to meet the criteria for application of Statement 71.

Accounting to Reflect the Discontinuation of Application of Statement 71

6. When an enterprise discontinues application of Statement 71 to all or part of its operations, that enterprise shall eliminate from its statement of financial position prepared for general-purpose external financial reporting the effects of any actions of regulators that had been recognized as assets and liabilities pursuant to Statement 71 but would not have been recognized as assets and liabilities by enterprises in general. However, the carrying amounts of plant, equipment, and inventory measured and reported pursuant to Statement 71[1] shall not be adjusted unless those assets are impaired, in which case the carrying amounts of those assets shall be reduced to reflect that impairment. Whether those assets have been impaired shall be

judged in the same manner as for enterprises in general. The net effect of the adjustments required by this Statement shall be included in income of the period in which the discontinuation occurs and shall be classified as an extraordinary item.

7. An enterprise that discontinues application of Statement 71 shall no longer recognize the effects of actions of a regulator as assets or liabilities unless the right to receive payment or the obligation to pay exists as a result of past events or transactions and regardless of future transactions.

Disclosures

8. For the period in which an enterprise reflects the discontinuation of application of Statement 71 to all or a separable portion of its operations, the enterprise shall disclose the reasons for the discontinuation and identify the portion of its operations to which the application of Statement 71 is being discontinued.

9. The disclosure requirements of APB Opinion No. 30, *Reporting the Results of Operations—Reporting the Effects of Disposal of a Segment of a Business, and Extraordinary, Unusual and Infrequently Occurring Events and Transactions,* for extraordinary items apply to the net adjustment reported in the statement of operations as a result of applying this Statement.

Amendment to Opinion 30

10. This Statement amends Opinion 30 only to the extent that classification of the net effect of discontinuing the application of Statement 71 as an extraordinary item pursuant to paragraph 6 of this Statement shall be made without regard to the criteria in paragraph 20 of that Opinion.

Effective Date and Transition

11. This Statement shall be effective for discontinuations of application of Statement 71 occurring in fiscal years ending after December 15, 1988. If an enterprise has issued financial statements in which the provisions of this Statement have not been applied to a discontinuation occurring in the fiscal year that includes December 15, 1988, the financial statements for the interim period of the discontinuation and subsequent interim periods within that

---

[1]The carrying amounts of plant, equipment, and inventory for enterprises applying Statement 71 differ from those for enterprises in general only because of the allowance for funds used during construction, intercompany profit, and disallowances of costs of recently completed plants. If any other amounts that would not be includable in the carrying amounts of plant, equipment, or inventory by enterprises in general (such as postconstruction operating costs capitalized pursuant to paragraph 9 of Statement 71) are included in or netted against the carrying amounts of plant, equipment, or inventory, those amounts shall be accounted for as this Statement prescribes for the effects of actions of a regulator.

fiscal year shall be restated. For discontinuations reported in fiscal years ending prior to December 15, 1988, retroactive application by restatement of the financial statements for the period including the date of discontinuation and periods subsequent to the date of discontinuation is permitted but not required. Any financial statements restated shall disclose the nature of the restatement and its effect on income before extraordinary items, extraordinary items, net income, and related per share amounts for each period restated. Interim and annual financial statements for periods that ended prior to the date of discontinuation of application of Statement 71 shall not be restated.

12. Enterprises with discontinuations occurring in fiscal years that include December 15, 1988 or December 15, 1989 may delay adopting this Statement until the issuance of annual financial statements for the fiscal year that includes December 15, 1989. Enterprises delaying adoption of this Statement shall, when adopting this Statement, restate their interim and annual financial statements for the period including the date of discontinuation and periods subsequent to that date and shall disclose the nature of the restatement and its effect on income before extraordinary items, extraordinary items, net income, and related per share amounts for each period restated.

The provisions of this Statement need not be applied to immaterial items.

This Statement was adopted by the affirmative vote of six members of the Financial Accounting Standards Board. Mr. Lauver dissented.

Mr. Lauver dissents from the issuance of this Statement because it does not require the effects of all specialized practices followed while an enterprise applied Statement 71 to be eliminated from the balance sheet at the time the enterprise discontinues application of that Statement. Specialized practices whose effects are not required to be eliminated upon discontinuing application of Statement 71 are capitalizing an allowance for earnings on shareholders' investment, capitalizing interest on bases different from those permitted by Statement 34, and capitalizing profits on intercompany sales. The effects of those specialized practices that are permitted to remain in the balance sheet have been reported as components of asset accounts (inventory and plant) that would have existed absent those components rather than in separate asset accounts and are said, therefore, not to represent assets resulting solely from actions of regulators. Mr. Lauver believes that the effects of all specialized

practices followed while applying Statement 71 are assets (or liabilities) resulting solely from actions of regulators, are substantively the same regardless of balance sheet classification, and should be eliminated to enhance subsequent comparability with other enterprises that are not subject to Statement 71 and to enhance distinctions from enterprises that continue to be subject to Statement 71.

As indicated herein, a rationale for conclusions expressed in this Statement is that, although conceptually correct to eliminate from the balance sheet all effects of the specialized practices followed while applying Statement 71, the cost of doing so, for the practices mentioned in the preceding paragraph, would exceed the benefits derived and that elimination is prohibited by this Statement. Although Mr. Lauver believes it is appropriate for a standard setter to refrain from requiring a conceptually correct solution when costs are judged to exceed benefits, he believes it is inappropriate to preclude a conceptually correct solution in financial statements of an enterprise that concludes that the benefits it perceives will exceed the costs that it alone will bear.

Members of the Financial Accounting Standards Board:

Dennis R. Beresford,
  Chairman
Victor H. Brown

Raymond C. Lauver
James J. Leisenring
C. Arthur Northrop

A. Clarence Sampson
Robert J. Swieringa

Appendix A

EXAMPLES OF THE APPLICATION OF THIS STATEMENT TO SPECIFIC SITUATIONS

CONTENTS

Appendix A

EXAMPLES OF THE APPLICATION OF THIS STATEMENT TO SPECIFIC SITUATIONS

13. This appendix provides examples of the application of this Statement to some specific situations. The examples do not address all possible applications of this Statement.

Assets Recorded Based Solely on Expected Future Revenue to Be Provided by the Regulator

14. Utility A operates solely in one regulatory jurisdiction. At December 31, 19X1, Utility A concludes, based on current market conditions, that it no longer meets the criteria for the application of Statement 71. Utility A's statement of financial position at December 31, 19X1 includes the following items:

a. Deferred purchased power costs (costs of power used for operations in prior periods that were expected to be recovered from customers as a result of an automatic adjustment clause)
b. Deferred costs of abandoned plant (costs for which recovery was being provided through rates)
c. Deferred costs of repairing storm damage.

How should those items be reported at December 31, 19X1?

15. All of those items should be eliminated from the enterprise's statement of financial position when it ceases to apply Statement 71. The resulting charge to income, net of any related tax effects, should be reported as an extraordinary item in the period that includes December 31, 19X1. The enterprise should no longer defer those costs and re-

port them as assets because they could not be reported as assets by enterprises in general. Enterprises in general would report a receivable for those items only if a right to receive payment exists as a result of past events or transactions and regardless of future transactions (such as future sales).

16. For example, a contract between a supplier and a customer for the sale of fuel oil may specify that next year's sales price will be adjusted based on the supplier's current-year cost of fuel oil. Even though it is probable that a future economic benefit (the ability to charge a higher price in the future) will result from the supplier's current-year cost of fuel oil, no asset exists at the end of the current year because the transactions (sales to the customer) that give the supplier control of the benefit are in the future. However, if the contract provides that the customer is obligated to pay additional amounts related to past purchases and regardless of future purchases, the supplier has an asset and it does not matter whether that payment is made in a single amount or when the customer will pay for next year's purchases.

Liabilities Recorded Based Solely on Actions of the Regulator

17. Utility B operates in two regulatory jurisdictions, State 1 and State 2. Forty percent of Utility B's operations are located in State 1 and 60 percent in State 2; system-wide assets, liabilities, and certain gains and losses are allocated 40 percent to State 1 and 60 percent to State 2. At December 31, 19X2, Utility B concludes, based on current and expected future market conditions in State 1, that it no longer meets the criteria for application of Statement 71 to its operations in State 1. No similar conditions exist in State 2, and actions of State 1's regulators are not expected to influence the decisions of regulators in State 2. Utility B's state-

ment of financial position at December 31, 19X2 includes the following items:

Deferred gain on restructuring debt, being amortized for rate-making purposes on an allocated basis by both states $50,000

Revenues collected subject to refund in prior years in State 1, expected to be refunded through future rates $75,000

How should those items be reported at December 31, 19X2?

18. The portion of the deferred gain allocable to State 1 (determined in the example to be 40 percent of $50,000, or $20,000), net of any related tax effects, should be eliminated from the enterprise's statement of financial position when it ceases to apply Statement 71 to its operations in State 1. No adjustment should be made for the deferred gain applicable to State 2. The regulatory-created accrual for revenues subject to refund in State 1, net of any related tax effects, should be eliminated. Whether any liability related thereto exists should be determined under generally accepted accounting principles for enterprises in general. For example, amounts that were collected in the current or prior periods for which refunds will be made *regardless of future sales* should continue to be re-

ported as liabilities after application of Statement 71 is discontinued. The credit to income resulting from the above adjustments, net of any related tax effects, should be reported as an extraordinary item in the period that includes December 31, 19X2.

Regulatory-Created Assets Resulting from the Recording of Deferred Income Taxes Not Recognized for Rate Making

19. Utility C operates solely in one regulatory jurisdiction. At June 30, 19X3, Utility C concludes, based on new legislation, that it no longer meets the criteria for application of Statement 71. Utility C had adopted FASB Statement No. 96, *Accounting for Income Taxes*, in 19X2 and because of applying Statement 71 had recorded a regulatory-created asset of $650,000 for deferred taxes resulting from temporary differences that had not been recognized in the rate-making process but that were expected to be recovered in the future. What reporting is required for that regulatory-created asset?

20. Utility C should eliminate that regulatory-created asset from its statement of financial position when the enterprise ceases to apply Statement 71. The charge to income, net of any related tax effects, should be reported as an extraordinary item in the period that includes June 30, 19X3.

Appendix B

BASIS FOR CONCLUSIONS

CONTENTS

Appendix B

BASIS FOR CONCLUSIONS

Introduction

21. This appendix summarizes considerations that were deemed significant by members of the Board in reaching the conclusions in this Statement. It in-

cludes reasons for accepting certain views and rejecting others. Individual Board members gave greater weight to some factors than to others.

22. An FASB Exposure Draft, *Regulated Enterprises—Accounting for the Discontinuation of Application of FASB Statement No. 71,* was issued for public comment on July 8, 1988. The Board received 81 letters of comment in response to the Exposure Draft. The Board concluded that it

could reach an informed decision on the basis of existing information without a public hearing.

Overall Conclusions on the Discontinuation of Application of Statement 71

23. For an enterprise with operations that meet the criteria for application of Statement 71, actions of a regulator may result in the recognition of assets and liabilities because the regulator may specify the amount and timing of recognition of allowable costs for rate-making purposes.

24. The conclusion that the criteria of Statement 71 are no longer met as a result of changes in circumstances is a significant event in terms of financial reporting for an enterprise. An objective of financial reporting is to achieve comparability of accounting information. Paragraph 119 of FASB Concepts Statement No. 2, *Qualitative Characteristics of Accounting Information,* states that this objective "is not to be attained by making unlike things look alike any more than by making like things look different." In this instance, achieving that objective requires reporting the effect of that significant event so that an enterprise that discontinues application of Statement 71 is distinguished from an enterprise that does not.

25. When an enterprise determines that it ceases to meet the criteria for application of Statement 71, assets and liabilities recognized solely because of judgments about the effects of actions of the regulator cease to meet the criteria for recognition. The Board concluded that the change in circumstances that led to the discontinuation of application of Statement 71 should be reported in financial statements. The approach set forth in the Exposure Draft required adjusting the financial statements of the enterprise so that they are comparable, at the date of the change and in future periods, with the financial statements of other enterprises that had never applied Statement 71.

26. Most respondents disagreed with the Exposure Draft's requirement to adjust the amounts recorded as plant, equipment, and inventory to the amounts that would have been recorded had the enterprise never applied Statement 71. The reasons given by those respondents for not adjusting the amounts recorded as plant, equipment, and inventory when discontinuing the application of Statement 71 included (a) viewing the allowance for funds used during construction as an acceptable substitute for interest that would have been capitalized under FASB Statement No. 34, *Capitalization of Interest Cost,* (b) the general notion, as expressed in paragraph 88 of FASB Concepts Statement No. 5, *Recognition and Measurement in Financial Statements of Business Enterprises,* that "once an asset or lia-

bility is recognized, it continues to be measured at the amount initially recognized until an event that changes the asset or liability or its amount occurs and meets the recognition criteria," (c) the precedent that the adoption of Statement 34 by enterprises in general was prospective, and (d) the assertion that the cost of obtaining the information necessary to adjust the amounts recorded as plant, equipment, and inventory exceeded the benefits derived from the adjustments.

27. Other respondents agreed with the Exposure Draft's requirement to adjust the amounts recorded as plant, equipment, and inventory to the amounts that would have been recorded had the enterprise never applied Statement 71. Those respondents viewed the differences in amounts recorded as plant, equipment, and inventory due to application of Statement 71 as no different from the separately identified effects of actions of a regulator recognized as assets and liabilities, such as deferred storm damage costs or deferred gains on reacquired debt. Those respondents agreed that those amounts should be eliminated upon the discontinuation of application of Statement 71.

28. Absent impairment, this Statement does not permit adjustment of the carrying amounts of plant, equipment, and inventory measured and recorded pursuant to Statement 71 when an enterprise discontinues application of Statement 71 to all or a portion of its operations. Some Board members agree that the allowances for funds used during construction were an acceptable substitute for the amounts of interest that would have been capitalized in accordance with Statement 34 and that once an asset is measured and recognized pursuant to generally accepted accounting principles, the cost basis of that asset, absent impairment or the occurrence of other events that change the asset or its amount, should not be adjusted. Other Board members believe that, in principle, the carrying amounts of plant, equipment, and inventory should be adjusted to the amounts that would have been recorded had Statement 71 never been applied but that the cost of determining and removing the allowance for funds used during construction and intercompany profit and of computing the interest that would have been capitalized in accordance with Statement 34 would exceed the benefits derived.

29. The Board considered permitting but not requiring enterprises that discontinue application of Statement 71 to adjust their carrying amounts of plant, equipment, and inventory to the amounts that would have been recorded had Statement 71 never been applied. Some Board members did not believe that adjustments to the carrying amounts of those assets were appropriate absent impair-

ment. Other Board members believed the advantages of prescribing a consistent method of discontinuing application of Statement 71 were sufficient to outweigh their concern about prohibiting an enterprise from using what those Board members believe to be the conceptually correct approach. For those reasons, this Statement does not permit enterprises that discontinue application of Statement 71 to adjust the carrying amounts of plant, equipment, and inventory to the amounts that would have been recorded had Statement 71 never been applied.

30. In determining the appropriate financial reporting for an enterprise that discontinues application of Statement 71, the Board considered whether the accounting for a change in circumstances should be based on the guidance contained in APB Opinion No. 20, *Accounting Changes.* The Board recognizes that the change from one accounting model to another is an unusual accounting event that is different from a discretionary change in accounting because the former is dictated by changed circumstances. That change is somewhat analogous to a "change in estimate effected by a change in accounting principle," described in paragraphs 11 and 32 of Opinion 20, that is required to be accounted for as a change in estimate. The Board concluded that, because the change in circumstances eliminates the justification for recognizing assets and liabilities whose recognition was based solely on judgments made about the effect of the rate-making process, that change should be reported as a separate component of net income of the period of the change.

31. The discontinuation of application of Statement 71 may, in some circumstances, not meet the criteria for extraordinary items in paragraph 20 of Opinion 30. The Board concluded that extraordinary-item treatment represents a practical and reasonable way to classify the adjustments resulting from the discontinuation of Statement 71 in a statement of operations. This Statement amends Opinion 30 to the extent that classification of the net effect of discontinuing the application of Statement 71 as an extraordinary item is made without regard to the criteria in paragraph 20 of that Opinion.

32. Some respondents asserted that an enterprise that discontinues the application of Statement 71 can justify continued recognition of assets and liabilities arising from the rate-making process because of judgments about the probability of their recovery from or payment to ratepayers. Those assertions were typically based on definitions of assets and liabilities in paragraphs 25 and 35 of FASB Concepts Statement No. 6, *Elements of Financial Statements,* which state:

> Assets are probable future economic benefits obtained or controlled by a particular entity as a result of past transactions or events.
>
> Liabilities are probable future sacrifices of economic benefits arising from present obligations of a particular entity to transfer assets or provide services to other entities in the future as a result of past transactions or events. [Footnote references omitted.]

33. Statement 71 recognizes that in certain circumstances the rate-making process provides a link between costs and revenues in one period and revenues in the future. When an enterprise meets the criteria for the application of Statement 71, the rate-making process can affect the recognition of assets and liabilities. The Board believes that continuing to recognize assets and liabilities based solely on judgments about the rate-making process is not appropriate when an enterprise ceases to meet the criteria for application of Statement 71. After an enterprise ceases to meet the criteria for application of Statement 71, it is in a position comparable to enterprises in a number of industries that are subject to regulation but do not apply Statement 71.

34. For enterprises that cease to meet the criteria for applying Statement 71 and continue to be subject to rate regulation, that regulation is similar to a contractual obligation to sell goods or services in the future at an established price or to other forms of price control. A contract that an enterprise in general believes is probable of generating higher than normal gross profits in the future does not provide a basis for the current recognition of an asset representing the anticipated "excess" gross profits related to that contract, nor does it provide a basis for deferring contract-related costs that would otherwise be charged to expense. Similarly, a contract that is probable of generating a lower than normal gross profit does not create a liability unless the contract meets the criteria of FASB Statement No. 5, *Accounting for Contingencies,* for accrual of a loss contingency.

35. This Statement does not provide detailed guidance for reaching judgments about whether application of Statement 71 should be discontinued. Similarly, Statement 71 does not provide detailed guidance for reaching judgments about whether it is appropriate to apply Statement 71. Because applicability of Statement 71 is and must remain a matter of judgment and because the objectives are clear, the Board decided that it was unnecessary to prescribe detailed guidance for reaching the judgments required by this Statement and by Statement 71.

36. Some respondents asked that this Statement define the term *costs* as it is used in the examples in paragraph 4. Some respondents argued it should be defined as "allowable costs" and other respondents argued it should be defined as "incurred costs." The term *costs* is used in paragraph 4 of this Statement consistent with its usage in paragraph 5 of Statement 71. As explained in paragraph 67 of the Basis for Conclusions to Statement 71, the term *costs* in paragraph 5 of Statement 71 is based on allowable costs.

Application of Overall Conclusions to Specific Items

37. The Board concluded that the approach required by this Statement would be easier to understand and implement with examples. Therefore, an appendix with examples is included.

38. The Exposure Draft included a reference to the use of estimates, averages, and computational shortcuts when implementing its provisions because of its requirement to adjust fixed assets to the amounts that would have been recorded had Statement 71 never been applied. This Statement requires significantly fewer adjustments to fixed assets than the approach in the Exposure Draft, and the Board concluded that the specific reference to the use of estimates, averages, and computational shortcuts was unnecessary.

39. Some respondents to the Exposure Draft disagreed with its application to "separable portions" of an enterprise's operation, and other respondents suggested that a separable portion of an enterprise should be no less than an enterprise's operations within a regulatory jurisdiction or a reportable segment as defined in FASB Statement No. 14, *Financial Reporting for Segments of a Business Enterprise.* Those respondents stated that discontinuing application of Statement 71 for a portion of an enterprise's operations or a portion of an enterprise's operations within a regulatory jurisdiction would not be meaningful and could be confusing to preparers and users of the financial statements. Other respondents agreed with discontinuing application of Statement 71 for separable portions of an enterprise's operations and indicated that this was consistent with the application of Statement 71. Paragraph 6 of Statement 71 states:

> If some of an enterprise's operations are regulated and meet the criteria of paragraph 5, this Statement shall be applied to only that portion of the enterprise's operations.

40. This Statement does not modify paragraph 6 of Statement 71. Statement 71 is applied to separable portions of an enterprise's operations, and therefore the discontinuation of application of Statement 71 should be applied to separable portions of an enterprise's operations. The separable portion may be an enterprise's operations within a regulatory jurisdiction or a smaller portion (such as a customer class within a regulatory jurisdiction), either of which could require the allocation of system-wide assets and liabilities.

41. This Statement does not modify FASB Statement No. 90, *Regulated Enterprises—Accounting for Abandonments and Disallowances of Plant Costs.* If the substance of the actions of the regulator for a separable portion of an enterprise's operations is an explicit, but indirect, disallowance of costs of a recently completed plant, that disallowance should be accounted for as prescribed by Statement 90. The application of Statement 71, as amended, is not optional. An enterprise's operations that meet the criteria for application of Statement 71 are required to be reported consistent with Statement 71, and an enterprise whose operations cease to meet the criteria for application of Statement 71 is required to discontinue application of Statement 71 as prescribed in this Statement.

42. This Statement requires that the carrying amounts of the plant, equipment, and inventory measured and recorded pursuant to Statement 71 not be adjusted unless those assets are impaired. Paragraph 7 of Statement 71 states:

> Authoritative accounting pronouncements that apply to enterprises in general also apply to regulated enterprises. However, enterprises subject to this Statement shall apply it instead of any conflicting provisions of standards in other authoritative pronouncements. [Footnote reference omitted.]

The carrying amounts of plant, equipment, and inventory for enterprises applying Statement 71 differ from those for enterprises in general only because of the allowance for funds used during construction, intercompany profit, and disallowances of costs of recently completed plants. If any other amounts that would not be includable in the carrying amounts of plant, equipment, or inventory by enterprises in general are included in or netted against the carrying amounts of plant, equipment, and inventory, those amounts should be separated from the carrying amounts of plant, equipment, and inventory and accounted for as prescribed in this Statement. For example, postconstruction operating costs that were capitalized pursuant to paragraph 9 of Statement 71 represent the effects of actions of a regulator regardless of their classification in the financial statements and should be accounted for as this Statement prescribes for the effects of actions of a regulator. Another example of the effect of actions of a regulator that would require adjustment is the cumulative difference, if any, between recorded depreciation and depreciation computed using a generally accepted method of depreciation.

43. Several respondents requested that this Statement address the accounting for reapplication of Statement 71 by an enterprise that had previously discontinued application of Statement 71 for all or a portion of its operations. The Board noted that the accounting for the initial application of Statement 71 has not been raised as an issue that needs to be addressed by the Board. In addition, some Board members believe that circumstances warranting reapplication of Statement 71 will occur rarely, if at all. The Board concluded that the accounting for the initial application or reapplication of Statement 71 is beyond the scope of this Statement.

44. Several respondents suggested that this Statement should require disclosures about the discontinuation of application of Statement 71, such as disclosing the reasons for the discontinuation and the portions of the enterprise's operations that do and do not apply Statement 71. In addition, for enterprises that discontinue application of Statement 71 but continue to be subject to rate regulation, some respondents suggested that the Statement require disclosure of the rate-making concepts used by the regulator and the factors that are considered in establishing rates and, to the extent that past events will be reflected in future prices, identify and quantify those regulatory actions.

45. The Board concluded that disclosure of the reasons for discontinuing application of Statement 71 and disclosure of the portion of an enterprise's operations for which the application of Statement 71 is being discontinued would provide useful information; therefore, this Statement requires disclosure of that information. The Board concluded that it would not be appropriate to require disclosure of the effects of regulation for enterprises that discontinue application of Statement 71 but continue to be subject to regulation without addressing disclosure requirements for enterprises that have never applied Statement 71 but are subject to regulation. However, the Board encourages disclo-

sures about the discontinuation of application of Statement 71 and the nature and effects of continuing regulation that would make the financial statements more informative and meaningful.

Effective Date and Transition

46. The Board considered whether this Statement should be applied retroactively to all enterprises that have previously discontinued application of Statement 71. The Board recognized that applying this Statement only to future discontinuations would diminish both comparability of financial statements among enterprises that have discontinued application of Statement 71 using different methods and consistency within an enterprise that reports discontinuations for portions of its operations in different periods using different methods. Although requiring restatement would increase comparability among companies discontinuing application of Statement 71 and consistency within a few enterprises that have previously discontinued the application of Statement 71 to a portion of their operations during fiscal years ending before December 15, 1988, the Board believes that those benefits do not justify the costs that would be incurred. Therefore, the Board decided that application of this Statement should be required for discontinuations occurring in annual periods ending after that date, with retroactive application to previously reported discontinuations permitted but not required. In no event should the interim or annual financial statements for periods that ended prior to the date of discontinuation of application of Statement 71 be restated.

47. Some respondents requested a delay of the effective date or a transition period to allow affected enterprises the time necessary to compute the effect of the discontinuation of application of Statement 71 pursuant to this Statement and, if necessary, time to resolve problems created by the accounting required by this Statement for loan indentures or other agreements. The Board believes that because plant, equipment, and inventory are not required to be restated for certain items as was required in the Exposure Draft, it would be rare that an enterprise would cease to meet the criteria for application of Statement 71 and would not know the accounting effect of the discontinuation. However, the Board concluded, primarily because this Statement is being issued late in the year in which it becomes effective, to allow for a delay in its required adoption.

Statement of Financial Accounting Standards No. 102
Statement of Cash Flows—Exemption of Certain Enterprises and Classification of Cash Flows from Certain Securities Acquired for Resale

an amendment of FASB Statement No. 95

STATUS

Issued: February 1989

Effective Date: For financial statements issued after February 28, 1989

Affects: Amends FAS 95, paragraphs 3, 15, 16(a), 16(b), 17(a), 17(b), 22(a), 23(a), 147, 148, and 149(a)

Affected by: Paragraph 8 and footnote 4 amended by FAS 115

SUMMARY

This Statement amends FASB Statement No. 95, *Statement of Cash Flows*, to exempt from the requirement to provide a statement of cash flows (a) defined benefit pension plans covered by FASB Statement No. 35, *Accounting and Reporting by Defined Benefit Pension Plans*, and certain other employee benefit plans and (b) highly liquid investment companies that meet specified conditions.

This Statement also requires that cash receipts and cash payments resulting from acquisitions and sales of (a) securities and other assets that are acquired specifically for resale and are carried at market value in a trading account and (b) loans that are acquired specifically for resale and are carried at market value or the lower of cost or market value be classified as operating cash flows in a statement of cash flows.

This Statement is effective for financial statements issued after February 28, 1989, with earlier application encouraged.

Statement of Financial Accounting Standards No. 102

Statement of Cash Flows—Exemption of Certain Enterprises and Classification of Cash Flows from Certain Securities Acquired for Resale

an amendment of FASB Statement No. 95

CONTENTS

INTRODUCTION

1. FASB Statement No. 95, *Statement of Cash Flows,* establishes standards for cash flow reporting and requires a statement of cash flows as part of a full set of financial statements for all business enterprises. Statement 95 supersedes APB Opinion No. 19, *Reporting Changes in Financial Position.*

2. FASB Statement No. 35, *Accounting and Reporting by Defined Benefit Pension Plans,* establishes specific financial reporting requirements for those plans and states that existing generally accepted accounting principles other than those discussed in that Statement may apply. The applicability of Statement 95 to defined benefit pension plans and other employee benefit plans is not specifically addressed by Statement 95.

3. Statement 95 acknowledges that information about the cash flows of certain investment companies may be less important than similar information for other enterprises, but the Board decided when that Statement was issued that investment companies should not be exempted from the requirement to provide a statement of cash flows because information about cash flows is relevant. Several representatives of investment companies requested that the Board reconsider the applicability of Statement 95 to those companies. Discussions with those representatives and others focused primarily on the usefulness of a statement of cash

flows for highly liquid investment companies with little or no debt.

4. Statement 95 requires business enterprises to present a statement of cash flows that classifies cash receipts and cash payments according to whether they result from operating, investing, or financing activities and provides a definition of each category. Statement 95 recognizes that certain cash receipts and cash payments may have aspects of more than one category of cash flows. For example, a cash payment may pertain to an item that, depending on the circumstances, could be either inventory or a productive asset. The Board was asked to address the appropriate classification of cash flows resulting from the active trading of securities in a trading account of a bank, broker and dealer in securities, or other enterprise.

STANDARDS OF FINANCIAL ACCOUNTING AND REPORTING

Exemptions from the Requirement to Provide a Statement of Cash Flows

5. A statement of cash flows is not required to be provided by a defined benefit pension plan that presents financial information in accordance with the provisions of Statement 35. Other employee benefit plans that present financial information similar to that required by Statement 35 (including

the presentation of plan investments at fair value) also are not required to provide a statement of cash flows. Employee benefit plans are encouraged to include a statement of cash flows with their annual financial statements when that statement would provide relevant information about the ability of the plan to meet future obligations (for example, when the plan invests in assets that are not highly liquid or obtains financing for investments).

6. Provided that the conditions in paragraph 7 are met, a statement of cash flows is not required to be provided by (a) an investment company that is subject to the registration and regulatory requirements of the Investment Company Act of 1940 (1940 Act), (b) an investment enterprise that has essentially the same characteristics as those subject to the 1940 Act, or (c) a common trust fund, variable annuity account, or similar fund maintained by a bank, insurance company, or other enterprise in its capacity as a trustee, administrator, or guardian for the collective investment and reinvestment of moneys.

7. For an investment enterprise specified in paragraph 6 to be exempt from the requirement to provide a statement of cash flows, all of the following conditions must be met:

a. During the period, substantially all of the enterprise's investments were highly liquid (for example, marketable securities and other assets for which a market is readily available).
b. Substantially all of the enterprise's investments are carried at market value.[1]
c. The enterprise had little or no debt, based on average debt outstanding[2] during the period, in relation to average total assets.
d. The enterprise provides a statement of changes in net assets.

Classification of Cash Flows from Acquisitions and Sales of Certain Securities and Other Assets

8. Banks, brokers and dealers in securities, and other enterprises may carry securities and other assets in a trading account.[3] Cash receipts and cash payments resulting from purchases and sales of securities and other assets shall be classified as operating cash flows if those assets are acquired specifically for resale and are carried at market value in a trading account.

9. Some loans are similar to securities in a trading account in that they are originated or purchased specifically for resale and are held for short periods of time. Cash receipts and cash payments resulting from acquisitions and sales of loans also shall be classified as operating cash flows if those loans are acquired specifically for resale and are carried at market value or at the lower of cost or market value.[4] Cash receipts resulting from sales of loans that were not specifically acquired for resale shall be classified as investing cash inflows. That is, if loans were acquired as investments, cash receipts from sales of those loans shall be classified as investing cash inflows regardless of a change in the purpose for holding those loans.

Amendments to Statement 95

10. Statement 95 is amended as follows:

a. The following footnote is added to the end of the first sentence of paragraph 3:

*A statement of cash flows is not required for defined benefit pension plans and certain other employee benefit plans or for certain investment companies as provided by FASB Statement No. 102, *Statement of Cash Flows—Exemption of Certain Enterprises and Classification of Cash Flows from Certain Securities Acquired for Resale.*

b. The following sentence is added to the end of paragraph 15:

Investing activities exclude acquiring and disposing of certain loans or other debt or equity instruments that are acquired specifically for resale, as discussed in Statement 102.

---

[1]Securities for which market value is determined using matrix pricing techniques, which are described in the AICPA Audit and Accounting Guide, *Audits of Investment Companies,* would meet this condition. Other securities for which market value is not readily determinable and for which fair value must be determined in good faith by the board of directors would not.

[2]For the purpose of determining average debt outstanding, obligations resulting from redemptions of shares by the enterprise, from unsettled purchases of securities or similar assets, or from covered options written generally may be excluded. However, any extension of credit by the seller that is not in accordance with standard industry practices for redeeming shares or for settling purchases of investments shall be included in average debt outstanding.

[3]Characteristics of trading account activities are described in FASB Statement No. 89, *Financial Reporting and Changing Prices,* and in the AICPA Industry Audit Guide, *Audits of Banks,* and Audit and Accounting Guide, *Audits of Brokers and Dealers in Securities.*

[4]Mortgage loans and mortgage-backed securities held for sale are required to be reported at the lower of cost or market value in accordance with FASB Statement No. 65, *Accounting for Certain Mortgage Banking Activities.*

c. The parenthetical comment in paragraphs 16(a) and 17(a) is superseded by the following:

(other than cash equivalents and certain debt instruments that are acquired specifically for resale)

d. The following parenthetical comment is added after the word *enterprises* in paragraphs 16(b) and 17(b):

(other than certain equity instruments carried in a trading account)

e. The following footnote is added after the word *goods* in paragraphs 22(a) and 23(a):

*The term *goods* includes certain loans and other debt and equity instruments of other enterprises that are acquired specifically for resale, as discussed in Statement 102.

f. The statement of cash flows and the reconciliation of net income to net cash provided by operating activities included in paragraph 147 of Example 3 of Appendix C is superseded by the statement of cash flows and the reconciliation of net income to net cash provided by operating activities included in paragraph 30 of Appendix B of this Statement. The statement of financial position and the statement of operations included in paragraph 148 and the transactions described in paragraph 149(a) of that example are superseded by the statement of financial position and the statement of operations included in paragraph 31 and the transactions described in paragraph 32 of Appendix B of this Statement.

Effective Date and Transition

11. This Statement is effective for financial statements issued after February 28, 1989. Earlier application is encouraged. Comparative amounts in financial statements for earlier periods shall be reclassified to comply with the requirements of this Statement.

This Statement was adopted by the affirmative votes of six members of the Financial Accounting Standards Board. Mr. Lauver dissented.

Mr. Lauver dissents from the issuance of this Statement because of the manner in which it exempts certain employee benefit plans and investment companies from the requirement to issue a statement of cash flows. Although it may be defensible to exempt certain enterprises from a requirement to issue a statement of cash flows, he believes that any exemption should be made by establishing criteria believed to indicate that a statement of cash flows provides little useful information to users and exempting all enterprises satisfying those criteria. He would not establish exemptions by selectively designating industries or types of businesses because that approach inevitably produces inequities and inconsistencies. For example, in the instances covered by this Statement, employee benefit plans that own illiquid assets and finance their investments in part with debt are exempted from issuing a statement of cash flows, but investment companies in a similar position are not exempted.

Members of the Financial Accounting Standards Board:

Dennis R. Beresford,	Raymond C. Lauver	A. Clarence Sampson
Chairman	James J. Leisenring	Robert J. Swieringa
Victor H. Brown	C. Arthur Northrop	

Statement of Cash Flows—Exemption of Certain Enterprises and Classification of Cash Flows from Certain Securities Acquired for Resale

FAS102

Appendix A

BACKGROUND INFORMATION AND BASIS FOR CONCLUSIONS

CONTENTS

Appendix A

BACKGROUND INFORMATION AND BASIS FOR CONCLUSIONS

Introduction

12. This appendix discusses factors deemed significant by members of the Board in reaching the conclusions in this Statement. It discusses reasons for accepting certain views and rejecting others. Individual Board members gave greater weight to some factors than to others. The Board concluded that it could reach an informed decision on the basis of existing information without a public hearing.

13. An FASB Exposure Draft, *Statement of Cash Flows—Exemption of Certain Enterprises and Classification of Cash Flows from Certain Securities Held for Resale,* was issued for public comment on November 30, 1988. The Board received 69 letters of comment in response to the Exposure Draft. Nearly all respondents supported the Board's conclusions, although some respondents addressed only specific issues. Some respondents suggested certain modifications that generally would clarify the Board's intent.

Employee Benefit Plans

14. The financial reporting requirements of defined benefit pension plans are addressed in Statement 35. Paragraph 6 of that Statement specifies that the annual financial statements of a plan shall include:

   a. A statement that includes information regarding the net assets available for benefits as of the end of the plan year
   b. A statement that includes information regarding the changes during the year in the net assets available for benefits

   c. Information regarding the actuarial present value of accumulated plan benefits as of either the beginning or end of the plan year
   d. Information regarding the effects, if significant, of certain factors affecting the year-to-year change in the actuarial present value of accumulated plan benefits. [Footnote reference omitted.]

Statement 35 also states that existing generally accepted accounting principles other than those discussed in that Statement may apply to the financial statements of defined benefit pension plans.

15. The Board concluded that paragraph 6 of Statement 35 presents a comprehensive list of the basic financial statements that defined benefit pension plans are required to provide, although additional financial information may be provided. Furthermore, the Board concluded that Statement 95 was not intended to modify the reporting requirements for those plans.

16. Other employee benefit plans that are not covered by Statement 35, such as health and welfare plans, may have characteristics similar to those of defined benefit pension plans and may present financial information similar to that required by Statement 35 (including the presentation of plan investments at fair value). The Board believes that those plans likewise should not be required to provide a statement of cash flows.

17. The Board does not prohibit the inclusion of a statement of cash flows with the annual financial statements of an employee benefit plan. In fact, the Board encourages plans to provide a statement of cash flows when that statement would provide relevant information about the ability of the plan to meet future obligations. For example, the Board believes that a statement of cash flows would pro-

vide relevant information about a plan's ability to meet future obligations when the plan invests in assets that are not highly liquid, such as real estate, or obtains financing for its investments.

Investment Companies

18. Before the issuance of Statement 95, the Board considered whether investment companies should be required to provide a statement of cash flows as part of a full set of financial statements. The Board recognized that information about the cash flows of certain investment companies may be less important than similar information for other enterprises, but the Board decided that information about cash flows is relevant and that investment companies should not be exempted from a requirement to provide a statement of cash flows.

19. While the Board continues to believe that information about cash flows is relevant for investment companies, the Board readdressed the need for highly liquid investment companies to provide a statement of cash flows under certain conditions. Highly liquid investment companies are those whose assets consist predominantly of cash, securities, and other assets for which a market is readily available. For example, open-end investment companies hold themselves out as being able to redeem their outstanding shares within seven days; therefore, they are required to maintain a portfolio of investments that enables them to fulfill that obligation.

20. For highly liquid investment companies that do not finance investments with debt, the Board concluded that the financial statements other than a statement of cash flows generally would provide sufficient information for users to assess the enterprises' liquidity, financial flexibility, profitability, and risk. However, for investment companies that invest in assets for which a market is not readily available or that finance investments with debt, the Board believes that a statement of cash flows would provide relevant information about the enterprises' investing and financing activities to assist users in those assessments.

21. Investment companies were not required to provide a statement of changes in financial position. Investment companies that are subject to the reporting requirements of the 1940 Act are required to provide a statement of changes in net assets. Net assets and changes in those net assets are relevant because net asset value per share is used by many investment companies to determine the price of shares redeemed and sold. Although the purpose and format of a statement of changes in net assets are different from those of a statement of cash flows, much of the information contained in those statements is similar. The Board concluded

that for investment companies that meet the conditions specified in paragraph 7, the cost of providing a statement of cash flows would exceed the benefits.

22. Certain investment enterprises may not be subject to the registration requirements of the 1940 Act either because the number of stockholders is limited or because they are otherwise exempted from the 1940 Act (for example, offshore funds, commodity pools, certain common trust funds of banks, or variable annuity accounts of life insurance companies). Because those investment enterprises have essentially the same characteristics as investment companies that are subject to the requirements of the 1940 Act, the Board concluded that the exemption also should apply to them provided they meet the conditions specified in paragraph 7.

Classification of Cash Flows from Acquisitions and Sales of Certain Securities and Other Assets

23. Statement 95 requires that cash flows be classified as investing, financing, or operating and provides a definition of each category. Paragraph 15 of Statement 95 defines investing activities to include:

> . . . making and collecting loans and acquiring and disposing of debt or equity instruments and property, plant, and equipment and other productive assets, that is, assets held for or used in the production of goods or services by the enterprise (other than materials that are part of the enterprise's inventory).

Operating activities include all transactions and other events that are not defined as investing or financing activities. Paragraph 21 of that Statement states that operating activities generally involve producing and delivering goods and providing services. Cash flows from operating activities are generally the cash effects of transactions and other events that enter into the determination of net income.

24. Paragraph 24 of Statement 95 recognizes that certain cash receipts and payments may have aspects of more than one category of cash flows. For example, a cash payment may pertain to an item that, depending on the circumstances, could be either inventory or a productive asset. Furthermore, paragraph 86 states that the three categories of operating, investing, and financing are not clearly mutually exclusive. For items at the margin, a reasonable case may be made for alternative classifications. Paragraph 87 notes that the Board recognizes that the most appropriate classification of items will not always be clear.

***Statement of Cash Flows—Exemption of Certain
Enterprises and Classification of Cash Flows
from Certain Securities Acquired for Resale***   **FAS102**

25. The definitions of operating and investing activities in Statement 95 provide flexibility for the appropriate classification of cash receipts and payments for assets that generally are productive assets but in certain cases may be inventory. For example, real estate generally is considered a productive asset, and a cash payment to purchase real estate generally is an investing cash outflow. However, if real estate is acquired by a real estate developer to be subdivided, improved, and sold in individual lots, then the cash payment to purchase that real estate would be classified as an operating cash flow because the real estate is acquired specifically for resale and is similar to inventory in other businesses.

26. For certain enterprises, purchases and sales of trading account assets have characteristics of both investing activities and operating activities. However, purchases and sales of debt and equity instruments of other enterprises are defined by Statement 95 as investing activities. The Board was asked to address the appropriate classification of cash flows from purchases and sales of securities in a trading account of a bank or a broker and dealer in securities. Because trading account assets are similar to inventory in other businesses in that they generally are acquired specifically for resale and are turned over very rapidly, the Board concluded that cash receipts and cash payments resulting from purchases and sales of securities and other assets that are acquired specifically for resale and are carried at market value in a trading account should be reported as operating cash flows.

27. Loans that are originated or purchased specifically for resale, are turned over rapidly, and are carried at market value or at the lower of cost or market value also are similar to inventory in other businesses. Therefore, the Board concluded that cash receipts and cash payments resulting from originations or purchases and sales of those loans also should be reported as operating cash flows.

28. The Board decided to require rather than permit cash flows from the activities described in paragraphs 26 and 27 to be classified as operating cash flows in order to achieve greater comparability among enterprises in classifying similar items.

29. When the Board addressed the issue of classification of cash flows resulting from the active trading of assets in a trading account, the Board also discussed whether additional net reporting of cash receipts and cash payments might be appropriate. The Board received several requests primarily from banks to reconsider the requirements of Statement 95 to report gross cash flows for various items for which they believe that the costs of accumulating the data exceed the benefits of the additional disclosures. Gross cash flows from trading activities were identified as particularly costly to accumulate. The Board concluded that the possibility of additional net reporting should be considered but that further research was required before a decision could be reached about the circumstances, if any, in which additional net reporting might be appropriate. That issue will be considered by the Board at a later date.

Appendix B

AMENDMENTS TO APPENDIX C OF STATEMENT 95

30. The statement of cash flows and the reconcilia-tion of net income to net cash provided by operating activities for Financial Institution, Inc., provided in paragraph 147 of Statement 95 are superseded by the following:

FINANCIAL INSTITUTION, INC.
STATEMENT OF CASH FLOWS
FOR THE YEAR ENDED DECEMBER 31, 19X1
Increase (Decrease) in Cash and Cash Equivalents

Cash flows from operating activities:		
Interest received	$ 5,350	
Fees and commissions received	1,320	
Proceeds from sales of trading securities	20,550	
Purchase of trading securities	(21,075)	
Financing revenue received under leases	60	
Interest paid	(3,925)	
Cash paid to suppliers and employees	(795)	
Income taxes paid	(471)	
Net cash provided by operating activities		$ 1,014
Cash flows from investing activities:		
Proceeds from sales of investment securities	2,225	
Purchase of investment securities	(4,000)	
Net increase in credit card receivables	(1,300)	
Net decrease in customer loans with maturities of 3 months or less	2,250	
Principal collected on longer term loans	26,550	
Longer term loans made to customers	(36,300)	
Purchase of assets to be leased	(1,500)	
Principal payments received under leases	107	
Capital expenditures	(450)	
Proceeds from sale of property, plant, and equipment	260	
Net cash used in investing activities		(12,158)
Cash flows from financing activities:		
Net increase in demand deposits, NOW accounts, and savings accounts	3,000	
Proceeds from sales of certificates of deposit	63,000	
Payments for maturing certificates of deposit	(61,000)	
Net increase in federal funds purchased	4,500	
Net increase in 90-day borrowings	50	
Proceeds from issuance of nonrecourse debt	600	
Principal payment on nonrecourse debt	(20)	
Proceeds from issuance of 6-month note	100	
Proceeds from issuance of long-term debt	1,000	
Repayment of long-term debt	(200)	
Proceeds from issuance of common stock	350	
Payments to acquire treasury stock	(175)	
Dividends paid	(240)	
Net cash provided by financing activities		10,965
Net decrease in cash and cash equivalents		(179)
Cash and cash equivalents at beginning of year		6,700
Cash and cash equivalents at end of year		$ 6,521

Statement of Cash Flows—Exemption of Certain Enterprises and Classification of Cash Flows from Certain Securities Acquired for Resale

FAS102

Reconciliation of net income to net cash provided by operating activities:

Net income		$1,056
Adjustments to reconcile net income to net cash provided by operating activities:		
Depreciation	$100	
Provision for probable credit losses	300	
Provision for deferred taxes	58	
Loss on sales of investment securities	75	
Gain on sale of equipment	(50)	
Increase in trading securities (including unrealized appreciation of $25)	(700)	
Increase in taxes payable	175	
Increase in interest receivable	(150)	
Increase in interest payable	75	
Decrease in fees and commissions receivable	20	
Increase in accrued expenses	55	
Total adjustments		(42)
Net cash provided by operating activities		$1,014

31. The statement of financial position and the statement of operations for Financial Institution, Inc., provided in paragraph 148 of Statement 95 are superseded by the following:

FINANCIAL INSTITUTION, INC.
STATEMENT OF FINANCIAL POSITION

	1/1/X1	12/31/X1	Change
Assets:			
Cash and due from banks	$ 4,400	$ 3,121	$ (1,279)
Federal funds sold	2,300	3,400	1,100
Total cash and cash equivalents	6,700	6,521	(179)
Trading securities	4,000	4,700	700
Investment securities	5,000	6,700	1,700
Credit card receivables	8,500	9,800	1,300
Loans	28,000	35,250	7,250
Allowance for credit losses	(800)	(850)	(50)
Interest receivable	600	750	150
Fees and commissions receivable	60	40	(20)
Investment in direct financing lease	–	421	421
Investment in leveraged lease	–	392	392
Property, plant, and equipment, net	525	665	140
Total assets	$52,585	$64,389	$11,804
Liabilities:			
Deposits	$38,000	$43,000	$ 5,000
Federal funds purchased	7,500	12,000	4,500
Short-term borrowings	1,200	1,350	150
Interest payable	350	425	75
Accrued expenses	275	330	55
Taxes payable	75	250	175
Dividends payable	–	80	80
Long-term debt	2,000	2,300	300
Deferred taxes	–	58	58
Total liabilities	49,400	59,793	10,393
Stockholders' equity:			
Common stock	1,250	2,100	850
Treasury stock	–	(175)	(175)
Retained earnings	1,935	2,671	736
Total stockholders' equity	3,185	4,596	1,411
Total liabilities and stockholders' equity	$52,585	$64,389	$11,804

Statement of Cash Flows—Exemption of Certain
Enterprises and Classification of Cash Flows **FAS102**
from Certain Securities Acquired for Resale

FINANCIAL INSTITUTION, INC.
STATEMENT OF OPERATIONS
FOR THE YEAR ENDED DECEMBER 31, 19X1

Revenues:
Interest income	$5,500	
Fees and commissions	1,300	
Net gain on sales of trading and investment securities	75	
Unrealized appreciation of trading securities	25	
Lease income	60	
Gain on sale of equipment	50	
Total revenues		$7,010

Expenses:
Interest expense	4,000	
Provision for probable credit losses	300	
Operating expenses	850	
Depreciation	100	
Total expenses		5,250
Income before income taxes		1,760
Provision for income taxes		704
Net income		$1,056

32. The transactions of Financial Institution, Inc., described in paragraph 149(a) of Statement 95 are superseded by the following:

Financial Institution sold trading securities with a carrying value of $20,400 for $20,550 and purchased trading securities for $21,075. Financial Institution recorded unrealized appreciation of trading securities of $25. Financial Institution also sold investment securities with a carrying value of $2,300 for $2,225 and purchased investment securities for $4,000.

(This page intentionally left blank.)

Statement of Financial Accounting Standards No. 103
Accounting for Income Taxes—Deferral of the Effective Date of FASB Statement No. 96

an amendment of FASB Statement No. 96

STATUS

Issued: December 1989

Effective Date: December 15, 1989

Affects: Amends FAS 96, paragraph 32
      Supersedes FAS 100

Affected by: Superseded by FAS 108 and FAS 109

(This page intentionally left blank.)

Statement of Financial Accounting Standards No. 104
Statement of Cash Flows—Net Reporting of Certain Cash Receipts and Cash Payments and Classification of Cash Flows from Hedging Transactions

an amendment of FASB Statement No. 95

STATUS

Issued: December 1989

Effective Date: For fiscal years ending after June 15, 1990

Affects: Amends FAS 95, paragraph 13
        Supersedes FAS 95, footnote 4

Affected by: No other pronouncements

SUMMARY

This Statement amends FASB Statement No. 95, *Statement of Cash Flows,* to permit banks, savings institutions, and credit unions to report in a statement of cash flows certain net cash receipts and cash payments for (a) deposits placed with other financial institutions and withdrawals of deposits, (b) time deposits accepted and repayments of deposits, and (c) loans made to customers and principal collections of loans.

This Statement also amends Statement 95 to permit cash flows resulting from futures contracts, forward contracts, option contracts, or swap contracts that are accounted for as hedges of identifiable transactions or events to be classified in the same category as the cash flows from the items being hedged provided that accounting policy is disclosed.

This Statement is effective for annual financial statements for fiscal years ending after June 15, 1990, with earlier application permitted. Separate early adoption of either the netting or hedging provisions is permitted. If the provisions of this Statement are elected, restatement or reclassification of comparative amounts in financial statements for earlier periods is required.

Statement of Financial Accounting Standards No. 104

Statement of Cash Flows—Net Reporting of Certain Cash Receipts and Cash Payments and Classification of Cash Flows from Hedging Transactions

an amendment of FASB Statement No. 95

CONTENTS

INTRODUCTION

Net Reporting of Certain Cash Receipts and Cash Payments

1. In FASB Statement No. 95, *Statement of Cash Flows,* the Board concluded that information about the gross amounts of cash receipts and cash payments during a period generally is more relevant than information about the net amounts of cash receipts and cash payments. However, for certain items, the net amount of cash receipts and cash payments may provide sufficient information. For example, Statement 95 provides that gross cash flows need not be reported for demand deposits of a bank or for investments, loans receivable, and debt of any enterprise if the original maturity of the asset or liability is three months or less.

2. The Board received several requests to reconsider the requirements of Statement 95 as they relate to banks. Those requests included assertions that the requirements of Statement 95 produce data that are of little or no value and are difficult and costly to accumulate. In particular, because deposit and lending activities generally involve high volumes of transactions, some assert that the cost incurred by the preparer to report gross cash flow information exceeds the benefit to users of the statement of cash flows.

3. This Statement modifies Statement 95 so that banks, savings institutions, and credit unions are not required to report gross amounts of cash receipts and cash payments for (a) deposits placed with other financial institutions and withdrawals of deposits, (b) time deposits accepted and repayments of deposits, and (c) loans made to customers and principal collections of loans. When those enterprises constitute part of a consolidated enterprise, net amounts of cash receipts and cash payments for deposit or lending activities of those enterprises shall be reported separate from gross amounts of cash receipts and cash payments for other investing and financing activities of the consolidated enterprise.

Classification of Cash Flows from Hedging Transactions

4. The Board received requests from various enterprises to reconsider the classification of cash flows from an item that is intended as a hedge of another item. Those requests generally focused on cash flows from a futures contract or forward contract that is accounted for as a hedge of an inventory transaction.

5. Footnote 4 of Statement 95 specified the classification of cash flows from a hedging instrument as follows:

> Each cash receipt or payment is to be classified according to its nature without regard to whether it stems from an item intended as a hedge of another item. For example, the

Statement of Cash Flows—Net Reporting of Certain
Cash Receipts and Cash Payments and Classification   **FAS104**
of Cash Flows from Hedging Transactions

proceeds of a borrowing are a financing cash inflow whether or not the debt is intended as a hedge of an investment, and the purchase or sale of a futures contract is an investing activity without regard to whether the contract is intended as a hedge of a firm commitment to purchase inventory.

6. This Statement modifies Statement 95 to permit cash flows resulting from futures contracts, forward contracts, option contracts, or swap contracts that are accounted for as hedges of identifiable transactions or events (for example, a cash payment from a futures contract that hedges a purchase or sale of inventory), including anticipatory hedges, to be classified in the same category as the cash flows from the items being hedged provided that accounting policy is disclosed. If for any reason hedge accounting for an instrument that hedges an identifiable transaction or event is discontinued, then any cash flows subsequent to the date of discontinuance shall be classified consistent with the nature of the instrument.

STANDARDS OF FINANCIAL ACCOUNTING AND REPORTING

Amendments to Statement 95

7. Statement 95 is amended as follows:

a. The following paragraph is added after paragraph 13:

Banks, savings institutions, and credit unions are not required to report gross amounts of cash receipts and cash payments for (a) deposits placed with other financial institutions and withdrawals of deposits, (b) time deposits accepted and repayments of deposits, and (c) loans made to customers and principal collections of loans. When those enterprises constitute part of a consolidated enterprise, net amounts of cash receipts and cash payments for deposit or lending activities of those enterprises shall be reported separate from gross amounts of cash receipts and cash payments for other investing and financing activities of the consolidated enterprise, including those of a subsidiary of a bank, savings institution, or credit union that is not itself a bank, savings institution, or credit union.

b. Footnote 4 is superseded by the following:

Generally, each cash receipt or payment is to be classified according to its nature without regard to whether it stems from an item intended as a hedge of another item. For example, the

proceeds of a borrowing are a financing cash inflow even though the debt is intended as a hedge of an investment, and the purchase or sale of a futures contract is an investing activity even though the contract is intended as a hedge of a firm commitment to purchase inventory. However, cash flows from futures contracts, forward contracts, option contracts, or swap contracts that are accounted for as hedges of identifiable transactions or events (for example, a cash payment from a futures contract that hedges a purchase or sale of inventory), including anticipatory hedges, may be classified in the same category as the cash flows from the items being hedged provided that accounting policy is disclosed. If for any reason hedge accounting for an instrument that hedges an identifiable transaction or event is discontinued, then any cash flows subsequent to the date of discontinuance shall be classified consistent with the nature of the instrument.

Effective Date and Transition

8. The provisions of this Statement are effective for annual financial statements for fiscal years ending after June 15, 1990, with earlier application permitted. Separate early adoption of either paragraph 7(a) or paragraph 7(b) is permitted. If the provisions of this Statement are elected, restatement or reclassification of comparative amounts in financial statements for earlier periods is required.

This Statement was adopted by the affirmative votes of five members of the Financial Accounting Standards Board. Messrs. Lauver and Swieringa dissented.

Messrs. Lauver and Swieringa dissent from the provision of this Statement that permits banks, savings institutions, and credit unions to report net cash receipts and cash payments for certain deposit and lending activities (paragraph 7(a) of this Statement). They continue to support the conclusion in paragraph 11 of Statement 95 that "generally, information about the gross amounts of cash receipts and cash payments during a period is more relevant than information about the net amounts of cash receipts and payments." Statement 95's permitted use of the indirect method is inconsistent with that conclusion because major classes of gross operating cash flows are not required to be reported separately. That permitted exception is now used to justify reporting net cash flows for certain investing and financing activities.

It is asserted that gross cash flow amounts for certain deposit and lending activities may be no more relevant than net cash flow amounts. Messrs. Lauver and Swieringa do not believe that that assertion is supportable. Consider, for example, one bank that adopted Statement 95 in 1988 and reported gross cash payments for loans originated or acquired of $14.9 billion, $10.8 billion, and $8.8 billion for 1988, 1987, and 1986, respectively. That bank also reported gross cash receipts for principal collected on loans of $14.3 billion, $10.4 billion, and $8.1 billion, respectively. Those gross cash flow amounts indicate a compound annual growth in those loan activities of over 30 percent over the 2-year period. Reporting gross amounts for lending activities provides information about events that occurred during a period that is not provided by net cash flows for those activities and is not provided elsewhere in the financial statements.

Moreover, Messrs. Lauver and Swieringa believe that reporting gross cash flow amounts is no less useful for banks, savings institutions, and credit unions than for finance companies, insurance companies, and other financial intermediaries. Paragraph 7(a) permits different cash flow reporting for enterprises that engage in essentially identical lending activities. Paragraph 7(a) also permits a consolidated enterprise to report net cash flows for the lending activities of its bank and savings institution subsidiaries even though it is required to report gross cash flows for the essentially identical lending activities of its finance, leasing, and insurance subsidiaries. Because paragraph 7(a) distinguishes among enterprises that engage in essentially identical lending transactions, Messrs. Lauver and Swieringa believe that exemption is inconsistent with the Board's stated mission to develop "neutral standards that result in accounting for similar transactions and circumstances similarly."

The Board's justification for the exemption provided to banks, savings institutions, and credit unions is that the costs of accumulating and reporting gross cash flow amounts are perceived to be larger for those enterprises than for finance companies, insurance companies, and other financial intermediaries that already voluntarily incur many of those costs as part of their reporting systems. The observation that "little incremental cost is required to develop gross cash flow information" by finance companies does not take into consideration the costs that those companies have already incurred to implement data-gathering systems that can be used to accumulate gross cash flow amounts. Messrs. Lauver and Swieringa believe that if cost-benefit judgments are to be used to justify an exemption, it is important to measure and consider all costs that are attributable to meeting a reporting requirement assuming equivalent data-gathering systems have been installed. Otherwise, individual enterprises or industries that have already installed those systems will be subjected to a reporting requirement, and enterprises or industries that have not already installed those systems will be exempted.

Mr. Lauver dissents from the provision of this Statement that permits classification of cash flows from certain hedging instruments in the same category as the cash flows from the items being hedged (paragraph 7(b) of this Statement). He believes that alternative does not enhance the objective of a statement of cash flows but has the objective of establishing net cash flow from operating activities as an alternative performance indicator, an objective that he believes is undesirable. Hedge accounting is an accounting technique whose objective is the reporting of entity performance. It is an optional accounting technique that associates two separate economic transactions, which in the aggregate are expected to mitigate the risk to the entity of either one alone, for the purpose of permitting the results of the two transactions to be reported in the statement of operations of a single fiscal period. In that way any gain on one transaction will counteract an anticipated loss on the other and vice versa.

Statement 95 states that the primary purpose of a statement of cash flows is to provide relevant information about cash receipts and cash payments of an enterprise during a period. Mr. Lauver finds it difficult to see how this purpose is enhanced, for example, by permitting cash flows from a futures contract for gold, an optional transaction, to be classified in the same category as the cash flows from the operation of a gold mine when hedge accounting is optionally elected. He believes that the ongoing activity of operating a mine and the optional, occasional entry of a position in a futures market based on anticipated future prices are not integral; that conclusion is especially clear because they are only regarded as being related when an accounting election is made. He believes that the objective of reporting cash flows should not be confused with the objective of reporting entity performance and that hedge accounting should not be used as a basis for establishing standards for providing a statement of cash flows whatever its merits for use in the statement of operations.

Further, Mr. Lauver believes, independent of the foregoing, that interest rate swap contracts should not be included in paragraph 7(b). He believes that when the objective of those contracts is to hedge net interest rate spreads, they do not hedge an identifiable transaction or event, and when the objective is that expressed in the last sentence of paragraph 40, the conclusion therein is inconsistent with paragraph 7(b) because that conclusion is not conditioned on the existence of a hedge.

Statement of Cash Flows—Net Reporting of Certain Cash Receipts and Cash Payments and Classification of Cash Flows from Hedging Transactions

FAS104

Appendix

BACKGROUND INFORMATION AND BASIS FOR CONCLUSIONS

CONTENTS

Appendix

BACKGROUND INFORMATION AND BASIS FOR CONCLUSIONS

Introduction

9. This appendix summarizes considerations that were deemed significant by members of the Board in reaching the conclusions in this Statement. It includes reasons for accepting certain views and rejecting others. Individual Board members gave greater weight to some factors than to others.

10. In response to requests that additional net reporting of cash receipts and cash payments be permitted under FASB Statement No. 95, *Statement of Cash Flows,* the Exposure Draft leading to FASB Statement No. 102, *Statement of Cash Flows—Exemption of Certain Enterprises and Classification of Cash Flows from Certain Securities Acquired for Resale,* invited interested parties to submit information about the circumstances in which additional net reporting might be appropriate. Requests for additional net reporting of cash flows focused generally on the banking industry and specifically on (a) deposits placed with banks, (b) deposits taken, (c) loans to customers, and (d) investment securities. There also were requests that the Board reexamine the classification requirement for cash flows resulting from an instrument that is intended as a hedge of another item. This Statement responds to those requests.

11. An FASB Exposure Draft, *Statement of Cash Flows—Net Reporting of Certain Cash Receipts and Cash Payments and Classification of Cash Flows from Hedging Transactions,* was issued for public comment on July 25, 1989. The Board received 112 letters of comment in response to the Exposure Draft. The Board concluded that it could reach an informed decision on the basis of existing information without a public hearing.

Net Reporting of Certain Cash Receipts and Cash Payments

12. In Statement 95, the Board concluded that information about gross amounts of cash receipts and cash payments during a period generally is more relevant than information about net amounts of cash receipts and cash payments. However, paragraph 76 of Statement 95 acknowledges that in certain circumstances, information about both cash receipts and cash payments may be no more relevant than information about only the net change.

13. Specifically, Statement 95 permits the reporting of net cash flows for (a) cash equivalents, (b) operating activities when the indirect method is used to report cash flows, (c) items in which the enterprise is substantially holding or disbursing cash on behalf of its customers, such as demand deposits of a bank and customer accounts payable of a broker-dealer, and (d) items for which the turnover is quick, the amounts are large, and the maturities are short. However, (d) above is limited to investments (other than cash equivalents), loans receivable, and debt providing that the original maturity of the asset or liability is three months or less.

14. The Exposure Draft proposed to amend Statement 95 to permit banks, savings institutions, and credit unions to report net cash flows for certain deposit and lending activities. Most respondents agreed with that proposal and contended that the requirements of Statement 95 for reporting cash flows for deposit and lending activities are costly for those enterprises to apply and that information about the gross cash flows for those activities is not useful. Representatives of the banking industry asserted that banks have had to spend an inappropriate amount of time and money to comply with the requirements for reporting cash flow information and that the additional costs include not only start-up costs or costs of modifying systems to adopt the standard but also ongoing costs of periodic reporting.

15. The Board concluded that for a bank, savings institution, or credit union information about gross cash flows for certain activities may be more difficult and costly to provide than for other enterprises, and the usefulness of this information may be questionable. The Board noted that major banking activities, such as deposit taking and lending, are required to be reported as investing or financing activities, while major activities of other enterprises, such as purchasing and selling goods and services, are reported as operating activities. Enterprises that report cash flows from operating activities using the indirect method are not required to report gross amounts of cash flows from those transactions. As noted in paragraph 109 of Statement 95, preparers of financial statements said that it would be costly for their enterprises to report gross operating cash receipts and cash payments and that they do not presently collect information in a manner that would allow them to determine amounts such as cash received from customers or cash paid to suppliers directly from their accounting systems. The Board gave particular consideration to that factor in deciding whether to permit use of the indirect method.

16. In addition, gross amounts of cash flows for certain banking activities may be difficult and costly to accumulate because of numerous noncash transactions. To report cash receipts and cash payments in a statement of cash flows, transactions that do not involve either a cash receipt or a cash payment must be eliminated from any totals. For example, when a loan is renewed or its terms are otherwise modified, the accounting records may indicate that the loan is repaid and a new loan is made. However, that transaction does not involve a cash flow and should not be reported in the statement of cash flows. The amount of effort currently required to separate cash transactions from noncash transactions is compounded by the high volume of transactions.

17. In determining the relevance of reporting gross cash flows, the Board considered comments from various users of banks' financial statements. Those users included financial analysts and individuals involved in mergers and acquisitions of financial institutions. While some users noted that a statement of cash flows for a bank may be important, particularly when determining whether an acquisition is economically sound, they generally agreed that the value of certain historical gross cash flow information is limited. Information about gross cash flows may provide a starting point or reference, but other information would be more relevant for analyzing liquidity or estimating future cash flows.

18. The high volume of transactions common to banks results in reporting gross amounts of cash flows that are large in relation to other cash flows. For example, gross cash flows pertaining to time deposits reported in the statement of cash flows of one major bank totaled more than 600 times the year-end balance of cash and cash equivalents. Banks generally have asserted that reporting gross cash flows of that magnitude tends to obscure more relevant data that may be included in the statement of cash flows. The Board generally believes that the size of a gross cash flow amount does not affect its relevance provided that amount is fairly reported.

19. Comparability of certain gross cash flow amounts among banks may be limited. Although Statement 95 permits the reporting of net cash flows when the original maturity of an asset or liability is three months or less, for practical reasons some enterprises have chosen to report gross cash flows for all such items rather than to separate them into those that qualify for net reporting and those that do not. In effect, gross cash flows and net cash flows may be reported differently, resulting in a lack of comparability.

20. Comparability also may be affected by internal accounting procedures because banks, savings institutions, and credit unions have the ability to create a reported cash flow through a debit or credit to a customer's demand deposit account. For example, if a customer rolls over a certificate of deposit upon maturity, a bank can record that transaction with or without making an entry to the customer's demand deposit account (that is, the bank may or may not debit and credit the demand deposit account), yet by definition one procedure results in a reported cash flow and the other does not. Thus, a bank that debits and credits a customer's demand deposit account when a loan or a certificate of deposit is renewed would report higher gross cash flow amounts relative to a bank that does not.

Statement of Cash Flows—Net Reporting of Certain
Cash Receipts and Cash Payments and Classification FAS104
of Cash Flows from Hedging Transactions

21. This Statement restricts the net reporting of lending activities to loans made to customers and to principal collections of loans. The Board believes that permitting net reporting of cash flows for all lending activities of banks would result in the loss of certain relevant gross cash flow information. For example, information about cash payments for purchases of loan portfolios or cash receipts from sales of loan portfolios provides relevant information about a bank's activities.[1] Furthermore, the Board believes that reporting gross cash flows for purchases or sales of loan portfolios should not be as difficult or costly as reporting gross cash flows for loans made or principal collections of loans. Purchases and sales of loan portfolios generally occur less frequently and are more centrally controlled. As a result, the Board concluded that net reporting of cash flows for lending activities of banks should be limited to cash payments for loans made to customers and principal collections of loans.

22. Some respondents stated that the Exposure Draft was not clear about whether a bank would be permitted to report net cash flows for principal collections attributable to purchased loans or for loans made to customers if those loans are subsequently sold. The amendment to Statement 95 in paragraph 7(a) of this Statement has been revised to clarify that net reporting of inflows of principal collections from purchased and originated loans and outflows for loan originations to customers irrespective of whether those loans are subsequently sold is permitted. (Refer to footnote 1.)

23. Statement 95 precludes reporting net cash flows for purchases and sales or maturities of investment securities. Some respondents to the Exposure Draft requested that the Board allow banks to classify cash flows from investment securities as operating activities or otherwise allow net reporting of those cash flows. However, investing in securities is not an activity that is unique to banks; similar activities occur in many other enterprises. These activities have been defined by Statement 95 as investing activities. The Board concluded that the cost and difficulty of reporting gross cash flow information for investment security transactions are less than for deposit and lending activities. Generally, investment activities are more centralized within the enterprise, the volume of transactions is smaller, and noncash transactions are less prevalent. Gross cash flow amounts may be useful because those amounts may enable users to assess investment portfolio turnover or to observe changes in an enterprise's investment strategies. The Board concluded that the benefit from reporting those amounts generally would exceed the cost.

24. Based on the factors discussed in paragraphs 14-20, the Board concluded that the cost for a bank, savings institution, or credit union to report gross amounts of cash receipts and cash payments for certain deposit and lending activities generally would exceed the benefit to users of the statement of cash flows. In response to comments, the Board also considered whether to permit finance companies, insurance companies, and other financial intermediaries to report net cash flows for their lending activities. A significant difference between those enterprises and banks, savings institutions, and credit unions is that generally finance companies, insurance companies, and other financial intermediaries cannot create reported cash flows by debiting and crediting customers' demand deposit accounts as discussed in paragraph 20. In addition, most finance companies presently accumulate loan origination or loan volume statistics for operating or other internal purposes. Accordingly, little incremental cost is required to develop gross cash flow information for external reporting. Because insurance companies generally do not engage in lending activities to the extent of banks, savings institutions, and credit unions, reporting gross cash flows for their lending activities should not be as costly. Thus, the Board concluded that for enterprises other than banks, savings institutions, and credit unions, the cost of reporting gross cash flows for lending activities generally would not exceed the benefit.

25. Some respondents requested that the Board define the transactions for which reporting net cash flows might be appropriate and allow that reporting for all enterprises that have those transactions. The Board concluded that while similar transactions generally should be accorded similar accounting treatment, in this circumstance cost-benefit considerations support different reporting based on the type of entity confronted with the transaction.

26. Consolidated enterprises frequently are engaged in various businesses in different industries. For example, a consolidated enterprise may include an industrial company, a finance company, a savings institution, and a leasing company. The Exposure Draft proposed that net cash flows may be reported for the specified activities of only a bank, savings institution, or credit union and not for those activities elsewhere within the consolidated enterprise. For example, net cash flow reporting of loans made to customers and principal collections of loans would not be permitted for a

---

[1]Statement 102, paragraph 9, specifies the reporting in a statement of cash flows for those loans acquired specifically for resale and carried at market value or at the lower of cost or market value.

finance company or leasing subsidiary of a bank, savings institution, or credit union. Furthermore, net cash flow amounts for deposit or lending activities of a subsidiary that is a bank or a savings institution should be reported separate from gross cash flow amounts for other investing and financing activities of the consolidated enterprise.

27. Some respondents to the Exposure Draft requested that the Board extend the net reporting of cash flows for deposit or lending activities to all similar activities within a consolidated reporting entity. In particular, they suggested that subsidiaries engaged in bank-related activities should be allowed to report on a basis consistent with that of a bank parent; otherwise, the financial statements would be inconsistent and confusing to users. However, bank-related subsidiaries often apply generally accepted accounting principles that differ from those of a bank subsidiary included in a consolidated group. For example, a bank may carry its investment securities at amortized cost, a broker-dealer subsidiary may carry its investment securities at market, and a venture capital subsidiary may carry its investment securities at fair value as determined by its board of directors. The Board noted that subsidiaries of a consolidated group often apply different, yet appropriate, accounting principles for similar transactions.

28. In response to requests by some respondents, the Board also considered whether the criteria for classifying cash flows should be modified to require that certain deposit and lending activities now classified as investing or financing activities be classified as operating activities. Although deposit and lending activities may be a bank's principal activities, they are not operating activities as described in Statement 95. Cash flows from operating activities include cash receipts and cash payments for purchases and sales of goods and services (inventory transactions), returns on investments, and all other cash receipts and payments not specifically defined as investing or financing activities.

29. The Board believes that a bank's deposit and lending activities are not analogous to inventory transactions in other business enterprises but are more analogous to the issuance of bonds by those enterprises to finance the construction of a new plant or the acquisition of a business. Similarly, gathering deposits is a financing activity. Cash received from customers is fungible and is commingled with the bank's other funds. Those deposits are available for a variety of purposes—to purchase trading or investment securities, to make loans, to pay operating expenses, or to redeem debt. Although deposit and lending activities may be a bank's principal activities, the Board believes

that they are appropriately classified as financing or investing activities.

Classification of Cash Flows from Hedging Transactions

30. Prior to the issuance of Statement 95, the Board addressed the classification of cash flows resulting from an instrument that is intended as a hedge of another item. The Board concluded that the cash flows from a hedging instrument should always be classified according to the nature of that instrument rather than in the same category as the cash flows of the item being hedged. The Board believed that the purchase or sale of a hedging instrument, such as a futures contract or a forward contract, is an investing activity. The Board also believed that implementation of an approach that classified the cash flows from a hedging instrument in the same category as the cash flows of the item being hedged would be more difficult and would require enterprises to maintain additional records.

31. After Statement 95 was issued, the Board received several inquiries about that classification requirement. Enterprises were particularly concerned about classifying cash flows from futures contracts or forward contracts that are accounted for as hedges of inventory transactions in a manner different from the cash flows from the purchase or sale of inventory. They indicated that the hedging transaction is integral to the inventory transaction and that the decision to purchase or sell futures contracts with the sole objective of reducing exposure to inventory price increases, establishing a profit floor, or locking in a gross margin is an operating decision by the enterprise to reduce the risks associated with its normal commercial operations of buying and selling goods. They urged the Board to allow cash flows from those types of hedges to be classified as operating cash flows and not as investing cash flows. They view that activity as being substantially different from an enterprise's typical investing activities. Some asserted that less effort would be required to classify the cash flows in the same category as the hedged item.

32. The Board readdressed the classification of cash flows from hedging instruments and reviewed examples from enterprises that engage in extensive hedging activities, primarily purchases or sales of futures contracts, related to their inventory transactions. The Board also considered foreign currency forward contracts related to a commitment to purchase or sell inventory or to a borrowing denominated in a foreign currency.

33. The Exposure Draft for this Statement proposed that cash flows from a futures contract, forward contract, or option contract that is accounted

Statement of Cash Flows—Net Reporting of Certain
Cash Receipts and Cash Payments and Classification   **FAS104**
of Cash Flows from Hedging Transactions

for as a hedge of an identifiable transaction or event be classified in the same category as the cash flows from the item being hedged.

34. The majority of the respondents to the Exposure Draft agreed that the cash flows of a hedging instrument that is accounted for as a hedge of an identifiable transaction or event should be classified in the same category as the cash flows from the item being hedged. They stated that a contract designed to lock in the future cost of a commodity is substantially different from an investment transaction. The objective of the hedging contract is to reduce the risk of price fluctuations and not to realize a profit. They asserted that the hedging contract is an integral part of the transaction and that reporting the cash flows of the hedge in the same category as the item being hedged would result in a more meaningful and understandable presentation.

35. However, some respondents opposed classifying cash flows from hedging instruments in the same category as the cash flows from the items being hedged. They cited increased cost in linking the two transactions together and commented that the hedging of a transaction is not a single economic event but two indirectly related transactions.

36. The Board believes that while generally each cash receipt or payment should be classified consistent with its nature, in some circumstances it may be appropriate to classify the cash flows from a hedging instrument in the same category as the cash flows from the item being hedged. For example, an enterprise may purchase a futures contract for the sole purpose of reducing exposure to increases in the price of a planned inventory purchase. The purchase of the hedging instrument may be considered integral to the subsequent purchase of the inventory. For this and similar instances when the hedging instrument is considered integral to the underlying transaction and is accounted for as a hedge, the Board believes that it may be appropriate to link the cash flows. The Board concluded that cash flows from certain contracts that are accounted for as hedges of identifiable transactions or events should be permitted to be classified in the same category as the cash flows from the items being hedged provided that accounting policy is disclosed. Changes in that policy are accounting changes to be reported in accordance with APB Opinion No. 20, *Accounting Changes.*

37. Hedge accounting reports gains or losses on the hedging instrument in the same period as the offsetting gains or losses of the item hedged. However, the cash flows from the hedging instrument may occur in a period different from the cash flows of the item hedged regardless of the amount of gain or loss that is hedged in a given year. In addition, a hedging instrument may be accounted for as a hedge for only a portion of the time that it is outstanding. Requiring the cash flows of an instrument designated as a hedge for a specified period to be linked with the item being hedged could entail significant costs. The Board is concerned that a requirement to classify the cash flows from a hedging instrument in the same category as the item being hedged may be difficult and costly.

38. For some hedging transactions, the cash flows cannot clearly be classified in the same category as the cash flows from the item being hedged. For example, an enterprise may hedge a net investment in a foreign operation with a borrowing that is denominated in the same currency as the net investment being hedged. Accounting for the borrowing as a hedge does not change the basic nature of the transaction; that is, it is still a borrowing. Furthermore, the cash flows from that foreign operation may include some cash flows that are properly classified as operating activities, some as investing activities, and some as financing activities. Accordingly, the cash receipts and payments from that borrowing cannot be identified with any specific cash flows from that operation and should be classified as financing activities.

39. Several respondents to the Exposure Draft suggested that the amendment to Statement 95 should encompass cash flows from hedging instruments other than futures contracts, forward contracts, and option contracts. Some requested that the amendment include cash flows from any instrument that would be considered a hedge of another transaction or event, while others specified that only cash flows from those instruments that qualify as hedges under current generally accepted accounting principles should be included. A few commented that the amendment should include cash flows from hedging instruments that may evolve in the future, and others requested that the Board clarify whether cash flows from swap contracts would be included.

40. The Board concluded that cash flows from swap contracts should be included within the scope of this Statement. Paragraph 17 of FASB Statement No. 52, *Foreign Currency Translation,* indicates that currency swaps are, in substance, essentially the same as forward contracts and should be accounted for the same as forward contracts. The Board also concluded that cash flows from an interest rate swap intended to effectively convert the interest rate of an asset or liability from variable to fixed or fixed to variable may be classified as operating cash flows consistent with the interest cash flows relating to the underlying asset or liability.

41. The Board believes the scope of this Statement should not be extended beyond the instruments named and conditions specified in paragraph 7(b). Otherwise, some may infer that the Board would endorse hedge accounting for any instrument that could be considered to reduce exposure to price or interest rate risk. This Statement does not address hedge accounting in the statement of financial position or the statement of operations. The Board is addressing the broader issues of hedge accounting as part of its project on financial instruments and off-balance-sheet financing.

Effective Date and Transition

42. The Exposure Draft would have been effective for annual financial statements for fiscal years ending after December 15, 1989, and would have required comparative amounts in financial statements for earlier periods to be reclassified. Because this Statement permits additional net reporting of certain cash flows, most of those responding to the Exposure Draft encouraged the Board to adopt the early effective date and commented that it would reduce cost and effort necessary to provide the information required to prepare the statement of cash flows. However, some requested that the Board delay the effective date to provide preparers of financial statements additional time to accumulate necessary information to modify the classification of cash flows from certain hedging transactions. The Board concluded, primarily because this Statement is being issued late in the year, to delay the effective date,

while allowing early adoption of either or both of the major provisions.

43. Some respondents suggested that reclassification of cash flows from hedging transactions for earlier periods should not be required. They indicated that the cost of reclassifying could exceed the benefits of additional comparability and that some enterprises may not have systems in place to accumulate the necessary information. Many of the concerns regarding requiring reclassification were in the context of an early implementation date and a requirement to modify the classification of cash flows from certain hedging transactions. Many of the respondents who agreed with the proposal to require consistent classification of cash flows from hedging transactions said that it would not be costly to report in that manner because their accounting records already link those transactions together.

44. Because modification of the classification of cash flows from certain hedging transactions is permitted and not required, the Board believes that when the option is elected, hedging cash flows for earlier periods should be reclassified to improve comparability. Also, hedging instruments and the items being hedged are linked for accounting purposes, and enterprises would have had to track them together for statement of financial position and statement of operations purposes. In addition, the Board believes that banks, savings institutions, and credit unions can restate without difficulty cash flows for the deposit and lending activities that this Statement allows to be reported net.

Statement of Financial Accounting Standards No. 105 Disclosure of Information about Financial Instruments with Off-Balance-Sheet Risk and Financial Instruments with Concentrations of Credit Risk

STATUS

Issued: March 1990

Effective Date: For fiscal years ending after June 15, 1990

Affects: Amends FAS 77, paragraph 9

Affected by: Paragraph 6 and footnotes 2 and 3 amended by FAS 107
    Paragraph 14(c) amended by FAS 111 and FAS 123
    Paragraph 14(e) superseded by FAS 125
    Paragraphs 17 and 18 and footnote 12 amended by FAS 119

Other Interpretive Pronouncement: FIN 39

Other Interpretive Release: FASB Special Report, *Illustrations of Financial Instrument Disclosures*

Issues Discussed by FASB Emerging Issues Task Force (EITF)

Affects: Partially resolves EITF Issue No. 84-23

Interpreted by: Paragraphs 20 and 22 interpreted by EITF Topic No. D-22

Related Issues: No EITF Issues

SUMMARY

This Statement establishes requirements for all entities to disclose information principally about financial instruments with off-balance-sheet risk of accounting loss. It is the product of the first phase on disclosure of information about financial instruments. This first phase focuses on information about the extent, nature, and terms of financial instruments with off-balance-sheet credit or market risk and about concentrations of credit risk for *all* financial instruments. Subsequent phases will consider disclosure of other information about financial instruments. The disclosure phases are interim steps in the Board's project on financial instruments and off-balance-sheet financing. Recognition and measurement issues are currently being considered in other phases of the project.

This Statement extends present disclosure practices of some entities for some financial instruments by requiring all entities to disclose the following information about financial instruments with off-balance-sheet risk of accounting loss:

- The face, contract, or notional principal amount
- The nature and terms of the instruments and a discussion of their credit and market risk, cash requirements, and related accounting policies

- The *accounting loss* the entity would incur if any party to the financial instrument failed completely to perform according to the terms of the contract and the collateral or other security, if any, for the amount due proved to be of no value to the entity
- The entity's policy for requiring collateral or other security on financial instruments it accepts and a description of collateral on instruments presently held.

This Statement also requires disclosure of information about significant concentrations of credit risk from an individual counterparty or groups of counterparties for all financial instruments.

This Statement is effective for financial statements issued for fiscal years ending after June 15, 1990.

(This page intentionally left blank.)

Statement of Financial Accounting Standards No. 105

Disclosure of Information about Financial Instruments with Off-Balance-Sheet Risk and Financial Instruments with Concentrations of Credit Risk

CONTENTS

INTRODUCTION

1. The FASB added a project on financial instruments and off-balance-sheet financing to its agenda in May 1986. The project is expected to develop broad standards to aid in resolving existing financial accounting and reporting issues and other issues likely to arise in the future about various financial instruments and related transactions. Issues to be considered include whether assets or liabilities should be recognized in financial statements of an entity as a result of certain transactions involving financial instruments; when assets should be considered sold and when liabilities should be considered settled; how to account for financial instruments that seek to transfer market and credit risks and for the underlying assets and liabilities to which the risk-transferring items are related; how financial instruments should be initially and subsequently measured; how entities that issue financial instruments with both liability and equity characteristics should account for them; and how best to disclose the potential favorable or unfavorable effects of financial instruments.

2. Because of the complexity of the issues on how financial instruments and transactions should be recognized and measured, Statements covering those issues will be developed only after extensive Board deliberations and after issuance of initial discussion documents, public hearings, and Exposure Drafts. The Board decided that as an interim step, pending completion of the recognition and measurement phases of the financial instruments project, improved disclosure of information about financial instruments is necessary. This Statement is the initial response to that need for improved disclosure of information.

3. Some disclosure of information about financial instruments has been required previously by generally accepted accounting principles. Some entities previously have disclosed additional information about financial instruments in their financial statements or elsewhere in annual reports to stockholders or regulators, either because of requirements of the Securities and Exchange Commission (SEC) or because of requirements of the regulators of particular industries or institutions. Moreover, some entities previously have disclosed additional information beyond that required by generally accepted accounting principles because they believe the information disclosed might be useful to investors, creditors, and other users in better understanding financial instruments and their effects on the entity. For many financial instruments, however, the

Disclosure of Information about Financial Instruments with Off-Balance-Sheet Risk and Financial Instruments with Concentrations of Credit Risk

FAS105

information disclosed in financial statements has been inadequate.

4. Many new financial instruments have been and will be created as responses to market volatility, deregulation, tax law changes, and other stimuli. The dynamic state of financial markets suggests the need to develop broad, general disclosure requirements about financial instruments. Generally accepted accounting principles and regulatory accounting requirements for financial instruments seem to have developed on an ad hoc basis, and only certain types of financial instruments or entities have been included within their scope. For example, FASB Statement No. 80, *Accounting for Futures Contracts,* applies primarily to only one type of financial instrument—futures contracts.

5. The Board initially concluded that the disclosure phase of the financial instruments project should take a broad approach to disclosure of information about financial instruments. However, after public comment on an initial Exposure Draft, *Disclosures about Financial Instruments,* issued November 30, 1987, the Board decided that the disclosure issues should be considered in separate phases. The first phase, which resulted in this Statement, includes financial instruments with off-balance-sheet credit or market risk and all financial instruments with concentrations of credit risk—areas many perceive as most in need of improvement. This Statement applies to all financial instruments with off-balance-sheet risk of accounting loss and all financial instruments with concentrations of credit risk except those specifically excluded by paragraphs 14 and 15. It applies to all entities. Subsequent phases will consider disclosure of other information about financial instruments.

STANDARDS OF FINANCIAL ACCOUNTING AND REPORTING

Definitions and Scope

6. A financial instrument is cash, evidence of an ownership interest in an entity, or a contract that both:

a. Imposes on one entity a contractual obligation[1] (1) to deliver cash or another financial instrument[2] to a second entity or (2) to exchange financial instruments on potentially unfavorable terms with the second entity
b. Conveys to that second entity a contractual right[3] (1) to receive cash or another financial instrument from the first entity or (2) to exchange other financial instruments on potentially favorable terms with the first entity.

7. The risk of accounting loss[4] from a financial instrument includes (a) the possibility that a loss may occur from the failure of another party to perform according to the terms of a contract (credit risk), (b) the possibility that future changes in market prices may make a financial instrument less valuable or more onerous (market risk),[5] and (c) the risk of theft or physical loss. This Statement addresses credit and market risk only.

8. Some financial instruments are recognized as assets, and the amount recognized reflects the risk of accounting loss to the entity. A receivable that is recognized and measured at the present value of future cash inflows, discounted at the historical interest rate (often termed *amortized cost*), is an example: the accounting loss that might arise from that account receivable cannot exceed the amount

---

[1]*Contractual obligations* encompass both those that are conditioned on the occurrence of a specified event and those that are not. All contractual obligations that are financial instruments meet the definition of *liability* set forth in FASB Concepts Statement No. 6, *Elements of Financial Statements,* although some may not be recognized as liabilities in financial statements—may be "off-balance-sheet"—because they fail to meet some other criterion for recognition. For some financial instruments, the obligation is owed to or by a group of entities rather than a single entity.

[2]The use of the term *financial instrument* in this definition is recursive (because the term *financial instrument* is included in it), but it is not circular. It requires a chain of contractual obligations that ends with the delivery of cash or an ownership interest in an entity. Any number of obligations to deliver financial instruments can be links in a chain that qualifies a particular contract as a financial instrument.

[3]*Contractual rights* encompass both those that are conditioned on the occurrence of a specified event and those that are not. All contractual rights that are financial instruments meet the definition of *asset* set forth in Concepts Statement 6, although some may not be recognized as assets in financial statements—may be "off-balance-sheet"—because they fail to meet some other criterion for recognition. For some financial instruments, the obligation is held by or due from a group of entities rather than a single entity.

[4]Accounting loss refers to the loss that may have to be recognized due to credit and market risk as a direct result of the rights and obligations of a financial instrument.

[5]A change in market price may occur (for example, for interest-bearing financial instruments) because of changes in general interest rates (interest rate risk), changes in the relationship between general and specific market interest rates (an aspect of credit risk), or changes in the rates of exchange between currencies (foreign exchange risk).

recognized as an asset in the statement of financial position.[6]

9. Some financial instruments that are recognized as assets entail conditional rights and obligations that expose the entity to a risk of accounting loss that may exceed the amount recognized in the statement of financial position; for example, an interest rate swap contract providing for net settlement of cash receipts and payments that conveys a right to receive cash at current interest rates may impose an obligation to deliver cash if interest rates change in the future. Those financial instruments have off-balance-sheet risk.[7]

10. Some financial instruments are recognized as liabilities, and the possible sacrifice needed to settle the obligation under the terms of the financial instrument cannot exceed the amount recognized in the statement of financial position. However, other financial instruments that are recognized as liabilities expose the entity to a risk of accounting loss because the ultimate obligation may exceed the amount that is recognized in the statement of financial position; for example, the ultimate obligation under a financial guarantee may exceed the amount that has been recognized as a liability. Those financial instruments have off-balance-sheet risk.

11. Still other financial instruments may not be recognized either as assets or as liabilities, yet may expose the entity to a risk of accounting loss; for example, a forward interest rate agreement that, unless a loss has been incurred, is not recognized until settlement. Those financial instruments also have off-balance-sheet risk.

12. This Statement requires disclosure of information about financial instruments that have off-balance-sheet risk and about financial instruments with concentrations of credit risk except as specifically modified by paragraphs 14 and 15. It does not change any requirements for recognition, measurement, or classification of financial instruments in financial statements.

13. Examples of financial instruments with off-balance-sheet risk that are included within the scope of this Statement are outstanding loan commitments written,[8] standby and commercial letters of credit written, financial guarantees written, options written, interest rate caps and floors written, recourse obligations on receivables sold, obligations to repurchase securities sold, outstanding commitments to purchase or sell financial instruments at predetermined prices, futures contracts, interest rate and foreign currency swaps, and obligations arising from financial instruments sold short. Appendix B provides additional examples of financial instruments that have and do not have off-balance-sheet risk.

14. The requirements of paragraphs 17, 18, and 20 do not apply to the following financial instruments, whether written or held:

a. Insurance contracts, other than financial guarantees and investment contracts, as discussed in FASB Statements No. 60, *Accounting and Reporting by Insurance Enterprises,* and No. 97, *Accounting and Reporting by Insurance Enterprises for Certain Long-Duration Contracts and for Realized Gains and Losses from the Sale of Investments*
b. Unconditional purchase obligations subject to the disclosure requirements of FASB Statement No. 47, *Disclosure of Long-Term Obligations*[9]
c. Employers' and plans' obligations for pension benefits, postretirement health care and life insurance benefits, employee stock option and stock purchase plans, and other forms of deferred compensation arrangements, as defined in FASB Statements No. 35, *Accounting and Reporting by Defined Benefit Pension Plans,* No. 87, *Employers' Accounting for Pensions,* No. 81, *Disclosure of Postretirement Health Care and Life Insurance Benefits,* No. 43, *Accounting for Compensated Absences,* as well as APB Opinions No. 25, *Accounting for Stock Issued to Employees,* and No. 12, *Omnibus Opinion—1967*
d. Financial instruments of a pension plan, includ-

---

[6]It is possible that an economic loss could exceed that amount if, for example, the current market value of an asset was higher than the amount recognized in the statement of financial position. This Statement, however, does not address that economic loss.

[7]In this Statement, off-balance-sheet risk is used to refer to off-balance-sheet risk of accounting loss.

[8]The off-balance-sheet risk from a commitment to lend cash at a floating interest rate is the exposure to credit loss arising from the obligation to fund a loan in accordance with the terms of the commitment.

[9]Unconditional purchase obligations not subject to the requirements of Statement 47 are included in the scope of this Statement. That is, unconditional purchase obligations that require the purchaser to make payment without regard to delivery of the goods or receipt of benefit of the services specified by the contract and are not within the scope of Statement 47 (because they were not negotiated as part of a financing arrangement, for example) are included in the scope of this Statement.

Disclosure of Information about Financial Instruments with Off-Balance-Sheet Risk and Financial Instruments with Concentrations of Credit Risk

FAS105

ing plan assets, when subject to the accounting and reporting requirements of Statement 87[10]

e. Substantively extinguished debt subject to the disclosure requirements of FASB Statement No. 76, *Extinguishment of Debt,* and any assets held in trust in connection with an in-substance defeasance of that debt.

15. The requirements of paragraphs 17 and 18 do not apply to the following instruments:

a. Lease contracts[11] as defined in FASB Statement No. 13, *Accounting for Leases*
b. Accounts and notes payable and other financial instrument obligations that result in accruals or other amounts that are denominated in foreign currencies and are included at translated or remeasured amounts in the statement of financial position in accordance with FASB Statement No. 52, *Foreign Currency Translation,* except (1) obligations under financial instruments that have off-balance-sheet risk from other risks in addition to foreign exchange risk and (2) obligations under foreign currency exchange contracts. Examples of the first exception include a commitment to lend foreign currency and an option written to exchange foreign currency for a bond (whether or not denominated in a foreign currency). Examples of the second exception include a forward exchange contract, a currency swap, a foreign currency futures contract, and an option to exchange currencies.

The requirements of paragraph 20 of this Statement do apply to the items described in subparagraphs (a) and (b) above.

16. Generally accepted accounting principles contain specific requirements to disclose information about the financial instruments noted in paragraphs 14 and 15, and this Statement does not change those require-

ments. For all other financial instruments, the requirements in this Statement are in addition to other disclosure requirements prescribed by generally accepted accounting principles.

Disclosure of Extent, Nature, and Terms of Financial Instruments with Off-Balance-Sheet Risk

17. For financial instruments with off-balance-sheet risk, except as noted in paragraphs 14 and 15, an entity shall disclose either in the body of the financial statements or in the accompanying notes the following information by class of financial instrument:[12]

a. The face or contract amount (or notional principal amount if there is no face or contract amount)
b. The nature and terms, including, at a minimum, a discussion of (1) the credit and market risk of those instruments, (2) the cash requirements of those instruments, and (3) the related accounting policy pursuant to the requirements of APB Opinion No. 22, *Disclosure of Accounting Policies.*[13]

Disclosure of Credit Risk of Financial Instruments with Off-Balance-Sheet Credit Risk

18. For financial instruments with off-balance-sheet credit risk, except as noted in paragraphs 14 and 15, an entity shall disclose either in the body of the financial statements or in the accompanying notes the following information by class of financial instrument:

a. The amount of accounting loss the entity would incur if any party to the financial instrument failed completely to perform according to the terms of the contract and the collateral or other security, if any, for the amount due proved to

---

[10]Financial instruments of a pension plan, other than the obligations for pension benefits, when subject to the accounting and reporting requirements of Statement 35 *are included* in the scope of this Statement.

[11]A contingent obligation arising out of a cancelled lease contract and a guarantee of a third-party lease obligation are not lease contracts and are included in the scope of this Statement.

[12]Practices for grouping and separately identifying—classifying—similar financial instruments in statements of financial position, in notes to financial statements, and in various regulatory reports have developed and become generally accepted, largely without being codified in authoritative literature. In this Statement, *class of financial instrument* refers to those classifications.

[13]Paragraph 12 of Opinion 22 as amended by FASB Statement No. 95, *Statement of Cash Flows,* says:

> Disclosure of accounting policies should identify and describe the accounting principles followed by the reporting entity and the methods of applying those principles that materially affect the determination of financial position, statement of cash flows, or results of operations. In general, the disclosure should encompass important judgments as to appropriateness of principles relating to recognition of revenue and allocation of asset costs to current and future periods; in particular, it should encompass those accounting principles and methods that involve any of the following:
>
> a. A selection from existing acceptable alternatives;
> b. Principles and methods peculiar to the industry in which the reporting entity operates, even if such principles and methods are predominantly followed in that industry;
> c. Unusual or innovative applications of generally accepted accounting principles (and, as applicable, of principles and methods peculiar to the industry in which the reporting entity operates).

be of no value to the entity

b. The entity's policy of requiring collateral or other security to support financial instruments subject to credit risk, information about the entity's access to that collateral or other security, and the nature and a brief description of the collateral or other security supporting those financial instruments.

19. An entity may find that disclosing additional information about the extent of collateral or other security for the underlying instrument indicates better the extent of credit risk. Disclosure of that additional information in those circumstances is encouraged.

Disclosure of Concentrations of Credit Risk of All Financial Instruments

20. Except as noted in paragraph 14, an entity shall disclose all significant concentrations of credit risk arising from *all* financial instruments, whether from an individual counterparty or groups of counterparties. *Group concentrations* of credit risk exist if a number of counterparties are engaged in similar activities and have similar economic characteristics that would cause their ability to meet contractual obligations to be similarly affected by changes in economic or other conditions. The following shall be disclosed about each significant concentration:

a. Information about the (shared) activity, region, or economic characteristic that identifies the concentration

b. The amount of the accounting loss due to credit risk the entity would incur if parties to the financial instruments that make up the concentration failed completely to perform according to the terms of the contracts and the collateral or other security, if any, for the amount due

proved to be of no value to the entity

c. The entity's policy of requiring collateral or other security to support financial instruments subject to credit risk, information about the entity's access to that collateral or other security, and the nature and a brief description of the collateral or other security supporting those financial instruments.

Amendment to Statement 77

21. This Statement amends FASB Statement No. 77, *Reporting by Transferors for Transfers of Receivables with Recourse.* In paragraph 9 of that Statement, the phrase *(b), if the information is available, the balance of the receivables transferred that remain uncollected at the date of each balance sheet presented* is superseded by *(b) information required by paragraphs 17, 18, and 20 of FASB Statement No. 105, Disclosure of Information about Financial Instruments with Off-Balance-Sheet Risk and Financial Instruments with Concentrations of Credit Risk.*

Effective Date and Transition

22. This Statement shall be effective for financial statements issued for fiscal years ending after June 15, 1990. Earlier application is encouraged. Disclosure in the year of transition of information required by paragraphs 17, 18, and 20 that previously has not been required to be reported need not be included in financial statements that are being provided for comparative purposes for fiscal years ending before the effective date of this Statement. For all subsequent fiscal years, the information required to be disclosed by this Statement shall be included for each year for which a statement of financial position is presented for comparative purposes.

> **The provisions of this Statement need not be applied to immaterial items.**

This Statement was adopted by the unanimous vote of the seven members of the Financial Accounting Standards Board:

Dennis R. Beresford,	Raymond C. Lauver	A. Clarence Sampson
Chairman	James J. Leisenring	Robert J. Swieringa
Victor H. Brown	C. Arthur Northrop	

*Disclosure of Information about Financial Instruments
with Off-Balance-Sheet Risk and Financial
Instruments with Concentrations of Credit Risk*   **FAS105**

Appendix A

ILLUSTRATIONS APPLYING THE DEFINITION OF A FINANCIAL INSTRUMENT

CONTENTS

Appendix A

ILLUSTRATIONS APPLYING THE DEFINITION OF A FINANCIAL INSTRUMENT

Introduction

23. This appendix provides a definition of a financial instrument and examples of instruments that are included in and excluded from the definition.

24. A financial instrument is cash, evidence of an ownership interest in an entity, or a contract that both:

a. Imposes on one entity a contractual obligation (1) to deliver cash or another financial instrument to a second entity or (2) to exchange financial instruments on potentially unfavorable terms with the second entity

b. Conveys to that second entity a contractual right (1) to receive cash or another financial instrument from the first entity or (2) to exchange other financial instruments on potentially favorable terms with the first entity.

Example 1—Cash

25. Currency[14] is a financial instrument even though generally the only contractual obligation placed on the issuing government is that it accept the currency as legal tender for payments due to it.

26. Demand deposits in banks are financial instruments of both the depositors and the banks. The depositors have a contractual right to receive currency on demand, and the banks have a contractual obligation to deliver currency on demand. The term *cash* as used in the definition includes both U.S. dollars and the currencies of other nations.

Example 2—Evidence of an Ownership Interest in an Entity

27. Common stock is a financial instrument that is evidence of an ownership interest in an entity, but others include preferred stock, partnership agreements, certificates of interest or participation, or warrants or options to subscribe to or purchase stock from the issuing entity.

Example 3—Contractual Right or Obligation to Receive or Deliver Cash

28. A contractual right to receive cash in the future is a financial instrument. Trade accounts, notes, loans, and bonds receivable all have that characteristic. An entity can have a contractual right to receive cash only if another entity has a contractual obligation to pay cash.

29. A contractual obligation to deliver cash in the future is also a financial instrument. Trade accounts, notes, loans, and bonds payable all have that characteristic. An entity can have a contractual obligation to pay cash only if another entity has the contractual right to receive cash.

---

[14]The definition of a financial instrument could be written to exclude currency but include other forms of cash (for example, cash deposits) since currency does not generally represent a promise to pay. The definition includes currency in cash primarily as a matter of convenience.

30. Physical assets such as inventory, property, plant, and equipment, and leased assets including their unguaranteed residuals, as well as intangibles such as patents, trademarks, and goodwill, do not meet the definition of a financial instrument. Each of those assets could eventually lead to the receipt of cash; however, because no other entity has a present obligation to deliver cash, the entity has no present right to receive cash.

Example 4—Contractual Right or Obligation to Receive or Deliver Goods or Services

31. The definition of a financial instrument excludes many assets that contain contractual rights, such as prepaid expenses and advances to suppliers, because their probable future economic benefit is receipt of goods or services instead of a right to receive cash or an ownership interest in another entity. It also excludes many liabilities that contain contractual obligations, such as deferred revenue, advances from suppliers, and most warranty obligations, because their probable economic sacrifice is delivery of goods or services instead of an obligation to deliver cash or an ownership interest in another entity.

32. The definition excludes contracts that either require or permit settlement by the delivery of commodities. Those contracts are excluded because the future economic benefit is receipt of goods or services instead of a right to receive cash or an ownership interest in an entity and the economic sacrifice is delivery of goods or services instead of an obligation to deliver cash or an ownership interest in an entity. For example, bonds to be settled in ounces of gold or barrels of oil rather than in cash are not financial instruments under the definition. Similarly, contracts that entitle the holder to receive from the issuer *either* a financial instrument (such as the face value of a bond) *or* a physical asset (such as a specified amount of gold or oil) do not meet the definition of a financial instrument (regardless of the probability of settlement in cash rather than in goods or services).

Example 5—Contractual Right or Obligation to Receive or Deliver Another Financial Instrument

33. Another financial instrument is one whose future economic benefit or sacrifice is receipt or delivery of a financial instrument other than cash. For example, a note that is payable in U.S. Treasury bonds gives the holder the contractual right to receive and the issuer the contractual obligation to deliver bonds, not cash. But the bonds are financial instruments because they represent obligations of the U.S. Treasury to pay cash. Therefore, the note is also a financial instrument of the note holder and the note issuer.

Example 6—Contractual Right or Obligation to Exchange Other Financial Instruments

34. Another financial instrument is one that gives an entity the contractual right or obligation to exchange other financial instruments on potentially favorable or unfavorable terms. An example is a call option to purchase a U.S. Treasury note for $100,000 in 6 months. The holder of the option has a contractual right to exchange the financial instruments on potentially favorable terms; if the market value of the note exceeds $100,000 six months later, the terms will be favorable to the holder who will exercise the option. The writer of the call option has a contractual obligation because the writer has an obligation to exchange financial instruments on potentially unfavorable terms if the holder exercises the option. The writer is normally compensated by the holder for undertaking that obligation. A put option to sell a Treasury note has similar but opposite effects. A bank's commitment to lend $100,000 to a customer at a fixed rate of 10 percent any time during the next 6 months at the customer's option is also a financial instrument.

35. A more complex example is a forward contract in which the purchasing entity promises to exchange $100,000 cash for a U.S. Treasury note and the selling entity promises to exchange a U.S. Treasury note for $100,000 cash 6 months later. During the six-month period, both the purchaser and the seller have a contractual right and obligation to exchange financial instruments. The market price for the Treasury note might rise above $100,000, which would make the terms favorable to the purchaser and unfavorable to the seller, or fall below $100,000, which would have the opposite effect. Therefore, the purchaser has both a contractual right (a financial instrument) similar to a call option held and a contractual obligation (a financial instrument) similar to a put option written; the seller has a contractual right (a financial instrument) similar to a put option held and a contractual obligation (a financial instrument) similar to a call option written.

36. An interest rate swap can be viewed as a series of forward contracts to exchange, for example, fixed cash payments for variable cash receipts computed by multiplying a specified floating-rate market index by a notional amount. Those terms are potentially favorable or unfavorable depending on subsequent movements in the index, and an interest rate swap is both a contractual right and a contractual obligation to both parties.

37. Options and contracts that contain the right or obligation to exchange a financial instrument for a physical asset are not financial instruments. For example, 2 entities may enter into sale-purchase con-

Disclosure of Information about Financial Instruments with Off-Balance-Sheet Risk and Financial Instruments with Concentrations of Credit Risk

FAS105

tracts in which the purchaser agrees to take delivery of gold or wheat 6 months later and pay the seller $100,000 on delivery. Because the sale-purchase contracts require the delivery of gold or wheat, which are not financial instruments, the sale-purchase contracts are not financial instruments.

Example 7—Contingent Rights or Obligations

38. Contingent items can be financial instruments under the definition. For example, in a typical financial guarantee, a borrower who borrows money from a lender simultaneously pays a fee to a guarantor; in return the guarantor agrees to pay the lender if the borrower defaults on the loan. The guarantee is a financial instrument of the guarantor (the contractual obligation to pay the lender if the borrower defaults) and a financial instrument of the lender (the contractual right to receive cash from the guarantor if the borrower defaults—normally reported together with the guaranteed loan).

39. Other contingent items that ultimately may require the payment of cash but do not as yet arise from contracts, such as contingent liabilities for tort judgments payable, are not financial instruments. However, when those obligations become enforceable by government or courts of law and are thereby contractually reduced to fixed payment schedules, the items would be financial instruments under the definition.

Appendix B

ILLUSTRATION APPLYING THE DEFINITION OF A FINANCIAL INSTRUMENT WITH OFF-BALANCE-SHEET RISK

40. A financial instrument has off-balance-sheet risk of accounting loss if the risk of accounting loss to the entity may exceed the amount recognized as an asset, if any, or if the ultimate obligation may exceed the amount that is recognized as a liability in the statement of financial position.

41. The risk of accounting loss from a financial instrument includes (a) the possibility that a loss may occur from the failure of another party to perform according to the terms of a contract (credit risk), (b) the possibility that future changes in market prices may make a financial instrument less valuable or more onerous (market risk), and (c) the risk of theft or physical loss. This Statement addresses credit and market risk only.

42. The following illustration presents some financial instruments that have and that do not have off-balance-sheet risk of accounting loss; it does not illustrate *all* financial instruments that are included in the scope of this Statement. Off-balance-sheet risk of accounting loss for similar financial instruments may differ among entities using different methods of accounting.

Illustration

	Off-Balance-Sheet (OBS) Risk of Accounting Loss					
	Holder[a]			Issuer[b]		
		Type of OBS Risk[c]			Type of OBS Risk[c]	
Financial Instrument	OBS Risk[d]	CR	MR	OBS Risk[d]	CR	MR
Traditional items:						
Cash	No					
Foreign currency	No					
Time deposits (non-interest bearing, fixed rate, or variable rate)	No			No		
Bonds carried at amortized cost (fixed or variable rate bonds, with or without a cap)	No			No		
Bonds carried at market (in trading accounts, fixed or variable rate bonds, with or without a cap)	No			No		
Convertible bonds (convertible into stock of the issuer at a specified price at option of the holder; callable at a premium to face at option of the issuer)	No			No		
Accounts and notes receivable/payable (non-interest bearing, fixed rate, or variable rate)	No			No		
Loans (fixed or variable rate, with or without a cap)	No			No		
Refundable (margin) deposits	No			No		
Accrued expenses receivable/payable (wages, etc.)	No			No		
Common stock (equity investments—cost method or equity method)[e]	No			No		
Preferred stock (convertible or participating)	No			No		
Preferred stock (nonconvertible or nonparticipating)	No			No		
Cash dividends declared	No			No		
Obligations arising from financial instruments sold short	No			Yes		X

***Disclosure of Information about Financial Instruments
with Off-Balance-Sheet Risk and Financial
Instruments with Concentrations of Credit Risk***   **FAS105**

Financial Instrument		Off-balance-sheet risk of accounting loss[d]	CR	MR
Innovative items:				
Increasing rate debt	No	No		
Variable coupon redeemable notes	No	No		
Collateralized mortgage obligations (CMOs):				
CMO accounted for as a borrowing by issuer	No	No		
CMO accounted for as a sale by issuer	No	No[f]		
Transfer of receivables:				
Investor has recourse to the issuer at or below the receivable carrying amount—accounted for as a borrowing by issuer	No	No		
Investor has recourse to the issuer—accounted for as a sale by issuer	No	Yes	X	
Investor has recourse to the issuer and the agreement includes a floating interest rate provision—accounted for as a sale by issuer	No	Yes	X	X
Investor has no recourse to the issuer—accounted for as a sale by issuer	No	No		
Securitized receivables		Same as transfer of receivables		
(Reverse) Repurchase agreements:				
Accounted for as a borrowing by issuer	No	No		
Accounted for as a sale by issuer	No	Yes	X	X

Note: Credit risk and market risk are present for many of the instruments included in this illustration. However, only those instruments with off-balance-sheet credit or market risk are denoted with an "X" (refer to footnote c).

[a] Holder includes buyer and investor.

[b] Issuer includes seller, borrower, and writer.

[c] An "X" in any of the columns (CR or MR) denotes the presence of the respective *off-balance-sheet* risk of accounting loss. The types of risk included are:
1. *Credit risk* (CR)—the possibility that a loss may occur from the failure of another party to perform according to the terms of a contract
2. *Market risk* (MR)—the possibility that future changes in market prices may make a financial instrument less valuable or more onerous.

[d] A "Yes" in this column denotes the presence of off-balance-sheet risk of accounting loss; a "No" denotes no off-balance-sheet risk of accounting loss.

[e] Many joint ventures or other equity method investments are accompanied by guarantees of the debt of the investee. Debt guarantees of this nature present off-balance-sheet risk of accounting loss due to credit risk and should be evaluated with other financial guarantees.

[f] Issuer refers to both the trust and the sponsor.

Continued on next page

Illustration—*Continued*

	Off-Balance-Sheet (OBS) Risk of Accounting Loss					
	Holder			Issuer		
		Type of OBS Risk			Type of OBS Risk	
Financial Instrument	OBS Risk	CR	MR	OBS Risk	CR	MR
Put option on stock (premium paid up front):						
Covered option	No			Yes		X
Naked option	No			Yes		X
Put option on interest rate contracts[g] (premium paid up front):						
Covered option	No			Yes	X	X
Naked option	No			Yes	X	X
Call option on stock, foreign currency, or interest rate contracts (premium paid up front):						
Covered option	No			Yes		X
Naked option	No			Yes		X
Loan commitments:						
Fixed rate	No			Yes	X	X
Variable rate	No			Yes	X	
Interest rate caps	No			Yes		X
Interest rate floors	No			Yes		X
Financial guarantees	No			Yes	X	
Note issuance facilities at floating rates	No			Yes	X	
Letters of credit (also standby letters of credit) at floating rates	No			Yes	X	

Financial Instrument	Off-Balance-Sheet Risk of Accounting Loss — Both Counterparties[h]		
	OBS Risk	Type of OBS Risk — CR	MR
Interest rate swaps—accrual basis:			
In a gain position	Yes		X
In a loss position	Yes		X
Gain or loss position netted: right of setoff exists[i]	Yes		X
Interest rate swaps—marked to market:			
In a gain position	Yes		X
In a loss position	Yes		X
Gain or loss position netted: right of setoff exists[i]	Yes		X
Currency swaps		Same as interest rate swaps	
Financial futures contracts—hedges (marked to market and gain or loss deferred—Statement 52 or 80 accounting):			
In a gain position	Yes		X
In a loss position	Yes		X
Multiple contracts settled net	Yes		X
Financial futures contracts—nonhedges (marked to market—Statement 52 or 80 accounting):			
In a gain position	Yes		X
In a loss position	Yes		X
Multiple contracts settled net	Yes		X
Forward contracts—hedges (marked to market and gain or loss deferred):			
In a gain position	Yes		X
In a loss position	Yes		X
Gain or loss position netted: right of setoff exists[i]	Yes		X
Forward contracts—nonhedges (marked to market and gain or loss recognized):			
In a gain position	Yes		X
In a loss position	Yes		X
Gain or loss position netted: right of setoff exists[i]	Yes		X
Forward contracts—not marked to market	Yes		X

[g] Put options on interest rate contracts have credit risk if the underlying instrument that might be put (a particular bond, for example) is subject to credit risk.

[h] Swaps, forwards, and futures are two-sided transactions; therefore, the holder and issuer categories are not applicable. Risks are assessed in terms of the position held by the entity.

[i] Netting of receivable and payable amounts when right of setoff does not exist is in contravention of APB Opinion No. 10, *Omnibus Opinion—1966*, paragraph 7, and FASB Technical Bulletin No. 88-2, *Definition of a Right of Setoff*.

Appendix C

ILLUSTRATIONS APPLYING THE DISCLOSURE REQUIREMENTS ABOUT FINANCIAL INSTRUMENTS WITH OFF-BALANCE-SHEET RISK AND CONCENTRATIONS OF CREDIT RISK

43. The examples that follow are guides to implementation of the disclosure requirements of this Statement. Entities are not required to display the information contained herein in the specific manner or in the degree of detail illustrated. Alternative ways of disclosing the information are permissible as long as they satisfy the disclosure requirements of this Statement.

Example 1—Nonfinancial Entity

44. This example illustrates the information that might be disclosed by CDA Corporation, a nonfinancial entity that has entered into interest rate swap agreements and foreign exchange contracts.[15] CDA Corporation has no significant concentrations of credit risk with any individual counterparty or groups of counterparties.

45. CDA Corporation might disclose the following:

Note U: Summary of Accounting Policies

[The accounting policies note to the financial statements might include the following.]

Interest Rate Swap Agreements

The differential to be paid or received is accrued as interest rates change and is recognized over the life of the agreements.

Foreign Exchange Contracts

The Corporation enters into foreign exchange contracts as a hedge against foreign accounts payable. Market value gains and losses are recognized, and the resulting credit or debit offsets foreign exchange gains or losses on those payables.

Note V: Interest Rate Swap Agreements[16]

The Corporation has entered into interest rate swap agreements to reduce the impact of changes in interest rates on its floating rate long-term debt. At December 31, 19XX, the Corporation had out-

standing 2 interest rate swap agreements with commercial banks, having a total notional principal amount of $85 million. Those agreements effectively change the Corporation's interest rate exposure on its $35 million floating rate notes due 1993 to a fixed 12 percent and its $50 million floating rate notes due 1998 to a fixed 12.5 percent. The interest rate swap agreements mature at the time the related notes mature. The Corporation is exposed to credit loss in the event of nonperformance by the other parties to the interest rate swap agreements. However, the Corporation does not anticipate nonperformance by the counterparties.

Note W: Foreign Exchange Contracts

At December 31, 19XX, the Corporation had contracts maturing June 30, 19X1 to purchase $12.9 million in foreign currency (18 million deutsche marks and 5 million Swiss francs at the spot rate on that date).

Example 2—Financial Entity

46. This example illustrates the information that might be disclosed by Bank of SLA, which has entered into the following financial instruments with off-balance-sheet risk: commitments to extend credit, standby letters of credit and financial guarantees written, interest rate swap agreements, forward and futures contracts, and options and interest rate caps and floors written. Bank of SLA has (a) significant concentrations of credit risk in the semiconductor industry in its home state and (b) loans to companies with unusually high debt to equity ratios as a result of buyout transactions.

47. Bank of SLA might disclose the following:

Note X: Summary of Accounting Policies

[The accounting policies note to the financial statements might include the following.]

Interest Rate Futures, Options, Caps and Floors, and Forward Contracts

The Corporation is party to a variety of interest rate futures, options, caps and floors, and forward contracts in its trading activities and in the management of its interest rate exposure.

Interest rate futures, options, caps and floors, and forward contracts used in trading activities are carried at market value. Realized and unrealized gains

---

[15]This example might apply also to a financial entity that has a limited number of financial instruments with off-balance-sheet risk.

[16]Placement within financial statements of the information that describes the extent of involvement an entity has in financial instruments with off-balance-sheet risk and the related nature, terms, and credit risk of those instruments is at the discretion of management. The example illustrates information that would be provided in a note "Interest Rate Swap Agreements." As an alternative, this same information could be included in the entity's note about long-term financing arrangements.

Disclosure of Information about Financial Instruments with Off-Balance-Sheet Risk and Financial Instruments with Concentrations of Credit Risk

FAS105

and losses are included in trading account profits.

Realized and unrealized gains and losses on interest rate futures, options, caps and floors, and forward contracts designated and effective as hedges of interest rate exposure are deferred and recognized as interest income or interest expense over the lives of the hedged assets or liabilities.

Interest Rate Swap Agreements

The Corporation is an intermediary in the interest rate swap market. It also enters into interest rate swap agreements both as trading instruments and as a means of managing its interest rate exposure.

As an intermediary, the Corporation maintains a portfolio of generally matched offsetting swap agreements. These swaps are carried at market value, with changes in value reflected in noninterest income. At inception of the swap agreements, the portion of the compensation related to credit risk and ongoing servicing is deferred and taken into income over the term of the swap agreements.

Interest rate swap agreements used in trading activities are valued at market. Realized and unrealized gains and losses are included in trading account profits. Unrealized gains are reported as assets and unrealized losses are reported as liabilities.

The differential to be paid or received on interest rate swap agreements entered into to reduce the impact of changes in interest rates is recognized over the life of the agreements.

Note Y: Financial Instruments with Off-Balance-Sheet Risk[17]

The Corporation is a party to financial instruments with off-balance-sheet risk in the normal course of business to meet the financing needs of its customers and to reduce its own exposure to fluctuations in interest rates. These financial instruments include commitments to extend credit, options written, standby letters of credit and financial guarantees, interest rate caps and floors written, interest rate swaps, and forward and futures contracts. Those instruments involve, to varying degrees, elements of credit and interest rate risk in excess of the amount recognized in the statement of financial position. The contract or notional amounts of those instruments reflect the extent of involvement the Corporation has in particular classes of financial instruments.

The Corporation's exposure to credit loss in the event of nonperformance by the other party to the financial instrument for commitments to extend credit and standby letters of credit and financial guarantees written is represented by the contractual notional amount of those instruments. The Corporation uses the same credit policies in making commitments and conditional obligations as it does for on-balance-sheet instruments. For interest rate caps, floors, and swap transactions, forward and futures contracts, and options written, the contract or notional amounts do not represent exposure to credit loss. The Corporation controls the credit risk of its interest rate swap agreements and forward and futures contracts through credit approvals, limits, and monitoring procedures.

Unless noted otherwise, the Corporation does not require collateral or other security to support financial instruments with credit risk.

	Contract or Notional Amount (in millions)
Financial instruments whose contract amounts represent credit risk:	
Commitments to extend credit	$ 2,780
Standby letters of credit and financial guarantees written	862
Financial instruments whose notional or contract amounts exceed the amount of credit risk:	
Forward and futures contracts	815
Interest rate swap agreements	10,520
Options written and interest rate caps and floors written	950

Commitments to extend credit are agreements to lend to a customer as long as there is no violation of any condition established in the contract. Commitments generally have fixed expiration dates or other termination clauses and may require payment of a fee. Since many of the commitments are expected to expire without being drawn upon, the total commitment amounts do not necessarily represent future cash requirements. The Corporation evaluates each customer's creditworthiness on a case-by-case basis. The amount of collateral obtained if deemed necessary by the Corporation upon extension of credit is based on management's credit evaluation of the counterparty. Collateral held varies but may include accounts receivable, inventory, property, plant, and equipment, and

---

[17]Placement within financial statements of the information that describes the extent of involvement an entity has in financial instruments with off-balance-sheet risk and the related nature, terms, and credit risk of those instruments is at the discretion of management. The example illustrates information that would be provided in a note "Financial Instruments with Off-Balance-Sheet Risk." An entity may decide, however, to disclose this information in several separate notes.

income-producing commercial properties.

Standby letters of credit and financial guarantees written are conditional commitments issued by the Corporation to guarantee the performance of a customer to a third party. Those guarantees are primarily issued to support public and private borrowing arrangements, including commercial paper, bond financing, and similar transactions. Except for short-term guarantees of $158 million, most guarantees extend for more than 5 years and expire in decreasing amounts through 20XX. The credit risk involved in issuing letters of credit is essentially the same as that involved in extending loan facilities to customers. The Corporation holds marketable securities as collateral supporting those commitments for which collateral is deemed necessary. The extent of collateral held for those commitments at December 31, 19XX varies from 2 percent to 45 percent; the average amount collateralized is 24 percent.

Forward and futures contracts are contracts for delayed delivery of securities or money market instruments in which the seller agrees to make delivery at a specified future date of a specified instrument, at a specified price or yield. Risks arise from the possible inability of counterparties to meet the terms of their contracts and from movements in securities values and interest rates.

The Corporation enters into a variety of interest rate contracts—including interest rate caps and floors written, interest rate options written, and interest rate swap agreements—in its trading activities and in managing its interest rate exposure. Interest rate caps and floors written by the Corporation enable customers to transfer, modify, or reduce their interest rate risk. Interest rate options are contracts that allow the holder of the option to purchase or sell a financial instrument at a specified price and within a specified period of time from the seller or "writer" of the option. As a writer of options, the Corporation receives a premium at the outset and then bears the risk of an unfavorable change in the price of the financial instrument underlying the option.

Interest rate swap transactions generally involve the exchange of fixed and floating rate interest payment obligations without the exchange of the underlying principal amounts. Though swaps are also used as part of asset and liability management, most of the interest rate swap activity arises when the Corporation acts as an intermediary in arranging interest rate swap transactions for customers. The Corporation typically becomes a principal in the exchange of interest payments between the parties and, therefore, is exposed to loss should one of the parties default. The Corporation minimizes this risk by performing normal credit reviews on its swap customers and minimizes its exposure to the interest rate risk inherent in intermediated swaps by entering into offsetting swap positions that essentially counterbalance each other.

Entering into interest rate swap agreements involves not only the risk of dealing with counterparties and their ability to meet the terms of the contracts but also the interest rate risk associated with unmatched positions. Notional principal amounts often are used to express the volume of these transactions, but the amounts potentially subject to credit risk are much smaller.

Note Z: Significant Group Concentrations of Credit Risk

Most of the Corporation's business activity is with customers located within the state. As of December 31, 19XX, the Corporation's receivables from and guarantees of obligations of companies in the semiconductor industry were $XX million.

As of December 31, 19XX, the Corporation was also creditor for $XX of domestic loans and other receivables from companies with high debt to equity ratios as a result of buyout transactions. The portfolio is well diversified, consisting of XX industries. Generally, the loans are secured by assets or stock. The loans are expected to be repaid from cash flow or proceeds from the sale of selected assets of the borrowers. Credit losses arising from lending transactions with highly leveraged entities compare favorably with the Corporation's credit loss experience on its loan portfolio as a whole. The Corporation's policy for requiring collateral is **[state policy, along with information about the entity's access to that collateral or other security and a description of collateral]**.

Example 3—Concentration of Credit Risk for Certain Entities

48. For certain entities, industry or regional concentrations of credit risk may be disclosed adequately by a description of the business. For example:

a. *A Retailer*—XYZ Corporation is a retailer of family clothing with three stores, all of which are located in Littletown. The Corporation grants credit to customers, substantially all of whom are local residents.

b. *A Bank*—ABC Bank grants agribusiness, commercial, and residential loans to customers throughout the state. Although the Bank has a diversified loan portfolio, a substantial portion of its debtors' ability to honor their contracts is dependent upon the agribusiness economic sector.

**Disclosure of Information about Financial Instruments
with Off-Balance-Sheet Risk and Financial
Instruments with Concentrations of Credit Risk**   **FAS105**

Appendix D

BACKGROUND INFORMATION AND BASIS FOR CONCLUSIONS

CONTENTS

Appendix D

**BACKGROUND INFORMATION AND
BASIS FOR CONCLUSIONS**

Introduction

49. This appendix summarizes considerations that were deemed significant by Board members in reaching the conclusions in this Statement. It includes reasons for accepting certain views and rejecting others. Individual Board members gave greater weight to some factors than to others.

Background Information

50. The Board added a project on financial instruments and off-balance-sheet financing to its agenda in May 1986. Some of the financial reporting issues that prompted the project were not new, but financial innovation had created many new problems and given a new sense of urgency to settling some older ones.

51. Deregulation, foreign exchange and interest rate volatility, and tax law changes are major causes of the creation of new financial instruments. Deregulation and competition have increasingly clouded once relatively distinct lines between various financial and predominantly nonfinancial entities and have resulted in the expansion of financial services and products. Many financial instruments have been developed to reduce an entity's interest rate and foreign exchange rate risk resulting from volatile markets by transferring risk to other entities; other instruments have been created to provide tax advantages. Many of the innovative financial instruments are a result of breaking apart or combining traditional instruments. In addition to the important economic incentives, some financial instruments have been favored because of their accounting implications.

52. Some financial reporting issues related to financial instruments have been resolved by the Board or its predecessors. The FASB Emerging Issues Task Force has reached consensuses on other issues. However, those decisions have often dealt narrowly with specific financial reporting issues. Consequently, the specific guidance often does not clearly apply to new financial instruments, or the guidance developed to resolve various specific issues may appear to be inconsistent if applied to similar, but not identical, financial reporting problems.

53. Innovative financial instruments, which gave rise to inconsistent accounting and solutions developed on an ad hoc basis, caused many, including the accounting profession, the SEC, bank regulators, and some providers of financial statements, to urge the Board to add to its agenda a major project dealing with financial instruments and off-balance-sheet financing.

54. The Board decided that recognition and measurement problems dealing with financial instruments should be considered as several separate, though related, issues, including:

a. Whether assets should be considered sold if there is recourse or other continuing involvement with them; whether liabilities should be considered settled when assets are dedicated to settle them; and other questions of derecognition, nonrecognition, and offsetting of related assets and liabilities
b. How to account for financial instruments and transactions that seek to transfer market and credit risks—for example, futures contracts, interest rate swaps, options, forward commitments, nonrecourse arrangements, and financial guarantees—and for the underlying assets or liabilities to which the risk-transferring items are related
c. How financial instruments should be measured—for example, at market value, amortized original cost, or the lower of cost or market
d. How issuers should account for financial instruments that have both debt and equity characteristics
e. Whether the creation of separate legal entities or trusts affects the recognition and measurement of financial instruments (which may not need to be included in the financial instruments project because it is already being addressed in the Board's project on the reporting entity).

55. Because of the complexity of those issues, Statements dealing with them will be issued only after extensive Board deliberation, including discussion documents, public hearings, and Exposure Drafts. As an interim measure, pending completion of the recognition and measurement phases of the financial instruments project, the Board decided that improved disclosure of information about financial instruments is necessary to provide better information about those instruments and to increase comparability of financial statements.

56. On November 30, 1987, the Board issued the Exposure Draft, *Disclosures about Financial Instruments.* That Exposure Draft defined financial instruments broadly to include both instruments for which the risk of loss is recognized in the statement of financial position (for example, bonds, loans, and trade receivables and payables) and instruments with potential risk of accounting loss that may substantially exceed the amount recognized, if any, in the statement of financial position (for example, interest rate swaps, forward contracts to buy or sell government bonds, and loan commitments). The latter instruments are often referred to as "off-balance-sheet"; however, that is an inaccurate description of the instruments as a class because many are recognized in the statement of financial position to some extent.

57. The 1987 Exposure Draft proposed to require for *all* financial instruments (both with and without off-balance-sheet risk) disclosure of information about their credit risk (maximum credit risk, probable and reasonably possible credit losses, and individual, industry, or geographic concentrations); market risk, including interest rate and foreign exchange risks (effective interest rates and contractual repricing or maturity dates); liquidity risk (contractual future cash receipts and payments); and current market values if they could be determined or estimated.

58. After issuing the 1987 Exposure Draft, the Board (a) worked with a group of companies and accounting firms that participated in a test application of the Exposure Draft's provisions, (b) met with financial analysts, accounting and other professional groups, and representatives of agencies that regulate financial institutions, and (c) analyzed approximately 450 letters of comment received on the Exposure Draft to obtain a better understanding of the feasibility of implementing the proposed disclosure requirements, the potential implementation costs, and the usefulness of the resulting information.

59. Overall, the Board found that most respondents agreed that improving disclosure of information about financial instruments, especially financial instruments with off-balance-sheet risk, is a useful interim step pending completion of the recognition and measurement phases of the financial instruments project. Respondents also agreed in general with the purposes of disclosure set forth in the 1987 Exposure Draft: to describe both recog-

nized and unrecognized items, to provide a useful measure of unrecognized items and other relevant measures of recognized items, and to provide information to help investors and creditors assess risks and potentials of both recognized and unrecognized items. Most respondents also agreed that the areas of risk identified in the Exposure Draft—market, credit, and liquidity risk—need more comparable disclosure of information.

60. However, many respondents also asserted that the proposed disclosure requirements were too extensive and that the cost of implementing them would be excessive. Many respondents suggested that the proposed requirements were overly quantitative and that more emphasis should be placed on supplementing or even replacing some proposed required quantitative information with narrative or qualitative descriptions of the nature, terms, and purposes of an entity's financial instruments.

61. Many respondents expressed concern that off-balance-sheet issues were not sufficiently considered in the Exposure Draft. They noted that many of the proposed requirements (for example, future contractual receipts and payments and information about interest rates and foreign exchange rates) could not be applied to some financial instruments with off-balance-sheet risk because of the contingent or conditional nature of those instruments. Some recommended that the Board concentrate on those off-balance-sheet issues as the area of most immediate concern.

62. After considering those responses, the Board concluded that the most expeditious way to deal with what many respondents perceive as the area most in need of improvement was to consider the disclosure issues discussed in the 1987 Exposure Draft in phases. The first phase, covered by this Statement, considers principally financial instruments with off-balance-sheet risk, focusing on disclosing information about the extent, nature, and terms of those instruments and about the credit risks associated with them. The first phase also addresses concentrations of credit risk for *all* financial instruments. Subsequent phases will consider disclosure of other information about financial instruments.

63. An advisory group was formed in October 1986 to advise the Board during the initial deliberations on the disclosure phase of the project. That group was subsequently replaced by a task force on the financial instruments project that was appointed in January 1989 to assist the Board in all aspects of the project. The need to improve the information disclosed, the purposes of disclosures, and possible disclosure of information about financial instruments were discussed at public meet-

ings of those groups and at several public Board meetings.

64. On July 21, 1989, the Board issued the revised Exposure Draft, *Disclosure of Information about Financial Instruments with Off-Balance-Sheet Risk and Financial Instruments with Concentrations of Credit Risk.* One hundred and eighty-eight comment letters were received. The Board concluded that it could reach an informed decision on the basis of existing information without a public hearing.

Need to Improve Information Disclosed about Financial Instruments

65. Financial statements and notes to those statements provide considerable descriptive information about financial instruments and the risks involved with them in addition to the information provided by the recognition of many financial instruments in statements of financial position. However, the Board concluded that not all relevant information about financial instruments has been adequately disclosed and not all information disclosed has been comparable.

66. Some entities have disclosed information not required by generally accepted accounting principles; others have disclosed information to comply with requirements of the SEC, or in reports required by those that regulate bank, savings and loan, insurance, and other industries or entities. But disclosure rules of the SEC apply only to public companies—some apply only to large banks and savings and loan holding companies—and the rules of other regulatory agencies apply only to specific regulated industries and only in special reports that, even if publicly available, are not distributed as widely as general-purpose financial statements.

67. Voluntary disclosures about financial instruments with off-balance-sheet risk and other information about recognized financial instruments differ, as might be expected, from entity to entity. Disclosure requirements of regulators tend to produce comparability within an industry, but different requirements for similar but separately regulated industries often do not. Comparability problems result from different time intervals used for disclosing information about future cash flows and interest rates, different principles in dealing with optional features of particular financial instruments, different measurement approaches, and other causes.

68. Each existing disclosure practice or rule may have responded to a particular perceived need when it was adopted. But the inadequacy of information disclosed about financial instruments and the lack

of comparability are inevitable consequences of the ad hoc way in which disclosure practices and requirements have evolved.

69. In response to those problems, the Board decided to seek improvements in information disclosed about financial instruments as the initial, interim step in its broad project on financial instruments and off-balance-sheet financing.

Approach Taken in Developing This Statement

70. The Board decided to improve information disclosed about financial instruments by extending and expanding practices presently existing within generally accepted accounting principles. The Board first considered the objectives of financial reporting, then the objectives or purposes of disclosures, and finally areas for improvement. The particular improvements identified in this Statement focus principally on financial instruments with off-balance-sheet risk.

Purposes of Disclosure

Objectives of Financial Reporting

71. The purposes of disclosure in financial reporting derive from the objectives of financial reporting. The objectives of financial reporting by business enterprises are based on the need to provide information that is useful to present and potential investors and creditors and other users in making rational investment, credit, and similar decisions about a particular enterprise. Since investors, creditors, and other users are interested in receiving cash from the enterprise, financial reporting should provide information to help them assess the amounts, timing, and uncertainty of prospective net cash flows of the enterprise because their prospects for receiving cash from investments in, loans to, or other participation in the enterprise depend significantly on its cash flow prospects. Financial reporting should respond to those user needs by providing information about the economic resources of an enterprise, the claims to those resources (its obligations to transfer resources to other entities and owners' equity), and the effects of transactions, other events, and circumstances that change resources and claims to those resources (FASB Concepts Statement No. 1, *Objectives of Financial Reporting by Business Enterprises,* paragraphs 34-40).

72. Similarly, the objectives of financial reporting by not-for-profit organizations are based on the need to provide information that is useful to present and potential resource providers and other users in making decisions about the allocations of resources to those organizations. Since resource providers and other users are interested in the success of the organization in carrying out its service objectives, financial statements should provide information to help them assess the services that a not-for-profit organization provides and its ability to continue to provide those services. Moreover, managers of a not-for-profit organization are accountable to resource providers and other users, not only for the custody and safekeeping of organization resources, but also for their efficient and effective use. Therefore, financial reporting should provide information useful in assessing how managers have discharged those responsibilities. Financial reporting should respond to those user needs by providing information about the economic resources, obligations, and net resources of a not-for-profit organization and the effects of transactions, events, and circumstances that change resources and interests in those resources (FASB Concepts Statement No. 4, *Objectives of Financial Reporting by Nonbusiness Organizations,* paragraphs 35-43).

Role of Financial Statements

73. Financial statements are a central feature of financial reporting. A full set of financial statements provides considerable information about an entity's economic resources (assets) and claims to those resources (liabilities and equity) and about the changes in those resources and claims. A full set of financial statements is necessary to satisfy the objectives of financial reporting. Further, a full set of financial statements requires notes or parenthetical disclosures to satisfy the objectives of financial reporting because of the practical limits on the information that can be conveyed in the body of financial statements.

Roles of Recognition and Disclosure

74. FASB Concepts Statement No. 5, *Recognition and Measurement in Financial Statements of Business Enterprises,* paragraph 6, says:

> Recognition is the process of formally recording or incorporating an item into the financial statements of an entity as an asset, liability, revenue, expense, or the like. Recognition includes depiction of an item in both words and numbers, with the amount included in the totals of the financial statements.

The words that describe a recognized item, or the category of like items that includes it, convey important information.

75. But recognition of an asset or liability, or of the effects of a transaction or other event, often does not disclose all the information financial reporting can and should provide for investors, creditors, and

other users. Disclosure of additional information often is necessary and commonly provided about recognized items. Moreover, many important items are not recognized as assets and liabilities in financial statements, and many transactions and other events are not recognized when they occur but only later when uncertainty about them is reduced sufficiently so that their effects are clear.

76. Concepts Statement 5, paragraph 7, develops the idea from Concepts Statement 1, paragraph 5, and Concepts Statement 4, paragraph 11:

. . . some useful information . . . is better provided, or can only be provided, by notes to financial statements or by supplementary information or other means of financial reporting:

a. Information disclosed in notes or parenthetically on the face of financial statements, such as significant accounting policies or alternative measures for assets or liabilities, amplifies or explains information recognized in the financial statements.[4] That sort of information is essential to understanding the information recognized in financial statements and has long been viewed as an integral part of financial statements prepared in accordance with generally accepted accounting principles.

[4]For example, notes provide essential descriptive information for long-term obligations, including when amounts are due, what interest they bear, and whether important restrictions are imposed by related covenants. . . .

77. The major purposes of disclosure identified by the Board based on the concepts summarized in the preceding paragraphs and its observations of present practices are (a) to describe both recognized and unrecognized items, (b) to provide a useful measure of unrecognized items and relevant measures of recognized items other than the measure recognized in the statement of financial position, and (c) to provide information to help investors and creditors assess risks and potentials of both recognized and unrecognized items. Those purposes are of primary importance for general-purpose external financial reporting, and they underlie most existing disclosure practices as well as the requirements of this Statement.

78. Another purpose underlying some disclosure requirements is to provide important information in the interim while other accounting issues are being studied in more depth. That purpose underlies, for example, FASB Statements No. 36, *Disclosure of Pension Information,* No. 47, *Disclosure of Long-Term Obligations,* and No. 81, *Disclosure of*

Postretirement Health Care and Life Insurance Benefits. It also underlies the requirements of this Statement.

Information Disclosed Provides Descriptions

79. One purpose of disclosure identified by the Board is to describe items recognized in the financial statements. The information conveyed by the brief description and the related amount recognized may suffice for a straightforward item like cash. However, additional descriptive information beyond that on the face of financial statements may need to be disclosed in notes or parenthetically for more complex items and for heterogeneous categories. For example, an explanatory disclosure about bonds payable might include a description of interest rates, maturity dates, and call provisions. For heterogeneous categories, such as portfolios of loans or common stocks, disclosure may include descriptions of the items or major subcategories of items combined in the category.

80. Information disclosed about financial instruments with off-balance-sheet risk describes characteristics that are not described in the statement of financial position. For example, disclosure of information about interest rate swaps might include the notional principal amounts, maturity dates, interest rates, dates on which interest rates change (if different from maturity), and perhaps other key features of the instruments or might illustrate the anticipated effects of those features. For conditional items, such as options written and financial guarantees, information disclosed might include the contract amounts or describe the reasons the entity engaged in those transactions and the conditions that would cause the entity to have an advantageous or disadvantageous result.

81. Information disclosed also commonly describes to some extent an entity's organizational structure, its accounting policies, events not recognized in its financial statements because they occurred after the financial statement date, and numerous other pertinent facts about the entity that may not be directly related to particular assets and liabilities or changes in them.

Information Disclosed May Provide Measures

82. For some financial instruments, the amount recognized, if any, in the entity's financial statements does not provide a measure of the instrument's risk of accounting loss. For example, an entity might recognize an asset or liability in connection with an interest rate swap contract. The risk of accounting loss could exceed the amount recognized as an asset in the statement of financial position, or the ultimate obligation could exceed the amount rec-

ognized as a liability in the statement of financial position. Unquantified descriptive information may be useful in helping investors and creditors to better understand the nature and terms of financial instruments with off-balance-sheet risk. However, it is also generally necessary to quantify in some way the entity's extent of involvement with financial instruments with off-balance-sheet risk and the entity's risk of accounting loss to give investors, creditors, and other users an idea of the relative importance of those instruments and their possible effects on the entity.

Information Disclosed Helps in Assessing Risks and Potentials

83. Whichever attribute of an asset or liability is measured in the financial statements, the amount recognized represents only a single point estimate of the future benefits or future sacrifices expected from the asset or liability. The amount recognized in the financial statements is determined with due care and regard to accounting standards, whose principal purpose is to guide or direct the determination of those amounts. However, a point estimate and a brief description can communicate only some of the information that investors, creditors, and other users need about future benefits embodied in assets or about future sacrifices embodied in liabilities. Additional information is generally necessary to help users assess the uncertainties that are present and the potential effects on the entity of the different possible outcomes. That need has been accepted in longstanding general practices of disclosure about loss and gain contingencies (codified in FASB Statement No. 5, *Accounting for Contingencies*, paragraphs 10 and 17(b)) and underlies many other present disclosure requirements and practices.

84. Benefit and sacrifice are not certain for most assets and many liabilities. For example, common stocks owned may go down, or up, in price before they are sold. Options written may require major outlays of cash or may expire unexercised depending principally on movements in the price of the underlying item. Investors, creditors, and other users trying to assess risks and potentials usually need information about all financial instruments to help them understand an entity's risk position.

85. Downside risk is perhaps of greater concern to investors and creditors than upside potential. While upside potential may increase profits, perhaps substantially, downside risk can eliminate profits, imperil creditors' likelihood of collection, or even destroy the entity. Financial instruments such as futures, forwards, swaps, options, and collars have the upside potential of producing gains and, through hedging, stabilizing an entity's finan-

cial position in an unstable market environment. But they also carry with them risks of sudden loss or failure if speculative positions are taken or if designated hedges prove not to be effective.

Consideration of Costs

86. While disclosures can produce benefits by providing descriptions and measures and can help in assessing risks and potentials, costs also must be considered in establishing standards that require disclosures. FASB Concepts Statement No. 2, *Qualitative Characteristics of Accounting Information,* paragraph 137, says:

> The costs of providing information are of several kinds, including costs of collecting and processing the information, costs of audit if it is subject to audit, costs of disseminating it to those who must receive it, costs associated with the dangers of litigation, and in some instances costs of disclosure in the form of a loss of competitive advantages vis-a-vis trade competitors, labor unions (with a consequent effect on wage demands), or foreign enterprises. The costs to the users of information, over and above those costs that preparers pass on to them, are mainly the costs of analysis and interpretation and may include costs of rejecting information that is redundant, for the diagnosis of redundancy is not without its cost.

Accordingly, disclosures should only be required if, in the Board's judgment, the benefits of the disclosures justify the related costs.

Disclosure of Information about Financial Instruments with Off-Balance-Sheet Risk and Financial Instruments with Concentrations of Credit Risk

87. When the Board decided to consider first the disclosure of information about financial instruments with off-balance-sheet risk and financial instruments with concentrations of credit risk, a primary objective was to improve the information disclosed about those instruments and to promote disclosure of comparable information in financial statements as quickly as possible. The Board also concluded that another primary objective of phase one was to bring the level of disclosure of information about financial instruments with off-balance-sheet risk at least up to that of existing disclosure requirements for on-balance-sheet financial instruments.

88. Consideration of the purposes of disclosure and observations of current practice and require-

Disclosure of Information about Financial Instruments with Off-Balance-Sheet Risk and Financial Instruments with Concentrations of Credit Risk

FAS105

ments led the Board to conclude that information about financial instruments with off-balance-sheet credit or market risk should disclose the extent, nature, and terms of an entity's financial instruments with off-balance-sheet risk, the cash requirements of those instruments, and the related credit risk of those instruments. The Board further concluded that financial statements should include information about financial instruments with concentrations of credit risk that would disclose the entity's exposure to credit risk due to changes in economic or other conditions. Paragraphs 89-112 provide the basis for the Board's conclusions about the specific information required to be disclosed by this Statement and about possible disclosures of information considered by the Board but not required. Areas to be considered in subsequent phases include disclosure of information about interest rates, future cash receipts and payments, and market value.

Extent, Nature, and Terms of an Entity's Financial Instruments with Off-Balance-Sheet Risk

89. The Board concluded that disclosing information about the face or contract amount (or notional principal amount) of financial instruments with off-balance-sheet risk provides a useful basis for assessing the extent to which an entity has open or outstanding contracts. The disclosure of that amount is intended to apprise investors, creditors, and other users that the entity is engaged in certain activities whose off-balance-sheet risk is beyond what is currently recognized in the statement of financial position. The face or contract amount gives investors and creditors an idea of the extent of involvement in transactions that have off-balance-sheet risk. That information conveys some of the same information provided by amounts recognized for on-balance-sheet instruments.

90. The July 1989 revised Exposure Draft included a requirement to disclose the amount recognized, if any, in the statement of financial position for instruments with off-balance-sheet risk. The Board asked for disclosure of amounts recognized in the statement of financial position because those amounts reduce the exposure to off-balance-sheet risk. Also, the Board was concerned that failure to disclose amounts already recognized for losses from risks may lead users to overestimate the risk of further losses that might be recognized.

91. Some respondents stated that to disclose the amount recognized in the statement of financial position applicable to financial instruments with off-balance-sheet risk is difficult if that amount is commingled with the allowance for loan losses and the entity assesses and recognizes the allowance for

the losses either on an overall basis or by counterparty rather than by class of financial instrument. For example, liabilities for losses on financial instruments with off-balance-sheet risk, such as standby commitments and guarantees, may be included in the allowance for loan losses rather than recognized as liabilities. After considering concerns of respondents about the practicability of identifying appropriate amounts in some cases, the Board decided not to require the disclosure of the amount recognized in the statement of financial position for instruments with off-balance-sheet risk. The Board continues to believe that disclosure of the amount recognized is often helpful to investors, creditors, and other users and therefore encourages entities to disclose those amounts.

92. Notwithstanding the above respondents' views about commingling of accounts in practice, the Board believes that probable credit losses, however assessed, either can be associated with or can be allocated for particular instruments. The Board believes that generally accepted accounting principles proscribe inclusion of an accrual for credit loss on a financial instrument with off-balance-sheet risk in a valuation account (allowance for loan losses) related to a recognized financial instrument.

93. The Board concluded that narrative descriptions of an entity's financial instruments with off-balance-sheet risk would help investors, creditors, and other users to understand better the effect that those instruments have on the entity. The Board concluded that a discussion of the credit and market risk and the cash requirements of those instruments and the entity's accounting policy for recognizing and measuring those instruments should be required for that purpose.

94. Some respondents previously had suggested requiring disclosure of information about the entity's purpose for holding or contracting financial instruments with off-balance-sheet risk, for example, whether a contract was intended to be a hedge or an investment. The Board concluded that the purpose of entering into a financial instrument may, in some cases, be self-evident from (a) the class of the instrument (for example, financial guarantees written or loan commitments or letters of credit written) or (b) the accounting policy (for example, the accounting policy may differ for those instruments designated as hedges and for those instruments designated as investment contracts). The Board concluded that a requirement to disclose the purpose of entering into certain financial instruments is not necessary because reporting entities are likely to disclose that information to explain more adequately the nature of risks of those instruments.

95. Some respondents suggested requiring disclosure of how an entity controls and monitors its off-balance-sheet risk. In part because it questioned whether the benefit of requiring that disclosure would justify the costs involved, the Board decided that that disclosure should not be required. The Board also was concerned that disclosure of that information might become "boilerplate" and thus of questionable relevance.

Credit Risk of Financial Instruments with Off-Balance-Sheet Credit Risk

96. The Board concluded that disclosure of information about amounts of credit risk and about collateral or other security should be required to help investors, creditors, and other users assess the credit risks of the entity.

Amounts of credit risk

97. Respondents to the revised Exposure Draft expressed concern about the requirement to disclose the amount that portrays the accounting loss the entity would incur if any party to the financial instrument failed completely to perform according to the terms of the contract and the collateral or other security, if any, for the amount due proved to be of no value to the entity. They stated that when the risk of loss is remote, disclosure is not required under Statement 5. Other respondents concurred with the Board's view that the amount to be disclosed should be conceptually the total amount that would be recognized (as an asset) if the instrument were an on-balance-sheet financial instrument. Collateral, if any, would not be considered, although it would be included in measuring any actual loss.

98. The Board concluded that disclosing the accounting credit risk exposure—the amount of accounting loss the entity would incur if the counterparty defaulted and the collateral or other security, if any, proved to be valueless—provides useful information for quantifying credit risk and should be required. That amount of exposure may not be a likely loss, but it delimits the total risk and provides a base point for analytical comparisons. Moreover, the amount of credit risk for financial instruments for which credit risk is not "off-balance-sheet" is recognized in the statement of financial position. For those instruments, the carrying amount in the statement of financial position defines the accounting loss the entity would incur due to complete counterparty failure. The Board concluded that the equivalent amount should be disclosed for financial instruments with off-balance-sheet risk.

Collateral

99. The Board concluded that disclosure of information about collateral or other security supporting financial instruments with off-balance-sheet risk is useful because collateral or other security generally reduces credit risk. The Board concluded that disclosing an entity's policy of requiring collateral or other security, and the entity's access to that collateral or security, along with a description of either the collateral or the security, would aid investors, creditors, and other users in assessing an entity's collateral policy and adequacy of the collateral in the event of default. The Board concluded also that while general information about collateral and other security may be useful and should be required, detailed information about the extent of coverage of potential loss may be difficult to quantify and should not be required. The Board decided to encourage disclosure of that information.

Concentrations of Credit Risk of All Financial Instruments

100. The Board concluded that disclosure of information about concentrations of credit risk resulting from exposures with an individual counterparty or groups of counterparties in the same industry or region or having similar economic characteristics should be required. Depending on the risks associated with an individual counterparty or groups of counterparties, a concentration of credit risk can be perceived as favorable or unfavorable, that is, as indicative of more or less credit risk. However, lack of diversification in a portfolio is generally considered—other factors being equal—to indicate greater exposure to credit risk. Concentration information also allows investors, creditors, and other users to make their own assessments of the credit risk associated with the area of concentration.

101. The Board considered specifying quantitative thresholds for determining reportable concentrations of credit risk with an individual counterparty or groups of counterparties. The Board concluded, however, that an entity should review its portfolio of financial instruments subjecting the entity to credit risk to determine if any significant concentrations of credit risk with an individual counterparty or groups of counterparties exist. Group concentrations of credit risk exist if a number of counterparties are engaged in similar activities or activities in the same region or have other similar economic characteristics that would cause their ability to meet contractual obligations to be similarly affected by changes in economic or other

Disclosure of Information about Financial Instruments with Off-Balance-Sheet Risk and Financial Instruments with Concentrations of Credit Risk

FAS105

conditions, for example, concentrations of credit risk resulting from loans to highly leveraged entities. The Board chose not to specify a threshold because "significance" depends, to a great extent, on individual circumstances.

102. In commenting on the revised Exposure Draft, some respondents suggested that additional guidance should be provided to define further group concentrations in similar activities, activities in the same region, or those having other similar economic characteristics. Others suggested that the Board should quantify *significant*. One reason given by some respondents was concern that the absence of more specific guidance allows room for "second-guessing" the conclusions reached by management after events have taken their course. While the Board understands those concerns, it finds persuasive the view that management judgment about concentrations and significance is in and of itself useful information. Therefore, the Board chose not to define further those terms.

103. Industry or regional concentrations often may be disclosed adequately by a description of the entity's principal activities, which may greatly reduce the cost of determining whether significant concentrations exist and of reporting their existence. For example, a local retail store may be able to disclose concentrations of credit risk adequately by describing its business, location, and the related granting of credit to local customers. In a similar manner, an entity whose principal activity consists of supplying parts to the computer industry may adequately disclose concentrations of credit risk by describing its principal activity and the related granting of credit to computer manufacturers. However, in other cases, a description of the principal activities may not provide sufficient information about concentrations of credit risk.

104. The Board considered requiring disclosure of concentrations of credit risk only for financial instruments with off-balance-sheet risk. However, the Board concluded that information about concentrations of credit risk is relevant only as related to an entity's entire credit risk portfolio. A judgment that a concentration exists is, in part, a judgment about significance and one that can be made only in the context of the total financial position of the entity. A judgment about concentrations within off-balance-sheet credit risk alone could result in disclosing information that is not significant in the context of the entity as a whole or in disclosing only a part of a concentration of the entity's credit risk thereby implying that no further risk of that kind exists. Therefore, the Board concluded that this Statement should require informa-

tion about concentrations of credit risk for *all* financial instruments.

105. Some respondents to the revised Exposure Draft suggested that information about lease receivables should be included in the disclosure of concentration information, primarily because leases constitute a significant element of credit risk for many entities. The Board decided to adopt that suggestion.

Exclusion of Certain Financial Instruments

106. The Board concluded that insurance contracts, other than financial guarantees and investment contracts, as discussed in Statements 60 and 97, should be excluded from this Statement's requirements because the significant business risks involved are generally other than credit and market risk. The risks associated with insurance contracts relate to cash surrender values, lapses, mortality, morbidity, and casualty risks.

107. The Board also excluded from this Statement's requirements (a) employers' and plans' obligations for pension benefits,[18] employers' and plans' obligations for postretirement health care and life insurance benefits, employer stock option and stock purchase plans for employees, employers' obligations for compensated absences, and other forms of deferred compensation, (b) financial instruments of a pension plan, including plan assets, when subject to the accounting and reporting requirements of Statement 87, (c) lease contracts (except for information about concentrations of credit risk), (d) unconditional purchase obligations subject to the disclosure requirements of Statement 47, and (e) extinguished debt subject to the disclosure requirements of Statement 76 and any assets held in trust in connection with an in-substance defeasance of that debt.

108. The Board or its predecessors previously have deliberated the information to be reported about those financial instruments with the exception of employers' accounting for postretirement health care and life insurance benefits, and adequate disclosure requirements exist. This Statement does not change the specific disclosure requirements for those financial instruments. As part of the Board's project on employers' accounting for postretirement health care and life insurance benefits, Statement 81 on disclosure of information was issued and should continue to be followed pending completion of the project.

109. Financial instruments of a pension plan, including plan assets, when subject to the accounting

---

[18]Contractual obligations other than those for pension benefits are not, however, excluded from this Statement's requirements.

and reporting requirements of Statement 87, are excluded from this Statement's requirements because of the financial reporting burden that would likely ensue. The Board was concerned that the information that otherwise would be required to be disclosed would not be easily determinable by employers and that the costs of compliance would be excessive. The Board considered but decided not to exclude from this Statement's requirements financial instruments of a pension plan, other than obligations for pension benefits, when the plan is subject to the accounting and reporting requirements of Statement 35. Concerns were not expressed about the cost and feasibility of compliance by employers for pension plans.

110. The Board developed the definition of financial instruments with off-balance-sheet risk of accounting loss to establish a scope that would include instruments that are generally considered to be off-balance-sheet instruments. The Board is aware that some instruments that may be considered to be on-balance-sheet have off-balance-sheet risk as defined by this Statement. Appendix B of the revised Exposure Draft included a list of financial instruments that have and do not have off-balance-sheet risk. The list of "traditional items" included "obligations receivable/payable in foreign currency" and indicated that those obligations do not result in off-balance-sheet risk to either the holder or the issuer. One respondent to the revised Exposure Draft observed that obligations payable denominated in foreign currency meet the definition of financial instruments with off-balance-sheet risk. The Board acknowledges that those obligations have off-balance-sheet risk of accounting loss as defined by this Statement.

111. In determining whether those instruments should be included in the disclosure requirements of this Statement for instruments with off-balance-sheet risk, the Board acknowledged that it had not previously contemplated that those instruments would be covered by this Statement. The Board noted that present practice generally includes disclosures about long-term debt denominated in foreign currency. Therefore, for practical reasons, the Board decided to exclude certain financial instrument obligations denominated in foreign currencies from the disclosure requirements for instruments with off-balance-sheet risk as described in paragraph 15(b) of this Statement.

112. The Board also noted that Appendix B of the revised Exposure Draft did not include the obligation arising when financial instruments are sold short as an example of an instrument with off-balance-sheet risk. The Board observed that those instruments do have off-balance-sheet market risk

and are subject to the disclosure requirements of this Statement.

Need for Judgment

113. Judgment will be needed in developing some of the information required to be disclosed by this Statement. The degree of judgment needed, for example, to identify significant industry or regional concentrations is similar to that needed to comply with other longstanding accounting and reporting requirements, such as determining allowances for losses on loans, inventory obsolescence, and litigation.

Application in Comparative Financial Statements

114. The Board decided that in the initial transitional year of applying the provisions of this Statement, disclosure of information beyond that already provided should be required only for the financial statements for the year of initial application. To obtain information retroactively that was not required for prior years might be difficult and costly for some entities, and the Board believes the benefits would not justify the costs.

115. The Board concluded that comparative disclosure of information about the extent, nature, and terms of financial instruments with off-balance-sheet risk would help investors, creditors, and other users assess any pertinent trends and the extent to which an entity is involved in investments with off-balance-sheet risk.

116. The Board also concluded that disclosure of information about the accounting loss an entity would incur if any party failed completely to perform according to a contract and information about collateral should be required on a comparative basis because that information is basically an extension of what is already generally provided about recognized financial instruments for each period included in comparative financial statements. Although no specific disclosure of information about collateral for recognized financial instruments is presently called for, the balance sheet description of certain financial instruments, for example, "real estate loans," "consumer loans," and "commercial loans," often gives a user an indication of whether the instrument is secured or collateralized. The Board concluded that the disclosure of comparative information also should extend to concentrations of credit risk so that an investor, creditor, or other user would have an indication of changes in that involvement.

117. The Board concluded that the requirement in this Statement to disclose that information on a comparative basis is consistent with ARB No. 43,

Chapter 2, "Form of Statements," and Concepts Statement 2:

> In any one year it is ordinarily desirable that the balance sheet, the income statement, and the surplus statement be given for one or more preceding years as well as for the current year. *Footnotes,* explanations, and accountants' qualifications *which appeared on the statements for the preceding years should be repeated,* or at least referred to, in the comparative statements to the extent that they continue to be of significance. [Chapter 2, Section A, paragraph 2, emphasis added.]

> Information about an enterprise gains greatly in usefulness *if it can be compared* with similar information about other enterprises and *with similar information about the same enterprise for some other period* or some other point in time. The significance of information, especially quantitative information, depends to a great extent on the user's ability to relate it to some benchmark. The comparative use of information is often intuitive, as when told that an enterprise has sales revenue of $1,000,000 a year, one forms a judgment of its size by ranking it with other enterprises that one knows. Investing and lending decisions essentially involve evaluations of alternative opportunities, and they cannot be made rationally if comparative information is not available.
> . . . the purpose of comparison is to detect and explain similarities and differences. Comparability should not be confused with identity, and sometimes more can be learned from differences than from similarities if the differences can be explained. The ability to explain phenomena often depends on the diagnosis of the underlying causes of differences or the discovery that apparent differences are without significance. [Concepts Statement 2, paragraphs 111 and 119, emphasis added.]

Applicability to Small, Nonpublic, or Nonfinancial Entities

118. The Board considered whether certain entities should be excluded from the scope of this Statement and concluded that the Statement should apply to all entities. In particular, the Board considered the usefulness of the disclosure of information for small, nonpublic, or predominantly nonfinancial entities. After considering the costs and benefits of the disclosure of information about financial instruments with off-balance-sheet risk and financial instruments with concentrations of credit risk required

by this Statement, the Board concluded that the disclosures are important for small and nonpublic entities and should be required. To the extent that a small or nonpublic entity has those instruments, some respondents have suggested that the disclosures required by this Statement may have a greater effect because, while many larger, public entities have disclosed information about financial instruments with off-balance-sheet risk voluntarily, few of the smaller or nonpublic entities have done so. The Board also observed that many small entities may have few, if any, financial instruments with off-balance-sheet risk.

119. The Board also considered whether the provisions of this Statement should apply to predominantly nonfinancial entities. The Board concluded that while this Statement likely would have its greatest effect on the financial reporting of entities whose assets and liabilities are primarily financial instruments, financial instruments with off-balance-sheet risk and financial instruments with concentrations of credit risk may constitute a significant part of the assets and liabilities of predominantly nonfinancial entities and disclosure of information about them is useful and should be required. Furthermore, in today's environment, distinguishing between financial entities and nonfinancial entities is often difficult.

Location of Information within Financial Reports

120. The Board considered whether the disclosure of information required by this Statement should be part of basic financial statements or should be provided as supplementary information. Concepts Statement 5 distinguishes between information that should be part of the basic financial statements and that which should be provided as supplementary information. Paragraph 7 of that concepts Statement emphasizes that information disclosed as part of the basic financial statements amplifies or explains information recognized in financial statements and is essential to understanding that information.

121. The disclosures required by this Statement build on the disclosures already included in basic financial statements and, like them, serve the major purposes of disclosure summarized in paragraph 77. In the past, requiring information as supplementary has also been a way of excluding certain entities from the scope of the requirements; however, as discussed in paragraphs 118 and 119, the Board concluded that the disclosures called for in this Statement should be provided by all entities. The Board concluded that there were no persuasive reasons for the disclosures about financial instruments to be outside the basic financial statements.

122. In responding to the revised Exposure Draft, certain investment companies observed that they already make extensive disclosure of information about financial instruments, including financial instruments subject to the disclosure requirements of this Statement. They observed further that those disclosures may appear in proxy materials or other materials outside the financial statements or in other documents separate from the financial statements. They asked that the Board consider permitting incorporation in the financial statements by reference in the notes to the financial statements. The Board does not object to incorporation of information by reference as long as that information is included elsewhere in the document containing the financial statements.

Effective Date

123. Prior to the release of the revised Exposure Draft, many constituents noted that completion of this phase of the disclosure project would be desirable as soon as practicable so that the Board could proceed to address remaining disclosure issues. Others commented that investors, creditors, and other users would be better prepared to respond to issues about financial instruments—both those about disclosure of information and those about recognition and measurement—with the benefit of the information about financial instruments required by this Statement.

124. Some had expressed concern, however, that some entities may not currently accumulate some of the required information. After consideration of those comments, the Board concluded that the effective date for all disclosure requirements of this Statement should be for financial statements issued for fiscal years ending after June 15, 1990. The Board, however, encourages entities to apply the disclosure requirements for financial statements issued for fiscal years ending on or before that date.

Statement of Financial Accounting Standards No. 106
Employers' Accounting for Postretirement Benefits
Other Than Pensions

STATUS

Issued: December 1990

Effective Date: For fiscal years beginning after December 15, 1992

Affects: Amends APB 12, paragraph 6
Supersedes APB 12, footnote 1
Amends APB 16, paragraph 88
Supersedes FAS 81
Amends FAS 87, paragraph 8
Supersedes FAS 87, footnote 3
Supersedes FTB 87-1

Affected by: No other pronouncements

Other Interpretive Releases: FASB Special Report, *A Guide to Implementation of Statement 106 on Employers' Accounting for Postretirement Benefits Other Than Pensions: Questions and Answers*
FASB Special Report, *A Guide to Implementation of Statement 87 on Employers' Accounting for Pensions: Questions and Answers*
FASB Special Report, *A Guide to Implementation of Statement 88 on Employers' Accounting for Settlements and Curtailments of Defined Benefit Pension Plans and for Termination Benefits: Questions and Answers*

Note: Although the Special Reports for Statements 87 and 88 do not specifically refer to postretirement benefits other than pensions, the user is referred to them because of the similarity in accounting.

Issues Discussed by FASB Emerging Issues Task Force (EITF)

Affects: Nullifies EITF Issue No. 86-20
Partially resolves EITF Issue No. 84-35
Resolves EITF Issue No. 86-19

Interpreted by: Paragraph 105 interpreted by EITF Issue No. 86-27
Paragraph 186 interpreted by EITF Topic No. D-36
Paragraphs 308 and 518 interpreted by EITF Issue No. 93-3

Related Issues: EITF Issues No. 88-23, 92-12, 92-13, and 96-5 and Topic No. D-27

SUMMARY

This Statement establishes accounting standards for employers' accounting for postretirement benefits other than pensions (hereinafter referred to as postretirement benefits). Although it applies to all forms of postretirement benefits, this Statement focuses principally on postretirement health care benefits. It will significantly change the prevalent current practice of accounting for postretirement benefits on a pay-as-you-go (cash) basis by requiring accrual, during the years that the employee renders the necessary service, of the expected cost of providing those benefits to an employee and the employee's beneficiaries and covered dependents.

The Board's conclusions in this Statement result from the view that a defined postretirement benefit plan sets forth the terms of an exchange between the employer and the employee. In exchange for the current services provided by the employee, the employer promises to provide, in addition to current wages and other benefits, health and other welfare benefits after the employee retires. It follows from that view that postretirement benefits are not gratuities but are part of an employee's compensation for services rendered. Since payment is deferred, the benefits are a type of deferred compensation. The employer's obligation for that compensation is incurred as employees render the services necessary to earn their postretirement benefits.

The ability to measure the obligation for postretirement health care benefits and the recognition of that obligation have been the subject of controversy. The Board believes that measurement of the obligation and accrual of the cost based on best estimates are superior to implying, by a failure to accrue, that no obligation exists prior to the payment of benefits. The Board believes that failure to recognize an obligation prior to its payment impairs the usefulness and integrity of the employer's financial statements.

The Board's objectives in issuing this Statement are to improve employers' financial reporting for postretirement benefits in the following manner:

a. To enhance the relevance and representational faithfulness of the employer's reported results of operations by recognizing net periodic postretirement benefit cost as employees render the services necessary to earn their postretirement benefits
b. To enhance the relevance and representational faithfulness of the employer's statement of financial position by including a measure of the obligation to provide postretirement benefits based on a mutual understanding between the employer and its employees of the terms of the underlying plan
c. To enhance the ability of users of the employer's financial statements to understand the extent and effects of the employer's undertaking to provide postretirement benefits to its employees by disclosing relevant information about the obligation and cost of the postretirement benefit plan and how those amounts are measured
d. To improve the understandability and comparability of amounts reported by requiring employers with similar plans to use the same method to measure their accumulated postretirement benefit obligations and the related costs of the postretirement benefits.

Similarity to Pension Accounting

The provisions of this Statement are similar, in many respects, to those in FASB Statements No. 87, *Employers' Accounting for Pensions,* and No. 88, *Employers' Accounting for Settlements and Curtailments of Defined Benefit Pension Plans and for Termination Benefits.* To the extent the promise to provide pension benefits and the promise to provide postretirement benefits are similar, the provisions of this Statement are similar to those prescribed by Statements 87 and 88; different accounting treatment is prescribed only when the Board has concluded that there is a compelling reason for different treatment. Appendix B identifies the major similarities and differences between this Statement and employers' accounting for pensions.

Basic Tenets

This Statement relies on a basic premise of generally accepted accounting principles that accrual accounting provides more relevant and useful information than does cash basis accounting. The importance of information about cash flows or the funding of the postretirement benefit plan is not ignored. Amounts funded or paid are given accounting recognition as uses of cash, but the Board believes that information about cash flows alone is insufficient. Accrual accounting goes beyond cash transactions and attempts to recognize the financial effects of noncash transactions and events as they occur. Recognition and measurement of the accrued obligation to provide postretirement benefits will provide users of financial statements with the opportunity to assess the financial consequences of employers' compensation decisions.

In applying accrual accounting to postretirement benefits, this Statement adopts three fundamental aspects of pension accounting: delayed recognition of certain events, reporting net cost, and offsetting liabilities and related assets.

Delayed recognition means that certain changes in the obligation for postretirement benefits, including those changes arising as a result of a plan initiation or amendment, and certain changes in the value of plan assets set aside to meet that obligation are not recognized as they occur. Rather, those changes are recognized systematically over future periods. All changes in the obligation and plan assets ultimately are recognized unless they are first reduced by other changes. The changes that have been identified and quantified but not yet recognized in the employer's financial statements as components of net periodic postretirement benefit cost and as a liability or asset are disclosed.

Net cost means that the recognized consequences of events and transactions affecting a postretirement benefit plan are reported as a single amount in the employer's financial statements. That single amount includes at least three types of events or transactions that might otherwise be reported separately. Those events or transactions—exchanging a promise of deferred compensation in the form of postretirement benefits for employee service, the interest cost arising from the passage of time until those benefits are paid, and the returns from the investment of plan assets—are disclosed separately as components of net periodic postretirement benefit cost.

Offsetting means that plan assets restricted for the payment of postretirement benefits offset the accumulated postretirement benefit obligation in determining amounts recognized in the employer's statement of financial position and that the return on those plan assets offsets postretirement benefit cost in the employer's statement of income. That offsetting is reflected even though the obligation has not been settled, the investment of the plan assets may be largely controlled by the employer, and substantial risks and rewards associated with both the obligation and the plan assets are borne by the employer.

Recognition and Measurement

The Board is sensitive to concerns about the reliability of measurements of the postretirement health care benefit obligation. The Board recognizes that limited historical data about per capita claims costs are available and that actuarial practice in this area is still developing. The Board has taken those factors into consideration in its decisions to delay the effective date for this Statement, to emphasize disclosure, and to permit employers to phase in recognition of the transition obligation in their statements of financial position. However, the Board believes that those factors are insufficient reason not to use accrual accounting for postretirement benefits in financial reporting. With increased experience, the reliability of measures of the obligation and cost should improve.

An objective of this Statement is that the accounting reflect the terms of the exchange transaction that takes place between an employer that provides postretirement benefits and the employees who render services in exchange for those benefits. Generally the extant written plan provides the best evidence of that exchange transaction. However, in some situations, an employer's cost-sharing policy, as evidenced by past practice or by communication of intended changes to a plan's cost-sharing provisions, or a past practice of regular increases in certain monetary benefits may indicate that the substantive plan—the plan as understood by the parties to the exchange transaction—differs from the extant written plan. The substantive plan is the basis for the accounting.

This Statement requires that an employer's obligation for postretirement benefits expected to be provided to or for an employee be fully accrued by the date that employee attains full eligibility for all of the benefits expected to be received by that employee, any beneficiaries, and covered dependents (the full eligibility date), even if the employee is expected to render additional service beyond that date. That accounting reflects the fact that at the full eligibility date the employee has provided all of the service necessary to earn the right to receive all of the benefits that employee is expected to receive under the plan.

The beginning of the attribution (accrual) period is the employee's date of hire unless the plan only grants credit for service from a later date, in which case benefits are generally attributed from the beginning of that credited service period. An equal amount of the expected postretirement benefit obligation is attributed to each year of service in the attribution period unless the plan attributes a disproportionate share of the expected benefits to employees' early years of service. The Board concluded that, like accounting for other deferred compensation agreements, accounting for postretirement benefits should reflect the explicit or implicit contract between the employer and its employees.

Single Method

The Board believes that understandability, comparability, and usefulness of financial information are improved by narrowing the use of alternative accounting methods that do not reflect different facts and circumstances. The Board has been unable to identify circumstances that would make it appropriate for different employers to use fundamentally different accounting methods or measurement techniques for similar postretirement benefit plans or for a single employer to use fundamentally different methods or measurement techniques for different plans. As a result, a single method is prescribed for measuring and recognizing an employer's accumulated postretirement benefit obligation.

Amendment to Opinion 12

An employer's practice of providing postretirement benefits to selected employees under individual contracts, with specific terms determined on an individual-by-individual basis, does not constitute a postretirement benefit *plan* under this Statement. This Statement amends APB Opinion No. 12, *Omnibus Opinion—1967*, to explicitly require that an employer's obligation under deferred compensation contracts be accrued following the terms of the individual contract over the required service periods to the date the employee is fully eligible for the benefits.

Transition

Unlike the effects of most other accounting changes, a transition obligation for postretirement benefits generally reflects, to a considerable extent, the failure to accrue the accumulated postretirement benefit obligation in earlier periods as it arose rather than the effects of a change from one acceptable accrual method of accounting to another. The Board believes that accounting for transition from one method of accounting to another is a practical matter and that a major objective of that accounting is to minimize the cost and mitigate the disruption to the extent possible without unduly compromising the ability of financial statements to provide useful information.

This Statement measures the transition obligation as the unfunded and unrecognized accumulated postretirement benefit obligation for all plan participants. Two options are provided for recognizing that transition obligation. An employer can choose to immediately recognize the transition obligation as the effect of an accounting change, subject to certain limitations. Alternatively, an employer can choose to recognize the transition obligation in the statement of financial position and statement of income on a delayed basis over the plan participants' future service periods, with disclosure of the unrecognized amount. However, that delayed recognition cannot result in less rapid recognition than accounting for the transition obligation on a pay-as-you-go basis.

Effective Dates

This Statement generally is effective for fiscal years beginning after December 15, 1992, except that the application of this Statement to plans outside the United States and certain small, nonpublic employers is delayed to fiscal years beginning after December 15, 1994. The amendment of Opinion 12 is effective for fiscal years beginning after March 15, 1991.

* * *

The Board appreciates the contributions of the many people and organizations that assisted the Board in its research on this project.

Statement of Financial Accounting Standards No. 106

Employers' Accounting for Postretirement Benefits Other Than Pensions

CONTENTS

INTRODUCTION

1. This Statement establishes standards of financial accounting and reporting for an employer that offers **postretirement benefits other than pensions**[1] (hereinafter referred to as **postretirement benefits**) to its employees.[2] The Board added a project on postemployment **benefits** other than pensions to its agenda in 1979 as part of its project on accounting for pensions and other postemployment benefits. In 1984, the subject of accounting for postemployment benefits other than pensions was identified as a separate project. As interim measures, FASB Statement No. 81, *Disclosure of Postretirement Health Care and Life Insurance Benefits,* was issued in November 1984, and FASB Technical Bulletin No. 87-1, *Accounting for a Change in Method of Accounting for Certain Postretirement Benefits,* was issued in April 1987.

2. Most employers have accounted for postretirement benefits on a pay-as-you-go (cash) basis. As the prevalence and magnitude of employers' promises to provide those benefits have increased, there has been increased concern about the failure of financial reporting to identify the financial effects of those promises.

3. The Board views a **postretirement benefit plan** as a deferred compensation arrangement whereby an employer promises to exchange future benefits for employees' current services. Because the obligation to provide benefits arises as employees render the services necessary to earn the benefits pursuant to the terms of the **plan,** the Board believes that the cost of providing the benefits should be recognized over those employee service periods.

4. This Statement addresses, for the first time, the accounting issues related to measuring and recognizing the exchange that takes place between an employer that provides postretirement benefits and the employees who render services in exchange for those benefits. The Board believes the accounting recognition required by this Statement should result in more useful and representationally faithful financial statements. However, this Statement is not likely to be the final step in the evolution of more useful accounting for postretirement benefit arrangements.

5. The Board's objectives in issuing this Statement are to improve employers' financial reporting for postretirement benefits in the following manner:

a. To enhance the relevance and representational faithfulness of the employer's reported results of operations by recognizing **net periodic postretirement benefit cost**[3] as employees render the services necessary to earn their postretirement benefits

b. To enhance the relevance and representational faithfulness of the employer's statement of financial position by including a measure of the obligation to provide postretirement benefits based on a mutual understanding between the employer and its employees of the terms of the underlying plan

c. To enhance the ability of users of the employer's financial statements to understand the extent and effects of the employer's undertaking to provide postretirement benefits to its employees by disclosing relevant information about the obligation and cost of the postretirement benefit plan and how those amounts are measured

d. To improve the understandability and comparability of amounts reported by requiring employers with similar plans to use the same method to measure their **accumulated postretirement benefit obligations** and the related costs of the postretirement benefits.

STANDARDS OF FINANCIAL ACCOUNTING AND REPORTING

Scope

6. This Statement applies to *all* postretirement benefits expected to be provided by an employer to current and former employees (including **retirees,** disabled employees,[4] and other former employees who are expected to receive postretirement benefits), their beneficiaries, and covered dependents, pursuant to the terms of an employer's undertak-

---

[1] Words that appear in the glossary are set in **boldface type** the first time they appear.

[2] The accounting for benefits paid after employment but before retirement (for example, layoff benefits) is a separate phase of the Board's project on accounting for postemployment benefits other than pensions. The fact that this Statement does not apply to those benefits should not be construed as discouraging the use of accrual accounting for those benefits.

[3] This Statement uses the term *net periodic postretirement benefit cost* rather than *net postretirement benefit expense* because part of the cost recognized in a period may be capitalized along with other costs as part of an asset such as inventory.

[4] The determination of disability benefits to be accrued pursuant to this Statement is based on the terms of the postretirement benefit plan defining when a disabled employee is entitled to postretirement benefits.

ing to provide those benefits. Postretirement benefits include, but are not limited to, postretirement health care;[5] life insurance provided outside a pension plan to retirees; and other welfare benefits such as tuition assistance, day care, legal services, and housing subsidies provided after retirement. Often those benefits are in the form of a reimbursement to plan participants or direct payment to providers for the cost of specified services as the need for those services arises, but they may also include benefits payable as a lump sum, such as death benefits. This Statement also applies to **settlement** of all or a part of an employer's accumulated postretirement benefit obligation or **curtailment** of a postretirement benefit plan and to an employer that provides postretirement benefits as part of a special **termination benefits** offer.

7. For the purposes of this Statement, a postretirement benefit plan is an arrangement that is mutually understood by an employer and its employees, whereby an employer undertakes to provide its current and former employees with benefits after they retire in exchange for the employees' services over a specified period of time, upon attaining a specified age while in service, or both. Benefits may commence immediately upon termination of service or may be deferred until retired employees attain a specified age.

8. An employer's practice of providing postretirement benefits may take a variety of forms and the obligation may or may not be funded. This Statement applies to any arrangement that is in substance a postretirement benefit plan, regardless of its form or the means or timing of its funding. This Statement applies both to written plans and to unwritten plans whose existence is discernible either from a practice of paying postretirement benefits or from oral representations made to current or former employees. Absent evidence to the contrary, it shall be presumed that an employer that has provided postretirement benefits in the past or is currently promising those benefits to employees will continue to provide those future benefits.

9. This Statement applies to deferred compensation contracts with individual employees if those contracts, taken together, are equivalent to a plan that provides postretirement benefits. It does not apply to an employer's practice of providing post-

retirement benefits to selected employees under individual contracts with specific terms determined on an individual-by-individual basis. Those contracts shall be accounted for individually, following the terms of the contract. To the extent the contract does not attribute the benefits to individual years of service, the expected future benefits should be accrued over the period of service required to be rendered in exchange for the benefits. (Refer to paragraph 13.)

10. A postretirement benefit plan may be part of a larger plan or arrangement that provides benefits currently to active employees as well as to retirees. In those circumstances, the promise to provide benefits to present and future retirees under the plan shall be segregated from the promise to provide benefits currently to active employees and shall be accounted for in accordance with the provisions of this Statement.

11. This Statement does not apply to pension or life insurance benefits provided through a pension plan. The accounting for those benefits is set forth in FASB Statements No. 87, *Employers' Accounting for Pensions,* and No. 88, *Employers' Accounting for Settlements and Curtailments of Defined Benefit Pension Plans and for Termination Benefits.*[6]

12. This Statement supersedes FASB Statement No. 81, *Disclosure of Postretirement Health Care and Life Insurance Benefits.* Paragraphs 13 and 114 of this Statement amend APB Opinion No. 12, *Omnibus Opinion—1967*; paragraph 14 amends Statement 87; and paragraph 89 amends APB Opinion No. 16, *Business Combinations.* Paragraph 115 rescinds FASB Technical Bulletin No. 87-1, *Accounting for a Change in Method of Accounting for Certain Postretirement Benefits.*

Amendment to Opinion 12

13. The following paragraphs and footnote replace the first four sentences and footnote of paragraph 6 of Opinion 12:

FASB Statement No. 87, *Employers' Accounting for Pensions,* or Statement No. 106, *Employers' Accounting for Postretirement Benefits Other Than Pensions,* applies to deferred

---

[5]Postretirement health care benefits are likely to be the most significant in terms of cost and prevalence, and certain of the issues that arise in measuring those benefits are unique. Therefore, much of the language of this Statement focuses on postretirement health care plans. Nevertheless, this Statement applies equally to all postretirement benefits.

[6]Two Special Reports prepared by the FASB staff, *A Guide to Implementation of Statement 87 on Employers' Accounting for Pensions,* and *A Guide to Implementation of Statement 88 on Employers' Accounting for Settlements and Curtailments of Defined Benefit Pension Plans and for Termination Benefits,* provide accounting guidance on implementation questions raised in connection with Statements 87 and 88. Many of the provisions in this Statement are the same as or are similar to the provisions of Statements 87 and 88. Consequently, the guidance provided in those Special Reports should be useful in understanding and implementing many of the provisions of this Statement.

compensation contracts with individual employees if those contracts, taken together, are equivalent to a postretirement income plan or a postretirement health or welfare benefit plan, respectively. Other deferred compensation contracts shall be accounted for individually on an accrual basis in accordance with the terms of the underlying contract.

To the extent the terms of the contract attribute all or a portion of the expected future benefits to an individual year of the employee's service, the cost of those benefits shall be recognized in that year. To the extent the terms of the contract attribute all or a portion of the expected future benefits to a period of service greater than one year, the cost of those benefits shall be accrued over that period of the employee's service in a systematic and rational manner. At the end of that period the aggregate amount accrued shall equal the then present value of the benefits expected to be provided to the employee, any beneficiaries, and covered dependents in exchange for the employee's service to that date.[*]

---

[*]The amounts to be accrued periodically shall result in an accrued amount at the full eligibility date (as defined in Statement 106) equal to the then present value of all of the future benefits expected to be paid. Paragraphs 413-416 of Statement 106 illustrate application of this paragraph.

Amendment to Statement 87

14. The following sentences replace the first two sentences and footnote of paragraph 8 of Statement 87:

This Statement does not apply to life insurance benefits provided outside a pension plan or to other postretirement health and welfare benefits. The accounting for those benefits is set forth in FASB Statement No. 106, *Employers' Accounting for Postretirement Benefits Other Than Pensions.*

Use of Reasonable Approximations

15. This Statement is intended to specify accounting objectives and results rather than computational means of obtaining those results. If estimates, averages, or computational shortcuts can reduce the cost of applying this Statement, their use is appropriate, provided the results are reasonably expected not to be materially different from the results of a detailed application.

Single-Employer Defined Benefit Postretirement Plans

16. This Statement primarily focuses on an employer's accounting for a **single-employer plan** that defines the postretirement benefits to be provided to retirees. For purposes of this Statement, a **defined benefit postretirement plan** is one that defines the postretirement benefits in terms of (a) monetary amounts (for example, $100,000 of life insurance) or (b) benefit coverage to be provided (for example, up to $200 per day for hospitalization, 80 percent of the cost of specified surgical procedures, and so forth). (Specified monetary amounts and benefit coverage are hereinafter collectively referred to as *benefits.*)

17. In some cases, an employer may limit its obligation through an individual or an aggregate "cap" on the employer's cost or benefit obligation. For example, an employer may elect to limit its annual postretirement benefit obligation for each retired plan participant to a maximum of $5,000. Or, an employer may elect to limit its share of the aggregate cost of covered postretirement health care benefits for a period to an amount determined based on an average per capita cost per retired plan participant. Plans of that nature are considered to be defined benefit postretirement plans. Paragraphs 472-478 illustrate measurement considerations for defined-dollar capped plans.

18. A postretirement benefit is part of the compensation paid to an employee for services rendered. In a defined benefit plan, the employer promises to provide, in addition to current wages and benefits, future benefits during retirement. Generally, the amount of those benefits depends on the **benefit formula** (which may include factors such as the number of years of service rendered or the employee's compensation before retirement or termination), the longevity of the retiree and any beneficiaries and covered dependents, and the incidence of events requiring benefit payments (for example, illnesses affecting the amount of health care required). In most cases, services are rendered over a number of years before an employee retires and begins to receive benefits or is entitled to receive benefits as a need arises. Even though the services rendered by the employee are complete and the employee has retired, the total amount of benefits the employer has promised and the cost to the employer of the services rendered are not precisely determinable but can be estimated using the plan's benefit formula and estimates of the effects of relevant future events.

Basic Elements of Accounting for Postretirement Benefits

19. Any method of accounting that recognizes the cost of postretirement benefits over employee service periods (before the payment of benefits to retirees) must deal with two factors that stem from the

nature of the arrangement. First, estimates or **assumptions** must be made about the future events that will determine the amount and timing of the benefit payments. Second, an **attribution** approach that assigns benefits and the cost of those benefits to individual years of service must be selected.

20. The **expected postretirement benefit obligation** for an employee is the **actuarial present value** as of a particular date of the postretirement benefits expected to be paid by the employer's plan to or for the employee, the employee's beneficiaries, and any covered dependents pursuant to the terms of the plan. Measurement of the expected postretirement benefit obligation is based on the expected amount and timing of future benefits, taking into consideration the expected future cost of providing the benefits and the extent to which those costs are shared by the employer, the employee (including consideration of contributions required during the employee's active service period and following retirement, deductibles, coinsurance provisions, and so forth), or others (such as through governmental programs).

21. The accumulated postretirement benefit obligation[7] as of a particular date is the actuarial present value of all future benefits attributed to an employee's service rendered to that date pursuant to paragraphs 43 and 44 and 52-55, assuming the plan continues in effect and that all assumptions about future events are fulfilled. Prior to the date on which an employee attains **full eligibility** for the benefits that employee is expected to earn under the terms of the postretirement benefit plan (the **full eligibility date**), the accumulated postretirement benefit obligation for an employee is a portion of the expected postretirement benefit obligation. On and after the full eligibility date, the accumulated postretirement benefit obligation and the expected postretirement benefit obligation for an employee are the same. Determination of the full eligibility date is affected by plan terms that provide incremental benefits expected to be received by or on behalf of an employee for additional years of service, unless those incremental benefits are trivial. Determination of the full eligibility date is not affected by plan terms that define when benefit payments commence or by an employee's current **dependency status.** (Paragraphs 397-408 illustrate determination of the full eligibility date.)

22. Net periodic postretirement benefit cost comprises several components that reflect different aspects of the employer's financial arrangements. The **service cost** component of net periodic postretirement benefit cost is the actuarial present value of benefits attributed to services rendered by employees during the period (the portion of the expected postretirement benefit obligation attributed to service in the period). The service cost component is the same for an unfunded plan, a plan with minimal funding, and a well-funded plan. The other components of net periodic postretirement benefit cost are **interest cost**[8] (interest on the accumulated postretirement benefit obligation, which is a discounted amount), **actual return on plan assets, amortization** of **unrecognized prior service cost,** amortization of the **transition obligation** or **transition asset,** and the **gain or loss component.**

Measurement of Cost and Obligations

Accounting for the substantive plan

23. An objective of this Statement is that the accounting reflect the terms of the exchange transaction that takes place between an employer that provides postretirement benefits and the employees who render services in exchange for those benefits, as those terms are understood by both parties to the transaction. Generally, the extant written plan provides the best evidence of the terms of that exchange transaction. However, in some situations, an employer's **cost-sharing** policy, as evidenced by past practice or by communication of intended changes to a plan's cost-sharing provisions (paragraphs 24 and 25), or a past practice of regular increases in certain monetary benefits (paragraph 26) may indicate that the **substantive plan**—the plan as understood by the parties to the exchange transaction—differs from the extant written plan. The substantive plan shall be the basis for the accounting.

24. Except as provided in paragraph 25, an employer's cost-sharing policy, as evidenced by the following past practice or communication, shall constitute the cost-sharing provisions of the substantive plan if either of the following conditions exist. Otherwise, the extant written plan shall be considered to be the substantive plan.

a. The employer has a past practice of (1) maintaining a consistent level of cost sharing between the employer and its retirees through

---

[7]The accumulated postretirement benefit obligation generally reflects a ratable allocation of expected future benefits to employee service already rendered in the attribution period; the accumulated benefit obligation under Statement 87 generally reflects the future benefits allocated to employee service in accordance with the benefit formula. In addition, unlike Statement 87, this Statement implicitly considers salary progression in the measurement of the accumulated postretirement benefit obligation of a pay-related plan.

[8]The interest cost component of postretirement benefit cost shall not be considered interest for purposes of applying FASB Statement No. 34, *Capitalization of Interest Cost.*

changes in deductibles, coinsurance provisions, retiree contributions, or some combination of those changes or (2) consistently increasing or reducing the employer's share of the cost of the covered benefits through changes in retired or **active plan participants'** contributions toward their retiree health care benefits, deductibles, coinsurance provisions, out-of-pocket limitations, and so forth, in accordance with the employer's established cost-sharing policy

b. The employer has the ability, and has communicated to affected **plan participants** its intent, to institute different cost-sharing provisions at a specified time or when certain conditions exist (for example, when health care cost increases exceed a certain level).

25. An employer's past practice of maintaining a consistent level of cost sharing with its retirees or consistently increasing or reducing its share of the cost of providing the covered benefits shall not constitute provisions of the substantive plan if accompanied by identifiable offsetting changes in other benefits or compensation[9] or if the employer incurred significant costs, such as work stoppages, to effect that cost-sharing policy.[10] Similarly, an employer's communication of its intent to institute cost-sharing provisions that differ from the extant written plan or the past cost-sharing practice shall not constitute provisions of the substantive plan (a) if the plan participants would be unwilling to accept the change without adverse consequences to the employer's operations or (b) if other modifications of the plan, such as the level of benefit coverage, or providing offsetting changes in other benefits, such as pension benefits, would be required to gain plan participants' acceptance of the change to the cost-sharing arrangement.

26. A past practice of regular increases in postretirement benefits defined in terms of monetary amounts may indicate that the employer has a present commitment to make future *improvements* to the plan and that the plan will provide monetary benefits attributable to prior service that are greater than the monetary benefits defined by the extant written plan. In those situations, the substantive commitment to increase those benefits shall be the basis for the accounting. Changes in the benefits, other than benefits defined in terms of monetary amounts, covered by a postretirement health care plan or by other postretirement benefit plans shall not be anticipated.

27. Contributions expected to be received from active employees toward the cost of their postretirement benefits and from retired plan participants are treated similarly for purposes of measuring an employer's expected postretirement benefit obligation. That obligation is measured as the actuarial present value of the benefits expected to be provided under the plan, reduced by the actuarial present value of contributions expected to be received from the plan participants during their remaining active service and postretirement periods. In determining the amount of the contributions expected to be received from those participants toward the cost of their postretirement benefits, consideration is given to any related substantive plan provisions, such as an employer's past practice of consistently increasing or reducing the contribution rates as described in paragraphs 24 and 25. An obligation to return contributions received from employees who do not attain eligibility for postretirement benefits and, if applicable, any interest accrued on those contributions shall be recognized as a component of an employer's postretirement benefit obligation.

28. Automatic benefit changes[11] specified by the plan that are expected to occur shall be included in measurements of the expected and accumulated postretirement benefit obligations and the service cost component of net periodic postretirement benefit cost. Also, **plan amendments** shall be included in the computation of the expected and accumulated postretirement benefit obligations once they have been contractually agreed to, even if

---

[9]For example, a past practice of increasing retiree contributions annually based on a specified index or formula may appear to indicate that the substantive plan includes a determinable indexing of the retirees' annual contributions to the plan. However, if that past practice of increasing retiree contributions is accompanied by identifiable offsetting changes in other benefits or compensation, those offsetting changes would indicate that the substantive plan incorporates only the *current* cost-sharing provisions. Therefore, future increases or reductions of those cost-sharing provisions should not be incorporated in measuring the expected postretirement benefit obligation.

[10]By definition, an employer does not have the unilateral right to change a collectively bargained plan. Therefore, if the postretirement benefits are the subject of collective bargaining, the extant written plan shall be the substantive plan unless the employer can demonstrate its ability to maintain (a) a consistent level of cost sharing or (b) a consistent practice of increasing or reducing its share of the cost of the covered benefits in past negotiations without making offsetting changes in other benefits or compensation of the affected plan participants or by incurring other significant costs to maintain that cost-sharing arrangement.

[11]For purposes of this Statement, a plan that promises to provide retirees a benefit in kind, such as health care benefits, rather than a defined dollar amount of benefit, is considered to be a plan that specifies automatic benefit changes. (The assumed rate of change in the future cost of providing health care benefits, the assumed health care cost trend rate, is discussed in paragraph 39.) Because automatic benefit changes are not conditional on employees rendering additional years of service, the full eligibility date is not affected by those changes. A benefit in kind includes the direct rendering of services, the payment directly to others who provide the services, or the reimbursement of the retiree's payment for those services.

some provisions take effect only in future periods. For example, if a plan amendment grants a different benefit level for employees retiring after a future date, that increased or reduced benefit level shall be included in current-period measurements for employees expected to retire after that date.

Assumptions

29. The Board believes that measuring the net periodic postretirement benefit cost and accumulated postretirement benefit obligation based on best estimates is superior to implying, by a failure to accrue, that no cost or obligation exists prior to the payment of benefits. This Statement requires the use of **explicit assumptions,** each of which individually represents the best estimate of a particular future event, to measure the expected postretirement benefit obligation. A portion of that expected postretirement benefit obligation is attributed to each period of an employee's service associated with earning the postretirement benefits, and that amount is accrued as service cost for that period.

30. The service cost component of postretirement benefit cost, any **prior service cost,** and the accumulated postretirement benefit obligation are measured using actuarial assumptions and present value techniques to calculate the actuarial present value of the expected future benefits attributed to periods of employee service. Each assumption used shall reflect the best estimate solely with respect to that individual assumption. All assumptions shall presume that the plan will continue in effect in the absence of evidence that it will not continue. Principal actuarial assumptions include the time value of money (**discount rates**); participation rates (for **contributory plans**); retirement age; factors affecting the amount and timing of future benefit payments, which for **postretirement health care benefits** consider past and present **per capita claims cost by age, health care cost trend rates, Medicare reimbursement rates,** and so forth; salary progression (for **pay-related plans**); and the probability of payment (turnover, dependency status, mortality, and so forth).

31. Assumed discount rates shall reflect the time value of money as of the **measurement date** in determining the present value of future cash outflows currently expected to be required to satisfy the postretirement benefit obligation. In making that assumption, employers shall look to rates of return on high-quality fixed-income investments cur-

rently available whose cash flows match the timing and amount of expected benefit payments. If settlement of the obligation with third-party insurers is possible (for example, the purchase of nonparticipating life insurance contracts to provide death benefits), the interest rates inherent in the amount at which the postretirement benefit obligation could be settled are relevant in determining the assumed discount rates. Assumed discount rates are used in measurements of the expected and accumulated postretirement benefit obligations and the service cost and interest cost components of net periodic postretirement benefit cost.

32. The **expected long-term rate of return on plan assets** shall reflect the average rate of earnings expected on the existing assets that qualify as **plan assets** and contributions to the plan expected to be made during the period. In estimating that rate, appropriate consideration should be given to the returns being earned on the plan assets currently invested and the rates of return expected to be available for reinvestment. If the return on plan assets is taxable to the trust or other fund under the plan, the expected long-term rate of return shall be reduced to reflect the related income taxes expected to be paid under existing law. The expected long-term rate of return on plan assets is used with the **market-related value of plan assets** to compute the **expected return on plan assets.** (Refer to paragraph 57.) There is no assumption of an expected long-term rate of return on plan assets for plans that are unfunded or that have no assets that qualify as plan assets pursuant to this Statement.

33. The service cost component of net periodic postretirement benefit cost and the expected and accumulated postretirement benefit obligations shall reflect future compensation levels to the extent the postretirement benefit formula defines the benefits wholly or partially as a function of future compensation levels.[12] For pay-related plans, assumed compensation levels shall reflect the best estimate of the actual future compensation levels of the individual employees involved, including future changes attributed to general price levels, productivity, seniority, promotion, and other factors. All assumptions shall be consistent to the extent that each reflects expectations about the same future economic conditions, such as future rates of inflation. Measuring service cost and the expected and accumulated postretirement benefit obligations based on estimated future compensation levels entails considering any indirect effects, such as

---

[12]For pay-related plans, salary progression is included in measuring the expected postretirement benefit obligation. For example, a postretirement health care plan may define the deductible amount or copayment, or a postretirement life insurance plan may define the amount of death benefit, based on the employee's average or final level of annual compensation.

benefit limitations, that would affect benefits provided by the plan.[13]

Assumptions unique to postretirement health care benefits

34. Measurement of an employer's postretirement health care obligation requires the use of several assumptions unique to health care benefits. Most significantly, it includes several assumptions about factors that will affect the amount and timing of future benefit payments for postretirement health care. Those factors include consideration of historical per capita claims cost by age, health care cost trend rates (for plans that provide a benefit in kind), and medical coverage to be paid by governmental authorities and other providers of health care benefits.

35. In principle, an employer's share of the expected future postretirement health care cost for a plan participant is developed by reducing the **assumed per capita claims cost** at each age at which the plan participant is expected to receive benefits under the plan by (a) the effects of coverage by Medicare and other providers of health care benefits, and (b) the effects of the cost-sharing provisions of the plan (deductibles, copayment provisions, out-of-pocket limitations, caps on the limits of the employer-provided payments, and retiree contributions).[14] The resulting amount represents the assumed **net incurred claims cost** at each age at which the plan participant is expected to receive benefits under the plan. If contributions are required to be paid by active plan participants toward their postretirement health care benefits, the actuarial present value of the plan participants' future contributions reduces the actuarial present value of the aggregate assumed net incurred claims costs.

36. The assumed per capita claims cost by age is the annual per capita cost, for periods after the measurement date, of providing the postretirement health care benefits covered by the plan from the earliest age at which an individual could begin to receive benefits under the plan through the remainder of the individual's life or the covered period, if shorter. The assumed per capita claims cost

shall be the best estimate of the expected future cost of the benefits covered by the plan.[15] It may be appropriate to consider other factors in addition to age, such as sex and geographical location, in developing the assumed per capita claims cost.

37. Past and present claims data for the plan, such as a historical pattern of gross claims by age (claims curve), should be used in developing the current per capita claims cost to the extent that those data are considered to be indicative of the current cost of providing the benefits covered by the plan. Those current claims data shall be adjusted by the assumed health care cost trend rate. The resulting assumed per capita claims cost by age, together with the **plan demographics,** determines the amount and timing of expected future **gross eligible charges.**

38. In the absence of sufficiently reliable plan data about the current cost of the benefits covered by the plan, the current per capita claims cost should be based, entirely or in part, on the claims information of other employers to the extent those costs are indicative of the current cost of providing the benefits covered by the plan. For example, the current per capita claims cost may be based on the claims experience of other employers derived from information in data files developed by insurance companies, actuarial firms, or employee benefits consulting firms. The current per capita claims cost developed on those bases shall be adjusted to best reflect the terms of the employer's plan and the plan demographics. For example, the information should be adjusted, as necessary, for differing demographics, such as the age and sex of plan participants, health care utilization patterns by men and women at various ages, and the expected geographical location of retirees and their dependents, and for significant differences between the nature and types of benefits covered by the employer's plan and those encompassed by the underlying data.

39. The assumption about health care cost trend rates represents the expected annual rates of change in the cost of health care benefits currently provided by the postretirement benefit plan, due to factors other than changes in the demographics of

---

[13]For example, a plan may define the maximum benefit to be provided under the plan (a fixed cap). In measuring the expected postretirement benefit obligation under that plan, the projected benefit payments would be limited to that cap. For a plan that automatically adjusts the maximum benefit to be provided under the plan for the effects of inflation (an adjustable cap), the expected postretirement benefit obligation would be measured based on adjustments to that cap consistent with the assumed inflation rate reflected in other inflation-related assumptions.

[14]In some cases, retiree contributions are established based on the average per capita cost of benefit coverage under an employer's health care plan that provides coverage to both active employees and retirees. However, the medical cost of the retirees may cause the average per capita cost of benefit coverage under the plan to be higher than it would be if only active employees were covered by the plan. In that case, the employer has a postretirement benefit obligation for the portion of the expected future cost of the retiree health care benefits that are not recovered through retiree contributions, Medicare, or other providers of health care benefits.

[15]If significant, the internal and external costs directly associated with administering the postretirement benefit plan also should be accrued as a component of assumed per capita claims cost.

the plan participants, for each year from the measurement date until the end of the period in which benefits are expected to be paid. Past and current health care cost trends shall be used in developing an employer's assumed health care cost trend rates, which implicitly consider estimates of health care inflation, changes in health care utilization or delivery patterns, technological advances, and changes in the health status of plan participants.[16] Differing services, such as hospital care and dental care, may require the use of different health care cost trend rates. It is appropriate for that assumption to reflect changes in health care cost trend rates over time. For example, the health care cost trend rates may be assumed to continue at the present level for the near term, or increase for a period of time, and then grade down over time to an estimated health care cost trend rate ultimately expected to prevail.

40. Certain medical claims may be covered by governmental programs under existing law or by other providers of health care benefits.[17] Benefit coverage by those governmental programs shall be assumed to continue as provided by the present law and by other providers pursuant to their present plans. Presently enacted changes in the law or amendments of the plans of other health care providers that take effect in future periods and that will affect the future level of their benefit coverage shall be considered in current-period measurements for benefits expected to be provided in those future periods. Future changes in laws concerning medical costs covered by governmental programs and future changes in the plans of other providers shall not be anticipated.

41. In some cases, determining the assumed per capita claims cost by age as described in paragraphs 36-38 may not be practical because credible historical information about the gross per capita cost of covered benefits may not be available or determinable to satisfy the stated measurement approach. However, credible historical information about **incurred claims costs** may be available. In those cases, an alternative method of developing the assumed per capita claims cost may be used provided the method results in a measure that is the best estimate of the expected future cost of the benefits covered by the plan. For example, the assumed health care cost trend rates may be determined by adjusting the expected change in the em-

ployer's share of per capita incurred claims cost by age by a factor that reflects the effects of the plan's cost-sharing provisions. However, an approach that projects net incurred claims costs using unadjusted assumed health care cost trend rates would implicitly assume changes in the plan's cost-sharing provisions at those assumed rates and, therefore, is not acceptable unless the plan's cost-sharing provisions are indexed in that manner or the substantive plan (paragraphs 24-26) operates in that manner.

42. Assumed discount rates include an inflationary element that reflects the expected general rate of inflation. Assumed compensation levels include consideration of future changes attributable to general price levels. Similarly, assumed health care cost trend rates include an element that reflects expected general rates of inflation for the economy overall and an element that reflects price changes of health care costs in particular. To the extent that those assumptions consider similar inflationary effects, the assumptions about those effects shall be consistent.

Attribution

43. An equal amount of the expected postretirement benefit obligation for an employee generally shall be attributed to each year of service in the **attribution period** (a benefit/years-of-service approach). However, some plans may have benefit formulas that attribute a disproportionate share of the expected postretirement benefit obligation to employees' early years of service. For that type of plan, the expected postretirement benefit obligation shall be attributed in accordance with the plan's benefit formula.

44. The beginning of the attribution period generally shall be the date of hire. However, if the plan's benefit formula grants credit only for service from a later date and that **credited service period** is not nominal in relation to employees' total years of service prior to their full eligibility dates, the expected postretirement benefit obligation shall be attributed from the beginning of that credited service period. In all cases, the end of the attribution period shall be the full eligibility date. (Paragraphs 409-412 illustrate the attribution provisions of this Statement.)

---

[16]An assumption about changes in the health status of plan participants considers, for example, the probability that certain claims costs will be incurred based on expectations of future events, such as the likelihood that some retirees will incur claims requiring technology currently being developed or that historical claims experience for certain medical needs may be reduced as a result of participation in a wellness program.

[17]For example, a retiree's spouse also may be covered by the spouse's present (or former) employer's health care plan. In that case, the spouse's employer (or former employer) may provide either primary or secondary postretirement health care benefits to the retiree's spouse or dependents.

Recognition of Net Periodic Postretirement Benefit Cost

45. As with other forms of deferred compensation, the cost of providing postretirement benefits shall be attributed to the periods of employee service rendered in exchange for those future benefits pursuant to the terms of the plan. That cost notionally represents the change in the **unfunded accumulated postretirement benefit obligation** for the period, ignoring employer contributions to the plan, plan settlements, and payments made by the employer directly to retirees. However, changes in that unfunded obligation that arise from experience gains and losses and the effects of changes in assumptions may be recognized as a component of net periodic postretirement benefit cost on a delayed basis. In addition, the effects of a plan initiation or amendment generally are recognized on a delayed basis.

46. The following components shall be included in the net postretirement benefit cost recognized for a period by an employer sponsoring a defined benefit postretirement plan:

a. Service cost (paragraph 47)
b. Interest cost (paragraph 48)
c. Actual return on plan assets, if any (paragraph 49)
d. Amortization of unrecognized prior service cost, if any (paragraphs 50-55)
e. **Gain or loss** (including the effects of changes in assumptions) to the extent recognized (paragraphs 56-62)
f. Amortization of the unrecognized obligation or asset existing at the date of initial application of this Statement, hereinafter referred to as the **unrecognized transition obligation**[18] or **unrecognized transition asset** (paragraphs 110 and 112).

Service cost

47. The service cost component recognized in a period shall be determined as the portion of the expected postretirement benefit obligation attributed to employee service during that period. The measurement of the service cost component requires identification of the substantive plan and the use of assumptions and an attribution method, which are discussed in paragraphs 23-44.

Interest cost

48. The interest cost component recognized in a period shall be determined as the increase in the accumulated postretirement benefit obligation to recognize the effects of the passage of time. Measuring the accumulated postretirement benefit obligation as a present value requires accrual of an interest cost at rates equal to the assumed discount rates.

Actual return on plan assets

49. For a funded plan, the actual return on plan assets shall be determined based on the **fair value** of plan assets (refer to paragraphs 65 and 66) at the beginning and end of the period, adjusted for contributions and benefit payments. If the fund holding the plan assets is a taxable entity, the actual return on plan assets shall reflect the tax expense or benefit for the period determined in accordance with generally accepted accounting principles. Otherwise, no provision for taxes shall be included in the actual return on plan assets.

Prior service cost

50. Plan amendments (including initiation of a plan) may include provisions that attribute the increase or reduction in benefits to employee service rendered in prior periods or only to employee service to be rendered in future periods. For purposes of measuring the accumulated postretirement benefit obligation, the effect of a plan amendment on a plan participant's expected postretirement benefit obligation shall be attributed to each year of service in that plan participant's attribution period, including years of service already rendered by that plan participant, in accordance with the attribution of the expected postretirement benefit obligation to years of service as discussed in paragraphs 43 and 44. If a plan is initiated that grants benefits solely in exchange for employee service after the date of the plan initiation or a future date, no portion of the expected postretirement benefit obligation is attributed to prior service periods because, in that case, the credited service period for the current employees who are expected to receive benefits under the plan begins at the date of plan initiation or the future date.

51. Plan amendments that improve benefits are granted with the expectation that the employer will realize economic benefits in future periods. Consequently, except as discussed in paragraph 54, this Statement does not permit the cost of benefit improvements (that is, prior service cost) to be included in net periodic postretirement benefit cost entirely in the year of the amendment. Rather, paragraph 52 provides for recognition of prior service

---

[18]Amortization of the unrecognized transition obligation or asset will be adjusted prospectively to recognize the effects of (a) a negative plan amendment pursuant to paragraph 55, (b) a constraint on immediate recognition of a net gain or loss pursuant to paragraph 60, (c) settlement accounting pursuant to paragraphs 92 and 93, (d) plan curtailment accounting pursuant to paragraphs 97-99, and (e) a constraint on delayed recognition of the unrecognized transition obligation pursuant to paragraph 112.

cost arising from benefit improvements during the remaining years of service to the full eligibility dates of those plan participants active at the date of the plan amendment. (Refer to paragraph 55 for plan amendments that reduce benefits.)

52. The cost of benefit improvements (including improved benefits that are granted to **fully eligible plan participants**) is the increase in the accumulated postretirement benefit obligation as a result of the plan amendment, measured at the date of the amendment. Except as specified in the next sentence and in paragraphs 53 and 54, that prior service cost shall be amortized by assigning an equal amount to each remaining year of service to the full eligibility date of each plan participant active at the date of the amendment who was not yet fully eligible for benefits at that date. If all or almost all of a plan's participants are fully eligible for benefits, the prior service cost shall be amortized based on the remaining life expectancy of those plan participants rather than on the remaining years of service to the full eligibility dates of the active plan participants.

53. To reduce the complexity and detail of the computations required, consistent use of an alternative amortization approach that more rapidly reduces unrecognized prior service cost is permitted. For example, a straight-line amortization of the cost over the average remaining years of service to full eligibility for benefits of the active plan participants is acceptable.

54. In some situations, a history of regular plan amendments and other evidence may indicate that the period during which the employer expects to realize economic benefits from an amendment that grants increased benefits is shorter than the remaining years of service to full eligibility for benefits of the active plan participants. Identification of those situations requires an assessment of the individual circumstances of the particular plan. In those circumstances, the amortization of prior service cost shall be accelerated to reflect the more rapid expiration of the employer's economic benefits and to recognize the cost in the periods benefited.

55. A plan amendment can reduce, rather than increase, the accumulated postretirement benefit obligation. A reduction in that obligation shall be used first to reduce any existing unrecognized prior service cost, then to reduce any remaining unrecognized transition obligation. The excess, if any, shall be amortized on the same basis as specified in paragraph 52 for prior service cost. Immediate recognition of the excess is not permitted.

Gains and losses

56. Gains and losses are changes in the amount of either the accumulated postretirement benefit obligation or plan assets resulting from experience different from that assumed or from changes in assumptions. This Statement generally does not distinguish between those sources of gains and losses. Gains and losses include amounts that have been realized, for example, by the sale of a security, as well as amounts that are unrealized. Because gains and losses may reflect refinements in estimates as well as real changes in economic values and because some gains in one period may be offset by losses in another or vice versa, this Statement does not require recognition of gains and losses as components of net postretirement benefit cost in the period in which they arise, except as described in paragraph 61. (Gain and loss recognition in accounting for settlements and curtailments is addressed in paragraphs 90-99.)

57. The expected return on plan assets shall be determined based on the expected long-term rate of return on plan assets (refer to paragraph 32) and the market-related value of plan assets. The market-related value of plan assets shall be either fair value or a calculated value that recognizes changes in fair value in a systematic and rational manner over not more than five years. Different methods of calculating market-related value may be used for different classes of assets (for example, an employer might use fair value for bonds and a five-year-moving-average value for equities), but the manner of determining market-related value shall be applied consistently from year to year for each class of plan assets.

58. Plan asset gains and losses are differences between the actual return on plan assets during a period and the expected return on plan assets for that period. Plan asset gains and losses include both (a) changes reflected in the market-related value of plan assets and (b) changes not yet reflected in the market-related value of plan assets (that is, the difference between the fair value and the market-related value of plan assets). Plan asset gains and losses not yet reflected in market-related value are not required to be amortized under paragraphs 59 and 60.

59. As a minimum, amortization of an **unrecognized net gain or loss** (excluding plan asset gains and losses not yet reflected in market-related value) shall be included as a component of net postretirement benefit cost for a year if, as of the beginning of the year, that unrecognized net gain

or loss exceeds 10 percent of the greater of the accumulated postretirement benefit obligation or the market-related value of plan assets. If amortization is required, the minimum amortization[19] shall be that excess divided by the average remaining service period of active plan participants. If all or almost all of a plan's participants are inactive, the average remaining life expectancy of the inactive participants shall be used instead of the average remaining service period.

60. Any systematic method of amortization of unrecognized gains and losses may be used in place of the minimum amortization specified in paragraph 59 provided that (a) the minimum amortization is recognized in any period in which it is greater (reduces the unrecognized amount by more) than the amount that would be recognized under the method used, (b) the method is applied consistently, (c) the method is applied similarly to both gains and losses, and (d) the method used is disclosed. If an enterprise uses a method of consistently recognizing gains and losses immediately, any gain that does not offset a loss previously recognized in income pursuant to this paragraph shall first offset any unrecognized transition obligation; any loss that does not offset a gain previously recognized in income pursuant to this paragraph shall first offset any unrecognized transition asset.

61. In some situations, an employer may forgive a retrospective adjustment of the current or past years' cost-sharing provisions of the plan as they relate to benefit costs *already incurred* by retirees[20] or may otherwise deviate from the provisions of the substantive plan to increase or decrease the employer's share of the benefit costs *incurred in the current or past periods*. The effect of a decision to temporarily deviate from the substantive plan shall be immediately recognized as a loss or gain.

62. The gain or loss component of net periodic postretirement benefit cost shall consist of (a) the difference between the actual return on plan assets and the expected return on plan assets, (b) any gain or loss immediately recognized or the amortization of the unrecognized net gain or loss from previous periods, and (c) any amount immediately recognized as a gain or loss pursuant to paragraph 61.

Measurement of Plan Assets

63. Plan assets are assets—usually stocks, bonds, and other investments (except certain **insurance contracts** as noted in paragraph 67)—that have been segregated and restricted (usually in a trust) to be used for postretirement benefits. The amount of plan assets includes amounts contributed by the employer, and by plan participants for a contributory plan, and amounts earned from investing the contributions, less benefits, income taxes, and other expenses incurred. Plan assets ordinarily cannot be withdrawn by the employer except under certain circumstances when a plan has assets in excess of obligations and the employer has taken certain steps to satisfy existing obligations. Securities of the employer held by the plan are includable in plan assets provided they are transferable.

64. Assets not segregated in a trust, or otherwise effectively restricted, so that they cannot be used by the employer for other purposes are not plan assets for purposes of this Statement, even though the employer may intend that those assets be used to provide postretirement benefits. Those assets shall be accounted for in the same manner as other employer assets of a similar nature and with similar restrictions. Amounts accrued by the employer but not yet paid to the plan are not plan assets for purposes of this Statement.

65. For purposes of the disclosures required by paragraph 74, plan investments, whether equity or debt securities, real estate, or other, shall be measured at their fair value as of the measurement date. The fair value of an investment is the amount that the plan could reasonably expect to receive for it in a current sale between a willing buyer and a willing seller, that is, other than in a forced or liquidation sale. Fair value shall be measured by the market price if an active market exists for the investment. If no active market exists for an investment but an active market exists for similar investments, selling prices in that market may be helpful in estimating fair value. If a market price is not available, a forecast of expected cash flows may aid in estimating

---

[19]The amortization must always reduce the beginning-of-the-year balance. Amortization of an unrecognized net gain results in a decrease in net periodic postretirement benefit cost; amortization of an unrecognized net loss results in an increase in net periodic postretirement benefit cost.

[20]For example, the terms of a substantive postretirement health care plan may provide that any shortfall resulting from current year benefit payments in excess of the employer's stated share of incurred claims cost and retiree contributions for that year is to be recovered from increased retiree contributions in the subsequent year. The employer may subsequently determine that increasing retiree contributions for the shortfall in the prior year would be onerous and make a decision to bear the cost of the shortfall for that year. The employer's decision to bear the shortfall represents a change in intent and the resulting loss shall be recognized immediately. Future decisions by the employer to continue to bear the shortfall suggest an amendment of the substantive plan that should be accounted for as described in paragraphs 50-55.

fair value, provided the expected cash flows are discounted at a current rate commensurate with the risk involved.[21] (Refer to paragraph 71.)

66. Plan assets used in plan operations (for example, buildings, equipment, furniture and fixtures, and leasehold improvements) shall be measured at cost less accumulated depreciation or amortization for all purposes.

Insurance Contracts

67. For purposes of this Statement, an insurance contract is defined as a contract in which an insurance company unconditionally undertakes a legal obligation to provide specified benefits to specific individuals in return for a fixed consideration or premium; an insurance contract is irrevocable and involves the transfer of significant risk from the employer (or the plan) to the insurance company.[22] Benefits covered by insurance contracts shall be excluded from the accumulated postretirement benefit obligation. Insurance contracts shall be excluded from plan assets, except as provided in paragraph 69 for the cost of **participation rights.**

68. Some insurance contracts **(participating insurance contracts)** provide that the purchaser (either the plan or the employer) may participate in the experience of the insurance company. Under those contracts, the insurance company ordinarily pays dividends to the purchaser, the effect of which is to reduce the cost of the plan. If the participating insurance contract causes the employer to remain subject to all or most of the risks and rewards associated with the benefit obligation covered or the assets transferred to the insurance company, that contract is not an insurance contract for purposes of this Statement, and the purchase of that contract does not constitute a settlement pursuant to paragraphs 90-95.

69. The purchase price of a participating insurance contract ordinarily is higher than the price of an equivalent contract without a participation right. The difference is the cost of the participation right. The cost of the participation right shall be recognized at the date of purchase as an asset. In subsequent periods, the participation right shall be measured at its fair value if the contract is such that fair value is reasonably estimable. Otherwise the participation right shall be measured at its amortized cost (not in excess of its net realizable value), and the cost

shall be amortized systematically over the expected dividend period under the contract.

70. To the extent that insurance contracts are purchased during the period to cover postretirement benefits attributed to service in the current period (such as life insurance benefits), the cost of those benefits shall be the cost of purchasing the coverage under the contracts, except as provided in paragraph 69 for the cost of a participation right. If all the postretirement benefits attributed to service in the current period are covered by **nonparticipating insurance contracts** purchased during that period, the cost of the contracts determines the service cost component of net postretirement benefit cost for that period. Benefits attributed to current service in excess of benefits provided by nonparticipating insurance contracts purchased during the current period shall be accounted for according to the provisions of this Statement applicable to plans not involving insurance contracts.

71. Other contracts with insurance companies may not meet the definition of an insurance contract because the insurance company does not unconditionally undertake a legal obligation to provide specified benefits to specified individuals. Those contracts shall be accounted for as investments and measured at fair value. If a contract has a determinable cash surrender value or conversion value, that is presumed to be its fair value. For some contracts, the best available estimate of fair value may be contract value.

Measurement Date

72. The measurements of *plan assets and obligations* required by this Statement shall be as of the date of the financial statements or, if used consistently from year to year, as of a date not more than three months prior to that date. Even though the postretirement benefit measurements are required as of a particular date, all procedures are not required to be performed after that date. As with other financial statement items requiring estimates, much of the information can be prepared as of an earlier date and projected forward to account for subsequent events (for example, employee service).

73. Measurements of *net periodic postretirement benefit cost* for both interim and annual financial statements generally shall be based on the assump-

---

[21]For an indication of factors to be considered in determining the discount rate, refer to paragraphs 13 and 14 of APB Opinion No. 21, *Interest on Receivables and Payables.* If significant, the fair value of an investment shall reflect the brokerage commissions and other costs normally incurred in a sale.

[22]If the insurance company providing the contract does business primarily with the employer and related parties (a **captive insurer**) or if there is any reasonable doubt that the insurance company will meet its obligations under the contract, the contract is not an insurance contract for purposes of this Statement.

tions at the beginning of the year (assumptions used for the previous year-end measurements of plan assets and obligations) unless more recent measurements of both plan assets and the accumulated postretirement benefit obligation are available. For example, if a significant event occurs, such as a plan amendment, settlement, or curtailment, that ordinarily would call for remeasurement, the assumptions used for those later measurements shall be used to remeasure net periodic postretirement benefit cost from the date of the event to the year-end measurement date.

Disclosures

74. This Statement requires disclosures about an employer's obligation to provide postretirement benefits and the cost of providing those benefits that are intended to enhance the usefulness of the financial statements to investors, creditors, and other users of financial information. An employer sponsoring one or more defined benefit postretirement plans (refer to paragraphs 77 and 78) shall disclose, if applicable, the following information about those plans:

a. A description of the substantive plan(s) that is the basis for the accounting (refer to paragraphs 23-28), including the nature of the plan, any modifications of the existing cost-sharing provisions that are encompassed by the substantive plan(s) (refer to paragraphs 24 and 25), and the existence and nature of any commitment to increase monetary benefits provided by the postretirement benefit plan (refer to paragraph 26), employee groups covered, types of benefits provided, **funding policy,** types of assets held and significant nonbenefit liabilities, and the nature and effect of significant matters affecting the comparability of information for all periods presented, such as the effect of a business combination or divestiture

b. The amount of net periodic postretirement benefit cost showing separately the service cost component, the interest cost component, the actual return on plan assets for the period, amortization of the unrecognized transition obligation or transition asset, and the net total of other components[23]

c. A schedule reconciling the funded status of the plan(s) with amounts reported in the employer's statement of financial position, showing separately:

(1) The fair value of plan assets

(2) The accumulated postretirement benefit obligation, identifying separately the portion attributable to retirees, other fully eligible plan participants, and other active plan participants

(3) The amount of unrecognized prior service cost

(4) The amount of unrecognized net gain or loss (including plan asset gains and losses not yet reflected in market-related value)

(5) The amount of any remaining unrecognized transition obligation or transition asset

(6) The amount of net postretirement benefit asset or liability recognized in the statement of financial position, which is the net result of combining the preceding five items

d. The assumed health care cost trend rate(s) used to measure the expected cost of benefits covered by the plan (gross eligible charges) for the next year and a general description of the direction and pattern of change in the assumed trend rates thereafter, together with the ultimate trend rate(s) and when that rate is expected to be achieved

e. The weighted-average of the assumed discount rate(s) and rate(s) of compensation increase (for pay-related plans) used to measure the accumulated postretirement benefit obligation and the weighted-average of the expected long-term rate(s) of return on plan assets and, for plans whose income is segregated from the employer's investment income for tax purposes, the estimated income tax rate(s) included in that rate of return

f. The effect of a one-percentage-point increase in the assumed health care cost trend rates for each future year on (1) the aggregate of the service and interest cost components of net periodic postretirement health care benefit cost and (2) the accumulated postretirement benefit obligation for health care benefits (For purposes of this disclosure, all other assumptions shall be held constant and the effects shall be measured based on the substantive plan that is the basis for the accounting.)

g. The amounts and types of securities of the employer and related parties included in plan assets, and the approximate amount of future an-

---

[23]The net total of other components is generally the net effect during the period of certain delayed recognition provisions of this Statement. That net total includes:

a. The net asset gain or loss during the period deferred for later recognition (in effect, an offset or a supplement to the actual return on plan assets)

b. Amortization of unrecognized prior service cost

c. Amortization of the net gain or loss from earlier periods

d. Any gain or loss recognized due to a temporary deviation from the substantive plan (paragraph 61).

nual benefits of plan participants covered by insurance contracts issued by the employer and related parties

h. Any alternative amortization method used pursuant to paragraphs 53 or 60

i. The amount of gain or loss recognized during the period for a settlement or curtailment and a description of the nature of the event(s) (Refer to paragraphs 90-99.)

j. The cost of providing special or contractual termination benefits recognized during the period and a description of the nature of the event(s). (Refer to paragraphs 101 and 102.)

Employers with Two or More Plans

75. Postretirement benefits offered by an employer may vary in nature and may be provided to different groups of employees. As discussed in paragraph 76, in some cases an employer may aggregate data from unfunded plans for measurement purposes in lieu of performing separate measurements for each unfunded plan (including plans whose designated assets are not appropriately segregated and restricted and thus have no plan assets as that term is used in this Statement). Net periodic postretirement benefit cost, the accumulated postretirement benefit obligation, and plan assets shall be determined for each separately measured plan or aggregation of plans by applying the provisions of this Statement to each such plan or aggregation of plans.

76. The data from all unfunded postretirement health care plans may be aggregated for measurement purposes if (a) those plans provide different benefits to the same group of employees or (b) those plans provide the same benefits to different groups of employees. Data from other unfunded postretirement welfare benefit plans may be aggregated for measurement purposes in similar circumstances, such as when an employer has a variety of welfare benefit plans that provide benefits to the same group of employees. However, a plan that has plan assets (as defined herein) shall not be aggregated with other plans but shall be measured separately.

77. Disclosures for plans with plan assets in excess of the accumulated postretirement benefit obligation generally may be aggregated with disclosures for plans that have accumulated postretirement benefit obligations that exceed plan assets. However, for purposes of the disclosures required by paragraph 74(c), the aggregate plan assets and the aggregate accumulated postretirement benefit obligation of the underfunded plans shall be separately disclosed. Otherwise, except as described in paragraph 78, the disclosures required by this Statement may be aggregated for all of an employ-

er's single-employer defined benefit plans, or plans may be disaggregated in groups to provide more useful information.

78. The disclosures required by this Statement shall be presented separately for the following:

a. Plans that provide primarily postretirement health care benefits and plans that provide primarily other postretirement welfare benefits if the accumulated postretirement benefit obligation of the latter plans is significant relative to the aggregate accumulated postretirement benefit obligation for all of the plans

b. Plans inside the United States and plans outside the United States if the accumulated postretirement benefit obligation of the latter plans is significant relative to the aggregate accumulated postretirement benefit obligation for all of the plans.

Multiemployer Plans

79. For purposes of this Statement, a **multiemployer plan** is a postretirement benefit plan to which two or more unrelated employers contribute, usually pursuant to one or more collective-bargaining agreements. A characteristic of multiemployer plans is that assets contributed by one participating employer may be used to provide benefits to employees of other participating employers since assets contributed by an employer are not segregated in a separate account or restricted to provide benefits only to employees of that employer.

80. A multiemployer plan usually is administered by a board of trustees composed of management and labor representatives and may also be referred to as a "joint trust" or "union plan." Generally, many employers participate in a multiemployer plan, and an employer may participate in more than one plan. The employers participating in multiemployer plans usually have a common industry bond, but for some plans the employers are in different industries, and the labor union may be their only common bond. Some multiemployer plans do not involve a union. For example, local chapters of a not-for-profit organization may participate in a plan established by the related national organization.

81. An employer participating in a multiemployer plan shall recognize as net postretirement benefit cost the required contribution for the period, which shall include both cash and the fair market value of noncash contributions, and shall recognize as a liability any unpaid contributions required for the period.

82. An employer that participates in one or more

multiemployer plans shall disclose the following separately from disclosures for a single-employer plan:

a. A description of the multiemployer plan(s) including the employee groups covered, the type of benefits provided (defined benefits or defined contribution), and the nature and effect of significant matters affecting comparability of information for all periods presented
b. The amount of postretirement benefit cost recognized during the period, if available. Otherwise, the amount of the aggregate required contribution for the period to the general health and welfare benefit plan that provides health and welfare benefits to both active employees and retirees shall be disclosed.

83. In some situations, withdrawal from a multiemployer plan may result in an employer's having an obligation to the plan for a portion of the plan's unfunded accumulated postretirement benefit obligation. If it is either probable or reasonably possible that (a) an employer would withdraw from the plan under circumstances that would give rise to an obligation or (b) an employer's contribution to the fund would be increased during the remainder of the contract period to make up a shortfall in the funds necessary to maintain the negotiated level of benefit coverage (a "maintenance of benefits" clause), the employer shall apply the provisions of FASB Statement No. 5, *Accounting for Contingencies.*

Multiple-Employer Plans

84. Some postretirement benefit plans to which two or more unrelated employers contribute are not multiemployer plans. Rather, those **multiple-employer plans** are in substance aggregations of single-employer plans, combined to allow participating employers to pool plan assets for investment purposes or to reduce the costs of plan administration. Those plans ordinarily do not involve collective-bargaining agreements. They may also have features that allow participating employers to have different benefit formulas, with the employer's contributions to the plan based on the benefit formula selected by the employer. Those plans shall be considered single-employer plans rather than multiemployer plans for purposes of this Statement, and each employer's accounting shall be based on its respective interest in the plan.

Postretirement Benefit Plans outside the United States

85. Except for its effective date (paragraph 108), this Statement includes no special provisions applicable to postretirement benefit arrangements outside the United States. Those arrangements are subject to the provisions of this Statement for purposes of preparing financial statements in accordance with accounting principles generally accepted in the United States. The applicability of this Statement to those arrangements is determined by the nature of the obligation and by the terms or conditions that define the amount of benefits to be paid, not by whether or how a plan is funded, whether benefits are payable at intervals or as a single amount, or whether the benefits are required by law or custom or are provided under a plan the employer has elected to sponsor.

Business Combinations

86. When an employer is acquired in a business combination that is accounted for by the purchase method under Opinion 16 and that employer sponsors a single-employer defined benefit postretirement plan, the assignment of the purchase price to individual assets acquired and liabilities assumed shall include a liability for the accumulated postretirement benefit obligation in excess of the fair value of the plan assets or an asset for the fair value of the plan assets in excess of the accumulated postretirement benefit obligation. The accumulated postretirement benefit obligation assumed shall be measured based on the benefits attributed by the acquired entity to employee service prior to the date the business combination is consummated, adjusted to reflect (a) any changes in assumptions based on the purchaser's assessment of relevant future events (as discussed in paragraphs 23-42) and (b) the terms of the substantive plan (as discussed in paragraphs 23-28) to be provided by the purchaser to the extent they differ from the terms of the acquired entity's substantive plan.

87. If the postretirement benefit plan of the acquired entity is amended as a condition of the business combination (for example, if the change is required by the seller as part of the consummation of the acquisition), the effects of any improvements attributed to services rendered by the participants of the acquired entity's plan prior to the date of the business combination shall be accounted for as part of the accumulated postretirement benefit obligation of the acquired entity. Otherwise, if improvements to the postretirement benefit plan of the acquired entity are not a condition of the business combination, credit granted for prior service shall be recognized as a plan amendment as discussed in paragraphs 50-55. If it is expected that the plan will be terminated or curtailed, the effects of those actions shall be considered in measuring the accumulated postretirement benefit obligation. Otherwise, no future changes to the plan shall be anticipated.

88. As a result of applying the provisions of para-

graphs 86 and 87, any previously existing unrecognized net gain or loss, unrecognized prior service cost, or unrecognized transition obligation or transition asset is eliminated for the acquired employer's plan. Subsequently, to the extent that the net obligation assumed or net assets acquired are considered in determining the amounts of contributions to the plan, differences between the purchaser's net periodic postretirement benefit cost and amounts it contributes will reduce the liability or asset recognized at the date of the combination.

Amendment to Opinion 16

89. The following footnote is added to the end of the last sentence of paragraph 88 of Opinion 16:

> *Paragraphs 86-88 of FASB Statement No. 106, *Employers' Accounting for Postretirement Benefits Other Than Pensions,* specify how the general guidelines of this paragraph shall be applied to assets and liabilities related to plans that provide postretirement benefits other than pensions.

Accounting for Settlement of a Postretirement Benefit Obligation

90. For purposes of this Statement, a settlement is defined as a transaction that (a) is an irrevocable action, (b) relieves the employer (or the plan) of primary responsibility for a postretirement benefit obligation, and (c) eliminates significant risks related to the obligation and the assets used to effect the settlement.[24] Examples of transactions that constitute a settlement include making lump-sum cash payments to plan participants in exchange for their rights to receive specified postretirement benefits and purchasing long-term nonparticipating insurance contracts for the accumulated postretirement benefit obligation for some or all of the plan participants.

91. A transaction that does not meet the three criteria of paragraph 90 does not constitute a settlement for purposes of this Statement. For example, investing in a portfolio of high-quality fixed-income securities with principal and interest payment dates similar to the estimated payment dates of benefits may avoid or minimize certain risks. However, that investment decision does not constitute a settlement because that decision can be reversed, and investing in that portfolio does not relieve the employer (or the plan) of primary responsibility for a postretirement benefit obligation nor does it eliminate significant risks related to that obligation.

92. For purposes of this Statement, the maximum gain or loss subject to recognition in income when a postretirement benefit obligation is settled is the unrecognized net gain or loss defined in paragraphs 56-60 plus any remaining unrecognized transition asset. That maximum gain or loss includes any gain or loss resulting from remeasurements of plan assets and the accumulated postretirement benefit obligation at the time of settlement.

93. If the entire accumulated postretirement benefit obligation is settled and the maximum amount subject to recognition is a gain, the settlement gain shall first reduce any remaining unrecognized transition obligation;[25] any excess gain shall be recognized in income.[26] If the entire accumulated postretirement benefit obligation is settled and the maximum amount subject to recognition is a loss, the maximum settlement loss shall be recognized in income. If only part of the accumulated postretirement benefit obligation is settled, the employer shall recognize in income the excess of the pro rata portion (equal to the percentage reduction in the accumulated postretirement benefit obligation) of the maximum settlement gain over any remaining unrecognized transition obligation or a pro rata portion of the maximum settlement loss.

94. If the purchase of a participating insurance contract constitutes a settlement (refer to paragraphs 67 and 90), the maximum gain (but not the maximum loss) shall be reduced by the cost of the participation right before determining the amount to be recognized in income.

---

[24]If an insurance contract is purchased from an insurance company controlled by the employer, the purchase of the contract does not constitute a settlement.

[25]As discussed in paragraph 112, in measuring the gain or loss subject to recognition in income when a postretirement benefit obligation is settled, it shall first be determined whether recognition of an additional amount of any unrecognized transition obligation is required.

[26]Because the plan is the unit of accounting, the determination of the effects of a settlement considers only the unrecognized net gain or loss and unrecognized transition obligation or asset related to the plan for which all or a portion of the accumulated postretirement benefit obligation is being settled.

95. If the cost of all settlements[27] in a year is less than or equal to the sum of the service cost and interest cost components of net postretirement benefit cost for the plan for the year, gain or loss recognition is permitted but not required for those settlements. However, the accounting policy adopted shall be applied consistently from year to year.

Accounting for a Plan Curtailment

96. For purposes of this Statement, a curtailment is an event that significantly reduces the expected years of future service of active plan participants or eliminates the accrual of defined benefits for some or all of the future services of a significant number of active plan participants. Curtailments include:

a. Termination of employees' services earlier than expected, which may or may not involve closing a facility or discontinuing a segment of a business
b. Termination or suspension of a plan so that employees do not earn additional benefits for future service. In the latter situation, future service may be counted toward eligibility for benefits accumulated based on past service.

97. The unrecognized prior service cost associated with the portion of the future years of service that had been expected to be rendered, but as a result of a curtailment are no longer expected to be rendered, is a loss. For purposes of measuring the effect of a curtailment, unrecognized prior service cost includes the cost of plan amendments and any remaining unrecognized transition obligation. For example, a curtailment may result from the termination of a significant number of employees who were plan participants at the date of a prior plan amendment.[28] The loss associated with that curtailment is measured as (a) the portion of the remaining unrecognized prior service cost related to that (and any prior) plan amendment attributable to the previously expected remaining future years of service of the employees who were terminated and (b) the portion of the remaining unrecognized transition obligation attributable to the previously

expected remaining future years of service of the terminated employees who were plan participants at the date of transition.

98. The accumulated postretirement benefit obligation may be decreased (a gain) or increased (a loss) by a curtailment.[29] That (gain) loss shall reduce any unrecognized net loss (gain).

a. To the extent that such a gain exceeds any unrecognized net loss (or the entire gain, if an unrecognized net gain exists), it is a curtailment gain.
b. To the extent that such a loss exceeds any unrecognized net gain (or the entire loss, if an unrecognized net loss exists), it is a curtailment loss.

For purposes of applying the provisions of this paragraph, any remaining unrecognized transition asset shall be treated as an unrecognized net gain and shall be combined with the unrecognized net gain or loss arising subsequent to transition to this Statement.

99. If the sum of the effects identified in paragraphs 97 and 98 is a net loss, it shall be recognized in income when it is probable that a curtailment will occur and the net effect is reasonably estimable. If the sum of those effects is a net gain, it shall be recognized in income when the related employees terminate or the plan suspension or amendment is adopted.

Relationship of Settlements and Curtailments to Other Events

100. A settlement and a curtailment may occur separately or together. If benefits expected to be paid in future periods are eliminated for some plan participants (for example, because a significant portion of the work force is dismissed or a plant is closed) but the plan remains in existence and continues to pay benefits, to invest assets, and to receive contributions, a curtailment has occurred but not a settlement. If an employer purchases nonparticipating insurance contracts for the accumulated postretirement benefit obligation and continues to

---

[27]For the following types of settlements, the cost of the settlement is:

a. For a cash settlement, the amount of cash paid to plan participants
b. For a settlement using nonparticipating insurance contracts, the cost of the contracts
c. For a settlement using participating insurance contracts, the cost of the contracts less the amount attributed to participation rights. (Refer to paragraphs 68 and 69.)

[28]A curtailment also may result from terminating the accrual of additional benefits for the future services of a significant number of employees. The loss in that situation is (a) a proportionate amount of the remaining unrecognized prior service cost based on the portion of the remaining expected years of service in the amortization period that originally was attributable to those employees who were plan participants at the date of the plan amendment and whose future accrual of benefits has been terminated and (b) a proportionate amount of the remaining unrecognized transition obligation based on the portion of the remaining years of service of all participants active at the date of transition that originally was attributable to the remaining expected future years of service of the employees whose future accrual of benefits has been terminated.

[29]Increases in the accumulated postretirement benefit obligation that reflect termination benefits are excluded from the scope of this paragraph. (Refer to paragraphs 101 and 102.)

provide defined benefits for future service, either in the same plan or in a successor plan, a settlement has occurred but not a curtailment. If a **plan termination** occurs (that is, the obligation is settled and the plan ceases to exist) and the plan is not replaced by a successor defined benefit plan, both a settlement and a curtailment have occurred (whether or not the employees continue to work for the employer).

Measurement of the Effects of Termination Benefits

101. Postretirement benefits offered as special or contractual termination benefits shall be recognized in accordance with paragraph 15 of Statement 88. That is, an employer that offers special termination benefits to employees shall recognize a liability and a loss when the employees accept the offer and the amount can be reasonably estimated. An employer that provides contractual termination benefits shall recognize a liability and a loss when it is probable that employees will be entitled to benefits and the amount can be reasonably estimated. A situation involving special or contractual termination benefits may also result in a curtailment to be accounted for under paragraphs 96-99 of this Statement.

102. The liability and loss recognized for employees who accept an offer of special termination benefits to be provided by a postretirement benefit plan shall be the difference between (a) the accumulated postretirement benefit obligation for those employees, assuming that those employees (active plan participants) not yet fully eligible for benefits would terminate at their full eligibility date and that fully eligible plan participants would retire immediately, without considering any special termination benefits and (b) the accumulated postretirement benefit obligation as measured in (a) adjusted to reflect the special termination benefits.

Disposal of a Segment

103. If the gain or loss measured in accordance with paragraphs 92-94, 97-99, or 101 and 102 is directly related to disposal of a segment of a business or a portion of a line of business, it shall be included in determining the gain or loss associated with that event. The net gain or loss attributable to the disposal shall be recognized pursuant to the requirements of APB Opinion No. 30, *Reporting the Results of Operations—Reporting the Effects of Disposal of a Segment of a Business, and Extraor-* *dinary, Unusual and Infrequently Occurring Events and Transactions.*

Defined Contribution Plans

104. For purposes of this Statement, a **defined contribution postretirement plan** is a plan that provides postretirement benefits in return for services rendered, provides *an individual account* for each participant, and has terms that specify how contributions to the individual's account are to be determined rather than the amount of postretirement benefits the individual is to receive.[30] Under a defined contribution plan, the postretirement benefits a plan participant will receive are limited to the amount contributed to the plan participant's account, the returns earned on investments of those contributions, and forfeitures of other plan participants' benefits that may be allocated to the plan participant's account.

105. To the extent a plan's defined contributions to an individual's account are to be made for periods in which that individual renders services, the net postretirement benefit cost for a period shall be the contribution called for in that period. If a plan calls for contributions for periods after an individual retires or terminates, the estimated cost shall be accrued during the employee's service period.

106. An employer that sponsors one or more defined contribution plans shall disclose the following separately from its defined benefit plan disclosures:

a. A description of the plan(s) including employee groups covered, the basis for determining contributions, and the nature and effect of significant matters affecting comparability of information for all periods presented
b. The amount of cost recognized during the period.

107. A postretirement benefit plan having characteristics of both a defined benefit plan and a defined contribution plan requires careful analysis. If the *substance* of the plan is to provide a defined benefit, as may be the case with some "target benefit" plans, the accounting and disclosure requirements shall be determined in accordance with the provisions of this Statement applicable to a defined benefit plan.

Effective Dates and Transition

108. Except as noted in the following sentences of this paragraph and in paragraphs 114 and 115, this

---

[30]For example, an employer may establish individual postretirement health care accounts for each employee, each year contributing a specified amount to each active employee's account. The balance in each employee's account may be used by that employee after the employee's retirement to purchase health care insurance or for other health care benefits. Rather than providing for defined health care benefits, the employer is providing a defined amount of money that may be used by retirees toward the payment of their health care costs.

Statement shall be effective for fiscal years beginning after December 15, 1992. For plans outside the United States and for defined benefit plans of employers that (a) are **nonpublic enterprises** and (b) sponsor defined benefit postretirement plan(s) with no more than 500 plan participants in the aggregate, this Statement shall be effective for fiscal years beginning after December 15, 1994. Earlier application is encouraged. Restatement of previously issued annual financial statements is not permitted. If a decision is made in other than the first interim period of an employer's fiscal year to apply this Statement early, previous interim periods of that year shall be restated.

109. If at the transition date an employer has excluded assets in a **postretirement benefit fund** from its statement of financial position and some or all of the assets in that fund do not qualify as plan assets as defined herein, the employer shall recognize in the statement of financial position the fair value of those nonqualifying assets as the employer's assets (not prepaid postretirement benefit cost) and an equal amount as an accrued postretirement benefit obligation pursuant to the transition to this Statement and before applying paragraph 110. Thereafter, those assets shall be accounted for in accordance with generally accepted accounting principles applicable to those types of assets, including their presentation in the employer's statement of financial position based on any restrictions on their use. The fair value of those assets at the transition date shall be used as their cost.

110. For a defined benefit plan, an employer shall determine as of the measurement date (paragraph 72) for the beginning of the fiscal year in which this Statement is first applied (the transition date), the amounts of (a) the accumulated postretirement benefit obligation and (b) the fair value of plan assets plus any recognized accrued postretirement benefit cost or less any recognized prepaid postretirement benefit cost. The difference between those two amounts, whether it represents a transition obligation or a transition asset, may be recognized either immediately in net income of the period of the change (paragraph 111) as the effect of a change in accounting principle,[31] or on a delayed basis (paragraph 112) as a component of net periodic postretirement benefit cost. Any transition obligation related to a defined contribution plan shall be recognized in the same manner. A single method of transition shall be elected at the date this Statement is initially applied for all defined benefit and defined contribution postretirement plans.

111. If immediate recognition of the transition obligation or asset is elected, the amount attributable to the effects of a plan initiation or any benefit improvements adopted after December 21, 1990 shall be treated as unrecognized prior service cost and excluded from the transition amount immediately recognized. In addition, an employer who chooses to immediately recognize the transition obligation or asset shall, at the date of transition, adjust as necessary the accounting for purchase business combinations consummated subsequent to December 21, 1990 to include in the assignment of the purchase price to assets acquired and liabilities assumed, recognition of the difference between the accumulated postretirement benefit obligation and the fair value of the plan assets, as described in paragraphs 87 and 88. If reliable information on which to base measurement of the assumed postretirement benefit obligation as of the date the business combination is consummated is not available, the purchaser shall retroactively adjust the purchase price allocation to recognize the obligation assumed or the asset acquired, using the best information available at the date of transition to this Statement. The cumulative effect on prior periods' income of that retroactive adjustment of the purchase price allocation, for example, increased amortization of goodwill associated with the business combination, and the amortization of prior service cost related to a plan initiation or amendment adopted after December 21, 1990, shall be recognized as part of the effect of the accounting change to adopt this Statement.

112. If delayed recognition is elected, the transition obligation or asset shall be amortized on a straight-line basis over the average remaining service period of active plan participants, except that (a) if the average remaining service period is less than 20 years, the employer may elect to use a 20-year period, and (b) if all or almost all of the plan participants are inactive, the employer shall use the average remaining life expectancy period of those plan participants. However, amortization of the transition obligation shall be accelerated if the cumulative benefit payments subsequent to the transition date to all plan participants exceed the cumulative postretirement benefit cost accrued subsequent to the transition date. In that situation, an additional amount of the unrecognized transition obligation shall be recognized equal to the excess cumulative benefit payments. For purposes of applying this provision, cumulative benefit payments shall be reduced by any plan assets or any recognized accrued postretirement benefit obligation at the transition date. Payments made pursuant to a settlement, as discussed in

---

[31]The effect of the accounting change and the related income tax effect shall be presented in the statement of income between the captions "extraordinary items" and "net income." The per share information presented on the statement of income shall include the per share effect of the accounting change.

paragraphs 90-94, shall be included in the determination of cumulative benefit payments made subsequent to the transition date.

113. If at the measurement date for the beginning of an employer's fiscal year it is expected that additional recognition of any remaining unrecognized transition obligation will be required pursuant to paragraph 112, amortization of the transition obligation for interim reporting purposes shall be based on the amount expected to be amortized for the year, except for the effects of applying paragraph 112 for any settlement required to be accounted for pursuant to paragraphs 90-94. Those effects shall be recognized when the related settlement is recognized. The effects of changes during the year in the initial assessment of whether additional recognition of the unrecognized transition obligation will be required for the year shall be recognized over the remainder of the year. The amount of the unrecognized transition obligation to be recognized for a year shall be finally determined at the measurement date for the end of the year based on the constraints on delayed recognition discussed in paragraph 112; any difference between the amortization of the transition obligation recognized during interim periods and the amount required to be recognized for the year shall be recognized immediately.

Effective Date and Transition—Amendment to Opinion 12

114. Paragraph 6 and the related footnote of APB Opinion No. 12, *Omnibus Opinion—1967,* are amended effective for fiscal years beginning after March 15, 1991. The effect of the amendment on existing individual deferred compensation contracts, other than those providing postretirement health or welfare benefits, shall be recognized as the effect of a change in accounting principle in accordance with paragraphs 17-21 of APB Opinion No. 20, *Accounting Changes.* Individual deferred compensation contracts that provide postretirement health or welfare benefits shall be subject to the general transition provisions and effective dates of this Statement.

Rescission of Technical Bulletin 87-1

115. Effective with the issuance of this Statement, FASB Technical Bulletin No. 87-1, *Accounting for a Change in Method of Accounting for Certain Postretirement Benefits,* is rescinded. If a change in method of accounting for postretirement benefits is adopted subsequent to the issuance of this Statement, the new method shall comply with the provisions of this Statement.

The provisions of this Statement need not be applied to immaterial items.

This Statement was adopted by the unanimous vote of the seven members of the Financial Accounting Standards Board:

Dennis R. Beresford, *Chairman*
Victor H. Brown

Raymond C. Lauver
James J. Leisenring
C. Arthur Northrop

A. Clarence Sampson
Robert J. Swieringa

Appendix A

BASIS FOR CONCLUSIONS

CONTENTS

Appendix A

BASIS FOR CONCLUSIONS

Introduction

116. This appendix summarizes considerations that were deemed significant by members of the Board in reaching the conclusions in this Statement. It includes reasons for accepting certain approaches and rejecting others. Individual Board members gave greater weight to some factors than to others.

117. This Statement addresses the accounting issues related to measuring and recognizing the exchange that takes place between an employer that promises to provide postretirement health care or other welfare benefits (postretirement benefits) and the employees who render services in exchange for those benefits. The Board's conclusion to recognize postretirement benefit promises on an accrual basis over employee service periods is not a new notion; rather, it is fundamental to accounting for all deferred compensation contracts.

Benefits and Costs

118. The mission of the FASB is to "establish and improve standards of financial accounting and reporting for the guidance and education of the public, including issuers, auditors, and users of financial statements" (FASB *Rules of Procedure,* page 2). In fulfilling that mission the Board follows certain precepts, including the precept to promulgate standards only when the expected benefits of the resulting information exceed the perceived costs. The Board strives to determine that a proposed standard will fill a significant need and that the costs imposed to meet that standard, as compared with other alternatives, are justified in relation to the overall benefits of the resulting information.

119. The objective, and implicit benefit, of issuing an accounting standard is the increased credibility and representational faithfulness of financial reporting as a result of the new or revised accounting. However, the value of that incremental improvement to financial reporting is impossible to quantify. Consequently, the Board's assessment of the benefit to preparers, creditors, investors, and other users of issuing an accounting standard is, unavoidably, subjective. Like the incremental benefit of issuing an accounting standard, the incremental costs imposed by a new accounting standard are diffuse. They are borne by users and attesters as well as preparers of financial statements. Some of those costs can be quantified, albeit imprecisely and with difficulty; but, most of the benefits and many of the costs of adopting a new accounting standard cannot be quantified. How does one measure the benefit of improved financial reporting? Or stated another way, how does one assess the cost of the failure to accrue an obligation?

120. FASB Concepts Statement No. 2, *Qualitative Characteristics of Accounting Information,* discusses the benefits and costs of accounting information. It states:

> The costs and benefits of a standard are both direct and indirect, immediate and deferred. They may be affected by change in circumstances not foreseen when the standard was promulgated. There are wide variations in the estimates that different people make about the dollar values involved and the rate of discount to be used in reducing them to a present value. . . . [It has been observed that] "the merits of any Standard, or of the Standards as a whole, can be decided finally only by judgments that are largely subjective. They cannot be decided by scientific test." [paragraph 142]

The Board believes those observations remain pertinent and accurately describe its process of considering benefits and costs.

121. An assessment of the benefits and costs of issuing an accounting standard is integral to the Board's decision-making process. Consideration of each individual issue includes the subjective weighing of the incremental improvement in financial reporting against the incremental cost of implementing the identified alternatives. At the end

of that process, the Board considers the accounting provisions in the aggregate and must conclude that issuance of the standard is a sufficient improvement in financial reporting to justify the perceived costs. Paragraphs 122-132 address the Board's overall assessment of possible benefits and costs. Various benefits and costs that were deemed significant in reaching the conclusions in this Statement are described in later paragraphs of this basis for conclusions.

122. The Board believes that this Statement will fill a significant need for information about the financial effects of postretirement benefits that have been exchanged for employee service. Those financial effects are currently omitted from most general-purpose financial statements. Pay-as-you-go (cash) basis accounting delays the recognition and measurement of those effects until postretirement benefits are paid; as a result, costs incurred currently are not recognized until future periods.

123. General-purpose financial statements imply completeness of information within the bounds of what is material and feasible. A material omission can rob financial statements of their credibility. Continuation of the present accounting practice for postretirement benefits would represent a material omission from the financial statements of many employers. That practice led some respondents to the February 1989 Exposure Draft, *Employers' Accounting for Postretirement Benefits Other Than Pensions,* to suggest immediate recognition of the currently existing obligation as the correction of an error.

124. This Statement fulfills a significant need for information by requiring the use of accrual accounting for postretirement benefits. Accrual accounting will more appropriately reflect the financial effects of an employer's existing promise to provide those benefits and the events that affect that promise in financial statements, as those events occur. That accounting will subject the employer's estimates and assumptions about the future events that will determine the amount and timing of future benefit payments to the discipline of accounting recognition and measurement, and to the independent review of auditors and others, thereby enhancing the utility of the information provided.

125. This Statement also fills the need for information by requiring descriptive disclosures about the postretirement benefit plan, current measures of the plan assets, obligations, and costs, and the effect on the employer's financial statements of the provisions for delayed recognition of certain events affecting those measures. Fulfilling the significant need for information comes at a cost—

namely, the incremental cost of developing, implementing, and maintaining a measurement and reporting system to support the required accrual accounting and disclosures and the cost of learning how to use the new information.

126. Many employers have not monitored and managed their postretirement benefit obligations and costs. Consequently, a significant portion of the incremental systems cost reflects costs that a prudent employer would incur in monitoring and managing the consequences of its postretirement benefit arrangement. The Board believes that those costs should be associated with the existence of those arrangements, rather than with the requirements of this Statement. The Board also believes that there will be relatively little incremental systems cost incurred to satisfy the disclosure requirements of this Statement because the necessary information already will be developed in order to meet the basic recognition and measurement requirements.

127. The incremental cost of the accounting and disclosure requirements of this Statement has been reduced by following, to a significant extent, the precedents in Statement 87 for pension accounting. Moreover, the general approach is similar in many respects to that used by consulting actuaries who have estimated postretirement benefit costs and obligations as part of special health care cost containment studies, employee termination incentive programs, restructurings, and mergers and business combinations.

128. The incremental cost of implementing the requirements of this Statement has been increased by alternative approaches that provide for the delayed recognition of employers' transition obligations and the effects of subsequent plan amendments and gains and losses. Those provisions generally increase the complexity of the requirements, reduce understandability and comparability, and create the need for additional disclosures. However, those provisions enhance the acceptability of this Statement to the extent they reflect the views of some constituents and minimize disruption.

129. This Statement provides both general objectives and provisions and detailed guidance and illustrations. Some respondents indicated that providing detailed guidance might increase the incremental cost of the requirements of this Statement. However, a lack of detailed guidance can result in incremental costs being incurred by employers, auditors, regulators, and others by implicitly requiring that they define issues, identify and debate alternatives, assess possible effects, and select and implement solutions. Those costs are often not readily apparent but, nevertheless, are sig-

nificant. Moreover, if different employers select different solutions in similar situations, with effects that are materially different, the resulting information lacks comparability, thereby reducing the benefits to investors and other users. Inevitably, critics, regulators, and other users demand elimination of alternatives, and additional costs would be incurred as those actions are taken.

130. Some believe that employers will change the designs of postretirement benefit plans or the way those plans are financed as a result of the new information about the financial effects of postretirement benefits. In addition, some believe that the new information may provide an additional impetus to federal legislation covering employers' obligations for those plans or the deductibility of employers' advance funding of those plans. Those actions, if taken, are not the direct result of a requirement to accrue postretirement benefits, but rather, may result from more relevant and useful information on which to base decisions.

131. The Board is sensitive to the consequences that are likely to occur as a result of the new information. However, the nature and extent of those consequences are highly uncertain and are difficult to isolate from the effects of other events that will occur independent of that new information. For example, the costs of providing health care benefits are significant and are increasing. Expected future changes in those costs are likely to affect the design and funding of postretirement benefit plans and federal legislation covering those plans, regardless of the issuance of this Statement.

132. Even if the Board could isolate the likely consequences of the information provided pursuant to this Statement from other events that produce change, enhancing or diminishing the possibility of those consequences is not the Board's objective. The information provided by general-purpose financial statements is a public good. That information is shared by many interested parties with disparate interests and forms the basis for contracts and for monitoring contract performance. Both the benefits and costs of the information provided pursuant to this Statement will be recognized over time and will affect many parties differently. Those parties and the contracts they enter into will benefit from more relevant and reliable information about the incidence of postretirement benefit costs. But improved financial information comes at a cost, and while some of those parties may not pay directly for the benefits they derive from that information, they are likely to bear indirectly some of its cost.

Scope

133. In considering the scope of the project, the Board discussed various benefits provided after retirement, such as postretirement health care benefits, and benefits offered after employment but before retirement, such as temporary benefits after a layoff. Postemployment benefits provided to nonretirees may have many of the same characteristics as postretirement benefits—they may be defined in kind rather than in fixed amounts and their legal status may be uncertain. However, while most postretirement benefits are provided for the lifetime of an eligible retiree and for some covered dependents, many nonretiree postemployment benefits are provided for a specified period of time, often based on years of service. But the most important difference may lie in the fundamentally different nature of the employer's promise. Nonretiree postemployment benefits are generally more like termination compensation—a payment for not working—than deferred compensation—a delayed payment of compensation for working.

134. The Board concluded that postretirement benefits, because of their prevalence and magnitude, should be addressed in the initial stages of the project. Upon completion of this first phase, the Board will consider the need to provide guidance for accounting for other benefits offered after employment but not pursuant to retirement.

135. This Statement covers all benefits, other than cash benefits and life insurance benefits paid by pension plans, provided to current or former employees, their beneficiaries, and covered dependents during the period following the employees' retirement. Benefits encompassed include, but are not limited to, postretirement health care; life insurance provided outside a pension plan; and other welfare benefits such as tuition assistance, day care, legal services, and housing subsidies provided after retirement. The Board's conclusion about accrual of an obligation over the period of employee service rendered in exchange for that benefit is applicable to all forms of compensation.

136. Health and other welfare benefits expected to be provided to employees deemed to be on a disability retirement are within the scope of this Statement. In many cases those employees will have permanently ceased active employment because of their disabilities and retired under the disability provisions of a postretirement benefit (pension) plan. In other cases those employees may have ceased permanent active employment because of their disabilities but not yet gone through formal

"retirement" procedures and are carried on nonretired status under the disability provisions of the plan solely to continue earning additional postretirement benefits such as pensions.

137. The determination of disability benefits to be accrued pursuant to this Statement is based on the terms of the postretirement benefit plan that define when a disabled employee is entitled to postretirement benefits. For example, the provisions of the postretirement health care plan may provide postretirement health care coverage after a disabled employee attains a specified number of years of credited service (which may include credit for periods after the employee is disabled), with a separate disability plan that provides health benefits prior to that date.[32] Or, the postretirement health care plan may have special provisions for disabled employees that entitle them to benefit coverage under the postretirement benefit plan at a date earlier than that coverage would commence for other employees who are not disabled. Including disability health and other welfare benefits provided to employees on a disability retirement within the scope of this Statement is consistent with past practice, most notably in the pension area. Disability benefits offered through a pension plan are covered by Statement 87 and FASB Statement No. 35, *Accounting and Reporting by Defined Benefit Pension Plans.*

138. The Board concluded that all promises to provide postretirement benefits should be accrued whether they are provided through a plan or through individual contracts. For purposes of this Statement, the Board has defined a plan as an arrangement whereby an employer undertakes to provide its employees with benefits after they retire (terminate their service after meeting specified age, service, or age and service requirements defined by the postretirement benefit plan) in exchange for their services over a specified period of time, upon attaining a specified age, or both. The amount of the benefits can be determined or estimated in advance from the provisions of a document or documents or from the employer's current and past practices. The plan may be written or unwritten. An employer's practice of providing postretirement benefits pursuant to informal guidelines is considered to be a plan for purposes of this Statement.

139. This Statement applies to deferred compensation contracts with individual employees if those contracts, taken together, are equivalent to a postretirement benefit plan. However, an employer's practice of providing postretirement benefits to selected employees under individual contracts, with specific terms determined on an individual-by-individual basis, does not constitute a postretirement benefit plan under this Statement. This Statement amends Opinion 12 to explicitly require that the employer's obligation under those contracts be accrued following the terms of the individual contract.

Evolutionary Changes in Accounting Principles

140. The Board concluded that the changes required by this Statement represent a significant improvement in financial reporting. Paragraph 2 of FASB Concepts Statement No. 5, *Recognition and Measurement in Financial Statements of Business Enterprises,* states that "the Board intends future change [in practice] to occur in the gradual, evolutionary way that has characterized past change." The Board realizes that the evolutionary change may have to be slower in some areas than in others.

141. Some Board members believe that it would be conceptually appropriate and preferable to (a) recognize an obligation for postretirement benefits that would not be less than the vested benefit obligation,[33] (b) immediately recognize the effects of plan initiations and amendments that are retroactive, and (c) immediately recognize gains and losses, perhaps with gains and losses reported currently in comprehensive income but not in earnings. However, the Board concluded that those alternatives should not be adopted at this time. Those alternatives would be a major change from current practice and from the standards adopted by the Board for employers' accounting for pensions.

---

[32]For example, an employer may promise to provide postretirement health care coverage to all employees who render 30 or more years of service. The employer may carry active employees who become disabled on active status so a disabled employee continues to accumulate credit toward postretirement benefits. Measurement of the expected postretirement benefit obligation should include an assumption that some employees who are expected to receive benefits under the postretirement benefit plan will become disabled and cease working prior to the date at which they otherwise would have been eligible for post-retirement health care benefits. The measurement of the postretirement benefits expected to be paid to disabled employees would encompass only those benefits expected to be paid during the period following what otherwise would have been their full eligibility date; in this case, the date at which the employee would have completed 30 years of service. That amount is attributed to an employee's service to the date the disability is assumed to occur.

[33]As used herein, *vested postretirement benefit obligation* refers to the actuarial present value as of a particular date of the benefits expected to be paid to or for retirees, former employees, and active employees assuming they terminated immediately, including benefits expected to be paid to or for beneficiaries and any covered dependents of those plan participants.

Improvements in Financial Reporting

142. This Statement represents the first authoritative accounting pronouncement that requires current recognition of the exchange transaction between an employer that promises to provide postretirement benefits and the employees who render service in exchange for the benefits promised. Employers have generally recognized the obligation and related costs arising from the exchange as the obligation was satisfied rather than when it was incurred. The Board concluded that the recognition required by this Statement should result in a more meaningful representation of the employer's financial position and results of operations at any point in time.

143. Certain aspects of the delayed recognition features of this Statement cause the obligation that is recognized to differ from the current measure of the unfunded obligation attributed to service in the current and prior years. However, that current measure of the obligation and the effect of delayed recognition in deriving the amount of that obligation that has been recognized are required to be disclosed.

144. This Statement requires recognition of a service cost component of net periodic postretirement benefit cost based on the actuarial present value of the portion of the expected postretirement benefit obligation attributed to service during the period. This Statement also requires disclosure of the other compensatory and financial components of postretirement benefit cost for the period in order to reflect the employer's net cost of the benefit promise. The Board concluded that disclosure of the components should significantly assist users in understanding the economic events that have occurred. Those disclosures also make it easier to understand why reported amounts change from period to period.

145. Some respondents argued that the uncertainties inherent in quantifying the obligation for postretirement benefits lead to the conclusion that the measurements are not sufficiently reliable for recognition in financial statements. They would prefer to disclose rather than recognize that obligation and the related cost. The Board does not find those arguments persuasive. The Board concluded that it is possible for employers to produce an estimate of that obligation that is sufficiently reliable and relevant to justify recognition in financial statements. The Board expects that with experience, the reliability of the measurement will be enhanced. The Board concluded that employers' current practice of not recognizing their postretirement benefit obligations and the related costs results in less reliable financial statements and impairs the usefulness and integrity of those financial statements.

Conclusions on Basic Issues—Single-Employer Defined Benefit Postretirement Plans

The Exchange

146. The Board's conclusions in this Statement derive from the view that a defined postretirement benefit is part of an exchange between the employer and the employee. In exchange for services provided by the employee, the employer promises to provide, in addition to current wages and other current and deferred benefits (such as a pension), health care and other welfare benefits during the employee's retirement period. Postretirement benefits are not gratuities but instead are part of an employee's compensation for services rendered. Since payment is deferred, the benefit is a type of deferred compensation. The employer's obligation for that compensation is incurred when the services exchanged for that benefit are rendered, not when an employee terminates or when a retiree receives benefits.

147. Postretirement benefits are a form of pension benefits in kind. Unlike traditional cash pension benefits, the employer promises to provide defined benefits or services as the need for those benefits or services arises or on the occurrence of a specified event. Typically, those postretirement benefits supplement cash benefits paid after retirement. Regardless of the form of the benefit—in cash or in kind—the underlying promise is the same. In exchange for service over a specified period, the employer will provide the employee and any covered dependents or beneficiaries with the defined postretirement benefits.

Funding and Accrual Accounting

148. This Statement relies on a basic premise of generally accepted accounting principles that accrual accounting provides more relevant and useful information than cash basis accounting. Accrual accounting goes beyond cash transactions and recognizes the financial effects on an entity of transactions and other events and circumstances that have future cash consequences as those events and transactions occur, rather than only when cash is received or paid by the entity. In particular, accrual accounting provides a link between an entity's operations (and other transactions, events, and circumstances that affect it) and its cash receipts and outlays. It provides information about an entity's assets and liabilities and changes in those amounts that cannot be obtained from information produced by accounting only for cash re-

ceipts and outlays. Because the Board views the event obligating the employer as the rendering of employee service in exchange for future (postretirement) benefits, this Statement rejects terminal accrual (accrual at retirement) and cash basis accounting. The Board concluded that for postretirement benefits, as in other areas, the information resulting from accrual accounting is more representationally faithful and more relevant to financial statement users than accounting information prepared solely on the basis of cash transactions.

149. This Statement reaffirms Board decisions that funding should not be used as the basis for accounting recognition of cost. However, the Board's conclusion that accounting information on an accrual basis is needed does not mean that accounting information and funding decisions are unrelated. Measurement and recognition of the accrued obligation to provide postretirement benefits will provide management and other users of financial statements with better information to assess the financial consequences of management's actions. That information about the postretirement benefit obligation will be a factor in determining the amount and timing of future contributions to the plan.

150. The decision of how or when to fund the obligation is not an accounting issue. It is a financing decision that is properly influenced by many factors (such as tax considerations and the availability of attractive investment alternatives) that are unrelated to how or when the postretirement benefit obligation is incurred. The amount funded (however determined) is, of course, given accounting recognition as a use of cash, but the Board concluded that this is one of many areas in which information about cash flows alone is not sufficient.

The Principal Issues

151. Among the many issues considered by the Board in this project, three stand out as central to the Board's extensive deliberations and to public debate. Those issues are (a) whether a postretirement benefit plan results in an obligation that meets the definition of a liability, (b) how and when the obligation and related cost should be measured and recognized, and (c) how and when any net obligation or net asset that exists when this Statement is first applied should be measured and recognized.

The liability

152. Liabilities are defined in paragraph 35 of FASB Concepts Statement No. 6, *Elements of Financial Statements,* as "probable future sacrifices of economic benefits arising from present obliga-

tions of a particular entity to transfer assets or provide services to other entities in the future as a result of past transactions or events" (footnote references omitted). Liabilities reflect the residual of certain transactions or events affecting an entity. For example, a liability for postretirement benefits reflects the interrelationship of the cumulative cost to an employer of an exchange transaction and the ultimate payment of benefits to the [former] employees—the other party to the exchange transaction.

153. The first characteristic of a liability is that it "embodies a present duty or responsibility to one or more entities that entails settlement by probable future transfer or use of assets at a specified or determinable date, on occurrence of a specified event, or on demand" (Concepts Statement 6, paragraph 36). The employer has a duty or requirement to sacrifice assets in the future—the essence of the first characteristic of a liability. That duty exists even though a benefit obligation may be satisfied by providing goods and services rather than cash and the amount and timing of the benefit payments are estimated.

154. An employer that promises to provide postretirement benefits almost certainly has assumed a responsibility to make future payments because at least some of the present employees will receive those benefits in the future. Measurement of the postretirement benefit obligation considers the likelihood that some employees will work to or beyond the date eligibility for some or all of the postretirement benefits is attained, while others will terminate prior to that date and forego any right to postretirement benefits.

155. The second characteristic of a liability is that "the duty or responsibility obligates a particular entity, leaving it little or no discretion to avoid the future sacrifice" (Concepts Statement 6, paragraph 36). Paragraph 36 also states that ". . . although most liabilities rest generally on a foundation of legal rights and duties, existence of a legally enforceable claim is not a prerequisite for an obligation to qualify as a liability if for other reasons the entity has the duty or responsibility to pay cash, to transfer other assets, or to provide services to another entity." Some respondents indicated that postretirement benefits do not meet this characteristic of a liability and consequently, in their view, need not be recognized. Some of those respondents argued that only legally enforceable claims should be reported as liabilities. Others noted that most employers have retained the right to terminate or amend their postretirement benefit promises and therefore believe those employers can avoid the obligation at their discretion.

156. Case law has not been unequivocal about the le-

gal enforceability or lack thereof of promises to provide postretirement benefits, although legal enforceability of certain claims has been demonstrated. However, in accordance with Concepts Statement 6, the Board has looked beyond the legal status of the promise to consider whether the liability is effectively binding on the employer because of past practices, social or moral sanctions, or customs.

157. An entity is not obligated to sacrifice assets in the future if it can avoid the future sacrifice at its discretion without significant penalty. The penalty to the employer need not be in the form of another liability but could be in the form of a reduction in the value of assets. Concepts Statement 6, paragraph 203, illustrates that notion as follows: "The example of an entity that binds itself to pay employees vacation pay or year-end bonuses by paying them every year even though it is not contractually bound to do so and has not announced a policy to do so has already been noted. . . . It could refuse to pay only by risking substantial employee-relations problems." As a practical matter, it is unlikely that an employer could terminate its existing obligations under a postretirement benefit plan without incurring some cost. Therefore, the Board concluded that in the absence of evidence to the contrary, an employer is presumed to have accepted responsibility to provide the promised benefits. Consequently, the accounting for postretirement benefit arrangements generally is based on the presumption that the plan will continue and that the benefits promised by the employer will be provided.

158. The third characteristic of a liability is that "the transaction or other event obligating the entity has already happened" (Concepts Statement 6, paragraph 36). This characteristic is met when the employee renders service in exchange for the future benefits. The Board concluded that, conceptually, compensation cost should be recognized in the period in which it is earned under the plan—that is, when the employee renders the required service, not when the need for the benefit arises (which is factored into measurement of the obligation). An objective of this Statement is to recognize the compensation cost of an employee's postretirement benefits over the employee's credited service period, even though the complexity of the postretirement benefit arrangement and the uncertainty of the amount and timing of the future payments may preclude complete recognition of the precise postretirement benefit cost and obligation over that period.

Criteria for recognition

159. Paragraph 63 of Concepts Statement 5, states that an item should be recognized when four

fundamental recognition criteria are met:

Definitions—The item meets the definition of an element of financial statements.
Measurability—It has a relevant attribute measurable with sufficient reliability.
Relevance—The information about it is capable of making a difference in user decisions.
Reliability—The information is representationally faithful, verifiable, and neutral.

160. Most respondents indicated that employee service pursuant to a postretirement benefit plan creates an obligation that meets the definition of a liability. Some of those respondents expressed concerns about an employer's ability to measure its obligation with sufficient reliability, while others questioned whether the costs outweigh the benefits of recognizing the liability and the related cost in the financial statements. However, a majority of the respondents supported recognizing an obligation for postretirement benefits. They indicated that reasonable estimates of the measure of an employer's postretirement benefit obligation can be developed and that recognition of a liability based on that best estimate is preferable to no recognition or to footnote disclosure in lieu of recognition.

161. Paragraph 46 of Concepts Statement 6 acknowledges that the effects of economic events are often uncertain and that the existence and amount of items need not be certain for them to qualify as assets and liabilities. Estimates and approximations are commonplace in financial statements. Paragraph 74 of Concepts Statement 5 states that "relevance should be evaluated in the context of the principal objective of financial reporting: providing information that is useful in making rational investment, credit, and similar decisions." Paragraph 59 of Concepts Statement 2 states that the reliability of a measurement of accounting information is dependent on the extent to which users can depend on it to represent the economic conditions or events that it purports to represent. That concepts Statement acknowledges that that is seldom a clear choice; rather, the issue is whether the accounting information is so relevant that some allowance ought to be made for some lack of reliability because the information provides a better representation of economic conditions than would be portrayed without the information.

162. Reliability may affect the timing of recognition. Paragraphs 76 and 77 of Concepts Statement 5 state:

. Information about some items that meet a definition may never become sufficiently reliable at a justifiable cost to recognize the item. For other items, those uncertainties are reduced as time passes, and reliability is increased as additional information becomes available.

. . . waiting for virtually complete reliability or minimum cost may make the information so untimely that it loses its relevance. At some intermediate point, uncertainty may be reduced at a justifiable cost to a level tolerable in view of the perceived relevance of the information.

163. The Board concluded that the obligation to provide postretirement benefits meets the definition of a liability (paragraphs 152-158), is representationally faithful, is relevant to financial statement users, and can be measured with sufficient reliability at a justifiable cost. To imply by a failure to accrue that no obligation exists prior to the payment of benefits is not a faithful representation of what the financial statements purport to represent. The Board concluded that failure to recognize the existence of the obligation significantly impairs the usefulness and credibility of the employer's financial statements.

Recognition versus disclosure

164. Some respondents agreed that better information about the cost of and obligation for postretirement benefits is needed but argued that the information would be just as useful if it were disclosed in the footnotes. In the Board's view, it is important that elements that qualify for recognition be recognized in the basic financial statements. Footnote disclosure is not an adequate substitute for recognition. The argument that the information is equally useful regardless of how it is presented could be applied to any financial statement element. The usefulness and integrity of financial statements are impaired by each omission of an element that qualifies for recognition. The incremental systems cost of recognition is insignificant. All of the costs of measuring the postretirement benefit obligation would be incurred to provide useful disclosures.

165. If disclosures and recognition are equally useful, then any asset or liability, or revenue or expense, could be reported with equal effect in either manner. Few would argue that disclosure is an alternative to recognition when discussing an entity's trade payables or cost of sales. If one accepts the view that an employer has a liability and cost for postretirement benefits exchanged for employees' current and past services, there is no substantive difference between postretirement benefits and other costs and liabilities other than the difficulty of measurement and the longer period of time over which the liability is paid. Although the "equal usefulness" argument may be valid for some sophisticated users, it may not hold for all or even most users. Those who assert that footnote disclosure or recognition would be equally useful, but argue only for disclosure, must believe that recognition and disclosure have different consequences.

Measurement of cost and obligations

166. The Board believes that the understandability, comparability, and usefulness of financial information are improved by narrowing the use of alternative accounting methods that do not reflect different facts and circumstances. Consequently, the Board has attempted to improve financial reporting by accounting for similar transactions similarly and by measuring enterprises' resources and claims to or interest in those resources on similar bases. Any method of accounting for postretirement benefits that recognizes the expected future cost during the service period must deal with two problems that stem from the nature of the arrangement. First, estimates or assumptions must be made about the future events that will determine the amount and timing of the benefit payments. Second, an approach must be selected for attributing the cost of those benefits to individual years of service.

167. The Board recognizes that uncertainty in measuring the benefit obligation for a single employee is greater than for a group because the future events that affect the amount and timing of future benefits, such as retirement date and life expectancy, can be more reliably estimated on a group basis. However, that uncertainty does not change the nature of the promise. Actuarial computations consider that some existing or future retirees will live longer than others and that some individuals will terminate employment before becoming eligible for the benefits or die before receiving any benefits. Those factors are appropriately considered in measuring the probable future sacrifice that will result from the present existing promise of benefits to former and current employees.

168. This Statement uses the term *expected postretirement benefit obligation* (a term not used in Statement 87) to describe the obligation for benefits expected to be received by plan participants. The expected postretirement benefit obligation is used as the basis for determining the benefit cost to be attributed to credited years of service. The term *accumulated postretirement benefit obligation* is used to describe the portion of the expected postretirement benefit obligation attributed to service to a measurement date. Since measurement of the expected postretirement benefit obligation includes an assumed salary progression for a pay-related plan, salary progression is, by definition, included in the accumulated benefit obligation for a pay-related postretirement benefit plan. Thus, the ac-

cumulated postretirement benefit obligation disclosed pursuant to this Statement is defined in terms notionally more comparable to the projected benefit obligation under Statement 87.

169. Since the accumulated benefit obligation defined by Statement 87 excludes assumed salary progression, the accumulated benefit obligation for a pay-related pension plan has no counterpart in this Statement. The Board concluded that it would be more confusing to define an additional measure of a benefit obligation, in addition to the expected and accumulated postretirement benefit obligations, under this Statement to compare with the accumulated benefit obligation for pay-related plans under Statement 87 than to measure the accumulated benefit obligation for those plans differently under the two Statements.

170. Despite that difference in the definition of the accumulated benefit obligation for a postretirement benefit plan and for a pension plan, service cost and interest cost are defined and measured in a similar fashion under both this Statement and Statement 87. Service cost under both Statements is the actuarial present value of benefits attributed to services rendered by plan participants during the period and includes consideration of salary progression for pay-related plans. Interest cost under this Statement is defined as the increase in the *accumulated* postretirement benefit obligation to recognize the effects of the passage of time; under Statement 87 interest cost is defined as the increase in the *projected* benefit obligation to recognize the effects of the passage of time.

171. In considering postretirement benefit plans, neither respondents nor the Board was able to identify fundamentally different circumstances that would make it appropriate for different employers to adopt different accounting methods or measurement techniques for similar plans or for a single employer to adopt different methods or measurement techniques for different plans. As a result, a single method is prescribed for measuring and recognizing an employer's obligation and the related net periodic cost. That method attributes the expected postretirement benefit obligation to employee service rendered to the date full eligibility for the postretirement benefits is attained. The method is intended to improve comparability and understandability of employers' financial statements in reporting the financial consequences of providing postretirement benefits. It generally is also consistent with accounting for other forms of deferred compensation earned by employees that are paid during retirement, such as pensions.

Accounting for the substantive plan

172. Many respondents to the Exposure Draft observed that employers' postretirement benefit promises (particularly for health care benefits) are evolving. They stated that employers will change their promises in reaction to expected future health care costs. They believe that because future costs are considered in postretirement benefit measurements, employers should be permitted to anticipate the changes to the plan that the employer would be likely to make in reaction to the expected future cost of the benefits currently covered by the plan. Some respondents suggested that a designated health care cost trend rate, such as the general inflation rate, be used to consider implicitly the future actions employers might take to control their postretirement health care costs. Other respondents suggested the use of more explicit approaches that would anticipate future plan amendments if certain conditions were met.

173. In response to those suggestions, the Board considered whether there are situations in which future plan changes should be anticipated for measurement purposes. Board members generally believed that when an employer has a present commitment to amend the plan, the extant written plan, amended to reflect that commitment, should be the basis for the accounting. The Board believed that evidence of an employer's commitment to amend the plan should include an employer's past practices of amending the plan, identification of strategies to effect future changes, and the assessment of the feasibility and likelihood of making those changes in light of the expected economic and social costs. Because the transaction that is the basis for the accounting is the result of an exchange between an employer and its employees, Board members believed that the substantive plan that is the basis for the accounting should be communicated to and understood by the plan participants as representing that exchange agreement.

174. Some Board members supported permitting the anticipation of changes, including changes in a plan's covered benefits, if certain conditions were met. The Board noted, however, that unlike changes in cost-sharing provisions, there would be no past practice of changing covered benefits that could be considered representative of the substantive plan. Once a benefit is eliminated, it cannot be eliminated again. In addition, given a choice of benefit changes that might occur, it is unlikely that employers could determine which would be most likely to occur. And, since different health care benefits may have different assumed health care

cost trend rates, the inability to determine the most likely change in the covered benefits would affect an employer's ability to measure its expected postretirement benefit obligation. The Board noted that those measurement concerns do not arise when benefits are defined solely in terms of monetary amounts. The Board concluded that changes in in-kind benefits covered by a postretirement health care plan or by other postretirement benefit plans should not be anticipated. The Board noted, however, that if an employer amends the benefits to be provided by the plan, the effect of the amendment is recognized immediately in measuring the employer's expected and accumulated postretirement benefit obligations, even if the effective date of the change in benefits is delayed until a specified date in the future.

175. Some Board members do not favor anticipating any future plan changes for purposes of measuring and recognizing an employer's postretirement benefit obligations. They note that financial statements are intended to present the financial effects of events and transactions that have already happened. In their view, future actions that change the promise should be recognized when the change occurs; to anticipate future changes is not a representationally faithful portrayal of the employer's current obligation. Therefore, they believe the obligation and cost to provide postretirement benefits should be measured as defined by the plan at the measurement date. Further, they believe the criteria to limit those plan changes that may be anticipated will prove to be unworkable, just as other attempts to account for management's intent have been unworkable. Other Board members believe that a plan's existing terms do not necessarily establish the substance of the current or past exchange transaction and therefore may not always provide the best basis for measuring an employer's current obligation.

176. The Board concluded that measures of an employer's postretirement benefit obligations should reflect the terms of the exchange transaction understood by an employer and its employees. To the extent that an employer has a past practice of maintaining a consistent level of cost sharing or consistently increasing or reducing the cost-sharing provisions of the plan that reflects the employer's cost-sharing policy, without offsetting identifiable changes in other benefits or compensation or other significant costs, that policy represents the substantive terms of the exchange transaction. Such a past practice would be indicated when the nature of the change and duration of the past practice are sufficient to warrant a presumption that it is understood by the plan participants. Similarly, if an employer has communicated its intent to institute different cost-sharing provisions of the plan at a

specified time or when specified conditions are met and those changes are likely to occur without adverse consequences to the employer's operations or offsetting changes in the plan participants' other benefits, those changes should be anticipated. The Board notes, however, that in most cases collectively bargained plans will be unable to anticipate plan changes because the employer does not have the unilateral ability to amend the plan and would most likely be unable to demonstrate a consistent past practice of cost-sharing changes without offsetting changes in other benefits. For that reason, some Board members believe there should be no possibility of an exception.

Contributory plans

177. Some employers may require that active employees contribute toward the cost of their postretirement benefits. Those contributions may be adjusted throughout the service period and may vary depending on the number of an employee's dependents. In addition, postretirement benefit plans may have cost-sharing provisions that require retired employees to share a portion of the cost of the benefits through contributions, copayment provisions, or deductibles. Because an employer's postretirement benefit obligation is measured as of a defined measurement date, the Exposure Draft proposed that for purposes of measuring the expected postretirement benefit obligation, employee contributions or cost-sharing provisions should be assumed using the rates or provisions required by the current plan benefit formula. Unless an employer had a history of regular increases in benefits indicative of a commitment to make future improvements to the plan, anticipating future changes to the plan would have been precluded for purposes of measuring the expected postretirement benefit obligation and net periodic postretirement benefit cost.

178. Contributions expected to be received from active employees toward the cost of their postretirement benefits and from retired plan participants are treated similarly for purposes of measuring an employer's expected postretirement benefit obligation. An employer's obligation to return contributions received from employees who do not attain eligibility for postretirement benefits, and, if applicable, any interest accrued on those contributions, should be recognized as a component of an employer's postretirement benefit obligation. Thus, an employer's statement of financial position should reflect an accrued obligation for postretirement benefits that includes (a) the accrued obligation to provide benefits to plan participants who are eligible for benefits or are expected to become eligible for benefits under the postretirement benefit plan and (b) the obligation to return accumulated contributions, plus any

interest thereon, to employees who are expected to terminate without attaining eligibility for the postretirement benefits.

Assumptions

179. Measurements of the actuarial present value of the expected and accumulated postretirement benefit obligations require actuarial assumptions. Those assumptions include discount rates, retirement age, the timing and amount of future benefits (which for postretirement health care benefits consider past and present per capita claims cost, health care cost trend rates, and medical coverage by governmental authorities and other providers of health care benefits), and the probability of payment (turnover, dependency status, mortality, and so forth). Measurement of the expected postretirement benefit obligation and the accumulated postretirement benefit obligation also considers salary progression when applicable. Many of the assumptions used in postretirement benefit measurements are similar to assumptions used in pension measurements.

180. This Statement requires that each significant assumption reflect the best estimate of the plan's future experience, solely with respect to that individual assumption (an "explicit" approach). All assumptions should assume that the plan will continue, absent compelling evidence to the contrary. The Board believes that an explicit approach results in more understandable and useful information about changes in the benefit obligation and the choice of significant assumptions used to determine the various measurements required by this Statement.

181. Some respondents argued that an implicit approach to assumptions, that combines the effect of two or more assumptions to approximate future experience, would improve comparability by reducing variability in employers' assumptions. Under an implicit approach, reliability of assumptions is judged in the aggregate, not individually. However, some respondents who supported an implicit approach seemed to favor uniformity of certain assumptions, such as the use of designated health care cost trend rates, rather than favoring the combination of two or more assumptions. Other respondents who supported an implicit approach seemed to support that approach because it would implicitly consider how the plan might be amended in the future to achieve a desired limit on cost increases. For example, some respondents supported measuring the employer's share of future incurred claims costs by projecting the increase in health care costs using the expected general inflation rate. They stated that applying the expected general inflation rate to the employer's share of per capita incurred claims costs (current cost) best reflects management's intent to control

those costs in the future within that limit. However, the Board believes that such an approach cannot be characterized as measuring the current promise or as being generally representative of a trend to limit an employer's commitment. If an employer has historically amended its plan to achieve a trend equal to the general inflation rate, the Board believes that that past practice is better considered explicitly in determining the substantive plan than implicitly through a surrogate health care cost trend rate.

182. The Board considered an implicit approach as an alternative for certain individual assumptions—for example, by measuring an employer's postretirement benefit obligation and cost using an assumed spread between the health care cost trend rate and the discount rate. An implicit approach was rejected because the Board concluded that users of financial statements are better able to make judgments about the measures presented if they are given the opportunity to compare employers' individual assessments of specific future events. Consequently, the Board concluded that employers should be required to measure their obligations using the best information and estimates available based on existing information and circumstances.

183. Measurement of an employer's postretirement benefit obligation is based on the current plan participants (a "closed group" approach) because it better recognizes the benefit obligation over the period in which employees render service in exchange for benefits. Accounting on the basis of an ongoing employee group (an "open group" approach) often defers recognition of part of the cost of employees' current service to later periods. That open group view provides no basis for recognizing the cost of benefits over the service periods related to the current work force and suggests by its application that employers have a cost and obligation for employees not yet hired.

184. The Board concluded that application of accrual accounting to postretirement benefit accounting requires that the cost of the benefits be recognized in the period in which the employer receives the associated economic benefits—as employee services are rendered. Employee compensation, whether paid currently or deferred, should be recognized when the services are rendered. The Board concluded that, in concept, the employer's obligation to an existing employee group is the sum of its obligations to individual employees, adjusted to reflect the present value of the amount of the obligation and the probability of payment (the actuarial present value).

185. Employers' postretirement benefit obligations will differ to the extent that their promises

are different. For example, some employers may fully reimburse the cost of nursing home care, while others may not provide for that care. Or, some employers may carve out Medicare benefits and provide a low level of supplementary health care coverage, while others may provide a more generous plan that coordinates benefits with Medicare. No standard plan design or package of postretirement benefits or a static set of circumstances exists that would call for all employers to use the same assumptions. Different types of benefits may have differing trend rate assumptions, and different employers may have differing expectations about benefit utilization. Because of differences in plan design and employer circumstances, including the expected demographics of the plan population, measurement assumptions about the timing and amount of future benefits should represent an employer's best estimate with respect to the factors affecting its particular promise.

186. The objective of selecting assumed discount rates is to measure the single amount that, if invested at the measurement date in a portfolio of high-quality debt instruments, would provide the necessary future cash flows to pay the accumulated benefits when due. Notionally, that single amount, the accumulated postretirement benefit obligation, would equal the current market value of a portfolio of high-quality zero coupon bonds whose maturity dates and amounts would be the same as the timing and amount of the expected future benefit payments. Because cash inflows would equal cash outflows in timing and amount, there would be no reinvestment risk in the yields to maturity of the portfolio. However, in other than a zero coupon portfolio, such as a portfolio of long-term debt instruments that pay semiannual interest payments or whose maturities do not extend far enough into the future to meet expected benefit payments, the assumed discount rates (the yield to maturity) need to incorporate expected reinvestment rates available in the future. Those rates should be extrapolated from the existing yield curve at the measurement date. Assumed discount rates should be reevaluated at each measurement date. If the general level of interest rates rises or declines, the assumed discount rates should change in a similar manner.

187. The Board concluded that, conceptually, the basis for determining the assumed discount rates for measuring the present value of the postretirement benefit obligation and the service cost component should be the same as the basis for determining the assumed discount rates for pension measurements. That is, conceptually, the selection of assumed discount rates should be based on the single sum that, if invested at the measurement date, would generate the necessary cash flows to pay the benefits when due.

188. Consistent with Statement 87, the Exposure Draft referred to "the interest rates inherent in the amount at which the postretirement benefit obligation could be effectively settled." Many respondents found that notion confusing because postretirement benefit obligations generally cannot be settled at the current time. However, as opposed to "settling" the obligation, which incorporates the insurer's risk factor, "effectively settling" the obligation focuses only on the time value of money and ignores the insurer's cost for assuming the risk of experience losses. Because of the misunderstanding of the meaning of "effectively settled," the Board concluded that reference to that phrase should be eliminated in order to clarify that the objective of the discount rate is to measure the time value of money. However, elimination of that phrase from this Statement is not intended to reflect a substantive difference between the requirements of Statement 87 and this Statement.

189. Some respondents to the Exposure Draft suggested that an indebtedness model approach that would consider the risk of default by an employer be used to discount an employer's postretirement benefit obligation. That approach suggests that the extent to which an employer chooses to fund its obligation in a trust or similar arrangement changes the value of the promise to retirees because the existence of the plan assets enhances the security of their benefit payments. Using that approach, two employers with identical postretirement benefit promises and plan demographics, but with different funding policies, would measure their expected postretirement benefit obligations differently.

190. The Board rejected the indebtedness model for postretirement benefit measurements. Measurement of pension obligations is not dependent on the level of plan assets, and the Board finds no reason for using different approaches to measure pension and postretirement benefit obligations. In addition, the Board notes that acceptance of the indebtedness model for discounting those obligations raises a broader issue that is beyond the scope of this Statement. The Board currently has a project on its agenda on present-value-based measurements; consideration of an indebtedness model will be encompassed by that project.

191. Most respondents who disagreed with the proposed discount rate favored basing assumed discount rates on company-specific rates, such as an entity's cost of capital or internal rate of return on assets or on shareholders' equity or a financing rate such as its incremental borrowing rate, or on "normalized" long-term interest rates. Generally, those respondents stated that the source of assets that will be used to satisfy an obligation should de-

termine the discount rate. Because most employers currently pay for postretirement benefits with cash generated from current operations or financing transactions, those respondents stated that the rate used to discount the obligation should be based on an employer's rate of return on shareholders' equity or its cost of financing. However, implementation of that approach would be difficult because there is no uniform method for determining a company's cost of capital and a negative rate of return on shareholders' equity would produce inexplicable results. Using a financing rate such as an entity's incremental borrowing rate for discounting purposes also would be difficult because the duration of existing debt is unlikely to be the period over which the postretirement benefits are expected to be paid.

192. Those respondents who advocated a "normalized" long-term rate stated that the use of a current rate for discounting introduces volatility into the measurement process that is unrelated to the postretirement benefit obligation. They recommended that some form of smoothing be used to reduce that volatility. However, the Board noted that smoothing only one assumption would not necessarily make the measurement less volatile because all of the other data and assumptions used in measuring an employer's postretirement benefit obligation and cost are updated annually and represent the best estimate of conditions at that point in time. Concerns about the volatility introduced by all assumptions are mitigated by the delayed recognition provisions provided for gains and losses, including the permitted use of a "corridor" to shield certain gains and losses from recognition. Furthermore, it is not the Board's intent to eliminate all volatility, particularly when it is representationally faithful of the phenomenon being reported.

193. The discounting approach prescribed by this Statement for employers' postretirement benefit obligations is consistent with the approach prescribed by Statement 87 for discounting employers' pension obligations. The Board's project on present-value-based measurements will consider alternative methods for discounting all of the obligations of an employer. In the interim, the approach required by this Statement should result in more comparable measures of the accumulated postretirement benefit obligation and of the service and interest cost components among employers than the other discounting alternatives considered.

194. Many of the other assumptions used in postretirement benefit measurements also are similar to assumptions used in pension measurements, but the sensitivity of the measures to changes in the assumptions may be more significant. For example, the turnover assumption may have a more signifi-

cant effect for postretirement benefits than for pension benefits because, in many cases, eligibility for postretirement benefits is an all-or-nothing proposition, while most pension plans provide reduced benefits for relatively short periods of service. The dependency status assumption also may have a more significant effect on postretirement benefit measurements than on pension measurements. Plan provisions that entitle an employee's spouse and other dependents to health care and other welfare benefits may substantially increase an employer's cost and obligation for postretirement benefits.

195. Postretirement benefit measurements are more sensitive to assumptions about retirement ages and the probability of retiring at each age than are pension measurements. For example, employer-provided postretirement health care benefits are significantly more expensive before Medicare coverage begins than after. Many pension arrangements provide for an actuarially reduced pension benefit for employees retiring before the normal retirement age; however, for an employee retiring early, there typically is no reduction in the postretirement benefit levels, and those benefits will be paid over a longer period of time and at a higher annual cost to the employer than if the employee retired at the normal retirement age. Similarly, postretirement benefit measurements are more sensitive than pension measurements to the life expectancy assumption. In particular, health care benefits are sensitive to that assumption because health care costs generally increase with age.

196. Postretirement health care and life insurance benefits may be based on an employee's final compensation. For example, an employer's postretirement health care plan may require retiree contributions based on the retiree's level of compensation at retirement, or a postretirement life insurance plan may provide a death benefit that is a multiple of final pay. As in employers' accounting for pensions, the Board concluded that assumed compensation levels should reflect the best estimate of participants' actual future compensation levels and should be consistent with assumed discount rates to the extent that both incorporate expectations about the same future economic conditions.

Assumptions unique to postretirement health care benefits

197. Measuring the expected postretirement benefit obligation for postretirement health care benefits includes making assumptions about the amount and timing of postretirement health care benefits expected to be paid in the future for current plan participants. Recent claims cost experience and the claims cost experience of other em-

ployers in the same industry or geographical location may provide useful information in developing the assumed per capita claims cost by age from the earliest age at which a plan participant could receive benefits under the plan to the longest life expectancy. Data files developed and maintained by insurers or benefits consultants about employers' claims costs for similar benefits programs and national or regional statistics about claims cost patterns also may provide information that may be used for developing the per capita claims cost by age.

198. The assumed health care cost trend rates consider the expected annual change in per capita claims costs due to all factors other than changes in the composition of the plan participants by age or dependency status. Changes in the cost of health care are influenced by numerous factors including changes in the cost of health care services, changes in the utilization pattern for health care services, changes in the nature and type of those services as medical practices change and new technology is developed, sociodemographic changes, and changes in public and private policy. Thus, in developing the assumed health care cost trend rates, the effects of medical care inflation, changes in medical care utilization or delivery patterns, technological advances, and changes in the health status of the covered population are all implicitly incorporated in the estimates. The effects of changes in enacted legislation are recognized as those changes occur.

199. Some respondents suggested that the health care cost trend rate would be more costly to develop than other estimates of future trends in costs, such as the general inflation rate. Consulting actuaries informed the Board that the health care cost trend rate per se is not significantly more costly to develop than other estimates of future costs. The more potentially significant cost is in the accumulation of the claims cost data to which any trend rate would be applied for measuring an employer's postretirement health care obligation and cost. (The measurement provisions of this Statement take into account employers' data limitations and the cost of measuring the employer's obligation and cost as described in paragraphs 38 and 41.) Consulting actuaries noted that the application of health care cost trend rates to the claims cost data produces a more relevant and representationally faithful measure of an employer's expected future cash outflows for postretirement health care benefits than would the use of alternative rates, at little or no incremental cost.

Attribution method

200. In the context of this Statement, attribution is the process of assigning the expected cost of ben-

efits to periods of employee service. The general objective is to assign to each year of service the cost of benefits earned or assumed to have been earned in that year. There are two broad groups, or families, of attribution methods—benefit approaches and cost approaches—and there are different attribution methods within those families.

201. Under Statement 87, pension benefits are attributed to employee service on the basis of the plan's benefit formula. A pension benefit formula is defined in paragraph 264 of that Statement as "the basis for determining payments to which participants may be entitled under a pension plan. Pension benefit formulas usually refer to the employee's service or compensation or both." For example, a benefit formula may be stated as: $Y\% \times$ number of years of service $\times$ final pay. The benefit formula method assigns benefits to periods of employee service based on the terms of the plan that define the benefits an employee will receive; the cost is calculated as the actuarial present value of the benefits assigned.

202. The Board believes that, normally, the terms of a plan (benefit formula) provide the most relevant basis for relating benefits promised to services rendered. The Board also believes that a single attribution method, normally based on the terms of the plan, should be prescribed to enhance comparability and understandability of financial statements. However, the Board considered whether the measurement approach should differ for plans that do not have a benefit formula that defines benefits in terms of the specific periods of service that must be rendered in exchange for the benefits. Noting that a difference in method might be warranted for those plans, the Board considered a variety of measurement approaches.

203. Arguments for a particular attribution method are usually based on which approach is perceived to best represent the underlying exchange between the employer and employee. The benefit approaches view the cost of the plan in terms of the benefits being earned each year, generally based on the terms of the plan (benefit formula). A distinct unit of retirement benefit is associated with each year of credited service; that is, those approaches assign benefits directly to years of service. The obligation measured under the benefit approaches is the actuarial present value of the benefits attributed to past and current employees' service to the reporting date, generally based on the terms of the plan.

204. The cost approaches view measurement of the obligation and cost on an annual basis as less important than the pattern of cost recognition from one period to another. Proponents of the

cost approaches generally take the view that an employer has career contracts with its employees. Thus, the cost of the plan is viewed in terms of the benefits expected to be earned over the entire working lives of the plan participants. That cost is allocated to years of service as a level amount that, if invested at the assumed discount rates, would equal the actuarial present value of those benefits at retirement, assuming no experience gains or losses. The costs assigned to each year may be level in dollar amounts or as a percentage of compensation. Proponents of cost approaches view the liability for an individual as measurable only at the date of hire or plan initiation (as zero) and at the retirement date (as the expected postretirement benefit obligation); at any interim date, only an arbitrary allocation is possible. The cost approaches produce an obligation for a group of employees with differing retirement dates that, at any point in time, can be described only as the result of the allocation that produced it. The accrued liability does not represent a measure of the benefits "earned" to date pursuant to the terms of the plan.

205. Because cost approaches assign a level amount of cost to each period, either as a percentage of compensation or in terms of dollars, they generally assign a greater percentage of the total cost of the benefit to earlier years of service in the attribution period than do benefit approaches. For postretirement benefit plans that have a level benefit formula, the benefit approaches assign a service cost to earlier periods of service in the attribution period that, when discounted, is less than that assigned during later years of service. Consequently, for those plans the benefit approaches typically result in lower charges than the cost approaches in early service periods offset by higher charges in later periods, and, in the absence of plan amendments, they generally result in a lower accrued liability at any point prior to the end of the attribution period.

206. For postretirement benefit plans that have a variable benefit formula,[34] cost approaches and benefit approaches may account for the benefit cost differently. Cost approaches generally project the expected postretirement benefit obligation at retirement and allocate an amount to each service period that is level in terms of dollars or percentage of compensation and that, together with interest at the assumed discount rates, will accumulate to the expected postretirement benefit obligation. Benefit approaches generally attribute different costs to different service periods when the benefit formula assigns different benefits to different periods of service.

207. The Board considered six methods for attributing postretirement benefits that are undefined in terms of the specified period of service to be rendered in exchange for the benefits. Those methods are described in paragraphs 180-186 of the Exposure Draft. Four of the methods were traditional approaches that incorporate the use of present value techniques, while the other two methods allocate the total benefit or cost on an undiscounted basis. The latter approaches attribute the expected postretirement benefits or cost to periods of service either as a level amount of benefit or cost or as a level percentage of compensation. Undiscounted approaches produce identical results under the benefit and cost methods.

208. The Board rejected the undiscounted approaches. Because the obligation is to provide benefits in the future, not currently, the Board concluded that the present value of the obligation expected to be paid is the most relevant and reliable measure of the obligation and of the cost of the services received. Discounting explicitly recognizes that the present value of an obligation payable in the future is less than that of an equal obligation payable currently. The Board concluded that recording an obligation at its ultimate cost without discounting is overly conservative and does not provide the information most relevant for decision making.

209. The Board rejected attribution on the basis of compensation because it does not faithfully represent how the cost is incurred under the terms of the plan. In cases in which compensation levels are a factor, years of service generally are also a consideration in determining the benefits to be provided because an employee would not be eligible for the benefits unless some period of service had been provided.

210. The Board was unable to identify a basis for attributing postretirement benefits that would be more appropriate, in most cases, than measurement of the current benefit cost and accumulated postretirement benefit obligation based on years of service. Statement 87 prescribes the attribution of pension benefits on the basis of years of service; compensation is considered for measuring the amount of the benefit to be attributed to each year of service when compensation levels are a factor in determining the amount of the pension benefit. The Board found no compelling reason to prescribe a different basis for attributing postretirement benefits than the basis used for attributing pension benefits.

---

[34]For example, the terms of the plan may state that retirees will receive an annual benefit that is equal to (a) 2.5 percent of covered benefits for each year of service through year 10, (b) 3.0 percent of covered benefits for each year of service in years 11-20, and (c) 3.5 percent of covered benefits for each year of service in years 21-30.

211. The Board's consideration therefore focused on two attribution approaches: a benefit/years-of-service approach and a cost/years-of-service approach. A benefit approach attributes benefits on the basis of individual plan participants; a cost approach may attribute either on an individual or on an aggregate basis. Of those alternative cost approaches, the Board focused on an aggregate approach. Since the objective of a cost method is the allocation of benefit costs, there is no reason to burden that method unnecessarily with complexities and computations that could not be supported as enhancing measurement of either the obligation at a point in time or the cost incurred for a period.

212. A benefit/years-of-service approach is viewed by the Board as more consistent with its conceptual framework's focus on measurement of assets and liabilities. An objective of a benefit approach is to fully accrue the expected postretirement benefit obligation for an employee by the end of the credited service period for that employee. Under an aggregate cost approach, cost is attributed based on the average remaining years of service of all active plan participants; consequently, the cost of the expected postretirement benefit obligation for an employee generally would be attributed to a period beyond the end of the credited service period for that employee.

213. The Board considers the benefit attribution pattern under a benefit approach to be more representative of how benefits are earned than the pattern under a cost approach. Assume, for example, that postretirement benefits are provided in exchange for 20 years of service. A benefit approach results in a level attribution of the *future* benefits, implying that the benefits are earned equally over the attribution period. An aggregate cost approach implicitly results in a declining *future* benefit attributed to years of service with the passing of time and approaching retirement, implying that proportionately more benefits are attributable to the early years of service than to the later years. Under both approaches, absent funding considerations, the cost of providing benefits rises with the passing of time as retirement is approached, although the increase is lower under the aggregate cost approach because the service cost component is a level amount or percentage.

214. When it began deliberations on the attribution method, the Board considered present plan designs as well as possible future plan designs. Because postretirement health care and other welfare benefits generally supplement pension benefits, the Board considered the likelihood that future postretirement benefit plan formulas will become more similar to pension plan formulas. That is, employers may promise postretirement benefits that vary based on individual years of service rather than promise the same benefits to all employees who become eligible for benefits. Since that time, various surveys have documented a trend in plan designs in that direction.

215. The Board noted that one particular aggregate cost approach is computationally less complex than a benefit approach because it does not attempt to differentiate between the causes of any unexpected changes in the unfunded accumulated benefit obligation; any unexpected change is recognized prospectively. The effects of plan amendments and gains and losses are incorporated into the unfunded expected postretirement benefit obligation for prospective recognition. However, the Board concluded that the computational advantages of that somewhat less complex aggregate cost approach did not outweigh the other considerations favoring a benefit/years-of-service approach.

216. A few respondents suggested that the Board not require the use of a single method of attributing the cost of postretirement benefits to periods of employee service but, rather, allow a choice among a number of acceptable actuarial methods. They noted that choices among accounting methods are allowed in other areas, including accounting for inventory and depreciation. They also suggested that a standardized method would not achieve comparability because of differences in assumptions or would impair comparability because it would obscure different circumstances that call for different approaches.

217. The Board is not convinced that differences in circumstances among employers require different methods for measuring the service cost component of net periodic postretirement benefit cost. Similar arguments were made about employers' accounting for pensions. However, respondents were unable to identify, and the Board was unable to develop, any basis to support the use of different methods. Differences in circumstances require the use of different assumptions or different attribution periods that appropriately result in different patterns of recognizing the cost of providing postretirement benefits.

218. Most respondents preferred a single attribution method based on the terms of the plan, similar to the approach prescribed by Statement 87. They maintained that that method would be more understandable and more useful than a less familiar method and would be less costly to implement than a new method. The Board agreed and concluded that a benefit/years-of-service approach should be prescribed. When a benefit formula does not define the specific years of service to be rendered in exchange for the benefits, the Board acknowledges

that an allocation of benefits to individual years of service in the attribution period has to be assumed. However, the Board believes that it would be inappropriate to develop an approach that is inconsistent with the benefit approach underlying Statement 87 unless that approach would significantly reduce implementation costs without unduly compromising the more conceptually appropriate approach, particularly since the Board views the promise for postretirement benefits to be similar to the promise for pension benefits.

Attribution period

219. A plan's benefit formula is the basis for determining the benefits to which plan participants may be entitled. The benefit formula specifies how plan participants attain eligibility for those benefits—the years of service to be rendered, the age to be attained while in service, or a combination of those factors. Consequently, a plan's benefit formula provides the most relevant and reliable basis for measuring the expected postretirement benefit obligation and for determining the period over which those benefits should be accrued.

220. The Board concluded that if the expected postretirement benefits promised pursuant to a plan are similar to a deferred vested pension benefit,[35] the benefit obligation should not be attributed beyond the date an employee has rendered the required service for full eligibility for the future benefits expected to be received by that employee. Full eligibility is attained by meeting specified age, service, or age and service requirements of the plan. The full eligibility date is the date at which an employee attains eligibility for all of the benefits that are expected to be received by that employee, including any benefits expected to be received by any beneficiaries or covered dependents.

221. For example, if a plan provides a postretirement health care or life insurance benefit to an employee who renders 10 years of service, the actuarial present value of that benefit should be fully accrued at the end of 10 years of service. Similarly, if a plan provides a postretirement benefit to an employee who attains age 55 while in service, the actuarial present value of that benefit should be fully accrued when the employee attains age 55. Whether benefits commence immediately or in the future does not change the employee's eligibility for postretirement benefits. The Board concluded that postretirement benefits should not be attrib-

uted beyond the date *full* eligibility for those benefits is attained.

222. The Exposure Draft proposed that, consistent with Statement 87, determination of the full eligibility date not be affected by measurement assumptions such as when benefit payments commence, dependency status, salary progression, and so forth. During its redeliberations, the Board again considered whether the full eligibility date should be affected by certain measurement assumptions. For example, for pay-related plans that define the benefit earned as a fixed percentage of final pay, an incremental benefit is earned each year for the effect of the change in an employee's pay rate for that year. Similarly, for plans that provide an indexed benefit that is "capped" at the indexed amount of the benefit at an employee's retirement, an incremental benefit equal to the effect of the annual change in that index is earned for each year of service. Board members believed the attribution period should include all employee service periods for which a nontrivial incremental postretirement benefit is earned. The Board recognized that consideration of those measurement assumptions in determining the full eligibility date would be inconsistent with how Statement 87 applies to certain pension plans with maximum credited service periods. Those situations are limited.

223. The Board concluded that it is willing to accept that inconsistency because considering all years of service that provide an incremental benefit in determining an employee's full eligibility date is both more understandable and more consistent with the accounting for other deferred compensation contracts under Opinion 12. Consequently, the full eligibility date is determined by plan terms that provide incremental benefits for additional service, such as benefits based on final pay or benefits that are indexed through an employee's active service period, unless those incremental benefits are trivial. Determination of the full eligibility date is *not* affected by plan terms that define when benefit payments commence or by an employee's current dependency status. (Paragraphs 397-408 illustrate determination of the full eligibility date.)

224. Respondents to the Exposure Draft generally disagreed with ending the attribution period at an employee's full eligibility date. Those respondents supported attributing benefits to an employee's full service period—ending with the expected retirement date—whether or not the benefit formula

---

[35]This Statement uses the term *vested benefits* in the accounting sense, not in the legal context. For accounting purposes, vesting refers to an employee's right to receive present or future benefits whether or not the employee remains in the service of the employer. The fact that the benefits do not commence until after the employee retires or that additional benefits may be earned by rendering additional service does not change the right to the benefits that have been earned and to which the employee would be entitled if the employee terminated.

defines the specific years of service to be rendered in exchange for the benefits. Many respondents indicated that, irrespective of the terms of the plan, attributing benefits to employees' full service periods reflects the employer's intent, asserting that the postretirement benefits promised to employees are substantially independent of their compensation levels or years of service. Other respondents indicated that attributing postretirement benefits to an employee's expected retirement date is more consistent with the attribution period for most pension benefits.

225. In its redeliberation of the attribution period, the Board observed the results of the field test of the Exposure Draft. Those results suggested that, for many employers who elect delayed recognition of the transition obligation, the difference in net periodic cost that results from attributing the expected postretirement benefit obligation to an employee's full eligibility date rather than the employee's expected retirement date is minimal. That is because, in those situations, net periodic cost reflects the interplay of service cost, interest cost, and amortization of an employer's transition obligation. If the expected postretirement benefit obligation is attributed to an employee's full eligibility date, the transition obligation that is recognized on a delayed basis in future periods is greater than if the benefit obligation is attributed over a longer period. In addition, if the benefit obligation is attributed to an employee's full eligibility date, there is no service cost for fully eligible plan participants. As a result of those effects, and the relative magnitude of interest cost, regardless of the attribution period, the net periodic cost for most employers is not likely to be significantly affected by attributing the expected postretirement benefit obligation over service to employees' full eligibility dates rather than over service to employees' expected retirement dates.

226. The Board observes that the terms of most pension plans result in attributing the pension benefits to the years of service to an employee's expected retirement date. Because most pension plans provide an incremental benefit for each year of service, the full eligibility date and retirement date are the same. Recent surveys suggest a trend among employers to amend their postretirement benefit plans to define the amount of benefits employees will receive based on the length of their service, similar to most pension plans. If that trend continues, the full eligibility date for many or most postretirement benefit plans also may be the employee's retirement date.

227. For postretirement benefit plans that are not pay-related or otherwise indexed during an employee's service period (most existing postretirement health care plans), attributing the benefits to an employee's full eligibility date *is* consistent with the attribution period for pension benefits; what may make the periods appear to be different is different plan terms that define when the benefits are earned. For postretirement benefit plans that are pay-related or that otherwise index benefits during employees' service periods to their retirement date, the full eligibility date and retirement date generally will be the same. The attribution period for those benefits will differ from the attribution period for a similarly defined pension benefit with a capped credited service period. (Refer to paragraphs 222 and 223.)

228. Ending the attribution period at an employee's full eligibility date is consistent with the plan terms, which, in the Board's view, provide the best evidence of the exchange transaction. The accounting for an exchange transaction should reflect the understanding of both parties to the transaction. If an employer were to change the eligibility requirements for postretirement benefits from 10 years of service and attainment of age 55 while in service to a requirement of 15 years of service and attainment of age 62 while in service, that would be a fundamentally different promise with an economic consequence for the employer and at least some employees. The Board believes it would not be representationally faithful to ignore the difference between those promises in determining the attribution period.

229. The Board considered attributing benefits beyond the full eligibility date in some, but not all, cases. Several criteria were considered in defining the conditions under which that should occur, such as whether eligibility for benefits is attained gradually or all at once, whether the benefit formula unambiguously defines the specific years of service to be rendered, whether a specific age must be attained while in service, and whether retirement from the company is required.

230. The Board considered an approach that would require attribution of benefits beyond a plan participant's full eligibility date to the participant's expected retirement date if all eligible plan participants receive the same benefit and if eligibility for the benefits is attained all at once upon attaining a specified age while in service, upon rendering a specified number of years of service, or a combination of both. However, the Board rejected that approach because it was troubled by the arbitrary nature of the resulting attribution period. For example, if a plan provides 60 percent of the cost of postretirement health care benefit coverage to all employees who render 25 or more years of service, that approach would require attribution over a 30-year period for an employee expected to

retire after 30 years of service. However, if a plan provides 40 percent of the cost of postretirement health care benefit coverage to all employees who render 20 years of service and an additional benefit of 4 percent for service in each of the following 5 years, the expected postretirement benefit obligation for an employee expected to render 30 years of service would be attributed to that employee's first 25 years of service. The accounting would attribute the benefits over different periods even though, in both cases, the benefit promise would be vested after 25 years of service and service beyond 25 years would not result in an incremental benefit.

231. The Board also considered an approach that would require attribution of benefits beyond the full eligibility date for those benefits if a plan's benefit formula does not unambiguously define the specific period of service to be rendered in exchange for the benefits. The Board rejected that condition because of the inconsistent results that would occur. For example, if one plan provides 75 percent of the cost of postretirement health care coverage to employees who render 30 years of service and a different plan provides the same benefits to employees who attain age 55 while in service and render at least 10 years of service, benefits would be attributed beyond the full eligibility date in the latter case but not the former. For an employee hired at age 25 who is expected to render 40 years of service, the benefits under the first plan would be attributed to the employee's first 30 years of service and the benefits under the second plan would be attributed to the employee's full service period, even though the same benefit is earned upon meeting the age and service conditions of the respective plans.

232. The Board also considered an approach that would require attribution of benefits beyond the full eligibility date if a plan's benefit formula requires attaining a specified age while in service. In that case, the credited service period is not unambiguously defined. The Board noted that the approach creates anomalies and rejected it as arbitrary for the reasons discussed in paragraphs 230 and 231.

233. The Board also considered an approach that would require attribution of benefits beyond the full eligibility date if an employee must meet the employer's criteria for retirement before termina-

tion in order to receive the benefits.[36] Under that approach, the benefit promise is viewed as an exchange for service over an employee's career, and retirement is viewed as the recognizable event. The Board rejected that approach for several reasons. While meeting the employer's criteria for retirement may define when postretirement benefit coverage is expected to commence, the act of retirement in and of itself does not reflect the exchange that takes place between the employer and an employee. It is the required employee service that is exchanged for postretirement benefits. In addition, an approach that attributes benefits beyond the full eligibility date based on the act of retirement would be inconsistent with accruing other deferred compensation contracts, including pensions, to the full eligibility date.

234. The need to be "retired" in order to receive benefits is not unique to other postretirement benefit plans. At the full eligibility date the employee has completed the contractual requirements for eligibility for all the postretirement benefits that employee is expected to receive and can terminate with entitlement to those benefits when a specified event occurs or the need for those benefits arises. An objective of accounting for deferred compensation contracts is to measure the accrued liability defined by the contract as reliably as possible and, therefore, to recognize cost over the periods in which the benefits are earned and the exchange takes place. Although for some contracts it may not be possible to determine the portion of the expected future benefits earned by an employee before that employee attains full eligibility for the benefits, no uncertainty remains at the full eligibility date. The total expected postretirement benefits have been earned at that date.

235. Attribution of postretirement benefits beyond the date full eligibility for the benefits is attained would suggest that there is a difference between "fully vested" pension benefits and "full eligibility" for other postretirement benefits. At the full eligibility date, the *right* to the benefits is not contingent upon rendering future service. Both vesting in pension benefits and attaining full eligibility for postretirement benefits are rights that are "earned" (exchanged) for meeting specified age, service, or age and service requirements. In both cases, an employee is not entitled to *receive* the benefits until after the employer-employee rela-

---

[36]For example, an employer may promise to provide postretirement health care coverage to all employees who retire from the company (terminate after meeting the age or service requirements that entitle an employee to immediate pension benefits); under the terms of the retirement plan, an employee may retire from the company early with 30 years of service or at the normal retirement age with less than 30 years of service. Consequently, for an employee hired at age 25 who renders 30 years of consecutive service, the employer has promised to provide postretirement benefit coverage upon that employee's termination (retirement) on or after rendering 30 years of service. Although that employee will render service beyond age 55, eligibility for the benefits is not conditional upon rendering additional service, and no incremental benefit is provided for doing so.

tionship is terminated. The Board saw no significant distinction between the two.

236. Paragraph 42(a) of Statement 87 states that "for benefits of a type includable in vested benefits,[9] [the benefits shall be considered to accumulate] in proportion to the ratio of the number of completed years of service to the number that will have been completed *when the benefit is first fully vested*" (emphasis added). Footnote 9 of Statement 87 describes a supplemental early retirement benefit that is vested after a stated number of years as an example of a benefit of a type includable in vested benefits. Paragraph 42(b) of Statement 87 states that "for benefits of a type not includable in vested benefits,[10] [the benefits shall be considered to accumulate] in proportion to the ratio of completed years of service to total projected years of service." Footnote 10 of Statement 87 describes a death or disability benefit that is payable only if death or disability occurs during active service as an example of a benefit of a type *not* includable in vested benefits. Most postretirement benefits are of a type includable in vested benefits.

237. The Board was unable to identify any approach that would, in its opinion, appropriately attribute benefits beyond the date full eligibility for those benefits is attained. Accordingly, the Board concluded that postretirement benefits should not be attributed to service beyond the date an employee attains full eligibility for those benefits. The Board also concluded that if the benefit formula defines the beginning of the credited service period, benefits generally should be attributed from that date. If the beginning of the credited service period is not defined, the beginning of the credited service period is deemed to be the date of hire, and benefits should be attributed from that date.

238. Some Board members disagree with ending the attribution period at the full eligibility date as defined in this Statement. They support attributing the expected postretirement benefit obligation from an employee's date of hire (or beginning of the credited service period, if later) to the date beyond which the employee's additional service will not change (neither increase nor decrease) the amount of benefits to which the employee will be entitled—usually the employee's retirement date. That approach would extend the attribution period to include any years of employee service during which the employer conceptually incurs a negative service cost because the employee, by electing to continue service after earning a vested postretirement benefit, gives back benefits that have been earned (refer to paragraphs 240-242). This Statement attributes the expected postretirement benefit obligation, rather than the vested postretirement benefit obligation, to years of credited

service and assigns no service cost to the years of service beyond the full eligibility date. Those Board members would attribute the expected postretirement benefit obligation on a pro rata basis to *all* years of service that change the amount of benefits an employee is entitled to receive, *including* those years in the giveback period.

239. Those Board members recognize that, depending on a plan's terms, an employee's full eligibility date may be the same as the employee's retirement date. In those instances there is no period during which the employer conceptually incurs a negative service cost. But for many existing plans, an employee's full eligibility date and retirement date differ. Those Board members are concerned with those latter plans. They observe that many existing plans provide benefits to employees "upon retirement" or "upon retiring from the company" without defining the specific years of service to be rendered in exchange for the benefits. Those Board members believe that, for those plans, ending the attribution period at the expected retirement date more appropriately reflects the understanding that postretirement benefits are exchanged for *all* years of employee service. Those Board members believe that attributing benefits to the date beyond which an employee's service will not change the amount of benefits to be received by the employee is a preferable, practical, and understandable approach to attributing the expected postretirement benefit obligation to years of service.

Amount attributed

240. Implicit in the Board's conclusion is the view that at the full eligibility date the employer has a measurable obligation to provide benefits in the future. The Board considered whether measurement of that obligation for a plan that provides benefits immediately after retirement should be based on (a) benefits the employee is expected to receive given the employee's expected retirement date (the expected postretirement benefit obligation) or (b) benefits the employee would be eligible to receive were the employee to retire (terminate) immediately (a vested postretirement benefit obligation). Under the latter approach, if the vested postretirement benefit obligation for an employee were attributed to service to the full eligibility date and that employee continued to render service rather than retire, a negative service cost would be recognized (for the reduction in the vested postretirement benefit obligation) during the subsequent service period as the employee foregoes a portion of the benefits that had been earned at the full eligibility date. Under either approach the same obligation—the expected postretirement benefit obligation—would be recognized at the employee's retirement date.

241. Attributing the vested postretirement benefit obligation to service to the full eligibility date is viewed as conceptually appropriate by some Board members. At that date, an obligation exists to provide postretirement benefits; that obligation is no longer contingent upon the employee rendering future service. Those Board members believe it is inconsistent to measure an obligation to which an employee is immediately eligible as the expected postretirement benefit obligation, which considers that benefits commence after additional future service, because no future service is required. They believe that a measurement based on rendering future service is not representationally faithful when a greater benefit has been earned that is not dependent upon the rendering of future service.

242. The ability to satisfy the benefit obligation at less than the "vested" amount is outside the control of an employer. Further, to attribute benefits on the basis of the expected postretirement benefit obligation anticipates an employee's election to remain in service and consequently give back a benefit. Certain Board members believe that, conceptually, that election should be accounted for as it is made. In their view, recognition of the vested postretirement benefit obligation at the full eligibility date and the subsequent giveback of benefits in the intervening period until retirement better reflects the exchange that has occurred. That is, the employer has promised to provide a specified level of benefit coverage in exchange for a minimum period of employee service or service to a specified attained age. During the service period subsequent to the full eligibility date, the economic benefit to the employee for continuing to work (and the employer's compensation cost) is the excess of the amount the employee receives for working over the amount the employee would have received had the employee not continued to work.

243. Despite the conceptual support that some Board members believe exists for attributing the vested postretirement benefit obligation over the service period to the full eligibility date, Board members recognized the difficulty of conveying to preparers and users of financial statements the notion of a negative service cost for some employees. Therefore, the Board concluded that the expected postretirement benefit obligation, rather than the vested postretirement benefit obligation, should be attributed to service to the full eligibility date.

244. The Board acknowledges that attribution of the expected postretirement benefit obligation to the full eligibility date may be viewed as being internally inconsistent because recognition and measurement are on different bases. Whereas recognition is based on service to the full eligibility date, measurement of the obligation considers service beyond that date be- cause an employer must consider when benefit payments are likely to commence in order to measure the expected postretirement benefit obligation that is to be attributed to employees' service periods. The Board notes that although some future events do not provide a basis for recognition of elements of financial statements, they may affect the measurement of recognized past events. The Board concluded that, absent a reconsideration of fundamental measurement and recognition concepts, attribution of the expected postretirement benefit obligation, rather than the vested postretirement benefit obligation, to the full eligibility date is preferable given the evolutionary state of accounting for postretirement benefits.

Attribution pattern

245. The Exposure Draft proposed attributing the expected postretirement benefit obligation to employee service using the benefit formula. That is, if the benefit formula attributes certain benefits to individual years or groups of years of service in the credited service period, the benefit formula generally would have been followed for attribution purposes. Otherwise, an equal amount of the expected benefits would have been assigned to each year of service in the attribution period. The Board believed then and continues to believe that the benefit formula is the most relevant basis for attributing benefits to years of service. However, it is particularly difficult to attribute benefits to years of service in accordance with the present terms of many postretirement health care plans. Frequently, the plan terms are ambiguous and quite difficult to apply at interim dates. For example, a plan may define different benefits for different years of service and have a separate age and service requirement that must be met to attain eligibility for any benefits.

246. Following a plan's benefit formula for attributing postretirement benefits to individual years of service in the attribution period adds a degree of complexity that the Board concluded was unnecessary. The Board believes that the primary objective of attribution is to have fully accrued the actuarial present value of the cost of the postretirement benefits expected to be provided to an employee pursuant to the terms of the contract (the expected postretirement benefit obligation) at the date the employee attains full eligibility for those benefits. Although following the benefit formula for attribution purposes would be more representationally faithful and consistent with Statement 87, the Board concluded that because postretirement benefits do not typically vest at interim dates during an employee's service period in the same manner as pension benefits, and because the terms of postretirement benefit plans generally are more complex than the terms of pension plans, the obligation ac-

crued at an interim date is not as relevant and reliable as the obligation accrued at the full eligibility date. Consequently, in order to reduce complexity, the Board concluded that the expected postretirement benefit obligation should be recognized by assigning an equal amount to each year of service in the attribution period, unless the plan's benefit formula attributes a disproportionate share of the expected postretirement benefit obligation to employees' early years of service.

Transition

247. The issues of how and when the transition amount should be recognized are sensitive ones to employers who face, for the first time, the prospect of accruing the cost of postretirement benefits exchanged for current service as well as accounting for the cost of those benefits exchanged for prior service. Unlike the effects of most other accounting changes, a transition obligation for postretirement benefits generally reflects, to some extent, the failure to accrue the obligation in the earlier periods in which it arose rather than the effects of a change from one accrual method of accounting to another.

248. An employer changing from the cash basis of accounting for postretirement benefits to the accrual basis required by this Statement has not recognized any of the cost of the benefits for active plan participants and only some portion of the cost of the benefits for retired plan participants—amounts that would have been recognized as the service and interest cost components of net periodic postretirement benefit cost in earlier periods. In addition, an indeterminate portion of the transition obligation may represent unrecognized prior service cost arising from a plan initiation or amendment, an unrecognized net gain or loss, or an unrecognized obligation from a prior business combination.

249. Determining the portion of the transition obligation that represents unrecognized service cost and interest cost of prior periods would require retroactively measuring the amount of benefit obligation that would have been recognized for each prior period by the employer had this Statement always been applied. To do that, an employer would have to determine the historical data and assumptions about the economic environment that would have been made at the date of plan adoption and at each subsequent measurement date. It is unlikely that the data necessary to measure the obligation at those dates exist, and it would be difficult, if not impossible, to develop assumptions that ignore the benefit of hindsight.

250. The Board concluded that transition is, to a significant extent, a practical matter. A major objective of transition is to minimize implementation costs and to mitigate disruption to the extent possible without unduly compromising the ability of financial statements to provide useful information. The Board also concluded that it would be confusing, complex, and inconsistent to measure the transition obligation differently from other measurements in accounting for postretirement benefits. The transition obligation is measured as the unrecognized unfunded accumulated postretirement benefit obligation, which is based on the portion of the expected postretirement benefit obligation attributed to each year of service rendered prior to a plan participant's full eligibility date. That measurement is consistent with the attribution of benefits to years of service, measurement of the effects of a plan initiation that grants retroactive benefits or a plan amendment, and the measurement of a postretirement benefit obligation assumed in a business combination accounted for as a purchase.

251. Changes from cash basis to accrual basis accounting are usually made retroactively. If the components of the transition obligation (asset) could be separately determined, it would be consistent with other provisions of this Statement to treat the unrecognized current service and interest cost as the cumulative effect of an accounting change (that is, to immediately recognize those components when this Statement is first applied), and retroactively remeasure prior purchase business combinations for postretirement benefit obligations assumed but not recognized. It also would be consistent to recognize at least some of the unrecognized prior service cost and unrecognized gain or loss prospectively, based on the delayed recognition afforded those components of postretirement benefit cost by this Statement. However, if the cumulative effect of the accounting change were required to be estimated, the cost of doing so could be prohibitive and the results questionable for the reasons discussed in paragraph 249.

252. Several alternatives to immediate recognition of the transition obligation or asset were considered. The Board believed that, conceptually, immediate recognition of the cumulative effect of the accounting change (as described in paragraph 251) would be most appropriate. The potential magnitude of the accumulated postretirement benefit obligation, particularly the obligation for postretirement health care benefits, suggests that any omission of that obligation would detract from the usefulness of the statement of financial position. However, the Board recognized that the magnitude of that obligation and the limited availability of historical data on which to base its measurement suggest the need for a more pragmatic approach. Those considerations led the Board to conclude in

the Exposure Draft that the initial emphasis of this Statement should be on disclosure of the transition obligation and that the subsequent recognition of that amount in the statement of financial position and in the statement of income should be phased in over future periods.

253. Respondents generally favored a transition period longer than the 15-year period proposed in the Exposure Draft. Some maintained that the magnitude of employers' transition obligations argues for a longer transition period to minimize disruption of current practice. Others noted that a longer transition period would better reflect the average remaining service period of the employee work force that will be entitled to the benefits. Because most existing plans do not give employees postretirement health care benefits unless they meet the company's criteria for retirement with an immediate pension benefit, the remaining service periods of participants in a postretirement health care plan is typically longer than the remaining service periods of participants in a pension plan. Employees who are eligible for postretirement health care benefits are generally only long-service employees, while employees are often entitled to a deferred vested pension benefit if they terminate at younger ages with shorter service periods. For a majority of the companies that participated in the field test of the Exposure Draft, the average remaining service period of the active participants in their postretirement benefit plans was between 18 years and 21 years; previous surveys of employers' pension plans indicated an average remaining service period of those plan participants that is several years shorter.

254. The Board concluded that employers whose plan participants' average remaining years of service is less than 20 years could elect to recognize their transition obligation or asset over 20 years, reflecting the average remaining service periods for participants in many other employers' postretirement benefit plans. However, the Board also concluded that phasing in recognition of a transition obligation should not result in slower recognition of an employer's postretirement benefit obligation than would result from continuation of the pay-as-you-go (cash basis) method. The Exposure Draft proposed that amortization of the transition obligation be accelerated if (a) cumulative benefit payments subsequent to the transition date to fully eligible plan participants at the transition date exceeded the sum of (1) the cumulative amortization of the entire transition obligation and (2) the cumulative interest on the unpaid transition obligation or (b) cumulative benefit payments subsequent to the transition date to all plan participants exceeded the cumulative postretirement benefit cost accrued subsequent to the transition date. As a result of the complexity as-

sociated with applying the first of those constraints, the Board concluded that recognition of the transition obligation should be accelerated only if the second constraint applies.

255. Although respondents to the Exposure Draft supported delayed recognition of the transition obligation as a practical approach to transition, most of those respondents also favored permitting (but not requiring) immediate recognition of the transition obligation or asset. They noted that FASB Technical Bulletin No. 87-1, *Accounting for a Change in Method of Accounting for Certain Postretirement Benefits,* permitted immediate recognition of the transition obligation in certain circumstances. They also noted that immediate recognition provides the simplest method of recognition that would most significantly improve financial reporting. Because a significant portion of the transition obligation is likely to relate to service and interest costs for prior periods, they argued that the Board should permit an employer to immediately recognize its transition obligation for postretirement benefits.

256. The Board's consideration of permitting immediate recognition of the transition obligation or asset focused on whether financial reporting would be enhanced by limiting alternatives, recognizing that in doing so, a conceptually defensible, and in some cases preferable, alternative might be eliminated. Some Board members believe that immediate recognition of the transition obligation or asset should not be permitted. They believe that the understandability and comparability of financial reporting, both in the year of adoption and in subsequent periods, would be improved by uniformly phasing in recognition of the transition obligation or asset for postretirement benefits for all employers. They also note that the actuarial techniques for measuring postretirement health care benefit obligations are still developing and should become more sophisticated and reliable with time and experience. They observe that near-term measures of the accumulated postretirement benefit obligation from which the transition obligation is derived will reflect the deficiencies of insufficient data collection in the past and the evolving actuarial practice in this area. They also note that subsequent adjustments to measures of the accumulated postretirement benefit obligation will be recognized in income through the gain or loss component of net periodic postretirement benefit cost.

257. Because an indeterminate portion of the transition obligation may relate to unrecognized prior service cost, an unrecognized net gain or loss, or the effects of a prior purchase business combination, immediate recognition of the transition obligation in its entirety would result in premature recognition of those amounts. Under the recogni-

tion provisions of this Statement, those effects are properly recognized in the results of operations for subsequent periods. Some Board members were troubled by that result. This Statement delays recognition of the effects of plan improvements, because they are granted with the expectation that the employer will realize economic benefits in the future, and of plan reductions and permits the delayed recognition of gains and losses. Opinion 16, as amended by this Statement, requires recognition of postretirement benefit obligations assumed in a purchase business combination in determining the cost of the assets acquired, including goodwill related to the purchase; that increase in the cost of the assets acquired is recognized as a charge against operations in future periods.

258. The Board concluded that an employer's transition obligation or asset may be recognized either on a delayed basis or immediately, subject to certain constraints. In reaching that conclusion, the Board recognized that complete comparability would not be achieved by proscribing immediate recognition of the transition obligation. A few companies have already adopted accrual accounting for postretirement benefits pursuant to Technical Bulletin 87-1 and have immediately recognized their transition obligations. Others would have the opportunity to do so before issuance of this Statement. Despite concerns about the availability and reliability of data on which to base measurement of an employer's accumulated postretirement benefit obligation, the Board believes that the delayed effective date of this Statement should provide for further development of actuarial techniques and the accumulation of more reliable data on which to base the measurements at the date of transition. The Board concluded that employers should not be precluded from recognizing their transition obligations in the manner that some believe most significantly improves financial reporting.

259. The Board considered limiting the immediate recognition of the postretirement benefit transition obligation to the amount in excess of any remaining unrecognized transition asset for pensions because the transition amounts result from similar standards for similar costs. Some Board members are concerned about the credibility of financial statements if income from the transition to one standard is included in income over time, while expense from the transition to a related standard is recognized all at once. Others believe that because the two standards relate to different subjects, credibility is not affected. The Board concluded that immediate recognition of the transition obligation for postretirement benefits should not be limited by any remaining transition asset for pensions. The Board observes that because transition is largely a practical matter, consideration should be

given to the facts and circumstances surrounding the issues addressed by the standard. In the case of postretirement benefits other than pensions, some Board members believe that a change from cash basis to accrual accounting is a circumstance sufficiently different from a change from one accrual method to another to justify a unique transition provision. They also believe that the transition obligation for postretirement benefits reflects service cost and interest cost attributable to prior periods to a much greater degree than the transition obligation for pensions.

260. Immediate recognition of an employer's transition obligation or asset is permitted only at the date of initial application of this Statement. The Board concluded that to permit immediate recognition at any subsequent time would result in too much variability in financial reporting for a long period of time. That option also would be inconsistent with some of the arguments in favor of immediate recognition and would introduce additional complexities in determining the amount that could be subsequently recognized.

261. The effect of immediately recognizing a transition obligation or asset and any related tax effect are to be reported separately in the statement of income as the effect of a change in accounting. To more closely approximate the measure of the cumulative effect of the accounting change, the amount immediately recognized in income is required to exclude certain effects that should, more appropriately, be reflected in determining future periods' income. Thus, the amount immediately recognized in income as the effect of the change in accounting is required to exclude the effects of (a) any previously unrecognized postretirement benefit obligation assumed in a business combination accounted for as a purchase, (b) a plan initiation, and (c) any plan amendment that improved benefits, to the extent that those events occur after the issuance of this Statement.

262. The Board considered excluding from the amount immediately recognized in income any significant portion of the transition obligation attributable to obligations assumed in past purchase business combinations or the effects of past plan initiations or amendments that improved benefits, in order to more reliably measure the effect of the accounting change. However, the Board believes that the data on which those measurements would be based for those past events are generally not available and would be costly, if not impossible, to develop. Some Board members believe that, at a minimum, the amounts related to any of those events that are known or are readily available should be excluded from any transition obligation immediately recognized in income. For primarily

practical reasons, the Board concluded that only the constraints identified in paragraph 261 should be applied.

263. The Board considered whether the effects of recognizing an employer's transition obligation or asset should be included in determining net income, as an adjustment of retained earnings, or as a component of comprehensive income, but not net income. Opinion 20 states that most changes in accounting should be recognized by including the cumulative effect of the change in accounting in net income of the period of change. The correction of an error and certain changes in accounting principles identified in that Opinion are recognized by restating prior periods, resulting in an adjustment of beginning retained earnings for the current period.

264. Some respondents favored recognizing the transition obligation (or asset) through a direct charge (or credit) to retained earnings because the amount relates primarily to past periods. However, recognition of the cumulative effect of an accounting change through income, as specified in Opinion 20, is a well-established principle. In addition, implementation issues would arise in recognizing the future effects of changes in the measure of the accumulated benefit obligation that is included in the transition obligation. One such issue would be how the effects of plan amendments that reduce benefits that existed at the transition date or the effects of settlements or curtailments and gains from experience different from that assumed should be reflected.

265. A few respondents supported a comprehensive income approach. Concepts Statement 5 discusses comprehensive income as a broad measure of the effects of all changes in an enterprise's equity for a period, other than from transactions resulting from investments by or distributions to owners. Earnings are described as a measure of performance for a period. Following a comprehensive income approach would include the effects of changes in accounting principles in comprehensive income but not in earnings. Respondents suggested establishing a separate, permanent component of equity to report the effect of recognizing the transition obligation either immediately or on a delayed basis. The suggested approach differs from certain existing separate components of equity (as described in FASB Statements No. 12, *Accounting for Marketable Securities,* and No. 52, *Foreign Currency Translation,* and Statement 87), that ultimately are reflected in determining net income of subsequent periods, if not offset by other events. The comprehensive income approach suggested by respondents would require separate Board consideration of how comprehensive income would be displayed, since Concepts State-

ment 5 does not address that issue. That consideration is beyond the scope of this Statement.

266. The Board concluded that, if an employer's transition obligation or asset is recognized immediately, the effect of that change in accounting should be recognized in a manner consistent with recognition of the effects of other changes in accounting. The Board believes that recognition of the effects of an accounting change through income is widely understood and accepted. To immediately recognize the effects of adopting this Statement in a different manner would be inconsistent with how subsequent adjustments of the transition obligation are recognized and would diminish the understandability and usefulness of the financial statements. Therefore, the Board concluded that the effects of an employer's election to immediately recognize its transition obligation or asset for postretirement benefits should be reported as the effect of an accounting change; employers that elect delayed recognition of the transition obligation or asset should report the recognition of that amount as a component of net periodic postretirement benefit cost, consistent with the manner of reporting the transition effects of Statement 87.

267. The Board also concluded that for individual deferred compensation contracts, the effects of a change in the measurement and recognition of an employer's obligation at the date the change in accounting is adopted should be recognized in a manner consistent with the nature of the benefit provided by the contract. Consequently, the effect of the change in accounting for individual contracts that provide postretirement health or other welfare benefits, measured at the date of the change, is subject to the general transition provisions and effective dates of this Statement (paragraphs 108-114). However, the effect of a change in accounting for other individual deferred compensation contracts is to be recognized as the cumulative effect of a change in accounting in accordance with Opinion 20, effective for fiscal years beginning after March 15, 1991. The Board believed that that delay in the effective date for those contracts should provide sufficient time for communication of the amendment of Opinion 12 to affected employers.

Components of Net Periodic Postretirement Benefit Cost

268. The Board concluded that an understanding of postretirement benefit accounting is facilitated by separately considering the components of net periodic postretirement benefit cost. Those components are service cost, interest cost, actual return on plan assets, amortization of unrecognized prior service cost, gain or loss recognition, and amorti-

zation of the transition obligation or asset for employers who elect delayed recognition of the unrecognized obligation or asset existing at the date of initial application of this Statement.

269. A plan with no plan assets, no plan amendments, no gains or losses, and no unrecognized transition amount would have two components of cost—service cost and interest cost. As employees work during the year in exchange for promised benefits, a *service cost* (compensation cost) accrues. Measurement of that component is discussed in the section on measurement of cost and obligations (paragraphs 166-246). Since the service cost component and the related obligation are measured on a present value basis under this Statement, a second component—*interest cost*—also must be accounted for. Measurement of that component is straightforward once the discount rates are determined; selection of appropriate discount rates is discussed in paragraphs 186-193.

270. A third component of cost exists for a funded plan—the *return* (or possibly loss) *on plan assets.* That component ordinarily reduces net periodic postretirement benefit cost. The interest cost and return on plan assets components represent financial items rather than employee compensation cost and are affected by changes in the employer's financing arrangements. For example, an employer can increase the return on plan assets by making additional contributions to a fund that is segregated and restricted for the payment of the postretirement benefits. An employer can decrease interest cost (and return on plan assets) by using plan assets to purchase nonparticipating life insurance contracts to settle part of the accumulated postretirement benefit obligation of a postretirement life insurance plan.

271. The fourth component of cost is the *amortization of unrecognized prior service cost,* which reflects the increase or decrease in compensation cost as a result of granting, improving, or reducing postretirement benefits attributed, pursuant to this Statement, to periods prior to the plan initiation or amendment. The amortization of unrecognized prior service cost that results from a plan initiation that grants retroactive benefits will increase net periodic postretirement benefit cost; amortization of prior service cost that results from a plan amendment will increase or decrease the net periodic postretirement benefit cost depending on whether the amendment increases or reduces (a negative plan amendment) benefits.

272. The fifth component of cost is the *gain or loss component*. That component either decreases or increases postretirement benefit cost depending on whether the net unrecognized amount is a gain

or a loss, whether the actual return on plan assets for a particular period is less than or greater than the expected return on plan assets, and whether an employer makes a decision to temporarily deviate from the substantive plan. That component combines gains and losses of various types and therefore includes both compensation and financial items that are not readily separable.

Conclusions on Other Issues—Single-Employer Defined Benefit Postretirement Plans

Fundamentals of Postretirement Benefit Accounting

273. In applying accrual accounting to postretirement benefits, this Statement accepts three fundamental ideas that are common to pension accounting: delayed recognition of certain events, reporting net cost, and offsetting liabilities and related assets. Those three features of practice have shaped financial reporting for pensions for many years even though they conflict in some respects with accounting principles applied elsewhere.

274. Delayed recognition means that certain changes in the obligation for postretirement benefits, including those changes that result from a plan initiation or amendment, and certain changes in the value of plan assets set aside to meet that obligation are not recognized as they occur. Rather, those changes are recognized systematically over future periods. All changes in the obligation and plan assets are ultimately recognized unless they are first offset by future changes. The changes that have been quantified but not yet recognized in the employer's financial statements as components of net periodic postretirement benefit cost and as a liability or asset are disclosed.

275. Net cost means that the recognized consequences of events and transactions that affect a postretirement benefit plan are reported as a single amount in the employer's financial statements. That net cost comprises at least three types of events or transactions that might otherwise be reported separately. Those events or transactions— exchanging a promise of deferred compensation in the form of postretirement benefits for employee service, the interest cost arising from the passage of time until those benefits are paid, and the returns from the investment of plan assets—are disclosed separately as components of net periodic postretirement benefit cost.

276. Offsetting means that the postretirement benefit obligation recognized in the employer's statement of financial position is reported net of amounts contributed to a plan specifically for the payment of that obligation and that the return on plan assets is offset in the employer's statement of

income against other components of net periodic postretirement benefit cost. That offsetting is reflected even though the obligation has not been settled, the investment of the plan assets may be largely controlled by the employer, and substantial risks and rewards associated with both the obligation and the plan assets are borne by the employer.

Recognition and Measurement of a Plan Initiation or Amendment

277. When a postretirement benefit plan is initiated or amended to increase benefits, credit may be explicitly granted for employee service rendered prior to the date of the plan initiation or amendment. However, a plan initiation or amendment may not explicitly grant prior service credit. Thus it may be unclear whether an obligation for prior service arises for all or some of the participants.

278. A plan initiation or amendment that provides benefits to current retirees can only grant the retirees credit for their prior service, since no future service can be required for them to be entitled to the new or amended benefits. Consequently, an obligation for prior service arises to the extent a plan initiation or amendment provides new or increased benefits to current retirees. A similar assessment can be made for a plan initiation or amendment that provides benefits to other plan participants who have rendered sufficient service to be fully eligible to receive the new or amended benefits. However, since some of those plan participants have not yet retired and are expected to render additional future service, some respondents argued that a plan initiation or amendment affecting active plan participants fully eligible for benefits may be viewed as prospective. That view acknowledges no obligation for prior service; any obligation would arise as the employees render future service in exchange for the benefits. As applied to active plan participants who are fully eligible for benefits, the latter argument appears to be consistent only with the use of an attribution period that would end at an active plan participant's retirement date, not with an attribution period ending at an active plan participant's full eligibility date.

279. When new or amended benefits are granted to active plan participants who are not yet fully eligible for benefits, the determination of whether those benefits are granted in exchange for past or future service is unclear unless specified by the plan initiation or amendment. Some respondents argued that because eligibility for the new or amended benefits is contingent on rendering future service, the plan initiation or amendment should be viewed only as prospective. Others argued that, consistent with the attribution approach that allocates an equal amount of benefit to each year of

service in the attribution period and assuming the plan's benefit formula does not specify the benefits earned for specific years of service, the granting of new or amended benefits should be viewed as partially retroactive, to the extent the benefits are attributable to prior service periods, and partially prospective.

280. The Board noted that if a plan initiation or amendment does not explicitly state whether the new or amended benefits are granted prospectively or retroactively, but affects retirees as well as active plan participants, the plan could be viewed as implicitly granting prior service credit to active plan participants expected to receive the new or amended benefits. Assigning new or amended benefits to prior periods acknowledges that benefits are provided in exchange for employee service over the total credited service period.

281. The Board considered whether a plan initiation should be given the same accounting treatment as a plan amendment. If a plan initiation is viewed as retroactive, presumably any subsequent plan amendment also should be viewed as retroactive unless the plan specifically ignores prior service in determining eligibility for the new or amended benefit. However, if a plan initiation is viewed as prospective, one could view a subsequent amendment to that plan either as retroactive to the date of plan initiation or as prospective.

282. In considering whether plan initiations and amendments should be viewed similarly (that is, both as retroactive or both as prospective), the Board acknowledged the potential difficulty in distinguishing between a plan initiation and plan amendment. For example, if an employer has a health care plan for retirees and decides to provide dental benefits to retirees, one can view the action as an amendment of the postretirement health care plan or as the initiation of a postretirement dental care plan. The Board also was concerned about accounting for other amendments that might be viewed as plan initiations. For example, if a plan providing nominal benefits was initiated on January 1 and then was amended a few months later to increase benefits, the amended plan could be viewed as the plan that was contemplated when initiated on January 1. The Board concluded that a plan initiation should be accounted for in a manner similar to a plan amendment, unless the plan specifically provides benefits solely in exchange for service after the date of the plan initiation or a future date.

283. The Board also considered whether the effects of a plan initiation or amendment on retirees and other fully eligible plan participants should be viewed as retroactive and the effects on other ac-

tive plan participants as prospective. In granting new or amended benefits to retirees and other fully eligible plan participants, an employer is implicitly, if not explicitly, granting credit for prior service. However, for active plan participants who have not yet attained full eligibility for those benefits, the new or amended benefits could be provided in exchange for their remaining service to full eligibility for benefits. Some interested parties, particularly consulting actuaries, advised the Board of the difficulties in measuring the service cost component of net periodic postretirement benefit cost and gains and losses if plan amendments were viewed as prospective for some plan participants.

284. Under a prospective approach, the benefits granted at plan initiation and with each subsequent amendment would need to be layered, requiring a repricing of each layer at each measurement date to determine service cost and gains or losses. That repricing could be particularly difficult when the plan does not define the specific periods of service to be rendered in exchange for the benefits and the benefits are defined in kind, rather than in terms of a fixed value or amount of benefit. In addition to the concerns expressed with prospective treatment of a plan initiation or amendment that affects certain active plan participants, the Board noted that negative plan amendments cannot logically be viewed as prospective for those plan participants. Given those factors, and the decision to reduce complexity by attributing the expected postretirement benefit obligation ratably to employees' years of service in the attribution period, the Board concluded that all plan amendments should be viewed as retroactive for all plan participants. Similarly, plan initiations generally should be viewed as retroactive unless the plan initiation specifically disregards prior service in determining eligibility for the new benefits.

Recognition of prior service cost

285. When a plan is amended to increase benefits or a plan is initiated and grants credit for prior service, the accumulated postretirement benefit obligation, based on retroactive allocation of benefits to service in prior years, is greater than before the plan initiation or amendment. As a result, the incremental obligation created by a plan initiation or amendment is reflected immediately as an increase in the accumulated postretirement benefit obligation. Whether that increase should be recognized (a) immediately as postretirement benefit cost for the year of the plan initiation or amendment or (b) on a delayed basis as part of postretirement benefit cost for future periods is arguable, particularly when the plan's terms attribute the increase to employees' prior service.

286. Some Board members support immediate recognition of prior service cost as an expense, particularly the portion related to existing retirees. Although some intangible economic benefits of a plan initiation or amendment may be received in future periods from benefit improvements for active plan participants, they believe that those intangible benefits do not qualify for recognition as an asset. Therefore, they believe there is little basis for delaying recognition of the underlying prior service cost to future periods. Other Board members believe that a plan initiation or amendment is made with a view to benefiting the employer's future operations through reduced employee turnover, improved productivity, or reduced demands for increases in cash compensation.

287. In its deliberations on Statement 87, the Board concluded that it is reasonable to assume that a plan amendment is the result of an economic decision and that a future economic benefit to the employer exists when benefit increases are granted to active plan participants and retirees. They observed that amortizing the cost of acquiring a future economic benefit over future periods is consistent with accounting practice in other areas. The Board also concluded that a requirement to charge the cost of a retroactive plan initiation or amendment immediately to net periodic pension cost would be an unacceptable change from prior practice. Accordingly, the Board concluded that the increase in the obligation resulting from a pension plan initiation or amendment should be recognized as a component of net periodic pension cost over a number of future periods as the anticipated benefit to the employer is expected to be realized.

288. In considering postretirement benefits, the Board found no compelling reason to recognize the cost of a retroactive plan initiation or amendment in a manner fundamentally different from that required by Statement 87. Thus, this Statement requires recognizing an equal amount of the prior service cost in each remaining year of service to the full eligibility date of each plan participant active at the date of the plan initiation or amendment who is not yet fully eligible for benefits at that date. Other alternatives provided under Statement 87 that recognize the prior service cost more rapidly, such as over the average remaining years of service to full eligibility for benefits of the active plan participants, also are permitted.

289. The Board recognizes that treating any plan amendment as retroactive, even if the new or amended benefits are provided solely in exchange for future service, results in a measure of the accumulated postretirement benefit obligation and of unrecognized prior service cost that may exceed

the measure that would result from following the plan terms. The effect of retroactive treatment, however, is consistent with the pattern of ratably attributing the expected postretirement benefit obligation to each year of service in the attribution period. The effects of a higher measure of the accumulated postretirement benefit obligation and unrecognized prior service cost in some cases, as a result of treating prospective changes as retroactive, are consequences that offset the benefits of the simpler methodology provided by a ratable attribution pattern. However, delayed recognition of prior service cost mitigates those effects and net periodic postretirement benefit cost is not expected to be significantly affected.

Recognition of the effect of a plan amendment that reduces benefits (negative plan amendment)

290. A plan amendment may reduce rather than increase benefits attributed to prior service. The Board concluded that, consistent with Statement 87, any decrement in the obligation for benefits attributable to prior service should first reduce any existing unrecognized prior service cost arising from the plan's initiation or subsequent benefit increases. Further, the Board concluded that any remaining effects of a negative plan amendment should next reduce any unrecognized transition obligation with any remaining credit generally recognized in a manner consistent with prior service cost; that is, over remaining years of service to full eligibility for benefits of the active plan participants. The Board concluded that those constraints on recognition of the effects of a negative plan amendment are necessary because the effects of reducing a plan promise should not be recognized before the original promise, including the unrecognized transition obligation, is recognized. Immediate recognition of the effects of a negative plan amendment also is precluded because future periods may be affected by an employer's decision to reduce benefits provided under the plan.

Delayed Recognition of Gains and Losses

291. Gains and losses, sometimes called actuarial gains and losses, are changes in either the accumulated postretirement benefit obligation or the fair value of plan assets arising from changes in assumptions and from experience different from that incorporated in the assumptions. For example, gains and losses include the effects on measurement of the accumulated postretirement benefit obligation that result from changes in the assumed health care cost trend rates for postretirement health care plans and actual returns on plan assets greater than or less than the expected rates of return.

292. Some respondents expressed concern about the volatility of a measure of an unfunded postretirement benefit obligation and the practical effects of incorporating that volatility into financial statements. The Board does not believe that volatility in financial statements is necessarily undesirable. If a financial measure purports to represent a phenomenon that is volatile, that measure must reflect the volatility or it will not be representationally faithful.

293. The Board acknowledges that, in the case of the accumulated postretirement benefit obligation, reported volatility may not be entirely a faithful representation of changes in the status of the obligation (the phenomenon represented). It also may reflect an unavoidable inability to predict accurately the future events that are anticipated in making period-to-period measurements. That may be particularly true for postretirement health care plans in light of the current inexperience in measuring the accumulated postretirement benefit obligation for those plans. The difference in periodic measures of the accumulated benefit obligation for a postretirement health care plan, and therefore the funded status of the plan, results partly from the inability to predict accurately for a period, or over several periods, annual expected claims costs, future trends in the cost of health care, turnover rates, retirement dates, dependency status, life expectancy, and other pertinent events. As a result, actual experience often differs significantly from what was estimated, which leads to changes in the estimates for future measurements. Recognizing the effects of revisions in estimates in full in the period in which they occur may produce financial statements that portray more volatility than is inherent in the employer's obligation.

294. The Board considered those views and concluded that, similar to employers' accounting for pensions, gains and losses should not be required to be recognized immediately as a component of net periodic postretirement benefit cost. Accordingly, this Statement provides for delayed recognition of gains (losses) over future periods to the extent they are not reduced by subsequent losses (gains). The effects of changes in the fair value of plan assets, including the indirect effect of those changes on the return-on-assets component of net periodic postretirement benefit cost, are recognized on a basis intended to reduce volatility. The method used was developed in Statement 87. Both the extent of reduction in volatility and the mechanism adopted to effect it are essentially practical decisions without conceptual basis. The Board believes that the market-related value of plan assets used in this Statement as a device to reduce the volatility of net periodic postretirement benefit cost is not as relevant as the fair value of those assets.

295. Unlike most pension plans, the return on postretirement benefit plan assets may be subject to income tax because of the lack of tax-exempt vehicles for funding those benefits. At present, even if postretirement benefit plan assets are restricted and segregated within a trust, the income generated by those assets generally is taxable. If the plan has taxable income, the assessed tax will reduce the returns available for payment of benefits or reinvestment. The Board concluded that when the trust or other entity holding the plan assets is taxed as a separate entity on the return on *plan assets* (as defined herein), the expected long-term rate of return should be determined by giving consideration to anticipated income taxes under enacted tax law. However, if the tax on income generated by plan assets is not a liability of the plan, but of the employer, the expected long-term rate of return should not anticipate a tax on those earnings, because that tax will be reflected in the employer's accounting for income taxes.

296. The Board had several reasons for adopting the approach required in this Statement for measuring and incorporating the return on plan assets into net periodic postretirement benefit cost. First, it is the same as that used in Statement 87 and is similar, mechanically, to actuarial practices intended to reflect the return on plan assets. As a result, it should be easier for those familiar with pension accounting or actuarial practices to understand and apply. Second, the use of explicit estimates of the return on plan assets avoids the use of discount rates, which are primarily relevant for measuring the accumulated postretirement benefit obligation, as part of a calculation related to the return on plan assets. Therefore, it reflects more clearly the Board's basic conclusion that information about a deferred compensation plan is more understandable if asset-related or financial features of the arrangement are distinguished from the liability-related and compensation cost features.

297. If assumptions prove to be accurate estimates of experience over a number of years, gains or losses in one year will be offset by losses or gains in subsequent periods. In that situation, all gains and losses would be offset over time, and amortization of unrecognized gains and losses would be unnecessary. The Board was concerned that the uncertainties inherent in assumptions could lead to gains or losses that increase rather than offset, and concluded that gains and losses should not be ignored completely. Actual experience will determine the final net cost of a postretirement benefit plan. The Board concluded that some amortization, at least when the net unrecognized gain or loss becomes significant, should be required.

298. Consistent with Statement 87, this Statement uses a "corridor" approach as a minimum amortization approach. That approach allows a reasonable opportunity for gains and losses to offset each other without affecting net periodic postretirement benefit cost. The Board also noted that the corridor approach is similar in some respects to methods used by some to deal with gains and losses on plan assets for funding purposes. The width of that corridor is related to the market-related value of plan assets and the amount of the accumulated postretirement benefit obligation because the gains and losses subject to amortization are changes in those two amounts. The Exposure Draft proposed that a net gain or loss equal to 10 percent of the greater of those two amounts should not be required to be amortized (and thus included in net periodic postretirement benefit cost). Thus, the width of the resulting corridor would be 20 percent (from 90 percent to 110 percent of the greater balance).

299. Respondents generally agreed with the proposal to shield from recognition gains and losses falling within a defined corridor. However, many of the respondents suggested a wider corridor. They stated that they believe there will be greater volatility of measurement of postretirement benefit obligations than of pension obligations. They suggested that that consideration and the inability to fund postretirement benefit plans (which they believed would provide offsetting asset-related gains and losses) warrant a wider corridor to further mitigate potential swings in net postretirement benefit cost from one period to the next.

300. The effects of widening the corridor to 20 percent of the greater of the accumulated postretirement benefit obligation or market-related value of plan assets were tested in a number of different scenarios. The results of that study showed that widening the corridor would have little effect on mitigating the volatility of net periodic postretirement benefit cost; the significant factor in mitigating that volatility is the period over which unrecognized gains or losses in excess of the corridor are recognized. The Board concluded that understandability and comparability would be enhanced by retaining the approach followed for pension accounting.

301. Gains and losses also may be recognized immediately or on a delayed basis using any systematic method of amortizing unrecognized gains and losses, provided the method is consistently followed and that it does not result in less rapid recognition of gains and losses than the minimum amortization discussed in paragraph 298. Amortization of unrecognized net gains or losses is based on beginning-of-year balances. If an employer elects to recognize gains and losses immediately, the amount of any net gain in excess of a net loss previously recognized in income shall first offset any

unrecognized transition obligation, and the amount of any net loss in excess of a net gain previously recognized in income shall first offset any unrecognized transition asset. That constraint was added because Board members believe that gains (losses) should not be recognized before the underlying unfunded (overfunded) accumulated postretirement benefit obligation is recognized.

302. In some cases an employer may assume a benefit obligation for current and past benefit payments that differs from the substance of the employer's commitment. For example, on the basis of the mutually understood terms of the substantive plan, an employer may anticipate for accounting purposes that any shortfall resulting from current year benefit payments in excess of the employer's substantive plan cost and participant contributions for the year will be recovered from increased participant contributions in the subsequent year. However, the employer may subsequently determine that increasing participant contributions for the prior year's shortfall is onerous and make a decision to bear the cost of the shortfall for that year. That is, an employer may make a decision not to retrospectively adjust participants' contributions to recover the shortfall. The Board concluded that the gain or loss from such a temporary deviation from the substantive plan should be immediately recognized as a gain or loss, without the benefit of the corridor or other delayed recognition alternatives. Because the effect of the deviation from the substantive plan has no future economic benefit to the employer; and relates to benefits already paid, the Board believes that delayed recognition of that effect would be inappropriate.

Minimum Liability

303. The Exposure Draft proposed that, similar to Statement 87, a minimum liability should be prescribed to limit the extent to which the delayed recognition of the transition obligation, plan amendments, and losses could result in omission of liabilities from an employer's statement of financial position. The minimum liability was defined as the unfunded accumulated postretirement benefit obligation for retirees and other fully eligible plan participants. The Board believed that that measurement represented a threshold below which the recognized liability would not be sufficiently representationally faithful. The proposed minimum liability provisions would have been effective five years after the effective date of this Statement.

304. Respondents generally disagreed with prescribing the minimum liability that should be recognized. They believed that the proposed minimum liability provision represented a departure from accrual ac-

counting and was inconsistent with the provisions of this Statement that provide for delayed recognition of gains and losses, prior service cost, and an employer's transition obligation. Respondents stated that unlike pensions, postretirement benefit obligations do not vest, as that term is used in its legal sense. They observed that the minimum liability provisions in Statement 87 approximate the statutory liability a U.S. employer would face if its pension plan were terminated. Currently, there are no similar statutory requirements for postretirement health care or welfare benefits. Some respondents also believed that the minimum liability provision would be confusing because it introduces an alternative measure of an employer's postretirement benefit obligation.

305. The Board concluded that this Statement should not require recognition of a minimum liability. The field test of the Exposure Draft provisions suggested that, ignoring the effects of gains and losses and plan amendments, the minimum liability provision for mature companies as defined in that study (companies with a ratio of one retiree to two to six active employees) generally would be inoperative after eight years. For companies with a higher retiree to active employee ratio, the field test suggested that the minimum liability provisions might be operative for more than 10 years. In other words, for possibly 10 or more years the minimum liability provisions could be effective solely as a result of phasing in recognition of the transition obligation. The Board concluded that the transition provisions of this Statement that provide for the delayed recognition of an employer's obligation for postretirement benefits at the date this Statement is initially applied should not be overridden by a requirement to recognize a liability that would accelerate recognition of that obligation in the statement of financial position.

306. The Board considered and decided not to amend Statement 87 to eliminate its minimum liability provision. Because most pension plans were thought to be adequately funded when Statement 87 was issued, the minimum liability provision served to identify those exceptional situations in which the pension plan was underfunded. However, it is widely acknowledged that postretirement benefit plans are significantly or totally underfunded. As a result, recognition of a minimum liability for such plans would be commonplace rather than an exception.

307. Some Board members believe that a liability that reflects only the accrued and unfunded postretirement benefit cost, in and of itself, is not a relevant or reliable representation of an employer's probable future sacrifice if recognition of significant losses, prior service costs, or the transition obliga-

tion has been delayed. They support retaining the minimum liability provision proposed in the Exposure Draft for the reasons described in paragraph 303. They observe that the liability for accrued and unfunded postretirement benefit cost does not purport to be a measure of the employer's present obligation in most cases; rather, it is the residual resulting from an allocation process. To the extent that one assumes that the employer is a going concern and that a postretirement benefit plan will continue, the employer's probable future sacrifice is represented by benefits to which retirees and other fully eligible plan participants are entitled and the portion of expected future benefits earned by other active plan participants. That probable future sacrifice can only be determined by considering the current funded status of the plan.

Measurement of Plan Assets

308. The Board considered whether employer assets intended to be used for the payment of postretirement benefits, including funds set aside in a separate trust or similar funding vehicle, should be included in plan assets. The Board concluded that if those assets can be used for other purposes at the employer's discretion, they should not be considered to be plan assets. In measuring the funded status of a postretirement benefit plan, the Board concluded that it is appropriate and consistent with pension accounting to include in plan assets only those assets that are restricted for the purpose of paying the plan's postretirement benefit obligations. Some respondents questioned whether certain funding vehicles can be restricted solely for the provision of postretirement benefits, as opposed to funding both active employees' and retirees' benefits, and would, therefore, qualify as plan assets. Whether a funding vehicle can be restricted solely for the payment of retirees' benefits is subject to legal, not accounting, interpretation.

309. The Board concluded that plan investments should be measured at fair value for purposes of this Statement, except as provided in paragraph 57 for purposes of determining the extent of delayed recognition of gains and losses. Fair value is the most relevant information that can be provided for assessing both the plan's ability to pay benefits as they come due and the future contributions necessary to provide for benefits already promised to employees. The relevance of fair value outweighs objections to its use based on difficulty of measurement. The same reasons led to a similar decision in Statements 35 and 87.

310. Measuring investments at fair value could introduce volatility into the financial statements as a result of short-term changes in fair values. Some respondents indicated that that volatility would be

meaningless or even misleading, particularly because of the long-run nature of the postretirement benefit commitment or because plan investments are often held for long periods, thus providing the opportunity for some gains or losses to reverse. As noted in paragraphs 58-60, the Board concluded that the difference between the actual return on plan assets and the expected return on plan assets could be recognized in net periodic postretirement benefit cost on a delayed basis. That conclusion was based on (a) the probability that at least some gains would be offset by subsequent losses, and vice versa, and (b) arguments that immediate recognition would produce unacceptable volatility and would be inconsistent with the present accounting model.

311. The Board also concluded that, similar to the conclusion in Statement 87, including accrued postretirement benefit costs as plan assets for purposes of the disclosure of funded status (paragraph 74(c)) (a) would be inappropriate because that amount has not been funded (contributed) and (b) would unnecessarily complicate the recognition and disclosure requirements of this Statement. Similarly, the Board concluded that elimination from plan assets of all securities of the employer held by the plan would be impractical and might be inappropriate absent a decision that the financial statements of the plan should be consolidated with those of the employer. However, the Board concluded that disclosure of the amount of those securities held is appropriate and should be required.

Measurement Date

312. The Board concluded that the prescribed measurement date should be responsive to the difficulties inherent in measurement of the accumulated postretirement benefit obligation as well as the time required to obtain actuarial valuation reports. The Board believed those considerations justified some flexibility in selecting the date at which the accumulated postretirement benefit obligation and plan assets should be measured.

313. Measuring plan assets as of the date of the financial statements does not present very significant or unusual problems; the difficulty arises primarily with measurement of the accumulated postretirement benefit obligation. The Board concluded that it should be feasible to provide information about the accumulated postretirement benefit obligation as of the date of the financial statements based on a valuation performed at an earlier date with adjustments for relevant subsequent events (especially employee service) after that date.

314. The Board concluded that the benefits of

having information on a timely basis and measured consistently with other financial information will usually outweigh the incremental costs. The Board acknowledges that practical problems may sometimes make it costly to obtain information, especially information about the accumulated postretirement benefit obligation and related components of net periodic postretirement benefit cost, as of the date of the financial statements. The Board concluded that the information required by this Statement should be as of a date not earlier than three months before the date of the financial statements. That measurement date is consistent with the measurement date prescribed by Statement 87. Measurements of postretirement benefit cost for interim and annual financial statements should be based on the assumptions used for the previous year-end financial reporting unless more recent measures of both plan assets and the accumulated postretirement benefit obligation are available, for example, as a result of a significant event, such as a plan amendment.

Settlements and Curtailments

315. This Statement provides for delayed recognition of the effects of plan initiations and amendments and gains and losses arising in the ordinary course of operations. In certain circumstances, however, recognition of some or all of those delayed effects may be appropriate. Paragraphs 316-332 discuss the basis for the Board's conclusions on settlement and curtailment accounting for postretirement benefit plans, which draw on the basis for conclusions in Statement 88. Except as discussed in paragraph 325, the Board's conclusions are the same as those prescribed in Statement 88 for a settlement or a curtailment of a defined benefit pension plan.

316. Settlements and curtailments are events that require income or expense recognition of previously unrecognized amounts and adjustments to liabilities or assets recognized in the employer's statement of financial position. The Board concluded that, similar to employers' accounting for pensions, previously unrecognized prior service cost, including any unrecognized transition obligation, and the previously unrecognized net gain (including any unrecognized transition asset) or loss should be recognized in the period when all of the following conditions are met:

a. All postretirement health care or other welfare benefit obligations under the plan are settled.
b. Defined benefits are no longer accrued under the plan.
c. The plan is not replaced by another defined benefit plan.
d. No plan assets remain.
e. The employees are terminated.
f. The plan ceases to exist as an entity.

317. It is not uncommon for some, but not all, of the above conditions to exist in a particular situation. For example, the accumulated postretirement benefit obligation may be settled without terminating the plan, or a plan may be suspended so that no further benefits will accrue for future services but its obligations are not settled. In other situations one or more of the above conditions may apply to only part of a plan. For example, one plan may be divided into two plans, one of which is then terminated, or one-half of the employees in a plan may terminate employment and the obligation for their benefits may be settled.

318. If recognition of previously unrecognized prior service cost and net gain or loss were required only when a plan is completely terminated and settled and if no recognition occurred when a plan is partially curtailed or an obligation is partially settled, anomalies and implementation problems would result. For example, if one employer had two plants with separate plans and another employer had two plants with a single plan, the accounting result of closing one plant and settling the related obligation would be a recognizable event for one employer but not for the other. If recognition were an all-or-nothing proposition, it would be necessary to determine when the extent of settlement or curtailment is sufficient for recognition. If all employees but one from a large group are terminated and obligations to the terminated employees are settled, presumably the accounting should reflect a plan termination. But it is not clear whether that accounting should apply if 5 percent, 10 percent, or 25 percent of the original group were to remain. The Board concluded in Statement 88 and reconfirmed in this Statement that a complete plan termination and settlement need not occur to recognize previously unrecognized amounts.

Settlement of the obligation

319. The Board concluded that settlement of all or part of the accumulated postretirement benefit obligation should be the event that requires recognition of all or part of the previously unrecognized net gain (including any unrecognized transition asset) or loss. Delayed recognition of gains and losses under this Statement is based in part on the possibility that gains or losses occurring in one period will be offset by losses or gains in subsequent periods. To the extent that the accumulated postretirement benefit obligation has been settled, the possibility of future gains and losses related to that obligation and the assets used to effect the settlement is eliminated.

320. Settlement of all or a large portion of the accumulated postretirement benefit obligation also may be viewed as realization of past gains or losses associated with that portion of the obligation and

the assets used to effect the settlement. That realization would not be affected by the employer's subsequent decision to undertake or not to undertake future defined benefit obligations.

321. The Board acknowledges that other actions an employer can take, especially those related to plan assets, can affect the possibility of a subsequent net gain or loss. For example, an employer may avoid or minimize certain risks by investing in a portfolio of high-quality fixed-income securities with principal and interest payment dates similar to the estimated payment dates of benefits, as with a dedicated bond portfolio.

322. Settlement differs from other actions in that (a) it is irrevocable, (b) it relieves the employer (or the plan) of primary responsibility for the obligation, and (c) it eliminates significant risks related to the obligation, such as the risk that participants will live longer than assumed, and to the assets used to effect the settlement. The decision to have a dedicated bond portfolio can be reversed, it does not relieve the employer of primary responsibility for the obligation, and such a strategy does not eliminate various risks, such as mortality risk and the escalating cost of providing the benefits. The Board concluded that the circumstances requiring gain or loss recognition should be defined narrowly.

323. The Board recognizes that changes in the previously estimated values of the accumulated postretirement benefit obligation and the plan assets may become evident at the time the obligation is settled. For example, the interest rates inherent in the price actually paid for insurance contracts that settle an obligation may be different from the assumed discount rates. Some respondents suggested that those changes should be recognized immediately in income as a gain or loss directly resulting from the settlement. The Board concluded that, based on the measurement principles adopted in this Statement, those changes reflect factors expected to be considered in the measurement of the postretirement benefit obligation and plan assets. The Board also concluded that those amounts should be included with the previously unrecognized net gain or loss before a pro rata portion of that amount is recognized.

324. This Statement requires measurement of a pro rata portion of the unrecognized net gain or loss based on the decrease in the accumulated postretirement benefit obligation resulting from a settlement. The Board acknowledges that a decrease in the amount of plan assets also can affect the possibility of future gains and losses. However, the Board concluded that it would be simpler and more practical to base the measurement only on the obligation settled.

325. Under Statement 88, a gain resulting from settlement of a pension obligation is measured without regard to any remaining unrecognized transition obligation. In contrast with the nature of the transition obligation that may arise under Statement 87, any unrecognized transition obligation for postretirement benefits is likely to include a significant amount of previously unrecognized current service cost and interest cost. For an ongoing plan, this Statement requires that for an employer that elects immediate recognition of gains or losses, any net gain for the year that does not offset a loss previously recognized in income must first reduce any remaining unrecognized transition obligation. Similarly, the Board has concluded that any gain arising from a settlement should be reduced by any unrecognized transition obligation; only the excess is recognized as a settlement gain. The Board concluded that an employer should not be permitted to accelerate recognition of gains if the underlying obligation that was remeasured, causing those gains to arise, has not yet been recognized.

Curtailment of the plan

326. One basis for delayed recognition of prior service cost is the likelihood of future economic benefits to the employer as a result of a plan initiation or amendment. Those benefits, in the Board's view, are derived from the future services of active plan participants, and the amortization of unrecognized prior service cost is based on those services. A curtailment, as defined in this Statement, is an event that significantly reduces the expected years of future service of present active plan participants or eliminates for a significant number of active plan participants the accrual of defined benefits for some or all of their future services.

327. The Board concluded that reduction of the expected years of future service of the work force or elimination of the accrual of defined postretirement benefits for a significant number of active plan participants raises doubt about the continued existence of the future economic benefits of unrecognized prior service cost. Therefore, the Board concluded that any remaining unrecognized prior service cost, including any unrecognized transition obligation, should be recognized when it is probable that a curtailment will occur, the effects are reasonably estimable, and the net result of the curtailment (as described in paragraphs 97 and 98) is a loss.

328. The Board also considered whether either the settlement or the termination of one plan and the adoption of a substantially equivalent replacement plan should trigger recognition of prior service cost. The Board concluded that neither of those events, absent a curtailment, raises sufficient

doubt as to the existence of future economic benefits to trigger that recognition.

329. A curtailment may directly cause a decrease in the accumulated postretirement benefit obligation (a gain) or an increase in the accumulated postretirement benefit obligation (a loss). For example, the accumulated postretirement benefit obligation may decline if active plan participants who are not yet eligible for benefits are terminated (a gain). On the other hand, the accumulated postretirement benefit obligation may increase if an event occurs that causes active plan participants fully eligible for benefits to leave earlier than previously expected (a loss).

330. Conceptually, the Board concluded that it would be appropriate to recognize those gains or losses immediately to the extent they do not represent the reversal of previously unrecognized losses or gains. However, the obligation eliminated or created by a curtailment may not be independent of previously unrecognized losses or gains. For example, part of that obligation could relate to past changes in actuarial assumptions about the discount rates that produced gains or losses not yet fully recognized. To illustrate, if in year 1 the employer reduces the assumed weighted-average discount rate from 9 percent to 8 percent, any accumulated postretirement benefit obligation is increased, resulting in an unrecognized loss. If in year 2 the employer terminates active plan participants, the obligation related to their nonvested accumulated benefits is eliminated and a gain arises, which is, at least in part, a reversal of the previously unrecognized loss.

331. The Board concluded that, similar to Statement 88, a curtailment gain or loss as defined in paragraph 97 (which does not include recognition of prior service cost) should first be offset to the extent possible against the plan's previously existing unrecognized net loss or gain. Any remainder of the curtailment gain or loss cannot, at least in an overall sense, be a reversal of unrecognized amounts, and, therefore, recognition of that remainder is appropriate.

332. The Board considered whether curtailment gains should be recognized before the curtailment occurs. It concluded that continuing the delayed recognition feature of this Statement for a curtailment gain should be retained until the related active plan participants terminate or the plan suspension or amendment is adopted. That is consistent with Statement 88 and Opinion 30 and avoids the inconsistent results that would otherwise occur if

the curtailment gain is directly related to a disposal of a segment of a business.

Measurement of Special Termination Benefits

333. FASB Statement No. 74, *Accounting for Special Termination Benefits Paid to Employees,* acknowledged that other benefits, in addition to pensions, may be offered pursuant to a special termination arrangement and should be included in measuring the termination expense. Statement 88, which superseded Statement 74, retains that scope and therefore applies to other benefits in addition to pensions. However, the Board concluded that reiterating the applicability of Statement 88 is necessary, since practice may have been to exclude postretirement health care costs from the measurement of termination benefits.

334. The primary conclusion of the Board in Statement 74 was that the cost of special termination benefits should be recognized as a liability and a loss when the employees accept the offer and the amount can be reasonably estimated. That conclusion is incorporated in Statement 88. The cost of other contractual termination benefits provided by the existing terms of a plan that are payable only in the event of employees' involuntary termination of service due to a plant closing or a similar event should be recognized when it is probable that employees will be entitled to benefits and the amount can be reasonably estimated.

335. Paragraph 3 of Statement 74 stated:

> The termination of employees under a special termination benefit arrangement may affect the estimated costs of other employee benefits, such as pension benefits, because of differences between past assumptions and actual experience. If reliably measurable, the effects of any such changes on an employer's previously accrued expenses for those benefits that result directly from the termination of employees shall be included in measuring the termination expense. [Footnote reference omitted.]

Statement 88 superseded that paragraph and provides that a gain or loss in a plan arising as a direct result of a curtailment, including a curtailment resulting from an offer of special termination benefits, is first offset against any previously existing unrecognized net loss or gain for that plan and any excess is then recognized (paragraph 13).

336. The Board considered the following three alternative measures of the termination expense[37]

---

[37] The cost of any related curtailment would be determined separately pursuant to paragraphs 97-99.

arising from the acceptance of an offer of special postretirement health care or other welfare termination benefits:

a. The difference between (1) the accumulated postretirement benefit obligation under the existing plan that would have been attributed to service to date assuming that active plan participants not yet fully eligible for benefits would terminate at their full eligibility date and that fully eligible active plan participants would retire immediately, without considering any special termination benefits, and (2) the remeasured accumulated postretirement benefit obligation based on the special termination benefits
b. The difference between (1) the accumulated postretirement benefit obligation attributed to service to date and (2) the remeasured accumulated postretirement benefit obligation based on the special termination benefits
c. The difference between (1) the actuarial present value of the postretirement benefits an employee would have received if the employee had terminated voluntarily immediately before the offer and (2) the actuarial present value of the postretirement benefits the employee is expected to receive after accepting the offer.

337. The Board concluded that the first alternative was appropriate because it better reflects the exchange. Unlike the second alternative, it recognizes the incentive offered in exchange for termination earlier than expected. The first alternative becomes more compelling when one considers the offer of special termination benefits for fully eligible active plan participants. For those employees, there may be no incentive in the form of benefits not already available. Under the first alternative, the effects of the change in the expected retirement dates for employees who accept the offer may be a curtailment loss pursuant to paragraphs 97-99.

338. In contrast, the third alternative ignores the notion that the obligation to provide postretirement benefits arises with the rendering of employee service. That notion underlies the accounting for all deferred compensation contracts. The Board also noted that the third alternative fails to recognize that the termination benefit incentive for an employee one year away from eligibility for retirement differs from the incentive for an employee five years away.

Disclosure

General considerations

339. Decisions on disclosure requirements require evaluating and balancing considerations of relevance, reliability, and cost. Relevance and reliability are characteristics that make information useful for making decisions and that make it beneficial to require disclosure of some information. Benefits to users that are expected to result from required disclosures must be compared with the costs of providing and assimilating that information. Evaluating individual disclosures relative to those criteria is generally a matter of judgment. Cost, for example, is affected by several factors, such as the number of different plans and the difficulty of aggregating or meaningfully summarizing some disclosures. As the total amount of disclosure increases, consideration must be given to whether the incremental cost to both preparers and users of additional disclosure may be greater than the benefit of the additional information. Conversely, there is also a cost of not disclosing information. The absence of certain disclosures may directly affect the ability of financial statement users to make well-informed decisions.

340. Many of the disclosure requirements arise as a result of provisions of this Statement that reflect practical, rather than conceptual, decisions. For example, the components of net periodic postretirement benefit cost are disclosed because the recognized consequences of events and transactions affecting a postretirement benefit plan are reported as a single amount that includes at least three types of transactions that conceptually should be reported separately. The effects of those events or transactions—the exchange of employee service for deferred compensation in the form of postretirement benefits, interest cost reflecting the passage of time until those benefits are paid, and the returns from the investment of plan assets—are therefore disclosed. Similarly, the reconciliation of the funded status of the plan(s) is disclosed as a result of the decision to exclude certain obligations and assets from the statement of financial position due to provisions that permit delayed recognition of (a) the transition obligation, (b) the effect of certain changes in the measure of an employer's accumulated postretirement benefit obligation, and (c) the effect of certain changes in the value of plan assets set aside to meet that obligation. Although those effects are identified and measured, they are not required to be recognized in the financial statements as they arise.

341. Many of the disclosures required by this Statement are similar to required disclosures for pension plans. Some studies of the pension disclosures required by Statement 87 have suggested they are valuable because of the information provided.

Specific disclosure requirements

Descriptive information

342. Respondents generally agreed with disclosure of information about plan provisions and employee groups. The Board concluded that a brief description of the plan that is the basis for the accounting (the substantive plan), including any modifications of the existing cost-sharing provisions or increases in monetary benefits that are encompassed by the substantive plan, the employee groups covered, and the types of benefits provided, could assist users in understanding the reported effects of the plan on the employer's financial statements. The Board also concluded that financial statements should disclose the nature and effects of significant changes in the factors affecting the computation of the accumulated postretirement benefit obligation and related cost recognized in the financial statements. Any other significant or unusual matters, such as the effect of a business combination, also should be disclosed to enhance a user's understanding of the impact of those matters on an employer's financial position and results of operations.

343. Many postretirement benefit plans currently in existence are unfunded. For those that are funded, the Board concluded that disclosure of the funding policy would be useful in understanding differences between funding and accounting for that plan. Information that highlights any changes in funding policies also can be useful in assessing future cash flows.

Net periodic postretirement benefit cost information

344. Most respondents indicated that information about an employer's net periodic postretirement benefit cost would be useful. As with pensions, the cost of providing postretirement benefits comprises several components. Disclosure of the components will, over time, increase the general understanding of the nature of postretirement benefit cost, the reasons for changes in that cost, and the relationship between financing activities and employee compensation cost.

Information about obligations and assets

345. Most respondents who addressed the proposed disclosures agreed with disclosures about the funded status of the postretirement benefit plan. They stated that it provides information that is important to an understanding of the economics of the plan. Some respondents indicated that as part of that disclosure, it is important to present the components of the accumulated postretirement benefit obligation. The Exposure Draft proposed disclosure of the vested postretirement benefit obligation to provide information about the employer's obligation to retirees and other former employees, and active employees assuming they terminated immediately. The Board believed the information required to measure the vested postretirement benefit obligation would be available and that no significant incremental cost would be associated with providing that disclosure.

346. Most respondents opposed disclosure of the vested postretirement benefit obligation. They said the disclosure would be misleading because the term *vested,* although used in its accounting sense, could be misunderstood to imply a legal obligation. Although an employer may have a social or moral obligation to provide the postretirement benefits that have been earned, employers indicated that they currently do not have a statutory requirement to provide those promised benefits, unlike their legal obligation to provide certain vested pension benefits. In addition, respondents observed that if a postretirement benefit plan were terminated, the actual liability would very likely differ from the amount proposed to be measured as the vested obligation.

347. The Board accepted those arguments and concluded that disclosure of the vested postretirement benefit obligation should not be required. However, the Board added paragraph 74(c)(2), which requires disaggregated information about the accumulated benefit obligation for retirees, other fully eligible plan participants, and other active plan participants. Respondents suggested those disclosures would be more useful.

348. Management has a stewardship responsibility for efficient use of plan assets just as it does for operating assets. The Board concluded that disclosure of general information about the major types of any plan assets (and nonbenefit liabilities, if any) and the actual amount of return on plan assets for the period is useful in assessing the profitability of investment policies and the degree of risk assumed.

349. The Board concluded that a reconciliation of the amounts included in the employer's statement of financial position to the funded status of the plan's accumulated postretirement benefit obligation is essential to understanding the relationship between the accounting for and the funded status of the plan. The Board acknowledges that the amount recognized in the financial statements as a net postretirement benefit liability or asset pursuant to this Statement generally will not fully reflect the underlying funded status of the plan, that is, the plan assets and the accumulated postretirement benefit obligation for an overfunded or underfunded plan.

Information about assumptions

350. The Exposure Draft proposed disclosure, if applicable, of the weighted-average assumed discount rate, rate of compensation increase, health care cost trend rate, expected long-term rate of return on plan assets, and, for plans whose income is segregated from the employer's income for tax purposes, the estimated income tax rate on the expected return on plan assets. Most respondents who addressed the disclosure issues supported disclosure of the significant assumptions used in measuring an employer's postretirement benefit obligation and cost. A few respondents, however, maintained that a more descriptive disclosure about the assumed health care cost trend rates would be more useful. They noted that a weighted-average rate can mask differences in an employer's assumptions about year-by-year health care cost trend rates. For example, two employers could report the same weighted-average health care cost trend rate even though they made significantly different assumptions about future trends in health care costs and have very different expected payment schedules.

351. The Board concluded that descriptive information about an employer's assumed health care cost trend rates would be more useful than disclosure of a weighted-average rate. Therefore, this Statement requires disclosure of the assumed health care cost trend rate(s) used to measure the expected cost of benefits covered by the plan (gross eligible charges) for the year following the measurement date and a more general description of the direction and pattern of change in the assumed trend rates thereafter. The Board believes that disclosure will result in more comparable and understandable information about the assumptions used by employers in measuring their postretirement benefit obligations and costs.

352. The Board concluded that the weighted-average assumed discount rate, rate of compensation increase, and long-term rate of return on plan assets should be required to be disclosed as proposed in the Exposure Draft. In determining those weighted averages, employers should consider both the timing and amount of the expected benefit payments, compensation increases, or return on plan assets. The weighted-average discount rate reflects an assumption that significantly affects the computation of the accumulated postretirement benefit obligation and net periodic postretirement benefit cost, as might the weighted-average rate of compensation increase for pay-related plans. Those disclosures assist in assessing the comparability of that information among employers. Because the weighted-average assumed long-term rate of return on plan assets is expected to differ from the weighted-average discount rate, the Board concluded that disclosure of that assumption should be required. As proposed in the Exposure Draft, disclosure of the estimated income tax rate on the return on plan assets is required for plans whose income is segregated from the employer's income for tax purposes.

353. This Statement also requires disclosure of the effect on the current measurement of the accumulated benefit obligation for postretirement health care benefits and the combined service cost and interest cost components of net periodic postretirement benefit cost, assuming a one-percentage-point increase in the health care cost trend rates for each year following the measurement date, holding all other assumptions constant. Respondents generally did not support disclosure of the sensitivity of reported amounts to particular assumptions. Some respondents asserted that disclosure of sensitivity information would diminish the credibility of the amounts reported in the financial statements and would ignore the effects of changes in other assumptions. They also noted that the effects of a one-percentage-point change are not linear, reducing, therefore, the predictive value of the information and its usefulness. Other respondents who supported sensitivity disclosures stated that the information would assist users in judging the sensitivity of the measures of an employer's postretirement benefit obligation and cost to changes in one of its significant underlying assumptions and would provide information about the potential impact of subsequent events different from that assumed.

354. Measuring the sensitivity of the accumulated postretirement benefit obligation and the combined service and interest cost components to a change in the assumed health care cost trend rates requires remeasuring the accumulated postretirement benefit obligation as of the beginning and end of the year. That measurement should be possible at minimal incremental cost as part of the actuarial valuation needed to develop the basic information required by this Statement. The Board concluded that requiring that sensitivity information will assist users in assessing the comparability of information reported by different employers as well as the extent to which future changes in assumptions or actual experience different from that assumed may affect the measurement of the obligation and cost. In addition, the sensitivity information may assist users in understanding the relative significance of an employer's cost-sharing policy as encompassed by the employer's substantive plan.

355. Sensitivity disclosures were initially proposed in accounting for pension costs. However, the Board ultimately decided not to require those disclosures for pensions because the cost of providing that information was viewed as outweighing the

benefits to users. The Board concluded that the need for sensitivity information is more compelling for postretirement health care measurements. Financial statement users are considerably less familiar with postretirement health care measurements than with pension measurements and with the subjectivity of the health care cost trend rate and the significant effect that assumption may have on measurement of the postretirement health care obligation. The Board acknowledges that the effects of percentage-point changes are not linear but concluded that the significance of the sensitivity disclosure outweighs concerns about users erroneously extrapolating from the amounts disclosed.

356. Some Board members believe the volume of disclosures required by this Statement is excessive and further contributes to the already extensive disclosures required in general-purpose financial statements. They believe that at some point the sheer volume of all required disclosures may overwhelm users' ability to assimilate information and focus on the more important matters. In particular, those Board members do not support the required sensitivity disclosures because they highlight only one aspect of the postretirement benefit obligation and cost. Similar sensitivity requirements could be imposed for other aspects of this Statement's requirements and, for that matter, any accounting estimate. They are also concerned that sensitivity disclosures may confuse or mislead users who attempt to use the information to make their own estimates of measures of the obligation and cost in different scenarios, without realizing the limitations of the disclosure.

Two or More Plans

357. Under certain circumstances, this Statement permits combining two or more *unfunded* plans for financial accounting and reporting purposes. Plans that provide different benefits to the same group of participants may be combined. For example, an employer may have separate medical care, dental care, and eye care plans that provide benefit coverage to all retirees of the company. Similarly, an employer may combine two or more unfunded plans that provide the same benefits to different groups of plan participants. For example, an employer may have identical postretirement medical care plans at each of its operating locations. This Statement permits combining plans in those situations because the differences in the plans are not substantive. Combining information in those cases results in combined measurements for accounting and disclosure purposes.

358. The Board concluded that an employer with one well-funded plan and another less well funded or unfunded plan is in a different position than an employer with similar obligations and assets in a single plan. Netting the plan assets of one plan against the net unfunded obligation of another would be an inappropriate disclosure of the unfunded obligation if those assets cannot be used to settle that obligation. That conclusion is consistent with existing generally accepted accounting principles that generally preclude offsetting assets and liabilities unless a right of setoff exists. The Exposure Draft proposed separate disclosure by over- and underfunded plans. However, the Board concluded that limiting the requirement for separate disclosure to the accumulated postretirement benefit obligation and the fair value of plan assets for plans with assets less than the accumulated postretirement benefit obligation (underfunded plans) would provide satisfactory information about the financial condition of an employer's plans and would reduce the cost of providing the required disclosures.

Different Accounting for Certain Small Employers

359. The 1985 FASB Exposure Draft, *Employers' Accounting for Pensions,* recognized that the cost of compliance with a pension standard was relatively greater for small employers than for large employers and more likely to exceed the perceived benefits. In that Exposure Draft, the Board tentatively concluded that the different relative costs and benefits might justify reduced disclosure requirements.

360. However, the Board ultimately concluded that the measurement of pension costs and recognition of pension liabilities should not differ for small or nonpublic employers, in part because evidence from users of financial statements of those employers did not support a different approach. Further, in the Board's view, the existence of a separate set of measurement requirements or a range of alternatives for certain employers probably would not reduce costs significantly, but would add complexity and reduce the comparability and usefulness of financial statements.

361. Similarly, the Board does not believe that postretirement benefit plans for small employers are sufficiently different from the plans of larger employers to warrant fundamentally different measurement and recognition or disclosure requirements. Although the costs of applying this Statement may be relatively higher for small employers, the postretirement benefit obligations of those employers are no different in nature from the postretirement benefit obligations of larger employers. The measurement provisions and effective date of this Statement take into account the data limitations of certain employers and the cost of measuring expected postretirement benefit

costs. Paragraph 38 provides for the use of claims experience of other employers in developing current per capita claims cost. Paragraph 41 permits the use of certain alternative approaches to developing assumed per capita claims cost. Therefore, the Board concluded that the requirements of this Statement should apply to all employers.

362. The Exposure Draft proposed a 2-year delay in the effective date for nonpublic employers whose plans all had fewer than 100 participants. Respondents generally agreed with the proposed delay in the effective date, although some suggested that the size criterion be increased to encompass larger groups of plan participants. Those respondents were concerned about the availability of data and the general lack of experience in measuring the postretirement benefit obligations for smaller plan populations.

363. The effective date of this Statement is delayed 2 years for those nonpublic employers whose plans in the aggregate have fewer than 500 participants. The size criterion was increased in response to the concerns expressed by respondents. The Board concluded that small employers and the professionals serving those employers may need additional time to obtain and evaluate the necessary data including, perhaps, tailoring data collected by actuaries or insurers for use in developing the assumed per capita claims cost by age. The Board concluded that a delayed effective date is a practical and appropriate means for facilitating adoption of this Statement by those employers.

Different Accounting for Certain Industries

364. For some employers subject to certain types of regulation (rate-regulated enterprises) or for employers that have certain types of government contracts for which reimbursement is a function of cost based on cash disbursements, the effects of the requirement to accrue the cost of postretirement benefits (the difference between the cost accrued and the pay-as-you-go cost for a period) may not be recoverable currently. The Board recognizes the practical concerns of those employers but concluded that the cost of a promise to provide postretirement benefits to qualifying employees is not changed by the circumstances described. The Board concluded that this Statement should include no special provisions for those employers. For some rate-regulated enterprises, FASB Statement No. 71, *Accounting for the Effects of Certain Types of Regulation,* may require that the difference between net periodic postretirement benefit cost as defined in this Statement and amounts of postretirement benefit cost considered for rate-making purposes be recognized as an asset or a liability created by the actions of the regulator.

Those actions of the regulator change the timing of recognition of net periodic postretirement benefit cost as an expense; they do not otherwise affect the requirements of this Statement.

Other Situations and Types of Plans

Contracts with Insurance Companies

365. The Board concluded that some contracts with insurance companies are in substance forms of investments and that the use of those funding arrangements should not affect the accounting principles for determining an employer's net periodic postretirement benefit cost. If those contracts have features linked with the insurance company's possible future obligation to pay benefits, their fair values may be difficult or impossible to determine. Although the Board concluded that fair value should be the measurement basis for all types of investments, it acknowledges that for some contracts the best available estimate of fair value may be contract value.

366. The Board recognizes that, except for single-premium life insurance contracts, there are few, if any, contracts at the present time that unconditionally obligate an insurance company to provide most forms of postretirement benefits. However, some insurance contracts, such as single-premium, nonparticipating life insurance contracts, do effectively transfer the primary obligation for payment of benefits from the employer (or the plan) to the insurance company. In those circumstances, the premium paid for the benefits attributed to the current period is an appropriate measure of postretirement benefit cost for that period. The Board concluded that the purchase of a nonparticipating insurance contract is a settlement of a postretirement benefit obligation rather than an investment.

367. Under some insurance contracts, the purchaser (either the plan or the employer) acquires the right to participate in the investment performance or experience of the insurance company (participating contracts). Under those contracts, if the insurance company has favorable experience, the purchaser receives dividends. For example, if the insurance company's investment return is better than anticipated, or perhaps if actual experience related to mortality or other assumptions is favorable, the purchaser will receive dividends that reduce the cost of the contract.

368. Participating contracts have some of the characteristics of an investment. However, the employer is as fully relieved of the obligation as with a nonparticipating contract, and a separate actuarial computation ordinarily would not be performed. The Board concluded that, except as indicated in

paragraphs 369, 370, and 374, it would be appropriate to treat a participating contract the same as a nonparticipating contract and to exclude the benefits covered from measures of the accumulated postretirement benefit obligation.

369. The Board was concerned that a participating contract could be structured in such a way that the premium would be significantly in excess of the cost of nonparticipating contracts because of the expectation of future dividends. If the full amount of the premium were recognized as service cost in the year paid and dividends were recognized as return on plan assets when received, the resulting measures of postretirement benefit cost would be unrelated to benefits earned by employees. If the employer had the ability to influence the timing of dividends, it would then be possible to shift cost among periods without regard to underlying economic events. The Board concluded that part of a participating contract (the participation right) is in substance an investment that should be recognized as an asset.

370. The Board concluded that, consistent with the measurement of other assets, the participation right should be measured at fair value in periods subsequent to its acquisition to the extent that fair value can be reasonably determined. The Board recognizes, however, that some participating contracts may not provide a basis for a better estimate of fair value than that provided by amortized cost and concluded that, in that situation, amortized cost should be used. That conclusion is not intended to permit use of amortized cost if that amount is in excess of net realizable value.

371. When it addressed employers' accounting for pensions, the Board was advised that the information needed to treat insurance contracts purchased from an insurance company affiliated with the employer as investments (that is, to include those contracts and covered benefits in plan assets and the accumulated postretirement benefit obligation, respectively) was not available and would not be cost beneficial to develop. The Board expects that also to be true for postretirement benefits. Therefore, this Statement requires only contracts purchased from a captive insurance subsidiary, and contracts purchased from an insurance company when there is reasonable doubt whether the insurance company will meet its obligations under the contract, to be treated as investments. However, because an employer remains indirectly at risk if insurance contracts are purchased from an affiliate, the Board concluded that disclosure of the approximate amount of annual benefits covered by those contracts should be required.

Insurance contracts used in settlements

372. As discussed in paragraph 368, an employer is as fully relieved of the accumulated postretirement benefit obligation by the purchase of a participating contract as it is by the purchase of a nonparticipating contract. Consequently, except as discussed in paragraphs 369 and 374, the Board concluded that it would be appropriate to treat a participating contract the same as a nonparticipating contract and to consider purchases of participating contracts as settlements of accumulated postretirement benefit obligations.

373. The Board recognizes that it is difficult to determine the extent to which a participating contract exposes the purchaser to the risk of unfavorable experience, which would be reflected in lower than expected future dividends or failure to recover the cost of the participation right. The Board also recognizes that under some insurance contracts described as participating, the purchaser might remain subject to all or most of the same risks and rewards of future experience that would have existed had the contract not been purchased. The Board also is aware that some participating contracts may require or permit payment of additional premiums if experience is unfavorable. The Board concluded that if a participating contract requires or permits payment of additional premiums because of experience losses, or if the substance of the contract is such that the purchaser retains all or most of the related risks and rewards, the purchase of that contract does not constitute a settlement.

374. If the purchase of a participating contract constitutes a settlement for purposes of this Statement, recognition of a previously unrecognized net gain or loss is required (paragraphs 93 and 94) except for settlement of a small portion of the accumulated postretirement benefit obligation (paragraph 95). However, the possibility of a subsequent loss is not completely eliminated with a participating contract because realization of the participation right is not assured. Because of the continuing risk of the participation right, this Statement requires that the maximum gain subject to recognition from a settlement (paragraph 94) be reduced by an amount equal to the cost of the participation right before determining the full or pro rata portion of that maximum gain (paragraph 93) to be recognized.

Multiemployer Plans

375. Generally, the employers that participate in multiemployer postretirement benefit plans are similar, in terms of both nature and industry affiliation, to employers that participate in multiem-

ployer pension plans. Although the plans provide defined benefits, they typically require a defined contribution from participating employers. Consequently, an employer's obligation to a multiemployer plan may be changed by events affecting other participating employers and their employees.

376. At present in the United States, the consequences of an employer's withdrawal from a multiemployer postretirement benefit plan are different from an employer's withdrawal from a multiemployer pension plan. In addition to any contractual requirements, withdrawal from a multiemployer pension plan is governed by the Multiemployer Pension Plan Amendments Act of 1980. An employer withdrawing from a multiemployer postretirement benefit plan is currently only subject to any contractual requirements.

377. In a multiemployer setting, eligibility for benefits is defined by the plan; retired employees continue to receive benefits whether or not their former employers continue to contribute to the plan. On the other hand, plan participants not yet eligible for benefits may lose accumulated postretirement benefits if their current or former employer withdraws from a plan unless they take or have a job with other employers who participate in the plan. While the plan may have the option of cancelling the accrued service credits that apply toward the required service, within the bargaining unit, of plan participants who were employed by a withdrawing employer and who become or are employed by another participating employer, that rarely occurs because of the difficulty of matching employees to specific employers. For example, in certain industries, an employee may work for more than one employer in a single day and different employers on different days, making it difficult to associate any portion of that employee's past service with a specific employer.

378. The Board considered the substantive differences between a multiemployer plan and a single-employer plan and concluded that separate disclosure for the two types of plans would enhance the understandability and usefulness of the information. This Statement requires disclosures that provide descriptive information about multiemployer plans and the cost recognized for the period. In some situations, employers participating in a multiemployer plan that provides health and welfare benefits to active employees and retirees may be unable to distinguish the portion of their required contribution that is attributable to postretirement benefits. In those situations, the amount of the aggregate contribution to the general health and welfare benefit plan is to be disclosed. The Board also noted that the provisions of FASB Statement No. 5, *Accounting for Contingencies,*

apply when additional liabilities, such as a withdrawal liability or increased contribution pursuant to a plan's "maintenance of benefits" clause, are probable and should be recognized, or are reasonably possible and, therefore, should be disclosed.

Multiple-Employer Plans

379. Some plans to which two or more unrelated employers contribute are not multiemployer plans. Rather, they are in substance more like aggregations of single-employer plans than like multiemployer plans. In a multiple-employer plan, the plan terms are defined by each participating employer. Whereas an employer's obligation to a multiemployer plan may be changed by events affecting other participating employers and their employees, an employer's accumulated postretirement benefit obligation in a multiple-employer plan is unchanged by those events. Therefore, the Board concluded that for purposes of this Statement, multiple-employer plans should be considered single-employer plans rather than multiemployer plans and each employer's accounting should be based on its respective interest in the plan.

Postretirement Benefit Plans outside the United States

380. The Board understands that employer-provided postretirement benefits currently are not prevalent outside the United States. In countries where those plans are provided, the Board believes that this Statement should be applied. The Board is not aware of extraordinary problems arising from the application of Statement 87 to foreign plans, and those requirements are based on actuarial calculations and assumptions similar to those needed to apply this Statement. Therefore, the provisions of this Statement are equally applicable to postretirement benefit plans in the United States and in other countries.

381. The Board concluded, however, that practical problems could arise in communicating the requirements of and obtaining the information necessary for initial application of this Statement to plans outside the United States. The Board concluded that allowing an extra two years before application is required would give employers time to make necessary arrangements in an orderly manner and would reduce the cost of transition. Unless the accumulated postretirement benefit obligation of the plans outside the United States is significant relative to the accumulated postretirement benefit obligation for all of an employer's postretirement benefit plans, the Board concluded that disclosures for those plans could be combined with disclosures for plans in the United States.

Defined Contribution Plans

382. The Board concluded that in most cases the formula in a defined contribution plan unambiguously assigns contributions to periods of employee service. The employer's present obligation under the terms of the plan is fully satisfied when the contribution for the period is made, provided that costs (defined contributions) are not being deferred and recognized in periods after the related service period of the individual to whose account the contributions are to be made. The Board concluded that defined contribution plans are sufficiently different from defined benefit plans that disclosures about the two types of plans should not be combined. The disclosures about defined contribution plans required by this Statement are limited to a description of the plan, the basis for determining contributions, the nature and effect of significant matters affecting comparability of information presented, and the cost recognized during the period.

Business Combinations

383. Opinion 16 requires that, in a business combination accounted for as a purchase, an acquiring company allocate the cost of an acquired company to the assets acquired and the obligations assumed. Paragraph 88 of that Opinion sets forth general guides for assigning amounts to the individual assets acquired and liabilities assumed, and includes in that list liabilities and accruals, such as deferred compensation, measured at the present value of the amounts to be paid determined at appropriate current interest rates. Practice has been mixed, with most acquiring companies assigning no value to those postretirement benefit obligations.

384. This Statement amends Opinion 16 to clarify that, in a business combination accounted for as a purchase, the purchaser recognize a postretirement benefit obligation (asset) for any assumed accumulated postretirement benefit obligation in excess of (less than) plan assets. That obligation (asset) is to be measured using the assumptions that reflect the purchaser's assessment of relevant future events. The terms of the substantive plan as determined by the purchaser may differ from the acquired company's plan if the criteria set forth in paragraph 24 for defining the substantive plan that is the basis of the accounting are satisfied. The Board concluded that those criteria apply equally in establishing an obligation that is assumed and an obligation that arises from the exchange of benefits for employee service.

385. Improvements to the acquired company's plan that are attributed to employee service prior to the date the business combination is consummated and that are conditions of the purchase agreement are not to be accounted for as prior service cost, but as part of the purchase agreement. Other improvements to the plan that are not part of the purchase agreement are to be accounted for as prior service cost to the extent they are attributable to employees' prior service pursuant to this Statement. If it is expected that the plan will be terminated or curtailed, the effects of those actions should be reflected in measuring the accumulated postretirement benefit obligation.

386. The Board concluded that measurement of the unfunded or overfunded accumulated postretirement benefit obligation defined by this Statement generally is consistent with measurement of a pension benefit obligation (or asset) assumed in a business combination accounted for as a purchase pursuant to paragraph 88 of Opinion 16, as amended by paragraph 75 of Statement 87. One result of the accounting required by this Statement is that the effects of plan amendments and gains and losses of the acquired company's plan that occurred before the acquisition are not a part of future postretirement benefit cost of the acquiring company. That is consistent with purchase accounting as defined by Opinion 16, which specifies that a new basis of accounting reflect the bargained (fair) value of assets acquired and liabilities assumed whether or not those values were previously reflected in the acquired company's financial statements.

387. The Board concluded that no recognition of additional liabilities for multiemployer plans should be required under Opinion 16 unless conditions exist that make an additional liability probable. The Board was not convinced that there ordinarily is an obligation for future contributions to a multiemployer plan or that recognition of any contractual withdrawal liability would provide useful information about such an obligation, absent a probable withdrawal.

Effective Dates

388. The Exposure Draft proposed that this Statement generally be effective for fiscal years beginning after December 15, 1991. Most respondents urged the Board to delay the proposed effective date for at least one year because of their concerns about the availability and reliability of data necessary to measure employers' postretirement benefit obligations and cost. Other respondents noted the significant improvement to financial statements resulting from adoption of the accounting required by this Statement and suggested accelerating the effective date.

389. The Board decided to allow more than the normal amount of time between issuance of this Statement and its required application to give employers

and their advisors time to assimilate the requirements and to obtain the information required. The Board concluded that an additional one-year delay in the general effective date to fiscal years beginning after December 15, 1992, is adequate for those purposes. As noted previously, the Board also allowed an addi- tional two years before employers are required to apply the provisions of this Statement to plans outside the United States and before certain small employers are required to apply those provisions. Paragraph 267 discusses the effective date for the amendment of Opinion 12.

Appendix B

COMPARISON OF EMPLOYERS' ACCOUNTING FOR OTHER POSTRETIREMENT BENEFITS WITH EMPLOYERS' ACCOUNTING FOR PENSIONS

390. This appendix provides a summary comparison of the major provisions of this Statement with the provisions of FASB Statement No. 87, *Employers' Accounting for Pensions*.

	Other Postretirement Benefit Plan	**Non-pay-related Pension Plan**
Basis for accounting	Extant written plan unless (a) past practice of maintaining a consistent level of cost sharing or consistently increasing or decreasing the cost-sharing provisions of the plan, (b) communication of intended changes to cost-sharing policy,* or (c) past practice of regular increases in monetary benefits indicates substantive plan differs from extant written plan; substantive plan is basis for accounting	Extant written plan unless a past practice of regular increases in non-pay-related benefits or benefits under career-average-pay plan indicates substantive commitment differs from extant written plan; if substantive commitment is basis for accounting
Attribution method and period	Benefit/years-of-service approach that attributes expected benefit obligation (EBO)† for postretirement benefits to years of service to date employee attains full eligibility for benefits expected to be provided to employee; beginning of attribution period is employee's date of hire unless plan only grants credit for service from a later date, in which case benefits are generally attributed from beginning of that credited service period; equal amount of EBO attributed to each year of service in attribution period	Benefit/years-of-service approach that attributes EBO to years of service in accordance with plan benefit formula

If plan benefit formula results in disproportionate attribution to later years of service, equal amount of EBO attributed to years of service to date employee attains full eligibility for those benefits |

Note: This appendix compares employers' accounting for a *postretirement benefit plan* with employers' accounting for a *non-pay-related pension plan* because most postretirement benefit plans (in particular, postretirement health care plans) do not have benefit formulas that are pay related.

*Conditions (a) and (b) are subject to the criteria in paragraph 25.

†*Expected benefit obligation (EBO)*—actuarial present value (APV) as of a particular date of postretirement benefits expected to be paid to or for a current plan participant.

Recognition of net cost	Other Postretirement Benefit Plan	Non-pay-related Pension Plan
Service cost	Actuarial present value (APV) of EBO allocated to a period of employee service during attribution period	Same as for other postretirement benefits
Interest cost	Accrual of interest to reflect effects of passage of time on the accumulated benefit obligation (ABO)‡	Same as for other postretirement benefits
Actual return on plan assets	Actual return based on fair value (FV) of plan assets at beginning and end of period, adjusted for contributions and benefit payments	Same as for other postretirement benefits
Prior service cost	Plan initiations and amendments treated as retroactive except for plan initiations that specifically provide new benefits only in exchange for future service	Retroactive benefits defined by plan initiation or amendment
Measurement	Change in ABO for new or amended benefits granted to plan participants	Same as for other postretirement benefits
Amortization	Delayed; equal amount assigned to each future year of service to full eligibility date of each active plan participant	Delayed; equal amount assigned to each future year of service of each active plan participant
	Presumption of economic benefit in future years; can overcome presumption if evidence that *increasing* plan benefits has no future economic benefit for the employer	Same as for other postretirement benefits
	If all or almost all participants are fully eligible for benefits, their remaining life expectancy used, rather than future service period	If all or almost all participants are inactive, their remaining life expectancy used, rather than remaining service period
	Alternative approaches permitted that more rapidly reduce unrecognized cost	Same as for other postretirement benefits
Negative plan amendment	Immediate recognition of effect precluded; initially offsets existing unrecognized prior service cost and unrecognized transition obligation, balance is amortized	Same treatment as pension benefit increase

Gains and losses	Changes in ABO and plan assets from experience different from that assumed or from changes in assumptions	Same as for other postretirement benefits
	Gain-loss component of net cost consists of (a) differences between actual and expected return on plan assets, (b) amortization of unrecognized net gain or loss, and (c) amount immediately recognized as a gain or loss due to decision to temporarily deviate from substantive plan; asset gains/losses not reflected in market-related value (MRV)§ not required to be amortized	Except for (c), same as for other postretirement benefits
Recognition	Either immediate or delayed; if immediate, gains (losses) that do not offset previously recognized losses (gains) first reduce any unrecognized transition obligation (asset)	Either immediate (without offsetting any unrecognized transition obligation or asset) or delayed
Minimum amortization	Unrecognized net gain or loss in excess of 10 percent of greater of ABO or MRV of plan assets, amortized over average remaining service period of active plan participants	Same as for other postretirement benefits
	If all or almost all participants are inactive, amortized over their average remaining life expectancy rather than over remaining service period	Same as for other postretirement benefits
Definition of plan assets	Assets segregated and restricted for sole purpose of providing the defined benefit	Same as for other postretirement benefits
Recognition of minimum liability	Recognition of minimum liability not required	ABO (for all plan participants) in excess of FV of plan assets
		If additional liability recognized, contra amount recognized first as intangible asset up to amount of unrecognized prior service cost and unrecognized transition obligation, with any excess reported as reduction of equity

‡*Accumulated benefit obligation (ABO)*—the portion of EBO attributed to service rendered to a specified date. That portion for a pension plan with a benefit formula that is pay related is referred to as the *projected benefit obligation*. However, for a pension plan with a benefit formula that excludes the effects of future compensation levels, the accumulated benefit obligation is the appropriate measure of the pension obligation for comparative purposes throughout this appendix.

§*Market-related value (MRV)*—either fair market value or a calculated value that recognizes changes in fair value in a systematic and rational manner over not more than five years.

	Other Postretirement Benefit Plan	Non-pay-related Pension Plan
Business combinations	Measure obligation assumed as unfunded ABO for all plan participants, using purchaser's assumptions	Same as for other postretirement benefits
Transition		
Measurement	Over- or underfunded ABO for all plan participants	Same as for other postretirement benefits
Recognition	Either immediate or delayed	Delayed recognition required
	If immediate, amount attributable to plan initiation or benefit improvements adopted after December 21, 1990 treated as unrecognized prior service cost and amount attributable to purchase business combinations consummated after December 21, 1990 treated as retroactive adjustment of purchase price allocation	Immediate recognition precluded
	If delayed, amortized on straight-line basis over average remaining service period of active plan participants; cannot be less rapid than pay-as-you-go cost	Amortized on a straight-line basis over average remaining service period of active plan participants
	If amortization period determined above is less than 20 years, may use a 20-year period	If amortization period determined above is less than 15 years, may use a 15-year period
	If all or almost all participants are inactive, their average remaining life expectancy used	Same as for other postretirement benefits
Disclosure	Similar to disclosures required by Statement 87, supplemented by disclosure of descriptive information about the substantive plan, amortization of transition obligation or asset, assumed health care cost trend rate, and the effect on the measure of the ABO and aggregate of service and interest cost components of net periodic cost of a one-percentage-point increase in the health care cost trend rate, holding all other assumptions constant	Disclosures required by Statement 87
	Disclosures for plans in and outside the United States may be combined unless ABO for plans outside the United States is significant relative to aggregate ABO	Disclosures for plans in and outside the United States may not be combined unless those plans use similar economic assumptions

Appendix C

ILLUSTRATIONS

CONTENTS

Appendix C

ILLUSTRATIONS

Introduction

391. This appendix provides additional discussion and examples that illustrate the application of certain requirements of this Statement to specific aspects of employers' accounting for postretirement benefits other than pensions. The illustrations are referenced to the applicable paragraph(s) of the standards section of this Statement where appropriate. Certain illustrations have been included to facilitate the understanding and application of certain provisions of this Statement that apply in specific circumstances that may not be encountered frequently by employers. The fact patterns shown may not be representative of actual situations but are presented only to illustrate those requirements.

392. Throughout these illustrations the accumulated postretirement benefit obligation and service cost are assumed as inputs rather than calculated based on some underlying population. For simplicity, benefit payments are assumed to be made at the end of the year, service cost is assumed to include interest on the portion of the expected postretirement benefit obligation attributed to the current year, and interest cost is based on the accumulated postretirement benefit obligation as of the beginning of the year. For unfunded plans, benefits are assumed to be paid directly by the employer and are reflected as a reduction in the accrued postretirement benefit cost. The required disclosure of the reconciliation of the funded status of the plan is illustrated in many of the cases; however, for simplicity, the components of the accumulated postretirement benefit obligation are not included in those reconciliations as required by paragraph 74(c)(2). In many of the cases, application of the underlying concepts has been simplified by focusing on a single employee for purposes of

illustration. In practice, the determination of the full eligibility date and the measurement of postretirement benefit cost and obligation are based on employee groups and consider various possible retirement dates and the probabilities associated with retirement at each of those dates.

Illustration 1—Illustration of Terms

Case 1A—Expected Postretirement Benefit Obligation and Accumulated Postretirement Benefit Obligation

393. This Statement uses two terms to describe certain measures of the obligation to provide postretirement benefits: *expected postretirement benefit obligation* and *accumulated postretirement benefit obligation*. The expected postretirement benefit obligation for an employee is the actuarial present value as of a measurement date of the postretirement benefits expected to be paid to or for the employee, the employee's beneficiaries, and any covered dependents. Prior to the date on which an employee attains full eligibility for the benefits that employee is expected to earn under the terms of the postretirement benefit plan (the full eligibility date), the accumulated postretirement benefit obligation for an employee is a portion of the expected postretirement benefit obligation. On and after the full eligibility date, the accumulated postretirement benefit obligation and the expected postretirement benefit obligation for an employee are the same. (Refer to paragraphs 20 and 21.) The following example illustrates the notion of the expected postretirement benefit obligation and the relationship between that obligation and the accumulated postretirement benefit obligation at various dates.

394. Company A's plan provides postretirement health care benefits to all employees who render at least 10 years of service and attain age 55 while in service. A 50-year-old employee, hired January 1, 1973 at age 30 and eligible for benefits upon attain-

ing age 55, is expected to terminate employment at age 62 and is expected to live to age 77. A discount rate of 8 percent is assumed.

At December 31, 1992, Company A estimates the expected amount and timing of benefit payments for that employee as follows:

Age	Expected Future Claims	Present Value at Age		
		50	53	55
63	$ 2,796	$1,028	$1,295	$1,511
64	3,093	1,052	1,326	1,547
65	856	270	339	396
66	947	276	348	406
67	1,051	284	357	417
68	1,161	291	366	427
69	1,282	297	374	436
70	1,425	306	385	449
71	1,577	313	394	460
72	1,744	321	404	471
73	1,934	329	415	484
74	2,137	337	424	495
75	2,367	346	435	508
76	2,620	354	446	520
77	3,899	488	615	717
	$28,889	$6,292	$7,923	$9,244

395. The expected and accumulated postretirement benefit obligations at December 31, 1992 (age 50) are $6,292 and $5,034 (20/25 of $6,292), respectively. An equal amount of the expected postretirement benefit obligation is attributed to each year of service from the employee's date of hire to the employee's full eligibility date (age 55) (paragraphs 43 and 44). Therefore, when the employee is age 50, the accumulated postretirement benefit obligation is measured as 20/25 of the expected postretirement benefit obligation, as the employee has rendered 20 years of the 25-year credited service period. Refer to Case 1B (paragraphs 397-408) for additional illustrations on the full eligibility date and Case 1C (paragraphs 409-412) for additional illustrations on attribution.

396. Assuming no changes in health care costs or other circumstances, the accumulated postretirement benefit obligation at December 31, 1995 (age 53) is $7,289 (23/25 of $7,923). At the end of the employee's 25th year of service and thereafter, the expected postretirement benefit obligation and the accumulated postretirement benefit obligation are equal. In this example, at December 31, 1997, when the employee is 55 and fully eligible for benefits, the accumulated and expected postretirement benefit obligations are $9,244. At the end of the 26th year of service (December 31, 1998) when the employee is 56, those obligations are $9,984 ($9,244 plus interest at 8 percent for 1 year).

Case 1B—Full Eligibility Date

397. The *full eligibility date* (paragraph 21) is the date at which an employee has rendered all of the service necessary to have earned the right to receive all of the benefits expected to be received by that employee under the terms of the postretirement benefit plan. Therefore, the present value of all of the benefits expected to be received by or on behalf of an employee is attributed to the employee's credited service period, which ends at the full eligibility date. Determination of an employee's full eligibility date is affected by plan terms that provide incremental benefits expected to be received by the employee for additional years of service, unless those incremental benefits are trivial. Determination of the full eligibility date is *not* affected by an employee's current dependency status or by plan terms that define when benefit payments commence. The following examples (paragraphs 398-408) are presented to assist in understanding the full eligibility date.

Plans that provide incremental benefits for additional years of service

Graded benefit formula

398. Some plans have benefit formulas that define different benefits for different years of service. To illustrate, assume a plan in which the percentage of

postretirement health care coverage to be provided by an employer is defined by groups of years of service. The plan provides 20 percent postretirement health care coverage for 10 years of service after age 35, 50 percent for 20 years of service after age 35, 70 percent for 25 years of service after age 35, and 100 percent for 30 years of service after age 35. The full eligibility date for an employee who was hired at age 35 and is expected to retire at age 62 is at age 60. At that date the employee has rendered 25 years of service after age 35 and is eligible to receive a benefit of 70 percent health care coverage after retirement. The employee receives no additional benefits for the last two years of service.

Pay-related plans

399. Some plans may base the amount of benefits or level of benefit coverage on employees' compensation, for example, as a percentage of their final pay. To the extent the plan's postretirement benefit formula defines benefits wholly or partially as a function of future compensation (that is, the plan provides incremental benefits for additional years of service when it is assumed that final pay will increase), determination of the full eligibility date for an employee is affected by those additional years of service the employee is expected to render (paragraph 21). In addition, measurements of the postretirement benefit obligation and service cost reflect the best estimate of employees' future compensation levels (paragraph 33).

400. For example, assume a plan provides life insurance benefits to employees who render 20 years of service and attain age 55 while in service; the benefit is equal to 20 percent of final pay. A 55-year-old employee, who currently earns a salary of $90,000, has worked 22 years for the company. The employee is expected to retire at age 60 and is expected to be earning $120,000 at that time. The employee is eligible for life insurance coverage under the plan at age 55, when the employee has met the age and service requirements. However, because the employee's salary continues to increase each year, the employee is not *fully eligible* for benefits until age 60 when the employee retires because the employee earns an incremental benefit for each additional year of service beyond age 55. That is, the employee earns an additional benefit equal to 20 percent of the increase in salary each year from age 55 to retirement at age 60 for service during each of those years.

Spousal coverage

401. Some postretirement benefit plans provide spousal or dependent coverage or both if the employee works a specified number of years beyond the date at which the employee attains eligibility for single coverage. For example, a postretirement health care plan provides single coverage to employees who work 10 years and attain age 50 while in service; the plan provides coverage for dependents if the employee works 20 years and attains age 60 while in service. Because the additional 10 years of service may provide an incremental benefit to employees, for employees expected to satisfy the age and service requirements and to have covered dependents during the period following the employee's retirement, their full eligibility date is the date at which they have both rendered 20 years of service and attained age 60 while in service. For employees not expected to have covered dependents after their retirement or who are not expected to render at least 20 years of service or attain age 60 while in service, or both, their full eligibility date is the date at which they have both rendered 10 years of service and attained age 50 while in service.

Single plan provides health care and life insurance benefits

402. Some postretirement benefit plans may have different eligibility requirements for different types of benefits. For example, assume a plan provides a postretirement death benefit of $100,000 to employees who render 20 or more years of service. Fifty percent health care coverage is provided to eligible employees who render 10 years of service, 70 percent coverage to those who render 20 years of service, and 100 percent coverage to those who render 30 years of service. Employees are eligible for the health care and death benefits if they attain age 55 while in service.

403. The full eligibility date for an individual hired at age 30 and expected to terminate employment at age 62 is the date on which that employee has rendered 30 years of service and attained age 55 while in service (age 60 in this example). At that date the employee is eligible for all of the benefits expected to be paid to or on behalf of that employee under the postretirement benefit plan ($100,000 death benefits and 100 percent health care coverage). The full eligibility date for an employee hired at age 37 and expected to retire at age 62 is the date on which that employee has rendered 20 years of service and attained age 55 while in service (age 57 in this example). At that date the employee is eligible for all of the benefits expected to be paid to or on behalf of that employee under the postretirement benefit plan ($100,000 death benefits and 70 percent health care coverage).

*Plans that provide benefits based on status
at date of termination*

404. Some postretirement benefit plans provide coverage for the spouse to whom an employee is married when the employee terminates service; that is, the marital status of an employee upon termination of employment determines whether single or spousal coverage is to be provided. In measuring the expected postretirement benefit obligation, consideration is given to factors such as when benefit coverage will commence, who will receive benefits (employee and any covered dependents), and the expected need for and utilization of benefit coverage. However, determination of an employee's full eligibility date is not affected by plan terms that define when payments commence or by an employee's current marital (or dependent) status (paragraph 21).

405. For example, assume a plan provides postretirement health care coverage to employees who render at least 10 years of service and attain age 55 while in service; health care coverage also is provided to employees' spouses at the date of the employees' retirement. A 55-year-old employee is single, has worked for the company for 30 years, and is expected to marry at age 59 and to retire at age 62. Although the employee is entitled to spousal coverage only if married at retirement, at age 55 the employee has earned the right to spousal coverage. The probability that the employee will be married when the employee retires is included in the actuarial assumptions developed to measure the expected postretirement benefit obligation for that plan participant. The full eligibility date (age 55 in this example) is not affected by that measurement assumption.

*Postretirement benefits to be received
by disabled plan participants*

406. Some plans provide postretirement benefits to disabled employees. For example, Company B provides disability income and health care benefits to employees who become disabled while in service and have rendered 10 or more years of service. Retiree health care benefits are provided to employees who render 20 or more years of service and attain age 55 while in service. Employees receiving disability benefits continue to accrue "credit" toward their eligibility for retiree health care benefits. Under this plan, an employee hired at age 25, who becomes permanently disabled at age 40, is entitled to receive retiree health care benefits commencing at age 55 (in addition to any disability income benefits commencing at age 40) because that employee worked for Company B for more than 10 years before becoming disabled. Under the terms of the plan the employee is given credit for working to age 55 even

though no actual service is rendered by the employee after the disabling event occurs.

407. Because the employee is permanently disabled, the full eligibility date is accelerated to recognize the shorter period of service required to be rendered in exchange for the retiree health care benefits—in this case the full eligibility date is age 40, the date of the disabling event. For a similar employee who is temporarily disabled at age 40 but returns to work and attains age 55 while in service, the full eligibility date is age 55. Company B's expected postretirement benefit health care obligation for the permanently disabled employee is based on the employee's expected health care costs commencing at age 55 and is attributed ratably to that employee's active service to age 40.

408. Only some employees become and remain disabled. Therefore, in measuring the expected postretirement benefit obligation and in determining the attribution period for plan participants expected to become disabled, the probability and timing of a disabling event is considered in determining whether employees are likely to become disabled and whether they will be entitled to receive postretirement benefits.

Case 1C—Attribution

Attribution period

409. Paragraph 44 states that the beginning of the *attribution period* shall be the date of hire unless the plan's benefit formula grants credit only for service from a later date, in which case benefits generally shall be attributed from the beginning of that credited service period. For example, for a plan that provides benefit coverage to employees who render 30 or more years of service or who render at least 10 years of service and attain age 55 while in service, without specifying when the credited service period begins, the expected postretirement benefit obligation is attributed to service from the date of hire to the earlier of the date at which a plan participant has rendered 30 years of service or has rendered 10 years of service and attained age 55 while in service. However, for a plan that provides benefit coverage to employees who render at least 20 years of service after age 35, the expected postretirement benefit obligation is attributed to a plan participant's first 20 years of service after attaining age 35 or after the date of hire, if later than age 35.

410. For a plan with a benefit formula that attributes benefits to a credited service period that is nominal in relation to employees' total years of service prior to their full eligibility dates, an equal

amount of the expected postretirement benefit obligation for an employee is attributed to each year of that employee's service from date of hire to date of full eligibility for benefits. For example, a plan with a benefit formula that defines 100 percent benefit coverage for service for the year in which employees attain age 60 has a 1-year credited service period. If plan participants are expected to have rendered an average of 20 years of service at age 60, the credited service period is nominal in relation to their total years of service prior to their full eligibility dates. In that case, the service cost is recognized from date of hire to age 60.

Attribution pattern

411. For all plans, except those that "frontload" benefits, the expected postretirement benefit obligation is attributed ratably to each year of service in the attribution period (paragraph 43). That is, an equal amount of the expected postretirement benefit obligation is attributed to each year of service from the employee's date of hire or beginning of the credited service period, if later, to the employee's full eligibility date unless (a) the credited service period is nominal relative to the total years of service prior to the full eligibility date (paragraph 410) or (b) the benefit formula frontloads benefits (paragraph 412).

Frontloaded plans

412. Some plans may have a benefit formula that defines benefits in terms of specific periods of service to be rendered in exchange for those benefits but attributes all or a disproportionate share of the expected postretirement benefit obligation to employees' early years of service in the credited service period. An example would be a life insurance plan that provides postretirement death benefits of $250,000 for 10 years of service after age 45 and $5,000 of additional death benefits for each year of service thereafter up to age 65 (maximum benefit of $300,000). For plans that frontload the benefit, the expected postretirement benefit obligation is attributed to employee service in accordance with the plan's benefit formula (paragraph 43). In this example, the actuarial present value of a $25,000 death benefit is attributed to each of the first 10 years of service after age 45, and the actuarial present value of an additional $5,000 death benefit is attributed to each year of service thereafter up to age 65.

Case 1D—Individual Deferred Compensation Contracts

413. An employer may provide postretirement benefits to selected employees under individual contracts with specific terms determined on an individual-by-individual basis. Paragraph 13 of this Statement amends APB Opinion No. 12, *Omnibus Opinion—1967,* to attribute those benefits to the individual employee's years of service following the terms of the contract. Paragraphs 414-416 illustrate the application of paragraph 13 for individual deferred compensation contracts.

Contract provides only prospective benefits

414. A company enters into a deferred compensation contract with an employee at the date of hire. The contract provides for a payment of $150,000 upon termination of employment following a minimum 3-year service period. The contract provides for a compensation adjustment for each year of service after the third year determined by multiplying $150,000 by the company's return on equity for the year. Also, each year after the third year of service, interest at 10 percent per year is credited on the amount due under the contract at the beginning of that year. Accordingly, a liability of $150,000 is accrued in a systematic and rational manner over the employee's first 3 years of service. Following the third year of service, the accrued liability is adjusted annually for accrued interest and the increased or decreased compensation based on the company's return on equity for that year. At the end of the third year and each subsequent year of the employee's service, the amount accrued equals the then present value of the benefit expected to be paid in exchange for the employee's service rendered to that date.

Contract provides retroactive benefits

415. A company enters into a contract with a 55-year-old employee who has worked 5 years for the company. The contract states that in exchange for past and future services and for serving as a consultant for 2 years after the employee retires, the company will pay an annual pension of $20,000 to the employee, commencing immediately upon the employee's retirement. It is expected that the future benefits to the employer from the consulting services will be minimal. Consequently, the actuarial present value of a lifetime annuity of $20,000 that begins at the employee's expected retirement date is accrued at the date the contract is entered into because the employee is fully eligible for the pension benefit at that date.

416. If the terms of the contract described in paragraph 415 had stated that the employee is entitled to the pension benefit only if the sum of the employee's age and years of service equal 70 or more at the date of retirement, the employee would be fully eligible for the pension benefit at age 60, after rendering 5 more years of service. The actuarial present value of a lifetime annuity of $20,000 that

begins at the expected retirement date would be accrued in a systematic and rational manner over the 5-year period from the date the contract is entered into to the date the employee is fully eligible for the pension benefit.

Illustration 2—Delayed Recognition and Reconciliation of Funded Status

417. Pursuant to the provisions of this Statement, the recognition of certain changes affecting measurement of the accumulated postretirement benefit obligation or the fair value of plan assets may be delayed. Those changes include plan amendments (paragraph 51) and gains and losses due to experience different from that assumed or from changes in assumptions (paragraph 56). Information about the effect of the changes that have been afforded delayed recognition is provided through disclosure of the reconciliation of the funded status of a plan to the accrued or prepaid postretirement benefit cost recognized in the employer's statement of financial position (paragraph 74(c)). The following cases (2A-2E, paragraphs 418-429) show how events that change the accumulated postretirement benefit obligation are reflected in that reconciliation.

Case 2A—Unrecognized Obligation at Date of Transition

418. For an unfunded plan with an accumulated postretirement benefit obligation of $600,000 at the date of transition (January 1, 1993), the reconciliation of the funded status of the plan with the

amount shown in the statement of financial position as of that date is as follows:

Accumulated postretirement benefit obligation	$(600,000)[a]
Plan assets at fair value	0
Funded status	(600,000)
Transition obligation at January 1, 1993	600,000
(Accrued)/prepaid postretirement benefit cost	$ 0

[a]The actuarial present value of the obligation for fully eligible plan participants' expected postretirement benefits and the portion of the expected postretirement benefit obligation for other active plan participants attributed to service to December 31, 1992. For example, assume a plan provides benefits to employees who render at least 20 years of service after age 35. For employees age 45 with 10 years of service at December 31, 1992, the accumulated postretirement benefit obligation is 50% of the expected postretirement benefit obligation for those employees. For employees age 55 or older who have rendered 20 or more years of service at December 31, 1992 and retirees (collectively referred to as fully eligible plan participants), the accumulated postretirement benefit obligation is the full amount of the expected postretirement benefit obligation for those employees.

419. The transition obligation or asset is the difference between (a) the accumulated postretirement benefit obligation and (b) the fair value of plan assets plus any recognized accrued postretirement benefit cost or less any recognized prepaid postretirement benefit cost at the date of transition (paragraph 110). If, as in this case, advance contributions were not made and postretirement benefit cost was not accrued in prior periods, there is no

accrued or prepaid postretirement benefit cost recognized in the statement of financial position, and, therefore, the transition obligation is equal to the unfunded status ($600,000).

Unrecognized amounts after date of transition

420. After the date of transition, any change in the accumulated postretirement benefit obligation or the plan assets (other than contributions and benefit payments) either is unrecognized, due to the delayed recognition provisions of this Statement, or is included in net periodic postretirement benefit cost. Contributions by the employer increase plan assets and decrease the accrued postretirement benefit cost or increase the prepaid postretirement benefit cost, subject to the provision of paragraph 112 requiring recognition of an addi-

tional amount of the unrecognized transition obligation in certain situations. All changes in the accumulated postretirement benefit obligation and plan assets are reflected in the reconciliation. Using Case 2A as the starting point, the following reconciliations (Cases 2B-2E) illustrate the effect of changes in assumptions or changes in the plan on measurement of the accumulated postretirement benefit obligation.

Case 2B—Employer Accrual of Net Periodic Postretirement Benefit Cost

421. Benefit payments of $42,000 are made at the end of 1993. Changes in accrued postretirement benefit cost, accumulated postretirement benefit obligation, and unrecognized transition obligation in 1993 are summarized as follows:

	Accrued Postretirement Benefit Cost	Accumulated Postretirement Benefit Obligation	Unrecognized Transition Obligation
Beginning of year	$ 0	$(600,000)	$600,000
Recognition of components of net periodic postretirement benefit cost:			
Service cost	(32,000)	(32,000)	
Interest cost[a]	(48,000)	(48,000)	
Amortization of transition obligation[b]	(30,000)		(30,000)
	(110,000)	(80,000)	(30,000)
Benefit payments	42,000	42,000	
Net change	(68,000)	(38,000)	(30,000)
End of year	$ (68,000)	$(638,000)	$570,000

[a]Assumed discount rate of 8% applied to the accumulated postretirement benefit obligation at the beginning of the year.

[b]The transition obligation of $600,000 is amortized on a straight-line basis over 20 years. Illustration 3, Case 3B, (paragraphs 435-442) illustrates the constraint on delayed recognition of the transition obligation pursuant to paragraph 112.

422. The funded status of the plan at January 1, 1993 and December 31, 1993 is reconciled with the amount shown in the statement of financial position at those dates as follows:

	1/1/93	Net Change	12/31/93
Accumulated postretirement benefit obligation	$(600,000)	$(38,000)	$(638,000)
Plan assets at fair value	0		0
Funded status	(600,000)	(38,000)	(638,000)
Unrecognized transition obligation	600,000	(30,000)	570,000
Accrued postretirement benefit cost	$ 0	$(68,000)	$ (68,000)

Case 2C—Plan Amendment That Increases Benefits

423. The plan is amended on January 2, 1994, resulting in a $90,000 increase in the accumulated postretirement benefit obligation. The effects of plan amendments are reflected immediately in measurement of the accumulated postretirement benefit obligation; however, the effects of the amendment are not recog-

nized immediately in the financial statements, but rather are recognized on a delayed basis (paragraph 52).

424. Benefit payments of $39,000 are made at the end of 1994. Changes in accrued postretirement benefit cost, accumulated postretirement benefit obligation, unrecognized transition obligation, and unrecognized prior service cost in 1994 are summarized as follows:

	Accrued Postretirement Benefit Cost	Accumulated Postretirement Benefit Obligation	Unrecognized Transition Obligation	Unrecognized Prior Service Cost
Beginning of year	$ (68,000)	$(638,000)	$570,000	$ 0
Plan amendment		(90,000)		90,000
Recognition of components of net periodic postretirement benefit cost:				
Service cost	(30,000)	(30,000)		
Interest cost[a]	(58,240)	(58,240)		
Amortization of transition obligation	(30,000)		(30,000)	
Amortization of prior service cost[b]	(9,000)			(9,000)
	(127,240)	(178,240)	(30,000)	81,000
Benefit payments	39,000	39,000		
Net change	(88,240)	(139,240)	(30,000)	81,000
End of year	$(156,240)	$(777,240)	$540,000	$81,000

[a]Assumed discount rate of 8% applied to the accumulated postretirement benefit obligation at the beginning of the year and to the increase in that obligation for the unrecognized prior service cost at the date of the plan amendment [($638,000 × 8%) + ($90,000 × 8%)].

[b]As permitted by paragraph 53, prior service cost of $90,000 is amortized on a straight-line basis over the average remaining years of service to *full eligibility* for benefits of the active plan participants (10 years in this example).

425. The funded status of the plan at December 31, 1993 and 1994 is reconciled with the amount shown in the statement of financial position at those dates as follows:

	12/31/93	Net Change	12/31/94
Accumulated postretirement benefit obligation	$(638,000)	$(139,240)	$(777,240)
Plan assets at fair value	0		0
Funded status	(638,000)	(139,240)	(777,240)
Unrecognized prior service cost	0	81,000	81,000
Unrecognized transition obligation	570,000	(30,000)	540,000
Accrued postretirement benefit cost	$ (68,000)	$ (88,240)	$(156,240)

Case 2D—Negative Plan Amendment

426. The plan is amended on January 4, 1995, resulting in a $99,000 reduction in the accumulated postretirement benefit obligation. As with a plan amendment that increases benefits, the effect of a negative plan amendment (an amendment that decreases benefits) is reflected immediately in the measurement of the accumulated postretirement benefit obligation. The effects of the negative plan amendment are recognized by first reducing any existing unrecognized prior service cost and then any existing unrecognized transition obligation; the remainder is recognized in the financial statements on a delayed basis.

427. Benefit payments in 1995 are $40,000. Changes in accrued postretirement benefit cost, accumulated postretirement benefit obligation, unrecognized transition obligation, and unrecognized prior service cost in 1995 are summarized as follows:

	Accrued Postretirement Benefit Cost	Accumulated Postretirement Benefit Obligation	Unrecognized Transition Obligation	Unrecognized Prior Service Cost
Beginning of year	$(156,240)	$(777,240)	$540,000	$ 81,000
Plan amendment[a]		99,000	(18,000)	(81,000)
Recognition of components of net periodic postretirement benefit cost:				
Service cost	(30,000)	(30,000)		
Interest cost[b]	(54,259)	(54,259)		
Amortization of transition obligation[c]	(29,000)		(29,000)	
Amortization of prior service cost	0			0
	(113,259)	14,741	(47,000)	(81,000)
Benefit payments	40,000	40,000		
Net change	(73,259)	54,741	(47,000)	(81,000)
End of year	$(229,499)	$(722,499)	$493,000	$ 0

---

[a]Paragraph 55 requires that the effects of a plan amendment that reduces the accumulated postretirement benefit obligation be used first to reduce any existing unrecognized prior service cost, then any unrecognized transition obligation. Any remaining effects are recognized on a delayed basis over the remaining years of service to full eligibility for those plan participants who were active at the date of the amendment. If all or almost all of the plan participants were fully eligible at that date, the remaining effects should be recognized over the remaining life expectancy of those plan participants.

[b]Assumed discount rate of 8% applied to the accumulated postretirement benefit obligation at the beginning of the year and to the decrease in that obligation at the date of the plan amendment [($777,240 × 8%) − ($99,000 × 8%)].

[c]Unrecognized transition obligation of $522,000 ($540,000 − $18,000) is amortized on a straight-line basis over the 18 years remaining in the transition period.

428. The funded status of the plan at December 31, 1994 and 1995 is reconciled with the amount shown in the statement of financial position at those dates as follows:

	12/31/94	Net Change	12/31/95
Accumulated postretirement benefit obligation	$(777,240)	$ 54,741	$(722,499)
Plan assets at fair value	0		0
Funded status	(777,240)	54,741	(722,499)
Unrecognized prior service cost	81,000	(81,000)	0
Unrecognized transition obligation	540,000	(47,000)	493,000
Accrued postretirement benefit cost	$(156,240)	$(73,259)	$(229,499)

Case 2E—Change in Assumption

429. The assumed health care cost trend rates are changed at December 31, 1995, resulting in a $55,000 increase in the accumulated postretirement benefit obligation. The net loss that results from a change in the health care cost trend rates assumption is reflected immediately in the measurement of the accumulated postretirement benefit obligation. However, as with most other gains and losses, the effect of a change in assumption may be recognized in the financial statements either immediately or on a delayed basis, as long as the recognition method is applied consistently.

	Before Change	Net Loss	After Change
Accumulated postretirement benefit obligation	$(722,499)	$(55,000)	$(777,499)
Plan assets at fair value	0		0
Funded status	(722,499)	(55,000)	(777,499)
Unrecognized net loss[a]	0	55,000	55,000
Unrecognized transition obligation	493,000		493,000
Accrued postretirement benefit cost	$(229,499)	$ 0	$(229,499)

[a]This Statement generally does not require recognition of gains and losses in the period in which they arise (paragraphs 56-61). However, at a minimum, amortization of an unrecognized net gain or loss is required to be recognized as a component of net periodic postretirement benefit cost for a year if, as of the beginning of the year, the unrecognized net gain or loss exceeds 10 percent of the greater of the accumulated postretirement benefit obligation or the market-related value of plan assets. Applications of those provisions are included in Illustration 5 (paragraphs 455-471).

Illustration 3—Transition—Determination of Amount and Timing of Recognition

430. This Statement provides two options for recognizing the transition obligation or asset in the statement of financial position and in the statement of income. An employer can phase in recognition of the transition obligation (asset) over future periods, as illustrated in Case 3A (paragraphs 432-434). However, phasing in recognition of a transition obligation should not result in less rapid recognition than would have resulted under pay-as-you-go accounting. That is, after the transition date, the cumulative postretirement benefit cost accrued should not be less than cumulative benefit payments (paragraph 112). Case 3B (paragraphs 435-442) illustrates a situation in which recognition of the transition obligation is accelerated as a result of that constraint.

431. Alternatively, an employer can recognize the transition obligation (asset) immediately in net income of the period of the change. However, if immediate recognition is elected, the amount attributable to the effects of a plan initiation or any benefit improvements adopted after December 21, 1990 is treated as prior service cost and excluded from the transition amount immediately recognized. In addition, an employer who chooses to immediately recognize its transition obligation shall, in accounting for any purchase business combination consummated after December 21, 1990, include in the purchase price allocation the unfunded accumulated postretirement benefit ob-

ligation assumed (paragraph 111). Case 3C (paragraphs 443-448) illustrates a situation in which those limitations apply.

Case 3A—Measuring the Transition Obligation and Delayed Recognition

432. Company C adopts this Statement for its financial statements for the year beginning January 1, 1993. Prior to adopting this Statement, Company C accrued postretirement benefit costs and made contributions to the plan to the extent those contributions were tax deductible. At January 1, 1993, the company had accrued postretirement benefit cost of $150,000 and plan assets of $180,000.

433. The transition obligation or asset is measured as the difference between (a) the accumulated postretirement benefit obligation and (b) the fair value of plan assets plus any recognized accrued postretirement benefit cost or less any recognized prepaid postretirement benefit cost as of the date of transition (paragraph 110). Company C's transition obligation is determined as follows:

Accumulated postretirement benefit obligation	$(465,000)
Plan assets at fair value	180,000
Accumulated postretirement benefit obligation in excess of plan assets	(285,000)
Accrued postretirement benefit cost	150,000
Transition obligation	$(135,000)

434. Company C elects to delay recognition of its transition obligation. Paragraph 112 permits straight-line amortization of the transition obligation or asset over the average remaining service period of plan par-

ticipants or 20 years, if longer. Company C estimates the average remaining service period of its active employees who are plan participants at the date of transition to be 10 years. Therefore, Company C can elect to amortize its transition obligation of $135,000 on a straight-line basis over either the average remaining service period of 10 years or 20 years. That amortization (either $13,500 for 10 years or $6,750 for 20 years) is included as a component of net periodic postretirement benefit cost. However, amortization of the transition obligation is accelerated when the constraint on delayed recognition described in paragraph 112 applies. (Refer to Case 3B, paragraphs 435-442.)

Case 3B—Constraint on Delayed Recognition of Transition Obligation

435. At December 31, 1992, the accumulated (and unrecognized) postretirement benefit obligation and plan assets of a defined benefit postretirement plan sponsored by Company D are as follows:

Accumulated postretirement benefit obligation	$(255,000)
Plan assets at fair value	0
Transition obligation	$(255,000)

436. Company D adopts this Statement for the year beginning January 1, 1993. At December 31, 1992, Company D has no prepaid or accrued postretirement benefit cost (postretirement benefit cost in prior years was accounted for on a pay-as-you-go basis). The average remaining service period of active plan participants at the date of transition is 17 years. Since the average remaining service period is less than 20 years, Company D may elect to amortize the transition obligation over 20 years

rather than 17 years (paragraph 112); Company D elects the 17-year period.

437. Benefit payments in 1993 are $45,000.

Changes in accrued postretirement benefit cost, accumulated postretirement benefit obligation, and unrecognized transition obligation in 1993 are summarized as follows:

	Accrued Postretirement Benefit Cost	Accumulated Postretirement Benefit Obligation	Unrecognized Transition Obligation
Beginning of year	$ 0	$(255,000)	$255,000
Recognition of components of net periodic postretirement benefit cost:			
Service cost	(30,000)	(30,000)	
Interest cost[a]	(20,400)	(20,400)	
Amortization of transition obligation[b]	(15,000)		(15,000)
	(65,400)	(50,400)	(15,000)
Benefit payments	45,000	45,000	
Net change	(20,400)	(5,400)	(15,000)
End of year	$(20,400)	$(260,400)	$240,000

[a]An 8% discount rate is assumed.

[b]$255,000 ÷ 17 years = $15,000 per year.

438. The funded status of the plan at January 1, 1993 and December 31, 1993 is reconciled with the amount shown in the statement of financial position at those dates as follows:

	1/1/93	Net Change	12/31/93
Accumulated postretirement benefit obligation	$(255,000)	$ (5,400)	$(260,400)
Plan assets at fair value	0		0
Funded status	(255,000)	(5,400)	(260,400)
Unrecognized transition obligation	255,000	(15,000)	240,000
Accrued postretirement benefit cost	$ 0	$(20,400)	$ (20,400)

439. In 1994, benefit payments increase to $95,000 and service cost increases to $35,000. Changes in accrued postretirement benefit cost, accumulated postretirement benefit obligation, and unrecognized transition obligation in 1994 are summarized as follows:

	Accrued Postretirement Benefit Cost	Accumulated Postretirement Benefit Obligation	Unrecognized Transition Obligation
Beginning of year	$(20,400)	$(260,400)	$240,000
Recognition of components of net periodic postretirement benefit cost:			
Service cost	(35,000)	(35,000)	
Interest cost	(20,832)	(20,832)	
Amortization of transition obligation[c]	(18,768)		(18,768)
	(74,600)	(55,832)	(18,768)
Benefit payments	95,000	95,000	
Net change	20,400	39,168	(18,768)
End of year	$ 0	$(221,232)	$221,232

[c]Amortization of the transition obligation in 1994 includes straight-line amortization of $15,000 plus additional recognition of $3,768. The additional recognition is required because in 1994 cumulative benefit payments subsequent to the January 1, 1993 transition date exceed cumulative postretirement benefit cost accrued subsequent to that date (paragraph 112). The additional transition obligation required to be recognized ($3,768) is determined as follows:

	1993	1994
Benefit payments:		
1/1/93 to beginning of current year		$ 45,000
Current year	$45,000	95,000
Cumulative 1/1/93 to end of current year	$45,000	$140,000
Postretirement benefit cost recognized:		
1/1/93 to beginning of current year		$ 65,400
Current year prior to recognition of any additional amount pursuant to paragraph 112	$65,400	70,832
Cumulative 1/1/93 to end of current year before applying paragraph 112 constraint	65,400	136,232
Additional amount required to be recognized pursuant to paragraph 112	0	3,768
Cumulative 1/1/93 to end of current year	$65,400	$140,000

440. The objective of the constraint on delayed recognition of the transition obligation (paragraph 112) is to preclude slower recognition of postretirement benefit cost (as a result of applying the delayed recognition provisions of this Statement) than would have resulted under pay-as-you-go accounting for costs. An indication that the constraint may apply is the existence of a prepaid postretirement benefit cost after the date of transition for an enterprise that prior to the application of this Statement was on a pay-as-you-go basis of accounting for other postretirement benefits. For example, in paragraph 439, if the employer had not recognized the additional $3,768 of transition obligation, the employer would have had a prepaid postretirement benefit cost equal to that amount.

441. The funded status of the plan at December 31, 1993 and 1994 is reconciled with the amount shown in the statement of financial position at those dates as follows:

	12/31/93	Net Change	12/31/94
Accumulated postretirement benefit obligation	$(260,400)	$ 39,168	$(221,232)
Plan assets at fair value	0		0
Funded status	(260,400)	39,168	(221,232)
Unrecognized transition obligation	240,000	(18,768)	221,232^d
Accrued postretirement benefit cost	$ (20,400)	$ 20,400	$ 0

^dIn 1995, the straight-line amortization of the unrecognized transition obligation will be $14,749 ($221,232 ÷ 15 years remaining in the transition period).

442. Paragraph 113 states that if at the measurement date for the beginning of an employer's fiscal year it is expected that additional recognition of any remaining unrecognized transition obligation will be required pursuant to paragraph 112, amortization of the transition obligation for interim reporting purposes shall be based on the amount expected to be amortized for the year, except for the effects of applying the constraint in paragraph 112 for any settlement required to be accounted for pursuant to paragraphs 90-94. Those effects shall be recognized when the related settlement is recognized. The effects of changes during the year in the initial assessment of whether additional recognition of the unrecognized transition obligation will be required for the year shall be recognized over the remainder of the year. The amount of the unrecognized transition obligation to be recognized for a year shall be finally determined at the end of the year (or the measurement date, if earlier) based on the constraints on delayed recognition discussed in paragraph 112; any difference between the amortization of the transition obligation recognized during interim periods and the amount required to be recognized for the year shall be recognized immediately.

Case 3C—Limitation on Immediate Recognition of Transition Obligation

443. Company F plans to adopt this Statement for its financial statements for the year beginning January 1, 1993. Company F's postretirement defined benefit health care plan is presently accounted for on a pay-as-you-go basis.

444. On January 1, 1991, Company F acquires Company G and accounts for the business combination as a purchase pursuant to APB Opinion No. 16, *Business Combinations*. Company G has a postretirement health care plan that Company F agrees to combine with its own plan. Company F assumes the accumulated postretirement benefit obligation of Company G's plan as part of the acquisition agreement. However, at the date the business combination is consummated, no liability is recognized for the postretirement benefit obligation assumed.

445. On July 3, 1992, Company F amends its postretirement benefit plan to provide postretirement life insurance benefits to its employees; employees are given credit for their service prior to that date. At the date of the plan amendment, prior service cost is estimated at $250,000. Average remaining years of service to the full eligibility dates of the plan participants active at the date of the amendment is 25 years.

446. At December 31, 1992, the accumulated postretirement benefit obligation is $2,000,000; there are no plan assets or accrued postretirement benefit cost. On January 1, 1993, when Company F adopts this Statement, it elects to recognize immediately the transition obligation. Because the plan amendment occurred after December 21, 1990, Company F must treat the effect of the amendment as unrecognized prior service cost (paragraph 111). Company F elects to recognize prior service cost on a straight-line basis over the average remaining years of service to full eligibility of the active plan participants as permitted by paragraph 53. Therefore, at December 31, 1992, the remaining prior service cost to be recognized over those plan participants' *future* years of service to their full eligibility dates is $245,000 ($250,000 less $5,000 retroactively recognized for the period from July 3, 1992 to December 31, 1992).

447. Because the purchase business combination also occurred after December 21, 1990, Company F must retroactively reallocate the purchase price to the assets acquired and obligations assumed to reflect the postretirement benefit obligation assumed. Company F determines that the postretirement benefit obligation it assumed with the acquisition of Company G, measured as of the date of the acquisition, was $800,000. The cumulative effect on statements of income for the period January 1, 1991 to December 31, 1992 is the amortization of additional goodwill ($40,000), which Company F recognizes in

1993 as part of the effect of the change in accounting (paragraph 111).

448. On January 1, 1993, Company F recognizes on its statement of financial position goodwill of $760,000 and an obligation for postretirement benefits of $1,755,000 ($2,000,000 unfunded postretirement benefit obligation less $245,000 unrecognized prior service cost). The difference of $995,000 ($1,755,000 − $760,000) is recognized in the statement of income as the effect of an accounting change and comprises the following:

Consequences of events affecting accumulated postretirement benefit obligation other than the business combination and plan amendment	$950,000
Amortization of goodwill for prior purchase business combination	40,000
Amortization of prior service cost for prior plan amendment	5,000
Effect of accounting change	$995,000

The unrecognized prior service cost ($245,000) will be recognized on a delayed basis over the remaining 24.5-year amortization period for the plan participants active at the date of the amendment.

Illustration 4—Plan Amendments and Prior Service Cost

449. This Statement requires that, at a minimum, prior service cost arising from a plan initiation or plan amendment be recognized by assigning an equal amount of the prior service cost to each remaining year of service to the full eligibility date of each plan participant active at the date of the plan initiation or amendment (paragraph 52). Consistent use of an alternative amortization method that more rapidly reduces the unrecognized prior service cost is permitted (paragraph 53).

450. Company H has a postretirement benefit plan that provides benefits to employees who render at least 20 years of service after age 35. On January 2, 1994, Company H amends its postretirement benefit plan to increase the lifetime cap on benefits provided, resulting in unrecognized prior service cost of $750,000 (the increase in the accumulated postretirement benefit obligation as a result of the plan amendment). Amortization of that unrecognized prior service cost is illustrated in

Cases 4A and 4B (paragraphs 451-454).

Case 4A—Equal Amount Assigned to Each Future Year of Service to Full Eligibility Date

451. The determination of the amortization of prior service cost is based on remaining years of service prior to the full eligibility date of each plan participant active at the date of the amendment but not yet fully eligible for benefits. (Refer to the glossary for the definition of plan participant.) Future years of service of active employees who are not plan participants are excluded. Each remaining year of service prior to the full eligibility date of each active plan participant not yet fully eligible for benefits is assigned an equal share of the prior service cost (paragraph 52). Thus, the portion of prior service cost to be recognized in each of those future years is weighted based on the number of those plan participants expected to render service in each of those future years.

452. At the date of the amendment (January 2, 1994), Company H has 165 employees of whom 15 are fully eligible for benefits, 10 are under age 35, and 40 are expected to terminate before becoming eligible for any benefits. Because the 10 employees under age 35 have not met the age requirements to participate in the plan (only service after age 35 is credited) and 40 employees are not expected to receive benefits under the plan, those 50 employees are not considered to be plan participants and, therefore, are excluded from the calculation. The 15 fully eligible plan participants also are excluded from the calculation because they do not have to render any additional service to earn the added benefits. The remaining 100 employees have not yet earned the full amount of the benefits they are expected to earn under the plan. Those employees are expected to become fully eligible for those benefits over the next 20 years. Their remaining years of service to full eligibility for benefits is the basis for amortization of the prior service cost.

453. The following schedules illustrate the calculation of the expected remaining years of service prior to full eligibility (Schedule 1) and the amortization schedule for recognizing the prior service cost (Schedule 2). Employees hired after the date of the plan amendment or who attain age 35 after the date of the plan amendment do not affect the amortization nor do revised estimates of remaining years of service, except those due to a curtailment.

Schedule 1—Determination of expected remaining years of service prior to full eligibility as of January 2, 1994

Indiv.	Remaining Years of Service Prior to Full Elig.	1994	1995	1996	1997	1998	1999	2000	2001	2002	2003	2004	2005	2006	2007	2008	2009	2010	2011	2012	2013	Total Remaining Years of Service Prior to Full Elig.
A1-A4	1	4																				4
B1-B6	2	6	6																			12
C1-C5	3	5	5	5																		15
D1-D5	4	5	5	5	5																	20
E1-E7	5	7	7	7	7	7																35
F1-F5	6	5	5	5	5	5	5															30
G1-G9	7	9	9	9	9	9	9	9														63
H1-H7	8	7	7	7	7	7	7	7	7													56
I1-I5	9	5	5	5	5	5	5	5	5	5												45
J1-J5	10	5	5	5	5	5	5	5	5	5	5											50
K1-K4	11	4	4	4	4	4	4	4	4	4	4	4										44
L1-L8	12	8	8	8	8	8	8	8	8	8	8	8	8									96
M1-M8	13	8	8	8	8	8	8	8	8	8	8	8	8	8								104
N1-N5	14	5	5	5	5	5	5	5	5	5	5	5	5	5	5							70
O1-O4	15	4	4	4	4	4	4	4	4	4	4	4	4	4	4	4						60
P1-P3	16	3	3	3	3	3	3	3	3	3	3	3	3	3	3	3	3					48
Q1-Q4	17	4	4	4	4	4	4	4	4	4	4	4	4	4	4	4	4	4				68
R1-R3	18	3	3	3	3	3	3	3	3	3	3	3	3	3	3	3	3	3	3			54
S1-S2	19	2	2	2	2	2	2	2	2	2	2	2	2	2	2	2	2	2	2	2		38
T1	20	1	1	1	1	1	1	1	1	1	1	1	1	1	1	1	1	1	1	1	1	20
Service Years Rendered		100	96	90	85	80	73	68	59	52	47	42	38	30	22	17	13	10	6	3	1	932
Amortization Fraction		$\frac{100}{932}$	$\frac{96}{932}$	$\frac{90}{932}$	$\frac{85}{932}$	$\frac{80}{932}$	$\frac{73}{932}$	$\frac{68}{932}$	$\frac{59}{932}$	$\frac{52}{932}$	$\frac{47}{932}$	$\frac{42}{932}$	$\frac{38}{932}$	$\frac{30}{932}$	$\frac{22}{932}$	$\frac{17}{932}$	$\frac{13}{932}$	$\frac{10}{932}$	$\frac{6}{932}$	$\frac{3}{932}$	$\frac{1}{932}$	

Note: To determine total remaining years of service prior to full eligibility, consideration is given to the remaining number of years of service to the full eligibility date of each plan participant or group of plan participants active at the date of the plan amendment who is not yet fully eligible for benefits. For example, in 1994, individuals A1-A4 meet the company's age and service requirements for full eligibility for the benefits they are expected to receive under the plan. Although it may be expected that those employees will work beyond 1994, benefits are not attributed to years of service beyond their full eligibility date (paragraph 21). Refer to Case 4B, paragraph 454, for less complex amortization approaches.

Schedule 2—Amortization of unrecognized prior service cost

Year	Beginning-of-Year Balance	Amortization Rate	Amortization	End-of-Year Balance
1994	$750,000	100/932	$80,472	$669,528
1995	669,528	96/932	77,253	592,275
1996	592,275	90/932	72,425	519,850
1997	519,850	85/932	68,401	451,449
1998	451,449	80/932	64,378	387,071
1999	387,071	73/932	58,745	328,326
2000	328,326	68/932	54,721	273,605
2001	273,605	59/932	47,479	226,126
2002	226,126	52/932	41,845	184,281
2003	184,281	47/932	37,822	146,459
2004	146,459	42/932	33,798	112,661
2005	112,661	38/932	30,579	82,082
2006	82,082	30/932	24,142	57,940
2007	57,940	22/932	17,704	40,236
2008	40,236	17/932	13,680	26,556
2009	26,556	13/932	10,461	16,095
2010	16,095	10/932	8,047	8,048
2011	8,048	6/932	4,828	3,220
2012	3,220	3/932	2,414	806
2013	806	1/932	806	0

Case 4B—Straight-Line Amortization over Average Remaining Years of Service to Full Eligibility Date

454. To reduce the complexity and detail of the computations shown in Case 4A (paragraph 453, Schedules 1 and 2), alternative amortization approaches that recognize prior service cost related to plan amendments more rapidly may be applied if used consistently (paragraph 53). For example, if Company H (Case 4A) elects to use straight-line amortization of prior service cost over the average remaining years of service prior to full eligibility for benefits of the active plan participants (932 future service years ÷ 100 employees = 9.32 years), the amortization would be as follows:

Year	Beginning-of-Year Balance	Amortization	End-of-Year Balance
1994	$750,000	$80,472[a]	$669,528
1995	669,528	80,472	589,056
1996	589,056	80,472	508,584
1997	508,584	80,472	428,112
1998	428,112	80,472	347,640
1999	347,640	80,472	267,168
2000	267,168	80,472	186,696
2001	186,696	80,472	106,224
2002	106,224	80,472	25,752
2003	25,752	25,752	0

[a]$750,000 ÷ 9.32 years = $80,472.

Note: Under this approach, the first year's amortization is the same as the first year's amortization under the weighted remaining years of service method illustrated in Case 4A (paragraph 453, Schedule 2). Thereafter, the amortization pattern will differ.

Illustration 5—Accounting for Gains and Losses and Timing of Measurements

455. Gains and losses include changes in the amount of the accumulated postretirement benefit obligation or plan assets resulting from experience different from that assumed or changes in assump- tions (paragraph 56). This illustration demonstrates the effects of gains and losses in accounting for postretirement benefits for Company I from 1993 to 1995. Case 5A (paragraphs 457-461) illustrates the accounting for a loss resulting from changes in assumptions in measuring the accumulated postretirement benefit obligation. Case 5B

(paragraphs 462-464) illustrates the effect of a gain when the return on plan assets exceeds projections. Case 5C (paragraphs 465-467) illustrates the accounting in a year when both gains and losses are experienced.

456. Company I adopts this Statement for the fiscal year beginning January 1, 1993 and elects a December 31 measurement date (date at which the accumulated postretirement benefit obligation and plan assets are measured). Alternatively, as discussed in paragraph 72, the company could

choose a measurement date not earlier than September 30. The company's accumulated postretirement benefit obligation on December 31, 1992 is $6,000,000, and the plan is unfunded. Beginning in 1993, and unless otherwise noted, the company funds at the end of each year an amount equal to the benefits paid that year plus the service cost and interest cost for that year. For illustrative purposes, the following assumptions are used to project changes in the accumulated postretirement benefit obligation and plan assets during the period 1993-1995:

	1993	1994	1995
Discount rate	9.5%	9.0%	9.0%
Expected long-term rate of return on plan assets		10.0%	10.0%
Average remaining years of service of active plan participants	12	12	12

Case 5A—Loss on Obligation

457. The reconciliation of the funded status of Company I's postretirement benefit plan with the amount shown in the statement of financial position at the date of transition (January 1, 1993) follows:

	Actual 1/1/93
Accumulated postretirement benefit obligation	$(6,000,000)
Plan assets at fair value	0
Funded status	(6,000,000)
Unrecognized transition obligation	6,000,000
(Accrued)/prepaid postretirement benefit cost	$ 0

458. Pursuant to paragraph 112, Company I elects to amortize the unrecognized transition obligation over a 20-year period rather than the average remaining service period of active plan participants at the date of transition (12 years).

Projected changes in prepaid postretirement benefit cost, accumulated postretirement benefit obligation, unrecognized transition obligation, and plan assets in 1993 are summarized as follows:

	Prepaid Postretirement Benefit Cost	Accumulated Postretirement Benefit Obligation	Unrecognized Transition Obligation	Plan Assets
Beginning of year	$ 0	$(6,000,000)	$6,000,000	$ 0
Recognition of components of net periodic postretirement benefit cost:				
Service cost	(300,000)	(300,000)		
Interest cost	(570,000)	(570,000)		
Amortization of transition obligation	(300,000)		(300,000)	
	(1,170,000)	(870,000)	(300,000)	
Assets contributed to plan	1,500,000			1,500,000
Benefit payments from plan		630,000		(630,000)
Net change	330,000	(240,000)	(300,000)	870,000
End of year—projected	$ 330,000	$(6,240,000)	$5,700,000	$ 870,000

459. When Company I's plan assets and obligations are measured at December 31, 1993, the accumulated postretirement benefit obligation is $760,000 greater than had been projected (a loss occurs) because the discount rate declined to 9 percent and for various other reasons not specifically identified. Company I elects to amortize amounts in excess of the "corridor" over the average remaining service period of active plan participants.[a]

460. The change in the funded status of the plan at December 31, 1993 from amounts projected and the reconciliation of the funded status of the plan with the amount shown in the statement of financial position at that date follow:

	Projected 12/31/93	Net Loss	Actual 12/31/93
Accumulated postretirement benefit obligation	$(6,240,000)	$(760,000)	$(7,000,000)
Plan assets at fair value	870,000		870,000
Funded status	(5,370,000)	(760,000)	(6,130,000)
Unrecognized net loss		760,000	760,000
Unrecognized transition obligation	5,700,000		5,700,000
Prepaid postretirement benefit cost	$ 330,000	$ 0	$ 330,000

461. In addition to the funded status reconciliation, the 1993 financial statements include the following disclosure of the components of net periodic postretirement benefit cost (as required by paragraph 74(b)):

Service cost	$ 300,000
Interest cost	570,000
Amortization of transition obligation	300,000
Net periodic postretirement benefit cost	$1,170,000

Case 5B—Gain on Assets

462. Changes in prepaid postretirement benefit cost, accumulated postretirement benefit obligation, unrecognized transition obligation, unrecognized net loss, and plan assets are projected at the beginning of the year. That projection serves as the basis for interim accounting until a subsequent event occurs requiring remeasurement. The projection at the beginning of 1994 follows:

---

[a]Paragraph 59 states that, at a minimum, amortization of an unrecognized net gain or loss is included as a component of net periodic postretirement benefit cost if, as of the beginning of the year, that unrecognized net gain or loss exceeds 10 percent of the greater of the accumulated postretirement benefit obligation or market-related value of plan assets. As used herein, *amounts in excess of the corridor* refers to the portion of the unrecognized net gain or loss in excess of the greater of those defined amounts.

	Prepaid Postretirement Benefit Cost	Accumulated Postretirement Benefit Obligation	Unrecognized Transition Obligation	Unrecognized Net Loss	Plan Assets
Beginning of year	$ 330,000	$(7,000,000)	$5,700,000	$760,000	$ 870,000
Recognition of components of net periodic postretirement benefit cost:					
Service cost	(320,000)	(320,000)			
Interest cost	(630,000)	(630,000)			
Amortization of transition obligation	(300,000)		(300,000)		
Amortization of unrecognized net loss[a]	(5,000)			(5,000)	
Expected return on plan assets[b]	87,000				87,000
	(1,168,000)	(950,000)	(300,000)	(5,000)	87,000
Assets contributed to plan	1,650,000				1,650,000
Benefit payments from plan		700,000			(700,000)
Net change	482,000	(250,000)	(300,000)	(5,000)	1,037,000
End of year—projected	$ 812,000	$(7,250,000)	$5,400,000	$755,000	$1,907,000

[a]Refer to Schedule 2 (paragraph 469) for computation.

[b]Refer to Schedule 1 (paragraph 468) for computation.

463. When Company I's plan assets and obligations are measured at December 31, 1994, the fair value of the plan assets is $150,000 greater than expected (an experience gain) because market performance was better than the 10 percent return that was assumed. The change in the funded status of the plan at December 31, 1994 from amounts projected and the reconciliation of the funded status of the plan with the amount shown in the statement of financial position at that date follow:

	Projected 12/31/94	Net Gain	Actual 12/31/94
Accumulated postretirement benefit obligation	$(7,250,000)		$(7,250,000)
Plan assets at fair value	1,907,000	$ 150,000[c]	2,057,000
Funded status	(5,343,000)	150,000	(5,193,000)
Unrecognized net (gain) or loss	755,000	(150,000)	605,000
Unrecognized transition obligation	5,400,000		5,400,000
Prepaid postretirement benefit cost	$ 812,000	$ 0	$ 812,000

[c]Refer to Schedule 1 (paragraph 468) for computation.

464. The 1994 financial statements include the following disclosure of the components of net periodic postretirement benefit cost:

Service cost	$ 320,000
Interest cost	630,000
Actual return on plan assets[d]	(237,000)
Amortization of transition obligation	300,000
Net amortization and deferral[e]	155,000
Net periodic postretirement benefit cost	$1,168,000

[d]Refer to Schedule 3 (paragraph 470) for computation.

[e]Refer to Schedule 4 (paragraph 471) for computation.

Case 5C—Loss on Assets and Gain on Obligation

465. Projected changes in prepaid postretirement benefit cost, accumulated postretirement benefit obligation, unrecognized transition obligation, unrecognized net loss, and plan assets for 1995 are summarized as follows:

	Prepaid Postretirement Benefit Cost	Accumulated Postretirement Benefit Obligation	Unrecognized Transition Obligation	Unrecognized Net Loss	Plan Assets
Beginning of year	$ 812,000	$(7,250,000)	$5,400,000	$605,000	$2,057,000
Recognition of components of net periodic postretirement benefit cost:					
Service cost	(360,000)	(360,000)			
Interest cost	(652,500)	(652,500)			
Amortization of transition obligation	(300,000)		(300,000)		
Amortization of unrecognized net loss[a]	0			0	
Expected return on plan assets[b]	193,700				193,700
	(1,118,800)	(1,012,500)	(300,000)	0	193,700
Assets contributed to plan	1,912,500				1,912,500
Benefit payments from plan		900,000			(900,000)
Net change	793,700	(112,500)	(300,000)	0	1,206,200
End of year—projected	$1,605,700	$(7,362,500)	$5,100,000	$605,000	$3,263,200

[a]Refer to Schedule 2 (paragraph 469) for computation.

[b]Refer to Schedule 1 (paragraph 468) for computation.

466. When Company I's plan assets and obligations are measured at December 31, 1995, both an asset loss of $220,360 and a liability gain of $237,260 are determined. The change in the funded status of the plan at December 31, 1995 from amounts projected and the reconciliation of the funded status of the plan with the amount shown in the statement of financial position at that date follow:

	Projected 12/31/95	Net Gain/Loss	Actual 12/31/95
Accumulated postretirement benefit obligation	$(7,362,500)	$ 237,260	$(7,125,240)
Plan assets at fair value	3,263,200	(220,360)[c]	3,042,840
Funded status	(4,099,300)	16,900	(4,082,400)
Unrecognized net (gain) or loss	605,000	(16,900)	588,100
Unrecognized transition obligation	5,100,000		5,100,000
Prepaid postretirement benefit cost	$ 1,605,700	$ 0	$ 1,605,700

[c]Refer to Schedule 1 (paragraph 468) for computation.

467. The 1995 financial statements include the following disclosure of the components of net periodic postretirement benefit cost:

Service cost	$ 360,000
Interest cost	652,500
Actual loss on plan assets[d]	26,660
Amortization of transition obligation	300,000
Net amortization and deferral[e]	(220,360)
Net periodic postretirement benefit cost	$1,118,800

[d]Refer to Schedule 3 (paragraph 470) for computation.

[e]Refer to Schedule 4 (paragraph 471) for computation.

Supporting Schedules

Schedule 1—Plan assets

468. This Statement requires use of an assumption about the long-term rate of return on plan assets and a market-related value of plan assets to calculate the expected return on plan assets. If the fund holding plan assets is a taxable entity, the expected long-term rate of return on plan assets is net of estimated income taxes, and the nonbenefit liability for accrued income taxes reduces plan assets. This Statement defines market-related asset value as either fair value or a calculated value that recognizes changes in fair value in a systematic and rational manner over not more than five years (paragraph 57). This schedule reflects the calculation of market-related value, the fair value of plan assets, the actual return on plan assets, and the deferred asset gain or loss for the year (the difference between actual and expected return on plan assets included in the net amortization and deferral component of net periodic postretirement benefit cost).

	1993	1994	1995
Expected long-term rate of return on plan assets		10.0%	10.0%
Beginning balance, market-related value[a]	$ 0	$ 870,000	$1,937,000
Contributions to plan (end of year)	1,500,000	1,650,000	1,912,500
Benefits paid by plan	(630,000)	(700,000)	(900,000)
Expected return on plan assets		87,000	193,700
	870,000	1,907,000	3,143,200
20% of each of last 5 years' asset gains (losses)		30,000	(14,072)
Ending balance, market-related value	$ 870,000	$1,937,000	$3,129,128
Beginning balance, fair value of plan assets	$ 0	$ 870,000	$2,057,000
Contributions to plan	1,500,000	1,650,000	1,912,500
Benefits paid	(630,000)	(700,000)	(900,000)
Actual return (loss) on plan assets[b]	0	237,000	(26,660)
Ending balance, fair value of plan assets	$ 870,000	$2,057,000	$3,042,840
Deferred asset gain (loss) for year[c]	$ 0	$ 150,000	$ (220,360)
Gain (loss) not included in ending balance market-related value[d]	$ 0	$ 120,000	$ (86,288)

[a]This example uses an approach that adds in 20% of each of the last 5 years' gains or losses.

[b]Refer to Schedule 3 (paragraph 470) for computation.

[c](Actual return on plan assets) − (expected return on plan assets).

[d](Ending balance, fair value of plan assets) − (ending balance, market-related value of plan assets).

Schedule 2—Test for amortization of unrecognized net gain or loss

469. This Statement generally does not require recognition of any of the gain or loss in the period in which it arises and permits a minimum amortization of an unrecognized net gain or loss whereby the net amount in excess of the "corridor" is amortized over the average remaining service period of active plan participants (paragraph 59 and paragraph 459, footnote a). That allows a reasonable opportunity for gains and losses to offset each other without affecting net periodic postretirement benefit cost.

	1993	1994	1995
10% of beginning balance of accumulated postretirement benefit obligation	$600,000	$700,000	$725,000
10% of beginning balance of market-related value of plan assets[e]	$ 0	$ 87,000	$193,700
Greater of the above	$600,000	$700,000	$725,000
Unrecognized net (gain) loss at beginning of year		$760,000	$605,000
Asset gain (loss) not included in beginning balance of market-related value[f]		0	120,000
Amount subject to amortization		$760,000	$725,000
Amount in excess of the corridor subject to amortization		$ 60,000	$ 0
Divided by average remaining service period (years)		12	
Required amortization		$ 5,000	

[e]Refer to Schedule 1 (paragraph 468) for calculation of market-related value of plan assets.

[f]Refer to Schedule 1 (paragraph 468) for calculation of gain or loss not included in prior year's ending balance market-related value.

Schedule 3—Determination of actual return or loss on plan assets

470. The determination of the actual return or loss on plan assets component of net periodic postretirement benefit cost is as follows:

	1993	1994	1995
Plan assets at fair value, beginning of year	$ 0	$ 870,000	$2,057,000
Plus: assets contributed to plan	1,500,000	1,650,000	1,912,500
Less: benefit payments from plan	(630,000)	(700,000)	(900,000)
	870,000	1,820,000	3,069,500
Less: plan assets at fair value, end of year	(870,000)	(2,057,000)	(3,042,840)
Actual (return) loss on plan assets	$ 0	$ (237,000)	$ 26,660

Schedule 4—Determination of net amortization and deferral

471. The net amortization and deferral component of net periodic postretirement benefit cost required to be disclosed pursuant to paragraph 74(b) is determined as follows:

	1994	1995
Amortization of unrecognized net (gain) or loss[g]	$ 5,000	$ 0
Deferred asset gain (loss) for year[h]	150,000	(220,360)
Net amortization and deferral	$155,000	$(220,360)

[g]Refer to Schedule 2 (paragraph 469) for computation.

[h]Refer to Schedule 1 (paragraph 468) for computation.

Illustration 6—Defined-Dollar Capped Plans

472. The following cases (6A and 6B, paragraphs 473-478) demonstrate the operation of defined-dollar capped plans and the possible effect of the "cap" on projecting costs for purposes of measuring the accumulated postretirement benefit obligation and net periodic postretirement benefit

cost. The examples are simplified and illustrate only one aspect of the measurement process (paragraph 17 and paragraph 33, footnote 13).

Case 6A—Dollar Cap Defined on Individual Coverage

473. Company J sponsors a postretirement health care plan for its salaried employees. The plan has an annual limitation (a "cap") on the dollar amount of the employer's share of the cost of covered benefits incurred by a plan participant. The retiree is responsible, therefore, for the amount by which the cost of the benefit coverage under the plan incurred during a year exceeds that cap. The company adjusts the cap annually for the effects of inflation. For 1993, the cap is $1,500; the inflation adjustment in 1994 and 1995 is assumed to be 4 percent. The employer's health care cost trend rate assumption is 13 percent for 1994 and 12 percent for 1995.

474. The employer's projected cost of providing benefit coverage in 1993-1995 for a 67-year-old retiree follows. Similar projections are made for each age at which a plan participant is expected to receive benefits under the plan. In this example, the incurred claims cost exceeds the cap on the employer's share of the cost in each year.

	Expected Cost for 67-Year-Old Retiree		
	1993	1994	1995
Gross eligible charges	$3,065	$3,463	$3,879
Medicare[a]	(890)	(1,003)	(1,125)
Deductible/coinsurance	(325)	(340)	(355)
Incurred claims cost	$1,850	$2,120	$2,399
Annual cap on employer's cost	$1,500	$1,560	$1,622
Employer's share of incurred claims cost	$1,500	$1,560	$1,622
Retiree's share of gross eligible charges[b]	$ 675	$ 900	$1,132

[a]The change in Medicare reflects the portion of the gross eligible charges for which Medicare is responsible under enacted Medicare legislation.

[b]Deductible/coinsurance plus share of incurred claims: 1993—[$325 + ($1,850 − $1,500)]; 1994—[$340 + ($2,120 − $1,560)]; 1995—[$355 + ($2,399 − $1,622)].

475. If, based on the health care cost trend rate assumptions, the employer's share of costs for each plan participant is not expected to be less than the cap in the future, Company J could measure its expected postretirement benefit obligation by projecting the annual cap. However, if per capita

claims data for some plan participants or estimates of the health care cost trend rate indicate that in the future the employer's share of the incurred claims cost will be less than the cap for at least some plan participants, the employer's obligation is to be measured as described in paragraphs 34-42.

Case 6B—Dollar Cap Defined in the Aggregate for the Retiree Group

476. Company K sponsors a contributory postretirement health care plan for its hourly employees. The plan has an annual limitation (a "cap") on the dollar amount of the employer's share of the cost of covered benefits incurred by the retiree group as a whole. The company agrees to bear annual costs equal to a specified dollar amount ($1,500 in 1993) multiplied by the number of retired plan participants (the employer contribution); participating retirees are required to contribute a stated amount

each year ($1,000 in 1993). The cap on the employer's share of annual costs and the retirees' contribution rates are increased 5 percent annually. The shortfall in a year (the amount by which incurred claims cost exceeds the combined employer and retiree contributions) is initially borne by the employer but is passed back to retirees in the subsequent year through supplemental retiree contributions for that year (a retrospective adjustment).

477. The employer projects the aggregate cost of benefits expected to be paid to current plan participants (40 retirees) in each future period as follows:

	1993	1994	1995
Gross eligible charges	$160,000	$215,000	$197,000
Medicare	(46,500)	(62,350)	(57,300)
Deductible/coinsurance	(20,750)	(27,440)	(24,700)
Incurred claims cost	$ 92,750	$125,210	$115,000
Retiree contributions[a]	$ 40,000	$ 42,000	$ 44,080
Maximum employer contribution[b]	60,000	63,000	66,160
	$100,000	$105,000	$110,240
Shortfall (to be recovered by additional retiree contributions in subsequent year)		$ 20,210	$ 4,760
Supplemental contribution from retirees due to shortfall in prior year			$ 20,210

[a]Per retiree: 1993—$1,000; 1994—$1,050; 1995—$1,102.

[b]Per retiree: 1993—$1,500; 1994—$1,575; 1995—$1,654.

478. If, as in this example, retirees absorb the entire shortfall in annual contributions and if there is a projected shortfall for all future years, the employer could measure its expected postretirement benefit obligation by projecting its annual contribution (contribution rate × expected number of retirees = expected obligation for the year).

Illustration 7—Disclosure Requirements

479. This Statement requires an employer to disclose information in its financial statements about the obligation to provide postretirement benefits and the cost of providing those benefits. Paragraph 74 describes the disclosures required for defined benefit postretirement plans (paragraphs 77 and 78 describe how those disclosures may be aggregated by an employer with more than one postretirement benefit plan), paragraph 106 describes the disclosures required for defined contribution plans, and paragraph 82 describes the disclosures required for multiemployer plans. The following cases (7A-7C, paragraphs 480-483) illustrate those disclosure requirements. For simplicity, comparative financial statements are assumed not to be presented.

Case 7A—Single-Employer Defined Benefit Postretirement Plan

480. Paragraph 78(a) permits an employer to combine the disclosures for health and other welfare benefit plans unless the accumulated postretirement benefit obligation of the plans that provide primarily other postretirement welfare benefits is significant relative to the aggregate accumulated postretirement benefit obligation of all the employer's postretirement benefit plans. For an employer that provides more than one defined benefit postretirement plan, the disclosure for the year ended December 31, 1993 would be as follows. Because the life insurance plan is not significant, it is combined with the health care plan for disclosure purposes as permitted by paragraph 78.

Note X: The company sponsors two defined benefit postretirement plans that cover both salaried and nonsalaried employees. One plan provides medical and dental benefits, and the other provides life insurance benefits. The postretirement health care plan is contributory, with retiree contributions adjusted annually; the life insurance plan is noncontributory. The accounting for the health care plan anticipates future cost-sharing changes to the written plan that are consistent with the company's expressed intent to increase retiree contributions each year by 50 percent of the excess of the expected general inflation rate over 6 percent. On July 24, 1993, the company amended its postretirement health care plan to provide vision coverage. Beginning in 1993, the company adopted a funding policy for its postretirement health care plan similar to its funding policy for its life insurance plan—an amount equal to a level percentage of the employees' salaries is contributed to the plan annually. For 1993, that percentage was 4.25, and the aggregate contribution for both plans was $34,000.

The following table sets forth the plans' combined funded status reconciled with the amount shown in the company's statement of financial position at December 31, 1993:

Accumulated postretirement benefit obligation:	
Retirees	$(187,000)
Fully eligible active plan participants	(100,000)
Other active plan participants	(297,400)
	(584,400)
Plan assets at fair value, primarily listed U.S. stocks and bonds	87,960
Accumulated postretirement benefit obligation in excess of plan assets	(496,440)
Unrecognized net gain from past experience different from that assumed and from changes in assumptions	(40,000)
Prior service cost not yet recognized in net periodic postretirement benefit cost	19,000
Unrecognized transition obligation	470,250
Accrued postretirement benefit cost	$ (47,190)

The company's postretirement health care plan is underfunded; the accumulated postretirement benefit obligation and plan assets for that plan are $552,400 and $36,800, respectively.

Net periodic postretirement benefit cost for 1993 included the following components:

Service cost—benefits attributed to service during the period	$15,000
Interest cost on accumulated postretirement benefit obligation	44,400
Actual return on plan assets	(3,960)
Amortization of transition obligation over 20 years	24,750
Net amortization and deferral	1,000
Net periodic postretirement benefit cost	$81,190

For measurement purposes, a 16 percent annual rate of increase in the per capita cost of covered health care benefits was assumed for 1994; the rate was assumed to decrease gradually to 6 percent for 2020 and remain at that level thereafter. The health care cost trend rate assumption has a significant effect on the amounts reported. To illustrate, increasing the assumed health care cost trend rates by 1 percentage point in each year would increase the accumulated postretirement benefit obligation as of December 31, 1993 by $73,000 and the aggregate of the service and interest cost components of net periodic postretirement benefit cost for the year then ended by $13,000.

The weighted-average discount rate used in determining the accumulated postretirement benefit obligation was 8 percent. The trust holding the plan assets is subject to federal income taxes at a 34 percent tax rate. The expected long-term rate of return on plan assets after estimated taxes was 6.6 percent.

Case 7B—Defined Contribution Plan

481. An illustration of the disclosure for a defined contribution plan follows:

Note X: The company sponsors a defined contribution postretirement health care plan covering substantially all of its employees in both its chemicals and automotive subsidiaries. The company's contributions and cost are determined annually as

1.5 percent of each covered employee's salary and totaled $569,000 in 1993.

Case 7C—Multiemployer Plan

482. An illustration of the disclosure for a multiemployer plan follows:

Note X: The company's trucking subsidiary participates in a multiemployer plan that provides defined postretirement health care benefits to substantially all unionized workers in that subsidiary. Amounts charged to postretirement benefit cost and contributed to the plan totaled $319,000 in 1993.

483. If the information regarding the amount of postretirement benefit cost recognized during the period (disclosed in paragraph 482) is not available and the postretirement health and welfare benefits are provided through a general health and welfare plan, the amount of the aggregate required contribution to the general health and welfare benefit plan should be disclosed as follows (paragraph 82(b)):

Note X: The company's trucking subsidiary participates in a multiemployer plan that provides substantially all unionized workers in that subsidiary with health care and other welfare benefits during their working lives and after retirement. Amounts charged to benefit cost and contributed to the health and welfare plan for those benefits totaled $400,000 in 1993.

Illustration 8—Accounting for Settlements

484. This Statement provides for delayed recognition of the effects of a plan initiation or a plan amendment, the transition obligation or transition asset, and gains or losses arising in the ordinary course of operations. In certain circumstances, how-

ever, recognition of some or all of those previously delayed amounts is appropriate. Settlements are events that may require income or expense recognition of certain previously unrecognized amounts and adjustments to liabilities or assets recognized in the employer's statement of financial position. The settlement of all or part of the accumulated postretirement benefit obligation is the event that requires recognition of all or part of a previously unrecognized net gain or loss and unrecognized transition asset. A settlement also may accelerate recognition of a transition obligation under the constraint in paragraph 112 (paragraphs 92 and 93). The following cases (8A-8C, paragraphs 485-495) illustrate the accounting for settlements in various circumstances.

*Case 8A—Settlement When an Unrecognized
Transition Obligation Exists*

485. Company L sponsors a postretirement life insurance plan. On January 1, 1993, the company adopts this Statement; prior to that date it accounted for postretirement benefits on a pay-as-you-go (cash) basis. On December 31, 1994, Company L settles the accumulated postretirement benefit obligation for its current retirees ($70,000) through the purchase of nonparticipating life insurance contracts.

486. In accounting for the settlement, Company L must determine whether recognition of an additional amount of any unrecognized transition obligation is required pursuant to the constraint on delayed recognition of the transition obligation (paragraphs 112 and 113). At December 31, 1994, the cumulative postretirement benefit cost accrued subsequent to the date of transition exceeds the cumulative benefits payments subsequent to that date (including payments made pur-

suant to the settlement); thus, the constraint on delayed recognition of the transition obligation is not operative. The results of the settlement are as follows:

| | December 31, 1994 | | |
	Before Settlement	Settlement	After Settlement
Accumulated postretirement benefit obligation	$(257,000)	$70,000	$(187,000)
Plan assets at fair value	73,000	(70,000)[a]	3,000
Funded status	(184,000)	0	(184,000)
Unrecognized net gain	(44,575)	12,124[a]	(32,451)
Unrecognized prior service cost	33,000		33,000
Unrecognized transition obligation	195,000	(12,124)[a]	182,876
Accrued postretirement benefit cost	$ (575)	$ 0	$ (575)

[a]The maximum settlement gain subject to recognition is the unrecognized net gain subsequent to transition plus any unrecognized transition asset ($44,575 + $0 = $44,575) (paragraph 92). If, as in this case, only part of the accumulated postretirement benefit obligation is settled, a pro rata portion of the maximum gain based on the relationship of the accumulated postretirement benefit obligation settled to the total accumulated postretirement benefit obligation ($70,000 ÷ $257,000 or 27.2%) is subject to recognition. That amount ($44,575 × 27.2% = $12,124) must first reduce any unrecognized transition obligation; any excess is recognized in income in the current period (paragraph 93). In this case, the settlement gain is entirely offset against the unrecognized transition obligation.

Case 8B—Settlement When an Unrecognized Transition Asset Exists

487. Company M sponsors a postretirement life insurance plan. On January 2, 1995, Company M settles the accumulated postretirement benefit obligation for its current retirees ($200,000) through the purchase of nonparticipating life insurance contracts.

488. Pursuant to paragraphs 92 and 93, a settlement gain of $78,506 is recognized, determined as follows:

| | January 2, 1995 | | |
	Before Settlement	Settlement	After Settlement
Accumulated postretirement benefit obligation	$(257,000)	$200,000	$(57,000)
Plan assets at fair value	350,900	(200,000)	150,900
Funded status	93,900	0	93,900
Unrecognized net gain	(44,575)	34,679[a]	(9,896)
Unrecognized prior service cost	33,000		33,000
Unrecognized transition asset	(56,333)	43,827[a]	(12,506)
Prepaid postretirement benefit cost	$ 25,992	$ 78,506	$104,498

[a]The maximum settlement gain is measured as the unrecognized net gain subsequent to transition plus the unrecognized transition asset ($44,575 + $56,333 = $100,908) (paragraph 92). Since only a portion of the accumulated postretirement benefit obligation is settled, a pro rata portion of the maximum gain based on the relationship of the accumulated postretirement benefit obligation settled to the total accumulated postretirement benefit obligation ($200,000 ÷ $257,000 or 77.8%) is subject to recognition. That amount ($100,908 × 77.8% = $78,506) must first reduce any unrecognized transition obligation ($0); any excess is recognized in income in the current period (paragraph 93). In this case, the entire settlement gain of $78,506 is recognized in income. The transition constraint of paragraph 112 that requires additional recognition of a *transition obligation* in certain circumstances is not applicable because there is an unrecognized *transition asset*.

Case 8C—Effect of Mid-Year Settlement on Transition Constraint

489. A settlement is an event that requires remeasurement of the accumulated postretirement benefit obligation prior to the settlement. This case illustrates the accounting for a settlement of part of the accumulated postretirement benefit obligation that occurs mid-year and the interaction between that event and other provisions of the Statement, such as the constraint on delayed recognition of the transition obligation.

490. Company N adopts this Statement for the fiscal year beginning January 1, 1993 and elects a year-end (December 31) measurement date. At the date of transition, the company's accumulated postretirement benefit obligation for its

postretirement life insurance plan is $6,000,000, and there are no plan assets. In 1993, the company establishes a policy of funding at the end of each year an amount equal to the benefits paid during the year plus the service and interest cost for the year. Benefits are paid at the end of each year and in 1993 are $630,000, which is less than the net periodic postretirement benefit cost accrued for the year ($1,170,000); thus, no additional transition obligation is recognized pursuant to paragraph 112. Company N elects to amortize net unrecognized gains and losses in excess of the "corridor" over the average remaining service period of plan participants (paragraph 59 and paragraph 459, footnote a).

491. At the beginning of 1994, Company N projects the life insurance benefits expected to be paid in 1994 to retirees' beneficiaries to determine whether recognition of an additional amount of

the unrecognized transition obligation will be required (paragraph 113). Although Company N is considering settling a portion of the accumulated postretirement benefit obligation, the effects of the settlement are not included in the projection because plan settlements are not anticipated for measurement or recognition prior to their occurrence. The projection indicates that no additional amount is required to be recognized. On June 30, 1994, Company N contributes additional funds ($1,430,000) and settles a portion ($1,900,000) of the accumulated postretirement benefit obligation for its current retirees through the purchase of nonparticipating life insurance contracts.

492. The changes in the funded status of the plan during the first six months of the year and a reconciliation of the funded status of the plan with the amount shown in the statement of financial position immediately prior to the settlement are as follows:

	Actual 12/31/93	Six Months Postretirement Benefit Cost	Assets Contributed to Plan	Effects of Remeasurement Immediately before Settlement	Before Settlement 6/30/94
Accumulated postretirement benefit obligation	$(6,600,000)	$(457,000)[a]		$420,000[b]	$(6,637,000)
Plan assets at fair value	870,000	43,500[c]	$1,430,000	0[b]	2,343,500
Funded status	(5,730,000)	(413,500)	1,430,000	420,000	(4,293,500)
Unrecognized net (gain) or loss	360,000	0		(420,000)[b]	(60,000)
Unrecognized transition obligation	5,700,000	(150,000)			5,550,000
Prepaid postretirement benefit cost	$ 330,000	$(563,500)	$1,430,000	$ 0	$ 1,196,500[d]

[a]Represents 6 months' service cost of $160,000 and interest cost of $297,000 on the accumulated postretirement benefit obligation for 1994, assuming a 9% discount rate.

[b]A gain results from the remeasurement of the accumulated postretirement benefit obligation immediately prior to the settlement as a result of a change in the assumed discount rates based on the interest rates inherent in the price at which the accumulated postretirement benefit obligation for the retirees will be settled. No gain or loss results from remeasurement of plan assets.

[c]Represents 6 months' return on plan assets, assuming a 10% return.

[d]Because there is a settlement (treated as a benefit payment) and a prepaid asset exists as a result of providing the funds to effect that settlement, the constraint on delayed recognition of the transition obligation pursuant to paragraph 112 may be applicable. The test to determine whether additional recognition is necessary should be done based on amounts for the full year (paragraph 494).

493. In accounting for a settlement, an employer must determine whether recognition of an additional amount of any unrecognized transition obligation is required pursuant to the constraint on delayed recognition (paragraph 112). Any additional

transition obligation required to be recognized as a result of a settlement is recognized when the related settlement is recognized (paragraph 113) as illustrated in the following table. Detailed calculations are presented in paragraph 494.

	June 30, 1994			
	Before Settlement	Settlement	Recognition of Transition Obligation	After Settlement
Accumulated postretirement benefit obligation	$(6,637,000)	$1,900,000		$(4,737,000)
Plan assets at fair value	2,343,500	(1,900,000)		443,500
Funded status	(4,293,500)	0		(4,293,500)
Unrecognized net (gain) or loss	(60,000)	17,160ᵉ		(42,840)
Unrecognized transition obligation	5,550,000	(17,160)ᵉ	$(718,822)	4,814,018
Prepaid postretirement benefit cost	$ 1,196,500	$　　　0	$(718,822)	$　 477,678

ᵉThe maximum settlement gain subject to recognition is the unrecognized net gain subsequent to transition plus any unrecognized transition asset ($60,000 + $0 = $60,000). If, as in this case, only part of the accumulated postretirement benefit obligation is settled, a pro rata portion of the maximum gain based on the relationship of the accumulated postretirement benefit obligation settled to the total accumulated postretirement benefit obligation ($1,900,000 ÷ $6,637,000 or 28.6%) is subject to recognition. That amount ($60,000 × 28.6% = $17,160) must first reduce any unrecognized transition obligation (paragraph 93); any excess is recognized. In this situation, the settlement gain is entirely offset against the unrecognized transition obligation.

494. When a settlement occurs in the middle of the year, as in this example, the additional transition obligation to be recognized, if any, pursuant to the constraint in paragraph 112 is determined based on projected amounts for the full year. In this case, at June 30, 1994, cumulative benefit payments from the date of transition (January 1, 1993) to December 31, 1994 are projected to exceed cumulative postretirement benefit cost accrued for that same period as illustrated in the following table. The additional transition obligation to be recognized is the amount by which cumulative benefit payments exceed cost accrued, or $718,822.

	Projected 12/31/94
Benefit payments:	
1/1/93 to beginning of 1994	$　 630,000
1994 excluding settlement	410,000
Settlement	1,900,000
Cumulative benefit payments	$2,940,000
Postretirement benefit cost recognized:	
1/1/93 to beginning of 1994	$1,170,000
1994	1,051,178ᶠ
Cumulative cost recognized	$2,221,178
Benefit payments in excess of cost recognized	$　718,822

ᶠ$563,500 for period 1/1/94-6/30/94 plus $487,678 for period 7/1/94-12/31/94. The net postretirement benefit cost of $487,678 recognized in the second half of 1994 (paragraph 495) includes amortization ($130,108) of the unrecognized transition obligation that remains after recognizing an additional portion ($718,822) of the unrecognized transition obligation pursuant to paragraph 112. Because determination of the additional portion of the transition obligation to be recognized and the transition obligation amortized in the second half of 1994 are interrelated, those amounts are determined in a single computation that is intended to result in unrecognized transition obligation at the end of the year that appropriately reflects the constraint of paragraph 112.

495. After the settlement, net periodic postretirement benefit cost for the remainder of the year is remeasured. The projected funded status of the plan reconciled to the projected amount to be shown in the statement of financial position follows:

	After Settlement 6/30/94	Six Months Postretirement Benefit Cost	Benefit Payments	Assets Contributed to Plan	Projected 12/31/94
Accumulated postretirement benefit obligation	$(4,737,000)	$(379,745)g	$410,000		$(4,706,745)
Plan assets at fair value	443,500	22,175h	(410,000)	$1,246,745	1,302,420
Funded status	(4,293,500)	(357,570)	0	1,246,745	(3,404,325)
Unrecognized net gain	(42,840)	0			(42,840)
Unrecognized transition obligation	4,814,018	(130,108)i			4,683,910
(Accrued)/prepaid postretirement cost	$ 477,678	$(487,678)	$ 0	$1,246,745	$ 1,236,745

gRepresents 6 months' service cost of $150,000 and interest cost of $229,745 on the accumulated postretirement benefit obligation, assuming a 9.7% discount rate.

hRepresents 6 months' return on plan assets, assuming a 10% return.

iUnrecognized transition obligation at 6/30/94 of $4,814,018 ÷ 18.5 years remaining in amortization period = $260,217; half-year amortization = $130,108.

Illustration 9—Accounting for Curtailments

496. This Statement provides for delayed recognition of the effects of a plan initiation or a plan amendment, the transition obligation or transition asset, and gains or losses arising in the ordinary course of operations. In certain circumstances, however, recognition of some or all of those previously delayed amounts is appropriate. Curtailments are events that may require income or expense recognition of certain previously unrecognized amounts and adjustments to liabilities or assets recognized in the employer's statement of financial position.

497. A curtailment is an event that significantly reduces the expected years of future service of active plan participants or eliminates the accrual of defined benefits for some or all of the future services of a significant number of active plan participants. Such a reduction or elimination raises doubt about the continued existence of the future economic benefits of prior plan amendments. Therefore, an appropriate portion of the remaining unrecognized prior service cost should be recognized when it is probable that a curtailment will occur, the effects are reasonably estimable, and the estimated effects of the curtailment are a net loss. When the estimated effects of a curtailment are a net gain, the gain should be recognized in income when the related employees terminate or the plan suspension or

amendment is adopted (paragraphs 97-99). For purposes of measuring those effects, any remaining unrecognized transition obligation is treated as unrecognized prior service cost. The following cases (9A and 9B, paragraphs 498-501) illustrate the accounting for curtailments.

Case 9A—Curtailment When an Unrecognized Gain and an Unrecognized Transition Obligation Exist

498. Company P sponsors a postretirement benefit plan. On October 29, 1994, Company P decides to reduce its operations by terminating a significant number of employees effective December 31, 1994. On October 29, 1994, it is expected that a curtailment gain will result from the termination. A consequence of the curtailment is a significant reduction in the number of employees accumulating benefits under the plan. The *remaining years of expected service* associated with those terminated employees who were plan participants at the date of transition is 22 percent of the remaining years of service of all plan participants at the date of transition. The *remaining years of service prior to full eligibility* associated with those terminated employees who were plan participants at the date of a prior plan amendment is 18 percent of the remaining years of service of all plan participants at the date of that plan amendment.

499. The sum of the effects of the plan curtailment is a gain of $5,160 that should be recognized in income when the related employees terminate (paragraph 99). That gain is determined as follows:

	December 31, 1994		
	Before Curtailment	**Curtailment**	**After Curtailment**
Accumulated postretirement benefit obligation	$(257,000)	$54,000[a]	$(203,000)
Plan assets at fair value	73,000		73,000
Funded status	(184,000)	54,000	(130,000)
Unrecognized net gain	(44,575)		(44,575)
Unrecognized prior service cost	33,000	(5,940)[a]	27,060
Unrecognized transition obligation	195,000	(42,900)[a]	152,100
(Accrued)/prepaid postretirement benefit cost	$ (575)	$ 5,160	$ 4,585

[a]The effect of the curtailment consists of two components:

1. The unrecognized transition obligation and unrecognized prior service cost associated with remaining years of service no longer expected to be rendered—measured as 22% (reduction in the remaining years of expected service associated with those terminated employees who were plan participants at the date of transition) of the unrecognized transition obligation of $195,000 ($42,900) and 18% (reduction in the remaining years of service prior to full eligibility for benefits associated with those terminated employees who were plan participants at the date of a prior plan amendment) of the unrecognized prior service cost of $33,000 related to that amendment ($5,940) (paragraph 97)

2. The gain from the decrease in the accumulated postretirement benefit obligation of $54,000 (due to the termination of employees whose accumulated benefits were not vested under the plan) in excess of the unrecognized net loss of $0, or $54,000 (paragraph 98(a)).

Case 9B—Curtailment Related to a Disposal of a Portion of the Business and an Unrecognized Loss and Unrecognized Transition Obligation Exist

500. Company R sponsors a postretirement benefit plan. On December 31, 1994, Company R sells a portion of its business at a gain of $100,000 before considering the effect of the related curtailment of its postretirement benefit plan. In connection with the sale, the number of employees accumulating benefits under the plan is significantly reduced; thus, a curtailment occurs. The *remaining years of expected service* associated with the terminated employees who were plan participants at the date of transition is 22 percent of the remaining years of service of all plan participants at the date of transition. The *remaining years of service prior to full eligibility* associated with the terminated employees who were plan participants at the date of that prior plan amendment is 18 percent of the remaining years of service of all plan participants at the date of that plan amendment.

501. The sum of the effects of the plan curtailment is a loss of $36,265 that should be recognized with the gain of $100,000 associated with Company R's sale of a portion of its business. The loss is determined as follows:

	December 31, 1994		
	Before Curtailment	Curtailment	After Curtailment
Accumulated postretirement benefit obligation	$(343,000)	$ 54,000[a]	$(289,000)
Plan assets at fair value	73,000		73,000
Funded status	(270,000)	54,000	(216,000)
Unrecognized net loss	41,425	(41,425)[a]	0
Unrecognized prior service cost	33,000	(5,940)[a]	27,060
Unrecognized transition obligation	195,000	(42,900)[a]	152,100
Accrued postretirement benefit cost	$ (575)	$(36,265)	$ (36,840)

---

[a]The effect of the curtailment consists of two components:

1. The unrecognized transition obligation and unrecognized prior service cost associated with remaining years of service no longer expected to be rendered—measured as 22% (reduction in the remaining years of expected service associated with those terminated employees who were plan participants at the date of transition) of the unrecognized transition obligation of $195,000 ($42,900) and 18% (reduction in the remaining years of service prior to full eligibility for benefits associated with those terminated employees who were plan participants at the date of a prior plan amendment) of the unrecognized prior service cost of $33,000 related to that amendment ($5,940) (paragraph 97)

2. The gain from the decrease in the accumulated postretirement benefit obligation of $54,000 (due to the termination of employees whose accumulated benefits were not vested under the plan) in excess of the unrecognized net loss of $41,425, or $12,575 (paragraph 98(a)).

Illustration 10—Accounting for a Partial Settlement and a Full Curtailment That Occur as a Direct Result of a Sale of a Line of Business

502. Company S sells a line of business on December 31, 1994; prior to that date, the company had no formal plan for disposal of those operations. Company S has a separate postretirement benefit plan that provides health care benefits to retirees of the division that is sold. In connection with that sale, (a) all of the employees of that division are terminated by Company S resulting in no further accumulation of benefits under the postretirement benefit plan (a full curtailment), (b) most of the terminated employees are hired by the acquiring company (some terminated employees fully eligible for benefits elect to retire immediately), (c) an accumulated postretirement benefit obligation of $80,000 for postretirement benefits related to the hired employees is assumed by the acquiring company (a partial settlement, since the obligation for

current retirees is retained by Company S), and (d) plan assets of $100,000, representing $80,000 for the settlement of the accumulated postretirement benefit obligation and $20,000 as an excess contribution, are transferred from the plan to the acquiring company. A $300,000 gain from the sale is calculated before considering the related effects on the plan.

503. The employer's accounting policy is to determine the effects of a curtailment before determining the effects of a settlement when both events occur simultaneously. Pursuant to paragraph 97, the unrecognized prior service cost associated with the portion of the future years of service that had been expected to be rendered, but as a result of a curtailment are no longer expected to be rendered, is a loss. When a full curtailment occurs, the entire remaining unrecognized prior service cost and unrecognized transition obligation is a loss because there are no future years of service to be rendered.

504. The net loss from the curtailment is $228,000, which is recognized with the $300,000 gain resulting from the disposal of the division. The effect of the curtailment is determined as follows:

	December 31, 1994		
	Before Curtailment	**Curtailment-Related Effects Resulting from Sale**	**After Curtailment**
Accumulated postretirement benefit obligation	$(257,000)	$ (10,000)[a]	$(267,000)
Plan assets at fair value	110,000		110,000
Funded status	(147,000)	(10,000)	(157,000)
Unrecognized net gain	(49,575)	10,000[a]	(39,575)
Unrecognized prior service cost	33,000	(33,000)[b]	0
Unrecognized transition obligation	195,000	(195,000)[c]	0
(Accrued)/prepaid postretirement benefit cost	$ 31,425	$(228,000)	$(196,575)

[a]The increase in the accumulated postretirement benefit obligation as a result of the fully eligible employees retiring earlier than expected is a loss of $10,000. That loss reduces the unrecognized net gain of $49,575; any excess (none in this case) would be recognized as the effect of a curtailment (paragraph 98).

[b]Measured as 100% (reduction in the remaining years of service prior to full eligibility for benefits associated with those terminated employees who were plan participants at the date of a prior plan amendment) of the unrecognized prior service cost of $33,000 related to that amendment (paragraph 97).

[c]Measured as 100% (reduction in the remaining years of expected service associated with those terminated employees who were plan participants at the date of transition) of the unrecognized transition obligation of $195,000 (paragraph 97).

505. The $8,128 loss related to the settlement and transfer of plan assets that is recognized with the gain from the sale is determined as follows:

	December 31, 1994		
	After Curtailment	**Settlement and Transfer of Plan Assets**	**After Settlement**
Accumulated postretirement benefit obligation	$(267,000)	$ 80,000[d]	$(187,000)
Plan assets at fair value	110,000	(100,000)[d]	10,000
Funded status	(157,000)	(20,000)	(177,000)
Unrecognized net gain	(39,575)	11,872[e]	(27,703)
Unrecognized prior service cost	0		0
Unrecognized transition obligation	0		0
Accrued postretirement benefit cost	$(196,575)	$ (8,128)	$(204,703)

[d]The accumulated postretirement benefit obligation for the employees hired by the purchaser is determined to be $80,000 and is settled when Company S transfers plan assets of an equal amount to the purchaser. In connection with the purchase agreement, Company S transfers an additional $20,000 of plan assets.

[e]Represents a pro rata amount of the maximum gain based on the relationship of the accumulated postretirement benefit obligation settled to the total accumulated postretirement benefit obligation ($80,000 ÷ $267,000 or 30%). The maximum gain is measured as the unrecognized net gain subsequent to transition plus any unrecognized transition asset ($39,575 + $0 = $39,575). The settlement gain is, therefore, 30% of $39,575, or $11,872; recognition of that gain is subject to first reducing any remaining unrecognized transition obligation. As there is no remaining unrecognized transition obligation (the remainder was recognized in connection with the curtailment), the gain of $11,872 is recognized together with the excess $20,000 transfer of plan assets as part of the net gain from the sale (paragraphs 92 and 93).

506. The sum of the effects related to postretirement benefits resulting from the sale is a loss of $236,128, the components of which are as follows:

Curtailment loss (paragraph 504)	$228,000
Settlement gain and loss from transfer of plan assets (paragraph 505)	8,128
Effects of sale	$236,128

Illustration 11—Accounting for the Effects of an Offer of Special Termination Benefits

507. The measurement of the effects of an offer of special termination benefits pursuant to paragraphs 101 and 102 and the accounting for the related curtailment are illustrated in the following paragraphs.

508. On January 16, 1995, Company T offers for a short period of time (until January 30, 1995) special benefits to its employees who elect voluntary termination of employment during that period (special termination benefits). As part of the offer, employees who voluntarily terminate will be credited with an additional five years of service and five years of age to determine eligibility for postretirement health care benefits. Employees are normally eligible for those benefits upon attaining age 55 and rendering at least 20 years of service.

509. On January 30, 1995, employees representing 18 percent of the work force accept the offer of special termination benefits. For those employees, the accumulated postretirement benefit obligation attributed to prior service periods based on their previously expected retirement dates (without consideration of the special offer) is $280,000. If those employees were assumed to terminate (retire) immediately upon attaining full eligibility for benefits (age 55 with 20 years of service), the accumulated postretirement benefit obligation for those employees would be $450,000. The accumulated postretirement benefit obligation for those employees after they accept the offer of the special termination benefits (full eligibility date accelerated, benefit coverage begins immediately) is $630,000.

510. The *remaining years of expected service* associated with the terminated employees who were plan participants at the date of transition is 24 percent of the remaining years of service of all plan participants at the date of transition. In addition, the portion of the unrecognized prior service cost arising from a prior plan amendment associated with the *remaining years of service prior to full eligibility* that are no longer expected to be rendered by the terminated employees is $25,000.

511. Pursuant to paragraph 99, if the sum of the effects resulting from a curtailment is a net loss, it shall be recognized in income when it is probable that a curtailment will occur and the effects are reasonably estimable. In this illustration, the effects resulting from the curtailment are not reasonably estimable until January 30, 1995, the acceptance date of the offer of special termination benefits. Consequently, at January 30, 1995, the

employer recognizes a loss of $453,400 that includes the cost of the special termination benefits ($180,000) and the net loss from the curtailment ($273,400) determined as follows:

	January 30, 1995			
	Before Employee Terminations	Special Termination Benefits	Effect of Curtailment	After Employee Terminations
Accumulated postretirement benefit obligation:				
Employees accepting offer	$(280,000)	$(180,000)[a]	$(170,000)[b]	$ (630,000)
Other employees	(633,000)			(633,000)
	(913,000)	(180,000)	(170,000)	(1,263,000)
Plan assets at fair value	141,000			141,000
Funded status	(772,000)	(180,000)	(170,000)	(1,122,000)
Unrecognized net gain	(88,000)		88,000[b]	0
Unrecognized prior service cost	148,500		(25,000)[c]	123,500
Unrecognized transition obligation	693,333		(166,400)[c]	526,933
Accrued postretirement benefit cost	$ (18,167)	$(180,000)	$(273,400)	$ (471,567)

[a]The loss from acceptance of the special termination benefits is $180,000 ($450,000 − $630,000), representing the difference between (1) the accumulated postretirement benefit obligation measured assuming that active plan participants not yet fully eligible for benefits would terminate employment at their full eligibility date and that fully eligible plan participants would retire immediately and (2) the accumulated postretirement benefit obligation reflecting the special termination benefits (paragraph 102).

[b]The increase in the accumulated postretirement benefit obligation as a result of the employees (fully eligible plan participants and other active plan participants not yet fully eligible for benefits) retiring at a date earlier than expected is a loss of $170,000 ($280,000 − $450,000). That amount is reduced by the unrecognized net gain of $88,000 (paragraph 98(b)) as part of the accounting for the curtailment.

[c]Additional effects of the curtailment are (1) the reduction of $25,000 in the unrecognized prior service cost (arising from a prior plan amendment) associated with the remaining years of service prior to full eligibility that are no longer expected to be rendered by the terminated employees and (2) the reduction of $166,400 in the unrecognized transition obligation associated with remaining years of service no longer expected to be rendered—measured as 24% (reduction in the remaining years of expected service associated with those employees affected by the early retirement who were plan participants at the date of transition) of the unrecognized transition obligation of $693,333 (paragraph 97).

Appendix D

BACKGROUND INFORMATION

512. In 1979, the Board added other postemployment benefits to its project on employers' accounting for pensions. The Board was concerned about the lack of information in financial statements about the cost of and obligation for other postemployment benefits. Evidence suggested that most large employers, as well as many smaller ones, provided health care and life insurance benefits to their retirees and were accounting for those benefits on a pay-as-you-go (cash) basis. Existing accounting pronouncements did not cover postretirement benefits provided outside a pension plan.

513. Other postemployment benefits were first considered in a 1981 FASB Discussion Memorandum, *Employers' Accounting for Pensions and Other Postemployment Benefits.* In its 1982 Preliminary Views, *Employers' Accounting for Pensions and Other Postemployment Benefits,* the Board tentatively concluded that the cost of postemployment health care and life insurance provided to retirees should be accrued during the service lives of the employees expected to receive benefits under those plans. The Board did not consider the cash basis and terminal accrual (accrual at retirement) methods to be acceptable methods for recognizing the cost of those benefits.

514. The Board based its tentative conclusion on its view that an employer has an obligation for promised postretirement benefits to the extent that future payments are probable and the service required of retirees and future retirees in exchange for those benefits has been rendered. That view led to the conclusion that postemployment benefits are a form of deferred compensation. Those views were reiterated in a 1983 FASB Discussion Memorandum, *Employers' Accounting for Pensions and Other Postemployment Benefits,* that addressed additional issues not raised in the 1981 Discussion Memorandum. However, in considering comments on that second Discussion Memorandum, the Board concluded that the accounting issues related to other postemployment benefits were being overshadowed by pension issues.

515. In February 1984, the Board concluded that

it should address employers' accounting for post-employment benefits other than pensions as a separate project. As an interim measure, in 1984 the Board issued FASB Statement No. 81, *Disclosure of Postretirement Health Care and Life Insurance Benefits*. In April 1987, FASB Technical Bulletin No. 87-1, *Accounting for a Change in Method of Accounting for Certain Postretirement Benefits*, was issued to provide temporary guidance to employers making a voluntary change in their method of accounting for postretirement health care benefits and postretirement life insurance benefits provided outside a pension plan.

516. A task force was appointed in December 1986. Employers' accounting for postretirement benefits was addressed at 29 public Board meetings and 3 public task force meetings between February 1987 and October 1988. In February 1989, the Board issued an Exposure Draft, *Employers' Accounting for Postretirement Benefits Other Than Pensions*. The Exposure Draft proposed standards of financial accounting and reporting for an employer that offers postretirement benefits other than pensions to its employees. Twenty-five companies participated in a field test of the Exposure Draft that was sponsored by the Financial Executives Research Foundation.

517. The Board received more than 475 comment letters in response to the Exposure Draft. Public hearings on the Exposure Draft were conducted in October and November 1989. Sixty-two organizations and individuals presented their views at the 5 days of hearings. Based on the information received in the comment letters and at the public hearings, the Board reconsidered its proposals in the Exposure Draft at 28 public Board meetings during the remainder of 1989 and 1990. The task force met at a public meeting in June 1990 to discuss the Board's tentative conclusions on employers' accounting for postretirement benefits. Appendix A discusses the basis for the Board's conclusions, including reasons for changes made to the provisions of the 1989 Exposure Draft.

Appendix E

GLOSSARY

518. This appendix contains definitions of certain terms used in accounting for postretirement benefits.

Accumulated postretirement benefit obligation
The actuarial present value of benefits attributed to employee service rendered to a particular date. Prior to an employee's full eligibility date, the accumulated postretirement benefit obligation as of a particular date for an employee is the portion of the expected postretirement benefit obligation attributed to that employee's service rendered to that date; on and after the full eligibility date, the accumulated and expected postretirement benefit obligations for an employee are the same.

Active plan participant
Any active employee who has rendered service during the credited service period and is expected to receive benefits, including benefits to or for any beneficiaries and covered dependents, under the postretirement benefit plan. Also refer to **Plan participant.**

Actual return on plan assets (component of net periodic postretirement benefit cost)
The change in the fair value of the plan's assets for a period including the decrease due to expenses incurred during the period (such as income tax expense incurred by the fund, if applicable), adjusted for contributions and benefit payments during the period.

Actuarial present value
The value, as of a specified date, of an amount or series of amounts payable or receivable thereafter, with each amount adjusted to reflect (a) the time value of money (through discounts for interest) and (b) the probability of payment (for example, by means of decrements for events such as death, disability, or withdrawal) between the specified date and the expected date of payment.

Amortization
Usually refers to the process of reducing a recognized liability systematically by recognizing revenues or of reducing a recognized asset systematically by recognizing expenses or costs. In accounting for postretirement benefits, amortization is also used to refer to the systematic recognition in net periodic postretirement benefit cost over several periods of previously *unrecognized* amounts, including unrecognized prior service cost, unrecognized net gain or loss, and any unrecognized transition obligation or asset.

Assumed per capita claims cost (by age)
The annual per capita cost, for periods after the measurement date, of providing the postretirement health care benefits covered by the plan from the earliest age at which an individual could begin to receive benefits under the plan through the remainder of the individual's life or the covered period, if shorter. To determine the assumed per capita claims cost, the per capita claims cost by age based on histori-

cal claims costs is adjusted for assumed health care cost trend rates. The resulting assumed per capita claims cost by age reflects expected future costs and is applied with the plan demographics to determine the amount and timing of future gross eligible charges. Also refer to **Gross eligible charges** and **Per capita claims cost by age.**

Assumptions

Estimates of the occurrence of future events affecting postretirement benefit costs, such as turnover, retirement age, mortality, dependency status, per capita claims costs by age, health care cost trend rates, levels of Medicare and other health care providers' reimbursements, and discount rates to reflect the time value of money.

Attribution

The process of assigning postretirement benefit cost to periods of employee service.

Attribution period

The period of an employee's service to which the expected postretirement benefit obligation for that employee is assigned. The beginning of the attribution period is the employee's date of hire unless the plan's benefit formula grants credit only for service from a later date, in which case the beginning of the attribution period is generally the beginning of that credited service period. The end of the attribution period is the full eligibility date. Within the attribution period, an equal amount of the expected postretirement benefit obligation is attributed to each year of service unless the plan's benefit formula attributes a disproportionate share of the expected postretirement benefit obligation to employees' early years of service. In that case, benefits are attributed in accordance with the plan's benefit formula. Also refer to **Credited service period.**

Benefit formula

The basis for determining benefits to which participants may be entitled under a postretirement benefit plan. A plan's benefit formula specifies the years of service to be rendered, age to be attained while in service, or a combination of both that must be met for an employee to be eligible to receive benefits under the plan. A plan's benefit formula may also define the beginning of the credited service period and the benefits earned for specific periods of service.

Benefits

The monetary or in-kind benefits or benefit coverage to which participants may be entitled under a postretirement benefit plan, including health care benefits, life insurance not pro-

vided through a pension plan, and legal, educational, and advisory services.

Captive insurer

An insurance company that does business primarily with related entities.

Contributory plan

A plan under which retirees or active employees contribute part of the cost. In some contributory plans, retirees or active employees wishing to be covered must contribute; in other contributory plans, participants' contributions result in increased benefits.

Cost-sharing (provisions of the plan)

The provisions of the postretirement benefit plan that describe how the costs of the covered benefits are to be shared between the employer and the plan participants. Cost-sharing provisions describe retired and active plan participants' contributions toward their postretirement health care benefits, deductibles, coinsurance, out-of-pocket limitations on participant costs, caps on employer costs, and so forth.

Credited service period

Employee service period for which benefits are earned pursuant to the terms of the plan. The beginning of the credited service period may be the date of hire or a later date. For example, a plan may provide benefits only for service rendered after a specified age. Service beyond the end of the credited service period does not earn any additional benefits under the plan. Also refer to **Attribution period.**

Curtailment (of a postretirement benefit plan)

An event that significantly reduces the expected years of future service of active plan participants or eliminates the accrual of defined benefits for some or all of the future services of a significant number of active plan participants.

Defined benefit postretirement plan

A plan that defines postretirement benefits in terms of monetary amounts (for example, $100,000 of life insurance) or benefit coverage to be provided (for example, up to $200 per day for hospitalization, 80 percent of the cost of specified surgical procedures, and so forth). Any postretirement benefit plan that is not a defined contribution postretirement plan is, for purposes of this Statement, a defined benefit postretirement plan.

Defined contribution postretirement plan

A plan that provides postretirement benefits in return for services rendered, provides an individual account for each plan participant, and specifies how contributions to the individual's account are to be determined rather than specifies the amount of benefits the individual is to receive. Under a defined contribution postretirement plan, the benefits a plan participant will receive depend solely on the amount contributed to the plan participant's account, the returns earned on investments of those contributions, and the forfeitures of other plan participants' benefits that may be allocated to that plan participant's account.

Dependency status

The status of a current or former employee having dependents (for example, a spouse or other relatives) who are expected to receive benefits under a postretirement benefit plan that provides dependent coverage.

Discount rates

The rates used to reflect the time value of money. Discount rates are used in determining the present value as of the measurement date of future cash flows currently expected to be required to satisfy the postretirement benefit obligation. Also refer to **Actuarial present value.**

Expected long-term rate of return on plan assets

An assumption about the rate of return on plan assets reflecting the average rate of earnings expected on existing plan assets and expected contributions to the plan during the period.

Expected postretirement benefit obligation

The actuarial present value as of a particular date of the benefits expected to be paid to or for an employee, the employee's beneficiaries, and any covered dependents pursuant to the terms of the postretirement benefit plan.

Expected return on plan assets

An amount calculated as a basis for determining the extent of delayed recognition of the effects of changes in the fair value of plan assets. The expected return on plan assets is determined based on the expected long-term rate of return on plan assets and the market-related value of plan assets.

Explicit (approach to) assumptions

An approach under which each significant assumption used reflects the best estimate of the plan's future experience solely with respect to that assumption.

Fair value

The amount that a plan could reasonably expect to receive for an investment in a current sale between a willing buyer and a willing seller, that is, other than a forced or liquidation sale.

Full eligibility (for benefits)

The status of an employee having reached the employee's full eligibility date. Full eligibility for benefits is achieved by meeting specified age, service, or age and service requirements of the postretirement benefit plan. Also refer to **Full eligibility date.**

Full eligibility date

The date at which an employee has rendered all of the service necessary to have earned the right to receive all of the benefits expected to be received by that employee (including any beneficiaries and dependents expected to receive benefits). Determination of the full eligibility date is affected by plan terms that provide incremental benefits expected to be received by or on behalf of an employee for additional years of service, unless those incremental benefits are trivial. Determination of the full eligibility date is *not* affected by plan terms that define when benefit payments commence or by an employee's current dependency status.

Fully eligible plan participants

Collectively, that group of former employees (including retirees) and active employees who have rendered service to or beyond their full eligibility date and who are expected to receive benefits under the plan, including benefits to their beneficiaries and covered dependents.

Funding policy

The program regarding the amounts and timing of contributions by the employer(s), plan participants, and any other sources to provide the benefits a postretirement benefit plan specifies.

Gain or loss

A change in the value of either the accumulated postretirement benefit obligation or the plan assets resulting from experience different from that assumed or from a change in an actuarial assumption, or the consequence of a decision to temporarily deviate from the substantive plan. Also refer to **Unrecognized net gain or loss.**

Gain or loss component (of net periodic postretirement benefit cost)

The sum of (a) the difference between the actual return on plan assets and the expected return on plan assets, (b) any gain or loss immediately recognized or the amortization of the unrecognized net gain or loss from previous periods, and (c) any amount immediately recognized as a gain or loss pursuant to a decision to temporarily deviate from the substantive plan. The gain or loss component is generally the net effect of delayed recognition of gains and losses (the net change in the unrecognized net gain or loss) except that it does not include changes in the accumulated postretirement benefit obligation occurring during the period and deferred for later recognition.

Gross eligible charges

The cost of providing the postretirement health care benefits covered by the plan to a plan participant, before adjusting for expected reimbursements from Medicare and other providers of health care benefits and for the effects of the cost-sharing provisions of the plan.

Health care cost trend rates

An assumption about the annual rate(s) of change in the cost of health care benefits currently provided by the postretirement benefit plan, due to factors other than changes in the composition of the plan population by age and dependency status, for each year from the measurement date until the end of the period in which benefits are expected to be paid. The health care cost trend rates implicitly consider estimates of health care inflation, changes in health care utilization or delivery patterns, technological advances, and changes in the health status of the plan participants. Differing types of services, such as hospital care and dental care, may have different trend rates.

Incurred claims cost (by age)

The cost of providing the postretirement health care benefits covered by the plan to a plan participant, after adjusting for reimbursements from Medicare and other providers of health care benefits and for deductibles, coinsurance provisions, and other specific claims costs borne by the retiree. Also refer to **Net incurred claims cost (by age).**

Insurance contract

A contract in which an insurance company unconditionally undertakes a legal obligation to provide specified benefits to specific individuals in return for a fixed consideration or premium. An insurance contract is irrevocable and involves the transfer of significant risk from the employer (or the plan) to the insurance company. If the insurance company providing the contract is a captive insurer, or if there is any reasonable doubt that the insurance company will meet its obligations under the contract, the contract is not an insurance contract for purposes of this Statement.

Interest cost (component of net periodic postretirement benefit cost)

The accrual of interest on the accumulated postretirement benefit obligation due to the passage of time.

Market-related value of plan assets

A balance used to calculate the expected return on plan assets. Market-related value can be either fair value or a calculated value that recognizes changes in fair value in a systematic and rational manner over not more than five years. Different methods of calculating market-related value may be used for different classes of plan assets, but the manner of determining market-related value shall be applied consistently from year to year for each class of plan asset.

Measurement date

The date of the financial statements or, if used consistently from year to year, a date not more than three months prior to that date, as of which plan assets and obligations are measured.

Medicare reimbursement rates

The health care cost reimbursements expected to be received by retirees through Medicare as mandated by currently enacted legislation. Medicare reimbursement rates vary by the type of benefits provided.

Multiemployer plan

A postretirement benefit plan to which two or more unrelated employers contribute, usually pursuant to one or more collective-bargaining agreements. A characteristic of multiemployer plans is that assets contributed by one participating employer may be used to provide benefits to employees of other participating employers since assets contributed by an employer are not segregated in a separate account or restricted to provide benefits only to employees of that employer. A multiemployer plan is usually administered by a board of trustees composed of management and labor representatives and may also be referred to as a "joint trust" or "union plan." Generally, many employers participate in a multiemployer plan, and an employer may participate in more than one plan. The employers participating in multiemployer plans usually have a common industry bond, but for some plans the employers are in different industries and the labor union may be their only common bond.

Multiple-employer plan

A postretirement benefit plan maintained by more than one employer but not treated as a multiemployer plan. Multiple-employer plans are generally not collectively bargained and are intended to allow participating employers, commonly in the same industry, to pool their plan assets for investment purposes and to reduce the cost of plan administration. A multiple-employer plan maintains separate accounts for each employer so that contributions provide benefits only for employees of the contributing employer. Multiple-employer plans may have features that allow participating employers to have different benefit formulas, with the employer's contributions to the plan based on the benefit formula selected by the employer.

Net incurred claims cost (by age)
The employer's share of the cost of providing the postretirement health care benefits covered by the plan to a plan participant; incurred claims cost net of retiree contributions. Also refer to **Incurred claims cost (by age).**

Net periodic postretirement benefit cost
The amount recognized in an employer's financial statements as the cost of a postretirement benefit plan for a period. Components of net periodic postretirement benefit cost include service cost, interest cost, actual return on plan assets, gain or loss, amortization of unrecognized prior service cost, and amortization of the unrecognized transition obligation or asset.

Nonparticipating insurance contract
An insurance contract that does not provide for the purchaser to participate in the investment performance or in other experience of the insurance company. Also refer to **Insurance contract.**

Nonpublic enterprise
An enterprise other than one (a) whose debt or equity securities are traded in a public market, either on a stock exchange or in the over-the-counter market (including securities quoted only locally or regionally), or (b) whose financial statements are filed with a regulatory agency in preparation for the sale of any class of securities.

Participating insurance contract
An insurance contract that provides for the purchaser to participate in the investment performance and possibly other experience (for example, morbidity experience) of the insurance company. Also refer to **Insurance contract.**

Participation right
A purchaser's right under a participating insurance contract to receive future dividends or retroactive rate credits from the insurance company.

Pay-related plan
A plan that has a benefit formula that bases benefits or benefit coverage on compensation, such as a final-pay or career-average-pay plan.

Per capita claims cost by age
The current cost of providing postretirement health care benefits for one year at each age from the youngest age to the oldest age at which plan participants are expected to receive benefits under the plan. Also refer to **Assumed per capita claims cost (by age).**

Plan
An arrangement that is mutually understood by an employer and its employees, whereby an employer undertakes to provide its employees with benefits after they retire in exchange for their services over a specified period of time, upon attaining a specified age while in service, or a combination of both. A plan may be written or it may be implied by a well-defined, although perhaps unwritten, practice of paying postretirement benefits or from oral representations made to current or former employees. Also refer to **Substantive plan.**

Plan amendment
A change in the existing terms of a plan. A plan amendment may increase or decrease benefits, including those attributed to years of service already rendered.

Plan assets
Assets—usually stocks, bonds, and other investments—that have been segregated and restricted (usually in a trust) to provide for postretirement benefits. The amount of plan assets includes amounts contributed by the employer (and by plan participants for a contributory plan) and amounts earned from investing the contributions, less benefits, income taxes, and other expenses incurred. Plan assets ordinarily cannot be withdrawn by the employer except under certain circumstances when a plan has assets in excess of obligations and the employer has taken certain steps to satisfy existing obligations. Assets not segregated in a trust, or otherwise effectively restricted, so that they cannot be used by the employer for other purposes are not plan assets, even though it may be intended that those assets be used to provide postretirement benefits. Amounts accrued by the employer as net periodic postretirement benefit cost but not yet paid to the plan are not plan assets. Securities of the employer held by the plan are includable in plan assets provided they are transferable. If a plan has liabilities other than for benefits, those nonbenefit obligations are considered as reductions of plan assets.

Plan demographics
The characteristics of the plan population including geographical distribution, age, sex, and marital status.

Plan participant
Any employee or former employee who has rendered service in the credited service period *and is expected to receive employer-provided benefits* under the postretirement benefit plan, including benefits to or for any beneficiaries and covered dependents. Also refer to **Active plan participant.**

Plan termination
An event in which the postretirement benefit plan ceases to exist and all benefits are settled by the purchase of insurance contracts or by other means. The plan may or may not be replaced by another plan. A plan termination with a replacement plan may or may not be in substance a plan termination for accounting purposes.

Postretirement benefit fund
Assets accumulated in the hands of a funding agency for the sole purpose of paying postretirement benefits when the claims are incurred or benefits are due. Those assets may or may not qualify as plan assets. Also refer to **Plan assets.**

Postretirement benefit plan
Refer to **Plan.**

Postretirement benefits
All forms of benefits, other than retirement income, provided by an employer to retirees. Those benefits may be defined in terms of specified benefits, such as health care, tuition assistance, or legal services, that are provided to retirees as the need for those benefits arises, such as certain health care benefits, or they may be defined in terms of monetary amounts that become payable on the occurrence of a specified event, such as life insurance benefits.

Postretirement benefits other than pensions
Refer to **Postretirement benefits.**

Postretirement health care benefits
A form of postretirement benefit provided by an employer to retirees for defined health care services or coverage of defined health care costs, such as hospital and medical coverage, dental benefits, and eye care.

Prior service cost
The cost of benefit improvements attributable to plan participants' prior service pursuant to a plan amendment or a plan initiation that provides benefits in exchange for plan participants' prior service. Also refer to **Unrecognized prior service cost.**

Retirees
Collectively, that group of plan participants that includes retired employees, their beneficiaries, and covered dependents.

Service cost (component of net periodic postretirement benefit cost)
The portion of the expected postretirement benefit obligation attributed to employee service during a period.

Settlement (of a postretirement benefit plan)
An irrevocable action that relieves the employer (or the plan) of primary responsibility for a postretirement benefit obligation and eliminates significant risks related to the obligation and the assets used to effect the settlement. Examples of transactions that constitute a settlement include (a) making lump-sum cash payments to plan participants in exchange for their rights to receive specified postretirement benefits and (b) purchasing nonparticipating insurance contracts for the accumulated postretirement benefit obligation for some or all of the plan participants.

Single-employer plan
A postretirement benefit plan that is maintained by one employer. The term also may be used to describe a plan that is maintained by related parties such as a parent and its subsidiaries.

Substantive plan
The terms of the postretirement benefit plan as understood by an employer that provides postretirement benefits and the employees who render services in exchange for those benefits. The substantive plan is the basis for the accounting for that exchange transaction. In some situations an employer's cost-sharing policy, as evidenced by past practice or by communication of intended changes to a plan's cost-sharing provisions, or a past practice of regular increases in certain monetary benefits may indicate that the substantive plan differs from the extant written plan.

Termination benefits
Benefits provided by an employer to employees in connection with their termination of employment. They may be either special termination benefits offered only for a short period of

time or contractual benefits required by the terms of a plan only if a specified event, such as a plant closing, occurs.

Transition asset

The unrecognized amount, as of the date this Statement is initially applied, of (a) the fair value of plan assets plus any recognized accrued postretirement benefit cost or less any recognized prepaid postretirement benefit cost in excess of (b) the accumulated postretirement benefit obligation.

Transition obligation

The unrecognized amount, as of the date this Statement is initially applied, of (a) the accumulated postretirement benefit obligation in excess of (b) the fair value of plan assets plus any recognized accrued postretirement benefit cost or less any recognized prepaid postretirement benefit cost.

Unfunded accumulated postretirement benefit obligation

The accumulated postretirement benefit obligation in excess of the fair value of plan assets.

Unrecognized net gain or loss

The cumulative net gain or loss that has not been recognized as a part of net periodic postretirement benefit cost or as a part of the accounting for the effects of a settlement or a curtailment. Also refer to **Gain or loss.**

Unrecognized prior service cost

The portion of prior service cost that has not been recognized as a part of net periodic postretirement benefit cost, as a reduction of the effects of a negative plan amendment, or as a part of the accounting for the effects of a curtailment.

Unrecognized transition asset

The portion of the transition asset that has not been recognized either immediately as the effect of a change in accounting or on a delayed basis as a part of net periodic postretirement benefit cost, as an offset to certain losses, or as a part of accounting for the effects of a settlement or a curtailment.

Unrecognized transition obligation

The portion of the transition obligation that has not been recognized either immediately as the effect of a change in accounting or on a delayed basis as a part of net periodic postretirement benefit cost, as an offset to certain gains, or as a part of accounting for the effects of a settlement or a curtailment.

Statement of Financial Accounting Standards No. 107
Disclosures about Fair Value of Financial Instruments

STATUS

Issued: December 1991

Effective Date: For fiscal years ending after December 15, 1992

Affects: Amends FAS 105, paragraph 6 and footnotes 2 and 3

Affected by: Paragraph 7 amended by FAS 126
Paragraph 8(a) amended by FAS 112 and FAS 123
Paragraph 8(b) superseded by FAS 125
Paragraphs 10 and 13 amended by FAS 119
Paragraph 28 amended by FAS 125

Other Interpretive Release: FASB Special Report, *Illustrations of Financial Instrument Disclosures*

Issues Discussed by FASB Emerging Issues Task Force (EITF)

Affects: No EITF Issues

Interpreted by: Paragraph 16 interpreted by EITF Topic No. D-29

Related Issues: No EITF Issues

SUMMARY

This Statement extends existing fair value disclosure practices for some instruments by requiring all entities to disclose the fair value of financial instruments, both assets and liabilities recognized and not recognized in the statement of financial position, for which it is practicable to estimate fair value. If estimating fair value is not practicable, this Statement requires disclosure of descriptive information pertinent to estimating the value of a financial instrument. Disclosures about fair value are not required for certain financial instruments listed in paragraph 8.

This Statement is effective for financial statements issued for fiscal years ending after December 15, 1992, except for entities with less than $150 million in total assets in the current statement of financial position. For those entities, the effective date is for fiscal years ending after December 15, 1995.

Statement of Financial Accounting Standards No. 107

Disclosures about Fair Value of Financial Instruments

CONTENTS

INTRODUCTION

1. The FASB added a project on financial instruments and off-balance-sheet financing to its agenda in May 1986. The project is expected to develop broad standards to aid in resolving existing financial accounting and reporting issues and other issues likely to arise in the future about various financial instruments and related transactions.

2. Because of the complexity of the issues about how financial instruments and transactions should be recognized and measured, the Board decided that, initially, improved disclosure of information about financial instruments is necessary. The first disclosure phase was completed in March 1990 with the issuance of FASB Statement No. 105, *Disclosure of Information about Financial Instruments with Off-Balance-Sheet Risk and Financial Instruments with Concentrations of Credit Risk*. The second phase, which resulted in this Statement, considers disclosures about fair value of all financial instruments, both assets and liabilities recognized and not recognized in the statement of financial position, except those listed in paragraph 8.

STANDARDS OF FINANCIAL ACCOUNTING AND REPORTING

Definitions and Scope

3. A financial instrument is defined as cash, evidence of an ownership interest in an entity, or a contract that both:

a. Imposes on one entity a contractual obligation[1] (1) to deliver cash or another financial instrument[2] to a second entity or (2) to exchange other financial instruments on potentially unfavorable terms with the second entity
b. Conveys to that second entity a contractual right[3] (1) to receive cash or another financial instrument from the first entity or (2) to exchange other financial instruments on potentially favorable terms with the first entity.

4. The definition in paragraph 3 is essentially the same as that in paragraph 6 of Statement 105, which is hereby amended to conform to this Statement. Appendix A of Statement 105 provides examples of instruments that are included in and

---

[1]*Contractual obligations* encompass both those that are conditioned on the occurrence of a specified event and those that are not. All contractual obligations that are financial instruments meet the definition of *liability* set forth in FASB Concepts Statement No. 6, *Elements of Financial Statements*, although some may not be recognized as liabilities in financial statements—may be "off-balance-sheet"—because they fail to meet some other criterion for recognition. For some financial instruments, the obligation is owed to or by a group of entities rather than a single entity.

[2]The use of the term *financial instrument* in this definition is recursive (because the term *financial instrument* is included in it), though it is not circular. The definition requires a chain of contractual obligations that ends with the delivery of cash or an ownership interest in an entity. Any number of obligations to deliver financial instruments can be links in a chain that qualifies a particular contract as a financial instrument.

[3]*Contractual rights* encompass both those that are conditioned on the occurrence of a specified event and those that are not. All contractual rights that are financial instruments meet the definition of *asset* set forth in Concepts Statement 6, although some may not be recognized as assets in financial statements—may be "off-balance-sheet"—because they fail to meet some other criterion for recognition. For some financial instruments, the right is held by or the obligation is due from a group of entities rather than a single entity.

excluded from the definition of a financial instrument.

5. For purposes of this Statement, the fair value of a financial instrument is the amount at which the instrument could be exchanged in a current transaction between willing parties, other than in a forced or liquidation sale. If a quoted market price is available for an instrument, the fair value to be disclosed for that instrument is the product of the number of trading units of the instrument times that market price.

6. Under the definition of fair value in paragraph 5, the quoted price for a single trading unit in the most active market is the basis for determining market price and reporting fair value. This is the case even if placing orders to sell all of an entity's holdings of an asset or to buy back all of a liability might affect the price, or if a market's normal volume for one day might not be sufficient to absorb the quantity held or owed by an entity.

7. This Statement requires disclosures about fair value for all financial instruments, whether recognized or not recognized in the statement of financial position, except for those specifically listed in paragraph 8. It applies to all entities. It does not change any requirements for recognition, measurement, or classification of financial instruments in financial statements.

8. The disclosures about fair value prescribed in paragraphs 10-14 are not required for the following:

a. Employers' and plans' obligations for pension benefits, other postretirement benefits including health care and life insurance benefits, employee stock option and stock purchase plans, and other forms of deferred compensation arrangements, as defined in FASB Statements No. 35, *Accounting and Reporting by Defined Benefit Pension Plans,* No. 87, *Employers' Accounting for Pensions,* No. 106, *Employers' Accounting for Postretirement Benefits Other Than Pensions,* and No. 43, *Accounting for Compensated Absences,* and APB Opinions No. 25, *Accounting for Stock Issued to Employees,* and No. 12, *Omnibus Opinion—1967*
b. Substantively extinguished debt subject to the disclosure requirements of FASB Statement No. 76, *Extinguishment of Debt,* and assets held in trust in connection with an in-substance defeasance of that debt
c. Insurance contracts, other than financial guarantees and investment contracts, as discussed in FASB Statements No. 60, *Accounting and Reporting by Insurance Enterprises,* and No. 97, *Accounting and Reporting by Insurance Enterprises for Certain Long-Duration Contracts*

and for Realized Gains and Losses from the Sale of Investments
d. Lease contracts as defined in FASB Statement No. 13, *Accounting for Leases* (a contingent obligation arising out of a cancelled lease and a guarantee of a third-party lease obligation are not lease contracts and are included in the scope of this Statement)
e. Warranty obligations and rights
f. Unconditional purchase obligations as defined in paragraph 6 of FASB Statement No. 47, *Disclosure of Long-Term Obligations*
g. Investments accounted for under the equity method in accordance with the requirements of APB Opinion No. 18, *The Equity Method of Accounting for Investments in Common Stock*
h. Minority interests in consolidated subsidiaries
i. Equity investments in consolidated subsidiaries
j. Equity instruments issued by the entity and classified in stockholders' equity in the statement of financial position.

9. Generally accepted accounting principles already require disclosure of or subsequent measurement at fair value for many classes of financial instruments. Although the definitions or the methods of estimation of fair value vary to some extent, and various terms such as market value, current value, or mark-to-market are used, the amounts computed under those requirements satisfy the requirements of this Statement and those requirements are not superseded or modified by this Statement.

Disclosures about Fair Value of Financial Instruments

10. An entity shall disclose, either in the body of the financial statements or in the accompanying notes, the fair value of financial instruments for which it is practicable to estimate that value. An entity also shall disclose the method(s) and significant assumptions used to estimate the fair value of financial instruments.

11. Quoted market prices, if available, are the best evidence of the fair value of financial instruments. If quoted market prices are not available, management's best estimate of fair value may be based on the quoted market price of a financial instrument with similar characteristics or on valuation techniques (for example, the present value of estimated future cash flows using a discount rate commensurate with the risks involved, option pricing models, or matrix pricing models). Appendix A of this Statement contains examples of procedures for estimating fair value.

12. In estimating the fair value of deposit liabilities, a financial entity shall not take into account the

value of its long-term relationships with depositors, commonly known as core deposit intangibles, which are separate intangible assets, not financial instruments. For deposit liabilities with no defined maturities, the fair value to be disclosed under this Statement is the amount payable on demand at the reporting date. This Statement does not prohibit an entity from disclosing separately the estimated fair value of any of its nonfinancial intangible and tangible assets and nonfinancial liabilities.

13. For trade receivables and payables, no disclosure is required under this Statement when the carrying amount approximates fair value.

14. If it is not practicable for an entity to estimate the fair value of a financial instrument or a class of financial instruments, the following shall be disclosed:

a. Information pertinent to estimating the fair value of that financial instrument or class of financial instruments, such as the carrying amount, effective interest rate, and maturity
b. The reasons why it is not practicable to estimate fair value.

15. In the context of this Statement, *practicable* means that an estimate of fair value can be made without incurring excessive costs. It is a dynamic concept: what is practicable for one entity might not be for another; what is not practicable in one year might be in another. For example, it might not be practicable for an entity to estimate the fair value of a class of financial instruments for which a quoted market price is not available because it has not yet obtained or developed the valuation model necessary to make the estimate, and the cost of obtaining an independent valuation appears excessive considering the materiality of the instruments to the entity. Practicability, that is, cost considerations, also may affect the required precision of the estimate; for example, while in many cases it might seem impracticable to estimate fair value on an individual instrument basis, it may be practicable for a class of financial instruments in a portfolio or on a portfolio basis. In those cases, the fair value of that class or of the portfolio should be disclosed. Finally, it might be practicable for an entity to estimate the fair value only of a subset of a class of financial instruments; the fair value of that subset should be disclosed.

Effective Dates and Transition

16. This Statement shall be effective for financial statements issued for fiscal years ending after December 15, 1992, except for entities with less than $150 million in total assets in the current statement of financial position. For those entities, the effective date shall be for financial statements issued for fiscal years ending after December 15, 1995. Earlier application is encouraged. In the initial year of application of this Statement, it need not be applied to complete interim financial statements.

17. Disclosures required by paragraphs 10-14 that have not previously been reported need not be included in financial statements that are being presented for comparative purposes for fiscal years ending before the applicable effective date of this Statement for an entity. For all subsequent fiscal years, the information required to be disclosed by this Statement shall be included for each year for which a statement of financial position is presented for comparative purposes.

The provisions of this Statement need not be applied to immaterial items.

This Statement was adopted by the unanimous vote of the six members of the Financial Accounting Standards Board:

Dennis R. Beresford,	Victor H. Brown	A. Clarence Sampson
Chairman	James J. Leisenring	Robert J. Swieringa
Joseph V. Anania		

Appendix A

EXAMPLES OF PROCEDURES FOR ESTIMATING FAIR VALUE

18. This appendix provides examples of procedures for estimating the fair value of financial instruments. The examples are illustrative and are not meant to portray all possible ways of estimating the fair value of a financial instrument in order to comply with the provisions of this Statement.

19. Fair value information is frequently based on information obtained from market sources. In broad terms, there are four kinds of markets in which financial instruments can be bought, sold, or originated; available information about prices differs by kind of market:

a. *Exchange market.* An exchange or "auction" market provides high visibility and order to the trading of financial instruments. Typically, closing prices and volume levels are readily available in an exchange market.
b. *Dealer market.* In a dealer market, dealers stand ready to trade—either buy or sell—for their own account, thereby providing liquidity to the market. Typically, current bid and asked prices are more readily available than information about closing prices and volume levels. "Over-the-counter" markets are dealer markets.
c. *Brokered market.* In a brokered market, brokers attempt to match buyers with sellers but do not stand ready to trade for their own account. The broker knows the prices bid and asked by the respective parties, but each party is typically unaware of another party's price requirements; prices of completed transactions are sometimes available.
d. *Principal-to-principal market.* Principal-to-principal transactions, both originations and resales, are negotiated independently, with no intermediary, and little, if any, information is typically released publicly.

Financial Instruments with Quoted Prices

20. As indicated in paragraph 11 of this Statement, quoted market prices, if available, are the best evidence of fair value of financial instruments. Prices for financial instruments may be quoted in several markets; generally, the price in the most active market will be the best indicator of fair value.

21. In some cases, an entity's management may decide to provide further information about the fair value of a financial instrument. For example, an entity may want to explain that although the fair value of its long-term debt is less than the carrying amount, settlement at the reported fair value may not be possible or may not be a prudent management decision for other reasons; or the entity may want to state that potential taxes and other expenses that would be incurred in an actual sale or settlement are not taken into consideration.

Financial Instruments with No Quoted Prices

22. For financial instruments that do not trade regularly, or that trade only in principal-to-principal markets, an entity should provide its best estimate of fair value. Judgments about the methods and assumptions to be used in various circumstances must be made by those who prepare and attest to an entity's financial statements. The following discussion provides some examples of how fair value might be estimated.

23. For some short-term financial instruments, the carrying amount in the financial statements may approximate fair value because of the relatively short period of time between the origination of the instruments and their expected realization. Likewise, for loans that reprice frequently at market rates, the carrying amount may normally be close enough to fair value to satisfy these disclosure requirements, provided there is no significant change in the credit risk of those loans.

24. Some financial instruments (for example, interest rate swaps and foreign currency contracts) may be "custom-tailored" and, thus, may not have a quoted market price. In those cases, an estimate of fair value might be based on the quoted market price of a similar financial instrument, adjusted as appropriate for the effects of the tailoring. Alternatively, the estimate might be based on the estimated current replacement cost of that instrument.

25. Other financial instruments that are commonly "custom-tailored" include various types of options (for example, put and call options on stock, foreign currency, or interest rate contracts). A variety of option pricing models that have been developed in recent years (such as the Black-Scholes model and binomial models) are regularly used to value options. The use of those pricing models to estimate fair value is appropriate under the requirements of this Statement.

26. For some predominantly financial entities, loans receivable may be the most significant category of financial instruments. Market prices may be more readily available for some categories of loans (such as residential mortgage loans) than for others. If no quoted market price exists for a category of loans, an estimate of fair value may be based on (a) the market prices of similar traded loans with similar credit ratings, interest rates, and

maturity dates, (b) current prices (interest rates) offered for similar loans in the entity's own lending activities, or (c) valuations obtained from loan pricing services offered by various specialist firms or from other sources.

27. An estimate of the fair value of a loan or group of loans may be based on the discounted value of the future cash flows expected to be received from the loan or group of loans. The selection of an appropriate current discount rate reflecting the relative risks involved requires judgment, and several alternative rates and approaches are available to an entity. A single discount rate could be used to estimate the fair value of a homogeneous category of loans; for example, an entity might apply a single rate to each aggregated category of loans reported for regulatory purposes. An entity could use a discount rate commensurate with the credit, interest rate, and prepayment risks involved, which could be the rate at which the same loans would be made under current conditions. An entity also could select a discount rate that reflects the effects of interest rate changes and then make adjustments to reflect the effects of changes in credit risk. Those adjustments could include (a) revising cash flow estimates for cash flows not expected to be collected, (b) revising the discount rate to reflect any additional credit risk associated with that group of loans, or some combination of (a) and (b).

28. A fair value for financial liabilities for which quoted market prices are not available can generally be estimated using the same techniques used for estimating the value of financial assets. For example, a loan payable to a bank could be valued at the discounted amount of future cash flows using an entity's current incremental rate of borrowing for a similar liability; alternatively, the discount rate could be the rate that an entity would have to pay to a creditworthy third party to assume its obligation, with the creditor's legal consent (sometimes referred to as the "settlement rate"), or the rate that an entity would have to pay to acquire essentially risk-free assets to extinguish the obligation in accordance with the requirements of Statement 76.

29. For deposit liabilities with defined maturities, such as certificates of deposit, an estimate of fair value might also be based on the discounted value of the future cash flows expected to be paid on the deposits. The discount rate could be the current rate offered for similar deposits with the same remaining maturities. For deposit liabilities with no defined maturities, paragraph 12 of this Statement requires that the fair value to be disclosed be the amount payable on demand at the reporting date.

Appendix B

ILLUSTRATIONS APPLYING THE DISCLOSURE REQUIREMENTS ABOUT FAIR VALUE OF FINANCIAL INSTRUMENTS

30. The examples that follow are guides to implementation of the disclosure requirements of this Statement. Entities are not required to display the information contained herein in the specific manner illustrated. Alternative ways of disclosing the information are permissible as long as they satisfy the disclosure requirements of this Statement. Paragraphs 12 and 21 of this Statement describe possible additional voluntary disclosures that may be appropriate in certain circumstances.

Example 1—Financial Entity

31. Bank A might disclose the following:

Note V: Disclosures about Fair Value of Financial Instruments

The following methods and assumptions were used to estimate the fair value of each class of financial instruments for which it is practicable to estimate that value:

Cash and short-term investments
For those short-term instruments, the carrying amount is a reasonable estimate of fair value.

Investment securities and trading account assets
For securities and derivative instruments held for trading purposes (which include bonds, interest rate futures, options, interest rate swaps, securities sold not owned, caps and floors, foreign currency contracts, and forward contracts) and marketable equity securities held for investment purposes, fair values are based on quoted market prices or dealer quotes. For other securities held as investments, fair value equals quoted market price, if available. If a quoted market price is not available, fair value is estimated using quoted market prices for similar securities.

Loan receivables
For certain homogeneous categories of loans, such as some residential mortgages, credit card receivables, and other consumer loans, fair value is estimated using the quoted market prices for securities backed by similar loans, adjusted for differences in loan characteristics. The fair value of other types of loans is estimated by discounting the future cash flows using the current rates at which similar loans would be made to borrowers with similar credit ratings and for the same remaining maturities.

Deposit liabilities
The fair value of demand deposits, savings accounts, and certain money market deposits is the amount payable on demand at the reporting date. The fair value of fixed-maturity certificates of deposit is estimated using the rates currently offered for deposits of similar remaining maturities.

Long-term debt
Rates currently available to the Bank for debt with similar terms and remaining maturities are used to estimate fair value of existing debt.

Interest rate swap agreements
The fair value of interest rate swaps (used for hedging purposes) is the estimated amount that the Bank would receive or pay to terminate the swap agreements at the reporting date, taking into account current interest rates and the current credit-worthiness of the swap counterparties.

Commitments to extend credit, standby letters of credit, and financial guarantees written
The fair value of commitments is estimated using the fees currently charged to enter into similar agreements, taking into account the remaining terms of the agreements and the present creditworthiness of the counterparties. For fixed-rate loan commitments, fair value also considers the difference between current levels of interest rates and the committed rates. The fair value of guarantees and letters of credit is based on fees currently charged for similar agreements or on the estimated cost to terminate them or otherwise settle the obligations with the counterparties at the reporting date.

The estimated fair values of the Bank's financial instruments are as follows:

	19X9		19X8	
	Carrying Amount	Fair Value	Carrying Amount	Fair Value
Financial assets:				
Cash and short-term investments	$XXX	$XXX	$XXX	$XXX
Trading account assets	XXX	XXX	XXX	XXX
Investment securities	XXX	XXX	XXX	XXX
Loans	XXX		XXX	
Less: allowance for loan losses	(XXX)		(XXX)	
Loans, net of allowance	XXX	XXX	XXX	XXX
Financial liabilities:				
Deposits	XXX	XXX	XXX	XXX
Securities sold not owned	XXX	XXX	XXX	XXX
Long-term debt	XXX	XXX	XXX	XXX
Unrecognized financial instruments:*				
Interest rate swaps:				
In a net receivable position	XXX	XXX	XXX	XXX
In a net payable position	(XXX)	(XXX)	(XXX)	(XXX)
Commitments to extend credit	(XXX)	(XXX)	(XXX)	(XXX)
Standby letters of credit	(XXX)	(XXX)	(XXX)	(XXX)
Financial guarantees written	(XXX)	(XXX)	(XXX)	(XXX)

*The amounts shown under "carrying amount" represent accruals or deferred income (fees) arising from those unrecognized financial instruments. Interest rate swaps and other derivative instruments entered into as trading activities are included in "trading account assets" or "securities sold not owned."

Example 2—Nonfinancial Entity

[In this example, it is assumed that the carrying amounts of the short-term trade receivables and payables approximate their fair values.]

32. Corporation B might disclose the following:

Note X: Disclosures about Fair Value of Financial Instruments

The following methods and assumptions were used to estimate the fair value of each class of financial instruments for which it is practicable to estimate that value:

Cash and short-term investments
The carrying amount approximates fair value because of the short maturity of those instruments.

Long-term investments
The fair values of some investments are estimated based on quoted market prices for those or similar investments. For other investments for which there are no quoted market prices, a reasonable estimate of fair value could not be made without incurring excessive costs. Additional information pertinent to the value of an unquoted investment is provided below.

Long-term debt
The fair value of the Corporation's long-term debt is estimated based on the quoted market prices for the same or similar issues or on the current rates offered to the Corporation for debt of the same remaining maturities.

Foreign currency contracts
The fair value of foreign currency contracts (used for hedging purposes) is estimated by obtaining quotes from brokers.

The estimated fair values of the Corporation's financial instruments are as follows:

	19X9		19X8	
	Carrying Amount	Fair Value	Carrying Amount	Fair Value
Cash and short-term investments	$XXX	$XXX	$XXX	$XXX
Long-term investments for which it is:				
• Practicable to estimate fair value	XXX	XXX	XXX	XXX
• Not practicable	XXX	—	XXX	—
Long-term debt	(XXX)	(XXX)	(XXX)	(XXX)
Foreign currency contracts	XXX	XXX	(XXX)	(XXX)

It was not practicable to estimate the fair value of an investment representing 12 percent of the issued common stock of an untraded company; that investment is carried at its original cost of $XXX (19X8, $XXX) in the statement of financial position. At year-end, the total assets reported by the untraded company were $XXX (19X8, $XXX) and the common stockholders' equity was $XXX (19X8, $XXX), revenues were $XXX (19X8, $XXX), and net income was $XXX (19X8, $XXX).

Example 3—Small Nonfinancial Entity

33. Corporation C, whose only financial instru-
ments are cash, short-term trade receivables and payables for which their carrying amounts approximate fair values, and long-term debt, might disclose the following:

Note Z: Long-Term Debt

Based on the borrowing rates currently available to the Corporation for bank loans with similar terms and average maturities, the fair value of long-term debt is $XXX (19X8, $XXX).

Appendix C

BACKGROUND INFORMATION AND BASIS FOR CONCLUSIONS

CONTENTS

Appendix C

BACKGROUND INFORMATION AND BASIS FOR CONCLUSIONS

Introduction

34. This appendix summarizes considerations that Board members deemed significant in reaching the conclusions in this Statement. It includes reasons for accepting certain views and rejecting others. Individual Board members gave greater weight to some factors than to others.

Background Information

35. Following the issuance of Statement 105 in March 1990, the Board decided to focus primarily on disclosures about fair value as the second phase in the disclosure part of the financial instruments project. Background information on the financial instruments project and on the purposes of disclosure is provided in Appendix D of Statement 105.

36. On December 31, 1990, after discussing the issues in five public Board meetings and two public task force meetings, the Board issued the Exposure Draft, *Disclosures about Market Value of Financial Instruments* (1990 Exposure Draft). The Board re-ceived 204 comment letters on that Exposure Draft and 19 organizations and individuals presented their views during public hearings held on May 29 and 30, 1991. Also, eight entities participated in a field test of the disclosures proposed in the 1990 Exposure Draft. The field test results, which are kept confidential at the entities' request, were used by the Board during its deliberations on scope, display, and other issues addressed by this Statement.

Terminology

37. Some respondents to the 1990 Exposure Draft suggested that use of the term *market value* did not reflect adequately the broad range of financial instruments covered by this Statement. Those respondents associate the term *market value* only with items that are traded on active secondary markets (such as exchange and dealer markets). As highlighted by the discussion in paragraph 19 of this Statement, the Board does not make that distinction. The term *market value,* as defined in paragraph 5 of the 1990 Exposure Draft, is applicable whether the market for an item is active or inactive, primary or secondary. The Board decided, however, to use the term *fair value* in this Statement to avoid further confusion and also to be consistent with the terminology used in similar disclosure proposals made recently by other national and international standard-setting organiza-

tions. The concept of fair value is the same as that of market value in the 1990 Exposure Draft; those who associate the term *market value* only with items that are traded in active secondary markets may however prefer to consider fair value as a broader concept that includes prices and rates obtained from both secondary and primary markets.

Disclosures about Fair Value of Financial Instruments

38. The Board decided to proceed with the second phase of the disclosure project because it has concluded that fair value provides a relevant measure for unrecognized financial instruments and another relevant measure for recognized financial instruments that are measured on other bases. The Board also concluded that the benefits of disclosing information about fair value, when practicable, justify the costs involved, except for certain financial instruments for which that information is not required by this Statement.

Relevance of Fair Value Information

39. Many respondents to the 1990 Exposure Draft questioned the relevance of measures of financial assets and liabilities based on fair values. The Board concluded that information about fair value of financial instruments meets the first objective of financial reporting stated in FASB Concepts Statement No. 1, *Objectives of Financial Reporting by Business Enterprises,* that is, to provide information that is useful to present and potential investors, creditors, and other users in making rational investment, credit, and similar decisions.

40. Fair values of financial instruments depict the market's assessment of the present value of net future cash flows directly or indirectly embodied in them, discounted to reflect both current interest rates and the market's assessment of the risk that the cash flows will not occur. Investors and creditors are interested in predicting the amount, timing, and uncertainty of future net cash inflows to an entity, as those are the primary sources of future cash flows from the entity to them. Periodic information about the fair value of an entity's financial instruments under current conditions and expectations should help those users both in making their own predictions and in confirming or correcting their earlier expectations.

41. Information about fair value better enables investors, creditors, and other users to assess the consequences of an entity's investment and financing strategies, that is, to assess its performance. For example, information about fair value shows the effects of a decision to borrow using fixed-rate rather than floating-rate financial instruments or

of a decision to invest in long-term rather than short-term instruments. Also, in a dynamic economy, information about fair value permits continuous reassessment of earlier decisions in light of current circumstances.

42. Finally, several articles and reports in recent years have indicated the potential usefulness of information about market value of financial instruments, particularly as an indicator of the solvency of financial institutions. For example, a report issued by the U.S. Department of the Treasury in February 1991, *Modernizing the Financial System,* discusses the possible advantages of market value information for regulatory supervision of financial institutions.

43. Some respondents to the 1990 Exposure Draft argued that information about fair value of financial instruments is not relevant if an entity intends to hold them for the long term. They contend that, in those cases, the only relevant measure for a financial instrument is carrying value based on the amount initially paid or received (or perhaps a lower recoverable amount for an asset). They further argue that carrying value based on historical cost or proceeds provides relevant information because it focuses on the decision that creates the asset or liability, the earning effects of that decision that will be realized over time, and the ultimate recoverable or settlement value of the financial asset or liability. They also question the relevance of fair value measures because those measures focus on the effects of transactions and events that do not involve the entity. They reflect only "opportunity" gains and losses; "opportunities" that are not relevant unless they are intended to be realized.

44. The Board concluded that information about fair value of financial instruments, combined with information about carrying value, is relevant in part because it reflects the effects of management's decisions to buy a financial asset or incur a financial liability at a specific time, and then to continue to hold an asset or owe a liability. Deciding first on the best timing, based on existing market conditions, to acquire an asset or incur a liability and then when and how to realize gains or losses are important parts of management's stewardship responsibility to an entity's owners. Movements in fair values, and thus in market returns, during the period that a financial asset is held or a financial liability is owed provide a benchmark with which to assess the results of management's decisions and its success in maximizing the profitable use of an entity's economic resources and in minimizing financing costs.

45. Some respondents to the 1990 Exposure Draft argued that the subjectivity inherent in estimating

the fair value of some financial assets and liabilities renders the information irrelevant and potentially misleading. Some also mentioned that many financial assets and liabilities are not readily marketable and that since it might be difficult or impossible to sell or settle them, information about their fair value is not useful.

46. The Board concluded that those arguments pertain more to the reliability of the estimates than to their relevance. In some cases, it may not be practicable to make a reasonable estimate of fair value. However, the Board expects that, in most cases, it will be practicable for an entity to make a reasonable estimate of fair value even of financial instruments that are not readily marketable.

47. Some have suggested that most or all financial instruments should be recognized and measured at their fair value in financial statements. The Board is considering recognition and measurement issues in other parts of the project on financial instruments. This Statement requires only disclosures about fair value.

48. The disclosures about fair value required by this Statement build on current practice and requirements. For example, FASB Statement No. 12, *Accounting for Certain Marketable Securities,* requires lower of cost or market measures and disclosure of the market value of certain equity securities traded on exchanges or in the over-the-counter markets, and FASB Statement No. 15, *Accounting by Debtors and Creditors for Troubled Debt Restructurings,* provides guidance on determining the fair value of assets without active markets when transferred in settlement of troubled debt.

49. Other accounting standard-setting organizations have also concluded that fair value information about financial instruments is relevant. In September 1991, the International Accounting Standards Committee (IASC) issued an Exposure Draft, *Financial Instruments,* which, among other things, proposes disclosures about fair value for all financial instruments. The Exposure Draft is the result of a joint effort with the Canadian Institute of Chartered Accountants (CICA), which also issued an Exposure Draft, *Financial Instruments,* in September 1991.

50. The disclosures about fair value proposed in the IASC Exposure Draft are essentially the same as those required by this Statement. The CICA Exposure Draft also proposes disclosures about fair value, but only for financial assets; however, disclosures about fair value of financial liabilities are encouraged.

Benefits and Costs

51. One of the precepts of the Board's mission is to promulgate standards only when the expected benefits of the resulting information exceed the perceived costs. The Board strives to determine that a proposed standard will fill a significant need and that the costs entailed in satisfying that need, as compared with other alternatives, are justified in relation to the overall benefits of the resulting information. The benefits of providing fair value information are discussed in paragraphs 38-46 of this Statement.

52. The benefits of providing fair value information about financial instruments come at a cost— principally, the incremental cost of developing, implementing, and maintaining a measurement and reporting system to generate the required disclosures. The Board believes that many entities already have some systems in place to monitor and manage the market risk of their portfolios of financial instruments. The Board also believes that the incremental costs of the disclosure requirements of this Statement have been reduced in various ways: by introducing a notion of practicability to ensure that excessive costs will not be incurred solely to comply with the provisions of this Statement; by giving only general guidance on how to estimate fair value, so that an entity can exercise judgment in determining the most cost-efficient way of obtaining the information; by excluding certain financial instruments from the scope of the Statement because the benefits of providing fair value information about those instruments are at least uncertain in relation to the costs involved; and by delaying the effective date of application of this Statement for smaller entities that may need more time to be able to comply with the provisions of this Statement.

53. The Board realizes that by reducing some of the incremental costs of the requirements of this Statement in those ways, it also has reduced some of the benefits and possibly increased other costs of those requirements. For example, by providing general rather than detailed guidance, it has potentially reduced the comparability of the fair value information among entities. At the same time, general guidance may increase the costs that will be incurred by preparers, auditors, regulators, and others as they evaluate and select appropriate approaches to assessing and disclosing fair value. Also, there will be a cost to users of financial statements as they attempt to make comparisons among entities of fair value information based on different methods and assumptions.

54. The Board is sensitive to the consequences that may occur as a result of the new information. For example, some respondents to the 1990 Exposure Draft and the 1987 Exposure Draft, *Disclosures about Financial Instruments,* mentioned that entities could possibly refrain from investing in financial instruments with significant market value volatility or in long-term instruments as a result of the required disclosures. Others mentioned that disclosing periodic changes in the fair value of all financial instruments of financial institutions might jeopardize the safety and soundness of the banking system as a whole. However, the nature and extent of those consequences are highly uncertain and are difficult to isolate from the effects of other events that will occur independent of that new information. For example, regulatory agencies for banks and thrifts recently have made and currently are considering further changes in regulations that may affect considerably the costs of doing business for those entities in the future. The Board's objective is not to enhance or diminish the possibility of those consequences but to improve disclosure of information about financial instruments so that users of financial statements may make better informed decisions.

Level of Guidance

55. Disclosures about fair value were originally proposed as part of a comprehensive set of disclosures about financial instruments included in the 1987 Exposure Draft. Some respondents to that Exposure Draft were concerned about the lack of specific guidance on how to estimate fair value. They maintained that different entities would disclose different market value estimates for similar financial instruments by using varying methods and assumptions, resulting in a lack of comparability between those entities' financial statements. Similar comments were made by some respondents to the 1990 Exposure Draft.

56. After considering those concerns, the Board reaffirmed its preference for general rather than detailed guidance in this Statement even though general guidance may result in disclosures that are less comparable from entity to entity. The Board concluded that the benefits to investors and creditors of having some timely information about fair value outweigh the disadvantage of that information being less than fully comparable. The Board noted that information about financial instruments based on historical prices also is not comparable from entity to entity. The Board also is aware that the current practices followed by entities that estimate fair value (as defined in this Statement) for internal management purposes vary and to impose specific methods or assumptions could increase the cost of compliance for at least some enti-

ties. Furthermore, those entities will be using methods they consider to be most pertinent to their situation. Finally, financial instruments have such diverse characteristics that the Board believes that it is not practicable at this time to prescribe detailed methods and assumptions to be used in estimating fair value.

Financial Instruments with Quoted Prices

57. The Board concluded that quoted market prices provide the most reliable measure of fair value. Quoted market prices are easy to obtain and are reliable and verifiable. They are used and relied upon regularly and are well understood by investors, creditors, and other users of financial information. In recent years, new markets have developed and some existing markets have evolved from thin to active markets, thereby increasing the ready availability of reliable fair value information.

58. Although many respondents to the 1990 and 1987 Exposure Drafts agreed with the usefulness of disclosing quoted market prices derived from active markets, some argued that quoted prices from thin markets do not provide relevant measures of fair value, particularly when an entity holds a large amount of a thinly traded financial instrument that could not be absorbed by the market in a single transaction. The Board considered this issue and reiterated its belief that quoted prices, even from thin markets, provide useful information because investors and creditors regularly rely on those prices to make their decisions. The Board noted that providing the liquidation value of a block of financial instruments is not the objective of this Statement. The Board also concluded that requiring the use of available quoted market prices would increase the comparability of the disclosures among entities.

Financial Instruments with No Quoted Prices

59. The Board realizes that estimating fair value when quoted market prices are unavailable may, in some cases, require considerable judgment. However, the Board noted that a considerable degree of judgment also is needed when complying with other longstanding accounting and reporting requirements.

60. Many respondents to the 1990 and 1987 Exposure Drafts commented that some valuation techniques require sophisticated assumptions (for example, expected prepayments on a portfolio of loans assuming various future levels of interest rates) that would force entities, particularly smaller ones, to incur significant additional costs. The Board believes that simplified assumptions may sometimes be used (with appropriate disclo-

sure) by an entity to provide a reliable estimate of fair value at a reasonable cost.

61. Paragraph 28 of the 1990 Exposure Draft stated that "an entity could also estimate market value by calculating separately (a) changes in market value due to changes in overall general interest rates and (b) changes in market value due to cash flows not expected to be collected and due to changes in market premiums for credit risk." Some respondents questioned whether that wording permitted the use of the allowance for loan losses in estimating the fair value of loans. Although the Board did not consider that specific issue at the Exposure Draft stage, some Board members believe that the use of the allowance for loan losses would not provide an acceptable estimate of fair value in most cases because, according to current accounting literature, the allowance does not take into account the timing of the expected losses and all the potential losses due to credit risk. On the other hand, the factors considered in determining an appropriate allowance for loan losses are considered in determining the effects of changes in credit risk when estimating fair value. The Board decided to provide general rather than detailed guidance by stating, in paragraph 27 of Appendix A of this Statement, that adjustments to reflect the effects of changes in credit risk could be made by revising cash flow estimates, revising the discount rate, or some combination of both.

62. The Board is aware that it is not always practicable for an entity to estimate the fair value of a financial instrument or a category of financial instruments. The Board concluded that, in such cases, an entity should disclose the reasons fair value was not estimated and certain descriptive information pertinent to the value of those financial instruments that would help investors and creditors make their decisions. Examples of that information are the carrying amount of a financial instrument, the expected maturity, and the effective interest rate of the instrument.

63. Paragraph 14(c) of the 1990 Exposure Draft would have required an entity to state whether it believes the carrying amount approximates fair value or is significantly higher or lower than fair value. Many respondents objected to that requirement because they believe that, in most situations where it is not practicable to estimate fair value, it also would not be practicable to make such a statement. Also, they mentioned the risk of litigation arising from such a subjective disclosure. Based on those arguments, the Board decided not to include that disclosure requirement in this Statement.

Financial Liabilities

64. Some respondents to the 1990 Exposure Draft proposed excluding all financial liabilities from the scope of this Statement. Although most existing disclosures about fair value, and most discussion of the need for additional disclosures, have focused on the values of assets, the Board concluded that disclosures about the fair value of financial liabilities are important because market price volatility, which creates economic gains and losses, affects financial liabilities as well as assets. For example, a decline in the market price of an entity's bonds may give the entity an opportunity to settle the debt at a price below the carrying amount and, thus, to recognize a gain.

65. Some respondents to the 1990 Exposure Draft questioned the relevance of fair value information for liabilities when an entity does not have the intent or the ability to settle the debt. Some respondents argued that even when an entity intends to settle a debt to realize a gain due to an increase in market interest rates, there would be no economic gain if the cash needed for settlement is obtained through issuance of other debt at current higher rates. The Board believes that fair value information also is relevant in those cases because it helps users of financial statements assess the effects on the entity of interest rate changes and the entity's ability to manage the related risk. The fair value of liabilities also provides information about the entity's success in minimizing financing costs on a continuing basis (for example, by timing borrowing decisions to take advantage of favorable market conditions). The Board noted that an entity does not necessarily need to settle a debt financed at a rate below prevailing market rates to realize a gain; the gain could be realized over the period of repayment of that debt. The Board also noted that under longstanding provisions of APB Opinion No. 26, *Early Extinguishment of Debt,* a gain is recognized in income if a debt is settled for less than its carrying amount, regardless of the source of the cash used to settle the debt.

66. Information about the fair values of both assets and liabilities is essential to permit an assessment of a financial institution's success in managing its financial assets and liabilities in a coordinated way. To limit potential net loss, financial institutions often seek to balance their asset and liability positions so that a decrease in the fair value of a financial asset is accompanied by a decrease in the fair value of a financial liability.

67. Some respondents, however, suggested that fair value information for liabilities of predominantly nonfinancial entities is not useful because

those entities hold relatively few financial assets. Also, those liabilities are often incurred to finance the acquisition of nonfinancial assets; disclosing the changes in the fair value of financial liabilities without the corresponding changes in the fair value of nonfinancial assets may be misleading. The Board considered those arguments and reiterated its belief that fair value information for liabilities in itself is relevant information and should be provided. The Board acknowledges that the usefulness of the fair value information for liabilities would be enhanced by fair value information for nonfinancial assets but those assets are outside the scope of this Statement. This Statement, however, emphasizes that an entity may voluntarily disclose information about the fair value of its nonfinancial assets and liabilities (paragraph 12).

68. The Board acknowledges that, as for assets with no quoted prices, variations in the methods used to estimate the fair value of liabilities with no quoted prices might reduce the comparability of fair value information among entities. Some entities will estimate fair value by using an incremental rate of borrowing that considers changes in an entity's own credit risk, while others will use a settlement rate that ignores at least part of those credit risk changes. However, the Board concluded that it should not, at this time, prescribe a single method to be used for all unquoted liabilities. The Board currently has a project on its agenda on the uses of interest methods of accounting that examines questions about accounting measurements based on the present value of future economic benefits or sacrifices, and it will consider the question of a single method as part of that project.[4]

Core Deposits

69. Some respondents to the 1990 Exposure Draft commented that a financial institution should consider the value of its long-term customer relationships (core deposit intangibles) in estimating the fair value of its deposits. The Board concluded that core deposit intangibles are separate intangible assets, not financial instruments, and are therefore outside the scope of this Statement. The Board noted that the accounting treatment for intangible assets similar to those identified by respondents as core deposit intangibles is partially addressed in FASB Statement No. 72, *Accounting for Certain Acquisitions of Banking or Thrift Institutions,* and the arguments used in Statement 72 support the conclusion reached by the Board in this Statement. The Board also noted that accounting standards do not prohibit voluntary disclosures about fair value of core deposit intangibles or any

other assets or liabilities that are not included in the scope of this Statement.

70. Some respondents asked whether the Board's intention, in the 1990 Exposure Draft, was to prescribe the disclosure of the carrying amount of deposit liabilities as an estimate of their fair value. Others mentioned that the fair value of deposit liabilities may differ from their carrying amount even when, as required by paragraph 12 of this Statement, the value of core deposit intangibles is not taken into consideration; they suggested that those deposits represent an inexpensive source of funds that will be available for a considerable period of time. The Board decided that for deposit liabilities with no defined maturities, the fair value to be disclosed should be the amount payable on demand at the reporting date. The Board disagreed with the view that deposit liabilities should be valued using the rates available on more expensive alternative sources of funds because those rates are not relevant to the markets for deposits; also, that approach does not consider all the costs related to servicing the deposits.

Exclusion of Certain Financial Instruments

71. This Statement does not require disclosures about fair value for (a) employers' and plans' obligations for pension benefits, employers' and plans' obligations for other postretirement benefits including health care and life insurance benefits, employee stock option and stock purchase plans, and other forms of deferred compensation arrangements, (b) substantively extinguished debt subject to the disclosure requirements of Statement 76 and assets held in trust in connection with an in-substance defeasance of that debt, (c) insurance contracts, other than financial guarantees and investment contracts, (d) lease contracts, (e) warranty obligations and rights, (f) unconditional purchase obligations as defined in Statement 47, (g) investments accounted for under the equity method, (h) minority interests in consolidated subsidiaries, (i) equity investments in consolidated subsidiaries, and (j) equity instruments issued by the entity and classified in stockholders' equity in the statement of financial position.

72. Some disclosures about fair value are already required by existing generally accepted accounting principles for some items included in category (a) of the previous paragraph. In addition, a project on employee stock compensation plans is currently on the Board's agenda. In Statement 76, the Board concluded that meeting specified conditions effectively immunizes the obligation against market risk.

---

[4]The Discussion Memorandum, *Present-Value-Based Measurements in Accounting,* was issued on December 7, 1990.

73. This Statement uses a definition of a financial instrument based on the definition contained in Statement 105. During the Board's deliberations on this phase of the disclosure project, some questions arose about the application of the definition to contracts that involve the future delivery of goods or services. For example, Statement 105 excludes from the definition a contract that either requires the exchange of a financial instrument for a nonfinancial commodity (a forward contract) or permits settlement of an obligation by delivery of a nonfinancial commodity (an option), because those contracts involve the required or optional future exchange or delivery of an item that is not a financial instrument. An alternative approach would separate those contracts into financial and nonfinancial components; for example, a forward contract to purchase goods could be viewed as both an obligation to pay cash—a financial instrument—and a right to receive goods—not a financial instrument. If the financial component of that contract were subject to the disclosure requirements of this Statement, a further question would be whether the estimate of the fair value of the financial component should take into account changes in value caused by changes in the price of the underlying commodity. If not, difficulties would arise in distinguishing between changes in the fair value of the financial component and changes in the fair value of the nonfinancial component of the contract.

74. The Board concluded that disclosures about fair value should not be required for insurance contracts, lease contracts, warranty obligations, and unconditional purchase obligations (such as take-or-pay contracts). The Board believes that definitional and valuation difficulties are present to a certain extent in those contracts and obligations, and that further consideration is required before decisions can be made about whether to apply the definition to components of those contracts and whether to require disclosures about fair value for the financial components. The Board noted that issues about the application of the definition of a financial instrument are addressed more comprehensively in the November 1991 FASB Discussion Memorandum, *Recognition and Measurement of Financial Instruments*.

75. The other instruments listed in paragraph 71(g)-(j) were added as a result of comments received from respondents on the scope of the Statement. The disclosures were intended to apply only to financial assets and liabilities; therefore, minority interests in consolidated subsidiaries and an entity's own equity instruments classified in stockholders' equity are exempt from the disclosure requirements. The Board also decided to clarify that there is no requirement to disclose the fair value of investments

in consolidated subsidiaries. Finally, the Board decided to exempt investments accounted for under the equity method from the disclosure requirements. The market value of those investments for which a quoted market price is available is already required to be disclosed under the provisions of Opinion 18, and the Board believes that the incremental benefits of estimating fair value for unquoted investments accounted for under the equity method do not outweigh the related costs.

76. Respondents to the 1990 Exposure Draft who proposed exempting other types of financial instruments from the disclosures required by this Statement were concerned about the difficulty or cost of estimating fair value. The Board concluded that no other type of financial instrument needs to be specifically excluded from the scope of this Statement because an entity will not be required to provide an estimate of fair value for a financial instrument if it is not practicable to do so.

Application in Comparative Financial Statements

77. The Board decided that, in the initial year of applying the provisions of this Statement, disclosures about fair value should be required as of the date of the latest statement of financial position. Obtaining prior-year fair value information not previously required might be difficult for many entities, and the Board believes the benefits would likely not justify the costs.

78. Although some respondents to the 1990 Exposure Draft suggested that the volume of disclosures would be unduly increased, the Board concluded that, after transition, comparative information about fair value should be provided for each year for which a statement of financial position is presented because that information is useful in assessing the management of market risk and pertinent trends.

Applicability to Small, Nonpublic, or Nonfinancial Entities

79. The Board considered whether certain entities should be excluded from the scope of this Statement. In particular, the Board considered the usefulness of the disclosures about fair value required by this Statement for small, nonpublic, or predominantly nonfinancial entities; a number of respondents to the 1990 Exposure Draft suggested exclusions on one or more of those bases. After considering the costs and benefits of those disclosures, the Board concluded that the disclosures are important and should be required for all entities, including small and nonpublic entities. The Board believes that the notion of "practicability" discussed in paragraph 15 ensures that excessive costs do not have to be incurred to comply with the dis-

closure requirements. In addition, the Board's decision to allow smaller entities additional time to apply the provisions of this Statement recognizes the fact that the costs of compliance can be reduced for those entities because the overall benefits of the information might be less than for larger entities.

80. The Board also concluded that while this Statement would likely have its greatest effect on the financial reporting of entities whose assets and liabilities are primarily financial instruments, financial instruments constitute an important part of the assets and liabilities of many predominantly nonfinancial entities as well, and disclosures about their fair value are useful and should be required. Furthermore, distinctions between financial and nonfinancial entities are becoming less pronounced.

81. The Board acknowledges that, for predominantly nonfinancial entities that have relatively few financial instruments, the benefits of disclosures about fair value might be less than for financial entities for which financial instruments are the most important part of their activities. However, the Board noted that the costs of compliance are relatively lower for those entities and that there are comparability benefits associated with having similar disclosure requirements apply to similar financial instruments. Accordingly, the Board decided that the disclosures required by this Statement should apply to all entities.

Location of Information within Financial Reports

82. The Board considered whether the disclosures required by this Statement should be part of the basic financial statements or should be provided as supplementary information. FASB Concepts Statement No. 5, *Recognition and Measurement in Financial Statements of Business Enterprises,* distinguishes between information that should be part of the basic financial statements and that which should be provided as supplementary information. Paragraph 7 of Concepts Statement 5 emphasizes that information disclosed as part of the basic financial statements amplifies or explains information recognized in financial statements and is essential to understanding that information.

83. Some respondents to the 1990 Exposure Draft suggested that the fair value information required by this Statement be disclosed as supplementary information because of the subjectivity associated with some estimates and to reduce the costs of compliance. Other respondents supported the Board's position in the Exposure Draft to allow entities enough flexibility to select the best way to disclose the information as part of the basic financial statements. Some also mentioned that the disclosures would be more credible if they are made as part of the basic financial statements.

84. The disclosures required by this Statement build on disclosures already included in basic financial statements and, like them, serve the major purposes of disclosure summarized in Appendix D of Statement 105; that is, to provide descriptions, to provide measures, and to help in assessing risks and potentials. In the past, requiring information to be supplementary has been done in conjunction with excluding certain entities from the scope of the requirements; however, as discussed in paragraphs 79-81, the Board concluded that the disclosures required by this Statement should be provided by all entities. The Board also concluded that all the disclosures about fair value of financial instruments should be included within the basic financial statements. The Board noted that having some fair value disclosures outside and others as part of the basic financial statements could potentially confuse the users of financial statements.

85. Some respondents believed that this Statement should require the fair value information to be disclosed in a tabular format in a single note to the financial statements. They believed that that approach would make the information more readily available and easier to understand by users of financial statements, thereby increasing the benefits of the disclosures. However, the Board concluded that entities should be allowed to determine the most appropriate way to disclose the fair value information in their financial statements.

Applicability to Interim Financial Statements

86. Some respondents to the 1990 Exposure Draft questioned whether the provisions of this Statement apply to interim financial statements. Paragraph 16 clarifies that disclosures about fair value are required to be made in all complete sets of interim financial statements, except in the initial year of application of this Statement. The minimum disclosure requirements for summarized interim financial information issued by publicly traded entities are established by APB Opinion No. 28, *Interim Financial Reporting.* Since the provisions of this Statement do not amend Opinion 28, summarized interim financial information need not include the disclosures required by this Statement.

Effective Dates and Transition

87. Some respondents to the 1987 Exposure Draft mentioned that completion of the disclosure part of the financial instruments project would be desirable as soon as practicable so that the Board could proceed to focus entirely on recognition and measure-

ment issues. On the other hand, many respondents expressed concern that some entities, particularly smaller ones, may not currently have in place the systems necessary to provide the required disclosures. After considering those comments, the Board proposed in the 1990 Exposure Draft that the effective date for larger entities, defined as entities with more than $100 million in total assets at the date of the latest statement of financial position, should be for financial statements issued for fiscal years ending after December 15, 1991. The Board also proposed to delay for one year the application of this Statement's requirements for entities that fall below that size criterion.

88. Many respondents to the 1990 Exposure Draft were concerned that they would not have sufficient time to prepare the required fair value information if a final Statement were issued late in 1991. Others

suggested that the size criterion used to determine which entities would have additional time to implement the provisions of this Statement should be increased; some noted that bank regulators require less extensive information for banks with less than $150 million in total assets. After considering those comments, the Board concluded that larger entities, defined as entities with more than $150 million in total assets in the current statement of financial position, should apply the provisions of this Statement in financial statements issued for fiscal years ending after December 15, 1992. The Board decided to delay the effective date for smaller entities by an additional three years to provide sufficient time for those entities to develop the systems necessary to provide the required disclosures, in light of the experience gained by larger entities on the use of various methods and assumptions for estimating fair value.

Statement of Financial Accounting Standards No. 108 Accounting for Income Taxes—Deferral of the Effective Date of FASB Statement No. 96

an amendment of FASB Statement No. 96

STATUS

Issued: December 1991

Effective Date: December 16, 1991

Affects: Amends FAS 96, paragraph 32
      Supersedes FAS 100
      Supersedes FAS 103

Affected by: Superseded by FAS 109

(The next page is 1412.)

Statement of Financial Accounting Standards No. 109
Accounting for Income Taxes

STATUS

Issued: February 1992

Effective Date: For fiscal years beginning after December 15, 1992

Affects: Amends ARB 43, Chapter 9C, paragraph 5
Supersedes ARB 43, Chapter 9C, paragraphs 11 through 13
Supersedes ARB 43, Chapter 10B
Supersedes ARB 43, Chapter 11B, paragraph 8
Supersedes ARB 44 (Revised) and related letter dated April 15, 1959
Supersedes APB 1
Supersedes APB 2, paragraph 16
Supersedes APB 6, paragraphs 20 through 23 and footnotes 7 and 8
Supersedes APB 11
Amends APB 16, paragraphs 87 and 88
Supersedes APB 16, paragraph 89
Amends APB 17, paragraph 30
Amends APB 21, footnote 8*
Amends APB 23, paragraphs 9, 13,* 21, and 23 and footnotes 7* and 9
Supersedes APB 23, paragraphs 10, 11, 14, and 24 and footnotes 3, 4, 6, and 10
Supersedes APB 24
Amends APB 25, paragraph 17
Amends APB 28, paragraphs 19* and 20 and footnotes 2 and 3
Amends APB 29, paragraph 27*
Amends APB 30, paragraph 7
Supersedes AIN-APB 4, Interpretations No. 4 and 6
Supersedes AIN-APB 11, Interpretations No. 1 through 25
Supersedes AIN-APB 15, Interpretations No. 13 and 16
Amends AIN-APB 18, Interpretations No. 1 and 2*
Supersedes AIN-APB 23, Interpretation No. 1
Amends AIN-APB 25, Interpretation No. 1
Amends FAS 12, paragraph 22*
Amends FAS 13, paragraph 47
Supersedes FAS 16, paragraph 11 and footnote 5
Amends FAS 16, paragraph 13 and footnotes 3 and 4
Amends FAS 19, paragraphs 61 and 62
Supersedes FAS 31
Supersedes FAS 37, paragraphs 4, 17, 18, and 26 through 29 and footnotes 1 through 3 and footnotes
(*) and (†) of paragraph 4
Amends FAS 37, paragraphs 19,* 20, 21,* 22,* 23, 24,* and 25*
Amends FAS 38, paragraphs 2 and 5
Supersedes FAS 38, footnote 2
Amends FAS 44, paragraph 6*
Amends FAS 52, paragraphs 22,* 23,* 24,* and 48
Amends FAS 57, paragraph 2
Supersedes FAS 60, paragraphs 55 through 58, 60(i), and 60(j) and footnote 8

---

*Result of the amendment, at least in part, described in paragraph 287.

Amends FAS 60, paragraph 59
Amends FAS 69, paragraphs 26, 30(c), 40, and 41
Supersedes FAS 71, paragraph 18 and footnote 12
Amends FAS 71, paragraph 46
Amends FAS 87, paragraph 37*
Amends FAS 89, paragraphs 33* and 96
Amends FAS 90, paragraphs 14 and 27*
Supersedes FAS 96
Supersedes FAS 100
Amends FAS 101, paragraph 19*
Supersedes FAS 103
Supersedes FAS 108
Amends FIN 18, paragraphs 6,* 8, 16, 18, 40 through 43, 46 through 55, 58, 65, 66, and 68 and
    footnotes 2,* 19, and footnote (*) of paragraph 47
Supersedes FIN 18, paragraphs 14, 15, 20, 23, 59 through 61, and 70 and footnotes 9 through 14, 18,
    21 through 23, and 25
Supersedes FIN 22
Supersedes FIN 25
Supersedes FIN 29
Amends FIN 30, paragraph 5*
Amends FIN 31, footnote 1
Supersedes FIN 32
Amends FTB 79-9, paragraph 3
Amends FTB 79-16 (Revised), paragraph 4
Supersedes FTB 81-2
Supersedes FTB 82-1, paragraph 5
Amends FTB 82-1, paragraph 7*
Supersedes FTB 83-1
Supersedes FTB 84-2
Supersedes FTB 84-3
Supersedes FTB 86-1
Supersedes FTB 87-2, paragraphs 9 through 11, 13, and 22 through 33 and footnotes 4 and 8
Amends FTB 87-2, paragraphs 14,* 18,* 34,* 35,* 36,* 40,* 45,* and 46*
Amends FTB 88-2, paragraph 4*

Affected by: Paragraph 36(b) amended by FAS 115
              Paragraph 36(e) amended by FAS 123

Other Interpretive Release: FASB Special Report, *A Guide to Implementation of Statement 109 on
                Accounting for Income Taxes: Questions and Answers*

Issues Discussed by FASB Emerging Issues Task Force (EITF)

  Affects: Nullifies EITF Issues No. 84-43, 85-3, 85-15, 85-33, 86-1, 86-4, 86-37, 86-41, and 86-42
            Partially nullifies EITF Issues No. 86-3 and 87-8
            Resolves EITF Issues No. 84-1, 84-2, 84-27, 85-5, 86-11, 87-28, and 91-3 and Topic No. D-7
            Partially resolves EITF Issues No. 85-41 and 88-5
            Affects EITF Issues No. 86-31, 88-19, and 91-8

---

*Result of the amendment, at least in part, described in paragraph 287.

Interpreted by: Paragraph 9 interpreted by EITF Topic No. D-31
Paragraph 9(f) interpreted by EITF Issues No. 92-8 and 93-9 and Topic No. D-56
Paragraph 11 interpreted by EITF Issue No. 93-9
Paragraphs 15 and 31 interpreted by EITF Issue No. 93-16
Paragraph 17 interpreted by EITF Issue No. 94-1 and Topic No. D-31
Paragraph 18 interpreted by EITF Issue No. 95-10
Paragraph 19 interpreted by EITF Issue No. 95-20
Paragraph 26 interpreted by EITF Issue No. 94-10
Paragraph 27 interpreted by EITF Issues No. 93-12 and 93-13 and Topic No. D-30
Paragraph 30 interpreted by EITF Issue No. 93-7
Paragraph 34 interpreted by EITF Issue No. 93-17
Paragraph 35 interpreted by EITF Issue No. 95-9 and Topic No. D-32
Paragraph 36 interpreted by EITF Issue No. 94-10 and Topic No. D-32
Paragraph 36(f) interpreted by EITF Issue No. 92-3
Paragraphs 37 and 38 interpreted by EITF Topic No. D-32
Paragraph 268 interpreted by EITF Topic No. D-33

Related Issues: EITF Issues No. 85-31, 86-9, 88-4, and 96-7

SUMMARY

This Statement establishes financial accounting and reporting standards for the effects of income taxes that result from an enterprise's activities during the current and preceding years. It requires an asset and liability approach for financial accounting and reporting for income taxes. This Statement supersedes FASB Statement No. 96, *Accounting for Income Taxes,* and amends or supersedes other accounting pronouncements listed in Appendix D.

Objectives of Accounting for Income Taxes

The objectives of accounting for income taxes are to recognize (a) the amount of taxes payable or refundable for the current year and (b) deferred tax liabilities and assets for the future tax consequences of events that have been recognized in an enterprise's financial statements or tax returns.

Basic Principles of Accounting for Income Taxes

The following basic principles are applied in accounting for income taxes at the date of the financial statements:

a. A current tax liability or asset is recognized for the estimated taxes payable or refundable on tax returns for the current year.
b. A deferred tax liability or asset is recognized for the estimated future tax effects attributable to temporary differences and carryforwards.
c. The measurement of current and deferred tax liabilities and assets is based on provisions of the enacted tax law; the effects of future changes in tax laws or rates are not anticipated.
d. The measurement of deferred tax assets is reduced, if necessary, by the amount of any tax benefits that, based on available evidence, are not expected to be realized.

Temporary Differences

The tax consequences of most events recognized in the financial statements for a year are included in determining income taxes currently payable. However, tax laws often differ from the recognition and measurement requirements of financial accounting standards, and differences can arise between (a) the amount of taxable income and pretax financial income for a year and (b) the tax bases of assets or liabilities and their reported amounts in financial statements.

APB Opinion No. 11, *Accounting for Income Taxes,* used the term *timing differences* for differences between the years in which transactions affect taxable income and the years in which they enter into the determination of pretax financial income. Timing differences create differences (sometimes accumulating over more than one year) between the tax basis of an asset or liability and its reported amount in financial statements. Other events such as business combinations may also create differences between the tax basis of an asset or liability and its reported amount in financial statements. All such differences collectively are referred to as *temporary differences* in this Statement.

Deferred Tax Consequences of Temporary Differences

Temporary differences ordinarily become taxable or deductible when the related asset is recovered or the related liability is settled. A deferred tax liability or asset represents the increase or decrease in taxes payable or refundable in future years as a result of temporary differences and carryforwards at the end of the current year.

Deferred Tax Liabilities

A deferred tax liability is recognized for temporary differences that will result in taxable amounts in future years. For example, a temporary difference is created between the reported amount and the tax basis of an installment sale receivable if, for tax purposes, some or all of the gain on the installment sale will be included in the determination of taxable income in future years. Because amounts received upon recovery of that receivable will be taxable, a deferred tax liability is recognized in the current year for the related taxes payable in future years.

Deferred Tax Assets

A deferred tax asset is recognized for temporary differences that will result in deductible amounts in future years and for carryforwards. For example, a temporary difference is created between the reported amount and the tax basis of a liability for estimated expenses if, for tax purposes, those estimated expenses are not deductible until a future year. Settlement of that liability will result in tax deductions in future years, and a deferred tax asset is recognized in the current year for the reduction in taxes payable in future years. A valuation allowance is recognized if, based on the weight of available evidence, it is *more likely than not* that some portion or all of the deferred tax asset will not be realized.

Measurement of a Deferred Tax Liability or Asset

This Statement establishes procedures to (a) measure deferred tax liabilities and assets using a tax rate convention and (b) assess whether a valuation allowance should be established for deferred tax assets. Enacted tax laws and rates are considered in determining the applicable tax rate and in assessing the need for a valuation allowance.

All available evidence, both positive and negative, is considered to determine whether, based on the weight of that evidence, a valuation allowance is needed for some portion or all of a deferred tax asset. Judgment must be used in considering the relative impact of negative and positive evidence. The weight given to the potential effect of negative and positive evidence should be commensurate with the extent to which it can be objectively verified. The more negative evidence that exists (a) the more positive evidence is necessary and (b) the more difficult it is to support a conclusion that a valuation allowance is not needed.

Changes in Tax Laws or Rates

This Statement requires that deferred tax liabilities and assets be adjusted in the period of enactment for the effect of an enacted change in tax laws or rates. The effect is included in income from continuing operations.

Effective Date

This Statement is effective for fiscal years beginning after December 15, 1992. Earlier application is encouraged.

Statement of Financial Accounting Standards No. 109

Accounting for Income Taxes

CONTENTS

INTRODUCTION

1. This Statement addresses financial accounting and reporting for the effects of **income taxes**[1] that result from an enterprise's activities during the current and preceding years.

2. FASB Statement No. 96, *Accounting for Income Taxes,* which was issued in December 1987, superseded APB Opinion No. 11, *Accounting for Income Taxes.* The effective date of Statement 96 was delayed to fiscal years that begin after December 15, 1992. In March 1989, the Board began consideration of requests to amend Statement 96 to (a) change the criteria for recognition and measurement of deferred tax assets and various other requirements of Statement 96 and (b) reduce complexity. This Statement is the result of that reconsideration.

STANDARDS OF FINANCIAL ACCOUNTING AND REPORTING

Scope

3. This Statement establishes standards of financial accounting and reporting for income taxes that are currently payable and for the tax consequences of:

a. Revenues, expenses, gains, or losses that are included in **taxable income** of an earlier or later year than the year in which they are recognized in financial income

b. Other **events** that create differences between the tax bases of assets and liabilities and their amounts for financial reporting

c. Operating loss or tax credit **carrybacks** for re-

---

[1]Words that appear in the glossary are set in **boldface type** the first time they appear.

funds of taxes paid in prior years and **carryforwards** to reduce taxes payable in future years.

This Statement supersedes Statement 96 and supersedes or amends other accounting pronouncements listed in Appendix D.

4. The principles and requirements of this Statement are applicable to:

a. Domestic federal (national) income taxes (U.S. federal income taxes for U.S. enterprises) and foreign, state, and local (including franchise) taxes based on income
b. An enterprise's[2] domestic and foreign operations that are consolidated, combined, or accounted for by the equity method
c. Foreign enterprises in preparing financial statements in accordance with U.S. generally accepted accounting principles.

5. This Statement does not address:

a. The basic methods of accounting for the U.S. federal investment tax credit (ITC) and for foreign, state, and local investment tax credits or grants (The deferral and flow-through methods as set forth in APB Opinions No. 2 and No. 4, *Accounting for the "Investment Credit,"* continue to be acceptable methods to account for the U.S. federal ITC.)
b. Discounting (Paragraph 6 of APB Opinion No. 10, *Omnibus Opinion—1966,* addresses that subject.)
c. Accounting for income taxes in interim periods (other than the criteria for recognition of tax benefits and the effect of enacted changes in tax laws or rates and changes in valuation allowances). (APB Opinion No. 28, *Interim Financial Reporting,* and other accounting pronouncements address that subject.)

Objectives and Basic Principles

6. One objective of accounting for income taxes is to recognize the amount of taxes payable or refundable for the current year. A second objective is to recognize **deferred tax liabilities and assets** for the future **tax consequences** of events[3] that have been recognized in an enterprise's financial statements or tax returns.

7. Ideally, the second objective might be stated more specifically to recognize the *expected* future tax consequences of events that have been recognized in the financial statements or tax returns. However, that objective is realistically constrained because (a) the tax payment or refund that results from a particular tax return is a joint result of all the items included in that return, (b) taxes that will be paid or refunded in future years are the joint result of events of the current or prior years and events of future years, and (c) information available about the future is limited. As a result, attribution of taxes to individual items and events is arbitrary and, except in the simplest situations, requires estimates and approximations.

8. To implement the objectives in light of those constraints, the following basic principles (the only exceptions are identified in paragraph 9) are applied in accounting for income taxes at the date of the financial statements:

a. A current tax liability or asset is recognized for the estimated taxes payable or refundable on tax returns for the current year.
b. A deferred tax liability or asset is recognized for the estimated future tax effects attributable to **temporary differences** and carryforwards.
c. The measurement of current and deferred tax liabilities and assets is based on provisions of the enacted tax law; the effects of future changes in tax laws or rates are not anticipated.
d. The measurement of deferred tax assets is reduced, if necessary, by the amount of any tax benefits that, based on available evidence, are not expected to be realized.

9. The only exceptions in applying those basic principles are that this Statement:

a. Continues certain exceptions to the requirements for recognition of deferred taxes for the areas addressed by APB Opinion No. 23, *Accounting for Income Taxes—Special Areas,* as amended by this Statement (paragraphs 31-34)
b. Provides special transitional procedures for temporary differences related to deposits in statutory reserve funds by U.S. steamship enterprises (paragraph 32)
c. Does not amend accounting for leveraged leases as required by FASB Statement No. 13, *Accounting for Leases,* and FASB Interpretation No. 21, *Accounting for Leases in a Business Combination* (paragraphs 256-258)
d. Prohibits recognition of a deferred tax liability or asset related to goodwill (or the portion

---

[2]The term *enterprise* is used throughout this Statement because accounting for income taxes is primarily an issue for business enterprises. However, the requirements of this Statement apply to the activities of a not-for-profit organization that are subject to income taxes.

[3]Some events do not have tax consequences. Certain revenues are exempt from taxation and certain expenses are not deductible. In the United States, for example, interest earned on certain municipal obligations is not taxable and fines are not deductible.

thereof) for which amortization is not deductible for tax purposes (paragraph 30)

e. Does not amend Accounting Research Bulletin No. 51, *Consolidated Financial Statements,* for income taxes paid on intercompany profits on assets remaining within the group, and prohibits recognition of a deferred tax asset for the difference between the tax basis of the assets in the buyer's tax jurisdiction and their cost as reported in the consolidated financial statements

f. Prohibits recognition of a deferred tax liability or asset for differences related to assets and liabilities that, under FASB Statement No. 52, *Foreign Currency Translation,* are remeasured from the local currency into the functional currency using historical exchange rates and that result from (1) changes in exchange rates or (2) indexing for tax purposes.

Temporary Differences

10. **Income taxes currently payable**[4] for a particular year usually include the tax consequences of most events that are recognized in the financial statements for that year. However, because tax laws and financial accounting standards differ in their recognition and measurement of assets, liabilities, equity, revenues, expenses, gains, and losses, differences arise between:

a. The amount of taxable income and pretax financial income for a year
b. The tax bases of assets or liabilities and their reported amounts in financial statements.

11. An assumption inherent in an enterprise's statement of financial position prepared in accordance with generally accepted accounting principles is that the reported amounts of assets and liabilities will be recovered and settled, respectively. Based on that assumption, a difference between the tax basis of an asset or a liability and its reported amount in the statement of financial position will result in taxable or deductible amounts in some future year(s) when the reported amounts of assets are recovered and the reported amounts of liabilities are settled. Examples follow:

a. *Revenues or gains that are taxable after they are recognized in financial income.* An asset (for example, a receivable from an installment sale) may be recognized for revenues or gains that will result in future taxable amounts when the asset is recovered.

b. *Expenses or losses that are deductible after they are recognized in financial income.* A liability (for example, a product warranty liability) may be recognized for expenses or losses that will result in future tax deductible amounts when the liability is settled.

c. *Revenues or gains that are taxable before they are recognized in financial income.* A liability (for example, subscriptions received in advance) may be recognized for an advance payment for goods or services to be provided in future years. For tax purposes, the advance payment is included in taxable income upon the receipt of cash. Future sacrifices to provide goods or services (or future refunds to those who cancel their orders) will result in future tax deductible amounts when the liability is settled.

d. *Expenses or losses that are deductible before they are recognized in financial income.* The cost of an asset (for example, depreciable personal property) may have been deducted for tax purposes faster than it was depreciated for financial reporting. Amounts received upon future recovery of the amount of the asset for financial reporting will exceed the remaining tax basis of the asset, and the excess will be taxable when the asset is recovered.

e. *A reduction in the tax basis of depreciable assets because of tax credits.*[5] Amounts received upon future recovery of the amount of the asset for financial reporting will exceed the remaining tax basis of the asset, and the excess will be taxable when the asset is recovered.

f. *ITC accounted for by the deferral method.* Under Opinion 2, ITC is viewed and accounted for as a reduction of the cost of the related asset (even though, for financial statement presentation, deferred ITC may be reported as deferred income). Amounts received upon future recovery of the reduced cost of the asset for financial reporting will be less than the tax basis of the asset, and the difference will be tax deductible when the asset is recovered.

g. *An increase in the tax basis of assets because of indexing whenever the local currency is the functional currency.* The tax law for a particular tax jurisdiction might require adjustment of the tax basis of a depreciable (or other) asset for the effects of inflation. The inflation-adjusted tax basis of the asset would be used to compute future tax deductions for depreciation or to compute gain or loss on sale of the asset. Amounts received upon future recovery of the local currency historical cost of the asset will be

---

[4]References in this Statement to income taxes currently payable and (total) **income tax expense** are intended to include also **income taxes currently refundable** and (total) **income tax benefit,** respectively.

[5]The Tax Equity and Fiscal Responsibility Act of 1982 provided taxpayers with the choice of either (a) taking the full amount of Accelerated Cost Recovery System (ACRS) deductions and a reduced tax credit (that is, investment tax credit and certain other tax credits) or (b) taking the full tax credit and a reduced amount of ACRS deductions.

less than the remaining tax basis of the asset, and the difference will be tax deductible when the asset is recovered.

h. *Business combinations accounted for by the purchase method.* There may be differences between the assigned values and the tax bases of the assets and liabilities recognized in a business combination accounted for as a purchase under APB Opinion No. 16, *Business Combinations.* Those differences will result in taxable or deductible amounts when the reported amounts of the assets and liabilities are recovered and settled, respectively.

12. Examples (a)-(d) in paragraph 11 illustrate revenues, expenses, gains, or losses that are included in taxable income of an earlier or later year than the year in which they are recognized in pretax financial income. Those differences between taxable income and pretax financial income also create differences (sometimes accumulating over more than one year) between the tax basis of an asset or liability and its reported amount in the financial statements. Examples (e)-(h) in paragraph 11 illustrate other events that create differences between the tax basis of an asset or liability and its reported amount in the financial statements. For all eight examples, the differences result in taxable or deductible amounts when the reported amount of an asset or liability in the financial statements is recovered or settled, respectively.

13. This Statement refers collectively to the types of differences illustrated by those eight examples and to the ones described in paragraph 15 as *temporary differences.* Temporary differences that will result in taxable amounts in future years when the related asset or liability is recovered or settled are often referred to in this Statement as **taxable temporary differences** (examples (a), (d), and (e) in paragraph 11 are taxable temporary differences). Likewise, temporary differences that will result in deductible amounts in future years are often referred to as **deductible temporary differences** (examples (b), (c), (f), and (g) in paragraph 11 are deductible temporary differences). Business combinations accounted for by the purchase method (example (h)) may give rise to both taxable and deductible temporary differences.

14. Certain basis differences may not result in taxable or deductible amounts in future years when the related asset or liability for financial reporting is recovered or settled and, therefore, may not be temporary differences for which a deferred tax lia-

bility or asset is recognized. One example under current U.S. tax law is the excess of cash surrender value of life insurance over premiums paid. That excess is a temporary difference if the cash surrender value is expected to be recovered by surrendering the policy, but is not a temporary difference if the asset is expected to be recovered without tax consequence upon the death of the insured (there will be no taxable amount if the insurance policy is held until the death of the insured).

15. Some temporary differences are deferred taxable income or tax deductions and have balances only on the income tax balance sheet and therefore cannot be identified with a particular asset or liability for financial reporting. That occurs, for example, when a long-term contract is accounted for by the percentage-of-completion method for financial reporting and by the completed-contract method for tax purposes. The temporary difference (income on the contract) is deferred income for tax purposes that becomes taxable when the contract is completed. Another example is organizational costs that are recognized as expenses when incurred for financial reporting and are deferred and deducted in a later year for tax purposes. In both instances, there is no related, identifiable asset or liability for financial reporting, but there is a temporary difference that results from an event that has been recognized in the financial statements and, based on provisions in the tax law, the temporary difference will result in taxable or deductible amounts in future years.

Recognition and Measurement

16. An enterprise shall recognize a deferred tax liability or asset for all temporary differences[6] and operating loss and tax credit carryforwards in accordance with the provisions of paragraph 17. **Deferred tax expense or benefit** is the change during the year in an enterprise's deferred tax liabilities and assets.[7] For deferred tax liabilities and assets acquired in a purchase business combination during the year, it is the change since the combination date. Total income tax expense or benefit for the year is the sum of deferred tax expense or benefit and income taxes currently payable or refundable.

Annual Computation of Deferred Tax Liabilities and Assets

17. Deferred taxes shall be determined separately for each tax-paying component (an individual en-

---

[6]Refer to paragraph 9. A deferred tax liability shall be recognized for the temporary differences addressed by Opinion 23 in accordance with the requirements of this Statement (paragraphs 31-34) and that Opinion, as amended.

[7]Paragraph 230 addresses the manner of reporting the transaction gain or loss that is included in the net change in a deferred foreign tax liability or asset when the reporting currency is the functional currency.

tity or group of entities that is consolidated for tax purposes) in each tax jurisdiction. That determination includes the following procedures:

a. Identify (1) the types and amounts of existing temporary differences and (2) the nature and amount of each type of operating loss and tax credit carryforward and the remaining length of the carryforward period
b. Measure the total deferred tax liability for taxable temporary differences using the applicable tax rate (paragraph 18)
c. Measure the total deferred tax asset for deductible temporary differences and operating loss carryforwards using the applicable tax rate
d. Measure deferred tax assets for each type of tax credit carryforward
e. Reduce deferred tax assets by a **valuation allowance** if, based on the weight of available evidence, it is *more likely than not* (a likelihood of more than 50 percent) that some portion or all of the deferred tax assets will not be realized. The valuation allowance should be sufficient to reduce the deferred tax asset to the amount that is more likely than not to be realized.

18. The objective is to measure a deferred tax liability or asset using the enacted tax rate(s) expected to apply to taxable income in the periods in which the deferred tax liability or asset is expected to be settled or realized. Under current U.S. federal tax law, if taxable income exceeds a specified amount, all taxable income is taxed, in substance, at a single flat tax rate. That tax rate shall be used for measurement of a deferred tax liability or asset by enterprises for which graduated tax rates are not a significant factor. Enterprises for which graduated tax rates are a significant factor shall measure a deferred tax liability or asset using the average graduated tax rate applicable to the amount of estimated annual taxable income in the periods in which the deferred tax liability or asset is estimated to be settled or realized (paragraph 236). Other provisions of enacted tax laws should be considered when determining the tax rate to apply to certain types of temporary differences and carryforwards (for example, the tax law may provide for different tax rates on ordinary income and capital gains). If there is a phased-in change in tax rates, determination of the applicable tax rate requires knowledge about when deferred tax liabilities and assets will be settled and realized.

19. In the U.S. federal tax jurisdiction, the applicable tax rate is the regular tax rate, and a deferred tax asset is recognized for alternative minimum tax credit carryforwards in accordance with the provisions of paragraph 17(d) and (e) of this Statement. If alternative tax systems exist in jurisdictions other than the U.S. federal jurisdiction, the applicable tax rate is determined in a manner consistent with the tax law after giving consideration to any interaction (that is, a mechanism similar to the U.S. alternative minimum tax credit) between the two systems.

20. All available evidence, both positive and negative, should be considered to determine whether, based on the weight of that evidence, a valuation allowance is needed. Information about an enterprise's current financial position and its results of operations for the current and preceding years ordinarily is readily available. That historical information is supplemented by all currently available information about future years. Sometimes, however, historical information may not be available (for example, start-up operations) or it may not be as relevant (for example, if there has been a significant, recent change in circumstances) and special attention is required.

21. Future realization of the tax benefit of an existing deductible temporary difference or carryforward ultimately depends on the existence of sufficient taxable income of the appropriate character (for example, ordinary income or capital gain) within the carryback, carryforward period available under the tax law. The following four possible sources of taxable income may be available under the tax law to realize a tax benefit for deductible temporary differences and carryforwards:

a. Future reversals of existing taxable temporary differences
b. Future taxable income exclusive of reversing temporary differences and carryforwards
c. Taxable income in prior carryback year(s) if carryback is permitted under the tax law
d. **Tax-planning strategies** (paragraph 22) that would, if necessary, be implemented to, for example:
   (1) Accelerate taxable amounts to utilize expiring carryforwards
   (2) Change the character of taxable or deductible amounts from ordinary income or loss to capital gain or loss
   (3) Switch from tax-exempt to taxable investments.

Evidence available about each of those possible sources of taxable income will vary for different tax jurisdictions and, possibly, from year to year. To the extent evidence about one or more sources of taxable income is sufficient to support a conclusion that a valuation allowance is not necessary, other sources need not be considered. Consideration of each source is required, however, to determine the amount of the valuation allowance that is recognized for deferred tax assets.

22. In some circumstances, there are actions (including elections for tax purposes) that (a) are prudent and feasible, (b) an enterprise ordinarily might not take, but would take to prevent an operating loss or tax credit carryforward from expiring unused, and (c) would result in realization of deferred tax assets. This Statement refers to those actions as *tax-planning strategies.* An enterprise shall consider tax-planning strategies in determining the amount of valuation allowance required. Significant expenses to implement a tax-planning strategy or any significant losses that would be recognized if that strategy were implemented (net of any recognizable tax benefits associated with those expenses or losses) shall be included in the valuation allowance. Refer to paragraphs 246-251 for additional guidance.

23. Forming a conclusion that a valuation allowance is not needed is difficult when there is negative evidence such as cumulative losses in recent years. Other examples of negative evidence include (but are not limited to) the following:

a. A history of operating loss or tax credit carryforwards expiring unused
b. Losses expected in early future years (by a presently profitable entity)
c. Unsettled circumstances that, if unfavorably resolved, would adversely affect future operations and profit levels on a continuing basis in future years
d. A carryback, carryforward period that is so brief that it would limit realization of tax benefits if (1) a significant deductible temporary difference is expected to reverse in a single year or (2) the enterprise operates in a traditionally cyclical business.

24. Examples (not prerequisites) of positive evidence that might support a conclusion that a valuation allowance is not needed when there is negative evidence include (but are not limited to) the following:

a. Existing contracts or firm sales backlog that will produce more than enough taxable income to realize the deferred tax asset based on existing sales prices and cost structures
b. An excess of appreciated asset value over the tax basis of the entity's net assets in an amount sufficient to realize the deferred tax asset
c. A strong earnings history exclusive of the loss that created the future deductible amount (tax loss carryforward or deductible temporary difference) coupled with evidence indicating that the loss (for example, an unusual, infrequent,

or extraordinary item) is an aberration rather than a continuing condition.

25. An enterprise must use judgment in considering the relative impact of negative and positive evidence. The weight given to the potential effect of negative and positive evidence should be commensurate with the extent to which it can be objectively verified. The more negative evidence that exists (a) the more positive evidence is necessary and (b) the more difficult it is to support a conclusion that a valuation allowance is not needed for some portion or all of the deferred tax asset.

A Change in the Valuation Allowance

26. The effect of a change in the beginning-of-the-year balance of a valuation allowance that results from a change in circumstances that causes a change in judgment about the realizability of the related deferred tax asset in future years ordinarily shall be included in income from continuing operations. The only exceptions are the initial recognition (that is, by elimination of the valuation allowance) of certain tax benefits that are allocated as required by paragraph 30 and paragraph 36 (items (c) and (e)-(g)). The effect of other changes in the balance of a valuation allowance are allocated among continuing operations and items other than continuing operations as required by paragraph 35.

An Enacted Change in Tax Laws or Rates

27. Deferred tax liabilities and assets shall be adjusted for the effect of a change in tax laws or rates. The effect shall be included in income from continuing operations for the period that includes the enactment date.

A Change in the Tax Status of an Enterprise

28. An enterprise's tax status may change from nontaxable to taxable or from taxable to nontaxable. An example is a change from a partnership to a corporation and vice versa. A deferred tax liability or asset shall be recognized for temporary differences in accordance with the requirements of this Statement at the date that a nontaxable enterprise becomes a taxable enterprise. A deferred tax liability or asset shall be eliminated at the date an enterprise ceases to be a taxable enterprise. In either case, the effect of (a) an election for a voluntary change in tax status is recognized on the approval date or on the filing date if approval is not necessary and (b) a change in tax status that results from a change in tax law is recognized on the enactment date. The effect of recognizing or elimi-

nating the deferred tax liability or asset shall be included in income from continuing operations.

Regulated Enterprises

29. Regulated enterprises that meet the criteria for application of FASB Statement No. 71, *Accounting for the Effects of Certain Types of Regulation,* are not exempt from the requirements of this Statement. Specifically, this Statement:

a. Prohibits net-of-tax accounting and reporting
b. Requires recognition of a deferred tax liability (1) for tax benefits that are flowed through to customers when temporary differences originate and (2) for the equity component of the allowance for funds used during construction
c. Requires adjustment of a deferred tax liability or asset for an enacted change in tax laws or rates.

If, as a result of an action by a regulator, it is probable that the future increase or decrease in taxes payable for items (b) and (c) above will be recovered from or returned to customers through future rates, an asset or liability is recognized for that probable future revenue or reduction in future revenue pursuant to paragraphs 9-11 of Statement 71. That asset or liability also is a temporary difference for which a deferred tax liability or asset shall be recognized.

Business Combinations

30. A deferred tax liability or asset shall be recognized in accordance with the requirements of this Statement for differences between the assigned values and the tax bases of the assets and liabilities (except the portion of goodwill for which amortization is not deductible for tax purposes, unallocated "negative goodwill," leveraged leases, and acquired Opinion 23 differences[8]) recognized in a purchase business combination (refer to paragraphs 259-272 for additional guidance). If a valuation allowance is recognized for the deferred tax asset for an acquired entity's deductible temporary differences or operating loss or tax credit carryforwards at the acquisition date, the tax benefits for those items that are first recognized (that is, by elimination of that valuation allowance) in financial statements after the acquisition date shall be applied (a) first to reduce to zero any goodwill related to the acquisition, (b) second to reduce to zero other noncurrent intangible assets related to the acquisition, and (c) third to reduce income tax expense.

Opinion 23 and U.S. Steamship Enterprise Temporary Differences

31. A deferred tax liability is not recognized for the following types of temporary differences unless it becomes apparent that those temporary differences will reverse in the foreseeable future:

a. An excess of the amount for financial reporting over the tax basis of an investment in a foreign subsidiary or a foreign corporate joint venture as defined in APB Opinion No. 18, *The Equity Method of Accounting for Investments in Common Stock,* that is essentially permanent in duration
b. Undistributed earnings of a domestic subsidiary or a domestic corporate joint venture that is essentially permanent in duration that arose in fiscal years beginning on or before December 15, 1992[9]
c. "Bad debt reserves" for tax purposes of U.S. savings and loan associations (and other "qualified" thrift lenders) that arose in tax years beginning before December 31, 1987 (that is, the base-year amount)
d. "Policyholders' surplus" of stock life insurance companies that arose in fiscal years beginning on or before December 15, 1992.

The indefinite reversal criterion in Opinion 23 shall not be applied to analogous types of temporary differences.

32. A deferred tax liability shall be recognized for the following types of taxable temporary differences:

a. An excess of the amount for financial reporting over the tax basis of an investment in a domestic subsidiary that arises in fiscal years beginning after December 15, 1992
b. An excess of the amount for financial reporting over the tax basis of an investment in a 50-percent-or-less-owned investee except as provided in paragraph 31(a) and (b) for a corporate joint venture that is essentially permanent in duration
c. "Bad debt reserves" for tax purposes of U.S. savings and loan associations (and other "qualified" thrift lenders) that arise in tax years beginning after December 31, 1987 (that is, amounts in excess of the base-year amount).

The tax effects of temporary differences related to deposits in statutory reserve funds by U.S. steamship enterprises that arose in fiscal years beginning on or before December 15, 1992 and that were not

---

[8]Acquired Opinion 23 differences are accounted for in accordance with the requirements of Opinion 23, as amended by this Statement.

[9]A last-in, first-out (LIFO) pattern determines whether reversals pertain to differences that arose in fiscal years beginning on or before December 15, 1992.

previously recognized shall be recognized when those temporary differences reverse or in their entirety at the beginning of the fiscal year for which this Statement is first applied.

33. Whether an excess of the amount for financial reporting over the tax basis of an investment in a more-than-50-percent-owned domestic subsidiary is a taxable temporary difference must be assessed. It is not a taxable temporary difference if the tax law provides a means by which the reported amount of that investment can be recovered tax-free and the enterprise expects that it will ultimately use that means. For example, under current U.S. federal tax law:

a. An enterprise may elect to determine taxable gain or loss on the liquidation of an 80-percent-or-more-owned subsidiary by reference to the tax basis of the subsidiary's net assets rather than by reference to the parent company's tax basis for the stock of that subsidiary.
b. An enterprise may execute a statutory merger whereby a subsidiary is merged into the parent company, the minority shareholders receive stock of the parent, the subsidiary's stock is cancelled, and no taxable gain or loss results if the continuity of ownership, continuity of business enterprise, and certain other requirements of the tax law are met.

Some elections for tax purposes are available only if the parent company owns a specified percentage of the subsidiary's stock. The parent company sometimes may own less than that specified percentage, and the price per share to acquire a minority interest may significantly exceed the per share equivalent of the amount reported as minority interest in the consolidated financial statements. In those circumstances, the excess of the amount for financial reporting over the tax basis of the parent's investment in the subsidiary is not a taxable temporary difference if settlement of the minority interest is expected to occur at the point in time when settlement would not result in a significant cost. That could occur, for example, toward the end of the life of the subsidiary, after it has recovered and settled most of its assets and liabilities, respectively. The fair value of the minority interest ordinarily will approximately equal its percentage of the subsidiary's net assets if those net assets consist primarily of cash.

34. A deferred tax asset shall be recognized for an excess of the tax basis over the amount for financial reporting of an investment in a subsidiary or corporate joint venture that is essentially permanent in duration only if it is apparent that the temporary difference will reverse in the foreseeable future. The need for a valuation allowance for that deferred tax asset and other deferred tax assets related to Opinion 23 temporary differences (for example, a deferred tax asset for foreign tax credit carryforwards or for a savings and loan association's bad-debt reserve for financial reporting) shall be assessed. Paragraph 21 identifies four sources of taxable income to be considered in determining the need for and amount of a valuation allowance for those and other deferred tax assets. One source is future reversals of temporary differences. Future reversals of taxable differences for which a deferred tax liability has not been recognized based on the exceptions cited in paragraph 31, however, shall not be considered. Another source is future taxable income exclusive of reversing temporary differences and carryforwards. Future distributions of future earnings of a subsidiary or corporate joint venture, however, shall not be considered except to the extent that a deferred tax liability has been recognized for existing undistributed earnings or earnings have been remitted in the past.

Intraperiod Tax Allocation

35. Income tax expense or benefit for the year shall be allocated among continuing operations, discontinued operations, extraordinary items, and items charged or credited directly to shareholders' equity (paragraph 36). The amount allocated to continuing operations is the tax effect of the pretax income or loss from continuing operations that occurred during the year, plus or minus income tax effects of (a) changes in circumstances that cause a change in judgment about the realization of deferred tax assets in future years (paragraph 26), (b) changes in tax laws or rates (paragraph 27), (c) changes in tax status (paragraph 28), and (d) tax-deductible dividends paid to shareholders (except as set forth in paragraph 36 for dividends paid on unallocated shares held by an employee stock ownership plan [ESOP] or any other stock compensation arrangement). The remainder is allocated to items other than continuing operations in accordance with the provisions of paragraph 38.

36. The tax effects of the following items occurring during the year are charged or credited directly to related components of shareholders' equity:

a. Adjustments of the opening balance of retained earnings for certain changes in accounting principles or a correction of an error
b. **Gains and losses included in comprehensive income but excluded from net income** (for example, translation adjustments under Statement 52 and changes in the carrying amount of marketable securities under FASB Statement No. 12, *Accounting for Certain Marketable Securities*)
c. An increase or decrease in contributed capital (for example, deductible expenditures reported

as a reduction of the proceeds from issuing capital stock)

d. An increase in the tax basis of assets acquired in a taxable business combination accounted for as a pooling of interests and for which a tax benefit is recognized at the date of the business combination

e. Expenses for employee stock options recognized differently for financial reporting and tax purposes (refer to paragraph 17 of APB Opinion No. 25, *Accounting for Stock Issued to Employees*)

f. Dividends that are paid on unallocated shares held by an ESOP and that are charged to retained earnings

g. Deductible temporary differences and carryforwards that existed at the date of a quasi reorganization (except as set forth in paragraph 39).

37. The tax benefit of an operating loss carryforward or carryback (other than those carryforwards referred to at the end of this paragraph) shall be reported in the same manner as the source of the income or loss in the current year and not in the same manner as (a) the source of the operating loss carryforward or taxes paid in a prior year or (b) the source of expected future income that will result in realization of a deferred tax asset for an operating loss carryforward from the current year. The only exceptions are as follows:

a. Tax effects of deductible temporary differences and carryforwards that existed at the date of a purchase business combination and for which a tax benefit is initially recognized in subsequent years in accordance with the provisions of paragraph 30

b. Tax effects of deductible temporary differences and carryforwards that are allocated to shareholders' equity in accordance with the provisions of paragraph 36 (items (c) and (e)-(g)).

38. If there is only one item other than continuing operations, the portion of income tax expense or benefit for the year that remains after the allocation to continuing operations is allocated to that item. If there are two or more items other than continuing operations, the amount that remains after the allocation to continuing operations shall be allocated among those other items in proportion to their individual effects on income tax expense or benefit for the year. When there are two or more items other than continuing operations, the sum of the separately calculated, individual effects of each item sometimes may not equal the amount of income tax expense or benefit for the year that remains after the allocation to continuing operations. In those circumstances, the procedures to allocate the remaining amount to items other

than continuing operations are as follows:

a. Determine the effect on income tax expense or benefit for the year of the total net loss for all net loss items

b. Apportion the tax benefit determined in (a) ratably to each net loss item

c. Determine the amount that remains, that is, the difference between (1) the amount to be allocated to all items other than continuing operations and (2) the amount allocated to all net loss items

d. Apportion the tax expense determined in (c) ratably to each net gain item.

Refer to paragraphs 273-276 for additional guidance.

Certain Quasi Reorganizations

39. The tax benefits of deductible temporary differences and carryforwards as of the date of a quasi reorganization as defined and contemplated in ARB No. 43, Chapter 7, "Capital Accounts," ordinarily are reported as a direct addition to contributed capital if the tax benefits are recognized in subsequent years. The only exception is for enterprises that have previously both adopted Statement 96 and effected a quasi reorganization that involves only the elimination of a deficit in retained earnings by a concurrent reduction in contributed capital prior to adopting this Statement. For those enterprises, subsequent recognition of the tax benefit of prior deductible temporary differences and carryforwards is included in income and reported as required by paragraph 37 (without regard to the referenced exceptions) and then reclassified from retained earnings to contributed capital. Those enterprises should disclose (a) the date of the quasi reorganization, (b) the manner of reporting the tax benefits and that it differs from present accounting requirements for other enterprises and (c) the effect of those tax benefits on income from continuing operations, income before extraordinary items, and on net income (and on related per share amounts).

Separate Financial Statements of a Subsidiary

40. The consolidated amount of current and deferred tax expense for a group that files a consolidated tax return shall be allocated among the members of the group when those members issue separate financial statements. This Statement does not require a single allocation method. The method adopted, however, shall be systematic, rational, and consistent with the broad principles established by this Statement. A method that allocates current and deferred taxes to members of the group by applying this Statement to each member

as if it were a separate taxpayer[10] meets those criteria. Examples of methods that are not consistent with the broad principles established by this Statement include:

a. A method that allocates only current taxes payable to a member of the group that has taxable temporary differences
b. A method that allocates deferred taxes to a member of the group using a method fundamentally different from the asset and liability method described in this Statement (for example, the Opinion 11 deferred method)
c. A method that allocates no current or deferred tax expense to a member of the group that has taxable income because the consolidated group has no current or deferred tax expense.

Certain disclosures are also required (paragraph 49).

Financial Statement Presentation

41. In a classified statement of financial position, an enterprise shall separate deferred tax liabilities and assets into a current amount and a noncurrent amount. Deferred tax liabilities and assets shall be classified as current or noncurrent based on the classification of the related asset or liability for financial reporting. A deferred tax liability or asset that is not related to an asset or liability for financial reporting (paragraph 15), including deferred tax assets related to carryforwards, shall be classified according to the expected reversal date of the temporary difference pursuant to FASB Statement No. 37, *Balance Sheet Classification of Deferred Income Taxes*. The valuation allowance for a particular tax jurisdiction shall be allocated between current and noncurrent deferred tax assets for that tax jurisdiction on a pro rata basis.

42. For a particular tax-paying component of an enterprise and within a particular tax jurisdiction, (a) all current deferred tax liabilities and assets shall be offset and presented as a single amount and (b) all noncurrent deferred tax liabilities and assets shall be offset and presented as a single amount. However, an enterprise shall not offset deferred tax liabilities and assets attributable to different tax-paying components of the enterprise or to different tax jurisdictions.

Financial Statement Disclosure

43. The components of the net deferred tax liability or asset recognized in an enterprise's statement of financial position shall be disclosed as follows:

a. The total of all deferred tax liabilities measured in procedure (b) of paragraph 17
b. The total of all deferred tax assets measured in procedures (c) and (d) of paragraph 17
c. The total valuation allowance recognized for deferred tax assets determined in procedure (e) of paragraph 17.

The net change during the year in the total valuation allowance also shall be disclosed. A **public enterprise** shall disclose the approximate tax effect of each type of temporary difference and carryforward that gives rise to a significant portion of deferred tax liabilities and deferred tax assets (before allocation of valuation allowances). A **nonpublic enterprise** shall disclose the types of significant temporary differences and carryforwards but may omit disclosure of the tax effects of each type. A public enterprise that is not subject to income taxes because its income is taxed directly to its owners shall disclose that fact and the net difference between the tax bases and the reported amounts of the enterprise's assets and liabilities.

44. The following information shall be disclosed whenever a deferred tax liability is not recognized because of the exceptions to comprehensive recognition of deferred taxes for any of the areas addressed by Opinion 23 (as amended by this Statement) or for deposits in statutory reserve funds by U.S. steamship enterprises:

a. A description of the types of temporary differences for which a deferred tax liability has not been recognized and the types of events that would cause those temporary differences to become taxable
b. The cumulative amount of each type of temporary difference
c. The amount of the unrecognized deferred tax liability for temporary differences related to investments in foreign subsidiaries and foreign corporate joint ventures that are essentially permanent in duration if determination of that lia-

---

[10]In that situation, the sum of the amounts allocated to individual members of the group may not equal the consolidated amount. That may also be the result when there are intercompany transactions between members of the group. The criteria are satisfied, nevertheless, after giving effect to the type of adjustments (including eliminations) normally present in preparing consolidated financial statements.

bility is practicable or a statement that determination is not practicable

d. The amount of the deferred tax liability for temporary differences other than those in (c) above (that is, undistributed domestic earnings, the bad-debt reserve for tax purposes of a U.S. savings and loan association or other qualified thrift lender, the policyholders' surplus of a life insurance enterprise, and the statutory reserve funds of a U.S. steamship enterprise) that is not recognized in accordance with the provisions of paragraphs 31 and 32.

45. The significant components of income tax expense attributable to continuing operations for each year presented shall be disclosed in the financial statements or notes thereto. Those components would include, for example:

a. **Current tax expense or benefit**
b. Deferred tax expense or benefit (exclusive of the effects of other components listed below)
c. Investment tax credits
d. Government grants (to the extent recognized as a reduction of income tax expense)
e. The benefits of operating loss carryforwards
f. Tax expense that results from allocating certain tax benefits either directly to contributed capital or to reduce goodwill or other noncurrent intangible assets of an acquired entity
g. Adjustments of a deferred tax liability or asset for enacted changes in tax laws or rates or a change in the tax status of the enterprise
h. Adjustments of the beginning-of-the-year balance of a valuation allowance because of a change in circumstances that causes a change in judgment about the realizability of the related deferred tax asset in future years.

46. The amount of income tax expense or benefit allocated to continuing operations and the amounts separately allocated to other items (in accordance with the provisions of paragraphs 35-39) shall be disclosed for each year for which those items are presented.

47. A public enterprise shall disclose a reconciliation using percentages or dollar amounts of (a) the reported amount of income tax expense attributable to continuing operations for the year to (b) the amount of income tax expense that would result from applying domestic federal statutory tax rates to pretax income from continuing operations. The "statutory" tax rates shall be the regular tax rates if there are alternative tax systems. The estimated amount and the nature of each significant reconciling item shall be disclosed. A nonpublic enterprise shall disclose the nature of significant reconciling items but may omit a numerical

reconciliation. If not otherwise evident from the disclosures required by this paragraph and paragraphs 43-46, all enterprises shall disclose the nature and effect of any other significant matters affecting comparability of information for all periods presented.

48. An enterprise shall disclose (a) the amounts and expiration dates of operating loss and tax credit carryforwards for tax purposes and (b) any portion of the valuation allowance for deferred tax assets for which subsequently recognized tax benefits will be allocated to reduce goodwill or other noncurrent intangible assets of an acquired entity or directly to contributed capital (paragraphs 30 and 36).

49. An entity that is a member of a group that files a consolidated tax return shall disclose in its separately issued financial statements:

a. The aggregate amount of current and deferred tax expense for each statement of earnings presented and the amount of any tax-related balances due to or from affiliates as of the date of each statement of financial position presented
b. The principal provisions of the method by which the consolidated amount of current and deferred tax expense is allocated to members of the group and the nature and effect of any changes in that method (and in determining related balances to or from affiliates) during the years for which the disclosures in (a) above are presented.

Effective Date and Transition

50. This Statement shall be effective for fiscal years beginning after December 15, 1992. Earlier application is encouraged. Financial statements for any number of consecutive fiscal years before the effective date may be restated to conform to the provisions of this Statement. Initial application of this Statement shall be as of the beginning of an enterprise's fiscal year (that is, if the Statement is adopted prior to the effective date and during an interim period other than the first interim period, all prior interim periods of that fiscal year shall be restated). Application of the requirements for recognition of a deferred tax liability or asset for a restated interim or annual period shall be based on the facts and circumstances as they existed at that prior date and without the benefit of hindsight.

51. The effect of initially applying this Statement shall be reported as the effect of a change in accounting principle in a manner similar to the cumulative effect of a change in accounting principle

(APB Opinion No. 20, *Accounting Changes,* paragraph 20) except for initially recognized tax benefits of the type required by this Statement to be excluded from comprehensive income. If the earliest year restated is not presented in the financial statements, the beginning balance of retained earnings and, if necessary, any other components of shareholders' equity for the earliest year presented shall be adjusted for the effect of the restatement as of that date. Paragraph 30 addresses the manner of reporting acquired tax benefits initially recognized subsequent to a business combination and paragraph 36 identifies five items ((c)-(g)) for which tax benefits are excluded from comprehensive income and allocated directly to contributed capital or retained earnings. Pro forma effects of retroactive application (Opinion 20, paragraph 21) are not required if statements of earnings presented for prior years are not restated.

52. When initially presented, the financial statements for the year this Statement is first adopted shall disclose:

a. The effect, if any, of adopting this Statement on pretax income from continuing operations (for example, the effect of adjustments for prior purchase business combinations and for regulated enterprises) for the year of adoption if restated financial statements for the prior year are not presented
b. The effect of any restatement on income from continuing operations, income before extraordinary items, and net income (and on related per share amounts) for each year for which restated financial statements are presented.

Prior Business Combinations

53. If financial statements for prior years are restated, all purchase business combinations that were consummated in those prior years shall be remeasured in accordance with the requirements of this Statement.

54. For a purchase business combination consummated prior to the beginning of the year for which this Statement is first applied, any balance remaining as of that date for goodwill or negative goodwill shall not be adjusted to equal the amount it would be if financial statements for the year of the combination and subsequent years were restated. However, except for leveraged leases and except as provided in paragraph 55, (a) remaining balances as of the date of initially applying this Statement for assets and liabilities acquired in that combination shall be adjusted from their net-of-tax amounts to their pretax amounts and (b) any differences between those adjusted remaining balances and their tax bases are temporary differences. A deferred tax liability or asset shall be recognized for those temporary differences pursuant to the requirements of this Statement as of the beginning of the year for which this Statement is first applied.

55. If, for a particular business combination, determination of the adjustment for any or all of the assets and liabilities referred to in paragraph 54 is impracticable, either because the necessary information is no longer available or because the cost to develop that information is excessive, none of the remaining balances of any assets and liabilities acquired in that combination shall be adjusted to pretax amounts, that is, all remaining amounts that were originally assigned on a net-of-tax basis pursuant to paragraph 89 of Opinion 16 shall not be adjusted. Any differences between those unadjusted remaining balances and their tax bases are temporary differences, and a deferred tax liability or asset shall be recognized for those temporary differences pursuant to the requirements of this Statement as of the beginning of the year for which this Statement is first applied.

56. The net effect of the adjustments required by paragraphs 54 and 55 shall be included in the effect of initially applying this Statement and reported in accordance with the provisions of paragraph 51.

Assets of Regulated Enterprises Reported on a Net-of-Tax or After-Tax Basis

57. Some regulated enterprises that apply Statement 71 have accounted for certain components of construction in progress on either a net-of-tax or after-tax basis, or both. Upon initial application of this Statement, those enterprises shall make appropriate adjustments required by this Statement to account for the net-of-tax and after-tax components of construction in progress as if the requirements of this Statement were applied to that construction in progress in all prior years. Except as provided in paragraph 58, the reported amount of plant in service at the beginning of the year for which this Statement is first applied shall be similarly adjusted.

58. If determination of the adjustment to plant in service referred to in paragraph 57 is impracticable, either because the necessary information is no longer available or because the cost to develop that information is excessive, any difference between the reported amount and the tax basis of that plant in service is a temporary difference, and a deferred tax liability shall be recognized for that temporary difference. If, as a result of an action by a regulator, it is probable that amounts required

for settlement of that deferred tax liability will be recovered from customers through future rates, an asset and the related deferred tax liability for that additional temporary difference shall be recognized for that probable future revenue.

59. The net effect of the adjustments required by paragraphs 57 and 58 shall be included in the effect of initially applying this Statement and reported in accordance with the provisions of paragraph 51.

> **The provisions of this Statement need not be applied to immaterial items.**

This Statement was adopted by the unanimous vote of the six members of the Financial Accounting Standards Board:

Dennis R. Beresford,	Victor H. Brown	A. Clarence Sampson
Chairman	James J. Leisenring	Robert J. Swieringa
Joseph V. Anania		

Appendix A

BASIS FOR CONCLUSIONS

CONTENTS

Appendix A

BASIS FOR CONCLUSIONS

Introduction

60. This appendix summarizes considerations that members of the Board deemed significant in reaching the conclusions in this Statement. It includes reasons for accepting certain views and rejecting others. Individual Board members gave greater weight to some factors than to others.

61. The tax consequences of most events affect taxable income for the year the events are recognized in the financial statements. The tax consequences of some events are deferred and will affect taxable income in future years. Events that have **deferred tax consequences** give rise to temporary differences. Paragraphs 10-15 discuss examples of temporary differences and describe how they originate and how they result in taxable or deductible amounts in future years.

62. The basic accounting issues about the effects of income taxes to be recognized in the financial statements for a period are as follows:

a. Whether the effects of income taxes recognized in the financial statements should be:
   (1) The amount of taxes payable for the period as determined by the tax return
   (2) The above plus the effect of all (comprehensive recognition) or at least some (partial recognition) temporary differences
   (3) The above plus the future tax benefit of operating loss and tax credit carryforwards

b. If recognized, whether the tax effects of temporary differences are:
   (1) Tax assets or liabilities to be recovered or settled in the future (the asset and liability approach)
   (2) Reductions in related assets and liabilities (the net-of-tax approach)
   (3) Deferred charges or deferred credits (the deferred approach)
   (4) A combination of the above based on the nature of the temporary differences
c. Whether measurement of the tax effects of temporary differences should be:
   (1) The incremental effect in the current year or the incremental effect in future years
   (2) Discounted
d. Whether deferred tax calculations are too complex, burdensome, and costly for:
   (1) Private and small public enterprises
   (2) All enterprises.

Conclusions on Basic Issues

63. The Board concluded that the financial statements should reflect the current and deferred tax consequences of all events[11] that have been recognized in the financial statements or tax returns. The Board believes that the asset and liability approach to accounting for income taxes is most consistent with the definitions in FASB Concepts Statement No. 6, *Elements of Financial Statements,* and with other parts of the conceptual framework. It also believes that the asset and liability approach produces the most useful and understandable information and that it is no more complex than any other approach to accounting for income taxes.

---

[11]Refer to paragraph 9.

64. The Board concluded that a current tax liability or asset should be recognized for taxes payable or refundable for the current year, and that a deferred tax liability or asset should be recognized for the deferred tax consequences of temporary differences and operating loss or tax credit carryforwards. The Board's reasons for rejecting partial or no recognition of deferred taxes are explained in paragraphs 200-205, and the reasons for rejecting the net-of-tax, deferred, and combination approaches are explained in paragraphs 206-222.

65. The Board believes that it would be desirable to measure a deferred tax liability or asset as the incremental effect on future cash flows for income taxes that will result from existing temporary differences and carryforwards. As a practical matter, however, the Board notes that the information needed for precise predictions about the future is not available. The Board concluded that certain simplifying assumptions and procedures are necessary.

66. Under the requirements of this Statement:

a. The enacted tax rate(s) expected to apply to taxable income in future years is used to measure:
   (1) The total deferred tax liability for taxable temporary differences
   (2) The total deferred tax asset for deductible temporary differences and operating loss carryforwards.
b. The total deferred tax asset is reduced by a valuation allowance if it is more likely than not that some portion or all of the asset will not be realized.
c. Deferred tax liabilities and assets are not discounted.

67. Measurement of current and deferred tax liabilities and assets is based on provisions of the enacted tax law; the effects of future changes in tax laws or rates are not anticipated. Calculations may often be complicated, but the Board believes that most of those complications are primarily attributable to applying the complexities in the tax law to complex business transactions. The Board concluded that complexities in the tax law do not justify different accounting for income taxes depending on an enterprise's size or ownership.

Benefits and Costs

68. The Board follows certain precepts, including the precept to promulgate standards only when the expected benefits of the resulting information exceed the perceived costs. The Board strives to determine that a proposed standard will fill a significant need and that the costs imposed to meet that standard, as compared with other alternatives, are justified in relation to the overall benefits of the resulting information.

69. Accounting for income taxes is a pervasive subject that affects most enterprises. Income taxes must be computed for complex business transactions within the context of voluminous, complicated, and constantly changing tax laws, rules, and regulations. Accounting requirements add additional complexities.

70. Opinion 11 was issued in 1967. Criticisms and concerns set forth in the accounting literature and in letters to the Board that requested reconsideration of Opinion 11 focused both on the complexity of the accounting requirements and on the relevance of the results of applying the requirements.

71. Numerous accounting pronouncements amended, interpreted, or supplemented Opinion 11 for areas that were not addressed or were not clear in that Opinion and for changes in the tax law. One criticism was that the various accounting requirements were inconsistent and that the results of applying them could only be described in terms of a mechanical process. Another criticism was that the time devoted to coping with the complexities and ambiguities of the requirements was not cost-beneficial when compared with the usefulness of the resulting information.

72. Criticisms and concerns also focused on the effect of applying Opinion 11 on the statement of financial position and on the increasing amounts of deferred tax credits reported by many enterprises. As measured and recognized under the requirements of Opinion 11, deferred tax credits and charges were not payables or receivables. Because those items were often considered to be only "bookkeeping" entries, some users of financial statements added deferred tax credits to shareholders' equity, and they also added the provision for deferred taxes back to earnings. Others did not. Uncertainty about the nature of those amounts created confusion for users.

73. Statement 96 was issued in December 1987. After it was issued, the Board received numerous requests to amend Statement 96. Those requests primarily focused on (a) changing the restrictive Statement 96 requirements for recognition of deferred tax assets to permit, in more instances, recognition of tax benefits that are expected to be realized and (b) reducing the complexity of scheduling the future reversals of temporary differences and considering hypothetical tax-planning strategies. The Board carefully considered the criticisms and concerns about the complexity of the requirements of Statement 96

and the understandability of the results of applying those requirements.

74. This Statement is the result of a comprehensive reconsideration of Opinion 11, Statement 96, and other related authoritative pronouncements. The Board believes that the requirements of this Statement produce results that are understandable and relevant. The Board also believes that the requirements are less complex than those of either Opinion 11 or Statement 96. Practical decisions, such as eliminating the proposal in the June 1991 FASB Exposure Draft, *Accounting for Income Taxes,* to recognize deferred taxes for certain temporary differences that are not timing differences, may reduce the cost and complexity of computing deferred taxes for many enterprises. Application of judgment to assess whether a valuation allowance is needed for deferred tax assets may sometimes be complex, but that complexity is the unavoidable result of the need for an informed decision about the effect of income taxes on an enterprise's financial position and results of operations.

A Deferred Tax Liability for Taxable Temporary Differences

75. The Board considered whether the deferred tax consequences of taxable temporary differences are a liability. Liabilities are defined in paragraph 35 of Concepts Statement 6 as "probable future sacrifices of economic benefits arising from present obligations of a particular entity to transfer assets or provide services to other entities in the future as a result of past transactions or events" (footnote references omitted).

76. The first characteristic of a liability is that it "embodies a present duty or responsibility to one or more other entities that entails settlement by probable future transfer or use of assets at a specified or determinable date, on occurrence of a specified event, or on demand" (Concepts Statement 6, paragraph 36). Taxes are a legal obligation imposed by a government, and an obligation for the deferred tax consequences of taxable temporary differences stems from the requirements of the tax law.

77. A government levies taxes on net taxable income. Temporary differences will become taxable amounts in future years, thereby increasing taxable income and taxes payable, upon recovery or settlement of the recognized and reported amounts of an enterprise's assets or liabilities.

78. The second characteristic of a liability is that "the duty or responsibility obligates a particular entity, leaving it little or no discretion to avoid the future sacrifice" (Concepts Statement 6, paragraph 36). An enterprise might be able to delay the future reversal of taxable temporary differences by delaying the events that give rise to those reversals, for example, by delaying the recovery of related assets or the settlement of related liabilities. A contention that those temporary differences will never result in taxable amounts, however, would contradict the accounting assumption inherent in the statement of financial position that the reported amounts of assets and liabilities will be recovered and settled, respectively; thereby making that statement internally inconsistent. For that reason, the Board concluded that the only question is when, not whether, temporary differences will result in taxable amounts in future years.

79. The third characteristic of a liability is that "the transaction or other event obligating the entity has already happened" (Concepts Statement 6, paragraph 36). Deferred tax liabilities result from the same past events that create taxable temporary differences.

A Deferred Tax Asset for Deductible Temporary Differences and Carryforwards

80. The Board considered whether the deferred tax consequences of deductible temporary differences and carryforwards are an asset. Assets are defined in paragraph 25 of Concepts Statement 6 as "probable future economic benefits obtained or controlled by a particular entity as a result of past transactions or events" (footnote reference omitted).

81. The first characteristic of an asset is that it "embodies a probable future benefit that involves a capacity, singly or in combination with other assets, to contribute directly or indirectly to future net cash inflows" (Concepts Statement 6, paragraph 26). Deductible temporary differences and carryforwards at the end of the current year that reduce taxable income and taxes payable in future years contribute indirectly to future net cash inflows. Alternatively, if loss carryback is permitted by the tax law, deductible temporary differences at the end of the current year that increase taxes refundable in future years contribute directly to future net cash inflows. In both circumstances, the first characteristic of an asset is met.

82. The second characteristic of an asset is that "a particular entity can obtain the benefit and control others' access to it" (Concepts Statement 6, paragraph 26). To the extent permitted by tax law, an enterprise has the ability to obtain the benefit that may result from existing deductible temporary differences and carryforwards by reducing taxes payable either for future years or for the current or preceding years by carryback refund. The enterprise has an exclusive right to that future benefit and therefore can control others' access to it.

83. The third characteristic of an asset is that "the transaction or other event giving rise to the entity's right to or control of the benefit has already occurred" (Concepts Statement 6, paragraph 26). The Board's conclusion in Statement 96 was that the critical past event is earning the income that permits realization of the benefit. Prior to earning income, deductible temporary differences and carryforwards were considered to be future tax benefits that are not yet recognizable in the financial statements.

84. The Statement 96 requirements for recognition of the tax benefit of deductible temporary differences and carryforwards were criticized by the Board's constituents. Many constituents stated that Statement 96 sometimes produced results that were not understandable or relevant. Some constituents were particularly concerned about the nonrecognition of tax benefits that are expected to be realized.

85. Upon reconsidering the requirements of Statement 96, the Board decided that the critical recognition event is the event that gives rise to deductible temporary differences and carryforwards. The Exposure Draft proposed, and most respondents agreed, that that event is the event that gives the enterprise a right to or control over the future tax benefits. Once that event has occurred, those tax benefits are recognizable in the financial statements.

86. A tax benefit will be realized, however, only if there is sufficient taxable income in particular future years. The existence or absence of future taxable income is critical to measurement of the amount of tax benefit that is recognized for deductible temporary differences and carryforwards at the end of the current year. The Board concluded that earning taxable income in future years (a) is the event that confirms the existence of a recognizable tax benefit at the end of the current year and (b) is not the prerequisite event that must occur before a tax benefit may be recognized as was the case under the requirements of Statement 96.

The Asset and Liability Approach to Accounting for Income Taxes

87. In concept, a deferred tax liability or asset represents the increase or decrease in taxes payable or refundable in future years as a result of temporary differences and carryforwards at the end of the current year. That concept is an incremental concept. A literal application of that concept would require measurement of:

a. The amount of taxes that *will* be payable or refundable in future years *inclusive* of reversing temporary differences and carryforwards

b. The amount of taxes that *would* be payable or refundable in future years *exclusive* of reversing temporary differences and carryforwards.

The incremental tax effect is the difference between those measurements.

88. As a practical matter, the Board believes that determination of the incremental difference between all future income tax cash flows with and without reversing temporary differences and carryforwards is impossible except in the simplest situations. For that reason, the Board decided to establish procedures (a) to measure deferred tax liabilities and assets using a tax rate convention and then (b) to assess whether a valuation allowance should be established for deferred tax assets.

Measurement

89. The Exposure Draft proposed that deferred tax liabilities and assets should be measured using the enacted tax rate expected to apply to the *last* dollars of taxable income in the periods in which the deferred tax liability or asset is expected to be settled or realized. Some respondents to the Exposure Draft disagreed. In their view, that approach would often overstate deferred tax liabilities and assets for enterprises for which graduated tax rates are a significant factor. For example, if the highest graduated tax rate is for taxable income in excess of $1,000, that tax rate would be the tax rate for measurement of deferred taxes if future annual taxable income is expected to be $1,001. However, lower graduated tax rates would actually apply to all but the last dollar of annual reversals of temporary differences in future years. For that reason, the Board decided to adopt the average graduated tax rate approach required by this Statement for enterprises for which graduated tax rates are a significant factor.

90. A few respondents to the Exposure Draft suggested measurement of deferred taxes using the lower alternative minimum tax (AMT) rate if an enterprise currently is an AMT taxpayer and expects to "always" be an AMT taxpayer. The Board believes that no one can predict whether an enterprise will always be an AMT taxpayer. Furthermore, it would be counterintuitive if the addition of AMT provisions to the tax law were to have the effect of reducing the amount of an enterprise's income tax expense for financial reporting, given that the provisions of AMT may be either neutral or adverse but never beneficial to an enterprise. It also would be counterintuitive to assume that an enterprise would permit its AMT credit carryforward to expire unused at the end of the life of the enterprise, which would have to occur if that enterprise was "always" an AMT taxpayer.

91. The Board concluded that all enterprises should measure deferred taxes for temporary differences using regular tax rates and assess the need for a valuation allowance for an AMT credit carryforward deferred tax asset using the guidance in this Statement. Otherwise, an enterprise's deferred tax liability could be understated for either of two reasons:

a. It could be understated if the enterprise currently is an AMT taxpayer because of temporary differences. Temporary differences reverse and, over the entire life of the enterprise, cumulative income will be taxed at regular tax rates.
b. It could be understated if the enterprise currently is an AMT taxpayer because of preference items but does not have enough AMT credit carryforward to reduce its deferred tax liability from the amount of regular tax on regular tax temporary differences to the amount of tentative minimum tax (TMT) on AMT temporary differences. In those circumstances, measurement of the deferred tax liability using AMT rates would anticipate the tax benefit of future special deductions, such as statutory depletion, which have not yet been earned.

Realizability of Deferred Tax Assets

92. The Board considered two basic approaches to the measurement of deferred tax assets. Under one approach, the "affirmative judgment" approach, a deferred tax asset is recognized for deductible temporary differences and carryforwards *if,* based on an affirmative judgment, that asset will be realized. Under the other approach, the "impairment" approach, a deferred tax asset is recognized for deductible temporary differences and carryforwards *unless* that asset is deemed to be impaired.

93. The Board also considered whether the criterion for either (a) future realization of the asset (under the affirmative judgment approach) or (b) impairment of the asset should be (1) "probable," (2) "more likely than not," or (3) something else.

94. Concepts Statement 6 defines assets and liabilities, in part, as *probable* future economic benefits and *probable* future sacrifices of economic benefits, respectively. But footnotes 18 and 21 explain that probable refers to "that which can reasonably be expected or believed on the basis of available evidence or logic but is neither certain nor proved" and is not used "in a specific accounting or technical sense (such as that in FASB Statement No. 5, *Accounting for Contingencies,* par. 3)."

95. For purposes of measurement of a deferred tax asset, the Board rejected *probable* as that term is used in Statement 5. The limited amount of information available about the future contributes to the following results of using that criterion in conjunction with each basic approach:

a. *Affirmative judgment approach.* A deferred tax asset would be recognized if it is probable that the asset *will* be realized. The problem is that recognition of a deferred tax asset that is *expected* to be realized is prohibited when the likelihood of realizing that asset is considered to be less than probable. The Board believes that result is unacceptable.
b. *Impairment approach.* A deferred tax asset would be recognized unless it is probable that the asset *will not* be realized. The problem is that recognition of a deferred tax asset that is not *expected* to be realized is nevertheless required when the likelihood of not realizing that asset is considered to be less than probable. The Board believes that result also is unacceptable.

96. The Board believes that the criterion required for measurement of a deferred tax asset should be one that produces accounting results that come closest to the expected outcome, that is, realization or nonrealization of the deferred tax asset in future years. For that reason, the Board selected *more likely than not* as the criterion for measurement of a deferred tax asset. Based on that criterion, (a) recognition of a deferred tax asset that is expected to be realized is required, and (b) recognition of a deferred tax asset that is not expected to be realized is prohibited.

97. The Board intends *more likely than not* to mean a level of likelihood that is more than 50 percent. Selection of more likely than not as the criterion for measurement of a deferred tax asset is intended to virtually eliminate any distinction between the impairment and affirmative judgment approaches. In practice, there should be no substantive difference between the accounting results of either:

a. Recognition of a deferred tax asset if the likelihood of realizing the future tax benefit is more than 50 percent (the affirmative judgment approach)
b. Recognition of a deferred tax asset unless the likelihood of not realizing the future tax benefit is more than 50 percent (the impairment approach).

98. The Board acknowledges that future realization of a tax benefit sometimes will be expected for a portion but not all of a deferred tax asset, and that the dividing line between the two portions may be unclear. In those circumstances, application of judgment based on a careful assessment of all available evidence is required to determine the

portion of a deferred tax asset for which it is more likely than not a tax benefit will not be realized. Most respondents to the Exposure Draft supported the impairment approach based on the criterion of more likely than not and believed that the guidance for exercise of judgment as provided in paragraphs 20-25 is sufficient.

Cumulative Losses in Recent Years

99. The Board considered whether there should be different requirements for recognition of a deferred tax asset for (a) deductible temporary differences and (b) tax loss carryforwards. The Board believes that, in substance, both are the same—both are amounts deductible on tax returns in future years. For example, a decision about whether to fund accrued pension costs currently will determine whether an enterprise has a tax loss carryforward or a deductible temporary difference if that enterprise otherwise has zero taxable income in the current year. The Board concluded that there should not be different requirements for recognition of a deferred tax asset for deductible temporary differences and tax loss carryforwards.

100. The Board also considered whether the criterion for recognition of a deferred tax asset should be at a higher level such as *assured beyond a reasonable doubt* when there is a cumulative pretax loss for financial reporting for the current and two preceding years. The rationale for that sort of requirement would be that cumulative losses in recent years is significant negative evidence about an enterprise's profitability that creates significant uncertainty about an enterprise's ability to earn taxable income and realize tax benefits in future years. When that condition exists, a more restrictive criterion for recognition of a deferred tax asset might be warranted to offset potential undue optimism concerning an enterprise's future profitability.

101. The Board is concerned, however, about the numerous implementation issues that would arise in applying a three-year cumulative loss test or some other similar test on a taxable entity by entity basis within consolidated financial statements. Implementation issues would include matters such as intercompany transactions, foreign operations, and business combinations accounted for by the purchase method. Numerous and detailed implementation rules for a three-year cumulative loss test would significantly increase the complexity of understanding and applying the requirements of this Statement.

102. The Board also is concerned about the effect on earnings when an enterprise moves into or out of a three-year cumulative loss status. When an enterprise moves into a three-year cumulative loss status, the assured beyond a reasonable doubt criterion ordinarily would (a) prohibit recognition of a tax benefit for the current year loss and (b) require recognition of a valuation allowance for deferred tax assets originally recognized in prior years. In those circumstances, deferred tax expense from elimination of the deferred tax asset would be added to a pretax loss to produce a larger net loss. Similarly, when an enterprise moves out of a three-year cumulative loss status, the more likely than not criterion might remove the need for a valuation allowance. In those circumstances, a deferred tax benefit from reinstatement of the deferred tax asset would be added to pretax income to produce a larger net income.

103. The Board believes that the more likely than not criterion required by this Statement is capable of appropriately dealing with all forms of negative evidence, including cumulative losses in recent years. That criterion requires positive evidence of sufficient quality and quantity to counteract negative evidence in order to support a conclusion that, based on the weight of *all* available evidence, a valuation allowance is not needed. A cumulative loss in recent years is a significant piece of negative evidence that is difficult to overcome. For that reason, the Board concluded that a more restrictive criterion such as assured beyond a reasonable doubt is not necessary.

Tax-Planning Strategies

104. Statement 96 prohibited anticipation of taxable income expected to be earned in future years for purposes of recognizing a tax benefit for deductible temporary differences and carryforwards at the end of the current year. Within the bounds of that constraint, however, Statement 96 required consideration of tax-planning strategies that maximize the amount of tax benefits recognizable in the current year. As a result, an enterprise was required to identify and recognize the effect of strategies that the enterprise did not expect to implement if it expected to be profitable in future years. Many of the Board's constituents believed that requirement for "hypothetical" strategies was complex and confusing.

105. This Statement requires consideration of future taxable income and other available evidence when assessing the need for a valuation allowance. Various assumptions and strategies (including elections for tax purposes) are implicit in estimates of expected future taxable income. The Board concluded that it should not try to establish detailed criteria and other rules and requirements for those types of assumptions and strategies.

106. A tax-planning strategy, as that term is used in this Statement, is a possible source of taxable in-

come that must be considered only in determining the amount of valuation allowance required. It is an action that an enterprise ordinarily might not implement but would implement, if necessary, to realize a tax benefit for an operating loss or tax credit carryforward before it expires. The existence of a tax-planning strategy demonstrates that a valuation allowance is not needed for some portion or all of a deferred tax asset.

107. A tax-planning strategy must be prudent and feasible. If an action is not prudent, management probably would not do it. If an action is not feasible, management does not have the ability to do it. Implementation of the tax-planning strategy must be primarily within the control of management but need not be within the unilateral control of management.

108. Statement 96 prohibited any tax-planning strategy that is expected to result in a significant cost. That requirement was consistent with the Statement 96 requirement to not anticipate any future events that are not inherently assumed in the financial statements. That requirement is not consistent, however, with this Statement's requirement to assess all available evidence to determine whether a valuation allowance is needed.

109. The Board concluded that tax-planning strategies that are expected to result in a significant cost should not be prohibited. The tax benefit recognized as a result of a tax-planning strategy, however, should be net of any significant expenses to implement that tax-planning strategy or any significant losses that would be recognized if that tax-planning strategy is implemented. The Board believes that it would be inappropriate to recognize a tax benefit in the current year and postpone recognition of any expenses or losses necessary to generate that tax benefit to a later year.

Change in Valuation Allowance

110. Some respondents to the Exposure Draft proposed that the current-year tax effect of a change in the valuation allowance for a deferred tax asset related to prior-year losses or expenses that were charged direct to equity pursuant to Statement 12, 52, or FASB Statement No. 60, *Accounting and Reporting by Insurance Enterprises,* also should be allocated direct to equity rather than to continuing operations. In effect, those respondents recommend a current-year correction of the after-tax amount of those losses or expenses originally reported in a prior year. But no respondent recommended current-year corrections of the after-tax amount of prior-year extraordinary gains or prior-year gains that were credited direct to equity. That situation could arise, for example, if the current-year loss from continuing operations

(a) offsets a deferred tax liability for a prior-year Statement 52 hedging gain or (b) results in a refund of taxes paid on a prior-year extraordinary gain.

111. The Board believes that there is no conceptual basis to require current-year corrections for the after-tax amount of prior-year losses or expenses while not requiring the same treatment of prior-year gains. Furthermore, current-year corrections of the after-tax amount of both gains and losses that occurred in prior years would be very complex. For those reasons, the Board decided that this Statement should retain the proposals in the Exposure Draft.

Changes in Tax Law and Tax Status

112. A change in tax law or rate or a change in the tax status of an enterprise is an event that has economic consequences for an enterprise in the year that the change occurs, that is, in the year that a change in tax law or rate is enacted or a change in tax status is approved. As a result of the change, deferred tax consequences become larger or smaller. Conceptually, it could be argued that an enterprise should anticipate the tax effect of an expected future change in tax law or rate or a change in tax status on its deferred tax liability or asset at the end of the current year. The Board believes, however, that recognition of those tax consequences in the year that a change occurs permits a more reliable measurement of the economic effects of an enacted change in tax law or rate or a change in the tax status of an enterprise.

113. Some respondents to the Exposure Draft proposed that the tax effect of an enacted change in tax rates on temporary differences related to a prior-year gain or loss that was reported as an extraordinary item, discontinued operations, or an item of comprehensive income excluded from net income should be reported in the same manner as that gain or loss was reported in the prior year. The Board concluded that it should not require reporting portions of the tax effect of an enacted change in tax rates (or a change in a valuation allowance as discussed above) as extraordinary items, and so forth, to remeasure in the current year the after-tax amount of gains and losses that occurred and were reported in prior years. The Board decided that the entire tax effect of a change in enacted tax rates should be allocated to continuing operations in order to avoid the sometimes complex problems of tracing back to events of prior years in conjunction with:

a. Many different types of temporary differences
b. Incremental tax rates (used for intraperiod allocation) that may be different from statutory tax rates

c. Operating loss and tax credit carrybacks and carryforwards.

Temporary Differences That Are Not Timing Differences

114. This Statement, and Statement 96 before it, requires recognition of a deferred tax liability or asset for temporary differences that are not timing differences under Opinion 11. Some of the Board's constituents objected to that requirement of Statement 96 for three particular types of temporary differences because of a perceived "conflict of concepts" with some other authoritative accounting pronouncement. The three types of differences and the perceived conflict of concepts for each are as follows:

a. *Deferred ITC.* Under Opinion 2, ITC is deferred and amortized over the life of the related asset, but Statement 96 required immediate recognition of a deferred tax asset for the difference between the book and tax basis of the related asset that results from deferral of ITC.
b. *Foreign nonmonetary assets.* Under Statement 52, exchange gains and losses are not recognized for foreign nonmonetary assets when the U.S. dollar is the functional currency, but Statement 96 required recognition of a deferred tax liability or asset for the difference between the book and tax basis of the related nonmonetary asset that results from a change in exchange rates.
c. *Intercompany sale of inventory or other assets.* Under ARB 51, taxes paid on intercompany profits are deferred, but Statement 96 required recognition of a deferred tax asset for the difference between the book and tax basis of the related asset that results from an intercompany sale.

115. The Board reconsidered whether to require recognition of deferred taxes for each of those three types of differences. The Board's reasons for continuing the requirement for deferred ITC and eliminating the requirement for foreign nonmonetary assets and intercompany sales are discussed below.

Deferred investment tax credit

116. The requirements for accounting for investment tax credits are contained in Opinions 2 and 4. In Opinion 2, the Accounting Principles Board (APB) concluded that:

a. The investment tax credit reduces the cost of the related asset, and for that reason, it should be deferred and amortized over the productive life of the related asset.
b. Display of the deferral in the statement of financial position as a reduction of the cost of the asset ordinarily is preferable.
c. Display of the deferral as deferred income is also permitted provided that the investment tax credit is accounted for as a reduction of the cost of the asset, that is, amortized over the productive life of the asset.

In Opinion 4, the APB concluded that:

(1) The essential nature of the investment tax credit is that it reduces the cost of the related asset, and the method of accounting for it in Opinion 2 is preferable.
(2) The flow-through method to account for the investment tax credit is also acceptable.

117. Accounting for an investment tax credit as required by Opinion 2 reduces the cost of the asset to less than its tax basis. The excess of tax basis over cost for financial reporting will be deductible in future years when the asset is recovered. Deferred tax accounting for that temporary difference does not change the accounting for the investment tax credit required by Opinion 2. The entire amount of the investment tax credit is still deferred at the outset and subsequently amortized over the life of the asset. The Board concluded that accounting for this temporary difference (a) is consistent with the basic principles of the Board's asset and liability approach to accounting for deferred *income taxes* and (b) is not a change in the deferred method of accounting for *investment tax credits* under Opinion 2.

Foreign nonmonetary assets

118. Statement 52 requires use of the U.S. dollar to measure the cost of foreign nonmonetary assets such as inventory, land, and depreciable assets when the U.S. dollar is the functional currency.[12] When exchange rates change, the amount of foreign currency revenues needed to recover the U.S. dollar cost of those assets also changes—but the foreign currency tax basis of those assets does not change. After a change in exchange rates, there will be a difference between (a) the amount of foreign currency needed to recover the U.S. dollar cost of those assets and (b) the foreign currency tax basis of those assets. Some believe that deferred taxes for those differences should be recognized in the period in which exchange rates change.

---

[12]Under Statement 52, another foreign currency could be the functional currency when the local currency is not the functional currency for a foreign entity. The requirements of this Statement and the basis for the Board's conclusions are the same for those situations as for when the U.S. dollar is the functional currency for a foreign entity.

119. Under Statement 96, that difference between the foreign currency equivalent of the U.S. dollar cost and the foreign tax basis of nonmonetary assets is accounted for as a temporary difference. Although that difference technically meets the definition of a temporary difference, the Board concluded that the substance of accounting for it as such is to recognize deferred taxes on exchange gains and losses that are not recognized under Statement 52. The Board decided to resolve that conflict between the requirements of Statements 96 and 52 by prohibiting recognition of deferred taxes for those differences. The Board believes that decision will significantly reduce complexity by eliminating cross-currency (U.S. dollar cost versus foreign tax basis) computations of deferred taxes for those differences.

120. The Board also considered indexing of foreign nonmonetary assets for tax purposes (to counter the effects of inflation) when the U.S. dollar is the functional currency. In most countries, indexing is "too little, too late." As a result, at least in part, of the Board's decision about Statement 52 differences discussed above, however, a comparison of indexed tax basis to local currency historical cost ordinarily would indicate an excess of tax over book basis and a potential deferred tax asset—a counterintuitive result in highly inflationary economies. For that reason, the Board decided to prohibit deferred tax accounting for differences that result from indexing for tax purposes whenever the U.S. dollar is the functional currency for a foreign entity.

Intercompany transfers of assets

121. An intercompany transfer of assets such as the sale of inventory or depreciable assets between tax jurisdictions is a taxable event that establishes a new tax basis for those assets in the buyer's tax jurisdiction. The new tax basis of those assets is deductible on the buyer's tax return when the cost of those assets as reported in the consolidated financial statements is recovered.

122. Paragraph 17 of ARB 51 requires deferral of income taxes paid by the seller on intercompany profits on assets remaining within the consolidated group. Under Statement 96, however, the tax paid by the seller is charged to expense, and a deferred tax asset is potentially recognizable for the excess of the buyer's tax basis over the cost of the assets as reported in the consolidated financial statements. As a result, under Statement 96, a tax benefit or tax expense attributable to transferred inventory may be recognized in a period before that inventory is sold to an unrelated third party.

123. This Statement changes that requirement of Statement 96. Some argued that the Board's con-

clusion to recognize a deferred tax asset for the seller's tax payments and to not recognize a deferred tax asset for the buyer's deductible temporary difference reflects a deferred approach that is inconsistent with the asset and liability approach to accounting for income taxes. An intercompany sale of inventory between tax jurisdictions changes the tax basis of the inventory and thereby creates a temporary difference that will result in tax deductions on the buyer's tax return when the cost of the inventory as reported in the consolidated financial statements is recovered. In this view, those deferred tax consequences should be recognized in the year they occur (usually the year of the intercompany sale) and not in the year that the inventory is sold to an unrelated third party.

124. The Board concluded that although the excess of the buyer's tax basis over the cost of transferred assets as reported in the consolidated financial statements technically meets the definition of a temporary difference, the substance of accounting for it as such is to recognize income taxes related to intercompany gains that are not recognized under ARB 51. The Board decided to resolve that conflict between the requirements of Statement 96 and ARB 51 by prohibiting recognition of a deferred tax asset in the buyer's tax jurisdiction for those differences. As a result, ARB 51 is unchanged, and the income taxes paid by the seller including the tax effect, in the seller's tax jurisdiction, of any reversing temporary differences as a result of that intercompany sale are deferred. The Board believes that that decision together with the decisions for Statement 52 and certain Opinion 23 differences should eliminate the need for complex cross-currency deferred tax computations for most enterprises.

Regulated Enterprises

125. When Statement 71 was issued, accounting for income taxes was a project on the Board's agenda, and the Board decided not to change regulated enterprises' accounting for income taxes until that project was completed. The general standards of accounting for the effects of regulation set forth in Statement 71 require recognition of a deferred tax liability or asset for the tax consequences of temporary differences because a regulator cannot relieve a regulated enterprise of a liability or asset that was not created by rate actions of the regulator. Those general standards require (a) recognition of an asset when a deferred tax liability is recognized if it is probable that future revenue will be provided for the payment of those deferred tax liabilities and (b) recognition of a liability when a deferred tax asset is recognized if it is probable that a future reduction in revenue will result when that deferred tax asset is realized. The Board concluded that this Statement should be ap-

plied to regulated enterprises consistent with the general standards of accounting for the effects of regulation set forth in Statement 71.

Leveraged Leases

126. The Board acknowledges that the accounting for income taxes related to leveraged leases set forth in Statement 13 and Interpretation 21 is not consistent with the requirements of this Statement. However, the Board concluded that it should not change the accounting for income taxes related to leveraged leases without considering the need to change leveraged lease accounting, and decided not to reopen the subject of leveraged lease accounting as part of this project. Therefore, this Statement does not change the requirements of Statement 13 or Interpretation 21. The Board also considered whether there should be any integration of (a) the results of accounting for income taxes related to leveraged leases with (b) the other results of accounting for income taxes as required by this Statement. Integration is an issue when all of the following exist:

(1) The accounting for a leveraged lease requires recognition of deferred tax credits.
(2) The requirements of this Statement limit the recognition of a tax benefit for deductible temporary differences and carryforwards not related to the leveraged lease.
(3) Unrecognized tax benefits in (b) could offset taxable amounts that result from future recovery of the net investment in the leveraged lease.

The Board concluded that, in those circumstances, integration should be required. However, consistent with the decision not to change leveraged lease accounting, the Board decided that integration should not override any results that are unique to income tax accounting for leveraged leases, for example, the manner of recognizing the tax effect of an enacted change in tax rates.

Business Combinations

127. Values are assigned to identified assets and liabilities when a business combination is accounted for as a purchase. The assigned values frequently will be different from the tax bases of those assets and liabilities. The Board concluded that a liability or asset should be recognized for the deferred tax consequences of differences between the assigned values and the tax bases of the assets and liabilities (other than nondeductible goodwill and leveraged leases) recognized in a purchase business combination.

128. The Board considered and rejected the approach that assigns net-of-tax values to those assets and liabilities. That approach mixes the normal amounts of expenses and revenues with their tax effects and thereby confuses the relationship between various items on the statement of earnings in subsequent years. For example, the relationship between sales and cost of sales is affected if cost of sales includes amounts that reflect the net-of-tax values assigned to acquired inventory or depreciable assets. Likewise, the relationship between pretax income from continuing operations and income tax expense is affected to the extent that pretax income from continuing operations includes any net-of-tax amounts.

129. Paragraph 89 of Opinion 16 stated that ". . . the fair value of an asset to an acquirer is less than its market or appraisal value if all or a portion of the market or appraisal value is not deductible for income taxes." The Board believes that the net result is the same whether amounts assigned to the individual assets acquired and liabilities assumed are pretax or net-of-tax. For example, assume (a) that the pretax market or appraisal value of depreciable assets acquired in a purchase business combination is $1,000, (b) that the tax basis of those assets is zero, and (c) that the enacted tax rate is 40 percent for all years. If net-of-tax, the assigned value of those assets would be $600. If pretax, the assigned value of those assets would be $1,000, and there would be a $400 deferred tax liability. Under either approach, the net result of allocating the purchase price is the same. The Board concluded that the amounts assigned to assets and liabilities in a purchase business combination should not be net of any related deferred tax liability or asset.

130. Paragraph 89 of Opinion 16 also stated that "the impact of tax effects on amounts assigned to individual assets and liabilities depends on numerous factors, including imminence or delay of realization of the asset value and the possible timing of tax consequences." That sentence has been interpreted to permit discounting the deferred tax effects of differences between the assigned amounts and the tax bases of the assets and liabilities in a purchase business combination. The issue of discounting a deferred tax liability or asset, however, has been excluded from the scope of this project. The Board decided that discounting deferred tax assets or liabilities should be prohibited for temporary differences (except for leveraged leases) related to business combinations as it is for other temporary differences.

131. Goodwill is recognized in a business combination accounted for as a purchase if the purchase price exceeds the assigned value of the identifiable net assets acquired. Conceptually, a deferred tax liability or asset always should be recognized for the deferred tax consequences of a difference between

the reported amount and the tax basis of goodwill. The requirements of this Statement differ, however, depending on whether amortization of goodwill is deductible for tax purposes. In tax jurisdictions where amortization of goodwill is not deductible, the Board believes that adjusting goodwill by an amount equal to the deferred tax liability or asset for the deferred tax consequences of recovering goodwill would not provide information that is particularly relevant. Furthermore, the computation of that adjustment often is very complex. For those reasons, the Board decided that a deferred tax liability or asset should not be recognized for goodwill temporary differences if amortization is not deductible.

132. Amortization of goodwill is deductible in certain tax jurisdictions. Nonrecognition of a deferred tax liability or asset would result in an uneven effective tax rate for financial reporting if the annual amount of amortization is different for financial reporting and tax purposes. For that reason, the Board concluded that a deferred tax liability or asset should be recognized for goodwill temporary differences in those tax jurisdictions.

133. Goodwill is not the only type of intangible asset for which amortization is not deductible in certain tax jurisdictions. The Board considered whether the exception to comprehensive recognition of deferred taxes that pertains to temporary differences related to goodwill should be extended to temporary differences related to other types of intangible assets. The Board decided that the exception should not be extended. Goodwill is a residual. It is the excess of purchase price over the assigned values of the identifiable net assets acquired. Other types of intangibles are not residuals. One reason for not recognizing deferred taxes related to goodwill is to avoid the gross-up of both sides of the statement of financial position that occurs because goodwill and the related deferred tax liability are mutually dependent on each other. That relationship does not exist for other types of intangible assets.

134. The other reason for not recognizing deferred taxes related to nondeductible goodwill is complexity. That complexity does not exist for other types of intangible assets. Furthermore, if amounts assigned to intangible assets, depreciable assets, or other types of assets acquired in a business combination exceed the tax basis of those assets, that excess will be taxable when those assets are recovered. The Board concluded that a deferred tax liability should be recognized for those taxable temporary differences regardless of whether the related assets are intangible assets or some other type of assets.

135. The tax law may permit operating loss or tax credit carryforwards of the acquiring or the acquired enterprise to reduce future taxable income or taxes payable attributable to the other enterprise if consolidated tax returns are filed subsequent to the acquisition. In those circumstances, the Board decided that any tax benefits recognizable by either enterprise as a result of the business combination should be included in accounting for the business combination. Goodwill is reduced, thereby reducing the annual charge to income for amortization of goodwill in subsequent years.

136. An acquired enterprise's deductible temporary differences and carryforwards are not included in measuring a purchase transaction if the criteria for recognition of tax benefits are not met. The Board decided against retroactive restatement of the purchase transaction and results of operations for intervening years if the criteria for recognition of tax benefits are met in subsequent periods. Recognition of a tax benefit in subsequent years is a consequence of either (a) earning income or (b) some other significant change in circumstances that causes a change in judgment about the need for a valuation allowance in those subsequent years. For that reason, the Board decided that (1) tax benefits should be accounted for in financial statements for the year in which the criteria for recognition of tax benefits are met, (2) the tax benefits should be applied first to reduce goodwill to zero and then to reduce other noncurrent intangible assets acquired in that business combination to zero, and (3) any additional tax benefits should be recognized as a reduction of income tax expense.

137. The Board decided that any noncurrent intangible assets other than goodwill should be reduced to zero before reducing income tax expense for acquired tax benefits that are recognized after the acquisition date for two reasons. One reason is that some of the Board's constituents were concerned that the opportunity to reduce income tax expense in future years for a portion of acquired tax benefits might sometimes influence purchase price allocations for business combinations. If amounts allocated to other noncurrent assets are increased, goodwill is reduced, thereby increasing the portion of acquired tax benefits that could reduce income tax expense in future years. Moreover, reliable fair values are sometimes difficult to obtain for noncurrent assets, particularly intangible assets. For those reasons, the Board concluded that both goodwill and other noncurrent intangible assets should be reduced to zero before the tax benefit of acquired deductible temporary differences and carryforwards are recognized as a reduction of income tax expense in future years.

138. Paragraph 72 of Statement 96 and the proposals in the Exposure Draft that preceded this Statement would have required, in certain limited circumstances, recognition of a tax benefit for the excess of an acquiring enterprise's tax basis of the stock of an acquired enterprise over the tax basis of the net assets of the acquired enterprise. The Board decided to eliminate that requirement because of changes in the U.S. federal tax law and the complexity of determining whether that requirement would be applicable in other tax jurisdictions.

Intraperiod Tax Allocation

139. The amount of tax expense or benefit for the year is allocated between pretax income or loss from continuing operations and other items that gave rise to the tax expense or benefit. Under Statement 96, the amount of tax expense or benefit allocated to continuing operations was determined without regard to any items that are reported apart from income or loss from continuing operations. Items reported apart from continuing operations were viewed as incremental, and their tax consequences were not considered in determining the amount of tax expense or benefit to be allocated to continuing operations.

140. This Statement, however, requires consideration of the tax consequences of events for which consideration was prohibited under Statement 96. Under this Statement, for example, taxable income expected in future years is considered for measurement of a deferred tax asset for the carryforward of a current-year loss from continuing operations. For that reason, the Board believes that it is also appropriate to consider an extraordinary gain in the current year for purposes of allocating a tax benefit to a current-year loss from continuing operations. The Board concluded that all items (for example, extraordinary items, discontinued operations, and so forth) should be considered for purposes of determining the amount of tax benefit that results from a loss from continuing operations and that should be allocated to continuing operations.

141. The Board concluded that the tax benefit of a loss or tax credit carryforward, if not recognized when the item arose, is not an extraordinary item when subsequently recognized because the tax benefit is neither unusual in nature nor infrequent in occurrence. That tax benefit results from both (a) earning income in the current year or the expectation of earning income in a future year and (b) incurring a loss in a prior year. The Board also considered whether the tax benefit should be reported in the same manner as the prior-year loss that gave rise to the carryforward. The Board decided that reporting the benefit of a loss or tax credit carryforward based on the event that occurred in the prior year would (1) produce less understandable results and (2) create the sometimes complex problem of tracing back to events of prior years.

142. The Board concluded that the amount of income taxes allocated to the beginning balance of retained earnings for a change in accounting principles should be measured as if the newly adopted accounting principles had been followed in prior years. If prior years are restated for a change in accounting principles or for a correction of an error, the related tax consequences also should be restated for those prior years.

143. The Board believes that the tax consequences of an event that increases or decreases contributed capital should be allocated directly to contributed capital. A tax deduction may be received for the difference between the exercise price of employee stock options and the fair value of the stock at the date of exercise. Because that difference between the exercise price and the fair value of the stock is not presently recognized as compensation expense in the financial statements, the Board believes that reporting the related tax benefit as a reduction of income tax expense would not be appropriate. Pending completion of the Board's project on accounting for employee stock options, the Board decided to make no changes to the requirements of Opinion 25 for reporting the tax effects of stock compensation plans.

144. The requirements of this Statement for reporting the tax benefit of tax-deductible dividends paid on allocated shares (that is, shares already earned by employees) of an employee stock ownership plan (ESOP) are the same as the requirements of Statement 96 for tax-deductible dividends paid to other shareholders. The Board also believes that the requirements of this Statement for tax-deductible dividends paid on shares held by an ESOP but not yet earned by employees are consistent with the requirements of Statement 96 and Opinion 25. An ESOP and a stock option plan are analogous. Both are compensatory arrangements and both sometimes result in tax deductions for amounts that are not presently recognized as compensation expense in the financial statements under existing generally accepted accounting principles. The tax benefits of both are reported as a credit to shareholders' equity.

145. The Board believes that a tax deduction received for the payment of dividends (exclusive of dividends paid on unallocated shares held by an ESOP) represents, in substance, an exemption from taxation of an equivalent amount of earnings. For that reason, the Board concluded that the tax benefit should be recognized as a reduction of tax expense and should not be allocated directly to

shareholders' equity. A tax benefit should not be recognized, however, for tax deductions or favorable tax rates attributable to future dividends of undistributed earnings for which a deferred tax liability has not been recognized under the requirements of Opinion 23. Favorable tax treatment would be reflected in measuring that unrecognized deferred tax liability for disclosure purposes.

146. The Board reconsidered the Statement 96 requirements for reporting tax benefits after a quasi reorganization. Statement 96 had different requirements for (a) quasi reorganizations that are only an elimination of a deficit in retained earnings by a concurrent reduction in contributed capital and (b) other quasi reorganizations. The Board concluded that after any quasi reorganization, including those that are only a deficit reclassification, the enterprise's accounting should be substantially similar to that appropriate for a new enterprise. The income reported by a new enterprise would not include tax benefits attributable to deductible temporary differences and carryforwards that arose prior to its organization date. Therefore, those tax benefits should be reported as a direct addition to contributed capital when recognized subsequent to the date of the quasi reorganization.

147. The Board is aware, however, that some enterprises effected a quasi reorganization that involved only a deficit reclassification and adopted Statement 96 based, at least in part, on reliance on the requirements for the manner of reporting those tax benefits under Statement 96. For that reason, although some noted that other changes to more restrictive requirements than Statement 96 have not received special treatment in this Statement and that this exception is inconsistent with other requirements of this Statement, the Board concluded that it is appropriate to provide an exception for those enterprises.

148. Statement 96 required and the Exposure Draft proposed that interest and penalities assessed on income tax deficiencies should not be reported as income tax expense. Some respondents cited the difficulty of separating the total accrual for an income tax "cushion" between taxes, interest, and penalties. Some financial statement users stated a preference for excluding interest on income tax deficiencies from other types of interest expense. Upon reconsideration, the Board decided to eliminate that proposed requirement.

Classification in a Statement of Financial Position

149. Statement 96 required that the current portion of a deferred tax liability or asset should be the deferred tax consequences of temporary differences that will result in taxable or deductible

amounts during the following year or operating cycle if longer than one year. Some of the Board's constituents believe that requirement increased complexity because it required a detailed analysis to determine the amount of next year's reversing temporary differences. For that reason, the Board considered two alternatives to the requirements of Statement 96. One alternative was to classify all deferred taxes as noncurrent. The other was to continue the requirements of Opinion 11 and Statement 37 and to allocate a valuation allowance between current and noncurrent deferred tax assets on a pro rata basis.

150. Some prefer the requirements of Statement 96. They believe that those requirements are consistent with the overall objective of and reinforce the concepts underlying an asset and liability approach to accounting for income taxes. Furthermore, application of those requirements would produce the information needed to determine the current and noncurrent portions of a valuation allowance so that allocation on a pro rata basis would be unnecessary. They also believe that most enterprises would spend very little time and effort on classification of deferred taxes because classification is not a significant issue for those enterprises. When classification is a significant issue, they believe any additional time and effort is entirely appropriate.

151. The first alternative, classify all deferred taxes as noncurrent, was not adopted because the Board believes that a deferred tax liability or asset should be classified as current or noncurrent in a classified statement of financial position. An inappropriate current ratio would result from noncurrent classification of the deferred tax consequences of temporary differences related to current assets and liabilities. The results of applying that alternative would be confusing for the users of financial statements.

152. The Board concluded, and most respondents to the Exposure Draft agreed, that the requirements for classification of deferred taxes in a classified statement of financial position should be the same as under Opinion 11 and Statement 37. The Board also concluded that a valuation allowance should be allocated on a pro rata basis. The reasons for those conclusions are:

a. The results from applying that alternative ordinarily should not be significantly different from the results from applying the requirements of Statement 96.
b. The requirements of that alternative are easier to understand and apply.
c. That alternative does not create the impression that detailed scheduling is required for situations in which it otherwise could be avoided.

153. The Board considered whether deferred tax assets and liabilities should be offset or presented separately. The Board decided to permit offset of deferred tax liabilities and assets for the same tax jurisdiction for purposes of presentation in the statement of financial position to avoid the detailed analyses necessary to determine whether reversing taxable and deductible temporary differences offset each other on a particular future tax return or in carryback or carryforward years. However, the Board decided to prohibit offset of deferred tax liabilities and assets attributable to different tax jurisdictions. Detailed analyses are not necessary to determine, for example, that a tax asset for German income taxes does not offset a tax liability for French income taxes.

Disclosures

154. The Board believes that the financial statement disclosures required by this Statement provide information that is useful in understanding the general effect of income taxes on a particular enterprise and that those disclosures can be prepared without encountering undue complexities or significant incremental costs.

155. Some respondents to the Exposure Draft recommended disclosure of additional information that might enable financial statement users to estimate the potential future effect of a change in tax laws or rates for each tax jurisdiction in which an enterprise has significant operations. The Board decided that this would require too much detail. In response to a similar recommendation by users of financial statements, however, the Board decided that a public enterprise should disclose the approximate total tax effect (not the separate tax effect for each tax jurisdiction) for each type of temporary difference and carryforward that gives rise to a significant portion of the enterprise's deferred tax liabilities and assets. The Board believes that this summarized information is useful and that it does not impose significant additional costs. This Statement also requires disclosure of the effect of enacted changes in tax laws or rates.

156. Some respondents to the Exposure Draft stated that disclosure of the amount of an enterprise's total deferred tax liabilities, deferred tax assets, and valuation allowances is of little value and potentially misleading. It might be misleading, for example, to continue to disclose a deferred tax asset and valuation allowance of equal amounts for a loss carryforward after operations are permanently terminated in a particular tax jurisdiction. The Board believes that it need not and should not develop detailed guidance for when to cease disclosure of the existence of a worthless asset. Some financial statement users, on the other hand, stated that disclosure of the total liability, asset, and valuation allowance as proposed in the Exposure Draft is essential for gaining some insight regarding management's decisions and changes in decisions about recognition of deferred tax assets. Other respondents recommended significant additional disclosures such as the extent to which net deferred tax assets are dependent on (a) future taxable income exclusive of reversing temporary differences or even (b) *each* of the four sources of taxable income cited in paragraph 21. After reconsideration, the Board concluded that disclosure of the total amounts as proposed in the Exposure Draft is an appropriate level of disclosure.

157. The Board considered and rejected a requirement for disclosure of the future maturities of a long-term deferred tax liability or asset. Disclosure of future maturities would require all enterprises with deferred tax liabilities or assets to analyze the distribution of taxable and deductible amounts among particular future years.

158. This Statement requires certain disclosures for an unrecognized deferred tax liability for temporary differences related to the areas addressed in Opinion 23 and deposits in statutory reserve funds by U.S. steamship enterprises. Those disclosure requirements are a result of the Board's decision to continue, in certain circumstances, the exception to comprehensive recognition of deferred taxes for those temporary differences.

159. This Statement does not prescribe a single method for recognition and measurement of income taxes in the separately issued financial statements of an entity that is a member of a group that files a consolidated tax return. It does, however, require certain criteria for the allocation method adopted (paragraph 40) and certain disclosures (paragraph 49) that previously were not required under Opinion 11 about the accounting for income taxes by such an entity. Some would have preferred to not require criteria for the allocation method because generally accepted accounting principles normally rely on disclosures under FASB Statement No. 57, *Related Party Disclosures,* and do not specify accounting requirements for related party transactions. The Board concluded, however, that those requirements are necessary (a) because an entity's reported results of operations and financial position can be significantly affected by those related-party transactions and (b) to obtain reported results that are closer to those that would be reported if the entity were an independent enterprise.

Effective Date and Transition

160. The Board considered and rejected a solely prospective application of the accounting stan-

dards required by this Statement. Continued recognition of deferred tax assets or liabilities computed under Opinion 11 or Statement 96 is inconsistent with the Board's present decisions about the deferred tax consequences of temporary differences. Furthermore, the cost and complexity of maintaining two systems of accounting for income taxes would not be justified.

161. The Exposure Draft proposed disclosure of the effect of adopting this Statement for the year of adoption if financial statements for the prior year are not restated. Some respondents to the Exposure Draft stated that the cost to develop that information would exceed the benefit of providing it. Two sets of deferred tax computations would be required for the year of adoption—one under the requirements of this Statement and another under the requirements of either Statement 96 or Opinion 11.

162. Upon reconsideration, the Board decided that it should not require two sets of deferred tax computations for a single year. However, this Statement does require disclosure of either (a) the current-year effect on pretax income (from adjustments for prior year business combinations and regulated enterprises) if prior-year financial statements are not restated or (b) the prior-year effect of restatement if prior-year financial statements are restated. Some users of financial statements study changes in the trend of pretax income, and the disclosure required in (a) above will identify the current-year impact on that trend as a result of adopting this Statement. The Board believes that the disclosures required in (b) above should not require excessive cost because that information already will have been developed as a result of restating prior-year financial statements.

163. The Board believes that restatement of financial statements for prior years would be desirable to provide useful information about income taxes for purposes of comparing financial data after the effective date of this Statement with data presented for earlier years. The Board recognizes, however, that the procedures required by this Statement sometimes would differ significantly from procedures followed in previous years and that restatement could be particularly complex and time-consuming for some enterprises. In addition, restatement requires the availability of records or information that an enterprise may no longer have or that its past procedures did not require. Therefore, the Board decided that restatement should be permitted but not required.

164. For similar reasons, the Board decided that the initial and subsequent accounting for purchase business combinations consummated in years prior to the year for which this Statement is first applied should not be restated.

165. For those purchase business combinations, the Board also considered whether to require adjustment of the remaining balances of assets (except for leveraged leases) and liabilities to pretax rather than net-of-tax amounts and recognition of a deferred tax liability or asset for the related temporary differences. The Board understands that for some prior business combinations, determination of those adjustments is impracticable, either because the necessary information is no longer available or because the cost to develop that information is excessive.

166. Statement 96 prohibited those adjustments in all instances. The purpose of that requirement was to eliminate the lack of comparability between the financial statements of enterprises that could and could not compute those adjustments. In reconsidering Statement 96, however, the Board decided to require those adjustments, if practicable, so that statements of financial position and statements of earnings will be more useful and representationally faithful (for both display and measurement) in future years. The Exposure Draft description of impracticable as involving "prohibitive" costs was changed to "excessive" costs to clarify that this is intended to be a "reasonable hurdle."

167. If determination of those adjustments is impracticable for a particular business combination, this Statement requires (except for leveraged leases) that any differences between the remaining balances of the assets and liabilities and their tax bases should be considered to be temporary differences and that a deferred tax liability or asset should be recognized for those temporary differences. For that calculation, the only information required for transition is the amounts of an enterprise's assets and liabilities for financial reporting and for tax purposes. That information should be available.

168. Similar considerations affected the Board's decisions about the method of transition for regulated enterprises. Upon initial application of this Statement, the reported amount of construction in progress is adjusted to the amount that would have resulted from applying this Statement to account for that construction in progress in all prior years. If construction is still in progress, the information needed to make that adjustment should be available. The information needed for plant that is already in service, however, might not be available. Upon initial application of this Statement, the reported amount of plant in service is adjusted to the amount that would have resulted from applying

this Statement in all prior years, if practicable. Otherwise, any difference between the reported amount and the tax basis of plant in service is accounted for as the temporary difference.

Exceptions to Comprehensive Recognition of Deferred Taxes

Opinion 23 and U.S. Steamship Enterprise Temporary Differences

169. Under Opinion 11 and Statement 96, there were certain exceptions to comprehensive recognition of deferred tax liabilities. A deferred tax liability was not recognized for the areas addressed by Opinion 23 and for deposits in statutory reserve funds by U.S. steamship enterprises. At the time of issuing Statement 96, the Board concluded that those temporary differences give rise to a recognizable deferred tax liability. However, the Board decided to continue those exceptions because of (a) the complexity of measuring the deferred tax liability for foreign undistributed earnings, (b) the need to compromise, and (c) the omission of discounting.

170. In reconsidering the requirements of Statement 96, the Board reconsidered whether the Opinion 23 and U.S. steamship enterprise temporary differences give rise to a recognizable deferred tax liability. The Board concluded that those temporary differences give rise to a recognizable deferred tax liability. Opinion 23 required partial recognition of deferred taxes—an approach to accounting for income taxes that the Board has rejected. The underlying rationale for Opinion 23 is based on an enterprise's ability and intent to control the timing of the events that cause temporary differences to reverse and result in taxable amounts in future years. The Board concluded that management's ability to determine the particular future year(s) in which a deferred tax liability will be settled does not eliminate the existence of that liability at the end of the current year.

171. Not recognizing a liability for the deferred tax consequences of Opinion 23 and U.S. steamship enterprise temporary differences overstates the shareholders' residual ownership interest in an enterprise's net earnings and net assets. The government has a claim (a right to collect taxes) that precludes shareholders from ever realizing a portion of the enterprise's net assets. A tax obligation is not a component of shareholders' equity.

172. The Board considered whether payment of income taxes for the Opinion 23 and U.S. steamship enterprise temporary differences might be a *contingency* as that term is used in Statement 5. The Board concluded that there is no uncertainty that a tax obligation has been incurred for those

temporary differences. The amount of the government's claim will never revert to the benefit of the shareholders unless there is a change in the tax law. The possibility of a change in the tax law in some future year is not an *uncertainty* as that term is used in Statement 5.

173. Complexity was one reason Statement 96 did not require recognition of a deferred tax liability for Opinion 23 and U.S. steamship enterprise temporary differences. Information received from constituents has convinced the Board that calculation of a deferred tax liability for undistributed foreign earnings that are or will be invested in a foreign entity indefinitely may sometimes be extremely complex. The hypothetical nature of those calculations introduces significant implementation issues and other complexities that occur less frequently in calculations of a deferred tax liability for an *expected* remittance of earnings from a foreign entity. For that reason, the Exposure Draft proposed to not require recognition of a deferred tax liability for undistributed earnings that are or will be invested in a foreign entity indefinitely. Based on respondents' concerns about complexity, however, the Board decided to extend that exception for foreign undistributed earnings to include the entire amount of a temporary difference between the book and tax basis of an investment in a foreign subsidiary or foreign corporate joint venture that is essentially permanent in duration regardless of the underlying reason(s) for that temporary difference.

174. A deferred tax liability is recognized for exempted taxable temporary differences if those temporary differences will reverse in the foreseeable future, and the Board decided that the same criterion should apply for recognition of a deferred tax asset for an excess of tax over the book basis of an investment in a foreign or domestic subsidiary or corporate joint venture that is essentially permanent in duration. The Exposure Draft proposed to prohibit recognition of a deferred tax asset for foreign tax credit carryforwards in excess of the amount by which those credits reduce the deferred tax liability recognized for undistributed foreign earnings and other foreign source income. Many respondents to the Exposure Draft objected to that limitation. After considering respondents' views, the Board decided to modify that limitation to permit recognition of the entire deferred tax asset so long as its future realization does not depend on either past or future Opinion 23 items (for example, undistributed earnings) for which a deferred tax liability either has not or will not be recognized.

175. Statement 96 required, in certain circumstances, disclosure of the amount of withholding taxes that would be payable upon remittance of

foreign earnings. Payment of withholding taxes may be avoided in many foreign jurisdictions if the parent's investment in the foreign entity is recovered by some means other than dividends, for example, by sale of the stock of that foreign entity. For that reason, the Board decided to eliminate the Statement 96 requirement for disclosure of withholding taxes.

176. The need to compromise was the second reason cited in Statement 96 for not requiring recognition of a deferred tax liability for Opinion 23 temporary differences. The Statement 96 requirements for recognition of deferred tax assets created the overriding reason for the need to compromise. The requirements of this Statement result in the recognition of deferred tax assets that could not be recognized under the requirements of Statement 96.

177. The omission of discounting was the third reason cited in Statement 96. This Statement prohibits discounting either deferred tax assets or deferred tax liabilities. The Board acknowledges that some of the types of deductible temporary differences that potentially give rise to the largest deferred tax assets are related to estimated liabilities (for example, other postretirement benefits) that are already discounted amounts. The Board notes, however, that an undiscounted deferred tax asset will sometimes be recognized for operating loss and tax credit carryforwards that may not be realized for up to 15 years into the future. Furthermore, discounting would usually require scheduling the reversals of temporary differences in future years.

178. Paragraph 2 of FASB Concepts Statement No. 5, *Recognition and Measurement in Financial Statements of Business Enterprises,* states that "the Board intends future change [in practice] to occur in the gradual, evolutionary way that has characterized past change." Thus, evolutionary change may have to be slower in some areas than in others. The Board concluded that, in this area, recognition of a deferred tax liability for *all* Opinion 23 and U.S. steamship enterprise temporary differences should not be required at this time. That requirement would be too great a change from present practice under either Opinion 11 or Statement 96. The Board also concluded that recognition of a deferred tax liability for those temporary differences on a *prospective* basis as required by this Statement is an evolutionary change in practice that results in a significant improvement in financial reporting.

179. The Board considered the cost and complexity that would result from recognition of a deferred tax liability for Opinion 23 and U.S. steamship enterprise temporary differences on a prospective basis. The Board concluded that, except for temporary differences between the book and tax basis of investments in foreign subsidiaries and foreign corporate joint ventures, any increase in cost or complexity as a result of that requirement would be minimal. For that reason, the Board decided to require recognition of a deferred tax liability for those temporary differences on a prospective basis.

180. Over the years, as a result of changes in the tax law, the particular tax benefits that gave rise to Opinion 23 temporary differences have been reduced for savings and loan associations (and other qualified thrift lenders) and have been eliminated for life insurance companies. Thus, eliminating those exceptions on a prospective basis should not have a significant effect for many of those enterprises. The tax law for recapture of a savings and loan association's bad-debt reserve for tax purposes changed for tax years beginning after December 31, 1987 and, for that reason, the Board chose that date for prospective recognition of a deferred tax liability for this type of temporary difference. The Exposure Draft proposed a limitation on recognition of a deferred tax asset for a savings and loan association's bad-debt reserve for financial reporting. Respondents disagreed because the effect of that limitation sometimes would be, in substance, the same as recognizing a deferred tax liability for tax bad-debt reserves that arose prior to tax years beginning after December 31, 1987. The Board decided to eliminate that limitation.

181. The Board sees little similarity between Opinion 23 differences and U.S. steamship enterprise differences. Opinion 23 differences reverse in indefinite future periods. U.S. steamship enterprise differences reverse in predictable future periods and, in substance, are no different from depreciation differences for which recognition of deferred taxes is required. For those reasons, the Exposure Draft proposed to eliminate the exception for U.S. steamship enterprises on a prospective basis. After consideration of responses to the Exposure Draft, however, the Board decided that recognition of the entire deferred tax liability for those temporary differences that exist at the beginning of the year for which this Statement is first applied also should be permitted.

182. A few respondents to the Exposure Draft proposed extending the Opinion 23 exception to comprehensive recognition of deferred taxes to certain analogous types of temporary differences, such as LIFO inventory temporary differences. The Board's reasons for concluding that Opinion 23 temporary differences give rise to a recognizable deferred tax liability equally apply to analogous types of temporary differences. The Board concluded that nonrecogni-

tion of a deferred tax liability for analogous types of temporary differences should be prohibited.

Tax Holidays

183. The Board considered whether a deferred tax asset ever should be recognized for the expected future reduction in taxes payable during a tax holiday. In most tax jurisdictions that have tax holidays, the tax holiday is "generally available" to any enterprise (within a class of enterprises) that chooses to avail itself of the holiday. The Board views that sort of exemption from taxation for a class of enterprises as creating a nontaxable status (somewhat analogous to S-corporation status under U.S. federal tax law) for which a deferred tax asset should not be recognized.

184. Some tax jurisdiction(s) may have a "unique" type of tax holiday that is *controlled* by the enterprise that qualifies for it (that is, a tax holiday that is not generally available to any enterprise within a class of enterprises that chooses to avail itself of the holiday). In those circumstances, conceptually, a deferred tax asset might be recognizable so long as (a) the enterprise has done whatever is necessary to qualify for the holiday and (b) the deferred tax asset recognized is net of the incremental cost of special requirements for future performance under the tax holiday agreement. The Board decided to prohibit recognition of a deferred tax asset for *any* tax holiday because of the practical problems in (1) distinguishing "unique" tax holidays (if any exist) for which recognition of a deferred tax asset might be appropriate from "generally available" tax holidays and (2) measuring the deferred tax asset.

The Incremental Effect of Future Losses

185. Conceptually, under an incremental approach, the tax consequences of tax losses expected in future years would be anticipated for purposes of:

a. Nonrecognition of a deferred tax liability for taxable temporary differences if there will be no future sacrifice because of future tax losses that otherwise would expire unused
b. Recognition of a deferred tax asset for the carryback refund of taxes paid for the current or a prior year because of future tax losses that otherwise would expire unused.

Nevertheless, the Board decided to prohibit anticipation of the tax consequences of future tax losses. That decision reduces the complexity of understanding and applying the requirements of this Statement.

Private and Small Public Enterprises

186. An issue in the August 1983 FASB Discussion Memorandum, *Accounting for Income Taxes,* is whether accounting requirements for income taxes should differ for private or small public enterprises. Most respondents to the Discussion Memorandum who addressed this issue opposed differential recognition or measurement. Respondents who could be identified as having a small enterprise perspective were rather evenly divided on this issue.

187. Under the asset and liability approach required by this Statement, measurement of a deferred tax liability or asset is based on the provisions of the tax law. Calculations may often be complicated, but the Board believes that many of those complications are primarily attributable to the tax law. Complexities in the tax law are applicable to small as well as to large enterprises. Those complexities must be dealt with for tax purposes regardless of what the accounting requirements might be. The Board believes that complexities in the tax law do not give rise to a need for different accounting requirements based on an enterprise's size or ownership.

188. The Board believes that accounting standards should establish requirements that result in accounting for similar transactions and circumstances similarly and for different transactions and circumstances differently. Different accounting standards for income taxes based on an enterprise's size or ownership would affect how financial statement amounts (for example, net income, total assets, and total liabilities) and relationships (for example, debt-to-equity ratio and times interest earned) are determined. The Board believes that the deferred tax consequences of temporary differences are recognizable liabilities or assets and nonrecognition of deferred taxes by some enterprises would deny the existence of deferred tax liabilities and assets. The Board believes that result would significantly reduce the credibility and usefulness of general-purpose external financial reporting.

189. The Board believes that the disclosure requirements of this Statement generally do not create significant new complexities or significant incremental costs. Paragraph 47 generally requires a numerical reconciliation between the reported amount of income tax expense and the amount that would result from applying domestic federal statutory tax rates. A numerical reconciliation was previously required only for public enterprises. The Board decided that nonpublic enterprises should disclose the reasons for significant differences but that a numerical reconciliation should

not be required. Similarly, paragraph 43 requires that nonpublic enterprises disclose the types of temporary differences, but not the tax effect of each, that give rise to significant portions of deferred tax liabilities and assets. In addition, the disclosures required when an enterprise's income is taxed directly to owners are applicable only for public enterprises. The Board decided that there should be no other differences between the disclosures required by this Statement for public enterprises and the disclosures required for nonpublic enterprises.

Interim Financial Reporting

190. The accounting requirements of Opinion 28 are based on a view that each interim period is primarily an integral part of the annual period. Tax expense for interim periods is measured using an estimated annual effective tax rate for the annual period. Opinion 28 rejects the discrete approach to interim reporting whereby the results of operations for each interim period would be determined as if the interim period were an annual period. The Board's asset and liability approach to accounting for income taxes for annual periods, however, is a discrete approach that measures a deferred tax liability or asset at a particular time.

191. The Board decided not to reopen the subject of interim accounting as part of this project and did not reconsider the general approach in Opinion 28 to accounting for income taxes in interim periods. As a result, most of the requirements in Opinion 28 remain unchanged. The Board concluded, however, that some changes were necessary because of the basic principles encompassed in this Statement.

192. In certain circumstances, Opinion 28 prohibits recognition of tax benefits unless future realization is assured beyond a reasonable doubt. That provision in Opinion 28 creates a conflict with the accounting requirements to be applied at the end of the year for annual reporting, and the Board decided to eliminate that provision.

193. Under the requirements of this Statement for annual reporting, the tax benefit of an operating loss carryforward is not reported as an extraordinary item unless realization of the carryforward results from an extraordinary gain. If realization of an operating loss carryforward that is attributable to losses in prior years is expected because of estimated "ordinary" income in the current year, the operating loss carryforward is included in the computation of the estimated annual effective tax rate the same as, for example, tax credit carryforwards.

194. Measurements of a deferred tax liability or asset for annual reporting are subject to change when enacted tax laws or rates change. Likewise, a valuation allowance is subject to change when a change in circumstances causes a change in judgment about the realizability of the related deferred tax asset in *future* years. For interim reporting, the Board believes that the effects of those changes should be recognized as of the enactment date for a change in tax law or rate or as of the date of a change in circumstances for a change in valuation allowance and should not be allocated to subsequent interim periods by an adjustment of the estimated annual effective tax rate for the remainder of the year. Thus, in effect, there is a catch-up adjustment for the cumulative effect as of the date of the change. The effect of changes in tax laws or rates and changes in judgment about the need for a valuation allowance on income or losses for future interim periods, however, is reflected by an adjustment of the estimated annual effective tax rate for the remainder of the year.

195. Paragraph 13 of FASB Statement No. 16, *Prior Period Adjustments,* identifies four items for which the results of prior interim periods should be restated. One of them encompasses the effects of new retroactive tax legislation. Subsequent to the issuance of Statement 16, however, restatement of prior interim periods has not been adopted in Board pronouncements addressing the tax effects of the 1979 U.K. tax legislation or the 1984 and 1986 U.S. tax legislation. Furthermore, that requirement of Statement 16 conflicts with the Board's decision that enactment of tax legislation is a discrete event and that the effects should be recognized in the period of enactment. The Board decided to amend Statement 16 to prohibit restatement of prior interim periods for the enactment of new tax legislation.

Issues Removed from the Scope of This Project

Accounting for the Investment Tax Credit

196. An issue in the 1983 Discussion Memorandum that preceded Statement 96 was the basic method for recognition of investment tax credits in financial income. The basic nature of the U.S. investment tax credit has been viewed in three different ways. Each view leads to different accounting for the investment tax credit. The three possibilities are that the investment tax credit:

a. Reduces the cost of the related asset (The investment tax credit is recognized in financial income as a reduction of depreciation over the productive life of the asset.)

b. Results in a liability because of the provision for recapture upon early disposal of the related asset (The investment tax credit is recognized in financial income as a reduction of tax expense for the years that the recapture periods lapse or ratably over the recapture period.)

c. Results in a reduction of tax expense. (The investment tax credit is recognized in financial income as a reduction of tax expense of the year that taxes payable are reduced.)

197. The Board believes that it would be desirable to have only one method to account for the investment tax credit. However, the Board decided not to address the issue of accounting for the investment tax credit for practical reasons including the Revenue Act of 1971.[13] As a result, the conclusions of the APB remain unchanged and both the deferral method (Opinion 2) and the flow-through method (Opinion 4) continue to be acceptable methods to account for the investment tax credit.

Discounting

198. Another issue in the 1983 Discussion Memorandum was whether measurement of a deferred tax liability or asset should reflect the time value of money, that is, whether a deferred tax liability or asset should be determined on a present value or discounted basis. Most respondents to the Discussion Memorandum opposed discounting deferred income taxes.

199. Conceptual issues, such as whether discounting income taxes is appropriate, and implementation issues associated with discounting income taxes are numerous and complex. Implementation issues include selection of the discount rate(s) and determination of the future years in which amounts will become taxable or deductible. The Board decided not to consider those issues at this time. If deferred income taxes were discounted, however, a detailed analysis of the future reversals of temporary differences would be routinely required and a frequent criticism of Statement 96 was the need for scheduling.

Proposals for Partial or No Recognition of Deferred Taxes That Were Rejected

Taxes Payable As Determined by the Tax Return

200. Some respondents to the Discussion Memorandum advocated that income tax expense for financial reporting should be the amount of taxes payable for the year as determined by the tax return. The rationale most frequently cited to support that proposal is summarized as follows:

a. The tax return determines the legal liability for income taxes.

b. Taxes are levied on aggregate taxable income, and individual events are merely indistinguishable pieces of the overall determination of aggregate taxable income.

c. Any tax payments for future years will be solely a consequence of generating taxable income in those future years.

d. Notional tax calculations based on the recognition and measurement of events for financial reporting are not appropriate.

e. All other approaches to accounting for income taxes are too complex.

201. The Board believes that the tax consequences of an individual event are separable from aggregate taxable income. For example, if the gain on an installment sale is taxable, both the sale and the tax consequences of the gain on the sale should be recognized in financial income for the same year. The tax law may permit an election to include some or all of the gain in the determination of taxable income in future years. That election, however, only affects when and not whether the gain will be included in determining taxable income. The tax consequences arose at the time of the sale and result from the gain on the sale.

202. As the installment sale receivable is collected, pro rata amounts of the gain are included in determining taxable income. Reporting the uncollected balance of the receivable at its net realizable value in the statement of financial position reflects an assumption that the receivable will be recovered and, therefore, that the gain will become taxable. Recognition of the sale and the gain on the sale on an accrual basis requires concurrent recognition of the tax consequences of the gain on the sale. For example, commission expense attributable to the installment sale is recognized on an accrual basis even if the commissions are paid as the receivable is collected and, likewise, income tax expense should also be recognized on an accrual basis. To do otherwise would result in accounting for the sale and the gain on an accrual basis and the related tax consequences on a cash basis—a result that the Board believes is inconsistent and inappropriate.

Partial Recognition of Deferred Taxes

203. Some respondents to the Discussion Memorandum suggested that the tax consequences of some events may never be paid and, therefore, should not be recognized as a tax liability. They

---

[13]The Revenue Act of 1971 states that no particular method to account for investment tax credit shall be required in taxpayers' reports to any federal agency.

stated that the aggregate of all timing differences or of timing differences for a particular type of recurring item such as depreciation usually keeps getting larger because new originating differences more than offset reversing differences. Their view is that since the cumulative amount of differences does not reverse, no future tax payment will arise, and a deferred tax liability should not be recognized.

204. The Board does not agree. The Board believes that a deferred tax liability will result in a future sacrifice even if the aggregate amount of temporary differences increases in future years.

205. Depreciation differences resulting from accelerated depreciation for tax purposes may be used as an example. The aggregate amount of depreciation differences may become larger in future years because of general price inflation, expansion of enterprise activities, or for other reasons. Nevertheless, the deferred tax consequences of a depreciation difference for a particular depreciable asset ordinarily will result in a sacrifice in future years. There will be a future sacrifice because an *individual* difference results in a taxable amount when revenue that recovers the reported amount of the depreciable asset exceeds its remaining tax basis. That taxable amount for a future year will result in a sacrifice in one of the following ways:

a. Increase taxable income and taxes payable if the enterprise earns net taxable income for that year
b. Reduce a tax loss and a loss carryback refund if the enterprise incurs a tax loss that offsets net taxable income of an earlier year
c. Reduce an operating loss carryforward, thereby increasing taxes payable if net taxable income is earned during the carryforward period.

The depreciation difference results in a future sacrifice in each of the three situations described above. The only circumstance in which there would be no future sacrifice is if, in situation (c) above, the enterprise does not pay taxes during the carryforward period.

Methods of Accounting for Income Taxes That Were Rejected

206. The Discussion Memorandum identified four basic approaches to accounting for income taxes. The conceptual nature of the resulting item in the statement of financial position is an important distinction among the four approaches. That item is viewed as:

a. A tax asset or liability under the asset and liability approach
b. A deferred credit or a deferred charge under the deferred approach

c. A reduction in related assets or liabilities under the net-of-tax approach
d. Either (b) or (c) above in combination with (a), depending on whether a difference between financial and taxable income results from an item that is recognized in financial income after or before it is included in determining taxable income.

This Statement requires the asset and liability approach to accounting for income taxes. The Board's reasons for rejecting the other approaches are discussed below.

The Deferred Approach to Accounting for Income Taxes

207. Opinion 11 required a deferred approach to accounting for income taxes. The objective was to match tax expense with related revenues and expenses for the year in which those revenues and expenses were recognized in pretax financial income. Differential calculations were used to measure the incremental effect on income tax expense resulting from either individual or groups of similar timing differences. Those calculations were based on either the gross change or the net change method. No adjustment was made to reflect changes in tax rates or laws in subsequent years. Deferred tax credits and charges in the statement of financial position represented the cumulative effect of interperiod tax allocation and were not receivables or payables.

208. The deferred method produces different results depending on whether the calculations are made by the gross change or the net change method in the following circumstances:

a. When tax rates change
b. When tax credits have statutory limitations
c. When an enterprise is significantly affected by graduated income tax rates
d. When originating timing differences affect one type of taxable income (for example, ordinary income) and the reversal affects a different type of taxable income (for example, capital gains).

209. Under the net change method, deferred tax balances may remain after the individual timing differences that gave rise to those balances have reversed if one of the situations described in paragraph 208 occurs. Those balances may continue to be reported in an enterprise's statement of financial position for as long as the particular type of timing difference exists. Those balances are not eliminated earlier than that because the objective of the deferred method is to measure the incremental effect on income tax expense as a result of tim-

ing differences in the year they originate; the objective is not to measure the cumulative amount of taxes payable or refundable when timing differences reverse in future years.

210. A criticism of the deferred method is its failure to recognize the consequences of an enacted change in tax laws or rates. The use of accelerated depreciation for taxes and straight-line depreciation for financial reporting is sometimes cited by advocates of the deferred approach as an example illustrating why that approach is appropriate. Advocates of the deferred approach state that a realized tax benefit for accelerated depreciation deductions cannot change as a result of a change in future tax rates. Under the deferred method, the realized benefit is reported in the statement of financial position pending allocation to reduce income tax expense in future years when the depreciation differences reverse. Measured and reported in that manner, deferred tax credits and charges do not meet the Board's definition of liabilities and assets in Concepts Statement 6.

211. A realized tax benefit for accelerated depreciation does not subsequently change if tax rates change. Depreciation differences, however, affect income taxes in two years—once in the year they originate and once again in the year they reverse. Revenues received in later years that recover the amount of depreciable assets reported in the financial statements are taxable. Taxable income as determined by the tax return is larger in later years because depreciation deductions for tax purposes have been used up. Taxes payable on that increased amount of taxable income will be determined by enacted tax rates for the year(s) the depreciation differences reverse and not for the year(s) that they originated. In the Board's opinion, measurements using enacted future tax rates provide more relevant information.

212. Other situations are not satisfactorily dealt with under a deferred approach that focuses on the statement of earnings and timing differences between financial and taxable income. Examples include:

a. A business combination gives rise to differences between the assigned values and the tax bases of an acquired enterprise's assets and liabilities that are not "timing" differences.
b. Deferred amounts may be affected by a change in the tax law such as the 1979 U.K. tax legislation regarding stock relief or the 1984 U.S. Tax Reform Act regarding taxation of Domestic International Sales Corporations and stock life insurance companies.

c. Deferred amounts may be affected when an enterprise changes its tax status and becomes or ceases to be a taxable entity.
d. Alternative minimum tax.

On the other hand, under a deferred approach that focuses on the statement of earnings and timing differences between financial and taxable income, the Board can see no reason for not recognizing the tax effects of timing differences for the areas addressed by Opinion 23 and for deposits in statutory reserve funds by U.S. steamship enterprises.

213. Some respondents to the Discussion Memorandum criticized the complexity of multiple with-and-without calculations particularly when deferred tax credits are eliminated and reinstated because of operating loss and tax credit carrybacks and carryforwards. The Board believes that the complexities arise because the issues pertain to amounts, deferred tax credits and charges, that can be described only in terms of the procedures by which the amounts were computed.

The Net-of-Tax Approach to Accounting for Income Taxes

214. The net-of-tax approach accounts for the effects of taxability and deductibility on assets and liabilities as reductions of the reported amounts of those assets and liabilities. The amount of accounts receivable from installment sales, for example, is reduced for the taxability of the cash receipts in the future years in which the receivables are collected. Depreciable assets, on the other hand, are viewed as providing future benefits from tax deductions and from use of the assets to provide a product or service. The cost of depreciable assets is allocated between the cost of future tax benefits and the cost of future benefits from use of the assets. As the tax deductibility of the assets is used up, a portion of the cost of the assets is used up and the reported amount of the assets is reduced.

215. Allocations of the cost of depreciable assets between tax benefits and benefits from use of the assets are subjective. Advocates of the net-of-tax approach propose that the portion of the cost of depreciable assets allocated to future tax benefits should be the amount of the tax benefits. The remaining cost of the assets is allocated to the future benefits from use of the assets. That approach appears to allocate too much cost to tax benefits and too little cost to benefits from use of the asset, but there may not be a workable solution to the problem that provides a better answer. An example of applying the net-of-tax method when there are depreciable assets is presented below. Equipment that costs $1,000 has a 4-year life. The tax rate is

40 percent. Tax deductions and their tax benefit are as follows:

	Tax Depreciation	Tax Benefit at 40 Percent
Year 1	$ 400	$160
Year 2	300	120
Year 3	200	80
Year 4	100	40
	$1,000	$400

Allocation of the cost of the equipment between the cost of future tax benefits and the cost of future benefits from use of the equipment, and the annual expiration of each of those components are as follows:

	Cost of Tax Benefits	Cost of Operation Benefits	Annual Expiration
Year 1	$160	$150	$ 310
Year 2	120	150	270
Year 3	80	150	230
Year 4	40	150	190
	$400	$600	$1,000

The reported amount of the equipment is reduced by $310 the first year, an additional $270 the second year, and so forth.

216. Straight-line depreciation for financial reporting would be $250 each year. In year 1, deferred tax expense would be $60 under either the deferred or the liability approach. An issue under the net-of-tax approach is whether the $310 expiration of the cost of depreciable assets in year 1 should be reported as $310 of depreciation or, alternatively, whether depreciation should be $250 and tax expense $60. The latter approach is recommended by most net-of-tax advocates. They cite some precedents for their approach and practical reasons why the other approach does not make sense. Nevertheless, application of the net-of-tax approach to depreciable assets is viewed as a cost allocation process.

217. Valuation accounts would be used to reduce assets and liabilities for the effects of their taxability or deductibility. The additional special procedures that are necessary to determine the amount of timing differences and their tax effects for each different asset or liability would be a practical problem. Another problem is that some timing differences cannot be identified with a specific asset or liability, for example, timing differences that result from (a) cash basis accounting for tax purposes and accrual accounting for financial reporting and (b) completed-contract accounting for tax purposes and percentage-of-completion accounting for financial reporting.

218. Reporting an enterprise's assets and liabilities net of their tax effects would make it difficult to understand an enterprise's overall tax situation, and those tax effects would have to be combined in financial statement disclosures. Financial statement disclosures that refer to income taxes that become payable or refundable in future years, however, would appear to contradict the underlying net-of-tax accounting. The Board believes that if recovery of an asset or settlement of a liability will result in amounts that are taxable or deductible, that fact is better communicated by reporting a deferred tax liability or asset rather than by reducing other assets and liabilities.

A Combination of Approaches to Accounting for Income Taxes

219. The net-of-tax or the deferred approach is sometimes proposed in combination with the asset and liability approach. Advocates believe that timing differences for items not yet included in the tax return give rise to an estimated future sacrifice or benefit that is a liability or an asset. Settlement of the estimated tax liability or asset occurs when the item enters the tax return. If the item has already been included in the tax return, advocates believe that the tax sacrifice or benefit has already occurred and that the tax effects should be deferred or applied to reduce a related asset or liability until the timing difference reverses.

220. The Board rejected use of either the deferred or the net-of-tax approach in combination with the asset and liability approach for the same reasons that the deferred and net-of-tax approaches were rejected as a single overall approach. The Board believes that the deferred tax consequences of temporary differences are recognizable liabilities and assets regardless of whether the item that created the temporary difference was first recognized in financial income or first included in taxable income.

221. Any combination of methods increases complexity. All of an enterprise's timing differences would have to be analyzed and sorted into two different groups. Different tax calculation procedures would then have to be applied to each group. In some instances, a single type of timing difference might have to be analyzed and sorted into both groups. For example, depreciation for some classes of assets is sometimes faster for financial reporting than for tax purposes. The underlying rationale for a combination of approaches does not permit offsetting those depreciation differ-

ences against excess tax depreciation in the early years for other classes of depreciable assets.

222. Amounts reported in the statement of financial position under a combination of approaches would be confusing. The tax effects of some differ-

ences would be reported as deferred tax liabilities or assets. The tax effects of other differences would be reported as deferred tax credits or charges, or as reductions of other assets and liabilities. Some sort of financial statement disclosure of an enterprise's overall tax status would be required.

Appendix B

APPLICATION OF THE STANDARDS TO SPECIFIC ASPECTS OF ACCOUNTING FOR INCOME TAXES

CONTENTS

Appendix B

APPLICATION OF THE STANDARDS TO SPECIFIC ASPECTS OF ACCOUNTING FOR INCOME TAXES

Introduction

223. This appendix provides additional discussion and examples[14] that illustrate application of the

standards to specific aspects of accounting for income taxes.

Recognition of Deferred Tax Assets and Deferred Tax Liabilities

224. A deferred tax liability is recognized for all taxable temporary differences,[15] and a deferred tax asset is recognized for all deductible temporary differences and operating loss and tax credit carryforwards. A valuation allowance is recognized if it

---

[14]The discussion and examples in this appendix assume that the tax law requires offsetting net deductions in a particular year against net taxable amounts in the 3 preceding years and then in the 15 succeeding years. Assumptions in this appendix about the tax law are for illustrative purposes only. The enacted tax law for a particular tax jurisdiction should be used for recognition and measurement of deferred tax liabilities and assets.

[15]Refer to paragraph 9.

is more likely than not that some portion or all of the deferred tax asset will not be realized.

225. The following example illustrates recognition of deferred tax assets and liabilities. At the end of year 3 (the current year), an enterprise has $2,400 of deductible temporary differences and $1,500 of taxable temporary differences.

A deferred tax liability is recognized at the end of year 3 for the $1,500 of taxable temporary differences, and a deferred tax asset is recognized for the $2,400 of deductible temporary differences. All available evidence, both positive and negative, is considered to determine whether, based on the weight of that evidence, a valuation allowance is needed for some portion or all of the deferred tax asset. If evidence about one or more sources of taxable income (refer to paragraph 21) is sufficient to support a conclusion that a valuation allowance is not needed, other sources of taxable income need not be considered. For example, if the weight of available evidence indicates that taxable income will exceed $2,400 in each future year, a conclusion that no valuation allowance is needed can be reached without considering the pattern and timing of the reversal of the temporary differences, the existence of qualifying tax-planning strategies, and so forth.

Similarly, if the deductible temporary differences will reverse within the next 3 years and taxable income in the current year exceeds $2,400, nothing needs to be known about future taxable income exclusive of reversing temporary differences because the deferred tax asset could be realized by carryback to the current year. A valuation allowance is needed, however, if the weight of available evidence indicates that some portion or all of the $2,400 of tax deductions from future reversals of the deductible temporary differences will not be realized by offsetting:

a. The $1,500 of taxable temporary differences and $900 of future taxable income exclusive of reversing temporary differences
b. $2,400 of future taxable income exclusive of reversing temporary differences

c. $2,400 of taxable income in the current or prior years by loss carryback to those years
d. $2,400 of taxable income in one or more of the circumstances described above and as a result of a qualifying tax-planning strategy (refer to paragraphs 246-251).

To the extent that evidence about one or more sources of taxable income is sufficient to eliminate any need for a valuation allowance, other sources need not be considered. Detailed forecasts, projections, or other types of analyses[16] are unnecessary if expected future taxable income is more than sufficient to realize a tax benefit. Detailed analyses are not necessary, for example, if the enterprise earned $500 of taxable income in each of years 1-3 and there is no evidence to suggest it will not continue to earn that level of taxable income in future years. That level of future taxable income is more than sufficient to realize the tax benefit of $2,400 of tax deductions over a period of at least 19 years (the year(s) of the deductions, 3 carryback years, and 15 carryforward years) in the U.S. federal tax jurisdiction.

226. The following example illustrates recognition of a valuation allowance for a portion of a deferred tax asset in one year and a subsequent change in circumstances that requires adjustment of the valuation allowance at the end of the following year. The assumptions are as follows:

a. At the end of the current year (year 3), an enterprise's only temporary differences are deductible temporary differences in the amount of $900.
b. Pretax financial income, taxable income, and taxes paid for each of years 1-3 are all positive, but relatively negligible, amounts.
c. The enacted tax rate is 40 percent for all years.

A deferred tax asset in the amount of $360 ($900 at 40 percent) is recognized at the end of year 3. If management concludes, based on an assessment of all available evidence (refer to guidance in paragraphs 20-25), that it is more likely than not that future taxable income will not be sufficient to realize a tax benefit for $400 of the $900 of deductible temporary differences at the end of the current year, a $160 valuation allowance ($400 at 40 percent) is recognized at the end of year 3.

---

[16]The terms *forecast* and *projection* refer to any process by which available evidence is accumulated and evaluated for purposes of estimating whether future taxable income will be sufficient to realize a deferred tax asset. Judgment is necessary to determine how detailed or formalized that evaluation process should be. Furthermore, information about expected future taxable income is necessary only to the extent positive evidence available from other sources (refer to paragraph 21) is not sufficient to support a conclusion that a valuation allowance is not needed. This Statement does not require either a *financial forecast* or a *financial projection* within the meaning of those terms in the Statements on Standards for Accountants' Services on Prospective Financial Information issued by the Auditing Standards Board of the American Institute of Certified Public Accountants.

Assume that pretax financial income and taxable income for year 4 turn out to be as follows:

Pretax financial loss	$ (50)
Reversing deductible temporary differences	(300)
Loss carryforward for tax purposes	$(350)

The $50 pretax loss in year 4 is additional negative evidence that must be weighed against available positive evidence to determine the amount of valuation allowance necessary at the end of year 4. Deductible temporary differences and carryforwards at the end of year 4 are as follows:

Loss carryforward from year 4 for tax purposes (see above)	$350
Unreversed deductible temporary differences ($900 − $300)	600
	$950

The $360 deferred tax asset recognized at the end of year 3 is increased to $380 ($950 at 40 percent) at the end of year 4. Based on an assessment of all evidence available at the end of year 4, management concludes that it is more likely than not that $240 of the deferred tax asset will not be realized and, therefore, that a $240 valuation allowance is necessary. The $160 valuation allowance recognized at the end of year 3 is increased to $240 at the end of year 4. The $60 net effect of those 2 adjustments (the $80 increase in the valuation allowance less the $20 increase in the deferred tax asset) results in $60 of deferred tax expense that is recognized in year 4.

Offset of Taxable and Deductible Amounts

227. The tax law determines whether future reversals of temporary differences will result in taxable and deductible amounts that offset each other in future years. The tax law also determines the extent to which deductible temporary differences and carryforwards will offset the tax consequences of income that is expected to be earned in future years. For example, the tax law may provide that capital losses are deductible only to the extent of capital gains. In that case, a tax benefit is not recognized for temporary differences that will result in future deductions in the form of capital losses unless those deductions will offset either (a) other existing temporary differences that will result in future capital gains, (b) capital gains that are expected to occur in future years, or (c) capital gains of the current year or prior years if carryback (of those capital loss deductions from the future reversal years) is expected.

Pattern of Taxable or Deductible Amounts

228. The particular years in which temporary differences result in taxable or deductible amounts generally are determined by the timing of the recovery of the related asset or settlement of the related liability. However, there are exceptions to that general rule. For example, a temporary difference between the tax basis and the reported amount of inventory for which cost is determined on a LIFO basis does not reverse when present inventory is sold in future years if it is replaced by purchases or production of inventory in those same future years. A LIFO inventory temporary difference becomes taxable or deductible in the future year that inventory is liquidated and not replaced.

229. For some assets or liabilities, temporary differences may accumulate over several years and then reverse over several years. That pattern is common for depreciable assets. Future originating differences for existing depreciable assets and their subsequent reversals are a factor to be considered when assessing the likelihood of future taxable income (paragraph 21(b)) for realization of a tax benefit for existing deductible temporary differences and carryforwards.

Change in Deferred Foreign Tax Assets and Liabilities

230. When the reporting currency (not the foreign currency) is the functional currency, remeasurement of an enterprise's deferred foreign tax liability or asset after a change in the exchange rate will result in a transaction gain or loss that is recognized currently in determining net income. Statement 52 requires disclosure of the aggregate transaction gain or loss included in determining net income but does not specify how to display that transaction gain or loss or its components for financial reporting. Accordingly, a transaction gain or loss that results from remeasuring a deferred foreign tax liability or asset may be included in the reported amount of deferred tax benefit or expense if that presentation is considered to be more useful. If reported in that manner, that transaction gain or loss is still included in the aggregate transaction gain or loss for the period to be disclosed as required by Statement 52.

Special Deductions

231. Statement 96 amended FASB Statement No. 19, *Financial Accounting and Reporting by Oil and Gas Producing Companies*, to require recognition of statutory depletion that would result from generating fu-

ture revenues exactly equal to the amount of the related assets (that is, the assets subject to statutory depletion) to the extent that the statutory depletion offsets a deferred tax liability for taxable temporary differences attributable to those assets. This Statement eliminates that amendment of Statement 19. The Board concluded that, under the basic approach to recognition of deferred tax benefits required by this Statement, the necessary past event for recognition of the tax benefit of statutory depletion is producing oil, mining copper, and so forth (or its subsequent sale). The tax benefit of statutory depletion and other types of special deductions such as those for Blue Cross-Blue Shield and small life insurance companies in future years should not be anticipated for purposes of offsetting a deferred tax liability for taxable temporary differences at the end of the current year.

232. As required above, the tax benefit of special deductions ordinarily is recognized no earlier than the year in which those special deductions are deductible on the tax return. However, some portion of the future tax effects of special deductions are implicitly recognized in determining (a) the average graduated tax rate to be used for measuring deferred taxes when graduated tax rates are a significant factor and (b) the need for a valuation allowance for deferred tax assets. In those circumstances, implicit recognition is unavoidable because (1) those special deductions are one of the determinants of future taxable income and (2) future taxable income determines the average graduated tax rate and sometimes determines the need for a valuation allowance.

Measurement of Deferred Tax Liabilities and Assets

233. The tax rate that is used to measure deferred tax liabilities and deferred tax assets is the enacted tax rate(s) expected to apply to taxable income in the years that the liability is expected to be settled or the asset recovered. Measurements are based on elections (for example, an election for loss carryforward instead of carryback) that are expected to be made for tax purposes in future years. Presently enacted changes in tax laws and rates that become effective for a particular future year or years must be considered when determining the tax rate to apply to temporary differences reversing in that year or years. Tax laws and rates for the current year are used if no changes have been enacted for future years. An asset for deductible temporary differences that are expected to be realized in future years through carryback of a future loss to the current or a prior year (or a liability for taxable temporary differences that are expected to reduce the refund claimed for the carryback of a future loss to the current or a prior year) is measured using tax laws and rates for the current or a prior year, that is, the year for which a

refund is expected to be realized based on loss carryback provisions of the tax law.

234. The following example illustrates determination of the tax rate for measurement of a deferred tax liability for taxable temporary differences when there is a phased-in change in tax rates. At the end of year 3 (the current year), an enterprise has $2,400 of taxable temporary differences, which are expected to result in taxable amounts of approximately $800 on the future tax returns for each of years 4-6. Enacted tax rates are 35 percent for years 1-3, 40 percent for years 4-6, and 45 percent for year 7 and thereafter.

The tax rate that is used to measure the deferred tax liability for the $2,400 of taxable temporary differences differs depending on whether the tax effect of future reversals of those temporary differences is on taxes payable for years 1-3, years 4-6, or year 7 and thereafter. The tax rate for measurement of the deferred tax liability is 40 percent whenever taxable income is expected in years 4-6. If tax losses are expected in years 4-6, however, the tax rate is:

a. 35 percent if realization of a tax benefit for those tax losses in years 4-6 will be by loss carryback to years 1-3
b. 45 percent if realization of a tax benefit for those tax losses in years 4-6 will be by loss carryforward to year 7 and thereafter.

235. The following example illustrates determination of the tax rate for measurement of a deferred tax asset for deductible temporary differences when there is a change in tax rates. The assumptions are as follows:

a. Enacted tax rates are 30 percent for years 1-3 and 40 percent for year 4 and thereafter.
b. At the end of year 3 (the current year), an enterprise has $900 of deductible temporary differences, which are expected to result in tax deductions of approximately $300 on the future tax returns for each of years 4-6.

The tax rate is 40 percent if the enterprise expects to realize a tax benefit for the deductible temporary differences by offsetting taxable income earned in future years. Alternatively, the tax rate is 30 percent if the enterprise expects to realize a tax benefit for the deductible temporary differences by loss carryback refund.

Assume that (a) the enterprise recognizes a $360 ($900 at 40 percent) deferred tax asset to be realized by offsetting taxable income in future years and (b) taxable income and taxes payable in each of years 1-3 were $300 and $90, respectively. Realization of a tax benefit of at least $270 ($900 at 30 percent) is assured because carryback refunds totalling $270 may be realized even if no taxable income is earned in future years. Recognition of a valuation allowance for the other $90 ($360 − $270) of the deferred tax asset depends on management's assessment of whether, based on the weight of available evidence, a portion or all of the tax benefit of the $900 of deductible temporary differences will not be realized at 40 percent tax rates in future years.

Alternatively, if enacted tax rates are 40 percent for years 1-3 and 30 percent for year 4 and thereafter, measurement of the deferred tax asset at a 40 percent tax rate could only occur if tax losses are expected in future years 4-6.

236. The following example illustrates determination of the average graduated tax rate for measurement of deferred tax liabilities and assets by an enterprise for which graduated tax rates ordinarily are a significant factor. At the end of year 3 (the current year), an enterprise has $1,500 of taxable temporary differences and $900 of deductible temporary differences, which are expected to result in net taxable amounts of approximately $200 on the future tax returns for each of years 4-6. Enacted tax rates are 15 percent for the first $500 of taxable income, 25 percent for the next $500, and 40 percent for taxable income over $1,000. This example assumes that there is no income (for example, capital gains) subject to special tax rates.

The deferred tax liability and asset for those reversing taxable and deductible temporary differences in years 4-6 are measured using the average graduated tax rate for the estimated amount of annual taxable income in future years. Thus, the average graduated tax rate will differ depending on the expected level of annual taxable income (including reversing temporary differences) in years 4-6. The average tax rate will be:

a. 15 percent if the estimated annual level of taxable income in years 4-6 is $500 or less
b. 20 percent if the estimated annual level of taxable income in years 4-6 is $1,000
c. 30 percent if the estimated annual level of taxable income in years 4-6 is $2,000.

Temporary differences usually do not reverse in equal annual amounts as in the example above, and a different average graduated tax rate might apply to reversals in different future years. However, a detailed analysis to determine the net reversals of temporary differences in each future year usually is not warranted. It is not warranted because the other variable (that is, taxable income or losses exclusive of reversing temporary differences in each of those future years) for determination of the average graduated tax rate in each future year is no more than an estimate. For that reason, an

aggregate calculation using a single estimated average graduated tax rate based on estimated average annual taxable income in future years is sufficient. Judgment is permitted, however, to deal with unusual situations, for example, an abnormally large temporary difference that will reverse in a single future year, or an abnormal level of taxable income that is expected for a single future year. The lowest graduated tax rate should be used whenever the estimated average graduated tax rate otherwise would be zero.

237. Deferred tax liabilities and assets are measured using enacted tax rates applicable to capital gains, ordinary income, and so forth, based on the expected type of taxable or deductible amounts in future years. For example, evidence based on all facts and circumstances should determine whether an investor's liability for the tax consequences of temporary differences related to its equity in the earnings of an investee should be measured using enacted tax rates applicable to a capital gain or a dividend. Computation of a deferred tax liability for undistributed earnings based on dividends should also reflect any related dividends received deductions or foreign tax credits, and taxes that would be withheld from the dividend.

Alternative Minimum Tax

238. Temporary differences such as depreciation differences are one reason why TMT may exceed regular tax. Temporary differences, however, ultimately reverse and, absent a significant amount of preference items, total taxes paid over the entire life of the enterprise will be based on the regular tax system. Preference items are another reason why TMT may exceed regular tax. If preference items are large enough, an enterprise could be subject, over its lifetime, to the AMT system; and the cumulative amount of AMT credit carryforwards would expire unused. No one can know beforehand which scenario will prevail because that determination can only be made after the fact. In the meantime, this Statement requires procedures that provide a practical solution to that problem.

239. Under the requirements of this Statement, an enterprise should:

a. Measure the total deferred tax liability and asset for regular tax temporary differences and carryforwards using the regular tax rate
b. Measure the total deferred tax asset for all AMT credit carryforward
c. Reduce the deferred tax asset for AMT credit carryforward by a valuation allowance if, based on the weight of available evidence, it is more likely than not that some portion or all of that deferred tax asset will not be realized.

Paragraph 21 identifies four sources of taxable income that should be considered in determining the need for and amount of a valuation allowance. No valuation allowance is necessary if the deferred tax asset for AMT credit carryforward can be realized:

1. Under paragraph 21(a), by reducing a deferred tax liability from the amount of regular tax on regular tax temporary differences to not less than the amount of TMT on AMT temporary differences
2. Under paragraph 21(b), by reducing taxes on future income from the amount of regular tax on regular taxable income to not less than the amount of TMT on AMT income
3. Under paragraph 21(c), by loss carryback
4. Under paragraph 21(d), by a tax-planning strategy such as switching from tax-exempt to taxable interest income.

Operating Loss and Tax Credit Carryforwards and Carrybacks

Recognition of a Tax Benefit for Carrybacks

240. An operating loss, certain deductible items that are subject to limitations, and some tax credits arising but not utilized in the current year may be carried back for refund of taxes paid in prior years or carried forward to reduce taxes payable in future years. A receivable is recognized for the amount of taxes paid in prior years that is refundable by carryback of an operating loss or unused tax credits of the current year.

Recognition of a Tax Benefit for Carryforwards

241. A deferred tax asset is recognized for an operating loss or tax credit carryforward.[17] In assessing the need for a valuation allowance, provisions in the tax law that limit utilization of an operating loss or tax credit carryforward are applied in determining whether it is more likely than not that some portion or all of the deferred tax asset will not be realized by reduction of taxes payable on taxable income during the carryforward period.

242. The following example illustrates recognition of the tax benefit of an operating loss in the loss year and in subsequent carryforward years when a valuation allowance is necessary in the loss year. The assumptions are as follows:

a. The enacted tax rate is 40 percent for all years.
b. An operating loss occurs in year 5.
c. The only difference between financial and taxable income results from use of accelerated depreciation for tax purposes. Differences that arise between the reported amount and the tax basis of depreciable assets in years 1-7 will result in taxable amounts before the end of the loss carryforward period from year 5.
d. Financial income, taxable income, and taxes currently payable or refundable are as follows:

	Year 1	Years 2-4	Year 5	Year 6	Year 7
Pretax financial income (loss)	$2,000	$5,000	$(8,000)	$ 2,200	$7,000
Depreciation differences	(800)	(2,200)	(800)	(700)	(600)
Loss carryback	—	—	2,800	—	—
Loss carryforward	—	—	—	(6,000)	(4,500)
Taxable income (loss)	$1,200	$2,800	$(6,000)	$(4,500)	$1,900
Taxes payable (refundable)	$ 480	$1,120	$(1,120)	$ —	$ 760

e. At the end of year 5, profits are not expected in years 6 and 7 and later years, and it is concluded that a valuation allowance is necessary to the extent realization of the deferred tax asset for the operating loss carryforward depends on taxable income (exclusive of reversing temporary differences) in future years.

---

[17]This requirement pertains to all ITC carryforwards regardless of whether the flow-through or deferral method is used to account for ITC.

The deferred tax liability for the taxable temporary differences is calculated at the end of each year as follows:

	Year 1	Years 2-4	Year 5	Year 6	Year 7
Unreversed differences:					
Beginning amount	$ —	$ 800	$3,000	$3,800	$4,500
Additional amount	800	2,200	800	700	600
Total	$800	$3,000	$3,800	$4,500	$5,100
Deferred tax liability (40 percent)	$320	$1,200	$1,520	$1,800	$2,040

The deferred tax asset and related valuation allowance for the loss carryforward are calculated at the end of each year as follows:

	Year 1	Years 2-4	Year 5	Year 6	Year 7
Loss carryforward for tax purposes	$—	$—	$6,000	$4,500	$—
Deferred tax asset (40 percent)	$—	$—	$2,400	$1,800	$—
Valuation allowance equal to the amount by which the deferred tax asset exceeds the deferred tax liability	—	—	(880)	—	—
Net deferred tax asset	$—	$—	$1,520	$1,800	$—

Total tax expense for each period is as follows:

	Year 1	Years 2-4	Year 5	Year 6	Year 7
Deferred tax expense (benefit):					
Increase in deferred tax liability	$320	$ 880	$ 320	$280	$ 240
(Increase) decrease in net deferred tax asset	—	—	(1,520)	(280)	1,800
	320	880	(1,200)	—	2,040
Currently payable (refundable)	480	1,120	(1,120)	—	760
Total tax expense (benefit)	$800	$2,000	$(2,320)	$ —	$2,800

In year 5, $2,800 of the loss is carried back to reduce taxable income in years 2-4, and $1,120 of taxes paid for those years is refunded. In addition, a $1,520 deferred tax liability is recognized for $3,800 of taxable temporary differences, and a $2,400 deferred tax asset is recognized for the $6,000 loss carryforward. However, based on the conclusion described in assumption (e), a valuation allowance is recognized for the amount by which that deferred tax asset exceeds the deferred tax liability.

In year 6, a portion of the deferred tax asset for the loss carryforward is realized because taxable income is earned in that year. The remaining balance of the deferred tax asset for the loss carryforward at the end of year 6 equals the deferred tax liability for the taxable temporary differences. A valuation allowance is not needed.

In year 7, the remaining balance of the loss carryforward is realized, and $760 of taxes are payable on net taxable income of $1,900. A $2,040 de-

ferred tax liability is recognized for the $5,100 of taxable temporary differences.

243. An operating loss or tax credit carryforward from a prior year (for which the deferred tax asset was reduced by a valuation allowance) may sometimes reduce taxable income and taxes payable that are attributable to certain revenues or gains that the tax law requires be included in taxable income for the year that cash is received. For financial reporting, however, there may have been no revenue or gain and a liability is recognized for the cash received. Future sacrifices to settle the liability will result in deductible amounts in future years. Under those circumstances, the reduction in taxable income and taxes payable from utilization of the operating loss or tax credit carryforward gives no cause for recognition of a tax benefit because, in effect, the operating loss or tax credit carryforward has been replaced by temporary differences that will result in deductible amounts when a nontax liability is settled in future years. The requirements for recognition of a tax benefit for de-

ductible temporary differences and for operating loss carryforwards are the same, and the manner of reporting the eventual tax benefit recognized (that is, in income or as required by paragraph 37) is not affected by the intervening transaction reported for tax purposes.

244. The following example illustrates the interaction of loss carryforwards and temporary differences that will result in net deductible amounts in future years. The assumptions are as follows:

a. The financial loss and the loss reported on the tax return for an enterprise's first year of operations are the same.
b. In year 2, a gain of $2,500 from a transaction that is a sale for tax purposes but a sale and leaseback for financial reporting is the only difference between pretax financial income and taxable income.

	Financial Income	Taxable Income
Year 1: Income (loss) from operations	$(4,000)	$(4,000)
Year 2: Income (loss) from operations	$ —	$ —
Taxable gain on sale		2,500
Taxable income before loss carryforward		2,500
Loss carryforward from year 1		(4,000)
Taxable income		$ —

The $4,000 operating loss carryforward at the end of year 1 is reduced to $1,500 at the end of year 2 because $2,500 of it is used to reduce taxable income. The $2,500 reduction in the loss carryforward becomes $2,500 of deductible temporary differences that will reverse and result in future tax deductions when lease payments are made. The enterprise has no deferred tax liability to be offset by those future tax deductions, the future tax deductions cannot be realized by loss carryback because no taxes have been paid, and the enterprise has had pretax losses for financial reporting since inception. Unless positive evidence exists that is sufficient to overcome the negative evidence associated with those losses, a valuation allowance is recognized at the end of year 2 for the full amount of the deferred tax asset related to the $2,500 of deductible temporary differences and the remaining $1,500 of operating loss carryforward.

Reporting the Tax Benefit of Operating Loss Carryforwards or Carrybacks

245. Except as noted in paragraph 37, the manner of reporting the tax benefit of an operating loss carryforward or carryback is determined by the source of the income or loss in the current year and not by (a) the source of the operating loss carryforward or taxes paid in a prior year or (b) the source of expected future income that will result in realization of a deferred tax asset for an operating loss carryforward from the current year. Deferred tax expense or benefit that results because a change in circumstances causes a change in judgment about the future realization of the tax benefit of an operating loss carryforward is allocated to continuing operations (refer to paragraph 26). Thus, for example:

a. The tax benefit of an operating loss carryforward that resulted from an extraordinary loss in a prior year and that is first recognized in the financial statements for the current year:
  (1) Is allocated to continuing operations if it offsets the current or deferred tax consequences of income from continuing operations
  (2) Is allocated to an extraordinary gain if it offsets the current or deferred tax consequences of that extraordinary gain
  (3) Is allocated to continuing operations if it results from a change in circumstances that causes a change in judgment about future realization of a tax benefit
b. The current or deferred tax benefit of a loss from continuing operations in the current year is allocated to continuing operations regardless of whether that loss offsets the current or deferred tax consequences of an extraordinary gain that:
  (1) Occurred in the current year
  (2) Occurred in a prior year (that is, if realization of the tax benefit will be by carryback refund)
  (3) Is expected to occur in a future year.

Tax-Planning Strategies

246. Expectations about future taxable income incorporate numerous assumptions about actions, elections, and strategies to minimize income taxes in future years. For example, an enterprise may have a practice of deferring taxable income whenever possible by structuring sales to qualify as installment sales for tax purposes. Actions such as that are not *tax-planning strategies*, as that term is used in this Statement, because they are actions that management takes in the normal course of business. For purposes of applying the require-

ments of this Statement, a *tax-planning strategy* is an action that management ordinarily might not take but would take, if necessary, to realize a tax benefit for a carryforward before it expires. For example, a strategy to sell property and lease it back for the expressed purpose of generating taxable income to utilize a carryforward before it expires is not an action that management takes in the normal course of business. A qualifying tax-planning strategy is an action that:

a. *Is prudent and feasible.* Management must have the ability to implement the strategy and expect to do so unless the need is eliminated in future years. For example, management would not have to apply the strategy if income earned in a later year uses the entire amount of carryforward from the current year.
b. *An enterprise ordinarily might not take, but would take to prevent an operating loss or tax credit carryforward from expiring unused.* All of the various strategies that are expected to be employed for business or tax purposes other than utilization of carryforwards that would otherwise expire unused are, for purposes of this Statement, implicit in management's estimate of future taxable income and, therefore, are not tax-planning strategies as that term is used in this Statement.
c. *Would result in realization of deferred tax assets.* The effect of qualifying tax-planning strategies must be recognized in the determination of the amount of a valuation allowance. Tax-planning strategies need not be considered, however, if positive evidence available from other sources (refer to paragraph 21) is sufficient to support a conclusion that a valuation allowance is *not* necessary.

247. Tax-planning strategies may shift estimated future taxable income between future years. For example, assume that an enterprise has a $1,500 operating loss carryforward that expires at the end of next year and that its estimate of taxable income exclusive of the future reversal of existing temporary differences and carryforwards is approximately $1,000 per year for each of the next several years. That estimate is based, in part, on the enterprise's present practice of making sales on the installment basis and on provisions in the tax law that result in temporary deferral of gains on installment sales. A tax-planning strategy to increase taxable income next year and realize the full tax benefit of that operating loss carryforward might be to structure next year's sales in a manner that does not meet the tax rules to qualify as installment sales. Another strategy might be to change next year's depreciation procedures for tax purposes.

248. Tax-planning strategies also may shift the estimated pattern and timing of future reversals of temporary differences. For example, if an operating loss carryforward otherwise would expire unused at the end of next year, a tax-planning strategy to sell the enterprise's installment sale receivables next year would accelerate the future reversal of *taxable* temporary differences for the gains on those installment sales. In other circumstances, a tax-planning strategy to accelerate the future reversal of *deductible* temporary differences in time to offset taxable income that is expected in an early future year might be the only means to realize a tax benefit for those deductible temporary differences if they otherwise would reverse and provide no tax benefit in some later future year(s). Examples of actions that would accelerate the future reversal of deductible temporary differences include:

a. An annual payment that is larger than an enterprise's usual annual payment to reduce a long-term pension obligation (recognized as a liability in the financial statements) might accelerate a tax deduction for pension expense to an earlier year than would otherwise have occurred.
b. Disposal of obsolete inventory that is reported at net realizable value in the financial statements would accelerate a tax deduction for the amount by which the tax basis exceeds the net realizable value of the inventory.
c. Sale of loans at their reported amount (that is, net of an allowance for bad debts) would accelerate a tax deduction for the allowance for bad debts.

249. A significant expense might need to be incurred to implement a particular tax-planning strategy, or a significant loss might need to be recognized as a result of implementing a particular tax-planning strategy. In either case, that expense or loss (net of any future tax benefit that would result from that expense or loss) reduces the amount of tax benefit that is recognized for the expected effect of a qualifying tax-planning strategy. For that purpose, the future effect of a differential in interest rates (for example, between the rate that would be earned on installment sale receivables and the rate that could be earned on an alternative investment if the tax-planning strategy is to sell those receivables to accelerate the future reversal of related taxable temporary differences) is not considered.

250. The following example illustrates recognition of a deferred tax asset based on the expected effect of a qualifying tax-planning strategy when a signif-

icant expense would be incurred to implement the strategy. The assumptions are as follows:

a. A $900 operating loss carryforward expires at the end of next year.
b. Based on historical results and the weight of other available evidence, the estimated level of taxable income exclusive of the future reversal of existing temporary differences and the operating loss carryforward next year is $100.
c. Taxable temporary differences in the amount of $1,200 ordinarily would result in taxable amounts of approximately $400 in each of the next 3 years.
d. There is a qualifying tax-planning strategy to accelerate the future reversal of all $1,200 of taxable temporary differences to next year.
e. Estimated legal and other expenses to implement that tax-planning strategy are $150.
f. The enacted tax rate is 40 percent for all years.

Without the tax-planning strategy, only $500 of the $900 operating loss carryforward could be realized next year by offsetting (a) $100 of taxable income exclusive of reversing temporary differences and (b) $400 of reversing taxable temporary differences. The other $400 of operating loss carryforward would expire unused at the end of next year. Therefore, the $360 deferred tax asset ($900 at 40 percent) would be offset by a $160 valuation allowance ($400 at 40 percent), and a $200 net deferred tax asset would be recognized for the operating loss carryforward.

With the tax-planning strategy, the $900 operating loss carryforward could be applied against $1,300 of taxable income next year ($100 of taxable income exclusive of reversing temporary differences and $1,200 of reversing taxable temporary differences). The $360 deferred tax asset is reduced by a $90 valuation allowance recognized for the net-of-tax expenses necessary to implement the tax-planning strategy. The amount of that valuation allowance is determined as follows:

Legal and other expenses to implement the tax-planning strategy	$150
Future tax benefit of those legal and other expenses—$150 at 40 percent	60
	$ 90

In summary, a $480 deferred tax liability is recognized for the $1,200 of taxable temporary differences, a $360 deferred tax asset is recognized for the $900 operating loss carryforward, and a $90 valuation allowance is recognized for the net-of-

tax expenses of implementing the tax-planning strategy.

251. Under this Statement, the requirements for consideration of tax-planning strategies pertain only to the determination of a valuation allowance for a deferred tax asset. A deferred tax liability ordinarily is recognized for all taxable temporary differences. The only exceptions are identified in paragraph 9. Certain seemingly taxable temporary differences, however, may or may not result in taxable amounts when those differences reverse in future years. One example is an excess of cash surrender value of life insurance over premiums paid (paragraph 14). Another example is an excess of the book over the tax basis of an investment in a domestic subsidiary (paragraph 33). The determination of whether those differences are taxable temporary differences does not involve a tax-planning strategy as that term is used in this Statement.

Regulated Enterprises

252. Paragraph 9 of Statement 71 requires a regulated enterprise that applies Statement 71 to capitalize an incurred cost that would otherwise be charged to expense if the following criteria are met:

a. It is probable that future revenue in an amount at least equal to the capitalized cost will result from inclusion of that cost in allowable costs for rate-making purposes.
b. Based on available evidence, the future revenue will be provided to permit recovery of the previously incurred cost rather than to provide for expected levels of similar future costs.

If the income taxes that result from recording a deferred tax liability in accordance with this Statement meet those criteria, an asset is recognized for those income taxes when the deferred tax liability is recognized. That asset and the deferred tax liability are not offset for general-purpose financial reporting; rather, each is displayed separately.

253. The following example illustrates recognition of an asset for the probable future revenue to recover future income taxes related to the deferred tax liability for the equity component of the allowance for funds used during construction (AFUDC). The assumptions are as follows:

a. During year 1, the first year of operations, total construction costs for financial reporting and tax purposes are $400,000 (exclusive of AFUDC).

b. The enacted tax rate is 34 percent for all future years.

c. AFUDC (consisting entirely of the equity component) is $26,000. The asset for probable future revenue to recover the related income taxes is calculated as follows:

34 percent of ($26,000 + A) = A (where A equals the asset for probable future revenue)

A = $13,394

At the end of year 1, the related accounts[18] are as follows:

Construction in progress	$426,000
Probable future revenue	$ 13,394
Deferred tax liability [34 percent of ($26,000 + $13,394)]	$ 13,394

254. The following example illustrates adjustment of a deferred tax liability for an enacted change in tax rates. The assumptions are the same as for the example in paragraph 253 except that a change in the tax rate from 34 percent to 30 percent is enacted on the first day of year 2. As of the first day of year 2, the related accounts are adjusted so that the balances are as follows:

Construction in progress	$426,000
Probable future revenue	$ 11,143
Deferred tax liability [30 percent of ($26,000 + $11,143)]	$ 11,143

255. The following example illustrates adjustment of a deferred tax liability for an enacted change in tax rates when that deferred tax liability represents amounts already collected from customers for the future payment of income taxes. In that case, there would be no asset for "probable future revenue." The assumptions are as follows:

a. Amounts at the end of year 1, the current year, are as follows:

Construction in progress for financial reporting	$400,000
Tax basis of construction in progress	$300,000
Deferred tax liability (34 percent of $100,000)	$ 34,000

b. A change in the tax rate from 34 percent to 30 percent is enacted on the first day of year 2. As a result of the reduction in tax rates, it is probable that $4,000 of the $34,000 (previously collected from customers for the future payment of income taxes) will be refunded to customers, together with the tax benefit of that refund, through a future rate reduction. The liability for the future rate reduction to refund a portion of the deferred taxes previously collected from customers is calculated as follows:

$4,000 + (30 percent of R) = R (where R equals the probable future reduction in revenue)

R = $5,714

As of the first day of year 2, the related accounts are adjusted so that the balances are as follows:

Construction in progress	$400,000
Probable reduction in future revenue	$ 5,714
Deferred tax liability [30 percent of ($100,000 − $5,714)]	$ 28,286

Leveraged Leases

256. This Statement does not change (a) the pattern of recognition of after-tax income for leveraged leases as required by Statement 13 or (b) the allocation of the purchase price in a purchase business combination to acquired leveraged leases as required by Interpretation 21. Integration of the results of income tax accounting for leveraged leases with the other results of accounting for income taxes under this Statement is required when deferred tax credits related to leveraged leases are the only source (refer to paragraph 21) for recognition of a tax benefit for deductible temporary differences and carryforwards not related to leveraged leases. A valuation allowance is not necessary if deductible temporary differences and carryforwards will offset taxable amounts from future recovery of the net investment in the leveraged lease. However, to the extent that the amount of deferred tax credits for a leveraged lease as determined under Statement 13 differs from the amount of the deferred tax liability related to the leveraged lease that would otherwise result from applying the requirements of this Statement, that difference is preserved and is not a source of taxable income for recognition of the tax benefit of deductible temporary differences and operating loss or tax credit carryforwards.

---

[18]In this example, if AFUDC had consisted entirely of a net-of-tax debt component in the amount of $26,000, the related accounts and their balances at the end of year 1 would be construction in progress in the amount of $439,394 and a deferred tax liability in the amount of $13,394.

257. Interpretation 21 requires that the tax effect of any difference between the assigned value and the tax basis of a leveraged lease at the date of a business combination not be accounted for as a deferred tax credit. This Statement does not change that requirement. Any tax effects included in unearned and deferred income as required by Interpretation 21 are not offset by the deferred tax consequences of other temporary differences or by the tax benefit of operating loss or tax credit carryforwards. However, deferred tax credits that arise after the date of a business combination are accounted for in the same manner as described above for leveraged leases that were not acquired in a purchase business combination.

258. The following example illustrates integration of the results of income tax accounting for leveraged leases with the other results of accounting for income taxes as required by this Statement.

a. At the end of year 1, the current year, an enterprise has two temporary differences. One temporary difference is for a leveraged lease that was entered into in a prior year. During year 1, the enacted tax rate for year 2 and thereafter changed from 40 percent to 35 percent. After adjusting for the change in estimated total net income from the lease as a result of the change in tax rates as required by Statement 13, the components of the investment in the leveraged lease at the end of year 1 are as follows:

Net rentals receivable plus residual value less unearned pretax income		$150,000
Reduced by:		
Deferred ITC	$ 9,000	
Deferred tax credits	39,000	48,000
Net investment in leveraged lease for financial reporting		$102,000

b. The other temporary difference is for a $120,000 estimated liability for warranty expense that will result in a tax deduction in year 5 when the liability is expected to be paid. Absent consideration of the deferred tax credits attributable to the leveraged lease, the weight of available evidence indicates that a valuation allowance is needed for the entire amount of the deferred tax asset related to that $120,000 deductible temporary difference.

c. The tax basis of the investment in the leveraged lease at the end of year 1 is $41,000. The amount of the deferred tax liability for that lev-

eraged lease that would otherwise result from the requirements of this Statement is determined as follows:

Net rentals receivable plus residual value less unearned pretax income	$150,000
Temporary difference for deferred ITC	9,000
	141,000
Tax basis of leveraged lease	41,000
Temporary difference	$100,000
Deferred tax liability (35 percent)	$ 35,000

d. Loss carryback (to year 2) and loss carryforward (to year 20) of the $120,000 tax deduction for warranty expense in year 5 would offset the $100,000 of taxable amounts resulting from future recovery of the net investment in the leveraged lease over the remainder of the lease term.

e. At the end of year 1, the enterprise recognizes a $42,000 ($120,000 at 35 percent) deferred tax asset and a related $7,000 valuation allowance. The effect is to recognize a $35,000 net deferred tax benefit for the reduction in deferred tax credits attributable to the leveraged lease. Deferred tax credits attributable to the leveraged lease determined under the requirements of Statement 13 are $39,000. However, the deferred tax liability determined under the requirements of this Statement is only $35,000. The $4,000 difference is not available for offsetting.

Business Combinations

259. This Statement requires recognition of deferred tax liabilities and deferred tax assets (and related valuation allowances, if necessary) for the deferred tax consequences of differences between the assigned values and the tax bases of the assets and liabilities recognized in a business combination accounted for as a purchase under Opinion 16. A deferred tax liability or asset is not recognized for a difference between the reported amount and the tax basis of goodwill or the portion thereof for which amortization is not deductible for tax purposes (paragraphs 262 and 263), unallocated "negative" goodwill, and leveraged leases (paragraphs 256-258). Acquired Opinion 23 differences are accounted for in accordance with the requirements of Opinion 23, as amended by this Statement (paragraphs 31-34).

Nontaxable Business Combinations

260. The following example illustrates recognition and measurement of a deferred tax liability and as-

set in a nontaxable business combination. The assumptions are as follows:

a. The enacted tax rate is 40 percent for all future years, and amortization of goodwill is not deductible for tax purposes.
b. An enterprise is acquired for $20,000, and the enterprise has no leveraged leases.
c. The tax basis of the net assets acquired is $5,000, and the assigned value (other than goodwill) is $12,000. Future recovery of the assets and settlement of the liabilities at their assigned values will result in $20,000 of taxable amounts and $13,000 of deductible amounts that can be offset against each other. Therefore, no valuation allowance is necessary.

The amounts recorded to account for the purchase transaction are as follows:

Assigned value of the net assets (other than goodwill) acquired	$12,000
Deferred tax liability for $20,000 of taxable temporary differences	(8,000)
Deferred tax asset for $13,000 of deductible temporary differences	5,200
Goodwill	10,800
Purchase price of the acquired enterprise	$20,000

Taxable Business Combinations

261. In a taxable business combination, the purchase price is assigned to the assets and liabilities recognized for tax purposes as well as for financial reporting. However, the amounts assigned to particular assets and liabilities may differ for financial reporting and tax purposes. A deferred tax liability and asset are recognized for the deferred tax consequences of those temporary differences in accordance with the recognition and measurement requirements of this Statement. For example, a portion of the amount of goodwill for financial reporting may be allocated to some other asset for tax purposes, and amortization of that other asset may be deductible for tax purposes. If a valuation allowance is recognized for that deferred tax asset at the acquisition date, recognized benefits for those tax deductions after the acquisition date should be applied (a) first to reduce to zero any

goodwill related to that acquisition, (b) second to reduce to zero other noncurrent intangible assets related to that acquisition, and (c) third to reduce income tax expense.

262. Amortization of goodwill is deductible for tax purposes in some tax jurisdictions. In those tax jurisdictions, the reported amount of goodwill and the tax basis of goodwill are each separated into two components as of the combination date for purposes of deferred tax calculations. The first component of each equals the lesser of (a) goodwill for financial reporting or (b) tax-deductible goodwill. The second component of each equals the remainder of each, that is, (1) the remainder, if any, of goodwill for financial reporting or (2) the remainder, if any, of tax-deductible goodwill. Any difference that arises between the book and tax basis of that first component of goodwill in future years is a temporary difference for which a deferred tax liability or asset is recognized based on the requirements of this Statement. No deferred taxes are recognized for the second component of goodwill. If that second component is an excess of tax-deductible goodwill over the reported amount of goodwill, the tax benefit for that excess is recognized when realized on the tax return, and that tax benefit is applied first to reduce to zero the goodwill related to that acquisition, second to reduce to zero other noncurrent intangible assets related to that acquisition, and third to reduce income tax expense.

263. The following example illustrates accounting for the tax consequences of goodwill when amortization of goodwill is deductible for tax purposes. The assumptions are as follows:

a. At the combination date, the reported amount and tax basis of goodwill are $600 and $800, respectively.
b. For tax purposes, amortization of goodwill will result in tax deductions of $400 in each of years 1 and 2. Those deductions result in a current tax benefit in years 1 and 2.
c. For financial reporting, amortization of goodwill is straight-line over years 1-4.
d. For purposes of simplification, the consequences of other temporary differences are ignored for years 1-4.
e. Income before amortization of goodwill and income taxes in each of years 1-4 is $1,000.
f. The tax rate is 40 percent for all years.

Income taxes payable for years 1-4 are:

	Year			
	1	**2**	**3**	**4**
Income before amortization of goodwill	$1,000	$1,000	$1,000	$1,000
Amortization of goodwill	400	400	—	—
Taxable income	$ 600	$ 600	$1,000	$1,000
Income taxes payable (40 percent)	$ 240	$ 240	$ 400	$ 400

At the combination date, goodwill is separated into two components as follows:

	Reported Amount	Tax Basis
First component	$600	$600
Second component	—	200
Total goodwill	$600	$800

A deferred tax liability is recognized at the end of years 1-3 for the excess of the reported amount over the tax basis of the first component of goodwill. A deferred tax asset is not recognized for the second component of goodwill; the tax benefit is allocated to reduce goodwill when realized on the tax returns for years 1 and 2.

The second component of goodwill is deductible $100 per year in years 1 and 2. Those tax deductions provide $40 ($100 at 40 percent) of tax benefits that are realized in years 1 and 2. Allocation of those realized tax benefits to reduce the first component of goodwill produces a deferred tax benefit by reducing the taxable temporary difference related to that component of goodwill. Thus, the total tax benefit allocated to reduce the first component of goodwill in each of years 1 and 2 is the sum of (a) the $40 realized tax benefit allocated to reduce goodwill and (b) the deferred tax benefit from reducing the deferred tax liability related to goodwill. That total tax benefit (TTB) is determined as follows:

$$TTB = \text{realized tax benefit plus (tax rate times TTB)}$$
$$TTB = \$40 + (.40 \times TTB)$$
$$TTB = \$67$$

Goodwill for financial reporting for years 1-4 is:

	Year			
	1	**2**	**3**	**4**
Balance at beginning of year	$600	$383	$188	$94
Amortization:				
$600 ÷ 4 years	150			
$383 ÷ 3 years		128		
$188 ÷ 2 years			94	94
Total tax benefit allocated to reduce goodwill	67	67	—	—
Balance at end of year	$383	$188	$ 94	$—

The deferred tax liability for the first component of goodwill and the related amount of deferred tax expense (benefit) for years 1-4 are:

	Year			
	1	**2**	**3**	**4**
Reported amount of goodwill at end of year	$383	$188	$ 94	$ —
Tax basis of goodwill (first component)	300	—	—	—
Taxable temporary difference	$ 83	$188	$ 94	$ —
Deferred tax liability:				
At end of year (40 percent)	$ 33	$ 75	$ 38	$ —
At beginning of year	—	33	75	38
Deferred tax expense (benefit) for the year	$ 33	$ 42	$(37)	$(38)

Income for financial reporting for years 1-4 is:

	Year			
	1	**2**	**3**	**4**
Income before amortization of goodwill and income taxes	$1,000	$1,000	$1,000	$1,000
Amortization of goodwill	150	128	94	94
Pretax income	850	872	906	906
Income tax expense (benefit):				
Current	240	240	400	400
Deferred	33	42	(37)	(38)
Benefit applied to reduce goodwill	67	67	—	—
Income tax expense	340	349	363	362
Net income	$ 510	$ 523	$ 543	$ 544

Carryforwards—Purchase Method

264. Accounting for a business combination should reflect any provisions in the tax law that restrict the future use of either of the combining enterprises' deductible temporary differences or carryforwards to reduce taxable income or taxes payable attributable to the other enterprise subsequent to the business combination. For example, the tax law may limit the use of the acquired enterprise's deductible temporary differences and carryforwards to subsequent taxable income of the acquired enterprise in a consolidated tax return for the combined enterprise. In that circumstance, or if the acquired enterprise will file a separate tax return, the need for a valuation allowance for some portion or all of the acquired enterprise's deferred tax assets for deductible temporary differences and carryforwards is assessed based on the acquired enterprise's *separate* past and expected future results of operations.

265. The following example illustrates (a) recognition of a deferred tax asset and the related valuation allowance for acquired deductible temporary differences at the date of a nontaxable business combination and in subsequent periods when (b) the tax law limits the use of an acquired enterprise's deductible temporary differences and carryforwards to subsequent taxable income of the acquired enterprise in a consolidated tax return. The assumptions are as follows:

a. The enacted tax rate is 40 percent for all future years.
b. The purchase price is $20,000, and the assigned value of the net assets acquired is also $20,000.
c. The tax basis of the net assets acquired is $60,000. The $40,000 ($60,000 − $20,000) of deductible temporary differences at the combination date is primarily attributable to an allowance for loan losses. Provisions in the tax law limit the use of those future tax deductions

to subsequent taxable income of the acquired enterprise.

d. The acquired enterprise's actual pretax results for the two preceding years and the expected results for the year of the business combination are as follows:

Year 1	$(15,000)
Year 2	(10,000)
Year 3 to the combination date	(5,000)
Expected results for the remainder of year 3	(5,000)

e. Based on assessments of all evidence available at the date of the business combination in year 3 and at the end of year 3, management concludes that a valuation allowance is needed at both dates for the entire amount of the deferred tax asset related to the acquired deductible temporary differences.

The acquired enterprise's pretax financial income and taxable income for year 3 (after the business combination) and year 4 are as follows:

	Year 3	Year 4
Pretax financial income	$15,000	$10,000
Reversals of acquired deductible temporary differences	(15,000)	(10,000)
Taxable income	$ —	$ —

At the end of year 4, the remaining balance of acquired deductible temporary differences is $15,000 ($40,000 − $25,000). The deferred tax asset is $6,000 ($15,000 at 40 percent). Based on an assessment of all available evidence at the end of year 4, management concludes that no valuation allowance is needed for that $6,000 deferred tax asset. Elimination of the $6,000 valuation allowance results in a $6,000 deferred tax benefit that is reported as a reduction of deferred income tax expense because there is no goodwill or other noncurrent intangible assets related to the acquisition. For the same reason, tax benefits realized in years 3 and 4 attributable to reversals of acquired deductible temporary differences are reported as a zero current income tax expense. The consolidated statement of earnings would include the following amounts attributable to the acquired enterprise for year 3 (after the business combination) and year 4:

	Year 3	Year 4
Pretax financial income	$15,000	$10,000
Income tax expense (benefit):		
Current	—	—
Deferred	—	(6,000)
Net income	$15,000	$16,000

266. The tax law in some tax jurisdictions may permit the future use of either of the combining enterprises' deductible temporary differences or carryforwards to reduce taxable income or taxes payable attributable to the other enterprise subsequent to the business combination. If the combined enterprise expects to file a consolidated tax return, a deferred tax asset (net of a valuation allowance, if necessary) is recognized for deductible temporary differences or carryforwards of either combining enterprise based on an assessment of the *combined* enterprise's past and expected future results of operations as of the acquisition date. This either reduces goodwill or noncurrent assets (except long-term investments in marketable securities) of the acquired enterprise or creates or increases negative goodwill.

267. The following example illustrates (a) elimination of the need for a valuation allowance for the deferred tax asset for an acquired loss carryforward based on offset against taxable temporary differences of the acquiring enterprise in a nontaxable business combination when (b) the tax law permits use of an acquired enterprise's deductible temporary differences and carryforwards to reduce taxable income or taxes payable attributable to the acquiring enterprise in a consolidated tax return. The assumptions are as follows:

a. The enacted tax rate is 40 percent for all future years.
b. The purchase price is $20,000. The tax basis of the identified net assets acquired is $5,000, and the assigned value is $12,000, that is, there are $7,000 of taxable temporary differences. The acquired enterprise also has a $16,000 operating loss carryforward, which, under the tax law, may be used by the acquiring enterprise in the consolidated tax return.

c. The acquiring enterprise has temporary differences that will result in $30,000 of net taxable amounts in future years.
d. All temporary differences of the acquired and acquiring enterprises will result in taxable amounts before the end of the acquired enterprise's loss carryforward period.

In assessing the need for a valuation allowance, future taxable income exclusive of reversing temporary differences and carryforwards (paragraph 21(b)) need not be considered because the $16,000 operating loss carryforward will offset (a) the *acquired* enterprise's $7,000 of taxable temporary differences and (b) another $9,000 of the *acquiring* enterprise's taxable temporary differences. The amounts recorded to account for the purchase transaction are as follows:

Assigned value of the identified net assets acquired	$12,000
Deferred tax liability recognized for the acquired company's taxable temporary differences ($7,000 at 40 percent)	(2,800)
Deferred tax asset recognized for the acquired loss carryforward based on offset against the acquired company's taxable temporary differences ($7,000 at 40 percent)	2,800
Deferred tax asset recognized for the acquired loss carryforward based on offset against the acquiring company's taxable temporary differences ($9,000 at 40 percent)	3,600
Goodwill	4,400
Purchase price of the acquired enterprise	$20,000

Subsequent Recognition of Carryforward Benefits—Purchase Method

268. If a valuation allowance is recognized for some portion or all of an acquired enterprise's deferred tax asset for deductible temporary differences and operating loss or tax credit carryforwards at the acquisition date, tax benefits for those items recognized in financial statements for a subsequent year(s) are:

a. First applied to reduce to zero any goodwill related to the acquisition
b. Second applied to reduce to zero other noncurrent intangible assets related to the acquisition
c. Third applied to reduce income tax expense.

Additional amounts of deductible temporary differences and operating loss or tax credit carryforwards may arise after the acquisition date and before recognition of the tax benefit of amounts existing at the acquisition date. Tax benefits are recognized in later years as follows:

a. The tax benefit of amounts existing at the acquisition date is first applied to reduce goodwill and other noncurrent intangible assets to zero. Any additional tax benefit reduces income tax expense.
b. The tax benefit of amounts arising after the acquisition date is recognized as a reduction of income tax expense.

Whether a tax benefit recognized in later years is attributable to an amount (for example, an operating loss carryforward) existing at or arising after the acquisition date is determined for financial reporting by provisions in the tax law that identify the sequence in which those amounts are utilized for tax purposes. If not determinable by provisions in the tax law, a tax benefit recognized for financial reporting is prorated between a reduction of (a) goodwill and other noncurrent intangible assets and (b) income tax expense.

269. The following example illustrates recognition of tax benefits subsequent to a business combination. The assumptions are as follows:

	Year 1	Year 2	Year 3
Pretax financial income (loss)	$(3,000)	$2,500	$1,500
Disposal of acquired identified net assets	(1,000)	—	—
Taxable income (loss) before loss carryforward	(4,000)	2,500	1,500
Loss carryforward (loss carryback not permitted)	4,000	(2,500)	(1,500)
Taxable income after loss carryforward	$ —	$ —	$ —

c. The tax rate is 40 percent for all years.
d. Based on an assessment of all available evidence, management reaches the following conclusions at the acquisition date and at the end of years 1 and 2:
  (1) At the acquisition date, the portion of the $1,000 of deductible temporary differences ($6,000 – $5,000) for which it is more likely than not that a tax benefit will not be realized is $500.
  (2) At the end of year 1, the portion of the $4,000 loss carryforward for which it is

a. A nontaxable business combination occurs on the first day of year 1. Before considering any acquired deferred tax assets, the purchase transaction is summarized as follows:

	Assigned Value	Tax Basis
Net assets acquired	$5,000	$6,000
Excess of purchase price over the fair value of the net assets acquired*	1,500	
Purchase price	$6,500	

*There are no other noncurrent intangible assets.

b. The only difference between pretax financial income and taxable income (amortization of goodwill is disregarded for this example) for years 1-3 is a $1,000 loss for tax purposes in year 1 from disposal of the acquired identified net assets at amounts equal to their $5,000 assigned value on the acquisition date.

more likely than not that a tax benefit will not be realized is $1,750.
  (3) At the end of year 2, it is more likely than not that a tax benefit will be realized for all of the remaining $1,500 of loss carryforward.

At the acquisition date, a $400 ($1,000 at 40 percent) deferred tax asset and a $200 ($500 at 40 percent) valuation allowance are recognized. The $200 net tax benefit reduces the excess of purchase price over the fair value of the net assets acquired from $1,500 to $1,300. Thus, the amount of goodwill recognized at the acquisition date is $1,300.

During year 1, the $1,000 of net deductible temporary differences at the acquisition date reverse and

are part of the $4,000 loss carryforward for tax purposes at the end of year 1. An analysis of the components of that $4,000 loss carryforward follows:

	Acquired Deductions	Loss in Year 1	Total
Tax loss carryforward	$1,000	$3,000	$4,000
Portion for which a tax benefit was recognized at the acquisition date	500	—	500
Remainder available for recognition of a tax benefit at the end of year 1	$ 500	$3,000	$3,500

Provisions in the tax law do not distinguish between those two components of the $3,500, and the component that is used first for tax purposes is indeterminable. However, the $500 of acquired deductions for which a tax benefit has not been recognized is one-seventh of the $3,500 total, and the $3,000 loss in year 1 is six-sevenths of the $3,500 total. The tax benefit of that $3,500 is prorated one-seventh to reduce goodwill and six-sevenths to reduce income tax expense when recognized in years 1 and 2.

At the end of year 1, a $1,600 ($4,000 at 40 percent) deferred tax asset and a $700 ($1,750 at 40 percent) valuation allowance are recognized. The tax benefit for the $700 increase in the net deferred

tax asset (from $200 at the acquisition date to $900 at the end of year 1) is prorated as follows:

a. One-seventh or $100 to reduce goodwill
b. Six-sevenths or $600 to reduce tax expense.

During year 2, $1,000 ($2,500 at 40 percent) of the deferred tax asset recognized at the end of year 1 is realized. In addition, a tax benefit is recognized for the remaining $1,750 of future tax deductions by eliminating the $700 valuation allowance. That tax benefit is prorated $100 to reduce goodwill and $600 to reduce tax expense. The combined effect of the changes in the deferred tax asset and the related valuation allowance during year 2 is illustrated below:

	Deferred Tax Asset		Tax Expense or (Benefit)
	Year 1	Year 2	
Deferred tax asset	$1,600	$600	$1,000
Valuation allowance	(700)	—	(700)
	$ 900	$600	300
Portion of $700 tax benefit allocated to reduce goodwill			100
Deferred tax expense for year 2			$ 400

The $600 deferred tax asset at the end of year 2 is realized in year 3, resulting in $600 of deferred tax expense for year 3. The consolidated statement of earnings would include the following amounts attributable to the acquired enterprise:

	Year 1	Year 2	Year 3
Pretax financial income (loss)	$(3,000)	$2,500	$1,500
Net deferred tax expense (benefit)	(600)	400	600
Net income (loss)	$(2,400)	$2,100	$ 900

Carryforwards—Pooling-of-Interests Method

270. The separate financial statements of combining enterprises for prior periods are restated on a combined basis when a business combination is accounted for by the pooling-of-interests method. For restatement of periods prior to the combination date, a combining enterprise's operating loss carryforward does not offset the other enterprise's taxable income because consolidated tax returns cannot be filed for those periods. However, provisions in the tax law may permit an operating loss carryforward of either of the combining enter-

prises to offset combined taxable income subsequent to the combination date.

271. If the combined enterprise expects to file consolidated tax returns, a deferred tax asset is recognized for either combining enterprise's operating loss carryforward in a prior period. A valuation allowance is necessary to the extent it is more likely than not that a tax benefit will not be realized for that loss carryforward through offset of either (a) the other enterprise's deferred tax liability for taxable temporary differences that will reverse subsequent to the combination date or (b) combined taxable income subsequent to the combination date. Determined in that manner, the valuation allowance may be less than the sum of the valuation allowances in the separate financial statements of the combining enterprises prior to the combination date. That tax benefit is recognized as part of the adjustment to restate financial statements on a combined basis for prior periods. The same requirements apply to deductible temporary differences and tax credit carryforwards.

272. A taxable business combination may sometimes be accounted for by the pooling-of-interests method. The increase in the tax basis of the net assets acquired results in temporary differences. The deferred tax consequences of those temporary differences are recognized and measured the same as for other temporary differences. As of the combination date, recognizable tax benefits attributable to the increase in tax basis are allocated to contributed capital. Tax benefits attributable to the increase in tax basis that become recognizable after the combination date (that is, by elimination of a valuation allowance) are reported as a reduction of income tax expense.

Intraperiod Tax Allocation

273. If there is only one item other than continuing operations, the portion of income tax expense or benefit for the year that remains after the allocation to continuing operations is allocated to that item. If there are two or more items other than continuing operations, the amount that remains after the allocation to continuing operations is allocated among those other items in proportion to their individual effects on income tax expense or benefit for the year.

274. The following example illustrates allocation of income tax expense if there is only one item

other than income from continuing operations. The assumptions are as follows:

a. The enterprise's pretax financial income and taxable income are the same.
b. The enterprise's ordinary loss from continuing operations is $500.
c. The enterprise also has an extraordinary gain of $900 that is a capital gain for tax purposes.
d. The tax rate is 40 percent on ordinary income and 30 percent on capital gains. Income taxes currently payable are $120 ($400 at 30 percent).

Income tax expense is allocated between the pretax loss from operations and the extraordinary gain as follows:

Total income tax expense	$120
Tax benefit allocated to the loss from operations	(150)
Incremental tax expense allocated to the extraordinary gain	$270

The effect of the $500 loss from continuing operations was to offset an equal amount of capital gains that otherwise would be taxed at a 30 percent tax rate. Thus, $150 ($500 at 30 percent) of tax benefit is allocated to continuing operations. The $270 incremental effect of the extraordinary gain is the difference between $120 of total tax expense and the $150 tax benefit from continuing operations.

275. The following example illustrates allocation of the tax benefit of a tax credit carryforward that is recognized as a deferred tax asset in the current year. The assumptions are as follows:

a. The enterprise's pretax financial income and taxable income are the same.
b. Pretax financial income for the year comprises $300 from continuing operations and $400 from an extraordinary gain.
c. The tax rate is 40 percent. Taxes payable for the year are zero because $330 of tax credits that arose in the current year more than offset the $280 of tax otherwise payable on $700 of taxable income.
d. A $50 deferred tax asset is recognized for the $50 ($330 − $280) tax credit carryforward. Based on the weight of available evidence, management concludes that no valuation allowance is necessary.

Income tax expense or benefit is allocated between pretax income from continuing operations and the extraordinary gain as follows:

Total income tax benefit		$ (50)
Tax expense (benefit) allocated to income from continuing operations:		
Tax (before tax credits) on $300 of taxable income at 40 percent	$120	
Tax credits	(330)	(210)
Tax expense allocated to the extraordinary gain		$160

Absent the extraordinary gain and assuming it was not the deciding factor in reaching a conclusion that

	Foreign Currency	Exchange Rate	Dollars
Unremitted earnings, beginning of year	1,000	FC1 = $1.20	1,200
Earnings for the year	600	FC1 = $1.10	660
Unremitted earnings, end of year	1,600	FC1 = $1.00	1,600

c. A $260 translation adjustment ($1,200 + $660 − $1,600) is charged to the cumulative translation adjustment account in shareholders' equity for year 2.
d. The U.S. parent expects that all of the foreign subsidiary's unremitted earnings will be remitted in the foreseeable future, and under Opinion 23, a deferred U.S. tax liability is recognized for those unremitted earnings.
e. The U.S. parent accrues the deferred tax liability at a 20 percent tax rate (that is, net of foreign tax credits, foreign tax credit carryforwards, and so forth). An analysis of the net investment in the foreign subsidiary and the related deferred tax liability for year 2 is as follows:

	Net Investment	Deferred Tax Liability
Balances, beginning of year	$1,200	$240
Earnings and related taxes	660	132
Translation adjustment and related taxes	(260)	(52)
Balances, end of year	$1,600	$320

f. For year 2, $132 of deferred taxes are charged against earnings, and $52 of deferred taxes are credited directly to the cumulative translation adjustment account in shareholders' equity.

a valuation allowance is not needed, the entire tax benefit of the $330 of tax credits would be allocated to continuing operations. The presence of the extraordinary gain does not change that allocation.

276. Income taxes are sometimes allocated directly to shareholders' equity. The following example illustrates the allocation of income taxes for translation adjustments under Statement 52 directly to shareholders' equity.

a. A foreign subsidiary has earnings of FC600 for year 2. Its net assets (and unremitted earnings) are FC1,000 and FC1,600 at the end of years 1 and 2, respectively.
b. The foreign currency is the functional currency. For year 2, translated amounts are as follows:

Appendix C

BACKGROUND INFORMATION

277. Opinion 11 was issued in 1967. Over the years that followed, it was the frequent subject of numerous criticisms and concerns that focused both on the complexity of the accounting requirements and on the meaningfulness of the results of applying the requirements.

278. In January 1982, the Board added a project to its agenda to reconsider accounting for income taxes, and a task force was appointed to advise the Board during its deliberations on this project. An FASB Research Report, *Accounting for Income Taxes: A Review of Alternatives,* prepared by Ernst & Whinney, was published in July 1983. The report discusses the accounting and reporting alternatives advanced in the accounting literature on income taxes.

279. The Discussion Memorandum on accounting for income taxes was issued in August 1983, and more than 400 comment letters were received. The Board conducted a public hearing on the Discussion Memorandum in April 1984, and 43 organizations and individuals presented their views at the 3-day hearing. In May 1984, the FASB sponsored three regional meetings to obtain the views of preparers, users, and auditors associated with the financial statements of small companies.

280. Accounting for income taxes was addressed at 20 public Board meetings and at 2 public task force meetings and, in September 1986, the Board issued an Exposure Draft, *Accounting for Income Taxes.* It proposed an asset and liability approach to account for the effects of income taxes that result from an enterprise's activities during the current and preceding years. The Board received more than 400 comment letters in response to the Exposure Draft.

281. In January 1987, the Board conducted a public hearing on the Exposure Draft. Fifty-one organizations and individuals presented their views at the 3-day hearing. Based on the information received in the comment letters and at the public hearing, the Board reconsidered its proposals in the Exposure Draft at 21 public Board meetings during 1987.

282. FASB Statement No. 96, *Accounting for Income Taxes,* was issued in December 1987 and the FASB Special Report, *A Guide to Implementation of Statement 96 on Accounting for Income Taxes,* was issued in March 1989. As issued, Statement 96 was effective for financial statements for fiscal years beginning after December 15, 1988, but the effective date was deferred three times, the last of which was to fiscal years beginning after December 15, 1992.

283. After the issuance of Statement 96, the Board received (a) requests for about 20 different limited-scope amendments to that Statement, (b) requests to change the criteria for recognition and measurement of deferred tax assets to anticipate, in certain circumstances, the tax consequences of future income, and (c) requests to reduce the complexity of scheduling the future reversals of temporary differences and considering hypothetical tax-planning strategies. The Board considered the requests to amend Statement 96 at 41 public Board meetings and 3 Implementation Group meetings starting in March 1989.

284. In June 1991, the Board issued an Exposure Draft, *Accounting for Income Taxes.* The Exposure Draft retained the asset and liability approach for financial accounting and reporting for income taxes as in Statement 96, but reduced the complexity of the standard and changed the criteria for recognizing and measuring deferred tax assets. During the comment period for the Exposure Draft, a limited-scope field test of the proposals in the Exposure Draft was completed, and an FASB-prepared seminar that explained and analyzed the proposals was presented by Board and staff members at nine locations throughout the country.

285. The Board received more than 250 comment letters in response to the Exposure Draft. In October 1991, the Board held a 3-day public hearing on the Exposure Draft, and 25 organizations and individuals presented their views. Based on the information received in the comment letters and at the public hearing, the Board reconsidered its proposals in the Exposure Draft at 12 public Board meetings. The basis for the Board's conclusions, including reasons for changes made to the provisions of the Exposure Draft, is set forth in Appendix A.

Appendix D

AMENDMENTS TO EXISTING PRONOUNCEMENTS

286. This Statement supersedes the following pronouncements:

a. Accounting Research Bulletin No. 44 (Revised), *Declining-balance Depreciation*
b. APB Opinion No. 1, *New Depreciation Guidelines and Rules*
c. APB Opinion No. 11, *Accounting for Income Taxes*
d. APB Opinion No. 24, *Accounting for Income Taxes—Investments in Common Stock Accounted for by the Equity Method (Other than Subsidiaries and Corporate Joint Ventures)*
e. FASB Statement No. 31, *Accounting for Tax Benefits Related to U.K. Tax Legislation concerning Stock Relief*
f. FASB Statement No. 96, *Accounting for Income Taxes*
g. FASB Statement No. 100, *Accounting for Income Taxes—Deferral of the Effective Date of FASB Statement No. 96*
h. FASB Statement No. 103, *Accounting for Income Taxes—Deferral of the Effective Date of FASB Statement No. 96*
i. FASB Statement No. 108, *Accounting for Income Taxes—Deferral of the Effective Date of FASB Statement No. 96*
j. AICPA Accounting Interpretations 4, "Change in Method of Accounting for Investment Credit," and 6, "Investment Credit in Consolidation," of APB Opinion No. 4, *Accounting for the "Investment Credit"*
k. AICPA Accounting Interpretations of APB Opinion No. 11, *Accounting for Income Taxes*
l. AICPA Unofficial Accounting Interpretations 13, "Subchapter S Corporations," and 16, "EPS for Extraordinary Items," of APB Opinion No. 15, *Earnings per Share*
m. AICPA Accounting Interpretations of APB Opinion No. 23, *Accounting for Income Taxes—Special Areas*

n. FASB Interpretation No. 22, *Applicability of Indefinite Reversal Criteria to Timing Differences*
o. FASB Interpretation No. 25, *Accounting for an Unused Investment Tax Credit*
p. FASB Interpretation No. 29, *Reporting Tax Benefits Realized on Disposition of Investments in Certain Subsidiaries and Other Investees*
q. FASB Interpretation No. 32, *Application of Percentage Limitations in Recognizing Investment Tax Credit*
r. FASB Technical Bulletin No. 81-2, *Accounting for Unused Investment Tax Credits Acquired in a Business Combination Accounted for by the Purchase Method*
s. FASB Technical Bulletin No. 83-1, *Accounting for the Reduction in the Tax Basis of an Asset Caused by the Investment Tax Credit*
t. FASB Technical Bulletin No. 84-2, *Accounting for the Effects of the Tax Reform Act of 1984 on Deferred Income Taxes Relating to Domestic International Sales Corporations*
u. FASB Technical Bulletin No. 84-3, *Accounting for the Effects of the Tax Reform Act of 1984 on Deferred Income Taxes of Stock Life Insurance Enterprises*
v. FASB Technical Bulletin No. 86-1, *Accounting for Certain Effects of the Tax Reform Act of 1986.*

287. Other pronouncements issued by the Accounting Principles Board and the Financial Accounting Standards Board refer to Opinion 11, Opinion 24, or Statement 96 or use the term *timing differences* as defined in Opinion 11. All such references appearing in paragraphs that establish standards or the scope of a pronouncement are hereby amended to refer instead to FASB Statement No. 109, *Accounting for Income Taxes,*[19] or to use the term *temporary differences.*

288. This Statement amends the following pronouncements:

a. Accounting Research Bulletin No. 43, *Restatement and Revision of Accounting Research Bulletins.* The following is added to the end of paragraph 5 of Chapter 9C:

The declining-balance method is one that meets the requirements of being systematic and rational.[2] If the expected productivity or revenue-earning power of the asset is relatively greater during the earlier years of its life, or where maintenance charges tend to increase during later years, the declining-balance method may provide the most satis-

factory allocation of cost. That conclusion also applies to other methods, including the sum-of-the-years'-digits method, that produce substantially similar results.

[2]Accounting Terminology Bulletin No. 1, *Review and Résumé,* paragraph 56.

Paragraphs 11-13 of Chapter 9C are replaced by the following:

11. Refer to FASB Statement No. 109, *Accounting for Income Taxes.*

Chapter 10B is deleted.

Paragraph 8 of Chapter 11B is deleted.

b. APB Opinion No. 2, *Accounting for the "Investment Credit."* Paragraph 16 is replaced by the following:

An investment credit should be reflected in the financial statements to the extent it has been used as an offset against income taxes otherwise currently payable or to the extent its benefit is recognizable under the provisions of FASB Statement No. 109, *Accounting for Income Taxes.* Refer to paragraph 48 of Statement 109 for required disclosures related to (a) tax credit carryforwards for tax purposes and (b) tax credit carryforwards for which a tax benefit has not been recognized for financial reporting.

c. APB Opinion No. 6, *Status of Accounting Research Bulletins.* Paragraphs 20-23 and footnotes 7 and 8 are deleted.

d. APB Opinion No. 16, *Business Combinations.* The last sentence in paragraph 87 is replaced by the following:

The tax basis of an asset or liability shall not be a factor in determining its fair value.

The last sentence in paragraph 88 is replaced by the following:

FASB Statement No. 109, *Accounting for Income Taxes,* paragraph 30, addresses accounting for the deferred tax consequences of the differences between the assigned values and the tax bases of assets and liabilities of an enterprise acquired in a purchase business combination.

[19]Except as in paragraph 288(dd).

Paragraph 89 is deleted.

e. APB Opinion No. 17, *Intangible Assets.* The last sentence in paragraph 30 is deleted.

f. APB Opinion No. 23, *Accounting for Income Taxes—Special Areas.* In paragraph 9, all words following *equity method* are deleted and replaced by *results in a temporary difference.*

Paragraph 10 is replaced by the following:

Temporary Difference. The Board believes it should be presumed that all undistributed earnings of a subsidiary will be transferred to the parent company. Accordingly, the undistributed earnings of a subsidiary included in consolidated income should be accounted for as a temporary difference unless the tax law provides a means by which the investment in a domestic subsidiary can be recovered tax free. However, for reasons described in FASB Statement No. 109, *Accounting for Income Taxes,* a deferred tax liability is not recognized for (a) an excess of the amount for financial reporting over the tax basis of an investment in a foreign subsidiary that meets the criteria in paragraph 12 of this Opinion and (b) undistributed earnings of a domestic subsidiary that arose in fiscal years beginning on or before December 15, 1992 and that meet the criteria in paragraph 12 of this Opinion. The criteria in paragraph 12 of this Opinion do not apply to undistributed earnings of domestic subsidiaries that arise in fiscal years beginning after December 15, 1992, and a deferred tax liability shall be recognized if the undistributed earnings are a taxable temporary difference.

Footnotes 3 and 4 are deleted.

Paragraph 11 is replaced by the following:

A deferred tax asset shall be recognized for an excess of the tax basis over the amount for financial reporting of an investment in a subsidiary in accordance with the requirements of paragraph 34 of Statement 109.

The last sentence of paragraph 13 is replaced by the following:

If a parent company recognizes a deferred tax liability for the temporary difference arising from its equity in undistributed earnings of a subsidiary and subsequently reduces its investment in the subsidiary through a taxable sale or other transaction, the amount of the temporary difference and the related deferred tax liability will change. An investment in common stock of an investee (other than a subsidiary or corporate joint venture) may change so that the investee becomes a subsidiary because the investor acquires additional common stock, the investee acquires or retires common stock, or other transactions affect the investment. A temporary difference for the investor's share of the undistributed earnings of the investee prior to the date it becomes a subsidiary shall continue to be treated as a temporary difference for which a deferred tax liability shall continue to be recognized to the extent that dividends from the subsidiary do not exceed the parent company's share of the subsidiary's earnings subsequent to the date it became a subsidiary.

Paragraph 14 is replaced by the following:

Disclosure. Statement 109 specifies the requirements for financial statement disclosures.

Footnote 6 is deleted.

In the second sentence in paragraph 21, *permanent differences* is replaced with *events that do not have tax consequences.*

The first and second sentences of paragraph 23 are deleted.

The first and second sentences in footnote 9 are deleted.

The third sentence of paragraph 23 is replaced by the following:

As described in Statement 109, a savings and loan association[9] should not provide deferred taxes on taxable temporary differences related to bad-debt reserves for tax purposes that arose in tax years beginning before December 31, 1987 (the base-year amount).

Paragraph 24 is replaced by the following:

Disclosure. Statement 109 specifies the requirements for financial statement disclosures.

Footnote 10 is deleted.

g. APB Opinion No. 25, *Accounting for Stock Issued to Employees.* In the second sentence of paragraph 17, (1) *are timing differences* is replaced by *result in temporary differences* and (2) *(APB Opinion No. 11, paragraphs 34 to 37)* is deleted and *in accordance with the provisions of FASB Statement No. 109, Accounting for Income Taxes* is added to the end of that sentence.

h. APB Opinion No. 28, *Interim Financial Reporting.* In footnote 2, *(see APB Opinion No. 11, paragraph 63)* is replaced by *(refer to FASB Statement No. 109, Accounting for Income Taxes, paragraph 47).*

In the first sentence of paragraph 20, (1) *(in the event carryback of such losses is not possible)* is deleted and (2) *realization is assured beyond any reasonable doubt (paragraph 45 of APB Opinion No. 11)* is replaced by *the tax benefits are expected to be (a) realized during the year or (b) recognizable as a deferred tax asset at the end of the year in accordance with the provisions of Statement 109.* In the second and third sentences of paragraph 20, *assured beyond reasonable doubt* is replaced by *more likely than not.* In footnote 3, *as is provided for in annual periods in paragraph 45 of APB Opinion No. 11* is deleted.

The last sentence in paragraph 20 is replaced by the following:

The tax effect of a valuation allowance expected to be necessary for a deferred tax asset at the end of the year for originating deductible temporary differences and carryforwards during the year should be included in the effective tax rate. The effect of a change in the beginning-of-the-year balance of a valuation allowance as a result of a change in judgment about the realizability of the related deferred tax asset in future years shall not be apportioned among interim periods through an adjustment of the effective tax rate but shall be recognized in the interim period in which the change occurs. The effects of new tax legislation shall not be recognized prior to enactment. The tax effect of a change in tax laws or rates on taxes currently payable or refundable for the current year shall be reflected after the effective dates prescribed in the statutes in the computation of the annual effective tax rate beginning no earlier than the first interim period that includes the enactment date of the new legislation. The effect of a change in tax laws or rates on a deferred tax liability or asset shall not be apportioned among interim periods through an adjustment of the annual effective tax rate. The tax effect of a change in tax laws or rates on taxes payable or refundable for a prior year shall be recognized as of the enactment date of the change as tax expense (benefit) for the current year.

i. APB Opinion No. 30, *Reporting the Results of Operations—Reporting the Effects of Disposal of a Segment of a Business, and Extraordinary, Unusual and Infrequently Occurring Events and Transactions.* In paragraph 7, *APB Opin-*

ion No. 11, Accounting for Income Taxes, paragraphs 45 and 61 is replaced by *FASB Statement No. 109, Accounting for Income Taxes, paragraph 37.*

j. AICPA Accounting Interpretations of APB Opinion No. 18, *The Equity Method of Accounting for Investments in Common Stock.* In the fourth sentence of the fifth paragraph of the interpretation section of Interpretation 1, the second half of the sentence beginning with *; for example* is deleted.

k. AICPA Accounting Interpretations of APB Opinion No. 25, *Accounting for Stock Issued to Employees.* In the last sentence of the last paragraph, the reference to paragraph 89 of Opinion 16 is deleted.

l. FASB Statement No. 12, *Accounting for Certain Marketable Securities.* The last sentence of paragraph 22 is deleted.

m. FASB Statement No. 13, *Accounting for Leases.* In paragraph 47, *, as prescribed in APB Opinion No. 11, "Accounting for Income Taxes," paragraphs 57, 59, and 64* is deleted.

n. FASB Statement No. 16, *Prior Period Adjustments.* Paragraph 11 is replaced by the following:

An item of profit and loss related to the correction of an error in the financial statements of a prior period[3] shall be accounted for and reported as a prior period adjustment[4] and excluded from the determination of net income for the current period.

Footnotes 3 and 4 are renumbered 4 and 3, respectively, and their positions are reversed. Footnote 5 is deleted. In the first sentence of paragraph 13, *(except for the effects of retroactive tax legislation)* is added after *taxes.* In the third sentence of paragraph 13, *new retroactive tax legislation or* is deleted.

o. FASB Statement No. 19, *Financial Accounting and Reporting by Oil and Gas Producing Companies.* In paragraph 61, *by the deferred method, as described in APB Opinion No. 11, "Accounting for Income Taxes,"* is replaced by *as described in FASB Statement No. 109, Accounting for Income Taxes,.* In the first sentence of paragraph 62, *the amount of income taxes otherwise payable shall not be taken into account* is replaced by *taxable income in future years shall be considered in determining whether it is more likely than not that the tax benefits of deferred tax assets will not be realized.* The second sentence is deleted. In the third sentence, (1) *Accordingly, the* is replaced by *However, the tax benefit of the*, (2) *shall be accounted for as a permanent difference in* is replaced by *shall not be recognized until*, and (3) *; it shall not be anticipated by recognizing interaction* is deleted.

p. FASB Statement No. 37, *Balance Sheet Classification of Deferred Income Taxes.* Paragraph 4 and the preceding caption and related footnotes are replaced by the following:

> 4. A temporary difference is related to an asset or liability if reduction* of the asset or liability causes the temporary difference to reverse. A deferred tax liability or asset for a temporary difference that is related to an asset or liability shall be classified as current or noncurrent based on the classification of the related asset or liability. A deferred tax liability or asset for a temporary difference not related to an asset or liability because (a) there is no associated asset or liability or (b) reduction of an associated asset or liability will not cause the temporary difference to reverse shall be classified based on the expected reversal date of the specific temporary difference. Such classification disregards any additional temporary differences that may arise and is based on the criteria used for classifying other assets and liabilities.

---

*As used here, the term *reduction* includes amortization, sale, or other realization of an asset and amortization, payment, or other satisfaction of a liability.

Paragraphs 17 and 18, the preceding caption, and footnote 1 are deleted.

In paragraph 19, the first and second references to *deferred income taxes* are replaced by *The deferred tax liability or asset* and *deferred tax liability or asset*, respectively.

In the illustration at the end of paragraph 20, *Accumulated Deferred Income Tax Debits Related to Accounting Change . . . $2,357,500* is replaced by *Deferred Tax Asset (40 percent is the enacted tax rate—no valuation allowance deemed necessary) . . . $2,050,000.*

In the first sentence of paragraph 21, *deferred income taxes do* is replaced by *deferred tax asset does*. In the second and third sentences, *deferred income tax debits* is replaced by *deferred tax asset*. At the end of the third sentence, *($261,944)* is replaced by *($227,778).*

In the second sentence of paragraph 22, *deferred income tax credits* is replaced by *temporary differences*. In the fourth and fifth sentences, *deferred income tax credits* is replaced by *deferred tax liability* and *deferred tax liabilities*, respectively.

In paragraphs 23-25, references to *deferred income tax credits* are changed to *deferred tax liability*. In the first sentence of paragraph 24, *do* is replaced by *does*.

Paragraphs 26-29, the captions preceding paragraphs 26 and 28, and footnotes 2 and 3 are deleted.

q. FASB Statement No. 38, *Accounting for Preacquisition Contingencies of Purchased Enterprises.* In the fourth sentence of paragraph 2, *benefits of preacquisition net operating loss carryforwards* is replaced by *effects of (a) temporary differences and carryforwards of the acquired enterprise that exist at the acquisition date and (b) income tax uncertainties related to the acquisition (for example, an uncertainty related to the tax basis of an acquired asset that will ultimately be agreed to by the taxing authority).* The last sentence of paragraph 2 is deleted. In the first sentence of paragraph 5, *tax benefit of a loss carryforward[2]* is replaced by *income tax effects referred to in paragraph 2 of this Statement[2].*

The first sentence of footnote 2 is replaced by the following:

> Those potential income tax effects shall be accounted for in accordance with the provisions of FASB Statement No. 109, *Accounting for Income Taxes.*

The second and third sentences of footnote 2 are deleted.

r. FASB Statement No. 52, *Foreign Currency Translation.* In paragraph 48, *deferred income taxes and* is deleted from the table in both places.

s. FASB Statement No. 57, *Related Party Disclosures.* The following item is added to the end of paragraph 2:

> (e) The information required by paragraph 49 of FASB Statement No. 109, *Accounting for Income Taxes.*

t. FASB Statement No. 60, *Accounting and Reporting by Insurance Enterprises.* Paragraph 55 is replaced by the following:

Except as noted in paragraph 59, a deferred tax liability or asset shall be recognized for the deferred tax consequences of temporary differences in accordance with FASB Statement No. 109, *Accounting for Income Taxes.*

Paragraphs 56-58 and footnote 8 are deleted.

The first and second sentences of paragraph 59 are deleted.

The third sentence of paragraph 59 is replaced by the following:

As described in Statement 109, a life insurance enterprise should not provide deferred taxes on taxable temporary differences related to "policyholders' surplus" that arose in fiscal years beginning on or before December 15, 1992.

Paragraph 60(i) is replaced by the following:

Statement 109 specifies the requirements for financial statement disclosures about income taxes.

Paragraph 60(j) is deleted.

u. FASB Statement No. 69, *Disclosures about Oil and Gas Producing Activities.* In the second sentence of paragraph 26 and the second sentence of paragraph 30(c), *permanent differences* is deleted and *tax deductions* is inserted before *tax credits and allowances.* In paragraphs 40 and 41 of Appendix A, *permanent differences* is replaced by *tax deductions.*

v. FASB Statement No. 71, *Accounting for the Effects of Certain Types of Regulation.* Paragraph 18 is replaced by the following:

A deferred tax liability or asset shall be recognized for the deferred tax consequences of temporary differences in accordance with FASB Statement No. 109, *Accounting for Income Taxes.*

Footnote 12 is deleted. In paragraph 46, (1) *as amended* is inserted after *Statement 16* and (2) *, adjustments that result from realization of income tax benefits of preacquisition operating loss carryforwards of purchased subsidiaries,* is deleted.

w. FASB Statement No. 89, *Financial Reporting and Changing Prices.* In paragraph 96, *De-*

ferred income tax charges[a]—Offsets to prospective monetary liabilities and *Deferred income tax credits[a]—Cash requirements will not vary materially due to changes in specific prices.* are replaced by *Deferred tax assets[a]* and *Deferred tax liabilities[a]*, respectively.

x. FASB Statement No. 90, *Regulated Enterprises—Accounting for Abandonments and Disallowances of Plant Costs.* The fifth and sixth sentences of paragraph 14 are replaced by the following:

Under FASB Statement No. 109, *Accounting for Income Taxes,* the tax effects of temporary differences are measured based on enacted tax laws and rates and are recognized based on specified criteria.

y. FASB Interpretation No. 18, *Accounting for Income Taxes in Interim Periods.* The following sentence is inserted after the second sentence in paragraph 8:

It also includes the effect of any valuation allowance expected to be necessary at the end of the year for deferred tax assets related to originating deductible temporary differences and carryforwards during the year.

Paragraph 14 is replaced by the following:

Recognition of the tax benefit of a loss. Paragraph 20 of Opinion 28 (as amended by Statement 109) provides that a tax benefit is recognized for a loss that arises early in a fiscal year if the tax benefits are expected to be (a) realized during the year or (b) recognizable as a deferred tax asset at the end of the year in accordance with the provisions of Statement 109. Paragraph 17(e) of Statement 109 requires that a valuation allowance be recognized if it is more likely than not that the tax benefit of some portion or all of a deferred tax asset will not be realized. Those limitations shall be applied in determining the estimated tax benefit of an "ordinary" loss for the fiscal year, used to determine the estimated annual effective tax rate described in paragraph 8 above, and the year-to-date tax benefit of a loss.

Footnotes 9-11 are deleted.

Paragraph 15 is replaced by the following:

Reversal of taxable temporary differences. A deferred tax liability related to existing taxable temporary differences is a source of evidence for recognition of a tax benefit when (a) an enterprise anticipates an "ordinary" loss for the fiscal year or has a year-to-date "ordinary" loss in excess of the anticipated "ordinary" loss for the fiscal year, (b) the tax benefit of that loss is not expected to be realized during the year, and (c) recognition of a deferred tax asset for that loss at the end of the fiscal year is expected to depend on taxable income from the reversal of existing taxable temporary differences (that is, a higher valuation allowance [paragraph 17(e) of Statement 109] would be necessary absent the existing taxable temporary differences). If the tax benefit relates to an estimated "ordinary" loss for the fiscal year, it shall be considered in determining the estimated annual effective tax rate described in paragraph 8 above. If the tax benefit relates to a year-to-date "ordinary" loss, it shall be considered in computing the maximum tax benefit that shall be recognized for the year-to-date.

Footnotes 12-14 are deleted.

In paragraph 16, the following sentence is inserted after the first sentence:

> Paragraph 20 of Opinion 28 (as amended) excludes the effects of changes in judgment about beginning-of-year valuation allowances and effects of changes in tax laws or rates from the estimated annual effective tax rate calculation.

The reference to *Paragraph 52 of APB Opinion No. 11*[18] in the third sentence is replaced by *Paragraphs 35-38 of Statement 109*. The fourth sentence and footnote 18 are deleted.

In the first sentence of paragraph 18, *shall not be recognized until it is realized or realization is assured beyond any reasonable doubt* is replaced by *shall be recognized when the tax benefit of the loss is expected to be (a) realized during the year or (b) recognizable as a deferred tax asset at the end of the year in accordance with the provisions of Statement 109*. The second sentence of paragraph 18 is deleted.

The third sentence of paragraph 18 is replaced by the following:

> Realization would appear to be more likely than not if future taxable income from (ordinary) income during the current year is expected based on an established seasonal pattern of loss in early interim periods offset by income in later interim periods.[19]

In footnote 19, *paragraph 47 of APB Opinion No. 11 (see Appendix A, paragraph 31) and* is deleted.

The fourth sentence in paragraph 18 is replaced by the following:

> If recognition of a deferred tax asset at the end of the fiscal year for all or a portion of the tax benefit of the loss depends on taxable income from the reversal of existing taxable temporary differences, refer to paragraph 15 above.

In the fifth sentence, *assured beyond any reasonable doubt* is replaced by *more likely than not* in all three places.

Paragraph 20 is replaced by the following:

> Paragraph 37 of Statement 109 requires that the manner of reporting the tax benefit of an operating loss carryforward recognized in a subsequent year generally is determined by the source of the income in that year and not by (a) the source of the operating loss carryforward or (b) the source of expected future income that will result in realization of a deferred tax asset for the operating loss carryforward. The tax benefit is allocated first to reduce tax expense from continuing operations to zero with any excess allocated to the other source(s) of income that provides the means of realization, for example, extraordinary items, discontinued operations, and so forth. That requirement also pertains to reporting the tax benefit of an operating loss carryforward in interim periods. The tax benefit of an operating loss carryforward from prior years shall be included in the effective tax rate computation if the tax benefit is expected to be realized as a result of "ordinary" income in the current year. Otherwise, the tax benefit shall be recognized in the manner described above in each interim period to the extent that income in the period and for the year to date is available to offset the operating loss carryforward or, in the case of a change in judgment about realizability of the related deferred tax asset in future years, the effect shall be recognized in the interim period in which the change occurs.

Footnotes 21-23 are deleted.

Paragraph 23 is replaced by the following:

Paragraph 20 of Opinion 28 (as amended by Statement 109) sets forth the requirements for recognition of the tax effects of a change in tax laws or rates. That paragraph refers to effective dates prescribed in the statutes. Paragraph 24 below describes the determination of when new legislation becomes effective.

Footnote 25 is deleted.

In the assumed facts for the examples in Appendix C, references in paragraphs 41, 43, 48, 49, 65, and 68 to *permanent differences* are replaced by references to *events that do not have tax consequences.* In the second sentence of the last subparagraph of paragraph 43, *assured of future realization beyond any reasonable doubt at year-end* is replaced by *recognizable at the end of the current year in accordance with the provisions of Statement 109.* The third and fourth sentences of that subparagraph are deleted.

The third sentence of paragraph 46 is replaced by the following:

Established seasonal patterns provide evidence that realization in the current year of the tax benefit of the year-to-date loss and of anticipated tax credits is more likely than not.

The third sentence of paragraph 47 is replaced by the following:

There is no established seasonal pattern and it is more likely than not that the tax benefit of the year-to-date loss and the anticipated tax credits will not be realized in the current or future years.

In footnote *, *realization of* is deleted and *assured beyond any reasonable doubt* is replaced by *expected to be (a) realized during the current year or (b) recognizable as a deferred tax asset at the end of the current year in accordance with the provisions of Statement 109.*

In the third subparagraph of paragraph 49, *If realization of the tax benefit of the loss and realization of tax credits were assured beyond any reasonable doubt* is replaced by *If there is a recognizable tax benefit for the loss and the tax credits pursuant to the requirements of Statement 109.* In the last sentence of paragraph 49, *assured beyond any reasonable doubt* is replaced by *expected to be (a) realized during the current year or (b) recognizable as a deferred*

tax asset at the end of the current year in accordance with the provisions of Statement 109.

The third sentence of paragraph 50 is replaced by the following:

The full tax benefit of the anticipated "ordinary" loss and the anticipated tax credits will be realized by carryback.

In paragraph 51, the third and fourth sentences are replaced by the following:

The full tax benefit of the anticipated "ordinary" loss and the anticipated tax credits will be realized by carryback. The full tax benefit of the maximum year-to-date "ordinary" loss can also be realized by carryback.

In the first sentence of paragraph 52, (1) *realization of, nor realization of,* and *assured beyond any reasonable doubt* are deleted, and (2) *nor* is added directly before, and *recognizable pursuant to Statement 109* is added directly after, *anticipated tax credits were.*

In the third sentence of paragraphs 53 and 54, (1) *Realization of* is replaced by *It is more likely than not that,* (2) *is assured beyond any reasonable doubt only to the extent* is replaced by *in excess,* and (3) *will not be realized* is added to the end of each sentence.

In the second sentence of paragraph 55, *are not assured beyond any reasonable doubt* is replaced by *exclusive of reversing temporary differences are unlikely.* In the third and fourth sentences of paragraph 55, (1) *credits* is replaced by *liabilities* and (2) *timing differences* is replaced by *existing net taxable temporary differences.* In the fifth sentence of paragraph 55, *(refer to paragraph 15 of this Interpretation)* is added after *to be used.* In the computation at the end of paragraph 55, (1) *credits* is replaced by *liabilities* and (2) *amortized* is replaced by *settled.*

The third sentence of paragraph 58 is replaced by the following:

The loss cannot be carried back, and available evidence indicates that a valuation allowance is needed for all of the deferred tax asset.

In the fourth sentence of paragraph 58, (1) *realization of* is deleted and (2) *not assured beyond any reasonable doubt except* is replaced by *recognized only.* Paragraphs 59-61 and the heading *Using a Prior Year Operating Loss Carryforward* are deleted.

In the fifth sentence of paragraph 66, (1) *Realization of* is replaced by *It is expected that* and (2) *is not assured beyond any reasonable doubt* is replaced by *will not be recognizable as a deferred tax asset at the end of the current year pursuant to Statement 109.*

Paragraph 70 and all references thereto are deleted.

z. FASB Interpretation No. 31, *Treatment of Stock Compensation Plans in EPS Computations.* In the last sentence of footnote 1, *as described in paragraph 36 of APB Opinion No. 11, Accounting for Income Taxes* is deleted.

aa. FASB Technical Bulletin No. 79-9, *Accounting in Interim Periods for Changes in Income Tax Rates.* The last sentence in paragraph 3 is deleted.

bb. FASB Technical Bulletin No. 79-16 (Revised), *Effect of a Change in Income Tax Rate on the Accounting for Leveraged Leases.* In paragraph 4, *paragraph 63 of APB Opinion No. 11, Accounting for Income Taxes* is replaced by *paragraph 47 of FASB Statement No. 109, Accounting for Income Taxes.*

cc. FASB Technical Bulletin No. 82-1, *Disclosure of the Sale or Purchase of Tax Benefits through Tax Leases.* Paragraph 5 is replaced by the following:

> Paragraph 47 of FASB Statement No. 109, *Accounting for Income Taxes,* requires that (a) the reported amount of income tax expense attributable to continuing operations for the year be reconciled to the amount of income tax expense that would result from applying domestic federal statutory tax rates to pretax income from continuing operations and (b) the estimated amount and the nature of each significant reconciling item be disclosed. Transactions involving the sale or purchase of tax benefits through tax leases may give rise to a significant reconciling item that should be disclosed pursuant to the requirements of Statement 109.

dd. FASB Technical Bulletin No. 87-2, *Computation of a Loss on an Abandonment.* Paragraphs 9-11 and 13 and footnote 4 are deleted. The first sentence of paragraph 18 is deleted. Appendix A is deleted. In Appendix B, in the second sentence of paragraph 36, the reference to *Opinion 11* should remain. In paragraph 40, the fifth, sixth, and seventh sentences should be deleted.

Appendix E

GLOSSARY

289. This appendix contains definitions of certain terms or phrases used in this Statement.

Carrybacks
Deductions or credits that cannot be utilized on the tax return during a year that may be carried back to reduce taxable income or taxes payable in a prior year. An operating loss carryback is an excess of tax deductions over gross income in a year; a tax credit carryback is the amount by which tax credits available for utilization exceed statutory limitations. Different tax jurisdictions have different rules about whether excess deductions or credits may be carried back and the length of the carryback period.

Carryforwards
Deductions or credits that cannot be utilized on the tax return during a year that may be carried forward to reduce taxable income or taxes payable in a future year. An operating loss carryforward is an excess of tax deductions over gross income in a year; a tax credit carryforward is the amount by which tax credits available for utilization exceed statutory limitations. Different tax jurisdictions have different rules about whether excess deductions or credits may be carried forward and the length of the carryforward period. The terms *carryforward, operating loss carryforward,* and *tax credit carryforward* refer to the amounts of those items, if any, reported in the tax return for the current year.

Current tax expense or benefit
The amount of income taxes paid or payable (or refundable) for a year as determined by applying the provisions of the enacted tax law to the taxable income or excess of deductions over revenues for that year.

Deductible temporary difference
Temporary differences that result in deductible amounts in future years when the related asset or liability is recovered or settled, respectively. Also refer to **Temporary difference.**

Deferred tax asset
The deferred tax consequences attributable to deductible temporary differences and carryforwards. A deferred tax asset is measured using the applicable enacted tax rate and provisions of the enacted tax law. A deferred tax asset is reduced by a valuation allowance if, based on the weight of evidence available, it is more likely than not that some portion or all of a deferred tax asset will not be realized.

Deferred tax consequences

The future effects on income taxes as measured by the applicable enacted tax rate and provisions of the enacted tax law resulting from temporary differences and carryforwards at the end of the current year.

Deferred tax expense or benefit

The change during the year in an enterprise's deferred tax liabilities and assets. For deferred tax liabilities and assets acquired in a purchase business combination during the year, it is the change since the combination date. Income tax expense or benefit for the year is allocated among continuing operations, discontinued operations, extraordinary items, and items charged or credited directly to shareholders' equity.

Deferred tax liability

The deferred tax consequences attributable to taxable temporary differences. A deferred tax liability is measured using the applicable enacted tax rate and provisions of the enacted tax law.

Event

A happening of consequence to an enterprise. The term encompasses both transactions and other events affecting an enterprise.

Gains and losses included in comprehensive income but excluded from net income

Under present practice, gains and losses included in comprehensive income but excluded from net income include certain changes in market values of investments in marketable equity securities classified as noncurrent assets, certain changes in market values of investments in industries having specialized accounting practices for marketable securities, adjustments from recognizing certain additional pension liabilities, and foreign currency translation adjustments. Future changes to generally accepted accounting principles may change what is included in this category.

Income taxes

Domestic and foreign federal (national), state, and local (including franchise) taxes based on income.

Income taxes currently payable (refundable)

Refer to **Current tax expense or benefit.**

Income tax expense (benefit)

The sum of current tax expense (benefit) and deferred tax expense (benefit).

Nonpublic enterprise

An enterprise other than one (a) whose debt or equity securities are traded in a public market, including those traded on a stock exchange or in the over-the-counter market (including securities quoted only locally or regionally), or

(b) whose financial statements are filed with a regulatory agency in preparation for the sale of any class of securities.

Public enterprise

An enterprise (a) whose debt or equity securities are traded in a public market, including those traded on a stock exchange or in the over-the-counter market (including securities quoted only locally or regionally), or (b) whose financial statements are filed with a regulatory agency in preparation for the sale of any class of securities.

Taxable income

The excess of taxable revenues over tax deductible expenses and exemptions for the year as defined by the governmental taxing authority.

Taxable temporary difference

Temporary differences that result in taxable amounts in future years when the related asset or liability is recovered or settled, respectively. Also refer to **Temporary difference.**

Tax consequences

The effects on income taxes—current or deferred—of an event.

Tax-planning strategy

An action (including elections for tax purposes) that meets certain criteria (paragraph 22) and that would be implemented to realize a tax benefit for an operating loss or tax credit carryforward before it expires. Tax-planning strategies are considered when assessing the need for and amount of a valuation allowance for deferred tax assets.

Temporary difference

A difference between the tax basis of an asset or liability and its reported amount in the financial statements that will result in taxable or deductible amounts in future years when the reported amount of the asset or liability is recovered or settled, respectively. Paragraph 11 cites 8 examples of temporary differences. Some temporary differences cannot be identified with a particular asset or liability for financial reporting (paragraph 15), but those temporary differences (a) result from events that have been recognized in the financial statements and (b) will result in taxable or deductible amounts in future years based on provisions of the tax law. Some events recognized in financial statements do not have tax consequences. Certain revenues are exempt from taxation and certain expenses are not deductible. Events that do not have tax consequences do not give rise to temporary differences.

Valuation allowance

The portion of a deferred tax asset for which it is more likely than not that a tax benefit will not be realized.

FAS110

Statement of Financial Accounting Standards No. 110
Reporting by Defined Benefit Pension Plans of
Investment Contracts

an amendment of FASB Statement No. 35

STATUS

Issued: August 1992

Effective Date: For financial statements for fiscal years beginning after December 15, 1992

Affects: Amends FAS 35, paragraph 11
   Supersedes FAS 35, paragraph 12 and footnote 6

Affected by: No other pronouncements

Issues Discussed by FASB Emerging Issues Task Force (EITF)

   Affects: Resolves EITF Issue No. 89-1

   Interpreted by: No EITF Issues

   Related Issues: No EITF Issues

SUMMARY

This Statement requires a defined benefit pension plan to report an investment contract issued by either an insurance enterprise or other entity at fair value. This Statement amends FASB Statement No. 35, *Accounting and Reporting by Defined Benefit Pension Plans,* to permit a defined benefit pension plan to report only contracts that incorporate mortality or morbidity risk at contract value.

This Statement is effective for fiscal years beginning after December 15, 1992. It need not be applied to deposit administration and immediate participation guarantee contracts entered into before March 20, 1992. Restatement of financial statements of prior years is required only if those statements are presented with statements for plan years beginning after December 15, 1992.

Statement of Financial Accounting Standards No. 110

Reporting by Defined Benefit Pension Plans of Investment Contracts

an amendment of FASB Statement No. 35

CONTENTS

INTRODUCTION

1. FASB Statement No. 35, *Accounting and Reporting by Defined Benefit Pension Plans,* establishes standards of financial accounting and reporting for the annual financial statements of a defined benefit pension plan. Paragraph 11 of Statement 35 states that "plan investments, whether equity or debt securities, real estate, or other (excluding contracts with insurance companies) shall be presented at their fair value at the reporting date." Paragraph 12 of that Statement states that "contracts with insurance companies shall be presented in the same manner as that contained in the annual report filed by the plan with certain governmental agencies pursuant to ERISA" (footnote reference omitted). The instructions to Forms 5500 and 5500-C permit unallocated contracts recognized as plan assets to be reported either at fair value or at amounts determined by the insurance company (that is, contract value).

2. Some have interpreted the exception in Statement 35 for contracts with insurance companies to allow guaranteed interest contracts, also referred to as "guaranteed investment contracts" or "GICs," to be reported at contract value. A GIC is a negotiated contract generally between an insurance enterprise (issuer) and an investor, typically a pension plan or savings and investment plan. GICs held by defined benefit pension plans generally provide for a specified return on principal invested over a specified period. Entities other than insurance enterprises have also offered instruments with similar characteristics. However, paragraph 11 of Statement 35 refers only to contracts with insurance companies. That reference raised questions about whether defined benefit pension plans that hold investments with characteristics similar to those of a GIC but issued by entities other than insurance enterprises may be permitted to report those investments at contract value.

3. The Emerging Issues Task Force (EITF) discussed the issue in EITF Issue No. 89-1, "Accounting by a Pension Plan for Bank Investment Contracts and Guaranteed Investment Contracts," but did not reach a consensus. As a result, the FASB added a project on pension plan accounting for investment contracts to its agenda.

STANDARDS OF FINANCIAL ACCOUNTING AND REPORTING

Reporting of Contracts

4. A defined benefit pension plan shall report investment contracts at fair value. A defined benefit pension plan shall report insurance contracts in the same manner as they are reported in the annual report filed by the plan with certain governmental agencies pursuant to the Employee Retirement Income Security Act of 1974 (ERISA). For purposes of this Statement, the terms *insurance contract* and *investment contract* are used as those terms are described for accounting purposes in FASB Statements No. 60, *Accounting and Reporting by Insurance Enterprises,* and No. 97, *Accounting and Reporting by Insurance Enterprises for Certain Long-Duration Contracts and for Realized Gains and Losses from the Sale of Investments.*

5. Paragraph 1 of Statement 60 describes insurance contracts:

The primary purpose of insurance is to provide economic protection from identified risks occurring or discovered within a specified period. Some types of risks insured include death, disability, property damage, injury to others, and business interruption. Insurance transactions may be characterized generally by the following:

a. The purchaser of an insurance contract makes an initial payment or deposit to the insurance enterprise in advance of the possible occurrence or discovery of an insured event.
b. When the insurance contract is made, the insurance enterprise ordinarily does not know if, how much, or when amounts will be paid under the contract.

6. Paragraphs 7 and 8 of Statement 97 describe insurance and investment contracts:

Long-duration contracts that do not subject the insurance enterprise to risks arising from policyholder mortality or morbidity are referred to in this Statement as investment contracts. A mortality or morbidity risk is present if, under the terms of the contract, the enterprise is required to make payments or forego required premiums contingent upon the death or disability (in the case of life insurance contracts) or the continued survival (in the case of annuity contracts) of a specific individual or group of individuals. A contract provision that allows the holder of a long-duration contract to purchase an annuity at a guaranteed price on settlement of the contract does not entail a mortality risk until the right to purchase is executed. If purchased, the annuity is a new contract to be evaluated on its own terms.

Annuity contracts may require the insurance enterprise to make a number of payments that are not contingent upon the survival of the beneficiary, followed by payments that are made if the beneficiary is alive when the payments are due (often referred to as *life-contingent payments*). Such contracts are considered insurance contracts under this Statement and Statement 60 unless (a) the probability that life-contingent payments will be made is remote or (b) the present value of the expected life-contingent payments relative to the present value of all expected payments under the contract is insignificant. [Footnote references omitted.]

Amendment to Statement 35

7. Statement 35 is amended as follows:

a. The parenthetical comment (*excluding contracts with insurance companies*) in paragraph 11 is replaced by (*excluding insurance contracts*).
b. Paragraph 12 is replaced by the following:

Insurance contracts shall be presented in the same manner as specified in the annual report filed by the plan with certain governmental agencies pursuant to ERISA; that is, either at fair value or at amounts determined by the insurance enterprise (contract value). A plan not subject to ERISA shall present its insurance contracts as if the plan were subject to the reporting requirements of ERISA.

Effective Date and Transition

8. This Statement is effective for financial statements for fiscal years beginning after December 15, 1992. Earlier adoption is encouraged. This Statement is not required to be applied to deposit administration and immediate participation guarantee contracts (as described in paragraphs 114-119 of Statement 35) entered into before March 20, 1992. Those contracts may continue to be presented in the same manner as insurance contracts as set forth in paragraph 12 of Statement 35 as amended by this Statement.

9. Accounting changes adopted to conform to the provisions of this Statement shall be made retroactively by restating the beginning balance of net assets available for plan benefits for the earliest period presented. Financial statements of prior plan years shall be restated to comply with the provisions of this Statement only if presented with financial statements for plan years beginning after December 15, 1992. If accounting changes are necessary to conform to the provisions of this Statement, the effect on the beginning balance of net assets available for benefits shall be disclosed in the financial statements for the year in which this Statement is first applied.

> The provisions of this Statement need not be applied to immaterial items.

This Statement was adopted by the unanimous vote of the seven members of the Financial Accounting Standards Board:

Dennis R. Beresford,	Victor H. Brown	A. Clarence Sampson
Chairman	James J. Leisenring	Robert J. Swieringa
Joseph V. Anania	Robert H. Northcutt, Jr.	

Appendix

BACKGROUND INFORMATION AND BASIS FOR CONCLUSIONS

CONTENTS

Appendix

BACKGROUND INFORMATION AND BASIS FOR CONCLUSIONS

Introduction

10. This appendix summarizes considerations that Board members deemed significant in reaching the conclusions in this Statement. It includes reasons for accepting certain views and rejecting others. Individual Board members gave greater weight to some factors than to others.

11. An FASB Exposure Draft, *Reporting by Defined Benefit Pension Plans of Investment Contracts,* was issued for public comment on March 20, 1992. The Board received 48 comment letters in response to that Exposure Draft. The Board concluded that it could reach an informed decision on the basis of existing information without a public hearing.

Background

12. Paragraph 5 of Statement 35 states that "the primary objective of a pension plan's financial statements is to provide financial information that is useful in assessing the plan's present and future ability to pay benefits when due" (footnote reference omit-

ted). The Board concluded that the reporting of plan investments at fair value provides the most relevant information about the resources of a plan. Statement 35 requires that defined benefit pension plans report investments at their fair value.

13. Although the Board recognized that there might be practical problems in determining the fair value of certain types of investments, it initially concluded that the relevance of fair value was sufficient to require its use. As a result, the July 1979 FASB Exposure Draft, *Accounting and Reporting by Defined Benefit Pension Plans,* that preceded Statement 35 required contracts with insurance companies to be reported at fair value. However, many respondents to that Exposure Draft expressed concerns about the complexity and feasibility of determining fair value for contracts with insurance companies.

14. Because the Board was concerned about delaying the issuance of Statement 35 to address those concerns, it concluded that contracts with insurance companies should be reported in the same manner as that required for filings under ERISA. The instructions to Form 5500 permit contracts with insurance companies to be reported at contract value. Therefore, in Statement 35, the Board permitted for practical reasons an exception to fair value reporting for contracts with insurance companies.

Application of Fair Value Exclusion to Insurance Contracts

15. Paragraph 74 of FASB Statement No. 107, *Disclosures about Fair Value of Financial Instruments,* states:

> The Board concluded that disclosures about fair value should not be required for insurance contracts. . . . The Board believes that definitional and valuation difficulties are present to a certain extent in those contracts and obligations, and that further consideration is required before decisions can be made about whether to apply the definition to components of those contracts and whether to require disclosures about fair value for the financial components.

16. The Board recognized in its discussions about investments held by defined benefit pension plans that it may be difficult to determine the fair value of an insurance contract that, as discussed in paragraph 1 of Statement 60 and paragraphs 7 and 8 of Statement 97, incorporates either a mortality or morbidity risk. The Board decided the fair value exclusion in Statement 35 should continue for insurance contracts as a result of the definitional and valuation difficulties.

17. Some respondents to the 1992 Exposure Draft argued that investment contracts with benefit-responsive provisions are insurance contracts or have valuation difficulties similar to insurance contracts with mortality or morbidity risk. Benefit-responsive investment contracts typically transfer investment-yield risk (that is, uncertainty as to the ultimate amount of investment income that will be earned on the net funds invested in the contract) and some principal payment timing risk to the issuer of the contract. However, the plan remains at risk for the ultimate amount of benefit payments. The Board concluded that a contract with benefit-responsive provisions should be reported as an investment contract if it cannot otherwise be considered an insurance contract as discussed in this Statement.

Reporting Investment Contracts at Fair Value

18. The Board considered whether the exception to fair value in Statement 35 should apply to investment contracts held by defined benefit pension plans. Paragraph 15 of Statement 97 states that "investment contracts issued by an insurance enterprise . . . do not incorporate significant insurance risk as that concept is contemplated in Statement 60 and shall not be accounted for as insurance contracts." Further, paragraph 39 of Statement 97 states that ". . . the Board concluded

that the accounting for investment contracts issued by insurance enterprises should be consistent with the accounting for interest-bearing and other financial instruments." Statement 107 requires holders of investment contracts, including defined benefit pension plans, to disclose the fair value of those contracts.

19. Several respondents to the 1992 Exposure Draft argued that contract value provides the most relevant information about a plan's ability to pay benefits when due because it represents the amount the plan will receive at the contract's maturity. Several respondents also questioned the relevance of reporting investment contracts at fair value. Because an established secondary market for investment contracts does not currently exist, the plan will be unable to realize fair value.

20. The Board continues to believe that fair value is more relevant as explained in paragraphs 105 and 107 of Statement 35 as follows:

> Plan administrators or other fiduciaries who manage plan assets are accountable not only for the custody and safekeeping of those [plan] assets but also for their efficient and profitable use in producing additional assets for use in paying benefits. Investment performance is an essential element of stewardship responsibility. Measuring changes in fair value provides information necessary for assessing annual investment performance and stewardship responsibility. Historical cost provides that information only when investments are sold.
>
> For fixed-income investments held to maturity, the Board recognizes that market fluctuations will reverse before maturity (assuming no defaults). However, at the reporting date, it is the fair value, not the historical cost or the expected value at maturity, that is relevant to an assessment of the plan's ability to pay benefits. Changes in value from period to period are relevant to an assessment of investment performance and discharge of stewardship responsibility. Presenting fixed-income investments at historical cost (whether or not the intent is to hold them to maturity) does not provide essential information about the effect on investment performance of the decision to hold. Further, it may be difficult to determine whether the plan has both the intent and ability to hold a particular fixed-income investment to maturity.

21. The Board understands that the lack of an active secondary market limits the ability of the

holder of an investment contract to realize fair value through a sale. However, it is inconsistent to require fixed-income investments that the plan has the ability and intent to hold to maturity to be reported at fair value and to allow investment contracts that generally have similar characteristics to be reported at contract value. In addition, reporting investment contracts at fair value based on current, not historical, interest rates is consistent with how the actuarial present value of accumulated plan benefits is measured.

22. The Board reaffirmed its belief that fair value provides the most relevant information about the resources of the plan and concluded it should require defined benefit pension plans to report investment contracts at fair value. The Board also concluded that investments with similar terms should be measured in a consistent manner whether an insurance enterprise or another entity issues the investment.

23. Several respondents to the 1992 Exposure Draft suggested that the Board provide additional guidance for determining the fair value of investment contracts. Those respondents expressed concern that the lack of an established secondary market would result in the determination of fair value based on subjective estimates that would result in inconsistent measurements. Other respondents suggested that if additional guidance is not provided by the Board, many plan trustees may inappropriately conclude that contract value equals fair value. The Board believes that the broad guidance provided in Statements 35 and 107, as noted in paragraph 26 of this Statement, should be sufficient to determine fair value. The Board realizes that it cannot anticipate the variety of terms that can be included in an investment contract and that application of this Statement may, in some cases, require considerable judgment. However, the Board noted, as it did when it issued Statement 107, that considerable judgment also is needed when complying with other longstanding accounting and reporting requirements.

Defined Contribution Plans

24. The Board discussed whether the project should include the reporting of investments held by defined contribution plans since a significant number of investment contracts are held by those plans. The Board has not previously addressed issues related to financial statements of defined contribution plans. The current authoritative guidance on the issue is the AICPA Audit and Accounting Guide, *Audits of Employee Benefit Plans.* That Guide follows the requirements of Statement 35 by requiring that investments held by defined contribution plans be reported at fair value except for

contracts with insurance companies, which are permitted to be reported at contract value.

25. The Board decided not to address the measurement of plan assets held by defined contribution plans in this project. Pursuing the differences between defined benefit pension plans and defined contribution plans would significantly expand the project. The issues that would have to be resolved before the Board could reach a conclusion about the appropriate measurement attribute would include the following: Who are the principal users of financial statements of defined contribution plans, what information is most relevant to their needs, and what are plan assets? Resolving those questions for all types of defined contribution plans, including those in which all investment decisions are made by the individual participants, would be time-consuming. The Board asked the AICPA, in view of its experience with defined contribution plans, to further address the appropriate reporting of investments held by defined contribution plans. The AICPA has undertaken a project to review the appropriate reporting for investment contracts held by defined contribution plans and health and welfare benefit plans.

Cost-Benefit Considerations

26. The benefits of this Statement are twofold. First, investment contracts held by defined benefit pension plans will be reported at fair value so that changes in the economic value of those contracts will be reflected in amounts reported to financial statement users. Second, the AICPA will be able to address defined contribution plan issues in light of the requirements of this Statement. However, those benefits have a cost; that is, the incremental cost of developing, implementing, and maintaining a system to generate the required valuations. The Board believes the cost of implementing this Statement is reduced by retaining the general guidance provided in paragraph 11 of Statement 35:

> If there is not an active market for an investment but there is such a market for similar investments, selling prices in that market may be helpful in estimating fair value. If a market price is not available, a forecast of expected cash flows may aid in estimating fair value, provided the expected cash flows are discounted at a rate commensurate with the risk involved. [Footnote reference omitted.]

In addition, Appendix A of Statement 107 provides examples of procedures for estimating fair value that are consistent with the general guidance provided in paragraph 11 of Statement 35.

Credit Quality Issues

27. The Board also discussed how to incorporate the credit quality of the issuer in determining the fair value for an investment that is not actively traded. Some plans may receive less than the amount that the issuer is legally obligated to pay due to the issuer's financial difficulties. The Board believes that the guidance provided in paragraph 11 of Statement 35 and by Statement 107 is appropriate for estimating fair value.

28. The credit quality of the issuer also must be evaluated when using contract value to report a contract with significant insurance risk. FASB Statement No. 5, *Accounting for Contingencies,* requires the accrual of a loss when both criteria of paragraph 8 of that Statement are met. The need to recognize a contingent loss always should be considered when there is an existing condition, situation, or set of circumstances involving uncertainty as to possible loss.

29. The Board noted that financial instruments held by a defined benefit pension plan are subject to the disclosure requirements of FASB Statement No. 105, *Disclosure of Information about Financial Instruments with Off-Balance-Sheet Risk and Financial Instruments with Concentrations of Credit Risk.*

Effective Date and Transition

30. The Board decided that some plans may need time to implement procedures necessary to determine fair value. Accordingly, this Statement is effective for fiscal years beginning after December 15, 1992.

31. In the basis for conclusions of Statement 35, the Board discussed the characteristics of both deposit administration and immediate participation guarantee contracts. Plan sponsors may have reported those contracts at contract value based on their discussion in Statement 35. The Board decided, for practical reasons, not to require the application of the provisions of this Statement to those contracts entered into before March 20, 1992. The 1992 Exposure Draft required deposit administration and immediate participation guarantee contracts entered into after March 19, 1992 to be reported at fair value. Several respondents to the 1992 Exposure Draft said that a few deposit administration and immediate participation guarantee contracts are still being issued and that some of those contracts may have significant insurance risk. The Board decided that any contract entered into after March 19, 1992 should be classified as either an insurance or investment contract pursuant to the requirements of this Statement and reported by the defined benefit pension plan accordingly.

Statement of Financial Accounting Standards No. 111
Rescission of FASB Statement No. 32 and Technical Corrections

STATUS

Issued: November 1992

Effective Date: November 30, 1992

Affects: Amends ARB 43, Chapter 1A, paragraph 1; Chapter 3A, paragraph 6(g); Chapter 7A, paragraph 10; Chapter 10A, paragraph 19; and Chapter 11B, paragraph 9
Supersedes ARB 43, Chapter 11B, footnotes 3 and 4
Supersedes ARB 51, footnote 1
Amends APB 6, paragraph 16
Amends APB 9, paragraph 17
Amends APB 10, paragraph 11(b)
Supersedes APB 12, footnote 1
Amends APB 15, paragraph 5 and Exhibit B of Appendix C
Amends APB 20, paragraphs 4, 7, 9, and 16 and footnote 4
Supersedes APB 20, footnotes 2 and 5
Amends APB 22, footnote 2
Supersedes AIN-ARB 51, Interpretation No. 1
Supersedes AIN-APB 4, Interpretation No. 5
Supersedes AIN-APB 7, Interpretation No. 1
Supersedes AIN-APB 8, Interpretations No. 1 through 28
Supersedes AIN-APB 9, Interpretation No. 2
Amends AIN-APB 15, Part I and Interpretations No. 2, 26, 30, 33, 56, and 92
Supersedes AIN-APB 15, Interpretations No. 10 and 38 and footnote 22
Amends AIN-APB 16, Interpretation No. 30
Amends AIN-APB 18, Interpretation No. 2
Supersedes AIN-APB 22, Interpretation No. 1
Amends AIN-APB 26, Interpretation No. 1
Amends FAS 5, paragraph 18
Amends FAS 14, paragraph 27(c)
Supersedes FAS 15, footnote 20
Amends FAS 15, footnote 26
Supersedes FAS 25, paragraphs 6 and 8
Supersedes FAS 32
Supersedes FAS 55
Supersedes FAS 56
Amends FAS 67, paragraph 2(b) and footnote 10
Amends FAS 76, paragraph 7
Supersedes FAS 83
Amends FAS 105, paragraph 14(c)
Supersedes FIN 18, footnote 5
Amends FIN 20, paragraph 5
Amends FTB 79-8, paragraphs 5 and 6
Amends FTB 80-1, paragraphs 1 through 4
Supersedes FTB 81-3
Supersedes FTB 85-2, footnote 9

Affected by: No other pronouncements

Issues Discussed by FASB Emerging Issues Task Force (EITF)

Affects: No EITF Issues

Interpreted by: No EITF Issues

Related Issue: EITF Topic No. D-1

SUMMARY

This Statement rescinds FASB Statement No. 32, *Specialized Accounting and Reporting Principles and Practices in AICPA Statements of Position and Guides on Accounting and Auditing Matters,* and its related pronouncements. The guidance in Statement 32, which specifies that the specialized accounting principles and practices contained in AICPA Statements of Position and Guides are preferable for purposes of justifying a change in accounting principles as required by APB Opinion No. 20, *Accounting Changes,* is no longer needed with the issuance of the AICPA's Statement on Auditing Standards (SAS) No. 69, *The Meaning of "Present Fairly in Conformity With Generally Accepted Accounting Principles" in the Independent Auditor's Report.* In general, SAS 69 *requires* an entity to adopt the accounting principles in pronouncements whose effective date is after March 15, 1992. An entity initially applying an accounting principle after that date (including those making an accounting change) must follow the applicable hierarchy set forth in SAS 69. An entity following an established accounting principle that was effective as of March 15, 1992 need not change its accounting until a new pronouncement is issued. This Statement also amends other existing authoritative literature to make various technical corrections.

This Statement is effective November 30, 1992.

Statement of Financial Accounting Standards No. 111

Rescission of FASB Statement No. 32 and Technical Corrections

CONTENTS

INTRODUCTION

Rescission of Statement 32

1. FASB Statement No. 32, *Specialized Accounting and Reporting Principles and Practices in AICPA Statements of Position and Guides on Accounting and Auditing Matters,* states that the specialized accounting principles contained in the AICPA Statements of Position (SOPs) and Guides on accounting and auditing matters listed in Appendix A of that Statement are preferable for the purpose of adopting a change in accounting principle under paragraphs 15 and 16 of APB Opinion No. 20, *Accounting Changes.*

2. The Board has amended that list twice with the issuance of FASB Statements No. 56, *Designation of AICPA Guide and Statement of Position (SOP) 81-1 on Contractor Accounting and SOP 81-2 concerning Hospital-Related Organizations as Preferable for Purposes of Applying APB Opinion 20* (issued February 1982), and No. 83, *Designation of AICPA Guides and Statement of Position on Accounting by Brokers and Dealers in Securities, by Employee Benefit Plans, and by Banks as Preferable for Purposes of Applying APB Opinion 20* (issued March 1985). Statements 56 and 83 added new AICPA audit and accounting Guides and SOPs to the Statement 32 list and eliminated those that had been superseded.

3. In January 1992, the AICPA Auditing Standards Board issued Statement on Auditing Standards (SAS) No. 69, *The Meaning of "Present Fairly in Conformity With Generally Accepted Ac-counting Principles" in the Independent Auditor's Report.* That Statement supersedes AU section 411 of the AICPA *Professional Standards.* SAS 69 revises the generally accepted accounting principles (GAAP) hierarchy by (a) adding a new category, (b) changing some of the sources of established accounting principles in two categories, and (c) designating which category is to be used when there is a conflict between categories. A summary of those categories is provided in paragraph 25.

4. The provisions of SAS 69 require that an affected entity must apply the provisions of pronouncements contained in categories *(b)-(d)* with an effective date after March 15, 1992. This will require a change in accounting principles by an entity not following such accounting. An entity initially applying an accounting principle after March 15, 1992 must follow the applicable hierarchy set forth in SAS 69. Special transition provisions apply to FASB Emerging Issues Task Force (EITF) consensus positions (refer to paragraph 18). An entity following an established accounting principle (in categories *(b)* and *(c)* under the previous GAAP hierarchy) that was effective as of March 15, 1992 need not change its accounting unless it chooses to make a change or unless a new pronouncement in categories *(b)-(d)* (under SAS 69) becomes effective after March 15, 1992. Since category *(b)* in SAS 69 contains the AICPA Guides and SOPs, the Board no longer needs to designate the specialized accounting and reporting principles and practices in AICPA Guides and SOPs that are preferable for the purpose of adopting a change in accounting principle under Opinion 20. This Statement rescinds Statement 32 and related pronouncements.

Technical Corrections

5. When the Board issues a pronouncement that contains amendments to prior pronouncements, the proposed amendments are reviewed by the Board and exposed for comment as part of the due process procedures. Over the years, the FASB staff and various constituents have identified instances where additional amendments should have been made explicit in certain pronouncements. Although, in general, those "effective" amendments have been appropriately indicated in the various editions of the FASB's *Original Pronouncements* and *Current Text* publications, those effective amendments were not subjected to the Board's review and due process procedures. This Statement identifies those effective amendments and establishes them as Board-approved amendments. In addition, this Statement amends existing authoritative literature (a) to correct references to AICPA guidance that has been revised or superseded since the issuance of that literature and (b) to extend certain provisions to reflect established practice.

STANDARDS OF FINANCIAL ACCOUNTING AND REPORTING

Rescission of Statement 32 and Related Pronouncements

6. This Statement rescinds the following pronouncements:

a. FASB Statement No. 32, *Specialized Accounting and Reporting Principles and Practices in AICPA Statements of Position and Guides on Accounting and Auditing Matters*
b. FASB Statement No. 56, *Designation of AICPA Guide and Statement of Position (SOP) 81-1 on Contractor Accounting and SOP 81-2 concerning Hospital-Related Organizations as Preferable for Purposes of Applying APB Opinion 20*
c. FASB Statement No. 83, *Designation of AICPA Guides and Statement of Position on Accounting by Brokers and Dealers in Securities, by Employee Benefit Plans, and by Banks as Preferable for Purposes of Applying APB Opinion 20.*

Amendments to Opinion 20

7. This Statement amends Opinion 20 as follows:

a. The second and third sentences of paragraph 4 are replaced by the following:

Each Statement and Interpretation of the Financial Accounting Standards Board (FASB), Opinion of the Accounting Principles Board, and AICPA Accounting Research Bulletin specifies its effective date and the manner of reporting a change to conform with the conclusions of that pronouncement. Other pronouncements of the FASB or other designated bodies as described in categories *(b)-(d)* of AICPA Statement on Auditing Standards (SAS) No. 69, *The Meaning of "Present Fairly in Conformity With Generally Accepted Accounting Principles" in the Independent Auditor's Report,* may also prescribe the manner of reporting a change in accounting principle.

b. Footnote 5 is deleted and the penultimate sentence of paragraph 16 is replaced by the following:

The issuance of a new pronouncement by the FASB or by other designated bodies as described in categories *(a)-(d)* of SAS 69 that creates a new accounting principle, interprets an existing principle, expresses a preference for an accounting principle, or rejects a specific principle *may require* an entity to adopt a change in accounting principle. The issuance of such a pronouncement is considered to constitute sufficient support for making a change in accounting principle provided that the hierarchy established by SAS 69 is followed.

Technical Corrections

8. This Statement amends the following pronouncements to make technical corrections to existing authoritative literature:

a. Accounting Research Bulletin No. 43, *Restatement and Revision of Accounting Research Bulletins.*

(1) The following is added after the second sentence of paragraph 1 of Chapter 1A (effectively amended by APB Opinion No. 10, *Omnibus Opinion—1966,* paragraph 12, which reaffirms that the installment method of recognizing revenue is generally not acceptable):

In the absence of the circumstances referred to above or other specific guidance, such as in FASB Statement No. 66, *Accounting for Sales of Real Estate,* the installment method is not acceptable.

(2) In paragraph 6 of Chapter 3A, *and certain types of research and development costs* is deleted from the last sentence (effectively superseded by FASB Statement No. 2, *Accounting for Research and Development*

Costs, paragraph 12, which requires that research and development costs be charged to expense when incurred).

(3) The following is added to the end of paragraph 10 of Chapter 7A (effectively amended by ARB No. 46, *Discontinuance of Dating Earned Surplus,* paragraph 2, which provides guidance as to when the dating of earned surplus should be discontinued):

The dating of earned surplus following a quasi reorganization would rarely, if ever, be of significance after a period of 10 years. There may be exceptional circumstances in which the discontinuance of the dating of earned surplus could be justified at the conclusion of a period less than 10 years.

(4) The last sentence of paragraph 19 of Chapter 10A is deleted (effectively superseded by FASB Statement No. 16, *Prior Period Adjustments,* paragraph 16(a), which amends the accounting for prior period adjustments).

(5) In paragraph 9 of Chapter 11B, everything following *income statement* in the second sentence through the end of that paragraph and footnotes 3 and 4 are deleted (effectively amended by Statement 16, paragraph 16(a), which amends the accounting for prior period adjustments).

b. ARB No. 51, *Consolidated Financial Statements.* Footnote 1 is deleted (effectively superseded by APB Opinion No. 16, *Business Combinations,* paragraph 7, which supersedes ARB No. 48, *Business Combinations*—referenced in footnote 1).

c. APB Opinion No. 6, *Status of Accounting Research Bulletins.* The last sentence of paragraph 16 is amended to refer to APB Opinion No. 18, *The Equity Method of Accounting for Investments in Common Stock* (effectively amended by FASB Statement No. 94, *Consolidation of All Majority-owned Subsidiaries,* paragraph 14, which supersedes paragraph 19 of ARB 51—referenced in paragraph 16).

d. APB Opinion No. 9, *Reporting the Results of Operations.* In paragraph 17, *described below* is deleted from the end of the second sentence (effectively superseded by Statement 16, paragraph 16(a), which deletes paragraphs 23 and 24 of Opinion 9—referenced by paragraph 17).

e. APB Opinion No. 10, *Omnibus Opinion—1966.* In paragraph 11(b), *as called for by paragraph 35 of APB Opinion No. 9,* is deleted

(effectively amended by APB Opinion No. 15, *Earnings per Share,* paragraph 3, which supersedes paragraph 35 of Opinion 9).

f. APB Opinion No. 12, *Omnibus Opinion—1967.* In paragraph 7, footnote 1 is replaced by the following (effectively superseded by FASB Statement No. 106, *Employers' Accounting for Postretirement Benefits Other Than Pensions,* paragraph 13):

The amounts to be accrued periodically shall result in an accrued amount at the full eligibility date (as defined in Statement 106) equal to the then present value of all of the future benefits expected to be paid. Paragraphs 413-416 of Statement 106 illustrate application of this paragraph.

g. APB Opinion No. 15, *Earnings per Share.*

(1) In paragraph 5, *and as described in paragraph 12 of FASB Statement No. 21, Suspension of the Reporting of Earnings per Share and Segment Information by Nonpublic Enterprises* is added at the end of the first sentence (effectively amended by Statement 21, paragraph 15, which amends the scope of Opinion 15).

(2) In Exhibit B of Appendix C, *bank prime rate* is replaced by *average Aa corporate bond yield as defined in FASB Statement No. 85, Yield Test for Determining whether a Convertible Security Is a Common Stock Equivalent* (effectively amended by Statement 85, paragraph 3, which amends the yield test for determining whether a convertible security is a common stock equivalent).

(3) Also in Exhibit B, *cash* is deleted from the term *cash yield* (effectively superseded by Statement 85, paragraph 4, which deletes *cash* from the term *cash yield* in paragraph 35 of Opinion 15).

h. APB Opinion No. 20, *Accounting Changes.* In paragraph 9, *; and a change in accounting for research and development expenditures, such as from recording as expense when incurred to deferring and amortizing the costs* is deleted (effectively amended by Statement 2, paragraph 12, which requires that research and development costs be expensed when incurred).

i. AICPA Accounting Interpretation 1, "Tax Allocation for DISCs," of ARB 51 is deleted (effectively superseded by paragraph 3 of APB Opinion No. 23, *Accounting for Income Taxes—Special Areas,* which supersedes paragraph 16 of ARB 51, the basis for the Interpretation, and by footnote 2 of Opinion 23, which addresses DISCs).

j. AICPA Accounting Interpretation 5, "Investment Credit Is Prior Period Adjustment," of APB Opinion No. 4, *Accounting for the "Investment Credit,"* is deleted (effectively superseded by Statement 16, paragraph 16(a), which amends the accounting for prior period adjustments).

k. AICPA Accounting Interpretation 1, "Accounting for Leases by Manufacturer or Dealer Lessors," of APB Opinion No. 7, *Accounting for Leases in Financial Statements of Lessors,* is deleted (effectively superseded by APB Opinion No. 27, *Accounting for Lease Transactions by Manufacturer or Dealer Lessors,* and Statement 13, paragraph 2, which supersedes Opinions 7 and 27).

l. AICPA Accounting Interpretations 1-28 of APB Opinion No. 8, *Accounting for the Cost of Pension Plans,* are deleted (effectively superseded by FASB Statement No. 87, *Employers' Accounting for Pensions,* paragraph 9, which supersedes Opinion 8).

m. AICPA Accounting Interpretation 2, "Revenue Ruling on LIFO Inventory of Subsidiary," of Opinion 9 is deleted (effectively superseded by Opinion 20, paragraph 5(c), which supersedes paragraph 25 of Opinion 9, which is the basis for the Interpretation).

n. AICPA Accounting Interpretations of Opinion 15.

  (1) In Part I and Interpretations 2, 26, 30, 33, and 92, the phrases *bank prime rate, bank prime interest rate*, and *the prime rate* are replaced with *average Aa corporate bond yield as defined in FASB Statement No. 85, Yield Test for Determining whether a Convertible Security Is a Common Stock Equivalent* (effectively amended by Statement 85, paragraph 3, which amends the yield test for determining whether a convertible security is a common stock equivalent).

  (2) Interpretation 10, "Closely Held Corporations," of Opinion 15 is deleted (effectively superseded by FASB Statement No. 21, *Suspension of the Reporting of Earnings per Share and Segment Information by Nonpublic Enterprises,* paragraph 12, which eliminates the requirements of Opinion 15 for nonpublic enterprises).

  (3) Interpretation 38, "Prime Rate Used in Yield Test," of Opinion 15 is deleted (effec-

tively superseded by Statement 85, paragraph 3, which deletes the use of the bank prime interest rate in yield tests).

o. AICPA Accounting Interpretation 30, "Representations in a Pooling," of Opinion 16. In the second sentence of the sixth paragraph, *paragraph 2 of ARB No. 50* is replaced by *paragraph 3(b) of FASB Statement No. 5, Accounting for Contingencies* (effectively amended by Statement 5, paragraph 7, which supersedes ARB No. 50, *Contingencies*).

p. AICPA Accounting Interpretation 2, "Investments in Partnerships and Ventures," of Opinion 18. In the fourth paragraph, *contrary to the provisions of paragraph 19-j (income taxes on undistributed earnings of subsidiaries),* is deleted (effectively amended by Opinion 23, paragraph 3, which supersedes paragraph 19-j of Opinion 18).

q. AICPA Accounting Interpretation 1, "Disclosure of 'Leveraged Lease' Transactions by Lessors," of APB Opinion No. 22, *Disclosure of Accounting Policies,* is deleted (effectively superseded by paragraphs 41-47 of Statement 13, which specify the accounting and disclosure requirements for lessors in leveraged lease transactions).

r. AICPA Accounting Interpretation 1, "Debt Tendered to Exercise Warrants," of APB Opinion No. 26, *Early Extinguishment of Debt.*

  (1) In the first paragraph, *before its scheduled maturity* is deleted (effectively amended by FASB Statement No. 76, *Extinguishment of Debt,* paragraph 9, which deletes this phrase from Opinion 26).

  (2) In the second paragraph, *"pursuant to the existing conversion privileges of the holder" (see paragraph 2 of the Opinion)* is deleted (effectively amended by Statement 76, paragraph 7, which supersedes paragraph 2 of Opinion 26).

s. FASB Statement No. 5, *Accounting for Contingencies.* The second sentence in paragraph 18 is replaced by the following (effectively amended because the documents referenced have been superseded):

  Subsequent Opinions issued by the Accounting Principles Board and Statements issued by the Financial Accounting Standards Board established more explicit disclosure requirements for a number of those items.

t. FASB Statement No. 14, *Financial Reporting for Segments of a Business Enterprise.* In paragraph 27(c), *unconsolidated subsidiaries and other* is deleted (effectively amended by Statement 94, paragraph 15, which deletes this phrase from Opinion 18).

u. FASB Statement No. 25, *Suspension of Certain Accounting Requirements for Oil and Gas Producing Companies.* Paragraphs 6 and 8 are deleted (effectively superseded by FASB Statement No. 69, *Disclosures about Oil and Gas Producing Activities,* paragraph 5, which deletes paragraphs in FASB Statement No. 19, *Financial Accounting and Reporting by Oil and Gas Producing Companies,* relating to disclosure requirements).

v. FASB Statement No. 55, *Determining whether a Convertible Security Is a Common Stock Equivalent,* is superseded (effectively superseded by Statement 85, paragraph 3, which amends the yield test for determining whether a convertible security is a common stock equivalent).

w. FASB Statement No. 67, *Accounting for Costs and Initial Rental Operations of Real Estate Projects.*

(1) In paragraph 2(b), the reference to FASB Statement No. 17, *Accounting for Leases—Initial Direct Costs,* and the last sentence are deleted and replaced by the following:

> FASB Statement No. 91, *Accounting for Nonrefundable Fees and Costs Associated with Originating or Acquiring Loans and Initial Direct Costs of Leases.* The accounting for initial direct costs is prescribed in FASB Statement No. 13, *Accounting for Leases,* as amended by Statement 91 and FASB Statement No. 98, *Accounting for Leases: Sale-Leaseback Transactions Involving Real Estate, Sales-Type Leases of Real Estate, Definition of the Lease Term, and Initial Direct Costs of Direct Financing Leases.*

(Paragraph 2(b) is effectively amended by Statement 91, paragraphs 24 and 25, which supersede Statement 17, amend the definition of initial direct costs, and amend the accounting for initial direct costs of direct financing leases, and by Statement 98, subparagraphs 22(h) and (i), which reflect the intent of the amendment made by Statement 91.)

(2) In footnote 10, the reference to Statement 17 is replaced by a reference to Statement 91

and *as amended by Statements 91 and 98* is added to the end of the second sentence.

x. FASB Statement No. 76, *Extinguishment of Debt.* The following is added to the end of paragraph 7 (effectively amended by FASB Statement No. 84, *Induced Conversions of Convertible Debt,* paragraph 5, which amends paragraph 2 of Opinion 26—referenced in paragraph 7):

> Also, this Opinion does not apply to a conversion of convertible debt when conversion privileges provided in the terms of the debt at issuance are changed (including changes that involve payment of consideration) to induce conversion of the debt to equity securities in accordance with the conditions of paragraph 2 of FASB Statement No. 84, *Induced Conversions of Convertible Debt.*

y. FASB Statement No. 105, *Disclosure of Information about Financial Instruments with Off-Balance-Sheet Risk and Financial Instruments with Concentrations of Credit Risk.* In paragraph 14(c), *No. 81, Disclosure of Postretirement Health Care and Life Insurance Benefits* is replaced by *No. 106, Employers' Accounting for Postretirement Benefits Other Than Pensions* (effectively amended by Statement 106, paragraph 12, which supersedes Statement 81).

z. FASB Interpretation No. 18, *Accounting for Income Taxes in Interim Periods.* Footnote 5 is deleted (effectively superseded by FASB Statement No. 97, *Accounting and Reporting by Insurance Enterprises for Certain Long-Duration Contracts and for Realized Gains and Losses from the Sale of Investments,* paragraph 28).

aa. FASB Technical Bulletin No. 79-8, *Applicability of FASB Statements 21 and 33 to Certain Brokers and Dealers in Securities.* In paragraphs 5 and 6, *statement of changes in financial position* is replaced by *statement of cash flows* (effectively amended by FASB Statement No. 95, *Statement of Cash Flows,* paragraph 152, which requires this change in other pronouncements).

bb. FASB Technical Bulletin No. 80-1, *Early Extinguishment of Debt through Exchange for Common or Preferred Stock.*

(1) In paragraphs 1-4, *early* is deleted (effectively amended by Statement 76, paragraph 9, which requires this change in Opinion 26).

(2) In the last sentence of paragraph 2, *before the scheduled maturity of the debt* and *early* is deleted (effectively amended by Statement 76, paragraph 8, which replaces the concept of early extinguishment).

(3) In the last sentence of paragraph 3, *as amended by FASB Statements No. 76, Extinguishment of Debt, and No. 84, Induced Conversions of Convertible Debt*, is added after *Opinion 26* (effectively amended by Statement 76, paragraph 7, and Statement 84, paragraph 5, which amend the applicability of Opinion 26).

(4) In paragraph 4, *a conversion by the holder pursuant to conversion privileges contained in the original debt issue* is replaced by the following (effectively amended by Statement 76, paragraph 7, and Statement 84, paragraph 5, which amend the applicability of Opinion 26):

a conversion of debt to equity securities of the debtor (a) pursuant to conversion privileges provided in the terms of the debt at issuance or (b) when conversion privileges provided in the terms of the debt at issuance are changed (including changes that involve payment of consideration) to induce conversion of the debt to equity securities in accordance with the conditions of paragraph 2 of Statement 84.

cc. FASB Technical Bulletin No. 81-3, *Multiemployer Pension Plan Amendments Act of 1980.* This Technical Bulletin is superseded (effectively superseded by Statement 87, paragraph 9, which supersedes Opinion 8).

dd. FASB Technical Bulletin No. 85-2, *Accounting for Collateralized Mortgage Obligations (CMOs).* Footnote 9 is deleted (effectively superseded by Statement 94, paragraph 13, which amends ARB 51 to require consolidation of all majority-owned subsidiaries).

9. This Statement amends the following pronouncements to delete or amend references to AICPA pronouncements that have been revised or superseded:

a. APB Opinion No. 20, *Accounting Changes.*

(1) In paragraph 7, the quotation marks in the second sentence and footnote 2 are deleted.

(2) In footnote 4, *Statement on Auditing Procedure No. 41, Subsequent Discovery of Facts Existing at the Date of the Auditor's Report* is replaced by *Section 561 of Statement on Auditing Standards No. 1, Codification of Auditing Standards and Procedures.*

b. APB Opinion No. 22, *Disclosure of Accounting Policies.* In footnote 2, *(see Statement on Auditing Procedure No. 38, paragraphs 5 and 6)* and *(see Statement on Auditing Procedure No. 33, Chapter 13, paragraphs 9 and 10)* are deleted.

c. AICPA Accounting Interpretation 56, "Fair Value Used If No Market Price," of Opinion 15. In the fourth paragraph, *Audits of Personal Financial Statements (an AICPA Industry Audit Guide published by the American Institute of CPAs in 1968)* is replaced by *Personal Financial Statements Guide (an Audit and Accounting Guide published by the American Institute of CPAs).*

d. FASB Statement No. 15, *Accounting by Debtors and Creditors for Troubled Debt Restructurings.*

(1) Footnote 20 is deleted (effectively superseded for finance companies by the AICPA Audit and Accounting Guide, *Audits of Finance Companies (Including Independent and Captive Financing Activities of Other Companies),* and for other entities by Statement 91).

(2) The last sentence in footnote 26 is deleted.

10. FASB Interpretation No. 20, *Reporting Accounting Changes under AICPA Statements of Position,* is amended to reflect established practice that has extended the provisions of Interpretation 20 to include AICPA Practice Bulletins, FASB Technical Bulletins, and EITF consensuses.

a. In the first sentence of paragraph 5, *or practice bulletin, an FASB technical bulletin, or a consensus of the FASB Emerging Issues Task Force (EITF)* is added after *statement of position* and at the end of the sentence *statement* is replaced by *pronouncement.*

b. The second sentence is replaced by the following:

If the pronouncement does not specify the manner of reporting a change in accounting principle to conform with its recommendations, an enterprise making a change in accounting principle to conform with the recommendations of the pronouncement shall report the change as specified by Opinion 20, except that EITF consensuses may be applied prospectively to future transactions unless otherwise stated.

The paragraph will then read as follows:

For purposes of applying *APB Opinion No. 20,* an enterprise making a change in accounting principle to conform with the recommendations of an AICPA statement of position or practice bulletin, an FASB technical bulletin, or a consensus of the FASB Emerging Issues Task Force (EITF) shall report the change as specified in the pronouncement. If the pronouncement does not specify the manner of reporting a change in accounting principle to conform with its recommendations, an enterprise making a change in accounting principle to conform with the recommendations of the pronouncement shall report the change as specified by Opinion 20, except that EITF consensuses may be applied prospectively to future transactions unless otherwise stated.

Effective Date

11. This Statement is effective November 30, 1992.

This Statement was adopted by the unanimous vote of the seven members of the Financial Accounting Standards Board:

Dennis R. Beresford,	Victor H. Brown	A. Clarence Sampson
Chairman	James J. Leisenring	Robert J. Swieringa
Joseph V. Anania	Robert H. Northcutt	

Appendix

BACKGROUND INFORMATION AND BASIS FOR CONCLUSIONS

Rescission of Statement 32

12. In 1979, the Board decided to exercise responsibility for all specialized accounting and reporting principles and practices in AICPA SOPs and Guides on accounting and auditing matters by extracting the specialized principles and practices from those documents and, after appropriate due process, issuing them as FASB Statements. That decision, made after extensive public comment, responded to a statement by the Securities and Exchange Commission in its 1978 report to Congress on its oversight of the accounting profession that "in the long run, the FASB should develop a mechanism for dealing . . . with accounting matters related to particular industries that are now covered by SOPs."

13. To clarify any uncertainty about the ongoing status of those specialized principles and practices and alleviate concern that those accounting principles would not be followed pending release of final FASB Statements, the Board in September 1979 issued Statement 32. Statement 32 designated the specialized[1] accounting and reporting principles in AICPA Guides and SOPs as preferable for purposes of justifying a change in accounting principles as required by Opinion 20.

14. Under the GAAP hierarchy that existed at the time Statement 32 was issued, as established by the AICPA in July 1975 in Statement on Auditing Standards No. 5, *The Meaning of "Present Fairly in Conformity With Generally Accepted Accounting Principles" in the Independent Auditor's Report,*[2] AICPA Guides, Interpretations, and SOPs together with FASB Technical Bulletins and widely recognized industry practice were considered secondary sources of established accounting principles—categories *(b)* and *(c).* If the accounting treatment of a transaction or event was not specified by a pronouncement covered by Rule 203 of the AICPA *Code of Professional Conduct,*[3] an established principle from any of those secondary sources could be used for financial reporting as long as it fairly presented the substance of the transaction.

15. Statement 32 did not require entities to change their specialized accounting and reporting practices to those contained in the AICPA Guides and SOPs. Statement 32 did, however, provide preferability status to the AICPA Guides and SOPs for

---

[1]The term *specialized* was used to refer to those current accounting and reporting principles and practices in existing AICPA Guides and SOPs that were neither superseded by nor contained in FASB Statements, FASB Interpretations, APB Opinions, and AICPA Accounting Research Bulletins.

[2]SAS 5 is codified in AICPA *Professional Standards,* Volume I, in AU section 411 and was superseded in January 1992 by SAS 69.

[3]Pronouncements covered by Rule 203—category *(a)*—of the AICPA *Code of Professional Conduct* include FASB Statements, FASB Interpretations, APB Opinions, and AICPA Accounting Research Bulletins.

the purpose of applying Opinion 20 so an entity electing to change its accounting treatment did not have to justify changing to the accounting specified by an AICPA Guide or SOP and an entity applying that accounting could not adopt a change to something less preferable. Likewise, an entity proposing a change to something other than a specialized accounting principle contained in an AICPA Guide or SOP had to justify that change.

16. Statement 32 lists the AICPA Guides and SOPs that contain specialized accounting and reporting principles considered preferable by the Board for the purpose of applying Opinion 20. The Board has amended Statement 32 twice, with the issuance of Statements 56 and 83, to add new audit and accounting Guides and SOPs issued by the AICPA and to delete those that have been superseded. The Board last amended Statement 32 in March 1985 (with the issuance of Statement 83) and has postponed subsequent amendments pending completion by the AICPA of its reexamination of the GAAP hierarchy. That reexamination resulted in SAS 69, issued in January 1992, which revises the GAAP hierarchy.

17. The revised GAAP hierarchy under SAS 69 (as summarized in paragraph 25) clearly indicates the accounting treatment required for a specific event or transaction when that event or transaction is not covered by Rule 203 guidance. SAS 69, paragraph 7, states:

> If the accounting treatment of a transaction or event is not specified by a pronouncement covered by rule 203, the auditor should consider whether the accounting treatment is specified by another source of established accounting principles. If an established accounting principle from one or more sources in category *(b)*, *(c)*, or *(d)* is relevant to the circumstances, the auditor should be prepared to justify a conclusion that another treatment is generally accepted. If there is a conflict between accounting principles relevant to the circumstances from one or more sources in category *(b)*, *(c)*, or *(d)*, the auditor should follow the treatment specified by the source in the higher category—for example, follow category *(b)* treatment over category *(c)*— or be prepared to justify a conclusion that a treatment specified by a source in the lower category better presents the substance of the transaction in the circumstances.

18. SAS 69 requires an entity to adopt a new pronouncement in categories *(b)-(d)* (as summarized in paragraph 25) that becomes effective after March 15, 1992. An entity following an established accounting principle (in categories *(b)* and *(c)* under the previous GAAP hierarchy) as of March 15, 1992 need not change its accounting treatment unless it chooses to make a change or unless a new pronouncement becomes effective in categories *(b)-(d)* (under SAS 69) after March 15, 1992. The transition provisions of SAS 69 state that an entity initially applying an accounting principle or making a change in accounting principle after March 15, 1992 must follow the applicable hierarchy as set forth in categories *(b)-(d)* except when initially applying FASB Emerging Issues Task Force consensus positions issued before March 16, 1992. Those consensuses "become effective in the hierarchy for initial application of an accounting principle after March 15, 1993."

19. With the issuance of SAS 69 the Board believes that there is no longer any uncertainty regarding the ongoing status of the specialized accounting and reporting principles and practices in AICPA Guides and SOPs. Consequently, the Board decided that the guidance provided by Statement 32 and related pronouncements is no longer needed and that those Statements should be rescinded.

Technical Corrections

20. At the time a pronouncement is developed by the Board, part of the process requires that a determination be made of the effect this new guidance will have on existing authoritative accounting pronouncements. If there is an effect, then the new pronouncement should amend or supersede the existing authoritative literature in detail so that there is (a) no doubt about what the amendment changes and (b) no conflict between the requirements of prior pronouncements and the requirements of the new pronouncement.

21. In the past, certain detailed amendments that could have been explicitly made to the authoritative literature were omitted. Those omissions occurred for various reasons. For example, because of a difference in style some pronouncements made general rather than specific amendments to prior pronouncements, and some needed technical amendments were overlooked when the new pronouncement was prepared.

22. As those omissions were discovered by the FASB staff or members of the accounting profession, corrections were made to the various editions of the FASB's *Original Pronouncements* and *Current Text* publications through effective amendments. However, those effective technical amendments have not been subjected to the Board's usual due process procedures. With the decision to issue a Statement to rescind Statement 32, the Board also decided to take this opportunity to identify

those effective amendments and issue them as Board-approved amendments.

23. The Board considered what parts of previously issued pronouncements to amend and decided that only the official guidance sections should be amended. The Board believes that the introduction, background information, and basis for conclusions paragraphs provide historical information that should not be amended or superseded unless the entire pronouncement is superseded. Those paragraphs are considered historical because they document the circumstances surrounding the development of a pronouncement. For example, they record (a) the reasons why the accounting requirements were considered to be necessary at that time, (b) what alternative guidance was considered, and (c) what the public comments were regarding the proposed requirements and how those comments were resolved.

24. In addition to the accounting guidance and historical paragraphs (described above), a pronouncement sometimes contains other paragraphs or appendixes. Those paragraphs or appendixes are ones that (a) state the scope of the pronouncement, (b) indicate substantive amendments to other existing pronouncements, (c) present examples or illustrations of application of the requirements of the pronouncement, and (d) present a glossary of the terms used in the pronouncement. The Board discussed the content of those various paragraphs and appendixes and decided that that material is part of the accounting guidance of the pronouncement and should be amended if the pronouncement is amended by a subsequent pronouncement. The Board further decided that when a pronouncement is superseded, the amendments made by that superseded pronouncement remain in effect unless they are explicitly amended.

Summary of GAAP Hierarchy under SAS 69

25. The chart below summarizes the GAAP hierarchy for financial statements of nongovernmental entities[4] under SAS 69.

Established Accounting Principles

Category *(a)*— FASB Statements and Interpretations, APB Opinions, and AICPA Accounting Research Bulletins

Category *(b)*— FASB Technical Bulletins, cleared[5] AICPA Industry Audit and Accounting Guides, and cleared AICPA Statements of Position

Category *(c)*— Consensus positions of the FASB Emerging Issues Task Force and cleared AICPA AcSEC Practice Bulletins

Category *(d)*— AICPA Accounting Interpretations, FASB Implementation Guides (Q&As), and widely recognized and prevalent industry practices

Other Accounting Literature

Other accounting literature, including FASB concepts Statements; APB Statements; AICPA Issues Papers; International Accounting Standards Committee Statements; GASB Statements, Interpretations, and Technical Bulletins; pronouncements of other professional associations or regulatory agencies; AICPA *Technical Practice Aids;* and accounting textbooks, handbooks, and articles.

Comments on Exposure Draft

26. The Board issued an Exposure Draft of a proposed Statement, *Rescission of FASB Statement No. 32 and Technical Corrections,* for comment on June 30, 1992 and received 21 letters of comment. Most of the respondents agreed that Statement 32 and related pronouncements should be rescinded.

27. Several respondents said that the guidance in Opinion 20, paragraph 4, which addresses scope, and paragraph 16 and footnote 5, which address the support needed to make a change in accounting principle, were confusing in view of the guidance

---

[4] "Rules and interpretive releases of the Securities and Exchange Commission (SEC) have an authority similar to category *(a)* pronouncements for SEC registrants. In addition, the SEC staff issues Staff Accounting Bulletins that represent practices followed by the staff in administering SEC disclosure requirements. Also, the Introduction to the FASB's *EITF Abstracts* states that the Securities and Exchange Commission's Chief Accountant has said that the SEC staff would challenge any accounting that differs from a consensus of the FASB Emerging Issues Task Force, because the consensus position represents the best thinking on areas for which there are no specific standards" (quoted from footnote 3 of SAS 69).

[5] As used in SAS 69, *cleared* means that the FASB has indicated that it does not object to the issuance of the proposed pronouncement. Footnote 4 of SAS 69 states that it should be assumed that such pronouncements have been cleared by the FASB unless the pronouncement indicates otherwise.

set forth in SAS 69. The Board agreed and has revised the amendment to Opinion 20 in paragraph 7 of this Statement to address this concern. In addition, the amendment to Interpretation 20 in paragraph 10 of this Statement was revised to clarify the application of EITF consensuses. Unless a consensus specifies the manner of reporting a change in accounting principle, an enterprise making a change in accounting principle to conform with an EITF consensus may apply the consensus prospectively to future transactions or may apply the provisions of Opinion 20 to prior transactions.

28. A majority of respondents agreed with the technical corrections. Several respondents indicated support for the practice of making needed technical corrections when they are identified and then formally issuing those corrections as Board-approved amendments after due process. A few respondents had suggestions for additional amendments. Because those suggested amendments were considered to be more substantive than technical corrections or were to sections of pronouncements that are not normally amended, they are not included in this Statement.

Statement of Financial Accounting Standards No. 112
Employers' Accounting for Postemployment Benefits

an amendment of FASB Statements No. 5 and 43

STATUS

Issued: November 1992

Effective Date: For fiscal years beginning after December 15, 1993

Affects: Amends FAS 5, paragraph 7
Amends FAS 43, paragraph 1
Supersedes FAS 43, paragraph 2
Amends FAS 107, paragraph 8(a)

Affected by: Paragraph 5(d) amended by FAS 123

Issues Discussed by FASB Emerging Issues Task Force (EITF)

Affects: No EITF Issues

Interpreted by: No EITF Issues

Related Issue: EITF Issue No. 96-5

SUMMARY

This Statement establishes accounting standards for employers who provide benefits to former or inactive employees after employment but before retirement (referred to in this Statement as *postemployment benefits*). Postemployment benefits are all types of benefits provided to former or inactive employees, their beneficiaries, and covered dependents. Those benefits include, but are not limited to, salary continuation, supplemental unemployment benefits, severance benefits, disability-related benefits (including workers' compensation), job training and counseling, and continuation of benefits such as health care benefits and life insurance coverage.

This Statement requires employers to recognize the obligation to provide postemployment benefits in accordance with FASB Statement No. 43, *Accounting for Compensated Absences,* if the obligation is attributable to employees' services already rendered, employees' rights to those benefits accumulate or vest, payment of the benefits is probable, and the amount of the benefits can be reasonably estimated. If those four conditions are not met, the employer should account for postemployment benefits when it is probable that a liability has been incurred and the amount can be reasonably estimated in accordance with FASB Statement No. 5, *Accounting for Contingencies.* If an obligation for postemployment benefits is not accrued in accordance with Statements 5 or 43 only because the amount cannot be reasonably estimated, the financial statements shall disclose that fact.

This Statement is effective for fiscal years beginning after December 15, 1993.

Statement of Financial Accounting Standards No. 112

Employers' Accounting for Postemployment Benefits

an amendment of FASB Statements No. 5 and 43

CONTENTS

INTRODUCTION

1. This Statement establishes standards of financial accounting and reporting for the estimated cost of benefits provided by an employer to former or inactive employees after employment but before retirement (referred to in this Statement as *postemployment benefits*). Postemployment benefits are all types of benefits provided to former or inactive employees, their beneficiaries, and covered dependents. Inactive employees are those who are not currently rendering service to the employer and who have not been terminated. They include those who have been laid off and those on disability leave, regardless of whether they are expected to return to active status. Postemployment benefits include, but are not limited to, salary continuation, supplemental unemployment benefits, severance benefits, disability-related benefits (including workers' compensation), job training and counseling, and continuation of benefits such as health care benefits and life insurance coverage.

2. Prior to this Statement, employers' accounting for the cost of postemployment benefits varied. Some employers accrued the estimated cost of those benefits over the related service periods of active employees. Other employers applied a terminal accrual approach and recognized the estimated cost of those benefits at the date of the event giving rise to the payment of the benefits (for example, the death of an active employee, the temporary or permanent disability of an active employee, or the layoff of an employee). Still other employers recognized the cost of postemployment benefits when they were paid (cash basis). Some employers may have used different methods of accounting for different types of benefits.

3. The Board concluded that postemployment benefits are part of the compensation provided to an employee in exchange for service. FASB Statement No. 43, *Accounting for Compensated Absences,* addresses amounts paid to active employees while on a compensated absence, such as for vacation, occasional sick days, and holidays. Other long-term fringe benefits and postemployment benefits, however, are specifically excluded from the scope of that Statement. In addition, all employment-related costs are excluded from the scope of FASB Statement No. 5, *Accounting for Contingencies.* This Statement affirms the Board's view that generally accepted accounting principles require recognition of the cost of postemployment benefits on an accrual basis and amends Statements 5 and 43 to include the accounting for postemployment benefits. Therefore, Statement 43 will (a) continue to specify the accounting for amounts paid to active employees while on a compensated absence, such as for vacation, occasional sick days, and holidays, (b) continue to not address other long-term fringe benefits provided to active employees, and (c) specify the accounting for postemployment benefits provided to former or inac-

tive employees prior to retirement that meet the conditions in paragraph 6. Statement 5 will specify the accounting for postemployment benefits that are not addressed by Statement 43 or by other FASB Statements or APB Opinions.

STANDARDS OF FINANCIAL ACCOUNTING AND REPORTING

Scope

4. This Statement applies to all types of postemployment benefits provided to former or inactive employees, their beneficiaries, and covered dependents after employment but before retirement, except as noted in the following paragraph. Benefits may be provided in cash or in kind and may be paid as a result of a disability, layoff, death, or other event. Benefits may be paid immediately upon cessation of active employment or over a specified period of time. Employees' rights to benefits may accumulate or vest as they render service.

5. This Statement does not apply to:

a. Postemployment benefits provided through a pension or postretirement benefit plan (FASB Statements No. 87, *Employers' Accounting for Pensions,* No. 88, *Employers' Accounting for Settlements and Curtailments of Defined Benefit Pension Plans and for Termination Benefits,* and No. 106, *Employers' Accounting for Postretirement Benefits Other Than Pensions,* specify the accounting for those costs.)
b. Individual deferred compensation arrangements that are addressed by APB Opinion No. 12, *Omnibus Opinion—1967,* as amended by Statement 106
c. Special or contractual termination benefits covered by Statements 88 and 106
d. Stock compensation plans that are addressed by APB Opinion No. 25, *Accounting for Stock Issued to Employees.*

Accounting for Postemployment Benefits

6. Postemployment benefits that meet the conditions in paragraph 6 of Statement 43 shall be accounted for in accordance with that Statement. Paragraph 6 of Statement 43 states:

An employer shall accrue a liability for employees' compensation for future absences if *all* of the following conditions are met:

a. The employer's obligation relating to employees' rights to receive compensa-

tion for future absences is attributable to employees' services already rendered,
b. The obligation relates to rights that vest or accumulate,
c. Payment of the compensation is probable, and
d. The amount can be reasonably estimated. [Footnote references omitted.]

Postemployment benefits that are within the scope of this Statement and that do not meet those conditions shall be accounted for in accordance with Statement 5. Paragraph 8 of Statement 5 states:

An estimated loss from a loss contingency (as defined in paragraph 1) shall be accrued by a charge to income if *both* of the following conditions are met:

a. Information available prior to issuance of the financial statements indicates that it is probable that an asset had been impaired or a liability had been incurred at the date of the financial statements. It is implicit in this condition that it must be probable that one or more future events will occur confirming the fact of the loss.
b. The amount of loss can be reasonably estimated. [Footnote references omitted.]

Disclosures

7. If an obligation for postemployment benefits is not accrued in accordance with Statements 5 or 43 only because the amount cannot be reasonably estimated, the financial statements shall disclose that fact.

Amendments to Existing Pronouncements

8. The following sentences are added to the end of paragraph 1 of Statement 43:

This Statement also applies to all forms of postemployment benefits, as defined in FASB Statement No. 112, *Employers' Accounting for Postemployment Benefits,* that meet the conditions in paragraph 6 of this Statement, except as noted in the following paragraph. Postemployment benefits that do not meet the conditions in paragraph 6 of this Statement shall be accounted for in accordance with FASB Statement No. 5, *Accounting for Contingencies,* as amended by Statement 112. This Statement does not address the accounting for benefits paid to active employees other than compensated absences.

9. The following paragraph replaces paragraph 2 of Statement 43:

This Statement does not apply to:

a. Postemployment benefits provided through a pension or postretirement benefit plan (FASB Statements No. 87, *Employers' Accounting for Pensions,* No. 88, *Employers' Accounting for Settlements and Curtailments of Defined Benefit Pension Plans and for Termination Benefits,* and No. 106, *Employers' Accounting for Postretirement Benefits Other Than Pensions,* specify the accounting for those costs.)

b. Individual deferred compensation arrangements that are addressed by APB Opinion No. 12, *Omnibus Opinion—1967,* as amended by Statement 106

c. Special or contractual termination benefits covered by Statements 88 and 106

d. Stock compensation plans that are addressed by APB Opinion No. 25, *Accounting for Stock Issued to Employees.*

This Statement does not address the allocation of costs of compensated absences to interim periods. The cost of postemployment benefits as determined under this Statement that is directly related to the disposal of a segment of a business or a portion of a line of business shall be recognized pursuant to the requirements of APB Opinion No. 30, *Reporting the Results of Operations—Reporting the Effects of Disposal of a Segment of a Business, and Extraordinary, Unusual and Infrequently Occurring Events and Transactions,* and included in determining the gain or loss associated with that event.

10. The last two sentences of paragraph 7 of Statement 5 are deleted and replaced by the following sentence:

Accounting for other employment-related costs is also excluded from the scope of this Statement except for postemployment benefits that become subject to this Statement through application of FASB Statement No. 112, *Employers' Accounting for Postemployment Benefits.*

11. In paragraph 8(a) of FASB Statement No. 107, *Disclosures about Fair Value of Financial Instruments,* the words *postemployment benefits,* are inserted after *other postretirement benefits including health care and life insurance benefits,* and No. 112, *Employers' Accounting for Postemployment Benefits,* is inserted after No. 106, *Employers' Accounting for Postretirement Benefits Other Than Pensions,* to exclude an employer's obligation for postemployment benefits from the requirements for disclosures about fair value.

Effective Date and Transition

12. This Statement shall be effective for fiscal years beginning after December 15, 1993. Earlier application is encouraged. The effect of initially applying this Statement shall be reported as the effect of a change in accounting principle in a manner similar to the cumulative effect of a change in accounting principle (APB Opinion No. 20, *Accounting Changes,* paragraph 20). Pro forma effects of retroactive application (Opinion 20, paragraph 21) are not required. Previously issued financial statements shall not be restated.

The provisions of this Statement need not be applied to immaterial items.

This Statement was adopted by the unanimous vote of the seven members of the Financial Accounting Standards Board:

Dennis R. Beresford,	Victor H. Brown	A. Clarence Sampson
Chairman	James J. Leisenring	Robert J. Swieringa
Joseph V. Anania	Robert H. Northcutt	

Appendix

BACKGROUND INFORMATION AND BASIS FOR CONCLUSIONS

CONTENTS

Introduction

13. This appendix summarizes considerations that were deemed significant by Board members in reaching the conclusions in this Statement. It discusses reasons for accepting certain views and rejecting others. Individual Board members gave greater weight to some factors than to others.

14. The Board issued the Exposure Draft, *Employers' Accounting for Postemployment Benefits,* for public comment on May 12, 1992. Fifty-nine comment letters were received and most respondents agreed with the Board that the cost of postemployment benefits should be accounted for on an accrual basis. The Board concluded that it could reach an informed decision on the basis of existing information without a public hearing.

Background

15. The project on employers' accounting for pensions and other postemployment benefits was initially added to the Board's agenda in 1979. In 1984, the Board concluded that it should address employers' accounting for postemployment benefits other than pensions as a separate project. In 1987, the Board deferred consideration of issues relating to benefits provided after employment but before retirement to focus its resources on postretirement benefits other than pensions. The Board excluded postemployment benefits from the scope of Statement 106:

> The accounting for benefits paid after employment but before retirement (for example, layoff benefits) is a separate phase of the Board's project on accounting for postemployment benefits other than pensions. The fact that this Statement does not apply to those benefits should not be construed as discouraging the use of accrual accounting for those benefits. [footnote 2]

Consequently, accounting for postemployment benefits other than retirement benefits is the final phase of the Board's project on employers' accounting for pensions and other postemployment benefits.

Applicability of Other Pronouncements

16. Certain postemployment benefits are covered by existing Statements or Opinions. Accounting for deferred compensation contracts is covered by Opinion 12 (as amended by Statement 106). Accounting for contractual and special termination benefits is covered by Statements 88 and 106. Accounting for the disposal of a segment of a business is covered by Opinion 30. Accounting for benefits paid after retirement is covered by Statements 87, 88, and 106. This Statement does not change the accounting for those benefits.

17. The Board considered whether guidance is needed in addressing employers' accounting for postemployment benefits. In the Board's view, Statements 5 and 43 specify appropriate accounting for postemployment benefits. However, postemployment benefits were specifically excluded from the scope of those Statements because at the time those Statements were issued the Board had a project on its agenda to address the accounting for pensions and other postemployment benefits. Since that time, the Board issued Statements that address postretirement benefits but none that address the accounting for postemployment benefits. The Board, therefore, concluded that it is appropriate to amend Statements 5 and 43 to include the accounting for postemployment benefits.

18. Several respondents to the Exposure Draft commented that it would be inappropriate to account for postemployment benefits by applying the criteria in Statement 43. They stated that postemployment benefits generally do not vest and if postemployment benefits do not vest, an employer does not have an obligation to provide benefits un-

til a future event occurs. The Board considered whether an employer's liability to provide nonvesting postemployment benefits arises only when a future event, such as termination or disability, occurs. If the rights to nonvesting postemployment benefits accumulate over the service period, then the event that creates a liability and affects the amount of benefits is the rendering of service by employees. If the payment of those benefits is probable and can be reasonably estimated, then the cost of those benefits should be recognized as they are earned by the employees. The Board concluded that if postemployment benefits meet the conditions in paragraph 6 of Statement 43, then the estimated cost of those benefits should be recognized in accordance with that Statement.

19. Some respondents noted that Statement 43 does not require employers to accrue a liability for nonvesting accumulating rights to receive sick pay benefits and questioned whether that exception would apply to nonvesting accumulating rights to receive postemployment benefits. In developing Statement 43, the Board concluded that probable payments for accumulating sick pay benefits would rarely be material unless they vest or are paid without an illness-related absence. The Board also noted that the lower degree of reliability associated with estimates of future sick pay and the cost of making and evaluating those estimates did not justify a requirement for an accrual.

20. Unlike nonvesting sick pay, nonvesting postemployment benefits may be material for certain employers, especially in certain industries, depending on many factors including, but not limited to, the duration of benefit payments and the incidence of events giving rise to the payment of benefits. In addition, the fact that there are employers currently accruing the estimated cost of those benefits, some over applicable employee service periods and others using a terminal accrual approach, suggests that sufficient information is available to many employers on which to develop a reliable estimate without significant cost. Accordingly, the Board concluded that the exception in Statement 43 should not be extended to postemployment benefits.

21. If postemployment benefits do not meet the conditions in paragraph 6 of Statement 43, then employers should recognize the estimated cost of those benefits in accordance with Statement 5. Statement 5 requires recognition of a loss contingency when it is probable that an asset has been impaired or a liability has been incurred and the amount of the loss can be reasonably estimated. Paragraph 59 of Statement 5 further clarifies the recognition of loss contingencies:

. . . even losses that are reasonably estimable should not be accrued if it is not probable that an asset has been impaired or a liability has been incurred at the date of an enterprise's financial statements because those losses relate to a future period rather than the current or a prior period.

22. For example, an employer may provide any former employee on permanent disability with continued medical insurance coverage until that employee meets the requirements for participation in the employer's postretirement medical plan. If the level of benefits provided is the same for any disabled employee regardless of years of service, the cost of those benefits should be recognized when the event causing a permanent disability occurs and a reasonable estimate can be made as specified by Statement 5.

23. Several respondents requested that this Statement provide guidance on how to measure an employer's postemployment benefit obligation. FASB Statements 87 and 106 discuss measurement issues extensively. To the extent that similar issues apply to postemployment benefit plans, employers may refer to those Statements for guidance in measuring their obligations in compliance with the requirements of this Statement. Respondents also asked the Board to provide explicit guidance on the applicability and use of discounting. Statements 5 and 43 do not provide explicit guidance and re-addressing those Statements is beyond the intended scope of this project. In addition, discounting is being addressed in the Board's existing project on present-value-based measurements. Accordingly, the Board decided not to provide explicit guidance on discounting in this Statement. As a result, the Board understands that the use of discounting in measuring postemployment benefit obligations will continue to be permitted but not required.

Disclosures

24. Statements 5 and 43 require disclosure if it is probable that an obligation has been incurred but it cannot be reasonably estimated. Statement 5 requires additional disclosures in other situations including when it is reasonably possible that a liability has been incurred. The Board decided not to apply the additional Statement 5 disclosures to postemployment benefit obligations because it believes that the additional cost of compliance is not warranted. Thus, this Statement requires disclosure only if an obligation for postemployment benefits is not accrued in accordance with Statements 5 or 43 solely because the amount cannot be reasonably estimated.

Effective Date and Transition

25. The effect of initially applying this Statement is to be reported as the effect of a change in accounting principle. Some respondents recommended that an option be provided to recognize that effect over future periods. The Board considered whether a provision for delayed recognition of the transition amount was needed. A major objective of transition is to minimize implementation costs and mitigate disruption without unduly compromising the ability of financial statements to provide useful information. An important factor considered by the Board was the potential magnitude of the unrecorded postemployment benefit obligation. Information made available to the Board indicated that postemployment benefits are generally not as significant as pension or other postretirement benefits. The Board concluded that a provision for delayed recognition was not needed to mitigate the financial statement impact of immediately recognizing the transition amount when this Statement is adopted. That provision would have added unnecessary complexity to the application of this Statement, reduced financial statement comparability, and been inconsistent with Statements 5 and 43, which do not provide for delayed recognition at transition.

Statement of Financial Accounting Standards No. 113
Accounting and Reporting for Reinsurance of
Short-Duration and Long-Duration Contracts

STATUS

Issued: December 1992

Effective Date: For financial statements for fiscal years beginning after December 15, 1992

Affects: Amends FAS 5, paragraph 44
   Supersedes FAS 60, paragraphs 38, 39, 40, and 60(f)
   Supersedes FAS 97, paragraph 27
   Amends FIN 39, paragraph 7

Affected by: Paragraph 6 amended by FAS 120

Other Interpretive Pronouncement: FIN 40

Other Interpretive Release: FASB Viewpoints, "Accounting for Reinsurance: Questions and Answers about
          Statement 113, " FASB *Status Report*, February 26, 1993

Issues Discussed by FASB Emerging Issues Task Force (EITF)

 Affects: No EITF Issues

 Interpreted by: Paragraph 21 interpreted by EITF Issue No. 93-6
       Paragraphs 22 through 24 interpreted by EITF Issue No. 93-6 and Topic No. D-54
       Paragraph 25 interpreted by EITF Issue No. 93-6

 Related Issue: EITF Topic No. D-35

SUMMARY

 This Statement specifies the accounting by insurance enterprises for the reinsuring (ceding) of insurance contracts. It amends FASB Statement No. 60, *Accounting and Reporting by Insurance Enterprises,* to eliminate the practice by insurance enterprises of reporting assets and liabilities relating to reinsured contracts net of the effects of reinsurance. It requires reinsurance receivables (including amounts related to claims incurred but not reported and liabilities for future policy benefits) and prepaid reinsurance premiums to be reported as assets. Estimated reinsurance receivables are recognized in a manner consistent with the liabilities relating to the underlying reinsured contracts.

 This Statement establishes the conditions required for a contract with a reinsurer to be accounted for as reinsurance and prescribes accounting and reporting standards for those contracts. The accounting standards depend on whether the contract is long duration or short duration and, if short duration, on whether the contract is prospective or retroactive. For all reinsurance transactions, immediate recognition of gains is precluded unless the ceding enterprise's liability to its policyholder is extinguished. Contracts that do not result in the reasonable possibility that the reinsurer may realize a significant loss from the insurance risk assumed generally do not meet the conditions for reinsurance accounting and are to be accounted for as deposits.

 This Statement requires ceding enterprises to disclose the nature, purpose, and effect of reinsurance transactions, including the premium amounts associated with reinsurance assumed and ceded. It also requires disclosure of concentrations of credit risk associated with reinsurance receivables and prepaid reinsurance premiums under the provisions of FASB Statement No. 105, *Disclosure of Information about Financial Instruments with Off-Balance-Sheet Risk and Financial Instruments with Concentrations of Credit Risk.*

 This Statement applies to financial statements for fiscal years beginning after December 15, 1992, with earlier application encouraged.

Statement of Financial Accounting Standards No. 113

Accounting and Reporting for Reinsurance of Short-Duration and Long-Duration Contracts

CONTENTS

INTRODUCTION

1. Insurance provides indemnification against loss or liability from specified events and circumstances that may occur or be discovered during a specified period. In exchange for a payment from the policyholder (a premium), an insurance enterprise agrees to pay the policyholder if specified events occur or are discovered. Similarly, the insurance enterprise may obtain indemnification against claims[1] associated with contracts it has written by entering into a reinsurance contract with another insurance enterprise (the **reinsurer**[2] or **assuming enterprise**). The insurer (or **ceding enterprise**) pays (cedes) an amount to the reinsurer, and the reinsurer agrees to reimburse the insurer for a specified portion of claims paid under the reinsured contracts. However, the policyholder usually is unaware of the reinsurance arrangement, and the insurer ordinarily is not relieved of its obligation to the policyholder. The reinsurer may, in turn, enter into reinsur-ance contracts with other reinsurers, a process known as retrocession.

2. FASB Statement No. 60, *Accounting and Reporting by Insurance Enterprises* (issued in 1982), specified the accounting by insurance enterprises for reinsurance contracts. Statement 60 is an extraction of requirements of the AICPA Industry Audit Guides, *Audits of Fire and Casualty Insurance Companies* and *Audits of Stock Life Insurance Companies* (1979 editions). It continued the long-established practice that originated in statutory accounting whereby ceding enterprises reported insurance activities net of the effects of reinsurance. If a reinsurance contract indemnified the ceding enterprise against loss or liability, Statement 60 required the ceding enterprise to reduce unpaid claim liabilities by related estimated amounts recoverable from reinsurers (ceded reserves or reinsurance recoverables) and to reduce

---

[1]The term *claim* is used in this Statement in the sense used in FASB Statement No. 60, *Accounting and Reporting by Insurance Enterprises,* to describe a demand for payment of a policy benefit because of the occurrence of an event insured by a long-duration or short-duration insurance contract.

[2]Words that appear in the glossary are set in **boldface type** the first time they appear.

unearned premiums by related amounts paid to reinsurers (ceded unearned premiums or prepaid reinsurance premiums).

3. APB Opinion No. 10, *Omnibus Opinion—1966,* paragraph 7, states, "It is a general principle of accounting that the offsetting of assets and liabilities in the balance sheet is improper except where a right of setoff exists." FASB Interpretation No. 39, *Offsetting of Amounts Related to Certain Contracts,* specifies criteria for determining whether a right of setoff exists but does not change the offsetting permitted or required by existing accounting pronouncements. Amounts payable to the policyholder and amounts receivable from the reinsurer do not meet the criteria for offsetting in Opinion 10 or Interpretation 39. Those criteria include the requirement that the reporting party have the legal right to set off the amount owed to one party with an amount receivable from that same party.

4. The issues of (a) whether net reporting of the effects of reinsurance is appropriate and (b) what is meant by indemnification against loss or liability under a reinsurance contract (generally referred to as risk transfer) have been studied by the insurance industry and the accounting and actuarial professions for some time. Interest in those issues has grown in recent years as a result of widespread public attention focused on failures of insurance enterprises. Risks associated with reinsurance have been cited as a contributing factor in several of those failures. Some commentators have observed that the offsetting of reinsurance-related assets and liabilities and inadequate reinsurance disclosures obscure risks associated with reinsurance. Others have observed that the accounting guidance in Statement 60 allows the use of reinsurance to accelerate the recognition of income relating to the reinsured contracts.

5. The increasing concerns about the effect of reinsurance accounting for contracts that do not indemnify the ceding enterprise against loss or liability, the limited accounting guidance on reinsurance in Statement 60, the lack of disclosure requirements for reinsurance transactions, and the inconsistency between the net accounting for reinsurance-related assets and liabilities and the established criteria for offsetting led the Board to reconsider the accounting and reporting for reinsurance required by Statement 60.

STANDARDS OF FINANCIAL ACCOUNTING AND REPORTING

Applicability and Scope

6. This Statement applies to all insurance enterprises to which Statement 60 applies. Insurers may enter into various types of contracts described as reinsurance, including those commonly referred to as **fronting arrangements.** This Statement provides guidance in paragraphs 8-13 on determining whether those contracts indemnify the ceding enterprise against loss or liability and therefore meet the conditions for reinsurance accounting. Contracts that meet those conditions shall be accounted for according to the provisions of paragraphs 14-26 of this Statement; other contracts with reinsurers are accounted for as deposits. The accounting provisions for reinsurance depend on whether the contract is long duration or short duration and, if short duration, on whether the contract is considered **prospective reinsurance** or **retroactive reinsurance.** Regardless of its form, any transaction that indemnifies an insurer against loss or liability relating to **insurance risk** shall be accounted for according to the provisions of this Statement.

7. This Statement does not address or change existing practice in accounting for reinsurance assumed, other than to provide guidance on indemnification against loss or liability relating to insurance risk in paragraphs 8-13 and require certain disclosures in paragraph 27.

Indemnification against Loss or Liability Relating to Insurance Risk

8. Determining whether a contract with a reinsurer provides indemnification against loss or liability relating to insurance risk requires a complete understanding of that contract and other contracts or agreements between the ceding enterprise and related reinsurers. A complete understanding includes an evaluation of all contractual features that (a) limit the amount of insurance risk to which the reinsurer is subject (such as through experience refunds, cancellation provisions, adjustable features, or additions of profitable lines of business to the reinsurance contract) or (b) delay the timely reimbursement of claims by the reinsurer (such as through payment schedules or accumulating retentions from multiple years).

Reinsurance of Short-Duration Contracts

9. Indemnification of the ceding enterprise against loss or liability relating to insurance risk in reinsurance of short-duration contracts requires both of the following, unless the condition in paragraph 11 is met:

a. The reinsurer assumes significant insurance risk under the reinsured portions of the underlying insurance contracts.
b. It is reasonably possible that the reinsurer may realize a significant loss from the transaction.

A reinsurer shall not be considered to have assumed significant insurance risk under the reinsured contracts if the probability of a significant variation in either the amount or timing of payments by the reinsurer is remote. Contractual provisions that delay timely reimbursement to the ceding enterprise would prevent this condition from being met.

10. The ceding enterprise's evaluation of whether it is reasonably possible for a reinsurer to realize a significant loss from the transaction shall be based on the present value of all cash flows between the ceding and assuming enterprises under reasonably possible outcomes, without regard to how the individual cash flows are characterized. The same interest rate shall be used to compute the present value of cash flows for each reasonably possible outcome tested.

11. Significance of loss shall be evaluated by comparing the present value of all cash flows, determined as described in paragraph 10, with the present value of the amounts paid or deemed to have been paid[3] to the reinsurer. If, based on this comparison, the reinsurer is not exposed to the reasonable possibility of significant loss, the ceding enterprise shall be considered indemnified against loss or liability relating to insurance risk only if substantially all of the insurance risk relating to the reinsured portions of the underlying insurance contracts has been assumed by the reinsurer.[4]

Reinsurance of Long-Duration Contracts

12. Indemnification of the ceding enterprise against loss or liability relating to insurance risk in reinsurance of long-duration contracts requires the reasonable possibility that the reinsurer may realize significant loss from assuming insurance risk as that concept is contemplated in Statement 60 and FASB Statement No. 97, *Accounting and Reporting by Insurance Enterprises for Certain Long-Duration Contracts and for Realized Gains and Losses from the Sale of Investments*. Statement 97 defines long-duration contracts that do not subject the insurer to mortality or morbidity risks as investment contracts. Consistent with that definition, a contract that does not subject the reinsurer to the reasonable possibility of significant loss from the events insured by the underlying insur-

ance contracts does not indemnify the ceding enterprise against insurance risk.

13. The evaluation of mortality or morbidity risk in contracts that reinsure policies subject to Statement 97 shall be consistent with the criteria in paragraphs 7 and 8 of that Statement. Evaluation of the presence of insurance risk in contracts that reinsure other long-duration contracts (such as those that reinsure ordinary life contracts or contracts that provide benefits related only to illness, physical injury, or disability) also shall be consistent with those criteria.

Reporting Assets and Liabilities Related to Reinsurance Transactions

14. Reinsurance contracts that are legal replacements of one insurer by another (often referred to as assumption and novation) extinguish the ceding enterprise's liability to the policyholder and result in removal of related assets and liabilities from the financial statements of the ceding enterprise. Reinsurance contracts in which a ceding enterprise is not relieved of the legal liability to its policyholder do not result in removal of the related assets and liabilities from the ceding enterprise's financial statements. Ceding enterprises shall report estimated **reinsurance receivables** arising from those contracts separately as assets. Amounts paid to the reinsurer relating to the unexpired portion of reinsured contracts (prepaid reinsurance premiums) also shall be reported separately as assets.

15. Amounts receivable and payable between the ceding enterprise and an individual reinsurer shall be offset only when a right of setoff exists, as defined in Interpretation 39.

16. The amounts of earned premiums ceded and recoveries recognized under reinsurance contracts either shall be reported in the statement of earnings, as separate line items or parenthetically, or those amounts shall be disclosed in the footnotes to the financial statements.

Recognition of Revenues and Costs

17. The financial reporting for a contract with a reinsurer depends on whether the contract is considered to be reinsurance for purposes of applying

---

[3]Payments and receipts under a reinsurance contract may be settled net. The ceding enterprise may withhold funds as collateral or may be entitled to compensation other than recovery of claims. Determining the amounts paid or deemed to have been paid (hereafter referred to as "amounts paid") for reinsurance requires an understanding of all contract provisions.

[4]This condition is met only if insignificant insurance risk is retained by the ceding enterprise on the reinsured portions of the underlying insurance contracts. The term *insignificant* is defined in paragraph 8 of FASB Statement No. 97, *Accounting and Reporting by Insurance Enterprises for Certain Long-Duration Contracts and for Realized Gains and Losses from the Sale of Investments*, to mean "having little or no importance; trivial" and is used in the same sense in this Statement.

this Statement. Paragraphs 8-13 identify the conditions necessary for a contract to be accounted for as reinsurance. Financial reporting for a reinsurance contract also depends on whether the contract reinsures short-duration or long-duration insurance contracts and, for short-duration contracts, on whether the contract is prospective or retroactive. Paragraphs 18-20 prescribe accounting standards applicable to all reinsurance contracts. Paragraphs 21-25 prescribe accounting standards specifically applicable to reinsurance of short-duration contracts, and paragraph 26 prescribes accounting standards for reinsurance of long-duration contracts.

18. This Statement does not specify the accounting for contracts that do not meet the conditions for reinsurance accounting, other than to incorporate the following provisions from paragraphs 39 and 40 of Statement 60, which continue in effect:

a. To the extent that a reinsurance contract does not, despite its form, provide for indemnification of the ceding enterprise by the reinsurer against loss or liability, the premium paid less the premium to be retained by the reinsurer shall be accounted for as a deposit by the ceding enterprise. A net credit resulting from the contract shall be reported as a liability by the ceding enterprise. A net charge resulting from the contract shall be reported as an asset by the reinsurer.

b. Proceeds from reinsurance transactions that represent recovery of acquisition costs shall reduce applicable unamortized acquisition costs in such a manner that net acquisition costs are capitalized and charged to expense in proportion to net revenue recognized.[5] If the ceding enterprise has agreed to service all of the related insurance contracts without reasonable compensation, a liability shall be accrued for estimated excess future servicing costs under the reinsurance contract. The net cost to the assuming enterprise shall be accounted for as an acquisition cost.

19. Reinsurance contracts do not result in immediate recognition of gains unless the reinsurance contract is a legal replacement of one insurer by another and thereby extinguishes the ceding enterprise's liability to the policyholder.

20. Reinsurance receivables shall be recognized in a manner consistent with the liabilities (including estimated amounts for claims incurred but not reported

and future policy benefits) relating to the underlying reinsured contracts. Assumptions used in estimating reinsurance receivables shall be consistent with those used in estimating the related liabilities.

Recognition of Revenues and Costs for Reinsurance of Short-Duration Contracts

21. Amounts paid for prospective reinsurance that meets the conditions for reinsurance accounting shall be reported as prepaid reinsurance premiums and amortized over the remaining **contract period** in proportion to the amount of insurance protection provided. If the amounts paid are subject to adjustment and can be reasonably estimated, the basis for amortization shall be the estimated ultimate amount to be paid.

22. Amounts paid for retroactive reinsurance that meets the conditions for reinsurance accounting shall be reported as reinsurance receivables to the extent those amounts do not exceed the recorded liabilities relating to the underlying reinsured contracts. If the recorded liabilities exceed the amounts paid, reinsurance receivables shall be increased to reflect the difference and the resulting gain deferred. The deferred gain shall be amortized over the estimated remaining **settlement period.** If the amounts and timing of the reinsurance recoveries can be reasonably estimated, the deferred gain shall be amortized using the effective interest rate inherent in the amount paid to the reinsurer and the estimated timing and amounts of recoveries from the reinsurer (the interest method). Otherwise, the proportion of actual recoveries to total estimated recoveries (the recovery method) shall determine the amount of amortization.

23. If the amounts paid for retroactive reinsurance exceed the recorded liabilities relating to the underlying reinsured contracts, the ceding enterprise shall increase the related liabilities or reduce the reinsurance receivable or both at the time the reinsurance contract is entered into, so that the excess is charged to earnings.

24. Changes in the estimated amount of the liabilities relating to the underlying reinsured contracts shall be recognized in earnings in the period of the change. Reinsurance receivables shall reflect the related change in the amount recoverable from the reinsurer, and a gain to be deferred and amortized, as described in paragraph 22, shall be adjusted or established as a result.[6] When changes in the estimated

---

[5]Paragraph 29 of Statement 60 addresses recognition of acquisition costs.

[6]Decreases in the estimated amount of the liabilities shall reduce the related amount recoverable from the reinsurer and accordingly reduce previously deferred gains. However, if the revised estimate of the liabilities is less than the amounts paid to the reinsurer, a loss shall not be deferred. The resulting difference shall be recognized in earnings immediately, as described in paragraph 23.

amount recoverable from the reinsurer or in the timing of receipts related to that amount occur, a cumulative amortization adjustment shall be recognized in earnings in the period of the change so that the deferred gain reflects the balance that would have existed had the revised estimate been available at the inception of the reinsurance transaction.

25. When practicable,[7] prospective and retroactive provisions included within a single contract shall be accounted for separately. If separate accounting for prospective and retroactive provisions included within a single contract is impracticable, the contract shall be accounted for as a retroactive contract provided the conditions for reinsurance accounting are met.

Recognition of Revenues and Costs for Reinsurance of Long-Duration Contracts

26. Amortization of the estimated cost of reinsurance of long-duration contracts that meets the conditions for reinsurance accounting depends on whether the reinsurance contract is long duration or short duration. The cost shall be amortized over the remaining life of the underlying reinsured contracts if the reinsurance contract is long duration, or over the contract period of the reinsurance if the reinsurance contract is short duration. Determining whether a contract that reinsures a long-duration insurance contract is long duration or short duration in nature is a matter of judgment, considering all of the facts and circumstances. The assumptions used in accounting for reinsurance costs shall be consistent with those used for the reinsured contracts. The difference, if any, between amounts paid for a reinsurance contract and the amount of the liabilities for policy benefits relating to the underlying reinsured contracts is part of the estimated cost to be amortized.

Disclosure

27. All insurance enterprises shall disclose the following in their financial statements:

a. The nature, purpose, and effect of ceded reinsurance transactions on the insurance enterprise's operations (Ceding enterprises also shall disclose the fact that the insurer is not relieved of its primary obligation to the policyholder in a reinsurance transaction.[8])
b. For short-duration contracts, premiums from direct business, reinsurance assumed, and reinsurance ceded, on both a written and an earned basis; for long-duration contracts, premiums and amounts assessed against policyholders from direct business, reinsurance assumed and ceded, and premiums and amounts earned
c. Methods used for income recognition on reinsurance contracts.

28. A ceding enterprise shall disclose concentrations of credit risk associated with reinsurance receivables and prepaid reinsurance premiums under the provisions of FASB Statement No. 105, *Disclosure of Information about Financial Instruments with Off-Balance-Sheet Risk and Financial Instruments with Concentrations of Credit Risk.*

Amendments to Other Pronouncements

29. This Statement supersedes paragraphs 38-40 and 60(f) of Statement 60, which address reinsurance, and incorporates the provisions of paragraphs 39 and 40 of Statement 60 in paragraph 18 of this Statement.

30. This Statement amends FASB Statement No. 5, *Accounting for Contingencies,* to include the following footnote at the end of paragraph 44:

*Paragraphs 8-13 of FASB Statement No. 113, *Accounting and Reporting for Reinsurance of Short-Duration and Long-Duration Contracts,* identify conditions that are required for a reinsurance contract to indemnify the ceding enterprise against loss or liability and to be accounted for as reinsurance. Any transaction between enterprises to which FASB Statement No. 60, *Accounting and Reporting by Insurance Enterprises,* applies must meet those conditions to be accounted for as reinsurance.

31. Paragraph 27 of Statement 97, which refers to the reinsurance guidance in Statement 60, is amended to read as follows:

The provisions of Statement 60 addressing loss recognition (premium deficiency) and financial statement disclosure, and the provisions of FASB Statement No. 113, *Accounting and Reporting for Reinsurance of Short-Duration and Long-Duration Contracts,* addressing reinsurance shall apply to limited-payment and universal life-type contracts addressed by this Statement.

---

[7]This term is used in the sense used in paragraph 15 of FASB Statement No. 107, *Disclosures about Fair Value of Financial Instruments,* to mean that the prospective and retroactive provisions can be accounted for separately without incurring excessive costs.

[8]As indicated in paragraph 16, the amount of recoveries recognized under reinsurance contracts also must be disclosed by the ceding enterprise if not reported separately in the statement of earnings.

32. Interpretation 39 does not modify the accounting prescribed by authoritative pronouncements in specific circumstances that result in offsetting or in a presentation that is similar to the effect of offsetting. Paragraph 7 of Interpretation 39 includes examples of that accounting and is amended to delete the reference to reinsurance in Statement 60.

Effective Date and Transition

33. This Statement is effective for financial statements for fiscal years beginning after December 15, 1992, with earlier application encouraged. The provisions of paragraphs 8-13 that establish the conditions for reinsurance accounting and paragraphs 17-26 that address recognition of revenues and costs of reinsurance need not be applied in financial statements for interim periods in the year of initial application, but amounts reported for those interim periods shall be restated if they are reported with annual financial statements for that fiscal year. Restatement of financial statements for earlier years to apply the provisions of paragraphs 8-13 and 17-26 is prohibited. Restatement of financial statements for earlier years to apply paragraphs 14-16 relating to gross reporting is encouraged but not required. The provisions of this Statement that establish the conditions for reinsurance accounting and address recognition of revenues and costs apply to reinsurance contracts entered into, renewed, amended,[9] or having an anniversary date in the year of adoption.

The provisions of this Statement need not be applied to immaterial items.

This Statement was adopted by the unanimous vote of the seven members of the Financial Accounting Standards Board:

Dennis R. Beresford,
  Chairman
Joseph V. Anania

Victor H. Brown
James J. Leisenring
Robert H. Northcutt

A. Clarence Sampson
Robert J. Swieringa

---

[9]Any change or adjustment of contractual terms is considered an amendment for purposes of applying this Statement.

Appendix A

BASIS FOR CONCLUSIONS

CONTENTS

Appendix A

BASIS FOR CONCLUSIONS

Introduction

34. This appendix summarizes considerations deemed significant by Board members in reaching the conclusions in this Statement. It includes reasons for accepting certain approaches and rejecting others. Individual Board members gave greater weight to some factors than to others.

35. An FASB Exposure Draft, *Accounting and Reporting for Reinsurance of Short-Duration and Long-Duration Contracts,* was issued for public comment in March 1992 and distributed to members of various industry organizations, in addition to the standard distribution, to encourage comment by those most affected by the proposal. Fifty-three comment letters were received in response to the Exposure Draft. The Board concluded that it could reach an informed decision without holding a public hearing. However, those who responded to the Exposure Draft were invited to participate in a public Board meeting, which took place in September 1992.

Background Information

36. For reinsurance contracts that indemnified the ceding enterprise against risk of loss or liability, Statement 60 continued the long-established practice that originated in statutory accounting whereby ceding enterprises reported insurance activities net of the effects of reinsurance. Unearned premiums and unpaid claim liabilities represent an insurance enterprise's obligation to policyholders at different times during the period of an insurance contract. Similarly, prepaid reinsurance premiums and reinsurance receivables represent probable future economic benefits to be received from a reinsurer. Statement 60 required insurance liabilities to be reported net of the related reinsurance amounts and also allowed reporting of earned premiums and claims costs net of reinsurance amounts in the statement of earnings.

37. Whether this offsetting of reinsurance amounts in financial statements of insurance enterprises should continue has been a recurring issue. Opinion 10 states, "It is a general principle of accounting that the offsetting of assets and liabilities in the balance sheet is improper except where a right of setoff exists." In issuing Interpretation 39, the FASB did not modify accounting treatments specified in

existing FASB and AICPA accounting pronouncements that result in offsetting, including the accounting for reinsurance under Statement 60.

38. How to determine whether a reinsurance contract indemnifies the ceding enterprise against loss or liability has been another recurring issue. Statement 5 requires deposit accounting for insurance and reinsurance contracts that do not indemnify the insured or ceding enterprise against loss or liability. Statement 60 incorporates that guidance for reinsurance contracts without specifying further the conditions under which loss or liability is indemnified. At the time Statement 60 was issued, the insurance industry and the accounting and actuarial professions were studying what circumstances constitute indemnification against loss or liability in a reinsurance transaction.

39. Many have expressed concern about the appropriateness of reporting the effects of reinsurance on a net basis, the effect of reinsurance accounting for contracts written as reinsurance that do not indemnify the ceding enterprise against loss or liability, the adequacy of reinsurance disclosures, and the limited accounting guidance for reinsurance contracts in Statement 60. In response to those concerns, the Board decided to reconsider the reinsurance provisions of Statement 60.

40. The Board had two objectives in adding this project to its agenda. The first objective was to consider the inconsistency between accounting for reinsurance and the established criteria for offsetting and to address the perceived deficiencies in the reporting of reinsurance transactions. Amounts recoverable from reinsurers are a very significant asset for some insurance enterprises. However, the netting provisions of Statement 60 and the exclusion of insurance contracts from Statement 105 have resulted in limited reporting about the amounts receivable from reinsurers, the effects of reinsurance on the reporting enterprise's operations, and the resulting exposure to credit risk. The second objective was to address the recognition of revenues and costs resulting from reinsurance transactions. The Board concluded that it was necessary to consider the lack of guidance in Statement 60 on recognition issues relating to reinsurance because of the increasing diversity and complexity of reinsurance arrangements and the proliferation of nontraditional reinsurance contracts. There also was an apparent inconsistency between the practice of immediately recognizing gains and losses on reinsurance contracts and the premise that reinsurance does not result in extinguishment of the related liabilities.

Benefits and Costs

41. The FASB's mission statement calls for the Board to determine whether a proposed standard will fill a significant need and whether the costs it imposes, compared with the possible alternatives, will be justified in relation to the overall benefits. The costs to implement an accounting standard and the benefits of reporting consistent, comparable, and reliable information in financial statements ordinarily must be assessed in general terms and cannot be quantified. There also is no common measure for objectively comparing those costs and benefits. Moreover, implementation costs are borne primarily by the preparers of financial statements rather than the broader constituency that also benefits from improved reporting. In establishing standards that are cost-effective, the Board must balance the diverse and often conflicting needs of a variety of constituents.

42. In addressing this project, the Board determined that the information provided to users about the effects of reinsurance transactions could be improved by (a) eliminating the industry practice of offsetting reinsurance assets and liabilities, (b) requiring disclosures about the credit risk associated with reinsurance receivables, and (c) limiting diversity among ceding enterprises in recognizing revenues and costs from reinsurance contracts.

43. The Board concluded that not all accounting issues relating to reinsurance contracts could be effectively addressed in this Statement. However, information provided to users about the effects of reinsurance could be improved and inconsistencies could be reduced by providing guidance for both short-duration and long-duration contracts. The Exposure Draft provided only general implementation guidance and did not attempt to identify and address all issues that could arise. Some respondents recommended that the Statement provide far more extensive implementation guidance and additional examples, particularly on applying the conditions for reinsurance accounting. Those requests were evaluated individually and, in certain instances, the Board concluded that additional guidance was warranted. However, because the Board believes that the cost of implementing very detailed standards for reinsurance accounting would outweigh the benefits, the overall approach of providing general rather than detailed guidance was retained. The Board believes the increased usefulness of the information provided on the effects of reinsurance transactions will exceed the costs of complying with this Statement.

44. The information required by this Statement should be readily available to the reporting enterprise because of similar regulatory reporting guidelines. Modification of existing systems may be required to facilitate reporting concentrations of credit risk and to comply with the provisions for recognizing revenues and costs required by this Statement. The Exposure Draft would have required prospective and retroactive elements of all reinsurance contracts to be accounted for separately. Respondents indicated that the cost of allocating amounts related to these provisions could be significant and that allocation might not always be practicable. To address these concerns, the Board concluded that contracts containing both prospective and retroactive elements should be accounted for as retroactive contracts when allocation is impracticable.

Scope

45. After reviewing current practice and the nature of reinsurance contracts, the Board concluded that an extensive reconsideration of the accounting for reinsurance is not necessary at this time; concerns could be addressed by modifying the standards of financial accounting and reporting for reinsurance in Statement 60 and by providing limited additional guidance. The guidance in paragraphs 39 and 40 of Statement 60 was not reconsidered and continues in effect. The provisions of those paragraphs have been incorporated in this Statement for convenience.

46. This Statement applies to any transaction that indemnifies an insurer against loss or liability relating to insurance risk. All transactions must meet the conditions in paragraphs 8-13 of this Statement to be accounted for as reinsurance. The Exposure Draft would have amended paragraph 44 of Statement 5 to indicate that similar conditions are required for an insurance policy to indemnify the insured against loss or liability. While that amendment was not expected to have a significant effect in practice, some respondents indicated its effect would be greater than anticipated. The Board decided not to extend the provisions in paragraphs 8-13 to primary insurance transactions. This potential inconsistency was accepted, even though paragraph 44 of Statement 5 suggests it is appropriate to apply a uniform concept of indemnification to both insurance and reinsurance, because the Board's intention was to not significantly change the accounting for primary insurance transactions in this narrow-scope project.

47. Likewise, the Board concluded that it was not necessary to address the accounting for reinsurance by the assuming enterprise. An assuming enterprise generally accounts for a reinsurance contract in the same manner as an insurance contract sold to an individual or noninsurance enterprise, as prescribed in Statements 60 and 97. Some constituents recommended that the Board specify the accounting by assuming enterprises and require symmetrical accounting by both parties to a reinsurance transaction. Those recommendations were not adopted because addressing the accounting for assuming enterprises would inevitably require a reconsideration of the accounting for primary insurance, which was beyond this project's scope. However, the conditions for reinsurance accounting in paragraphs 8-13 and certain disclosure requirements apply to both ceding and assuming enterprises.

48. Some respondents to the Exposure Draft asked that certain types of entities or transactions be excluded from the scope. The Board was urged to limit the scope to loss portfolio transfers or other transactions that some consider prone to abusive accounting under current standards. The Board considered and rejected that approach because it perceived the need for improved accounting and reporting guidance for reinsurance in general. The transactions in question also could not be distinguished conceptually from other reinsurance transactions. Insurers may enter into various transactions with reinsurers that serve legitimate business purposes but do not meet the conditions for reinsurance accounting in this Statement. The Board's objective was only to specify the accounting standards for reinsurance, as distinct from other transactions.

49. For similar reasons, fronting arrangements are included within the scope of this Statement. Some insurance enterprises currently do not report fronting arrangements as reinsurance contracts. However, the ceding enterprise in a fronting arrangement retains the same risks associated with any other type of reinsurance contract and is not relieved of its obligation to the policyholders.

50. Several respondents questioned whether servicing carriers for involuntary risk pools should be included in the Statement's scope. Servicing carriers generally retain the primary obligation to the policyholder and have no right to offset claim liabilities against amounts due from other pool participants. Although the credit risk associated with involuntary pools may be reduced because of the pool membership's joint and several liability, the servicing carrier is still dependent on the ability of other pool members to pay their proportionate share of claims. State authorities oversee such pools and may act to support the solvency of a pool, but that action generally is voluntary. The Board concluded that it was unable to effectively distinguish servicing carrier business from other types of reinsurance for accounting purposes. Separate presentation or disclosure of servicing carrier activity is not precluded by this Statement.

51. Some respondents asked the Board to limit the Statement's scope to short-duration contracts, citing a perceived lack of accounting abuse related to long-duration contracts and the differences between the long-duration and short-duration insurance models. However, reinsurance of long-duration contracts sometimes is used to accelerate income recognition by effectively unlocking the assumptions used in estimating benefit reserves. In addition, reinsurance of long-duration contracts is not unique and the specific questions raised by respondents about how the standard would be applied to long-duration contracts were not so complex or difficult as to justify a separate project to develop additional detailed guidance for reinsurance of long-duration contracts.

52. Reinsurance contracts sometimes are used to "sell" a line of business by coinsuring all or substantially all of the risks related to the line. Some respondents asked that those contracts be exempt from the requirements of this Statement. The Board concluded that unless the ceding enterprise is legally relieved of its liability to the policyholder, as described in paragraph 19, such reinsurance does not constitute a sale and immediate recognition of a gain should be precluded.

53. Some respondents asked whether structured settlement transactions are included within the scope of this Statement. Structured settlements may, in some circumstances, legally replace one insurer by another and thereby extinguish the primary insurer's liability to the policyholder. This Statement requires that an immediate gain or loss be recognized when such an extinguishment occurs. A structured settlement transaction that does not constitute an extinguishment is accounted for as reinsurance if the annuity funding the settlement meets the conditions for reinsurance accounting. Otherwise, the transaction is accounted for in accordance with paragraph 18 of this Statement. Whether a ceding enterprise has been legally relieved of its entire obligation to the policyholder under a structured settlement is a factual question that depends on the settlement's terms.

54. This Statement applies only to enterprises to which Statement 60 applies and, thus, continues the exemption in Statement 60 for mutual life insurance enterprises. The Board specifically considered whether that exemption is appropriate in accounting and reporting for reinsurance. Mutual life insurance enterprises are included within the scope of Interpretation 39 and Opinion 10, suggesting that they also should be required to separately report assets and liabilities arising from reinsurance. However, the Board observed that this Statement's provisions on reporting revenues and costs are closely linked to the accounting model for

long-duration contracts found in Statement 60. Determining how those provisions would apply to enterprises that do not follow the Statement 60 model might be time-consuming and could involve considering the appropriate accounting for insurance contracts by mutual life insurance enterprises.

55. The Board also noted that it has asked the AICPA to expeditiously complete its project on the accounting for insurance activities, including reinsurance, by mutual life insurance enterprises. Accordingly, the Board did not expand this Statement's scope to encompass those topics, and concluded that this Statement should apply only to enterprises to which Statement 60 applies.

Indemnification against Loss or Liability Relating to Insurance Risk

56. This Statement incorporates the provisions of paragraph 40 of Statement 60 that require deposit accounting for reinsurance contracts that do not indemnify the ceding enterprise against loss or liability. Those provisions incorporate without change the guidance in paragraph 44 of Statement 5. Determining whether a reinsurance contract indemnifies the ceding enterprise against loss or liability has been controversial and problematic in practice. The Board concluded that this Statement should provide general guidance on the circumstances under which reinsurance contracts provide indemnification against loss or liability and therefore meet the conditions for reinsurance accounting.

57. Transactions other than reinsurance may provide indemnification against various types of loss or liability. Under this Statement, the distinguishing characteristic of reinsurance is indemnification against loss or liability related to insurance risk. As contemplated in Statements 60 and 97, insurance risk is the risk associated with the occurrence of insured events under an insurance contract. Those risks include the uncertainties relating to both the ultimate amount of payments and the timing of those payments. Risks other than those associated with the occurrence of insured events under an insurance contract, such as the risk that investment income will vary from expectations, are not elements of insurance risk. Although insurers may face significant exposure to risks other than insurance risk, indemnification against loss or liability in a reinsurance transaction is a function of the insurance risk assumed by the reinsurer.

58. Determining whether a reinsurance contract indemnifies the ceding enterprise against loss or liability relating to insurance risk requires a complete understanding of all contracts or agreements with related reinsurers. Although an individual contract may appear to indemnify the ceding enterprise, the risk assumed

by the reinsurer through one reinsurance contract may have been offset by other contracts or agreements. A contract does not meet the conditions for reinsurance accounting if features of the reinsurance contract or other contracts or agreements directly or indirectly compensate the reinsurer or related reinsurers for losses. That compensation may take many forms, and an understanding of the substance of the contracts or agreements is required to determine whether the ceding enterprise has been indemnified against loss or liability relating to insurance risk. For example, contractual features may limit the reinsurer's exposure to insurance risk or delay the reimbursement of claims so that investment income mitigates exposure to insurance risk. Examples of those contractual features, which are not intended to be all-inclusive, are included in paragraph 8 of this Statement.

59. Reinsurance programs often entail the reinsurance of various layers of exposure through multiple reinsurance contracts. The Board concluded that indemnification against loss or liability relating to insurance risk should be determined in relation to the provisions of the individual reinsurance contract being evaluated. That is, to meet the conditions for reinsurance accounting, the terms of the individual reinsurance contract must indemnify the ceding enterprise against loss or liability relating to insurance risk.

60. Several respondents to the Exposure Draft observed that this requirement could result in different accounting for similar transactions depending on the contractual structure of the transactions. Those respondents recommended that the conditions for reinsurance accounting be evaluated based on whether a reinsurance program, taken as a whole, indemnifies the insurer against loss or liability related to insurance risk. That approach was rejected because it would not have been practicable to define what constitutes a reinsurance program. Further, contracts that are not, in substance, reinsurance could meet the conditions for reinsurance accounting by being designated as part of a program that, as a whole, met those conditions.

Reinsurance of Short-Duration Contracts

61. A short-duration insurance contract requires that an insurer make payments to the policyholder because insured events occurred during the contract period. However, an insurer's exposure to risk does not end with the close of the contract pe-

riod. Exposure to risk extends beyond that date to the date when the last claim is settled and paid. During that period, many factors may affect the ultimate claims paid. Policyholders may discover and assert more claims than expected or may assert them more quickly than expected. The costs of individual claims may exceed the insurer's expectations. Courts and legislative bodies may extend the insurer's exposure beyond that originally contemplated. A reinsurance contract may limit the insurer's exposure to some or all of those circumstances. The extent of protection provided may range from very little to a considerable amount.

62. The Board concluded that two conditions must be met for reinsurance of a short-duration contract to indemnify the ceding enterprise against loss or liability relating to insurance risk. First, the reinsurer must assume significant insurance risk under the reinsured portions[10] of the underlying contracts. Implicit in this condition is the requirement that both the amount and timing of the reinsurer's payments depend on and directly vary with the amount and timing of claims settled under the reinsured contracts. Contractual features that delay timely reimbursement to the ceding enterprise prevent the reinsurer's payments from directly varying with the claims settled under the reinsured contracts.

63. Second, even if the first condition is met, the contract does not indemnify the ceding enterprise against loss or liability relating to insurance risk unless either (a) it is reasonably possible that the assuming enterprise may realize a significant loss[11] from the transaction or (b) the contract fulfills the condition described in paragraph 11.

64. The Exposure Draft did not specify how to determine exposure to significant loss, and a number of respondents asked for additional guidance in this area. Paragraph 10 requires that significance be determined based on the present value of all cash flows between the ceding and assuming enterprise under reasonably possible outcomes. All cash flows are included because payments that effectively represent premiums or refunds of premiums may be described in various ways under the terms of a reinsurance contract. The way a cash flow is characterized does not affect whether it should be included in determining the reinsurer's exposure to loss. Consistent with Statement 5, an outcome is reasonably possible if its probability is more than remote.

---

[10]A ceding enterprise may reinsure only part of the risks associated with the underlying contracts. For example, a proportionate share of all risks or only specified risks may be reinsured. The conditions for reinsurance accounting are evaluated in relation to the reinsured portions of the underlying insurance contracts, rather than all aspects of those contracts.

[11]The Exposure Draft would have required the possibility of significant gain or loss. Based on comments received, the Board concluded that possibility of loss is the essential condition for indemnification and deleted the reference to gain from this Statement.

65. Respondents asked for more guidance about the benchmark for measuring significance. The Board clarified this provision to indicate that significance of loss is evaluated in relation to the present value of the amounts paid to the reinsurer.

66. The cash flows between the ceding and assuming enterprise and the amounts paid to the reinsurer are compared at their present values to achieve a consistent temporal frame of reference. A constant interest rate is used in determining those present values because the possibility of investment income varying from expectations is not an element of insurance risk. The Board concluded that it was not necessary to specify in detail the interest rate used in the calculation; judgment is required to identify a reasonable and appropriate rate.

67. Under very limited circumstances, the reinsurer need not be exposed to the reasonable possibility of significant loss for a contract to meet the conditions for reinsurance accounting. For example, applying the "reasonable possibility of significant loss" condition is problematic when the underlying insurance contracts themselves do not result in the reasonable possibility of significant loss to the ceding enterprise.[12] The Board concluded that, when the reinsurer has assumed substantially all of the insurance risk in the reinsured portions of the underlying policies,[13] even if that risk does not result in the reasonable possibility of significant loss, the transaction meets the conditions for reinsurance accounting. In this narrow circumstance, the reinsurer's economic position is virtually equivalent to having written the insurance contract directly. The risks retained by the ceding enterprise are insignificant, so that the reinsurer's exposure to loss is essentially the same as the insurer's.

Reinsurance of Long-Duration Contracts

68. The Board considered the concept of insurance risk as it relates to certain long-duration contracts when it deliberated Statement 97 and concluded that, to be considered insurance, those contracts must subject the insurance enterprise to mortality or morbidity risk. Indemnification of a ceding enterprise against loss or liability relating to insurance risk under a related reinsurance contract requires that the reinsurer be subject to those same risks. Even though other risks, such as investment yield risk, are significant business elements of a long-duration insurance contract, those risks are not unique to insurance or reinsurance. Consistent with Statement 97, reinsurance of long-duration contracts that does not subject the reinsurer to mortality or morbidity risks associated with the underlying reinsured contracts is, in substance, an investment contract. The Board also concluded that for a long-duration contract to meet the conditions for reinsurance accounting, the contract must subject the reinsurer to the reasonable possibility of significant loss from the insurance risk assumed.

69. Statement 97 focuses on certain life insurance-type contracts and excludes various other types of long-duration contracts, such as health and disability insurance contracts. The Board concluded that the conditions for reinsurance accounting for other types of long-duration contracts should be consistent with those described in paragraph 68 of this Statement. To be accounted for as reinsurance, the contract must subject the reinsurer to the risks insured by the underlying reinsured contracts.

Reporting Assets and Liabilities Related to Reinsurance Transactions

70. The Actuarial Standards Board's Actuarial Standard of Practice No. 11, *The Treatment of Reinsurance Transactions in Life and Health Insurance Company Financial Statements,* acknowledges the need to evaluate the gross liability to policyholders in establishing an appropriate net liability under a reinsurance contract. Auditing guidance issued by the AICPA identifies reinsurance as an area with potential for increased audit risk and emphasizes the exposure associated with the gross insurance liability. However, some observers have expressed concern that actuarial and audit practices sometimes focus on net exposures and may fail to adequately assess and analyze gross exposures.

71. The Board determined that the net reporting of assets and liabilities related to reinsurance is inconsistent with the established conditions for offsetting and does not result in a meaningful presentation in financial statements of insurance enterprises. Some respondents to the Exposure Draft objected to gross reporting on the basis that disclosure is adequate to ensure a meaningful presentation. However, disclosure of offsetting amounts is not equivalent to the recognition of assets and liabilities in the statement of financial position. In addition, some reinsurance disclosures are not easily understood or comparable with disclosures of other insurance enterprises.

72. The net accounting for reinsurance prescribed in Statement 60 also may obscure the required ac-

---

[12]Most commonly, this arises when an individual risk or insurance contract, rather than a group of risks or contracts, is reinsured. The probability of loss from any individual short-duration insurance contract generally is considered to be remote. Therefore, outcomes that would expose the assuming enterprise to risk of significant loss ordinarily could not be characterized as reasonably possible.

[13]It is presumed that those policies qualify as insurance for accounting purposes.

counting for the underlying reinsured contracts. A number of constituents indicated that the current practice of reporting insurance net of reinsurance activity is consistent with the way insurers view and manage their businesses. These constituents maintained that reporting the net exposure from the reinsured contracts appropriately reflects the role of reinsurance in mitigating risk. However, the existence of a reinsurance contract does not alter the measurement of the liabilities that should be recognized on the underlying reinsured contracts. The Board concluded that separate reporting of reinsurance receivables and the related liabilities will provide a more relevant and representationally faithful presentation of the effects of reinsurance. The additional disclosures required for reinsurance transactions in paragraph 27 should provide users of financial statements with information about the purpose of reinsurance and its role in mitigating risk.

73. The Board also concluded that reinsurance receivables should be recognized consistent with recognition of the liabilities related to the underlying reinsured contracts. Because the valuation of reinsurance receivables depends on the terms of the reinsurance contract and on estimates used in measuring the liabilities relating to the reinsured contracts, the Board chose not to stipulate a specific valuation method. However, the ceding enterprise must assess the collectibility of those receivables in accordance with Statement 5.

74. Some respondents to the Exposure Draft disputed the Board's characterization of reinsurance receivables on unpaid claims as assets. In their view, the reporting of a claim is the event triggering asset recognition; otherwise, the reinsurer has no contractual obligation to the ceding enterprise. However, reinsurance receivables on unpaid claims represent probable future economic benefits controlled by the ceding enterprise as a result of the payment of a reinsurance premium and the occurrence of an insured event. The entity that controls the economic benefit need not have the ability to convert it to cash or another asset immediately, through sale or assertion of a contractual right, to meet the established criteria for recognition. Reporting and settlement of claims relate to measurement of the asset rather than the criteria for recognition. Those events represent the conditions[14] necessary to establish the ultimate amount of the asset and the timing of its collection.

75. Some respondents suggested that reinsurance recoverables be reported as valuation accounts associated with the claim liability. FASB Concepts Statement No. 6, *Elements of Financial Statements,* paragraph 43, describes a liability valuation account:

> A separate item that reduces or increases the carrying amount of a liability is sometimes found in financial statements. For example, a bond premium or discount increases or decreases the face value of a bond payable to its proceeds or present value. Those "valuation accounts" are part of the related liability and are neither liabilities in their own right nor assets.

Reinsurance receivables are an asset, not a liability valuation account. Valuation accounts exist only as part of a measurement of a liability, not as a complete measurement of a liability.

76. Amounts recoverable from reinsurers on unasserted claims may be included with other reinsurance receivables in the statement of financial position. Some respondents objected to the combined presentation because users of financial statements might find that presentation confusing. However, similar concerns could be expressed about other balances typically reported in an insurer's financial statements. For example, claim liabilities generally include amounts relating to both reported and unreported claims. Although this Statement requires amounts recoverable on unasserted claims to be reported as reinsurance receivables, it does not preclude separate presentation or disclosure of various types of receivables.

77. Statement 60 requires that unearned premiums received by an insurance enterprise relating to the unexpired portion of short-duration contracts be reported separately from other liabilities. The Board concluded that a ceding enterprise should likewise report amounts paid to reinsurers relating to the unexpired portion of short-duration contracts (referred to in Statement 60 as ceded unearned premiums) separately from reinsurance receivables. Those amounts represent prepaid premiums on prospective reinsurance contracts.

78. Several balances may arise between the ceding and assuming enterprise in a reinsurance contract, including funds withheld on ceded premiums, commissions, unsettled claims, and funds advanced by the assuming enterprise. Those items may qualify for offsetting under the conditions established by Interpretation 39, and this Statement does not preclude offsetting when appropriate.

---

[14]Among the transactions specifically addressed by Interpretation 39 is the offsetting of amounts related to conditional contracts, whose obligations or rights depend on the occurrence of some specified future event that is not certain to occur.

However, an insurance enterprise must evaluate each situation in light of the conditions required for offsetting in determining the appropriate financial statement presentation.

79. Some respondents suggested that gross reporting of amounts related to reinsurance would result in less useful financial statements. Those respondents generally maintained that users of financial statements are more interested in the net exposure, consistent with the way management views its business. Some were concerned that enterprises engaging heavily in reinsurance transactions will be perceived as being financially stronger because of the correspondingly larger assets and liabilities that will be reported. Others stated that financial ratios and trend data used by analysts will be adversely affected by the change. Respondents also suggested that commingling assets and liabilities related to servicing carrier business with other types of reinsurance will diminish the usefulness of financial statements. However, a number of respondents indicated that gross information would be more useful than net information.

80. The comments on usefulness often referred to the perceived relevance and representational faithfulness of net reporting. The Board carefully considered those comments and concluded that financial statements from which significant amounts of assets and liabilities are omitted generally lack relevance and are not representationally faithful. Offsetting reinsurance assets against the related liabilities implies a relationship between those assets and liabilities that does not exist unless the established criteria for offsetting are met. Further, offsetting reinsurance receivables against the related liabilities obscures the credit risk associated with reinsurance.

81. Examples of other accounting literature in which net reporting is permitted, such as pension accounting and leveraged leases, were cited by some respondents as a basis for continuing the practice of net reporting of reinsurance transactions. Interpretation 39 did not modify the accounting treatment of those transactions. The Board decided to include the exemptions in Interpretation 39 as a practical matter to avoid disturbing certain longstanding accounting practices without full exploration of the issues involved. Having addressed those issues for reinsurance, the Board concluded that the benefits of reporting reinsurance assets and liabilities separately are sufficient to justify the change.

82. A number of respondents asked the Board to consider allowing reinsurance recoverables on unpaid claims to be reported as a contraliability against claim reserves, rather than as an asset. Many of the same arguments made against gross reporting were provided as reasons for a contraliability presentation.

83. Advocates of a contraliability presentation also observed that the amount recoverable from the reinsurer and the related claim liabilities are difficult to measure. In their view, the volatile nature of the reinsured risks renders the gross amounts unreliable, but the presence of reinsurance permits measurement of a net exposure with more reliability. Contraliability presentation would minimize the effect of that volatility by presenting the reinsurance recoverable and the related liabilities together.

84. Advocates of a contraliability presentation also cited the linkage between the reinsured liabilities and the amounts recoverable from the reinsurer. In reinsurance, the asset arises from and is dependent on the same transaction as the liability for both the amount and timing of its realization. These respondents believe that relationship is more faithfully represented by displaying those amounts together rather than as a separate asset and liability.

85. The Board acknowledged the potential volatility of the estimates and the close linkage between the asset and liability but rejected the contraliability approach. Reinsurance recoverables on unpaid claims meet the qualifications for recognition as an asset and should be reported as such. Contraliabilities are not considered a financial statement element under the Board's conceptual framework. The Board also was not persuaded that the characteristics of a reinsurance transaction are sufficiently different from other transactions to justify a presentation other than that prescribed in Interpretation 39. The additional disclosure requirements this Statement prescribes, including the requirement to disclose the nature, purpose, and effect of reinsurance on the enterprise's operations, should provide users of financial statements with additional information to assess the effect of volatility and the ability of reinsurance to mitigate it.

86. Paragraph 38 of Statement 60 allowed, but did not require, amounts paid to reinsurers and reinsurance recoveries to be netted against related earned premiums and incurred claim costs in the statement of earnings. Most enterprises report those amounts on a net basis consistent with the presentation in the statement of financial position. The Board determined that reporting gross amounts in the statement of earnings would be preferable. However, the Board acknowledged that the reasons for gross reporting in the statement of earnings are less compelling. Opinion 10 and Interpretation 39 address only the offsetting of assets and liabilities. Further, unlike the statement of financial position, the statement of earnings does not convey information about credit risk.

87. As proposed in the Exposure Draft, enterprises could have reported the effects of reinsurance on earned premiums and claim costs (that is, the amount by which earned premiums are reduced by amounts paid or payable to reinsurers, and the amount by which claim costs are reduced by amounts received or receivable from reinsurers) either as separate line items or parenthetically within the statement of earnings. Appendix B illustrates those presentations. Respondents recommended that the Board also allow those amounts to be reported net, with appropriate footnote rather than parenthetical disclosure. The Board agreed that earned premiums ceded and reinsurance recoveries may be disclosed rather than reported separately in the statement of earnings.

Recognition of Revenues and Costs

88. Accounting for the effects of reinsurance contracts on the revenues and costs of the ceding enterprise is complicated because reinsurance contracts serve various objectives. An insurance enterprise may purchase reinsurance to reduce exposure to losses from the events it has agreed to insure, similar to a direct insurance contract purchased by an individual or noninsurance enterprise. The insurance enterprise also may contract with a reinsurer to facilitate the writing of contracts larger than those normally accepted, to obtain or provide assistance in entering new types of business, or to accomplish tax or regulatory objectives. It is not practicable to identify and separately account for each individual element of a reinsurance contract, and the guidance in Statement 60 is inadequate to result in consistent accounting for the payments and proceeds resulting from reinsurance contracts. The Board determined that this Statement should prescribe in more detail the accounting for revenues and costs of reinsurance contracts.

89. Although a contract may meet the conditions for reinsurance accounting, the difference between the amount paid to the reinsurer and the liabilities related to the reinsured contracts may result from underwriting, investment, service, sales, or financing activities. Varying applications of the provisions of Statement 60 have sometimes resulted in immediate recognition of a gain or loss equal to that difference. The Exposure Draft concluded that immediate recognition of gains or losses from reinsurance contracts generally is inappropriate and inconsistent with the premise that the insurance enterprise has not been relieved of its obligations to the holders of the reinsured contracts.[15]

90. Some constituents stated that it would be appropriate to recognize the effects of reinsurance in income immediately, referring to reinsurance as a sale or a form of extinguishment of debt. Others stated that, when the ceding enterprise has been indemnified against loss or liability relating to insurance risk, sufficient risk has been transferred to the reinsurer to result in immediate recognition. However, in the Board's view, immediate recognition is not appropriate unless an extinguishment has taken place. The conditions necessary for indemnification against insurance risk are considerably less stringent than those required for extinguishment, which occurs only when the ceding enterprise has been entirely relieved of its obligations to the policyholder.

91. A few respondents stated that the reinsurance transaction is a significant event that should result in remeasurement of the related liabilities and recognition of the effects of remeasurement in income. The Board concluded that reinsurance does not alter the nature or amount of the obligations owed to the policyholder. Rather, the ceding enterprise has acquired a separate asset—the right to recoveries from the reinsurer.

92. Some respondents said that the significant gains sometimes recognized by ceding enterprises under the current standards result from an accounting anomaly, and the Board's proposed accounting would not resolve that anomaly. The amounts paid to the reinsurer may reflect the time value of money as an element of pricing. The ceding enterprise's gains occur at least partly because the related liabilities are not stated at present value under current accounting standards. Several constituents recommended that the Board defer reaching a conclusion about reinsurance until the fundamental question of the role of discounting in measuring assets and liabilities is resolved. Those constituents correctly described the nature of the issue, but the Board decided that delaying resolution of the inconsistencies in reinsurance accounting would not be appropriate.

93. The Board concluded that estimated reinsurance receivables should be recognized in a manner consistent with the related liability. The accounting for amounts that represent recovery of acquisition costs is addressed in paragraph 39 of Statement 60 and incorporated in paragraph 18 of this Statement. Other amounts paid or received, other than advances or forms of collateral, are presumed to be part of the net cost of reinsurance discussed in paragraphs 94-109.

---

[15]The Board decided, as a number of respondents to the Exposure Draft recommended, that losses relating to retroactive contracts should be distinguished from other gains and losses arising from reinsurance transactions. The accounting for retroactive contracts is described in paragraphs 22-24.

*Recognition of Revenues and Costs for
Reinsurance of Short-Duration Contracts*

94. Contracts that meet the conditions for reinsurance accounting also may include elements of a financing arrangement. Existing accounting pronouncements do not provide guidance that would allow an insurer to identify the separate elements and costs of reinsurance. If a reinsurance contract is prospective, reinsurance activities affect the results of the ceding enterprise while the reinsured contracts are in force (the contract period) and during the subsequent period over which claims are settled. If a reinsurance contract is retroactive, the coverage period is closed and the reinsurance contract can affect only the remaining settlement period.

95. The distinction between prospective and retroactive reinsurance contracts is based on whether the contract reinsures future or past insured events covered by the underlying contracts. For example, in occurrence-based insurance, the insured event is the occurrence of a loss covered by the insurance contract. In claims-made insurance, the insured event is the reporting to the insurer, within the period specified by the policy, of a claim for a loss covered by the insurance contract. A claims-made reinsurance contract that reinsures claims asserted to the reinsurer in a future period as a result of insured events that occurred prior to entering into the reinsurance contract is a retroactive contract.

96. Some constituents stated that, in their view, the distinction between prospective and retroactive contracts is unnecessary because all reinsurance transactions that indemnify the ceding enterprise against loss or liability relating to insurance risk should be treated alike. However, the Board was not prepared to impose settlement period accounting on all reinsurance transactions without a more complete exploration of the insurance accounting model.

97. Some would prefer that the distinction between prospective and retroactive contracts be based on the event covered by the reinsurance contract rather than the insured event under the insurance contract. Others recommended using management's intentions to determine whether the contract is prospective or retroactive. The Board concluded that the significant distinction in reinsurance is whether an insured event has occurred under the underlying insurance contracts. The nature of the risks assumed by the reinsurer is fundamentally different when an insured event has already occurred. The Board also believes that management's intentions do not determine whether a contract is retroactive or prospective.

98. Reinsurance contracts may include both prospective and retroactive provisions. For example, a reinsurance contract that reinsures liabilities relating to contracts written during one or more prior years also may reinsure losses on contracts to be written during one or more future years. Reinsurance also may be acquired some time after the reinsured contract has been written, but before the close of the coverage period for that contract, and be made effective as of the beginning of the contract period. This may result in a reinsurance contract with prospective and retroactive provisions that relate to a single contract year.[16]

99. A troublesome issue for the Board was deciding whether and how to separate the various elements of such mixed contracts. The Exposure Draft proposed separate accounting for the prospective and retroactive elements of all contracts having elements of both. Respondents observed that the cost to separate these elements could be significant and separation would not be practicable in all circumstances. They generally would have resolved this problem by making the classification based on the contract's predominant characteristics. The Board rejected that approach because the criterion for making the determination was vague and could require extremely detailed implementation guidance. When practicable, separate accounting is required for the prospective and retroactive provisions of the contract. Otherwise, the contract is classified as retroactive.

100. The Board concluded that amounts paid for prospective reinsurance should be amortized over the contract period in proportion to the amount of insurance protection provided. This approach ignores the protection provided by reinsurance over the remaining settlement period but is consistent with the basic insurance accounting model in Statement 60 for short-duration contracts, which recognizes estimated revenues and costs over the contract period. Subsequent changes in estimates are recognized in income of the period in which the estimates are changed.

101. The amounts paid for retroactive reinsurance are made up of various elements of the reinsurance contract. The primary elements are the implicit discounting of the related liabilities and a premium for indemnification against loss from adverse development on the reinsured contracts. It generally is not practicable to identify the effect of each element, and the Board has not required these elements to be accounted for separately. However, the amount paid to the reinsurer for retroactive reinsurance may ex-

---

[16]It is not uncommon for a reinsurance arrangement to be initiated before the beginning of a policy period but not finalized until after the policy period begins. Whether there was agreement in principle at the beginning of the policy period and, therefore, the contract is substantively prospective must be determined based on the facts and circumstances.

ceed the recorded liabilities relating to the reinsured contracts. In the Exposure Draft, the Board concluded that amounts paid for a reinsurance contract in excess of the related liabilities either may result from significant risk of future adverse development under the reinsured contracts or may indicate that the liabilities are understated. The Exposure Draft would have permitted amounts in excess of the recorded liabilities to be recognized as an asset to the extent they represented protection against future adverse development.

102. Respondents who addressed this issue generally disagreed with the Board's conclusion. Some pointed out that, when such differences arise from retroactive transactions, the reinsured events have already occurred. The uncertainty that is being reinsured is the estimation of the liabilities relating to those past events, and the amount paid to the reinsurer in excess of the recorded liabilities may be viewed as representing at least the minimum liability that should be accrued. Otherwise, the amount does not reflect anticipated future recoveries from the reinsurer and should not be recorded as an asset. The Board concluded that amounts paid for retroactive reinsurance in excess of recorded liabilities should be charged to expense at the inception of the reinsurance contract. The offsetting adjustment may increase the liability, reduce the amount recoverable from the reinsurer, or both, depending on the facts and circumstances. Recognizing an appropriate liability for the claims relating to the underlying reinsured contracts may require a charge to expense greater than the amount paid in excess of the recorded liabilities, but the charge to expense will not be less than that amount.

103. The Board concluded that costs and revenues of retroactive reinsurance other than amounts in excess of the recorded liabilities should be accounted for over the settlement period of the underlying insurance contracts. Unlike prospective reinsurance, a retroactive reinsurance contract cannot provide protection over the coverage period. That period is past, and any protection provided by retroactive reinsurance must relate to the remaining settlement period.

104. Some respondents objected to the inconsistency between settlement period accounting for retroactive contracts and the contract period accounting required by the insurance accounting model. However, the Board observed that resolving that inconsistency would entail a comprehensive review of insurance accounting, including reconsideration of revenue and expense recognition, measurement (discounting), and financial statement presentation. One solution to the inconsistency that likely would be considered if such a comprehensive review were undertaken is accounting for all insurance and reinsurance contracts over the settlement period. Although the Board has not deliberated this issue, some believe that the settlement period best represents the period over which services are provided by insurers and reinsurers and, therefore, is the appropriate period over which all revenues and costs should be recognized. The Board concluded that the concerns raised in this project are not sufficient to expand the scope to a general reconsideration of insurance accounting and that users would be better served by a more timely resolution of concerns specific to reinsurance reporting.

105. The Board faced similar issues in defining the amortization method for gains deferred for retroactive reinsurance contracts. To the extent the deferred gain arises from the implicit discounting of liabilities, amortization using the interest method would appear appropriate. However, the difference being amortized is the net accounting effect of all elements of the reinsurance contract, including the effects of discounting and of the premium paid for indemnification against loss or liability relating to insurance risk. Separate identification and accounting for each element is not considered feasible and would have greatly increased the complexity of this Statement. The interest method also requires estimates of the amount and timing of payments, which may not be practicable in some circumstances. Consequently, the Exposure Draft would have permitted ratable recognition as amounts are recovered under the reinsurance contract (the recovery method) or on a straight-line basis.

106. The Board's decision to eliminate the deferral of amounts in excess of recorded liabilities (as described in paragraph 23) made the straight-line method unnecessary. Many respondents to the Exposure Draft found that method objectionable on conceptual grounds. A number of respondents also recommended that the interest method be required when practicable. Upon reconsideration, the Board agreed to require the interest method when the amount and timing of the recoveries can be reasonably estimated and require the recovery method in other circumstances.

107. Amortization of deferred amounts arising from retroactive reinsurance under both the interest method and the recovery method is based on the ceding enterprise's estimates of the expected timing and total amount of cash flows. The Board concluded that the timing of changes in those estimates should not alter the recognition of the revenues and costs of reinsurance. Therefore, this Statement requires changes in estimates of the amount recoverable from the reinsurer to be ac-

counted for consistently both at the inception of and after the reinsurance transaction.

108. Establishing an amount recoverable from a reinsurer may result in a deferred gain, reflecting the amount by which the recorded liabilities exceed the amounts paid to the reinsurer. Likewise, a change in the estimate of the amount recoverable from a reinsurer after the inception of the reinsurance transaction results in or adjusts the amount of a deferral. Previously deferred amounts are reduced when the estimate is decreased. However, if the revised estimate of the related liabilities is less than the amounts paid to the reinsurer, a loss is not deferred. The resulting difference is charged to expense, as described in paragraph 23.

109. Changes in the estimated amount recoverable from a reinsurer or the timing of receipts related to those amounts affect amortization through a catch-up adjustment. When the change in estimate is recognized, the deferral is adjusted to the balance that would have existed had the revised estimate been available at the inception of the reinsurance transaction, with an offsetting charge or credit to income.

Recognition of Revenues and Costs for Reinsurance of Long-Duration Contracts

110. When a long-duration contract is reinsured, there may be a difference between the amounts paid for the reinsurance contract and the amount of liabilities related to the underlying reinsured contracts. That difference results from differences between the assumptions used by the ceding enterprise and those used by the reinsurer in estimating the future performance of the reinsured contracts.

111. The Board concluded that the difference between the amounts paid for a reinsurance contract and the amount of liabilities related to the underlying long-duration contracts should be considered part of the net cost of the reinsurance at the time it is acquired. The cost of reinsurance should be recognized over the remaining life of the underlying reinsured contracts unless the reinsurance contract is short duration in nature, when the cost should be recognized over the period of the reinsurance contract. Determining whether reinsurance of a long-duration contract is short duration in nature is a matter of judgment. For example, some contracts described as yearly renewable term may be, in substance, long-duration contracts, depending on their terms and how they are priced. Paragraphs 7 and 8 of Statement 60 provide guidance on distinguishing between short-duration and long-duration contracts.

Disclosure

112. Statement 60 required disclosure of the nature and significance of reinsurance transactions to the enterprise's operations, including total reinsurance premiums assumed and ceded, and estimated amounts recoverable from reinsurers, which are offset against claim liabilities. Current reinsurance disclosures are not comparable, are often difficult to understand, and are not as useful as they could be in assessing the effect of reinsurance on the operating results of an insurance enterprise. Moreover, disclosures about the credit risk associated with reinsurance receivables currently are not provided.

113. This Statement supersedes the disclosure requirements in paragraph 60(f) of Statement 60. Because of the complexities of reinsurance, the Board concluded that the gross amounts reported in the financial statements should be supplemented by disclosure about the nature, purpose, and effect of reinsurance transactions on the ceding enterprise. However, because the uses of reinsurance are varied, the Board did not specify what information is useful in assessing the effect of reinsurance, other than to require an indication by ceding enterprises that reinsurance does not relieve the insurer of its obligation to the policyholder. Appendix B provides some illustrations of disclosures required by this Statement. The Board determined that information about the significance of reinsurance, as reflected in the total amount of reinsurance premiums ceded and assumed, should be provided, including information about both written and earned premiums relating to short-duration contracts (if the difference is significant).

114. In reviewing current disclosure practices, the Board observed that credit risk associated with amounts due from reinsurers, although significant to some insurance enterprises, is not disclosed. Insurance contracts were among the financial instruments excluded from the scope of Statement 105, because the significant business risks involved generally are other than credit and market risk, namely, uncertainty about the ultimate timing and amount of claims. Because receivables and payables that result from insurance contracts are not subject to the same insurance risks that persuaded the Board to exclude insurance contracts from Statement 105, the Board concluded that Statement 105 disclosures are required for concentrations of credit risk for reinsurance receivables and prepaid reinsurance premiums.

115. The Board considered whether disclosures about the extent to which reinsurance contracts indemnify the ceding enterprise against loss or liability relating to insurance risk would be useful in as-

sessing the viability of an insurance enterprise and the objectives of reinsurance. The Board decided that a specific disclosure requirement should not be imposed in this Statement. The extent to which risk is transferred between enterprises has broader implications than reinsurance. For example, those disclosures would be relevant for insurance purchased by any enterprise and for transactions that purport to hedge financial positions. Developing verifiable and reliable disclosures may be difficult, but the Board encourages appropriate disclosure of indemnification policies as part of this Statement's required disclosure about the nature and effect of reinsurance transactions.

116. Some respondents asked the Board to consider requiring numerous additional disclosures other than those included in the Exposure Draft. Several of these would have imposed more stringent requirements on insurers than are imposed on other enterprises in the same circumstances. For example, a number of respondents suggested additional disclosures about credit risk that would have effectively amended Statement 105 to result in stricter requirements for insurers. The Board rejected these suggestions because it believes disclosures applicable to all enterprises should be applied consistently across industries. In considering requests for additional disclosures, the Board also balanced concerns about "disclosure overload" with requests from some respondents for additional disclosures that financial statement users might find useful. The Board concluded that the disclosures required in this Statement achieve an appropriate balance between those concerns.

Effective Date and Transition

117. The Board concluded that this Statement should be applied in a manner that will minimize the accounting changes that must be made for existing reinsurance contracts. The Board discussed effective dates intended to allow insurance enterprises sufficient time to gather the required information for restatement of assets and liabilities of prior periods, if desired. Because information similar to that required by this Statement must be reported under current regulatory requirements and should be available to the reporting enterprise and because constituents indicated that improved reporting in this area is needed as soon as is practicable, the Board concluded that this Statement should be effective for fiscal years beginning after December 15, 1992. However, to allow more time for adoption, the provisions of this Statement relating to indemnification against loss or liability relating to insurance risk and recognition of revenues and costs need not be applied in financial statements for interim periods in the year of adoption.

If those interim amounts are reported with annual financial statements for that fiscal year, restatement is required.

118. The Exposure Draft would have allowed restatement of previously reported revenues and costs if the financial statements also were restated to report gross amounts. Upon reconsideration, the Board concluded that restatement was not appropriate because of the significance of management's intentions in determining whether and when to enter into a reinsurance transaction. Prohibiting restatement of revenues and costs also will result in more consistent reporting during the transition period and will lessen implementation costs for some enterprises.

119. The Exposure Draft would have applied to transactions entered into or renewed in the year of adoption. Respondents asked how this provision should be applied to continuous and multiple-year contracts and to contract amendments. The Board concluded that this Statement should apply to transactions having an anniversary date in the year of adoption, effectively subjecting all in-force reinsurance contracts to its provisions. The Board also concluded that this Statement should apply to all contract amendments, including amendments of contracts that were otherwise excluded from this Statement under the transition provisions. However, because financial statements will not be restated to reflect the provisions on recognition of revenues and costs, previously recognized amounts relating to existing contracts are not affected by this Statement.

Appendix B

ILLUSTRATIONS

Introduction

120. This appendix contrasts reporting of gross amounts for reinsurance contracts, as required by this Statement, and reporting of net amounts for those contracts, as previously required by Statement 60. The requirements of this Statement are applied to a property-casualty insurance enterprise that issues short-duration contracts in Illustration 1 and to a life insurance enterprise that issues long-duration contracts in Illustration 2. The illustrations include examples of reinsurance disclosures that would be appropriate under the provisions of this Statement. Significant judgment is required in assessing the adequacy of disclosures. These examples are not intended to incorporate all possible types of disclosure that may be relevant.

Illustration 1

The Property-Casualty Insurance Company
Statement of Financial Position (in millions)

	Gross	Net[a]
Assets:		
Investments	$ 8,500	$ 8,500
Cash	20	20
Receivables:		
Reinsurance[b]	1,400	100
Other	1,900	1,900
Deferred policy acquisition costs	300	300
Prepaid reinsurance premiums[c]	250	—
Other assets	1,400	1,400
Total assets	$13,770	$12,220
Liabilities and equity:		
Liabilities for claims and claim settlement expenses	$ 7,600	$ 6,300
Unearned premiums	1,700	1,450
Other liabilities	2,300	2,300
Equity	2,170	2,170
Total liabilities and equity	$13,770	$12,220

The Property-Casualty Insurance Company
Statement of Earnings (in millions)

	Gross	Net[a]
Revenues:		
Premiums earned	$3,350	$2,900
Premiums ceded[d]	(450)	—
Net premiums earned	2,900	2,900
Net investment income	1,700	1,700
Other revenues	400	400
Total revenues	5,000	5,000
Expenses:		
Claims and claim settlement expenses	2,200	1,900
Reinsurance recoveries[d]	(300)	—
Net claims and claim settlement expenses	1,900	1,900
Policy acquisition costs	1,450	1,450
Other expenses	1,150	1,150
Total expenses	4,500	4,500
Earnings before tax	$ 500	$ 500

[a]Net numbers are presented for illustrative comparison and are not required by this Statement.

[b]Under Statement 60 requirements, typically only the amount receivable for paid claims and claim settlement expenses would be reported as a reinsurance receivable. This Statement requires that estimated amounts receivable from reinsurers include amounts related to paid and unpaid claims and claims incurred but not reported. Details of the amounts comprising reinsurance receivables may be presented separately.

[c]Prepaid reinsurance premiums include amounts paid to reinsurers relating to the unexpired portion of reinsured policies, often referred to as ceded unearned premiums.

[d]Alternatively, the effect of reinsurance on premiums earned and claim costs may be shown parenthetically or may be disclosed. For example, following is an illustration of a parenthetical presentation:

Premiums earned (net of premiums ceded totaling $450)	$2,900
Claims and claim settlement expenses (net of reinsurance recoveries totaling $300)	$1,900

The Property-Casualty Insurance Company
Notes to Financial Statements

Summary of Significant Accounting Policies

In the normal course of business, the Company seeks to reduce the loss that may arise from catastrophes or other events that cause unfavorable underwriting results by reinsuring certain levels of risk in various areas of exposure with other insurance enterprises or reinsurers.

Amounts recoverable from reinsurers are estimated in a manner consistent with the claim liability associated with the reinsured policy. The amount by which the liabilities associated with the reinsured policies exceed the amounts paid for retroactive reinsurance contracts is amortized in income over the estimated remaining settlement period using the interest method. The effects of subsequent changes in estimated or actual cash flows are accounted for by adjusting the previously deferred amount to the balance that would have existed had the revised estimate been available at the inception of the reinsurance transactions, with a corresponding charge or credit to income.

Reinsurance

Reinsurance contracts do not relieve the Company from its obligations to policyholders. Failure of reinsurers to honor their obligations could result in losses to the Company; consequently, allowances are established for amounts deemed uncollectible. The Company evaluates the financial condition of its reinsurers and monitors concentrations of credit risk arising from similar geographic regions, activities, or economic characteristics of the reinsurers to minimize its exposure to significant losses from reinsurer insolvencies. At December 31, 19X3, reinsurance receivables with a carrying value of $260 million and prepaid reinsurance premiums of $45 million were associated with a single reinsurer. The Company holds collateral under related reinsurance agreements in the form of letters of credit totaling $150 million that can be drawn on for amounts that remain unpaid for more than 120 days.

The effect of reinsurance on premiums written and earned is as follows (in millions):

	Written	Earned
Direct	$2,880	$2,730
Assumed	630	620
Ceded	(470)	(450)
Net premiums	$3,040	$2,900

Illustration 2

The Life Insurance Company
Statement of Financial Position (in millions)

	Gross	Net[a]
Assets:		
Investments	$13,100	$13,100
Cash	20	20
Receivables:		
Reinsurance[b]	1,400	100
Other	1,900	1,900
Deferred policy acquisition costs	300	300
Other assets	1,400	1,400
Total assets	$18,120	$16,820
Liabilities and equity:		
Liability for policy benefits	$ 7,200	$ 6,300
Policyholders' contract deposits	5,000	4,600
Other liabilities	3,750	3,750
Equity	2,170	2,170
Total liabilities and equity	$18,120	$16,820

The Life Insurance Company
Statement of Earnings (in millions)

	Gross	Net[a]
Revenues:		
Premiums and policyholder fees earned	$3,350	$2,900
Premiums ceded[c]	(450)	—
Net premiums and policyholder fees earned	2,900	2,900
Net investment income	1,700	1,700
Other revenues	400	400
Total revenues	5,000	5,000
Expenses:		
Policyholder benefits	2,200	1,900
Reinsurance recoveries[c]	(300)	—
Net policyholder benefits	1,900	1,900
Amortization of deferred policy acquisition costs	950	950
Other expenses	1,650	1,650
Total expenses	4,500	4,500
Earnings before tax	$ 500	$ 500

[a]Net numbers are presented for illustrative comparison and are not required by this Statement.

[b]Under Statement 60 requirements, typically only the amount receivable for benefits and expenses paid would be reported as a reinsurance receivable. This Statement requires that estimated amounts receivable from reinsurers include amounts related to paid and unpaid benefits, including amounts related to liabilities recognized for future policy benefits. Details of the amounts comprising reinsurance receivables may be presented separately.

[c]Alternatively, the effect of reinsurance on premiums earned and benefit costs may be shown parenthetically or may be disclosed. For example, following is an illustration of a parenthetical presentation:

Premiums and policyholder fees earned (net of premiums ceded totaling $450) $2,900

Benefits (net of reinsurance recoveries totaling $300) $1,900

The Life Insurance Company
Notes to Financial Statements

Summary of Significant Accounting Policies

In the normal course of business, the Company seeks to limit its exposure to loss on any single insured and to recover a portion of benefits paid by ceding reinsurance to other insurance enterprises or reinsurers under excess coverage and coinsurance contracts. The Company retains a maximum of $500,000 of coverage per individual life.

Amounts paid or deemed to have been paid for reinsurance contracts are recorded as reinsurance receivables. The cost of reinsurance related to long-duration contracts is accounted for over the life of the underlying reinsured policies using assumptions consistent with those used to account for the underlying policies.

Reinsurance

Reinsurance contracts do not relieve the Company from its obligations to policyholders. Failure of reinsurers to honor their obligations could result in losses to the Company; consequently, allowances are established for amounts deemed uncollectible. The Company evaluates the financial condition of its reinsurers and monitors concentrations of credit risk arising from similar geographic regions, activities, or economic characteristics of the reinsurers to minimize its exposure to significant losses from reinsurer insolvencies. At December 31, 19X3, reinsurance receivables with a carrying value of $260 million were associated with a single reinsurer. The Company holds collateral under related reinsurance agreements in the form of letters of credit totaling $150 million that can be drawn on for amounts that remain unpaid for more than 120 days.

The effect of reinsurance on premiums and amounts earned is as follows (in millions):

Direct premiums and amounts assessed against policyholders	$2,730
Reinsurance assumed	620
Reinsurance ceded	(450)
Net premiums and amounts earned	$2,900

Appendix C

GLOSSARY

121. This appendix defines certain terms as they are used in this Statement. Various other terms common to the insurance industry are defined in Appendix A of Statement 60.

Assuming enterprise
The party that receives a reinsurance premium in a reinsurance transaction. The assuming enterprise (or reinsurer) accepts an obligation to reimburse a ceding enterprise under the terms of the reinsurance contract.

Ceding enterprise
The party that pays a reinsurance premium in a reinsurance transaction. The ceding enterprise receives the right to reimbursement from the assuming enterprise under the terms of the reinsurance contract.

Contract period
The period over which insured events that occur are covered by the reinsured contracts. Commonly referred to as the coverage period or period that the contracts are in force.

Fronting arrangements
Reinsurance arrangements in which the ceding enterprise issues a policy and reinsures all or substantially all of the insurance risk with the assuming enterprise.

Insurance risk
The risk arising from uncertainties about both (a) the ultimate amount of net cash flows from premiums, commissions, claims, and claim settlement expenses paid under a contract (often referred to as underwriting risk) and (b) the timing of the receipt and payment of those cash flows (often referred to as timing risk). Actual or imputed investment returns are not an element of insurance risk. Insurance risk is fortuitous—the possibility of adverse events occurring is outside the control of the insured.

Prospective reinsurance
Reinsurance in which an assuming enterprise agrees to reimburse a ceding enterprise for losses that may be incurred as a result of future insurable events covered under contracts subject to the reinsurance. A reinsurance contract may include both prospective and retroactive reinsurance provisions.

Reinsurance receivables
All amounts recoverable from reinsurers for paid and unpaid claims and claim settlement expenses, including estimated amounts receivable

for unsettled claims, claims incurred but not reported, or policy benefits.

Reinsurer
Refer to **Assuming enterprise.**

Retroactive reinsurance
Reinsurance in which an assuming enterprise agrees to reimburse a ceding enterprise for liabilities incurred as a result of past insurable events covered under contracts subject to the reinsurance. A reinsurance contract may include both prospective and retroactive reinsurance provisions.

Settlement period
The estimated period over which a ceding enterprise expects to recover substantially all amounts due from the reinsurer under the terms of the reinsurance contract.

Statement of Financial Accounting Standards No. 114
Accounting by Creditors for Impairment of a Loan

an amendment of FASB Statements No. 5 and 15

STATUS

Issued: May 1993

Effective Date: For fiscal years beginning after December 15, 1994

Affects: Amends FAS 5, paragraph 23
   Amends prospectively FAS 15, paragraphs 1, 33, 34, and 42
   Supersedes prospectively FAS 15, paragraphs 30 through 32, 35 through 37, 40(a), and 41 and
    footnotes 18, 19, 21, 24, and 25
   Amends FAS 60, paragraph 47
   Amends FAS 91, paragraph 14
   Supersedes FTB 79-6
   Supersedes FTB 79-7

Affected by: Paragraphs 8 and 11 through 15 amended by FAS 118
    Paragraphs 17 through 20 and 65 superseded by FAS 118

Other Interpretive Pronouncement: FTB 94-1

Issues Discussed by FASB Emerging Issues Task Force (EITF)

 Affects: Nullifies EITF Issues No. 87-5 and 89-9 and Topic No. D-37

 Interpreted by: No EITF Issues

 Related Issues: EITF Issues No. 84-4, 84-19, 85-44, 87-18, 87-19, 94-8, and 96-22

SUMMARY

  This Statement addresses the accounting by creditors for impairment of certain loans. It is applicable to all creditors and to all loans, uncollateralized as well as collateralized, except large groups of smaller-balance homogeneous loans that are collectively evaluated for impairment, loans that are measured at fair value or at the lower of cost or fair value, leases, and debt securities as defined in FASB Statement No. 115, *Accounting for Certain Investments in Debt and Equity Securities.* It applies to all loans that are restructured in a troubled debt restructuring involving a modification of terms.

  It requires that impaired loans that are within the scope of this Statement be measured based on the present value of expected future cash flows discounted at the loan's effective interest rate or, as a practical expedient, at the loan's observable market price or the fair value of the collateral if the loan is collateral dependent.

  This Statement amends FASB Statement No. 5, *Accounting for Contingencies,* to clarify that a creditor should evaluate the collectibility of both contractual interest and contractual principal of all receivables when assessing the need for a loss accrual. This Statement also amends FASB Statement No. 15, *Accounting by Debtors and Creditors for Troubled Debt Restructurings,* to require a creditor to measure all loans that are restructured in a troubled debt restructuring involving a modification of terms in accordance with this Statement.

  This Statement applies to financial statements for fiscal years beginning after December 15, 1994. Earlier application is encouraged.

Statement of Financial Accounting Standards No. 114

Accounting by Creditors for Impairment of a Loan

an amendment of FASB Statements No. 5 and 15

CONTENTS

INTRODUCTION

1. The FASB was asked by the AICPA's Accounting Standards Executive Committee (AcSEC), the Federal Deposit Insurance Corporation (FDIC), and others to address in what circumstances, if any, a creditor should measure impairment of a loan based on the present (discounted) value of expected future cash flows related to the loan. AcSEC originally addressed the issue of accounting for loan impairment in an effort to reconcile certain AICPA Audit and Accounting Guides for different types of financial institutions, which provide inconsistent guidance for the application of FASB Statement No. 5, *Accounting for Contingencies,* to the loan portfolio of a financial institution. That inconsistent guidance has resulted in significant differences in when and how different types of financial institutions recognize losses for impaired loans.

2. This Statement amends Statement 5 to clarify that a creditor should evaluate the collectibility of both contractual interest and contractual principal of all receivables when assessing the need for a loss accrual.

3. This Statement also amends FASB Statement No. 15, *Accounting by Debtors and Creditors for Troubled Debt Restructurings,* to require creditors to measure all loans that are restructured in a trou-

bled debt restructuring involving a modification of terms in accordance with this Statement.

STANDARDS OF FINANCIAL ACCOUNTING AND REPORTING

Definitions and Scope

4. For purposes of this Statement, a loan is a contractual right to receive money on demand or on fixed or determinable dates that is recognized as an asset in the creditor's statement of financial position. Examples include but are not limited to accounts receivable (with terms exceeding one year) and notes receivable.

5. This Statement applies to all creditors. It addresses the accounting by creditors for impairment of a loan by specifying how allowances for credit losses related to certain loans should be determined. This Statement also addresses the accounting by creditors for all loans that are restructured in a troubled debt restructuring involving a modification of terms of a receivable, except restructurings of loans excluded from the scope of this Statement in paragraph 6(b)-(d), including those involving a receipt of assets in partial satisfaction of a receivable. The term *troubled debt restructuring* is used in this Statement consistent with its use in Statement 15.

6. This Statement applies to all loans that are identified for evaluation, uncollateralized as well as collateralized, except:

a. Large groups of smaller-balance homogeneous loans that are collectively evaluated for impairment. Those loans may include but are not limited to credit card, residential mortgage, and consumer installment loans.
b. Loans that are measured at fair value or at the lower of cost or fair value, for example, in accordance with FASB Statement No. 65, *Accounting for Certain Mortgage Banking Activities*, or other specialized industry practice.
c. Leases as defined in FASB Statement No. 13, *Accounting for Leases*.
d. Debt securities as defined in FASB Statement No. 115, *Accounting for Certain Investments in Debt and Equity Securities*.

7. This Statement does not specify how a creditor should identify loans that are to be evaluated for collectibility.[1] A creditor should apply its normal loan review procedures in making that judgment. This Statement does not address when a creditor should record a direct write-down of an impaired loan, nor does it address how a creditor should assess the overall adequacy of the allowance for credit losses. In addition to the allowance calculated in accordance with this Statement, a creditor should continue to recognize an allowance for credit losses necessary to comply with Statement 5.

Recognition of Impairment

8. A loan is impaired when, based on current information and events, it is probable that a creditor will be unable to collect all amounts due according to the contractual terms of the loan agreement. As used in this Statement and in Statement 5, as amended, *all amounts due according to the contractual terms* means that both the contractual interest payments and the contractual principal payments of a loan will be collected as scheduled in the loan agreement. This Statement does not specify how a creditor should determine that it is probable that it will be unable to collect all amounts due according to the contractual terms of a loan. A creditor should apply its normal loan review procedures in making that judgment. An insignificant delay or insignificant shortfall in amount of payments does not require application of this Statement. A loan is not impaired during a period of delay in payment if the creditor expects to collect all amounts due including interest accrued at the contractual interest rate for the period of delay. Thus, a demand loan or other loan with no stated maturity is not impaired if the creditor expects to collect all amounts due including interest accrued at the contractual interest rate during the period the loan is outstanding.

9. Usually, a loan whose terms are modified in a troubled debt restructuring already will have been identified as impaired because the condition specified in paragraph 8 will have existed before a formal restructuring. However, if a loan is excluded from the scope of this Statement under paragraph 6(a), a creditor may not have accounted for that loan in accordance with this Statement before the loan was restructured. The creditor shall apply the provisions of this Statement to that loan when it is restructured.

10. The term *probable* is used in this Statement consistent with its use in Statement 5, which defines probable as an area within a range of the likelihood that a future event or events will occur confirming the fact of the loss. That range is from probable to remote, as follows:

Probable. The future event or events are likely to occur.
Reasonably possible. The chance of the future event or events occurring is more than remote but less than likely.
Remote. The chance of the future event or events occurring is slight.

The term probable is further described in paragraph 84 of Statement 5, which states:

The conditions for accrual in paragraph 8 [of Statement 5] are not inconsistent with the accounting concept of conservatism. *Those conditions are not intended to be so rigid that they require virtual certainty before a loss is accrued.* [Emphasis added.] They require only that it be *probable* that an asset has been impaired or a liability has been incurred and that the amount of loss be *reasonably* estimable. [Emphasis in original.]

---

[1]Sources of information useful in identifying loans for evaluation that are listed in the AICPA's Auditing Procedure Study, *Auditing the Allowance for Credit Losses of Banks,* include a specific materiality criterion; regulatory reports of examination; internally generated listings such as "watch lists," past due reports, overdraft listings, and listings of loans to insiders; management reports of total loan amounts by borrower; historical loss experience by type of loan; loan files lacking current financial data related to borrowers and guarantors; borrowers experiencing problems such as operating losses, marginal working capital, inadequate cash flow, or business interruptions; loans secured by collateral that is not readily marketable or that is susceptible to deterioration in realizable value; loans to borrowers in industries or countries experiencing economic instability; and loan documentation and compliance exception reports.

Measurement of Impairment

11. Measuring impaired loans requires judgment and estimates, and the eventual outcomes may differ from those estimates. Creditors should have latitude to develop measurement methods that are practical in their circumstances. Paragraphs 12-16 address those measurement methods.

12. Some impaired loans have risk characteristics that are unique to an individual borrower, and the creditor will apply the measurement methods described in paragraphs 13-16 on a loan-by-loan basis. However, some impaired loans may have risk characteristics in common with other impaired loans. A creditor may aggregate those loans and may use historical statistics, such as average recovery period and average amount recovered, along with a composite effective interest rate as a means of measuring those impaired loans.

13. When a loan is impaired as defined in paragraph 8 of this Statement, a creditor shall measure impairment based on the present value of expected future cash flows discounted at the loan's effective interest rate, except that as a practical expedient, a creditor may measure impairment based on a loan's observable market price, or the fair value of the collateral if the loan is collateral dependent. Regardless of the measurement method, a creditor shall measure impairment based on the fair value of the collateral when the creditor determines that foreclosure is probable. A loan is collateral dependent if the repayment of the loan is expected to be provided solely by the underlying collateral. The creditor may choose a measurement method on a loan-by-loan basis. A creditor shall consider estimated costs to sell, on a discounted basis, in the measure of impairment if those costs are expected to reduce the cash flows available to repay or otherwise satisfy the loan. If the measure of the impaired loan is less than the recorded investment in the loan[2] (including accrued interest, net deferred loan fees or costs, and unamortized premium or discount), a creditor shall recognize an impairment by creating a valuation allowance with a corresponding charge to bad-debt expense or by adjusting an existing valuation allowance for the impaired loan with a corresponding charge or credit to bad-debt expense.

14. If a creditor measures an impaired loan using a present value amount, the creditor shall calculate

that present value amount based on an estimate of the expected future cash flows of the impaired loan, discounted at the loan's effective interest rate. The effective interest rate of a loan is the rate of return implicit in the loan (that is, the contractual interest rate adjusted for any net deferred loan fees or costs, premium, or discount existing at the origination or acquisition of the loan).[3] The effective interest rate for a loan restructured in a troubled debt restructuring is based on the original contractual rate, not the rate specified in the restructuring agreement. If the loan's contractual interest rate varies based on subsequent changes in an independent factor, such as an index or rate (for example, the prime rate, the London interbank offered rate, or the U.S. Treasury bill weekly average), that loan's effective interest rate may be calculated based on the factor as it changes over the life of the loan or may be fixed at the rate in effect at the date the loan meets the impairment criterion in paragraph 8. The creditor's choice shall be applied consistently for all loans whose contractual interest rate varies based on subsequent changes in an independent factor. Projections of changes in the factor should not be made for purposes of determining the effective interest rate or estimating expected future cash flows.

15. If a creditor measures an impaired loan using a present value calculation, the estimates of expected future cash flows shall be the creditor's best estimate based on reasonable and supportable assumptions and projections. All available evidence, including estimated costs to sell if those costs are expected to reduce the cash flows available to repay or otherwise satisfy the loan, should be considered in developing the estimate of expected future cash flows. The weight given to the evidence should be commensurate with the extent to which the evidence can be verified objectively. If a creditor estimates a range for either the amount or timing of possible cash flows, the likelihood of the possible outcomes shall be considered in determining the best estimate of expected future cash flows.

16. Subsequent to the initial measurement of impairment, if there is a significant change (increase or decrease) in the amount or timing of an impaired loan's expected future cash flows, or if actual cash flows are significantly different from the cash flows previously projected, a creditor shall recalculate the impairment by applying the procedures specified in paragraphs 12-15 and by adjust-

---

[2]The term *recorded investment in the loan* is distinguished from *net carrying amount of the loan* because the latter term is net of a valuation allowance, while the former term is not. The recorded investment in the loan does, however, reflect any direct write-down of the investment.

[3]A loan may be acquired at a discount because of a change in credit quality or rate or both. When a loan is acquired at a discount that relates, at least in part, to the loan's credit quality, the effective interest rate is the discount rate that equates the present value of the investor's estimate of the loan's future cash flows with the purchase price of the loan.

ing the valuation allowance. Similarly, a creditor that measures impairment based on the observable market price of an impaired loan or the fair value of the collateral of an impaired collateral-dependent loan shall adjust the valuation allowance if there is a significant change (increase or decrease) in either of those bases. However, the net carrying amount of the loan shall at no time exceed the recorded investment in the loan.

Income Recognition

17. The present value of an impaired loan's expected future cash flows will change from one reporting period to the next because of the passage of time and also may change because of revised estimates in the amount or timing of those cash flows. A creditor shall recognize the change in present value in accordance with either (a) or (b) as follows:

a. The increase in present value of the expected future cash flows that is attributable to the passage of time shall be reported as interest income accrued on the net carrying amount of the loan at the effective interest rate used to discount the impaired loan's estimated future cash flows. The change in present value, if any, that is attributable to changes in the amount or timing of expected future cash flows shall be reported as bad-debt expense in the same manner in which impairment initially was recognized or as a reduction in the amount of bad-debt expense that otherwise would be reported.
b. The entire change in present value shall be reported as bad-debt expense in the same manner in which impairment initially was recognized or as a reduction in the amount of bad-debt expense that otherwise would be reported.

18. A creditor that recognizes income in accordance with paragraph 17(a) shall apply that method to all loans for which impairment is measured based on the present value of expected future cash flows discounted at the loan's effective interest rate and shall apply that method consistently from one reporting period to the next.

19. The observable market price of an impaired loan or the fair value of the collateral of an impaired collateral-dependent loan may change from one reporting period to the next. A creditor that measures impairment on either of those bases shall report a decrease in the measure of the impaired loan as bad-debt expense in the same manner in which impairment initially was recognized. An increase in the measure of the impaired loan shall be reported as a reduction in the amount of bad-debt expense that otherwise would be reported.

Disclosures

20. A creditor shall disclose, either in the body of the financial statements or in the accompanying notes, the following information:

a. As of the date of each statement of financial position presented, the recorded investment in the loans for which impairment has been recognized in accordance with this Statement and the total allowance for credit losses related to those impaired loans
b. For each period for which results of operations are presented, the activity in the allowance for credit losses account, including the balance in the allowance for credit losses account at the beginning and end of each period, additions charged to operations, direct write-downs charged against the allowance, and recoveries of amounts previously charged off
c. The creditor's income recognition policy (paragraph 17(a) or (b)). A creditor that recognizes income in accordance with paragraph 17(a) also shall disclose the amount of interest income recognized in accordance with that paragraph.

Amendments to Existing Pronouncements

21. The first sentence of paragraph 23 of Statement 5 is replaced by the following:

If, based on current information and events, it is probable that the enterprise will be unable to collect all amounts due according to the contractual terms of the receivable, the condition in paragraph 8(a) is met. As used here, *all amounts due according to the contractual terms* means that both the contractual interest payments and the contractual principal payments will be collected as scheduled according to the receivable's contractual terms. However, a creditor need not consider an insignificant delay or insignificant shortfall in amount of payments as meeting the condition in paragraph 8(a).

22. Statement 15 is amended prospectively as follows:

a. The second sentence in paragraph 1 is replaced by:

A creditor in a troubled debt restructuring involving a modification of terms shall account for the restructured loan in accordance with the provisions of FASB Statement No. 114, *Accounting by Creditors for Impairment of a Loan,* except that a troubled debt restructuring involving a modification of terms before the effective date of Statement 114 may continue to be accounted for and disclosed in accordance with this Statement as long as the restructured loan is not impaired based on the terms of the restructuring agreement.

b. Paragraph 30 is replaced by the following:

A creditor in a troubled debt restructuring involving only a modification of terms of a receivable—that is, not involving receipt of assets (including an equity interest in the debtor)—shall account for the troubled debt restructuring in accordance with the provisions of Statement 114.

c. In the second sentence of paragraph 33, *paragraphs 30-32* is deleted and replaced by *Statement 114*. The third and fourth sentences are deleted.

d. In paragraph 34, the following is added after *foreclosure by the creditor,*:

that is, the creditor receives physical possession of the debtor's assets regardless of whether formal foreclosure proceedings take place,

e. In the third sentence of paragraph 42, *according to the provisions of paragraphs 30-32* is replaced by *as prescribed in Statement 114*. In the fourth sentence, *Those paragraphs* is replaced by *That Statement*.

f. Paragraphs 31, 32, 35-37, 40(a), 41, and footnotes 18, 19, 21, 24, and 25 are superseded prospectively. (Refer to paragraph 27 of this Statement.)

23. In the last sentence of paragraph 47 of FASB Statement No. 60, *Accounting and Reporting by Insurance Enterprises,* the phrase *realized gains and losses* is replaced by *income as prescribed in FASB Statement No. 114, Accounting by Creditors for Impairment of a Loan.*

24. In the first sentence of paragraph 14 of FASB Statement No. 91, *Accounting for Nonrefundable Fees and Costs Associated with Originating or Acquiring Loans and Initial Direct Costs of Leases,* the phrase *for purposes of applying paragraph 30 of that Statement* is deleted.

25. FASB Technical Bulletins No. 79-6, *Valuation Allowances Following Debt Restructuring,* and No. 79-7, *Recoveries of a Previous Writedown under a Troubled Debt Restructuring Involving a Modification of Terms,* are superseded by this Statement.

Effective Date and Transition

26. This Statement shall be effective for financial statements for fiscal years beginning after December 15, 1994. Earlier application is encouraged. Previously issued annual financial statements shall not be restated. Initial application of this Statement shall be as of the beginning of an enterprise's fiscal year (that is, if the Statement is adopted prior to the effective date and during an interim period other than the first interim period, all prior interim periods of that fiscal year shall be restated).

27. This Statement applies to all troubled debt restructurings involving a modification of terms. However, if a loan that was restructured in a troubled debt restructuring involving a modification of terms before the effective date of this Statement is not impaired based on the terms specified by the restructuring agreement, a creditor may continue to account for the loan in accordance with the provisions of Statement 15 prior to its amendment by this Statement.

> **The provisions of this Statement need not be applied to immaterial items.**

This Statement was adopted by the affirmative votes of five members of the Financial Accounting Standards Board. Messrs. Leisenring and Swieringa dissented.

Messrs. Leisenring and Swieringa disagree with the measurement of impaired loans required by paragraphs 13 and 14 of this Statement. They believe that if a loan is impaired, a new direct measurement of the loan at fair value should be recognized. That fair value should be measured by the market value of the loan or similar asset if an active market exists. If no market value is readily available, a creditor should use a forecast of expected future cash flows to estimate the fair value of the impaired loan, provided that those cash flows are discounted at a rate or rates commensurate with the risk involved.

Messrs. Leisenring and Swieringa disagree that this Statement has improved the information provided to users about impaired loans by eliminating inconsistencies in the accounting for those loans by different types of creditors for similar loans (paragraph 33). Paragraph 13 permits three different measures of impairment to be used by a given creditor for similar loans. The measures based on an observable market price of the loan or the fair value of the collateral of an impaired collateral-dependent loan are inconsistent with the Board's objective to measure only the loss due to credit deterioration (paragraph 51). Those two measurements reflect changes in market rates of interest or other factors that may cause a change in the fair value of an impaired loan. Messrs. Leisenring and Swieringa believe that a fair value objective or notion should underlie the measurement of all loan impairments. An impaired loan is a risky asset. Not only are expected future cash flows likely to differ from contractual amounts, there is risk that they will differ from actual future cash flows, in some cases dramatically. They believe that measuring that risky asset at its fair value provides the most relevant information about expected future cash flows and the riskiness of those cash flows.

Messrs. Leisenring and Swieringa also disagree with the requirement in paragraph 14 to discount expected future cash flows at the loan's effective interest rate if a creditor chooses to measure an impaired loan using a present value amount. As suggested above, they believe that expected future cash flows of an impaired loan should be discounted at market interest rates that reflect current economic events and conditions and that are commensurate with the risks involved; that is, current rates that would be charged under current conditions for a new loan with similar terms and expected future cash flows rather than at the loan's historical effective interest rate. The historical ef-

fective interest rate reflects the risk characteristics of the loan at the time it was originated or acquired, but not at the time it is impaired. In addition, they believe that use of an historical effective interest rate would overstate the charge to bad-debt expense if the effective rate is higher than current market rates. They believe that the charge to income for impairment losses should not exceed the charge to income that would be necessary for the net carrying amount to equal the loan's fair value.

Messrs. Leisenring and Swieringa disagree with the Board's conclusions about a troubled debt restructuring involving a modification of terms as defined in paragraph 5(c) of Statement 15. They believe that if a troubled loan is formally restructured, the terms of the original loan agreement and the loan's historical effective interest rate cease to be relevant and that the loan should be remeasured at fair value to reflect the risk characteristics of the loan and the market conditions at the time of the restructuring.

Finally, Mr. Leisenring disagrees with the conclusion in paragraph 27 that allows loans that were restructured before the effective date of this Statement and are not impaired based on the terms of the restructuring agreement to be accounted for in accordance with Statement 15. Mr. Leisenring believes that loans that were restructured prior to the effective date of this Statement should be remeasured at the market rate of interest in effect at the time the loan was restructured. If it is not practicable to determine the market rate in effect at that time, the current market rate of interest could be used.

Appendix

BACKGROUND INFORMATION AND BASIS FOR CONCLUSIONS

CONTENTS

Appendix

BACKGROUND INFORMATION AND BASIS FOR CONCLUSIONS

Introduction

28. This appendix summarizes considerations that were deemed significant by Board members in reaching the conclusions in this Statement. It includes reasons for accepting certain approaches and rejecting others. Individual Board members gave greater weight to some factors than to others.

29. An FASB Exposure Draft, *Accounting by Creditors for Impairment of a Loan,* was issued for public comment in June 1992. The Board received approximately 160 comment letters, and 17 organizations and individuals presented their views during a public hearing held on November 3 and 9, 1992. Also, four entities participated in a field test of the provisions of the Exposure Draft. Members of the Board visited six other entities to discuss the provisions of the Exposure Draft with chief executive officers, chief financial officers, and credit officers. The field test results and the results of the meetings, which are confidential at the entities' request, were useful to the Board during its deliberations of the issues addressed by this Statement.

Background Information

30. The Board accelerated part of the financial instruments project to address in what circum-

stances, if any, a creditor should measure the impairment of a loan based on the present value of expected future cash flows related to the loan. This acceleration was undertaken in part at the urging of AcSEC. AcSEC had previously considered this issue as part of a proposed Statement of Position that also considered how to determine whether collateral for a loan has been in-substance foreclosed and how to account for foreclosed assets. (AcSEC's consideration resulted in Practice Bulletin No. 7, *Criteria for Determining Whether Collateral for a Loan Has Been In-Substance Foreclosed,* and AICPA Statement of Position 92-3, *Accounting for Foreclosed Assets.*) However, AcSEC informed the Board that it could not develop a solution to the loan impairment issue that would achieve consensus and requested the Board to resolve the issue.

31. AcSEC originally undertook its deliberations in an effort to reconcile the inconsistent guidance existing in certain AICPA Audit and Accounting Guides. The Guides address, among other things, the application of Statement 5 to a financial institution's loan portfolio. The most significant inconsistency in the guidance relates to the inclusion of interest in the valuation of troubled loans. The AICPA Audit and Accounting Guide, *Audits of Savings Institutions,* and AICPA Statement of Position 75-2, *Accounting Practices of Real Estate Investment Trusts,* call for interest to be included in the measurement of troubled loans—a discounted cash flow concept—but other AICPA Guides are silent on that point. This inconsistent guidance led to different accounting among the different types

of financial institutions. The Securities and Exchange Commission, the Federal Home Loan Bank Board, and the FDIC also urged reconciliation of this diverse guidance.

Benefits and Costs

32. The FASB's mission statement charges the Board to determine that a proposed standard will fill a significant need and that the costs it imposes, compared with possible alternatives, will be justified in relation to the overall benefits. Fulfilling that charge can be problematic since there is no common gauge by which to judge objectively the costs to implement a standard against the need to report consistent, comparable, and reliable information in financial statements. The challenge is amplified because the costs to implement a new standard are not borne directly by some of those who derive the benefits of improved reporting. In establishing standards that are cost-effective, the Board must balance the diverse and often conflicting needs of a wide cross section of constituents.

33. The Board determined that the information provided to users about impaired loans could be improved by eliminating inconsistencies in the accounting among different types of creditors for similar loans. As discussed in FASB Concepts Statement No. 2, *Qualitative Characteristics of Accounting Information,* providing comparable financial information enables users to identify similarities in and differences between two sets of economic events. Therefore, to the extent that similar loans are subject to the same requirements for measuring impaired loans, financial reporting would be improved.

34. The benefits of eliminating inconsistencies in the accounting among different types of creditors come with a cost to some creditors—principally, the incremental cost of developing, implementing, and maintaining a measurement and reporting system to generate the required present values, observable market prices, or fair value of the collateral of collateral-dependent loans. However, the Board believes the cost of implementing this standard will be minimized because the Statement does not specify how a creditor should identify loans that are to be evaluated for collectibility or how a creditor should determine that it is probable that it will be unable to collect all amounts due according to the loan's contractual terms. Rather, the Statement provides that a creditor should apply its normal loan review procedures in making those judgments. In addition, the Board believes that prescribing a loan's effective interest rate as the appropriate discount rate will minimize implementation costs because that rate is readily available.

35. Application of judgment to determine expected future cash flows may be complex, but that complexity is the unavoidable result of the need for information about the effect of impaired loans on a creditor's financial position and results of operations. Practical decisions, such as permitting a creditor to recognize an observable market price of the loan or the fair value of the collateral of a collateral-dependent loan as alternatives to discounting and eliminating the proposed requirement in the Exposure Draft to recognize separately the two components of the change in present value, were made to reduce the cost and complexity of applying this Statement. Additionally, permitting a creditor to aggregate loans and use historical experience in calculating the present value of expected future cash flows also may reduce the cost and complexity of applying this Statement. The Board believes that the benefits of this Statement will exceed the costs of implementation.

Definitions and Scope

36. The Board believes that accounting for impaired loans should be consistent among all creditors and for all types of lending except for loans that are measured at fair value or at the lower of cost or fair value in accordance with specialized industry practice. (For example, Statement 65 specifies that mortgage loans held for sale should be accounted for at the lower of cost or market value, and venture capital investment companies generally account for loans at fair value.) Fair value accounting or the lower of cost or fair value accounting obviates the need for accounting guidance for impairment associated with those loans.

37. The Board was unable to identify any compelling reasons to support a conclusion that the lending process for consumer, mortgage, commercial, and other loans, whether uncollateralized or collateralized, is fundamentally different. Neither was the Board able to identify any compelling reasons to suggest that different types of creditors should account for impaired loans differently or that financial statement users for a particular industry or size of entity would be better served by accounting that differs from that of other creditors.

38. The Board concluded that this Statement should not apply to large groups of smaller-balance homogeneous loans that are collectively evaluated for impairment. In situations in which all or a portion of a loan portfolio consists of a large number of small-dollar-value homogeneous loans (such as consumer installment loans, residential mortgages, or credit card loans), creditors typically use a formula based on various factors to estimate an allowance for loan losses. Those factors include past loss

experience, recent economic events and current conditions, and portfolio delinquency rates. The Board recognizes the established practice of using a formula approach for estimating losses related to these types of loans and does not intend for this Statement to change that approach. The Board presumes that while a formula approach does not explicitly discount expected future cash flows, it results in a measure of impairment that implicitly discounts expected future cash flows.

39. The Exposure Draft would have applied to all loans that are individually and specifically evaluated for impairment but not to loans that are accounted for at fair value or at the lower of cost or fair value. It also did not address large groups of smaller-balance homogeneous loans that are collectively evaluated for impairment. Some respondents said that it was unclear whether the Exposure Draft applied to medium-balance loans. By deleting the reference to loans that are individually and specifically evaluated for impairment, the Board clarified that the only loans it did not intend to address were large groups of smaller-balance loans that are collectively evaluated for impairment. This Statement does not apply to leases or debt securities.

Recognition of Impairment

Discounted or Undiscounted Measurement of Impairment

40. An assumption inherent in a creditor's statement of financial position prepared in accordance with generally accepted accounting principles is that the reported amounts of assets will be recovered. However, as discussed in paragraph 31, different types of creditors have applied the guidance in Statement 5 about collectibility of receivables differently in measuring the amount of loan impairment. Some creditors have recognized impairment of a loan only when *undiscounted* expected future cash inflows are less than the loan's net carrying amount. Others have recognized impairment when *discounted* expected future cash inflows are less than the loan's net carrying amount.

41. The threshold issue is whether impaired loans should be carried at discounted or undiscounted amounts. The Board observed that a creditor's recorded investment in a loan both at origination and subsequently during the life of the loan, as long as the loan performs according to its contractual terms, is the sum of the present values of the future cash flows that are designated as interest and the future cash flows that are designated as principal, including any amount due at maturity, discounted at the effective interest rate implicit in the loan. The effective interest rate implicit in the loan may be the same as or may differ from the in-

terest rate stated in the agreement. If the effective interest rate differs from the stated interest rate, the recorded investment in the loan is the face amount plus net deferred loan costs and unamortized premium or less net deferred loan fees and unamortized discount.

42. The Board concluded that a loan that becomes impaired should continue to be carried at an amount that considers the present value of all expected future cash flows, in a manner consistent with the loan's measurement before it became impaired. The Board concluded that because loans are recorded originally at discounted amounts, the ongoing assessment for impairment should be made in a similar manner.

43. The Board recognizes that expected future cash flows from impaired loans are usually uncertain and creditors will be required to exercise significant judgment in developing the estimates of expected future cash flows. The Board believes that existing methods of measuring impaired loans and determining the adequacy of the allowance for credit losses already consider the uncertainty of expected future cash flows. The Board concluded that this uncertainty of expected future cash flows is not a valid reason to ignore discounting and that failure to measure impaired loans on a discounted basis would not only be inconsistent with the manner in which unimpaired loans are measured but also would inappropriately ignore the time value of money. If impaired loans were measured on an undiscounted basis, two loans could be carried at the same amount although one is performing fully and the other is a loan for which no cash flows are expected to be received for several years. In the Board's view, this is an unreasonable result both in terms of the appropriate measure of the two loans in the statement of financial position and in terms of the appropriate measurement of the event of impairment.

44. Some respondents interpreted the Exposure Draft to require an estimate of a specific amount of expected future cash flows for each impaired loan for each reporting period. The Board clarified this Statement to indicate that estimates of expected future cash flows may represent a creditor's best estimate within a range of possibilities.

45. Some respondents suggested that impaired loans could be aggregated as a means of measuring the present value of the expected future cash flows. In the Board's view, some impaired loans have risk characteristics that are unique to the borrower, and it is appropriate to measure those impaired loans on a loan-by-loan basis. However, some impaired loans may have risk characteristics in common with other impaired loans. The Board concluded that it is appropriate to use aggregation techniques

in measuring those impaired loans at the present value of the expected future cash flows. Past experience with loans with similar risk characteristics may provide an indication of the average time it takes to work out an impaired loan and the average amount the creditor will recover. The Board concluded that making estimates of the expected future cash flows and calculating the present value of the expected future cash flows based on the creditor's experience with loans with similar risk characteristics is consistent with the requirement for a creditor to make its best estimate of expected future cash flows. The Board acknowledges that actual cash flows will seldom, if ever, be exactly the same in timing and amount as the projections of expected future cash flows.

46. This Statement requires that a creditor consider estimated costs to sell, on a discounted basis, in the creditor's measure of impairment if those costs are expected to reduce the cash flows available to repay or otherwise satisfy the loan. For example, if repayment of a loan is dependent on the sale of the collateral, a creditor that uses a discounted cash flow method to measure impairment should reduce its estimate of expected future cash flows by its estimates of costs to sell. Likewise, if a creditor uses the fair value of the collateral to measure impairment of a collateral-dependent loan and repayment or satisfaction of a loan is dependent on the sale of the collateral, the fair value of the collateral should be adjusted to consider estimated costs to sell. However, if repayment or satisfaction of the loan is dependent only on the operation, rather than the sale, of the collateral, the measure of impairment would not incorporate estimated costs to sell the collateral.

47. The Board's conclusion that impaired loans should be carried at discounted amounts is not intended to signal a similar conclusion in the Board's project on accounting for impairment of long-lived assets. Loans and long-lived assets are similar in that both are intended to be cash-generating assets and both are subject to impairment. However, basic differences between loans and long-lived assets may or may not lead the Board to different conclusions about discounting in the project on impairment of long-lived assets.

48. The Board observed that other standard-setting organizations also have concluded that it is appropriate to measure impaired loans based on discounted expected future cash flows. In November 1992, the Canadian Institute of Chartered Accountants issued an Exposure Draft, *Impaired Loans,* which proposes that an impaired loan or group of loans be measured as the estimated future cash flows discounted at the effective interest rate

inherent in the loan agreement. At its March 1993 meeting, the International Accounting Standards Committee (IASC) considered comments received on E40, *Financial Instruments.* The IASC concluded that its final standard on financial instruments should indicate that the carrying amount of an impaired financial asset (including impaired and restructured loans) should be the present value of the estimated future cash flows discounted at the effective interest rate.

49. The Board also considered whether the loss threshold for recognition of loan impairment should be changed from the Statement 5 definition of probable to some other threshold. The United States General Accounting Office asserted in its April 1991 report, *Failed Banks: Accounting and Auditing Reforms Urgently Needed,* that "'probable' . . . has, in the case of banks, come to mean 'virtually certain,' rather than 'more likely than not,'" and "the 'probable' requirement as it is sometimes applied has unduly delayed loss recognition . . . of problem assets." The Board did not intend "probable" to mean "virtually certain to occur." The Statement 5 definition of probable states that "the future event or events are *likely to occur*" (emphasis added). The Board recognizes that application of the term probable in practice requires judgment, and to clarify its intent the Board has reiterated the guidance in paragraph 84 of Statement 5 in paragraph 10 of this Statement. The term probable is used in this Statement consistent with its use in Statement 5. This Statement does not specify how a creditor should determine that it is probable that it will be unable to collect all amounts due according to a loan's contractual terms.

Appropriate Discount Rate

50. This Statement specifies that when a loan is impaired, a creditor should measure impairment based on the present value of expected future cash flows discounted at the loan's effective interest rate. As a practical expedient, a creditor may measure impairment based on the loan's observable market price or the fair value of the collateral if the loan is collateral dependent. The Board understands that estimates of expected future cash flows from impaired loans require judgment and that the eventual outcomes may differ from those estimates. The Board does not believe that the judgment inherent in the estimates is a valid reason to ignore discounting. However, the Board does believe that the judgment inherent in the estimates is sufficient to permit the use of observable market price or fair value of the collateral of a collateral-dependent loan as practical alternatives to the present value of expected future cash flows discounted at the loan's effective rate.

51. The Board concluded that a loan impairment measurement should reflect only a deterioration of credit quality, which is evidenced by a decrease in the estimate of expected future cash flows to be received from the loan. The Board believes that the measure of an impaired loan should recognize the change in the net carrying amount of the loan based on new information about expected future cash flows rather than record a new direct measurement. The Board, therefore, concluded that the loan impairment measurement should not reflect changes in market rates of interest that may cause a change in the fair value of an impaired loan.

52. Because the Board believes that only the loss due to credit deterioration should be measured, the Board concluded that the expected future cash flows should be discounted at the loan's effective interest rate. The effective interest rate of a loan is the rate of return implicit in the loan (that is, the contractual interest rate adjusted for any net deferred loan fees or costs, premium, or discount). The Board observed that the recorded amount of an unimpaired loan, as long as the loan performs according to its contractual terms, is the present value of the contractual future cash inflows—both those designated as principal and as interest—discounted at the loan's historical or effective rate. Thus, the measurement basis for an impaired loan will be the same as the measurement basis for the same loan before it became impaired. As a practical expedient, the Board concluded that for a loan whose stated rate varies based on subsequent changes in an independent factor, creditors should be permitted to fix the rate at the rate in effect at the date the loan meets the impairment criterion.

53. Some respondents suggested that creditors be permitted to recognize an observable market price of the loan or the fair value of the collateral of an impaired collateral-dependent loan as alternatives to discounting. Some respondents suggested that creditors be required to recognize the fair value of the collateral if a loan is collateral dependent. For regulatory reporting purposes, banks and other depository institutions are required to recognize the fair value of the collateral of an impaired collateral-dependent loan. As a practical expedient, the Board decided to permit a creditor to recognize an observable market price for the loan or the fair value of the collateral of a collateral-dependent loan as alternatives to estimating and discounting the expected future cash flows for the loan. The Board expects that the measurement method for an individual impaired loan would be applied consistently to that loan and that a change in method would be justified by a change in circumstance.

54. The Board concluded that impairment of a loan is not an event that should result in a new di-

rect measurement of the loan at fair value at the date impairment is recognized. Under that approach, an impaired loan's expected future cash flows would be discounted at a market interest rate commensurate with the risks involved to arrive at a measure of the loan's fair value. Noting that unimpaired loans are not carried at fair value after origination, the Board concluded that loan impairment should be recognized based solely on deterioration of credit quality evidenced by a decrease in expected future cash flows rather than on changes in both expected future cash flows and other current economic events, such as changes in interest rates. In addition, the Board observed that if a market rate were specified, questions could be raised about whether a new measurement would be required if the creditor's estimate of expected future cash flows remained constant but current market interest rates changed.

55. Some respondents observed that fair value is widely used in a variety of situations and could be implemented with minimal cost to financial statement preparers because it is consistent with the values disclosed in accordance with FASB Statement No. 107, *Disclosures about Fair Value of Financial Instruments.* The Board noted that many creditors make the disclosures required under Statement 107 on a portfolio basis; they do not make separate disclosures for impaired loans. Furthermore, the Board understands that there are practical difficulties in determining a market rate for an impaired loan.

56. The Board also considered whether an impaired loan's expected future cash flows should be discounted at the creditor's cost-of-funds interest rate. A cost-of-funds interest rate would reflect the time value of money to a specific creditor and would reflect the creditor's cost to carry an impaired loan (a cost-recovery notion). Under that approach, interest would be one of a creditor's costs to carry an impaired loan. This method is consistent with current requirements of the AICPA Guide on savings institutions and SOP 75-2, which require discounting at a rate that would correspond to an expected average rate to be paid during the estimated holding period. The Board believes that impairment should be measured by looking only at the loan and that a loan's net carrying amount should not be affected by the credit standing of the creditor and the interest rate it pays on its debt or by whether the creditor has outstanding debt.

57. The Board also considered whether an impaired loan's expected future cash flows should be discounted at a risk-free interest rate. A risk-free interest rate would reflect at least the minimum interest that could have been earned if the funds were not invested in the impaired loan. The Board concluded that the risk-free rate has no relationship to

the impaired loan being measured and, therefore, would be an irrelevant discount rate to use in measuring an impaired loan.

Income Recognition

58. When an asset is carried on a discounted basis, the present value of expected future cash flows will increase from one reporting period to the next as a result of the passage of time (assuming that the timing and amount of expected future cash flows remain constant). The change in present value from one reporting period to the next may result not only from the passage of time but also from changes in estimates of the timing or amount of expected future cash flows. Similarly, the observable market price of an impaired loan or the fair value of the collateral of an impaired collateral-dependent loan may change from one reporting period to the next. Because the Board believes that the net carrying amount of an impaired loan should be the present value of expected future cash flows (or the observable market price or the fair value of the collateral) not only at the date at which impairment initially is recognized but also at each subsequent reporting period, the Board concluded that changes in that measure should be recognized.

59. The Exposure Draft would have required the change in present value attributable to the passage of time to be reported as interest income and the change in present value, if any, attributable to changes in the amount or timing of expected future cash flows to be reported as bad-debt expense or as a reduction in the amount of bad-debt expense that otherwise would be reported. Some respondents stated that the change in present value attributable to the passage of time should be reported as a reduction of bad-debt expense because that approach could be implemented with less cost to financial statement preparers. The Board concluded that a creditor that measures impairment based on the present value of expected future cash flows should be permitted to report the entire change in present value as bad-debt expense but that a creditor that wishes to report the change in present value attributable to the passage of time as interest income should not be proscribed from doing so. Because some financial analysts indicated that knowing that information is important, the Board concluded that creditors that choose the latter alternative should disclose the amount of interest income that represents the change in present value attributable to the passage of time. For practical reasons, the Board concluded that changes in observable market prices or the fair value of the collateral should be reported as bad-debt expense or a reduction in bad-debt expense.

60. The Board considered and rejected an approach under which the change in present value would be reported as a separate amount such as "accrual of interest on impaired loans" because that presentation does not identify the reason for the change in present value. The Board reasoned that changes in a present-value-based measurement of loan impairment must be either interest or part of bad-debt expense.

61. The Board also considered whether loan impairment should be recorded through a valuation allowance or through a direct write-down that would establish a new cost basis for the impaired loan. The Board concluded that because of the subjectivity inherent in the valuation of an impaired loan and because estimates of the timing and amount of an impaired loan's cash flows, an observable market price, or the fair value of the collateral may change, impairment should be recorded through a valuation allowance that subsequently may change to reflect changes in the measure of the impaired loan. However, the net carrying amount of the loan shall at no time exceed the recorded investment in the loan.

Troubled Debt Restructurings

62. The Exposure Draft would have required a formal loan restructuring (a troubled debt restructuring involving a modification of terms as defined in paragraph 5(c) of Statement 15) to be remeasured at a current fair value to recognize that the terms of the original loan agreement cease to be relevant. Some respondents indicated that a troubled debt restructuring does not result in a new loan but rather represents part of a creditor's ongoing effort to recover its investment in the original loan. Therefore, the interest rate used to discount expected future cash flows on a restructured loan should be the same interest rate used to discount expected future cash flows on an impaired loan. Some respondents stated that requiring a different interest rate to discount the expected future cash flows on impaired loans and restructured loans would give creditors the incentive to accelerate or delay the timing of a troubled debt restructuring to achieve an accounting result. Some respondents stated that the Board would have to provide guidance on when a restructuring had occurred in substance. Based on those considerations, the Board concluded that it is appropriate to use the effective interest rate in the original loan agreement to discount the expected future cash flows on an impaired loan and a restructured loan.

63. The Board recognizes that this Statement introduces asymmetry between creditors' and

debtors' accounting for troubled debt restructurings involving a modification of terms. However, the Board concluded that this Statement should address only creditors' accounting and that debtors' accounting should not be considered because expanding the scope of this Statement to address debtors' accounting likely would delay issuance of the final Statement.

Disclosures

64. The Board believes that the financial statement disclosures required by this Statement provide information that is useful in understanding a creditor's accounting for impaired loans. The Board concluded that the recorded investment in the impaired loans, the total allowance for credit losses related to those impaired loans, an analysis of the activity in a creditor's allowance for credit losses account, and the creditor's income recognition policy are information relevant to financial statement users. The Board also concluded that the disclosures previously required by paragraphs 40(a) and 41 of Statement 15 are no longer necessary because all loans that are restructured in troubled debt restructurings will meet the definition of impairment and, therefore, will be subject to the disclosure requirements of paragraph 20 of this Statement except as discussed in the following paragraph.

65. Some respondents asked whether the requirement in paragraph 20(a) to disclose the recorded investment in the loans for which impairment has been recognized in accordance with this Statement applies to a restructured loan if the creditor has written down the loan and the present value of the expected future cash flows, or the observable market price, or the fair value of the collateral is equal to or greater than the recorded investment in the loan. As noted in paragraph 9, usually a loan whose terms are modified in a troubled debt restructuring already will be impaired because the condition specified in paragraph 8 will have existed before a formal restructuring. However, if the creditor has written down a loan and the measure of the restructured loan under paragraph 13 is equal to or greater than the recorded investment in the loan, there would be no impairment to be recognized in accordance with this Statement. The creditor is not required to disclose the recorded investment in that loan in years after the write-down but is required under paragraph 20(b) to disclose the amount of the write-down and is required under paragraph 20(a) to disclose the recorded investment in the year of the write-down. Some respondents asked a similar question for loans that have not been restructured, but for which the creditor has taken a direct write-down. In that situation, if the measure of the loan under paragraph 13 is equal to or greater than the recorded investment in the loan, there is no impairment to be recognized in accordance with this Statement, and the creditor is not required to disclose the recorded investment in the loan in years after the write-down.

66. The Exposure Draft would have required a creditor to disclose reversals of the allowance for interest (that is, the change in present value attributable to the passage of time) and reversals of the allowance attributable to increases in estimates of expected future cash flows. The Board agreed with respondents who indicated that the information might be excessive for a creditor that recognizes income in accordance with paragraph 17(b) and should not be required. The Board agreed with respondents who said that a creditor that recognizes interest income in accordance with paragraph 17(a) should disclose the amount of interest income that is accrued on the net carrying amount of an impaired loan.

67. Additionally, paragraph 21 of the Exposure Draft reiterated a disclosure requirement that already exists under paragraph 32 of FASB Statement No. 95, *Statement of Cash Flows;* that paragraph, but not the requirement in Statement 95, was deleted and is not repeated in this Statement.

Amendments to Existing Pronouncements

68. The impairment recognition criterion in paragraph 8 of this Statement is similar to that of paragraph 23 of Statement 5, which describes the application of the Statement 5 conditions for accrual of loss contingencies to the collectibility of all receivables. That paragraph states that ". . . based on available information, it is probable that the enterprise will be unable to collect all amounts due." The Board recognizes that in practice, "all amounts due" has not always been interpreted to include both the future contractual interest and the contractual principal of a loan. Thus, this Statement amends paragraph 23 of Statement 5 to clarify that "all amounts due" refers to both principal and interest. The Board believes this is the appropriate interpretation because, as illustrated in Appendix A of APB Opinion No. 21, *Interest on Receivables and Payables,* the recorded amount of a loan is the present value of the contractual principal and interest cash flows discounted at the loan's effective interest rate. While this Statement requires a creditor to consider collectibility of both principal and interest for all receivables, it specifies the method to be used to measure impairment only for impaired loans that are within the scope of this Statement.

69. After considering comments received, the Board decided that when a creditor determines that foreclosure is probable, a creditor should remeasure

the loan at the fair value of the collateral so that loss recognition is not delayed until actual foreclosure. The Board believes that the requirement in this Statement to discount expected future cash flows will reduce the amount of loss that would be recognized when foreclosure is probable compared with the loss that would be recognized for the same loan under the current undiscounted measure of loan losses. However, the requirement to discount may not preclude the need to recognize additional loss when foreclosure is probable because estimates of expected future cash flows are not remeasured using a market rate and because estimates of expected future cash flows may change when a creditor determines that foreclosure is probable.

70. This Statement amends paragraph 34 of Statement 15 to clarify the applicability of that paragraph. Paragraph 34 was intended to apply to a narrow set of circumstances; that is, a troubled debt restructuring or other circumstance in which a debtor surrendered property to the creditor and the creditor was in possession of the asset with or without having to go through formal foreclosure procedures. Paragraph 84 of the basis for conclusions in Statement 15 states, "The Board agreed that a restructuring may be in substance a foreclosure, repossession, or other transfer of assets even though formal foreclosure or repossession proceedings are not involved." The amendment to paragraph 34 of Statement 15 clarifies that intent.

71. The Board recognizes that in practice paragraph 34 of Statement 15 and the term *in-substance foreclosure* are applied in situations other than troubled debt restructurings or situations in which a debtor surrenders property to the creditor. Under the SEC's Financial Reporting Release No. 28, *Accounting for Loan Losses by Registrants Engaged in Lending Activities,* and Practice Bulletin 7, a creditor is required to account for the operations of the collateral underlying some loans, even though the creditor has not taken possession of collateral, as if foreclosure had occurred. The Board recognizes the practical problems of accounting for the operations of an asset the creditor does not possess and concluded, therefore, that a loan for which foreclosure is probable should continue to be accounted for as a loan.

Effective Date and Transition

72. The Board decided to prohibit retroactive application of the Statement. Because the measurement of impaired loans is based on estimates that are likely to change, the Board questioned the relevance of restatement. The Board recognizes the benefits of comparative financial statements, but it questions the ability of a creditor to "re-create"

historical estimates of the timing and amounts of cash flows, the observable market price, or the fair value of the collateral that would be necessary for restatement. For those reasons, the Board concluded that retroactive application of the Statement should be prohibited. The Board also discussed accounting for loans that were restructured in troubled debt restructurings before the effective date of this Statement. The Exposure Draft would have applied to all loans restructured before the effective date. Some respondents indicated that the final Statement should not apply to restructurings before the effective date because those transactions were entered into based on the accounting rules at the time. Some respondents said that previously restructured loans should be accounted for under the final Statement only if they are currently or subsequently impaired based on the restructured terms or subsequently are restructured again. The Board concluded that troubled debt restructurings before the effective date of this Statement are required to be accounted for in accordance with this Statement only if the restructured loans are impaired; that is, if they are not performing in accordance with the contractual terms of the restructuring agreement.

73. Some respondents requested a one-year delay in the effective date to give them time to develop techniques for estimating expected future cash flows and to develop systems to calculate present value. Bank regulators also requested a one-year delay so that their examiners could be adequately trained. The Board believes that changes made to the provisions of the Exposure Draft—in particular, permitting creditors to recognize the observable market price of the loan or the fair value of the collateral of a collateral-dependent loan and permitting use of aggregation techniques—will minimize the implementation burden. However, the Board decided to delay the effective date proposed in the Exposure Draft.

74. The Exposure Draft would have required a creditor to report the effect of initially applying this Statement as the effect of a change in accounting principle in a manner similar to the cumulative effect of a change in accounting principle as described in paragraph 20 of APB Opinion No. 20, *Accounting Changes.* The Board decided that the cost of isolating a "cumulative effect" would exceed the related benefit of that information and that a creditor should report the effect of initially applying this Statement as bad-debt expense or as an adjustment to bad-debt expense in accordance with paragraph 13. This Statement does not preclude a creditor from disclosing in the notes to the financial statements the effect of initially applying this Statement if the creditor believes it is practical to do so.

Statement of Financial Accounting Standards No. 115
Accounting for Certain Investments in Debt and Equity Securities

STATUS

Issued: May 1993

Effective Date: For fiscal years beginning after December 15, 1993

Affects: Amends ARB 43, Chapter 3A, paragraph 4
    Amends APB 18, paragraph 19(l)
    Supersedes FAS 12
    Supersedes FAS 60, paragraphs 45 and 46 and footnote 7
    Amends FAS 60, paragraphs 50 and 51
    Amends FAS 65, paragraphs 4 through 8, 9(a), 9(c), 12, 17, 28, and 29
    Amends FAS 80, paragraph 5
    Amends FAS 91, paragraphs 3 and 27(a)
    Amends FAS 97, paragraph 28
    Amends FAS 102, paragraph 8 and footnote 4
    Amends FAS 109, paragraph 36(b)
    Supersedes FIN 11
    Supersedes FIN 12
    Supersedes FIN 13
    Supersedes FIN 16
    Amends FIN 40, paragraphs 4 and 5
    Amends FTB 79-19, paragraph 1
    Supersedes FTB 79-19, paragraph 6
    Amends FTB 85-1, paragraph 3

Affected by: Paragraph 4 amended by FAS 124
    Paragraph 7 amended by FAS 125

Other Interpretive Pronouncement: FTB 94-1

Other Interpretive Release: FASB Special Report, *A Guide to Implementation of Statement 115 on Accounting for Certain Investments in Debt and Equity Securities: Questions and Answers*

Issues Discussed by FASB Emerging Issues Task Force (EITF)

  Affects: EITF Issues No. 85-25, 86-40, 89-18, and 91-5

  Interpreted by: Paragraph 3 interpreted by EITF Topic No. D-39
    Paragraph 7 interpreted by EITF Issue No. 96-10 and Topic No. D-39
    Paragraph 9 interpreted by EITF Topic No. D-51
    Paragraph 13 interpreted by EITF Topic No. D-41
    Paragraph 16 interpreted by EITF Issue No. 93-18 and Topic No. D-44
    Paragraph 115 interpreted by EITF Issue No. 96-15

  Related Issues: EITF Issues No. 84-20, 85-23, 85-39, 87-1, 89-4, 94-8, 96-11, and 96-12
    and Topics No. D-11 and D-40

SUMMARY

This Statement addresses the accounting and reporting for investments in equity securities that have readily determinable fair values and for all investments in debt securities. Those investments are to be classified in three categories and accounted for as follows:

- Debt securities that the enterprise has the positive intent and ability to hold to maturity are classified as *held-to-maturity securities* and reported at amortized cost.
- Debt and equity securities that are bought and held principally for the purpose of selling them in the near term are classified as *trading securities* and reported at fair value, with unrealized gains and losses included in earnings.
- Debt and equity securities not classified as either held-to-maturity securities or trading securities are classified as *available-for-sale securities* and reported at fair value, with unrealized gains and losses excluded from earnings and reported in a separate component of shareholders' equity.

This Statement does not apply to unsecuritized loans. However, after mortgage loans are converted to mortgage-backed securities, they are subject to its provisions. This Statement supersedes FASB Statement No. 12, *Accounting for Certain Marketable Securities,* and related Interpretations and amends FASB Statement No. 65, *Accounting for Certain Mortgage Banking Activities,* to eliminate mortgage-backed securities from its scope.

This Statement is effective for fiscal years beginning after December 15, 1993. It is to be initially applied as of the beginning of an enterprise's fiscal year and cannot be applied retroactively to prior years' financial statements. However, an enterprise may elect to initially apply this Statement as of the end of an earlier fiscal year for which annual financial statements have not previously been issued.

(This page intentionally left blank.)

Statement of Financial Accounting Standards No. 115

Accounting for Certain Investments in Debt and Equity Securities

CONTENTS

INTRODUCTION

1. This Statement addresses the accounting and reporting for certain investments in **debt securities**[1] and **equity securities.** It expands the use of **fair value** accounting for those securities but retains the use of the amortized cost method for investments in debt securities that the reporting enterprise has the positive intent and ability to hold to maturity.

2. This Statement was undertaken mainly in response to concerns expressed by regulators and others about the recognition and measurement of investments in debt securities, particularly those held by financial institutions. They questioned the appropriateness of using the amortized cost method for certain investments in debt securities in light of certain trading and sales practices. Their concerns also were prompted by the existence of inconsistent guidance on the reporting of debt securities held as assets in various AICPA Audit and Accounting Guides. The AICPA's Accounting Standards Executive Committee (AcSEC) and the major CPA firms, among others, urged the Board

to reexamine the accounting for certain investments in **securities.**

STANDARDS OF FINANCIAL ACCOUNTING AND REPORTING

Scope

3. Except as indicated in paragraph 4, this Statement establishes standards of financial accounting and reporting for investments in equity securities that have readily determinable fair values and for all investments in debt securities.

a. The fair value of an equity security is readily determinable if sales prices or bid-and-asked quotations are currently available on a securities exchange registered with the Securities and Exchange Commission (SEC) or in the over-the-counter market, provided that those prices or quotations for the over-the-counter market are publicly reported by the National Association of Securities Dealers Automated Quotations

---

[1]Words that appear in the glossary in Appendix C are set in **boldface type** the first time they appear.

systems or by the National Quotation Bureau. Restricted stock[2] does not meet that definition.

b. The fair value of an equity security traded only in a foreign market is readily determinable if that foreign market is of a breadth and scope comparable to one of the U.S. markets referred to above.

c. The fair value of an investment in a mutual fund is readily determinable if the fair value per share (unit) is determined and published and is the basis for current transactions.

4. This Statement does not apply to investments in equity securities accounted for under the equity method nor to investments in consolidated subsidiaries. This Statement does not apply to enterprises whose specialized accounting practices include accounting for substantially all investments in debt and equity securities at market value or fair value, with changes in value recognized in earnings (income) or in the change in net assets. Examples of those enterprises are brokers and dealers in securities, defined benefit pension plans, and investment companies. This Statement also does not apply to not-for-profit organizations; however, it does apply to cooperatives and mutual enterprises, including credit unions and mutual insurance companies.

5. This Statement supersedes FASB Statement No. 12, *Accounting for Certain Marketable Securities,* and supersedes or amends other accounting pronouncements listed in Appendix B.

Accounting for Certain Investments in Debt and Equity Securities

6. At acquisition, an enterprise shall classify debt and equity securities into one of three categories: held-to-maturity, available-for-sale, or trading. At each reporting date, the appropriateness of the classification shall be reassessed.

Held-to-Maturity Securities

7. Investments in debt securities shall be classified as *held-to-maturity* and measured at amortized cost in the statement of financial position only if the reporting enterprise has the positive intent and ability to hold those securities to maturity.

8. The following changes in circumstances, however, may cause the enterprise to change its intent to hold a certain security to maturity without calling into question its intent to hold other debt securities to maturity in the future. Thus, the sale or transfer of a held-to-maturity security due to one of the following changes in circumstances shall not be considered to be inconsistent with its original classification:

a. Evidence of a significant deterioration in the issuer's creditworthiness

b. A change in tax law that eliminates or reduces the tax-exempt status of interest on the debt security (but not a change in tax law that revises the marginal tax rates applicable to interest income)

c. A major business combination or major disposition (such as sale of a segment) that necessitates the sale or transfer of held-to-maturity securities to maintain the enterprise's existing interest rate risk position or credit risk policy

d. A change in statutory or regulatory requirements significantly modifying either what constitutes a permissible investment or the maximum level of investments in certain kinds of securities, thereby causing an enterprise to dispose of a held-to-maturity security

e. A significant increase by the regulator in the industry's capital requirements that causes the enterprise to downsize by selling held-to-maturity securities

f. A significant increase in the risk weights of debt securities used for regulatory risk-based capital purposes.

In addition to the foregoing changes in circumstances, other events that are isolated, nonrecurring, and unusual for the reporting enterprise that could not have been reasonably anticipated may cause the enterprise to sell or transfer a held-to-maturity security without necessarily calling into question its intent to hold other debt securities to maturity. All sales and transfers of held-to-maturity securities shall be disclosed pursuant to paragraph 22.

9. An enterprise shall not classify a debt security as held-to-maturity if the enterprise has the intent to hold the security for only an indefinite period. Consequently, a debt security should not, for example, be classified as held-to-maturity if the enterprise anticipates that the security would be available to be sold in response to:

a. Changes in market interest rates and related changes in the security's prepayment risk

b. Needs for liquidity (for example, due to the withdrawal of deposits, increased demand for loans, surrender of insurance policies, or payment of insurance claims)

---

[2]*Restricted stock,* for the purpose of this Statement, means equity securities for which sale is restricted by governmental or contractual requirement (other than in connection with being pledged as collateral) except if that requirement terminates within one year or if the holder has the power by contract or otherwise to cause the requirement to be met within one year. Any portion of the security that can be reasonably expected to qualify for sale within one year, such as may be the case under Rule 144 or similar rules of the SEC, is not considered restricted.

c. Changes in the availability of and the yield on alternative investments

d. Changes in funding sources and terms

e. Changes in foreign currency risk.

10. Although its asset-liability management may encompass consideration of the maturity and repricing characteristics of all investments in debt securities, an enterprise may decide that it can accomplish the necessary adjustments under its asset-liability management without having all of its debt securities available for disposition. In that case, the enterprise may choose to designate certain debt securities as unavailable to be sold to accomplish those ongoing adjustments deemed necessary under its asset-liability management, thereby enabling those debt securities to be accounted for at amortized cost on the basis of a positive intent and ability to hold them to maturity.

11. Sales of debt securities that meet either of the following two conditions may be considered as maturities for purposes of the classification of securities under paragraphs 7 and 12 and the disclosure requirements under paragraph 22:

a. The sale of a security occurs near enough to its maturity date (or call date if exercise of the call is probable) that interest rate risk is substantially eliminated as a pricing factor. That is, the date of sale is so near the maturity or call date (for example, within three months) that changes in market interest rates would not have a significant effect on the security's fair value.

b. The sale of a security occurs after the enterprise has already collected a substantial portion (at least 85 percent) of the principal outstanding at acquisition due either to prepayments on the debt security or to scheduled payments on a debt security payable in equal installments (both principal and interest) over its term. For variable-rate securities, the scheduled payments need not be equal.

Trading Securities and Available-for-Sale Securities

12. Investments in debt securities that are not classified as held-to-maturity and equity securities that have readily determinable fair values shall be classified in one of the following categories and measured at fair value in the statement of financial position:

a. *Trading securities.* Securities that are bought and held principally for the purpose of selling them in the near term (thus held for only a short period of time) shall be classified as *trading securities.* Trading generally reflects active and frequent buying and selling, and trading securities are generally used with the objective of generating profits on short-term differences in price. Mortgage-backed securities that are held for sale in conjunction with mortgage banking activities, as described in FASB Statement No. 65, *Accounting for Certain Mortgage Banking Activities,* shall be classified as trading securities. (Other mortgage-backed securities not held for sale in conjunction with mortgage banking activities shall be classified based on the criteria in this paragraph and paragraph 7.)

b. *Available-for-sale securities.* Investments not classified as trading securities (nor as held-to-maturity securities) shall be classified as *available-for-sale securities.*

Reporting Changes in Fair Value

13. Unrealized **holding gains and losses** for trading securities shall be included in earnings. Unrealized holding gains and losses for available-for-sale securities (including those classified as current assets) shall be excluded from earnings and reported as a net amount in a separate component of shareholders' equity until realized. Paragraph 36 of FASB Statement No. 109, *Accounting for Income Taxes,* provides guidance on reporting the tax effects of unrealized holding gains and losses reported in a separate component of shareholders' equity.

14. Dividend and interest income, including amortization of the premium and discount arising at acquisition, for all three categories of investments in securities shall continue to be included in earnings. This Statement does not affect the methods used for recognizing and measuring the amount of dividend and interest income. Realized gains and losses for securities classified as either available-for-sale or held-to-maturity also shall continue to be reported in earnings.

Transfers between Categories of Investments

15. The transfer of a security between categories of investments shall be accounted for at fair value.[3] At the date of the transfer, the security's

---

[3]For a debt security transferred into the held-to-maturity category, the use of fair value may create a premium or discount that, under amortized cost accounting, shall be amortized thereafter as an adjustment of yield pursuant to FASB Statement No. 91, *Accounting for Nonrefundable Fees and Costs Associated with Originating or Acquiring Loans and Initial Direct Costs of Leases.*

unrealized holding gain or loss shall be accounted for as follows:

a. For a security transferred from the trading category, the unrealized holding gain or loss at the date of the transfer will have already been recognized in earnings and shall not be reversed.
b. For a security transferred into the trading category, the unrealized holding gain or loss at the date of the transfer shall be recognized in earnings immediately.
c. For a debt security transferred into the available-for-sale category from the held-to-maturity category, the unrealized holding gain or loss at the date of the transfer shall be recognized in a separate component of shareholders' equity.
d. For a debt security transferred into the held-to-maturity category from the available-for-sale category, the unrealized holding gain or loss at the date of the transfer shall continue to be reported in a separate component of shareholders' equity but shall be amortized over the remaining life of the security as an adjustment of yield in a manner consistent with the amortization of any premium or discount. The amortization of an unrealized holding gain or loss reported in equity will offset or mitigate the effect on interest income of the amortization of the premium or discount (discussed in footnote 3) for that held-to-maturity security.

Consistent with paragraphs 7-9, transfers from the held-to-maturity category should be rare, except for transfers due to the changes in circumstances identified in subparagraphs 8(a)-8(f). Given the nature of a trading security, transfers into or from the trading category also should be rare.

Impairment of Securities

16. For individual securities classified as either available-for-sale or held-to-maturity, an enterprise shall determine whether a decline in fair value below the amortized cost basis is other than temporary. For example, if it is probable that the investor will be unable to collect all amounts due according to the contractual terms of a debt security not impaired at acquisition, an other-than-temporary impairment shall be considered to have occurred.[4] If the decline in fair value is judged to be other than temporary, the cost basis of the individual security shall be written down to fair value as a new cost basis and the amount of the write-down shall be included in earnings (that is, accounted for as a realized loss). The new cost basis shall not be changed for subsequent recoveries in fair value. Subsequent increases in the fair value of available-for-sale securities shall be included in the separate component of equity pursuant to paragraph 13; subsequent decreases in fair value, if not an other-than-temporary impairment, also shall be included in the separate component of equity.

Financial Statement Presentation

17. An enterprise that presents a classified statement of financial position shall report all trading securities as current assets and shall report individual held-to-maturity securities and individual available-for-sale securities as either current or noncurrent, as appropriate, under the provisions of ARB No. 43, Chapter 3A, "Working Capital—Current Assets and Current Liabilities."[5]

18. Cash flows from purchases, sales, and maturities of available-for-sale securities and held-to-maturity securities shall be classified as cash flows from investing activities and reported gross for each security classification in the statement of cash flows. Cash flows from purchases, sales, and maturities of trading securities shall be classified as cash flows from operating activities.

Disclosures

19. For securities classified as available-for-sale and separately for securities classified as held-to-maturity, all reporting enterprises shall disclose the aggregate fair value, gross unrealized holding gains, gross unrealized holding losses, and amortized cost basis by major security type as of each date for which a statement of financial position is

---

[4]A decline in the value of a security that is other than temporary is also discussed in AICPA Auditing Interpretation, *Evidential Matter for the Carrying Amount of Marketable Securities,* which was issued in 1975 and incorporated in Statement on Auditing Standards No. 1, *Codification of Auditing Standards and Procedures,* as Interpretation 20, and in SEC Staff Accounting Bulletin No. 59, *Accounting for Noncurrent Marketable Equity Securities.*

[5]Chapter 3A of ARB 43 indicates in paragraph 4 that "the term *current assets* is used to designate cash and other assets or resources commonly identified as those which are reasonably expected to be realized in cash or sold or consumed during the normal operating cycle of the business." That paragraph further indicates that the term also comprehends "marketable securities representing the investment of cash available for current operations." Paragraph 5 indicates that "a one-year time period is to be used as a basis for the segregation of current assets in cases where there are several operating cycles occurring within a year."

presented. In complying with this requirement, financial institutions[6] shall include in their disclosure the following major security types, though additional types also may be included as appropriate:

a. Equity securities
b. Debt securities issued by the U.S. Treasury and other U.S. government corporations and agencies
c. Debt securities issued by states of the United States and political subdivisions of the states
d. Debt securities issued by foreign governments
e. Corporate debt securities
f. Mortgage-backed securities
g. Other debt securities.

20. For investments in debt securities classified as available-for-sale and separately for securities classified as held-to-maturity, all reporting enterprises shall disclose information about the contractual maturities of those securities as of the date of the most recent statement of financial position presented. Maturity information may be combined in appropriate groupings. In complying with this requirement, financial institutions shall disclose the fair value and the amortized cost of debt securities based on at least 4 maturity groupings: (a) within 1 year, (b) after 1 year through 5 years, (c) after 5 years through 10 years, and (d) after 10 years. Securities not due at a single maturity date, such as mortgage-backed securities, may be disclosed separately rather than allocated over several maturity groupings; if allocated, the basis for allocation also shall be disclosed.

21. For each period for which the results of operations are presented, an enterprise shall disclose:

a. The proceeds from sales of available-for-sale securities and the gross realized gains and gross realized losses on those sales
b. The basis on which cost was determined in computing realized gain or loss (that is, specific identification, average cost, or other method used)
c. The gross gains and gross losses included in earnings from transfers of securities from the available-for-sale category into the trading category
d. The change in net unrealized holding gain or loss on available-for-sale securities that has been included in the separate component of shareholders' equity during the period
e. The change in net unrealized holding gain or loss on trading securities that has been included in earnings during the period.

22. For any sales of or transfers from securities classified as held-to-maturity, the amortized cost amount of the sold or transferred security, the related realized or unrealized gain or loss, and the circumstances leading to the decision to sell or transfer the security shall be disclosed in the notes to the financial statements for each period for which the results of operations are presented. Such sales or transfers should be rare, except for sales and transfers due to the changes in circumstances identified in subparagraphs 8(a)-8(f).

Effective Date and Transition

23. This Statement shall be effective for fiscal years beginning after December 15, 1993. Except as indicated in the following paragraph, initial application of this Statement shall be as of the beginning of an enterprise's fiscal year; at that date, investments in debt and equity securities owned shall be classified based on the enterprise's current intent. Earlier application as of the beginning of a fiscal year is permitted only in financial statements for fiscal years beginning after issuance of this Statement. This Statement may not be applied retroactively to prior years' financial statements.

24. For fiscal years beginning prior to December 16, 1993, enterprises are permitted to initially apply this Statement as of the end of a fiscal year for which annual financial statements have not previously been issued. This Statement may not be applied retroactively to the interim financial statements for that year.

25. The effect on retained earnings of initially applying this Statement shall be reported as the effect of a change in accounting principle in a manner similar to the cumulative effect of a change in accounting principle as described in paragraph 20 of APB Opinion No. 20, *Accounting Changes*. That effect on retained earnings includes the reversal of amounts previously included in earnings that would be excluded from earnings under this Statement (refer to paragraph 13). The unrealized holding gain or loss, net of tax effect, for securities classified as available-for-sale as of the date that this Statement is first applied shall be an adjustment of the balance of the separate component of equity. The pro forma effects of retroactive application (discussed in paragraph 21 of Opinion 20) shall not be disclosed.

The provisions of this Statement need not be applied to immaterial items.

---

[6]For purposes of the disclosure requirements of paragraphs 19 and 20, the term *financial institutions* includes banks, savings and loan associations, savings banks, credit unions, finance companies, and insurance companies, consistent with the usage of that term in AICPA Statement of Position 90-11, *Disclosure of Certain Information by Financial Institutions About Debt Securities Held as Assets*.

This Statement was adopted by the affirmative votes of five members of the Financial Accounting Standards Board. Messrs. Sampson and Swieringa dissented.

Messrs. Sampson and Swieringa disagree with the accounting treatment prescribed in paragraphs 6-18 of this Statement because it does not resolve two of the most important problems that caused the Board to address the accounting for certain investments in debt and equity securities—namely, accounting based on intent, and gains trading. They believe that those problems can only be resolved by reporting all securities that are within the scope of this Statement at fair value and by including unrealized changes in fair value in earnings.

This Statement requires that debt securities be classified as held-to-maturity, available-for-sale, or trading and that securities in each classification be accounted for differently. As a result, three otherwise identical debt securities could receive three different accounting treatments within the same enterprise. Moreover, classification of debt securities as held-to-maturity is based on management's positive intent and ability to hold to maturity. The notion of intent to hold to maturity (a) is subjective at best, (b) is not likely to be consistently applied, (c) given the provisions in paragraphs 8-11, is not likely to be descriptive of actual transactions and events, and (d) disregards the best available information about the present value of expected future cash flows from a readily marketable debt security—namely, its observable market price. Effective management of financial activities increasingly requires a flexible approach to asset and liability management that is inconsistent with a hold-to-maturity notion.

This Statement also requires that certain debt securities classified as held-to-maturity be reported at amortized cost and that certain debt and equity securities classified as available-for-sale be reported at fair value with unrealized changes in fair value excluded from earnings. Those requirements provide the opportunity for the managers of an enterprise to manage its earnings by selectively selling securities and thereby selectively including realized gains in earnings and selectively excluding unrealized losses from earnings. An impressive amount of empirical evidence indicates that many financial institutions have engaged in that behavior. That behavior undermines the relevance and reliability of accounting information.

The Board concluded that unrealized changes in fair value for trading securities should be reported in earnings because that reporting reflects the economic consequences of the events of the enterprise (such as changes in fair values) as well as the transactions (such as sales of securities) when those events and transactions occur and results in more relevant reporting (paragraph 92). However, the Board concluded that similar reporting of unrealized changes in fair value for available-for-sale securities has the potential for significant earnings volatility that is unrepresentative of both the way enterprises manage their businesses and the impact of economic events on the overall enterprise and, therefore, decided that those changes should be excluded from earnings (paragraphs 93 and 94). Those conclusions do not alleviate the potential for volatility in reported earnings; rather, they provide the opportunity for selective volatility in reported earnings—that is, the volatility in reported earnings that results from the recognition of unrealized changes in fair value in earnings through selective sales of securities.

Reporting all securities that are within the scope of this Statement at fair value and including unrealized changes in fair value in earnings would result in reflecting the consequences of economic events (price changes) in the periods in which they occur rather than when managers wish to selectively recognize those consequences in earnings. Messrs. Sampson and Swieringa believe that this reporting is the only way to resolve the problems of accounting based on intent and gains trading that have raised concerns about the relevance and credibility of accounting for certain investments in debt and equity securities.

In addition, Mr. Sampson is concerned that the conclusions adopted in this Statement may, in some cases, portray unrepresentative volatility in capital because enterprises are not permitted to recognize the unrealized changes in fair value of the liabilities that are related to investments accounted for as available-for-sale securities.

Appendix A

BACKGROUND INFORMATION AND BASIS FOR CONCLUSIONS

CONTENTS

Appendix A

BACKGROUND INFORMATION AND BASIS FOR CONCLUSIONS

Introduction and Overview

26. This appendix summarizes considerations that Board members deemed significant in reaching the conclusions in this Statement. It includes reasons for accepting certain views and rejecting others. Individual Board members gave greater weight to some factors than to others.

27. The Board tried to resolve several problems with the current accounting and reporting practices for debt and equity securities. Those problems, which are discussed in greater detail in this appendix, are summarized as follows:

a. *Inconsistent literature.* The authoritative literature on investments in debt securities is incon-

sistent among different industries and has resulted in diversity in reporting.

b. *LOCOM not evenhanded.* The current requirement to use the lower-of-cost-or-market (LOCOM) method for debt securities held for sale and for noncurrent marketable equity securities is not evenhanded because it recognizes the net diminution in value but not the net appreciation in the value of those securities.

c. *Greater relevance of fair value information.* Some believe that fair value information about debt securities is more relevant than amortized cost information in helping users and others assess the effect of current economic events on the enterprise.

d. *Gains trading.* The current requirement to use the amortized cost method permits the recognition of holding gains through the selective sale of appreciated securities but does not require the concurrent recognition of holding losses.

e. *Accounting based on intent.* Current accounting for a debt security is based not on the characteristics of the asset but on management's plans for holding or disposing of the investment. Intent-based accounting impairs comparability.

28. After concluding that the project would not prescribe the comprehensive use of fair value accounting for all securities and related liabilities, the Board supported an approach that resolves the first two problems listed in paragraph 27. It partially addresses the third issue and leaves the last two problems unresolved, although required disclosures will at least highlight situations where gains trading exists. Nevertheless, because the disparities among industries and the differences in recognizing unrealized gains and unrealized losses are eliminated, the Board considers this standard to be an improvement in financial reporting.

Background Information

29. In May 1986, the Board added to its agenda a project to reexamine the accounting for financial instruments, including issues involving off-balance-sheet financing. The Board focused initially on disclosures, resulting in the issuance of FASB Statements No. 105, *Disclosure of Information about Financial Instruments with Off-Balance-Sheet Risk and Financial Instruments with Concentrations of Credit Risk,* in March 1990 and No. 107, *Disclosures about Fair Value of Financial Instruments,* in December 1991.

30. Regulators and others have expressed concerns about the recognition and measurement of investments in debt securities, particularly those held by financial institutions. In 1988, the Office of the Comptroller of the Currency issued a banking circular that identified certain investment practices deemed to be unsuitable and specified that securities acquired in connection with those practices generally should not be classified in the investment portfolio. That same year the Federal Home Loan Bank Board released a proposed statement of policy that addressed the classification of securities as held for investment, held for sale, and held for trading.

31. Those regulators questioned the appropriateness of using the amortized cost method rather than the LOCOM method when trading and sales practices were inconsistent with the amortized cost method. They expressed specific concerns about "gains trading" by financial institutions, an activity implying that decisions to sell certain securities are based on being able to report gains in the financial statements. In gains trading, appreciated securities are sold to recognize gains, but securities with unrealized losses are held and, because the amortized cost method is used, unrealized losses are not recognized. Those practices suggest that, rather than being held for investment, the securities in the portfolio are being held for sale, in which case the

LOCOM method is usually considered to be more appropriate. Some regulators also expressed concern about an institution's ability to "defer" the recognition of losses by using the amortized cost method even though they did not engage in gains-trading activities.

32. Those concerns, along with inconsistent guidance on the reporting of debt securities held as assets in the AICPA Audit and Accounting Guides, prompted AcSEC to undertake a project on the measurement and reporting of debt securities held as assets by financial institutions. That project led to the exposure for comment of a proposed Statement of Position (SOP), *Reporting by Financial Institutions of Debt Securities Held as Assets,* in May 1990.

33. In September 1990, the chairman of the SEC emphasized some of the shortcomings of reporting investments at amortized cost and indicated that, for banks and thrift institutions, "serious consideration must be given to reporting all investment securities at market value." In October 1990, AcSEC concluded that the project on debt securities held as assets by financial institutions could be most effectively dealt with by the FASB and urged the FASB to undertake a limited-scope project on the recognition and measurement of investment securities. AcSEC indicated that "an objective standard, such as one based on market value measurements, may be more appropriate. . . ." AcSEC noted that current economic developments suggested that, in addition to depository institutions, it might be desirable to include insurance companies, mortgage bankers, finance companies, and other commercial enterprises in the scope of any FASB Statement. In November 1990, the major CPA firms advised the FASB that they endorsed AcSEC's recommendations.

34. As an interim measure, AcSEC issued Statement of Position 90-11, *Disclosure of Certain Information by Financial Institutions About Debt Securities Held as Assets,* in November 1990. That SOP requires disclosure of, among other things, the estimated market values, gross unrealized gains, and gross unrealized losses, by pertinent category, for debt securities held as assets by financial institutions. That SOP was initially effective for 1990 calendar-year reporting.

35. Although AcSEC's focus was on the accounting for investments in debt securities, AcSEC also suggested that the FASB could conform the accounting for debt securities and equity securities by amending Statement 12 to include debt securities.

36. Early in the development of the project, the Board and staff members held meetings with repre-

sentatives of banks, thrifts, insurance enterprises, industrial enterprises, and regulators to better understand why investments in debt and equity securities are held and how they are used in managing interest rate risk. During the course of the project, the Board and staff members consulted frequently with the Financial Accounting Standards Advisory Council (FASAC), the Financial Instruments Task Force, professional groups, regulators, users of financial statements, and other interested parties.

37. In September 1992, the Board issued an Exposure Draft, *Accounting for Certain Investments in Debt and Equity Securities,* for a 90-day comment period. Approximately 600 organizations and individuals responded to the Exposure Draft, many with multiple letters. In November and December 1992, members of the Board and staff also conducted eight field visits to constituents to discuss the Exposure Draft. The results of those visits were useful to the Board during its deliberations of the issues addressed by this Statement.

38. In December 1992 and January 1993, the Board held a public hearing on the proposals in the Exposure Draft. Twenty-eight individuals and firms presented their views at the 3-day public hearing. In March 1993, the Board's Financial Instruments Task Force met and discussed, among other things, the Exposure Draft and a staff draft of possible revisions to reflect the Board's redeliberations to that date.

Relevance of Fair Values of Investments in Securities

39. Some Board members believe that measuring all investments in debt and equity securities at fair value in the financial statements is relevant and useful to present and potential investors, creditors, and others in making rational investment, credit, and similar decisions—the first objective of financial reporting, as discussed in FASB Concepts Statement No. 1, *Objectives of Financial Reporting by Business Enterprises.* Other Board members are uncertain about the relevance of measuring those investments at fair value and believe that the relevance of that information should be evaluated after the results of applying Statement 107 are analyzed.

40. Some Board members believe the fair value of debt and equity securities is useful because it assists investors, creditors, and other users in evaluating the performance of an enterprise's investment strategies. Investors are interested in assessing the amounts, timing, and uncertainty of prospective net cash inflows to an enterprise, since those are also the main source of cash flows from the enter-

prise to them. Fair value portrays the market's estimate of the present value of the net future cash flows of those securities, discounted to reflect both the current interest rate and the market's estimate of the risk that the cash flows will not occur. Other Board members believe that fair value information is less relevant for debt securities that will be held to maturity.

41. Several articles and reports in recent years have indicated the potential usefulness of information about the market value of investment securities, particularly as an indicator of the solvency of financial institutions. Those articles indicate that some depository institutions have failed, or experienced impairment of earnings or capital, because of speculative securities activities and that other institutions have experienced an erosion of the liquidity of their securities portfolios as a result of decreases in the market value of those securities. In a liquidity shortage, the fair value of investments, rather than their amortized cost, is the amount available to cover an enterprise's obligations.

42. Some persons question the relevance of fair value measures for investments in securities, arguing in favor of reporting based on amortized cost. They believe that amortized cost provides relevant information because it focuses on the decision to acquire the asset, the earning effects of that decision that will be realized over time, and the ultimate recoverable value of the asset. They argue that fair value ignores those concepts and focuses instead on the effects of transactions and events that do not involve the enterprise, reflecting opportunity gains and losses whose recognition in the financial statements is, in their view, not appropriate until they are realized.

43. Opponents of fair value reporting also challenge the subjectivity that may be necessary in estimating fair values and question the usefulness of reporting fair values for securities if they are not readily marketable. They argue that the questionable reliability impairs the relevance of the fair value information. The Board understands that reliability is an important factor in financial reporting and, therefore, decided that for equity securities the scope be limited to those that have readily determinable fair values. The scope of this Statement includes only those debt instruments that are securities. The Board believes that sufficiently reliable estimates of fair value can be made for those instruments. The Board also believes that the increased use of fair values in financial reporting, partially reflecting the requirements in Statement 107 and SOP 90-11, will result in increased availability and reliability of fair value information.

Scope and Project Approach

44. The Board decided to limit the scope of the project because of its desire to expedite resolution of the problems with the current accounting and reporting practices for investment securities. Accordingly, the Board decided to address the accounting for only certain financial assets and not to change the accounting for financial liabilities nor include other assets.

Financial Assets

45. In deciding which assets to include in the scope of the Statement, the Board excluded receivables that are not securities because of concerns about the effort and cost required in some cases to make a reasonable estimate of fair value. Examples of receivables that are not securities include commercial accounts receivable, consumer installment loans, commercial real estate loans, residential mortgage loans, and checking account overdraft advances.

46. The Board decided to model the definition of *security* (paragraph 137) after the definition provided in the Uniform Commercial Code. The Board decided not to use the definition provided in the Securities Exchange Act of 1934 because that definition is too broad; it encompasses instruments that the Board concluded should not be included in the scope of this Statement, such as notes for routine personal bank loans.

47. The Board decided to include certain equity securities in the scope of this Statement because the relevance of fair value is at least as great for those equity securities as for debt securities, since equity securities can be converted to cash only through sale at fair value. The Board decided the scope should include only equity securities with readily determinable fair values because a broader scope would include equity instruments that would present significant valuation problems, such as investments in closely held companies and partnerships. By including only equity securities with readily determinable fair values, this Statement addresses the same investments in marketable equity securities as addressed in Statement 12.

48. Some respondents noted that the definition of *equity security* in Statement 12 included stock warrants and other options to acquire or dispose of equity securities, whereas the definition in the Exposure Draft did not. Those respondents suggested that the definition be consistent with Statement 12. The Board agreed and has revised the definition of *equity security* to include those options.

Financial Liabilities

49. Some enterprises, particularly financial institutions, manage their interest rate risk by coordinating their holdings of financial assets and financial liabilities. This practice would suggest that, in order for the financial statements to present a more accurate view of an enterprise's exposure to risk, some liabilities should be reported at fair value if some investments are required to be reported at fair value. The Board considered in significant detail whether enterprises should be permitted the option of reporting at fair value the liabilities that are related to the investments in debt securities that are reported at fair value.

50. The valuation of liabilities was considered as an option rather than as a requirement because the Board understood that many enterprises that typically invest their resources primarily in physical assets or intangible assets rather than in financial assets do not manage interest rate risk by relating their financial assets and liabilities.

51. The Board believes it would be preferable to permit certain related liabilities to be reported at fair value especially if all investments in debt securities were required to be reported at fair value. However, the Board was unable to identify, and respondents did not propose, any approach for valuing liabilities that the Board considered workable and not unacceptably complex or permissive. Because many enterprises manage interest rate risk on an overall basis for all financial assets and liabilities rather than for specific financial assets and specific liabilities, difficulties arose in trying to identify which liabilities should be considered as related to the debt securities being reported at fair value.

52. The Board also was unable to agree on how deposit liabilities of banks and thrifts should be valued. Some Board members believe that the fair value of a deposit liability should be based on the terms of the obligation, that is, if the deposit is payable on demand, the fair value cannot be less than the amount that could be withdrawn. That amount represents the settlement amount with the counterparties and is consistent with the Board's decision in Statement 107 that the unit of measure for financial instruments generally should be the individual instrument rather than the portfolio. Other Board members would anticipate the depositor's probable forbearance in exercising its right to withdraw the funds on deposit; thus, in their view, the fair value of the deposit liability should be based on the probable timing of the expected future cash outflows—which essentially incorporates

the institution's core deposit intangible into the valuation of deposit liabilities. The value associated with the probable timing of those expected cash flows is currently recognized in purchase business combinations, but as an intangible asset.

53. Similar difficulties exist for the valuation of certain liabilities of life insurance companies. Differing views exist about how the fair value of liabilities would be determined. For example, some respondents believe the fair value of an insurer's liabilities depends on what assets it holds, whereas others believe the fair value of the insurer's obligations to make future cash outflows should be determined independent of the composition of its assets. In addition, some believe that a life insurer's liabilities for policy reserves should not be less than the amount payable on demand at the policyholder's option for the cash surrender value, particularly since most life insurance policies result in the payment of the cash value at surrender rather than in the payment of death benefits. Others believe the cash surrender value should not be a minimum level for the fair value of the liabilities.

54. Because the Board was unable to develop a workable approach for identifying specific related liabilities and determining their fair value once identified, it decided not to require that all investments in debt securities be reported at fair value and, in replacing the LOCOM method with fair value for certain securities, decided not to include their unrealized changes in fair value in earnings. Instead, the Board agreed to an approach that would introduce more fair value into the financial reporting for investments in debt and equity securities but not change the valuation of related liabilities. The Board believes that the approach in this standard is appropriate because it is built on existing practice, which does not involve the valuation of liabilities.

55. Many respondents, principally bankers and insurers, commented that the approach in the Exposure Draft was unfair because it was one-sided, applying fair value to only some financial assets and no liabilities. Those respondents indicated that if the Board requires that securities be reported at fair value, it should also require (or at least permit) enterprises to report the related liabilities at fair value to avoid unrepresentative volatility in their financial statements. The Board believes that unrepresentative volatility (as well as unrepresentative smoothing) may also result from the use of historical cost accounting when securities are selectively sold and gains or losses are recognized. That volatility may be more acceptable to some because management can control it by deciding which securities to sell and when.

56. As indicated previously, the Board believes it would be preferable to permit certain related liabilities to be reported at fair value if all investments in debt securities were required to be reported at fair value. But this Statement does not broadly expand the use of fair value in reporting securities, and current practice recognizes the net diminution in fair value of securities held for sale (through the LOCOM method) without considering changes in the value of any liabilities. Consequently, the Board believes it is not essential to address the valuation of liabilities in this Statement and that the changes required by this Statement will provide more relevant, reliable, and useful information.

The Approach in This Statement

57. In developing this Statement, the Board considered two frequently heard criticisms of fair value accounting for debt and equity securities: (a) fair values are not as relevant for debt securities that are held to maturity and (b) the valuation of only some assets, without related liabilities, could result in inappropriate volatility of reported earnings. Those two criticisms prompted the Board to consider both retaining the use of amortized cost accounting for debt securities that are held to maturity and reporting the unrealized holding gains and losses on securities available for sale outside earnings.

Investments being held to maturity

58. Some persons believe that amortized cost is a more relevant measure of debt securities because, if a debt security is held to maturity, that cost will be realized, absent default, and any interim unrealized gains and losses will reverse. The Board concluded that amortized cost is most likely to be relevant for those debt securities that will be held to maturity and decided to prescribe different accounting for those debt securities. This criterion is consistent with the provisions of the AICPA Audit and Accounting Guide, *Audits of Savings Institutions,* which requires "the intent and ability to hold to maturity" as a prerequisite for use of the amortized cost method. The use of the amortized cost method in FASB Statement No. 60, *Accounting and Reporting by Insurance Enterprises,* also is based on the ability and intent to hold debt securities to maturity, whereas the guidance for banks is based on the ability and intent to hold securities on a long-term basis.

59. The Board deliberately chose to make the *held-to-maturity* category restrictive because it believes that the use of amortized cost must be justified for each investment in a debt security. At acquisition, an enterprise should determine if it has the positive intent and ability to hold a security to *maturity,*

which is distinct from the mere absence of an intent to sell. The Board believes that, if management's intention to hold a debt security to maturity is uncertain, it is not appropriate to carry that investment at amortized cost; amortized cost is relevant only if a security is actually held to maturity. In establishing intent, an enterprise should consider pertinent historical experience, such as sales and transfers of debt securities classified as held-to-maturity. A pattern of sales or transfers of those securities is inconsistent with an expressed current intent to hold similar debt securities to maturity.

60. The Board decided that a debt security that is available to be sold in response to changes in market interest rates, changes in the security's prepayment risk, the enterprise's need for liquidity, changes in foreign exchange risk, or other similar factors should not be included in the held-to-maturity category because the possibility of a sale is indicative that the enterprise does not have a positive intent and ability to hold the security to maturity. A debt security that is considered available to be sold as part of an enterprise's asset-liability management activities should not be classified as held-to-maturity. Similarly, an enterprise that maintains a dynamic hedging program in which changes in external factors require that certain securities be sold to maintain an effective hedge would not have the intent and ability to hold those securities to maturity.

61. In articulating the views expressed in the preceding paragraph, the Exposure Draft used the phrase *might be sold*. Many respondents misunderstood the Board's intended meaning of that phrase, extracting it from its context and emphasizing the uncertainty of future events—that anything "might" happen. The Board expects that extremely remote "disaster scenarios" (such as a run on a bank or an insurance company) would not be anticipated by an enterprise in deciding whether it had the positive intent and ability to hold a debt security to maturity. This Statement does not use the phrase *might be sold* to avoid the potential for misunderstanding.

62. The Board believes that an enterprise's decision to classify a security as held-to-maturity implies that during the term of the security the enterprise's decisions about continuing to hold that security will not be affected by changes in market interest rates or the security's prepayment risk. That decision is consistent with the view that a change in fair value, which would reflect a change in market interest rates or prepayment risk, is not relevant for a security that will be held to maturity. The Board believes that the classification of a debt security as held-to-maturity is theoretically incompatible with the subsequent designation of a fu-

tures contract or other financial instrument as a hedge of that debt security's interest rate risk. That designation is the basis for hedge accounting (that is, deferring and amortizing the change in value due to changes in market interest rates), which effectively reflects an alteration in the characteristics of the debt security (as though a new synthetic instrument has been created).

63. Because of that theoretical incompatibility, the Board proposed in the Exposure Draft that, subsequent to a debt security's classification as held-to-maturity, hedge accounting could not be achieved by designating a futures contract as a hedge of that security. Respondents generally opposed the proposed restriction on the use of hedge accounting as unnecessary and contrary to the Board's current efforts to address hedging issues on a comprehensive basis. The Board decided that, even though a theoretical incompatibility may exist for subsequent hedges of held-to-maturity securities, the proposed restriction on using hedge accounting should not be included in the final standard because the accounting for all hedging transactions is currently being addressed by the Board in a separate project. The Board also noted that hedge accounting does not provide the same accounting results as the sale of the security because it does not result in immediate recognition of the security's unrealized holding gain or loss.

64. The Exposure Draft indicated that "the sale of a debt security near enough to its maturity (for example, within 30 days) that interest rate risk is substantially eliminated as a pricing factor shall be considered in substance held to maturity." A number of respondents requested that the example of 30 days be changed to 90 days, many noting that the guidance regarding cash equivalents in FASB Statement No. 95, *Statement of Cash Flows,* applies a 3-month cutoff in determining whether securities are "so near their maturity that they present insignificant risk of changes in value because of changes in interest rates." The Board agreed with the suggestion and changed the example of "30 days" to "three months."

65. Some respondents commented that interest rate risk is also substantially eliminated as a pricing factor near to a call date when the issuer is expected to exercise the call option. Those respondents suggested that the standard also address the sale of a callable debt security near to the call date if exercise of the call is probable. The Board agreed with that suggestion.

66. A few respondents reported that many banks routinely sell their investments in mortgage-backed securities after a substantial portion of the principal has been recovered through prepayments. They

explained that the "tail" portion of a mortgage-backed security is sold because it no longer represents an efficient investment to the enterprise mainly due to the economic costs of accounting for remnants of the original issue. They requested that the Board consider permitting enterprises to sell securities classified as held-to-maturity prior to their maturity when prepayments have reduced the remaining principal to low levels. The Board decided for practical reasons that selling a debt security after a substantial portion of the principal has been collected should be considered equivalent to holding the security to maturity. The Board decided that the collection of 85 percent of the principal outstanding at acquisition (not the principal outstanding at issuance for securities purchased in the secondary market) constituted a reasonable threshold of what represents a "substantial portion of the principal." However, the Board limited application of this practical exception to collections of principal due either to prepayments on the debt security or to scheduled payments on a security payable in equal installments (both principal and interest) over its term (except that the scheduled payments need not be equal for variable-rate debt).

67. Some respondents indicated that, although they have the intent to hold the vast majority of their investments to maturity, they do not know at acquisition which specific securities will or will not be sold. Having to classify securities upon acquisition does not, in their opinion, provide the desired degree of flexibility to manage their portfolio. The Board considered two approaches that would potentially address those concerns.

68. The Board considered an approach that would eliminate the need to classify specific debt securities as available-for-sale or held-to-maturity. Instead, enterprises would designate the percentage of the securities acquired each year that would not be held to maturity and, at each reporting date, recognize a pro rata portion of the unrealized holding gain or loss on all securities. The Board rejected that approach because it would obscure the reporting of discrete investments. Under that approach, no specific debt security would be reported at fair value; instead, the carrying amount of the available-for-sale securities would be a blended amount—an allocation of portfolio totals—that, in the Board's view, would not be useful to users of financial statements. The Board also noted that the approach would continue to limit management's discretion in selling securities.

69. The Board also considered whether the standard should permit enterprises to sell without justification some specified amount of held-to-maturity securities without calling into question the enterprise's intent to hold other debt securities

to maturity. The Board rejected that approach as being inconsistent with the premise underlying the use of amortized cost—that management intends to hold all such securities to maturity. However, the Board decided that the sale of a held-to-maturity security due to events that are isolated, nonrecurring, and unusual for the reporting enterprise that could not have been reasonably anticipated should not necessarily call into question the enterprise's intent to hold other debt securities to maturity. But if the sale of a held-to-maturity security occurs without justification, the materiality of that contradiction of the enterprise's previously asserted intent must be evaluated.

70. The Board recognizes that the intent to hold a security to maturity is not absolute and that in some circumstances management's intent could change for certain securities. The Exposure Draft acknowledged that, for example, management might decide to sell a security because of either an increase in the security's credit risk or a change in the tax law that eliminates the tax-exempt status of interest on that security. Respondents identified a variety of other circumstances that they believed should justify the sale of a security classified as held-to-maturity.

71. Some respondents believed that enterprises should be permitted to sell held-to-maturity securities to generate taxable gains to offset existing taxable losses, or vice versa. Some respondents also desired to be able to sell those securities in response to changes in the enterprise's anticipated future profitability. It was suggested, for example, that if taxable losses were expected for the next several years, the enterprise should be permitted to sell tax-exempt securities classified as held-to-maturity. The Board rejected those suggested reasons for selling held-to-maturity securities. Securities that may need to be sold to implement tax-planning strategies should be classified as available-for-sale, not held-to-maturity.

72. Some respondents suggested that the standard permit the sale of a held-to-maturity security in advance of any deterioration in the creditworthiness of the issuer, perhaps based solely on industry statistics. The Board believes that the sale must be in response to an actual deterioration, not mere speculation. That deterioration should be supported by evidence about the issuer's creditworthiness; however, the enterprise need not await an actual downgrading in the issuer's published credit rating or inclusion on a "credit watch" list.

73. Some respondents suggested that major business combinations and major dispositions should be identified as circumstances that would justify being able to sell a held-to-maturity security. The

Board agreed that, following a pooling of interests, the continuing management may need to sell or transfer some held-to-maturity securities to maintain the enterprise's existing credit risk policy, foreign exchange risk exposure, or interest rate risk position under its asset-liability management policy. Similarly, following a major purchase acquisition, some of the acquiring enterprise's held-to-maturity securities may need to be transferred or sold because of the nature of the liabilities assumed—even though all of the acquired securities are classified anew following such a business combination.

74. The Board acknowledged that, after a major disposition, some held-to-maturity securities may need to be transferred or sold to maintain the interest rate risk exposure that predated the disposition. In considering those issues, the Board rejected a suggestion to automatically permit investment portfolio restructurings after a business combination or disposition. The Board believes that held-to-maturity securities should be transferred or sold only when the transfer or sale is necessary to maintain a particular risk exposure consistent with the enterprise's risk posture prior to the business combination or disposition. Furthermore, the Board believes those necessary transfers or sales should occur concurrent with or shortly after the business combination or disposition.

75. Some respondents suggested that the transfer or sale of a held-to-maturity security should be permitted in response to changes in the regulatory environment. The Board believes that if an enterprise is forced to dispose of a held-to-maturity security because a change in statutory or regulatory requirements significantly modifies what constitutes a permissible investment, that disposition should not call into question management's intent to hold the remaining securities in that category to maturity. Similarly, if a change in statutory or regulatory requirements significantly reduces the maximum level of investment that the enterprise can make in certain kinds of securities or in securities with a specified low credit quality, the sale of held-to-maturity securities to comply with that newly imposed maximum also should not call into question the classification of other held-to-maturity securities. The Board also agreed that if regulators significantly increase the risk weights of certain debt securities used for risk-based capital purposes, the sale of held-to-maturity securities with those recently increased risk weights should not call into question the classification of other held-to-maturity securities.

76. Some respondents suggested that the sale of held-to-maturity securities should always be permitted to meet regulatory capital requirements.

The Board rejected blanket approval for those sales. It noted that an enterprise's ability and intent to hold securities to maturity would be called into question by the sale of held-to-maturity securities to realize gains to replenish regulatory capital that had been reduced by a provision for loan losses. The Board believes that gains trading with held-to-maturity securities to meet an enterprise's capital requirements is inconsistent with the held-to-maturity notion. In contrast, if an enterprise chooses to downsize to comply with a significant increase in the industry's capital requirements, the sale of one or more held-to-maturity securities in connection with that downsizing would not call into question the classification of other held-to-maturity securities.

77. In some circumstances it may not be possible to hold a security to its original stated maturity, such as when the security is called by the issuer prior to maturity. The issuer's exercise of the call option effectively accelerates the security's maturity and should not be viewed as inconsistent with classification in the held-to-maturity category.

Investments not being held to maturity

78. For investments in debt securities that management does not have the positive intent and ability to hold to maturity, and for investments in equity securities with readily determinable fair values, the Board concluded that fair value information is more relevant than amortized cost information, in part because it reflects the effects of management's decision to buy a financial asset at a specific time and then continue to hold it for an unspecified period of time. For example, if an enterprise invests in a fixed-rate security and interest rates fall, the enterprise is in a better position than if it had invested in a variable-rate security. Movements in fair values, and thus market returns, during the period that a debt or equity security is held also provide a benchmark from which to assess the results of management's decisions and its success in maximizing the profitable use of the enterprise's economic resources. That success, or failure, is relevant and should be reflected in the financial statements in the period that the event (that is, the change in interest rates) occurs.

79. The Board decided that those investments in debt and equity securities should be reported at fair value. However, because of concerns about the potential volatility that would result from reporting the fair value changes of only some assets, and no liabilities, in earnings, the Board determined that the unrealized holding gains and losses for available-for-sale securities should be excluded from earnings. The basis for that conclusion is discussed in paragraphs 90-95.

80. The Board concluded that investments that are bought and held principally for the purpose of selling them in the near term should be classified as *trading* securities. Trading generally reflects active and frequent buying and selling, and trading securities generally are used with the objective of generating profits on short-term differences in price. The designation of trading securities under this Statement is the same as present practice by depository institutions.

81. Some respondents suggested that the criteria for classifying assets as current or noncurrent be used to distinguish between trading securities and available-for-sale securities. The Board disagreed because that suggestion is inconsistent with the character of trading securities, which are acquired generally with the objective of generating profits on short-term differences in price. Other respondents suggested that all securities classified as current should be classified as trading securities. The Board believes that available-for-sale securities should not be automatically transferred to the trading category because the passage of time has caused the maturity date to be within one year or because management intends to sell the security within one year.

82. All investments in debt and equity securities that are valued at fair value and are not classified as trading securities would be classified as *available-for-sale securities*. This category would include marketable equity securities previously covered by Statement 12, except to the extent that the investor classifies some of them as trading securities. Additionally, the available-for-sale category will include debt securities that are being held for an unspecified period of time, such as those that the enterprise would consider selling to meet liquidity needs or as part of an enterprise's risk management program.

83. At acquisition, an investor should determine and document the classification of debt and equity securities into one of the three categories—held-to-maturity, available-for-sale, or trading. At each reporting date, the appropriateness of the classification must be reassessed. For example, if an enterprise no longer has the ability to hold securities to maturity, their continued classification as held-to-maturity would not be appropriate.

Transfers between categories of investments

84. Many respondents noted that the Exposure Draft's proposed requirement to account for transfers at fair value and recognize in earnings any unrealized holding gains and losses existing at the date of a transfer would facilitate gains trading; a change in management's intent would cause an appreciated security to be transferred, resulting in immediate recognition of the gain in earnings. Respondents urged the Board not to provide that opportunity, especially in a standard that they expected would help resolve the gains trading issue, not aggravate it. Some respondents suggested that all unrealized holding gains or losses on transferred securities be deferred in a separate component of equity. Others supported an approach that reported unrealized holding gains and losses in a manner consistent with the category into which the security has been transferred.

85. The Board acknowledged that the proposed accounting for transfers would have permitted discretionary adjustments to earnings that could weaken the credibility of reported earnings. To avoid that potential consequence, the Board decided that unrealized holding gains and losses would be recognized in earnings only if the security were transferred into the trading category. Otherwise, the unrealized holding gains and losses that had not yet been recognized in earnings would be reported in a separate component of equity. In certain respects, this approach is similar to the notion of recognizing unrealized gains and losses in a manner consistent with the category into which the security has been transferred. Because the Board expects transfers from the held-to-maturity category to be rare, special disclosures about the circumstances that resulted in the transfers are required.

Comments on the approach in this statement

86. As stated previously, some Board members would have preferred to require the use of fair value for all investments in debt and equity securities, even if the Board was unable to resolve at this time how to deal with the option to account for related liabilities at their fair values. Other Board members would have preferred to require the use of fair value for all securities, but only if it were practicable to permit the valuation of liabilities at their fair values. Other Board members, as well as many respondents, believe that consideration of the use of fair value for all investments in debt and equity securities should be delayed until the results of applying Statement 107 can be analyzed.

87. Despite those various views, Board members believe that the existing diversity in guidance must be addressed and that an interim solution is appropriate at this point, given the present status of the overall project on the recognition and measurement of financial instruments. The Board expects that the use of fair value measurements for financial instruments will be reassessed at an appropriate future point in the financial instruments project. This reassessment would likely include an evaluation of the relevance, reliability, and use of

fair values based on experience from applying Statement 107 and this Statement. The Board has no preconceived views about the outcome of that consideration.

88. The Board also recognizes that the classification of investments in debt securities into three categories and the use of management intent as a criterion to distinguish among the categories present some difficulties. The classification of debt securities into three categories, each of which has different accounting, could result in comparability problems among enterprises. Enterprises with virtually identical securities may account for those securities differently. Additionally, basing the distinction in accounting treatment on management intent could result in an inconsistent application of the standard and contribute to comparability difficulties. Some constituents as well as some Board members question the relevance of accounting that results from using the intent of management as a criterion.

89. While the Board recognizes that there are some difficulties associated with the use of management intent as a criterion, and with the classification of identical instruments into several categories, it believes that this standard will improve financial reporting overall because it will standardize for all enterprises the criterion for when a debt security should be reported at amortized cost and specify a more evenhanded approach for recognizing unrealized gains and unrealized losses.

Reporting Changes in Fair Value

90. This Statement provides requirements for reporting changes in the fair value of investments in securities. The total change in fair value consists of both the unpaid interest income earned on a debt security (or the unpaid accrued dividends on an equity security) and the remaining change in fair value that results from holding a security, known as the *unrealized holding gain or loss*. The reporting requirements for unrealized holding gains and losses depend on the classification of securities as trading or available-for-sale, as outlined in paragraph 13. This Statement does not change the current practice of including interest income in earnings, regardless of a security's classification.

91. For trading securities, the Board decided that unrealized holding gains and losses should be included in the determination of earnings, consistent with present accounting. The Board also decided that unrealized holding gains and losses on available-for-sale securities should be excluded from the determination of earnings. The unrealized holding gains and losses should be reported as a net amount in a separate component of shareholders'

equity until the holding gains and losses are realized or a provision for impairment is recognized.

92. For securities that are actively managed, the Board believes that financial reporting is improved when earnings reflect the economic consequences of the events of the reporting enterprise (such as changes in fair value) as well as the transactions (such as purchases and sales of securities) that occur. Including changes in fair value in the determination of earnings results in more relevant financial information to current shareholders, whose composition typically changes to some degree from one reporting period to the next. Including unrealized changes in fair value in earnings provides a more equitable reporting of results and changes in shareholders' equity among the different shareholder groups over the period that a security is held by recognizing in each reporting period the effects of economic events occurring in those periods. Thus, the Board concluded that unrealized changes in value on trading securities should be reported in earnings.

93. However, some enterprises, particularly financial institutions, that consider both their investments in securities and their liabilities in managing interest rate risk contend that reporting unrealized holding gains and losses on only the investments, and not related liabilities, in earnings has the potential for significant volatility that is unrepresentative of both the way they manage their business and the impact of economic events on the overall enterprise.

94. Based principally on those concerns, the Board decided that unrealized holding gains and losses on debt and equity securities that are available for sale but that are not actively managed in a trading account should be reported outside earnings—a method of reporting currently used for some securities under Statement 12. That reporting would alleviate the potential for volatility in reported earnings resulting from a requirement to value some assets at fair value without at least permitting fair-value-based accounting for related liabilities. It also would mitigate concerns about reporting the fluctuation in fair value of long-term investments in earnings. However, the Board recognizes that volatility in earnings can still result from the sale of securities. Furthermore, the approach does not resolve concerns about gains trading.

95. Many respondents, particularly bankers and insurers, emphasized that reporting the unrealized holding gains and losses for available-for-sale securities in a separate component of equity would create volatility in reported capital. The Board acknowledges that reporting those securities at fair

value will cause greater volatility in total share-holders' equity than use of the amortized cost method would, but believes that the greater relevance of fair value for those securities significantly outweighs the disadvantages of that potential volatility in equity. Furthermore, the Board believes those disadvantages are mitigated by the supplemental disclosures of fair value for other financial assets and liabilities pursuant to Statement 107.

Benefits and Costs

96. In accomplishing its mission, the Board follows certain precepts, including the precept to promulgate standards only when the expected benefits of the information exceed the perceived costs. The Board endeavors to determine that a proposed standard will fill a significant need and that the costs imposed to meet that standard, as compared to other alternatives, are justified in relation to the overall benefits of the resulting information.

97. The benefits of reporting debt and equity securities at fair value are discussed in paragraphs 39-43 of this Statement. Furthermore, in eliminating the inconsistencies in the existing authoritative literature, this Statement is beneficial in avoiding the diversity and confusion resulting from the current accounting guidance. It also eliminates the un-evenhandedness of LOCOM, which recognizes the net diminution in value of securities but not the net appreciation in value.

98. The incremental costs of the accounting and disclosure requirements of this Statement have been minimized in several ways. The Board has been informed that many enterprises already have systems in place to manage the market risk of their portfolios and that those systems provide much of the information that is necessary to comply with this Statement. Additionally, the required disclosures in Statement 107 provide much of the information required in this Statement. For financial institutions, the incremental burden is further minimized by the existing disclosure requirements of SOP 90-11 and regulatory reporting requirements. Furthermore, because the LOCOM method is not used, enterprises will not be required to combine portfolios of investments of various subsidiaries.

99. The Board is sensitive to the economic consequences that may result from the new information. For example, many respondents commented that enterprises may no longer invest in long-term instruments, such as long-term U.S. Treasury securities and corporate bonds, to reduce the potential for volatility in reported capital. They further suggested that such discontinued investment could jeopardize the market for those long-term securities. Some respondents also predicted that this Statement would exacerbate the credit crunch by causing financial institutions to make fewer loans, particularly long-term loans.

100. However, the nature and extent of those consequences are highly uncertain and are difficult to isolate from the effects of other events that will occur independent of that new information. For example, regulatory agencies are continuing to make changes in regulations that may affect the future costs of doing business for certain enterprises. Even if the Board could isolate the likely consequences of the information provided pursuant to this Statement from other events that produce change, it is outside the Board's role to deal with those possible consequences. The Board's objective in this pronouncement is to improve the consistency in how information about investments in securities is determined so that users of financial statements may make better-informed decisions.

Enterprises Included in Scope

101. Although the issues that gave rise to the Board's consideration of this Statement were raised in the context of financial institutions, particularly depository institutions, the Board believes that this Statement should not be limited to the accounting by those institutions. The Board's approach to standard setting generally has been to consider the accounting for a specific transaction or financial instrument and not to try to develop specialized accounting methods for different industries, particularly for transactions that are not unique to a specific industry.

102. The Board considered whether certain enterprises should be excluded from the scope of this Statement based on industry, size, or nonpublic status and concluded that any enterprise that chooses to invest in marketable securities should be able to make or gain access to a reasonable estimate of fair value. Deregulation and market forces have blurred the distinction between industries and have heightened desires for greater comparability between financial statements of enterprises nominally in different industries. Those factors reinforced the Board's belief that all enterprises with identical financial instruments should account for those instruments in the same manner.

103. Some respondents suggested that nondepository financial institutions (particularly life insurance companies) be exempted from this Statement. The Board believes that distinguishing between nondepository financial institutions and other financial institutions is not warranted because both types of institutions invest their resources primarily in financial assets and the fair value of invest-

ments in debt and equity securities of all financial institutions is similarly affected by changes in market interest rates. Furthermore, Statement 60 already requires that the use of amortized cost in accounting for debt securities held by insurance companies be based on the ability and intent to hold the securities to maturity.

104. Other respondents suggested that nonfinancial institutions be exempted from this Statement. The Board believes that a distinction between financial and nonfinancial institutions is not warranted even though commercial and industrial companies invest their resources primarily in physical assets rather than financial assets. To the extent that those enterprises invest in debt and equity securities, those financial assets have the same future economic benefits as when held by a financial institution.

105. Respondents, principally bankers, also suggested that smaller and nonpublic enterprises be exempted because they lack the capabilities or resources necessary to provide estimates of fair values. The Board believes that prudent investment management normally warrants knowledge of market estimates, and smaller enterprises should have access to those estimates. Additionally, the fair value of investments in debt and equity securities owned by smaller or nonpublic enterprises is affected by changes in market interest rates in the same manner as those owned by large or public enterprises. The Board notes that even small, nonpublic banks have been required for many years to disclose the market value of their investments in securities.

106. The Board also considered exempting not-for-profit organizations, such as health and welfare organizations, hospitals, colleges and universities, religious institutions, trade associations, and private foundations, from the scope of this Statement. The Board believes that for those organizations not currently reporting their investments at fair value, the measurement standards in this Statement would probably be an improvement to the current accounting for investments in debt and equity securities, such as those held in endowment funds. At issue is whether those requirements should be articulated in this Statement or in a later Statement after the Board resolves its agenda project on financial statement display by not-for-profit organizations. The Board decided it was more efficient to solicit and consider comments only on the accounting by enterprises other than not-for-profit organizations. Accordingly, not-for-profit organizations are not required to apply the provisions in this Statement. The Board intends to address the issue of accounting for investments by not-for-profit organizations within its separate overall project on not-for-profit organizations.

107. Some respondents questioned whether a credit union was included in the scope as a financial institution or excluded as a not-for-profit organization. FASB Concepts Statement No. 4, *Objectives of Financial Reporting by Nonbusiness Organizations,* states in paragraph 7, "Examples of organizations that clearly fall outside the focus of this Statement include all investor-owned enterprises and other types of organizations, such as mutual insurance companies and other mutual cooperative entities that provide dividends, lower costs, or other economic benefits directly and proportionately to their owners, members, or participants." Accordingly, because credit unions, like mutual insurance companies, provide economic benefits to their members, they are not considered nonbusiness or not-for-profit organizations and, thus, are *not* excluded from the scope of this Statement.

108. The Board understands that enterprises in certain industries apply specialized accounting practices that include accounting for substantially all investments in debt and equity securities at market value or fair value, with the changes in those values recognized in earnings or in changes in net assets. The Board decided not to change the accounting by those enterprises because it believes that, for those enterprises, that accounting provides more relevant information for users of their financial statements. Consequently, those enterprises, such as brokers and dealers in securities, defined benefit pension plans, and investment companies, are excluded from the scope of this Statement.

Other Issues

Terminology

109. The Board decided to use the term *fair value* in this Statement to avoid confusion between the terms *fair value* and *market value;* some constituents associate the term *market value* only with items that are traded on active secondary markets (such as exchange and dealer markets). However, the Board does not make that distinction, intending the term to be applicable whether the market for an item is active or inactive, primary or secondary. The Board decided to use the term *fair value* also to maintain consistency with the terminology in Statement 107 and the financial instrument proposals made recently by the International Accounting Standards Committee and the Canadian Institute of Chartered Accountants. Those proposals would require disclosures of fair value for financial assets and financial liabilities.

Determining Fair Values

110. The Board concluded that quoted market prices, if available, provide the most reliable meas-

ure of fair value. Quoted market prices are easy to obtain and are reliable and verifiable. They are used and relied upon regularly and are well understood by investors, creditors, and other users of financial information.

111. Although quoted market prices are not available for all debt securities, the Board believes that a reasonable estimate of fair value can be made or obtained for the remaining debt securities required to be valued at fair value by this Statement. Some respondents mentioned the difficulty of reliably estimating the fair value of local municipal bonds; however, because municipal bonds are often intended to be held to maturity, to that extent, they are not reported at fair value. For debt securities that do not trade regularly or that trade only in principal-to-principal markets, a reasonable estimate of fair value can be made using a variety of pricing techniques, including, but not limited to, discounted cash flow analysis, matrix pricing, option-adjusted spread models, and fundamental analysis. The Board realizes that estimating fair value may require judgment but noted that a considerable degree of judgment is also needed when complying with other long-standing accounting and reporting requirements.

Impairment of Securities

112. The Board concluded that it is important to recognize in earnings all declines in fair value below the amortized cost basis that are considered to be other-than-temporary; a loss inherent in an investment security should be recognized in earnings even if it has not been sold. This is consistent with the other-than-temporary-impairment notion that was included in Statement 12.

113. The Board recognizes that the impairment provisions of this Statement differ from those in FASB Statement No. 114, *Accounting by Creditors for Impairment of a Loan,* which indicates that a loan is impaired when it is probable that the creditor (investor) will be unable to collect all amounts due according to the contractual terms of the loan agreement. This Statement requires that the measure of impairment be based on the fair value of the security, whereas Statement 114 permits measurement of an unsecuritized loan's impairment based on either fair value (of the loan or the collateral) or the present value of the expected cash flows discounted at the loan's effective interest rate. The Board recognizes that a principal difference between securities and unsecuritized loans is the relatively greater and easier availability of reliable market prices for securities, which makes it more practical and less costly to require use of a fair value approach. In addition, some Board members believe that securities are distinct from receivables

that are not securities and that securities warrant a different measure of impairment—one that reflects both current estimates of the expected cash flows from the security and current economic events and conditions.

114. During the course of this project, some have urged the Board to develop guidance that would resolve recent practice problems about the application of other-than-temporary impairment. Although the Board believes that other-than-temporary impairment exists if it is probable that the investor will be unable to collect all amounts due according to the contractual terms of the security, the Board believes that providing comprehensive guidance on other-than-temporary impairment involves issues beyond the scope of this Statement.

Financial Instruments Used to Hedge Investments at Fair Value

115. This Statement does not address the accounting for other financial instruments used to hedge investments in securities. However, the accounting for those instruments may be affected if they are hedges of securities whose accounting is changed by this Statement. Gains and losses on instruments that hedge securities classified as trading would be reported in earnings, consistent with the reporting of unrealized gains and losses on the trading securities. Gains and losses on instruments that hedge available-for-sale securities are initially reported in a separate component of equity, consistent with the reporting for those securities, but then should be amortized as a yield adjustment. The reporting of available-for-sale securities at fair value does not change the recognition and measurement of interest income.

Amendment of Statement 91

116. Some respondents noted that the change from LOCOM to fair value for reporting available-for-sale securities would cause FASB Statement No. 91, *Accounting for Nonrefundable Fees and Costs Associated with Originating or Acquiring Loans and Initial Direct Costs of Leases,* to no longer apply to those securities. Paragraph 3 of Statement 91 indicates that it does not apply to loans and securities reported at fair value. The Board noted that the intent of that provision was to exclude only the loans and securities whose changes in value were included in earnings, not those loans and securities whose changes in value are reported in a separate component of shareholders' equity. Consequently, the Board agreed to amend Statement 91 to clarify that only loans and securities reported at fair value with changes in value reported in earnings are excluded from that Statement's scope. Thus, Statement 91 would continue to apply to available-for-sale securi-

ties that previously were reported at amortized cost or LOCOM.

Financial Statement Presentation and Disclosure

117. The Board decided not to require the presentation of individual amounts for the three categories of investments on the face of the statement of financial position, provided the information is presented in the notes. Thus, enterprises that report certain investments in debt securities as *cash equivalents* in accordance with the provisions of Statement 95 can continue that practice, provided that the notes reconcile the reporting classifications used in the statement of financial position.

118. Some respondents asked how the cash flows from purchases, sales, and maturities of trading and available-for-sale securities should be classified in the statement of cash flows. Because trading securities are bought and held principally for the purpose of selling them in the near term, the cash flows from purchases and sales of trading securities should be classified as cash flows from operating activities. However, available-for-sale securities are not acquired for that purpose. The Board believes that cash flows from purchases, sales, and maturities of available-for-sale securities should be classified as cash flows from investing activities and reported gross in the statement of cash flows.

119. The Board believes that the financial statement disclosures required by this Statement provide information that is useful in analyzing an enterprise's investment strategies and exposures to risk. Gross unrealized gains and losses may indicate the results of hedging activities. Information about the sale or transfer of securities, including information on realized gains and losses, would reveal reallocations of the enterprise's resources and would help identify gains-trading activity. In considering the disclosures to be required, the Board consulted with representative organizations of users of financial statements. Respondents were generally supportive of the disclosures proposed in the Exposure Draft.

Effective Date and Transition

120. The Board proposed that this Statement should be effective for fiscal years beginning after December 15, 1993 for all enterprises. The Board considered whether to permit a delayed effective date for smaller enterprises (as provided in Statement 107) but decided that extra time was not required to develop the fair value information required by this Statement. In contrast, Statement 107 required disclosure of the fair value of all financial instruments, some of which are more difficult to value. The Board noted that smaller financial insti-

tutions are already required by SOP 90-11 to disclose the market value of their investments in debt securities. Respondents generally concurred with the proposed effective date, indicating that no deferral of the effective date was needed.

121. Some respondents requested that application of the new standard in 1993 financial statements be permitted, in part to enable them to include the cumulative effect of the accounting change in the income statement for 1993 rather than 1994. The Board decided to permit enterprises, for fiscal years beginning prior to December 16, 1993, to initially apply this Statement as of the end of a fiscal year for which annual financial statements have not previously been issued.

122. Because the classification of securities among the three categories is based on the enterprise's current intent, the Board decided that retroactive application of the provisions of this Statement is inappropriate. Except as permitted in the preceding paragraph, this Statement should be applied prospectively as of the beginning of the fiscal year.

123. As indicated in paragraph 23, at the date of initial application of this Statement, the enterprise's investments in debt and equity securities shall be classified based on the enterprise's current intent. The classification at initial application should not be considered a transfer between categories; thus, the accounting for transfers in paragraph 15 is not relevant to the initial application of this Statement. At the date of initial application, the unrealized holding gain or loss, net of tax effect, for securities classified as available-for-sale should be reported in the separate component of shareholders' equity. The unrealized holding gains and losses, net of tax effect, previously included in earnings that would be excluded from earnings under this Statement would be reversed in the income statement as the cumulative effect of a change in accounting principle.

Appendix B

AMENDMENTS TO EXISTING PRONOUNCEMENTS

124. This Statement supersedes Statement 12 and related FASB Interpretations No. 11, *Changes in Market Value after the Balance Sheet Date,* No. 12, *Accounting for Previously Established Allowance Accounts,* No. 13, *Consolidation of a Parent and Its Subsidiaries Having Different Balance Sheet Dates,* and No. 16, *Clarification of Definitions and Accounting for Marketable Equity Securities That Become Nonmarketable.*

Statement of Financial Accounting Standards No. 116
Accounting for Contributions Received and Contributions Made

STATUS

Issued: June 1993

Effective Date: For fiscal years beginning after December 15, 1994

Affects: No other pronouncements

Affected by: No other pronouncements

Other Interpretive Pronouncement: FIN 42

Other Interpretive Release: FASB *Highlights,* "Time for a Change—Implementing FASB Statements 116 and 117," January 1995

SUMMARY

This Statement establishes accounting standards for contributions and applies to all entities that receive or make contributions. Generally, contributions received, including unconditional promises to give, are recognized as revenues in the period received at their fair values. Contributions made, including unconditional promises to give, are recognized as expenses in the period made at their fair values. Conditional promises to give, whether received or made, are recognized when they become unconditional, that is, when the conditions are substantially met.

This Statement requires not-for-profit organizations to distinguish between contributions received that increase permanently restricted net assets, temporarily restricted net assets, and unrestricted net assets. It also requires recognition of the expiration of donor-imposed restrictions in the period in which the restrictions expire.

This Statement allows certain exceptions for contributions of services and works of art, historical treasures, and similar assets. Contributions of services are recognized only if the services received (a) create or enhance nonfinancial assets or (b) require specialized skills, are provided by individuals possessing those skills, and would typically need to be purchased if not provided by donation. Contributions of works of art, historical treasures, and similar assets need not be recognized as revenues and capitalized if the donated items are added to collections held for public exhibition, education, or research in furtherance of public service rather than financial gain.

This Statement requires certain disclosures for collection items not capitalized and for receipts of contributed services and promises to give.

This Statement is effective for financial statements issued for fiscal years beginning after December 15, 1994, except for not-for-profit organizations with less than $5 million in total assets and less than $1 million in annual expenses. For those organizations, the Statement is effective for fiscal years beginning after December 15, 1995. Earlier application is encouraged. This Statement may be applied either retroactively or by recognizing the cumulative effect of the change in the year of the change. The provisions for recognition of expirations of restrictions may be applied prospectively.

125. The following is added to paragraph 4 of Chapter 3A of ARB 43 following *operations* in subitem (f):

, including investments in debt and equity securities classified as trading securities under FASB Statement No. 115, *Accounting for Certain Investments in Debt and Equity Securities*

126. The following sentence is added to the end of paragraph 19(l) of APB Opinion No. 18, *The Equity Method of Accounting for Investments in Common Stock:*

FASB Statement No. 115, *Accounting for Certain Investments in Debt and Equity Securities,* addresses the accounting for investments in equity securities with readily determinable fair values that are not consolidated or accounted for under the equity method.

127. FASB Statement 60 is amended as follows:

a. Paragraph 45 is replaced by the following:

All investments in debt securities and investments in equity securities that have readily determinable fair values, as defined by FASB Statement No. 115, *Accounting for Certain Investments in Debt and Equity Securities,* shall be accounted for in accordance with the provisions of that Statement.

b. Paragraph 46 is replaced by the following:

Investments in equity securities that are not addressed by Statement 115 because they do not meet the criteria in paragraph 3 of that Statement shall be reported at fair value, and changes in fair value shall be recognized as unrealized gains and losses and reported, net of applicable income taxes, in a separate component of equity.

c. The last two sentences of paragraph 50 and footnote 7 to that paragraph are deleted.

d. The first sentence of paragraph 51 is replaced by the following:

If a decline in the fair value of an equity security that is not addressed by Statement 115 because it does not meet the criteria in paragraph 3 of that Statement is considered to be other than temporary, the investment shall be reduced to its net realizable value, which becomes its new cost basis.

128. Statement 65 is amended as follows:

a. In paragraph 4, *and mortgage-backed securities* is deleted and the following is added at the end of the paragraph:

Mortgage-backed securities held for sale in conjunction with mortgage banking activities shall be classified as trading securities and reported at fair value in accordance with the provisions of FASB Statement No. 115, *Accounting for Certain Investments in Debt and Equity Securities.*

b. In paragraph 5, *and mortgage-backed securities* is deleted.

c. In the first sentence of paragraph 6, *or mortgage-backed security* is deleted. In the last sentence of paragraph 6, *or mortgage-backed security* and *or security* are deleted. The following is added to paragraph 6 immediately after the first sentence:

The securitization of a mortgage loan held for sale shall be accounted for as the sale of the mortgage loan and the purchase of a mortgage-backed security classified as a trading security at fair value.

d. In paragraph 7, all references to *or mortgage-backed security* and *or security* are deleted.

e. In the last sentence of paragraph 8, *as being held for sale* is replaced by *as being either mortgage loans held for sale or mortgage-backed securities classified as trading securities under Statement 115.*

f. In the first sentence of paragraph 9(a), *and mortgage-backed securities* is deleted. The following is added to the end of paragraph 9(a):

If the fair value of a mortgage-backed security subject to an investor purchase commitment exceeds the commitment price, the implicit loss on the commitment shall be recognized.

g. In each sentence of paragraph 9(c), the first usage of *market value* is replaced by *fair value.*

h. In paragraph 12, all references to *or mortgage-backed securities* and *or securities* are deleted.

i. The following is added to the penultimate sentence in paragraph 17 after *investor*:

(or fair value of the mortgage loan at the time it is securitized)

j. In paragraphs 28 and 29, *and mortgage-backed securities* is deleted.

129. In the last sentence of paragraph 5 of FASB Statement No. 80, *Accounting for Futures Contracts,* the phrase *until it is amortized or* is added after *equity.*

130. Statement 91 is amended as follows:

a. In paragraph 3, *if the changes in market value are included in earnings* is added at the end of the last sentence.

b. In paragraph 27(a), which amends paragraph 6 of Statement 65, *or security* is deleted.

131. In paragraph 28 of FASB Statement No. 97, *Accounting and Reporting by Insurance Enterprises for Certain Long-Duration Contracts and for Realized Gains and Losses from the Sale of Investments,* the phrase *investments that are classified as trading securities and* is added after *except* in the parenthetical expression of the amendment of Statement 60 in the fourth sentence of that paragraph.

132. FASB Statement No. 102, *Statement of Cash Flows—Exemption of Certain Enterprises and Classification of Cash Flows from Certain Securities Acquired for Resale,* is amended as follows:

a. The following sentence is added to the end of paragraph 8:

Cash flows from purchases, sales, and maturities of available-for-sale securities shall be classified as cash flows from investing activities and reported gross in the statement of cash flows.

b. In footnote 4 to paragraph 9, *and mortgage-backed securities* is deleted.

133. In paragraph 36(b) of Statement 109, *changes in the carrying amount of marketable securities under FASB Statement No. 12, Accounting for Certain Marketable Securities* is replaced by *changes in the unrealized holding gains and losses of securities classified as available-for-sale under FASB Statement No. 115, Accounting for Certain Investments in Debt and Equity Securities.*

134. In paragraphs 4 and 5 of FASB Interpretation No. 40, *Applicability of Generally Accepted Accounting Principles to Mutual Life Insurance and Other Enterprises,* the references to Statement 12 are deleted.

135. FASB Technical Bulletin No. 79-19, *Investor's Accounting for Unrealized Losses on Marketable Securities Owned by an Equity Method Investee,* is amended as follows:

a. In paragraph 1, *accumulated changes in the valuation allowance for marketable equity securities* is replaced by *unrealized holding gains or losses on investments in debt and equity securities.*

b. Paragraph 6 is replaced by the following:

If a subsidiary or other investee that is accounted for by the equity method is required to include unrealized holding gains and losses on investments in debt and equity securities in the stockholders' equity section of the balance sheet pursuant to the provisions of Statement 115, the parent or investor shall adjust its investment in that investee by its proportionate share of the unrealized gains and losses and a like amount shall be included in the stockholders' equity section of its balance sheet.

136. In paragraph 3 of FASB Technical Bulletin No. 85-1, *Accounting for the Receipt of Federal Home Loan Mortgage Corporation Participating Preferred Stock,* the phrase *a marketable equity security that subsequently should be reported in accordance with Statement 12 (at the lower of cost or market)* is replaced by *an equity security that subsequently should be reported at fair value in accordance with FASB Statement No. 115, Accounting for Certain Investments in Debt and Equity Securities.*

Appendix C

GLOSSARY

137. This appendix contains definitions of terms or phrases as used in this Statement.

Debt security

Any security representing a creditor relationship with an enterprise. It also includes (a) preferred stock that by its terms either must be redeemed by the issuing enterprise or is redeemable at the option of the investor and (b) a collateralized mortgage obligation (CMO) (or other instrument) that is issued in equity form but is required to be accounted for as a nonequity instrument regardless of how that instrument is classified (that is, whether equity or debt) in the issuer's statement of financial position. However, it excludes option contracts, financial futures contracts, forward contracts, and lease contracts.

- Thus, the term *debt security* includes, among other items, U.S. Treasury securities, U.S. government agency securities, municipal securities, corporate bonds, convertible debt, commercial paper, all securitized debt instruments, such as CMOs and real estate mortgage investment conduits (REMICs), and interest-only and principal-only strips.
- Trade accounts receivable arising from sales on credit by industrial or commercial enterprises and loans receivable arising from consumer,

commercial, and real estate lending activities of financial institutions are examples of receivables that do not meet the definition of *security;* thus, those receivables are not debt securities (unless they have been securitized, in which case they would meet the definition).

Equity security

Any security representing an ownership interest in an enterprise (for example, common, preferred, or other capital stock) or the right to acquire (for example, warrants, rights, and call options) or dispose of (for example, put options) an ownership interest in an enterprise at fixed or determinable prices. However, the term does not include convertible debt or preferred stock that by its terms either must be redeemed by the issuing enterprise or is redeemable at the option of the investor.

Fair value

The amount at which a financial instrument could be exchanged in a current transaction between willing parties, other than in a forced or liquidation sale. If a quoted market price is available for an instrument, the fair value to be used in applying this Statement is the product of the number of trading units of the instrument times its market price.

Holding gain or loss

The net change in fair value of a security exclusive of dividend or interest income recognized but not yet received and exclusive of any write-downs for other-than-temporary impairment.

Security

A share, participation, or other interest in property or in an enterprise of the issuer or an obligation of the issuer that (a) either is represented by an instrument issued in bearer or registered form or, if not represented by an instrument, is registered in books maintained to record transfers by or on behalf of the issuer, (b) is of a type commonly dealt in on securities exchanges or markets or, when represented by an instrument, is commonly recognized in any area in which it is issued or dealt in as a medium for investment, and (c) either is one of a class or series or by its terms is divisible into a class or series of shares, participations, interests, or obligations.

125. The following is added to paragraph 4 of Chapter 3A of ARB 43 following *operations* in subitem (f):

> , including investments in debt and equity securities classified as trading securities under FASB Statement No. 115, *Accounting for Certain Investments in Debt and Equity Securities*

126. The following sentence is added to the end of paragraph 19(l) of APB Opinion No. 18, *The Equity Method of Accounting for Investments in Common Stock:*

> FASB Statement No. 115, *Accounting for Certain Investments in Debt and Equity Securities,* addresses the accounting for investments in equity securities with readily determinable fair values that are not consolidated or accounted for under the equity method.

127. FASB Statement 60 is amended as follows:

a. Paragraph 45 is replaced by the following:

> All investments in debt securities and investments in equity securities that have readily determinable fair values, as defined by FASB Statement No. 115, *Accounting for Certain Investments in Debt and Equity Securities,* shall be accounted for in accordance with the provisions of that Statement.

b. Paragraph 46 is replaced by the following:

> Investments in equity securities that are not addressed by Statement 115 because they do not meet the criteria in paragraph 3 of that Statement shall be reported at fair value, and changes in fair value shall be recognized as unrealized gains and losses and reported, net of applicable income taxes, in a separate component of equity.

c. The last two sentences of paragraph 50 and footnote 7 to that paragraph are deleted.

d. The first sentence of paragraph 51 is replaced by the following:

> If a decline in the fair value of an equity security that is not addressed by Statement 115 because it does not meet the criteria in paragraph 3 of that Statement is considered to be other than temporary, the investment shall be reduced to its net realizable value, which becomes its new cost basis.

128. Statement 65 is amended as follows:

a. In paragraph 4, *and mortgage-backed securities* is deleted and the following is added at the end of the paragraph:

> Mortgage-backed securities held for sale in conjunction with mortgage banking activities shall be classified as trading securities and reported at fair value in accordance with the provisions of FASB Statement No. 115, *Accounting for Certain Investments in Debt and Equity Securities.*

b. In paragraph 5, *and mortgage-backed securities* is deleted.

c. In the first sentence of paragraph 6, *or mortgage-backed security* is deleted. In the last sentence of paragraph 6, *or mortgage-backed security* and *or security* are deleted. The following is added to paragraph 6 immediately after the first sentence:

> The securitization of a mortgage loan held for sale shall be accounted for as the sale of the mortgage loan and the purchase of a mortgage-backed security classified as a trading security at fair value.

d. In paragraph 7, all references to *or mortgage-backed security* and *or security* are deleted.

e. In the last sentence of paragraph 8, *as being held for sale* is replaced by *as being either mortgage loans held for sale or mortgage-backed securities classified as trading securities under Statement 115.*

f. In the first sentence of paragraph 9(a), *and mortgage-backed securities* is deleted. The following is added to the end of paragraph 9(a):

> If the fair value of a mortgage-backed security subject to an investor purchase commitment exceeds the commitment price, the implicit loss on the commitment shall be recognized.

g. In each sentence of paragraph 9(c), the first usage of *market value* is replaced by *fair value.*

h. In paragraph 12, all references to *or mortgage-backed securities* and *or securities* are deleted.

i. The following is added to the penultimate sentence in paragraph 17 after *investor*:

> (or fair value of the mortgage loan at the time it is securitized)

j. In paragraphs 28 and 29, *and mortgage-backed securities* is deleted.

129. In the last sentence of paragraph 5 of FASB Statement No. 80, *Accounting for Futures Contracts,* the phrase *until it is amortized or* is added after *equity.*

130. Statement 91 is amended as follows:

a. In paragraph 3, *if the changes in market value are included in earnings* is added at the end of the last sentence.

b. In paragraph 27(a), which amends paragraph 6 of Statement 65, *or security* is deleted.

131. In paragraph 28 of FASB Statement No. 97, *Accounting and Reporting by Insurance Enterprises for Certain Long-Duration Contracts and for Realized Gains and Losses from the Sale of Investments,* the phrase *investments that are classified as trading securities and* is added after *except* in the parenthetical expression of the amendment of Statement 60 in the fourth sentence of that paragraph.

132. FASB Statement No. 102, *Statement of Cash Flows—Exemption of Certain Enterprises and Classification of Cash Flows from Certain Securities Acquired for Resale,* is amended as follows:

a. The following sentence is added to the end of paragraph 8:

Cash flows from purchases, sales, and maturities of available-for-sale securities shall be classified as cash flows from investing activities and reported gross in the statement of cash flows.

b. In footnote 4 to paragraph 9, *and mortgage-backed securities* is deleted.

133. In paragraph 36(b) of Statement 109, *changes in the carrying amount of marketable securities under FASB Statement No. 12, Accounting for Certain Marketable Securities* is replaced by *changes in the unrealized holding gains and losses of securities classified as available-for-sale under FASB Statement No. 115, Accounting for Certain Investments in Debt and Equity Securities.*

134. In paragraphs 4 and 5 of FASB Interpretation No. 40, *Applicability of Generally Accepted Accounting Principles to Mutual Life Insurance and Other Enterprises,* the references to Statement 12 are deleted.

135. FASB Technical Bulletin No. 79-19, *Investor's Accounting for Unrealized Losses on Marketable Securities Owned by an Equity Method Investee,* is amended as follows:

a. In paragraph 1, *accumulated changes in the valuation allowance for marketable equity securities* is replaced by *unrealized holding gains or losses on investments in debt and equity securities.*

b. Paragraph 6 is replaced by the following:

If a subsidiary or other investee that is accounted for by the equity method is required to include unrealized holding gains and losses on investments in debt and equity securities in the stockholders' equity section of the balance sheet pursuant to the provisions of Statement 115, the parent or investor shall adjust its investment in that investee by its proportionate share of the unrealized gains and losses and a like amount shall be included in the stockholders' equity section of its balance sheet.

136. In paragraph 3 of FASB Technical Bulletin No. 85-1, *Accounting for the Receipt of Federal Home Loan Mortgage Corporation Participating Preferred Stock,* the phrase *a marketable equity security that subsequently should be reported in accordance with Statement 12 (at the lower of cost or market)* is replaced by *an equity security that subsequently should be reported at fair value in accordance with FASB Statement No. 115, Accounting for Certain Investments in Debt and Equity Securities.*

Appendix C

GLOSSARY

137. This appendix contains definitions of terms or phrases as used in this Statement.

Debt security

Any security representing a creditor relationship with an enterprise. It also includes (a) preferred stock that by its terms either must be redeemed by the issuing enterprise or is redeemable at the option of the investor and (b) a collateralized mortgage obligation (CMO) (or other instrument) that is issued in equity form but is required to be accounted for as a nonequity instrument regardless of how that instrument is classified (that is, whether equity or debt) in the issuer's statement of financial position. However, it excludes option contracts, financial futures contracts, forward contracts, and lease contracts.

- Thus, the term *debt security* includes, among other items, U.S. Treasury securities, U.S. government agency securities, municipal securities, corporate bonds, convertible debt, commercial paper, all securitized debt instruments, such as CMOs and real estate mortgage investment conduits (REMICs), and interest-only and principal-only strips.
- Trade accounts receivable arising from sales on credit by industrial or commercial enterprises and loans receivable arising from consumer,

commercial, and real estate lending activities of financial institutions are examples of receivables that do not meet the definition of *security;* thus, those receivables are not debt securities (unless they have been securitized, in which case they would meet the definition).

Equity security

Any security representing an ownership interest in an enterprise (for example, common, preferred, or other capital stock) or the right to acquire (for example, warrants, rights, and call options) or dispose of (for example, put options) an ownership interest in an enterprise at fixed or determinable prices. However, the term does not include convertible debt or preferred stock that by its terms either must be redeemed by the issuing enterprise or is redeemable at the option of the investor.

Fair value

The amount at which a financial instrument could be exchanged in a current transaction between willing parties, other than in a forced or liquidation sale. If a quoted market price is available for an instrument, the fair value to be used in applying this Statement is the product of the number of trading units of the instrument times its market price.

Holding gain or loss

The net change in fair value of a security exclusive of dividend or interest income recognized but not yet received and exclusive of any write-downs for other-than-temporary impairment.

Security

A share, participation, or other interest in property or in an enterprise of the issuer or an obligation of the issuer that (a) either is represented by an instrument issued in bearer or registered form or, if not represented by an instrument, is registered in books maintained to record transfers by or on behalf of the issuer, (b) is of a type commonly dealt in on securities exchanges or markets or, when represented by an instrument, is commonly recognized in any area in which it is issued or dealt in as a medium for investment, and (c) either is one of a class or series or by its terms is divisible into a class or series of shares, participations, interests, or obligations.

Statement of Financial Accounting Standards No. 116
Accounting for Contributions Received and Contributions Made

STATUS

Issued: June 1993

Effective Date: For fiscal years beginning after December 15, 1994

Affects: No other pronouncements

Affected by: No other pronouncements

Other Interpretive Pronouncement: FIN 42

Other Interpretive Release: FASB *Highlights,* "Time for a Change—Implementing FASB Statements 116 and 117," January 1995

SUMMARY

This Statement establishes accounting standards for contributions and applies to all entities that receive or make contributions. Generally, contributions received, including unconditional promises to give, are recognized as revenues in the period received at their fair values. Contributions made, including unconditional promises to give, are recognized as expenses in the period made at their fair values. Conditional promises to give, whether received or made, are recognized when they become unconditional, that is, when the conditions are substantially met.

This Statement requires not-for-profit organizations to distinguish between contributions received that increase permanently restricted net assets, temporarily restricted net assets, and unrestricted net assets. It also requires recognition of the expiration of donor-imposed restrictions in the period in which the restrictions expire.

This Statement allows certain exceptions for contributions of services and works of art, historical treasures, and similar assets. Contributions of services are recognized only if the services received (a) create or enhance nonfinancial assets or (b) require specialized skills, are provided by individuals possessing those skills, and would typically need to be purchased if not provided by donation. Contributions of works of art, historical treasures, and similar assets need not be recognized as revenues and capitalized if the donated items are added to collections held for public exhibition, education, or research in furtherance of public service rather than financial gain.

This Statement requires certain disclosures for collection items not capitalized and for receipts of contributed services and promises to give.

This Statement is effective for financial statements issued for fiscal years beginning after December 15, 1994, except for not-for-profit organizations with less than $5 million in total assets and less than $1 million in annual expenses. For those organizations, the Statement is effective for fiscal years beginning after December 15, 1995. Earlier application is encouraged. This Statement may be applied either retroactively or by recognizing the cumulative effect of the change in the year of the change. The provisions for recognition of expirations of restrictions may be applied prospectively.

Statement of Financial Accounting Standards No. 116

Accounting for Contributions Received and Contributions Made

CONTENTS

INTRODUCTION

1. This Statement establishes standards of financial accounting and reporting for **contributions**[1] received and contributions made. Accounting for contributions is an issue primarily for **not-for-profit organizations** because contributions are a significant source of revenues for many of those organizations. However, this Statement applies to all entities (not-for-profit organizations and business enterprises) that receive or make contributions. This Statement also establishes standards for recognizing expirations of restrictions on contributions received and for accounting for **collections** of works of art, historical treasures, and similar assets acquired by contribution or by other means.

2. Guidance for accounting for contributions received by not-for-profit organizations is currently provided primarily by the AICPA Guides and Statement of Position (SOP) listed in Appendix A. This Statement is part of a broader FASB agenda project that considers several inconsistencies in that guidance. Because this Statement establishes standards for accounting for contributions, provisions in the Guides and SOP that are inconsistent with this Statement are no longer acceptable *specialized*[2] accounting and reporting principles and practices. This Statement's consideration of the classification of receipts of donor-restricted contributions and the recognition and display of expirations of donor restrictions is within the general framework for financial reporting

---

[1]Words that appear in the glossary are set in **boldface type** the first time they appear.

[2]The term *specialized* is used to refer to those current accounting and reporting principles and practices in the existing AICPA Guides and SOPs that are neither superseded by nor contained in the Accounting Research Bulletins, APB Opinions, FASB Statements, and FASB Interpretations.

as set forth in FASB Statement No. 117, *Financial Statements of Not-for-Profit Organizations.*

STANDARDS OF FINANCIAL ACCOUNTING AND REPORTING

Scope

3. This Statement applies to contributions[3] of cash and other assets, including **promises to give**. It does not apply to transfers of assets that are in substance purchases of goods or services—exchange transactions in which each party receives and sacrifices commensurate value. However, if an entity voluntarily transfers assets to another or performs services for another in exchange for assets of substantially lower value and no unstated rights or privileges are involved, the contribution inherent in that transaction is within the scope of this Statement.

4. This Statement does not apply to transfers of assets in which the reporting entity acts as an agent, trustee, or intermediary, rather than as a donor or donee. It also does not apply to tax exemptions, tax incentives, or tax abatements, or to transfers of assets from governmental units to business enterprises.

Definitions

5. A contribution is an unconditional transfer of cash or other assets to an entity or a settlement or cancellation of its liabilities in a voluntary **nonreciprocal transfer** by another entity acting other than as an owner. Other assets include securities, land, buildings, use of facilities or utilities, materials and supplies, intangible assets, services, and **unconditional promises to give** those items in the future.

6. A promise to give is a written or oral agreement to contribute cash or other assets to another entity; however, to be recognized in financial statements there must be sufficient evidence in the form of verifiable documentation that a promise was made and received. A communication that does not indicate clearly whether it is a promise is considered an unconditional promise to give if it indicates an unconditional intention to give that is legally enforceable.

7. A **donor-imposed condition** on a transfer of assets or a promise to give specifies a future and uncertain event whose occurrence or failure to occur gives the promisor a right of return of the assets transferred or releases the promisor from its obligation to transfer assets promised. In contrast, a **donor-imposed restriction** limits the use of contributed assets; it specifies a use that is more specific than broad limits resulting from the nature of the organization, the environment in which it operates, and the purposes specified in its articles of incorporation or bylaws or comparable documents for an unincorporated association.

Contributions Received

8. Except as provided in paragraphs 9 and 11, contributions received shall be recognized as revenues or gains in the period received and as assets, decreases of liabilities, or expenses depending on the form of the benefits received. Contributions received shall be measured at their fair values. Contributions received by not-for-profit organizations shall be reported as **restricted support** or **unrestricted support** as provided in paragraphs 14-16.

Contributed Services

9. Contributions of services shall be recognized if the services received (a) create or enhance nonfinancial assets or (b) require specialized skills, are provided by individuals possessing those skills, and would typically need to be purchased if not provided by donation. Services requiring specialized skills are provided by accountants, architects, carpenters, doctors, electricians, lawyers, nurses, plumbers, teachers, and other professionals and craftsmen. Contributed services and promises to give services that do not meet the above criteria shall not be recognized.

10. An entity that receives contributed services shall describe the programs or activities for which those services were used, including the nature and extent of contributed services received for the period and the amount recognized as revenues for the period. Entities are encouraged to disclose the fair value of contributed services received but not recognized as revenues if that is practicable.

Contributed Collection Items

11. An entity need not recognize contributions of works of art, historical treasures, and similar assets if

---

[3]This Statement also uses terms such as *gift* and *donation* to refer to a contribution; however, it generally avoids terms such as *awards, grants, sponsorships,* and *appropriations* that often are more broadly used to refer not only to contributions but also to assets transferred in exchange transactions in which the *grantor, sponsor,* or *appropriator* expects to receive commensurate value.

Accounting for Contributions Received and

the donated items are added to collections that meet all of the following conditions:

a. Are held for public exhibition, education, or research in furtherance of public service rather than financial gain
b. Are protected, kept unencumbered, cared for, and preserved
c. Are subject to an organizational policy that requires the proceeds from sales of collection items to be used to acquire other items for collections.

12. For purposes of initial application of this Statement, entities are encouraged either to capitalize retroactively collections acquired in previous periods[4] or to capitalize collections on a prospective basis. Capitalization of selected collections or items is precluded.

13. Contributed collection items shall be recognized as revenues or gains if collections are capitalized and shall not be recognized as revenues or gains if collections are not capitalized. An entity that does not recognize and capitalize its collections or that capitalizes collections prospectively shall disclose the additional information required by paragraphs 26 and 27.

Reporting by Not-for-Profit Organizations

14. A not-for-profit organization shall distinguish between contributions received with **permanent restrictions**, those received with **temporary restrictions**, and those received without donor-imposed restrictions. A restriction on an organization's use of the assets contributed results either from a donor's explicit stipulation or from circumstances surrounding the receipt of the contribution that make clear the donor's implicit restriction on use. Contributions with donor-imposed restrictions shall be reported as restricted support; however, donor-restricted contributions whose restrictions are met in the same reporting period may be reported as unrestricted support provided that an organization reports consistently from period to period and discloses its accounting policy. Restricted support increases **permanently restricted net assets** or **temporarily restricted net assets**.

Contributions without donor-imposed restrictions shall be reported as unrestricted support that increases **unrestricted net assets**.

15. Receipts of unconditional promises to give with payments due in future periods shall be reported as restricted support unless explicit donor stipulations or circumstances surrounding the receipt of a promise make clear that the donor intended it to be used to support activities of the current period. For example, receipts of unconditional promises to give cash in future years generally increase temporarily restricted net assets.

16. Gifts of long-lived assets received without stipulations about how long the donated asset must be used shall be reported as restricted support if it is an organization's accounting policy to imply a time restriction that expires over the useful life of the donated assets. Organizations that adopt a policy of implying time restrictions also shall imply a time restriction on long-lived assets acquired with gifts of cash or other assets restricted for those acquisitions. In the absence of that policy and other donor-imposed restrictions on use of the asset, gifts of long-lived assets shall be reported as unrestricted support. An organization shall disclose its accounting policy.

Expiration of Donor-imposed Restrictions

17. A not-for-profit organization shall recognize the expiration of a donor-imposed restriction on a contribution in the period in which the restriction expires. A restriction expires when the stipulated time has elapsed, when the stipulated purpose for which the resource was restricted has been fulfilled, or both.[5] If an expense is incurred for a purpose for which both unrestricted and temporarily restricted net assets are available, a donor-imposed restriction is fulfilled to the extent of the expense incurred unless the expense is for a purpose that is directly attributable to another specific external source of revenue. For example, an expense does not fulfill an existing donor restriction if that expense is incurred for a purpose that is directly attributable to and reimbursed by a sponsored exchange agreement or a conditional

---

[4]Collections of works of art, historical treasures, and similar assets acquired in previous periods but not capitalized as assets may be retroactively capitalized at their cost or fair value at date of acquisition, current cost, or current market value, whichever is deemed most practical.

[5]If two or more temporary restrictions are imposed on a contribution, the effect of the expiration of those restrictions is recognized in the period in which the last remaining restriction has expired. Temporarily restricted net assets with time restrictions are not available to support expenses until the time restrictions have expired. Time restrictions implied on gifts of long-lived assets expire as the economic benefits of the acquired assets are used up; that is, over their estimated useful lives. In the absence of donor stipulations specifying how long donated assets must be used or an organization's policy of implying time restrictions, restrictions on long-lived assets, if any, or cash to acquire long-lived assets expire when the assets are placed in service.

award from a government agency, private foundation, or others. Pursuant to paragraph 19 of Statement 117, expirations of donor-imposed restrictions that simultaneously increase one class of net assets and decrease another (reclassifications) are reported separately from other transactions.

Contributions Made

18. Contributions made shall be recognized as expenses in the period made and as decreases of assets or increases of liabilities depending on the form of the benefits given. For example, gifts of items from inventory held for sale are recognized as decreases of inventory[6] and contribution expenses, and unconditional promises to give cash are recognized as payables and contribution expenses. Contributions made shall be measured at the fair values of the assets given or, if made in the form of a settlement or cancellation of a donee's liabilities, at the fair value of the liabilities canceled.

Measurement at Fair Value

19. Quoted market prices, if available, are the best evidence of the fair value of monetary and nonmonetary assets, including services. If quoted market prices are not available, fair value may be estimated based on quoted market prices for similar assets, independent appraisals, or valuation techniques, such as the present value of estimated future cash flows. Contributions of services that create or enhance nonfinancial assets may be measured by referring to either the fair value of the services received or the fair value of the asset or of the asset enhancement resulting from the services. A major uncertainty about the existence of value may indicate that an item received or given should not be recognized.[7]

20. The present value of estimated future cash flows using a discount rate commensurate with the risks involved is an appropriate measure of fair value of unconditional promises to give cash.[8] Subsequent accruals of the interest element shall be accounted for

as contribution income by donees and contribution expense by donors. Not-for-profit organizations shall report the contribution income as an increase in either temporarily or permanently restricted net assets if the underlying promise to give is donor restricted.

21. Unconditional promises to give that are expected to be collected or paid in less than one year may be measured at net realizable value (net settlement value) because that amount, although not equivalent to the present value of estimated future cash flows, results in a reasonable estimate of fair value.

Conditional Promises to Give

22. **Conditional promises to give**, which depend on the occurrence of a specified future and uncertain event to bind the promisor, shall be recognized when the conditions on which they depend are substantially met, that is, when the conditional promise becomes unconditional. A conditional promise to give is considered unconditional if the possibility that the condition will not be met is remote. For example, a stipulation that an annual report must be provided by the donee to receive subsequent annual payments on a multiyear promise is not a condition if the possibility of not meeting that administrative requirement is remote. A transfer of assets with a conditional promise to contribute them shall be accounted for as a refundable advance until the conditions have been substantially met.

23. Determining whether a promise is conditional or unconditional can be difficult if it contains donor stipulations that do not clearly state whether the right to receive payment or delivery of the promised assets depends on meeting those stipulations. It may be difficult to determine whether those stipulations are conditions or restrictions. In cases of ambiguous donor stipulations, a promise containing stipulations that are not clearly unconditional shall be presumed to be a conditional promise.

---

[6]If the fair value of an asset transferred differs from its carrying amount, a gain or loss should be recognized on the disposition of the asset (APB Opinion No. 29, *Accounting for Nonmonetary Transactions*, paragraph 18).

[7]Contributed tangible property worth accepting generally possesses the common characteristic of all assets—future economic benefit or service potential. The future economic benefit or service potential of a tangible item usually can be obtained by exchanging it for cash or by using it to produce goods or services. However, if an item is accepted solely to be saved for its potential future use in scientific or educational research and has no alternative use, it may have uncertain value, or perhaps no value, and should not be recognized.

[8]An entity may estimate the future cash flows of a portfolio of short-term promises resulting from a mass fund-raising appeal by using experience it gained from similar appeals.

Disclosures of Promises to Give

24. Recipients of unconditional promises to give shall disclose the following:

a. The amounts of promises receivable in less than one year, in one to five years, and in more than five years
b. The amount of the allowance for uncollectible promises receivable.

25. Recipients of conditional promises to give shall disclose the following:

a. The total of the amounts promised
b. A description and amount for each group of promises having similar characteristics, such as amounts of promises conditioned on establishing new programs, completing a new building, and raising matching gifts by a specified date.

Financial Statement Presentation and Disclosure for Collections

26. An entity that does not recognize and capitalize its collections shall report the following on the face of its statement of activities, separately from revenues, expenses, gains, and losses:

a. Costs of collection items purchased as a decrease in the appropriate class of net assets
b. Proceeds from sale of collection items as an increase in the appropriate class of net assets
c. Proceeds from insurance recoveries of lost or destroyed collection items as an increase in the appropriate class of net assets.

Similarly, an entity that capitalizes its collections prospectively shall report proceeds from sales and insurance recoveries of items not previously capitalized separately from revenues, expenses, gains, and losses.

27. An entity that does not recognize and capitalize its collections or that capitalizes collections prospectively shall describe its collections, including their relative significance, and its accounting and stewardship policies for collections. If collection items not capitalized are deaccessed during the period, it also shall (a) describe the items given away, damaged, destroyed, lost, or otherwise deaccessed during the pe-

riod or (b) disclose their fair value. In addition, a line item shall be shown on the face of the statement of financial position that refers to the disclosures required by this paragraph. That line item shall be dated if collections are capitalized prospectively, for example, "Collections acquired since January 1, 1995 (Note X)."

Effective Date and Transition

28. This Statement shall be effective for financial statements issued for fiscal years beginning after December 15, 1994 and interim periods within those fiscal years, except for not-for-profit organizations with less than $5 million in total assets and less than $1 million in annual expenses. For those organizations, the effective date shall be for fiscal years beginning after December 15, 1995. Earlier application is encouraged.

29. Unless this Statement is applied retroactively under the provisions of paragraph 30, the effect of initially applying this Statement shall be reported as the effect of a change in accounting principle in a manner similar to the cumulative effect of a change in accounting principle (APB Opinion No. 20, *Accounting Changes,* paragraph 19). The amount of the cumulative effect shall be based on a retroactive computation, except that the provisions of paragraph 17 for recognition of expirations of restrictions may be applied prospectively. A not-for-profit organization shall report the cumulative effect of a change in accounting on each class of net assets in the statement of activities between the captions "extraordinary items," if any, and "change in unrestricted net assets," "change in temporarily restricted net assets," and "change in permanently restricted net assets." A business enterprise shall report the amount of the cumulative effect in the income statement between the captions "extraordinary items" and "net income" (Opinion 20, paragraph 20).

30. This Statement may be applied retroactively by restating opening net assets for the earliest year presented or for the year this Statement is first applied if no prior years are presented. The provisions of paragraph 17 for recognition of expirations of restrictions may be applied prospectively. In the period that this Statement is first applied, a not-for-profit organization shall disclose the nature of any restatement and its effect on the change in net assets

for each period presented. A business enterprise shall account for any restatement as a change in accounting principle applied retroactively (Opinion 20, paragraphs 27 and 28).

> **The provisions of this Statement need not be applied to immaterial items.**

This Statement was adopted by the affirmative votes of six members of the Financial Accounting Standards Board. Mr. Beresford dissented.

Mr. Beresford dissents from the issuance of this Statement because it requires recipients of unconditional promises to give to recognize assets and revenues in the period the promise is received. In particular, he questions whether the recognition of revenues for restricted gifts, especially for promises collectible in the distant future, results in more meaningful financial reporting. Further, Mr. Beresford believes there is too much subjectivity involved in distinguishing between promises to give and other communications of intentions to give. He suggests that, until these matters are satisfactorily resolved, improving disclosures about promises and precluding their recognition would be a better step.

Mr. Beresford is troubled by the potential for misunderstanding of financial information resulting from the requirement. Currently, most organizations that recognize promises to give also recognize deferred revenue. Organizations, particularly those that rely heavily on annual pledge drives, will report large increases in net assets if promises are recorded. He is concerned that the amounts will be regarded as surplus resources or otherwise misinterpreted by financial statement users.

It is not clear to Mr. Beresford that the distinction between a promise to give and a communication of intention to give is an appropriate basis for distinguishing an asset from a "nonasset." Both are communications that a donor will provide cash in the future for the support of the organization. The only difference may be in the percentage of the communications that ultimately results in future cash receipts, and this difference may be slight in many cases.

Mr. Beresford believes that it will be difficult to differentiate between promises and intentions in many cases. He is troubled that the subjectivity involved in making the distinction will result in an unacceptable level of inconsistency and that the motivations of some preparers of financial statements will increase that level of inconsistency. That inconsistency, when combined with the requirement to recognize revenues for unconditional promises to give, would make it difficult, if not impossible, for donors and other users of financial statements to compare different organizations' statements of activities and make informed resource allocation decisions. Therefore, Mr. Beresford would preclude recognition of promises to give to enhance comparability. He believes a period of experience with improved disclosures would allow time to resolve implementation concerns and to gain experience in using the information.

Members of the Financial Accounting Standards Board:

Dennis R. Beresford,	Victor H. Brown	A. Clarence Sampson
Chairman	James J. Leisenring	Robert J. Swieringa
Joseph V. Anania	Robert H. Northcutt	

Appendix A

BACKGROUND INFORMATION

31. In March 1986, the Board added a project to its agenda to establish standards needed to resolve certain inconsistent accounting and reporting practices of not-for-profit organizations. The project has three parts: accounting for contributions, display of information in financial statements, and accounting for depreciation. The Board completed the part on depreciation in 1987 when it issued FASB Statement No. 93, *Recognition of Depreciation by Not-for-Profit Organizations.*

32. In October 1990, the Board issued an Exposure Draft of a proposed Statement, *Accounting for Contributions Received and Contributions Made and Capitalization of Works of Art, Historical Treasures,*

and Similar Assets. Many respondents to that Exposure Draft suggested that because the parts on accounting for contributions and on financial statement display are interrelated, it would be more productive if they were combined or more closely coordinated. The Board agreed and coordinated this Statement with Statement No. 117, *Financial Statements of Not-for-Profit Organizations.*

33. Accounting for contributions is described in the following AICPA documents:

a. *Audits of Colleges and Universities,* 1973
b. *Audits of Voluntary Health and Welfare Organizations,* 1974
c. SOP 78-10, *Accounting Principles and Reporting Practices for Certain Nonprofit Organizations,* 1978
d. *Audits of Providers of Health Care Services,* 1990.

The requirements for accounting for contributions in those documents are similar in some respects. In other respects they differ from each other and from generally accepted accounting principles applicable to other entities.

34. For example, guidance for recognizing restricted contributions is inconsistent. The colleges and universities Guide and the health care services Guide suggest accounting for those contributions as direct additions to restricted fund balances (net assets). Both Guides suggest that temporarily restricted contributions be recognized as "revenues" when the restrictions are met. The health and welfare Guide suggests accounting for purpose-restricted contributions as revenues of a restricted fund and time-restricted contributions as deferred revenues. SOP 78-10 suggests accounting for current restricted contributions as liabilities until the restrictions on the gifts are met.

35. Guidance for recognizing certain other contributions also has been inconsistent. For example, page 14 of the health and welfare Guide says, "In the absence of clear evidence as to a specified program period, donations and pledges should be recorded as support when received." However, paragraph 65 of SOP 78-10 says, "In the absence of a specified support period, . . . [legally enforceable] pledges scheduled to be received over a future period should be assumed to be support for that period and should be accounted for as deferred support in the balance sheet." Paragraph 7.18 of the health care services Guide provides similar guidance for unrestricted pledges. The colleges and universities Guide differs significantly, since it permits but does not require recognition of a pledge as an asset or as revenue.

36. Criteria for recognition of contributed services also differ among the Guides. The health and welfare Guide requires recognition of revenue and expense under certain specified conditions and does not preclude recognition of other services received. The health care services Guide provides similar guidance. In contrast, SOP 78-10 precludes recognition of services other than those meeting conditions similar to the other Guides. The colleges and universities Guide does not provide criteria for recognition of contributed services.

37. Although generally accepted accounting principles require recognition of contributions of tangible assets at their fair value at date of receipt, SOP 78-10 permits an exception. Paragraph 114 of SOP 78-10 says the ". . . contributed value of current-period accessions . . . should be disclosed in the financial statements." SOP 78-10 has been interpreted as allowing disclosure as an alternative to recognition of revenues in financial statements of museums, art galleries, botanical gardens, libraries, and similar entities that receive contributions of property for their "inexhaustible collections."

38. Further, the specialized industry guidance of SOP 78-10, paragraph 113, encourages but does not require capitalization of "inexhaustible collections owned by museums, art galleries, botanical gardens, libraries, and similar entities." The Board added this issue to the scope of this Statement as a result of responses to the Exposure Draft that led to Statement 93. In paragraph 39 of Statement 93, the Board indicated that the Statement on recognition of depreciation need not cover recognition of assets but that the Board would consider recognition of "collections," both contributed and purchased, as part of its project on accounting for contributions. Accordingly, in addition to addressing recognition of contributions, this Statement considers accounting for works of art, historical treasures, and similar assets whether acquired by contribution or by other means.

39. The Board discussed how to resolve the inconsistencies in accounting for contributions at public Board meetings and public meetings of the FASB Task Force on Accounting Issues for Not-for-Profit Organizations. In October 1990, the Board issued its first Exposure Draft on contributions. More than 1,000 organizations and individuals provided written

comments. Forty respondents presented their views at a public hearing in July 1991, and most agreed that there is a need to establish consistent standards for accounting for contributions.

40. The Board reconsidered the proposals in that Exposure Draft at public meetings of the Board and of the task force. The major changes resulting from the Board's redeliberations were:

a. Works of art, historical treasures, and similar items need not be capitalized if they are added to collections that are held for public exhibition, education, or research in furtherance of public service rather than financial gain. Disclosures about collections that are not capitalized are required.
b. Criteria for recognition of contributed services were made more restrictive, and recognition of contributed services that do not meet the revised criteria is precluded rather than encouraged.
c. Provisions for recognizing expirations of donor-imposed restrictions may be applied prospectively
d. Disclosures about receipts of promises to give are required.

41. In November 1992, the Board issued a revised Exposure Draft, *Accounting for Contributions Received and Contributions Made*, which incorporated the above changes and certain other revisions. The Board received more than 280 comment letters on that revised Exposure Draft. In October 1992, the Board also issued a related Exposure Draft, *Financial Statements of Not-for-Profit Organizations*. Twenty-four organizations and individuals presented their views at a 2-day public hearing held in February 1993. That hearing was held to obtain additional information from participants about the proposals for financial statements of not-for-profit organizations; however, participants also were encouraged to comment on the revised proposals for contributions. Most participants commented on provisions in both Exposure Drafts.

42. Twenty organizations also participated in a field test of the proposed Statements on financial statements and on accounting for contributions. Those organizations shared their recasted financial statements with 39 users of financial statements who also participated in the field test. The field test results, the details of which are confidential at the request of some participants, and the written comments and public hearing testimony of respondents to both proposed Statements were considered by the Board during its deliberations of the issues addressed by this Statement. The major issues and concerns raised by respondents and field test participants and the basis for the Board's conclusions on those issues and concerns are discussed in Appendix B.

Appendix B

BASIS FOR CONCLUSIONS

CONTENTS

Appendix B

BASIS FOR CONCLUSIONS

Introduction

43. This appendix summarizes considerations that Board members deemed significant in reaching the conclusions in this Statement. It includes reasons for accepting certain views and rejecting others. Individual Board members gave greater weight to some factors than to others.

Objectives

44. To accomplish its mission, the FASB strives to improve the usefulness of financial reporting by fo-

cusing on the primary characteristics of relevance and reliability and on the qualities of comparability and consistency. The usefulness of information about an entity increases if that information can be compared with similar information about other entities or about the same entity in other periods. To the extent that similar contributions are subject to the same requirements for recognition and disclosure, financial reporting will be improved. In return for some sacrifice of freedom of choice, adherence to externally imposed standards brings a gain from greater comparability and consistency and also a gain in credibility (FASB Concepts Statement No. 2, *Qualitative Characteristics of Accounting Information,* paragraph 16).

Benefits and Costs

45. A major benefit of this Statement is the increased comparability, consistency, and credibility of financial reporting that will result from eliminating some of the inconsistencies in current guidance (Appendix A). The Board believes that financial reporting of not-for-profit organizations will significantly improve by consistently recognizing (a) restricted contributions as revenues, (b) unconditional promises to give as assets and revenues or as liabilities and expenses, and (c) certain contributed services. Increased disclosure of information about receipts of contributed services and conditional promises to give and about collections also will improve financial reporting.

46. The Board believes that consistent standards for recognizing contributions are needed. However, the value of the incremental improvement to financial reporting is impossible to quantify. Because there is no common gauge by which to judge objectively the costs to implement a standard against the need to improve information in financial statements, the Board's assessment of the costs and benefits is unavoidably subjective. Moreover, because the costs to implement a new standard are not borne directly by those who derive the benefits of the improved reporting, the Board must balance the diverse and often conflicting needs of preparers, investors, donors, creditors, and others who use financial statements.

47. The Board believes that the incremental costs of the requirements of this Statement have been reduced in various ways: by not requiring contributions of works of art, historical treasures, and similar items to be capitalized if they are held in collections as defined; by restricting the criteria for recognition of contributed services; by allowing prospective appli-

cation of provisions for expirations of restrictions; by extending the effective date of this Statement; and by allowing an additional one-year extension for small not-for-profit organizations. Reducing some of the incremental costs of the requirements of this Statement in those ways may reduce some of the benefits and possibly increase other costs. For example, allowing alternatives to capitalization of collections may increase the costs incurred by users of financial statements as they evaluate differing information about those items. The Board concluded that the overall benefits of the information provided by applying this Statement justify the costs of complying with these standards.

Distinguishing Contributions from Other Transactions

48. The Board focused on three characteristics that help distinguish contributions from other transactions—contributions (a) are nonreciprocal transfers, (b) are transfers to or from entities acting other than as owners, and (c) are made or received voluntarily. Those characteristics distinguish contributions from exchange transactions, which are reciprocal transfers in which each party receives and sacrifices approximately equal value; from investments by owners and distributions to owners, which are nonreciprocal transfers between an entity and its owners; and from other nonreciprocal transfers, such as impositions of taxes or fines and thefts, which are not voluntary transfers.

Distinguishing Contributions from Exchange Transactions

49. Because some exchange transactions may appear to be much like contributions, a careful assessment of the characteristics of the transaction is required to determine whether the recipient of a transfer of assets has given up an asset or incurred a liability of commensurate value. The Board believes that assessing the characteristics of transactions from the perspectives of both the resource provider and the recipient is necessary to determine whether a contribution has occurred.

50. For example, a resource provider may sponsor research and development activities at a research university and retain proprietary rights or other privileges, such as patents, copyrights, or advance and exclusive knowledge of the research outcomes. The research outcomes may be intangible, uncertain, or difficult to measure, and may be perceived by the

university as a sacrifice of little or no value; however, their value often is commensurate with the value that a resource provider expects in exchange. Similarly, a resource provider may sponsor research and development activities and specify the protocol of the testing so the research outcomes are particularly valuable to the resource provider. Those transactions are not contributions if their potential public benefits are secondary to the potential proprietary benefits to the resource providers.

51. Moreover, a single transaction may be in part an exchange and in part a contribution. For example, if a donor transfers a building to an entity at a price significantly lower than its market value and no unstated rights or privileges are involved, the transaction is in part an exchange of assets and in part a contribution to be accounted for as required by this Statement.

Distinguishing Contributions from Agency and Similar Transactions

52. A transfer of assets also may appear to be a contribution when a donor uses an intermediary organization as its agent or trustee to transfer assets to a third-party donee, particularly if the agent indirectly achieves its mission by disbursing the assets. Although the transaction between the donor and the donee may be a contribution, the transfer of assets from the donor is not a contribution received by the agent, and the transfer of assets to the donee is not a contribution made by the agent.

53. The recipient of assets who is an agent or trustee has little or no discretion in determining how the assets transferred will be used. For example, if a recipient receives cash that it must disburse to *any* who meet guidelines specified by a resource provider or return the cash, those receipts may be deposits held by the recipient as an agent rather than contributions received as a donee. Similarly, if a recipient receives cash that it must disburse to individuals identified by the resource provider or return the cash, neither the receipt nor the disbursement is a contribution for the agent, trustee, or intermediary.

54. In contrast, if the resource provider allows the recipient to establish, define, and carry out the programs that disburse the cash, products, or services to the recipient's beneficiaries, the recipient generally is involved in receiving and making contributions.

Exclusion of Certain Transactions

55. Some respondents to the 1990 Exposure Draft asked whether the scope of this Statement was intended to include accounting for certain transfers that might be considered both voluntary and nonreciprocal, such as tax incentives, tax abatements, and transfers of land, buildings, or other assets by governments to entice businesses to their communities. The Board concluded that those transactions present specific complexities that may need special study and therefore excluded them from the scope of this Statement.

56. Some respondents to the 1992 Exposure Draft asked the Board to exclude all governmental transfers. Many colleges and universities, in particular, said determining whether specific grants, appropriations, loan guarantees, and similar governmental transfers are exchange transactions or are voluntary and nonreciprocal transfers—contributions—is difficult and often arbitrary. Some asserted that governmental transfers are never voluntary contributions. They suggested that all governmental transfers be reported as a separate category of revenue and be excluded from the scope of this Statement to allow their industry associations or the AICPA to provide industry-specific guidance. The Board believes that whether a grant is from a government agency, private foundation, or corporation, the difficulties in determining whether a transfer is an exchange transaction or a contribution are substantially the same. The Board acknowledges that to apply the provisions of this Statement requires a careful assessment of the characteristics of the transfers as discussed in paragraphs 48-54; however, it concluded that excluding all governmental transfers is neither necessary nor desirable because that would further delay improvements to practice.

Distinguishing Donor-imposed Restrictions from Conditions

57. This Statement distinguishes between unrestricted gifts, restricted gifts, and transfers of cash or other assets with conditions, which are similar to conditional promises to give. A donor-imposed restriction limits the use of donated assets; however, a condition creates a barrier that must be overcome before assets transferred or promised become contributions received or made. The distinction between a restriction and a condition, although clear in concept, sometimes is obscure in practice.

58. The Board concluded that a donor-imposed restriction, which limits or directs the use of donated assets, is not fundamentally different from an explicit or implied stipulation that donated assets be used to

support an organization's broad charitable, educational, religious, or similar purposes. Both are expressions or directives that the donated assets be used to support an organization's activities, and both are gifts that increase the organization's capacity to provide services. A donor's directive may be more prescriptive; for example, that donated assets be used to support a particular program service, to support the acquisition of long-lived assets, or to create a permanent endowment or term-endowment fund. That prescription, however, does not change the fundamental and underlying event—the voluntary nonreciprocal transfer of economic benefits from a donor to a donee.

59. The Board also concluded that although an unrestricted gift and a restricted gift are similar events, information about the nature and extent of donor-imposed restrictions is relevant to users of financial statements (paragraphs 145-148). A donor-imposed restriction imposes special responsibilities on the management of an organization to ensure that it uses donated assets as stipulated. The limits imposed by those restrictions may impinge upon an organization's performance and its ability to provide a satisfactory level of services.

60. The Board concluded that a transfer of cash or other assets with a stipulation that the assets be returned if a specified future and uncertain event occurs or fails to occur is fundamentally different from both an unrestricted gift and a restricted gift. Imposing a condition creates a barrier that must be overcome before the recipient of the transferred assets has an unconditional right to retain those promised assets. For example, a transfer of cash with a promise to contribute that cash if a like amount of new gifts are raised from others within 30 days and a provision that the cash be returned if the gifts are not raised imposes a condition on which a promised gift depends.

61. By imposing a condition, the transferor of assets not only retains a right of return of the transferred assets, but also casts doubt on whether the intent of the transfer was to make a gift, to conditionally promise a gift, or, at the extreme, not to make a gift. Because donors impose very different kinds of conditions, the likelihood of meeting a condition can range from probable to remote. The Board concluded that if a transferor imposes a condition, a reasonable possibility exists that the condition will not occur and the transferred assets will be returned and, thus, should be accounted for as a refundable advance.

62. Some respondents to the 1992 Exposure Draft, particularly foundations, said this Statement should

make clear whether imposing administrative requirements, such as requiring routine annual reporting as a "condition" of a multiyear grant, would preclude recognition of an otherwise unconditional promise to give. Some also expressed concern that donors and donees may avoid recognition of unconditional promises to give by adding *trivial* conditions or requesting that they be added. Paragraph 22 clarifies that a promise to give is considered unconditional if the possibility that the condition will not be met is remote. Conditions on transfers of assets as described in this Statement are similar to those described in federal income tax laws and regulations. Title 26 of the Code of Federal Regulations says that if "a transfer for charitable purposes is dependent upon the performance of some act or the happening of a precedent event in order that it might become effective, no deduction is allowable unless the possibility that the charitable transfer will not become effective is so remote as to be negligible" (26 CFR Sec.1.170A-1(e)).

63. Private foundations, governmental agencies, and some business enterprises transfer cash or other assets with both donor-imposed restrictions and stipulations that impose a condition on which a gift depends. Certain not-for-profit organizations use fund accounting and reporting methods that emphasize accountability for all funds received but may not distinguish between transfers of cash received with donor-imposed restrictions and those with conditions. This Statement, however, makes that distinction and provides that when a restriction and a condition exist, the transfer be accounted for as a refundable advance until the condition on which it depends is substantially met.

64. Some respondents to the 1990 and 1992 Exposure Drafts said that the distinction between a donor-imposed restriction and a condition is not significant. Many of those respondents said because donated assets received with a restriction would be returned if a restriction was not met, those transfers also should be accounted for as refundable advances (liabilities) until the restrictions are met. Others said that transfers of assets with restrictions are similar to advance payments for services to be rendered and should be accounted for as "deferred revenues" (liabilities). A few respondents that would not distinguish between restrictions and conditions said that transfers of assets with donor-imposed restrictions or conditions should be accounted for as refundable advances but that both should be recognized as contributions received when it becomes *probable* that the restrictions or conditions will be met.

65. Failures to comply with donors' restrictions, although rare, do occur, sometimes as a result of events occurring subsequent to receiving a contribution. The Board continues to believe that a presumption that an organization will use donated assets in accordance with the limitations specified is inherent in the acceptance of a contribution. Donors and donees both expect donors' directives will be carried out.

66. The Board concluded that to require ongoing assessments of the probability of meeting a restriction in order to determine when to recognize a restricted gift is neither necessary nor practical. FASB Statement No. 5, *Accounting for Contingencies,* applies if a subsequent event raises the possibility that an organization may not satisfy a restriction. Paragraph 8 of Statement 5 requires that an estimated loss be recognized if information available prior to issuance of the financial statements indicates that it is probable an asset had been impaired or a liability had been incurred at the date of the financial statements and the amount of the loss can be reasonably estimated.

67. The Board believes that a gift of cash or other assets given to increase an organization's ability to carry out its charitable purposes differs significantly from an advance payment for services to be rendered in exchange. A donor's restriction may emphasize specific program services that the donor wishes to support; however, designating that donated assets be used to support services provided to an organization's beneficiaries, although viewed as "deferred revenues" by some respondents to the Exposure Drafts, is not the equivalent of an advance payment in exchange for services to be received. FASB Concepts Statement No. 6, *Elements of Financial Statements,* states that a restricted contribution involves a fiduciary responsibility, not an obligation:

> The essence of a not-for-profit organization is that it obtains and uses resources to provide specific types of goods or services, and the nature of those goods or services is often critical in donors' decisions to contribute cash or other assets to a particular organization. Most donors contribute assets (restricted as well as unrestricted) to an organization to increase its capacity to provide those goods or services, and receipt of donated assets not only increases the assets of the organization but also imposes a fiduciary responsibility on its management to use those assets effectively and efficiently in pursuit of those service objectives.

That responsibility pertains to all of the organization's assets and does not constitute an equitable or constructive obligation .... In other words, a not-for-profit organization's fiduciary responsibility to use assets to provide services to beneficiaries does not itself create a duty of the organization to pay cash, transfer other assets, or provide services to one or more creditors. Rather, an obligation to a creditor results when the organization buys supplies for a project, its employees work on it, and the like, and the organization therefore owes suppliers, employees, and others for goods and services they have provided to it.

A donor's restriction focuses that fiduciary responsibility on a stipulated use for specified contributed assets but does not change the basic nature of the organization's fiduciary responsibility to use its assets to provide services to beneficiaries. A donor's gift ... imposes a responsibility to spend the cash or use the asset in accordance with the donor's instructions. In its effect on the liabilities of the organization, a donor's restriction is essentially the same as management's designating a specified use for certain assets. That is, the responsibility imposed by earmarking assets for specified uses is fundamentally different, both economically and legally, from the responsibility imposed by incurring a liability, which involves a creditor's claim. [Paragraphs 56-58, footnote reference omitted.]

68. The Board concluded that the distinction between donor-imposed restrictions and conditions is relevant to users of financial statements. The Board reaffirmed its conclusion that donor-imposed restrictions place limits on the use of contributed resources, but those limits do not create liabilities. To treat all restricted contributions as liabilities merely because a few may be returned would overstate an organization's liabilities. The Board also concluded that conditions cast significant doubts that assets will be retained, and those doubts are a cause for delaying recognition of a gift (paragraphs 75-81). The Board believes that consistent application of this distinction will result in a significant improvement over the current inconsistent accounting practices for restricted gifts and transfers of assets with conditional promises to contribute them.

Ambiguous Donor Stipulations

69. The distinction between a condition and a restriction, although clear in concept, may not be clear in practice because of ambiguous donor stipulations. For example, a restricted contribution may appear to also be conditional if it contains stipulations that do not clearly state whether the right to retain assets transferred or to receive the promised assets is dependent on fulfilling the stipulation.

70. To minimize implementation problems, the Board concluded that a presumption is necessary when ambiguous donor stipulations cannot be resolved by a review of facts and circumstances surrounding the gift or communications with the donor. Paragraph 23 of this Statement provides that a promise that contains stipulations that are not clearly unconditional shall be presumed to be a conditional promise. A few respondents to the 1992 Exposure Draft requested further clarification for promises to give services. The Board believes promises to give services generally involve personal services that, if not explicitly conditional, are often implicitly conditioned upon the future and uncertain availability of specific individuals whose services have been promised. The Board also clarified that organizations may not recognize the receipt of an unconditional promise to give services of the kind that do not meet the criteria in paragraph 9.

71. Absence of a specified time for transfer of cash or other assets, by itself, does not necessarily lead to a determination that a promise to give is ambiguous. If the parties fail to express the time or place of performance and performance is unconditional, performance within a reasonable time after making a promise is an appropriate expectation; similarly, if a promise is conditional, performance within a reasonable time after fulfilling the condition is an appropriate expectation. The Board concluded that promises to give that are silent about payment terms but otherwise are clearly unconditional should be accounted for as unconditional promises to give.

Recognition, Measurement, and Disclosure of Contributions

72. Some not-for-profit organizations have disclosed information about certain noncash contributions and unconditional promises to give in notes to financial statements but have not recognized those gifts as revenues. The Board believes that nonrecognition or delayed recognition generally omits relevant informa-

tion about an entity's economic resources and obligations and about its activities during a period, making financial statements unnecessarily incomplete. The Board concluded that disclosures about contributions are not a satisfactory substitute for financial statement recognition.

Criteria for Recognition

73. The Board considered when contributions should be recognized. Paragraph 63 of FASB Concepts Statement No. 5, *Recognition and Measurement in Financial Statements of Business Enterprises,* states that an item should be recognized in financial statements when four fundamental criteria are met:

Definitions—The item meets the definition of an element of financial statements.
Measurability—It has a relevant attribute measurable with sufficient reliability.
Relevance—The information about it is capable of making a difference in user decisions.
Reliability—The information is representationally faithful, verifiable, and neutral.

All four criteria are subject to a pervasive cost-benefit constraint. To be useful and worth providing, the expected benefits of information should justify the perceived costs of providing and using it.

74. Difficulty in measuring reliably and uncertainty of realization are sometimes cited as reasons for not recognizing certain contributions received. It is sometimes suggested that accounting and financial reporting should reflect "conservatism" whenever uncertainties exist. Those arguments suggest that if significant doubt exists about whether to recognize an item, financial reporting should err on the side of understating assets or overstating liabilities. However, accounting procedures that deliberately err in the direction of understatement of net assets introduce a bias into financial reporting. Deliberate bias conflicts with representational faithfulness, neutrality, and comparability. Thus, the doctrine of conservatism cannot be used to justify deferring recognition of revenues or gains beyond the time that adequate evidence of their existence becomes available, or to justify recognizing expenses or losses before adequate evidence that they have been incurred becomes available.

Effects of Conditions on Timing of Recognition

75. In certain circumstances, uncertainties may be so significant that recognition of an asset or liability must be delayed until there is adequate evidence that it exists, has value, and can be reliably measured. If an asset or liability is recognized before uncertainty is sufficiently resolved, the resulting information may be unreliable. Paragraph 76 of Concepts Statement 5 states:

> Reliability may affect the timing of recognition. The first available information about an event that may have resulted in an asset, liability, or change therein is sometimes too uncertain to be recognized: it may not yet be clear whether the effects of the event meet one or more of the definitions or whether they are measurable, and the cost of resolving those uncertainties may be excessive. Information about some items that meet a definition may never become sufficiently reliable at a justifiable cost to recognize the item. For other items, those uncertainties are reduced as time passes, and reliability is increased as additional information becomes available.

76. Uncertainty is inherent in a transfer of assets with a conditional promise to contribute those assets. Until the specified condition occurs, it is uncertain whether the transfer will become a right to retain those assets or an obligation to relinquish them. Several factors affect whether a condition will be met. They include whether the condition of the promise is an event outside the organization's control and whether work necessary to meet the condition requires additional funding from other sources. These factors make it difficult to determine reliably when, if at all, the conditional promise will become a right giving the promisee sufficient control of the promised asset and a duty making the promisor unable to avoid future sacrifice.

77. Uncertainties about meeting a condition typically diminish over time. Makers of conditional promises generally can avoid a future sacrifice of assets if they provide promisees with timely notification of the cancellation of their conditional promise. However, as time passes that ability diminishes. Case law and public policy suggest that once a promisee has begun efforts in reliance on a conditional promise, both parties should be held to their promises. Promisors generally are not allowed to escape their promises until and unless a reasonable period of time

has elapsed for the promisee to meet the condition, and promisees generally are held to their part of the agreement, which includes meeting the condition. However, until the specified future and uncertain event that is the subject of the condition occurs or fails to occur, a promisee does not have an unconditional right to retain the assets transferred or to demand payment.

78. Some respondents to the 1990 and 1992 Exposure Drafts said delaying recognition until a conditional right becomes unconditional defers recognition of conditional transfers of assets and conditional promises to give beyond the time that adequate evidence of the existence of the asset is available. They said that evidence of a probable future economic benefit is sufficient to recognize an asset. Some said that at a minimum, recognition of an asset on a percentage-of-completion basis should be allowed.

79. The Board believes that until the condition is substantially met, there is insufficient basis to make a presumption about the expected outcome. Doubt remains about whether all or none of the promised assets will be realized. Presently, there are no cost-effective techniques to measure with sufficient reliability the value of a conditional right to receive a promised gift or a conditional obligation to deliver a promised gift. The Board concluded that substantially meeting the condition is the underlying event resulting in a contribution to the promisee from the promisor and until that event occurs a contribution should not be recognized, regardless of whether the promisor has already transferred the assets or has promised to transfer the assets in the future.

80. The Board noted, however, that certain promises become unconditional in stages because they are dependent on several or a series of conditions—milestones—rather than on a single future and uncertain event and are recognized in increments as each of the conditions is met. Similarly, other promises are conditioned on promisees' incurring certain qualifying expenses (or costs). Those promises become unconditional and are recognized to the extent that the expenses are incurred. The accounting for that type of conditional promise results in recognition of assets and revenues as allowable costs are incurred, which resembles contractor accounting for government cost plus fixed fee arrangements where the contractor's right to partial payment becomes unconditional in advance of delivery of a finished product.

81. The Board considered whether a waiver of a condition is implicit in a promisor's decision to transfer assets after a conditional promise was made but before the condition is substantially met. It concluded that a change in the original conditions of the agreement between promisor and promisee should not be implied without an explicit waiver. A transfer of assets after a conditional promise to give is made and before the conditions are met is the same as a transfer of assets with a conditional promise to contribute those assets. By imposing a condition, a promisor retains its right of return of its assets if the condition is not met. It is reasonable to believe that by imposing a condition rather than promising unconditionally, a promisor has evidenced a strong and continuing interest in seeing that the specified condition occurs.

Basic Conclusions about Recognition and Measurement

82. Information about contributions of assets generally is relevant and should be recognized in financial statements. To be recognized in financial statements an item also must have a relevant attribute that is measurable with reasonable reliability and information about it must be representationally faithful, verifiable, and neutral.

83. The Board concluded that the fair value of the asset transferred, liability incurred, or liability canceled or settled is the relevant attribute for measuring contributions received or made. That conclusion reaffirms the conclusion reached in APB Opinion No. 29, *Accounting for Nonmonetary Transactions,* and the relevant AICPA Guides and SOP 78-10.[9] Specifically, Opinion 29 provides that

> . . . a nonmonetary asset received in a nonreciprocal transfer should be recorded at the fair value of the asset received. A transfer of a nonmonetary asset . . . in a nonreciprocal transfer should be recorded at the fair value of the asset transferred, and a gain or loss should be recognized on the disposition of the asset. [paragraph 18]

The Board also concluded that contributions generally are measurable with sufficient reliability. Contributions of monetary assets generally do not cause measurability problems, and although contributions of nonmonetary assets may present difficulties, they generally are measurable by both donors and donees.

84. However, a major uncertainty about the existence of value may indicate that a specific item received or given should not be recognized. If an item is accepted solely for a potential educational value or historical significance and has no alternative use, it may have uncertain value, or no value, and should not be recognized. For example, contributions of flora, fauna, photographs, and objects that are identified with historic persons, places, or events often have no value or have highly restricted alternative uses. The benefits of information about items, received or given, that may not have values are negligible.

85. Based on its considerations about the relevance of information about contributions and the measurability of contributed assets, the Board reached the following basic conclusions:

a. A contribution made and a corresponding contribution received should be recognized by both the donor and the donee at the same time, that is, upon occurrence of the underlying event—the nonreciprocal transfer of an economic benefit.

b. Donor-imposed restrictions place limits on the use of contributed resources and may affect an entity's performance and its ability to provide services. However, limitations on the use of donated resources do not change the fundamental nature of the contribution transaction or conclusions about when to recognize the underlying event.

c. Certain forms of contributed resources may be more difficult to measure reliably than others, but the form of the contributed resources alone should not change conclusions about whether to recognize the underlying event.

86. The Board considered whether those basic conclusions about recognition and measurement should be applied to all contributions received or whether certain exceptions permitted by the Guides and SOP 78-10 should continue. The Board specifically considered the recognition of promises to give, contributed services, and contributed works of art, historical treasures, and similar assets.

Promises to Give

87. This Statement defines the term *promise to give* using the common meaning of the word promise—a

---

[9] The AICPA's health care services Guide, paragraph 2.07, the colleges and universities Guide, page 48, the health and welfare Guide, page 20, and SOP 78-10, paragraph 71, generally specify that gifts of nonmonetary assets received should be measured at the fair value of the item received at the date of gift.

written or oral agreement to do (or not to do) something. A promise to give is a written or oral agreement to contribute cash or other assets to another entity. A promise carries rights and obligations—the recipient of a promise to give has a right to expect that the promised assets will be transferred in the future, and the maker has a social and moral obligation, and generally a legal obligation, to make the promised transfer.

88. Other sources have used other terms to describe promises to give. For example, legal treatises often use the term *subscription,* as in *charitable subscription,* as does the colleges and universities Guide. A similar promise made by corporate and governmental entities has sometimes been described as a *grant agreement, grant award,* or *sponsored agreement;* however, those terms have also been used for exchange contracts.

89. The 1990 Exposure Draft used the term *pledge* to describe a promise to give, as do the health care services and health and welfare Guides and SOP 78-10. However, some respondents to that Exposure Draft said that they use that term to describe promises as well as other indications of intentions to give that are not promises. Although the Board continues to believe that most pledges are promises to give, this Statement avoids use of the term *pledge* because it may be misinterpreted.

90. Paragraph 6 of this Statement provides additional guidance to minimize implementation concerns raised by respondents to the Exposure Drafts. First, it clarifies that sufficient evidence in the form of verifiable documentation must exist to recognize a promise to give. That clarification is intended to mitigate concerns that accounting results may be manipulated by recognizing potentially nonexistent assets; however, it does not preclude recognition of verifiable oral promises, such as those documented by tape recordings, written registers, or other means that permit subsequent verification. This Statement also clarifies that a written or oral communication that does not indicate clearly whether it is a promise is considered an unconditional promise to give if it indicates an unconditional intention to give that is legally enforceable. The Board decided that presumption is necessary to resolve ambiguities that cannot otherwise be resolved by a review of the facts and circumstances or by communications with the other party. The Board believes that in those circumstances it is reasonable to assume that a communication is a promise if it is legally enforceable.

91. The Board concluded that promises to give should be recognized on a basis consistent with recognition of other contributions. The making or receiving of an unconditional promise to give is an event that meets the fundamental recognition criteria. Accordingly, this Statement requires the promisee to recognize the promise as an asset and a contribution revenue or gain and the promisor to recognize the promise as a liability and a contribution expense. A conditional promise to give, like a transfer of assets with a conditional promise to contribute them, is recognized as a contribution at the time the condition is substantially met.

Meeting the definition of an asset or a liability

92. The Board concluded that an unconditional promise to give meets the definition of an asset when received and the definition of a liability when made. Concepts Statement 6 says that "assets are probable future economic benefits obtained or controlled by a particular entity as a result of past transactions or events" and "liabilities are probable future sacrifices of economic benefits arising from present obligations of a particular entity to transfer assets or provide services to other entities in the future as a result of past transactions or events" (paragraphs 25 and 35, footnote references omitted). Concepts Statement 6 discusses the three essential characteristics of assets and liabilities.

93. The first essential characteristic of an asset is that "it embodies a probable future benefit that involves a capacity, singly or in combination with other assets, to contribute directly or indirectly to future net cash inflows" (Concepts Statement 6, paragraph 26). Similarly, the first essential characteristic of a liability is that "it embodies a present duty or responsibility to one or more other entities that entails settlement by probable future transfer or use of assets at a specified or determinable date, on occurrence of a specified event, or on demand" (Concepts Statement 6, paragraph 36).

94. A promise by one entity to make a nonreciprocal transfer of assets to another entity in the future has the first essential characteristic of an asset and of a liability. That promise reflects a clear duty or requirement of the promisor to transfer promised assets in the future at a specified or determinable date or, if conditional, upon occurrence of a specified event.

95. In addition, an unconditional promise clearly is a precursor of a probable future benefit to the promisee. Inherent in that promise to give is a reasonable

expectation that the promisor will deliver and the promisee will receive, and evidence suggests that promises to give generally are kept. A conditional pledge, which involves future and uncertain events, raises significant uncertainties about obtaining the economic benefits promised.

96. The second essential characteristic of an asset is that "a particular entity can obtain the benefit and control others' access to it"; the second essential characteristic of a liability is that "the duty or responsibility obligates a particular entity, leaving it little or no discretion to avoid the future sacrifice" (Concepts Statement 6, paragraphs 26 and 36).

97. The Board believes that because of social and moral sanctions promisors commonly feel bound by their unconditional promises, regardless of their legal status. Paragraph 40 of Concepts Statement 6 states:

> . . . although most liabilities stem from legally enforceable obligations, some liabilities rest on equitable or constructive obligations. . . . Liabilities stemming from equitable or constructive obligations are commonly paid in the same way as legally binding contracts, but they lack the legal sanction that characterizes most liabilities and may be binding primarily because of social or moral sanctions or custom. An equitable obligation stems from ethical or moral constraints rather than from rules of common or statute law, that is, from a duty to another entity to do that which an ordinary conscience and sense of justice would deem fair, just, and right—to do what one ought to do rather than what one is legally required to do.

The equitable obligation that results from making a promise gives the promisee the ability to obtain the future benefit of the promised assets regardless of the legal status of the promise.

98. The availability of legal remedies provides another means of obtaining control over the promised assets, even if those legal remedies are seldom exercised. The Board consulted lawyers and reviewed the research of others[10] about the legal enforceability of promises to give. It understands that charitable promises generally have been enforced in this country, with the courts often applying the principles of con-

tract law. Promises are universally enforced if some consideration exists; some courts go far in their efforts to discover consideration sufficient to support a promise to give. Other courts, to make a promise enforceable, adopt the doctrine of promissory estoppel as the equivalent of consideration; that is, the promisor is estopped from raising the defense of lack of consideration if the promisor makes a promise that should reasonably be expected to induce action or forbearance of a substantial character on the part of a promisee. Still other courts will uphold a promise to give as valid and enforceable as a matter of public policy.

99. The Board concluded that unconditional promises result in equitable or legal obligations; conditional promises may not. Promisors may not feel bound by their conditional promises until the promisee begins meeting the condition or until the condition has been met.

100. The third essential characteristic of an asset is that "the transaction or other event giving rise to the entity's right to or control of the benefit has already occurred"; the third essential characteristic of a liability is that "the transaction or other event obligating the entity has already happened" (Concepts Statement 6, paragraphs 26 and 36). For unconditional promises, the Board concluded that the transaction or other event—the promise—giving rise to the entity's right to the benefit has already occurred. For conditional promises, the Board concluded that the event that should result in recognition is substantially meeting the condition.

Measurability, relevance, and reliability

101. The Board concluded that unconditional promises to give also meet the criteria of measurability, relevance, and reliability. The Board concluded that promises to give generally are measurable with sufficient reliability and, consistent with measuring contributions received at their fair value at date of gift, those receivables and payables should be measured at their fair value at the date the promise is received.

102. The Board concluded that information about promises to give, whether received or made, is relevant. Donors, creditors, and other users are interested in information about probable future transfers

---

[10]M. F. Budig, G. T. Butler, and L. M. Murphy, *Pledges to Non-Profit Organizations: Are They Enforceable and Must They Be Enforced?* New York University. In press.

of cash or other economic resources. That information is useful in assessing an entity's financial position and ability to generate public support and continue to operate. If the promisor is a not-for-profit organization whose primary purpose is to make contributions to others in the furtherance of its own mission, information about promises made is helpful in assessing the organization's performance. Thus, information about promises to give meets the test of relevance since it is "capable of making a difference in a decision by helping users to form predictions about the outcomes of past, present, and future events or to confirm or correct expectations" (Concepts Statement 2, paragraph 47).

Respondents' comments about recognition of promises to give

103. Most respondents to the 1990 Exposure Draft, including users of financial statements, said that not-for-profit organizations should not be required to recognize promises to give. Some of those respondents suggested that the Board establish standards to improve the disclosures of information about receipts of promises to give (pledges) and permit rather than require recognition of those promises as assets in financial statements.

104. The Board concluded that to permit rather than require recognition of unconditional promises to give would not improve existing practice. Since the 1970s, the Guides have required recognition of pledges by hospitals, voluntary health and welfare organizations, and most organizations other than colleges and universities. In 1979, the FASB designated that guidance as the preferred specialized industry practices for organizations considering a change in their accounting practice. The Board is aware that large numbers of colleges and universities and religious organizations do not recognize pledges receivable as assets although most maintain records of their pledges.[11] The Board believes that to permit, rather than require, recognition of pledges receivable would not further comparability between organizations and thus would not improve practice. The Board also concluded that disclosures that provide relevant in-

formation about an organization's future cash flows would be a useful improvement to practice and the 1992 Exposure Draft proposed that all organizations that receive promises to give provide the information required by paragraphs 24 and 25 of this Statement. Considerably fewer comments were received on the 1992 Exposure Draft; however, most of those respondents also disagreed with this Statement's required recognition of unconditional promises.

105. The Board also considered whether, as a few respondents suggested, it should preclude recognition of unconditional promises to give. The Board concluded that precluding recognition of unconditional promises to give would not faithfully represent an entity's assets or liabilities at the end of a period or its revenues or expenses during a period. That omission of relevant information about an entity's assets or liabilities and its revenues or expenses would make financial statements of all organizations unnecessarily incomplete. Furthermore, precluding recognition of unconditional promises to give would not improve comparability; rather, that would make unlike circumstances appear the same.

106. Some respondents said that promises to give that are binding primarily because of social and moral sanctions are indistinguishable from statements of intent to give and that making a distinction between the two will result in similar transactions being accounted for differently. Most would not recognize promises or statements of intent; a few would recognize both. Because social and moral sanctions obligate a promisor, the Board concluded that if a communication of intention to give is in substance a promise, it should be recognized. The Board does not intend, however, that entities recognize communications that clearly are not promises.

107. Several other respondents to the 1990 Exposure Draft said that only legally enforceable promises to give should be recognized. Many of those respondents contended that promises to give generally are not legally enforceable. The 1992 Exposure Draft noted that research examined by the Board indicates

---

[11] A 1985 survey and review of college and university annual reports found that of the 344 private institutions reviewed, only 10 percent recognized pledges receivable as assets in their balance sheet, 37 percent disclosed information about their pledges in notes to their financial statements, and more than 50 percent did neither, possibly because the pledges were not material (*Principles & Presentation: Higher Education,* [New York, Peat, Marwick, Mitchell & Co.: 1985], 39). A September 1987 survey conducted by the FASB staff had similar findings for colleges and universities and for religious organizations (9 percent and 18 percent, respectively, recognizing unrestricted pledges as assets) but noted that most (67 percent) hospitals recognized their unrestricted pledges and almost all organizations (more than 94 percent) maintained records of their pledges (Adams, Bossio, and Rohan, FASB Special Report, *Accounting for Contributed Services: Survey of Preparers and Users of Financial Statements of Not-for-Profit Organizations,* 52).

that most courts enforce promises to give, although in a few states promises are not enforceable except under the doctrine of promissory estoppel. The Board considered whether *only* legally enforceable promises to give should be recognized, and concluded that doing so would result in recognizing transactions with the same economic substance differently because of the differences in states' laws.

108. Many of the respondents to the 1990 Exposure Draft said that unconditional promises to give are not assets because donees would not use legal remedies to enforce a promise. They said that legal remedies are inconsistent with the nature of a contribution or that enforcement would jeopardize future fund raising. The Board acknowledges that legal remedies are often impractical; however, legal remedies seldom are necessary because promises generally are kept. Further, it is the *availability* of legal remedies, rather than the intent to use them, that provides an entity with an additional means of obtaining the future benefit. Although few respondents to the 1992 Exposure Draft asserted that unconditional promises are not assets, many respondents continued to recommend limiting recognition to only legally enforceable promises.

109. A few respondents to the 1990 and 1992 Exposure Drafts said an unconditional promise to give is similar to a purchase order. They said that both are legally enforceable and are indications of future cash flows. They suggested that, like purchase orders, promises to give should not be recognized before they are partially executed. The critical difference is that a promise to give is a nonreciprocal transfer, while a purchase order is part of an exchange transaction. To a seller, a purchase order involves a right to receive cash and an obligation to deliver goods or services in the future in approximately offsetting amounts. An unconditional promise to give involves a right to receive assets without an obligation to deliver assets or services.

110. Some respondents to the 1990 Exposure Draft contended that complying with recognition requirements for promises to give would hinder fund-raising efforts. This was the most frequently cited concern of respondents to the 1992 Exposure Draft. Some said recognition of unconditional promises to give would make entities appear to have excess spendable funds and, thus, have a reduced need for contributions. Others said that documenting information so that promises to give can be distinguished from other communications would damage trusting relationships

between an entity and its donors. Still others asserted that requiring donors to recognize multiyear unconditional promises would discourage that kind of long-term giving. The extent of those consequences is highly uncertain. The Board concluded that donors and other users need information about promises to give to make informed decisions about allocation of resources to not-for-profit organizations and the information must report promises as faithfully as possible without coloring the image it communicates for the purpose of influencing behavior in any particular direction.

Measurement of unconditional promises to give

111. The Board considered whether, as suggested by respondents to the 1990 Exposure Draft, it should provide further guidance on measuring the fair value of unconditional promises to give. The 1990 Exposure Draft said that APB Opinion No. 21, *Interest on Receivables and Payables,* provides the relevant standards for discounting future receipts or payments. Several respondents to that Exposure Draft said further guidance on measuring the fair value of unconditional promises to give is necessary or would be helpful. The 1992 Exposure Draft proposed and the Board concluded in this Statement that the present value of estimated future cash flows using a discount rate commensurate with the risks involved is an appropriate measure of fair value for unconditional promises to give cash.

112. Several respondents to the Exposure Drafts said that the undiscounted amount of cash promised should be used to measure all promises to give or all promises due within a period of no more than 5 years. Some of those respondents said that although a zero percent interest rate is unreasonable in a bargained-for exchange, that rate is appropriate to measure a promise to give because it is a voluntary nonreciprocal transfer. Others said the sum of the undiscounted promised cash flows is consistent with the amount the donor intended as a contribution. Still others said discounting would add costs and complexities without providing sufficiently useful information for promises that are due within relatively short periods (up to five years). The Board believes that failure to discount a promise to give does not faithfully represent its fair value. Cash to be received or paid in the future does not have the same value or utility as cash that is available now.

113. This Statement permits measuring unconditional promises to give that are expected to be collected or paid within one year at their net realizable

value because that amount, although not equivalent to the present value of estimated future cash flows, results in a reasonable estimate of fair value. That provision, which was not in the 1990 Exposure Draft, was added for practical reasons. The Board concluded that the requirements for measuring promises to give should be no more stringent than requirements for measuring trade receivables.

114. This Statement also permits measuring a portfolio of short-term promises to give that result from mass fund-raising appeals by using estimates of future cash flows based on experience gained from similar appeals. Annual campaigns, mail solicitations, telethons, or phonathons generally result in many promises of small dollar amounts that are due in less than one year and are unconditional. To measure individually the present value of estimated cash flows for promises to give resulting from those campaigns generally is impracticable. Measurement difficulties are compounded because the solicitation process may result in some spurious promises. The Board concluded that an entity may estimate the cash flows of a portfolio of short-term promises from mass fund-raising appeals using collection experience gained in previous similar appeals and that the promises may be measured at net realizable value because that measurement results in a reasonable estimate of fair value.

115. The 1992 Exposure Draft proposed that, consistent with guidance in Opinion 21, the subsequent accrual of the interest element on a multiyear promise to give should be reported as interest income by the donee and interest expense by the donor. A significant majority of respondents commenting on that proposal disagreed, including those that support recognition of promises to give at their present value. Some said that the interest element is a component of the contribution or that donors perceive it as part of their contribution. They contend that reporting that component as interest would add confusion that would exceed any potential benefit. The Board reconsidered its decision and concluded that the interest element should be accounted for as contribution income by donees and contribution expense by donors. The Board agreed that is likely to result in more understandable reporting. It also notes that reporting the interest element as a component of contribution income or contribution expense is consistent with accounting for the element of interest involved in certain other transactions; such as, the costs of pensions or of other postretirement benefits.

Disclosures

116. The 1992 Exposure Draft proposed that recipients be required to provide information about both promises to give and unrecognized communications that indicate an intention to give. The Board concluded that information about both would be useful in assessing a not-for-profit organization's ability to provide services in the future. The Board also concluded that this Statement should not require disclosures for makers of promises and indications of intentions to give because Statement 5 and Statement No. 47, *Disclosure of Long-Term Obligations,* provide the relevant standards.

117. Many respondents to the 1992 Exposure Draft said that the proposed disclosures for intentions to give would provide information of dubious value that would not justify the costs to provide that information. The Board continues to believe that information about intentions to give may be helpful to users of financial statements, especially if significant difficulties and uncertainties are encountered in distinguishing intentions to give from receipts of promises to give or when intentions to give are regularly solicited. However, the Board is sensitive to concerns raised about the costs of quantifying and verifying amounts of intentions to give, including negative consequences that might result from required audit procedures imposed during a delicate gift solicitation (precommitment) phase. The Board decided that this Statement should neither require nor preclude disclosures for intentions to give because it is not clear, at this time, that the potential benefits of information about the amount of intentions to give would justify the costs to provide that information.

Contributed Services

118. Most not-for-profit organizations receive and use contributed services in their operations, but few recognize them as revenues and expenses. The health and welfare Guide says that "because of the difficulty of placing a monetary value on donated services, and the absence of control over them, the value of these services often is not recorded as contributions [revenue] and expense" (page 21). However, the Guide requires recognition of revenue and expense under certain specified conditions, and although it does not encourage recognition of services received under other conditions, it does not preclude their recognition. In contrast, SOP 78-10, paragraph 67, precludes recognition of services not meeting similar conditions, and it has been interpreted by some as permitting rather than requiring recognition of contributed services meeting its conditions.

119. The Board considered that guidance, and the 1990 Exposure Draft proposed conditions for recognition of contributed services that generally are measurable with sufficient reliability. That Exposure Draft also encouraged recognition of other contributed services if they could be measured with sufficient reliability and at a reasonable cost. Permitting entities to recognize other measurable services was believed to be a reasonable step to allow practice to continue to evolve.

120. Some respondents to the 1990 Exposure Draft said that recognition of contributed services should not be required under any circumstances because the benefits of reporting information about their fair values would not exceed the cost to provide that information. Some respondents suggested recognizing only services that are donated by qualified entities if they would normally be purchased or suggested other conditions that focused on services integral to an organization's mission. Still other respondents, including users of financial statements, expressed concern about encouraging recognition of measurable services that did not meet the conditions. They questioned whether those services would be measured reliably and said standards are necessary to limit rather than encourage diverse recognition practices.

121. Because of user skepticism about the information provided by recognizing most contributed services and concerns raised about the cost to provide that information, the Board decided to revise the recognition criteria proposed by the 1990 Exposure Draft. The Board believes the conditions of paragraph 9 of this Statement limit recognition to only those services that will provide information that is clearly relevant, clearly measurable, and obtainable at a cost that does not exceed the benefits of the information provided. By drawing on existing industry guidance, the revised criteria should help minimize disruption to practice yet also should improve practice by eliminating certain inconsistencies in the existing guidance.

122. The Board also decided, for practical reasons, to preclude recognition of contributed services received that do not meet the conditions of paragraph 9 of this Statement. Respondents to the 1990 Exposure Draft expressed strong concerns about any permissive recognition. They said that methods of measurement and assumptions would vary considerably between entities, that resulting financial information often would not be reliable, or that discretionary recognition would lead to differing accounting practices

or perhaps practices biased toward presenting favorable ratios of program or fund-raising cost to total expenses. The Board believes that the disadvantages of inconsistent recognition practices outweigh the advantages of permitting discretionary recognition as a means for practice to evolve.

123. The Board also concluded that nonmonetary information about the nature and extent of contributed services received is useful in understanding an organization's operations, including its dependence on contributed services. Accordingly, the Board decided that organizations should describe the programs or activities for which contributed services are received and used. Nonmonetary information, such as the number and trends of donated hours received or service outputs provided by volunteer efforts, may be helpful in assessing the success and long-term viability of the organization. Other monetary information about contributed services received also may be helpful, such as the fair values of contributed services not recognized or the dollar amount of contributions raised by volunteers.

124. Views of respondents to the 1992 Exposure Draft differed on recognition of contributed services. Some said that the revised criteria are a significant improvement over the original proposal. Others said the criteria are too restrictive and preclude recognition of some contributed services that are both relevant and measurable with sufficient reliability. Some reiterated concerns raised in paragraph 120. The Board considered those comments and concluded that the criteria in paragraph 9 are necessary to limit recognition to only those services that are clearly relevant and measurable at a cost that does not exceed the benefits of the information provided.

Collection Items

125. This Statement considers certain specialized industry practices that permit but do not require certain organizations to capitalize works of art, historical treasures, and similar items held in their inexhaustible collections (paragraphs 37 and 38). In 1978, the accounting standards division of the AICPA said:

> . . . it is often impracticable to determine a value for [inexhaustible] collections [owned by museums, art galleries, botanical gardens, libraries, and similar entities] and accordingly [the division] has concluded that they need not be capitalized. If records and values do exist for the collections, the division encourages capitalization, at cost, if purchased, and

at a fair value, if acquired by donation. If historical cost is indeterminable, the alternative methods of valuing described in the section on fixed assets should be used. . . .

The nature and the cost or contributed value of current-period accessions and the nature of and proceeds from deaccessions should be disclosed in the financial statements. [SOP 78-10, paragraphs 113 and 114]

Some museums and similar entities recognize their "inexhaustible collections" as assets; however, most do not.

126. The 1990 Exposure Draft generally would have required all entities to recognize works of art, historical treasures, and similar items as assets in the period acquired and retroactively capitalize those items. The few respondents that supported that proposal generally said that recognition of these items as assets in financial statements is necessary to provide users of financial statements with information to assess an entity's financial position, the results of its operations, and how its managers have discharged their responsibilities for the custody and safekeeping of the entity's assets. However, almost all of the other respondents said that for most museums and similar entities that hold collections, the costs to capitalize works of art, historical treasures, and similar assets would outweigh the benefits of the information that capitalization would provide.

127. The Board reaffirmed its conclusion that works of art, historical treasures, and similar items are assets, regardless of the owner or the owner's intent to sell or hold the items as part of a collection. The Board also concluded, however, that because information necessary to recognize those items was not compiled in the past and may no longer be available or may be too costly to obtain, the incremental benefits of the information gained by recognizing works of art, historical treasures, and similar items held in "collections" as assets often would not justify the cost to provide that information. Accordingly, the 1992 Exposure Draft proposed that under certain specific circumstances entities need not recognize as assets works of art, historical treasures, and similar items held as part of a collection.

Definition of a collection

128. The Board's objective in defining collections (paragraph 11) is to exempt from recognition only those works of art, historical treasures, and similar as-

sets that are held for public exhibition, education, or research in furtherance of public service and that are to be preserved and protected. Collections, as used in this Statement, generally are held by museums, botanical gardens, libraries, aquariums, arboretums, historic sites, planetariums, zoos, art galleries, nature, science and technology centers, and similar educational, research, and public service organizations that have those divisions; however, the definition is not limited to those entities nor does it apply to all items held by those entities.

129. This Statement's definition of a collection is based on the American Association of Museums' *Code of Ethics for Museums* (1991) and its "Accreditation: Self-Study" (1989). The definitions in those documents are widely used by the kinds of organizations for which the Board believes the relevant cost and benefit problem exists. The Board decided that having an organizational policy that requires that the proceeds from collection items sold be used to acquire other items for collections demonstrates a commitment and a probability that the collections will and can be maintained. The Board believes that commitment is particularly relevant to its considerations about both the benefits and costs of providing information about those assets.

Collection items are assets

130. Collection items, although generally held for long periods of time and seldom sold, are assets that continue to provide economic benefit or service potential through their use. In a not-for-profit organization, that service potential or future economic benefit is used to provide desired or needed goods or services to beneficiaries. Those items also provide future cash flows from admissions, rentals, and royalties, and often are the reason for contributions in support of the entity's mission. The Board concluded that collection items have the common characteristics possessed by all assets—the scarce capacity to provide services or benefits to the entity that uses those items (Concepts Statement 6, paragraph 28).

131. Some respondents said that works of art, historical treasures, and similar assets that are part of "collections" are "held in trust" for the public and are not assets of the collectors. Many equated the "inability" to sell items from collections with forgoing the economic benefit inherent in those items. The Board concluded, however, that holders of collection items continue to reap economic benefits from those assets and it would be inappropriate to preclude their recognition and capitalization as assets.

Benefits and costs of capitalizing collections

132. Respondents to the 1990 Exposure Draft provided information useful to the Board in considering the benefits and costs of recognizing collection items. Most respondents said that they had experienced little or no demand for information about the value of collections held by museums and similar entities. Many also said that because of the extraordinarily long lives of most collection items, measures of their cost or fair value at date of gift are irrelevant. Although current values for collections or selected items may be of interest to an organization's managers, particularly in relation to decisions about the level of protection or insurance for assets, most respondents said to maintain current values on an annual basis would be cost prohibitive. The Board believes that information about the existence of collection items and changes in the nature of those assets is relevant to many, if not most, users of financial statements. However, the Board is unaware of a significant demand among external users of general-purpose financial statements for dollar-value information about collection items.[12]

133. Almost all respondents to the 1990 Exposure Draft said that the cost to retroactively capitalize collections would be excessive because records of the cost of purchased items or of the fair value at the date of contribution of donated items generally do not exist. They also said that the extraordinary human resources required to value the large collections of most organizations are neither currently available nor likely to be affordable in the future. Further, some said that galleries would have to be closed to the public to appraise objects on display and that removing objects from storage and returning them to storage would require additional cost and involve risk of damage.

134. The Board concluded that the cost of retroactively capitalizing collections often would exceed the incremental benefit of the information gained, especially for entities that have been in existence for several decades or more. The Board also concluded that the disclosures required by paragraphs 26 and 27 of this Statement, which were proposed by the 1992 Exposure Draft, will provide information that is useful in assessing how managers of an entity are discharging their responsibilities for the custody and safekeeping of collections without imposing significant costs to provide that information. The Board believes that this disclosure alternative to required recognition is a practical step that will improve current reporting practices.

135. The Board also concluded that works of art, historical treasures, and similar items that are not part of a collection should be recognized as assets in financial statements. Some entities that hold these items do not espouse the mission of public education, exhibition, and research and the attendant responsibilities to protect, keep unencumbered, care for, and preserve the items, and some entities that do maintain collections have some items that are not part of its collections. The Board found no reason to exempt items that are not part of a collection from recognition as assets.

Capitalization of collections is encouraged

136. The Board believes that, although often not practical, retroactive capitalization is conceptually the proper accounting for works of art, historical treasures, and similar assets and encourages entities that have capitalized their collections to continue that practice. However, the Board also believes that it would be inappropriate and potentially confusing to users of financial statements if entities selectively capitalize or omit some gifts or some purchases of collection items. Accordingly, an entity that has capitalized only a portion of its collections should assess the costs and benefits of capitalization and determine whether (a) recognition of all gifts and purchases either retroactively or prospectively from a date of adoption or (b) no capitalization and no recognition of gifts is most appropriate.

137. To assist entities that are considering retroactive capitalization, the Board decided to permit entities to measure collection items acquired in previous periods at their cost or fair value at date of acquisition, current cost, or current market value, whichever is deemed most practical. The Board expects that individual entities will use the measure that is most readily determinable with reasonable reliability. Additionally, the Board decided to permit entities to

---

[12]In response to a 1989 FASB survey of users and potential users of financial statements, some users said that information about the dollar amount of donated collection items could be useful in evaluating a museum; however, most did not believe the usefulness of information gained by retroactive capitalization of prior acquisitions would exceed the costs to provide that information.

Interviews of users conducted by others "uncovered no evidence of the usefulness of dollar-value information about collections" (Henry R. Jaenicke and Alan S. Glazer, *Accounting for Museum Collections and Contributions of Collection Items* [Washington, D.C.: American Association of Museums, 1991], 4 and 75-78).

measure one attribute of some collection items or groups of items and a different attribute of other collection items or groups of items if that would be practical. Flexibility in the attributes used to measure the amount to be capitalized will reduce the usefulness of the information provided; however, the Board decided that allowing entities a one-time option to capitalize collection items at the measure they deem most practical is a reasonable step to help reduce the costs of retroactive capitalization.

138. Many, if not most, respondents to the 1990 Exposure Draft that hold collections said they are unwilling to retroactively capitalize their collections because the costs of doing so would outweigh the benefits of information gained. However, the substantial one-time costs and disruptions that often make retroactive capitalization impracticable generally do not exist at the time donated items are received, and no costs or disruptions are associated with capitalizing purchased items. Because the Board believes that collection items are assets and are measurable and that information about collections generally is relevant and reliable, it decided to permit prospective recognition provided an entity capitalizes all collection items acquired after the date of initial adoption of this Statement.

139. The Board also considered whether to permit or preclude recognition of revenues for contributed collection items if an entity does not capitalize collections. The Board believes recognition of revenues for contributed collection items would be confusing if the amount recognized is also reported as a decrease in net assets rather than as an asset. Further, the Board believes that if an entity decides to incur the costs necessary to report contribution revenues, that entity should capitalize its collections, either prospectively or retroactively. Thus, the Board concluded that con-

tributed collection items shall be recognized as revenues or gains if collections are capitalized and shall not be recognized as revenues or gains if collections are not capitalized.

Disclosures required if collections are not capitalized retroactively

140. Several respondents to the 1990 Exposure Draft, including the American Association of Museums' Accounting for Contributions Task Force, suggested disclosures that might compensate for weaknesses in financial reporting that result from not capitalizing collections. The Board concluded that the disclosures required by paragraphs 26 and 27 of this Statement are necessary to overcome financial reporting weaknesses and anomalies that result from not capitalizing collections. For example, an entity that does not capitalize collections reports its purchases of collection items as a decrease to its net assets in the statement of activities, but that decrease is neither an expense nor a loss. Under generally accepted accounting principles, an expenditure for the acquisition of a long-lived tangible asset does not result in a decrease in net assets. Further, an entity might fail to report information about gifts made to other entities and uninsured losses from fires, thefts, or impairments of assets because the items have no carrying value.

141. The Board decided that certain transactions involving collection items should be reported separately from items of revenues, gains, expenses, and losses to reduce confusion resulting from the anomalies that result from not capitalizing collection items. The following illustrates one possible format[13] that may be used to satisfy the financial disclosure provisions of this Statement.

---

[13]Appendix C of Statement 117 contains illustrations of several formats of statements of activities that might be adapted to comply with the provisions of this Statement.

Organization M
Statement of Activities
For the Year Ended June 30, 19XX

	Unrestricted	Temporarily Restricted	Permanently Restricted	Total
Revenues and other support	XXX	XXX	XXX	XXX
Gain on sale of art that is not held in a collection	1			1
Net assets released from restrictions	XXX	(XXX)		
Total revenues, gains, and other support	XXX	XX	XXX	XXX
Expenses	XXX			XXX
Change in net assets before changes				
related to collection items not capitalized	XX	XX	XXX	XXX
Change in net assets related to collection items not capitalized:				
Proceeds from sale of collection items	5		10	15
Proceeds from insurance recoveries on				
destroyed collection items			1	1
Collection items purchased but not				
capitalized			(25)	(25)
	5		(14)	(9)
Change in net assets	XX	XX	XXX	XXX

142. The Board concluded that users need additional disclosures if collections are not capitalized. To increase users' understanding of the size and significance of the collections and management's responsibilities for the collections, the Board decided to require a general description of the collection and its significance and a description of management's stewardship efforts. To ensure that users of the financial statements understand that significant assets of the entity are omitted, the Board decided to require disclosure of accounting policies for collections and a line item on the face of the statement of financial position that refers to all required note disclosures. To provide information about losses or impairments of collection items if those items were not capitalized, the Board decided to require a description of items given away, damaged, destroyed, lost, or otherwise deaccessed or disclosure of their fair value.

143. The Board also considered the suggestion by some respondents that the Board require all entities that do not capitalize their collections to provide a schedule that reconciles from period to period the number of items held in each of their major collections. The Board decided not to require that reconciliation because it believes that other forms of disclosure may be more useful than item counts.

144. Most museums and other respondents to the 1992 Exposure Draft that commented on the provisions for recognition of and disclosures about collections supported the provisions in this Statement. Some museums that endorse the provisions of paragraphs 11(a) and (b) but are not committed to reinvesting proceeds from sales of collection items to acquire other items for collections (paragraph 11(c)) asked the Board to allow nonrecognition of their collection items. Having an organizational policy and demonstrated commitment to reinvest in collection items is particularly relevant to the Board's conclusions about collection assets.

Reporting Information about Donor-imposed Restrictions

145. Contributions are a primary source of revenues for many not-for-profit organizations; often they are donor restricted. Donor-imposed restrictions place limits on the use of assets received that affect the types and levels of service that an organization can provide. Because those limitations generally are pervasive, recurring, and sometimes permanent, the Board believes that financial reporting should reflect the extent and nature of donor-imposed limits and changes in them.

Information about Three Classes of Net Assets

146. Some restrictions limit the organization's ability to sell or exchange the asset received; more commonly, the restriction applies to an amount of net assets. Some donor-imposed restrictions impose limits that are permanent, for example, stipulating that resources be invested in perpetuity (not used up). Others are temporary, for example, stipulating that resources may be used only after a specified date, for particular programs or services, or to acquire buildings and equipment. The nature and extent of the limits resulting from donor-imposed restrictions are relevant to donors and other users, as well as management, when making their resource allocation decisions. The Board concluded that not-for-profit organizations should distinguish between contributions received that increase permanently restricted net assets, that increase temporarily restricted net assets, and that increase unrestricted net assets (paragraph 14).

147. Donors, creditors, and other resource providers are interested in knowing not only that an organization's net assets have increased (or decreased) but also how and why. Concepts Statement 6 says:

> Since donor-imposed restrictions affect the types and levels of service a not-for-profit organization can provide, whether an organization has maintained certain classes of net assets may be more significant than whether it has maintained net assets in the aggregate. For example, if net assets were maintained in a period only because permanently restricted endowment contributions made up for a decline in unrestricted net assets, information focusing on the aggregate change might obscure the fact that the organization had not maintained the part of its net assets that is fully available to support services in the next period. [paragraph 106]

148. The Board believes that information about a minimum of three classes of net assets, based on the presence or absence of donor-imposed restrictions and their nature, generally is necessary to gain an adequate understanding of the financial position and results of operations of a not-for-profit organization. Information about permanent restrictions is useful in determining the extent to which an organization's net assets are not a source of cash for payments to present or prospective lenders, suppliers, or employees and thus are not expected to be directly available

for providing services or paying creditors. Information about the extent of unrestricted net assets and of temporarily restricted net assets is useful in assessing an organization's ability and limitations on its ability to allocate resources to provide services or particular kinds of services or to make cash payments to creditors in the future.

Implicit Donor Restrictions

149. The 1990 Exposure Draft said that donor-imposed restrictions result from either a donor's explicit stipulation or a donee's explicit representation to donors. Some respondents noted that certain contributions contain implicit donor restrictions and asked whether those contributions would be reported as donor restricted. The Board clarified that donor-imposed restrictions also may result from circumstances at the time a gift is received that make clear a donor's implicit restriction of the use of contributed assets. The Board identified two situations in which it believes implied donor restrictions exist—contributions of unconditional promises to give with payments due in future periods and contributions of long-lived assets.

150. The Board concluded that a time restriction is implicit in an unconditional promise to give with payments due in future periods. That time restriction is implied unless a donor explicitly states that the gift is to support current activities or other circumstances make that clear. The Board believes that it is reasonable to assume that by specifying future payment dates donors indicate that their gift is to support activities in each period in which a payment is scheduled.

151. The 1992 Exposure Draft also proposed that time restrictions be implied on gifts of long-lived assets unless the donor explicitly states that the donated asset is to be sold to provide proceeds for unrestricted use or other circumstances make that clear. A significant majority of the respondents to the 1992 Exposure Draft did not comment on whether a time restriction is implicit in a gift of a long-lived asset, perhaps indicating tacit agreement with the proposal. However, nearly all of the minority of respondents commenting on this matter disagreed with the Exposure Draft.

152. Some respondents said that implying a time restriction is inconsistent with the Board's fundamental conclusion that donor-imposed restrictions result from either a donor's explicit stipulation or a donee's

explicit representation to donors. Those respondents agreed that a donor restriction exists on gifts of cash or other assets to acquire long-lived assets; however, they said those are explicit restrictions that are satisfied when the stipulated acquisition occurs. Others said that implying a time restriction adds unnecessary recordkeeping costs for long-lived assets that are acquired with multiple sources of funding and raises other accounting complexities for the gifted portion. Still others said the Board should make clear that the implied time restriction is required only in circumstances where donor-restricted amounts are material in relation to total funding sources for long-lived assets.

153. The Board continues to believe that it is reasonable to assume that by contributing long-lived assets without saying they may be sold immediately, donors indicate that those assets are to be used to provide services in future periods and that a similar implicit restriction exists for gifts of cash or other assets restricted to acquisition of long-lived assets. However, in light of the implementation concerns raised and the lack of a compelling legal basis or general acceptance for implying a time restriction on gifts of long-lived assets, the Board concluded that without further study it would be inappropriate to require or preclude organizations from applying that accounting convention. Accordingly, paragraph 16 of this Statement permits but does not require organizations to adopt a policy of implying a time restriction for donations of long-lived assets and because that choice is allowed, organizations must disclose the policy adopted.

Exception to Reporting Gifts as Donor Restricted

154. Some respondents to the 1992 Exposure Draft suggested that broadly restricted contributions—for activities that ordinarily occur in the normal course of operations—should be classified as unrestricted revenues. They said information about *restricted* gifts would be more meaningful if only donor-restricted gifts that permit the organization to undertake activities it would not otherwise conduct were separately reported as restricted gifts. They also said defining donor restrictions in that way would avoid reporting of virtually automatic reclassifications for expirations of restrictions that they contend provides information of little value and adds unnecessary bookkeeping.

155. The Board concluded there is no need to redefine donor restrictions. However, it decided, for practical reasons, to permit contributions with restrictions that are met in the same reporting period to be re-

ported as unrestricted support provided that an organization reports consistently from period to period and discloses its accounting policy (paragraph 14). That reporting, if elected, would not affect the reported amounts for change in temporarily restricted net assets for the period or temporarily restricted net assets at the end of a period. Thus, the expected benefits from applying the basic provisions of this Statement are not reduced significantly by the allowed exception, which the Board believes could help reduce the costs of implementing this Statement.

Expiration of Restrictions

Recognition of the Expiration

156. The Board concluded that an expiration of a donor-imposed restriction on a not-for-profit organization's net assets is an event that affects the entity and that financial statements should recognize the effects of that event in the period in which it occurs (paragraph 17). Information about the expiration of restrictions is useful in assessing the extent to which a not-for-profit organization used resources obtained in past periods for activities of the current period. Additionally, recognizing expirations of restrictions is necessary in determining the nature and extent to which net assets remain restricted at the end of the period.

157. Some respondents to the 1990 Exposure Draft asked the Board to clarify whether its intent was to specify that temporarily restricted net assets should be decreased when both unrestricted and purpose-restricted net assets are available for the same expenditure. Some, but not all of those respondents said that if both unrestricted and purpose-restricted net assets are available, restrictions expire when management identifies an expense with a restricted gift. They said that this method reflects the way that the organization's managers have discharged their stewardship responsibilities. The Board rejected that method of reporting, which it believes would result in different accounting for similar events because of differences in management objectives.

158. Other respondents said that donors assume that their gifts will be spent after unrestricted funds allocated to the same purpose have been exhausted, that is, that they have given incremental funds. The Board believes that restrictions should not be implied unless circumstances make clear that the donor restricted use of the contribution. The Board does not believe that it is reasonable to imply that a donor prevents use of contributed resources until unrestricted resources are exhausted.

159. The 1992 Exposure Draft retained the provision of the 1990 Exposure Draft that would require recognition of the expiration of a donor-imposed restriction when that event occurs and clarified that the recognition of an expense that satisfies a donor-imposed restriction decreases temporarily restricted net assets. The 1992 Exposure Draft also noted that this Statement would not specify or limit management discretion in determining which source of temporarily restricted net assets is decreased if an expense is incurred for a purpose for which more than one source of temporarily restricted net assets is available.

160. A minority of respondents to the 1992 Exposure Draft, mostly colleges and universities, said that the additional guidance provided about when donor restrictions expire is inadequate, too prescriptive, or too difficult to implement. Generally, they repeated previous suggestions that organizations be allowed to recognize expirations of donor restrictions when the institutional fiduciary charged with executing the terms of the gift determines an expense has been incurred for the specified purpose. The Board continues to reject that suggestion. The Board believes that this Statement's permitted exception for gifts with restrictions received and met in the same period may help reduce implementation concerns raised by those respondents.

161. Paragraph 17 of this Statement also provides that if an expense is incurred for a purpose for which both unrestricted and temporarily restricted net assets are available, a donor-imposed restriction is fulfilled to the extent of the expense incurred *unless the expense is for a purpose that is directly attributable to another specific external source of revenue.* The latter provision and an example were added to avoid unintended negative economic consequences that could result from the more prescriptive guidance of the 1992 Exposure Draft.

Reporting Expiration of Restrictions

162. This Statement specifies when to recognize expirations of donor-imposed restrictions, and Statement 117 specifies how to report the effects of those expirations in financial statements. The latter Statement specifies that expirations of restrictions that simultaneously decrease restricted net assets and increase unrestricted net assets (reclassifications) are reported separately from other transactions.

163. Some respondents to the 1990 Exposure Draft said that reporting expirations of restrictions in financial statements is unnecessary or potentially confusing. Generally, those respondents suggested reporting restricted contributions as deferred revenue until the restriction is met, thereby avoiding the need for reclassifications among classes of net assets. They also said that delaying recognition of the revenue from restricted contributions would achieve a better "match" of revenues and expenses. Some respondents to the 1992 Exposure Draft reiterated those comments.

164. The Board concluded that information about the relationship between inflows and outflows of a period and the relationship between restricted resources and the expenses or other activities they support generally is useful in assessing whether activities during a period have drawn upon, or contributed to, past or future periods. The Board also concluded that delaying recognition of revenue from a restricted gift is not necessary to provide information about those relationships. Further, as discussed in paragraphs 57-68, restricted contributions do not result in deferred revenues. Nonreciprocal transfers seldom involve matching procedures because "nonreciprocal transfers to an entity rarely result directly and jointly from the same transactions as expenses [and] most contributions and expenses are much more closely related to time periods than to each other" (Concepts Statement 6, paragraph 151).

165. The Board believes that reporting the relationship between gifts restricted to support specific program expenses and the expenses they support can be achieved by reporting expirations of donor-imposed restrictions. First, reporting the relationship of gifts to periods is achieved by recognizing contributions in the period received. Second, the relationship between the restricted contribution and the expense it supports is reported because a restriction generally expires in the period when the specified expense occurs. For example, an expiration of a purpose restriction decreases temporarily restricted net assets and increases unrestricted net assets at the same time as the expense that satisfies the restriction is reported as a decrease in unrestricted net assets. Thus, the relationship is reported in the unrestricted class of net assets in the period the restricted resources are used to support expenses.

166. That same type of relationship is reported with gifts that are time restricted. For example, a gift of a term endowment that is to be invested for five years is recognized as restricted support (revenue or gain) in the period it is received. In year 5, when that term

endowment becomes unrestricted, a reclassification is reported to reflect the decrease in temporarily restricted net assets and the increase in unrestricted net assets. Thus, the related effects of that time-restricted gift are reported in the period of receipt as well as the period in which the nature of the restriction changes.

167. The Board also believes that its clarification of expirations of restrictions and its conclusions about implicit restrictions on unconditional promises to give and on gifts of long-lived assets may help eliminate other "matching" concerns raised by some respondents. Most unconditional promises to give with payments due in future periods will be recognized as temporarily restricted support with time restrictions that expire in the periods those payments are due. That recognition should avoid misunderstandings that some respondents said would occur if promises to give due in future periods were recognized as unrestricted revenue and were perceived by users of financial statements as currently available funds.

168. Some respondents said misunderstanding would occur if gifts of long-lived assets (or long-lived assets acquired with restricted gifts of cash) were reported as current revenues or perceived to result in currently available funds. Some of those respondents would initially report those gifts as so-called capital contributions, or report the contributions and assets in a discrete fund group, or both. The Board believes that with appropriate labeling of land, buildings, equipment, and other long-lived assets in statements of financial position, users of financial statements will understand that those assets differ from cash and other liquid assets, whether or not they are initially reported as contributions that increase unrestricted net assets. The Board also concluded reporting long-lived assets in a separate fund group is not necessary. Nonetheless, this Statement allows organizations the option to recognize most gifts of long-lived assets as temporarily restricted support with implied time restrictions and report the expirations of those restrictions over the useful life of the assets. That reporting option provides a means to avoid the potential misunderstandings that are of concern to some respondents.

Effective Date and Transition

169. The 1992 Exposure Draft proposed that this Statement generally be effective for annual financial statements issued for fiscal years beginning after December 15, 1994. The Board believes that providing ample time before this Statement becomes effective is desirable so organizations can coordinate its implementation with Statement 117.

170. The Board also concluded that a delay to fiscal years beginning at least one year (and up to 18 months) after the date of this Statement's issuance would be reasonable for most not-for-profit organizations. The Board believes that this Statement's effective date (fiscal years beginning after December 15, 1994) would allow many small not-for-profit organizations and their external advisors sufficient time to assimilate the requirements of this Statement, obtain information that may be required, and put in place the systems necessary to gather required information.

171. Nonetheless, a national association representing more than 400 human services organizations (and a few other respondents) requested an additional one-year delay for small not-for-profit organizations. About one-third of the association's members have annual budgets of less than $1 million and the association said the extended transition period would allow them sufficient time to utilize the initial experience gained by larger organizations and CPAs. They believe that experience could help them find cost-effective ways to implement this Statement and Statement 117. Board members believe a further delay generally is not necessary. However, because small organizations are often dependent on outside volunteers and are particularly sensitive to any incremental one-time costs, the Board decided to grant a one-year delay for organizations with less than $5 million in total assets and less than $1 million in annual expenses.

172. Earlier application of this Statement is encouraged where practicable. Applying this Statement early may result in some loss of comparability of reporting among organizations during the transition period; however, the Board concluded that the benefits of the information gained by permitting early application outweigh its disadvantages. Because retroactive application of the provisions of paragraph 17 may be difficult, and perhaps impossible, if an organization no longer has the necessary records or past procedures did not require those records, the Board decided to permit rather than require retroactive application of the provisions of that paragraph. Respondents to the 1992 Exposure Draft generally agreed with its proposed effective date and transition provisions.

Appendix C

EXAMPLES OF THE APPLICATION OF THIS STATEMENT TO SPECIFIC SITUATIONS

CONTENTS

Appendix C

EAMPLES OF THE APPLICATION OF THIS STATEMENT TO SPECIFIC SITUATIONS

Introduction

173. This appendix provides additional discussion and examples that illustrate application of this Statement to some specific situations. The examples do not address all possible applications of this Statement and assume that all items addressed are material.

Scope and Definition

174. Some transfers of assets that are exchange transactions may appear to be contributions if the services or other assets given in exchange are perceived to be a sacrifice of little value and the exchanges are compatible with the recipient's mission. Furthermore, a single transaction may be in part an exchange and in part a contribution. A careful assessment of the characteristics of the transaction, from the perspectives of both the resource provider and the recipient, is necessary to determine whether a contri-

bution has occurred. Examples 1 and 2 illustrate the need to assess the relevant facts and circumstances to distinguish between the receipt of resources in an exchange and the receipt of resources in a contribution.

175. A transfer of assets also may appear to be a contribution when a donor uses an agent, a trustee, or an intermediary to transfer assets to a donee. Receipts of resources as an agent, trustee, or intermediary of a donor are not contributions received to the agent. Deliveries of resources as an agent, trustee, or intermediary of a donor are not contributions made by the agent. Similarly, contributions of services (time, skills, or expertise) between donors and donees that are facilitated by an intermediary are not contributions received or contributions made by the intermediary. Examples 3-5 illustrate the need to assess the relevant facts and circumstances to distinguish between the receipt of resources as a donee and the receipt of resources as an agent, a trustee, or an intermediary organization.

Example 1—Receipt of Resources in an Exchange

176. University A, a large research university with a cancer research center, regularly conducts research to

discover more effective methods of treating cancer and often receives contributions to support its efforts. University A receives resources from a pharmaceutical company to finance the costs of a clinical trial of an experimental cancer drug the company developed. The pharmaceutical company specifies the protocol of the testing, including the number of participants to be tested, the dosages to be administered, and the frequency and nature of follow-up examinations. The pharmaceutical company requires a detailed report of the test outcome within two months of the test's conclusion. Because the results of the clinical trial have particular commercial value for the pharmaceutical company, receipt of the resources is not a contribution received by University A, nor is the disbursement of the resources a contribution made by the pharmaceutical company.

Example 2—Receipt of Resources Partially in Exchange and Partially as a Contribution

177. Charitable Organization B receives $100,000 in cash from a donor under a charitable remainder annuity trust agreement designating Organization B as the trustee and charitable remainder beneficiary—a donee. The terms of the trust agreement require that Organization B, as trustee, invest the trust assets and pay $5,000 each year to an annuitant (an income beneficiary specified by the donor) for the remainder of the annuitant's life. Upon death of the annuitant, Organization B may use its remainder interest for any purpose consistent with its mission.

178. Organization B, as a donee, would recognize the contribution received as revenue in the period the trust is established. The transfer is partially an exchange transaction—an agreement for annuity payments to a beneficiary over time—and partially a contribution. The contribution received by Organization B is the unconditional right to receive the remainder interest of the annuity trust. The amount of the contribution received by Organization B is the fair value of the trust assets ($100,000 cash transferred) less the fair value of the estimated annuity payments (the present value of $5,000 to be paid annually over the expected life of the annuitant). Because Organization B must invest the underlying donated assets until the annuitant's death, the revenue recognized for this type of contribution—temporarily restricted support—should be distinguished from revenues from gifts that are either unrestricted or permanently restricted (paragraph 14). The death of the annuitant determines when the required annuity payments cease and when the trust expires and effec-

tively removes all restrictions on the net assets of Organization B. If the terms of this agreement had specified that upon death of the annuitant Organization B is to use its remainder interest to establish a permanent endowment, the revenue would be recognized as permanently restricted support rather than temporarily restricted support.

Example 3—Receipt of Resources as an Agent Rather Than as a Donee

179. Organization C receives relief supplies from Individual D with instructions to deliver the supplies to specified third-party beneficiaries. Organization C accepts responsibility for delivering those supplies because it has a distribution network and a mutual interest in serving the needs of the specified beneficiaries. Organization C has no discretion in determining the parties to be benefited; it must deliver the resources to the specified beneficiaries. Receipt of those goods is not a contribution received to Organization C, nor is the delivery of those goods to the beneficiaries a contribution made by Organization C. Rather, a contribution of goods is made by Individual D and received by the third-party beneficiaries.

Example 4—Intermediary between Donor and Donee

180. Organization E develops and maintains a list of lawyers and law firms that are interested in providing services without charge to charitable organizations and certain individuals. Organization E encourages individuals in need of free legal services to contact Organization E for referral to lawyers in the individual's community that may be willing to serve them. The decision about whether and how to serve a specific individual rests with the lawyer. Under those circumstances, Organization E merely acts as an intermediary in bringing together a willing donor and donee. The free legal services are not a contribution received by Organization E.

Example 5—Intermediary between Government Provider and Its Beneficiary

181. Hospital F provides health care services to patients that are entitled to Medicaid assistance under a joint federal and state program. The program sets forth various administrative and technical requirements covering provider participation, payment mechanisms, and individual eligibility and benefit provisions. Medicaid payments made to Hospital F on behalf of the program beneficiaries are third-party

payments for patient services rendered. Hospital F provides patient care for a fee—an exchange transaction—and acts as an intermediary between the government provider of assistance and the eligible beneficiary. The Medicaid payments are not contributions to Hospital F.

Contributions Received

182. Contributions are received in several different forms. Most often the item contributed is an asset, but it also can be forgiveness of a liability. The types of assets commonly contributed include cash, marketable securities, land, buildings, use of facilities or utilities, materials and supplies, other goods or services, and unconditional promises to give those items in the future. This Statement requires entities receiving contributions to recognize them at the fair values of the assets received. However, recognition of contributions of works of art, historical treasures, and similar assets is not required if the donated items are added to collections (paragraph 11). Recognition of contributions of services is required for those contributed services received that meet one of the specified conditions of paragraph 9 of this Statement and is precluded for contributed services that do not. Examples 6-16 illustrate application of the recognition and measurement principles in this Statement.

Example 6—Contribution of Real Property

183. Mission G, a religious organization, receives a building (including the land on which it was constructed) as a gift from a local corporation with the understanding that the building will be used principally as an education and training center for organization members or for any other purpose consistent with the organization's mission. Educating and training its members is an important activity of the mission.

184. Mission G would recognize the contributed property as an asset and as support and measure that property at its fair value (paragraph 8). Information necessary to estimate the fair value of that property could be obtained from various sources, including (a) amounts recently paid for similar properties in the locality, (b) estimates of the market value of the property by local appraisers or real estate brokers, (c) an estimate of the fair value of the property by the local tax assessor's office, or (d) estimates of its replacement cost (paragraph 19). This contribution is unrestricted support because the donated assets may be used for any purpose and Mission G does not have a

policy of implying time restrictions on gifts of long-lived assets (paragraph 16). If Mission G's policy is to imply a time restriction, the contribution is temporarily restricted support and the restriction expires over the useful life of the building.

Example 7—Contribution of a Work of Art

185. Museum H, which preserves its collections as described in paragraph 11, receives a gift of a valuable painting from a donor. The donor obtained an independent appraisal of the fair value of the painting for tax purposes and furnished a copy to the museum. The museum staff evaluated the painting to determine its authenticity and worthiness for addition to the museum's collection. The staff recommended that the gift be accepted, adding that it was not aware of any evidence contradicting the fair value provided by the donor and the donor's appraiser.

186. If Museum H capitalizes its collections, Museum H would recognize the fair value of the contributed work of art received as revenue and capitalize it as an asset at its fair value (paragraphs 13 and 19). The staff of Museum H is qualified to estimate the fair value of the contributed painting and evidence of its fair value exists. If Museum H does not capitalize its collections, Museum H is precluded from recognizing the contribution (paragraph 13) and would provide the information required by paragraphs 26 and 27.

187. If Museum H accepted the painting with the donor's understanding that it would be sold rather than added to its collection, Museum H would recognize the contribution of the painting received as unrestricted revenue and as an asset at its fair value (paragraphs 8 and 16).

Example 8—Contribution of Historical Objects

188. Historical Society I receives several old photographs as a gift from a long-time local resident. The photographs depict a particular area as it was 75 years ago. After evaluating whether the photographs were worthy of addition to the historical society's collection, the staff concluded the photographs should be accepted solely because of their potential historical and educational use; that is, the photographs may be of interest to future researchers, historians, or others interested in studying the area. The photographs are not suitable for display and no alternative use exists.

189. Regardless of whether Historical Society I capitalizes its collections, Historical Society I would

not recognize the contributed photographs in this example as assets because there is major uncertainty about the existence of value and no alternative use exists (paragraph 19).

Example 9—Contribution of Utilities

190. Foundation J operates from a building it owns in City K. The holding company of a local utility has been contributing electricity on a continuous basis subject to the donor's cancellation.

191. The simultaneous receipt and use of electricity or other utilities is a form of contributed assets and not services. Foundation J would recognize the fair value of the contributed electricity as both revenue and expense in the period it is received and used (paragraph 8). Foundation J could estimate the fair value of the electricity received by using rates normally charged to a consumer of similar usage requirements.

Example 10—Contribution of Use of Property

192. Charity L receives the free use of 10,000 square feet of prime office space provided by a local company. The local company has informed Charity L that it intends to continue providing the space as long as it is available, and although it expects it would be able to give the charity 30 days advance notice, it may discontinue providing the space at any time. The local company normally rents similar space for $14 to $16 annually per square foot, the going market rate for office space in the area. Charity L decides to accept this gift—the free use of office space—to conduct its daily central administrative activities.

193. The simultaneous receipt and use of facilities is a form of contributed assets and not services. Charity L would recognize the fair value of the contributed use of facilities as both revenue and expense in the period it is received and used (paragraph 8).

194. If the local company explicitly and unconditionally promises the use of the facility for a specified period of time (for example, five years), the promise would be an unconditional promise to give. In that case, Charity L would recognize the receipt of the unconditional promise as a receivable and as restricted support at its fair value. The donor would recognize the unconditional promise when made as a payable and an expense at its fair value (paragraph 18).

Example 11—Contribution of Services

195. Institute M decides to construct a building on its property. It obtains the necessary architectural plans and specifications and purchases the necessary continuing architectural services, materials, permits, and so forth at a total cost of $400,000. A local construction company contributes the necessary labor and equipment. An independent appraisal of the building (exclusive of land), obtained for insurance purposes, estimates its fair value at $725,000.

196. Institute M would recognize the services contributed by the construction company because the contributed services received meet condition (a)—the services received create or enhance nonfinancial assets—or because the services meet condition (b)—the services require specialized skills, are provided by individuals possessing those skills, and would typically need to be purchased if not provided by donation (paragraph 9). Contributions of services that create or enhance nonfinancial assets may be measured by referring to either the fair value of the services received or the fair value of the asset or of the asset enhancement resulting from the services (paragraph 19). In this example, the fair value of the contributed services received could be determined by subtracting the cost of the purchased services, materials, and permits ($400,000) from the fair value of the asset created ($725,000), which results in contributed services received of $325,000. Alternatively, the amount the construction company would have charged could be used if more readily available.

197. If some of the labor did not require specialized skills and was provided by volunteers, those services still would be recognized because they meet condition (a).

Example 12—Contribution of Services

198. Faculty salaries are a major expense of University N. The faculty includes both compensated faculty members (approximately 80 percent) and uncompensated faculty members (approximately 20 percent) who are associated with religious orders and contribute their services to the university. The performance of both compensated and uncompensated faculty members is regularly and similarly evaluated; both must meet the university's standards and both provide services in the same way.

199. University N would recognize both revenue and expense for the services contributed by the uncompensated faculty members because the contribution meets condition (b) of paragraph 9. Teaching requires specialized skills; the religious personnel are qualified and trained to provide those skills; and University N typically would hire paid instructors if the

religious personnel did not donate their services. University N could refer to the salaries it pays similarly qualified compensated faculty members to determine fair value of the services received.

200. Similarly, if the uncompensated faculty members in this example were given a nominal stipend to help defray certain of their out-of-pocket expenses, University N still would recognize both revenue and expense for the services contributed. The contribution received would be measured at the fair value of the services received less the amount of the nominal stipend paid.

Example 13—Contribution of Services

201. A member of the Board of Trustees of Civic Organization O is a lawyer and from time to time in the capacity of a trustee provides advice on general business matters, including questions about business opportunities and risks and ethical, moral, and legal matters. The advice provided on legal matters is provided as a trustee in the role of a trustee, not as a lawyer, and the opinions generally are limited to routine matters. Generally, the lawyer suggests that Civic Organization O seek the opinion of its attorneys on substantive or complex legal questions. All of the organization's trustees serve without compensation, and most trustees have specialized expertise (for example, a chief executive officer, a minister, a physician, a professor, and a public accountant) that makes their advice valuable to Civic Organization O. The trustee-lawyer also serves without compensation as a trustee for two other charitable organizations.

202. Civic Organization O would be precluded from recognizing the contributed services it receives from its trustee-lawyer or its other trustees because the services contributed do not meet either of the conditions of paragraph 9 of this Statement. Condition (a) is not relevant. The trustee-lawyer's services do not meet condition (b) because the substantive or complex legal questions that require the specialized skills of a lawyer are referred to the organization's attorneys or because the advice provided by trustees typically would not be purchased if not provided by donation.

Example 14—Contribution of Services

203. Hospital P provides short-term inpatient and outpatient care and also provides long-term care for the elderly. As part of the long-term care program, the hospital has organized a program whereby local high school students may contribute a minimum of 10 hours a week, from 3:00 p.m. to 6:00 p.m., to the hospital. These students are assigned various duties, such as visiting and talking with the patients, distributing books and magazines, reading, playing chess, and similar activities. The hospital does not pay for these services or similar services. The services are accepted as a way of enhancing or supplementing the quality of care and comfort provided to the elderly long-term care patients.

204. Hospital P would be precluded from recognizing the contributed services because the services contributed do not meet either of the conditions of paragraph 9 of this Statement. Condition (a) is not relevant. Condition (b) has not been met because the services the students provide do not require specialized skills nor would they typically need to be purchased if not provided by donation.

Example 15—Contribution of Services

205. College Q conducts an annual fund-raising campaign to solicit contributions from its alumni. In prior years, College Q recruited unpaid student volunteers to make phone calls to its alumni. This year, a telemarketing company, whose president is an alumnus of College Q, contributed its services to College Q for the annual alumni fund-raising campaign. The company normally provides telemarketing services to a variety of clients on a fee basis. College Q provided the company with a list of 10,000 alumni, several copies of a typed appeal to be read over the phone, and blank contribution forms to record pledges received. The company contacted most of the 10,000 alumni.

206. College Q would be precluded from recognizing the contributed services of the telemarketing company. Condition (a) of paragraph 9 is not relevant. Condition (b) has not been met because the services do not require specialized skills or because College Q typically would not need to purchase the services if they were not provided by donation. College Q normally conducts its campaign with untrained students in a manner similar to the manner used by the telemarketing firm.

Example 16—Contribution of an Interest in an Estate

207. In 19X0, Individual R notifies Church S that she has remembered the church in her will and provides a written copy of the will. In 19X5, Individ-

ual R dies. In 19X6, Individual R's last will and testament enters probate and the probate court declares the will valid. The executor informs Church S that the will has been declared valid and that it will receive 10 percent of Individual R's estate, after satisfying the estate's liabilities and certain specific bequests. The executor provides an estimate of the estate's assets and liabilities and the expected amount and time for payment of Church S's interest in the estate.

208. The 19X0 communication between Individual R and Church S specified an intention to give. The ability to modify a will at any time prior to death is well established; thus in 19X0 Church S did not receive a promise to give and did not recognize a contribution received. When the probate court declares the will valid, Church S would recognize a receivable and revenue for an unconditional promise to give at the fair value of its interest in the estate (paragraphs 8 and 19-21). If the promise to give contained in the valid will was instead conditioned on a future and uncertain event, Church S would recognize the contribution when the condition was substantially met. A conditional promise in a valid will would be disclosed in notes to financial statements (paragraph 25).

Appendix D

GLOSSARY

209. This appendix contains definitions of certain terms used in this Statement.

Collections

Works of art, historical treasures, or similar assets that are (a) held for public exhibition, education, or research in furtherance of public service rather than financial gain, (b) protected, kept unencumbered, cared for, and preserved, and (c) subject to an organizational policy that requires the proceeds of items that are sold to be used to acquire other items for collections.

Conditional promise to give

A promise to give that depends on the occurrence of a specified future and uncertain event to bind the promisor.

Contribution

An unconditional transfer of cash or other assets to an entity or a settlement or cancellation of its liabilities in a voluntary nonreciprocal transfer by another entity acting other than as an owner.

Donor-imposed condition

A donor stipulation that specifies a future and uncertain event whose occurrence or failure to occur gives the promisor a right of return of the assets it has transferred or releases the promisor from its obligation to transfer its assets.

Donor-imposed restriction

A donor stipulation that specifies a use for the contributed asset that is more specific than broad limits resulting from the nature of the organization, the environment in which it operates, and the purposes specified in its articles of incorporation or bylaws or comparable documents for an unincorporated association. A restriction on an organization's use of the asset contributed may be temporary or permanent.

Nonreciprocal transfer

A transaction in which an entity incurs a liability or transfers an asset to another entity (or receives an asset or cancellation of a liability) without directly receiving (or giving) value in exchange.

Not-for-profit organization

An entity that possesses the following characteristics that distinguish it from a business enterprise: (a) contributions of significant amounts of resources from resource providers who do not expect commensurate or proportionate pecuniary return, (b) operating purposes other than to provide goods or services at a profit, and (c) absence of ownership interests like those of business enterprises. Not-for-profit organizations have those characteristics in varying degrees (Concepts Statement 4, paragraph 6). Organizations that clearly fall outside this definition include all investor-owned enterprises and entities that provide dividends, lower costs, or other economic benefits directly and proportionately to their owners, members, or participants, such as mutual insurance companies, credit unions, farm and rural electric cooperatives, and employee benefit plans (Concepts Statement 4, paragraph 7).

Permanent restriction

A donor-imposed restriction that stipulates that resources be maintained permanently but permits the organization to use up or expend part or all of the income (or other economic benefits) derived from the donated assets.

Permanently restricted net assets

The part of the net assets of a not-for-profit organization resulting (a) from contributions and other inflows of assets whose use by the organization is limited by donor-imposed stipulations that neither expire by passage of time nor can be fulfilled or otherwise removed by actions of the organization, (b) from other asset enhancements and diminishments subject to the same kinds of stipulations, and (c) from reclassifications from (or to) other classes of net assets as a consequence of donor-imposed stipulations (Concepts Statement 6, paragraph 92).

Promise to give

A written or oral agreement to contribute cash or other assets to another entity. A promise to give may be either conditional or unconditional.

Restricted support

Donor-restricted revenues or gains from contributions that increase either temporarily restricted net assets or permanently restricted net assets. Also refer to **Unrestricted support**.

Temporarily restricted net assets

The part of the net assets of a not-for-profit organization resulting (a) from contributions and other inflows of assets whose use by the organization is limited by donor-imposed stipulations that either expire by passage of time or can be fulfilled and removed by actions of the organization pursuant to those stipulations, (b) from other asset enhancements and diminishments subject to the same kinds of stipulations, and (c) from reclassifications to (or from) other classes of net assets as a consequence of donor-imposed stipulations, their expiration by passage of time, or their fulfillment and removal by actions of the organization pursuant to those stipulations (Concepts Statement 6, paragraph 93).

Temporary restriction

A donor-imposed restriction that permits the donee organization to use up or expend the donated assets as specified and is satisfied either by the passage of time or by actions of the organization.

Unconditional promise to give

A promise to give that depends only on passage of time or demand by the promisee for performance.

Unrestricted net assets

The part of net assets of a not-for-profit organization that is neither permanently restricted nor temporarily restricted by donor-imposed stipulations (Concepts Statement 6, paragraph 94).

Unrestricted support

Revenues or gains from contributions that are not restricted by donors. Also refer to **Restricted support.**

Statement of Financial Accounting Standards No. 117
Financial Statements of Not-for-Profit Organizations

STATUS

Issued: June 1993

Effective Date: For fiscal years beginning after December 15, 1994

Affects: Amends FAS 95, paragraphs 3, 18, 19, 27(b), 28 through 30, 32, and 130 and footnote 12

Affected by: Paragraph 168 amended by FAS 124

Other Interpretive Release: FASB *Highlights*, "Time for a Change—Implementing FASB Statements 116 and 117," January 1995

Issues Discussed by FASB Emerging Issues Task Force (EITF)

Affects: No EITF Issues

Interpreted by: Paragraph 22 interpreted by EITF Topic No. D-49

Related Issues: No EITF Issues

SUMMARY

This Statement establishes standards for general-purpose external financial statements provided by a not-for-profit organization. Its objective is to enhance the relevance, understandability, and comparability of financial statements issued by those organizations. It requires that those financial statements provide certain basic information that focuses on the entity as a whole and meets the common needs of external users of those statements.

This Statement requires that all not-for-profit organizations provide a statement of financial position, a statement of activities, and a statement of cash flows. It requires reporting amounts for the organization's total assets, liabilities, and net assets in a statement of financial position; reporting the change in an organization's net assets in a statement of activities; and reporting the change in its cash and cash equivalents in a statement of cash flows.

This Statement also requires classification of an organization's net assets and its revenues, expenses, gains, and losses based on the existence or absence of donor-imposed restrictions. It requires that the amounts for each of three classes of net assets—permanently restricted, temporarily restricted, and unrestricted—be displayed in a statement of financial position and that the amounts of change in each of those classes of net assets be displayed in a statement of activities.

This Statement amends FASB Statement No. 95, *Statement of Cash Flows,* to extend its provisions to not-for-profit organizations and to expand its description of cash flows from financing activities to include certain donor-restricted cash that must be used for long-term purposes. It also requires that voluntary health and welfare organizations provide a statement of functional expenses that reports expenses by both functional and natural classifications.

This Statement is effective for annual financial statements issued for fiscal years beginning after December 15, 1994, except for organizations with less than $5 million in total assets and less than $1 million in annual expenses. For those organizations, the Statement is effective for fiscal years beginning after December 15, 1995. Earlier application is encouraged.

Statement of Financial Accounting Standards No. 117

Financial Statements of Not-for-Profit Organizations

CONTENTS

INTRODUCTION

1. This Statement establishes standards for general-purpose external financial statements provided by a **not-for-profit organization**.[1] It specifies that those statements include a statement of financial position, a statement of activities, and a statement of cash flows. This Statement also amends FASB Statement No. 95, *Statement of Cash Flows*, to extend its provisions to not-for-profit organizations. It also specifies that **voluntary health and welfare organizations** continue to provide a statement of functional expenses, which is useful in associating expenses with service efforts and accomplishments of not-for-profit organizations.

2. Not-for-profit organizations currently provide financial statements that differ in their form and content. For example, most hospitals, trade associations, and membership organizations provide a statement of financial position and a statement of activities (or statement of revenues and expenses) that report their financial position and results of operations for the entity as a whole. In contrast, universities, museums, religious organizations, and certain other not-for-profit organizations often provide financial statements that report the financial position and changes in financial position of individual fund groups, but many do not report financial position and results of operations for the entity as a whole. Recently, some not-for-profit organizations have begun reporting cash flow information, but most do not. Further, voluntary health and welfare organizations and certain other charitable organizations generally provide a statement that reports expenses by **functional classification** and by

---

[1]Words that appear in the glossary are set in **boldface type** the first time they appear.

natural classification, but most other not-for-profit organizations do not.

3. This Statement is part of a project that has been considering those and other inconsistent practices of not-for-profit organizations, including accounting and reporting principles and practices that are incorporated in several of the audit Guides of the American Institute of Certified Public Accountants (Appendix A). Because this Statement now establishes standards for reporting certain basic information in financial statements that are applicable to all not-for-profit organizations, provisions in AICPA Guides and Statements of Position that are inconsistent with this Statement are no longer acceptable *specialized*[2] accounting and reporting principles and practices. Within the parameters of this Statement, the AICPA or another appropriate body, following the process described in AICPA Statement on Auditing Standards (SAS) No. 69, *The Meaning of "Present Fairly in Conformity With Generally Accepted Accounting Principles" in the Independent Auditor's Report,* may provide more specific reporting guidance for certain not-for-profit organizations.

STANDARDS OF FINANCIAL ACCOUNTING AND REPORTING

Purpose of a Set of Financial Statements

4. The primary purpose of financial statements is to provide relevant information to meet the common interests of donors, members, creditors, and others who provide resources to not-for-profit organizations. Those external users of financial statements have common interests in assessing (a) the services an organization provides and its ability to continue to provide those services and (b) how managers discharge their stewardship responsibilities and other aspects of their performance.

5. More specifically, the purpose of financial statements, including accompanying notes, is to provide information about:

a. The amount and nature of an organization's assets, liabilities, and net assets
b. The effects of transactions and other events and circumstances that change the amount and nature of net assets

c. The amount and kinds of inflows and outflows of economic resources during a period and the relation between the inflows and outflows
d. How an organization obtains and spends cash, its borrowing and repayment of borrowing, and other factors that may affect its liquidity
e. The service efforts of an organization.

Individual financial statements provide different information, and the information each statement provides generally complements information in other financial statements.

Scope

6. A complete set of financial statements of a not-for-profit organization shall include a statement of financial position as of the end of the reporting period, a statement of activities and a statement of cash flows for the reporting period, and accompanying notes to financial statements.

7. This Statement specifies certain basic information to be reported in financial statements of not-for-profit organizations. Its requirements generally are no more stringent than requirements for business enterprises. A set of financial statements includes, either in the body of financial statements or in the accompanying notes, that information required by generally accepted accounting principles that do not specifically exempt not-for-profit organizations and required by applicable specialized accounting and reporting principles and practices. For example, not-for-profit organizations should apply the disclosure and display provisions for financial instruments; loss contingencies; extraordinary, unusual, and infrequently occurring events; and accounting changes.

8. This Statement discusses how to report assets, liabilities, net assets, revenues, expenses, gains, and losses in financial statements; however, it does not specify when to recognize or how to measure those elements. The degree of aggregation and order of presentation of items of assets and liabilities in statements of financial position or of items of revenues and expenses in statements of activities of not-for-profit organizations, although not specified by this Statement, generally should be similar to those required or permitted for business enterprises. Appendix C includes financial statements that illustrate some of the ways that the requirements of this Statement may be met.

---

[2] The term *specialized* is used to refer to those current accounting and reporting principles and practices in existing AICPA Guides and Statements of Position that are neither superseded by nor contained in the Accounting Research Bulletins, APB Opinions, FASB Statements, and FASB Interpretations.

Statement of Financial Position

Purpose and Focus of a Statement of Financial Position

9. The primary purpose of a statement of financial position is to provide relevant information about an organization's assets, liabilities, and net assets and about their relationships to each other at a moment in time. The information provided in a statement of financial position, used with related disclosures and information in other financial statements, helps donors, members, creditors, and others to assess (a) the organization's ability to continue to provide services and (b) the organization's liquidity, financial flexibility,[3] ability to meet obligations, and needs for external financing.

10. A statement of financial position shall focus on the organization as a whole and shall report the amounts of its total assets, liabilities, and net assets.

Classification of Assets and Liabilities

11. A statement of financial position, including accompanying notes to financial statements, provides relevant information about liquidity, financial flexibility, and the interrelationship of an organization's assets and liabilities. That information generally is provided by aggregating assets and liabilities that possess similar characteristics into reasonably homogeneous groups. For example, entities generally report individual items of assets in homogeneous groups, such as cash and cash equivalents; accounts and notes receivable from patients, students, members, and other recipients of services; inventories of materials and supplies; deposits and prepayments for rent, insurance, and other services; marketable securities and other investment assets held for long-term purposes; and land, buildings, equipment, and other long-lived assets used to provide goods and services. Cash or other assets received with a **donor-imposed restriction** that limits their use to long-term purposes should not be classified with cash or other assets that are unrestricted and available for current use.[4]

12. Information about liquidity shall be provided by one or more of the following:

a. Sequencing assets according to their nearness of conversion to cash and sequencing liabilities according to the nearness of their maturity and resulting use of cash

b. Classifying assets and liabilities as current and noncurrent, as defined by Accounting Research Bulletin No. 43, Chapter 3A, "Working Capital—Current Assets and Current Liabilities"

c. Disclosing in notes to financial statements relevant information about the liquidity or maturity of assets and liabilities, including restrictions on the use of particular assets.

Classification of Net Assets as Donor Restricted or Unrestricted

13. A statement of financial position provided by a not-for-profit organization shall report the amounts for each of three classes of net assets—**permanently restricted net assets, temporarily restricted net assets**, and **unrestricted net assets**—based on the existence or absence of donor-imposed restrictions.

14. Information about the nature and amounts of different types of **permanent restrictions** or **temporary restrictions** shall be provided either by reporting their amounts on the face of the statement or by including relevant details in notes to financial statements. Separate line items may be reported within permanently restricted net assets or in notes to financial statements to distinguish between permanent restrictions for holdings of (a) assets, such as land or works of art, donated with stipulations that they be used for a specified purpose, be preserved, and not be sold or (b) assets donated with stipulations that they be invested to provide a permanent source of income. The latter result from gifts and bequests that create permanent **endowment funds**.

15. Similarly, separate line items may be reported within temporarily restricted net assets or in notes to financial statements to distinguish between temporary restrictions for (a) support of particular operating

---

[3]Liquidity reflects an asset's or liability's nearness to cash. Financial flexibility is the ability of an entity to take effective actions to alter amounts and timing of cash flows so it can respond to unexpected needs and opportunities. Information about the nature and amount of restrictions imposed by donors on the use of contributed assets, including their potential effects on specific assets and on liabilities or classes of net assets, is helpful in assessing the financial flexibility of a not-for-profit organization.

[4]ARB No. 43, Chapter 3A, "Working Capital—Current Assets and Current Liabilities," paragraph 6, says that the "concept of the nature of current assets contemplates the exclusion from that classification of . . . cash and claims to cash which are restricted as to withdrawal or use for other than current operations, are designated for expenditure in the acquisition or construction of noncurrent assets, or are segregated[1] for the liquidation of long-term debts," and footnote 1 explains that "even though not actually set aside in special accounts, funds that are clearly to be used in the near future for the liquidation of long-term debts, payments to sinking funds, or for similar purposes should also . . . be excluded from current assets."

activities, (b) investment for a specified term, (c) use in a specified future period, or (d) acquisition of long-lived assets. Donors' temporary restrictions may require that resources be used in a later period or after a specified date (time restrictions), or that resources be used for a specified purpose (purpose restrictions), or both. For example, gifts of cash and other assets with stipulations that they be invested to provide a source of income for a specified term and that the income be used for a specified purpose are both time and purpose restricted. Those gifts often are called *term endowments.*

16. Unrestricted net assets generally result from revenues from providing services, producing and delivering goods, receiving unrestricted contributions, and receiving dividends or interest from investing in income-producing assets, less expenses incurred in providing services, producing and delivering goods, raising contributions, and performing administrative functions. The only limits on the use of unrestricted net assets are the broad limits resulting from the nature of the organization, the environment in which it operates, and the purposes specified in its articles of incorporation or bylaws and limits resulting from contractual agreements with suppliers, creditors, and others entered into by the organization in the course of its business. Information about those contractual limits that are significant, including the existence of loan covenants, generally is provided in notes to financial statements. Similarly, information about self-imposed limits that may be useful, including information about voluntary resolutions by the governing board of an organization to designate a portion of its unrestricted net assets to function as an endowment (sometimes called a *board-designated endowment*), may be provided in notes to or on the face of financial statements.

Statement of Activities

Purpose and Focus of a Statement of Activities

17. The primary purpose of a statement of activities is to provide relevant information about (a) the effects of transactions and other events and circumstances that change the amount and nature of net assets, (b) the relationships of those transactions and

other events and circumstances to each other, and (c) how the organization's resources are used in providing various programs or services. The information provided in a statement of activities, used with related disclosures and information in the other financial statements, helps donors, creditors, and others to (1) evaluate the organization's performance during a period, (2) assess an organization's service efforts and its ability to continue to provide services, and (3) assess how an organization's managers have discharged their stewardship responsibilities and other aspects of their performance.

18. A statement of activities provided by a not-for-profit organization shall focus on the organization as a whole and shall report the amount of the change in net assets for the period. It shall use a descriptive term such as *change in net assets* or *change in equity.*[5] The change in net assets should articulate to the net assets or equity reported in the statement of financial position.

Changes in Classes of Net Assets

19. A statement of activities shall report the amount of change in permanently restricted net assets, temporarily restricted net assets, and unrestricted net assets for the period. Revenues, expenses, gains, and losses increase or decrease net assets and shall be classified as provided in paragraphs 20-23. Other events, such as expirations of donor-imposed restrictions, that simultaneously increase one class of net assets and decrease another (reclassifications) shall be reported as separate items. Information about revenues, expenses, gains, losses, and reclassifications generally is provided by aggregating items that possess similar characteristics into reasonably homogeneous groups.

Classification of Revenues, Expenses, Gains, and Losses

20. A statement of activities shall report revenues as increases in unrestricted net assets unless the use of the assets received is limited by donor-imposed restrictions. For example, fees from rendering services and income from investments generally are unrestricted; however, income from donor-restricted permanent or term endowments may be donor restricted

---

[5]This Statement does not use the terms *fund balance* or *changes in fund balances* because in current practice those terms are commonly used to refer to individual groups of assets and related liabilities rather than to an entity's net assets or changes in net assets taken as a whole. Reporting by fund groups is not a necessary part of external financial reporting; however, this Statement does not preclude providing disaggregated information by fund groups.

and increase either temporarily restricted net assets or permanently restricted net assets. A statement of activities shall report expenses as decreases in unrestricted net assets.

21. Pursuant to FASB Statement No. 116, *Accounting for Contributions Received and Contributions Made,* in the absence of a donor's explicit stipulation or circumstances surrounding the receipt of the contribution that make clear the donor's implicit restriction on use, contributions are reported as unrestricted revenues or gains (**unrestricted support**), which increase unrestricted net assets. Donor-restricted contributions are reported as restricted revenues or gains (**restricted support**), which increase temporarily restricted net assets or permanently restricted net assets depending on the type of restriction. However, donor-restricted contributions whose restrictions are met in the same reporting period may be reported as unrestricted support provided that an organization reports consistently from period to period and discloses its accounting policy.

22. A statement of activities shall report gains and losses recognized on investments and other assets (or liabilities) as increases or decreases in unrestricted net assets unless their use is temporarily or permanently restricted by explicit donor stipulations or by law. For example, net gains on investment assets, to the extent recognized in financial statements, are reported as increases in unrestricted net assets unless their use is restricted to a specified purpose or future period. If the governing board determines that the relevant law requires the organization to retain permanently some portion of gains on investment assets of endowment funds, that amount shall be reported as an increase in permanently restricted net assets.

23. Classifying revenues, expenses, gains, and losses within classes of net assets does not preclude incorporating additional classifications within a statement of activities. For example, within a class or classes of changes in net assets, an organization may classify items as *operating* and nonoperating, expendable and nonexpendable, earned and unearned, recurring and nonrecurring, or in other ways. This Statement neither encourages nor discourages those further classifications. However, because terms such as *operating income, operating profit, operating surplus, operating deficit,* and *results of operations* are used with different meanings, if an intermediate measure of *operations* (for example, excess or deficit of *operating* revenues over expenses) is reported, it shall be in a financial statement that, at a minimum, reports the change in unrestricted net assets for the period. If an organization's use of the term *operations* is not apparent from the details provided on the face of the statement, a note to financial statements shall describe the nature of the reported measure of operations or the items excluded from operations.

Information about Gross Amounts of Revenues and Expenses

24. To help explain the relationships of a not-for-profit organization's ongoing major or central operations and activities, a statement of activities shall report the gross amounts of revenues and expenses. However, investment revenues may be reported net of related expenses, such as custodial fees and investment advisory fees, provided that the amount of the expenses is disclosed either on the face of the statement of activities or in notes to financial statements.

25. A statement of activities may report gains and losses as net amounts if they result from peripheral or incidental transactions or from other events and circumstances that may be largely beyond the control of the organization and its management. Information about their net amounts generally is adequate to understand the organization's activities. For example, an entity that sells land and buildings no longer needed for its ongoing activities commonly reports that transaction as a net gain or loss, rather than as gross revenues for the sales value and expense for the carrying value of the land and buildings sold. The net amount of those peripheral transactions, used with information in a statement of cash flows, usually is adequate to help assess how an entity uses its resources and how managers discharge their stewardship responsibilities.

Information about an Organization's Service Efforts

26. To help donors, creditors, and others in assessing an organization's service efforts, including the costs of its services and how it uses resources, a statement of activities or notes to financial statements shall provide information about expenses reported by their functional classification such as major classes of program services and supporting activities. Voluntary health and welfare organizations shall report that information as well as information about expenses by their natural classification, such as salaries, rent, electricity, interest expense, depreciation, awards and

grants to others, and professional fees, in a matrix format in a separate financial statement. Other not-for-profit organizations are encouraged, but not required, to provide information about expenses by their natural classification.

27. Program services are the activities that result in goods and services being distributed to beneficiaries, customers, or members that fulfill the purposes or mission for which the organization exists. Those services are the major purpose for and the major output of the organization and often relate to several major programs. For example, a large university may have programs for student instruction, research, and patient care, among others. Similarly, a health and welfare organization may have programs for health or family services, research, disaster relief, and public education, among others.[6]

28. Supporting activities are all activities of a not-for-profit organization other than program services. Generally, they include management and general, fund-raising, and membership-development activities. Management and general activities include oversight, business management, general recordkeeping, budgeting, financing, and related administrative activities, and all management and administration except for direct conduct of program services or fund-raising activities. Fund-raising activities include publicizing and conducting fund-raising campaigns; maintaining donor mailing lists; conducting special fund-raising events; preparing and distributing fund-raising manuals, instructions, and other materials; and conducting other activities involved with soliciting contributions from individuals, foundations, government agencies, and others. Membership-development activities include soliciting for prospective members and membership dues, membership relations, and similar activities.

Statement of Cash Flows

Purpose of a Statement of Cash Flows

29. The primary purpose of a statement of cash flows is to provide relevant information about the cash receipts and cash payments of an organization during a period. Statement 95 discusses how that in-

formation helps investors, creditors, and others and establishes standards for the information to be provided in a statement of cash flows of a business enterprise.

Amendments to Statement 95

30. Statement 95 is amended to extend its provisions to not-for-profit organizations as follows:

a. In the first sentence of paragraph 3, *or not-for-profit organization* is added after *business enterprise*.

b. In paragraph 3, the following is added after the first sentence:

> In this Statement *enterprise* encompasses both business enterprises and not-for-profit organizations, and the phrase *investors, creditors, and others* encompasses donors. The terms *income statement* and *net income* apply to a business enterprise; the terms *statement of activities* and *change in net assets* apply to a not-for-profit organization.

c. In paragraph 18, the following is added after *investment;*:

> receiving restricted resources that by donor stipulation must be used for long-term purposes;

d. In paragraph 19, the following is added to the end of the list:

> c. Receipts from contributions and investment income that by donor stipulation are restricted for the purposes of acquiring, constructing, or improving property, plant, equipment, or other long-lived assets or establishing or increasing a permanent endowment or term endowment.

e. In paragraph 27(b), the following footnote is added after *received*:

> *Interest and dividends that are donor restricted

---

[6]Information about an organization's major programs (or segments) can be enhanced by reporting the interrelationships of program expenses and program revenues. For example, a university might report expenses for its instruction and other academic services with related revenues from student tuition and expenses for its housing and food services with related revenues from room and board fees. Related nonmonetary information about program inputs, outputs, and results also is helpful; for example, information about applications, acceptances, admissions, enrollment and occupancy rates, and degrees granted. Generally, reporting that kind of information is feasible only in supplementary information or management explanations or by other methods of financial reporting.

for long-term purposes as noted in paragraphs 18 and 19(c) are not part of operating cash receipts.

f. In paragraphs 28, 29, and 30 and in footnote 12, the following is added after each reference to *net income*:

of a business enterprise or change in net assets of a not-for-profit organization

g. In the third sentence of paragraph 32, the following is added after *lease;*:

obtaining a building or investment asset by receiving a gift;

h. In paragraph 130, the following is added to the end of the first sentence:

of business enterprises. Appendix C of Statement No. 117, *Financial Statements of Not-for-Profit Organizations,* provides illustrations for the preparation of statements of cash flows for a not-for-profit organization.

Effective Date and Transition

31. This Statement shall be effective for annual financial statements issued for fiscal years beginning after December 15, 1994, except for organizations with less than $5 million in total assets and less than $1 million in annual expenses. For those organizations, the effective date shall be for fiscal years beginning after December 15, 1995. Earlier application is encouraged. This Statement need not be applied in financial statements for interim periods in the initial year of application, but information for those interim periods shall be reclassified if reported with annual financial statements for that fiscal year. If comparative annual financial statements are presented for earlier periods, those financial statements shall be reclassified (or restated) to reflect retroactive application of the provisions of this Statement. In the year that this Statement is first applied, the financial statements shall disclose the nature of any restatements and their effect, if any, on the change in net assets for each year presented.

The provisions of this Statement need not be applied to immaterial items.

This Statement was adopted by the unanimous vote of the seven members of the Financial Accounting Standards Board:

Dennis R. Beresford, *Chairman*	Victor H. Brown	A. Clarence Sampson
Joseph V. Anania	James J. Leisenring	Robert J. Swieringa
	Robert H. Northcutt	

Appendix A

BACKGROUND INFORMATION

32. This Statement considers and sets standards to resolve inconsistencies in financial statement display practices of not-for-profit organizations and has been coordinated with Statement 116 that considers accounting for contributions. This Statement also considers the specialized accounting and reporting principles of not-for-profit organizations that are described in the following AICPA documents:

a. *Audits of Colleges and Universities,* 1973
b. *Audits of Voluntary Health and Welfare Organizations,* 1974

c. Statement of Position 78-10, *Accounting Principles and Reporting Practices for Certain Nonprofit Organizations,* 1978
d. *Audits of Providers of Health Care Services,* 1990.

33. In March 1986, the Board added a project to its agenda to establish standards needed to resolve certain inconsistent accounting and reporting practices of not-for-profit organizations. Initially the project had two major parts: accounting for contributions and accounting for depreciation. The Board completed the depreciation part in 1987 when it issued FASB Statement No. 93, *Recognition of Depreciation by Not-for-Profit Organizations.*

34. In April 1986, with the Board's encouragement, the AICPA agreed to undertake a project to study

matters of financial statement display. The AICPA's Accounting Standards Executive Committee (AcSEC) established a Not-for-Profit Organizations Task Force to prepare a report on display issues. In December 1988, AcSEC submitted its task force's report, *Display in the Financial Statements of Not-for-Profit Organizations,* to the Board. In February 1989, the Board added financial statement display as a third part of its project to establish standards for not-for-profit organizations.

35. In August 1989, the Board issued an Invitation to Comment, *Financial Reporting by Not-for-Profit Organizations: Form and Content of Financial Statements,* that included the AICPA task force report and requested comments on issues raised by that report. It identified 26 issues, many of which included one or more subordinate issues. The Board received more than 150 written responses to the Invitation to Comment. The AICPA task force report and the responses to the issues it raised provided useful information that assisted the Board in its deliberations. The major issues and the basis for the Board's conclusions on those issues are discussed in Appendix B.

36. In October 1992, the Board issued the Exposure Draft, *Financial Statements of Not-for-Profit Organizations.* The Board received more than 280 comment letters on that Exposure Draft, and 24 organizations and individuals presented their views during a public hearing held on February 25 and 26, 1993. In November 1992, the Board also issued a related revised Exposure Draft, *Accounting for Contributions Received and Contributions Made.* Twenty organizations participated in a field test of these proposed Statements. Those organizations shared their recasted financial statements with 39 users of financial statements who also participated in this field test. The field test results, the details of which are confidential at the request of some participants, and the written comments and public hearing testimony of respondents to both proposed Statements were considered by the Board at a number of public Board meetings and at public meetings of the FASB Task Force on Accounting Issues for Not-for-Profit Organizations. That 17-member task force has provided advice on technical matters and about the priorities of the issues considered during all stages of the project.

Appendix B

BASIS FOR CONCLUSIONS

CONTENTS

Appendix B

BASIS FOR CONCLUSIONS

Introduction

37. This appendix summarizes considerations that Board members deemed significant in reaching the conclusions in this Statement. It includes reasons for accepting certain views and rejecting others. Individual Board members gave greater weight to some factors than to others.

Benefits and Costs

38. The mission of the FASB is to establish and improve standards of financial accounting and reporting for the guidance and education of the public, including issuers, auditors, and users of financial information. In fulfilling that mission the Board strives to determine that a proposed standard will fill a significant need and that the costs imposed to meet that standard, as compared with other alternatives, are justified in relation to the overall benefits of the resulting information. Because there is no common gauge by which to judge objectively the costs to implement a standard against the need to improve information in financial statements, the Board's assessment of the costs and benefits of issuing an accounting standard is unavoidably subjective. Moreover, because the costs to implement a new standard are not borne directly by those who derive the benefits of the improved reporting, the Board must balance the diverse and often conflicting needs of preparers, investors, donors, creditors, and others who use financial statements.

39. The Board's objective in issuing this Statement is to improve the relevance, understandability, and comparability of general-purpose financial statements issued by not-for-profit organizations. Those organizations currently provide financial statements that differ in their form and content. The Board believes that this Statement fills a significant need by requiring information that meets the objectives of financial reporting for not-for-profit organizations, by defining what constitutes a complete set of general-purpose financial statements for those organizations, and by requiring methods of reporting that information that are comprehensive, understandable, useful for decisions by present and potential resource providers, and consistent with the Board's conceptual framework.

40. The Board concluded that the overall benefits of the information provided by applying this Statement justify the costs that this Statement may impose. Although there will be transitional costs as not-for-profit organizations apply the requirements of this Statement, the Board believes that those organizations generally have the information systems that are needed to meet those requirements and that the ongoing costs should not be significantly greater than for existing requirements. The Board also believes that some of the costs this Statement imposes have been reduced in various ways: by limiting the provisions of this Statement to requirements that are generally no more stringent than those for business enterprises, by providing broad guidance and allowing some latitude in how information is reported in financial statements, and by extending the effective date of application of this Statement.

Framework for Considering Issues on Financial Statement Display

41. The Board's consideration about what information should be reported in financial statements provided by not-for-profit organizations and how it should be displayed benefited from initial research contained in the report of the AICPA task force, which was included in the Invitation to Comment. The issues identified in that report, as well as the comments received, provided a framework for considering the kind of information that might be required or permitted to be reported or precluded from being reported in financial statements.

42. Several respondents to the Invitation to Comment suggested that the Board focus its efforts on fundamental issues and the Board agreed. It concluded that the reporting standards in this Statement generally should focus on information that is essential in meeting the financial reporting objectives applicable to all not-for-profit organizations and should be no more stringent than requirements for business enterprises.

Objectives of General-Purpose External Financial Reporting

43. The Board reaffirms that general-purpose external financial reporting should focus on the interests of present and potential resource providers. Paragraph 9 of FASB Concepts Statement No. 4, *Objectives of Financial Reporting by Nonbusiness Organizations*, says:

> The objectives [of financial reporting by not-for-profit organizations] stem from the

common interests of those who provide resources to [not-for-profit] organizations in the services those organizations provide and their continuing ability to provide services. In contrast, the objectives of financial reporting [of business enterprises] stem from the interests of resource providers in the prospects of receiving cash as a return of and return on their investment. Despite different interests, resource providers of all entities look to information about economic resources, obligations, net resources, and changes in them for information that is useful in assessing their interests. All such resource providers focus on indicators of organization performance and information about management stewardship. [Footnote reference omitted.]

44. Thus, financial reporting by both not-for-profit organizations and business enterprises focuses on providing information that is useful to resource providers in deciding whether to provide resources to an entity. More specifically, Concepts Statement 4 says:

Financial reporting should provide information about an organization's economic resources, obligations, and net resources. That information helps resource providers and others identify the organization's financial strengths and weaknesses, evaluate information about the organization's performance during the period . . . , and assess its ability to continue to render services. [paragraph 44]

Periodic measurement of the changes in the amount and nature of the net resources of a [not-for-profit] organization and information about the service efforts and accomplishments of an organization together represent the information most useful in assessing its performance. [paragraph 47]

Financial reporting should provide information about the amounts and kinds of inflows and outflows of resources during a period. It should distinguish resource flows that change net resources, such as inflows of fees or contributions and outflows for wages and salaries, from those that do not change net resources, such as borrowings or purchases of buildings. It also should identify inflows and outflows of restricted resources. [paragraph 48]

Financial reporting should provide information about the relation between inflows and outflows of resources during a period. [paragraph 49]

Financial reporting should provide information about the service efforts of a [not-for-profit] organization. Information about service efforts should focus on how the organization's resources . . . are used in providing different programs or services. [paragraph 52]

Financial reporting should provide information about how an organization obtains and spends cash or other liquid resources, about its borrowing and repayment of borrowing, and about other factors that may affect its liquidity. [paragraph 54]

45. The objectives and capabilities of general-purpose external financial statements are limited; they do not and cannot satisfy all potential users equally well. They are useful to groups of external users, such as donors and creditors, that generally have similar needs. Regulatory bodies, such as departments of health, education, and consumer affairs, although interested in financial information, often have special-purpose needs that general-purpose financial statements cannot provide. They also have the authority to require information to meet their needs.

46. Individual financial statements also have practical limits. Generally, dissimilar information cannot be combined in a single statement without complicating the information, obscuring the statement's purpose, or both. For example, a single statement of "funds flows" might report and measure changes in economic resources of current funds as well as changes in other economic resources; however, that statement might unnecessarily confuse items of revenue with transfers from noncurrent funds or items of expense with expenditures to acquire noncurrent assets. This Statement considers whether that information is essential and should be presented in a single financial statement or in separate financial statements.

Broad Standards for Basic Information

47. Several respondents to the Invitation to Comment urged the Board to establish broad standards directed at the "critical" issues and to allow organizations sufficient latitude to report relevant information

in ways they believe are most useful to present and potential users of their financial statements. Some respondents also suggested that that approach might allow more possibility for certain not-for-profit organizations, such as hospitals and universities, to report in ways that are comparable to similar profit-making or governmental entities. The Board agreed that broad standards that allow, within certain parameters, the exercise of judgment in determining how to best communicate meaningful information have certain advantages.

48. The Board believes that this Statement's broad general standards for reporting information in financial statements provided by not-for-profit organizations represent a significant step toward improving the comparability of those financial statements. Those standards also allow for future changes in financial statement display practices to occur in the gradual, evolutionary way that has characterized past changes in practices of both business enterprises and not-for-profit organizations. The Board believes that, at this time, broad general standards are preferable to narrow prescriptive standards that could unnecessarily inhibit the evolutionary development of meaningful financial reporting. Those respondents to the Exposure Draft who commented on this matter generally supported this fundamental approach and the reporting flexibility that this Statement permits.

49. The AICPA and other respondents, including members of the FASB's task force, asked the Board to clarify whether future Guides could establish more specific guidance than the broad reporting standards established by this Statement. Paragraph 3 of this Statement indicates that within the parameters of this Statement, the AICPA or another appropriate body, following the process described in AICPA Statement on Auditing Standards (SAS) No. 69, *The Meaning of "Present Fairly in Conformity With Generally Accepted Accounting Principles" in the Independent Auditor's Report,* may provide more specific reporting guidance for certain not-for-profit organizations. SAS 69 requires that an entity adopt *cleared* AICPA Industry Audit and Accounting Guides, and *cleared* AICPA Statements of Position that become effective after March 15, 1992. As used in SAS 69, *cleared* means that the FASB has indicated that it does not object to the issuance of the proposed pronouncement.

50. A national association representing colleges and universities and other respondents also asked the Board to clarify whether existing fund accounting requirements in Chapters 3-10 of *Audits of Colleges and Universities* are superseded by this Statement. Footnote 5 to paragraph 18 clarifies that reporting by fund groups is not required or precluded for purposes of external financial reporting. However, how an organization maintains its internal accounting and recordkeeping systems is a matter outside the purview of the FASB.

Complete Set of Financial Statements

51. The Invitation to Comment asked what basic financial statements, at a minimum, should be required parts of a complete set of general-purpose external financial statements for a not-for-profit organization. Most respondents agreed with the advisory recommendation of the AICPA task force that a balance sheet (statement of financial position), a statement of changes in net assets (statement of activities), and a statement of cash flows should be required parts of a complete set of financial statements.

52. The Board agreed; it concluded that three financial statements are necessary to provide the variety of information needed to meet the financial reporting objectives of a not-for-profit organization and to report that information in ways that are both comprehensive and understandable. A statement of financial position, a statement of activities, and a statement of cash flows, used with related disclosures, provide information that is useful in assessing (a) the services an organization provides and its ability to continue to provide those services and (b) how managers discharge their stewardship responsibilities and other aspects of their performance. A majority of respondents agreed that the three basic financial statements should be required. However, some respondents to the Exposure Draft said that a statement of cash flows should not be a required part of a set of financial statements. They said that the additional information it provides may not be sufficiently useful to justify the added cost or may add confusion. However, most users of financial statements that participated in the field test found the statement of cash flows helpful or said the statement enhanced their understanding of the organization.

53. The Board concluded that the changes required by this Statement will result in greater comparability, completeness, and clarity in the financial statements issued by not-for-profit organizations, which should enhance significantly the understanding of the information provided by their financial statements. The direct beneficiaries of that information are likely to

be present and potential donors, members, and creditors of not-for-profit organizations, which include individuals, foundations, and government granting agencies. Indirectly, not-for-profit organizations and society are likely to benefit from improved information that may lead to more efficient and effective decisions about how resources are allocated. The Board believes that not-for-profit organizations generally have management information systems that provide the basic information needed to prepare a set of financial statements that conform to the provisions of this Statement and that the benefits of the information provided generally exceed the costs to provide that information.

54. The Board continues to believe that "ideally, financial reporting also should provide information about the service accomplishments of a [not-for-profit] organization" (Concepts Statement 4, paragraph 53). However, this Statement emphasizes information to be reported in financial statements. Since information about service accomplishments generally is not measurable in units of money, it cannot be included and reported in the totals of the financial statements.

Other Financial Statements

55. Some respondents to the Invitation to Comment and to the Exposure Draft said that one or more additional financial statements are necessary to report or measure other essential information. Some respondents said that a statement that reports expenses by both functional and natural classifications is necessary. Others said that a statement that reports operating revenues and expenses separate from other revenues and expenses should be required. Still others said that comparative financial statements for the prior period should be a required part of a complete set of financial statements.

Statement of Functional Expenses

56. The Board considered whether all not-for-profit organizations should provide information about expenses by (a) functional classification, (b) natural classification, (c) either functional or natural classification at the option of the organization, or (d) both functional and natural classification. It also considered whether they should provide that information in a financial statement or in notes to financial statements.

Reporting expenses by functional classification

57. The Board concluded that information about expenses by function, such as major programs or serv-

ices and major classes of supporting services, is necessary to an understanding of a not-for-profit organization's service efforts and that a set of financial statements should include that information. Requiring that information also is a step toward providing information that may be useful in associating an organization's expenses with its accomplishments. The Board concluded that information about an organization's expenses by function may be meaningfully communicated either in a statement of activities or in notes to financial statements.

58. The Board also concluded that information about the costs of significant programs or services are both relevant and measurable with sufficient reliability. Many costs are directly related to a major program or service or to a supporting activity. Some costs relate to two or more major programs and may require allocations. Techniques for allocating costs among significant programs or services are reasonably well developed; allocating costs among segments, products or services, and accounting periods are common in general-purpose accounting and reporting, managerial accounting, tax accounting, and contract accounting of all entities.

59. This Statement provides latitude for organizations to define their major programs and determine the degree of aggregation used when reporting expenses of major programs. That latitude has several advantages. Foremost, it allows organizations to report in ways that they believe are meaningful, related to their service efforts, and consistent with internal management information systems. That latitude allows organizations to use existing cost-allocation systems to provide the information necessary to comply with this Statement.

60. This Statement describes program services (paragraph 27) and supporting activities (paragraph 28) broadly. The Board believes those descriptions are consistent with functional reporting practices commonly used by most not-for-profit organizations for general-purpose reporting, regulatory filings, or sometimes both. By conforming to predominant existing practices of classification, this Statement should minimize disruption to the continuity of financial reporting by not-for-profit organizations and minimize transitional costs.

61. Some respondents to the Exposure Draft said reporting expenses by function should not be required because that would be more stringent than reporting required of business enterprises. The Board concluded, however, that this difference, which stems

from different indicators of performance of not-for-profit organizations and business enterprises, is appropriate and necessary. Paragraph 9 of Concepts Statement 4 explains that not-for-profit organizations "generally have no single indicator of performance comparable to a business enterprise's profit. Thus, other indicators of performance are usually needed." It adds that those indicators are "information about the nature of and relation between inflows and outflows of resources and information about *service efforts* and accomplishments" (emphasis added). Furthermore, the Board observes that a requirement for information about a not-for-profit organization's expenses by function is similar to standards that require information about a business enterprise's industry segments.

Reporting expenses by natural classification

62. The Board decided not to require not-for-profit organizations to provide an analysis of expenses by natural classification. Some respondents said that information about expenses by natural classification may be essential in understanding the ability of an organization to continue to provide services and about the nature of the costs of providing those services. They noted that information about relatively fixed costs, such as salaries, versus discretionary costs, such as grants to subrecipients or awards to others, can be particularly useful. The Board agrees that information about expenses by natural classification often is useful and encourages organizations to provide that information. However, it also believes that information about expenses by natural classification may not be essential in understanding the service efforts of all not-for-profit organizations or in assessing the ability of all organizations to continue to provide services.

Reporting by voluntary health and welfare organizations

63. The Board indicated in the Exposure Draft that it believes that current specialized accounting and reporting principles and practices that require certain organizations to provide information about their expenses by both functional and natural classifications are not inconsistent with the requirements of this Statement. Thus, those specialized requirements continue in effect. It also noted that not-for-profit organizations often provide that information in regulatory filings to the Internal Revenue Service and certain state agencies, which are available to the public. Nonetheless, some respondents said the status of current AICPA requirements was unclear because this Statement encourages but does not require information about expense by natural classification. Respondents who use the financial statements of voluntary health and welfare organizations and other not-for-profit organizations expressed strong concern that they might lose meaningful information that currently is available to them if the Board did not clarify the status of the statement of functional expenses.

64. This Statement requires that voluntary health and welfare organizations continue to provide a statement that reports expenses by their functional and natural classifications in a matrix format. The Board believes that requirement is appropriate to prevent the loss of information that voluntary health and welfare organizations and users of their financial statements generally have found to be useful. The Board concluded that before extending that requirement to other organizations, further study is necessary to determine whether other cost-beneficial means of reporting information useful in associating expenses with service efforts might be developed.

Operating Statement

65. Some respondents to both the Invitation to Comment and the Exposure Draft suggested that a statement of activities should be divided into two parts, a statement of "operations" and a statement of other changes in net assets. They generally suggested that the first statement would report "operating" revenues and expenses and would be accompanied by another statement that would report all other revenues, gains, expenses, and losses and the change in net assets for the organization as a whole. They said that a separate operating statement is needed with a "bottom line" different from change in net assets. However, the respondents who expressed that view differed on how to define an operating measure and on which revenues and expenses would be included in or excluded from "operations." For example, some would include in "operations" all gifts that are available for current period use, whether restricted or not. Others would exclude gifts restricted to specified operating purposes if those purposes were not met in the current period. Some would exclude from "operations" revenues, gains, or losses from nonrecurring, unexpected, or unusual events such as a very large bequest, an insurance gain on a fire loss, or an unexpected loss contingency. Others would include some or all of those items.

66. The AICPA task force also considered whether a distinction should be made between operating and

nonoperating activities and, if so, whether it should be accomplished within a statement of changes in net assets or through separate statements. In paragraph 124 of its report, the task force said that as it "tried to find a universal definition of 'operations' in a not-for-profit environment, differences in the use of that term became more apparent. In fact, it became clear that distinctions based on operations tend to be arbitrary." That observation is not limited to the not-for-profit sector. To define "operations" for business enterprises has proved equally problematic.

67. The Board decided to neither require nor preclude a not-for-profit organization from classifying its revenues, expenses, gains, and losses as operating or nonoperating within its statement of activities. Present standards neither require nor preclude a business enterprise from classifying its revenues, expenses, gains, and losses in that way, and the Board found no compelling reason to prescribe more specific display standards for not-for-profit organizations.

68. The Board believes that within the parameters of this Statement, not-for-profit organizations should have the same latitude as a business enterprise to make distinctions that they believe will provide meaningful information. Most respondents to the Exposure Draft that commented on this matter agreed that this Statement should not preclude making so-called operating or nonoperating or other distinctions within each of this Statement's required classes of net assets. A few respondents and FASB task force members suggested, however, that because terms such as *operating income, operating profit, operating surplus, operating deficit,* and *results of operations* are used with different meanings, some constraints are necessary to avoid focusing on undefined measures that may be misunderstood. The Board decided that if an intermediate measure of *operations* is reported, it should be in a financial statement that, at a minimum, reports the change in unrestricted net assets for the period. This Statement also specifies that if an organization's use of the term *operations* is not apparent from the details provided on the face of the statement, a note to financial statements should describe the nature of the reported measure of operations or

the items excluded from operations. Appendix C illustrates how an intermediate measure of operations might be presented in financial statements.

Comparative Financial Statements

69. The Invitation to Comment asked whether a complete set of financial statements should include prior-year comparative information in essentially the same form as financial statements for the current period. Most respondents agreed with the AICPA task force advisory conclusion that prior-year comparative information should be encouraged but not required and that if presented, prior-year information should comply with the minimum requirements for a set of financial statements.

70. The Board concluded that the existing standard provided by ARB No. 43, Chapter 2A, "Form of Statements—Comparative Financial Statements," which encourages but does not require comparative financial statements, is relevant to all entities. The usefulness of information about an entity increases if that information can be compared with similar information for other periods, but at times it may be impractical or impossible to provide comparative information on a fully consistent basis of accounting. For example, if a business enterprise or not-for-profit organization changes from a cash basis to an accrual basis of accounting, comparable information for periods before the change may be impossible or too expensive to obtain because of the way accounts were kept. The Board found no reason to impose a more stringent standard for reporting by not-for-profit organizations. Most respondents to the Exposure Draft agreed; others generally said that comparative financial statements should be required.

Aggregation and Classification of Information

71. The Board believes that if financial statements are to be useful, data must be simplified, condensed, and aggregated into meaningful totals.[7] Many not-for-profit organizations are complex entities with multiple program services and diverse, complex, and sometimes unpredictable sources of funding. Their transactions and events are voluminous and must be

---

[7]"It is a very fundamental principle indeed that knowledge is always gained by the *orderly* loss of information, that is, by condensing and abstracting and indexing the great buzzing confusion of information that comes from the world around us into a form which we can appreciate and comprehend" (Kenneth E. Boulding, *Economics as a Science* [New York: McGraw-Hill Book Company, 1970], 2, emphasis added).

combined and condensed to be reported in financial statements in ways that are understandable to external resource providers and others. That fact leads to a number of considerations.

Aggregated Information Focusing on an Entity

72. The Board believes that aggregated information about an entity as a whole facilitates an overall understanding of its financial position, results of its operations, and its cash flows. It concluded that reporting certain basic totals, such as total assets, liabilities, net assets, change in net assets, cash and cash equivalents, and change in cash and cash equivalents, will improve the understandability, usefulness, and completeness of financial reporting by not-for-profit organizations. It also believes that that basic information is necessary to an overall understanding of the entity's financial position, results of its operations, and its cash flows.

73. Summary amounts also are useful in assessing an entity's financial strengths and weaknesses over periods of time, and they provide a basis for further inquiry and analysis of the reasons why its net assets increased or decreased, the causes of the changes in its cash and other liquid assets, and so forth. Summary amounts also are helpful in comparing a not-for-profit organization with other organizations, including similar entities in the profit-making or governmental sectors.

74. In assessing the financial position or performance of a not-for-profit organization, however, the Board believes it is important to avoid focusing attention almost exclusively on net assets, change in net assets, total assets, or other highly simplified and aggregated amounts. For example, in Concepts Statement No. 6, *Elements of Financial Statements,* paragraph 106, the Board says, "Since donor-imposed restrictions affect the types and levels of service a not-for-profit organization can provide, whether an organization has maintained certain classes of net assets may be more significant than whether it has maintained net assets in the aggregate." Similarly, it is important to avoid focusing attention almost exclusively on "the bottom line" or other highly simplified and condensed information about business enterprises. Accordingly, this Statement requires not only summary amounts that focus on a not-for-profit organization as a whole but also information about items and components of those amounts; for example, it generally requires reporting information about the gross amounts of items of revenues and expenses and of cash receipts and cash payments.

Classification of Information

75. The Board concluded that the usefulness of information provided by financial statements of not-for-profit organizations could be vastly improved if certain basic information is classified in comparable ways. The Board decided that all not-for-profit organizations should:

a. Report assets and liabilities in reasonably homogeneous groups and sequence or classify them in ways that provide relevant information about their interrelationships, liquidity, and financial flexibility.
b. Classify and report net assets in three groups—permanently restricted, temporarily restricted, and unrestricted—based on the existence or absence of donor-imposed restrictions and the nature of those restrictions.
c. Aggregate items of revenues, expenses, gains, and losses into reasonably homogeneous groups and classify and report them as increases or decreases in permanently restricted, temporarily restricted, or unrestricted net assets.
d. Classify and report cash receipts and cash payments as resulting from investing, financing, or operating activities.

The Board concluded that those broad classifications are among the minimum requirements necessary to meet the objectives of financial reporting by not-for-profit organizations (paragraphs 43 and 44).

76. Classifying and aggregating items with similar characteristics into reasonably homogeneous groups and separating items with differing characteristics is a basic reporting practice that increases the usefulness of information. For example, cash collections of receivables from patients, students, or other service recipients may differ significantly in continuity, stability, and risk from cash collections of pledges made to a special-purpose fund-raising campaign. Classifying and reporting those receivables and collections of receivables as separate groups of assets and of cash inflows facilitates financial statement analysis aimed at objectives such as predicting amounts, timing, and uncertainty of future cash flows.

77. Perhaps the most prevalent problem in current practice is that not-for-profit organizations report their financial position and the effects of transactions, events, and circumstances that change the amount and nature of their net assets in significantly different ways. Many not-for-profit organizations report information for groups of assets and related liabilities of

four or more individual fund groups, either in several columns on a single page or in statements on separate pages. Some also include a total column or measures of total assets, liabilities, and net assets of the organization; however, many do not.

78. Although disaggregated information can be useful, differing definitions and terminology for reporting disaggregated fund groups make current financial reporting by not-for-profit organizations difficult to understand. Some organizations use internally defined fund groups that focus on measures of importance to an organization's managers rather than on the common information needs of external users of its financial statements. Other organizations focus on measures or fund groups unique to their particular industry.

79. Differing definitions and fund groups often result in financial statements with objectives or measurement focuses that are unclear, misunderstood, or both. For example, the Guide for colleges and universities explicitly says, "The statement of current funds revenues, expenditures, and other changes is a statement unique to educational and similar institutions. . . . It does not purport to present the results of operations or the net income or loss for the period as would a statement of income or a statement of revenues and expenses" (pages 55 and 56). That statement of current funds revenues, expenditures, and other changes measures the change in current funds, which is similar to a measure of change in working capital. Nonetheless, it often is said to be an "operating statement" or said to present the operating surplus, deficit, or "bottom line" for the period.

80. The Board believes this Statement's basic requirements for classifying information in financial statements will lead to more relevant, comparable, and understandable financial reporting by not-for-profit organizations. More prescriptive standards that require information to be classified in ways that go beyond the minimum requirements of this Statement may result in further improvements. However, because not-for-profit organizations are diverse and many are complex entities, the Board decided that it is best at this time to allow sufficient latitude for financial reporting practices to continue to evolve. The Board also believes that AICPA Guides and industry groups are likely, as in the past, to provide guidance to meet more specific needs for disaggregated information that may arise in practice.

Format of Financial Statements

81. The Invitation to Comment raised several questions about whether specified financial statement formats should be required, permitted, or precluded. For example, the AICPA task force suggested that information about revenues, expenses, gains, and losses for each of three classes of net assets should be allowed to be reported on a single page with no organization-wide totals for each item. That task force also suggested that a standardized format should not be required. Views of respondents to the Invitation to Comment were divided. Most would require columnar formats, although a large minority would not. Many would require totals for items of an entity's revenues, expenses, gains, and losses, but many would not. Many of those that would require or preclude particular formats are concerned that unstructured disaggregated information may obscure other essential and meaningful information.

82. Except as noted in paragraph 68, the Board decided to neither prescribe nor prohibit particular formats for a statement of financial position, a statement of activities, or a statement of cash flows, in part because similar prescriptions and proscriptions do not exist for business enterprises. The Board also concluded that standards for reporting financial information should focus on the content of financial statements, that is, on the basic information to be provided in financial statements. Most respondents to the Exposure Draft agreed. The Board expects this Statement's focus on certain basic aggregated information will place practical limits on the number of differing ways information is formatted and that those practical limits will eliminate most concerns about highly disaggregated information. The Board also expects that, as in the past, industry associations will encourage their member organizations to adopt, within the parameters of this Statement, reasonably common and preferable practices for reporting information in financial statements.

Statement of Financial Position

83. The Board concluded that a statement of financial position (balance sheet) should provide relevant information about an organization's assets, liabilities, and net assets. Information that helps resource providers and others identify the organization's financial strengths and weaknesses, evaluate its performance during the period, and assess its ability to continue to render services is relevant.

Display of Aggregated Totals

84. The Board concluded that a statement of financial position should report the aggregated totals for an organization's assets, liabilities, and net assets. These totals are helpful in assessing the interrelationship of an organization's assets and liabilities and, together with information about the components of assets, liabilities, and net assets, are necessary to an understanding of an organization's financial position. In paragraph 103 of its report, the AICPA task force explicitly recommended that the aggregated total of an organization's net assets be presented in a statement of financial position. Respondents to the Invitation to Comment generally agreed.

85. The Invitation to Comment did not ask whether not-for-profit organizations should report aggregated totals for assets and liabilities. However, the AICPA task force recommended that amounts for items of assets, liabilities, and net assets be presented as a self-balancing group of amounts in a single column, which suggests that highly aggregated totals would be presented. A single group of amounts also implies exclusion or elimination of interfund amounts that could overstate an organization's total assets and total liabilities.[8] Most respondents to the Invitation to Comment and to the Exposure Draft supported reporting assets, liabilities, and net assets in one self-balancing group of amounts in a single column.

86. This Statement emphasizes the need for information about both aggregated totals for assets, liabilities, and net assets and about reasonably homogeneous groups of items of assets and liabilities. Because the Board decided not to emphasize or preclude specific statement formats, this Statement permits a left-to-right or top-to-bottom "balanced" format as well as single-column, multicolumn, single-page, or multipage formats. The Board believes that the provisions of this Statement applied with other generally accepted accounting principles will provide relevant information about the amounts and nature of differing kinds of assets and liabilities, either through disclosures in a statement of financial position or in accompanying notes to financial statements.

Classification of Assets and Liabilities

87. The Invitation to Comment asked whether not-for-profit organizations should classify items of assets and liabilities as current or long-term or should use another classification method, such as nearness to cash, to provide information about liquidity. The AICPA task force recommended that not-for-profit organizations be required to either provide a classified statement of financial position (current and noncurrent assets and liabilities) or highlight illiquid assets by displaying in the net asset section the amount of the entity's fixed assets less related liabilities (sometimes called the *net investment in plant* or *net equity invested in property, plant, and equipment*). A significant majority of respondents disagreed with that recommendation. Some respondents said that the requirements should be more permissive, but many others said that they should be more prescriptive. For example, many agreed that a classified statement of financial position should be permitted but they would not require that or the alternative breakout of the net asset section. Many others said a classified statement should be required. Others said that a nearness to cash method of classification should be required.

88. The Board concluded that reporting the net equity invested in property, plant, and equipment within the net asset section is not a substitute for arranging or classifying items of assets and liabilities in ways that provide information about liquidity. The Board believes that essential information about liquidity and an organization's financial flexibility can be provided either by classifying assets and liabilities as current and noncurrent or by sequencing assets according to their nearness of conversion to cash and liabilities according to the nearness of their maturity and resulting use of cash. Each method has advantages and practical limitations.

---

[8]This Statement does not preclude display of interfund items in a statement of financial position; rather, its requirement to display total assets and liabilities results in certain practical limits on how interfund items are displayed in a financial statement. For example, because receivables and payables between fund groups are not organizational assets or liabilities, a statement of financial position must clearly label and arrange those interfund items to eliminate their amounts when displaying total assets or liabilities.

89. Classifying assets and liabilities as current and noncurrent, although not required by generally accepted accounting principles, is a common reporting practice of both business enterprises and not-for-profit organizations. As others have noted,[9] this classification alone generally does not provide users of financial statements with the liquidity information they need. Thus, other disclosures must be added to the financial statement or notes to financial statements. More recently, financial reporting has emphasized information about changes in cash and cash equivalents, and that new emphasis obviates the need for a rigid requirement to classify and report amounts of current assets and current liabilities.

90. For many small or less-complex organizations, grouping homogeneous items of assets and liabilities and sequencing them according to nearness of cash or maturity is sufficient. Further distinctions at higher degrees of aggregation, such as current and noncurrent assets and liabilities, generally would be unnecessary. Board members also noted that since the issuance of FASB Statement No. 94, *Consolidation of All Majority-Owned Subsidiaries*, many entities have been experimenting with differing degrees of aggregating and displaying information about their assets and liabilities. They believe that at this time it is best to avoid prescriptive standards that might stand in the way of those evolving reporting practices.

91. Some relevant information about the liquidity or maturity of assets and liabilities cannot be adequately communicated solely by classification methods, such as current and noncurrent, or by sequencing information in financial statements. This Statement and generally accepted accounting principles provide latitude, in those circumstances, to disclose information in notes to financial statements. For example, organizations that receive significant amounts of multiyear pledges or that finance their cash needs by borrowing long term generally must use notes to their statements to provide information about expected cash inflows from receivables or expected cash outflows to satisfy long-term borrowings. The Board decided that to report relevant information about liquidity and the interrelationship of assets and liabilities, not-for-profit organizations should have latitude to select classification methods, levels of aggregation, and disclosure techniques that are most meaningful and practical for their circumstances.

92. The Board also considered whether more specific standards are necessary to provide information about the nature and amount of donor-imposed restrictions on the use of contributed assets. A majority of respondents to the Invitation to Comment agreed with the AICPA task force advisory recommendation that not-for-profit organizations be permitted but not required to disaggregate and report assets and liabilities by their related classes of net assets. Respondents that disagreed were divided. Some would preclude that kind of disaggregation and others would require it. A few respondents to the Invitation to Comment and to the Exposure Draft said restrictions on gifts that create permanent endowments or that require acquisition of land, buildings, and other long-lived assets differ significantly from other donor restrictions and that those assets must be reported in a separate statement of financial position.

93. Donor-imposed restrictions may influence the liquidity or cash flow patterns of certain assets and that kind of information may be helpful in assessing the financial flexibility of a not-for-profit organization. For example, a donor stipulation that donated cash be used to acquire land and buildings limits an organization's ability to take effective actions to respond to unexpected opportunities or needs, such as emergency disaster relief. On the other hand, some donor-imposed restrictions have little or no influence on cash flow patterns or an organization's financial flexibility. For example, a gift of cash with a donor stipulation that it be used for emergency-relief efforts has a negligible impact on an organization if emergency relief is one of its major ongoing programs.

94. The Board decided to permit but not require not-for-profit organizations to disaggregate and report assets and liabilities by donor-restricted and unrestricted classes or fund groups. It believes that not-for-profit organizations generally can provide relevant information about liquidity and financial flexibility by aggregating assets and liabilities into reasonably homogeneous groups that include the effects of donor-imposed restrictions as well as other contractual restrictions. Classifying and labeling assets in ways that include the effects of restrictions on

---

[9]"New business practices, new methods of financing, and new methods of accounting have resulted in balance sheet accounts that defy classification as current or noncurrent.

"Perhaps one of the most significant changes that has occurred is the change in attitudes toward disclosure of financial information. Financial statement users demand, and companies are willing to disclose, much more detailed information about their financial affairs in supporting schedules and notes to financial statements than at the time accountants began to classify assets and liabilities as current or noncurrent" (Loyd C. Heath, Accounting Research Monograph 3, *Financial Reporting and the Evaluation of Solvency* [New York, AICPA, 1978], 74).

liquidity is a long-established practice. For example, cash and claims to cash restricted as to withdrawal or use for other than current operations, whether actually set aside in a special account or not, are excluded from current assets of a business enterprise. Similarly, amounts of cash restricted to a permanent endowment should be excluded from aggregated amounts of cash and cash equivalents for current operations of a not-for-profit organization because they are not homogeneous items.

Classification of Net Assets

95. The Invitation to Comment asked if not-for-profit organizations should report amounts for classes of net assets and, if so, how they should label those amounts. The AICPA task force recommended that not-for-profit organizations report three classes of net assets (or equity)—unrestricted, temporarily restricted, and permanently restricted—as defined by Concepts Statement 6. It also said organizations should use those terms in their financial statements. Respondents generally agreed with the first recommendation; however, views differed about how to label the three classes of net assets.

96. The Board concluded that information about the effects of donor-imposed restrictions on net assets is relevant to users of financial statements of not-for-profit organizations. Donors' restrictions impose special responsibilities on management of an organization to ensure that it uses donated assets as stipulated. Because they also place limits on the use of resources, donors' restrictions may impinge upon an organization's performance and its ability to provide a satisfactory level of services. Information about how managers discharge their stewardship responsibilities for donor-restricted resources also is useful in assessing an organization's performance.

97. Although respondents to the Invitation to Comment generally supported requiring a minimum of three classes of net assets, the Board also considered whether fewer or more classes of net assets would be appropriate. For example, the Board considered whether reporting unrestricted net assets and donor-restricted net assets would suffice. The Board also considered the present practices of not-for-profit organizations that provide disaggregated information through the use of several fund groups. The Board believes that aggregation in financial statements at a level higher than that commonly found in practice would improve financial reporting by not-for-profit organizations and an understanding of the financial

position of those organizations. Important details about differing kinds of donor-restricted classes of net assets also can be provided in notes to financial statements.

98. The Board concluded that consistent with Concepts Statement 6, information about a minimum of three classes of net assets, based on the presence or absence of donor-imposed restrictions and their nature, generally is necessary to gain an adequate understanding of the financial position of a not-for-profit organization, including its financial flexibility and ability to continue to render services. Information about permanent restrictions is useful in determining the extent to which an organization's net assets are not a source of cash for payments to present or prospective lenders, suppliers, or employees and thus are not expected to be directly available for providing services or paying creditors. Information about the extent of unrestricted net assets and of temporarily restricted net assets is useful in assessing an organization's ability and limitations on its ability to allocate resources to provide services or particular kinds of services or to make cash payments to creditors in the future. The Board believes that aggregated information about the three component parts of an organization's net assets is especially important to both donors and creditors and that that information is best provided by display of their amounts in a statement of financial position. Most respondents to the Exposure Draft expressed similar views; others said that amounts for fund balances should be required for fund groups, such as operating, plant, endowment, and other funds.

99. The Board also considered comments raised about how to label the three classes of net assets. Several representatives of health care providers said that single equity line items, identified as unrestricted, temporarily restricted, and permanently restricted are sufficient but that specific terms should not be required. Other respondents said organizations should have sufficient latitude to use other terms, such as unrestricted fund balance, temporarily restricted fund balance, and permanently restricted fund balance.

100. The Board concluded that while definitions are necessary to make the distinctions required by this Statement, stringent requirements to use specific terms are not necessary to faithfully represent those distinctions. As illustrated in Appendix C, this Statement encourages the use of the terms unrestricted, temporarily restricted, and permanently restricted net assets; however, the Board knows that other labels

exist. For example, *equity* may be used for net assets, and *other* or *not donor-restricted* may be used with care to distinguish unrestricted net assets from the temporarily and permanently restricted classes of net assets. For example, the net asset section might be arranged as follows:

Donor restricted:		
Permanently	$XXX	
Temporarily	XXX	
Other:		
Designated by the Board		
for [*purpose*]	$XXX	
Undesignated	XXX	XXX
Net assets		$XXX

At a minimum, the amounts for each of the three classes of net assets and the total of net assets must be reported in a statement of financial position and the captions used to describe those amounts must correspond with their meanings, as defined by this Statement. A few respondents to the Exposure Draft suggested that organizations should be required to report separate amounts of unrestricted net assets designated by the governing board for long-term investment or for investment in plant. The Board concluded that those disclosures are not essential and that organizations should be permitted but not required to provide those or other disclosures on the face of financial statements or in notes to financial statements.

Disclosures about Composition of Assets in Accordance with Donor Restrictions

101. The Invitation to Comment asked whether an organization that does not maintain an appropriate composition of assets (usually cash and marketable securities) in amounts needed to comply with all donor restrictions should report that noncompliance. It also asked if that reporting should be accomplished by (a) explicit disclosure in notes to financial statements, (b) displaying self-balancing fund groups for each significant type of donor restriction, or (c) other means. The AICPA task force recommended that if an organization does not maintain an appropriate composition of assets in amounts needed to comply with all donor restrictions, the amounts and circumstances involved should be disclosed. Respondents to the Invitation to Comment generally agreed; however, some respondents suggested that existing ac-

counting and auditing standards adequately address this matter.

102. In their May 7, 1992 letter responding to a request of the FASB about the adequacy of existing accounting and auditing standards, the AICPA's Not-for-Profit Organizations Committee and Not-for-Profit Organizations Guide Task Force said:

> We believe [FASB Statement No. 5, *Accounting for Contingencies,* AICPA Statements on Auditing Standards No. 47, *Audit Risk and Materiality in Conducting an Audit,* and No. 54, *Illegal Acts by Clients*] require that noncompliance with donor-imposed restrictions be disclosed if there is a reasonable possibility that a material contingent liability has been incurred at the date of the financial statements or there is at least a reasonable possibility that the noncompliance could lead to a material loss of revenue, or can cause an entity not to be able to continue as a going concern.

They also said that existing AICPA Guides for not-for-profit organizations provide relevant guidance and they will consider developing further guidance as part of a Guide revision project to be completed after the FASB issues this Statement. Accordingly, the Board concluded that this Statement, which emphasizes how and what information to provide in financial statements, need not explicitly consider this matter of compliance and related disclosure issues raised by the Invitation to Comment.

Statement of Activities

103. The Board concluded that a statement of activities should provide relevant information about the effects of transactions and other events and circumstances that change the amount and nature of an organization's net assets. This Statement affirms that information about revenues, expenses, gains, and losses is relevant and emphasizes four measures of their effects—change in the amount of an organization's net assets and change in the amounts of an organization's permanently restricted net assets, temporarily restricted net assets, and unrestricted net assets. The Board believes those measures together with information about their components are essential to resource providers and others in evaluating an organization's performance during the period. Respondents to the Exposure Draft generally agreed.

Display of Aggregated Totals

104. The Invitation to Comment requested comments about the appropriate level of aggregation or disaggregation in reporting the amounts for items of revenues, expenses, gains, and losses, and the change in net assets. Several interrelated questions asked whether certain disaggregated information and certain aggregated totals about those items should be required or permitted to be reported or precluded from being reported in a statement of changes in net assets (statement of activities). It also raised several questions about how to format those items in a statement of changes in net assets.

105. In paragraph 225 of its report, the AICPA task force said that among other things it "believes that the statement of changes in net assets should . . . include . . . revenues, expenses, gains, and losses and their components classified into the appropriate class of net assets—permanently restricted, temporarily restricted, and unrestricted [and] the change for the period in each of the three classes of net assets. . . ." In paragraph 226 the task force also said that "a total for each element [revenues, expenses, gains, and losses] should not be required to be displayed" and it summarized more specifically the ways it believes the content of a statement of changes in net assets should be presented, including how specific line items should be sequenced and how statements should be formatted, to best achieve the objectives of financial reporting by not-for-profit organizations. The Board decided that at this time it would be preferable to focus on requirements for reporting certain basic and essential information by all not-for-profit organizations rather than how specific line items are sequenced or how statements are formatted.

Change in net assets and change in classes of net assets

106. The AICPA task force recommended that a statement of changes in net assets include measures of change in permanently restricted net assets, change in temporarily restricted net assets, and change in unrestricted net assets. The task force was divided on whether change in net assets for the organization as a whole should be displayed; the majority of its members said display of that measure should be permitted and a significant minority said it should be required. A majority of respondents supported the AICPA recommendation to classify revenues, expenses, gains, and losses and their components into permanently restricted, temporarily

restricted, and unrestricted net assets and report the change for each of the three classes of net assets. Some respondents who disagreed would require totals for the activity of the organization as a whole or would classify revenues, expenses, gains, and losses in other ways, such as by an "operating" and nonoperating classification or by "managed fund groups" as defined by the organization.

107. The Board concluded that not-for-profit organizations should report the amounts for the change in net assets for the organization as a whole and the change in permanently restricted net assets, temporarily restricted net assets, and unrestricted net assets. The Board concluded that those four measures of the effects of revenues, expenses, and other transactions, events, and circumstances are necessary to evaluate an organization's performance during the period and they are useful in assessing its ability to continue to render services. This Statement also affirms the conclusions in paragraphs 9 and 47 of Concepts Statement 4 that not-for-profit organizations "generally have no single indicator of performance comparable to a business enterprise's profit" and that "periodic measurement of the changes in the amount and nature of the net resources of a [not-for-profit] organization and information about the service efforts and accomplishments of an organization together represent the information most useful in assessing its performance."

108. Measures of the change in an organization's net assets and its classes of net assets are useful individually and collectively. Paragraphs 103-106 of Concepts Statement 6 explain that a measure of the amount of periodic change in net assets is useful in assessing whether an organization is maintaining its net assets, drawing upon resources received in past periods, or adding resources that can be used to support future periods. That measure provides information useful in assessing an organization's overall ability to continue to provide satisfactory levels of services. Periodic measures of change in net assets are also useful in assessing trends over time.

109. Moreover, not-for-profit organizations receive significant amounts of contributed resources and because donor-imposed restrictions often affect the types and level of service they can provide, information about changes in the nature of net assets of not-for-profit organizations is useful, particularly in assessing their ability to respond to short-term needs for differing types or higher levels of services. For example, if an organization maintained its net assets

solely because it received a significant permanently restricted endowment contribution that made up for a significant decrease in unrestricted net assets, measures of the change in the permanently restricted and unrestricted classes of net assets would be informative in assessing the organization's long-run and short-run ability to provide comparable types or levels of services in the future. Similarly, if the organization received significant restricted contributions in response to a building campaign, a measure of the change in the temporarily restricted class of net assets may be useful in assessing the extent to which the organization maintained the part of net assets that is restricted to specific uses and is not fully available to support services of the next period. While each of the four required measures provide useful information, because of their interrelationships, they also provide information by complementing each other.

110. Furthermore, the Board believes that requiring not-for-profit organizations to distinguish between transactions and other events without donor-imposed restrictions and those with temporary or permanent restrictions imposes no more stringent standards on those organizations than exist for business enterprises. Rather, the distinctions required of not-for-profit organizations and of business enterprises reflect differences in their characteristics and objectives of financial reporting. Business enterprises must distinguish between owner and nonowner transactions that change their net assets, a distinction that generally is not relevant to not-for-profit organizations, and not-for-profit organizations must distinguish between transactions without donor-imposed restrictions and those with permanent and temporary restrictions, a distinction that generally is not relevant to business enterprises.

A measure of "operating income" or similar measures

111. As discussed in paragraphs 65-68, the Board also considered whether to require distinctions between "operating" revenues, expenses, gains, and losses and other transactions that change an organization's net assets. Some respondents to the Invitation to Comment and to the Exposure Draft said that there is a strong need for a measure of how an organization is managing or maintaining the resources available for its "operations" or its "current operations." Others characterized that as a need for a measure similar to a business enterprise's "net income," "operating income," or "income from continuing operations." A

few others said that unusually large gifts should be classified as nonoperating revenues or capital contributions if the organization's governing board designates those gifts for long-term investment. However, most respondents to the Exposure Draft suggested that the Board not define or proscribe a so-called operating measure for all or specific types of not-for-profit organizations.

112. The Board believes that change in unrestricted net assets, which measures whether an organization has maintained the part of its net assets that is fully available to support services in the next period, may serve as an *operating measure* as that term is used by some respondents. The Board also believes that this Statement provides ample latitude to sequence items of revenues and expenses in ways that permit organizations to report subtotals similar to other respondents' descriptions of "operating income" or "current operating income." Thus, this Statement should not inhibit an evolution toward reporting the so-called operating measure if all or certain kinds of not-for-profit organizations or industries find that measure desirable for their specific circumstances.

113. The Board also considered whether to preclude or limit the use of terms such as *operating income* or *operating surplus or deficit.* Some FASB task force members and others said that this Statement allows too much flexibility and that the term *operating income* may be used inconsistently. They suggested specifying that if an *operating* label is used, it should only be used for the measure of unrestricted net assets as defined by this Statement or for an intermediate component of unrestricted net assets that excludes a few specified items, such as extraordinary items, the effects of discontinued operations, the cumulative effect of accounting changes, and perhaps certain gains and losses on investment assets.

114. The Board concluded that there is no compelling reason to prescribe the display of another measure similar to but not identical to a measure of change in unrestricted net assets. The Board observes that generally accepted accounting principles and the application of paragraph 7 of this Statement require display of an appropriately labeled subtotal for change in a class of net assets before the effects of an extraordinary item, the discontinuance of an operating segment, or an accounting change. For example, using the columnar Format B in Appendix C, a statement of activities would report the effects of an extraordinary item as follows:

	Unrestricted	Temporarily Restricted	Permanently Restricted	Total
Change in net assets before extraordinary items	$11,558	$(1,128)	$5,020	$15,450
Extraordinary items (Note X)	xxx	xxx	xxx	xxx
Change in net assets	$xx,xxx	$(x,xxx)	$x,xxx	$xx,xxx

Because generally accepted accounting principles require that these captions be modified appropriately when an organization reports the cumulative effect of an accounting change or the effects of disposal of a segment of its operations that may affect any one or more classes of its net assets, there is no need for this Statement to require the use of a specific label for the unrestricted or any one class of net assets. That would impose a standard more stringent than those that exist for business enterprises. The results of the Board's field test revealed that about half of the participants chose to report an intermediate measure of operations; however, they differed significantly in how they defined and described that measure. In its redeliberations of the Exposure Draft, the Board decided to add the disclosure and reporting requirements of paragraph 23 of this Statement.

115. The Board also reaffirmed its decision not to prescribe, at this time, whether to report gains and losses from investments in a particular sequence, in an intermediate measure of net assets, or as a specified component of change in net assets. The Board intends to consider the issue of accounting for investments by not-for-profit organizations, including how to measure investment assets and whether to recognize unrealized gains and losses, in a subsequent part of its project on not-for-profit organizations. The Board considered similar accounting and reporting issues for business enterprises in Statement No. 115, *Accounting for Certain Investments in Debt and Equity Securities.*

Totals for revenues, expenses, gains, and losses

116. The AICPA task force recommended that organizations be permitted but not required to display totals for the aggregated amounts of their revenues, expenses, gains, or losses. Most respondents to the Invitation to Comment agreed with that recommendation; almost all of the respondents that disagreed with that recommendation would require display of those totals. The Board concluded that totals for each element are not essential. That requirement would be more stringent than display requirements for business enterprises and could inhibit meaningful financial reporting by not-for-profit organizations. The Board believes that the measures of change in net assets and classes of net assets required by this Statement provide the necessary and relevant aggregated information about the effects of a not-for-profit organization's revenues, expenses, gains, and losses.

117. The Invitation to Comment also asked if the activity for the three classes of net assets is reported separately, whether organization-wide totals should be required for each line item of revenues, expenses, gains, and losses. Almost half of the respondents to the Invitation to Comment would require those totals; others were nearly evenly divided between precluding and permitting totals.

118. The Board concluded, and most respondents to the Exposure Draft agreed, that organization-wide totals are not necessary for individual line items of revenues, expenses, gains, or losses. It believes information about reasonably homogeneous components of revenues, such as unrestricted contributions available to support current expenses and restricted contributions to be used to acquire land and buildings, generally is more meaningful than the aggregated total of those components. Disaggregated information that permits users of financial information to relate components of revenues to components of expenses also is often preferable to information provided by their aggregated amounts. For example, information that permits analysis of the levels of revenues from tuition in relation to expenses for instruction and other academic services and of revenues from room and board fees in relation to expenses for housing and food services generally is more meaningful than totals of aggregated items of revenues, such as student tuition and fees, or aggregated items of expenses, such as salaries, heat, electricity, or supplies. The Board believes that those who prepare financial statements generally are best able to make judgments about the extent to which financial statements or notes to financial statements should provide disaggregated information about various items of revenues or expenses and that this Statement need not limit those judgments.

Classification of Items as Donor Restricted or Unrestricted

119. This Statement generally specifies reporting an item of revenue, expense, gain, or loss as an increase or decrease in unrestricted net assets unless the use of the asset received is limited by donor-imposed restrictions. That provision is consistent with and stems from decisions reached in Statement 116, which establishes the standards for recognizing, measuring, and classifying contributions received. Paragraph 21 of this Statement describes the basic guidance for classifying donor-restricted and unrestricted contributions. Paragraphs 120-137 discuss considerations about two classification issues that were raised by the Invitation to Comment: classifying net appreciation on endowments and classifying expenses.

Classification of net appreciation on investments of donor-restricted endowments

120. The Invitation to Comment requested comments about the classification of net appreciation on investments of donor-restricted endowments. It asked whether not-for-profit organizations should initially display gains and losses as permanently restricted or initially display net appreciation in excess of original principal as unrestricted or temporarily restricted, depending on the purposes and uses specified by the donor.

121. In paragraph 187 of its report, the AICPA task force recommended that "gains and losses on investments of permanently restricted net assets should be displayed initially as permanently restricted, and the amount of net gains available for use by the organization should be disclosed in the notes to the financial statements." It also said, "To the extent that accumulated net gains are appropriated for use by the organization in accordance with the law, such amounts should be displayed as capital reclassifications." Most respondents to the Invitation to Comment agreed with the recommendation for initial display and disclosure, but some of those respondents and others said certain amounts subsequently appropriated by the organization's governing board are "operating reclassifications" rather than "capital reclassifications."

122. Respondents who disagreed with the AICPA recommendation to initially display net gains as permanently restricted challenged the appropriateness of that classification and necessity for a subsequent reclassification. Those respondents generally said that

if net gains are available for use by the organization, those gains are not permanently restricted and classifying those gains as permanently restricted would be misleading. The Board agreed and concluded that there is no need to delay recognizing available net gains in unrestricted or temporarily restricted net assets until such time as the organization's governing board acts to appropriate them for use. Decisions about when to spend resources generally do not bear on the issue, which is whether the resources are available for spending.

123. The Board concluded that not-for-profit organizations should classify gains and losses on permanent endowments consistent with the Board's fundamental conclusions for contributions received. That is, restricted net assets result only from a donor's stipulation that limits the organization's use of net assets or from a law that extends the donor's stipulation to enhancements (including holding gains) and diminishments of those net assets.

124. The Board believes that there is general agreement that, for example, if a donor stipulates that net gains be added to the principal of its gift until that endowed gift plus accumulated gains increases to a specified dollar level, the gains are permanently restricted. Support for that view also exists in the comments to Section 3 of the Uniform Management of Institutional Funds Act (Uniform Act), which since its development in 1972 has been adopted in varying forms in at least 29 states and the District of Columbia. The Uniform Act says, "If a gift instrument expresses or otherwise indicates the donor's intention that the governing board may not appropriate the net appreciation in the value of the fund, his wishes will govern." Section 3 also prohibits implying a restriction on the expenditure of net appreciation from a common set of words often used in gift instruments:

> A restriction upon the expenditure of net appreciation may not be implied from a designation of a gift as an endowment, or from a direction or authorization in the applicable gift instrument to use only "income," "interest," "dividends," or "rents, issues or profits," or "to preserve the principal intact," or a direction which contains other words of similar import.

125. The Board believes that the relevant issue is one of fact. Do donor-imposed restrictions exist that preclude the use of gains and losses (net appreciation) on permanent endowments, either as a result of

explicit or clear implicit donor stipulations or by law? The Board believes that because donor stipulations and laws vary, not-for-profit organizations must assess the relevant facts and circumstances for their endowment gifts and their relevant laws to determine if net appreciation on endowments is available for spending or is permanently restricted.

126. Some business officers of colleges and universities have expressed strong concern that institutions in the same state will interpret the state laws differently. They attribute that concern to differing interpretations about the provisions of the Uniform Act, particularly those of Section 2, "Appropriation of Appreciation," and Section 6, "Standard of Conduct." The Board considered that concern and it specifically considered the Uniform Act. Sections 2 and 6 of the Uniform Act provide that:

> The governing board may appropriate for expenditure for the uses and purposes for which an endowment fund is established so much of the net appreciation, realized and unrealized, in the fair value of the assets of an endowment fund over the historic dollar value of the fund as is prudent under the standard established by Section 6.
>
> In the administration of the powers to appropriate appreciation, . . . members of a governing board shall exercise ordinary business care and prudence under the facts and circumstances prevailing at the time of the action or decision. In so doing they shall consider long and short term needs of the institution in carrying out its educational, religious, charitable, or other eleemosynary purposes, its present and anticipated financial requirements, expected total return on its investments, price level trends, and general economic conditions.

127. Interpretations differ about the extent to which, if at all, the standard of ordinary business care and prudence precludes an institution's use of net appreciation. Some constituents believe that the Uniform Act supports the traditional view that gains on investments of endowments are not expendable unless the governing board makes an affirmative judgment that it is prudent to spend those gains. Others, including Board members, believe that the responsibility to exercise ordinary business care and prudence in determining whether to spend net appreciation is similar to the fiduciary responsibilities that exist for all charitable resources under an organization's control. That

latter view is consistent with page 5 of the Prefatory Note to the Uniform Act, which says:

> The Uniform Act authorizes expenditure of appreciation subject to a standard of business care and prudence. It seems unwise to fix more exact standards in a statute. To impose a greater constriction would hamper adaptation by different institutions to their particular needs.
>
> The standard of care is that of a reasonable and prudent director of a nonprofit corporation—similar to that of a director of a business corporation—which seems more appropriate than the traditional Prudent Man Rule applicable to private trustees. . . .

128. Some states have adopted modified forms of the Uniform Act and in some cases those modifications may be substantive and relevant to the classification of net gains. For example, at least one state (Rhode Island) provides that the "historic dollar value" of an endowment fund, as defined in the Uniform Act, shall be adjusted to reflect the change, if any, in the purchasing power of the historic dollar value of the fund. This modification is substantive because it requires changes to the measure of the original historic dollar value. Thus, the portion of net appreciation in excess of the original historic dollar value that is necessary to cover the purchasing power adjustments must be retained and, considering past economic history and prospects for continued inflation, interpreting and classifying that amount as permanently restricted would be a fair representation. Most states, however, have not adopted explicit provisions that fix more exacting standards or impose a greater constriction than the standard of ordinary business care and prudence quoted above.

129. The Board concluded that a definitive interpretation of the Uniform Act is not necessary or critical to the issue. The Board decided that this Statement should require reporting of gains and losses on endowments that faithfully represents the relevant facts and circumstances. Accordingly, the Board concluded that if the law of the relevant jurisdiction, as interpreted by an organization's governing board, places permanent restrictions on some part of the net appreciation, that amount should be reported as permanently restricted net assets in the organization's financial statements. In the absence of such a law or a donor's explicit or clear implicit permanent restriction, net appreciation should be reported as unrestricted if the endowment's income is unrestricted or

temporarily restricted if the endowment's income is temporarily restricted by the donor.

130. The Board also concluded that to implement the provisions of this Statement, latitude for interpretation by an institution's governing board is necessary for both conceptual and practical reasons, especially for institutions in Uniform Act states. Section 1(5) of the Uniform Act defines the "historic dollar value" of an endowment fund and includes comments that provide additional guidance. It also provides that "the determination of historic dollar value made in good faith by the institution is conclusive." Accordingly, the Board believes that it is appropriate that this Statement provide that net appreciation be classified in accordance with those conclusive good-faith determinations made by an institution's governing board.

131. Respondents to the Exposure Draft that commented on the provisions of paragraph 22 of this Statement expressed differing views; although most agreed, many continue to believe that the Uniform Act requires retention of some gains or that interpretations of the Uniform Act will be inconsistent. At this time, the Board has no reason to believe that governing boards will interpret similar facts and circumstances, including state statutes, in significantly differing ways. Rather, the Board believes that ample opportunities exist for the directors and officers of colleges, universities, museums, and other organizations to avoid that perceived problem. Consultations with others, including corporate counsel, outside auditors, industry associations, attorneys general, state societies of CPAs, and other institutions generally result in common understandings and conclusions about matters of state and local law.

132. Some respondents raised questions about reporting losses on investments and requested guidance for display if the law requires repatriation from unrestricted assets of previously appropriated earnings. Their questions generally relate to specific facts and circumstances and the display generally would follow from the requirements, if any, of the relevant laws. The Board plans to consider those and other issues of accounting for investments in a subsequent part of its project on not-for-profit organizations.

Classification of expenses as unrestricted

133. The Invitation to Comment asked whether all expenses should be classified as decreases in unrestricted net assets or, if not, whether expenses financed by restricted resources should be reported as decreases in the permanently or temporarily restricted class of net assets. The AICPA task force recommended that all expenses be shown in the unrestricted class of net assets. Paragraph 193 of its report said, "Some members believe all expenses should be presented in the unrestricted [class of net assets] because expenses are the using up of resources, causing any restrictions related to them to expire." The task force also noted that a reclassification of resources from temporarily restricted net assets to unrestricted net assets could be presented when restricted resources are used to finance expenses of a restricted grant.

134. Respondents to the Invitation to Comment expressed mixed views. Although many agreed with the AICPA task force advisory recommendation, most did not. Those who disagreed generally said that (a) the related reclassifications are confusing and that a direct decrease to temporarily restricted net assets is easy to understand, (b) the revenues and expenses relate to each other and should be presented together, or (c) certain specific exceptions should be allowed.

135. The Board concluded that not-for-profit organizations should report expenses as decreases in unrestricted net assets. Identifying or designating sources of donor-restricted revenues to be used to finance specific expenses does not make an expense donor restricted. Rather, expenses result from the decisions of an organization's managers about the activities to be carried out and about how and when particular resources are to be used. The Board believes that the perceived confusion about reclassifications can be avoided by appropriate labeling in financial statements and by reporting those items separately and in reasonably homogeneous groups as required by paragraph 19.

136. Further, although some respondents to the Invitation to Comment and the Exposure Draft said reporting certain expenses as a decrease in the restricted class of net assets is simpler or more understandable, the Board believes that reporting has disadvantages that outweigh the perceived simplicity. Because expenses often occur months or years after the related restricted support is received and recognized in financial statements, reporting an expense in the restricted class of net assets would not necessarily achieve the "match" of revenues and expenses that some respondents desire. Moreover, reporting current period expenses in the temporarily restricted

class of net assets with restricted support for gifts restricted for use in a future period may cause greater confusion, particularly for those users of financial statements that believe revenues and expenses of a period are necessarily directly related to each other.

137. A few respondents to the Exposure Draft said that certain information currently available to them may be lost if all expenses are reported in the unrestricted class of net assets. Generally, they expressed concern that the extent to which an organization's expenses are dependent on restricted contributions may no longer be clear from its financial statements. The Board believes those concerns generally are satisfied by this Statement's requirements to distinguish between donor-restricted and unrestricted revenues and gains and present those and other items in reasonably homogeneous groups.

Reporting Gross Amounts of Revenues for Special Events

138. Paragraph 24 of this Statement requires reporting of gross amounts of revenues and expenses. The Board concluded that information about those amounts is essential to "provide information about the amounts and kinds of inflows and outflows of resources during a period" (Concepts Statement 4, paragraph 48). That information is helpful to users of financial statements in understanding and assessing an organization's ongoing major or central operations and activities. A few respondents to the Exposure Draft said that the current practice of netting the revenues and direct costs of *special events* should be permitted. As paragraph 25 explains, organizations may report net amounts for their special events if they result from peripheral or incidental transactions. However, so-called special events often are ongoing and major activities; if so, organizations should report the gross revenues and expenses of those activities.

Statement of Cash Flows

139. The Board concluded that a statement of cash flows should provide relevant information about the cash receipts and cash payments of an organization during a period. Statement 95 established standards for the information to be provided in a statement of cash flows of a business enterprise. Paragraph 69 of Statement 95 says the "exclusion of not-for-profit organizations from the scope of [Statement 95] means only that the Board has not yet decided whether not-for-profit organizations should be re-

quired to provide a statement of cash flows." The Board concluded, in this Statement, that the provisions of Statement 95 generally are applicable to not-for-profit organizations.

140. The Invitation to Comment requested comments on provisions of Statement 95 and whether to apply or amend those provisions to make them applicable to not-for-profit organizations. The AICPA task force recommended applying most of the provisions of Statement 95. Respondents to the Invitation to Comment generally agreed as did most respondents to the Exposure Draft.

Amendment to Description of Financing Cash Flows

141. The Invitation to Comment asked whether items identified by the AICPA task force as "capital cash flows" should be reported as operating, investing, or as a separate category of cash flows. The AICPA task force recommended that a fourth category be created to display capital cash flows, which it defined in paragraph 255 of its report to "include all permanently restricted gifts and temporarily restricted cash receipts from donors for property, plant, and equipment, and those that are not immediately available for operations, such as term endowments, and gifts subject to a life interest." Most respondents to the Invitation to Comment agreed; however, several respondents, including an organization representing institutional lending officers, said that a new category could be misinterpreted and confusing, and is not necessary.

142. In paragraph 254 of its report, the AICPA task force said that "transactions involving changes in permanently restricted and temporarily restricted net assets for which the restrictions are likely to last for an extended period of time . . . may not easily fit into the categories prescribed in FASB Statement No. 95." Those who disagreed with the task force's recommendation generally said that "capital cash flows" can be appropriately reported as financing activities. Some also suggested that the financing cash flows could be presented in two sections: debt financing cash flows and capital cash flows.

143. The Board concluded that creating a fourth category of cash flows to accommodate the cash inflows of not-for-profit organizations described by the AICPA task force as capital cash flows is neither necessary nor desirable. The Board believes that a new

category would create new differences in terminology and definitions between not-for-profit organizations and business enterprises, and between not-for-profit organizations and governmental entities, and those differences could cause more confusion than clarity. Paragraph 15 of GASB Statement No. 9, *Reporting Cash Flows of Proprietary and Nonexpendable Trust Funds and Governmental Entities That Use Proprietary Fund Accounting,* which requires governmental entities to classify cash receipts and cash payments as resulting from operating, noncapital financing, capital and related financing, or investing activities, uses similar terms that have definitions that differ from those in Statement 95 and those recommended by the AICPA task force.

144. The Board concluded that comparability of reporting will be enhanced if both business enterprises and not-for-profit organizations report their cash flows using the same classifications and definitions. Common definitions and reporting will help enhance users' understandings of information provided in statements of cash flows. Although GASB Statement 9 provides different definitions, colleges, universities, hospitals, and other organizations may, under this Statement, subdivide categories of cash flows to provide information in their statement of cash flows that is reasonably comparable to if not the same as governmental entities.

145. To implement the Board's conclusion, this Statement amends Statement 95 to extend its scope to not-for-profit organizations and to expand the description of financing activities in paragraph 18 of Statement 95 to encompass receipts of resources that by donor stipulation must be used for long-term purposes. That category of transactions was not considered when Statement 95 was issued. This Statement also amends paragraph 19 to include among its list of cash inflows from financing activities receipts from contributions and investment income that by donor stipulation are restricted for the purposes of acquiring, constructing, or improving property, plant, equipment, or other long-lived assets or establishing or increasing a permanent endowment or term endowment.

Reporting Net Cash Flows from Operating Activities

146. The Invitation to Comment asked whether not-for-profit organizations should be required to report cash flows from operating activities using the direct method and, if so, whether they should provide a rec-

onciling statement. The AICPA task force discussed the advantages of the direct method and the indirect method of presenting cash flows from operating activities and, in paragraph 260, the task force said that it "believes that the direct method of reporting would be more useful to preparers and users of not-for-profit organization's financial statements." It recommended that not-for-profit organizations be required to present their statements of cash flows using the direct method of presentation. A significant majority of respondents disagreed. Respondents generally said that the option of presenting net cash flows from operating activities using the indirect method as permitted for business enterprises should be allowed for not-for-profit organizations for reasons similar to those discussed in Statement 95.

147. The Board agreed with those respondents and concluded that, consistent with Statement 95, not-for-profit organizations should be encouraged to use the direct method of reporting net cash flows from operating activities and allowed to use the indirect method. The advantages and disadvantages of each method and the Board's considerations of each are discussed in paragraphs 106-121 of Statement 95. More specifically, paragraph 119 says:

> The Board believes that both the direct and the indirect methods provide potentially important information. The more comprehensive and presumably more useful approach would be to use the direct method in the statement of cash flows and to provide a reconciliation of net income and net cash flow from operating activities in a separate schedule—thereby reaping the benefits of both methods while maintaining the focus of the statement of cash flows on cash receipts and payments. This Statement therefore encourages enterprises to follow that approach. But most providers and users of financial statements have little or no experience and only limited familiarity with the direct method, while both have extensive experience with the indirect method. Not only are there questions about the ability of enterprises to determine gross amounts of operating cash receipts and payments, . . . but also little information is available on which specific categories of operating cash receipts and payments would be most meaningful.

148. The Board concluded that those observations also apply to not-for-profit organizations, which generally have little experience presenting statements of

cash flows. This Statement also clarifies that not-for-profit organizations that present a reconciling schedule when using the direct method or that use the indirect method should reconcile the change in net assets as reported in a statement of activities to net cash flows from operating activities. The Board believes that reconciling from the change in net assets is consistent with reporting information that focuses on cash flows for the entity as a whole.

Reporting Cash Flows from Purchases and Sales of Investment Securities

149. A few respondents to the Exposure Draft said that the reporting of gross amounts of cash from purchasing and selling securities, particularly those of endowment funds, may be misleading, inappropriate, or both. Some suggested that because permanent endowments require reinvestment of cash inflows from selling securities, the cash outflows, which are nondiscretionary expenditures to maintain the existing endowment, are not available and the appearance of those inflows and outflows in a statement of cash flows can easily mislead users. The Board believes that reporting those cash flows as investing activities—not operating activities—is appropriate and is generally understood by users of financial statements. Furthermore, the Board believes that, for reasons similar to those discussed in paragraphs 97-99 of Statement 95, allocating transactions for pooled investments between nondiscretionary transactions to maintain or expand the permanent endowments and discretionary expenditures to maintain or expand board-designated endowment funds would necessarily be arbitrary and add additional costs that would exceed the benefits provided.

Effective Date and Transition

150. The Exposure Draft proposed that this Statement generally be effective for annual financial statements issued for fiscal years beginning after December 15, 1994. The Board decided to provide ample time before this Statement becomes effective primarily to coordinate its implementation with Statement 116. The Board also noted that that extended time may be helpful to organizations that have not determined the historic dollar value of their permanent endowment funds. Most respondents agreed that the proposed effective date would provide adequate time for organizations to update systems and gather information necessary to report the basic information required by this Statement.

151. Nonetheless, a national association representing over 400 human services organizations (and a few other respondents) requested an additional one-year delay for small not-for-profit organizations. About one-third of the association's members have annual budgets of less than $1 million and the association said an extended transition period would allow them sufficient time to utilize the initial experience gained by larger organizations and CPAs. They believe that experience could help them find cost-effective ways to implement this Statement and Statement 116. Board members believe a further delay generally is not necessary. However, because small organizations are often dependent on outside volunteers and are particularly sensitive to any incremental one-time costs, the Board decided to grant a one-year delay for organizations with less than $5 million in total assets and less than $1 million in annual expenses.

152. Earlier application of this Statement is encouraged. Applying this Statement early may result in some erosion in comparability of reporting during the transition period; however, the Board concluded that the benefits of the information gained by permitting early application outweigh its disadvantages. Respondents to the Exposure Draft generally agreed.

Appendix C

ILLUSTRATIVE EXAMPLES

153. This appendix provides illustrations of statements of financial position, statements of activities, and statements of cash flows. These illustrations are intended as examples only; they present only a few of the permissible formats. Other formats or levels of detail may be appropriate for certain circumstances. Organizations are encouraged to provide information in ways that are most relevant and understandable to donors, creditors, and other external users of financial statements. The Board encourages organizations to provide comparative financial statements; however, for simplicity, the illustrative statements of activities and statements of cash flows provide information for a single period.

154. The illustrations also include certain notes to the financial statements for matters discussed in this Statement. The illustrative notes are not intended to illustrate compliance with all generally accepted accounting principles and specialized accounting and reporting principles and practices.

155. Shading* is used to highlight certain basic totals that must be reported in financial statements to comply with the provisions of this Statement. This Statement requires not only reporting those certain basic totals but also reporting components of those aggregates; for example, it requires reporting information about the gross amounts of items of revenues and expenses and cash receipts and payments.

Statement of Financial Position

156. A statement of financial position that sequences assets and liabilities based on their relative liquidity is presented. For example, cash and contributions receivable restricted by donors to investment in land, buildings, and equipment are not included with the line items "cash and cash equivalents" or "contributions receivable." Rather, those items are reported as "assets restricted to investment in land, buildings, and equipment" and are sequenced closer to "land, buildings, and equipment"; cash and cash equivalents of permanent endowment funds held temporarily until suitable long-term investment opportunities are identified are included in the classification "long-term investments." Assets and liabilities also may be arrayed by their relationship to net asset classes, classified as current and noncurrent, or arranged in other ways. Comparative statements of financial position are provided to facilitate understanding of the statement of cash flows.

Not-for-Profit Organization
Statements of Financial Position
June 30, 19X1 and 19X0
(in thousands)

	19X1	19X0
Assets:		
Cash and cash equivalents	$　　75	$　　460
Accounts and interest receivable	2,130	1,670
Inventories and prepaid expenses	610	1,000
Contributions receivable	3,025	2,700
Short-term investments	1,400	1,000
Assets restricted to investment in land, buildings, and equipment	5,210	4,560
Land, buildings, and equipment	61,700	63,590
Long-term investments	218,070	203,500
[Total assets	$292,220]	$278,480
Liabilities and net assets:		
Accounts payable	$　2,570	$　1,050
Refundable advance		650
Grants payable	875	1,300
Notes payable		1,140
Annuity obligations	1,685	1,700
Long-term debt	5,500	6,500
[Total liabilities	10,630]	12,340
Net assets:		
[Unrestricted	115,228	103,670
Temporarily restricted (Note B)	24,342	25,470
Permanently restricted (Note C)	142,020	137,000
Total net assets	281,590]	266,140
Total liabilities and net assets	$292,220	$278,480

---

*Editor's Note: In this edition, the totals are highlighted by being enclosed in brackets rather than by shading.

Statement of Activities

157. Three formats of statements of activities are presented. Each format has certain advantages. Format A reports information in a single column. That format most easily accommodates presentation of multiyear comparative information. Format B reports the same information in columnar format with a column for each class of net assets and adds an optional total column. That format makes evident that the effects of expirations on donor restrictions result in reclassifications between classes of net assets. It also accommodates presentation of aggregated information about contributions and investment income for the entity as a whole. Format C reports information in two statements with summary amounts from a statement of revenues, expenses, and other changes in unrestricted net assets (Part 1 of 2) articulating with a statement of changes in net assets (Part 2 of 2). Alternative formats for the statement of changes in net assets—a single column and a multicolumn—are illustrated. The two-statement approach of Format C focuses attention on changes in unrestricted net assets. That format may be preferred by organizations that view their *operating* activities as excluding receipts of donor-restricted revenues and gains from contributions and investment income. To facilitate comparison of the formats, the same level of aggregation is used in each of the statements of activities.

158. The three illustrative statements of activities show items of revenues and gains first, then expenses, then losses; reclassifications, which must be shown separately, are reported with revenues and gains. Those items could be arranged in other ways and other subtotals may be included. For example, the items may be sequenced as (a) revenues, expenses, gains and losses, and reclassifications shown last or (b) certain revenues, less directly related expenses, followed by a subtotal, then other revenues, other expenses, gains and losses, and reclassifications. Paragraph 167 provides an example that shows how items may be sequenced to distinguish between operating and nonoperating activities or to make other distinctions, if desired.

159. Although the illustrative statements of activities report expenses by function, expenses may be reported by natural classification in the statements with functional classification disclosed in the notes.

Format A

Not-for-Profit Organization
Statement of Activities
Year Ended June 30, 19X1
(in thousands)

Changes in unrestricted net assets:
  Revenues and gains:

Contributions	$ 8,640
Fees	5,400
Income on long-term investments (Note E)	5,600
Other investment income (Note E)	850
Net unrealized and realized gains on long-term investments (Note E)	8,228
Other	150
Total unrestricted revenues and gains	28,868

Net assets released from restrictions (Note D):

Satisfaction of program restrictions	11,990
Satisfaction of equipment acquisition restrictions	1,500
Expiration of time restrictions	1,250
Total net assets released from restrictions	14,740
Total unrestricted revenues, gains, and other support	43,608

Expenses and losses:

Program A	13,100
Program B	8,540
Program C	5,760
Management and general	2,420
Fund raising	2,150
Total expenses (Note F)	31,970
Fire loss	80
Total expenses and losses	32,050
[Increase in unrestricted net assets	11,558]

Changes in temporarily restricted net assets:

Contributions	8,110
Income on long-term investments (Note E)	2,580
Net unrealized and realized gains on long-term investments (Note E)	2,952
Actuarial loss on annuity obligations	(30)
Net assets released from restrictions (Note D)	(14,740)
[Decrease in temporarily restricted net assets	(1,128)]

Changes in permanently restricted net assets:

Contributions	280
Income on long-term investments (Note E)	120
Net unrealized and realized gains on long-term investments (Note E)	4,620
Increase in permanently restricted net assets	5,020
Increase in net assets	15,450
Net assets at beginning of year	266,140
Net assets at end of year	$281,590

Format B

Not-for-Profit Organization
Statement of Activities
Year Ended June 30, 19X1
(in thousands)

	Unrestricted	Temporarily Restricted	Permanently Restricted	Total
Revenues, gains, and other support:				
Contributions	$ 8,640	$ 8,110	$ 280	$ 17,030
Fees	5,400			5,400
Income on long-term investments (Note E)	5,600	2,580	120	8,300
Other investment income (Note E)	850			850
Net unrealized and realized gains on				
long-term investments (Note E)	8,228	2,952	4,620	15,800
Other	150			150
Net assets released from restrictions				
(Note D):				
Satisfaction of program restrictions	11,990	(11,990)		
Satisfaction of equipment acquisition				
restrictions	1,500	(1,500)		
Expiration of time restrictions	1,250	(1,250)		
Total revenues, gains, and other support	43,608	(1,098)	5,020	47,530
Expenses and losses:				
Program A	13,100			13,100
Program B	8,540			8,540
Program C	5,760			5,760
Management and general	2,420			2,420
Fund raising	2,150			2,150
Total expenses (Note F)	31,970			31,970
Fire loss	80			80
Actuarial loss on annuity obligations		30		30
Total expenses and losses	32,050	30		32,080
[Change in net assets	11,558	(1,128)	5,020	15,450]
Net assets at beginning of year	103,670	25,470	137,000	266,140
Net assets at end of year	$115,228	$ 24,342	$142,020	$281,590

Format C, Part 1 of 2

Not-for-Profit Organization
Statement of Unrestricted Revenues, Expenses, and
Other Changes in Unrestricted Net Assets
Year Ended June 30, 19X1
(in thousands)

Unrestricted revenues and gains:	
Contributions	$ 8,640
Fees	5,400
Income on long-term investments (Note E)	5,600
Other investment income (Note E)	850
Net unrealized and realized gains on long-term investments (Note E)	8,228
Other	150
Total unrestricted revenues and gains	28,868
Net assets released from restrictions (Note D):	
Satisfaction of program restrictions	11,990
Satisfaction of equipment acquisition restrictions	1,500
Expiration of time restrictions	1,250
Total net assets released from restrictions	14,740
Total unrestricted revenues, gains, and other support	43,608
Expenses and losses:	
Program A	13,100
Program B	8,540
Program C	5,760
Management and general	2,420
Fund raising	2,150
Total expenses (Note F)	31,970
Fire loss	80
Total unrestricted expenses and losses	32,050
Increase in unrestricted net assets	$11,558

Format C, Part 2 of 2

Not-for-Profit Organization
Statement of Changes in Net Assets
Year Ended June 30, 19X1
(in thousands)

Unrestricted net assets:	
Total unrestricted revenues and gains	$ 28,868
Net assets released from restrictions (Note D)	14,740
Total unrestricted expenses and losses	(32,050)
[Increase in unrestricted net assets	11,558]
Temporarily restricted net assets:	
Contributions	8,110
Income on long-term investments (Note E)	2,580
Net unrealized and realized gains on long-term investments (Note E)	2,952
Actuarial loss on annuity obligations	(30)
Net assets released from restrictions (Note D)	(14,740)
[Decrease in temporarily restricted net assets	(1,128)]
Permanently restricted net assets:	
Contributions	280
Income on long-term investments (Note E)	120
Net unrealized and realized gains on long-term investments (Note E)	4,620
Increase in permanently restricted net assets	5,020]
[Increase in net assets	15,450]
Net assets at beginning of year	266,140
Net assets at end of year	$281,590

Format C, Part 2 of 2 (Alternate)

Not-for-Profit Organization
Statement of Changes in Net Assets
Year Ended June 30, 19X1
(in thousands)

	Unrestricted	Temporarily Restricted	Permanently Restricted	Total
Revenues, gains, and other support:				
Unrestricted revenues, gains, and other support	$ 28,868			$ 28,868
Restricted revenues, gains, and other support:				
Contributions		$ 8,110	$ 280	8,390
Income on long-term investments (Note E)		2,580	120	2,700
Net unrealized and realized gains on long-term investments (Note E)		2,952	4,620	7,572
Net assets released from restrictions (Note D)	14,740	(14,740)		
Total revenues, gains, and other support	43,608	(1,098)	5,020	47,530
Expenses and losses:				
Unrestricted expenses and losses	32,050			32,050
Actuarial loss on annuity obligations		30		30
Total expenses and losses	32,050	30		32,080
[Change in net assets	11,558	(1,128)	5,020	15,450]
Net assets at beginning of year	103,670	25,470	137,000	266,140
Net assets at end of year	$115,228	$ 24,342	$142,020	$281,590

(This page intentionally left blank.)

Statement of Cash Flows

160. Statements of cash flows are illustrated using both the direct and indirect methods of reporting cash flow from operating activities.

Direct Method

Not-for-Profit Organization
Statement of Cash Flows
Year Ended June 30, 19X1
(in thousands)

Cash flows from operating activities:	
Cash received from service recipients	$ 5,220
Cash received from contributors	8,030
Cash collected on contributions receivable	2,615
Interest and dividends received	8,570
Miscellaneous receipts	150
Interest paid	(382)
Cash paid to employees and suppliers	(23,808)
Grants paid	(425)
[Net cash used by operating activities	(30)]
Cash flows from investing activities:	
Insurance proceeds from fire loss on building	250
Purchase of equipment	(1,500)
Proceeds from sale of investments	76,100
Purchase of investments	(74,900)
[Net cash used by investing activities	(50)]
Cash flows from financing activities:	
Proceeds from contributions restricted for:	
Investment in endowment	200
Investment in term endowment	70
Investment in plant	1,210
Investment subject to annuity agreements	200
	1,680
Other financing activities:	
Interest and dividends restricted for reinvestment	300
Payments of annuity obligations	(145)
Payments on notes payable	(1,140)
Payments on long-term debt	(1,000)
	(1,985)
Net cash used by financing activities	(305)
Net decrease in cash and cash equivalents	(385)
Cash and cash equivalents at beginning of year	460
Cash and cash equivalents at end of year	$ 75

Reconciliation of change in net assets to net cash used by operating activities:

[Change in net assets	$ 15,450]
Adjustments to reconcile change in net assets to net cash used by operating activities:	
Depreciation	3,200
Fire loss	80
Actuarial loss on annuity obligations	30
Increase in accounts and interest receivable	(460)
Decrease in inventories and prepaid expenses	390
Increase in contributions receivable	(325)
Increase in accounts payable	1,520
Decrease in refundable advance	(650)
Decrease in grants payable	(425)
Contributions restricted for long-term investment	(2,740)
Interest and dividends restricted for long-term investment	(300)
Net unrealized and realized gains on long-term investments	(15,800)
[Net cash used by operating activities	$ (30)]

Supplemental data for noncash investing and financing activities:

Gifts of equipment	$140
Gift of paid-up life insurance, cash surrender value	80

Indirect Method

Not-for-Profit Organization
Statement of Cash Flows
Year Ended June 30, 19X1
(in thousands)

Cash flows from operating activites:

[Change in net assets	$ 15,450]
Adjustments to reconcile change in net assets to net cash used by operating activities:	
Depreciation	3,200
Fire loss	80
Actuarial loss on annuity obligations	30
Increase in accounts and interest receivable	(460)
Decrease in inventories and prepaid expenses	390
Increase in contributions receivable	(325)
Increase in accounts payable	1,520
Decrease in refundable advance	(650)
Decrease in grants payable	(425)
Contributions restricted for long-term investment	(2,740)
Interest and dividends restricted for long-term investment	(300)
Net unrealized and realized gains on long-term investments	(15,800)
[Net cash used by operating activities	(30)]
Cash flows from investing activities:	
Insurance proceeds from fire loss on building	250
Purchase of equipment	(1,500)
Proceeds from sale of investments	76,100
Purchase of investments	(74,900)
[Net cash used by investing activities	(50)]
Cash flows from financing activities:	
Proceeds from contributions restricted for:	
Investment in endowment	200
Investment in term endowment	70
Investment in plant	1,210
Investment subject to annuity agreements	200
	1,680
Other financing activities:	
Interest and dividends restricted for reinvestment	300
Payments of annuity obligations	(145)
Payments on notes payable	(1,140)
Payments on long-term debt	(1,000)
	(1,985)
Net cash used by financing activities	(305)
Net decrease in cash and cash equivalents	(385)
Cash and cash equivalents at beginning of year	460
Cash and cash equivalents at end of year	$ 75
Supplemental data:	
Noncash investing and financing activities:	
Gifts of equipment	$140
Gift of paid-up life insurance, cash surrender value	80
Interest paid	382

Notes to Financial Statements

161. Illustrative Note A provides required policy disclosures (paragraphs 14 and 16 of Statement 116) that bear on the illustrated statements and Notes B and C provide information required by this Statement. Notes D through F provide information that not-for-profit organizations are encouraged to disclose. However, paragraph 26 requires voluntary health and welfare organizations to provide the information in Note F in a statement of functional expenses. All amounts are in thousands.

Note A

The Organization reports gifts of cash and other assets as restricted support if they are received with donor stipulations that limit the use of the donated assets. When a donor restriction expires, that is, when a stipulated time restriction ends or purpose restriction is accomplished, temporarily restricted net assets are reclassified to unrestricted net assets and reported in the statement of activities as net assets released from restrictions.

The Organization reports gifts of land, buildings, and equipment as unrestricted support unless explicit donor stipulations specify how the donated assets must be used. Gifts of long-lived assets with explicit restrictions that specify how the assets are to be used and gifts of cash or other assets that must be used to acquire long-lived assets are reported as restricted support. Absent explicit donor stipulations about how long those long-lived assets must be maintained, the Organization reports expirations of donor restrictions when the donated or acquired long-lived assets are placed in service.

Note B

Temporarily restricted net assets are available for the following purposes or periods:

Program A activities:	
Purchase of equipment	$ 3,060
Research	4,256
Educational seminars and publications	1,520
Program B activities:	
Disaster relief	2,240
Educational seminars and publications	2,158
Program C activities: general	2,968
Buildings and equipment	2,150
Annuity trust agreements	2,850
For periods after June 30, 19X1	3,140
	$24,342

Note C

Permanently restricted net assets are restricted to:

Investment in perpetuity, the income from which is expendable to support:	
Program A activities	$ 27,524
Program B activities	13,662
Program C activities	13,662
Any activities of the organization	81,972
	136,820
Endowment requiring income to be added to original gift until fund's value is $2,500	2,120
Paid-up life insurance policy that will provide proceeds upon death of insured for an endowment to support general activities	80
Land required to be used as a recreation area	3,000
	$142,020

Note D

Net assets were released from donor restrictions by incurring expenses satisfying the restricted purposes or by occurrence of other events specified by donors.

Purpose restrictions accomplished:

Program A expenses	$ 5,800
Program B expenses	4,600
Program C expenses	1,590
	11,990
Program A equipment acquired and placed in service	1,500

Time restrictions expired:

Passage of specified time	850
Death of annuity beneficiary	400
	1,250
Total restrictions released	$14,740

Note E

Investments are carried at market or appraised value, and realized and unrealized gains and losses are reflected in the statement of activities. The Organization invests cash in excess of daily requirements in short-term investments. At June 30, 19X1, $1,400 was invested short term, and during the year short-term investments earned $850. Most long-term investments are held in two investment pools. Pool A is for permanent endowments and the unappropriated net appreciation of those endowments. Pool B is for amounts designated by the board of trustees for long-term investment. Annuity trusts, term endowments, and certain permanent endowments are separately invested. Long-term investment activity is reflected in the table below:

	Pool A	Pool B	Other	Total
Investments at beginning of year	$164,000	$32,800	$6,700	$203,500
Gifts available for investment:				
Gifts creating permanent endowment	200		80	280
Gifts creating term endowments			70	70
Gifts creating annuity trusts			200	200
Amount withdrawn at death of annuitant			(400)	(400)
Investment returns (net of expenses of $375):				
Dividends, interest, and rents	6,000	2,000	300	8,300
Realized and unrealized gains	12,000	3,800		15,800
Total return on investments	18,000	5,800	300	24,100
Amounts appropriated for current operations	(7,500)	(2,000)		(9,500)
Annuity trust income for current and future payments			(180)	(180)
Investments at end of year	$174,700	$36,600	$6,770	$218,070

The participation in the pools and ownership of the other investments at June 30, 19X1 is shown in the table below:

	Pool A	Pool B	Other	Total
Permanently restricted net assets	$136,820		$2,200	$139,020
Temporarily restricted net assets	10,752		4,570	15,322
Unrestricted net assets	27,128	$36,600		63,728
	$174,700	$36,600	$6,770	$218,070

The board of trustees has interpreted state law as requiring the preservation of the purchasing power (real value) of the permanent endowment funds unless explicit donor stipulations specify how net appreciation must be used. To meet that objective, the

Organization's endowment management policies require that net appreciation be retained permanently in an amount necessary to adjust the historic dollar value of original endowment gifts by the change in the Consumer Price Index. After maintaining the real value of the permanent endowment funds, any remainder of total return is available for appropriation. In 19X1, the total return on Pool A was $18,000 (10.6 percent), of which $4,620 was retained permanently to preserve the real value of the original gifts. The remaining $13,380 was available for appropriation by the board of trustees. State law allows the board to appropriate so much of net appreciation as is prudent considering the Organization's long- and short-term needs, present and anticipated financial requirements, expected total return on its investments, price level trends, and general economic conditions. Under the Organization's endowment spending policy, 5 percent of the average of the market value at the end of the previous 3 years is appropriated, which was $7,500 for the year ended June 30, 19X1.

Note F

Expenses incurred were for:

		Program			Management	Fund
	Total	**A**	**B**	**C**	**and General**	**Raising**
Salaries, wages, and benefits	$15,115	$ 7,400	$3,900	$1,725	$1,130	$ 960
Grants to other organizations	4,750	2,075	750	1,925		
Supplies and travel	3,155	865	1,000	490	240	560
Services and professional fees	2,840	160	1,490	600	200	390
Office and occupancy	2,528	1,160	600	450	218	100
Depreciation	3,200	1,440	800	570	250	140
Interest	382				382	
Total expenses	$31,970	$13,100	$8,540	$5,760	$2,420	$2,150

Transactions Reported in the Illustrative Financial Statements

162. The following facts and transactions are reflected in the illustrative financial statements. The transactions are presented by class of net assets to facilitate locating their effects in the statements and notes.

The following transactions affect unrestricted net assets:

a. The organization invested cash in excess of daily requirements in short-term investment instruments. Interest earned on these investments totaled $850. The governing board has designated a portion of unrestricted net assets for long-term investment. Those assets earned $2,000.

b. The organization received unrestricted contributions of the following: cash, $5,120; recognizable contributed services, $300; other consumable assets, $1,410; equipment, $140; and unconditional promises to give to support activities of 19X1, $1,020.

c. Equipment with an original cost of $660 and accumulated depreciation of $330 was destroyed in a fire. Insurance proceeds of $250 were received. The equipment was originally purchased with unrestricted assets.

d. All conditions of a prior year's grant of $650 were substantially met. The grant proceeds were originally recorded as a refundable advance.

e. The organization made a payment of $425 on its prior year unconditional grant to an unrelated agency.

f. The organization repaid $1,140 of its notes payable. Interest of $32 was incurred and paid on these notes.

g. The organization repaid $1,000 of its long-term debt. Interest of $350 was incurred and paid on the debt.

h. Depreciation amounted to $3,200.

The following transactions affect temporarily restricted net assets:

i. The organization received temporarily restricted contributions as follows:

Restricted to:	Cash	Consumable Assets	Promises to Give
Program purposes	$2,170	$960	$ 990
Use in future periods	740		930
Acquisition of land, buildings, and equipment	770		1,380

j. In addition, a donor transferred cash of $200 to set up an annuity trust having a related annuity obligation with a present value of $100. Upon the death of the beneficiary, the remaining interest will be used for a donor-stipulated purpose.

k. In addition, a donor contributed cash of $70 to create a term endowment. At the end of 15 years the endowment assets can be used to support the organization's operations.

l. The organization made payments of $145 to beneficiaries of annuity trust agreements.

The following transactions affect permanently restricted net assets:

m. A donor contributed a paid-up life insurance policy with a cash surrender value of $80. Upon the death of the insured, the death benefit must be used to create a permanent endowment. There was no change in the cash surrender value between the date of the gift and the end of the fiscal year.

n. A donor contributed cash of $200 to create a permanent endowment fund. The income is restricted to use for Program A activities.

The following transactions affect more than one class of net assets:

o. The organization collected promises to give of $3,055: $980 of amounts for unrestricted purposes, $610 of amounts restricted to future periods, $1,025 of amounts restricted to program purposes, and $440 of amounts for acquisition of land, buildings, and equipment.

p. The organization utilized all of the $1,410 consumable assets contributed for unrestricted purposes, and $350 of the $960 consumable assets contributed for program purposes.

q. A trust annuitant died and the $400 remainder interest became available for the unrestricted use of the organization. Management decided to invest the remainder interest in short-term investments. The actuarial gain on death of the annuitant is included in the actuarial loss on annuity obligations.

r. The organization acquired and placed in service $1,500 of equipment for Program A; temporarily restricted net assets were available at the time the equipment was purchased.

s. The net gain, unrealized and realized, on unrestricted net assets designated by the governing board for long-term investment of $3,800 was recognized. The net gain, unrealized and realized, on permanent endowments and the unappropriated net appreciation of those endowments of $12,000 was recognized. The governing board has interpreted the law in its jurisdiction as requiring preservation of purchasing power. The governing board has selected the CPI as the measure of changes in purchasing power. The CPI has changed by 3.5 percent over the year. The index-adjusted original gift amount of the endowment at the end of the previous year was $132,000.

t. The organization reinvested the yield of $120 on a permanent endowment that requires income to be added to the original gift until the fund's value is $2,500.

Statement of Activities with Additional Classifications

163. This Statement neither encourages nor discourages organizations from classifying items of revenues, expenses, and other changes in net assets as operating and nonoperating, expendable and nonexpendable, earned and unearned, recurring and nonrecurring, or in other ways. Rather, the requirements of this Statement provide a few broad constraints for a statement of activities and allow not-for-profit organizations latitude to make distinctions that they believe will provide meaningful information to users of their financial statements. Like business enterprises, that latitude allows organizations to report an undefined intermediate measure of operations. That latitude also allows reporting practices to develop in an evolutionary manner for all or certain kinds of not-for-profit organizations.

164. Entities that use terms such as *operating income, operating profit, operating surplus, operating*

deficit, and *results of operations* often use those terms with different meanings. Business enterprises that choose to make an operating and nonoperating distinction do so within an income statement (statement of earnings) that at a minimum reports net income for the period as well as an intermediate measure of income before the effects of a discontinued operating segment, extraordinary items, or an accounting change, if any.

165. Paragraph 23 imposes a similar constraint on not-for-profit organizations that choose to use similar terms. If an organization reports an intermediate measure of *operations,* it must do so within a financial statement that, at a minimum, reports the change in unrestricted net assets for the period. Paragraph 23 also specifies that if an organization's use of the term *operations* is not apparent from the details provided on the face of the statement, a note to financial statements should describe the nature of the reported measure of operations or the items excluded from operations.

166. A statement of unrestricted revenues, expenses, and other changes in unrestricted net assets that subdivides all transactions and other events and circumstances to make an operating and nonoperating distinction is illustrated. This example uses part 1 of 2 of Format C of the previously illustrated statements of activities to show a measure of operations—change in unrestricted net assets from operations.

167. The shaded* areas depict the constraints imposed by this Statement and by generally accepted accounting principles to report appropriately labeled subtotals for changes in classes of net assets before the effects of discontinued operating segments, extraordinary items, or accounting changes, if any. The unshaded areas depict areas within the statement for which there is latitude to sequence and classify items of revenues and expenses. Other formats also may be used. For example, the single-statement approach of Format B may be helpful in describing an organization's ongoing major or central operations if that organization's view of operating activities includes receiving donor-restricted revenues from contributions and investment income.

Other Not-for-Profit Organization
Statement of Unrestricted Revenues, Expenses, and
Other Changes in Unrestricted Net Assets
Year Ended June 30, 19X1
(in thousands)

Operating revenues and support:	
Fees from providing services	$ X,XXX
Operating support	X,XXX
Net assets released from restrictions	X,XXX
Total operating revenues and support	XX,XXX
Operating expenses:	
Programs	XX,XXX
Management and general	X,XXX
Fund raising	X,XXX
Total operating expenses	XX,XXX
Change in unrestricted net assets from operations	X,XXX
Other changes:	
[Items considered to be nonoperating	X,XXX
(paragraphs 65-68 and 111-115).]	X,XXX
Change in net assets before effects of discontinued operations,	
extraordinary items, and changes in accounting principles	XX,XXX
Discontinued operations	X,XXX
Extraordinary items	X,XXX
Changes in accounting principles	X,XXX
Change in net assets	XX,XXX
Net assets at beginning of year	XXX,XXX
Net assets at end of year	$XXX,XXX

---

*Editor's Note: In this edition, the areas are highlighted by being enclosed in brackets rather than by shading.

1656

Appendix D

GLOSSARY

168. This appendix contains definitions of certain terms or phrases used in this Statement.

Donor-imposed restriction
A donor stipulation that specifies a use for a contributed asset that is more specific than broad limits resulting from the nature of the organization, the environment in which it operates, and the purposes specified in its articles of incorporation or bylaws or comparable documents for an unincorporated association. A restriction on an organization's use of the asset contributed may be temporary or permanent.

Endowment fund
An established fund of cash, securities, or other assets to provide income for the maintenance of a not-for-profit organization. The use of the assets of the fund may be permanently restricted, temporarily restricted, or unrestricted. Endowment funds generally are established by donor-restricted gifts and bequests to provide a permanent endowment, which is to provide a permanent source of income, or a term endowment, which is to provide income for a specified period. The principal of a permanent endowment must be maintained permanently—not used up, expended, or otherwise exhausted—and is classified as permanently restricted net assets. The principal of a term endowment must be maintained for a specified term and is classified as temporarily restricted net assets. An organization's governing board may earmark a portion of its unrestricted net assets as a board-designated endowment (sometimes called funds functioning as endowment or quasi-endowment funds) to be invested to provide income for a long but unspecified period. The principal of a board-designated endowment, which results from an internal designation, is not donor restricted and is classified as unrestricted net assets.

Functional classification
A method of grouping expenses according to the purpose for which costs are incurred. The primary functional classifications are program services and supporting activities.

Not-for-profit organization
An entity that possesses the following characteristics that distinguish it from a business enterprise: (a) contributions of significant amounts of resources from resource providers who do not expect commensurate or proportionate pecuniary return, (b) operating purposes other than to provide goods or services at a profit, and (c) absence of ownership interests like those of business enterprises. Not-for-profit organizations have those characteristics in varying degrees (Concepts Statement 4, paragraph 6). Organizations that clearly fall outside this definition include all investor-owned enterprises and entities that provide dividends, lower costs, or other economic benefits directly and proportionately to their owners, members, or participants, such as mutual insurance companies, credit unions, farm and rural electric cooperatives, and employee benefit plans (Concepts Statement 4, paragraph 7).

Permanent restriction
A donor-imposed restriction that stipulates that resources be maintained permanently but permits the organization to use up or expend part or all of the income (or other economic benefits) derived from the donated assets.

Permanently restricted net assets
The part of the net assets of a not-for-profit organization resulting (a) from contributions and other inflows of assets whose use by the organization is limited by donor-imposed stipulations that neither expire by passage of time nor can be fulfilled or otherwise removed by actions of the organization, (b) from other asset enhancements and diminishments subject to the same kinds of stipulations, and (c) from reclassifications from (or to) other classes of net assets as a consequence of donor-imposed stipulations (Concepts Statement 6, paragraph 92).

Restricted support
Donor-restricted revenues or gains from contributions that increase either temporarily restricted net assets or permanently restricted net assets. Also refer to **Unrestricted support**.

Temporarily restricted net assets

The part of the net assets of a not-for-profit organization resulting (a) from contributions and other inflows of assets whose use by the organization is limited by donor-imposed stipulations that either expire by passage of time or can be fulfilled and removed by actions of the organization pursuant to those stipulations, (b) from other asset enhancements and diminishments subject to the same kinds of stipulations, and (c) from reclassifications to (or from) other classes of net assets as a consequence of donor-imposed stipulations, their expiration by passage of time, or their fulfillment and removal by actions of the organization pursuant to those stipulations (Concepts Statement 6, paragraph 93).

Temporary restriction

A donor-imposed restriction that permits the donee organization to use up or expend the donated assets as specified and is satisfied either by the passage of time or by actions of the organization.

Unrestricted net assets

The part of net assets of a not-for-profit organization that is neither permanently restricted nor temporarily restricted by donor-imposed stipulations (Concepts Statement 6, paragraph 94).

Unrestricted support

Revenues or gains from contributions that are not restricted by donors. Also refer to **Restricted support.**

Voluntary health and welfare organizations

Organizations formed for the purpose of performing voluntary services for various segments of society. They are tax exempt (organized for the benefit of the public), supported by the public, and operated on a "not-for-profit" basis. Most voluntary health and welfare organizations concentrate their efforts and expend their resources in an attempt to solve health and welfare problems of our society and, in many cases, those of specific individuals. As a group, voluntary health and welfare organizations include those not-for-profit organizations that derive their revenue primarily from voluntary contributions from the general public to be used for general or specific purposes connected with health, welfare, or community services (*Audits of Voluntary Health and Welfare Organizations*, preface).

Statement of Financial Accounting Standards No. 118
Accounting by Creditors for Impairment of a Loan— Income Recognition and Disclosures

an amendment of FASB Statement No. 114

STATUS

Issued: October 1994

Effective Date: For fiscal years beginning after December 15, 1994

Affects: Amends FAS 114, paragraphs 8 and 11 through 15
Supersedes FAS 114, paragraphs 17 through 20 and 65

Affected by: No other pronouncements

Issues Discussed by FASB Emerging Issues Task Force (EITF)

Affects: No EITF Issues

Interpreted by: Paragraph 6(i) interpreted by EITF Issue No. 96-22

Related Issues: No EITF Issues

SUMMARY

This Statement amends FASB Statement No. 114, *Accounting by Creditors for Impairment of a Loan,* to allow a creditor to use existing methods for recognizing interest income on an impaired loan. To accomplish that, it eliminates the provisions in Statement 114 that described how a creditor should report income on an impaired loan (paragraphs 17-19).

This Statement does not change the provisions in Statement 114 that require a creditor to measure impairment based on the present value of expected future cash flows discounted at the loan's effective interest rate, or as a practical expedient, at the observable market price of the loan or the fair value of the collateral if the loan is collateral dependent.

This Statement amends the disclosure requirements in Statement 114 to require information about the recorded investment in certain impaired loans and about how a creditor recognizes interest income related to those impaired loans.

This Statement is effective concurrent with the effective date of Statement 114, that is, for financial statements for fiscal years beginning after December 15, 1994, with earlier application encouraged.

Statement of Financial Accounting Standards No. 118

Accounting by Creditors for Impairment of a Loan—Income Recognition and Disclosures

an amendment of FASB Statement No. 114

CONTENTS

INTRODUCTION AND BACKGROUND

1. FASB Statement No. 114, *Accounting by Creditors for Impairment of a Loan,* was issued in May 1993 and addresses the accounting by creditors for impairment of certain loans. Statement 114 is effective for financial statements for fiscal years beginning after December 15, 1994.

2. The Board received several requests to delay the effective date of Statement 114 and to clarify how that Statement should be implemented. A delay was requested to allow more time to resolve implementation questions about the application of the income recognition provisions in paragraphs 17-19 of Statement 114 and to make the necessary changes to accounting systems.

3. This Statement amends Statement 114 to allow a creditor to use existing methods for recognizing interest income on impaired loans. To accomplish this, it eliminates the income recognition provisions in paragraphs 17-19 of Statement 114. As amended, Statement 114 does not address how a creditor should recognize, measure, or display interest income on an impaired loan. This Statement amends the disclosure requirements in Statement 114 to require information about the recorded investment in certain impaired loans and about how a creditor recognizes interest income related to those impaired loans.

4. Prior to the issuance of this Statement, Statement 114 provided for two alternative income recognition methods to be used to account for changes in the net carrying amount of an impaired loan subsequent to the initial measure of impairment. Under the first income recognition method, a creditor would accrue interest on the net carrying amount of the impaired loan and report other changes in the net carrying amount of the loan as an adjustment to bad-debt expense. Under the second income recognition method, a creditor would recognize all changes in the net carrying amount of the loan as an adjustment to bad-debt expense. While those income recognition methods are no longer required, this Statement does not preclude a creditor from using either of those methods.

5. Statement 114 requires that a creditor recognize impairment of a loan *if* the present value of expected future cash flows discounted at the loan's effective interest rate (or, alternatively, the observable market price of the loan or the fair value of the collateral) is less than the recorded investment in the impaired loan. If the present value of expected future cash

flows (or, alternatively, the observable market price of the loan or the fair value of the collateral) is equal to or greater than the recorded investment in the impaired loan, no impairment is recognized. This Statement does not change those requirements. When the net carrying amount of an impaired loan equals the present value of expected future cash flows (or, alternatively, the observable market price of the loan or the fair value of the collateral), this Statement will affect only the *classification* of income (or expense) that results from changes in the measure of an impaired loan, not the total *amount* of income (or expense) recognized within a given reporting period. However, when a creditor's policies for recognizing interest income and for charging off loans result in a recorded investment in an impaired loan that is less than the present value of expected future cash flows discounted at the loan's effective interest rate (or, alternatively, the observable market price of the loan or the fair value of the collateral), this Statement will cause both the classification and the total amount of income (or expense) recognized within a given reporting period to be different from that which would have been determined in accordance with paragraphs 17-19 of Statement 114.

STANDARDS OF FINANCIAL ACCOUNTING AND REPORTING

Amendments to Statement 114

6. Statement 114 is amended as follows:

a. The following sentence is added after the second sentence of paragraph 8:

> For a loan that has been restructured in a troubled debt restructuring, *the contractual terms of the loan agreement* refers to the contractual terms specified by the original loan agreement, not the contractual terms specified by the restructuring agreement.

b. In the first sentence of paragraph 11, *impaired loans* is replaced by *impairment of a loan.*

c. In the last sentence of paragraph 12, *those impaired loans* is replaced by *impairment of those loans.*

d. In the last sentence of paragraph 13, *measure of the impaired loan* is replaced by *present value of expected future cash flows (or, alternatively, the observable market price of the loan or the fair value of the collateral).*

e. In the first sentence of paragraph 14, *measures an impaired loan using* is replaced by *bases its measure of loan impairment on.*

f. In the first sentence of paragraph 15, *measures an impaired loan using* is replaced by *bases its measure of loan impairment on.*

g. Paragraph 17 is replaced by the following:

> This Statement does not address how a creditor should recognize, measure, or display interest income on an impaired loan. Some accounting methods for recognizing income may result in a recorded investment in an impaired loan that is less than the present value of expected future cash flows (or, alternatively, the observable market price of the loan or the fair value of the collateral). In that case, while the loan would meet the definition of an impaired loan in paragraph 8, no additional impairment would be recognized. Those accounting methods include recognition of interest income using a cost-recovery method, a cash-basis method, or some combination of those methods. The recorded investment in an impaired loan also may be less than the present value of expected future cash flows (or, alternatively, the observable market price of the loan or the fair value of the collateral) because the creditor has charged off part of the loan.

h. Paragraphs 18 and 19 are deleted.

i. Paragraph 20 is replaced by the following paragraphs:

> A creditor shall disclose, either in the body of the financial statements or in the accompanying notes, the following information about loans that meet the definition of an impaired loan in paragraph 8 of this Statement:

> a. As of the date of each statement of financial position presented, the total recorded investment in the impaired loans at the end of each period and (1) the amount of that recorded investment for which there is a related allowance for credit losses determined in accordance with this Statement and the amount of that allowance and (2) the amount of that recorded investment for which there is no related allowance for credit losses determined in accordance with this Statement

b. The creditor's policy for recognizing interest income on impaired loans, including how cash receipts are recorded

c. For each period for which results of operations are presented, the average recorded investment in the impaired loans during each period, the related amount of interest income recognized during the time within that period that the loans were impaired, and, unless not practicable, the amount of interest income recognized using a cash-basis method of accounting during the time within that period that the loans were impaired.

Information about an impaired loan that has been restructured in a troubled debt restructuring involving a modification of terms need not be included in the disclosures required by paragraphs 20(a) and 20(c) in years after the restructuring if (i) the restructuring agreement specifies an interest rate equal to or greater than the rate that the creditor was willing to accept at the time of the restructuring for a new loan with comparable risk and (ii) the loan is not impaired based on the terms specified by the restructuring agreement. That exception shall be applied consistently for paragraphs 20(a) and 20(c) to all loans restructured in a troubled debt restructuring that meet the criteria in (i) and (ii).

For each period for which results of operations are presented, a creditor also shall disclose the activity in the total allowance for credit losses related to loans, including the balance in the allowance at the beginning and end of each period, additions charged to operations, direct write-downs charged against the allowance, and recoveries of amounts previously charged off. The total allowance for credit losses related to loans includes those amounts that have been determined in accordance with FASB Statement No. 5, *Accounting for Contingencies,* and with this Statement.

j. Paragraph 65 is deleted.

Effective Date and Transition

7. This Statement is effective concurrent with the effective date of Statement 114. Statement 114 is effective for financial statements for fiscal years beginning after December 15, 1994, with earlier application encouraged.

The provisions of this Statement need not be applied to immaterial items.

This Statement was adopted by the affirmative votes of five members of the Financial Accounting Standards Board. Messrs. Leisenring and Swieringa dissented.

Messrs. Leisenring and Swieringa disagree that paragraphs 17-19 of Statement 114 should have been eliminated. Those paragraphs permitted a choice between two methods for recognizing income on impaired loans. They do not believe that those methods are complex or that complex guidance would have been necessary to implement those methods. The Board was aware that changes in accounting systems would be needed to implement those methods when it issued Statement 114 and that the accounting for impaired loans required by bank and thrift regulators was inconsistent with the income recognition provisions in paragraphs 17-19.

Messrs. Leisenring and Swieringa agree that the elimination of the income recognition provisions in Statement 114 will affect only the classification of income and not the total amount of income recognized within a given reporting period if the recorded investment in an impaired loan is equal to or greater than the present value of expected future cash flows (or, alternatively, the observable market price of the loan or the fair value of the collateral). However, the accounting for impaired loans currently required by bank and thrift regulators includes recognition of interest income using a cost-recovery method, a cash-basis method, or some combination of those accounting methods. Those methods can result in a recorded investment in an impaired loan that is less than the present value of expected future cash flows (or, alternatively, the observable market price of the loan or the fair value of the collateral). In that circumstance, income effects of the passage of time and changes in estimates, that otherwise would be recognized currently, are recognized in later periods. Messrs. Leisenring and Swieringa believe that that result is inconsistent with the fundamental premise in Statement 114 that loans should be carried at the present value of expected future cash flows (or, alternatively, the observable market price of the loan or the fair value of the collateral).

The cost-recovery method is intended to address the uncertainty of expected future cash flows from impaired loans by delaying income recognition. The measure of impairment under Statement 114 takes into account the uncertainty of expected future cash flows. The Board concluded in Statement 114 that impairment of a loan should be based on the present value of expected future cash flows (or, alternatively, the observable market price of the loan or the fair value of the collateral) and that changes in estimates (or, alternatively, in market prices or fair values) should be recognized currently (paragraphs 40-43 and 58 of Statement 114). As a result, Messrs. Leisenring and Swieringa believe that the cost-

recovery method is not acceptable under Statement 114, and they disagree with the amendment because it would permit the use of that method under that Statement.

Messrs. Leisenring and Swieringa are concerned that the amendment will allow the net carrying amount of a loan to be any amount as long as it does not exceed the present value of expected cash flows (or, alternatively, the observable market price of the loan or the fair value of the collateral). They believe that paragraphs 17-19 of Statement 114 could have been amended to eliminate inconsistencies in accounting for income on impaired loans by specifying a single method for recognizing interest income on an impaired loan. They would have delayed the effective date of Statement 114 if the Board needed time to develop a single method.

Members of the Financial Accounting Standards Board:

Dennis R. Beresford,	Anthony T. Cope	Robert H. Northcutt
Chairman	John M. Foster	Robert J. Swieringa
Joseph V. Anania	James J. Leisenring	

Appendix A

BACKGROUND INFORMATION AND BASIS FOR CONCLUSIONS

8. This appendix summarizes considerations that were deemed significant by Board members in reaching the conclusions in this Statement. It includes reasons for accepting certain approaches and rejecting others. Individual Board members gave greater weight to some factors than to others. The Board concluded that it could reach an informed decision on the basis of existing information without a public hearing.

9. Statement 114 requires that a creditor measure impairment of a loan based on the present value of expected future cash flows discounted at the loan's effective interest rate or, as a practical expedient, at the observable market price of the loan or the fair value of the collateral if the loan is collateral dependent. Prior to the issuance of this Statement, Statement 114 provided for two alternative income recognition methods to be used to account for changes in the net carrying amount of the loan subsequent to the initial measure of impairment. Under the first income recognition method, a creditor would accrue interest on the net carrying amount of the impaired loan and report other changes in the net carrying amount of the

loan as an adjustment to bad-debt expense. Under the second income recognition method, a creditor would recognize all changes in the net carrying amount of the loan as an adjustment to bad-debt expense. A creditor would have been precluded from using a cost-recovery or a cash-basis method of accounting. The two measurement methods that were allowed as practical expedients and the second income recognition method were not included in the Exposure Draft that resulted in Statement 114 and were added during the deliberations leading to that Statement because commentators said those provisions would facilitate implementation.

10. The Board received several requests to delay the effective date of Statement 114 and to clarify how that Statement should be implemented. The requests stated that more time was needed to resolve implementation issues about the application of the income recognition provisions in paragraphs 17-19. The requests also stated that the accounting for impaired loans currently required by bank and thrift regulators is inconsistent with the provisions in those paragraphs. The requests stated that enterprises under the jurisdiction of those regulators would be required to make significant changes to their accounting systems to comply with the income recognition provisions in paragraphs 17-19 and that the implementation issues could not be resolved in time to make the necessary changes to accounting systems.

11. Statement 114 addresses the measurement of loan impairment. While income recognition was addressed in paragraphs 17-19 of Statement 114, the Board considered those provisions to be secondary in importance to the provisions that addressed measurement of loan impairment. The requests to delay the effective date were based on implementation issues related to those income recognition provisions, not on the measurement provisions.

12. An FASB Exposure Draft, *Accounting by Creditors for Impairment of a Loan—Income Recognition,* was issued on March 31, 1994. In the deliberations that preceded that Exposure Draft, the Board considered delaying the effective date of Statement 114 and issuing guidance for implementing the provisions in paragraphs 17-19 of Statement 114. The Board concluded that the implementation guidance would be complex and that constituents might be required to make costly changes to their accounting systems to implement that guidance; those systems changes could require further modifications if regulators issued accounting guidance in response to the provisions of Statement 114. Furthermore, implementation of the income recognition provisions in paragraphs 17-19 of Statement 114 would not have eliminated inconsistencies in the accounting for income on impaired loans because those provisions permitted a choice between two methods for recognizing income on impaired loans. Accordingly, the Board concluded that, to avoid a delay in the effective date of the measurement provisions of Statement 114, it would be preferable to allow creditors to use existing accounting methods for recognizing interest income and to eliminate the income recognition provisions.

13. The Board received 57 comment letters on the Exposure Draft. Some respondents to the Exposure Draft agreed that the income recognition provisions in paragraphs 17-19 of Statement 114 should be eliminated but gave other reasons for delaying the effective date. Some stated that the effective date should be delayed to give regulators time to resolve regulatory accounting and disclosure issues related to impaired loans. Some stated that a delay would give creditors time to modify accounting systems and policies. Some stated that more time would be needed to implement the disclosure requirements proposed in the Exposure Draft. After considering those comments, the Board concluded that the most significant implementation issues would be resolved by the elimination of paragraphs 17-19 of Statement 114 and by the simplification of certain disclo-

sure requirements that were proposed in the Exposure Draft of this Statement. The Board also concluded that a creditor should implement Statement 114 for fiscal years beginning after December 15, 1994.

14. Some respondents asked whether the amendment to Statement 114 would allow a creditor to use the methods for recognizing interest income that were described in paragraphs 17-19 of Statement 114. While those income recognition methods are no longer required by Statement 114, the Board concluded that a creditor should not be precluded from using those methods.

15. Some respondents said that the elimination of the income recognition provisions in paragraphs 17-19 of Statement 114 would result in inconsistent application of that Statement. Implementation of the income recognition provisions in paragraphs 17-19 would not have eliminated inconsistencies in income recognition on impaired loans, since the provisions in those paragraphs permitted a choice between two methods for recognizing income. Moreover, because not all impaired loans are within the scope of Statement 114, creditors could recognize interest income using existing accounting methods for some impaired loans. That is, a creditor could use a cost-recovery or cash-basis method of accounting for recognizing income on impaired loans that are excluded from the scope of Statement 114 because they are smaller-balance homogeneous loans that are collectively evaluated for impairment.

16. Statement 114, as amended by this Statement, does not address how a creditor should recognize, measure, or display interest income on an impaired loan. However, users of financial statements have told the Board that it is important to know how a creditor recognizes interest and records cash receipts related to impaired loans. The Board decided that a creditor should disclose its accounting policies for recognizing interest income on impaired loans, including its policy for recording cash receipts.

17. The Exposure Draft would have required that a creditor quantify and disclose the amount of interest income recognized, including the amount of cash receipts recorded as interest on an impaired loan and the amount of interest income that would have been recognized according to the contractual terms of the original loan agreement. Some respondents indicated that the information required to make those disclosures was not readily available and that it would be

costly to develop accounting systems to gather that information. In response to those comments, the Board decided to simplify the disclosures that were proposed in the Exposure Draft by requiring that a creditor disclose the average recorded investment in the impaired loans during the reporting period and the related amount of interest income recognized during the time within that period that those loans were impaired. The Board believes that those disclosures will provide financial statement users with useful information about how a creditor recognized interest income on impaired loans. This Statement does not specify how a creditor should calculate the average recorded investment in the impaired loans during the reporting period. The Board believes that a creditor should develop an appropriate method and that averages based on month-end balances may be considered an appropriate method.

18. The Board believes that disclosure of the amount of interest income recognized on impaired loans using a cash-basis method of accounting also will provide financial statement users with valuable information about how cash receipts were recorded. The Board understands that this information generally is available and believes that a creditor should provide that information unless it is not practicable to do so.

19. Paragraph 20(a) of Statement 114 (prior to amendment) required that a creditor disclose the recorded investment in the loans for which impairment had been recognized in accordance with Statement 114 and the total allowance related to those impaired loans. Paragraph 65 of Statement 114 explained that if the creditor had written down a loan so that the present value of expected future cash flows (or, alternatively, the observable market price of the loan or the fair value of the collateral) was equal to or greater than the recorded investment in the loan, no impairment would be recognized. In those situations, the creditor would not have been required to disclose the recorded investment in the loan in years after the write-down. Respondents indicated that that disclosure would confuse financial statement users because information would not be provided about the total population of loans that meet the definition of an impaired loan in paragraph 8 of Statement 114. They said that information about the total population of impaired loans could be provided easily. This Statement eliminates paragraph 65 of Statement 114 and amends the disclosure provisions in paragraph 20 of that Statement to require that a creditor disclose the total recorded investment in loans that meet the definition of an impaired loan in paragraph 8 of State-

ment 114 at the end of the reporting period, the recorded investment in those impaired loans for which there is a related allowance for credit losses, and the recorded investment in those impaired loans for which there is no related allowance for credit losses. Those disclosures should be provided for impaired loans that have been charged off partially. Those disclosures cannot be provided for loans that have been charged off fully because both the recorded investment and the allowance for credit losses will equal zero.

20. A troubled debt restructuring need not be included in the disclosures required by paragraphs 20(a) and 20(c) of Statement 114 (as amended) if the restructuring agreement specifies an interest rate equal to or greater than the rate that the creditor was willing to accept at the time of the restructuring for a new loan with comparable risk and the loan is not impaired based on the terms specified by the restructuring agreement. Although troubled debt restructurings meet the definition of an impaired loan in paragraph 8 of Statement 114, this treatment is consistent with the disclosure requirements (prior to amendment) in paragraph 40(a) of FASB Statement No. 15, *Accounting by Debtors and Creditors for Troubled Debt Restructurings,* and should limit the cost of providing those disclosures.

21. Some respondents indicated that the scope of paragraph 20(b) of Statement 114 (prior to amendment) was unclear. Some stated that they believed that the intent of that paragraph was to require that a creditor provide information about the activity for the total allowance for credit losses, including amounts determined in accordance with Statement 5. Others stated that they believed that the scope of paragraph 20(b) was limited to the allowances determined in accordance with Statement 114. The Board believes that the creditor should provide information about the activity for the total allowance for credit losses, including amounts determined in accordance with Statement 5.

22. The Exposure Draft would have amended the scope of paragraph 20(c) of Statement 114 to apply to "loans that are impaired (or, alternatively, for all loans for which a creditor has credit concerns)." The alternative scope for the disclosures was included in the Exposure Draft to help reduce the cost of implementing the disclosure requirements. However, some respondents stated that the alternative scope would not reduce the cost of implementation and would result in inconsistent disclosure practices. The Board

decided to delete the phrase *(or, alternatively, for all loans for which a creditor has credit concerns).*

23. Some respondents asked whether a loan should be considered to meet the definition of an impaired loan in paragraph 8 of Statement 114 if it was restructured in a troubled debt restructuring and is not impaired based on the terms specified by the restructuring agreement. The Board concluded in Statement 114 that a loan restructured in a troubled debt restructuring is an impaired loan. It should not be accounted for as a new loan because a troubled debt restructuring is part of a creditor's ongoing effort to recover its investment in the original loan. A loan usually will have been identified as impaired because the condition specified in paragraph 8 of State-ment 114 will have existed before a formal restructuring. Although certain troubled debt restructurings may be excluded from the disclosures required by paragraphs 20(a) and 20(c) of Statement 114 (as amended), for a restructured loan that has not been excluded from the scope of Statement 114 because of the transition provisions in paragraph 27 of Statement 114, the measurement provisions of Statement 114 should be applied when it is probable that a creditor will be unable to collect all amounts due according to the contractual terms of the *original* loan agreement. Likewise, a creditor should use existing accounting methods for recognizing interest income on impaired loans for that loan; the income recognition provisions (prior to amendment) in paragraph 30 of Statement 15, need not be applied.

(This page intentionally left blank.)

Appendix B

THE SCOPE OF THE DISCLOSURE REQUIREMENTS IN PARAGRAPH 20(a) OF STATEMENT 114, AS AMENDED

24. The following table summarizes the scope of the disclosure requirements in paragraph 20(a) of Statement 114, as amended by this Statement.

Description of Loans	Required Disclosures about the Recorded Investment in Loans That Meet the Definition of an Impaired Loan in Paragraph 8 of Statement 114		
	(A) The Total Recorded Investment in the Impaired Loans	(B) The Amount of the Recorded Investment in (A) for Which There Is a Related Allowance for Credit Losses	(C) The Amount of the Recorded Investment in (A) for Which There Is No Related Allowance for Credit Losses
1. Loans that meet the definition of an impaired loan in paragraph 8 of Statement 114 and that have *not* been charged off fully	Included. The amount disclosed in (A) must equal the sum of (B) and (C).	Included if there is a related allowance for credit losses.	Included if there is no related allowance for credit losses.
2. Loans that meet the definition of an impaired loan in paragraph 8 of Statement 114 and that have been charged off fully	Excluded. The recorded investment and allowance for credit losses are equal to zero.		
3. Loans restructured in a troubled debt restructuring before the effective date of Statement 114 that are not impaired based on the terms specified by the restructuring agreement	Excluded. Disclosures should be provided in accordance with Statement 15.		

4. Loans restructured in a troubled debt restructuring before the effective date of Statement 114 that are impaired based on the terms specified by the restructuring agreement	Refer to items 1 and 2 above.
5. Loans restructured in a troubled debt restructuring after the effective date of Statement 114	May be excluded in years after the restructuring if (a) the restructuring agreement specifies an interest rate equal to or greater than the rate that the creditor was willing to accept at the time of the restructuring for a new receivable with comparable risk and (b) the loan is not impaired based on the terms specified by the restructuring agreement. Otherwise, refer to items 1 and 2 above.
6. Large groups of smaller-balance homogeneous loans that are collectively evaluated for impairment and other loans that are excluded from the scope of Statement 114 as defined in paragraph 6 of that Statement	Excluded unless restructured in a troubled debt restructuring (refer to items 3-5 above and paragraph 9 of Statement 114 for requirements for a restructured loan).

Statement of Financial Accounting Standards No. 119
Disclosure about Derivative Financial Instruments
and Fair Value of Financial Instruments

STATUS

Issued: October 1994

Effective Date: For fiscal years ending after December 15, 1994

Affects: Amends FAS 105, paragraphs 17 and 18 and footnote 12
Amends FAS 107, paragraphs 10 and 13

Affected by: No other pronouncements

Other Interpretive Release: FASB Special Report, *Illustrations of Financial Instrument Disclosures*

Issues Discussed by FASB Emerging Issues Task Force (EITF)

Affects: Partially nullifies EITF Issue No. 91-4

Interpreted by: No EITF Issues

Related Issues: No EITF Issues

SUMMARY

This Statement requires disclosures about derivative financial instruments—futures, forward, swap, and option contracts, and other financial instruments with similar characteristics. It also amends existing requirements of FASB Statement No. 105, *Disclosure of Information about Financial Instruments with Off-Balance-Sheet Risk and Financial Instruments with Concentrations of Credit Risk,* and FASB Statement No. 107, *Disclosures about Fair Value of Financial Instruments.*

This Statement requires disclosures about amounts, nature, and terms of derivative financial instruments that are not subject to Statement 105 because they do not result in off-balance-sheet risk of accounting loss. It requires that a distinction be made between financial instruments held or issued for trading purposes (including dealing and other trading activities measured at fair value with gains and losses recognized in earnings) and financial instruments held or issued for purposes other than trading. It also amends Statements 105 and 107 to require that distinction in certain disclosures required by those Statements.

For entities that hold or issue derivative financial instruments for trading purposes, this Statement requires disclosure of average fair value and of net trading gains or losses. For entities that hold or issue derivative financial instruments for purposes other than trading, it requires disclosure about those purposes and about how the instruments are reported in financial statements. For entities that hold or issue derivative financial instruments and account for them as hedges of anticipated transactions, it requires disclosure about the anticipated transactions, the classes of derivative financial instruments used to hedge those transactions, the amounts of hedging gains and losses deferred, and the transactions or other events that result in recognition of the deferred gains or losses in earnings. This Statement also encourages, but does not require, quantitative information about market risks of derivative financial instruments, and also of other assets and liabilities, that is consistent with the way the entity manages or adjusts risks and that is useful for comparing the results of applying the entity's strategies to its objectives for holding or issuing the derivative financial instruments.

This Statement amends Statement 105 to require disaggregation of information about financial instruments with off-balance-sheet risk of accounting loss by class, business activity, risk, or other category that is consistent with the entity's management of those instruments. This Statement also amends Statement 107 to require that fair value information be presented without combining, aggregating, or netting the fair value of derivative financial instruments with the fair value of nonderivative financial instruments and be presented together with the related carrying amounts in the body of the financial statements, a single footnote, or a summary table in a form that makes it clear whether the amounts represent assets or liabilities.

This Statement is effective for financial statements issued for fiscal years ending after December 15, 1994, except for entities with less than $150 million in total assets. For those entities, this Statement is effective for financial statements issued for fiscal years ending after December 15, 1995.

Statement of Financial Accounting Standards No. 119

**Disclosure about Derivative Financial Instruments
and Fair Value of Financial Instruments**

CONTENTS

INTRODUCTION

1. The Board added a project on financial instruments and off-balance-sheet financing to its technical agenda in May 1986. The project's objective is to develop broad standards to aid in resolving existing financial accounting and reporting issues and other issues likely to arise in the future about various financial instruments and related transactions.

2. Due to the complexity of the issues about how financial instruments and related transactions should be recognized and measured, and the likelihood that it will take time to resolve those issues, the Board decided that improved disclosure of information about financial instruments was necessary in the meantime. FASB Statement No. 105, *Disclosure of Information about Financial Instruments with Off-Balance-Sheet Risk and Financial Instruments with Concentrations of Credit Risk,* was issued in March 1990 and FASB Statement No. 107, *Disclosures about Fair Value of Financial Instruments,* was issued in December 1991.

3. Since the issuance of Statements 105 and 107, several parties have called for further improvements in disclosure about derivative financial instruments. This Statement responds to those requests. Some have called for voluntary disclosures like those already provided by a few entities, while others have urged the Board to enhance existing disclosure requirements. Some also have suggested that the Board should improve the clarity of the disclosures about fair value required for all financial instruments. As a result of those requests, the Board decided that further improvements in disclosures about derivative financial instruments and fair value of financial instruments are necessary.

4. The Board concluded that more disclosure about derivative financial instruments is needed because they are increasingly important in business and finance but are as yet not well understood by many investors, creditors, and others. Investors and creditors need information about derivative financial instruments, specifically, information about the purposes for which derivative financial instruments are held or

issued. The information they need—and the ability of entities to provide that information—varies depending on an entity's purpose for holding or issuing the derivatives.

STANDARDS OF FINANCIAL ACCOUNTING AND REPORTING

Definitions and Scope

5. *Financial instrument* is defined in Statement 107. For purposes of this Statement, a *derivative financial instrument* is a futures, forward, swap, or option contract, or other financial instrument with similar characteristics.

6. Examples of other financial instruments with characteristics similar to option contracts include interest rate caps or floors and fixed-rate loan commitments. Those instruments have characteristics similar to options in that they provide the holder with benefits of favorable movements in the price of an underlying asset or index with limited or no exposure to losses from unfavorable price movements, generally in return for a premium paid at inception by the holder to the issuer. Variable-rate loan commitments and other variable-rate financial instruments also may have characteristics similar to option contracts. For example, contract rate adjustments may lag changes in market rates or be subject to caps or floors. Examples of other financial instruments with characteristics similar to forward contracts include various kinds of commitments to purchase stocks or bonds, forward interest rate agreements, and interest rate collars. Those instruments are similar to forwards in that they provide benefits of favorable movements in the price of an underlying asset or index and exposure to losses from unfavorable price movements, generally with no payments at inception.

7. The definition of *derivative financial instrument* in paragraph 5 excludes all on-balance-sheet receivables and payables, including those that "derive" their values or contractually required cash flows from

the price of some other security or index, such as mortgage-backed securities, interest-only and principal-only obligations, and indexed debt instruments. It also excludes optional features that are embedded within an on-balance-sheet receivable or payable, for example, the conversion feature and call provisions embedded in convertible bonds.

Disclosure about All Derivative Financial Instruments

8. For many derivative financial instruments, information about their amounts, nature, and terms is required to be disclosed because those instruments are included in the scope of Statement 105. For options held and other derivative financial instruments not included in the scope of Statement 105 (because they do not have *off-balance-sheet risk of accounting loss,* as defined in Statement 105), an entity shall disclose either in the body of the financial statements or in the accompanying notes the following information by *category of financial instrument:*[1]

a. The face or contract amount (or notional principal amount if there is no face or contract amount)[2]
b. The nature and terms, including, at a minimum, a discussion of (1) the credit and market risk of those instruments, (2) the cash requirements of those instruments, and (3) the related accounting policy pursuant to the requirements of APB Opinion No. 22, *Disclosure of Accounting Policies.*

Disclosure about Purposes for Which Derivative Financial Instruments Are Held or Issued

9. The disclosures required in paragraph 8 of this Statement shall distinguish between derivative financial instruments held or issued for:

a. *Trading purposes,* including dealing and other trading activities measured at fair value with gains and losses recognized in earnings

---

[1]In this Statement, *category of financial instrument* refers to class of financial instrument, business activity, risk, or other category that is consistent with the management of those instruments. If disaggregation of financial instruments is other than by class, the entity also shall describe for each category the classes of financial instruments included in that category.

[2]Disclosure of the face or contract amount of financial instruments, including those within the scope of Statement 105, may be misleading when the instruments are leveraged and the leverage features are not adequately disclosed. For example, the notional amounts of an interest rate swap may be misleading if the contract's settlement payments are based on a formula that multiplies the effect of interest rate changes. Disclosure of the nature and terms of those instruments requires a discussion of the leverage features and their general effects on (a) the credit and market risk, (b) the cash requirements, and (c) the related accounting policy.

b. *Purposes other than trading.*

Disclosure about Derivative Financial Instruments Held or Issued for Trading Purposes

10. Entities that hold or issue derivative financial instruments for *trading purposes* shall disclose, either in the body of the financial statements or in the accompanying notes, the following:

a. The average fair value of those derivative financial instruments during the reporting period,[3] presented together with the related end-of-period fair value, distinguishing between assets and liabilities
b. The net gains or losses (often referred to as net trading revenues) arising from trading activities during the reporting period disaggregated by class, business activity, risk, or other category that is consistent with the management of those activities and where those net trading gains or losses are reported in the income statement. If the disaggregation is other than by class, the entity also shall describe for each category the classes of derivative financial instruments, other financial instruments, and nonfinancial assets and liabilities from which the net trading gains or losses arose.

Entities that trade other types of financial instruments or nonfinancial assets are encouraged, but not required, to present a more complete picture of their trading activities by also disclosing average fair value for those assets and liabilities.

Disclosure about Derivative Financial Instruments Held or Issued for Purposes Other Than Trading

11. Entities that hold or issue derivative financial instruments for *purposes other than trading* shall disclose the following:

a. A description of the entity's objectives for holding or issuing the derivative financial instruments, the context needed to understand those objectives, and its strategies for achieving those objectives, including the classes of derivative financial instruments used[4]
b. A description of how each class of derivative financial instrument is reported in the financial statements including the policies for recognizing (or reasons for not recognizing) and measuring the derivative financial instruments held or issued, and when recognized, where those instruments and related gains and losses are reported in the statements of financial position and income
c. For derivative financial instruments that are held or issued and accounted for as hedges of anticipated transactions (both firm commitments and forecasted transactions for which there is no firm commitment), (1) a description of the anticipated transactions whose risks are hedged, including the period of time until the anticipated transactions are expected to occur, (2) a description of the classes of derivative financial instruments used to hedge the anticipated transactions, (3) the amount of hedging gains and losses explicitly deferred,[5] and (4) a description of the transactions or other events that result in the recognition in earnings of gains or losses deferred by hedge accounting.

Encouraged Disclosure about All Derivative Financial Instruments Held or Issued

12. Entities are encouraged, but not required, to disclose quantitative information about interest rate, foreign exchange, commodity price, or other market risks of derivative financial instruments that is consistent with the way the entity manages or adjusts those risks and that is useful for comparing the results of applying the entity's strategies to its objectives for holding or issuing the derivative financial instruments. Quantitative disclosures about the risks of derivative financial instruments are likely to be even

---

[3]The calculation of average fair value based on daily balances is preferable to a calculation based on less frequent intervals. It is, however, sufficient to disclose average fair value based on the most frequent interval that a trader's systems generate for management, regulatory, or other reasons.

[4]For example, if an entity's objective for a derivative position is to keep a risk arising from the entity's nonderivative assets below a specified level, the context would be a description of those assets and their risks, and a strategy might be purchasing put options in a specified proportion to the assets at risk.

[5]For purposes of the disclosure of hedging gains and losses, the term *explicitly deferred* refers to deferrals in separate accounts in the manner required by FASB Statement No. 80, *Accounting for Futures Contracts,* for hedges of anticipated transactions and by FASB Statement No. 52, *Foreign Currency Translation,* for hedges of firm commitments. Those deferrals are in contrast to implicit deferrals that are (a) embedded in related carrying amounts for hedges of recognized assets and liabilities or (b) not recorded because changes in the value of the hedging instrument are not recognized.

more useful, and less likely to be perceived to be out of context or otherwise misunderstood, if similar information is disclosed about the risks of other financial instruments or nonfinancial assets and liabilities to which the derivative financial instruments are related by a risk management or other strategy.

13. Appropriate ways of reporting the quantitative information encouraged in paragraph 12 will differ for different entities and will likely evolve over time as management approaches and measurement techniques evolve. Possibilities include disclosing (a) more details about current positions and perhaps activity during the period, (b) the hypothetical effects on equity, or on annual income, of several possible changes in market prices, (c) a gap analysis of interest rate repricing or maturity dates, (d) the duration of the financial instruments, or (e) the entity's value at risk from derivative financial instruments and from other positions at the end of the reporting period and the average value at risk during the year. This list is not exhaustive, and entities are encouraged to develop other ways of reporting the quantitative information.

Amendments to Existing Pronouncements

14. Statement 105 is amended as follows:

a. In paragraph 17, the following footnote is added after *financial instruments with off-balance-sheet risk*:

> *Similar disclosures are required for derivative financial instruments without off-balance-sheet risk in paragraph 8 of FASB Statement No. 119, *Disclosure about Derivative Financial Instruments and Fair Value of Financial Instruments*.

b. In paragraphs 17 and 18, *class* is replaced by *category*.

c. The following paragraph is inserted at the beginning of footnote 12:

> In this Statement, *category of financial instrument* refers to class of financial instrument, business activity, risk, or other category that is consistent with the management of those instruments. If disaggregation of financial instruments is other than by class, the entity also shall describe for each category the classes of financial instruments included in that category.

d. The following paragraph is added after paragraph 17:

> The disclosures required in paragraph 17 shall distinguish between financial instruments with off-balance-sheet risk held or issued for trading purposes, including dealing and other trading activities measured at fair value with gains and losses recognized in earnings, and financial instruments with off-balance-sheet risk held or issued for purposes other than trading.

15. Statement 107 is amended as follows:

a. In paragraph 10, the following footnote is added after *either in the body of the financial statements or in the accompanying notes*:

> *If disclosed in more than a single note, one of the notes shall include a summary table. The summary table shall contain the fair value and related carrying amounts and cross-references to the location(s) of the remaining disclosures required by this Statement, as amended.

b. In paragraph 10, the following is added after the first sentence:

> Fair value disclosed in the notes shall be presented together with the related carrying amount in a form that makes it clear whether the fair value and carrying amount represent assets or liabilities and how the carrying amounts relate to what is reported in the statement of financial position.

c. The following is added to the end of paragraph 10:

> The disclosures shall distinguish between financial instruments held or issued for trading purposes, including dealing and other trading activities measured at fair value with gains and losses recognized in earnings, and financial instruments held or issued for purposes other than trading.

d. The following paragraph and footnote are added after paragraph 13:

> In disclosing the fair value of a derivative financial instrument,[*] an entity shall not (a) combine, aggregate, or net that fair value with the fair

value of nonderivative financial instruments or (b) net that fair value with the fair value of other derivative financial instruments—even if those nonderivative or derivative financial instruments are considered to be related, for example, by a risk management strategy—except to the extent that the offsetting of carrying amounts in the statement of financial position is permitted under the general principle in paragraphs 5 and 6 of FASB Interpretation No. 39, *Offsetting of Amounts Related to Certain Contracts,* or the exception for master netting arrangements in paragraph 10 of Interpretation 39.

---

*For purposes of this Statement, *derivative financial instrument* is used in the same sense as in paragraph 5 of FASB Statement No. 119, *Disclosure about Derivative Financial Instruments and Fair Value of Financial Instruments.*

Effective Dates and Transition

16. This Statement shall be effective for financial statements issued for fiscal years ending after De-cember 15, 1994, except for entities with less than $150 million in total assets in the current statement of financial position. For those entities, this Statement shall be effective for financial statements issued for fiscal years ending after December 15, 1995. Earlier application is encouraged. In the initial year of application, this Statement need not be applied to complete interim financial statements.

17. Disclosures required by paragraphs 8-11 and paragraphs 14 and 15 that have not previously been reported need not be included in financial statements that are presented for comparative purposes for fiscal years ending before the applicable effective date of this Statement. For all subsequent fiscal years, the information required to be disclosed by paragraph 10(b) of this Statement shall be included for each year for which an income statement is presented for comparative purposes, and all other information required to be disclosed by this Statement shall be included for each year for which a statement of financial position is presented for comparative purposes.

> **The provisions of this Statement need not be applied to immaterial items.**

This Statement was adopted by the unanimous vote of the seven members of the Financial Accounting Standards Board:

Dennis R. Beresford,	Anthony T. Cope	Robert H. Northcutt
Chairman	John M. Foster	Robert J. Swieringa
Joseph V. Anania	James J. Leisenring	

Appendix

BACKGROUND INFORMATION AND BASIS FOR CONCLUSIONS

CONTENTS

Appendix

BACKGROUND INFORMATION AND BASIS FOR CONCLUSIONS

Introduction

18. This appendix summarizes considerations that Board members deemed significant in reaching the conclusions in this Statement. It includes reasons for accepting certain views and rejecting others. Individual Board members gave greater weight to some factors than to others.

Background Information

19. The Board added a project on financial instruments to its agenda in 1986. As an early step in that project the Board focused on disclosures, resulting in FASB Statement No. 105, *Disclosure of Information about Financial Instruments with Off-Balance-Sheet Risk and Financial Instruments with Concentrations* of Credit Risk, which became effective in 1990, and FASB Statement No. 107, *Disclosures about Fair Value of Financial Instruments,* which became effective for larger entities in 1992. Background information on the overall project and the early disclosure work is provided in Appendix D of Statement 105 and Appendix C of Statement 107.

20. The Board received requests from many different constituents for further improvements in disclosures about *derivatives,* generally meaning futures, forward, swap, and option contracts and the like. Some called for voluntary action such as the added disclosures already being provided by a few institutions, while others urged the Board to enhance existing requirements as a further intermediate step in its project on financial instruments. Many urged that this be done quickly.

21. For example, in its July 1993 study *Derivatives: Practices and Principles,* the Group of Thirty, a private, independent, nonprofit body that examines financial issues, called for disclosure of information

about management's attitude toward financial risks, how derivatives are used and how risks are controlled, accounting policies, management's analysis of positions at the balance sheet date and the credit risk inherent in those positions, and, for dealers, additional information about the extent of activities in derivatives. Derivatives also were the subject of major studies prepared by several federal agencies, all of which cited the need for improvements in financial reporting for derivatives.

22. Several government officials expressed concern about derivatives, including financial reporting for them, in speeches and in writings. SEC commissioners and staff members suggested that the Board and the SEC must do more given the lack of transparency in financial statements of entities with derivative notional amounts far in excess of their capital. They also recommended that entities should strive to provide investors with as much information about off-balance-sheet items used to manage on-balance-sheet assets and liabilities as is already being disclosed for the on-balance-sheet items. Federal banking regulators called for modernization of accounting and disclosure standards to address new products and new risk management techniques. Those regulators cited serious deficiencies in the disclosures noted in the Group of Thirty study, especially the absence of a summary measure of market-risk exposure, and called for a "no surprises" policy on derivatives. They also issued directives to banks on that subject and considered requiring improved disclosure in regulatory reports. Extensive news reports cited those concerns and publicized difficulties encountered by several dealers and end-users of derivatives. Congressional hearings and proposed legislation were a further demonstration of concern.

23. Investors and creditors also expressed concern. For example, in its 1993 position paper, *Financial Reporting in the 1990s and Beyond,* the Association for Investment Management and Research (AIMR) noted that:

> Analysts also are confounded by the interrelationships and complexity of financial instruments. . . . Those risks are at least to be disclosed under the provisions of FASB Statement 105, but the disclosures are scattered throughout the financial statement notes and are completely understood only by relatively sophisticated and tenacious financial statement readers. [page 30]

24. The AICPA Special Committee on Financial Reporting told the Board that investors and creditors it interviewed almost uniformly complained of being mystified and frustrated about the effects of derivatives on the companies they follow and supported the AIMR position, rating the general category of off-balance-sheet exposures from financial instruments as one of their top priorities for improvement in financial reporting.

25. Concern about the financial reporting for derivatives is an international phenomenon. The International Accounting Standards Committee, in its revised Exposure Draft E48, *Financial Instruments,* proposes extensive disclosure about derivatives and other financial instruments, some of which goes beyond what is currently required in the United States.

26. After considering those concerns, in November 1993 the FASB staff solicited comments from the Financial Instruments Task Force, the Emerging Issues Task Force, and the Financial Accounting Standards Advisory Council to help in the prompt formulation of a recommendation to the Board on the need for action. After receiving comments from members of those bodies and from others who had expressed interest and weighing its other priorities, the Board decided in December 1993 to redirect some of its efforts on financial instruments toward enhanced disclosure about derivatives.

27. Following that decision, the Board held an open meeting with interested parties to discuss what disclosures needed to be improved and how the improvements might be accomplished.

28. The Board established both general and specific objectives for this Statement. The general objectives are the same as the objectives for disclosures of financial instruments explored in paragraphs 129-139 of the 1987 Exposure Draft, *Disclosures about Financial Instruments.* Those objectives, later summarized in paragraphs 79-85 of Statement 105, include: to describe items recognized in the financial statements, to provide appropriate measures of financial assets and financial liabilities, and to help users assess the risks and potentials that are present and the effects on the entity of different possible outcomes. The more specific objectives of this Statement are (a) to enhance disclosure about derivative financial instruments, (b) to make technical improvements to the disclosure of information about fair value of financial instruments, and (c) to accomplish (a) and (b) in time to improve 1994 year-end financial reporting. This Statement will not resolve all of the concerns expressed. In particular, the Board is aware that

the disclosures required by this Statement are likely to be of only limited value to regulators and others concerned about the "systemic risk" of derivatives.

29. The Board issued the Exposure Draft, *Disclosure about Derivative Financial Instruments and Fair Value of Financial Instruments,* in April 1994. The Board received 144 comment letters on that Exposure Draft. In June 1994, the Board met with interested parties to discuss derivative disclosures made for 1993 year-end financial reporting and how improvements might be made to the disclosures proposed in the Exposure Draft. The Board concluded that it could reach an informed decision on the basis of existing information without a public hearing.

30. The Board concluded that (a) the main focus of this Statement should be set by the term *derivative financial instrument,* (b) information about amounts, nature, and terms should be disclosed for all derivative financial instruments, not just for those with off-balance-sheet risk of accounting loss, (c) disclosure about derivative financial instruments should distinguish between, and report different kinds of information for, derivative financial instruments held or issued for trading purposes and those held or issued for purposes other than trading, (d) disclosure of quantitative information about risks of derivative financial instruments and their role in managing other risks should be encouraged, though not required at this time, and (e) Statements 105 and 107 should be amended to improve the disclosures they require. The remaining sections of this appendix discuss those conclusions in more detail.

Definitions and Scope

31. The Board concluded that for purposes of this Statement a derivative financial instrument is a futures, forward, swap, or option contract, or other financial instrument with similar characteristics.

32. That definition of *derivative financial instrument* builds on the definition of a *financial instrument* in Statements 105 and 107. That definition excludes contracts that either require the exchange of a financial instrument for a nonfinancial commodity or permit settlement of an obligation by delivery of a nonfinancial commodity, because those contracts involve the required or optional future exchange or delivery

of an item that is not a *financial instrument.* Some respondents suggested that the scope of this Statement should be expanded to include commodity contracts.[6] In some cases, commodity contracts and some other contractual arrangements have characteristics similar to derivative financial instruments in that they are used interchangeably, present somewhat similar risks and potentials, and are not always well disclosed.

33. The Board considered suggestions from respondents to include those items within the definition of *derivative* but was concerned about the complexities and complications, both known and unknown, that a more expanded scope might entail. The Board also was concerned that a more expanded scope might be inconsistent with the Board's objective of improving 1994 year-end financial reporting. The Board, therefore, concluded that the definition of *derivative* for the purposes of this Statement should be limited by the definition of *financial instrument.*

34. Some respondents questioned whether the term *derivative financial instrument* should include such on-balance-sheet receivables and payables as mortgage-backed securities, interest-only and principal-only obligations, and debt instruments indexed to the price of precious metals or common stock. They noted that all of those on-balance-sheet receivables and payables "derive" their values or required cash flows from the price of some other security or index. Others suggested that the term should include optional features that are embedded within an on-balance-sheet receivable or payable, for example, the conversion feature and call provisions embedded in convertible bonds. While better information about those items may be needed, the widespread concern that led to this Statement was more narrowly focused. Moreover, the Board was concerned that a more expanded scope might be inconsistent with the Board's objective of improving 1994 year-end financial reporting. The Board, therefore, decided that this Statement should follow a narrower usage of the term *derivative* that includes futures, forward, swap, and option contracts, and other financial instruments with similar chararacteristics, and excludes on-balance-sheet receivables and payables and optional features that are embedded in those receivables and payables.

---

[6]The definition of *financial instrument* in Statements 105 and 107 excludes many types of commodity-based derivative contracts, for example, most futures contracts for petroleum products. That definition, however, includes other commodity contracts, for example, most oil swaps, because they must be settled in cash.

35. The definition of *derivative financial instrument* includes *other financial instruments with similar characteristics*. Examples of other financial instruments with characteristics similar to option contracts include interest rate caps or floors and fixed-rate loan commitments. Some respondents objected to those examples. They argued that fixed-rate loan commitments are not typically considered derivatives and should be excluded from the definition. The Board believes that fixed-rate loan commitments have characteristics similar to option contracts in that they provide the holder with benefits of favorable movements in the price of an underlying asset or index with limited or no exposure to losses from unfavorable price movements. Like option contracts, they subject the issuer to market risk. The Board decided that those financial instruments should be included within the definition of *derivative financial instrument* and subject to the disclosures required by this Statement.

36. Variable-rate loan commitments and other variable-rate financial instruments also may include terms that subject the issuer to market risk. For example, contract rate adjustments may lag changes in market rates or be subject to caps or floors. Those financial instruments have characteristics similar to option contracts and, therefore, are subject to the disclosures required by this Statement.

Disclosure about All Derivative Financial Instruments

37. For many derivative financial instruments, certain information already is required to be disclosed because those instruments are included within the scope of Statement 105. Statement 105 requires all entities to disclose information about the extent, nature, terms, and credit risk of financial instruments with off-balance-sheet risk of accounting loss and the concentrations of credit risk for all financial instruments. Paragraph 62 of Statement 105 explains that the goal in limiting the scope of Statement 105 to "principally financial instruments with off-balance-sheet risk" resulted from a Board conclusion that that was "the most expeditious way to deal with what many respondents perceive as the area most in need of improvement."

38. The Board was concerned that because Statement 105's scope generally excludes financial instruments that do not have off-balance-sheet risk of accounting loss, some entities have omitted disclosures of significant positions in certain derivative financial instruments. Frequently cited examples include op-

tions held, interest rate caps and floors held, and loan commitments held. If financial statements fail to disclose those instruments, investors and creditors may be less likely to understand an entity's purpose for holding or issuing the instruments that are disclosed.

39. The Board concluded that information about the face or contract amount (or notional principal amount) of derivative financial instruments not within the scope of Statement 105, when coupled with the Statement 105 disclosures, will more effectively communicate the relative significance of an entity's entire derivative financial instrument position and may facilitate an understanding of the purpose for which the instruments are held or issued. The Board also concluded that disclosures that discuss the credit, market, and liquidity risk and the related accounting policy of an entity's derivative financial instruments that are not within the scope of Statement 105 should help investors and creditors to better understand those positions.

40. Some respondents suggested that more disclosure should be required about the credit risk of derivative financial instruments that are not within the scope of Statement 105. Paragraphs 18 and 19 of Statement 105 require credit risk disclosures for derivative financial instruments with off-balance-sheet credit risk of accounting loss. For a derivative financial instrument that is not within the scope of Statement 105, such as an option held, the credit risk of accounting loss is on-balance-sheet and reflected in the carrying amount of the assets recognized in the statement of financial position. Derivative financial instruments, however, can present economic credit risk on unrealized gains from past favorable price movements that have not yet been recognized in the financial statements or from possible future favorable price movements. Those economic credit risks are not risks of accounting loss and are not necessarily reported in the Statement 105 disclosures or elsewhere. Moreover, it is unclear how financial statements could disclose those risks, other than, perhaps, in disclosing fair value.

41. Statement 107 already requires disclosures about fair value of derivative financial instruments. In addition, paragraph 20 of Statement 105 already requires disclosures of significant concentrations of credit risk for *all* financial instruments. The Board concluded that this Statement need not require more disclosure about credit risk of derivative financial instruments not within the scope of Statement 105.

Disclosure about Purposes for Which Derivative Financial Instruments Are Held or Issued

42. One factor that contributes to the confusion and concern about derivative financial instruments is that financial statements omit or inadequately explain why entities hold or issue various types of derivatives. The Board concluded in the Exposure Draft that disclosures of derivative financial instruments should be separated into two categories based on the reasons that entities hold or issue the derivatives. The Exposure Draft proposed that disclosures distinguish between derivative financial instruments held or issued for *trading purposes,* including dealing or other activities reported in a trading account and measured at fair value, and *purposes other than trading.* The Board agreed that that distinction would be meaningful and readily understood by most financial statement users.

43. Most respondents supported the Exposure Draft's distinction between *trading purposes* and *purposes other than trading.* Some respondents, however, stated that those two categories did not accurately reflect derivatives activity. They suggested that the disclosures would be more realistic if separated into three categories: dealing, speculative position taking, and risk management. The Board considered that alternative but was concerned about the inherent difficulties in defining and distinguishing between those categories, particularly speculative position taking and risk management.

44. Some respondents stated that the distinction should be based on how derivatives are accounted for rather than on their purpose. They suggested that it would be more appropriate to distinguish between derivatives measured at fair value with gains and losses recognized in earnings and all other derivatives. The Board, however, concluded that a distinction based on accounting method, although possibly easier to apply, would not be as useful in providing an indication of why derivatives are held or issued.

45. Some respondents asked that the trading purposes category be clarified. They asked whether *trading* has the same meaning as in *trading securities* in FASB Statement No. 115, *Accounting for Certain Investments in Debt and Equity Securities.* Paragraph 12(a) of Statement 115 defines *trading securities* as "securities that are bought and held principally for the purpose of selling them in the near term (thus held for only a short period of time)." The Board decided that that definition would not always readily

apply to derivative financial instruments because some traders of swaps and other less liquid customized derivatives commonly maintain those positions for longer periods but report them as part of their trading portfolios.

46. Paragraph 12(a) of Statement 115, however, also states: "Trading generally reflects active and frequent buying and selling, and trading securities are generally used with the objective of generating profits on short-term differences in price." Those types of activities in derivative financial instruments generally indicate that the instruments are held or issued for *trading purposes.*

47. Some respondents asked whether derivative financial instruments used to hedge dealing activities also are considered held or issued for *trading purposes.* The Board concluded that for purposes of this Statement, *dealing* is the activity of standing ready to trade—either buying or selling—for the dealer's own account, thereby providing liquidity to the market. To facilitate this activity, dealers commonly hold contracts with customers for derivative financial instruments for indefinite periods and enter into other contracts to manage the risks arising from their trading account assets and liabilities. All of those activities are considered dealing for purposes of this Statement, and dealing is included as one component of *trading purposes.*

48. Some respondents asked that the Board clarify whether all derivative financial instruments that are measured at fair value should be categorized as held or issued for *trading purposes.* In the Exposure Draft, *trading purposes* included "other activities reported in a trading account and measured at fair value." The Board believes that some derivative financial instruments may be measured at fair value but not considered held or issued for *trading purposes.* For example, some hedging activities may entail the use of foreign exchange contracts that fail to meet the criteria for deferral accounting under FASB Statement No. 52, *Foreign Currency Translation.* Those derivative financial instruments, although measured at fair value, may be categorized as held or issued for *purposes other than trading.*

49. Some respondents asked that the Board clarify whether all derivative financial instruments that are measured at fair value but not reported in an established trading account should be categorized as held or issued for *purposes other than trading.* As noted in paragraph 48, the Exposure Draft defined *trading*

purposes as including "other activities reported in a *trading account* and measured at fair value" (emphasis added). Some respondents suggested that the term *trading account* had common usage and meaning in only some industries. The Board, therefore, decided that *trading purposes* should include "dealing and other trading activities measured at fair value with gains and losses recognized in earnings."

Disclosure about Derivative Financial Instruments Held or Issued for Trading Purposes

50. Fair value of derivative financial instruments at the end of the reporting period already is required to be disclosed under Statement 107. However, trading positions typically fluctuate, and the ending balance may not always be representative of the range of balances and related risks that an entity has assumed during a period. The Exposure Draft proposed that for derivative financial instruments held or issued for *trading purposes,* an entity should disclose the average, maximum, and minimum aggregate fair value of each class of derivative financial instrument, distinguished between assets and liabilities. The Board concluded that that information would provide investors and creditors with a better indication of the level of risk assumed by an entity when holding or issuing derivative financial instruments for *trading purposes.*

51. Some respondents stated that maximum and minimum balances are not currently captured or used for management purposes and that significant time and costs would be required to collect and maintain that information. Some also questioned the usefulness of that information. In response to those and other concerns, the Board decided not to require disclosures of maximum and minimum aggregate fair value. The Board believes disclosures of the average fair value when coupled with comparable period-end balances, as required by Statement 107, as amended, will enhance the information about an entity's activities during the reporting period.

52. Some respondents stated that while some traders are required to collect average balance information for regulatory purposes, that information generally is not collected by class of financial instrument, in part, because of the complications created by cross-product master netting agreements. The Board concluded that it was more important to disclose average fair value consistent with the period-end disclosures required by Statement 107, as amended, than to focus on disclosures limited by class and, consequently, decided not to require disclosures of average fair value by class of derivative financial instrument.

53. The Board also considered whether the average fair value of trading positions should be based on daily balances. As indicated by the Group of Thirty study, many banks, broker-dealers, and other kinds of entities currently have systems in place to accumulate daily information for management purposes. Moreover, they may be required to report that information to regulators. Some traders may not be subject to those regulations and may not otherwise have the systems in place to generate daily balances. The Board concluded that while information based on daily balances is preferable to less frequent intervals, it is sufficient to disclose average fair value based on the most frequent interval that a trader's systems generate for management, regulatory, or other reasons.

54. Information about average fair value is potentially useful for investors and creditors of any entity with a position in derivatives, whether for trading purposes or for purposes other than trading. The Board decided to require those disclosures for trading purposes because the information needed is generally available. For example, the Group of Thirty study strongly recommended daily market valuation of derivative positions as best practice for dealers, and its survey indicated that the vast majority already follow that practice. In contrast, that study recommended regular, rather than daily, market valuation by end-users of derivatives, and its survey indicated that most end-users currently do not regularly value their positions. Thus, the necessary data may be less likely to be available for derivative financial instruments held or issued for purposes other than trading, and the Board decided not to require average fair value for those derivatives.

55. Trading activities of many entities include both derivative financial instruments and other kinds of financial instruments or nonfinancial assets or liabilities that are not derivative financial instruments. Currently, most entities with trading operations are required by their regulators to report total net trading gains or losses from all sources. The Exposure Draft proposed that entities disclose "the net gains or losses . . . arising from derivative financial instrument trading activities. . . ." The Board had concluded that disclosing net trading gains or losses from derivative trading activities separately would help users better understand the magnitude of those activities. In addition, a comparison of the changes in net trading gains or losses from period to period would illustrate the degree of volatility inherent in the operations.

56. Some respondents stated that to be more meaningful and operational the disclosure of net trading

gains or losses must reflect the way the trading activities are managed. For management purposes, net trading gains or losses are generally disaggregated by business activity, risk, or some other category. Each category may include net trading gains or losses from derivative financial instruments, other financial instruments, commodity contracts, and other nonfinancial assets and liabilities. After considering those comments, the Board decided not to require the disclosure of net trading gains or losses solely from derivative financial instruments. The Board concluded that the amount of net trading gains or losses should be disclosed by whatever categories are consistent with the management of those activities. The Board also concluded that for each category the entity should provide a qualitative disclosure describing the classes of derivative financial instruments, other financial instruments, and nonfinancial assets and liabilities from which the net trading gains or losses arose.

57. The Board acknowledges that this Statement's required disclosures may not be representative of an entity's overall trading activities. However, the main concern of those who called for improved disclosure is the inadequacy of information about derivatives. This Statement responds to that concern. The Board concluded that entities that trade other financial instruments or nonfinancial assets should be encouraged, but not required, to present a more complete picture of their trading activities by also disclosing average fair value for those items and any other information that may improve financial statement users' understanding of the entity's overall trading activities.

Disclosure about Derivative Financial Instruments Held or Issued for Purposes Other Than Trading

All purposes other than trading

58. The Board believes that for derivatives held or issued for purposes other than trading, such as risk management, qualitative disclosures should be required to help investors and creditors understand what an entity is trying to accomplish with its derivatives. The Board concluded that an entity should disclose its objectives for holding or issuing derivative financial instruments, the context needed to understand those objectives, and its strategies for achieving those objectives.

59. The Exposure Draft proposed that the objectives, context, and strategies be disclosed by class of derivative financial instrument held or issued for purposes other than trading. Some respondents noted that disclosure by class would require unnecessary detail and might be inconsistent with the way in which the entity is managed. In response to those comments, the Board decided not to require disclosure of the objectives, context, and strategies by class of derivative financial instrument.

60. Existing disclosure of accounting policies in response to the requirements of APB Opinion No. 22, *Disclosure of Accounting Policies,* could be more helpful in assisting investors, creditors, and others in understanding how derivative financial instruments held or issued for purposes other than trading are reported in the financial statements. The Board concluded that this Statement should emphasize the disclosure of the policies for recognizing (or not recognizing) and measuring the derivative financial instruments held or issued, and when recognized, where those instruments and related gains and losses are reported in the statements of financial position and income.

61. Some respondents suggested that disclosure of the portion of earnings attributable to derivative financial instruments held for purposes other than trading, such as hedging or risk management activities, should be required. They argued that that information is necessary to assess the profitability and cash flows of an entity's core business before the effects of hedging or risk management. However, the Board was concerned about the difficulty of defining *hedging* or *risk management.* Further, even if *hedging* or *risk management* was adequately defined, many entities would not have systems in place to identify and accumulate the portion of earnings generated from those activities. Moreover, some suggested that even if those systems did exist, the amounts disclosed would be incomplete and possibly misleading if limited solely to earnings from derivative financial instruments, since those instruments are held or issued to hedge or in some way manage risks arising from an entity's other activities, not necessarily to produce profits. For all of those reasons, the Board concluded that those disclosures should not be required.

Hedging

62. The Board considered whether current hedging-related disclosures should provide additional information to enable investors, creditors, and other users of financial statements to understand an entity's risk exposures and its techniques for managing those risks. Disclosures previously have been required for

some hedges. FASB Statement No. 80, *Accounting for Futures Contracts,* requires certain disclosures about hedging with exchange-traded futures contracts. In addition, EITF Issue No. 91-4, "Hedging Foreign Currency Risks with Complex Options and Similar Transactions," requires certain disclosures for currency options, option combinations, and similar instruments used to hedge anticipated transactions. Many of the instruments currently used for hedging, however, such as most forwards, most options, and all interest rate swaps, are not explicitly covered by any disclosure requirement.

63. The Board concluded that four additional disclosures should be required for derivative financial instruments that are held or issued for the purpose of hedging anticipated transactions (both firm commitments and forecasted transactions for which there is no firm commitment): (a) a description of the anticipated transactions whose risks are hedged with derivative financial instruments, including the period of time until the anticipated transactions are expected to occur, (b) a description of the classes of derivative financial instruments used to hedge the anticipated transactions, (c) the amount of hedging gains and losses explicitly deferred, and (d) a description of the transactions or other events that result in the recognition in earnings of gains or losses deferred by hedge accounting. The Board concluded that those disclosures would assist investors, creditors, and other users of financial statements in evaluating an entity's success in hedging anticipated transactions and the importance of that activity to the entity.

64. The Board considered whether additional disclosures also should be required for deferred gains and losses on hedges of existing assets and liabilities because disclosures only about hedging anticipated transactions might present an incomplete picture of an entity's overall hedging activities. Previous accounting standards have not required that deferrals on hedging of existing assets and liabilities be reported separately from the hedged items. For example, Statement 80 requires that a change in the market value of a futures contract that qualifies as a hedge of an existing asset or liability be recognized as an adjustment of the carrying amount of the item being hedged. Thus, it may not be easy to separate deferred hedging gains or losses from the carrying amount of an item that has been hedged more than once. Similarly, if a deferred gain or loss has been recognized by adjusting the carrying amount of an interest-bearing asset and has been factored into that asset's effective yield, after a time the amount remaining to be recog-

nized may not be readily identifiable. Those disclosures will become feasible only if accounting standards for deferred hedging gains and losses are modified so that those gains and losses are separately distinguishable from the related hedged positions. The Board concluded that it should not require entities to provide information about gains and losses deferred as a result of hedge accounting of existing assets and liabilities.

65. The Board also considered whether it should require disclosure of hedging gains and losses that are implicitly deferred because changes in value of the hedging instrument are not recognized. The Board concluded that it should not require disclosure of implicit deferrals primarily for cost-benefit reasons, because it is not convinced that most entities have systems capable of identifying and accounting for those amounts. Furthermore, Statement 107, as amended by this Statement, requires the disclosure of the fair value of derivative financial instruments to be presented together with the related carrying amounts. That disclosure may in some cases be a useful indication of hedging gains and losses that have been implicitly deferred.

66. The Board also considered whether it should require an analysis of the changes in deferred gains and losses associated with hedging transactions that have occurred during the period. The analysis might be required to show (a) the beginning and ending amounts of deferred losses recognized as assets in the financial statements, deferred gains recognized as liabilities in the financial statements, and net deferred gains or losses recognized as a separate component of equity, indicating the category in the statement of financial position within which those deferred gains or losses are reported, (b) additions to deferred gains and losses and removals from deferred gains and losses during the period, and (c) the amount of the change in deferred gains or losses recognized in income during the period and a discussion of the events and transactions that result in recognition in income. The Board is not convinced that the benefits from disclosing that information justify the preparation costs and the costs to users of trying to interpret the data. The Board concluded that those disclosures should not be required.

Encouraged Disclosure about All Derivative Financial Instruments Held or Issued

67. One major use for derivatives is to manage interest rate, foreign exchange, commodity price, and other market risks. Few requirements for disclosure

about market risks of derivative financial instruments have been codified in the accounting literature. Existing requirements include the disclosure required by Statement 105 about off-balance-sheet risk of accounting loss, which requires face or contract or notional principal amounts and a discussion of the market risk of those instruments. While that information should be useful in assessing market risk, comments of investors, creditors, and other users of financial statements suggest that the resulting disclosure is insufficient for understanding the risk management activities of entities that hold or issue derivative financial instruments for purposes other than trading. The Group of Thirty study and other recent studies that have focused attention on the risk management activities of traders of derivative financial instruments suggest that information disclosed about those activities also is insufficient.

68. Other information about market risks also has been disclosed in management discussion and analysis sections of SEC filings and in bank call reports and in other reports required by regulators. The comments of financial statement users and from recent studies and press reports suggest that even those additional data have not been fully responsive to concerns of investors, creditors, regulators, and other users of financial statements.

69. Several different kinds of quantitative information about market risks of derivative financial instruments are used by management and are sometimes disclosed in practice. Possible approaches for reporting that information in financial statements include disclosing:

a. More details about current positions—An example for an entity with a small number of swaps might include disclosure of the fixed rates, the floating index, and the term of each swap. Entities, however, that use a large number of derivative financial instruments for managing or adjusting risk may find disclosure about each derivative impractical.
b. The hypothetical effects of several possible changes in market prices—An example of the effects of several possible changes in market prices might be disclosure of the effects of ± 100 and ± 200 basis point shifts in all interest rates; flattening of the yield curve by an increase in short rates or a decrease in long rates, or conversely, steepening of the curve; ± 10 percent shifts in all ex-

change rates against the reporting currency; or ± 20 percent shifts in prices of commodities that the entity purchases regularly. The indicated amounts of change ± are only illustrative. Entities choosing this disclosure would show some of the changes in market prices that they actually use in managing or adjusting risk. Some respondents suggested that this disclosure would be of limited value, since it would simply represent a "snapshot" of the portfolio on a given date. The Board is aware of that limitation but notes that most financial information is reported as of a balance sheet date or for a previous year and, therefore, is subject to the same kind of limitation.

c. A gap analysis—Gap analysis is an approach to the measurement of interest rate risk. The carrying amounts of rate-sensitive assets and liabilities, and the notional principal amounts of swaps and other unrecognized derivatives, are grouped by expected repricing or maturity date. The results are summed to show a cumulative interest sensitivity "gap" between assets and liabilities. Some form of gap analysis has been disclosed by some financial entities for several years. Some respondents suggested that gap analysis is losing its popularity as a management tool for financial entities because it fails to capture the effect of options and because it can be misleading unless all of the instruments in the analysis are denominated in a single currency.

d. The duration of instruments—Duration is the result of a calculation based on the timing of future cash flows and can be thought of as the life, in years, of a notional zero-coupon bond whose fair value would change by the same amount as the real bond or portfolio in response to a change in market interest rates. Only a few institutions have reported duration information. The usefulness of information about the duration of a bond or portfolio might be enhanced by also disclosing the convexity, which is the extent to which duration itself changes as prices change.

e. The entity's value at risk—Value at risk is the expected loss from an adverse market movement with a specified probability over a period of time. For example, based on a simulation of a large number of possible scenarios, an entity can determine with 97.5 percent probability (corresponding to calculations using about 2 standard deviations) that any adverse change in the portfolio value over 1 day will not exceed a calculated amount, the value at risk. Value at risk is used by dealers in managing risk of derivative financial instruments, and the Group of Thirty study recommended its use as best practice. Some suggested that value at risk might have some relation to a minimum safe level of capital. Value at risk has the disadvantage of being little known among investors, creditors, preparers, and indeed financial entities that are not derivative dealers. Some respondents suggested that although value at risk is an appropriate measure, most banks and other entities do not yet have the measurement or reporting systems to support that disclosure.

70. The Exposure Draft would have encouraged, but would not have required, disclosure of quantitative information about interest rate or other market risks of derivative financial instruments. Most respondents favored that approach. Others, including some commissioners and staff of the SEC, suggested that the encouraged quantitative information should be required. Some said that required disclosure of that information would better facilitate risk assessment, particularly for end-users of derivatives, than would the disclosures required by this Statement.

71. The Board, however, was concerned about requiring disclosure of quantitative information about risks using approaches that were not well defined, that were not well understood, and that could not easily be explained or calculated. The Board also was concerned about the various shortcomings of the different approaches. The Board considered requiring entities that hold or issue derivative financial instruments to disclose quantitative information using one or more of the approaches identified in the Exposure Draft. It also considered requiring disclosure of whichever approach is consistent with the technique an entity uses to manage its market risks.

72. The Board believes that the continuing evolution of approaches to risk management limits the ability to clearly define the most useful approach to disclosing quantitative information about market risks and that encouraging disclosure will aid that evolution. Even if an approach could be defined, the Board is concerned about the difficulty, at least for some entities, of gathering and calculating the information for 1994 year-end financial reporting purposes. For those and other reasons, the Board concluded that the disclosure of quantitative information about risks should be encouraged rather than required.

73. Some respondents argued that the encouraged disclosure, if provided, will include forward-looking information. They suggested that that information has potential legal ramifications if actual outcomes

were to differ from estimates disclosed. The Board disagrees that the encouraged disclosure must include forward-looking information. The quantitative disclosures encouraged in this Statement, depending on the approach chosen, could measure either an entity's current risk position or its success in achieving prior objectives. The Board believes that disclosure of both kinds of information may be useful and that neither kind of information necessitates disclosure of forward-looking information.

74. Some entities use one approach to manage risk in one part of their business and a different approach to manage risk in other parts of their business. The Board encourages those entities to provide separate disclosure for each part of their business.

75. The quantitative disclosures encouraged in this Statement, if limited solely to the risks of derivative financial instruments, may present an unbalanced view of an entity's overall market risk. The Board encourages entities to disclose similar information about the risks of other financial instruments or nonfinancial assets and liabilities to which the derivative financial instruments are related by a risk management or other strategy.

Amendments to Existing Pronouncements

76. Statement 105 requires an entity to disclose the extent, nature, and terms of financial instruments with off-balance-sheet risk of accounting loss. Paragraph 94 of Statement 105 states that some respondents to the 1989 revised Exposure Draft, *Disclosure of Information about Financial Instruments with Off-Balance-Sheet Risk and Financial Instruments with Concentrations of Credit Risk,* had suggested that the Board require:

> ... disclosure of information about the entity's purpose for holding or contracting financial instruments with off-balance-sheet risk. ... The Board concluded that a requirement to disclose the purpose of entering into certain financial instruments is not necessary because reporting entities are likely to disclose that information to explain more adequately the nature of risks of those instruments.

In developing this Statement, the Board became aware that since the adoption of Statement 105 many entities have not chosen to explain their purposes for entering into financial instruments with off-balance-sheet risk of accounting loss, including derivative financial instruments. The Board and most respondents agreed that disclosure about financial instruments with off-balance-sheet risk would be more useful to investors, creditors, and other users of financial statements if information about purposes was provided.

77. The Board concluded that to be consistent with the other disclosures required by this Statement, Statement 105 should be amended to require that the disclosure of the extent, nature, and terms of financial instruments with off-balance-sheet risk distinguish between instruments held or issued for trading purposes and instruments held or issued for purposes other than trading. For similar reasons, the Board also concluded that Statement 107 should be amended to require that the disclosures about fair value of financial instruments be categorized in the same manner.

78. Some respondents objected to the requirement in Statement 105 to disclose the face or contract amount (or notional principal amount) of financial instruments with off-balance-sheet risk. Some respondents suggested that those amounts are not useful and could be misleading, particularly in the case of leveraged instruments when the amount disclosed may not be representative of the risks of the instrument.

79. The Board understands that disclosure of the face or contract amount is an imperfect measure of market or credit risk for some financial instruments. Those amounts, however, provide an indication of the presence of those risks and of the volume of derivative activity. The Board continues to believe that that information is useful to investors and creditors. The Board agrees that the face or contract amount of some financial instruments may be misleading, particularly if the instruments are leveraged and information about the leverage features of those instruments is not provided. The Board concluded that entities are required to disclose the general effects of the leverage features of financial instruments as part of the description of the nature and terms of those instruments required by paragraph 17 of Statement 105 and paragraph 8 of this Statement.

80. Some respondents disagreed with the provision in the Exposure Draft that information should be provided by class of financial instrument, as required by Statement 105. Some argued that disclosure of the face or contract amount by class is not useful and that some other categorization would better indicate the risk exposures of those instruments. In response to those concerns, the Board decided that disclosure by class for purposes of Statement 105 should be optional and that the disclosure could instead be disag-

gregated by whatever category is consistent with the management of those instruments. The Board also decided that if the disaggregation is other than by class of financial instrument, the entity should provide a qualitative description of the classes of financial instruments included in each category. The Board believes that, overall, this amendment should improve the usefulness of the Statement 105 disclosure by allowing entities to provide the information in the manner in which it is most meaningful.

81. Statement 107 requires that an entity disclose, either in the body of the financial statements or in the accompanying notes, the fair value of financial instruments for which it is practicable to estimate that value. Entities also are required to disclose the methods and significant assumptions used to estimate the fair value of those financial instruments. Statement 107 provides illustrations that some have used as a guide for implementing the disclosure requirements. However, Statement 107 permits various ways of disclosing the information.

82. Statement 107 became effective for larger entities in late 1992. Based on the first two years of application, some have said that the disclosures are not as useful as they could have been. Some specifically asked the Board to improve those disclosures. Others suggested that the Board wait and allow higher quality disclosures to emerge in response to market forces. The Board concluded that disclosures about fair value of financial instruments should be improved by amending Statement 107 to provide more guidance on how to present the required information.

83. The disclosures required by Statement 107 are not limited to derivative financial instruments. This Statement presents an opportunity to improve those disclosures. The Board believes this Statement will enable investors, creditors, and other users to better understand the Statement 107 disclosures and better assess the consequences of an entity's investment and financing strategies.

84. Paragraph 10 of Statement 107 permitted disclosures "either in the body of the financial statements or in the accompanying notes." In that Statement, the Board concluded that entities should be allowed to determine the most appropriate way to disclose the fair value information in their financial statements. The Board reconsidered that earlier conclusion in light of observed practices and concluded in the Exposure Draft that an approach that put the disclosures in the body of the financial statements or in "one location" in the accompanying notes would be more

likely to achieve the objective of meaningful and useful financial reporting.

85. Some respondents disagreed with the Board's conclusion, arguing that *one location* was undefined and, therefore, the intent and effect of requiring disclosures in one location were unclear. Other respondents argued that it was more meaningful to include disclosures of fair value in several footnotes where they could be combined with related information. In its redeliberations, the Board considered requiring that the disclosures be presented in a single footnote to the financial statements. That approach, however, would be impractical in some cases due to the breadth of the disclosures and their interrelationship with the disclosures of Statement 105 and the other disclosures required by this Statement. The Board, therefore, concluded that if the disclosures are provided in more than a single footnote, one of the notes should contain a summary table. The summary table should contain the fair value and related carrying amounts and cross-references to the location(s) of the remaining disclosures required by Statement 107, as amended.

86. Some respondents said that disclosures that present fair value and net carrying amounts together were easier to use than those that made no reference to carrying amounts. The presentation of net carrying amounts is already suggested, although not required, by Statement 107. Paragraph 44 of Statement 107 states:

> The Board concluded that information about fair value of financial instruments, combined with information about carrying value, is relevant in part because it reflects the effects of management's decisions to buy a financial asset or incur a financial liability at a specific time, and then to continue to hold an asset or owe a liability.

In addition, the disclosure of carrying values is illustrated in the examples in Appendix B of Statement 107. Based on comments received and observation of practice, the Board concluded that it should specifically require that presentation.

87. The Board was concerned that in some Statement 107 disclosures it was impossible to determine whether fair value amounts disclosed for such "off-balance-sheet" items as interest rate swaps were favorable (representing unrecognized assets) or unfavorable (representing unrecognized liabilities) to the

entity. That ambiguity limited the usefulness of those disclosures for investors and creditors who were interested in aggregating the values of recognized and unrecognized financial instruments. The Exposure Draft proposed that the disclosures make clear whether the amounts disclosed are "favorable (assets) or unfavorable (liabilities)."

88. Some respondents suggested that the Exposure Draft's use of the words *favorable* and *unfavorable* could potentially be confusing, particularly in the case of certain futures contracts when the carrying amount may be recorded as a deferred gain or loss. In response to those concerns, the Board decided to delete those words in its amendment to Statement 107.

89. The Exposure Draft would have amended Statement 107 to require that in disclosing the fair value of a class of off-balance-sheet derivative financial instruments an entity should not combine, aggregate, or net the fair value of separate financial instruments of a different class, even if those instruments are considered to be related, for example, by a risk management strategy. The Exposure Draft also would have prohibited the netting of the fair value of financial instruments within a single class, except to the extent that the offsetting of carrying amounts was permitted by FASB Interpretation No. 39, *Offsetting of Amounts Related to Certain Contracts.*

90. Some respondents stated that the Exposure Draft's proposed amendment was confusing and inconsistent with the requirements of Interpretation 39. Others suggested that the proposed amendment would be misleading unless the disclosures were accompanied by a narrative description of the relationships between amounts disaggregated by this proposed amendment. Interpretation 39 permits the offsetting of the carrying amount of on-balance-sheet derivative financial instruments if the contracts are executed with the same counterparty under a master netting arrangement. The Board was concerned that the amendment as proposed would have permitted less offsetting in the footnote disclosures than is permitted in the statement of financial position. Furthermore, some entities had modified their information systems to comply with Interpretation 39 and might have had to modify those systems again to comply with this proposed amendment. The Board decided to revise the amendment to prohibit the combining, aggregating, or netting of the fair value of derivative financial instruments with the fair value of nonderivative financial instruments and the netting of derivative financial instruments with other derivative financial instruments, except to the extent that the

offsetting of carrying amounts in the statement of financial position is permitted by Interpretation 39. The Board also concluded that if some entities believe that additional disclosures are necessary to prevent the disaggregated fair value amounts from being misleading, this Statement would not prohibit those disclosures.

91. Some respondents also suggested that Statement 107 should be amended to require standardization of methods and assumptions used in estimating fair value. That Statement currently does not prescribe standard methods or assumptions. The Board's reasons are stated in paragraph 56 of Statement 107:

> ... the Board reaffirmed its preference for general rather than detailed guidance in this Statement even though general guidance may result in disclosures that are less comparable from entity to entity. The Board concluded that the benefits to investors and creditors of having some timely information about fair value outweigh the disadvantage of that information being less than fully comparable. . . . The Board also is aware that the current practices followed by entities that estimate fair value . . . for internal management purposes vary and to impose specific methods or assumptions could increase the cost of compliance for at least some entities. . . . Finally, financial instruments have such diverse characteristics that the Board believes that it is not practicable at this time to prescribe detailed methods and assumptions to be used in estimating fair value.

The Board believes that those reasons remain persuasive and decided not to amend Statement 107 to require standardization of methods and assumptions.

92. Some respondents also suggested that Statement 107 should be amended to require more detailed disclosures of the methods and assumptions for determining fair value. Paragraph 10 of Statement 107 already calls for the kind of disclosures being requested. It states that "an entity also shall disclose the method(s) and significant assumptions used to estimate the fair value of financial instruments." The illustrations in Appendix B of Statement 107 provide detailed disclosures of methods and assumptions. The Board decided that a further evaluation of the extent of the problem and potential solutions would be necessary before considering any amendment to Statement 107 to require more detailed disclosures of methods and assumptions.

Cost-Benefit Considerations

93. One of the precepts of the Board's mission is to promulgate standards only when the expected benefits of the resulting information exceed the perceived costs. The Board strives to determine that a proposed standard will fill a significant need and that the costs entailed in satisfying that need, as compared with other alternatives, are justified in relation to the overall benefits of the resulting information. The benefits of providing information about derivative financial instruments and improving the disclosures about derivative financial instruments with off-balance-sheet risk and the fair value of financial instruments are discussed in earlier paragraphs of this Statement, in paragraphs 71-85 of Statement 105, and in paragraphs 51-54 of Statement 107.

94. The benefits of providing information about derivative financial instruments and improving the disclosures of other financial instruments come at a cost—namely, the incremental cost of developing, implementing, and maintaining a system to generate the required disclosures. Many entities, particularly those who hold derivatives for trading purposes, already have systems in place to monitor and manage their derivative activities. The Board has attempted to contain any incremental costs of the disclosure requirements of this Statement by (a) giving only general guidance on the quantitative and qualitative disclosures about the purposes for which derivative financial instruments are held or issued so that an entity can exercise its judgment in determining the most cost-effective way of obtaining the information, (b) excluding certain proposed trading-purposes disclosures (paragraphs 50-56) and hedging-related disclosures (paragraphs 64-66) from this Statement because the benefits of providing that information are at least uncertain in relation to the costs involved, and (c) encouraging rather than requiring the disclosure of quantitative information about market risks of derivative financial instruments, in part because the measurement tools are still evolving.

Applicability to Certain Entities

95. The Board considered whether certain entities should be excluded from the scope of this Statement. In particular, the Board considered the usefulness of the disclosures about derivative financial instruments required by this Statement for small or predominantly nonfinancial entities. The Board also considered the usefulness of the disclosures for investment companies.

96. Many small entities have few, if any, derivative financial instruments, so costs of compliance to them may be minimal. Moreover, the decision to allow small entities additional time to apply the provisions of this Statement recognizes that the initial costs of compliance for those small entities that hold or issue more than a few derivative financial instruments may be higher than those for larger entities.

97. The Board also concluded that while this Statement would likely have its greatest impact on the financial reporting of entities whose assets and liabilities are primarily financial instruments, many predominantly nonfinancial entities have financial instruments, including derivative financial instruments, as an important part of their assets and liabilities. Disclosures about their identity, measurement, and the purposes for which they are held or issued are useful and should be required.

98. The Board acknowledged that for predominantly nonfinancial entities that have relatively small amounts of derivative financial instruments in proportion to their total assets or liabilities, the benefits of this Statement's disclosures to the users of their financial statements may be less than those for financial entities for which derivative financial instruments are a more important part of their activities. However, the costs of compliance are relatively lower for those entities, and there are comparability benefits associated with having similar disclosure requirements apply to similar financial instruments. Accordingly, the Board decided that the disclosures required by this Statement should apply to all entities.

99. Some respondents to the Exposure Draft questioned whether this Statement should apply to investment companies, for example, mutual funds. Those respondents said that the disclosures required by this Statement would duplicate the information that they are already required to provide, such as the disclosures required in Management's Discussion and Analysis (MD&A). The Board considered those comments but believes that some of the disclosures required by this Statement extend beyond what investment companies currently disclose. Moreover, the Board noted that if current MD&A disclosures satisfy the requirements of this Statement, those disclosures could be included in the basic financial statements through incorporation by reference to MD&A. Accordingly, the Board decided that the disclosures required by this Statement also should apply to investment companies.

Location of Information within Financial Reports

100. The Board considered whether the disclosures required by this Statement should be a part of the basic financial statements or whether they should be provided in MD&A or as other supplementary information. FASB Concepts Statement No. 5, *Recognition and Measurement in Financial Statements of Business Enterprises,* distinguishes between information that should be a part of the basic financial statements and that which should be provided as supplementary information. Paragraph 7 of Concepts Statement 5 emphasizes that information disclosed as part of the basic financial statements amplifies or explains information recognized in financial statements and is essential to understanding that information.

101. Some respondents suggested that the qualitative information required by this Statement should be disclosed in MD&A. They argued that entities would be less constrained and the disclosures could be better integrated with related disclosures about trading and risk management activities. Other respondents suggested that the Board should not place the disclosures in MD&A. They argued that MD&A is required only by the SEC and thus is only applicable to public companies, while some of the significant dealers and users of derivative financial instruments are nonpublic companies. Others suggested that the Board has no authority to prescribe requirements for MD&A.

102. Some respondents suggested that the qualitative information required by this Statement should be disclosed as other supplementary information because of the subjectivity associated with describing the purposes for which derivative financial instruments are held and the difficulty in auditing that information. Others suggested that the accuracy and quality of the disclosures would suffer if the information was permitted to be supplementary. Still others argued that since the information is important and related to the Statement 105 and 107 disclosures, it should be included in footnotes to the basic financial statements.

103. The Board has never addressed the issue of whether it could require disclosures in MD&A. Because the scope of this project is narrowly focused, the Board decided not to address that issue in this Statement. As noted in paragraph 99, however, the Board decided that, in order to limit redundancy, it

would be appropriate for entities to include the disclosures required by this Statement in the basic financial statements through incorporation by reference to MD&A.

104. In prior standards, the Board has required information to be supplementary partly as a way of excluding certain entities from the scope of the requirements. However, as discussed in paragraphs 95-99, the Board concluded that the disclosures required by this Statement should be provided by all entities.

105. The disclosures required by this Statement build on disclosures already included in the basic financial statements and, like them, serve the major purposes of disclosure summarized in Appendix D of Statement 105; that is, to provide descriptions, to provide measures, and to help in assessing risks and potentials. The Board concluded that there are no persuasive reasons for the disclosures about derivative financial instruments to be outside the basic financial statements. The Board also observed that information encouraged, but not required, by paragraphs 12 and 13 of this Statement could be disclosed within or outside the basic financial statements.

Applicability to Interim Financial Statements

106. Some respondents questioned whether the provisions of this Statement should apply to interim financial statements. Paragraph 16 of this Statement clarifies that disclosures are required for all complete sets of interim financial statements, except in the initial year of application of this Statement. The minimum disclosure requirements for summarized interim financial information issued by publicly traded entities that are established by APB Opinion No. 28, *Interim Financial Reporting,* are not affected by this Statement.

Effective Dates and Transition

107. The Board decided that, in the initial year of applying the provisions of this Statement, all newly required disclosures about all derivative financial instruments, about purposes for which derivative

financial instruments are held or issued, and of the amendments to existing pronouncements should be required only as of the date of the latest statement of financial position. Disclosures of prior-year information also would be helpful. The Board concluded that obtaining prior-year information for many of the disclosures might be difficult for many entities and impossible for others and that the benefits may likely not justify the costs. The Board observed that the transition for this Statement is similar to that used in Statements 105 and 107.

108. The Board concluded that, after transition, comparative information should be provided because that information is useful in assessing the management of market risk and pertinent trends.

109. Some larger reporting entities expressed concern that certain disclosures proposed in the Exposure Draft, particularly those applicable to derivatives held or issued for trading purposes, could not be provided without significant systems changes. In response to those and other concerns, the Board decided not to require certain disclosures for which information was not available nor readily calculable (paragraphs 50-56). For that and other reasons, the Board concluded that the proposed effective date would not unduly burden larger reporting entities.

110. Statement 107 became effective for larger entities, defined as entities with $150 million or more in total assets in the current statement of financial position, for financial statements issued for fiscal years ending after December 15, 1992. For smaller entities, Statement 107 becomes effective for financial statements issued for fiscal years ending after December 15, 1995. Because this Statement amends Statement 107, the Board decided to delay the effective date for smaller entities by one year to coincide with the effective date of Statement 107 for those entities. While the other provisions of this Statement could perhaps be made effective earlier for smaller entities, the Board believes a single delayed effective date will be simpler and will allow smaller entities more time to develop the required disclosures, in light of the experience gained by larger entities.

Statement of Financial Accounting Standards No. 120
Accounting and Reporting by Mutual Life Insurance Enterprises and by Insurance Enterprises for Certain Long-Duration Participating Contracts

an amendment of FASB Statements No. 60, 97, and 113 and Interpretation No. 40

STATUS

Issued: January 1995

Effective Date: For fiscal years beginning after December 15, 1995

Affects: Amends FAS 60, paragraph 6
Amends FAS 97, paragraphs 6 and 11
Amends FAS 113, paragraph 6
Effectively amends FIN 40, paragraph 5
Amends FIN 40, paragraph 7

Affected by: No other pronouncements

SUMMARY

This Statement extends the requirements of FASB Statements No. 60, *Accounting and Reporting by Insurance Enterprises,* No. 97, *Accounting and Reporting by Insurance Enterprises for Certain Long-Duration Contracts and for Realized Gains and Losses from the Sale of Investments,* and No. 113, *Accounting and Reporting for Reinsurance of Short-Duration and Long-Duration Contracts,* to mutual life insurance enterprises, assessment enterprises, and fraternal benefit societies (all of which are hereafter referred to as mutual life insurance enterprises). The AICPA has established accounting for certain participating life insurance contracts of mutual life insurance enterprises in its Statement of Position 95-1, *Accounting for Certain Insurance Activities of Mutual Life Insurance Enterprises,* that should be applied to those contracts that meet the conditions in this Statement. This Statement also permits stock life insurance enterprises to apply the provisions of the SOP to participating life insurance contracts that meet the conditions in this Statement. This Statement is effective for financial statements issued for fiscal years beginning after December 15, 1995.

This Statement also amends FASB Interpretation No. 40, *Applicability of Generally Accepted Accounting Principles to Mutual Life Insurance and Other Enterprises,* to defer the effective date of the general provisions of that Interpretation to fiscal years beginning after December 15, 1995. This Statement does not change the disclosure and other transition provisions of Interpretation 40.

Accounting and Reporting by Mutual Life Insurance
Enterprises and by Insurance Enterprises for
Certain Long-Duration Participating Contracts

FAS120

Statement of Financial Accounting Standards No. 120

Accounting and Reporting by Mutual Life Insurance Enterprises and by Insurance Enterprises for Certain Long-Duration Participating Contracts

an amendment of FASB Statements No. 60, 97, and 113 and
Interpretation No. 40

CONTENTS

INTRODUCTION

1. FASB Statements No. 60, *Accounting and Reporting by Insurance Enterprises,* No. 97, *Accounting and Reporting by Insurance Enterprises for Certain Long-Duration Contracts and for Realized Gains and Losses from the Sale of Investments,* and No. 113, *Accounting and Reporting for Reinsurance of Short-Duration and Long-Duration Contracts,* exempted mutual life insurance enterprises from the requirements of those Statements. FASB Interpretation No. 40, *Applicability of Generally Accepted Accounting Principles to Mutual Life Insurance and Other Enterprises,* did not address or change the existing exemptions of mutual life insurance enterprises from those Statements. Because of the lack of accounting guidance for the insurance and reinsurance activities of those enterprises, the Board asked the AICPA to reactivate and expeditiously complete its project on that issue. The Board's discussions with the AICPA emphasized that any guidance should be within the parameters of Statements 60, 97, and 113.

2. This Statement extends the requirements of Statements 60, 97, and 113 to mutual life insurance enterprises, assessment enterprises, and fraternal benefit societies. The AICPA has established accounting for certain participating life insurance contracts of those enterprises in its Statement of Position 95-1, *Accounting for Certain Insurance Activities of Mutual Life Insurance Enterprises,* that should be applied to those contracts that meet the conditions in this Statement. This Statement also permits stock life insurance enterprises to apply the provisions of the SOP to participating life insurance contracts that meet the conditions in this Statement. This Statement and the SOP are effective for fiscal years beginning after December 15, 1995.

3. This Statement also amends Interpretation 40 to defer the effective date of the general provisions of that Interpretation to fiscal years beginning after December 15, 1995, so that Interpretation 40, this Statement, and the SOP are concurrently effective. This Statement does not change the disclosure and other transition provisions of Interpretation 40.

STANDARDS OF FINANCIAL ACCOUNTING AND REPORTING

Accounting and Reporting by Mutual Life Insurance Enterprises

4. Mutual life insurance enterprises, assessment enterprises, and fraternal benefit societies (all of which

are hereafter referred to as mutual life insurance enterprises) shall apply Statements 60 and 97, except as noted in the following paragraph, and shall apply Statement 113 in reporting their insurance and reinsurance activities in financial statements prepared in conformity with generally accepted accounting principles.

Accounting and Reporting by Insurance Enterprises for Certain Long-Duration Participating Contracts

5. Mutual life insurance enterprises shall apply Statement 60 or 97, as appropriate, to participating life insurance contracts unless those contracts meet both of the following conditions:[1]

a. The contracts are long-duration participating contracts that are expected to pay dividends to policyholders based on actual experience of the insurer.
b. Annual policyholder dividends are paid in a manner that identifies divisible surplus and distributes that surplus in approximately the same proportion as the contracts are considered to have contributed to divisible surplus (commonly referred to in actuarial literature as the contribution principle).

6. Stock life insurance enterprises with participating life insurance contracts that meet the conditions in paragraph 5 of this Statement are permitted to account for those contracts in accordance with the SOP. The same accounting policy shall be applied consistently to all those participating life insurance contracts. Disclosure of the specific accounting policy applied to those contracts shall be made in accordance with APB Opinion No. 22, *Disclosure of Accounting Policies.*

Amendments to Statements 60, 97, and 113 and Interpretation 40

7. Paragraph 6 of Statement 60 is amended as follows:

a. In the first sentence, *and title insurance enterprises* is replaced by *title insurance enterprises, mutual life insurance enterprises, assessment enterprises, and fraternal benefit societies.*

b. The last sentence is replaced by:

FASB Statement No. 120, *Accounting and Reporting by Mutual Life Insurance Enterprises and by Insurance Enterprises for Certain Long-Duration Participating Contracts,* addresses the accounting for certain long-duration participating life insurance contracts.

8. Statement 97 is amended as follows:

a. In paragraph 6, *and FASB Statement No. 120, Accounting and Reporting by Mutual Life Insurance Enterprises and by Insurance Enterprises for Certain Long-Duration Participating Contracts,* is added to the end of the last sentence.

b. In paragraph 11, *and Statement 120* is added to the end of the second sentence.

9. The following is added at the end of the first sentence of paragraph 6 of Statement 113:

and to participating life insurance contracts that meet the conditions in paragraph 5 of FASB Statement No. 120, *Accounting and Reporting by Mutual Life Insurance Enterprises and by Insurance Enterprises for Certain Long-Duration Participating Contracts.*

10. The first sentence of paragraph 7 of Interpretation 40 is replaced by the following:

The general provisions of this Interpretation are effective for financial statements issued for fiscal years beginning after December 15, 1995, and the disclosures specified in paragraphs 5 and 6 are effective for annual statements for fiscal years beginning after December 15, 1992.

Effective Date and Transition

11. This Statement shall be effective for financial statements for fiscal years beginning after December 15, 1995, with earlier application encouraged. The effect of initially applying this Statement shall be reported retroactively through restatement of all previously issued annual financial statements presented for comparative purposes for fiscal years beginning after December 15, 1992. Previously issued financial statements for any number of consecutive annual pe-

---

[1]The AICPA's SOP establishes the accounting for those participating life insurance contracts of mutual life insurance enterprises that meet the conditions in paragraph 5 of this Statement. Because the accounting for those contracts is not specified in any of the officially established accounting principles in category (a) of AICPA Statement on Auditing Standards No. 69, *The Meaning of "Present Fairly in Conformity With Generally Accepted Accounting Principles" in the Independent Auditor's Report,* SAS 69 recognizes the SOP as generally accepted accounting principles (category (b)) for those contracts.

Accounting and Reporting by Mutual Life Insurance Enterprises and by Insurance Enterprises for Certain Long-Duration Participating Contracts

FAS120

riods preceding that date may be restated to conform to the provisions of this Statement. The cumulative effect of adopting this Statement shall be included in the earliest year restated.

> **The provisions of this Statement need not be applied to immaterial items.**

This Statement was adopted by the affirmative votes of six members of the Financial Accounting Standards Board. Mr. Leisenring dissented.

Mr. Leisenring disagrees with the deferral of the effective date of Interpretation 40. He believes that by delaying the effective date of Interpretation 40 the Board is allowing a practice to continue that it observed was unacceptable for the reasons described in that Interpretation. He believes that no events or circumstances have arisen since the issuance of Interpretation 40 that warrant a delay in the effective date of that Interpretation.

Mr. Leisenring believes that users of financial statements that are described as having been prepared in conformity with generally accepted accounting principles should expect that all appropriate accounting pronouncements have been applied. Interpretation 40 does not change the accounting for transactions, events, or circumstances under generally accepted accounting principles, but clarifies that those pronouncements must be applied when the financial statements have been described as being prepared in conformity with those standards. He believes that the effective date of Interpretation 40 should not be deferred because that Interpretation will improve the comparability of financial reporting among insurance enterprises for transactions and events other than those specifically addressed in Statements 60, 97, and 113 and the SOP for mutual life insurance enterprises that decide to prepare financial statements in conformity with generally accepted accounting principles.

Members of the Financial Accounting Standards Board:

Dennis R. Beresford, *Chairman*	Anthony T. Cope	Robert H. Northcutt
	John M. Foster	Robert J. Swieringa
Joseph V. Anania	James J. Leisenring	

Appendix

BACKGROUND INFORMATION AND BASIS FOR CONCLUSIONS

CONTENTS

Appendix

BACKGROUND INFORMATION AND BASIS FOR CONCLUSIONS

Introduction

12. This appendix summarizes considerations that were deemed significant by Board members in reaching the conclusions in this Statement. It includes reasons for accepting certain views and rejecting others. Individual Board members gave greater weight to some factors than to others.

13. An FASB Exposure Draft, *Accounting and Reporting by Mutual Life Insurance Enterprises and by Insurance Enterprises for Certain Long-Duration Participating Contracts,* was issued for public comment on March 24, 1994, and distributed to members of various industry organizations, in addition to the standard distribution, to encourage comment from those most affected by the proposal. The Board received 31 comment letters in response to that Exposure Draft. The Board concluded that it could reach an informed decision on the basis of existing information without a public hearing.

Background Information

14. In 1972, the AICPA published an Industry Audit Guide, *Audits of Stock Life Insurance Companies.* That Guide did not apply to mutual life insurance enterprises. The AICPA Insurance Companies Committee subsequently formed a task force to address accounting and reporting by mutual life insurance enterprises but later suspended that project.

15. In 1982, the Board issued Statement 60 which extracted the specialized accounting practices from the Guide. Statement 60 specifically exempted mutual life insurance enterprises from its requirements because the issue of which insurance accounting and reporting principles should be applied to those entities still had not been resolved. In 1987, Statement 97 was issued and also excluded mutual life insurance enterprises for the same reason. Statement 113, issued in 1992, continued the exemption of mutual life insurance enterprises.

16. In 1993, Interpretation 40 was issued. Interpretation 40 clarified that mutual life insurance enterprises that issue financial statements described as prepared "in conformity with generally accepted accounting principles" are required to apply all applicable authoritative accounting pronouncements in preparing those statements.

17. Interpretation 40 did not address or change the existing exemptions of mutual life insurance enterprises from Statements 60, 97, and 113. Interpretation 40, originally effective for fiscal years beginning after December 15, 1994, highlighted the need to definitively resolve the accounting and reporting requirements for the insurance activities of mutual life insurance enterprises.

18. Mutual life insurance enterprises primarily issue participating life insurance contracts. Participating life insurance contracts provide policyholders with certain guaranteed benefits and allow policyholders to share in the experience of the enterprise through dividends. Dividends are paid periodically and generally reflect the experience and performance of the enterprise for investment activity, mortality experience, and contract administration for each particular class of contracts. The determination and distribution of dividends distinguish participating life insurance contracts from nonparticipating life insurance contracts.

19. The AICPA identified certain participating life insurance contracts that have features of the policies addressed by both Statements 60 and 97. Those contracts are different from other forms of participating contracts because dividends paid by those contracts are adjusted to reflect actual company experience. The features of those contracts that are similar to the contracts addressed by Statement 60 include individual contract functions that are not separately displayed to policyholders nor explicitly stated in the policy, a pattern of premiums that is specified in the policy and that is generally level and fixed over the contract's life, and the lack of an explicit policyholder account balance. Those contracts also have features that provide a measure of flexibility and discretion to the insurance enterprise that is similar to those found in universal life-type contracts addressed by Statement 97. For example, dividends on participating life insurance contracts are adjusted by the insurer to reflect actual company performance. In effect, those contracts contain similar provisions to Statement 60 contracts but function like Statement 97 contracts. Accordingly, the AICPA decided that those contracts should receive specialized accounting treatment to reflect the features of those contracts.

20. The AICPA has issued SOP 95-1 that requires mutual life insurance enterprises to apply the SOP's

Accounting and Reporting by Mutual Life Insurance Enterprises and by Insurance Enterprises for Certain Long-Duration Participating Contracts

FAS120

accounting to participating life insurance contracts that meet the conditions in paragraph 5 of the SOP and to apply Statement 60 or 97 to all other life insurance policies in reporting their insurance activities in financial statements prepared in conformity with generally accepted accounting principles. Statement 113 applies to all reinsurance activities of mutual life insurance enterprises.

21. The AICPA asked the Board to remove the exemption for mutual life insurance enterprises from Statements 60, 97, and 113 and to require stock life insurance enterprises that have participating life insurance contracts that meet the conditions in paragraph 5 of the SOP to apply the accounting in the SOP to those policies in reporting their insurance activities in financial statements prepared in conformity with generally accepted accounting principles.

22. The Board considered the SOP and the AICPA's requests and decided to issue this Statement to address accounting and reporting principles for the insurance and reinsurance activities of mutual life insurance enterprises and to permit rather than require stock life insurance enterprises to apply the accounting in the SOP to participating life insurance contracts that meet the conditions in paragraph 5 of this Statement.

Applicability of Other Pronouncements

23. After considering the nature of insurance and reinsurance contracts of mutual life insurance enterprises, the AICPA concluded that Statements 60, 97, and 113 generally provide an appropriate model for the accounting and reporting of insurance and reinsurance activities of mutual life insurance enterprises. Based on that conclusion, the AICPA decided that requiring mutual life insurance enterprises to apply the provisions of those Statements to the insurance and reinsurance activities of those enterprises, except for participating life insurance contracts that meet the conditions in paragraph 5 of this Statement, would improve the comparability and understandability of financial reporting among insurance enterprises for insurance and reinsurance activities. Accordingly, the AICPA requested that the Board remove the exemptions of mutual life insurance enterprises from Statements 60, 97, and 113.

24. After considering the AICPA's conclusions, the Board decided that a general consideration of accounting and reporting by mutual life insurance enterprises was not necessary at this time. The Board

agreed with the AICPA and decided to remove the exemptions of mutual life insurance enterprises from Statements 60, 97, and 113.

25. Most respondents to the March 1994 Exposure Draft supported the overall approach of applying Statements 60, 97, and 113 to mutual life insurance enterprises. A few respondents suggested that the needs of policyowners, regulators, and the accounting profession would be better served by developing a universal accounting model for mutual life insurance enterprises that incorporates the best practices of statutory and generally accepted accounting principles. Such an approach would entail a comprehensive review of insurance accounting and reporting. The Board concluded that the concerns raised by those respondents do not warrant general reconsideration of insurance accounting and reporting at this time. The Board believes that the needs of users would be better served by providing mutual life insurance enterprises that elect to adopt generally accepted accounting principles with a more timely resolution of insurance accounting and reporting issues that is based on the existing framework of those principles.

Accounting for Certain Long-Duration Participating Life Insurance Contracts

26. The AICPA also concluded that the accounting for certain long-duration participating life insurance contracts of mutual life insurance enterprises should be addressed separately. The AICPA decided that considering separately the accounting for participating life insurance contracts that meet the conditions in paragraph 5 of this Statement was warranted because of the contractual differences between those contracts and other types of participating life insurance contracts.

27. The Board believes that the accounting in the SOP is reasonable for participating life insurance contracts that meet the conditions in paragraph 5 of this Statement. The Board acknowledges that the SOP will establish accounting principles for those contracts that differ from those applied to other types of participating life insurance contracts, but the Board believes that differences in the features of those contracts justify differences in accounting. The Board believes that the accounting in the SOP reasonably reflects the features of those contracts within the parameters of Statements 60 and 97.

28. A few respondents to the Exposure Draft disagreed with the AICPA's and the Board's conclusion

on that issue. Those respondents stated that participating life insurance contracts that meet the conditions in paragraph 5 of this Statement should be accounted for using a Statement 60 methodology because those contracts are similar to other life insurance contracts accounted for in accordance with Statement 60. In its redeliberations on the SOP, the AICPA reconsidered that approach and concluded that the accounting in the SOP more closely reflects the features of those contracts than a Statement 60 methodology. The Board concurs with the AICPA that for participating life insurance contracts that meet the conditions in paragraph 5 of this Statement the accounting in the SOP is more appropriate than the accounting under a Statement 60 approach.

29. The Board considered two approaches to include the SOP's accounting for participating life insurance contracts that meet the conditions in paragraph 5 of this Statement in the framework of generally accepted accounting principles. One approach would have referred to the SOP as a source of established accounting principles for those contracts. The other approach would have included the SOP's accounting requirements (paragraphs 11-24 of the SOP) in this Statement, making this Statement the source of accounting principles for those contracts.

30. The Board decided that the SOP should be referred to in this Statement as the source of established accounting principles for those contracts. The Board understands that including the SOP's accounting in this Statement would have established that accounting as category (a) accounting principles and would have integrated the SOP's accounting into FASB literature, thereby facilitating retrieval of that information. However, including the SOP's accounting in this Statement would have required the Board to deliberate the SOP's accounting, and the Board decided that that was not warranted at this time. The Board also concluded that this Statement and AICPA Statement on Auditing Standards No. 69, *The Meaning of "Present Fairly in Conformity With Generally Accepted Accounting Principles" in the Independent Auditor's Report,* will appropriately establish the SOP's accounting in the body of generally accepted accounting principles. The Board believes that financial statement users, preparers, and auditors will have reasonable access to the SOP and that reference to the SOP will provide adequate notice about the SOP's applicability to those contracts.

31. The Board also considered whether stock life insurance enterprises with participating life insurance contracts that meet the conditions in paragraph 5 of

this Statement should be required or permitted to apply the SOP's accounting to those contracts. Stock life insurance enterprises currently are required to apply Statement 60 to those contracts. The AICPA requested that the Board amend Statement 60 to require stock life insurance enterprises having that type of contract to apply the accounting in the SOP to those contracts.

32. The Board recognizes that the information provided to users about the insurance and reinsurance activities of life insurance enterprises could be improved by limiting the diversity among insurance enterprises in accounting and reporting for those activities. The Board acknowledges that permitting stock life insurance enterprises with participating life insurance contracts that meet the conditions in paragraph 5 of this Statement to apply the accounting in the SOP to those contracts may cause inconsistencies between insurance enterprises in their accounting for those contracts. The Board believes, however, that there are likely to be only a limited number of stock life insurance enterprises with material amounts of those contracts and decided not to require those enterprises to comply with the SOP.

33. In addition, the Board agreed that requiring stock life insurance enterprises to comply with the SOP would require the Board to deliberate the SOP's accounting and include that accounting in this Statement. The Board decided that the limited inconsistencies that may arise by permitting stock life insurance enterprises to apply the accounting in the SOP do not warrant further Board consideration at this time. The Board believes that the disclosures required by this Statement and Opinion 22 will provide sufficient information to assist users in understanding differences in accounting (between insurance enterprises) for participating life insurance contracts that meet the conditions in paragraph 5 of this Statement.

34. Most respondents to the Exposure Draft that addressed that issue agreed with the Board's conclusion to permit stock life insurance enterprises to apply the SOP to participating contracts that meet the conditions in paragraph 5 of this Statement. Some respondents stated that consistency and comparability in financial reporting among insurance enterprises would be improved if stock life insurance enterprises were either precluded from applying or required to apply the accounting in the SOP to those contracts. The Board reconsidered that issue but continues to believe that the accounting in the SOP reasonably reflects the features of those contracts and should be

Accounting and Reporting by Mutual Life Insurance
Enterprises and by Insurance Enterprises for
Certain Long-Duration Participating Contracts   **FAS120**

available to stock life insurance enterprises. The Board also believes that a decision to require stock life insurance enterprises to apply the SOP's accounting to those contracts would necessitate adding the accounting conclusions in the SOP to this Statement thereby requiring time-consuming deliberations. The Board decided not to require stock life insurance enterprises to apply the provisions of the SOP because the overall benefits of providing timely guidance on the accounting and reporting of insurance activities by mutual life insurance enterprises outweigh the incremental improvement in the consistency and comparability of financial reporting among insurance enterprises that would result from requiring stock life insurance enterprises to apply the SOP's accounting. Accordingly, the Board decided to retain the provision to permit stock life insurance enterprises to apply the accounting in the SOP.

Effective Date and Transition

35. Adoption of the provisions of this Statement is likely to establish a fundamentally different basis of accounting for insurance and reinsurance activities of mutual life insurance enterprises that currently prepare financial statements based on statutory accounting practices. Therefore, the Board decided that retroactive restatement is the appropriate method of reporting the effect of initially applying this Statement. Requiring a uniform transition method will improve the understandability and comparability of financial statements of mutual life insurance enterprises, both in the year of adoption and in subsequent periods. The Board recognizes that restatement of all years may be costly and may require information that mutual life insurance enterprises may no longer have or that was not previously required. The Board concluded that transition is, to a significant extent, a practical matter and therefore limited the requirement to restate previously issued annual financial statements that are presented for comparative purposes to fiscal years beginning after December 15, 1992, consistent with reporting the effect of initially applying Interpretation 40.

36. The Exposure Draft and Interpretation 40 provided only general implementation guidance and did not attempt to identify and address all issues that could arise from the adoption of multiple accounting standards. A few respondents asked the Board to provide more detailed implementation guidance. Those respondents stated that the financial information provided to users could be improved and inconsistencies could be reduced by providing more extensive guid-

ance. The Board considered those requests but concluded that delaying timely resolution of the accounting and reporting of insurance activities of mutual life insurance enterprises to undertake the time-consuming effort to identify all potential implementation issues and provide detailed implementation guidance was not warranted. The Board decided that for practical reasons the overall approach of providing general guidance should be retained and that this Statement should not address detailed implementation issues that may result from its requirements or those of Interpretation 40.

37. The Exposure Draft would have required that this Statement be effective for fiscal years beginning after December 15, 1994. The Board had previously stated its intention to address the accounting and reporting of insurance and reinsurance activities of mutual life insurance enterprises within the parameters of Statements 60, 97, and 113. Accordingly, the Board believed that that effective date would provide sufficient time to assimilate the requirements of this Statement and the SOP and to obtain the required information. The Board also concluded that the provisions of the proposed Statement and Interpretation 40 should be concurrently effective.

38. Many respondents urged the Board to delay the proposed effective date in the Exposure Draft. They pointed out that the Statement and SOP establish a fundamentally different basis of accounting for those mutual life insurance enterprises that currently prepare financial statements based on statutory accounting practices that differ significantly from generally accepted accounting principles. Respondents indicated that applying the Statement and the SOP to 1995 financial statements would be difficult if the final pronouncements were not issued until late 1994.

39. In its redeliberations, the Board discussed effective dates that would allow mutual life insurance enterprises sufficient time to assimilate the requirements of this Statement and the SOP, obtain the required information, and develop systems to meet ongoing accounting and reporting requirements. The Board decided that a one-year delay of the proposed effective date to fiscal years beginning after December 15, 1995 would be adequate for that purpose. The AICPA similarly deferred the effective date of the SOP.

Deferral of the Effective Date of Interpretation 40

40. As issued, the general provisions of Interpretation 40 are effective for fiscal years beginning after

December 15, 1994. Most respondents to the Exposure Draft that commented on the effective date agreed with the Board that this Statement, the SOP, and Interpretation 40 should be effective concurrently. Many respondents indicated that because the initial adoption of multiple accounting pronouncements is complex, the pronouncements should be adopted in the same reporting period. That complexity is primarily attributable to the interaction of insurance and noninsurance accounting standards. Also, several respondents stated that the understandability and comparability of financial statements of enterprises affected by this Statement, the SOP, and Interpretation 40 would be improved by concurrent adoption of all applicable authoritative accounting pronouncements in preparing financial statements in accordance with generally accepted accounting principles. Some respondents stated that because of limited accounting and actuarial resources, deferral of the effective date of Interpretation 40 would allow for a more orderly implementation of the provisions of this Statement, the SOP, and Interpretation 40.

41. The Board continues to believe that the understandability and comparability of financial reporting among insurance enterprises that elect to adopt generally accepted accounting principles would be improved by concurrent initial adoption of insurance and noninsurance accounting pronouncements. The Board concluded that the disadvantages to preparers,

users, and auditors that would be caused by required adoption of Interpretation 40 one year before the required adoption of this Statement and the SOP outweigh the disadvantages of a one-year delay in the effective date of that Interpretation.

42. On September 30, 1994, the Board issued the Exposure Draft, *Applicability of Generally Accepted Accounting Principles to Mutual Life Insurance and Other Enterprises—Deferral of the Effective Date of FASB Interpretation No. 40,* which proposed deferring the effective date of Interpretation 40 by one year to fiscal years beginning after December 15, 1995. The Board received 10 comment letters on that Exposure Draft. A large majority of respondents supported the deferral. A few respondents repeated suggestions that were included in their comment letters on the March 1994 Exposure Draft and that are addressed in this basis for conclusions.

43. The Board concluded that (a) it could reach an informed decision on that Exposure Draft on the basis of existing information without a public hearing, (b) deferral of the general provisions of Interpretation 40 is necessary and a one-year deferral to fiscal years beginning after December 15, 1995 is appropriate, and (c) the amendment of Interpretation 40 as specified in paragraph 10 is appropriately included in this Statement. The Board emphasized that the disclosures specified in paragraphs 5 and 6 of Interpretation 40 remain in effect.

Statement of Financial Accounting Standards No. 121 Accounting for the Impairment of Long-Lived Assets and for Long-Lived Assets to Be Disposed Of

STATUS

Issued: March 1995

Effective Date: For fiscal years beginning after December 15, 1995

Affects: Supersedes APB 16, paragraph 88(d)
    Amends APB 17, paragraph 31
    Amends APB 18, paragraph 19(h)
    Amends AIN-APB 30, Interpretation No. 1
    Amends FAS 15, paragraphs 28 and 33
    Amends FAS 19, paragraph 62
    Amends FAS 34, paragraph 19
    Amends FAS 51, paragraph 14
    Amends FAS 60, paragraph 48
    Amends FAS 61, paragraph 6
    Supersedes FAS 66, footnote 5
    Amends FAS 67, paragraphs 3, 24, and 28
    Supersedes FAS 67, paragraphs 16 and 25
    Amends FAS 71, paragraphs 9 and 10
    Amends FAS 101, paragraph 6

Affected by: No other pronouncements

Issues Discussed by FASB Emerging Issues Task Force (EITF)

Affects: Resolves EITF Issue No. 84-28
    Partially resolves EITF Issue No. 85-36
    Affects EITF Issues No. 90-16, 93-4, and 93-11

Interpreted by: Paragraphs 6 and 10 interpreted by EITF Issue No. 95-23
    Paragraphs 15, 34, and 35 interpreted by EITF Topic No. D-45

Related Issues: EITF Issues No. 87-11, 89-13, 90-6, 94-3, 95-21, 96-2, and 97-4

SUMMARY

This Statement establishes accounting standards for the impairment of long-lived assets, certain identifiable intangibles, and goodwill related to those assets to be held and used and for long-lived assets and certain identifiable intangibles to be disposed of.

This Statement requires that long-lived assets and certain identifiable intangibles to be held and used by an entity be reviewed for impairment whenever events or changes in circumstances indicate that the carrying amount of an asset may not be recoverable. In performing the review for recoverability, the entity should estimate the future cash flows expected to result from the use of the asset and its eventual disposition. If the sum of the expected future cash flows (undiscounted and without interest charges) is less than the carrying amount of the asset, an impairment loss is recognized. Otherwise, an impairment loss is not recognized. Measurement of an impairment loss for long-lived assets and identifiable intangibles that an entity expects to hold and use should be based on the fair value of the asset.

This Statement requires that long-lived assets and certain identifiable intangibles to be disposed of be reported at the lower of carrying amount or fair value less cost to sell, except for assets that are covered by APB Opinion No. 30, *Reporting the Results of Operations—Reporting the Effects of Disposal of a Segment of a Business, and Extraordinary, Unusual and Infrequently Occurring Events and Transactions.* Assets that are covered by Opinion 30 will continue to be reported at the lower of carrying amount or net realizable value.

This Statement also requires that a rate-regulated enterprise recognize an impairment for the amount of costs excluded when a regulator excludes all or part of a cost from the enterprise's rate base.

This Statement is effective for financial statements for fiscal years beginning after December 15, 1995. Earlier application is encouraged. Restatement of previously issued financial statements is not permitted. Impairment losses resulting from the application of this Statement should be reported in the period in which the recognition criteria are first applied and met. The initial application of this Statement to assets that are being held for disposal at the date of adoption should be reported as the cumulative effect of a change in accounting principle.

Statement of Financial Accounting Standards No. 121

Accounting for the Impairment of Long-Lived Assets and for Long-Lived Assets to Be Disposed Of

CONTENTS

INTRODUCTION

1. This Statement establishes accounting standards for the impairment of long-lived assets, certain identifiable intangibles, and goodwill related to those assets to be held and used and for long-lived assets and certain identifiable intangibles to be disposed of.

2. Long-lived assets such as plant and equipment generally are recorded at cost, which is usually fair value at the date of acquisition. The original cost usually is reduced over time by depreciation (amortization) so that the cost of the asset is allocated to the periods in which the asset is used. That practice has been modified in some circumstances when an asset has been determined to be impaired, in which case the asset has been written down to a new carrying amount that is less than the remaining cost and a loss has been recognized. Accounting standards generally have not addressed when impairment losses should be recognized or how impairment losses should be measured. As a result, practice has been diverse.

STANDARDS OF FINANCIAL ACCOUNTING AND REPORTING

Scope

3. This Statement applies to long-lived assets, certain identifiable intangibles, and goodwill related to those assets to be held and used and to long-lived assets and certain identifiable intangibles to be disposed of. The Statement applies to all entities. This Statement does not apply to financial instruments, long-term customer relationships of a financial institution (for example, core deposit intangibles and credit cardholder intangibles), mortgage and other servicing rights, deferred policy acquisition costs, or deferred tax assets. It also does not apply to assets whose accounting is prescribed by:

a. FASB Statement No. 50, *Financial Reporting in the Record and Music Industry*
b. FASB Statement No. 53, *Financial Reporting by Producers and Distributors of Motion Picture Films*

c. FASB Statement No. 63, *Financial Reporting by Broadcasters*

d. FASB Statement No. 86, *Accounting for the Costs of Computer Software to Be Sold, Leased, or Otherwise Marketed*

e. FASB Statement No. 90, *Regulated Enterprises—Accounting for Abandonments and Disallowances of Plant Costs.*

Appendix B contains a list of certain pronouncements that refer to impairment or disposal of assets and indicates which pronouncements are amended by this Statement and which pronouncements remain as authoritative literature. All references to an asset in this Statement also refer to groups of assets representing the lowest level of identifiable cash flows as described in paragraph 8.

Assets to Be Held and Used

Recognition and Measurement of Impairment

4. An entity shall review long-lived assets and certain identifiable intangibles to be held and used for impairment whenever events or changes in circumstances indicate that the carrying amount of an asset may not be recoverable.

5. The following are examples of events or changes in circumstances that indicate that the recoverability of the carrying amount of an asset should be assessed:

a. A significant decrease in the market value of an asset

b. A significant change in the extent or manner in which an asset is used or a significant physical change in an asset

c. A significant adverse change in legal factors or in the business climate that could affect the value of an asset or an adverse action or assessment by a regulator

d. An accumulation of costs significantly in excess of the amount originally expected to acquire or construct an asset

e. A current period operating or cash flow loss combined with a history of operating or cash flow losses or a projection or forecast that demonstrates continuing losses associated with an asset used for the purpose of producing revenue.

6. If the examples of events or changes in circumstances set forth in paragraph 5 are present or if other events or changes in circumstances indicate that the carrying amount of an asset that an entity expects to hold and use may not be recoverable, the entity shall estimate the future cash flows expected to result from the use of the asset and its eventual disposition. Future cash flows are the future cash inflows expected to be generated by an asset less the future cash outflows expected to be necessary to obtain those inflows. If the sum of the expected future cash flows (undiscounted and without interest charges) is less than the carrying amount of the asset, the entity shall recognize an impairment loss in accordance with this Statement. Otherwise, an impairment loss shall not be recognized; however, a review of depreciation policies may be appropriate.[1]

7. An impairment loss recognized in accordance with paragraph 6 shall be measured as the amount by which the carrying amount of the asset exceeds the fair value of the asset. The fair value of an asset is the amount at which the asset could be bought or sold in a current transaction between willing parties, that is, other than in a forced or liquidation sale. Quoted market prices in active markets are the best evidence of fair value and shall be used as the basis for the measurement, if available. If quoted market prices are not available, the estimate of fair value shall be based on the best information available in the circumstances. The estimate of fair value shall consider prices for similar assets and the results of valuation techniques to the extent available in the circumstances. Examples of valuation techniques include the present value of estimated expected future cash flows using a discount rate commensurate with the risks involved, option-pricing models, matrix pricing, option-adjusted spread models, and fundamental analysis.

8. In estimating expected future cash flows for determining whether an asset is impaired (paragraph 6), and if expected future cash flows are used in measur-

---

[1]Paragraph 10 of APB Opinion No. 20, *Accounting Changes,* addresses the accounting for changes in depreciation estimates, and paragraph 32 addresses the accounting for changes in the method of depreciation. Whenever there is reason to assess the recoverability of the carrying amount of an asset under paragraphs 4 and 5 of this Statement, there may be reason to review the depreciation estimates and method under paragraphs 10 and 32 of Opinion 20. However, an impairment loss that results from applying this Statement should be recognized prior to performing that review. The provisions of Opinion 20 apply to the reporting of changes in the depreciation estimates and method regardless of whether an impairment loss is recognized under paragraph 6 of this Statement.

ing assets that are impaired (paragraph 7), assets shall be grouped at the lowest level for which there are identifiable cash flows that are largely independent of the cash flows of other groups of assets.

9. Estimates of expected future cash flows shall be the best estimate based on reasonable and supportable assumptions and projections. All available evidence should be considered in developing estimates of expected future cash flows. The weight given to the evidence should be commensurate with the extent to which the evidence can be verified objectively. If a range is estimated for either the amount or timing of possible cash flows, the likelihood of possible outcomes shall be considered in determining the best estimate of future cash flows.

10. In limited circumstances, the test specified in paragraph 6 will be applicable at only the entity level because the asset being tested for recoverability does not have identifiable cash flows that are largely independent of other asset groupings. In those instances, if the asset is not expected to provide any service potential to the entity, the asset shall be accounted for as if abandoned or held for disposal in accordance with the provisions of paragraph 15 of this Statement. If the asset is expected to provide service potential, an impairment loss shall be recognized if the sum of the expected future cash flows (undiscounted and without interest charges) for the entity is less than the carrying amounts of the entity's assets covered by this Statement.

11. After an impairment is recognized, the reduced carrying amount of the asset shall be accounted for as its new cost. For a depreciable asset, the new cost shall be depreciated over the asset's remaining useful life. Restoration of previously recognized impairment losses is prohibited.

Goodwill

12. If an asset being tested for recoverability was acquired in a business combination accounted for using the purchase method, the goodwill that arose in that transaction shall be included as part of the asset grouping (paragraph 8) in determining recoverability. If some but not all of the assets acquired in that transaction are being tested, goodwill shall be allocated to the assets being tested for recoverability on a pro rata basis using the relative fair values of the long-lived assets and identifiable intangibles acquired at the acquisition date unless there is evidence to suggest that some other method of associating the goodwill with those assets is more appropriate. In instances where goodwill is identified with assets that are subject to an impairment loss, the carrying amount of the identified goodwill shall be eliminated before making any reduction of the carrying amounts of impaired long-lived assets and identifiable intangibles.

Reporting and Disclosure

13. An impairment loss for assets to be held and used shall be reported as a component of income from continuing operations before income taxes for entities presenting an income statement and in the statement of activities of a not-for-profit organization. Although there is no requirement to report a subtotal such as "income from operations," entities that present such a subtotal must include the impairment loss in that subtotal.

14. An entity that recognizes an impairment loss shall disclose all of the following in financial statements that include the period of the impairment write-down:

a. A description of the impaired assets and the facts and circumstances leading to the impairment
b. The amount of the impairment loss and how fair value was determined
c. The caption in the income statement or the statement of activities in which the impairment loss is aggregated if that loss has not been presented as a separate caption or reported parenthetically on the face of the statement
d. If applicable, the business segment(s) affected.

Assets to Be Disposed Of

Recognition and Measurement

15. APB Opinion No. 30, *Reporting the Results of Operations—Reporting the Effects of Disposal of a Segment of a Business, and Extraordinary, Unusual and Infrequently Occurring Events and Transactions,* requires that certain assets to be disposed of be measured at the lower of carrying amount or net realizable

value.[2] All long-lived assets and certain identifiable intangibles to be disposed of that are not covered by that Opinion and for which management, having the authority to approve the action, has committed to a plan to dispose of the assets, whether by sale or abandonment, shall be reported at the lower of carrying amount or fair value less cost to sell. The fair value of the assets to be disposed of shall be measured in accordance with paragraph 7 of this Statement.

16. Cost to sell an asset to be disposed of generally includes the incremental direct costs to transact the sale of the asset such as broker commissions, legal and title transfer fees, and closing costs that must be incurred before legal title can be transferred. Costs generally excluded from cost to sell an asset to be disposed of include insurance, security services, utility expenses, and other costs of protecting or maintaining an asset. However, if a contractual agreement for the sale of an asset obligates an entity to incur costs in the future to effect the ultimate sale, those costs shall be included as adjustments to the cost to sell an asset to be disposed of. If the fair value of an asset is measured by the current market value or by using the current selling price for a similar asset, that fair value shall be considered to be a current amount and that fair value and cost to sell shall not be discounted. If the fair value of an asset is measured by discounting expected future cash flows and if the sale is expected to occur beyond one year, the cost to sell also shall be discounted. Assets to be disposed of covered by this Statement shall not be depreciated (amortized) while they are held for disposal.

17. Subsequent revisions in estimates of fair value less cost to sell shall be reported as adjustments to the carrying amount of an asset to be disposed of, provided that the carrying amount of the asset does not exceed the carrying amount (acquisition cost or other basis less accumulated depreciation or amortization) of the asset before an adjustment was made to reflect the decision to dispose of the asset.

Reporting and Disclosure

18. An entity that holds assets to be disposed of that are accounted for in accordance with paragraphs 15-17 of this Statement shall report gains or losses resulting from the application of those paragraphs as a component of income from continuing operations before income taxes for entities presenting an income statement and in the statement of activities of a not-for-profit organization. Although entities are not required to report a subtotal such as "income from operations," entities that present such a subtotal must include the gains or losses resulting from the application of paragraphs 15-17 in that subtotal.

19. An entity that accounts for assets to be disposed of in accordance with paragraphs 15-17 shall disclose all of the following in financial statements that include a period during which those assets are held:

a. A description of assets to be disposed of, the facts and circumstances leading to the expected disposal, the expected disposal date, and the carrying amount of those assets
b. If applicable, the business segment(s) in which assets to be disposed of are held
c. The loss, if any, resulting from the application of paragraph 15 of this Statement
d. The gain or loss, if any, resulting from changes in the carrying amounts of assets to be disposed of that arises from application of paragraph 17 of this Statement
e. The caption in the income statement or statement of activities in which the gains or losses in (c) and (d) are aggregated if those gains or losses have not been presented as a separate caption or reported parenthetically on the face of the statement
f. The results of operations for assets to be disposed of to the extent that those results are included in the entity's results of operations for the period and can be identified.

---

[2]Paragraphs 13-16 of Opinion 30 prescribe the accounting for the disposal of a segment of a business. Paragraph 13 defines a segment of a business as "a component of an entity whose activities represent a separate major line of business or class of customer." Paragraph 15 of that Opinion prescribes the determination of a gain or loss on the disposal of a segment of a business and states:

In the usual circumstance, it would be expected that the plan of disposal would be carried out within a period of one year from the measurement date and that such projections of operating income or loss would not cover a period exceeding approximately one year. [Footnote reference omitted.]

Amendments to Existing Pronouncements

20. Paragraph 88(d) of APB Opinion No. 16, *Business Combinations,* is replaced by the following:

> d. Plant and equipment: (1) to be used, at the current replacement cost for similar capacity[11] unless the expected future use of the assets indicates a lower value to the acquirer, and (2) to be sold, at fair value less cost to sell.

21. The following sentence is added to the beginning of paragraph 31 of APB Opinion No. 17, *Intangible Assets,* immediately following the heading:

> Identifiable intangible assets not covered by FASB Statement No. 121, *Accounting for the Impairment of Long-Lived Assets and for Long-Lived Assets to Be Disposed Of,* and goodwill not identified with assets that are subject to an impairment loss shall be evaluated as follows.

22. In the first sentence of paragraph 19(h) of APB Opinion No. 18, *The Equity Method of Accounting for Investments in Common Stock,* the phrase *the same as a loss in value of other long-term assets* is deleted.

23. The last question and its interpretation of AICPA Accounting Interpretation 1, "Illustration of the Application of APB Opinion No. 30," are superseded by this Statement.

24. FASB Statement No. 15, *Accounting by Debtors and Creditors for Troubled Debt Restructurings,* is amended as follows:

a. The following sentence is added after the first sentence in paragraph 28:

> A creditor that receives long-lived assets that will be sold from a debtor in full satisfaction of a receivable shall account for those assets at their fair value less cost to sell, as that term is used in paragraphs 15-17 of FASB Statement No. 121, *Accounting for the Impairment of Long-Lived Assets and for Long-Lived Assets to Be Disposed Of.*

b. The last sentence of paragraph 28 is replaced by the following:

> The excess of (i) the recorded investment in the receivable[17] satisfied over (ii) the fair value of assets received (less cost to sell, if required above) is a loss to be recognized. For purposes of this paragraph, losses, to the extent they are not offset against allowances for uncollectible amounts or other valuation accounts, shall be included in measuring net income for the period.

c. In the second sentence of paragraph 33, *at their fair values* is deleted and *less cost to sell* is inserted after *reduced by the fair value.*

25. The following new paragraph and heading are added after paragraph 62 of FASB Statement No. 19, *Financial Accounting and Reporting by Oil and Gas Producing Companies:*

> **Impairment Test for Proved Properties and Capitalized Exploration and Development Cost**
>
> The provisions of FASB Statement No. 121, *Accounting for the Impairment of Long-Lived Assets and for Long-Lived Assets to Be Disposed Of,* are applicable to the costs of an enterprise's wells and related equipment and facilities and the costs of the related proved properties. The impairment provisions relating to unproved properties referred to in paragraphs 12, 27-29, 31(b), 33, 40, 47(g), and 47(h) of this Statement remain applicable to unproved properties.

26. The following sentence is added to the end of paragraph 19 of FASB Statement No. 34, *Capitalization of Interest Cost:*

> The provisions of FASB Statement No. 121, *Accounting for the Impairment of Long-Lived Assets and for Long-Lived Assets to Be Disposed Of,* apply in recognizing impairment of assets held for use.

27. The first two sentences of paragraph 14 of FASB Statement No. 51, *Financial Reporting by Cable*

Television Companies, are replaced by the following:

Capitalized plant and certain identifiable intangible assets are subject to the provisions of FASB Statement No. 121, *Accounting for the Impairment of Long-Lived Assets and for Long-Lived Assets to Be Disposed Of.*

28. FASB Statement No. 60, *Accounting and Reporting by Insurance Enterprises,* is amended as follows:

a. In the first sentence of paragraph 48, *and an allowance for any impairment in value* is deleted.

b. In the last sentence of paragraph 48, *Changes in the allowance for any impairment in value relating to real estate investments* is replaced by *Reductions in the carrying amounts of real estate investments resulting from the application of FASB Statement No. 121, Accounting for the Impairment of Long-Lived Assets and for Long-Lived Assets to Be Disposed Of.*

29. FASB Statement No. 61, *Accounting for Title Plant,* is amended as follows:

a. In the first and second sentences of paragraph 6, *value* is replaced by *carrying amount.*

b. The last sentence of paragraph 6 is replaced by the following:

Those events or changes in circumstances, in addition to the examples in paragraph 5 of FASB Statement No. 121, *Accounting for the Impairment of Long-Lived Assets and for Long-Lived Assets to Be Disposed Of,* indicate that the carrying amount of the capitalized costs may not be recoverable. Accordingly, the provisions of Statement 121 apply.

30. Footnote 5 to paragraph 21 of FASB Statement No. 66, *Accounting for Sales of Real Estate,* is replaced by the following:

Paragraph 24 of FASB Statement No. 67, *Accounting for Costs and Initial Rental Operations of Real Estate Projects,* as amended by FASB Statement No. 121, *Accounting for the Impairment of Long-Lived Assets and for Long-Lived Assets to Be Disposed Of,* specifies the account-ing for property that has not yet been sold but is substantially complete and ready for its intended use.

31. FASB Statement No. 67, *Accounting for Costs and Initial Rental Operations of Real Estate Projects,* is amended as follows:

a. In paragraph 3, *costs in excess of estimated **net realizable value*** is replaced by *reductions in the carrying amounts of real estate assets prescribed by FASB Statement No. 121, Accounting for the Impairment of Long-Lived Assets and for Long-Lived Assets to Be Disposed Of.*

b. Paragraph 16 is deleted.

c. The first and second sentences of paragraph 24 are replaced by the following:

A real estate project, or parts thereof, that is substantially complete and ready for its intended use* shall be accounted for at the lower of carrying amount or fair value less cost to sell as prescribed in paragraphs 15-17 of Statement 121. The recognition and measurement principles contained in paragraphs 4-7 of that Statement shall apply to real estate held for development and sale, including property to be developed in the future as well as that currently under development. Determining whether the carrying amounts of real estate projects require write-downs shall be based on an evaluation of individual projects.

---

*Refer to footnote 5.

d. Paragraph 25 is replaced by the following:

Paragraph 5 of Statement 121 provides examples of events or changes in circumstances that indicate that the recoverability of the carrying amount of an asset should be assessed. Insufficient rental demand for a rental project currently under construction is an additional example that indicates that the recoverability of the real estate project should be assessed in accordance with paragraph 6 of Statement 121.

e. In paragraph 28, the term *net realizable value* and its definition are deleted.

32. FASB Statement No. 71, *Accounting for the Effects of Certain Types of Regulation,* is amended as follows:

a. The following sentence is added to the end of paragraph 9:

If at any time the incurred cost no longer meets the above criteria, that cost shall be charged to earnings.

b. Paragraph 10 is amended as follows:

(1) The second and third sentences are replaced by:

If a regulator excludes all or part of a cost from allowable costs, the carrying amount of any asset recognized pursuant to paragraph 9 of this Statement shall be reduced to the extent of the excluded cost.

(2) In the fourth sentence, *the asset has* is replaced by *other assets have* and the following phrase is added to the end of that sentence after the footnote added by FASB Statement No. 90, *Regulated Enterprises—Accounting for Abandonments and Disallowances of Plant Costs:*

and FASB Statement No. 121, *Accounting for the Impairment of Long-Lived Assets and for Long-Lived Assets to Be Disposed Of,* shall apply.

c. The following new paragraph is added after paragraph 10:

If a regulator allows recovery through rates of costs previously excluded from allowable costs, that action shall result in recognition of a new asset. The classification of that asset shall be consistent with the classification that would

have resulted had those costs been initially included in allowable costs.

33. The following phrase is added to the end of the third sentence of paragraph 6 of FASB Statement No. 101, *Regulated Enterprises—Accounting for the Discontinuation of Application of FASB Statement No. 71:*

and FASB Statement No. 121, *Accounting for the Impairment of Long-Lived Assets and for Long-Lived Assets to Be Disposed Of,* shall apply, except for the provisions for income statement reporting in paragraph 13 of that Statement.

Effective Date and Transition

34. This Statement shall be effective for financial statements for fiscal years beginning after December 15, 1995. Earlier application is encouraged. Restatement of previously issued financial statements is not permitted. Impairment losses resulting from the application of this Statement shall be reported in the period in which the recognition criteria are first applied and met.

35. The initial application of this Statement to assets that are being held for disposal at the date of adoption shall be reported as the cumulative effect of a change in accounting principle, as described in APB Opinion No. 20, *Accounting Changes.* A business enterprise shall report the amount of the cumulative effect in the income statement between the captions "extraordinary items," if any, and "net income" (Opinion 20, paragraph 20). A not-for-profit organization shall report the cumulative effect of a change in accounting on each class of net assets in the statement of activities between the captions "extraordinary items," if any, and "change in unrestricted net assets," "change in temporarily restricted net assets," and "change in permanently restricted net assets." The pro forma effects of retroactive application (Opinion 20, paragraph 21) are not required to be disclosed.

> **The provisions of this Statement need not be applied to immaterial items.**

This Statement was adopted by the affirmative votes of five members of the Financial Accounting Standards Board. Messrs. Anania and Northcutt dissented.

Messrs. Anania and Northcutt disagree with this Statement's conclusion in paragraph 7 that an impairment loss should be measured as the amount by which the carrying amount of an asset exceeds the asset's fair value. The Board concluded that a decision to continue to operate rather than sell an impaired asset is economically similar to a decision to invest in that asset and, therefore, the impaired asset should be measured at its fair value. Messrs. Anania and Northcutt do not agree with the rationale of that conclusion. In their view, fair value, which is predicated on the concept of an exchange in a current transaction between willing parties, is not an appropriate measure of impairment because (1) there has been no exchange transaction with an independent party and (2) the asset will continue to be used in operations.

Mr. Anania believes that an impaired asset should be measured at its recoverable cost including the time value of money. In Mr. Anania's view, that approach is the appropriate improvement within the historical cost model to resolve the inconsistent accounting practices that currently exist. Mr. Anania would accept an incremental borrowing rate to determine the present value of estimated future cash flows from an impaired asset that does not have a quoted market price. However, he also would support a discount rate based on rates of return on high-quality, fixed-income investments, with cash flows matching the timing of the asset's expected cash flows. Mr. Anania believes that use of the latter rate would provide greater comparability when similar assets are owned by different entities that have different debt capacities. The recoverable cost including interest approach is discussed in paragraphs 82-85.

In addition, Mr. Anania believes that a forecast of expected cash flows will be the only available information to determine fair value for assets of an entity-specific nature, such as special-purpose structures and customized equipment. In Mr. Anania's view, the requirement to discount those cash flows at a rate commensurate with the risks involved, as discussed in paragraphs 92 and 93, imposes an unnecessary burden to determine that rate when there is clearly no plan or intent to sell the asset.

Mr. Northcutt believes that this Statement's requirement to measure an impaired asset at fair value is a precedent-setting departure from the transaction-based historical cost model. In Mr. Northcutt's view, the requirement to recognize an impairment loss is not an event or transaction that warrants the adoption of a new basis of accounting at fair value. He does not believe that a fair value measure provides the most relevant and reliable information for users of financial statements, and he finds little relevance in using that measure for an impaired asset that will continue to be held and used. Further, Mr. Northcutt believes that using fair value to measure an impaired

asset fails to recognize the nature of that asset, permits "fresh-start" accounting based on management's decision to keep an asset rather than sell it, and usually results in an excessive loss in the current period and an excessive profit in future periods.

Under the present accounting model, a long-lived asset is initially recognized and measured at cost, which is also presumed to be fair value. All subsequent measurements of that asset are the result of a process of allocation through depreciation or amortization. The carrying amount of the asset never purports to reflect anything other than the unallocated balance of the asset's original cost. Mr. Northcutt agrees with the impairment recognition test in paragraph 6 of this Statement and believes that when the carrying amount of an asset cannot be recovered through future operations, an impairment loss should be recognized. However, he believes that an impairment loss should reflect the cost of the asset that will not be recovered from the future operation and subsequent disposal of the asset. Thus, an impaired asset should be written down to its recoverable cost excluding interest. Mr. Northcutt views interest cost as a period cost. For the same reasons as those cited in the dissent to FASB Statement No. 34, *Capitalization of Interest Cost,* he believes that interest cost should not be included as part of an impairment loss regardless of whether the interest is an accrual of actual debt costs or the result of discounting expected future cash flows at some debt rate.

Mr. Northcutt further believes that the use of a fair value measurement, which is based on the notion of an exchange transaction between a willing buyer and a willing seller, fails to consider the nature of the asset in question. He believes that measurement at fair value is not operational. Clearly, the test for recoverability in paragraph 6 of this Statement is an entity-specific test. The estimate of future cash flows expected to result from the use of the asset reflects many aspects that are unique to the specific plans and operations of the entity. That estimate depends on assumptions about many variables, such as the efficiency of the entity's work force, the effectiveness of its marketing efforts, the creativity of its engineers, and management's willingness to invest additional capital. Estimating expected future cash flows is a very subjective process at best, but is probably within the capabilities of an entity's management if it is in the context of that entity's specific plans and operations.

Mr. Northcutt believes that while it may be possible to estimate the timing of expected future cash flows and then discount those cash flows at a rate "commensurate with the risks," it is presumptuous to believe that the result approximates fair value, as defined. In paragraph 70, the Board argues that the decision to continue to use rather than sell an impaired asset is presumably based on a comparison of expected future cash flows from alternative courses of action and is essentially a capital investment decision. The Board further presumes that no entity would decide to continue to use an asset unless that alternative was expected to produce more in terms of expected future cash flows or service potential than the alternative of selling it and reinvesting the proceeds. Mr. Northcutt believes that the Board's rationale demonstrates that the entity-specific cash flows are not the same as the market-based cash flows used to estimate fair value and that both sets of cash flows must be determined.

Mr. Northcutt believes that due to the nature of the long-lived assets subject to this Statement, quoted market prices in active markets will rarely be available and that the use of other valuation techniques will be required. Prices of similar assets, rental cash flows, and appraisals may produce reasonable fair value estimates for certain assets, such as an office building, but are unavailable for unique assets, such as manufacturing facilities or industrial equipment. Mr. Northcutt believes that cash flows used to estimate fair value must be based on some notion of "market" cash flows. He doubts the operationality of this Statement when the only available information is an entity's own cash flows expected from an asset's use and disposition. In Mr. Northcutt's view, a measure that uses entity-specific assumptions about an asset's expected future cash flows does not represent fair value.

Mr. Northcutt disagrees with the use of a fair value measurement that will yield variable results for identical assets. For example, consider two identical assets subject to different depreciation methods that result in different carrying amounts. It is possible that one asset could fail the impairment test in paragraph 6 of this Statement, whereas the other asset could pass, with the difference attributed solely to management's choice of a depreciation method. One asset would be written down to its fair value in accordance with paragraphs 7-11, whereas the other asset would remain at its carrying amount. Mr. Northcutt does not believe that those significantly different outcomes for the two assets, solely based on the depreciation method that was selected, produce decision-useful information for comparing the performance of different entities. In Mr. Northcutt's view, an asset's depreciation method does not influence management's decision to continue to use the asset or to dispose of the asset. He believes that if the recoverable cost approach was permitted, the resulting write-down would appropriately reflect a depreciation "catch-up" adjustment and that future depreciation would be based on the asset's new recoverable cost.

Mr. Northcutt also disagrees with this Statement's requirement that long-lived assets to be disposed of that are not covered by Opinion 30 be measured at the lower of carrying amount or fair value less cost to sell. Consistent with his view on assets to be held and used, Mr. Northcutt believes that a long-lived asset to be disposed of also should be written down to its recoverable cost—its net realizable value. In his view, net realizable value is a market value notion because it represents the net proceeds expected to be received when an asset is sold. The only difference between the fair value less cost to sell measure and the net realizable value measure is the consideration of the time value of money. The fair value less cost to sell measure requires that the expected net proceeds be discounted.

The Board decided to include assets to be disposed of in the scope of this Statement to preclude an entity from avoiding recognition of a larger fair value impairment loss by declaring an impaired asset as held for disposal and writing it down to its net realizable value. That decision illustrates that the measurements of impaired assets and assets to be disposed of are interrelated. Mr. Northcutt agrees that the measurements are interrelated but believes that the appropriate measure for an impaired asset is recoverable cost and, therefore, the appropriate measure for an asset to be disposed of is net realizable value.

Furthermore, Mr. Northcutt believes that measuring assets to be disposed of at the lower of carrying amount or fair value less cost to sell will not produce the best decision-useful information for users of financial statements because that measure usually results in a higher current-period loss and higher future-period income. According to paragraph 17, the carrying amount of an asset to be disposed of must be adjusted each reporting period for all revisions to the estimate of fair value less cost to sell. If the estimate of future net proceeds does not change, the passage of time will result in the carrying amount of the asset being adjusted to reflect the time value of money by a credit to income. Mr. Northcutt believes that a present decision to dispose of an asset at a loss should not result in income in future periods.

Appendix A

BACKGROUND INFORMATION AND BASIS FOR CONCLUSIONS

CONTENTS

Appendix A

BACKGROUND INFORMATION AND BASIS FOR CONCLUSIONS

Introduction

36. This appendix summarizes considerations that Board members deemed significant in reaching the conclusions in this Statement. It includes reasons for accepting certain approaches and rejecting others. Individual Board members gave greater weight to some factors than to others.

37. Accounting standards generally have not addressed when impairment losses for long-lived assets, identifiable intangibles, and goodwill related to those assets should be recognized or how those losses should be measured. As a result, practice has

been diverse. This Statement provides accounting guidance for the recognition and measurement of impairment losses for long-lived assets, certain identifiable intangibles, and goodwill related to those assets to be held and used. This Statement also addresses the accounting for long-lived assets and certain identifiable intangibles to be disposed of.

Background Information

38. In July 1980, the Accounting Standards Executive Committee of the AICPA (AcSEC) sent the Board the AICPA Issues Paper, *Accounting for the Inability to Fully Recover the Carrying Amounts of Long Lived Assets.* AcSEC urged the Board to consider issues raised in the Issues Paper and to provide specific accounting guidance for the impairment of assets.

39. In 1980, the Financial Accounting Standards Advisory Council (FASAC) also discussed accounting for impairment of long-lived assets and advised the Board to continue its work on the conceptual framework project and other agenda topics before adding a project on impairment of assets. The Board agreed and in November 1980 decided not to add a project on impairment of assets to its agenda.

40. The FASB Emerging Issues Task Force (EITF) discussed the issue of impairment at its meetings in October 1984, December 1985, and February 1986. EITF members noted that there were divergent measurement practices in accounting for impairment of assets and a significant increase in the size and frequency of write-downs of long-lived assets. However, members were not able to reach a consensus on any of the impairment issues and urged the Board to add a project on impairment of assets to its agenda.

41. In a March 1985 survey about potential new agenda issues, FASAC members cited impairment of assets as the second most important issue for the Board to address. In September 1986, responding to a similar survey, most FASAC members supported adding a project on impairment to the FASB technical agenda. Many members stated that the problem of large, "surprise" write-downs of assets was significant enough to justify consideration by the Board.

42. Also in September 1986, the Committee on Corporate Reporting of the Financial Executives Institute (FEI) published the results of its "Survey on Unusual Charges," which was conducted at the request of the

Board to assist in exploring current accounting practices for impairment of long-lived assets. The study indicated divergent reporting and measurement practices. In 1991, the FEI updated the survey and found that divergent reporting and measurement practices persisted.

43. In May 1987, the Institute of Management Accountants (IMA), formerly the National Association of Accountants, with the encouragement of the Board, approved a research study to examine accounting for impairment of assets. The IMA research report, *Impairments and Writeoffs of Long-Lived Assets,* published in May 1989, noted a variety of disclosure practices and a steady increase in the number of write-downs. The report suggested that authoritative guidance on the accounting for impairment of long-lived assets was needed.

44. The Board added a project to its agenda in November 1988 to address accounting for the impairment of long-lived assets and identifiable intangibles. A task force was formed in May 1989 to assist with the preparation of a Discussion Memorandum and to advise the Board. The FASB Discussion Memorandum, *Accounting for the Impairment of Long-Lived Assets and Identifiable Intangibles,* was issued in December 1990. The Board received 146 comment letters on the Discussion Memorandum, and 20 individuals and organizations presented their views at a public hearing that was held in August 1991. In January 1992, the Board began deliberating the issues at its public meetings. The Board also discussed those issues at a public meeting of the task force.

45. In November 1993, the Board issued an Exposure Draft, *Accounting for the Impairment of Long-Lived Assets.* The Board received 147 comment letters on the Exposure Draft, and 15 individuals and organizations presented their views at a public hearing that was held in May 1994. The Board reconsidered the proposals in the Exposure Draft at its public meetings. The Board also discussed possible revisions to the Exposure Draft at a public meeting of the task force.

46. In November 1994, the results of a field test of the Exposure Draft were published in an FASB Special Report, *Results of the Field Test of the Exposure Draft on Accounting for the Impairment of Long-Lived Assets.* The field test was conducted jointly by the Asset Impairment Subcommittee of the Financial Executives Institute's Committee on Corporate Re-

porting and the FASB. Ten entities participated in the field test by completing a comprehensive questionnaire. That questionnaire asked participants to detail the accounting policies and procedures used in the recognition and measurement of previous impairment losses and adjustments to the carrying amounts of assets to be disposed of. The questionnaire also asked what the effects would have been had the provisions of the Exposure Draft been applied to the same losses and adjustments. The field test results were considered by the Board during its redeliberations of the issues addressed by this Statement.

Scope

47. The original scope of the project was limited to accounting for the impairment of long-lived assets and identifiable intangibles. The Discussion Memorandum did not address accounting for goodwill, long-lived assets to be disposed of, or depreciation. It also did not address joint or common costs, cash flow estimation techniques, or discounting. It did, however, invite comments on the tentative decision to exclude goodwill, assets to be disposed of, and depreciation from the scope of the project. Based on comments received, the Board decided to include goodwill related to impaired assets in the scope of the Exposure Draft and this Statement. It concluded that long-lived assets and identifiable intangibles could not be tested for impairment without also considering the goodwill arising from the acquisition of those assets. The Board also decided that accounting for long-lived assets and identifiable intangibles to be disposed of should be included in the scope of the Exposure Draft and this Statement. In the Board's view, if those assets were not addressed, an entity could potentially avoid the recognition of an impairment loss for assets otherwise subject to an impairment write-down by declaring that those assets are held for sale.

48. The Board decided not to expand the scope of the project to include depreciation. The choice of depreciation method and estimates of useful life and salvage value can have an impact on whether an impairment exists and, when it does, the amount. The Board believes that an asset's depreciation method, estimated useful life, and estimated salvage value should be reviewed periodically and should be changed if current estimates are significantly different from previous estimates. Paragraph 32 of Opinion 20 addresses the accounting for changes in the method of depreciation; paragraph 10 of Opinion 20 addresses the accounting for changes in estimates.

The Board agreed that a review of depreciation policies is necessary when considering impairment and included reference to that review in paragraph 6 of this Statement.

49. The Board believes that an impairment condition—the inability to recover fully the carrying amount of an asset—is different from the need to review an asset's depreciation method and estimates of useful life and salvage value. As stated in paragraph 5 of ARB No. 43, Chapter 9C, "Emergency Facilities: Depreciation, Amortization and Income Taxes," depreciation accounting is "a system of accounting which aims to distribute the cost or other basic value of tangible capital assets, less salvage (if any), over the estimated useful life of the unit (which may be a group of assets) in a systematic and rational manner. It is a process of allocation, not of valuation." It is important to recognize that depreciation accounting is used to distribute or allocate asset carrying amounts that are recoverable. Perhaps the period of recovery may be longer or shorter than previously estimated. Perhaps an alternative depreciation method may be more appropriate. Yet, in using depreciation accounting, it is inherently assumed that the carrying amount of the asset will be recovered.

50. This Statement does not apply to financial instruments, long-term customer relationships of a financial institution (for example, core deposit intangibles and credit cardholder intangibles), mortgage and other servicing rights, deferred policy acquisition costs, or deferred tax assets. Financial instruments (including investments in equity securities accounted for under the cost or equity method), mortgage servicing rights, and other servicing rights are excluded from this Statement because they are under study in other agenda projects. This Statement does not apply to core deposit intangibles and credit cardholder intangibles because they have characteristics that make their measurements similar to measurements that are used for financial instruments.

51. The Board chose not to include accounting for leases in the scope of the Exposure Draft because FASB Statement No. 13, *Accounting for Leases,* discusses leases in detail. Most respondents who commented on the treatment of leases in the Exposure Draft suggested that the scope should include all capital leases of lessees, and the Board agreed to include those leases in this Statement. The Board also agreed that assets of lessors subject to operating leases are within the scope of this Statement. The Board did not include deferred tax assets in the scope

of this Statement because they are addressed in FASB Statement No. 109, *Accounting for Income Taxes.*

52. The Exposure Draft would not have applied to assets whose accounting is prescribed by FASB Statement No. 60, *Accounting and Reporting by Insurance Enterprises.* In part, Statement 60 addresses the accounting by insurance enterprises for deferred policy acquisition costs and real estate investments. Several respondents questioned whether that scope exclusion applied to both of those types of assets. The Board intended to exclude only deferred policy acquisition costs. Deferred policy acquisition costs are often considered to be related to other assets and liabilities of insurance enterprises, and as a result, the accounting for those costs is unique to the insurance industry. Statement 60 and FASB Statement No. 97, *Accounting and Reporting by Insurance Enterprises for Certain Long-Duration Contracts and for Realized Gains and Losses from the Sale of Investments,* address the impairment of those costs. Therefore, the Board concluded that deferred policy acquisition costs, but not real estate investments or other assets covered by Statement 60, should be excluded from the scope of this Statement. The Board also decided to exclude from the scope of this Statement assets addressed in Statements that apply to certain specialized industries, specifically the record and music, motion picture, broadcasting, and software industries.

53. This Statement applies to long-lived assets and certain identifiable intangibles to be disposed of that are not covered by Opinion 30. The Board decided not to reconsider the conclusions of Opinion 30 because it did not wish to undertake an examination of all of the issues contained in that Opinion.

54. The Board decided to include impairment of regulatory assets in the scope of this Statement. The Board concluded that a distinction should be made between a regulated enterprise's plant and other fixed assets that any other enterprise would recognize as assets and its regulatory assets that any other enterprise would charge to expense as incurred.

55. Some respondents to the Exposure Draft suggested that not-for-profit organizations should not be included in the scope of the Statement because some assets may not have independent cash flows at a level lower than the total organization. The Board has provided further guidance in paragraph 10 to address those assets, whether held by business enterprises or

by not-for-profit organizations. Accordingly, not-for-profit organizations are included in the scope of this Statement.

When to Test for Impairment

56. Respondents to the Discussion Memorandum stressed that requiring a specific periodic impairment test for all assets would be unnecessary and cost prohibitive. They favored limiting impairment testing to when events or changes in circumstances indicate that an impairment test is necessary. They suggested that the impairment indicators contained in the Discussion Memorandum, which had been suggested in the Issues Paper, would be useful examples of events or changes in circumstances that indicate that an impairment assessment is warranted.

57. The Board concluded in the Exposure Draft that management has the responsibility to consider whether an asset is impaired but that to test each asset each period would be too costly. Existing information and analyses developed for management review of the entity and its operations generally will be the principal evidence needed to determine when an impairment exists. Indicators of impairment, therefore, are useful examples of events or changes in circumstances that suggest that the recoverability of the carrying amount of an asset should be assessed. The examples in paragraph 5 of this Statement were derived from the following list in the Issues Paper:

a. Reduction in the extent to which a plant is used
b. Dramatic change in the manner in which an asset is used
c. Substantial drop in the market value of an asset
d. Change in law or environment
e. Forecast showing lack of long-term profitability
f. Costs in excess of amount originally expected to acquire or construct an asset.

58. The Board considered suggestions that the list of impairment indicators should be definitive, that is, the existence of one or more indicators should determine whether an impairment exists. Because Board members were convinced that the list could never be complete, they concluded that it would best serve as examples of events or changes in circumstances that might suggest an impairment loss exists. The Board sought additional examples of impairment indicators in its review of comment letters and public hearing testimony on the Exposure Draft and during meetings with constituent organizations. Some respondents suggested that the list of examples should ad-

dress events or changes in circumstances that might suggest an impairment loss exists when past events or changes in circumstances also are considered, such as a current period operating or cash flow loss combined with a history of operating or cash flow losses. Other respondents suggested that an impairment assessment is warranted if a regulator excludes a cost from a regulated enterprise's rate base. The Board agreed and incorporated additional examples into paragraph 5 of this Statement, such as a significant physical change in an asset, an adverse action or assessment by a regulator, and a current period operating or cash flow loss combined with a history of operating or cash flow losses.

Recognition of an Impairment Loss

59. The Board considered the alternative recognition criteria identified and discussed in the Discussion Memorandum and used in practice: economic impairment, permanent impairment, and probability of impairment.

60. The economic criterion calls for loss recognition whenever the carrying amount of an asset exceeds the asset's fair value. It is an approach that would require continuous evaluation for impairment of long-lived assets similar to the ongoing lower-of-cost-or-market measurement of inventory. The economic criterion is based on the measurement of the asset. Using the same measure for recognition and measurement assures consistent outcomes for identical fact situations. However, the economic criterion presupposes that a fair value is available for every asset on an ongoing basis. Otherwise, an event or change in circumstance would be needed to determine which assets needed to be measured and in which period. Some respondents to the Discussion Memorandum indicated that the results of a measurement should not be sufficient reason to trigger recognition of an impairment loss. They favored using either the permanence or probability criterion to avoid recognition of write-downs that might result from measurements reflecting only temporary market fluctuations.

61. The permanence criterion calls for loss recognition when the carrying amount of an asset exceeds the asset's fair value and the condition is judged to be permanent. Some respondents to the Discussion Memorandum indicated that a loss must be permanent rather than temporary before recognition should occur. In their view, a high hurdle for recognition of an impairment loss is necessary to prevent premature write-offs of productive assets. Others stated that re-

quiring the impairment loss to be permanent makes the criterion too restrictive and virtually impossible to apply with any reliability. Still others noted that the permanence criterion is not practical to implement; in their view, requiring management to assess whether a loss is permanent goes beyond management's ability to apply judgment and becomes a requirement for management to predict future events with certainty.

62. The probability criterion, initially presented in the Issues Paper, calls for loss recognition based on the approach taken in FASB Statement No. 5, *Accounting for Contingencies*. Using that approach, an impairment loss would be recognized when it is deemed probable that the carrying amount of an asset cannot be fully recovered. Some respondents to the Discussion Memorandum stated that assessing the probability that an impairment loss has occurred is preferable to other recognition alternatives because it is already required by Statement 5. Most respondents to the Discussion Memorandum supported the probability criterion because, in their view, it best provides for management judgment.

63. A practical approach to implementing a probability criterion was presented at the public hearing on the Discussion Memorandum. That approach uses the sum of the expected future cash flows (undiscounted and without interest charges) to determine whether an asset is impaired. If that sum exceeds the carrying amount of an asset, the asset is not impaired. If the carrying amount of the asset exceeds that sum, the asset is impaired and the recognition of a new cost basis for the impaired asset is triggered.

64. The Exposure Draft included an undiscounted cash flows recognition criterion, and most respondents supported that criterion. Some respondents expressed concern about situations where small differences in cash flow estimates might result in a large loss being recognized in one instance and no loss being recognized in another. Other respondents suggested that the recognition criteria should be more flexible; management should be able to choose the recognition criteria to be used in impairment situations. Some respondents suggested that fair value be used for both recognition and measurement purposes. Still other respondents suggested using the present value of expected future cash flows discounted at the entity's incremental borrowing rate for both recognition and measurement purposes.

65. The Board affirmed its conclusion that an impairment loss should be recognized whenever the

sum of the expected future cash flows (undiscounted and without interest charges) resulting from the use and ultimate disposal of an asset is less than the carrying amount of the asset. The Board believes that the approach is consistent with the definition of an impairment as the inability to fully recover the carrying amount of an asset and with a basic presumption underlying a statement of financial position that the reported carrying amounts of assets should, at a minimum, be recoverable.

66. The Board adopted the recoverability test that uses the sum of the expected future cash flows (undiscounted and without interest charges) as an acceptable approach for identifying when an impairment loss must be recognized. In many cases, it may be relatively easy to conclude that the amount will equal or exceed the carrying amount of an asset without incurring the cost of projecting cash flows.

67. The recognition approach adopted by the Board must be operational in an area of significant uncertainty. The Board's approach requires the investigation of potential impairments on an exception basis. An asset must be tested for recoverability only if there is reason to believe that the asset is impaired as evidenced by events or changes in circumstances. If that test indicates that the sum of the expected future cash flows (undiscounted and without interest charges) to be generated by the asset is insufficient to recover the carrying amount of the asset, the asset is considered impaired. That approach uses information that the Board believes is generally available to an entity.

68. The Board acknowledges that some object to this approach because they believe that relatively minor changes in cash flow estimates, which may be imprecise, could result in significant differences in the carrying amount of an asset. The Board considered that objection in evaluating whether it was appropriate to use undiscounted cash flows as a recoverability test. The Board concluded that the potential usefulness, from a practical standpoint, of that test was sufficient to overcome that objection.

Measurement of an Impairment Loss

69. An impairment loss is not recognized unless the carrying amount of an asset is no longer recoverable using a test of recoverability—the sum of the expected future cash flows (undiscounted and without interest charges). When an asset's carrying amount is not recoverable using that measure, the Board be-

lieves that a new cost basis for the impaired asset is appropriate. The Board concluded that a decision to continue to operate rather than sell an impaired asset is economically similar to a decision to invest in that asset and, therefore, the impaired asset should be measured at its fair value. The amount of the impairment loss should be the amount by which the carrying amount of the impaired asset exceeds the fair value of the asset. That fair value then becomes the asset's new cost basis.

70. When an entity determines that expected future cash flows from using an asset will not result in the recovery of the asset's carrying amount, it must decide whether to sell the asset and use the proceeds for an alternative purpose or to continue to use the impaired asset in its operations. The decision presumably is based on a comparison of expected future cash flows from those alternative courses of action and is essentially a capital investment decision. In either alternative, proceeds from the sale of the impaired asset are considered in the capital investment decision. Consequently, a decision to continue to use the impaired asset is equivalent to a new asset purchase decision, and a new basis of fair value is appropriate.

71. Some respondents to the Exposure Draft disagreed with using fair value to measure impairment. The Board considered those views, but it concluded that the fair value of an impaired asset is the best measure of the cost of continuing to use that asset because it is consistent with management's decision process. Presumably, no entity would decide to continue to use an asset unless that alternative was expected to produce more in terms of expected future cash flows or service potential than the alternative of selling it and reinvesting the proceeds. The Board also believes that using fair value to measure the amount of an impairment loss is not a departure from the historical cost principle. Rather, it is a consistent application of principles practiced elsewhere in the current system of accounting whenever a cost basis for a newly acquired asset must be determined.

72. The Board believes that fair value is an easily understood notion. It is the amount at which an asset could be bought or sold in a current transaction between willing parties. The fair value measure is basic to economic theory and is grounded in the reality of the marketplace. Fair value estimates are readily available in published form for many assets, especially machinery and equipment. For some assets, multiple, on-line database services provide up-to-

date market price information. Estimates of fair value also are subject to periodic verification whenever assets are exchanged in transactions between willing parties.

73. The Exposure Draft included an approach for measuring an asset's fair value that was based on paragraph 13 of FASB Statement No. 15, *Accounting by Debtors and Creditors for Troubled Debt Restructurings*. That approach was not clear about whether the results of valuation techniques could be considered only if selling prices in an active market for similar assets did not exist. Further, some respondents to the Exposure Draft indicated that assumptions developed from selling prices for similar assets are sometimes included in valuation techniques that also consider expected future cash flows. The Board decided to include an approach for measuring the fair value of an asset that would be broadly applicable to other assets in addition to those covered by this Statement.

74. The Board concluded that quoted market prices in active markets are the most objective and relevant measure of an asset's fair value and should be used, if available. If quoted market prices are not available, the estimate of fair value should be based on the best information available in the circumstances. The estimate of fair value should consider prices for similar assets and the results of valuation techniques to the extent available in the circumstances. Valuation techniques for measuring an asset covered by this Statement should be consistent with the objective of measuring fair value and should incorporate assumptions that market participants would use in their estimates of the asset's fair value.

75. The Board recognizes that there may be practical problems in determining the fair value of certain types of assets covered by this Statement that do not have quoted market prices in active markets. While the objective of using a valuation technique is to determine fair value, the Board acknowledges that in some circumstances, the only information available without undue cost and effort will be the entity's expected future cash flows from the asset's use.

Alternative Measures of an Impairment Loss

76. The Board considered approaches other than fair value that also are possible within the historical cost framework for determining the amount of an impairment loss. Those approaches are recoverable cost and recoverable cost including interest.

Recoverable Cost

77. Recoverable cost is measured as the sum of the undiscounted future cash flows expected to be generated over the life of an asset. For example, if an asset has a carrying amount of $1,000,000, a remaining useful life of 5 years, and expected future cash flows over the 5 years of $180,000 per year, the recoverable cost would be $900,000 (5 × $180,000), and the impairment loss would be $100,000 ($1,000,000 − $900,000).

78. The Board did not adopt recoverable cost as the measure of an impairment loss. Proponents of the recoverable cost measure believe that impairment is the result of the inability to recover the carrying amount of an asset. They do not view the decision to retain an impaired asset as an investment decision; rather, they view the recognition of an impairment loss as an adjustment to the historical cost of the asset. They contend that recoverable cost measured by the sum of the undiscounted expected future cash flows is the appropriate carrying amount for an impaired asset and the amount on which the impairment loss should be determined.

79. Proponents of the recoverable cost measure do not believe that the fair value of an asset is a relevant measure unless a transaction or other event justifies a new basis for the asset at fair value. They do not view impairment to be such an event.

80. Some proponents of the recoverable cost measure assert that measuring an impaired asset at either fair value or a discounted present value results in an inappropriate understatement of net income in the period of the impairment and an overstatement of net income in subsequent periods. The Board did not agree with that view. Board members noted that measuring an impaired asset at recoverable cost could result in reported losses in future periods if the entity had incurred debt directly associated with the asset.

81. Proponents of the recoverable cost measure view interest cost as a period cost that should not be included as part of an impairment loss regardless of whether the interest is an accrual of actual debt costs or the result of discounting expected future cash flows using a debt rate.

Recoverable Cost including Interest

82. Recoverable cost including interest generally is measured as either (a) the sum of the undiscounted expected future cash flows including interest costs on actual debt or (b) the present value of expected future cash flows discounted at some annual rate such as a debt rate. For example, if an asset has a carrying value of $1,000,000, a remaining useful life of 5 years, expected future cash flows (excluding interest) over the 5 years of $180,000 per year, and a debt rate of 6 percent, recoverable cost including interest would be $758,225 (4.21236 × $180,000), and the impairment loss would be $241,775 ($1,000,000 − $758,225).

83. The Board did not adopt recoverable cost including interest as an appropriate measure of an impairment loss. Proponents of the recoverable cost including interest measure agree that the time value of money should be considered in the measure, but they view the time value of money as an element of cost recovery rather than as an element of fair value. Proponents believe that the measurement objective for an impaired asset should be recoverable cost and not fair value. However, they believe that interest should be included as a carrying cost in determining the recoverable cost. To them, the objective is to recognize the costs (including the time value of money) that are not recoverable as an impairment loss and to measure an impaired asset at the costs that are recoverable.

84. Because of the difficulties in attempting to associate actual debt with individual assets, proponents of the recoverable cost including interest measure believe that the present value of expected future cash flows using a debt rate such as an incremental borrowing rate is a practical means of achieving their measurement objective. They recognize that an entity that has no debt may be required to discount expected future cash flows. They believe that the initial investment decision would have included consideration of the debt or equity cost of funds.

85. The Board believes that use of the recoverable cost including interest measure would result in different carrying amounts for essentially the same impaired assets because they are owned by different entities that have different debt capacities. The Board does not believe that discounting expected future cash flows using a debt rate is an appropriate measure for determining the value of those assets.

Different Measures for Different Impairment Losses

86. The Board also considered but did not adopt an alternative approach that would require different measures for different impairments. At one extreme, an asset might be impaired because depreciation assumptions were not adjusted appropriately. At the other extreme, an asset might be impaired because of a major change in its use. Some believe that the first situation is similar to a depreciation "catch-up" adjustment and that an undiscounted measure should be used. They believe that the second situation is similar to a new investment in an asset with the same intended use and that a fair value measure should be used. The Board was unable to develop a workable distinction between the first and second situations that would support the use of different measures.

Cash Flows

87. The Board recognizes that judgments, estimates, and projections will be required for measuring impaired assets and that precise information about the relevant attributes of those assets seldom will be available. Partly as a result, the Board decided that the measurement guidance provided in this Statement should be general.

88. The Board agreed that one method of obtaining an appropriate measure in some situations is to project expected future cash flows and to discount those cash flows at a current rate that considers the risks inherent in those cash flows. The Board decided not to address issues about how to project cash flows or what interest rate should be associated with those cash flows. The Board currently has a separate project on present-value-based measurements in accounting on its agenda to consider the latter issue.

89. The Board acknowledges that the language in paragraph 9 allows the use of either the single most likely estimate of expected future cash flows or a range that considers the probability of the possible outcomes. The Board concluded that it would be more useful to permit entities to use cash flow estimation techniques that are currently available and to allow for the use of new techniques that may be developed in the future rather than to prescribe specific techniques in this Statement.

90. The Board considered imposing specific limits on assumptions used to estimate expected future cash flows, such as limiting volume and price assumptions to current levels. The Board decided not to include limits on assumptions because specific limits may be inconsistent with the assumptions that market participants would use in their estimates of an asset's fair value.

91. The Exposure Draft used the term *net* cash flows in certain instances to describe the expected future cash flows used to test the recoverability of an asset in paragraph 6 and to measure an impaired asset in paragraph 7. In this Statement, the reference to *net* cash flows has been eliminated to be consistent with descriptions of cash flows used to determine the fair value of an asset in other pronouncements. The Board's intended meaning of *net*—future cash inflows expected to be generated by an asset should be reduced by the future cash outflows expected to be necessary to obtain those inflows—has been added to paragraph 6 of this Statement.

Discount Rate

92. If quoted market prices for an asset are not available, paragraph 7 of this Statement allows for the consideration of the results of valuation techniques in estimating the fair value of the asset. If such techniques are used, the estimate of fair value may be based on the present value of expected future cash flows using a discount rate commensurate with the risks involved.

93. The discount rate commensurate with the risks involved is a rate that would be required for a similar investment with like risks. That rate is the asset-specific rate of return expected from the market—the return the entity would expect if it were to choose an equally risky investment as an alternative to operating the impaired asset. For some entities that have a well-developed capital budgeting process, the hurdle rate used to make investment decisions might be useful in estimating that rate.

94. Several respondents to the Exposure Draft said that disclosure of the discount rate used to determine the present value of the estimated expected future cash flows should not be required. The Board decided that disclosure of the discount rate without disclosure of the other assumptions used in estimating expected future cash flows generally would not be

meaningful to financial statement users. Therefore, this Statement does not require disclosure of the discount rate.

Grouping for Recognition and Measurement of an Impairment Loss

95. The Board concluded that for testing whether an asset is impaired and for measuring the amount of the impairment loss, assets should be grouped at the lowest level for which there are identifiable cash flows that are largely independent of the cash flows generated by other asset groups. The issue underlying the grouping of assets is when, if ever, it is appropriate to offset the unrealized losses on one asset with the unrealized gains on another. In the Board's view, for determining whether to recognize and how to measure an impairment loss, assets should be grouped when they are used together; that is, when they are part of the same group of assets and are used together to generate joint cash flows.

96. In deciding the appropriate grouping of assets for impairment consideration, the Board reviewed a series of examples that demonstrated the subjectivity of the grouping issue. Varying facts and circumstances introduced in the cases inevitably justified different groupings. Although most respondents to the Discussion Memorandum generally favored grouping at the lowest level for which there are identifiable cash flows for recognition and measurement of an impairment loss, determining that lowest level requires considerable judgment.

97. The Board considered a case that illustrated the need for judgment in grouping assets for impairment. In that case, an entity operated a bus company that provided service under contract with a municipality that required minimum service on each of five separate routes. Assets devoted to serving each route and the cash flows from each route were discrete. One of the routes operated at a significant deficit that resulted in the inability to recover the carrying amounts of the dedicated assets. The Board concluded that the five bus routes would be an appropriate level at which to group assets to test for and measure impairment because the entity did not have the option to curtail any one bus route.

98. The Board concluded that the grouping issue requires significant management judgment within certain parameters. Those parameters are that the assets

should be grouped at the lowest level for which there are cash flows that are identifiable and that those cash flows should be largely independent of the cash flows of other groupings of assets.

99. Not-for-profit organizations that rely in part on contributions to maintain their assets may need to consider those contributions in determining the appropriate cash flows to compare with the carrying amount of an asset. Some respondents to the Exposure Draft stated that the recognition criteria in paragraph 6 would be problematic for many not-for-profit organizations because it may be difficult, if not impossible, for them to identify expected future cash flows with specific assets or asset groupings. In other cases, expected future cash flows can be identified with asset groups. However, if future unrestricted contributions to the organization as a whole are not considered, the sum of the expected future cash flows may be negative, or positive but less than the carrying amount of the asset. For example, the costs of administering a museum may exceed the admission fees charged, but the organization may fund the cash flow deficit with unrestricted contributions.

100. Other respondents indicated that similar difficulties would be experienced by business enterprises. For example, the cost of operating assets such as corporate headquarters or centralized research facilities may be funded by revenue-producing activities at lower levels of the enterprise. Accordingly, in limited circumstances, the lowest level of identifiable cash flows that are largely independent of other asset groups may be the entity level. The Board concluded that the recoverability test in paragraph 6 should be performed at the entity level if an asset does not have identifiable cash flows lower than the entity level. The cash flows used in the recoverability test should be reduced by the carrying amounts of the entity's other assets that are covered by this Statement to arrive at the cash flows expected to contribute to the recoverability of the asset being tested. Not-for-profit organizations should include unrestricted contributions to the organization as a whole that are a source of funds for the operation of the asset.

101. If an impairment write-down is not required, the entity should review the asset's depreciation method, estimated useful life, and estimated salvage value to determine if any adjustments are necessary. However, if the asset does not have any future service potential to the entity, it should be accounted for at the lower of carrying amount or fair value less cost to sell as if the asset had been abandoned or will be

disposed of. Paragraph 28 of FASB Concepts Statement No. 6, *Elements of Financial Statements,* defines service potential as "the scarce capacity to provide services or benefits to the entities that use them."

102. The Exposure Draft would have required entities that follow the successful efforts method of accounting prescribed by FASB Statement No. 19, *Financial Accounting and Reporting by Oil and Gas Producing Companies,* to group, for impairment purposes, those capitalized costs of an entity's wells and related equipment and facilities and the costs of related proved properties in the same manner as those costs are grouped, for amortization purposes, under paragraphs 30 and 35 of that Statement. That provision was included in the Exposure Draft so that entities that follow the successful efforts method of accounting would not need to group cash flows at a level lower than the level at which the applicable costs are being amortized. However, many respondents to the Exposure Draft objected to singling out the oil and gas industry for special grouping provisions. Although the Board agreed to delete that requirement in this Statement because there is no reason to provide an exception to the general grouping provision, the Board did not endorse the view of many respondents that oil and gas companies should group their assets in the same manner as those assets are managed or on a country-by-country basis. The Board concluded that all entities should group assets at the lowest level for which there are identifiable cash flows that are largely independent of the cash flows of other groups of assets.

103. The Board considered requests for a limited exception to the fair value measurement for impaired long-lived assets that are subject to nonrecourse debt. Some believe that the nonrecourse provision is effectively a put option for which the borrower has paid a premium. They believe that the impairment loss on an asset subject entirely to nonrecourse debt should be limited to the loss that would occur if the asset were put back to the lender.

104. The Board decided not to provide an exception for assets subject to nonrecourse debt. The recognition of an impairment loss and the recognition of a gain on the extinguishment of debt are separate events, and each event should be recognized in the period in which it occurs. The Board believes that the recognition of an impairment loss should be based on the measurement of the asset at its fair value and that the existence of nonrecourse debt should not influence that measurement. The Board further believes

that a gain on the extinguishment of debt should be recognized in the period in which it occurs and that it should continue to be classified as an extraordinary gain in accordance with FASB Statement No. 4, *Reporting Gains and Losses from Extinguishment of Debt.*

Restoration of Impairment Losses

105. The Board considered whether to prohibit or require restoration of previously recognized impairment losses. It decided that an impairment loss should result in a new cost basis for the impaired asset. That new cost basis puts the asset on an equal basis with other assets that are not impaired. In the Board's view, the new cost basis should not be adjusted subsequently other than as provided under the current accounting model for prospective changes in the depreciation estimates and method and for further impairment losses. Most respondents to the Exposure Draft agreed with the Board's decision that restoration should be prohibited.

Goodwill

106. The Exposure Draft proposed that goodwill identified with potentially impaired long-lived assets and identifiable intangibles be combined with those assets when testing for impairment. If the test indicates that an impairment exists, the carrying amount of the identified goodwill would be eliminated before making any reduction of the carrying amounts of impaired long-lived assets and identifiable intangibles. Several respondents to the Exposure Draft objected to the allocation of goodwill to the asset groups on the basis that goodwill is a residual that results from a business combination accounted for under the purchase accounting method. Some respondents suggested that the residual should be evaluated on its own merits, without describing how that evaluation might be accomplished. Others said that goodwill should be evaluated apart from long-lived assets and identifiable intangibles. They suggested excluding goodwill completely from the scope of this Statement, leaving all goodwill subject to the provisions of APB Opinion No. 17, *Intangible Assets.*

107. The Board decided to retain the provisions of the Exposure Draft to include goodwill identified with a potentially impaired asset with the carrying amount of that asset in performing the impairment test in paragraph 6 and in measuring an impairment loss in accordance with paragraph 7. The amount of the impairment loss should equal the difference between an asset's carrying amount, including identified goodwill, and the asset's fair value. If the carrying amount of an impaired asset, excluding identified goodwill, exceeds the asset's fair value, the identified goodwill should be eliminated and the asset should be written down to its fair value. If the fair value of an impaired asset exceeds the asset's carrying amount, excluding identified goodwill, the identified goodwill should be written down to an amount equal to that excess. The Board concluded that in the absence of evidence to support a more appropriate association, goodwill should be attributed to long-lived assets and identifiable intangibles that were acquired in a business combination using a pro rata allocation based on the relative fair values of those assets at the date of acquisition. Goodwill that is not identified with impaired assets should continue to be accounted for under Opinion 17.

Reporting and Disclosure of Impairment Losses

108. The Board considered the alternative ways described in the Discussion Memorandum for reporting an impairment loss: reporting the loss as a component of continuing operations, reporting the loss as a special item outside continuing operations, or separate reporting of the loss without specifying the classification in the statement of operations. The Board concluded that an impairment loss should be reported as a component of income from continuing operations before income taxes for entities that present an income statement and in the statement of activities of a not-for-profit organization. If no impairment had occurred, an amount equal to the impairment loss would have been charged to operations over time through the allocation of depreciation or amortization. That depreciation or amortization charge would have been reported as part of continuing operations of a business enterprise or as an expense in the statement of activities of a not-for-profit organization. Further, an asset that is subject to a reduction in its carrying amount due to an impairment loss will continue to be used in operations. The Board concluded that an impairment loss does not have characteristics that warrant special treatment, for instance, as an extraordinary item.

109. The Board believes that financial statements should include information on impairment losses that would be most useful to users. After considering responses to the Exposure Draft, the Board concluded that an entity that recognizes an impairment loss should describe the assets impaired and the facts and circumstances leading to the impairment; disclose the

amount of the loss and how fair value was determined; disclose the caption in the income statement or the statement of activities in which the loss is aggregated unless that loss has been presented as a separate caption or reported parenthetically on the face of the statement; and, if applicable, disclose the business segment(s) affected. The Board decided not to require further disclosures, such as the assumptions used to estimate expected future cash flows and the discount rate used when fair value is estimated by discounting expected future cash flows.

Early Warning Disclosures

110. In 1985, the AICPA established a task force to consider the need for improved disclosures about risks and uncertainties that affect companies and the manner in which they do business. In July 1987, the task force published *Report of the Task Force on Risks and Uncertainties,* which concluded that companies should make early warning disclosures in their financial statements. In December 1994, AcSEC issued AICPA Statement of Position 94-6, *Disclosure of Certain Significant Risks and Uncertainties.* That SOP requires entities to include in their financial statements disclosures about (a) the nature of operations, (b) the use of estimates in the preparation of financial statements, (c) certain significant estimates, and (d) current vulnerability due to certain concentrations.

111. The Board observed that early warning disclosures would be useful for certain potential impairments. However, most respondents to the Exposure Draft said that the Statement should not require early warning disclosures. The Board observed that SOP 94-6 uses essentially the same events or changes in circumstances as those in paragraph 5 of this Statement to illustrate when disclosures of certain significant estimates should be made for long-lived assets. Therefore, the Board concluded that it was not necessary for this Statement to require early warning disclosures.

Assets to Be Disposed Of

112. The Board agreed that accounting for long-lived assets and certain identifiable intangibles to be disposed of should be addressed by this Statement. In the Board's view, if those assets were not addressed, an entity could potentially avoid the recognition of an impairment loss for assets otherwise subject to an impairment write-down by declaring that those assets are held for sale. Existing guidance for assets to be disposed of that constitute a segment of a business is provided by Opinion 30. Some believe that Opinion 30 requires the use of a net realizable value measure because it anticipates a relatively short holding period for the assets to be disposed of. The last sentence of paragraph 15 of the Opinion states:

> In the usual circumstance, it would be expected that the plan of disposal would be carried out within a period of one year from the measurement date and that such projections of operating income or loss would not cover a period exceeding approximately one year. [Footnote reference omitted.]

113. The net realizable value measure of Opinion 30 seems to anticipate that the disposal of an asset will be completed within approximately one year and does not consider the time value of money. However, a measurement principle for assets to be disposed of that assumes a disposal period of one year or less often is not realistic. For example, concerns about environmental liabilities, such as remediation costs that must be incurred before legal title can be transferred, often extend the period of time necessary to dispose of an asset well beyond one year. The Board considered several alternative measures. For reasons similar to the conclusions reached for assets held for use, the Board concluded that the appropriate measure for assets to be disposed of is the lower of carrying amount or fair value less cost to sell. If the fair value of an asset is measured by the current market value or by using the current selling price for a similar asset, that fair value should be considered to be a current amount and that fair value and cost to sell should not be discounted. If the fair value of an asset is measured by discounting expected future cash flows and if the sale is expected to occur beyond one year, the cost to sell also should be discounted.

114. Opinion 30 applies to assets to be disposed of in a limited context. The Board realizes that potential inconsistencies might arise if fair value is used to measure impairment losses for assets held for use and net realizable value is used to measure certain assets to be disposed of. Several respondents to the Exposure Draft suggested that the Board consider the issues related to Opinion 30 in a separate project. Others suggested that the Board modify Opinion 30 to provide consistency between the provisions for disposal of a segment of a business and those for all other assets to be disposed of.

115. The Board considered amending Opinion 30 to change the lower of carrying amount or net realizable value measure to the lower of carrying amount or fair value less cost to sell measure. However, the Board did not wish to expand the scope of this Statement and undertake an examination of all the issues contained in Opinion 30 on the expected disposal of a segment of a business. Those issues include the calculation of operating results during the holding period, the presentation of operating results in the income statement, and the netting of operating income or loss with adjustments to the carrying amounts of assets held for disposal. The Board decided not to amend Opinion 30 and concluded that long-lived assets and certain identifiable intangibles to be disposed of that are not covered by that Opinion should be measured at the lower of carrying amount or fair value less cost to sell.

116. The Board concluded that the cost to sell an asset to be disposed of generally includes the incremental direct costs to transact the sale of the asset. Cost to sell is deducted from the fair value of an asset to be disposed of to arrive at the current value of the estimated net proceeds to be received from the asset's future sale. The Board decided that costs incurred during the holding period to protect or maintain an asset to be disposed of generally are excluded from the cost to sell an asset because those costs usually are not required to be incurred in order to sell the asset. However, the Board believes that costs required to be incurred under the terms of a contract for an asset's sale as a condition of the buyer's consummation of the sale should be included in determining the cost to sell an asset to be disposed of.

117. Some respondents to the Exposure Draft objected to the elimination of the last question and its interpretation of AICPA Accounting Interpretation 1, "Illustration of the Application of APB Opinion No. 30." Those respondents said that the Interpretation's guidance for disposals of assets that do not meet the requirements of Opinion 30 has been helpful in practice. Other respondents stated that the guidance was too permissive and agreed that it should be superseded. Interpretation 1 is not specific as to the grouping of assets to which it applies, is not clear in its definitions of gains and losses and holding period, and provides no guidance on how to distinguish a portion of a segment of a business from other assets.

118. Because of the ambiguities associated with the Interpretation, the Board concluded that it was not feasible to amend the Interpretation to conform its requirements to this Statement. The Board decided that the only practical solution was to supersede the last question and its interpretation of Interpretation 1 and that all long-lived assets and certain identifiable intangibles to be disposed of not covered by Opinion 30 should be covered by this Statement. The Board agreed that applying this Statement to assets not already covered by Opinion 30, leaving that Opinion unchanged, and superseding the portion of the Interpretation that specified another accounting treatment for a portion of a line of business to be disposed of would enhance reporting and disclosure consistency for assets to be disposed of.

119. This Statement addresses the measurement of long-lived assets and certain identifiable intangibles to be disposed of not covered by Opinion 30 and whether those assets should be depreciated (amortized) during the holding period. This Statement also provides guidance on the cost to sell an asset to be disposed of, including the determination of the cost to sell an asset when a contractual obligation for an asset's sale requires an entity to incur certain costs during the holding period. This Statement does not address the general issue of accounting for the results of operations of assets to be disposed of during the holding period.

120. In March 1994, the EITF began discussing EITF Issue No. 94-3, "Liability Recognition for Certain Employee Termination Benefits and Other Costs to Exit an Activity (including Certain Costs Incurred in a Restructuring)." The EITF completed its discussion of the issues in January 1995 after reaching a number of consensuses. Certain consensuses address the issue of when an entity should recognize a liability for costs, other than employee termination benefits, that are directly associated with a plan to exit an activity. In part, the consensuses establish certain criteria that must be met in order for an entity to recognize a liability for those costs and require the results of operations of an activity that will be exited to be recognized in the periods in which the operations occur. The Board believes that the consensuses provide useful guidance about the accounting for the results of operations of an asset to be disposed of when the planned disposal also involves an exit from an activity.

Depreciation of Assets to Be Disposed Of

121. The Board considered whether assets to be disposed of that are carried at the lower of carrying amount or fair value less cost to sell should be depreciated while they are held for disposal. Depreciation

is the systematic allocation of an asset's cost over the asset's service period. Some believe that depreciation accounting is inconsistent with the notion of assets to be disposed of and with the use of the lower of carrying amount or fair value less cost to sell measure for those assets. They believe that assets to be disposed of are equivalent to inventory and should not be depreciated. Others believe that all operating assets should be depreciated and that no exception should be made for operating assets held for disposal.

122. The Board concluded that assets to be disposed of covered by this Statement should not be depreciated during the period they are held. Because the assets will be recovered through sale rather than through operations, accounting for those assets is a process of valuation rather than allocation. An asset to be disposed of will not be reported at carrying amount but at the lower of carrying amount or fair value less cost to sell and fair value less cost to sell will be evaluated each period to determine if it has changed.

Goodwill Related to Assets to Be Disposed Of

123. Goodwill related to assets to be disposed of by an entity should be accounted for under the provisions of Opinion 17, paragraph 32, which states:

> Ordinarily goodwill and similar intangible assets cannot be disposed of apart from the enterprise as a whole. However, a large segment or separable group of assets of an acquired company or the entire acquired company may be sold or otherwise liquidated, and all or a portion of the unamortized cost of the goodwill recognized in the acquisition should be included in the cost of the assets sold.

Real Estate Development

124. The Exposure Draft proposed amending FASB Statements No. 66, *Accounting for Sales of Real Estate*, and No. 67, *Accounting for Costs and Initial Rental Operations of Real Estate Projects*, to change the lower of carrying amount or net realizable value measure to the lower of carrying amount or fair value less cost to sell measure. The Board initially decided to amend those Statements to conform the measurement of assets subject to those Statements with the measurement of assets to be disposed of.

125. Some real estate development organizations objected to the proposed amendments in the Exposure Draft. They questioned why the scope of a project on long-lived assets included real estate development. They argued that real estate development assets are more like inventory and, therefore, the lower of carrying amount or net realizable value measure is more relevant. They did not address, however, why that measure would be more appropriate for real estate inventory than the lower of cost or market measure required for inventory under paragraph 4 of ARB No. 43, Chapter 4, "Inventory Pricing."

126. Others disagreed with the inventory argument, asserting that although real estate development assets will eventually be disposed of, the provisions of the Exposure Draft would have required long-term real estate projects to recognize impairments far too frequently. They said that nearly all long-term projects, regardless of their overall profitability, would become subject to write-downs in their early stages of development, only to be reversed later in the life of the project due to revised estimates of fair value less cost to sell. The Board considered alternative approaches to measuring those real estate assets. The Board decided to apply the provisions of paragraphs 4-7 to land to be developed and projects under development and to apply paragraphs 15-17 to completed projects. The Board believes that assets under development are similar to assets held for use, whereas completed projects are clearly assets to be disposed of.

Regulated Enterprises

127. FASB Statement No. 71, *Accounting for the Effects of Certain Types of Regulation*, establishes the accounting model for certain rate-regulated enterprises. Because the rates of rate-regulated enterprises generally are designed to recover the costs of providing regulated services or products, those enterprises are usually able to recover the carrying amounts of their assets. Paragraph 10 of Statement 71 states that when a regulator excludes a cost from rates, "the carrying amount of any related asset shall be reduced to the extent that the asset has been impaired. Whether the asset has been impaired shall be judged the same as for enterprises in general" (footnote reference omitted). Statement 71 does not provide any guidance about when an impairment has, in fact, oc-

curred or about how to measure the amount of the impairment.

128. The Board considered whether the accounting for the impairment of long-lived assets and identifiable intangibles by rate-regulated enterprises that meet the criteria for applying Statement 71 should be the same as for enterprises in general. In March 1993, the EITF discussed incurred costs capitalized pursuant to the criteria of paragraph 9 of Statement 71. The EITF reached a consensus in EITF Issue No. 93-4, "Accounting for Regulatory Assets," that a cost that does not meet the asset recognition criteria in paragraph 9 of Statement 71 at the date the cost is incurred should be recognized as a regulatory asset when it does meet those criteria at a later date. The EITF also reached a consensus that the carrying amount of a regulatory asset should be reduced to the extent that the asset has been impaired with impairment judged the same as for enterprises in general; the provisions of this Statement nullify that consensus.

129. The Board considered several approaches to recognizing and measuring the impairment of long-lived assets and identifiable intangibles of rate-regulated enterprises. One approach the Board considered was to apply paragraph 7 of FASB Statement No. 90, *Regulated Enterprises—Accounting for Abandonments and Disallowances of Plant Costs,* to all assets of a regulated enterprise and not just to costs of recently completed plants. That paragraph requires that an impairment loss be recognized when a disallowance is probable and the amount can be reasonably estimated. If a regulator explicitly disallows a certain dollar amount of plant costs, an impairment loss should be recognized for that amount. If a regulator explicitly but indirectly disallows plant costs (for example, by excluding a return on investment on a portion of plant costs), an impairment loss should be recognized for the effective disallowance by estimating the expected future cash flows that have been disallowed as a result of the regulator's action and then computing the present value of those cash flows. That approach would recognize a probable disallowance as an impairment loss, the amount of the loss would be the discounted value of the expected future cash flows disallowed, and the discount rate would be the same as the rate of return used to estimate the expected future cash flows.

130. A second approach the Board considered was to supersede paragraph 7 of Statement 90 and apply this Statement's requirements to all plant costs. A disallowance would result in costs being excluded from the rate base. The recognition and measurement requirements of this Statement would be applied to determine whether an impairment loss would be recognized for financial reporting purposes.

131. A third approach the Board considered was to apply the general impairment provisions of this Statement to all assets of a regulated enterprise except for disallowances of costs of recently completed plants, which would continue to be covered by paragraph 7 of Statement 90. A disallowance would result in the exclusion of costs from the rate base. That disallowance would result in an impairment loss for financial reporting purposes if the costs disallowed relate to a recently completed plant. If the costs disallowed do not relate to a recently completed plant, the recognition and measurement requirements of this Statement would be applied to determine whether and how much of an impairment loss would be recognized for financial reporting purposes.

132. A fourth approach the Board considered was to apply the general impairment standard to all assets of a regulated enterprise except (a) regulatory assets that meet the criteria of paragraph 9 of Statement 71 and (b) costs of recently completed plants that are covered by paragraph 7 of Statement 90. Impairment of regulatory assets capitalized as a result of paragraph 9 of Statement 71 would be recognized whenever the criteria of that paragraph are no longer met.

133. The Board decided that the fourth approach should be used in accounting for the impairment of all assets of a rate-regulated enterprise. The Board amended paragraph 9 of Statement 71 to provide that a rate-regulated enterprise should charge a regulatory asset to earnings if and when that asset no longer meets the criteria in paragraph 9(a) and (b) of that Statement. The Board also amended paragraph 10 of Statement 71 to require that a rate-regulated enterprise recognize an impairment for the amount of costs excluded when a regulator excludes all or part of a cost from rates, even if the regulator allows the rate-regulated enterprise to earn a return on the remaining costs allowed.

134. The Board believes that because a rate-regulated enterprise is allowed to capitalize costs that enterprises in general would otherwise have charged to expense, the impairment criteria for those assets should be different from enterprises in general. The Board believes that symmetry should exist between the recognition of those assets and the subsequent

impairment of those assets. The Board could see no reason that an asset created as a result of regulatory action could not be impaired by the actions of the same regulator. Other assets that are not regulatory assets covered by Statement 71 or recently completed plant costs covered by Statement 90, such as older plants or other nonregulatory assets of a rate-regulated enterprise, would be covered by the general provisions of this Statement.

135. Some respondents to the Exposure Draft also asked that the Board clarify the accounting for previously disallowed costs that are subsequently allowed by a regulator. The Board decided that previously disallowed costs that are subsequently allowed by a regulator should be recorded as an asset, consistent with the classification that would have resulted had those costs initially been included in allowable costs. Thus, plant costs subsequently allowed should be classified as plant assets, whereas other costs (expenses) subsequently allowed should be classified as regulatory assets. The Board amended Statement 71 to reflect this decision. The Board decided to restore the original classification because there is no economic change to the asset—it is as if the regulator never had disallowed the cost. The Board determined that restoration of cost is allowed for rate-regulated enterprises in this situation, in contrast to other impairment situations, because the event requiring recognition of the impairment resulted from actions of an independent party and not management's own judgment or determination of recoverability.

Loan Impairment

136. In May 1993, the Board issued FASB Statement No. 114, *Accounting by Creditors for Impairment of a Loan,* which requires certain impaired loans to be measured based on the present value of expected future cash flows, discounted at the loan's effective interest rate, or as a practical expedient, at the loan's observable market price or the fair value of the collateral if the impaired loan is collateral dependent. Regardless of the measurement method, a creditor should measure impairment based on the fair value of the collateral when the creditor determines that foreclosure is probable. A creditor should consider estimated costs to sell, on a discounted basis, in the measure of impairment if those costs are expected to reduce the cash flows available to repay or otherwise satisfy the loan.

137. As suggested by one commentator to the Exposure Draft, the Board decided to amend Statement 15

to make the measurement of long-lived assets that are received in full satisfaction of a receivable and that will be sold consistent with the measurement of other long-lived assets under this Statement. The amendment requires that those assets be measured at fair value less cost to sell. The Board considered amending Statement 15 to address shares of stock or equity interests in long-lived assets that are received in full satisfaction of a receivable and that will be sold, but it determined that those items are outside the scope of this Statement.

138. Loans and long-lived assets are similar in that both are cash-generating assets that are subject to impairment. However, inherent differences between monetary and nonmonetary assets have resulted in different accounting treatments for them under the current reporting model.

Benefits and Costs

139. In establishing standards that are cost-effective, the Board must balance the diverse and often conflicting needs of constituents. The Board must conclude that a proposed standard will fulfill a need and that the costs it imposes, compared with possible alternatives, will be justified in relation to the overall benefits. There is no objective way to determine the costs to implement a standard and weigh them against the need to report consistent, comparable, relevant, and reliable information in the financial statements.

140. The Board determined that the information provided to users about impaired long-lived assets could be improved by increasing comparability in the recognition, measurement, display, and disclosure of impairment among entities. As discussed in FASB Concepts Statement No. 2, *Qualitative Characteristics of Accounting Information,* comparable financial information enables users to compare one entity's response to economic or other forces with the response of another. Therefore, to the extent that similar situations for impairment of long-lived assets are subject to the same requirements for recognition, measurement, display, and disclosure, financial reporting would be improved.

141. The Board believes that using the examples provided in paragraph 5 of events or changes in circumstances that might suggest a lack of recoverability will help maximize the use of information already known by management. Comment letters and public hearing testimony on the Discussion Memorandum

and the Exposure Draft clearly indicated that a requirement to specifically test each asset or group of assets for impairment each period would not be cost-effective.

142. Determination of an asset's fair value is required only if the asset's carrying amount, including identified goodwill, cannot be recovered. The Board believes that information necessary to perform the recoverability test is generally available from budgets and projections used by management in the decision-making process. Grouping assets at the lowest level of identifiable cash flows minimizes the offsetting of unrealized losses on one asset with the unrealized gains on another without requiring the complexities and costs of attributing interdependent cash flows to individual assets.

Effective Date and Transition

143. The Exposure Draft proposed that this Statement be effective for financial statements for fiscal years beginning after December 15, 1994. Some respondents requested a delay in the effective date to allow for a reasonable amount of time for entities to develop appropriate accounting policies and procedures. The Board agreed and decided that this Statement should be effective for financial statements for fiscal years beginning after December 15, 1995. The Board believes that the effective date provides adequate time for entities to make modifications to their procedures for reviewing long-lived assets and certain identifiable intangibles to conform with this Statement. The Board encourages early adoption of this Statement.

144. The recognition provisions of this Statement should be applied based on the facts and circumstances existing at the date of adoption. The continuing effect of events or changes in circumstances that occurred prior to the Statement's adoption should be considered when this Statement is initially applied. For example, the recoverability of an asset should be tested, in accordance with paragraph 6, on the date the Statement is adopted if that asset experienced a significant decrease in market value in a prior period and the market value of that asset has not recovered.

145. The Board considered requests to provide for a cumulative effect of a change in accounting principle adjustment for impairment losses that have not been previously recognized but are recognized at the time this Statement is implemented. The Board decided to prohibit the cumulative effect adjustment and retro-active application of this Statement's requirements for assets to be held and used because measurement of an impaired asset is based on estimates that are likely to change and management's assessment of events and circumstances is subjective and not readily subject to retroactive review. Impairment losses resulting from the application of this Statement should be reported in the period in which the recognition criteria are first applied and met.

146. The initial application of this Statement to assets that are being held for disposal at the date of adoption should be reported as the cumulative effect of a change in accounting principle, as described in Opinion 20. The pro forma effects of retroactive application (Opinion 20, paragraph 21) are not required to be disclosed. The Board concluded that the effect of applying this Statement to assets to be disposed of represents a change in measurement principle and does not affect when management identifies an asset for future disposal. The Board decided to prohibit retroactive application of this Statement's requirements for assets to be disposed of because that approach would require an entity to derive fair values for assets that had been disposed of in periods prior to the Statement's initial application.

Appendix B

REFERENCES TO PRONOUNCEMENTS

147. There are many references in the existing authoritative literature to impairment of assets and disposal of assets. Paragraphs 20-33 indicate the amendments to existing pronouncements. The Board decided that the scope of this Statement should exclude financial instruments, long-term customer relationships of a financial institution (for example, core deposit intangibles and credit cardholder intangibles), mortgage and other servicing rights, deferred policy acquisition costs, and deferred tax assets. The Board also decided that assets whose accounting is specifically addressed in Statements covering certain specialized industries, specifically the record and music, motion picture, broadcasting, and software industries, would remain subject to the various requirements of the existing literature for those assets. The following table indicates (a) certain pronouncements that refer to impairment of assets and disposal of assets and (b) which of those pronouncements will apply this Statement and which will continue to apply the existing requirements.

(This page intentionally left blank.)

Pronouncement	Title	Apply General Impairment Standard	Apply Existing Requirement	Existing Requirement Paragraph Number
APB Opinion No. 17	*Intangible Assets*			
	• Identifiable intangibles specifically excluded from the scope of this Statement (long-term customer relationships of a financial institution [for example, core deposit intangibles and credit card-holder intangibles])		X	31
	• All other identifiable intangibles	X		
	• Goodwill identified with assets included in the scope of this Statement	X		
	• Goodwill identified with assets not included in the scope of this Statement		X	31
APB Opinion No. 18	*The Equity Method of Accounting for Investments in Common Stock*		X	19(h) (as amended by this Statement)
APB Opinion No. 30	*Reporting the Results of Operations—Reporting the Effects of Disposal of a Segment of a Business, and Extraordinary, Unusual and Infrequently Occurring Events and Transactions*		X	14, 15
FASB Statement No. 7	*Accounting and Reporting by Development Stage Enterprises*	X		
FASB Statement No. 13	*Accounting for Leases*			
	• Capital leases of lessees	X		
	• Sales-type, direct financing, and leveraged leases of lessors		X	17
	• Assets of lessors subject to operating leases	X		

FASB Statement No. 19	*Financial Accounting and Reporting by Oil and Gas Producing Companies*		
	• Unproved properties	X	12, 27-29, 31(b), 33, 40, 47(g), 47(h)
	• Proved properties, wells and related equipment and facilities	X	
FASB Statement No. 34	*Capitalization of Interest Cost*	X	
FASB Statement No. 44	*Accounting for Intangible Assets of Motor Carriers*	X	3-7
FASB Statement No. 50	*Financial Reporting in the Record and Music Industry*	X	11
FASB Statement No. 51	*Financial Reporting by Cable Television Companies*	X	
FASB Statement No. 53	*Financial Reporting by Producers and Distributors of Motion Picture Films*	X	16-17
FASB Statement No. 60	*Accounting and Reporting by Insurance Enterprises*		
	• Deferred policy acquisition costs	X	32-37
	• All other assets	X	
FASB Statement No. 61	*Accounting for Title Plant*	X	
FASB Statement No. 63	*Financial Reporting by Broadcasters*	X	7
FASB Statement No. 65	*Accounting for Certain Mortgage Banking Activities*	X	7
FASB Statement No. 66	*Accounting for Sales of Real Estate*	X	

Pronouncement	Title	Apply General Impairment Standard	Apply Existing Requirement	Existing Requirement Paragraph Number
FASB Statement No. 67	*Accounting for Costs and Initial Rental Operations of Real Estate Projects*	X		
FASB Statement No. 71	*Accounting for the Effects of Certain Types of Regulation*	X		
FASB Statement No. 86	*Accounting for the Costs of Computer Software to Be Sold, Leased, or Otherwise Marketed*		X	10
FASB Statement No. 90	*Regulated Enterprises—Accounting for Abandonments and Disallowances of Plant Costs*		X	7
FASB Statement No. 97	*Accounting and Reporting by Insurance Enterprises for Certain Long-Duration Contracts and for Realized Gains and Losses from the Sale of Investments* • Deferred policy acquisition costs		X	25, 27
FASB Statement No. 101	*Regulated Enterprises—Accounting for the Discontinuation of Application of FASB Statement No. 71*	X		
FASB Statement No. 109	*Accounting for Income Taxes*		X	20-26
FASB Statement No. 114	*Accounting by Creditors for Impairment of a Loan*		X	8-16
FASB Statement No. 115	*Accounting for Certain Investments in Debt and Equity Securities*		X	16

Statement of Financial Accounting Standards No. 122
Accounting for Mortgage Servicing Rights

an amendment of FASB Statement No. 65

STATUS

Issued: May 1995

Effective Date: Prospectively for fiscal years beginning after December 15, 1995

Affects: Amends FAS 65, paragraphs 1, 10, 15, 19, and 30
  Supersedes FAS 65, paragraphs 16 through 18 and footnote 6
  Supersedes FTB 87-3, paragraph 9

Affected by: Superseded by FAS 125

Issues Discussed by FASB Emerging Issues Task Force (EITF)

  Affects: Nullifies EITF Issues No. 86-39 and 92-10
    Partially nullifies EITF Issue No. 86-38

(The next page is 1754.)

Statement of Financial Accounting Standards No. 123
Accounting for Stock-Based Compensation

STATUS

Issued: October 1995

Effective Date: For fiscal years beginning after December 15, 1995

Affects: Amends ARB 43, Chapter 13B, paragraph 2
Supersedes ARB 43, Chapter 13B, paragraph 15
Amends APB 25, paragraph 4
Supersedes APB 25, paragraph 19 and footnote 5
Supersedes APB 29, footnote 4
Amends AIN-APB 25, Interpretation No. 1
Amends FAS 5, paragraph 7
Amends FAS 21, footnote 3
Amends FAS 43, paragraph 2
Amends FAS 105, paragraph 14(c)
Amends FAS 107, paragraph 8(a)
Amends FAS 109, paragraph 36(e)
Amends FAS 112, paragraph 5(d)
Amends FIN 28, paragraph 2
Amends FIN 31, footnote 1
Amends FIN 38, paragraph 2
Supersedes FTB 82-2

Affected by: Paragraph 49 superseded by FAS 128
Paragraphs 50, 357, and 358 amended by FAS 128
Paragraphs 359 through 361 and footnote 26 superseded by FAS 128

Issues Discussed by FASB Emerging Issues Task Force (EITF)

Affects: EITF Issue No. 84-8

Interpreted by: Paragraph 8 interpreted by EITF Issue No. 96-3

Related Issue: EITF Issue No. 96-18

SUMMARY

This Statement establishes financial accounting and reporting standards for stock-based employee compensation plans. Those plans include all arrangements by which employees receive shares of stock or other equity instruments of the employer or the employer incurs liabilities to employees in amounts based on the price of the employer's stock. Examples are stock purchase plans, stock options, restricted stock, and stock appreciation rights.

This Statement also applies to transactions in which an entity issues its equity instruments to acquire goods or services from nonemployees. Those transactions must be accounted for based on the fair value of the consideration received or the fair value of the equity instruments issued, whichever is more reliably measurable.

Accounting for Awards of Stock-Based Compensation to Employees

This Statement defines a *fair value based method* of accounting for an employee stock option or similar equity instrument and encourages all entities to adopt that method of accounting for all of their employee stock compensation plans. However, it also allows an entity to continue to measure compensation cost for those plans using the *intrinsic value based method* of accounting prescribed by APB Opinion No. 25, *Accounting for Stock Issued to Employees.* The fair value based method is preferable to the Opinion 25 method for purposes of justifying a change in accounting principle under APB Opinion No. 20, *Accounting Changes.* Entities electing to remain with the accounting in Opinion 25 must make pro forma disclosures of net income and, if presented, earnings per share, as if the fair value based method of accounting defined in this Statement had been applied.

Under the fair value based method, compensation cost is measured at the grant date based on the value of the award and is recognized over the service period, which is usually the vesting period. Under the intrinsic value based method, compensation cost is the excess, if any, of the quoted market price of the stock at grant date or other measurement date over the amount an employee must pay to acquire the stock. Most fixed stock option plans—the most common type of stock compensation plan—have no intrinsic value at grant date, and under Opinion 25 no compensation cost is recognized for them. Compensation cost is recognized for other types of stock-based compensation plans under Opinion 25, including plans with variable, usually performance-based, features.

Stock Compensation Awards Required to Be Settled by Issuing Equity Instruments

Stock Options

For stock options, fair value is determined using an option-pricing model that takes into account the stock price at the grant date, the exercise price, the expected life of the option, the volatility of the underlying stock and the expected dividends on it, and the risk-free interest rate over the expected life of the option. Nonpublic entities are permitted to exclude the volatility factor in estimating the value of their stock options, which results in measurement at *minimum value.* The fair value of an option estimated at the grant date is not subsequently adjusted for changes in the price of the underlying stock or its volatility, the life of the option, dividends on the stock, or the risk-free interest rate.

Nonvested Stock

The fair value of a share of nonvested stock (usually referred to as restricted stock) awarded to an employee is measured at the market price of a share of a nonrestricted stock on the grant date unless a restriction will be imposed after the employee has a vested right to it, in which case fair value is estimated taking that restriction into account.

Employee Stock Purchase Plans

An employee stock purchase plan that allows employees to purchase stock at a discount from market price is not compensatory if it satisfies three conditions: (a) the discount is relatively small (5 percent or less satisfies this condition automatically, though in some cases a greater discount also might be justified as noncompensatory), (b) substantially all full-time employees may participate on an equitable basis, and (c) the plan incorporates no option features such as allowing the employee to purchase the stock at a fixed discount from the lesser of the market price at grant date or date of purchase.

Stock Compensation Awards Required to Be Settled by Paying Cash

Some stock-based compensation plans require an employer to pay an employee, either on demand or at a specified date, a cash amount determined by the increase in the employer's stock price from a specified level. The entity must measure compensation cost for that award in the amount of the changes in the stock price in the periods in which the changes occur.

Disclosures

This Statement requires that an employer's financial statements include certain disclosures about stock-based employee compensation arrangements regardless of the method used to account for them.

The pro forma amounts required to be disclosed by an employer that continues to apply the accounting provisions of Opinion 25 will reflect the difference between compensation cost, if any, included in net income and the related cost measured by the fair value based method defined in this Statement, including tax effects, if any, that would have been recognized in the income statement if the fair value based method had been used. The required pro forma amounts will not reflect any other adjustments to reported net income or, if presented, earnings per share.

Effective Date and Transition

The accounting requirements of this Statement are effective for transactions entered into in fiscal years that begin after December 15, 1995, though they may be adopted on issuance.

The disclosure requirements of this Statement are effective for financial statements for fiscal years beginning after December 15, 1995, or for an earlier fiscal year for which this Statement is initially adopted for recognizing compensation cost. Pro forma disclosures required for entities that elect to continue to measure compensation cost using Opinion 25 must include the effects of all awards granted in fiscal years that begin after December 15, 1994. Pro forma disclosures for awards granted in the first fiscal year beginning after December 15, 1994, need not be included in financial statements for that fiscal year but should be presented subsequently whenever financial statements for that fiscal year are presented for comparative purposes with financial statements for a later fiscal year.

Statement of Financial Accounting Standards No. 123

Accounting for Stock-Based Compensation

CONTENTS

INTRODUCTION

1. This Statement establishes a **fair value**[1] based method of accounting for **stock-based compensation plans.** It encourages entities to adopt that method in place of the provisions of APB Opinion No. 25, *Accounting for Stock Issued to Employees,* for all arrangements under which employees receive shares of stock or other equity instruments of the employer or the employer incurs liabilities to employees in amounts based on the price of its stock.

2. This Statement also establishes fair value as the measurement basis for transactions in which an entity acquires goods or services from nonemployees in exchange for equity instruments. This Statement uses the term *compensation* in its broadest sense to refer to the consideration paid for goods or services, regardless of whether the supplier is an employee or not. For example, employee compensation includes both cash salaries or wages and other consideration that may be thought of more as means of attracting, retaining, and motivating employees than as direct payment for services rendered.

---

[1] Terms defined in Appendix E, the glossary, are set in **boldface type** the first time they appear.

3. Opinion 25, issued in 1972, requires compensation cost[2] for stock-based employee compensation plans to be recognized based on the difference, if any, between the quoted market price of the stock and the amount an employee must pay to acquire the stock. Opinion 25 specifies different dates for the pertinent quoted market price of the stock used in measuring compensation cost, depending on whether the terms of an award[3] are fixed or variable, as those terms are defined in Opinion 25.

4. Since 1972, **stock options** and other forms of stock-based employee compensation plans have become increasingly common. Also, option-pricing models have become widely used for measuring the value of stock options and similar equity instruments other than those issued to employees as compensation. Opinion 25 has been criticized for producing anomalous results and for providing little general guidance to use in deciding how to account for new forms of stock-based employee compensation plans. Several FASB Interpretations and Technical Bulletins have dealt with specific kinds of plans, and the Emerging Issues Task Force has considered numerous related issues.

5. Because of the perceived deficiencies in Opinion 25, early in the 1980s the AICPA's Accounting Standards Executive Committee, the staff of the Securities and Exchange Commission, most of the larger accounting firms, industry representatives, and others asked the Board to reconsider the accounting specified in Opinion 25. This Statement, which is the result of that reconsideration, establishes an accounting method based on the fair value of equity instruments awarded to employees as compensation that mitigates many of the deficiencies in Opinion 25. The Board encourages entities to adopt the new method. However, this Statement permits an entity in determining its net income to continue to apply the accounting provisions of Opinion 25 to its stock-based employee compensation arrangements. An entity that continues to apply Opinion 25 must comply with the disclosure requirements of this Statement, which supersede the disclosure requirements of paragraph 19 of Opinion 25. This Statement also supersedes or amends other accounting pronouncements listed in Appendix D. Appendix A explains the reasons the Board decided not to require recognition of compensation cost for stock-based employee compensation arrangements measured in accordance with the fair value based method described in this Statement.

STANDARDS OF FINANCIAL ACCOUNTING AND REPORTING

Scope and Alternative Accounting Methods

6. This Statement applies to all transactions in which an entity acquires goods or services by issuing equity instruments[4] or by incurring liabilities to the supplier in amounts based on the price of the entity's common stock or other equity instruments. Therefore, it applies to all transactions in which an entity grants shares of its common stock, stock options, or other equity instruments to its employees, except for equity instruments held by an employee stock ownership plan.[5]

7. The accounting for all stock-based compensation arrangements with employees or others shall reflect the inherent rights and obligations, regardless of how those arrangements are described. For example, the rights and obligations embodied in a transfer of stock to an employee for consideration of a nonrecourse note are substantially the same as if the transaction were structured as the grant of a stock option, and the transaction shall be accounted for as such. The terms of the arrangement may affect the fair value of the

---

[2]This Statement refers to recognizing *compensation cost* rather than *compensation expense* because part of the amount recognized in a period may be capitalized as part of the cost to acquire an asset, such as inventory.

[3]This Statement uses the term *award* as the collective noun for multiple instruments with the same terms granted at the same time either to a single employee or to a group of employees. An award may specify multiple vesting dates, referred to as graded vesting, and different parts of an award may have different expected lives.

[4]An entity may conditionally transfer an equity instrument to another party under an arrangement that permits that party to choose at a later date or for a specified time whether to deliver the consideration for it or to forfeit the right to the conditionally transferred instrument with no further obligation. In that situation, the equity instrument is not *issued* until the issuing entity has received the consideration, such as cash, an enforceable right to receive cash, other financial instruments, goods, or services, agreed to by the parties to the transaction. For that reason, this Statement does not use the term *issued* for the grant of stock options or other equity instruments subject to service or performance conditions (or both) for vesting.

[5]AICPA Statement of Position No. 93-6, *Employers' Accounting for Employee Stock Ownership Plans*, specifies the accounting by employers for employee stock ownership plans.

stock options or other equity instruments and shall be appropriately reflected in determining that value. For example, whether an employee who is granted an implicit option structured as the exchange of shares of stock for a nonrecourse note is required to pay nonrefundable interest on the note affects the fair value of the implicit option.

Accounting for Transactions with Other Than Employees

8. Except for transactions with employees that are within the scope of Opinion 25, all transactions in which goods or services are the consideration received for the issuance of equity instruments shall be accounted for based on the fair value of the consideration received or the fair value of the equity instruments issued, whichever is more reliably measurable. The fair value of goods or services received from suppliers other than employees frequently is reliably measurable and therefore indicates the fair value of the equity instruments issued. The fair value of the equity instruments issued shall be used to measure the transaction if that value is more reliably measurable than the fair value of the consideration received.[6] A common example of the latter situation is the use of the fair value of tradable equity instruments issued in a purchase business combination to measure the transaction because the value of the equity instruments issued is more reliably measurable than the value of the business acquired.

9. This Statement uses the term *fair value* for assets and financial instruments, including both liability and equity instruments, with the same meaning as in FASB Statement No. 121, *Accounting for the Impairment of Long-Lived Assets and for Long-Lived Assets to Be Disposed Of*. Statement 121 says that the fair value of an asset is

> . . . the amount at which the asset could be bought or sold in a current transaction between willing parties, that is, other than in a forced or liquidation sale. Quoted market prices in active markets are the best evidence of fair value and shall be used as the basis for the measurement, if available. If quoted market prices are not available, the estimate of

fair value shall be based on the best information available in the circumstances. The estimate of fair value shall consider prices for similar assets and the results of valuation techniques to the extent available in the circumstances. Examples of valuation techniques include the present value of estimated expected future cash flows using a discount rate commensurate with the risks involved, option-pricing models, matrix pricing, option-adjusted spread models, and fundamental analysis. [paragraph 7]

10. If the fair value of the goods or services received is not reliably measurable, paragraph 8 of this Statement requires that the measure of the cost of goods or services acquired in a transaction with other than an employee be based on the fair value of the equity instruments issued. However, this Statement does not prescribe the **measurement date,** that is, the date of the stock price on which the fair value of the equity instrument is based, for a transaction with a nonemployee (paragraphs 70-73).

Accounting for Transactions with Employees

11. This Statement provides a choice of accounting methods for transactions with employees that are within the scope of Opinion 25. Paragraphs 16-44 of this Statement describe a method of accounting based on the fair value, rather than the **intrinsic value,** of an employee stock option or a similar equity instrument. The Board encourages entities to adopt the fair value based method of accounting, which is preferable to the Opinion 25 method for purposes of justifying a change in accounting principle under APB Opinion No. 20, *Accounting Changes*.[7] However, an entity may continue to apply Opinion 25 in accounting for its stock-based employee compensation arrangements. An entity that does so shall disclose pro forma net income and, if presented, earnings per share, determined as if the fair value based method had been applied in measuring compensation cost (paragraph 45).

12. The fair value based method described in paragraphs 16-44 of this Statement applies for (a) measuring stock-based employee compensation cost by an

---

[6]The consideration received for issuing equity instruments, like the consideration involved in a repurchase of treasury shares, may include intangible rights. FASB Technical Bulletin No. 85-6, *Accounting for a Purchase of Treasury Shares at a Price Significantly in Excess of the Current Market Price of the Shares and the Income Statement Classification of Costs Incurred in Defending against a Takeover Attempt*, provides pertinent guidance.

[7]Opinion 20, paragraph 8, provides that initial adoption of an accounting principle for a transaction that the entity has not previously had to account for is not a change in accounting principle.

entity that adopts that method for accounting purposes and (b) determining the pro forma disclosures required of an entity that measures stock-based employee compensation cost in accordance with the intrinsic value based method in Opinion 25. Neither those paragraphs (16-44) nor subsequent paragraphs (45-54) of this Statement affect application of the *accounting* provisions of Opinion 25 by an entity that continues to apply it in determining reported net income.

13. For convenience, in describing the fair value based method, paragraphs 16-44 of this Statement refer only to *recognition* or *accounting* requirements. However, those provisions apply equally in determining the pro forma amounts that must be disclosed if an entity continues to apply Opinion 25.

14. An entity shall apply the same accounting method—either the fair value based method described in this Statement or the intrinsic value based method in Opinion 25—in accounting for all of its stock-based employee compensation arrangements. Once an entity adopts the fair value based method for those arrangements, that election shall not be reversed.[8]

15. Equity instruments granted or otherwise transferred directly to an employee by a **principal stockholder** are stock-based employee compensation to be accounted for by the entity under either Opinion 25 or this Statement, whichever method the entity is applying, unless the transfer clearly is for a purpose other than compensation.[9] The substance of a transaction in which a principal stockholder directly transfers equity instruments to an employee as compensation is that the principal stockholder makes a capital contribution to the entity and the entity awards equity instruments to its employee. An example of a situation in which a direct transfer of equity instruments to an employee from a principal stockholder is not compensation cost is a transfer to settle an obligation of the principal stockholder unrelated to employment by the reporting entity.

Valuation of Equity Instruments Issued for Employee Services

Measurement Basis

16. Frequently, part or all of the consideration received for equity instruments issued to employees is past or future employee services. Equity instruments issued to employees and the cost of the services received as consideration shall be measured and recognized based on the fair value of the equity instruments issued. The portion of the fair value of an equity instrument attributed to employee services is net of the amount, if any, that employees pay for the instrument when it is granted. Paragraphs 17-25 of this Statement provide guidance on how to measure the fair value of stock-based employee compensation. Paragraphs 26-33 provide guidance on how to attribute compensation cost to the periods in which employees render the related services. Appendix B, which is an integral part of this Statement, provides additional guidance on both measurement and attribution of employee compensation cost.

Measurement Objective and Date

17. The objective of the measurement process is to estimate the fair value, based on the stock price at the **grant date,** of stock options or other equity instruments to which employees become entitled when they have rendered the requisite service and satisfied any other conditions necessary to earn the right to benefit from the instruments (for example, to exercise stock options or to sell shares of stock). Restrictions that continue in effect after employees have earned the rights to benefit from their instruments, such as the inability to transfer **vested** employee stock options to third parties, affect the value of the instruments actually issued and therefore are reflected in estimating their fair value. However, restrictions that stem directly from the forfeitability of instruments to which employees have not yet earned the right, such as the inability either to exercise a nonvested option or to sell **nonvested stock,** do not affect the value of the instruments issued at the vesting date, and their effect therefore is not included in that

---

[8]APB Opinion No. 22, *Disclosure of Accounting Policies*, requires an entity to include a description of all significant accounting policies as an integral part of the financial statements. The method used to account for stock-based employee compensation arrangements is an accounting policy to be included in that description.

[9]That accounting has been required since 1973 in accordance with AICPA Accounting Interpretation 1, "Stock Plans Established by a Principal Stockholder," of Opinion 25.

value. Instead, no value is attributed to instruments that employees forfeit because they fail to satisfy specified service- or performance-related conditions.

Measurement Methods

Awards that call for settlement by issuing equity instruments

18. The fair value of a share of nonvested stock awarded to an employee shall be measured at the market price (or estimated market price, if the stock is not publicly traded) of a share of the same stock as if it were vested and issued on the grant date. Nonvested stock granted to employees usually is referred to as **restricted stock,** but this Statement reserves that term for shares whose sale is contractually or governmentally restricted after the shares are vested and fully outstanding. The fair value of a share of restricted stock awarded to an employee, that is, a share that will be restricted after the employee has a vested right to it, shall be measured at its fair value, which is the same amount as a share of similarly restricted stock issued to nonemployees.

19. The fair value of a stock option (or its equivalent) granted by a **public entity** shall be estimated using an option-pricing model (for example, the Black-Scholes or a binomial model) that takes into account as of the grant date the exercise price and expected life of the option, the current price of the underlying stock and its expected **volatility,** expected dividends on the stock (except as provided in paragraphs 32 and 33), and the risk-free interest rate for the expected term of the option. For options that a U.S. entity grants on its own stock, the risk-free interest rate used shall be the rate currently available on zero-coupon U.S. government issues with a remaining term equal to the expected life of the options. Guidance on selecting other assumptions is provided in Appendix B. The fair value of an option estimated at the grant date shall not be subsequently adjusted for changes in the price of the underlying stock or its volatility, the life of the option, dividends on the stock, or the risk-free interest rate.

20. A **nonpublic entity** shall estimate the value of its options based on the factors described in the preceding paragraph, except that a nonpublic entity need not consider the expected volatility of its stock over the expected life of the option. The result of excluding volatility in estimating an option's value is an amount commonly termed **minimum value.**

21. It should be possible to reasonably estimate the fair value of most stock options and other equity instruments at the date they are granted. Appendix B illustrates techniques for estimating the fair values of several options with complicated features. However, in unusual circumstances, the terms of a stock option or other equity instrument may make it virtually impossible to reasonably estimate the instrument's fair value at the date it is granted. For example, it may be extremely difficult, if not impossible, to reasonably estimate the fair value of a stock option whose exercise price decreases (or increases) by a specified amount with specified changes in the price of the underlying stock. Similarly, it may not be possible to reasonably estimate the value of a convertible instrument if the conversion ratio depends on the outcome of future events.

22. If it is not possible to reasonably estimate the fair value of an option or other equity instrument at the grant date, the final measure of compensation cost shall be the fair value based on the stock price and other pertinent factors at the first date at which it is possible to reasonably estimate that value. Generally, that is likely to be the date at which the number of shares to which an employee is entitled and the exercise price are determinable. Estimates of compensation cost for periods during which it is not possible to determine fair value shall be based on the current intrinsic value of the award, determined in accordance with the terms that would apply if the option or similar instrument had been currently exercised.

Employee stock purchase plans

23. If an employee stock purchase plan satisfies all of the following criteria, the plan is not compensatory. Therefore, the discount from market price merely reduces the proceeds from issuing the related shares of stock.

a. The plan incorporates no option features other than the following, which may be incorporated:
   (1) Employees are permitted a short period of time—not exceeding 31 days—after the purchase price has been fixed to enroll in the plan.
   (2) The purchase price is based solely on the stock's market price at date of purchase, and employees are permitted to cancel participation before the purchase date and obtain a refund of amounts previously paid (such as those paid by payroll withholdings).

b. The discount from the market price does not exceed the greater of (1) a per-share discount that would be reasonable in a recurring offer of stock to stockholders or others or (2) the per-share amount of stock issuance costs avoided by not having to raise a significant amount of capital by a public offering. A discount of 5 percent or less from the market price shall be considered to comply with this criterion without further justification.

c. Substantially all full-time employees that meet limited employment qualifications may participate on an equitable basis.

24. A plan provision that establishes the purchase price as an amount based on the lesser of the stock's market price at date of grant or its market price at date of purchase is, for example, an option feature that causes the plan to be compensatory. Similarly, a plan in which the purchase price is based on the stock's market price at date of grant and that permits a participating employee to cancel participation before the purchase date and obtain a refund of amounts previously paid is a compensatory plan.

Awards that call for settlement in cash

25. Some awards of stock-based compensation result in the entity's incurring a liability because employees can compel the entity to settle the award by transferring its cash or other assets to employees rather than by issuing equity instruments. For example, an entity may incur a liability to pay an employee either on demand or at a specified date an amount to be determined by the increase in the entity's stock price from a specified level. The amount of the liability for such an award shall be measured each period based on the current stock price. The effects of changes in the stock price during the **service period** are recognized as compensation cost over the service period in accordance with the method illustrated in FASB Interpretation No. 28, *Accounting for Stock Appreciation Rights and Other Variable Stock Option or Award Plans.* Changes in the amount of the liability due to stock price changes after the service period are compensation cost of the period in which the changes occur.

Recognition of Compensation Cost

26. The total amount of compensation cost recognized for an award of stock-based employee compensation shall be based on the number of instruments that eventually vest. No compensation cost is recognized for awards that employees forfeit either because they fail to satisfy a service requirement for vesting, such as for a **fixed award,** or because the entity does not achieve a **performance condition,** unless the condition is a target stock price or specified amount of intrinsic value on which vesting or exercisability is conditioned. For awards with the latter condition, compensation cost shall be recognized for awards to employees who remain in service for the requisite period regardless of whether the target stock price or amount of intrinsic value is reached.[10] Previously recognized compensation cost shall not be reversed if a vested employee stock option expires unexercised.

27. For purposes of this Statement, a stock-based employee compensation award becomes vested when an employee's right to receive or retain shares of stock or cash under the award is not contingent on the performance of additional services. Typically, an employee stock option that is vested also is immediately exercisable. However, if performance conditions affect either the exercise price or the exercisability date, the service period used for attribution purposes shall be consistent with the assumptions used in estimating the fair value of the award. Paragraphs 309 and 310 in Appendix B illustrate how to account for an option whose exercise price depends on a performance condition.

28. An entity may choose at the grant date to base accruals of compensation cost on the best available estimate of the number of options or other equity instruments that are expected to vest and to revise that estimate, if necessary, if subsequent information indicates that actual forfeitures are likely to differ from initial estimates. Alternatively, an entity may begin accruing compensation cost as if all instruments granted that are subject only to a service requirement are expected to vest. The effect of actual forfeitures would then be recognized as they occur. Initial accruals of compensation cost for an award with a performance condition that will determine the number of options or shares to which all employees receiving the award will be entitled shall be based on the best estimate of the outcome of the performance condition, although forfeitures by individual employees

---

[10]The existence of a target stock price that must be achieved to make an option exercisable generally affects the value of the option. Option-pricing models have been adapted to value many of those *path-dependent* options.

may either be estimated at the grant date or recognized only as they occur.[11]

29. Compensation cost estimated at the grant date for the number of instruments that are expected to vest based on performance-related conditions, as well as those in which vesting is contingent only on future service for which the entity chooses to estimate forfeitures at the grant date pursuant to paragraph 28, shall be adjusted for subsequent changes in the expected or actual outcome of service- and performance-related conditions until the vesting date. The effect of a change in the estimated number of shares or options expected to vest is a change in an estimate, and the cumulative effect of the change on current and prior periods shall be recognized in the period of the change.

30. The compensation cost for an award of equity instruments to employees shall be recognized over the period(s) in which the related employee services are rendered by a charge to compensation cost and a corresponding credit to equity (paid-in capital) if the award is for future service. If the service period is not defined as an earlier or shorter period, the service period shall be presumed to be the period from the grant date to the date that the award is vested and its exercisability does not depend on continued employee service (paragraph 27). If an award is for past services, the related compensation cost shall be recognized in the period in which it is granted.

31. Compensation cost for an award with a graded vesting schedule shall be recognized in accordance with the method described in Interpretation 28 if the fair value of the award is determined based on different expected lives for the options that vest each year, as it would be if the award is viewed as several separate awards, each with a different vesting date. If the expected life or lives of the award is determined in another manner, the related compensation cost may be recognized on a straight-line basis. However, the amount of compensation cost recognized at any date must at least equal the value of the vested portion of the award at that date. Appendix B illustrates application of both attribution methods to an award accounted for by the fair value based method.

32. Dividends or dividend equivalents paid to employees on the portion of an award of stock or other equity instruments that vests shall be charged to retained earnings. Nonforfeitable dividends or dividend equivalents paid on shares of stock that do not vest shall be recognized as additional compensation cost. The choice of whether to estimate forfeitures at the grant date or to recognize the effect of forfeitures as they occur described in paragraph 28 also applies to recognition of nonforfeitable dividends paid on shares that do not vest.

33. If employees receive only the dividends declared on the class of stock granted to them after the stock becomes vested, the value of the award at the grant date shall be reduced by the present value of dividends expected to be paid on the stock during the vesting period, discounted at the appropriate risk-free interest rate. The fair value of an award of stock options on which dividend equivalents are paid to employees or are applied to reduce the exercise price pursuant to antidilution provisions shall be estimated based on a dividend payment of zero.

Additional Awards and Modifications of Outstanding Awards

34. The fair value of each award of equity instruments, including an award of **reload options,** shall be measured separately based on its terms and the current stock price and related factors at the date it is granted.

35. A modification of the terms of an award that makes it more valuable shall be treated as an exchange of the original award for a new award. In substance, the entity repurchases the original instrument by issuing a new instrument of greater value, incurring additional compensation cost for that incremental value. The incremental value shall be measured by the difference between (a) the fair value of the modified option determined in accordance with the provisions of this Statement and (b) the value of the old option immediately before its terms are modified, determined based on the shorter of (1) its remaining expected life or (2) the expected life of the modified option. Appendix B provides further guidance on and illustrates the accounting for modifications of both vested and nonvested options.

36. Exchanges of options or changes to their terms in conjunction with business combinations, spinoffs, or other equity restructurings, except for those made

---

[11]For convenience, the remainder of this document refers to options or shares *expected to vest* because referring specifically to both acceptable methods of accounting for forfeitures by individual employees each time the point is mentioned would be too unwieldy.

to reflect the terms of the exchange of shares in a business combination accounted for as a pooling of interests, are modifications for purposes of this Statement. However, a change to the terms of an award in accordance with antidilution provisions that are designed, for example, to equalize an option's value before and after a stock split or a stock dividend is not a modification of an award for purposes of this Statement.

Settlements of Awards

37. An entity occasionally may repurchase equity instruments issued to employees after the employees have vested rights to them. The amount of cash or other assets paid (or liabilities incurred) to repurchase an equity instrument shall be charged to equity, provided that the amount paid does not exceed the value of the instruments repurchased. For example, an entity that repurchases for $10 a share of stock on the date it becomes vested does not incur additional compensation cost if the market price of the stock is $10 at that date. However, if the market price of the stock is only $8 at that date, the entity incurs an additional $2 ($10 − $8) of cost. An entity that settles a nonvested award for cash has, in effect, vested the award, and the amount of compensation cost measured at the grant date but not yet recognized shall be recognized at the date of repurchase.

38. For employee stock options, the incremental amount, if any, to be recognized as additional compensation cost upon cash settlement shall be determined based on a comparison of the amount paid with the value of the option repurchased, determined based on the remainder of its original expected life at that date. As indicated in paragraph 37, if stock options are repurchased before they become vested, the amount of unrecognized compensation cost shall be recognized at the date of the repurchase.

39. The accounting shall reflect the terms of a stock-based compensation plan as those terms are mutually understood by the employer and the employees who receive awards under the plan. Generally, the written plan provides the best evidence of its terms. However, an entity's past practice may indicate that the **substantive terms** of a plan differ from its written terms. For example, an entity that grants a **tandem award** consisting of either a stock option or a cash stock appreciation right (SAR) is obligated to pay cash on demand if the choice is the employee's, and the entity thus incurs a liability to the employee. In contrast, if the choice is the entity's, it can avoid

transferring its assets by choosing to settle in stock, and the award qualifies as an equity instrument. However, if an entity that nominally has the choice of settling awards by issuing stock generally settles in cash, or if the entity generally settles in cash whenever an employee asks for cash settlement, the entity probably is settling a substantive liability rather than repurchasing an equity instrument. The substantive terms shall be the basis for the accounting.

40. To restrict control to a limited group, for example, the members of a particular family, a nonpublic entity may obligate itself to repurchase its equity instruments for their fair value at the date of repurchase. In practice, such an obligation is not deemed to convert the stock to a liability. This Statement is not intended to change that view of the effect of a fair value repurchase agreement for a nonpublic entity. Thus, a nonpublic entity may grant or otherwise issue to employees equity instruments subject to such a repurchase agreement. The repurchase agreement does not convert those equity instruments to liabilities, provided that the repurchase price is the fair value of the stock at the date of repurchase.

Accounting for Tax Consequences of Equity Instruments Awarded to Employees

41. Income tax regulations specify allowable tax deductions for stock-based employee compensation arrangements in determining an entity's income tax liability. Compensation cost recognized under this Statement is measured based on the fair value of an award to an employee. Under existing U.S. tax law, allowable tax deductions are generally measured at a specified date as the excess of the market price of the related stock over the amount the employee is required to pay for the stock (that is, at intrinsic value). The **time value** component of the fair value of an option is not tax deductible. Therefore, tax deductions generally will arise in different amounts and in different periods from compensation cost recognized in financial statements.

42. The cumulative amount of compensation cost recognized for a stock-based award that ordinarily results in a future tax deduction under existing tax law shall be considered to be a deductible temporary difference in applying FASB Statement No. 109, *Accounting for Income Taxes*. The deferred tax benefit (or expense) that results from increases (or decreases) in that temporary difference, for example, as additional service is rendered and the related cost is recognized, shall be recognized in the income statement.

Recognition of compensation cost for an award that ordinarily does not result in tax deductions under existing tax law shall not be considered to result in a deductible temporary difference in applying Statement 109. A future event, such as an employee's disqualifying disposition of stock under existing U.S. tax law, can give rise to a tax deduction for an award that ordinarily does not result in a tax deduction. The tax effects of such an event shall be recognized only when it occurs.

43. Statement 109 requires a deferred tax asset to be evaluated for future realization and to be reduced by a valuation allowance if, based on the weight of the available evidence, it is more likely than not that some portion or all of the deferred tax asset will not be realized. Differences between (a) the deductible temporary difference computed pursuant to paragraph 42 and (b) the tax deduction inherent in the current fair value of the entity's stock shall not be considered in measuring either the gross deferred tax asset or the need for a valuation allowance for a deferred tax asset recognized under this Statement.

44. If a deduction reported on a tax return for a stock-based award exceeds the cumulative compensation cost for that award recognized for financial reporting, the tax benefit for that excess deduction shall be recognized as additional paid-in capital. If the deduction reported on a tax return is less than the cumulative compensation cost recognized for financial reporting, the write-off of a related deferred tax asset in excess of the benefits of the tax deduction, net of the related valuation allowance, if any, shall be recognized in the income statement except to the extent that there is remaining additional paid-in capital from excess tax deductions from previous stock-based employee compensation awards accounted for in accordance with the fair value based method in this Statement. In that situation, the amount of the write-off shall be charged against that additional paid-in capital.

Disclosures

45. Regardless of the method used to account for stock-based employee compensation arrangements, the financial statements of an entity shall include the disclosures specified in paragraphs 46-48. In addition, an entity that continues to apply Opinion 25 shall disclose for each year for which an income statement is provided the pro forma net income and, if earnings per share is presented, pro forma earnings per share, as if the fair value based accounting method in this Statement had been used to account for stock-based compensation cost. Those pro forma amounts shall reflect the difference between compensation cost, if any, included in net income in accordance with Opinion 25 and the related cost measured by the fair value based method, as well as additional tax effects, if any, that would have been recognized in the income statement if the fair value based method had been used. The required pro forma amounts shall reflect no other adjustments to reported net income or earnings per share.

46. An entity with one or more stock-based compensation plans shall provide a description of the plan(s), including the general terms of awards under the plan(s), such as vesting requirements, the maximum term of options granted, and the number of shares authorized for grants of options or other equity instruments. An entity that uses equity instruments to acquire goods or services other than employee services shall provide disclosures similar to those required by this paragraph and paragraphs 47 and 48 to the extent that those disclosures are important in understanding the effects of those transactions on the financial statements.

47. The following information shall be disclosed for each year for which an income statement is provided:

a. The number and weighted-average exercise prices of options for each of the following groups of options: (1) those outstanding at the beginning of the year, (2) those outstanding at the end of the year, (3) those exercisable at the end of the year, and those (4) granted, (5) exercised, (6) forfeited, or (7) expired during the year.

b. The weighted-average grant-date fair value of options granted during the year. If the exercise prices of some options differ from the market price of the stock on the grant date, weighted-average exercise prices and weighted-average fair values of options shall be disclosed separately for options whose exercise price (1) equals, (2) exceeds, or (3) is less than the market price of the stock on the grant date.

c. The number and weighted-average grant-date fair value of equity instruments other than options, for example, shares of nonvested stock, granted during the year.

d. A description of the method and significant assumptions used during the year to estimate the fair values of options, including the following weighted-average information: (1) risk-free interest rate, (2) expected life, (3) expected volatility, and (4) expected dividends.

e. Total compensation cost recognized in income for stock-based employee compensation awards.

f. The terms of significant modifications of outstanding awards.

An entity that grants options under multiple stock-based employee compensation plans shall provide the foregoing information separately for different types of awards to the extent that the differences in the characteristics of the awards make separate disclosure important to an understanding of the entity's use of stock-based compensation. For example, separate disclosure of weighted-average exercise prices at the end of the year for options with a fixed exercise price and those with an indexed exercise price is likely to be important, as would segregating the number of options not yet exercisable into those that will become exercisable based solely on employees' rendering additional service and those for which an additional condition must be met for the options to become exercisable.

48. For options outstanding at the date of the latest statement of financial position presented, the range of exercise prices (as well as the weighted-average exercise price) and the weighted-average remaining contractual life shall be disclosed. If the range of exercise prices is wide (for example, the highest exercise price exceeds approximately 150 percent of the lowest exercise price), the exercise prices shall be segregated into ranges that are meaningful for assessing the number and timing of additional shares that may be issued and the cash that may be received as a result of option exercises. The following information shall be disclosed for each range:

a. The number, weighted-average exercise price, and weighted-average remaining contractual life of options outstanding

b. The number and weighted-average exercise price of options currently exercisable.

Earnings per Share Implications

49. APB Opinion No. 15, *Earnings per Share*, requires that employee stock options, nonvested stock, and similar equity instruments granted to employees be treated as common stock equivalents in computing earnings per share. The number of nonvested equity instruments used in computing primary earnings per share shall be the same as the number that are used in measuring the related compensation cost in accordance with this Statement. Fully diluted earnings per share shall continue to be based on the actual number of options or shares granted and not yet forfeited, unless doing so would be antidilutive. If vesting is contingent on other factors, such as the level of future earnings, the shares or options shall be treated as contingent shares in accordance with paragraph 62 of Opinion 15. AICPA Accounting Interpretation 91, "Earnings Conditions," of Opinion 15 provides additional guidance on applying paragraph 62 of Opinion 15 to stock-based employee compensation plans. If stock options or other equity instruments are granted during a period, the shares issuable shall be weighted to reflect the portion of the period during which the equity instruments were outstanding.

50. In applying the treasury stock method of Opinion 15, the assumed proceeds shall be the sum of (a) the amount, if any, the employee must pay, (b) the amount of compensation cost attributed to future services and not yet recognized, and (c) the amount of tax benefits, if any, that would be credited to additional paid-in capital. FASB Interpretation No. 31, *Treatment of Stock Compensation Plans in EPS Computations*, provides detailed examples of the treatment of stock compensation plans accounted for under Opinion 25 in earnings per share computations. Although the related cost and tax amounts will differ if the fair value based accounting method in this Statement is applied, the principles in Interpretation 31 remain applicable.

Effective Date and Transition

51. The requirement in paragraph 8 of this Statement shall be effective for transactions entered into after December 15, 1995.

52. The recognition provisions of this Statement may be adopted upon issuance. Regardless of when an entity initially adopts those provisions, they shall be applied to all awards granted after the beginning of the fiscal year in which the recognition provisions are first applied. The recognition provisions shall not be applied to awards granted in fiscal years before the year of initial adoption except to the extent that prior years' awards are modified or settled in cash after the beginning of the fiscal year in which the entity adopts the recognition provisions. Accounting for modifications and settlements of awards initially accounted for in accordance with Opinion 25 is discussed and illustrated in Appendix B.

53. The disclosure requirements of this Statement shall be effective for financial statements for fiscal years beginning after December 15, 1995, or for the

fiscal year for which this Statement is initially adopted for recognizing compensation cost, whichever comes first. The disclosure requirements need not be applied in an interim report unless a complete set of financial statements is presented for that period. Pro forma disclosures required by paragraph 45 of this Statement shall include the effects of all awards granted in fiscal years that begin after December 15, 1994. Pro forma disclosures for awards granted in the first fiscal year beginning after December 15, 1994 need not be included in financial statements for that fiscal year but shall be presented subsequently whenever financial statements for that fiscal year are presented for comparative purposes with financial statements for a later fiscal year.

54. During the initial phase-in period, the effects of applying this Statement for either recognizing compensation cost or providing pro forma disclosures are not likely to be representative of the effects on reported net income for future years, for example, because options vest over several years and additional awards generally are made each year. If that situation exists, the entity shall include a statement to that effect. The entity also may wish to provide supplemental disclosure of the effect of applying the fair value based accounting method to all awards made in fiscal years beginning before the date of initial adoption that were not vested at that date.

The provisions of this Statement need not be applied to immaterial items.

This Statement was adopted by the affirmative votes of five members of the Financial Accounting Standards Board. Messrs. Foster and Leisenring dissented.

Messrs. Foster and Leisenring dissent from the issuance of this Statement because they believe that the compensation associated with employee stock options should be recognized as a cost in the financial statements and disagree with the decision to permit that cost to be reflected only in pro forma disclosures. They agree with the Board's conclusion that employee stock options represent compensation and that the amount of associated cost can be determined with sufficient reliability for recognition in financial statements. Messrs. Foster and Leisenring believe that, having reached those conclusions, the Board should accept the conclusion of paragraph 9 of FASB Concepts Statement No. 5, *Recognition and Measurement in Financial Statements of Business Enterprises,* that disclosure is not a substitute for recognition in financial statements for items that meet recognition criteria.

Messrs. Foster and Leisenring believe that a high level of controversy and a perceived threat to accounting standard setting in the private sector as discussed in paragraphs 57-62 are inappropriate reasons for not requiring recognition in financial statements of an item that meets the recognition criteria of Concepts Statement 5.

Messrs. Foster and Leisenring further believe that the effect of this Statement on improving disclosure of compensation cost for those entities that choose not to adopt the fair value based method is substantially diminished because the Statement does not require disclosure of the pro forma effect on net income and earnings per share in summarized interim financial data required by APB Opinion No. 28, *Interim Financial Reporting.* They believe that comparable data presented on a quarterly basis is important to financial analysis.

While Messrs. Foster and Leisenring concur with the conclusion that fair value of employee stock options is the appropriate measure of compensation cost, they do not agree that the grant date method of accounting as described in paragraphs 16-44 results in the best measure of that cost. As discussed in paragraphs 155-160, the Board's decision to look to certain events that occur after the grant date in measuring compensation cost, by, for example, adjusting for forfeitures after that date, is inconsistent with its decision to base compensation cost on a grant date stock price. Messrs. Foster and Leisenring believe that a more understandable, representationally faithful, and consistent measure of the compensation granted in an employee stock option would be achieved by measuring the fair value of all vested options at the vesting date. As explained in paragraphs 96 and 167, employee stock options are not issued until the vesting date. At that date, the employer and employee have fulfilled their obligations under the agreement that offers the stock options and consequently the options are issued and can then be measured.

Despite their belief that vesting date measurement would result in a superior measure of compensation cost, Messrs. Foster and Leisenring would have accepted the modified grant date method and assented to issuance of this Statement if the cost determined under that method was required to be recognized rather than only disclosed. Notwithstanding the shortcomings of the modified grant date method of measuring compensation expense, it is significantly better than the continued failure to recognize compensation cost in financial statements—the result of applying Opinion 25.

Members of the Financial Accounting Standards Board:

Dennis R. Beresford,	Anthony T. Cope	Robert H. Northcutt
Chairman	John M. Foster	Robert J. Swieringa
Joseph V. Anania	James J. Leisenring	

Appendix A

BASIS FOR CONCLUSIONS

CONTENTS

Appendix A

BASIS FOR CONCLUSIONS

Introduction

55. This appendix summarizes considerations that Board members deemed significant in reaching the conclusions in this Statement. It includes reasons for accepting certain approaches and rejecting others. Individual Board members gave greater weight to some factors than to others.

56. Accounting for stock-based employee compensation plans is a pervasive subject that affects most public entities and many nonpublic entities. Opinion 25 continues to be criticized for producing anomalous results and for lacking an underlying conceptual rationale that helps in resolving implementation questions or in deciding how to account for

stock-based compensation plans with new features. A frequently cited anomaly is that the requirements of Opinion 25 typically result in the recognition of compensation cost for performance options but no cost is recognized for fixed options that may be more valuable at the grant date than performance options. Critics of Opinion 25 also note that long-term fixed options granted to employees are valuable financial instruments, even though they carry restrictions that usually are not present in other stock options. Financial statements prepared in accordance with the requirements of Opinion 25 do not recognize that value. The resulting financial statements are less credible than they could be, and the financial statements of entities that use fixed employee options extensively are not comparable to those of entities that do not make significant use of fixed options. Because of the various criticisms of Opinion 25, in March 1984, the Board added a project to its agenda to reconsider accounting by employers for stock-based compensation plans.

Why the Board Decided Not to Require Fair Value Accounting

57. In June 1993, the Board issued an Exposure Draft on accounting for stock-based compensation that would have replaced Opinion 25 with an accounting method based on recognizing the fair value of equity instruments issued to employees, regardless of whether the instrument was a share of stock, a fixed or performance option, or some other instrument, with measurement based on the stock price at the date the instrument was granted. Requiring all entities to follow the fair value based method in the Exposure Draft would have (a) resulted in accounting for stock-based employee compensation that was both internally consistent and also consistent with accounting for all other forms of compensation, (b) "leveled the playing field" between fixed and variable awards, and (c) made the accounting for equity instruments issued to employees more consistent with the accounting for all other free-standing equity instruments[12] and the related consideration received.

58. That Exposure Draft was extraordinarily controversial. The Board's due process is intended to ensure that the views of all interested parties are heard and fully considered. The Board not only expects but actively encourages debate of the issues and proposals in an Exposure Draft, and the final Statement generally benefits from information the Board receives during that debate. Both the Board and its constituents usually learn from the debate, with the result that the Board's views and the views of many of its constituents generally move closer together during the debate.

59. Unlike other highly controversial topics, the controversy on accounting for stock-based compensation escalated throughout the exposure process. The main point of contention was whether compensation cost should be recognized for stock options with fixed terms that are at-the-money[13] at the date they are granted. Constituents gave different reasons for opposing cost recognition, with many expressing concerns about whether the fair value of employee stock options at the grant date can be estimated with sufficient reliability. Most respondents urged the Board to expand disclosures about stock-based employee

compensation arrangements rather than to change the basic accounting method in Opinion 25. The specific comments of respondents to the Exposure Draft and later comments made as the Board redeliberated the issues are discussed later in this appendix.

60. The debate on accounting for stock-based compensation unfortunately became so divisive that it threatened the Board's future working relationship with some of its constituents. Eventually, the nature of the debate threatened the future of accounting standards setting in the private sector.

61. The Board continues to believe that financial statements would be more relevant and representationally faithful if the estimated fair value of employee stock options was included in determining an entity's net income, just as all other forms of compensation are included. To do so would be consistent with accounting for the cost of all other goods and services received as consideration for equity instruments. The Board also believes that financial reporting would be improved if all equity instruments granted to employees, including instruments with variable features such as options with performance criteria for vesting, were accounted for on a consistent basis. However, in December 1994, the Board decided that the extent of improvement in financial reporting that was envisioned when this project was added to its technical agenda and when the Exposure Draft was issued was not attainable because the deliberate, logical consideration of issues that usually leads to improvement in financial reporting was no longer present. Therefore, the Board decided to specify as preferable and to encourage but not to require recognition of compensation cost for all stock-based employee compensation, with required disclosure of the pro forma effects of such recognition by entities that continue to apply Opinion 25.

62. The Board believes that disclosure of the pro forma effects of recognizing compensation cost according to the fair value based method will provide relevant new information that will be of value to the capital markets and thus will achieve some but not all of the original objectives of the project. However, the Board also continues to believe that disclosure is not an adequate substitute for recognition of assets, liabilities, equity, revenues, and expenses in financial

---

[12]A *free-standing* equity instrument is one that is not embedded in a compound instrument with other, nonequity, components. For example, convertible debt is a compound instrument with both liability and equity components. The call option on common stock that is part of convertible debt is not a free-standing equity instrument, and it is not currently accounted for separately from the liability component.

[13]For convenience, this appendix uses the terms *at-the-money, out-of-the-money,* and *in-the-money* commonly used by option traders to denote an option with an exercise price that *equals, exceeds,* or *is less than,* respectively, the current price of the underlying stock.

statements, as discussed more fully later in this appendix. The Board chose a disclosure-based solution for stock-based employee compensation to bring closure to the divisive debate on this issue—not because it believes that solution is the best way to improve financial accounting and reporting.

Alternative Accounting Methods

63. When the Board decided not to require recognition of compensation cost determined by the fair value based method, it also decided that it was important to avoid explicitly or implicitly endorsing arguments against the Exposure Draft that the Board did not find credible. For example, endorsing the argument that an at-the-money option has no value or that financial statements should exclude the values of financial instruments that are difficult to measure would misrepresent the Board's views and likely would impede efforts to improve financial reporting in other areas—especially for other financial instruments, some of which are more complex and may be more difficult to value than employee stock options. The Board's reasons for rejecting those arguments are discussed in paragraphs 76-117 of this appendix.

64. The Board also decided that improved disclosure alone—regardless of the nature of the disclosure—is not sufficient. The Board thus encourages entities to adopt the fair value based accounting method described in this Statement. That method permits an entity to avoid in its financial statements the effects of Opinion 25 that encourage fixed plans and discourage plans with variable, performance-based features. Providing an alternative accounting method does not achieve as level a playing field for fixed and performance-based plans as the Board and some of its constituents would like. However, it establishes a mechanism that can result in a more level playing field over time if many entities eventually choose the fair value based accounting method. It also provides a means by which improved accounting for stock-based employee compensation can evolve through the voluntary actions of entities and their advisors without the Board's having to undertake another reconsideration of this topic.

65. Some respondents asked the Board to permit a plan-by-plan choice between the intrinsic value based method in Opinion 25 and the fair value based method established by this Statement. Those respondents argued that permitting a choice on a plan-by-plan basis would result in a more level playing field than this Statement does because entities could

avoid the volatility in compensation cost for performance-based awards that often results from Opinion 25's requirements while continuing to report zero expense for most fixed awards.

66. The Board decided not to permit a plan-by-plan choice of accounting method. The overriding objective of this project was to improve the accounting for stock-based employee compensation by superseding Opinion 25's inconsistent requirements for fixed and variable awards with accounting standards that would result in more relevant and representationally faithful financial statements. That overriding objective could not be achieved without developing an internally consistent accounting method for all stock-based employee compensation awards, which in turn would result in a more level playing field for fixed and performance-based awards. Providing a plan-by-plan choice would permit an entity to choose whichever method it expected to produce the lower reported cost for each award. Permitting that choice was not among the objectives of this project.

67. The Board notes that permitting a plan-by-plan choice of accounting method would still be biased in favor of fixed awards and therefore would not level the playing field because entities would continue to be required to report compensation cost for performance-based awards while reporting no cost for fixed, at-the-money stock options. Permitting a plan-by-plan choice of method also would eliminate any possibility that evolution alone, perhaps including the development of improved methods of valuing employee stock options, would eventually result in better accounting for stock-based employee compensation.

68. Permitting a plan-by-plan choice also would result in more complicated financial statements. Entities would need to explain which method was used for which plans and why, as well as provide disclosures to help users of the financial statements understand the effects of the accounting choices and to put all entities' reporting on a comparable basis.

Pro Forma Disclosure of the Effects of Applying Fair Value Based Accounting

69. Because this Statement permits an entity to choose either of two different methods of accounting for its stock-based employee compensation arrangements, pro forma disclosures of net income and earnings per share computed as if the fair value based method had been applied are required in the financial

statements of an entity that chooses to continue to apply Opinion 25. Those disclosures will give investors, creditors, and other users of the financial statements more comparable information, regardless of the accounting method chosen. The pro forma disclosures also will make available better information than Opinion 25 provides about the costs of stock-based employee compensation.

Accounting for Equity Instruments Issued for Consideration Other Than Employee Services

70. The Exposure Draft was the result of a comprehensive reconsideration of accounting issues related to the measurement and recognition of stock-based compensation paid to employees for their services. The Board's deliberations that led to the Exposure Draft also considered current accounting principles for other issuances of equity instruments. The Exposure Draft covered accounting for all issuances of equity instruments for consideration other than cash, which may consist of goods, services, or noncash financial instruments. Issuances of equity instruments for cash rarely raise significant accounting issues.

71. That the cost of employee services measured by the fair value of equity instruments issued in exchange for them should be recognized in determining the employer's net income is not a new notion. Indeed, recognition of consideration received and the cost incurred as that consideration is used in an entity's operations is fundamental to the accounting for equity instruments. Therefore, the Board decided that the choice of continuing to apply Opinion 25 should be limited to issuances of equity instruments for employee services that fall within the scope of Opinion 25. All other issuances of equity instruments should be recognized based on the fair value of the consideration received or the fair value of the equity instrument issued, whichever is more reliably measurable.

72. The appropriate date at which to measure an issuance of equity instruments for consideration other than employee services usually is a relatively minor issue. Generally, an issuer of equity instruments receives the consideration for them—whether it is cash, another financial instrument, or an enforceable right to receive financial instruments, goods, or services in the future—almost immediately after the parties agree to the transaction. If a longer time elapses between agreement and receipt of consideration, neither the issuer nor the other party may have a unilateral obligation under the contract during that period.

That is, the distinction between grant date and vesting date may not be clearly present in many situations other than stock-based employee compensation. For some transactions, such as business combinations, in which the measurement date can be a significant issue, other accounting pronouncements specify the date of the stock price on which the measurement should be based. Therefore, this Statement does not specify the measurement date for determining the fair value of equity instruments issued to other than employees.

73. An initial draft of portions of this Statement was distributed for comment to task force members and other constituents. That draft would have excluded stock options issued to independent contractors from the transactions to which an entity may apply Opinion 25 in determining net income. Some respondents objected to that exclusion because, in practice, the scope of Opinion 25 has been extended to include many option recipients treated as independent contractors for tax purposes. Some Board members believe that application of Opinion 25 to service providers that are not employees is inappropriate. However, the Board decided that resolving the issue of whether Opinion 25 has been applied correctly is outside the scope of this Statement. The Board expects to consider at a future date the need for a pronouncement about the scope of Opinion 25.

Why Stock-Based Employee Compensation Is a Cost That Should Be Recognized in Financial Statements

74. Paragraphs 75-117 of this appendix discuss the reasons for the Board's principal conclusions on recognition and measurement issues, which support the Board's belief that recognition of stock-based employee compensation cost determined according to the fair value based method is preferable to continued application of Opinion 25 with only pro forma disclosures of the effect of recognizing stock-based employee compensation cost. That discussion begins with the basic issue of why employee stock options give rise to recognizable compensation cost.

75. The Board's conclusion that recognizing the costs of all stock-based employee compensation, including fixed, at-the-money stock options, is the preferable accounting method stems from the following premises:

a. Employee stock options have value.

b. Valuable financial instruments given to employees give rise to compensation cost that is properly included in measuring an entity's net income.

c. The value of employee stock options can be estimated within acceptable limits for recognition in financial statements.

Employee Stock Options Have Value

76. An option or warrant to buy an entity's stock for a fixed price during an extended future time period is a valuable right, even if the ways in which the holder can exercise the right are limited. Investors pay cash to buy stock options and warrants that generally have fewer restrictions than employee stock options, and unrestricted options and warrants are traded daily in financial markets. The additional restrictions inherent in employee stock options, such as the inability to transfer the option to a third party for cash, cause the value of an employee stock option to be less than the value of an otherwise identical tradable option at any time before the expiration date, but the restrictions do not render employee stock options valueless.

77. Employees rarely pay cash to acquire their employee stock options. Instead, employees provide services to their employer in exchange for cash, stock options, and other employee benefits. Even if employees are required to pay a nominal amount of cash for their options, it usually is far less than the fair value of the options received. The majority of the consideration an employer receives for employee stock options is employee services. Nonrecognition of compensation cost implies either that employee stock options are free to employees or that the options have no value—neither of which is true.

78. Some respondents argued that an employee stock option has value only if the employee ultimately realizes a gain from it. The Board does not agree. Many traded options ultimately expire worthless; that does not mean that the options had no value either when they were written or at any other time before they expired. An employee stock option has value when it is granted regardless of whether, ultimately, (a) the employee exercises the option and purchases stock worth more than the employee pays for it or (b) the option expires worthless at the end of the option period. The grant date value of a stock option is the value *at that date* of the right to purchase an entity's stock at a fixed price for an extended time period. Investors pay cash to acquire that right—employees provide services to acquire it.

Valuable Financial Instruments Given to Employees Give Rise to Compensation Cost That Is Properly Included in Measuring an Entity's Net Income

79. Employees provide services for which employers pay compensation. The components of an employee's total compensation package are, to some extent, flexible. The compensation package, for example, might include more cash and less health insurance, or the package might include stock options and less cash. Some employers even offer employees a choice between predetermined amounts of cash and stock options.

80. Large employers have included stock options in the compensation packages of upper echelon management for many years, and some employers recently have adopted broad-based plans that cover most of their full-time employees. A stated objective of issuing stock options is to align employee interests with those of shareholders and thereby motivate employees to work to maximize shareholder value. In addition, many start-up and other cash-poor entities provide stock options to make up for cash wages and other benefits that are less than those available elsewhere. Many respondents from younger, rapidly growing entities said that their success was attributable in large part to their extensive use of stock options; without stock options, they could not have attracted and retained the employees they needed.

81. Some respondents said that stock options are not direct compensation for services rendered and thus are not comparable to cash salaries and wages. Rather, stock options usually have other objectives, such as to attract valuable employees and to encourage them to stay with the employer by requiring a period of service before their options vest and become exercisable. Stock options, like other forms of incentive compensation, also are intended to motivate employees to perform better than they might have without the incentive. Stock-based compensation awards often are intended to compensate employees for incremental efforts beyond the basic performance required to earn their salaries or wages. Respondents that made those points generally said that the value of stock options is not a compensation cost that should be recognized in the entity's financial statements.

82. The Board acknowledges that employee stock options, as well as other forms of stock-based compensation, usually are not direct substitutes for a

stated amount of cash salaries. That does not, however, imply that the value of options issued to employees is not a recognizable cost. Group medical and life insurance, disability insurance, employer-paid memberships in health clubs, and the like also are not direct compensation like cash salaries because the amount of benefit that an individual employee may receive does not necessarily vary directly with either the amount or the quality of the services rendered. However, virtually everyone agrees that the costs of those benefits are properly deducted in determining the entity's net income. Like employee stock options, benefits such as medical insurance and pensions are compensation in the broad sense of costs incurred to attract, retain, and motivate employees. It has long been an established practice that, even if employee benefits are paid—directly or indirectly—with shares of the employer's stock, the value of the stock issued to the employee or the service provider is a cost to be reported in the employer's income statement.

83. Some opponents of recognizing compensation cost for stock options acknowledge that stock options are recognizable compensation, but they say that a requirement to recognize that compensation would have adverse economic consequences because many entities would reduce or eliminate their stock option programs. However, some of the same respondents also said that Opinion 25's bias in favor of fixed awards at the expense of awards with performance conditions, options with indexed exercise prices, and the like should be eliminated because that bias has undesirable economic consequences. It deters employers from using more performance-based awards, which those respondents consider preferable to fixed options in many situations.

84. The Board's operating precepts require it to consider issues in an even-handed manner, without intentionally attempting to encourage or to discourage specific economic actions. That does not imply that improved financial reporting should not have economic consequences; a change in accounting standards that makes available more relevant and representationally faithful financial information often will have economic consequences. For example, the availability of the new information resulting from application of this Statement may lead an entity to reassess the costs and benefits of its existing stock option plans. If a reassessment reveals that the expected benefits of a stock option plan do not justify its costs, a rational response would be to revise or eliminate the plan. However, an entity presumably would not

restrict or eliminate a stock option program whose motivational effect on employees is expected to make a net contribution to reported results of operations. To do so would not be rational because continuing the plan would be expected to increase revenues (or to decrease other expenses) more than enough to offset the reported compensation cost. In addition, many small, emerging entities told the Board that stock options often substitute for higher cash wages or other benefits, such as pensions. Significantly reducing those option programs would not make economic sense if employees would demand equal or greater cash wages or other benefits to replace the lost stock options.

85. Some people told the Board that a requirement to recognize compensation cost might bring additional discipline to the use of employee stock options. Unless and until the stock price rises sufficiently to result in a dilutive effect on earnings per share, the current accounting for most fixed stock options treats them as though they were a "free good." Stock options have value—employee stock options are granted as consideration for services and thus are not free.

86. Some respondents said that recognizing the compensation cost stemming from stock options would, by itself, raise the cost of capital of all entities that use options extensively. An individual entity's cost of capital would rise only if its lenders or buyers and sellers of its stock had previously been misled by the accounting under Opinion 25 to believe that fixed, at-the-money employee stock options have no value and thus impose no cost on the entity. If that were the situation for an individual entity or a group of entities, any increase in cost of capital would result from new, relevant information. Making available at an acceptable cost information that is helpful in making investment, credit, and similar decisions is the overriding objective of financial reporting.

87. Some respondents that agreed with the Board's conclusion that accounting standards, by themselves, are highly unlikely to have negative economic consequences noted that the market abhors uncertainty. Reducing uncertainty can reduce the cost of capital. Therefore, recognizing in financial statements the cost of all stock-based compensation measured in a reasonable and internally consistent manner might lower rather than raise an entity's cost of capital. Financial statement users no longer would have to decide how to consider the cost of stock options in their analysis of an entity, knowing that whatever method they chose would be based on inadequate information. With amounts recognized and measured on a

reasonable and consistent basis that takes into account detailed information generally available only to the entity, users might still choose to modify or use the available information in different ways, but they would have a reasonable starting point for their analysis.

Expenses and capital transactions

88. Some respondents pointed out that the definition of expenses in FASB Concepts Statement No. 6, *Elements of Financial Statements,* says that expenses result from outflows or using up of assets or incurring of liabilities (or both). They asserted that because the issuance of stock options does not result in the incurrence of a liability, no expense should be recognized. The Board agrees that employee stock options are not a liability—like stock purchase warrants, employee stock options are equity instruments of the issuer. However, equity instruments, including employee stock options, are valuable financial instruments and thus are issued for valuable consideration, which often is cash or other financial instruments but for employee stock options is employee services. Using in the entity's operations the benefits embodied in the asset received results in an expense, regardless of whether the consideration is cash or other financial instruments, goods, or services.[14] Moreover, even if shares of stock or other equity instruments are donated to a charity, the fair value of the instruments issued is recognized together with other charitable contributions in determining the issuer's net income. The Board recently reaffirmed that general principle in FASB Statement No. 116, *Accounting for Contributions Received and Contributions Made.*

89. Others noted that the issuance of an employee stock option is a capital transaction. They contended that capital transactions do not give rise to expenses. As discussed in paragraph 88, however, issuances of equity instruments result in the receipt of cash, other financial instruments, goods, or services, which give rise to expenses as they are used in an entity's operations. Accounting for the consideration received for issuing equity instruments has long been fundamental to the accounting for all free-standing equity instruments except one—fixed stock options subject to the requirements of Opinion 25.

90. Some respondents also asserted that the issuance of an employee stock option is a transaction directly

between the recipient and the preexisting stockholders in which the stockholders agree to share future equity appreciation with employees. The Board disagrees. Employees provide services to the entity—not directly to the individual stockholders—as consideration for their options. Carried to its logical conclusion, that view would imply that the issuance of virtually any equity instrument, at least those issued for goods or services rather than cash or other financial instruments, should not affect the issuer's financial statements. For example, no asset or related cost would be reported if shares of stock were issued to acquire legal or consulting services, tangible assets, or an entire business in a business combination. Moreover, in practice today, even if a stockholder directly pays part of an employee's cash compensation (or other corporate expenses), the transaction and the related costs are reflected in the entity's financial statements, together with the stockholder's contribution to paid-in capital. To omit such costs would give a misleading picture of the entity's financial performance.

91. The Board sees no conceptual basis that justifies different accounting for the issuance of employee stock options than for all other transactions involving either equity instruments or employee services. As explained in paragraphs 57-62, the Board's decision not to require recognition of compensation expense based on the fair value of options issued to employees was not based on conceptual considerations.

Prepaid compensation

92. The Exposure Draft proposed that an asset, prepaid compensation, be recognized at the date stock-based employee compensation awards are granted; the prepaid compensation would represent the value already conveyed to employees for services to be received in the future. Later, compensation cost would have been incurred as the benefits embodied in that asset were used up; that is, as the employees rendered service during the vesting period.

93. Many respondents objected to the recognition of prepaid compensation at the grant date. They said that, unlike most other amounts paid to suppliers before services are received, the proposed prepaid compensation for nonvested stock-based employee compensation did not meet the definition of an asset in paragraph 25 of Concepts Statement 6, which defines

---

[14]Concepts Statement 6, paragraph 81, footnote 43, notes that, in concept, most expenses decrease assets. However, if receipt of an asset, such as services, and its use occur virtually simultaneously, the asset often is not recorded.

assets as "probable future economic benefits obtained or controlled by a particular entity as a result of past transactions or events" (footnote reference omitted). Prepaid fees for legal services, consulting services, insurance services, and the like represent probable future economic benefits that are controlled by the entity because the other party to the transaction has entered into a contract to provide services to earn the fees. The service provider is not entitled to walk away from its obligation to render the services that are the subject of the contract by merely foregoing collection of the fee for services not rendered. Although courts rarely enforce specific performance under a service contract, a construction contractor, for example, cannot decide unilaterally not to finish a building after digging the foundation without being subject to legal action for monetary damages by the other party to the contract. Contracts sometimes specify the damages to be paid if the contract is broken. In other circumstances, such as prepaid rent or insurance, the purchaser of the service may be able to successfully sue for specific performance—the right to occupy an office or to be reimbursed for fire damage, for example.

94. Those respondents said that employee stock options do not represent probable future benefits that are controlled by the employer at the date the options are granted because employees are not obligated to render the services required to earn their options. The contract is unilateral—not bilateral—because the entity has only conditionally transferred forfeitable equity instruments and is obligated to issue the instruments *if and when* the employee has rendered the specified service or satisfied other conditions. However, the employee is not obligated to perform the services and may leave the employer's service without being subject to damages beyond the loss of the compensation that would have been paid had the services been rendered.

95. The Board agreed that an entity does not obtain an asset for future service to be rendered at the date employee stock options are granted. Therefore, this Statement does not require recognition of prepaid compensation at the grant date. Rather, the cost of the related services is accrued and charged to compensation cost only in the period or periods in which the related services are received. At the grant date, awards of stock-based employee compensation are fully executory contracts. Once employees begin to render the services necessary to earn the compensation, execution of the contracts has begun, and recognition of the services already received is appropriate. The

Board's conclusions on how to attribute compensation cost to the periods in which the entity receives the related employee services are discussed further in paragraphs 196-203.

96. An equity instrument may be conditionally transferred to another party under an agreement that allows that party to choose at a later date whether to deliver the agreed consideration for it, which may be goods or services rather than cash or financial instruments, or to forfeit the right to the instrument conditionally transferred, with no further obligation. In that situation, the equity instrument is not *issued* for accounting purposes until the issuing entity has received consideration for it and the condition is thus satisfied. The grant of an employee stock option subject to vesting conditions is an example of such a conditional transfer. For that reason, this Statement does not use the term *issued* to refer to the grant of a stock option or other equity instrument that is subject to service or performance conditions for vesting. The Board's conclusion that the entity receives no asset at the date employee stock options are granted is consistent with that use of the term *issued*. That conclusion about the issuance date of employee stock options, in turn, has implications for the appropriate date at which to measure the value of the equity instruments issued. This Statement requires a measurement method that combines attributes of both grant date and vesting date measurement. The Board's conclusions on measurement date and method are discussed in paragraphs 149-154.

The usefulness and integrity of the income statement

97. An entity's income statement reports the revenues from and the costs of its operations. Under Opinion 25, part of a cost, compensation to employees, is not reported in the income statements of most entities that issue fixed stock options. Some entities use fixed stock options more extensively than other entities do, and reported operating expenses thus are understated to differing degrees. Comparisons between entities of profit margins, rates of return, income from operations, and the like are impaired to the extent that entities continue to account for their stock-based employee compensation according to the provisions of Opinion 25.

98. To illustrate the lack of comparability under Opinion 25, assume that Companies A, B, and C each report $6 million of total compensation cost. Company A does not grant fixed stock options to its

employees, but Companies B and C do. The value of fixed stock options as a percentage of the total compensation package for employees of Companies B and C are 20 percent and 40 percent, respectively. Total compensation cost for Company A is $6 million, as reported in its financial statements. Although Companies B and C report the same amount of compensation cost as Company A, actual compensation is $7.5 million for Company B and $10 million for Company C. The three companies are not competing for capital on a level playing field because their financial statements are not comparable.

99. Some opponents of recognizing compensation cost for stock options are concerned about the adverse effect they contend it would have on their income statements. The effect of recognizing compensation cost for employee stock options should be neither more nor less adverse than the effect of recognizing a comparable amount of depreciation (or any other) cost. Recognition of depreciation always reduces a company's profit or increases its loss. Entities would look more profitable on paper if they discontinued depreciating their assets, but no one recommends not recognizing depreciation to eliminate its adverse effect on the income statement. The Board believes that the rationale that a potentially adverse effect on income statements argues against recognition is no more compelling for compensation than it is for any other cost.

The cost of employee stock options is not "recognized" in earnings per share

100. Primary earnings per share represents the entity's earnings (the numerator) divided by the number of common and common equivalent shares outstanding (the denominator). Some respondents that opposed recognizing compensation cost for employee stock options said that to do so would "double count" the effect of issuing stock options. The dilutive effect of any in-the-money stock options is included in the denominator of earnings per share, and a reduction in net income (the numerator) would, in their view, create an inappropriate dual effect.

101. The Board disagrees. A transaction that results in an expense and also increases, actually or potentially, the number of shares outstanding properly affects both the numerator and denominator of the earnings per share calculation. If an entity issues stock, stock options, or stock purchase warrants for cash and uses the cash received to pay expenses, earnings are reduced and more common equivalent shares are outstanding. Even in applying the requirements of Opinion 25, granting nonvested (so-called restricted) stock decreases the numerator (earnings) and increases the denominator (shares outstanding). In both of those examples, the effect on income appropriately reflects the use of the consideration received (either cash or employee services) for issuing equity instruments.

Disclosure is not a substitute for recognition

102. FASB Concepts Statement No. 5, *Recognition and Measurement in Financial Statements of Business Enterprises,* says:

> Since recognition means depiction of an item in both words and numbers, with the amount included in the totals of the financial statements, disclosure by other means is *not* recognition. Disclosure of information about the items in financial statements and their measures that may be provided by notes or parenthetically on the face of financial statements, by supplementary information, or by other means of financial reporting is not a substitute for recognition in financial statements for items that meet recognition criteria. [paragraph 9]

103. Many respondents contended that improved disclosures about employee stock options in the notes to financial statements would be as useful as recognition of compensation cost in the income statement. A specific disclosure proposal submitted by a group of providers and users of financial statements and endorsed by the largest accounting firms was illustrated in Appendix E of the Exposure Draft. Most respondents, including some that had previously endorsed that proposal, agreed that the proposed disclosures were too extensive and included some items that more properly belong in a proxy statement. The Board received several other proposals for disclosures in lieu of recognition during the exposure period and during its redeliberations of the conclusions in the Exposure Draft. Some of those proposals included a measure of the value of options granted during the year, but most focused largely on greatly expanding the detailed data disclosed about stock-based employee compensation plans.

104. As discussed in paragraphs 57-62, the Board's decision to encourage but not to require recognition of compensation cost for the fair value of stock-based

employee compensation was not based on acceptance of the view that disclosure is an adequate substitute for recognition in the financial statements. If disclosure and recognition were equal alternatives, the arguments for only disclosing either detailed information about stock-based employee compensation awards or the amount of unrecognized cost would apply equally to other costs such as depreciation, warranties, pensions, and other postretirement benefits.

105. The Board believes that the pro forma disclosures required by this Statement will mitigate to some extent the disadvantages of permitting disclosure in lieu of recognition. To disclose only additional details about options granted, vested, forfeited, exercised, expired, and the like would permit only the most sophisticated users of financial statements to estimate the income statement impact of recognizing all compensation costs. Many individual investors and other users of financial statements could not, and even the more sophisticated users would have available less information than the entity itself has on which to base estimates of value and related compensation cost related to employee stock options. The Board's continuing belief that disclosure is not an adequate substitute for recognition of items that qualify for recognition in financial statements is the reason for this Statement's establishment of the fair value based accounting method as preferable for purposes of justifying an accounting change and for encouraging entities to adopt it.

106. The Board did not specifically address during its formal deliberations whether pro forma disclosures of the effects on net income and earnings per share of applying the fair value based method should be included in summarized interim financial data required by APB Opinion No. 28, *Interim Financial Reporting.* That question arose late in the process of drafting this Statement when some Board members noted that comparable information about earnings and earnings per share presented on a quarterly basis would be important to financial analysis. Other Board members agreed but thought that it was too late in this extraordinarily controversial project to add a requirement for pro forma disclosures in summarized interim financial data. Therefore, this Statement does not require those disclosures. If a need for pro forma disclosures on a quarterly basis becomes apparent, the Board will consider at a later date whether to require those disclosures.

The Value of Employee Stock Options Can Be Estimated within Acceptable Limits for Recognition in Financial Statements

107. The value of employee services rendered is almost always impossible to measure directly. For that reason, accounting for the cost of employee services is based on the value of compensation paid, which is presumed to be an adequate measure of the value of the services received. Compensation cost resulting from employee stock options is measured based on the value of stock options granted rather than on the value of the services rendered by the employee, which is consistent with the accounting for other forms of employee compensation.

108. Trading of options in the financial markets has increased significantly in the last 20 years. During that time, mathematical models to estimate the fair value of options have been developed to meet the needs of investors. Some employers and compensation consultants have used variations of those models in considering how much of a compensation package should consist of employee stock options and in determining the total value of a compensation package that includes stock options. Many that have been using option-pricing models for those purposes said that the existing models are not sufficiently accurate for accounting purposes, although they are adequate for comparing the value of compensation packages across entities and for estimating the value of options in designing compensation packages. Those respondents generally said that a more precise measure is needed for measuring compensation cost in the income statement than for comparing the value of total compensation, including options, paid by various entities or in determining how many options to grant an employee.

109. The Board disagrees with the distinction made by those respondents. One important use of financial statements is to compare the relative attractiveness of investment and lending opportunities available in different entities. Therefore, increasing the comparability of financial statements is a worthy goal, even if all entities use a measurement method that is less precise than the Board or its constituents might prefer.

110. The derivative markets have developed rapidly with the introduction of new kinds of options and option-like instruments, many of which are long term and nontraded—or even nontransferable. For example, interest rate caps and floors, both of which are forms of options, are now common. Often, option

components are embedded in other instruments, and both the seller and the purchaser of the instrument need to evaluate the value added by each component of a compound instrument. Mathematical models that extend or adapt traditional option-pricing models to take into account new features of options and other derivative securities also continue to be developed. Sometimes decisions have been made based on inadequate analysis or incomplete models, resulting in large and highly publicized losses for one party to a contract. Those instances usually lead to additional analysis of the instruments in question and further refinement of the models. However, market participants—whether they consider themselves to be traders, investors, or hedgers—continue to commit billions of dollars to positions in options and other derivatives, based at least in part on analysis using mathematical pricing models that are not perfect.

111. The Exposure Draft noted that uncertainties inherent in estimates of the fair value of employee stock options are generally no more significant than the uncertainties inherent in measurements of, for example, loan loss reserves, valuation allowances for deferred tax assets, and pension and other postretirement benefit obligations. All estimates, because they are estimates, are imprecise. Few accrual-based accounting measurements can claim absolute reliability, but most parties agree that financial statement recognition of estimated amounts that are approximately right is preferable to the alternative—recognizing nothing—which is what Opinion 25 accounting recognizes for most employee stock options. Zero is not within the range of reasonable estimates of the value of employee stock options at the date they are granted, the date they vest, or at other dates before they expire, with the possible exception of deep-out-of-the-money options that are near expiration. Even those latter options generally have a nominal value until very shortly before expiration.

112. Many respondents said that the Exposure Draft inappropriately compared the imprecision in estimating the value of employee stock options with similar imprecisions inherent in estimating, for example, the amount of an entity's obligation to provide postretirement health care benefits. They said that because postretirement health care benefits eventually result in cash payments by the entity, the total obligation and related cost are "trued up" over the entity's life. In contrast, the value of employee stock options estimated at the grant date is not trued up to reflect the actual gain, if any, that an employee realizes from an award of employee stock options. Those respondents

asserted that the lack of true-up makes it necessary for the estimated value of employee stock options that forms the basis for recognizing the related compensation cost to be more precise than an estimate of the value of the same entity's obligation for postretirement health care benefits.

113. The Board questions that perceived distinction between the relative importance of the precision of estimates of the value of employee stock options and the precision of other estimates inherent in financial statements. Although the total amount of any expense that is ultimately paid in cash will necessarily equal the total of the amounts attributed to each of a series of years, the appropriate amount to attribute to any individual year is never trued up. Nor can the precision of the reported total obligation be determined at any date while it is being incurred. For example, the total cost of a postretirement health care plan will be trued up only if the plan is terminated. Investors, creditors, and other users of financial statements must make decisions based on a series of individual years' financial statements that covers less than the entire life of the entity. For costs such as postretirement health care benefits, the true-up period for an individual employee (or group of similar employees) may be decades, and even then the total amount cannot be separated from amounts attributed to other employees. Concern about the reliability of estimates of the value of employee stock options and the related cost seem equally applicable to annual estimates of, for example, obligations for postretirement benefits and the related cost.

114. The respondents that emphasized the importance of truing up the total cost of a stock-based employee compensation award generally were adamantly opposed to exercise date accounting—the only accounting method for employee stock options that would true up interim cost estimates to equal the total gain, if any, an employee realizes. The Board rejected exercise date accounting for conceptual reasons, as discussed in paragraph 149. However, deferring final measurement of a transaction until enough of the related uncertainties have been resolved to make reasonably reliable measurement possible is the usual accounting response to measurement difficulties for virtually all other transactions except an award to an employee of fixed stock options.

115. The standard Black-Scholes and binomial option-pricing models were designed to estimate the value of transferable stock options. The value of transferable stock options is more than the value of

employee stock options at the date they are granted primarily for two reasons. First, transferable stock options can be sold, while employee stock options are not transferable and can only be exercised. Second, an employee can neither sell nor exercise nonvested options. Nonvested employee options cannot be exercised because the employee has not yet fully paid for them and is not obligated to do so. Options other than employee options rarely include a lengthy period during which the holder may choose to walk away from the right to the options.

116. The measurement method in this Statement reduces the estimated value of employee stock options below that produced by an option-pricing model for nonforfeitable, transferable options. Under the method in this Statement, the recognized value of an employee stock option that does not vest—and thus is never issued to the employee—is zero. In addition, the estimated value of an employee stock option is based on its expected life rather than its maximum term, which may be considerably longer. Paragraphs 155-173 explain why the Board believes those adjustments are appropriate and sufficient to deal with the forfeitability and nontransferability of employee stock options.

117. The Board continues to believe that use of option-pricing models, as modified in this Statement, will produce estimates of the fair value of stock options that are sufficiently reliable to justify recognition in financial statements. Imprecision in those estimates does not justify failure to recognize compensation cost stemming from employee stock options. That belief underlies the Board's encouragement to entities to adopt the fair value based method of recognizing stock-based employee compensation cost in their financial statements.

The Major Measurement Issues

118. Having concluded that stock-based compensation awards, including fixed employee stock options, give rise to compensation cost that should be measured and recognized, the Board considered more detailed measurement and recognition issues.

Measurement Date for Compensation Cost

119. The measurement date for equity instruments awarded to employees is the date at which the stock price that determines the measurement of the transaction is fixed. The Board decided to retain the provisions of the Exposure Draft that the measurement date for equity instruments awarded to employees (and subsequently issued to them if vesting conditions are satisfied) and the related compensation cost is to be measured based on the stock price at the grant date. The Board also decided that the measurement method for public entities should be fair value. The reasons for those conclusions are discussed in paragraphs 120-153.

Alternative measurement dates

120. Possible measurement dates[15] include the date an award of employee stock options or similar instruments is granted *(grant date)*, the date on which an employee has completed the service period necessary for the award to vest *(vesting date)*, the dates on which an employee renders the related services *(service date)*, the date on which all service-related conditions expire *(service expiration date)*, and the date an award is exercised or expires *(exercise date)*.

Grant date

121. Advocates of grant date measurement note that the employer and employee come to a mutual understanding of the terms of a stock-based compensation award at the grant date and that the employee begins to render the service necessary to earn the award at that date. They therefore consider use of the grant date stock price appropriate in measuring the transaction. In deciding whether to grant shares of stock, for example, and how many shares to award an individual employee, both parties to the agreement presumably have in mind the current stock price—not the possible stock price at a future date. If compensation cost were measured based on the stock price at a later date, such as the date at which the award vests, the amount of compensation cost that could result from an award would not be known when an entity decides how many shares to grant.

122. Advocates of grant date measurement also consider it to be consistent with generally accepted concepts and practices applied to other equity instruments. They note that changes in the price of an issuer's stock after the parties agree to the terms of a transaction in which equity instruments are issued

---

[15]The various measurement dates discussed refer to the dates of the stock price on which fair value and the related cost are based—not the date at which accounting based on estimates begins. For example, most advocates of vesting date measurement would begin accruing compensation cost as soon as employees begin to render the service necessary to earn their awards.

generally do not affect the amount at which the transaction is recognized. Grant date measurement is based on the view that equity instruments are issued to employees—not just conditionally transferred to them—at the grant date because the entity becomes unilaterally obligated at that date. To be fully consistent with that premise, application of grant date measurement would reflect at the grant date the effect of all restrictions inherent in vesting requirements in estimating the value of the instrument considered to be effectively issued at the grant date. For example, the value of an option with a performance vesting condition would be reduced to reflect both the likelihood that the performance condition will not be satisfied and the likelihood that an employee will not continue in service until the end of the vesting period. Because the option is considered to have been issued to the employee at the grant date, initial estimates would not be subsequently adjusted to reflect differences between estimates and experience.

123. To illustrate, if an employee stock option is considered to be issued at the grant date, the effects of its forfeitability, nonexercisability, and any other restrictions that are in effect during the vesting period but that are removed after the equity instrument vests would be estimated at the grant date and not subsequently adjusted. Changes in the value of an entity's equity instruments, whatever the source, are not reflected in its income statement. For example, if an entity grants 10,000 options, of which 8,000 are expected to vest, the final measurement of compensation cost in accordance with a strict application of grant date measurement would be based on the value of 8,000 options estimated at the grant date, regardless of whether all 10,000 options or only 4,000 options eventually vested.

Vesting date

124. Proponents of measuring the value of equity instruments awarded to employees and the related compensation cost based on the stock price at the date the award vests note that employees have not earned the right to retain their shares or options until that date. They suggest that a more descriptive term for the *grant date* would be *offer date* because the entity makes an offer at that date and becomes unilaterally obligated to issue equity instruments to employees if the employees render the necessary service or satisfy other conditions for vesting. Employees effectively accept the offer by fulfilling the requisite conditions (generally rendering services) for vesting. Proponents contend that the transaction between the

employer and employee should not be finally measured until both parties have fulfilled their obligations under the agreement because the employee has only a conditional right to the equity instruments and the instruments thus are not actually issued until that date.

125. Advocates of vesting date measurement consider that method to be consistent with accounting for the issuance of similar equity instruments to third parties for either cash or an enforceable right to receive cash or other assets in the future. At the date a stock purchase warrant, for example, is issued and measured, the investor need not satisfy obligations to provide further assets or services to the issuer to become eligible to retain and exercise the warrant. For the same reason, vesting date advocates do not think that measurement of the transaction should be held open after the vesting date. Once an employee stock option becomes vested, they contend that the employee is in much the same position as a third-party holder of a stock purchase warrant.

Service date

126. Service date measurement can be described as a variation of vesting date measurement because, in both methods, measurement of the transaction between an employer and its employees is held open until employees have rendered the services necessary to earn their awards. Advocates of service date measurement, however, point out that the earning of a stock-based compensation award—like the earning of other forms of compensation—is a continuous process. They say that the related compensation cost should be measured based on the stock prices during the period the service is rendered—not solely on the stock price at either the beginning or the end of that period.

127. Advocates of service date measurement prefer it to vesting date measurement because the latter adjusts the value (and related cost) of the service received in, for example, year 1 of a two-year vesting period based on stock price changes that occur in year 2. Moreover, the increment (or decrement) in value attributable to year 1's service is recognized in year 2. In their view, to retroactively adjust the value of consideration (in this situation, employee services) already received for future issuance of an equity instrument is to treat awards of equity instruments to employees as if they were liabilities until the employees have vested rights to them. Because an entity that grants stock options is obligated only to issue its own

stock, not to transfer its assets, those that favor service date accounting contend that measuring nonvested awards as if they were liabilities is inappropriate.

128. Under service date measurement, a proportionate number of the shares in a grant of shares of stock subject to vesting requirements, for example, would in concept be measured based on the stock price each day that an employee renders service. In practice, the results of daily accrual probably would be reasonably approximated by basing the amount of compensation cost recognized each accounting period on the average stock price for that period.

Service expiration date

129. The service expiration date, sometimes referred to as the *portability date,* is the date at which all service-related conditions that may change the terms under which employees may exercise their stock options expire. Awards of employee stock options generally specify a limited period of time, often 90 days but sometimes a shorter or even no period, after termination of service during which employees with vested options may exercise them. The options are canceled if they are not exercised by the end of that period. If the exercise period is 90 days after termination, the service expiration or portability date is 90 days before the maximum term of the options expires. If the options are exercised before then, the exercise date would be the measurement date. (For an award of stock subject to vesting requirements, the service expiration date is the date at which service-related restrictions on the sale of the stock lapse, which usually would be the same as the vesting date.)

130. Advocates of service expiration date measurement argue that a limitation on exercise of an option after termination of service, say to 90 days, effectively reduces the term of a vested option to 90 days. On the day that an employee's rights to that option vest, the employee holds an option whose effective term is 90 days, regardless of its stated term. Each additional day of service until the service expiration date extends the life of the option by one day. Advocates also generally note that equity of an entity arises from transactions between the entity and its owners in their role as owners, not as suppliers, employees, creditors, or some other role. Advocates of service expiration date measurement do not consider an employee stock option to be an outstanding equity instrument as long as the employee must render additional service to extend the term of the option. Until

then, the ongoing transaction is one between an entity and its employees in their role as employees in which the entity incurs a liability to pay for employee services. Thus, they say that it is appropriate to treat the option as a liability until all service-related restrictions expire (or the option is exercised, whichever comes first).

131. Supporters of service expiration date measurement also note that it would be easier to apply than earlier measurement dates. If the period after which service-related conditions expire is short, such as 90 days, most of the option's value at that time is likely to be made up of its intrinsic value, which is readily measurable. If the option has no intrinsic value at that time, its total value also is likely to be low, and concerns about how well traditional option-pricing models measure that value would be mitigated by the short life of the option.

Exercise date

132. Some that favor exercise date measurement of stock-based employee compensation awards do so because they consider call options written by an entity on its stock to be liabilities rather than equity instruments. They acknowledge that those options, including both employee stock options and stock purchase warrants, do not qualify as liabilities under the definition in paragraph 35 of Concepts Statement 6 because they do not obligate the entity to transfer its assets to the holder and thus lack an essential characteristic of a liability. Those that hold this view generally favor revising the conceptual distinction between liabilities and equity instruments so that an obligation to issue stock at a fixed price would qualify as a liability.

133. Advocates of exercise date measurement note that an obligation to issue stock at a price that may be less than its market price at the date of the transaction has the potential to transfer value from the preexisting stockholders to holders of the call options. In their view, that potential makes the obligation a liability of the entity, even though the entity is not obligated to transfer its own assets to the holders of the options. Other advocates of exercise date measurement contend that the gain, if any, that an employee realizes upon exercise of a stock option appropriately measures the total compensation paid. They are less concerned about the conceptual distinction between liabilities and equity because they see little, if any, practical difference between an employee stock option and a cash bonus indexed to the price of the entity's stock.

134. Exercise date advocates also note that measurement at that date is simple and straightforward. Concerns about how to apply option-pricing models initially developed for traded options to forfeitable, nontransferable employee options, how to estimate expected long-term volatility, and the like do not apply if final measurement is based on the gain, if any, that an employee realizes by exercising an option. The usual response to major problems in measuring the effects of a transaction is to defer final measurement until the difficulties are resolved. Exercise date measurement might be appropriate for that reason, regardless of more conceptual considerations.

Measurement Method for Compensation Cost

135. This Statement specifies fair value as the basic method for measuring awards of equity instruments, including stock options, to employees as compensation. Not only the appropriate measurement method but also the meaning of *fair value*—especially at the grant date—were contentious issues during the exposure period. Moreover, respondents' views on the measurement method often were closely linked to their views on the measurement date question. The possible measurement methods, together with differences, if any, in how they might be applied at various possible measurement dates are discussed in paragraphs 136-148. The reasons for the Board's conclusions on measurement date and method are then explained.

Intrinsic value

136. The intrinsic value of an option at any point during its term is the difference between its exercise price and the current price of the underlying stock. Intrinsic value thus excludes the value of the right to purchase the underlying stock at a fixed price for a specified future period—its time value. Respondents that favored measuring employee stock options at their intrinsic value generally said that intrinsic value is easily measured and understood. Some also noted that employees cannot convert the time value of their options to cash.

137. Intrinsic value measurement might be combined with any of the measurement dates discussed in paragraphs 120-134. However, the vast majority of the advocates of intrinsic value would accept only intrinsic value measurement at the grant date. They generally said that Opinion 25 has "worked well" and that the Board should not change its requirements but merely supplement them with additional disclosures.

However, some respondents went further and said that grant date-intrinsic value accounting—Opinion 25's method for fixed plans—should be applied to variable plans as well. Adopting that suggestion would result in recognition of no compensation cost for all options that are at-the-money when granted, implying that at-the-money options have no value. The inaccuracy of that implication already has been discussed (paragraphs 76-78).

138. Respondents that favored extending grant date-intrinsic value measurement to variable plans said that the result would be a level playing field for fixed and variable plans. The Board believes that adopting a grant date-intrinsic value method for all options would level the playing field at the cost of making financial statements even less relevant and representationally faithful than they are when Opinion 25 is the basis of measuring stock-based employee compensation cost. That is not an acceptable outcome of a project that was undertaken with the overriding objective of improving financial reporting. An *exercise date*-intrinsic value method also would level the playing field, and some Board members think that it would enhance the relevance and representational faithfulness of financial statements.

Minimum value

139. The so-called minimum value method derives its name from the theory underlying its calculation. The idea is that a person who wishes to purchase a call option on a given stock would be willing to pay *at least* (perhaps more important, the option writer would demand *at least*) an amount that represents the benefit (sacrifice) of the right to defer payment of the exercise price until the end of the option's term. For a dividend-paying stock, that amount is reduced by the present value of the expected dividends because the holder of an option does not receive the dividends paid on the underlying stock.

140. Minimum value thus can be determined by a present value calculation. It is (a) the current price of the stock reduced by the present value of the expected dividends on the stock, if any, during the option's term minus (b) the present value of the exercise price. Present values are based on the risk-free rate of return. For a 10-year option with an exercise price of $50 on a stock with a current price of $50 and expected dividends of $.25 paid at the end of each quarter—an expected annual dividend yield of 2 percent—minimum value is computed as shown below. The risk-free interest rate available for 10-year investments is 7 percent.

Current stock price	$50.00
Minus:	
Present value of exercise price[16]	24.83
Present value of expected dividends	7.21
Minimum value	$17.96

Investing $24.83 at a 7 percent risk-free interest rate for 10 years would give the investor $50, which is the amount needed to exercise the option. However, an investor who held the stock rather than the option would receive dividends during the term of the option with a present value of $7.21. The net benefit from deferring payment of the exercise price thus is $17.96.

141. Minimum value also can be computed using an option-pricing model and an expected volatility of effectively zero. (Standard option-pricing models do not work if the volatility input is zero because the models use volatility as a divisor, and zero cannot be a divisor. Using an expected volatility of, say, 0.001 avoids that problem.) In the above example, using an option-pricing model with an expected volatility of effectively zero, a risk-free rate of 7 percent, an expected dividend yield of 2 percent, and an option term of 10 years results in a minimum value of $16.11. That is lower than the amount calculated using simple present value techniques ($16.11 versus $17.96) because the calculations inherent in option-pricing models assume that both the stock price and dividends will grow at the same rate (if the dividend assumption is stated as a constant yield). The assumed growth rate is the difference between the risk-free interest rate and the dividend rate, which is 5 percent (7 percent – 2 percent) in this example.

142. For a stock that pays no dividends, minimum value is the same regardless of which method is used, and the lower the expected dividend yield, the less difference between the results of the two methods. This Statement permits only nonpublic entities to measure their options at minimum value (paragraphs 174-178 explain the Board's conclusions on nonpublic entities), and many of the nonpublic entities that use employee stock options extensively pay either no or relatively low dividends. Moreover, the expected life of employee stock options with a contractual term of 10 years often is substantially shorter, which also reduces the amount of potential difference. In addition, models are available that compute

value based on a fixed dividend amount, rather than a constant dividend yield. Therefore, the Board acceded to the request of some respondents to permit either method of computing minimum value.

Fair value

143. Because it ignores the effect of expected volatility, the minimum value method differs from methods designed to estimate the fair value of an option, such as the Black-Scholes and binomial option-pricing models and extensions or modifications of those original models. Expected volatility provides much of the value of options—especially relatively short-term options. Even for longer term options such as most employee stock options, the level of expected volatility accounts for a significant part of the difference in the values of options on different stocks. Option holders benefit from the volatility of stocks because they have the right to capture increases in the price of (and related return on) the underlying stock during the term of the option without having to bear the full risk of loss from stock price decreases. The maximum amount that the holder of a call option can lose is the premium paid to the option writer—which represents the right to benefit from price increases without the corresponding risk of loss from price decreases during the option term. In contrast, the holder of a share of the underlying stock can lose the full value of the share.

144. The fair value of the option whose minimum value was computed in paragraphs 140 and 141 thus is more than either $17.96 or $16.11. The fair value of that option depends on the expected volatility of the underlying stock. If the expected long-term volatility of the stock in the example is 35 percent, the fair value of the option is approximately $23.08. Volatility and its effect on option value are defined and explained more fully in Appendixes E and F.

What is the fair value of an employee stock option?

145. The Exposure Draft applied to employee stock options the same definition of fair value that is used elsewhere in the authoritative literature. That definition and the related guidance, which are quoted in paragraph 9, focus first on the price at which a willing buyer and a willing seller would be willing to exchange an item in other than a forced or liquidation

---

[16]Present value calculations reflect daily compounding.

sale and require the use of quoted market prices for the same or similar items if they are available. However, the definition mentions several valuation techniques, including option-pricing models, that are acceptable for estimating fair value if quoted market or other exchange prices for the item or a similar item are not available.

146. Some respondents apparently focused solely on the part of the definition that refers to the price a willing buyer would pay for an item. They said that the objective of determining the fair value of an employee stock option should be to determine the amount of cash compensation employees would be willing to trade for their stock options. Those respondents mentioned several reasons, such as the relatively large amount of most employees' personal financial wealth that is tied to the fortunes of their employer or employees' need for cash to pay current expenses, that might make most employees unwilling to pay as much as a third party might pay for a given stock option.

147. The Board rejected that view of the meaning of the *fair value* of an employee stock option. The fair values of other financial instruments do not take into account either the source of the funds with which a buyer might pay for the instrument or other circumstances affecting individual buyers. A logical extension of that view could result in a different "fair value" for identical options in a single grant for each employee who receives an award, even if the expected life is the same for each option.

148. Moreover, the definition of fair value places equal emphasis on the amount a willing (and presumably rational) seller would demand for the item. The estimated fair value of employee stock options, like the estimated fair value of other financial instruments for which market prices are not available, may not reflect all of the factors that an individual willing buyer or willing seller would consider in establishing an exchange price. That does not make it inappropriate to estimate the fair value of the item using a valuation technique that takes into account the theoretical effect on buyers and sellers as a group of the various features of the instrument. In addition, market prices are usually set at the margin. An option writer would seek the highest bidder with the capacity to buy the option. That bidder would be the pertinent "willing buyer."

Conclusions on Measurement Date and Method

149. After considering both the written responses to the Discussion Memorandum, *Distinguishing between Liability and Equity Instruments and Accounting for Instruments with Characteristics of Both,* and comments made at the public hearing on that document (refer to Appendix C), the Board decided early in 1992 not to pursue possible changes to the conceptual definitions of liabilities and equity. Instead, the Board decided to seek resolution of issues on accounting for stock-based compensation within the context of the conceptual definitions set forth in Concepts Statement 6 under which a call option written by an entity on its stock is an equity instrument rather than a liability. The Board decided not to pursue exercise date measurement on conceptual grounds because it is more consistent with viewing call options written as liabilities.

150. Each of the other possible measurement dates had advocates among the Board members in deliberations preceding issuance of the Exposure Draft. Even at that time, most Board members thought that a reasonable conceptual case could be made for either the vesting date or the service date. On balance, however, the Board agreed that a variation of grant date measurement was appropriate, and that was what the Exposure Draft proposed. In reaching that conclusion, Board members generally found persuasive the argument that measurement at the grant date bases the compensation cost stemming from a stock-based compensation award on the stock price at the date the parties agree to its terms. As discussed in paragraphs 92-96, the Board also concluded in the Exposure Draft that an asset—prepaid compensation—should be recognized at the grant date because the Board was persuaded at that time that a forfeitable equity instrument conditionally transferred to an employee could be considered "issued," which is an important part of the rationale for grant date accounting. However, Board members subsequently agreed with the majority of respondents that said that an entity that grants stock-based compensation does not receive an enforceable right to employee services at the grant date. That conclusion raises an additional question about the appropriateness of grant date accounting versus some version of vesting date accounting.

151. An overwhelming majority of respondents favored grant date measurement. They generally emphasized the importance of basing the measure of the related cost on the stock price at the date the parties

agree to the terms of an award. Most of those respondents, however, did not support the fair value based measurement method in the Exposure Draft. Most that opposed the Exposure Draft on that basis said that traditional option-pricing models, even modified to take into account the effect of forfeitability and nontransferability, did not fully reflect all of the factors that would affect the fair value of an employee stock option at the grant date. For example, an employee or a third party to whom an option is issued that is neither exercisable nor transferable for the first part of its life presumably would want to pay less for the option because of those restrictions. Similarly, many respondents pointed out that liquidity adds value and that the fair value of shares of "restricted" or "letter" stock is less than the value of unrestricted stock of the same entity.

152. Most respondents that took that view favored continued measurement of employee stock options at intrinsic value on the grounds that fair value could not be measured with reasonable reliability at the grant date. Others, however, suggested reducing the estimated fair value of both stock options and nonvested stock at the grant date to reflect additional restrictions during the vesting period. For example, some suggested a reduction in value by an arbitrary percentage, say, 10 percent for each year of the vesting period. The Board considered both that and other possible, but more complicated, ways of taking restrictions during the vesting period into account.

153. The Board reaffirmed its conclusion in the Exposure Draft that public entities should account for their stock options and other equity instruments at fair value. A fair value basis is consistent with the measurement principles applied to other issuances of equity instruments and to other forms of compensation paid to employees. Equity instruments other than employee stock options and the consideration received for them are recognized at their fair values on the dates the instruments are issued. For example, the initial recognition of debt issued with detachable stock purchase warrants is based on the relative fair values of the debt and the warrants at the date of issuance—not on a calculated minimum value of the warrants. Similarly, a share of stock or a warrant issued to settle an obligation to pay for services other than employee services would be measured at fair value. Other forms of compensation paid to employees, including cash, other assets, pension benefits, and the like are initially measured at the fair value of the asset given up or the liability incurred. The Board does not believe that concerns about measurement

are a sufficient reason to measure compensation paid in stock options on a different basis.

154. Paragraphs 165-173 discuss the modifications to standard option-pricing models to take into account the nontransferability of vested employee stock options. The Board's intent in this Statement is for the guidance in both the standards section and the guidance and illustrations in Appendix B to be sufficiently broad that employers may adopt future refinements in models that improve their application to employee stock options without requiring the Board to amend this Statement.

Restrictions that apply only during the vesting period

155. This Statement requires recognition of no compensation cost for awards that do not vest, as proposed in the Exposure Draft. Even so, some respondents said that an additional reduction in value is needed for awards of employee stock options that do vest to reflect their nonexercisability before they vested. Those respondents did not consider the use of expected life sufficient to reflect both the nontransferability and nonexercisability of nonvested options.

156. Board members generally agreed that investors who might purchase equity instruments with restrictions similar to those in a nonvested award of employee stock compensation (including nonvested shares of stock, which in effect are options for which the entire exercise price is employee services) would take those restrictions into account in determining how much they would be willing to pay for the instruments. However, employees do not pay the full value of their options at the grant date, although they may pay a nominal amount for each option granted. If they fully paid for their options at the grant date, the options would not be subsequently forfeitable, and the restrictions stemming from forfeitability would not exist. An investor who pays cash or other enforceable consideration for an option subject to restrictions similar to those in a nonvested employee stock option could not be required subsequently to forfeit entirely any benefit inherent in the instrument if the investor did not fulfill additional requirements.

157. Restrictions that apply to awards of stock-based employee compensation only during the period before they become vested stem entirely from the forfeitability of nonvested awards, which in turn stems from employees' not yet having satisfied the conditions necessary to earn their awards and having no

enforceable obligation to do so. That conclusion is consistent with not recognizing prepaid compensation at the grant date. Some Board members believe that conclusion calls for measuring both the value of the equity instrument and the related compensation cost based on the stock price at the vesting date—the date the instrument is issued. Other Board members agree that vesting date measurement may be conceptually appropriate; nevertheless, they consider it important to base the measure of compensation cost stemming from awards of employee stock options on the stock price at the date the entity decides how many options to award to an employee—the grant date.

158. Respondents' overwhelming opposition to vesting date measurement and the potential resulting volatility in reported net income during the vesting period would make it less likely that entities would voluntarily adopt the fair value based method if it were based on the stock price at the vesting date. The choice of accounting methods in this Statement provides an opportunity for entities to improve their accounting for employee stock options. Therefore, on balance, the Board decided to retain the Exposure Draft's provision that compensation cost should be measured based on the stock price at the grant date. However, the Board does not consider it necessary also to reflect in the measurement of fair value restrictions that no longer apply after employee stock options become vested and nonforfeitable. To do so would be inconsistent with the employee stock options' being issued at the vesting date (paragraph 96). The measurement method in the Exposure Draft combined features of both grant date and vesting date measurement because it adjusted for the effect of the difference, if any, between estimated and actual forfeitures due to failure to render the requisite service or to satisfy performance conditions. The measurement method in this Statement also is a hybrid of grant date and vesting date accounting for the same reason.

159. Some respondents that favored reducing the value of nonvested employee stock options for restrictions that stem from their forfeitability were opposed to similar reductions in the value of shares of nonvested stock. They noted similar situations in which the value of shares of an entity's stock that are involved in other employee compensation or benefit arrangements is not reduced below the market price of an unrestricted share at the date compensation is measured even though individual employees may not be able to realize the value of the stock for many

years. Examples are stock transferred to employee stock ownership plans, an entity's contributions of its own stock to either defined benefit or defined contribution pension plans, and deferred compensation arrangements designed to permit employees to defer payment of income taxes.

160. As mentioned earlier, the Board views shares of nonvested stock as employee stock options in which the exercise price consists entirely of employee services. Therefore, the Board believes that any reduction in the value of stock-based compensation to reflect restrictions during the vesting period would have to apply to both nonvested options and nonvested shares of stock. The Board is concerned that applying such a reduction to the stock-based employee compensation covered by this Statement would raise questions about the appropriateness of making similar value reductions in other situations in which shares of an entity's stock are used to provide employee benefits.

Option-pricing models and fair value

161. A quoted market price, if one is available, is the best measure of the fair value of an asset, liability, or equity instrument. In its deliberations leading to this Statement, the Board was not able to identify currently available quoted market prices or negotiated prices for employee stock options that would qualify as a price at which a willing buyer and a willing seller would exchange cash for an option. Some employers have offered employees a choice between a specified amount of cash or a specified number of options on the employer's stock. However, the Board understands that the terms of those arrangements generally do not result from negotiation between the employer and employee(s). The Board also was told that employers often offer a relatively low alternative cash amount to induce employees to choose options.

162. Market prices for employee stock options may become available in the future, perhaps through arrangements that permit employees to purchase their options by trading a specified amount of cash compensation for them on clearly unbiased terms. If so, the foregone cash compensation—not an estimated fair value of the options—would be recognized as compensation cost, and no adjustments for expected option forfeitures and nontransferability would be needed.

163. It also is conceivable, although unlikely, that options between parties other than employers and

employees that are subject to essentially the same restrictions as employee stock options might be developed and traded. For example, a third-party option might in concept be made forfeitable under certain conditions, and the option contract might specify that the options can only be exercised—not transferred to another party. The provisions of this Statement are not intended to preclude use of quoted market prices to determine the fair values of employee stock options if such prices become available. However, various implementation questions would need to be considered, such as how to treat options that are forfeited. Because neither quoted nor negotiated market prices existed when the Board developed this Statement, it has not considered those issues. This Statement specifies the basic method and assumptions to be used in estimating the fair values of employee stock options in the absence of a quoted market price. Specifically, this Statement requires the use of an option-pricing model, and it also specifies how to reduce the amount resulting from use of a traditional option-pricing model to reflect the unique restrictions inherent in employee stock options.

164. The Board recognizes that many entities and their auditors are not familiar with option-pricing models and the inherent mathematics. However, software to apply the models is widely available and easy to use for one who is familiar with electronic spreadsheets and similar tools. Selecting the appropriate assumptions to use as inputs to the models is not easy, but entities and their advisors must select similar assumptions about the future in many other areas of accounting. Understanding the details of the inherent mathematical formulas is not necessary, just as it is not necessary for an entity to understand the precise computations an actuary might use to estimate the amount of a liability for pension benefits.

Adapting option-pricing models for employee stock options

165. Paragraphs 166-173 explain the reasons for the specified adjustments to the results of standard option-pricing models to reflect differences between the terms of employee stock options and the traded options for which option-pricing models were initially developed.

Forfeitures before vesting

166. This Statement uses the term *forfeiture* to refer only to an employee's failure to earn a vested right to a stock-based employee compensation award be-

cause the specified vesting requirements are not satisfied. In other words, a vested award is no longer subject to forfeiture as this Statement uses that term, although the term of a vested award may be truncated by termination of service. Some respondents said that previously recognized compensation cost should be reversed to income if an option expires unexercised because its exercise price exceeds the market price of the stock. Some of those respondents interpreted the notion of forfeiture to include all situations in which employees do not realize gains on their options—for whatever reason. This Statement does not permit reversal of compensation cost in that situation because to do so would be inconsistent with the nature of an employee stock option (an equity instrument of the employer) and with both grant date and vesting date accounting. As with other equity instruments, the cost recognized for an employee stock option stems from use of the consideration received—not from subsequent changes in the value of the equity instrument. Moreover, to be internally consistent, recognizing income when an option expires out-of-the-money would call for recognizing additional compensation cost when the stock price increases as well—the result would be exercise date accounting.

167. This Statement requires that the compensation cost for an award of employee stock options reflect the number of options that actually vest. That is the same as the provision of the Exposure Draft, although the rationale is somewhat different. The Exposure Draft explained that provision as a means of adjusting the grant date value of an award of forfeitable stock-based employee compensation to reflect the risk of forfeiture. The measurement method in this Statement is intended to be consistent with an entity's having no enforceable right to future employee services or other consideration for forfeitable awards. An award of stock-based employee compensation does not result in the issuance of equity instruments until the award is vested. Recognizing compensation cost only for the number of instruments actually issued (vested) is consistent with that view of the nature of a nonvested award.

168. The Exposure Draft proposed that an entity be required to estimate expected forfeitures at the grant date, with subsequent adjustments if actual forfeitures differed from estimates. Some respondents said that permitting accrual of compensation cost for all awards not yet forfeited, with reversals of previously accrued compensation cost for subsequently forfeited awards, would reduce the implementation cost of this

Statement. The Board decided to permit that method of accounting for forfeitures for cost-benefit reasons. However, accrual of compensation cost during the service period based on expected forfeitures, with subsequent adjustments as necessary, remains an acceptable method. Respondents asked how changes in estimates of forfeitures (and performance outcomes) during the vesting period should be attributed. The Board concluded that the effects of retroactively applying a change in estimate during the vesting period should be recognized at the date of the change.

Inability to transfer vested employee stock options to third parties

169. The value of a transferable option is based on its maximum term because it rarely is economically advantageous to exercise, rather than sell, a transferable option before the end of its contractual term. Employee stock options differ from most other options in that employees cannot sell their options—they can only exercise them.[17] To reflect the effect of employees' inability to sell their vested options, this Statement requires that the value of an employee stock option be based on its expected life rather than its maximum term.

170. For example, a 10-year option with an exercise price of $50 on a stock with a market price of $50 might be valued at $25.89, assuming that the stock's volatility is 30 percent, it pays a dividend of 1 percent, and the risk-free interest rate is 7.5 percent. After 5 years, when the stock price has risen to $75, an option holder might wish to realize the gain on the option, thereby terminating exposure to future price changes. The fair value of a 5-year option with an intrinsic value of $25 ($75 - $50) on the same stock is $39.86, assuming that the stock's volatility is now 35 percent, the dividend yield remains at 1 percent, and the current risk-free rate for 5-year maturities is 7 percent. If the option is transferable, the holder could sell it for $39.86 rather than exercise it and receive only the intrinsic value of $25. An employee who does not wish to remain exposed to future price changes in the underlying stock after 5 years can only exercise the option and sell the stock obtained upon exercise—realizing only the gain of $25 in intrinsic

value. The employee is unable to realize the option's remaining time value of $14.86 ($39.86 - $25) because of its nontransferability. In other words, an employee who exercises an option with a contractual term of 10 years after only 5 years receives the benefit of only a 5-year option. Because the economic effect of holding a nontransferable rather than a transferable option is to make early exercise significantly more likely, the Board's conclusion stated in the Exposure Draft was that estimating the fair value of an employee stock option based on its expected life, later adjusted to actual life, rather than its maximum term is a logical and practical means of reducing the option's value to reflect its nontransferability.

171. Many respondents objected to the Exposure Draft's proposed subsequent adjustment of expected life to actual life. They generally pointed to the resulting counterintuitive effect that higher expense would be recognized for an option that runs for its full contractual term because its exercise price always exceeds the stock price than for an option that is exercised relatively early in its contractual term because the stock price increased rapidly.

172. As discussed in Appendix C, the Board held a roundtable discussion in April 1994. Participants were invited to submit papers and discuss with other participants, the Board, and its staff potential changes to the measurement method proposed in the Exposure Draft. The papers presented by academic researchers generally agreed that use of expected life is the appropriate way to adjust for the nontransferability of employee stock options. They also agreed with other respondents that the expected life estimated at the grant date should not be subsequently adjusted if actual life differs from expected life because that would produce a counterintuitive result. The participants in the roundtable also discussed several features that affect the expected life of an employee stock option, such as the relationship between expected life and expected volatility and the effect of the nonlinear relationship between option value and option life. Several factors considered helpful in estimating expected life are incorporated in the guidance on selecting assumptions in Appendix B.

---

[17]Some employees may be permitted to place their nontransferable options in a trust for the benefit of family members or otherwise to transfer vested options to family members. However, the options remain nontransferable in the hands of the trust or family member. The transfer thus does not affect the value of the option—both the option holder and the option writer (the employer) know it may be economically advantageous for the holder to exercise the options before maturity because exercise remains the only available means to terminate exposure to future price changes.

173. The Board reaffirmed its conclusion in the Exposure Draft that the appropriate way to reflect the effect on an option's fair value of an employee's inability to sell vested options is to use the option's expected life rather than its contractual term in estimating fair value using an option-pricing model. However, the Board also agreed with respondents and researchers that the Exposure Draft's requirement to adjust compensation cost to reflect the effect of a difference between expected life and actual life should be eliminated. The Board believes that eliminating that requirement will reduce the costs of complying with this Statement. Not adjusting option value to reflect differences between initial estimates and later estimates or outcomes—at least not after the vesting date—also is generally consistent with the Board's conclusion that equity instruments awarded to employees are issued at the vesting date. The value recognized for equity instruments issued in other situations is not changed by subsequent events. An argument could be made that changes in expected life should be reflected until the vesting date, but to do so without also reflecting changes in the price of the underlying stock during the vesting period would have the same counterintuitive results as the Exposure Draft's requirement to reflect differences between expected life and actual life.

Nonpublic Entities

Measurement

174. An emerging entity whose stock is not yet publicly traded may offer stock options to its employees. In concept, those options also should be measured at fair value at the grant date. However, the Board recognizes that estimating expected volatility for the stock of a newly formed entity that is rarely traded, even privately, is not feasible. The Board therefore decided to permit a nonpublic entity to omit expected volatility in determining a value for its options. The result is that a nonpublic entity may use the *minimum value* method discussed and illustrated in paragraphs 139-142. Options granted after an entity qualifies as a public entity must be measured using the procedures specified for public entities. Paragraphs 273-287 in Appendix B provide guidance on how to determine the assumptions required by option-pricing models, including expected volatility for a publicly traded stock that has little, if any, trading history.

175. The Exposure Draft included a provision that permitted a nonpublic entity to use the minimum value method except when its stock was traded with sufficient frequency to reasonably estimate expected volatility. Several respondents to the Exposure Draft thought that "traded with sufficient frequency" would be difficult to judge and that few nonpublic entities would likely incorporate volatility into their measurements on that basis. The Board decided to permit any nonpublic entity to exclude volatility from its measurement of option value. However, a nonpublic entity may incorporate volatility if it desires to do so.

176. Some respondents to the Exposure Draft suggested that there is no reason for different measurement methods for public and nonpublic entities. They believe all entities should use the same method and that requiring public entities to report higher compensation cost based on fair value creates a bias against them. Some respondents endorsed using minimum value for all entities. Others said that the need for special guidance for nonpublic entities was additional evidence that the Exposure Draft's proposals were flawed and that the Board should abandon its approach.

177. A solution suggested by other respondents was to require all entities to use the same expected volatility, such as the historical volatility of a market index. They believe that would ease application of the Statement, mitigate the differences in an entity's transition from nonpublic to public, and improve comparability by reducing the subjectivity of the estimate of volatility.

178. The Board believes that mandating the same estimate of expected volatility for use by all entities would impair, rather than improve, comparability because the volatilities of different entities differ. The use of minimum value by nonpublic entities is a practical solution to the difficulties of estimating expected volatility for a nonpublic entity. For a public entity, estimating the fair value of its options is practicable because an estimate of expected volatility can be made.

Definition of a public entity

179. The Exposure Draft defined a public entity consistent with definitions used in FASB Statements, except that an entity with only publicly traded debt, not equity securities, would be classified as a nonpublic entity. The Exposure Draft definition also drew from the definition in AICPA Statement on Auditing Standards No. 26, *Association with Financial Statements,* which makes it clear that a subsidiary of a

public entity also is a public entity. Some respondents objected to considering a subsidiary of a public entity that, by itself, would not meet that definition to be a public entity for purposes of this Statement. They believe that whether an entity is owned by a public entity is not relevant to the measure of a nonpublic subsidiary's options. They also said that awards related to the subsidiary's stock may be better employee incentives than awards related to the parent company's stock.

180. The Board recognizes that the accounting consequences of classifying a subsidiary as a public entity may limit the types of award that it chooses to grant. For example, an entity might choose not to grant an option on the stock of a wholly owned subsidiary combined with a repurchase agreement for the stock issued upon exercise because that award would be treated as a liability in consolidated financial statements. If classification as nonpublic were extended to subsidiaries, the effect of the provisions of paragraph 40 that permit nonpublic entities with mandatory fair value stock repurchase agreements to treat them as equity instruments even though the entity is effectively obligated to transfer its assets to the holder would be to permit a consolidated public entity to treat effective liabilities to employees of those subsidiaries as if they were equity instruments. The Board believes that would be an inappropriate result. The Board notes that an award of the parent's equity instruments could include a subsidiary performance criterion, at least partially achieving the goal of relating incentive compensation of subsidiary employees to subsidiary performance.

181. Some respondents to the Exposure Draft suggested that a newly public entity should continue to be classified as nonpublic for some period. Others suggested that a public entity whose stock is thinly traded should be classified as nonpublic. In contrast, some respondents suggested that a nonpublic entity that expected to go public within a certain period should be classified as a public entity. The Board decided that the most straightforward approach would be to determine public or nonpublic status based on an entity's characteristics at the date an award is granted.

Other Measurement Issues

Reload Options and Options with a Reload Feature

182. Reload options are granted upon exercise of previously granted options whose original terms pro-

vide for the use of shares of stock that the employee has held for a specified period of time, referred to as *mature shares*, rather than cash to satisfy the exercise price. At the time of exercise using mature shares, the employee is automatically granted a reload option for the same number of shares used to exercise the original option. The exercise price of the reload option is the market price of the stock at the date the reload option is granted; its term is equal to the remainder of the term of the original options.

183. Because a reload feature is part of the options initially awarded, the Board believes that the value added to those options by the reload feature ideally should be considered in estimating the fair value of the initial award at its grant date. However, the Board understands that no reasonable method currently exists to estimate the value added by a reload feature.

184. Some respondents to the Exposure Draft suggested that an option with a reload feature can be valued at the grant date as a "forward start option" commencing at the date or dates that the option is "reloaded." The forward start option's value would be added to the value of the option granted with a reload feature to determine the total value of the award. However, the forward start option formula calls for a number of subjective inputs, such as the number of expected reloads, the expected timing of each reload, and the expected total rate of return on the stock. Also, because an employee can take advantage of the reload feature only with shares already held, the employer would need to estimate (a) the number of employees who are expected to pay the exercise price with those shares rather than with cash and (b) their holdings of mature shares.

185. Others suggested that a reload feature be treated as if it merely extended the life of an option to its maximum term because the term of a reload option granted upon exercise of an option with mature shares cannot extend beyond the expiration date of the original option. Under that view, the fair value of an option with a reload feature would be estimated based on its maximum term, regardless of the expected life of the original option. However, that method understates the value of the reload feature because the value of an option on a dividend-paying stock is reduced by the present value of the dividends expected to be paid during the term of the option. The holder of an option subject to a reload feature, however, receives the dividends paid on stock obtained by exercising the option early and also is granted a reload option. Further, the holder of a reload option

can effectively realize a gain by selling the stock acquired on exercise without forfeiting the opportunity to benefit from future increases in the price of the underlying stock, which also makes the reload option worth more than an otherwise identical option without a reload feature even if its value is based on its contractual life.

186. The Board continues to believe that, ideally, the value of an option with a reload feature should be estimated at the grant date, taking into account all of its features. However, at this time, it is not feasible to do so. Accordingly, the Board concluded that the best way to account for an option with a reload feature is to treat both the initial grant and each subsequent grant of a reload option separately.

Modifications of Awards

187. An employer and employee may agree to modify the terms of an award of stock options or similar instruments. The Board concluded that the effects of a modification of terms are indistinguishable from the effects of an exchange of the existing equity instrument for a new instrument. For example, the same transaction might be described either as a decrease in the exercise price of an outstanding option or as the repurchase (and subsequent cancellation) of the existing option in exchange for a new option with a lower exercise price. The economics of the transaction are the same regardless of how it is described. In effect, the employee surrenders, and the employer repurchases, the existing instrument in exchange for another instrument.

188. The repurchase of an equity instrument generally is accounted for based on the fair values of the instrument repurchased and the consideration paid for it. For example, if an entity repurchases shares of common stock at an amount significantly in excess of the current market price of the shares, the excess is presumed to be attributable to stated or unstated rights the issuer receives in addition to the shares surrendered, such as an agreement that the stockholder will not purchase additional shares. The Board concluded that a modification of the terms of a stock-based compensation award should be accounted for based on a comparison of the fair value of the modified option at the date it is granted and the value at that date of the old option that is repurchased (immediately before its terms are modified) determined based on the shorter of (a) its remaining initially estimated expected life or (b) the expected life of the modified option. If the fair value of the modified option exceeds the value of the old option repurchased, the entity recognizes additional compensation cost for the difference.

189. The method in the Exposure Draft for determining the additional compensation cost arising from a modification of an award was revised based on comments received and because of changes in the proposed measurement method for measuring compensation cost. As discussed in paragraph 173, under the measurement method in this Statement, the expected life estimated at the grant date is not subsequently adjusted to the actual life in determining the value of options granted. The "true-up" approach in the Exposure Draft significantly influenced the proposed method for modifications, which based the fair value of the original option on its remaining contractual life at the date of modification. However, under this Statement's requirements, no changes are made to the value of an instrument determined at the grant date. Therefore, the Board believes that determining the value of the original option at the date of modification using the shorter of the expected life of the modified option or the remaining portion of the expected life of the original option is consistent with not truing up the initial measure of compensation cost for a change in option life. It also precludes the possibility of a counterintuitive result, namely, a reduction of compensation cost, which some respondents said could result from certain minor modifications. Using the shorter of the expected life of the modified option or the remaining portion of the expected term of the original option precludes net credits to compensation cost arising from modifications of an award.

190. An employee generally will accept a modification only if its effect is to increase the value of the instrument the employee holds. For example, the maximum term of an award of stock options may be extended or the exercise price may be lowered. Some respondents asked that the Statement address the accounting for cancellations of existing awards or for modifications of existing awards that reduce the value of the instrument held by the employee. The Board discussed those situations and believes that the circumstances under which an employer could unilaterally cancel or reduce the value of an award to an employee without substituting another form of compensation would be rare. The Board decided that it was not practical to consider the appropriate accounting for such an unusual—perhaps nonexistent—transaction except in the context of a specific set of facts.

191. Exchanges of equity instruments or changes to their terms in conjunction with a business combination accounted for as a pooling of interests are not considered modifications for purposes of this Statement. The Board recognizes that entities have essentially no discretion in revising the terms of outstanding equity awards if the business combination is to qualify as a pooling of interests. However, there are no similar criteria for other equity transactions, such as a business combination accounted for as a purchase. Therefore, an exchange or modification of an equity instrument as a result of a purchase business combination, spinoff, or other equity restructuring is considered a modification for purposes of this Statement. The terms of an equity instrument also may be modified pursuant to a stock dividend or a stock split without changing the value of the instruments that the employee holds. For example, an adjustment to an option's exercise price designed to equalize the holder's value before and after a stock split or a stock dividend is not a modification for purposes of this Statement.

192. Some respondents suggested that the criteria in EITF Issue No. 90-9, "Changes to Fixed Employee Stock Option Plans as a Result of Equity Restructuring," should be used to determine whether additional compensation should be recognized for equity restructurings under the fair value based method in this Statement. EITF Issue 90-9 is written in the context of Opinion 25's intrinsic value measurement method. The Board believes that the requirements in this Statement for accounting for modifications of awards, including those resulting from equity restructurings, are more appropriate for the fair value based method because those requirements are based on comparing fair values before and after a modification. As with all other Opinion 25-related authoritative literature, the consensus on EITF Issue 90-9 continues to apply for an entity that recognizes compensation cost based on Opinion 25.

193. Some respondents requested additional guidance on the accounting for cash settlements or modifications of nonvested awards. Paragraphs 35-40 of this Statement provide that guidance, and Appendix B illustrates the accounting for cash settlements and modifications.

194. Appendix B also illustrates accounting for cash settlements and modifications of options granted before or after initial application of this Statement. Generally, whether the entity has chosen to recognize compensation cost under the fair value based method

or to disclose the pro forma effects of that method does not affect the illustrations.

195. An entity that has disclosed the pro forma effects of adopting this Statement for several years may choose to adopt the cost recognition method in this Statement. In that situation, subsequent modifications of awards for which pro forma disclosures were made should be accounted for as if cost had been recognized under the fair value based method as shown in the illustrations for modifications of awards granted after adoption of this Statement (Illustrations 5(a)-5(d)). Doing so will make the financial statements for periods after adoption more consistent for comparative purposes with the pro forma disclosures made for any prior years presented.

Recognizing Compensation Cost over the Service Period

Attribution Period

196. This Statement continues the provisions of Opinion 25 and Interpretation 28 that stock-based compensation cost is to be recognized over the period or periods during which the employee performs the related services. If the service period is not defined as an earlier or shorter period, the service period is presumed to be the vesting period. If the award is for past service, compensation cost is recognized when the award is granted.

197. The Board considered whether the attribution period for employee stock options should extend beyond the vesting date, perhaps to the service expiration date (paragraphs 129-131), even though the measurement date is the grant date. Advocates of that method, which might be considered consistent with amortization of postretirement health care benefits over the period to *full eligibility date*, contend that employees have not earned the full benefit to which they are entitled until termination of service no longer shortens the life of the option. They would use the longer attribution period to allocate the time value of an option.

198. Most respondents that addressed this issue agreed with the Exposure Draft that the attribution period should not extend beyond the vesting date. However, some respondents suggested attribution over the option's expected life, which would be consistent with the method described in paragraph 197. They believe that the option serves as an incentive during its entire life and that attribution over the longer period "better matches" revenues and costs.

199. Although amortization of the time value of an option beyond the vesting date has some conceptual appeal, the Board concluded that no compelling reason exists to extend the attribution period beyond the period now used for stock options that give rise to compensation cost. The Board notes that the decision on when to exercise a vested option is the employee's. The right to exercise an option has been earned by the date the option becomes vested.

200. As discussed in paragraph 96, options are issued to employees at the vesting date. Some advocates of vesting date accounting say that a logical extension of that view would call for recognition of the full amount of the compensation cost at the vesting date, once the equity instrument has been fully earned and issued to the employee. However, the cost of services received in exchange for other employee benefits with a vesting period, such as pensions and other postemployment benefits, generally is recognized in the periods in which the services are received even if the benefits are not yet vested. Although those employee benefit plans generally result in the incurrence of liabilities rather than the issuance of equity instruments, the Board decided that the form of eventual settlement should not change the general principle that the costs of employee services are recognized over the periods in which employees are required to render service to earn the right to the benefit.

Awards with Graded Vesting

201. Interpretation 28 requires that compensation cost for a variable award with a graded vesting schedule, such as an award that vests 25 percent per year over 4 years, be accrued as if the grant were a series of awards rather than a single award. Each award in the series is accounted for as if it had its own separate service period and vesting date. That method attributes a higher percentage of the reported cost to the earlier years than to the later years of the service period because the early years of service are part of the vesting period for later awards in the series. For example, cost attributed to the first year of service includes not only the amount that vests in that year but also one-half of the award that vests in the second year, one-third of the award that vests in the third year, and so on.

202. The Exposure Draft acknowledged that the Interpretation 28 method of recognizing compensation cost is more complicated than others and may be considered illogical if an award with graded vesting is viewed as a single award rather than a series of linked awards. Therefore, it proposed that an award with graded vesting would be attributed ratably to individual years of service. Some respondents recommended that the cost of awards that vest in a graded pattern should be attributed using the method in Interpretation 28.

203. As noted in paragraph 31, an entity may estimate the fair value of an award of stock options with graded vesting using different estimated lives for each group of options depending on the length of the vesting period for that group. If the entity uses that method, the Board concluded that it would be logically consistent to require the attribution pattern specified by Interpretation 28. If the entity does not use different estimated lives but rather uses either an average life for the entire award or different lives based on considerations other than the vesting period for each group, it may use either the Interpretation 28 approach or an approach that ratably allocates compensation cost over the service period. However, to be consistent with the attribution pattern required for other employee benefit plans, the cumulative compensation cost recognized at any date must at least equal the value of the portion of the award that is vested. For example, if an award vests over 3 years, with 50 percent vested after the first year, and 25 percent in each of the next 2 years, cost accrued by the end of the first year must at least equal the amount attributable to 50 percent of the award.

Dividends

204. This Statement requires that dividends paid on shares of nonvested stock that are not expected to, and do not, vest be recognized as additional compensation cost during the vesting period. If an employee terminates service and forfeits nonvested stock but is not required to return dividends paid on the stock during the vesting period, the Board concluded that recognizing those dividends as additional compensation is appropriate.

205. The fair value of a share of stock in concept equals the present value of the expected future cash flows to the stockholder, which includes dividends. Therefore, additional compensation does not arise from dividends on nonvested shares that eventually vest. Because the measure of compensation cost for those shares is their fair value at the grant date, recognizing dividends as additional compensation would effectively double count the dividends.

206. The recipient of an award of nonvested stock may not receive dividends paid on the stock during the vesting period. In that situation, the Board concluded that the value of the award at the grant date should be the fair value of a dividend-paying share of the stock reduced for the present value of the dividends that will not be received during the vesting period.

207. Some employee stock options are *dividend protected,* which means that the exercise price is adjusted downward during the term of the option to take account of dividends paid on the underlying stock that the option holder does not receive. The effect of that adjustment of the exercise price is to remove the effect of dividends as a factor that reduces the value of a stock option on a dividend-paying stock. The usual method of applying an option-pricing model to estimate the value of a dividend-protected option is to assume a dividend payment of zero on the underlying stock, and this Statement requires use of that method.

Settlements of Stock-Based Compensation Awards

208. This Statement deals primarily with equity instruments, such as stock options, issued to employees as compensation. Ordinarily, an entity settles stock options upon exercise by issuing stock rather than by paying cash. However, an entity sometimes may choose to repurchase an employee stock option for a cash payment equal to the intrinsic value of the option when it is exercised.

209. Under some stock-based compensation plans, an entity incurs a liability to its employees, the amount of which is based on the price of the entity's stock. An example of the latter is a cash SAR under which an employee receives upon "exercise" a cash payment equal to the increase in the price of the employer's common stock from a specified level. For example, if the price of the stock increases from $25 to $35 per share, employees receive a $10 cash payment for each SAR held.

210. In addition, some tandem plans offer employees a choice of receiving either cash or shares of stock in settlement of their stock-based compensation awards. For example, an employee may be given an award consisting of a cash SAR and a stock SAR with the same terms. A stock SAR is the same as a cash SAR except that it calls for settlement in shares of stock with an equivalent value. Exercise of one cancels the other. The employee can demand settlement either in cash or in shares of stock.

211. Opinion 25 provides that the amount of cash paid to settle an earlier award of stock or stock options is the final measure of the related compensation cost. An entity's repurchase of stock shortly after the employee acquired that stock upon exercise of an option is considered *cash paid to settle an earlier award,* and compensation cost is adjusted accordingly. Under Opinion 25, a stock SAR is a variable award because the number of shares to which an employee is entitled cannot be determined at the grant date. Compensation cost for a stock SAR thus is finally measured when the SAR is exercised, which produces the same compensation as for a cash SAR. However, a stock SAR and a stock option with similar terms, both of which qualify as equity instruments under the definitions in Concepts Statement 6, result in different amounts of compensation cost under Opinion 25. For example, no compensation cost is recognized for an award of 100 stock options at $25 per share if the market price of the stock is $25 at the grant date even if the stock price is $35 when the options are exercised. However, if an identical transaction involved an award of stock SARs rather than stock options, compensation cost of $1,000 [100 shares × ($35 − $25)] is recognized.

212. One reason for the Board's undertaking a comprehensive review of Opinion 25 was a concern that the differing results produced for stock-based compensation awards that call for settlement by issuing stock and those that call for settlement in cash were, at best, difficult to understand and explain. While it may be appropriate for cash plans and stock plans to result in different total charges to income, no common thread to distinguish between cash and stock plans is apparent in Opinion 25. For example, some awards that result in the entity's issuing equity instruments, such as stock SARs, are treated as if the entity had incurred a liability. Similar awards, such as stock options, are treated as equity instruments unless they are eventually settled in cash, at which time the accounting is adjusted to produce the same results as if the entity had incurred a liability rather than issued an equity instrument at the grant date.

213. Some constituents contend that the amount of compensation cost recognized for stock-based compensation awards should not differ solely because one award calls for settlement in stock and another calls for settlement in an equivalent amount of cash. Others are not concerned with differing results for

stock plans and cash plans, but they note that the provisions of Opinion 25 sometimes produce results that are inconsistent with those for similar transactions in equity instruments issued to outside parties. For example, the repurchase of stock from an investor who recently acquired it by exercising a stock purchase warrant would not be accounted for as if it were the settlement of a liability.

214. As discussed in Appendix C, late in 1988 the Board set aside work on stock compensation issues to await progress on its broader project on distinguishing between liability and equity instruments. The main reason for that decision was concern about whether applying the current distinction between liabilities and equity instruments and the different effects on income stemming from repurchase of an equity instrument versus settlement of a liability produced appropriate results for stock-based compensation plans. Because the Board subsequently decided not to pursue substantive changes to the conceptual definitions of liabilities and equity, it considered accounting for stock-based compensation awards in the context of the definitions in Concepts Statement 6.

215. Concepts Statement 6 distinguishes between liabilities and equity on the basis of whether an instrument obligates the issuer to transfer its assets (or to use its assets in providing services) to the holder. A liability embodies such an obligation, while an equity instrument does not. A call option that an entity writes on its own stock, such as an employee stock option, is an equity instrument because its settlement requires only the issuance of stock, which is not the issuer's asset. The entity's obligation under a cash SAR, on the other hand, is a liability because its settlement requires the transfer of assets to the holder.

216. Whether an instrument qualifies as a liability or an equity instrument of its issuer depends on the nature of the obligation embodied in it—not on the means by which it is actually settled. In other words, the characteristics of a liability are present from the date it is incurred. Settlement of a liability by issuing equity instruments, such as shares of stock, whose value is the same as the amount of the liability does not change the nature of the obligation settled—the transaction is the settlement of a liability. Similarly, the repurchase of an equity instrument for cash does not convert the equity instrument to a liability—the transaction still is the repurchase of an equity instrument.

217. The Board decided that the principles outlined in paragraph 216 apply to obligations incurred to employees under stock-based compensation awards as well as to similar obligations incurred to other parties. Those principles provide the basis for dealing with both awards that call for settlement in stock and awards that call for settlement in cash (or other assets of the entity). The former are equity instruments when issued, and their subsequent repurchase for cash equal to their value does not call for an adjustment to previously recognized compensation cost. The latter are liabilities, and their settlement calls for an adjustment to previously recognized compensation cost if the settlement amount differs from the carrying amount of the liability.

218. The Board also concluded that the conceptual distinctions between liabilities and equity instruments provide a reasonable way of accounting for tandem plans that offer a choice of settlement in stock or in cash. An entity that grants a tandem award consisting of either a stock option or a cash SAR, for example, is obligated to pay cash upon demand if the choice of settlement is the employee's. The contract gives the entity no discretion to avoid transferring its assets to the employee if the employee elects settlement in cash. The entity thus has incurred a liability. If the choice is the entity's, however, it can avoid transferring assets simply by electing to issue stock, and the award results in the issuance of an equity instrument. However, this Statement requires accounting for the substantive terms of a plan. If an entity nominally has the choice of settling awards under a tandem plan by issuing stock but regularly does so by paying cash, or if the entity settles awards in cash whenever employees ask for cash settlement, the instrument awarded likely is a substantive liability of the entity.

Stock Repurchase Agreements of Closely Held Entities

219. Many respondents to the Discussion Memorandum on distinguishing between liabilities and equity noted that closely held entities commonly specify that shares of stock granted or otherwise issued to employees cannot be transferred to a third party but can only be sold to the issuer. Often, the holder is required to sell, and the issuer is required to repurchase, the stock at a price that reasonably approximates fair value at the date of repurchase. In a family-owned entity, a repurchase agreement may apply to all of the

stock outstanding, or it may apply only to shares held by employees and others that are not members of the founding family.

220. In concept, stock that its issuer must repurchase for fair value at the date of repurchase is a liability rather than an equity instrument because the issuer is obligated to transfer its assets to the holder. To treat all of those instruments as liabilities, however, would be troublesome because an entity with repurchase agreements for all of its common stock would report no equity. In practice, the existence of a mandatory fair value repurchase agreement, by itself, is not considered to convert to a liability an instrument that otherwise would qualify as equity. Future work on the Board's liability-equity project will consider the effect of a mandatory fair value repurchase agreement. The Board therefore concluded that this Statement should not change current practice concerning the effect of a mandatory fair value repurchase agreement applicable to the stock of a nonpublic entity.

221. Some respondents to the Exposure Draft asked that mandatory repurchases under all formula-based plans be considered repurchases at fair value that are accounted for as the repurchase of an equity instrument. Others requested that additional criteria be provided to establish whether the formula in a plan produces a repurchase price equivalent to fair value. The Board believes that the terms of formula value repurchase plans are too diverse to specify the circumstances, if any, in which a formula-based value might be fair value. Whether the terms of a particular plan produce a repurchase price that is a reasonable estimate of fair value and whether the plan is subject to additional compensation cost needs to be assessed on a case-by-case basis (paragraphs 37-40).

Accounting for Tax Effects of Stock Compensation Awards

222. The provisions of the Exposure Draft on accounting for the tax effects of awards of stock-based employee compensation were based on recognizing an asset, prepaid compensation, for the fair value of an award at the grant date. For awards of stock options, the financial reporting basis of that asset generally would exceed its tax basis at the grant date because the time value component of an option's value is not tax deductible. Therefore, a temporary difference would arise for which a deferred tax liability would be recognized under Statement 109. Because the Board decided that prepaid compensation should not be recognized at the grant date, the proposed tax accounting no longer could be applied.

223. Statement 109 retained Opinion 25's provisions on accounting for the income tax effects of stock-based employee compensation. The Board considered whether it should fundamentally change those requirements and decided not to, for the reasons explained in paragraphs 225-231.

224. The Board believes that recognition of deferred tax benefits related to stock-based awards for financial reporting should be based on provisions in the tax law that govern the deductibility of stock-based compensation. Some stock-based compensation plans result in tax deductions. Examples under existing U.S. tax law are so-called nonstatutory stock options (which are options that do not qualify for preferential tax treatment as incentive stock options) and nonvested stock. However, under existing U.S. tax law, an entity does not receive tax deductions for so-called incentive stock options (provided that employees comply with the requisite holding periods).

225. The Board believes that the recognition of compensation cost in an entity's income statement for an award that ordinarily results in tax deductions creates a deductible temporary difference for which deferred taxes are recognized under Statement 109. Paragraph 15 of Statement 109 describes temporary differences that are not associated with a particular asset or liability for financial reporting but that result from an event that has been recognized in the financial statements and, based on the provisions in the tax law, will result in deductible amounts in future years. Normally, tax deductions ultimately recognized for a stock option accounted for under this Statement will differ in amount from the compensation cost recognized for financial reporting. Compensation cost recognized for financial reporting under this Statement is measured as the fair value of the award at the grant date, which includes a time value component that is never tax deductible. Changes in the market value of the stock after the grant date do not affect the measurement of compensation cost recognized. Tax deductions are generally based on the intrinsic value of the award measured as the excess of the market price of the stock over the price, if any, the employee pays for the stock at a specified date. Changes in the market price of the stock between the date an award is granted and the exercise date directly affect the amount of the entity's tax deduction.

226. The Board decided that the amount of the temporary difference should be determined based on the compensation cost recognized for financial reporting

rather than by reference to the expected future tax deduction (which would be estimated by the current intrinsic value of the award). The Board believes that approach is preferable because it is less complex to apply, will produce less volatility in reported net income, and will be consistent with the recognition of the tax effects of stock-based awards for those employers that continue to apply Opinion 25 for their stock-based employee compensation plans.

227. The temporary difference related to a stock-based award is measured by the cumulative compensation cost recognized rather than the expected future tax deduction based on the present intrinsic value of the award. Therefore, a deferred tax asset recognized for that temporary difference should be reduced by a valuation allowance only if, based on the weight of the available evidence, the entity expects future taxable income will be insufficient to recover the deferred tax asset in the periods the tax deduction for the stock-based award will be recognized or in an applicable carry-back or carry-forward period.

228. The amount of stock-based compensation that is deducted on the tax return may exceed the compensation cost recognized for financial reporting. This Statement requires that the tax benefits of deductions in excess of compensation cost be recognized as additional paid-in capital when they are initially recognized. The Board agrees with the conclusion of the Accounting Principles Board in Opinion 25 that the additional tax benefits are attributable to an equity transaction.

229. Alternatively, the deductible amount on the tax return may be less than the cumulative compensation cost recognized for a particular stock-based award. The Board concluded that the write-off of the related deferred tax asset in that situation should be recognized in the income statement except to the extent that there is paid-in capital arising from excess tax deductions from previous awards under stock-based employee compensation arrangements accounted for using the fair value based method described in this Statement. The Board believes that it would be inappropriate for an entity to use credits to paid-in capital from awards accounted for under Opinion 25 to offset the write-off of a deferred tax asset related to compensation cost measured using the fair value based method in this Statement because those credits generally result from awards for which no compensation cost has been recognized. To use those credits would overstate an entity's cumulative net income.

230. This Statement does not permit retroactive application to determine the fair value of stock-based awards granted before this Statement's effective date. The Board believes that it would not be practical to determine the appropriate amount of excess tax deductions that would have been credited to paid-in capital had the fair value based method been applied to awards granted before the effective date of this Statement. After the effective date of this Statement, entities that continue to apply Opinion 25 are required to determine not only the pro forma net income effects of the fair value based method but also the pro forma equity effects in determining the tax benefits for excess tax deductions that would have been recognized in paid-in capital had the fair value based method in this Statement been applied to recognize compensation cost. Paid-in capital for tax benefits resulting from awards granted before the effective date of this Statement are still available for applying paragraph 17 of Opinion 25 because this Statement does not change the accounting for tax effects under Opinion 25. Entities also are precluded from offsetting the write-off of a deferred tax asset against the tax benefits of excess deductions or tax credits reported as paid-in capital from stock-based arrangements that are outside the scope of this Statement, such as employee stock ownership plans.

231. An entity sometimes may realize tax benefits for an award that ordinarily does not result in a tax deduction because an employee receiving the stock does not comply with a holding period required by the tax law for favorable tax treatment for the recipient. The Board decided that the resulting tax benefit from such a disqualifying disposition should be recognized in the period that the event occurs. The benefit of any deduction recognized in the income statement is limited to the tax benefit for the cumulative compensation cost previously recognized for financial reporting. Any excess benefit should be recognized as an increase to paid-in capital.

Employee Stock Purchase Plans and Other Broad-Based Plans

232. The Exposure Draft applied to broad-based employee stock option plans and broad-based plans that permit employees to purchase stock at a discount from market value (*employee stock purchase plans*) the same recognition and measurement provisions as those proposed for all other stock-based plans. Many respondents said that broad-based plans should be

exempted from the proposed requirement to recognize compensation cost for the fair value of the benefit given to employees. They noted that Opinion 25, paragraph 7, considers broad-based plans that meet certain specified criteria to be *noncompensatory*, with no compensation cost recognized even if the purchase price is less than the price of the underlying stock at the measurement date. Respondents also pointed out that Opinion 25 cites an employee stock purchase plan that qualifies under Section 423 of the Internal Revenue Code as an example of a noncompensatory plan.

233. The Internal Revenue Code provides that employees will not be immediately taxed on the difference between the market price of the stock purchased and a discounted purchase price if several requirements in Section 423 are met. The requirements are generally the same as those in paragraph 7 of Opinion 25, with the following additions:

a. The option price may not be less than the lesser of (1) 85 percent of the market price when the option is granted or (2) 85 percent of the price at exercise.
b. The term of the option cannot exceed 5 years from the grant date if the purchase price is 85 percent or more of the market price at the exercise date. If the purchase price can turn out to be less than 85 percent of the stock price at exercise, the term of the option cannot exceed 27 months from the grant date. For example, 27 months is the maximum term of a *look-back option* in which the purchase price equals the lower of 85 percent of the stock price at the grant date or at the exercise date.

234. In the past few years, some employers have granted fixed, 10-year stock options to substantially all employees. Those awards differ from Section 423 employee stock purchase plans because the exercise price usually equals the stock price at the date of grant and the term is longer. Although those options generally do not qualify as *noncompensatory* under Opinion 25, no compensation cost is typically recognized for them because of the intrinsic value method specified in Opinion 25. In this Statement, the phrase *broad-based* plans includes long-term fixed stock options issued to substantially all of an entity's employees as well as Section 423 plans.

235. In supporting the noncompensatory treatment of broad-based plans, respondents said that the primary purpose of those plans is not to compensate employees for services rendered. Rather, broad-based plans are aimed at encouraging employees to become stakeholders, thereby leading to greater employee loyalty and an interest in increasing shareholder value, and at raising capital over time without incurring the stock issuance costs related to a public offering. Many respondents asserted that the purchase discount offered to employees was comparable to the stock issuance costs avoided by issuing the stock to employees rather than to the public. The purchase discount is viewed as an inducement for employees to participate in the plans or as a cost of raising capital. Some respondents suggested that the noncompensatory provisions of Opinion 25 should be not only retained but also broadened to encompass options with a 10-year term.

236. The Board found merit in the argument that a small percentage discount in a broad-based plan offered to employees is an inducement that is analogous to a discount routinely offered to stockholders and others or to avoided stock issuance cost. The Board decided that the purchase discount in a broad-based plan is noncompensatory if the discount from the market price does not exceed the greater of the following two thresholds:

a. The per-share discount that would be reasonable in a recurring offer of stock to stockholders or others. For example, some entities offer a purchase discount to shareholders participating in a dividend reinvestment program. The Board related this threshold to a recurring discount because it did not want a percentage discount justified by an isolated rights offering that might involve an above-normal discount.
b. The per-share amount of stock issuance costs avoided by not having to raise a significant amount of capital by a public offering. Some respondents suggested that this threshold should be based on the per-share avoided stock issuance costs for a public offering of only the number of shares expected to be issued to the employees. The Board rejected that suggestion. Per-share amounts would tend to be higher for a small public offering because many of the costs are more fixed than variable. The Board agreed to include this threshold in the standard because of the long-term impact of broad-based plans, which some respondents indicated provide a significant source of capital *over time*. The Board does not want this threshold used to justify a higher percentage discount as noncompensatory simply based on a short-term focus.

237. Some constituents expressed concern about the effort and related costs to justify the purchase discount granted to employees. The Board discussed whether a specified discount should be established for cost-benefit reasons as a safe harbor for a noncompensatory discount. It decided to specify that a purchase discount of 5 percent or less automatically complies with the Statement's limitations on the amount of purchase discount allowed for noncompensatory broad-based plans. The Board chose 5 percent because, based on available data, it believes that amount is closer to the average cost of most public offerings than is the 15 percent discount effectively used as a safe harbor under Opinion 25. A discount in excess of 5 percent is permitted if an entity can justify it under the criteria in paragraph 23.

238. Having decided that a reasonable percentage discount (such as 5 percent) can be included in a noncompensatory broad-based plan, the Board considered how compensation cost should be determined for a broad-based plan that includes a higher percentage discount than could be considered noncompensatory. Should the cost computation include the entire discount or only the portion that exceeds the amount that would, by itself, qualify as noncompensatory? The Board decided that if an employee stock purchase plan includes an excessively high discount that cannot be justified under the criteria in paragraph 23(b), the plan is compensatory and the entire discount should be used in determining compensation cost. The Board rejected the notion that an employee stock purchase plan could be accounted for as partially compensatory and partially noncompensatory.

239. The Board considered respondents' requests that broad-based plans with look-back options be considered noncompensatory and noted that a look-back option can have substantial value because it enables the employee to purchase the stock for an amount that could be significantly less than the market price at date of purchase. A look-back option is not an essential element of a broad-based plan aimed at promoting broad employee stock ownership; a purchase discount also provides inducement for participation. The Board concluded that broad-based plans that contain look-back options cannot be treated as noncompensatory. The consequences of other option features are discussed in paragraphs 240 and 241.

240. Under some employee stock purchase plans, the purchase price is fixed at the grant date (for example, as a percentage of the market price at the grant

date) and an enrollment period is provided for employees to decide whether to participate. Technically, the availability of an enrollment period after the purchase price has been fixed constitutes an option feature that has time value. However, for practical reasons, the Board decided that an enrollment period not in excess of 31 days is not a disqualifying option feature that would otherwise preclude a plan from being treated as noncompensatory.

241. To facilitate employee participation and eliminate the need for lump-sum payments, employee stock purchase plans typically stipulate that participating employees pay for stock purchases by payroll withholding during a period preceding the date of purchase. Under some plans, employees are permitted to cancel their participation in the plan before the purchase date and obtain a refund of amounts previously withheld. If a plan permits a participating employee to cancel participation in the plan after the purchase price has been fixed, that cancellation ability is an option feature. The Board decided that a plan in which the purchase price is fixed at the grant date and participating employees may cancel their participation before the purchase date and obtain a refund of previous withholdings is indistinguishable from a fixed-price option and therefore should be treated as compensatory. In contrast, a plan in which the purchase price is based *solely* on the *purchase-date* market price embodies no valuable option feature. Even if the plan enables participating employees to cancel their participation before the purchase date and obtain a refund of previous withholdings, that plan might qualify as noncompensatory.

242. The Board considered attempting to simplify determining the fair value of an employee stock purchase plan that incorporates a look-back option by establishing a specified percentage of the stock price at the grant date, such as 20 percent, that could be considered fair value. The Board rejected that idea largely because determining an appropriate percentage that would produce a reasonable substitute for fair value for a wide variety of plans did not seem feasible. Moreover, the Board understands that, given the choice of using a specified amount or determining an amount based on its own circumstances, many entities do not select the specified amount without first determining the alternative amount.

Disclosures

243. Paragraphs 244-261 discuss the basis for the Board's conclusions on the required disclosures of

this Statement other than the pro forma disclosures required by paragraph 45. The basis for the Board's conclusions on those pro forma disclosures is discussed in paragraph 69.

244. Some respondents suggested that the Board provide percentage guidelines to specify when both the pro forma disclosures of the effects of applying the fair value based method and the disclosures in paragraphs 46-48 could be omitted on the grounds of immateriality. The Board decided not to do so because it believes an entity can best determine the materiality of the disclosures in its individual circumstances. In addition, different percentage criteria likely would be needed for different disclosures, for example, the materiality of some items might be best evaluated in terms of the effect on reported net income, while the materiality of other items might be better evaluated in the context of number of shares outstanding. Specifying those guidelines for individual disclosures could unduly complicate this Statement. The Board notes, however, that the general guidance provided at the end of each Statement on application of its provisions to immaterial items applies to both accounting and disclosure requirements.

Disclosures Similar to Those Required by Opinion 25

245. The Board concluded that the disclosures specified in paragraphs 46-48 should be required for all entities regardless of the method used to account for stock-based employee compensation. The disclosures required by Opinion 25 thus are superseded by this Statement, regardless of the method an entity uses to account for stock-based employee compensation cost.

246. The Exposure Draft proposed continuing the disclosures required by Opinion 25, including the number of shares under option, the option price, the number of shares for which options are exercisable, the number of shares exercised, and the exercise prices. In applying Opinion 25, many entities have disclosed only the range of exercise prices of options, which is not very helpful in understanding the potential increase in outstanding shares by option exercises, especially if the range is wide. The Exposure Draft proposed disclosing the weighted-average exercise prices of options outstanding, granted, and exercised.

247. Many respondents expressed support for the proposed disclosures. Others said that additional information about options outstanding at the date of the financial statements would be useful. They generally requested more information helpful in evaluating "potential future dilution," "option overhang," or potential capital contributions from outstanding options. They suggested the need for more information about options whose exercise prices are greater than, equal to, or less than the current stock price. Those respondents said that weighted-average information, although important, is not sufficient for those assessments because, by itself, it provides no information helpful in evaluating the likelihood that options will be exercised in the future. Disclosure of the number of options outstanding at each exercise price, or at least by ranges of exercise prices, was suggested.

248. The Board concurred and decided to require disclosure of the range of exercise prices (as well as the weighted-average exercise price) and the weighted-average remaining contractual life for the options outstanding as of the date of the latest statement of financial position presented. If the overall range of exercise prices is wide (for example, the highest exercise price exceeds approximately 150 percent of the lowest exercise price), the Board decided to require further segregation of those prices into narrower ranges that are meaningful for assessing the likelihood and consequences of future exercises. The Board also decided that the number and weighted-average exercise price of options that are currently exercisable at that date should be disclosed for each range.

249. The Board decided not to specify strict criteria for when further segregation should be required. The 150 percent example in paragraph 48 is meant to be a guideline. An entity should exercise its judgment in providing the most meaningful disclosures.

Disclosures of Method and Significant Assumptions Used to Determine Fair Value

250. The Exposure Draft proposed requiring disclosure of the method and significant assumptions used to estimate the fair value of options. About half of the respondents that commented on the proposed disclosures supported that requirement; others considered those disclosures unnecessary if compensation cost is recognized. Many respondents opposed disclosure of expected dividends, and a fewer number also opposed disclosure of the expected volatility. They said they feared that those disclosures raised the potential for future litigation if the disclosures were misconstrued as a commitment to declare future dividends

or a forecast of future stock prices. Others suggested that disclosure of assumptions should not be required because entities might have to reveal confidential information about possible future changes in dividend rates and the like.

251. As explained in paragraphs 273-287 of Appendix B, the assumptions about expected volatility and dividends needed to comply with this Statement generally should be based on historical experience, adjusted for *publicly available information* that may indicate ways in which the future is reasonably expected to differ from the past. In addition, required disclosures of potentially sensitive assumptions in other areas, such as expected rates of salary increases used in measuring pension cost for a period, apparently have not led to litigation or other problems. Moreover, after the Exposure Draft was issued, the SEC began requiring registrants to disclose the underlying assumptions, including expected volatility and dividends, if they choose to comply with the recently expanded proxy disclosures about the value of options granted to executives by disclosing the "present value" of the options at the grant date.

252. The Exposure Draft did not propose requiring disclosure of expected lives of stock options, principally because that assumption was required to be subsequently adjusted to actual life in measuring compensation cost. Some respondents said that disclosure of expected lives would be useful, especially should the Board decide not to require "true up" of expected life to actual life—which is the conclusion that the Board reached (paragraph 173).

253. The Board therefore concluded that disclosure of the method and significant assumptions used in estimating the fair values of stock options should be required. The assumptions used in an option-pricing model can significantly affect the estimated value of stock options, and therefore disclosure of the assumptions used will assist in understanding the information provided by entities in their financial statements.

Other Required Disclosures

254. The Exposure Draft proposed requiring entities with both fixed and indexed or performance-based plans to provide separate disclosures for the different types of plans. Some respondents to the Exposure Draft requested additional guidance on the situations in which separate disclosures would be necessary and what information should be provided separately for fixed plans and other plans. The Board decided that separate disclosures should be provided to the extent that differences in the characteristics of the awards make those disclosures important to an understanding of the entity's use of stock-based compensation. This Statement gives examples of such circumstances rather than specifying detailed requirements. The Board recognizes that entities differ in the extent to which they use various forms of stock-based employee compensation. An entity should exercise its judgment in providing detailed information that is useful in its own situation.

255. The Exposure Draft proposed, and this Statement retains, required disclosure of the weighted-average fair values of options granted during the year, along with the weighted-average exercise prices. That disclosure will allow a reader to compute the ratio of option value to stock value at grant date, which is commonly used for comparisons between entities and in assessing the perceived reasonableness of option valuations. Reference to a ratio helps in comparing, for example, the estimated value of an option on a $20 stock with one on a $90 stock. However, that ratio generally is used only for options whose exercise prices equal the stock price at the grant date.

256. For example, if both the $20 stock and the $90 stock paid dividends of approximately 1.5 percent and other factors such as expected lives of the options, historical stock price volatility, and future prospects were similar, one might question estimated fair values of options on the 2 stocks with similar terms if the ratio of fair value to stock price is 20 percent for the $20 stock and 40 percent for the $90 stock. Those ratios might be comparable, however, if the exercise price of the first option is $20 (equal to the stock price at grant date) but the exercise price of the second option is $75 ($15 less than the stock price at grant date). To combine in the same ratio options with exercise prices that equal, exceed, and are less than the stock price at the grant date would produce a meaningless amount. Accordingly, this Statement requires separate disclosure of weighted-average fair values and exercise prices of options granted at exercise prices that equal the stock price at the grant date and those whose exercise prices differ from the grant date stock price.

257. During the Board's redeliberations of the proposals in the Exposure Draft, questions arose about whether the disclosures required by this Statement were generally consistent with current disclosures for

other potentially dilutive financial instruments. APB Opinion No. 15, *Earnings per Share,* says:

> The use of complex securities complicates earnings per share computations and makes additional disclosures necessary. The Board has concluded that financial statements should include a description, in summary form, sufficient to explain the pertinent rights and privileges of the various securities outstanding. Examples of information which should be disclosed are dividend and liquidation preferences, participation rights, call prices and dates, conversion or exercise prices or rates and pertinent dates, sinking fund requirements, unusual voting rights, etc. [paragraph 19]

That paragraph could be interpreted to apply to employee stock options, although entities generally have not done so because Opinion 25 specifically deals with stock-based awards to employees. The Board believes that the disclosures required by this Statement are generally consistent with disclosures long required for other potentially dilutive securities.

258. During its deliberations leading to the Exposure Draft, the Board received several proposals for disclosures in lieu of cost recognition for stock-based compensation, the most comprehensive of which was submitted by a group of preparers and users of financial statements and was endorsed by the six largest accounting firms. That proposal was included in the Exposure Draft as Appendix E.

259. As discussed earlier, many respondents to the Exposure Draft supported additional disclosures as a substitute for measurement and recognition of compensation cost. The notice to recipients asked whether any of the additional disclosure items in Appendix E should be added to the required disclosures, assuming that recognition of compensation cost was required. Few respondents suggested additional disclosure items, and some said that none of the additional disclosure items in Appendix E's example were warranted. The Board therefore did not expand the required disclosures to include items from Appendix E of the Exposure Draft.

260. During its deliberations, especially after the Board had initially decided to require disclosure of pro forma information rather than recognition of compensation cost determined by the fair value based method, some constituents asserted that disclo-

sure of a single point estimate of the fair value of employee stock options was not appropriate. They said that the assumptions used in option-pricing models are too subjective or that available option-pricing models are inappropriate for estimating the fair value of employee stock options with their inherent differences from tradable options. They suggested that the Board require only disclosure of a range of possible values for employee stock options.

261. As discussed earlier in this appendix and in Appendix B, the Board believes that option-pricing models, adjusted as this Statement specifies for the differences between the typical employee stock option and a tradable option for which the models were initially developed, will produce estimated values for employee stock options that will be within acceptable limits for recognition in financial statements. The Board also believes that it has required disclosure of the basic information needed to understand the effects of stock-based compensation plans. An entity may, of course, disclose additional information it considers pertinent to readers of its financial statements. For example, an entity may disclose supplemental information, such as a range of values calculated on the basis of different assumptions, provided that the supplemental information is reasonable and does not discredit the information required by this Statement (paragraph 364).

Benefits and Costs

262. The mission of the FASB is to "establish and improve standards of financial accounting and reporting for the guidance and education of the public, including issuers, auditors, and users of financial information" (FASB *Rules of Procedure,* page 1). In fulfilling that mission the Board strives to determine that the expected benefits of the information resulting from a new standard will exceed the perceived costs. The objective and implicit benefit of issuing an accounting standard are the increased credibility and representational faithfulness of financial reporting as a result of the new or revised accounting. However, the value of that incremental improvement to financial reporting and most of the costs to achieve it are subjective and cannot be quantified. Likewise, the costs of *not* issuing an accounting standard are impossible to quantify.

263. The Board's consideration of each individual issue in a particular project includes the subjective weighing of the incremental improvement in financial reporting against the incremental cost of implementing the identified alternatives. At the end of that

process, the Board considers the accounting provisions in the aggregate and must conclude that issuance of the standard is a sufficient improvement in financial reporting to justify the related costs.

264. The Board concluded that the expected benefits resulting from this Statement will exceed the related costs. Although required recognition using the fair value based method of determining compensation cost for stock-based employee compensation would have provided greater benefits, the representational faithfulness and credibility of the information provided by the financial statements and notes, taken as a whole, will be improved even if the results of that method are only reflected in disclosure of pro forma information. Entities that choose to adopt the fair value based method will be better able to establish plans that they believe provide the best incentives with less need to "design around" accounting standards. Opinion 25's distinction between fixed and variable awards effectively encourages fixed stock options and discourages performance awards. Encouraging one form of award at the expense of another not only imposes the cost of treating accounting requirements as a significant factor in plan design but also may encourage selection of plans that an entity might not otherwise choose.

265. The Board has attempted to mitigate the incremental costs of complying with this Statement wherever possible without detracting from its objectives. For example:

a. A nonpublic entity is permitted to use the so-called minimum value method to value its options. *

b. Entities may choose to estimate the number of options or other equity instruments that are expected to vest and to revise that estimate, if necessary, if subsequent information indicates that actual forfeitures are likely to differ from initial estimates. Alternatively, an entity may begin recognizing compensation cost as if all instruments granted are expected to vest, with recognition of actual forfeitures as they occur.

c. The grant-date estimate of expected option life is not adjusted to actual outstanding life, as was proposed in the Exposure Draft. The Board believes that elimination of that requirement will reduce the costs of complying with this Statement.

d. If there is a range of reasonable assumptions about the factors that are used in option-pricing models, entities are to use the low end of the range. That should somewhat simplify the decisions involved in determining appropriate assumptions.

Effective Dates and Transition

266. The Exposure Draft proposed two effective dates: one for its disclosure provisions, including pro forma disclosures of its effects on net income and earnings per share, and a later date for adopting its recognition provisions in the financial statements. Because this Statement does not require an entity to adopt the fair value based method of accounting for stock-based employee compensation (although the Board encourages entities to do so), the question of effective date pertains almost entirely to the required pro forma disclosures. An entity may adopt the fair value based method of accounting for its stock-based employee compensation cost as soon as the Statement is issued or at any date thereafter. The only restriction is that the new method must be applied *as of* the beginning of the fiscal year in which it is adopted.

267. The Board decided that a lengthy transition period for the required pro forma disclosures is not necessary. The fair value based method to be used in those disclosures has been debated and widely publicized for several years. The measurement method in this Statement is similar to the one in the Exposure Draft, and the areas of change, such as not adjusting for the effect of a difference between initially estimated expected and actual lives of options, should ease implementation. Therefore, the Board decided that the required pro forma disclosures should begin with awards granted in fiscal years beginning after December 15, 1994 (that is, awards granted in 1995 fiscal years). However, the Board recognizes that the issuance of this Statement relatively late in 1995 might make it difficult for some entities with fiscal years ending in December to gather the information necessary to disclose pro forma information in their 1995 financial statements. The Board thus decided that required presentation of pro forma information should begin with financial statements for 1996, which also should include the pro forma disclosures for 1995 if comparative financial information is presented.

268. This Statement deals separately with issuances of equity instruments to acquire employee services in transactions that are included in the scope of Opinion 25 and other issuances of equity instruments to acquire goods or services. For the latter transactions, this Statement essentially codifies current best practice, which is to measure the transaction at the fair value of the consideration received or the fair value of the equity instrument issued, whichever is more

reliably measurable. The Board decided that the effective date of that provision should be transactions entered into after December 15, 1995, because the provisions are not expected to result in a significant change in practice.

269. The Exposure Draft proposed prospective application of the new method of accounting for stock-based employee compensation plans, that is, the new method would be applied only to awards granted after a specified date. This Statement retains prospective application. Some respondents were concerned about the inherent "ramp-up" effect on compensation cost as additional awards are granted and the first awards to which the new method applies move through their vesting periods. Those respondents generally suggested either requiring or permitting retroactive application to all awards that are not vested at the effective date.

270. The Board recognizes the potential for misleading implications caused by the ramp-up effect of prospective application of a new accounting or pro forma disclosure requirement for a recurring transac-

tion. However, the Board continues to question the feasibility of retroactive application of the fair value based method of accounting, which could involve several years depending on the length of the vesting period. (Some constituents even objected to having to apply the fair value based method to awards granted in 1995, but before this Statement was issued.) For example, field test participants reported that estimating what assumptions they might have used for expected option lives, volatility, or dividends for grants made several years in the past was problematical. The Board decided that requiring retroactive application would be excessively burdensome. Permitting either retroactive or prospective application would detract from the comparability of the information reported by different entities. Instead, the Board decided that entities should be required to alert readers of the financial statements if amounts of compensation cost determined using the fair value based method that are reflected in the pro forma disclosures or recognized are not indicative of future amounts when the new method will apply to all outstanding, nonvested awards.

Appendix B

ILLUSTRATIVE GUIDANCE FOR APPLYING THE STANDARDS

CONTENTS

Appendix B

ILLUSTRATIVE GUIDANCE FOR APPLYING THE STANDARDS

Introduction

271. This appendix, which is an integral part of the requirements of this Statement, discusses further the fair value based method of accounting for stock-based employee compensation and illustrates its application to specific awards. The examples and related assumptions in this appendix are illustrative only; they may not represent actual situations.

272. The guidance in paragraphs 273-287 on selecting assumptions for use in an option-pricing model applies equally to (a) an entity that applies the fair value based method in accounting for its stock-based employee compensation cost and (b) an entity that accounts for its stock-based employee compensation in accordance with Opinion 25 and discloses the pro forma information required by paragraph 45. Except

where noted, the illustrations in paragraphs 288-356 assume that the reporting entity had adopted the fair value based method of accounting for compensation cost before the transactions illustrated. However, had the entity continued to account for its stock-based employee compensation cost in accordance with Opinion 25, it would follow the same procedures in preparing the pro forma disclosures required by this Statement.

Selecting Assumptions for Use in an Option-Pricing Model

273. This Statement requires a public entity to estimate the fair value of an employee stock option using a pricing model that takes into account the exercise price and expected life of the option, the current price of the underlying stock, its expected volatility, the expected dividends on the stock, and the current risk-free interest rate for the expected life of the option. As indicated in paragraph 19, a U.S. entity issuing an option on its own stock must use as the risk-free interest rate the implied yield currently available on zero-coupon U.S. government issues with a remaining term equal to the expected life of the option that is

being valued. Guidance on selecting the other assumptions listed in paragraph 19 is provided in the following paragraphs.[18]

274. In estimating the expected volatility of and dividends on the underlying stock, the objective is to approximate the expectations that likely would be reflected in a current market or negotiated exchange price for the option. Similarly, the objective in estimating the expected lives of employee stock options is to approximate the expectations that an outside party with access to detailed information about employees' exercise behavior likely would develop based on information available at the grant date.

275. The Board recognizes that in most circumstances there is likely to be a range of reasonable expectations about future volatility, dividends, and option life. If one amount within the range is a better estimate than any other amount, that amount should be used. If no amount within the range is a better estimate than any other amount, it is appropriate to use an estimate at the *low* end of the range for expected volatility and expected option life, and an estimate at the *high* end of the range for expected dividends. (Computed option value varies directly with expected volatility and life, but it varies inversely with expected dividends.) That approach is similar to the one used in FASB Interpretation No. 14, *Reasonable Estimation of the Amount of a Loss,* which requires accrual of the minimum amount in a range of reasonable estimates of the amount of a loss if no amount within the range is a better estimate than any other amount.

276. Expectations about the future generally are based on past experience, modified to reflect ways in which currently available information indicates that the future is reasonably expected to differ from the past. In some circumstances, identifiable factors may indicate that unadjusted historical experience is a relatively poor predictor of future experience. For example, if an entity with two distinctly different lines of business disposes of the one that was significantly less volatile and generated more cash than the other, historical volatility, dividends, and perhaps lives of stock options from the predisposition period are not likely to be the best information on which to base reasonable expectations for the future.

277. In other circumstances, historical information may not be available. For example, an entity whose common stock has only recently become publicly traded will have little, if any, historical data on the volatility of its own stock. In that situation, expected volatility may be based on the average volatilities of similar entities for an appropriate period following their going public. Similarly, an entity whose common stock has been publicly traded for only a few years and has generally become less volatile as more trading experience has been gained might appropriately place more weight on the more recent experience. It also might consider the stock price volatilities of similar entities.

278. Not all of the general guidance on selecting assumptions provided in paragraphs 273-277 is repeated in the following discussion of factors to be considered in selecting specific assumptions. However, the general guidance is intended to apply to each individual assumption. The Board does *not* intend for an entity to base option values on historical average option lives, stock volatility, or dividends (whether stated as a yield or a dollar amount) without considering the extent to which historical experience reasonably predicts future experience.

Expected Lives of Employee Stock Options

279. The value of an award of employee stock options may be based either on an appropriately weighted average expected life for the entire award or on appropriately weighted lives for subgroups of the award based on more detailed data about employees' exercise behavior. Paragraphs 281 and 282 each discuss a different way to incorporate a range of expected lives in estimating option value rather than effectively assuming that all employees hold their options for the weighted-average life.

280. Factors to consider in estimating the expected life of an award of stock options include:

a. The vesting period of the grant. The expected life must at least include the vesting period. In addition, if all other factors are equal, the length of time employees hold options after they first become exercisable may vary inversely with the length of the vesting period. For example, employees may be more likely to exercise options

[18]The guidance on assumptions in this Statement, especially the expected lives of employee stock options, benefited from several working papers discussed at an informal roundtable discussion on measuring the value of employee stock options the Board held on April 18, 1994. Some of those papers have subsequently been published.

shortly after the options vest if the vesting period is four years than if the vesting period is only two years.

b. The average length of time similar grants have remained outstanding in the past.

c. Expected volatility of the underlying stock. On average, employees may tend to exercise options on highly volatile stocks earlier than on stocks with low volatility.

281. Segregating options into groups for employees with relatively homogeneous exercise behavior may also be important. Option value is not a linear function of option term; value increases at a decreasing rate as the term lengthens. For example, a two-year option is worth less than twice as much as a one-year option if all other assumptions are equal. That means that calculating estimated option value based on a single weighted-average life that includes widely differing individual lives will overstate the value of the entire award. Segregating options granted into several groups, each of which has a relatively narrow range of lives included in its weighted-average life, reduces that overstatement. For example, the experience of an entity that grants options broadly to all levels of employees might indicate that top-level executives tend to hold their options longer than middle-management employees hold theirs and that hourly employees tend to exercise their options earlier than any other group. In addition, employees who are encouraged or required to hold a minimum amount of their employer's equity instruments, including options, might on average exercise options later than employees not subject to that provision. In those situations, segregating options by groups of recipients with relatively homogeneous exercise behavior and determining the related option values based on appropriate weighted-average expected lives for each group will result in an improved estimate of the fair value of the total award.

282. Rather than estimating expected life directly, an entity may wish to estimate it indirectly, using an option-pricing model that has been modified to compute an option value using an assumed stock price at which the options would be expected to be exercised. For example, an entity's experience might show a large increase in option exercises when the stock price first reaches 200 percent of the exercise price. If so, that entity might compute an option value using a pricing model that implicitly determines a weighted-average life based on exercise at an assumed price of 200 percent of the exercise price. The model would assume exercise of the option at each point on the in-

herent probability distribution of possible stock prices at which the expected price at exercise is first reached. On branches of the binomial tree on which the stock price does not reach 200 percent of the exercise price but is in-the-money at the end of the contractual term, the model would assume exercise at that date. The expected life is then computed as the weighted-average life of the resulting binomial tree. That method recognizes that employees' exercise behavior is related to the path of the stock price.

283. Segregating options into groups based on the exercise behavior of the recipients also may be important if the technique in paragraph 282 is used. For example, an employer's experience might indicate that hourly employees tend to exercise for a smaller percentage gain than do more highly compensated employees.

Expected Volatility

284. Volatility is a measure of the amount by which a price has fluctuated or is expected to fluctuate during a period. The measure of volatility used in the Black-Scholes option-pricing model is the annualized standard deviation of the continuously compounded rates of return on the stock over a period of time. Generally, at least 20 to 30 price observations made at regular intervals are needed to compute a statistically valid standard deviation. For long-term options, historical volatility generally should be calculated based on more—probably many more—than 30 observations. The concept of volatility is defined more fully in the glossary. One method of calculating historical average annualized volatility based on weekly price observations is illustrated in Appendix F. As discussed further in the following paragraph, an entity may need to adjust historical average annualized volatility to estimate a reasonable expected volatility over the expected life of an option.

285. Factors to consider in estimating expected volatility include:

a. The historical volatility of the stock over the most recent period that is generally commensurate with the expected option life.

b. The length of time an entity's stock has been publicly traded. If that period is shorter than the expected life of the option, historical volatility should be computed for the longest period for which trading activity is available. A newly public entity also should consider the historical volatility of similar entities following a comparable period in their lives. For example, an entity that has been publicly traded for only one year that grants options with an average expected life of five years might consider the pattern and level of historical volatility of more mature entities in the same industry for the first six years the stocks of those entities were publicly traded.

c. The mean-reversion tendency of volatilities. For example, an entity with insufficient trading history on which to base an estimate of historical volatility might take into account mean-reversion tendencies (sometimes called *shrinkage*). A newly public entity with a trading history of only 1 year might have a historical volatility of 60 percent, while the mean volatility of an appropriate peer group is only 35 percent. Until a longer series of historical data is available, the entity might use an expected volatility of approximately 47.5 percent [(.60 + .35) ÷ 2]. A more mature entity also should consider mean-reversion tendencies and other reasons for which expected future volatility may differ from past volatility. For example, if an entity's stock was extraordinarily volatile for some identifiable period of time because of a failed takeover bid or a major restructuring, that period might be disregarded in computing historical average annual volatility.

d. Appropriate and regular intervals for price observations. In general, weekly price observations should be sufficient for computing long-term historical volatility. The price observations should be consistent from period to period. For example, an entity might use the closing price for each week or the highest price for the week, but it should not use the closing price for some weeks and the highest price for other weeks.

Expected Dividends

286. Standard option-pricing models generally call for expected dividend yield. However, the models may be modified to use an expected dividend amount rather than a yield. An entity may use either its expected yield or its expected payments. If the latter, the entity's historical pattern of increases in dividends should be considered. For example, if an entity's policy generally has been to increase dividends by approximately 3 percent per year, its estimated option value should not assume a fixed dividend amount throughout the expected life unless there is evidence that supports that assumption.

287. Generally, the assumption about expected dividends should be based on publicly available informa-

tion. An entity that does not pay dividends and has no plans to do so would assume an expected dividend yield of zero. However, an emerging entity with no history of paying dividends might expect to begin paying dividends during the expected lives of its employee stock options. Those entities may use an average of their past dividend yield (zero) and the mean dividend yield of an appropriately comparable peer group. For example, it would not be appropriate for a young, rapidly growing entity to base its expected dividend yield on the average dividend yield of the entities in the Standard & Poor's 500 Index.

Illustrative Computations

Illustration 1—Fixed Stock Option

288. Company S, a public entity, grants options with a maximum term of 10 years to its employees. The exercise price of each option equals the market price of its stock on the grant date. All options vest at the end of three years (cliff vesting). The options do not qualify for tax purposes as incentive stock options. The corporate tax rate is 34 percent.

289. The following table shows assumptions and information about options granted on January 1, 2000.

Options granted	900,000
Employees granted options	3,000
Expected forfeitures per year	3%
Stock price	$50
Exercise price	$50
Expected life of options	6 years
Risk-free interest rate	7.5%
Expected volatility	30%
Expected dividend yield	2.5%

290. Using as inputs the last 6 items from the table above, the Black-Scholes option-pricing model modified for dividends determines a fair value of $17.15 for each option. Using the same assumptions, a binomial model produces a value of $17.26. A difference between a Black-Scholes model and a binomial model grant-date valuation of an option generally arises from the binomial model's fully reflecting the benefit in limited circumstances of being able to exercise an option on a dividend-paying stock before its expiration date when it is economic to do so. (If Company S paid no dividends, both the Black-Scholes and the binomial models would determine a fair value of $22.80, holding other assumptions constant.) Although some available software modifies

the Black-Scholes model to attempt to take that benefit into account, the result may not be exactly the same as a binomial model. The following illustrations use a fair value of $17.15, but $17.26 is equally acceptable.

291. Total compensation cost recognized over the vesting period will be the fair value of all options that actually vest, determined based on the stock price at the grant date. This Statement allows an entity either to estimate at the grant date the number of options expected to vest or to recognize compensation cost each period based on the number of options not yet forfeited. An adjustment to eliminate compensation cost previously recognized for options that were subsequently forfeited is recognized when the forfeitures occur. This example assumes that Company S estimates at the grant date the number of options that will vest and subsequently adjusts compensation cost for changes in the assumed rate of forfeitures and differences between expectations and actual experience. None of the compensation cost is capitalized as part of the cost to produce inventory or other assets.

292. The estimate of the expected number of forfeitures considers historical employee turnover rates and expectations about the future. Company S has experienced historical turnover rates of approximately 3 percent per year for employees at the grantees' level having nonvested options, and it expects that rate to continue. Therefore, Company S estimates the total value of the award at the grant date based on an expected forfeiture rate of 3 percent per year. Actual forfeitures are 5 percent in 2000, but no adjustments to cost are recognized in 2000 because Company S still expects actual forfeitures to average 3 percent per year over the 3-year vesting period. During 2001, however, management decides that the rate of forfeitures is likely to continue to increase through 2002, and the assumed forfeiture rate for the entire award is changed to 6 percent per year. Adjustments to cumulative cost to reflect the higher forfeiture rate are made at the end of 2001. At the end of 2002 when the award becomes vested, actual forfeitures have averaged 6 percent per year, and no further adjustment is necessary.

Cliff vesting

293. The first set of calculations illustrates the accounting for the award of options on January 1, 2000,

assuming that the entire award vests at the end of three years, that is, the award provides for cliff vesting rather than graded vesting. (Paragraphs 298-305 illustrate the accounting for an award assuming graded vesting in which a specified portion of the award vests at the end of each year.) The number of options expected to vest is estimated at the grant date to be 821,406 (900,000 × .97 × .97 × .97). Thus, as shown in Table 1, the estimated value of the award at January 1, 2000 is $14,087,113 (821,406 × $17.15), and the compensation cost to be recognized during each year of the 3-year vesting period is $4,695,704 ($14,087,113 ÷ 3). The journal entries to recognize compensation cost follow.

For 2000:

Compensation cost	4,695,704	
Additional paid-in capital— stock options		4,695,704

To recognize compensation cost.

Deferred tax asset	1,596,539	
Deferred tax expense		1,596,539

To recognize the deferred tax asset for the temporary difference related to compensation cost ($4,695,704 × .34 = $1,596,539).

The net after-tax effect on income of recognizing compensation cost for 2000 is $3,099,165 ($4,695,704 − $1,596,539).

294. In the absence of a change in estimate or experience different from that initially assumed, the same journal entries would be made to recognize compensation cost and related tax effects for 2001 and 2002, resulting in a net after-tax cost for each year of $3,099,165. However, at the end of 2001, management changes its estimated employee forfeiture rate from 3 percent to 6 percent per year. The revised number of options expected to vest is 747,526 (900,000 × .94 × .94 × .94). Accordingly, the revised total compensation cost to be recognized by the end of 2002 is $12,820,071 (747,526 × $17.15). The cumulative adjustment to reflect the effect of adjusting the forfeiture rate is the difference between two-thirds of the revised cost of the award and the cost already recognized for 2000 and 2001. The related journal entries and the computations follow.

At December 31, 2001 to adjust for new forfeiture rate:

Revised total compensation cost	**$12,820,071**
Revised cumulative cost as of 12/31/01 ($12,820,071 × ⅔)	$ 8,546,714
Cost already recognized in 2000 and 2001 ($4,695,704 × 2)	9,391,408
Adjustment to cost at 12/31/01	$ (844,694)

The related journal entries are:

Additional paid-in capital— stock options	844,694	
Compensation cost		844,694

To adjust compensation cost and equity already recognized to reflect a higher estimated forfeiture rate.

Deferred tax expense	287,196	
Deferred tax asset		287,196

To adjust the deferred tax accounts to reflect the tax effect of increasing the estimated forfeiture rate ($844,694 × .34 = $287,196).

For 2002:

Compensation cost	4,273,357	
Additional paid-in capital— stock options		4,273,357

To recognize compensation cost ($12,820,071 ÷ 3 = $4,273,357).

Deferred tax asset	1,452,941	
Deferred tax expense		1,452,941

To recognize the deferred tax asset for additional compensation cost ($4,273,357 × .34 = $1,452,941).

At December 31, 2002, the entity would examine its actual forfeitures and make any necessary adjustments to reflect compensation cost for the number of shares that actually vested.

Table 1—Fixed Stock Option—Cliff Vesting

Year	Total Value of Award	Pretax Cost for Year	Cumulative Pretax Cost
2000	$14,087,113 (821,406 × $17.15)	$4,695,704 ($14,087,113 ÷ 3)	$4,695,704
2001	$12,820,071 (747,526 × $17.15)	$3,851,010 [($12,820,071 × ⅔) – $4,695,704]	$8,546,714
2002	$12,820,071 (747,526 × $17.15)	$4,273,357 ($12,820,071 ÷ 3)	$12,820,071

295. For simplicity, the illustration assumes that all of the options are exercised on the same day and that Company S has already recognized its income tax expense for the year without regard to the effects of the exercise of the employee stock options. In other words, current tax expense and current taxes payable were recognized based on income and deductions before consideration of additional deductions from exercise of the employee stock options. The amount credited to common stock (or other appropriate equity account) for the exercise of the options is the sum of (a) the cash proceeds received and (b) the amounts credited to additional paid-in capital for services received earlier that were charged to compensation cost. At exercise, the stock price is assumed to be $70.

At exercise:

Cash (747,526 × $50)	37,376,300	
Additional paid-in capital—stock options	12,820,071	
Common stock		50,196,371

To recognize the issuance of stock upon exercise of options.

1811

296. The difference between the market price of the stock and the exercise price on the date of exercise is deductible for tax purposes because the options do not qualify as incentive stock options. The benefit of tax return deductions in excess of compensation cost recognized results in a credit to additional paid-in capital. Tax return deductions that are less than compensation cost recognized result in a debit to additional paid-in capital to the extent that the benefit of tax deductions from stock-based compensation awards in excess of compensation cost recognized based on the fair value method have been previously credited to capital. To the extent that insufficient credits are available in additional paid-in capital, a charge is made to income tax expense in the period of exercise (paragraph 44). With the stock price at $70 at exercise, the deductible amount is $14,950,520 [747,526 × ($70 – $50)]. The entity has sufficient taxable income, and the tax benefit realized is $5,083,177 ($14,950,520 × .34).

At exercise:

Deferred tax expense	4,358,824	
Deferred tax asset		4,358,824

To write off deferred tax asset related to deductible stock options at exercise ($12,820,071 × .34 = $4,358,824).[19]

Current taxes payable	5,083,177	
Current tax expense		4,358,824
Additional paid-in capital—stock óptions		724,353

To adjust current tax expense and current taxes payable to recognize the current tax benefit from deductible compensation cost upon exercise of options. The credit to additional paid-in capital is the tax benefit of the excess of the deductible amount over the compensation cost recognized: [($14,950,520 – $12,820,071) × .34 = $724,353].

297. If instead the options had expired unexercised, the additional paid-in capital—stock options account would have been closed to other paid-in capital. Previously recognized compensation cost would not be reversed. Similar to the adjustment for the actual tax deduction realized described in paragraph 296, whether part or all of the deferred tax asset of $4,358,824 is charged to additional paid-in capital or to income tax expense is determined by applying paragraph 44.

Graded vesting

298. Paragraph 31 of this Statement provides for use of either the attribution method described in Interpretation 28 or a straight-line method for awards with graded vesting depending on the approach used to estimate the value of the option award. Both methods are illustrated and use the same assumptions that follow. Company S awards 900,000 options on January 1, 2000, that vest according to a graded schedule of 25 percent for the first year of service, 25 percent for the second year, and the remaining 50 percent for the third year. Each employee is granted 300 options.

299. Table 2 shows the calculation of the number of employees and the related number of options expected to vest. Using the expected 3 percent annual forfeiture rate, 90 employees are expected to terminate during 2000 without having vested in any portion of the award, leaving 2,910 employees to vest in 25 percent of the award. During 2001, 87 employees are expected to terminate, leaving 2,823 to vest in the second 25 percent of the award. During 2002, 85 employees are expected to terminate, leaving 2,738 employees to vest in the last 50 percent of the award. That results in a total of 840,675 options expected to vest from the award of 900,000 options with graded vesting. As provided in paragraph 28, Company S could have chosen to recognize cost based on the number of options granted and recognized forfeitures as they occur; that method is not illustrated.

---

[19]Individual entries to the deferred tax asset account do not add to $4,358,824 due to rounding differences.

Table 2—Fixed Stock Option—Graded Vesting—Expected Amounts

Year	Number of Employees	Number of Vested Options
	Total at date of grant 3,000	
2000	3,000 – 90 (3,000 × .03) = 2,910	2,910 × 75 (300 × 25%) = 218,250
2001	2,910 – 87 (2,910 × .03) = 2,823	2,823 × 75 (300 × 25%) = 211,725
2002	2,823 – 85 (2,823 × .03) = 2,738	2,738 × 150 (300 × 50%) = 410,700
		Total vested options 840,675

Circumstances in which Interpretation 28 attribution is required

300. If the value of the options that vest over the three-year period is estimated by separating the total award into three groups according to the year in which they vest because the expected life for each group differs significantly, the fair value of the award and its attribution would be determined as follows. (Paragraphs 281 and 283 discuss segregation of options into groups that vest.) The estimated weighted-average expected life of the options that vest in 2000 is assumed to be 2.5 years, resulting in a value of $11.33 per option.[20] The estimated weighted-average expected life of the options that vest in 2001 is assumed to be 4 years, resulting in a value of $14.32 per option. The estimated weighted-average expected life of the options that vest in 2002 is assumed to be 5.5 years, resulting in a value of $16.54 per option. Table 3 shows the estimated compensation cost for the options expected to vest.

Table 3—Fixed Stock Option—Graded Vesting—Expected Cost

Year	Vested Options	Expected Life	Value per Option	Compensation Cost
2000	218,250	2.5 years	$11.33	$ 2,472,773
2001	211,725	4.0 years	14.32	3,031,902
2002	410,700	5.5 years	16.54	6,792,978
	840,675			$12,297,653

301. Compensation cost is recognized over the periods of service during which each group of options is earned. Thus, the $2,472,773 cost attributable to the 218,250 options that vest in 2000 is allocated to the year 2000. The $3,031,902 cost attributable to the 211,725 options that vest at the end of 2001 is allocated over their 2-year vesting period (2000 and 2001). The $6,792,978 cost attributable to the 410,700 options that vest at the end of 2002 is allocated over their 3-year vesting period (2000, 2001, and 2002).

302. Table 4 shows how the $12,297,653 expected amount of compensation cost determined at the grant date is attributed to the years 2000, 2001, and 2002.

---

[20]To simplify the illustration, the fair value of each of the 3 groups of options is based on the same assumptions about expected volatility, expected dividend yield, and the risk-free interest rate used to determine the value of $17.15 for the cliff-vesting options (paragraph 290). In practice, each of those assumptions would be related to the expected life of the group of options being valued, which means that at least the risk-free interest rate and perhaps all three assumptions would differ for each group.

Table 4—Fixed Stock Option—Graded Vesting—
Computation of Expected Cost

	Pretax Cost to Be Recognized		
	2000	**2001**	**2002**
Options vesting in 2000	$2,472,773		
Options vesting in 2001	1,515,951	$ 1,515,951	
Options vesting in 2002	2,264,326	2,264,326	$ 2,264,326
Cost for the year	$6,253,050	$ 3,780,277	$ 2,264,326
Cumulative cost	$6,253,050	$10,033,327	$12,297,653

Circumstances in which straight-line attribution is permitted

303. Company S assumes a single weighted-average expected life of five years for the entire award of graded vesting options because the expected lives of each group of options that vest are not expected to be significantly different. Other assumptions except for expected life are the same as in the previous illustration. Company S elects to recognize compensation cost on a straight-line basis.

304. Using an estimated weighted-average expected life of 5 years results in a value of $15.87 per option. The same number of options are expected to vest as shown in the previous illustration, 840,675, based on estimated forfeitures. Total compensation cost to be attributed in a straight-line pattern over the 3-year vesting period is $13,341,512 (840,675 × $15.87). Compensation cost recognized at any date must be at least equal to the amount attributable to options that are vested at that date. For example, if this same option award vested 50 percent in the first year of the 3-year vesting period, at least $6,670,756 ($13,341,512 × 50%) would be recognized in the first year.

305. The estimated value of the award is adjusted to reflect differences between expected and actual forfeitures as illustrated for the cliff-vesting options, regardless of which method described in paragraph 31 is used to estimate value and attribute cost for the graded vesting options. For example, if the actual forfeiture rate is 5 percent rather than 3 percent in 2000, the compensation cost for the options that vest in 2000 (attributed under the Interpretation 28 method) is adjusted to $2,421,788 (2,850 × 75 × $11.33), reflecting the reduction in the number of employees [2,850 = 3,000 – (3,000 × .05)] whose first 75 options became vested at December 31, 2000. Compensation

cost for the options expected to vest in 2001 and 2002 also is recomputed to reflect the actual forfeitures in 2000. Similar adjustments are made to reflect differences, if any, between expected and actual forfeitures in those years. Total compensation cost at the end of 2002 reflects the number of vested options at that date.

Illustration 2—Performance-Based Stock Option

Illustration 2(a)—Option award under which the number of options to be earned varies

306. Illustration 2(a) shows the computation of compensation cost if Company S grants a performance-based stock option award instead of a fixed stock option award. Under the plan, employees vest in differing numbers of options depending on the increase in market share of one of Company S's products over a three-year period. On January 1, 2000, Company S grants to each of 1,000 employees an award of up to 300 10-year options on shares of its common stock. If by December 31, 2002, market share increases by at least 5 percentage points, each employee vests in at least 100 options at that date. If market share increases by at least 10 percentage points, another 100 options vest, for a total of 200. If market share increases by more than 20 percentage points, each employee vests in 300 options. Company S's stock price on January 1, 2000, is $50, and other assumptions are the same as in Illustration 1. The fair value at the grant date of an option expected to vest is $17.15. The estimated fair value of the entire performance-based award depends on the number of options that are expected to be earned during the vesting period. Accruals of cost are based on the best estimate of market share growth over the three-year vesting period, and adjusted for subsequent changes in the expected or actual market share growth. Paragraph 28 requires accruals of cost to be

based on the best estimate of the outcome of the performance condition. Therefore, Company S is not permitted to estimate a percentage likelihood of achieving a performance condition and base accruals on an amount that is not a possible outcome.

307. Table 5 shows the compensation cost recognized in 2000, 2001, and 2002 if Company S estimates at the grant date that it is probable that market share will increase between 10 and 20 percentage points. That estimate remains reasonable until the end of 2002, when Company S's market share has increased over the 3-year period by more than 20 percentage points. Thus, each employee vests in options on 300 shares.

308. As in Illustration 1, Company S experiences actual forfeiture rates of 5 percent in 2000, and in 2001 changes its estimate of forfeitures for the entire award from 3 percent to 6 percent per year. In 2001, cumu-

lative compensation cost is adjusted to reflect the higher forfeiture rate. By the end of 2002, a 6 percent forfeiture rate has been experienced, and no further adjustments for forfeitures are necessary. Through 2000, Company S estimates that 913 employees $(1,000 \times .97 \times .97 \times .97)$ will remain in service until the vesting date. At the end of 2001, the number of employees estimated to vest is adjusted for the higher forfeiture rate, and the number of employees expected to vest in the award is 831 $(1,000 \times .94 \times .94 \times .94)$. The value of the award is estimated initially based on the number of options expected to vest, which in turn is based on the expected level of performance, and the fair value of each option. Compensation cost is initially recognized ratably over the three-year vesting period, with one-third of the value of the award recognized each year, adjusted as needed for changes in the estimated and actual forfeiture rates and for differences between estimated and actual market share growth.

Table 5—Performance-Based Stock Option—Number of Options Varies

Year	Total Value of Award	Pretax Cost for Year	Cumulative Pretax Cost
2000	$3,131,590 ($17.15 × 200 × 913)	$1,043,863 ($3,131,590 ÷ 3)	$1,043,863
2001	$2,850,330 ($17.15 × 200 × 831)	$856,357 [($2,850,330 × 2/3) – $1,043,863]	$1,900,220
2002	$4,275,495 ($17.15 × 300 × 831)	$2,375,275 ($4,275,495 – $1,900,220)	$4,275,495

Illustration 2(b)—Option award under which the exercise price varies

309. Illustration 2(b) shows the computation of compensation cost if Company S grants a performance-based stock option award under which the exercise price, rather than the number of shares, varies depending on the level of performance achieved. On January 1, 2000, Company S grants to its chief executive officer (CEO) 10-year options on 10,000 shares of its common stock, which are immediately exercisable. The stock price at the grant date is $50, and the initial exercise price also is $50. However, that price decreases to $30 if the market share of Company S's products increases by at least 10 per-

centage points by December 31, 2001, and provided that the CEO continues to be employed by Company S.

310. Company S estimates at the grant date the expected level of market share growth, the exercise price of the options, and the expected life of the options. Other assumptions, including the risk-free interest rate and the service period over which the cost is attributed, need to be consistent with those estimates. Company S estimates at the grant date that its market share growth will be at least 10 percentage points over the 2-year performance period, which means that the expected exercise price of the options is $30, resulting in an estimated option value of

$22.64.[21] Compensation cost of $226,400 (10,000 × $22.64) would be accrued over the expected 2-year service period. Paragraph 19 of this Statement requires the value of both fixed and performance awards to be estimated as of the date of grant. Paragraph 26, however, calls for recognition of cost for the number of instruments that actually vest. For this performance award, Company S also selects the expected assumptions at the grant date if the performance goal is not met. If market share growth is not at least 10 percentage points over the 2-year period, Company S estimates that the CEO will exercise the options with a $50 exercise price in 5 years. All other assumptions would need to be consistent, resulting in an estimated option value of $15.87.[22] (For convenience, the illustration assumes that all options are expected to be exercised on the same date.) Total compensation cost to be recognized if the performance goal is not met would be $158,700 (10,000 × $15.87). During the two-year service period, adjustments to expected amounts for changes in estimates or actual experience are made and cost recognized by the end of that period reflects whether the performance goal was met.

Illustration 3—Stock Option with Indexed Exercise Price

311. Company S instead might have granted stock options whose exercise price varies with an index of the stock prices of a group of entities in the same industry. Assume that on January 1, 2000, Company S grants 100 options on its stock with a base exercise price of $50 to each of 1,000 employees. The options have a maximum term of 10 years. The exercise price of the options increases or decreases on December 31 of each year by the same percentage that the index has increased or decreased during the year. For example, if the peer group index increases by 10 percent in 2000, the exercise price of the options during 2001 increases to $55 ($50 × 1.10). The assumptions about the risk-free interest rate and expected life, dividends, volatility, and forfeiture rates are the same as in Illustration 1. On January 1, 2000, the peer group index is assumed to be 400. The dividend yield on the index is assumed to be 1.25 percent.

312. Each indexed option may be analyzed as an option to exchange 0.1250 (50 ÷ 400) "shares" of the peer group index for a share of Company S stock, that is, to exchange one noncash asset for another noncash asset. An option to purchase stock for cash also can be thought of as an option to exchange one asset (cash in the amount of the exercise price) for another (the share of stock). The gain on a cash option equals the difference between the price of the stock upon exercise and the amount—the "price"—of the cash exchanged for the stock. The gain on an option to exchange 0.1250 "shares" of the peer group index for a share of Company S stock also equals the difference between the prices of the 2 assets exchanged.

313. To illustrate the equivalence of an indexed option and the option above, assume that an employee exercises the indexed option when Company S's stock price has increased 100 percent to $100 and the peer group index has increased 75 percent, from 400 to 700. The exercise price of the indexed option thus is $87.50 ($50 × 1.75). The employee's realized gain is $12.50.

Price of Company S stock	$100.00
Less: Exercise price of option	87.50
Gain on indexed option	$ 12.50

That is the same as the gain on an option to exchange 0.1250 "shares" of the index for one share of Company S stock:

Price of Company S stock	$100.00
Less: Price of a "share" of the peer group index (.1250 × $700)	87.50
Gain on exchange	$ 12.50

314. The Black-Scholes or binomial option-pricing models can be extended to value an option to exchange one asset for another. The principal extension is that the volatility of an option to exchange two noncash assets is based on the relationship between the volatilities of the prices of the assets to be exchanged—their **cross-volatility.** In a cash option, the amount of cash to be paid involves no risk, that is, it is not volatile, so that only the volatility of the stock needs to be considered in estimating the option's value. In contrast, the value of an option to exchange two noncash assets depends on possible movements

---

[21]Option value is determined using a $50 stock price, $30 exercise price, 3-year expected life, 6.5 percent risk-free interest rate, 2.5 percent dividend yield, and .30 volatility.

[22]Option value is determined using a $50 stock price, $50 exercise price, 5-year expected life, 7.5 percent risk-free interest rate, 2.5 percent dividend yield, and .30 volatility.

in the prices of both assets—in this example, a "share" of the peer group index and a share of Company S stock. Historical cross-volatility can be computed directly by measuring the stock price in "shares" of the peer group index. For example, the stock price was 0.1250 "shares" at the grant date and 0.1429 (100 ÷ 700) "shares" at the exercise date. Those share amounts then are used to compute cross-volatility. Cross-volatility also can be computed indirectly based on the respective volatilities of Company S stock and the peer group index and the correlation between them. The cross-volatility between Company S stock and the peer group index is assumed to be 26.5 percent.

315. In a cash option, the assumed risk-free interest rate (discount rate) represents the return on the cash that will not be paid until exercise. In this example, an equivalent "share" of the index, rather than cash, is what will not be "paid" until exercise. The dividend yield on the peer group index of 1.25 percent therefore is used in place of the risk-free interest rate as an input to the Black-Scholes model.

316. The exercise price for the indexed option is the value of an equivalent "share" of the peer group index, which is $50 (0.1250 × 400). The fair value of each option granted is $9.78 based on the following inputs:

Stock price	$50
Exercise price	$50
Dividend yield	2.50%
Discount rate	1.25%
Volatility	26.5%
Expected life	6 years

The value of the entire award would be based on the number of options expected to vest. That cost would be recognized over the service period as shown in Illustration 1.

Illustration 4—Option with Exercise Price That Increases by a Fixed Amount or a Fixed Percentage

317. Some entities grant options with exercise prices that increase by a fixed amount or a constant percentage periodically rather than by the percentage change in an index. For example, the exercise price of the options in Illustration 1 might increase by a fixed amount of $2.50 per year. Binomial option-pricing models can be adapted to accommodate exercise prices that change over time.

318. Options with exercise prices that increase by a constant percentage also can be valued using an option-pricing model that accommodates changes in exercise prices. Alternatively, those options can be valued by deducting from the discount rate the annual percentage increase in the exercise price. That method works because a decrease in the risk-free interest rate and an increase in the exercise price have a similar effect—both reduce the option value. For example, the exercise price of the options in Illustration 1 might increase at the rate of 5 percent annually. For that example, Company S's options would be valued based on a risk-free interest rate of 2.5 percent (7.5% − 5%). Holding all other assumptions constant from Illustration 1, the value of each option granted by Company S would be $12.34.

Illustration 5—Modifications and Cash Settlements

Illustration 5(a)—Modification of vested options granted after adoption of this Statement

319. The following examples of accounting for modifications of the terms of an award are based on Illustration 1, in which Company S granted its employees 900,000 options with an exercise price of $50 on January 1, 2000. At January 1, 2004, after the options have vested, the market price of Company S stock has declined to $40 per share, and Company S decides to reduce the exercise price of the outstanding options to $40. In effect, Company S issues new options with an exercise price of $40 and a contractual term equal to the remaining contractual term of the original January 1, 2000, options, which is 6 years, in exchange for the original vested options. Company S incurs additional compensation cost for the excess of the fair value of the modified options issued over the value of the original options at the date of the exchange measured as shown in paragraph 320. The modified options are immediately vested, and the additional compensation cost is recognized in the period the modification occurs.

320. The fair value on January 1, 2004, of the modified award, based on a 3-year expected life, $40 current stock price, $40 exercise price, 7 percent risk-free interest rate, 35 percent volatility, and a 2.5 percent dividend yield, is $10.82. To determine the amount of additional compensation cost arising from the modification, the value of the original vested options assumed to be repurchased is computed based on the shorter of (a) the remaining expected life of the original options or (b) the expected

life of the modified options. In this example, the remaining expected life of the original options is two years, which is shorter than the expected life of the modified options (three years). The resulting computed value at January 1, 2004, of the original options based on a $40 current stock price, a $50 exercise price, a risk-free interest rate of 7 percent, expected volatility of 35 percent, and a 2.5 percent dividend yield is $5.54 per option. Thus, the additional compensation cost stemming from the modification is $5.28 per option, determined as follows:

Fair value of modified option at January 1, 2004	$10.82
Less: Value of original option at January 1, 2004	5.54
Additional compensation cost to be recognized	$ 5.28

Compensation cost already recognized during the vesting period of the original award is $12,820,071 for 747,526 vested options (refer to Illustration 1). For simplicity, it is assumed that no options were exercised before the modification. Previously recognized cost is not adjusted. Additional compensation cost of $3,946,937 (747,526 vested options × $5.28) is recognized on January 1, 2004, because the modified options are fully vested.

Illustration 5(b)—Cash settlement of vested options granted after adoption of this Statement

321. Rather than modify the option terms, Company S offers to settle the original January 1, 2000 options for cash at January 1, 2004. The value of each option is estimated in the same way as illustrated in the preceding example, resulting in a value of $5.54. Company S recognizes the settlement as the repurchase of an outstanding equity instrument, and no additional compensation cost is recognized at the date of settlement unless the cash payment exceeds $5.54. Previously recognized compensation cost for the fair value of the original options is not adjusted.

Illustration 5(c)—Modification of nonvested options granted after adoption of this Statement

322. This example assumes that Company S granted its employees 900,000 options with an exercise price of $50, as in Illustration 1. At January 1, 2001, 1 year into the 3-year vesting period, the market price of Company S stock has declined to $40 per share, and Company S decides to reduce the exercise price of the options to $40. The 3-year cliff-vesting requirement is not changed. In effect, Company S grants new options with an exercise price of $40 and a contractual term equal to the 9-year remaining contractual term of the options granted on January 1, 2000, in exchange for the original nonvested options. The expected life of the repriced options is five years. Company S incurs additional compensation cost for the excess of the fair value of the modified options issued over the value of the original options at the date of the exchange determined in the manner set forth in paragraph 320. Company S adds that incremental amount to the remaining unrecognized compensation cost for the original options at the date of modification and recognizes the total amount over the remaining two years of the three-year vesting period.

323. The fair value at January 1, 2001, of the modified options, based on a 5-year expected life, $40 current stock price, $40 exercise price, 7 percent risk-free interest rate, 35 percent volatility, and a 2.5 percent dividend yield, is $13.60 per option. The computed value of the original options at the date of modification used to measure additional compensation cost is based on an expected life of five years because the remaining expected life of the original options and the expected life of the modified options both are five years. The resulting value of the original options, based on a current stock price of $40 and an exercise price of $50, with other assumptions the same as those used to determine the fair value of the modified options, is $10.77. Thus, the additional compensation cost stemming from the modification is $2.83, determined as follows:

Fair value of modified option at January 1, 2001	$13.60
Less: Value of original option at January 1, 2001	10.77
Incremental value of modified January 1, 2001, option	$ 2.83

324. On January 1, 2001, the remaining balance of unrecognized compensation cost for the original op-

tions is $11.43 per option.[23] The total compensation cost for each modified option that is expected to vest is $14.26, determined as follows:

Incremental value of modified option	$ 2.83
Unrecognized compensation cost for original option	11.43
Total compensation cost to be recognized	$14.26

That amount is recognized during 2001 and 2002, which are the two remaining years of the service period.

Illustration 5(d)—Cash settlement of nonvested options granted after adoption of this Statement

325. Rather than modify the option terms, Company S offers to settle the original January 1, 2000 grant of options for cash at January 1, 2001. Because the stockprice decreased from $50 at the grant date to $40 at the date of settlement, the estimated fair value of each option is the same as in Illustration 5(c), $10.77. If Company S pays $10.77 per option, it would recognize that cash settlement as the repurchase of an outstanding equity instrument and total compensation cost would not be remeasured. However, the cash payment for the options effectively vests them. Therefore, the remaining unrecognized compensation cost of $11.43 per option also would be recognized at the date of settlement.

Illustration 5(e)—Modification of vested options granted before adoption of this Statement

326. This example assumes that a modification similar to Illustration 5(a) above occurred on January 1, 1998, and that the original award was granted before Company S adopted this Statement.[24] Thus, Company S recognized no compensation cost for the original options accounted for in accordance with Opinion 25 because the exercise price equaled the stock price at the measurement (grant) date. To better illustrate the accounting distinction, all other assumptions are the same as in Illustration 5(a). Therefore, the fair value of the modified option is assumed to be $10.82, as determined in paragraph 320.

327. Because no compensation cost was recognized for the original options, the modified options are treated as a new grant. Compensation cost of $10.82 is recognized for each outstanding option at the date of the modification. However, if immediately before their terms were modified, the original options had been in-the-money and thus had intrinsic value at the date of modification, that intrinsic value would be excluded from the amount of compensation cost recognized. For example, if a modification of terms occurred in conjunction with a spinoff, the original options might have intrinsic value of, say, $2 each, just before their terms are modified. In that situation, if the fair value of a modified option is $16.50, only $14.50 ($16.50 − $2) of compensation cost would be recognized at the date of the modification. The intrinsic value is excluded from compensation cost because the employees could have exercised their options immediately before the modification and received the intrinsic value without affecting the amount of compensation cost recognized. Only the time value of the modified options is additional compensation cost.

Illustration 5(f)—Modification of nonvested options granted before adoption of this Statement

328. This example of a modification of an option assumes that an award originally accounted for according to Opinion 25 is not yet vested when it is modified. Company S grants an option with an exercise price of $47 when the stock price is $50 and the option cliff-vests after 3 years. Opinion 25 requires compensation cost of $3 ($50 − $47) to be recognized over the vesting period at the rate of $1 per year. After two years of that three-year cliff-vesting period, Company S adopts the accounting method for cost recognition encouraged by this Statement. It also decides to reduce the exercise price of the options to $40, which is the current price of the stock. For convenience, the value of the modified option on the date of the modification is again assumed to be $10.82 (paragraph 320), which consists entirely of time value.

329. Company S had recognized compensation cost of $2 under Opinion 25 at the date of modification for each option that had not been forfeited. After the

---

[23]Using a value of $17.15 for the original option as in Illustration 1 results in recognition of $5.72 ($17.15 ÷ 3) per year. The unrecognized balance at January 1, 2001 is $11.43 ($17.15 − $5.72) per option.

[24]For purposes of the pro forma disclosures required by paragraph 45 of this Statement, the method in Illustrations 5(e) through 5(g) applies only to modifications and cash settlements of awards granted before the beginning of the fiscal year for which that paragraph is initially applied. A modification or cash settlement of an award for which compensation cost has been included in pro forma disclosures since it was granted would be treated in the pro forma disclosures in the same manner as in Illustrations 5(a) through 5(d).

modification, the remaining amount of compensation cost to be recognized during the final year of the 3-year service period is $9.17 for each option that vests, determined as follows:

Fair value of modified option	$10.82
Less: Value of original option, based on 1-year remaining life[25]	2.65
Incremental value of modified option	8.17
Plus: Remaining unrecognized cost for original option	1.00
Compensation cost to be recognized	$ 9.17

The value of the original option deducted from the fair value of the modified option to determine the amount of compensation cost to recognize is based on a one-year life because that is the remaining term of the vesting period. To maintain consistency with (a) the requirements of this Statement for accounting for plan modifications and (b) the principal difference between this Statement and Opinion 25—accounting for the time value of an option—the vesting period is used as the expected life of the original option. The life of an option beyond the vesting period is not pertinent to the accounting under Opinion 25.

Illustration 5(g)—Cash settlement of vested options granted before adoption of this statement

330. This example assumes that a cash settlement of the options described in Illustration 5(a) above occurred on January 1, 1998, and that the original options were granted before Company S adopted the accounting method for cost recognition encouraged by this Statement. Thus, Company S recognized no compensation cost for the original award accounted for in accordance with Opinion 25 because the exercise price equaled the stock price at the measurement (grant) date. All other assumptions are the same as in Illustration 5(a). Therefore, the amount of the cash payment and the fair value of the out-of-the-money option at the date of cash settlement are $10.82, as determined in paragraph 320.

331. Because no cost was recognized for the original award, the cash settlement of the out-of-the-money options for $10.82 each is treated as a new grant. Compensation cost of $10.82 is recognized for each outstanding option at the date of settlement. However, if the original options had been in-the-money and thus had intrinsic value immediately before the

settlement, that intrinsic value would be excluded from the amount of compensation cost recognized for the reasons cited in Illustration 5(e), paragraph 327.

Illustration 6—Options Granted by a Nonpublic Entity

332. Company P, a nonpublic entity, grants 100 stock options on its stock to each of its 100 employees. The options cliff-vest after three years. The fair value of the stock and the exercise price of the options is $5, the expected life of the options is 8 years, and the risk-free interest rate is 7.5 percent. Company P calculates a *minimum value* for each option. The so-called minimum value does not take into account the expected volatility of the underlying stock.

Fair value of stock	$5.00
Present value of exercise price (compounded daily)	2.74
Minimum value of each option	$2.26

333. An option-pricing model can also be used to compute the minimum value of Company P's options if the volatility assumption is set to near zero (say, 0.001), resulting in the same $2.26. If Company P expected to pay dividends, the minimum value of the options would be further reduced to reflect the present value of the expected dividends that the option holder will not receive. Assuming a 1 percent dividend yield over the 8-year expected life of the options, an option-pricing model results in a minimum value of $1.87.

334. Alternatively, the present value of the expected dividends would be computed as $.30, using 32 quarterly (8-year expected life) payments of $.0125 [($5.00 × .01) ÷ 4], and a quarterly interest rate of 1.875 percent (7.5 percent annual rate). That amount would be deducted from the minimum value of an option on a stock that pays no dividends computed in paragraph 332, resulting in a minimum value of $1.96 ($2.26 − $.30). The $0.39 present value of the dividends computed using the option-pricing model ($2.26 − $1.87) differs from the $0.30 present value computed by directly discounting dividend payments because the option-pricing model assumes that dividends will grow with increases in the stock price (if

---

[25]Other assumptions are $40 stock price, $47 exercise price, expected volatility of 30 percent, risk-free interest rate of 5 percent, and dividend yield of 2.5 percent.

the dividend assumption is stated as a constant yield). The assumed growth rate is the difference between the risk-free interest rate and the dividend rate. In this example, that difference is 6.5 percent (7.5% – 1%). Either method of computing minimum value is acceptable in applying this Statement.

Illustration 7—Tandem Plan—Stock Options or Cash SARs

335. A plan in which employees are granted awards with two separate components, in which exercise of one component cancels the other, is referred to as a tandem plan. In contrast, a **combination plan** is an award with two separate components, both of which can be exercised.

336. The following illustrates the accounting for a tandem plan in which employees have a choice of either stock options or cash SARs. Company S grants to its employees an award of 900,000 stock options or 900,000 cash SARs on January 1, 2000. The award vests on December 31, 2002, and has a contractual life of 10 years. If an employee exercises the SARs, the related stock options are canceled. Conversely, if an employee exercises the options, the related SARs are canceled.

337. The tandem award results in Company S's incurring a liability because the employees can demand settlement in cash, and Company S therefore is obligated to pay cash upon demand. If Company S could choose whether to settle the award in cash or by issuing stock, the award would be an equity instrument because Company S would have the discretion to avoid transferring its assets to employees (unless Company S's past practice is to settle most awards in cash, indicating that Company S has incurred a substantive liability as indicated in paragraph 39). In this illustration, however, Company S incurs a liability to pay cash, which it will recognize over the service period. The amount of the liability will be adjusted each year to reflect the current stock price. If employees choose to exercise the options rather than the SARs, the liability is settled by issuing stock.

338. In concept, the fair value of the expected liability at the grant date is $14,087,113 as computed in Illustration 1 because the value of the SARs and the value of the stock options are equal. However, this Statement does not require accounting for the time value of the cash SARs at the grant date because the compensation cost stemming from the award must be finally measured as the intrinsic value of the SARs at

the exercise (or expiration) date. Accordingly, at the end of 2000, when the stock price is $55, the amount of the liability is $4,107,030 (821,406 cash SARs expected to vest × $5 increase in stock price). One-third of that amount, $1,369,010, is recognized as compensation cost for 2000. At the end of each year during the vesting period, the expected liability is remeasured based on the current stock price. As provided in paragraph 28, Company S has the choice of estimating forfeitures at the grant date or accruing cost for the total grant and adjusting for forfeitures as they occur. After the vesting period, the expected liability is remeasured for all outstanding vested awards.

Illustration 8—Tandem Plan—Phantom Shares or Stock Options

339. The illustration that follows is for a tandem plan in which the components have different values after the grant date, depending on the movement in the price of the entity's stock. The employee's choice of which component to exercise will depend on the relative values of the components when the award is exercised.

340. Company S grants to its CEO an immediately vested award consisting of two measurable parts:

a. 1,000 phantom stock units (units) whose value is always equal to the value of 1,000 shares of Company S's common stock.
b. Options on 3,000 shares of Company S stock with an exercise price of $50 per share.

At the grant date, Company S's stock price is $50 per share. The CEO may choose whether to exercise the options or to cash in the units at any time during the next five years. Exercise of all of the options cancels all of the units, and cashing in all of the units cancels all of the options. The cash value of the units will be paid to the CEO at the end of five years if the option component of the tandem award is not exercised before then.

341. With a 3-to-1 ratio of options to units, exercise of 3 options will produce a higher gain than receipt of cash equal to the value of 1 share of stock if the stock price appreciates from the grant date by more than 50 percent. Below that point, one unit is more valuable than the gain on three options. To illustrate that relationship, the results if the stock price increases 50 percent to $75 are:

	Units		**Exercise of Options**	
Market value	$75,000	($75 × 1,000)	$225,000	($75 × 3,000)
Purchase price	0		150,000	($50 × 3,000)
Net cash value	$75,000		$ 75,000	

342. If the price of Company S's common stock increases from $50 to $75, each part of the tandem grant will produce the same net cash inflow (ignoring transaction costs) to the CEO. If the price increases only to $74, the value of 1 share of stock exceeds the gain on exercising 3 options, which would be $72 [3 × ($74 − $50)]. But if the price increases to $76, the gain on exercising 3 options, $78 [3 × ($76 − $50)], exceeds the value of 1 share of stock.

343. At the grant date, the CEO could take $50,000 cash for the units and forfeit the options. Therefore, the total value of the award at the grant date must exceed $50,000 because at stock prices above $75, the CEO receives a higher amount than would the holder of 1 share of stock. To exercise the 3,000 options, the CEO must forfeit the equivalent of 1,000 shares of stock, in addition to paying the total exercise price of $150,000 (3,000 × $50). In effect, the CEO receives only 2,000 shares of Company S stock upon exercise. That is the same as if the option component of the tandem award consisted of options to purchase 2,000 shares of stock for $75 per share.

344. The cash payment obligated by the units qualifies the award as a liability of Company S. The maximum amount of the cash liability, which is indexed to the price of Company S's common stock, is $75,000 because at stock prices above $75, the CEO will exercise the options.

345. In measuring compensation cost, the award may be thought of as a *combination*—not tandem—grant of (a) 1,000 units with a value at grant of $50,000 and (b) 2,000 options with a strike price of $75 per share. Compensation cost is measured as the combined value of the two parts.

346. The expected volatility of Company S stock is assumed to be 30 percent, the risk-free interest rate is 7 percent, Company S stock pays no dividend, and the expected life of the options is 5 years. Using those assumptions, the fair value of an option with an exercise price of $75 is $12.13 when the price of Com-

pany S's stock price is $50. Therefore, the total value of the award at the grant date is:

Units (1,000 × $50)	$50,000
Options (2,000 × $12.13)	24,260
Value of award	$74,260

347. Compensation cost recognized at the date of grant (the award is immediately vested) therefore would be $74,260. That amount is more than either of the components by itself, but less than the total cost that would be computed if both components (1,000 units and 3,000 options with an exercise price of $50) were exercisable. Because granting the units creates a liability, changes in the liability that result from increases or decreases in the price of Company S's stock price would be recognized each period until exercise, except that the amount of the liability would not exceed $75,000.

Illustration 9—"Look-Back" Options

348. Some entities offer options to employees under Section 423 of the Internal Revenue Code, which provides that employees will not be immediately taxed on the difference between the market price of the stock and a discounted purchase price if several requirements are met. One requirement is that the option price may not be less than the smaller of (a) 85 percent of the market price when the option is granted or (b) 85 percent of the price at exercise. An option that provides the employee the choice of (a) or (b) may not have a term in excess of 27 months. Options that provide for the more favorable of two (or more) exercise prices are referred to as "look-back" options. A look-back option with a 15 percent discount from the market price at either grant or exercise is worth more than a fixed option to purchase stock at 85 percent of the current market price because the holder of the look-back option cannot lose. If the price rises, the holder benefits to the same extent as if the exercise price were fixed at the grant date. If the

stock price falls, the holder still receives the benefit of purchasing the stock at a 15 percent discount from its price at the date of exercise.

349. For example, on January 1, 2000, when its stock price is $50, Company S offers its employees the opportunity to sign up for a payroll deduction to purchase its stock at either 85 percent of the stock's current price or 85 percent of the price at the end of the year when the options expire, whichever is lower. The exercise price of the options is the lesser of (a) $42.50 ($50 × .85) or (b) 85 percent of the stock price at the end of the year when the option is exercised. For simplicity, the first set of calculations assumes that Company S pays no dividends, its expected volatility is .30, and the risk-free interest rate available for the next 12 months is 6.8 percent.

350. The value of that look-back option can be estimated at the grant date by breaking it into its components and valuing the option as a combination position. In this situation, the components are:

• 0.15 of a share of nonvested stock
• 0.85 of a 1-year call option held with an exercise price of $50.

Supporting analysis for the two components is discussed below.

351. Beginning with the first component, an option with an exercise price that equals 85 percent of the value of the stock at the exercise date will always be worth 15 percent (100% – 85%) of the stock price upon exercise. For a stock that pays no dividends, that option is the equivalent of 15 percent of a share of the stock. The holder of the look-back option will receive *at least* the equivalent of 0.15 of a share of stock upon exercise, regardless of the stock price at that date. For example, if the stock price falls to $40, the exercise price of the option will be $34 ($40 × .85), and the holder will benefit by $6 ($40 – $34), which is the same as receiving 0.15 of a share of stock for each option.

352. If the stock price upon exercise is more than $50, the holder of the look-back option receives a benefit that is worth more than 15 percent of a share of stock. At prices of $50 or more, the holder receives a benefit for the difference between the stock price upon exercise and $42.50—the exercise price of the option (.85 × $50). If the stock price is $60, the holder benefits by $17.50 ($60 – $42.50). However, the holder cannot receive *both* the $17.50 value of an

option with an exercise price of $42.50 *and* 0.15 of a share of stock. In effect, the holder gives up 0.15 of a share of stock worth $7.50 ($50 × .15) if the stock price is above $50 at exercise. The result is the same as if the exercise price of the option were $50 ($42.50 + $7.50), and the holder of the look-back option held 85 percent of a 1-year call option with an exercise price of $50 in addition to 0.15 of a share of stock that will be received if the stock price is $50 or less upon exercise.

353. A standard option-pricing model can be used to value the 1-year call option on 0.85 of a share of stock represented by the second component. Therefore, the compensation cost for the look-back option at the grant date is:

• 0.15 of a share of nonvested stock ($50 × 0.15)	$ 7.50
• Call on 0.85 of a share of stock, exercise price of $50 ($7.56 × .85)	6.43
Total grant date value	$13.93

354. For a look-back option on a dividend-paying stock, both the value of the nonvested stock component and the value of the option component would be adjusted to reflect the effect of the dividends that the employee does not receive during the life of the option. The present value of the dividends expected to be paid on the stock during the life of the option, which is one year in the example, would be deducted from the value of a share that receives dividends. One way to accomplish that is to base the value calculation on shares of stock rather than dollars by assuming that the dividends are reinvested in the stock.

355. For example, if Company S pays a quarterly dividend of 0.625 percent (2.5% ÷ 4) of the current stock price, 1 share of stock would grow to 1.0252 (the future value of 1 using a return of 0.625 percent for 4 periods) shares at the end of the year if all dividends are reinvested. Therefore, the present value of 1 share of stock to be received in 1 year is only 0.9754 of a share today (again applying conventional compound interest formulas compounded quarterly) if the holder does not receive the dividends paid during the year.

356. The value of the option component is easier to compute; the appropriate dividend assumption is used in the option-pricing model in determining the

value of an option on a whole share of stock. Thus, the compensation cost for the look-back option if Company S pays quarterly dividends at the annual rate of 2.5 percent is:

- 0.15 of a share of nonvested stock
  ($50 × 0.15 × 0.9754) $ 7.32
- Call on 0.85 of a share of stock,
  $50 exercise price, 2.5% dividend
  yield ($6.78 × 0.85)   5.76

Total grant date value $13.08

The first component, which is worth $7.32 at the grant date, is the minimum amount the holder benefits regardless of the price of the stock at the exercise date. The second component, worth $5.76 at the grant date, represents the additional benefit to the holder if the stock price is above $50 at the exercise date.

Illustration of the Earnings per Share Computation

357. An illustration of the computation of earnings per share follows. Under Opinion 15 and FASB Interpretation No. 31, *Treatment of Stock Compensation Plans in EPS Computations,* stock options, stock appreciation rights, and other awards to be settled in stock are common stock equivalents for purposes of computing earnings per share. In applying the treasury stock method, all dilutive common stock equivalents, regardless of whether they are exercisable, are treated as if they had been exercised. The treasury stock method assumes that the proceeds upon exercise are used to repurchase the entity's stock, reducing the number of shares to be added to outstanding common stock in computing earnings per share. The proceeds assumed to be received upon exercise include the exercise price that the employee pays, the amount of compensation cost measured and attributed to future services but not yet recognized, and the amount of any tax benefits upon assumed exercise that would be credited to additional paid-in capital. The assumed proceeds exclude any future tax benefits related to compensation cost to be recognized in income.

358. Under paragraph 28 of this Statement, an entity has the choice of estimating forfeitures in advance or recognizing forfeitures as they occur. The same number of options used to measure compensation cost should be used in the calculation of primary earnings per share. The following computation of the number of incremental shares to be considered outstanding in computing primary earnings per share assumes that options have been granted in the current year and prior years and that the entity anticipates the effect of future forfeitures. For this illustration, a total of 4,600,000 options are assumed to be outstanding from current year's and prior years' grants, of which 4,500,000 are expected to vest. The weighted-average exercise price of outstanding options is assumed to be $40. The average stock price during 2000 is assumed to be $52. The year-end stock price is $55. To simplify the illustration, it is assumed that (a) all outstanding options are the type that upon exercise give rise to deductible compensation cost for income tax purposes, and (b) no tax benefit upon exercise would be credited to additional paid-in capital; that is, the tax deduction based on current intrinsic value is less than the amount of cost recognized for financial statement purposes.

359. Computation of assumed proceeds for primary earnings per share:

- Amount employees would pay if all options expected to vest were exercised using weighted-average exercise price (4,500,000 × $40) $180,000,000
- Average unrecognized compensation balance during year[26]   16,000,000

Assumed proceeds $196,000,000

360. Assumed repurchase of shares:

- Repurchase shares at average market price during the year
  ($196,000,000 ÷ $52)   3,769,231
- Incremental shares to be added
  (4,500,000 − 3,769,231)   730,769

361. The number of shares to be added to outstanding shares for purposes of the primary earnings per share calculation is 730,769. The computation of fully diluted earnings per share would be based on the same method illustrated above. However, the total number of options outstanding, rather than the number of options expected to vest, would be used,

---

[26]Average unrecognized compensation balance is determined by averaging the beginning-of-the-year balance of cost measured and unrecognized and the end-of-the-year balance of cost measured and unrecognized. The assumed amount is $16,000,000 based on ongoing cost recognition for stock options granted in the current year and prior years.

and the average and year-end net unrecognized compensation cost would be adjusted to reflect the inclusion of options not expected to vest. The year-end unrecognized compensation cost and the year-end stock price would be used in computing fully diluted earnings per share if they result in a more dilutive calculation than use of average unrecognized compensation and the average stock price for the year.

Illustrative Disclosures

362. An illustration of disclosures of an entity's compensation plans follows. The illustration assumes that compensation cost has been recognized in accordance with the provisions of this Statement for several years. The amount of compensation cost recognized each year includes both costs from that year's grants and from prior years' grants. The number of options outstanding, exercised, forfeited, and expired each year includes options granted in prior years. The additional disclosures that would be required if the entity had elected to continue to recognize compensation cost in accordance with Opinion 25 are presented in paragraph 363.

* * *

Stock Compensation Plans

At December 31, 2006, the Company has four stock-based compensation plans, which are described below. The Company accounts for the fair value of its grants under those plans in accordance with FASB Statement 123. The compensation cost that has been charged against income for those plans was $23.3 million, $28.7 million, and $29.4 million for 2004, 2005, and 2006, respectively.

Fixed Stock Option Plans

The Company has two fixed option plans. Under the 1999 Employee Stock Option Plan, the Company may grant options to its employees for up to 8 million shares of common stock. Under the 2004 Managers' Incentive Stock Option Plan, the Company may grant options to its management personnel for up to 5 million shares of common stock. Under both plans, the exercise price of each option equals the market price of the Company's stock on the date of grant and an option's maximum term is 10 years. Options are granted on January 1 and vest at the end of the third year under the 1999 Plan and at the end of the second year under the 2004 Plan.

The fair value of each option grant is estimated on the date of grant using the Black-Scholes option-pricing model with the following weighted-average assumptions used for grants in 2004, 2005, and 2006, respectively: dividend yield of 1.5 percent for all years; expected volatility of 24, 26, and 29 percent, risk-free interest rates of 6.5, 7.5, and 7 percent for the 1999 Plan options and 6.4, 7.4, and 6.8 percent for the 2004 Plan options; and expected lives of 6, 5, and 5 years for the 1999 Plan options and 5, 4, and 4 years for the 2004 Plan options.

A summary of the status of the Company's two fixed stock option plans as of December 31, 2004, 2005, and 2006, and changes during the years ending on those dates is presented below:

Fixed Options	2004 Shares (000)	2004 Weighted-Average Exercise Price	2005 Shares (000)	2005 Weighted-Average Exercise Price	2006 Shares (000)	2006 Weighted-Average Exercise Price
Outstanding at beginning of year	4,500	$34	4,600	$38	4,660	$42
Granted	900	50	1,000	55	950	60
Exercised	(700)	27	(850)	34	(800)	36
Forfeited	(100)	46	(90)	51	(80)	59
Outstanding at end of year	4,600	38	4,660	42	4,730	47
Options exercisable at year-end	2,924		2,873		3,159	
Weighted-average fair value of options granted during the year	$15.90		$17.46		$19.57	

The following table summarizes information about fixed stock options outstanding at December 31, 2006:

Range of Exercise Prices	Options Outstanding Number Outstanding at 12/31/06	Options Outstanding Weighted-Average Remaining Contractual Life	Options Outstanding Weighted-Average Exercise Price	Options Exercisable Number Exercisable at 12/31/06	Options Exercisable Weighted-Average Exercise Price
$25 to 33	1,107,000	3.6 years	$29	1,107,000	$29
39 to 41	467,000	5.0	40	467,000	40
46 to 50	1,326,000	6.6	48	1,326,000	48
55 to 60	1,830,000	8.5	57	259,000	55
$25 to 60	4,730,000	6.5	47	3,159,000	41

Performance-Based Stock Option Plan

Under its Goals 2010 Stock Option Plan adopted in 2002, each January 1 the Company grants selected executives and other key employees stock option awards whose vesting is contingent upon increases in the Company's market share for its principal product. If at the end of 3 years market share has increased by at least 5 percentage points from the date of grant, one-third of the options under the award vest to active employees. However, if at that date market share has increased by at least 10 percentage points, two-thirds of the options under the award vest, and if market share has increased by 20 percentage points or more, all of the options under the award vest. The number of shares subject to options under this plan cannot exceed 5 million. The exercise price of each option, which has a 10-year life, is equal to the market price of the Company's stock on the date of grant.

The fair value of each option grant was estimated on the date of grant using the Black-Scholes option-pricing model with the following assumptions for 2004, 2005, and 2006, respectively: risk-free interest rates of 6.5, 7.6, and 7.4 percent; dividend yield of 1.5 percent for all years; expected lives of 6, 6, and 7 years; and volatility of 24, 26, and 29 percent.

A summary of the status of the Company's performance-based stock option plan as of December 31, 2004, 2005, and 2006, and changes during the years ending on those dates is presented below:

Performance Options	2004 Shares (000)	2004 Weighted-Average Exercise Price	2005 Shares (000)	2005 Weighted-Average Exercise Price	2006 Shares (000)	2006 Weighted-Average Exercise Price
Outstanding at beginning of year	830	$46	1,635	$48	2,533	$51
Granted	850	50	980	55	995	60
Exercised	0		0		(100)	46
Forfeited	(45)	48	(82)	50	(604)	51
Outstanding at end of year	1,635	48	2,533	51	2,824	55
Options exercisable at year-end	0		780	46	936	47
Weighted-average fair value of options granted during the year	$16.25		$19.97		$24.32	

As of December 31, 2006, the 2.8 million performance options outstanding under the Plan have exercise prices between $46 and $60 and a weighted-average remaining contractual life of 7.7 years. The Company expects that approximately one-third of the nonvested awards at December 31, 2006, will eventually vest based on projected market share.

Employee Stock Purchase Plan

Under the 1987 Employee Stock Purchase Plan, the Company is authorized to issue up to 10 million shares of common stock to its full-time employees, nearly all of whom are eligible to participate. Under the terms of the Plan, employees can choose each year to have up to 6 percent of their annual base earnings withheld to purchase the Company's common stock. The purchase price of the stock is 85 percent of the lower of its beginning-of-year or end-of-year market price. Approximately 75 to 80 percent of eligible employees have participated in the Plan in the last 3 years. Under the Plan, the Company sold 456,000 shares, 481,000 shares, and 503,000 shares to employees in 2004, 2005, and 2006, respectively. Compensation cost is recognized for the fair value of the employees' purchase rights, which was estimated using the Black-Scholes model with the following assumptions for 2004, 2005, and 2006, respectively: dividend yield of 1.5 percent for all years; an expected life of 1 year for all years; expected volatility of 22, 24, and 26 percent; and risk-free interest rates of 5.9, 6.9, and 6.7 percent. The weighted-average fair value of those purchase rights granted in 2004, 2005, and 2006 was $11.95, $13.73, and $15.30, respectively.

* * *

363. If compensation cost has been determined by applying Opinion 25 as permitted by this Statement (paragraph 5), the total compensation cost disclosed in the first paragraph of the illustrative disclosures would need to be revised to reflect the cost recognized under Opinion 25. The following paragraph would replace that paragraph; all other disclosures about the plans and related assumptions would be required.

* * *

At December 31, 2006, the Company has four stock-based compensation plans, which are described below. The Company applies APB Opinion 25 and related Interpretations in accounting for its plans. Accordingly, no compensation cost has been recognized for its fixed stock option plans and its stock purchase plan. The compensation cost that has been charged against income for its performance-based plan was $6.7 million, $9.4 million, and $0.7 million for 2004, 2005, and 2006, respectively. Had compensation cost for the Company's four stock-based compensation plans been determined based on the fair value at the grant dates for awards under those plans consistent with the method of FASB Statement 123, the Company's net income and earnings per share would have been reduced to the pro forma amounts indicated below:

		2004	2005	2006
Net income	As reported	$347,790	$407,300	$479,300
	Pro forma	$336,828	$394,553	$460,398
Primary earnings per share	As reported	$1.97	$2.29	$2.66
	Pro forma	$1.91	$2.22	$2.56
Fully diluted earnings per share	As reported	$1.49	$1.73	$2.02
	Pro forma	$1.44	$1.68	$1.94

* * *

Supplemental Disclosures

364. In addition to the information required by this Statement, an entity may disclose supplemental information that it believes would be useful to investors and creditors, such as a range of values calculated on the basis of different assumptions, provided that the supplemental information is reasonable and does not discredit the information required by this

Statement. The alternative assumptions should be described to enable users of the financial statements to understand the basis for the supplemental information. For example, if in the previous example the Company estimated in 2004 that its expected stock price volatility over the next 6 years was within a range of 24 to 32 percent in which no amount was a better estimate than any other amount, its use of a 24 percent volatility assumption is consistent with paragraph 275, which indicates that using an estimate at the low end of the range for expected volatility is appropriate in that circumstance. The Company could, however, choose to disclose supplementally the weighted-average fair value of stock options granted during the year (and related effect on the pro forma disclosures) based on the midpoint or the high end of the range of expected volatility. However, presenting supplemental disclosures based on, for example, an expected volatility assumption of 18 percent would not be appropriate because the Company had already concluded in making its calculations that an 18 percent assumption is below the range of reasonable assumptions. Presenting supplemental disclosures of the value of stock options based on an approach contrary to the methodology specified in this Statement, such as reflecting an additional discount related to the nontransferability of nonvested stock options, is similarly inappropriate. However, the Company's supplemental disclosures could include the intrinsic value of stock options exercised during the year.

Appendix C

BACKGROUND INFORMATION

365. In 1984, the Board added to its agenda a project to reconsider APB Opinion No. 25, *Accounting for Stock Issued to Employees.* On May 31, 1984, an FASB Invitation to Comment, *Accounting for Compensation Plans Involving Certain Rights Granted to Employees,* was issued based on the November 4, 1982, AICPA Issues Paper, *Accounting for Employee Capital Accumulation Plans.* The Board received 144 letters of comment.

366. From 1985 through 1988, the Board considered accounting for stock-based compensation and conducted research on various aspects of those plans, including how existing option-pricing models might be adapted to measure the fair value of employee stock options.

367. The issues were complex and highly controversial. Still, each time the issue was raised, Board members voted unanimously that employee stock options result in compensation cost that should be recognized in the employer's financial statements.

368. As with all FASB projects, the Board's discussions of stock compensation were open to public observation, and its tentative conclusions on individual issues were reported in its weekly *Action Alert.* During the Board's deliberations from 1985 to 1988, more than 200 letters were received that commented on, and usually objected to, tentative conclusions reported in *Action Alert.* That was unusual because most of the Board's constituents await publication of an Exposure Draft before they submit comments.

369. Some Board members and others were troubled by the differing results of stock-based compensation plans that called for settlement in cash and those that called for settlement in stock. But exercise date accounting for all plans is the only way to achieve consistent results between cash and stock plans, and that accounting was not considered to be consistent with the definitions of liabilities and equity in FASB Concepts Statement No. 6, *Elements of Financial Statements.* It also would be inconsistent with current accounting for stock purchase warrants, which are similar to employee stock options except that warrants are issued to outsiders rather than to employees.

370. A part of the financial instruments project on the Board's agenda considers whether changes to the concepts of liabilities and equity are needed. Late in 1988, the Board decided to set aside specific work on stock compensation while it considered broader questions of how to distinguish between liabilities and equity and the implications of that distinction.

371. In August 1990, a Discussion Memorandum, *Distinguishing between Liability and Equity Instruments and Accounting for Instruments with Characteristics of Both,* was issued. The Discussion Memorandum framed and discussed numerous issues, some of which bear directly on deciding how to account for employee stock options. The Board received 104 comment letters and in March 1991 held a public hearing on the issues, at which 14 commentators appeared.

372. More than 90 percent of the respondents to the Discussion Memorandum said that an entity's obligation to issue its own stock is an equity instrument because the entity does not have an obligation to transfer its assets (an entity's own stock is not its asset), which is an essential characteristic of a liability. In February 1992, the Board decided not to pursue possible changes to the conceptual distinction between liabilities and equity and to resume work on the stock compensation project within the present conceptual framework.

373. In March 1992, the Board met with several compensation consultants and accountants to discuss

current practice in valuing employee stock options and accounting for stock compensation. The compensation consultants generally agreed that current accounting provisions heavily affect the design of stock compensation plans. They said that there were far fewer variable (or performance) plans than fixed plans because of the required accounting for variable plans. The compensation consultants also said that the Black-Scholes and other option-pricing models were used to value various types of employee stock options for purposes other than accounting. Grant date measures were relied on to provide comparisons to other compensation arrangements.

374. A task force of accountants, compensation consultants, industry representatives, and academics was formed to assist in the project. Accounting for stock compensation was addressed at 19 public Board meetings and at 2 public task force meetings in 1992 and 1993. The Board's tentative conclusions on individual issues were reported in *Action Alert*. During 1992 and the first part of 1993, more than 450 comment letters were received, mostly objecting to the tentative conclusions. Many of the letters proposed disclosure in lieu of cost recognition for stock compensation. Several of the commentators submitted alternatives to the Board; the most comprehensive disclosure proposal was included as an appendix to the Exposure Draft.

375. In June 1993, the Board issued an FASB Exposure Draft, *Accounting for Stock-based Compensation*, that would have required recognizing compensation cost for all awards of stock-based compensation that eventually vest, based on their fair value at the grant date. The Board and KPMG Peat Marwick conducted a field test of the provisions of the Exposure Draft. In addition, other organizations provided information about their own test applications of the Exposure Draft.

376. As discussed in Appendix A, the Exposure Draft was extraordinarily controversial. The Board received 1,786 comment letters, including approximately 1,000 form letters, on the Exposure Draft. The vast majority of respondents objected to the recognition of compensation cost for fixed employee stock options—sometimes for reasons that had little to do with accounting. In March 1994, the Board held six days of public hearings in Connecticut and California. Representatives from 73 organizations presented testimony at those hearings. Several legislative proposals were introduced in Congress, both opposing and supporting proposals in the Exposure

Draft. A Sense of the Senate resolution was passed that the FASB "should not at this time change the current generally accepted accounting treatment of stock options and stock purchase plans." However, a second resolution was passed that "Congress should not impair the objectivity or integrity of the FASB's decisionmaking process by legislating accounting rules."

377. In April 1994, the Board held a public round-table discussion with academic researchers and other participants on proposals the participants had submitted to improve the measure of the value of stock options. Also during 1994, the Board discussed accounting for stock-based compensation at 13 public Board meetings and at 1 public task force meeting.

378. In December 1994, the Board discussed the alternatives for proceeding with the project on accounting for stock-based compensation in light of the comment letters, public hearing testimony, and various meetings held to discuss the project. The Board decided to encourage, rather than require, recognition of compensation cost based on a fair value method and to pursue expanded disclosures. Employers would be permitted to continue to apply the provisions of Opinion 25. Employers that continued to apply Opinion 25 would be required to disclose the pro forma effects on net income and earnings per share if the new accounting method had been applied.

379. The Board discussed the details of the disclosure-based approach at six Board meetings in 1995. In 1995, 131 comment letters were received on the disclosure-based approach. In May 1995, an initial draft of the standards section and some of the other parts of this Statement were distributed to task force members and other interested parties that requested the draft; 34 comment letters were received. Appendix A discusses the basis for the Board's conclusions, including reasons for changes made to the provisions of the 1993 Exposure Draft.

Appendix D

AMENDMENTS TO EXISTING PRONOUNCEMENTS

380. FASB Technical Bulletin No. 82-2, *Accounting for the Conversion of Stock Options into Incentive Stock Options as a Result of the Economic Recovery Tax Act of 1981*, is superseded.

381. This Statement amends ARB No. 43, Chapter 13B, "Compensation Involved in Stock Option and Stock Purchase Plans," as follows:

a. The following sentences are added to the end of paragraph 2:

> FASB Statement No. 123, *Accounting for Stock-Based Compensation*, specifies a fair value based method of accounting for stock-based compensation plans and encourages entities to adopt that method for all arrangements under which employees receive shares of stock or other equity instruments of the employer or the employer incurs liabilities to employees in amounts based on the price of the employer's stock. However, Statement 123 permits an employer in determining its net income to continue to apply the accounting provisions of this section and Opinion 25 to all its stock-based employee compensation arrangements. Entities that continue to apply this section and Opinion 25 shall comply with the disclosure requirements of Statement 123.

b. Paragraph 15 is deleted.

382. APB Opinion No. 25, *Accounting for Stock Issued to Employees*, is amended as follows:

a. The following sentences are added to the end of paragraph 4:

> FASB Statement No. 123, *Accounting for Stock-Based Compensation*, specifies a fair value based method of accounting for stock-based compensation plans and encourages entities to adopt that method in place of the provisions of this Opinion for all arrangements under which employees receive shares of stock or other equity instruments of the employer or the employer incurs liabilities to employees in amounts based on the price of the employer's stock. Statement 123 permits an entity in determining its net income to continue to apply the accounting provisions of Opinion 25. If an entity makes that election, it shall apply Opinion 25 to all its stock-based employee compensation arrangements. If an entity elects to apply Statement 123, that election shall not be reversed. Entities that continue to apply Opinion 25 shall comply with the disclosure requirements of Statement 123.

b. Paragraph 19 is replaced by the following:

Disclosure. Paragraphs 45-48 of FASB Statement No. 123, *Accounting for Stock-Based Compensation*, specify the disclosures related to stock-based employee compensation arrangements that shall be made in the financial statements.

c. Footnote 5 is deleted.

383. Footnote 4 of APB Opinion No. 29, *Accounting for Nonmonetary Transactions*, is replaced by the following:

> FASB Statement No. 123, *Accounting for Stock-Based Compensation*, applies to all transactions in which an entity acquires goods or services by issuing equity instruments or by incurring liabilities to the supplier in amounts based on the price of the entity's common stock or other equity instruments.

384. The following is added as a footnote to the end of the penultimate paragraph of AICPA Accounting Interpretation 1, "Stock Plans Established by a Principal Stockholder," of Opinion 25:

> *FASB Statement No. 123, *Accounting for Stock-Based Compensation*, specifies a fair value based method of accounting for stock-based compensation plans and encourages entities to adopt that method in place of the provisions of Opinion 25 for all arrangements under which employees receive shares of stock or other equity instruments of the employer or the employer incurs liabilities to employees in amounts based on the price of the employer's stock. Paragraph 15 of Statement 123 adopts the substance of this Interpretation regardless of the method chosen to account for stock-based compensation.

385. In the fourth sentence of paragraph 7 of FASB Statement No. 5, *Accounting for Contingencies*, the phrase *APB Opinion No. 25, Accounting for Stock Issued to Employees*, is replaced by *FASB Statement No. 123, Accounting for Stock-Based Compensation*.

386. In footnote 3 to paragraph 12 of FASB Statement No. 21, *Suspension of the Reporting of Earnings per Share and Segment Information by Nonpublic Enterprises*, the phrase *paragraph 15 of Chapter 13B, "Compensation Involved in Stock Option and Stock Purchase Plans," of ARB No. 43* is replaced by *paragraphs 45-48 of FASB Statement No. 123, Accounting for Stock-Based Compensation*.

387. In paragraph 2 of FASB Statement No. 43, *Accounting for Compensated Absences*, as amended by FASB Statement No. 112, *Employers' Accounting for Postemployment Benefits*, the phrase *APB Opinion No. 25, Accounting for Stock Issued to Employees*, is replaced by *FASB Statement No. 123, Accounting for Stock-Based Compensation*.

388. In paragraph 14(c) of FASB Statement No. 105, *Disclosure of Information about Financial Instruments with Off-Balance-Sheet Risk and Financial Instruments with Concentrations of Credit Risk*, the phrase *as well as APB Opinions No. 25, Accounting for Stock Issued to Employees, and No. 12* is replaced by *and No. 123, Accounting for Stock-Based Compensation, and APB Opinion No. 12*.

389. Paragraph 8(a) of FASB Statement No. 107, *Disclosures about Fair Value of Financial Instruments*, as amended by Statement 112, is amended as follows:

a. The phrase *No. 123, Accounting for Stock-Based Compensation*, is added before *and No. 43*.
b. The phrase *APB Opinions No. 25, Accounting for Stock Issued to Employees, and No. 12* is replaced by *APB Opinion No. 12*.

390. In paragraph 36(e) of FASB Statement No. 109, *Accounting for Income Taxes*, the phrase *paragraphs 41-44 of FASB Statement No. 123, Accounting for Stock-Based Compensation, and* is added after *refer to*.

391. In paragraph 5(d) of Statement 112, the phrase *APB Opinion No. 25, Accounting for Stock Issued to Employees*, is replaced by *FASB Statement No. 123, Accounting for Stock-Based Compensation*.

392. The following is added as a footnote to the end of the second sentence of paragraph 2 of FASB Interpretation No. 28, *Accounting for Stock Appreciation Rights and Other Variable Stock Option or Award Plans:*

> *FASB Statement No. 123, *Accounting for Stock-Based Compensation*, specifies a fair value based method of accounting for stock-based compensation plans (including those that involve variable plan awards) and encourages entities to adopt that method in place of the provisions of Opinion 25 for all arrangements under which employees receive shares of stock or other equity instruments of the employer or the

employer incurs liabilities to employees in amounts based on the price of the employer's stock. Statement 123 permits an entity in determining its net income to continue to apply the accounting provisions of Opinion 25. If an entity makes that election, it shall apply Opinion 25 (including this Interpretation) to all its stock-based employee compensation arrangements.

393. The following is added to the end of footnote 1 to paragraph 3 of FASB Interpretation No. 31, *Treatment of Stock Compensation Plans in EPS Computations:*

> FASB Statement No. 123, *Accounting for Stock-Based Compensation*, specifies a fair value based method of accounting for stock-based compensation plans (including those that involve variable plan awards) and encourages entities to adopt that method in place of the provisions of Opinion 25.

394. The following is added as a footnote at the end of paragraph 2 of FASB Interpretation No. 38, *Determining the Measurement Date for Stock Option, Purchase, and Award Plans Involving Junior Stock:*

> *FASB Statement No. 123, *Accounting for Stock-Based Compensation*, specifies a fair value based method of accounting for stock-based compensation plans (including those that involve variable plan awards) and encourages entities to adopt that method in place of the provisions of Opinion 25.

Appendix E

GLOSSARY

395. This appendix contains definitions of certain terms or phrases used in this Statement.

Combination plan
> An award with two (or more) separate components, all of which can be exercised. Each part of the award is actually a separate grant, and compensation cost is measured and recognized for each grant.

Cross-volatility
> A measure of the relationship between the volatilities of the prices of two assets taking into account the correlation between price movements in the assets.

Fair value

The amount at which an asset could be bought or sold in a current transaction between willing parties, that is, other than in a forced or liquidation sale. Quoted market prices in active markets are the best evidence of fair value and are to be used as the basis for measurement, if available. If quoted market prices are not available, the estimate of fair value is based on the best information available in the circumstances. The estimate of fair value considers prices for similar assets and the results of valuation techniques to the extent available in the circumstances. Examples of valuation techniques include the present value of estimated expected future cash flows using a discount rate commensurate with the risks involved, option-pricing models, matrix pricing, option-adjusted spread models, and fundamental analysis.

Fixed award

An award of stock-based employee compensation for which vesting is based solely on an employee's continuing to render service to the employer for a specified period of time, that is, an award that does not specify a performance condition for vesting. This Statement uses the term *fixed award* in a somewhat different sense than Opinion 25 uses the same or similar terms because Opinion 25 distinguishes between fixed awards and variable awards, while this Statement only distinguishes between fixed awards and performance awards. For example, Opinion 25 does not consider stock appreciation rights (SARs), regardless of whether they call for settlement in stock or in cash, to be fixed awards because the number of shares to which an employee is entitled is not known until the exercise date. This Statement considers an SAR that calls for settlement in stock to be substantially the same as a fixed stock option. A cash SAR is an indexed liability pursuant to this Statement, and the measurement date is the settlement (exercise) date because that is consistent with accounting for similar liabilities—not because a cash SAR is a variable award.

Grant date

The date at which an employer and an employee have a mutual understanding of the terms of a stock-based compensation award. The employer becomes contingently obligated on the grant date to issue equity instruments or transfer assets to employees who fulfill vesting requirements. Awards made under a plan that is subject to shareholder approval are not deemed to be granted until that approval is obtained unless approval is essentially a formality, for example, management and the members of the board of directors control enough votes to approve the plan. The grant date of an award for current service may be the end of a fiscal period instead of a subsequent date when an award is made to an individual employee if (a) the award is provided for by the terms of an established formal plan, (b) the plan designates the factors that determine the total dollar amount of awards to employees for that period (for example, a percentage of net income), and (c) the award is attributable to the employee's service during that period.

Intrinsic value

The amount by which the market price of the underlying stock exceeds the exercise price of an option. For example, an option with an exercise price of $20 on a stock whose current market price is $25 has an intrinsic value of $5.

Issuance of an equity instrument

An equity instrument is issued when the issuing entity receives the agreed-upon consideration, which may be cash, an enforceable right to receive cash or another financial instrument, goods, or services. An entity may conditionally transfer an equity instrument to another party under an arrangement that permits that party to choose at a later date or for a specified time whether to deliver the consideration or to forfeit the right to the conditionally transferred instrument with no further obligation. In that situation, the equity instrument is not *issued* until the issuing entity has received the consideration. For that reason, this Statement does not use the term *issued* for the grant of stock options or other equity instruments subject to service or performance conditions (or both) for vesting.

Measurement date

The date at which the stock price that enters into measurement of the fair value of an award of employee stock-based compensation is fixed.

Minimum value

An amount attributed to an option that is calculated without considering the expected volatility of the underlying stock. Minimum value may be computed using a standard option-pricing model and a volatility of effectively zero. It also may be computed as (a) the current price of the stock reduced to exclude the present value of any expected dividends during the option's life minus (b) the present value of the exercise price. Different methods of reducing the current price of the stock for the present value of the expected dividends, if any, may result in different computed minimum values.

Nonpublic entity

Any entity other than one (a) whose equity securities trade in a public market either on a stock exchange (domestic or foreign) or in the over-the-counter market, including securities quoted only locally or regionally, (b) that makes a filing with a regulatory agency in preparation for the sale of any class of equity securities in a public market, or (c) that is controlled by an entity covered by (a) or (b).

Nonvested stock

Shares of stock that cannot currently be sold because the employee to whom the shares were granted has not yet satisfied the vesting requirements necessary to earn the right to the shares. The restriction on sale of nonvested stock is due to the forfeitability of the shares. A share of nonvested stock also can be described as a nonvested employee stock option with a cash exercise price of zero—employee services are the only consideration the employer has received for the stock when the option is "exercised," and the employer issues vested, unrestricted shares to the employee.

Performance condition or performance award

An award of stock-based employee compensation for which vesting depends on both (a) an employee's rendering service to the employer for a specified period of time and (b) the achievement of a specified performance target, for example, attaining a specified growth rate in return on assets or a specified percentage increase in market share for a specified product. A performance condition might pertain either to the performance of the enterprise as a whole or to some part of the enterprise, such as a division.

Principal stockholder

One who either owns 10 percent or more of an entity's common stock or has the ability, directly or indirectly, to control or significantly influence the entity.

Public entity

Any entity (a) whose equity securities trade in a public market either on a stock exchange (domestic or foreign) or in the over-the-counter market, including securities quoted only locally or regionally, (b) that makes a filing with a regulatory agency in preparation for the sale of any class of equity securities in a public market, or (c) that is controlled by an entity covered by (a) or (b).

Reload option and option granted with a reload feature

An option with a reload feature is one that provides for automatic grants of additional options whenever an employee exercises previously granted options using shares of stock, rather than cash, to satisfy the exercise price. At the time of exercise using shares, the employee is automatically granted a new option, called a *reload option* for the same number of shares used to exercise the previous option. The number of reload options granted is the number of shares tendered, and the exercise price of the reload option is the market price of the stock on the date the reload option is granted. All terms of the reload option, such as expiration date and vesting status, are the same as the terms of the previous option.

Restricted stock

Shares of stock for which sale is contractually or governmentally restricted for a given period of time. Most stock grants to employees are better termed *nonvested stock* because the limitation on sale stems solely from the forfeitability of the shares before employees have satisfied the necessary service or performance requirements to earn the rights to the shares. Restricted stock issued for consideration other than employee services, on the other hand, is fully paid for immediately, that is, there is no period analogous to a vesting period during which the issuer is unilaterally obligated to issue the stock when the purchaser pays for it, but the purchaser is not obligated to buy the stock. This Statement uses the term *restricted stock* to refer only to fully vested and outstanding stock whose sale is contractually or governmentally restricted. (Refer to the definition of *nonvested stock*.)

Service period

The period or periods during which the employee performs the service in exchange for stock options or similar awards. If the service period is not defined as an earlier or shorter period, the service period is presumed to be the vesting period. However, if performance conditions affect either the exercise price or the exercisability date, this Statement requires that the service period over which compensation cost is attributed be consistent with the related assumption used in estimating the fair value of the award. Doing so will require estimates at the grant date, which will be subsequently adjusted as necessary to reflect experience that differs from initial expectations.

Stock option

A contract that gives the holder the right, but not the obligation, either to purchase or to sell a certain number of shares of stock at a predetermined price for a specified period of time.

Stock-based compensation plan

A compensation arrangement under which one or more employees receive shares of stock, stock options, or other equity instruments, or the employer incurs a liability(ies) to the employee(s) in amounts based on the price of the employer's stock.

Substantive terms

The terms of a stock-based compensation plan as those terms are mutually understood by the employer and the employee who receives a stock-based award under the plan. Although the written terms of a stock-based compensation plan usually provide the best evidence of the plan's terms, an entity's past practice may indicate that some aspects of the substantive terms differ from the written terms.

Tandem plan

An award with two (or more) components in which exercise of one part cancels the other(s).

Time value

The portion of the fair value of an option that exceeds its intrinsic value. For example, an option with an exercise price of $20 on a stock whose current market price is $25 has intrinsic value of $5. If the fair value of that option is $7, the time value of the option is $2 ($7 − $5).

Vest or Vested

To earn the rights to. An employee's award of stock-based compensation becomes vested at the date that the employee's right to receive or retain shares of stock or cash under the award is no longer contingent on remaining in the service of the employer or the achievement of a performance condition (other than the achievement of a target stock price or specified amount of intrinsic value). Typically, an employee stock option that is vested also is immediately exercisable.

Volatility

A measure of the amount by which a price has fluctuated (historical volatility) or is expected to fluctuate (expected volatility) during a period. The volatility of a stock is the standard deviation of the continuously compounded rates of return on the stock over a specified period. That is the same as the standard deviation of the differences in the natural logarithms of the stock prices plus dividends, if any, over the period. The higher the volatility, the more the returns on the stock can be expected to vary—up or down. Volatility is typically expressed in annualized terms that are comparable regardless of the time period used in the calculation, for example, daily, weekly, or monthly price observations.

The *rate of return* (which may be positive or negative) on a stock for a period measures how much a stockholder has benefited from dividends and appreciation (or depreciation) of the share price. Return on a stated rate increases as compounding becomes more frequent, approaching e^{rate} as a limit as the frequency of compounding approaches continuous. For example, the continuously compounded return on a stated rate of 9 percent is $e^{(.09)}$. (The base of the natural logarithm system is e, which is a constant, transcendental number, the first 5 digits of which are 2.7183.) Stock price changes are log-normally distributed, but continuously compounded rates of return on stocks are normally distributed.

The expected annualized volatility of a stock is the range within which the continuously compounded annual rate of return is expected to fall roughly two-thirds of the time. For example, to say that a stock with an expected continuously compounded rate of return of 12 percent has a volatility of 30 percent means that the probability that the rate of return on the stock for 1 year will fall between -18 percent (12% – 30%) and 42 percent (12% + 30%) is approximately two-thirds. If the stock price is $100 at the beginning of the year and it does not pay dividends, the year-end price would be expected to fall between $83.53 ($100 × e^{(-.18)}) and $152.20 ($100 × e^{(.42)}) approximately two-thirds of the time.

For the convenience of those who are not familiar with the concept of volatility, Appendix F provides more information on volatility and shows one way in which an electronic spreadsheet may be used to calculate historical volatility based on weekly price observations.

Appendix F

CALCULATING HISTORICAL VOLATILITY

Introduction

396. As discussed in paragraphs 273-278 of Appendix B, estimating expected long-term future volatility generally begins with calculating historical volatility for a similar long-term period and then considering the effects of ways in which the future is reasonably expected to differ from the past. For some mature entities, unadjusted long-term historical volatility may be the best available predictor of future long-term volatility. However, this appendix should be read in the context of paragraphs 284 and 285 of Appendix B, which mention factors that should be considered in determining whether historical volatility is a reasonable indicator of expected future volatility.

397. The concept of volatility and the reason that it is an important factor in estimating the fair value of an option is well explained in various texts on option-pricing models and the use of derivative financial instruments. However, those texts are generally directed more at mathematicians than at accountants, and one without an extensive background in statistics and mathematics may find them difficult to understand. During the exposure process and the field test, the staff received numerous requests for help in understanding the notion of volatility, especially for an illustration of how to compute historical volatility. This appendix responds to that request.

398. The goal of this appendix is not to explain the development of traditional option-pricing models and why they are valid. Sources for that information are

available. Several currently available articles and texts that explain option-pricing models and the place of volatility in option value are listed at the end of this appendix. This appendix is intended to help someone familiar with the use of electronic spreadsheets to compute historical volatility in three common situations. The illustrations do not provide a rigorous explanation of the mathematical concepts underlying the computations. In addition, the illustrations do not illustrate the only possible way of calculating historical volatility; for example, observations at daily or monthly, rather than weekly, intervals might have been used.

399. This appendix also is not intended to deemphasize the importance of adjusting historical volatility, however computed, to reflect ways in which future volatility is reasonably expected to differ from historical volatility for entity-specific reasons.

Volatility Is a Standard Deviation

400. The needed assumption about expected volatility for use in the traditional Black-Scholes and binomial option-pricing models is the *annualized* standard deviation of the differences in the natural logarithms of the possible future stock prices. Natural logarithms are needed to compute the continuous rate of return reflected in the change from one stock price to another, plus dividends, if any. A standard deviation is a statistical method used to convert a series of natural logarithms of stock price changes into a single, usable statistic—volatility. Like rates of return, volatility can be measured over any time period. For convenience and consistency, volatility is generally expressed on an annual basis even if the measurement period is longer or shorter than one year.

Computing Historical Volatility for a Stock That Pays No Dividends

401. The first step in computing historical volatility is to gather the necessary stock prices. The expected lives of employee stock options generally are several years long, so weekly (perhaps even monthly) stock price observations generally should be sufficient. (Volatility estimates for shorter-term options, such as 30-, 60-, or 90-day options commonly traded on exchanges, generally rely on daily, or even more frequent, stock price observations). The consistency of the time intervals between observations is critical—determining the frequency of the observations is not as critical, although the frequency of observations

likely will affect the computed volatility. The time intervals between price observations should be as uniform as possible; for example, the weekly stock closing price could be used for all observations. It would not be appropriate to use the weekly closing price for some observations and, for example, the average weekly price for other observations in the same calculation.

402. The Board is not aware of any research that demonstrates conclusively how long the historical period used to estimate expected long-term future volatility should be. However, informal tests and preliminary research tends to confirm the intuitive expectation that long-term historical volatility generally predicts long-term future volatility better than short-term historical volatility predicts long-term future volatility. Paragraph 285 of this Statement says that estimates of expected future long-term volatility should be based on historical volatility for a period that approximates the expected life of the option being valued. For example, if the expected life of an employee stock option is three years, historical volatility might be based on weekly closing stock prices for the most recent three years. In that situation, approximately 157 weekly stock price observations would be needed (52 observations per year for 3 years plus the initial observation).

403. For convenience, the illustrative calculations are based on only 20 price observations, which is generally considered to be the minimum number of sample observations necessary to compute a statistically valid estimate of standard deviation. Therefore, the table shows the calculation of the annualized historical volatility based on 19 weeks of stock price activity. More than 20 price observations would be necessary for long-term employee stock options; more observations also would improve the statistical validity of the estimate of expected volatility.

404. In the following table, column B contains the 20 stock price observations for the 19-week period. Each cell in column C contains the ratio of the stock price at the end of that week to the stock price at the end of the preceding week. That is designated by the symbol P_n/P_{n-1}. For example, in week 4, the number in column C is computed as the week 4 stock closing price ($48.50) divided by the week 3 stock closing price ($51.00), or 0.95098. Column D is the natural logarithm (the mathematical expression *Ln*) of the amount computed in column C. The weekly volatility estimate is the standard deviation of the amounts shown in column D. Most, if not all, electronic spreadsheets include a standard deviation function that will automatically compute the standard deviation of a series of amounts.

Table 1

A	B	C	D
Date	Stock Price	P_n/P_{n-1}	$Ln(P_n/P_{n-1})$
Week 0	$50.00		
Week 1	51.50	1.030000	0.029559
Week 2	52.00	1.009709	0.009662
Week 3	51.00	0.980769	-0.019418
Week 4	48.50	0.950980	-0.050262
Week 5	46.50	0.958763	-0.042111
Week 6	45.75	0.983871	-0.016261
Week 7	50.50	1.103825	0.098782
Week 8	53.50	1.059406	0.057708
Week 9	51.75	0.967290	-0.033257
Week 10	53.25	1.028986	0.028573
Week 11	54.50	1.023474	0.023203
Week 12	56.00	1.027523	0.027151
Week 13	53.50	0.955357	-0.045670
Week 14	52.00	0.971963	-0.028438
Week 15	55.00	1.057692	0.056089
Week 16	56.25	1.022727	0.022473
Week 17	58.00	1.031111	0.030637
Week 18	55.50	0.956897	-0.044060
Week 19	56.00	1.009009	0.008969
Weekly Volatility			**0.041516**
Annualized Volatility	$0.041516\sqrt{52}$		**0.299**

405. Weekly volatility must be converted to an annualized measure of volatility before it can be used in most option-pricing models. To convert from periodic to annualized volatility, the periodic volatility is multiplied by the square root of the number of periods in a year. In this example, weekly observations are used. There are 52 weeks in a year, so weekly volatility is multiplied by the square root of 52 to convert it to annualized volatility. If monthly stock price observations were used, the monthly volatility would be multiplied by the square root of 12 to convert to annualized volatility. Likewise, daily volatility would be multiplied by the square root of the number of trading days in the year to compute annualized volatility (about 260). The annualization calculation is independent of the number of observations used to compute the periodic historical volatility. For example, whether 20 or 157 weeks of data are used to compute weekly volatility, that weekly volatility must be multiplied by the square root of 52 to convert it to annual volatility.

Computing Historical Volatility for a Dividend-Paying Stock

406. Computing volatility for a dividend-paying stock is very similar to computing volatility for a stock that does not pay dividends. The only difference is an adjustment for dividends paid. Because volatility is defined as the standard deviation of the total return on a stock, dividend payments, which are part of the total return, affect the computation. The price change resulting solely from the effect of dividend payment on the stock price must be removed from the price observations used to calculate volatility.

407. As discussed in paragraph 401, stock price observations used in the calculations should be separated by uniform time periods. When gathering data, it is important to observe the payment of dividends. If an ex-dividend date occurs between two price observations, the per-share dollar amount of the dividends should be noted. For example, if the ex-dividend date for a dividend of one dollar occurs between the third and fourth weekly price observations, that payment should be noted when gathering stock price observations. In computing historical volatility, dividends must be added to the stock price after the ex-dividend date before the ratio in column C (the price after the dividend to the price before the dividend) is computed. Note that the market reflects the effect of a dividend payment on the stock price on the ex-dividend date, not the date of the cash distribution, because the ex-dividend date is the last date that a seller, rather than a purchaser, of stock is entitled to the dividend.

408. The following table illustrates the computation of historical volatility based on weekly stock closing prices for a company that pays a dividend of $1 between both the week 3 and week 4 price observations and the week 15 and week 16 price observations.

Table 2

A	B	C	D
Date	**Stock Price**	P_n/P_{n-1}	$Ln(P_n/P_{n-1})$
Week 0	$50.00		
Week 1	51.50	1.030000	0.029559
Week 2	52.00	1.009709	0.009662
Week 3	51.00	0.980769	-0.019418
Week 4	48.50		
Dividend Adjusted	49.50	0.970588	-0.029853
Week 5	46.50	0.958763	-0.042111
Week 6	45.75	0.983871	-0.016261
Week 7	50.50	1.103825	0.098782
Week 8	53.50	1.059406	0.057708
Week 9	51.75	0.967290	-0.033257
Week 10	53.25	1.028986	0.028573
Week 11	54.50	1.023474	0.023203
Week 12	56.00	1.027523	0.027151
Week 13	53.50	0.955357	-0.045670
Week 14	52.00	0.971963	-0.028438
Week 15	55.00	1.057692	0.056089
Week 16	56.25		
Dividend Adjusted	57.25	1.040909	0.040094
Week 17	58.00	1.031111	0.030637
Week 18	55.50	0.956897	-0.044060
Week 19	56.00	1.009009	0.008969
Weekly Volatility			**0.040799**
Annualized Volatility	$.040799\sqrt{52}$		**0.294**

409. The only difference between Table 2 and Table 1 is the necessary adjustment in Table 2 for the dividend payments made between the week 3 and week 4 observations and between the week 15 and week 16 observations. In each case, the ratio of the current period stock price to the prior period stock price must be adjusted for the dividend payment. For example, the pre-dividend week 3 observation is used in the ratio of the week 3 stock price to the week 2 stock price. Then, the post-dividend week 4 stock price must be adjusted by the amount of the dividend payment before the ratio of the week 4 stock price to the week 3 stock price is computed in column C (both stock prices in the ratio must be either pre-dividend or post-dividend). That adjustment is necessary to isolate the price change effect in the change from week 3 to week 4 that is independent from the stock price decrease caused by the dividend payment.

Computing Historical Volatility for a Stock That Has Split

410. If a stock split occurs during the historical period over which volatility is to be calculated, an adjustment much like the one for a dividend payment is required for that split. For computing the ratio of the stock prices around the period of the split, the prices must be shown in consistent form, that is, either pre-split or post-split. For example, in Table 2, if a stock split had occurred between the week 16 and week 17 stock price observations, the price observed in week 17 would be $29 instead of the $58 shown in the table. For computing column B, the ratio of the week 16 stock price to the week 15 stock price would be unchanged, but the ratio of the week 17 to the week 16 price would need adjustment. The split-adjusted week 17 stock price of $29 should be divided by the split-adjusted week 16 stock price, which is $28.125. After the adjustment is made for the stock split, the calculation of historical volatility

is the same as in Table 2. If the only difference from the Table 2 stock price changes is the stock split, the historical volatility would be the same as the volatility computed in Table 2 because the stock split would not alter the relative size of the random stock price changes that volatility measures.

Sources for Further Information about Option-Pricing Models and Volatility

411. The following sources provide further information on option-pricing models and the relationship of volatility to option value:

- Black, Fischer, and Myron Scholes. "The Pricing of Options and Corporate Liabilities." *The Journal of Political Economy 81*, 3 (May-June 1973): 637-654.
- Cox, John C., and Mark Rubinstein. *Option Markets*. Englewood Cliffs, N.J.: Prentice-Hall, Inc., 1985.
- Figlewski, Stephen, William L. Silber, and Marti G. Subrahmanyam, eds. *Financial Options: From Theory to Practice*. New York: New York University, Business One Irwin, 1990.
- Hull, John C. *Options, Futures, and Other Derivative Securities*. Englewood Cliffs, N.J.: Prentice-Hall, Inc., 1993.
- Smithson, Charles W., Clifford W. Smith, Jr., and D. Sykes Wilford. *Managing Financial Risk*. New York: Richard D. Irwin, Inc., 1995.

Those sources include the classic works in which the Black-Scholes and binomial option-pricing models were first developed and other sources that may be useful.

Statement of Financial Accounting Standards No. 124
Accounting for Certain Investments Held by Not-for-Profit Organizations

STATUS

Issued: November 1995

Effective Date: For fiscal years beginning after December 15, 1995

Affects: Amends FAS 60, paragraph 45
Supersedes FAS 60, paragraph 46
Amends FAS 65, paragraph 4
Amends FAS 91, paragraph 3
Amends FAS 115, paragraph 4
Amends FAS 117, paragraph 168

Affected by: No other pronouncements

Issues Discussed by FASB Emerging Issues Task Force (EITF)

Affects: No EITF Issues

Interpreted by: Paragraph 11 interpreted by EITF Topic No. D-49

Related Issues: No EITF Issues

SUMMARY

This Statement establishes standards for accounting for certain investments held by not-for-profit organizations. It requires that investments in equity securities with readily determinable fair values and all investments in debt securities be reported at fair value with gains and losses included in a statement of activities. This Statement requires certain disclosures about investments held by not-for-profit organizations and the return on those investments.

This Statement also establishes standards for reporting losses on investments held because of a donor's stipulation to invest a gift in perpetuity or for a specified term.

This Statement is effective for annual financial statements issued for fiscal years beginning after December 15, 1995. Earlier application is encouraged. This Statement is applied either by restating the financial statements of all prior years presented or by recognizing the cumulative effect of the change in the year of the change. The expiration of restrictions on previously unrecognized net gains may be recognized prospectively.

Statement of Financial Accounting Standards No. 124

Accounting for Certain Investments Held by Not-for-Profit Organizations

CONTENTS

INTRODUCTION

1. This Statement establishes standards of financial accounting and reporting for certain investments in **securities**[1] and establishes disclosure requirements for most investments held by not-for-profit organizations.

2. Guidance for accounting for and reporting of investments held by not-for-profit organizations is currently provided primarily by the AICPA Guides listed in paragraph 22. This Statement is part of a broader FASB agenda project that considers several inconsistencies in that guidance. In addition, this Statement considers many of the same concerns that were examined for business enterprises in FASB Statement No. 115, *Accounting for Certain Investments in Debt and Equity Securities*. Because this Statement establishes standards for certain investments, provisions in the AICPA Guides that are inconsistent with this Statement are no longer acceptable *specialized*[2] accounting and reporting principles and practices.

STANDARDS OF FINANCIAL ACCOUNTING AND REPORTING

Scope

3. The measurement standards of paragraph 7 apply to investments in **equity securities** that have readily determinable fair values, except those described in paragraph 5, and to all investments in **debt securities.** For purposes of this Statement, the **fair value** of an equity security is readily determinable if one of the following three criteria is met:

a. Sales prices or bid-and-asked quotations for the security are currently available on a securities exchange registered with the Securities and Exchange Commission (SEC) or in the over-the-counter market, provided that those prices or quotations for the over-the-counter market are publicly reported by the National Association of Securities Dealers Automated Quotations systems

---

[1]Words that appear in the glossary are set in **boldface type** the first time they appear.

[2]The term *specialized* is used to refer to the current accounting and reporting principles and practices in the existing AICPA Guides and Statements of Position that are neither superseded by nor contained in Accounting Research Bulletins, APB Opinions, FASB Statements, or FASB Interpretations.

or by the National Quotation Bureau. Restricted stock[3] does not meet that definition.

b. For an equity security traded only in a foreign market, that foreign market is of a breadth and scope comparable to one of the U.S. markets referred to above.

c. For an investment in a mutual fund, the fair value per share (unit) is determined and published and is the basis for current transactions.

4. The reporting standards of paragraphs 8-16 apply to all investments held by not-for-profit organizations, except those described in paragraph 5.

5. This Statement does not apply to investments in equity securities that are accounted for under the equity method or to investments in consolidated subsidiaries.

6. Generally accepted accounting principles other than those discussed in this Statement also apply to investments held by not-for-profit organizations. For example, not-for-profit organizations must disclose information required by FASB Statements No. 105, *Disclosure of Information about Financial Instruments with Off-Balance-Sheet Risk and Financial Instruments with Concentrations of Credit Risk,* No. 107, *Disclosures about Fair Value of Financial Instruments,* and No. 119, *Disclosure about Derivative Financial Instruments and Fair Value of Financial Instruments.*

Accounting for Investments in Debt Securities and Certain Equity Securities

7. Investments in equity securities with readily determinable fair values and all investments in debt securities shall be measured at fair value in the statement of financial position.

Reporting Investment Gains, Losses, and Income

8. Pursuant to paragraph 22 of FASB Statement No. 117, *Financial Statements of Not-for-Profit Organizations,* gains and losses on investments shall be reported in the statement of activities as increases or decreases in unrestricted net assets unless their use is temporarily or permanently restricted by explicit donor stipulations or by law.

9. Pursuant to paragraph 20 of Statement 117, dividend, interest, and other investment income shall be reported in the period earned as increases in unrestricted net assets unless the use of the assets received is limited by donor-imposed restrictions. Donor-restricted investment income is reported as an increase in temporarily restricted net assets or permanently restricted net assets, depending on the type of restriction. This Statement does not specify methods to be used for measuring the amount of dividend and interest income.

10. Gains and investment income that are limited to specific uses by donor-imposed restrictions may be reported as increases in unrestricted net assets if the restrictions are met in the same reporting period as the gains and income are recognized, provided that the organization has a similar policy for reporting contributions received, reports consistently from period to period, and discloses its accounting policy.

Donor-Restricted Endowment Funds

11. A donor's stipulation that requires a gift to be invested in perpetuity or for a specified term creates a **donor-restricted endowment fund.** Unless gains and losses are temporarily or permanently restricted by a donor's explicit stipulation or by a law that extends a donor's restriction to them, gains and losses on investments of a donor-restricted endowment fund are changes in unrestricted net assets. For example, if a donor states that a specific investment security must be held in perpetuity, the gains and losses on that security are subject to that same permanent restriction unless the donor specifies otherwise. However, if a donor allows the organization to choose suitable investments, the gains are not permanently restricted unless the donor or the law requires that an amount be retained permanently. Instead, those gains are unrestricted if the investment income is unrestricted or are temporarily restricted if the investment income is temporarily restricted by the donor.

12. In the absence of donor stipulations or law to the contrary, losses on the investments of a donor-restricted endowment fund shall reduce temporarily restricted net assets to the extent that donor-imposed temporary restrictions on net appreciation of the fund have not been met before the loss occurs. Any remaining loss shall reduce unrestricted net assets.

---

[3]For the purpose of this Statement, *restricted stock* means equity securities for which sale is restricted at acquisition by governmental or contractual requirement (other than in connection with being pledged as collateral) except if that requirement terminates within one year or if the holder has the power by contract or otherwise to cause the requirement to be met within one year. Any portion of the security that can be reasonably expected to qualify for sale within one year, such as may be the case under Rule 144 or similar rules of the SEC, is not considered restricted.

13. If losses reduce the assets of a donor-restricted endowment fund below the level required by the donor stipulations or law,[4] gains that restore the fair value of the assets of the endowment fund to the required level shall be classified as increases in unrestricted net assets.

Disclosures

14. For each period for which a statement of activities is presented, a not-for-profit organization shall disclose:

a. The composition of investment return including, at a minimum, investment income, net realized gains or losses on investments reported at other than fair value, and net gains or losses on investments reported at fair value
b. A reconciliation of investment return to amounts reported in the statement of activities if investment return is separated into operating and nonoperating amounts, together with a description of the policy used to determine the amount that is included in the measure of operations and a discussion of circumstances leading to a change, if any, in that policy.

15. For each period for which a statement of financial position is presented, a not-for-profit organization shall disclose:

a. The aggregate carrying amount of investments by major types, for example, equity securities, U.S. Treasury securities, corporate debt securities, mortgage-backed securities, oil and gas properties, and real estate
b. The basis for determining the carrying amount for investments other than equity securities with readily determinable fair values and all debt securities
c. The method(s) and significant assumptions used to estimate the fair values of investments other

than financial instruments[5] if those other investments are reported at fair value
d. The aggregate amount of the deficiencies for all donor-restricted endowment funds for which the fair value of the assets at the reporting date is less than the level required by donor stipulations or law.

16. For the most recent period for which a statement of financial position is presented, a not-for-profit organization shall disclose the nature of and carrying amount for each individual investment or group of investments that represents a significant concentration of market risk.[6]

Effective Date and Transition

17. This Statement shall be effective for fiscal years beginning after December 15, 1995, and interim periods within those fiscal years. Earlier application is encouraged.

18. Unless this Statement is applied retroactively under the provisions of paragraph 19, the effect of initially applying this Statement shall be reported as the effect of a change in accounting principle in a manner similar to the cumulative effect of a change in accounting principle (APB Opinion No. 20, *Accounting Changes,* paragraph 19). The amount of the cumulative effect shall be based on a retroactive computation, except that the expiration of restrictions on previously unrecognized gains and losses may be recognized prospectively.[7] A not-for-profit organization shall report the cumulative effect of a change in accounting on each class of net assets in the statement of activities between the captions "extraordinary items," if any, and "change in unrestricted net assets," "change in temporarily restricted net assets," and "change in permanently restricted net assets."

19. This Statement may be applied retroactively by restating the beginning net assets for the earliest year presented or, if no prior years are presented, for the

---

[4]Donors that create endowment funds can require that their gifts be invested in perpetuity or for a specified term. Some donors may require that a portion of income, gains, or both be added to the gift and invested subject to similar restrictions. It is generally understood that at least the amount of the original gift(s) and any required accumulations is not expendable, although the value of the investments purchased may occasionally fall below that amount. Future appreciation of the investments generally restores the value to the required level. In states that have enacted its provisions, the Uniform Management of Institutional Funds Act describes "historic dollar value" as the amount that is not expendable.

[5]Paragraph 10 of Statement 107 requires organizations to disclose the method(s) and significant assumptions used to estimate the fair value of *financial instruments.*

[6]Paragraph 20 of Statement 105 requires organizations to disclose all significant concentrations of *credit risk* arising from financial instruments, whether from an individual counterparty or groups of counterparties.

[7]Paragraph 17 of FASB Statement No. 116, *Accounting for Contributions Received and Contributions Made,* establishes standards for recognizing the expiration of donor-imposed restrictions. Those standards also apply to the expiration of donor-imposed restrictions on investment income, gains, and losses. A similar provision permitting prospective recognition of the expirations of restrictions is included in paragraphs 29 and 30 of Statement 116.

year this Statement is first applied. The expiration of restrictions on previously unrecognized gains and losses may be recognized prospectively. In the period that this Statement is first applied, a not-for-profit or-ganization shall disclose the nature of any restatement and its effect on the change in net assets and on each class of net assets for each period presented.

> **The provisions of this Statement need not be applied to immaterial items.**

This Statement was adopted by the affirmative votes of five members of the Financial Accounting Standards Board. Messrs. Beresford and Northcutt dissented.

Mr. Beresford disagrees with the standard in paragraph 7 that requires all investments in debt securities to be measured at fair value. Mr. Beresford believes this Statement should require a two-category approach. Under that approach, debt securities that an organization has the positive intent and ability to hold to maturity would be reported at amortized cost. Other debt securities and equity securities with readily determinable fair values would be reported at fair value. If a debt security is held to maturity, interim changes in that security's market value do not affect either the amount or timing of net cash flows to the entity. Consequently, Mr. Beresford agrees with the Board's conclusion in paragraph 58 of Statement 115 that "amortized cost is most likely to be relevant for those debt securities that will be held to maturity," and he believes that different accounting treatment is warranted for those debt securities. He believes that not-for-profit organizations should have the same ability as business enterprises to measure those securities at amortized cost.

Mr. Beresford also believes that more restrictive display requirements are necessary when amounts computed under a spending-rate or other budgetary method are included within an organization's measure of operations. He believes that users of financial statements might be misled if the amount reported within an operating measure is greater than the actual return for the period. He would limit the amount reported within the operating measure to actual gains and losses for the period—those amounts are based on the nature of the underlying transactions rather than on spending-rate or budgetary designations.

Mr. Northcutt disagrees with the standards in paragraphs 11-13, which prescribe the accounting for losses on the investments of donor-restricted endowment funds. Mr. Northcutt believes this Statement should require the method described in paragraphs 78 and 79, in which losses on investments of perma-nently restricted endowment funds reduce the net asset classes in which unappropriated net appreciation of the fund is reported and any additional losses reduce permanently restricted net assets. In Mr. Northcutt's view, the method required by paragraphs 11-13 has three main problems.

First, Mr. Northcutt believes that the method required by this Statement fails to acknowledge that not-for-profit organizations identify the assets of each endowment fund and the investment income earned by those assets because they have fiduciary responsibilities and must be able to demonstrate that they are complying with the donors' stipulations and applicable laws. Because the assets of an endowment fund are known, classification of the net assets related to those assets is straightforward. First, the portion of the net assets that may never be spent because of donor or legal restrictions should be classified as permanently restricted net assets. Next, net appreciation for which restrictions on expenditure have not yet been met should be classified as temporarily restricted net assets. Finally, the remaining portion of net appreciation should be classified as unrestricted net assets. If a loss reduces the value of the assets of an endowment fund, the classification of the net assets related to the remaining assets follows the same procedure. If a loss reduces the assets of an endowment fund below the amount that must be maintained in perpetuity (historic dollar value), those assets are entirely unexpendable and all the net assets of that endowment fund should be classified as permanently restricted.

Mr. Northcutt acknowledges that the method he prefers must either define the assets of the fund or tolerate the effects of differing definitions. A definition requires a method for identifying when assets are removed from the fund for spending and thus are no longer present to absorb losses. Mr. Northcutt accepts the method provided in the Uniform Management of Institutional Funds Act for removing net appreciation—appropriation. He would define the assets of an endowment fund using appropriation because he believes the effects of management's discretion on classification of net assets are limited. An appropriation for expenditure does not change the class of net assets in which the appropriated amount is reported. An appropriation does not change when restrictions on net appreciation expire. When a loss occurs, only one classification of net assets is possible because an appropriation either was made or was not made prior to the loss. An appropriation can be made only when the fund has available net appreciation, and amounts appropriated may not be returned to the fund. The appropriation determines only the amount of net appreciation of a donor-restricted endowment fund that is available to absorb a future loss.

Mr. Northcutt recognizes that attributing significance to the act of appropriation for purposes of classifying losses on endowment funds may be viewed as inconsistent with the Board's decisions in Statements 116 and 117. He would be willing to amend Statement 117 to allow an exception only for this case.

Second, Mr. Northcutt believes that the method of accounting for losses described in this Statement can result in the classification of permanently restricted net assets and unrestricted net assets in a manner that is inconsistent with the definitions of those classes of net assets. That method can result in an overstatement of permanently restricted net assets, which could lead users to believe that there are more assets generating income for support of the organization than there actually are. That method also can result in an understatement of the net resources that an organization as a whole has available to meet current operating needs.

Third, Mr. Northcutt believes that the method described in paragraphs 11-13 of this Statement misclassifies the gains that restore the fair value of the assets of the endowment fund to the level required by donor stipulations or law. That method would report future gains as increases in unrestricted net assets, even though the amount of net resources that are expendable for current operating needs is unchanged. In effect, gains that must be retained in perpetuity because of a donor-imposed restriction will be reported as increases in unrestricted net assets, which makes sense only because it corrects the erroneous reporting of the year of the loss.

Appendix A

BACKGROUND INFORMATION

20. In March 1986, the Board added a project to its agenda to resolve certain inconsistent accounting practices of not-for-profit organizations. The Board identified five areas of inconsistency that persist, in part, because the specialized accounting principles and practices in the AICPA Guides for not-for-profit organizations contain inconsistent requirements. Accounting for investments, one of the five areas, was initially included in the financial instruments project, which was added to the Board's agenda in May 1986.

21. FASB Statement No. 115, *Accounting for Certain Investments in Debt and Equity Securities*, issued in May 1993, specifically excluded not-for-profit organizations from its scope. The Board decided to consider the issues about investments held by not-for-profit organizations after it resolved its agenda projects on accounting for contributions and financial statement display by those organizations. FASB Statements No. 116, *Accounting for Contributions Received and Contributions Made*, and No. 117, *Financial Statements of Not-for-Profit Organizations*, were issued in June 1993. In February 1994, the Board began deliberations to establish standards for reporting investments held by not-for-profit organizations.

22. Current guidance for accounting for and reporting of investments held by not-for-profit organizations is provided by the following four AICPA Guides:

a. *Audits of Colleges and Universities*
b. *Audits of Voluntary Health and Welfare Organizations*
c. *Audits of Providers of Health Care Services*
d. *Audits of Certain Nonprofit Organizations.*

The requirements in those Guides are similar in some respects. In other respects they differ from each other and from generally accepted accounting principles applicable to other entities. The inconsistencies lead to differences in accounting practices and, hence, to comparability and understandability problems. Further, three of the Guides permit accounting alternatives that lead to further inconsistencies within the subsector they cover.

23. In addition to the inconsistencies in the Guides, the Board identified other problems that this project should attempt to resolve:

a. *Greater relevance of fair value information.* Some believe that fair value information about investments is a more relevant measure of the ability of the organization's assets to support operations than cost-based information.
b. *LOCOM is not evenhanded.* The lower-of-cost-or-market method, which is required by one Guide and permitted by another, is not evenhanded because it recognizes the net diminution in value but not the net appreciation in the value of investments.
c. *Managing change in net assets.* Cost-based measures create situations in which decisions to sell certain securities may be based on the sale's effect on the change in net assets. Organizations may choose to sell appreciated securities to recognize the unrealized gains while choosing to retain other securities with unrealized losses. Similarly, organizations may choose to sell securities with unrealized losses while choosing to retain appreciated securities to reduce the change in net assets.

d. *Accounting based on intent.* Accounting standards based on the intent of management make the accounting treatment depend on the plans of management rather than the economic characteristics of an asset. Intent-based accounting impairs comparability.

24. The Board discussed the resolution of those problems at a number of public Board meetings. In March 1995, the Board issued the Exposure Draft, *Accounting for Certain Investments Held by Not-for-Profit Organizations.* The Board and staff analyzed the 86 comment letters received and obtained additional information from a field test of the proposed requirements for classification of losses on investments of endowment funds and from a meeting with rating agency analysts, officers of grant-making foundations, and others who use the financial statements of not-for-profit organizations. The concerns raised by respondents, field test participants, and users of financial statements were considered by the Board at additional public Board meetings. Throughout the project, the Board and staff consulted with the members of the FASB Task Force on Accounting Issues for Not-for-Profit Organizations, including discussing the Board's tentative decisions at a June 1994 public meeting. The Board decided that it could reach an informed decision without holding a public hearing.

Appendix B

BASIS FOR CONCLUSIONS

CONTENTS

Appendix B

BASIS FOR CONCLUSIONS

Introduction

25. This appendix summarizes considerations that Board members deemed significant in reaching the conclusions in this Statement. It includes reasons for accepting certain views and rejecting others. Individual Board members gave greater weight to some factors than to others.

Benefits and Costs

26. The mission of the Board is to establish and improve standards of financial accounting and reporting for the guidance and education of the public, including issuers, auditors, and users of financial information. In fulfilling that mission, the Board strives to determine that a proposed standard will fill a significant need and that the costs imposed to meet that standard, as compared with other alternatives, are justified in relation to the overall benefits of the resulting infor-

mation. Present and potential donors, creditors, members, and others all benefit from improvements in financial reporting; however, the costs to implement a new standard may not be borne evenly by all parties. Further, the costs of not issuing a standard are impossible to quantify. Because there is no common gauge by which to judge objectively the costs to implement a standard against the need to improve information in financial statements, the Board's assessment of the costs and benefits of issuing an accounting standard is unavoidably subjective.

27. The benefits of reporting debt and certain equity securities at fair value are discussed in paragraphs 33-40. In addition to those benefits, fair value measurement resolves for those investments each of the problems discussed in paragraph 23 of Appendix A. This Statement enhances comparability by eliminating the inconsistencies in the current guidance for reporting carrying amounts of equity securities with readily determinable fair values and all debt securities. For those securities, this Statement also removes the bias implicit in LOCOM accounting, precludes opportunities for managing change in net assets through selective sale of securities, and

eliminates the subjectivity of accounting based on management's intent.

28. The Board concluded that the overall benefits of the information provided by applying this Statement justify the costs that this Statement may impose. Because the AICPA Guides and FASB Statement No. 107, *Disclosures about Fair Value of Financial Instruments,* require that not-for-profit organizations disclose fair value information for investments reported at cost, organizations generally have the information systems that are needed to meet the requirements of this Statement. Although there will be transitional costs as not-for-profit organizations apply the requirements, the Board believes that the ongoing costs of applying this Statement should not be significantly greater than for existing requirements. The Board also believes that some of the costs this Statement imposes have been reduced in various ways: by limiting the scope of the measurement standards to equity securities whose fair values are readily determinable and to debt securities, by providing broad guidance and allowing some latitude in how information is reported in financial statements, and by eliminating requirements to disclose cost-based information for investments reported at fair value.

Scope

29. This Statement provides measurement standards for most investments held by not-for-profit organizations. Some not-for-profit organizations have more complex investment portfolios that include investments that are outside the scope of this Statement. A broader scope would have included investments such as interests in trusts, joint-venture agreements, oil and gas properties, real estate, and investments in closely held companies and partnerships. Those investments could have raised significant valuation issues that might not have been resolved in time to coordinate the implementation of this Statement with the implementation of Statements 116 and 117.

30. Most respondents to the Exposure Draft agreed with the Board's decision to limit the scope of this Statement. A few of those respondents said that the Board should consider carefully any requests to expand the scope to include investments that are not readily marketable. They were troubled by the subjectivity that may be necessary in estimating fair values. The Board understands that reliability is an important factor in financial reporting and, therefore, limited the scope for equity securities to those that have readily determinable fair values. The scope of this Statement includes all debt instruments that are securities because the Board believes that sufficiently reliable estimates of fair value can be made for those instruments.

31. A few other respondents indicated that the scope should be expanded to include either all investments or all financial instruments. Provisions of the AICPA Guides remain in effect for measuring investments that are not within the scope of this Statement, including impairment of investments reported using cost-based measures. Where permitted by the relevant AICPA Guide, the Board does not discourage not-for-profit organizations from using fair value to measure investments that are outside the scope of this Statement; the Board limited the scope for practical reasons.

32. The Board decided to use the definitions of *security, equity security, debt security,* and *readily determinable fair value* that were developed in Statement 115 to ensure that this Statement and Statement 115 apply to the same investments. In the future, the Board expects to consider the accounting for other financial instruments held by business enterprises and not-for-profit organizations within the financial instruments project that is currently on its technical agenda.

Accounting for Certain Investments in Debt and Equity Securities

Relevance of Fair Values of Investments in Securities

33. The Board concluded that measuring investments in debt and equity securities at fair value in the financial statements provides information that is relevant and useful to present and potential donors, creditors, and others in making rational decisions about the allocation of resources to not-for-profit organizations—the first objective of financial reporting discussed in FASB Concepts Statement No. 4, *Objectives of Financial Reporting by Nonbusiness Organizations.*

34. Measuring those investments at fair value also serves to achieve the second objective of financial reporting—providing information that is useful in assessing the ability of the organization to provide services. Fair value more accurately measures the resources available to provide mission-related services because it portrays the market's estimate of the net

future cash flows of those securities, discounted to reflect both time value and risk. "The assessment of cash flow potential is important because it relates directly to the organization's ability to provide the goods and services for which it exists" (Concepts Statement 4, paragraph 45).

35. Fair value information assists users in assessing management's stewardship and performance—thus helping to meet the third objective of financial reporting discussed in Concepts Statement 4. Management must continually decide whether to hold an investment or to sell the investment and redirect resources to other investments or other uses. Fair value reports information useful in evaluating the performance of management in dynamic market conditions.

36. Many respondents to the Exposure Draft agreed with the Board about the relevance of fair value information. Creditors, rating agencies, regulators, and others that use the financial statements of not-for-profit organizations said fair value measures provide information that is useful to them in comparing and evaluating organizations and their managements. Because the goal of investing is to maximize returns commensurate with the risks undertaken, the only way to evaluate performance is to compare returns, adjusted for risk, to that of other entities or to common market indicators. Those financial statement users said that comparisons are reasonable only when securities and their returns are measured using fair value measures.

37. The ability to make meaningful comparisons between organizations is enhanced when securities are measured at fair value. Cost-based measures of the same security can vary significantly from organization to organization; fair value measures vary little, if at all. The value of securities, and all financial instruments, comes from the ability to convert them to their promised cash flows and to use the resulting cash to purchase the services, goods, and long-lived assets that the organization needs to conduct its activities. The cash flows associated with the securities do not depend on which organization owns them; thus, the measures of securities should not vary from organization to organization.

38. Some respondents were concerned primarily about reporting unrealized changes in fair value in their financial statements. Some that supported fair value measures said that changes in the fair values of securities should not be reported in the statement of activities until realized. They argued that the volatility that results from reporting unrealized gains and losses in change in net assets is unrepresentative of the results of operations of the organization and presents a false picture of the organization's stewardship abilities. Other respondents that favored cost-based measures said that not-for-profit organizations invest for long-term returns that support program activities and that temporary fluctuations in market values are irrelevant to managing the organization or its investment portfolio. They argued that fair value measures ignore those considerations. In their view, fair value measures focus on the effects of transactions and events that do not involve the organization and report opportunity gains and losses that should not be recognized until realized.

39. The Board concluded that to delay recognition of gains and losses until they are realized omits relevant information from the financial statements of not-for-profit organizations. To ignore fluctuations that actually occur fails to represent faithfully the risks inherent in investing activities, and to fail to report increases and decreases in value in periods when market conditions change impairs the credibility of financial statements. Recognizing only realized gains and losses in financial statements does not eliminate volatility in the change in net assets; instead, it provides opportunities to use selective sales of securities to manage that volatility. This Statement attempts to reduce opportunities to manage the reported change in net assets by selective sales of securities.

40. The requirement to report investments in equity securities with readily determinable fair values and all debt securities at fair value builds on current and evolving practices and requirements. Three of the four AICPA Guides permit organizations to report investments at fair value, and all four Guides require disclosure of fair value if investments are reported using a cost-based measure. FASB Statement No. 35, *Accounting and Reporting by Defined Benefit Pension Plans,* requires that all plan investments be reported at fair value because that reporting provides the most relevant information about the resources of a plan and its present and future ability to pay benefits when due. Statements 107, 115, and 119 also require that entities report fair value information about their financial instruments because that information is relevant to users of financial statements.

Consideration of Whether to Amend Statement 115

41. The Board considered amending Statement 115 to include not-for-profit organizations within its

scope. In addition to not-for-profit organizations, Statement 115 excludes from its scope enterprises whose specialized accounting practices include accounting for substantially all investments in debt and equity securities at market or fair value, with changes in value recognized in earnings (income) or in change in net assets. Those enterprises (principally brokers and dealers in securities, defined benefit pension plans, and investment companies) are excluded because the Board believes that their current accounting practices provide more relevant information for users of their financial statements. The specialized accounting practices of most not-for-profit organizations permit reporting investments at fair value with changes in fair value recognized in change in net assets, and a significant number of not-for-profit organizations presently do so. Accordingly, the Board considered whether an approach similar to those specialized accounting practices or the approach used in Statement 115 would result in more relevant information for the users of the financial statements of not-for-profit organizations.

42. Statement 115 identifies three categories of investments into which an enterprise classifies its investments. The accounting and reporting differ by category. Investments in debt securities that the enterprise has the positive intent and ability to hold to maturity are classified as *held-to-maturity securities* and are reported at amortized cost. Debt and equity securities that are bought and held principally for the purpose of selling them in the near term are classified as *trading securities* and reported at fair value, with unrealized holding gains and losses included in earnings.[8] Debt and equity securities not classified as either held-to-maturity securities or trading securities are classified as *available-for-sale securities* and reported at fair value, with unrealized holding gains and losses excluded from earnings and reported in a separate component of shareholders' equity.

43. The approach in Statement 115 resulted from a need to accommodate situations that are largely nonexistent in not-for-profit organizations. Some enterprises affected by Statement 115 (principally banks, thrifts, credit unions, and insurance companies) manage their interest rate risk by coordinating the maturity and repricing characteristics of their investments and their liabilities. Reporting unrealized holding gains and losses on only the investments, and not the

related liabilities, could cause volatility in earnings that is not representative of how financial institutions are affected by economic events. The Board concluded that accommodations similar to those in Statement 115 were unnecessary for not-for-profit organizations because (a) the purposes for which not-for-profit organizations hold investments generally do not relate investments to liabilities and (b) the change in net assets is not a performance measure comparable to earnings of a business enterprise.

44. Respondents to the Exposure Draft and task force members helped the Board identify the purposes for which not-for-profit organizations hold investments. Three of the primary purposes identified were endowment, funded depreciation, and short-term investment of operating cash surpluses. Organizations usually do not relate investment assets to liabilities when investing for those purposes. However, organizations may relate investment assets to specific liabilities when investing for other purposes. For many of those other purposes, the related liability is measured and periodically remeasured at the present value of estimated future cash flows using a discount rate commensurate with the risks involved. For example, the obligation to the beneficiary of an annuity agreement is measured at the present value of the payments to be made, the obligation to employees covered by a funded postretirement benefit plan is measured at the actuarial present value of the expected benefits attributed to periods of employee service, and the obligation to provide future service in continuing care retirement communities is measured at the present value of future net cash flows. This Statement's requirement to measure investment securities at fair value will eliminate situations where the adjustment of the liability is included in the change in net assets, but the change in the value of related investments is not.

45. In other identified relationships, such as many debt service funds, this Statement requires that the investments be measured at fair value, although the related liability is reported at historical proceeds. However, most respondents that supported a Statement 115 approach or its held-to-maturity category indicated that they did not coordinate maturities of the investments with the related liabilities. The Board concluded that the possibility for volatility that is not representative of how not-for-profit organizations are

---

[8]In addition to securities that are acquired with the purpose of selling them in the near term, Statement 115 also permits an enterprise to classify securities that it plans to hold for a longer period as *trading securities.* However, the decision to classify a security as trading should occur at acquisition; transfers into or out of the trading category should be rare.

affected by economic events is limited, both in the number of not-for-profit organizations potentially affected and in the amounts of investments and liabilities involved.

46. The Board also noted that the distinctions between the three categories of investments of Statement 115 are less relevant for not-for-profit organizations because the change in net assets is not a performance measure equivalent to earnings of a business enterprise. "[Not-for-profit] organizations generally have no single indicator of performance comparable to a business enterprise's profit" (Concepts Statement 4, paragraph 9). Although the magnitude of profits is generally indicative of how successfully a business enterprise performed, the same relationship is not true of a not-for-profit organization. The magnitude of change in net assets does not indicate how successfully a not-for-profit organization performed in providing goods and services. Further, because donor-imposed restrictions affect the types and levels of service a not-for-profit organization can provide, the change in each class of net assets may be more significant than the change in net assets for the organization as a whole (FASB Concepts Statement No. 6, *Elements of Financial Statements,* paragraph 106).

47. Because change in net assets is not a performance measure, the distinction between trading securities and available-for-sale securities is less relevant for not-for-profit organizations in reporting changes in fair value than that distinction is for business enterprises. Business enterprises distinguish between components of comprehensive income,[9] reporting certain changes in equity (net assets) in an income statement and other changes in net assets in a separate component of equity. The trading and available-for-sale categories are used to make those differentiations. In contrast, the statement of activities of a not-for-profit organization is like a statement of comprehensive income; it reports all changes in net assets. Reporting in a manner similar to Statement 115 introduces unnecessary complications by introducing separate components of equity within the three classes of net assets.

48. The Board concluded that fair value is more relevant to donors and other users of a not-for-profit organization's financial statements than the approach used in Statement 115. The Board decided that use of the three categories of investments prescribed in Statement 115 would add complexity without returning sufficient benefits for measurement or reporting purposes of not-for-profit organizations.

49. Some respondents, primarily health care organizations and their auditors, said that because Statement 115 requires business enterprises to report changes in fair value of available-for-sale securities in a separate category of equity and to report held-to-maturity securities at amortized cost, users would be unable to make meaningful comparisons when not-for-profit organizations and business enterprises are engaged in the same industry. This Statement allows an organization with those comparability concerns to report in a manner similar to business enterprises by identifying securities as available-for-sale or held-to-maturity and excluding the unrealized gains and losses on those securities from an operating measure within the statement of activities.

Debt Securities Held to Maturity

50. In addition to the three-category approach used in Statement 115, the Board considered a two-category approach. Under that approach, debt securities that the organization has the positive intent and ability to hold to maturity would be reported at amortized cost. Other debt securities and equity securities with readily determinable fair values would be reported at fair value. Two of the AICPA Guides permit the use of amortized cost for debt securities if a not-for-profit organization has the intent and ability to hold those securities to maturity. The Board considered whether that practice should continue and decided that amortized cost should not be permitted.

51. Respondents to the Exposure Draft that favored a two-category approach said that fair value information is less relevant for debt securities that are being held to maturity. They said that amortized cost provides relevant information because it focuses on the decision to acquire the asset, the earning effects of that decision that will be realized over time, and the ultimate recoverable value of the asset. If a debt security is held to maturity, the face value of the security will be realized, unless the issuer defaults, and all interim unrealized gains and losses will be reversed. In their view, increases and decreases in the fair value of

---

[9]Comprehensive income includes all changes in equity during a period except those resulting from investments by owners and distributions to owners (Concepts Statement 6, paragraph 70).

the debt security are not true gains and losses in investment value because the organization's cash flows are "locked in" at purchase.

52. Other respondents said that fair value information is as relevant for debt securities that are being held to maturity as it is for other investments. Increases or decreases in fair value reflect the success or failure of the strategy of purchasing and holding a longer-term rather than a shorter-term debt security in an environment of changing interest rates. For example, if an organization invests in a fixed-rate debt security and interest rates rise, the organization generally will receive less cash than if it had invested in a variable-rate security. That success (or failure) in maximizing the return on the organization's resources is relevant and should be reflected in the financial statements in the period the event (that is, the change in interest rates) occurs. In addition, fair value also reflects the risk that the cash flows will not be received as expected.

53. Some respondents that favored fair value measures mentioned that effective management of financial activities often requires a flexible investment strategy that is inconsistent with a held-to-maturity notion. They said that although many investment policies are based on long-term strategies, market fluctuations impact decisions to buy or sell specific instruments in order to achieve the organization's overall objectives. The Board believes that if an organization would sell a debt security to achieve its investment objectives, the organization does not have the positive intent to hold the security to maturity.

54. Other respondents that favored a two-category approach said they use a buy-and-hold strategy or "ladder" the maturities of their debt securities so that the organization can hold debt securities to maturity. Many of those respondents were concerned about volatility in the change in net assets, which would result if debt securities could not be reported at amortized cost when market interest rates changed. However, respondents that expressed that concern indicated that debt securities being held to maturity represent only a small portion of their portfolios. The Board noted that unless a portfolio was composed completely of debt securities being held to maturity, a two-category approach would not resolve concerns about volatility in change in net assets.

55. Respondents also said that not-for-profit organizations should have the same ability as business enterprises to report debt securities classified as held-to-maturity securities at amortized cost. Measuring an investment at (a) amortized cost if the organization has the positive intent and ability to hold it to maturity or (b) fair value if the organization does not have that intent bases the measurement on the intent of management rather than on the economic characteristics of the asset. Measurement based on the intent of management is one of the problems that this Statement attempts to resolve.

56. Statement 115 did not resolve the problem of accounting by intent. As discussed in paragraphs 43-48 of this Statement, the approach in Statement 115 resulted from a need to accommodate situations that are largely nonexistent in not-for-profit organizations. Thus, the Board concluded that allowing a not-for-profit organization to account for investments based on management's intent is unwarranted and that investments in equity securities with readily determinable fair values and all debt securities should be reported at fair value.

Determining Fair Values

57. The Board decided to use the term *fair value* in this Statement to avoid confusion between the terms *fair value* and *market value;* some constituents associate the term *market value* only with items that are traded on active secondary markets (such as exchange and dealer markets). However, the Board does not make that distinction and intends the term to be applicable whether the market for an item is active or inactive, primary or secondary.

58. The fair value of an asset is the amount at which the asset could be bought or sold in a current transaction between willing parties, that is, other than in a forced or liquidation sale. Quoted market prices in active markets are the best evidence of fair value and should be used as the basis for measurement, if available. Quoted market prices are easy to obtain and are reliable and verifiable. They are used and relied upon regularly and are well understood by donors, creditors, and other users of financial information.

59. Although quoted market prices are not available for all debt securities, the Board believes that a reasonable estimate of fair value can be made or obtained for the remaining debt securities required to be reported at fair value by this Statement. For debt securities that do not trade regularly or that trade only in principal-to-principal markets, the estimate of fair value should be based on the best information available in the circumstances. The estimate of fair value

should consider market prices for similar debt securities and the results of valuation techniques to the extent available in the circumstances. Examples of valuation techniques include the present value of estimated expected future cash flows using a discount rate commensurate with the risks involved, option-pricing models, matrix pricing, option-adjusted spread models, and fundamental analysis. The Board realizes that estimating fair value may require judgment but notes that a considerable degree of judgment also is needed when complying with other long-standing accounting and reporting requirements.

Financial Statement Presentation

Reporting Investment Gains, Losses, and Income

60. This Statement provides requirements for reporting changes in the fair value of investments in securities. The total change in fair value consists of both the change in the unpaid interest income on a debt security (or the unpaid accrued dividends on an equity security until the ex-dividend date) and the change in fair value that results from holding a security—the gain or loss, which can be either realized or unrealized. Gains and losses are recognized as changes in net assets in the periods in which they occur, and investment income is recognized as revenue in the period earned. Delaying recognition of restricted gains, losses, and income until the restrictions are met is inappropriate. The requirements of this Statement clarify, but do not change, the requirements of Statement 117.

61. Statement 117 establishes broad standards directed at critical display issues and allows organizations latitude to present information in a form that management believes is most meaningful to financial statement users. The Board decided that display guidance in this Statement also should focus on critical information that is essential in meeting the financial reporting objectives for all not-for-profit organizations.

62. The Board concluded that the most critical information—investment gains, losses, and investment income—should be recognized and reported

in the statement of activities. Other critical information about the types of investments, their risks, and their returns should be disclosed, but organizations can decide whether that information is disclosed on the face of the statements or in the notes to financial statements.

63. The Board considered whether more restrictive display requirements were necessary for realized gains and losses, unrealized gains and losses, investment return, or the amounts computed under a spending-rate or other budgetary method for reporting endowment returns. By not prescribing specific standards in this Statement, the Board recognizes that differing financial statement display practices are probable. Statement 117 is not yet in effect for most organizations, and they are just beginning to explore reporting that complies with its requirements and responds to its flexibility. The Board believes that it is premature to conclude that reporting differences will be undesirable and that at this time it is best to allow latitude so that financial reporting practices may continue to evolve.

64. Most respondents supported the reporting flexibility that this Statement permits. However, several respondents said that users of financial statements might be misled if organizations use a spending-rate or total return policy[10] that reports in an operating measure an amount that exceeds the total investment return for the year. The Board noted that those respondents were not similarly concerned about reporting less than the total investment return in an operating measure, nor were they concerned about reporting net realized gains in an operating measure and net unrealized losses outside that measure, although the reporting in that latter case also may result in including an amount in an operating measure that exceeds the total investment return for the year. A few respondents said that distinctions between realized and unrealized amounts are acceptable because those distinctions are based on the underlying nature of the transaction, but spending-rate and total return amounts are computed using formulas. In general, the Board agrees that amounts reported in an organization's financial statements should be based on the nature of the underlying transactions

---

[10]In managing their endowment funds, some organizations use a spending-rate or total return policy. Those policies consider total investment return—investment income (interest, dividends, rents, and so forth) plus net realized and unrealized gains (or minus net losses). Typically, spending-rate or total return policies emphasize (a) the use of prudence and a rational and systematic formula to determine the portion of cumulative investment return that can be used to support operations of the current period and (b) the protection of endowment gifts from a loss of purchasing power as a consideration in determining the formula to be used.

rather than on budgetary designations—to report otherwise suggests the reported operating measure is being managed. In this case only, the Board agreed that amounts based on budgetary designations may be displayed because the necessary constraints are provided by the disclosures required by paragraph 14 of this Statement and paragraph 23 of Statement 117 (including its requirement that an operating measure, if reported, must appear in a financial statement that, at a minimum, reports the change in unrestricted net assets for the period).

Reporting Losses on Endowment Funds

65. Statement 117 requires that gains and losses be classified based on the existence or absence of donor-imposed restrictions or law that limits their use. Paragraph 129 of that Statement explains the application of that requirement to the net appreciation of endowment funds:

> . . . the Board concluded that if the law of the relevant jurisdiction, as interpreted by an organization's governing board, places permanent restrictions on some part of the net appreciation, that amount should be reported as permanently restricted net assets in the organization's financial statements. In the absence of such a law or a donor's explicit or clear implicit permanent restriction, net appreciation should be reported as unrestricted if the endowment's income is unrestricted or temporarily restricted if the endowment's income is temporarily restricted by the donor.

Some respondents to the Exposure Draft of Statement 117 raised questions about reporting losses on investments of endowments. The Board deferred consideration of those issues to this Statement.

66. The Board limited its consideration to losses on investments of endowment funds that are created by donor stipulations requiring that the gifts be invested in perpetuity or for a specified term. The classification of losses on investments of an endowment fund created by a board designation of unrestricted funds is straightforward; the losses are classified as reductions in unrestricted net assets because all sources of that endowment fund—original amount, gains and losses, and interest and dividends—are free of donor restrictions.

67. The classification of losses on investments of an endowment fund created by a donor also is straightforward if the donor explicitly states in the gift agreement what is to occur in the event of a loss; the losses are classified in accordance with the donor stipulations. Similarly, a donor's explicit requirement that an organization hold a specific donated asset in perpetuity implies that the enhancements and diminishments of that asset (gains and losses) are subject to the same permanent restriction. In the absence of donor stipulations or law to the contrary, the Board concluded that losses on investments of a donor-restricted endowment fund should reduce temporarily restricted net assets to the extent that donor-imposed temporary restrictions on net appreciation of the fund have not been met before the loss occurs and that any remaining loss should reduce unrestricted net assets.

Fundamental conclusions about the classification of losses

68. In determining the method to be used to classify losses in the absence of explicit donor stipulations or law, the Board considered the Uniform Management of Institutional Funds Act (Uniform Act), which has been adopted in varying forms in at least 38 states and the District of Columbia. It says:

> The governing board may appropriate for expenditure for the uses and purposes for which an endowment fund[11] is established so much of the net appreciation, realized and unrealized, in the fair value of the assets of an endowment fund over the historic dollar value[12] of the fund as is prudent. . . .
>
> Unrealized gains and losses must be combined with realized gains and losses to insure

---

[11]The Uniform Act uses the term *endowment fund* to describe a fund with characteristics of a donor-restricted endowment fund, as defined in this Statement. Section 1(3) of the Uniform Act defines an endowment fund as:

> . . . an institutional fund, or any part thereof, not wholly expendable by the institution on a current basis under the terms of the applicable gift instrument.

[12]The Uniform Act defines *historic dollar value* in Section 1(5) as:

> . . . the aggregate fair value in dollars of (i) an endowment fund at the time it became an endowment fund, (ii) each subsequent donation to the fund at the time it is made, and (iii) each accumulation made pursuant to a direction in the applicable gift instrument at the time the accumulation is added to the fund.

that the historic dollar value is not impaired. [Section 2 and the comment to that section, footnotes added.]

Although the Uniform Act indicates that losses should be netted against gains and that realized and unrealized amounts should be considered equally in applying its provisions, the Act is silent about an organization's responsibility to restore a decrease in the value of the assets of an endowment fund. The Board concluded that a method for classifying losses of a donor-restricted endowment fund should not define an organization's fiduciary responsibilities to maintain the assets of the fund; each organization should determine its responsibilities in accordance with donor-imposed restrictions and law.

69. The Board also considered different interpretations of "the assets of an endowment fund," in part because the Uniform Act does not define that phrase. Different interpretations result in different determinations of which investment losses are losses of a donor-restricted endowment fund and how much of prior periods' appreciation can be netted with losses of the fund in the current period. Respondents' interpretations of the phrase differed. For example, some organizations that participated in the field test of the Exposure Draft interpreted the phrase to mean that assets purchased with a gift and assets purchased with its net appreciation are part of the endowment fund until a portion of the assets is removed by an appropriation for expenditure. Other participants said that in addition to those assets, assets purchased with investment income are part of the fund. Another participant said that assets purchased with net appreciation are not part of the fund at all. Without case law to help interpret the Uniform Act, the Board has no basis to adopt one interpretation and reject all others. The Board concluded that a method for classifying losses should accommodate different interpretations of "the assets of an endowment fund" but minimize the effects of differing interpretations on the classification of net assets.

70. The Board considered whether the ability to "appropriate for expenditure" granted by the Uniform Act should influence the classification of losses. Attributing significance to an act of appropriation would allow management's intent to influence the classification of net assets and is inconsistent with the Board's conclusions in Statements 116 and 117. Statement 116 requires that a restriction on temporarily restricted net appreciation expire when an expense is incurred for the restricted purpose, regard-

less of whether an amount is appropriated. In Statement 117, the Board concluded that decisions about when to appropriate resources should not influence their classification—net gains are reported in unrestricted or temporarily restricted net assets unless permanently restricted by the donor or law. The Board concluded that appropriation of a portion of net appreciation should not change the classification of a loss on an endowment fund.

71. The Board believes that inconsistent classification of net assets would result if it did not specify a method for classifying losses on investments of donor-restricted endowment funds. Donors generally are silent about losses on the investments of the funds they establish, and the Uniform Act is unclear about an organization's responsibilities when a loss occurs. Without explicit donor stipulations or law to determine the classification of losses on investments of endowment funds, organizations could arrive at different answers in similar circumstances.

72. The Board considered the three methods for classifying losses on investments of donor-restricted endowment funds that are discussed in paragraphs 73-82, as well as variations of those methods. All of the methods considered had some drawbacks. The Board believes that the method in this Statement for classifying losses is simple to apply and will result in greater comparability and consistency in classification of net assets so that users of financial statements may make better-informed decisions.

Method used in this Statement for classifying losses

73. The Board concluded that, in the absence of donor stipulations or law to the contrary, losses on the investments of a donor-restricted endowment fund reduce temporarily restricted or unrestricted net assets. The Board concluded that if a donor requires an endowment fund to be invested in perpetuity, permanently restricted net assets should equal the historic dollar value of the fund. The Uniform Act says, "Accounting entries recording realization of gains or losses to the fund have no effect upon historic dollar value. No increase or decrease in historic dollar value of the fund results from the sale of an asset held by the fund and the reinvestment of the proceeds in another asset" (comment to Section 1(5)). Unless historic dollar value changes, such as when a donor directs that gains be accumulated in the fund, neither gains nor losses affect permanently restricted net assets.

74. Whether a loss reduces temporarily restricted net assets, unrestricted net assets, or both depends on where the net appreciation of the fund is classified at the time the loss occurs. First, to the extent that donor-imposed temporary restrictions on net appreciation have not been met prior to the loss, the loss reduces temporarily restricted net assets. The remaining loss reduces unrestricted net assets, which can be viewed as reducing any net appreciation classified in that net asset class and then reducing unrestricted net assets for any excess loss (that is, the amount by which the fair value of the assets of the fund is less than the historic dollar value). In other words, when losses exceed the net appreciation classified in temporarily restricted and unrestricted net assets, the excess loss reduces unrestricted net assets.

75. The Board concluded that the method used in this Statement is most consistent with the fundamental conclusions described in paragraphs 68-72. Under that method, different interpretations of "the assets of an endowment fund," especially differences in how and when net appreciation is removed from the fund, have a lesser effect on the classification of net assets. A loss that reduces the fair value of the assets of the endowment fund to historic dollar value and a loss that reduces the fair value below historic dollar value reduce the same net asset class, unrestricted net assets, unless restrictions on net appreciation have not been met prior to the loss. The effects of appropriation are minimized because the amounts appropriated for expenditure also are classified in unrestricted net assets (or will be reclassified to that net asset class shortly because the donor-imposed restrictions will be met when the amounts are spent).

76. A drawback of that method is that excess losses decrease unrestricted net assets even if the organization is not required by a donor-imposed restriction or law to use its unrestricted resources to restore immediately the value of the endowment fund to the level required by donor stipulations or law. Some respondents said that that drawback could be mitigated by requiring organizations to disclose the amount of the deficiency when the fair value of the assets of a donor-restricted endowment fund is less than the level required by the donor's restriction or law. The Board agreed and added that requirement. However, the field test results indicated that, except in the early years of an endowment fund, incidences of excess losses will be few because organizations generally accumulate net appreciation through policies that preserve and grow their endowment funds.

77. Because unrestricted net assets are reduced for the excess loss when the fair value of the assets of the endowment fund falls below the fund's historic dollar value, this Statement requires that unrestricted net assets be restored from future gains for that reduction. Some respondents said that that classification was confusing and that they would expect those gains to be classified as increases in permanently restricted net assets because they cannot be appropriated for expenditure. However, because the prior loss did not reduce permanently restricted net assets, the classification suggested by respondents would increase the amount of permanently restricted net assets beyond the level required by donor restrictions or law. Thus, gains that restore the fair value of the assets of the endowment fund to the fund's required level (historic dollar value) should be classified as increases to the same class of net assets that was previously reduced for the excess loss—unrestricted net assets. After the fair value of the assets of the endowment fund equals the required level, gains are again available for expenditure, and those gains that are restricted by the donor are classified as increases in temporarily restricted net assets.

Other methods considered

78. The Board also considered a method in which losses would reduce temporarily restricted and unrestricted net assets to the extent that unappropriated net appreciation is classified in those net asset classes, but the excess loss would reduce permanently restricted net assets if the donor required the fund to be invested in perpetuity or would reduce temporarily restricted net assets if the donor required the fund to be invested for a specified term. Most respondents that commented on the endowment loss provisions preferred that method.

79. That method would result in the same classification of net assets as this Statement except when the fair value of the assets of the endowment fund is less than historic dollar value. However, it cannot accommodate differing interpretations of "the assets of an endowment fund." Unless all organizations interpret the phrase in the same way, the calculation of the excess loss could differ, resulting in different classifications of net assets in similar circumstances. In addition, how and when an organization removes net appreciation from the fund also can affect classification of net assets. If an organization determines that appropriated amounts are unavailable to absorb losses on the investments of an endowment fund, an action of the governing board to appropriate an

amount forces a larger reduction in permanently restricted net assets than would have occurred if that amount had not been appropriated. The Board concluded that it is unacceptable to have differing classifications of net assets result from an action of the governing board. The Board rejected that method after evaluating it in light of the fundamental conclusions in paragraphs 68-72.

80. The Board also considered a second method that would allocate income, gains, and losses between the classes of net assets based on the proportionate interests of those classes in the investment pool—or the investments of each fund if investments were not pooled. Each time the fair value of the units related to permanently restricted net assets increased beyond historic dollar value, units with a value equal to the net appreciation would be transferred to temporarily restricted net assets (or unrestricted net assets if the donor did not restrict the use of income from the endowment). Each time a restriction expired, units with a value equal to the expired amount would be transferred from temporarily restricted net assets to unrestricted net assets. Income and gains on the units related to permanently restricted net assets would be classified as increases in temporarily restricted net assets if restricted by the donor to a specific use; otherwise, they would increase unrestricted net assets in accordance with paragraphs 8 and 9 of this Statement. Losses on those units would decrease permanently restricted net assets. Income, gains, and losses on the units related to unrestricted and temporarily restricted net assets would increase or decrease those net asset classes.

81. That second method results in similar classifications of net assets regardless of the interpretation of "the assets of an endowment fund" or whether amounts were appropriated. Further, it is the only method considered by the Board that does not reduce unrestricted net assets for a loss on investments of permanently restricted net assets. The method in this Statement and the other methods considered by the Board result in restriction of previously unrestricted gains when a loss occurs.

82. However, because that method allocates gains, losses, and income based on the proportionate interests of each net asset class, it can be inconsistent with some organizations' interpretations of their fiduciary responsibilities to maintain the assets of the endowment fund and to use the income earned by those assets in accordance with the donors' stipulations. That method's classification of losses is most consistent

with an interpretation that an organization's fiduciary responsibilities do not extend to net appreciation of previous periods; that is, net appreciation is not included in "the assets of an endowment fund." The Board rejected the second method after evaluating it in light of the fundamental conclusions in paragraphs 68-72.

Disclosures

83. Using an approach of broad standards for basic information similar to that used in Statement 117, the Board determined the information that is required to be disclosed without prescribing whether it should be disclosed on the face of the statements or in the notes. That approach allows an organization's management to report the information in a manner that is most useful to users of its financial statements. The disclosure requirements are not intended to limit the amount of detail or the manner of providing information; additional classifications and subclassifications may be useful.

84. The Board developed the disclosure requirements after consulting with its task force and with users of financial statements of not-for-profit organizations. It also considered existing disclosure requirements for investments reported at fair value, especially those found in Statements 35 and 115. The Board believes that the required disclosures provide information that is useful in assessing management's stewardship and the organization's liquidity and exposure to risk.

85. Some respondents questioned the need for the information about the composition of investment return or the reconciliation required if investment return is separated into operating and nonoperating amounts. Disclosures required for investment return reinforce the requirements of Statement 117 to (a) report information about revenues, gains, and losses by aggregating items into relatively homogeneous groups and (b) disclose information about the nature of a reported measure of operations if the definition of operations is not apparent from the face of the statement of activities. Users of financial information indicated that the disclosures required by paragraph 14 were especially useful in their work. The Board retained those requirements.

86. A few respondents suggested that additional guidance should be provided for the disclosure about "significant concentration of market risk or risk of physical loss" that was proposed in the Exposure

Draft. Others suggested that the Board should quantify *significant*. The Board believes that management's judgment about concentrations and significance is in itself useful information. Therefore, the Board chose not to define further those terms. The Board concluded that an entity should review its portfolio of investments to determine if any significant concentrations of market risk result from the nature of the investments or from a lack of diversity of industry, currency, or geographic location. The Board decided to delete the requirement to disclose information about the risk of physical loss.

87. The Board concluded that disclosure of realized gains and losses is necessary when investments that are reported at measures other than fair value are sold. Without that disclosure, information about total investment return may be misleading to donors, creditors, and other users of financial statements because the realized gains or losses reported will represent the activity of more than a single period; that is, the organization's change in net assets will include unrealized gains and losses accumulated in previous periods but not recognized until the year of sale.

88. However, the Board is not convinced that information about realized gains and losses or about the historical cost of investments is relevant and useful for investments reported at fair value when the changes in their fair values are reported in a statement of activities. Most respondents agreed. Both realized and unrealized net gains on endowment funds may be prudently spent in accordance with the Uniform Act. Thus, distinguishing between them does not enhance a user's assessment of an organization's ability to provide mission-related services and to pay debtors. Both realized and unrealized gains and losses are included in a statement of activities, and opportunities for managing change in net assets through selective sale of securities are greatly reduced by the requirements of this Statement. A user, therefore, does not need information about realized and unrealized gains and losses and about the historical cost of investments to determine if selective sales are occurring. Further, a user does not need the information to determine the potential tax consequences of management's decisions to sell or hold investments; realization of gains and losses has no tax consequences for most not-for-profit organizations.

89. The Board recognizes that information about realized and unrealized gains and losses and about historical costs of investments may be useful in some circumstances. For example, if a state adopted a modified form of the Uniform Act that allows a not-for-profit organization to spend only realized gains or if an organization pays taxes on realized gains and losses, information that distinguishes between realized and unrealized amounts may be useful. Thus, this Statement does not preclude disclosing that information.

90. The Exposure Draft would have required that organizations disclose information about their investment objectives and about the contractual maturities of debt securities. Many respondents, including users of financial statements, asked the Board not to require those disclosures. Some said that information about investment objectives should not be required of not-for-profit organizations because Statement 115 does not require business enterprises to make that disclosure. Others said that organizations may have different objectives for different investment portfolios and that, as an organization's policies become more complex, investment objectives become more difficult to summarize. Still others said that the resulting disclosures might be "boilerplate" or would be meaningless without an accompanying disclosure of investment performance. A number of respondents said that information about contractual maturities was unnecessary when debt securities are reported at fair value. The Board decided that the information need not be disclosed.

Effective Date and Transition Method

91. The Board concluded that this Statement should be effective for fiscal years beginning after December 15, 1995. That effective date corresponds to the later effective date of Statements 116 and 117, which are effective for fiscal years beginning after December 15, 1995, for organizations with less than $5 million in total assets and $1 million in revenues. It was not possible to require the implementation of this Statement for the earlier effective date of Statements 116 and 117 (fiscal years beginning after December 15, 1994).

92. A few respondents said that smaller organizations might have difficulty implementing this Statement by its effective date. Because the AICPA Guides and Statement 107 require disclosure of the fair value of investments, organizations already have the necessary information systems in place. In addition, many not-for-profit organizations already report investments at fair value. Thus, the Board concluded that there is adequate time to develop the information required by this Statement. The Statement should not

be difficult to implement, except perhaps for the release of restrictions on investment appreciation.

93. The Board decided to allow prospective treatment for the release of restrictions on previously unrecognized gains and losses. Determining the expiration of restrictions may be difficult or impossible if an organization no longer has the necessary records or if past procedures did not require those records. The Board permits similar treatment for expiration of restrictions on contributions in Statement 116.

94. Early application of this Statement is encouraged whenever practicable. Some respondents said that applying this Statement early may result in some loss of comparability of reporting between organizations during the transition period; however, the Board concluded that the benefits of early application outweigh its disadvantages. In addition, allowing early implementation will allow organizations that must implement Statements 116 and 117 on the earlier effective date to implement this Statement in the same fiscal year.

Appendix C

ILLUSTRATIVE EXAMPLES

Example of Classification of an Endowment Fund Loss

95. This example illustrates the classification prescribed by this Statement of a loss on investments of a donor-restricted endowment fund. Paragraph 12 of this Statement requires that in the absence of donor stipulations or law to the contrary, losses on the investments of a donor-restricted endowment fund reduce temporarily restricted net assets to the extent that donor-imposed temporary restrictions on net appreciation of the fund have not been met before the loss occurs. Any remaining loss reduces unrestricted net assets. Paragraph 13 requires that if losses reduce the assets of a donor-restricted endowment fund below the level required by donor stipulations or law, gains that restore the fair value of the assets of the endowment fund to the required level are classified as increases in unrestricted net assets.

Year 1

96. At the beginning of year 1, NFP Organization received a gift of $1,000,000. The donor specified that the gift be used to create an endowment fund that will be invested in perpetuity with income to be used for the support of Program A. The investments purchased with the gift earned $30,000 of investment income. NFP Organization spent that income plus an additional $20,000 of unrestricted resources on Program A during the year. At the end of the year, the fair value of the investments was $1,047,000.

Transactions for year 1 are classified as increases or decreases in permanently restricted net assets, temporarily restricted net assets, or unrestricted net assets as follows:

	Net Assets			
Transactions	**Unrestricted**	**Temporarily Restricted**	**Permanently Restricted**	**Total**
Activity of Program A				
Board-designated resources[a]	$ 20,000			$ 20,000
Investment income		$ 30,000		30,000
Expenses	(50,000)			(50,000)
Release restriction[b]	30,000	(30,000)		
Subtotal	0	0		0
Investments				
Gift			$1,000,000	1,000,000
Gains[c]		47,000		47,000
Release restriction[b]	20,000	(20,000)		
Subtotal	20,000	27,000	1,000,000	1,047,000
End of year	$ 20,000	$ 27,000	$1,000,000	$1,047,000

a. The governing board designates $20,000 of unrestricted resources of the organization to be spent in support of Program A.

b. When $50,000 is spent in support of Program A, restrictions are released on the $30,000 of income and $20,000 of temporarily restricted gains according to the provisions of Statement 116. The restrictions on the gains expire even though the governing board chose to use unrestricted resources rather than sell some investments and use the proceeds for Program A.

c. The $47,000 gain is restricted to the same purpose as the income in accordance with the Uniform Act.

Year 2

97. On January 1, in accordance with its spending policy, the governing board of NFP Organization sold some investments for $25,000 and spent the proceeds on Program A. The remaining investments earned $30,000 of investment income, which NFP Organization also spent on Program A. At the end of the year, the fair value of the investments was $1,097,000.

Transactions for year 2 are classified as follows:

		Net Assets		
Transactions	**Unrestricted**	**Temporarily Restricted**	**Permanently Restricted**	**Total**
Activity of Program A				
Spending policy[d]		$ 25,000		$ 25,000
Investment income		30,000		30,000
Expenses	$(55,000)			(55,000)
Release restriction	55,000	(55,000)		0
Subtotal	0	0		0
Investments				
Spending policy[d]		(25,000)		(25,000)
Gains		75,000		75,000
Beginning of year	20,000	27,000	$1,000,000	1,047,000
End of year	$ 20,000	$ 77,000	$1,000,000	$1,097,000

d. When the governing board sells investments and uses the proceeds for the donor's specified purpose, the historic dollar value of the endowment fund does not change. Neither the decision by the governing board to appropriate net appreciation nor the sale of the investments changes the class of net assets in which the appropriated amount is reported. The $25,000 is classified as temporarily restricted net assets until the restriction is met by spending on Program A.

Year 3

98. On January 1, in accordance with its spending policy, the governing board of NFP Organization sold some investments for $28,000 and spent the proceeds on Program A. The remaining investments earned $30,000 of investment income, which NFP Organization also spent on Program A. At the end of the year, the fair value of the investments was $975,000.

Transactions for year 3 are classified as follows:

		Net Assets		
Transactions	**Unrestricted**	**Temporarily Restricted**	**Permanently Restricted**	**Total**
Activity of Program A				
Spending policy		$ 28,000		$ 28,000
Investment income		30,000		30,000
Expenses	$(58,000)			(58,000)
Release restriction	58,000	(58,000)		0
Subtotal	0	0		0
Investments				
Spending policy		(28,000)		(28,000)
Losses[e]	(45,000)	(49,000)		(94,000)
Beginning of year	20,000	77,000	$1,000,000	1,097,000
End of year[f]	$(25,000)	$ 0	$1,000,000	$ 975,000

e. According to the provisions of paragraph 12, the decline in the fair value of the assets of the endowment fund reduces temporarily restricted net assets by $49,000. The remaining loss reduces unrestricted net assets.

f. According to the provisions of paragraph 15(d), NFP Organization would disclose the $25,000 deficiency between the fair value of the investments of the endowment fund at the end of the year and the level required by donor stipulations or law. If NFP Organization had other donor-restricted endowment funds in deficit positions, it would disclose the aggregate amount of the deficiencies.

Year 4

99. On January 1, the governing board of NFP Organization could not apply its spending policy because the fair value of the investments was less than the historic dollar value of the fund; thus, no appreciation was available for expenditure. The investments earned income of $27,000, which NFP Organization spent on Program A. At the end of the year, the fair value of the investments was $1,005,000.

Transactions for year 4 are classified as follows:

		Net Assets		
Transactions	**Unrestricted**	**Temporarily Restricted**	**Permanently Restricted**	**Total**
Activity of Program A				
Investment income		$ 27,000		$ 27,000
Expenses	$(27,000)			(27,000)
Release restriction	27,000	(27,000)		0
Subtotal	0	0		0
Investments				
Gains[g]	25,000	5,000		30,000
Beginning of year	(25,000)	0	$1,000,000	975,000
End of year	$ 0	$ 5,000	$1,000,000	$1,005,000

g. According to the provisions of paragraph 13 of this Statement, because losses have reduced the assets of a donor-restricted endowment fund below the level required by donor stipulations or law ($1,000,000), the gains ($25,000) that restore the fair value of the assets of the endowment fund to the required level are classified as increases in unrestricted net assets. The remaining gains ($5,000) are available to be spent on Program A.

Example of an Organization That Separates Investment Return into Operating and Nonoperating Amounts

100. This example illustrates the disclosures required by paragraph 14 and a statement of activities that reports a portion of investment return within a measure of operations. Paragraph 14(a) requires an organization to disclose the composition of investment return including, at a minimum, investment income, net realized gains or losses on investments reported at other than fair value, and net gains or losses on investments reported at fair value. Paragraph 14(b) requires a reconciliation of investment return to amounts reported in the statement of activities if investment return is separated into operating and nonoperating amounts, together with a description of the policy used to determine the amount that is included in the measure of operations and a discussion of circumstances leading to a change, if any, in that policy. The reconciliation need not be provided if an organization includes all investment return in its measure of operations or excludes it from that measure entirely.

101. Statement 117 neither encourages nor discourages organizations from classifying items of revenues, expenses, and other changes in net assets as operating and nonoperating, but it requires that if an organization reports an intermediate measure of operations, it must do so within a financial statement that, at a minimum, reports the change in unrestricted net assets for the period. Statement 117 also specifies that if an organization's use of the term *operations* is not apparent from the details provided on the face of the statement of activities, a note to financial statements should describe the nature of the reported measure of operations or the items excluded from operations.

102. This example is illustrative only; it does not indicate a preferred method of reporting investment return or defining operations. Organizations may separate investment return into operating and non-operating amounts in ways that they believe will provide meaningful information to users of their financial statements. Distinctions may be based on:

a. The nature of the underlying transactions, such as classifying realized amounts as operating and unrealized amounts as nonoperating

b. Budgetary designations, such as classifying amounts computed under a spending-rate or total return policy as operating and the remainder of investment return as nonoperating

c. The reporting requirements for categories of investments used in Statement 115, such as classifying investment income, realized gains and losses, unrealized gains and losses on trading securities, and other-than-temporary impairment losses on securities (that is, all items included in net income of a business enterprise) as operating and classifying the remainder of investment return as nonoperating

d. Other characteristics that provide information that is relevant and understandable to donors, creditors, and other users of financial statements.

103. A statement of activities of Not-for-Profit Organization is illustrated below. Not-for-Profit Organization invests cash in excess of daily requirements in short-term investments; during the year, those investments earned $1,275. Most long-term investments of Not-for-Profit Organization's endowments are held in an investment pool, which earned income of $11,270 and had net gains of $15,450. Certain endowments are separately invested because of donors' requirements. The investments of those endowments earned income of $1,000 and increased in value by $1,500. One donor required that the net gains be added to the original endowment gift; that endowment's investment in the pool increased in value by $180.

Not-for-Profit Organization
Statement of Activities
Year Ended June 30, 19X1

	Unrestricted	Temporarily Restricted	Permanently Restricted	Total
Operating revenues, gains, and other support:				
Contributions	$ x,xxx	$ x,xxx		$xx,xxx
Fees	x,xxx			x,xxx
Investment return designated for current operations	11,025	4,500		15,525
Other	xxx			xxx
Net assets released from restrictions	xx,xxx	(xx,xxx)		
Total operating revenues, gains, and other support	xx,xxx	(x,xxx)		xx,xxx
Operating expenses and losses:				
Program A	xx,xxx			xx,xxx
Program B	x,xxx			x,xxx
Program C	x,xxx			x,xxx
Management and general	x,xxx			x,xxx
Fund raising	x,xxx			x,xxx
Total operating expenses	xx,xxx			xx,xxx
Change in net assets from operations	x,xxx	(x,xxx)		x,xxx
Other changes:				
Investment return in excess of amounts designated for current operations	10,992	3,798	$180	14,970
[Other items considered to be nonoperating]	x,xxx	x,xxx		x,xxx
	xxx	xxx	xxx	xxx
Change in net assets	$xx,xxx	$ x,xxx	$xxx	$xx,xxx

104. Not-for-Profit Organization would add the following illustrative text to its note to the financial statements that describes the measure of operations:

The board of trustees designates only a portion of the Organization's cumulative investment return for support of current operations; the remainder is retained to support operations of future years and to offset potential market declines. The amount computed under the endowment spending policy of the investment pool and all investment income earned by investing cash in excess of daily requirements are used to support current operations.

105. The following illustrative text and schedule would be added to a note to the financial statements about investments to provide the information about the composition of return and the reconciliation of investment return required by paragraph 14:

State law allows the board to appropriate so much of the net appreciation as is prudent considering the Organization's long- and short-term needs, present and anticipated financial requirements, expected total return on its investments, price level trends, and general economic conditions. Under the Organization's endowment spending policy, 5 percent of the average of the fair value at the end of the previous 3 years is appropriated to support current operations. The following schedule summarizes the investment return and its classification in the statement of activities:

	Unrestricted	Temporarily Restricted	Permanently Restricted	Total
Dividends, interest, and rents (net of expenses of $565)	$ 8,400	$ 3,870		$ 12,270
Net realized and unrealized gains	12,342	4,428	$180	16,950
Return on long-term investments	20,742	8,298	180	29,220
Interest on short-term investments	1,275			1,275
Total return on investments	22,017	8,298	180	30,495
Investment return designated for current operations	(11,025)	(4,500)		(15,525)
Investment return in excess of amounts designated for current operations	$ 10,992	$ 3,798	$180	$ 14,970

106. Often, as in the example above, the amount of investment return designated for current operations is less than the total return on investments for the year. An organization may be able to designate an amount for the support of operations even if the total investment return for the year is less than the amount computed under a spending-rate policy; for example, when the organization designates part of its cumulative investment return from prior years to support its current operations. In that case, the operating and nonoperating amounts should be labeled to faithfully represent their natures. For example, the amount excluded from operations, which is negative, might be labeled "Investment return reduced by the portion of cumulative net appreciation designated for current operations."

Appendix D

AMENDMENTS TO EXISTING PRONOUNCEMENTS

107. FASB Statement No. 60, *Accounting and Reporting by Insurance Enterprises,* as amended by FASB Statement No. 115, *Accounting for Certain Investments in Debt and Equity Securities,* is amended as follows:

a. The following sentence is added at the end of paragraph 45:

A not-for-profit organization that conducts insurance activities should account for those investments in accordance with FASB Statement No. 124, *Accounting for Certain Investments Held by Not-for-Profit Organizations.*

b. Paragraph 46 is replaced by the following:

Investments in equity securities that are not addressed by Statement 115 or Statement 124 because they do not have "readily determinable fair values" as defined by those Statements shall be reported at fair value. A business enterprise shall recognize changes in fair value as unrealized gains and losses reported, net of applicable income taxes, in a separate component of equity. A not-for-profit organization shall recognize the change in fair value in its statement of activities.

108. The following sentence is added at the end of paragraph 4 of FASB Statement No. 65, *Accounting*

for Certain Mortgage Banking Activities, as amended by Statement 115:

> Mortgage-backed securities held by not-for-profit organizations shall be reported at fair value in accordance with the provisions of FASB Statement No. 124, *Accounting for Certain Investments Held by Not-for-Profit Organizations.*

109. In paragraph 3 of FASB Statement No. 91, *Accounting for Nonrefundable Fees and Costs Associated with Originating or Acquiring Loans and Initial Direct Costs of Leases,* as amended by Statement 115, *of a business enterprise or change in net assets of a not-for-profit organization* is added at the end of the last sentence.

110. The last sentence of paragraph 4 of Statement 115 is replaced by the following:

> This Statement applies to cooperatives and mutual enterprises, including credit unions and mutual insurance companies, but does not apply to not-for-profit organizations. FASB Statement No. 124, *Accounting for Certain Investments Held by Not-for-Profit Organizations,* establishes standards for not-for-profit organizations.

111. In paragraph 168 of FASB Statement No. 117, *Financial Statements of Not-for-Profit Organizations,* the definition of *endowment fund* is replaced by the following:

> An established fund of cash, securities, or other assets to provide income for the maintenance of a not-for-profit organization. The use of the assets of the fund may be permanently restricted, temporarily restricted, or unrestricted. Endowment funds generally are established by donor-restricted gifts and bequests to provide a permanent endowment, which is to provide a permanent source of income, or a term endowment, which is to provide income for a specified period. The portion of a permanent endowment that must be maintained permanently—not used up, expended, or otherwise exhausted—is classified as permanently restricted net assets. The portion of a term endowment that must be maintained for a specified term is classified as temporarily restricted net assets. An organization's governing board may earmark a portion of its unrestricted net assets as a board-designated endowment (sometimes called funds functioning as endowment or quasi-endowment funds) to be invested to provide income for a long but unspecified period. A board-designated endowment, which results from an internal designation, is not donor restricted and is classified as unrestricted net assets.

Appendix E

GLOSSARY

112. This appendix contains definitions of terms or phrases as used in this Statement.

Debt security
Any security representing a creditor relationship with an enterprise. It also includes (a) preferred stock that by its terms either must be redeemed by the issuing enterprise or is redeemable at the option of the investor and (b) a collateralized mortgage obligation (CMO) (or other instrument) that is issued in equity form but is required to be accounted for as a nonequity instrument regardless of how that instrument is classified (that is, whether equity or debt) in the issuer's statement of financial position. However, it excludes option contracts, financial futures contracts, forward contracts, lease contracts, and swap contracts.

- Thus, the term *debt security* includes, among other items, U.S. Treasury securities, U.S. government agency securities, municipal securities, corporate bonds, convertible debt, commercial paper, all securitized debt instruments, such as CMOs and real estate mortgage investment conduits (REMICs), and interest-only and principal-only strips.
- Trade accounts receivable arising from sales on credit and loans receivable arising from consumer, commercial, and real estate lending activities of financial institutions and not-for-profit organizations are examples of receivables that do not meet the definition of *security;* thus, those receivables are not debt securities (unless they have been securitized, in which case they would meet the definition).

Donor-restricted endowment fund
An endowment fund that is created by a donor stipulation requiring investment of the gift in perpetuity or for a specified term. Also refer to **Endowment fund.**

Endowment fund

An established fund of cash, securities, or other assets to provide income for the maintenance of a not-for-profit organization. The use of the assets of the fund may be permanently restricted, temporarily restricted, or unrestricted. Endowment funds generally are established by donor-restricted gifts and bequests to provide a permanent endowment, which is to provide a permanent source of income, or a term endowment, which is to provide income for a specified period. The portion of a permanent endowment that must be maintained permanently—not used up, expended, or otherwise exhausted—is classified as permanently restricted net assets. The portion of a term endowment that must be maintained for a specified term is classified as temporarily restricted net assets. An organization's governing board may earmark a portion of its unrestricted net assets as a board-designated endowment (sometimes called funds functioning as endowment or quasi-endowment funds) to be invested to provide income for a long but unspecified period. A board-designated endowment, which results from an internal designation, is not donor restricted and is classified as unrestricted net assets.

Equity security

Any security representing an ownership interest in an enterprise (for example, common, preferred, or other capital stock) or the right to acquire (for example, warrants, rights, and call options) or dispose of (for example, put options) an ownership interest in an enterprise at fixed or determinable prices. However, the term does not include convertible debt or preferred stock that by its terms either must be redeemed by the issuing enterprise or is redeemable at the option of the investor.

Fair value

The amount at which an asset could be bought or sold in a current transaction between willing parties, that is, other than in a forced or liquidation sale. If a quoted market price is available for a financial instrument, the fair value to be used in applying this Statement is the product of the number of trading units of the instrument times the market price per unit.

Security

A share, participation, or other interest in property or in an enterprise of the issuer or an obligation of the issuer that (a) either is represented by an instrument issued in bearer or registered form or, if not represented by an instrument, is registered in books maintained to record transfers by or on behalf of the issuer, (b) is of a type commonly dealt in on securities exchanges or markets or, when represented by an instrument, is commonly recognized in any area in which it is issued or dealt in as a medium for investment, and (c) either is one of a class or series or by its terms is divisible into a class or series of shares, participations, interests, or obligations.

Statement of Financial Accounting Standards No. 125
Accounting for Transfers and Servicing of Financial Assets and Extinguishments of Liabilities

STATUS

Issued: June 1996

Effective Date: For transfers and servicing of financial assets and extinguishments
of liabilities occurring after December 31, 1996

Affects: Supersedes APB 26, paragraph 3(a)
Amends FAS 13, paragraph 20
Amends FAS 22, footnote 1
Amends FAS 65, paragraphs 1, 6, 9(a), 10, 15, and 34
Supersedes FAS 65, paragraphs 8, 11, 16 through 19, 30 and the paragraphs added by FAS 122,
and footnotes 4 and 6
Supersedes FAS 76
Supersedes FAS 77
Supersedes FAS 105, paragraph 14(e)
Supersedes FAS 107, paragraph 8(b)
Amends FAS 107, paragraph 28
Amends FAS 115, paragraph 7
Supersedes FAS 122
Supersedes FTB 84-4
Supersedes FTB 85-2
Supersedes 86-2, paragraph 12
Supersedes FTB 87-3, paragraphs 1 through 7 and 9

Affected by: Paragraph 19 superseded by FAS 127

Issues Discussed by FASB Emerging Issues Task Force (EITF)

Affects: Nullifies EITF Issues No. 85-40, 86-39, 89-2, 92-10, and 94-9 and Topics No. D-13 and D-48
Partially nullifies EITF Issues No. 84-5, 85-25, 86-18, 86-38, 87-30, 88-11, 88-17, 88-22,
89-4, 90-2, 92-2, and 96-10
Resolves EITF Issues No. 84-21, 84-26, 85-26, 85-30, 85-34, 87-18, 87-25, and 94-4
Partially resolves EITF Issues No. 84-20 and 87-20 and Topic No. D-14

Interpreted by: Paragraph 9 interpreted by EITF Topic No. D-51

Related Issues: EITF Issues No. 84-15, 85-13, 86-8, 86-24, 86-36, 87-34, 88-18, 88-20, 90-18, 90-19,
90-21, 95-5, 95-15, 96-19, 96-20, and 97-3

SUMMARY

This Statement provides accounting and reporting standards for transfers and servicing of financial assets and extinguishments of liabilities. Those standards are based on consistent application of a *financial-components approach* that focuses on control. Under that approach, after a transfer of financial assets, an entity recognizes the financial and servicing assets it controls and the liabilities it has incurred, derecognizes financial assets when control has been surrendered, and derecognizes liabilities when extinguished. This Statement provides consistent standards for distinguishing transfers of financial assets that are sales from transfers that are secured borrowings.

A transfer of financial assets in which the transferor surrenders control over those assets is accounted for as a sale to the extent that consideration other than beneficial interests in the transferred assets is received in exchange. The transferor has surrendered control over transferred assets if and only if all of the following conditions are met:

a. The transferred assets have been isolated from the transferor—put presumptively beyond the reach of the transferor and its creditors, even in bankruptcy or other receivership.
b. Either (1) each transferee obtains the right—free of conditions that constrain it from taking advantage of that right—to pledge or exchange the transferred assets or (2) the transferee is a qualifying special-purpose entity and the holders of beneficial interests in that entity have the right—free of conditions that constrain them from taking advantage of that right—to pledge or exchange those interests.
c. The transferor does not maintain effective control over the transferred assets through (1) an agreement that both entitles and obligates the transferor to repurchase or redeem them before their maturity or (2) an agreement that entitles the transferor to repurchase or redeem transferred assets that are not readily obtainable.

This Statement requires that liabilities and derivatives incurred or obtained by transferors as part of a transfer of financial assets be initially measured at fair value, if practicable. It also requires that servicing assets and other retained interests in the transferred assets be measured by allocating the previous carrying amount between the assets sold, if any, and retained interests, if any, based on their relative fair values at the date of the transfer.

This Statement requires that servicing assets and liabilities be subsequently measured by (a) amortization in proportion to and over the period of estimated net servicing income or loss and (b) assessment for asset impairment or increased obligation based on their fair values.

This Statement requires that debtors reclassify financial assets pledged as collateral and that secured parties recognize those assets and their obligation to return them in certain circumstances in which the secured party has taken control of those assets.

This Statement requires that a liability be derecognized if and only if either (a) the debtor pays the creditor and is relieved of its obligation for the liability or (b) the debtor is legally released from being the primary obligor under the liability either judicially or by the creditor. Therefore, a liability is not considered extinguished by an in-substance defeasance.

This Statement provides implementation guidance for assessing isolation of transferred assets and for accounting for transfers of partial interests, servicing of financial assets, securitizations, transfers of sales-type and direct financing lease receivables, securities lending transactions, repurchase agreements including "dollar rolls," "wash sales," loan syndications and participations, risk participations in banker's acceptances, factoring arrangements, transfers of receivables with recourse, and extinguishments of liabilities.

This Statement supersedes FASB Statements No. 76, *Extinguishment of Debt,* and No. 77, *Reporting by Transferors for Transfers of Receivables with Recourse.* This Statement amends FASB Statement No. 115, *Accounting for Certain Investments in Debt and Equity Securities,* to clarify that a debt security may not be classified as held-to-maturity if it can be prepaid or otherwise settled in such a way that the holder of the security would not recover substantially all of its recorded investment. This Statement amends and extends to all servicing assets and liabilities the accounting standards for mortgage servicing rights now in FASB Statement No. 65, *Accounting for Certain Mortgage Banking Activities,* and supersedes FASB Statement No. 122, *Accounting for Mortgage Servicing Rights.* This Statement also supersedes Technical Bulletins No. 84-4, *In-Substance Defeasance of Debt,* No. 85-2, *Accounting for Collateralized Mortgage Obligations (CMOs),* and No. 87-3, *Accounting for Mortgage Servicing Fees and Rights.*

This Statement is effective for transfers and servicing of financial assets and extinguishments of liabilities occurring after December 31, 1996, and is to be applied prospectively. Earlier or retroactive application is not permitted.

Statement of Financial Accounting Standards No. 125

Accounting for Transfers and Servicing of Financial Assets and Extinguishments of Liabilities

CONTENTS

INTRODUCTION AND SCOPE

1. The Board added a project on financial instruments and off-balance-sheet financing to its agenda in May 1986. The project is intended to develop standards to aid in resolving existing financial accounting and reporting issues and other issues likely to arise in the future about various financial instruments and related transactions. The November 1991 FASB Discussion Memorandum, *Recognition and Measurement of Financial Instruments,* describes the issues to be considered. This Statement focuses on the issues of accounting for **transfers**[1] and servicing of **financial assets** and extinguishments of liabilities.

2. Transfers of financial assets take many forms. Accounting for transfers in which the **transferor** has no continuing involvement with the transferred assets or with the **transferee** has not been controversial. However, transfers of financial assets often occur in which the transferor has some continuing involvement either with the assets transferred or with the transferee. Examples of continuing involvement are **recourse,** servicing, agreements to reacquire, options written or held, and pledges of **collateral.** Transfers of financial assets with continuing involvement raise issues about the circumstances under which the transfers should be considered as sales of all or part of the assets or as secured borrowings and about how transferors and transferees should account for sales and secured borrowings. This Statement establishes standards for resolving those issues.

3. An entity may settle a liability by transferring assets to the creditor or otherwise obtaining an unconditional release. Alternatively, an entity may enter into other arrangements designed to set aside assets dedicated to eventually settling a liability. Accounting for those arrangements has raised issues about when a liability should be considered extinguished. This Statement establishes standards for resolving those issues.

---

[1]Terms defined in Appendix D, the glossary, are set in **boldface type** the first time they appear.

4. This Statement does not address transfers of custody of financial assets for safekeeping, contributions,[2] or investments by owners or distributions to owners of a business enterprise. This Statement does not address subsequent measurement of assets and liabilities, except for (a) **servicing assets and servicing liabilities** and (b) **interest-only strips,** securities, loans, other receivables, or retained interests in securitizations that can contractually be prepaid or otherwise settled in such a way that the holder would not recover substantially all of its recorded investment. This Statement does not change the accounting for employee benefits subject to the provisions of FASB Statement No. 87, *Employers' Accounting for Pensions,* No. 88, *Employers' Accounting for Settlements and Curtailments of Defined Benefit Pension Plans and for Termination Benefits,* or No. 106, *Employers' Accounting for Postretirement Benefits Other Than Pensions.* This Statement does not change the provisions relating to leveraged leases in FASB Statement No. 13, *Accounting for Leases,* or money-over-money and wrap lease transactions involving nonrecourse debt subject to the provisions of FASB Technical Bulletin No. 88-1, *Issues Relating to Accounting for Leases.* This Statement does not address transfers of nonfinancial assets, for example, servicing assets, or transfers of unrecognized financial assets, for example, minimum lease payments to be received under operating leases.

5. The Board concluded that an objective in accounting for transfers of financial assets is for each entity that is a party to the transaction to recognize only assets it controls and liabilities it has incurred, to **derecognize** assets only when control has been surrendered, and to derecognize liabilities only when they have been extinguished. Sales and other transfers frequently result in a disaggregation of financial assets and liabilities into components, which become separate assets and liabilities. For example, if an entity sells a portion of a financial asset it owns, the portion retained becomes an asset separate from the portion sold and from the assets obtained in exchange.

6. The Board concluded that another objective is that recognition of financial assets and liabilities should not be affected by the sequence of transactions that result in their acquisition or incurrence unless the ef-

fect of those transactions is to maintain effective control over a transferred financial asset. For example, if a transferor sells financial assets it owns and at the same time writes a put option (such as a guarantee or recourse obligation) on those assets, it should recognize the put obligation in the same manner as would another unrelated entity that writes an identical put option on assets it never owned. Similarly, a creditor may release a debtor on the condition that a third party assumes the obligation and that the original debtor becomes secondarily liable. In those circumstances, the original debtor becomes a guarantor and should recognize a guarantee obligation in the same manner as would a third-party guarantor that had never been primarily liable to that creditor, whether or not explicit consideration was paid for that guarantee. However, certain agreements to repurchase or redeem transferred assets maintain effective control over those assets and should therefore be accounted for differently than agreements to acquire assets never owned.

7. Previous accounting standards generally required that a transferor account for financial assets transferred as an inseparable unit that had been either entirely sold or entirely retained. Those standards were difficult to apply and produced inconsistent and arbitrary results. For example, whether a transfer "purported to be a sale" was sufficient to determine whether the transfer was accounted for and reported as a sale of receivables under one accounting standard or as a secured borrowing under another.

8. Previous standards did not accommodate recent innovations in the financial markets. After studying many of the complex developments that have occurred in financial markets during recent years, the Board concluded that previous approaches that viewed each financial asset as an indivisible unit do not provide an appropriate basis for developing consistent and operational standards for dealing with transfers and servicing of financial assets and extinguishments of liabilities. To address those issues adequately and consistently, the Board decided to adopt as the basis for this Statement a *financial-components approach* that focuses on control and recognizes that financial assets and liabilities can be divided into a variety of components.

---

[2]Contributions—unconditional nonreciprocal transfers of assets—are addressed in FASB Statement No. 116, *Accounting for Contributions Received and Contributions Made.*

STANDARDS OF FINANCIAL ACCOUNTING AND REPORTING

Accounting for Transfers and Servicing of Financial Assets

9. A transfer of financial assets (or all or a portion of a financial asset) in which the transferor surrenders control over those financial assets shall be accounted for as a sale to the extent that consideration other than **beneficial interests** in the transferred assets is received in exchange. The transferor has surrendered control over transferred assets if and only if all of the following conditions are met:

a. The transferred assets have been isolated from the transferor—put presumptively beyond the reach of the transferor and its creditors, even in bankruptcy or other receivership (paragraphs 23 and 24).
b. Either (1) each transferee obtains the right—free of conditions that constrain it from taking advantage of that right (paragraph 25)—to pledge or exchange the transferred assets or (2) the transferee is a qualifying special-purpose entity (paragraph 26) and the holders of beneficial interests in that entity have the right—free of conditions that constrain them from taking advantage of that right (paragraph 25)—to pledge or exchange those interests.
c. The transferor does not maintain effective control over the transferred assets through (1) an agreement that both entitles and obligates the transferor to repurchase or redeem them before their maturity (paragraphs 27-29) or (2) an agreement that entitles the transferor to repurchase or redeem transferred assets that are not readily obtainable (paragraph 30).

10. Upon completion of any transfer of financial assets, the transferor shall:

a. Continue to carry in its statement of financial position any retained interest in the transferred assets, including, if applicable, servicing assets (paragraphs 35-41), beneficial interests in assets transferred to a qualifying special-purpose entity in a **securitization** (paragraphs 47-58), and retained **undivided interests** (paragraph 33)

b. Allocate the previous carrying amount between the assets sold, if any, and the retained interests, if any, based on their relative **fair values** at the date of transfer (paragraphs 31-34).

11. Upon completion[3] of a transfer of assets that satisfies the conditions to be accounted for as a sale (paragraph 9), the transferor (**seller**) shall:

a. Derecognize all assets sold
b. Recognize all assets obtained and liabilities incurred in consideration as **proceeds** of the sale, including cash, put or call options held or written (for example, guarantee or recourse obligations), forward commitments (for example, commitments to deliver additional receivables during the revolving periods of some securitizations), swaps (for example, provisions that convert interest rates from fixed to variable), and servicing liabilities, if applicable (paragraphs 31, 32, and 35-41)
c. Initially measure at fair value assets obtained and liabilities incurred in a sale (paragraphs 42-44) or, if it is not practicable to estimate the fair value of an asset or a liability, apply alternative measures (paragraphs 45 and 46)
d. Recognize in earnings any gain or loss on the sale.

The transferee shall recognize all assets obtained and any liabilities incurred and initially measure them at fair value (in aggregate, presumptively the price paid).

12. If a transfer of financial assets in exchange for cash or other consideration (other than beneficial interests in the transferred assets) does not meet the criteria for a sale in paragraph 9, the transferor and transferee shall account for the transfer as a secured borrowing with pledge of collateral (paragraph 15).

Recognition and Measurement of Servicing Assets and Liabilities

13. Each time an entity undertakes an obligation to service financial assets it shall recognize either a servicing asset or a servicing liability for that servicing contract, unless it securitizes the assets, retains all of the resulting securities, and classifies them as debt securities held-to-maturity in accordance with FASB Statement No. 115, *Accounting for Certain*

---

[3]Although a transfer of securities may not be considered to have reached completion until the settlement date, this Statement does not modify other generally accepted accounting principles, including FASB Statement No. 35, *Accounting and Reporting by Defined Benefit Pension Plans*, and AICPA Statements of Position and audit and accounting Guides for certain industries, that require accounting at the trade date for certain contracts to purchase or sell securities.

Investments in Debt and Equity Securities. If the servicing asset or liability was purchased or assumed rather than undertaken in a sale or securitization of the financial assets being serviced, it shall be measured initially at its fair value, presumptively the price paid. A servicing asset or liability shall be amortized in proportion to and over the period of estimated net servicing income (if servicing revenues exceed servicing costs) or net servicing loss (if servicing costs exceed servicing revenues). A servicing asset or liability shall be assessed for impairment or increased obligation based on its fair value (paragraphs 35-38).

Financial Assets Subject to Prepayment

14. Interest-only strips, loans, other receivables, or retained interests in securitizations that can contractually be prepaid or otherwise settled in such a way that the holder would not recover substantially all of its recorded investment shall be subsequently measured like investments in debt securities classified as available-for-sale or trading under Statement 115, as amended by this Statement (paragraph 233).[4]

Secured Borrowings and Collateral

15. A debtor may grant a **security interest** in certain assets to a lender (the secured party) to serve as collateral for its obligation under a borrowing, with or without recourse to other assets of the debtor. An obligor under other kinds of current or potential obligations, for example, interest rate swaps, also may grant a security interest in certain assets to a secured party. If collateral is transferred to the secured party, the custodial arrangement is commonly referred to as a pledge. Secured parties sometimes are permitted to sell or repledge (or otherwise transfer) collateral held under a pledge. The same relationships occur, under different names, in transfers documented as sales that are accounted for as secured borrowings (paragraph 12). The accounting for collateral by the debtor (or obligor) and the secured party depends on whether the secured party has taken control over the collateral and on the rights and obligations that result from the collateral arrangement:

a. If (1) the secured party is permitted by contract or custom to sell or repledge the collateral and (2) the debtor does not have the right and ability to redeem the collateral on short notice, for example, by substituting other collateral or terminating the contract, then

   (i) The debtor shall reclassify that asset and report that asset in its statement of financial position separately (for example, as securities receivable from broker) from other assets not so encumbered.

   (ii) The secured party shall recognize that collateral as its asset, initially measure it at fair value, and also recognize its obligation to return it.

b. If the secured party sells or repledges collateral on terms that do not give it the right and ability to repurchase or redeem the collateral from the transferee on short notice and thus may impair the debtor's right to redeem it, the secured party shall recognize the proceeds from the sale or the asset repledged and its obligation to return the asset to the extent that it has not already recognized them. The sale or repledging of the asset is a transfer subject to the provisions of this Statement.

c. If the debtor defaults under the terms of the secured contract and is no longer entitled to redeem the collateral, it shall derecognize the collateral, and the secured party shall recognize the collateral as its asset to the extent it has not already recognized it and initially measure it at fair value.

d. Otherwise, the debtor shall continue to carry the collateral as its asset, and the secured party shall not recognize the pledged asset.

Extinguishments of Liabilities

16. A debtor shall derecognize a liability if and only if it has been extinguished. A liability has been extinguished if either of the following conditions is met:

a. The debtor pays the creditor and is relieved of its obligation for the liability. *Paying the creditor* includes delivery of cash, other financial assets, goods, or services or reacquisition by the debtor of its outstanding debt securities whether the securities are canceled or held as so-called treasury bonds.

---

[4]As a result of that amendment to Statement 115, securities that were previously classified as held-to-maturity may need to be reclassified. Reclassifications of interest-only strips or other securities from held-to-maturity to available-for-sale required to initially apply this Statement would not call into question an entity's intent to hold other debt securities to maturity in the future.

b. The debtor is legally released[5] from being the primary obligor under the liability, either judicially or by the creditor.

Disclosures

17. An entity shall disclose the following:

a. If the entity has entered into repurchase agreements or securities lending transactions, its policy for requiring collateral or other security

b. If debt was considered to be extinguished by in-substance defeasance under the provisions of FASB Statement No. 76, *Extinguishment of Debt,* prior to the effective date of this Statement, a general description of the transaction and the amount of debt that is considered extinguished at the end of the period so long as that debt remains outstanding

c. If assets are set aside after the effective date of this Statement solely for satisfying scheduled payments of a specific obligation, a description of the nature of restrictions placed on those assets

d. If it is not practicable to estimate the fair value of certain assets obtained or liabilities incurred in transfers of financial assets during the period, a description of those items and the reasons why it is not practicable to estimate their fair value

e. For all servicing assets and servicing liabilities:

(1) The amounts of servicing assets or liabilities recognized and amortized during the period

(2) The fair value of recognized servicing assets and liabilities for which it is practicable to estimate that value and the method and significant assumptions used to estimate the fair value

(3) The risk characteristics of the underlying financial assets used to stratify recognized servicing assets for purposes of measuring impairment in accordance with paragraph 37

(4) The activity in any valuation allowance for impairment of recognized servicing

assets—including beginning and ending balances, aggregate additions charged and reductions credited to operations, and aggregate direct write-downs charged against the allowances—for each period for which results of operations are presented.

Implementation Guidance

18. Appendix A describes certain provisions of this Statement in more detail and describes their application to certain types of transactions. Appendix A is an integral part of the standards provided in this Statement.

Effective Date and Transition

19. This Statement shall be effective for transfers and servicing of financial assets and extinguishments of liabilities occurring after December 31, 1996, and shall be applied prospectively. Earlier or retroactive application of this Statement is not permitted.

20. For each servicing contract in existence before January 1, 1997, previously recognized servicing rights and "excess servicing" receivables that do not exceed **contractually specified servicing fees** shall be combined, net of any previously recognized servicing obligations under that contract, as a servicing asset or liability. Previously recognized servicing receivables that exceed contractually specified servicing fees shall be reclassified as interest-only strips receivable. Thereafter, the subsequent measurement provisions of this Statement shall be applied to the servicing assets or liabilities for those servicing contracts (paragraph 37) and to the interest-only strips receivable (paragraph 14).

21. The provisions of paragraph 14 and the amendment to Statement 115 (paragraph 233) shall be effective for financial assets held on or acquired after January 1, 1997.

> The provisions of this Statement need not be applied to immaterial items.

---

[5]If nonrecourse debt (such as certain mortgage loans) is assumed by a third party in conjunction with the sale of an asset that serves as sole collateral for that debt, the sale and related assumption effectively accomplish a legal release of the seller-debtor for purposes of applying this Statement.

This Statement was adopted by the affirmative votes of six members of the Financial Accounting Standards Board. Mr. Foster dissented.

Mr. Foster dissents from the issuance of this Statement because he believes that the notion of effective control that is applied to repurchase agreements, including dollar rolls, and securities lending transactions should be applied consistently to other transfers of financial assets, including securitization transactions. Furthermore, he believes that in those instances where the financial-components approach is applied, all rights (assets) and obligations (liabilities) that are recognized by the transferor after a sale or securitization has occurred should be measured at fair value.

Under paragraphs 9(a) and 9(b) of this Statement, control is deemed to have been surrendered if the transferred assets have been legally isolated from the transferor and the transferee has the right to pledge or exchange the transferred assets. That notion of control is the cornerstone of the financial-components approach. However, the Board considered that approach inappropriate to account for certain transactions, such as those involving repurchase agreements, including dollar rolls, and securities lending transactions, where legal control over the assets has been surrendered, but where the Board believes that effective control still exists. For those transactions, paragraph 9(c) was specifically crafted to override the criteria for transfers of legal control in paragraphs 9(a) and 9(b). Paragraph 9(c), however, was designed to provide an exception only for certain transactions resulting in inconsistent application of the control notion: one set of transfers of financial assets—securitizations—is accounted for using a narrow, legal definition of control while others are accounted for using a broad notion of effective control. Mr. Foster favors an approach that encompasses the broader notion of effective control. He questions why, if the financial-components approach is inappropriate to account for all transfers of financial assets, it is appropriate to apply it to securitizations. He believes that if the entirety of the arrangement is considered, certain securitization transactions, such as those having a revolving-period agreement, also result in effective control being retained by the transferor and accordingly those transactions should be accounted for as secured borrowings.

In securitizations having a revolving-period agreement, which are described in paragraphs 130-133, the transferor generally continues to collect the cash from the transferred receivables, commingles that cash with its own cash, invests the cash for its own benefit, and uses the cash to buy additional receivables from itself that it selects. As a result of those features, the future benefits of the receivables (the cash flows to be received from them) that inure to the transferor are little different, if at all, from the future benefits that the transferor would obtain from receivables that it holds for its own account. Mr. Foster believes that in those transactions effective control of the receivables has not been surrendered and that the transferred receivables continue to be assets of the transferor.

Paragraph 26 of FASB Concepts Statement No. 6, *Elements of Financial Statements,* states, "An asset has three essential characteristics: (a) it embodies a probable future benefit that involves a capacity, singly or in combination with other assets, to contribute directly or indirectly to future net cash inflows, (b) a particular entity can obtain the benefit and control others' access to it, and (c) the transaction or other event giving rise to the entity's right to or control of the benefit has already occurred." Mr. Foster believes that in securitizations having revolving-period agreements, the transferred receivables meet each of those criteria from the perspective of the transferor. The transferred receivables directly or indirectly contribute to the transferor's cash inflows—it generally receives and retains all of the cash inflows during the term of the arrangement subject only to payment of what amounts to interest on the investment of the holders of beneficial interests—and the transferor can and does obtain and control others' access to both the receivables and the cash inflows by its structuring of the transaction and retention of most of the cash flows until termination of the arrangement. Paragraph 131 of this Statement asserts that the cash obtained by the transferor in those securitizations is received in exchange for new receivables and is not obtained as a benefit attributable to its previous ownership of the transferred receivables. In substance, however, the transfer of new receivables is little different from the substitution of collateral prevalent in many secured loan arrangements. In short, the transferred receivables have all of the attributes of assets controlled by the transferor.

As described below, the principal criteria cited in the basis for conclusions for treating repurchase agreements and securities lending transactions as secured borrowings apply equally to many securitizations, particularly those having a revolving-period agreement.

The inability of the transferor in a transfer with a revolving-period agreement to sell new receivables elsewhere because it has contracted to sell those new receivables on prearranged terms at times that it does not determine or have much influence over is asserted to be significant in paragraph 131. However, within fairly wide latitude, the transferor in those circumstances has retained the right to change the interest rate (the price) on both the previously transferred receivables and receivables to be transferred in the future. Mr. Foster believes that that right substantially diminishes any disadvantage of not being able to sell the receivables elsewhere and substantially negates any effect, favorable or onerous, on the transferor as a result of changes in market conditions as asserted in paragraph 50. In fact, any effects on the transferor result solely from having financed the receivables at whatever rate is paid the beneficial owners of the securities. Furthermore, the transferor of assets transferred under repurchase agreements or in securities lending transactions cannot sell those assets elsewhere.

Two reasons advanced in support of the treatment of repurchase agreements and securities lending transactions as secured borrowings are that (a) those transactions are difficult to characterize because they have attributes of both borrowings and sales and (b) supporting arguments can be found for accounting for those transactions as borrowings or sales. Those two reasons are equally applicable to securitization transactions having a revolving-period agreement—they are treated as sales for purposes of marketing to investors and as borrowings for tax purposes, and legal opinions and the prospectuses for those transactions acknowledge that their treatment as sales may not be sustained in a legal dispute.

The only supporting arguments cited for the treatment of repurchase agreements and securities lending transactions as secured borrowings that are not equally applicable to certain securitizations are that (a) forward contracts that are fully secured should be treated differently than those that are unsecured and (b) making a change in existing accounting practice would have a substantial impact on the reported financial position of certain entities and on the markets in which they participate. Mr. Foster does not believe that the existence of security in support of a transaction should determine its accounting treatment and notes that extension of the reasoning in paragraph 141 would lead to lenders not recognizing loans receivable that are unsecured. While it may be necessary to consider prior accounting treatment and the effect a change in accounting practice would have

on certain entities, Mr. Foster believes that those factors should carry relatively little weight in determining what is an appropriate accounting standard.

Paragraph 18 of Opinion 29 states, "The Board concludes that in general accounting for nonmonetary transactions should be based on the fair values of the assets (or services) involved which is the same basis as that used in monetary transactions. Thus, the cost of a nonmonetary asset acquired in exchange for another nonmonetary asset is the fair value of the asset surrendered to obtain it . . ." (footnote reference omitted). The conclusion embodied in that language is that the accounting for both monetary and nonmonetary transactions acquired in an exchange should be based on the fair values of the assets (or services) involved. Mr. Foster believes that in securitization transactions in which control is deemed under this Statement to be surrendered and in partial sales of financial assets, assets (or rights) are surrendered in exchange for cash and other rights and obligations, all of which are new.[6] The new assets (rights) received are part of the proceeds of the exchange, and any liabilities (obligations) incurred are a reduction of the proceeds. As such, those new assets and liabilities should be measured at their fair values as they are in all other exchange transactions.

This Statement contends that in those transactions certain components of the original assets have not been exchanged. If that is one's view, however, it is clear that a transaction of sufficient significance to result in the derecognition of assets has occurred. Furthermore, the event of securitization results in a change in the form and value of assets— securities are generally more easily sold or used as collateral and thus are more valuable than receivables. Mr. Foster believes that a securitization transaction, like the initial recognition of an asset or liability and derecognition of assets and liabilities where it is clear an exchange has occurred, is also sufficiently significant that the resulting, or remaining components of, assets and liabilities should be recorded at fair value.

Mr. Foster also notes, as described in paragraphs 182-184, that the distinctions made in paragraphs 10 and 11 between (a) assets retained and (b) assets obtained and liabilities incurred are arbitrary. For example, one could easily argue that beneficial interests acquired in a transfer of receivables have different rights and obligations than the receivables and accordingly should be accounted for

---

[6]In the case of a partial sale of a financial asset, the transferor generally has reduced the marketability of the asset because it can no longer sell the entire asset—it can only sell part of that asset. Consequently, the partial interest in the original asset has different rights and privileges than those embodied in the original asset and, therefore, is a new asset—different from the original asset.

not as retained assets, but as new and different assets, and, arguably, the rights inherent in derivatives arising in a securitization transaction, which are considered new rights (assets) in this Statement, were embedded, albeit in an obscure form, in the transferred assets and could be as readily identified as retained portions of them. That the Board needed to make those distinctions arbitrarily begs for a consistent measurement attribute—fair value—for all of the rights and obligations held by the transferor subsequent to the transfer.

Members of the Financial Accounting Standards Board:

Dennis R. Beresford,	Anthony T. Cope	Robert H. Northcutt
Chairman	John M. Foster	Robert J. Swieringa
Joseph V. Anania	James J. Leisenring	

Appendix A

IMPLEMENTATION GUIDANCE

CONTENTS

Appendix A

IMPLEMENTATION GUIDANCE

Introduction

22. This appendix describes certain provisions of this Statement in more detail and describes how they apply to certain types of transactions. This appendix discusses generalized situations. Facts and circumstances and specific contracts need to be considered carefully in applying this Statement. This appendix is an integral part of the standards provided in this Statement.

Isolation beyond the Reach of the Transferor and Its Creditors

23. The nature and extent of supporting evidence required for an assertion in financial statements that transferred financial assets have been isolated—put presumptively beyond the reach of the transferor and its creditors, either by a single transaction or a series of transactions taken as a whole—depend on the facts and circumstances. All available evidence that either supports or questions an assertion shall be considered. That consideration includes making judgments about whether the contract or circumstances permit the transferor to revoke the transfer. It also may include making judgments about the kind of bankruptcy or other receivership into which a transferor or special-purpose entity might be placed, whether a transfer of financial assets would likely be deemed a true sale at law, whether the transferor is affiliated with the transferee, and other factors pertinent under applicable law. Derecognition of transferred assets is appropriate only if the available evidence provides reasonable assurance that the transferred assets would be beyond the reach of the powers of a bankruptcy trustee or other receiver for the transferor or any of its affiliates, except for an affiliate that is a qualifying special-purpose entity designed to make remote the possibility that it would enter bankruptcy or other receivership (paragraph 57(c)).

24. Whether securitizations isolate transferred assets may depend on such factors as whether the securitization is accomplished in one step or two steps (paragraphs 54-58). Many common financial transactions, for example, typical repurchase agreements and securities lending transactions, isolate transferred assets from the transferor, although they may not meet the other criteria for surrender of control.

Conditions That Constrain a Transferee

25. Many transferor-imposed or other conditions on a transferee's contractual right to pledge or exchange a transferred asset constrain a transferee from taking advantage of that right. However, a transferor's right of first refusal on a bona fide offer from a third party, a requirement to obtain the transferor's permission to sell or pledge that shall not be unreasonably withheld, or a prohibition on sale to the transferor's competitor generally does not constrain a transferee from pledging or exchanging the asset and, therefore, presumptively does not preclude a transfer containing such a condition from being accounted for as a sale. For example, a prohibition on sale to the transferor's competitor would not constrain the transferee if it were able to sell the transferred assets to a number of other parties; however, it would be a constraint if that competitor were the only potential willing buyer.

Qualifying Special-Purpose Entity

26. A qualifying special-purpose entity[7] must meet both of the following conditions:

a. It is a trust, corporation, or other legal vehicle

---

[7]The description of a special-purpose entity is restrictive. The accounting for transfers of financial assets to special-purpose entities should not be extended to any entity that does not satisfy all of the conditions articulated in this paragraph.

whose activities are permanently limited by the legal documents establishing the special-purpose entity to:

(1) Holding title to transferred financial assets
(2) Issuing beneficial interests (If some of the beneficial interests are in the form of debt securities or equity securities, the transfer of assets is a securitization.)
(3) Collecting cash proceeds from assets held, reinvesting proceeds in financial instruments pending distribution to holders of beneficial interests, and otherwise servicing the assets held
(4) Distributing proceeds to the holders of its beneficial interests.

b. It has standing at law distinct from the transferor. Having standing at law depends in part on the nature of the special-purpose entity. For example, generally, under U.S. law, if a transferor of assets to a special-purpose trust holds all of the beneficial interests, it can unilaterally dissolve the trust and thereby reassume control over the individual assets held in the trust, and the transferor "can effectively assign his interest and his creditors can reach it."[8] In that circumstance, the trust has no standing at law, is not distinct, and thus is not a qualifying special-purpose entity.

Agreements That Maintain Effective Control over Transferred Assets

27. An agreement that both entitles and obligates the transferor to repurchase or redeem transferred assets from the transferee maintains the transferor's effective control over those assets, and the transfer is therefore to be accounted for as a secured borrowing, if and only if all of the following conditions are met:

a. The assets to be repurchased or redeemed are the same or substantially the same as those transferred (paragraph 28).
b. The transferor is able to repurchase or redeem them on substantially the agreed terms, even in the event of default by the transferee (paragraph 29).
c. The agreement is to repurchase or redeem them before maturity, at a fixed or determinable price.
d. The agreement is entered into concurrently with the transfer.

28. To be substantially the same,[9] the asset that was transferred and the asset that is to be repurchased or redeemed need to have all of the following characteristics:

a. The same primary obligor (except for debt guaranteed by a sovereign government, central bank, government-sponsored enterprise or agency thereof, in which case the guarantor and the terms of the guarantee must be the same)
b. Identical form and type so as to provide the same risks and rights
c. The same maturity (or in the case of mortgage-backed pass-through and pay-through securities have similar remaining weighted-average maturities that result in approximately the same market yield)
d. Identical contractual interest rates
e. Similar assets as collateral
f. The same aggregate unpaid principal amount or principal amounts within accepted "good delivery" standards for the type of security involved.

29. To be able to repurchase or redeem assets on substantially the agreed terms, even in the event of default by the transferee, a transferor must at all times during the contract term have obtained cash or other collateral sufficient to fund substantially all of the cost of purchasing replacement assets from others.

30. A call option or forward contract that entitles the transferor to repurchase, prior to maturity, transferred assets not readily obtainable elsewhere maintains the transferor's effective control, because it would constrain the transferee from exchanging those assets, unless it is only a **cleanup call.**

Measurement of Interests Held after a Transfer of Financial Assets

Assets Obtained and Liabilities Incurred as Proceeds

31. The proceeds from a sale of financial assets consist of the cash and any other assets obtained in the transfer less any liabilities incurred. Any asset obtained that is not an interest in the transferred asset is part of the proceeds from the sale. Any liability incurred, even if it is related to the transferred assets, is a reduction of the proceeds. Any **derivative financial**

---

[8]*Scott's Abridgement of the Law on Trusts*, 156 (Little, Brown and Company, 1960), 296.
[9]In this Statement, the term *substantially the same* is used consistently with the usage of that term in the AICPA Statement of Position 90-3, *Definition of the Term Substantially the Same for Holders of Debt Instruments, as Used in Certain Audit Guides and a Statement of Position.*

instrument entered into concurrently with a transfer of financial assets is either an asset obtained or a liability incurred and part of the proceeds received in the transfer. All proceeds and reductions of proceeds from a sale shall be initially measured at fair value, if practicable.

Illustration—Recording Transfers with Proceeds of Cash, Derivatives, and Other Liabilities

32. Company A sells loans with a fair value of $1,100 and a carrying amount of $1,000. Company A retains no servicing responsibilities but obtains an option to purchase from the transferee the loans sold or similar loans and assumes a recourse obligation to repurchase delinquent loans. Company A agrees to provide the transferee a return at a floating rate of interest even though the contractual terms of the loan are fixed rate in nature (that provision is effectively an interest rate swap).

Fair Values

Cash proceeds	$1,050
Interest rate swap	40
Call option	70
Recourse obligation	60

Net Proceeds

Cash received	$1,050
Plus: Call option	70
Interest rate swap	40
Less: Recourse obligation	(60)
Net proceeds	$1,100

Gain on Sale

Net proceeds	$1,100
Carrying amount of loans sold	1,000
Gain on sale	$ 100

Journal Entry

Cash	1,050	
Interest rate swap	40	
Call option	70	
Loans		1,000
Recourse obligation		60
Gain on sale		100
To record transfer		

Retained Interests

33. Other interests in transferred assets—those that are not part of the proceeds of the transfer—are retained interests over which the transferor has not relinquished control. They shall be measured at the date of the transfer by allocating the previous carrying amount between the assets sold, if any, and the retained interests, based on their relative fair values. That procedure shall be applied to all transfers in which interests are retained, even those that do not qualify as sales. Examples of retained interests include securities backed by the transferred assets, undivided interests, servicing assets, and cash reserve accounts and residual interests in securitization trusts. If a transferor cannot determine whether an asset is a retained interest or proceeds from the sale, the asset shall be treated as proceeds from the sale and accounted for in accordance with paragraph 31.

Illustration—Recording Transfers of Partial Interests

34. Company B sells a pro rata nine-tenths interest in loans with a fair value of $1,100 and a carrying amount of $1,000. There is no servicing asset or liability, because Company B estimates that the **benefits of servicing** are just adequate to compensate it for its servicing responsibilities.

Fair Values

Cash proceeds for nine-tenths interest sold	$990
One-tenth interest retained $[(\$990 \div \frac{9}{10}) \times \frac{1}{10}]$	110

Carrying Amount Based on Relative Fair Values

	Fair Value	Percentage of Total Fair Value	Allocated Carrying Amount
Nine-tenths interest sold	$ 990	90	$ 900
One-tenth interest retained	110	10	100
Total	$1,100	100	$1,000

Gain on Sale

Net proceeds	$990
Carrying amount of loans sold	900
Gain on sale	$ 90

Journal Entry

Cash	990	
Loans		900
Gain on sale		90
To record transfer		

Servicing Assets and Liabilities

35. Servicing of mortgage loans, credit card receivables, or other financial assets includes, but is not limited to, collecting principal, interest, and escrow payments from borrowers; paying taxes and insurance from escrowed funds; monitoring delinquencies; executing foreclosure if necessary; temporarily investing funds pending distribution; remitting fees to guarantors, trustees, and others providing services; and accounting for and remitting principal and interest payments to the holders of beneficial interests in the financial assets. Servicing is inherent in all financial assets; it becomes a distinct asset or liability only when contractually separated from the underlying assets by sale or securitization of the assets with servicing retained or separate purchase or assumption of the servicing.

36. An entity that undertakes a contract to service financial assets shall recognize either a servicing asset or a servicing liability, unless the transferor securitizes the assets, retains all of the resulting securities, and classifies them as debt securities held-to-maturity in accordance with Statement 115, in which case the servicing asset or liability may be reported together with the asset being serviced. Each sale or securitization with servicing retained or separate purchase or assumption of servicing results in a servicing contract. A servicer of financial assets commonly receives the benefits of servicing—revenues from contractually specified servicing fees, late charges, and other ancillary sources, including "float," all of which it is entitled to receive only if it performs the servicing—and incurs the costs of servicing the assets. Each servicing contract results in a servicing asset or servicing liability. Typically, the benefits of servicing are expected to be more than **adequate compensation** to the servicer for performing the servicing, and the contract results in a servicing asset. However, if the benefits of servicing are not expected to adequately compensate the servicer for performing the servicing, the contract results in a servicing liability.

37. A servicer that recognizes a servicing asset or servicing liability shall account for the contract to service financial assets separately from those assets, as follows:

a. Report servicing assets separately from servicing liabilities in the statement of financial position (paragraph 13).
b. Initially measure servicing assets retained in a sale or securitization of the assets being serviced at their allocated previous carrying amount based on relative fair values, if practicable, at the date of the sale or securitization (paragraphs 10, 33, 34, and 42-46).
c. Initially measure servicing assets purchased or servicing liabilities assumed at fair value (paragraph 13).
d. Initially measure servicing liabilities undertaken in a sale or securitization at fair value, if practicable (paragraphs 11(b), 11(c), and 42-46).
e. Account separately for rights to future interest income from the serviced assets that exceeds contractually specified servicing fees. Those rights are not servicing assets; they are financial assets, effectively interest-only strips to be accounted for in accordance with paragraph 14 of this Statement.
f. Subsequently measure servicing assets by amortizing the amount recognized in proportion to and over the period of estimated net servicing income—the excess of servicing revenues over servicing costs (paragraph 13).
g. Subsequently evaluate and measure impairment of servicing assets as follows:
   (1) Stratify servicing assets based on one or more of the predominant risk characteristics of the underlying financial assets. Those characteristics may include financial asset type,[10] size, interest rate, date of origination, term, and geographic location.
   (2) Recognize impairment through a valuation allowance for an individual stratum. The amount of impairment recognized shall be the amount by which the carrying amount of servicing assets for a stratum exceeds their fair value. The fair value of servicing assets that have not been recognized shall not be used in the evaluation of impairment.
   (3) Adjust the valuation allowance to reflect changes in the measurement of impairment subsequent to the initial measurement of impairment. Fair value in excess of the carrying amount of servicing assets for that stratum, however, shall not be recognized. This Statement does not address when an entity should record a direct write-down of recognized servicing assets (paragraph 13).
h. Subsequently measure servicing liabilities by amortizing the amount recognized in proportion to and over the period of estimated net servicing loss—the excess of servicing costs over servicing revenues. However, if subsequent events have increased the fair value of the liability above the carrying amount, for example, because of significant changes in the amount or timing of actual or expected future cash flows from the cash flows previously projected, the servicer shall revise its earlier estimates and recognize the increased obligation as a loss in earnings (paragraph 13).

38. As indicated above, transferors sometimes agree to take on servicing responsibilities when the future benefits of servicing are not expected to adequately compensate them for performing that servicing. In that circumstance, the result is a servicing liability rather than a servicing asset. For example, if in the transaction illustrated in paragraph 32 the transferor had agreed to service the loans without explicit compensation and it estimated the fair value of that servicing obligation at $50, net proceeds would be reduced to $1,050, gain on sale would be reduced to $50, and the transferor would report a servicing liability of $50.

Illustration—Sale of Receivables with Servicing Retained

39. Company C originates $1,000 of loans that yield 10 percent interest income for their estimated lives of 9 years. Company C sells the $1,000 principal plus the right to receive interest income of 8 percent to another entity for $1,000. Company C will continue to service the loans and the contract stipulates that its compensation for performing the servicing is the right to receive half of the interest income not sold. The remaining half of the interest income not sold is considered an interest-only strip receivable. At the date of the transfer, the fair value of the loans, including servicing, is $1,100. The fair value of the servicing asset is $40.

---

[10]For example, for mortgage loans, financial asset type refers to the various conventional or government guaranteed or insured mortgage loans and adjustable-rate or fixed-rate mortgage loans.

Fair Values

Cash proceeds	$1,000
Servicing asset	40
Interest-only strip receivable	60

Carrying Amount Based on Relative Fair Values

	Fair Value	Percentage of Total Fair Value	Allocated Carrying Amount
Loans sold	$1,000	91	$ 910
Servicing asset	40	3.6	36
Interest-only strip receivable	60	5.4	54
Total	$1,100	100	$1,000

Gain on Sale

Net proceeds	$1,000
Carrying amount of loans sold	910
Gain on sale	$ 90

Journal Entries

Cash	1,000	
Loans		910
Gain on sale		90
To record transfer		
Servicing asset	36	
Interest-only strip receivable	54	
Loans		90
To record servicing asset and interest-only strip receivable		
Interest-only strip receivable	6	
Equity		6
To begin to subsequently measure interest-only strip receivable like an available-for-sale security (paragraph 14)		

40. The previous illustration demonstrates how a transferor would account for a simple sale or securitization in which servicing is retained. Company C might instead transfer the financial assets to a corporation or a trust that is a qualifying special-purpose entity. If the qualifying special-purpose entity securitizes the loans by selling beneficial interests to the public, it in turn becomes a transferor of securities to investors. The qualifying special-purpose entity pays the cash proceeds to the original transferor, which accounts for the transfer as a sale and derecognizes the financial assets assuming that the criteria in paragraph 9 are met. Securitizations often combine the elements shown in paragraphs 32, 34, and 39, as illustrated below.

Illustration—Recording Transfers of Partial Interests with Proceeds of Cash, Derivatives, Other Liabilities, and Servicing

41. Company D originates $1,000 of prepayable loans that yield 10 percent interest income for their

9-year expected lives. Company D sells nine-tenths of the principal plus interest of 8 percent to another entity. Company D will continue to service the loans, and the contract stipulates that its compensation for performing the servicing is the 2 percent of the interest income not sold. Company D retains an option to purchase the loans sold or similar loans and a recourse obligation to repurchase delinquent loans.

Fair Values

Cash proceeds	$900
Call option	70
Recourse obligation	60
Servicing asset	90
One-tenth interest retained	100

Net Proceeds

Cash received	$900
Plus: Call option	70
Less: Recourse obligation	(60)
Net proceeds	$910

Carrying Amount Based on Relative Fair Values

	Fair Value	Percentage of Total Fair Value	Allocated Carrying Amount
Interest sold	$ 910	83	$ 830
Servicing asset	90	8	80
One-tenth interest retained	100	9	90
Total	$1,100	100	$1,000

Gain on Sale

Net proceeds	$910
Carrying amount of loans sold	830
Gain on sale	$ 80

Journal Entries

Cash	900	
Call option	70	
Loans		830
Recourse obligation		60
Gain on sale		80
To record transfer		

Servicing asset	80	
Loans		80
To record servicing asset		

At the time of the transfer, Company D reports its one-tenth retained interest in the loans at its allocated carrying amount of $90.

Fair Value

42. The fair value of an asset (or liability) is the amount at which that asset (or liability) could be bought (or incurred) or sold (or settled) in a current transaction between willing parties, that is, other than in a forced or liquidation sale. Quoted market prices in active markets are the best evidence of fair value and shall be used as the basis for the measurement, if available. If a quoted market price is available, the fair value is the product of the number of trading units times market price.

43. If quoted market prices are not available, the estimate of fair value shall be based on the best information available in the circumstances. The estimate of fair value shall consider prices for similar assets and liabilities and the results of valuation techniques to the extent available in the circumstances. Examples of valuation techniques include the present value of estimated expected future cash flows using a discount rate commensurate with the risks involved, option-pricing models, matrix pricing, option-adjusted spread models, and fundamental analysis. Valuation techniques for measuring financial assets and liabilities and servicing assets and liabilities shall be consistent with the objective of measuring fair value. Those techniques shall incorporate assumptions that market participants would use in their estimates of values, future revenues, and future expenses, including assumptions about interest rates, default, prepayment, and volatility. In measuring **financial liabilities** and servicing liabilities at fair value by discounting estimated future cash flows, an objective is to use discount rates at which those liabilities could be settled in an arm's-length transaction.

44. Estimates of expected future cash flows, if used to estimate fair value, shall be the best estimate based on reasonable and supportable assumptions and pro-jections. All available evidence shall be considered in developing estimates of expected future cash flows. The weight given to the evidence shall be commensurate with the extent to which the evidence can be verified objectively. If a range is estimated for either the amount or timing of possible cash flows, the likelihood of possible outcomes shall be considered in determining the best estimate of future cash flows.

If It Is Not Practicable to Estimate Fair Values

45. If it is not practicable to estimate the fair values of assets, the transferor shall record those assets at zero. If it is not practicable to estimate the fair values of liabilities, the transferor shall recognize no gain on the transaction and shall record those liabilities at the greater of:

a. The excess, if any, of (1) the fair values of assets obtained less the fair values of other liabilities incurred, over (2) the sum of the carrying values of the assets transferred
b. The amount that would be recognized in accordance with FASB Statement No. 5, *Accounting for Contingencies*, as interpreted by FASB Interpretation No. 14, *Reasonable Estimation of the Amount of a Loss.*

Illustration—Recording Transfers If It Is Not Practicable to Estimate a Fair Value

46. Company E sells loans with a carrying amount of $1,000 to another entity for cash plus a call option to repurchase the loans sold or similar loans and incurs a recourse obligation to repurchase any delinquent loans. Company E undertakes to service the transferred assets for the other entity. In Case 1, Company E finds it impracticable to estimate the fair value of the servicing contract, although it is confident that servicing revenues will be more than adequate compensation for performing the servicing. In Case 2, Company E finds it impracticable to estimate the fair value of the recourse obligation.

Fair Values	Case 1	Case 2
Cash proceeds	$1,050	$1,050
Servicing asset	XX*	40
Call option	70	70
Recourse obligation	60	XX*
Fair value of loans transferred	1,100	1,100

*Not practicable to estimate fair value.

Net Proceeds	Case 1	Case 2
Cash received	$1,050	$1,050
Plus: Call option	70	70
Less: Recourse obligation	(60)	XX
Net proceeds	$1,060	$1,120

Carrying Amount Based on Relative Fair Values (Case 1)

	Fair Value	Percentage of Total Fair Value	Allocated Carrying Amount
Loans sold	$1,060	100	$1,000
Servicing asset	0	0	0
Total	$1,060	100	$1,000

Carrying Amount Based on Relative Fair Values (Case 2)

	Fair Value	Percentage of Total Fair Value	Allocated Carrying Amount
Loans sold	$1,120	97	$ 970
Servicing asset	40	3	30
Total	$1,160	100	$1,000

Journal Entries	Case 1		Case 2	
Cash	1,050		1,050	
Servicing asset	0*		30	
Call option	70		70	
Loans		1,000		1,000
Recourse obligation		60		150†
Gain on sale		60		0
To record transfer				

*Assets shall be recorded at zero if an estimate of the fair value of the assets is not practicable.
†The amount recorded as a liability in this example equals the sum of the known assets less the fair value of the known liabilities, that is, the amount that results in no gain or loss.

Securitizations

47. Financial assets such as mortgage loans, automobile loans, trade receivables, credit card receivables, and other revolving charge accounts are assets commonly transferred in securitizations. Securitizations of mortgage loans may include pools of single-family residential mortgages or other types of real estate mortgage loans, for example, multifamily residential mortgages and commercial property mortgages. Securitizations of loans secured by chattel mortgages on automotive vehicles as well as other equipment (including direct financing or sales-type

leases) also are common. Both financial and nonfinancial assets can be securitized; life insurance policy loans, patent and copyright royalties, and even taxi medallions also have been securitized. But securitizations of nonfinancial assets are outside the scope of this Statement.

48. An originator of a typical securitization (the transferor) transfers a portfolio of financial assets to a special-purpose entity, commonly a trust. In "pass-through" and "pay-through" securitizations, receivables are transferred to the special-purpose entity at the inception of the securitization, and no further

transfers are made; all cash collections are paid to the holders of beneficial interests in the special-purpose entity. In "revolving-period" securitizations, receivables are transferred at the inception and also periodically (daily or monthly) thereafter for a defined period (commonly three to eight years), referred to as the revolving period. During the revolving period, the special-purpose entity uses most of the cash collections to purchase additional receivables from the transferor on prearranged terms.

49. Beneficial interests in the qualifying special-purpose entity are sold to investors and the proceeds are used to pay the transferor for the assets transferred. Those beneficial interests may comprise either a single class having equity characteristics or multiple classes of interests, some having debt characteristics and others having equity characteristics. The cash collected from the portfolio is distributed to the investors and others as specified by the legal documents that established the qualifying special-purpose entity.

50. Pass-through, pay-through, and revolving-period securitizations that meet the criteria in paragraph 9 qualify for sale accounting under this Statement. All financial assets obtained or retained and liabilities incurred by the originator of a securitization that qualifies as a sale shall be recognized and measured as provided in paragraph 11; that includes the implicit forward contract to sell new receivables during a revolving period, which may become valuable or onerous to the transferor as interest rates and other market conditions change.

Revolving-Period Securitizations

51. The value of the forward contract implicit in a revolving-period securitization arises from the difference between the agreed-upon rate of return to investors on their beneficial interests in the trust and current market rates of return on similar investments. For example, if the agreed-upon annual rate of return to investors in a trust is 6 percent, and later market rates of return for those investments increased to 7 percent, the forward contract's value to the transferor (and burden to the investors) would approximate the present value of 1 percent of the amount of the investment for each year remaining in the revolving structure after the receivables already transferred have been collected. If a forward contract to sell receivables is entered into at the market rate, its value at inception may be zero. Changes in the fair value of the forward contract are likely to be greater if

the investors receive a fixed rate than if the investors receive a rate that varies based on changes in market rates.

52. Gain or loss recognition for revolving-period receivables sold to a securitization trust is limited to receivables that exist and have been sold. Recognition of servicing assets or liabilities for revolving-period receivables is similarly limited to the servicing for the receivables that exist and have been transferred. As new receivables are sold, rights to service them become assets or liabilities and are recognized.

53. Revolving-period securitizations may use either a discrete trust, used for a single securitization, or a master trust, used for many securitizations. To achieve another securitization using an existing master trust, a transferor first transfers additional receivables to the trust and then sells additional ownership interests in the trust to investors. Adding receivables to a master trust, in itself, is neither a sale nor a secured borrowing under paragraph 9, because that transfer only increases the transferor's beneficial interest in the trust's assets. A sale does not occur until the transferor receives consideration other than beneficial interests in the transferred assets. Transfers that result in an exchange of cash, that is, either transfers that in essence replace previously transferred receivables that have been collected or sales of beneficial interests to outside investors, are transfers in exchange for consideration other than beneficial interests in the transferred assets and thus are accounted for as sales (if they satisfy all the criteria in paragraph 9) or as secured borrowings.

Isolation of Transferred Assets in Securitizations

54. A securitization, carried out in one transfer or a series of transfers, may or may not isolate the transferred assets beyond the reach of the transferor and its creditors. Whether it does depends on the structure of the securitization transaction taken as a whole, considering such factors as the type and extent of further involvement in arrangements to protect investors from credit and interest rate risks, the availability of other assets, and the powers of bankruptcy courts or other receivers.

55. In certain securitizations, a corporation that, if it failed, would be subject to the U.S. Bankruptcy Code transfers financial assets to a special-purpose trust in exchange for cash. The trust raises that cash by issuing to investors beneficial interests that pass through all cash received from the financial assets, and the

transferor has no further involvement with the trust or the transferred assets. The Board understands that those securitizations generally would be judged as having isolated the assets, because in the absence of any continuing involvement there would be reasonable assurance that the transfer would be found to be a true sale at law that places the assets beyond the reach of the transferor and its creditors, even in bankruptcy or other receivership.

56. In other securitizations, a similar corporation transfers financial assets to a special-purpose entity in exchange for cash and beneficial interests in the transferred assets. That entity raises the cash by issuing to investors commercial paper that gives them a senior interest in cash received from the financial assets. The beneficial interests retained by the transferring corporation represent a junior interest to be reduced by any credit losses on the financial assets in trust. The commercial paper interests are highly rated by credit rating agencies largely because the transferor is highly rated. Depending on facts and circumstances, the Board understands that those "single-step" securitizations often would be judged in the United States as not having isolated the assets, because the nature of the continuing involvement may make it difficult to obtain reasonable assurance that the transfer would be found to be a true sale at law that places the assets beyond the reach of the transferor and its creditors in U.S. bankruptcy (paragraph 83). If the transferor fell into bankruptcy and the transfer was found not to be a true sale at law, investors in the transferred assets might be subjected to an automatic stay that would delay payments due them, and they might have to share in bankruptcy expenses and suffer further losses if the transfer was recharacterized as a secured loan.

57. Still other securitizations use two transfers intended to isolate transferred assets beyond the reach of the transferor and its creditors, even in bankruptcy. In those "two-step" structures:

a. First, the corporation transfers financial assets to a special-purpose corporation that, although wholly owned, is so designed that the possibility that the transferor or its creditors could reclaim the assets is remote. This first transfer is designed to be judged to be a true sale at law, in part because the transferor does not provide "excessive" credit or yield protection to the special-purpose corporation, and the Board understands that transferred assets are likely to be judged beyond the reach of the transferor or the transferor's creditors even in bankruptcy.

b. Second, the special-purpose corporation transfers the assets to a trust, with a sufficient increase in the credit or yield protection on the second transfer (provided by a junior retained beneficial interest or other means) to merit the high credit rating sought by third-party investors who buy senior beneficial interests in the trust. Because of that aspect of its design, that second transfer might not be judged to be a true sale at law and, thus, the transferred assets could at least in theory be reached by a bankruptcy trustee for the special-purpose corporation.

c. However, the special-purpose corporation is designed to make remote the possibility that it would enter bankruptcy, either by itself or by substantive consolidation into a bankruptcy of its parent should that occur. For example, its charter forbids it from undertaking any other business or incurring any liabilities, so that there can be no creditors to petition to place it in bankruptcy. Furthermore, its dedication to a single purpose is intended to make it extremely unlikely, even if it somehow entered bankruptcy, that a receiver under the U.S. Bankruptcy Code could reclaim the transferred assets because it has no other assets to substitute for the transferred assets.

The Board understands that the "two-step" securitizations described above, taken as a whole, generally would be judged under present U.S. law as having isolated the assets beyond the reach of the transferor and its creditors, even in bankruptcy or other receivership.

58. A securitization by an entity subject to a possible receivership under procedures different from the U.S. Bankruptcy Code may isolate transferred assets from the transferor and its creditors even though it uses only one transfer directly to a special-purpose entity that issues beneficial interests to investors and the transferor provides credit or yield protection. For example, the Board understands that assets transferred by a U.S. bank are not subject to an automatic stay under Federal Deposit Insurance Corporation (FDIC) receivership and could only be obtained by the receiver if it makes the investors completely whole, that is, the investors must be paid compensation equivalent to all the economic benefits contained in the transferred assets, including bargained-for yield, before the FDIC could obtain those assets. Those limited powers appear insufficient to place the transferred assets within reach of the receiver. The powers of other receivers for entities not subject to the U.S. Bankruptcy Code, and of bankruptcy trustees in other

jurisdictions, vary considerably, and therefore some receivers may be able to reach transferred financial assets, and others may not.

Sales-Type and Direct Financing Lease Receivables

59. Sales-type and direct financing receivables secured by leased equipment, referred to as gross investment in lease receivables, are made up of two components: minimum lease payments and residual values. Minimum lease payments are requirements for lessees to pay cash to lessors and meet the definition of a financial asset. Thus, transfers of minimum lease payments are subject to the requirements of this Statement. Residual values represent the lessor's estimate of the "salvage" value of the leased equipment at the end of the lease term and may be either guaranteed or unguaranteed; they meet the definition of financial assets *if they are guaranteed*. Thus, transfers of guaranteed residual values also are subject to the requirements of this Statement. Unguaranteed residual values do not meet the definition of financial assets, and transfers of them are not subject to the requirements of this Statement. Transfers of unguaranteed residual values continue to be subject to Statement 13, as amended. Because guaranteed residual value interests are treated as financial assets, increases to their estimated value over the life of the related lease are recognized. Entities selling or securitizing lease financing receivables shall allocate the gross investment in receivables between minimum lease payments and unguaranteed residual values using the individual carrying amounts of those components at the date of transfer. Entities also shall record a servicing asset or liability in accordance with paragraphs 10 and 13, if appropriate.

Illustration—Recording Transfers of Lease Financing Receivables with Residual Values

60. At the beginning of the second year in a 10-year sales-type lease, Company F sells for $505 a nine-tenths interest in the minimum lease payments and retains a one-tenth interest in the minimum lease payments and a 100 percent interest in the unguaranteed residual value of leased equipment. Company F receives no explicit compensation for servicing, but estimates that the other benefits of servicing are just adequate to compensate it for its servicing responsibilities, and hence records no servicing asset or liability. The carrying amounts and related gain computation are as follows:

Carrying Amounts

Minimum lease payments		$ 540
Unearned income related to minimum lease payments		370
Gross investment in minimum lease payments		910
Unguaranteed residual value	$ 30	
Unearned income related to residual value	60	
Gross investment in residual value		90
Total gross investment in financing lease receivable		$1,000

Gain on Sale

Cash received		$ 505
Nine-tenths of carrying amount of gross investment in minimum lease payments	$819	
Nine-tenths of carrying amount of unearned income related to minimum lease payments	333	
Net carrying amount of minimum lease payments sold		486
Gain on sale		$ 19

Journal Entry

Cash	505	
Unearned income	333	
Lease receivable		819
Gain on sale		19

To record sale of nine-tenths of the minimum lease
payments at the beginning of year 2

Securities Lending Transactions

61. Securities lending transactions are initiated by broker-dealers and other financial institutions that need specific securities to cover a short sale or a customer's failure to deliver securities sold. Transferees ("borrowers") of securities generally are required to provide "collateral" to the transferor ("lender") of securities, commonly cash but sometimes other securities or standby letters of credit, with a value slightly higher than that of the securities "borrowed." If the "collateral" is cash, the transferor typically earns a return by investing that cash at rates higher than the rate paid or "rebated" to the transferee. If the "collateral" is other than cash, the transferor typically receives a fee. Securities custodians or other agents commonly carry out securities lending activities on behalf of clients. Because of the protection of "collateral" (typically valued daily and adjusted frequently for changes in the market price of the securities transferred) and the short terms of the transactions, most securities lending transactions in themselves do not impose significant credit risks on either party. Other risks arise from what the parties to the transaction do with the assets they receive. For example, investments made with cash "collateral" impose market and credit risks on the transferor.

62. In some securities lending transactions, the criteria in paragraph 9 are met, including the third criterion. Those transactions shall be accounted for (a) by the transferor as a sale of the "loaned" securities for proceeds consisting of the "collateral"[11] and a forward repurchase commitment and (b) by the transferee as a purchase of the "borrowed" securities in exchange for the "collateral" and a forward resale commitment. During the term of that agreement, the transferor has surrendered control over the securities

transferred and the transferee has obtained control over those securities with the ability to sell or transfer them at will. In that case, creditors of the transferor have a claim only to the "collateral" and the forward repurchase commitment.

63. However, many securities lending transactions are accompanied by an agreement that entitles and obligates the transferor to repurchase or redeem the transferred assets before their maturity under which the transferor maintains effective control over those assets (paragraphs 27-30). Those transactions shall be accounted for as secured borrowings, in which cash (or securities that the holder is permitted by contract or custom to sell or repledge) received as "collateral" is considered the amount borrowed, the securities "loaned" are considered pledged as collateral against the cash borrowed, and any "rebate" paid to the transferee of securities is interest on the cash the transferor is considered to have borrowed. Collateral provided in securities lending transactions that are accounted for as secured borrowings shall be reported in the statement of financial position like other collateral, as set forth in paragraph 15.

64. The transferor of securities being "loaned" accounts for cash received (or for securities received that may be sold or repledged and were obtained under agreements that are not subject to repurchase or redemption on short notice, for example, by substitution of other collateral or termination of the contract) in the same way whether the transfer is accounted for as a sale or a secured borrowing. The cash (or securities) received shall be recognized as the transferor's asset—as shall investments made with that cash, even if made by agents or in pools with other securities lenders—along with the obligation to return the cash (or securities).

---

[11]If the "collateral" is a financial asset that the holder is permitted by contract or custom to sell or repledge and the debtor does not have the right and ability to redeem the collateral on short notice, for example, by substituting other collateral or terminating the contract, that financial asset is proceeds of the sale of the "loaned" securities. To the extent that the "collateral" consists of letters of credit or other financial instruments that the holder is not permitted by contract or custom to sell or pledge, a securities lending transaction does not satisfy the sale criteria and is accounted for as a loan of securities by the transferor to the transferee.

Illustration—Securities Lending Transaction Treated as a Secured Borrowing

65. Accounting for a securities lending transaction treated as a secured borrowing:

> **Facts**
>
> | | |
> |---|---:|
> | Transferor's carrying amount and fair value of security loaned | $1,000 |
> | Cash "collateral" | 1,020 |
> | Transferor's return from investing cash collateral at a 5 percent annual rate | 5 |
> | Transferor's rebate to the borrower at a 4 percent annual rate | 4 |

The loaned securities cannot be redeemed on short notice, for example, by substitution of other collateral. For simplicity, the fair value of the security is assumed not to change during the 35-day term of the transaction.

> **Journal Entries for the Transferor**
>
> *At inception:*
>
> | | | |
> |---|---:|---:|
> | Cash | 1,020 | |
> | Payable under securities loan agreements | | 1,020 |
> | To record the receipt of cash collateral | | |
> | | | |
> | Securities loaned to broker | 1,000 | |
> | Securities | | 1,000 |
> | To reclassify loaned securities that cannot be redeemed on short notice | | |
> | | | |
> | Money market instrument | 1,020 | |
> | Cash | | 1,020 |
> | To record investment of cash collateral | | |
>
> *At conclusion:*
>
> | | | |
> |---|---:|---:|
> | Cash | 1,025 | |
> | Interest | | 5 |
> | Money market instrument | | 1,020 |
> | To record results of investment | | |
> | | | |
> | Securities | 1,000 | |
> | Securities loaned to broker | | 1,000 |
> | To record return of security | | |
> | | | |
> | Payable under securities loan agreements | 1,020 | |
> | Interest ("rebate") | 4 | |
> | Cash | | 1,024 |
> | To record repayment of cash collateral plus interest | | |

Journal Entries for the Transferee

At inception:

Receivable under securities loan agreements	1,020	
Cash		1,020
To record transfer of cash collateral		

Securities	1,000	
Obligation to return borrowed securities		1,000
To record receipt of borrowed securities that cannot be redeemed on short notice		

At conclusion:

Obligation to return borrowed securities	1,000	
Securities		1,000
To record the return of securities		

Cash	1,024	
Receivable under securities loan agreements		1,020
Interest revenue ("rebate")		4
To record the receipt of cash collateral and rebate interest		

Repurchase Agreements and "Wash Sales"

66. Government securities dealers, banks, other financial institutions, and corporate investors commonly use repurchase agreements to obtain or use short-term funds. Under those agreements, the transferor ("repo party") transfers a security to a transferee ("repo counterparty" or "reverse party") in exchange for cash[12] and concurrently agrees to reacquire that security at a future date for an amount equal to the cash exchanged plus a stipulated "interest" factor.

67. Repurchase agreements can be effected in a variety of ways. Some repurchase agreements are similar to securities lending transactions in that the transferee has the right to sell or repledge the securities to a third party during the term of the repurchase agreement. In other repurchase agreements, the transferee does not have the right to sell or repledge the securities during the term of the repurchase agreement. For example, in a tri-party repurchase agreement, the transferor transfers securities to an independent third-party custodian that holds the securities during the term of the repurchase agreement. Also, many repurchase agreements are for short terms, often overnight, or have indefinite terms that allow either party to terminate the arrangement on short notice. However, other repurchase agreements are for longer terms, sometimes until the maturity of the transferred asset. Some repurchase agreements call for repurchase of securities that need not be identical to the securities transferred.

68. If the criteria in paragraph 9 are met, including the third criterion, the transferor shall account for the repurchase agreement as a sale of financial assets and a forward repurchase commitment, and the transferee shall account for the agreement as a purchase of financial assets and a forward resale commitment. Other transfers that are accompanied by an agreement to repurchase the transferred assets that shall be accounted for as sales include transfers with agreements to repurchase at maturity and transfers with repurchase agreements in which the transferee has not obtained collateral sufficient to fund substantially all of the cost of purchasing replacement assets.

69. Furthermore, "wash sales" that previously were not recognized if the same financial asset was purchased soon before or after the sale shall be accounted for as sales under this Statement. Unless there is a concurrent contract to repurchase or redeem the transferred financial assets from the transferee, the transferor does not maintain effective control over the transferred assets.

---

[12]Other securities or letters of credit rarely are exchanged in repurchase agreements instead of cash.

70. As with securities lending transactions, under many agreements to repurchase transferred assets before their maturity the transferor maintains effective control over those assets. Repurchase agreements that do not meet all the criteria in paragraph 9 shall be treated as secured borrowings. Fixed-coupon and dollar-roll repurchase agreements, and other contracts under which the securities to be repurchased need not be the same as the securities sold, qualify as borrowings if the return of substantially the same (paragraph 28) securities as those concurrently transferred is assured. Therefore, those transactions shall be accounted for as secured borrowings by both parties to the transfer.

71. If a transferor has transferred securities to an independent third-party custodian, or to a transferee, under conditions that preclude the transferee from selling or repledging the assets during the term of the repurchase agreement (as in most tri-party repurchase agreements), the transferor has not surrendered control over those assets. In those circumstances, the transferee does not acquire the right to sell or repledge the securities during the term of the repurchase agreement; therefore, it does not have access to the benefits embodied in those assets. The transferee shall not record those assets as its own, nor shall transferor derecognize those assets.

Loan Syndications

72. Borrowers often borrow amounts greater than any one lender is willing to lend. Therefore, it is common for groups of lenders to jointly fund those loans. That may be accomplished by a syndication under which several lenders share in lending to a single borrower, but each lender loans a specific amount to the borrower and has the right to repayment from the borrower.

73. Each lender in the syndication shall account for the amounts it is owed by the borrower. Repayments by the borrower may be made to a lead lender that then distributes the collections to the other lenders of the syndicate. In those circumstances, the lead lender is simply functioning as a servicer and, therefore, shall not recognize the aggregate loan as an asset.

Loan Participations

74. Groups of banks or other entities also may jointly fund large borrowings through loan participations in which a single lender makes a large loan to a borrower and subsequently transfers undivided interests in the loan to other entities.

75. Transfers by the originating lender may take the legal form of either assignments or participations. The transfers are usually on a nonrecourse basis, and the transferor ("originating lender") continues to service the loan. The transferee ("participating entity") may or may not have the right to sell or transfer its participation during the term of the loan, depending upon the terms of the participation agreement.

76. If the loan participation agreement gives the transferee the right to pledge or exchange those participations and the other criteria in paragraph 9 are met, the transfers to the transferee shall be accounted for by the transferor as sales of financial assets. A transferor's right of first refusal on a bona fide offer from a third party, a requirement to obtain the transferor's permission that shall not be unreasonably withheld, or a prohibition on sale to the transferor's competitor is a limitation on the transferee's rights but presumptively does not constrain a transferee from exercising its right to pledge or exchange. However, if the loan participation agreement constrains the transferees from pledging or exchanging their participations, the transferor has not relinquished control over the loan and shall account for the transfers as secured borrowings.

Banker's Acceptances and Risk Participations in Them

77. Banker's acceptances provide a way for a bank to finance a customer's purchase of goods from a vendor for periods usually not exceeding six months. Under an agreement between the bank, the customer, and the vendor, the bank agrees to pay the customer's liability to the vendor upon presentation of specified documents that provide evidence of delivery and acceptance of the purchased goods. The principal document is a draft or bill of exchange drawn by the customer that the bank stamps to signify its "acceptance" of the liability to make payment on the draft on its due date.

78. Once the bank accepts a draft, the customer is liable to repay the bank at the time the draft matures. The bank recognizes a receivable from the customer and a liability for the acceptance it has issued to the vendor. The accepted draft becomes a negotiable financial instrument. The vendor typically sells the accepted draft at a discount either to the accepting bank or in the marketplace.

79. A risk participation is a contract between the accepting bank and a participating bank in which the

participating bank agrees, in exchange for a fee, to reimburse the accepting bank in the event that the accepting bank's customer fails to honor its liability to the accepting bank in connection with the banker's acceptance. The participating bank becomes a guarantor of the credit of the accepting bank's customer.

80. An accepting bank that obtains a risk participation shall not derecognize the liability for the banker's acceptance because the accepting bank is still primarily liable to the holder of the banker's acceptance even though it benefits from a guarantee of reimbursement by a participating bank. The accepting bank shall not derecognize the receivable from the customer because it controls the benefits inherent in that receivable and it is still entitled to receive payment from the customer. The accepting bank shall, however, record the guarantee purchased, and the participating bank shall record a liability for the guarantee issued.

Illustration—Banker's Acceptance with a Risk Participation

81. An accepting bank assumes a liability to pay a customer's vendor and obtains a risk participation from another bank. The details of the banker's acceptance are provided below:

Facts

Face value of the draft provided to vendor	$1,000
Term of the draft provided to vendor	90 days
Commission with an annual rate of 10 percent	25
Fee paid for risk participation	10

Journal Entries for Accepting Bank

At issuance of acceptance:

Receivable from customer	1,000	
Cash	25	
Time draft payable to vendor		1,000
Deferred acceptance commission revenue		25

At purchase of risk participation from a participating bank:

Guarantee purchased	10	
Cash		10

Upon presentation of the accepted time draft:

Time draft payable to vendor	1,000	
Deferred acceptance commission revenue	25	
Cash		1,000
Acceptance commission revenue		25

Upon collection from the customer (or the participating bank, if the customer defaults):

Cash	1,000	
Guarantee expense	10	
Receivable from customer		1,000
Guarantee purchased		10

Journal Entries for Participating Bank

Upon issuing the risk participation:

Cash	10	
Guarantee liability		10

Upon payment by the customer to the accepting bank:

Guarantee liability	10	
Guarantee revenue		10

OR:

In the event of total default by the customer:

Guarantee loss	990	
Guarantee liability	10	
Cash (paid to accepting bank)		1,000

Factoring Arrangements

82. Factoring arrangements are a means of discounting accounts receivable on a nonrecourse, notification basis. Accounts receivable are sold outright, usually to a transferee (the factor) that assumes the full risk of collection, without recourse to the transferor in the event of a loss. Debtors are directed to send payments to the transferee. Factoring arrangements that meet the criteria in paragraph 9 shall be accounted for as sales of financial assets because the transferor surrenders control over the receivables to the factor.

Transfers of Receivables with Recourse

83. In a transfer of receivables with recourse, the transferor provides the transferee with full or limited recourse. The transferor is obligated under the terms of the recourse provision to make payments to the transferee or to repurchase receivables sold under certain circumstances, typically for defaults up to a specified percentage. The effect of a recourse provision on the application of paragraph 9 may vary by jurisdiction. In some jurisdictions, transfers with full recourse may not place transferred assets beyond the reach of the transferor and its creditors, but transfers with limited recourse may. A transfer of receivables with recourse shall be accounted for as a sale, with the proceeds of the sale reduced by the fair value of the recourse obligation, if the criteria in paragraph 9 are met. Otherwise, a transfer of receivables with recourse shall be accounted for as a secured borrowing.

Extinguishments of Liabilities

84. If a creditor releases a debtor from primary obligation on the condition that a third party assumes the obligation and that the original debtor becomes secondarily liable, that release extinguishes the original debtor's liability. However, in those circumstances, whether or not explicit consideration was paid for that guarantee, the original debtor becomes a guarantor. As a guarantor, it shall recognize a guarantee obligation in the same manner as would a guarantor that had never been primarily liable to that creditor, with due regard for the likelihood that the third party will carry out its obligations. The guarantee obligation shall be initially measured at fair value, and that amount reduces the gain or increases the loss recognized on extinguishment.

Appendix B

BACKGROUND INFORMATION AND BASIS FOR CONCLUSIONS

CONTENTS

Appendix B

BACKGROUND INFORMATION AND BASIS FOR CONCLUSIONS

Introduction

85. This appendix summarizes considerations that were deemed significant by Board members in reaching the conclusions in this Statement. It includes reasons for accepting certain approaches and rejecting others. Individual Board members gave greater weight to some factors than to others.

Background

86. In recent years, transfers of financial assets in which the transferor has some continuing involvement with the transferred assets or with the transferee have grown in volume, variety, and complexity. Those transfers raise the issues of whether transferred financial assets should be considered to be sold and a related gain or loss recorded, whether the assets should be considered to be collateral for borrowings, or whether the transfer should not be recognized.

87. A transferor may sell financial assets and receive in exchange cash or other assets that are unrelated to the assets sold so that the transferor has no continuing involvement with the assets sold. Alternatively, an entity may borrow money and pledge financial assets as collateral, or a transferor may engage in any of a variety of transactions that transfer financial assets to another entity with the transferor having some continuing involvement with the assets transferred. Examples of continuing involvement are recourse or guarantee obligations, servicing, agreements to repurchase or redeem, and put or call options on the assets transferred.

88. Many transactions disaggregate financial assets into separate components by creating undivided interests in pools of financial assets that frequently reflect multiple participations (often referred to as tranches) in a single pool. The components created may later be recombined to restore the original assets or may be combined with other financial assets to create still different assets.

89. An entity also may enter into transactions that change the characteristics of an asset that the entity continues to hold. An entity may sell part of an asset, or an undivided interest in the asset, and retain part of the asset. In some cases, it has not been clear what the accounting should be.

90. An entity may settle a liability by transferring assets to a creditor and obtaining an unconditional release from the obligation. Alternatively, an entity may arrange for others to settle or set aside assets to settle a liability later. Those alternative arrangements have raised issues about when a liability is extinguished.

91. The Board previously provided guidance for two specific types of transfers of financial assets in FASB Statement No. 77, *Reporting by Transferors for Transfers of Receivables with Recourse,* and in FASB Technical Bulletin No. 85-2, *Accounting for Collateralized Mortgage Obligations (CMOs).* Confusion and inconsistency in accounting practices developed because the provisions of those two pronouncements provided seemingly conflicting guidance. In practice, if an entity sold financial assets to a special-purpose entity that issued debt securities, the guidance under Technical Bulletin 85-2 would be applied, and if any of those securities were obtained by the seller, the transaction would be accounted for as a borrowing. However, if the interests issued by the special-purpose entity were designated as participations instead of debt securities, the guidance in Statement 77 would be applied, and the transaction would be accounted for as a sale even if the seller retained recourse on some of the participations. Further, accounting for other types of transfers, whether developed by analogy to Statement 77 or Technical Bulletin 85-2, in industry practices codified in various AICPA audit and accounting Guides, in consensuses of the Emerging Issues Task Force (EITF), or in other ways, added to the confusion and inconsistency.

92. FASB Statement No. 76, *Extinguishment of Debt,* established accounting practices that (a) treat liabilities that are not fully settled as if they had been extinguished and (b) derecognize assets transferred to a trust even though the assets continue to benefit the transferor. Some criticized Statement 76 as being inconsistent with Statement 77; others disagreed.

93. The Board decided that it was necessary to reconsider Statements 76 and 77, Technical Bulletin 85-2, and other guidance and to develop new standards for transfers of financial assets and extinguishments of liabilities.

94. The Board added a project to its agenda in May 1986 to address those and other problems in accounting for financial instruments and off-balance-sheet financing. This Statement, as part of that

project, focuses on accounting for transfers and servicing of financial assets and extinguishments of liabilities. The Financial Instruments Task Force, which was formed in January 1989, assisted in the preparation of a Discussion Memorandum on those issues and advised the Board in its deliberations. The FASB Discussion Memorandum, *Recognition and Measurement of Financial Instruments,* was issued in November 1991. The Board received 96 comment letters on the Discussion Memorandum. During 1994 and 1995, the Board discussed issues about transfers and servicing of financial assets and extinguishments of liabilities at numerous public meetings. The Financial Instruments Task Force reviewed drafts of the proposed Statement and discussed it with the Board at a public meeting in February 1995. The Financial Accounting Standards Advisory Council discussed a draft of the proposed Statement and advised the Board at public meetings. The Board also received requests from constituents to discuss issues about credit card securitizations and securities lending transactions and repurchase agreements. The Board met with constituents interested in those issues at public meetings in November 1994 and April 1995.

95. In October 1995, the Board issued an Exposure Draft, *Accounting for Transfers and Servicing of Financial Assets and Extinguishments of Liabilities.* The Board received 112 comment letters on the Exposure Draft, and 24 individuals and organizations presented their views at a public hearing held in February 1996. In addition, 10 enterprises participated in limited field-testing of the provisions of the Exposure Draft. The comments and test results were considered by the Board during its redeliberations of the issues addressed by the Exposure Draft in public meetings in 1996. The Financial Instruments Task Force reviewed a draft of the final Statement. This Statement is a result of those Board meetings and deliberations.

Benefits and Costs

96. The Board's mission statement charges the Board to determine that a proposed standard will fill a significant need and that the costs it imposes will be justified in relation to the overall benefits.

97. Previous practices in accounting for transfers of financial assets were inconsistent about the circumstances that distinguish sales from secured borrowings. The result was confusion on the part of both users and preparers of financial statements. This Statement eliminates that inconsistency and should reduce that confusion by distinguishing sales from secured borrowings based on the underlying contractual commitments and customs that determine substance. Much of the information needed to implement the accounting required by this Statement is substantially the same as that required for previous accounting and, therefore, should be available. Some of the information may not have been collected in accounting systems but is commonly obtained by sellers and buyers for use in negotiating transactions. Although there will be one-time costs for systems changes needed to apply the accounting required by this Statement, the benefits in terms of more credible, consistent, and understandable information will be ongoing.

98. In addition, in developing this Statement, the Board considered how the costs incurred to implement the requirements of this Statement could be minimized by, for example, (a) not requiring retroactive application of the initial measurement provisions of this Statement to existing servicing rights and excess servicing receivables, (b) carrying over without change the subsequent measurement (amortization and impairment) provisions of FASB Statement No. 122, *Accounting for Mortgage Servicing Rights,* which mortgage servicers have recently implemented, (c) not requiring allocation of previous carrying amounts of assets partially sold based on relative fair values at acquisition, but rather at the date of transfer, and (d) not requiring additional disclosures for transfers such as securitizations beyond those currently presented within the financial statements. The Board is confident that the benefits derived from the accounting required by this Statement will outweigh the costs of implementation.

Approaches Considered

99. The Board noted that the most difficult questions about accounting for transfers of financial assets concern the circumstances in which it is appropriate to remove previously recognized financial assets from the statement of financial position and to recognize gain or loss. One familiar approach to those questions views each financial asset as a unit that should not be derecognized until the risks and rewards that are embodied in that asset have been surrendered. Variations on that approach attempt to choose which risks and rewards are most critical and whether all or some major portion of those risks and rewards must be surrendered to allow derecognition.

100. In addition to reviewing U.S. accounting literature, the Board reviewed the approach described

by the International Accounting Standards Committee (IASC) in its Proposed International Accounting Standard, *Financial Instruments,* Exposure Draft E40 (1992), later revised as Exposure Draft E48 (1994). In E40, derecognition of financial assets and liabilities would have been permitted only upon the transfer to others of the underlying risks and rewards, presumably all risks and rewards. That approach could have resulted in an entity's continuing to recognize assets even though it had surrendered control over the assets to a successor entity. The approach in E40 was similar to that taken in Technical Bulletin 85-2. The Board concluded that the approaches proposed in E40 and provided in Technical Bulletin 85-2 were unsatisfactory because the result does not faithfully represent the effects of the transfer of assets and because of the potential for inconsistencies.

101. In response to comments received on E40, the IASC proposal was revised in E48 to require the transfer of *substantially all* risks and rewards. That modification did not overcome the inconsistency noted in paragraphs 97 and 100 of this Statement and added the prospect of difficulties in application because of the need to identify, measure, and weigh in the balance each of possibly many and varied risks and rewards embodied in a particular financial asset. The number of different risks and rewards would vary depending on the definitions used. Questions would arise about whether each identified risk and reward should be substantially surrendered to allow derecognition, whether all risks should be aggregated separately from all rewards, and whether risks and rewards should somehow be offset and then combined for evaluation. That modification also might lead to wide variations in practice depending on how various entities interpreted *substantially all* in the necessarily subjective evaluation of the aggregated, offset, and combined risks and rewards. Moreover, viewing each financial asset as an indivisible unit is contrary to the growing practice in financial markets of disaggregating individual financial assets or pools of financial assets into components. The IASC is continuing to study that issue in its financial instruments project.

102. The Board also noted that application of a risks-and-rewards approach for derecognizing financial assets would be highly dependent on the sequence of transactions leading to their acquisition. For example,

if Entity A initially acquired an undivided subordinated interest in a pool of financial assets, it would recognize that subordinated interest as a single asset. If, on the other hand, Entity B initially acquired a pool of financial assets identical to the pool in which Entity A participates, then sold a senior interest in the pool and continued to hold a subordinated interest identical to the undivided interest held by Entity A, Entity B might be judged under a risks-and-rewards approach to have retained substantially all the risks of the entire pool. Thus, Entity B would carry in its statement of financial position the entire pool of financial assets as well as an obligation equal to the proceeds from the sale of the undivided senior interest, while Entity A would report its identical position quite differently. Those accounting results would disregard one of the fundamental tenets of the Board's conceptual framework; that is, "accountants must not disguise real differences nor create false differences."[13]

103. The Board also considered the approach required by the United Kingdom's Accounting Standards Board in Financial Reporting Standard No. 5, *Reporting the Substance of Transactions,* a variation of the risks-and-rewards approach that requires the surrender of substantially all risks and rewards for derecognition of financial assets but permits, in limited circumstances, the use of a *linked presentation.* Use of the linked presentation is restricted to circumstances in which an entity borrows funds to be repaid from the proceeds of pledged financial assets, any excess proceeds go to the borrower, and the lender has no recourse to other assets of the borrower. In those circumstances, the pledged assets remain on the borrower's statement of financial position, but the unpaid borrowing is reported as a deduction from the pledged assets rather than as a liability; no gain or loss is recognized. That approach had some appeal to the Board because it would have highlighted significant information about transactions that many believe have characteristics of both sales and secured borrowings. The Board observed, however, that the linked presentation would not have dealt with many of the problems created by the risks-and-rewards approach. Further, the Board concluded that it is not appropriate for an entity to offset restricted assets against a liability or to derecognize a liability merely because assets are dedicated to its repayment, as discussed in paragraphs 218-221.

---

[13]FASB Concepts Statement No. 2, *Qualitative Characteristics of Accounting Information,* par. 119.

104. Statement 77 based the determination of whether to derecognize receivables on transfer of control instead of on evaluation of risks and rewards. This Statement takes a similar approach. However, Statement 77 was narrowly focused on sales of receivables with recourse and did not address other transfers of financial assets. Also, the derecognition of receivables under that Statement could depend on the sequence of transactions that led to their acquisition or on whether any options were involved. The Board concluded that simply superseding Technical Bulletin 85-2 and allowing Statement 77 to remain in effect would not have dealt adequately with the issues about transfers of financial assets.

105. Statement 76 followed a risks-and-rewards approach in requiring that (a) it be probable that a debtor would not be required to make future payments with respect to the debt under any guarantees and (b) an in-substance defeasance trust be restricted to owning only monetary assets that are risk free with cash flows that approximately coincide, as to timing and amount, with the scheduled interest and principal payments on the debt being extinguished. The Board concluded (paragraphs 218-221) that that approach was inconsistent with the financial-components approach that focuses on control developed in this Statement. As a result, the Board decided to supersede Statement 76 but to carry forward those of its criteria that could be modified to conform to the financial-components approach.

106. The considerations discussed in paragraphs 99-105 led the Board to seek an alternative to the risks-and-rewards approach and variations to that approach.

Objectives of the Financial-Components Approach

107. The Board concluded that it was necessary to develop an approach that would be responsive to current developments in the financial markets to achieve consistent accounting for transfers and servicing of financial assets and extinguishments of liabilities. That approach—the financial-components approach—is designed to:

a. Be consistent with the way participants in the financial markets deal with financial assets, including the combination and separation of components of those assets

b. Reflect the economic consequences of contractual provisions underlying financial assets and liabilities
c. Conform to the FASB conceptual framework.

108. The approach analyzes a transfer of a financial asset by examining the component assets (controlled economic benefits) and liabilities (obligations for probable future sacrifices of economic benefits) that exist after the transfer. Each party to the transfer recognizes the assets and liabilities that it controls after the transfer and no longer recognizes the assets and liabilities that were surrendered or extinguished in the transfer. That approach has some antecedents in existing accounting guidance, for example, in EITF Issue No. 88-11, "Allocation of Recorded Investment When a Loan or Part of a Loan Is Sold." The Board identified the concepts set forth in paragraphs 109-111 as an appropriate basis for the financial-components approach.

Conceptual Basis for the Financial-Components Approach

109. FASB Concepts Statement No. 6, *Elements of Financial Statements,* states the following about assets:

Assets are probable future economic benefits obtained or controlled by a particular entity as a result of past transactions or events. [Paragraph 25, footnote reference omitted.]
Every asset is an asset of some entity; moreover, no asset can simultaneously be an asset of more than one entity, although a particular physical thing or other agent [e.g., contractual rights and obligations] that provides future economic benefit may provide separate benefits to two or more entities at the same time. . . . To have an asset, an entity must control future economic benefit to the extent that it can benefit from the asset and generally can deny or regulate access to that benefit by others, for example, by permitting access only at a price.
Thus, *an asset of an entity is the future economic benefit that the entity can control and thus can, within limits set by the nature of the benefit or the entity's right to it, use as it pleases.* The entity having an asset is the one that can exchange it, use it to produce goods or services, exact a price for others' use of it,

use it to settle liabilities, hold it, or perhaps distribute it to owners.

The definition of assets focuses primarily on the future economic benefit to which an entity has access and only secondarily on the physical things and other agents that provide future economic benefits. *Many physical things and other agents are in effect bundles of future economic benefits that can be unbundled in various ways, and two or more entities may have different future economic benefits from the same agent at the same time or the same continuing future economic benefit at different times.* For example, two or more entities may have undivided interests in a parcel of land. Each has a right to future economic benefit that may qualify as an asset under the definition in paragraph 25, even though the right of each is subject at least to some extent to the rights of the other(s). Or, one entity may have the right to the interest from an investment, while another has the right to the principal. [Paragraphs 183-185; emphasis added.]

110. Concepts Statement 6 states the following about liabilities:

Liabilities are probable future sacrifices of economic benefits arising from present obligations of a particular entity to transfer assets or provide services to other entities in the future as a result of past transactions or events. [Paragraph 35, footnote references omitted.]

Most liabilities are obligations of only one entity at a time. Some liabilities are shared—for example, two or more entities may be "jointly and severally liable" for a debt or for the unsatisfied liabilities of a partnership. But most liabilities bind a single entity, and those that bind two or more entities are commonly ranked rather than shared. For example, *a primary debtor and a guarantor may both be obligated for a debt, but they do not have the same obligation—the guarantor must pay only if the primary debtor defaults and thus has a contingent or secondary obligation,* which ranks lower than that of the primary debtor.

Secondary, and perhaps even lower ranked, obligations may qualify as liabilities under the definition in paragraph 35, but recognition considerations are highly significant in deciding whether they should for-

mally be included in financial statements because of the effects of uncertainty (paragraphs 44-48). For example, the probability that a secondary or lower ranked obligation will actually have to be paid must be assessed to apply the definition. [Paragraphs 204 and 205; emphasis added.]

111. Financial assets and liabilities are assets and liabilities that qualify as financial instruments as defined in paragraph 3 of FASB Statement No. 107, *Disclosures about Fair Value of Financial Instruments:*

A financial instrument is defined as cash, evidence of an ownership interest in an entity, or a contract that both:

a. Imposes on one entity a contractual obligation (1) to deliver cash or another financial instrument to a second entity or (2) to exchange other financial instruments on potentially unfavorable terms with the second entity

b. Conveys to that second entity a contractual right (1) to receive cash or another financial instrument from the first entity or (2) to exchange other financial instruments on potentially favorable terms with the first entity. [Footnote references omitted.]

112. Based on the concepts and definitions cited in paragraphs 109-111, the Board concluded that the key to applying the financial-components approach can be summarized as follows:

a. The economic benefits provided by a financial asset (generally, the right to future cash flows) are derived from the contractual provisions that underlie that asset, and the entity that controls those benefits should recognize them as its asset.

b. A financial asset should be considered sold and therefore should be derecognized if it is transferred and control is surrendered.

c. A transferred financial asset should be considered pledged as collateral to secure an obligation of the transferor (and therefore should not be derecognized) if the transferor has not surrendered control of the financial asset.

d. Each liability should be recognized by the entity that is primarily liable and, accordingly, an entity that guarantees another entity's obligation should recognize only its obligation to perform on the guarantee.

e. The recognition of financial assets and liabilities should not be affected by the sequence of transactions that led to their existence unless as a result of those transactions the transferor maintains effective control over a transferred asset.

f. Transferors and transferees should account symmetrically for transfers of financial assets.

113. Most respondents to the Exposure Draft generally supported the financial-components approach, especially as it applies to securitization transactions.

114. The concepts underlying the financial-components approach could be applied by analogy to accounting for transfers of nonfinancial assets and thus could result in accounting that differs significantly from that required by existing standards and practices. However, the Board believes that financial and nonfinancial assets have significantly different characteristics, and it is not clear to what extent the financial-components approach is applicable to nonfinancial assets. Nonfinancial assets have a variety of operational uses, and management skill plays a considerable role in obtaining the greatest value from those assets. In contrast, financial assets have no operational use. They may facilitate operations, and financial assets may be the principal "product" offered by some entities. However, the promise embodied in a financial asset is governed by contract. Once the contract is established, management skill plays a limited role in the entity's ability to realize the value of the instrument. Furthermore, the Board believes that attempting to extend this Statement to transfers of nonfinancial assets would unduly delay resolving the issues for transfers of financial assets, because of the significant differences between financial assets and nonfinancial assets and because of the significant unresolved recognition and measurement issues posed by those differences. For those reasons, the Board concluded that existing accounting practices for transfers of nonfinancial assets should not be changed at this time. The Board further concluded that transfers of servicing assets and transfers of property subject to operating leases are not within the scope of this Statement because they are nonfinancial assets.

115. The following paragraphs discuss the application of the concepts and principles described in paragraphs 109-114. First, circumstances that require derecognition of transferred assets and recognition of assets and liabilities received in exchange are discussed in the paragraphs about sales of financial assets, transfers to special-purpose entities, and other transfers (paragraphs 116-175). Then, the measurement of assets controlled and liabilities incurred (paragraphs 176-214) and subsequent measurement (paragraphs 215-217) are discussed. Finally, extinguishments of liabilities are discussed (paragraphs 218-224).

Sales of Financial Assets

116. If an entity transfers financial assets, surrenders control of those assets to a successor entity, and has no continuing involvement with those assets, accounting for the transaction as a sale and derecognizing the assets and recognizing the related gain or loss is not controversial. However, accounting for transfers of financial assets has been controversial and inconsistent in circumstances in which an entity transfers only a partial interest in a financial asset or has some other continuing involvement with the transferred asset or the transferee.

117. Under the financial-components approach, the accounting for a transfer is based on whether a transferor surrenders control of financial assets. Paragraph 3 of Statement 77 states, "This Statement establishes standards of financial accounting and reporting by transferors for transfers of receivables with recourse that *purport to be sales* of receivables" (emphasis added). The Board believes that, while it may have some significance at law, a more exacting test than whether a transaction purports to be a sale is needed to conclude that control has been surrendered in a manner that is consistent with the definitions in Concepts Statement 6. The Board concluded that a sale occurs only if control has been surrendered to another entity or group of entities and that surrender of control depends on whether (a) transferred assets have been isolated from the transferor, (b) transferees have obtained the right to pledge or exchange either the transferred assets or beneficial interests in the transferred assets, and (c) the transferor does not maintain effective control over the transferred assets through an agreement to repurchase or redeem them before their maturity.

118. The Board developed its criterion that transferred assets must be isolated—put presumptively beyond the reach of the transferor and its creditors, even in bankruptcy or other receivership (paragraph 9(a))—in large part with reference to securitization practices. Credit rating agencies and investors in securitized assets pay close attention to (a) the possibility of bankruptcy or other receivership of the transferor, its affiliates, or the special-purpose entity,

even though that possibility may seem unlikely given the present credit standing of the transferor, and (b) what might happen in such a receivership, because those are major areas of risk for them. If certain receivers can reclaim securitized assets, investors will suffer a delay in payments due them and may be forced to accept a pro rata settlement. Credit rating agencies and investors commonly demand transaction structures that minimize those possibilities and sometimes seek assurances from attorneys about whether entities can be forced into receivership, what the powers of a receiver might be, and whether the transaction structure would withstand receivers' attempts to reach the securitized assets in ways that would harm investors. Unsatisfactory structures or assurances commonly result in credit ratings that are no higher than those for the transferor's liabilities and in lower prices for transferred assets.

119. Because legal isolation of transferred assets has substance, the Board decided that it could and should serve as an important part of the basis for determining whether a sale should be recognized. Some constituents expressed concern about the feasibility of an accounting standard based on those legal considerations, but the Board concluded that having to consider only the evidence available should make that requirement workable.

120. Respondents to the Exposure Draft raised several questions about the application of the isolation criterion in paragraph 9(a) to existing securitization structures. The questions included whether it was necessary to consider separately the accounting by the first-tier special-purpose entity, whose transfer to the second-tier trust taken by itself might not satisfy the isolation test. After considering those comments and consulting with respondents who specialize in the structure of securitization transactions, the Board concluded that related language in Appendix A should be revised to explain that that criterion can be satisfied either by a single transaction or by a series of transactions considered as a whole. As discussed in paragraphs 54-58, the Board understands that the series of transactions in a typical two-tier structure taken as a whole may satisfy the isolation test because the design of the structure achieves isolation.

121. The Board understands that a one-tier structure with significant continuing involvement by a transferor subject to the U.S. Bankruptcy Code might not satisfy the isolation test, because a trustee in bankruptcy has substantial powers that could alter amounts that investors might receive and thus it may

be difficult to conclude that control has been relinquished. Some respondents argued that a one-tier structure with continuing involvement generally should be adequate if the transferor's credit rating is sufficiently high that the chance of sudden bankruptcy is remote. The Board did not accept that view because isolation should not depend on the credit standing of the transferor. The Board believes that a one-tier structure may satisfy the isolation test despite continuing involvement if the transferor is subject to receivership by receivers with more limited powers over transferred assets, for example, the FDIC. The Board understands that the FDIC, unlike a receiver in bankruptcy, cannot impose an automatic stay. However, it can terminate the transaction by paying investors compensation equivalent to all principal and interest earned to date, in effect making the investors whole.

122. The second criterion (paragraph 9(b)) for a transfer to be a sale focuses on whether the transferee has the right—free of conditions that constrain it from taking advantage of that right—to pledge or exchange the transferred assets. That criterion is consistent with the idea that the entity that has an asset is the one that can use it in the various ways set forth in Concepts Statement 6, paragraph 184 (quoted in paragraph 109 of this Statement). A transferee may be able to use a transferred asset in some of those ways but not in others. Therefore, establishing criteria for determining whether control has been relinquished to a transferee necessarily depends in part on identifying which ways of using the kind of asset transferred are the decisive ones. In the case of transfers of financial assets, the transferee holds the assets, but that is not necessarily decisive because the economic benefits of financial assets consist primarily of future cash inflows. The Board concluded that the ways of using assets that are important in determining whether a transferee holding a financial asset controls it are the ability to exchange it or pledge it as collateral and thus obtain all or most of the cash inflows that are the primary economic benefits of financial assets. As discussed in paragraph 127, if the transferee is a special-purpose entity, the ultimate holders of the assets are the beneficial interest holders, and the important rights concern their ability to exchange or pledge their interests.

123. The Exposure Draft proposed that a transferee be required to have the right—free of transferor-imposed conditions—to pledge or exchange the transferred assets for a transfer to qualify as a sale. Respondents to the Exposure Draft observed that

some transferor-imposed conditions may not indicate that the transferor retains control over the assets transferred. The respondents suggested that some conditions are imposed for business or competitiveness purposes, not to keep control over future economic benefits of the transferred assets, and that those conditions should not preclude a transfer from being accounted for as a sale. Other respondents noted that not all conditions that might limit a transferee's ability to take advantage of a right to pledge or exchange transferred assets were necessarily imposed by the transferor. The Board decided that the criterion should not be restricted to being transferor imposed and that some conditions, described in paragraph 25, should not disqualify a transaction, so long as those conditions do not constrain the transferee from taking advantage of its right to pledge or exchange the transferred assets.

Settlement Date and Trade Date Accounting

124. Many transfers of financial assets have been and, under this Statement, will be recognized at the settlement date. During its redeliberations, the Board discussed the implications of this Statement on trade date accounting for certain securities transactions, and concluded that this project did not set out to address that issue. Therefore, the Board decided that this Statement should not modify generally accepted accounting principles, including FASB Statement No. 35, *Accounting and Reporting by Defined Benefit Pension Plans,* and AICPA Statements of Position and audit and accounting Guides for certain industries, that require accounting at the trade date for certain contracts to purchase or sell securities. The Board observes that the AICPA's Securities Contracts Task Force is currently developing a proposed Statement of Position that would clarify for all entities the date at which to recognize (or derecognize) contracts to purchase or sell securities in (or from) the statement of financial position.

Transfers to Qualifying Special-Purpose Entities, Including Securitizations

125. Many transfers of financial assets are to qualifying special-purpose entities of the type described in paragraph 26. After those transfers, the qualifying special-purpose entity holds legal title to the transferred assets but does not have the right to pledge or exchange the transferred assets. Rather, the activities of the qualifying special-purpose entity are limited to carrying out the provisions of the legal documents that established it. One significant purpose of those

limitations on activities often is to make remote the possibility that a qualifying special-purpose entity could enter bankruptcy or other receivership, even if the transferor were to enter receivership.

126. Some respondents asked whether the special-purpose entity criteria apply to entities formed for purposes other than transfers of financial assets. The Board decided that the description of a special-purpose entity in paragraph 26 is restrictive. Transfers to entities that meet all of the conditions in paragraph 26 qualify for sale accounting under paragraph 9 of this Statement. Other entities with some similar characteristics also might be broadly described as "special-purpose." For example, an entity might be formed for the purpose of holding specific nonfinancial assets and liabilities or carrying on particular commercial activities. The Board decided that those entities are not qualifying special-purpose entities as the term is used in this Statement, and the accounting for transfers of financial assets to special-purpose entities should not be extended to transfers to any entity that does not satisfy all of the conditions in paragraph 26.

127. Qualifying special-purpose entities issue beneficial interests of various kinds—variously characterized as debt, participations, residual interests, and otherwise—as required by the provisions of those agreements. Holders of beneficial interests in the qualifying special-purpose entity have the right to pledge or exchange those interests but do not control the individual assets held by the qualifying special-purpose entity. The effect of establishing the qualifying special-purpose entity is to merge the contractual rights in the transferred assets and to allocate undivided interests in them—the beneficial interests. Therefore, the right of holders to pledge or exchange those beneficial interests is the counterpart of the right of a transferee to pledge or exchange the transferred assets themselves.

128. Sometimes financial assets, especially mortgage loans, are securitized and the transferor retains all of the beneficial interests in the qualifying special-purpose entity as securities. The objective is to increase financial flexibility because securities are more liquid and can more readily be sold or pledged as collateral to secure borrowings. In some cases, securitization may reduce regulatory capital requirements. The Board concluded that transfers of financial assets to a qualifying special-purpose entity, including securitizations, should qualify as sales only to the extent that consideration other than beneficial interests in the transferred assets is received.

129. The Board observes that a special-purpose entity that has distinct standing at law may still be an affiliate of the transferor, and therefore its assets and liabilities may be required to be included with those of the transferor in consolidated financial statements. That issue is dealt with in generally accepted accounting principles for consolidated financial statements. Many respondents maintained that existing principles are not clear and asked the Board to develop within this Statement additional consolidation guidance for special-purpose entities. The Board concluded that this Statement is not intended to change existing generally accepted accounting principles for consolidation issues. However, the Board acknowledges that consolidation of special-purpose entities is an issue that merits further consideration and is committed to deliberating that issue in its current project on consolidated financial statements.

Securitizations with Revolving-Period Features

130. As noted in paragraph 48, in some securitizations, short-term receivables are transferred to a special-purpose entity, and the special-purpose entity then issues long-term beneficial interests. Collections from transferred receivables are used to purchase additional receivables during a defined period called the revolving period. Thereafter, the collections are used to redeem beneficial interests in due course. Some have questioned the propriety of sales treatment in those securitizations because much of the cash collected during the revolving period is returned to the transferor. The Board decided that sales treatment was appropriate for transfers with revolving-period features because the transferor surrenders control of the assets transferred. While the revolving-period agreement requires that the transferor sell receivables to the trust in exchange for cash on prearranged terms, sales of additional receivables during the revolving period are separate transactions from the original sale.

131. The transferor in a transfer with a revolving-period agreement, such as a credit card securitization, must sell receivables to the securitization trust on prearranged terms. The transferor can perhaps predict the timing of transfers, but the actual timing depends primarily on borrower behavior. If not bound by that contract, the transferor could sell its new receivables elsewhere, possibly on better terms. The transferor obtains the cash as proceeds in exchange for new receivables transferred under the revolving-period agreement, not as benefits from its previous ownership of the receivables or its residual interest in the securitization trust.

132. The revolving-period agreement is an implicit forward contract, with rights and obligations on both sides. The transferor has little or no discretion to avoid its obligations under the revolving-period agreement and would suffer adverse consequences for failure to deliver receivables to the trust during the revolving period. For example, if the transferor were to take deliberate actions to avoid its obligations to sell receivables by triggering the agreement's "early amortization" provisions, the transferor would be exposed to litigation for not honoring its commitment. The transferor also could suffer if it later tried to sell its receivables in the securitization market: the transferor would probably have to offer wary investors a higher return. Deliberate early termination by the transferor is rare in practice because of those adverse consequences. Similarly, the securitization trust and investors cannot avoid the obligation to purchase additional receivables. For those reasons, the revolving-period agreement does not provide control over receivables previously sold but rather is an implicit forward contract for future sales of receivables.

133. Some respondents to the Exposure Draft proposed that existing revolving-period securitizations should continue to apply previous accounting standards for all transfers into an existing trust after the effective date of this Statement. Several respondents asked about the effect of the provisions of this Statement on transfers into a master trust that is used for a series of securitizations. They pointed out that it would be difficult to change the present structure of those trusts in response to new accounting standards. Others observed that because master trusts have very long or indefinite lives, "grandfathering" transfers to existing trusts would result in noncomparable financial statements for a long time to come. After considering those arguments, the Board decided to retain the proposed requirement that this Statement apply to all transfers of assets after its effective date, in order to minimize the noncomparability caused by the transition. However, the Board also responded to respondents' questions about accounting for master trusts by clarifying in paragraph 53 that a transfer into a master trust in exchange for beneficial interests is neither a sale nor a secured borrowing under the provisions of paragraph 9.

Other Transfers of Financial Assets

Repurchase Agreements and Securities Lending Transactions

134. The Exposure Draft proposed that transfers of financial assets with repurchase commitments, such as repurchase agreements and securities lending transactions, should qualify as secured borrowings only if the transfer was *assuredly temporary*—the period until repurchase is less than three months or the period is indefinite but the contracts are repriced daily at overnight market rates and can be terminated by either party on short notice. It also proposed that the assets to be repurchased had to be the same (for example, U.S. securities having the same CUSIP number) as those transferred. Respondents generally disagreed with those provisions of the Exposure Draft about these ambiguous transactions, and the Board changed those provisions in its redeliberations.

Legal and economic ambiguity of these transactions

135. Repurchase agreements and securities lending transactions are difficult to characterize because those transactions are ambiguous: they have attributes of both sales and secured borrowings. Repurchase agreements typically are documented as sales with forward purchase contracts and generally are treated as sales in bankruptcy law and receivers' procedures, but as borrowings in tax law, under court decisions that cite numerous economic and other factors. Repurchase agreements are commonly characterized by market participants as secured borrowings, even though one reason that repurchase agreements arose is that selling and then buying back securities, rather than borrowing with those securities as collateral, allows many government agencies, banks, and other active participants in the repurchase agreement market to stay "within investment and borrowing parameters that delineate what they may or may not do."[14] Securities loans are commonly documented as loans of securities collateralized by cash or by other securities or by letters of credit, but the "borrowed" securities are invariably sold, free of any conditions, by the "borrowers," to fulfill obligations under short sales or customers' failure to deliver securities they have sold; securities loans are generally treated as sales

under U.S. bankruptcy and tax laws (but only as they relate to income distributions).

136. Previous accounting practice generally has treated repurchase agreements as secured borrowings, although "repos-to-maturity" and certain other longer term repurchase agreements have been treated as sales. Previous accounting practice has not recognized some securities lending transactions, because the transactions were executed by an entity's custodian or other agent, and has treated others as secured borrowings. Supporting arguments exist for accounting for both kinds of transactions as borrowings, both kinds as sales, or some as borrowings and others as sales.

137. The American Law Institute[15] describes the legal status of a securities lending transaction as follows:

> The securities lender does not retain any property interest in the securities that are delivered to the borrower. The transaction is an outright transfer in which the borrower obtains full title . . . the borrower needs the securities to transfer them to someone else . . . if the securities borrower defaults on its redelivery obligation, the securities lender has no property interest in the original securities that could be asserted against any person to whom the securities borrower may have transferred them. . . . The securities lender's protection is its right to foreclose on the collateral given to secure the borrower's redelivery obligation. Perhaps the best way to understand securities lending is to note that the word "loan" in securities lending transactions is used in the sense it carries in loans of money, as distinguished from loans of specific identifiable chattels. Someone who lends money does not retain any property interest in the money that is handed over to the borrower.

138. While that description focuses on securities lending, much of it appears applicable to repurchase agreements as well. If judged by the criteria in paragraphs 9(a) and 9(b) and the legal reasoning in paragraph 137, financial assets transferred under typical repurchase or securities lending agreements would qualify for derecognition as having been sold for

[14]Marcia Stigum, *The Repo and Reverse Markets* (Homewood, Ill.: Dow Jones-Irwin, 1989), 313.
[15]*Uniform Commercial Code, Revised Article 8, Investment Securities,* Proposed Final Draft (Philadelphia: American Law Institute, 1994), 18 and 19.

proceeds consisting of cash and a forward purchase contract. During the term of the agreement, the transferred assets are isolated from the transferor, are placed in the hands of a transferee that can—and typically does—obtain their benefits by selling or pledging them, and are readily obtainable in the market.

139. The Board considered requiring sales treatment for all of those transactions. The Board also considered an approach that would have recognized the effects of the transaction in the statement of financial position (recognizing the proceeds received as cash or securities and a forward purchase contract) without characterizing the transaction as a sale. The Board ultimately decided, for both conceptual and practical reasons, that secured borrowing treatment should be retained for most of those transactions.

140. In concept, having a forward purchase contract—a right and obligation to buy an asset—is not the same as owning that asset. Dividends or interest on securities are paid by the issuer to the current security holder, that is, to whoever may now hold the securities transferred in the repurchase agreement or loan, while the transferor has at most only the contractual right to receive—from the transferee—payments in lieu of dividends or interest. In addition, the voting rights reside not with the transferor but with the current security holder, because those rights generally cannot be contractually released.

141. However, the commitments entered into in a repurchase or securities lending agreement are more extensive than a common forward purchase contract. The transferor has agreed to repurchase the security, often in as little as a day, at a fixed price that differs from the sale price by an amount that is essentially interest on the cash transferred. The transferor also commonly receives payments in lieu of interest or dividends and has protection of collateral that is valued daily and adjusted frequently for changes in the market value of the transferred asset—collateral that the transferor is entitled to use to purchase replacement securities should the transferee default, even in the event of bankruptcy or other receivership. Those arrangements are not typical of forward purchase contracts and suggest that having a repurchase agreement or securities lending contract to repurchase a transferred asset before its maturity is much like still owning that asset.

142. Practically, participants in the very large markets for repurchase agreements and securities lending transactions are, for the most part, unaccustomed to treating those transactions as sales, and a change to sale treatment would have a substantial impact on their reported financial position. Given the difficulty in characterizing those ambiguous transactions, the decision to treat all of those transactions as sales would be a close call, and the Board was not convinced that the benefits of a change based on that close call would justify the costs.

143. The Exposure Draft proposed that transfers of financial assets with repurchase commitments, such as repurchase agreements and securities lending transactions, should be accounted for as secured borrowings if the transfers were assuredly temporary, and as sales if the transfers were not assuredly temporary. As proposed, to be assuredly temporary, the period until repurchase would have had to be short enough not to diminish assurance that the contract and arrangements backing it up would prove effective, that is, with maturities either under three months or indefinite and terminable by either party on short notice. Also, to be assuredly temporary, the entity would have had to be entitled and obligated to repurchase the same assets. After considering comment letters and testimony at the public hearing, the Board decided to change both of those proposed requirements.

The period until repurchase

144. The Exposure Draft proposed that transfers of financial assets should qualify as borrowings if the period until repurchase is less than three months or the period is indefinite but the contracts are repriced daily at overnight market rates and can be terminated by either party on short notice. A three-month limit was arbitrary, but based on its initial inquiries, the Board tentatively concluded that three months would be a clear and workable time limit that should not present difficulty, because it understood that most repurchase agreements and securities loans are for periods much shorter than three months or are indefinite, and almost all of the others are for periods much longer than three months.

145. Respondents generally disagreed with that provision of the Exposure Draft. They argued that the arbitrary three-month limit would not be effective and that entities could alter the accounting for a transfer by adding or subtracting one or two days to or from the term of the agreement. While some offered other arbitrary time limits, many respondents argued that all transfers accompanied by a forward contract to repurchase the transferred assets before maturity

should be accounted for as secured borrowings. In their view, most repurchase agreements represent a temporary transfer of only some elements of control over the transferred assets.

146. After considering those comments, the Board decided to remove the proposed requirement that the period until repurchase be less than three months. Board members concluded that any distinction based on the specified time until repurchase would not be workable. As outlined in paragraph 141, the elements of control by the transferee over assets obtained in a typical securities lending or repurchase agreement are both temporary and limited. The Board concluded that the contractual obligation and right to repurchase an asset before its maturity effectively bind the asset transferred back to the transferor.

147. Some respondents suggested a distinction based on a different time period, or on the proportion of the life of the asset transferred, but the Board rejected those possibilities. Any other time period would have the same faults as the three-month limit proposed in the Exposure Draft: it would be arbitrary, with no meaningful distinction between transactions just on one side of the limit and those just on the other side. Similarly, the Board concluded that the only meaningful distinction based on required repurchase at some proportion of the life of the assets transferred is between a "repo-to-maturity," in which the typical settlement is a net cash payment, and a repurchase before maturity, in which the portion of the asset that remains outstanding is indeed reacquired in an exchange.

Substantially the same assets

148. The Exposure Draft proposed that a repurchase agreement would have to require return of the same asset (for example, U.S. securities having the same CUSIP number) for the transfer to be treated as a borrowing. In the Exposure Draft, the Board reasoned that agreements to acquire securities that—while perhaps similar—are not the same as those transferred do not maintain any kind of control over the transferred securities. Most repurchase agreements require return of the same asset. Some are less rigid. For example, some mortgage-backed instruments are transferred in a class of repurchase agreements known as *dollar rolls*. There are several procedural differences between dollar-roll transactions and ordinary repurchase agreements. However, the most significant difference is the agreement that assets returned need not be the same as those transferred.

Instead, the transferor agrees to accept back assets with characteristics that are substantially the same within limits established by the market.

149. While a few respondents supported the Exposure Draft's reasoning, most did not. Respondents argued that the economic differences between the assets initially transferred and assets to be reacquired under a dollar-roll transaction that meets the existing accounting criteria for being substantially the same are, as the term implies, not substantial and should not result in an accounting difference. They argued that existing accounting guidance found in AICPA Statement of Position No. 90-3, *Definition of the Term Substantially the Same for Holders of Debt Instruments, as Used in Certain Audit Guides and a Statement of Position*, has proven adequate to constrain the characteristics of assets that are to be reacquired. After redeliberation, the Board accepted those arguments and decided that if the assets to be repurchased are the same or substantially the same as those concurrently transferred, the transaction should be accounted for as a secured borrowing. The Board also decided to incorporate the definition in SOP 90-3 in this Statement. The Board noted that not all contracts in the dollar-roll market require that the securities involved have all of the characteristics of "substantially the same." If the contract does not require that, the transferor does not maintain effective control.

The importance of the right and obligation to repurchase, collateral, and symmetry

150. The Board based its decisions about agreements that maintain effective control over transferred assets in part on observation of contracts and practices that prevail in the repurchase agreement and securities lending markets. Concerns of market participants about risk of default by the parties to the contract, rights at law in the event of default, and credit risk of transferred assets, among other factors, have led to several contractual features intended to assure that the transferors indeed maintain effective control.

151. The Board decided that to maintain effective control the transferor must have *both* the contractual right *and* the contractual obligation to reacquire securities that are identical to or substantially the same as those concurrently transferred. Transfers that include only the right to reacquire, at the option of the transferor or upon certain conditions, or only the obligation to reacquire, at the option of the transferee or

upon certain conditions, generally do not maintain the transferor's control, because the option might not be exercised or the conditions might not occur. Similarly, expectations of reacquiring the same securities without any contractual commitments, as in "wash sales," provide no control over the transferred securities.

152. The Board also decided that the transferor's right to repurchase is not assured unless it is protected by obtaining collateral sufficient to fund substantially all of the cost of purchasing identical replacement securities during the term of the contract so that it has received the means to replace the assets even if the transferee defaults. Judgment is needed to interpret the term *substantially all* and other aspects of the criterion that the terms of a repurchase agreement do not maintain effective control over the transferred asset. However, arrangements to repurchase or lend readily obtainable securities, typically with as much as 98 percent collateralization (for entities agreeing to repurchase) or as little as 102 percent overcollateralization (for securities lenders), valued daily and adjusted up or down frequently for changes in the market price of the security transferred and with clear powers to use that collateral quickly in event of default, typically fall clearly within that guideline. The Board believes that other collateral arrangements typically fall well outside that guideline.

153. Some respondents argued for a continuation of previous asymmetrical practices in accounting for dollar rolls. In previous practice, transferors have accounted for dollar-roll agreements as borrowing transactions, while dealers who receive the transferred assets have accounted for them as purchases. The Board observed that the same transaction cannot in concept or simple logic be a borrowing-lending arrangement to the transferor and a purchase-sale transaction to the transferee. The Exposure Draft would have resolved that asymmetry by requiring that transferors account for the transactions as sales. In response to respondents' concerns about transferors' accounting, this Statement instead calls for transferors to account for qualifying dollar-roll transactions as secured borrowings and requires that dealers account for the same transactions as secured loans.

Agreements Entitling the Transferor to Repurchase or Redeem Assets That Are Not Readily Obtainable

154. The Board considered whether to allow sale treatment if a transferor of financial assets concurrently acquires from the transferee a call option on the assets sold. Some questioned whether the transferor that holds a call option has surrendered control of the assets to the transferee. Some believe that an entity that holds an option to acquire a financial asset controls that asset. However, the holder of a call option does not receive interest or dividends generated by the asset, cannot exercise any voting rights inherent in the asset, may not be aware of the location or present custody of the asset, and is not able to sell the asset and deliver it without first exercising the call. And it may never exercise the call. If an entity that holds a call option on an asset controls that asset, then it follows that the entity should recognize the asset under the call option at the time the call option is acquired. However, two parties would then recognize the same asset—the entity that holds the call option and either the writer of the call option or the party from whom the writer plans to acquire the asset if the call is exercised.

155. The Board concluded that sale treatment should not be precluded in instances in which the transferor simultaneously obtains a call option on the asset sold, provided that the asset is readily obtainable. The writer of a call option on a financial asset may choose not to own the asset under the call option if it is readily obtainable; it may instead plan to acquire that asset if the call is exercised and delivery is demanded. In those circumstances, it is realistic to assume that the transferee can sell or repledge the asset to a third party and, at the same time, in good faith write a call option on that asset.

156. The Board concluded that a sale should not be recognized in instances in which the transferor simultaneously obtains a call on a transferred asset that is not readily obtainable. The resulting accounting treatment of an option on a not-readily-obtainable asset that is obtained as part of a transfer of financial assets is different from the accounting treatment generally accorded to the same option that is purchased for cash. From the transferor's viewpoint, that difference in accounting treatment between an option purchased and an option obtained as part of a transfer of assets conflicts with the principle that the recognition of financial assets and liabilities should not be affected by the sequence of transactions that led to their existence. However, as noted in paragraph 25, if the option is a component of a transfer of financial assets, and it does not constrain the transferee from selling or repledging the asset, that should not preclude the transfer from being accounted for as a sale. If the existence of an option constrains the transferee from

selling or repledging the transferred asset (because the asset is not readily obtainable to satisfy the option if exercised), then the transferor has not relinquished effective control over the asset and thus should not derecognize it.

Assets Obtained as Collateral That Can Be Sold or Repledged

157. The Exposure Draft proposed that for transactions involving collateral, including securities lending transactions and repurchase agreements, secured parties should recognize all cash collateral received as well as all other financial instruments received as collateral that they have the ability by contract or custom to sell or repledge prior to the debtor's default, because they have important rights over that collateral. Secured parties in those positions are entitled and able to use the cash received as collateral, or the cash they can obtain by selling or repledging other collateral, for their own purposes. Therefore, in the Exposure Draft, the Board concluded that that collateral is the secured party's asset, along with an obligation to return the collateral that is the secured party's liability. In the Exposure Draft, the Board reasoned that if that collateral was permitted to be excluded from the statement of financial position, assets that secured parties can use to generate income would not be recognized. Reporting income but not the assets that generate it could understate a secured party's assets (and liabilities) as well as overstate its return on assets. In contrast, noncash collateral that secured parties are not able to sell or repledge cannot be used to generate cash or otherwise benefit the secured party (other than by reducing the credit risk on the financial asset it secures, an effect already recognized in measuring that financial asset) and is not the secured party's asset.

158. The Board noted that the accounting proposed was consistent with Governmental Accounting Standards Board (GASB) Statement No. 28, *Accounting and Financial Reporting for Securities Lending Transactions,* that was issued in May 1995. GASB Statement 28 also required, for reasons similar to those noted in this Statement, that securities lenders record noncash collateral if the contract specifically allows the governmental entity to pledge or sell the collateral before a debtor defaults.

159. Many respondents objected to recognition of collateral because they contended that the proposed accounting would result in the same asset being recognized by two entities. As discussed in paragraph 172 and in the Exposure Draft, while the secured party reports the security as its asset, the transferor reports a different asset, a receivable for the return of the collateral from the secured party. Respondents also argued that recognizing the collateral implies that the secured party expects all the benefits of that asset, whereas it typically is not entitled to retain dividends, interest, or benefits from appreciation. Respondents who objected to recognizing collateral generally preferred that secured parties disclose collateral received. Other respondents suggested that it was not clear that the collateral provisions applied not only to a secured borrowing but also to collateral pledged in all other kinds of transactions.

160. The Board reconsidered the provisions of the Exposure Draft in light of those comments. To improve clarity and refine its conclusions, the Board focused on four circumstances in which a secured party arguably should recognize collateral it has received: (a) cash collateral, (b) collateral securing obligations in default, (c) other collateral that the secured party has sold or repledged, and (d) other collateral that the secured party can sell or repledge.

Cash collateral

161. Some respondents objected to recording any asset received as collateral, even cash, on the grounds that it remains the asset of the party posting it as collateral and is therefore not the secured party's asset. Other respondents agreed that cash collateral should be recognized because transfers of financial assets in exchange for cash collateral cannot be distinguished from borrowing cash and because cash is fungible. It is therefore impossible to determine whether it has been used by the secured party. The Board concluded for the latter reason that all cash collateral should be recorded as an asset by the secured party, together with a liability for the obligation to return it to the transferor, whose asset is a receivable.

Collateral securing obligations in default

162. Many respondents pointed out that collateral securing an obligation becomes the property of the secured party upon default on the secured obligation. A respondent argued differently, maintaining that a defaulting debtor does not relinquish control over the collateral until it no longer has an opportunity to redeem the collateral by curing the default. The Board agreed that the secured party should recognize collateral to the extent it has not already recognized the collateral if the debtor defaults and is no longer entitled to redeem it.

*Other collateral that the secured party
has sold or repledged*

163. Some respondents who agreed that cash collateral should be recognized argued that the secured party should not recognize other collateral unless the debtor had defaulted, no matter what powers it has over that collateral, again because in their view the transferred assets remain the assets of the transferor. Others argued that while it may make sense for the secured party to recognize an obligation if collateral is sold, as is common practice in some industries, it is not common practice for broker-dealers and others to recognize an asset and a liability when they repledge collateral. Respondents from the broker-dealer community noted that they regularly repledge substantial amounts of collateral in conjunction with loans secured by customer margin balances and "borrow versus pledge" matched securities transactions and that that collateral activity has not been recognized under previous practice, although it has been disclosed. After considering those arguments, the Board concluded that collateral should be considered for recognition when it is sold or repledged, because the ability to pledge or exchange an asset is the benefit that the Board determined constitutes control over a financial asset, as set forth in paragraph 9(b) and discussed in paragraphs 122 and 123.

164. One respondent observed that the documentation supporting some transactions preserves the transferor's legal right to redeem its collateral, even though the transferee has repledged the assets to a third entity. In those instances, should the transferee default, the transferor has rights to redeem its collateral directly from the third entity to which the initial transferee repledged it. The respondent argued that a transferee with that right has not surrendered control over the assets. The Board agreed with that reasoning and adopted it. Because the status of the right to redeem may not always be clear, the Board chose to implement it by requiring recognition of collateral by the secured party if it sells or repledges collateral on terms that do not enable it to repurchase or redeem the collateral from the transferor on short notice. One result is that broker-dealers and others who obtain financial assets in reverse repurchase agreements, securities loans, or as collateral for loans and then sell or repledge those assets will in some cases recognize under this Statement assets and liabilities that previously went unrecognized. The Board noted that obligations to return to the transferor assets borrowed and then sold have sometimes been effectively recognized as part of a liability for securities sold but not yet purchased, and did not require change in that practice.

*Other collateral that the secured party can
sell or repledge*

165. The Exposure Draft called for recognition of collateral that the secured party can repledge or exchange but has not yet used. Some argued that secured parties should not be required to recognize any unused collateral, reasoning that the collateral and related obligation did not meet the definition of an asset or a liability of the secured party. They contended that to be considered an asset of the secured party the collateral must embody a probable future economic benefit that contributes directly or indirectly to future net cash inflows and that in the case of many kinds of collateral, there is only a possible benefit that has not been realized until that collateral is sold or repledged. The Board disagreed, noting that collateral that can be sold or repledged has a capacity to contribute directly to future cash inflows—from a sale or secured borrowing—and that the obligation to return the collateral when reclaimed will require a future economic sacrifice—the relinquishing of control. The Board also observed that broker-dealers and others are able to benefit from collateral in various ways and that the right to benefit from the use of a financial asset is, in itself, an asset.

166. A respondent pointed out that the right to repledge or exchange is significantly constrained if the transferor has the right and ability to redeem the collateral on short notice, for example, by substituting other collateral or terminating the contract on short notice, and thereby demand the return of the particular security pledged as collateral. The Board agreed, reasoning that a transferor that can redeem its pledged collateral on short notice has not surrendered control of the transferred assets. The transferee will be able to use the transferred assets in certain ways to earn a return during the period of the agreement, but the value of its asset may be very limited because of the transferor's rights to substitute or cancel.

167. The Board considered an approach that would have recorded only the net value of the specific rights that the secured party has over the collateral. That approach might have been consistent with the financial-components approach, and several respondents asked the Board to consider it. However, no one, including the Board, was able to identify a method that the Board judged to be sound for separating the collateral into components.

168. Another possibility considered would have been to recognize the transfer of control over the collateral and for the two parties each to report their mutual rights and obligations under the contract net, that is, for the debtor to net its receivable for the transferred security against its obligation under the secured borrowing and for the secured creditor to net its obligation to return the security against its secured loan receivable. The only change to the statement of financial position would have been the difference in carrying amounts, if any, with a note disclosing the details. That approach is different from present practice in its details but would have produced similar total assets and liabilities. It arguably would have been more consistent with the financial-components approach that focuses on control and would have simplified the accounting. While this approach appealed to some Board members, the Board ultimately rejected it. The approach would have been inconsistent with other pronouncements that govern offsetting, because in this case there is no intent to settle net.

169. After considering comments and testimony on those matters, the Board decided that financial assets transferred as collateral in a secured borrowing should be recognized by the secured party as an asset with a corresponding liability for the obligation to return the collateral if the secured party is permitted by contract or custom to sell or repledge the collateral and the transferor does not have the right and ability to redeem the collateral on short notice, for example, by substituting other collateral or terminating the contract.

170. In addition, because there appears to be significant variation in practice, the Board decided to require entities to disclose their policies for requiring collateral or other security for securities lending transactions and repurchase agreements to inform users about the credit risk that entities assume in those transactions. Respondents did not object to that proposed disclosure.

Security Interests, Custodial Arrangements,
Contributions, and Other Transfers That
Do Not Qualify as Sales

171. The Board concluded that a borrower that grants a security interest in financial assets should not derecognize the financial assets during the term of the secured obligation. Although the borrower's rights to those assets are restricted because it cannot sell them until the borrowing is repaid, it has not surrendered control if the lender cannot sell or repledge

the assets unless the borrower defaults. That assets subject to a security interest have been pledged, and are therefore collateral in the possession of the lender or the lender's agent, does not affect recognition by the debtor because effective control over those assets remains with the debtor in the absence of default under the terms of the borrowing.

172. To maintain symmetry in the accounting of secured parties and debtors (paragraphs 157-170), the Board decided that debtors should redesignate in their statements of financial position collateral that has been put into the hands of a secured party that is permitted by contract or custom to sell or repledge it and which they are not entitled and able to redeem on short notice, for example, by substituting other collateral or terminating the arrangement. That redesignation avoids a situation in which two or more entities report the same assets as if both held them (as could occur under previous accounting practices).

173. Under previous practice, financial assets transferred to another party for safekeeping or custody continue to be carried as assets by the transferor. The only consideration exchanged in those transfers is, perhaps, payment of a fee by the transferor to the custodian for the custodial services. The custodian does not control the assets but must follow the transferor's instructions. The Board concluded that existing practice should continue and that this Statement need not deal with transfers of custody for safekeeping.

174. Some transfers of financial assets are unconditional nonreciprocal transfers that are contributions. The Board did not address them in this Statement because accounting for contributions is addressed in FASB Statement No. 116, *Accounting for Contributions Received and Contributions Made.*

175. Some transfers of financial assets will fail to meet the criteria specified in paragraph 9 to be accounted for as sales even though they might be structured as and purport to be sales. The Board concluded that those transfers should be accounted for as secured borrowings.

Measurement under the Financial-Components Approach

176. Following a transfer of financial assets that qualifies as a sale, assets retained or obtained and liabilities incurred by the transferor could at first be measured at either (a) fair value at the date of the transfer or (b) an allocated portion of the transferor's carrying amount for the assets transferred.

177. The usual initial measure of assets and liabilities is the price in an exchange transaction or the equivalent fair value. Paragraph 88 of FASB Concepts Statement No. 5, *Recognition and Measurement in Financial Statements of Business Enterprises,* states:

> Initial recognition of assets acquired and liabilities incurred generally involves measurement based on current exchange prices at the date of recognition. Once an asset or a liability is recognized, it continues to be measured at the amount initially recognized until an event that changes the asset or liability or its amount occurs and meets the recognition criteria.

178. In APB Opinion No. 29, *Accounting for Nonmonetary Transactions,* the Accounting Principles Board, in prescribing the basis for measurement of assets received in nonmonetary exchanges, states:

> . . . in general accounting for nonmonetary transactions should be based on the fair values of the assets (or services) involved which is the same basis as that used in monetary transactions. [Paragraph 18, footnote reference omitted.]

179. The Board believes that those concepts should be applied to new interests obtained or incurred in transfers of financial assets. At issue is whether the financial assets controlled and liabilities incurred in a transfer of financial assets that qualifies as a sale are new to the transferor and thus are part of the proceeds from the transfer, subject to initial measurement using the concepts summarized in paragraphs 177 and 178, or instead are retained beneficial interests over which the transferor has not surrendered control that need not be subject to new measurement under those concepts. The Board concluded that the answer depends on the type of financial instrument or other interest held or incurred.

180. The Board decided that a distinction can and should be made between new assets and liabilities that are part of the proceeds from the transfer and continuing interests in retained assets held in a new form. Cash received as proceeds for assets sold has no continuing connection with those assets and is clearly a new asset. Unrelated assets obtained also are clearly new assets, for example, a government bond received in exchange for transferred accounts receivable. Any asset received that is not an interest in the transferred asset is new to the transferor and thus is part of the proceeds from the sale. Any liability incurred, even if it is related to the transferred assets, is an obligation that is new to the transferor and thus a reduction of proceeds. Therefore, all of those new assets and liabilities should be initially measured at fair value. The issue becomes more challenging for assets controlled after a sale that are related to the assets sold.

Measuring Liabilities and Derivative Financial Instruments Related to Assets Sold at Fair Value

181. An entity that sells a financial asset may incur liabilities that are related to the assets sold. A common example of a liability incurred by the transferor is a recourse or guarantee obligation. Certain risks, such as recourse or guarantees, are inherent in the original financial asset before it is transferred, which might seem to support carrying over the prior carrying amount. However, before the transfer, the transferor has no obligation to another party; after the transfer, it does. The Board concluded that liabilities incurred in a transfer of financial assets are therefore new and should be initially measured at fair value.

182. An entity that sells a financial asset may enter into derivative financial instrument contracts that are related to the assets sold, for example, options, forwards, or swaps. One example of a related contract is an option that allows purchasers of receivables to put them back to the transferor, which is similar to a recourse obligation. Another example is a repurchase commitment held by the seller in a repurchase agreement that is accounted for as a sale,[16] which is a kind of forward contract. A third example is an agreement similar to an interest rate swap in which the transferor receives from a securitization trust the fixed interest amounts due on securitized receivables and pays the trust variable amounts based on a floating interest rate index. Under present practice, a party to an option or a forward purchase or sale commitment generally does not recognize the acquisition or disposition of the underlying assets until and unless delivery occurs. A party to a swap recognizes net amounts receivable or payable under the swap rather than the

---

[16]Accounting for repurchase agreements is discussed in paragraphs 66-71.

full notional amounts of the reference contracts. Options, forward commitments, swaps, and other derivative contracts are financial assets or liabilities separate and apart from the underlying asset. For that reason and because of the practical need to make a workable distinction, the Board concluded that derivative financial instruments entered into by a seller in an exchange for a financial asset are newly created in the transaction and should be considered part of the proceeds and initially measured at fair value at the date of exchange.

183. Respondents to the Exposure Draft asked the Board to provide more detailed guidance on how they should differentiate between an asset or liability that is part of the proceeds of a transfer and a retained interest in transferred assets. The Board acknowledges that, at the margin, it may be difficult to distinguish between a retained interest in the asset transferred and a newly created asset. The Board believes that it is impractical to provide detailed guidance that would cover all possibilities. A careful examination of cash flows, risks, and other provisions should provide a basis for resolving most questions. However, the Board agrees that it would be helpful to provide guidance if an entity cannot determine how to classify an instrument and decided that in that case the instrument should be considered to be a new asset and thus part of the proceeds of the sale initially measured at fair value.

Measuring Retained Interests in Assets Sold at Allocated Previous Carrying Amount

184. The Board decided that all other interests in the transferred financial assets held after a securitization or other transfer of financial assets should be measured at their previous carrying amount, allocated between the assets sold, if any, and the retained interests, if any, based on their relative fair values at the date of the transfer. Retained interests in the transferred assets continue to be assets of the transferor, albeit assets of a different kind, because they never left the possession of the transferor and, thus, a surrender of control cannot have occurred. Therefore, the retained interests should continue to be carried at their allocated previous carrying amount, with no gain or loss recognized. Defining this category as the residual set of interests in transferred instruments held after the transfer (those interests that are neither derivatives nor liabilities of the transferor) establishes a clearer distinction between assets and liabilities that are part of the proceeds of the transfer and retained interests.

Other Alternatives Considered

185. In developing the Exposure Draft, the Board considered several alternative measurement approaches including (a) measuring all assets held after a securitization or sale of a partial undivided interest (either a pro rata interest or a nonproportional interest) initially at fair value, (b) measuring interests held after a securitization at fair value and measuring retained undivided interests at allocated previous carrying amounts, and (c) measuring all interests in transferred financial assets held after a transfer at their allocated previous carrying amounts. Some respondents to the Exposure Draft supported each of those approaches. However, most respondents agreed with the Board's reasoning that a retained interest in a transferred asset represents continuing control over a previous asset, albeit in different form, and thus should not be remeasured at fair value. Most respondents also accepted the approach proposed in the Exposure Draft as workable.

186. Another possibility that was rejected by the Board was to allocate the carrying amount between the portion of an asset sold and the portion of an asset retained based on relative fair values at the date the receivable was originated or acquired by the transferor, adjusted for payments and other activity from the date of acquisition to the date of transfer. The consensus reached in EITF Issue No. 88-11, "Allocation of Recorded Investment When a Loan or Part of a Loan Is Sold," required use of that acquisition date method unless it is not practical, in which case the allocation should be based on relative fair values at the date of sale. In its deliberations on this Statement, the Board decided to require allocation based on fair values at the date of sale or securitization because it is more representative of the asset's value and the cost of re-creating the information from the date of acquisition would exceed the perceived benefits. The Board decided that the acquisition date method was not clearly superior in concept to an allocation based on fair values at the date of sale or securitization and, based in part on practices under that consensus, that that method was so often impractical because of recordkeeping difficulties that it was not useful as a general principle. No other possible methods of allocation appeared likely to produce results that were significantly more relevant.

Servicing Assets and Servicing Liabilities

187. Previously, net "mortgage servicing rights" were recognized as assets and those rights were accounted for in accordance with FASB Statements No. 65, *Accounting for Certain Mortgage Banking Activities,* and No. 91, *Accounting for Nonrefundable Fees and Costs Associated with Originating or Acquiring Loans and Initial Direct Costs of Leases,* and Statements 115 and 122. The amount recognized as net mortgage servicing rights was based on the fair value of certain expected cash inflows net of expected cash outflows. The expected cash inflows—future servicing revenues—included a normal servicing fee,[17] expected late charges, and other ancillary revenues. The expected cash outflows—future servicing costs—included various costs of performing the servicing. A separate "excess servicing fee receivable" was recognized if the servicer expected to receive cash flows in excess of a normal servicing fee, and a liability was recognized if the servicer expected to receive less than a normal servicing fee or if the entity's servicing costs were expected to exceed normal costs. The servicing rights asset was subsequently measured by amortization and assessment for impairment based on its fair value. That set of procedures has been called the mortgage servicing method.

188. Servicing assets and obligations for other assets sold or securitized were either accounted for like mortgage servicing or, more commonly, remained unrecognized until amounts were received and services were provided. Attempts have been made in practice to extend the mortgage servicing method to the servicing of other financial assets. However, identifying a normal servicing fee and other aspects of the mortgage servicing method have been difficult and disparate practices have resulted. The Board concluded it was necessary to address in this project accounting for servicing of all kinds of financial assets.

189. In October 1993, the Board decided to reconsider the accounting for mortgage servicing activities established in Statement 65. The primary thrust of that project was to resolve differences in the accounting for purchased versus originated mortgage servicing. Statement 122 was the result of that effort. In February 1995, the Board decided that accounting for excess mortgage servicing receivables and other

servicing issues should be dealt with, to the extent necessary, not in that project but rather in this one, because those issues largely arise in transfers of financial assets and possible answers are necessarily interrelated. The Board considered alternative methods of accounting for servicing (the mortgage servicing method required by Statement 65, as amended by Statement 122, as well as a gross method and a right or obligation method) and chose a method that combines the best features of the mortgage servicing method and other possible methods.

Alternatives to the Mortgage Servicing Method

190. The mortgage servicing method described in paragraph 187 was required by Statement 65, as amended by Statement 122, for mortgage servicing rights. While that method was familiar to mortgage servicers and had certain advantages over other methods, the distinction between normal and excess servicing and other complexities of the method make it difficult to apply for some other kinds of servicing.

191. The Board considered a gross method that would have required that a servicer recognize both a servicing receivable asset consisting of expected future servicing revenues and a servicing obligation liability for the servicing work to be performed. The Board decided that it was questionable whether a receivable for servicing not yet rendered met the definition of an asset and that, given the conceptual questions, that method did not merit the large change in practice that it would have required.

192. The Board also considered a right or obligation method that would have recognized a single item, commonly an asset but occasionally a liability, for each servicing contract. That asset or liability would have been the net of the gross asset and liability that would have been reported separately under the gross approach. The resulting asset would have been subsequently measured like an interest-only strip, that is, at fair value with unrealized gains and losses recognized in equity if available-for-sale. Some respondents suggested that servicing rights should be subsequently measured in that way, because reporting servicing rights at fair value would be more useful to investors and other financial statement users than the historical cost amortization and impairment methods of the mortgage servicing approach. Furthermore,

---

[17]Statement 65 defined a current (normal) servicing fee rate as "a servicing fee rate that is representative of servicing fee rates most commonly used in comparable servicing agreements covering similar types of mortgage loans." FASB Technical Bulletin No. 87-3, *Accounting for Mortgage Servicing Fees and Rights,* clarified what rate a seller-servicer should use as a servicing fee rate as described in Statement 65.

under an approach like that in Statement 115, unrealized gains and losses would not have been recognized in earnings, but rather in a separate component of shareholders' equity.

193. The Board considered the right or obligation method well suited in several respects to the range of mortgage and other servicing contracts that now exist or might arise. However, the Board did not choose that method in part for the practical reason of avoiding an early change from the recently adopted provisions of Statement 122. Instead, the Board chose to combine the best features of that method—the simplicity of reporting only a single asset or liability for each servicing contract and not having to distinguish between normal and excess servicing—with the best features of the mortgage servicing method.

Recognition and Measurement of Servicing Assets and Servicing Liabilities

194. The method adopted in this Statement carries forward the amortization and impairment provisions that were required under the mortgage servicing method in Statements 65 and 122. The Board considers those subsequent measurement provisions workable. However, changes to the mortgage servicing method are necessary to adapt the accounting for mortgage servicing to all servicing assets and servicing liabilities, to reduce complexities for financial statement preparers and users, and to be compatible with the other recognition and initial measurement principles in this Statement.

195. One change is the elimination of the distinction between normal and excess servicing. The Board decided that that distinction has been too difficult to make except in markets as liquid as the market for residential mortgage servicing. The Board considered two ways in which normal and excess servicing might be retained in accounting for those liquid markets.

196. One way would have been to leave in place the accounting for servicing of mortgages as required in Statement 65, as amended by Statement 122, while using a different method that was not dependent on determining a normal servicing fee for all other servicing. However, the Board concluded that comparability of financial statements would have suffered if the accounting for essentially similar servicing activities differed depending on the type of asset serviced. Another way would have been to revise the definition of normal servicing fee rates so that servicers could

determine a normal servicing fee rate in the absence of a developed secondary market for servicing. That change would have provided servicers of other types of loans or receivables (such as auto loans and credit card balances) with an opportunity to establish normal servicing rates and apply the mortgage servicing method to other servicing rights, rather than be subject to recognizing less gain or more loss on the sale of receivables because normal servicing was unknown. The Board considered that method but concluded that that alternative might result in continuing questions about what are normal servicing fees for different types of servicing.

197. The Board also noted that the distinction between normal and excess servicing, even in liquid markets, is no longer relevant for financial reporting because under current market practices, excess and normal servicing assets, which arise from a single contract, generally cannot be sold separately after the sale or securitization of the underlying financial assets. The excess servicing receivable, like normal servicing, will be collected only if the servicing work is performed satisfactorily. In addition, accounting based on that distinction is unduly complex and often results in several assets and liabilities being recognized for one servicing contract. While excess servicing continues to resemble an interest-only strip in some respects, the Board concluded in light of the lessened distinction between normal and excess servicing that it was more useful to account for all servicing assets and servicing liabilities in a similar manner.

198. The Board chose instead to distinguish only between the benefits of servicing—amounts that will be received only if the servicing work is performed to the satisfaction of the assets' owner or trustee—and other amounts retained after a securitization or other transfer of financial assets. A consequence of that method is that interest-only strips retained in securitizations, which do not depend on the servicing work being performed satisfactorily, are subsequently measured differently from servicing assets that arise from the same securitizations. That difference in accounting could lead transferors that retain an interest in transferred assets to select a stated servicing fee that results in larger servicing assets and lower retained interests (or vice versa) with an eye to subsequent accounting. The Board believes, however, that the potential accounting incentives for selecting a higher or lower stated servicing fee largely will counterbalance each other.

199. Most respondents agreed with the Board's decision to eliminate the distinction between excess and normal servicing. Some respondents to the Exposure Draft asked for further explanation of the new terms it used for accounting for servicing and about how they differed from the terminology of the mortgage servicing approach used in prior pronouncements. In response, this Statement defines the terms *adequate compensation* for servicing, *benefits of servicing,* and *contractually specified servicing fees* in the glossary and discusses them more completely in paragraphs 36-38.

200. The Exposure Draft proposed that an entity account for all servicing assets in the same manner because rights to service financial assets, while they may differ in the particulars of the servicing, in the extent of compensation, and in liquidity, are in essence the same. As with other retained interests in transferred assets, valid arguments can be made for measuring servicing assets either at allocated previous carrying amount or at fair value. However, the Board saw no reason to treat retained servicing assets differently than other retained interests and therefore decided that they should be initially measured at their allocated previous carrying amount.

201. For similar reasons, the Board viewed servicing liabilities as new obligations arising from a transfer and decided to account for them like other liabilities incurred upon sale or securitization, at fair value.

202. Some respondents questioned how to apply the transition provisions to servicing rights and excess servicing receivables in existence as of this Statement's effective date. The Board considered those comments and as a result decided to change paragraph 20 to (a) not permit retroactive application of this Statement to ensure comparability between entities and (b) clarify how this Statement should be applied to previous balances.

Financial Assets Subject to Prepayment

203. Paragraph 233 of this Statement amends Statement 115 to eliminate the use of the *held-to-maturity* category for securities subject to substantial prepayment risk, thereby requiring that they be classified as either available-for-sale or trading and subsequently measured at fair value. Paragraph 14 extends that measurement principle to interest-only strips, loans, other receivables, and retained interests in securitizations subject to substantial prepayment risk.

204. The justification for using historical-cost-based measurement for debt securities classified as held-to-maturity is that no matter how market interest rates fluctuate, the holder will recover its recorded investment and thus realize no gains or losses when the issuer pays the amount promised at maturity. The same argument is used to justify historical-cost-based measurement for other receivables not held for sale. That justification does not extend to receivables purchased at a substantial premium over the amount at which they can be prepaid, and it does not apply to instruments whose payments derive from prepayable receivables but have no principal balance, as demonstrated by large losses realized in recent years by many holders of interest-only strips and other mortgage derivatives. As a result, the Board concluded that those receivables must be subsequently measured at fair value with gains or losses being recognized either in earnings (if classified as trading) or in a separate component of shareholders' equity (if classified as available-for-sale). The Board, by deciding that a receivable may not be classified as held-to-maturity if it can be prepaid or otherwise settled in such a way that the holder of the asset would not recover *substantially all* of its recorded investment, left room for judgment, so that investments in mortgage-backed securities or callable securities purchased at an insubstantial premium, for example, are not necessarily disallowed from being classified as held-to-maturity.

205. Some respondents to the Exposure Draft agreed with the Board's conclusions about financial assets subject to prepayment when applied to interest-only strips but questioned the application of those conclusions to loans, other receivables, and retained interests in securitizations. They maintained that the nature of the instrument and management's intent should govern classification rather than actions that a borrower might take under the contract.

206. The Board did not agree with those arguments. A lender that holds a portfolio of prepayable loans or bonds at par will realize the carrying amount of its investment if the borrowers prepay. However, if the lender originated or acquired those loans or bonds at a substantial premium to par, it may lose some or all of that premium and thus not recover a substantial portion of its recorded investment if borrowers prepay. The potential loss is less drastic for premium loans or bonds than for interest-only strips, but it can still be substantial. The Board concluded that the rationale outlined in paragraph 204 extends to any situation in which a lender would not recover substantially all of its recorded investment if borrowers were to exercise prepayment or other rights granted to

them under the contracts. The Board also concluded that the provisions of paragraph 14 do not apply to situations in which events that are not the result of contractual provisions, for example, borrower default or changes in the value of an instrument's denominated currency relative to the entity's functional currency, cause the holder not to recover substantially all of its recorded investment.

207. Other respondents asked that the Board clarify the term *substantially all*. Some suggested that the Board use the 90 percent test found in APB Opinion No. 16, *Business Combinations*. Although applying the term *substantially all* requires judgment about how close to 100 percent is close enough, the Board decided to leave the language of paragraphs 14 and 233 unchanged rather than to require a specific percentage test that would be inherently arbitrary.

Fair Value

208. The Board decided to include an approach for measuring fair value that would be broadly applicable. The definition of fair value in paragraphs 42-44 is consistent with that included in other recent Statements.[18] The Board found no compelling reason to redefine *fair value* under the financial-components approach.

209. Many of the assets and liabilities held after a sale by a transferor with continuing involvement are not traded regularly. Because quoted market values would not be available for those assets and liabilities, fair values would need to be determined by other means in applying the financial-components approach. There was concern that, in some cases, the best estimate of fair value would not be sufficiently reliable to justify recognition in earnings of a gain following a sale of financial assets with continuing involvement, because errors in the estimate of asset value or liability value might result in recording a nonexistent gain. The Board considered requiring that fair value be verifiable to achieve a higher degree of reliability to justify recognition in earnings of a gain following a sale of financial assets with continuing involvement. However, to promote consistency between its Statements, the Board decided not to introduce a new notion of fair value based on reliability.

210. The Exposure Draft proposed that gain recognition following a sale with continuing involvement

should be allowed only to the extent that it is practicable to estimate fair values for assets obtained and liabilities incurred in sales with continuing involvement. To accomplish that, the Board concluded that if it is not practicable to estimate their fair values, assets should be measured at zero and liabilities at the greater of the amount called for under Statement 5, as interpreted by Interpretation 14, or the excess, if any, of the fair value of the assets obtained less the fair value of the other liabilities incurred over the sum of the carrying values of the assets transferred. That requirement was intended to prevent recognition of nonexistent gains through underestimating liabilities. The Board considered whether the practicability exception should be extended to the transferee's accounting and decided not to allow such an exception. The Board concluded that because the transferee is the purchaser of the assets, it should be able to value all assets and any liabilities it purchased or incurred, presumptively based on the purchase price paid. In addition, because the transferee recognizes no gain or loss on the transfer, there is no possibility of recognizing a nonexistent gain.

211. Respondents to the Exposure Draft asked the Board to clarify the meaning of the term *practicable*, especially in relation to the use of the same term in Statement 107. The comment letters also revealed a considerable range of interpretation of that provision among respondents. Some suggested that the provision would apply to all but the most common transactions. Others suggested that the provision would seldom apply and alluded to the relatively few entities that have used the practicability exception in Statement 107.

212. Because no practicability exception is used, for example, in the June 1996 FASB Exposure Draft, *Accounting for Derivative and Similar Financial Instruments and for Hedging Activities*, the Board considered whether to expand the discussion of practicability, or to remove it from the document. The Board ultimately concluded that the October 1995 Exposure Draft's practicability provisions should remain unchanged in this Statement for the reason noted in paragraphs 209 and 210.

213. Other respondents suggested that this Statement should include a limit on the amount of gain that can be recognized in a transfer of financial assets. Several suggested the limitation found in EITF

---

[18]FASB Statements No. 121, *Accounting for the Impairment of Long-Lived Assets and for Long-Lived Assets to Be Disposed Of*, par. 7, and No. 122, *Accounting for Mortgage Servicing Rights*, par. 3(f).

Issue 88-11. In that Issue, the Task Force reached a consensus that "the amount of any gain recognized when a portion of a loan is sold should not exceed the gain that would be recognized if the entire loan was sold." Respondents maintained that a limitation would meet the Board's objective of preventing recognition of nonexistent gains through underestimating liabilities.

214. The Board rejected the suggested limitation for several reasons. First, it was not clear that the limitation in Issue 88-11 could have been applied across a wide range of transactions. The limitation presumes that a market price exists for transfers of whole assets, but one reason that securitization transactions take place is because sometimes no market exists for the whole assets being securitized. Second, the limitation would have required that accountants ignore the added value that many maintain is created when assets are divided into their several parts. Third, the use of relative fair values at the date of transfer, rather than relative fair values on initial acquisition as in Issue 88-11, would have mitigated many of the concerns that appear to have prompted the Task Force to adopt a limitation. Finally, the Board was concerned that a gain limitation might have obscured the need to consider whether the transaction gives rise to a loss.

Subsequent Measurement

215. The provisions of this Statement focus principally on the initial recognition and measurement of assets and liabilities that result from transfers of financial assets. This Statement does not address subsequent measurement except for servicing assets and servicing liabilities and financial assets subject to prepayment.

216. Several respondents to the Exposure Draft asked the Board to include guidance about subsequent measurement in this Statement. They observed that the financial-components approach leads to recognition of assets and liabilities that were not recognized under previous standards. They also observed that accountants who draw analogies to existing accounting practices may find a variety of equally plausible approaches to subsequent measurement.

217. The Board is sensitive to concerns about subsequent measurement, especially to the possibility of emerging diversity in practice. However, attempting to address subsequent measurement would have expanded significantly the scope of this project. In addition, any guidance on subsequent measurement in this project would have applied only to assets and liabilities that emerge from a transfer of financial assets. Accounting for similar assets and liabilities not connected with a transfer of financial assets would have continued to follow existing practice; if so, diversity would have continued to exist. On balance, the Board concluded that it was better to complete this project without providing guidance on subsequent measurement and leave reconsideration of existing standards and practices for subsequent measurement for future segments of the Board's financial instruments project or other projects.

Extinguishments of Liabilities

218. Statement 76 required that a debtor treat a liability as if extinguished if it completed an in-substance defeasance. Under that Statement, a debtor derecognized a liability if it transferred essentially risk-free assets to an irrevocable defeasance trust and the cash flows from those assets approximated the scheduled interest and principal payments of the debt that was being extinguished. Under that Statement, the debtor also derecognized the assets that were set aside in the trust.

219. Derecognition of liabilities after an in-substance defeasance has been controversial. A number of respondents to the Exposure Drafts that led to Statement 76 and subsequent Board requests for comment have criticized the transactions as having insufficient economic substance to justify derecognition or gain recognition. Researchers and analysts have demonstrated that in-substance defeasance transactions conducted after interest rates have risen, which resulted in an accounting gain under Statement 76, have economic impact; those transactions constitute an economic loss to shareholders.[19] That research and analysis suggest that derecognition of liabilities and recognition of a gain in those circumstances may not be representationally faithful.

---

[19]The research referred to includes John R. M. Hand, Patricia J. Hughes, and Stephan E. Sefcik, "In-Substance Defeasances: Security Price Reactions and Motivations," *Journal of Accounting and Economics* (May 1990): 47-89; Judy Beckman, J. Ralph Byington, and Paul Munter, "Extinguishment of Debt by In-Substance Defeasance: Managerial Perspectives," *Journal of Corporate Accounting and Finance* (Winter 1989/90): 167-174; Bruce R. Gaumnitz and Joel E. Thompson, "In-Substance Defeasance: Costs, Yes; Benefits, No," *Journal of Accountancy* (March 1987): 102-105; and Abraham M. Stanger, "Accounting Developments: In-Substance Defeasance—Reality or Illusion?" *The Corporation Law Review* (Summer 1984): 274-277.

220. Under the financial-components approach, an in-substance defeasance transaction does not meet the derecognition criteria for either the liability or the asset. The transaction lacks the following critical characteristics:

a. The debtor is not released from the debt by putting assets in the trust; if the assets in the trust prove insufficient, for example, because a default by the debtor accelerates its debt, the debtor must make up the difference.

b. The lender is not limited to the cash flows from the assets in trust.

c. The lender does not have the ability to dispose of the assets at will or to terminate the trust.

d. If the assets in the trust exceed what is necessary to meet scheduled principal and interest payments, the transferor can remove the assets.

e. Neither the lender nor any of its representatives is a contractual party to establishing the defeasance trust, as holders of interests in a qualifying special-purpose entity or their representatives would be.

f. The debtor does not surrender control of the benefits of the assets because those assets are still being used for the debtor's benefit, to extinguish its debt, and because no asset can be an asset of more than one entity, those benefits must still be the debtor's assets.

221. The Board concluded that the previous treatment of in-substance defeasance was inconsistent with the derecognition criteria of the financial-components approach and that the provisions on in-substance defeasance in Statement 76 should be superseded by this Statement. Respondents to the Exposure Draft generally accepted that change, although some disagreed, citing arguments similar to those made in Statement 76 and refuted, in the Board's view, by the critical characteristics cited in paragraph 220.

222. Paragraph 3(a) of Statement 76 required derecognition of the transferred assets and the liability by the debtor if a debtor transfers assets to its creditor in exchange for a release from all further obligation under the liability. That provision has not been controversial and is consistent with the financial-components approach. Accordingly, paragraph 3(a) of Statement 76 was incorporated substantially unchanged as paragraph 16(a) of this Statement.

223. Paragraph 3(b) of Statement 76 stated, "The debtor is legally released from being the primary obligor under the debt either judicially or by the creditor *and it is probable that the debtor will not be required to make future payments with respect to that debt under any guarantees*" (emphasis added; footnote references omitted). Except for the italicized portion, paragraph 3(b) was carried forward as paragraph 16(b) of this Statement. Some respondents to the Exposure Draft disagreed with that change, arguing that the revised provision was too lenient in that it might allow, for example, derecognition of liabilities and inappropriate gain recognition when entities are replaced as primary obligor by entities with little economic substance. However, the italicized phrase is omitted from this Statement because it is contrary to the financial-components approach. If an entity is released from being a primary obligor and becomes a secondary obligor and thus effectively a guarantor of that liability, it should recognize that guarantee in the same manner as a third-party guarantor that was never the primary obligor. The Board noted, however, that concerns about inappropriate gains are unwarranted: if an entity with little substance were to become a primary obligor, a guarantor of that obligation would have to recognize a liability almost as great as if it were the primary obligor. To emphasize those matters, the Board included a discussion of the secondary obligor's liability in Appendix A.

224. The Board concluded that the basic principle that liabilities should be derecognized only if the debtor pays the creditor or is legally released from its obligation applies not just to debt securities but to all liabilities. Accordingly, this Statement broadens the scope of paragraphs 3(a) and 3(b) of Statement 76 to include all liabilities not excluded from this Statement's scope by paragraph 4 and to delete the reference to sales in the public market.

Disclosures

225. The Board decided that this Statement should continue to require disclosure of debt defeased in accordance with Statement 76 before the effective date of this Statement because this Statement does not change the accounting for those defeasance transactions. The Board also decided to require that an entity disclose assets restricted to the repayment of particular debt obligations, for example, in in-substance defeasance transactions after this Statement becomes effective, because while that restriction is insufficient cause to derecognize the assets, that information is useful in determining what resources are unavailable to general creditors and for general operations. The

Board decided that an entity should disclose its policies for requiring collateral or other securities in repurchase agreements and securities lending transactions accounted for as borrowings. The Board believes that that information is useful for assessing the amount of risk that an entity assumes in repurchase agreements and securities lending transactions, which appears to vary considerably in practice.

226. The Board also decided to carry forward the disclosures required by Statement 122 and extend them to all servicing rights, because those disclosures provide information financial statement users need to make independent judgments about the value of servicing rights and obligations and the related risks.

227. In addition, the Board decided to require that an entity describe items for which it is impracticable to measure their fair value and disclose why the fair value of an asset obtained or liability incurred could not be estimated, despite the concerns of some Board members that this requirement was unnecessary and might lead to uninformative disclosures.

228. The Board decided that only those additional disclosures should be required because sufficient disclosures are currently in place for transfers and servicing of financial assets, extinguishments of liabilities, and the components resulting from those transfers and extinguishments. For example, transfers of financial assets in exchange for cash must appear in the statement of cash flows, while information about any noncash exchanges must appear in related disclosures, under the provisions of FASB Statement No. 95, *Statement of Cash Flows*. The Board also considered various disclosures now required for certain specialized industries by AICPA Guides and other pronouncements and decided that the potential benefits of requiring those disclosures in this Statement did not justify the costs involved.

Effective Date and Transition

229. The Board proposed in the Exposure Draft that this Statement should be effective for transfers and servicing of financial assets and extinguishments of liabilities occurring after December 31, 1996, and the Board did not change that effective date. While many respondents accepted and some even urged adoption on that date, some respondents expressed concern about the ability to carry out certain of this Statement's provisions by that date, including systems changes needed to keep track of supporting data efficiently. The Board concluded that some of those concerns should be ameliorated by the effects of changes from the Exposure Draft on the accounting for repurchase agreements, securities lending, loan participations, and collateral, and that in other cases data adequate for external financial reporting could be obtained in other ways while systems changes were being completed.

230. The Exposure Draft proposed that this Statement should be applied prospectively to achieve consistency in accounting for transfers of financial assets. That requirement also will ensure that all entities entering into a given transaction report that transaction under the same guidance. If entities were permitted to implement early or implement at the beginning of fiscal years that did not coincide, opportunities might arise to structure transactions in ways that result in the same assets and liabilities being reported in the financial statements of both parties or in the financial statements of neither party. The Board found that possibility undesirable. Most respondents to the Exposure Draft generally accepted that conclusion.

231. The Board also decided that retroactive implementation for all entities was not feasible and that allowing voluntary retroactive implementation was unwise because it would impair comparability of financial statements by permitting disparate accounting treatment for similar transactions reported in previous periods. The Board concluded that those considerations outweighed the lack of consistency within an entity's financial statements for transactions occurring before and after the effective date of this Statement. In addition, the Board concluded that the benefits of retroactive application of the provisions of this Statement would not justify the considerable cost of doing that. Respondents generally accepted that conclusion.

Appendix C

AMENDMENTS TO EXISTING PRONOUNCEMENTS

232. This Statement supersedes FASB Statements No. 76, *Extinguishment of Debt*, No. 77, *Reporting by Transferors for Transfers of Receivables with Recourse*, and No. 122, *Accounting for Mortgage Servicing Rights*, and FASB Technical Bulletins No. 84-4, *In-Substance Defeasance of Debt*, and No. 85-2, *Accounting for Collateralized Mortgage Obligations (CMOs)*.

233. The following sentence is added to the end of paragraph 7 of FASB Statement No. 115, *Accounting for Certain Investments in Debt and Equity Securities:*

A security may not be classified as held-to-maturity if that security can contractually be prepaid or otherwise settled in such a way that the holder of the security would not recover substantially all of its recorded investment.

234. Paragraph 3(a) of APB Opinion No. 26, *Early Extinguishment of Debt,* as amended by Statement 76, is replaced by the following:

Extinguishment of liabilities. FASB Statement No. 125, *Accounting for Transfers and Servicing of Financial Assets and Extinguishments of Liabilities,* defines transactions that the debtor shall recognize as an extinguishment of a liability.

235. In the last sentence of paragraph 20 of FASB Statement No. 13, *Accounting for Leases,* as amended by Statement 77, the reference to Statement 77 is replaced with a reference to FASB Statement No. 125, *Accounting for Transfers and Servicing of Financial Assets and Extinguishments of Liabilities.*

236. The last sentence of footnote 1 of FASB Statement No. 22, *Changes in the Provisions of Lease Agreements Resulting from Refundings of Tax-Exempt Debt,* as amended by Statement 76, is deleted.

237. FASB Statement No. 65, *Accounting for Certain Mortgage Banking Activities,* is amended as follows:

a. The second sentence of paragraph 6 that was added by Statement 115 is replaced by the following:

After the securitization of a mortgage loan held for sale, the mortgage-backed security shall be classified as a trading security.

b. Paragraph 8, as amended by Statement 115, is deleted.

c. The last sentence of paragraph 9(a) is deleted.

d. In paragraph 10, *(paragraphs 16 through 19)* is deleted and replaced by *(paragraph 13 of FASB*

Statement No. 125, Accounting for Transfers and Servicing of Financial Assets and Extinguishments of Liabilities).

e. Paragraph 11 and footnote 4 are deleted.

f. In paragraph 15, the reference to paragraph 18 (as amended by Statement 122) is deleted and the following is added to the end of paragraph 15 replacing the sentence added by Statement 122:

The rate used to determine the present value shall be an appropriate long-term interest rate. For this purpose, estimates of future servicing revenue shall include expected late charges and other ancillary revenue. Estimates of expected future servicing costs shall include direct costs associated with performing the servicing function and appropriate allocations of other costs. Estimated future servicing costs may be determined on an incremental cost basis. The amount capitalized shall be amortized in proportion to, and over the period of, estimated net servicing income—the excess of servicing revenues over servicing costs.

g. Paragraphs 16-19 and 30 and footnote 6, as amended by Statement 122, are deleted.

h. The three paragraphs added by Statement 122 to paragraph 30 are deleted.

i. In paragraph 34, the terms *current (normal) servicing fee rate* and *servicing* and their definitions are deleted.

238. This Statement carries forward certain amendments that Statement 122 made to Statement 65. Those amendments are:

a. In the first sentence of paragraph 1, *origination or acquisition* is replaced by *purchase or acquisition.*

b. In the first sentence of paragraph 10, *of existing* is replaced by *or origination of.*

239. Paragraph 14(e) of FASB Statement No. 105, *Disclosure of Information about Financial Instruments with Off-Balance-Sheet Risk and Financial Instruments with Concentrations of Credit Risk,* is replaced by the following:

Substantively extinguished debt subject to the disclosure requirements of FASB Statement

No. 125, *Accounting for Transfers and Servicing of Financial Assets and Extinguishments of Liabilities.*

240. FASB Statement No. 107, *Disclosures about Fair Value of Financial Instruments,* is amended as follows:

a. Paragraph 8(b) of FASB Statement 107 is replaced by the following:

> Substantively extinguished debt subject to the disclosure requirements of FASB Statement No. 125, *Accounting for Transfers and Servicing of Financial Assets and Extinguishments of Liabilities*

b. In the last sentence of paragraph 28, *, or the rate that an entity would have to pay to acquire essentially risk-free assets to extinguish the obligation in accordance with the requirements of Statement 76* is deleted.

241. Paragraph 12 of FASB Technical Bulletin No. 86-2, *Accounting for an Interest in the Residual Value of a Leased Asset: Acquired by a Third Party or Retained by a Lessor That Sells the Related Minimum Rental Payments,* is replaced by the following:

> Yes. A residual value of a leased asset is a financial asset to the extent of the guarantee of the residual value. Accordingly, increases to its estimated value over the remaining lease term should be recognized.

242. FASB Technical Bulletin No. 87-3, *Accounting for Mortgage Servicing Fees and Rights,* is amended as follows:

a. Paragraphs 1-7 are deleted.

b. Paragraph 9, as amended by Statement 122, is replaced by the following:

> An enterprise may acquire servicing assets or liabilities by purchasing or originating financial assets with servicing rights retained or by purchasing the servicing rights separately. Servicing assets and liabilities are amortized in proportion to, and over the period of, estimated net servicing income—the excess of servicing revenues over servicing costs.

Appendix D

GLOSSARY

243. This appendix defines terms or phrases used in this Statement.

Adequate compensation
The amount of benefits of servicing that would fairly compensate a substitute servicer should one be required, which includes the profit that would be demanded in the marketplace.

Beneficial interests
Rights to receive all or portions of specified cash inflows to a trust or other entity, including senior and subordinated shares of interest, principal, or other cash inflows to be "passed-through" or "paid-through," premiums due to guarantors, and residual interests.

Benefits of servicing
Revenues from contractually specified servicing fees, late charges, and other ancillary sources, including "float."

Cleanup call
An option held by the servicer, which may be the transferor, to purchase transferred financial assets when the amount of outstanding assets falls to a level at which the cost of servicing those assets becomes burdensome.

Collateral
Personal or real property in which a security interest has been given.

Contractually specified servicing fees
All amounts that, per contract, are due to the servicer in exchange for servicing the financial asset and would no longer be received by a servicer if the beneficial owners of the serviced assets or their trustees or agents were to exercise their actual or potential authority under the contract to shift the servicing to another servicer. Depending on the servicing contract, those fees may include some or all of the difference between the interest rate collectible on the asset being serviced and the rate to be paid to the beneficial owners of those assets.

Derecognize

Remove previously recognized assets or liabilities from the statement of financial position.

Derivative financial instrument

A futures, forward, swap, or option contract, or other financial instrument with similar characteristics (Statement 119, paragraph 5).

Fair value

Refer to paragraphs 42-44.

Financial asset

Cash, evidence of an ownership interest in an entity, or a contract that conveys to a second entity a contractual right (a) to receive cash or another financial instrument from a first entity or (b) to exchange other financial instruments on potentially favorable terms with the first entity (Statement 107, paragraph 3(b)).

Financial liability

A contract that imposes on one entity a contractual obligation (a) to deliver cash or another financial instrument to a second entity or (b) to exchange other financial instruments on potentially unfavorable terms with the second entity (Statement 107, paragraph 3(a)).

Interest-only strip

A contractual right to receive some or all of the interest due on a bond, mortgage loan, collateralized mortgage obligation, or other interest-bearing financial asset.

Proceeds

Cash, derivatives, or other assets that are obtained in a transfer of financial assets, less any liabilities incurred.

Recourse

The right of a transferee of receivables to receive payment from the transferor of those receivables for (a) failure of debtors to pay when due, (b) the effects of prepayments, or (c) adjustments resulting from defects in the eligibility of the transferred receivables.

Securitization

The process by which financial assets are transformed into securities.

Security interest

A form of interest in property that provides that upon default of the obligation for which the security interest is given, the property may be sold in order to satisfy that obligation.

Seller

A transferor that relinquishes control over financial assets by transferring them to a transferee in exchange for consideration.

Servicing asset

A contract to service financial assets under which the estimated future revenues from contractually specified servicing fees, late charges, and other ancillary revenues are expected to more than adequately compensate the servicer for performing the servicing. A servicing contract is either (a) undertaken in conjunction with selling or securitizing the financial assets being serviced or (b) purchased or assumed separately.

Servicing liability

A contract to service financial assets under which the estimated future revenues from stated servicing fees, late charges, and other ancillary revenues are not expected to adequately compensate the servicer for performing the servicing.

Transfer

The conveyance of a noncash financial asset by and to someone other than the issuer of that financial asset. Thus, a transfer includes selling a receivable, putting it into a securitization trust, or posting it as collateral but excludes the origination of that receivable, the settlement of that receivable, or the restructuring of that receivable into a security in a troubled debt restructuring.

Transferee

An entity that receives a financial asset, a portion of a financial asset, or a group of financial assets from a transferor.

Transferor

An entity that transfers a financial asset, a portion of a financial asset, or a group of financial assets that it controls to another entity.

Undivided interest

Partial legal or beneficial ownership of an asset as a tenant in common with others. The proportion owned may be pro rata, for example, the right to receive 50 percent of all cash flows from a security, or non–pro rata, for example, the right to receive the interest from a security while another has the right to the principal.

Statement of Financial Accounting Standards No. 126
Exemption from Certain Required Disclosures about
Financial Instruments for Certain Nonpublic Entities

an amendment of FASB Statement No. 107

STATUS

Issued: December 1996

Effective Date: For fiscal years ending after December 15, 1996

Affects: Amends FAS 107, paragraph 7

Affected by: No other pronouncements

SUMMARY

This Statement amends FASB Statement No. 107, *Disclosures about Fair Value of Financial Instruments*, to make the disclosures about fair value of financial instruments prescribed in Statement 107 optional for entities that meet all of the following criteria:

a. The entity is a nonpublic entity.
b. The entity's total assets are less than $100 million on the date of the financial statements.
c. The entity has not held or issued any derivative financial instruments, as defined in FASB Statement No. 119, *Disclosure about Derivative Financial Instruments and Fair Value of Financial Instruments*, other than loan commitments, during the reporting period.

This Statement shall be effective for fiscal years ending after December 15, 1996. Earlier application is permitted in financial statements that have not been issued previously.

Statement of Financial Accounting Standards No. 126

Exemption from Certain Required Disclosures about Financial Instruments for Certain Nonpublic Entities

an amendment of FASB Statement No. 107

CONTENTS

INTRODUCTION

1. The FASB received requests that it exempt certain entities from the requirements of FASB Statement No. 107, *Disclosures about Fair Value of Financial Instruments*. The Board concluded that the disclosures required by Statement 107 should be optional for certain nonpublic entities. The basis for the Board's conclusions is presented in the appendix to this Statement.

STANDARDS OF FINANCIAL ACCOUNTING AND REPORTING

2. Disclosures about the fair value of financial instruments prescribed in Statement 107 shall be optional for an entity that meets all of the following criteria:

a. The entity is a nonpublic entity.
b. The entity's total assets are less than $100 million on the date of the financial statements.
c. The entity has not held or issued any derivative financial instruments as defined in FASB Statement No. 119, *Disclosure about Derivative Financial Instruments and Fair Value of Financial Instruments*, other than loan commitments, during the reporting period.

The criteria shall be applied to the most recent year presented in comparative financial statements to determine applicability of this Statement. If disclosures are not required in the current period, the disclosures for previous years may be omitted if financial statements for those years are presented for comparative purposes. If disclosures are required in the current period, disclosures about the fair value of financial instruments prescribed in Statement 107 that have not been reported previously need not be included in financial statements that are presented for comparative purposes.

3. For purposes of this Statement, a nonpublic entity is any entity other than one (a) whose debt or equity securities trade in a public market either on a stock exchange (domestic or foreign) or in the over-the-counter market, including securities quoted only locally or regionally, (b) that makes a filing with a regulatory agency in preparation for the sale of any class of debt or equity securities in a public market, or (c) that is controlled by an entity covered by (a) or (b).

4. This Statement does not change the requirements of FASB Statements No. 115, *Accounting for Certain Investments in Debt and Equity Securities*, and No. 124, *Accounting for Certain Investments Held by Not-for-Profit Organizations* (including disclosures about financial instruments other than equity and debt securities that are measured at fair value in the statement of financial position), or any requirements,

other than those specified in paragraph 2, for recognition, measurement, classification, or disclosure of financial instruments in financial statements.

Amendment to Statement 107

5. The following is added at the end of the second sentence of paragraph 7 of Statement 107:

> but is optional for those entities covered by FASB Statement No. 126, *Exemption from Certain*

Required Disclosures about Financial Instruments for Certain Nonpublic Entities.

Effective Date

6. This Statement shall be effective for fiscal years ending after December 15, 1996. Earlier application is permitted in financial statements that have not been issued previously.

> **The provisions of this Statement need not be applied to immaterial items.**

This Statement was adopted by the unanimous vote of the seven members of the Financial Accounting Standards Board:

Dennis R. Beresford,
   Chairman
Joseph V. Anania

Anthony T. Cope
John M. Foster
Gaylen N. Larson

James J. Leisenring
Gerhard G. Mueller

Appendix

BACKGROUND INFORMATION AND BASIS FOR CONCLUSIONS

CONTENTS

Appendix

BACKGROUND INFORMATION AND BASIS FOR CONCLUSIONS

Introduction

7. This appendix summarizes considerations that were deemed significant by Board members in reaching the conclusions in this Statement. It discusses reasons for accepting certain views and rejecting others. Individual Board members gave greater weight to some factors than to others.

8. The Board issued an Exposure Draft, *Elimination of Certain Disclosures about Financial Instruments by Small Nonpublic Entities,* on September 20, 1996. The Exposure Draft proposed making the disclosures prescribed by Statement 107 optional for nonpublic

entities with total assets of less than $10 million that do not hold or issue derivative instruments during the reporting period. The Board received 76 comment letters. The Board considered those comments and revised the Exposure Draft by clarifying this Statement's applicability and modifying the criteria for determining if the disclosures required by Statement 107 are optional. The Board concluded that it could reach an informed decision on the basis of existing information without a public hearing.

Benefits and Costs

9. The mission of the Board is to establish and improve standards of financial accounting and reporting for the guidance and education of the public, including issuers, auditors, and users of financial information. In fulfilling that mission, the Board strives to determine that a proposed standard will fill a significant need and that the costs imposed to meet that standard, as compared with other alternatives, are justified in relation to the overall benefits of the resulting information. Present and potential investors, creditors, and others benefit from improvements in financial reporting; however, the costs to implement a new standard may not be borne evenly by all parties. Further, the costs of not issuing a standard are impossible to quantify. Because there is no common gauge by which to judge objectively the costs to implement a standard against the need to improve information in financial statements, the Board's assessment of the costs and benefits of issuing an accounting standard is unavoidably subjective.

10. The Board has a commitment to consider potential disclosure differences between small and large companies on a case-by-case basis.[1] The Board recognizes that there is an incremental cost of applying Statement 107. The Board has long acknowledged that the cost of any accounting requirement falls disproportionately on small entities because of their limited accounting resources and need to rely on outside professionals.[2]

11. In paragraph 79 of Statement 107, the Board observed:

> The Board considered whether certain entities should be excluded from the scope of this Statement. In particular, the Board con-

sidered the usefulness of the disclosures about fair value required by this Statement for small, nonpublic, or predominantly nonfinancial entities; a number of respondents to the 1990 Exposure Draft suggested exclusions on one or more of those bases. After considering the costs and benefits of those disclosures, the Board concluded that the disclosures are important and should be required for all entities, including small and nonpublic entities. The Board believes that the notion of "practicability" discussed in paragraph 15 ensures that excessive costs do not have to be incurred to comply with the disclosure requirements. In addition, the Board's decision to allow smaller entities additional time to apply the provisions of this Statement recognizes the fact that the costs of compliance can be reduced for those entities because the overall benefits of the information might be less than for larger entities.

12. Public accountants who serve smaller nonpublic entities informed the Board that the practicability provisions of Statement 107 have been useful in reducing the costs of complying with the Statement. However, they also reported that there is a cost of documenting compliance with the Statement, including the reasons why an entity concludes that estimating fair value is impracticable.

13. This Statement will result in some loss of information provided by the financial statements of certain nonpublic entities. However, the Board views that loss as temporary. The Board currently plans to address a number of issues involving the recognition and measurement of financial instruments. As those issues are resolved, the disclosures required by Statement 107 will change. The Board will have the opportunity to consider whether the entities to which this Statement applies should make the revised disclosures.

Fair Value Information in the Financial Statements of Smaller Nonpublic Entities

14. The Board has concluded in its Exposure Draft, *Accounting for Derivative and Similar Financial Instruments and for Hedging Activities,* that fair value is the most relevant measure for financial instruments. Nothing in this Statement changes that view.

---

[1]"Board Responds to Concerns about 'Standards Overload,' " FASB *Status Report,* No. 150, November 22, 1983.

[2] "FASB Analyzes Small Business Concerns about Accounting Standards," FASB *Status Report,* No. 181, November 3, 1986.

However, the Board concluded that the disclosures required by Statement 107 likely have limited utility to users of the financial statements of certain nonpublic entities. In reaching that conclusion, the Board considered (a) the types of financial instruments held by smaller nonpublic entities, (b) the extent to which those entities' financial statements already provide information about the fair value of financial instruments, and (c) the extent to which those entities make use of Statement 107's practicability provisions.

Types of Financial Instruments

15. Smaller nonpublic entities are less likely than larger entities to engage in complex financial transactions. Apart from cash and trade receivables, their financial assets tend to be traded securities, investments in other closely held entities, and balances with related parties. Their financial liabilities tend to be trade payables, variable-rate loans, and fixed-rate loans. In contrast, entities that engage in complex financial transactions or that have substantial risk associated with changes in the fair values of financial instruments are likely to use derivative financial instruments. This Statement does not apply to entities that held or issued derivative financial instruments, other than loan commitments, during the reporting period.

Information Already Provided in Financial Statements

16. The financial statements of entities covered by this Statement generally provide significant information about fair value of financial instruments, even without the requirements of Statement 107. Trade receivables and payables and variable-rate instruments are already carried at amounts that approximate fair value. Investments in securities addressed by Statements 115 and 124 are carried at fair value (as trading or available-for-sale) or, if carried at cost, the fair values are disclosed. Existing disclosures about fixed-rate long-term debt include information about interest rates and repayment terms. That information should allow users to estimate whether the fair value of the long-term debt is significantly different from the carrying amount.

Use of the Practicability Exception

17. The Board has been informed that smaller entities make frequent use of Statement 107's practicability exception when considering whether to disclose the fair value of many financial instruments,

especially investments in other closely held entities and balances with related parties.

18. After considering the issues discussed in paragraphs 14-17, the Board concluded that, pending resolution of the underlying recognition and measurement issues, certain entities should have the option of not making disclosures mandated by Statement 107.

Factors Considered in Determining Scope

19. In considering which entities might be removed from the scope of Statement 107, the Board considered questions of size, financial activity, and ownership.

20. Previous FASB Statements that provided differential disclosure requirements have done so based on whether the entity is nonpublic. That criterion alone would have removed many large, nonpublic entities with complicated financial activities from the scope of Statement 107. The Board does not believe that it is appropriate to exempt those entities from the scope of Statement 107.

21. The Board decided that a size criterion was necessary to supplement the nonpublic criterion used in earlier pronouncements. The Exposure Draft proposed $10 million of total assets. The majority of the respondents to the Exposure Draft said that that amount was too low. The Board considered the nature of financial instruments in smaller nonpublic firms that do not use derivative financial instruments and decided that a higher threshold was acceptable. The Board settled on $100 million of total assets as an amount. In reaching its decision, the Board noted that exempting certain entities from current fair value disclosures is a practical matter and that the criteria used in paragraph 2 of this Statement are not meant to carry over into or influence future considerations about the usefulness of disclosures about financial instruments or other matters.

22. Some respondents said that total-asset size was not the best indicator of the relevance of disclosures about financial instruments. Some firms would not qualify for exemption as a result of having significant inventory or other physical assets. The Board considered changing the criterion to total financial instruments or to the amount of financial instruments not included within the scope of Statement 115 or Statement 124. While a criterion based on financial instruments may be more pertinent to the decision to exempt certain entities from the disclosure requirements in Statement 107, the Board decided that such

a criterion would unnecessarily complicate the standard. The objective of this Statement is to reduce complexity for certain entities, and requiring them to make decisions as to what is and what is not a financial instrument would not contribute to that objective. A total-asset criterion is easier to apply and could accomplish much of the same effect.

23. A larger total-asset criterion also exempts more financial institutions and other entities with higher concentrations of financial instruments. Some Board members were concerned that disclosures about fair values of financial instruments are particularly relevant for those entities. However, the Board decided to exempt entities with less than $100 million of total assets that meet the other criteria in this Statement. In reaching that decision, the Board considered (a) available evidence about the composition of assets at smaller financial institutions and (b) regulatory requirements for reporting fair values to the Federal Deposit Insurance Corporation.

24. The Board had concluded in the Exposure Draft that an entity that uses derivative financial instruments subject to the requirements of Statement 119 should remain within the scope of Statement 107.

Statements 119 and 107 interact with one another, and their requirements are not easily separated. More important, an entity that uses derivative financial instruments is not, by virtue of its utilization of complex financial instruments, the type of entity to which this Statement is intended to apply. Several respondents to the Exposure Draft indicated that the definition of derivative financial instruments in Statement 119 includes loan commitments and, as such, many entities would be precluded from applying this Statement. The Board agreed that loan commitments should not preclude entities from applying the provisions of this Statement.

25. Some respondents noted that the Exposure Draft was not clear on whether disclosures are required when previous periods are presented for comparative purposes. The Board determined that it would not be cost beneficial to provide information for periods presented for comparative purposes unless those disclosures were presented in prior periods and the disclosures prescribed by Statement 107 are required in the current period. The following table presents the requirements for disclosures when prior periods are presented in comparative financial statements.

If Disclosures for the Current Period Are:	And Disclosures for Prior Periods Were:	Then Disclosures for Prior Periods Presented in Comparative Statements Are:
Optional	Optional	Optional
Optional	Required	Optional
Required	Optional	Optional
Required	Required	Required

Statement of Financial Accounting Standards No. 127
Deferral of the Effective Date of Certain Provisions
of FASB Statement No. 125

an amendment of FASB Statement No. 125

STATUS

Issued: December 1996

Effective Date: December 31, 1996

Affects: Supersedes FAS 125, paragraph 19

Affected by: No other pronouncements

SUMMARY

FASB Statement No. 125, *Accounting for Transfers and Servicing of Financial Assets and Extinguishments of Liabilities,* was issued in June 1996 and establishes, among other things, new criteria for determining whether a transfer of financial assets in exchange for cash or other consideration should be accounted for as a sale or as a pledge of collateral in a secured borrowing. Statement 125 also establishes new accounting requirements for pledged collateral. As issued, Statement 125 is effective for all transfers and servicing of financial assets and extinguishments of liabilities occurring after December 31, 1996.

The Board was made aware that the volume and variety of certain transactions and the related changes to information systems and accounting processes that are necessary to comply with the requirements of Statement 125 would make it extremely difficult, if not impossible, for some affected enterprises to apply the transfer and collateral provisions of Statement 125 to those transactions as soon as January 1, 1997. As a result, this Statement defers for one year the effective date (a) of paragraph 15 of Statement 125 and (b) for repurchase agreement, dollar-roll, securities lending, and similar transactions, of paragraphs 9-12 and 237(b) of Statement 125.

This Statement provides additional guidance on the types of transactions for which the effective date of Statement 125 has been deferred. It also requires that if it is not possible to determine whether a transfer occurring during calendar-year 1997 is part of a repurchase agreement, dollar-roll, securities lending, or similar transaction, then paragraphs 9-12 of Statement 125 should be applied to that transfer.

All provisions of Statement 125 should continue to be applied prospectively, and earlier or retroactive application is not permitted.

Statement of Financial Accounting Standards No. 127

Deferral of the Effective Date of Certain Provisions of FASB Statement No. 125

an amendment of FASB Statement No. 125

CONTENTS

INTRODUCTION

1. FASB Statement No. 125, *Accounting for Transfers and Servicing of Financial Assets and Extinguishments of Liabilities,* was issued in June 1996. That Statement establishes, among other things, new criteria for determining whether a transfer of financial assets should be accounted for as a sale or as a pledge of collateral in a secured borrowing. Statement 125 also establishes new accounting requirements for pledged collateral.

2. As issued, Statement 125 is effective for all transfers and servicing of financial assets and extinguishments of liabilities occurring after December 31, 1996, and is to be applied prospectively. Earlier or retroactive application of Statement 125 is not permitted.

3. The Board was made aware that the volume and variety of certain transactions and the related changes to information systems and accounting processes that are necessary to comply with the requirements of Statement 125 would make it extremely difficult, if not impossible, for some affected enterprises to apply the transfer and collateral provisions of Statement 125 to those transactions as soon as January 1, 1997. As a result, this Statement defers for one year the effective date (a) of paragraph 15 of Statement 125 and (b) for repurchase agreement, dollar-roll, securities lending, and similar transactions, of paragraphs 9-12 and 237(b) of Statement 125. The provisions of Statement 125 will continue to be applied prospectively, and earlier or retroactive application is not permitted.

4. To defer the effective date of paragraphs 9-12 and 237(b) of Statement 125 only for certain transactions, the Board has grouped all transfers of financial assets into two broad categories: (a) repurchase agreement, dollar-roll, securities lending, and similar transactions and (b) all other transfers and servicing of financial assets. As discussed in paragraph 14 of this Statement, the Board recognizes that it may be difficult to determine the appropriate categorization of certain transactions for purposes of determining the effective date of Statement 125 and therefore has provided guidance for those circumstances.

STANDARDS OF FINANCIAL ACCOUNTING AND REPORTING

Amendment to Statement 125

5. Paragraph 19 of Statement 125 is replaced by the following:

> This Statement shall be effective for transfers and servicing of financial assets and extinguishments of liabilities occurring after December 31, 1996, except that:
>
> a. Paragraph 15 shall be effective for all transfers of financial assets occurring after December 31, 1997.

b. For repurchase agreement, dollar-roll, securities lending, and similar transactions, paragraphs 9-12 and 237(b) shall be effective for transfers of financial assets occurring after December 31, 1997.

If it is not possible to determine whether a transfer occurring during calendar-year 1997 is covered by paragraph 19(b), then paragraphs 9-12 and 237(b) shall be applied to that transfer. All provisions of this Statement shall be applied prospectively, and earlier or retroactive application is not permitted.

Effective Date

6. This Statement is effective December 31, 1996.

> **The provisions of this Statement need
> not be applied to immaterial items.**

This Statement was adopted by the unanimous vote of the seven members of the Financial Accounting Standards Board:

Dennis R. Beresford,	Anthony T. Cope	James J. Leisenring
Chairman	John M. Foster	Gerhard G. Mueller
Joseph V. Anania	Gaylen N. Larson	

Appendix

BACKGROUND INFORMATION AND BASIS FOR CONCLUSIONS

7. Statement 125 was issued in June 1996 and as issued is effective for transfers and servicing of financial assets and extinguishments of liabilities occurring after December 31, 1996. As discussed in paragraph 229 of Statement 125, some respondents to the Exposure Draft had expressed concern about their ability to apply certain provisions of Statement 125 by that date, including making the changes to information and accounting systems needed to apply the newly established accounting requirements and efficiently track supporting data. The Board concluded that some of those concerns should be ameliorated by the effects of changes from the Exposure Draft and that in other cases data adequate for external financial reporting could be obtained in other ways while systems changes were being completed.

8. After Statement 125 was issued, however, representatives from various enterprises, particularly those representing brokers and dealers in securities, continued to express to the Board concerns about the effective date of Statement 125. On October 16, 1996, the Board met with representatives from interested enterprises to discuss those concerns, which focused on the volume and variety of repurchase agreement, dollar-roll, securities lending, and similar transactions. The Board became convinced that, for those transactions, substantial changes to information systems and accounting processes were essential for brokers and dealers in securities and other enterprises to comply with Statement 125. The requisite changes and the volume and variety of those transactions would make it extremely difficult, if not impossible, for some affected enterprises to account for those transfers of financial assets and apply the secured borrowing and collateral provisions of Statement 125 as soon as January 1, 1997.

9. The Board appreciated the concerns expressed by those enterprises that attempting to account for those types of transactions manually until appropriate modifications could be made to information systems and accounting processes might lead to a significant temporary deterioration in the financial controls over and quality of financial information reported by the affected enterprises. Those enterprises informed the Board that a one-year delay for those transactions would provide an appropriate period of time for modifying information systems and accounting processes.

10. In November 1996, the Board issued an Exposure Draft, *Deferral of the Effective Date of Certain Provisions of FASB Statement No. 125,* that proposed deferring for one year the effective date of paragraph 15 (addressing secured borrowings and collateral) of Statement 125 for all transactions and of paragraphs 9-12 (addressing transfers of financial assets) only for transfers of financial assets that are part

of repurchase agreement, dollar-roll, securities lending, and similar transactions. The Board did not believe that it was necessary or appropriate to defer the effective date of the other provisions of Statement 125 for other types of transactions because those provisions and transactions do not involve so great a volume or variety, nor do they involve such extensive changes to information systems and accounting processes. The Board received letters of comment from 29 respondents, a large majority of whom supported the Exposure Draft. The comments were considered by the Board during its redeliberations in a public meeting in December 1996, and the Board concluded that it could reach an informed decision on the basis of existing information without a public hearing.

11. The Board recognized that some enterprises that enter into repurchase agreement, dollar-roll, securities lending, and similar transactions and into collateral arrangements do so in volumes and varieties that would permit them to apply paragraphs 9-12 and 15 of Statement 125 to those transactions beginning on January 1, 1997, with little difficulty. However, the Board decided to require deferral rather than allow optional deferral because the Board continues to believe, for reasons discussed in paragraph 230 of Statement 125, that all parties should consistently apply Statement 125 to the same types of transactions and as of the same date.

12. To facilitate the deferral of the effective date of paragraphs 9-12 and 237(b) of Statement 125 for only the specified transactions, transfers of financial assets have been grouped into two broad categories. Transfers in the first category—repurchase agreement (refer to paragraphs 66-68 and 71 of Statement 125), dollar-roll (refer to paragraph 70 of Statement 125), securities lending (refer to paragraphs 61-64 of Statement 125), and similar transactions—frequently involve an agreement that both entitles and obligates the transferor to repurchase or redeem the same or substantially the same (refer to paragraphs 27 and 28 of Statement 125) financial assets before their maturity. Other similar transactions include "buy-sell" agreements and certain other transfers of financial assets that are very similar to repurchase agreement, dollar-roll, and securities lending transactions in both form and objectives.

13. Transfers in the second category include securitizations (as defined in paragraph 243 of Statement 125) and other transfers of financial assets that,

prior to the effective date of Statement 125, are accounted for in accordance with FASB Statements No. 77, *Reporting by Transferors for Transfers of Receivables with Recourse,* and No. 65, *Accounting for Certain Mortgage Banking Activities,* as amended by FASB Statement No. 122, *Accounting for Mortgage Servicing Rights,* and FASB Technical Bulletin No. 85-2, *Accounting for Collateralized Mortgage Obligations (CMOs).* Transfers in the second category also include, but are not limited to, wash sales, loan syndications and participations, bankers' acceptances, and factoring arrangements (as discussed in Appendix A to Statement 125).

14. The Board recognized that in some cases it may be difficult to determine whether a transaction is better included in one category or the other for purposes of determining the effective date of Statement 125. As indicated in paragraph 5 of this Statement, if it is not possible to determine the category in which a transfer occurring during calendar-year 1997 should be included, then paragraphs 9-12 and 237(b) of Statement 125 should be applied to that transfer. That guidance is intended to be restrictive and does not allow an enterprise the option of including a transaction in one category or the other. The Board continues to believe that the effective date of Statement 125 should be the same for similar transactions, particularly for all parties to the same transaction.

Other Possibilities Considered

15. The Board considered not deferring any portion of Statement 125 for any type of transfer of financial assets. However, the Board concluded that that option would be unresponsive to a valid concern of some of its constituents. The Board then considered several possibilities for deferring the effective date of Statement 125. One possibility was deferring the effective date of the entire Statement for all transactions. Board members noted that that approach would be simpler. However, a number of constituents desire and have incurred significant effort and expense to apply the provisions of Statement 125 to securitizations, sales of mortgages and other receivables, and other transactions occurring after December 31, 1996. For that reason, the Board concluded that prohibiting those enterprises from applying the provisions associated with transfers and servicing of financial assets to those transactions as of the original effective date of Statement 125 would be undesirable.

16. The Board also considered permitting the choice of earlier or retroactive application. However, the

Board continues to believe that, for the reasons discussed in paragraphs 230 and 231 of Statement 125, that would be undesirable.

17. The Board also considered deferring the effective date of Statement 125 with earlier implementation encouraged and requiring that the cumulative effect of applying Statement 125 to all transfers of financial assets and extinguishments of liabilities occurring after December 31, 1996 be recognized in the year beginning after December 15, 1997. The Board determined, however, that an approach that includes a cumulative-effect adjustment would not sufficiently alleviate the systems and administrative problems that the Board was attempting to respond to because it would continue to be necessary for affected enterprises to capture and process accounting information beginning with transfers occurring as soon as January 1, 1997.

18. The Board also considered deferring the effective date only for paragraph 15 of Statement 125. While that solution would perhaps be simpler than the other options that were considered and would address a portion of the problems raised by the affected enterprises, it would not address the information systems and accounting process requirements for a large volume and variety of transactions. Therefore, the Board concluded that deferring the effective date of only paragraph 15 was less desirable than the approach in this Statement.

Statement of Financial Accounting Standards No. 128
Earnings per Share

STATUS

Issued: February 1997

Effective Date: For financial statements for both interim and annual periods ending after December 15, 1997

Affects: Supersedes APB 15
  Amends APB 18, paragraph 18
  Supersedes APB 18, footnote 8
  Amends APB 20, paragraphs 20, 21, 42 through 44, and 46 through 48
  Supersedes APB 28, paragraph 30(b)
  Amends APB 30, paragraph 9
  Supersedes APB 30, paragraph 12 and footnote 3
  Supersedes AIN-APB 15, Interpretations No. 1 through 102
  Supersedes AIN-APB 20, Interpretations No. 1 and 2
  Amends FAS 21, paragraphs 12 and 14
  Supersedes FAS 21, footnote 3
  Supersedes FAS 85
  Supersedes FAS 123, paragraphs 49 and 359 through 361 and footnote 26
  Amends FAS 123, paragraphs 50, 357, and 358
  Supersedes FIN 28, paragraph 6
  Supersedes FIN 31
  Supersedes FIN 38, paragraph 7
  Amends FTB 79-8, paragraph 2

Affected by: No other pronouncements

Issues Discussed by FASB Emerging Issues Task Force (EITF)

  Affects: Partially nullifies EITF Issues No. 85-18 and 90-4
      Partially resolves EITF Issue No. 96-13

  Interpreted by: No EITF Issues

  Related Issues: EITF Issues No. 84-22, 90-19, and 92-3 and Topics No. D-15, D-42, and D-53

SUMMARY

This Statement establishes standards for computing and presenting earnings per share (EPS) and applies to entities with publicly held common stock or potential common stock. This Statement simplifies the standards for computing earnings per share previously found in APB Opinion No. 15, *Earnings per Share,* and makes them comparable to international EPS standards. It replaces the presentation of primary EPS with a presentation of basic EPS. It also requires dual presentation of basic and diluted EPS on the face of the income statement for all entities with complex capital structures and requires a reconciliation of the numerator and denominator of the basic EPS computation to the numerator and denominator of the diluted EPS computation.

Basic EPS excludes dilution and is computed by dividing income available to common stockholders by the weighted-average number of common shares outstanding for the period. Diluted EPS reflects the potential dilution that could occur if securities or other contracts to issue common stock were exercised or converted into common stock or resulted in the issuance of common stock that then shared in the earnings of the entity. Diluted EPS is computed similarly to fully diluted EPS pursuant to Opinion 15.

This Statement supersedes Opinion 15 and AICPA Accounting Interpretations 1-102 of Opinion 15. It also supersedes or amends other accounting pronouncements listed in Appendix D. The provisions in this Statement are substantially the same as those in International Accounting Standard 33, *Earnings per Share,* recently issued by the International Accounting Standards Committee.

This Statement is effective for financial statements issued for periods ending after December 15, 1997, including interim periods; earlier application is not permitted. This Statement requires restatement of all prior-period EPS data presented.

Statement of Financial Accounting Standards No. 128

Earnings per Share

CONTENTS

INTRODUCTION

1. This Statement specifies the computation, presentation, and disclosure requirements for **earnings per share**[1] (EPS) for entities with publicly held **common stock** or **potential common stock.** This Statement's objective is to simplify the computation of earnings per share and to make the U.S. standard for computing earnings per share more compatible with the EPS standards of other countries and with that of the International Accounting Standards Committee (IASC).

2. In 1969, the AICPA issued APB Opinion No. 15, *Earnings per Share,* and by 1971 had published 102 Accounting Interpretations of Opinion 15. Given the widespread use of EPS data, the objective of Opinion 15 was to provide a standard so that earnings per share would be computed on a consistent basis and presented in the most meaningful manner. That objective also underlies this Statement.

3. Opinion 15 permitted a single presentation of "earnings per common share" for entities with simple

---

[1]Terms defined in Appendix E, the glossary, are set in **boldface type** the first time they appear.

capital structures. That presentation was similar to **basic EPS,** which is a common presentation outside the United States. However, Opinion 15 required that entities with complex capital structures present both "primary" and "fully diluted" EPS on the face of the income statement. The primary EPS computation included "common stock equivalents" in the denominator (the number of common shares outstanding). Only two other countries require presentation of primary EPS; all other countries that have EPS requirements require presentation of only basic EPS or both basic and fully diluted EPS.

4. In October 1993, the IASC issued a draft Statement of Principles, *Earnings per Share,* for public comment. Because earnings per share is one of the most widely used financial statistics, the IASC's goal was to initiate a common approach to the determination and presentation of earnings per share that would permit global comparisons. Even though EPS data may have limitations because of the different national methods for determining "earnings," the IASC and the FASB believe that a consistently determined denominator will be a significant improvement in international financial reporting.

5. The Board pursued its EPS project concurrently with the IASC to help achieve international harmonization of the accounting standards for computing earnings per share. The focus of the project was on the denominator of the EPS computation, not on issues about the determination of earnings. The IASC issued IAS 33, *Earnings per Share,* concurrently with the issuance of this Statement; the provisions in that Standard are substantially the same as those in this Statement.

STANDARDS OF FINANCIAL ACCOUNTING AND REPORTING

Scope

6. This Statement requires presentation of earnings per share by all entities that have issued common stock or potential common stock (that is, **securities** such as **options, warrants, convertible securities,** or **contingent stock agreements)** if those securities

trade in a public market either on a stock exchange (domestic or foreign) or in the over-the-counter market, including securities quoted only locally or regionally. This Statement also requires presentation of earnings per share by an entity that has made a filing or is in the process of filing with a regulatory agency in preparation for the sale of those securities in a public market. This Statement does not require presentation of earnings per share for investment companies[2] or in statements of wholly owned subsidiaries. Any entity that is not required by this Statement to present earnings per share in its financial statements that chooses to present earnings per share in its financial statements shall do so in accordance with the provisions of this Statement.

7. This Statement supersedes Opinion 15, AICPA Accounting Interpretations 1-102 of Opinion 15, AICPA Accounting Interpretations 1, "Changing EPS Denominator for Retroactive Adjustment to Prior Period," and 2, "EPS for 'Catch-up' Adjustment," of APB Opinion No. 20, *Accounting Changes,* FASB Statement No. 85, *Yield Test for Determining whether a Convertible Security Is a Common Stock Equivalent,* and FASB Interpretation No. 31, *Treatment of Stock Compensation Plans in EPS Computations.* It also amends other accounting pronouncements listed in Appendix D.

Basic Earnings per Share

8. The objective of basic EPS is to measure the performance of an entity over the reporting period. Basic EPS shall be computed by dividing **income available to common stockholders** (the numerator) by the **weighted-average number of common shares outstanding** (the denominator) during the period. Shares issued during the period and shares reacquired during the period shall be weighted for the portion of the period that they were outstanding.

9. Income available to common stockholders shall be computed by deducting both the dividends declared in the period on **preferred stock** (whether or not paid) and the dividends accumulated for the period on cumulative preferred stock (whether or not earned)[3] from income from continuing operations (if

---

[2]That is, investment companies that comply with the requirements of the AICPA Audit and Accounting Guide, *Audits of Investment Companies,* to present selected per-share data.

[3]Preferred dividends that are cumulative only if earned shall be deducted only to the extent that they are earned.

that amount appears in the income statement)[4] and also from net income. If there is a loss from continuing operations or a net loss, the amount of the loss shall be increased by those preferred dividends.

10. Shares issuable for little or no cash consideration upon the satisfaction of certain conditions (**contingently issuable shares**) shall be considered outstanding common shares and included in the computation of basic EPS as of the date that all necessary conditions have been satisfied (in essence, when issuance of the shares is no longer contingent). Outstanding common shares that are contingently returnable (that is, subject to recall) shall be treated in the same manner as contingently issuable shares.[5]

Diluted Earnings per Share

11. The objective of **diluted EPS** is consistent with that of basic EPS—to measure the performance of an entity over the reporting period—while giving effect to all **dilutive** potential common shares that were outstanding during the period. The computation of diluted EPS is similar to the computation of basic EPS except that the denominator is increased to include the number of additional common shares that would have been outstanding if the dilutive potential common shares had been issued. In addition, in computing the dilutive effect of convertible securities, the numerator is adjusted to add back (a) any convertible preferred dividends and (b) the after-tax amount of interest recognized in the period associated with any convertible debt. The numerator also is adjusted for any other changes in income or loss that would result from the assumed conversion of those potential common shares, such as profit-sharing expenses. Similar adjustments also may be necessary for certain contracts that provide the issuer or holder with a choice between settlement methods.

12. Diluted EPS shall be based on the most advantageous **conversion rate** or **exercise price** from the standpoint of the security holder. Previously reported

diluted EPS data shall not be retroactively adjusted for subsequent conversions or subsequent changes in the market price of the common stock.

No Antidilution

13. The computation of diluted EPS shall not assume conversion, exercise, or **contingent issuance** of securities that would have an **antidilutive** effect on earnings per share. Shares issued on actual conversion, exercise, or satisfaction of certain conditions for which the underlying potential common shares were antidilutive shall be included in the computation as outstanding common shares from the date of conversion, exercise, or satisfaction of those conditions, respectively. In determining whether potential common shares are dilutive or antidilutive, each issue or series of issues of potential common shares shall be considered separately rather than in the aggregate.

14. Convertible securities may be dilutive on their own but antidilutive when included with other potential common shares in computing diluted EPS. To reflect maximum potential dilution, each issue or series of issues of potential common shares shall be considered in sequence from the most dilutive to the least dilutive. That is, dilutive potential common shares with the lowest "earnings per incremental share" shall be included in diluted EPS before those with a higher earnings per incremental share.[6] Illustration 4 in Appendix C provides an example of that provision.

15. An entity that reports a discontinued operation, an extraordinary item, or the cumulative effect of an accounting change in a period shall use income from continuing operations[7] (adjusted for preferred dividends as described in paragraph 9) as the "control number" in determining whether those potential common shares are dilutive or antidilutive. That is, the same number of potential common shares used in computing the diluted per-share amount for income from continuing operations shall be used in computing all other reported diluted per-share amounts even

---

[4]An entity that does not report a discontinued operation but reports an extraordinary item or the cumulative effect of an accounting change in the period shall use that line item (for example, *income before extraordinary items* or *income before accounting change*) whenever the line item *income from continuing operations* is referred to in this Statement.

[5]Thus, contingently issuable shares include shares that (a) will be issued in the future upon the satisfaction of specified conditions, (b) have been placed in escrow and all or part must be returned if specified conditions are not met, or (c) have been issued but the holder must return all or part if specified conditions are not met.

[6]Options and warrants generally will be included first because use of the treasury stock method does not impact the numerator of the computation.

[7]Refer to footnote 4.

if those amounts will be antidilutive to their respective basic per-share amounts.[8]

16. Including potential common shares in the denominator of a diluted per-share computation for continuing operations always will result in an antidilutive per-share amount when an entity has a *loss* from continuing operations or a *loss* from continuing operations available to common stockholders (that is, after any preferred dividend deductions). Although including those potential common shares in the other diluted per-share computations may be dilutive to their comparable basic per-share amounts, no potential common shares shall be included in the computation of any diluted per-share amount when a loss from continuing operations exists, even if the entity reports net income.

Options and Warrants and Their Equivalents

17. The dilutive effect of outstanding **call options** and warrants (and their equivalents) issued by the reporting entity shall be reflected in diluted EPS by application of the **treasury stock method** unless the provisions of paragraphs 24 and 50-53 require that another method be applied. Equivalents of options and warrants include nonvested stock granted to employees, stock purchase contracts, and partially paid stock subscriptions.[9] Under the treasury stock method:

a. Exercise of options and warrants shall be assumed at the beginning of the period (or at time of issuance, if later) and common shares shall be assumed to be issued.
b. The proceeds from exercise shall be assumed to be used to purchase common stock at the average market price during the period.[10]
c. The incremental shares (the difference between the number of shares assumed issued and the number of shares assumed purchased) shall be included in the denominator of the diluted EPS computation.[11]

18. Options and warrants will have a dilutive effect under the treasury stock method only when the average market price of the common stock during the period exceeds the exercise price of the options or warrants (they are "in the money"). Previously reported EPS data shall not be retroactively adjusted as a result of changes in market prices of common stock.

19. Dilutive options or warrants that are issued during a period or that expire or are canceled during a period shall be included in the denominator of diluted EPS for the period that they were outstanding. Likewise, dilutive options or warrants exercised during the period shall be included in the denominator for the period prior to actual exercise. The common shares issued upon exercise of options or warrants shall be included in the denominator for the period after the exercise date. Consequently, incremental shares assumed issued shall be weighted for the period the options or warrants were outstanding, and common shares actually issued shall be weighted for the period the shares were outstanding.

Stock-based compensation arrangements

20. Fixed awards and nonvested stock (as defined in FASB Statement No. 123, *Accounting for Stock-Based Compensation*) to be issued to an employee[12]

---

[8]For example, assume that Corporation X has income from continuing operations of $2,400, a loss from discontinued operations of $(3,600), a net loss of $(1,200), and 1,000 common shares and 200 potential common shares outstanding. Corporation X's basic per-share amounts would be $2.40 for continuing operations, $(3.60) for the discontinued operation, and $(1.20) for the net loss. Corporation X would include the 200 potential common shares in the denominator of its diluted per-share computation for continuing operations because the resulting $2.00 per share is dilutive. (For illustrative purposes, assume no numerator impact of those 200 potential common shares.) Because income from continuing operations is the control number, Corporation X also must include those 200 potential common shares in the denominator for the other per-share amounts, even though the resulting per-share amounts [$(3.00) per share for the loss from discontinued operation and $(1.00) per share for the net loss] are antidilutive to their comparable basic per-share amounts; that is, the loss per-share amounts are less.

[9]Refer to paragraph 64.

[10]Refer to paragraphs 21, 47, and 48.

[11]Consider Corporation Y that has 10,000 warrants outstanding exercisable at $54 per share; the average market price of the common stock during the reporting period is $60. Exercise of the warrants and issuance of 10,000 shares of common stock would be assumed. The $540,000 that would be realized from exercise of the warrants ($54 × 10,000) would be an amount sufficient to acquire 9,000 shares ($540,000/$60). Thus, 1,000 incremental shares (10,000 − 9,000) would be added to the outstanding common shares in computing diluted EPS for the period.

A shortcut formula for that computation follows (note that this formula may not be appropriate for stock-based compensation awards [refer to paragraph 21]):

Incremental shares = [(market price − exercise price)/market price] × shares assumed issued under option; thus, [($60 − $54)/$60] × 10,000 = 1,000 incremental shares.

[12]The provisions in paragraphs 20-23 also apply to stock-based awards issued to other than employees in exchange for goods and services.

under a stock-based compensation arrangement are considered options for purposes of computing diluted EPS. Such stock-based awards shall be considered to be outstanding as of the grant date for purposes of computing diluted EPS even though their exercise may be contingent upon vesting. Those stock-based awards are included in the diluted EPS computation even if the employee may not receive (or be able to sell) the stock until some future date. Accordingly, all shares to be issued shall be included in computing diluted EPS if the effect is dilutive. The dilutive effect of stock-based compensation arrangements shall be computed using the treasury stock method. If the stock-based awards were granted during the period, the shares issuable must be weighted to reflect the portion of the period during which the awards were outstanding.

21. In applying the treasury stock method described in paragraph 17, the assumed proceeds shall be the sum of (a) the amount, if any, the employee must pay upon exercise, (b) the amount of compensation cost attributed to future services and not yet recognized,[13] and (c) the amount of tax benefits (both deferred and current), if any, that would be credited to additional paid-in capital assuming exercise of the options. Assumed proceeds shall not include compensation ascribed to past services. The tax benefit is the amount resulting from a tax deduction for compensation in excess of compensation expense recognized for financial reporting purposes. That deduction arises from an increase in the market price of the stock under option between the measurement date and the date at which the compensation deduction for income tax purposes is determinable. The amount of the tax benefit shall be determined by a "with-and-without" computation. Paragraph 17 of APB Opinion No. 25, *Accounting for Stock Issued to Employees,* states that in some instances the tax deduction for compensation may be less than the compensation expense recognized for financial reporting purposes. If the resulting difference in income tax will be deducted from capital in accordance with that paragraph, such taxes to be deducted from capital shall be treated as a reduction of assumed proceeds.

22. If stock-based compensation arrangements are payable in common stock or in cash at the election of either the entity or the employee, the determination of whether such stock-based awards are potential common shares shall be made based on the provisions in paragraph 29. If an entity has a tandem plan (as defined in Statement 123) that allows the entity or the employee to make an election involving two or more types of equity instruments, diluted EPS for the period shall be computed based on the terms used in the computation of compensation expense for that period.

23. Performance awards (as defined in Statement 123) shall be included in diluted EPS pursuant to the contingent share provisions in paragraphs 30-35 of this Statement. As discussed in paragraph 26 of Statement 123, targeted stock price options are not considered to be a performance award. However, because options with a target stock price have a market price contingency, the contingent share provisions of this Statement shall be applied in determining whether those options are included in the computation of diluted EPS.

Written put options

24. Contracts that require that the reporting entity repurchase its own stock, such as written **put options** and forward purchase contracts, shall be reflected in the computation of diluted EPS if the effect is dilutive. If those contracts are "in the money" during the reporting period (the exercise price is above the average market price for that period), the potential dilutive effect on EPS shall be computed using the **reverse treasury stock method.** Under that method:

a. Issuance of sufficient common shares shall be assumed at the beginning of the period (at the average market price during the period) to raise enough proceeds to satisfy the contract.

b. The proceeds from issuance shall be assumed to be used to satisfy the contract (that is, to buy back shares).

c. The incremental shares (the difference between the number of shares assumed issued and the

---

[13]This provision applies only to those stock-based awards for which compensation cost will be recognized in the financial statements in accordance with APB Opinion No. 25, *Accounting for Stock Issued to Employees,* or Statement 123.

number of shares received from satisfying the contract) shall be included in the denominator of the diluted EPS computation.[14]

Purchased options

25. Contracts such as purchased put options and **purchased call options** (options held by the entity on its own stock) shall not be included in the computation of diluted EPS because including them would be antidilutive. That is, the put option would be exercised only when the exercise price is higher than the market price and the call option would be exercised only when the exercise price is lower than the market price; in both instances, the effect would be antidilutive under both the treasury stock method and the reverse treasury stock method, respectively.

Convertible Securities

26. The dilutive effect of convertible securities shall be reflected in diluted EPS by application of the **if-converted method.** Under that method:

a. If an entity has convertible preferred stock outstanding, the preferred dividends applicable to convertible preferred stock shall be added back to the numerator.[15]

b. If an entity has convertible debt outstanding, (1) interest charges applicable to the convertible debt shall be added back to the numerator, (2) to the extent nondiscretionary adjustments based on income[16] made during the period would have been computed differently had the interest on convertible debt never been recognized, the numerator shall be appropriately adjusted, and (3) the numerator shall be adjusted for the income tax effect of (1) and (2).

c. The convertible preferred stock or convertible debt shall be assumed to have been converted at the beginning of the period (or at time of issuance, if later), and the resulting common shares shall be included in the denominator.

27. In applying the if-converted method, conversion shall not be assumed for purposes of computing diluted EPS if the effect would be antidilutive. Convertible preferred stock is antidilutive whenever the amount of the dividend declared in or accumulated for the current period per common share obtainable on conversion exceeds basic EPS. Similarly, convertible debt is antidilutive whenever its interest (net of tax and nondiscretionary adjustments) per common share obtainable on conversion exceeds basic EPS.

28. Dilutive convertible securities that are issued during a period in circumstances where conversion options lapse, preferred stock is redeemed, or related debt is extinguished shall be included in the denominator of diluted EPS for the period that they were outstanding. Likewise, dilutive convertible securities converted during a period shall be included in the denominator for the period prior to actual conversion. The common shares issued upon actual conversion shall be included in the denominator for the period after the date of conversion. Consequently, shares assumed issued shall be weighted for the period the convertible securities were outstanding, and common shares actually issued shall be weighted for the period the shares were outstanding.

Contracts That May Be Settled in Stock or Cash

29. If an entity issues a contract that may be settled in common stock or in cash at the election of either the entity or the holder, the determination of whether that contract shall be reflected in the computation of diluted EPS shall be made based on the facts available each period.[17] It shall be presumed that the contract will be settled in common stock and the resulting potential common shares included in diluted EPS (in accordance with the relevant provisions of this Statement) if the effect is more dilutive. A contract that is reported as an asset or liability for accounting purposes may require an adjustment to the numerator for any changes in income or loss that would result if the contract had been reported as an equity instrument for accounting purposes during the period. That

---

[14]For example, Corporation Z sells 100 put options with an exercise price of $25; the average market price for the period is $20. In computing diluted EPS at the end of the period, Corporation Z assumes it issues 125 shares at $20 per share to satisfy its put obligation of $2,500. The difference between the 125 shares issued and the 100 shares received from satisfying the put option (25 incremental shares) would be added to the denominator of diluted EPS.

[15]The amount of preferred dividends added back will be the amount of preferred dividends for convertible preferred stock deducted from income from continuing operations (and from net income) in computing income available to common stockholders pursuant to paragraph 9.

[16]Nondiscretionary adjustments include any expenses or charges that are determined based on the income (loss) for the period, such as profit-sharing and royalty agreements.

[17]An example of such a contract is a written put option that gives the holder a choice of settling in common stock or in cash. Stock-based compensation arrangements that are payable in common stock or in cash at the election of either the entity or the employee shall be accounted for pursuant to this paragraph.

adjustment is similar to the adjustments required for convertible debt in paragraph 26(b). The presumption that the contract will be settled in common stock may be overcome if past experience or a stated policy provides a reasonable basis to believe that the contract will be paid partially or wholly in cash.

Contingently Issuable Shares

30. Shares whose issuance is contingent upon the satisfaction of certain conditions shall be considered outstanding and included in the computation of diluted EPS as follows:

a. If all necessary conditions have been satisfied by the end of the period (the events have occurred), those shares shall be included as of the beginning of the period in which the conditions were satisfied (or as of the date of the contingent stock agreement, if later).

b. If all necessary conditions have not been satisfied by the end of the period, the number of contingently issuable shares included in diluted EPS shall be based on the number of shares, if any, that would be issuable if the end of the reporting period were the end of the contingency period (for example, the number of shares that would be issuable based on current period earnings or period-end market price) and if the result would be dilutive. Those contingently issuable shares shall be included in the denominator of diluted EPS as of the beginning of the period (or as of the date of the contingent stock agreement, if later).[18]

Paragraphs 31-34 provide general guidelines that shall be applied in determining the EPS impact of different types of contingencies that may be included in contingent stock agreements.

31. If attainment or maintenance of a specified amount of earnings is the condition and if that amount has been attained, the additional shares shall be considered to be outstanding for the purpose of computing diluted EPS if the effect is dilutive. The diluted EPS computation shall include those shares that would be issued under the conditions of the contract based on the assumption that the current amount of earnings will remain unchanged until the end of the agreement, but only if the effect would be dilutive. Because the amount of earnings may change in a future period, basic EPS shall not include such con-

tingently issuable shares because all necessary conditions have not been satisfied. Illustration 3 in Appendix C provides an example of that provision.

32. The number of shares contingently issuable may depend on the market price of the stock at a future date. In that case, computations of diluted EPS shall reflect the number of shares that would be issued based on the current market price at the end of the period being reported on if the effect is dilutive. If the condition is based on an average of market prices over some period of time, the average for that period shall be used. Because the market price may change in a future period, basic EPS shall not include such contingently issuable shares because all necessary conditions have not been satisfied.

33. In some cases, the number of shares contingently issuable may depend on both future earnings and future prices of the shares. In that case, the determination of the number of shares included in diluted EPS shall be based on both conditions, that is, earnings to date and current market price—as they exist at the end of each reporting period. If *both* conditions are not met at the end of the reporting period, no contingently issuable shares shall be included in diluted EPS.

34. If the contingency is based on a condition other than earnings or market price (for example, opening a certain number of retail stores), the contingent shares shall be included in the computation of diluted EPS based on the assumption that the current status of the condition will remain unchanged until the end of the contingency period. Illustration 3 in Appendix C provides an example of that provision.

35. Contingently issuable potential common shares (other than those covered by a contingent stock agreement, such as contingently issuable convertible securities) shall be included in diluted EPS as follows:

a. An entity shall determine whether the potential common shares may be assumed to be issuable based on the conditions specified for their issuance pursuant to the contingent share provisions in paragraphs 30-34.

b. If those potential common shares should be reflected in diluted EPS, an entity shall determine

---

[18]For year-to-date computations, contingent shares shall be included on a weighted-average basis. That is, contingent shares shall be weighted for the interim periods in which they were included in the computation of diluted EPS.

their impact on the computation of diluted EPS by following the provisions for options and warrants in paragraphs 17-25, the provisions for convertible securities in paragraphs 26-28, and the provisions for contracts that may be settled in stock or cash in paragraph 29, as appropriate.[19]

However, exercise or conversion shall not be assumed for purposes of computing diluted EPS unless exercise or conversion of similar outstanding potential common shares that are not contingently issuable is assumed.

Presentation on Face of Income Statement

36. Entities with simple capital structures, that is, those with only common stock outstanding, shall present basic per-share amounts for income from continuing operations[20] and for net income on the face of the income statement. All other entities shall present basic and diluted per-share amounts for income from continuing operations and for net income on the face of the income statement with equal prominence.

37. An entity that reports a discontinued operation, an extraordinary item, or the cumulative effect of an accounting change in a period shall present basic and diluted per-share amounts for those line items either on the face of the income statement or in the notes to the financial statements. Per-share amounts not required to be presented by this Statement that an entity chooses to disclose shall be computed in accordance with this Statement and disclosed only in the notes to the financial statements; it shall be noted whether the per-share amounts are pretax or net of tax.[21]

Periods Presented

38. Earnings per share data shall be presented for all periods for which an income statement or summary of earnings is presented. If diluted EPS data are reported for at least one period, they shall be reported for all periods presented, even if they are the same amounts as basic EPS. If basic and diluted EPS are

the same amount, dual presentation can be accomplished in one line on the income statement.

Terminology

39. The terms *basic EPS* and *diluted EPS* are used in this Statement to identify EPS data to be presented and are not required to be captions used in the income statement. There are no explicit requirements for the terms to be used in the presentation of basic and diluted EPS; terms such as *earnings per common share* and *earnings per common share—assuming dilution,* respectively, are appropriate.

Disclosure Requirements

40. For each period for which an income statement is presented, an entity shall disclose the following:

a. A reconciliation of the numerators and the denominators of the basic and diluted per-share computations for income from continuing operations.[22] The reconciliation shall include the individual income and share amount effects of all securities that affect earnings per share.[23] Illustration 2 in Appendix C provides an example of that disclosure.

b. The effect that has been given to preferred dividends in arriving at income available to common stockholders in computing basic EPS.

c. Securities (including those issuable pursuant to contingent stock agreements) that could potentially dilute basic EPS in the future that were not included in the computation of diluted EPS because to do so would have been antidilutive for the period(s) presented.

41. For the latest period for which an income statement is presented, an entity shall provide a description of any transaction that occurs after the end of the most recent period but before issuance of the financial statements that would have changed materially the number of common shares or potential common shares outstanding at the end of the period if the transaction had occurred before the end of the period.

---

[19]Neither interest nor dividends shall be imputed for the additional contingently issuable convertible securities because any imputed amount would be reversed by the if-converted adjustments for assumed conversions.

[20]Refer to footnote 4.

[21]Paragraph 33 of FASB Statement No. 95, *Statement of Cash Flows,* prohibits reporting an amount of cash flow per share.

[22]Refer to footnote 4.

[23]An entity is encouraged to refer to pertinent information about securities included in the EPS computations that is provided elsewhere in the financial statements as prescribed by FASB Statement No. 129, *Disclosure of Information about Capital Structure,* and other accounting pronouncements.

Examples of those transactions include the issuance or acquisition of common shares; the issuance of warrants, options, or convertible securities; the resolution of a contingency pursuant to a contingent stock agreement; and the conversion or exercise of potential common shares outstanding at the end of the period into common shares.

Computational Guidance

42. The determination of EPS data as required by this Statement considers the complexities of the capital structures of some entities. The calculations also shall give effect to matters such as stock dividends or splits and business combinations. Guidelines for dealing with some common computational matters and some complex capital structures are set forth in Appendix A. That appendix is an integral part of the requirements of this Statement.

Effective Date and Transition

43. This Statement shall be effective for financial statements for both interim and annual periods ending after December 15, 1997. Earlier application is not permitted. However, an entity is permitted to disclose pro forma EPS amounts computed using this Statement in the notes to the financial statements in periods prior to required adoption. After the effective date, all prior-period EPS data presented shall be restated (including interim financial statements, summaries of earnings, and selected financial data) to conform with the provisions of this Statement.

The provisions of this Statement need not be applied to immaterial items.

This Statement was adopted by the unanimous vote of the seven members of the Financial Accounting Standards Board:

Dennis R. Beresford,	Anthony T. Cope	James J. Leisenring
Chairman	John M. Foster	Gerhard G. Mueller
Joseph V. Anania	Gaylen N. Larson	

Appendix A

COMPUTATIONAL GUIDANCE

CONTENTS

Appendix A

COMPUTATIONAL GUIDANCE

Introduction

44. This appendix, which is an integral part of the requirements of this Statement, provides general guidance to be used in the computation of earnings per share.

Computing a Weighted Average

45. The weighted-average number of shares discussed in this Statement is an arithmetical mean average of shares outstanding and assumed to be outstanding for EPS computations. The most precise average would be the sum of the shares determined on a daily basis divided by the number of days in the period. Less-precise averaging methods may be used, however, as long as they produce reasonable results. Methods that introduce artificial weighting, such as the "Rule of 78" method, are not acceptable for computing a weighted-average number of shares for EPS computations.

Applying the Treasury Stock Method

Year-to-Date Computations

46. The number of incremental shares included in quarterly diluted EPS shall be computed using the average market prices during the three months included in the reporting period. For year-to-date diluted EPS, the number of incremental shares to be included in the denominator shall be determined by computing a year-to-date weighted average of the number of incremental shares included in each quarterly diluted EPS computation. Illustration 1 (Full Year 20X1, footnote a) in Appendix C provides an example of that provision.

Average Market Price

47. In applying the treasury stock method, the average market price of common stock shall represent a meaningful average. Theoretically, every market transaction for an entity's common stock could be included in determining the average market price. As a practical matter, however, a simple average of weekly or monthly prices usually will be adequate.

48. Generally, closing market prices are adequate for use in computing the average market price. When prices fluctuate widely, however, an average of the high and low prices for the period that the price represents usually would produce a more representative price. The method used to compute the average market price shall be used consistently unless it is no longer representative because of changed conditions. For example, an entity that uses closing market prices to compute the average market price for several years of relatively stable market prices might need to change to an average of high and low prices if prices start fluctuating greatly and the closing market prices no longer produce a representative average market price.

Options and Warrants and Their Equivalents

49. Options or warrants to purchase convertible securities shall be assumed to be exercised to purchase the convertible security whenever the average prices of both the convertible security and the common stock obtainable upon conversion are above the exercise price of the options or warrants. However, exercise shall not be assumed unless conversion of similar outstanding convertible securities, if any, also is assumed. The treasury stock method shall be applied to determine the incremental number of convertible securities that are assumed to be issued and immediately converted into common stock. Interest or dividends shall not be imputed for the incremental convertible securities because any imputed amount would be reversed by the if-converted adjustments for assumed conversions.

50. Paragraphs 51-53 provide guidance on how certain options, warrants, and convertible securities should be included in the computation of diluted EPS. Conversion or exercise of the potential common shares discussed in those paragraphs shall not be reflected in diluted EPS unless the effect is dilutive. Those potential common shares will have a dilutive effect if (a) the average market price of the related common stock for the period exceeds the exercise price or (b) the security to be tendered is selling at a price below that at which it may be tendered under the option or warrant agreement and the resulting discount is sufficient to establish an effective exercise price below the market price of the common stock obtainable upon exercise. When several conversion alternatives exist, the computation shall give effect to the alternative that is most advantageous to the holder of the convertible security. Similar treatment shall be given to preferred stock that has similar provisions or

to other securities that have conversion options that permit the investor to pay cash for a more favorable conversion rate.

51. Options or warrants may permit or require the tendering of debt or other securities of the issuer (or its parent or its subsidiary) in payment of all or a portion of the exercise price. In computing diluted EPS, those options or warrants shall be assumed to be exercised and the debt or other securities shall be assumed to be tendered. If tendering cash would be more advantageous to the option holder or warrant holder and the contract permits tendering cash, the treasury stock method shall be applied. Interest (net of tax) on any debt assumed to be tendered shall be added back as an adjustment to the numerator. The numerator also shall be adjusted for any nondiscretionary adjustments based on income (net of tax). The treasury stock method shall be applied for proceeds assumed to be received in cash.

52. The underlying terms of certain options or warrants may require that the proceeds received from the exercise of those securities be applied to retire debt or other securities of the issuer (or its parent or its subsidiary). In computing diluted EPS, those options or warrants shall be assumed to be exercised and the proceeds applied to purchase the debt at its average market price rather than to purchase common stock under the treasury stock method. The treasury stock method shall be applied, however, for excess proceeds received from the assumed exercise. Interest, net of tax, on any debt assumed to be purchased shall be added back as an adjustment to the numerator. The numerator also shall be adjusted for any nondiscretionary adjustments based on income (net of tax).

53. Convertible securities that permit or require the payment of cash by the holder of the security at conversion are considered the equivalent of warrants. In computing diluted EPS, the proceeds assumed to be received shall be assumed to be applied to purchase common stock under the treasury stock method and the convertible security shall be assumed to be converted under the if-converted method.

Restatement of EPS Data

Stock Dividends or Stock Splits

54. If the number of common shares outstanding increases as a result of a stock dividend or stock split[24]

or decreases as a result of a reverse stock split, the computations of basic and diluted EPS shall be adjusted retroactively for all periods presented to reflect that change in capital structure. If changes in common stock resulting from stock dividends, stock splits, or reverse stock splits occur after the close of the period but before issuance of the financial statements, the per-share computations for those and any prior-period financial statements presented shall be based on the new number of shares. If per-share computations reflect such changes in the number of shares, that fact shall be disclosed.

Rights Issues

55. A **rights issue** whose exercise price at issuance is less than the fair value of the stock contains a bonus element that is somewhat similar to a stock dividend. If a rights issue contains a bonus element and the rights issue is offered to all existing stockholders, basic and diluted EPS shall be adjusted retroactively for the bonus element for all periods presented. If the ability to exercise the rights issue is contingent on some event other than the passage of time, the provisions of this paragraph shall not be applicable until that contingency is resolved.

56. The number of common shares used in computing basic and diluted EPS for all periods prior to the rights issue shall be the number of common shares outstanding immediately prior to the issue multiplied by the following factor: (fair value per share immediately prior to the exercise of the rights)/(theoretical ex-rights fair value per share). Theoretical ex-rights fair value per share shall be computed by adding the aggregate fair value of the shares immediately prior to the exercise of the rights to the proceeds expected from the exercise of the rights and dividing by the number of shares outstanding after the exercise of the rights. Illustration 5 in Appendix C provides an example of that provision. If the rights themselves are to be publicly traded separately from the shares prior to the exercise date, fair value for the purposes of this computation shall be established at the close of the last day on which the shares are traded together with the rights.

Prior-Period Adjustments

57. Certain APB Opinions and FASB Statements require that a restatement of the results of operations of a prior period be included in the income statement or

---

[24]Refer to ARB No. 43, Chapter 7B, "Capital Accounts—Stock Dividends and Stock Split-Ups."

summary of earnings. In those instances, EPS data given for the prior period or periods shall be restated. The effect of the restatement, expressed in per-share terms, shall be disclosed in the period of restatement.

58. Restated EPS data shall be computed as if the restated income or loss had been reported originally in the prior period or periods. Thus, it is possible that common stock assumed to be issued upon exercise, conversion, or issuance of potential common shares in accordance with the provisions of this Statement may not be included in the computation of restated EPS amounts. That is, retroactive restatement of income from continuing operations could cause potential common shares originally determined to be dilutive to become antidilutive pursuant to the control number provision in paragraph 15. The reverse also is true. Retroactive restatement also may cause the numerator of the EPS computation to change by an amount that differs from the amount of the retroactive adjustment.

Business Combinations and Reorganizations

59. When common shares are issued to acquire a business in a transaction accounted for as a purchase business combination, the computations of earnings per share shall recognize the existence of the new shares only from the acquisition date. When a business combination is accounted for as a pooling of interests, EPS computations shall be based on the aggregate of the weighted-average outstanding shares of the constituent businesses, adjusted to equivalent shares of the surviving business for all periods presented. In reorganizations, EPS computations shall be based on analysis of the particular transaction and the provisions of this Statement.

Participating Securities and Two-Class Common Stock

60. The capital structures of some entities include:

a. Securities that may participate in dividends with common stocks according to a predetermined formula (for example, two for one) with, at times, an upper limit on the extent of participation (for example, up to, but not beyond, a specified amount per share)

b. A class of common stock with different dividend rates from those of another class of common stock but without prior or senior rights.

61. The if-converted method shall be used for those securities that are convertible into common stock if the effect is dilutive. For those securities that are not convertible into a class of common stock, the "two class" method of computing earnings per share shall be used. The two-class method is an earnings allocation formula that determines earnings per share for each class of common stock and participating security according to dividends declared (or accumulated) and participation rights in undistributed earnings. Under that method:

a. Income from continuing operations (or net income) shall be reduced by the amount of dividends declared in the current period for each class of stock and by the contractual amount of dividends (or interest on participating income bonds) that must be paid for the current period (for example, unpaid cumulative dividends).[25]

b. The remaining earnings shall be allocated to common stock and participating securities to the extent that each security may share in earnings as if all of the earnings for the period had been distributed. The total earnings allocated to each security shall be determined by adding together the amount allocated for dividends and the amount allocated for a participation feature.

c. The total earnings allocated to each security shall be divided by the number of outstanding shares of the security to which the earnings are allocated to determine the earnings per share for the security.

d. Basic and diluted EPS data shall be presented for each class of common stock.

For the diluted EPS computation, outstanding common shares shall include all potential common shares assumed issued. Illustration 6 in Appendix C provides an example of that provision.

Securities of Subsidiaries

62. The effect on consolidated EPS of options, warrants, and convertible securities issued by a subsidiary depends on whether the securities issued by the subsidiary enable their holders to obtain common

---

[25]Dividends declared in the current period do not include dividends declared in respect of prior-year unpaid cumulative dividends. Preferred dividends that are cumulative only if earned are deducted only to the extent that they are earned.

stock of the subsidiary company or common stock of the parent company. The following general guidelines shall be used for computing consolidated diluted EPS by entities with subsidiaries that have issued common stock or potential common shares to parties other than the parent company:[26]

a. Securities issued by a subsidiary that enable their holders to obtain the subsidiary's common stock shall be included in computing the subsidiary's EPS data. Those per-share earnings of the subsidiary shall then be included in the consolidated EPS computations based on the consolidated group's holding of the subsidiary's securities. Illustration 7 in Appendix C provides an example of that provision.

b. Securities of a subsidiary that are convertible into its parent company's common stock shall be considered among the potential common shares of the parent company for the purpose of computing consolidated diluted EPS. Likewise, a subsidiary's options or warrants to purchase common stock of the parent company shall be considered among the potential common shares of the parent company in computing consolidated diluted EPS. Illustration 7 in Appendix C provides an example of that provision.

As noted in paragraph 18 of APB Opinion No. 18, *The Equity Method of Accounting for Investments in Common Stock,* as amended by this Statement, the above provisions are applicable to investments in common stock of corporate joint ventures and investee companies accounted for under the equity method.

63. The if-converted method shall be used in determining the EPS impact of securities issued by a parent company that are convertible into common stock of a subsidiary company or an investee company accounted for under the equity method. That is, the securities shall be assumed to be converted and the numerator (income available to common stockholders) adjusted as necessary in accordance with the provisions in paragraph 26(a) and (b). In addition to those adjustments, the numerator shall be adjusted appropriately for any change in the income recorded by the parent (such as dividend income or equity method income) due to the increase in the number of common shares of the subsidiary or equity method investee outstanding as a result of the assumed conversion. The denominator of the diluted EPS computation would not be affected because the number of shares of parent company common stock outstanding would not change upon assumed conversion.

Partially Paid Shares and Partially Paid Stock Subscriptions

64. If an entity has common shares issued in a partially paid form[27] and those shares are entitled to dividends in proportion to the amount paid, the common-share equivalent of those partially paid shares shall be included in the computation of basic EPS to the extent that they were entitled to participate in dividends. Partially paid stock subscriptions that do not share in dividends until fully paid are considered the equivalent of warrants and shall be included in diluted EPS by use of the treasury stock method. That is, the unpaid balance shall be assumed to be proceeds used to purchase stock under the treasury stock method. The number of shares included in diluted EPS shall be the difference between the number of shares subscribed and the number of shares assumed to be purchased.

---

[26]Refer to paragraphs 140 and 141.

[27]Issuing common shares that are not fully paid is permitted in some countries.

Appendix B

BACKGROUND INFORMATION AND BASIS FOR CONCLUSIONS

CONTENTS

Appendix B

BACKGROUND INFORMATION AND BASIS FOR CONCLUSIONS

Introduction

65. This appendix summarizes considerations that were deemed significant by Board members in reaching the conclusions in this Statement. It includes reasons for accepting certain views and rejecting others. Individual Board members gave greater weight to some factors than to others.

Background Information

66. In 1991, the Board issued a plan for international activities (which was updated in 1995) that describes

the FASB's role in international activities and proposes steps to increase the range and intensity of its international activities.[28] An objective of the plan is to make financial statements more useful for investors and creditors by increasing the international comparability of accounting standards concurrent with improving the quality of accounting standards. One element of the plan is for the FASB to work toward greater international comparability of accounting standards by identifying projects that potentially could achieve broad international agreement in a relatively short time and by initiating cooperative international standards-setting projects.

67. An FASB Prospectus, *Earnings per Share*, was distributed for public comment in June 1993. The objective of the Prospectus was to inform the Board's constituents of a potential EPS project and to obtain information from them about the scope and importance of that project. The Prospectus explained that Opinion 15, as amended and interpreted, often had been criticized for having complex and arbitrary provisions and that, over the years, the FASB had received requests to reconsider EPS issues. In addition, it mentioned that the IASC had an EPS project on its agenda that provided an opportunity for the FASB to work with that international group toward achieving greater international comparability of EPS data.

68. The Prospectus explained that an EPS project would lend itself to a relatively narrow selection of issues and would not involve profound or divisive theoretical issues; thus, the Board concluded that an EPS project was a potential candidate for a successful cooperative international project. A majority of respondents to the Prospectus favored the Board's adding the project to its agenda in light of the agenda criteria. Most respondents indicated that the potential for international comparability should be an important consideration in the Board's agenda decision.

69. In March 1994, the Board added a project on earnings per share to its technical agenda to be pursued concurrently with the similar project of the IASC. The objective of the project was twofold: (a) to improve and simplify U.S. generally accepted accounting principles and (b) to issue a standard that would be compatible with international standards.

70. The IASC added an EPS project to its agenda in 1989 and issued a draft Statement of Principles, *Earnings per Share*, for public comment in

October 1993. In June 1994, the IASC approved a Statement of Principles to be used as the basis for an IASC Exposure Draft. In November 1995, the IASC approved an Exposure Draft of a proposed International Accounting Standard, *Earnings per Share*, which was issued in January 1996.

71. In January 1996, the FASB issued an Exposure Draft, *Earnings per Share and Disclosure of Information about Capital Structure*. Part I of the Exposure Draft proposed computation, presentation, and disclosure requirements for earnings per share by entities with publicly held common stock or potential common stock, and Part II proposed disclosures about an entity's capital structure applicable to all entities. Part I was substantially the same as the IASC Exposure Draft. The Board received 104 comment letters in response to the FASB Exposure Draft. Most letters were supportive of the proposal. The IASC received 75 comment letters in response to its Exposure Draft. The concerns raised by respondents to both Exposure Drafts and the concerns expressed by the IASC were considered by the Board at public meetings in 1996. No formal field test was conducted on the FASB Exposure Draft; however, six respondents to the Exposure Draft noted that they had applied the provisions in Part I to their company's capital structure and generally had found that the requirements were not difficult to apply and resulted in minor changes, if any, from their current EPS computations.

72. The Board decided to issue the two parts of the Exposure Draft as separate Statements because of the differences in scope. That is, the Board did not want nonpublic entities that were excluded from the scope of Part I of the Exposure Draft to have to concern themselves with numerous provisions that were not applicable to them. FASB Statement No. 129, *Disclosure of Information about Capital Structure*, was issued concurrently with this Statement. The provisions of Statement 129 are essentially unchanged from those proposed in Part II of the Exposure Draft.

73. The FASB and the IASC exchanged information on the progress of their respective EPS projects during the deliberation and redeliberation processes, and the FASB considered the tentative decisions reached by the IASC on all issues. In addition, members of the IASC Steering Committee on Earnings per Share

---

[28]FASB *Highlights*, "FASB's Plan for International Activities," January 1995.

and the IASC staff participated in FASB meetings to discuss the differences between the tentative conclusions of the two standards-setting bodies. Similarly, members of the FASB and its staff participated in IASC meetings to discuss those differences. Both the FASB and the IASC agreed to modifications of their initial positions on issues that were not considered critical. In addition, some of the conclusions reached by the FASB were influenced by how those conclusions would simplify the computation of earnings per share. The FASB decided it could reach an informed decision on the project without holding a public hearing. In January 1997, the IASC approved IAS 33, *Earnings per Share,* which was issued about the same time as this Statement.

Benefits and Costs

74. One of the precepts of the Board's mission is to promulgate standards only when the expected benefits of the resulting information exceed the perceived costs of providing that information. The Board strives to determine that a proposed standard will fill a significant need and that the costs entailed in satisfying that need, as compared with other alternatives, are justified in relation to the overall benefits of the resulting information.

75. The Board concluded that EPS information provided to users in financial statements could be improved by simplifying the existing computational guidance, revising the disclosure requirements, and increasing the comparability of EPS data on an international basis. Some of the changes made to the EPS guidance in an effort to simplify the computation include (a) not considering common stock equivalents in the computation of basic EPS, (b) eliminating the modified treasury stock method and the 3 percent materiality provision, and (c) revising the contingent share provisions (including eliminating the requirement to restate prior EPS data in certain situations) and the supplemental EPS data requirements.

76. The Board expects that the costs to implement this Statement will include initial costs for education and the redesign of procedures used to compute EPS data but that any ongoing costs should be minimal. The Board believes that the benefits of simplifying the EPS computation and harmonizing with national and international standards-setting bodies will outweigh the costs of implementing this Statement.

Conclusions on Basic Issues

Scope

77. This Statement, which provides computation, presentation, and disclosure requirements for earnings per share, requires presentation of earnings per share by entities with publicly held common stock or potential common stock and by entities that are in the process of selling that stock to the public. Nonpublic entities are excluded from the scope because, generally, those entities have simple capital structures and few common stockholders; thus, EPS data may not be meaningful for users of their financial statements. In addition, nonpublic entities were excluded from the scope of Opinion 15 (as amended by FASB Statement No. 21, *Suspension of the Reporting of Earnings per Share and Segment Information by Nonpublic Enterprises*), and the Board was not aware of any new information that would suggest that those entities should be required to report EPS data. For similar reasons, the Board decided not to include in the scope of this Statement entities whose publicly traded securities include only debt. However, any entity that chooses to present EPS data should do so in accordance with this Statement.

78. Few respondents commented on the proposed scope of the Statement. Those that did suggested that the scope exemption in the Exposure Draft for investment companies registered under the Investment Company Act of 1940 be expanded to include investment companies, such as offshore mutual funds, that are not registered under the 1940 Act but that provide the same selected per-share data (in accordance with the AICPA Audit and Accounting Guide, *Audits of Investment Companies*). The Board agreed to make that change.

Objective of the Earnings per Share Computations

79. In discussing various issues about the computation of diluted EPS, the Board found it helpful to identify the objective of both basic and diluted EPS in order to reach consistent conclusions on those issues. The Board concluded that the objective of basic EPS is to measure the performance of an entity over the reporting period and that the objective of diluted EPS should be consistent with the basic EPS objective while giving effect to all dilutive potential common shares that were outstanding during the period.

80. Other objectives of diluted EPS that the Board considered and rejected were that it should be a predictor of dilution—a forward-looking number as opposed to one based on historic numbers—or that it should maximize dilution. In concluding that diluted EPS should be an extension of basic EPS—a historic, "for the period" number—the Board looked to FASB Concepts Statement No. 1, *Objectives of Financial Reporting by Business Enterprises,* which discusses the historical nature of accounting information, and FASB Concepts Statement No. 2, *Qualitative Characteristics of Accounting Information,* which discusses the "predictive value" of financial information. Concepts Statement 1 explains that users of financial statements may make predictions using financial information—information that is historical. Paragraph 53 of Concepts Statement 2 states in part:

> Users can be expected to favor those sources of information and analytical methods that have the greatest predictive value in achieving their specific objectives. Predictive value here means value as an *input* [emphasis in original] into a predictive process, *not value directly as a prediction.* [Emphasis added.]

81. The IASC initially concluded that the objective of diluted EPS should be to indicate the potential variability or risk attached to basic EPS as a consequence of the issue of potential common shares or to act as a warning signal of the potential dilution of basic EPS. Following that objective, diluted EPS would be computed using end-of-period shares and stock prices. The Board considers that objective to be relevant and useful but believes that it is preferable for diluted EPS to be computed in a manner consistent with the computation of basic EPS. After much discussion, the IASC agreed to require that diluted EPS be computed following the FASB objective because (a) diluted EPS computed following a performance objective can be presented in a time series and compared with diluted EPS of other periods and (b) a "warning signal" objective can be adequately conveyed through supplementary note disclosure.

82. To accommodate the concerns of the IASC, both the FASB and the IASC Exposure Drafts included disclosure requirements related to the IASC's warning signal objective. More than half of the respondents to the FASB Exposure Draft who commented on those disclosure requirements stated that they did not believe that the warning signal objective was relevant or useful, and some found the related disclosures

confusing. Respondents to the IASC Exposure Draft made similar comments; they also encouraged the IASC to choose one objective. The FASB and the IASC decided to eliminate those disclosure requirements in response to the comments received.

Basic Earnings per Share

83. One of the main objectives of the Board's project on earnings per share was to issue a standard that would be compatible with those of the IASC and national standards-setting bodies. The biggest difference between Opinion 15 and other EPS standards is that Opinion 15 required presentation of primary EPS, which includes the dilutive effect of common stock equivalents. Currently, only two other countries require that primary EPS be presented. Thus, the first issue that the Board had to address was whether to eliminate the requirement to present primary EPS and replace it with a computation that does not consider the effects of common stock equivalents.

84. In making its decision to replace primary EPS with basic EPS, the Board considered the requirements of Opinion 15 to compute primary EPS, the criticisms about primary EPS, the arguments in favor of basic EPS, and the comments it had received from constituents prior to adding the project to its agenda.

Primary earnings per share

85. The rules used to compute primary EPS (Opinion 15 and its amendments and interpretations) had been criticized as being extremely complex and containing a number of arbitrary provisions. Those criticisms largely focused on the determination of convertible securities as common stock equivalents, specifically, the use of the Aa corporate bond rate for the common stock equivalency test, the two-thirds yield test for common stock equivalency, and the classification of a security as a common stock equivalent at issuance without regard to later events.

86. The complexity of Opinion 15 may have contributed to errors or to inconsistency in its application. Several empirical studies indicated that EPS rules often are misunderstood by preparers and auditors and are not always applied correctly. The primary EPS statistic itself had been widely criticized as not being useful. Considerable evidence showed that many users of financial statements think that primary EPS is based on an undiluted weighted-average number of common shares outstanding; that is, they think that primary EPS is computed without giving effect to common stock equivalents.

87. Because primary EPS assumes exercise and conversion of dilutive common stock equivalents, it includes a certain amount of dilution. Some said that the endpoints on the scale of dilution—from zero dilution to maximum dilution—would convey better information to financial statement users. Those critics said that the rules of Opinion 15 conceal part of the total potential dilution by presenting two numbers that include dilution rather than an undiluted and a diluted number.

88. Opinion 15 had drawn its strongest criticism from users (primarily financial analysts) and academics. Analysts' interest stemmed from the use of EPS in the computation of the price-earnings ratio, perhaps the most frequently cited statistic in the business of equity investment. In addition, analysts' earnings projections almost always are presented on a per-share basis. The Board did not receive many requests from other parties to comprehensively reconsider Opinion 15; therefore, it appeared that preparers and auditors had assimilated and accepted the rules. Most respondents to the EPS Prospectus agreed that basic EPS would be a simpler and more useful statistic than primary EPS. Most respondents to the Exposure Draft agreed that disclosing the full range of possible dilution using basic EPS and diluted EPS would reveal more useful information than the partial range of dilution disclosed with primary EPS and fully diluted EPS under Opinion 15. However, some respondents noted that that they did not find basic EPS to be a useful statistic and thought that users would focus only on diluted EPS.

89. The Board decided to replace primary EPS with basic EPS for the following reasons:

a. Presenting undiluted and diluted EPS data would give users the most factually supportable *range* of EPS possibilities. The spread between basic and diluted EPS would provide information about an entity's capital structure by disclosing a reasonable estimate of how much potential dilution exists.
b. Use of a common international EPS statistic has become even more important as a result of database-oriented financial analysis and the internationalization of business and capital markets.
c. The notion of common stock equivalents as used in primary EPS is viewed by many as not operating effectively in practice, and "repairing" it does not appear to be a feasible option.
d. The primary EPS computation is complex, and

there is some evidence that the current guidance is not well understood and may not be consistently applied.
e. If basic EPS were to replace primary EPS, the criticisms about the arbitrary methods by which common stock equivalents are determined would no longer be an issue. If entities were required to disclose the details of their convertible securities, the subjective determination of the likelihood of conversion would be left to individual users of financial statements.

Computation of basic earnings per share

Weighted-average number of shares

90. In computing basic (and diluted) EPS, the Board agreed that use of a weighted-average number of shares is necessary so that the effect of increases or decreases in outstanding shares on EPS data will be related to the portion of the period during which the related consideration affected operations.

Contingently issuable shares

91. Contractual agreements (usually associated with purchase business combinations) sometimes provide for the issuance of additional common shares contingent upon certain conditions being met. The Board concluded that (a) consistent with the objective that basic EPS should represent a measure of the performance of an entity over a specific reporting period, contingently issuable shares should be included in basic EPS only when there is no circumstance under which those shares would not be issued and (b) basic EPS should not be restated for changed circumstances.

92. A few respondents to the Exposure Draft suggested that contingently issuable shares should never be included in the computation of basic EPS because basic EPS is supposed to be an EPS ratio with no dilution. They said that the denominator should include only actual shares outstanding. The Board considered that view but decided to retain the provision that "vested" contingently issuable shares should be considered in the computation of basic EPS because consideration for those shares has been received. The Board also agreed to retain the provision that contingently returnable shares should be treated in the same manner as contingently issuable shares. The IASC agreed to include a similar provision in IAS 33 in response to the comments received on its Exposure Draft (which did not include such a provision).

Diluted Earnings per Share

93. Securities (such as options, warrants, convertible debt, and convertible preferred stock) that do not have a current right to participate fully in earnings but that may do so in the future by virtue of their option or conversion rights are referred to in this Statement as potential common shares or potentially dilutive shares. That "potential dilution" is relevant to users because it may reduce the per-share amount of current earnings to be distributed by way of dividends in the future and may increase the number of shares over which the total market value of an entity is divided.

94. Whether option or conversion rights of potential common shares actually will be exercised is usually not determinable at an entity's reporting date. However, with the use of assumptions, it is possible to arrive at a reasonable estimate of what earnings per share would have been had common stock been issued for those securities. The Board concluded that the treasury stock method and the if-converted method prescribed in Opinion 15 should continue to be used in computing diluted EPS.

No antidilution

95. In computing diluted EPS, only potential common shares that are dilutive—those that reduce earnings per share or increase loss per share—are included. Exercise of options and warrants or conversion of convertible securities is not assumed if the result would be antidilutive, such as when a loss from continuing operations is reported. The sequence in which potential common shares are considered may affect the amount of dilution that they produce. The sequence of the computation was not specifically addressed in Opinion 15, but the IASC proposed that in order to maximize the dilution of earnings per share, each issue or series of potential common shares should be considered in sequence from the most dilutive to the least dilutive. The Board agreed with the IASC that that is a reasonable approach and included a similar provision in this Statement. Most respondents to the Exposure Draft agreed that sequencing potential common shares from the most dilutive to the least dilutive is a workable approach.

96. The Board also concluded that the "control number" for determining whether including potential common shares in the diluted EPS computation would be antidilutive should be *income from continuing operations* (or a similar line item above net in-

come if it appears on the income statement). As a result, if there is a loss from continuing operations, diluted EPS would be computed in the same manner as basic EPS is computed, even if an entity has net income after adjusting for a discontinued operation, an extraordinary item, or the cumulative effect of an accounting change. Similarly, if an entity has income from continuing operations but its preferred dividend adjustment made in computing *income available to common stockholders* in accordance with paragraph 9 results in a "loss from continuing operations available to common stockholders," diluted EPS would be computed in the same manner as basic EPS.

97. If *net income* were the control number as it was under Opinion 15, diluted EPS often would be the same number as basic EPS. The Board decided to change the control number to income from continuing operations because in the United States net losses are often the result of discontinued operations, extraordinary items, or accounting changes reported by the cumulative-effect method. The Board agreed that if an entity had income from continuing operations but had an accounting change that resulted in a net loss, its diluted net loss per share *should* include potential common shares (even though their effect would be antidilutive) and should not be the same as its basic net loss per share that does not include potential common shares. With income from continuing operations as the control number, the diluted net loss per share in that case would reflect the effect of potential common shares.

98. In addition, EPS data are more comparable over time if income from continuing operations is used as the control number. That is, for an entity that reports a net loss in the period solely because of the cumulative effect of an accounting change upon adopting a new accounting standard, that period's diluted net loss per share would reflect no dilution if net income were the control number and, thus, diluted net loss per share for the period would not be comparable with past or future diluted net income per-share amounts (which would reflect some dilution). The same would be true for an entity that makes a voluntary accounting change, reports discontinued operations, or reports extraordinary items that result in a net loss.

99. Respondents to the Exposure Draft agreed with the change in the control number from *net income* under Opinion 15 to *income from continuing operations* in this Statement. The IASC did not include a

control number provision in its Exposure Draft. In response to the comments received on the FASB Exposure Draft and the few comments on the issue received in response to the IASC Exposure Draft, the IASC agreed to include a provision in IAS 33 that requires *net profit from continuing ordinary activities* to be used as the control number in establishing whether potential common shares are dilutive or antidilutive.

Options and warrants and their equivalents

100. The issuance of common stock upon exercise of options and warrants produces cash inflows for the issuing entity but does not affect income. In computing earnings per share, an assumed issuance of stock increases the denominator but does not affect the numerator. The resulting reduction in earnings per share could be considered excessive if there were no adjustment for the use of the cash proceeds. The treasury stock method was meant to adjust for that situation by assuming that the cash proceeds from issuing common stock are used to acquire treasury shares. Thus, only the *net* assumed issuance of shares (common shares issued upon exercise less treasury shares acquired) is reflected in the denominator of the diluted EPS computation. Other methods that the Board considered in determining how to reflect the potential dilution of options and warrants in the computation of diluted EPS are discussed in paragraphs 101-104.

Imputed earnings method

101. Some countries use an imputed earnings method to compute diluted EPS. That method assumes that the proceeds from exercise of options and warrants are used to repay debt or are invested, for example, in government securities, rather than used to purchase treasury shares. Following the imputed earnings method, either the amount of interest that would have been saved (if the debt were repaid) or the income that would have been earned (on the investment) is added to the numerator of the computation, and the denominator is adjusted for the number of shares assumed to have been issued upon exercise of the options or warrants. The disadvantages of that method are that it requires an arbitrary assumption about the appropriate rate of earnings, it overstates dilution because it treats antidilutive potential common shares as if they were dilutive, and it gives the

same effect to all options and warrants regardless of the current market price.

Treasury stock method with a discounted exercise price

102. Another method that the Board considered was to discount the expected proceeds from exercise of options or warrants with long exercise periods to reflect the time value of money prior to applying the treasury stock method. The argument for that method is that because contracts with long exercise periods are not likely to be exercised for a considerable period of time, the exercise price should be discounted to its fair value at the balance sheet date, reflecting "time value" as one component of the value of an option or warrant. The main disadvantage of that method is that the determination of (a) the time periods over which to discount the options or warrants and (b) the applicable discount rate is subjective.

Maximum dilution method

103. The maximum dilution method assumes that all options and warrants are exercised and that the common shares issued upon exercise are added to the denominator with no change in the numerator. The principal disadvantage of that method is that an assumption that all potential common shares will convert without a change in earnings is both counterintuitive and unrealistic. It also would give the same effect to all options and warrants regardless of the current market price.

Graham-Dodd method

104. In computing diluted EPS, the Graham-Dodd method[29] takes into consideration all options and warrants, including those whose exercise price exceeds the market price of common stock. That method assumes that options and warrants are equivalent to additional outstanding common shares with the same aggregate market value as that of the options or warrants issued. The computation divides the total market value of all options and warrants by the current market price of the common stock to determine the number of additional common shares that would be equivalent to the value of outstanding options and warrants. Those additional common shares would be included in the denominator of the diluted EPS computation. In addition to showing the dilutive

---

[29]The method is described in Graham, Dodd, and Cottle, *Security Analysis: Principles and Technique,* 4th ed. (New York: McGraw-Hill, 1962).

effect of "out of the money" options and warrants, the Graham-Dodd method reflects more dilution as the value of options and warrants increases relative to the value of common stock. That method requires the use of option-pricing models at each reporting period to value options and warrants that are not traded.[30]

Treasury stock method

105. The Board decided to retain the treasury stock method from Opinion 15 because of its use in present practice, its relative simplicity and lack of subjectivity, and its adoption by the IASC (although the method is described differently in IAS 33). The method also reflects more dilution as the value of options and warrants increases relative to the value of common stock. That is, as the average market price of the stock increases, the assumed proceeds from exercise will buy fewer shares, thus, increasing the EPS denominator. The Board was concerned that the treasury stock method understates potential dilution because it gives no dilutive effect to options and warrants whose exercise prices exceed current common stock prices and, therefore, are antidilutive under the treasury stock method but may be dilutive sometime in the future. However, the Board was unable to identify another method that would address that concern that did not have its own set of disadvantages. To offset that concern, the Board decided to require disclosure in the notes to the financial statements of potential common shares not included in the computation of dilutive EPS because their impact would be antidilutive based on current market prices.

106. Another common criticism of the treasury stock method that the Board considered is that it assumes a hypothetical purchase of treasury stock. The Board recognizes that the funds obtained by issuers from the exercise of options and warrants are used in many ways with a wide variety of results that cannot be anticipated. Application of the treasury stock method in EPS computations represents a practical approach to reflecting the dilutive effect that would result from the issuance of common stock under option and warrant agreements at an effective price below the current market price.

107. The Board made one change to the treasury stock method prescribed in Opinion 15. This Statement requires that the average stock price for the period always be used in determining the number of

treasury shares assumed purchased with the proceeds from the exercise of options or warrants rather than the higher of the average or ending stock price as prescribed by Opinion 15. The Board believes that use of the average stock price is consistent with the objective of diluted EPS to measure earnings per share for the period based on period information and that use of end-of-period data or estimates of the future is inconsistent with that objective. If purchases of treasury shares actually were to occur, the shares would be purchased at various prices, not at the price at the end of the period. In addition, use of an average stock price eliminates the concern that end-of-period fluctuations in stock prices could have an undue effect on diluted EPS if an end-of-period stock price were required to be used. Respondents to the Exposure Draft generally agreed with the requirement to use the average stock price.

108. Opinion 15 required that the "modified treasury stock" method be used if the number of shares of common stock obtainable upon exercise of outstanding options and warrants in the aggregate is more than 20 percent of the number of common shares outstanding at the end of the period. The Board found that the modified treasury stock method prescribed in Opinion 15 was not widely used in practice because few entities ever met the 20 percent test. For that reason, and in an effort to simplify the EPS computation and to be consistent with the IASC Standard, the Board decided not to include that method in this Statement. Respondents to the Exposure Draft generally agreed with the elimination of the modified treasury stock method.

Stock-based compensation arrangements

109. Fixed employee stock options (fixed awards) and nonvested stock (including restricted stock) are included in the computation of diluted EPS based on the provisions for options and warrants in paragraphs 17-25. Even though their issuance may be contingent upon vesting, they are not considered to be "contingently issuable shares" as that term is used in this Statement because to consider them contingently issuable shares would be a change from present practice and the provisions of IAS 33. However, because issuance of performance-based stock options (and performance-based nonvested stock) is contingent upon satisfying conditions in addition to

---

[30]Statement 123 generally requires that valuation only at the grant date.

the mere passage of time, those options and non-vested stock are considered to be contingently issuable shares in the computation of diluted EPS. The Board decided that a distinction should be made only between time-related contingencies and contingencies requiring specific achievement.

110. The guidance in paragraph 21 for determining the assumed proceeds when applying the treasury stock method to an entity that has stock-based compensation arrangements is based on similar guidance in Statement 123, which was based on the provisions in paragraph 3 of FASB Interpretation No. 31, *Treatment of Stock Compensation Plans in EPS Computations.* The Board agreed that it would be appropriate to carry forward the remainder of the relevant guidance in paragraphs 4-6 of Interpretation 31 into this Statement. That guidance has been incorporated into paragraphs 20, 22, and 29 of this Statement. Examples 1 and 2 from Appendix B of Interpretation 31 are included in Illustration 8 in Appendix C.

Written put options and purchased options

111. A number of respondents to the Exposure Draft requested that the Board address how written put options, purchased put options, and purchased call options should be included in the computation of diluted EPS. Emerging Issues Task Force (EITF) Issue No. 87-31, "Sale of Put Options on Issuer's Stock," addresses put options sold by a company for cash that enable the holder to sell shares of the company's stock at a fixed price to the company. The EITF reached a consensus that the reverse treasury stock method should be used in computing the impact of those options on earnings per share. Under that method, the incremental number of shares to be added to the denominator is computed as the excess of shares that will be issued for cash at the then current market price to obtain cash to satisfy the put obligation over the shares received from satisfying the puts. The Board agreed to include that approach in this Statement for "in the money" contracts that require that the reporting entity repurchase its own stock.

112. The Board concluded that neither purchased put options nor purchased call options should be reflected in diluted EPS because their effect would be antidilutive. A few respondents stated that entities should be permitted to aggregate the calls held by an entity on its own stock (purchased calls) with the options or warrants it is attempting to hedge. Those re-spondents suggested that the Board modify the treasury stock method to require that proceeds assumed to be received from the exercise of options be used to pay the strike price on the call option that the entity holds on its own stock (rather than assume that the proceeds received will be used to purchase treasury shares as required by the treasury stock method). The Board confirmed its position that securities that would have an antidilutive effect should not be included in the diluted EPS computation and that securities should be considered separately rather than in the aggregate in determining whether their effect on diluted EPS would be dilutive or antidilutive.

Convertible securities

113. Other securities that could result in the issuance of common shares, in addition to options and warrants, are debt and preferred stock that are convertible into common stock. The impact of those potential common shares on diluted EPS is determined by use of the if-converted method. That method recognizes that the holders of convertible preferred stock cannot share in distributions of earnings available to common stockholders unless they relinquish their right to senior distributions. Conversion is assumed, and income available to common stockholders is determined before distributions are made to holders of those securities. Likewise, the if-converted method recognizes that convertible debt can participate in earnings through interest or dividends, either as a senior security or as common stock, but not both.

114. The Board chose to retain the if-converted method prescribed in Opinion 15 in this Statement. There have been few criticisms of that method, and it is the method used by the IASC. One common criticism of the if-converted method is that conversion may be assumed when a convertible security appears likely to remain a senior security.

Contracts that may be settled in stock or cash

115. As discussed in paragraph 110, the guidance in Interpretation 31 has been brought forward into this Statement. Paragraph 6 of that Interpretation established a rebuttable presumption that when stock appreciation rights and other variable plan awards may be settled in stock or cash (at the election of either the holder or the reporting entity), the entity should presume settlement in common stock and the dilutive potential common shares should be included in the EPS computation unless the presumption is overcome. The Board agreed that that guidance was

equally appropriate for other contracts that could be settled in stock or cash and thus included that guidance in paragraph 29 of this Statement. The Board believes that that approach is consistent with the objective of diluted EPS to reflect potential dilution that existed during the period. In circumstances in which the contract is reported as an asset or liability for accounting purposes (as opposed to an equity instrument) but the contract is presumed to be settled in common stock for EPS purposes, the Board believes it is appropriate to adjust income available to common stockholders for any changes in the fair value of the contract that had been recognized in income. Although all such contracts that provide the issuer or holder with a choice between settlement methods may not meet the definition of an option, warrant, convertible security, or contingently issuable share, they do meet the definition of potential common stock in paragraph 171 of this Statement.

Contingently issuable shares

116. In discussing the issue of the impact of contingently issuable shares on diluted EPS, the Board chose not to retain the requirements in Opinion 15 to (a) increase the numerator of the computation for possible future earnings levels and (b) restate prior EPS data for differences in actual and assumed earnings levels. The Board concluded that making assumptions about future earnings and restating for events that occur after the end of a period would be inconsistent with a "historic" objective. Thus, the Board decided to include contingently issuable shares in the computation of diluted EPS based only on current earnings (which are assumed to remain unchanged until the end of the contingency period) and to prohibit restatement.

117. The Board also was not in favor of permitting restatement of EPS data due to changes in market prices. The Board noted that restatement was prohibited for the impact of changes in market prices on the number of shares included in the denominator as a result of applying the treasury stock method. The Board decided to include shares contingent on market price in diluted EPS based on the end-of-period market price and to prohibit restatement.

118. Contingent stock agreements sometimes provide for shares to be issued in the future pending the satisfaction of conditions unrelated to earnings or market value (for example, opening a certain number of retail locations). Similar to its other conclusions, the Board decided (a) to include contingent shares in the computation of diluted EPS based on the assumption that the current status of the condition will remain unchanged until the end of the contingency period and (b) to prohibit restatement. Thus, if only half of the requisite retail locations have been opened, then no contingent shares would be included in the diluted EPS computation.

119. The Board considered including contingent shares on a pro rata basis based on the current status of the condition (such as half of the contingent shares for the example in paragraph 118). However, the Board was concerned that a pro rata approach would not be implemented easily and that it might make little sense in many instances, such as when it is readily apparent that the condition will not be met.

120. Some Board members were concerned about the inconsistency in when compensation cost for performance awards is included in the numerator of the diluted EPS computation (pursuant to Statement 123) and when the related contingent shares are included in the denominator of the same computation (pursuant to this Statement). The initial accruals of compensation cost for performance awards are based on the best estimate of the outcome of the performance condition. That is, compensation cost is estimated at the grant date for the options that are expected to vest based on performance-related conditions and that are accrued over the vesting period. However, pursuant to this Statement, diluted EPS would reflect only those shares (stock options) that would be issued if the end of the reporting period were the end of the contingency period. In most cases, performance awards will not be reflected in diluted EPS until the performance condition has been satisfied. The Board observed that (a) the focus of this Statement is the denominator of the EPS computation, not the determination of earnings, and (b) that treatment is consistent with current practice when compensation is associated with a contingent award.

121. Most respondents to the Exposure Draft agreed with the changes proposed for contingent stock agreements. A few respondents requested that the Board clarify as of what date contingently issuable shares should be included in the computations of basic and diluted EPS. The Board concluded that contingent shares should be deemed to be issued when all of the necessary conditions have been met and that those shares should be included in basic EPS on a weighted-average basis. In most cases, the shares would be included only as of the last day of the period because whether the condition has been satisfied

may not be certain until the end of the period. The Board concluded that contingent shares should be included in the denominator of the diluted EPS computation in a manner similar to other potential common shares; that is, as if the shares were issued at the beginning of the period (or as of the date of the contingent stock agreement, if later). However, for year-to-date computations, the Board agreed that contingent shares should be included on a weighted-average basis. That approach is similar to the method used for including incremental shares in year-to-date computations when applying the treasury stock method.

Presentation on Face of Income Statement

122. The Board agreed that EPS data should be presented prominently in the financial statements because of the significance attached by investors and others to EPS data and because of the importance of evaluating the data in conjunction with the financial statements. Thus, the Board concluded that both basic and diluted per-share amounts should be presented on the face of the income statement for income from continuing operations and net income. The Board agreed that, at a minimum, those per-share amounts should be presented on the face of the income statement to help users determine the impact of items reported "below-the-line."

123. The Board decided to give entities the option of presenting basic and diluted per-share amounts for discontinued operations, extraordinary items, and the cumulative effect of an accounting change either on the face of the income statement or in the notes to financial statements to address the concern that some constituents had with excessive information on the income statement. The extent of the data presented and the captions used will vary with the complexity of an entity's capital structure and the presence of transactions outside continuing operations.

124. The IASC Exposure Draft required presentation of only basic and diluted net income per share on the face of the income statement and encouraged presentation of other per-share amounts. Most respondents to the FASB Exposure Draft agreed with the requirements related to presentation of per-share amounts on the face of the income statement and in the notes to the financial statements and stated that the IASC should adopt the FASB's presentation approach. The IASC decided not to change its presentation requirements in its EPS standard but acknowledged that it will have to address presentation of per-share amounts other than net income per share as part of other related projects on its agenda.

125. The June 1996 FASB Exposure Draft, *Reporting Comprehensive Income,* would require presentation of a per-share amount for comprehensive income on the face of the statement of financial performance in which comprehensive income is reported. Per-share amounts are not required by that Exposure Draft for subtotals resulting from classifications within other comprehensive income. If that Exposure Draft is finalized as proposed, the Board will have to determine how comprehensive income per share should be computed to be in accordance with the provisions of this Statement.

126. The Board's decision to require a dual EPS presentation (basic and diluted EPS) for entities with complex capital structures regardless of the variance between basic and diluted EPS is a change from Opinion 15. Opinion 15 provided that fully diluted EPS did not have to be presented if the dilution caused by including all potential common shares in the computation was less than 3 percent of "simple" EPS, which includes no dilution. Similarly, primary EPS could be presented as simple EPS if the dilution caused by including common stock equivalents in the computation was less than 3 percent of simple EPS.

127. The Board decided to eliminate what is referred to as the "materiality threshold" for presentation of diluted EPS because (a) the requirement was used inconsistently, (b) in many cases, an entity had to compute fully diluted EPS to determine whether it met the 3 percent test, and (c) in any period that an entity's earnings per share fell out of the 3 percent range, Opinion 15 required fully diluted EPS to be shown for all periods presented. The Board concluded that requiring a dual presentation at all times by all entities with complex capital structures places all of the facts in the hands of users of financial statements at minimal or no cost to preparers and gives users an understanding of the extent and trend of potential dilution. The Board also noted that many entities currently present fully diluted EPS even when it does not differ by 3 percent from simple or primary EPS because when fully diluted EPS is compared over time, small differences may be relevant in assessing relative changes between periods.

128. Most respondents to the Exposure Draft agreed with the Board's conclusion that presenting both basic and diluted EPS on the face of the income statement would result in minimal or no additional cost to the preparer. However, many of those respondents requested that the Board retain a materiality threshold

similar to that in Opinion 15. They stated that presentation of diluted EPS when it is not materially different from basic EPS is an immaterial disclosure that could cause confusion (that is, multiple EPS amounts on the face of the income statement might be confusing to users). Some respondents also stated that the marginal costs of dual presentation would exceed the marginal benefits to the user community.

129. Because of those comments and the view of some respondents that diluted EPS is the more useful statistic, the Board initially decided that if only one per-share amount were to be required to be presented on the face of the income statement it should be diluted EPS, not basic EPS. The Board reasoned that a single presentation would eliminate any confusion that unsophisticated users might have with multiple EPS amounts and any confusion over which EPS number databases should include. In addition, presenting only diluted EPS on the face of the income statement would display the most meaningful information in the primary financial statements and would be another step toward simplification of the EPS guidance. The Board acknowledged the usefulness of providing a range of potential dilution and, therefore, agreed to retain the requirement that basic EPS should be presented in the notes to the financial statements as part of the required reconciliation of basic and diluted EPS.

130. Because of the international harmonization goal of the project, the FASB presented its initial decisions on income statement presentation to the IASC Steering Committee on Earnings per Share and the IASC Board in September 1996 as preliminary conclusions. The FASB indicated that it would reconsider those decisions based on the IASC's level of support for making similar changes to its proposed standard. The IASC decided to retain its requirement for equal prominence of basic and diluted EPS on the face of the income statement because it believes that there is valuable information content in the difference between the two numbers. The users in the United States with whom the FASB discussed its preliminary conclusions shared that view.

131. In the interest of international harmonization, the Board ultimately decided to retain the dual presentation requirement proposed in the Exposure Draft. The Board acknowledged that if it were to stay with its "diluted EPS only" preliminary conclusion, the resulting FASB and IASC EPS standards would have been substantially the same because EPS would be *computed* in the same manner even though it would not be *presented* in the same manner. However, the Board believes it is most important to achieve harmonization in all aspects with the IASC, especially because the difference is only one of display, not one of a conceptual nature.

132. Consequently, both the FASB and the IASC agreed that dual presentation of basic and diluted EPS should be required in all instances, regardless of the difference between the two numbers. As noted in paragraph 89(a), the Board believes that, when compared with diluted EPS, basic EPS is useful as a benchmark for determining the amount of potential dilution. If basic and diluted EPS are the same amount, dual presentation can be accomplished in one line on the income statement. In response to the concerns of some respondents to the Exposure Draft that removal of the 3 percent materiality threshold will result in more variations in the concept of materiality than currently exists, the Board noted that the materiality box that states "The provisions of this Statement need not be applied to immaterial items" does not apply to the difference between two numbers.

Conclusions on Other Issues

Stock Dividends or Stock Splits

133. This Statement requires an entity that has a stock dividend, stock split, or reverse stock split after the close of the period but before issuance of the financial statements to compute basic and diluted EPS in those financial statements based on the new number of shares because those per-share amounts would have to be restated in the subsequent period. The IASC Exposure Draft proposed computing earnings per share in those situations based on the shares actually existing at the date of the financial statements. It also proposed disclosing a description of the subsequent event and pro forma EPS amounts in the financial statements of the period prior to the actual event.

134. Most respondents to the FASB Exposure Draft preferred the FASB restatement requirement over the IASC disclosure approach. Those respondents noted that reflecting the subsequent event in the current period would provide more useful, relevant, and meaningful information and would obviate the need for later restatement. In response to the comments it received on that issue and in the interest of harmonization, the IASC agreed to change from a disclosure approach to a requirement to restate, similar to that in this Statement.

Rights Issues

135. The IASC Exposure Draft proposed using the "theoretical ex-rights method" for adjusting EPS data for a bonus element contained in a rights issue offered to all existing stockholders. The FASB Exposure Draft proposed that the treasury stock method be used for making that adjustment. The Board initially decided not to use the IASC's proposed method because of the complexity of that method and the familiarity in the United States with the treasury stock method and because the treasury stock method achieves quite similar results. As noted by a few respondents to the Exposure Drafts, rights offerings are much more common outside the United States and use of the ex-rights method is established in international practice. In the interest of harmonization, the Board decided to accept the IASC's position on that issue and require use of the ex-rights method when adjusting both basic and diluted EPS for the bonus element in a rights issue.

Supplemental Earnings per Share Data

136. Opinion 15 required disclosure of supplemental EPS data. The purpose of those disclosures was to show what primary EPS would have been if the conversions or sales of securities had occurred at the beginning of the period being reported on rather than during the period. The Board concluded that requiring disclosure of similar information in this Statement was not consistent with the objective of basic and diluted EPS and, thus, decided not to include that requirement in this Statement. However, the Board agreed that it would be useful for financial statements to include a description of transactions that occur after the balance sheet date but before issuance of the financial statements that would have resulted in a material change in the number of common or potential common shares outstanding at the end of the period. Including that information will provide those that want to compute "pro forma" EPS information with the necessary data. Some respondents to the Exposure Draft suggested that information about post-balance-sheet transactions that occurred in periods other than the most recent period would not be useful. The Board decided to require disclosure of that information only for the current reporting period rather than, as proposed in the Exposure Draft, for all periods for which an income statement is presented.

Disclosure Requirements

137. The Board decided to require a reconciliation of the numerators and denominators of the basic and diluted EPS computations in this Statement because the reconciliation is simple and straightforward and will help users better understand the dilutive effect of certain securities included in the EPS computations. SEC Regulation S-K requires presentation of a statement that reasonably details the computation of earnings per share unless the computation can be clearly determined from the material contained in the annual report. The reconciliation required by this Statement should satisfy the SEC requirement and should not result in additional costs to preparers. The Board agreed that disclosing the nature and impact of each dilutive potential common share (or series of shares) included in the diluted EPS computation, as well as separately identifying those antidilutive potential common shares that could dilute earnings per share in the future, allows users to exercise their own judgment as to the "likely" EPS number.

138. Some respondents to the Exposure Draft did not support the reconciliation requirement and stated that (a) the costs to prepare it would exceed the benefit to users, (b) it would be complex and confusing, and (c) it is already required by the SEC. A number of respondents observed that the SEC has proposed eliminating its similar reconciliation requirement in Regulation S-K. The SEC has decided to postpone acting on that proposal in light of comments it has received regarding the usefulness of the reconciliation to investors and financial analysts and the similar proposed requirement in the FASB Exposure Draft. The comments received by the SEC reinforced the Board's position that the reconciliation contains information that is very useful to users of financial statements. However, in response to some of the comments it received, the Board agreed that insignificant reconciling items need not be itemized as part of the reconciliation and could be combined (aggregated).

139. The Exposure Draft would have required disclosure of information that would assist users of financial statements in assessing how basic EPS may be affected in the future due to the potential common shares still outstanding at the balance sheet date as well as the common stock price at that date. Those requirements were referred to as the "warning signal" disclosures because they were meant to address the IASC's warning signal objective for diluted EPS.

However, as noted in paragraph 82, many respondents who commented on the warning signal disclosure requirement in the Exposure Draft stated that they did not believe that the warning signal objective was relevant or useful, and some found the related disclosures confusing. Those respondents generally stated that the costs of the related disclosures would exceed the benefits and that those disclosures would be too complex. A number of respondents to the IASC Exposure Draft made similar comments, and some suggested that the disclosure requirement be made optional. Respondents also noted that some of the information is already required to be disclosed in the financial statements pursuant to other IASC standards. After reconsideration, both the FASB and the IASC agreed to eliminate the warning signal disclosure requirements from their respective standards.

Securities of Subsidiaries

140. This Statement is based on the current practice of deducting income attributable to the noncontrolling interest (minority interest) to arrive at consolidated net income in the consolidated financial statements. The October 1995 FASB Exposure Draft, *Consolidated Financial Statements: Policy and Procedures,* would change that practice to require that net income attributable to the noncontrolling interest be deducted from consolidated net income to arrive at an amount called *net income attributable to the controlling interest.* In addition, that Exposure Draft states that the computation of earnings per share in consolidated financial statements that include subsidiaries that are not wholly owned should be based on and designated as the amount of net income attributable to the controlling interest. Although consolidated net income would include the results of all consolidated operations, the EPS computation would continue to be based only on net income attributable to the controlling interest.

141. The consolidations Exposure Draft would not require disclosure of "income from continuing operations attributable to the controlling interest" if a noncontrolling interest exists. If that Exposure Draft is finalized as proposed, the Board will have to determine what the control number should be for entities that are required to present earnings per share for net income attributable to the controlling interest. Those and other related issues will be addressed before the Board finalizes its redeliberations on the proposed Statement on consolidated financial statements.

Effective Date and Transition

142. The Board decided that this Statement should be effective for financial statements issued for periods ending after December 15, 1997, including interim periods. The Board believes that that effective date provides adequate time for entities to make any needed modifications to their systems and procedures to conform with the provisions of this Statement. For comparability, the Board decided to require restatement of all prior-period EPS data presented (including interim and summary financial information) in the period of adoption.

143. Earnings per share is a widely quoted statistic; therefore, to enhance comparability among entities, the Board decided to prohibit early adoption of this Statement. Thus, entities are prohibited from presenting EPS data computed in accordance with this Statement on the face of the income statement prior to the required adoption date. However, the Board decided to permit entities to disclose pro forma EPS data in the notes to the financial statements prior to that date.

144. Most respondents to the Exposure Draft agreed with the proposed effective date; however, some respondents suggested that this Statement be effective as of the beginning of the year (for calendar-year entities) rather than as of the end of the year. Most respondents agreed with the Board that the benefits of restatement would exceed the related costs and that both the requirement to restate and the prohibition on early adoption would enhance the consistency and comparability of financial reporting. Due to the prohibition on early adoption, the Board decided to retain the effective date proposed in the Exposure Draft so that calendar-year entities will not have to wait until 1998 to adopt this Statement. That is, calendar-year entities will have to implement the Statement in the fourth quarter of 1997 (and restate back to January 1, 1997). An entity with a June 30, 1997 year-end will have to implement the Statement in its second quarter, the quarter ending December 31, 1997 (and restate its first-quarter results).

145. Some respondents indicated that restatement of all EPS data presented would be impracticable in some situations, especially for entities that present tables of 10-year selected data or that have had a number of changes in capital structure due to mergers or acquisitions. The Board acknowledged that it might be difficult to restate EPS data for 10 years, especially if there have been changes in capital structures. However, the Board decided to retain the

requirement for restatement because it believes that the benefits far outweigh the costs. In conjunction with that decision, the Board noted that this Statement does not require presentation of EPS data for 10 years. It requires only that if EPS data are presented, those data must be computed in accordance with the provisions of this Statement. Thus, entities that choose to present EPS data in summaries of earnings or selected financial data must restate that EPS data.

Other Literature on Earnings per Share

146. A number of respondents to the Exposure Draft suggested that the Board address changes to or con-

tinuation of other authoritative guidance on earnings per share, including that of the SEC and the EITF. Because one of the objectives of the EPS project was to simplify the EPS literature, the Board agreed to include in this Statement a table listing all non-FASB authoritative EPS literature and this Statement's impact, if any, on that literature. That table is presented in Appendix F as a reference tool. The Board did not deliberate any of the issues discussed in the other literature, except where specifically noted.

Appendix C

ILLUSTRATIONS

CONTENTS

Appendix C

ILLUSTRATIONS

Introduction

147. This appendix illustrates this Statement's application to entities with complex capital structures. Certain assumptions have been made to simplify the computations and focus on the issue at hand in each illustration.

Illustration 1—Computation of Basic and Diluted Earnings per Share and Income Statement Presentation

148. This example illustrates the quarterly and annual computations of basic and diluted EPS in the year 20X1 for Corporation A, which has a complex capital structure. The control number used in this illustration (and in Illustration 2) is income before extraordinary item and accounting change because Corporation A has no discontinued operations. Paragraph 149 illustrates the presentation of basic

and diluted EPS on the face of the income statement. The facts assumed are as follows:

Average market price of common stock. The average market prices of common stock for the calendar-year 20X1 were as follows:

First quarter	$59
Second quarter	$70
Third quarter	$72
Fourth quarter	$72

The average market price of common stock from July 1 to September 1, 20X1 was $71.

Common stock. The number of shares of common stock outstanding at the beginning of 20X1 was 3,300,000. On March 1, 20X1, 100,000 shares of common stock were issued for cash.

Convertible debentures. In the last quarter of 20X0, 4 percent convertible debentures with a principal amount of $10,000,000 due in 20 years were sold for cash at $1,000 (par). Interest is payable semiannually on November 1 and May 1. Each $1,000 debenture is convertible into 20 shares of common stock. No debentures were converted in 20X0. The entire issue was converted on April 1, 20X1, because the issue was called by the Corporation.

Convertible preferred stock. In the second quarter of 20X0, 600,000 shares of convertible preferred stock were issued for assets in a purchase transaction. The quarterly dividend on each share of that convertible preferred stock is $0.05, payable at the end of the quarter. Each share is convertible into one share of common stock. Holders of 500,000 shares of that convertible preferred stock converted their preferred stock into common stock on June 1, 20X1.

Warrants. Warrants to buy 500,000 shares of common stock at $60 per share for a period of 5 years were issued on January 1, 20X1. All outstanding warrants were exercised on September 1, 20X1.

Options. Options to buy 1,000,000 shares of common stock at $85 per share for a period of 10 years were issued on July 1, 20X1. No options were exercised during 20X1 because the exercise price of the options exceeded the market price of the common stock.

Tax rate. The tax rate was 40 percent for 20X1.

Year 20X1	Income (Loss) before Extraordinary Item and Accounting Change[a]	Net Income (Loss)
First quarter	$3,000,000	$ 3,000,000
Second quarter	4,500,000	4,500,000
Third quarter	500,000	(1,500,000)[b]
Fourth quarter	(500,000)	3,750,000[c]
Full year	$7,500,000	$ 9,750,000

[a]This is the control number (before adjusting for preferred dividends). Refer to paragraph 15.

[b]Corporation A had a $2 million extraordinary loss (net of tax) in the third quarter.

[c]Corporation A had a $4.25 million cumulative effect of an accounting change (net of tax) in the fourth quarter.

(This page intentionally left blank.)

First Quarter 20X1

Basic EPS Computation

Net income	$3,000,000
Less: Preferred stock dividends	(30,000)[a]
Income available to common stockholders	$2,970,000

Dates Outstanding	Shares Outstanding	Fraction of Period	Weighted-Average Shares
January 1–February 28	3,300,000	2/3	2,200,000
Issuance of common stock on March 1	100,000		
March 1–March 31	3,400,000	1/3	1,133,333
Weighted-average shares			3,333,333

Basic EPS $0.89

The equation for computing basic EPS is:

$$\frac{\text{Income available to common stockholders}}{\text{Weighted-average shares}}$$

---

[a]600,000 shares × $0.05

1972

First Quarter 20X1

Diluted EPS Computation

Income available to common stockholders		$2,970,000
Plus: Income impact of assumed conversions		
Preferred stock dividends	$ 30,000[a]	
Interest on 4% convertible debentures	60,000[b]	
Effect of assumed conversions		90,000
Income available to common stockholders + assumed conversions		$3,060,000
Weighted-average shares		3,333,333
Plus: Incremental shares from assumed conversions		
Warrants	0[c]	
Convertible preferred stock	600,000	
4% convertible debentures	200,000	
Dilutive potential common shares		800,000
Adjusted weighted-average shares		4,133,333

Diluted EPS $0.74

The equation for computing diluted EPS is:

$$\frac{\text{Income available to common stockholders} + \text{Effect of assumed conversions}}{\text{Weighted-average shares} + \text{Dilutive potential common shares}}$$

---

[a] 600,000 shares × $0.05

[b] ($10,000,000 × 4%) ÷ 4; less taxes at 40%

[c] The warrants were not assumed exercised because they were antidilutive in the period ($60 exercise price > $59 average price).

Second Quarter 20X1

Basic EPS Computation

Net income	$4,500,000
Less: Preferred stock dividends	(5,000)[a]
Income available to common stockholders	$4,495,000

Dates Outstanding	Shares Outstanding	Fraction of Period	Weighted-Average Shares
April 1	3,400,000		
Conversion of 4% debentures on April 1	200,000		
April 1–May 31	3,600,000	2/3	2,400,000
Conversion of preferred stock on June 1	500,000		
June 1–June 30	4,100,000	1/3	1,366,667
Weighted-average shares			3,766,667

Basic EPS $1.19

The equation for computing basic EPS is:

Income available to common stockholders

_____

Weighted-average shares

---

[a] 100,000 shares × $0.05

Second Quarter 20X1

Diluted EPS Computation

Income available to common stockholders		$4,495,000
Plus: Income impact of assumed conversions		
Preferred stock dividends	$ 5,000[a]	
Effect of assumed conversions		5,000
Income available to common stockholders + assumed conversions		$4,500,000
Weighted-average shares		3,766,667
Plus: Incremental shares from assumed conversions		
Warrants	71,429[b]	
Convertible preferred stock	433,333[c]	
Dilutive potential common shares		504,762
Adjusted weighted-average shares		4,271,429

Diluted EPS $1.05

The equation for computing diluted EPS is:

$$\frac{\text{Income available to common stockholders} + \text{Effect of assumed conversions}}{\text{Weighted-average shares} + \text{Dilutive potential common shares}}$$

---

[a] 100,000 shares × $0.05

[b] $60 × 500,000 = $30,000,000; $30,000,000 ÷ $70 = 428,571; 500,000 − 428,571 = 71,429 shares **OR** [($70 − $60) ÷ $70] × 500,000 shares = 71,429 shares

[c] (600,000 shares × 2/3) + (100,000 shares × 1/3)

Third Quarter 20X1

Basic EPS Computation

Income before extraordinary item	$ 500,000
Less: Preferred stock dividends	(5,000)
Income available to common stockholders	495,000
Extraordinary item	(2,000,000)
Net loss available to common stockholders	$(1,505,000)

Dates Outstanding	Shares Outstanding	Fraction of Period	Weighted-Average Shares
July 1–August 31	4,100,000	2/3	2,733,333
Exercise of warrants on September 1	500,000		
September 1–September 30	4,600,000	1/3	1,533,333
Weighted-average shares			4,266,666

Basic EPS

Income before extraordinary item	**$ 0.12**
Extraordinary item	$(0.47)
Net loss	$(0.35)

The equation for computing basic EPS is:

$$\frac{\text{Income available to common stockholders}}{\text{Weighted-average shares}}$$

Third Quarter 20X1

Diluted EPS Computation

Income available to common stockholders		$ 495,000
Plus: Income impact of assumed conversions		
Preferred stock dividends	$ 5,000	
Effect of assumed conversions		5,000
Income available to common stockholders + assumed conversions		500,000
Extraordinary item		(2,000,000)
Net loss available to common stockholders + assumed conversions		$(1,500,000)
Weighted-average shares		4,266,666
Plus: Incremental shares from assumed conversions		
Warrants	51,643[a]	
Convertible preferred stock	100,000	
Dilutive potential common shares		151,643
Adjusted weighted-average shares		4,418,309

Diluted EPS

Income before extraordinary item	**$ 0.11**
Extraordinary item	**$(0.45)**
Net loss	**$(0.34)**

The equation for computing diluted EPS is:

$$\frac{\text{Income available to common stockholders} + \text{Effect of assumed conversions}}{\text{Weighted-average shares} + \text{Dilutive potential common shares}}$$

Note: The incremental shares from assumed conversions are included in computing the diluted per-share amounts for the extraordinary item and net loss even though they are antidilutive. This is because the control number (income before extraordinary item, adjusted for preferred dividends) was income, not a loss. (Refer to paragraphs 15 and 16.)

---

[a][($71 − $60) ÷ $71] × 500,000 = 77,465 shares; 77,465 × 2/3 = 51,643 shares

Fourth Quarter 20X1

Basic and Diluted EPS Computation

Loss before accounting change	$ (500,000)
Plus: Preferred stock dividends	(5,000)
Loss available to common stockholders	(505,000)
Accounting change	4,250,000
Net income available to common stockholders	$3,745,000

Dates Outstanding	Shares Outstanding	Fraction of Period	Weighted- Average Shares
October 1–December 31	4,600,000	3/3	4,600,000
Weighted-average shares			4,600,000

Basic and Diluted EPS

Loss before accounting change	**$(0.11)**
Accounting change	**$ 0.92**
Net income	**$ 0.81**

The equation for computing basic (and diluted) EPS is:

$$\frac{\text{Income available to common stockholders}}{\text{Weighted-average shares}}$$

Note: The incremental shares from assumed conversions are not included in computing the diluted per-share amounts for the accounting change and net income because the control number (loss before accounting change, adjusted for preferred dividends) was a loss, not income. (Refer to paragraphs 15 and 16.)

Full Year 20X1

Diluted EPS Computation

Income available to common stockholders		$ 7,455,000
Plus: Income impact of assumed conversions		
Preferred stock dividends	$ 45,000	
Interest on 4% convertible debentures	60,000	
Effect of assumed conversions		105,000
Income available to common stockholders + assumed conversions		7,560,000
Extraordinary item		(2,000,000)
Accounting change		4,250,000
Net income available to common stockholders + assumed conversions		$ 9,810,000
Weighted-average shares		3,991,666
Plus: Incremental shares from assumed conversions		
Warrants	30,768[a]	
Convertible preferred stock	308,333[b]	
4% convertible debentures	50,000[c]	
Dilutive potential common shares		389,101
Adjusted weighted-average shares		4,380,767

Diluted EPS

Income before extraordinary item and accounting change	$ 1.73
Extraordinary item	$(0.46)
Accounting change	$ 0.97
Net income	$ 2.24

The equation for computing diluted EPS is:

$$\frac{\text{Income available to common stockholders} + \text{Effect of assumed conversions}}{\text{Weighted-average shares} + \text{Dilutive potential common shares}}$$

---

[a](71,429 shares × 3/12) + (51,643 shares × 3/12)

[b](600,000 shares × 5/12) + (100,000 shares × 7/12)

[c]200,000 shares × 3/12

149. The following illustrates how Corporation A might present its EPS data on its income statement. Note that the per-share amounts for the extraordinary item and the accounting change are not required to be shown on the face of the income statement.

	For the Year Ended 20X1
Earnings per common share	
Income before extraordinary item and accounting change	$ 1.87
Extraordinary item	(0.50)
Cumulative effect of a change in accounting principle	1.06
Net income	$ 2.43
Earnings per common share—assuming dilution	
Income before extraordinary item and accounting change	$ 1.73
Extraordinary item	(0.46)
Cumulative effect of a change in accounting principle	0.97
Net income	$ 2.24

150. The following table includes the quarterly and annual EPS data for Corporation A. The purpose of this table is to illustrate that the sum of the four quarters' EPS data will not necessarily equal the annual EPS data. This Statement does not require disclosure of this information.

	First Quarter	Second Quarter	Third Quarter	Fourth Quarter	Full Year
Basic EPS					
Income (loss) before extraordinary item and accounting change	$0.89	$1.19	$ 0.12	$(0.11)	$ 1.87
Extraordinary item	—	—	(0.47)	—	(0.50)
Accounting change	—	—	—	0.92	1.06
Net income (loss)	$0.89	$1.19	$(0.35)	$ 0.81	$ 2.43
Diluted EPS					
Income (loss) before extraordinary item and accounting change	$0.74	$1.05	$ 0.11	$(0.11)	$ 1.73
Extraordinary item	—	—	(0.45)	—	(0.46)
Accounting change	—	—	—	0.92	0.97
Net income (loss)	$0.74	$1.05	$(0.34)	$ 0.81	$ 2.24

Illustration 2—Earnings per Share Disclosures

151. The following is an illustration of the reconciliation of the numerators and denominators of the basic and diluted EPS computations for "income before extraordinary item and accounting change" and other related disclosures required by paragraph 40 for Corporation A in Illustration 1. **Note:** Statement 123 has specific disclosure requirements related to stock-based compensation arrangements.

	For the Year Ended 20X1		
	Income **(Numerator)**	**Shares** **(Denominator)**	**Per-Share** **Amount**
Income before extraordinary item and accounting change	$7,500,000		
Less: Preferred stock dividends	(45,000)		
Basic EPS			
Income available to common stockholders	7,455,000	3,991,666	$1.87
Effect of Dilutive Securities			
Warrants		30,768	
Convertible preferred stock	45,000	308,333	
4% convertible debentures	60,000	50,000	
Diluted EPS			
Income available to common stockholders + assumed conversions	$7,560,000	4,380,767	$1.73

Options to purchase 1,000,000 shares of common stock at $85 per share were outstanding during the second half of 20X1 but were not included in the computation of diluted EPS because the options' exercise price was greater than the average market price of the common shares. The options, which expire on June 30, 20Y1, were still outstanding at the end of year 20X1.

Illustration 3—Contingently Issuable Shares

152. The following example illustrates the contingent share provisions described in paragraphs 10 and 30-35. The facts assumed are as follows:

- Corporation B had 100,000 shares of common stock outstanding during the entire year ended December 31, 20X1. It had no options, warrants, or convertible securities outstanding during the period.
- Terms of a contingent stock agreement related to a recent business combination provided the following to certain shareholders of the Corporation:
  - 1,000 additional common shares for each new retail site opened during 20X1
  - 5 additional common shares for each $100 of consolidated, after-tax net income in excess of $500,000 for the year ended December 31, 20X1.
- The Corporation opened two new retail sites during the year:
  - One on May 1, 20X1.
  - One on September 1, 20X1.
- Corporation B's consolidated, year-to-date after-tax net income was:
  - $400,000 as of March 31, 20X1
  - $600,000 as of June 30, 20X1
  - $450,000 as of September 30, 20X1
  - $700,000 as of December 31, 20X1.

Note: In computing diluted EPS for an interim period, contingent shares are included as of the beginning of the period. For year-to-date computations, footnote 18 of this Statement requires that contingent shares be included on a weighted-average basis.

	First Quarter	Second Quarter	Third Quarter	Fourth Quarter	Full Year
Basic EPS Computation					
Numerator	$400,000	$200,000	$(150,000)	$250,000	$700,000
Denominator:					
Common shares outstanding	100,000	100,000	100,000	100,000	100,000
Retail site contingency	0	667[a]	1,333[b]	2,000	1,000[c]
Earnings contingency[d]	0	0	0	0	0
Total shares	100,000	100,667	101,333	102,000	101,000
Basic EPS	$ 4.00	$ 1.99	$ (1.48)	$ 2.45	$ 6.93

	First Quarter	Second Quarter	Third Quarter	Fourth Quarter	Full Year
Diluted EPS Computation					
Numerator	$400,000	$200,000	$(150,000)	$250,000	$700,000
Denominator:					
Common shares outstanding	100,000	100,000	100,000	100,000	100,000
Retail site contingency	0	1,000	2,000	2,000	1,250[e]
Earnings contingency	0[f]	5,000[g]	0[h]	10,000[i]	3,750[j]
Total shares	100,000	106,000	102,000	112,000	105,000
Diluted EPS	$ 4.00	$ 1.89	$ (1.47)[k]	$ 2.23	$ 6.67

---

[a] 1,000 shares × 2/3

[b] 1,000 shares + (1,000 shares × 1/3)

[c] (1,000 shares × 8/12) + (1,000 shares × 4/12)

[d] The earnings contingency has no effect on basic EPS because it is not certain that the condition is satisfied until the end of the contingency period (paragraphs 10 and 31). The effect is negligible for the fourth-quarter and full-year computations because it is not certain that the condition is met until the last day of the period.

[e] (0 + 1,000 + 2,000 + 2,000) ÷ 4

[f] Corporation B did not have $500,000 year-to-date, after-tax net income at March 31, 20X1. Projecting future earnings levels and including the related contingent shares are not permitted by this Statement.

[g] [($600,000 − $500,000) ÷ $100] × 5 shares

[h] Year-to-date, after-tax net income was less than $500,000.

[i] [($700,000 − $500,000) ÷ $100] × 5 shares

[j] (0 + 5,000 + 0 + 10,000) ÷ 4

[k] Loss during the third quarter is due to a change in accounting principle; therefore, antidilution rules (paragraph 15) do not apply.

Illustration 4—Antidilution Sequencing

153. The following example illustrates the antidilution sequencing provisions described in paragraph 14 for Corporation C for the year ended December 31, 20X0. The facts assumed are as follows:

- Corporation C had income available to common stockholders of $10,000,000 for the year 20X0.
- 2,000,000 shares of common stock were outstanding for the entire year 20X0.
- The average market price of the common stock was $75.

- Corporation C had the following potential common shares outstanding during the year:
  - Options (not compensation related) to buy 100,000 shares of common stock at $60 per share.
  - 800,000 shares of convertible preferred stock entitled to a cumulative dividend of $8 per share. Each preferred share is convertible into 2 shares of common stock.
  - 5 percent convertible debentures with a principal amount of $100,000,000 (issued at par). Each $1,000 debenture is convertible into 20 shares of common stock.
- The tax rate was 40 percent for 20X0.

Determination of Earnings per Incremental Share

	Increase in Income	Increase in Number of Common Shares	Earnings per Incremental Share
Options	0	20,000[a]	—
Convertible preferred stock	$6,400,000[b]	1,600,000[c]	$4.00
5% convertible debentures	3,000,000[d]	2,000,000[e]	1.50

Computation of Diluted Earnings per Share

	Income Available	Common Shares	Per Share	
As reported	$10,000,000	2,000,000	$5.00	
Options	0	20,000		
	10,000,000	2,020,000	4.95	Dilutive
5% convertible debentures	3,000,000	2,000,000		
	13,000,000	4,020,000	3.23	Dilutive
Convertible preferred stock	6,400,000	1,600,000		
	$19,400,000	5,620,000	3.45	Antidilutive

Note: Because diluted EPS *increases* from $3.23 to $3.45 when convertible preferred shares are included in the computation, those convertible preferred shares are antidilutive and are ignored in the computation of diluted EPS. Therefore, diluted EPS is reported as $3.23.

---

[a] $[(\$75 - \$60) \div \$75] \times 100,000$
[b] 800,000 shares × $8
[c] 800,000 shares × 2
[d] ($100,000,000 × 5%) less taxes at 40%
[e] 100,000 debentures × 20

Illustration 5—Rights Issues

154. The following example illustrates the provisions for stock rights issues that contain a bonus element as described in paragraphs 55 and 56. The facts assumed are as follows:

- Net income was $1,100 for the year ended December 31, 20X0.
- 500 common shares were outstanding for the entire year ended December 31, 20X0.
- A rights issue was offered to all existing shareholders in January 20X1. The last date to exercise the rights was March 1, 20X1. The offer provided 1 common share for each 5 outstanding common shares (100 new shares).
- The exercise price for the rights issue was $5 per share acquired.

- The fair value of 1 common share was $11 at March 1, 20X1.
- Basic EPS for the year 20X0 (prior to the rights issuance) was $2.20.

As a result of the bonus element in the January 20X1 rights issue, basic and diluted EPS for 20X0 will have to be adjusted retroactively. The number of common shares used in computing basic and diluted EPS is the number of shares outstanding immediately prior to the rights issue (500) multiplied by an *adjustment factor*. Prior to computing the adjustment factor, the *theoretical ex-rights fair value per share* must be computed. Those computations follow:

Theoretical ex-rights fair value per share[a]	$10	=	$\dfrac{(500 \times \$11) + (100 \times \$5)}{(500 + 100)}$
Adjustment factor[b]	1.1	=	$11 ÷ $10
Denominator for restating basic EPS	550	=	500 × 1.1
Restated basic EPS for 20X0	$2.00	=	$1,100 ÷ 550

Diluted EPS would be adjusted retroactively by adding 50 shares to the denominator that was used in computing diluted EPS prior to the restatement.

---

[a]The equation for computing the theoretical ex-rights fair value per share is:

$$\frac{\text{Aggregate fair value of shares prior to exercise of rights } + \text{ Proceeds from exercise of rights}}{\text{Total shares outstanding after exercise of rights}}$$

[b]The equation for computing the adjustment factor is:

$$\frac{\text{Fair value per share immediately prior to exercise of rights}}{\text{Theoretical ex-rights fair value per share}}$$

Illustration 6—Two-Class Method

155. The two-class method of computing basic EPS for an entity that has more than one class of nonconvertible securities is illustrated in the following example. This method is described in paragraph 61; as noted in that paragraph, diluted EPS would be computed in a similar manner. The facts assumed for the year 20X0 are as follows:

- Net income was $65,000.
- 10,000 shares of $50 par value common stock were outstanding.

- 5,000 shares of $100 par value nonconvertible preferred stock were outstanding.
- The preferred stock was entitled to a noncumulative annual dividend of $5 per share before any dividend is paid on common stock.
- After common stock has been paid a dividend of $2 per share, the preferred stock then participates in any additional dividends on a 40:60 *per-share* ratio with common stock. (That is, after preferred and common stock have been paid dividends of $5 and $2 per share, respectively, preferred stock participates in any additional dividends at a rate of

two-thirds of the additional amount paid to common stock on a per-share basis.)
- Preferred stockholders have been paid $27,000 ($5.40 per share).
- Common stockholders have been paid $26,000 ($2.60 per share).

Basic EPS for 20X0 would be computed as follows:

Net income		$65,000
Less dividends paid:		
Preferred	$27,000	
Common	26,000	53,000
Undistributed 20X0 earnings		$12,000

Allocation of undistributed earnings:

To preferred:

$0.4(5,000) \div [0.4(5,000) + 0.6(10,000)] \times \$12,000 = \$3,000$
$\$3,000 \div 5,000 \text{ shares} = \$0.60 \text{ per share}$

To common:

$0.6(10,000) \div [0.4(5,000) + 0.6(10,000)] \times \$12,000 = \$9,000$
$\$9,000 \div 10,000 \text{ shares} = \$0.90 \text{ per share}$

Basic per-share amounts:

	Preferred Stock	Common Stock
Distributed earnings	$5.40	$2.60
Undistributed earnings	0.60	0.90
Totals	$6.00	$3.50

Illustration 7—Securities of a Subsidiary: Computation of Basic and Diluted Earnings per Share

156. The following example illustrates the EPS computations for a subsidiary's securities that enable their holders to obtain the subsidiary's common stock based on the provisions in paragraph 62. This example is based on current practice. Based on the provisions in the consolidations Exposure Draft, the presentation of earnings per share would differ from that illustrated in this example for an entity that includes subsidiaries that are not wholly owned. The facts assumed are as follows:

Parent corporation:

- Net income was $10,000 (excluding any earnings of or dividends paid by the subsidiary).
- 10,000 shares of common stock were outstanding; the parent corporation had not issued any other securities.
- The parent corporation owned 900 common shares of a domestic subsidiary corporation.
- The parent corporation owned 40 warrants issued by the subsidiary.
- The parent corporation owned 100 shares of convertible preferred stock issued by the subsidiary.

Subsidiary corporation:

- Net income was $3,600.
- 1,000 shares of common stock were outstanding.
- Warrants exercisable to purchase 200 shares of its common stock at $10 per share (assume $20 average market price for common stock) were outstanding.
- 200 shares of convertible preferred stock were outstanding. Each share is convertible into two shares of common stock.
- The convertible preferred stock paid a dividend of $1.50 per share.
- No intercompany eliminations or adjustments were necessary except for dividends.
- Income taxes have been ignored for simplicity.

Subsidiary's Earnings per Share

Basic EPS	$3.30	Computed:	$(\$3,600^a - \$300^b) \div 1,000^c$
Diluted EPS	$2.40	Computed:	$\$3,600^d \div (1,000 + 100^e + 400^f)$

Consolidated Earnings per Share

Basic EPS	$1.31	Computed:	$(\$10,000^g + \$3,120^h) \div 10,000^i$
Diluted EPS	$1.27	Computed:	$(\$10,000 + \$2,160^j + \$48^k + \$480^l) \div 10,000$

---

[a] Subsidiary's net income

[b] Dividends paid by subsidiary on convertible preferred stock

[c] Shares of subsidiary's common stock outstanding

[d] Subsidiary's income available to common stockholders ($3,300) increased by $300 preferred dividends from applying the if-converted method for convertible preferred stock

[e] Incremental shares from warrants from applying the treasury stock method, computed: $[(\$20 - \$10) \div \$20] \times 200$

[f] Shares of subsidiary's common stock assumed outstanding from conversion of convertible preferred stock, computed: 200 convertible preferred shares × conversion factor of 2

[g] Parent's net income

[h] Portion of subsidiary's income to be included in consolidated basic EPS, computed: $(900 \times \$3.30) + (100 \times \$1.50)$

[i] Shares of parent's common stock outstanding

[j] Parent's proportionate interest in subsidiary's earnings attributable to common stock, computed: $(900 \div 1,000) \times (1,000$ shares $\times \$2.40$ per share$)$

[k] Parent's proportionate interest in subsidiary's earnings attributable to warrants, computed: $(40 \div 200) \times (100$ incremental shares $\times \$2.40$ per share$)$

[l] Parent's proportionate interest in subsidiary's earnings attributable to convertible preferred stock, computed: $(100 \div 200) \times (400$ shares from conversion $\times \$2.40$ per share$)$

Illustration 8—Application of the Treasury Stock Method for Stock Appreciation Rights and Other Variable Stock Option Award Plans

157. The following examples illustrate the provisions in paragraphs 20-22 for computing the effect on diluted EPS of stock appreciation rights and other variable stock option or award plans when the service period is presumed to be the vesting period. The examples do not comprehend all possible combinations of circumstances. Amounts and quantities have been rounded for simplicity. The following examples are based on the examples in Appendix B of Interpretation 31, which is superseded by this Statement. Accordingly, the terminology and compensation cost is based on the guidance in Opinion 25 and related literature.

The provisions of the agreements are as follows:

Date of grant	January 1, 1999
Expiration date	December 31, 2008
Vesting	100% at the end of 2002
Number of shares under option	1,000
Option exercise price	$10 per share
Quoted market price at date of grant	$10 per share

- Stock appreciation rights are granted in tandem with stock options for market value appreciation in excess of the option price.
- Exercise of the rights cancels the options for an equal number of shares and vice versa.
- Share appreciation is payable in stock, cash, or a combination of stock and cash at the entity's election.

The facts assumed are as follows:

- There are no circumstances in these two examples that would overcome the presumption that the rights are payable in stock (refer to paragraph 29).
- The tax deduction for compensation will equal the compensation recognized for financial reporting purposes.
- The quoted market prices of common stock on December 31 of the years 1999–2004 were as follows:

1999	$11
2000	$12
2001	$15
2002	$14
2003	$15
2004	$18

FASB Statement of Standards

Example 1

158. The following example illustrates the annual computation of incremental shares for the above-described stock appreciation right plan. A single annual computation is shown for simplicity in this and in the following example. Normally, a computation would be done monthly or quarterly.

Date	Market Price	Compensation			Compensation Accrued to Date	Measurable Compensation Attributed to Future Periods[d]	Amount to Be Paid by Employee	Assumed Proceeds	Additional Shares for Diluted EPS			
		Per Share[a]	Aggregate[b]	Percentage Accrued[c]					Shares Issuable[e]	Treasury Shares Assumed Repurchased[f]		Incremental Shares
12/31/99	$11	$1	$1,000	25%	$ 250	$ 750	—	$ 750	47	35		12
12/31/00	12	2	2,000	50	1,000	1,000	—	1,000	130	76		54
12/31/01	15	5	5,000	75	3,750	1,250	—	1,250	259	83		176
12/31/02	14	4	4,000	100	4,000	0	—	0	310[g]	43[g]		267[g]
12/31/03	15	5	5,000	100	5,000	0	—	0	310	0		310
12/31/04	18	8	8,000	100	8,000	0	—	0	394	0		394

[a]Market price less exercise price ($10).

[b]Aggregate compensation for unexercised shares to be allocated to periods in which service is performed (shares under option × compensation per share).

[c]The percentage accrued is based on the four-year vesting period.

[d]Unaccrued compensation in this example.

[e]Average aggregate compensation ÷ average market price.

[f]Average assumed proceeds ÷ average market price.

[g]Illustration of computation of additional shares for one year (2002) follows:

Date	Market Price	Aggregate Compensation	Assumed Proceeds
12/31/01	$15.00	$5,000	$1,250
12/31/02	14.00	4,000	0
Average	14.50	4,500	625

Additional shares for diluted EPS:

Shares issuable	310	(4,500 ÷ $14.50)
Treasury shares	(43)	(625 ÷ $14.50)
Incremental shares	267	

Example 2

159. If the stock appreciation rights vested 25 percent per year commencing in 1999, the annual computation of incremental shares for diluted EPS in Example 1 would change as illustrated in the following example. The computation of compensation expense is explained in FASB Interpretation No. 28, *Accounting for Stock Appreciation Rights and Other Variable Stock Option or Award Plans*, Appendix B, Example 2.

The additional facts assumed are as follows:

- On December 31, 2001, the employee exercises the right to receive share appreciation on 300 shares.
- On March 15, 2002, the employee exercises the right to receive share appreciation on 100 shares; quoted market price $15 per share.
- On June 15, 2003, the employee exercises the right to receive share appreciation on 100 shares; quoted market price $16 per share.
- On December 31, 2003, the employee exercises the right to receive share appreciation on 300 shares.
- On December 31, 2004, the employee exercises the right to receive share appreciation on 200 shares.

Date	Transaction	Number of Shares under Option	Market Price	Compensation Per Share[a]	Aggregate[b]	Percentage Accrued[c]	Compensation Accrued to Date	Measurable Compensation Attributed to Future Periods[d]	Amount to Be Paid by Employee	Assumed Proceeds	Shares Issuable[e]	Treasury Shares Assumed Repurchased[f]	Incremental Shares	Weighted-Average Shares Outstanding[g]	Total Shares
12/31/99			$11	$1	$1,000	52%	$ 520	$480	—	$480	47	22	25	—	25
12/31/00			12	2	2,000	79	1,580	420	—	420	130	39	91	—	91
12/31/01			15	5	5,000	94	4,700	300	—	300	259	26	233	—	233
12/31/01	SAR	300	15	5											
3/15/02	SAR	100	15	5											
12/31/02	SAR	100	14	4	2,400	100	2,400	0	—	0	193	10	183	126	309
6/15/03	SAR	100	16	6											
12/31/03	SAR	100	15	5	2,500	100	2,500	0	—	0	170[h]	0	170	153[i]	323
12/31/03	SAR	300	15	5											
12/31/04	SAR	300	18	8	1,600	100	1,600	0	—	0	78	0	78	270	348
12/31/04	SAR	200	18	8											

Transaction code:
SAR—Exercise of a stock appreciation right.

[a] Market price for the year less exercise price ($10).
[b] Aggregate compensation for unexercised shares to be allocated to periods in which the service is performed (shares under option × compensation per share).
[c] Refer to the schedule in paragraph 24 of Interpretation 28.
[d] Unaccrued compensation in this example.
[e] Average aggregate compensation ÷ average market price, weighted for portion of period during which rights were unexercised.
[f] Average assumed proceeds ÷ average market price.
[g] Shares issued upon exercise of stock appreciation rights. These would be included in the enterprise's total weighted-average shares outstanding.
[h] Illustration of computation of shares issuable for one year (2003) follows:

	Number of Shares under Option	Average Compensation per Share	Average Aggregate Compensation	Average Market Price	Aggregate Shares Issuable	Weighing Factor	Shares Issuable
Rights outstanding:							
Entire year 2003	500	$4.50	$2,250	$14.50	155	12/12	155
1/1-6/15	100	5.00	500	15.00	33	5.5/12	15
							170

[i] Illustration of computation of weighted-average shares outstanding for one year (2003) follows:

	Number of Shares under Option	Compensation per Share	Aggregate Compensation	Market Price	Aggregate Shares Outstanding	Weighing Factor	Weighted-Average Shares Outstanding
Shares issued:							
12/31/01	300	$5	$1,500	$15	100	12/12	100
3/15/02	100	5	500	15	33	12/12	33
6/15/03	100	6	600	16	38	6.5/12	20
							153

Appendix D

AMENDMENTS TO EXISTING PRONOUNCEMENTS

160. This Statement supersedes the following pronouncements:

a. APB Opinion No. 15, *Earnings per Share*
b. AICPA Accounting Interpretations 1-102 of Opinion 15
c. AICPA Accounting Interpretations 1, "Changing EPS Denominator for Retroactive Adjustment to Prior Period," and 2, "EPS for 'Catch-up' Adjustment," of APB Opinion No. 20, *Accounting Changes*
d. FASB Statement No. 85, *Yield Test for Determining whether a Convertible Security Is a Common Stock Equivalent*
e. FASB Interpretation No. 31, *Treatment of Stock Compensation Plans in EPS Computations.*

161. This Statement also amends other pronouncements issued by either the Accounting Principles Board or the Financial Accounting Standards Board that refer to Opinion 15. All such references appearing in paragraphs that establish standards or the scope of a pronouncement are hereby amended to refer instead to FASB Statement No. 128, *Earnings per Share.*

162. The last sentence of paragraph 18 and footnote 8 of APB Opinion No. 18, *The Equity Method of Accounting for Investments in Common Stock,* are replaced by the following:

An investor's *share of the earnings or losses* of an investee should be based on the shares of *common* stock held by an investor.[8]

_____
[8]Paragraph 62 of FASB Statement No. 128, *Earnings per Share,* discusses the treatment of common shares or potential common shares for purposes of computing consolidated EPS. The provisions of that paragraph also apply to investments in common stock of corporate joint ventures and investee companies accounted for under the equity method.

163. Opinion 20 is amended as follows:

a. The last sentence of paragraph 20 is replaced by the following:

Presentation of per-share amounts for the cumulative effect of an accounting change shall be made either on the face of the income statement or in the related notes.

b. The parenthetical phrase in the second sentence of paragraph 21 is replaced by the following:

(basic and diluted, as appropriate under FASB Statement No. 128, *Earnings per Share*)

c. In paragraphs 42 and 46, *(which are not common stock equivalents)* is deleted.

d. In the comparative statements in paragraphs 43, 44, and 47, in Note A in paragraph 47, and in the five-year summary in paragraph 48, *full* in *assuming full dilution* is deleted.

164. Paragraph 30(b) of APB Opinion No. 28, *Interim Financial Reporting,* is replaced by the following:

Basic and diluted earnings per share data for each period presented, determined in accordance with the provisions of FASB Statement No. 128, *Earnings per Share.*

165. APB Opinion No. 30, *Reporting the Results of Operations—Reporting the Effects of Disposal of a Segment of a Business, and Extraordinary, Unusual and Infrequently Occurring Events and Transactions,* is amended as follows:

a. Paragraph 9 is amended as follows:

(1) In the first sentence, *APB Opinion No. 15,* is replaced by *FASB Statement No. 128, Earnings per Share.*

(2) Footnote 3 is deleted.

b. Paragraph 12 is replaced by the following:

Earnings per share data for extraordinary items shall be presented either on the face of the income statement or in the related notes, as prescribed by Statement 128.

166. FASB Statement No. 21, *Suspension of the Reporting of Earnings per Share and Segment Information by Nonpublic Enterprises,* is amended as follows:

a. Paragraph 12 is amended as follows:

(1) In the first sentence, *APB Opinion No. 15[3] and* is deleted.

(2) In the second sentence, *Opinion No. 15 and* is deleted.

(3) Footnote 3 is deleted.

b. In paragraph 14, *earnings per share and* and *APB Opinion No. 15 and* are deleted.

167. FASB Statement No. 123, *Accounting for Stock-Based Compensation*, is amended as follows:

a. Paragraph 49 is replaced by the following:

FASB Statement No. 128, *Earnings per Share*, requires that employee stock options, nonvested stock, and similar equity instruments granted to employees be treated as potential common shares in computing diluted earnings per share. Diluted earnings per share shall be based on the actual number of options or shares granted and not yet forfeited, unless doing so would be anti-dilutive. If vesting is contingent upon factors other than continued service, such as the level of future earnings, the shares or options shall be treated as contingently issuable shares in accordance with paragraphs 30-35 of Statement 128. If stock options or other equity instruments are granted during a period, the shares issuable shall be weighted to reflect the portion of the period during which the equity instruments were outstanding.

b. Paragraph 50 is amended as follows:

(1) In the first sentence, *Opinion 15* is replaced by *Statement 128*.

(2) In the second sentence, *FASB Interpretation No. 31, Treatment of Stock Compensation Plans in EPS Computations,* is replaced by *Statement 128*.

(3) In the third sentence, *Interpretation 31* is replaced by *Statement 128*.

c. Paragraph 357 is amended as follows:

(1) In the second sentence, *Under Opinion 15 and FASB Interpretation No. 31, Treatment of Stock Compensation Plans in EPS Computations* is replaced by *Under FASB Statement No. 128, Earnings per Share* and *common stock equivalents* is replaced by *potential common shares.*

(2) In the third sentence, *common stock equivalents* is replaced by *potential common shares.*

d. Paragraph 358 is amended as follows:

(1) The first three sentences are deleted.

(2) In the fourth sentence, *, of which 4,500,000 are expected to vest* is deleted.

(3) The seventh sentence is deleted.

e. Paragraph 359 and footnote 26 are replaced by the following:

Computation of assumed proceeds for diluted earnings per share:

• Amount employees would pay if all options outstanding were exercised using the weighted-average exercise price (4,600,000 × $40)	$184,000,000
• Average unrecognized compensation balance during year[26]	17,700,000
Assumed proceeds	$201,700,000

---

[26]Average unrecognized compensation balance is determined by averaging the beginning-of-the-year balance of cost measured and unrecognized and the end-of-the-year balance of cost measured and unrecognized. The assumed amount is $17,700,000 based on ongoing cost recognition for stock options granted in the current year and prior years.

f. Paragraph 360 is replaced by the following:

Assumed repurchase of shares:

• Repurchase shares at average market price during the year ($201,700,000 ÷ $52)	3,878,846
• Incremental shares to be added (4,600,000 − 3,878,846)	721,154

The number of shares to be added to outstanding shares for purposes of the diluted earnings per share calculation is 721,154.

g. Paragraph 361 is deleted.

168. Paragraph 6 of FASB Interpretation No. 28, *Accounting for Stock Appreciation Rights and Other Variable Stock Option or Award Plans,* is replaced by the following:

Stock appreciation rights and other variable plan awards are included in the computation of diluted earnings per share pursuant to the provisions of paragraphs 20-23 of FASB Statement No. 128, *Earnings per Share*.

169. Paragraph 7 of FASB Interpretation No. 38, *Determining the Measurement Date for Stock Option, Purchase, and Award Plans Involving Junior Stock*, is replaced by the following:

Paragraphs 20-23 of FASB Statement No. 128, *Earnings per Share*, provide guidance on when and how junior stock plans should be reflected in the diluted earnings per share computation.

170. In the first sentence of paragraph 2 of FASB Technical Bulletin No. 79-8, *Applicability of FASB Statements 21 and 33 to Certain Brokers and Dealers in Securities, and APB Opinion No. 15, Earnings per Share*, is deleted.

Appendix E

GLOSSARY

171. This appendix contains definitions of certain terms or phrases used in this Statement.

Antidilution (antidilutive)
An increase in earnings per share amounts or a decrease in loss per share amounts.

Basic earnings per share (basic EPS)
The amount of earnings for the period available to each share of common stock outstanding during the reporting period.

Call option
A contract that allows the holder to buy a specified quantity of stock from the writer of the contract at a fixed price for a given period. Refer to **option** and **purchased call option**.

Common stock (common shares)
A stock that is subordinate to all other stock of the issuer.

Contingent issuance
A possible issuance of shares of common stock that is dependent on the satisfaction of certain conditions.

Contingent stock agreement
An agreement to issue common stock (usually in

connection with a business combination accounted for by the purchase method) that is dependent on the satisfaction of certain conditions. Refer to **contingently issuable shares**.

Contingently issuable shares (contingently issuable stock)
Shares issuable for little or no cash consideration upon the satisfaction of certain conditions pursuant to a contingent stock agreement. Refer to **contingent stock agreement**.

Conversion rate (conversion ratio)
The ratio of the number of common shares issuable upon conversion to a unit of a convertible security. For example, $100 face value of debt convertible into 5 shares of common stock would have a conversion ratio of 5 to 1.

Convertible security
A security that is convertible into another security based on a conversion rate; for example, convertible preferred stock that is convertible into common stock on a two-for-one basis (two shares of common for each share of preferred).

Diluted earnings per share (diluted EPS)
The amount of earnings for the period available to each share of common stock outstanding during the reporting period and to each share that would have been outstanding assuming the issuance of common shares for all dilutive potential common shares outstanding during the reporting period.

Dilution (dilutive)
A reduction in earnings per share resulting from the assumption that convertible securities were converted, that options or warrants were exercised, or that other shares were issued upon the satisfaction of certain conditions.

Earnings per share (EPS)
The amount of earnings attributable to each share of common stock. For convenience, the term is used in this Statement to refer to either earnings or loss per share.

Exercise price
The amount that must be paid for a share of common stock upon exercise of an option or warrant.

If-converted method

A method of computing EPS data that assumes conversion of convertible securities at the beginning of the reporting period (or at time of issuance, if later).

Income available to common stockholders

Income (or loss) from continuing operations or net income (or net loss) adjusted for preferred stock dividends.

Option

Unless otherwise stated in this Statement, a call option that gives the holder the right to purchase shares of common stock from the reporting entity in accordance with an agreement upon payment of a specified amount. As used in this Statement, options include, but are not limited to, options granted to employees and stock purchase agreements entered into with employees. Options are considered "securities" in this Statement. Refer to **call option.**

Potential common stock

A security or other contract that may entitle its holder to obtain common stock during the reporting period or after the end of the reporting period.

Preferred stock

A security that has rights that are preferential to common stock.

Purchased call option

A contract that allows the reporting entity to buy a specified quantity of its own stock from the writer of the contract at a fixed price for a given period. Refer to **call option.**

Put option

A contract that allows the holder to sell a specified quantity of stock to the writer of the contract at a fixed price during a given period.

Reverse treasury stock method

A method of recognizing the dilutive effect on earnings per share of satisfying a put obligation. It assumes that the proceeds used to buy back common stock (pursuant to the terms of a put option) will be raised from issuing shares at the average market price during the period. Refer to **put option.**

Rights issue

An offer to existing shareholders to purchase additional shares of common stock in accordance with an agreement for a specified amount (which is generally substantially less than the fair value of the shares) for a given period.

Security

The evidence of debt or ownership or a related right. For purposes of this Statement, it includes options and warrants as well as debt and stock.

Treasury stock method

A method of recognizing the use of proceeds that could be obtained upon exercise of options and warrants in computing diluted EPS. It assumes that any proceeds would be used to purchase common stock at the average market price during the period.

Warrant

A security that gives the holder the right to purchase shares of common stock in accordance with the terms of the instrument, usually upon payment of a specified amount.

Weighted-average number of common shares outstanding

The number of shares determined by relating (a) the portion of time within a reporting period that common shares have been outstanding to (b) the total time in that period. In computing diluted EPS, equivalent common shares are considered for all dilutive potential common shares.

Appendix F

OTHER LITERATURE ON EARNINGS PER SHARE

172. The following table addresses changes to or continuation of other authoritative guidance on earnings per share, including that of the SEC and the EITF. For each item, this table either discusses the impact of this Statement, if any, or indicates reasons that specific items are beyond the scope of this Statement. This table is presented in this Statement for use as a reference tool. The Board did not deliberate any of the issues contained in the literature listed in this table, except where specifically noted.

Note: Current SEC, EITF, and AICPA guidance has been quoted, paraphrased, or restated to facilitate the reader's understanding of the effect of this Statement.

Status after Statement 128	Current Guidance	Effect of Statement 128
N/A	**Staff Accounting Bulletin (SAB) 64 Topic 3C: Redeemable Preferred Stock** SAB 64 states that if the initial fair value of redeemable preferred stock is less than the mandatory redemption amount, the carrying amount of the stock should be increased to the mandatory redemption amount through periodic accretions charged against retained earnings. Those periodic accretions are treated in the same manner as a dividend on nonredeemable preferred stock for EPS computations. That is, dividends on the preferred stock and accretions of their carrying amounts cause income or loss available to common stockholders (the EPS numerator) to be less than reported income.	The Board expects to address the accounting for preferred stock in its project on distinguishing between liability and equity instruments. Statement 128 does not address numerator issues relating to the EPS computation. Statement 128 permits an adjustment only for preferred dividends in computing income available to common stockholders. The SEC guidance for redeemable preferred stock continues to apply. [9]
N/A	**Topic 6B: Accounting Series Release (ASR) No. 280—*General Revision of Regulation S-X*** ASR 280 states that income or loss available to common stockholders should be reported on the face of the income statement when it is materially different in quantitative terms from reported net income or loss or when it is indicative of significant trends or other qualitative considerations.	The disclosure requirement is due, in part, to the provisions in Topic 3C; similar provisions are not included in Statement 128. Statement 128 does not require income available to common stockholders to be presented on the face of the income statement. The SEC disclosure guidance continues to apply.

SAB 68
Topic 5Q: Increasing Rate Preferred Stock

N/A

SAB 68 states that the discount resulting from the issuance of increasing rate preferred stock should be amortized over the period preceding commencement of the perpetual dividend through a charge to retained earnings and a corresponding increase in the carrying amount of the preferred stock. Those periodic increases are treated in the same manner as a dividend on nonredeemable preferred stock for EPS computations. That is, dividends on the preferred stock and accretions of their carrying amounts cause income or loss available to common stockholders (the EPS numerator) to be less than reported income.

The Board expects to address the accounting for preferred stock in its project on distinguishing between liability and equity instruments. Statement 128 does not address numerator issues relating to the EPS computation. Statement 128 permits an adjustment only for preferred dividends in computing income available to common stockholders. The SEC guidance for increasing rate preferred stock continues to apply. [9]

Status Legend:

Affirmed = Consensus is carried forward (with or without modifications).

N/A = Issue is either outside the scope of or unaffected by Statement 128.

Nullified = Consensus is overturned (either entirely or partially, as noted).

Pending = The SEC staff has indicated that it will consider amending or rescinding the guidance prior to the effective date of Statement 128.

Resolved = Guidance is provided by Statement 128 on issues previously unresolved by EITF.

Bold numbers in brackets refer to related paragraphs in Statement 128.

Status after Statement 128	Current Guidance	Effect of Statement 128
	SAB 83 **Topic 4D: Earnings per Share Computations in an Initial Public Offering**	
Pending	The guidance in SAB 83 is applicable to registration statements filed in connection with an initial public offering (IPO) of common stock. SAB 83 states that potentially dilutive instruments with exercise prices below the IPO price that are issued within a one-year period prior to the initial filing of the IPO registration statement should be treated as outstanding for all reported periods (current and prior), in the same manner as shares issued in a stock split are treated. However, in determining the dilutive effect of the issuances, a treasury stock approach may be used.	Statement 128 would permit those potentially dilutive common shares to be included only in the computation of *diluted* EPS and only from the date of issuance. In essence, SAB 83 permits an entity involved in an IPO to treat those potentially dilutive common shares as outstanding common shares in the computation of both basic and diluted EPS for all reported periods. [17]
	This method should be applied in the computation of EPS for all prior periods, including loss years in which the impact of the incremental shares is antidilutive.	Statement 128 does not permit incremental shares to be included in the computation of diluted EPS when an entity has a loss from continuing operations (as the effect is antidilutive). [13, 15, 16] The SEC guidance continues to apply to SEC registrants involved in an IPO that have issued such potentially dilutive common shares.

EITF Topic No. D-15—Earnings-per-Share Presentation for Securities Not Specifically Covered by APB Opinion No. 15

N/A

Topic D-15 (an SEC Observer announcement) states that when situations not expressly covered in Opinion 15 occur, they should be dealt with according to their substance. It also provides the two following general principles that must be considered in analyzing new securities in order to reflect the most appropriate EPS presentation.

Although not expressly stated, this broad concept is implicit in Statement 128.

Pending

1. Securities that enable the holder to participate with common shareholders in dividends over a significant period of time should be reflected in EPS using the two-class method if that method is more dilutive than other methods.

Statement 128 requires use of the two-class method for participating securities that are not convertible into common stock (the if-converted method should be used for all convertible securities). **[60, 61]**

Pending

2. Contingent issuances should be reflected in fully diluted EPS if those contingent issuances have at least a reasonable possibility of occurring.

The contingent-share provisions in Statement 128 are fairly specific and do not permit an entity to consider the probability of a contingent issuance occurring. **[30]**

Status after Statement 128	Current Guidance	Effect of Statement 128
N/A	**EITF Topic No. D-42—The Effect on the Calculation of Earnings per Share for the Redemption or Induced Conversion of Preferred Stock** Topic D-42 (an SEC Observer announcement) states that if a registrant redeems its preferred stock, the excess of the fair value of the consideration transferred to the holders of the preferred stock over the carrying amount of the preferred stock should be subtracted from net income to arrive at net income available to common stockholders in the computation of EPS. Similarly, if convertible preferred stock is converted to other securities issued by the registrant pursuant to an inducement offer, the excess of the fair value of all securities and other consideration transferred to the holders of the convertible preferred stock over the fair value of securities issuable pursuant to the original conversion terms should be subtracted from net income to arrive at net income available to common stockholders.	The Board expects to address the accounting for preferred stock in its project on distinguishing between liability and equity instruments. Statement 128 does not address numerator issues relating to the EPS computation. Statement 128 permits an adjustment only for preferred dividends in computing income available to common stockholders. The SEC guidance for redemption or induced conversion of preferred stock continues to apply. [9]
N/A	**EITF Topic No. D-53—Computation of Earnings per Share for a Period That Includes a Redemption or an Induced Conversion of a Portion of a Class of Preferred Stock** Topic D-53 (an SEC Observer announcement) is related to Topic D-42. Topic D-53 states that if a registrant effects a redemption or induced conversion of only a *portion* of the outstanding securities of a class of preferred stock, any excess consideration should be attributed to those shares that are redeemed or converted.	The Board expects to address the accounting for preferred stock in its project on distinguishing between liability and equity instruments. Statement 128 does not address numerator issues relating to the EPS computation. The SEC guidance for redemption or induced conversion of preferred stock continues to apply.

For purposes of determining whether the "if converted" method is dilutive for the period, the shares redeemed or converted should be considered separately from those shares that are not redeemed or converted.

The "if converted" provisions in Statement 128 do not address how to determine whether a convertible security is antidilutive when there has been a partial conversion. [26-28]

EITF Issue No. 85-18—Earnings-per-Share Effect of Equity Commitment Notes

Nullified

Issue 85-18 states that shares contingently issuable under equity commitment notes and equity contracts should *not* be included in EPS computations. Those shares are considered contingently issuable because the company has an option of paying in cash or stock.

Statement 128 contradicts the consensus reached. Statement 128 states that contracts that may be settled in stock or cash should be presumed to be settled in stock and reflected in the computation of diluted EPS unless past experience or a stated policy provides a reasonable basis to believe otherwise. [29]

Affirmed

Issue 85-18 states that equity contracts that specifically require the issuance of common stock to repay debt should be included in the EPS computations as potentially dilutive securities.

Statement 128 supports the consensus reached; equity contracts that require payment in stock should be considered potentially dilutive securities (convertible debt). [26-28]

EITF Issue No. 87-31—Sale of Put Options on Issuer's Stock

Affirmed

Issue 87-31 prescribes use of the reverse treasury stock method to account for the dilutive effect of written put options that are "in the money" during the period.

In computing diluted EPS, Statement 128 requires use of the reverse treasury stock method to account for the dilutive effect of written put options and similar contracts that are "in the money" during the reporting period. [24]

Note: The EITF combined the consensuses in this Issue with the consensuses in Issue No. 96-13, "Accounting for Derivative Financial Instruments Indexed to, and Potentially Settled in, a Company's Own Stock."

Status after Statement 128	Current Guidance	Effect of Statement 128
N/A	**EITF Issue No. 88-9—Put Warrants** The EITF superseded its consensus on this Issue for companies with publicly traded stock in Issue 96-13.	N/A
Nullified	**EITF Issue No. 90-4—Earnings-per-Share Treatment of Tax Benefits for Dividends on Stock Held by an Employee Stock Ownership Plan (ESOP)** Issue 1: Dividends on preferred stock held by an ESOP should be deducted from net income, net of any applicable income tax benefit, when computing primary EPS. Issue 2: The second issue was addressed by the EITF in Issue No. 92-3, "Earnings-per-Share Treatment of Tax Benefits for Dividends on Unallocated Stock Held by an Employee Stock Ownership Plan (Consideration of the Implications of FASB Statement No. 109 on Issue 2 of EITF Issue No. 90-4)."	Statement 128 has no provisions related to primary EPS and, thus, nullifies the consensus of Issue 90-4. However, it seems appropriate to make a similar deduction for dividends on preferred stock held by an ESOP when computing both basic and diluted EPS if that preferred stock is considered outstanding (that is, if the ESOP shares are allocated).
	EITF Issue No. 90-19—Convertible Bonds with Issuer Option to Settle for Cash upon Conversion Issue 90-19 provides EPS guidance for companies that issue debt instruments that are convertible into a fixed number of common shares. Upon conversion, the issuer either is required or has the option to satisfy all or part of the obligation in cash as follows:	

Affirmed*

Instrument A: If the issuer must satisfy the obligation entirely in cash, the instrument does not have an impact on primary or fully diluted EPS other than that the conversion spread must be recognized as a charge to income.

Statement 128 implicitly supports the consensus reached; this type of security does not meet the definition of potential common stock. [171]

Affirmed*

Instrument B: If the issuer may satisfy the entire obligation in either stock or cash equivalent to the conversion value, the instrument is treated as convertible debt for purposes of computing primary and fully diluted EPS.

Statement 128 implicitly supports the consensus reached. Contracts that may be settled in stock or cash should be presumed to be settled in stock and reflected in the computation of diluted EPS unless past experience or a stated policy provides a reasonable basis to believe otherwise. [29]

Affirmed*

Instrument C: If the issuer must satisfy the accreted value of the obligation in cash and may satisfy the conversion spread in either cash or stock, the instrument does not have an impact on primary EPS but impacts fully diluted EPS as convertible debt.

Statement 128 implicitly supports the consensus reached for diluted EPS. [29]

---

*The guidance related to primary EPS is nullified because Statement 128 eliminates the presentation of primary EPS.

Status after Statement 128	Current Guidance	Effect of Statement 128
N/A	**EITF Issue No. 92-3—Earnings-per-Share Treatment of Tax Benefits for Dividends on Inoculated Stock Held by an Employee Stock Ownership Plan (Consideration of the Implications of FASB Statement No. 109 on Issue 2 of EITF Issue No. 90-4)** Issue 92-3 states that tax benefits related to dividends paid on unallocated common stock held by an ESOP, which are charged to retained earnings, should not be an adjustment to net income for purposes of computing EPS. SOP 93-6 was issued in November 1993. Under SOP 93-6, dividends paid on unallocated ESOP shares are not treated as dividends for financial reporting purposes and, therefore, do not affect the if-converted EPS computations.	Statement 128 provides no guidance on common stock held by an ESOP. The guidance in AICPA Statement of Position (SOP) 93-6, *Employers' Accounting for Employee Stock Ownership Plans*, continues to apply as does the consensus in EITF Issue 92-3. AICPA Statement of Position 76-3, *Accounting Practices for Certain Employee Stock Ownership Plans*, continues to apply for "grandfathered" shares.

EITF Issue No. 94-7—Accounting for Financial Instruments Indexed to, and Potentially Settled in, a Company's Own Stock

Resolved

Issue 94-7 addresses the classification of certain contracts (forward sales, forward purchases, purchased put options, and purchased call options) that are settled in a variety of ways (physical, net share, or net cash) as equity instruments or assets-liabilities and specifies the treatment of changes in the fair value of those instruments. The Issue does not address EPS treatment.

Note: The EITF combined the consensuses in this Issue with the consensuses in Issue 96-13.

Statement 128 states that contracts that may be settled in stock or cash should be presumed to be settled in stock and reflected in the computation of diluted EPS unless past experience or a stated policy provides a reasonable basis to believe otherwise. [29]

In computing diluted EPS, Statement 128 requires use of the reverse treasury stock method to account for the dilutive effect of written put options and similar contracts that are "in the money" during the reporting period. Statement 128 states that purchased options should not be reflected in the computation of diluted EPS because to do so would be antidilutive. [24, 25]

EITF Issue No. 96-1—Sale of Put Options on Issuer's Stock That Require or Permit Cash Settlement

Resolved

Issue 96-1 provides guidance similar to Issue 94-7 and relates only to written put options settled in a variety of ways. The Issue does not address EPS treatment.

Note: The EITF combined the consensuses in this Issue with the consensuses in Issue 96-13.

Refer to discussion on Issue 94-7.

**Status after
Statement 128**

Current Guidance

Effect of Statement 128

Resolved

EITF Issue No. 96-13—Accounting for Derivative Financial Instruments Indexed to, and Potentially Settled in, a Company's Own Stock

Issue 96-13 codifies the consensuses provided in Issues 87-31, 94-7, and 96-1 into a framework that can be applied to a variety of similar financial instruments settled in a variety of different ways. With the exception of the consensus on use of the reverse treasury stock method in Issue 87-31, Issue 96-13 does not address EPS treatment.

Refer to discussion on Issue 94-7.

Statement of Financial Accounting Standards No. 129
Disclosure of Information about Capital Structure

STATUS

Issued: February 1997

Effective Date: For financial statements for periods ending after December 15, 1997

Affects: Supersedes APB 10, paragraphs 10 and 11
Supersedes FAS 47, paragraph 10(c)

Affected by: No other pronouncements

Issues Discussed by FASB Emerging Issues Task Force (EITF)

Affects: No EITF Issues

Interpreted by: No EITF Issues

Related Issue: EITF Issue No. 86-32

SUMMARY

This Statement establishes standards for disclosing information about an entity's capital structure. It applies to all entities. This Statement continues the previous requirements to disclose certain information about an entity's capital structure found in APB Opinions No. 10, *Omnibus Opinion—1966*, and No. 15, *Earnings per Share*, and FASB Statement No. 47, *Disclosure of Long-Term Obligations*, for entities that were subject to the requirements of those standards. This Statement eliminates the exemption of nonpublic entities from certain disclosure requirements of Opinion 15 as provided by FASB Statement No. 21, *Suspension of the Reporting of Earnings per Share and Segment Information by Nonpublic Enterprises*. It supersedes specific disclosure requirements of Opinions 10 and 15 and Statement 47 and consolidates them in this Statement for ease of retrieval and for greater visibility to nonpublic entities.

This Statement is effective for financial statements for periods ending after December 15, 1997. It contains no change in disclosure requirements for entities that were previously subject to the requirements of Opinions 10 and 15 and Statement 47.

Statement of Financial Accounting Standards No. 129

Disclosure of Information about Capital Structure

CONTENTS

INTRODUCTION

1. In conjunction with its project to supersede the provisions for computing earnings per share (EPS) found in APB Opinion No. 15, *Earnings per Share,* the Board reviewed the disclosure requirements specified in that Opinion. The Board noted that although some of the disclosures were not necessarily related to the computation of earnings per share, they provided useful information. Because nonpublic entities were excluded from the scope of Opinion 15 and that Opinion's disclosure requirements regarding capital structure are not required elsewhere, the Board decided to include those disclosure requirements in this Statement and make them applicable to all entities. In addition, the Board decided to incorporate related disclosure requirements from other Opinions or Statements into this Statement for ease of use. The specific disclosures required by this Statement were previously required by APB Opinion No. 10, *Omnibus Opinion—1966,* Opinion 15, and FASB Statement No. 47, *Disclosure of Long-Term Obligations,* for entities that were subject to the requirements of those standards.

2. The following terms and definitions are used in this Statement:

a. *Securities*—the evidence of debt or ownership or a related right. For purposes of this Statement, the term *securities* includes options and warrants as well as debt and stock.

b. *Participation rights*—contractual rights of security holders to receive dividends or returns from the security issuer's profits, cash flows, or returns on investments.

c. *Preferred stock*—a security that has preferential rights compared to common stock.

STANDARDS OF FINANCIAL ACCOUNTING AND REPORTING

Scope

3. This Statement applies to all entities, public and nonpublic, that have issued securities addressed by this Statement.

Information about Securities

4. An entity shall explain, in summary form within its financial statements, the pertinent rights and privileges of the various securities outstanding. Examples of information that shall be disclosed are dividend and liquidation preferences, participation rights, call prices and dates, conversion or exercise prices or rates and pertinent dates, sinking-fund requirements, unusual voting rights, and significant terms of contracts to issue additional shares.[1]

---

[1]Disclosure of this information about securities previously was required by Opinion 15, paragraph 19.

5. An entity shall disclose within its financial statements the number of shares issued upon conversion, exercise, or satisfaction of required conditions during at least the most recent annual fiscal period and any subsequent interim period presented.[2]

Liquidation Preference of Preferred Stock

6. An entity that issues preferred stock (or other senior stock) that has a preference in involuntary liquidation considerably in excess of the par or stated value of the shares shall disclose the liquidation preference of the stock (the relationship between the preference in liquidation and the par or stated value of the shares).[3] That disclosure shall be made in the equity section of the statement of financial position in the aggregate, either parenthetically or "in short," rather than on a per-share basis or through disclosure in the notes.

7. In addition, an entity shall disclose within its financial statements (either on the face of the statement of financial position or in the notes thereto):

a. The aggregate or per-share amounts at which preferred stock may be called or is subject to redemption through sinking-fund operations or otherwise; and

b. The aggregate and per-share amounts of arrearages in cumulative preferred dividends.[4]

Redeemable Stock

8. An entity that issues redeemable stock shall disclose the amount of redemption requirements, separately by issue or combined, for all issues of capital stock that are redeemable at fixed or determinable prices on fixed or determinable dates in each of the five years following the date of the latest statement of financial position presented.[5]

Amendments to Existing Pronouncements

9. Paragraphs 10 and 11 of Opinion 10 are deleted as well as the heading preceding paragraph 10.

10. Paragraph 10(c) of Statement 47 is deleted.

Effective Date and Transition

11. This Statement shall be effective for financial statements for periods ending after December 15, 1997. It contains no change in disclosure requirements for entities that were previously subject to the requirements of Opinions 10 and 15 and Statement 47.

**The provisions of this Statement need
not be applied to immaterial items.**

This Statement was adopted by the unanimous vote of the seven members of the Financial Accounting Standards Board:

Dennis R. Beresford, *Chairman*	Anthony T. Cope	James J. Leisenring
Joseph V. Anania	John M. Foster	Gerhard G. Mueller
	Gaylen N. Larson	

---

[2]Disclosure of this information about changes in securities previously was required by Opinion 15, paragraph 20. Footnote 5 to Opinion 15 referred to paragraph 10 of APB Opinion No. 12, *Omnibus Opinion—1967*. That paragraph requires, among other things, disclosure of the changes in the number of shares of equity securities during at least the most recent annual fiscal period and any subsequent interim period presented to make the financial statements sufficiently informative. The disclosure required by paragraph 5 of this Statement meets that requirement.
[3]Disclosure of this information about liquidation preferences previously was required by Opinion 10, paragraph 10.
[4]Disclosure of this information about preferred stock previously was required by Opinion 10, paragraph 11.
[5]Disclosure of this information about redemption requirements previously was required by Statement 47, paragraph 10(c).

Appendix

BACKGROUND INFORMATION AND BASIS FOR CONCLUSIONS

CONTENTS

Appendix

BACKGROUND INFORMATION AND BASIS FOR CONCLUSIONS

Introduction

12. This appendix summarizes considerations that were deemed significant by Board members in reaching the conclusions in this Statement. It includes reasons for accepting certain views and rejecting others. Individual Board members gave greater weight to some factors than to others.

Background Information

13. In March 1994, the Board added a project on earnings per share to its technical agenda to be pursued concurrently with a similar project of the International Accounting Standards Committee (IASC). The objective of the Board's project was twofold: (a) to improve and simplify U.S. generally accepted accounting principles and (b) to issue a standard that would be compatible with international standards.

14. In January 1996, the Board issued an FASB Exposure Draft, *Earnings per Share and Disclosure of Information about Capital Structure*. Part I of the proposed Statement included provisions related to the computation and presentation of earnings per share and was not applicable to nonpublic entities. Part II of the proposed Statement included disclosure requirements for information about capital structure and was applicable to all entities. The Board received 104 comment letters on the Exposure Draft, most of which commented only on the earnings per share provisions in Part I. The few letters that addressed Part II generally supported the Board's intent to centralize capital structure disclosure requirements.

15. The Board decided to issue Part II as a separate Statement because of its applicability to nonpublic entities. The Board was concerned that if it included those disclosure requirements in the final Statement on computing earnings per share, nonpublic entities might not be aware of the existence of those disclosure requirements and their wider applicability.

Conclusions on Basic Issues

Scope

16. This Statement is applicable to all entities that have issued securities addressed by this Statement. The Board believes that all of the required disclosures will be useful to users of financial statements of entities that have issued any type of security covered by this Statement, whether or not those securities are publicly held. The scope of this Statement is unchanged from that of the standards that previously contained its disclosure requirements (Opinions 10 and 15 and Statement 47), except for the elimination of the exemption of nonpublic entities from the provisions of Opinion 15. That exemption was provided by FASB Statement No. 21, *Suspension of the Reporting of Earnings per Share and Segment Information by Nonpublic Enterprises,* which was amended by FASB Statement No. 128, *Earnings per Share.*

Disclosure Requirements

17. Opinion 15 required disclosure of descriptive information about securities that is not necessarily related to the computation of earnings per share. The Board considered limiting that disclosure to information about only those securities that affect or could affect the computation of basic and diluted EPS. However, the Board decided not to limit the disclosure requirement because it contains useful information about the capital structure of an entity that is not required elsewhere.

18. This Statement also requires disclosure of information about (a) the liquidation preference of preferred stock and (b) redeemable stock that previously had been required to be disclosed by Opinion 10 and Statement 47, respectively. Those disclosure requirements were incorporated into this Statement because the Board believes that it is useful to include all disclosure requirements related to an entity's capital structure in the same standard.

Effective Date

19. The Board decided that this Statement should be effective for financial statements for periods ending after December 15, 1997. That effective date corresponds to the effective date of Statement 128. This Statement contains no change in disclosure requirements for entities that were previously subject to the requirements of Opinions 10 and 15 and Statement 47.

(Refer to Volume II of the *Original Pronouncements* for the appendixes and topical index.)